Alternative Dispute Resolution

Strategies for Law and Business

ANDERSON'S

Law School Publications

ADMINISTRATIVE LAW ANTHOLOGY
by Thomas O. Sargentich

ADMINISTRATIVE LAW: CASES AND MATERIALS
by Daniel J. Gifford

ALTERNATIVE DISPUTE RESOLUTON: STRATEGIES FOR LAW AND BUSINESS
by E. Wendy Trachte-Huber and Stephen K. Huber

AN ADMIRALTY LAW ANTHOLOGY
by Robert M. Jarvis

ANALYTIC JURISPRUDENCE ANTHOLOGY
by Anthony D'Amato

AN ANTITRUST ANTHOLOGY
by Andrew I. Gavil

APPELLATE ADVOCACY: PRINCIPLES AND PRACTICE (Second Edition)
Cases and Materials
by Ursula Bentele and Eve Cary

A CAPITAL PUNISHMENT ANTHOLOGY (and Electronic Caselaw Appendix)
by Victor L. Streib

CASES AND PROBLEMS IN CRIMINAL LAW (Third Edition)
by Myron Moskovitz

THE CITATION WORKBOOK
by Maria L. Ciampi, Rivka Widerman, and Vicki Lutz

CIVIL PROCEDURE: CASES, MATERIALS, AND QUESTIONS
by Richard D. Freer and Wendy C. Perdue

COMMERCIAL TRANSACTIONS: PROBLEMS AND MATERIALS
Vol. 1: Secured Transactions Under the UCC
Vol. 2: Sales Under the UCC and the CISG
Vol. 3: Negotiable Instruments Under the UCC and the CIBN
by Louis F. Del Duca, Egon Guttman, and Alphonse M. Squillante

COMMUNICATIONS LAW: MEDIA, ENTERTAINMENT, AND REGULATION
by Donald E. Lively, Allen S. Hammond, Blake D. Morant, and Russell L. Weaver

A CONSTITUTIONAL LAW ANTHOLOGY
by Michael J. Glennon

CONSTITUTIONAL LAW: CASES, HISTORY, AND DIALOGUES
by Donald E. Lively, Phoebe A. Haddon, Dorothy E. Roberts, and Russell L. Weaver

THE CONSTITUTIONAL LAW OF THE EUROPEAN UNION
by James D. Dinnage and John F. Murphy

CONSTITUTIONAL TORTS
by Sheldon H. Nahmod, Michael L. Wells, and Thomas A. Eaton

CONTRACTS
Contemporary Cases, Comments, and Problems
by Michael L. Closen, Richard M. Perlmutter, and Jeffrey D. Wittenberg

A CONTRACTS ANTHOLOGY (Second Edition)
by Peter Linzer

CORPORATE AND WHITE COLLAR CRIME: AN ANTHOLOGY
by Leonard Orland

A CRIMINAL LAW ANTHOLOGY
by Arnold H. Loewy

CRIMINAL LAW: CASES AND MATERIALS
by Arnold H. Loewy

A CRIMINAL PROCEDURE ANTHOLOGY
by Silas J. Wasserstrom and Christie L. Snyder

CRIMINAL PROCEDURE: ARREST AND INVESTIGATION
by Arnold H. Loewy and Arthur B. LaFrance

CRIMINAL PROCEDURE: TRIAL AND SENTENCING
by Arthur B. LaFrance and Arnold H. Loewy

ECONOMIC REGULATION: CASES AND MATERIALS
by Richard J. Pierce, Jr.

ELEMENTS OF LAW
by Eva H. Hanks, Michael E. Herz, and Steven S. Nemerson

ENDING IT: DISPUTE RESOLUTION IN AMERICA
Descriptions, Examples, Cases and Questions
by Susan M. Leeson and Bryan M. Johnston

ENVIRONMENTAL LAW (Second Edition)
Vol. 1: Environmental Decisionmaking: NEPA and the Endangered Species Act
Vol. 2: Water Pollution
Vol. 3: Air Pollution
Vol. 4: Hazardous Wastes
by Jackson B. Battle, Robert L. Fischman, Maxine I. Lipeles, and Mark S. Squillace

AN ENVIRONMENTAL LAW ANTHOLOGY
by Robert L. Fischman, Maxine I. Lipeles, and Mark S. Squillace

ENVIRONMENTAL PROTECTION AND JUSTICE
Readings and Commentary on Environmental Law and Practice
by Kenneth A. Manaster

AN EVIDENCE ANTHOLOGY
by Edward J. Imwinkelried and Glen Weissenberger

FEDERAL EVIDENCE COURTROOM MANUAL
by Glen Weissenberger

FEDERAL RULES OF EVIDENCE (Second Edition)
Rules, Legislative History, Commentary and Authority
by Glen Weissenberger

FEDERAL RULES OF EVIDENCE FOR UNITED STATES COURTS AND MAGISTRATES
by Publisher's Staff

FIRST AMENDMENT ANTHOLOGY
by Donald E. Lively, Dorothy E. Roberts, and Russell L. Weaver

INTERNATIONAL ENVIRONMENTAL LAW ANTHOLOGY
by Anthony D'Amato and Kirsten Engel

INTERNATIONAL HUMAN RIGHTS: LAW, POLICY AND PROCESS
Problems and Materials
by Frank C. Newman and David Weissbrodt

INTERNATIONAL INTELLECTUAL PROPERTY ANTHOLOGY
by Anthony D'Amato and Doris Estelle Long

INTERNATIONAL LAW ANTHOLOGY
by Anthony D'Amato

INTERNATIONAL LAW COURSEBOOK
by Anthony D'Amato

INTRODUCTION TO THE STUDY OF LAW: CASES AND MATERIALS
by John Makdisi

JUDICIAL EXTERNSHIPS: THE CLINIC INSIDE THE COURTHOUSE
by Rebecca A. Cochran

JUSTICE AND THE LEGAL SYSTEM
A Coursebook
by Anthony D'Amato and Arthur J. Jacobson

THE LAW OF DISABILITY DISCRIMINATION
by Ruth Colker

Continued

THE LAW OF MODERN PAYMENT SYSTEMS AND NOTES
by Fred H. Miller and Alvin C. Harrell

LAWYERS AND FUNDAMENTAL MORAL RESPONSIBILITY
by Daniel R. Coquillette

MICROECONOMIC PREDICATES TO LAW AND ECONOMICS
by Mark Seidenfeld

PATIENTS, PSYCHIATRISTS AND LAWYERS
Law and the Mental Health System
by Raymond L. Spring, Roy B. Lacoursiere, M.D., and Glen Weissenberger

PROBLEMS AND SIMULATIONS IN EVIDENCE (Second Edition)
by Thomas F. Guernsey

A PRODUCTS LIABILITY ANTHOLOGY
by Anita Bernstein

PROFESSIONAL RESPONSIBILITY ANTHOLOGY
by Thomas B. Metzloff

A PROPERTY ANTHOLOGY
by Richard H. Chused

THE REGULATION OF BANKING
Cases and Materials on Depository Institutions and Their Regulators
by Michael P. Malloy

A SECTION 1983 CIVIL RIGHTS ANTHOLOGY
by Sheldon H. Nahmod

SPORTS LAW: CASES AND MATERIALS (Second Edition)
by Raymond L. Yasser, James R. McCurdy, and C. Peter Goplerud

A TORTS ANTHOLOGY
by Lawrence C. Levine, Julie A. Davies, and Edward J. Kionka

TRIAL PRACTICE
by Lawrence A. Dubin and Thomas F. Guernsey

TRIAL PRACTICE AND CASE FILES
by Edward R. Stein and Lawrence A. Dubin

TRIAL PRACTICE AND CASE FILES with *Video* Presentation
by Edward R. Stein and Lawrence A. Dubin

FORTHCOMING PUBLICATIONS

BASIC ACCOUNTING PRINCIPLES FOR LAWYERS:
With Present Value and Expected Value
by C. Steven Bradford and Gary A. Ames

CONSTITUTIONAL CONFLICTS
by Derrick A. Bell, Jr.

A CONSTITUTIONAL LAW ANTHOLOGY (Second Edition)
by Donald E. Lively, Michael J. Glennon, Phoebe A. Haddon, Dorothy E. Roberts and Russell L. Weaver

A JUVENILE LAW ANTHOLOGY
by Victor L. Streib and Lynn Sametz

EUROPEAN COMMUNITY LAW ANTHOLOGY
by Anthony D'Amato and Karen V. Kole

INTERNATIONAL HUMAN RIGHTS: LAW POLICY, AND PROCESS (Second Edition)
by Frank C. Newman and David Weissbrodt

PRINCIPLES OF EVIDENCE (Third Edition)
by Irving Younger, Michael Goldsmith, and David A. Sonenshein

UNINCORPORATED BUSINESS ENTITIES
by Larry E. Ribstein

ALTERNATIVE DISPUTE RESOLUTION

STRATEGIES FOR LAW AND BUSINESS

E. WENDY TRACHTE-HUBER

Director and Executive Professor,
A.A. White Dispute Resolution Institute
College of Business Administration
University of Houston

and

STEPHEN K. HUBER

Professor of Law and Director,
LL.M. Program
University of Houston Law Center

ANDERSON PUBLISHING CO.
CINCINNATI, OHIO

ALTERNATIVE DISPUTE RESOLUTION: STRATEGIES FOR LAW AND BUSINESS

2035 Reading Road / Cincinnati, Ohio 45202
800 582 7295 / e-mail andpubco@aol.com / Fax 513 562 5430

ISBN: 0-87084-032-0

DEDICATION

To Jennifer and Robert with Love

E.W.T-H. & S.K.H.

TABLE OF CONTENTS

PREFACE .... **xxvii**
ACKNOWLEDGEMENTS .... **xxxi**
TABLE OF CASES .... **xxxiii**

PART I. DISPUTE RESOLUTION: GENERAL CONSIDERATIONS

CHAPTER 1: AN OVERVIEW OF DISPUTE RESOLUTION **3**

A. Introduction 3
B. The Dispute Settlement Continuum 4
1. Chart adapted from E. Wendy Trachte, NEGOTIATION: STRATEGIES FOR LAW & BUSINESS 9 (1994) 4
2. Comments and Questions 5
C. The Modern ADR Movement: Alternative to What? 5
1. Comments and Questions 5
2. William Twining, *Alternatives to What: Theories of Litigation, Procedure and Dispute Settlement in Anglo-American Jurisprudence: Some Neglected Classics,* 56 MODERN L. REV. 380, 380-383 (1993) 6
D. Thinking About the Alternatives 7
1. Comments and Questions 7
2. Frank E.A. Sander, *Alternative Methods of Dispute Reolution: An Overview,* 37 FLA. L. REV. 1 (1985) 8
3. Harry T. Edwards, *Alternative Dispute Resolution: Panacea or Anathema?,* 99 HARV. L. REV. 668 (1986) 20
4. Jethro K. Lieberman & James F. Henry, *Lessons From the Alterntive Dispute Resolution Movement,* 53 U. CHI. L. REV. 424, 424-432 (1986) 27
E. Alternative Dispute Resolution in Earlier America 29
1. Comments and Questions 29
2. Bruce H. Mann, *The Formalization of Informal Law: Arbitration Before the American Revolution,* 59 N.Y.U. L. REV. 443 (1984) 30

CHAPTER 2: COMMUNICATIONS: THEORY AND PRACTICE **39**

A. Introduction 39
B. Effective Communication 40
1. Eastwood Atwater, I HEAR YOU 1-3, 65-74 (1992) 40
2. David A. Binder, Paul Bergman & Susan C. Price, LAWYERS AS COUNSELORS 35-44 (1991) 41
3. Comments and Questions 47
4. Kathleen Kelley Reardon, THEY DON'T GET IT, DO THEY? COMMUNICATION IN THE WORKPLACE—CLOSING THE GAP BETWEEN MEN AND WOMEN 40-45 (1995) 48

C. Eliciting Information: Questions 49
1. John M. Haynes, THE FUNDAMENTALS OF FAMILY MEDIATION 185-186 (1994) 49
2. David A. Binder, Paul Bergman & Susan C. Price, LAWYERS AS COUNSELORS 69-81, 237-56 (1991) 51
D. Context of Communications 67
1. Comments and Questions 67
2. Franz Lieber, LEGAL AND POLITICAL HERMENEUTICS 17-19 (3d ed. 1880) 68
3. *Frigaliment Importing Co. v. B.N.S. International Sales Co.*, 190 F. Supp. 116 (S.D.N.Y. 1960) 68
4. Comments and Questions 72
E. The Management of Impressions 73
1. William Sansom, A CONTEST OF LADIES 230-32 (Hogarth 1956) 73
2. Comments and Questions 73
3. Jean Paul Sartre, BEING AND NOTHINGNESS 59 (1956) 74
4. Comments and Questions 74
5. Erving Goffman, THE PRESENTATION OF SELF IN EVERYDAY LIFE 1-8 (1959) 75

CHAPTER 3: THEORETICAL APPROACHES TO DISPUTES AND DISPUTING 77

A. Introduction 78
B. Competition and Cooperation 79
1. Comments and Questions 79
2. Adam Smith, AN INQUIRY INTO THE NATURE AND CAUSES OF THE WEALTH OF NATIONS 118-119 (1776) (Penguin 1986) 79
3. Garrett Hardin, *The Tragedy of the Commons*, SCIENCE, Vol. 162, at 1243, 1244 (13 December, 1968) 80
4. The Prisoner's Dilemma 81
5. Comments and Questions 82
C. Economics and Game Theory 83
1. Comments and Questions 83
2. Steven Shavell, *Alternative Dispute Resolution: An Economic Analysis*, 24 J. LEGAL STUDIES 1 (1995) 83
3. Comments and Questions 93
4. H. Scott Bierman & Luis Fernandez, GAME THEORY WITH ECONOMIC APPLICATIONS 68-70 (1993) 94
5. Howard Raiffa, THE ART AND SCIENCE OF NEGOTIATION 52-54 (1982) 95
D. Agency Theory 96
1. Comments and Questions 96
2. Ronald J. Gilson & Robert H. Mnookin, *Disputing Through Agents: Cooperation and Conflict Between Lawyers in Litigation*, 94 COLUM. L. REV. 509 (1994) 97
E. Learning Theory and Psychology 112
1. Lyonel Festinger, AN INTRODUCTION TO THE THEORY OF COGNITIVE DISSONANCE 1-6, 261-267 (1957) 112
2. Comments and Questions 113

3. Barry M. Staw, *The Escalation of Commitment to a Course of Action*, ACADEMY OF MANAGEMENT REVIEW, October 1981 at 577 114
4. Phyllis Beck Kritek, NEGOTIATING AT AN UNEVEN TABLE: DEVELOPING MORAL COURAGE IN RESOLVING OUR CONFLICTS 55-64 (1994) 119
5. Cognitive Barriers and Reactive Devaluation 123

F. Anthropology 123
1. Sally Engle Merry, DISPUTING WITHOUT CULTURE [Review of Stephen B. Goldberg, Eric D. Green & Frank E.A. Sander DISPUTE RESOLUTION (1985)], 100 HARV. L. REV. 2057 (1987) 123
2. Laura Nader, *Controlling Processes in the Practice of Law: Hierachy and Pacification in the Movement to Re-Form Dispute Ideoalogy*, 9 OHIO ST. J. ON DISP. RESOL. 1 (1993) 131
3. Carrie Menkel-Meadow, *The Many Ways of Mediation: The Transformation of Traditions, Ideoalogies, Paradigms, and Practices*, 1995 NEGOTIATION J. 217, 233 138
4. Comments and Questions 139
5. William Twining, *Alternatives to What: Theories of Litigation, Procedure and Dispute Settlement in Anglo-America Jurisprudence: Some Neglected Classics*, 56 MODERN L. REV. 380, 385-87 (1993) 139
6. Comments and Questions 141
7. Karl N. Llewellyn & E. Adamson Hoebel, THE CHEYENNE WAY 20-22 (1941) 141

PART II. NEGOTIATION

CHAPTER 4: THE NEGOTIATION PROCESS 145

A. Introduction 146
B. Models of Negotiations 146
1. Comments and Questions 146
2. P.H. Gulliver, DISPUTES AND NEGOTIATIONS: A CROSS-CULTURAL PERSPECTIVE xiii-xv, 79-80, (1979) 146
3. John S. Murray, *Understanding Competing Theories of Negotiation*, 1986 NEGOTIATION J. 179, 179-82 149
4. Comments and Questions 150
5. Carrie Menkel-Meadow, *Toward Another View of Legal Negotiation: The Structure of Problem Solving*, 31 UCLA L. REV. 754, 760-762 (1984) 151

C. The Negotiation Environment 151
1. David A. Lax & James K. Sebenius, THE MANAGER AS NEGOTIATOR 339 (1986) 151
2. Comments and Questions 152
3. Robert H. Mnookin and Lewis Kornhauser, *Bargaining in the Shadow of the Law: The Case of Divorce*, 88 YALE L.J. 950 (1979) 152

D. Strategies for Successful Negotiation 168
1. David A. Lax & James K. Sebenius, *Interests: The Measure of Negotiation*, 2 NEGOTIATION J. 73 (1986) 168
2. Donald G. Gifford, *A Context-Based Theory of Strategy Selection in Legal Negotiation*, 46 OHIO ST. L.J., 45-58 (1985) 170

E. The Search for "Win-Win" Solutions 177
1. Comments and Questions 177
2. Adam Smith, AN INQUIRY INTO THE NATURE AND CAUSES OF THE WEALTH OF NATIONS 4-5 (1776) (Penguin 1986) 178
3. David A. Lax & James K. Sebenius, THE MANAGER AS NEGOTIATOR (1986) 178
4. *James J. White, Review Essay: The Pros and Cons of "Getting to YES"* by Roger Fisher & William Ury, 31 J. LEGAL EDUCATION 115 (1981) 179
5. Roger Fisher, *Comment on James White's Review of "Getting to YES,"* 31 J. LEGAL EDUCATION 128 (1981) 182
F. Barriers to Settlement 186
1. Comments and Questions 186
2. Robert H. Mnookin, *Why Negotiations Fails: An Exploration of Barriers to the Resolution of Conflict,* 8 OHIO ST. J. ON DISP. RESOL. 235 (1993) 186
G. Women as Negotiators 192
1. Comments and Questions 192
2. Charles B. Craver, *The Impact of Gender on Clinical Negotiating Achievement,* 6 OHIO STATE J. ON DISP. RESOL. 1 (1990) 193

CHAPTER 5: TRANS-NATIONAL AND CROSS-CULTURAL PERSPECTIVES 203
A. Introduction 203
B. Dispute Settlement Among Closely Knit Groups 204
1. Comments and Questions 204
2. Jerold Auerbach, JUSTICE WITHOUT LAW? 3 (1981) 205
3. Diane LeResche, *A Comparison of the American Mediation Process with a Korean-American Harmony Restoration, Process,* 9 MEDIATION Q. 323 (1992) 205
C. Prejudice and ADR Processes 215
1. Richard Delgado, et al., *Fairness and Formality: Minimizing the Risk of Prejudice in Alternative Dispute Resolution,* 1985 WIS. L. REV. 1359, 1387-1404 215
2. Comments and Questions 222
D. Dispute Settlement Among Native Americans 223
1. Comments and Questions 223
2. Robert Yazzie, "Traditional Navajo Dispute Resolution in the Navajo Peacemaker Court," NIDR Forum, Spring 1995, at 4 224
E. Negotiating in Japan: A Primer for Americans 234
1. Comments and Questions 234
2. Glen Fisher, INTERNATIONAL NEGOTIATION: A CROSS-CULTURAL PERSPECTIVE (1980) 235
3. Dean Allen Foster, BARGAINING ACROSS BORDERS: HOW TO NEGOTIATE BUSINESS SUCCESSFULLY ANYWHERE IN THE WORLD, 264-293 (1992) 236
4. Robert M. March, THE JAPANESE NEGOTIATOR: SUBTLETY AND STRATEGY BEYOND WESTERN LOGIC 15-17 (1990) 237

5. Sanjyot P. Dunung, DOING BUSINESS IN ASIA: THE COMPLETE GUIDE 1-50 (1995) 238
6. Boye Lafayette DeMente, HOW TO DO BUSINESS WITH THE JAPANESE: A COMPLETE GUIDE TO JAPANESE CUSTOMS AND BUSINESS PRACTICES 6-8, 47-49, 57-58 (1993) 239
7. Philip R. Harris & Robert T. Moran, MANAGING CULTURAL DIFFERENCE 393-405 (1991) 241
F. Pricing Services: A Cross-Cultural Exercise 241
1. Shaiva Naipaul, NORTH OF SOUTH: AN AFRICAN JOURNEY 47-52 (1978) 241
2. Comments and Questions 243

CHAPTER 6: NEGOTIATION APPLICATIONS 245
A. Introduction 245
B. Settlement of Business Disputes 245
1. Arthur Allen Leff, *Injury, Ignorance and Spite: The Dynamics of Coercive Collection,* 80 YALE L.J. 1, 25-26 (1970) 245
2. Comments and Questions 247
3. E. Wendy Trachte, NEGOTIATION: STRATEGIES FOR LAW & BUSINESS 80-84 (1994) 248
C. Negotiation of Criminal Charges: Plea Bargaining 252
1. Comments and Questions 252
2. Abraham S. Blumberg, *The Practice of Law as a Confidence Game,* 1 LAW & SOC'Y REV. 15, 18-31 (1967) 253
3. Donald G. Gifford, *A Context-Based Theory of Strategy Selection,* 46 OHIO ST. L.J. 41, 73-82 (1985) 259
D. Negotiations Within Legislative Bodies 265
1. Tom Melling, *Dispute Resolution Within Legislative Institutions,* 46 STAN. L. REV. 1677 (1994) 265
2. Comments and Questions 272

PART III: MEDIATION

CHAPTER 7: THE MEDIATION PROCESS 275
A. Introduction 276
B. Reflections on Mediation in Modern America 277
1. Lon L. Fuller, *Mediation—Its Forms and Functions,* 44 S. CAL. L. REV. 305 (1970) 277
2. Robert A. Baruch Bush & Joseph P. Folger, THE PROMISE OF MEDIATION: RESPONDING TO CONFLICT THROUGH EMPOWERMENT AND RECOGNITION 15-27 (1994) 288
3. James J. Alfini, *Trashing, Bashing, and Hashing It Out: Is this the End of "Good Mediation"?,* 19 FLA. ST. U. L. REV. 47, 66-73 (1991) 293
C. Basics of the Mediation Process 294
1. Christopher W. Moore, MEDIATION 1-7, 10-16 (U.S. Army Corps Of Engineers 1991) (IWR Pamphlet 91-ADR-P-3) 294

2. Eric Galton, REPRESENTING CLIENTS IN MEDIATION 25-53 (1995) 302
3. James P. Groton, GETTING THE MEDIATION PROCESS STARTED, in Alan E. Harris, Charles M. Sink & Randall W. Wulff, ADR: A PRACTICAL GUIDE TO RESOLVE CONSTRUCTION DISPUTES 77-86 (1994) 315

D. Strategies for Success in Mediation 319
1. Eric Galton, REPRESENTING CLIENTS IN MEDIATION 69-72 (1994) 319
2. Stephen P. Morrell & William Baker, SUCCEEDING IN MEDIATION, in Alan E. Hanes, Charles M. Sink & Randall W. Wulff 101-114 ADR: A PRACTICAL GUIDE TO RESOLVE CONSTRUCTION DISPUTES (1994) 321
3. Tom Arnold, *Twenty Common Errors in Mediation Advocacy,* ADR TODAY, Spring 1995, at 2 329
4. Eileen Miggins Hohlt, EFFECTIVE USE OF CAUCUS (1993) 335
5. Kimberlee K. Kovach, MEDIATION: PRINCIPLES AND PRACTICE 108-10 (1994) 337

E. Impasse—And What to Do About It 337
1. Christopher W. Moore, *Techniques to Break Impasse,* in Jay Folberg & Ann Milne, DIVORCE MEDIATION 251-75 (1988) 337
2. Eric Galton, REPRESENTING CLIENTS IN MEDIATION 104-112 (1995) 350

F. Mediation as Healing/Therapy and Empowerment 353
1. Comments and Questions 353
2. Lois Gold, *Influencing Unconscious Influences: The Healing Dimension of Mediation,* 11 MEDIATION QUART. 55 (1993) 353
3. Robert A. Baruch Bush, *Efficiency and Protection, or Empowerment and Recognition?: The Mediator's Role and Ethical Standards in Mediation,* 41 FLA. L. REV. 253, 267-86 (1989) 361

G. Closing Considerations 369
1. Eric R. Galton, MEDIATION CHECKLIST (1995) 369
2. Recent Developments in the States 375

CHAPTER 8: DIVORCE AND FAMILY MEDIATION 379

A. Introduction 379

B. How Family Mediation Works 380
1. Phyllis Gangel-Jacob, *Some Words of Caution About Divorce Mediation,* 23 HOFSTRA L. REV. 825 (1995) 380
2. Comments and Questions 381
3. John M. Haynes, THE FUNDAMENTALS OF FAMILY MEDIATION (1994) 381
4. Alison Taylor, *A General Theory of Divorce Mediation,* in Jay Folberg & Ann Milne, DIVORCE MEDIATION 61-82 (1988) 381
5. Robert Tompkins, *Parenting Plans: A Concept Whose Time Has Come,* 33 FAMILY & CONCILIATION COURTS REVIEW 286 (1995) 395

C. Are Women Disadvantaged in Family Mediation 400
1. Trina Grillo, *The Mediation Alternative: Process Dangers For Women,* 100 YALE L.J. 1545 (1991) 400
2. Comments and Questions 417
3. Joshua D. Rosenberg, *In Defense of Mediation,* 33 ARIZ. L. REV. 467 (1991) 417
4. Diane Neumann, *How Mediation Can Effectively Address the Male-Female Power Imbalance in Divorce,* 9 MEDIATION QUART. 227 (1992) 429

5. Anne Field, *Divorce Mediation and Other (Cheap) Ways to Split*, COSMPOLITAN, August 1995 at 136 436
6. Comments and Questions 438
D. Lawyer Participation in Divorce Mediation 439
1. Comments and Questions 439
2. Craig A. McEwen, Nancy H. Rogers, & Richard J. Maiman, *Bring In the Lawyers: Challenging the Dominant Approaches to Ensuring Fairness in Divorce Mediation*, 79 MINN. L. REV. 1317 (1995) 439
E. Duty of Mediators to Promote Fair Results 458
1. Scott H. Hughes, *Elizabeth's Story: Exploring Power Imbalances in Divorce Mediation*, 8 GEO. J. LEGAL ETHICS 553, 584-595 (1995) 458
2. Comments and Questions 462

CHAPTER 9: MEDIATION APPLICATIONS 465
A. Introduction 466
B. Mediation of Bioethical Disputes 466
1. Comments and Questions 466
2. Nancy N. Dubler & Leonard J. Marcus, MEDIATING BIOETHICAL DISPUTES 33-58 (1994) (United Hospital Fund of New York) 467
C. Victim-Offender Mediation 474
1. Jennifer Gerarda Brown, *The Use of Mediation to Resolve Criminal Cases: A Procedural Critique*, 43 EMORY L.J. 1247, 1248-1266, 1308-1309 (1994) 474
2. Mark S. Umbright, MEDIATING INTERPERSONAL CONFLICTS: A PATHWAY TO PEACE 135-163 (1995) 482
3. Comments and Questions 482
D. Farmer-Lender Mediation 483
1. Leonard L. Riskin, *Two Concepts of Mediation in the FmHA Farmer-Lender Mediation Program*, 45 ADMIN. L. REV. 21 (1993) 483
2. Comments and Questions 500
E. Commercial Disputes 501
1. American Arbitration Association, Mediation Rules for Commercial Financial Disputes (1993) 501
2. Comments and Questions 504
F. Regulating Mediation: Analysis and Proposal 504
1. Nancy H. Rogers & Craig A. McEwen, MEDIATION LAW, POLICY & PRACTICE §§13:02 to 13.03 (2d ed. 1994) 504
2. Comments and Questions 510

PART IV: ARBITRATION

CHAPTER 10: THE ARBITRATION PROCESS 513
A. Introduction 514
B. Arbitration of Commercial Disputes 516
1. Soia Mentschikoff, *Commercial Arbitration*, 61 COLUM. L. REV. 846 (1961) 516

2. Comments and Questions 524
3. William L.D. Barrett, *Arbitration of a Complex Commercial Case: Practical Guidelines for Arbitrators and Counsel,* ARBITRATION J., December 1986, at 15 524

C. American Arbitration Association: Administered Arbitration 532
1. Comments and Questions 532
2. American Arbitration Association, Arbitration Rules for Commercial Disputes [with AAA Commentary] (1993) 532

D. CPR Institute for Dispute Resolution, CPR Non-Administered Arbitration Rules and Commentary (1995) 555

E. Non-Binding Arbitration 567
1. Lester Edelman et al., NON-BINDING ARBITRATION 1-5, 8-12 (U.S. Army Corps of Engineers 1990) (IWR Pamphlet 90-ADR-P-2) 567
2. Comments and Questions 572

F. Drafting of Provisions Related to Arbitration 572
1. Comments and Questions 572
2. CPR Institute for Dispute Resolution, Standard Arbitration Clauses (1995) 573
3. American Arbitration Association, Drafting Dispute Resolution Clauses: A Practical Guide (1993) 574
4. Tom Arnold, A VOCABULARY OF ALTERNATIVE DISPUTE RESOLUTION PROCEDURES, footnote 37 (1995) 591

CHAPTER 11: THE LAW OF ARBITRATION 597

A. Introduction 598

B. Early Anglo-American Arbitration Law 600
1. Comments and Questions 600
2. *Kulukundis Shipping Co., S/A v. Amtorg Trading Corp.,* 126 F.2d 978, 982-985 (2d Cir. 1942) (Judge Jerome Frank) 601
3. Soia Mentschikoff, *Commercial Arbitration,* 61 COLUM. L. REV. 846 (1961) 602
4. John R. Van Winkle, *An Analysis of the Arbitration Rule of the Indiana Rules of Alternative Dispute Resolution,* 27 IND. L. REV. 735 (1994) 603

C. The Federal Arbitration Act [United States Code Title 9] 604
1. Comments and Questions 604
2. The FAA [Unabridged] 605
   a. General Provisions 605
   b. Convention on the Recognition and Enforcement of Foreign Arbitral Awards [New York Convention] 609
   c. Inter-American Convention on International Commercial Arbitration [Panama Convention] 610
3. Scope of the Federal Arbitration Act 612
   a. *Allied-Bruce Terminix Companies, Inc. v. Dobson,* 115 S. Ct. 834 (1995) 612
   b. Comments and Questions 618

D. State Arbitration Legislation 619
1. Comments and Questions 619
2. The Uniform Arbitration Act [Unabridged] 620

3. John R. Van Winkle, *An Analysis of the Arbitration Rule of the Indiana Rules of Alternative Dispute Resolution,* 27 IND. L. REV. 735 (1994) 625
4. Comments and Questions 632
E. Who Determines Arbitrability, And by What Standard? 632
1. *AT&T Technologies, Inc. v. Communications Workers of America,* 475 U.S. 643 (1986) 632
2. Comments and Questions 636
3. *Shearson Lehman Hutton, Inc. v. Wagoner,* 944 F.2d 114 (2d Cir. 1991) 636
4. *First Options of Chicago v. Kaplan,* 115 S. Ct. 1920 (1995) 639
F. When Does Federal Law Preempt State Law? 642
1. *Perry v. Thomas,* 482 U.S. 483 (1987) 642
2. *In the matter of Smith Barney, Harris Upham & Co. v. Luckie,* 647 N.E.2d 1308 (N.Y. 1995) 645
3. Comments and Questions 649
4. *Mastrobuono v. Shearson Lehman Hutton, Inc.,* 115 S. Ct. 1212 (1995) 649
5. Comments and Questions 654
6. Preemption Under the Railway Labor Act: *Hawaiian Airlines, Inc. v. Norris,* 114 S. Ct. 2239 (1994) 654
G. Judicial Review of Remedies Ordered by an Arbitrator 657
1. Remedial Authority of Arbitrators Under New York Law [As Viewed by the New York Court of Appeals] 657
a. Why Focus on New York Law? 657
b. *In the Matter of the Arbitration between Stanley J. Staklinski and Pyramid Electric Co.,* 160 N.E.2d 78 (N.Y. 1959) 657
c. *In the Matter of the Arbitration between Grayson-Robinson Store Inc. and Iris Construction Corp.,* 8 N.Y.2d 133, 168 N.E.2d 377, 202 N.Y.S.2d 303 (1960) 659
d. Comments and Questions 662
e. *Garrity v. Stuart,* 353 N.E.2d 793 (1976) 662
f. Comments and Questions 665
g. *In the Matter of the Arbitration between SCM Corp. and Fisher Park Lane Co.,* 358 N.E.2d 1024 (N.Y. 1976) 666
2. Remedial Authority of Arbitrators in General 670
a. Comments and Questions 670
b. *In re Arbitration Between Tretina Printing, Inc. v. Fitzpatrick & Assocs., Inc.,* 640 A.2d 788 (N.J. 1994) 670
c. *Advanced Micro Devices, Inc. v. Intel Corp.,* 885 P.2d 994 (Cal.1994) 680
d. Comments and Questions 691
H. Mixture of Arbitrable and Nonarbitrable Claims 692
1. *Dean Witter Reynolds v. Byrd,* 470 U.S. 213 (1985) 692
2. *Volt Information Sciences, Inc. v. Stanford University,* 489 U.S. 468 (1989) 695
3. Comments and Questions 699
I. Arbitration of Antitrust Claims 699
1. *Mitsubishi Motors Corp. v. Soler Chrysler-Plymouth, Inc.,* 473 U.S. 614 (1985) 699

2. Comments and Questions 705
3. *Coors Brewing Co. v. Molson Breweries*, 51 F.3d 1511 (10th Cir. 1995) 705
4. Antitrust Arbitration in America 708
a. *Nghiem v. NEC Electronics, Inc.*, 25 F.3d 1437 (9th Cir. 1994) 708
b. *Kotam Electronics, Inc. v. JBL Consumer Products, Inc.*, 59 F.3d 1155 (11th Cir. 1995) 710
c. Comments and Questions 711
J. Predispute Agreements to Arbitrate Securities Claims 712
1. *Shearson/American Express, Inc. v. McMahon*, 482 U.S. 220 (1987) 712
2. Racketeering [RICO] Claims 718
3. *Rodriguez de Quijas v. Shearson/American Express, Inc.*, 490 U.S. 477 (1989) 718
4. Comments and Questions 722

CHAPTER 12: ARBITRATION APPLICATIONS 723
A. Introduction 724
B. Enforcement of Arbitration Clauses in Contracts Between Businesses and Their Consumer Customers: Banking Institutions 725
1. Comments and Questions 725
2. Mark E. Budnitz, *Arbitration of Disputes Between Consumers and Financial Institutions: A Serious Threat to Consumer Protection*, 10 OHIO ST. J. ON DISP. RESOL. 267 (1995) 725
3. Arbitration Provisions: Bank of America 737
4. Arbitration Provisions: Zions First National Bank 738
5. Comments and Questions 740
C. Arbitration of Employment Disputes 741
1. The Steelworkers Trilogy 741
2. Role of the Arbitrator in Labor Disputes 742
a. Comments and Questions 742
b. Lon L. Fuller, *Collective Bargaining and the Arbitrator*, 1963 WIS.L.REV. 3 742
3. Arbitration of Employment Discrimination Claims 756
a. *Alexander v. Gardner-Denver Co.*, 415 U.S. 36 (1974) 756
b. *Gilmer v. Interstate/Johnson Lane Corp.*, 500 U.S. 20 (1991) 760
c. Comments and Questions 766
d. Christine Godsil Cooper, *Where Are We Going With* Gilmer?—*Some Ruminations on the Arbitration of Discrimination Claims*, 11 ST. LOUIS U. PUB. L. REV. 302, 237-40 (1992) 766
e. Stephen L. Hayford & Michael J. Evers, *The Interaction Between the Employment-at-Will Doctrine and Employer-Employee Agreements to Arbitrate Statutory Fair Employment Practices Claims: Difficult Choices for At-Will Employers*, 73 N.C. L. REV. 443 (1995) 768
f. Comments and Questions 773
g. Michele M. Buese, *Contracting Employment Disputes Out of the Jury System: Analysis of the Implementation of Binding Arbitration*

in the Non-Union Workplace and Proposals to Reduce the Harsh Effects of a Non-Appealable Award, 22 PEPP. L. REV. 1485 (1995) 773
h. Comments and Questions 775
4. Use of ADR Procedures, Notably Arbitration, for Equal Employment Opportunity Claims 775
a. General Accounting Office, Health, Education, & Human Services Division, B-257171, July 5, 1995 775
b. Comments and Questions 781
D. Therapeutic Values of Arbitration 781
1. Comments and Questions 781
2. Roger I. Abrams, Frances E. Abrams & Dennis R. Nolan, *Arbitral Therapy*, 46 RUTGERS L. REV. 1751 (1994) 782
E. Arbitration in the Securities Industry 794
1. Comments and Questions 794
2. National Association of Securities Dealers, REPORT OF THE ARBITRATION POLICY TASKFORCE (1996) 794

PART V: ADDITIONAL ADR APPROACHES

CHAPTER 13: HYBRIDS AND OTHER ADR PROCEDURES 805
A. Introduction 805
B. A Taxonomy of ADR Procedures 806
1. Comments and Questions 806
2. Tom Arnold, A VOCABULARY OF ALTERNATIVE DISPUTE RESOLUTION PROCEDURES (1995) 806
C. Mediation and Arbitration Hybrids 816
1. Comments and Questions 816
2. Tom Arnold, A VOCABULARY OF ALTERNATIVE DISPUTE RESOLUTION PROCEDURES (1995) 816
D. Mini-Trial 820
1. Jethro K. Lieberman & James F. Henry, *Lessons From the Alternative Dispute Resolution Movement*, 53 U. CHI. L. REV. 424, 427-429 (1986) 820
2. Tom Arnold A VOCABULARY OF ALTERNATIVE DISPUTE RESOLUTION PROCEDURES (1995) 821
3. Lester Edelman et al., *The Mini-Trial* 1-6, 9-17 (U.S. Army Corps of Engineering 1989) (IWR Pamphlet 89-ADR-P-1) 823
4. CPR Institute for Dispute Resolution, CPR Minitrial Model Procedure and Commentary (1995) 827
E. Ombudsman 833
1. Tom Arnold, A VOCABULARY OF ALTERNATIVE DISPUTE RESOLUTION PROCEDURES (1995) 833
2. Mary B. Rowe, *Options, Functions, and Skills: What an Organizational Ombudsman Might Want to Know*, 11 NEGOTIATION J. 103 (1995) 834
3. Comments and Questions 843

CHAPTER 14: DISPUTE RESOLUTION BY ADMINISTRATIVE AGENCIES 845

A. Introduction..845
B. ADR Services Provided by Federal Agencies 846
1. Comments and Questions..846
2. William E. Simkin & Nicholas A. Fidandis, MEDIATION AND THE DYNAMICS OF COLLECTIVE BARGAINING 37-39, 195-207 (1986) 847
3. Comments and Questions..854
4. Reba Page & Wesley C. Jockisch, *The Corps of Engineers Board of Contract Appeals Use of Alternative Dispute Resolution,* 24 PUBLIC CONTRACT L.J. 453 (1995) 854
C. Adjudication: Judicial Review..860
1. *Johnson v. Robison,* 415 U.S. 361 (1974) 860
2. Comments and Questions..861
3. Access to the Federal Court System 861
a. *Walters v. National Association of Radiation Survivors,* 473 U.S. 305 (1985)..861
b. Jerry L. Mashaw, DUE PROCESS IN THE ADMINISTRATIVE STATE 264-267 (1985)..868
c. Lawyers and Judicial Review to the Rescue 869
d. *Thomas v. Union Carbide Agricultural Products Co.,* 473 U.S. 568 (1985)..869
e. Comments and Questions..872
D. Agency Adjudication as ADR: Public Benefits Cases 873
1. Comments and Questions..873
2. *Goldberg v. Kelly,* 397 U.S. 254 (1970)..873
3. Comments and Questions..876
4. *Richardson v. Perales,* 402 U.S. 389 (1971)..877
5. *Heckler v. Campbell,* 461 U.S. 458 (1983)..880
6. Comments and Questions..883
E. Agency-Mandated ADR 883
1. Comments and Questions..883
2. Harold H. Bruff, *Public Programs, Private Deciders; The Constitutionality of Arbitration in Federal Programs,* 67 TEX. L. REV. 441 (1989) 883
3. Stephen K. Huber, *Administrative Dispute Resolution Act of 1990* (1996)..890
4. Cynthia B. Dauber, *The Ties That Do Not Bind: Nonbinding Arbitration in Federal Administrative Agencies,* 9 ADMIN. L.J. AM. U. 165 (1995)..890
5. U.S. Department of Justice, Order No. 1160.1 (1995), SUBJECT: PROMOTING THE BROADER APPROPRIATE USE OF ALTERNATIVE DISPUTE RESOLUTION TECHNIQUES..892
F. Rulemaking..894
1. Stephen K. Huber, *The Negotiated Rulemaking Act of 1990* (1996)..894
2. David M. Pritzker, *The Blossoming of Reg-Neg,* NIDR News, August 1995, at 6..895

3. Comments and Questions 897
4. R. Shep Melnick, *Administrative Law and Bureaucratic Reality*, 44 ADMIN. L. REV. 245 (1992) 898

PART VI: ADR IN THE JUDICIAL SYSTEM

CHAPTER 15: COURT-ANNEXED ADR PROCEDURES 907
A. Introduction 908
B. Early Neutral Evaluation 908
1. Comments and Questions 908
2. Tom Arnold, A VOCABULARY OF ALTERNATIVE DISPUTE RESOLUTION PROCEDURES (1995) 909
3. Joshua D. Rosenberg & H. Jay Folberg, *Alternative Dispute Resolution: An Empirical Analysis*, 46 STAN. L. REV. 1487 (1994) 910
C. Summary Jury Trial 924
1. *Strandell v. Jackson County*, 838 F.2d 884 (7th Cir. 1988) 924
2. Comments and Questions 925
3. *Cincinnati Gas and Electric Co. v. General Electric Co.*, 854 F.2d 900 (6th Cir. 1988) 925
4. Neil Vidmar & Jeffrey Rice, *Jury Determined Settlements, and Summary Jury Trials*, 19 FLA. ST. U. L. REV. 89, 95-103 (1991) 928
5. Lucille M. Ponte, *Putting Mandatory Summary Jury Trial Back on the Docket: Recommendations on the Exercise of Judicial Authority*, 63 FORDHAM L. REV. 1069 (1995) 932
6. Comments and Questions 934
D. Court Annexed Arbitration 935
1. Lisa Bernstein, *Understanding the Limits of Court-Connected ADR: A Critique of Federal Court-Annexed Arbitration Programs*, 141 U. PA. L. REV. 2169, 2177-2186 (1993) 935
2. *Firelock, Inc. v. District Court*, 776 P.2d 1090 (Colo. 1989) (en banc) 937
3. Comments and Questions 945
4. *United States v. Joseph Gullo*, 672 F.Supp. 99 (W.D.N.Y. 1987) 945
E. Screening Panels: Medical Malpractice Claims 947
1. Comments and Questions 947
2. Jean A. Macchiaroli, *Medical Malpractice Screening Panels: Proposed Model Legislation to Cure Judicial Ills*, 58 GEO. WASH. L. REV. 181, 186-97, 239-60 (1990) 947
F. ADR in Appeals Courts: Appellate Mediation 961
1. Comments and Questions 961
2. Irving R. Kaufman, *Reform for A System in Crisis: Alternative Dispute Resolution in the Federal Courts*, 59 FORDHAM L. REV. 1 (1990) 962
3. Susan FitzGibbon, *Appellate Settlement Conference Programs: A Case Study*, 1993 J. DISPUTE RES. 57 (1993) 963

CHAPTER 16: COURT-ANNEXED ADR: ISSUES AND OPTIONS..........979
A. Introduction....................980
B. Constitutional Limitation on Compulsory Court-Annexed ADR....................980
1. Dwight Golann, *Making Alternative Dispute Resolution Mandatory: The Constitutional Issues,* 68 OR. L. REV. 487 (1989)....................980
2. Lucy V. Katz, *Compulsory Alternative Dispute Resolution and Voluntarism: Two-Headed Monster or Two Sides of the Coin?,* 1993 J. DISP. RESOL. 1, 22-31....................992
3. Comments and Questions....................995
C. Judicial Settlement Conference....................995
1. Succeeding in Settlement Conferences....................995
a. Comments and Questions....................995
b. Wayne D. Brazil, *Effective Lawyering in Judicially Hosted Settlement Conferences,* 1988 J. DISP. RESOL. 1, 22-31....................995
2. In Person Appearance of Private Parties....................1005
a. *G. Heileman Brewing Co., Inc. v. Joseph Oat Corp.,* 871 F.2d 648 (7th Cir. 1989) (en banc)....................1005
b. Rule 16, Federal Rules of Civil Procedure (1993 Version)....................1012
c. Comments and Questions....................1013
3. Settlement Authority of Government Representatives....................1014
a. *In re Stone,* 986 F.2d 898 (5th Cir. 1993)....................1014
b. Comments and Questions....................1017
D. Is There a Duty of Good Faith Participation in Mandatory ADR?....................1019
1. *Decker v. Lindsay,* 824 S.W.2d 247 (Tex. Civ. App. 1992)....................1019
2. Edward F. Sherman, *Court-Mandated Alternative Dispute Resolution: What Form of Participation Should be Required?,* 46 SMU L. REV. 2079 (1993)....................1022
3. Comments and Questions....................1034
E. Conflicts Between State and Federal ADR Policies....................1035
1. Comments and Questions....................1035
2. *Woods v. Holy Cross Hospital,* 591 F.2d 1164 (5th Cir. 1979)....................1036
3. Comments and Questions....................1041
4. Lucy V. Katz, *Compulsory Alternative Dispute Resolution and Voluntarism: Two-Headed Monster or Two Sides of the Coin?,* 1993 J. DISP. RESOL. 1....................1041
5. Dwight Golann, *Making Alternative Dispute Resolution Mandatory: The Constitutional Issues,* 68 OR. LAW REV. 487 (1989)....................1042

CHAPTER 17: SETTLEMENT LAW AND POLICY....................1045
A. Introduction....................1046
B. The Great Settlement Debate....................1046
1. Owen M. Fiss, *Against Settlement,* 93 YALE L.J. 1073 (1984)....................1046
2. Comments and Questions....................1053
3. Andrew W. McThenia & Thomas L. Shaffer, *For Reconciliation,* 94 YALE L.J. 1660 (1985)....................1054

4. Owen M. Fiss, *Out of Eden* 94 YALE L.J. 1669 (1985) 1057
5. Jethro K. Lieberman & James F. Henry, *Lessons From the Alternative Dispute Resolution Movement,* 53 U. CHI. L. REV. 424, 432-435 (1986) 1060
6. Marc Galanter & Mia Cahill, *"Most Cases Settle": Judicial Promotion and Regulation of Settlement,* 46 STAN. L. REV. 1339 (1994) 1061

C. Enforcement of Proffered Settlement Agreements 1064
1. Comments and Questions 1064
2. *Ames v. Ames,* 860 S.W.2d 590 (Tex. Civ. App. 1993) 1065
3. *Cary v. Cary,* 894 S.W.2d 111 (Tex. Civ. App. 1995) 1066
4. *Padilla v. LaFrance,* 907 S.W. 2d 454 (Tex. 1995) 1068
5. Comments and Questions 1072
6. Texas Family Code Amendment 1072
7. Comments and Questions 1073

D. Discovery of ADR and Settlement Communications 1073
1. Comments and Questions 1073
2. *National Labor Relations Board v. Macaluso,* 618 F.2d 51 (9th Cir. 1980) 1074
3. Eric D. Green, *A. Heretical View of the Mediation Privilege,* 2 OHIO ST. J. ON DISP. RESOL. 1 (1986) 1077
4. Wayne D. Brazil, *Protecting the Confidentiality of Settlement Negotiations,* 39 HASTINGS L.J. 955 (1988) 1080
5. Kristina M. Kerwin, *"The Discoverability of Settlement and ADR Communications: Federal Rule of Evidence 408 and Beyond,* 12 REV. LITIG. 665 (1993) 1089

E. ADR, Confidentiality, and Federal Administrative Law 1091
1. Administrative Conference of the United States, Encouraging Settlements by Protecting Mediator Confidentiality, Recommendation 88-11, 1 CFR § 305.88-11 (1988) 1091
2. Comments and Questions 1095
3. Administrative Dispute Resolution Act of 1990, 5 USC §§ 571, 574 1095
4. Comments and Questions 1097

F. Multiple Forums, Multiple Parties, Nonparties 1097
1. Comments and Questions 1097
2. *Flynn v. Gorton,* 255 Cal. Rptr. 768 (Cal. App. 1989) 1098
3. *Haworth, Inc. v. Steelcase, Inc.,* 12 F.3d 1090 (Fed. Cir. 1994) 1100

CHAPTER 18: ADR AND ADJUDICATION: POLICY IMPLICATIONS 1105

A. Introduction 1106

B. Courts in Crisis: Is ADR a Solution? 1106
1. Irving R. Kaufman, *Reform for A System in Crisis: Alternative Dispute Resolution in the Federal Courts,* 59 FORDHAM L. REV. 1 (1990) 1106
2. Comments and Questions 1108
3. Donna Stienstra & Thomas E. Willging, ALTERNATIVES TO LITIGATION: DO THEY HAVE A PLACE IN THE FEDERAL COURTS (Federal Judicial Center 1995) 1109

C. Court Bureaucracy, Civil Cases, and ADR 1112
1. Patrick E. Longan, *Bureaucratic Justice Meets ADR: The Emerging Role For Magistrates as Mediators*, 73 NEB. L. REV. 712 (1994) .. 1112
2. Comments and Questions 1122
D. Cooptation of ADR Into the Legal System 1123
1. Carrie Menkel-Meadow, *Pursuing Settlement in an Adversary Culture: A Tale of Innovation Co-opted or "The Law of ADR,"* 19 FLA. ST. U. L. REV. 1, 1-5, 39-45 (1991) 1123
2. Comments and Questions 1128
E. Too Much ADR, Too Little Adjucation? 1128
1. Judith Resnik, *Many Doors? Closing Doors? Alternative Dispute Resolution and Adjudication,* 10 OHIO ST. J. ON DISP. RESOL. 211 (1995) 1128
2. Comments and Questions 1137

PART VII: DISPUTE RESOLUTION PROFESSIONALS

CHAPTER 19: PROFESSIONAL QUALIFICATIONS, PROFESSIONAL LIABILITY 1141
A. Introduction 1141
B. Should Government Regulate Dispute Resolution Professionals? 1142
1. Typology of Approaches to Professional Regulation 1142
a. Registration 1142
b. Certification 1143
c. Licensure 1143
2. Walter Gellhorn, *The Abuse of Occupational Licensure,* 44 U. CHI. L. REV. 6 (1976) 1143
3. Comments and Questions 1150
4. Nancy H. Rogers & Craig A. McEwen, MEDIATION LAW, POLICY & PRACTICE §§ 11:04 to 11:07 (2d ed 1994) 1151
5. Comments and Questions 1153
C. Qualifications for Neutrals 1153
1. Alison Taylor, *The Four Foundations of Family Mediation: Implications for Training and Ceritification,* 12 MEDIATION QUARTERLY 77 (1994) 1153
2. Barbara Diamond, *ADR Programs in Other States* (July 12, 1994) (Memo to the Structure and Finance Subcommittee, State Bar of Massachusetts Standing Committee on Dispute Resolution) 1162
3. National Association of Securities Dealers, REPORT OF THE ARBITRATION POLICY TASKFORCE 88-112 (1996) 1165
D. Liability for Professional Negligence: Malpractice 1175
1. Nancy H. Rogers & Craig A. McEwen, MEDIATION LAW, POLICY & PRACTICE § 11.03 (2d ed. 1994) 1175
2. Comments and Questions 1177
E. Immunity from Suit by Association with Judicial Process 1177
1. *Butz v. Economou,* 438 U.S. 478 (1978) 1177

2. *Davis v. Scherer,* 468 U.S. 183 (1984) 1181
3. Comments and Questions 1181
4. *Howard v. Drapkin,* 271 Cal. Rptr. 893 (Cal. App. 1990) 1182
5. *Wagshal v. Foster,* 28 F.3d 1249 (D.C. Cir. 1994), cert. denied, 115 S. Ct. 1314 (1995) 1189
6. Nancy H. Rogers & Craig A. McEwen, MEDIATION LAW, POLICY & PRACTICE § 11.03, Mediator Immunity (2d ed. 1994) 1192

CHAPTER 20: PROFESSIONAL RESPONSIBILITY: ETHICAL ISSUES IN ADR 1195

A. Introduction 1196
B. Overview of Professional Responsibility Issues 1196
1. Comments and Questions 1196
2. Standards for All Neutrals 1196
a. Ethical Standards of Professional Conduct for Members of the Society of Professionals in Dispute Resolution [SPIDR] (1987) 1196
b. Draft Ethical Standards for Neutrals Providing ADR Services to State Trial Courts in Massachusetts (1995) 1199
3. Standards for Mediators 1205
a. AAA/ABA/SPIDR, STANDARDS OF CONDUCT FOR MEDIATORS (1994) 1205
b. Robert B. Moberly, *Ethical Standards For Court-Appointed Mediators and Florida's Mandatory Mediation Experiment,* 21 FLA. ST. U. L. REV. 701 (1994) 1208
c. National Association of Social Workers, STANDARDS OF PRACTICE FOR SOCIAL WORK MEDIATORS 1213
4. Standards for Arbitrators 1216
a. AAA/ABA, THE CODE OF ETHICS FOR ARBITRATORS IN COMMERCIAL DISPUTES 1216
b. Nonneutral Neutrals: Party-Appointed Arbitrators 1220
C. Puffing, Deception and Lying in Negotiations 1220
1. James J. White, *Machiavelli and the Bar: Ethical Limitations on Lying in Negotiation,* 1980 AMERICAN BAR FOUNDATION RESEARCH J. 921 1220
2. Walter W. Steele, *Deceptive Negotiating and High-Tones Morality,* 39 VAND. L. REV. 1387 (1986) 1228
3. Comments and Questions 1234
D. Confidentiality 1234
1. Comments and Questions 1234
2. Kevin Gibson, *Confidentiality in Mediation: A Moral Reassessment,* 1992 J. DISP. RESOL. 25 1235
E. Seeking Business: Advertising and Solicitation 1240
1. Comments and Questions 1240
2. Richard C. Hile *Rules Regulating Advertisements and Written Solicitation Communications: An Overview,* 58 TEXAS BAR JOURNAL 595 (1995) 1241
F. Professional Ethics and the Neutral Lawyer 1243
1. Comments and Questions 1243

2. Leonard L. Riskin, *Toward New Standards for the Neutral Lawyer in Mediation,* 26 ARIZ. L. REV. 329 (1984) 1244
3. Comments and Questions 1254

CHAPTER 21: PLANNING FOR AND AVOIDING DISPUTES: SYSTEMS DESIGN 1255

A. Introduction 1256
B. Main Elements of an ADR System Design 1257
1. E. Wendy Trachte-Huber, ADR SYSTEM DESIGN: THE PRE-LITIGATION OPTION (THE ATTORNEY AS CONSULTANT) (1993) 1257
2. Cathy A. Costantino & Christina Sickles Merchant, DESIGNING CONFLICT MANAGEMENT SYSTEMS — A GUIDE TO CREATING PRODUCTIVE AND HEALTHY ORGANIZATIONS 19-32, 117-33 (1995) 1259
3. William R. Potapchuk et.al., *Getting to the Table: A Guide for Senior Managers* (1990), U.S. Army Corps of Engineers Working Paper No. 3 [IWR Working Paper 90-ADR-WP-3], Appendix A 1267
4. Comments and Questions 1271
C. Total Quality Management (TQM) 1272
1. Comments and Questions 1272
2. E. Wendy Trachte-Huber, ADR SYSTEM DESIGN: THE PRE-LITIGATION OPTION (THE ATTORNEY AS CONSULTANT) (1993) 1272
D. Labor-Management Relationships 1273
1. Comments and Questions 1273
2. Executive Order No. 12,871 (October 1, 1993) (President Clinton), 58 Fed. Reg. 52,201 (1993) 1273
3. U.S. Army Corps. Of Engineers, *Partnership Councils: Building Successful Labor-Management Relationships,* IWR Working Paper 94-ADR-WP-5 (1994) 1275
4. William L. Bedman, *From Litigation to ADR: Brown & Root's Experience,* DISPUTE RES.J., VOL. 50, OCT.-DEC.1995, AT 8 1280
5. Mobility of Lawyers and Other Professionals 1286
E. Partnering 1286
1. Tom Arnold, A VOCABULARY OF ALTERNATIVE DISPUTE RESOLUTION PROCEDURES (1995) 1286
2. Lester Edelman et.al., *Partnering* 1-5, 7-10 17-20 (U.S. Army Corps of Engineering 1991) (IWR Pamphlet 91-ADR-P-4) 1287
3. Partnering Experiences: Oliver Lock and Dam Replacement 1294

APPENDIX: EXERCISES & PROBLEMS & ROLE PLAYS

INDEX

PREFACE

This book can be used for a variety of courses including Introduction to ADR, Negotiation, Mediation, and Arbitration. The materials are designed for use in graduate level courses in law schools, business schools, and the social sciences. Our thoughts for the parts of these materials to focus on for each type of course are contained in the accompanying Teacher's Manual.

Some of the cases and materials included in our book are heavily edited, but lengthy excerpts from many are used. Most footnotes from articles and cases, and citations within the text of cases, are omitted without specific notation. Footnote numbers are retained from the original material. Omissions from text are indicated by ellipses.

These materials include numerous cases compared to other ADR materials, but few cases compared to a typical law school course (and also law courses taught elsewhere in a university setting). The majority of the cases are in the materials on arbitration. For teachers who want to undertake serious case law analysis, two lines of arbitration cases are presented. One is a group of cases decided by the New York Court of Appeals, which presents a state law perspective, and the other is composed of (mostly) recent U.S. Supreme Court decisions. In the context of negotiation, mediation, and hybrid ADR procedures, there is less case law, but that fact means these decisions are of particular importance. Important cases, and debates about major ADR issues, are presented at length to allow for detailed class discussion.

We decided against providing a bibliography (even though we both require one in student papers). Written work about ADR and related topics is far too extensive to make the inclusion of a bibliography a worthwhile endeavor. This point is illustrated by Charles J. Coleman & Theodora T. Haynes, LABOR ARBITRATION: AN ANNOTATED BIBLIOGRAPHY (1994), a 269 page work that covers over 1,300 books and articles about labor arbitration. An entire issue of the Ohio State Journal of Dispute Resolution is given over to a bibliography [Volume 9, at pages 433-619 (1994)], which in turn is an update of a 1989 bibliography issue. The full text of the cases and articles presented in the pages that follow will provide the interested reader with a wealth of citations to the relevant literature.

Many of the authors whose works appear in this book have strong views on issues, and no effort is made to hide them. Indeed, many of the pieces were selected precisely because they represent diverse points of view. We have exercised "best efforts" to present works that are serious and accurate, but the reader must also remember that often authors are advocates for particular positions.

The intended audience for this book is graduate students, but one of the authors is using them for an upper division college course at Rice University. The primary focus, reflecting our teaching background, is law and business students but our classes have included students from social work, psychology, political science, economics, and sociology. Other subject areas also recognize the importance and value of ADR. At the University of Houston, great interest in ADR has come from the Hilton College of Hotel & Restaurant Management. Given the need in the hospitality industry to avoid disputes with customers and employees (hotels and restaurants are staff intensive operations), and rapid adjustment of those that do arise, this interest makes sense. Dispute resolution is increasingly seen as an integral part of a sound education for middle school and high school students, as well as for school administrators, so colleges of education have evinced a serious interest in ADR.

Senior administrators from all types of organizations (large corporations, small businesses, universities, hospitals, family courts) and with every imaginable educational background, have taken the 40 hour Mediation training course at the A.A. White Dispute Resolution Institute. Our experience has been that the mixture of persons from diverse backgrounds and organizations improves the teaching process and course quality. Particularly with adult students, much is learned from other students rather than the teacher. Indeed, an important aspect of teaching adults is to provide an environment that draws on the experience of the students and facilitates learning from fellow students.

Graduate students from different disciplines can usefully be placed together in a single course. The benefits from the different knowledge bases and outlooks that the students bring to the course far exceed the problems. We have found the experience to be a refreshing challenge, that is far more enervating than the conveying of doctrine and examination of narrow issues that occupies much graduate law and business study. [The "mail box rules" that are a staple of contracts and business law courses come immediately to mind.] Sadly, constraints of university structure, subject disciplines, and scheduling make it almost impossible to teach a course that attracts students from several graduate disciplines. [At the University of Houston, it is possible — not easy, but possible — to teach joint business and law courses only because the buildings that house the two colleges are a mere 100 yards apart.]

This book is divided into seven parts, each consisting of three chapters. After a brief description of the contents, we will briefly discuss using the for law school, business school, and social science courses. We have many additional ideas for teaching mixed groups of students, which we will be glad to share with anyone who is interested. We are just an E-mail away.

Part I provides a general introduction to, and overview of, dispute resolution. In this part we offer an introduction to dispute resolution in general, and cover basic material that is of importance in negotiation, and to the many forms of dispute settlement. Chapter One considers the Alternative Dispute Resolution movement, and asks to what ADR is an alternative. We also seek to make it clear to students that ADR is old as well as new, and that alternatives to litigation played a central role in America before the United States was a nation.

Communications is the topic of Chapter Two. Outside the natural sciences and engineering, few if any graduate students, as a group, have less experience with gathering information from other human beings than law students. This chapter is designed to introduce students to communications, with a bit of theory, some practical "how to" tips, and exercises that involve actual information gathering. This material may seem superficial to those with a background in psychology, communications, and similar topics. Chapter Three is titled Theoretical and Nonlaw Approaches to Disputing. It presents a theoretical (but not mathematical) approach to disputing behavior, largely from the social sciences.

Parts II, III, and IV are devoted to the three basic ADR processes: negotiation, mediation, and arbitration. Each part consists of three chapters. The first is a process chapter that introduces the subject, and provides specifics about how the process actually works. While these materials have a heavy theoretical component, they are designed for use by persons who will actually participate in negotiation, mediation, and (to a lesser extent) arbitration. Participatory exercises are provided in the Appendix. Confidential facts for different parties, and additional exercises, are found in the Teacher's Manual.

The third chapter of each part presents applications. The objective is to provide context and deepen understanding. These materials can be discussed at length, or assigned for reading with little class consideration. [We operate on the assumption that graduate students are capable of reading and understanding even complicated written materials, and of taking the initiative to ask questions when something is not understood.]

The middle chapter in each of these three parts is devoted to in-depth consideration of a particular aspect of negotiation, mediation, and arbitration. The subjects are, respectively:

1. Trans-national and cross-cultural negotiation;
2. Family mediation; and
3. The law of arbitration.

Part V provides an introduction to ADR processes beyond the "big three" of arbitration, mediation, and negotiation. Many are special or hybrid processes developed for particular classes of problems. Court annexed processes are introduced here, and then considered at length in Part VI. These additional processes are the subject of Chapter 13.

The subject of Chapter 14 is administrative agencies (mainly federal). This chapter is based on the perhaps controversial premise that the processing of disputes by administrative agencies, both through adjudication and rulemaking, is itself an important form of ADR. [Consider this single fact: each year the number of contested disability claims adjudicated by the Social Security Administration is larger than the number of cases decided by the entire federal court system.] Use of the ADR procedures already discussed by administrative agencies is also considered in depth, because the federal government has been a leader in the innovative (and conventional) use of ADR.

Part VI consists of four chapters that consider the use of ADR in the judicial system. Chapter 15 provides an in-depth consideration of the most important court-annexed ADR procedures:

1. Early Neutral Evaluation;
2. Summary Jury Trial;
3. Court-Annexed Arbitration;
4. Medical Malpractice Screening Panels; and
5. Appellate Mediation.

Chapter 16 addresses policy questions associated with compulsory participation in court-annexed ADR, including the following:

1. Constitutional limits on court-ordered ADR;
2. Judicial settlement conferences, notably the settlement authority of private parties and government representatives;
3. Good faith participation in mandatory ADR; and
4. Conflicts between federal and state ADR policy.

Chapter 17 deals with settlement law and policy. This topic is of enormous importance because, as everyone knows, most cases settle (and most disputes settle before ever becoming cases). We begin with a well-known essay by Owen Fiss, "Against Settlement," and some of the responses it has engendered. The remainder of the chapter is devoted to legal issues regarding settlement, such as:

1. Enforcement of purported settlement agreements;
2. Discovery of ADR and settlement communications;
3. Confidentiality in administrative proceedings; and
4. Problems due to multiple forums or multiple parties.

Chapter 18 considers the policy implications of the growing use of ADR by courts, particularly the federal courts.

Part VII is titled Dispute Resolution Professionals. The focus here shifts from ADR processes to the persons who implement them. Chapter 19 examines questions associated with professional qualifications, including the following:

1. Should government establish (end enforce) minimum standards for dispute resolution professionals?
2. If the answer to the previous question is yes, what sort of standards are appropriate?
3. What should be the consequences of failing to comply with government established (professional liability)?

Also considered are issues related to potential legal liability of dispute resolution professionals.

Chapter 20 covers ethical issues in ADR, both in the general sense of ethical behavior, and the specific sense of compliance with standards in professional codes of conduct. Several ethical codes adopted by private organizations are presented for students to consider and compare. Particular attention is given to two problem situations: deception/puffing/lying in negotiations, and confidentiality of ADR processes (and related disclosures).

Chapter 21 is devoted to Systems Design, which is planning at an organizational level for the avoidance of disputes, and for dealing with disputes that do arise. Of course, the prevention and resolution of disputes is a central theme throughout the book; the focus here is doing so in a systematic manner for an entire organization. Particular attention is given to the labor-management and construction settings (partnering), where the use of sophisticated pre-dispute arrangements is a common practice.

The Appendix presents exercises, problems, and role plays, along with some suggestions for their use. Further guidance on the use of this material, confidential facts for participants, and additional "hands on" exercises and problems are found in the manual for teachers that accompanies this book.

ACKNOWLEDGEMENTS

This book would not exist without the extraordinary assistance of three persons at the University of Houston: Robyn Pietsch, Harriet Richman, and Beverly Ward. Our daughter Jennifer, a trained middle school peer mediator, provided much greater assistance than could be expected from someone of her tender years. Several leaders in the ADR community also are personal friends of one or both of the authors: Judge Nancy Atlas, Tom Arnold, Dick Buckley, Ambassador Pru Bushnell, Frank Evans, Eric Galton, several Steve Goldbergs, Nat Gozansky, Kim Kovach, Randy Lowry, Craig McEwen, Judge Margaret Mirabal, Sharon Press, Alan Rau, Len Riskin, Nancy Rogers, Frank Sander, Ed Sherman, Ruby Sondock, Charles Wiggins, and Alvin Zimmerman. We also wish to acknowledge our recently deceased friend and colleague, Maurice Rosenberg. We are grateful to our many colleagues and students at the University of Houston colleges of law and business, who have contributed so greatly to our education over the years.

We are indebted to the authors whose articles are excerpted here. In many instances, we do not know the authors except by the excellence of their writings. In the process of producing this book, the authors have read many thousands of pages of materials related to ADR. On balance, we were struck by the high quality of this work, and many excellent works had to be omitted due to lack of space.

Much assistance was provided by the good people at Anderson Publishing particularly our editor, Sean Caldwell. We are in the debt of all the persons mentioned above, and many others too, but of course we alone are responsible for any errors and omissions.

The materials by other writers used in this book are more oriented to law than the authors wanted, because book publishers generally refused permission to reprint excerpts without payment of high (per page) charges (if they deigned to respond at all). This response perhaps was to be expected from commercial publishers, but we did anticipate a more favorable reception from academic presses. Social science journals also required payments, but less than for books. By contrast, law reviews gave permission to reprint articles (to the extent they held the copyright) in every instance. Obtaining permissions from individual authors who hold copyrights to law review articles required additional effort, but these permissions also were forthcoming in every instance.

Our quest for permissions produced an occasional irony. As background on the topic of professional licensure, we planned to use two pieces: a Chapter from CAPITALISM AND FREEDOM by the distinguished economist Milton Friedman, and an article by Walter Gellhorn. Both were published by the University of Chicago. The same person signed letters on behalf of the University granting permission to use the Gellhorn piece without charge, but offering use of the Friedman piece only upon payment of $500 (and then only upon obtaining permission from the author). As a result, we used excerpts from Gellhorn but not Friedman.

Few observations are truly original, and most of what one knows represents the ideas of others, or at least is based on what one hears and reads. We cannot do better than to borrow from Rudyard Kipling, who limned the classic acknowledgement of obligations to others.

When 'Omer Smote 'is Bloomin Lyre

When 'Omer smote 'is bloomin lyre,
He'd 'heard men sing by land an' sea;
An' what he though 'e might require,
'E went an' took — the same as me!

The market girls an' fisherman,
The shepards an' the sailors too,
They 'eard old songs turn up again,
But kept it quiet — same as you!

They knew 'e stole; 'e knew they knowed.
They didn't tell, nor make a fuss,
But winked at 'Omer down the road,
An' 'e winked back — the same as us!

Strikingly, Kipling chose this poem, rather than his much more famous Recessional, as the final piece in his collected poems.

TABLE OF CASES

Advanced Micro Devices v. Intel, 680
Alexander v. Gardner-Denver Co., 756
Allied-Bruce Terminex Companies v. Dobson, 612
Aluminum Company of America v. Essex Group, 1257
Ames v. Ames, 1065
AT&T Technologies v. Communications Workers, 632
Bankers Life & Casualty v. Crenshaw, 989
Bernhardt v. Polygraph Co. of America, 1042
Butz v. Economou, 1177
Capital Traction v. Hof, 982
Cary v. Cary, 1066
Cincinnati Gas & Electric v. General Electric, 925
Colgrove v. Battin, 933
Commodity Futures Trading Comm. v. Schor, 887
Coors Brewing v. Molson Breweries, 705
Davis v. Scherer, 1181
Dean Witter Reynolds v. Byrd, 692
Decker v. Lindsay, 1019, 1033
Erie Railroad v. Tompkins, 957, 1035, 1036
Firelock, Inc. v. District Court, 937
First Option of Chicago v. Kaplan, 639
Flynn v. Gorton, 1098
Frigaliment Importing Co. v. B.N.S. Int'l Sales Co., 68
G. Heileman Brewing v. Joseph Oat Corp., 936, 1005
Garrity v. Stuart, 662
Gilmer v. Interstate/Johnson Lane Corp., 760
Goldberg v. Kelly, 868, 873
Goldfarb v. Virginia State Bar, 1147
Grayson-Robinson v. Iris Construction, 659
Hawaiian Airlines, Inc. v. Norris, 654
Haworth, Inc. v. Steelcase, Inc. 1100
Heckler v. Campbell, 880
Howard v. Drabkin, 1182
In re Stone, 1014
Jacobellis v. Ohio, 1035
Jarndyce v. Jarndyce, 691
Johnson v. Robison, 860
Kotam Electronics v. JBL Consumer Products, 710
Kulukundis Shipping Co. v. Amtorg Trading, 601
Lange v. Marshall, 1175
Mastrobuono v. Shearson Lehman Hutton, Inc., 649
Mathews v. Eldridge, 876

Meyer Goldberg Inc. v. Fisher Foods, Inc., 1101
Mitsubishi Motors v. Solar Chrysler-Plymouth, 699
National Labor Relations Board v. Macaluso, 1074
Ngiem v. NEC Electronics, 708
Padilla v. LaFrance, 1068
Parker v. Brown, 1147
Perry v. Thomas, 642
Pierson v. Post, 3
Richardson v. Perales, 877
Rodriguez de Quijas v. Shearson/American Express, 718
San Juan v. American Board of Psychiatry, 712
SCM Corp. v. Fisher Park Lane Co., 666
Shearson v. Wagoner, 636
Shearson/American Express v. McMahon, 712
Silberg v. Anderson, 1184
Smith Barney v. Luckie, 645
Staklinski v. Pyramid Electric Co., 657
Steelworkers Trilogy, 741
(In re) Stone, 1014
Strandell v. Jackson, 924, 1032
Tarasoff v. Regents, 1235
Thomas v. Union Carbide, 869, 886, 984
Tretina Printing v. Fitzpatrick & Assoc., 670
United States v. Joseph Gullo, 945
United Steelworkers Trilogy, 741
Volt Information Services v. Stanford, 695
Wagshal v. Foster, 1189
Walters v. Nat'l Ass'n of Radiation Survivors, 861, 986
Wilko v. Swan, 714, 721, 1131
Woods v. Holy Cross Hospital, 1036

Part I

Dispute Resolution: General Considerations

Chapter 1

An Overview of Dispute Resolution

CASE STUDY

(Adapted from *Pierson v. Post*, (1805))

Lodowick Post was a hunter. Mr. Post enjoyed participating in fox hunts, and owned hunting dogs trained for these events. It seems that one day Mr. Post was fox hunting on public land when he and his dogs came upon a wild fox. Mr. Post, in a wild and desperate attempt to kill the fleeing fox, took aim and fired his rifle. The shot hit the fox, although the blow was not fatal—the fox continued to run.

Mr. Pierson had been watching Post's hunt from a distance. As luck would have it, the fox, fleeing from Mr. Post, came near Mr. Pierson. With full knowledge of Post's pursuit, Mr. Pierson killed the fox and made off with the carcass. Post saw Pierson carry off "his" fox, and brought suit against him for the value of the fox. Post claimed that he had acquired a right to the animal by his act of pursuit.

[Legal History: The trial court awarded Post the value of the fox. However, the New York Supreme Court did not agree. A majority of the court held that Post had no cognizable claim because mere pursuit of a wild animal did not amount to "occupancy." The court stated that to hold otherwise "would prove a fertile source of quarrels and litigation." The court went on to hold that it is necessary to bring the animal within one's possession or control in order to acquire a right to the animal.]

A. Introduction

This chapter presents an overview of the multiple ways that disputes arise and are resolved. Since the central focus of this book is alternative dispute resolution (ADR), it is necessary to address the question, alternative to what? A large part of the answer is judicial trials, but this approach is both over-inclusive and under-inclusive. Sections C and D address the scope of ADR and the alternative to what question. The central options, moving from the least to the most formal, are: negotiation, mediation and arbitration. There also are an assortment of processes that are variants or hybrids of the main approaches, often with fancy names like ombudsperson and summary jury trial. A more detailed array of the dispute settlement options is presented in section B, but discussion of the various processes is reserved for subsequent chapters.

Today ADR is often considered as a species of modern reform agenda, whose origin is commonly traced to the Pound Conference in 1976. While the expanded use of ADR since 1976 has indeed been impressive, resort to ADR has a long history in America. Earlier ADR developments are mentioned in many places in this book. In the present chapter, we limit ourselves to an article about ADR in Connecticut before the Revolutionary War.

ADR is widely thought and spoken of as a movement and a cause to be promoted. The existence of a common classification does not mean that participants in the ADR movement agree on what it is, where it is going, or how it should evolve. Indeed, some of the most acrimonious disputes are between insiders who want to shape the contours and direction of the movement. Examination of these debates must await an introduction to the basics of ADR, which is the purpose of this Chapter.

B. The Dispute Settlement Continuum

1. Chart adapted from E. Wendy Trachte, Negotiation: Strategies for Law & Business 9 (1994)*

There is a broad variety of responses to problems or disputes, that can be arrayed along a continuum from the least to the most intrusive, from voluntary to involuntary, and from non-binding to binding. [The listing below does not fully take account of all three factors.] This listing is offered only as an introductory aid for readers, and the placement of various options should be regarded as an approximation.

DISPUTE RESOLUTION CONTINUUM

Default Position: Conflict Avoidance

—DIRECT COMMUNICATION—

Discussion Between Principals

Discussion Through Agents

Negotiation

—INTERVENTION BY THIRD PARTY—

Ombudsman

Conciliation

Mediation

Moderated Settlement Conference

Private Judging

Non-Binding Arbitration

*Reprinted with permission.

Early Neutral Evaluation

Mini-Trial

Summary Jury Trial

—BINDING PROCESSES—

Administrative Action/Hearing

Binding Arbitration

Litigation

—EXTRA-LEGAL PROCESSES—

Non-Violent Direct Action

Violence/War

2. Comments and Questions

a. These processes (and others as well) will be discussed at length later in this book. Also considered will be hybrids that combine features of various ADR processes. Indeed, one of the advantages of ADR is that dispute resolution processes can be custom designed to fit particular situations and needs.

b. The various dispute resolution options considered in this course are dealt with largely on an instrumental basis, with much attention given to the advantages and disadvantages of various processes. You should not, however, lose sight of the broader implications for a society of choices about disputes and disputing.

> The varieties of dispute settlement, and the socially sanctioned choices in any culture, communicate the ideals people cherish, their perceptions of themselves, and the quality of their relationships with others. They indicate whether people wish to avoid or encourage conflict, suppress it, or resolve it amicably. Ultimately the most basic values of society are revealed in its dispute-settlement procedures. Although every society provides institutions for dispute settlement, by no means are these necessarily, or exclusively, legal institutions. Conceptions of the role of law change, and assessments of the advantages and disadvantages of submitting disputes to its processes not only shift, but exist in perpetual tension.

Jerold Auerbach, JUSTICE WITHOUT LAW 1 (1981).

C. The Modern ADR Movement: Alternative to What?

1. Comments and Questions

a. ADR is not simply a set of options; there is a "movement," with believers in the cause and zealous advocates. There also is a body of literature and some specialized vocabulary. The modern ADR movement is commonly dated from the Pound Conference sponsored by the American Bar Association in 1976, the bi-centennial of the Declaration of Independence. Jerold Auerbach, JUSTICE WITHOUT LAW? 123-24 (1981). The conference was named after Dean Roscoe Pound in recognition of the 70th anniversary of his famous speech to the ABA: "The Causes of Popular Dissatisfaction with the Administration of Justice." 29 A.B.A. 295 (1906).

b. Professor Laura Nader also dates the modern ADR movement to the Pound Conference. *See* Chapter 3, section F. As long as one recognizes the artificiality of tracing the origin of a movement to a particular event or point in time, dating the modern ADR movement from the Pound Conference is convenient and useful.

c. Reference is made to the "modern" ADR movement, because ADR has a long and varied past in America. *See generally* Jerold Auerbach, JUSTICE WITHOUT LAW? (1981). See also the Mann article in section F of this Chapter. The early history of arbitration is discussed at Chapter 11, section B.

d. The implicit answer to the "alternative to what?" question is alternative to formal legal process, but that response is both overinclusive and underinclusive. Indeed the very question is grounded in a legal perspective. An anthropologist would say that if the topic is dealing with disputes, formal law and courts is merely one of the alternatives. *See* Sally Merry, in Chapter 3, section F. How would you respond to the "alternative to what" question? You should revisit this question after you have learned more about ADR processes.

e. In the next piece William Twining considers the contents of ADR, and seeks to place it in a jurisprudential context. Twining is a distinguished British law professor, and a close observer of the American legal scene. Among his numerous legal publications is a biography of Karl Llewellyn. Another part of this article is reprinted in Chapter 3, section F.

2. William Twining, *Alternatives to What: Theories of Litigation, Procedure and Dispute Settlement in Anglo-American Jurispurdence: Some Neglected Classics*, 56 MODERN L. REV. 380, 380-383 (1993)*

Concern with different institutions and methods of dispute settlement has a long history. But the rapid growth in lawyers' interest in "alternative dispute resolution" (ADR) is widely perceived to have gathered momentum in the late 1960s in the United States. [Since then] . . . there has indeed been a remarkable growth in the "ADR industry," exemplified by the development of organizations, courses within law schools, continuing legal education and an extensive literature. The main stimuli appear to have been largely pragmatic and political rather than theoretical or "scientific." Three particular concerns seem to have predominated: a feeling on the part of the American legal establishment that the court system was becoming intolerably overloaded by an increased volume of civil claims and criminal prosecutions; a felt need, on the part of professionals and others, for specialized private fora to serve particular interests (e.g. commercial arbitration); and a view that over and above the concomitant increase in congestion, delay and expense, the system was incapable in more fundamental ways of living up to the ideals of "access to justice" for all.

*Reprinted with permission.

When a "movement" relating to law develops in the United States, one outcome is almost invariably a massive, confusing and largely unsystematic body of literature of variable quality. The ADR movement is no exception. In so far as any general patterns can be discussed from the American ADR literature, perhaps three main strands can be differentiated: first, a body of writing that is concerned with institutional design, in which the central questions relate to the appropriateness of different methods of dispute resolution to various types of dispute. The pioneering work of Lon Fuller in the latter phases of his career is a prominent example.

Second, there has been a series of essentially political debates about the desirability and necessity of encouraging and developing ADR on a large scale. The diagnosis, prescriptions and the motives of the enthusiasts were challenged by skeptics of varying political persuasions: for example, radical critics, . . . while doubting that "justice" was routinely achieved in litigation, argued that the alternatives prescribed by advocates of ADR were no more likely to enhance either access to or delivery of justice in practice and that the net effect of the movement would be to discourage the disadvantaged from trying to assert their legal rights. From a rather different perspective, Owen Fiss argued forcefully "against settlement" not only on the grounds that negotiation and mediation tend to favour the powerful, but also because the development of alternatives would undermine the creative role of the courts in developing public policy and inventing new solutions—an optimistic (and perhaps prototypically American) conception of the political role and importance of courts.

A third strand of literature is specifically educational. While some of the most prominent educational works deal with broad issues of institutional design and its political implications, the main thrust is to prepare lawyers for participation in these alternative modes by developing "skills" in respect of such matters as counselling, interviewing, negotiation, mediation and non-curial advocacy.

The vast bulk of these three bodies of literature is atheoretical. By and large it represents a series of pragmatic and ad hoc reactions to some specific perceived problems in the American legal system at a particular period in history. There are two main exceptions to this broad generalization: first, quite extensive reference is made to the specialized and generally excellent literature of legal anthropology exemplified by such writers as Malinowski, Llewellyn and Hoebel, Gluckman, Gulliver, and Nader. Second, a substantial body of detailed empirical research has been done on criminal process, civil litigation and some alternative processes. Most of this research has been informed by contemporary social science methodology and fits within the kind of theoretical framework that is associated with "the process school" in American jurisprudence—that is to say, a perspective that views litigation and other legal processes as a largely linear and discrete series of decisions and events involving a variety of participants, arenas, procedures, discourses and outcomes.

This characterization of a vast and complex body of American literature is, of course, a great simplification. However, in so far as it is broadly correct it suggests that this heritage has two characteristics that need to be borne in mind by outsiders. First, it focuses on concerns, institutions and phenomena that are specifically American, despite the de-parochialising influence of anthropology. Second, it is largely divorced from what is widely perceived to be "mainstream" Anglo-American jurisprudence as exemplified, on the one hand, by English positivists in the tradition of Bentham, Austin, Hart and Raz, and by their, largely American, critics such as Rawls and Dworkin. The two main exceptions are . . . Lon Fuller and Karl Llewellyn. However, there is, or at least there is generally thought to be, a disjuncture between these two jurists "sociological" writings about dispute settlement and their most memorable contributions to mainstream jurisprudence. Only a tenuous connection is perceived between Fuller's writings on mediation and adjudication and his attacks on positivism; similarly, Llewellyn's reputation as the spokesman and interpreter of Legal Realism, the architect of the Uniform Commercial Code and the author of *The Common Law Tradition* is generally treated as separate from *The Cheyenne Way* and his "law-jobs theory." . . .

In so far as there is a perceived disjuncture between the literature on ADR and mainstream Anglo-American jurisprudence, this is puzzling because one of the most persistent concerns of our legal theorists has been about the nature of adjudication. Twentieth-century Anglo-American jurisprudence has been extraordinarily court-centered, with many of the main debates focusing on the role of judges and reasoning about questions of law in hard cases. If *alternative* dispute resolution is mainly concerned with alternatives to civil adjudication, it seems strange that mainstream theories of adjudication do not feature prominently in discussions of ADR.

Two related factors may help to explain this disjuncture, at least in part. First, Anglo-American legal scholarship and legal education have tended to focus on analysis, exposition and argumentation about legal doctrine. In respect of this, the most visible and interesting issues tend to surface in atypical arenas, notably appellate courts. This sometimes obscures the obvious point that in only a tiny percentage of litigated cases is an adjudicative decision required; only a small percentage of adjudicative decisions involve disputed questions of law rather than of fact or disposition; and the percentage of cases that are appealed is strikingly small. The vast majority of civil cases is settled or abandoned before trial; and an even greater percentage of criminal cases involves a guilty plea which precludes an adjudicative decision on either the facts or the law. Accordingly, in so far as a great deal of Anglo-American jurisprudence focuses on the roles and reasonings of appellate judges on questions of law, and treats such judges as the center-point not only of litigation, but of law in general, it treats statistically insignificant and atypical decisions as central.

The phrase "alternative dispute resolution" is revealing. The word "alternative" implies exceptional or secondary or even deviant in contrast with something that is normal or standard or ordinary. But alternative to what? To litigation? Hardly, for some of the standard alternatives such as negotiation, compromise and mediation regularly feature as phases *within* litigation. To adjudication? If so, it is not just our theorists who are obsessed with the atypical; rather, court-centered thinking and discourse are deeply ingrained in our legal culture.

For closely related reasons, those enclaves of legal theory which have focused more directly on non-curial legal activities and phenomena—sociology of law, legal anthropology and its precursor historical jurisprudence—have generally been marginalized in our legal culture. Thus, the main parts of our theoretical heritage that are seen as relevant to dispute settlement are largely outside the mainstream of jurisprudence. . . .

D. Thinking About the Alternatives

1. Comments and Questions

a. The three pieces in this section provide an introduction to what constitutes ADR, and to issues surrounding the use of ADR. The objective is to provide the reader with a view of the forest, as a prelude to examing particular aspects thereof in far greater detail.

b. The author of the first reading, Professor Frank Sander of Harvard Law School, presented an important and influential paper at the Pound Conference. Sander suggested a multi-door court house that served as a dispute-resolution center. Disputants would be channeled by a screening clerk into the appropriate process (arbitration, mediation, ombudsman, litigation). Sander thought that too much dispute settlement was directed to courts, and that many matters should be dealt with by processes other than a trial, or at least other settlement processes should be used prior to a court hearing.

2. Frank E.A. Sander, *Alternative Methods of Dispute Resolution: An Overview*, 37 Fla. L. Rev. 1 (1985)*

Perhaps a good place to begin is with some definitions. What exactly do we mean by "alternative dispute resolution mechanisms" (ADRMs)? Alternative to what? Presumably "alternative" is used as a substitute for the traditional dispute resolution mechanism, the court. Interestingly enough, however, courts do not resolve most disputes. The literature on dispute processing and dispute transformation has delineated ways in which grievances may be turned into ongoing disputes, and the myriad ways in which disputes may be resolved by means other than court adjudication. In fact, disputes that cannot be readily adjusted may be presented initially to a whole host of dispute processors such as arbitrators, mediators, fact-finders or ombudsmen. If the dispute is ultimately filed in court, approximately 90-95 percent of these disputes are settled by negotiation, with little or no court litigation. Hence, the argument for "alternatives" is not based on the need to find a substitute for court adjudication. Rather, it is based on the need to gain a better understanding of the functioning of these alternative mechanisms and processes.

Alternatives to courts are not a new phenomenon. Yet, the current resurgence of alternative dispute resolution seems to have a freshness about it. The movement appears to have a much broader theoretical and practical base. It might therefore be useful briefly to speculate on the confluence of events that have led to the current renewal of interest in alternatives.

The sixties were characterized by considerable strife and conflict, emanating in part from the civil rights struggles and the Vietnam War protests. An apparent legacy of those times was a lessened tolerance and a greater tendency to turn grievances into disputes. Also relevant was a significant increase in the statutory creation of new causes of action.

A noteworthy development from these events was that courts found themselves inundated with new filings, triggering cries of alarm from the judicial administration establishment. This judicial congestion led to claims that equal access to justice had been denied. Spurred in part by these conditions, parties attempted to resolve some of these disputes through alternative dispute resolution mechanisms. In the 1964 Civil Rights Act Congress established the Community Relations Service in the United States Department of Justice to aid courts and others in settling intractable racial and community disputes. The Ford Foundation established the National Center for Dispute Settlement and the Institute of Mediation and Conflict Resolution to study dispute settlement mechanisms.

---

*Reprinted with permission.

Any attempt to isolate the roots of a complex and ill-understood movement is bound to suffer from oversimplification. One can readily identify a number of other social forces that contributed to the recent flowering of the alternatives movement. One contributor is the waning role of some of society's traditional mediating institutions such as the family, the church, and the wardheeler. A second influence is the discernible recent mood of anti-professionalism. Both these conditions point towards the creation of alternative indigenous mechanisms such as community mediation centers and family dispute settlement tribunals. Of course, need alone does not always lead to constructive solutions. Fortunately, for the alternatives movement, the Law Enforcement Assistance Administration (LEAA) took a firm interest in developing and testing ADRMs, even if the required nexus with the criminal law system at times distorted the proper emphasis.

Certain intellectual developments paralleled these social forces. Over the past 15-20 years some cultural anthropologists have attempted to apply their study of foreign dispute settlement to the local scene. Contemporaneous with that effort has been the work of other legal scholars, most notably the late Lon Fuller, who have attempted to analyze characteristics of various dispute processes such as mediation and arbitration. These scholars proposed some useful conclusions about the strengths and limitations of particular processes for particular types of disputes.

From this brief and fragmentary history, four goals of the alternatives movement emerge:

1) to relieve court congestion, as well as undue cost and delay;
2) to enhance community involvement in the dispute resolution process;
3) to facilitate access to justice;
4) to provide more "effective" dispute resolution.

These goals might overlap and conflict. Consider, for example, the problem of "excessive" access. If society is too ready to provide access for all kinds of disputes, this will lengthen the queue and aggravate the congestion problem. Similarly, measures aimed at relieving court congestion would take a very different form from measures designed to enhance community control over dispute settlement. Hence, it is essential to think clearly and precisely about the reasons for pursuing ADRMs. . . .

II. CURRENT TYPES OF DISPUTE AND PROGRAMS

This section presents a brief overview of the rich variety of ADRMs presently in use. Of necessity the picture will be somewhat fragmentary and conclusory. Because many mechanisms involve a blend or sequence of different dispute processes, it might be useful first to provide a brief restatement of the basic processes.

The most common and familiar form of dispute settlement between two parties is bargaining or negotiation. Negotiation offers the great advantage of allowing the parties themselves to control the process and the solution. Sometimes, however, disputants are unable to settle the dispute, and a third party must be engaged. If a third party joins the negotiations, the parties must determine whether he or she has power to impose a solution on the parties, or whether the third party is simply to help the disputants arrive at their own solution. The latter role is commonly referred to as conciliation or mediation. The former might entail some form of adjudication, by a court, an administrative agency, or a private adjudicator, also known as an arbitrator.

A. Labor Mediation and Arbitration

The model for many of the current mechanisms is the system developed during World War II for handling grievances arising under collective bargaining agreements. Typically, such agreements provide for a series of steps whereby an employee with a grievance first complains to his foreman. Next a meeting occurs between the Union Committee and the Plant Committee. Finally, if the matter cannot be resolved within the plant by negotiation, the parties select an outside arbitrator, often with the assistance of the American Arbitration Association or the Federal Mediation and Conciliation Service. This procedure is comparatively expeditious and inexpensive, even though recent complaints suggest it is becoming more formal, costly, and time-consuming. In short, it is too much like the court system it was originally designed to circumvent.

This procedure for dealing with disputes arising under collective bargaining agreements should be contrasted with disputes which arise in reaching such agreements. With collective bargaining, negotiation and mediation are the principal dispute settlement tools because economic terms of employment are rarely externally imposed on the parties. Hence, if an agreement cannot be achieved by these means, the principal economic weapon, the strike, might be deemed necessary. However, in certain public sector industries where strikes cannot be tolerated—fire departments, police departments and schools—compulsory arbitration is sometimes utilized.

Troublesome questions have also been raised when employees present claims arising under recent enactments guaranteeing non-discrimination on account of sex, race or age. Such cases have often created bitter contests, with sharply differing factual assertions. Therefore, some commentators have suggested that adjudication is unsuitable because of its "win-lose" nature and have argued for resolving some of these cases by a process of mediation.

B. Commercial Arbitration

Long before the rise of labor arbitration, commercial contract disputes were submitted to arbitration by a panel of experts in the industry. This mechanism works particularly well in industries where a continuing relationship exists between the parties. Such cases necessitate an expeditious and amicable method by which one or more individuals familiar with the trade practices can resolve the disputes. The American Arbitration Association now handles close to 10,000 of these disputes each year. In addition, an untold number are handled similarly under private industry agreements.

C. Consumer Disputes

In a sense, consumer disputes could be subsumed under the category of commercial arbitration. Consumer disputes, however, typically involve smaller claims. Additionally, consumer contract agreements [outside of securities, banking and insurance] rarely provide for arbitration of disputes.

In recent years several mechanisms have been developed for extrajudicial handling of consumer disputes. Some states have created consumer protection divisions within the attorney general's office, where such claims are sought to be mediated, often by volunteers. Likewise, some industry groups, such as the Better Business Bureaus, have established procedures for arbitrating such claims. Some industries (*e.g.*, automobiles and major appliances) even set up panels providing free arbitration of the consumer's claim. Of course, consumer claims also can be presented in small claims court and, where available, to media action programs such as Call for Action, where the service provided is not really dispute resolution but information and referral. Because of the clout wielded by these latter groups, they sometimes act in effect like mediators or ombudsmen in adjusting consumer grievances. A recent study, however, suggests the effectiveness and accessibility of some of these mechanisms may be suspect.

D. Interpersonal Disputes

One of the best examples of the need for new dispute resolution mechanisms can be seen with respect to various types of interpersonal disputes. Here, the tendency of courts to look backwards and produce winners and losers is least responsive to the needs of the parties, who usually are seeking to resolve present controversies and avoid future disputes. Mediation, which helps the parties settle their problems jointly, is far more suited to this task than adjudication.

1. Neighborhood Justice Centers

In the past decade well over two hundred community dispute centers have been created. These are known by various names, ranging from "citizen complaint center" to "neighborhood justice center." These centers are either freestanding institutions or are affiliated with the court. Center referrals are received from the court, prosecutor, police or other community agencies; some disputants also come on a walk-in basis. The kinds of cases handled varies widely, from landlord-tenant disputes to domestic and neighbor quarrels.

Although dispute centers vary greatly, two differing prototypes deserve exploration. One, commonly attached to a prosecutor's office, features rapid screening of a large number of cases to determine whether quick settlement might be possible and desirable. These programs involve high-volume processing in very short sessions, which law students often conduct. Whether this process should be viewed as true mediation is open to question.

In contrast to this approach is the more typical mediation, conducted by a professionally trained mediator or by a person drawn from the neighborhood who has received mediation training. Two or three mediators often conduct these mediations, which typically last three to four hours. These meetings allow disputants a full opportunity to present their views, and permit the mediators to meet with each of the disputants separately before attempting to reach agreement.

On the whole, the experience with these projects has been encouraging, although further public education is needed to stimulate greater resort to these unfamiliar institutions. Americans appear too prone to presume that anyone engaged in a dispute should take it to a lawyer or court. Ironically, the individuals who do use the new projects find them helpful and satisfying, and the agreements reached appear to endure. New York recently became the first state to recognize the value of these agencies by providing public funding for them.

2. Divorce Mediation

Although some neighborhood justice centers handle divorces, these cases often present more challenging problems of dispute settlement because complex legal and tax issues arise, as well as difficult questions of child custody. In 1981, California became the first state to require mediation to resolve all child custody disputes. In a number of other jurisdictions, mediation services are available in court-connected agencies. The principal development in divorce mediation, however, has occurred outside the courts, as lawyers and mental health professionals perform mediation as a private service. Although public interest in this alternative to the traditional legal process is widespread, the institution of divorce mediation remains in a state of infancy. Questions yet to be resolved include: Who should be the mediators? What kind of training should they receive? How should their services be compensated? How, if at all, will representative lawyers fit into this process? Should a new form of regulation be developed for this newly emerging profession?

3. Parent/Child Disputes

Another subcategory of cases that might be heard in neighborhood justice centers, but is sometimes handled in separate projects, involves various types of parent/child disputes. A recent study attempted to inventory such projects. One such project is the Children's Hearing Project in Cambridge Massachusetts, which is patterned on a similar proceeding in Scotland. Both projects utilize citizens from the community to help parents and children settle their disputes.

E. Intra-Institutional Disputes

Some institutions have recently applied the grievance machinery model of the labor sector to their intra-institutional settings. For example, a California prison established a grievance committee comprising prisoners and supervisory personnel to air prisoner complaints. If the case could not be resolved internally it would be submitted, at least in an advisory capacity, to an outside arbitrator. This process features initial consideration by a group with representation from both sides, and the possibility of ultimate submission to an outside authority. This process has been replicated in other correctional facilities and other institutional settings, such as schools.

Despite the analogy to the collective bargaining context, there are obvious differences between labor and prison contexts. In the prison all power is on one side, and that side is often reluctant to surrender any power, even to an outside arbiter's advisory review. Hence, the success of grievance mechanisms in the more complex prison setting has been questioned. Alternative ways of resolving prisoner disputes, which make up a very large proportion of the recent caseload growth in the federal courts, are voluntary mediation of prisoner grievances, and ombudsman mechanisms. The latter method involves a third party of great ability and integrity who is empowered to investigate complaints or grievances. Following completion of the inquiry, the ombudsman makes recommendations to the individual in charge of the institution. Usually an ombudsman has no coercive power, but if he is highly regarded, his judgment is given considerable respect. It would be difficult for the institution's presiding authority wholly to ignore a prestigious ombudsman's report that a meritorious grievance had been unfairly ignored. Therein, of course, lies a principal reason for institutional resistance to this mechanism.

F. Claims Against the Government

The ombudsman institution first arose in Scandinavia in response to citizen's complaints against the government. A number of American states and municipalities now have ombudsmen. An analogue of the ombudsman concept has been the development of media action lines such as Call for Action on television.

G. Public Disputes

Most of the controversies considered previously involve two disputants, with relatively concrete, defined concerns. In recent years, however, more large-scale disputes have arisen involving a multiplicity of parties and interests. Examples of such disputes are community conflicts over whether a facility should be built in the area, certain racial controversies, major claims to land holdings by Native Americans, and environmental disputes. Such cases have proved to be far more intractable, and have often required a combination of litigation and mediation. A number of organizations, most of them privately sponsored, have sought to develop special expertise in the handling of such cases.

H. Court-Annexed Mechanisms

Most of the mechanisms discussed thus far are primarily found in the private dispute resolution sector and are not a part of the formal court structure. In an attempt to make courts more responsive to the emerging alternatives movement, ADRMs have been incorporated in one way or another into the court system.

1. Small Claims Adjudication and Mediation

Over fifty years ago courts were recognized as too elaborate and expensive for simple cases involving only small claims. This led to the creation of small claims court, where litigants themselves, without lawyers, can present their disputes. These actions normally involve claims of not more than $1,000 and result in a type of quick, rough justice. Some scholars have recently raised serious questions about the efficacy of small claims courts. Nevertheless, the institution appears to be an essentially durable one that has carved a place in the catalog of useful dispute settlement mechanisms. An interesting recent variant has been utilization of mediation in small claims court.

2. Compulsory Arbitration

Following a 1950's experiment in Philadelphia, a number of jurisdictions have recently passed legislation requiring all monetary claims cases up to a certain limit (generally around $10,000-$15,000) to be initially processed by arbitration. In view of the prevailing right to trial by jury, a right to de novo review must then be accorded in the courts. However, such recourse to the courts might be subjected to cost sanctions if the petitioner does not prevail in court. Absent such a sanction, the net result might be to substitute two proceedings for the previous one. A similar program was begun on an experimental basis in three federal district courts. Preliminary data from these experiments are encouraging, and show that even where a sizeable percentage of the cases are appealed to court, very few proceed to trial.

3. Malpractice Screening

Following the malpractice "crisis" in the mid-seventies, a number of states set up special procedures for malpractice actions. Often the parties are initially required to arbitrate their differences. In other jurisdictions, such as Massachusetts, a screening panel is established, consisting of a doctor, lawyer and judge. The panel determines whether a prima facie case is established. If not the plaintiff may proceed only by putting up a bond for the defendant's costs. The success of these experiments has varied. In some states, the special procedures have been abandoned or declared unconstitutional. In others, the mechanisms have worked well to screen out spurious claims.

4. Large Litigation

Many of the devices discussed above are applicable only to what has sometimes been referred to as "minor disputes." Some devices have also been developed to deal specifically with large and complex litigation.

a. *Rent-a-Judge*

Arbitration often employs experienced individuals such as retired judges to arbitrate difficult cases. Such use of arbitration, by consent of the parties, is quite different from that discussed in Section 2 above, where reference to arbitration is compulsory rather than consensual.

A variant of this practice has developed in some jurisdictions, notably California. It calls for parties to select a retired judge to hear the case, much as an arbitrator would. The procedures applied are the same as those that would apply in court, except as otherwise modified by the parties. Most notably, the judge's decision has the same force and effect as a judgment entered by a regular court.

The Rent-a-Judge procedure raises important policy questions. For example, should parties be able to hire the best available judges under circumstances where the decision has the full force of law, just as if the case had been decided in court? How does this practice square with the notion of equal access to the courts regardless of means? What will be the impact of such a practice on the regular judiciary? These questions and others deserve more discussion than they have received thus far.

b. *Mini-Trial*

Ten years ago some imaginative litigants in the federal district court in California developed an innovative extrajudicial mechanism to aid in the settlement of complex and protracted litigation. The procedure calls for the parties to select an experienced individual to preside at a two-day information exchange. Each party has one day to present its case in any form it desires, including questions for the opposing side. The highest official of each party, assuming a corporate litigant, must attend this hearing. At the end of the proceeding, the two top officials confer, without their lawyers, to evaluate the case. In the seminal case utilizing this innovative procedure, the parties promptly settled. If an agreement is not reached, then the presiding official will give his view concerning how the case would be resolved in court. The parties then use this additional information to discuss settlement. If settlement is not achieved, the procedure has no evidentiary effect and the case returns to court. In virtually all cases which have utilized this procedure, however, settlement has been achieved. The procedure has the additional virtue that it can be readily adapted to different situations (e.g., the presider can be dispensed with, more or less time can be allowed for the presentations).

III. PROBLEMS AND PROSPECTS

A. Relation of ADRMs to Each Other and to the Court System

Implicit in the preceding discussion is the notion that dispute resolution mechanisms are dispersed throughout the social fabric. The mechanisms are either public or private, mandatory or optional. Wherever disputes arise among individuals or organizations, a complex network of possible grievance mechanisms appears to be available for the venting of these grievances. The question which naturally arises is what, if any, relationship should exist among the different types of mechanisms. This question assumes importance not only for the disputant who might benefit from some guidance concerning where to take any particular dispute, but also for a society seeking to provide a coherent response to these grievances.

One can envision a system possessing a hierarchy and structure within the formal public dispute resolution system, complemented by a vast and ill-understood network of indigenous dispute mechanisms. In essence, that is our present system. Disputants might first try to utilize the array of informal mechanisms provided in the particular arena where the dispute arises. Then, as a last resort, disputants might take the controversy to the public forum, the court. That is the paradigm but in fact, informal private mechanisms are frequently not available, or if they are, they are not resorted to. The result is often the typically American tendency to take the case immediately to court. The net effect is that many disputes presented to court are not appropriate for court adjudication and could be better handled by some other mechanism.

This situation led me to suggest, in a paper delivered at the Pound Conference in 1976, a more comprehensive and diverse mechanism known as a Dispute Resolution Center. This center would provide a variety of dispute resolution processes, according to the needs of the particular dispute. This concept was later termed "the multi-door courthouse" (MDC).

What would such an institution look like? A provisional first-step type of MDC could consist essentially of a screening and referral clerk who would seek to diagnose incoming cases and refer them to the most suitable ADRMs. Depending on the available mechanisms in the particular community, referrals might be made to mediation, arbitration, court adjudication, fact finding, malpractice screening, media action lines or an ombudsman. Such a model would be subject to all the familiar deficiencies of a referral scheme. For example, slippage often occurs between the act of referral and the receiving agency's actual handling of the case.

A more ideal model would contain all the "doors" under one roof, as part of an integrated dispute resolution center. Such a mansion might feature the following doors:

(1) effective and accessible small claims adjudication;
(2) services for family, landlord/tenant, and other continuing relations cases;
(3) ombudsmen for the processing of disputes between citizens and large bureaucracies;
(4) social service agencies providing mental health counseling and treatment of alcohol and drug related problems;
(5) trial court of general jurisdiction for novel statutory and constitutional claims, as well as major criminal cases; and
(6) compulsory arbitration for small monetary claims.

Additional dispute processing forums might include those mediating or arbitrating juvenile matters and those handling ordinance violations such as bad checks and health code and building code violations.

An integrated multi-door courthouse would have a number of benefits as well as potential pitfalls. First, such a full-service MDC would provide an efficient way of availing a wide range of dispute processes. It could also serve as a major source of information and referral, transcending the particular "doors" that are available. Second, bringing such diverse ADRMs under the court umbrella would solve the increasingly difficult question of how to fund alternative mechanisms. Likewise, it would avoid the pro-court adjudication bias inherent in the present system where the state pays the costs of court adjudication but not those of other, often more suitable, mechanisms.

Third, because of the predominant emphasis on courts in our society, most alternatives are seldom used. This caseload drought is ironic in light of the generally high satisfaction rate among those parties using alternative mechanisms. Thus, a major difficulty appears to be popular unfamiliarity with these mechanisms. This requires additional public education, but it also argues for building ARDMs into an expanded court system.

These are some of the substantial benefits that might be derived from such an ADRM experiment. However, major obstacles exist as well. A critical feature would be the initial screening which would require a highly skilled intake worker rather than a bureaucratic court functionary. Accordingly, a crucial question is whether ADRM specialists presently have sufficient knowledge of the particular characteristics of various dispute processes and mechanisms. This knowledge is necessary to confidently refer particular types of cases to one or another mechanism. While this science is at a primitive stage, one could posit a number of plausible criteria for determining the suitability of various dispute mechanisms.

1. Nature of Case

ADRMs should be designed to handle a novel claim challenging the constitutionality of a statute quite differently from a claim applying established principles to a specific set of facts. Only the former merits the unique skills and resources of a court. The latter can be more expeditiously and inexpensively dealt with by arbitration.

2. Relationship of Disputants

Adjudication typically seeks to make a definitive determination with respect to past events, while mediation attempts to restructure the relationship of the disputants. Thus, mediation best resolves cases involving long-term relationships extending into the future. For example, a mediator is more likely to resolve effectively a mid-contract dispute between a landlord and tenant, or even a divorce, than is a judge. Not only will a mediator be better equipped to restructure future relationships, but the open-ended and non-coercive process of mediation is also more likely to teach the parties to recognize and resolve future controversies. Mediation thus gives maximum durability to the settlement the parties have created.

A significant qualification, however, is presented in the case where the two disputants have substantially disparate bargaining power. In such a case, mediation is either pointless, or worse yet, threatens to take undue and unfair advantage of the weaker party. ADRM specialists must learn far more about the optional combination of formal adjudicative and informal mediation processes for this type of case.

3. Size and Complexity of Claim

Society has already taken some account of the size and complexity criterion in establishing, on an optional basis, small claims courts for the processing of minor disputes. Some states have even experimented with the use of different tracks for cases of different complexity. Generally, however, transaction costs in processing disputes have largely been ignored. To be sure, certain cases (e.g., a serious crime or a major constitutional challenge) should not be measured by the amount in controversy. Beyond those cases and others raising similar considerations, however, should not we lawyers be more attuned to the immense public cost every time a lawsuit is processed in court? If a case involves only $1000 and does not raise larger issues of public policy, should society not require such a case to be processed in small claims court or its functional equivalent? The counterargument, of course, is that for the low-income consumer a claim of $1000 over his defective refrigerator is as important as a multi-million dollar claim is for General Motors. That argument, however, misses the point. If the larger claim is also a straightforward collection action, it also does not deserve access to the deluxe adjudication model. These factors and others need further exploration. Indeed, one of the potential benefits of such a tentative typology is that it will permit the acquisition of significant additional data to test some of the stated hypotheses.

In addition to the cited general criteria, certain programmatic channels might also be proposed. For example, medical malpractice claims would be directed to the appropriate screening tribunal. Prisoners' claims might be sent to an internal grievance mechanism to be initially processed. And if the jurisdiction had an ombudsman, claims against the government would be directed there.

As appealing and efficient as such a scheme might be, it would undoubtedly have its costs. First, intelligent central referral presumes the intake official is completely aware of all the facts. However, disputants are often notoriously inarticulate in voicing their real grievances. In such a case, the true complaint does not surface until much later in the proceeding. Second, any new institution also runs the risk of sinking to the lowest bureaucratic level, and thereby eliminating the benefits that emanate from decentralized, indigenous dispute resolution. A related bureaucratic nightmare has the MDC simply shunting difficult and undesirable cases to an endless series of "alternatives" from which the disputants emerge dissatisfied and disillusioned.

A final question is whether the referral process should be optional or compulsory. A system of mandatory referral raises different questions of law and policy than would a merely advisory reference. No single uniform answer to this question is required. At the outset, referral should undoubtedly be voluntary, while necessary information is obtained about the workings of the system. But once that level of experience and understanding is attained with respect to a particular class of cases, that particular referral process might become mandatory. For example, sufficient data now exists to warrant the initial compulsory referral of small monetary claims to arbitration. However, ADRM specialists must first learn more about what types of cases are particularly suitable for such treatment, and what types of cases are not.

B. Data Drought

Despite all of the recent developments in alternative modes of dispute settlement, relatively little is known about the critical questions of ADRMs. For example, ADRM specialists have essentially no sophisticated data concerning the relative time and cost of alternative dispute settlement mechanisms such as arbitration and mediation. No doubt this problem is due to the difficult questions that would be posed by such an inquiry. What, for example, are the appropriate ingredients of cost? What is the aggregate cost to the system? What is the cost to the parties? And how does one determine the comparative cost of a case in court? Should cost be determined on a marginal or an average basis? What is the appropriate time frame?

Suppose, for example, that a particular court case cost $462, while a mediated solution cost $597. Does this show that mediation is more costly, even if the effect of the mediation were not only to settle the present dispute but to prevent future ones? This question suggests the difficulty of measuring potential benefits to be derived from particular forms of dispute settlement. Perhaps these questions explain why so little sophisticated research has been published.

C. Critiques

In recent years the alternatives movement has been severely attacked from a number of quarters. Perhaps the most pervasive of these has emanated from the political left. The argument suggests that providing ADRMs for the poor and powerless constitutes the establishment's attempt to "cool out" legitimate grievances by negotiating or mediating away poor people's legal rights. To the extent that this argument rests on implicit premises of distributive justice, it goes well beyond the issues of formal versus informal justice. In fact, little evidence suggests that the courts can, barring very exceptional situations, bring about major redistributions of wealth and power. Indeed, given the existing constraints of restricted access to the courts and the summary treatment accorded many litigants, it is far from clear that disputants fare less well in the informal system. Moreover, the limited empirical evidence supports the conclusion that disputants prefer the informal system. Perhaps, from a radical perspective, this only proves that the courts themselves are an instrument of capitalist domination. However, that argument takes us considerably beyond the issue of formal versus informal justice.

If the focus is narrowed to the actual operation of the informal system, a number of legitimate issues arise. Particularly where alternatives are considered for minor criminal cases, questions arise concerning the availability of various procedural and constitutional protections. Perhaps this question becomes essentially one of fair notice and free choice. If the "defendant" prefers the informal process after having been fully apprised of the protections and consequences in each system, there can be little complaint. This goal, however, might be difficult to achieve in practice. In fact, some programs fail to fully disclose the different procedures and consequences of each system. Occasionally, those programs effectively push the complainee into the informal system, for example, by sending him a letter on District Attorney stationery so "suggesting." Where the program is overtly compulsory, in court-annexed arbitration, different types of issues arise, such as whether the legally required right of access to the courts, following exhaustion of the alternative mechanism, can be significantly burdened, as by imposing various "costs" on the judicial petitioner.

Other problems stem from inadequate conceptualization of ADRM processes. For example, if a substantial power disparity exists between disputants then mediation will be inappropriate because it threatens to exploit the apparent powerlessness of one disputant. Perhaps here again it is largely a question of full information coupled with free choice. Or, as noted with respect to a comparable situation in an environmental dispute, we need to learn more about the optimal interrelationship between the formal and the informal legal processes.

ADRM specialists should strive to combine the court's power-equalizing role with the greater participation, flexibility and range of choices offered by the mediative process.

D. Role of Lawyers in ADRMs

What is the proper role of attorneys in alternative dispute resolution mechanisms? First, ADRMs must distinguish between a lawyer's role as a representative of the disputants, and a lawyer's role as a dispute resolver. With respect to the former, much turns on the nature of the proceeding. If, for example, the dispute is a low-key squabble between two neighbors, lawyers might not be needed. However, if the dispute is a complex divorce case involving technical issues in a zero sum context, the argument for legal representation becomes much more compelling. In short, the issue of legal representation in ADRMs is not unlike that in court. The mere fact that the alternative process is nonadversary does not necessarily indicate that lawyers have no legitimate role.

When the lawyer's role as dispute resolver is considered, the lawyer's claimed expertise must rest on a different footing. Unfortunately, much of a law student's training is in adversary dispute settlement rather than accommodative problem-solving. This situation is rapidly changing, however. Increasingly, legal education encompasses mediation and other ADRM training. Hence, lawyers should be neither specially qualified or disqualified for alternative dispute resolution. Depending on the case in question, lawyers with appropriate training might often possess excellent credentials for alternative dispute resolution.

The new roles outlined above present an exciting challenge to the legal community. If it is to be successfully met, the new system will require:

1) the continued support of the legal education community (including the continuing legal education establishment);
2) an open mind on the part of the legal ethics committees who will be asked to sanction the work done by these newly created professionals;
3) some institutional mechanisms capable of providing training and possibly financial support to aid traditional lawyers in making appropriate vocational changes; and
4) possible regulation and certification of the new professionals.

3. Harry T. Edwards*, *Alternative Dispute Resolution: Panacea or Anathema?*, 99 HARV. L. REV. 668 (1986)**

I. THE PROBLEM IN PERSPECTIVE

If alternative dispute resolution mechanisms are most significant as substitutes for traditional litigation, then it is important to assess the specific problems facing our judicial system that ADR seeks to address. Fortunately, the literature on this subject is so extensive that it is unnecessary here to rehash the issues or to resolve the ongoing debate as to whether we are truly an overly litigious society. It is enough to note that, in recent years, the cost of litigation has substantially increased and the number of cases filed in state and federal courts has mushroomed. . . .

---

*Edwards is a judge on the D.C. Circuit court of appeals. Before that he was a distinguished law professor, and the co-author with James White of the first ADR Casebook.

Given the inadequacy of traditional responses to the manifold problems with our court systems, it is not surprising that many commentators believe that we must develop new approaches for dispute resolution in lieu of litigation. Generally, I concur, but I think that there are two critical threshold inquires that we must make before we leap to embrace any system of ADR. First, we should consider whether an ADR mechanism is being proposed to facilitate existing court procedures, or as an alternative wholly separate from the established system. Second, we must consider whether the disputes that will be resolved pursuant to an ADR system will involve significant public rights and duties. In other words, we must determine whether ADR will result in an abandonment of our constitutional system in which the "rule of law" is created and principally enforced by legitimate branches of government and whether rights and duties will be delimited by those the law seeks to regulate. . . .

Obviously, many disputes cannot be easily classified as solely private disputes that implicate no constitutional or public law. Many commentators have tried to distinguish "public" and "private" disputes; but, in my view, no one has been fully successful in this effort. The problem is that hidden in many seemingly private disputes are often difficult issues of public law. In this Commentary, I offer no easy solution to the definitional problem of public/private disputes. I do suggest, however, that there are a number of public law cases that are easily identifiable as such. These include constitutional issues, issues surrounding existing government regulation, and issues of great public concern. The latter category might include, for example, the development of a legal standard of strict liability in products liability cases. Although less easily identifiable than constitutional and regulatory issues, such issues of great public concern can be accommodated so long as ADR mechanisms are created as adjuncts to existing judicial or regulatory systems, or if these issues can be relitigated in court after initial resolution pursuant to ADR.

II. THE ROLE OF ADR WITHIN THE TRADITIONAL COURT SYSTEM

One way to deal with the caseload problem is simply to divert cases from litigation by limiting the jurisdiction of the courts. There are two difficulties with such a "demand-side" approach. First, limiting the jurisdiction of courts may result in diminished rights for minorities and other groups, whose cases in areas like civil rights, prisoner suits, and equal employment are likely to be the first removed from the courts. Second, the jurisdiction-limiting solution fails to recognize the potential role of ADR within the traditional court systems. If we rush to limit the substantive jurisdiction of our courts, we may lose our best opportunity to experiment with the promise of ADR.

Implicitly recognizing these two difficulties, many ADR advocates have suggested the use of ADR as an adjunct to federal and state court systems. ADR would not replace litigation, but instead would be used to make our traditional court systems work more efficiently and effectively. Because the vast majority of all court cases are settled rather than adjudicated, many commentators believe that ADR has an enormous potential for reducing caseloads by enhancing the effectiveness of settlement; at the same time, because ADR would be under the careful supervision of courts, there is far less danger that ADR would become a nefarious scheme for diminishing the rights of the underprivileged in our society.

There are several ways in which the enormous settlement-enhancing potential of ADR can be tapped. Many lawyers insist that a neutral, penetrating, and analytical assessment of a case greatly enhances the prospects of a successful negotiation by offering a realistic view of what could transpire if a case goes to full-blown adjudication. Furthermore, because too many lawyers view the suggestion of compromise as an admission of weakness, mechanisms that place the onus of suggesting settlement negotiations on neither party have tremendous potential for initiating settlement at much earlier stages in the litigation.

Indeed, many private litigants and courts already use ADR because it offers such a neutral assessment and requires parties to think about compromise at earlier stages in the litigation. For example, several corporations have pioneered the resolution of large and complicated business disputes by mini-trials. Although the result is nonbinding, mini-trials have been tremendously successful in settling cases quickly. Business litigants frequently find the opinion of a third party invaluable in deciding how best to settle many quite complicated cases. The mini-trials also have the virtue of forcing corporate litigants to confront the weaknesses in their cases. Unfortunately, however, mini-trials are a realistic option only for the wealthy, and the success of mini-trials may result from the fact that they are initiated by the parties, who thereby show their predisposition to settle.

Court-annexed arbitration—quickly being adopted in many state and federal courts—may offer a "poor man's mini-trial." Many jurisdictions have compulsory arbitration for particular classes of cases—primarily tort and contract disputes with potential damage awards below an established dollar ceiling. Critically, therefore, court-annexed arbitration is most often used to resolve private disputes rather than difficult public law issues. Indeed, by diverting private disputes to arbitration, federal and state courts may be able to expend more time and energy resolving difficult public law problems.

The experience in most state court-annexed arbitration programs is very encouraging. A large percentage of the disputants accept the arbitrated settlements and express satisfaction with the arbitration process. In Pittsburgh, for example, court-annexed arbitration ends three-quarters of all cases without appeal, and the median time to a hearing is three months, in marked contrast to an eighteen-month wait for trial. In Michigan, although disputants accept the arbitration award in less than half of the cases, only seven percent of all cases in which the arbitration award is rejected actually go to trial.

Of course, in the excitement over the docket-clearing potential of court-annexed arbitration, we must not make the mistake of ignoring the quality of arbitration outcomes. . . .

The seventh amendment right to a jury trial requires that arbitrated settlements be nonbinding, unless the parties agree otherwise. In cases seen to be very important to the litigants—whether for monetary reasons or otherwise—losing parties are rarely willing to accept the result of arbitration as long as a trial de novo remains available and they have so little to lose by resorting to full-blown litigation. Only if parties agree beforehand to waive their jury rights can arbitration be fully effective.

Even with this problem of finality, court-annexed arbitration has increased the ease with which cases are settled. Most parties that reject arbitration decisions eventually settle—often earlier than they would have in the absence of arbitration. Even if parties do not accept the outcome of arbitration, the arbitrator's decision forces both parties to focus on a neutral third-party's realistic assessment of the case.

As our experience with court-annexed arbitration demonstrates, federal and state courts are striving mightily to accommodate and encourage the development of demonstrably effective dispute resolution mechanisms, especially in cases involving private disputes. At the same time, because these alternatives allow for careful supervision by the judiciary, there is less danger that the poor will find no room on the docket. And most importantly, under these ADR mechanisms, which function as adjuncts to existing court systems, there is little likelihood that we will see the creation or development of public law by private parties. By focusing on that quadrant of the matrix offering the least concern—the resolution of mostly private disputes by ADR systems that act as adjuncts to courts—programs such as court-annexed arbitration may diminish the pressure on courts to reduce substantive rights in response to perceived or actual excessive case-loads.

III. THE ROLE OF ADR AS AN "ALTERNATIVE" SYSTEM

It is clear, however, that a number of ADR proponents have a far more ambitious vision of ADR than that set forth so far. Some, such as Jerold Auerbach, seem to favor community resolution of disputes using community values instead of the rule of law. Others, such as Chief Justice Burger, complain that "there is some form of mass neurosis that leads many people to think courts were created to solve all the problems of mankind," and believe that ADR must be used to curb the "flood" of "new kinds of conflicts" . . . that have purportedly overwhelmed the judicial system. In either case, these ADR advocates propose a truly revolutionary step—the resolution of cases through ADR mechanisms free from any judicial monitoring or control.

If we can assume that it is possible to finance and administer truly efficient systems of dispute resolution, then there would appear to be no significant objections to the use of even wholly independent ADR mechanisms to resolve private disputes that do not implicate important public values. For instance, settling minor grievances between neighbors according to local mores or resolving simple contract disputes by commercial norms may lead to the disposition of more disputes and the greater satisfaction of the participants. In strictly private disputes, ADR mechanisms such as arbitration often are superior to adjudication. Disputes can be resolved by neutrals with substantive expertise, preferably chosen by the parties, and the substance of disputes can be examined without issue-obscuring procedural rules. Tens of thousands of cases are resolved this way each year by labor and commercial arbitration, and even more private disputes undoubtedly could be better resolved through ADR than by adjudication.

However, if ADR is extended to resolve difficult issues of constitutional or public law—making use of nonlegal values to resolve important social issues or allowing those the law seeks to regulate to delimit public rights and duties— there is real reason for concern. An oft-forgotten virtue of adjudication is that it ensures the proper resolution and application of public values. In our rush to embrace alternatives to litigation, we must be careful not to endanger what law has accomplished or to destroy this important function of formal adjudication. [Judge Edwards then presents the settlement views of Owen Fiss.] . . .

The concern here is that ADR will replace the rule of law with nonlegal values. . . . For example, many environmental disputes are now settled by negotiation and mediation instead of adjudication. Indeed, as my colleague Judge Wald recently observed, there is little hope that Superfund legislation can solve our nation's toxic waste problem unless the vast bulk of toxic waste disputes are resolved through negotiation, rather than litigation. Yet, as necessary as environmental negotiation may be, it is still troubling. When Congress or a government agency has enacted strict environmental protection standards, negotiations that compromise these strict standards with weaker standards result in the application of values that are simply inconsistent with the rule of law. Furthermore, environmental mediation and negotiation present the danger that environmental standards will be set by private groups without the democratic checks of governmental institutions. . . .

A subtle variation on this problem of private application of public standards is the acceptance by many ADR advocates of the "broken-telephone" theory of dispute resolution that suggests that disputes are simply "failures to communicate" and will therefore yield to "repair service" by the expert "facilitator.". . .

[M]utual understanding and good feeling among disputants obviously facilitates intelligent dispute resolution, but there are some disputes that cannot be resolved simply by mutual agreement and good faith. It is a fact of political life that many disputes reflect sharply contrasting views about fundamental public values that can never be eliminated by techniques that encourage disputants to "understand" each other. Indeed, many disputants understand their opponents all too well. Those who view tobacco as an unacceptable health risk, for example, can never fully reconcile their differences with the tobacco industry, and we should not assume otherwise. One essential function of law is to reflect the public resolution of such irreconcilable differences; lawmakers are forced to choose among these differing visions of the public good. A potential danger of ADR is that disputants who seek only understanding and reconciliation may treat as irrelevant the choices made by our lawmakers and may, as a result, ignore public values reflected in rules of law.

We must also be concerned lest ADR becomes a tool for diminishing the judicial development of legal rights for the disadvantaged. . . . ADR may result in the reduction of possibilities for legal redress of wrongs suffered by the poor and underprivileged, "in the name of increased access to justice and judicial efficiency." Inexpensive, expenditious, and informal adjudication is not always synonymous with fair and just adjudication. The decisionmakers may not understand the values at stake and parties to disputes do not always possess equal power and resources. Sometimes because of this inequality and sometimes because of deficiencies in informal processes lacking procedural protections, the use of alternative mechanisms will produce nothing more than inexpensive and ill-informed decisions. And these decisions may merely legitimate decisions made by the existing power structure within society. Additionally, by diverting particular types of cases away from adjudication, we may stifle the development of law in certain disfavored areas of law. Imagine, for example, the impoverished nature of civil rights law that would have resulted had all race discrimination cases in the sixties and seventies been mediated rather than adjudicated. The wholesale diversion of cases involving the legal rights of the poor may result in the definition of these rights by the powerful in our society rather than by the application of fundamental societal values reflected in the rule of law.

Family law offers one example of this concern that ADR will lead to "second-class justice." In the last ten years, women have belatedly gained many new rights, including new laws to protect battered women and new mechanisms to ensure the enforcement of child-support awards. There is a real danger, however, that these new rights will become simply a mirage if all "family law" disputes are blindly pushed into mediation. The issues presented extend beyond questions of unequal bargaining power. For example, battered women often need the batterer ordered out of the home or arrested—goals fundamentally inconsistent with mediation.

Some forms of mediation, however, would protect the public values at stake. Professors

Mnookin and Kornhauser suggest, for example, that divorce settlements can be be mediated successfully despite disparities in bargaining power by requiring court review of settlements that deviate from a predefined norm. Additionally, some disputes that are not otherwise subject to court review also might be well suited for mediation. Many cases, however, may require nothing less than judicial resolution. At the very least we must carefully evaluate the appropriateness of ADR in the resolution of particular disputes.

Even with these concerns, however, there are a number of promising areas in which we might employ ADR in lieu of traditional litigation. Once a body of law is well developed, arbitration and other ADR mechanisms can be structured in such a way that public rights and duties would not be defined and delimited by private groups. The recent experience of labor arbitrators in the federal sector, who are required to police compliance with laws, rules, and regulations, suggests that the interpretation and application of law may not lie outside the competence of arbitrators. So long as we restrict arbitrators to the application of clearly defined rules of law, and strictly confine the articulation of public law to our courts, ADR can be an effective means of reducing mushrooming caseloads. Employment discrimination cases offer a promising example. Many employment discrimination cases are highly fact-bound and can be resolved by applying established principles of law. Others, however, present novel questions that should be resolved by a court. If the more routine cases could be certified to an effective alternative dispute resolution system that would have the authority to make some final determinations, the courts could devote greater attention to novel legal questions, and the overall efficiency of an anti-discrimination law might be enhanced.

In other areas, we could capitalize on the substantive expertise and standards developed by well-established ADR mechanisms. For example, the experience and standards developed through decades of labor arbitration and mediation could prove particularly useful in settling disputes between nonunionized employees and their employers in cases of "unjust dismissal." Labor arbitrators have developed fine-tuned standards for just-cause terminations, which they could easily transfer to the nonunion workplace, thus providing similar protection to nonunion employees. Similarly, the expertise developed over the years by commercial arbitrators could be used to settle other business disputes, which now often require years of litigation. We should also encourage more private parties to accept binding arbitration voluntarily. Recently, the SEC and the securities industry developed a system of securities arbitration used in thousands of securities law cases. If this system is fair to investors and to broker-dealers, perhaps we should permit investors to commit themselves by contract to binding arbitration.

Additionally, the qualities of labor arbitration that make it so successful in the context of collective bargaining are readily transferable to other fields of law. The presence of a skilled neutral with substantive expertise, the avoidance of issue-obscuring procedural rules, the arbitrator's freedom to exercise common sense, the selection of arbitrators by the parties, and the tradition of limited judicial review of arbitral decisions—factors that make arbitration superior to litigation in labor cases—would make arbitration superior to litigation in other contexts as well. Although the labor context has the benefit of a collective bargaining agreement providing rules not subject to arbitrary change by one party, the experience with federal employees demonstrates that arbitration can achieve substantial benefits even when it is limited to the interpretation of rules imposed unilaterally. Perhaps arbitration could prove useful in moderating disagreements between citizens, in resolving grievances of citizens against social service agencies, and in resolving complaints of prisoners over conditions of confinement.

Finally, there are some disputes in which community values—coupled with the rule of law—may be a rich source of justice. Mediation of disputes between parents and schools about special education programs for handicapped children has been very successful. A majority of disputes have been settled by mediation, and parents are generally positive about both the outcome and the process. At issue in these mediations is the appropriate education for a child, a matter best resolved by parents and educators—not courts. Similarly, many landlord-tenant disputes can ultimately be resolved only by negotiation. Most tenant "rights" are merely procedural rather than substantive. Yet tenants desire substantive improvement in housing conditions or assurances that they will not be evicted. Mediation of landlord-tenant disputes, therefore, can be very successful—often more successful than adjudication—because both parties have much to gain by agreement.

In both of these examples, however, the option of ultimate resort to adjudication is essential. It is only because handicapped children have a statutory right to education that parent-school mediation is successful. It is only because tenants have procedural rights that landlords will bargain at all.

ADR can thus play a vital role in constructing a judicial system that is both more manageable and more responsive to the needs of our citizens. It is essential—as the foregoing examples illustrate—that this role of ADR be strictly limited to prevent the resolution of important constitutional and public law issues by ADR mechanisms that are independent of our courts. Fortunately, few ADR programs have attempted to remove public law issues from the courts. Although this may merely reflect the relative youth of the ADR movement, it may also manifest an awareness of the danger of public law resolution in nonjudicial fora.

IV. OVERRIDING CONSIDERATIONS

Apart from the issues concerning the appropriate application of ADR mechanisms, two additional overriding considerations should affect the employment of ADR. One has to do with research and appraisal, the other with the training and expertise of those who will serve as neutrals in ADR systems. . . .

There are a number of ADR proponents who appear to believe that a good neutral can resolve any issue without regard to substantive expertise. Our experience with arbitrators and mediators in collective bargaining proves the folly of this notion. The best neutrals are those who understand the field in which they work. Yet, the ADR movement often seeks to replace issue-oriented dispute resolution mechanisms with more generic mechanisms without considering the importance of substantive expertise.

Some would respond that judges are generalists and yet we trust our state and federal judiciary to resolve a broad range of disputes. This argument, however, is deceptive because judges are specialists in resolving issues of law. Law aims to resolve disputes on the basis of rules, whereas alternative dispute resolution mechanisms turn to nonlegal values. If disputes are to be resolved by rules of law, the legal experts designated by our state and federal constitutions—that is, the judges—should resolve them. If nonlegal values are to resolve disputes, we should recognize the need for substantive expertise. . . .

4. Jethro K. Lieberman & James F. Henry, *Lessons From the Alternative Dispute Resolution Movement*, 53 U. Chi. L. Rev. 424, 424-432 (1986)*

I. WHAT IS ADR?

The ADR roster includes such well-known processes as arbitration, mediation, conciliation, and, perhaps, negotiation. These processes can be used to settle existing disputes or to prevent disputes from developing. There are also new hybrid devices that borrow from courtroom procedure—including, most prominently, the mini-trial. The roster may also be expanded to include the roles played by certain officials and quasi-officials (such as court-appointed masters, special masters, and neutral experts), by private persons retained as neutrals, by ombudsmen, and by private judges. Changes in procedural rules to provide incentives to the parties to settle (for example, further penalizing parties who turn down reasonable settlement offers) and the greater use of partial summary judgment might also be viewed as ADR techniques.

It is easier to point to discrete practices than to discern the entire direction of the new movement. ADR has no generally accepted abstract or theoretical definition. But it does have a fundamental premise: it is worthwhile both to reduce the costs of resolving disputes, however this can be accomplished, and to improve the quality of the final outcome. We offer a working definition of ADR as a starting point for analysis: ADR is a set of practices and techniques that aim (1) to permit legal disputes to be resolved outside the courts for the benefit of all disputants; (2) to reduce the cost of conventional litigation and the delays to which it is ordinarily subject; or (3) to prevent legal disputes that would otherwise likely be brought to the courts. . . .

The "disputes" with which ADR is centrally concerned should be distinguished from "problems," "grievances," or "claims." Problems are the troubles that affect the human lot, such as damage from storms or sudden illness. Grievances are those problems that affect a particular person, but which may or may not have a particular person or group as the cause of the distress. When the sufferer asks the person thought to be causing the grievance to forbear, the grievance has become a claim or complaint. But a dispute arises only when the one against whom the complaint is lodged fails to respond satisfactorily to the aggrieved party. And a "legal" dispute arises only when the claim is grounded in a legal entitlement. ADR, then, should be viewed as a set of practices that are truly alternatives to the courts for the resolution of disputes that could legitimately be disposed of by judicial decree.

Finally, ADR can be "alternative" in one of two senses: because the parties privately choose to avoid litigation (or to terminate it short of judgment), or because legal rules require or permit the courts to send the dispute elsewhere (as in court-annexed arbitration). The analysis that follows largely takes the perspective of parties who have privately and voluntarily chosen to resolve their disputes outside the formal procedures of adjudication. . . .

What often prevents disputes from being resolved is a failure to communicate stemming from a lack of trust between the parties. ADR is premised on the hypothesis that if the parties could overcome this distrust, they could voluntarily reach a settlement as just as the result a court would impose.

The adversary process—the engine of the adjudicatory system—operates on a theory of fundamental distrust: Never put faith in the adversary. Litigation thus becomes formal, tricky,

*Reprinted with permission.

divisive, time-consuming, and distorting. These characteristics are reflected in the common image of discovery in large-scale commercial cases that takes years to conduct, in the careful coaching and preparation of witnesses, and in the skillful impeachment of sound witnesses during cross-examination. In contrast, the creation of trust is central to the design of many ADR processes. . . .

Mediation leads to the building of trust . . . [by permitting] a neutral to learn intimate facts from both sides that they would never have shared with each other in the course of trial preparation. By building on the parties' trust in the mediator, the process thus allows the parties to explore workable options. With the knowledge that he gains, the mediator can learn how far apart the parties are and devise ways of bridging the gap.

One lesson that ADR teaches, then, is that processes designed to restore and build trust can overcome the suspicion and mutual hostility fostered by the adversary system and can lead the parties to settle their differences. When the substantive outcome is compared to the likely result in court—and the costs of continued litigation are weighed in the balance—both parties generally benefit from ADR.

A working hypothesis of ADR is that the results of ADR are often superior to court judgments—and even more clearly superior to conventional settlements. Although the hypothesis is difficult to test, it is supported by several considerations.

First, adjudication is characterized by a "winner-take-all" outcome. This cannot be wholly true, for jury damage awards can work compromises, and the parties can shape consent decrees through bargaining. Nevertheless, in many cases, the fundamental issue of liability can be resolved only by holding for the plaintiff or the defendant. ADR, by contrast, is not bound by the zero-sum game of adjudication. While we have defined ADR as concerned with "legal disputes,'" participants in ADR are free to go beyond the legal definition of the scope of their dispute. They can search for creative solutions to the problem that gave rise to the dispute, and those solutions may be far more novel than any remedy a court has the power to provide. . . .

Second, in classes of cases involving complex institutions, negotiations conducted by executives are likely to yield results superior to those conducted by the lawyers. The executives are far more familiar than their lawyers with the nuances of their business and can respond more quickly and creatively to proposals raised by their counterparts. We do not mean to diminish the role or responsibilities of lawyers in the negotiations; their legal knowledge will often be crucial to successful settlements and good lawyer-negotiators may be more skillful than poorly trained executive-negotiators. Nevertheless, the business executive may be presumed to be less distracted by the shadow the law casts over the dispute; the executive will look at the complete business picture, unconstrained by the narrow parameters imposed by legal doctrine.

Third, direct involvement by the client can obviate or minimize difficulties arising from the self-interest of lawyers. This point may be particularly instructive for judges. By requiring clients to attend pretrial conferences, judges can be sure that the clients know and approve of the propositions their lawyers will assert in court on their behalf.

Fourth, ADR techniques and processes can be far more systematic than the horsetrading of conventional settlement negotiations. Settlement negotiations are often perceived as consisting of sharp tactics and bluff. "Unprincipled" negotiations occur in large part because the parties lack a means of communicating with each other. ADR processes permit realistic assessments of whether offers and counteroffers are in good faith.

Fifth, properly designed ADR processes make it more likely that settlement decisions will be based on the merits of disputes. . . . [V]arious factors may contribute to more or less settlement. Delay in the judicial system tends to "increase[] the likelihood of settlement by reducing the stakes in the case," in part because delay diminishes the present value of the ultimate award. Other factors include rules governing prejudgment interest and the availability of pretrial discovery. This analysis could lead the courts to advocate policies that would increase delay (or other costs of litigation) in order to prompt settlement. The resulting settlements would not necessarily be just, however, because they would not have taken account of power disparities. The party with the more meritorious claim might not prevail because he is too poor to amass the requisite evidence through the discovery process. Society may have the power to foster higher settlement rates by manipulating the factors that induce people to stay out of court, but many proponents of ADR would not view such policies as consonant with the ADR philosophy. A dispute should not merely be settled; it should be settled justly. . . .

Finally, a sixth reason to think that ADR leads to "better" outcomes is that the use of private neutrals permits the parties to submit their dispute to one with greater expertise in their particular subject than does the luck of the draw in the courtroom. Many complex disputes involve data and concepts that lie beyond the knowledge of generalist judges (and of all juries). The ADR neutral can be selected for a particular expertise, thus saving the parties the cost of educating the fact-finder (and the risk of failing to do so). Moreover, if the parties have personally participated in selecting the neutral, they may be psychologically disposed to accept his statement of the case, whether it is a binding decision (as in arbitration) or an advisory opinion (as in a mini-trial).

E. Alternative Dispute Resolution in Earlier America

1. Comments and Questions

a. The use of ADR is not a new, or even recent, development. One ancient example that will be familiar to readers is the dispute between two women over a baby that was settled by King Solomon. ADR has been widely used in America long before the present ADR movement, which is commonly dated to the Pound Conference in 1976. Congress adopted the Federal Arbitration Act in 1925. Mediation and arbitration have been in regular use throughout the 20th century to resolve labor-management disputes. Merchants have used mediation and arbitration (often through trade or industry bodies) for centuries, an approach that was already established in England when the United States was still a colony.

b. Professor Jerold Auerbach's JUSTICE WITHOUT LAW? (1981) is an excellent history of the dispute settlement approaches adopted by discrete and insular groups in America, which struck them as more congenial than resort to the judicial system provided by government.

c. A wonderful article by Professor Bruce Mann will suffice to demonstrate that ADR of the most formal sort—arbitration—was commonly used in America long before the Revolutionary War. You should not assume that the "arbitration" of 250 or 300 years ago is the same thing as "arbitration" today. Look for similarities and differences. Mann notes that the role of arbitration in early Connecticut changed as the society changed.

2. Bruce H. Mann, *The Formalization of Informal Law: Arbitration Before the American Revolution*, 59 N.Y.U. L. Rev. 443 (1984)*

Zephaniah Swift, a Connecticut jurist of the early republic, described arbitration as "an amicable and neighbourly mode of settling personal controversies." Arbitrators, he wrote, "are not tied down to the same strictness, formality and precision as courts of late. While they have greater latitude in the mode of proceeding than courts of law, they have ampler powers to do compleat and perfect justice between the parties in the decision of the matters in dispute."... Long before Swift wrote [in 1796] arbitration played a significant role in resolving the disputes of people who preferred not to go to law. Unlike litigation, arbitration was inexpensive, expeditious, and private. Above all, it was, as Swift recognized, "neighbourly"—uniquely tied to and shaped by the communities in which it functioned. The community ties were an essential part of arbitration. Without them, arbitration would not have been the popular and effective alternative to formal legal process that it was.

Although we customarily think of arbitration as nonlegal in nature, the relationship between arbitration and the legal system has always been strong. It became stronger in early America as the communities that had nurtured arbitration grew less communal. In time, the legal system appropriated arbitration to itself and turned it into a formal process that differed little from legal adjudication. The transformation was particularly clear in Connecticut, where it was part of a general pattern of legal change in America before the Revolution. . . .

THE ENGLISH BACKGROUND

To begin, we must first understand the forms of arbitration in English law that were current in the seventeenth century and thus familiar to the colonists. Common law arbitration was sufficiently developed by the seventeenth century for John March to devote part of a treatise to the subject. Parties who decided to submit their differences to arbitration rather than to law would select two or more men as arbitrators and instruct them on settlement of the dispute. The instructions would take the form of an oral or written submission setting forth the nature and limits of the dispute, charging and empowering the arbitrators to hear the parties and their evidence, and to "make end" of their differences. The instructions, or "submissions," often stipulated a time limit within which the arbitrators had to make their decision and the form, whether written or oral, the decision had to take. Submission of the dispute to arbitration was, of course, voluntary, at least in the sense that it was not compelled by legal authority.

Voluntariness, in fact, permeated the process. For example, because executory oral contracts were unenforceable, either party to an oral submission could revoke the submission, and thus the authority of the arbitrators, with impunity. Disputants sought to correct this problem by submitting to arbitration on written instruments called deeds, which both parties signed. But submission by deed offered little deterrence to revocation. The aggrieved party whose opponent had revoked a written submission could bring an action of debt, for nonperformance of the obligation in the deed. Courts, however, would award only nominal damages for the breach—after all, how much damage could a person sustain whose only "injury" was having to "seek the king's justice?" Thus, despite their coercive intent, deeds did little to impair the voluntariness of the process.

The submission was not the only part of the process that relied on the continuing commitment of the parties to a resolution. Even when the parties stood firm to the conclusion, there was no guarantee that they would abide by the award. For all practical purposes, arbitration awards were unenforceable. Arbitrators did not have legal process at their disposal to enforce their awards, nor could courts issue writs of execution on them. If the award required one party to pay money, the party in whose favor the arbitrators had awarded could bring an action of debt or of assumpsit against his opponent. Neither action, however, made the award itself enforceable. Moreover, each action was so hedged with procedural limitations that it was often simpler to sue on the underlying dispute. Successful arbitration thus rested on the good faith of the parties rather than on legal sanctions.

II. ARBITRATION AND COMMUNITY IN SEVENTEENTH-CENTURY CONNECTICUT

Connecticut in the seventeenth century was a small society. The universe for most people was the town in which they lived. It is difficult now to imagine what this meant. The average town contained perhaps a hundred families, five or six hundred people, most of whom lived within a few hundred yards of the center of town. Where houses stopped, field and forest began. People not only knew one another, they knew one another in a variety of contexts. . . . [T]he interdependence of the early settlers, born as it was partly of choice and partly of necessity, gave the first towns a powerful cohesiveness. A voluntary process such as arbitration could work in such communities either because of trust, which one would expect in covenanted communities, or because of naked self-interest, which one would expect in all communities in which survival depended on cooperation.

One should not, of course, equate community with a utopia free of conflict. . . . The web of interpersonal relationships that characterized such communities served both as a wellspring of cohesion and as a fertile source of quarrels. Disputes could be particularly nasty and enduring precisely because personal relations were close and frequent. . . .

Arbitration in Connecticut before 1700 was a community affair. . . . The community nexus of arbitration should not surprise us. Arbitration was, after all, a consensual process. No one compelled disputants to submit their differences to the judgment of arbitrators whose only authority came from the parties themselves. People did not sacrifice the compulsory process of law for the voluntariness of arbitration when they were strangers—the vagaries of the results could be too great. They chose arbitration over law when they knew one another and trusted each other to treat as final an award that was legally unenforceable. They also chose arbitration for its relative speed, inexpensiveness, and informality. . . .

Merely by virtue of living in the same community, disputants had a joint past and an expectation or necessity of continued relations. Their disputes thus had to be handled in a way that would enable them to resume their normal neighborly relations, even if only under a flag of truce. Arbitration was well-suited to the task of blurring the distinction between victor and vanquished so that the parties could continue their relations within the community. . . .

Everything about arbitration emphasized its ties to the community. . . . Arbitrators . . . tended to be from the same town as the disputants or from neighboring towns. Arbitration thus offered disputants a method of resolving their differences that was intimately linked to the communities in which they lived. This bond between arbitration and community explains why the unenforeceability of arbitration awards caused few problems in the first decades of settlement. . . . Once disputants had submitted to arbitration . . . the party that openly repudiated the award risked community disapproval. Arbitration awards did not have to be legally enforceable as long as community sanctions sufficed. . . .

The absence of evidentiary strictures, the power of the parties to define the scope of the inquiry, the availability of remedies that common law courts did not have, the spirit of compromise implicit in the submission, the ability to choose arbitrators, the mutuality of awards, the privacy of the process—these qualities made arbitration attractive in situations where the parties, for whatever reasons, had to be able to continue to deal with one another. In short, arbitration in 17th century Connecticut was a uniquely community-based form of handling disputes and was well suited to the needs of the communities it served. But communities are not static. They grow and change, often to the dismay of their inhabitants. When communities changed, as they inevitably did, arbitration had to change too.

III. ARBITRATION AND COMMUNITY IN CONNECTICUT: 1700-1750

A. The Changing Character of Community

[Most of] the twenty-nine towns incorporated in Connecticut from 1686 to 1734 did not share the communitarian impulses of their predecessors. . . . They were settled by farmers whose primary interest was in making a living for themselves and their families. The settlers doubtless expected to created stable communities, but . . . they did not start out with communities in place. The absence of a group-minded community meant that one of the conditions that encouraged voluntary arbitration was absent.

As new towns appeared, population growth and migration weakened cohesiveness of the towns settled earlier. . . . [B]etween 1670 and 1700 . . . population density increased by half. There was thus less land to go around. Fewer fathers in the second generation than in the first could endow their sons with enough land to enable them to remain in the community. Landless sons migrated elsewhere or took up a trade. Population growth and the settlement of outlying areas within towns drew people away from the central common. As settlement within towns dispersed, outlying areas acquired the trappings of community and won incorporation as separate ecclesiastical societies, or parishes, with their own ministers and meetinghouses. Town populations were swelled by people who did not share the communitarian ideals of the first inhabitants, either because they had different backgrounds or because children do not always accept the values of their parents. Towns became less insular. People still had continuing relationships that they wished to preserve, but those relationships increasingly crossed town boundaries.

B. New Arbitration Techniques: Methods of Submission and Problems of Enforcement

. . . . All arbitrations mentioned in petitions to the Assembly before 1700 involved disputants from the same town or the same family. For the next half-century, the proportion of such arbitrations dropped to 57 percent. People continued to use arbitration in the eighteenth century, but as the bonds of community weakened, far fewer people could rely on community support to assure voluntary compliance with awards. The legal unenforceability of arbitration awards now became troublesome. In response, disputants adopted various devices that in time changed the nature of arbitration itself.

The first such device was submitting to arbitration by deed. . . . In Connecticut, deeds took the form of a written submission, signed by both parties, containing a promise that the party who failed to perform the award would forfeit a penalty sum. . . . Deeds . . . suffered the double disadvantage of presupposing the absence of the trust necessary for oral submissions without adding significantly to the enforceability of arbitration awards. An action on the case for breach of promises made in a deed of submission was not a sufficiently predictable method of assuring compliance with an award that one party was inclined to ignore.

A second device, submitting to arbitration on conditioned bonds, followed as a consequence of the weakness of deeds. The shift from deeds to bonds coincided with the shift in the residence patterns of parties to arbitration at the turn of the century. The parties would execute bonds in each other's favor for a penal amount conditioned on nonperformance of any award granted by arbitrators named in the bonds. They would then exchange bonds and proceed to arbitration. Conditioned bonds had long been a mainstay of bilateral contracts at English law. As used in arbitration, they raised the cost of ignoring an award by creating an enforceable debt obligation. A person who refused to perform an award risked being sued for the full penal sum of the bond he had given. . . .

The reign of conditioned bonds in arbitration did not last long in Connecticut. . . . By 1730, they had been replaced by promissory notes that the parties executed in favor of each other and deposited with the arbitrators as pledges to perform the award. After making the award, the arbitrators could either return the notes to their makers or turn them both over to the party in whose favor they had decided. . . . Promissory notes offered several advantages over the now-emasculated conditioned bonds. First, they were simple enough for parties to draft themselves without the aid of a scrivener. Second, unlike conditioned bonds, they were absolute in form, which, at least initially, made them even more difficult to defend against. Third, and most importantly, promissory notes gave arbitrators a means of securing compliance with their awards that they did not have before. This last point was crucial. . . .

As long as arbitrators had possession of the notes, they could compel compliance with their awards. They could return the notes to their makers or give both notes to the person in whose favor they had awarded. They could turn the loser's note over to the winner immediately, or, if they were of a mind to give him time to perform the award, they could wait. They could endorse the loser's note down to the amount of the award before delivering it to the winner for collection, or they could deliver it unendorsed and thereby enable the victor to sue for the full face amount. These powers amounted to private enforcement of arbitration awards. Promissory notes gave arbitrators a source of power that was independent of any personal prestige they might have. Whereas before the shift to promissory notes arbitrators had only their social authority in the community to persuade disputants to accept their awards, now they had a means of legal compulsion.

By the 1730's, then, arbitration, which once had been a voluntary process from beginning to end, was voluntary only in its beginning—in the decision to submit to arbitration. Its end was now coercive.

C. Arbitration and Legal Structure

The changes in arbitration discussed thus far, shifts in the residence patterns of the parties and in the forms of submission, were essentially external changes. To understand the position of arbitration in the larger legal structure and how that position changed, we must look at why people chose arbitration in the first place and whether it fulfilled their expectations.

Although litigation occasionally afforded some of the social benefits of arbitration, people who chose arbitration rather than law seemed to believe that arbitration offered advantages that were unobtainable elsewhere. . . . One source of the belief that arbitration could achieve what law could not was that arbitration awards could, in fact, offer remedies that judgments at law could not. Early arbitration awards sometimes resembled decrees in equity, with instructions that amounted to injunctive relief. For example, in 1679 the arbitrators in a long and bitter dispute between Francis Hall of Stratford and his son, Isaac, confirmed Isaac in the possession of land he then held, fixed the rent he should pay to his father for it, directed Francis to confirm the reversion of the land to Isaac so that title would pass to Isaac when Francis died, ordered the cancellation of all accounts between them (except an account for cattle, which Isaac was to repay within three years), and directed Isaac to return to Francis the jointure under which he had claimed additional land belonging to Francis. . . .

In the eighteenth century, however, arbitration lost its ability to do equity between disputants. The omnibus awards that had made arbitration so effective in addressing disputes in all their ramifications . . . were replaced by purely monetary awards that partook more of damages awarded at law than of remedies tailored to the social circumstances of individual disputes. Why this shift to monetary awards occurred is unclear. . . .

The growing prominence of monetary awards in the eighteenth century also reflected the declining community basis of arbitration. The large proportion of arbitrations between disputants from different towns after 1700 indicated the geographic dispersal and consequent attenuation of the underlying social relations. Disputes in such circumstances tended not to be played out against a complex range of relations between the parties but instead focused rather narrowly on the individual transactions in question. . . . Arbitration had clearly become more law-like by the middle of the 18th century. . . .

IV. THE FORMALIZATION OF ARBITRATION AFTER 1750

Arbitration in Connecticut underwent one final change before the Revolution. The most visible sign of the change was a statute enacted in 1753 that created for the first time a formal legal framework for arbitration. In a larger sense, however, the statute was simply an extension of the long-standing effort to secure compliance with arbitration awards. It completed the formalization of what had once been a rather neighborly way of handling disputes.

The Connecticut statute was a variant of the English Arbitration Act. . . . Although in form the English act applied to all disputes, it particularly addressed the need of the mercantile community for arbitration that rested on something more than the good faith of the parties. The Connecticut statute, like the English act, addressed commercial needs for more secure arbitration. To appreciate its significance, we must first understand the special role of arbitration in the mercantile community.

A. Commerce and Arbitration

There is little formal evidence of commercial arbitration in Connecticut before 1750 . . ., [but that] can hardly mean that merchants and traders in Connecticut did not resort to arbitration. The few that we do see depict arbitration as a standard method of settling disagreements between merchants. It seems more likely that so few traces of commercial arbitration appear in the court record because, by and large, commercial arbitration succeeded.

Merchants have always formed communities defined by common interests, common goals, trade usages, and the like. Like all professionals, lawyers included, merchants developed shorthand styles of ordering their world and the transactions within it—styles that doubtless seemed obscure to outsiders, but that streamlined and rationalized merchants' dealings among themselves. . . . Part of the strength of the law merchant was that it left the adjudication of mercantile questions to merchants. Arbitration, which allowed parties to choose their own judges, offered the same advantage and thus played a favored role in the resolution of commercial disputes. . . .

[T]he institutions and special jurisdictions that supported the law merchant in England did not cross the Atlantic. Instead, colonial merchants were left largely to their own devices. Arbitration was a readily available substitute. The only authority arbitrators needed to settle disputes was that conferred by the parties in their submission. Moreover, until the middle of the eighteenth century, the mercantile community retained enough community of interest that the procedural mechanisms for enforcing arbitration awards were both unnecessary and inappropriate.

[Merchants dealt with each other repeatedly, and so] developed a stake in the continuation of the relationship that diminished the significance of differences over individual transactions. Merchants could no more afford disruption of a trading relationship than towns could afford rifts in the multilayered relationships that bound their inhabitants together. They therefore tended to act with restraint in their dealings with one another. When merchants could no longer forbear disputing, the compromise implicit in arbitration suited their needs. For merchants, as for nonmerchants, arbitration enabled disputing parties to continue their relations within the community. . . .

Toward the middle of the eighteenth century, however, the mercantile community began to change. Connecticut had undergone an economic transformation in the first half of the century. . . . As trade expanded, so did the ranks of merchants. . . . The commercialization of the economy not only meant that more people were engaged in trade, but also that more of them were newcomers who did not appreciate the norms of the business community. At the same time, the increased opportunity for business-related disputes made commercial arbitration all the more desirable for its speed and choice of judges. New traders and established merchants, however, did not have the community of interest that enabled commercial arbitration to function as smoothly as it had when merchants were a more homogeneous group. These changes in the business community explain the sharp increase in the number of failed commercial arbitrations mentioned in the petitions after mid-century. They also explain why merchants saw in the English Arbitration Act a possible solution to the weaknesses of arbitration and urged a similar statute upon the General Assembly.

B. Codification and Its Aftermath: New Forms of Submission

The Connecticut arbitration statute of 1753 permitted parties to have their submission to arbitration made a rule of court. They would then be under court order to submit to arbitration and to abide by the award, with failure to do either punishable by contempt process.

More importantly, when parties had made their submission a rule of court, the statute empowered the arbitrators to file a return of their award with the county court, which could then grant a writ of execution to collect the award "in case of disobedience of either party." The statute thus made arbitration awards directly enforceable by legal process. Parties still could not enforce executory promises to arbitrate, but disputants who invoked the statute and submitted to arbitration under a rule of court lost the power to change their minds.

Not all disputants, however, invoked the statute. Only nineteen percent of the noncommercial arbitrations and forty percent of the commercial arbitrations mentioned in petitions to the Assembly between 1753 and 1775 were under a rule of court. This does not mean that the statute was ineffectual. On the contrary, it appears to have spurred the development of yet another form of submission—one that took the salient features of submission by rule of court and improved upon them. In the new form, disputants would execute promissory notes, confess judgment on the notes before a justice of the peace, and take out executions on the judgments, which they then deposited with the arbitrators. When the arbitrators made their award, they would endorse the execution against the loser down to the amount of the award and deliver it to the victor. Pledging executions had the same practical effect as submission by rule of court, since both made execution process available on the award . . . but . . . was faster and more convenient. . . .

Other significant changes in arbitration also occurred after 1753. For example, parties took to naming justices of the peace as arbitrators. The presence of a sworn judicial officer, even one who in theory was not acting in his official capacity, gave the proceedings a more formal, legalistic tone. After 1753, one finds for the first time parties testifying under oath at arbitration hearings and lawyers participating as counsel to the disputants. . . .

The enforceability of arbitration awards after the statute made procedural formalization inevitable. There is an inverse relationship between the enforceability of awards and the freedom of arbitrators to decide without reference to rules of law. Arbitrators have greater discretion when their awards are not readily enforceable, for their discretion is bounded only by the parties' perceptions of the fairness of the award. Parties who believe an award is unjust can choose to ignore it. But when awards become more like legal judgments in their consequences for the parties, as they did with the extension of execution process, the community requires that they be governed by similar legal standards.

The factors that led to procedural formalization also produced a substantive formalization of awards. The trend toward exclusively monetary awards was now complete. None of the awards in the petitions after 1753 have the variety or complexity of awards from earlier in the century. There is none of the joinder of issues or mixture of remedies that characterized early awards. Arbitrators lost the discretion to fashion remedies that differed from those available at common law. Because executions were levied for money rather than for specific articles, arbitration backed by execution process favored monetary awards. Although disputants still spoke of submitting to arbitration to achieve "an equitable settlement" or a resolution "according to the rules of equity and justice," it is clear that little equity remained in the process, at least in the remedies that arbitrators applied. A process that once had directed parties to perform executory contracts now offered only monetary awards much like any court of law . . . .

The transformation of arbitration awards into legal judgments permitted a measure of direct enforcement that arbitration had never before enjoyed. However, the new-found legalization of arbitration was not without a price. Arbitration, which had always been adjudicatory in nature, became downright legalistic. Not only were the awards different, but the hearing process itself had changed. After the statute, arbitrators looked more like judges than they did before. Indeed, many of them were judges. They presided over proceedings that resembled formal hearings. . . . The process itself still went by the name arbitration, but it was no longer what the name had once implied. . . . It was, as Zephaniah Swift later wrote, "a court created, constituted, and appointed by the parties." There are limits to how much a process can change before it becomes transformed. The statute made arbitration awards enforceable at law, which had been the goal of secured submissions. But the changes set in motion by the search for enforceability transformed arbitration from a voluntary, communal form of settling disputes into a pale imitation of legal adjudication.

Chapter 2

Communications: Theory and Practice

CASE STUDY

Ms. Mozart, a female associate at the law firm of Vivaldi & Brahms, L.L.P., was subjected to repeated instances of sexual harassment by Mr. Vivaldi, a partner at the firm. Ms. Mozart claims that the harassment included lewd comments, invitations out for dinner and drinks, physical contact in the workplace, and other inappropriate conduct. Ms. Mozart made numerous attempts to report the situation to the male colleague who served as her supervisor, but the supervisor took no action to alleviate her fears. Ms. Mozart alleges that her supervisor ignored her reports in an effort to avoid any friction with Mr. Vivaldi, from whom they were attempting to secure an assignment at the time of the incident.

Ms. Mozart and her supervisor had been lobbying very hard to work on an important case with Mr. Vivaldi. In fact, the supervisor agreed to discuss the case over a weekend tennis match with Mr. Vivaldi. Ms. Mozart said that she felt she needed to make a similar contribution to the case. As a result, Ms. Mozart made it clear to Mr. Vivaldi that she was willing to work as hard as her male colleagues to see that the case came to a resolution.

The harassment culminated in a single event whereby Mr. Vivaldi took her up on her offer and suggested that they discuss the case that night over drinks. Mr. Vivaldi then proceeded to proposition Ms. Mozart relentlessly, which prompted her to storm out of the bar and bring this lawsuit against Mr. Vivaldi and the firm. Although Ms. Mozart was disgusted by Mr. Vivaldi's behavior, she enjoyed her job with the firm and had a good relationship with her other colleagues. In addition, Ms. Mozart was frequently commended on the quality of her work and was considered a valuable asset to the firm.

A. Introduction

Communication is integral to the settlement of disputes, but it is integral to much else in life — indeed, to leading a meaningful life at all. So, the reader might reasonably ask, why a chapter on communication in a set of materials on ADR that is addressed to graduate students? Formal education spends much time on the tools of communication (vocabulary, grammar), and on writing skills, but little on two-way oral communication. Those who participate in forensics learn to argue effectively, which requires skills of persuasion, but not an exchange of information. One can obtain an excellent college education without ever being required to collect information from another individual, let alone one who is a participant in a serious and upsetting dispute. In addition, even people who have excellent communications skills can learn more.

Strong communications skills are essential for effective participation in any dispute resolution process, whether as negotiator, counsel, or decider. The focus here is on matters that are not commonly taught, so written communication is largely ignored and particular emphasis is placed on nonverbal communication.

B. Effective Communication

1. Eastwood Atwater, I Hear You 1-3, 65-74 (1992)*

Whatever Happened to Listening?

Despite the amount of time spent in listening, the average person does not listen very well. Immediately after hearing someone talk, we generally understand and remember only about half of what was said. Within the next forty eight hours we forget half of that again, so that we retain only 25 percent of what we originally heard. . . .

How Well Do You Listen?

To find out how well or poorly you listen, you might try this: The next time someone initiates a conversation with you, ask yourself, "Am I really listening or am I thinking of what I want to say next?" . . . Use this simple exercise to become more aware of your listening habits, especially the difficulty of listening well. . . . How would you rate yourself as a listener? How do you think others would rate you? Ask a friend, someone at work, or your spouse or child for their opinions.

Faulty Listening Habits

Often we fail to listen well for some rather obvious reasons. Many times we are too busy talking to listen, or we may be preoccupied or distracted. Sometimes we are simply too tired or too lazy to listen. After all, listening is hard work because it requires concentration. But most often it's because of our faulty listening habits.

Think of the worst listeners you know and describe their listening habits. Robert L. Montgomery found that the poor listener (commonly): interrupts; jumps to conclusions; finishes the speaker's sentences; is inattentive; changes the subject; writes everything down; doesn't give any responses; is impatient; loses his or her temper; and fidgets nervously.

Sound familiar? Probably so, because each of us has engaged in some of these practices at one time or another. However, when we exhibit any of these at least 40 percent of the time, others tend to see them as habitual or characteristic of us. . . .

Nonverbal Communication

Our awareness of nonverbal communication is reflected in many of our popular figures of speech. We speak of happy people being "filled with joy" or "bursting with pride." We see fearful people as "paralyzed" or "frozen" with fear. Angry people may be described as "trembling with rage" . . . . or "ready to explode." Tense people are portrayed as "biting their lips." In each of these examples, people are expressing their feelings through their bodies as well as their

*Reprinted with permission.

words. While experts differ in their estimates, it is safe to say that more than half of our face-to-face communication is nonverbal. Listening to the speaker's message, then, means learning how to read his or her body language as well and responding appropriately. . . .

Vocal Expressions

A good listener . . . hears more than the speaker's words. He also hears the speaker's pitch, tone of voice, and rate of speech. He notices the variations of speech, like failing to complete a sentence and/or pausing frequently. . . . Tone of voice is an especially valuable clue to feelings. Rollo May, a famous psychotherapist, often asks himself "What does the voice say when I stop listening to the words and listen only to the tone?" . . . From the listener's standpoint, anger and sadness are usually the easiest to recognize, while nervousness and jealousy are among the most difficult.

The volume and pitch of the speaker's voice, how high or low, or how loud or soft it sounds, are also helpful in decoding the speaker's message. Some emotions like enthusiasm, joy, and disbelief are usually delivered in a high pitch. Anger and fear are also expressed in a high pitch, as well as in a wider range of tone and pitch of volume. On the other hand, apathy and emotions like sadness and grief are usually expressed softly and in a low pitch, especially toward the end of each sentence.

The rate of speech also tells us something about the speaker's feelings. People talk faster when they are excited or anxious, or when they are speaking about a personal problem or something that is threatening to them. People are also apt to speak faster when they are trying to persuade us or sell us something. . . . [P]eople usually talk more slowly when they are depressed, grief-stricken, disgusted, contemptuous, or tired. . . .

2. David A. Binder, Paul Bergman & Susan C. Price, Lawyers as Counselors 35-44 (1991)*

4. INHIBITORS

The seven inhibitors described below are common in lawyer-client dialogues. While other phenomena may also inhibit active client participation, these seven operate across a wide range of client personality types. Though the discussion treats each inhibitor as a separate phenomenon, in practice each often intertwines with others. Of the seven inhibitors, the first two—ego threat and case threat—probably play the most pervasive role in blocking full communication.

A. Ego Threat

Clients tend to withhold information which they perceive as threatening to their self-esteem. The requested information may relate either to past or anticipated behavior, and the feelings that a question may arouse can range from mild embarrassment to a strong sense of guilt or shame. If a client believes that a truthful response will lead you to evaluate the client negatively, such a response threatens the client's self-esteem; the response is "ego threatening." Rather than risk your negative evaluation, the client may answer falsely, or become reluctant to participate in the conversation. . . .

Ego threat may at times arise not because a client fears your personal negative evaluation

*Reprinted with permission of the West Publishing Corporation.

but because a client fears that certain information may become public. In other words, a client may fear that disclosing information may lead friends, relatives or others to think ill of the client. In such a situation, a client may admit damaging information as long as the client believes that you will keep the information confidential.

B. Case Threat

A second major factor tending to inhibit client communication is "case threat." A client may believe that revealing information will "hurt my case." For example, an innocent criminal defendant may not want to reveal to you that she was near the scene of a crime because she fears that if the judge and jurors find it out she will lose. Alternatively, the client may fear that revealing the information will cause you to believe that the case is a loser and to fail to pursue it zealously. (In such situations, ego threat may be present as well. If the client believes that revealing that she was at the scene of the crime will cause the lawyer to disbelieve her claim of innocence, the potential loss of self-esteem may well inhibit a truthful response.) . . .

Similarly, assume that in a civil matter you ask a client about the whereabouts of a business document. If the client fears that information on the document contains damaging information, case threat may lead the client not to reveal its whereabouts.

"Case threat" may also inhibit clients who have transactional matters. Assume that Jean consults you in connection with a proposal to lease space in an office building. During a conversation about negotiation strategy, you inquire about the maximum length lease that Jean will accept. Jean is willing to accept a ten year lease, but she hopes the owner will agree to a five-year term. Jean may be unwilling to reveal her willingness to accept a ten year deal, feeling that once you know her "bottom line," you will not press as hard as you otherwise might for a shorter lease term.

C. Role Expectations

Role expectations often affect communication between lawyers and clients. Most of us have sets of beliefs about what kind of behavior is appropriate within the confines of particular relationships. For example, most people think there are certain ways that one should (or should not) behave when interacting with parents. Similarly, most people have beliefs about how employers should relate to employees. We may each have different sets of beliefs, but most of us do approach many relationships with preset expectations.

Beliefs about what constitutes proper behavior are "expectations." Since the expectations under discussion here pertain to what a person believes constitutes proper behavior in a particular relationship, the entire phenomenon may be labeled "role expectations." The effect of role expectations is that when a person interacts with another about whom the person has preset role expectations, those beliefs may (if only unconsciously) come into play and cause the person to modify his or her behavior to conform with the beliefs.

Role expectations develop from a variety of sources, from both actual and vicarious experiences. Family, friends, associates, news media, institutions and the like constantly deliver messages about what constitutes appropriate behavior when one assumes a particular position. In short, role expectations are learned and shaped by life experiences.

In most relationships, one person assumes a position of authority or leadership over the other. Therefore, when people initially enter into a particular relationship, they often expect to be in either a dominant or subordinate position. If one is a parent one expects to dominate;

if one is a child, one expects to be dominated. Teachers often see their students as occupying subordinate roles. Again, these beliefs develop unconsciously from years of cultural infusion. Undoubtedly, people might be better off if they saw more relationships as involving shared responsibility, but the fact is that frequently they do not. Rather, they see relationships in terms of dominant and subordinate positions.

What does this phenomenon have to do with lawyers and clients? Clients will frequently enter your office with a set of expectations about what constitutes appropriate "client behavior." The expectations will vary from client to client; not all clients will have acquired their expectations from the same learning sources. In many instances, however, clients think of their lawyers as occupying positions of authority. Such clients may be somewhat reluctant to communicate fully in the belief that you know what subjects are deserving of inquiry. Thus, if you fail to broach a topic which a client feels is important, the client may assume (again, either consciously or intuitively) that the topic is not a significant one.

Interestingly, many clients have an opposite set of beliefs. This second group of clients tends to believe that a lawyer's role is limited to carrying out their wishes and that it is their privilege to speak their minds about any and all topics. In short, these clients see themselves in a dominant position vis-a-vis their counsel, and they are often not interested in fully responding to inquiries they perceive as unimportant.

The closer a client's expectations come to either extreme of the dominant-subordinate spectrum, the more difficulties you may expect to encounter in developing full information. The subordinate client must be motivated to talk much more freely; after all, not even the most brilliant lawyer will be able to think of everything relevant to the best possible resolution for a client's problem. On the other hand, you must provide a "dominating" client with the impetus to speak about topics you deem important.

D. Etiquette Barrier

A fourth inhibitor is the "etiquette barrier." Often, an individual has information that he or she will freely provide to some persons but not to others. For example, there are things that women tell women but not men; that blacks tell blacks, but not whites; that students tell students, but not teachers; that doctors tell doctors, but not patients. Information is perceived to be appropriate for peers but not for those in other groups or roles. The etiquette barrier arises from people's desires not to shock, embarrass, offend or discomfort. It reflects a person's thinking about the effect of information on a listener, not a person's thinking about how the listener will view him or her. Hence, loss of self-esteem is not a component of the etiquette barrier.

For example, assume that you represent a juvenile charged with murder. The client insists that a member of a rival gang was the actual culprit and that the client had heard this other person swearing and making threats toward the victim. But when you ask your client what swear words the actual killer uttered, the client becomes reluctant to talk. The etiquette barrier may be at the heart of this reluctance. The client would probably have little difficulty uttering or repeating profanity to his peers, but may feel that profanity is improper in a conversation with a lawyer.

When you sense that a client feels that a topic is "taboo," you need to convey the idea that the topic is open for discussion. If you do not take the initiative in granting permission, a client affected by the "etiquette barrier" will usually continue to withhold the data.

E. Trauma

This phenomenon occurs when you ask a client to recall an experience which evokes unpleasant feelings. Many events cause people to experience such negative feelings as fear, anger, humiliation, and sadness. When you ask clients to recall such events, they may reexperience the negative feelings. . . . Likewise, an estate planning client who is considering disinheriting a close relative may for similar reasons be reluctant to talk about the reasons he or she wants to disinherit the person.

F. Perceived Irrelevancy

This inhibitor is often more difficult to recognize, as it does not involve any feelings of discomfort or threat. The feeling involved here is one of "no reason to provide that data." A client feels that nothing will be gained by providing the information you request and so is reluctant to provide it.

An interview of a parent accused of child abuse provides an illustration. Those who have worked in the area of child abuse have observed that battering parents tend to be individuals who have very few and infrequent social contacts. If you represent a parent accused of child abuse, therefore, you may wish to uncover information about the nature and extent of the client's social contacts. However, to a parent accused of child abuse, questions about the general nature of the parent's social activities are quite likely to seem irrelevant, if not frivolous. The questions are not concerned with the relationship between the parent and the child. They seemingly have nothing to do with the case. As a consequence, the client may feel little motivation to provide a detailed response.

"Perceived irrelevancy" is just as likely to arise in a transactional context. Assume you represent a partnership which has asked you to negotiate the purchase of a building. You may ask the partners for information about why the owner wants to sell, so that in problem solving fashion you can structure the deal in such a way that it meets both your clients' and the seller's needs. But the clients, perhaps seeing little importance in exploring the seller's needs, may provide only perfunctory information.

G. Greater Need

The last inhibitor is "greater need." This situation is characterized by a client's need or desire to talk about a subject other than that which is of immediate interest to you. As a consequence, the client cannot concentrate on your question, and full and accurate information is not forthcoming. For example, an incarcerated defendant concerned primarily with bail or O.R. [own recognizance] release will often be unable to turn full attention to questions relating to the underlying charge. Similarly, a tenant threatened with eviction may be more concerned with when and where he can move than with inquiries related to a potential "habitability defense."

In such situations, your questions are not perceived as irrelevant or threatening. Rather, the client is simply concerned with a subject which, while perhaps secondary to you, is primary to the client.

5. FACILITATORS

The five facilitators described below encourage clients to participate fully in counseling dialogues. . . . [N]ote that you typically may employ facilitators without waiting for client reluctance to rear its annoying head. That is, you routinely incorporate the facilitators into all dialogues, whether the clients are enthusiastic or reluctant participants.

A. Empathic Understanding

Empathic understanding typically gives clients feelings of trust and confidence in an attorney-client relationship and thereby motivates clients to participate fully in conversations. Despite the motivational power of empathic understanding, lawyers commonly fail to utilize it when talking with clients.

People have limited opportunities in our society to express their thoughts and feelings to someone who is willing to (1) listen, (2) understand, and (3) at the same time, not judge. . . . Providing advice or analysis, even if done with a genuine desire to be of help, ironically tends to give an individual little impetus to delve further into a subject. There is little point in expressing your ideas and feelings if all you get in return is lay psychoanalysis or advice on how to change or ignore your feelings.

However, in the presence of . . . [a] nonjudgmental listener who provides empathic responses, most people are strongly motivated to continue communicating. Almost without realizing it, people will tend to provide an ever-increasing amount of information. Precisely why nonjudgmental understanding results in increased inducement to communicate is not known. However, many experts in the field of psychology have stressed the fact that it does have this self-propelling effect.

The opportunities for you to utilize empathic understanding are endless. Clients almost always are emotionally involved in their problems, and thus repeatedly express feelings about what has occurred or is likely to occur. Their recitals of information are likely to be accompanied by and intertwined with feelings about such diverse matters as: (1) how they felt at the time an event occurred; (2) how they feel about people or institutions involved in their problem; (3) why events have unfolded, and why people have behaved as they have; (4) how they feel about an event at present; and (5) how they feel about what is likely to happen in the future. . . .

B. Fulfilling Expectations

The phenomenon of "fulfilling expectations" refers to people's tendencies to want to satisfy the perceived expectations of those with whom they interact. Your simply communicating, verbally or nonverbally, your expectations will often be the catalyst that motivates a client to undertake a particular discussion.

This facilitator is especially useful when you sense that certain inhibitors are making a client reluctant to provide information. On sensing the reluctance, you can verbally convey a strong expectation that the sought data should be revealed. The client's need to conform to your expectations may well be stronger than whatever needs have given rise to the reluctance to respond. In such situations, the inhibitors will be overcome and the information revealed.

Note two additional points about fulfilling expectations. First, the phenomenon can be useful in overcoming memory difficulties as well as inhibitors. Second, the phenomenon can be inadvertently employed to create an expectation that the sought data need not be revealed. The following example will help you consider both points.

Assume that a client has indicated that she cannot remember much of what occurred at a meeting held two years earlier. You may convey your expectation that by probing her memory further, the client will be able to recollect more information:

> "I understand how hard it is to recall; I've often had that difficulty myself. Often I find, however, that if I concentrate for a while things start to come back. Why don't you think about it a little more?"

This statement employs two facilitators. First, you empathize; you articulate your understanding of the difficulty. Additionally, you convey your expectation that with more effort, the client will be able to provide more information. Your message is, "though the task may be difficult, I expect that you will attempt it."

Unfortunately, you may inadvertently convey an expectation that a client need make no further effort to recall information. For example, assume that in the example above you had said:

> "I understand that it is difficult to remember the details of an event that happened so long ago."

This statement does nothing more than empathize with the client's difficulty, and standing alone it may be counterproductive. While you convey understanding of the client's dilemma, you also convey the idea that you do not expect an answer.

C. Recognition

Human beings often need attention and recognition from people outside their close circle of family and friends. They enjoy feeling important and seek the attention and esteem of outsiders. Thus, giving an interviewee "recognition" motivates the interviewee to be more cooperative and open.

Assuming you are not a client's close friend or relative, you may supply "recognition" simply by sincerely praising a client's cooperation or help: "Your giving me that information is very helpful." "That was very important information you just gave me." "You're really doing a good job of setting out the consequences of not demanding an option to renew at this time."

D. Altruistic Appeals

People often need to identify with a high value or cause that is beyond their immediate self-interest. This need may be a form of identification with the objectives of a large social group. A person's performance of altruistic deeds usually increases the person's self-esteem. Thus, clients are often motivated to participate fully when doing so makes them feel altruistic. . . .

E. Extrinsic Reward

Realizing that certain behavior is in their self-interest usually motivates people to engage in that behavior. Thus, a person with the mind set, "what's in it for me?" at times is reluctant to provide information. Hence, you may facilitate disclosure of information that a client seems reluctant to discuss by pointing out why the sought data may aid in resolving the client's problem. You thereby indicate that providing the information is in the client's best interest.

As the term "extrinsic" may suggest, this facilitator differs in an important way from those previously discussed. The earlier phenomena drew their motivational strength from satisfying clients' psychological needs within the counseling interaction itself. Use of extrinsic reward, on the other hand, achieves motivational force from a client's realizing how participation in the interview will satisfy needs external to the interview—i.e., a favorable resolution of a client's matter. A client's reward comes from outside the interview: "Mr. Edwards, if you will tell me a bit more about your investments, I'll be able to draft the trust in a way that minimizes taxes."

6. SUMMARY

As the common inhibitors and facilitators are referred to frequently throughout the remainder of this book, we list them all together:

INHIBITORS	FACILITATORS
Ego Threat	Empathic Understanding
Case Threat	Fulfilling Expectations
Role Expectations	Recognition
Etiquette Barrier	Altruistic Appeals
Trauma	Extrinsic Reward
Perceived Irrelevancy	
Greater Need	

7. PERSONALITY CONFLICTS

Though this chapter has described a number of psychological phenomena, you have perhaps noted that it has not mentioned one factor that all would recognize as important to the interaction of any two people—their personalities. All of us are more comfortable with some people than with others. Thus, lawyer-client communications are often inhibited by some degree of personality conflict. If a client, for one reason or another, perceives you as someone with whom he or she is not comfortable, or someone who is too aggressive or too passive to handle a matter effectively, the client may feel reluctant to participate fully. By the same token, you may, for one reason or another, perceive a client as too aggressive, passive, unscrupulous, or disorganized; and such perceptions may inhibit your interaction with the client.

3. Comments and Questions

a. Do men and women, as a class, communicate differently in important ways, and if so what are the differences? This is a much debated topic that is of obvious relevance for negotiation, but on which firm answers cannot be ventured with confidence. To the extent there are important differences, there remains the question of what, if anything, is called for in the way of a policy response by government or the private sector. Even if systematic aggregate differences between men and women are shown, this does not tell us how specific individuals will respond in particular situations.

b. Much of the literature is polemical, and much is driven by various ideological agendas. Some useful books in the area are Carol Gilligan, IN A DIFFERENT VOICE (1982); Pat Heim & Susan Golant, HARDBALL FOR WOMEN (1992); P. J. Kalbfleisch & M. J. Cody (eds.), WOMEN'S STYLE IN PROBLEM SOLVING INTERACTIONS: POWERLESS OR SIMPLY FEMININE? (1995); Rosabeth Moss Kantor, MEN AND WOMEN OF THE CORPORATION (1993); Felice N. Schwartz, BREAKING WITH TRADITION (1992); Deborah Tannen, YOU JUST DON'T UNDERSTAND: WOMEN AND MEN IN CONVERSATION (1990).

c. We are concerned with the narrower issues, of what differences there are between sexes for purposes of negotiation, mediation, and other aspects of ADR, and how those differences matter. It is widely thought that battered wives should not be required to mediate with their husbands in divorce proceedings, but this a very different matter from styles of talking.

(Violence might usefully be defined as a form of "communication" for some purposes, but the term in used in a narrower sense in this Chapter.)

d. Consider women as negotiators. Are women, as a class, better or worse negotiators than men? What is the basis for your conclusion? Empirical research on this topic is presented in Chapter 3, section E. Do you think women, as a class, are at a communication disadvantage in divorce mediation, and why? This question is considered at length in Chapter 8, section C.

e. The following excerpt addresses the business arena, and raises the concern that women do not get ahead because they do not communicate in the same way as men, and that the male pattern of communication is dominant.

4. Kathleen Kelley Reardon, They Don't Get It, Do They? Communication in the Workplace — Closing the Gap Between Men and Women 40-45(1995)*

Turning Around Dysfunctional Communications Patterns

Communication patterns between men and women have not kept pace with women's progress. Women are past ready for leadership positions, even in the largest companies, but the communication scripts they bring to work are often at odds with those that men are accustomed to using. With such an imperfect fit, the efforts of men and women to work together at senior levels have yielded disappointing results. Their communication is clumsy and often nonproductive. It leads to misunderstandings and, on the part of both women and men, alienation and anger. . . .

Dysfunctional communication patterns (DCP) can't be eradicated unless women are willing to risk altering them. When an interaction emanates from an outmoded stereotype, speaking up and exiting are two approaches women can take to improve the communication cultures in which they work. . . .

Speaking up has gotten an undeserved bad reputation, especially for women. The truth is that a wide range of communication strategies exists between demure and abrasive. Clinging to either end of the range is a recipe for failure.

A Common Dysfunctional Communication Pattern

The following scenario demonstrates what to look for and how to change a negative interaction.

Michael: You came on a bit strong in that meeting.
Jessica: I was just trying to make a point.
Michael: Well, you sure did that.
Jessica: Do you think I overdid it?
Michael: It isn't what I think that counts.
Jessica: Did Al say anything to you about what I said?
Michael: He didn't have to. Didn't you see his eyes?

In this DCP, Jessica gave that power to Michael. When she said, "I was just trying to make a point," her defensive stance signaled to Michael that she was willing to participate in the DCP he had started. When she later said, "Do you think I overdid it?" she confirmed his control

*Reprinted with permission.

over the definition of her actions and reinforced the direction of the DCP. She prolonged the process by asking, "Did Al say anything about it?"

This interaction would have been quite different had Jessica been unwilling to let Michael's definition of her actions survive unscathed. Consider this possibility:

Michael: You came on a bit strong in that meeting.

Jessica: Somebody had to. The project is too important to worry about making everyone feel cozy. . . .

In the above example, Jessica's response is swift, short, and unexpected. It pulls the two communicators out of the scripted DCP and into new territory—one more positive and professional. It also conveys that Jessica is confident and that she has a persuasive, legitimate, work-related reason for her actions. Her conviction signals to Michael that she won't yield to his definition of her actions at the meeting.

People often retry initiating a DCP when others have refused to cooperate. Despite Jessica's assertive reply, Michael might try to throw her off track with this statement:

Michael: Well, you sure made your point.

Again, Jessica has a choice. She can participate in a negative DCP or respond in a way that is unexpected, positive, and likely to bring the interaction to a close. The following is an example:

Michael: Well, you sure made your point.

Jessica: Thank you.

Jessica has refused to participate in the DCP. Even if Jessica is concerned about the reactions others at the meeting might have had to her assertive comments, she needn't convey the message that she is worried. It just encourages people to continue emphasizing differences in a negative manner.

C. Eliciting Information: Questions

1. John M. Haynes, The Fundamentals of Family Mediation 185-186 (1994)*

USING QUESTIONS

Ideally, the mediator's work is conducted in the question form. When asking questions the mediator cannot give advice or instructions on what to do. The clients provide the answers and therefore tend to own the answers. Using questions is one way of helping the clients maintain control of the content.

Different types of questions are useful at different stages of the process, and different question types are used for specific purposes. Here are question forms that help to keep the session moving:

Opening questions: Help to get things started

What is the current situation?

What are going to be the major issues in the mediation?

What worries you the most about the mediation/negotiations?

What experience do you have in dealing with this type of problem?

Information questions: Obtain facts and/or opinions
Who is living in the house now?
What is your mortgage payment?
Where will the children go to school?

Clarifying questions: Make abstract and general ideas more specific
What do you mean by "everything"?
When do you want this to end?

Justifying questions: Clarify the reasons one party holds a position
Why do you think . . .?
How will this solve the problem?
How will it work on a daily basis?

Hypothetical questions: Introduce ideas into the discussion
Suppose you tried this option, what do you think would happen?
If you could write the script, what would it be?

Leading questions: Suggest an idea within the questions
Given the nature of the problem, is it possible to . . .?
Is this the only option worth considering?
I was wondering whether what another couple considered might be useful to you.

Stimulating questions: Encourage new ideas
Are there other ways to solve this problem?
What happens if you don't reach agreement on this problem?

Participation questions: Encourage expression of ideas/needs
What do you think about that, Mary?
How does that idea strike you, John?

Focusing questions: Bring the discussion back to the core issues
Where do we go from here?
How does this relate to the issue of the children?

Alternative questions: Compare two or more alternatives
Which of these two options do you think is better?
Do both work well for both of you?

Closure questions: Encourage making the decision
Have we spent enough time on this issue?
Do you want to think about it and decide next week?
Have we agreed to the following . . .?

Evaluation questions: Help the couple assess their progress and future:
Why do you think we are blocked on this issue?
What will happen if we do this?

2. David A. Binder, Paul Bergman & Susan C. Price, Lawyers as Counselors 69-81, 237-56 (1991)*

QUESTIONING

. . . The information you get from clients, their motivation to speak and their attitudes towards you are all influenced to some degree by the kinds of questions that you ask. Of course, human behavior is too complex to conclude that a particular form of question will always generate the same type of client response. Nonetheless, research and experience demonstrate that different forms of questions are likely to alter the amount, nature and quality of information that you receive. By understanding the forms of questions, and the typical consequences each is likely to produce, you can make explicit questioning choices tailored to your goals, the type of information you are seeking and the particular client with whom you are dealing.

2. FORMS OF QUESTIONS

A. Generally

Questions come in a variety of forms, ranging from open to leading. No hard and fast line separates one form from another. But the principal touchstone that distinguishes forms of questions is the degree of freedom a question allows in a response. For example, consider the following questions:

1. "Tell me about the car."
2. "Tell me about the color of the car."
3. "Tell me whether the car was red."

On the surface, each question seems pretty much like the others; each begins with "Tell me" and asks about a car. But further analysis demonstrates that the questions differ in the freedom of response they allow. The first question allows a client to discuss any or all characteristics about the car that the client wishes. The second question restricts the client's discussion to characteristics pertaining to the car's color. The third question allows no description at all; it restricts the client to verifying whether the car was red.

The freer a client is to choose the scope of a response, the more "open" a question is. And the more a question restricts a response, the more "closed" it is. Neither form of question is necessarily more effective than the other. Given how clients typically react to open and closed questions, each has its purposes.

B. Open Questions

Open questions allow clients substantial latitude to select the content and wording of a response. Open questions indicate your expectation that a client respond at some length and allow a client to respond in his or her own words. At their broadest, open questions even allow a client to choose the subject matter of a response.

Examine the following questions:

1. "Tell me what brought you in here."

---

*Reprinted with permission of the West Publishing Corporation.

2. "Tell me about your family."
3. "What happened after the meeting?"
4. "What took place during the conversation."
5. "How will your employees react if you move the business to a new location?"

Each question is open. Each invites a lengthy response, on a variety of potential topics, and in words of the clients' own choosing.

Even within the open question category, you find distinctions. No. 1 imposes no subject matter restriction at all. Granted, a client will probably talk about a legal problem, rather than, say, an insight into the poetry of Byron. But the question allows the client to describe the problem in any way he or she sees fit, and to delve into whatever aspects seem most important to the client.

No. 2 imposes some subject matter limitation—-the client is limited to a discussion of "family." But its openness allows the client to talk about family heritage; occupations of family members; statistical data such as names, addresses and ages; personality traits of family members, and the like. Also, the client can decide whether the term "family" means "immediate family" or includes cousins, nieces and nephews.

No. 3 imposes a chronological limitation—the client is limited to talking about what took place "after the meeting." But which post-meeting events to discuss are entirely up to the client.

No. 4 imposes a different sort of limitation—-the client's response is limited to a single conversation. Yet, this question too is open. The client may talk about the parties to the conversation, what they said, and/or what activities took place during the conversation.

Lastly, No. 5 asks the client to discuss possible consequences of a proposed decision on a group of employees. Its openness allows the client to discuss a variety of possible consequences, to differentiate among different groups of employees, and perhaps to talk about the client's long-range business goals.

C. Closed Questions

Closed (narrow) questions select the subject matter of a client's response and also limit the scope of a reply. Closed questions seek specific data. Examples of closed questions include:

1. "In which hand was she holding the gun?"
2. "How fast was the blue car going?"
3. "Just where did the chicken cross the road?"
4. "How many employees are likely to quit if you move the business to a new location?"

D. Yes-No Questions

"Yes-No" questions are a commonly employed form of closed question. Yes-No questions even more severely limit the scope of a client's response by including in the question all the information you seek and asking the client only to confirm or deny it. All closed questions can, of course, be restated in Yes-No form. Thus, the Yes-No versions of the closed questions above are:

1. "Was she holding the gun in her left hand?"
2. "Was the blue car exceeding the speed limit?"
3. "Did the chicken cross the road at the crosswalk?"

4. "Will some employees quit if you move the business to a new location?"

E. Leading Questions

As you are no doubt aware, leading questions not only provide all the information that you seek but also suggest the desired answer. Leading questions are little more than outright assertions, accompanied either by a tone of voice or language clue that you desire a particular answer. They are closed questions in assertive form. For example, in leading form the closed questions from subsection (C) are as follows:

1. "She was holding the gun in her left hand?"
2. "The blue car was going over 65, correct?"
3. "The chicken crossed the road at the crosswalk, didn't it?"
4. "I take it you'll lose some employees if you move the business to a new location?"

The rather dramatic "Isn't it true. . . ." phrase that cross-examiners tend to use during trial is certainly not a necessary characteristic of leading questions. Questions two and three have other and less dramatic verbal clues, while the first and fourth rely on voice intonation.

3. ADVANTAGES AND DISADVANTAGE OF DIFFERENT FORMS OF QUESTIONS

In addition to delineating the scope of a response, a question's form can also impact a client's ability and willingness to recall and provide information. This section examines this impact.

A. Open Questions

1. Open Questions Often Motivate Full Client Participation

a. Because they allow clients to decide what information is significant, open questions provide "recognition." You show confidence in their ability to know what information is significant. Both the recognition and the fact that they are talking about what they see as important tend to provide motivation.

b. Open questions typically avoid potential inhibitors. The primary inhibitors that open questions avoid are ego threat, case threat, and the etiquette barrier. Often clients are uncomfortable about certain aspects of their problems and are therefore reluctant to talk about those aspects. A closed question seeking information about an uncomfortable topic may therefore harm rapport by forcing a client either to talk about an uncomfortable topic or consciously avoid it. Open questions leave clients free to avoid talking about threatening subjects.

As a lawyer, you often have to ask clients about sensitive subjects. When planning a client's estate, for example, you may raise the possibility that a client's child may predecease the client. Talking to a business client, you may ask about the integrity of the client's partner or office manager. As a criminal defense lawyer, you may ask about a client's mental state and past criminal record. Clients may be uncomfortable and reluctant to talk if, with a closed question, you directly seek such sensitive information. Open questions allow clients to discuss sensitive information in their own way and when they are ready to do so.

Similarly, open questions also tend to overcome the inhibitor of "greater need." Since open questions allow clients to talk about what to them seems most important, you avoid any reluctance that would be created were you to ask closed questions about topics that a client regarded as of secondary importance.

2. Open Questions Often Facilitate Your Gaining Complete Data

a. Because both problems and clients' experiences are unique, you almost never will be able to think of everything that might be important to achieving a satisfactory solution. As one author has put it, "Qualitative answers—feelings, reasons, other experiences—can only come when the question is open-ended, not closed, and when the answer must be a paragraph, not a word." For example, whether the issue is past events giving rise to a lawsuit, or potential consequences of a proposed resolution, you usually cannot think of all the factors that might bear on the issue. Thus, you cannot rely on closed questions to elicit all important data.

b. Open questions promote completeness by preserving clients' trains of thought. When clients are allowed to describe matters in their own words, their paths of association remain intact and they tend to recall data that they might not mention in response to closed questions.

c. Open questions also promote the accuracy of information. Psychological research has shown that answers to open questions are more accurate than answers to closed questions.

d. Open questions tend to be more efficient in terms of time than closed questions. Even if you could think of everything that might affect a client's matter, pursuing each and every detail with closed questions would consume an inordinate amount of time. An answer to a single open question will often cover the same ground as the answers to a series of closed questions.

However, . . . be warned that a number of disadvantages are associated with [open questions].

3. Open Questions Sometimes Inhibit Full Client Participation

Open questions put much of the burden for recalling and describing information on a client. Many people are not comfortable in the conversational limelight and will prefer you to carry the load. In such situations, open questions may elicit only short, minimal responses.

4. Open Questions Are Not Sufficient for Gaining Complete Data

a. Open questions do little to stimulate memory. As a noted psychologist suggests, "Compared to other forms of report, narrative reports . . . tend to be less complete. . . . [A] narrative produces much higher accuracy but much lower quantity." As a result, events or other information known to a client typically remain undisclosed in response to open questions. . . .

Thus, to get complete data you typically have to ask a combination of open and closed questions. Because of their ability to call specific data to a client's attention, closed questions are generally more successful than open ones at stimulating a client's recall. For example, the closed question, "Did you talk about precise geographical limits during conversation A?" may remind the client of details that did not emerge in the answer to the open question. In short, in response to closed questions, clients often recognize data that they do not recall in response to open ones.

b. Open questions may also fail to elicit information that clients do remember, but which they do not recognize as being legally salient. When a client is mistaken about or unaware of legal requirements, the client may well omit information from a narrative response in the belief that the information is without legal significance.

5. Open Questions Are Sometimes Inefficient

Open questions may not be effective with clients who ramble or are extremely verbose. Certain clients may regard a question such as, "What happened since our last meeting?" as an invitation to describe irrelevant events in great detail, and to vilify all with whom they disagree. Asking open questions of such clients may be the equivalent of pouring gasoline on a fire.

B. Closed Questions

The typical advantages of closed questions are as follow:

1. Closed Questions Elicit Details

Perhaps the most important advantage of closed questions is that they allow you to elicit details. . . .

2. Closed Questions Sometimes Motivate Clients

Some clients may be uncertain of how to respond to an open question. For example, a question such as, "What consequences do you see if we reject the proposal?" may confuse some clients. Does the question call for every possible consequence, or only for the most significant ones? How much elaboration do you expect? Does the question somehow "test" the client to see how many consequences the client can identify? Clients for whom open questions create such thoughts will probably be reluctant to answer fully and openly. Such clients may find closed questions "easier" to answer: their topics are readily identifiable, their scope is readily apparent, and a client has only to produce a limited amount of information. Therefore, for such clients, closed questions may provide greater motivation to answer.

Closed questions may provide greater motivation than open questions in other contexts as well. Recall the suggestion that open questions often motivate clients by allowing them to postpone mention of sensitive topics until the client feels comfortable doing so. You may employ closed questions to delay discussion of sensitive matters as well. Closed questions allow you to "tippy toe" either into or around sensitive topics. When you know or strongly suspect that a client will be reluctant to discuss a particular topic, through closed questions you can pursue the topic a small bit at a time, and stop at the point that a client becomes obviously reluctant to proceed further. . . .

Alas, as you undoubtedly suspect, closed questions also have disadvantages:

3. Too Many Closed Questions May Harm Rapport

Over-reliance on closed questions may result in clients leaving meetings feeling that they never had a chance to say what was really on their minds. The more you ask questions which limit the scope of a response, the less likely are you to learn everything that a client thinks is important. In turn, a client is likely to be less engaged in identifying a problem and actively participating in its resolution.

4. Closed Questions Often Prevent You From Learning Important Information

Asking numerous closed questions is likely to cause you to miss both trees and the forest. You miss trees, because in any matter there are too many for you to find with closed questions. Moreover, clients tend not to volunteer information when faced with a plethora of closed questions, figuring that if a bit of data is important, surely you will seek it out.

At the same time, your focus on individual trees is likely to obscure your view of the forest. The immersion in bits of detail frustrates your learning a client's overall story.

Unfortunately, lawyers tend to ask far too many closed questions. Despite the advantages of open questions, lawyers traditionally favor closed questions. One reason may be the "filling" phenomenon. None of us approaches an event from a totally neutral perspective. We carry around "schema" which allow our past experiences to make sense of new ones. We ordinarily apply these schema unconsciously, in order to make sense of daily life. Think how complicated life would be if each trip to a supermarket, say, were a completely new and unique experience. In turn, our schema often lead us to "fill in" the details of an event based on our expectations of how such events usually occur. . . .

The tendency of lawyers to ask too many closed questions may also be a product of "premature diagnosis." The traditional pigeonholes of legal analysis are powerful. When a client begins to discuss a matter, a lawyer may automatically begin to pigeonhole it as a "products liability" case, an "inter vivos trust" matter, or a "securities issuance" problem. The initial pigeonhole is often premature—your diagnosis may be inaccurate, or at least incomplete. But once you place a problem into a pigeonhole, you then turn to gathering data that fits the matter into that pigeonhole. From there, it is but a short step to using closed questions that elicit the specific data you need to process the matter.

As with filling, inoculating yourself against the tendency to engage in premature diagnosis may be impossible. Be aware of the tendency, but try not to let initial pigeonholes foreclose the way you think about ways a client's problem might be resolved. For example, the legal reality that a client may be entitled in a lawsuit only to monetary damages should not foreclose you from asking, "If you could write your own ticket, what result would you like to see?"

5. Closed Questions Can Create Inaccurate Responses

Closed questions tend to produce more erroneous information than open questions. One potential reason may be a combination of the motivational factor, "fulfilling expectations," and the "filling" phenomenon. When you ask closed questions seeking details, clients usually try to fulfill your expectations by supplying such details. But because of the "filling" phenomenon, the answers may come not from clients' recollection of actual events, but from clients' past experiences. Therefore, clients who are asked for details may well respond with what their schemas tell them probably occurred, not what actually did occur.

Closed questions may distort responses in another way. Because closed questions define the topics for clients to a greater extent than do open questions, closed questions usually reflect a lawyer's choice of vocabulary, not a client's. For instance, compare the open question, "Describe his behavior" with the closed question, "Was he angry?" The closed question not only identifies a specific emotion, it also attaches a label to it. And closed questions' verbal labels often distort responses.

In one study, for example, changing a word in a question from "frequently" to "occasionally" produced markedly different results. In this study, which has been replicated often, one group of random respondents was asked, "Do you get headaches frequently and, if so, how often?" Another group was asked, "Do you get headaches occasionally, and, if so, how often?" The first group reported an average of 2.2 headaches per week; the second group only 0.7 headaches per week. . . .

C. Leading Questions

Although the term "leading question" is often accompanied by or greeted with sneers, such questions are sometimes proper and necessary for eliciting a full picture of a client's problem.

1. Leading Questions Sometimes Overcome Potential Inhibitors

Leading questions sometimes help you to overcome the inhibitors of ego threat, case threat and the etiquette barrier. These inhibitors sometimes make clients reluctant to disclose matters they perceive as sensitive. Hence, when a discussion may touch on a sensitive matter, use of leading questions suggests that you already know about the troublesome data, that the client need not fear letting the cat out of the bag, and that you are prepared to talk about it in a forthright manner. . . . The examples below illustrate how leading questions may overcome embarrassment in two typical legal situations. Compare the following sets of questions:

A. 1. "Have you ever been arrested before?"
   2. "I guess you've had some problems with the police before?"
B. 1. "Do you see any problems in letting them look at your books?"
   2. "The acquiring company's examination of your books will bring to light things like allowing employees to use company cars for personal use. How should we talk to them about these matters?"

Assuming that you strongly suspect that the troublesome conduct has in fact occurred, the use of leading questions may overcome these clients' fear and embarrassment, and consequent reluctance to talk openly and honestly. However, as the sneer that often accompanies or greets the term "leading" suggest, leading questions are not without their disadvantages.

2. Leading Questions Sometimes Prevent You From Learning Important Data

A leading question often reflects your ardent desire to have facts come out in a way favorable to a client. For example, if an appellate case or a statute uses a word, you might want a client to use precisely that word in recounting a past event. Hence, you incorporate that word in a leading question. Though that word may be an inaccurate label, the leading question may cause a client, consciously or unconsciously, to affirm it. You may thereby introduce inaccuracy into a discussion. When you later discover the inaccuracy (or have it pointed out to you by another party), it may be too late to seek solutions which you and a client might have pursued if the true data were known earlier.

3. Leading Questions May Be Ethically Improper

Use of leading questions in your office sometimes is even more improper than it may be at trial. Generally, you cannot ethically suggest "correct" answers to clients. For example, assume that a couple consults you about a new house that they purchased, based in part on their understanding that the roof on the house was brand new. When it later turns out that the roof is old and needs replacing, the clients seek advice about what they should do. Might you ask, "I take it that the seller actually told you that the roof was new?" The answer is clear—such a question does nothing except tell the clients what to say. Absent unusual circumstances, the question is improper.

4. Conclusion

As you can see, motivating clients to participate fully and gathering complete data usually requires you to employ each form of question. However, even employing the "correct" form of question at the "correct" time is no guarantee that motivation and complete, accurate data will result. Because no single client is typical in all respects, a question that motivates one client may inhibit another. Moreover, some clients will treat a yes-no question as little different than an open one, while others will respond quite literally. Lastly, any one client may respond to the same form of question differently at different times. Thus, you need to adapt the forms of questions to the dynamics of individual conversations. . . .

GATHERING INFORMATION FROM ATYPICAL AND DIFFICULT CLIENTS

2. RELUCTANCE TO DISCUSS PARTICULAR TOPICS

. . . [Some] clients are reluctant to discuss particular matters that arise in the course of discussion. This type of client is generally forthcoming and responsive, but changes noticeably when a topic which to the client is unpleasant or threatening comes along. This is a common reaction. . . .

B. Techniques For Responding to Client Reluctance

[W]hether you anticipate reluctance or become aware of it in the course of discussion, your choices are to (1) ignore the problem and press on with the topic; (2) postpone consideration of the topic until a future time when greater rapport or some other factor will overcome the client's reluctance; or (3) mention the problem of reluctance and seek to overcome it through discussion. In the abstract, no choice is inherently likely to be better than another. Considering such factors as a client's personality and your need for immediate discussion of a topic will at least insure that your choice is professionally responsible. Below, consider a few techniques for employing option No. 3, directly raising a client's reluctance.

1. Motivational Statements

Motivational statements explicitly recognize or anticipate a client's reluctance and invite a client to talk about it. One type of motivational statement consists of two parts. The first part attempts to overcome the inhibiting factor by conveying empathic understanding of the client's anxiety or discomfort. The second part utilizes a facilitator, and typically points out the benefit the client is likely to gain by overcoming the inhibitor and discussing a topic openly.

For example, return to the client whose spouse recently died as the result of alleged medical malpractice. Assume you anticipate the client's reluctance to describe the deceased spouse's deathbed conversations with the physician, and you decide to make a motivational statement in advance. The motivational statement may be along these lines:

> "Ms. Bridges, I'd like to turn next to conversations your husband had with his physician after his surgery and before his death. I realize that this may not be easy for you; it may cause you to relive some very painful memories. But I'll be in the best position to help you if you tell me as much as you can recall."

Here you not only acknowledge that the topic will not be easy, but also identify a reason that it may not be easy: "it may cause you to relive some very painful memories." You may have chosen to omit this segment, since by including it you run the risk of playing "amateur psychologist." However, since just about everybody would agree that talking about the recent death of a spouse is likely to be painful, there is little risk to such a statement. As for the second, "reward," portion of the statement, it is a generic statement of potential benefit, not keyed in to this or any other client in particular. As such, you may employ this form of remark in most motivational statements.

Consider next the client faced with foreclosure. Assume that you do not anticipate client reluctance to discuss conversations with the mortgage loan broker. But after broaching the subject, you realize that the client seems uneasy and unwilling to talk about it. Since you did not anticipate reluctance, you may be unable to reflect the client's precise feelings. Hence, you might simply try to recognize the client's discomfort with a statement such as, "You look uncomfortable. It seems like something is bothering you." This remark is empathic to a degree; it recognizes the client's discomfort. However, it may suggest criticism and therefore may make the client feel defensive. The client may respond in self-defense: "I don't feel uncomfortable. What makes you say that?" Or, the client's may be vague: "I guess I'm just uncomfortable talking to a lawyer."

Hence, when a client seems uncomfortable, but you are uncertain of the reason, you may want to try other forms of motivational statements. One alternative is a normalizing response. A normalizing response tends not to make clients defensive because it spreads the client's feelings over a large group of clients. For example, you might say,

> "You seem a bit uncomfortable. You know, many people feel there are things they would rather not tell their lawyers. I understand that; after all, we do not know each other very well yet, and I can understand that many people find it difficult to confide in someone else who is a relative stranger. But only if I have all the information can I fully protect your interests."

Here too, you point out the client's discomfort. But by also stating that many people feel just as the client seems to, you avoid direct criticism. Again, you conclude with a generic statement of reward and a desire to help.

A second form of motivational statement you may use when uncertain of the basis of reluctance is a request for corrective feedback. Here, you take personal responsibility for a client's discomfort. A normalizing response puts the focus on the client; a request for corrective feedback places it on you. For example, again in the context of the foreclosure matter, you might say,

> "I have the sense there is some difficulty here. Perhaps something I've said has made

you uncomfortable, or maybe even something that I've failed to say. Is there anything you want to tell me? I hope you'll let me know if I'm doing something that makes you feel uncomfortable."

Though a client's reluctance may have nothing to do with what you have said or failed to say, such a remark conveys empathy without making a client defensive. It may even encourage a client to describe the underlying source of concern: "No, it's nothing you've done. It's just that I think maybe I should have asked about a balloon payment, and I'm feeling kind of dumb."

2. Confidentiality

When utilizing motivational statements, you may also want to stress attorney-client confidentiality:

> "Remember, unless you tell me you're planning to rob a bank or something like that, everything you tell me is confidential. I cannot and will not divulge anything you say without your express permission."

3. Changing the Pattern of Questions

Facing a reluctant client, another option is to change your questioning pattern. . . . [W]hile open questions do motivate many people to provide narrative-type responses, there are clients for whom this is not true. Even clients who are generally forthcoming in response to open questions may become reluctant to talk about an anxiety-producing event. Such clients may respond better to narrow questions which can help ease a client into an event by eliciting information one step at a time. Narrow questions can remove some of the burden of disclosure by moving into a topic "bit by bit." . . .

3. RELUCTANCE TO COMMENCE AN INTERVIEW

A type of reluctance which may seem strange to you is reluctance to commence an interview. . . . For many people, beginnings are difficult. Moreover, sometimes clients do not come to see you entirely of their own volition; they are in your office physically, but not mentally. . . .

Empathizing with a client's discomfort, making a normalizing remark and emphasizing confidentiality may help a client get started. Likewise, a shift to closed questions may take the conversational onus off the client at least temporarily. Especially if the questions seek non-threatening, statistical-type information, a client can ease into supplying data. . . .

If you sense that a client's reluctance stems from uncertainty about whether to get enmeshed at all with a lawyer, statements such as, "Only if I have all the information can I adequately protect your interests" may further inhibit client cooperation. The client may feel that supplying information is a commitment to forging ahead before the client has decided to do so. To prevent this reaction, you may want to make a "reward" statement such as, "Only if I first have some basic information can we decide together whether it makes sense for you to go ahead."

Another motivational approach you can employ when reluctance appears at the outset of a meeting is to ask, "Perhaps you have a question or two you want to ask me?" Asking such a question may ferret out the reason for reluctance. However, be aware that many people are not comfortable asking questions.

4. COMMUNICATING WITH AGED AND INFIRM CLIENTS

You may have difficulty getting information from some clients not because of reluctance, but because it is difficult for them to communicate. Common barriers to satisfactory communication include advanced age and medical infirmity. Certainly not every older person will have difficulty recalling and conveying information. But when the situation does arise, you want to be prepared to surmount it.

One skill you need to draw upon to interview and counsel clients with such difficulties is patience. What initially seems a client's marginal ability to respond may be little more than a relaxed style of speech. But when a client has genuine difficulty understanding and responding, you will need more than patience.

One simple technique is to ask closed questions. Clients who have difficulty communicating are more likely to respond to closed questions than open ones. However, you must be careful. The more difficulty a client is having, the more likely are you to ask questions that are leading. The leading questions may be unethical, and a client's responses may in turn mislead you. . . .

5. RAMBLING CLIENTS

Perhaps every lawyer's worst fear is a rambling client, a client who views a question as little more than a momentary interruption in an excursion into details that seemingly have little to do with the problem at hand. There may be many reasons for lawyers' typically strong reactions to ramblers. Perhaps lawyers are uncomfortable with the feeling that they have lost control over an interview. Or perhaps ramblers simply consume too much of that most precious commodity, time. Finally, rambling may cut against the grain of those trained in the virtues of precision.

From clients' perspectives, a variety of factors may produce rambling responses. First, recognize that a client may actually be describing relevant, important data; only "premature diagnosis" stamps the description as rambling. Beyond that, clients may ramble because a topic is threatening, or because of a "greater need" to discuss their own subject. Finally, some clients, due to an emotional reaction to events or because of underlying personality factors, may have difficulty sticking to topics.

The initial decision is whether to respond to a client's rambling behavior. For instance, assume a client does respond adequately to questions, but in addition rambles into irrelevant areas. Would your tendency be to ignore the rambling responses or to attempt to confine the client in the future to relevant responses? Obviously no formula points to an unerring approach. Your judgment in an individual case will be based on such factors as time pressures, overall rapport, and the extent of the rambling. You may well decide to ignore the rambling. Indeed, even where a client's responses consist of little more than rambling you may choose to ignore it, perhaps on the theory that the client will eventually wear down and respond to ensuing inquiries.

When you decide to confront a rambling client, the following considerations may help. First, you may respond by empathizing with the client's concerns as evidenced in the rambling statements. Often, a client will ramble continuously about the same limited subject matter. Yet, aware that the topics have nothing to do with the client's legal concerns, you repeatedly fail to respond to what the client is saying. The dialogue resembles two ships passing in the night: you ask questions which are not answered, the client makes statements which are ignored. By simply empathizing with the client's concerns, you may satisfy a client's need to be heard and thereby diminish a client's tendency to ramble. . . .

If rambling persists despite your empathetic response, you may employ a series of closed questions. Their limited focus of inquiry offers clients less opportunity to ramble. Once you get a client back on a non-rambling track, you may even revert to a more open questioning pattern.

A final approach, which you can use when speaking with talkative clients who you anticipate are likely to get off track, is to alert the client in advance to your need to interrupt. To apologize in advance, you might make a comment along the following lines.

> "I want to apologize in advance for any interruptions I may make in our conversation if I feel we're getting off track. I don't like to interrupt but I find that in many instances it helps us use our time together more effectively."

Such an apology is usually well received. Typical client responses are, "You're right; I'm just so upset it's hard to stop myself" and "I know I'm a real talker, so go ahead and speak up when you need me to stop."

6. CLIENTS WHO ARE HOSTILE, ANGRY AND EXPLOSIVE

Sometimes clients' inner pressures escalate to the point that clients explode into fits of anger, hurt or hostility. In some clients, a fit takes the form of tears; in others, it takes the form of complaints, threats or accusations. Though you may think such fits are confined to inherently emotional matters such as child custody disputes, in fact outbursts are possible even in seemingly mundane settings. . . .

If an outburst occurs without warning, active listening is a powerful skill for responding with compassion. You may not be able to immediately take away a client's hurt and anger, but you can let clients know that you understand and accept how upset they are feeling. . . . Another tactic is to allow a client a "cooling off" period following an emotional outburst. It is often unrealistic to expect that an active listening response will instantly defuse a client's anger and allow you to continue on as if nothing had happened. Offer a client a chance to relax with a soft drink or fruit juice.

Finally, help a client recover from an outburst by offering a face-saving, "normalizing" response. After an outburst, most clients feel sheepish, embarrassed or ashamed. As a result, some will try to make light of their discomfort. For example, the client above might say, "Well, my friends always say I have a short fuse." Control the impulse to tease back: "Short? More like invisible!" Instead, offer a response that generalizes and normalizes a client's feelings: "All of us blow up once in a while when we're under pressure," or "I know that many [individuals] faced with your situation feel like they're being screwed over by the legal system." Then, reaffirm your desire to help: "When you're feeling ready, we can talk some more. I want to help you find every way we can to make the best of a bad situation."

Working with hostile, angry clients is neither easy nor pleasant. However, most clients respond to coping skills such as active listening, cooling off periods, normalizing replies, and affirmations of your desire to help.

7. FABRICATION

One of the more vexing problems is talking to clients who you strongly suspect of lying.

Lying may be active or passive: a client may either supply false information, or withhold information. Obviously the line between a client who may be mistaken and who is lying, or one who is simply reluctant to supply information and one who consciously withholds it, is not a bright one. The matter is one of degree, rooted in a client's conscious intent. You have to rely on your judgment as to which side of the line a client's conduct falls.

A. Indicia of Fabrication

Typically, the inhibitors of ego threat and case threat are the root cause of fabrication. Clients may lie in the belief (probably often correct) that truthful information will hurt their cause. They also may lie because they are ashamed or guilty about what really happened, or because they believe you would not respect them if you knew the true facts. Such feelings are not limited to clients: How freely do you share information that casts you in a negative light?

The bases upon which you might detect fabrication are the stuff of the literature of cross-examination, a full discussion of which is beyond the scope of this book. Generally, inconsistencies are one clue to possible fabrication. A client's statement to you conflicts with what the client previously told somebody else; bad luck if the somebody else is a police officer. Or, a story may have internal inconsistencies—one portion does not square with another. For example, a client states at one point that he was driving late at night; at another point, he states that his car lights were not on.

Implausibilities also suggest fabrication. For example, in an actual case, a client testified, "James is fine now, but when I took his temperature, it was so high that it broke the thermometer." Common sense and experience suggest that the story is implausible. Not only are extremely high temperatures usually fatal, but also they rarely result in broken thermometers.

On other occasions, a story may conflict in some way with a more believable story. For example, a client tells you that a 6-month-old child's broken leg was caused by the child falling off a sofa onto a carpeted floor. The story conflicts with the medical expert, who concludes that the X-rays indicate a spiral fracture of the leg, and that spiral fractures can be caused only by a great deal of rotational force, not by a fall from a sofa.

These are some of the more common factors that are likely to lead you to suspect fabrication. Below, consider potential responses you might make.

B. Responding to Suspected Fabrication

Even an indirect suggestion that you suspect a client of lying can severely damage an attorney-client relationship. Therefore, first be reasonably confident of your diagnosis of fabrication. Movies have fostered an image of streetwise lawyers who can unerringly spot a lie and immediately force people to "come clean" with a statement such as: "Come on, nobody would believe that. I haven't believed something like that since I was 3 years old. Now, tell me what really happened." Most of us, however, are not blessed with such blinding certainty. Better to eliminate other possible explanations before leaping to the conclusion that a client is lying. After all, it may be that the third party, supposedly neutral witness, is mistaken, not your client. Perhaps the doctor in the spiral fracture case above misread the X-rays or picked up the wrong X-rays. Perhaps the client has made an honest mistake. You should at least consider such possibilities before you employ the following techniques.

1. Prevention

Hopefully, one benefit of a client-centered approach itself is reduced fabrication. The more rapport you have with a client, the less likely a client will lie. But in particular, three other devices may help to prevent fabrication. One is "topic avoidance." If you delay discussion of critical points which are most likely to lead to fabrication until after you have had a chance to build rapport, you may reduce the chance that a client will lie. Many criminal defense attorneys employ this technique, intentionally postponing discussion of what happened prior to an arrest until one or two meetings with their clients have taken place.

A second device is "disclosure." By disclosing data already in your possession which is especially case or ego threatening, you lessen the risk that a client will deny its existence. This device is one frequently used by parents of young children. Assume that a father enters a room and finds an overturned beaker of milk in the middle of the living room rug moments after the father saw his six-year-old daughter Melinda playing in the living room. The father might confront Melinda with a question such as, "Melinda, did you spill the milk?" But that question is prone to elicit a defensive, deceitful response from Melinda. Instead, the father might say, "Melinda, it seems you've spilt that milk you were drinking. Why don't you tell me what happened." This remark discloses that the father already knows "the worst" and is likely to elicit a more honest response provided the father's tone of voice and body language indicate he is not threatening punishment.

You too will frequently be aware of negative information concerning clients. Perhaps you will know that a client seeking advice about a business venture has previously declared bankruptcy. Or, that a doctor who is a defendant in a wrongful death case has previously been discharged from the staffs of two hospitals. In each case, a question which puts the onus on the client to be the first to reveal the information may elicit an evasive, misleading or dishonest reply. Instead, a remark such as, "I understand you have had some problems in a couple of hospitals in the past. Can you tell me something about that?" may ease the client towards a full and forthright reply.

A "war story" is a third device you may employ to prevent fabrication. A war story is simply a tale drawn from your prior experience. Sometimes, you tell a war story simply to entertain or impress a client with the depth of your experience. In this instance, you tell a war story to illustrate the pitfalls of dishonesty. For example, assume that you represent the owner of a restaurant who is applying for a liquor license. You are aware that the client has two "silent partners" . . . who are said to have ties to organized crime. Such information, if true, would in all likelihood prevent issuance of the liquor license. If you fear that the client will lie when asked about connections with [the silent partners] you may tell a war story as follows:

> "I've handled a number of cases in which clients have sought liquor licenses, and issues concerning an applicant's associates arise frequently. Unfortunately, sometimes clients do not level with me completely, and information is concealed which, had I known about it earlier, could have been easily met and overcome. For instance, a couple of years ago a client of mine was seeking a liquor license, and there was some question about whether she had sold liquor to a minor in another state. When I asked her about it before we went before the Board, she assured me that she had never been licensed anywhere, that there must be some confusion. Then the Board came

up with a record showing she had been licensed. As it turned out, she had signed the application in the other state simply to help out a friend; she never took an active role in the liquor business and had I known about it we could have explained what happened and she would have gotten her license. As it was, the license was denied. For the next few minutes I'll be asking you for information about your business operations because these applications for liquor licenses are pretty thorough. As we go through the application, be sure to tell me everything so if there's any problem in the offing we can try to think of ways to solve it."

Here, you tell a war story aimed at impressing the client with the need to be accurate. The message is that even if the information may be in some way negative, you may nevertheless produce a successful result. Thus, the war story is also motivational.

2. Confrontation

When despite your best preventative efforts you are convinced a client is lying, and you want to uncover the actual facts, you must confront a client. Available confrontational techniques range from indirect to direct, the latter consisting of an explicit statement of disbelief. Consider here four confrontational techniques, beginning with the most indirect.

a. Request for Clarification

A request for clarification phrases the confrontation in terms of your own confusion, rather than the client's misstatements. Explicitly point out what troubles you, and ask the client to clarify. For example, you might state,

"I'm a bit confused. You've told me that minimum pricing was discussed at the meeting; but your own employee's memo summarizing the meeting makes no mention of that. Can you clarify this point for me?"

"I'm a little confused. According to the accident report, you told the officer you were going home at the time of the incident. But just a short time earlier, you told me that you were on your way to a doctor's appointment. Could you clarify this difference for me?"

Note that the requests for clarification do not overtly indicate your disbelief. And often, disbelief is premature. The first client may explain, "The employee had to leave the meeting for about 20 minutes to talk to the shop foreperson. Thinking back on it, that's when we talked about minimum pricing." The second may respond, "I was going home after the doctor's office and I guess I was nervous and just left out the part about the doctor."

b. The Omniscient Third Party

Another method of probing suspected fabrication while attempting to preserve rapport involves ascribing your need to broach a possible untruth to a non-present yet powerful and critically important third party. The third party is, of course, not present at your conversation and therefore is in no position to dispute the position you ascribe to it. Potential third party "whipping people" include opposing counsel, a judge, or even "law firm policy."

For example, you may take the role of opposing counsel, and ask the client why the client's version of events is more likely to be believed than the adversary's. By stressing that "this is what our opponent is going to say," you confront a client's story without personally indicating your disbelief. The tactic often impels a client either to provide explanations (which you then investigate), or to admit that the original story was not entirely accurate.

Assume for instance that you represent a salesperson sued by a former employer for unlawfully taking that employer's customer list and using it on behalf of a new employer. The salesperson's story, which you find unbelievable, is that the salesperson did not take the customer list but has developed the customers on the salesperson's own. You may confront the client with the adversary's story as follows:

> "Pat, let's look at what the attorney for A. Co. (the former employer) is going to say. They will say that you worked for them for 14 years; that you were given monthly customer lists; that you agreed to turn over all customer lists to A. Co. if you left employment; that after you left you called on exactly the same customers you did when you worked for A. Co., and that you even showed one of these customers that you still had the A. Co. list. How are we going to overcome this story?"

A somewhat difficult variation of this technique is for you to ask a client to help you figure out what story an adversary is likely to present, and how to refute it. To establish an adversary's story, you typically need to work with a client by suggesting some possibilities. If a client has difficulty refuting the adversary's story, a client may understand the weakness of his or her own story, and perhaps tell a more truthful one. On the other hand, if a client too readily refutes an adversary's story, you may point out that the adversary is unlikely to rely on such an easily refuted story. Then, continue to work with a client to develop a story an adversary is more likely to tell. You may continue this process until you and a client arrive at a more realistic version. When the client cannot refute an adversary's ultimate story, the client may tell a more truthful version.

A third variation of this technique is a mock cross examination. You question a client as though you were opposing counsel on cross. Often, until a role play exercise such as this forces a client to confront a story in a dynamic setting, clients do not face up to the obvious weaknesses in their false stories.

c. *Silence*

Alone or following the use of other techniques, silence can be a powerful indication of disbelief. Though you say little or nothing, your body language conveys your lack of belief and your expectation that a client will tell the truth. You need not have Shakespearian training to carry out this technique. Direct eye contact, a facial expression that is both serious and indicative of disbelief, and perhaps a few shakes of the head are often more than sufficient.

d. *Direct Verbal Confrontation*

Direct confrontation involves starkly telling a client that (a) a story is not believable and (b) why you disbelieve it. Consider this example:

> "Mr. Thomas, I simply do not believe what you are telling me. According to you, your brother failed to repay the $100,000 when it was due and you did not realize it until over a year later. People whose brothers owe them $100,000 by a certain date don't forget such a date for a whole year. I'd like the truth."

Directly confronting a client is difficult. A client may get angry, accuse you of misdeeds, and terminate the relationship. Thus, you should make such a statement only if you are quite certain a client is indeed lying. Keep in mind, however, that the statement's purpose is to help a client tell the truth. Therefore, your own conduct should be consistent with this goal. Your demeanor when making the statement, for example, should indicate your concern and desire to help. And, you might include a motivational statement, such as advising a client that the truth is likely to be in the client's best interest. In addition, you may let the client know that you will continue to accept the client even if the client admits to having lied. Thus, in the debt example above, you might have preceded the confrontational statement with a motivational statement as follows:

> "Mr. Thomas, I'd like to help you, and I think I can help you, but only if you are honest with me. Unfortunately, in my experience clients sometimes are less than totally honest. I'm used to that, and if it turns out that's occurred here it will in no way interfere with my willingness to help you. But frankly, I simply do not believe . . ."

Do not expect results, if any there are, instantly. A client may need time before realizing that admitting to fabrication and telling a truthful story is in his or her best interests. Perhaps more meetings will take place before a client "comes clean." You may even have to repeat the motivational and confrontational statements. But short of terminating the attorney-client relationship, this is about as forceful as you can be when confronting a possibly fabricated story.

Ultimately if a client sticks with a story and your suspicions continue, you will have to consider whether you need to withdraw.

D. Context of Communications

1. Comments and Questions

a. How much is one ton? Is a ton exclusively a measure of weight, or can it be a measure of volume? The answer depends on which unit of weight or volume is under consideration, and there are more options than you might have imagined:

1. long ton or metric ton (2,240 pounds);
2. short ton (2,000 pounds);
3. register ton (100 cubic feet of cargo space in a ship);
4. freight ton (40 cubic feet); or
5. long ton of seawater (35 cubic feet).

The related concept of tonnage, meaning the carrying capacity of a ship, also varies. In England, tonnage is measured in the actual tons that the vessel can safely transport; in the U.S., tonnage is based on the cubic capacity of the hold. Tonnage as a measure of weight is sometimes measured in hundredweights, which is 100 pounds for a short ton but 112 pounds for a long ton.

b. Words take their meaning in part from the context in which they are used. This illustration, and the two items that follow, are designed to show the difficulties of clear and precise communication.

c. Similar issues are addressed by writers about meaning in literature and in law. *See e.g.*, Stanley E. Fish, IS THERE A TEXT IN THIS CLASS? (1980); Richard Posner, LAW AND LITERATURE (1988).

2. Franz Lieber, Legal and Political Hermeneutics 17-19 (3d ed. 1880)

Let us take an instance of the simplest kind, to show in what degree we are continually obliged to resort to interpretation. Suppose a housekeeper says to a domestic: fetch some soup meat, accompanying the act with giving some money to the latter. Common sense and good faith will tell the domestic:

1. he should go immediately, or as soon as his other occupations are finished;
2. that the money handed him by the housekeeper is intended to pay for the meat thus ordered, and not as a present to him;
3. that he should buy such meat and of such parts of the animal as has commonly been used at the house for making soup;
4. that he should go to the butcher that normally provides the family, or to some convenient stall, and not to an unnecessarily distant place;
5. that he return the rest of the money;
6. that he bring the meat home without adding anything injurious or disagreeable; and
7. that he fetch the meat for the use of the family and not for himself.

(Many more instructions might be added.) We are constrained, then, always to leave a large part of our meaning to be discovered by interpretation, which in many cases must necessarily cause some obscurity with regard to the exact meaning which our words were intended to convey (and which they in fact convey) to the other party.

3. *Frigaliment Importing Co. v. B.N.S. International Sales Co.*, 190 F. Supp. 116 (S.D.N.Y. 1960)

Friendly, Circuit Judge.

The issue is, what is chicken? Plaintiff says "chicken" means a young chicken, suitable for broiling and frying. Defendant says "chicken" means any bird of that genus that meets contract specifications on weight and quality, including what it calls "stewing chicken" and plaintiff pejoratively terms "fowl." Dictionaries give both meanings, as well as some others not relevant here. To support it, plaintiff sends a number of volleys over the net; defendant essays to return them and adds a few serves of its own. . . . I have concluded that plaintiff has not sustained its burden of persuasion that the contract used "chicken" in the narrower sense.

The action is for breach of the warranty that goods sold shall correspond to the description. Two contracts are in suit. In the first, dated May 2, 1957, defendant, a New York sales corporation, confirmed the sale to plaintiff, a Swiss corporation, of:

"US Fresh Frozen Chicken, Grade A, Government Inspected, Eviscerated
2 1/2-3 lbs. and 1 1/2-2 lbs. each all chicken individually wrapped in cryovac packed in secured fiber cartons or wooden boxes, suitable for export
75,000 lbs. 2.5-3 lbs. . ..@$33.00
25,000 lbs. 1.5-2 lbs. . ..@$36.50
per 100 lbs. FAS New York
scheduled May 10, 1957 pursuant to instructions from Penson & Co., New York."

The second contract . . . was identical save that only 50,000 lbs. of the heavier "chicken" were called for, the price of the smaller birds was $37 per 100 lbs., and shipment was scheduled for May 30. The initial shipment under the first contract was short but the balance was shipped on May 17. When the initial shipment arrived in Switzerland, plaintiff found, on May 28, that the 2.5-3 lbs. birds were not young chicken suitable for broiling and frying but stewing chicken or "fowl;" indeed, many of the cartons and bags plainly so indicated. Protests ensued. Nevertheless, shipment under the second contract was made on May 29, the 2.5-3 lbs. birds again being stewing chicken. Defendant stopped the transportation of these at Rotterdam.

This action followed. . . . [N]otwithstanding that acceptance was in Switzerland, New York law controls. . . .

Since the word "chicken" standing alone is ambiguous, I turn first to see whether the contract itself offers any aid to its interpretation. Plaintiff says the 1.5-2 lbs. birds necessarily had to be young chicken since the older birds do not come in that size, hence the 2.5-3 lbs. birds must likewise be young. This is unpersuasive — a contract for "apples" of two different sizes could be filled with different kinds of apples even though only one species came in both sizes. Defendant notes that the contract called not simply for chicken but for "US Fresh Frozen Chicken, Grade A, Government Inspected." It says the contract thereby incorporated by reference the Department of Agriculture's regulations, which favor its interpretation; I shall return to this after reviewing plaintiffs' other contentions.

The first hinges on an exchange of cablegrams which preceded execution of the formal contracts. The negotiations leading up to the contracts were conducted in New York between defendant's secretary, Ernest R. Bauer, and a Mr. Stovicek, who was in New York for the Czechoslovak government at the World Trade Fair. A few days after meeting Bauer at the fair, Stovicek telephoned and inquired whether defendant would be interested in exporting poultry to Switzerland. Bauer then met with Stovicek, who showed him a cable from plaintiff dated April 26, 1957, announcing that they "are buyer" of 25,000 lbs. of chicken 2.5-3 lbs. weight, Cryovac packed, grade A Government inspected, at a price up to 33 cents per pound, for shipment on May 10, to be confirmed by the following morning, and were interested in further offerings. After testing the market for price, Bauer accepted, and Stovicek sent a confirmation that evening. Plaintiff stresses that, although these and subsequent cables between plaintiff and defendant, which laid the basis for the additional quantities under the first and for all of the second contract, were predominantly in German, they used the English word "chicken;" it claims this was done because it understood "chicken" meant young chicken whereas the German word, "Huhn," included both "Brathuhn" (broilers) and "Suppenhuhn" (stewing chicken), and that defendant, whose officers were thoroughly conversant with German, should have realized this. Whatever force this argument might otherwise have is largely drained away by Bauer's testimony that he asked Stovicek what kind of chickens were wanted, received the answer "any kind of chickens," and then, in German, asked whether the cable meant "Huhn" and received an affirmative response. Plaintiff attacks this as contrary to what Bauer testified on his deposition in March, 1959, and also on the ground that Stovicek had no authority to interpret the meaning of the cable. The first contention would be persuasive if sustained by the record, since Bauer was free at the trial from the threat of contradiction by Stovicek as he was not at the time of the deposition; however review of the deposition does not convince me of the claimed inconsistency. As to the second contention, it may well be that Stovicek lacked authority to commit plaintiff for prices or delivery dates other than those specified in the cable; but plaintiff cannot at the same time rely on its cable to Stovicek as its dictionary to the meaning of the contract and repudiate the interpretation given the dictionary by the man in whose hands it was put. Plaintiff's reliance on the fact that the contract forms contain the words "through the intermediary of: _______," with the blank not filled, as negating agency, is wholly unpersuasive; the purpose of this clause was to permit filling in the name of an intermediary to whom a commission would be payable, not to blot out what had been the fact.

Plaintiff's next contention is that there was a definite trade usage that "chicken" meant "young chicken." Defendant showed that it was only beginning in the poultry trade in 1957, thereby bringing itself within the principle that "when one of the parties is not a member of the trade or other circle, his acceptance of the standard must be made to appear" by proving either that he had actual knowledge of the usage or that the usage is "so generally known in the community that his actual individual knowledge of it may be inferred." 9 Wigmore, Evidence (3d ed. 1940) § 2464. Here, there was no proof of actual knowledge of the alleged usage; indeed, it is quite plain that defendant's belief was to the contrary. In order to meet the alternative requirement, the law of New York demands a showing that "the usage is of so long continuance, so well established, so notorious, so universal and so reasonable itself, as that the presumption is violent that the parties contracted with reference to it, and made it a part of their agreement." *Walls v. Bailey*, 1872, 49 N.Y. 464, 472-473.

Plaintiff endeavored to establish such a usage by the testimony of three witnesses and certain other evidence. Strasser, resident buyer in New York for a large chain of Swiss cooperatives, testified that "on chicken I would definitely understand a broiler." However,the force of this testimony was considerably weakened by the fact that in his own transactions the witness, a careful businessman, protected himself by using "broiler" when that was what he wanted and "fowl" when he wished older birds. . . . [A] witness' consistent failure to rely on the alleged usage deprives his opinion testimony of much of its effect. Niesielowski, an officer of one of the companies that had furnished the stewing chicken to defendant, testified that "chicken" meant "the male species of the poultry industry. That could be a broiler, a fryer or a roaster," but not a stewing chicken; however, he also testified that upon receiving defendant's inquiry for "chickens", he asked whether the desire was for "fowl or frying chickens" and, in fact, supplied fowl, although taking the precaution of asking defendant, a day or two after plaintiffs acceptance of the contracts in suit, to change its confirmation of its order from "chickens," as defendant had originally prepared it, to "stewing chickens." Dates, an employee of Urner-Barry Company, which publishes a daily market report on the poultry trade, gave it as his view that the trade meaning of "chicken" was "broilers and fryers." In addition to this opinion testimony, plaintiff relied on the fact that the Urner-Barry service, the Journal of Commerce, and Weinberg Bros. & Co. of Chicago, a large supplier of poultry, published quotations in a manner which, in one way or another, distinguish between "chicken," comprising broilers, fryers and certain other categories, and "fowl," which, Bauer acknowledged, included stewing chickens. This material would be impressive if there were nothing to the contrary. However, there was, as will now be seen.

Defendant's witness Weininger, who operates a chicken eviscerating plant in New Jersey, testified "Chicken is everything except a goose, a duck, and a turkey. Everything is a chicken, but then you have to say, you have to specify which category you want or that you are talking about." Its witness Fox said that in the trade "chicken" would encompass all the various classifications. Sadina, who conducts a food inspection service, testified that he would consider any bird coming within the classes of "chicken" in the Department of Agriculture's regulations to be a chicken. The specifications approved by the General Services Administration include fowl as well as broilers and fryers under the classification "chickens." Statistics of the Institute of American Poultry Industries use the phrases "young chickens" and "mature chickens," under the general heading "Total chickens" and the Department of Agriculture's daily and weekly price reports avoid use of the word "chicken" without specification.

Defendant advances several other points which it claims affirmatively support its construction. Primary among these is the regulation of the Department of Agriculture, 7 C.F.R. § 70.300 et. seq. entitled, "Grading and Inspection of Poultry and Edible Products Thereof," and in particular § 70.301 which recited: "Chickens. The following are the various classes of chickens:"

(a) Broiler or fryer

(b) Roaster . .

(c) Capon . . .

(d) Stag . . .

(e) Hen or stewing chicken or fowl . . .

(f) Cock or old rooster

Defendant argues . . . that the contract incorporated these regulations by reference. Plaintiff answers that the contract provision related simply to grade and Government inspection and did not incorporate the Government definition of "chicken," and also that the definition in the Regulations is ignored in the trade. However, the latter contention was contradicted by Weininger and Sadina; and there is force in defendant's argument that the contract made the regulations a dictionary, particularly since the reference to Government grading was already in plaintiff's initial cable to Stovicek.

Defendant makes a further argument based on the impossibility of its obtaining broilers and fryers at the 33¢ price offered by plaintiff for the 2.5-3 lbs. birds. There is no substantial dispute that, in late April, 1957, the price for 2.5-3 lbs. broilers was between 35 and 37 cents per pound, and that when defendant entered into the contracts, it was well aware of this and intended to fill them by supplying fowl in these weights. It claims that plaintiff must likewise have known the market since plaintiff had reserved shipping space on April 23, three days before plaintiff's cable to Stovicek, or, at least, that Stovicek was chargeable with such knowledge. It is scarcely an answer to say, as plaintiff does in its brief, that the 33 cents price offered by the 2.5-3 lbs. "chickens" was closer to the prevailing 35 cents price for broilers than to the 30 cents at which defendant procured fowl. Plaintiff must have expected defendant to make some profit — certainly it could not have expected defendant deliberately to incur a loss.

Finally, defendant relies on conduct by the plaintiff after the first shipment had been received. On May 28 plaintiff sent two cables complaining that the larger birds in the first shipment constituted "fowl." Defendant answered with a cable refusing to recognize plaintiff's objection and announcing "We have today ready for shipment 60,000 lbs. chicken 2.5-3 lbs. 25,000 lbs. broilers 1.5-2 lbs., these being the goods procured for shipment under the second contract, and asked immediate answer whether we are to ship this merchandise to you and whether you will accept the merchandise." After several other cable exchanges, plaintiff replied on May 29, "Confirm again that merchandise is to be shipped since resold by us if not enough pursuant to contract chickens are shipped the missing quantity is to be shipped within ten days stop we resold to our customers pursuant to your contract chickens grade A you have to deliver us said merchandise we again state that we shall make you fully responsible for all resulting costs." Defendant argues that if plaintiff was sincere in thinking it was entitled to young chickens, plaintiff would not have allowed the shipment under the second contract to go forward, since the distinction between broilers and chickens drawn in defendant's cablegram must have made it clear that the larger birds would not be broilers. However, plaintiff answers that the cables show plaintiff was insisting on delivery of young chickens and that defendant shipped old ones at its peril. . . . Defendant points out also that plaintiff proceeded to deliver some of the larger birds in Europe, describing them as "poulets"; defendant argues that it was only when plaintiff's customers complained about this that plaintiff developed the idea that "chicken" meant "young chicken." There is little force in this in view of plaintiff's immediate and consistent protests.

When all the evidence is reviewed, it is clear that defendant believed it could comply with the contracts by delivering stewing chicken in the 2.5-3 lbs. size. Defendant's subjective intent would not be significant if this did not coincide with an objective meaning of "chicken." Here it did coincide with one of the dictionary meanings, with the definition in the Department of Agriculture Regulations to which the contract made at least oblique reference, with at least some usage in the trade, with the realities of the market, and with what plaintiff's spokesman had said. Plaintiff asserts it to be equally plain that plaintiff's own subjective intent was to obtain broilers and fryers; the only evidence against this is the material as to market prices and this may not have been sufficiently brought home. In any event it is unnecessary to determine that issue. For plaintiff has the burden of showing that "chicken" was used in the narrower rather than in the broader sense, and this it has not sustained.

4. Comments and Questions

a. Arthur L. Corbin's view of the *Frigaliment* decision was based on his rural upbringing. "For ten years on a Kansas farm it had been a regular job to 'feed the chickens' with no suggestion that the old hens and roosters were to be excluded." CORBIN ON CONTRACTS, § 543B (1960). This was written a short time before Corbin's death. Corbin objected to the search for an "objective" meaning of "chicken."

It seems, however, that Friendly (apart from being unable to resist the opportunity to show off his extraordinary judicial virtuosity) was looking for objective sources that might have been used by the parties as the basis of their bargain. Friendly sought (without success) to determine what these sophisticated merchants meant by the word "chicken" by examining possible sources of trade usage.

b. There is an objective approach that is more useful and realistic than to identify the meaning of chicken by reference to words, usage, or interpretation — and that is to apply economic criteria to this contract between organizations experienced in international chicken transactions.

c. *Frigaliment* could not be disposed of solely on the basis of burden of proof, because the first shipment was accepted and used, so buyer clearly owes something to seller. Assume that the first shipment was not paid for, seller sues for payment, and buyer (plaintiff in Frigaliment) raises the defense of breach of contract by seller. What result and why?

E. The Management of Impressions

1. William Sansom, A Contest of Ladies 230-32 (Hogarth 1956)

[Preedy is an Englishman, on summer holiday in Spain. Sansom describes Preedy making his first appearance on the beach of his hotel.] But in any case he took care to avoid catching anyone's eye. First of all, he had to make it clear to those potential companions of his holiday that they were of no concern to him whatsoever. He stared through them, round them, over them—eyes lost in space. The beach might have been empty. If by chance a ball was thrown his way, he looked surprised; then let a smile of amusement lighten his face (Kindly Preedy), looked round dazed to see that there were people on the beach, tossed it back with a smile to himself and not a smile at the people, and then resumed carelessly his nonchalant survey of space.

But it was time to institute a little parade, the parade of the Ideal Preedy. By devious handling he gave any who wanted to look a chance to see the title of his book—a Spanish translation of Homer, classic thus, but not daring, cosmopolitan too—and then gathered together his beach-wrap and bag into a neat sand-resistant pile (Methodical and Sensible Preedy), rose slowly to stretch at ease his huge frame (Big-Cat Preedy), and tossed aside his sandals (Carefree Preedy, after all).

The marriage of Preedy and the sea! There were alternative rituals. The first involved the stroll that turns into a run and a dive straight into the water, thereafter smoothing into a strong splashless crawl towards the horizon. But of course not really to the horizon. Quite suddenly he would turn on to his back and thrash great white splashes with his legs, somehow thus showing that he could have swum further had he wanted to, and then would stand up a quarter out of water for all to see who it was.

The alternative course was simpler, it avoided the cold-water shock and it avoided the risk of appearing too high-spirited. The point was to appear to be so used to the sea, the Mediterranean, and this particular beach, that one might as well be in the sea as out of it. It involved a slow stroll down and into the edge of the water—not even noticing his toes were wet, land and water all the same to him—with his eyes up at the sky gravely surveying portents, invisible to others, of the weather (Local Fisherman Preedy).

2. Comments and Questions

a. Preedy does not come off well from this description. What we learn is that Preedy is vain, perhaps foolish, and unduly concerned about appearances. (Others might use different terms, but they would not be admiring ones.) What is striking about this passage is its careful depiction of the impressions that a person is seeking to make about himself.

b. People engaged in dispute resolution procedures commonly pay considerable attention to appearances. Defense lawyers tell their clients to be well dressed when they appear in court, and may even help with the selection of an appropriate outfit. It is common to have families of parties seated in the courtroom.

c. Many an unpresupposing physical specimen of a judge is impressive indeed when wearing robes (in England, a wig as well), and sitting above the proceedings below — after all have risen, at the order of the bailiff, for the entry of the judge. (Would it be far fetched to suggest an analogy to the Wizard of Oz?)

d. In a negotiation, both parties go to considerable efforts to present themselves as being in a strong position, and unlikely to come down very far from their asking price. Their position is likely to include claims or requests that they are quite prepared to bargain away, and may even have been included for that purpose. Perhaps we were a bit too hasty in judging Preedy so harshly.

3. Jean Paul Sartre, Being And Nothingness 59 (1956)

The Waiter

Let us consider this waiter in the cafe. His movement is quick and forward, a little too precise, a little too rapid. He comes toward the patrons with a step a little too quick. He bends forward a little too eagerly; his voice, his eyes express an interest a little too solicitous for the order of the customer. Finally there he returns, trying to imitate in his walk the inflexible stiffness of some kind of automaton while carrying his tray with the recklessness of a tightrope-walker by putting it in a perpetually unstable, perpetually broken equilibrium which he perpetually reestablishes by a light movement of the arm and hand. All his behavior seems to us a game. He applies himself to chaining his movements as if they were mechanisms, the one regulating the other; his gestures and even his voice seem to be mechanisms; be gives himself the quickness and pitiless rapidity of things. He is playing, he is amusing himself. But what is he playing? We need not watch long before we can explain it: he is playing at being a waiter in a cafe. There is nothing there to surprise us. The game is a kind of marking out and investigation. The child plays with his body in order to explore it, to take inventory of it; the waiter in the cafe plays with his condition in order to realize it. This obligation is not different from that which is imposed on all tradesmen. Their condition is wholly one of ceremony. The public demands of them that they realize it as a ceremony; there is the dance of the grocer, of the tailor, of the auctioneer, by which they endeavor to persuade their clientele that they are nothing but a grocer, an auctioneer, a tailor. A grocer who dreams is offensive to the buyer, because such a grocer is not wholly a grocer. Society demands that he limit himself to his function as a grocer. . . .

4. Comments and Questions

a. The making of legislation has also been described as similar to a dance, by no less an eminence than Professor Woodrow Wilson (the same Wilson who subsequently became President). This analogy is often used in describing negotiation and mediation.

b. To what extent do attorneys participating in a dispute resolution process engage in ceremonies? Does the practiced trial lawyer or mediator know what is "real" and what is role? In this regard, consider the following from the philosopher Santayana:

> Masks are arrested expressions and admirable echoes of feeling, at once faithful, discreet, and superlative. Living things in contact with the air must acquire a cuticle, and it is not urged against cuticles that they are not hearts; yet some philosophers seem to be angry with images for not being things, and with words for not being feelings. Words and images are like shells, no less integral parts of nature than are the substances they cover, but better addressed to the eye and more open to observation. I would not say that substance exists for the sake of appearance, or faces for the sake

> of masks, or the passions for the sake of poetry and virtue. Nothing arises in nature for the sake of anything else; all these phases and products are involved equally in the round of existence.

George Santayana, SOLILOQUIES IN ENGLAND AND LATER SOLILOQUIES 131-132 (1992)

c. To what extent does Sartre's description of the waiter apply to a mediator or other third party neutral? Describe the role expectations of arbitrators, mediators, and negotiators. To what extent can one sensibly offer such a description apart from the background and setting of a particular situation?

d. How people present themselves will have an impact on how others perceive them. At the same time, the recipient of impressions knows that the other person may be putting on a show for their benefit, and they may respond in kind. In the next piece, Erving Goffman examines the dynamic of making impressions.

5. Erving Goffman, THE PRESENTATION OF SELF IN EVERYDAY LIFE 1-8 (1959)

When an individual enters the presence of others, they commonly seek to acquire information about him or to bring into play information about him already possessed. . . . Information about the individual helps to define the situation, enabling others to know in advance what he will expect of them and what they may expect of him. Informed in these ways, the others will know how best to act in order to call forth a desired response from him.

If unacquainted with the individual, observers can glean clues from his conduct and appearance which allow them to apply their previous experience with individuals roughly similar to the one before them or, more important, to apply untested stereotypes to him. They can also assume from past experience that only individuals of a particular kind are likely to be found in a given social setting. . . .

However, during the period in which the individual is in the immediate presence of the others, few events may occur which directly provide the others with the conclusive information they will need if they are to direct wisely their own activity. Many crucial facts lie beyond the time and place of interaction or lie concealed within it. For example, the "true" or "real" attitudes, beliefs, and emotions of the individual can be ascertained only indirectly, through his avowals or through what appears to be involuntary expressive behavior. Similarly, if the individual offers the others a product or service, they will often find that during the interaction there will be no time and place immediately available for eating the pudding that the proof can be found in. They will be forced to accept some events as conventional or natural signs of something not directly available to the senses. . . .

Let us now turn from the others to the point of view of the individual who presents himself before them. He may wish them to think highly of him or to think that he thinks highly of them, or to perceive how in fact he feels toward them, or to obtain no clear-cut impression; he may wish to ensure sufficient harmony so that the interaction can be sustained, or to . . . confuse, mislead, antagonize, or insult them. Regardless of the particular objective which the individual has in mind and of his motive for having this objective, it will be in his interest to control the conduct of the others, especially their responsive treatment of him. This control is achieved largely by influencing the definition of the situation which the others come to formulate, and he can influence this definition by expressing himself in such a way as to give them the kind of impression that will lead them to act voluntarily in accordance with his own plan. Thus, when an individual appears in the presence of others, there will usually be some reason for him to mobilize his activity so that it will convey an impression to others which it is in his interests to convey. . . .

The others of course may sense that the individual is manipulating the presumably spontaneous aspects of his behavior, and seek in this very act of manipulation some shading of conduct that the individual has not managed to control. This again provides a check upon the individual's behavior, thus reestablishing the asymmetry of the communication process. Here I would like only to add the suggestion that the arts of piercing an individual's effort at calculating unintentionality seem better developed than our capacity to manipulate our own behavior, so that regardless of how many steps have occurred in the information game, the witness is likely to have the advantage over the actor. . . .

Chapter 3

Theoretical Approaches to Disputes and Disputing

CASE STUDY

In 1992, the Texas alternative rock band "Speakeasy" recorded their first album called "1st Song." In order to record this album, the four members recruited the help of Lou Diamond, a friend of theirs for many years. Diamond created a record company called Bulldog Records, completely funded with his own money, and orally contracted with Speakeasy for its first recording deal. Since the members of Speakeasy and Diamond were close friends, many terms of the agreement were not addressed nor written into contract form.

"1st Song" was recorded and released in a few short weeks and a single pressing (a pressing is 10,000 copies) of the CD was produced and delivered to regional radio stations and local music stores. The band aggressively promoted their CD with club dates, regional tours and college radio promotions. Before they knew it, Speakeasy was taking off. Their success was primarily due to their live shows and a song that was on "1st Song" called "Home." Album sales were rising, but they were not making a great deal of money. Late in 1993, only 4,000 copies of "1st Song" remained on the shelves. At this point, Diamond and Speakeasy decided that it would not be prudent to invest the money to produce another pressing and Speakeasy and Diamond ended their business relationship and eventually all copies of "1st Song" disappeared from the shelves.

Speakeasy continued to promote the CD in the local clubs and was eventually approached by Jim Weitz of Superscope Records, one of the music industry's newest major labels that had made its mark by signing some of the best up and coming new bands. Superscope offered Speakeasy a three record deal and immediately sent them into the studio to record their second CD, "2nd Song." The form contract they signed with Superscope contained a clause which assigned to Superscope all rights to any recorded material the band has produced. It is Superscope's position that this clause assigns the rights to "1st Song" over to them.

Since the song "Home" was such a success, Superscope insisted that Speakeasy include it on "2nd Song." Superscope aggressively promoted the band and the song, sending copies of the CD to all of the major radio stations in the nations and sending Speakeasy on tours across the U.S. and Canada with some of their more established bands. The result was that the song "Home" was climbing the charts and Speakeasy had become an overnight sensation.

While on tour in New York, approximately one year after Superscope and Speakeasy signed their contract, Speakeasy's drummer was in a record store and saw several copies of "1st Song" in the bins behind the copies of "2nd Song." This struck him as odd since the first CD was released only in Texas and because all copies had been sold over a year ago. He discussed this with the store manager and discovered that the store had received a shipment of 100 copies only the week before from Bulldog Records. The CD was marked with a label stating "Featuring the new hit song...Home!"

The drummer promptly reported his finding to Weitz. Upon further investigation, Weitz discovered that Diamond and Bulldog had sent over 200,000 copies of "1st Song" to various record stores in the U.S. and Canada. Superscope's attorney immediately filed an application for injunctive relief, and the injunction was granted until the rights of the parties can be established. The injunction prohibits Bulldog Records from further distribution and the 175,000 copies of "1st Song" that remained on the shelves were returned to Bulldog Records. The injunction also prohibits Superscope from producing and marketing "1st Song."

Superscope and Speakeasy then filed this action against Bulldog Records seeking 2 million dollars in damages for copyright infringement, unauthorized sales and intentional interference with a contractual relationship. Bulldog Records denies that Superscope or Speakeasy have any rights in "1st Song" because Diamond produced the CD entirely with his own funds and because Speakeasy told him that "they did not care what he did with 1st Song." It is Bulldog's position that Speakeasy surrendered it's rights to the CD with that statement. The agreement between Bulldog and Speakeasy was oral.

A. Introduction

The purpose of this Chapter is to provide an introduction to social science research that offers helpful insights on disputing and the resolution of disputes. The following subject areas are examined here (without accompanying mathematics):

1. Competition and Cooperation
2. Economics and Game Theory
3. Agency Theory
4. Learning Theory and Psychology
5. Anthropology

The discussion in this Chapter addresses disputing generally. Application of social science theory to specific dispute resolution procedures will be considered later, in conjunction with the discussion of the particular procedures.

B. Competition and Cooperation

1. Comments and Questions

a. This section focuses attention on the seemingly obvious insight that interactions between people with divergent goals involve elements of both cooperation and competition. Each is important, and both are beneficial.

b. The settlement of disputes presents elements of both competition and cooperation. The parties are disputing, yet they must cooperate in order to terminate their dispute. In trying to achieve a (nonimposed) settlement, the parties cooperate to create the best set of options, while competing over how the available spoils will be divided. To put the matter colloquially, the parties cooperate to make the pie as large as possible, but compete over how to divide the pie.

c. This brings us to the eve of the Industrial Revolution, and the publication of Adam Smith, AN INQUIRY INTO THE NATURE AND CAUSES OF THE WEALTH OF NATIONS (1776). Before Smith, exchange transactions were regarded as sterile because no net benefit resulted; one person's gain equalled the other person's loss. (In modern terminology, exchange was seen as a "zero sum game.") It was Smith's great insight to prove to the world that exchanges benefitted both parties (else they would not occur). Value was personal to individuals, and often related to one's stock of resources, so both parties to an exchange could benefit.

d. In a competitive economy, people acting in their own self-interest will produce an economically efficient system. In Smith's memorable phrase, this will occur as if people's conduct was guided by "an invisible hand." And, Smith, trained in moral philosophy, noted the paradox that selfish behavior, while a private vice, is a public virtue.

e. Smith's work in the sphere of economics suggests that the solutions parties work out for their disputes will be for the best, both in terms of the individuals and the society — and this is often the case. In other instances, however, the result of action based on individual self-interest may be dreadful for the larger society — and even bad for the individuals involved.

f. An introduction to these difficulties is provided by the Prisoner's Dilemma and the Parable of the Commons. These themes will be revisited often in the ensuing chapters.

2. Adam Smith, AN INQUIRY INTO THE NATURE AND CAUSES OF THE WEALTH OF NATIONS 118-119 (1776) (Penguin 1986)

The division of labour, from which so many advantages are derived, is not originally the effect of any human wisdom, which foresees and intends that general opulence to which it gives occasion. It is the necessary, though very slow and gradual consequence of a certain propensity in human nature which has in view no such extensive utility; the propensity to truck, barter, and exchange one thing for another.

Whether this propensity be one of those original principles in human nature of which no further account can be given; or whether, as seems more probable, it be the necessary consequence of the faculties of reason and speech, it belongs not to our present subject to inquire. It is common to all men, and to be found in no other race of animals, which seem to know neither this nor any other species of contracts. Two grey-hounds, in running down the same hare, have sometimes the appearance of acting in some sort of concert. Each turns her towards his companion, or endeavors to intercept her when his companion turns her toward himself. This, however, is not the effect of any contract, but of the accidental concurrence of their passions in the same object at that particular time. Nobody ever saw a dog make a fair and deliberate exchange of one bone for another with another dog. Nobody ever saw one animal by its gestures and natural cries signify to another, this is mine, that yours; I am willing to give this for that. When an animal wants to obtain something either of a man or of another animal, it has no other means of persuasion but to gain the favour of those whose service it requires. A puppy fawns upon its dam, and a spaniel endeavors by a thousand attractions to engage the attention of its master who is at dinner, when it wants to be fed by him. Man sometimes uses the same arts with his brethren, and when he has no other means of engaging them to act according to his inclinations, endeavors by every servile and fawning attention to obtain their good will. He has not time, however, to do this upon every occasion. In civilized society he stands at all times in need of the cooperation and assistance of great multitudes, while his whole life is scarce sufficient to gain the friendship of a few persons. In almost every other race of animals the individual, when it is grown up to maturity, is entirely independent, and in its natural state has occasion for the assistance of no other living creature. But man has almost constant occasion for the help of his brethren, and it is in vain for him to expect it from their benevolence only. He will be more likely to prevail if he can interest their self-love in his favour, and show them that it is for their own advantage to do for him what he requires of them. Whoever offers to another a bargain of any kind, proposes to do this. Give me that which I want, and you shall have this which you want, is the meaning of every such offer; and it is in this manner that we obtain from one another the far greater part of those good offices which we stand in need of. It is not from the benevolence of the butcher, the brewer or the baker that we expect our dinner, but from their regard to their own interest. We address ourselves, not to their humanity but to their self-love, and never talk to them of our own necessities but of their advantages. Nobody but a beggar chooses to depend chiefly upon the benevolence of his fellow-citizens. . . .

3. Garrett Hardin, *The Tragedy of the Commons*, SCIENCE, Vol. 162, at 1243, 1244 (13 December, 1968)*

Tragedy of Freedom in a Commons

The tragedy of the commons develops in this way. Picture a pasture open to all. It is to be expected that each herdsman will try to keep as many cattle as possible on the commons. Such an arrangement may work reasonably satisfactorily for centuries because tribal wars, poaching, and disease keep the numbers of both man and beast well below the carrying capacity of the land. Finally, however, comes the day of reckoning, that is, the day when the long-desired goal of social stability becomes a reality. At this point, the inherent logic of the commons remorselessly generates tragedy.

As a rational being, each herdsman seeks to maximize his gain. Explicitly or implicitly, more or less consciously, he asks, "What is the utility to me of adding one more animal to my herd?" This utility has one negative and one positive component.

1) The positive component is a function of the increment of one animal. Since the herdsman receives all the proceeds from the sale of the additional animal, the positive utility is nearly +1.
2) The negative component is a function of the additional overgrazing created by one more animal. Since, however, the effects of overgrazing are shared by all the herdsmen, the negative utility for any particular decisionmaking herdsman is only a fraction of −1.

Adding together the component partial utilities, the rational herdsman concludes that the only sensible course for him to pursue is to add another animal to his herd. And another; and another. . . . But this is the conclusion reached by each and every rational herdsman sharing a commons. Therein is the tragedy. Each man is locked into a system that compels him to increase his herd without limits—in a world that is limited. Ruin is the destination toward which all men rush, each pursuing his own best interest in a society that believes in the freedom of the commons. Freedom in a common brings ruin to all.

4. The Prisoner's Dilemma

The Prisoner's Dilemma arises in the following manner. Two persons (A and B) commit a bank robbery. They are subsequently arrested, and are immediately placed in two different locations in order to prevent communication between them. The District Attorney (DA) knows that A and B committed the bank robbery, but she lacks adequate evidence to convict them of this crime. The DA does, however, have sufficient evidence to convict both A and B of a lesser offense, illegal possession of a firearm, for which the sentence is one year. (The Prisoner's Dilemma story comes in many different versions, but they are all variants on the same basic theme.)

The DA decides to make identical offers to both A and B, in an attempt to induce confessions. (The analysis that follows is for Prisoner A only, but that for Prisoner B is identical.) The following are the exclusive sentencing options (rules):

1. If A and B both decline to confess, then neither will be convicted of bank robbery, but each will receive a sentence of one year imprisonment for the lesser offense.
2. If A confesses and B does not confess, then A goes free and B will receive a sentence of ten years imprisonment.
3. If A does not confess and B confesses, than B goes free and A will receive a sentence of ten years imprisonment.
4. If A and B both confess, then each will receive a sentence of seven years imprisonment.

Now, we are ready for Prisoner A to make a rational and self-interested response to the choices offered by the DA. The options for both A and B are simple, and two in number: confess ("defect") or remain silent. In order for A to make a sensible decision, account must also be taken of what B will do. Let us consider the outcome for each option, assuming first that B confesses and then that B remains silent:

1. B Confesses. If A remains silent, then A goes to jail for ten years. If A also confesses, then A goes to jail for seven years. So, assuming B confesses, A is better off by confessing than by remaining silent.
2. B is Silent. If A confesses, then A is set free. If A also remains silent, then A goes to jail for one year (the lesser charge). So, assuming B remains silent, A is better off by confessing than remaining silent.

Under either possible response by B, Prisoner A is best off by confessing. Prisoner B, applying the same analysis, will also decide to confess. Put the two results together, and we have the "solution" to the Prisoner's Dilemma. Both parties confess, and each goes to jail for seven years. At the risk of pointing out the obvious, the reader will observe that maximizing behavior on the part of A and B does not produce an optimum result for A and B taken together, or even for A and B taken individually.

5. Comments and Questions

a. Imagine that you are having dinner with several friends, and there is an (unspoken) agreement that the bill will be shared equally. The individual, by ordering a sumptuous feast, can benefit from a "free rider" effect, while the "responsible" member of the group who orders an inexpensive meal will incur increased costs. This situation represents an everyday example of the idea that what is in the self-interest of the individual at a particular time is not necessarily in the best interest of the group, and may not even be in the long-run best interest of the individual.

b. Once the number of persons in the group and the meal options are specified, a mathematical model of the Restaurant "game" can be mapped. If the game is played only once, the rational participant in the Restaurant will "defect" and maximize individual good rather than group benefit. But, since everyone faces the same calculus, all will eat expensively and all will face a higher bill than any of them individually or as a group would desire. Even with repetitions expected, defections are likely to occur in the absence of group action.

c. If one were so inclined, this situation might be called the Tragedy of the Restaurant. Make this a two-person game, and we have a variant that might be called the Diner's Dilemma.

d. Now, let us suppose that our diners, after several high-dollar dinners seek to find a less costly solution, without giving up the "all-for-one and one-for-all" conviviality associated with sharing the dinner check. (That is, the group does not want to abandon the dinner game by adopting a pay your own bill approach.) What suggestions can you offer? Play the options you generate as new iterations of the Restaurant game.

e. Suppose the group wants to try a modified version of the game, by splitting into two (adjoining) tables, with separate group bills for the persons at each table. How might the groups be configured to achieve maximum fairness? These and related issues are discussed in Natalie S. Glance & Bernardo A. Huberman, *The Dynamics of Social Dilemmas*, SCIENTIFIC AMERICAN, March 1994, at 75.

C. Economics and Game Theory

1. Comments and Questions

a. Economics and game theory are presented together because of their common intellectual roots, the emphasis on formal assumptions and structured (usually mathematical) mode of analysis, and the central focus on questions of distribution that are important for dispute resolution.

b. Whatever definitions one uses for economics and game theory (contentious matters we avoid), there is a large overlap between them. A person could not claim to be a serious student of either subject, without extensive knowledge about the other. The growing use of game theory by economists has led to near agreement among the best graduate programs that a professional economics education is incomplete without a firm understanding of this new tool. *See,* H. Scott Bierman & Luis Fernandez, GAME THEORY WITH ECONOMIC APPLICATIONS iii (1993) (college course for economics majors).

c. An interest in analytical models based on rigorous assumptions known to be at variance with reality does not evidence a disinterest in reality, or a disinclination to solve messy "real world" problems that do not comport with assumptions drawn on paper.

2. Steven Shavell, *Alternative Dispute Resolution: An Economic Analysis*, 24 J. LEGAL STUDIES 1 (1995)*

When parties need to resolve a dispute, they may often turn not only to the state-sanctioned method of dispute resolution — trial before a court — but also to alternatives, notably, to arbitration, abbreviated trial procedures, or mediation. Although particular methods of alternative dispute resolution (which will be referred to collectively as ADR) vary from one another, they share the feature that a third party is involved who offers an opinion or communicates information about the dispute to the disputants. In addition, the formality, length, and complexity of ADR are usually less than those of official proceedings.

Interest in ADR has grown over the years, and today utilization of ADR is widespread. Moreover, ADR is increasingly encouraged by courts and legislation; in various areas of dispute, plaintiffs and defendants are required to use ADR before they are given recourse to trial. Alternative dispute resolution is now part of the law school curriculum; casebooks on ADR have been published; and journals devoted to it have been established. Indeed, the group of lawyers, arbitrators, academics, and jurists fostering ADR has taken on some of the aspects of a social movement.

Why, exactly, is ADR employed? What are its advantages to private parties and to society? Should ADR be subsidized, provided, or mandated by the state? In examining these questions in this article, I apply the economic approach in that I assume that parties take rational account of the effects of ADR on the likely disposition of their disputes, and for clarity I consider stylized models of parties' behavior. I make a basic distinction in the analysis between ex ante agreements to employ ADR (arrangements made before disputes arise), and ex post resort to ADR (use of ADR after disputes have arisen).

---

*Reprinted with permission.

Ex ante ADR agreements are treated in Section I of this article. Here, ADR may be adopted because it is to the mutual benefit of the parties to a contract or to those who have some other relationship with each other. Three reasons why ADR may be mutually beneficial are discussed. First, ADR may lower the cost of resolving disputes or risk. Second, ADR may engender superior incentives through greater accuracy of result or other characteristics. Suppose, for instance, that substandard performance of a contract would be correctly assessed by expert arbitrators under ADR but not by courts. Then the parties to the contract might well prefer to adopt ADR because it would induce good performance, thereby raising the willingness of the promisee to pay for the contract. Third, ADR may result in improved incentives to engage in disputes or to refrain from that. For example, it may be that the number of disputes brought under the legal process would be excessive, dissipating substantial resources of the parties without instigating mutually desirable changes in behavior; thus an ADR agreement that would serve to limit the number of disputes would be advantageous.

Such benefits of ex ante ADR agreements cannot generally be obtained by means of ex post agreements to use ADR. Where courts are not able to ascertain substandard performance and this occurs, the parties will hardly have any reason at that point to adopt ADR—it will be too late to induce good performance. The advantages of ex ante ADR agreements, combined with the frequent inability to secure them through ex post ADR agreements, explain why parties will often want to make ex ante ADR agreements.

Because ex ante ADR agreements made by knowledgeable parties raise their well-being, the agreements raise social welfare (in the absence of external effects). Thus, it is suggested that ex ante ADR agreements should ordinarily be enforced by the legal system. At the same time, there is no general call for ex ante ADR to be subsidized or otherwise aided by the state.

Ex post ADR agreements are considered in Section II of this article. Parties will tend to make ex post ADR agreements when, after a dispute arises, ADR would produce mutual gains. This can come about in two major ways: through promotion of settlement, and through reduction of dispute resolution costs. To determine how ADR functions in these respects, I append ADR to the standard economic model of litigation. Specifically, I assume that a potential plaintiff decides whether to sue, and if so, he either goes immediately to trial, agrees to a settlement, or engages in binding or nonbinding ADR. Alternative dispute resolution is assumed to be cheaper than trial and possibly to convey information about what would occur at trial. Two ADR regimes are studied: where the use of ADR is voluntary, and where nonbinding ADR is required before there can be a trial. I compare outcomes in these regimes with that where ADR is unavailable.

The main descriptive conclusions are readily summarized. First, the tendency to bring suit is not affected by ADR where its use is voluntary. A person will bring suit in the model only if he has a credible threat to proceed thereafter. If ADR is voluntary, the defendant can always refuse to engage in ADR, so that the plaintiff must be willing to go to trial to have a credible threat, which is exactly his situation in the absence of ADR. When, however, nonbinding ADR is required before trial, the situation is altered. For example, since ADR is cheaper than trial, it may be that a party who would not be willing to go to trial would be willing to engage in nonbinding ADR and thus to bring suit. But it may also be that the tendency to sue would be decreased because, to go to trial, a party must incur ADR costs plus trial costs rather than just the latter.

Second, given that suit has been brought, the availability of ADR tends to reduce the frequency of both trial and of immediate settlement. Being a kind of substitute for trial and being cheaper than trial, parties may elect ADR rather than go to trial. Similarly, parties may elect ADR rather than settle since ADR constitutes an inexpensive form of legal combat; the costs of ADR are lower than those of trial and may not be high enough to discourage the parties from use of ADR. It will be seen in the analysis that these conclusions, along with those concerning the election of binding versus nonbinding ADR, depend significantly on how well ADR predicts trial outcomes.

Following the descriptive analysis of ex post ADR, I consider its private and social value. I observe that the private value of ex post ADR does not incorporate its incentive effects on parties' behavior; only ex ante ADR agreements reflect incentive effects. Consequently, it is not clear in principle that even voluntary ex post ADR agreements enhance individuals' welfare, and there is no apparent basis for the state's requiring nonbinding ADR before trial. (Indeed, such mandatory ADR can have the perverse effect of increasing the cost of litigation, by adding another layer to it, without promoting settlement.) This raises questions about the general wisdom of public policies requiring or otherwise furthering use of ADR.

I. EX ANTE AGREEMENTS TO USE ALTERNATIVE DISPUTE RESOLUTION

A. Ex Ante Alternative Dispute Resolution Agreements and Mutual Benefits

Suppose that two parties are in contact with each other before adverse events that could lead to legal disputes arise. The parties might be in a contractual relationship (including that between employer and employee) and be considering the problem of inadequate performance or breach. . . . Let us now briefly consider the three sources of mutual advantage mentioned in the introduction.

B. Reduction in Dispute Resolution Costs or in Risk

If adoption of ADR would lead to a reduction in the total costs to the parties of dispute resolution, then it would obviously be in their interests to make an ex ante ADR agreement. If, for example, the costs for each party were reduced by one-third in every dispute, then they each would want to employ ADR, other things being equal. Note, though, that in principle the parties would not need to make an ex ante agreement to obtain the one-third reduction in costs. They can wait until disputes arise and then adopt ADR and still reduce their costs by one-third. Thus, while reduction in costs is an advantage of ex ante ADR agreements, it is equally an advantage of ex post ADR agreements.

Similarly, if ADR would lower the risks attending disputes (because, for instance, exposure to unreliable jury verdicts could be avoided), the parties would tend to find ADR mutually beneficial if one or the other is risk averse. And, as with cost reduction, this benefit can be obtained by parties after disputes arise, so that it is a source of advantage for both ex post and ex ante ADR agreements.

C. Improvement in Incentives

A different way in which ADR may be of aid to parties is that it may induce a change in behavior that benefits both, by increasing the joint value that their relationship produces. . . . [A]rbitrators who can discern substandard contractual performance . . . better than it would be in court. More generally, ADR could lead to improved incentives for other reasons, such as that a different legal rule is employed from that which would be applied in court. As long as ADR leads to changes in behavior that raise joint value for parties, there will be a mutually beneficial agreement that they can make involving ADR rather than the legal system.

It should be emphasized that, as a general matter, ADR that improves incentives must be agreed to ex ante because the parties would not obtain joint benefits from an ADR agreement ex post. [T]here would obviously be no joint advantage to be gained by adopting ADR . . . [after] substandard performance has occurred, [because] it is too late to affect incentives to induce good performance.

D. Beneficial Changes in the Frequency of Disputes

A third route by which ADR may produce gains for the parties is by bringing about a change in the frequency of disputes. It could be that, given the applicable law, too many actions would be brought in the sense that they would absorb resources in the form of dispute resolution costs but not produce any (or, more generally, much) benefit in behavior. In such a case, the two sides would elect to make an ADR agreement that reduces the frequency of disputes. . . .

Observe as well that the parties must make an ex ante ADR agreement to reduce the frequency of disputes. They will not make an ex post ADR agreement; their whole problem is that, if they wait until a dispute arises, the harmed party will have a reason to bring an action.

While in the above example the problem was that too many suits would be brought in the absence of ADR, another possibility is that the frequency of disputes would be too low in the absence of ADR, in that more actions would improve incentives and increase joint value by an amount exceeding the change in dispute resolution costs. And here, too, only an ex ante ADR agreement would be helpful to the parties.

E. Ex Ante Alternative Dispute Resolution Agreements and Social Policy

When parties elect to use ADR, they are both made better off, so that social welfare must rise, other things being equal. Accordingly, the general policy of the law should be to enforce ex ante ADR agreements. This statement is, of course, subject to the two usual qualifications about the desirability of enforcement of any agreements. First, it may be that a party to an agreement was not properly informed about relevant information—in the present context, information about the legal process or the character of ADR. Second, it may be that an agreement to use ADR would negatively affect third parties (e.g., children in a divorce). Either problem could provide grounds for not enforcing an ex ante ADR agreement.

Although the state should enforce private ADR agreements, this does not imply that it should subsidize or otherwise actively encourage ADR agreements. No general basis for such a policy is evident. But, again, this statement is subject to two standard qualifications. It could be that parties have inadequate information about the benefits of ADR and that this information cannot effectively be communicated to them (if the information could be communicated to the parties, they could decide whether they want to use ADR). The second conventional qualification is that ADR might positively affect third parties. These qualifications could justify promoting or requiring ADR.

Another qualification, special to the context of legal disputes, is that parties who use the courts do not at present pay the full costs of the public services that are thereby rendered to them, whereas one presumes parties do pay the full costs of ADR. Thus, ADR appears more expensive in comparison to the courts than it really is, and ADR might thus be used less often relative to the courts than would be best. (Suppose, for instance, that use of the court truly costs $1,000 and ADR $500, but that parties pay only $250 to use the courts; then ADR appears twice as costly as the courts even though it is really half as costly.) As an antidote to this problem of relative pricing, ADR could be subsidized. But that would not offer a full solution to a problem that emanates from failure to charge completely for use of the courts: if ADR is subsidized along with the courts, both methods of dispute resolution will be cheaper to use than they truly are for society to provide, leading to over-utilization of each. Other things being equal, the appropriate policy would seem to be to subsidize neither.

A final observation is that there is no paradox represented by the conclusion that the law should ordinarily enforce ex ante ADR agreements, which is to say, the law should enforce agreements that bypass the legal process. . . . [T]he parties themselves know much about their own situations; typically, they know their situations far better than the courts could. Hence, it is not surprising that parties should be able to choose for themselves a better method of dispute resolution than the legal process would offer, and that the courts should respect such choices.

II. EX POST AGREEMENTS TO USE ALTERNATIVE DISPUTE RESOLUTION

A. Ex Post Alternative Dispute Resolution Agreements and Mutual Benefits

Parties who are in a dispute will decide to make an ADR agreement if this will be to their mutual benefit. The main reasons why ADR may appeal jointly to parties ex post is that it may constitute a cheap substitute for trial or that it may provide them with information about the trial outcome and thus make settlement more likely. In both ways ADR may serve to lower the expected costs of dispute resolution. ADR may also lower risk, as I will discuss in a later subsection dealing with risk aversion. In the next subsection, I review the standard model of litigation without ADR. I then introduce voluntary ADR into the standard model, and, following that, I examine mandatory nonbinding ADR. In the final subsection, I consider social policy and ex post ADR.

Before proceeding, several comments about ex post ADR and ex ante ADR are worth making. First, any mutual advantage that parties can obtain through an ex post ADR agreement can also be obtained through an ex ante ADR agreement—they need merely specify ADR appropriately in an ex ante agreement. . . . Second, parties may not be able to make ex ante ADR agreements because they are not in contact ex ante; this is true by definition for strangers who happen to have a dispute. Or, even if parties are in contact, they may decide it is not worth the trouble to make an ex ante agreement because the odds of a dispute are low and because, if a dispute arises, they can make an ex post agreement to gain the advantage they would have from an ex ante agreement.

B. Standard Model of Litigation

. . . According to the standard model of litigation, the plaintiff first decides whether or not to bring suit, and then, if he does, he and the defendant either settle or proceed to trial. Trial is assumed to involve a cost for each side, but, for simplicity, suit is taken to be costless.

In this model, it is supposed that a plaintiff will bring suit if and only if he would have a credible threat thereafter to go to trial. (The motivation is that otherwise the defendant would refuse to pay anything in settlement to the plaintiff.) Assuming, as I shall, that parties are risk neutral, this implies that the plaintiff will bring suit if and only if his expected judgment would exceed his trial cost. If, for instance, the plaintiff would win $10,000 with likelihood 80 percent and his trial cost would be $2,000, his expected judgment would be $8,000, so he would bring suit, but he would not do this if his chance of prevailing were only 10 percent and his expected judgment therefore would be only $1,000.

Given that suit is brought, it is supposed that there will be a settlement if and only if there exists a settlement agreement that both parties would prefer to trial. This will be true if the minimum settlement acceptable to the plaintiff is less than the maximum settlement acceptable to the defendant. . . .

Now append to the model the possibility that the parties may agree to ADR, which may either be binding on the parties or nonbinding. After nonbinding ADR, the parties either settle or go to trial. . . . Alternative dispute resolution is assumed to involve a cost for each party, but it is smaller than that of trial (notably, because of the procedural simplicity of ADR).

As in the standard model, it is assumed that the plaintiff will bring a suit if and only if he would then have a credible threat against the defendant. Note that since ADR is voluntary, the defendant is free to refuse ADR. Accordingly, the plaintiff will have a credible threat if and only if he is willing to go to trial. Thus, as before, the plaintiff will bring suit if and only if his expected gain from trial would exceed his trial cost. The availability of ADR therefore does not affect the conditions under which suit will be brought. (This conclusion would not necessarily hold in a model allowing for asymmetry of information and including a cost of bringing suit. In such a model, plaintiffs might bring suit even though they would be unwilling to go to trial because defendants might mistakenly think they would be willing to go to trial.)

To determine what will occur if suit is brought, we must be explicit about the nature of ADR. I will suppose that the parties hold probabilistic beliefs about the outcome of ADR and that ADR will result in either a plaintiff victory or a defendant victory, with the magnitude of the possible ADR judgment being known by both parties to equal that which would be awarded at trial. (In other words, any uncertainty attending ADR or trial is about liability, not damages.) Also, the ADR outcome may alter the parties' probabilistic beliefs about what would occur at trial. In this regard, I consider two polar cases.

One case is that ADR perfectly predicts trial outcomes. If so, then, if ADR results in a plaintiff victory, the parties will know that trial would result in the same, and if ADR results in a plaintiff loss, the parties will know that that would happen at trial. In this case, a party's probability that he will win in ADR must equal his probability that he will win at trial since he believes that ADR perfectly predicts trial. . . . [T]he ADR outcome is by hypothesis independent of the trial outcome.

The opposing case is that ADR has no predictive value. If so, the parties' beliefs about the trial outcome after ADR will be precisely what they were before ADR. In this case, a party's probability that he will win in ADR need have no particular relationship to his probability of winning at trial. . . .

Of course, in general, ADR will have some, but not perfect, predictive value; thus ADR will change parties' beliefs, but they will not know for sure what will happen at trial after they learn ADR results. This general case is best addressed after the two polar cases are analyzed.

1. THE CASE WHERE ADR PERFECTLY PREDICTS TRIAL OUTCOMES. Our object is to determine which of the four possible outcomes will occur — immediate settle-

ment, immediate trial, binding ADR, or nonbinding ADR. Observe first that immediate trial will never occur because the parties would prefer binding ADR to trial, as binding ADR is cheaper but otherwise equivalent to trial.

With regard to nonbinding ADR, note that, after such ADR, the parties will definitely settle, for at that point they will agree on what would happen at trial. In particular, if the plaintiff loses in ADR, the parties will both believe that the plaintiff would definitely lose at trial, so the plaintiff will not pursue the matter, in effect settling for zero. If the plaintiff wins in ADR, the parties will both believe that the plaintiff would surely win at trial, so they will settle for some quantity approximating the judgment amount, and for simplicity I assume they will settle for exactly the judgment amount. . . . On reflection, therefore, nonbinding ADR is seen to be essentially equivalent to binding ADR. Under both, the plaintiff obtains nothing if he loses in ADR, and he obtains his judgment if he wins — either in a settlement, under nonbinding ADR, or as an award, under binding ADR.

The remaining possibility is immediate settlement. This the parties may decide upon—yet only if settlement is mutually preferable not only to trial but also to ADR. Recall from Section IIB above that the parties will prefer settlement to trial if and only if the plaintiff's expected judgment exceeds the defendant's by less than the sum of trial costs. By the same logic, the parties will prefer settlement to binding (and thus to nonbinding) ADR if and only if the plaintiff's expected judgment exceeds the defendant's by less than the sum of ADR costs. Since ADR costs are lower than trial costs, if the parties prefer settlement to ADR, they will also prefer settlement to trial, but if they prefer settlement to trial, they might still prefer ADR to settlement. . . .

In summary, the parties will never go to trial. They will settle immediately if and only if the plaintiff's expected judgment exceeds the defendant's by less than the sum of ADR costs. Otherwise, the parties will elect either binding or nonbinding ADR, the two being equivalent. If they choose nonbinding ADR, they will settle afterward. There are two differences between the outcome here and that in which ADR is not available: there are no trials, and immediate settlement occurs less often because ADR sometimes occurs instead.

2. THE CASE WHERE ADR HAS NO PREDICTIVE VALUE. In this case, the parties will never choose nonbinding ADR since after such ADR their beliefs will not be changed, and they will thus be in the same position as before yet have incurred costs. Binding ADR, however, might be chosen by the parties because it may serve as a cheap substitute for trial (even though it does not predict trial outcomes). . . .

More generally, binding ADR might be preferred to trial not only because it is cheaper but also because the plaintiff's and defendant's beliefs about ADR may diverge more than they diverge about trial (and thus ADR may provide them, in effect, with a better bet).

Settlement may also be preferred to trial and to binding ADR. Settlement will be preferred to trial if the divergence in expected judgments from trial is less than the sum of trial costs. Settlement will be preferred to binding ADR if the divergence in expected ADR awards exceeds the sum of ADR costs. If both of these conditions hold true, then settlement will be elected by the parties.

To summarize, the parties might go immediately to trial, settle, or engage in binding ADR, but never in nonbinding ADR. Comparing the outcomes to those when ADR is not available, there will be trial, but less often than before, and there will be settlement, but less often than before. Binding ADR will to some extent be chosen instead of settlement or trial.

3. THE CASE WHERE ADR IS AN IMPERFECT PREDICTOR OF TRIAL OUTCOMES. In this case, if there is nonbinding ADR, it may or may not be followed by settlement, depending on how parties' beliefs are affected by the ADR outcome. . . .

[I]t is possible for nonbinding ADR to be followed always by settlement, by settlement only if there is a plaintiff win in ADR or only if there is a defendant win, or never to be followed by settlement. The analysis of binding ADR, immediate trial, and immediate settlement is essentially the same as in the previous two cases. Any of the four possible outcomes may occur, and the factors that lead to each can be understood by reference to the discussion above.

D. Model of Litigation with Nonbinding Alternative Dispute Resolution Required before Trial

Assume next that the option of immediate trial is not open; that is, assume that parties must engage in nonbinding ADR before they can proceed to trial. (They can, of course, settle immediately or decide to employ binding ADR rather than nonbinding ADR.) . . . Because the plaintiff's threat in this situation is to engage in nonbinding ADR, the plaintiff will bring suit if and only if his expected gain resulting from nonbinding ADR exceeds his costs. His expected gain from nonbinding ADR will be investigated below; as we will see, it can be greater or less than what it would be from immediate trial, so that the incentive to sue can be larger or smaller than in the absence of required nonbinding ADR before trial.

1. THE CASE WHERE ADR PERFECTLY PREDICTS TRIAL OUTCOMES. In this case, given that suit is brought, recall that the parties would never elect to go to trial immediately, so that the requirement that they use nonbinding ADR before trial will never constrain what they would otherwise do. Hence, given that suit is brought, the parties will behave as described earlier. They will either settle immediately, if the difference in expected judgments is less than the sum of ADR costs, or they will engage in ADR. And if they engage in ADR, they will be indifferent between binding and nonbinding ADR.

We can, however, say something about the tendency of the plaintiff to bring suit. As we discussed, if the plaintiff engages in nonbinding ADR and prevails, he will then settle for an amount equal to the judgment. Hence, the expected gross return to the plaintiff from ADR is the same as that from trial, but ADR costs less; the plaintiff's net return will therefore exceed that from going to trial. Consequently, suit will be more frequent than when ADR was not required. . . .

The reason that the plaintiff will sue more often is, in essence, that ADR provides a cheap substitute for trial to which the defendant must submit if the plaintiff wants. Before, since the defendant could refuse to participate in this cheap substitute for trial, the plaintiff did not sue as often.

2. THE CASE WHERE ADR HAS NO PREDICTIVE VALUE. In this case, the conclusion from Section IIC above was that the parties might go immediately to trial, settle, or engage in binding ADR, but the parties would never engage in nonbinding ADR because this would not change their beliefs, only absorb resources. Consequently, preventing the parties from going immediately to trial may alter what occurs given that suit is brought. In particular, parties may decide to use nonbinding ADR if, in the absence of the requirement to do so, they would have elected to go immediately to trial. When that is so, they now will have to, in effect, pay larger trial costs since now they will have to bear the costs of ADR plus the costs of trial in order to go to trial. They may be willing to do this if the difference in their expected beliefs

is large enough. Otherwise, they will settle immediately or use binding ADR.

With regard to the propensity to bring suit, it can be demonstrated that suit will be less frequent than when ADR is not required before trial. A person who is contemplating suit knows that his threat is to use nonbinding ADR. But since this might be followed by trial, the cost he would face to go to trial is the cost of ADR plus the cost of trial. Hence, if ADR would be followed by trial, he will bring suit only if the expected judgment exceeds the sum of the cost of ADR and the cost of trial. Thus, he will bring suit less often than if his cost were only the cost of trial, the situation when ADR was not required.

3. THE CASE WHERE ADR IS AN IMPERFECT PREDICTOR OF TRIAL OUTCOMES. With regard to this case, it is apparent that, given that suit is brought, the requirement may or may not affect the outcome, depending on whether immediate trial would or would not have been chosen, as described earlier. Immediate trial would have been chosen, roughly, if ADR would be a relatively poor predictor of trial outcomes and if there was an initially large difference in beliefs between plaintiff and defendant. Also, the plaintiff's tendency to bring suit will tend to be increased by the nonbinding ADR requirement if ADR is fairly informative and often leads to settlement; otherwise, the frequency of suit will tend to be reduced by the ADR requirement.

E. Comparison of Regimes without Alternative Dispute Resolution, with Voluntary Alternative Dispute Resolution, and with Nonbinding Alternative Dispute Resolution Required before Trial

I can summarize as follows. The propensity to sue is the same in regimes without ADR and with voluntary ADR, for under both the plaintiff must be willing to go to trial to have a credible threat against the defendant. But when nonbinding ADR must precede trial, the tendency to sue is different; the plaintiff will sue if he would be willing to engage in nonbinding ADR. This means that the tendency to sue is greater than otherwise if ADR would be followed by settlement, something that is likely if ADR predicts trial outcomes. But it means that the tendency to bring suit will be less than otherwise if ADR would not be followed by settlement and would therefore merely add costs to the litigation process; this is likely if ADR does not predict trial outcomes very well.

Given that suit is brought, ADR leads to substitution away from both trial and settlement and toward ADR. The specifics of the substitution depend, as explained, on the costs of ADR, on how informative ADR is of trial outcomes, and on whether nonbinding ADR is required before trial.

F. Risk Aversion

To this point, it has been assumed that parties are risk neutral. If one or both are risk averse and suit has been brought, immediate settlement becomes more attractive because it reduces risk. Specifically, if there is an immediate settlement, parties bear no risk, whereas they would bear risk not only if they went to trial, but also if they engaged in ADR. Alternative dispute resolution obviously involves risk if it is binding. If ADR is nonbinding but has some predictive value about trial, it also involves risk, for even if there is a settlement after ADR, the settlement amount will be affected by the ADR outcome.

Of course, even though settlement is more attractive in the presence of risk aversion, the parties may not settle. If they do not, then risk aversion may make binding ADR more attractive than it would otherwise be. If, unlike in the model I examined, the amount of damages is uncertain, but less subject to variation under ADR than under trial, binding ADR will reduce risk for the parties. Another point is that risk aversion means that nonbinding ADR is more likely to be followed by settlement than we had shown.

The general conclusion is then that risk aversion makes both immediate settlement and, possibly, binding ADR, more desirable than otherwise and thus reduces the frequency of trial from what it would otherwise be. With regard to whether suit will be brought, risk aversion generally reduces the bringing of suits. This is because the prospect of trial (or of nonbinding ADR where this is required before trial) becomes less attractive, so the plaintiff would have a credible threat against the defendant less often.

G. Ex Post Alternative Dispute Resolution Agreements and Social Policy

As mentioned in the introduction, when parties decide whether or not to adopt ADR after disputes have arisen, they have no reason to take into account the fact that the prospect of ADR may affect their behavior in an undesirable way. For instance, ADR agreements that plaintiffs and defendants rationally agree to when disputes arise may reduce defendants' payments to plaintiffs. Anticipating this, defendants' incentives to prevent injuries will therefore be reduced, and that could lower plaintiffs' well-being. Thus, we do not know that ADR agreements made ex post will advance parties' welfare.

This means that, in principle, we cannot say that ADR agreements made ex post should be enforced. Nevertheless, one suspects that the advantages of ex post ADR agreements often outweigh the possible disadvantages attending parties' failure to take incentive effects into account when they decide ex post about ADR.

In any case, there is again no clear argument for the state's encouraging the use of ADR, notably, for it to insist on nonbinding ADR before trial. Not only do we not know what effect this has on behavior, we have seen in the analysis that it can have effects on legal costs and the tendency to bring suit that could be disadvantageous. Required nonbinding ADR can for instance reduce the incentive to sue and raise the cost of litigation in situations where neither would be desirable.

III. CONCLUDING REMARKS

Among the issues omitted from the analysis is that concerning the exchange of information during ADR. If ADR alters parties' opinions about trial outcomes, often bringing them close enough to promote settlement, then it must be that ADR results in a party obtaining information that it would not otherwise learn. One wonders why, exactly, this should be true. Why should ADR result in parties learning more than they would through voluntary exchange of information and the discovery process? It is sometimes said that ADR provides parties new information because they hear the opinion of a neutral outsider, yet it would seem that parties could always consult individually with outsiders without adopting ADR. It is sometimes suggested as well that ADR may furnish clients a unique chance to understand the character of their cases and thereby help to defeat client-lawyer agency problems. Whatever is the truth of the matter, it warrants investigation.

Another issue of interest not addressed above is why there is strong support for public encouragement of ADR. A major explanatory element, if not the principal one, is no doubt the simple fact that ADR is cheaper than trial. Thus, whenever a dispute is resolved through

ADR instead of trial, dispute resolution costs are lowered. What may frequently not be given due weight are two other facts. First, as elaborated here, ADR can influence the frequency of suit and leads many parties who would have settled instead to engage in ADR — raising dispute resolution costs. Second, private parties have strong motives of their own to elect ADR, and special arguments are required to justify public promotion of it.

3. Comments and Questions

a. Game theory is about games of strategy. The word "game" is not used in the sense of amusement or entertainment. Many "games" that people play are not "games" as defined by game theory. Conversely, such serious matters as business and even war are games. (The field might better have been named "strategy theory.") Games involve interactive situation where the choice by one person will have an impact on another person, who may respond in a manner which promotes the second person's interests.

The approach of game theory is to seek insight about complex interactions by examining structured, abstracted, and simplified versions of decisions that include a strategic component. The prototype situation is a two-person, one-issue game. (The introduction of even a single additional party or issue makes the analysis far more complex.) Two-players (often, a buyer and a seller) seek to assign a value of some continuous variable (money) that they can mutually adjust. (The value reflects the thing being bargained about, but the measurement is in money.)

b. Game theory builds on decision theory. The following brief summation of decision theory is from an advanced college textbook:

> Decision theory is a set of methods by which a single, isolated decision maker can reach intelligent decisions when faced with a complex sequence of choices. The larger the number of decisions you must make, or that are made by someone . . . else, the larger the number of branches on the (decision) tree. In order to be unambiguous, decision trees must satisfy four rules: (1) Every node must have a parent, (2) no node can come before itself, (3) every node must have an ancestor that is an initial node, and (4) this initial node must be the only initial node of the tree.
>
> Backward induction provides a simple algorithm for finding the optimal sequence of decisions in a multistage decision tree. This algorithm embodies an overriding principle of decision theory: look before you leap.

H. Scott Bierman & Luis Fernandez, GAME THEORY WITH ECONOMIC APPLICATIONS (1993).

c. The seminal work on game theory is John Von Neumann & Oskar Morgenstern, THEORY OF GAMES AND ECONOMIC BEHAVIOR (1944). The seminal work on the application of game theory to negotiation is Howard Raiffa, THE ART AND SCIENCE OF NEGOTIATION (1982). Game theory is characterized by high levels of abstraction, and the leading work is a branch of advanced mathematics. Von Neumann & Morgenstern begin by telling us, in the first sentence of their preface, that they are presenting an exposition of "a mathematical theory of games." (p. v) The first sentence of Raiffa's prologue tells us that he became interested in the theory of games while a graduate student in mathematics. (p. 1)

d. The basic description of a simple two-party game must be detailed and specific — in effect, mathematical relationships are being stated in words. To address this simple two-party situation, game theory requires strict assumptions (rules of the game), which include the following:

1. There are only two parties to the negotiation;
2. There is no neutral third party (mediator);
3. A continuous variable (money but not a child);
4. Each bargainer is monolithic (able to make a binding decision);
5. The bargainers are concerned about this deal only, thus eliminating such factors as:
   a. linkage to other transactions;
   b. linkage to other outstanding problems;
   c. consideration of past or future dealings; and
   d. setting of a precedent;
6. Time is not a factor;
7. Contracts are inviolable and enforceable;
8. A single threat environment (terminate negotiations, with restoration of the status quo ante — apart from the costs of undertaking the negotiation and not succeeding);
9. Each bargainer knows her reservation price, but has only a probabilistic knowledge of the other party's reservation price; and
10. The setting, language, and individual variables are all irrelevancies.

This model assumes that bargaining is done directly by the parties, and not through agents. The introduction of action through agents raises a whole new set of problems, which are addressed by agency theory. (See the Gilson & Mnookin article in section D of this Chapter, which makes extensive use of the Prisoner's Dilemma as a heuristic device.) Finally, note that the tenth item assumes away most of disciplines such as anthropology, sociology, psychology, and communication theory.

e. The rules of a game, such as the sentencing options in the Prisoner's Dilemma (see Section B, above), may not be "adjusted" any more than the rules of chess may be "adjusted" by permitting pawns to jump over other pieces in specified circumstances. To pursue the chess analogy, the only objective statement to be made about a game in which pawns jump over other pieces is that this game is not chess, because the game is defined by its rules. If one were inclined toward normative judgments, one might conclude that the new game is "better" than chess, but that game is not chess.

f. In repeated two-player games, studies have demonstrated that "tit-for-tat" is the most effective strategy: cooperate the first time, and then do whatever the other person did in the prior iteration of the game. With multiple players, however, this strategy generally will not produce optimum results.

4. H. Scott Bierman & Luis Fernandez, Game Theory with Economic Applications 68-70 (1993)

The Elements of A Game

Game theory is concerned with how individuals make decisions when they are aware that their actions affect each other and when each individual takes this into account. It is the interaction between individual decision makers, all of who are behaving purposefully, and whose decisions have implications for other people, that makes strategic decisions different from other decisions. . . . A game . . . consists of the following:

(1) a set of players,
(2) an order of play,
(3) a description of the information available to any player at any point during the game,
(4) a set of actions available to each player whenever called upon to make a decision,
(5) the outcome that results from every possible sequence of actions by the players, and
(6) a utility ranking for every player over the set of outcomes.

The ranking of an outcome to a player is that player's payoff. Any description of a strategic situation must have all six elements to be considered well defined. . . .

[D]ecision makers are assumed to make their choices according to internally consistent criteria. Such behavior is called rational behavior. Game theorists also assume that all players are rational. In addition, however, they have found it necessary to make two additional assumptions. The first assumption is that the rationality of every player is common knowledge. . . . The second assumption . . . is that the complete description of the game—players, actions, strategies, order of play, information, and pay-offs—is also common knowledge. This second assumption is very strong—much stronger than simply assuming that every player is rational . . . .

5. Howard Raiffa, The Art and Science of Negotiation 52-54 (1982)

Analytical Models and Empirical Results

In one interesting experiment . . . many pairs of subjects were each asked to divide $2 between themselves; no agreement meant no money. In the symmetrical version, practically all settled on the $1 focal point. In some pairs, one party was secretly prompted to hold out for $1.20 and to hold firm; as expected, the reactions of the opposing parties were also firm —they would rather take nothing than 80 cents. Would this be your preference, too, if you had to share $200 and someone demanded $120?

The subjects were next told to share $2 but they were each penalized 5 cents for every minute it took them to decide on their sharing rule. They quickly jumped to the $1 focal point. Then came an interesting variation: Party A was penalized 5 cents per minute of negotiations, whereas Party B was penalized 10 cents per minute. Clearly Party A had a strategic advantage. But what had become the natural focal point? The surprising thing is that empirically, averaging over many subjects, Party A (the stronger party) in this variation did worse—not better, as might have been expected. Once symmetry was destroyed it invited power confrontations, and the seemingly advantaged Party A ended up, on the average, worse off than he had been in the symmetric case.

There is a famous example used by game theorists: How should a rich man and a poor man agree to share $200? The rich man could argue for a $150-to-$50 split in his favor because it would grieve the poor man more to lose $50 than the rich man to lose $150. Of course, an arbitrator, keeping in mind the needs of the rich man and the poor man, might suggest the reverse apportionment. The rich man could also argue for an even split on the grounds that it would be wrong to mix business and charity: "Why should I be asked to give charity to this poor man? I would rather get my fair share of $100 and give charity to a much poorer person."

Instead of dividing up $200, let's introduce another asymmetry by having two bargainers divide up 200 poker chips; as before, no agreement means no chips to either. Suppose further that Player A can convert the chips to dollars in equal amounts—one chip equals one dollar—but that Player B is given a complicated nonlinear schedule for converting chips to dollars. . . . This is analogous to the rich man's claiming that the real currency involved in his negotiation with the poor man should be after-tax dollars; and because he is in a higher tax bracket than the poor man, he should get more than $100 in a "symmetric" split of $200.

Another way of disturbing an apparently symmetric strategic situation is to have different numbers of people on each side of the bargaining situation. A simple case might be one in which Party A and Party B have to divide $200. No agreement means no money. But now let Party A comprise two people (A' and A") who have agreed to their share, and let B represent one person. At one focal point, $100 could go to Party A and $100 to Party B; A's $100 could then be split, $50 to A' and $50 to A". At another focal point, each of the three could get $66.66; each one, after all, has full veto power.

This compendium of possible asymmetries is far from complete, but the examples it presents are instructive: differences in initial endowments or wealth, differences in time-related costs, differences in perceived determination or aggressiveness, differences in marginal valuations (as in tax brackets), differences in needs, and differences in the number of people comprising each side. There are, of course, many others.

The notion of symmetry and focal points is often associated by bargainers with their notion of "fairness." But one person's symmetry is frequently another's asymmetry, and the discussion of what is symmetric can be divisive. Even in the extremely simple case of two-party distributive bargaining, in which each side knows the other's reservation price and in which a zone of agreement is known to exist, there is a possibility that the players might not agree to an apportionment of the potential surplus.

D. Agency Theory

1. Comments and Questions

a. When a principal has to act through an agent, as happens constantly in an industrialized society, the actions of the agent may be at variance with the desires of the principal. That is, the interests of the agent may be less than completely congruent with those of the principal, and the action of the agent may vary accordingly. Employment of lawyers is a classic principal-agent situation, and the ensuing article examines agency theory in this context.

b. A distinct message to be taken from the Gilson & Mnookin article relates to their use of the Prisoner's Dilemma as a heuristic tool. In the classic version, as presented in section B above, the Prisoner's Dilemma no doubt struck the reader as cleverly illustrating a fairly simple idea about human behavior. This article demonstrates advanced use of the Prisoner's Dilemma.

c. Students of politics have long been interested in agency theory, because it reflects a fundamental concern about representative government. Public choice theory argues that legislators and bureaucracies often will act in their own interests, which may not be identical with that of the public. So too do interest groups, which obtain benefits through the intervention of government. For an introduction to the literature, see Daniel A. Farber & Philip P. Frickey,

LAW AND PUBLIC CHOICE (1991); Glen O. Robinson, AMERICAN BUREAUCRACY: PUBLIC CHOICE AND PUBLIC LAW (1991).

d. A certain similarity to agency theory is found in the concept of "moral hazard" that is a central concern for vendors of insurance. The problem is that people who purchase insurance will behave less carefully than those who are not insured, with attendant costs to the insurer. There is a vast amount of evidence that demonstrates the "moral hazard" phenomenon, and it does not include fraudulent claims or intentional activity such as arson. (For this reason, the word "moral" is a misnomer.)

2. Ronald J. Gilson & Robert H. Mnookin, *Disputing Through Agents: Cooperation and Conflict Between Lawyers in Litigation*, 94 COLUM. L. REV. 509 (1994)*

Introduction

Do lawyers facilitate dispute resolution or do they instead exacerbate conflict and pose a barrier to the efficient resolution of disputes? A distinctive characteristic of our formal mechanisms of conflict resolution is that clients carry on their disputes through lawyers. Yet, at a time when the role of lawyers in dispute resolution has captured not only public but political attention, social scientists have remained largely uninterested in the influence of lawyers on the disputing process. . . . Economists have developed an extensive literature that models one or another aspect of the litigation and settlement process. But the economic literature, with rare exceptions, shares a troublesome feature. Almost by convention, litigation is modeled as a two-person game between principals, thereby abstracting away the legal system's central institutional characteristic—litigation is carried out by agents.

While any model must make concessions to tractability, this simplifying assumption is especially troublesome because lawyers have long been considered to have a special influence on how litigation is conducted, even if there has been no consensus on whether lawyers dampen or exacerbate conflict in litigation. Today, the dominant popular view is that lawyers magnify the inherent divisiveness of dispute resolution. According to this vision, litigators rarely cooperate to resolve disputes efficiently. Instead, shielded by a professional ideology that is said to require zealous advocacy, they endlessly and wastefully fight in ways that enrich themselves but rarely advantage the clients. . . .

Purveyor of needless conflict need not be the only vision of the lawyer's role in litigation. Over a century ago, Abraham Lincoln suggested that lawyers can play an extraordinarily constructive role in disputes—as peacemakers who facilitate efficient and fair resolution of conflict when their clients could not do so for themselves. From this perspective, a central characteristic of the formal legal system—that clients carry on their dispute through lawyers who are their agents—has the potential for damping rather than exacerbating the conflictual character of litigation. In this Article we offer a conceptual foundation for this alternative perspective—a foundation that rests on the idea that lawyers may allow clients to cooperate in circumstances when their clients could not do so on their own. We construct this foundation using basic notions drawn from game theory and agency theory.

---

*Reprinted with permission.

We begin by using the prisoner's dilemma as a heuristic to understand better the circumstances of disputants locked in a legal conflict in an abstract world in which there are no lawyers—only the parties themselves and a judge. In Part I, we describe a litigation game in which each disputant faces a single choice: she can either cooperate by volunteering all relevant information to the other side or defect by using the discovery process in an adversarial manner to hide unfavorable information. We analyze litigation initially in the form of this one-round, two-person prisoner's dilemma, in which the inability of parties to commit effectively to cooperation results in dominant strategies that yield suboptimal results. Because a single lawsuit has a number of strategic interactions, we then analyze litigation as a finite number of repeated games, each of which is structured as a prisoner's dilemma. Our primary message in Part I is that in many legal conflicts each disputant may feel compelled to make a contentious move in order to avoid being exploited by, and to take advantage of any weakness in, the other side. Nevertheless, the net result of contentious moves by both may be an outcome that is less efficient than if the disputants had cooperated.

In Part II, we explore the role that lawyers might play in overcoming the prisoner's dilemma. Our analysis in this Part, unlike most game theoretic models of the litigation process, acknowledges the central institutional characteristic of the legal system—litigation is carried out by lawyers on behalf of their clients. We suggest that, in contrast to clients who are unlikely to litigate against one another ever again, lawyers are repeat players who have the opportunity to establish reputations. At the core of our story is the potential for disputing parties to avoid the prisoner's dilemma inherent in much litigation by selecting cooperative lawyers whose reputations credibly commit each party to a cooperative strategy.

At this point, we introduce a dialectical tension between game theory and agency theory. On the one hand, we suggest that the possibility for commitment to cooperation exists because the incentives for a cooperative lawyer, who is a repeat player concerned with maintaining her reputation over time, differ from those of her client, who as a one-shot litigant may be tempted to defect. On the other hand, we suggest that because the interests of the client (as principal) and the interests of her lawyer (as agent) diverge in some respects, cooperation may be undermined in two very different ways. One danger is that the agents may "collude" to exacerbate conflict when that behavior serves their own interests. Alternatively, a principal may persuade a previously cooperative agent to defect in order to increase the principal's payoff.

I. LITIGATION AS A PRISONER'S DILEMMA

The prisoner's dilemma provides a useful heuristic to illuminate a common characteristic of dispute settlement through litigation. In many disputes, each litigant may feel compelled to make a contentious move either to exploit, or to avoid exploitation by, the other side. Yet, the combination of contentious moves by both results in a less efficient outcome than if the litigants had been able to cooperate.

In this Part we first describe a litigation game with all the required characteristics of a one-round prisoner's dilemma, so as to expose this tension inherent in many legal disputes. Next, we analyze the assumptions underlying a prisoner's dilemma to expose both the opportunities and limits of using it as a heuristic for the litigation process. Finally, we complicate the analysis by drawing on research that explores the multi-round prisoner's dilemma. We treat a single lawsuit as analogous to the same players playing a finite number of games, each round of which is structured as a prisoner's dilemma.

A. The Litigation Game. A One-Round Prisoner's Dilemma

Consider the following "litigation game," a highly abstracted model of litigation possessing the attributes of a one-round prisoner's dilemma. Able and Baker dispute the proper division of $100 according to some legal standard. For the moment, assume that litigation does not involve lawyers, but only the two parties and a judge. Each party holds information not known by the other side. Some of this information is favorable and some of it is unfavorable. Before the judge decides the case, there is a one-stage simultaneous disclosure process in which each party hands to the judge and the opposing party a sealed envelope containing information. Only two moves are possible, and neither player can know in advance what the other will do. One move is cooperation: a player voluntarily (and at no cost to the other side) discloses to the other side and to the judge all material information in her possession. The second option, defection, involves the adversarial use of the disclosure process to hide unfavorable information. As a consequence, the other side must spend $15 to force disclosure of some but not all of the information withheld. After the envelope exchange and the "purchase" of some of the withheld information, the judge resolves the dispute based on the information disclosed.

With the payoff structure indicated by the following matrix, this game poses a prisoner's dilemma. If both players cooperate, there are no discovery expenses for either side and we will assume the Judge awards $50 to Able and $50 to Baker. If both players defect, each must spend $15 to pry out some but not all of the unfavorable information possessed by the other side. Although the judge lacks complete information, we assume that she divides the $100 in the same ratio; the net recovery to the parties is now $35 to Able and $35 to Baker. The third scenario, in which one player defects while the other cooperates, provides the defector with a higher payoff ($70) and hurts the "sucker" in two ways. First, because the cooperating player has disclosed all of its unfavorable information while the defecting party has only disclosed some of the information unfavorable to it, the judge awards the sucker a gross recovery of only $30. Second, the sucker has spent $15 to get less than all of the information unfavorable to the other side before the judge (without which his recovery would be even lower). Thus, the sucker's net recovery is only $15.

In this litigation game, Able's best response to whatever strategy Baker chooses is to defect. In other words, defection is Able's dominant strategy. The same, of course, is true for Baker. Defect-Defect, therefore, is a "dominant strategy equilibrium," even though this result guarantees each party only $35, rather than the $50 produced by a strategy of mutual cooperation. If there is no way for the disputants to bind each other to make a cooperative move, rational actors end up with less than "fools" who simply cooperate.

B. Is the Prisoner's Dilemma an Appropriate Model for Litigation?

To what extent does the prisoner's dilemma represent an appropriate, albeit highly simplified, model of the litigation process? Focus first on the payoff structure. In a prisoner's dilemma, the best payoff for a player occurs when that player defects and the other player cooperates. The worst payoff results when a player cooperates while the other player defects. The other two outcomes fall between these extremes, with the reward for mutual cooperation better than the payoff for mutual defection. This means that a prisoner's dilemma cannot be a zero sum or purely distributive game: the total combined payoff from mutual cooperation must exceed the total combined payoff from mutual defection. Indeed, in a symmetric prisoner's dilemma, each player's payoff from mutual cooperation must be greater than each player's payoff from mutual defection.

How realistic is it to assume that in litigation the payoff structure takes this form? In many disputes, the assumption that mutual cooperation might benefit both sides seems entirely plausible. Mutual cooperation involves lower total litigation costs than mutual defection. Moreover, when parties share information, reveal their true underlying interests, and engage in collaborative problem-solving, they may sometimes develop new options that "create value" or "expand the pie" for both disputants in comparison to the result flowing from mutual defections. Both parties may sometimes gain from a negotiated resolution that takes a form a judge could not impose. For example, both parties may prefer exchanging a property that the plaintiff values more highly than the defendant over a judicially determined damage award. It also seems plausible that the best and worst individual outcomes will occur when one party cooperates and the other does not. In many disputes, because of the adversarial nature of litigation, cooperative moves by one litigant, if not reciprocated by the other, can lead to exploitation and something akin to a sucker's payoff. Unbalanced discovery, where only one side discloses unfavorable information, yields this result.

Not every legal dispute involves the sort of payoff structure required by the prisoner's dilemma. . . . In some disputes the very best payoff for one or both players occurs when both players cooperate. In other cases, mutual defection may yield the best payoff for a defendant interested in delay because interest earned by putting off the damage payment may exceed any differential in transaction costs. This suggests the importance of exploring in particular legal contexts whether the payoff assumptions for the prisoner's dilemma are, in fact, appropriate.

The rules of the game for a prisoner's dilemma also require that each player remains ignorant of what the other player will do before making a move: enforceable commitments or contracts are not possible and thus the parties cannot credibly bind themselves to cooperate. At first glance, this restrictive assumption seems entirely inappropriate. Disputants in litigation can enter into enforceable agreements with respect to future conduct. The prisoner's dilemma disappears if the parties can, at reasonable cost, spell out the terms of an enforceable agreement to cooperate in the litigation, and thereby bind each other to exchange all relevant information so as to decrease litigation costs.

The problem is that in many cases, particularly complex ones, the parties may not be able to specify fully the terms of such an agreement in advance. Agreements with respect to certain aspects of litigation—for example, limiting the number of depositions, or adopting a particular discovery schedule—may be easy to write and enforce, but it may be very difficult or expensive to specify fully a contract to "conduct a lawsuit cooperatively" or "to disclose all material information." Moreover, even if the terms can be specified, it may be very difficult to determine whether a defection has occurred. Even where a breach of such a contract is observable by the parties, a violation may be difficult to verify to a judge, thus making enforcement problematic.

Discovery disputes in contentious cases reveal the severity of these problems. If one party claims that the other party has breached an agreement by engaging in abusive discovery practices, a judge often faces substantial evidentiary difficulties. Typically, the judge knows little about the information available to either the responding or the requesting party. . . .[26]

In sum, the payoff structure specified for a prisoner's dilemma seems appropriate for many disputes. Moreover, verification problems make the adequate enforcement of binding general commitments to cooperate in litigation (whether imposed by contract or rule) highly problematic. Therefore, despite its restrictive assumptions about payoffs and blind action, the prisoner's dilemma game is a powerful heuristic for understanding the barriers to cooperation in litigation.

C. Litigation as a Multi-Round Prisoner's Dilemma Game

At first glance, litigation between principals who are unlikely to sue each other again appears to be a one-round game. However, one can view a single lawsuit as consisting of a number of strategic encounters: each discovery request, the scheduling of depositions, and each motion might be seen as a separate game between the same parties. If each of these many tactical encounters during a lawsuit has the structure of a prisoner's dilemma, does the fact that the same parties play each other on multiple occasions over the course of a single lawsuit provide an opportunity for cooperation that is not available to players in a one-round game?

The answer seems to be no, although the explanation is more complicated than it once appeared. There is a rich theoretical literature analyzing "repeated games," which explores how rational players might behave in the context of a long-term relationship. Duncan Luce and Howard Raiffa demonstrated some time ago that, so long as the prisoner's dilemma game is played a known finite number of times, rational players still have no incentive to cooperate. The reasoning is straightforward. In the last round, both players recognize that there is no incentive to cooperate because the final game is identical to the one-round game described above. Now consider the next-to-last round. Because the players know that both will defect in the last round, the next-to- last round is no different from the last. Reasoning backwards round by round, the multi-round game unravels all the way back to the first round.

More recent research, however, suggests that cooperative behavior can develop in a multi-round prisoner's dilemma under certain conditions. Suppose that, instead of a known finite number of rounds, there is only a known probability that the game will end before infinite time has passed. If there is a high enough probability in each round that the parties will play an additional round, the prospect of future dealings can induce cooperation, depending upon the payoff function. Robert Axelrod studied the question of what would be a good strategy if players were confronted with an iterated prisoner's dilemma. Axelrod invited game theorists to participate in a computer tournament in which each submitted a strategy that was paired off with every other submission. "Amazingly enough, the winner was the simplest of all strategies submitted. This was TIT FOR TAT, the strategy which cooperates on the first move and

---

[26]As Judge Easterbrook has stated:

Judges can do little about impositional discovery when parties control the legal claims to be presented and conduct the discovery themselves. . . . The judicial officer always knows less than the parties. . . . We cannot prevent what we cannot detect; we cannot detect what we cannot define; we cannot define "abusive" discovery except in theory, because in practice we lack essential information.

Frank H. Easterbrook, Comment, *Discovery as Abuse,* 69 B.U. L. REV. 635, 638-39 (1989).

then does whatever the other player did on the previous move." [When the tournament was replayed after the participants were advised of the inital winner and allowed to alter their strategies in light of that outcome, tit-for-tat won again.] Other theoretical research suggests that cooperation may be sustained even in games of a known number of rounds, provided the number of rounds is large enough and the players believe there are at least a few players in the population who will always play cooperatively.

Together, this work indicates that there may be circumstances under which the parties can escape the prisoner's dilemma if there are significantly high prospects that they will have a large number of future dealings with each other and that they care enough about the outcomes of those future dealings. Unfortunately, the conditions necessary for cooperation in the course of a single lawsuit, even when broken down into a series of subgames, are sufficiently rigorous that the one-shot prisoner's dilemma remains the correct heuristic with which to explore the potential for lawyers to facilitate cooperation.

First, unlike the multi-round games considered in the theoretical literature, the aggregate payoff to the subgames of the decomposed litigation remains reasonably fixed. Also, the number of subgames in litigation, while perhaps unspecifiable ex ante, has predictable finite limits. To be more precise, because players can locate with reasonable precision the final round of a lawsuit, unraveling may begin. In this sense, a lawsuit is unlike a repeated game in which there is simply a finite probability that the game may end after any given round. Finally, the strategies that induce cooperation in repeated games require that each party know after each round whether an opponent cooperated or defected. In litigation, where even cooperative behavior occurs in the context of a competitive environment, the risk of misunderstanding an opponent's move is significant. In the prisoner's dilemma, each player has only two basic moves: cooperation or defection. In litigation, there are many gray tones between the black and white of these two pure moves. The opposing party often takes an action that must be evaluated by degree: Was the action too competitive and therefore a defection? Mistakes and misunderstandings can lead to conflictual outcomes even when both parties seek to follow a cooperative strategy.[36]

II. THE ROLE LAWYERS MIGHT PLAY IN OVERCOMING THE PRISONER'S DILEMMA

We are now ready to introduce individual lawyers into the clients' prisoner's dilemma model of litigation. Assuming the particular litigation game has the payoff structure of a prisoner's dilemma, each client would prefer mutual cooperation to mutual defection. However, each lacks the means credibly to commit to her good intentions. In this Part, we show how disputing through lawyers may provide a means to make such a commitment: Lawyers, acting as agents, have the potential to solve the game theoretic problem of mutual defection. We then consider the first level of the game theory-agency theory dialectic: how use of an agent to pre-

[36]Even if both players are following a strategy of tit-for-tat, the game can deteriorate into alternating defections if the parties mistake cooperation for defection with sufficient frequency. *See* Jonathan Bendor et al., *When in Doubt . . . Cooperation in a Noisy Prisoner's Dilemma,* 35 J. CONFLICT RESOL. 691, 691-706 (1991).

commit to cooperate creates its own set of agency problems. Initially we consider a world of sole practitioners—all lawyers practice alone.

A. The Pre-Litigation Game: Choosing Lawyers

Assume that both clients must litigate through a lawyer (an assumption that, for a change, is descriptively accurate). Further suppose that there exists a class of sole practitioners who have reputations for cooperation which assure that, once retained, they will conduct the litigation in a cooperative fashion. Three final assumptions define our "pre-litigation game." First, clients disclose their choice of lawyer—and thus, whether they have chosen a cooperative lawyer—prior to the beginning of the litigation game. Second, if one client chooses a cooperative lawyer and her opponent does not, the client choosing a cooperative lawyer can change her mind without cost before the litigation game begins. Third, after the litigation game begins, clients cannot change lawyers.

Under these assumptions, disputing through lawyers provides an escape from the prisoner's dilemma. As we have defined the pre-litigation game, each client's dominant strategy is to choose a cooperative lawyer because the choice of a cooperative lawyer binds each client to a cooperative strategy. If client A chooses a cooperative lawyer and client B also chooses a cooperative lawyer, both clients receive the higher cooperative payoff. Alternatively, if client B does not choose a cooperative lawyer, client A is no worse off having initially chosen to cooperate. In that event, client A replaces her cooperative lawyer with a gladiator and is in the same position as if she had chosen a gladiator in the first instance. Thus, her dominant strategy is to choose a cooperative lawyer and to switch if her opponent does not adopt a parallel strategy. Of course, client B confronts the same choices and has the same dominant strategy. The result is a cooperative equilibrium because the introduction of lawyers has transformed the prisoner's dilemma payoff structure into a game in which the only choices are mutual cooperation or mutual defection. Mutual cooperation obviously has the higher payoff for each party.

This is the easy part. Designing a game in which the players can credibly commit is not difficult if one assumes the availability of commitment techniques. What makes the game interesting from a policy perspective is the extent to which its assumptions are consistent with institutional patterns. This consistency is what interests us about lawyers as sources of credible commitments: We believe the assumptions that define the pre-litigation game are roughly consistent with the way litigation occurs.

In the pre-litigation game, we first required clients to disclose their choice of lawyer before the game began. In real litigation, plaintiffs must typically disclose their choice of lawyer at the outset of litigation: the lawyer's name is, quite literally, the first thing that appears on the complaint. Similarly, the defendant must have a lawyer to respond to the complaint, and even to request an extension of the time in which to file an answer to the complaint. Again, this discloses the identity of the lawyer chosen.

We next assumed that a plaintiff choosing a cooperative lawyer could costlessly switch to a gladiator upon learning that her opponent had chosen a gladiator. In the real world, there are costs in switching lawyers, but these costs are likely to be low at the outset. A client will have expended little on her lawyer by the time the identity of her opponent's lawyer is revealed. Thus, for practical purposes, the game's assumption of a costless opportunity to switch lawyers on the disclosure of opposing counsel is roughly consistent with real litigation patterns.

The third assumption—that clients cannot change lawyers during the litigation game—is more problematic. At first glance, the assumption seems patently false; a client may discharge counsel at any time. On closer examination, the presence of substantial switching costs may provide a reasonable proxy for a prohibition against discharging cooperative counsel once the litigation is well underway. As litigation proceeds, a lawyer expends substantial time becoming familiar with the law and especially the facts of the case. The client pays for the lawyer's acquisition of this knowledge. The client's investment in the lawyer's knowledge is relationship-specific in the extreme; that is, it is of no value to the client if the lawyer is fired. Thus, the price of firing the lawyer is the cost of bringing another lawyer up to speed in the litigation. While not a prohibition on changing lawyers, switching costs impose a substantial penalty on defection. Indeed, the longer the litigation continues, the more switching will cost.

Thus, the special assumptions underlying our pre-litigation game are not implausible. What remains, however, is the most critical of the assumptions on which lawyers' potential to facilitate cooperation depends: the existence of lawyers with reputations for cooperation. How and why are such reputations created and sustained? How do clients learn which lawyers are cooperative?

B. A Reputation Market for Cooperative Lawyers

The preceding discussion suggests why there might be a demand for cooperative lawyers. Both parties to a lawsuit with a prisoner's dilemma payoff schedule would like to hire cooperative lawyers because that allows them to commit to a cooperative strategy. Clients should therefore be willing to pay a premium for such lawyers, reflecting a portion of the amount by which the cooperative payoff exceeds the noncooperative payoff.

Establishing the supply side is also straightforward. Lawyers would be willing to invest in achieving a reputation for cooperation because they would receive a return on that investment by virtue of the premium fees clients would be willing to pay. As in standard reputation models, the lawyer's investment in reputation serves two functions. First, it identifies the lawyer as one who possesses the desired, but otherwise, unobservable, attribute; the client must be able to find a cooperative lawyer. Second, it represents the penalty that the market will impose if the lawyer treats his reputation as bait rather than as bond by turning into a gladiator at the request of an opportunistic client. Noncooperative behavior would forfeit the lawyer's investment in a cooperative reputation. Thus, so long as the lawyer's possible loss of investment in reputation exceeds the size of the bribe an opportunistic client would be willing to pay, cooperative lawyers will not be suborned and a market for cooperative lawyers should be available.

However, establishing that clients would demand demonstrably cooperative lawyers and that lawyers would want to supply that service is not sufficient to assure that the market operates. The key word in the previous sentence is "demonstrably." The linchpin of this model is that the lawyer's cooperative or noncooperative behavior be observable. What makes the client's commitment credible is that her lawyer will lose his investment in reputation if he behaves noncooperatively. But this penalty cannot be imposed if the noncooperative behavior cannot be observed. Thus, the structure fails if an erstwhile cooperative lawyer can behave noncooperatively and get away with it.

For this purpose it is critical to . . . return to the distinction between observable and verifiable misconduct noted earlier. That misconduct be observable requires only that the party suffering the affront know with confidence that it occurred. For misconduct to be verifiable, in contrast, the party suffering the affront must be able to demonstrate to an enforcement agency, such as a court, that the misconduct occurred. The difference is important. Verification requires formal proof of misconduct sufficient to meet judicial thresholds. It is commonplace that misconduct which is observable—known to the participants—nonetheless may not be verifiable either because there is no extrinsic proof and the misbehaving party can simply deny the allegations, because the cost of verifying the misconduct is too high, or because the difficulty of defining misconduct limits the legal standard to extreme cases.

In our case, noncooperative conduct by one client's lawyer may not be verifiable, but may nonetheless be readily observable by the lawyer on the other side. Recall that the outcome of the pre-litigation game is that both clients retain cooperative lawyers. Thus, one lawyer's subsequent misconduct must, in the first instance, be observable only to the opposing lawyer, not to the client. A trained litigator, himself pursuing a cooperative strategy and completely familiar with the facts of the case, should be able to detect a change in the behavior of opposing counsel. After all, in litigation, noncooperative behavior by one lawyer must operate initially through its impact on the other side's lawyer. The lawyer can then pass on to the client the fact of noncooperative conduct—the reputation violation—following which both lawyer and client can impose the penalty of lost reputation on the misbehaving lawyer by distributing the information to the legal community.[49]

Thus, the conditions necessary for the operation of a reputation market for cooperative lawyers are plausible, at least at this level of abstraction.

C. Agency Problems that May Subvert Cooperation

The employment of lawyers with identifiable reputations does have the potential to facilitate cooperation between clients in litigation. However, the use of agents to make credible the commitment to cooperate itself poses two potential agency problems. First, the two lawyer-agents may "conspire" to maximize their incomes at the expense of their clients through noncooperative behavior that prolongs the litigation and increases legal fees. When each lawyer stands as gatekeeper against the other lawyer's individual noncooperative misconduct, what protects both clients from the lawyers' joint determination to behave noncooperatively? Second, a client may subvert a lawyer with a reputation for cooperation. This second problem represents the converse of the first. For a lawyer with a limited number of clients, a particular client may be so important that the threat of withdrawn patronage may induce the lawyer to risk his cooperative reputation by behaving noncooperatively. In other words, there may be circumstances in which incentives may induce a lawyer to abandon his cooperative reputation. . . .

III. UNDERSTANDING THE LANDSCAPE OF LITIGATION

This Part draws on our analysis to understand better the distribution of cooperation across practice settings. We first consider a practice area in which cooperation seems to be dimin-

[49]Given the way we have defined the pre-litigation game, the information concerning the misconduct of a previously cooperative lawyer need only circulate within the community of cooperative lawyers. Recall that after the clients disclose their selection of lawyers, any client that has selected a cooperative lawyer may change counsel if her opponent has selected a gladiator. If a "cooperative" lawyer later defects, knowledge of this misconduct within the community of cooperative lawyers would impose the necessary reputational penalty if that lawyer would no longer be considered cooperative. This coutcome depends on the loyalty of the nondefecting cooperative lawyer to spread the word within the community.

ishing—commercial litigation. Does the prisoner's dilemma heuristic help us better understand the clear public and professional perception that the conduct of large-scale commercial litigation has dramatically deteriorated? We then turn to a practice area in which one can observe persistent pockets of cooperation — family law practice. In each case, the inquiry centers on the characteristics that the prisoner's dilemma heuristic has identified as crucial to a cooperative role for lawyers: the litigation payoff structure and the existence of a workable reputation market. With respect to the former, there must be gains from cooperation. With respect to the latter, the issues revolve about what one might call the costs of scrutiny—the ease with which both clients and lawyers can observe lawyers' reputations and, correspondingly, lawyers' difficulty in credibly establishing reputations for cooperation and their relative gains and losses from breaking these reputations.

A. Understanding the Contentiousness of Commercial Litigation

Viewing the perceived deterioration in the conduct of commercial litigation through the lens of the prisoner's dilemma suggests two explanations for the increase in contentiousness: a change in the character of the litigation itself; and the impact of growth in the size of the legal community upon the formation and maintenance of reputations for cooperation.

1. The Changing Payoff Structure in Litigation. — Two conclusions about the character of large commercial litigation have emerged in recent years, one empirical and relating to its frequency, the second subjective and relating to its conduct. Recent studies have documented a dramatic increase in the amount of commercial litigation after 1970. . . .

Over the same period, commercial litigators attested to the increasingly uncivil conduct of civil litigation. The phenomenon of discovery abuse was the most obvious manifestation. Overreaching requests for production were met with dogged resistance to any but perfunctory compliance, and the liberal discovery contemplated by the Federal Rules of Civil Procedure—which aimed to eliminate surprise and facilitate a resolution of the merits based on full information— led instead to trench warfare. Motion and counter-motion, each accompanied by requests for sanctions, created multiple satellite litigation that pushed the merits into the background.

The prisoner's dilemma heuristic suggests a possible link between the empirical fact of increased commercial litigation and the subjective fact that litigation behavior has become significantly more contentious. Recall that in order for lawyers to allow clients credibly to precommit to a cooperative solution the payoffs in the lawsuit must take the form of a prisoner's dilemma: mutual cooperation must have a bigger payoff for each player than mutual defection. If some commercial litigation has payoffs in which one party does not gain from mutual cooperation, such litigation would suffer from defections and be more conflictual. One or both parties would choose gladiators in the pre-litigation game even if that party knew the result would be that the other party would respond in kind.

At least some of the increase in commercial litigation stems from lawsuits in which there were no gains from cooperation. In his study of New York commercial litigation, William Nelson notes that during the 1970s the statutory prejudgment interest rate . . . was no higher than 6%. In contrast, the market rate of interest over the 1974-1980 period ranged from 10.5% at the end of 1974 to 21.5% at the end of 1980, a spread over the statutory rate ranging from 4.5% to 15.5%. Now consider the payoff to a litigation game in which one player owes the other money. As the interest rate spread increases, it becomes more likely that the defendant's dominant strategy will be noncooperation because the gains from the spread outweigh the transaction costs of conflict: the more conflictual the litigation, the longer the process takes, and the longer the defendant earns the interest rate spread. . . .

This example suggests that the payoff structure of commercial litigation is hardly immutable, and change may well affect the frequency of cooperation. Changes in economic conditions or the rules concerning prejudgment interest can affect the payoff structure of commercial litigation. Some jurisdictions now have rules imposing market-level prejudgment interest in some disputes, and it is plain that, as legal fees have increased and interest rates have fallen, there may be fewer disputes in which delay so clearly serves one party's interest. Thus, it may be no coincidence that large corporations became much more interested in Alternative Dispute Resolution (ADR) in the 1980s when interest rates were falling and legal costs were increasing.

While the interest rate spread that drove the increase in noncooperative litigation during the 1970s has abated, the phenomenon of strategic litigation, which can have the same payoff pattern, may have replaced it. In this context, litigation is strategic when it seeks not to vindicate a substantive legal right, but when the client uses it as a device to secure a business advantage by imposing costs on the opposing party. Examples include litigation brought by a target company simply to delay a hostile takeover, or trade secret litigation brought against former employees of a high technology company who leave to form a start-up venture, with the goal of creating sufficient uncertainty that financing is unavailable and the venture fails. As with strategies exploiting a positive interest rate spread, the payoff structure in this type of litigation is such that for one party the dominant strategy is noncooperation. . . .

2. The Size of the Legal Community and Reputations for Cooperation. — Central to the potential for lawyers to facilitate a cooperative solution to a prisoner's dilemma litigation game is an effective reputation market for lawyers. Lawyers must be able to earn and maintain observable reputations for cooperation, and lawyers must be able to observe breaches of reputation by opposing counsel and have an interest in reporting these breaches. There is reason to believe that the enormous growth in size of the large law firms that provide legal representation in most substantial commercial litigation has undermined the effectiveness of the reputation market. . . .

Thus, the information structure of the litigation game can explain the presence of significant conflict in litigation even though most lawyers claim to play tit-for-tat. Litigation is quite "noisy." Clearly identifying whether the other side has cooperated or defected in a competitive environment where cooperation is defined as being not too conflictual, is often quite difficult. For example, not all objections to discovery requests are defections.

Uncertainty over the character of the game compounds the uncertainty over whether an opponent has cooperated or defected in a particular round. Recall that only some litigation has the payoff structure of a prisoner's dilemma. Evaluating an opponent's action also requires correctly evaluating the litigation itself—noncooperation does not constitute defection if there is no possibility of gaining from cooperation.

When there is uncertainty about both the players' moves and the nature of the game, a tit-for-tat strategy results in more conflict rather than less. Moreover, because of the tendency for a noisy prisoner's dilemma game between two tit-for-tat players to degenerate into repeated defection following an initial mistake, the systemic increase in conflict is exacerbated by increases in the percentage of tit-for-tat players in the environment. . . .

The same problem also hinders the maintenance of reputations. For a reputation market to work, defections by cooperative lawyers must be observable. However, both aspects of noise we have considered—a mixed environment of cooperative and noncooperative litigation, and the difficulty of evaluating whether a particular action by an opponent is cooperative when the standard for cooperation is being not too competitive—makes observation of defection more difficult.

B. Understanding the Presence of Cooperation in Family Law Practice

We now consider whether one can also apply the prisoner's dilemma to help understand a practice setting in which, unlike large commercial litigation, cooperation between opposing counsel is plainly observable—matrimonial practice. Given the different institutional characteristics in commercial litigation on the one hand, and divorce law on the other, does the prisoner's dilemma heuristic explain different levels of cooperation?

1. The Payoff Structure in Divorce. — The first step in applying the prisoner's dilemma heuristic to family law practice is analysis of the payoff structure. If lawyers are to have the potential to credibly commit their clients to cooperate, there must be gains from cooperation (and the risk of loss if the other party defects). Put in context, divorce litigation must be more than a zero-sum game in which the couple's property and children are simply divided.

Divorce bargaining is sometimes seen as a purely distributive (zero-sum) game in which any benefit to the wife necessarily comes at the husband's expense, and vice versa. Both the money issues and the custody issues do have distributive elements with zero-sum characteristics. When a divorcing couple divides $2,000 in a checking account, a $100-larger share to the wife necessarily results in a $100-smaller share to the husband. Similarly, if a father must transfer more of his paycheck to the mother's household by way of support, there are fewer funds available to spend on himself. Division of the child's time also displays this distributive feature. When a child spends more time in one household, this necessarily reduces the time potentially spent in the other.

But divorce bargaining is hardly a zero-sum game in its entirety: in many circumstances, cooperation can "create value" and improve the outcome from each party's point of view. First, and most fundamentally, not all of the father and mother's interests are at odds. Parents often share a fundamental interest in the well-being of their child. If the child does well, both parents are better off. Therefore, devising an arrangement that benefits the child potentially creates joint gains for both parents. Parental cooperation in co-parenting may improve opportunities for the children, and thus both parents may benefit. Even if childless, a divorcing couple may have other shared interests as well. Reducing the costs of divorce—financial and emotional—once again may benefit both parties. To the extent that the parties can reduce the transaction costs of divorce, they obviously increase the financial and emotional resources available to build new lives. In addition to other interests the divorcing spouses may share, there are potential gains realizable from the parties' preferences and the differences in relative values that they may attach to different assets or activities. "This means that there can be gains—and value created—through trades." Cooperation allows divisions to be based upon the parties' personal preferences, rather than the impersonal relative valuations of the market or a court.

While it is obvious that divorcing parents can sometimes themselves devise arrangements that benefit both themselves and their children, a number of potential barriers to cooperation make the divorce lawyer's role critical. For one thing, the strong emotions attending divorce may pose a formidable barrier to collaborative rational problem-solving.

Joint problem-solving and negotiation work best with clear communication and good listening skills. Many couples lacked these skills during the marriage itself, and divorce is obviously an extremely difficult time to develop them. Indeed, many couples may replay in the divorce process old and dysfunctional patterns of dealing with each other during the marriage, and these patterns may make cooperation difficult or impossible.

When inexperience, inability, or a soured relationship prevent divorcing spouses from cooperating themselves, the payoff structure of divorce proceedings may frequently take the form of the prisoner's dilemma. Cooperative divorce lawyers may therefore provide an escape: by credibly committing their clients to cooperate, the lawyers as intermediaries may be able to create gains that the spouses could not realize alone.

The potential for the sucker's payoff is also present. In the divorce process, cooperative moves by one side—if not reciprocated by the other side—may lead to exploitation. Opportunities for strategic behavior likewise exist because the parties often will not know with certainty (1) the other side's true preferences regarding the allocation of assets; (2) the other spouse's preferences or attitudes toward risk; and (3) the likely outcome in court if they do not settle their disputes. Some matrimonial lawyers are known as "bombers," or Rambo types who will defect in a variety of ways: by contesting custody on behalf of a client who is really interested in simply paying less support; by vigorously resisting the disclosure of relevant financial information; and by generally using discovery requests and responses, depositions, and motions to wear down the other side in what amounts to a war of attrition.

2. The Institutional Structure of the Divorce Bar. — Not only is the payoff structure in divorce proceedings consistent with a cooperative role for lawyers, but the institutional structure of family law practice appears to allow lawyers, at least in some instances, to create and sustain reputations for cooperation (and non-cooperation). Family law practice tends to be both localized and specialized. A divorcing husband and wife usually hire attorneys in the same legal community. Increasingly, some lawyers have tended to specialize in family practice, especially in metropolitan areas. Typically, over a period of time, these local specialists repeatedly deal with one another. Through this repeated exposure lawyers can develop and sustain their reputations.

Professional organizations for family law specialists appear to facilitate this process of reputation development and maintenance. For example, the American Academy of Matrimonial Lawyers, a self-anointed elite of the family law bar, seems to exist for the principal purpose of providing an efficient reputational network among family lawyers. All of its members are specialists who are frequently involved in divorces of wealthy individuals.

Interviews with California family law specialists suggest that a reputational market does exist; that some lawyers cultivate reputations as cooperative problem-solvers, while others are viewed as more adversarial, both by themselves and others; and that, as suggested by our prelitigation game, there is a substantial amount of self-selection both by clients and attorneys. The small sample size and the informal methodology of our survey mean that one should view our conclusions only as suggestive, but the anecdotal evidence we have gathered seems consistent with our framework.

Not surprisingly, the Academy members that we interviewed all knew each other from prior first-hand dealings; they readily and consistently characterized each other either as cooperative problem-solvers or as more adversarial gladiators. The lawyers interviewed suggested that most Northern California members of the Academy have a problem-solving orientation, at least when involved in a case in which opposing counsel was also an Academy member. However, the members consistently described a smaller number of members as being more adversarial.

All of the cooperative problem-solvers whom we interviewed reported that over half of their practice (as measured in terms of income) involved cases in which an Academy member also represented the other spouse. With the exception of cases involving known gladiators, members of the Academy typically voluntarily exchanged information and documents reciprocally and informally. Because opposing counsel knew and trusted each other, they rarely insisted on interrogatories, depositions, or engaged in protracted formal discovery.

Not surprisingly, the interviews suggested that cooperative problem-solvers much preferred dealing with lawyers who shared their orientation. A great deal of sorting and self-selection appears to occur based on reputation. Lawyers who saw themselves as cooperative said they would describe their problem-solving orientation during initial meetings with clients. They reported that their clients often were seeking lawyers with a particular orientation. Several cooperative lawyers reported that they regularly turned away clients who sought highly adversarial representation. As one stated, "If a client is hell bent upon hiring an advocate to disembowel the adverse party, I direct them elsewhere." They also suggested that such clients rarely approached them in the first place. . . .

A final feature of matrimonial practice may also facilitate cooperation. Unlike a commercial litigator, a family law specialist is usually not unduly dependent upon a single client for his or her livelihood. This should make it easier for a cooperative problem-solver to resist client pressure to defect after the case is underway.

We do not mean for our analysis of family law practice to suggest that matrimonial practice is exclusively or even predominantly cooperative. Instead, we use matrimonial practice to illustrate that reputational markets presently exist that permit clients to commit to cooperative strategies in circumstances in which the clients themselves might have great difficulty doing so. Our informal survey of San Francisco matrimonial specialists strongly suggests that the relationship between lawyers known to each other to have cooperative, problem-solving orientations facilitates dispute resolution. . . .

IV. FACILITATING COOPERATION

We have suggested through application of the prisoner's dilemma heuristic that in many circumstances lawyers may help clients achieve cooperation when the clients cannot do so themselves. In this account the relationship between the lawyers is critical. The game theory-agency theory dialectic, in turn, highlights the barriers to lawyers credibly committing their clients to cooperation. We now take up some of the normative implications of our analysis: What institutional reforms hold promise for reducing the barriers to lawyers facilitating cooperation between their clients? First, we survey norms of professional conduct to determine whether the governing rules create space for cooperative practice—can a reputation for cooperation be established and maintained if litigation requires zealous advocacy? . . .

Traditional norms of professional conduct are insistently client-centered. As in other professional relationships, the lawyer's technical skills and regulatory monopoly provide both a means to advance the client's interest in a specialized environment and a facade behind which the lawyer can favor herself at the client's expense. Professional responsibility, like other forms of fiduciary obligation, seeks to disarm that conflict by imposing a duty of loyalty that privileges the client's interest over that of the lawyer. In the litigation context, the client's preferred position is given shape through the norm of zealous advocacy: the lawyer must vigorously assert the client's interests; the final authority on important issues of strategy rests with the client; and the client may discharge his lawyer at will, but the lawyer has only limited ability to withdraw from representation. . . .

This picture of client-centered advocacy presents a serious problem for the lawyer seeking to establish or maintain a reputation for cooperation. The zealous advocacy model views litigation from the client's perspective: as a one-round game. But in establishing and maintaining the reputation necessary to facilitate cooperation between clients, a lawyer necessarily plays a multi-round game for different clients. The lawyer may have to forgo litigation tactics that are both lawful and in the client's best interest in a particular lawsuit to allow the lawyer effectively to commit other clients to cooperate in other lawsuits. More concretely, if the payoff structure in a lawsuit takes the form of a prisoner's dilemma, the lawyer may best serve the client's interests by mid-stream defection, even though the lawyer thereby destroys her privately and socially valuable reputation for cooperation. Is zealous advocacy therefore inconsistent with reputation-based cooperation? Can a lawyer decline to defect even if defection is otherwise lawful? Can she withdraw if the client insists on defection? Can the lawyer and client agree at the outset of the representation that the lawyer will adopt a cooperative rather than a zealous advocacy litigation style? Each of these questions raises important issues of professional responsibility. Our goal here is not to resolve those issues . . . but to highlight the potential of professional norms to be a barrier to commitments to cooperate.

CONCLUSION

Our story weaves together three principal ideas: (a) the prisoner's dilemma offers a suggestive and powerful metaphor for some aspects of litigation; (b) a lawyer's reputation may serve to bond a client's cooperation in the litigation process, thereby resolving the prisoner's dilemma; and (c) principal-agent conflicts . . . create incentives that sometimes facilitate cooperation in litigation but that, at other times, undermine cooperation. Our message is that the relationship between opposing lawyers and their capacity to establish credible reputations for cooperation have profound implications for dispute resolution: if the payoff structure establishes cooperation as the most desirable strategy and supportive institutional structures exist, lawyers may be able to damp conflict, reduce transaction costs, and facilitate dispute resolution.

Our story rests fundamentally on the idea that lawyers develop reputations, and that the reputation for being a cooperative problem-solver may be a valuable asset. When opposing lawyers know and trust each other, we believe there often will be substantial opportunities for both parties to benefit by reducing transaction costs. . . .

Theory suggests that a reputational market would operate most effectively when the size of the legal community is comparatively small. The actions of lawyers can then be well publicized, and lawyers can expect to face each other repeatedly in the future. Thus our analysis at least suggests why small-town lawyers may be less prone to exacerbate disputes with one another than are big-city lawyers, and also why one might expect to see a greater degree of cooperation within certain specialties than within the general community of attorneys. . . .

We began our inquiry by asking whether lawyers facilitate dispute resolution or instead exacerbate conflict. Common sense and anecdotal observation together suggest that lawyers sometimes help and sometimes hurt. Our goal has been to provide a theoretical framework to understand better when conflict and cooperation occur and how we can facilitate greater cooperation.

E. Learning Theory and Psychology

1. Lyonel Festinger, An Introduction to the Theory of Cognitive Dissonance 1-6, 261-267 (1957)

[T]he individual strives toward consistency within himself. His opinions and attitudes . . . tend to exist in clusters that are internally consistent. . . . Granting that consistency is the usual thing, perhaps overwhelmingly so, what about these exceptions which come to mind so readily? Only rarely, if ever, are they accepted psychologically as inconsistencies by the person involved. Usually more or less successful attempts are made to rationalize them.

But persons are not always successful in explaining away or in rationalizing inconsistencies to themselves. For one reason or another, attempts to achieve consistency may fail. The inconsistency then simply continues to exist. Under such circumstances, there is psychological discomfort [dissonance]. The basic hypotheses I wish to state are as follows:

1. The existence of dissonance, being psychologically uncomfortable, will motivate the person to try to reduce the dissonance and achieve consonance.
2. When dissonance is present, in addition to trying to reduce it, the person will actively avoid situations and information which would likely increase the dissonance.

In short, I am proposing that dissonance . . . is a motivating factor in its own right. Cognitive dissonance can be seen as an antecedent condition which leads to activity oriented toward dissonance reduction just as hunger leads to activity oriented toward hunger reduction. . . .

If dissonance is to be reduced or eliminated by changing one or more cognitive elements, it is necessary to consider how resistant these cognitive elements are to change. . . . What, then, are the circumstances that make it difficult for the person to change his actions?

1. The change may be painful or avoid loss. . . .
2. The present behavior may be otherwise satisfying. . . .
3. Making the change may simply not be possible. . . . Some behavior, especially emotional reactions, may not be under the voluntary control of the person. . . .

The core of the theory of dissonance which we have stated is rather simple. It holds that:

1. There may exist dissonant or "nonfitting" relations among cognitive elements.
2. The existence of dissonance gives rise to pressures to reduce the dissonance and to avoid increases in dissonance.
3. Manifestations of the operation of these pressures include behavior changes, changes of cognition, and new opinions.

Although the core of the theory is simple, it has rather wide implications and applications to a variety of situations which on the surface look very different. . . .

Decisions Resulting in Dissonance

Although psychologists have paid a great deal of attention to the decision-making process, there has only been occasional recognition of the problems that ensue when a decision has been made. One of the major consequences of having made a decision is the existence of dissonance. . . .

[A] number of situations have been denoted as implying the existence of cognitive dissonance.

1. Dissonance almost always exists after a decision has been made between two or more alternatives. The cognitive elements corresponding to positive characteristics of the rejected alternatives, and those corresponding to negative characteristics of the chosen alternative, are dissonant with the knowledge of the action that has been taken. Those cognitive elements corresponding to positive characteristics of the chosen alternative and negative characteristics of the rejected alternative are consonant with the cognitive elements corresponding to the action which has been taken.
2. Dissonance almost always exists after an attempt has been made, by offering rewards or threatening punishment, to elicit overt behavior that is at variance with private opinion. If the overt behavior is successfully elicited, the person's private opinion is dissonant with his knowledge concerning his behavior; his knowledge of the reward obtained or of the punishment avoided is consonant with his knowledge concerning his behavior. If the overt behavior is not successfully elicited, then his private opinion is consonant with his knowledge of what he has done, but the knowledge of the reward not obtained or of the punishment to be suffered is dissonant with his knowledge of what he has done.
3. Forced or accidental exposure to new information may create cognitive elements that are dissonant with existing cognition. . . .

2. Comments and Questions

a. Festinger's work is a classic in psychology. In other parts of the book he discusses how people learn to rationalize discordant information. People who keep using tobacco despite its devastating and well-known health hazards offer an obvious example, and it is striking that Festinger was already employing this example in 1957.

b. What does the theory of cognitive dissonance have to do with dispute resolution? How might it be applied before, during, and after a negotiation?

c. Individual responses to dissonance vary, with a picture showing approximately a normal curve. Just as some persons are more "risk adverse" than others, it is reasonable to suppose that some persons are less tolerant of dissonance than others. Thus, different people will respond in various ways to the same change in dissonance, risk, and most other types of change.

d. In the ensuing article, Professor Staw examines the consequences of commitment to a position, and the impediment to new evidence and change that can result. This is an important matter because major decisions are commonly arrived at over a period of time, and may be composed of many sub-decisions. How is Staw's analysis related to cognitive dissonance?

3. Barry M. Staw, *The Escalation of Commitment to a Course of Action*, Academy of Management Review, October 1981 at 577*

Many of the most difficult decisions an individual must make are choices not about what to do in an isolated instance but about the fate of an entire course of action. This is especially true when the decision is whether to cease a questionable line of behavior or to commit more effort and resources into making that course of action pay off. Do individuals in such cases cut their losses or escalate their commitment to the course of action? Consider the following examples:

1. An individual has spent three years working on an advanced degree in a field with minimal job prospects. The individual chooses to . . . finish the degree rather than switching to an entirely new field of study. Having obtained the degree, the individual is faced with the options of unemployment, working under dissatisfying conditions, such as part time or temporary status, or starting anew in a completely unrelated field.
2. An individual purchased a stock at $50 a share, but the price has gone down to $20. Still convinced about the merit of the stock, he buys more shares at this lower price. Soon the price declines further and the individual is again faced with the decision to buy more, hold what he already has, or sell out entirely. . . .
3. A city spends a large amount of money to improve its sewer and drainage system . . . [that] involves digging 131 miles of tunnel shafts, reservoirs, and pumping stations. The excavation is only 10 percent completed and is useless until it is totally finished. The project will take the next 20 years to complete and will cost $11 billion. Unfortunately, the deeper the tunnels go, the more money they cost, and the greater are the questions about the wisdom of the entire venture.
4. A company overestimates its capability to build an airplane brake that will meet certain technical specifications at a given cost. Because it wins the government contract, the company is forced to invest greater and greater effort into meeting the contract terms. As a result of increasing pressure to meet specifications and deadlines, records and tests of the brake are misrepresented to government officials. Corporate careers and company credibility are increasingly staked to the airbrake contract, although many in the firm know the brake will not work effectively. At the conclusion of the construction period, the government test pilot flies the plane; it skids off the runway and narrowly misses injuring the pilot.
5. At an early stage of the U.S. involvement in the Vietnam War, George Ball, then Undersecretary of State, wrote the following in a memo to President Johnson: "The decision you face now is crucial. Once large numbers of U.S. troops are committed to direct combat, they will begin to take heavy casualties in a war they are ill equipped to fight in a noncooperative if not downright hostile countryside. Once we suffer large casualties, we will have started a well-nigh irreversible process. Our involvement will be so great that we cannot — without national humiliation — stop short of achieving our complete objectives. Of the two possibilities, I think humiliation would be more likely than the achievement of our objectives — even after we have paid terrible costs.

As evidenced in the above examples, many of the most injurious personal decisions and

*Reprinted with permission.

most glaring policy disasters can come in the shape of sequential and escalating commitments. Judging by popular press accounts and the observation of everyday events, it appears that individuals may have a tendency to become locked in to a course of action, throwing good money after bad or committing new resources to a losing course of action. The critical question from an analytical point of view is whether these everyday examples denote a syndrome of decisional errors or are just a post hoc reconstruction of events. That is, do decisions about commitment to a course of action inherently lead individuals to errors of escalation or are we, as observers, simply labeling a subset of decisions whose outcomes turned out to be negative?

THE FALLIBLE DECISION MAKER

In the psychological literature, there have been two primary ways of explaining decisional errors. One is to point to individual limitations in information processing. Individuals are limited in their ability and desire to search for alternatives and input information, recall information from memory, and to compare alternatives on multiple criteria. Because of the limitations to individual ability at each phase of cognitive information processing, the end product of individual decisions may optimize neither personal utility nor collective welfare. A second way to explain decisional errors is to attribute a breakdown in rationality to interpersonal elements, such as social power or group dynamics. . . . Cohesive groups may . . . suppress dissent, censor information, create illusions of invulnerability, and stereotype enemies. Any of these by-products of social interaction may, of course, hinder rational decision making and lead individuals or groups to decisional errors.

Although the limitations to rationality posed by the group dynamics and information processing literatures can be relevant to commitment decisions they do not seem to capture the central element of the commitment dilemma. A salient feature of the preceding case examples is that a series of decisions is associated with a course of action, rather than an isolated choice. The consequences of any single decision, therefore, can have implications about the utility of previous choices as well as determine future events or outcomes. This means that sunk costs may not be sunk psychologically but may enter into future decisions.

Under traditional models of economic rationality, resources should be allocated and decisions entered into when future benefits are greater than future costs. Losses or costs that may have been experienced in the past but that are not expected to recur should not (at least from a normative perspective) enter into decision calculations. However, individuals may be motivated to rectify past losses as well as to seek future gain. One source of this motivation may be a desire on the part of individuals to appear rational in their decision making. The literature on self-justification processes [e.g., Festinger, 1957] supports this proposition and at least some of the tendency to escalate commitment may be explained by self-justification motives.

RESEARCH ON THE ESCALATION OF COMMITMENT

Self-Justification in Commitment Decisions

The largest and most systematic source of data on the justification of behavior is provided by the social psychological literature on forced compliance. Typically, in forced compliance studies an individual is induced to perform an unpleasant or dissatisfying act when no compensating external rewards are present. It is generally predicted that individuals will bias their attitudes on the experimental task in a positive direction so as to justify their previous behavior. Such biasing of attitudes is most likely to occur when individuals feel personally responsible for negative consequences, and when these consequences are difficult to undo.

In a series of research studies, my associates and I also used a self-justification framework in investigating whether decision makers can become overcommitted to a course of action. However, the assumption underlying these studies was that individuals may go beyond the passive distortion of adverse consequences in an effort to rationalize a behavioral error. By committing new and additional resources, an individual who has suffered a setback could attempt to "turn the situation around" or to demonstrate the ultimate rationality of his or her original course of action. . . .

External v. Internal Justification

Although research on commitment has emphasized the role of justification, these studies have chiefly tapped what could be labeled an internal justification process. When justification is considered primarily as an intra-individual process, individuals are posited to attend to events and to act in ways to protect their own self-images. But within most social settings, justification may also be directed externally. When faced with an external threat or evaluation, individuals may be motivated to prove to others that they were not wrong in an earlier decision and the force for such external justification could well be stronger than the protection of self-esteem. . . .

Norms for Consistency

In addition to the internal and external forms of justification, norms for consistency in action may be another major source of commitment. A lay theory may exist in our society, or at least within many organizational settings, that administrators who are consistent in their actions are better leaders than those who switch from one line of behavior to another. . . .

Evidence for a preference or norm for consistency is also seen in the results of a national political survey. In a Gallup poll on President Carter's popularity after his first year in office, respondents who were dissatisfied with the president were asked why they felt this way. "Indecisiveness" was the second-most-frequent response given by the public and the only response that could be coded as a general pattern of behavior (the others were related to specific issues of the economy, foreign policy, campaign promises, etc.).

. . . [S]urvey and anecdotal data point to the possibility of an implicit theory of leadership according to which effective administrators are fully committed to and steadfast in a course of action. In order to test for the existence of such a lay theory, Ross and I conducted an experiment on the reactions of individuals to selected forms of administrative behavior. Subjects included practicing managers, undergraduates in business, and undergraduates in a psychology course. Results showed that administrators were rated highest when they followed a consistent course of action and were ultimately successful. . . . This . . . supported a predicted "hero effect" for the administrator who remained committed through two apparent failures of a course of action, only to succeed in the end. Finally, the effect of consistency on ratings of the administrator was shown to vary by subject group, being strongest among practicing administrators, next strong among business students, and weakest among psychology undergraduates. These results suggest not only that consistency in action is perceived to be part of effective leadership but that this perception may be acquired through socialization in business and governmental roles.

TOWARD A THEORETICAL MODEL

. . . [M]otivation to justify decisions can be seen as a function of responsibility for negative consequences as well as both internal and external demands for competence. . . . [R]esponsibility for negative consequences leads to a motivation to justify previous decisions, if there is a need to demonstrate competence to oneself or others. . . . [T]he traditional literature on dissonance and self-justification considers only the desire of individuals to be correct or accurate in decision making for reasons of self-esteem, but the need to demonstrate competence to external parties may also be a potent force. . . .

Such predictions may be culture bound; but emphases on individual rationality and competence are so strong in Western societies that they are likely to foster concomitant needs for rationalizing one's actions. Likewise, because norms for rationality are so dominant in business and governmental organizations, decision makers in these settings may also find it necessary to justify their actions to constituents within and outside the organization. In sum, it is ironic that both internal and external needs to demonstrate competence can lead to justification, because justification is exactly what may detract from the rational or competent decision making that both individuals and organizations seek to achieve. . . .

Prospective vs. Retrospective Rationality

[F]orces for justification can lead to a form of "retrospective rationality." The individual, when motivated by a need to justify, seeks to appear competent in previous as opposed to future actions. In contrast, SEU (subjective expected utility) models of behavior posit that the individual is prospectively rational, seeking to maximize future utility. What adds to the complexity of decision making is the fact that both forces may operate in commitment decisions.

As determinants of prospective rationality, some set of perceived probabilities and values should affect resource allocation decisions. Already within commitment situations, we have validated the effects of the efficacy of resources and the causal persistence of a setback. However, it is possible that individual perceptions of the likelihood and value of various outcomes are also influenced by nonobjective factors. . . . [A]s shown in an experiment by Fox, individuals make more use of information that exonerates them for an earlier error than information that is implicating. Thus, it can be expected that motivation to justify decisions will affect the search for and storage of information by individuals. Likewise, having been responsible for negative consequences may make the achievement of future outcomes all the more important. The value of future returns may intensify if they are needed to cover past losses. . . .

In addition to the confluence of retrospective and prospective rationality, there is probably a third force of major importance to commitment decisions. Individuals can become committed to a course of action simply because they believe consistency in action is an appropriate form of behavior. Individuals sometimes model their own behavior on those they see as successful within organizations and society in general. These effects may be time dependent inasmuch as high-level administrators model their behavior on leadership stereotypes that exist in the culture at a given time in history. These effects can also be noncognitive, since behavior may be modeled without a direct calculation of costs and benefits. . . . Likewise, norms for consistency can be viewed as an outgrowth of individual needs for cognitive consistency [Festinger, 1957] or socialization for consistency within the general society. . . .

AN ASSESSMENT OF THE COMMITMENT PROCESS

This article began with a series of examples and an inquiry into whether commitment situations can inherently lead individuals into errors of escalation. The examples were tilted in the direction of an escalation of commitment and in each case the escalation seemed to lead to further problems or losses. Obviously, it is also possible that escalation of commitment can bring a turnaround of results and positive as well as negative consequences. But this is not the point. The crucial issue is whether there is a tendency to escalate commitment above and beyond what would be warranted by the "objective" facts of the situation. From our research, the answer to this question must be a qualified Yes.

If a decision maker were to escalate commitment only when the facts warranted it, there should be no effects of justification or norms for consistency on commitment. The only variables of relevance to "objective" commitment decisions would be factors influencing the probability and value of future outcomes. However, knowledgeable observers of a commitment situation do not generally reach the same decisions as do actors who have experienced losses. In addition, there may be a simple preference on the part of individuals for consistency in behavior even when it is not warranted by the facts of a commitment situation. Thus, motivation to justify and norms for consistency may each contribute to a general tendency to escalate. . . .

IMPLICATIONS

If we accept the conclusion that there is a tendency to escalate on the part of individuals, what are its implications? Perhaps the most likely victims of an escalation tendency will be behaviors that are perceptually associated as parts of a single course of action. In such sequences of behavior, both justification and consistency influences have been found to override more objective elements of the situation. Prime candidates for escalation therefore include resource allocation or investment decisions that are identified by an entering and exit value, life choices that are linked together with the label of a career, and policy decisions for which administrators are held accountable by others in an organization or by the general public. In these situations, one must be especially wary of escalation tendencies and perhaps take counteractions to restore balance to decision making.

In counterbalancing an escalation tendency, . . . individuals should seek and follow the advice of outsiders who can assess the relevant issues of a decision situation without being responsible for previous losses or subject to internal or external needs to justify past actions. Likewise, organizations that have experienced losses from a given investment or course of action should rotate or change those in charge of allocating resources. One applied instance of such a counterbalancing strategy was recently uncovered . . . in a comparative case study of procedures in two banks for coping with the problem of delinquent loans. The more financially aggressive bank, which had issued loans with greater risk, utilized separate departments for lending and "workout," the latter department being in charge of efforts to recover the bank's investment from problem accounts. In contrast, the more conservative bank, which had fewer delinquent loans, had developed no formal procedure for separating responsibility for lending and workout, the original loan officer being charged with all phases of the loan relationship.

[In summary,] . . . our research has shown that administrators sometimes become trapped in a course of action by external demands for success, and administrative experimentation is often viewed as an inappropriate form of leadership behavior. Thus, it may be important to revamp performance evaluation systems facing administrators so that the motivation for action will shift from the defense of past actions to attainment of future gain (e.g., from a retrospective to a prospective basis). It may also be necessary to retrain administrators and resocialize students entering governmental and business organizations about the merits of experimentation versus consistency. In each of these ways, the actions of decision makers can perhaps be directed away from the tendency to escalate.

4. Phyllis Beck Kritek,* Negotiating at an Uneven Table: Developing Moral Courage in Resolving Our Conflicts 55-64 (1994)**

Imagining Alternatives

As a youngster I was advised that if I found a prevailing norm troublesome, it was my job to find a credible alternative. This was a useful lesson. Since I clearly find our culture's fixation on dominance power troublesome, I have spent some time searching for alternative assumptions about what is of worth and value. I am recording these here since they demonstrate the possibility of discovering antidotes to our fixation on dominance power, and since they are the context within which I respond to uneven tables.

I think conflict is a dimension of the human condition, one of the givens we find waiting for us when we arrive on the planet. We also find a myriad of emotional responses to this conflict. Thus, when we try to resolve our conflicts, we often find ourselves so enmeshed in the emotions of the conflict that imagining new ways of approaching it seems like a luxury. It is not an optimal time for stretching our imaginations. Prior reflection may thus be helpful.

Accepting Mystery

When we do stretch our imaginations, we find that our minds take in that which we have not yet experienced. This transition is at first a confrontation with mystery. Mystery fascinates us. Part of what we like about mysteries is following them along and finally seeing them "solved," testing our own cleverness against the challenge. We like mysteries, but only if we can hope to solve them. Lurking mysteries without solutions remind us of our limits and can thus irritate or intimidate us. At some level, we would secretly like to have all the answers.

One of the most predictable things about books is that most authors write like they have solved a mystery, no matter what the topic. Authors feel safer writing in this manner, and it reassures readers. We cheer on the author, grateful that someone has put that nagging question to rest.

Unfortunately, I'm not able to do this with this book—or with just about anything else. Every good answer today has lurking in it the next good question. I believe that's how knowledge "is." I think that the good tough questions get us closer to understanding than dogma or "right" answers. Hence, this book lacks "the-one-best-way" formulas, but it does try to honestly raise important questions and honor mysteries when they show up. Mysteries are a door-

---

*Phyllis Beck Kritek is professor and chair of psychosocial nursing and leadership development at the University of Texas Medical Branch at Galveston School of Nursing, where she also serves as director of doctoral program development.

**Reprinted with permission.

way to the profound, and lift me well beyond the simplistic repetitiousness of sparring for dominance power.

The closer I get to important truths, the more I feel paradox lurking, and it keeps me reluctant to promise more than I can deliver. Books as recipes scare me. So I am saying, "Here are some ideas to play with; see how they work for you; let me know." Accepting mystery can be an asset in creating dialogues. It also frees us to continue to learn and grow without feeding the illusion that we can know everything or the compulsion to appear as if we do.

Creating Metaphors

Cognitive scientists, over the last few decades, have revealed that we can better understand human behavior and learning by better understanding the function of metaphors. When we are trying to tell someone about an experience we've had that they've never had, we use metaphors as a bridge. . . .

Metaphors . . . give us access to new things. But the new things have their own power to disrupt our lives. Sometimes the metaphor is useful, helping us to test out a new idea under somewhat safe circumstances. "Try this it tastes just like cherry candy"—the most popular lie that parents in the United States tell toddlers taking their first liquid penicillin. This is how we try to slide in new information with metaphors.

As we soon discover, however, the new information can rise up like a tornado and cause all manner of mischief. It may not fit where I have put it, or it may not even want to be seen in the company of the other facets of my world. It may want a new place, its own place, or it may want to change everything else in the system. It can become a quite frustrating and unwelcome guest. So the metaphor is useful but can become risky on occasion.

Sometimes we tell it to settle down and quit being such a bother. Other times we try to cut a deal with it, and talk it into being the idea we had wanted it to be. Sometimes we put it in exile. Sometimes none of this works, and we must simply overhaul the system because it is unwilling to respond to even our most gracious and sincere efforts at taming.

This explains both the attraction and the danger of a metaphor when we use it to learn. It unveils the deep dangers embedded in poetry. It could let things in we never meant to let in; once there, it can create havoc. Plato knew this.

As you may now see, the metaphor has enormous power. The metaphor can say more than the "facts." I can say I went to a family reunion or I can say I spent eight hours sorting through the human networks of my autobiography. The message of the metaphor carries more impact, says more, does more. . . .

The Metaphor of War

I believe . . . that [war] is our central metaphor. War, of course, encompasses more than frank battle with instruments of destruction. It includes conflict, argument, contest, the clear designation of winners and losers. . . There are rules, time limits, and the victors and vanquished when it is done. The centrality of this metaphor in our culture is not difficult to document. When I discovered that health care advertising was identifying its "target" audience, I knew we had hit a new level of confusion. We also "conquer" disease and "attack" pathogens. We "destroy" cancerous cells using "weapons" against tumors. We lament that AIDS is a loss of the body's "defenses" against "invading" organisms. Medicine is war.

So is advertising, business, sports, news, science, politics, economics . . . this list can go on and on. We have even mounted "wars" against poverty, drugs, violence, and AIDS. I have spent about ten years now observing this metaphor, trying to develop a sensitivity toward it and trying to find alternate metaphors that both communicate and provide a different frame for reality. Every day I find I still use the war metaphor somewhere; every day I find myself stumbling about in the darkness failing to generate the new and useful metaphors.

Further exemplars may be useful. Here are some key words and phrases that help give a sense of how we culturally use war as a metaphor: defend, attack, protect, strategize, outflank, line of resistance, retreat, reconnoiter, defeat, surrender, give in, fight back, conquer, vanquish, target, weapon, arsenal, win, fail, promote, prevail, humiliate, vindicate, disarm, imprison, hit the ground running, orders, shooting, fired, fired on, casualties, assault, bludgeon, squabble, mission, guard, dispute, strong arm . . . this list is not exhaustive. One can replicate it by locating it where I did, in a single edition of a local newspaper. Articles included ones on the assault of a severe storm, conflicts among various organized religions, filming a new video, and the casualties in a domestic environment.

If war is not the predominant metaphor, it is assuredly a central one. And it supports a habit of mind and heart that assumes conflict, competition, and adversarialness. It frames how we view much of life. And that, of course, has an impact. Certainly, if this is the primary metaphor used to clarify the nature of a conflict, one might understand this. If it is less consciously the primary metaphor used to resolve conflict, it is less helpful. In essence, the metaphor is sustained and strengthened because no alternate metaphor is provided to enable conflicting parties to envision a new reality.

The metaphor of war is used to explain most conflicts and their resolution. This too is not difficult to document. War and adversarialness are implicitly assumed to be the "given" of the species. The war described is usually discord based on power experienced as dominance. The solutions sustain this primary metaphor and usually only peripherally acknowledge alternate models of conflict or its resolution. In my experience, many people struggle when they try to sensitize themselves to this troublesome insight. Nonetheless, it is clear that power can also be exercised as moral agency, that some conflicts involve a struggle for self-reliance, and that human love is a powerful alternative model for conflict resolution that is rarely acknowledged

Examining Myths

Joseph Campbell, perhaps inadvertently, has turned us all into amateur mythologists of a sort, either through personal study of his works or the effort to deal with those who have. The men's movements have evolved largely from an initial focus on mythopoetic dimensions of what it means to be a man. The women's movements reflect this same interest in the mythopoetic. Jungian psychology is grounded in such myths, and the meeting between Eastern and Western philosophies is largely a mythic conversation. Something important is emerging from these discussions about myths. They apparently have meaning for us.

Evolutionary developments like this are always a bit unsettling. One can never quite squeeze them into the right place, since they have no place. They come largely to unsettle us, to disrupt our lives and demand some new growth of us. They are rarely totally welcome. When I was a child, a myth was something used to show me the unreal, to explain to me the virtues of rationality and materialism. Much of our current meandering in the mythic seems to represent a return to our roots. We are also discovering replications or re-expressions of our myths in our history and in our daily lives.

The heightening of consciousness about myth seems often to be a function of an overall heightening of consciousness in general as an evolutionary task of the times. Imagining alternatives to various wars is one such task. We have for decades conducted a war on nature; now we advise people to be good to their mother, the earth. Imagining alternatives to armed conflict is an analogous task, and the images here may or may not prove mythic in nature. Disarmament is not the creation of peace. Often conflict resolution sustains the traditional myth of war even as it attempts to address the limits of such myths.

I think it is important for us to begin to comprehend and respect the impact of our mythic roots. This process helps us understand the metaphors we live by; it helps us understand our own propensities and tendencies much better. There are many dimensions to this comprehension and respect. My list is not exhaustive, but bears scrutiny: religious, cultural, societal, ethnic, national, familial, and personal. All, of course, occur in a historical context. All frame our beliefs, thoughts, feelings, emotions, hopes, and dreams. They also feed and sustain these expressions of ourselves, and they are the content and the context of our daily lives. They are the templates for how we create and sustain our realities.

Some people want to create new myths. I like this idea, but I always have a lurking sense that the tougher task is confronting the ones that hold us in thrall at this time. These we live out unconsciously, sustaining and maintaining them. If we engaged in an honest scrutiny of these myths, we might begin to ask useful questions about them. We might even take responsibility for the inevitable consequences of the choices we have made. We might then imagine new choices, and find and create the myths that enable us to sustain the consequences of these new choices.

Many of the proponents of conflict resolution simply ignore the impact of the dominant myths in our culture. Yet effective resolution of conflict implicitly assumes one is willing to live with the negotiated agreement. If the agreement is contrary to some central myth in my life, I may give the veneer of concurrence to demonstrate that I am a good person, or to avoid censure, but I will not really have dealt with the conflict. I will merely have veiled it, or walled it off only to have it emerge later with some new ugly face. Suppression is not resolution. Myths revisit us, whether we invite them or not.

I have always been moved by Socrates' comment that the unexamined life is not worth living. It is only recently that I clearly understood that he said this shortly before he drank the hemlock. I had wanted his comment to be a guide for living; now it seems more a reflection designed to affirm the life he led. The fact that it ended as it ended may explain why so many people squirm at the thought of examining their lives. Maybe we're all afraid of what we will find. We hide things behind walls and pretend they cannot harm us since we have sequestered them so well. This is an illusion. They will come out and will have their way with us, one way or another, now and later.

Myths seem such forces to me, and while the examining of the myths is difficult, sometimes harrowing, ignoring them is equally dangerous and has the added embarrassment of being stupid. So I vote with Socrates, hemlock and all, liking the integrity and autonomy afforded me by the examination. But such examination is not fun or easy, and it stands in sharp contrast to the more hedonistic models in vogue today: the avoidance of reflection or the cheap quick trick of emotive, sentimental, and superficial self-appraisal.

Myths shape everything. This is worrisome, of course, If you don't know your myths, you are busy shaping without knowing exactly what you're shaping. At the very least, this should evoke a certain nervousness. Folks end up saying things that they never meant to say. Conflict resolution efforts often seem this way to me. People of good faith, with good intentions, keep saying and doing things that seem to represent unexamined life at its best. Such people accept mythic assumptions and sanitize them for their purposes rather than scrutinizing and perhaps even transforming them. As a result, the mythic assumptions of the conflict become the mythic assumptions of the outcomes, and all parties fail to imagine that alternate mythic images might serve them better. Einstein once said that imagination is more important than knowledge. Conflict resolution often seems more intent on knowledge than on imagination, more on facticity than wisdom.

This is inherently contradictory, since the generation of options is a central task of negotiation. Such option generation seems to me the most creative and fun part of conflict resolution. If facticity and the sustaining of central myths are placed as constraints on this task, the options will be narrow and unimaginative and will further perpetuate the problems that gave rise to the conflict. This seems difficult to confront. When I have seen efforts made to do so, they are often dismissed as trivial. When I have tried to do so myself with very accomplished negotiators, I sense an inner conflict in such persons. They seem to say, "Yes, you are right, but there is no solution to this quandary, and besides, it scares me and I don't want to look at it or think about it, even a little. Please go away!"

This is not comforting to me. It also creates waves of self doubt. It makes me more careful in my reflections. It has not, however, silenced the inner voice that tells me that conflict resolution has not yet arrived at the soul of the matter. What is perhaps more ominous is the sense that there is no intention of ever getting there. Often people merely fine-tune the superficial layers of a problem, avoiding the deeper issues implicit in conflict resolution. Myth is a central issue in this regard. It is an American myth that if it works for you it must not be broke and if it ain't broke, you shouldn't fix it. Imagining airplanes or electricity did not emerge from this myth.

The myths of our past take us to the heart of any matter. The myths of our future are the outpourings of imagination. Both are integral to the tough task of creating desired outcomes when we're confronted with a conflict. Neither seem to me to be adequately acknowledged in current explorations of conflict resolution. Intuitively, one or another negotiator may "cheat" and use these gifts at a given moment. This does not make the negotiators credible, but rather examples of deviance. This is not enough for me.

5. Cognitive Barriers and Reactive Devaluation

These topics are discussed by Professor Robert Mnookin at Chapter 4, section F.

F. Anthropology

1. Sally Engle Merry,* Disputing Without Culture [Review of Stephen B. Goldberg, Eric D. Green & Frank E.A. Sander Dispute Resolution (1985)], 100 Harv. L. Rev. 2057 (1987)**

*The author, an anthropologist, is a Professor at Wellesley College.

I. INTRODUCTION

. . . ADR challenges traditional understandings of the centrality of adjudication to the maintenance of social order in modern society. It expresses an anti-law ideology, claiming that non-adversarial ways of resolving conflict can create a better world. ADR urges the legal profession to move away from its exclusive focus on the use of courts to resolve conflicts and to consider a broader spectrum of problem-solving approaches. . . .

Used initially in the labor-management field, mediation and arbitration have expanded to new arenas: smaller civil disputes, divorces, child custody disputes, consumer problems, environmental conflicts, job discrimination complaints, prisoner grievances, integovernmental disputes, and international conflicts. Not only are new dispute resolution arenas constantly opening up, but . . . established ADR processes are becoming institutionalized, with ongoing, sometimes public, funding, established procedures and models, and more professionalized third-party roles characterized by higher training standards, codes of ethics, professional associations, and concerns about certification or licensing. . . . Ironically, as ADR expands, the alternatives are gradually becoming more closely tied to the courts and to legal professionals, and the programs themselves are becoming professionalized. . . .

Dispute Resolution is a "how-to" book: it describes each potential dispute resolution process, analyzes its strengths and weaknesses, and offers some guidelines about the kinds of cases for which it may be effective. It delineates techniques for resolving disputes and criteria for tailoring these techniques to particular problems. The authors evaluate effectiveness primarily in terms of efficiency—measured in cost and speed—and participant "satisfaction"—measured by asking users whether they considered the process fair and whether they were satisfied with its outcome.

Yet this approach produces a technocratic preoccupation with appropriate forums. Because the book offers a tool kit of techniques along with rules about when each tool should be employed, the complexity of actual situations and the surrounding social fabric fades into the background. Exercises in bargaining for law students have the same abstract unreality. At best, this simplification gives students a false sense of easily being able to get to the bottom of issues and settle cases; at worst, it fosters the kind of quick typification and routine treatment of cases that, ironically, ADR advocates often cite as the central problem with conventional adjudication.

Dispute Resolution does not consider the ADR movement in the context of contemporary American society. The book ignores the social, cultural, and political dimensions of ADR, but this neglect accurately represents the unreflective nature of the ADR movement as a whole. After discussing the intellectual origins of the ADR movement in the anthropology of law, this Review examines four premises of the ADR movement as embodied in this book that deserve further scrutiny. It concludes by considering the broader cultural implications of the current interest in alternative dispute resolution.

II. CROSS-CULTURAL STUDY OF DISPUTE RESOLUTION

. . . Legal anthropology turns the legal paradigm upside down: instead of looking at the different ways law handles conflicts, anthropologists examine the various ways conflicts are resolved, with law representing only one possible approach. Thus, anthropologists view law as the alternative mode of settling disputes, not the other way around. Yet much of the ADR movement ignores the central insight provided by the anthropological study of disputing: the interactive relationship between dispute resolution and cultural practice. Anthropological studies that examine the processes by which law-like tasks are carried out are premised on the concept of the dispute or trouble-case as a social event, embedded within a structure of social relationships and a cultural world of rules, practices of handling conflict, and normative principles within which positions are phrased in the course of disputing. The dispute itself is a social construct, whose definition shifts with the audience to whom it is presented, who may actively redefine it.

A dispute can be defined as a confrontation that has escalated into a public arena. The way a dispute is handled depends on the structure of the society in which it arises and the social relationship between the disputing parties. . . . In general, anthropological studies indicate that when disputants are bound together by multi-stranded social relationships, they will seek to compromise their differences, but when they have only single-stranded social ties, they will seek victory in adversarial contests rather than attempt to reach compromise.

In their enthusiasm over the discovery that law is only one mode among many for dealing with disputes, proponents of ADR tend to ignore the important role that law and legal consciousness play in American culture and the social differences between American society and small-scale societies in which processes like mediation exist naturally. For example, many of these societies either do not have a state at all, or if one exists, it is remote from day-to-day village life. In contrast, the state plays a central role in ordering details of neighborhood, family, and community life in modern America and in structuring the shape of the economy and society. Small-scale societies also do not usually have a highly developed cultural awareness of legal rights, equality, or the rights to legal participation that are characteristic of American society. Dispute Resolution discusses the way various forms of dispute resolution can be adapted to particular situations, but it does not consider the importance of the underlying structure of social relations in American society or the extent to which resistance to ADR is engendered by Americans' widespread cultural conceptions of legal solutions to problems.

III. PREMISES OF THE ADR MOVEMENT

A. The Model of Disputing

The ADR movement, as exemplified in Dispute Resolution, is premised on an implicit model of the nature of disputing. The ADR approach assumes that dispute resolution is a rational and instrumental process in which actors seek to maximize their self-interests. They make calculated choices about dispute resolution techniques based on cost, speed, and anticipated outcomes. Under this model, actors are expected to flock to more efficient forums.

Given this model, one of the stubborn problems for proponents of the ADR movement, particularly for proponents of mediation services for people with minor interpersonal disputes, is explaining why such services are rarely sought voluntarily. Because recent studies suggest that people who mediate their disputes are more often satisfied than those with similar problems who go to court, one would expect many to choose mediation voluntarily. Yet most people, given the choice, prefer court resolution of minor interpersonal disputes over mediation. The most common explanation given for this reluctance to choose mediation is that most people are not familiar with it but are inundated with messages about courts. Although ignorance of the process of mediation clearly discourages its use, other factors that are more closely connected to the way in which participants actually view disputes are also significant.

The problem with the ADR model is that it does not describe the way people behave. It views disputes as disembodied events separated from the social world. Disputing, however, is cultural behavior, informed by participants' moral views about how to fight, the meaning participants attach to going to court, social practices that indicate when and how to escalate disputes to a public forum, and participants' notions of rights and entitlement. Parties to a dispute operate within systems of meaning; they seek ways of doing things that seem right, normal, or fair, often acting out of habit or moral conviction. The normative framework shapes the way people conceptualize problems, the ways they pursue them, and the kinds of solutions they look for.

The working-class and middle-class Americans that Susan Silbey and I interviewed in a study of neighborhood and family disputing indicated that they preferred to talk over problems rather than to turn to court, which they regarded as a last resort. They were not initially litigious, in the sense of being eager to run to court, and seemed quite reluctant to take a step that they saw as serious and likely to escalate the dispute significantly. By the time a dispute is serious enough to warrant outside intervention by a public third party, the disputing parties have often come to view the problem in terms of rights and principles and no longer want the opportunity to discuss the dispute informally. Naive users of the courts typically expect that the law exists to protect them and that it will be applied to their particular problem firmly and powerfully.

One of the pressing research tasks for the ADR movement should be to chart the actions of experienced mediation clients to see what they do when the next problem comes along. These are people who obviously know what mediation is and what it can do for them, and it would be of great value to know if they seek out mediation for their next dispute or if they go to court. My limited observations of disputants in two neighborhood justice center programs indicates that they return to court.

B. Classifying Processes and the Problem of "Fit"

The project enunciated in Dispute Resolution is one of matching problems to processes. Yet the processes are presented in overly simplified and static ways that highlight only their formal structure. The categories most commonly employed to describe dispute resolution processes refer only to the structures and procedures of dispute resolution. Each dispute resolution process—negotiation, mediation, arbitration, and so forth—contains highly diverse ideologies of conflict which stem from the ways the actors conceive of their tasks and their prerogatives. Dispute resolution is shaped by the culture of those who practice it. In order to understand disputing or any other social process, an observer must get "inside the heads" of the actors to discover what they think they are doing and what it means to them. The ideological definition of the process, springing from its social and cultural context, exerts a powerful influence on the behavior of those who carry it out. For example, a third party who believes that she is balancing demands based on contradictory rights will define the dispute resolution project differently than one who thinks that she is overcoming misunderstandings. A person who views her task as one of restoring peace or "making the balance" will have a different vision of the job than one who defines it as punishing rulebreakers. Some mediators, for example, understand their role to be bargaining between the contending parties, while others conceptualize the task as facilitating communication and allowing a therapeutic venting of feelings. Dispute resolution has a chameleonlike quality, whose character shifts with the perceptions of its participants. Thus, determining which process is most appropriate based only on its formal structure will ignore a great deal of variation in practice within a single process.

Furthermore, dispute resolution processes exist within a sequence of events unfolding over time. Disputes are not always settled when they are brought to dispute handling forums. Rather, they often continue in new forms or with new definitions for prolonged periods, with the public processing simply a point at which the dispute enters a new phase or becomes transformed in some way. Social science research on disputing generally talks about dispute processing rather than dispute resolution. Dispute Resolution, however, presents the alternatives statically, viewing them for the most part as a set of cubbyholes into which disputes are sent for processing. In the social world, these procedures are linked together into regular, patterned sequences, and the nature of any process depends on where it is in a particular sequence. Each domain of disputing has its own sequence, its own set of expectations about how one moves from one stage to another along with attached cultural meanings to moving, failing to move, jumping stages, or timing shifts from one stage to another. Knowledge of the next stage, with its associated costs, possible outcome, and cultural meaning, is a critical part of each disputant's assessment of her situation, as is the question of what happens if the parties fail to settle.

Although the analytic framework of Dispute Resolution sees these processes as alternatives rather than as stages, its case studies clearly illustrate the importance of linkages over time. For example, the option of going to arbitration has a "chilling effect" on labor negotiations, negotiation itself is intimately linked to a litigation strategy, and the fact of filing a case in small claims court affects the bargaining leverage of the disputants in mediation. Some of the hybrids depend upon these linkages. For example, the mini-trial . . . would be quite different without the prospect of a full trial down the road.

. . . No process exists separately from its place in the unfolding sequence of stages, which gives it meaning and force. If parties are aware that a more coercive process will ensue if mediation fails, the dynamics of the mediation will differ sharply from "pure mediation," because the expectation of an imposed settlement will inevitably alter the meaning of the event for all the actors.

Moreover, disputes themselves change over time and change as they are processed. For example, the young man who refuses to leave his young girlfriend alone and is dragged into court by her father presents a different problem the first time he appears than he does three years later when the father is lodging his third criminal complaint.

If disputes are to be assigned to appropriate resolution processes, who is going to make that decision and on what basis? Dispute Resolution cites the need for further research to help develop guidelines and concludes with a plea for that research as an aide to designing an adjudicatory tracking system suggesting that the problem is one of expertise, not politics. Yet directing disputes to different forums involves political decisions about how to define the problems, what kinds of coercive force to impose on parties, and what value society should place on problems of each type. Dispute Resolution ignores the political nature of the fitting process: the possible use of unrecognized criteria such as race, gender, and class, and the typical neglect of other criteria, such as disputants' preferences, for determining "appropriateness."

As courts and legislatures move to make alternatives mandatory, the ability to choose forums is being transferred from individual disputants to the institutions that assign cases to particular forums. Some clients voluntarily choose to use an alternative to courts because of the high costs of litigation—as in divorce, environmental, or commercial disputes—while others are increasingly urged or even required to use mediation instead of courts, particularly for disputes involving interpersonal issues or small amounts of money—cases which are usually handled in low-cost small claims, criminal, and juvenile courts. In fact, the large majority of people who use the courts for any reasons go to the lower courts, and it is here that the average citizen's ideas about the legitimacy of the legal order are formed and transformed. The criticism that ADR provides second-class justice applies primarily to these disputants, many of whom are poorer and less able to afford legal help than those who choose alternatives to bypass expensive litigation. In short, much of the successful growth and application of ADR has been among the more affluent disputants, whereas it has been less popular among users who are being encouraged to substitute these services for low cost court services.

C. The Novelty of ADR Reforms

Dispute Resolution contains little discussion of historical parallels to similar reforms, nor has there been such discussion within the ADR movement. Yet similar developments have arisen during the twentieth century. There seems to be an historical pattern of oscillation between formal systems of dispute resolution and informal reforms that gradually became more formalized, leading to new calls for informal reforms of the now calcified older reforms. Many of the Progressive Era reformers of the early twentieth century, for example, advocated reforms similar to ADR processes. The evolution of the juvenile court system, a reform instituted in this period, provides one of the more vivid illustrations of this process. Developed as an informal alternative to the adult criminal court at the turn of the century, the juvenile court system was dedicated to an ideology of treatment and cure rather than punishment. It was designed to consider the best interest of the child rather than to evaluate evidence of wrongdoing. Critics of the reforms, however, charged that the juvenile courts failed to protect the rights of juveniles adequately. A landmark Supreme Court decision in 1967, In re Gault, provided greater legal protection for juveniles, enhancing the formalistic and legalistic character of juvenile hearings. Yet, by the 1980s, social agencies in at least two states (New York and Massachusetts) had again begun to create informal alternatives to the juvenile courts for status offenders. . . .

The ADR movement seems to be the most recent manifestation of this historical pattern, an effort to create informal systems outside the legal system that eventually come to incorporate many of its characteristics. As each alternative gradually comes to look more like the legal system it has replaced, routine treatment, delay, and impersonality are likely to reemerge. This transformation is already occurring in the ADR movement. . . . It is assuming more legalistic, formal characteristics as it becomes more closely integrated into the courts. We should not be surprised.

D. The Indifferent State

Not only does the ADR movement lack an historical perspective; it also presumes an indifferent state. Nineteenth century chiefs ruling over the powerful Ashanti state in Ghana had their own "litigation fetishes," over which they poured offerings of palm oil while intoning prayers to the deities to bring them cases: "Case-hearing rock, these days of hunger are killing us, let me get cases to settle." Cases meant both wealth and power: a local adage went, "If the chief tries to conciliate parties in a street quarrel, he will soon be starving." The ability to settle disputes is an important source of power for any state. Studies of dispute settlement in several European nations during the early modern period also reveal ambitious kings attempting to control existing forms of dispute resolution and outlawing indigenous systems such as feuds and duels as they endeavored to consolidate power. In his historical study of patterns of court litigation in St. Louis over the past 150 years, Wayne McIntosh points out that the state is always a competitor in the marketplace of disputes, endeavoring to dominate other institutions that provide dispute resolution services.

If governments typically have an interest in exercising substantial control over dispute resolution, how will they regard the creation of alternative forms of dispute resolution outside their power? It seems likely that political leaders will resist the creation of autonomous dispute resolution institutions, drawing those that are formed into the orbit of existing state-run institutions or relegating to the consideration of ADR only those cases that are deemed trivial.

Developments in ADR suggest that both of these phenomena are occurring. In the arena of interpersonal disputes, for example, independent, autonomous programs are struggling for funding and cases, while programs firmly attached to courts are inundated with referrals and are far more likely to be supported by public funds. Programs sometimes find that courts are reluctant to relinquish control over cases referred to mediation and wish to retain final oversight, unless the problems are regarded as trivial. . . .

Moreover, state-supported ADR programs are less likely to provide a dispute resolution process or form of authority that is significantly different from that which their users would encounter in court. The power of the third party to impose a decision differs between mediation and court processing, but the interpretive processes that take place in both mediation and lower court case processing exhibit substantial similarities. A comparison of the way interpersonal cases are handled in court-annexed mediation and the processing they receive in court suggests that both involve similar processes of informal negotiation, situational assessment of the cases, and outcomes that include some kind of ongoing supervision. High-volume mediation programs also experience problems of routinization and burnout of mediators not unlike the problems plaguing the lower courts.

Critics of the ADR movement argue that it represents an extension of state power through nonstate means: the control of the state over the details of people's daily lives is expanded, but under the guise of a participatory, consensual, and voluntary process. Although it is hard to see capitalist conspiracy in the efforts of well-meaning citizens who devote an evening every few weeks to helping others less fortunate and educated than themselves to resolve problems of drinking, violence, or unruly children and neighbors, in the aggregate the political meaning of the movement is inescapable. Dispute Resolution and some segments of the ADR movement seem naive about the political implications of alternative processes, failing to question sufficiently for whom these processes are designed, whose interests they serve, and what politically significant differences exist between forms and applications of ADR.

The book provides no discussion of the state's interest in these dispute resolution processes, despite evidence that the state tends either to eliminate competing processes or to control those which it supports, both through funding and referral of cases. The reformers of the Progressive Era shared a similar naivete about the interests of the state, also assuming, as David Rothman puts it, a shared interest between the kept and the keeper as they expanded institutions for keeping. Just as juvenile court, probation, parole, and indeterminate sentencing reforms widened the scope of state supervision over citizens in the early twentieth century, so, too, have the contemporary neighborhood justice centers. The expansion of control and pressures to use alternatives are obviously far more salient for poorer, more vulnerable users who are least likely to be voluntary users or to have any alternatives they can afford. They apply more to the multi-door courthouse than to the mini-trial.

The failure of Dispute Resolution to consider the political significance of the ADR movement, in the sense of its impact on the distribution of power in American society, is illustrated by the book's neglect of the question of who should be responsible for fitting actual disputes to appropriate processes. The ability to take an inchoate problem, frame it as suitable for one process or another, and send it to a process that exists in a larger sequence of predetermined stages is an important source of power.

IV. ADR AND THE AMERICAN CULTURE OF LITIGIOUSNESS

One of the most intriguing questions raised by Dispute Resolution and, indeed, by the whole ADR movement, is why the idea of ADR took hold in America at this precise historical moment. What does it say about American society, about our attitudes toward law and courts, and about our sense of ourselves and our communities that we are so attracted by ways of dealing with differences that promise reconciliation rather than a contest over rights? This perspective on the role of law in enhancing social justice is very different from the one that prevailed in the 1960's and 1970's. ADR is usually justified by the congestion of the courts and the demand placed upon them by ordinary persons. The overuse of the courts to resolve family, neighborhood, and other "minor" problems is often blamed on the breakdown of community and the erosion of authority of home, school, religion, and other institutions. Yet there is no clear evidence that the backlogs plague the lower courts; instead, they seem to occur largely in the higher courts.

Proponents of the notion that the courts are too congested, and therefore that new alternatives are necessary, may be responding to the presence of new users in the courts who are considered undesirable and who present frustrating and unrewarding problems—people making claims about domestic violence, neighborhood harassment, sexual harassment on the job, discrimination, faulty goods, shoddy medical service, and deteriorated rental housing. These users are making difficult demands for protection from the courts. Their use of legal institutions, however, is a response to the new legal entitlements of the 1960's and to the expansion of access to the courts produced through the vigorous legal services and legal advocacy of the same period. More rights were created and more people were invited to use the courts to claim these rights, including women, minorities, prisoners, workers, and consumers.

Are people indeed so eager to take their personal problems to court? My research suggests that ordinary people go to court because they have an understanding of themselves as endowed with rights and entitled to the protection of the state against intolerable harassment and attacks by spouses, friends, and neighbors. Yet they go reluctantly, after a prolonged period of difficulty, and only as a last resort. They have learned how to use the courts and have heard the message that they, too, are members of American society, entitled to benefit from its legal system and the services it offers. Indeed, fighting with law is viewed as more civilized than fighting with fists or knives in several of the working-class neighborhoods I studied.

ADR invites these people out of the courts and encourages them to use alternative dispute resolution processes. Further, it provides an ideological justification for sending them away because their problems are defined as "inappropriate" for legal forums. Having absorbed the pervasive legal ideology of American society and come to see themselves as full and entitled participants in that society, working-class Americans are being discouraged from using the very institutions they now see as their own, perhaps because their problems seem insolvable or unrewarding to the courts. The ADR movement has done well for the well-to-do. Its advocates must now address the broader problems of ADR's involuntary users, for whom the conflicts that must be "resolved" run far deeper than whatever immediate confrontation brought them into the dispute processing system. . . .

2. Laura Nader,* *Controlling Processes in the Practice of Law: Hierarchy and Pacification in the Movement to Re-Form Dispute Ideology*, 9 Ohio St. J. on Disp. Resol. 1 (1993)**

I. INTRODUCTION

. . . I will argue in this article that harmony ideology—the use of a rhetoric of peace through consensus—finds fertile ground within the legal profession through cultural control. Social control relates to "intense influence," working extraordinarily long hours with little contact with the outside world, and also focuses on hierarchy: The Chief Justice does not have to present evidence for lawyers to believe him. Social and cultural power mechanisms amount to controlling processes. Such control mechanisms have received inadequate attention both within and without the legal profession. . . . What anthropologists have learned over the past fifty years is that it is exactly those symbols, placed by any society outside the jurisdiction of its formal social control systems (what Aldous Huxley in 1958 called "impersonal forces"), that we find control operating most adamantly. Yet, there is no compatible body of laws or activist concern with covert power mechanisms—such as group think or ideological control—which are so central a part of modernity, and which are accelerated by commercial media and political organizations.

Legal scholars and lawyers should pay more attention to controlling processes not only because of increasing incidences of thought control allegations in legal suits involving cult and cult-like activities, but also because the exercise of intense influence is so pervasive in late twentieth-century America. Even lawyers and judges may be subjected to intense influence under certain conditions.

Over the past twenty years lawyers and judges in the United States have been pummeled in the popular media and in dispute resolution journals by an accelerating wave of antagonism toward litigation and the adversarial process. During the same period, enthusiasm for alternative dispute resolution (ADR) has promoted these mechanisms as being efficient, as providing access to resolution, and as exalting harmony rather than rights. The intensity was striking and so was the impact. So successful has the movement against litigation and the adversary process been, that there has been widespread acceptance of a legal harmony model of law as an answer to the concerns of how to deliver justice to the many.

The movement was not about theory. It was directed towards practice. ADR was on the agenda of legal practitioners. Trial lawyers met to ponder their complicitous part as promulgators of anger and the adversary process. Federal judges bought into the reframing of what is wrong with our legal system, and often indiscriminately accepted the ADR analysis. Even

---

*Laura Nader is a Professor of Anthropology, University of California, Berkeley.

**Reprinted with permission.

stranger were the 1960's activist lawyers, who are now born-again mediators who accept ADR forums and use them to erase issues of class, gender, and race, to "treat people equally." By 1993, ADR has become a major industry, which includes social workers, mental health professionals, lawyers, behavioral scientists, and dozens of journals where ADR is formalized.

The ADR rhetoric of the past two decades was a response to the law reform discourse of the 1960s, a discourse concerned with justice and root causes, and with debates over right and wrong. In the early 1970s, when the justice talk of the various rights movements (civil rights, consumer rights, environmental rights, etc.) was replaced by talk of harmony and efficiency, the public debate was over the question of "too much litigation." A change in the manner of thinking about rights and justice was shaped through a new discourse, and by means of this discourse produced a movement against the contentious or adversarial qualities of American law. In some ways, it was a rebellion against law and lawyers—often by lawyers themselves. A movement to control litigation was being constructed to replace justice and rights talk with what I call harmony ideology, the belief that harmony in the guise of compromise or agreement is ipso facto better than an adversary posture. . . .

After I summarize the components that became the centerpiece of the ADR movement, I will focus on the questions: Why have so many people in the legal profession fallen prey to ADR rhetoric? Why did members of the legal elite accept this ideological takeover of their profession with such placidity? I argue that harmony ideology—manifested in the reluctance of many lawyers to defend their profession against this ADR onslaught—finds fertile ground through mechanisms of hierarchy and coercive harmony. . . .

Working extraordinarily long hours, with little contact with the outside world, lawyers are particularly susceptible to the kinds of control effects documented in cults. The cultural control works first by playing on a rhetoric of peace and harmony, a rhetoric with historic roots in American civic culture, and also through training in hierarchy which begins with lawyers' first acquaintances with law in law school and continues throughout their professional careers. Both hierarchy and harmony discourse constitute a movement to covert power mechanisms that have received inadequate attention in writings about the legal profession.

II. THE ADR EXPLOSION

Today ADR has a history and a scholarship. People from fields as disparate as anthropology, history, psychology, law, and political science have been piecing together the story of the movement. [T]he following questions are often shared: By what means was an ADR movement launched in a country where the rule of law was paramount? What have been the consequences of the shift from adversarial to harmony ideology in terms of the expressed purpose of law in the United States? What is the meaning of harmony ideology in relation to unequal relationships, and more broadly in terms of creating a culture of harmony which may be coercive, repressive, and basically undemocratic? It is the third question that is of interest in this paper.

Some might say that ADR is a hegemonic movement, in which the exercise of political control working through a combination of persuasion and force makes it appear as if persuasion is the predominant feature. The movement was one based on rhetoric and style at first, only later becoming legal practice. Acceptance of the rhetoric led to institution building. By means of new apparatuses changes in the handling of civil cases came about, changes that functioned to suppress the realities of class, gender, and racial antagonisms in the United States, while affording efficiency and often cheaper dispute resolution for business. The image was of a reformed and informal law unfractured by power differences. In so far as it realized the opposite of its stated purpose, it was an unreal law reform movement.

For my research, the turning point was 1976, the year of the bicentennial celebration of the United States. During that year, the Roscoe Pound Conference, "Perspectives on Justice in the Future," was held in St. Paul, Minnesota, where Roscoe Pound delivered his long-remembered 1906 talk to the American Bar Association on "The Causes of Popular Dissatisfaction with the Administration of Justice." [29 A.B.A. 295 (1906)]. The Pound Conference brought together judges and staff from all of our fifty states in what became a key social drama, the beginning of a serious attack on the adversary process. The Conference was described as serving "to arouse a new spirit . . . a new optimism about the possibility of creative innovation in the administration of justice." The presenters were law-trained, and their messages covered the common theme of procedural reform from adversarial to alternative dispute resolution. . . .

In the years following the Pound Conference, the public was immersed in alternative dispute resolution rhetoric, which by the end of the decade had the quality of discursive cement. Chief Justice Warren Burger had set the tone for a change. In his work he was aided by members of the American judiciary, leaders of the American Bar Association, and the growing group of alternative dispute resolution professionals. The rhetoric was restricted and formulaic, and its users were assertive and repetitive. They made broad generalizations, invoked authority and danger, and presented values as facts. The Chief Justice warned that adversarial modes of conflict resolution were tearing the country apart, and that there had to be a better way. He claimed that Americans were inherently litigious, and that ADR was more civilized than the adversary process. His "Isn't There a Better Way?" speeches followed the peremptory style of assertive rhetoric, grounding the use of arbitration with reference to the time of Homer and Athenian law. Pointing to the early uses of arbitration, he said lawyers should be healers, rather than warriors, procurers, or hired guns. He also repeated that Americans were the most litigious people on the globe. During his time as Chief Justice, Burger continued to speak about lawyers as healers, and plaintiffs as patients needing treatment; there was little talk of rights, remedies, injustice, prevention, or unequal power.

The framework of a harmony law model took hold. Justice Burger was quoted as saying that "the nation was plagued with an almost irrational focus — virtually a mania — on litigation as a way to solve all problems." Although there was common sense in Burger's speeches, the fact that many of his declarations were not supportable did not seem to matter. There was a momentum building. The ideology of harmony began to be believed and to be institutionalized. By the late 1980s, the newspapers, the major political speeches, the evangelical radio stations, the latest insurance copy, all had some comment on the litigation explosion and anti-litigation. The rhetoric was part of the formula central to building a movement that would implement a harmony ideology of legal reform. It did not hurt that there was a close fit between the rhetoric, the ethic of Christian harmony, the interests of corporations in cutting legal fees, psychologists and other therapists, the woman's movement, and a myriad of vested interests. The harmony law model was for some anti-law, anti-confrontation, anti-anger, and for many a response to the "too many rights" movement. Furthermore, the ADR movement was being spearheaded by the Chief Justice of the U.S. Supreme Court.

III. THE CRITICS OF ADR

Critics of the alternative reform movement since the mid 1970s are abundant, many of them seeking to separate myth and rhetoric from substantiated evidence. Because there are summaries of the leading critical works elsewhere, let me simply say here that a number of critics provided evidence that challenged the assumptions of the Burger rhetoric. They compared the United States with other European industrial democracies and concluded that the U.S. system of justice had inadequate public investment. Half as much was spent per capita on U.S. courts than in West Germany from 1960 to 1973. Two widely influential articles questioned the assumption of a litigation explosion and concluded there was no litigation explosion despite noticeable perceptions. The same studies found that per capita use of regular civil courts in the U.S. was comparable to that of England, Australia, Denmark, and New Zealand, although somewhat higher than Germany and Sweden and far higher than Japan, Spain, and Italy. According to these and other studies, the "litigation explosion" is more folklore than fact.

Others asked what is so good about settlement or conversely, what is so bad about litigation? After all, written law represents important normative conclusions about substantive justice which ADR circumvents. Other critics follow the contours and broader significance of the change and ask, as did Richard Abel, "[i]s the ambit of state control contracting or expanding?" Consumers wrote outraged letters asking, when is arbitration really arbitration in referring to the conflict of interest when arbitration panels are sponsored, funded, and staffed by manufacturers and dealers. In many cases, the consumer was "complaining to Ford about Ford." Clearly, we need to differentiate more clearly when it is that we are improving dispute resolution and when we are being subjected to intimidation, because the more general finding is that successes in the field of alternatives are rare. . . .

When mediation becomes a process of communication, justice is measured by implicit standards of conformity and . . . issues of what is just become irrelevant. The potential plaintiff becomes the victim (or the patient), and the ethic of treatment prevails. Furthermore, treatment by means of mediation fictionalizes the conflict. The reformulation of disputes shifts attention from employer negligence in workers' compensation to the injured worker, in the context of a privatized justice. Other studies began to show that, with the exception perhaps of intracorporate cases, ADR processes were not being used as widely as they might be.

The hard sell stage was initiated to overcome public hesitancy and resistance to using ADR. ADR became mandatory in many states, and its ideology spread into the schools, therapy, business organizations, hospitals, and every level of American life from the living room to the board rooms, and even into the White House (where observers regularly praise presidents for harmonious or mediating styles, rather than for assertive leadership). Professors in universities are negatively measured on their level of contentiousness, as are workers in white collar jobs, irrespective of work performance. Both style and organizational changes are imbued with conformist ideology, intolerant of dissent, what I have called coercive harmony.

Cultural imperialism, the struggle for the control and the construction of ideas for mind colonization purposes, is normally difficult to track. But in the case of harmony law, it is easier to comprehend because much of what I describe is articulated in public spaces by means of professional and media formats. The Pound Conference was published and is now part of the public record. What has been less in the public eye is how it works, the "it" in this case referring to an ideology constructed with a practical purpose in mind. ADR was not meant to be abstract. A body of critical work dealt with whether and how real is the litigation explosion, or how great is the need for litigation. . . . In the examples that follow, the main features of selection have been hierarchy and "soft" violence (where the manufacture of consent induces a moral panic that covers up unequal power relations, such as between men and women or junior and senior partners). I speak here about the kind of indirect control that serves to make people mute or afraid or both. Such control is exquisite as a powerful silencing technique. . . .

IV. HOW ADR AND HIERARCHY WORK AS "SOFT" VIOLENCE: MEDIATION

When Chief Justice Warren Burger mentioned healing as more civilized behavior than contentiousness, he was, probably unwittingly, reiterating a European imperialist tradition that used a hierarchy of manners and public gesture to domesticate the subordinated and to insure the absence of contestation in the colonies. Burger's phrases might appear trivial at first, but socializing people to silence by means of culture is rarely trivial, especially in a democracy constructed around ideas of free, open, and untrammeled debate. The manner in which ADR exploded onto the national scene, and the rhetoric by which Justice Burger promoted ADR, was seductive. Who could be against harmony or civilized behavior or healing or efficiency? The appeal was to a broad audience, and many, especially women, were attracted to the soft or gentle aspects of an informal justice.

The women's movement of the 1970s and 1980s, replete with a rhetoric of equality and relationships, was attracted to contextual rather than rule-centered, abstract thought. Many women had voiced criticisms of the family court system in the United States as a forum that couldn't produce just results in a respectful and humane manner. Indeed, mediation was put forward as an alternative because it promised to be a feminist alternative to the patriarchally inspired adversary system. Mediation of family cases spread throughout the country and became mandatory in many states, including California.

In 1991, Trina Grillo, a law professor and mediator, published the first seething critique of mandatory mediation in relation to the inherently dangerous aspects of what she calls "process dangers" for women. The fact that her article appeared in the Yale Law Journal is important because of its visibility and prestige. Central to Grillo's critique is the relation of law to the promises of mediation in family disputes involving men, women, and the custody of their children. Grillo measures the promise of the form, in this case mediation, against real cases and not abstract rules and hypothetical cases. She also measures mediation against adversarial justice in court trials.

Mediation promised centrality accorded to context; it was to have a place for emotion as well as rationality, and the parties were supposed to participate in determining their future. However, Grillo's work is about how mediation operates as control, control in defining the problem, control of speech and expression, and control over public record. Mediation is a process that is confidential rather than public. Her analysis is both cultural and legal. She is pointed in her assessment of formal equality as a destroyer of social context and speaks of the destruction of rights that accompanies the limitation of discussion of fault and past facts in the case. She is most concerned with what happens when mediators frame cases between partners as equal control, when there is unequal responsibility. Important also are her observations on the suppression of anger in mediation sessions, especially the prohibitions on female anger. Grillo calls our attention to the notion of separateness that accompanies the expression of anger in a society where the idea of "the couple" prevails in definitions of male-female relations. Finally, she states that choice of process is sabotaged by forced engagement; she sees mandatory mediation as a dangerous environment within which patriarchy and prejudice can flourish.

Grillo's paper is brilliant because it requires a certain openness and brightness of mind to grasp indirect control patterns and to articulate their functioning. As noted earlier, Grillo is both a law professor and a mediator, but not everybody makes such a powerful argument against mandatory mediation, or for a mediation that meets the truth in advertising standard. The model she is attacking is less one of law than of therapy, for as she notes "[t]he movement for voluntary mediation of divorce disputes began several decades ago as lawyers and therapists offered to help their clients settle their cases in a nonadversarial manner." For the mediation movement, the point was not just to help clients, but to help them in a nonadversarial manner. It was the forum that attained first importance.

. . . Josh Rosenberg, also a law professor and mediator, writes a critique of Grillo's article called In Defense of Mediation. In his work, Rosenberg uses the same formulaic Burger rhetoric: "[m]ediation has won praise from the bar, from numerous participants and practitioners and from scholars as a tremendous breakthrough in dispute resolution." He uses metaphoric imagery in referring to "Grillo's horror stories," and a rhetorical trick to dismiss serious discussion of consequences: "[T]here is much in life that has the potential to do great damage."

Mandatory mediation abridges American freedom because it is often outside the law, eliminates choice of procedure, removes equal protection before an adversary law, and is generally hidden from view. The situation is much like that in psychotherapy, little regulation and little accountability. Mind control activities operate best in isolation, and those who have read the literature on influence understand that people in life crises are vulnerable to coercive influence. Divorce is one such life crisis. The mediation model described by Grillo is one belonging to the mental health professionals, so it is not surprising that the civil plaintiff becomes a patient.

The informal law of mediation is unwritten, which adds to the potential for abuse, and is for the most part unconsciously perceived. It is a process that often operates with the notion of moral minimalism "in which people prefer the least extreme reactions to offenses and are reluctant to exercise any social control against one another at all." Under such conditions, couples are treated as if they were equal and it becomes irrelevant whether one member had abused, deceived, or otherwise oppressed the other. Discussion of blame or rights is avoided and replaced by the rhetoric of compromise and relationship; cultural notions of justice are factored out. As Grillo says, mediation becomes a "mutually regulated dance between oppressor and oppressed," thereby obscuring issues of unequal social power.

In a manner that is gripping, Grillo describes the exercise of a technique which discourages people from asserting their rights when they have been injured. She reminds us that rights assertion cannot flourish when discussion of fault and the past are not permitted. A sense of disentitlement flattens the desire to seek redress. Like psychotherapy, the mediation model focuses on the individual, and assumes that the parties, as opposed to social ills, are responsible for all family problems. Flattening by insistence on formal equality is a subtle and powerful control because it is supported by American equality ideology.

It is assumed, for example, that both parents are equally competent to take care of the children because discussion of fault and past is limited. . . . The consequences can be devastating for both mother and child. Grillo notes, "[t]he insistence of a mother that a young child not be permitted to stay overnight with an alcoholic father who smokes in bed might be characterized as a mother needing to stay in control." Her observation that mediation does not take anger seriously enough is also arresting because today mainstream America assumes that anger is bad.

While there is in practice a possibility for the expression of anger in the adversarial context because anger is often a key component in the adversarial fight, in mediation sessions, expression of anger is discouraged and its suppression is particularly directed at women. Grillo finds this suppression destructive of energy needed for coping with crisis. Her discussion of the social prohibitions against female anger, particularly against women of color, are astute observations from one who understands . . . that there are limits to particular forums. In Grillo's work, she argues that there are limits to what one can accomplish with suppressing protest, or what conversely is possible from legitimate expression of anger. Suppression of anger often leads to individual paralysis, self- hatred, depression, or worse. Grillo's case against mandatory mediation is a case against mind colonization, or intense influence publicly condoned in private spaces. . . .

VII. CONCLUDING REMARKS

In conclusion, I return to the opening paragraphs. Why are members of the bench and bar so vulnerable to believing the rhetoric put forth by Chief Justice Warren Burger and his associates? Why did they not challenge his statements that the use of the courts is excessive or that Americans are too litigious or that informal justice is more just? While conceding that not all or maybe even most lawyers fell prey to the rhetoric, they were silent, and silence helped the drum beat along. The silence continues, in spite of refutation by legal scholars, the U.S. General Accounting Office, the Rodino Committee Report that showed no explosion of tort actions, Business Week, and the National Center for State Courts. Why have our lawyers and judges not corrected the record, when they see the business of their own courts being distorted and when they hear American companies speak as if the American judiciary were a part of the radical left? Many actually did believe the rhetoric, allowed it to prevail, and participated in its dissemination, but the answer goes beyond the hierarchical structures of our law schools and undemocratic corporate law firms.

Most certainly moral minimalism results from an absence of critical thinking, or perhaps it is a result of a profession in which individuals are trained to do but not to think; or from a population immersed in therapeutic modes of thought. The lack of critical thinking also has to do with the way in which lawyers use the concept of evidence, the meaning of which is antithetical to its use in the natural and behavioral sciences. Evidence is used to win, and not necessarily to find the "truth" about a case, to separate fact from fiction, to challenge basic assumptions. Thus, along with lessons in neutralizing emotions and moral issues an absence of critical use of evidence leads to the "pack" mentality; follow the herd becomes the rule.

Take, for example, the issue of medical malpractice and the notion that medical malpractice awards are out of control. The idea that juries are increasingly moving toward bigger jury awards, although asserted, is not supported by the empirical literature, which supports a picture of medical malpractice at substantial variance with both the popular press and law review articles. The Medical Malpractice Project at Duke University Law School does not support the criticisms leveled against juries in medical malpractice cases. . . .

The drum beat serves as a battering ram to reduce the rights of victims in order to sue perpetrators of harm and to pacify the public at large. . . . By itself, the concept of cultural control leads neither to explanation nor to understanding; there is no political or ideological institution which does not exercise control, nor is there indication in the phrase of who the agents of control are. Here Antonio Gramsci's idea of hegemony is useful in forcing us to look at the institutions through which dominant belief systems are transmitted. Concepts like the informal state, or economic government help us to visualize the motivation of organizations and professionals who seek control through pacification; but to understand pacification or the struggle for freedom and autonomy, empirical research might be useful.

In many American towns and cities, law avoidance and law aversion were important historically for community survival. Consensus and harmony were used by small religious and ethnic communities to survive in the culture at large. But the United States is no longer a place of isolated communities. Nevertheless, in planning the 1976 Pound Conference, Chief Justice Burger built an ethic out of nostalgic elements available in the culture at large and so developed a strategy that transformed the conflict of the 1960s and 1970s so that it did not effectively threaten opposing state and corporate interests, nor did it expose the corporate drive to restrict victims' rights through "tort reform."

The effectiveness of thought control is generally measured in relation to freedom from state coercion. People who use such terms as "manufacturing consent," as most recently Noam Chomsky, or "engineering of consent," are speaking about thought controls and mind colonization. Consent is not manufactured out of thin air; therein lies its power. It is pieced together from the culture at hand, and as David Noble put it in the title of his first book, it becomes America By Design. The examples articulated in this paper speak of a diverse group of people in the practice of law affected by intense influence or mind colonization. Some of these people are elites and considered powerful while some were in the category of litigant or subordinate worker. Intense influence is found at all levels. As we learned by comments from uncensored workers, there is still a critical sense at large, a "surprise factor." Without a critical sense in law, lawyers become commodities, unable to distinguish fact from fiction. Our vision of freedom atrophies while the. . . body of law and a legal education that recognizes the dangers of intense influence remains unrealized.

3. Carrie Menkel-Meadow, *The Many Ways of Mediation: The Transformation of Traditions, Ideologies, Paradigms, and Practices*, 1995 Negotiation J. 217, 233

LITIGATION ROMANTICISM

In my view, Laura Nader's otherwise superb anthropological work outside the United States seems somewhat shadowed, in the United States, . . . by a devotion to the "litigation romanticism" of her consumer activist brother, Ralph Nader. Litigation has its place — but how often has the "little consumer" really had an empowering democratic encounter in a courtroom with one of the three major car companies? The few exceptions do not illustrate the conditions for "ideal speech conditions" in a society of either formal legal participation or more local "popular justice." Individualized communication may not be the only way to empower communities. But, if we cannot learn to have conversations with one another, to define issues, discuss problems, express needs and rights at the individualized level, I do not understand how either mass movements or professionalized (lawyer-led) litigation will fare better.

4. Comments and Questions

a. Extensive parts of the Grillo and Rosenberg articles discussed by Professor Nader are reprinted in Chapter 8.

b. This is no place to tackle the arguments related to the severity and dimensions of the purported "litigation crisis," but it is worth pointing out some possible explanations for why participants in the debate keep talking past each other. All agree that there has been a dramatic increase in lawsuits filed at all levels of the federal courts, both in absolute numbers and per judge. The article by Judge Irving R. Kaufman, at Chapter 18, section B, provides some numbers, and he does not even discuss the U.S. Supreme Court. On that subject, *see* Peter L. Strauss, *One Hundred Fifty Cases Per Year: Some Implications of the Supreme Court's Limited Resources for Judicial Review of Agency Action*, 87 COLUM. L. REV. 1093 (1987).

However, the vast majority of litigation takes place in courts established pursuant to state law. What counts as litigation is another contentious issue. Does one count limited jurisdiction truibunals such as small claims courts and Justices of the Peace? What of adjudications by administrative agencies? The Social Security Admininstration alone processes some 1.3 million contested proceedings annually.

5. William Twining, *Alternatives to What: Theories of Litigation, Procedure and Dispute Settlement in Anglo-America Jurispurdence: Some Neglected Classics*, 56 MODERN L. REV. 380, 385-87 (1993)*

Llewellyn's Law-Jobs Theory and Some Successors

Karl Llewellyn's "law-jobs" theory . . . represents a relatively neglected part of his thought. [See especially Karl Llewellyn, *The Normative, the Legal and the Law-Jobs*, 49 YALE L.J. 1355 (1940).] It is relevant in the present context because it places dispute prevention and dispute settlement at the centre of a general sociological theory of law-government. The outline of the theory can be summarized as follows: All of us are members of groups, such as a family, a club, a teenage gang, a school or commercial organization, a trade union, a political party, a nation state, the world community. In order to survive and to achieve its aims, in so far as it has aims, any human group has to meet certain needs or ensure that certain jobs are done. The first, perhaps the most important, of these jobs is to channel behavior and expectations of members of the group in order to avoid conflicts or disputes within it. Second, when disputes arise, they have to be resolved or, at least, be kept at a tolerably low level, or else the group will disintegrate or its objectives will be frustrated or impaired. Third, as the circumstances of the group change, so the behavior and expectations of members of the group have to be adjusted to such changes in order to avoid conflicts and disappointments. Fourth, decision-making in the group needs to be regulated both in respect of who has power and authority to participate in decisions and in respect of the procedures by which decisions are arrived at. This allocation of authority and power is typically the primary function of a "constitution" of, for example, a club or a nation state. Fifth, in any group, but especially in complex groups, techniques, practices, skills and devices need to be developed for satisfactorily meeting the first four needs. Channelling behavior, settling disputes, making smooth adjustments to change and providing

*Reprinted with permission.

for acceptable ways of reaching decisions can often be difficult tasks, involving high levels of skill or quite refined or sophisticated devices and institutions.

First, the theory boldly claims to apply to all human groups, from a two-person unit (such as a motor-racing team or a one-parent family) to the world community. It includes submarines, prisons, clubs, tribes, villages and multinational corporations, and regional groupings as well as nation states. Controversy has surrounded how useful it is to treat all human groups as comparables, but in so far as one can ask certain standard questions about how disputes are avoided and handled in any group its claim to comprehensiveness is particularly significant. For example, it helps to free legal theory from focusing exclusively on the nation state and it thus provides a starting point for theories of legal pluralism and "non-state law."

Second, the theory provides one escape route from obsessive concern with the definition of law. For Llewellyn, "the institution of law-government" was the main, but not the only, institution specialized to performing the law jobs in those groups we choose to call societies; conversely, the law jobs are the main, but not the only, functions of that institution. In specific contexts for particular purposes, it may be useful to distinguish between the "legal" and "non-legal," but these are merely secondary issues of taxonomy. From this perspective it matters little whether, for example, the Kpelle moot, a university disciplinary committee, an Ifugao "go-between," a marriage guidance bureau, or a "rent-a-judge trial" are labelled as "legal" or not—they are all institutionalized dispute-processing mechanisms that can be compared and contrasted within a single framework.

Third, Llwellyn claimed that all of the law-jobs are essential to group survival and successful achievement of collective goals. But any particular task can bc done by a variety of means, singly or in combination. Dispute prevention in most societies, for example, is served by a complex mixture of formal and informal norms, education, rewards and incentives, hedges, barbed wire, physical force and other means of social control. Similarly, in any group, one should expect dispute settlement to be achieved by a variety of means. In a famous passage, Llewellyn summed up the basic insight, which he credited to Max Weber:

> The jobs to be done are jobs to be done: modern complexity of institution serves merely to highlight processes which require to be gone through, in some fashion, in any group. The jobs, therefore, get themselves done after some fashion always — or the group simply is no more. Hence if the officially announced imperatives fail to put themselves over, one must look elsewhere for the doing of the jobs . . . Hence to see a legal regulation which is not working is promptly to face a problem of further inquiry: What is working and how?

Finally, as this passage suggests, the law-jobs theory is a contextual theory which requires that any particular institution, device, "case" or other phenomenon should be viewed in the context of a larger whole. Any decision or event in a process such as litigation should be viewed in the context of the process as a whole. Thinking in terms of total pictures and total processes was part of the basic methodology of Llewellyn's realism. This leads naturally to one of the basic insights and truisms of modern dispute settlement theory: that in any given society only a tiny proportion of all disputes are likely ever to reach those institutions we choose to call "courts" or even those processes which might be included within the sphere of "litigation." A natural starting point for the consideration of any particular dispute settlement method or institution is a realistic demographic total picture of all disputes in the society or group and how they are presently being resolved. . . .

6. Comments and Questions

a. Such limited knowledge as American lawyers have about traditional "law ways" among indiginous American communities is likely come to from Karl N. Llewellyn & E. Adamson Hoebel, THE CHEYENNE WAY (1941). Llewellyn's work is summarized in Professor Twining's article. Hoebel was a distinguished anthropologist. They came together because Llewellyn recognized the central truth known to anthropologists: reasonable success in addressing disputes is a central task for any society or culture, else it will cease to exist.

b. Llewellyn's views about the role of disputes and disputing was stated succinctly in a speech to first year law students:

> What, then, is this law business about? It is about the fact that our society is honeycombed with disputes. Disputes actual and potential; disputes to be settled and disputes to be prevented; both appealing to law, both making up the business of the law. But obviously those which most violently call for attention are the actual disputes. . . . Actual disputes call for somebody to do something about them. First, so that there may be peace, for the disputants; for other persons whose ears and toes disputants are disturbing. And, secondly, so that the dispute may really be put to rest, which means, so that a solution may be achieved which, at least in the main, is bearable to the parties and not disgusting to the lookers-on. This doing something about disputes, this doing of it reasonably, is the business of the law.

Karl Llewellyn, THE BRAMBLE BUSH: ON OUR LAW AND ITS STUDY 12 (1930). Note the absence of any mention of a sovereign power, an army to enforce rules, or written law. The Llewellyn view of law is further explained in the Cheyenne Way (the fractured prose is vintage Llewellyn).

7. Karl N. Llewellyn & E. Adamson Hoebel, THE CHEYENNE WAY 20-22 (1941)

Law has as one of its main purposes to make men go around in more or less clear ways; law does in fact to some extent make men go round in more or less clear ways. Law purposes to channel behavior in such manner as to prevent or avoid conflict; and law does in important degree so channel behavior. Without the purpose attribute, law is unthinkable; without the effect attribute, law cannot be said to "prevail" in a culture, to have "being" in it.

But there is more to law than intended and largely effective regulation and prevention. Law has the peculiar job of cleaning up social messes when they have been made. Law thus exists also for the event of breach of law and has a major portion of its essence in the doing of something about such a breach. . . .

What has been said lays out three roads into exploration of the law-stuff of a culture. The one road is ideological and goes to "rules" which are felt as proper for channeling and controlling behavior. Students of ethics and legal philosophers are likely to call these felt standards for proper behavior "norms." . . . The second road is descriptive; it deals with practice. It explores the patterns according to which behavior actually occurs. The third road is a search for instances of hitch, dispute, grievance, trouble, and inquiry into what the trouble was and what was done about it. . . .

The three approaches are related; indeed they flow each into the other. For it is rare in a simple group or society that "norms" which are felt or know as the proper ones to control behavior are not made in the image of at least some of the actually prevalent behavior; and it is rare, on the other hand, that they do not to some extent become active in their turn and aid in patterning behavior further. . . .

The three approaches are thus related; nor can any of them be understood without the others. . . . [N]orms for conduct differ in quality and in power according as they do or do not coincide with the clearer practices of life. Practices, in turn, have variant meaning not only according to the degree, range, and sharpness of their existence, but according to the kind and power of norms which sustain or oppose them. Further, norms and practices alike take flavor from the frequency of breach and from the nature and regularity of what is done in case of trouble. . . . Even as what is done in trouble-cases draws inspiration, in its nature and in its extent, from what are known as practices or are felt as norms, so also what has been done in trouble-cases shapes later living in its image. The three, then, are intimately related.

Part II

Negotiation

Chapter 4

The Negotiation Process

CASE STUDY

(Adapted from *Woodruff v. Clark County Farm Bureau Coop.)*

Mr. Woodruff, who had been in the poultry business for fifteen years, sought to phase out his broiler business and begin raising chickens for the production of eggs. Representatives of the defendant, ("Farm Bureau") contacted him regarding the purchase of chickens from Farm Bureau. Woodruff met with them at two of Farm Bureau's facilities where he observed, and mentioned to them, that their flocks of chickens were in bad condition. He testified that Farm Bureau assured him on both occasions that he would get only the good chickens, and that the bad chickens would be culled. While at Farm Bureau he did not ask about vaccination or mortality rates because he had confidence in Farm Bureau and considered it customary for chicken farmers to vaccinate against coccidiosis while the chickens were young. Woodruff then orally agreed to purchase the chickens for $1.55 each. Thereafter, a delivery man brought 7,622 chickens to Woodruff, and both men culled over 1400 of the unacceptable chickens. At that time, Woodruff was advised that the chickens would develop in the proper manner, i.e., that they would "bloom out or straighten up and fly right."

Woodruff signed delivery receipts which contained disclaimers of warranties regarding freedom from disease and provided that the chickens were accepted "as is" unless culled and returned. He testified that the delivery man did not alert him to the disclaimer, he did not read the receipts and did not remember signing them. The new chickens began dying, and the Farm Bureau representatives who came to inspect them asked Woodruff if he was adding any coccidiosis treatment to the feed. Woodruff replied that they were too old for such treatment, and any reputable company would treat its chickens for coccidiosis before they are 22 weeks old. The Farm Bureau representatives then left (apparently hastily) without giving Woodruff any other information.

Woodruff's chickens continued to die, and eventually his business lost $45,000 in gross income because the chickens never exceeded 60% of production capability.

[Legal History: The trial judge granted Farm Bureau's motion for summary judgement because (1) Woodruff could have culled the unacceptable birds and sent them back before acceptance, and (2) based on the disclaimers in the receipts. The court of appeals reversed and remanded, holding (1) that warranties of merchantability and fitness for a particular purpose were implied as a matter of law under the U.C.C., (2) the disclaimers in the receipts were inadequate because they were not conspicuous and did not mention "merchantability," (3) material fact issues existed as to whether Farm Bureau had made express warranties, and (4) disclaimers are nullified to the extent they conflict with express warranties.]

A. Introduction

Just as we have been speaking prose most of our lives, we have been negotiating since we were small children. Much of our interaction with other people, whether face-to-face or through some other medium of communication, can be characterized as negotiation. Even if the scope of negotiation is limited to disputes and planning, this still covers much activity. The purpose of this chapter is to provide a framework for reflecting upon a form of activity with which you already have considerable experience, and to raise some of the issues and problems that arise in negotiation. Attention also is given to negotiation strategy. The objective is to improve both your understanding of negotiation, and your ability to put that knowledge to use.

The most fundamental concepts are the hardest to define, but a brief effort may be helpful. To negotiate means to discuss or meet about a present or potential question or problem. There are three essential elements:

1. Two (or more) parties;
2. The matter(s) under consideration; and
3. Interaction regarding a topic or topics.

A broader term, such as negotiation activity or behavior, includes related activities like preparation for a negotiation and taking action with respect to the matter under consideration.

Negotiation is the primary activity engaged in by attorneys and managers. Negotiation is the primary method used by managers, and even by lawyers, to address issues and solve problems. (Except in television shows, lawyers spend little time in court. Even full-time litigators spend 95 percent of their time in preparation for trials or appeals.)

The chapter begins with models of negotiation, which in turn sets the stage for a consideration of the environment in which negotiation takes place and strategies for success in negotiation. The search for "win-win" solutions is considered next, followed by an examination of barriers to settlement. The final section addresses the question of whether there are significant differences in negotiation behavior, or results achieved, between men and women.

B. Models of Negotiations

1. Comments and Questions

a. List the skills you think are necessary to effectively negotiate?

b. Outline your last three negotiations. How, if at all did you prepare for each of them?

c. What is your next negotiation opportunity? How will you apply knowledge about the process and theory of negotiation?

2. P. H. Gulliver, Disputes and Negotiations: A Cross-Cultural Perspective xiii-xv, 79-80, (1979)

Negotiation is one kind of problem-solving process — one in which people attempt to reach a joint decision on matters of common concern in situations where they are in disagreement and conflict. . . . In their disagreement or competition with each other, they neither seek the deciding judgment of a third party nor resort to the sheer force of violence against each other. Rather, by the exchange of information, they explore the nature and extent of their differences and the possibilities open to them, they seek to induce or persuade each other to modify their expectations and requirements, and they search for an outcome that is at least satisfactory enough to both parties. . . . [T]he outcome is frequently some kind of compromise. However, compromise is not at all inevitable: The negotiators may be able to discover some acceptable outcome that they had not originally conceived of or considered, which offers advantage to both of them. . . .

DISPUTES AND NEGOTIATIONS: KEY TERMS

A *dispute* begins when two parties become unable or unwilling to deal with problems and disagreement in their relationship by dyadic adjustment in private and when, therefore, one or both put the matter into a public domain. At that time, other people take cognizance and they become involved, as supporters, representatives, or third parties, in one or more meetings in some agreed arena. Some result, an *outcome,* is eventually reached. This may be positive agreement on some or all of the issues in dispute, but it may be a deadlock or an uncontrollable default by one party from which the outcome is the retention of the status quo.

Negotiations are processes of interaction between disputing parties whereby, without compulsion by a third-party adjudicator, they endeavor to come to an interdependent, *joint decision* concerning the terms of agreement on the issues between them. This joint decision is one that, in the end, is agreeable to and accepted by both parties after each has brought influence and persuasion to bear on the other and, most probably, after both have experienced influence from other sources. . . . It often represents a compromise between the parties' initial demands and expectations, but there may be, in part or whole, the joint creation of some new terms not originally conceived of by either party. The outcome reflects the relative strengths of the parties in terms of their resources of material and symbolic power and the constraints of moral and practical rules and values in the society.

Negotiations proceed through the *exchange of information* between the parties, and between them and third parties. Information is verbal and nonverbal, including evidence, argument, appeals to rules and ideology, expressions of strength and proposals of terms for agreement. This exchange permits a *learning* process by which each party formulates, modifies, and readjusts expectations, preferences, and proposals. In consequence, the parties are able to approach agreement on an outcome. . . .

Professor Gulliver, a Canadian anthropologist who has studied dispute settlement among many groups, notably the Warusha tribe in Tanzania, has developed a multiple-phase model of the negotiation process. He begins with a dispute; one might add one or more phases for gaining acknowledgement from both parties of the existence of a dispute that required their joint attention. Of course, the phases do not always take place in this order, and there is overlap among them. "Phase" is a better term than step precisely because the later is more suggestive of separation, while "phase" suggests imprecision at the edges, and overlap.

1. The search for an arena. A forum where negotiations can occur needs to be accepted. Addressing problems that are not easily resolved commonly involves one or more in-person meetings, but the forum could be the telephone or even the Internet.

2. Composition of agenda and definition of issues. While the parties have acknowledged the existence of a dispute, and are prepared to do something about it, there commonly is disagreement, or at least a lack of clarity about the agenda and issues.

3. Establishing maximal limits to issues in dispute. In this phase, the parties limit issues and stake out their positions. Gulliver makes a point of rejecting the proposition that this is the beginning of "real" negotiations, because negotiation over substance often takes place during the negotiation over ground rules for the negotiation.

4. Narrowing the differences. In this phase the parties come together, and differences are narrowed. The emphasis, and often the tone, shifts from differences and antagonism to coordination and even cooperation. The transition to this phase may be gradual or abrupt (as when one party makes a significant concession or the first realistic offer). Several strategies are commonly employed to narrow differences where multiple issues are outstanding:

(a) the simple agenda method;
(b) focus on the one or two most important issues;
(c) reduce issues to the attributes of a single objective;
(d) solve the less difficult issues; and
(e) trading and package deals.

The very fact of selecting one of these approaches will result in simplifying the issues and providing a focus to the negotiation.

5. Preliminaries to Final Bargaining. With the issues defined in scope and limited in number, the differences between the parties are more starkly revealed. This focusing process is a necessary predicate for serious bargaining. Such a sharpening of the issues sometimes will make the ultimate solution clear to the parties, whereupon they can proceed with relative ease to a final disposition. The opposite can occur as well, and it may be appreciated for the first time that a problem exists that cannot easily be compromised.

This stage encompasses other matters that must be addressed before a final bargain can be made. Much needed information is exchanged, and sub-issues are addressed. In a labor-management negotiation, for example, even if the basic wage rate has been agreed upon, there may still be issues about adjustments for different types of work, skill level, seniority, various types of overtime, holiday pay, productivity bonuses, etc. Formulas may be devised, and trade-offs made that bring the parties closer to agreement.

6. Final bargaining. This is when the parties close the deal, disposing of the few issues or problems that remain unsettled. [In a listing of negotiating steps, final bargaining seems to lead inevitably to a bargain, but it is well to remember the wisdom of that great American philosopher Lawrence G. (Yogi) Berra: "It ain't over till it's over."]

7. Ritual Affirmation. Rituals are grist for the mill of anthropologists, while they are an extra-legal irrelevance if not a distraction to lawyers. (In earlier days, rituals were of legal consequence, because the ritual was evidence of agreement.) The rituals best known in modern America are hand-shaking after a deal has been made, and kissing by spouses after the person presiding has declared them married. Religious ceremonies and parties are common, and in some instances gifts are given to commemorate the event. More dramatically, an agreement to end hostilities may be accompanied by the exchange of prisoners.

This model of negotiation, like the economist's model of a competitive market, is an "ideal-type;" it is not an operative description of what typically happens in human interactions, or a description of any particular interaction. Such models are useful in thinking about human behavior precisely because they filter out "noise," the variables of specific instances that can get in the way of thinking clearly about the process.

3. John S. Murray, *Understanding Competing Theories of Negotiation*, 1986 NEGOTIATION J. 179, 179-82*

Negotiation theorists appear to be deeply divided between proponents of competitive and problem-solving theories. . . . Many teachers—and most students—of negotiation are confused by the often polemical dialogue between opposing theorists. Adding to this confusion is the lack of precision with which theorists and practitioners use terms theory, strategy and style. Commentators representing separate disciplines have referred to many different negotiation theories and models:

1. competitive and coordinative;
2. competitive and cooperative;
3. adversarial and problem-solving;
4. hard, soft and principled;
5. distributive and integrative; and
6. functional and developmental.

Although these multiple references appear to sift naturally into the two competing camps that I am calling competitive and problem-solving, the confusion remains. Are there really two competing theories that explain realities in the negotiating setting? Should there be just one? If there are two, do the strategies that each favors necessarily conflict? What behavioral characteristics does each explain, and what are the downside risks that are hidden within each? . . .

The stereotypical competitive negotiator is a zealous advocate: tough, clever, thorough, articulate, unemotional, demanding, aggressive and unapproachable, . . . the type who achieves victory by defeating his opponent. The problem-solver is also thorough and articulate, but in addition: personable, cooperative, firm, principled, concerned about the other side's interests, and committed to fairness and efficiency. . . . Even terminology reflects the distance between the patterns. A competitive bargainer . . . negotiates **against** an opponent; a problem-solver negotiates **with** the other side. . . . Each of these views has a significant and distinct impact on the behavior of negotiators who accept it.

The competitive negotiator appears to have a narrow perspective on the negotiation as a whole, but broad and flexible standards for selecting strategies and manipulating the process. Competitive theory is reflected in behavior when the negotiator:

1. Maximizes own return in present transaction.
2. Considers needs/interests/attitudes of opponent as not legitimate, and only relevant when usable to achieve #1.

---

*Reprinted with permission.

3. Views all disputing processes and strategies as equally valuable and useful if helpful in achieving #1.
4. Behaves cooperatively only if it helps achieve #1.
5. Chooses processes and strategies similar to military maneuvers. The focus is on the process of winning, not the resolution of disputes.
6. Presents a strong defense against opponent's tactics.
7. Must control the negotiation process for proper manipulation.

The problem-solving negotiator, on the other hand, holds a broad perspective on the negotiation as a whole, combined with more rigid limits on strategy and conduct. Some of the key behavioral elements for the problem-solvers are:

1. Maximizes own return within the larger time and community context.
2. Considers needs/interests/attitudes of other side as both relevant and legitimate to resolving the dispute.
3. Is competitive but not antagonistic.
4. Tries to discover and share any joint gains available.
5. Concentrates on the substance of the dispute or decision.
6. Considers negotiation and other voluntary processes as superior to nonvoluntary methods (adjudication).

4. Comments and Questions

a. You should consider the questions raised by Murray about negotiation theories now, and then reconsider them after completing the chapters on negotiation.

b. The focus on winning and losing that is common to competitive negotiating is badly misplaced, according to those who prefer a predominantly problem-solving approach. Roger Fisher & William L. Ury, GETTING TO YES 154 (1981) conclude:

> In most instances to ask a negotiator "Who's winning?" is as inappropriate as to ask who's winning a marriage. If you ask that question about your marriage, you have already lost the most important negotiation—the one about what kind of game to play, about the way you deal with each other and your shared and differing interests.

Are you persuaded by the analogy of negotiating to a marriage? What are the major factors you considered in arriving at an answer?

c. Do you find the analogy between competitive negotiation and military tactics helpful? Is it persuasive?

d. Based on Murray's explanation of the two forms of negotiating behavior, which do you think he favors? Here is the final paragraph of the article (p. 186):

> The conclusion may be unavoidable that only the problem-solving theory satisfies all three quality standards for a general theory: it describes negotiation realities with reasonable accuracy, is useful in developing strategies, and provides consistently good outcomes for the competent negotiator. The recognizable competitive variant may just reflect different negotiator personality and style characteristics, and the quality and consistency of outcomes may depend partly on the relative levels of negotiator competence.

A statement that employs the qualifier "may" three times in two sentences is too hedged for evaluation. Absent those qualifiers, do you agree with Murray's conclusion, and why?

5. Carrie Menkel-Meadow, *Toward Another View of Legal Negotiation: The Structure of Problem Solving*, 31 UCLA L. Rev. 754, 760-762 (1984)*

The primary, but not exclusive, criterion for evaluation of a negotiation model is the quality of the solution produced. This includes the extent to which the process utilized contributes to or hinders the search for "quality" solutions. In elaborating on approaches to negotiation I shall consider the following criteria of evaluation:

1. Does the solution reflect the client's total set of "real" needs, goals and objectives, in both the short and the long term?
2. Does the solution reflect the other party's full set of "real" needs, goals and objectives, in both the short and long term?
3. Does the solution promote the relationship the client desires with the other party?
4. Have the parties explored all the possible solutions that might either make each better off or one party better off with no adverse consequences to the other party?
5. Has the solution been achieved at the lowest possible transaction costs relative to the desirability of the result?
6. Is the solution achievable, or has it only raised more problems that need to be solved? Are the parties committed to the solution so it can be enforced without regret?
7. Has the solution been achieved in a manner congruent with the client's desire to participate in and affect the negotiation?
8. Is the solution "fair" or "just"? Have the parties considered the legitimacy of each other's claims and made any adjustments they feel are humanely or morally indicated?

Criteria one through seven are all based on a utilitarian justification of negotiation. By satisfying these criteria, a negotiation may produce results which are more satisfactory to the parties, thus enhancing commitment to and enforcement of the agreement. The final criterion is applicable to those negotiators who wish to consider the effects of their solution on the other party from a humanitarian or ethical perspective.

C. The Negotiation Environment

1. David A. Lax & James K. Sebenius, The Manager as Negotiator 339 (1986)

THE MANAGER IS ALWAYS IN THE MIDDLE

Former Secretary of Labor John Dunlop once remarked that any bargain really involves three separate transactions: one across the table and one on each side of it. Making a deal with the "other" side is normally only part of the process; often the interplay with one's "own" side is as difficult or even more so. Straightforward dealings like collective bargaining or industrial procurement often place the manager in the familiar "middle" between the "internal" and "external" negotiations, that is, the linked bargains in and outside the organization. . . . A moment's thought, however, suggests that this same structure characterizes much of a manager's job as well. Inside hierarchies and within networks, the issues are linked, requiring negotiations that are at once "upwards and downwards," or "side to side."

---

2. Comments and Questions

a. As indicated by the last selection, in any moderately complex negotiation situation, there are three negotiations going on at once: that between the parties, and among the two parties being represented. Within a labor union, the younger workers are likely to be interested largely in present cash income, while older workers will be more concerned about health care and the retirement plan. Within a business, there may divergent opinions from the sales, credit, and legal departments. Can you identify other examples, from your personal experience or topics that you have studied in school?

b. An important backdrop for bargaining is the position taken by the legal system about a matter in dispute, so the bargaining is said to take place "in the shadow of the law." The next reading provides an in-depth examination of this insight. To what extent are the observations made in the divorce context applicable to business and employment negotiations?

3. Robert H. Mnookin and Lewis Kornhauser, *Bargaining in the Shadow of the Law: The Case of Divorce*, 88 Yale L.J. 950 (1979)*

This article suggests an alternative way of thinking about the role of law at the time of divorce. It is concerned primarily with the impact of the legal system on negotiations and bargaining that occur *outside* the courtroom. We see the primary function of contemporary divorce law not as imposing order from above, but rather as providing a framework within which divorcing couples can themselves determine their post-dissolution rights and responsibilities. This process by which parties to a marriage are empowered to create their own legally enforceable commitments is a form of "private ordering."

Available evidence concerning how divorce proceedings actually work suggests that a reexamination from the perspective of private ordering is timely. "Typically, the parties do not go to court at all, until they have worked matters out and are ready for the rubber stamp." Both in the United States and in England, the overwhelming, majority of divorcing couples resolve distributional questions concerning marital property, alimony, child support, and custody without bringing any contested issue to court for adjudication.

This new perspective and the use of the term "private ordering" are not meant to suggest an absence of important social interests in how the process works or in the fairness of its outcomes. The implicit policy questions are ones of emphasis and degree: to what extent should the law permit and encourage divorcing couples to work out their own arrangements? Within what limits should parties be empowered to make their own law by private agreement? What procedural or substantive safeguards are necessary to protect various social interests?

Nor is this perspective meant to imply that law and the legal system are unimportant. To divorcing spouses and their children, family law is inescapably relevant. The legal system affects *when* a divorce may occur, *how* a divorce must be procured, and *what* the consequences of divorce will be. Our primary purpose is to develop a framework within which to consider how the rules and procedures used in court for adjudicating disputes affect the bargaining process that occurs between divorcing couples *outside* the courtroom.

In this article we first examine the degree to which the law today authorizes private ordering at the time of divorce: to what extent can divorcing spouses create their own legally

---

*Reprinted by permission of The Yale Law Journal Company and Fred B. Rothman & Company.

enforceable commitments? In this context, we will also explain why we think the legal system should provide divorcing couples broad power to resolve the various questions that arise. Second, we develop a simple bargaining model to suggest how the legal system affects negotiations between spouses and their representatives at the time of divorce. Finally, we apply this framework to several issues that have dominated much of the academic discussion concerning family law during recent years: (1) the advantages and disadvantages of discretion-conferring legal standards for child custody; (2) Goldstein, Freud, and Solnit's proposed visitation standard; [omitted] (3) the role of lawyers in the divorce process; and (4) the role of courts in "undisputed" divorces.

I. PRIVATE ORDERING IN DIVORCE

A. Existing Limits on Private Ordering

A legal system might allow varying degrees of private ordering upon dissolution of the marriage. Until recently, divorce law attempted to restrict private ordering severely. Divorce was granted only after an official inquiry by a judge, who had to determine whether "appropriate grounds"—very narrowly defined in terms of marital offenses—existed. When a divorce was granted, the state asserted broad authority to structure the economic relationship of the spouses and to maintain regulatory jurisdiction over the children and their relationship to the parents. Doctrines such as collusion, connivance, and condonation were meant to curtail the degree to which parties themselves could bring about a divorce through agreement; the procedural requirements reflected the view that everyone was "a suspicious character." Obviously, the marital-offense regime could not, even at its most restrictive, eliminate collusion entirely. Some divorcing spouses worked things out for themselves and then (with their lawyers' help) staged a carefully rehearsed and jointly produced play for the court. Nevertheless, the legal system was structured to minimize private ordering.

Dramatic changes in divorce law . . . now permit a substantial degree of private ordering. The "no-fault revolution" has made divorce largely a matter of private concern. Parties to a marriage can now explicitly create circumstances that will allow divorce. Indeed, agreement between spouses is not necessary in most states; either spouse can unilaterally create the grounds for dissolution simply by separation for a sufficient period of time.

The parties' power to determine the consequences of divorce depends on the presence of children. When the divorcing couple has no children, the law generally recognizes the power of the parties upon separation or divorce to make their own arrangements concerning marital property and alimony. A spousal agreement may be subject to some sort of judicial proceeding—or, in England, submission to a Registrar—but on both sides of the Atlantic the official review appears to be largely perfunctory. In some American states a couple may make its agreement binding and final—i.e., not subject to later modification by a court.

In families with minor children, existing law imposes substantial doctrinal constraints. For those allocational decisions that directly affect children—that is, child support, custody, and visitation—parents lack the formal power to make their own law. Judges, exercising the state's *parens patriae* power, are said to have responsibility to determine who should have custody and on what conditions. Private agreements concerning these matters are possible and common, but agreements cannot bind the court, which, as a matter of official dogma, is said to have an independent responsibility for determining what arrangement best serves the child's welfare. Thus, the court has the power to reject a parental agreement and order some other level of child support or some other custodial arrangement it believes to be more desirable. Moreover, even if the parties' initial agreement is accepted by the court, it lacks finality. A court may at any time during the child's minority reopen and modify the initial decree in light of any subsequent change in circumstances. The parties entirely lack the power to deprive the court of this jurisdiction.

On the other hand, available evidence on how the legal system processes undisputed divorce cases involving minor children suggests that parents actually have broad powers to make their own deals. Typically, separation agreements are rubber stamped even in cases involving children. A study of custody in England suggests, for example, that courts rarely set aside an arrangement acceptable to the parents. Anecdotal evidence in America suggests that the same is true here.

The parents' broad discretion is not surprising for several reasons. First, getting information is difficult when there is no dispute. The state usually has very limited resources for a thorough and independent investigation of the family's circumstances. Furthermore, parents may be unwilling to provide damaging information that may upset their agreed arrangements. Second, the applicable legal standards are extremely vague and give judges very little guidance as to what circumstances justify overriding a parental decision. Finally, there are obvious limitations on a court's practical power to control the parents once they leave the courtroom. For all these reasons, it is not surprising that most courts behave as if their function in the divorce process is dispute settlement, not child protection. When there is no dispute, busy judges or registrars are typically quite willing to rubber stamp a private agreement, in order to conserve resources for disputed cases.

B. The Advantages of Private Ordering

Before proceeding further, we should make clear the reasons why we think the law should give divorcing spouses broad powers to make their own agreement. There are obvious and substantial savings when a couple can resolve distributional consequences of divorce without resort to courtroom adjudication. The financial cost of litigation, both private and public, is minimized. The pain of a formal adversary proceeding is avoided. Recent psychological studies indicate that children benefit when parents agree on custodial arrangements. Moreover, a negotiated agreement allows the parties to avoid the risks and uncertainties of litigation, which may involve all-or-nothing consequences. Given the substantial delays that often characterize contested judicial proceedings, agreement can often save time and allow each spouse to proceed with his or her life. Finally, a consensual solution is by definition more likely to be consistent with the preferences of each spouse, and acceptable over time, than would a result imposed by a court.

In divorces that involve no minor children, divorcing couples should have very broad powers to make their own arrangements; significant limitations are inconsistent with the premises of no-fault divorce. After all, who can better evaluate the comparative advantages of alternative arrangements than the parties themselves? Courts should not, of course, enforce agreements that reflect fraud or overreaching. Nor do we wish to minimize the importance of appropriate standards for alimony and marital property, for . . . these standards very much affect negotiated outcomes. Nonetheless, against a backdrop of fair standards, parties should be encouraged to settle these economic issues for themselves. The state should provide an efficient and fair mechanism for enforcing such agreements and for settling disputes when the parties are unable to agree.

When there are minor children, the state obviously has broader interests than simple dispute settlement. The state also has a responsibility for child protection. To acknowledge this responsibility, however, is not to define its limits. Indeed, the critical questions concern the proper scope of the child-protection function at the time of divorce and the mechanisms that best perform this function. . . .

[T]he actual determination of what is in fact in a child's best interest is ordinarily quite indeterminate. It requires predictions beyond the capacity of the behavioral sciences and involves imposition of values about which there is little consensus in our society. Thus, the fundamental question is: who gets to decide on behalf of the child? To what extent should the child's parents be given the freedom to decide between themselves how responsibility for their children is to be allocated following divorce?

We believe divorcing parents should be given considerable freedom to decide custody matters—subject only to the same minimum standards for protecting the child from neglect and abuse that the state imposes on *all* families. A negotiated resolution is desirable from the child's perspective for several reasons. First, a child's social and psychological relationships with both parents ordinarily continue after the divorce. A process that leads to agreement between the parents is preferable to one that necessarily has a winner and a loser. A child's future relationship with each of his parents is better ensured and his existing relationship less damaged by a negotiated settlement than by one imposed by a court after an adversary proceeding. Notions of child protection hardly justify general judicial suspicion of parental agreements; the state's interest in the child's well-being in fact implies a concomitant interest in facilitating parental agreement.

Second, the parents will know more about the child than will the judge, since they have better access to information about the child's circumstances and desires. Indeed, a custody decision privately negotiated by those who will be responsible for care after the divorce seems much more likely than a judicial decision to match the parents' capacities and desires with the child's needs.

If parents have the authority to decide custodial arrangements, there is no doubt that parents may make mistakes. But so may judges. More fundamentally, given the epistemological problems inherent in knowing what is best for a child, there is reason to doubt our capacity to know whether any given decision is a mistake. Therefore, the possibility that negotiated agreements may not be optimal for the child hardly can be a sufficient argument against a preference for private ordering. Moreover, because parents, not state officials, are primarily responsible for the day-to-day child-rearing decisions both before and after divorce, parents, not judges, should have primary authority to agree on custodial arrangements. This means that courts should not second-guess parental agreements unless judicial intervention is required by the narrow child-protection standard implicit in neglect laws. This is not to suggest that the state does not have an important responsibility to inform parents concerning the child's needs during and after divorce; nor does it mean that the state does not have an important interest in facilitating parental agreement. Nevertheless, the law in action, which acknowledges substantial parental power, seems preferable to existing doctrine, which imposes substantial restrictions on the parents' power to decide for themselves.

II. THE ELEMENTS OF A BARGAINING MODEL

Whether or not one accepts the desirability of private ordering, it is clear that most divorcing couples do not require adjudication of their disputes. It is therefore appropriate to analyze how the legal system affects the bargaining behavior of divorcing couples.

A. Doctrinal Divisions from a Bargaining Perspective

Legal doctrine separates the potential consequences of divorce into four distributional questions: (1) how should the couple's property—the stock of existing wealth owned separately or together—be divided? (marital property law); (2) what ongoing claims should each spouse have on the future earnings of the other? (alimony law); (3) what ongoing claims should a child have for a share of the earnings or wealth of each of his parents? (child-support law); and (4) how should the responsibilities and opportunities of child rearing be divided in the future? (child-custody and visitation law).

These four strands of law, and the procedural mechanisms for their implementation, are conventionally seen by legal commentators from a highly regulatory perspective. Analysis seems premised on the notion that the distributional consequences of divorce should be determined through judicial or administrative proceedings in which legal standards are imposed from above on the divorcing spouses. Moreover, it is generally assumed that the doctrinal boundaries between these four issues are clear.

Reexamination from the perspective of spouses who are negotiating their own settlements suggests three important conclusions. First, marital property, alimony, and child-support issues are all basically problems of money, and the distinctions among them become very blurred. Each can be translated into present dollar values. Although there are differences among the three with respect to termination and enforcement risks, the value of different bundles of the three elements can be compared. Second, custodial arrangements can often be divided in a wide variety of ways. Third, the money and custody issues are inextricably linked.

1. The Money Elements of the Bargain

a. Alimony and Child Support

From the economic perspective of bargaining spouses, alimony and child support seem fungible: both involve periodic money payments and, indeed, will often be paid by a single check from the noncustodial parent. A father may find it psychologically easier to pay child support, which will presumably only help his children, than alimony, which explicitly helps his former spouse. But this characterization hardly imposes much of a practical constraint. A custodial spouse is not required to keep track of how child-support money is spent, and the courts do not supervise child-support expenditures once a payment has been made. Even if a court were concerned with how transfer payments are spent, accounting would be extremely difficult. Many tangible goods and services in a family setting have some element of "joint consumption." For example, the custodial spouse and the child will generally share housing. This makes it impossible to provide high-quality housing for the child without also providing it for the custodial spouse. Similarly, it would be difficult and expensive to provide the custodian and child with different diets and different social milieux. Consequently, child-support payments that are used for housing and feeding the child will inevitably inure to the benefit of the custodial spouse.

Joint consumption may also create a normative dilemma with respect to alimony and child-support standards. Divorce or separation typically occasions an economic loss that must be borne by someone. Our legal and cultural norms reflect the notion that children should not bear the economic loss, and that, other things being equal, the spouses should bear the loss equally. Because joint consumption implies that the custodial parent and children must essentially share the same standard of living, a dilemma arises: either the children must bear some part of the economic loss, or the noncustodial parent must bear much more of the extra financial burdens imposed by divorce than the custodial spouse.

Financial provision for a spouse terminates automatically on remarriage or death, while child-support normally ends when a child reaches his majority or is emancipated. The parents will know how many years remain before a child will reach majority; however, there may be considerable uncertainty about the probability that a spouse who is receiving alimony will remarry. Therefore, the characterization of the elements of payments will probably affect a party's calculation of the risks concerning how long a payment will last and how easily it can be modified in the future. The characterization of the elements may also affect the tax consequences. However, the tax laws give divorcing spouses broad power to control by their own agreement the characterization, and hence tax consequences, of support payments. Presumably, each spouse is only interested in the risk-adjusted flow of his or her net income after taxes, taking into account the receipt or payment of interspousal money transfers. Thus, to the extent that the different consequences of alternative legal characterizations can be known and evaluated in advance, alimony and child support remain largely fungible for bargaining purposes.

b. Lump-Sum Payments versus Payments over Time

From a bargaining perspective, the more important distinction will be between a lump-sum transfer of money or property, which is typical of marital property, and payments over time, whether alimony, child support, or a combination of the two. Inflation aside, receiving $100 today is preferable for several reasons to receiving a promise of $10 each year for ten years. First, the present value of any stream of future payments must reflect a discount for the fact that the total amount is unavailable to invest or spend during the entire ten-year period. Second, when a recipient is receiving money over time, he or she faces the risk that the promise may be broken, or may be enforceable only at considerable expense. Periodic alimony or child-support payments thus pose risks of noncollection that are avoided by a lump-sum settlement. Finally, lump-sum and periodic transfers are taxed differently under the Internal Revenue Code.

Despite these important differences, it would not seem especially difficult during bargaining to convert lump-sum offers into offers involving flows over time. For any set of time preferences, one spouse can in principle convert a money flow over time into a present-value equivalent. Moreover, a recipient can always discount the value of a promise to reflect the perceived risks that the full amount may never be received. Finally, the tax consequences of alternatives can be evaluated and compared.

This ability to compare different packages has obvious implications for private bargaining, at least when the couple has sufficient economic resources. Sophisticated parties and their lawyers will attempt to seek out circumstances in which a different characterization, because of tax effects or differences in risk or time preferences of the parties, can make both spouses better off.

2. Custody

The remaining element of the bargain concerns the custodial duties and rights of the parents. By varying the time the child spends with each parent, and by assigning particular child-rearing tasks to one parent or the other, a divorce settlement may divide prerogatives in many different ways. . . .

3. The Relationship of Custody and Money

The preceding analysis suggests that, to a considerable degree, it is possible to reduce the concerns of divorce bargaining into two elements: money and custody. From a bargaining perspective, even these two elements are inextricably linked for two reasons: over some range of alternatives, each parent may be willing to exchange custodial rights and obligations for income or wealth, and parents may tie support duties to custodial prerogatives as a means of enforcing their rights without resort to court.

Economic analysis suggests that a parent may, over some range, trade custodial rights for money. . . . Suggesting the possibility of such trade-offs does *not* mean that the parent would be willing to relinquish all time with the child for a sufficiently large sum of money. Indeed, with a minimum level of resources, a parent may have a parallel minimum of custodial rights for the reduction of which no additional payment, however large, could be adequate compensation.

The negotiating process itself provides many opportunities for the parties to link money and custody issues. The most obvious opportunity exists in the context of enforcement of support or visitation. The legal system does not permit these connections in most states: in a suit brought to collect overdue support payments, a father cannot defend on the ground that his ex-wife did not permit visitation. Nor have courts permitted a custodial parent to cut off visitation because of a failure to pay support. Nevertheless, it is often time consuming and expensive to enforce promises in court. There can be substantial advantages, therefore, from the perspective of one or both bargainers, in having piecemeal bargains that spread support payments over time and, as a practical matter, link the custody issue, especially visitation, with the financial issues. If a father who values visitation fails to make support payments, then, quite apart from the mother's ability to enforce his promise in court (which may often be too slow and expensive to be effective), the mother may believe that she can retaliate by informally cutting off the father's visitation or making it more difficult. Even though this tactic has no legal validity, it is nevertheless likely to be faster, cheaper, and more effective than court enforcement. Similarly, a father may believe that his ability to cut off support will ensure that the mother will keep her word concerning visitation.

The links between support and visitation are nurtured not only by the parties' power to take self-help measures, but also by important cultural values. Many believe that support obligations and visitation rights are inextricably tied together in terms of what it means to be a parent. A father who fails to support his children, at least when he has the financial capacity to do so, may in popular perception no longer be entitled to maintain a relationship with his minor children if the custodial mother objects. Similarly, a mother who purposely prevents a father from maintaining his relationship with his children after a divorce may be viewed as no longer entitled to his support.

B. Toward a Theory of Divorce Bargaining

Ideally, a bargaining theory would allow us to predict how alternative legal rules would affect negotiations between particular spouses and the deal, if any, they would strike. Such a theory might be combined with knowledge of how the characteristics that determine bargaining behavior are distributed among divorcing couples. Alternative rules and procedures could then be compared by evaluating the patterns of bargains that would result under each. Unfortunately, no existing theory of bargaining allows confident prediction of how different legal rules and procedures would influence outcomes; nor is there much information about current patterns and outcomes of the bargaining process.

What follows is not a complete theory. Instead, we identify five factors that seem to be important influences or determinants of the outcomes of bargaining, and then offer some observations on the bargaining process. The factors are (1) the preferences of the divorcing parents; (2) the bargaining endowments created by legal rules that indicate the particular allocation a court will impose if the parties fail to reach agreement; (3) the degree of uncertainty concerning the legal outcome if the parties go to court, which is linked to the parties' attitudes towards risk; (4) transaction costs and the parties' respective abilities to bear them; and (5) strategic behavior.

1. Parental Preferences

Parental preferences vary with regard to money and child-rearing responsibilities. Ordinarily, economists assume that a person's tastes for most goods and services are insatiable: no matter how much a person has, he will see himself as better off with more. This is certainly a reasonably apt description of most people's taste for money; other things being equal, nearly everyone would prefer having more money to having less. This is not to say, of course, that people view the relative importance of money in the same way.

Preferences with regard to custody, however, probably vary a great deal more from person to person. Many individuals like spending time with their children and are willing to sacrifice a great deal in order to have child-rearing responsibilities. Sadly, some parents might pay a great deal to avoid child-rearing tasks altogether. There are also a wide variety of prerogatives and duties associated with child rearing, and parental preferences may vary among them. A parent may value very highly some tasks, like reading the child a bedtime story, and place negative value on others, like shopping for school clothes. Preferences may vary depending on how much custody a parent has; a parent will not necessarily prefer more. Some parents with limited child-rearing responsibilities may be willing to sacrifice money for additional custody up to a certain point; but once they have "enough" custody, they may be willing to give up money to avoid additional responsibility. For other parents, no amount of money can adequately compensate for a reduction in custody below a certain minimum level. Above that point, however, trade-offs between money and custody would be consistent with their tastes.

Informed bargaining requires a parent to assess accurately his or her own preferences concerning custodial alternatives. Yet the assessments are difficult and complicated. The information each parent has relates to the actual division of child-rearing tasks in an ongoing family. Dissolution or divorce inevitably alters this division, and the parent may discover new advantages or disadvantages to child-rearing responsibilities. Moreover, the parents' own needs may alter drastically after divorce. A parent interested in dating may find the child an intrusion in a way that the child never was during marriage. Additionally, a parent's interest in children may vary according to their age. Because children and parents both change, and changes may be unpredictable, projecting parental preferences for custody ten years into the future is a formidable task. Nevertheless, most parents have some self-awareness, however imperfect, and no third party (such as a judge) is likely to have better information about a parent's tastes, present or future.

Parental preferences, of course, will not generally be determined solely by self-interested judgments; a bargaining theory must take note of possible altruism or spite. One hopes that parental preferences reflect a desire for their children's happiness and well-being, quite apart from any parental advantage.

For example, a father may commit himself to child-support payments beyond what he predicts a court would require, simply because he does not want his children to suffer economic detriment from a divorce. A mother may agree to substantial visitation for the father because she thinks this is good for the children, even though she personally despises the father and wants nothing more to do with him. Similarly, either or both spouses may have preferences that attach great weight to the happiness and desires of their former spouse.

At the other extreme, one can easily imagine preferences that reflect spite and envy. A spouse may simply have a strong wish to punish the other spouse, regardless of the detriment to himself or to the children. An angry parent may engage in a protracted and largely hopeless custody fight, exhausting his financial reserves and bringing emotional torment to the children, simply to punish his spouse.

2. How Legal Rules Create Bargaining Endowments

Divorcing parents do not bargain over the division of family wealth and custodial prerogatives in a vacuum; they bargain in the shadow of the law. The legal rules governing alimony, child support, marital property, and custody give each parent certain claims based on what each would get if the case went to trial. In other words, the outcome that the law will impose if no agreement is reached gives each parent certain bargaining chips—an endowment of sorts.

A simplified example may be illustrative. Assume that in disputed custody cases the law flatly provided that all mothers had the right to custody of minor children and that all fathers only had the right to visitation two weekends a month. Absent some contrary agreement acceptable to both parents, a court would order this arrangement. Assume further that the legal rules relating to marital property, alimony, and child support gave the mother some determinate share of the family's economic resources. In negotiations under this regime, neither spouse would ever consent to a division that left him or her worse off than if he or she insisted on going to court. The range of negotiated outcomes would be limited to those that leave both parents as well off as they would be in the absence of a bargain.

If private ordering were allowed, we would not necessarily expect parents to split custody and money the way a judge would if they failed to agree. The father might well negotiate for more child-time and the mother for less. This result might occur either because the father made the mother better off by giving her additional money to compensate her for accepting less child-time, or because the mother found custody burdensome and considered herself better off with less custody. Indeed, she might agree to accept less money, or even to pay the father, if he agreed to relieve her of some child-rearing responsibilities. In all events, because the parents' tastes with regard to the trade-offs between money and child-time may differ, it will often be possible for the parties to negotiate some outcome that makes both better off than they would be if they simply accepted the result a court would impose.

3. Private Ordering Against a Backdrop of Uncertainty

Legal rules are generally not as simple or straightforward as is suggested by the last example. Often, the outcome in court is far from certain, with any number of outcomes possible. Indeed, existing legal standards governing custody, alimony, child support, and marital property are all striking for their lack of precision and thus provide a bargaining backdrop clouded by uncertainty. The almost universal judicial standard for resolving custody disputes is the "best interests of the child." Except in situations when one parent poses a substantial threat to the child's well-being, predicting who will get custody under this standard is difficult indeed, especially given the increasing pressure to reject any presumption in favor of maternal custody. Similarly, standards governing alimony and child support are also extraordinarily vague and allow courts broad discretion in disputed cases.

Analyzing the effects of uncertainty on bargaining is an extremely complicated task. It is apparent, however, that the effects in any particular case will depend in part on the attitudes of the two spouses toward risk—what economists call "risk preferences." . . .

4. Transaction Costs

Costs are involved in resolving the distributional consequences of separation or divorce, and in securing the divorce itself. The transaction costs that the parties must bear may take many forms, some financial and some emotional. The most obvious and tangible involve the expenditure of money. Professional fees—particularly for lawyers—must be paid by one or both parties. In addition, there are filing fees and court costs. More difficult to measure, but also important, are the emotional and psychological costs involved in the dispute-settlement process. Lawsuits generally are emotionally burdensome; the psychological costs imposed by bargaining (and still more by litigation) are particularly acute in divorce.

The magnitude of these transaction costs, both actual and expected, can influence negotiations and the outcome of bargaining. In the dissolution process, one spouse, and that spouse's attorney, can substantially affect the magnitude of the transaction costs that must be borne by the other spouse. As is generally the case, the party better able to bear the transaction costs, whether financial or emotional, will have an advantage in divorce bargaining.

In divorce, transaction costs will generally tend to be (1) higher if there are minor children involved, because of the additional and intensely emotional allocational issues to be determined; (2) an increasing function of the amount of property and income the spouses have, since it is rational to spend more on negotiation when the possible rewards are higher; and (3) higher when there is a broad range of possible outcomes in court.

5. Strategic Behavior

The actual bargain that is struck through negotiations—indeed, whether a bargain is struck at all—depends on the negotiation process. During this process, each party transmits information about his or her own preferences to the other. This information may be accurate or intentionally inaccurate; each party may promise, threaten, or bluff. Parties may intentionally exaggerate their chances of winning in the court in the hope of persuading the other side to accept less, or may threaten to impose substantial transaction costs—economic or psychological—on the other side. In short, there are a variety of ways in which the parties may engage in strategic behavior during the bargaining process.

Opportunities for strategic behavior exist because the parties often will not know with certainty (1) the other side's true preferences with regard to the allocational outcomes; (2) the other spouse's preferences or attitudes towards risk; and (3) what the outcome in court will be or even what the actual odds in court are. Although parents may know a great deal about each other's preferences for money and children, complete knowledge of the other spouse's attitudes is unlikely.

How do parties and their representatives actually behave during the process? Two alternative models are suggested by the literature: (1) a *Strategic Model,* which would characterize the process as "a relatively norm-free process centered on the transmutation of underlying bargaining strength into agreement by the exercise of power, horse-trading, threat, and bluff"; and (2) a *Norm-Centered Model,* which would characterize the process by elements normally associated with adjudication—the parties and their representatives would invoke rules, cite precedents, and engage in reasoned elaboration. Anecdotal observation suggests that each model captures part of the flavor of the process. The parties and their representatives do make appeals to legal and social norms in negotiation, but they frequently threaten and bluff as well.

C. The Task Facing the Spouses and the Process of Negotiation

The task facing divorcing spouses can be summarized, based on the preceding analysis, as one of attempting through bargaining to divide money and child-rearing responsibilities to reflect personal preferences. Even though the interests of the two parents may substantially conflict, opportunities for making both parents better off through a negotiated agreement will exist to the extent that parental preferences differ.

This analysis suggests why most divorcing couples never require adjudication for dispute settlement. The parties gain substantial advantages when they can reach an agreement concerning the distributional consequences of divorce. They can minimize the transaction costs involved in adjudication. They can avoid its risks and uncertainties, and negotiate an agreement that may better reflect their individual preferences.

Furthermore, divorcing spouses usually have no incentive to take cases to court for their precedential value. Unlike insurance companies, public-interest organizations, and other "repeat players," a divorcing spouse will generally have no expectation that an adjudicated case will create precedent, or that any precedent created will be of personal benefit in future litigation.

Given the advantages of negotiated settlements, why do divorcing spouses ever require courtroom adjudication of their disputes? There are a variety of reasons why some divorce cases will be litigated:

1. Spite. One or both parties may be motivated in substantial measure by a desire to punish the other spouse, rather than simply to increase their own net worth.

2. Distaste for Negotiation. Even though it costs more, one or both parties may prefer the adjudicative process (with third-party decision) to any process that requires a voluntary agreement with the other spouse. Face-to-face contact may be extremely distasteful, and the parties may not be able to negotiate—even with lawyers acting as intermediaries—because of distrust or distaste.

3. *Calling the Bluff—The Breakdown of Negotiations.* If the parties get heavily engaged in strategic behavior and get carried away with making threats, a courtroom battle may result, despite both parties' preference for a settlement. Negotiations may resemble a game of "chicken" in which two teenagers set their cars on a collision course to see who turns first. Some crack-ups may result.

4. *Uncertainty and Risk Preferences.* The exact odds for any given outcome in court are unknown, and it has been suggested that litigants typically overestimate their chances of winning. To the extent that one or both of the parties typically overestimate their chances of winning, more cases will be litigated than in a world in which the outcome is uncertain but the odds are known. In any event, when the outcome is uncertain, settlement prospects depend on the risk preferences of the two spouses.

5. *No Middle Ground.* If the object of dispute cannot be divided into small enough increments—whether because of the law, the practical circumstances, or the nature of the subject at issue—there may be no middle ground on which to strike a feasible compromise. Optimal bargaining occurs when, in economic terminology, nothing is indivisible.

These points can be illustrated through a simple example. Assume a divorcing couple has no children and the only issue is how they will divide 100 shares of stock worth $10,000. Let us further assume that it would cost each spouse $1,000 to have a court decide this issue, and that each spouse must pay his own litigation costs.

If the outcome in court were entirely certain, would the parties ever litigate? Suppose it were clear that a court would inevitably award one-half of the stock; to each spouse because it would be characterized as community property. If the issue were litigated, each spouse would end up with only $4,000. A spouse would therefore never accept a settlement offer of less than $4,000. One might expect that the parties would normally simply settle for $5,000, and save the costs of litigation. Taking the issue to court would substitute an expensive mode of dispute resolution—adjudication—for a cheaper mode—negotiation.

Even when the outcome in court is certain, litigation is still possible. A spouse might engage in strategic behavior and threaten to litigate in order to get more than half. Suppose the husband threatened to litigate unless the wife agreed to accept a settlement of $4,500. The wife might accept $4,500 but only if she believed the threat. She would know with proper legal advice that her husband would only end up with $4,000 if he litigated. Therefore the threat ordinarily would not be credible. She might call his bluff and tell him to sue. If the wife were convinced, however, that her husband was motivated by spite and in fact preferred to litigate rather than accept less than $5,500, she might accept $4,500. If the outcome in court is certain, then, absent spite, strategic behavior, or a distaste for negotiations, adjudication should not generally occur. . . .

What about cases in which the result in court is uncertain? Assume, for example, that there is a fifty percent chance that the husband will get all $10,000, and a fifty percent chance that the wife will get all $10,000. Settlement in these circumstances obviously depends on the risk preferences of the two spouses. If both are risk neutral, then both will negotiate the same way as they would if they knew for certain that a court would award each of them $5,000—the "expected" value of the litigation in this case.

To the extent that the parties are both risk-averse—each is prepared to accept less than $5,000 to avoid the risks of litigation—the parties have a broader range of possible settlements that both would prefer to the risks of litigation. This may facilitate agreement.

Conversely, if both parties are risk preferrers—each prefers the gamble to an offer of the expected value of $5,000—all cases are likely to be litigated. When one party is a risk preferrer and the other is risk-averse, it is difficult to predict the effect on the rate of litigation. In any negotiated outcome, a risk preferrer will have an advantage over the party who is risk-averse.

III. THE BARGAINING FRAMEWORK APPLIED

A. Custody Standards: The Rule/Discretion Debate Revisited

There has been considerable debate about the advantages and disadvantages of legal standards that confer broad discretionary power on decision-makers. But analysis has generally focused, both in the family law context and elsewhere, on the effects of discretion on the decision-making behavior of officials. We would like to suggest a different perspective, focusing on the implications of discretionary standards when they serve as the backdrop for out-of-court negotiations by the parties themselves.

The effect on the process of divorce bargaining of having more or less precise standards can be fruitfully explored by comparing and contrasting the effects of three different custody standards, each of which has proponents in current policy discussion:

1. A maternal-preference rule creates a strong presumption in favor of giving custody to a mother, with the father having limited visitation rights. Until recently, this was the dominant standard.
2. The best interests of the child standard calls for a highly individualized determination, confers broad discretion on the judge, and gives no automatic preference to either parent simply on the basis of the parent's or the child's sex. This standard seems to be the dominant one today. We will assume that ordinarily the parent who is awarded custody will have care and control of the child for all but two weekends a month, during which time the other spouse will have visitation rights.
3. A joint custody rule provides that in disputed cases each parent will have care and control of a child for half the time. Although it has been seriously proposed, no jurisdiction has adopted this rule.

Each of these three custody standards creates its own set of bargaining endowments. Because different rules give various amounts of bargaining chips to the parties, changing the standard would affect each party's relative bargaining power and would therefore influence the range and frequency of possible negotiated outcomes.

For example, if the legal standard were changed from a maternal-preference rule to a standard that gave no preference based on parental sex, then a father's chances of winning custody in a contested case would be improved. This in turn would affect the outcomes reached through negotiation, since it would generally increase the bargaining power of fathers as a class and decrease the bargaining power of mothers. Because of differences in parental preferences, however, not all fathers would end up with more child-time: some might simply pay less in alimony or child support. Thus, our analysis suggests that recent changes in custody law giving fathers more equal claims to custody, and in alimony law limiting the extent and availability of permanent alimony, have strengthened the relative bargaining power of husbands.

Both the best interests standard and the joint-custody rule are "neutral" as between the sexes; nevertheless, they have very different implications for bargaining. Under the best interests principle the outcome in court will often be uncertain: each spouse may be able to make a plausible claim for custody, and it may be impossible to predict how a court would decide a disputed case. Under the joint-custody standard, on the other hand, the parties both know what will happen in court: each will be responsible for the child half the time. Thus, comparison of these two standards allows us to explore further the effects of uncertainty on the bargaining process.

Uncertainty has several important effects on the relative bargaining power of the parties. As suggested earlier, if there is substantial variance among the possible court-imposed outcomes, the relatively more risk-averse party is comparatively disadvantaged. The important policy implications of this fact are illustrated by the following example.

Assume that both the parents would like to have custody. The father is risk-neutral; he would be indifferent if given a choice between (1) having custody of his child half the time; or (2) being exposed to adjudication under the best interests standard and having a fifty percent chance of winning full custodial rights and a fifty percent chance of only having visitation rights. The mother, on the other hand, we will assume is risk-averse; she would much prefer the certainty of half the child's time to the risk of adjudication with a fifty percent chance that she might end up only with visitation.

We would predict that under the best interests standard the mother, because she is risk-averse, will accept less in order to avoid the gamble inherent in adjudication. Both custody standards are "sex neutral," yet the best interests standard disadvantages a risk-averse parent and the joint-custody rule does not. The fact that uncertainty about the outcome in court concerning custody disadvantages the relatively more risk-averse parent is a peculiarly ironic and tragic result. Most of us would assume that a good parent would be unwilling to take a gamble in which one outcome would substantially diminish his or her relationship with the child. And yet the consequence of a vague, discretionary rule is to disadvantage such a parent if he or she is negotiating with a spouse who is more of a gambler.

Vague legal standards have other effects on the parties' relative bargaining power and on negotiations. Uncertainty about the outcome in court probably increases transaction costs. . . . It would also seem that vague legal standards give a relative advantage to the more able negotiator. As the dispersion among possible outcomes in court becomes wider, there will be a greater premium on bargaining skills, since there will be greater opportunities for strategic behavior and a wider range of possible negotiated outcomes that might leave a party better off than possible court-imposed outcomes. . . .

Evaluation of the joint-custody rule suggests another dilemma: a standard may have good characteristics as a background rule for private ordering but may nevertheless be unacceptable as a standard for adjudicating disputed cases. The advantages of the joint-custody rule from the perspective of bargaining are that it does not disadvantage the relatively risk-averse parent, reduces the scope for strategic behavior, and imposes lower transaction costs. Nevertheless, it would probably be disastrous to impose joint custody on the parties if they could not agree to it themselves, since joint custody normally requires a very high degree of parental cooperation. Without such cooperation, the substantial contact both parents would have with the child, and necessarily with each other, would create endless possibilities for antagonism between the parents, with predictably detrimental effects on the child's well-being. Ordering joint custody may be very much like carrying out Solomon's threat to cut the child in half. . . .

C. Lawyers in the Dispute Settlement Process

Private ordering suggests new perspectives on the role of lawyers in divorce. Lawyers perform a number of functions in the divorce process:

a. Source of information. Lawyers can provide the basic information about each spouse's bargaining endowment—the applicable legal norms and the probable outcome in court if the case is litigated. Indeed, as noted earlier, imprecision in the applicable legal standards increases one's need for legal advice. A rational client will want an accurate assessment of the possible costs of alternative modes of dispute settlement. Lawyers are also an important source of information about transaction costs, a major element of which will be legal fees.

b. Counselor. The lawyer may help the parties determine what their real interests are. Divorcing spouses may not have carefully examined the financial questions or their own preferences for childrearing responsibilities.

c. Clerk. To secure a divorce, even when there is no dispute, it is typically necessary for certain legal procedures to be followed and for various forms to be completed. To the extent the forms and the procedures are intricate, divorcing couples may require legal assistance even though there is no dispute whatsoever.

d. Negotiator. Lawyers can serve as negotiators with the other spouse or the other spouse's lawyer. Some parties may find negotiation extremely difficult, particularly given the anger and sense of guilt that often accompany divorce. Negotiators can be hired in the marketplace for legal services.

e. Litigator. When there is a dispute that must go to court, the lawyer has responsibility for marshaling and presenting relevant evidence and making the necessary legal arguments.

2. Evaluating the Lawyer's Role

If one accepts the proposition that the primary function of the legal system should be to facilitate private ordering and dispute resolution, then several important questions come into sharp focus. To what extent does the participation of lawyers facilitate dispute resolution? Are there fairer and less costly procedures in which lawyers would play a lesser role?

Many observers are very critical of the way some lawyers behave in divorce negotiations. Lawyers may make negotiations more adversarial and painful, and thereby make it more difficult and costly for the spouses to reach agreement. Indeed, lawyers may be more likely than lay people to adopt negotiating strategies involving threats and the strategic misrepresentation of their clients' true preferences in the hope of reaching a more favorable settlement for the client. . . . The participation of lawyers in the divorce process may on balance lead to more disputes and higher costs without improving the fairness of outcomes.

Yet, there are also arguments that lawyers facilitate dispute settlement. Lawyers may make negotiations more rational, minimize the number of disputes, discover outcomes preferable to both parties, increase the opportunities for resolution out of court, and ensure that the outcomes reflect the applicable legal norms.

In view of the critical role of lawyers and the disparate functions they may perform, it is startling how little we know about how lawyers actually behave. Obviously, lawyers are not all the same. Their styles and talents differ. Some lawyers are known within the profession as negotiators who strive to find middle ground acceptable to both sides; others are fighters who love the courtroom battle. Research could usefully explore how much specialization there is and, more importantly, the extent to which clients, when they are choosing a lawyer at the time of divorce, have any notion at all of their lawyers' skills or preferences for these various roles. More generally, systematic empirical research might illustrate how often, and in what circumstances, lawyers facilitate dispute settlement at the time of divorce, and how often, and in what circumstances, they hinder it.

This framework also suggests how timely it is to reexamine the question of why the legal profession should have a monopoly on these roles and the extent to which it does have such a monopoly. How well are lawyers trained to perform these various roles? Other professionals or paraprofessionals might serve some of these functions as well as lawyers at a substantially lower cost. This is most obviously the case when there is no dispute, and the attorney's role is essentially that of a clerk. . . .

E. The Role of Courts

Because divorce has become so widespread in this country, it is probably the most common occasion for ordinary citizens to interact with courts and the legal system. These contacts, to the extent they seem superfluous and unduly unpleasant, may contribute to public cynicism about law and its processes. Consideration of the issue from our perspective of private ordering highlights the need for general reform and gives specific support to the oft-asserted desirability of removing undisputed divorce cases from court dockets.

Obviously, the state should provide some mechanism for dispute settlement when the parties have not been able to agree. Having courts adjudicate disputed cases is certainly one plausible way to do this, although alternatives are possible. A striking feature of the present system, however, is the requirement that undisputed cases also pass through court. Every state requires a court proceeding as part of the divorce process, with a narrow exception in California.

This requirement is understandable from a historical perspective: it represented a regulatory mechanism to ensure that divorces were only granted in narrowly defined circumstances. Before the no-fault revolution, dispute settlement was not the primary function of divorce proceedings. The no-fault revolution has now empowered either spouse unilaterally to create the circumstances for divorce. Ironically, however, the shell of the same administrative and regulatory mechanism has been preserved. This regulatory mechanism comes at a high price. The requirement of a judicial proceeding probably imposes significant transaction costs, both public and private. . . .

The requirement of judicial review in all divorce cases involving children may, ironically, send inappropriate signals to parents at the time of divorce: it may suggest to them that because of the divorce they are no longer trusted to be adequate parents, and the state will now assume on an ongoing basis special responsibility for their children. Such signals are not only gratuitously insulting, but wrong: the state does not and cannot assume broad child-rearing responsibilities after divorce.

Conclusion

Viewing the process of divorce from the perspective of private ordering does not make previously intractable family law problems disappear. If anything, the world seems even more complex, since the analysis requires us to examine the effects of alternative rules and procedures on informal and formal bargaining about which we have little understanding. There now exists no bargaining theory that can yield accurate predictions of the expected outcomes with different legal rules, even when rational, self-interested parties are only negotiating over money issues. Divorce bargaining is often considerably more complex.

Given the absence of powerful theory or systematic data, this essay makes no claims to being definitive. It instead suggests a theoretical perspective that permits a broader analysis of the probable consequences of family law rules and procedures. It also more sharply exposes a set of questions of enormous social importance. If one accepts the proposition that the role of the legal system in determining the consequences of divorce should reflect an emphasis on dispute settlement, then the inadequacies of our current system are readily apparent. The analysis does not imply that the state should simply withdraw all resources from the process and leave it to the divorcing spouses to work things out on their own, unassisted by any professional help or legal protection. Instead, this inquiry should emphasize the desirability of learning more about how alternative procedural mechanisms might facilitate dispute resolution during a typically difficult and painful time in the lives of parents and children alike.

The perspective certainly has implications far broader than family law. Individuals in a wide variety of contexts bargain in the shadow of the law. Few automobile accident claims are ever tried; most are settled out of court. Criminal prosecutions are typically resolved by a plea bargain. Most administrative proceedings result in consent agreements rather than trials. In each of these contexts, the preferences of the parties, the entitlements created by law, transaction costs, attitudes toward risk, and strategic behavior will substantially affect the negotiated outcomes. Indeed, we hope this article will stimulate and encourage further work by others in a variety of contexts. Theoretical and empirical research concerning how people bargain in the shadow of the law should provide us with a richer understanding of how the legal system affects behavior, and should allow a more realistic appraisal of the consequences of reform proposals.

D. Strategies for Successful Negotiation

1. David A. Lax & James K. Sebenius, *Interests: The Measure of Negotiation*, 2 Negotiation J. 73 (1986)*

People negotiate to further their interests. And negotiation advisors urge attention to interests. . . . Yet the classic admonition to "know thyself" surely scoops any late twentieth century advice of this sort. . . . [N]egotiators often focus on interests, but conceive of them too nar-

*Reprinted with permission.

rowly; we will argue for a more expansive conception. . . . [I]nterests often conflict, so negotiators need ways to assess the relative importance of their various interests. . . .

As hard as it may be to sort out one's own interests, understanding how others see theirs — their subjective scheme of values are perceived through their peculiar psychological filters — can be extraordinarily difficult. Obviously, suggesting a stretch "in the other person's shoes" is good advice; equally obviously, it is only a starting point. . . .

GENERAL LESSONS FOR ASSESSING INTERESTS

In contrast to the apparent crispness of the issues, interests are often vaguer. There may be no apparent scale with which to measure say, precedent or organizational status. Yet the same logic that is useful for making issue tradeoffs can apply to assuring the relative impact of interests. The generic steps are as follows:

- Identify the interests that may be at stake.
- For each interest, imagine the possible packages that serve it best and worst; for example, imagine the range of precedents that might follow from the negotiation. This roughly defines the increment of value associated with each interest.
- The importance of each interest depends on the relative importance of its increment compared to those of the other interests; for example, how does the gain from the worst to the best possible precedent compare with the gain from the worst to the best possible monetary outcome?

The currency of negotiation generally involves positions on issues but the results are measured by how well underlying interests are furthered. As such, it is helpful constantly to shuttle back and forth between abstract interests and more specific issues, both to check for consistency and to keep real concerns uppermost in mind.

Finally, . . . a negotiator should constantly assess his counterparts' interests and preferences. Beyond various ways of trying to put oneself in the other's shoes, assessment of another's interests may be improved by investigating:

- Past behavior in related settings, both in style and substance.
- Training and professional affiliation: engineers and financial analysts will often have quite difference modes of perception and approaches to potential conflict from, say, lawyers and insurance adjusters.
- Organizational position and affiliation. Those in the production department will often see long, predictable manufacturing runs as the company's dominant interest while marketers will opt for individual tailoring to customer specs and deep inventories for rapid deliveries. This is another example of the old and wise expression "where you stand depends on where you sit."
- Whom they admire, whose advice carries weight, and to whom they tend to defer on the kind of issues at stake.

In the end, interests are bound up with psychology and culture.

ASSESSING WHICH INTERESTS ARE AT STAKE

- Beyond the obvious tangible interests that may be affected by issues to be discussed, consider subtler interests in reputation, precedent, relationships, strategy, fairness, and the like.

- Distinguish underlying interests from the issues under discussion and the positions taken on them.
- Distinguish between intrinsic and instrumental reasons for valuing interests, especially some of the subtler ones.
- In seeking to understand others' interests, remember that interests depend on perceptions, that perceptions are subjective, and thus that to assess interests is to probe psyches. This process can be aided by clear communication, the advice of third parties, role playing, and taking into account past behavior, training, professional affiliation, organizational position, as well as those to whom the others defer.
- Keep in mind that interests and issues can change on purpose or accidentally as the parties learn, events occur, or certain tactics are employed.

ASSESSING TRADEOFFS

- Tradeoffs are as important to interests as proportions are to recipes.
- To assess tradeoffs among intangible interests, it is sometimes helpful to imagine services one could buy otherwise to satisfy the same interests.
- To assess tradeoffs among issues:
  - — Specify the worst and best possible outcomes on each issue to define the possible increments.
  - — Compare the increments by thinking hard about underlying interests and which increments are most valued.
  - — Break the increments into smaller pieces and similarly compare their relative valuation.
  - — Change assessments as more is learned about how different positions on the issues affect interests.
  - — Assess interest tradeoffs using the same logic.

Negotiation is a process of potentially opportunistic interaction in which two or more parties with some apparently conflicting interests seek to do better by jointly decided action than they could otherwise. For evaluating alternatives and creating agreements, interests are the measure and raw material. The alternatives to negotiated agreement or what the parties could each do alone define the threshold of value that any agreement must exceed. The potential of negotiation is bounded only by the quality of the agreements that can be devised. The processes of negotiation are creating and claiming value. . . .

2. Donald G. Gifford, *A Context-Based Theory of Strategy Selection in Legal Negotiation*, 46 Ohio St. L.J. 41, 45-58 (1985)*

The type of negotiation strategy likely to yield the most favorable outcome for a client is an important question, because the attorney is professionally obligated to seek an advantageous result for her client in all negotiations. . . . This section defines the characteristics of three primary negotiation strategies and suggests that the negotiator's view of his relationship with the other party is the primary determinant that identifies each theory and distinguishes it from the others. The competitive negotiator seeks to force opposing party to a settlement favorable to

*Reprinted with permission.

the negotiator by convincing the opponent that his case is not as strong as previously thought and that he should settle the case. The cooperative strategy mandates that the negotiator make concessions to build trust in the other party and encourage further concessions on his part. The third strategy, integrative bargaining, seeks to find solutions to the conflict which satisfy the interests of both parties. . . .

A negotiation strategy is a separate and distinct concept from the negotiator's personal characteristics; a strategy is the negotiator's planned and systematic attempt to move the negotiation process toward a resolution favorable to his client's interests. Negotiation strategy consists of the decisions made regarding the opening bid and the subsequent modifications of proposals. Admittedly, strategy and personal style are frequently intertwined. A negotiator who has a "forceful, aggressive, and attacking" personal style frequently will succeed in causing an opponent to lose confidence in himself or his case thereby inducing substantial unilateral concessions, a goal of the competitive strategy. In another instance, however, a negotiator who is "courteous, personable, and friendly" may, through competitive strategic moves such as high opening demands and infrequent concessions, be even more successful in destroying the opponent's confidence in his case and inducing unilateral concessions from the opponent. Usually, a negotiator's personal characteristics positively correlate with his preferred negotiating strategy. Separating personal style and negotiation strategies, however, yields new flexibility for the negotiator. It is possible for negotiators with cooperative personal characteristics to adopt a competitive strategy when it would be advantageous, and naturally competitive individuals can adopt a cooperative strategy. Further, a negotiator should often make competitive, cooperative, and integrative moves within a single negotiation. If negotiation strategies are recognized as something distinct from the personal style of negotiators, then the essential elements of each strategy can be disseminated in writing and taught to prospective negotiators. Short of psychoanalysis, however, it might be difficult or impossible to transform a naturally "courteous, personable, and friendly" individual, even temporarily, into someone who is "attacking, forceful, and aggressive."

A. The Competitive Strategy

The competitive negotiator tries to maximize the benefits for his client by convincing his opponent to settle for less than she otherwise would have at the outset of the negotiation process. The basic premise underlying the competitive strategy is that all gains for one's own client are obtained at the expense of the opposing party. The strategy aims to convince the opposing party that her settlement alternative is not as advantageous as she previously thought. Competitive tactics are designed to lessen the opponent's confidence in her case, thereby inducing her to settle for less than she originally asked. The competitive negotiator moves "psychologically against the other person," with behavior designed to unnerve the opponent. Competitive negotiators expect similar behavior from their opponents and therefore mistrust them. In undermining their opponents' confidence, competitive negotiators employ a strategy which often includes the following tactics:

1. a high initial demand;
2. limited disclosure of information regarding facts and one's own preferences;
3. few and small concessions;
4. threats and arguments; and
5. apparent commitment to positions during the negotiating process.

A negotiator who utilizes the competitive strategy begins with a high initial demand. Empirical research repeatedly demonstrates a significant positive relationship between a negotiator's original demand and his payoff. A high initial demand conceals the negotiator's minimum settlement point and allows the negotiator to grant concessions during the negotiating process and still achieve a favorable result. The negotiator's opening position may also include a false issue—a demand that the negotiator does not really care about, but one that can be traded for concessions from the opponent during the negotiation. Generally, the more that the negotiator insists upon a particular demand early in the negotiation, the larger the concession that ultimately will be obtained from the opponent in exchange for dropping that demand. In addition, the opponent may have evaluated the negotiator's case more favorably than the negotiator has; a high demand protects the negotiator from quickly agreeing to a less favorable settlement than one which he might later obtain. If the demand is high but credible, the opponent's response to the demand may also educate the negotiator about how the opponent evaluates her own case.

The competitive negotiator selectively and strategically shares information with his opponent. He does not disclose the least favorable terms to which his client would agree, that is, his minimum reservation point. He prefers to obtain an even more favorable settlement in excess of his reservation point. If the negotiator reveals his reservation point too quickly, the opponent has no incentive to offer anything more than the reservation price. Therefore, the competitive negotiator carefully hides not only his reservation point, but also any information which would allow the opponent to determine his true reservation point. For example, in a criminal case, the prosecutor might conceal from the defense attorney information regarding her caseload, her familiarity with the case, her own vacation plans, and the attitude of the victim toward the case. Conversely, the competitive negotiator selectively discloses information which strengthens his case and which undermines the opponent's case. The competitive negotiator should also pursue tactics that glean information about his opponent's reservation price, his opponent's attitude toward the case, and specific facts about the case.

The competitive strategy of negotiations mandates that the party make as few concessions as possible. If a concession must be made, it should be as small as possible. The competitive negotiator makes concessions reluctantly, because concessions may weaken one's position through both "position loss" and "image loss." Position loss occurs because in most negotiations a norm exists against withdrawing a concession. Further, an early concession results in an opportunity loss for something that might have been extracted in exchange for the concession later in the negotiation process. Image loss occurs because after a concession, the opponent perceives that the negotiator is flexible; in the opponent's mind this may suggest that further concessions can be obtained. Obviously, however, concessions are generally an inevitable part of the negotiating process. Concessions made by a negotiator build an expectation of reciprocity and lead to further concessions by the opponent which bring the parties closer to agreement. Granting concessions prevents premature deadlock and impasse and maintains goodwill with the adversary. This may be necessary to complete the negotiations or to foster a continued cooperative venture in the future. When possible, the competitive negotiator seeks to create the illusion in his opponent's eye that he is making a concession without diminishing his own satisfaction. This is done by either conceding on an issue the negotiator does not care about or appearing to make a concession without really making one.

The competitive negotiator obviously strives to force his opponent into making as many and as large concessions as possible while he makes few concessions, small in degree. To force concessions from his opponent, he employs both arguments and threats. In negotiations, arguments are communications intended to persuade the opponent to draw logical inferences from known data. For example, a plaintiff's attorney might describe a favorable eyewitness account of a collision and ask the defense counsel to infer the probability that her client will be found liable. Arguments should suggest to the opponent that her case is weaker than she previously thought and, therefore, that she should make new concessions. A threat, on the other hand, is a communication intended to inform the opponent that unless she agrees to a settlement acceptable to the negotiator, the negotiator or his client will act to the opponent's detriment. For example, a union negotiator might threaten that the union will strike if management refuses to make wage concessions.

The competitive negotiator not only uses offensive tactics to force concessions from his opponent, but he also makes as few concessions as possible. The competitive negotiator ignores both arguments and threats, believing that this is the best response. When the negotiator must make a concession, the competitive strategist suggests that the negotiator give the opponent a "positional commitment," a reason why he is not conceding more. Without such a positional commitment, according to the competitive strategist, the opponent will perceive the grant of a concession as a weakness and will expect further concessions. The negotiator's resolve to concede nothing more can be substantiated by linking the concession to a principle, to the negotiator's personal reputation, or to a threat of ending negotiations.

To the extent that the success of a negotiation strategy is measured by the payoff in a single negotiation involving the division of limited resources between two parties, studies of simulated negotiations suggest that the competitive strategy yields better results than other strategies for the negotiator. However, the competitive strategy suffers severe disadvantages. The likelihood of impasse is much greater for negotiators who employ the competitive strategy than for those who use other approaches. Competitive tactics engender tension and mistrust between the parties, which can give the appearance that the parties are farther apart than they really are. These negative attitudes may carry over into matters other than the current negotiation and may make continuing relationships difficult.

B. The Cooperative Strategy

A view of human nature different than that upon which the competitive strategy is premised, with its emphasis on undermining the confidence of opposing counsel, underlies most collaborative interaction. In everyday events, even when they are deciding how to divide a limited resource between them, two negotiators often seek to reach an agreement which is fair and equitable to both parties and seek to build an interpersonal relationship based on trust. This approach to negotiation can be designated the cooperative strategy. The cooperative negotiator initiates granting concessions in order to create both a moral obligation to reciprocate and a relationship built on trust that is conducive to achieving a fair agreement.

The cooperative negotiator does not view making concessions as a necessity resulting from a weak bargaining position or a loss of confidence in the value of her case. Rather, she values concessions as an affirmative negotiating technique designed to capitalize on the opponent's desire to reach a fair and just agreement and to maintain an accommodative working relationship. Proponents of the cooperative strategy believe that negotiators are motivated not only by individualistic or competitive desires to maximize their own utilities, but also by collectivistic desires to reach a fair solution. Cooperative negotiators assert that the competitive strategy often leads to resentment between the parties and a breakdown of negotiations.

According to Professor Otomar Bartos, an originator of the cooperative strategy, the negotiator should begin negotiations not with a maximalist position, but rather with a more moderate opening bid that is both favorable to him and barely acceptable to the opponent. Once two such opening bids are on the table, the negotiators should determine the midpoint between the two opening bids and regard it as a fair and suitable outcome. External facts, such as how large a responsive concession the negotiator expects from the opponent, whether she is representing a tough constituency that would view large concessions unfavorably, and whether she is under a tight time deadline and wants to expedite the process by making a large concession, affect the size of the negotiator's first concession. According to Professor Bartos, the negotiator should then expect the opponent to reciprocate with a concession of similar size so that the midpoint between the parties' positions remains the same as it was after the realistic opening bids were made. The concessions by the parties are fair, according to Bartos, as long as the parties do not need to revise their initial expectations about the substance of the agreement.

The term cooperative strategy embraces a larger variety of negotiation tactics than Bartos' detailed model. Cooperative strategies include any strategies that aim to develop trust between the parties and that focus on the expectation that the opponent will match concessions ungrudgingly. Endemic to all cooperative strategies is the question of how the negotiator should respond if the opponent does not match her concessions and does not reciprocate her goodwill. The major weakness of the cooperative approach is its vulnerability to exploitation by the competitive negotiator. The cooperative negotiator is severely disadvantaged if her opponent fails to reciprocate her concessions. Cooperative negotiation theorists suggest a variety of responses when concessions are not matched. Professor Bartos recommends that the negotiator "stop making further concessions until the opponent catches up."

Because of its vulnerability to exploitation, the cooperative theory may not initially appear to be a viable alternative to the competitive strategy. As mentioned previously, in tightly controlled experiments with simulated negotiations, the competitive strategy generally produces better results. However, in actual practice, the competitive approach results in more impasses and greater distrust between the parties. Furthermore, most people tend to be cooperative in orientation and trusting of others. Professor Williams found that sixty-five percent of the attorneys he surveyed used a cooperative approach. This, of course, means that in a majority of cases the cooperative negotiator will not be exploited by her opponent, because the opponent also uses a cooperative approach. Most cooperative negotiators probably would not feel comfortable using the competitive negotiators' aggressive tactics, which are designed to undermine the opponent and his case. Nor would they relish living and working in the mistrustful milieu which may result from the use of the competitive strategy.

C. The Integrative Strategy

Both the competitive and cooperative strategies focus on the opposing positions of the negotiators—each negotiator attempts to achieve as many concessions from the other as possible. These concessions move the negotiations closer to an outcome favorable to the negotiator; however, each concession diminishes the opponent's satisfaction with the potential agreement. Integrative bargaining, on the other hand, attempts to reconcile the parties' interests and thus provides high benefits to both. Integrative bargaining is usually associated with a situation in which the parties' interests are not directly opposed and the benefit of one widget for one party does not necessarily result in the loss of one widget for the opponent. Instead, the parties use a problem-solving approach to invent a solution which satisfies the interests of both parties.

Integrative bargaining recently has received widespread attention as the result of; the publication of Professors Roger Fisher and William Ury's popular text, *Getting to Yes: Negotiating Agreement Without Giving In.* Professors Fisher and Ury's negotiation strategy is largely based on integrative bargaining theory, although it goes beyond integrative theory in important ways. The authors call their strategy principled negotiation and identify four basic points to this approach:

People: Separate the people from the problem.
Interests: Focus on interests, not positions.
Options: Generate a variety of possibilities before deciding what to do.
Criteria: Insist that the result be based on some objective standard.

The first point distinguishes integrative bargaining from both cooperative bargaining and competitive bargaining, according to Professors Fisher and Ury. The competitive bargainer believes that his relationship with the opponent is important, because he seeks to change the opponent's position through sheer willpower. The cooperative negotiator builds trust in order to reach a fair agreement. In contrast, Professors Fisher and Ury's principled negotiator attempts to separate the interpersonal relationship between the negotiators from the merits of the problem or conflict.

Professors Fisher and Ury's second and third points are the standard components of integrative bargaining theory. The negotiation dance of concession matching or positioning, which is a part of both competitive and cooperative behavior, often obscures the parties' real interests. A major component of integrative bargaining is the free exchange of information between the negotiators so that each party's motives, goals, and values are understood and appreciated.

Integrative bargaining attempts to locate a solution that satisfies both parties' respective interests. Professor Dean Pruitt, a social psychologist, identifies several types of integrative agreements. The most dramatic integrative solution emerges when the parties "brainstorm" and develop a new option that satisfies the significant needs of both parties. The second type of integrative bargaining is often referred to as "logrolling." In logrolling, each negotiator agrees to make concessions on some issues while his counterpart concedes on other issues; the agreement reconciles the parties' interests to the extent that the parties have different priorities on the issues. For example, a plea bargaining agreement might provide that the defendant will plead guilty to a felony, and the prosecutor will recommend that the defendant receive probation. Defendants are often most concerned with the possibility of imprisonment; the prosecutor, in a particular case, may care more about securing a felony conviction than she does about the defendant's sentence.

Another form of integrative bargaining is described by Professor Pruitt as "cost cutting." [Dean Pruitt, NEGOTIATION BEHAVIOR (1981).] A negotiator, in order to reach an agreement, may find ways to diminish the tangible or intangible costs to the opponent when the opponent accepts an agreement that satisfies the negotiator. For example, a management attorney who agrees to the wage demands of a certain type of worker might be concerned that in the future the union will expect similarly generous agreements for other workers. The union negotiator may reassure management that she understands that this wage agreement for certain employees stems from special circumstances, such as historical inequities, and that similar wage concessions should not be expected for other employees.

Several procedures facilitate reaching an integrative agreement. The free exchange of information and brainstorming efforts to invent options for mutual gains were discussed previously. In addition, the possibility of logrolling suggests that disputed issues should be considered simultaneously rather than sequentially. The negotiator should also develop a set of goals and other requirements in order to generate and screen alternative proposals. To the extent that the parties exchange negotiating proposals, the integrative negotiator should try to incorporate into his proposal some element of an opponent's previously suggested solution. Finally, the negotiator should continually alter his own proposal incrementally so he only gradually reduces the level of benefit to be realized by his client. This behavior is referred to by Professor Pruitt as "heuristic trial and error."

Traditional integrative bargaining strategy does not have universal applicability. The strategy is utilized most easily when the parties share a problem-solving orientation, and either an identifiable mutual gain option is available or multiple issues which can be traded off against one another exist. It is less useful when the parties disagree on only a single issue and the parties' interests are inherently opposed. Examples of situations that present direct conflicts include personal injury litigation and plea bargaining.

Professors Fisher and Ury urge the "principled negotiator" to insist upon a result based on objective criteria when the parties' interests seem to directly conflict and no mutually advantageous solution appears to be available. In this situation, they recommend the following steps:

1. Frame each issue as a joint search for objective criteria.
2. Reason and be open to reason as to which standards are most appropriate and how they should be applied.
3. Never yield to pressure, only to principle.

By stressing the desirability of reaching a fair decision, Professors Fisher and Ury appear to be borrowing from the principles of the cooperative strategists, especially from Professor Otomar Bartos. With this addition to traditional integrative bargaining, Professors Fisher and Ury claim to have found an "all-purpose strategy" that can be used in any negotiation regardless of the number of issues, the nature of the issues, or the orientation of the opposing party.

D. The Strategic Choice Model

The three negotiation strategies outlined above are not mutually exclusive; frequently a negotiator will use more than one strategy in a single negotiation. Some issues in a negotiation may lend themselves to an integrative approach, while others must be resolved through competitive or cooperative bargaining. Furthermore, most negotiations that begin with competitive approaches will culminate prior to agreement with either cooperative or integrative bargaining. Social psychologist Professor Dean Pruitt, in his strategic choice model of negotiation, recognizes that various negotiation strategies will be used in the same negotiation. The strategic choice model suggests that the negotiator must choose between engaging in competitive behavior, making a unilateral concession, and suggesting an integrative proposal at every point in the negotiation process. These alternative tactics correspond closely with the competitive, cooperative, and integrative strategies previously outlined.

Professor Pruitt further suggests that negotiations frequently will progress from a competitive stage to what he refers to as a coordinative stage. During the competitive stage, the negotiator tries to persuade the opponent to move toward the negotiator's position and to convince the opponent that the negotiator's own position is firm. Eventually, however, if the parties are to agree, they must engage in either cooperative or integrative bargaining. The competitive antagonism between the parties diminishes as each negotiator's own goals and expectations are tempered by realism; trust is engendered as the negotiators recognize that the opponent's expectations have also been lowered. At this point, the parties are psychologically ready to trade concessions or engage in problem-solving in order to resolve the conflict.

Often, competitive behavior and cooperative behavior alternate within a single negotiation or even occur simultaneously; different issues will be at varying stages of resolution, and agreements resulting from cooperative or integrative bargaining will often produce new issues to be resolved by the parties. Negotiators, however, cannot easily shift between competitive tactics and cooperative or integrative tactics in all instances. Successful competitive tactics, which attack the opponent and his case, jeopardize the positive working relationships necessary for the cooperative and integrative strategies. The combination of competitive strategies and cooperative or integrative strategies will typically occur only at different phases of a negotiation process or on easily separable and distinct issues. . . .

[In the remainder of the article, Professor Gifford applies his theory in several contexts. See Chapter 6, section C for his discussion of plea bargaining.]

E. The Search for "Win-Win" Solutions

1. Comments and Questions

a. Here we turn again to the dual theme of competition and cooperation, both of which are central aspects of negotiation. In view of the disparaging reaction to the work of Adam Smith represented by the Parable of the Commons and the Prisoner's Dilemma (see Chapter 3, section B), Smith must receive his due. There is no better example of the benefits of cooperation than the pin factory immortalized by Smith in the early pages of the Wealth of Nations.

b. The duality of creating value, and competing to obtain the largest share thereof, is called the negotiator's dilemma by Lax and Sebenius. A fundamental difficulty here is that seeking a larger share may impede the creation of potential wealth (increasing the size of the pie), while a focus on the creation of wealth may allow the other party to appropriate most of the wealth that has been created.

c. With this background, we are ready to consider the ideas embodied in the best known and best selling book about negotiation: Roger Fisher & William Ury, GETTING TO YES: NEGOTIATING AGREEMENT WITHOUT GIVING IN (1981). (A second, and expanded, edition was published in 1991, with Bruce Patton added as a co-author). In terms of the competing theories of negotiating discussed by Professor Murray in section B, above, Fisher and Ury favor integrative bargaining (synonyms include cooperative and problem-solving bargaining).

d. Professor Gifford's discussion of strategy selection in the previous section provides a summary of GETTING TO YES, so we turn directly to the most critical review received by the book, by Professor James J. White and the response by Roger Fisher. Whatever one thinks of the tone of White's review, his views are entitled to serious consideration. White is perhaps the leading commercial law scholar in America, and the co-author (with Harry Edwards) of the first casebook on negotiation.

e. Make a list of the areas of disagreement between White and Fisher & Ury. In each instance, who do you think has the better of the arguments?

2. Adam Smith, AN INQUIRY INTO THE NATURE AND CAUSES OF THE WEALTH OF NATIONS 4-5 (1776) (Penguin 1986)

To take an example . . . from a very trifling manufacture; but one in which the division of labour has been very often taken notice of, the trade of the pin-maker. A workman not educated to this business, nor acquainted with the machinery employed in it . . . could scarce, perhaps, with his utmost industry, make one pin in a day, and certainly could not make twenty. But in the way in which this business is now carried on, not only the whole work is a peculiar trade, but it is divided into a number of branches, of which the greater part are likewise peculiar trades. One man draws out the wire, another straights it, a third cuts it, a fourth points it, a fifth grinds it at the top for receiving the head; to make the head requires two or three distinct operations; to put it on is a peculiar business, to whiten the pins is another; it is even a trade by itself to put them into the paper; and the important business of making a pin is, in this manner, divided into about eighteen distinct operations, which, in some manufactories, are all performed by distinct hands, though in others the same man will sometimes perform two or three of them. I have seen a small manufactory of this kind where ten men only were employed, and where some of them consequently performed two or three distinct operations. But though they were very poor, and therefore but indifferently accommodated with the necessary machinery, they could, when they exerted themselves, make among them about twelve pounds of pins in a day. There are in a pound upwards of four thousand pins of a middling size. Those ten persons, therefore, could make among them upwards of forty-eight thousand pins in a day. Each person, therefore, making a tenth part of forty-eight thousand pins, might be considered as making four thousand eight hundred pins in a day. But if they had all wrought separately and independently, and without any of them having been educated to this peculiar business, they certainly could not each of them have made twenty, perhaps not one pin in a day; that is, certainly, not the two hundred and fortieth, perhaps not the four thousand eight hundredth part of what they are at present capable of performing, in consequence of a proper division and combination of other different operations.

3. David A. Lax & James K. Sebenius, THE MANAGER AS NEGOTIATOR (1986)

THE NEGOTIATOR'S DILEMMA: CREATING AND CLAIMING VALUE

. . . We assume that each negotiator strives to advance his interests, whether they are narrowly conceived or include such concerns as improving the relationship, acting in accord with conceptions of equity, or furthering the welfare of others. Negotiators must learn, in part from each other, what is jointly possible and desirable. To do so requires some degree of cooperation. But, at the same time, they seek to advance their individual interests. This involves some degree of competition.

. . . [C]ompetitive and cooperative elements are inextricably entwined. In practice, they cannot be separated. This bonding is fundamentally important to the analysis, structuring, and conduct of negotiation. There is a central, inescapable tension between cooperative moves to create value jointly and competitive moves to gain individual advantage. This tension affects virtually all tactical and strategic choice.

1. What precisely does it mean to create value? Where do joint gains really come from? What tactics are required to realize them?
2. What do we mean by claiming value? What tactics are appropriate?
3. If negotiation involves an inescapable tension between competitive and cooperative impulses, how can one manage it effectively?
4. Can't we manage this tension by separating the creating from the claiming? Why not do all the creating first and then just divide the cleverly created joint gains? Or, why not get the hard claiming out of the way and then try to find all the available joint gains? What other choices do we have?

4. James J. White, *Review Essay: The Pros and Cons of "Getting to YES" by Roger Fisher & William Ury*, 31 J. Legal Education 115 (1981)*

Getting to YES is a puzzling book. On the one hand it offers a forceful and persuasive criticism of much traditional negotiating behavior. It suggests a variety of negotiating techniques that are both clever and likely to facilitate effective negotiation. On the other hand, the authors seem to deny the existence of a significant part of the negotiation process, and to oversimplify or explain away many of the most troublesome problems inherent in the art and practice of negotiation. The book is frequently naive, occasionally self-righteous, but often helpful.

Initially, one should understand what the book is and what it is not. It is not a scholarly work on negotiation. . . . The book is not rigorous and analytical, rather it is anecdotal and informative. It does not add fundamentally to our understanding of the negotiation process. Rather it points to a need for change in our general conception of negotiation, and points out errors of emphasis that exist in much of the thinking about negotiation. The book's thesis is well summarized by the following passage:

> Behind opposed positions lie shared and compatible interests, as well as conflicting ones. We tend to assume that because the other side's positions are opposed to ours, their interests must also be opposed. If we have an interest in defending ourselves, then they must want to attack us. If we have an interest in minimizing the rent, then their interest must be to maximize it. In many negotiations, however, a close examination of the underlying interests will reveal the existence of many more interests that are shared or compatible than ones that are opposed (p. 43).

This point is useful for all who teach or think about negotiation. The tendency of those deeply involved in negotiation or its teaching is probably to exaggerate the importance of negotiation on issues where the parties are diametrically opposed and to ignore situations where the parties' interests are compatible. By emphasizing that fact, and by making a clear articulation of the importance of cooperation, imagination, and the search for alternative solutions, the authors teach helpful lessons. The book therefore provides worthwhile reading for every pro-

---

*Reprinted with permission.

fessional negotiator and will make sound instruction for every tyro.

Unfortunately the book's emphasis upon mutually profitable adjustment, on the "problem solving" aspect of bargaining, is also the book's weakness. It is a weakness because emphasis of this aspect of bargaining is done to almost total exclusion of the other aspect of bargaining, "distributional bargaining," where one for me is minus one for you. . . . [S]tudents of negotiation have long distinguished between that aspect of bargaining in which modification of the parties' positions can produce benefits for one without significant cost to the other, and on the other hand, cases where benefits to one come only at significant cost to the other. They have variously described the former as "exploring for mutual profitable adjustments," "the efficiency aspect of bargaining," or "problem solving." The other has been characterized as "distributional bargaining" or "share bargaining." Thus some would describe a typical negotiation as one in which the parties initially begin by cooperative or efficiency bargaining, in which each gains something with each new adjustment without the other losing any significant benefit.

Eventually, however, one comes to bargaining in which added benefits to one impose corresponding significant costs on the other. For example, in a labor contract one might engage in cooperative bargaining by the modification of a medical plan so that the employer could engage a less expensive medical insurance provider, yet one that offered improved services. Each side gains by that change from the old contract. Ultimately parties in a labor negotiation will come to a raw economic exchange in which additional wage dollars for the employees will be dollars subtracted from the corporate profits, dollars that cannot be paid in dividends to the shareholders.

One can concede the authors' thesis (that too many negotiators are incapable of engaging in problem solving or in finding adequate options for mutual gain), yet still maintain that the most demanding aspect of nearly every negotiation is the distributional one in which one seeks more at the expense of the other. My principal criticism of the book is that it seems to overlook the ultimate hard bargaining. Had the authors stated that they were dividing the negotiation process in two and were dealing with only part of it, that omission would be excusable. That is not what they have done. Rather they seem to assume that a clever negotiator can make any negotiation into problem solving. . . . To my mind this is naive. By so distorting reality, they detract from their powerful and central thesis.

Chapter 5, entitled "Insist on Objective Criteria," is a particularly naive misperception or rejection of the guts of distributive negotiation. Here, as elsewhere, the authors draw a stark distinction between a negotiator who simply takes a position without explanation and sticks to it as a matter of "will," and the negotiator who is reasonable and insists upon "objective criteria." Of course the world is hardly as simple as the authors suggest. Every party who takes a position will have some rationale for that position; every able negotiator rationalizes every position that he takes. Rarely will an effective negotiator simply assert "X" as his price and insist that the other party meet it.

The suggestion that one can find objective criteria (as opposed to persuasive rationalizations) seems quite inaccurate. . . . The distributive aspect of the negotiation often turns on the relative power of the parties. One who could sell his automobile to a particular person for $6,000 could not necessarily sell it for more than $5,000 to another person, not because of principle, but because of the need of the seller to sell and the different need of the two buyers to buy. To say that there are objective criteria that call for a $5,000 or $6,000 price, or in the case of a personal injury suit for a million dollars or an $800,000 judgment, is to ignore the true dynamics of the situation and to exaggerate the power of objective criteria.

Any lawyer who has been involved in a personal injury suit will marvel at the capacity of an effective plaintiff's lawyer to appear to do what the authors seem to think impossible, namely to give the superficial appearance of certainty and objectivity to questions that are inherently imponderable. For example, an effective plaintiff's lawyer will sometimes fix a certain dollar amount per week for the pain and suffering which one might suffer. He will then multiply that amount by the number of weeks per year and the number of years in the party's life expectancy. Thus he produces a series of tables and columns full of "hard" numbers. These have the appearance of objectivity, but in fact they are subjective, based (if on anything) on a judgment about how a jury would react to the case. Every lawyer who has ever been involved in a lawsuit in which experts have been hired by each side will have a deep skepticism about the authors' appeal to scientific merit as a guide in determining a fair outcome in the negotiation of any hotly disputed problem.

In short, the authors' suggestion in Chapter 5 that one can avoid "contests of will" and thereby eliminate the exercise of raw power is at best naive and at worst misleading. Their suggestion that the parties look to objective criteria to strengthen their cases is a useful technique used by every able negotiator. Occasionally it may do what they suggest: give an obvious answer on which all can agree. Most of the time it will do no more than give the superficial appearance of reasonableness and honesty to one party's position.

The authors' consideration of "dirty tricks" in negotiation suffers from more of the same faults found in their treatment of objective criteria. At a superficial level I find their treatment of dirty tricks to be distasteful because it is so thoroughly self-righteous. The chapter is written as though there were one and only one definition of appropriate negotiating behavior handed down by the authors.

Apart from the rather trivial concern about their self-righteousness, their discussion is troublesome because it discloses an ignorance of, or a disregard for, the subtleties involved in distinguishing between appropriate and inappropriate conduct in negotiation. There is no concession to the idea that certain forms of behavior may be acceptable within certain regional or ethnic groups; that Jews may negotiate differently than Quakers, or city people differently than those in the country. There is no recognition that the setting, participants, or substance may impose a set of rules. Rather a whole host of things labeled "dirty tricks, deliberate deception, psychological warfare, and positional pressure" are out of bounds. Consider their treatment of threats:

> Good negotiators rarely resort to threats. They do not need to; there are other ways to communicate the same information. If it seems appropriate to outline the consequences of the other side's action, suggest those that will occur independently of your will rather than those you could choose to bring about. Warnings are much more legitimate than threats and are not vulnerable to counter threats: "Should we fail to reach agreement, it seems highly probable to me that the news media would insist on publishing the whole sordid story. In a matter of this much public interest I don't see how we could legitimately suppress information. Do you?" (p. 143).

The statement which they approve (and label as a "warning" and not a "threat") would likely be construed as a threat. One who wishes to threaten his opponent in a negotiation is not likely to say, "If we do not reach agreement I will see to it that the information concerning your client becomes public." Rather he is likely to say what the authors suggest, "In a matter of this much public interest, I don't see how we could legitimately suppress information, do you?" In fact the authors have suggested merely a more subtle and more Machiavellian form of threat.

The question of deception is dealt with in the same facile way:

> Less than full disclosure is not the same as deception. Deliberate deception as to facts or one's intentions is quite different from not fully disclosing one's present thinking. Good faith negotiation does not require total disclosure. Perhaps the best answer to questions such as "What is the most you would be willing to pay if you had to?" would be along the following lines: "Let's not put ourselves under such a strong temptation to mislead. If you think no agreement is possible, and that we may be wasting our time, perhaps we could disclose our thinking to some trustworthy third party, who can tell us whether there is a zone of potential agreement." In this way it is possible to behave with full candor about information that is not being disclosed (p. 140).

The authors seem not to perceive that between "full disclosure" and "deliberate deception" lies a continuum, not a yawning chasm. They seem to ignore the fact that in one sense the negotiator's role is, at least passively, to mislead his opponent about his settling point while at the same time to engage in ethical behavior. Most who have engaged in significant negotiation will concede the tension between those two responsibilities. . . .

Finally, because the book almost totally disregards distributive bargaining, it necessarily ignores a large number of factors that probably have a significant impact on the outcome of negotiations. For example, Karrass and Ross suggest that a party's aspiration level is an important factor in determining the outcome of a negotiation, other things being equal. There is evidence that the level of the first offer, and the pace and form of concessions all affect the outcome of negotiation, yet there is no consideration of those matters. . . . No book of 163 pages can be expected to deal with every aspect of negotiation. . . .

Marvin Mindes identifies three prominent images of lawyers: hero, helper, and trickster. From Machiavelli onward much classical negotiating behavior could certainly be classified as trickster behavior, yet the trickster is the most pejorative of the various lawyer models. In a sense *Getting to YES* may be regarded as a plea for the recognition that a lawyer can be a good negotiator without deviating at all from his role as "helper." I believe that the authors are fundamentally mistaken about that. Anyone who would maximize his potential as a negotiator must occasionally do things that would cause others to classify him as a "trickster," whether he so classifies himself or not. To suggest that the world is otherwise is to mislead the reader. . . .

5. Roger Fisher, *Comment on James White's Review of "Getting to YES,"* 31 J. Legal Education 128 (1981)*

The editor has kindly invited me not to "respond" to Jim White's review, but rather to clarify areas of disagreement between us, and to suggest where my own thinking has changed since Bill Ury and I wrote *Getting to YES*. But for the editor's fortunate prohibition, there would be a tendency to react to a review that describes oneself or one's book as distasteful, self-righteous, not rigorous, not scholarly, distorting, and naive. Although I do not agree with those adjectives, I, too, see some inadequacies in the book. On the first day of my most recent negotiation course I tore a paperback copy in half to convince students how much work we had yet to do.

*Reprinted with permission.

Although clearer, I believe, than most books on negotiation, concepts such as "position" and "power" are not presented as precisely as they might be, nor is it made sufficiently clear how using objective criteria to talk about fairness can be combined with being an advocate. *Getting to YES,* however, is beyond recall. With twelve foreign editions and a third of a million copies in print, the book will have to take care of itself. Far more important is jointly working to improve our collective analysis and understanding of the negotiation process.

Different purposes? To some extent, I believe, White is more concerned with the way the world is, and I am more concerned with what intelligent people ought to do. One task is to teach the truth — to tell students the unpleasant facts of life, including how people typically negotiate. But I want a student to negotiate better than his or her father. I see my task as to give the best possible prescriptive advice, taking into account the way other human beings are likely to behave as well as one's own emotions and psychological state.

Suppose a husband and wife come to an expert in negotiation asking advice on how best to negotiate the terms of a separation agreement that will involve children and jointly-held property. What is the best advice that such an expert could give to both about the process — about the manner of negotiating that would be most likely to produce a wise and fair outcome while maximizing their ability to deal with future problems, and minimizing their costs in terms of time, resources, and emotional stress? If one of them alone asked for such advice, in what ways would wise recommendations differ? These are the questions I am interested in.

The world is a rough place. It is also a place where, taken collectively, we are incompetent at resolving our differences in ways that efficiently and amicably serve our mutual interests. It is important that students learn about bluffing and hard bargaining, because they will certainly encounter it. It is also important that our students become more skillful and wise than most people in dealing with differences. Thus, to some extent, White and I are emphasizing different aspects of what needs to be taught.

Are distributional issues amenable to joint problem solving? The most fundamental difference between White's way of thinking and mine seems to concern the negotiation of distributional issues "where one for me is minus one for you." We agree on the importance of cooperation, imagination, and the search for creative options where the task is to reconcile substantive interests that are compatible. White, however, sees the joint problem-solving approach as limited to that area. In his view, the most demanding aspect of nearly every negotiation is the distributional one in which one seeks more at the expense of the other. Distributional matters, in his view, must be settled by the ultimate hard bargaining. He regards it as a distortion of reality to suggest that problem solving is relevant to distributional negotiation.

Here we differ. By focusing on the substantive issues (where the parties' interests may be directly opposed), White overlooks the shared interest that the parties continue to have in the process for resolving that substantive difference. How to resolve the substantive difference is a shared problem. Both parties have an interest in identifying quickly and amicably a result acceptable to each, if one is possible. How to do so is a problem. A good solution . . . requires joint action.

The guts of the negotiation problem, in my view, is not who gets the last dollar, but what is the best process for resolving that issue. It is certainly a mistake to assume that the only process available for resolving distributional questions is hard bargaining over positions. In my judgment it is also a mistake to assume that such hard bargaining is the best process for resolving differences efficiently and in the long-term interest of either side.

Two men in a lifeboat quarreling over limited rations have a distributional problem. One approach to resolving that problem is to engage in hard bargaining. A can insist that he will sink the boat unless he gets 60 percent of the rations. B can insist that he will sink the boat unless he gets 80 percent of the rations. But A's and B's shared problem is not just how to divide the rations; rather it is how to divide the rations without tipping over the boat and while getting the boat to safer waters. In my view, to treat the distributional issue as a shared problem is a better approach than to treat it as a contest of will in which a more deceptive, more stubborn, and less rational negotiator will tend to fare better. Treating the distributional issue as a problem to be solved ("How about dividing the rations in proportion to our respective weights?" or "How about a fixed portion of the rations for each hour that one of us rows?") is likely to be better for both than a contest over who is more willing to sink the boat.

Objective criteria. It is precisely in deciding such distributional issues that objective criteria can play their most useful role. Here is a second area of significant disagreement. White finds it useful to deny the existence of objective standards: "The suggestion that one can find objective criteria (as opposed to persuasive rationalizations) seems quite inaccurate." To his way of thinking the only approach is for a negotiator first to adopt a position and later to develop rationalizations for it: ". . . every able negotiator rationalizes every position that he takes."

No one has suggested that in most negotiations there is a single objective criterion that both parties will quickly accept as determinative. The question is rather what should be treated as the essence of the negotiation, and what attitude should be taken toward arguments advanced in the discussion. White thinks it better to treat positions of the parties as the essence of the negotiation, and objective standards advanced by either party as mere rationalizations. That is one approach. A different approach is possible and, I believe, preferable.

Two judges, in trying to reach agreement, will be looking for standards that should decide the case. They may have their predispositions and even strongly-held views, but they will jointly look for an agreed basis for decision. Each will typically advance law, precedent, and evidence not simply as rationalizations for positions adopted for other reasons, but honestly, as providing a fair basis for decision. White's example of litigation is the very one I would advance to demonstrate that, however great the disagreement, the wise approach is to insist upon using objective criteria as the basis for decision. It is better for the parties in court to be advancing objective standards which they suggest ought to be determinative than to be telling the court that they won't take less (or pay more) than so many dollars. The same, I believe, is true for negotiators.

Two negotiators can be compared with two judges, trying to decide a case. There won't be a decision unless they agree. It is perfectly possible for fellow negotiators, despite their self-interest, to behave like fellow judges, in that they advance reasoned arguments seriously, and are open to persuasion by better arguments. They need not advance standards simply as rationalizations for positions, but as providing a genuine basis for joint decision.

What we are suggesting is that in general a negotiator should seek to persuade by coming up with better arguments on the merits rather than by simply trying to convince the other side that he is the more stubborn. A good guideline is for a negotiator to advance arguments as though presenting them to an impartial arbitrator, to press favorable bases for decision, but none so extreme as to damage credibility. (On the receiving side, a good guideline is for a negotiator to listen to arguments as though he were an impartial arbitrator, remaining open to persuasion despite self-interest and preconceptions.) My experience suggests that this method is often more efficient and amicable than hard positional bargaining and more often leads to satisfactory results for both parties.

Power. White seems to find the concept of "raw power" useful for a negotiator. I do not. For a negotiator, the critical questions of power are (1) how to enhance one's ability to influence favorably a negotiator on the other side, and (2) how to use such ability as one has. My ability to exert influence depends upon the cumulative impact of several factors: skill and knowledge, the state of our relationship, the legitimacy of our respective interests, the elegance of a proposed solution, my willingness and ability to commit myself, and the relative attractiveness to each side of its best alternative. In advance of a negotiation I can work to enhance each of those elements. During a negotiation I can orchestrate my use of these factors so that they reenforce and augment each other, or I can use some elements in ways that undermine others. Unless I am careful, a threat to use "raw power" will weaken rather than enhance my total ability to influence the other side, since it is likely to deprive me of knowledge, damage a relationship, and undercut my legitimacy.

Incidentally, I consider warnings (of what it will be in my interest to do, or of what will happen independent of my action) to be not simply a more Machiavellian form of threat. Being more legitimate than a threat (of harm I could cause you), a warning tends to exert more influence.

Deception. White correctly calls attention to the difficult issue of ethical behavior, where disclosure of what a negotiator would be willing to do if he or she had to in order to reach agreement would be damaging to self-interest. The problem is particularly acute if the substance of the negotiation is haggling over positions—over statements of what one is willing or unwilling to do. With such positional bargaining in mind White sees the negotiator's role as being "to mislead his opponent about his settling point while at the same time to engage in ethical behavior."

I believe White fails to appreciate the extent to which the ethical problem is reduced if instead of negotiating by making a series of offers and counteroffers (each often intended to deceive the other as to what one is really willing to do), one treats negotiation as a joint search for an appropriate objective basis for decision, taking into account legitimate interest. If one tries to persuade the other side on the merits, as one would try to persuade an arbitrator, the rewards for — and need for — misleading are far less.

Changed thinking. Getting to YES says "Don't Bargain Over Positions." [T]here are categories of negotiations where positional bargaining is the best way to proceed. On single-issue negotiations among strangers where the transaction costs of exploring interests would be high and where each side is protected by competitive opportunities, haggling over positions may work better than joint problem solving. A typical case would be negotiating a sale on the New York Stock Exchange.

Another chapter heading, "Separate the People from the Problem," also puts the matter too broadly. In some cases the people are the problem; negotiating a good relationship with them may be more important than the substantive outcome of any one negotiation. And good relations can ease future substantive negotiations. I still think that relationship issues and substantive issues should be separated to the following extent: One should not threaten a relationship as a means of trying to coerce a substantive concession; nor should one make an otherwise unjustified concession in hopes of buying a good relationship.

Getting to YES as a whole, I believe, blurs a desirable distinction between descriptive analysis and prescriptive advice. Descriptively, it sorts facts into useful categories: positions vs. interests; people issues vs. substantive ones; inventing vs. deciding; discussing what negotiators will or won't do vs. discussing what they ought to do. Those distinctions, like distinctions between reptiles and mammals, or between short snakes and long snakes, are objectively true and, despite possible difficulties in drawing lines, exist as facts in the real world. Whether or not they are useful is another question.

We go beyond suggesting these descriptive categories by advancing some prescriptive rules of thumb, indicated by the chapter headings in the book. These are not advanced as guidelines that will in every case produce the desired result. No such guidelines can exist, since negotiators who deal with each other often desire different results. The rules of thumb we advanced are the best we could come up with. Without knowing the particular subject matter of a negotiation or the identity of the people on the other side, what is the best advice one can give to a negotiator? People may prefer to ask different questions, but I have not yet heard better answers to the question on which we were and are working.

F. Barriers to Settlement

1. Comments and Questions

a. The following speech by Professor Mnookin considers the application of game theory, economic analysis, agency theory, and psychology to negotiation. These topics should be familiar from the readings in Chapter 3, but here these ideas are applied to the specific context of negotiation.

b. To what extent are the observations made by Mnookin specific to negotiation, and to what extent are more broadly applicable to other dispute settlement contexts?

c. For each of the barriers discussed by Mnookin, consider what might be done in actual negotiation contexts to address the barrier? (Telling people they are being irrational or foolish is almost never a useful approach.)

2. Robert H. Mnookin, *Why Negotiations Fails: An Exploration of Barriers to the Resolution of Conflict*, 8 Ohio St. J. On Disp. Resol. 235 (1993)*

I. INTRODUCTION

Conflict is inevitable, but efficient and fair resolution is not. Conflicts can persist even though there may be any number of possible resolutions that would better serve the interests of the parties . . . . In our everyday personal and professional lives, we have all witnessed disputes where the absence of a resolution imposes substantial and avoidable costs on all parties. Moreover, many resolutions that are achieved — whether through negotiation or imposition — conspicuously fail to satisfy the economist's criterion of Pareto efficiency. . . . Why is it that under circumstances where there are resolutions that better serve disputants, negotiations often fail to achieve efficient resolutions? In other words, what are the barriers to the negotiated resolution of conflict?

---

*Reprinted with permission.

II. BARRIERS TO THE NEGOTIATED RESOLUTION OF CONFLICT

. . . I will explore four such barriers. Each of these barriers reflect somewhat different theoretical perspectives on negotiation and dispute resolution. The first barrier is a strategic barrier, which is suggested by game theory and the economic analysis of bargaining. The barrier relates to an underlying dilemma inherent in the negotiation process. Every negotiation characteristically involves a tension between: (a) discovering shared interests and maximizing joint gains, and (b) maximizing one's own gains where more for one side will necessarily mean less for the other. The second barrier arises as a result of the principal/agent problem. In many disputes, principals do not negotiate on their own behalf but instead act through agents who may have somewhat different incentives than their principals. This work draws on research concerning the "principal/agent" problem in law and economics and transaction cost economics. The third barrier is cognitive, and relates to how the human mind processes information, especially in evaluating risks and uncertainty. My discussion here draws on recent work in cognitive psychology, especially the pathbreaking research of Amos Tversky and Daniel Kahneman. The fourth and final barrier, "reactive devaluation," draws on the social psychological research of . . . Lee Ross, and relates to the fact that bargaining is an interactive social process in which each party is constantly drawing inferences about the intentions, motives, and good faith of the other. . . .

[M]y purpose is to show that the concept of barriers provides a useful and necessarily interdisciplinary vantage point for exploring why negotiations sometimes fail. After describing these four barriers and their relevance to the study of negotiation, I will briefly suggest a variety of ways that neutral third parties might help overcoming each of these barriers.

A. Strategic Barriers

The first barrier to the negotiated resolution of conflict is inherent in a central characteristic of negotiation. Negotiation can he metaphorically compared to making a pie and then dividing it up. The process of conflict resolution affects both the size of the pie, and who gets what size slice.

The disputants' behavior may affect the size of the pie in a variety of ways. On the one hand, spending on avoidable legal fees and other process costs shrinks the pie. On the other hand, negotiators can together "create value" and make the pie bigger by discovering resolutions in which each party contributes special complementary skills that can be combined in a synergistic way, or by exploiting differences in relative preferences that permit trades that make both parties better off. Books like "Getting to Yes" and proponents of "win-win negotiation" emphasize the potential benefits of collaborative problem-solving approaches to negotiation which allow parties to maximize the size of the pie.

Negotiation also involves issues concerning the distribution of benefits, and, with respect to pure distribution, both parties cannot be made better off at the same time. Given a pie of fixed size, a larger slice for you means a smaller one for me.

Because bargaining typically entails both efficiency issues (that is, how big the pie can be made) and distributive issues (that is, who gets what size slice), negotiation involves an inherent tension — one that David Lax and James Sebenius have dubbed the "negotiator's dilemma." In order to create value, it is critically important that options be created in light of both parties' underlying interests and preferences. This suggests the importance of openness and disclosure, so that a variety of options can be analyzed and compared from the perspectives of all concerned. However, when it comes to the distributive aspects of bargaining, full disclosure — particularly if unreciprocated by the other side — can often lead to outcomes in which the more open party receives a comparatively smaller slice. To put it another way, unreciprocated approaches to creating value leave their maker vulnerable to claiming tactics. On the other hand, focusing on the distributive aspects of bargaining can often lead to unnecessary deadlocks and, more fundamentally, a failure to discover options or alternatives that make both sides better off. A simple example can expose the dilemma. . . . [It] involves what game theorists call "information asymmetry." This simply means each side to a negotiation characteristically knows some relevant facts that the other side does not know.

Suppose I have ten apples and no oranges, and Nancy Rogers has ten oranges and no apples. (Assume apples and oranges are otherwise unavailable to either of us.) I love oranges and hate apples. Nancy likes them both equally well. I suggest to Nancy that we might both be made better off through a trade. If I disclose to Nancy that I love oranges and don't eat apples, and Nancy wishes to engage in strategic bargaining, she might simply suggest that her preferences are the same as mine, although, in truth, she likes both. She might propose that I give her nine apples (which she says have little value to her) in exchange for one of her very valuable oranges. Because it is often very difficult for one party to know the underlying preferences of the other party, parties in a negotiation may puff, bluff, or lie about their underlying interests and preferences. Indeed, in many negotiations, it may never be possible to know whether the other side has honestly disclosed its interests and preferences. I have to be open to create value, but my openness may work to my disadvantage with respect to the distributive aspect of the negotiation.

Even when both parties know all the relevant information, and that potential gains may result from a negotiated deal, strategic bargaining over how to divide the pie can still lead to deadlock (with no deal at all) or protracted and expensive bargaining, thus shrinking the pie. For example, suppose Nancy has a house for sale for which she has a reservation price of $245,000. I am willing to pay up to $295,000 for the house. Any deal within a bargaining range from $245,000 to $295,000 would make both of us better off than no sale at all. Suppose we each know the other's reservation price. Will there be a deal? Not necessarily. If we disagree about how the $50,000 "surplus" should be divided (each wanting all or most of it), our negotiation may end in a deadlock. We might engage in hardball negotiation tactics in which each tried to persuade the other that he or she was committed to walking away from a beneficial deal, rather than accept less than $40,000 of the surplus. Nancy might claim that she won't take a nickel less than $285,000, or even $294,999 for that matter. Indeed, she might go so far as to give a power of attorney to an agent to sell only at that price, and then leave town in order to make her commitment credible. Of course, I could play the same type of game and the result would then be that no deal is made and that we are both worse off. In this case, the obvious tension between the distribution of the $50,000 and the value creating possibilities inherent in any sale within the bargaining range may result in no deal.

Strategic behavior — which may be rational for a self-interested party concerned with maximizing the size of his or her own slice — can often lead to inefficient outcomes. Those subjected to claiming tactics often respond in kind, and the net result typically is to push up the cost of the dispute resolution process. . . . Parties may be tempted to engage in strategic behavior, hoping to get more. Often all they do is shrink the size of the pie. Those experienced in the civil litigation process see this all the time. One or both sides often attempt to use pretrial discovery as leverage to force the other side into agreeing to a more favorable settlement. Often the net result, however, is simply that both sides spend unnecessary money on the dispute resolution process.

B. The Principal/Agent Problem

The second barrier is suggested by recent work relating to transaction cost economics, and is sometimes called the "principal/agent" problem. . . . The basic problem is that the incentives for an agent (whether it be a lawyer, employee, or officer) negotiating on behalf of a party to a dispute may induce behavior that fails to serve the interests of the principal itself. The relevant research suggests that it is no simple matter — whether by contract or custom — to align perfectly the incentives for an agent with the interests of the principal. This divergence may act as a barrier to efficient resolution of conflict.

Litigation is fraught with principal/agent problems. In civil litigation, for example — particularly where the lawyers on both sides are being paid by the hour — there is very little incentive for the opposing lawyers to cooperate, particularly if the clients have the capacity to pay for trench warfare and are angry to boot. Commentators have suggested that this is one reason many cases settle on the courthouse steps, and not before: for the lawyers, a late settlement may avoid the possible embarrassment of an extreme outcome, while at the same time providing substantial fees. . . . [Principal-agent problems are discussed at greater length in Chapter 3, section D.]

C. Cognitive Barriers

The third barrier is a by-product of the way the human mind processes information, deals with risks and uncertainties, and makes inferences and judgments. Research by cognitive psychologists during the last fifteen years suggests several ways in which human reasoning often departs from that suggested by theories of rational judgment and decision making. Daniel Kahneman and Amos Tversky have done research on a number of cognitive biases that are relevant to negotiation. . . . I [will] focus on two aspects of their work: those relating to loss aversion and framing effects.

Suppose everyone attending this evening's lecture is offered the following happy choice: At the end of my lecture you can exit at the north end of the hall or the south end. If you choose the north exit, you will be handed an envelope in which there will be a crisp new twenty dollar bill. Instead, if you choose the south exit, you will be given a sealed envelope randomly pulled from a bin. One quarter of these envelopes contain a $100 bill, but three quarters are empty. In other words, you can have a sure gain of $20 if you go out the south door, or you can instead gamble by choosing the south door where you will have a 25% chance of winning $100 and a 75% chance of winning nothing. Which would you choose? A great deal of experimental work suggests that the overwhelming majority of you would choose the sure gain of $20, even though the "expected" value of the second alternative, $25, is slightly more. This is a well known phenomenon called "risk aversion." The principle is that most people will take a sure thing over a gamble, even where the gamble may have a somewhat higher "expected" payoff.

Daniel Kahneman and Amos Tversky have advanced our understanding of behavior under uncertainty with a remarkable discovery. They suggest that, in order to avoid what would otherwise he a sure loss, many people will gamble, even if the expected loss from the gamble is larger. Their basic idea can be illustrated by changing my hypothetical. Although you didn't know this when you were invited to this lecture, it is not free. At the end of the lecture, the doors are going to be locked. If you go out the north door, you'll be required to pay $20 as an exit fee. If you go out the south door, you'll participate in a lottery by drawing an envelope. Three quarters of the time you're going to be let out for free, but one quarter of the time you're going to be required to pay $100. . . . What do you choose? There's a great deal of empirical research, based on the initial work of Kahneman and Tversky, suggesting that the majority of this audience would choose the south exit — i.e., most of you would gamble to avoid having to lose $20 for sure. Kahneman and Tversky call this "loss aversion."

Now think of these two examples together. Risk aversion suggests that most of you would not gamble for a gain, even though the expected value of $25 exceeds the sure thing of $20. On the other hand, most of you would gamble to avoid a sure loss, even though, on the average, the loss of going out the south door is higher. Experimental evidence suggests that the proportion of people who will gamble to avoid a loss is much greater than those who would gamble to realize a gain.

Loss aversion can act as a cognitive barrier to the negotiated resolution of conflict for a variety of reasons. For example, both sides may fight on in a dispute in the hope that they may avoid any losses, even though the continuation of the dispute involves a gamble in which the loss may end up being far greater. . . . [N]egotiators may, in some circumstances, be adverse to offering a concession in circumstances where they view the concession as a sure loss. Indeed, the notion of rights or entitlements may be associated with a more extreme form of loss aversion that Kahneman and Tversky call "enhanced loss aversion," because losses "compounded by outrage are much less acceptable than losses that are caused by misfortune or by legitimate actions of others."

One of the most striking features of loss aversion is that whether something is viewed as a gain or loss — and what kind of gain or loss it is considered — depends upon a reference point, and the choice of a reference point is sometimes manipulable. Once again, a simple example suggested by Kahneman and Tversky, can illustrate.

Suppose you and a friend decide to go to Cleveland for a big night out on the town. You've made reservations at an elegant restaurant that will cost $100 a couple. In addition, you've bought two superb seats — at $50 each — to hear the Cleveland orchestra. You set off for Cleveland, thinking you have your symphony tickets and $100, but no credit cards.

Imagine that you park your car in Cleveland and make a horrifying discovery — you've lost the tickets. Assume that you cannot he admitted to the symphony without tickets. Also imagine that someone is standing in front of the Symphony Hall offering to sell two tickets for $100. You have a choice. You can use the $100 you intended for the fancy dinner to buy the tickets to hear the concert, or you can skip the concert and simply go to dinner. What would you do?

Consider a second hypothetical. After you park your car, you look in your wallet and you realize to your horror that the $100 is gone, but the tickets are there. In front of the Symphony Hall is a person holding a small sign indicating she would like to buy two tickets for $100. What do you do? Do you sell the tickets and go to dinner? Or do you instead skip dinner and simply go to the concert?

Experimental research suggests that in the first example many more people will skip the symphony and simply go out to dinner, while in the second example, the proportions are nearly reversed; most people would skip dinner and go to the concert. The way we keep our mental accounts is such that, in the first instance, to buy the tickets a second time would somehow be to overspend our ticket budget. And, yet, an economist would point out that the two situations are essentially identical because there is a ready and efficient market in which you can convert tickets to money or money to tickets.

The purpose of the hypothetical is to suggest that whether or not an event is framed as a loss can often affect behavior. This powerful idea concerning "framing" has important implications for the resolution of disputes to which I will return later.

D. "Reactive Devaluation" of Compromises and Concessions

The final barrier I wish to discuss, "reactive devaluation," is an example of a social/psychological barrier that arises from the dynamics of the negotiation process and the inferences that negotiators draw from their interactions. My Stanford colleague, psychology Professor Lee Ross, and his students have done experimental work to suggest that, especially between adversaries, when one side offers a particular concession or proposes a particular exchange of compromises the other side may diminish the attractiveness of that offer or proposed exchange simply because it originated with a perceived opponent. The basic notion is a familiar one, especially for lawyers. How often have you had a client indicate to you in the midst of litigation, "If only we could settle this case for $7,000. I'd love to put this whole matter behind me. "Lo and behold, the next day, the other side's attorney calls and offers to settle for $7,000. You excitedly call your client and say, "Guess what the other side has just offered to settle this case for $7,000." You expect to hear jubilation on the other end of the phone, but instead there is silence. Finally, your client says, "Obviously they must know something we don't know. If $7,000 is a good settlement for them, it can't be a good settlement for us."

Both in laboratory and field settings, Ross and his colleagues have marshalled interesting evidence for "reactive devaluation. " They have demonstrated both that a given compromise proposal is rated less positively when proposed by someone on the other side than when proposed by a neutral or an ally. They also demonstrated that a concession that is actually offered is rated lower than a concession that is withheld, and that a compromise is rated less highly after it has been placed on the table by the other side than it was beforehand. . . .

Ross has described a range of cognitive and motivational processes that may account for the reactive devaluation phenomenon. Whatever its roots, reactive devaluation certainly can act as a barrier to the efficient resolution of conflict. It suggests that the exchange of proposed concessions and compromises between adversaries can he very problematic. When one side unilaterally offers a concession that it believes the other side should value and the other side reacts by devaluing the offer, this can obviously make resolution difficult. The recipient of a unilateral concession is apt to believe that her adversary has given up nothing of real value and may therefore resist any notion that she should offer something of real value in exchange. On the other hand, the failure to respond may simply confirm the suspicions of the original offeror, who will believe that her adversary is proceeding in bad faith and is being strategic.

III. OVERCOMING STRATEGIC BARRIERS: THE ROLES OF NEGOTIATORS AND MEDIATORS

The study of barriers can do more than simply help us understand why negotiations sometimes fail when they should not. It can also contribute to our understanding of how to overcome these barriers. Let me illustrate this by using the preceding analysis of four barriers briefly to explore the role of mediators, and to suggest why neutrals can often facilitate the efficient resolution of disputes by overcoming these specific barriers.

First, let us consider the strategic barrier. To the extent that a neutral third party is trusted by both sides, the neutral may be able to induce the parties to reveal information about their underlying interests, needs, priorities, and aspirations that they would not disclose to their adversary. This information may permit a trusted mediator to help the parties enlarge the pie in circumstances where the parties acting alone could not. Moreover, a mediator can foster a problem-solving atmosphere and lessen the temptation on the part of each side to engage in strategic behavior. A skilled mediator can often get parties to move beyond political posturing and recriminations about past wrongs and to instead consider possible gains from a fair resolution of the dispute.

A mediator also can help overcome barriers posed by principal/agent problems. A mediator may bring clients themselves to the table, and help them understand their shared interest in minimizing legal fees and costs in circumstances where the lawyers themselves might not be doing so. In circumstances where a middle manager is acting to prevent a settlement that might benefit the company, but might be harmful to the manager's own career, an astute mediator can sometimes bring another company representative to the table who does not have a personal stake in the outcome.

A mediator can also promote dispute resolution by helping overcome cognitive barriers. Through a variety of processes, a mediator can often help each side understand the power of the case from the other side's perspective. Moreover, by reframing the dispute and suggesting a resolution that avoids blame and stresses the positive aspects of a resolution, a mediator may be able to lessen the effects of loss aversion. . . . Tversky thinks that cognitive barriers are like optical illusions — knowing that an illusion exists does not necessarily enable us to see things differently. Nevertheless, I believe that astute mediators can dampen loss aversion through reframing, by helping a disputant reconceptualize the resolution. By emphasizing the potential gains to both sides of the resolution and de-emphasizing the losses that the resolution is going to entail, mediators (and lawyers) often facilitate resolution.

With respect to the fourth barrier, reactive devaluation, mediators can apply an important and quite obvious role. Reactive devaluation can often be sidestepped if the source of a proposal is a neutral — not one of the parties. Indeed, one of the trade secrets of mediators is that after talking separately to each side about what might or might not be acceptable, the mediator takes responsibility for making a proposal. This helps both parties avoid reactive devaluation by allowing them to accept as sensible a proposal that they might have rejected if it had come directly from their adversary. . . .

G. Women as Negotiators

1. Comments and Questions

a. Do women, on average, negotiate as well as men? Do specific subsets of women, such as law students, negotiate as effectively (judged by bottom line results) as similarly situated men? Is there cause for concern about women being able to participate effectively in the myriad personal and business negotiations that are part of daily life?

b. To the extent there are substantial differences between men and women in negotiation behavior, what should government or society at large do about the situation?

c. The related topic of participation by women in divorce mediation, particularly where the woman is a battered spouse, is discussed at Chapter 8, section C.

d. A few recent books relating to women and negotiation that will provide a useful introduction to the subject (and a wealth of additional citations) are Carol Gilligan, IN A DIFFERENT VOICE (1982); Pat Heim & Susan Golant, HARDBALL FOR WOMEN (1992); P. J. Kalbfleisch & Cody (eds.), GENDER, POWER, AND COMMUNICATIONS (1995); Kathleen Kelly Reardon, THEY DON'T GET IT, DO THEY? (1995); Felice N. Schwartz, BREAKING WITH TRADITION (1992); Deborah Tannen, YOU JUST DON'T UNDERSTAND (1990).

2. Charles B. Craver, *The Impact of Gender on Clinical Negotiating Achievement*, 6 OHIO STATE J. ON DISP. RESOL. 1 (1990)*

I. INTRODUCTION

Imagine a spectrum with two images at either extreme. At one end sits the image of Woman, embodying qualities associated with generations of women who themselves had little hand in shaping the image. She lacks public power. She serves other people. She is expected to be and often succeeds in being caring, empathetic, cooperative, and generous. At the opposite end stands the figure of Lawyer, as molded by previous generations of men. He is powerful, instrumental, and adversarial.

During the past twenty-five years, there has been a substantial increase in the number of women entering the legal profession. In 1964, 4 percent of law students were female. As recently as 1970, women constituted only 4.7 percent of legal practitioners. By the late 1980's, women comprised 41 percent of law students and 16 percent of practicing attorneys. Despite the significant increase in the number of female lawyers, many individuals continue to believe that male and female practitioners behave differently. They think that gender differences render women less effective in highly competitive encounters. Consequently, these individuals suspect that female attorneys are less successful negotiators than their male counterparts.

This article will empirically compare the results achieved by male and female students in clinical negotiation exercises. It will initially examine the perceived differences between male and female behavior. Statistically established distinctions relevant to negotiation interactions will be explored, and unsupportable stereotypes will be discussed. Comparisons will be made concerning the manner in which men and women deal with the stress of highly competitive situations.

A statistical comparison will then be made between the results achieved by male and female students during the past sixteen years in the negotiation exercises employed in my Legal Negotiating course. Despite the fact that stereotypical beliefs would suggest that women would not be as effective as their male cohorts in such competitive encounters, my anecdotal experiences have not disclosed any apparent differences regarding the results attained by male and female students. I have thus hypothesized that I would find no statistically significant difference between the settlements achieved by the men and women in my Legal Negotiating course. This null hypothesis includes two critical components. First, that

---

*Reprinted with permission.

the average results obtained by male and female students would be approximately equal. Second, that there would be no evidence to suggest that male negotiators have employed a more competitive approach that might produce similar means, but more skewed results.

II. REAL AND PERCEIVED GENDER DIFFERENCES

Men and women are usually perceived as being quite different, with these role expectations creating gender-based stereotypes. Generally, men are described by a series of traits that reflect competence, rationality, and assertiveness. Men, for example, are viewed as independent, objective, active, competitive, adventurous, self-confident, and ambitious. Women are seen as possessing the opposite of each of these traits. They are characterized as dependent, subjective, passive, not competitive, not adventurous, not self-confident, and not ambitious. Men are thought to be rational and logical, while women are considered emotional and intuitive. Men are expected to emphasize objective factors, with women focusing upon relationships. As a result, men are considered more likely to define issues in abstract terms, and to resolve them through application of reasoning based upon justice and rights. Men are thought more likely to rely upon legal principles than are women.

Men are expected to be dominant and authoritative, while women are viewed as passive and submissive. When the sexes interact, men tend to speak for longer periods and to interrupt more frequently than women. Men usually exert more control over the subjects being discussed. This masculine tendency to dominate male-female interactions could provide men with an inherent advantage during negotiations by enabling them to control the agenda and direct the discussions.

When Hanisch and Carnevale studied the mediative styles of male and female subjects, they found that men were more confident of their ability to influence the negotiators. Female mediators sent fewer verbal signals to the negotiators, and they evidenced a greater desire to obtain the approval of the involved parties. Professor Gilligan has suggested that perceived gender differences may be attributed to the fact that American women have historically felt less powerful than their male cohorts. This phenomenon has often caused women to be less confident regarding their ability to influence others and more concerned with the manner in which others view their performance.

Male and female self-concepts are affected by the stereotypical way in which others view their performance. When men are successful, their performance tends to be attributed to intrinsic factors such as intelligence and hard work. When women are successful, however, their performance is usually attributed to extrinsic variables such as luck or the actions of others. This phenomenon enhances male self-confidence by permitting them to accept credit for their achievements, and it undermines the confidence of successful women by attributing their accomplishments to external considerations.

When men and women encounter competition, they may behave differently. It has been suggested that "women are more likely [than men] to avoid competitive situations, less likely to acknowledge competitive wishes, and not likely to do as well in competition." Many women are apprehensive regarding the negative consequences that they associate with competitive achievement. "Again and again women report the feeling that a successful woman alienates herself from both women and men." This phenomenon may be attributed to the different acculturation process for boys and girls.

Boys have traditionally been exposed to competitive situations at an early age. They have been encouraged to participate in little league baseball, basketball, soccer and other competitive athletic endeavors. These activities introduce boys to the "thrill of victory and the agony of defeat" during their formative years. "Traditional girls' games like jump rope and hopscotch are turn-taking games, where competition is indirect since one person's success does not necessarily signify another's failure." While directly competitive games teach boys how to resolve the disputes that inevitably arise, girls rarely have the opportunity to learn such informal adjudicative skills. By adulthood, men are much more likely to have become accustomed to the rigors of overt competition and familiar with the application of societal rules to resolve inter-competitor controversies.

Competitive games teach boys that it is more enjoyable to win than to lose. They learn that a positive mental attitude is likely to enhance their probability of success. It is thus not surprising that college men generally exude greater confidence in problem-solving situations than college women. Men expect to achieve more advantageous results than their female cohorts. This factor would suggest that college males would be more successful than college females with respect to competitive interactions, such as those involving negotiating exercises. Those individuals who begin bargaining encounters with greater confidence and higher aspiration levels tend to attain more favorable agreements.

In competitive situations, males are generally expected to behave more aggressively than females. Boys usually receive parental approval for aggressive and competitive tendencies, while girls are encouraged to be passive and dependent. During interpersonal transactions, men are more likely to employ "highly intense language" to persuade others, and they tend to be more effective when utilizing this approach. Women, on the other hand, are more likely to use less intense language during persuasive encounters, and they are inclined to be more effective behaving in that manner. Females tend to employ language containing more disclaimers than their male cohorts, which may be perceived by the recipients as an indication of less confidence. When women eschew traditionally feminine conduct and behave in a stereotypically masculine fashion, they are usually not rewarded. They are instead criticized for deviating from conventional male-female role expectations.

When men negotiate, they generally endeavor to maximize their return, while women are inclined to emphasize the maintenance of relationships. This phenomenon may explain why women tend to employ more accommodating strategies than men in resolving conflicts. One might expect that the tendency of men to seek maximum results and the inclination of women to resort to accommodating behavior would provide men with an advantage during bargaining transactions.

Empirical evidence indicates that women are not as effective at deception. Studies have shown that men are more comfortable in situations in which they are expected to dissemble, and they find it easier to behave in a Machiavellian manner. These factors should further benefit male negotiators, since individuals involved in the legal negotiation process are usually endeavoring to mislead their opponents.

On the one hand the negotiator must be fair and truthful; on the other he must mislead his opponent. "Like the poker player, a negotiator hopes that his opponent will overestimate the value of his hand. Like the poker player, in a variety of ways he must facilitate his opponent's inaccurate assessment. The critical difference between those who are successful negotiators and those who are not lies in this capacity both to mislead and not to be misled."

Despite the various factors that would support the theory that male negotiators would achieve more beneficial results than female negotiators, empirical studies involving competitive interactions do not consistently substantiate this supposition. Psychologists endeavoring to measure male-female differences during competitive encounters most frequently employ variations of the "Prisoner's Dilemma" exercise. The most basic formulation involves two participants who simultaneously select option A or option B, for a possible reward of 1, 5, or 10 points. Each party's result depends on the interaction between their choice and the option selected by their opponent.

A/A is the cooperative choice, since this combination permits both participants to maximize their joint gain over repeated trials. Either person may "defect" and select "B" hoping to obtain a reward of 10, compared to their opponent's 1. The party's short-term benefit is likely to be offset by the fact that the other participant will probably respond by shifting from "A" to "B" to minimize his or her future exposure. Cooperative behavior ensures a diminished, but safer, return for both.

Based upon the stereotypical belief that men are more competitive than women, one might reasonably expect men to behave more competitively when participating in the Prisoner's Dilemma game. Men would be more likely to establish higher aspiration levels, and they would probably endeavor to take advantage of the perceived feminine trait of accommodation. The various Prisoners Dilemma studies have, however, discerned little or no gender differences. Many of the cited studies found no statistically significant gender difference concerning competitive tendencies. Of those experiments that did discern different behavior, some found males to be more competitive and some found females to be more competitive. Almost identical findings were obtained with respect to cooperative behavior. Most studies discovered no difference based upon participant gender, while others obtained mixed results.

Various factors might explain why the anticipated gender differences did not materialize. In their study, Grant and Sermat found that women could be both more cooperative and more competitive, without being submissive. Furthermore, when men and women interact in a competitive environment, men occasionally make the mistake of assuming that the women will not be as competitive. Men who make assumptions based on this stereotype simply provide the female participants with an inherent advantage. In addition, women who encounter men in competitive environments often work more diligently to achieve optimal results. It is as if the men are "brought down" by the women and the women are "brought up" by the men.

Other important gender differences occur when men and women interact in competitive settings. Although women tend to employ less powerful language when they are in less powerful roles, they utilize forceful language when they are in a position of equality. During most of the Prisoner's Dilemma studies, the male and female participants were placed in positions of relative equality.

Another factor that may explain the lack of gender differences is the role of education. "When individuals are trained to perform a specific role, gender communication-behavior differences disappear." Highly educated professionals exhibit a similar trend, with women adopting a more masculine style of communication. These findings would suggest that if professionals are trained in mediating or negotiating skills, gender-based communication differences would be minimized. This would not, however, guarantee that male and female subjects would be viewed identically even when they behave similarly. Male-female stereotypes could still cause many observers to perceive women participants as less controlling and less influential than male participants, even in settings in which the women were objectively exhibiting dominant behavior.

One might reasonably expect gender-based communication stereotypes to place women at a disadvantage in legal negotiation exercises. They would be perceived as less dominant and thus less forceful. They would be expected to be less logical and more emotional. Nonetheless, two important factors counter-balance these stereotypes. The advanced education possessed by law students and the specific training received in a legal negotiating course would minimize the gender-based communication differentials. The female negotiators may also benefit from the established fact that women are typically more sensitive to nonverbal messages than their male cohorts. Since a significant amount of critical communication during interpersonal transactions is nonverbal, the enhanced ability of female negotiators to decode such signals could offset any disadvantage associated with latent stereotyping.

Professor Deaux succinctly recognized that behavioral predictions based upon stereotypical beliefs regarding men and women are likely to be of questionable validity in most settings.

> [D]espite the persistence of stereotypes, the studies of social behavior suggest that there are relatively few characteristics in which men and women consistently differ. Men and women both seem to be capable of being aggressive, helpful, and alternately cooperative and competitive. In other words, there is little evidence that the nature of women and men is so inherently different that we are justified in making stereotyped generalizations.

If Professor Deaux's assessment is correct, one should not expect to find any statistically significant difference between the results achieved by men and women in clinical negotiating exercises.

III. CLINICAL NEGOTIATING COURSE METHODOLOGY

Since the vast majority of legal problems are resolved by negotiated agreements, instead of adjudicative decisions, the development of bargaining skills should substantially enhance one's ability to practice law. During the 1960's, innovative law professors began to recognize that simulated exercises could be employed in clinical courses to teach students about the negotiation process. James J. White at the University of Michigan, and Cornelius J. Peck and Robert L. Fletcher at the University of Washington developed simulation models designed to improve the bargaining competence of future legal practitioners.

Since 1973, I have regularly taught a Legal Negotiating course based upon the White-Peck-Fletcher models. During the first half of the semester, the class explores theoretical and practical concepts pertaining to the negotiation process. . . . The impact of verbal and nonverbal communication and psychological factors upon the negotiation process is studied. The manner in which the personal needs of the clients and attorneys and the different types of legal problems and relationships involved influence the bargaining transaction is discussed. The various phases of the negotiation process are examined, along with the different techniques that negotiators are likely to encounter. The way in which cultural differences and gender role expectations affect bargaining relationships is also considered. Specific issues pertaining to such topics as the commencement of litigation, settlement discussions, judicial settlement conferences, telephone negotiations, and the enhancement of seemingly weak positions are examined.

While the negotiation process is being formally explored, the students are required to engage in three or four negotiation exercises. The class is divided into groups of two or four.

The groups are each instructed to seek a negotiated resolution of an identical legal problem. At the conclusion of each exercise, the various results are disclosed and individual negotiations are evaluated in an effort to determine which techniques were successfully and unsuccessfully employed. I endeavor to integrate the theoretical concepts with the students' simulated experiences.

During the second half of the semester, class members engage in five negotiation exercises which count towards two-thirds of their course grade. Each problem is structured in a duplicate bridge format. Everyone receives the same "General Information" describing the specific dispute that needs to be resolved. All of the individuals on the same side are provided with the identical "Confidential Information" apprising them of their client's goals and the manner in which they will be evaluated if they achieve a settlement or fail to do so. Each side consists of two students, in an effort to demonstrate that lawyers must not only negotiate with their opponents, but also with their own clients. For each exercise, participants are randomly assigned different partners and different opponents. The results of each exercise are rank-ordered from high to low for each side based upon the team's results measured against the confidential scoring information provided prior to the exercise. This ordering scheme is used to grade each team's performance. In an effort to induce students to focus on the impact of theoretical concepts upon their negotiating exercises, each student is required to prepare a twelve to fifteen page paper exploring this interrelationship. This paper accounts for one-third of the course grade.

The environment in my Legal Negotiating class is highly competitive. Each group is evaluated solely by its performance vis-a-vis the other groups representing the same side of the problem. Although opposing parties are encouraged to maximize their joint return through cooperative bargaining, they realize that it is their own respective point totals that will determine their group placement and, ultimately, their individual grades. The class members are usually second semester, third-year students. I frequently remind them that if they consider the pressure generated by this course to be high, they should contemplate their reaction to situations in which their clients' money or freedom will be involved.

At the beginning of this research project, I discussed my work with Dr. Peggy McIntosh of the Wellesley College Center for Research on Women. She appropriately noted that my course evaluation structure reflected the mores indigenous to the white, male-dominated legal profession. Dr. McIntosh suggested that the model might be different if it had been developed by women or minorities. She further indicated that my statistical assessment could not determine whether my former male and female students employed identical negotiation styles.

Over the past fifteen years, I have made presentations on legal negotiating to numerous attorneys in thirty states, Washington, D.C., Canada, and the People's Republic of China. Many practitioners, particularly older men, have asked whether female negotiators can be as effective as their male cohorts. These attorneys have often cited the stereotypical assumptions that females will not be as aggressive or competitive as males. I have generally responded with my overall impression that men and women students appear to achieve similar outcomes in my Legal Negotiating course.

This study is not being conducted to demonstrate that men and women behave identically in negotiations. It is being carried out to determine whether, once the evaluative criteria are defined, male and female students are able to obtain similar results. While I recognize that the men and women in my course may occasionally employ gender-specific styles, these differences may not necessarily generate different outcomes. As Professor MacKinnon has observed from a feminist perspective: "In academic and professional areas, it's: you define what merit is, we will meet it."

IV. STATISTICAL FINDINGS

My database included fifteen Legal Negotiating classes at five different law schools. Since I was comparing male and female clinical negotiating achievement, only the student negotiation exercise placements were used. The means and standard deviations were calculated for males and females in each of the fifteen classes. A t-test was then performed for each class to determine if there was a statistically significant difference between the male and female means for any class. T-probability values of 0.10 or lower would establish statistical significance at the 0.10 level, while t-probability values of 0.05 or lower would demonstrate significance at the 0.05 level. Since I hypothesized that no statistically significant difference would be found and had no reason to suspect that if any difference was found it would favor males or females, two-tailed t-probability values were employed. . . .

For seven classes, the means for the male students were slightly higher than the means for the female students, while the female means were somewhat above the male means with respect to the other eight classes. A review of the t-probability values further demonstrates the absence of any statistically significant gender-based difference. No statistically significant difference was found at the 0.05 level for any class. A significant difference was only ascertained for one class (1981) at the 0.10 level. These findings would strongly suggest that there is no correlation between gender and clinical negotiating achievement.

As the number of female law students increased during the 1970's and early 1980's, one might wonder whether women students became more competitive as they became acculturated to the traditional, male-dominated law school environment. This phenomenon might be suspected, for example, if the data indicated that female means rose vis-a-vis male means with the passage of time. An examination of the data shows no such trend. The female means exceeded the male means for 1973, 1977, 1980, and 1981, while the male means were higher in 1976, 1979, and 1982.

Although the t-test calculations failed to establish a statistically significant difference between the average results achieved by male and female negotiators, it is possible that the actual results obtained by men were different from those attained by women. For example, if the men were more competitive, their results might have been more skewed than those of the women. Competitive men might have endeavored to obtain total "victory" and been forced to accept complete "defeat" (i.e., a nonsettlement) if they were unable to attain their ultimate objective. The more accommodating females, on the other hand, would have tended to cluster around the mean.

If the male results were more skewed than the female results, the male standard deviations would be substantially higher than the female standard deviations. A review of the different standard deviations does not reveal any skewing. For most classes, the male and female standard deviations are approximately equal. Furthermore, while the male standard deviations were higher for eight classes, the female standard deviations were higher for the other seven classes. These figures would warrant rejection of the theory that men are more likely to behave in a "win-lose" competitive manner while women are more likely to act in a "win-win" cooperative fashion.

V. DISCUSSION OF FINDINGS

During the past sixteen years, I have discovered that practitioners and law students of both sexes permit gender-based stereotypes to influence their negotiating interactions with persons of the opposite gender and people of the same gender. Many individuals assume that men will be highly competitive negotiators who will always endeavor to achieve maximum results. Women negotiators, on the other hand, are expected to be more accommodating and less competitive.

On those occasions in my Legal Negotiating class when two women have been paired against two other women, they have often permitted stereotypical beliefs to affect their transaction. They have regularly expressed the preliminary view that their interaction would be more pleasant, due to the absence of the overt "win-lose" competitiveness that they attribute to their male classmates. Once their bargaining encounters have commenced, however, they have generally been as competitive as the men.

This empirical study was undertaken to test the validity of practitioner and student assumptions regarding the impact of gender upon negotiation results. Based upon my previous course observations, I hypothesized that there was no difference with respect to the negotiation outcomes obtained by male and female negotiators. The fifteen years of data warrant acceptance of the null hypothesis. The t-test calculations disclosed no statistically significant difference between the mean results achieved by male and female negotiators. A review of the standard deviations pertaining to each class failed to show that male students achieved skewed results. This would negate the stereotypical belief that men are more competitive "win-lose" negotiators than their female cohorts.

The absence of any statistically significant difference between the results attained by male and female students in my Legal Negotiating course exercises should not be surprising. Law students are a self-selecting group of highly intelligent and highly competitive individuals. It is thus possible that an analogous study of the results achieved by undergraduate or high school students on clinical negotiating exercises might indicate the influence of gender-based differences.

It would be beneficial for legal negotiating professors at other law schools to engage in similar research to determine whether they would find any statistically significant gender differences. It would also be informative for professors of other clinical skills courses, such as trial practice, mediation, and client counseling, to compare the performances of their students to ascertain the presence or absence of any gender-based distinctions.

Legal negotiating professors should examine our own gender-based stereotypical beliefs to ensure that we are not subconsciously encouraging male and female students to behave differently. We should be careful not to permit individuals to suggest that women cannot achieve substantive results as favorable as those attained by men.

Legal practitioners must acknowledge the impact that gender-based stereotypes may exert upon negotiating interactions. Male attorneys who believe that female lawyers will not be as competitive or Machiavellian as their male cohorts will simply provide women opponents with an inherent advantage. Female lawyers must also eschew reliance upon such stereotypical opinions with respect to both their male and female opponents. Women practitioners who conclude that adversaries are treating them lightly because of their gender should not hesitate to take advantage of the situation. Their favorable outcomes will teach their chauvinistic opponents a lesson, while simultaneously benefiting their own clients.

VI. CONCLUSION

Fifteen years of empirical data have demonstrated the absence of any statistically significant difference between the clinical negotiating results achieved by male and female law students. This finding should induce students, teachers, and practitioners to reassess the validity of their stereotypical beliefs concerning the behavior of men and women attorneys in competitive interactions. There is simply no reason to suspect that female lawyers cannot attain outcomes as beneficial as those obtained by their male counterparts in any bargaining setting.

Chapter 5

Trans-National and Cross-Cultural Perspectives

CASE STUDY

(Adapted from *Dodge v. Giant Foods, Inc.*)

Stephen Dodge, plaintiff, was an employee of Giant Food, defendant. Giant Food has grooming regulations which prohibit long hair for men and provides that women must secure their long hair. Mr. Dodge sued on behalf of all male employees of Giant Food who have been discharged or assigned to unfavorable positions because they chose to wear their hair longer than permitted by Giant's grooming regulations. Mr. Dodge filed an action claiming that Giant's grooming regulations violate the prohibition against sex discrimination contained in Title VII of the Civil Rights Act. The court noted that the regulations obviously distinguish between long and short haired males as well as treating long haired males differently from long haired females. However, the court noted that distinctions based upon sex do not necessarily violate Title VII unless a harm can be shown. This was not done here. Additionally, the court pointed out that Giant Food enforced strict grooming regulations against women's hair length. The court proceeded to go into a detained analysis of cases which have considered regulations which embody a distinction based on sex. The court concluded that Title VII was never intended to encompass sexual classifications having only an indirect effect on employment opportunities. Regulations, such as hair length restrictions, are classifications by sex which do not limit employment opportunities by making distinctions on unalterable personal characteristics. The regulations do not represent an attempt by Food Giant to prevent employment of a particular sex and they do not pose distinct disadvantages for one sex.

A. Introduction

This chapter examines private trans-national and cross-cultural negotiation among individuals. The negotiators may represent organizations and the stakes may be large, but the number of parties is limited. The term culture is used broadly to encompass a set of values, norms, and standard practices commonly (not universally) used by a group. Generalizations about groups are just that — general statements. A pejorative label for such classification is stereotyping. Max Weber used the term "ideal type" (with ideal meaning "archetype" rather than expressing a value judgment). Group membership neither defines nor limits a person, but it often provides a convenient way to identify information about a person with whom one negotiates. Even if additional information is available, acquisition thereof is costly and may be precluded by time constraints.

The cross-cultural offerings in this Chapter are not designed to make you an expert on harmony restoration among Korean-Americans, traditional dispute resolution among the Navajo, or negotiating in Japan, although you will learn a good bit about each of these matters. Rather, the purpose is to sensitize you to cultural differences, and to adjust to such differences. While the differences between the examples just cited and ordinary everyday negotiations in familiar surroundings is large, different cultures are all around us.

If you want to make a sale or resolve a problem, it helps to understand the values, background, and aspirations of the party with which you are dealing. It has become common to talk about "corporate culture." Understanding the culture of the business or individual you are working with often is helpful in reaching a desired goal.

Richard Delgado raises a different and distinctly more ominous cultural concern about ADR processes, which is that prejudice may undermine their value, and therefore their legitimacy, for the poor and minorities. The context of his comments largely are ADR procedures with third party intervention, rather than direct negotiation. The concerns he raises are important, and they fit better in the cross-cultural context than anywhere else in the book.

International negotiation is too important to ignore, but far too large a topic for even cursory coverage. Accordingly, discussion is limited to negotiating in a single important country: Japan. Readers will not become experts on Japan, but should get a sense of major differences.

It may be helpful in thinking about culture to give brief consideration to an important indigenous American culture that is a central topic of this book: the culture of commerce (which itself is composed of many subcultures). Business entities have long been major users of ADR processes. Calvin Coolidge, in perhaps his only memorable observation, stated that "the business of America is business." What do most adults know about the world of letters of credit (both commercial and standby), bills of lading (both straight and negotiable), holders in due course, perfected security interests, conditions (precedent, concurrent, and subsequent, not to mention those that are precedent in fact but subsequent in form and vice-versa), bulk sales, CIF and FAS terms (acronyms too well known to spell out), the midnight deadline, and the perfect tender rule? These are aspects of a culture about which most newly minted college graduates (especially if they were not business majors) are blissfully ignorant — probably far more so than about discrimination against ethnic minorities, oppression of women, and the beleaguered white male.

B. Dispute Settlement Among Closely Knit Groups

1. Comments and Questions

a. It is commonly noted that closely knit communities, of which immigrant ethnic groups are a notable example, are particularly likely to favor nonlegal dispute resolution. Professor Auerbach cites examples going back through American history.

b. Diane LeReche examines a contemporary immigrant group, Korean-Americans, and how traditional processes of dispute settlement are retained in a new country. Casual observation, common sense, and empirical research all show a strong tendency of immigrant groups in this country to make modified use of the customs from which their family emigrated, including those for dealing with discord, which diminishes over time.

c. One impact of mass media (notably radio and television), along with institutions such as the public schools, is to speed the acculturation of immigrants, and the pace of absorption of at least the second generation into the dominant culture. Before one becomes too nostalgic for the fine traditions of the old country, it should be noted that there are costs as well as benefits to the preservation of "traditional norms" and an absence of "outside scrutiny" on members of immigrant communities, particularly the least skilled, least educated, and women (not mutually exclusive categories).

2. Jerold Auerbach, JUSTICE WITHOUT LAW? 3 (1981)

From the Dutch in New Amsterdam [the early name for New York City] to the Jews of the Lower East Side, in a wide geographical arc that encompassed Scandanavians in the Midwest and the Chinese on the West Coast, some newcomers from other cultures and traditions tried to place their disputes as far beyond the reach of American law as possible. Aliens in a hostile land, they encountered a society whose legal institutions were overtly biased against them or, at best, indifferent to their distinctive values. Their own indigenous method of dispute settlement, centuries old in some instances, shielded them from outside scrutiny and enabled them to inculcate and preserve their traditional norms. . . .

3. Diane LeResche, A *Comparison of the American Mediation Process with a Korean-American Harmony Restoration Process*, 9 MEDIATION Q. 323 (1992)*

Scholars have shown that there are cultural variations in perceptions of conflicts and conflict resolution processes. We have not known explicitly to what extent the process used by community mediation centers is similar to those commonly used by various American ethnic groups.

To begin the work of assessing how similar the typical American community-based mediation center procedure is to the customary process of resolving interpersonal conflict employed by some ethnic groups, a study was conducted using interviews with some Korean-Americans and material from a sampling of mediator training workshops. This article provides an introduction to the findings of the study. . . .

Data Collection

Information about process used by the American community-based mediation centers was derived from a content analysis of data collected from a national sampling of private, nonprofit mediation centers. Three modes of data collection were utilized: (1) training manuals employed to train volunteer and paid mediators, (2) participant observation in mediator training workshops, and (3) ten public relations and educational videotapes describing and demonstrating the mediation process. Five centers were studied in depth. . . .

A profile and description of Korean-American interpersonal conflicts and the third-party-

---

assisted process for handling them was elicited from content analyses of case-historical data. The information was collected during face-to-face, in-depth, semi-structured, open-ended interviews with thirty-five adult self-identified English-speaking Koreans who resided in the Washington, D.C., metropolitan area. They were asked to talk only about conflicts among Korean-Americans. The sample was one of convenience and snowballing. Ages ranged from eighteen to thirty-five; the mean age was thirty-one. About half were women. About three-fourths of the interviewees were first generation. They were predominantly in professional occupations or university students. None . . . had any previous knowledge or use of American mediation services. Koreans in America were selected because no relevant literature exists for them and because they are one of the fastest growing immigrant groups in the United States.

Framework for Comparing Processes

A framework for comparing processes was derived from a merging of indigenous categories that resulted from the content analyses of the information gathered about the two processes studied. . . . The framework is designed for comparing more than just customary ways of handling conflicts. It was evident from the research that it is also very important to portray perceptions of what is and is not considered to be a conflict and what people believe causes conflicts; these beliefs not only vary but also influence how people respond to interpersonal situations. The framework includes the following nine categories:

1. Concepts of conflicts
2. Perceptions of the derivation of conflicts
3. How the process is initiated
4. Roles and responsibilities of the people in conflict
5. Characteristics, roles, and responsibilities of a third party
6. Third-party preparation
7. Third-party meetings with the conflicting parties
8. Generation and selection of solutions
9. How the process is concluded.

Profile of Korean-American Harmony Restoration. The sequential phases of a process, as described by the Korean-Americans interviewed, are labeled according to descriptions the Korean-Americans provided:

1. Getting respected person
2. Knowing about relationships and proper conduct
3. Contemplation and planning
4. Go-between advising and suggesting solutions
5. Having an understanding
6. Restoring harmony.

Profile of the American Community-Based Mediation Procedure. The categories profiling an American community-based mediation procedure are as follows:

1. Community outreach, education, and public relations
2. Intake, receiving referrals, getting parties to the table
3. Mediator premediation session preparation
4. The mediation session(s)

a. Opening statements and procedural ground rules
b. Defining the problem
c. Creating optional solutions
d. Selecting solutions
e. Writing an agreement
f. Closing

5. Evaluation of the session(s)
6. Follow-up with the parties.

Comparing Concepts of Conflict and of Derivation of Conflicts

The basic assumption of the American mediation centers is that conflict is a natural phenomenon. It is neither positive nor negative; it simply exists. Although conflicts can be disruptive, they are not considered totally bad. They may even be viewed as good, insofar as they can result in circumstances changing from unhealthy to healthy ones.

The Koreans in America, on the other hand, tend to perceive conflicts as negative situations that represent a shameful inability to maintain harmonious relationships with others. A conflict is not an acceptable condition; hence careful attention must be paid to avoidance of any activity that may cause discord. Prevention and an emphasis on minimizing attention to frictions are the first action and reaction to any disruption in harmony. Patience, tolerance, and accommodation follow, to the extent that they are emotionally feasible.

In general mediation centers see interpersonal conflicts as problems in communication between people. Poor communication leads to misunderstandings, both between persons who have known each other for long periods and between persons known to one another solely in the immediate situation. Conflicts are considered to be ubiquitous.

Korean-Americans, by contrast, posit that conflicts occur when at least one person does not behave in the proper manner toward another. When someone is selfish or insults another person, a conflict is created. Insults are actions that reflect that one is not showing the respect another is entitled to receive. Insults are offensive attacks. Conflicts occur between persons within a familial or social network. Because Korean-Americans rarely interact with people they consider to be outside their networks, they do not realize conflicts with those with whom they have no connections. These distinct variations in the values attached to interpersonal conflicts and their causes lead to some contrasting views of the purpose of resolving conflicts, as well as how to do so.

There are similarities also in the objectives and goals of the two resolution processes. The ultimate goal of an American mediation center process is to obtain a formal agreement that specifies which of the parties will take what future actions where and when to remedy the issues discerned during the mediation sessions. The written agreement is to have been created by the parties so that it will be mutually acceptable and beneficial and therefore endure. There are competing demands that the goal be relationship centered or agreement centered. Both are deemed desirable and sometimes possible to achieve, but the nurturance of the relationship between the parties is usually the ultimate goal.

Secondary goals are to show the parties a method of focusing on their interests and needs in the generation and selection of solutions to conflicts and to teach effective communication skills in order to prevent conflicts in the future.

Objectives linked to the goals are to intervene quickly in conflicts before they escalate to violence, to provide an efficient means of resolving conflicts (that is, low cost, time saving, and convenient for the parties), and to offer a confidential and private process. By advocating the use of a rational, collaborative process the centers also attempt to empower people to resolve their own conflicts now and in the future. . . .

The centers do not aim to determine who is at fault, to assess blame, or to punish. The process used by Korean-Americans is similar in not seeking to assign blame, although it expects apologies to be made. However, since all persons involved in the conflict are seen to have contributed to it in some way, each one acknowledges and offers apologies for mistakes made during the course of the unharmonious state.

The supreme goal for Korean-Americans is to have harmonious relations among all persons within one's network of family, friends, and colleagues. Hence the main purpose of a conflict resolution procedure is to restore harmony where it does not exist. This purpose entails the reconciliation of people through helping them understand their relationships. The Korean-American process is centered on future relationships between those directly, and less directly, involved in the conflict more than on details of a contract.

An objective of the process is to find a solution that does not engender bitterness for the long term, helps all to save face, and preserves customary proper conduct between people in defined role relationships. A concomitant objective is for the intermediary to convince the conflicting persons to accept a reasonable solution, which means making necessary adjustments in their behavior, coping with a difficult situation, accommodating to others in the short term, and compromising, especially for the good of the whole group, even to the neglect of self. These are the objectives of making hwa hae (harmony).

How the Process Is Initiated

There are virtually no commonalities in how the two procedures are initiated. . . . The chief distinction is that the focus of the American center is on how to get the parties to come to the mediation table; for Korean-Americans, it is on how a suffering person can find the most suitable intermediary.

Efforts are made by people affiliated with the American mediation center to inform people of their services . . . through impersonal outreach, advertising, education, and public relations. Social service agencies are appealed to for referrals to the center. When a conflict is manifested, persons may refer themselves to the center or make contact on the advice of someone else. A request for information or an appointment for help may be initiated by one or more of the actual parties in conflict. A staff person at the center questions the "complainant" and initiates contact with the other party in an effort to get everyone to come into the center for a meeting with mediators. The intake worker makes an official appointment at a time convenient to all concerned and informs the parties about the mediation process, the fees for the service, and the need to sign a contract agreeing to participate in mediation.

A Korean-American generally launches a semiformal resolution process when all patience and attempts at handling the situation have been exhausted. He or she probably considers the potential ramifications of asking various persons to assist as an intermediary, narrows the choice to the most appropriate person, and then carefully approaches that person, politely and submissively requesting guidance. The person asked to assist may be reluctant to do so and will not be unduly pressured to perform this role. Unspoken responsibilities to assist one another in times of need are understood by all involved.

Roles and Responsibilities of Parties in Conflict

The persons at the heart of the conflict have different roles to play and different responsibilities in each of these processes. When taking part in American community-based mediation, the parties are expected to generate potential solutions, make their own decisions about acceptable outcomes, and act on their own behalf. They are to be rational, control their emotions, and behave in an orderly, restrained manner, separating mind, body, and spirit. The parties are to take turns telling their views of the conflict situation and their interests and needs in relation to it. They are urged to be direct and verbal, disclosing themselves fully and acting in good faith.

Thoughts are to be conveyed in a relatively formal, businesslike manner. The focus of discussion is to be on those aspects of one's life that are central to the immediate conflict; in other words, one's personal, political, social, and economic realms are to be kept separate. Parties are expected to work at finding a solution. . . .

Parties are to agree to and abide by ground rules established by the mediators. It is considered a virtue to be assertive and to claim one's rights with regard to terms of the agreement. One may demand and be aggressive for what one believes is a fair and just outcome, but one is to conform to the process managed by the mediators. Similar conformity and assertiveness are also evidenced by Koreans in America.

Koreans in America are more passive, however, in generating potential solutions to the conflict at this stage (for they have already made extensive attempts before enlisting the intermediary's help). They are expected to listen carefully to the intermediary, consider seriously the advice offered, consult with others in their network about proposed solutions, taking the kibun (similar to the English concepts of morale, face, self-esteem, state of mind) and wishes of others into account before acquiescing to the intermediary. Feelings and intuitions are as fundamental to their actions, as is information. . . . One remembers that the social, personal, political, and economic aspects of life are interrelated, so that decisions made and actions taken have many far-reaching effects.

A person is not expected to interact in the same way with everyone. Although there is some reciprocity, there are basic inequalities and differences in how persons relate to one another. The hierarchical, paternalistic design of Confucius for relationship behaviors is adhered to, sometimes subconsciously. Hence role behaviors depend on the relationship and context of each conflict. Loyalty, trust, and deference to intermediaries is probably consistently the norm.

The Korean-Americans follow the lead of their intermediaries, waiting for the solution offered, the reasons for selecting it, and the persuasive comments about embracing what is necessary to make hwa hae. Those participating in the American mediation centers are very actively involved in creating and choosing the solutions relevant to their personal needs; they attend only to their mediators' directions about the steps to follow in the process.

Characteristics, Roles, and Responsibilities of Third Party

The Korean-American intermediary takes an active part in almost all dimensions of the lives of those he or she is working with in order to restore harmony. The intermediary's responsibilities are many and taken quite seriously, for the harmony of the larger groups to which they all belong is at stake. It is a temporary role, which he or she has felt an obligation to perform for persons in some way personally related. The intermediary has an informal relationship with the conflicting persons, having been personally known to each of them, in fact often interacting with them in other situations.

The ideal intermediary is wise, intelligent, experienced, and fair. He or she has the ability to use nunch'i ("eyeing the situation," an ability to pick up the subtle cues that reveal how someone is feeling; being perceptive about the emotions and attitudes of another person and knowing how to respond sensitively to that person), does not disturb anyone's kibun, and is respectful of people. These abilities are all informally learned. The intermediary has had no formal training in being a third party, but has demonstrated in some way a capacity to fill the roles of fact finder, planner, thinker, diplomat, persuader, adviser, generator of reasonable solutions, go-between, and arranger of social events.

In contrast, mediators in the American conflict resolution center have been trained specifically to fill the role of process manager, facilitator of communication, and advocate for a collaborative process. They have received some training in listening effectively, guiding the parties sequentially through their tasks, keeping them attuned to the ground rules and focused on reaching an agreement. The relationship between mediators and the parties is a contractual one, for they are operating in a professional, official capacity as third parties and do not interact with the parties in other contexts. They are frequently part-time volunteers at the mediation center. They are required to be able to demonstrate empathy, neutrality, and impartiality and to advocate and use a collaborative process for resolving conflicts. . . .

The dominant parallels between the two types of dispute resolvers are, first, the third parties are respected and trusted by those in conflict (with Korean-Americans, they are also highly respected by the broader community) and, second, the third parties exhibit respect for the people, acting to minimize anxieties, fears, and uneasiness. In both cases, they are responsible for the comfort of the parties and the atmosphere in which the conflict and solutions are discussed. Both act as "agents of reality," helping parties to assess costs and benefits of an ongoing conflict, versus a swift resolution, and to evaluate the viability of solutions. On the surface, these features appear to be very similar. However, the ways in which they are displayed vary. The traits that make a third party respected and trusted are not the same for each group. Methods of alleviating anxieties differ. . . .

Differences between the two third parties are even more numerous. Korean-Americans prefer intermediaries who are personally known to them, have substantial knowledge of their life circumstances, and who can encourage people to do good and behave properly. It is important that they give advice—sound advice. Mediators in American conflict resolution centers are trained not to offer solutions or any other type of advice. The third party in the mediation center is seen as a resource person for the parties, someone knowledgeable and skilled about a process for resolving conflicts. Korean-Americans consult the third party for his or her knowledge about proper actions to take in troubled situations, for substantive guidance to the best decisions. . . .

Third-Party Preparation

In general, preparation by mediators in the community-based centers is concentrated in their formal training for the position of mediator. That preparation is considered to be adequate for any type of conflict case they may mediate. A Korean-American intermediary does fresh, extensive personal preparation during each phase of every actual conflict situation.

American mediation centers emphasize the adequacy of mediator training as preparation for all types of conflict cases because they believe in treating all persons equally, in individuals' responsibility for their own resolutions. The mediator's role is to manage the general process rather than to be intimately involved in the substantive issues. Training in communication skills and the sequential aspects of the mediation process is considered the foundation that will carry the mediator through each case. Mediators do not need to be experts on the issues of concern to the parties. They do spend some time just before the mediation session reviewing very basic information about each of the parties and a synopsis of the conflict issues, as presented on the intake form. They may review their training manual in order to remember what steps to follow, the ground rules to use, and suggested phrases. They gather additional information about the parties and the conflict itself only during the sessions, when the parties tell their stories. If the mediators are unsure how to proceed with a session, they may have brief private caucuses with co-mediators to discuss and plan alternative actions to help the parties (for example, how to balance powers between the parties, especially to empower a weaker one, or what to do in a deadlock situation). Mediators spend very little time reflecting on the case when they are not face to face with the parties. Preparing the appropriate atmosphere for the sessions is generally limited to making sure that the furniture in the office is adequately arranged. There is a strong belief that by plugging into the general process and techniques learned in the training workshops, the mediators can handle any conflict case efficiently.

It is not essential for the Korean-American intermediary to be efficient. Rather, thorough and thoughtful preparation is highly valued. The ideal intermediary is planning throughout the process, which begins with fact finding about the wider relationships between or among the groups of which the conflicting persons are members (historical, current, and potential future interactions), the opinions of others about the conflict, and the characters of those involved. Preparation includes seeking a profound understanding of the conditions of the parties involved, their expected behaviors, their characters, and the social context in which they live and will live. They draw on the teachings of others, their own experiences, what the sages have said about proper conduct in society, and other relevant material. The Korean-American process considers contemplation to find optimal solutions, the best presentation of a solution, and the most persuasive arguments for appropriate behavior. Preparation also comprises making arrangements for meeting with people at various locations and times, such as for the concluding social occasion in which harmony is restored.

Third-Party Meetings with Conflicting Parties

Contrasts are apparent in the pattern of activities when the third party and those central to the conflict convene. An important area of difference is in structural features, for example, where they meet (in an office or an informal setting), who is present (third party and conflicting parties; face-to-face or separate meetings with the go-between; only the immediate parties present or extended family and friends also permitted), and the duration and pace of the meetings (relatively few lively meetings or numerous meetings and gradual progress over a period of time).

The degree of structure and the atmosphere of the meetings are different. The gathering in the mediation center is very structured and businesslike, with a stress on hard work and confidentiality regarding all that is said. The tone is serious; light humor is used primarily to ease tensions. Displays of emotions by all are controlled and limited by the mediator. A definite sequence is followed: the announcement of ground rules, uninterrupted story telling, the generation of optional solutions, discussion and negotiation of the final terms of agreement, the joint signing of a written contractual agreement. All is done through what is usually designated as a collaborative problem-solving approach. The process used in the mediation center is very action oriented, that is, the pace is deliberately kept active and little time is allowed for contemplation by anyone.

The Korean-American process allows more time for thoughtful discussion and individual contemplation by the third party as well as by those considered to be suffering the conflict. The structure is less formal, partly because the go-between meets separately with each person when their kibuns are most likely to be receptive to the type of discussion he or she wants to have with them, initially to gather information, later to give advice and encourage them to accept a solution. Neither the process as a whole nor the individual meetings have a clear time frame. Each meeting may last for minutes or for several hours. It may take several weeks or months until understanding occurs and *hwa hae* is achieved. There are no set days of the week, hours, or locations in which the meetings may take place. The process is fluid and flexible.

The mediation center's process is virtually always a face-to-face interaction of the parties, in which they do most of the talking directly to each other. The mediators direct them to address certain topics and move the discussion from stage to stage. The Korean-American intermediary, meeting individually with each of the persons in the conflict, probably talks more than they do: describing the solution and reasons for recommending it, trying to convince each person of the benefits of accommodating or compromising, and relaying the thoughts of the other persons with whom he or she has been conferring. Emotional outbursts by those in conflict tend to be accepted and left to run their own course.

In both processes, effective communication is valued. The emphasis for the center's mediators is on listening skill. Although being a good listener is also considered important for both the Korean-American intermediaries and the persons they are speaking to, effective speaking skills (primarily connoting the sensitive phrasing of ideas) are emphasized more. In the mediation center, direct communication among all present is the modus operandi, whereas among Korean-Americans, use of indirect communication is more prevalent and is the accepted norm. One of the ways in which Yum (1988) differentiates between these two communication styles is by noting that for East Asians, communication cannot be compartmentalized; it is an ongoing, infinite process of interpretation between people. The North American orientation, on the other hand, is to perceive communication as the transfer of messages during a short-term, discontinuous relationship.

The mediation centers emphasize the importance of giving all parties the opportunity for full and open expression of their views of the conflict and what they want to do about it. Korean-Americans interviewed did not mention this goal at all.

The content of the discussions is also different in each procedure. The Korean-Americans are more likely to talk of the moral dilemmas involved, proper conduct, the rights and wrongs of individual behaviors, duties and considerations for other people, and one's obligations to the harmonious functioning of society. Deliberations can be lengthy and philosophical. The mediators in the community-based centers keep the discussions on a more matter-of-fact level, circumscribed essentially by the immediate situations of the parties and the conflict.

In both processes, all parties try to discover what ingredients are necessary to end the conflict and accept that the ultimate responsibility for making the final decisions belongs to those engaged in the conflict, not to the third parry.

Generation and Selection of Solutions

The Korean-Americans interviewed stressed that they want the advice of an intermediary about the best way for each of them to handle the conflict. They believe that if they need help, it is because their emotions are inhibiting their abilities to make good decisions, and that the intermediary is the objective analyst they require. Although they may contribute ideas to the intermediary, they rely on his or her thoughtful guidance to generate viable solutions.

The philosophy of the American mediation center is that people need to create their own solutions, because they know better than the third parry what is feasible for resolving the conflict, and because solutions generated by the parties are more likely to be sustained than those generated by someone else: the parties must "own" the agreement. The self-generation approach follows from the American accent on self-reliance.

The plan of the mediation center process is for the parties to the conflict to define the issues clearly and identify their respective needs and underlying interests, before seeking potential solutions. The mediator leads the parties through the steps: brainstorming potential options, establishing criteria for selecting the best ones, negotiating something for each person, and then narrowing the list of possibilities to the final selection and refinements. Mediators may suggest ideas if the parties seem unable to produce any acceptable to both sides. They may also query the parties to do some reality checking about the solutions proposed. Mediators remind the parties that solutions should concentrate on the immediate and short-term actions. Solutions may or may not include a component of restitution. Ideally, the moral solution to the conflict will be a win-win option with something for everyone, so that no one loses.

The Korean-American intermediary gathers ideas from the parties in order to generate possible solutions. The intermediary's own experiences and the words of respected sages are also considered in the search for solutions appropriate to a particular configuration of symbiotic relationships. Thus no one's allegiance to a group is questioned, face-saving is maintained or restored, and the persons in the dispute can find ways to come together ideologically. The intermediary contemplates and composes one or more solutions to propose to each person, along with reasons why they should be seriously considered. In effect, he or she negotiates with each person and, as go-between, refines and builds an understanding acceptable to both. The solution need not be innovative; it may be patterned on precedents, and it may mean learning to cope with an existing situation.

There is very likely more emphasis on conformity in the Korean-American process than in solutions generated by the mediation center process. Final understandings will be those that make the persons concerned feel best, feel most in harmony with one another. Restoration of harmony is more important than resolution of material issues. Complementary relations mean that no one loses, for each person has some type of protracted obligation to the other that may not be evidenced in the immediate situation or even in this generation. The binding understanding is based on a long-term perspective of the common good. For the short term, self-interests may be subordinated to the honor and well-being of one's family and other relevant groups. People neither owe nor own anything by themselves.

In the process advocated by the mediation centers, although there is an expression of interest in the relationship between the parties, a decision on a fair distribution of resources is an important part of the agreement. It is assumed that relationships are relatively transient; the conflict may, in fact, pertain to the dissolution of a relationship.

Concluding the Process

The final phases of the Korean-American process are not events that explicitly announce the conclusion or the definitive resolution of the conflict. They incorporate a more intuitive recognition that an understanding has been reached and harmony has been restored. There is a social occasion in which the reestablishment of harmonious relationships is unofficially observed. The Korean-American understanding is oral. Apologies are important components. The celebration of restored harmony takes place in a relaxed social atmosphere, with gaiety, refreshments, and probably the ritual of sharing a glass.

On the other hand, the conclusion of the conflict resolution procedure used by the American mediation centers is solemnized in at least three undisguised steps: the writing and signing of an agreement, closing statements, and a follow-up with the parties by a center staff person to determine the status of the agreement. The formal agreement (usually on a special form) specifies in detail who will do what, when, and how. Copies are given to each party, and one is kept in the center's files. A relatively cursory evaluation of the case may also be done by the mediators.

In both processes, the third party acknowledges in some fashion the positive aspects of what has occurred: for example, the mediator congratulates the parties on reaching an agreement and for working hard to do so; the Korean-American intermediary affirms the fine character of each person as shown by what each has done for the good of the larger group. . . .

Conclusions

Many differences were found between . . . an American mediation and a Korean-American harmony restoration process, . . . as well as in the perceptions of types of conflicts and their origins. Particular contrasts were identified in the goals and objectives of the processes, how they are initiated, the roles and responsibilities of the people in conflict and of the third parties, the type and extent of third-party preparation, the structure of third-party meetings with the conflicting parties, the generation and selection of solutions, and how processes are concluded.

The findings provide a point of departure for exploration and discussion of what mediation centers can do if they are chartered to serve entire communities, and if they are not intent on imposing one basic process on all persons. Some mediation centers may decide to serve only those who find the standard mediation process acceptable.

Others may want to design their programs to meet the process preferences of a broader group. Instead of providing "an alternative" (that is, mediation), they may want to provide "optional processes." They will need to garner information in depth about diversity in their neighborhoods and, actively involving the people who may seek assistance with conflicts, develop relevant services and training for third parties. If conflicts in multi-ethnic communities are to be handled effectively, third parties must, at a minimum, become knowledgeable about different conflict values and forums, so that they can respond flexibly and competently when persons different from themselves request assistance.

The ethics of mediation centers are also at issue. Each person's values, attitudes, and behaviors should be respected. No one should be coerced into a process that violates values or embarrasses individuals. A deeper understanding of diversity is needed, one that goes beyond the customs that are readily manifested. An additional caveat: degrees of assimilation vary by individual, making prejudging and stereotyping very hazardous and inappropriate. Documenting an ethnic group's general orientation toward interpersonal conflicts and methods for handling them is only the initial step in preparing a full complement of true alternative dispute resolution services. Identifying intragroup preferences will allow us to move toward offering help with both intragroup and intergroup conflicts.

C. Prejudice and ADR Processes

1. Richard Delgado, et al., *Fairness and Formality: Minimizing the Risk of Prejudice in Alternative Dispute Resolution*, 1985 Wis. L. Rev. 1359, 1387-1404*

III. THEORIES OF PREJUDICE AND ADR

E. The Optimal Setting for the Reduction of Prejudice:
Formal vs. Informal Dispute Resolution

The selection of one mode or another of dispute resolution can do little, at least in the short run, to counter prejudice that stems from authoritarian personalities or historical currents. Prejudice that results from social-psychological factors is, however, relatively controllable. Much prejudice is environmental—people express it because the setting encourages or tolerates it. In some settings people feel free to vent hostile or denigrating attitudes toward members of minority groups; in others they do not.

[S]ocial-psychological theories of prejudice indicate that prejudiced persons are least likely to act on their beliefs if the immediate environment confronts them with the discrepancy between their professed ideals and their personal hostilities against out-groups. According to social psychologists, once most persons realize that their attitudes and behavior deviate from what is expected, they will change or suppress them.

Given this human tendency to conform, American institutions have structured and defined situations to encourage appropriate behavior. Our judicial system, in particular, has incorporated societal norms of fairness and even-handedness into institutional expectations and rules of procedure at many points. These norms create a "public conscience and a standard for expected behavior that check overt signs of prejudice." They do this in a variety of ways. First, the formalities of a court trial—the flag, the black robes, the ritual—remind those present that the occasion calls for the higher, "public" values, rather than the lesser values embraced during moments of informality and intimacy. In a courtroom trial the American Creed, with its emphasis on fairness, equality, and respect for personhood, governs. Equality of status, or something approaching it, is preserved—each party is represented by an attorney and has a prescribed time and manner for speaking, putting on evidence, and questioning the other side.

Equally important, formal adjudication avoids the unstructured, intimate interactions that, according to social scientists, foster prejudice. The rules of procedure maintain distance between the parties. Counsel for the parties do not address one another, but present the issue to the trier of fact. The rules preserve the formality of the setting by dictating in detail how this confrontation is to be conducted.

That the formality of adversarial adjudication deters prejudice is borne out by the few empirical studies that have investigated the question. An experiment conducted by Walker and his colleagues showed that subjects viewed adversarial procedures as "the most preferable and the fairest mode of dispute resolution," a preference that may even extend to persons in countries that do not use an adversarial system of justice. Another experiment placed subjects in a laboratory setting behind a "veil of ignorance" and asked them to choose among a variety of procedural alternatives. Almost all the subjects chose the adversarial system. The authors concluded that the adversary system introduces a systematic evidentiary bias in favor of the weaker party.

Another experiment showed that the "competitive presentation of evidence counteracts decisionmaker bias. . . ." In one experiment, subjects were presented with a test case; they were given a list of both "lawful" and "unlawful" factors, but were told to consider only the "lawful" ones in making a decision. The results showed that in a simulated adversarial framework, even those subjects predetermined to be biased gave less weight to unlawful factors in their decisionmaking. The authors hypothesized that adversarial procedure counteracts decisionmaker bias because it combats the natural human tendency to "judge too swiftly in terms of the familiar that which is not yet fully known." The human propensity to prejudge and make irrational categorizations is thus checked by procedural safeguards found in an adversarial system.

Formality and adversarial procedures thus counteract bias among legal decisionmakers and disputants. But it seems likely that those factors increase fairness in yet a third way—by strengthening the resolve of minority disputants to pursue their legal rights.

F. Dispute Resolution and the Minority Disputant

Early in life, minority children become aware of themselves as different, especially with respect to skin color. This awareness is often not merely neutral, but associated with feelings of inferiority. Separate studies by psychologists Kenneth Clark and Mary Goodman in which minority children were presented with dolls of various colors illustrate this graphically. For example, when asked to make a choice between a white and black doll, "the doll that looks like you," most black children chose the white doll. A black child justified his choice of the white doll over the black doll as a friend because "his feet, hands, ears, elbows, knees, and hair are clean." In another experiment, a black child hated her skin color so much that she "vigorously lathered her arms and face with soap in an effort to wash away the dirt." As minority children grow, they are "likely to experience a long series of events, from exclusion from play groups and cliques to violence and threats of violence, that are far less likely to be experienced by the average member of the majority group." Against a background of "slights, rebuffs, forbidden opportunities, restraints, and often violence . . . the minority group member shapes that fundamental aspect of personality—a sense of oneself and one's place in the total scheme of things."

Discriminatory treatment can trigger a variety of responses. Writers identify three main reactions: avoidance, aggression, and acceptance. A minority group member may display one or more of these responses, depending on the setting. In some situations, victims of discrimination are likely to respond with apathy or defeatism; in others, the same individuals may forthrightly and effectively assert their interests. In general, when a person feels "he is the master of his fate, that he can control to some extent his own destiny, that if he works hard things will go better for him, he is then likely to achieve more. . . ." That is, minority group members are more apt to participate in processes which they believe will respond to reasonable efforts. They are understandably less likely to participate in proceedings where the results are random and unpredictable.

Thus, it is not surprising that a favored forum for redress of race-based wrongs has been the traditional adjudicatory setting. Minorities recognize that public institutions, with their defined rules and formal structure, are more subject to rational control than private or informal structures. Informal settings allow wider scope for the participants' emotional and behavioral idiosyncrasies; in these settings majority group members are most likely to exhibit prejudicial behavior. Thus, a formal adjudicative forum increases the minority group member's sense of control and, therefore, may be seen as the fairer forum. This perception becomes self-fulfilling: minority persons are encouraged to pursue their legal rights as though prejudice were unlikely and thus the possibility of prejudice is in fact lessened.

IV. THE LEFT CRITIQUE OF ADR

Many commentators who have criticized ADR have expressed concerns associated with the "left"—concerns for the unempowered, the poor and other disadvantaged groups. This section canvasses the thoughts of these commentators, in particular objections that informalism (i) solidifies control by capital and the state; (ii) disadvantages "weaker" parties; (iii) expands state control; (iv) deflects energy away from collective action; and (v) promotes law without justice. As we shall see, the political critique of ADR, although based on different premises and couched in different terms, comes to the same general conclusion as the psychological critique: ADR is no safe haven for the poor and powerless.

Some commentators have criticized informalism for reinforcing powerful or authoritarian forces in society—capital, the state, formal legal institutions, or the wealthy. The most representative of these writers is Richard Abel, a member of the Critical Legal Studies Conference.

In an early article, Abel writes that informalism inhibits social change by persuading disputants with legitimate grievances to sacrifice their grievances in the interests of peace and cooperation. Informalism "presupposes a high degree of normative consensus on the substantive norms that control behavior outside the legal system" and views dispute resolution as a process by which a third party works to get the opposing parties to acknowledge their shared values and resolve their dispute on the basis of those values. The flaw in this view, according to Abel, is that instead of consensus there is disagreement about social and political values; by concealing this dissensus, ADR curbs efforts by have-nots to improve their position.

Abel's later views take on a decidely more Marxist cast. In *Conservative Conflict and the Reproduction of Capitalism: The Role of Informal Justice,* Abel argues that the rise of informalism indicates a shift of power to the more powerful elements in society—capital and the state—a shift whose source lies in the "backlash to the 'rights explosion' of the last few decades." Abel contrasts formalism, a product of classical liberal theory that has worked to protect the oppressed, with informalism, which:

> expresses positivist theories . . . which justify domination, authority, [and] the exercise of

> control from above . . . Classic liberalism is the ideology of the revolutionary phase of capitalism, whereas positivism is the ideology of capitalism triumphant. The movement from formalism to informalism thus reflects and carries forward a shift in power from the less privileged to the more.

In a third article, Abel argues that "informal institutions neutralize conflict by responding to grievances in ways that inhibit their transformation into serious challenges to the domination of state and capital." This neutralization occurs in a number of ways. First, informalism allows the state to extend its control to new areas of conflict. It does this by attracting to formal institutions disputes that otherwise would have been settled outside the system had not informal mechanisms reduced the workload of formal institutions, and by attracting to informal forums disputes that would have been settled outside the system had those informal forums not been available. Further, by seeming to proffer solicitude, informalism fosters dependence, thereby strengthening the state's and capital's control over conflict in society.

Thus, by directing conflict into safe channels, capital and the state are able to render conflict "conservative," i.e., safe, repetitive, and homeostatic. By creating an environment that emphasizes cooperation and imposing that on the disputants, ADR denies the existence of many conflicts and transforms others into simple misunderstandings. When informalism is unable to suppress conflict completely, it channels it so as to minimize its political and structural aspects. It does this by defining "who can claim and what they can claim," by defining "the locus of significant conflict—typically the neighborhood," and by defining "the adversaries against whom claims can be made." Informalism directs attention to interpersonal, intra-neighborhood, and intra-class disagreements, ignoring the conflicts that are important to the oppressed (and likely to threaten the powerful)—conflicts between labor and capital, consumer and producer, polluter and inhabitants of polluted environments.

Others have expressed similar concerns about informalism. For example, Auerbach, in *Justice Without Law?*, charges that informal alternatives were more or less consciously designed to siphon discontent from courts. Alternative processes reduce the danger of political confrontation and thus preserve the power of legal institutions and the stability of the social system.

In addition to the macropolitical concerns just reviewed, critics have also expressed microinstrumental concerns for the individuals who use ADR. Abel who is also a principal spokesperson for this view, observes that formal legal institutions begin with a presumption of inequality between the parties and construct elaborate rules and mechanisms to protect weaker parties. Informal systems deemphasize these concerns—they presume "that the people or entities that interact outside formal legal institutions are roughly equal in political power, wealth, and social status." However, according to Abel, this is an erroneous presumption—there is no such equality—with the result that informal forums greatly disadvantage weaker parties.

Mark Lazerson comes to the same conclusion, based on studies of landlord-tenant relations. He argues that "procedural formality recognizes inequality and attempts to compensate for it by making both parties conform to the same standards." If the procedural formalities are withdrawn, the weaker party stands little or no chance of succeeding in litigation. Hofrichter and [Laura] Nader level similar criticism, the former based on his studies of neighborhood justice centers; the latter, on her examination of consumer complaint mechanisms.

For some, the tension between informalism and justice is unresolvable: "Without legal power the imbalance between aggrieved individuals and corporations, or government agencies cannot be redressed." One cannot have equity and informality at the same time.

A third criticism is that informalism extends the state's control over members of disadvantaged classes. This happens in two ways. First, "[b]ecause informal state institutions reduce or disguise coercion[,] they can . . . review behavior that presently escapes state control." In our society the reach of coercive institutions is limited by formal rights and individual resistance to coercion. Institutions that appear noncoercive circumvent formal rights and undermine resistance, and are thus able to bring new types of dispute within the ambit of state control.

Second, the "creation of informal institutions increases the quantum of state resources devoted to social control." By relieving the courts of some of their burden, informal mechanisms free up resources which the courts can then use to process more cases. And, because informal forums attract disputes that would not otherwise have been handled by the state, they increase the areas of life subject to state coercion.

Informalism thus extends state control. While this is worrisome, it does not in itself imply bias against minorities, the poor, and the politically unempowered. However, this increased state control does implicate such bias because informal procedures, like formal ones, are often directed toward the economically, socially, and politically oppressed. This is evidenced, for instance, by the location of NJCs in neighborhoods with disproportionate numbers of these groups' members. Moreover, the differing ways in which the poor and the privileged use legal institutions make the poor especially susceptible to state control. The poor use law "to settle disputes, enhance their authority, or demonstrate conformity to norms [and] do so in controversies with equals or inferiors, not against superiors." The privileged, by contrast, use law "to control inferiors but protect one another from state intervention."

Hofrichter echoes many of these criticisms, but adds a new twist. He argues that informal dispute resolution processes are more intrusive than those associated with formal adjudication. For example, he points to mediation and the freewheeling, "therapeutic" inquiry that characterizes it, an inquiry whose "openness magnifies the extent to which the state penetrates the lives of disputants: Their deepest emotions and most personal problems become part of the process of conflict resolution. This intervention itself is regulation, regardless of its effect on the outcome." Informal institutions can also expand state control by referring disputants to other state agencies for further, sometimes extended, monitoring, in the course of which detailed records are often kept.

Commentators also criticize informalism for draining energy from collective action that would be of greater benefit to disadvantaged groups than would a series of individual decisions. First, informalism may attract disputes that otherwise would have led to collective action. Second, by handling problems on a case-by-case basis, informalism ignores the class basis of many kinds of conflict: "[T]he content of conflict is divorced from collective interests, segregated from similar cases, and limited to the immediate relationship between the disputants. Consumers may "win" cases as individuals . . . but lose as members of a wider social class. . . ." And Nader, examining consumer complaints, observes:

> Disputing without law is not a very satisfactory experience for most consumers and citizens in this country, yet it is unlikely that the force of law can be marshalled to address "little injustices" unless they are reconceptualized as collective harms. For official action in that direction to have any likelihood of yielding more than symbolic victories, an active and vital grass-roots citizen and consumer movement must be encouraged.

A final criticism is that informalism serves private interests at the expense of public ones. This works to the detriment of minorities, the poor, women, and other disadvantaged groups to the extent that they benefit most from the public policies underlying formal legal processes. The principal spokesperson for this view is Owen Fiss. [See Chapter 17, section B.]

V. PREJUDICE IN ADR—ASSESSING AND BALANCING THE RISKS

ADR increases the risk of prejudice toward vulnerable disputants. Our review of social science writings on prejudice reveals that the rules and structures of formal justice tend to suppress bias, whereas informality tends to increase it. The social science findings are reinforced, on a sociopolitical level, by ADR's left wing critics, who see ADR as increasing the power of authoritarian social institutions over individuals, extending state coercive power into new areas of citizens' lives, and discouraging collective action.

This part assumes that the social-science and left wing critiques are at least partly valid—that ADR does indeed increase the risk of unfair treatment for minority disputants, women and the poor. From this it proceeds to address two final questions: (i) How much weight should be assigned to such a risk? and (ii) Can the risk be minimized without forfeiting the benefits and advantages of ADR?

A. The Ideal of Fairness in American Procedure

If ADR increases the risk of prejudice or bias in adjudication, it does not follow immediately that ADR should be curtailed. Equity concerns are only one value among many; conceivably, the gains in flexibility, speed, and economy that ADR's proponents cite could override moderate losses in fairness. A survey of the role of the ideal of fairness in American procedural law suggests, however, that the balance should be struck on the side of fairness.

American procedural law's history evidences a strong and steady evolution toward fairness, an evolution that has at times overshadowed the impulse toward economy and efficiency. Over a century ago, the Field code simplified pleading rules, largely to eliminate traps for the unwary and to render legal paper work intelligible to ordinary persons. The great procedural reforms of this century, civil discovery and long-arm jurisdiction, were likewise intended to equalize power and opportunity among litigants. Discovery enables litigants of modest means to learn facts about the dispute that might otherwise remain in the exclusive possession of the more powerful party. Long-arm jurisdiction enables citizens injured by corporations and other powerful entities to bring them to account where the injury occurred, instead of being forced to sue where the defendant is found.

Civil and criminal reforms have made access to court cheaper and more readily available to all. Public defenders and legal aid attorneys represent individuals who cannot afford the costs of a private lawyer. Transcripts on appeal in some cases have been held a defendant's constitutional right. A panoply of rules and procedures, reviewed earlier, have developed to assure fairness, despite the added costs they impose. Many of these are minor, such as the rule permitting modification of time rules for good cause. Others are broader, cutting across areas and stages of litigation, such as the requirement of trial by jury. Although efficiency and fairness are often in tension, our jurisprudence regards fairness in litigation as an important ideal not to be discarded lightly—and certainly not in broad based, systemic fashion. The next section addresses the question of how best to preserve that value in informal proceedings without sacrificing the benefits of informality.

Striking the Balance: Protecting Against Prejudice Without Sacrificing the Benefits of ADR

ADR offers a number of clear-cut benefits. It can shape a decree flexibly so as to protect a continuing relationship between the parties. It is low-cost, speedy, and, for some at least, non-intimidating. Yet there is little benefit for a minority disputant in a quick, painless hearing that renders an adverse decision tainted by prejudice.

Part III showed that the risk of prejudice is greatest when a member of an in-group confronts a member of an out-group; when that confrontation is direct, rather than through intermediaries; when there are few rules to constrain conduct; when the setting is closed and does not make clear that "public" values are to preponderate; and when the controversy concerns an intimate, personal matter rather than some impersonal question. Our review also indicated that many minority participants will press their claims most vigorously when they believe that what they do and say will make a difference, that the structure will respond, and that the outcome is predictable and related to effort and merit.

It follows that ADR is most apt to incorporate prejudice when a person of low status and power confronts a person or institution of high status and power. In such situations, the party of high status is more likely than in other situations to attempt to call up prejudiced responses; at the same time, the individual of low status is less likely to press his or her claim energetically. The dangers increase when the mediator or other third party is a member of the superior group or class. Examples of ADR settings that may contain these characteristics are prison and other institutional review boards, consumer complaint panels, and certain types of cases referred to an ombudsman. In these situations, minorities and members of other out-groups should opt for formal in-court adjudication, and the justice system ought to avoid pressuring them to accept an alternate procedure. ADR should be reserved for cases in which parties of comparable power and status confront each other.

ADR also poses heightened risks of prejudice when the issue to be adjudicated touches a sensitive or intimate area of life, for example, housing or culture-based conduct. Thus, many landlord-tenant, interneighbor, and intrafamilial disputes are poor candidates for ADR. When the parties are of unequal status and the question litigated concerns a sensitive, intimate area, the risks of an outcome colored by prejudice are especially great. If, for reasons of economy or efficiency ADR must be resorted to in these situations, the likelihood of bias can be reduced by providing rules that clearly specify the scope of the proceedings and forbid irrelevant or intrusive inquiries, by requiring open proceedings, and by providing some form of higher review. The third-party facilitator or decisionmaker should be a professional and be acceptable to both parties. Any party desiring one should be provided with an advocate, ideally an attorney, experienced with representation before the forum in question. To avoid atomization and lost opportunities to aggregate claims and inject public values into dispute resolution, ADR mechanisms should not be used in cases that have a broad societal dimension, but forward them to court for appropriate treatment.

Would measures like these destroy the very advantages of economy, simplicity, speed, and flexibility that make ADR attractive? Would such measures render ADR proceedings as expensive, time-consuming, formalistic, and inflexible as trials? These measures do increase the costs, but, on balance, those costs seem worth incurring. The ideal of equality before the law is too insistent a value to be compromised in the name of more mundane advantages. Continued growth of ADR consistent with goals of basic fairness will require two essential adjustments: (1) It will be necessary to identify those areas and types of ADR in which the dangers of prejudice are greatest and to direct those grievances to formal court adjudication; (2) In those areas in which the risk of prejudice exists, but is not so great as to require an absolute ban, checks and formalities must be built into ADR to ameliorate these risks as much as possible. With both inquiries, the preliminary investigations and tentative identifications of troublesome areas made in this Article may prove useful starting points.

2. Comments and Questions

a. Do you believe that "the adversary system introduces a systematic evidentiary bias in favor of the weaker party?" Do you think that Delgado believes this proposition? (He cites this conclusion from a study, without questioning it.) Note that Delgado does not simply argue the clearly true proposition that the legal system sometimes favors the weak, but that the adversary introduces a "systematic bias" in favor of weaker parties.

b. Professor Menkel-Meadow has dubbed this position "litigation romanticism," and asks this question: How often has the "little consumer" really had an empowering democratic encounter in a courtroom with one of the three major car companies? Carrie Menkel-Meadow, *The Many Ways of Mediation: The Transformation of Traditions, Ideologies, Paradigms, and Practices,* 1995 NEGOTIATION J. 217, 233. Are there good answers to her question?

c. What sort of evidence, either current or historical might be marshalled to support Professor Delgado's assertion? For some possibilities, see the Laura Nader article in Chapter 3, section F, and the material on women being disadvantaged in divorce mediation in Chapter 8, section C.

d. The rapid growth in the use of arbitration clauses by businesses in contracts with their customers and employees suggests that large organizations prefer to avoid a judicial forum. It does not, however, follow that therefore consumers and employees should prefer access to courts. There is considerable evidence that the "game" of litigation is a "lose-lose" situation, compared to mediation and arbitration.

e. The conventional wisdom among scholars from all over the ideological spectrum is that the legal system reflects power relationships, notably economic interests, within the society. Lawrence Friedman in his much acclaimed A HISTORY OF AMERICAN LAW put the matter this way: "The basic premise of this book is that, despite a strong dash of history and idiosyncracy, the strongest ingredient in American law, at any given time, is the present: current emotions, real economic interests, concrete political groups." Lawrence M. Friedman, A HISTORY OF AMERICAN LAW 14 (1973).

f. Suppose Delgado's views about prejudice in ADR are substantially correct, along with the similar views of those who argue that mediation (and perhaps other ADR processes) are bad for women (the majority), at least in the divorce context. What then? What does Delgado suggest? What do you think?

g. Delgado observes that: "ADR is most apt to incorporate prejudice when a person of low status and power confronts a person or institution of high status and power." Do you agree? Now substitute litigation for ADR. Is your answer to this question different from your answer to the previous question? Is it likely that whatever the regime of rules, and whatever the arena, persons of "high status and power" will generally "win" over persons of "low status and power?"

h. The dramatic cuts in funding for legal aid programs make access to civil courts ever less realistic for the indigent, and even middle income persons.

i. In evaluating ADR, it is important to consider the "compared to what" question. For most people, the alternative to an ADR process is not a full blown due process trial with a team of the finest lawyers in the land. For them, the choices often are to do nothing, or to go into debt to hire a relatively inexpensive attorney.

j. Upon examination, some of the criticism of ADR cited by Delgado is based on the success of ADR in settling disputes. For example, "informalism" is criticized "for draining energy from collective action" by the settlement of individual grievances, which if unsettled would lead to collective action "that would be of greater benefit to disadvantaged groups. . . ." That is a fair enough point from the perspective of a political organizer, but it hardly follows that therefore the informal process is defective. Rather the complaint is that by resolving individual disputes more effectively, opposition to the system is reduced.

k. Even if one succeeded in showing that ADR is no worse than litigation or other options in terms of the prejudice faced by minorities, immigrants, or other disfavored classes this is hardly a large compliment. Professor Delgado's title states a goal that clearly is desirable: "minimizing the risk of prejudice in ADR." Seriously addressing that objective requires a deeper understanding of ADR procedures and the differences between them. Achieving such an understanding is a central goal of this course.

D. Dispute Settlement Among Native Americans

1. Comments and Questions

a. The purpose of this section is to introduce you to a different legal tradition and another way of thinking about dispute resolution, not to educate you about "legal" principles employed by Navajos or Native Americans. Even the word "legal" is a cultural artifact, because the very idea of a clearly defined separate domain of law and lawyers is by no means the norm in other countries, or even in sub-communities within the United States.

b. The study of dispute settlement in the absence of a formal government structure and legal system has been conducted largely by anthropologists rather than lawyers. See the materials in Chapter 3, section F. If one defines law as the command of the sovereign supported by a sanction, as do the legal positivists, many societies do not have "law." Admittedly, these societies deal with disputes, but that is not the domain of law and lawyers.

c. Of what relevance is the Navajo peacemaking experience to an urban America in the age of computers?

2. Robert Yazzie, "Traditional Navajo Dispute Resolution in the Navajo Peacemaker Court," NIDR Forum, Spring 1995, at 4*

[The Honorable Robert Yazzie is Chief Justice of the Navajo Nation.]

INTRODUCTION - CENTURIES OF MISUNDERSTANDING

Before explaining how traditional Navajo dispute resolution works, we must consider an ancient problem. On August 9, 1555, Holy Roman Emperor Charles the Fifth issued a decree. It said that the "good laws of Indians" must be "honored and obeyed." Why is it that today, Americans know nothing about "the good laws of Indians?" Many people do not know that traditional Indian law still exists. We of the Navajo Nation courts believe that the Navajo Peacemaker Court is an exceptional justice method. It uses our "good laws." We believe they must be "honored and obeyed."

There is another conflict: while the Indian nations of the United States have had their own courts for over one hundred years, Indian judges have problems getting respect. While there are over two hundred tribal courts in the United States, they are ignored. Some people say they do not trust tribal court decisions; that somehow an Indian court does not offer due process or assure equal protection of law. Those are false assumptions.

I will describe our law and the workings of the Navajo Peacemaker Court. There is nothing mysterious about it, because it makes a lot of sense. You will see why we feel it is not "alternative dispute resolution," but the best way to deal with human conflict. To us it is "O.D.R."—"original dispute resolution."

THE DEFINITION OF LAW

People think they know what the word law means. However, when you talk about "traditional Indian law" or "Indian common law," you lose them. People do not have the slightest idea what you mean.

What is law? One definition is that it consists of three things: norms, institutions, and force.

The first element is norms. A norm is a feeling of ought—one ought to do this or ought not do that.

The second is institutions. A norm becomes a law when it is restated as a rule and enforced by an institution. Most people think of that as police and courts.

The third element is coercion or force. Many definitions of law insist that without force or the ability to punish, there can be no law.

This is a non-Indian definition. It insists that there must be rules and punishment. This kind of law can only hurt; it cannot heal. Navajos do not believe in powerful authority figures who judge others. Navajos cannot accept punishment as an effective way to deal with bad conduct. To understand those beliefs, let us look at law from the Navajo viewpoint.

We too accept the approach that law is norms in institutions. When I first heard the definition above, I felt something was missing. I asked the person who gave it to me if human emotions should be an element. Aren't emotions a part of the process? Shouldn't they be? The Navajo language describes our norms, and Navajos say, "words are powerful." Each word tells something exactly. Many have strong connotations. A connotation is an emotional message.

*Reprinted with permission.

For example, let's take the Navajo word for lawyer. In Navajo, it is "'agha'diit'aahii." Some translate it as "one who can never lose an argument." What connotation does that carry? It is someone who is skilled in advocating a point of view to sell it to others. The actual translation is, "one who pushes out with words." The Navajo connotation is that such a person is pushy and bossy; not a very nice person at all. Navajos so respect individuality that they feel it is not polite to boss others around.

When Navajos define law, we use the norms element. A norm is a value and shared feeling about the way to do things. Sometimes, Navajos say "hozhigo" or "do things in a good way." We know what it means to "do things in a good way," because our language and education tells us how to feel that way and we know what it means. Navajos go beyond the idea of norms as an element of law to insist that moral values are an element. The Navajo word for law is "bee-haz'aanii." It means something fundamental, something that exists from the beginning of time, something that is absolutely there.

We say that the Holy People "put it there for us from the time of beginning" for better thinking, planning and guidance. We say, "life comes from it," because it nourishes our life. It is not simply rules to guide our daily lives, but the essence of life. The first element of our definition of law is strong shared feelings about the basics. It is something more—shared feelings about the right path. To us, the end goal of law is "hozho."

Given emotion in word connotations, it is difficult to translate that word into English. It is "the perfect state." It is when people come together and deal with each other well. Navajos believe that everything is a part of creation or reality, so hozho is when everyone and everything is in good relations. Sometimes the word is translated as harmony. It is much more. It is the goal of peacemaking—our justice and harmony ceremony. It means that "there is a place for everything in reality, and there is hozho when everything is in its proper place, functioning well with everything else." Our teachings and beliefs are designed to guide people toward that state. That kind of justice works, because it is a complete view of life and not a process where an individual wins or loses.

Navajos also believe that institutions are an element of law. To understand the Navajo definition, you must know about our traditional institutions. My relationships begin with my immediate family, but I also have obligations to my clan relatives through both my mother and father.

Navajo law builds on relationships. It works because of them. People's conduct is guided by family and clan relationships. Therefore, a clan is a legal institution, and I introduce myself by clan to tell you who I am.

If you are a Navajo, you also introduce yourself to me by clan, so we can tell how we are related to each other. That tells us both what our obligations are to each other. I have obligations to my relatives, but I also have obligations to strangers. We say, "treat strangers like they were a relative." Our law comes from relationships—from the most immediate to everyone and everything. I imagine that I am at the center of a circle, and my relations grow as I go out to the rim. If I am in a good state, so is my family. If my family functions well, so will its clans. If the clans work together, the Navajo Nation is well. If the Navajo Nation is strong, America is strong too. The good radiates out, if we all want it that way.

Navajos believe that every person is a judge. A judge is someone who sees a situation and applies values to tell people what to do about it. Each Navajo carries values inside. When there is trouble, Navajos use them to deal with it. Even when two people deal with each other, they are a legal institution. I will give you an example: An anthropologist by the name of Downs mentions a case where a man stole a woman's blanket and jewelry so he could sell them to buy wine. The woman suspected him and confronted him the next day. The man immediately admitted what he had done and gave the woman enough sheep to make up for the loss.

They used Navajo moral principles and emotions to do things "in a good way." The woman suspected the man and demanded nalyeeh. That is a word which asks for compensation for a wrong, and it is also a demand to do things in the proper way. The man knew what he did, and replied honestly. Why? Because good relationships are a basic value. He had to "do things in a good way" by making up for the theft, because that is a shared moral value. Also, Navajos live in small communities. If I get into an argument with someone, I still have to live in the same community with him.

How much compensation is due under our law? Enough "so there will be no hard feelings." The focus is not on money or amounts of money. It is on good feelings and relationships, while doing things in the good way.

Navajos part ways with their Anglo friends on the issue of whether force, coercion, or punishment are elements of law. We don't believe in it. Force, coercion, and punishment are not necessary to have law. We do not have institutions to punish. We have them to keep us together, not pull us apart through force or revenge. We do punish in our courts. We send people to jail, make them do community service, or impose fines on them. Those are modern practices. There were severe punishments in the old days. One of them was shunning, where everyone turned their backs on a repeat offender or someone who committed an outrageous crime. The worst punishment for a Navajo is for his family, clan and neighbors to shut him out. One of our judges says that someone who was shunned might commit suicide out of shame. Traditional Navajo law provided the death penalty, although it was unusual. It was used to punish incest, witchcraft or treason.

Early European explorers often said, "Indians have no law." Why? They didn't see police; didn't find courts; they saw no uniforms, jails, or trappings of power. They couldn't understand traditional leadership, so they couldn't see the elders or clan mothers, who are so important to native legal institutions. They couldn't identify Indian legal institutions, and thus assumed Indians had no law. They didn't see Indian due process in action, and that is still true today.

Misunderstandings come from the idea that you must have force and punishment to have law. Adjudication uses authority, rank and power, but that does not necessarily work. I can try to make someone else obey the rules using force. I can make a threat to punish, but what happens when I go away? When I turn my back, that person will usually return to what he was doing in the first place.

What if I deal with that person in a different way? Instead of threatening to punish, I deal with that person as an equal. Also, I bring in others to address the problem. We all talk out what it is and have an opinion about it. We speak with the wrongdoer, give our opinions, and ask him to respond back. We use our relationship with him to come to agreements.

Then, when I walk away, everyone knows what was said: everyone agrees on an outcome. I can turn my back, because everyone who was there knows the agreement and is there to enforce it. It's not a matter of threats—it's an agreement everyone knows and follows.

The agreement works without using force because of what we call "k'e." That is another word which is hard to translate. I usually translate it as respect. Others say it means solidarity. It is respect in the sense that Navajos have respect for others and for a decision made by the group. . . . K'e is a deep feeling of responsibilities to others and the duty to live in good relations with them. It has to do with the importance of relationships to foster consensus and healing. . . .

Another difference between the way you might look at institutions and the way Navajos see them is how we view leadership. In the Anglo way, a judge is one who knows the law and uses that knowledge to make decisions for others. A judge is supposed to be wise to decide things well. In an Anglo courtroom, a judge uses wisdom or knowledge of the law to announce the reasons for a decision. A judge sits over others and decides things for them. To make that appear fair, a judge fits the decision into the framework of the law to explain what he or she did.

Navajos see judges in a different way. In the traditional Navajo way, a judge is one who has the problem. The people involved in a dispute make a decision about what to do to resolve it. Everyone knows the law and the people who have the dispute talk about it to solve their own problem.

In Anglo dispute resolution, only those who are immediately involved in the dispute participate. In a courtroom, that is the plaintiff and the defendant. In alternative dispute resolution, it is only the people who are directly connected with the dispute. For example, in a divorce case, it is only the husband and wife. Aren't other people affected by divorce? What about the children? What about the couple's parents? What about neighbors? What about co-workers? Marital discord affects them too.

Think of a legal conflict as a "zone of dispute.". . . In Navajo law the couple's children, parents, and others are a part of the problem—or are affected by it—so they are also within the zone of dispute. They are there, because they are a part of it all. They all have opinions which come from their values, so they are all judges in the process.

If someone hurts me, my family is involved and part of the zone of dispute because I am hurt. My family relies on me for support, so an injury to me is an injury to them. My family owes me an obligation to protect me from others. My family participates in those impacts and duties. On the other hand, if I hurt someone and I am obliged to pay compensation to make up for an injury and make sure there are no hard feelings, my family is involved. It owes a duty to others to help pay it. That duty comes from the obligation to help me and the duty of clans as groups to work with each other.

When there is a dispute, everyone affected by conflict participates. We discuss our values and the moral principles which apply to the problem. We then come to an agreement about what to do that benefits everyone. Once that is done, there is a judgment everyone knows. We live by it. That is one of the ways Navajo relationships work as a legal system.

Having relatives involved in a dispute is fundamental. A non-Indian family court judge in Albuquerque, New Mexico likes to use Navajo peacemaking techniques in her domestic relations cases. In one case, involving child custody and visitation, the parties were Navajos. The judge called in a Navajo law school graduate to talk to them. She lectured away, with no success. Later, the judge brought in the parents of the couple to talk about custody and visitation. The child's grandparents settled the case. They influenced the fighting parents, because grandparents have an interest in their grandchild.

In another case, a young Navajo woman took a man to court for a declaration of paternity. The man denied he was the father. The judge sent the case to our Navajo Peacemaker Court. The couple's parents attended. The discussion was no longer about whether the man was the father, but what the families were going to do about the well-being of their child. The grandparents knew what was going on all the time. It is hard to hide things in a small community, and family members have an interest in their children.

We share a similar definition of law, but use it in a different way. Navajos use their language to convey values. We carry our law in our heads, not in law books. Navajos know their language, ceremonies, prayers, and the stories of how we came to be. We apply their values in our traditional institutions where everyone knows the law and how to use it to make decisions. Now, let's address a more familiar figure in institutions—a leader.

LEADERSHIP

What if I have a dispute with another and we can't agree? What if we bring in our family members and we still can't agree? We then turn to a leader for help, but there is another way to look at leadership. Agreement comes from shared values. We agree something is right. We agree something should be done. If we do not agree, then we must turn to someone else for guidance. Where would our group go for it? We would seek out someone we believe in; someone we trust. . . .

We have a Navajo name for an "intelligent man" (or woman) whom we respect: it is "naat'aanii"—someone who speaks strongly, wisely, and well—someone who plans. A naat'aanii is our traditional civic leader. Sometimes people translate the word as "peace chief." That is not accurate. Navajos did not have chiefs in the sense of someone who made decisions for others. Our leaders make decisions with others. We respect people who have wisdom and who share it.

A naat'aanii is also our law and justice leader. In the Anglo way, a judge is a wise person who makes decisions for others and gives good reasons for the decision. You seldom hear an American judge teach people in the courtroom or guide them from the bench. In the Navajo way, our leaders teach and guide others. A naat'aanii shares wisdom to help people make plans and resolve their troubles. He does not make decisions for people, but with them.

Other Indian nations call such persons elders. An elder isn't simply someone who is older and thus wiser—it is someone who gives guidance: someone people listen to out of respect. There are elders for civic matters and guides for spiritual development. In the Indian way, we usually do not separate the two, although that is modern practice. For that reason, we of the Navajo Nation courts are trying to reintroduce spirituality and traditional religion to our work.

HOZHOOJI NAAT'AANII - THE JUSTICE AND HARMONY CEREMONY

It is a process of discussion to reach consensus. To us, it is a ceremony. What is a ceremony? A philosopher once said that what really sets humans apart from animals is ceremony; that humans are the ceremonial animal. A ceremony is . . . something that has dignity; something sacred. Hozhooji naat'aanii is a phrase that refers to talking and planning to restore damaged relationships or build new ones. It is guided by a person with wisdom—a naat'aanii—who helps plan things using k'e (respect and solidarity) to regain hozho. We call it peacemaking in English.

The elements or phases of peacemaking are: First, prayer; Second, the expression of feelings by everyone within the zone of dispute; Third, the "lecture;" Fourth, discussion; Fifth, consensus about a plan; Sixth, reconciliation; and Seventh, closure with prayer.

PRAYER

The Indian world is not solely a material world. There is a spiritual dimension to life. Many Indian groups are not secular societies; they do not separate spirituality from everyday life. In general Indian belief, the people of the spirit world are very much a part of daily life; they actively participate in it. You can ask them for help. Prayer is the way you seek that guidance and help.

Put in a more secular and western way, prayer helps set the tone to make people more receptive. It touches their attitudes to prompt a positive approach to the process. We say, "put your anger outside the door." We ask people to come in with a positive attitude, using prayer. Even Alcoholics Anonymous speaks about the "Higher Power" as part of its curing techniques.

EMOTION

Imagine the case of someone who has a whiplash because a drunk driver rear ended her at a stop sign. What happens if the driver wants to tell a court about the pain and anger over being injured? "Objection! Sustained." What if the drunk driver apologizes at the scene? That is used against him.

Navajo legal procedure in peacemaking lets people express their emotions, and it doesn't penalize them for being human. One of the things we say about the Navajo Peacemaker Court is that the most important piece of paper it uses is the Kleenex tissue paper for drying tears. . . . There is a place for people to express how they feel without rules of evidence. In courtrooms, people cannot say how they feel. However, bearing emotions is an essential part of our process.

When I disagree with someone, I do something very human. I quickly attribute a bad motive to that person's conduct. "He did it because he's a bad person." I make an assumption about another's behavior, just as he assumes things about me. I probably won't understand the fact that the person feels there were good reasons for doing what he did. Clearing up misunderstandings is often our hardest job. They cause conflict. Conflict requires healing, and we think our justice and harmony ceremony is a healing ceremony.

In Navajo ceremonial practice, you identify what is inside. You bring it out so you can deal with it. That is why we not only allow but encourage expressions of feelings — to bring them out. We also know that healing comes from making the patient feel part of the group. It helps our hurt to know that others care and are there to help us. We allow venting to use those dynamics.

Here is how we say it in Navajo: "Watch your words. Watch what you say." Remember, words are very powerful. The Holy People gave them to us, and they created us to communicate. That is why you must think and speak in a positive way. Be gentle with your words. Do not gossip or accuse. Gossip has a name. It has a mind, eyes and a voice. It is a being. It can cause you as much trouble as you make by calling it, so do not call it to you. It is a living monster because it gets in the way of a successful life. The same is true when you accuse. If you have no respect for others, they will not respect you. As we and our young Anglo friends say, "What goes around comes around.". . . These sayings are very powerful in the Navajo language, and that is why our language is law.

Everyone gets to express their feelings to start the process. They are cautioned to be careful in doing so. Everyone gets to explain how they feel about the problem. They get to relate what they think caused it. Our procedure is different, because people can go back a long way to tell what they think went wrong. Sometimes, people will go back for generations to describe some ancient wrongdoing and a history of relationships. That is proper, because it gets to the bottom of things. At the end of the venting process, we know everyone's attitude about each other and their feelings about what happened. It is then time for the "lecture."

THE LECTURE

When the participants have told their stories and expressed their emotions, it is time for the naat'aani to become more actively involved. His wisdom is a resource for people to use. The lecture is a major part of our idea of justice. For example, when Navajos call the police on a family member, they do not always want an arrest. Most often, the family asks the officer to "talk to" or lecture the offender. When people go into peacemaking, they expect a naat'aanii to do the same. We use our wise people to help by sharing their knowledge and experience.

When the prayers have been said; when emotions have been expressed; and when the people have told their stories, a naat'aanii gives guidance. He (or she) offers it from stories, prayers, traditions and ceremonies which apply to the situation. Navajos have great respect for traditions. They are the law, which everyone knows is binding from their rearing in its values. The lecture is not just a sermon about doing good and avoiding evil. It is a very practical discussion of the problem at hand. The naat'aanii will relate the values and how they apply to the dispute. That is done to educate everyone about how they should proceed. If there are bad attitudes or misunderstandings, the lecture highlights them and shows how they vary from Navajo values.

The lecture is information, wisdom, teaching. It gives the disputants the tools they need to go on to the next stage of the ceremony: discussion.

DISCUSSION

There is a popular saying which describes the Navajo process of discussion. The saying goes, "If you're not part of the solution, you're part of the problem." That is very true. What are the major barriers to finding a solution? People's attitudes toward each other can be a barrier. Misunderstandings prevent agreement. There are also the emotions of denial, minimalization and externalization.

Denial is something we see each day in our courts. As many as one-third of Navajo Nation criminal cases involve driving while intoxicated charges. When the defendant goes before the bench, he denies having a problem. He says, "I was just unlucky to get picked up for DWI last Saturday night; I don't have a drinking problem."

Minimalization is another obstacle to solving problems. Take the usual domestic violence case: the defendant says "It's no big deal." Or, "Everybody does it, so it's O.K." In our courts, a defendant will sometimes say, "It's traditional for an Indian to beat his wife." In sex abuse cases we may hear, "It's traditional to have sex with a young woman when she reaches puberty." Or "It's part of our tradition to have sex with a foster child." Those are all false stereotypes. We try to defeat excuses which make light of violent conduct—that it is permissible to abuse women or children. In Navajo society, we work to educate people that violence toward women or sexual abuse have nothing to do with our traditions.

The third barrier, externalization, is equally wrong. It is blaming. "It is your fault," they say. "It's someone else's fault, not mine." "If she didn't nag me all the time, I wouldn't have to beat her." Or, "Its not my fault; I was drunk." Or, "I can't help it; I'm an alcoholic." Or, "It's the system that's to blame." People try to shift blame to others or claim bad luck. "Don't blame me," they say; or "Oh, poor me!"

Those psychological states are ignorant. They are bad attitudes. They are misinformation. They are stereotypes. How do we deal with them? I was a trial judge for many years, and I used to hear these excuses. I had a heavy caseload, so how could I get underneath them? If a defendant in a DWI case says, "I don't have a drinking problem," how can I know if that is true? If a domestic violence defendant says, "She started it and I had to defend myself," how do I know if that is a lie? When a carload of teenagers are charged with possession of liquor, each will say "it was the other guy's beer and I didn't know about it." How do I know? Peacemaking deals with excuses nicely.

Let's take a closer look at our DWI example: we can believe the defendant or not. If we believe him, he will drive drunk again and possibly end up killing someone. If we don't believe him, and send him into an alcohol program, it won't work. If someone has the attitude that they don't have a problem, they will not own up to the truth. Alcohol programs do not work for someone in denial. In Navajo peacemaking, a DWI defendant doesn't tell his story to the judge. He tells it to his family. He tells it to his spouse, to his mother, to his brothers and sisters, and to those who know him best. They know what is really going on and set him straight.

What about domestic violence? Some people say that you cannot use mediation to deal with it. That is true for one-on-one settings. Peacemaking is not mediation, because it involves the entire family. Family members know how to deal with denial, minimalization, and externalization. For example, there was a domestic violence case in our Tuba City court where a young defendant used all the usual excuses. He did not admit his conduct or see its effects. His sister sat and listened, and when the young man was through, she gave him some reality therapy. He trusted her, so he listened.

The sister told him that he was an abuser; that he had no right to abuse his wife; and that while he was an alcoholic, that was no excuse. She told him he was violent and that he must do something about his attitudes and his drinking. She explained the traditional Navajo principles he violated—that Navajos believe in the dignity of women, so he must not hurt them. She then offered her love and her help to work with him. She broke down his barriers and used her influence as a sister to deal with the underlying problem.

Relatives are present to separate truth from fiction and to stop the excuses. They are also there to assist victims and protect them from being abused again. Discussion by everyone involved separates truth from fiction; reality from unreality. Discussion works, because it uses a Navajo healing technique. We use the same principles in both traditional healing and traditional justice. Peacemaking works because it gets underneath the surface of a problem to get at its causes.

Here is another example of Navajo legal thinking. In Navajo, the word nayee means monster. Our creation account tells of the time when monsters roamed Navajoland and hunted down Navajos. Two Navajo heroes killed some monsters and weakened others, and we still tell the stories of how the twins dealt with the monsters. The word nayee means something deeper, as is most often true in our language. It also means "that which gets in the way of a successful life." A monster is very real to us.

Denial is a monster, as are minimalization and externalization. Alcoholism is a monster. Depression, which causes people to use alcohol to kill the pain, is a monster. Family strife is a monster. What do you do with a "monster" or "that which gets in the way of a successful life?" You identify it. You bring it out in the open. You put it before you to examine it. What is it? How does it work? What does it do? What are the effects of alcohol abuse or family violence on those who are related to you? Psychiatrists say that traditional Navajo healing works because you objectify a problem to deal with it. The discussion phase brings all of that out. . . .

One of our retired judges used to sit as a trial judge in Chinle, a traditional area in the center of the Navajo Nation. On occasion, when he would look deeper into an assault case, he would find that it was caused by a grazing dispute. (While the Navajo Nation is the biggest Indian nation in the United States, it is very dry and does not support large livestock herds. There is a land shortage for our traditional grazing economy.)

On recognizing the cause of the assault, the judge would ask everyone in the neighborhood to come in to talk about the grazing dispute. They would assemble in the courtroom and talk it out. Once the people settled how they would use grazing permits in the area, the judge would dismiss the criminal charges.

There is another healing dynamic we use. The psychiatrists call it solidarity. You can heal by reuniting the sick with the well and by letting the patient know others are there for them. That's just another way of saying that k'e works.

People come to agreement through discussion. They identify the problem and the solutions to it. They eliminate the problem by making certain that everyone is part of the solution. They do it using consensus.

CONSENSUS

Consensus is where everyone agrees on what to do. Navajos now have representative democracy, where a majority elects people to a council, and where council decisions are reached by majority vote. However, the traditional Navajo political form was direct democracy, where everyone took part in making important decisions. They were not made by majority vote. They were made by consensus, where everyone agreed. Peacemaking removes the barriers to decision. It relies on respect and that elusive emotion we call k'e to bring about consensus. A full discussion of problems, in light of reality, produces a good plan. That is why we sometimes call our justice procedure "talking things out." The final decision works because we reconcile people in continuing relationships using respect. The closing prayer is like a seal on an agreement. It prompts everyone to remember what was agreed and to commit themselves to carry out the agreement.

RECONCILIATION

The "winner take all" system of justice produces its own problems. One of our judges described it as one party going out of the courtroom with his tail in the air, and the other going out with his tail between his legs. If, instead, you use methods which promote reconciliation, you will resolve the conflicts which underlie ongoing problems. A judgment in a "win-lose" system tells people what they must do. An agreement in peacemaking commits them to what they will do. An agreement is better than a judgment.

DUE PROCESS AND EQUAL PROTECTION

If due process is fairness, what is fair? What does it mean for people to be equal to afford "equal protection of the law?" One of the major mistakes of the Indian Civil Rights Act, which imposes most of the U.S. Bill of Rights protections on Indian nations, is that those are cultural notions. That is, different cultures have different ways of looking at "fairness" and "equality."...

Does Navajo peacemaking afford due process of law? Yes. The major elements of due process procedure are (1) notice of the nature of claims and when and where they will be decided; (2) an opportunity to be heard in a meaningful way and at a meaningful time; (3) the right to the assistance of counsel and witnesses; (4) and the right to an impartial decision-maker.

In peacemaking, everyone involved in the problem receives notice of the nature of the dispute and where and when it will be talked out. In the old days, that was done by word of mouth and a summons by a naat'aanii's town crier or assistant. Today we give it in writing.

Everyone has an opportunity to be heard, because anyone who is interested can speak. There are no rules of evidence to limit what may be said. "Talking things out" means just that—everyone talks until the subject is completely exhausted. People can speak in a meaningful way and at a meaningful time and place.

The rights to counsel and the attendance of witnesses are slightly different under Navajo common law. Navajos always have the right to have someone speak for them. That may be a relative who speaks well or who is respected. Under our Peacemaker Court rules, lawyers have to stand outside when peacemaking is taking place; they are not allowed in peacemaking. However, a victim who is weak or inarticulate can have someone there to speak on their behalf. Such is not advocacy, as you know it, but effective speech to give the victim's views and feelings. As for the right to witnesses, those who know what happened are part of the discussion.

There is no decision-maker more impartial than yourself. A final agreement is the product of each person's commitment to abide by the group decision. If you do not like it, you don't have to agree to it. There will be no binding decision until there is agreement. You may be called upon to say why you don't agree, but that gives an additional opportunity to persuade the others. It also allows you to see how you are wrong and gracefully agree to something you can then live with.

I like to say that Navajo due process affords more protection than adjudication. After all, you have a more complete opportunity to speak, involve anyone you like, have someone speak for you, and help produce the final decision. Adjudication takes power out of the hands of the people. Peacemaking puts control in the people's hands. It is not a matter of a stranger making a decision for you; particularly one which may punish.

Now, let's consider Navajo equal protection. What does it mean when people are equal before the law? We believe that Navajos are equal in it, because they know it. Navajos believe it is wrong to use coercion on another, so the legal process requires consensus among equals. Each person enters peacemaking as an equal and participates in it as an equal. Decisions are the product of consensus, sometimes prompted by the wisdom of a naat'aanii. There is equality in participation, and equality in outcomes.

Equality in outcomes most often means a form of sharing where people lower their demands or do what they might not otherwise do. In one peacemaking case, involving a truck driver who killed some sheep, the driver's grandfather agreed to pay for the damage done to the grandson's pickup and give the herders some rams and ewes to replace some of the herd. The grandfather had no obligation to do so, but assured equality in the outcome by offering to pay. In that case, the parties reached a compromise to get a result which benefitted everyone. The technical term for that is distributive justice. The popular word is sharing.

SUMMING UP

So, what is peacemaking? It is the path to justice. It is a balance of individual rights and the needs of the group. The two seemingly opposite goals are reconciled, because individual needs are tied to group success. We say of individual rights, "It's up to him," but the individual does not want it said that he "acts as if he had no relatives." There is almost complete freedom, but we cannot be free unless others benefit too.

E. Negotiating in Japan: A Primer for Americans

1. Comments and Questions

a. There seems to be an almost endless number of recent books about doing business throughout the world, that are written in English and addressed to an American audience. Some of this work is simply dreadful. One book about doing business internationally, after some general analysis, proceeds through the continents (not countries) seriatim, with Asia being dispatched in nine pages! Several recent books can be found about any nation that is of major economic importance to the United States.

b. Any acceptably concise discussion of negotiating in other countries, and the negotiating style of people from other nations, runs the grave risk of being inaccurate, shallow, naive, and racist (anyway, ethnocentric).

c. Our response to this quandary is to provide a series of short readings on doing business and negotiating in a single country. Japan was selected because of its homogeneity (thus making generalization easier than about countries like Canada or India); the importance of political and economic ties between the U.S. and Japan; the difficulties in trade negotiations between Americans and Japanese at the individual, firm, and national level; and the availability of relevant materials.

d. A key to successful negotiation in another country is to speak the local language, as well as understanding local customs, but that is not the American way.

e. One theme that is clear from even a cursory consideration of business negotiations in Japan is that attorneys play little if any role. Bringing counsel to a meeting will be treated as evidence of distrust, and is far more likely to derail negotiations than to move them forward.

2. Glen Fisher, International Negotiation: A Cross-Cultural Perspective (1980)

Westerners who negotiate with Japanese feel that the whole idea of holding a formal session specifically to negotiate is somewhat foreign to many Japanese. Americans are frustrated when their counterparts do not enter into an expected give-and-take. . . .

There is little in Japanese culture to make Japanese feel comfortable with articulate advocacy in polite company, most especially in formal settings. They see such as the occasion to ceremonially adopt what has already been worked out in a patient consensus-generating process. To openly disagree at a formal stage is distasteful and embarrassing, like enduring a husband and wife spat at a dinner party. Certainly the Japanese are not prepared to change their position in such a setting. . . . Nor is it easy for them to tolerate the surprises that are normally a part of adversary proceedings. One [State Department] officer recalled his acute embarrassment when, after carefully going over the text of his ambassador's speech in advance with his Japanese counterparts precisely to provide a smooth no-surprises session, the ambassador on the spur of the moment discarded the speech and spoke extemporaneously. The substance was not changed, but the credibility of the working level officer was set back severely.

Harmony is important to Japanese. They still use go-betweens to assure smoothness in social relations in all kinds of dealings from arranging weddings to making political accommodations. . . .

Most of all, Americans see negotiating sessions as problem-solving exercises, and "problems" are precisely the dragons that Americans take joy in slaying. In the State Department, I recall officers accusing a Country Director of being prepared to create crises when none existed because he so enjoyed meeting crises. Hardly a Japanese outlook!

A Japanese team presents more of a closed circle. . . . The progression to leadership and status is by professional competence, but also very much by seniority and experience. Hence, the team leader might be only marginally competent in the specific subject matter under negotiation, but still be the obvious head. He holds his position by being the representative of a consensus process through which the negotiating position has been derived. . . . The Japanese system disallows flexibility at the negotiating table and requires long periods of time to consider new proposals. . . . [I]t is a decisionmaking process where ideas and supporting decisions tend to come from the bottom up, or at least from mid-level up rather than from the top down. The negotiator speaks from the authority of a consensus, something that cannot be easily changed in the give-and-take of negotiation.

In Japan, new initiatives depend heavily on middle-level technical experts, and their superiors tend to accept their judgements. Their accumulation of data and information serves both the deliberation process and implementation. . . . [T]op managers . . . serve as prestigeful representatives of the structure over which they preside, avoiding the stance of the dynamic decision-making executive. . . .

In any case, to the Japanese a negotiated agreement is seen as an indication of the direction to be taken, with adjustments and modifications to be made according to conditions and consensus among the parties. Thus a U.S. expectation of contractual finality is uncongenial to Japanese institutional culture. And the Japanese inclination to suggest "sensible" changes after a contract is signed is seen from the U.S. side as devious.

3. Dean Allen Foster, BARGAINING ACROSS BORDERS: HOW TO NEGOTIATE BUSINESS SUCCESSFULLY ANYWHERE IN THE WORLD, 264-293 (1992)

The Basic Concept of the Negotiation

The very definition of negotiating can vary culture to culture. . . . [M]any cultures view negotiation primarily as an opportunity to build a relationship; resolving a particular issue is simply not the first goal. Such cultures often view the initial meeting as the beginning of a larger negotiation encompassing many meetings. . . . The Japanese view the negotiation as a collaborative process of "mind-meeting," which can mandate several meetings before substantive issues are even discussed. Americans who have traveled halfway around the world to meet their Japanese counterparts for the first time in Tokyo on Monday and expect to be back in their office in Detroit on Friday with a signed deal will surely be disappointed. . . .

Americans tend to view negotiating as a competitive process of offers and counteroffers, while the Japanese tend to view the negotiation as an opportunity for information-sharing. . . . At the beginning of a business relationship between an American and a Japanese, the immediate substantive issue is simply not on the table as far as the Japanese are concerned. . . . For the Japanese, bargaining too soon can be a sign of untrustworthiness. It is for this reason that Americans in the now classic Japanese-American cross-cultural business scenario lose the deal by bargaining about price just because they are made anxious by Japanese silence. . . .

[C]ultures such as Japan . . . view conflict at the table as dysfunctional. Correspondingly, these cultures seek to avoid conflict and are indirect, as opposed to confrontational, in their response to it. The maintenance of wa, or harmony, in Japan is such a basic and critical value that it significantly affects much of the behavior during negotiation, as well as determines attitudes toward it. In their effort to maintain harmony, to avoid conflict at the table, the Japanese will employ indirect and avoidant behavior. They will also place priority on face-saving, status acknowledgment, and the establishment of an ongoing system of mutual obligation, expectation, and fulfillment, as symbolized by their often elaborate (and expensive) gift-giving and hosting customs.

The Selection of the Negotiators

Because the Japanese choose their chief negotiators on the basis of status and seniority, these people may not be the ones most informed about the details necessary to make a decision. In fact, their assistants may be better equipped with the facts to respond to your question. However, assistants are not usually empowered to approve decisions. . . .

In Japan, cards are exchanged upon meeting in order for the individuals to learn many things about each other, not the least being status. . . . In Japan, cards are received with two hands, lovingly examined, and carefully arranged in front of you on the table, in an order that represents the seating of your opposite numbers. They must never be mishandled, written upon, folded, or put in one's back pocket to be sat upon. . . . Many hotels in Japan will translate your business card for you, for a small fee, if you send it to them in advance of your trip.

Group Versus Individual Orientation

In Japan, "the nail that sticks up gets hammered down"; that is, the individual who brings attention to himself or herself will be sharply put back in his or her place. . . .

Group or individual orientation . . . affects the negotiation process in a number of ways. In group-oriented societies, the other side will probably be a team, as opposed to an individual or a few individuals. Decisions will probably not be made at the table, but rather will be discussed among the group members after the meeting is over.

The time the Japanese take to make their decisions may seem interminable to the Americans awaiting a decision, but the information exchanged at the table must be taken back to all parties concerned and decided upon in many mini-meetings among themselves. This Japanese decision-making system is known as *ringi seido,* or "reverential inquiry about superior's intentions from below.". . . [T]he Japanese retain today the need to have the entire group in agreement (harmony, again) on an issue before it is implemented. . . . Traditionally (and this is changing, too, depending on the industry), lower levels "inquire" about the intentions of the next level up. Ideas and decisions move from the bottom up, with each level seeking approval from the next higher level. At each step upward, consensus must be reached by the players before the issue is "recommended" upward again. The final form reaches the decision makers at the top, who then put their stamp of approval (often literally) on it.

By this time, of course, all players have discussed the issue at length and have "bought in." Therefore, although the decision-making time in Japan may seem extremely long to the impatient American, once the decision is made, implementation is usually quite rapid, since all concerned with the project are already intimately familiar with it. And it is at this point that the Japanese get their turn to complain about how slowly the Americans move. For Americans may make decisions more quickly, may even decide them directly at the table, but then the project, once decided upon by the top, must move back down through the organization, getting everyone's "buy-in," understanding, and compliance along the way—usually after the decision is made. . . .

4. Robert M. March, The Japanese Negotiator: Subtlety and Strategy Beyond Western Logic 15-17 (1990)

Among themselves, the truth is that the Japanese do not like negotiation. It has disagreeable connotations of confrontation, to be avoided whenever possible. The Japanese instinct is for agreements worked out behind the scenes on the basis of give and take, harmony and long-term interest. In fact . . . very few Japanese even know how to negotiate in the Western sense. In everyday life in Japan, there is little experience of bargaining to buy household goods at lower prices, or even of using arguments in a debating fashion to win points. The common Western ideal of a persuasive communicator—one who is highly skilled in argumentation, who overcomes objections with verbal flair, who is an energetic extrovert—would be regarded by most Japanese as superficial, insincere, and . . . a little vulgar. What the Japanese learn in their culture is that vagueness in discussion is a virtue. They learn to involve others, to listen to their views, and, when no strongly dissenting views remain, a decision is made. It is noteworthy that nobody seems to make the actual decision, rather it just seems to "happen." As for individual involvement, as a Japanese everyone knows that as long as you remain silent, you project a favorable impression and are assumed to be thinking deeply about the problem. . . .

The culturally approved use of ambiguity in Japan extends even to the business setting, where it is linked in the Japanese mind to the issue of personal trust. Whereas . . . American negotiators may develop bargaining ranges and strategic options as a matter of course in their pre-negotiation planning, this is still rare among the Japanese. This is especially true when the foreigner adopts a bargaining or "horse trading" approach. One or two counterproposals may be in order, but an invitation to "horse trade" provokes in many Japanese a certain aristocratic disdain for the merchant mind. . . .

[I]t is still commonly accepted that if two parties trust each other, money and other details need not be discussed. Thus, in many industries in Japan neither contracts nor invoices or even product catalogs are used. On occasions when contracts are used, a point will be made of not reading the fine print, for to do so would imply a lack of trust. . . .

Despite this, the Japanese employ an array of means to influence others and achieve their goals, means that if not completely unknown in the West, are often carried to extremes that seem bizarre or undignified to Westerners. The reason behind such behavior is that they are doing everything they can to avoid appearing either self-centered (as they fear they would were they to speak about the merits or superiority of their company or their products) or coldly rational (as they also fear they would were they to concentrate only on economic or business issues, without relating sympathetically to the other side). There are powerful injunctions in Japanese society against both of these attitudes, and their behavior will make better sense if this is understood. . . .

5. Sanjyot P. Dunung, Doing Business in Asia: The Complete Guide 1-50 (1995)

The Japanese place a very high importance on personal interactions and spend a great deal of their time building relationships and developing trust. . . . Accordingly, there is very little cold calling in Japan. All new contacts are developed via introductions by third parties. . . . You will find that having a strong personal connection with a highly respected third party who acts as your introducer, will give you a better chance of achieving business success, especially if the person you want to meet has a sense of obligation to your introducer. The introducer (shokaisha) can also function as a trusted and respected go-between and may be called upon later to advise both sides or act as a mediator during a difficult negotiation. . . .

Most Japanese are not accustomed to dealing with women in business situations. As international business has increased, the frequency of business interactions involving Japanese men and non-Japanese women has increased, but not significantly. If you are a foreign woman . . . , with patience and gentle persistence you will be able to gradually win their respect and business, but do not expect close relationships with them. . . . Some, particularly younger, Japanese will be able to deal with you better than their older colleagues. . . .

In Japan, age is synonymous with wisdom and experience. Consequently, the Japanese often have a difficult time negotiating or conducting business with foreigners who appear substantially younger and inexperienced. . . .

In Japanese business, a man's marital status may influence his career path. Traditionally, while it is acceptable for a man to remain a bachelor until his late twenties, he faces distinct social and professional pressure to find a wife soon after turning thirty. An unmarried man over thirty may be bypassed for promotion and suffer poor postings or assignments, because the Japanese view marriage and family as symbols of stability and maturity. . . .

No matter how hard you work at building your relationship, remember that you, as a non-Japanese, will always be perceived as a . . . foreigner to the Japanese. . . . Foreigners should not let this reality obstruct business relationships, but simply recognize that the concept of close business relationships will take on a new and more formal dimension in Japan. . . .

One Japanese concept that is particularly difficult for non-Japanese to comprehend is *honne* and *tatemae.* Honne refers to the substance or real or inner truth of an issue, and tatemae is the public, diplomatic truth or official position. This important concept helps the Japanese to maintain harmony. The Japanese will avoid voicing their true feelings or honne in order to preserve harmony. The best way to counter this problem is to ask more questions to get a better sense of an issue. Remember to keep the questions nonoffensive and somewhat indirect to avoid causing any embarrassment to your Japanese counterpart. . . .

The Japanese often avoid sustained eye contact as it can be considered intimidating. Junior people are less likely to make eye contact and will keep their visual focus low out of respect for the speaker. Westerners should not assume that this posture implies a lack of trust, honest, or sincerity.

Do not try to fill up the silent gaps during a conversation. Silence usually means the Japanese are seriously contemplating the issue. The Japanese rarely ever say "No" outright. A blunt "No" is considered rude, almost like an opinion on a person rather than on his idea. Other expressions that can mean "No" include . . . it is difficult, I am not sure, I will think about it, and [apparent affirmations followed by "but"].

If you need to say "No," do so in a similarly roundabout manner to avoid a confrontation and offending your counterpart. Never say "No" outright, as it may cause your counterpart to lose face. . . .

The Japanese routinely engage in a verbal and physical gesture that is best described as a guttural moan with the tilt of the head. This is usually done in a situation in which they feel uncomfortable. . . . The nervous laugh or smile can also indicate difficulty. The Japanese also indicate "No" by placing their hand perpendicular to their face and waiving it rapidly back and forth.

6. Boye Lafayette DeMente, How to do Business with the Japanese: A Complete Guide to Japanese Customs and Business Practices 6-8, 47-49, 57-58 (1993)

There are three basic principles to business success in Japan. You must have a product or service that the Japanese want to buy; you must have an extensive network of contacts in Japan that you can orchestrate to achieve your goals; and you must have sufficient cross-cultural skills to gain the confidence and good-will of the Japanese and make them comfortable dealing with you.

It helps tremendously if you are starting out with a product that has been successful in the American market. Often, the first criterion the Japanese apply to any foreign-made product is how successful it has been in its own home market. In Japan, even more so than in the United States, every product has a distinctive identity, image, acceptable role, and what Japan marketing specialist Earle Okumura calls its "contact infrastructure." . . . One of the major differences between the Japanese market and the American market is that the contact infrastructure in Japan tends to be far more deeply entrenched and more influential in the marketing of any product. . . . Once you have established your network, it is also necessary to spend more time nurturing it to keep it working smoothly. . . .

The first characteristic of business in Japan is its personal nature. The second characteristic . . . is its competitiveness—fierce competition that drives the engine of the economy domestically as well as internationally. . . . The obsession for exquisite design, high quality, an almost unlimited amount of aftermarket service, and a steady stream of new product makes the Japanese marketplace the most competitive in the world. . . .

Cultural insensitivity and casual-to-arrogant attitudes remain the greatest handicaps afflicting many foreigners . . . interested in the Japanese market. Americans in particular. Americans generally rank at or near the bottom in sensitivity to other cultures. We continue to downplay the importance or ignore the importance of speaking the language of people we want to do business with. We do not give sufficient value to the life-styles, habits, likes, and dislikes of Japanese consumers. . . .

Japanese Business Values

The guiding principle of most Westerners is that profit must be made. This standard pervades virtually all our endeavors and actions. We give only secondary consideration to the needs of our employees. We tend to look upon society at large and our government as separate entities and we often think of government as an adversary.

Leading Japanese businessmen, on the other hand, automatically identify themselves as Japanese first and entrepreneurs second. Their guiding principles are (1) their overall responsibility to Japan, (2) their responsibilities to their employees, and (3) the need to be successful in business to fulfill the first two obligations. . . .

This is not to suggest . . . that the Japanese do not try to make a profit. But time and again, in situations in which the Westerner's behavior is determined entirely by profit, the Japanese businessman's behavior is determined largely by other considerations. He will strive to maintain harmony in the company, in the market, or in the country; avoid laying off employees; or enhancing his reputation. . . .

Most Japanese businessmen identify very closely with their government. They consider their interests and those of the government to be essentially the same, and they expect the government to exercise significant control over their industry. Where the government has not taken a direct hand in the conduct of business, the businessmen have formed associations and cartels with others in the same industry and then sought government approval and guidance. . . .

The Japanese View of Contracts

Japanese businessmen do not like to sign detailed, restrictive contracts. To them, no agreement is final for the simple reason that circumstances change, and they want to be able to change with them. They prefer a loose arrangement based on sincerity and goodwill. . . .

The flexibility provided by this type of contractual arrangement gives the Japanese a tremendous advantage over those who are bound by tightly limiting contracts. If they do sign an American contract with lots of fine print, they will usually abide by the terms until conditions change; then they renegotiate.

The Japanese do not use lawyers in their negotiations and seldom consult them in case of disputes (there are only some 16,000 attorneys in the country. . . .) Disliking the legalistic approach to contracts or business, they have taken a very strong position against foreign legal firms operating in Japan. . . .

7. Philip R. Harris & Robert T. Moran, MANAGING CULTURAL DIFFERENCE 393-405 (1991)

Tips for Business Interactions with the Japanese

1. Saving face and achieving harmony are more important factors in business dealings for the Japanese than achieving higher sales and profits.
2. Third party introductions are important. They prefer this indirect approach whereby you use a go-between or arbitrator who may be involved until the conclusion of the negotiation.
3. Whomever you approach in the organization, do so at the highest level; the first person contacted is also involved throughout the negotiation.
4. Avoid direct communication on money; leave this to the go-between or lower echelon staff.
5. Never put a Japanese in a position where he must admit failure or impotency.
6. Avoid praise of your product or services; let your literature or go-between do that.
7. Use business cards with your titles, preferably both in Japanese and English.
8. The logical, cognitive, or intellectual approach is insufficient; the emotional level of communications is considered important (as in dealing with a known business associate vs. a stranger).
9. Formality prevails in senior staff meetings with interpreters present. The more important the meeting, the more senior executives present.
10. Wait patiently for meetings to move beyond preliminary tea and inconsequential talk.

F. Pricing Services: A Cross-Cultural Exercise

1. Shaiva Naipaul, NORTH OF SOUTH: AN AFRICAN JOURNEY 47-52 (1978)

[The author, brother of the far better known V. S. Naipaul, was of Indian descent, born and raised in Trinidad, spent many years in England, and traveled extensively throughout Africa. The Kikuyu are the largest tribal group in Kenya. Kenyatta Avenue is one of the main thoroughfares in Nairobi, the capital and largest city in Kenya.]

A certain embarrassment had so far prevented me from making use of the service offered by the shoeshine boys who line Kenyatta Avenue. The occupation had too many unpleasant associations. But observation had shown that my reservations were not shared by many people. My scruples were rapidly eroded. My chosen shoeshine "boy" was not a boy at all—though, I should add, many of the fraternity literally are. He was a gray-headed, rheumy-eyed Kikuyu. He wagged his head and clucked his tongue when he saw the state of my shoes. . . .

"Expensive," he said, kneading the leather and nodding appreciatively.

"Not very," I said cautiously.

"I am first-class shoeshine boy. I will make them be like new for you. They will shine just like mirror. I am best shoeshine boy in the whole of Nairobi. Many years' experience." He began loosening the laces.

"What's your charge?"

"Charge?"

"How much will I have to pay you? How many shillings?" He waived his arms airily.

"Don't worry about charge."

"But I do worry."

He sighed. It was as though I had caused him profound spiritual pain. "Worries no good for the heart. I ask reasonable price. No need to worry." He produced a bottle containing a yellowish liquid. . . . This he applied liberally, rubbing it in with vigor.

"Is that polish?"

"Special ingredient," he said, switching his attention from one shoe to the other. "Secret formula. Highly secret formula."

I started to feel uneasy. It occurred to me that I had behaved extremely foolishly. I should have insisted on settling what the price would be before allowing him to start.

He explained that the treatment he was giving me would make any further polishing unnecessary for one whole year. "You just take a soft cloth and wipe it over. It will shine just like mirror. I give you full guarantee."

"Nonsense."

"Not nonsense," he replied equably. "True. This is Deluxe Special I give you. Not nonsense."

I withdrew my foot completely.

"Look . . ." He took a crumpled sheet of paper from his shirt pocket and handed it to me. "Read what it says there."

It was a typewritten testimonial. "This is to certify that I did not need to have my shoes polished for one year after receiving the Deluxe Special. During all that time my shoes shone like a mirror." The scrawled signature was impossible to decipher.

"Do you expect me to believe this rubbish?" I examined my shoes. The kerosene-soaked leather had gone dull and blotchy.

He watched me composedly. "You cannot meet your friends with your shoes looking like that."

I saw his point: I was trapped. I surrendered my feet to him. "Remember—no more secret ingredients and formulas. Just polish."

"Just polish," he repeated. "You are hard man to please, bwana."

With swift dispatch he polished and shined, coaxing out an indifferent gleam from the damaged leather. It would have to do.

I held out five shillings, thinking myself more than generous in the circumstances; I did not want to create a scene. He looked at the money; he looked at me.

"What is that for?"

"For your labor."

He laughed the way one laughs at an obvious absurdity. "Bwana . . . bwana . . ."

"Are you trying to tell me that you expect to be paid more than five shillings for destroying my shoes?"

He nodded.

"How much?"

"Sixty shillings, bwana." He folded his arms across his chest. He showed me a neatly typewritten card . . . that . . . listed the various services he claimed to provide and their cost.

Super Deluxe Special: 100 shillings
Deluxe Special: 80 shillings
Deluxe Ordinary: 50 shillings
Special: 35 shillings
Ordinary: 20 shillings
Quick polish: 5 shillings
Quick brush: 3 shillings

"Which one of these am I supposed to have had?

"You had the Deluxe Special for eighty shillings. But (he looked furtively at my shoes). . . . I give you discount price."

I returned the card. "Five shillings or nothing."

"The card, bwana. Read what the card says."

"I don't care what it says. Five shillings or nothing."

He ran to the neighboring shoeshine boy. The Kikuyu, gabbling now in his native tongue, pointed at the card, then at me, then at my shoes. He was the very picture of outraged virtue. His ally glowered at me. I went over to them.

"What is he saying?"

"He is saying," the ally replied, "that you are refusing to pay him. He is saying he will call the police for you." He was grim; unfriendly.

I looked up and down the avenue. There was not a policeman in sight. The Kikuyu was gabbing again, pointing at the card and at me. I too now sought an ally. I approached one of the passersby and asked what he normally paid to have his shoes shined. He shrugged and continued on his way. I asked another. He was no more helpful. An absurd panic gripped me. I offered ten shillings. The Kikuyu refused, folding his arms across his chest. I offered fifteen. He refused that too. I flung the fifteen shillings on his stand and walked away with as much resolution as I could summon. The Kikuyu pursued me down the avenue.

"I call the police for you. They throw you in jail. They beat you up. They kill you. I myself kill you."

I fled into the safety of the first hotel I came to.

2. Comments and Questions

a. How much should Naipaul pay for the shoeshine? Whether the theory is contract or restitution, he received a service that had value and was rendered at his request. When price is not agreed upon, the vendor is entitled to receive the "fair market value" for the goods or services in question. That, of course, is a difficult matter. The problem also allows an exploration of warranty issues.

b. One of the authors (a former resident of East Africa) has used this situation for some years in teaching Contracts, as a device to drive home the importance for buyers for prior agreement on the price term. The exotic (to American students) setting for the shoeshine problem, and the diverse backgrounds of the parties, has never been a barrier to the contract law analysis.

c. How is the shoeshine problem different from the dispute that can (and often does) occur when a person uses an unlicensed taxi in any major city (in America or elsewhere), and does not determine the price prior to commencing the ride?

d. At the end of this discussion of cultural differences it bears remembering that, while sensitivity is required, success in negotiation still can be achieved.

Chapter 6

Negotiation Applications

CASE STUDY

(Adapted from *Moser v. U.S. Steel Corporation*, 676 S.W.2d 99 (1984))

The Mosers and the Gefferts were the owners of neighboring tracts of land. Originally, the boundary between the two properties was a winding road. In 1949, the road was straightened. As a result, each party had approximately 6 acres of his neighbor's land on his side of the road. Being congenial neighbors, the Mosers and Gefferts granted deeds conveying the surface estates of the pieces of land to the other one. Each party, however, retained their rights to the mineral estates on the conveyed land. Shortly thereafter, uranium was discovered on the tract of land granted to the Mosers. The Gefferts insisted that the uranium was part of the mineral estate, and therefore belonged to them. However, since the uranium was near the surface, the Mosers naturally insisted that it was part of the surface estate conveyed to them.

[Actual Legal History: The Mosers sued the Gefferts to establish ownership of the uranium. Ultimately, the Texas Supreme Court decided that the uranium was part of the mineral estate, and awarded its ownership to the Gefferts.]

A. Introduction

This chapter considers negotiation in three contexts: the settlement of business disputes, plea bargaining in criminal cases, and the adoption of legislation. Additional case studies abound. One good source is a major Sunday newspaper, which should generate several interesting topics for discussion.

B. Settlement of Business Disputes

1. Arthur Allen Leff, *Injury, Ignorance and Spite: The Dynamics of Coercive Collection*, 80 Yale L.J. 1, 25-26 (1970)

The "solution" to many of the diverse disputes between businessmen takes the form of some variation on one of the following scenarios. The scene of each is simple: split screen, two telephones:

1. Buyer: Hello, Morris? Those widgets you sent us. They're breaking every minute. You want me to pay for such junk?
   Seller: Look, if your men don't know how to use widgets right, what do you want from me? They're just what you ordered, Grade A-2 stainless steel widgets.
   Buyer: Stainless steel they're not. Swiss cheese maybe, orange-crate wood, but not steel.
   Seller: Look, Kevin, maybe we've been having a little quality control problem—just temporary. Do the best you can and we'll make it up next time.
   Buyer: OK, but don't forget. The noise of popping widgets my partner doesn't have to hear.

---

2. Seller: Hello, Kevin? So what's with our last bill?
   Buyer: My bookkeeper's been sick.
   Seller: Uh huh. Your hand cramps when you pick up a pen?
   Buyer: Soon, Morris.
   Seller: How soon? Tomorrow?
   Buyer: Come on, Morris; did I make such a stink when you were shipping out those cardboard widgets?
   Seller: OK, OK. Maybe I'll give you a couple of weeks more. You're not really in trouble are you?
   Buyer: Absolutely not. I got plenty of orders. Go check with some of the other guys.
   Seller: Don't worry. I already did. OK, take a couple of weeks. Give my get-wells to your bookkeeper.
   Buyer: Hah!

---

3. Seller: So Kevin? Morris. Where's the money?
   Buyer: Soon.
   Seller: It's been soon a long time. Now it's now.
   Buyer: Look Morris, I could have gotten the stuff from Acme or Nadir cheaper. I gave you the trade.
   Seller: Now you're giving me the business. Now! Or there'll be trouble.
   Buyer: Tell you what I'll do. I'll pay you today, right now, what I could've got the merchandise for from Acme.
   Seller: Tell you what I'll do. I'll break your head is what I'll do. We got a goddam contract Kevin, and you pay the goddam contract price.
   Buyer: Morris, you don't like my deal, sue me with your contract.
   Seller: I may and I may not. But one thing I know I'll do; anyone asks me if you pay your bills the answer is no. [The last clause is delivered in a high-pitched shriek of absolute credibility.]
   Buyer: Morris? Half today, the rest at the end of the month?
   Seller: OK.

2. Comments and Questions

a. The three brief negotiations described by Professor Leff teach us much about relations between commercial sellers and buyers. The disputes portrayed are the most serious problems faced by each type of party. The fundamental concern of sellers is that buyers will not make full and timely payment, with total nonpayment being the ultimate horrible. The range of potential problems that might strike buyers is greater, but defective goods (breach of warranty) is unquestionably the most significant.

b. Buyers and sellers are merchants. In the vocabulary of the Uniform Commercial Code (UCC), a "merchant" is a person who deals in goods of the kind in the transaction at issue. UCC, § 2-104. One is not a merchant in the abstract, but only with respect to a particular transaction. Merchants are experienced and expert with regard to widgets, or whatever other input is the subject of a transaction. Merchants are expert about two related aspects of the thing being bought or sold: the product itself, and the market for that product.

c. Merchants are "repeat players," frequently engaging in particular types of transactions. This has two consequences in terms of knowledge about the type of transaction, including the sorts of things that can go awry. First, the merchant becomes expert simply by repetition. Even the least observant person or firm learns a good bit from doing something twenty or fifty times, be it riding a bicycle, mediating a child custody case, or purchasing a truckload of widgets. Second, the per transaction cost of investing in information drops as the number of instances increases, making it rational for a merchant to pay (whether in money or in time) to acquire further information about commonly engaged in transactions.

d. Businesses that deal regularly with a product (be it finished goods, semi-finished, or raw materials) become expert in addressing problems that arise commonly. Imperfect widgets usually are not a calamity—a zero defects approach makes sense only for the space shuttle and a few other special situations. Where parties deal regularly with one another, as commonly occurs, the possibility for trade-offs arise, as Leff's examples illustrate. The buyer makes do with less than perfect widgets, the seller is patient about receiving payment.

e. One aspect of expertise is the ability to distinguish between minor or temporary problems and serious ones. A buyer can find out from other buyers about their experience with the quality of seller's goods, responsiveness when problems arise, willingness to be flexible in accommodating buyer's needs, etc. Similarly, a seller that is not being paid can find out if a buyer has serious problems, or just temporary difficulty. Recall from Leff's second negotiation: the seller asks whether the buyer is really in trouble, and the buyer responds no, you can check with others. The seller's answer is, "Don't worry. I already did."

Expertise about problems means that fewer arise, and those that do often can be solved more easily—particularly when the parties have dealt with one another before and plan to do so again. An established business relationship is not to be severed casually. This supplier or customer may be imperfect, but the alternative could be worse. Even if the alternative is not "worse," there are costs associated with making a change and adjusting to a new situation.

f. Merchants often do not need the assistance of third parties to resolve disputes, because they have access to very effective informal sanctions. In Leff's third dialogue, when buyer suggest that seller is welcome to sue, seller's response is to threaten the far more effective sanction of telling others in the trade know that buyer does not pay his debts. (There are often more formal mechanisms for broadcasting credit information, ranging from credit bureaus to trade organizations.) Of course, the ultimate informal sanction for seller is to decline to sell to buyer, or do so only on a cash basis, but that "solution" carries costs in lost business.

Where buyer is the aggrieved party, its informal sanction is both simple and highly effective: take its business elsewhere. In unusual instances, the alternatives are few or inconvenient, but normally there will be several other sellers who are willing and able to serve the buyer's needs. The rational strategy for buyer is to switch rather than to fight.

g. The matters at issue in business disputes are largely about economic relationships. It is a mistake to think matters like ego and friendship are irrelevant, but compared to divorce and child custody problems, the noneconomic aspects of the dispute normally are minor. The importance of the matter negotiated about also is modest in most instances; the worst case scenario for the wronged party just is not very bad.

h. Not all business negotiations are as easily dispatched as those in Leff's dialogues. A small debt is a problem primarily for the debtor. A large debt is a problem for the creditor. Small firms with limited capital lack the leverage available to a large firm. No firm wants to be dependent on a single customer. A sound rule for long time survival of a firm (and a lot less worry for its senior managers) is to avoid having any customer represent more than five percent of its business. From the perspective of the customer, being the dominant customer of a supplier has the benefit of leverage over the supplier, and excellent service, but this approach also raises the risk of dislocation in the event the supplier goes out of business or has severe quality problems. In this circumstance, litigation is unlikely to be helpful, because the most likely consequence is to drive the supplier to a bankruptcy court filing. Even if the customer was awarded a substantial money judgment, it almost certainly would be uncollectible. A judgment creditor is a species of unsecured creditor, and such claims get paid last—if at all.

i. Business contracts often provide for resort to ADR mechanisms if informal settlement does not work. Solutions short of litigation nearly always suffice, because of the situational characteristics described above. Disputes between merchants and consumers, who are "one-shot players," do not settle so easily. In what fundamental ways is the consumer transaction different from the transaction between merchants, and how do these differences impact potential settlement of buyer-seller disputes? How should these differences influence the design of a dispute settlement regime for consumer purchases of "big ticket" items?

3. E. Wendy Trachte, Negotiation: Strategies for Law & Business 80-84 (1994)*

ANNOTATED NEGOTIATION CHECKLIST FOR COMMERCIAL TRANSACTIONS

Preparation & Planning

☐ Determine the appropriate parties to the negotiation. (Who will be necessary to make a decision regarding this transaction?)

*Reprinted with permission.

- ☐ Determine your "Best Alternative To a Negotiated Agreement" (BATNA). (What are your alternatives if the negotiation is unsuccessful?)
- ☐ Consider all the options available in the negotiation. (What are your alternatives in this transaction, e.g. tax ramifications, sales terms, etc.?)
- ☐ What is the remedy available? (There must be a valid contract in order to obtain damages, specific performance, or an injunction. If no contract, remedy will be limited to quantum meruit, rescission, or reformation.)
- ☐ Is the contract enforceable? (It must meet certain requirements such as: the statute of frauds; mutual assent; lawful object of the contract; two or more parties; legal consideration; enforceable by party, lawful assignees or third-party beneficiary.)
- ☐ Is the Uniform Commercial Code (U.C.C.) applicable? (Article 2 of the U.C.C. applies if the negotiation involves a sale of goods that are existing and movable at the time of the contract.)
- ☐ If the U.C.C. is not applicable, are the elements of a valid contract present? (Is the contract lawful or based on legal consideration? Are the requirements of the statute of frauds met, i.e. writing containing: the identity of the parties; object of the contract; all the essential terms; signature of the party to be held liable. Note: Oral contracts may be admitted under certain circumstances.)
- ☐ Are the parties competent? (Parties such as infants, insane persons, intoxicated persons, and corporations may not be competent.)
- ☐ Is there mutual assent? (The elements of mutual assent include: offer; acceptance; absence of mistake; fraud; or duress; meeting of the minds.)
- ☐ Is there consideration? (Present or future benefit or detriment not already contracted for in a prior transaction.)
- ☐ Are all elements considered under U.C.C.?
  - ☐ Statute of frauds requirements (U.C.C. §§ 2-201, 2-202, 2-104(1))
  - ☐ Mutual assent including offer (U.C.C. §§ 2-204, 2-205, 2-305); counter-offer (U.C.C. § 2- 207); acceptance (U.C.C. § 2-206)
  - ☐ Unconscionability (U.C.C. § 2-302)
  - ☐ Impossibility (U.C.C. §§ 2.306, 2-615)
  - ☐ Consideration (U.C.C. §§ 2-209(1) & (3), 2-203)
  - ☐ Shipment (U.C.C. § 2-308)
  - ☐ Warranty (U.C.C. §§ 2-312 to 2-318)
  - ☐ Title (U.C.C. § 2-312)
  - ☐ Title (U.C.C. § 2-403)
  - ☐ Statute of limitations (U.C.C. § 2-725)
  - ☐ Conditions (U.C.C. §§ 2-324, 2-326, 2-327)
  - ☐ Assignment (U.C.C. § 2-210)
  - ☐ Damages (U.C.C. §§ 2-703 to 2-708, 2-710 to 2-715)
- ☐ Determine the other side's "Best Alternative To A Negotiated Agreement (BATNA). (What are the other side's alternatives if the negotiation is unsuccessful, e.g. competition?)
- ☐ Determine your negotiation strategy. (Allow yourself a range of strategies so that you remain flexible in the process.)

- ☐ Determine all points of the negotiation that are not negotiable. (On which points are there options and on which points are you firm?)
- ☐ Provide written pre-negotiation proposals to the other side. (Title the contract a "working draft" so that revisions are negotiable.)
- ☐ Determine the appropriate timing for your negotiation. (If your negotiation settlement requires approval by parties not present, you should allow sufficient time to seek such approval.)
- ☐ Determine who will be the negotiator for your side. (You may use a team approach but this still needs some organization, e.g. who will open the negotiation; who will close the negotiation.)
- ☐ Keep a file on the negotiation process with all relevant documents. (Keep all correspondence, proposals, contracts, etc.)
- ☐ Develop a negotiation agenda. (What are the issues you wish to consider and in which order would you like to consider them?)
- ☐ Determine the strengths and weaknesses on your side. (What are the reasons this deal should be made from your perspective?)
- ☐ Determine a list of appropriate experts. (In the event experts are necessary, you will have already studied the options.)
- ☐ Determine your first offer. (What is the "reasonable" offer to maximize your client's level of satisfaction?)
- ☐ Decide the best location for the negotiation. (Consider your office, a neutral location, and finally the other side's location.)
- ☐ Make necessary travel and accommodation arrangements (if you plan on going out of town or your client needs to travel).
- ☐ Identify any parties who should be contacted or invited to the negotiation (a behind-the-scenes decision maker, often the chief financial officer).

Actual Negotiation

- ☐ Before the negotiation begins, review the location. (Who will sit where and what are the logistics, e.g. phone, FAX, copy machine, bathroom facility, food.)

The Meeting

- ☐ Determine if the parties present have the authority to negotiate. (If other approval is required for action, determine if representative will be available for consultation during the negotiation.)
- ☐ Determine the other side's method of negotiating. (Is the approach cooperative, aggressive, or competitive?)
- ☐ Stay calm. (Do not allow your emotions or those of your client to surface.)
- ☐ Move the negotiation through your agenda as developed in the preparation phase. (Guide discussion to the issues you wish considered.)
- ☐ Make certain you understand the other side's position. (Use communication skills such as "reframing" to test whether you have heard what you thought you heard.)

- ☐ Stay flexible. (Adjust your original negotiation strategy after you recognize your original strategy may not work.)

Dealing with Impasse

- ☐ Information disclosure. (Recall that you need to have some level of trust to disclose information that may be valuable to opposing counsel and detrimental to you.)
- ☐ Fact clarification. (You may wish to show proof of your facts through documentation or other methods.)
- ☐ Face saving. (Give a reason for your demand, concession or change in position.)
- ☐ Consider a new or different issue. (If you are not moving then change subjects.)
- ☐ Rank the issues. (Decide which issues are most important to you and the other side.)
- ☐ Focus on the negotiation process. (Remind the parties present that sticking to the agenda is important.)
- ☐ Use of allies. (Remind the parties that there are others similarly situated, e.g. class action or other buyers or sellers.)
- ☐ Use of media for community pressure. (Suggest you might contact the media.)
- ☐ Mediation or other ADR process. (Suggest a mediator be invited to facilitate the negotiation process.)
- ☐ Change negotiators. (Have another person serve as primary negotiator.)
- ☐ Redefine the issues. (Use a flip chart or other method to re-evaluate and prioritize the issues.)
- ☐ Switch to a principled negotiation style. (Utilize a win-win approach in the negotiation process.)
- ☐ Adjourn the negotiation either temporarily or permanently. (Stop the process so that all parties can regroup and rest.)
- ☐ Select a compromise solution. (In negotiating a relationship, compromises often start a positive cooperative relationship.)
- ☐ Brainstorm. (Recall that all ideas are discussed with no commitment by any party to accept the options generated.)

Closing the Negotiation

- ☐ Close at the appropriate time. (Once the issues have been discussed and a basic agreement is reached, it is appropriate to close the deal.)
- ☐ Decide whether to give a final concession or offer. (Recall that ultimatums are often difficult to recant.)
- ☐ Decide who will write the formal documents. (You may wish to write out major agreed-upon points and then use that as the basis for any formal agreement.)
- ☐ Recap the points agreed upon. (Use a product that allows you to place major points on a board that can then be copied so each party has an exact duplicate of what has been agreed upon.)

- ☐ In event that an agreement has not been reached, leave room to resume negotiations at a later date. (Just because you were unable to reach agreement today does not mean you may not reach agreement tomorrow.)

Formalizing Settlement

- ☐ Draft a document that incorporates the terms of the agreement reached. (Avoid using boilerplate language as this is often contrary to what has been agreed upon.)
- ☐ Include a dispute resolution clause. (You may select mediation, arbitration, or even negotiation in the event a dispute arises among the parties.)
- ☐ Do not include terms that were not agreed upon or you will risk ruining the agreement. (If you must include a provision that was not discussed in the negotiation, tell the other side before they find it and think you are tricking them.)
- ☐ Use plain English. (Avoid legalese.)
- ☐ Contract clauses that may need to included:
    - ☐ Preamble, including parties' intentions
    - ☐ Definitions such as subject matter; territory; net income; fair market value; affiliates; collateral; or security; or security
    - ☐ Payment
    - ☐ Reporting/Audits
    - ☐ Tax consequences
    - ☐ Inspection/Acceptance
    - ☐ Warranties
    - ☐ Delivery
    - ☐ Most Favored Nation clause
    - ☐ Third-party rights
    - ☐ Changes in the agreement
    - ☐ Government regulations
    - ☐ Diligence
    - ☐ Closing
    - ☐ Confidentiality
    - ☐ Publicity
    - ☐ Termination
    - ☐ Default
    - ☐ No competition
    - ☐ Compliance with law
    - ☐ Conditions precedent
    - ☐ Notice

C. Negotiation of Criminal Charges: Plea Bargaining

1. Comments and Questions

a. The vast majority of persons accused of a crime do not receive a trial. Instead, the accused pleads guilty to an agreed upon offense, commonly to a lesser offense than would be charged at trial, and the sentence that the prosecutor will recommend to the judge is also agreed upon. Judges are not bound by sentencing deals struck between the prosecutor and the accused, but the prosecutor's recommendation is nearly always followed.

b. Counsel for defendants are part of the assembly line processing that constitutes the criminal law system. Our plea bargaining system is widely regarded as an abomination, both inside and outside the United States, but that is a topic for another book.

c. Professor Blumberg characterizes this system as a confidence game, in which the accused is the victim and the (usually appointed) attorney is not the friend that the role would suggest. Professor Gifford discusses negotiation strategies for plea bargaining. You should consider to what extent the same strategies are applicable in other negotiation situations, and to what extent they are special to the criminal law context.

d. The related topic of victim-offender mediation is considered at Chapter 9, section C.

2. Abraham S. Blumberg, *The Practice of Law as a Confidence Game*, 1 Law & Soc'y Rev. 15, 18-31 (1967)*

In numerous criminal decisions, the Supreme Court reiterates the traditional legal conception of a defense lawyer based on the ideological perception of a criminal case as an adversary, combative proceeding, in which counsel for the defense assiduously musters all the admittedly limited resources at his command to defend the accused. . . . Does the Supreme Court's conception of the role of counsel in a criminal case square with social reality? . . .

COURT STRUCTURE DEFINES ROLE OF DEFENSE LAWYER

The overwhelming majority of convictions in criminal cases (usually over 90 per cent) are not the product of a combative, trial-by-jury process at all, but instead merely involve the sentencing of the individual after a negotiated, bargained-for plea of guilty has been entered. . . . [S]cant attention has been paid to the organizational structure and personnel of the criminal court itself. Indeed, the extremely high conviction rate produced without the features of an adversary trial in our courts would tend to suggest that the "trial" becomes a perfunctory reiteration and validation of the pretrial interrogation and investigation.

The institutional setting of the court defines a role for the defense counsel in a criminal case radically different from the one traditionally depicted. Sociologists and others have focused their attention on the deprivations and social disabilities of such variables as race, ethnicity, and social class as being the source of an accused person's defeat in a criminal court. Largely overlooked is the variable of the court organization itself, which possesses a thrust, purpose, and direction of its own. It is grounded in pragmatic values, bureaucratic priorities, and administrative instruments. These exalt maximum production and the particularistic career designs of organizational incumbents, whose occupational and career commitments tend to generate a set of priorities. These priorities exert a higher claim than the stated ideological goals of "due process of law," and are often inconsistent with them.

Organizational goals and discipline impose a set of demands and conditions of practice on

---

*Reprinted by permission of the Law and Society Association.

the respective professions in the criminal court, to which they respond by abandoning their ideological and professional commitments to the accused client, in the service of these higher claims of the court organization. All court personnel, including the accused's own lawyer, tend to be coopted to become agent-mediators who help the accused redefine his situation and restructure his perceptions concomitant with a plea of guilty.

Of all the occupational roles in the court the only private individual who is officially recognized as having a special status and concomitant obligations is the lawyer. His legal status is that of "an officer of the court" and he is held to a standard of ethical performance and duty to his client as well as to the court. . . . However, lawyers, whether privately retained or of the legal-aid, public defender variety, have close and continuing relations with the prosecuting office and the court itself through discreet relations with the judges via their law secretaries or "confidential" assistants. Indeed, lines of communication, influence and contact with those offices, as well as with the Office of the Clerk of the Court, Probation Division, and with the press, are essential to present and prospective requirements of criminal law practice. . . .

Accused persons come and go in the court system schema, but the structure and its occupational incumbents remain to carry on their respective career, occupational and organizational enterprises. The individual stridencies, tensions, and conflicts a given accused person's case may present to all the participants are overcome, because the formal and informal relations of all the groups in the court setting require it. The probability of continued future relations and interaction must be preserved at all costs.

This is particularly true of the "lawyer regulars" i.e., those defense lawyers, who by virtue of their continuous appearances in behalf of defendants, tend to represent the bulk of a criminal court's non-indigent case workload, and those lawyers who are not "regulars," who appear almost casually on behalf of an occasional client. Some of the "lawyer regulars" are highly visible as one moves about the major urban centers of the nation; their offices line the back streets of the courthouses, at times sharing space with bondsmen. Their political "visibility" in terms of local club house ties, reaching into the judge's chambers and prosecutor's office, are also deemed essential to successful practitioners. Previous research has indicated that the "lawyer regulars" make no effort to conceal their dependence upon police, bondsmen, and jail personnel. Nor do they conceal the necessity for maintaining intimate relations with all levels of personnel in the court setting as a means of obtaining, maintaining, and building their practice. These informal relations are the sine qua non not only of retaining a practice, but also in the negotiation of pleas and sentences.

The client, then, is a secondary figure in the court system as in certain other bureaucratic settings. He becomes a means to other ends of the organization's incumbents. He may present doubts, contingencies, and pressures which challenge existing, informal arrangements or disrupt them; but these tend to be resolved in favor of the continuance of the organization and its relations as before. There is a greater community of interest among all the principal organizational structures and their incumbents than exists elsewhere in other settings. The accused's lawyer has far greater professional, economic, intellectual and other ties to the various elements of the court system than he does to his own client. In short, the court is a closed community.

This is more than just the case of the usual "secrets" of bureaucracy which are fanatically defended from an outside view. Even all elements of the press are zealously determined to report on that which will not offend the board of judges, the prosecutor, probation, legal-aid, or other officials, in return for privileges and courtesies granted in the past and to be granted in the future. Rather than any view of the matter in terms of some variation of a "conspiracy" hypothesis, the simple explanation is one of an ongoing system handling delicate tensions, managing the trauma produced by law enforcement and administration, and requiring almost pathological distrust of "outsiders" bordering on group paranoia.

The hostile attitude toward "outsiders" is in large measure engendered by a defensiveness itself produced by the inherent deficiencies of assembly line justice, so characteristic of our major criminal courts. Intolerably large caseloads . . . [that] must be disposed of in an organizational context of limited resources and personnel, potentially subject the participants in the court community to harsh scrutiny from appellate courts, and other public and private sources of condemnation. As a consequence, an almost irreconcilable conflict is posed in terms of intense pressures to process huge numbers of cases on the one hand, and the stringent ideological and legal requirements of "due process of law," on the other hand. A rather tenuous resolution of the dilemma has emerged in the shape of a large variety of bureaucratically ordained and controlled short cuts, deviations, and outright rule violations adopted as court practice in order to meet production norms. Fearfully anticipating criticism on ethical as well as legal grounds, all the significant participants in the court's social structure are bound into an organized system of complicity. This consists of a work arrangement in which the patterned, covert, informal breaches, and evasions of "due process" are institutionalized, but are, nevertheless, denied to exist.

These institutionalized evasions will be found to occur to some degree, in all criminal courts. Their nature, scope and complexity are largely determined by the size of the court, and the character of the community in which it is located, e.g., whether it is a large, urban institution, or a relatively small rural county court. In addition, idiosyncratic, local conditions may contribute to a unique flavor in the character and quality of the criminal law's administration in a particular community. . . . A wide variety of coercive devices are employed against an accused-client, couched in a depersonalized, instrumental, bureaucratic version of due process of law, and which are in reality a perfunctory obeisance to the ideology of due process. These include some very explicit pressures which are exerted in some measure by all court personnel, including judges, to plead guilty and avoid trial. In many instances the sanction of a potentially harsh sentence is utilized as the visible alternative to pleading guilty. . . . Too often, the discretionary power as to bail is part of the arsenal of weapons available to collapse the resistance of an accused person. . . .

The defense attorneys, therefore, whether of the legal-aid, public defender variety, or privately retained, although operating in terms of pressures specific to their respective role and organizational obligations, ultimately are concerned with strategies which tend to lead to a plea. It is the rational, impersonal elements involving economies of time, labor, expense and a superior commitment of the defense counsel to these rationalistic values of maximum production of court organization that prevail, in his relationship with a client. The lawyer "regulars" are frequently former staff members of the prosecutor's office and utilize the prestige, know-how and contacts of their former affiliation as part of their stock in trade. Close and continuing relations between the lawyer "regular" and his former colleagues in the prosecutor's office generally overshadow the relationship between the regular and his client. The continuing colleagueship of supposedly adversary counsel rests on real professional and organizational needs of a quid pro quo, which goes beyond the limits of an accommodation or modus vivendi one might ordinarily expect under the circumstances of an otherwise seemingly adversary relationship. Indeed, the adversary features which are manifest are for the most part muted and exist even in their attenuated form largely for external consumption. The principals, lawyer and assistant district attorney, rely upon one another's cooperation for their continued professional existence, and so the bargaining between them tends usually to be "reasonable" rather than fierce. . . .

FEE COLLECTION AND FIXING

Defense lawyers condition even the most obtuse clients to recognize that there is a firm interconnection between fee payment and the zealous exercise of professional expertise, secret knowledge, and organizational "connections" in their behalf. Lawyers, therefore, seek to keep their clients in a proper state of tension, and to arouse in them the precise edge of anxiety which is calculated to encourage prompt fee payment. Consequently, the client attitude in the relationship between defense counsel and an accused is in many instances a precarious admixture of hostility, mistrust, dependence, and sycophancy. By keeping his client's anxieties aroused to the proper pitch, and establishing a seemingly causal relationship between a requested fee and the accused's ultimate extrication from his onerous difficulties, the lawyer will have established the necessary preliminary groundwork to assure a minimum of haggling over the fee and its eventual payment. . . .

At the outset, because there are great risks of nonpayment of the fee, due to the impecuniousness of his clients, and the fact that a man who is sentenced to jail may be a singularly unappreciative client, the criminal lawyer collects his fee in advance. . . . The criminal lawyer must serve three major functions, or stated another way, he must solve three problems. First, he must arrange for his fee; second, he must prepare and then, if necessary, "cool out" his client in case of defeat (a highly likely contingency); third, he must satisfy the court organization that he has performed adequately in the process of negotiating the plea, so as to preclude the possibility of any sort of embarrassing incident which may serve to invite "outside" scrutiny.

In assuring the attainment of one of his primary objectives, his fee, the criminal lawyer will very often enter into negotiations with the accused's kin, including collateral relatives. In many instances, the accused himself is unable to pay any sort of fee or anything more than a token fee. It then becomes important to involve as many of the accused's kin as possible in the situation. This is especially so if the attorney hopes to collect a significant part of a proposed substantial fee. It is not uncommon for several relatives to contribute toward the fee. The larger the group, the greater the possibility that the lawyer will collect a sizable fee by getting contributions from each. . . .

. . . But the larger the fee the lawyer wishes to exact, the more impressive his performance must be, in terms of his stage managed image as a personage of great influence and power in the court organization. Court personnel are keenly aware of the extent to which a lawyer's stock in trade involves the precarious stage management of an image which goes beyond the usual professional flamboyance, and for this reason alone the lawyer is "bound in" to the authority system of the court's organizational discipline. Therefore, to some extent, court personnel will aid the lawyer in the creation and maintenance of that impression. There is a tacit commitment to the lawyer by the court organization, apart from formal etiquette, to aid him in this. Such augmentation of the lawyer's stage managed image as this affords, is the partial basis for the quid pro quo which exists between the lawyer and the court organization. It tends to serve as the continuing basis for the higher loyalty of the lawyer to the organization; his relationship with his client, in contrast, is transient, ephemeral and often superficial.

DEFENSE LAWYER AS DOUBLE AGENT

The lawyer has often been accused of stirring up unnecessary litigation, especially in the field of negligence. . . . The strong incentive of possible fees motivates the lawyer to promote litigation which would otherwise never have developed. However, the criminal lawyer develops a vested interest of an entirely different nature in his client's case: to limit its scope and duration rather than do battle. Only in this way can a case be "profitable." Thus, he enlists the aid of relatives not only to assure payment of his fee, but he will also rely on these persons to help him in his agent-mediator role of convincing the accused to plead guilty, and ultimately to help in "cooling out" the accused if necessary.

It is at this point that an accused-defendant may experience his first sense of "betrayal." While he had perhaps perceived the police and prosecutor to be adversaries, or possibly even the judge, the accused is wholly unprepared for his counsel's role performance as an agent mediator. In the same vein, it is even less likely to occur to an accused that members of his own family or other kin may become agents, albeit at the behest and urging of other agents or mediators, acting on the principle that they are in reality helping an accused negotiate the best possible plea arrangement under the circumstances. Usually, it will be the lawyer who will activate next of kin in this role, his ostensible motive being to arrange for his fee. But soon latent and unstated motives will assert themselves, with entreaties by counsel to the accused's next of kin, to appeal to the accused to "help himself" by pleading. . . .

In effect, in his role as double agent, the criminal lawyer performs an extremely vital and delicate mission for the court organization and the accused. Both principals are anxious to terminate the litigation with a minimum of expense and damage to each other. There is no other personage or role incumbent in the total court structure more strategically located, who by training and in terms of his own requirements, is more ideally suited to do so than the lawyer. In recognition of this, judges will cooperate with attorneys in many important ways. For example, they will adjourn the case of an accused in jail awaiting plea or sentence if the attorney requests such action. While explicitly this may be done for some innocuous and seemingly valid reason, the tacit purpose is that pressure is being applied by the attorney for the collection of his fee, which he knows will probably not be forthcoming if the case is concluded. Judges are aware of this tactic on the part of lawyers, who, by requesting an adjournment, keep an accused incarcerated awhile longer as a not too subtle method of dunning a client for payment. . . .

The judge will help an accused's lawyer in still another way. He will lend the official aura of his office and courtroom so that a lawyer can stage manage an impression of an "all out" performance for the accused in justification of his fee. The judge and other court personnel will serve as a backdrop for a scene charged with dramatic fire which the accused's lawyer makes a stirring appeal in his behalf. With a show of restrained passion, the lawyer will intone the virtues of the accused and recite the social deprivations which have reduced him to his present state. The speech varies somewhat, depending on whether the accused has been convicted after trial or has pleaded guilty. In the main, however, the incongruity, superficiality, and ritualistic character of the total performance is underscored by a visibly impassive, almost bored reaction on the part of the judge and other members of the court retinue.

Afterward, there is a hearty exchange of pleasantries between the lawyer and district attorney, wholly out of context in terms of the supposed adversary nature of the preceding events. The fiery passion in defense of his client is gone, and the lawyers for both sides resume their offstage relations, chatting amiably and perhaps including the judge in their restrained banter. No other aspect of their visible conduct so effectively serves to put even a casual observer on notice, that these individuals have claims upon each other. These seemingly innocuous actions are indicative of continuing organizational and informal relations, which, in their intricacy and depth, range far beyond any priorities or claims a particular defendant may have.

The "cop-out" ceremony, in which the court process culminates, is not only invaluable for redefining the accused's perspectives of himself, but also in reiterating publicly in a formally structured ritual the accused person's guilt for the benefit of significant "others" who are observing. The accused not only is made to assert publicly his guilt of a specific crime, but also a complete recital of its details. He is further made to indicate that he is entering his plea of guilty freely, willingly, and voluntarily, and that he is not doing so because of any promises or in consideration of any commitments that may have been made to him by anyone. This last is intended as a blanket statement to shield the participants from any possible charges of "coercion" or undue influence that may have been exerted in violation of due process requirements. Its function is to preclude any later review by an appellate court on these grounds, and also to obviate any second thoughts an accused may develop in connection with his plea.

However, for the accused, the conception of self as a guilty person is in large measure a temporary role adaptation. His career socialization as an accused, if it is successful, eventuates in his acceptance and redefinition of himself as a guilty person. However, the transformation is ephemeral, in that he will, in private, quickly reassert his innocence. Of importance is that he accept his defeat, publicly proclaim it, and find some measure of pacification in it. Almost immediately after his plea, a defendant will generally be interviewed by a representative of the probation division in connection with a presentence report which is to be prepared. The very first question to be asked of him by the probation officer is: "Are you guilty of the crime to which you pleaded?" This is by way of double affirmation of the defendant's guilt. Should the defendant now begin to make bold assertions of his innocence, despite his plea of guilty, he will be asked to withdraw his plea and stand trial on the criminal charges. Such a threatened possibility is, in most instances, sufficient to cause an accused to let the plea stand and to request the probation officer to overlook his exclamations of innocence. . . .

[The author then discusses a study of persons who pleaded guilty.] It would be well to observe at the outset, that of the 724 defendants who pleaded guilty before trial, only 43 (6 per cent) . . . had confessed prior to their indictment. Thus, the ultimate judicial process was predicated upon evidence independent of any confession of the accused. . . .

In order to determine which agent-mediator was most influential in altering the accused's perspectives as to his decision to plead or go to trial (regardless of the proposed basis of the plea), the same sample of defendants were asked to indicate the person who first suggested to them that they plead guilty. They were also asked to indicate which of the persons or officials who made such suggestion, was most influential in affecting their final decision to plead.

It is popularly assumed that the police, through forced confessions, and the district attorney, employing still other pressures, are most instrumental in the inducement of an accused to plead guilty. . . . [I]t is actually the defendant's own counsel who is most effective in this role. Further, this phenomenon tends to reinforce the extremely rational nature of criminal law administration, for an organization could not rely upon the sort of idiosyncratic measures employed by the police to induce confessions and maintain its efficiency, high production and overall rational-legal character. The defense counsel becomes the ideal agent-mediator since, as "officer of the court" and confidant of the accused and his kin, he lives astride both worlds and can serve the ends of the two as well as his own. . . .

The overwhelming majority of accused persons . . . related a specific incident which indicated an urging or suggestion, either during the course of the first or second contact, that they plead guilty to a lesser charge if this could be arranged. Of all the agent-mediators, it is the lawyer who is most effective in manipulating an accused's perspectives, notwithstanding pressures that may have been previously applied by police, district attorney, judge or any of the agent-mediators that may have been activated by them. . . .

[T]he lawyer's role as agent-mediator may be seen as unique in that he is in effect a double agent. Although, as "officer of the court" he mediates between the court organization and the defendant, his roles with respect to each are rent by conflicts of interest. Too often these must be resolved in favor of the organization which provides him with the means for his professional existence. Consequently, in order to reduce the strains and conflicts imposed in what is ultimately an overdemanding role obligation for him, the lawyer engages in the lawyer-client "confidence game" so as to structure more favorably an otherwise onerous role system.

CONCLUSION

[D]ecisions of the Supreme Court, in the area of criminal law administration and defendant's rights, fail to take into account three crucial aspects of social structure which may tend to render the more libertarian rules as nugatory. The decisions overlook (1) the nature of courts as formal organizations; (2) the relationship that the lawyer-regular actually has with the court organization; and (3) the character of the lawyer-client relationship in the criminal court (the routine relationships, not those unusual ones that are described in "heroic" terms in novels, movies, and TV).

Courts, like many other modern large-scale organizations possess a monstrous appetite for the cooptation of entire professional groups as well as individuals. Almost all those who come within the ambit of organizational authority, find that their definitions, perceptions and values have been refurbished, largely in terms favorable to the particular organization and its goals. . . .

3. Donald G. Gifford, *A Context-Based Theory of Strategy Selection*, 46 OHIO ST. L.J. 41, 73-82 (1985)*

[In earlier parts of this article, Professor Gifford discussed strategy selection. See excerpt at Chapter Four, section 2. Then he applies the model in several legal contexts, including plea bargaining.]

---

*Reprinted with permission.

B. The Defense Attorney's Strategy in Plea Bargaining

It is possible to recommend a plea bargaining strategy likely to be effective in most cases, because the plea bargaining process generally exhibits certain characteristics that determine which strategy is likely to succeed, even though the specific mechanics of plea bargaining and behavior patterns of prosecutors and defense attorneys vary from one locality to another and from one case to another. The defense attorney's negotiation strategy is construed broadly here to include not only formal plea discussions, but also tactical considerations in deciding whether to file particular motions, how to handle discovery and the exchange of information in plea bargaining, the timing of the guilty plea, and all informal discussions with the prosecutor.

The first factor a defense attorney should consider in choosing a negotiation strategy is the strategy of the opponent—the prosecutor. Although few prosecutors consciously design a purposeful negotiation strategy, an identifiable pattern exists in most prosecutors' opening demands and concessions. This pattern can usefully be identified as a strategy. Even though the exact concessions granted by prosecutors in plea bargaining are characterized by prosecutor individuality, the prosecutor's overall strategy, in most cases, is substantially defined by certain characteristics of the criminal justice system and the prosecutor's role in it.

The charges initially filed against the defendant, together with the probable sentence after conviction, determine the prosecutor's opening demand in plea bargaining negotiations. In almost all cases, the prosecutor's opening demand mirrors what would be expected from a negotiator who follows the competitive strategy: a high, but credible, demand. The initial charge is usually a high demand both because the prosecutor has overcharged and because legislatively defined criminal sentences are generally unrealistically lengthy. Overcharging allows the prosecutor to make concessions, in the form of reduced charges, to the defendant in order to encourage him to plead guilty. The initial charge also is a threat to the defendant: if he does not enter into an agreement, then he might be convicted on more serious charges and serve a longer sentence.

Although the prosecutor's strategy may include both competitive and cooperative tactics as plea bargaining proceeds, her strategy will probably become predominantly cooperative. The primary factor accounting for the frequency of a cooperative strategy among prosecutors in the later stages of plea bargaining is the prosecutor's unique role as a "minister of justice." The prosecutor's goal is not to maximize the length of the defendant's sentence or even the severity of the crime to which the defendant pleads. Empirical studies suggest that a prosecutor's attempt to individualize justice by considering equitable factors about the circumstances of the offense and the characteristics of the offender, such as the youth of the defendant, the lack of a prior criminal record, and provocation by the victim, provides the primary motivation for a prosecutor to make bargaining concessions. The prosecutor's orientation in bargaining, therefore, parallels that of the cooperative negotiator, who attempts to achieve a fair solution. Other factors contribute to the prosecutor's cooperative orientation. These factors include her continuing relationship with defense attorneys, pressures from judges to reach agreement, large caseloads, and the prevailing cooperative norms of plea bargaining. Finally, in most cases the prosecutor can afford to adopt a noncompetitive rather than a competitive strategy because she is not highly accountable to a constituent. Unlike the defense attorney, whose concessions in plea bargaining must be ratified by his client, the prosecutor makes independent decisions about bargaining concessions. In any particular case, specific circumstances may influence the prosecutor to adopt a competitive strategy. However, the pattern of prosecutorial conduct discussed above is prevalent enough to strongly influence the defense attorney's selection of a negotiation strategy.

The second factor a defense attorney should consider in choosing a negotiation strategy is the relative bargaining power of the defense attorney compared to that of the prosecutor. In most cases, the prosecutor possesses much greater power in plea bargaining than does the defense attorney. The consequences for the defendant of failing to achieve an agreement with the prosecutor, that is, the defendant's "best alternative to a negotiated agreement," are not attractive. Most defendants have little chance of being acquitted if they proceed to trial. According to Professor Milton Heumann, "[M]ost of the defendants are factually guilty and have no legal grounds to challenge the state's evidence." If convicted after trial, most defendants will receive a sentence considerably longer than if they had pleaded guilty.

The defense attorney's plea bargaining strategy frequently will be affected by his desire to maintain good working relationships with the prosecutor and the judge. Professor Abraham Blumberg, after his exhaustive study of the criminal justice system in an urban setting, noted that "lines of communication, influence, and contact with those offices . . . are essential to the practice of criminal law." According to Professor Blumberg, the lawyer who regularly works with criminal cases needs to develop "an ongoing 'account' with the prosecution office which he can draw upon from time to time to meet the exigencies of a particular case." This need for a continuing positive working relationship coupled with the necessity of disposing of a large number of cases leads to symbiotic relationships among the prosecutor defense attorney, and judge. Professors Arthur Rosett and Donald Cressey describe the group comprised of these three actors as the "committee on criminal justice." According to Professors Rosett and Cressey, these parties develop an accommodative working relationship: "Day by day, judges, prosecutors, defenders, and probation officers encounter the same basic types of cases. . . . In time, courthouse workers develop a group sense of justice. They come to understand each other and learn to take each other's views into account."

A primary reason for the courthouse subculture is the defense attorney's need, as well as the prosecutor's, to dispose of cases quickly. This pressure to reach agreement is an additional, independent reason to adopt a cooperative approach. Defense attorneys cannot afford to use competitive tactics and risk stalemate, because their time limitations permit them to try only a few cases. Professors Rosett and Cressey state that if plea bargaining participants were to employ competitive strategies, then "the workday of the courthouse would be so crammed with bluffs, counter bluffs, and counter-counter bluffs, that there would be no time for dispositions."

Although many of the described factors may suggest the adoption of a noncompetitive strategy, the defense attorney's need to maintain good rapport with a client who is hostile toward the prosecutor may lead him to employ a different approach. A competitive strategy is probably advantageous to convince the client that the attorney is "on his side." Defendants are very critical of plea bargaining, usually because they perceive that their attorneys are insufficiently adversarial in representing their interests and are too inclined to sell-out their interests. One defendant in a survey conducted by Professor Jonathan Casper complained that the public defender's first thought is to "cop out." This attitude may be exacerbated if the defense attorney adopts a noncompetitive strategy.

Finally, in choosing between a competitive and a noncompetitive strategy, the defense attorney should consider the norms that govern the tenor of the relationship between the prosecutor and the defense attorney in plea bargaining. Generally, prosecutors expect that defense attorneys will be cooperative in plea bargaining; they punish attorneys who are too adversarial in representing their clients by refusing to grant the typical plea bargaining concessions to these attorneys' clients.

The issues negotiated in plea bargaining are predominantly zero-sum issues, but some opportunities for integrative bargaining may exist. At first glance, it appears inherently difficult to reconcile the interests of an accused murderer and a prosecutor, pressured by an outraged community to convict the defendant, and to find a solution that will benefit both negotiators. Most cases, however, will offer some potential for integrative bargaining, because the prosecutor and the defendant prioritize the issues at stake differently. Prosecutors are most interested in obtaining a conviction, while defendants are most interested in minimizing the length of the sentence. Guilty plea agreements that allow the prosecutor to convict a defendant on a charge which accurately reflects the seriousness of the crime but that provides for a comparatively light sentence (that is, a light sentence recommendation or a light sentence contained in the statute to which the defendant pleads guilty) may serve the interests of both the prosecutor and the defendant. All parties may also want to avoid the expense, anxiety, and time consumed by litigation. Finally, an inventive defense attorney can use the integrative techniques of brainstorming to generate nonincarceration sanctions, such as restitution.

Application of the factors used in choosing a negotiation strategy to the situation generally facing the defense attorney in plea bargaining suggests the adoption of a predominantly cooperative strategy coupled with some early competitive tactics and integrative solutions whenever feasible. Of course, other factors in a particular case that are inconsistent with the characteristics of the typical plea bargaining system described above, such as a case in which there is a good chance of acquittal at trial or a case that involves a prosecutor who is personally very competitive or antagonistic, should cause an attorney to modify the recommended strategy. Nevertheless, in the same way that cross-examination tactics recommended by trial practice teachers can be generally followed by the trial attorney, the recommendations for a plea bargaining strategy discussed above should form the foundation for a defense attorney's effective plea bargaining strategy. Of course, the defense attorney's negotiation strategy always must be determined within the parameters established by the client.

In the early phases of the negotiation, the defense attorney should begin with a competitive strategy, but in a cooperative style. Even though several practice manuals suggest that defense attorneys should be extremely cooperative and seek to achieve a guilty plea agreement early in plea bargaining, negotiation theory establishes at least four reasons that the defense attorney's early tactics should be competitive. First, the government's opening demand, usually characterized by overcharging and excessively long legislatively-determined prison sentences, is very competitive. As previously discussed, a negotiator who uses a cooperative strategy against a competitive negotiator is severely disadvantaged. Thus, a defense attorney risks exploitation if he begins negotiations with a cooperative strategy. Second, the defendant usually has low bargaining power; some social scientists recommend that the less powerful negotiator begin competitively and become more cooperative later in the negotiation. Third, it may be necessary to adopt a competitive strategy initially to communicate to the prosecutor that the attorney intends to zealously represent the client and that he will not "cave in" because of his caseload or other personal or institutional pressures. Finally, early competitive moves often convince the client that his attorney intends to represent him vigorously; this improves client relations.

A competitive strategy is recommended for the defense attorney early in plea bargaining but the question remains: What specific competitive tactics should be used? The defense attorney should attempt to obtain unilateral concessions from the prosecutor by asking the prosecutor about her sense of "what the case is worth" and what charge reductions she can make, without indicating the defendant's willingness to plead to any charge at all. Similarly, in the early stages of negotiation, the defense attorney should seek the fullest possible discovery from the prosecutor. At the same time, he should withhold, or only selectively disclose, his client's version of the facts and other evidence available to him. The attorney can also reduce the prosecutor's power advantage by insisting that the prosecutor deal only with provable offenses and with a realistic penalty, instead of with overcharges and the statutorily defined penalty maximums.

Most important, defense attorneys should raise with the prosecutor valid defenses, motions, and other issues as part of their negotiation strategy. Doing so, however, can entail considerable risks and costs for defense attorneys. Judges and prosecutors sometimes view such motions and legal challenges with hostility, and they may retaliate against the defense attorney later in the plea bargaining process by refusing to make discretionary reductions based on the equities of the case. Defense attorneys who file motions that prosecutors view as frivolous may never get a break in plea bargaining. Accordingly, the defense attorney should pursue viable legal issues, but should try to maintain a cooperative relationship with the prosecutor. Sometimes the defense attorney can informally raise legal challenges to the government's case. If legal challenges are presented in this manner, the prosecutor is often more willing to make appropriate dismissals or reductions than if a formal motion is filed in court. In addition, the defense attorney can often place on an obstreperous client the responsibility for competitive tactics, such as refusing to enter pleas or raising certain defenses, and still maintain a cordial personal working relationship with the prosecutor.

It is important to reiterate the distinction between negotiation strategy and negotiation style. If an attorney hopes to appeal to the prosecutor's equitable discretion later in the negotiation, his personal style should be accommodative, not antagonistic. The defense attorney should attempt to argue defenses and other legal issues vigorously, while maintaining cordial personal relationships. An attorney with an accommodative personal style can often switch from a competitive to a cooperative strategy during a negotiation. It is more difficult for an antagonistic attorney to build a relationship on trust and seek discretionary favors from a prosecutor later in a negotiation.

Following the initial stages of plea bargaining, virtually all the factors discussed previously suggest adopting a noncompetitive strategy for plea bargaining. Usually the cooperative strategy will be more effective than the integrative strategy, although some opportunities for integrative solutions may exist. The following factors suggest the adoption of a noncompetitive strategy:

(1) the prosecutor will probably use a cooperative strategy;

(2) the prosecutor has greater bargaining power;

(3) an amicable continuing relationship between the defense attorney and the prosecutor should be maintained;

(4) various pressures to reach agreement exist; and

(5) the prevailing norms in plea bargaining mandate the use of cooperative tactics.

The prosecutor's use of a cooperative strategy supports the adoption of a noncompetitive strategy. In most cases, the prosecutor views her role as one requiring her to individualize justice by taking into account the circumstances of the offense and the characteristics of the offender. Prosecutors will react more favorably in this role if defense attorneys appear to be working with them to evaluate the culpability of the defendant. If the probable outcome of the case is a plea by the defendant, the defense attorney should share information freely with the prosecutor and seek to identify those mitigating factors that would induce the prosecutor to make bargaining concessions.

Finally, the defense attorney should urge integrative solutions whenever feasible. Often plea bargaining is not a zero-sum situation, and the defense attorney should seek agreements in appropriate cases that allow the prosecutor to obtain a conviction at the same time that the client is protected from a long prison term. Restitution and other alternatives to incarceration may satisfy both the prosecutor's need for a sanction and the defendant's desire to avoid incarceration.

Both the competitive and the noncompetitive strategies have advantages and disadvantages in plea bargaining. In a particular case, one aspect of the bargaining context may suggest the adoption of one strategy over the other. If the prosecutor's case is weak and conviction is unlikely, the use of a competitive strategy becomes more attractive. If an inexperienced prosecuting attorney wants to gain more trial experience, a defense attorney's cooperative strategy is unlikely to yield substantial concessions. When deciding on a negotiating strategy, the defense attorney should always determine the factors that distinguish the instant case from the usual plea bargaining situation. If these factors are important, the attorney may want to modify the suggested strategy. Even if the attorney modifies the recommended strategy in a particular case with unusual characteristics, however, this recommendation at least provides the criminal defense attorney with a starting point. Thus, this proposed strategy is a more useful tool for the practicing criminal defense attorney than either a mere list of factors to be applied on an ad hoc basis or the admonishment that he will learn to plea bargain as he gains experience.

In summary, negotiation theory suggests that the plea bargaining strategy most likely to succeed in a typical case is one which begins with a competitive approach and progresses to a cooperative approach as negotiations continue. To accomplish this strategy switch, the defense attorney should attempt to maintain a cordial and accommodative relationship with the prosecutor, even during the early phases of bargaining. It is difficult to compare this strategy with the "state of the art" recommendations of practicing criminal defense attorneys, because practicing lawyers give inconsistent advice. Some commentators recommend a cooperative strategy designed to reach an agreement as quickly as possible; others suggest that cooperating with the prosecutor is equivalent to selling out. The strategy recommended above, however, appears likely to be the most effective in the plea bargaining context.

D. Negotiations Within Legislative Bodies

1. Tom Melling, *Dispute Resolution Within Legislative Institutions*, 46 STAN. L. REV. 1677 (1994)*

INTRODUCTION

. . . While legal literature abounds with dispute resolution techniques for our court system, scholars have neglected to analyze their importance for the legislative process. Instead, scholars study the content of statutes, their application, and legislative history, but ignore the process that produced the legislation. Similarly, practicing lawyers clamor to learn about ADR techniques that substitute for litigation, yet they know little about how the legislative process affects the formation of statutes.

This failure to evaluate the legislative process from the perspective of dispute resolution is surprising, given the modern importance of statutory law and the role that lawyers, lobbyists, and legislators play in drafting and passing statutes. Lawyers can better advance their clients' interests if they understand the barriers to collaborative legislative decision-making. By understanding different dispute resolution techniques, legislators can build consensus among competing interest groups and achieve more favorable results. Judges can also interpret statutes better by studying the legislative process. Moreover, cooperative approaches to legislative decision-making are increasingly important as competing interest groups have nearly mired the federal government in gridlock. Because the legislative process is naturally flexible and receptive to innovation, legislative dispute resolution techniques deserve study.

This note applies dispute resolution theory to legislative conflict. The focal point of the analysis is a case study of the Central Utah Project Completion Act (CUP)[14] — a monumental legislative settlement that revolutionizes water management in Utah. Western water policy is particularly apt for the study of dispute resolution because Western farmers, environmentalists, and cities are continually fighting over this vital but finite resource. Although this conflict continues, Utah's environmentalists and water users worked together to craft novel solutions, making the CUP the "reform model" for future water planning. . . .

II. OVERCOMING LEGISLATIVE BARRIERS: EXAMPLES OF DISPUTE RESOLUTION STRATEGIES

The preceding section identified three barriers to the cooperative resolution of conflict within legislative institutions: strategic voting and institutional structure, bargaining through the mass media, and bargaining through elected representatives. Understanding these barriers can do more than just explain why negotiations fail; it can help us devise strategies to overcome the barriers. This Part describes [an] example where legislators and disputing parties used three dispute resolution techniques to overcome these barriers. The techniques used were a unanimous decision rule, negotiation in private, and mediation by a politician. A unan-

---

[14]Pub. L. No. 102-575, 106 Stat. 4600 (1992) (codified as amended in scattered sections of 43 U.S.C.). *See generally,* Tom Melling, *The CUP Holds the Solution: Utah's Hybrid Alternative to Water Markets,* 13 J. OF ENERGY, NAT. RESOURCES & ENVTL L. 159 (1993).

imous decision rule eliminates the instability and chaos of cyclical voting by compelling the parties to develop a mutually beneficial solution through cooperative bargaining. Negotiation in private eliminates the politician's dilemma by eliminating the use of the media as a bargaining weapon. Mediation by a politician or a group of politicians encourages interest groups to come to the bargaining table and to resolve their disputes face to face.

A. The CUP: A Case Study of Water Policy Reform

For Utahns, the CUP Completion Act is perhaps the most important legislation enacted by the United States Congress in the last decade. It authorizes the expenditure of nearly $1 billion to complete a water project that will deliver water to urban areas along the Wasatch Front and to farmers in Central Utah. Despite Utah's position as the second most arid state, the CUP will allow the state's economy to grow well into the twenty-first century.

The CUP was originally designed to solve a difficult predicament in Utah. If past trends continue, virtually all population and economic growth will occur in the Salt Lake Valley corridor of North-Central Utah. Yet Utah's most abundant water resource, the Colorado River, lies on the state's eastern border, shielded by a mountain range that rises to 12,000 feet. Thus, in 1956, Congress approved the CUP. It was designed to divert water from fifteen tributaries of the Colorado River through the range of separating mountains to the state's population and agricultural centers.

The massive scale of the project nearly caused its demise. By 1987, twenty-one years after construction began, cost overruns approached $500 million. In addition, the environmental impacts were profound. The CUP dewatered or seriously degraded approximately 245 miles of streams, riparian areas, and associated wetlands, destroying thousands of acres of wildlife habitat. The Bureau of Reclamation added to the problem by delaying the project's environmental mitigation far behind project construction.

In 1988, the funds authorized by Congress to complete the project ran out. The CUP was less than 50 percent complete; yet it had not delivered one drop of water from the Colorado River tributaries. Realizing that the CUP was in danger of becoming a white elephant, Utah's congressional delegation tried to obtain additional funds. They introduced a one-paragraph reauthorization bill requesting an additional $750 million. The leadership of the House Interior Committee, however, refused to move the bill because it lacked genuine fiscal and environmental reforms. The Committee's rejection set the stage for four years of difficult negotiations.

The legislative dispute concerned two broad issues—fiscal and environmental reform. The substantive issues were complex, but the parties fell into several identifiable groups. Environmental organizations led the demand for fiscal and environmental reform. On the other side, agricultural interests and water users fought these reforms, arguing that Congress should keep its commitment to complete the project. At the political level, Utah's congressional delegation split along party lines. The Republicans supported agricultural interests and opposed environmental reforms. Utah's Republicans, however, could not move the bill through the Democratically controlled House without the support of Representative Wayne Owens, the sole Democrat in Utah's congressional delegation. Representative Owens supported the environmentalists' call for fiscal and environmental reform; nevertheless, he needed the project completed for his own political survival.

Round one: 1988-1990. For over two years, Utah's politicians tried to redesign the project themselves. The negotiations were combative and bitter, spearheaded primarily by Utah Senator Jake Garn and Representative Owens. Both sides played political hardball. Representative Owens enlisted the General Accounting Office to investigate past expenditures sponsored by Senator Garn, undermining the Senator's credibility in the eyes of the House and Senate committee chairmen. Senator Garn enlisted the Utah Republican Party to file an ethics complaint against Representative Owens alleging improper congressional behavior.

In early 1990, Utah's congressional delegation finally reached a compromise and again submitted legislation to the Interior Committee. Despite several fiscal and environmental improvements, national environmental organizations remained opposed to the bill, claiming it had "serious problems." Because of this opposition, the chairman of the Interior Committee once again refused to move the bill.

Round two: 1990-1991. Water users still desperately wanted to get the CUP reauthorized. Environmentalists were equally eager to remedy the damage caused by $1 billion of unfinished construction. Given this glimmer of mutual interest, Representative Owens used his influence with national environmental organizations and with Utah's water community to bring these traditional foes together. In this new round of negotiations, the politicians took a back seat. With Representative Owens acting as a mediator, the groups discovered many common interests. Two and a half months later, the parties signed an agreement that became the blueprint for the CUP Completion Act.

The redesigned CUP contains unprecedented reforms that make it the most fiscally responsible and environmentally progressive federal water project in the West. The CUP's water conservation program significantly increases state cost-sharing requirements and thus sets the standard for future reclamation financing. To address the environmental damage caused by the project's construction, the CUP removes the lackluster Bureau of Reclamation from the task of environmental mitigation and replaces it with a new environmental commission that oversees all mitigation and habitat restoration. In short, by working together, the parties found ways to deliver the water and to protect the environment in a way that made all the parties better off. This agreement, forged during the second round of negotiations, was not fortuitous; it was the result of a specific process that created a cooperative negotiating environment. The three procedural strategies identified earlier helped the parties to overcome legislative barriers and to bargain cooperatively.

1. A Unanimous Decision Rule

When the Utah congressional delegation initially requested additional funds to complete the CUP in 1988, the House Interior Committee chairman stipulated that all affected parties must support the legislation before he would move it out of the committee. This meant that the entire Utah congressional delegation, national and local environmental organizations, the governor of Utah, public power interests, and the North Ute Indian Tribe all had to support the bill.

In multiparty negotiations, parties must manage the decision-making process, either explicitly or implicitly, by adopting decision rules. Although a majority decision rule generally governs our democratic processes, the CUP experience suggests that the use of a consensus process can help overcome the barrier of strategic voting and institutional structure.

A unanimous decision rule was critical to the negotiation process for several reasons. First, it encouraged reluctant parties to come to the bargaining table. Although the environmentalists might have blocked a reauthorization of the project, either by lobbying Congress or by challenging the project in court, the chairman's requirement of unanimous agreement eliminated any concern that they would lose their leverage or be ignored if they entered negotiations. As a result, they were able to devote their energies to resolving problems rather than to fighting reauthorization.

In addition to fostering greater participation, a unanimous decision rule eliminated the instability associated with shifting coalitions and strategic voting. Rather than seeking proposals to create a majority coalition, the parties sought solutions that everyone could support. Therefore, the negotiation environment fostered brainstorming and compromise, not strategic behavior and splintered coalitions. Ultimately, the parties discovered subtle alternatives that "enlarged the pie." As dispute resolution scholars have asserted: "Consensus, defined and developed by the stakeholders, is more likely to resolve a dispute than a vote of a legislative body, a decision by an administrative agency, or a court decree because it is likely to meet more of their interests."

Finally, the unanimous decision rule helped create a more stable and lasting agreement. Since all parties participated in crafting the solution, they all worked for its passage. Significantly, the parties agreed not to sabotage the bill with floor amendments, eliminating a fear that often clouds legislative negotiations. In addition, because the parties left the process satisfied with their result, they have continued to consult each other, identifying and solving potential problems before they arise.

Recent empirical studies of group negotiation explain why a unanimous decision rule can overcome the barrier of strategic voting and institutional structure. One study found that groups using a unanimous decision rule were more likely to achieve higher joint outcomes, to integrate the interests of group members, and to distribute resources more equitably than groups using a majority decision rule. A majority decision rule creates fewer opportunities for the parties to discover the priorities of others, which can impede problem-solving activities that maximize the combined utility of group members. A majority decision rule can also be vulnerable to paradoxes of voting that result in inefficient outcomes. Under a unanimous decision rule, the parties have more control over the process and feel more satisfied with and committed to the group's decision.

Empirical studies of jury decisions confirm the advantages of a unanimous decision rule. Although the choice of decision rule generally does not affect the outcomes of jury verdicts, it does affect the nature of jury deliberations. Juries operating under a majority decision rule rarely reach a consensus. Jurors in the minority generally participate less in the decision-making process and are significantly more dissatisfied with the deliberative process and outcome. Finally, . . . under a majority rule jurors may have "polite and academic conversation" rather than "earnest and robust argument," once the majority makes up its mind.

Obviously, however, several factors must be present for a unanimous decision rule to be practical. Most important, the prospect of no agreement must be worse for all parties than a negotiated settlement. This was critical to the CUP negotiations. If the parties had not reached an agreement, the water users would have wasted millions of dollars and would still not have received any water. For the environmentalists, an unfinished project would have made permanent over $1 billion of construction scars and degradation. The Northern Ute Indian Tribe would have lost its water rights without receiving any compensation. Public power groups would have undermined their relationship with a politically valuable ally, agricultural interests. Finally, an unfinished project would have jeopardized the careers of Utah politicians. Thus, all parties had strong incentives to reach an agreement.

A great risk of requiring unanimity is that each party receives veto power. This increases the bargaining power of weaker parties who may be tempted to prevent resolution. For example, studies have shown that juries operating under a unanimous decision rule "hang" more often. Because of this possibility, some researchers believe that, in a zero-sum negotiation, a majority decision rule may work better than a requirement of unanimity.

Under a unanimous decision rule, parties may also threaten to veto to gain strategic advantage. During the CUP negotiations, a couple of parties threatened to oppose the bill if others did not acquiesce to their demands. While these threats initially caused great concern, other parties exercised strong group pressure that encouraged the threatening parties to back down. While the effectiveness of group pressure has never been studied with juries, there are several reasons why group pressure in the political arena may be highly effective at decreasing the danger of threats. First, most government officials are repeat players; therefore, wielding veto power against other parties has long-term reputational consequences. Second, if a party actually carries out a veto threat, the public will blame that party for creating gridlock. In the case of the CUP, no party wanted to be targeted as responsible for killing the project.

Other concerns may also make a unanimous decision rule impractical. As the number of negotiating parties increases, a majority decision rule becomes more efficient. Jury studies have shown that impasse becomes more frequent, and deliberations take longer, in larger groups. All parties that can realistically block an agreement must participate in the negotiation process. If an important group is left out—especially a powerful party—any agreement may be meaningless. In the first round of CUP negotiations, Utah's politicians did not include the national environmental groups. Although the Utah political delegation reached a consensus, the environmental groups blocked the agreement and another round of negotiations began. On the other hand, the parties excluded the Bureau of Reclamation, the original architects and builders of the project. Making an "end run" around the Bureau allowed the parties to craft historic reforms to complete the project. The Bureau opposed the second agreement because it was "not a party involved in the development of the [new bill] but could not stop its passage." Excluding the Bureau was possible only because Senator Garn had considerable clout with the Bush administration. Ultimately, he had to appeal to President Bush's Chief of Staff, John Sununu, to fend off the Bureau's attempt to sabotage the reauthorization bill.

2. Negotiation In Private

The bargaining atmosphere during the two rounds of CUP negotiations demonstrates how the politician's dilemma creates a barrier to the cooperative resolution of conflict. During the first round of negotiations, parties used the press to stake out positions, to make threats, and to attack other parties. Tensions escalated, and the parties overlooked many mutually beneficial solutions. For example, when Senator Garn publicly opposed Representative Owens' proposal to create a fund for future environmental repairs, he took a rigid bargaining position, making future negotiation more difficult. The press focused on this single issue, causing the parties to ignore other relevant considerations. For Senator Garn and Representative Owens, going to the press became the dominant strategy, since each felt compelled to protect his position and to take advantage of any exploitable weakness. This approach wasted time and resources that could have been used to research or discuss alternatives.

When the second round of negotiations began, the CUP parties agreed to a truce. They no longer relied on the press to influence the negotiation; they bargained in private. When they reached closure on an issue, the parties would address the press together. Removing the press from the decision-making process helped to "smooth out the playing field," making a search for joint solutions possible. It eliminated the temptation to use outside strategies and hence eliminated the politician's dilemma.

Some may contend that, although the media hinder cooperative bargaining, it is better for society to involve the press in every step of the legislative process because the press squares government policies with popular opinion and discourages unethical or disingenuous behavior by elected officials. This argument should not prevent private political negotiation. First, if the parties operate under a unanimous decision rule, and if all of the affected parties are included in the negotiation, a watchdog like the press is not needed. Even if a party is left out of the bargaining process, the proposed bill must pass through Congress. During congressional debate, there is more than ample time for the press to scrutinize a bill and to alert the public to problems in the legislative process. For example, Congress took over thirty months to enact the CUP Completion Act after the parties reached the agreement they made public.

3. Mediation By A Politician

The CUP experience suggests an unorthodox role for politicians: the mediation of disputes between conflicting interest groups. When the CUP conflict began in 1988, Representative Owens played the role of an active advocate. Motivated by the need to move the bill out of the House Subcommittee on Water, Power, and Offshore Energy Resources, he spearheaded environmental reform efforts. After two years of protracted, frustrating, and disappointing bargaining, Representative Owens had achieved significant environmental reforms. Nevertheless, environmental organizations refused to support the result. They sought greater environmental protections, as well as slightly different objectives. In other words, the water users and environmentalists failed to reach an agreement because of the elected representative barrier.

In the second round of negotiations, the water users and environmentalists eliminated this problem by negotiating directly, with Representative Owens acting as a mediator. Because Representative Owens enjoyed the respect of all the parties, he was able to persuade them to begin a new round of negotiations. Once the environmentalists became directly involved in the negotiation process, they could express and achieve their objectives directly.

By stepping into the role of mediator, Representative Owens not only eliminated the elected representative barrier but also assisted the dispute resolution process. During the negotiations, he helped create viable alternatives and guided the parties towards agreement. Sometimes he acted as a facilitator, helping to sustain the bargaining process. He organized meetings, facilitated communication, and kept notes during the negotiations "which went on to five o'clock in the morning." At other times, he was an "activist mediator." When the parties could not agree on several issues, they "looked to somebody who would resolve those issues." Because both sides respected his judgment, they accepted Representative Owens' position as the final settlement. On more than one occasion, both sides nearly walked out. Without Representative Owens acting as a mediator, "the process probably would have failed." Each time, he succeeded in persuading the frustrated party to stay and resolve the problem.

There are several good reasons for politicians to remove themselves from the traditional role of an agent and step into the role of mediator. Many of the typical characteristics of politicians make them effective mediators. Mediators must have intelligence, stamina, energy, patience, a sense of humor, persuasiveness, credibility, and impartiality. Except perhaps for impartiality, these are valuable skills for anyone who hopes to win a grueling campaign for elected office. Without these skills, Representative Owens would not have been nearly as successful in bringing the groups together and mediating the dispute. For example, his sense of humor often kept disagreements from escalating out of control.

In addition to possessing traits needed to play the role of mediator, politicians bring a special advantage to the position of mediator: Their stature gives them influence over the parties. For example, the parties to the CUP dispute valued their relationship with Representative Owens and consequently were willing to work with him and to accept his position as the mediated solution to an impasse when necessary. Jacob Bercovitch refers to the mediator's ability to influence the outcome as "leverage." Elected officials tend automatically to have a certain amount of leverage, making them well positioned to mediate disputes. Bercovitch, a critic of the traditional emphasis on impartial mediation, argues that mediators need leverage to achieve their primary tasks of reframing and persuasion.

On the other hand, some politicians may not be well-suited to the role of mediator. Usually, politicians define themselves to their constituents as advocates for specific policies or popular legislation. Many politicians believe the only thing in the middle of the road is yellow paint and dead chickens. [The Texas version of this adage is, yellow stripes and dead armadillos.] Thus, politicians may develop such strong reputations for their positions that they lose their ability to act as neutral third parties. Often a politician's outsized personality cannot fit into the mediator's "ego container, an imaginary box to constrain one's self-importance." Politicians may also try to take advantage of their power to unfairly mediate a dispute. But credibility may be the greatest barrier to mediation by politicians. To be effective, a mediator must build trust and maintain the respect of the parties. In the world of politics, past voting records, well-publicized opinions, and affiliation with political parties shape political credibility. Although Representative Owens was clearly not entirely neutral in the CUP dispute, both the water users and the environmentalists trusted him to set aside his substantive goals and to devote his attention to helping the parties resolve the dispute. . . .

III. AFTER CONFLICT RESOLUTION WITHIN LEGISLATIVE INSTITUTIONS: THE IMPORTANCE OF STATUTORY INTERPRETATION

. . . If administrative agencies and courts misunderstand or ignore the special processes that enabled disputing parties to find a solution—often a fragile compromise-they may misinterpret the statute and undermine the collaborative solution.

Obviously, legislation that resolves a conflict should bring an end to the immediate threat of litigation. Moreover, dispute resolution techniques in a legislative forum can foster a new level of cooperation between former adversaries, further decreasing the likelihood of future litigation. For example, the legislative process culminating in the CUP Completion Act not only ended a longstanding, contentious conflict but also created working relationships between water users and environmentalists. As unforeseen problems have arisen in the implementation and construction of the CUP, both sides have been able to communicate freely, identify common ground, and peaceably find solutions without resorting to the courts. Nevertheless, as time passes and situations change, conflicts will inevitably arise that cannot be resolved through cooperative action. Because any legislative solution may at some point be subject to litigation, and because administrative agencies may administer a statute contrary to the parties' collaborative agreement, the disputing parties should protect their agreements from later misinterpretation.

Parties can protect their agreements in several ways. First, parties can incorporate a nonseverability clause, which will prevent courts from altering a few sections of a statute and disrupting a delicate, balanced agreement. For example, farming, mining, and urban advocates were concerned that state courts might declare sections of the Arizona Groundwater Management Act unconstitutional. They overcame this concern by using a nonseverability clause "under which the entire Act would fall if any part of the Act were to be declared unconstitutional." Another protective strategy is to minimize conflicting sources of legislative history. Legislators can incorporate detailed explanations of a bill into a single report or document, thereby minimizing the risk of conflicting legislative history. The CUP Completion Act illustrates this approach. The only legislative history that explains and clarifies the Act is the House Report from the Interior and Insular Affairs Committee. Courts thus have no other interpretive tool outside the Report and the statute themselves. Legislators who are involved in the process can also agree not to offer floor statements or amendments that could be used to shape future interpretation of the statute. . . .

2. Comments and Questions

a. Melling certainly is correct that the ADR literature has largely ignored legislatures, perhaps following the injunction that there are two things that one does not want to see made — sausage and legislation. Political scientists have long been interested in the legislative process although, like so much of the social sciences, recent writings are so full of specialized vocabulary and mathematics as to be incomprehensible to the uninitiated.

b. Many people think that the best single work on how the legislative process works at the federal level still is Eric Redman, THE DANCE OF LEGISLATION (1973). Redman takes his title from the writing of a distinguished political science professor, Woodrow Wilson: "Once you begin the dance of legislation, and you must struggle through its mazes as best you can to the breathless end — if any end there be."

c. It is striking that the metaphor of legislation as dance can be traced back at least as far as Wilson, because settlement negotiations, both facilitated and directly between parties, is commonly spoken of as a dance toward an agreed solution.

Part III

Mediation

Chapter 7

The Mediation Process

CASE STUDY

(Adapted from: *Wylie v. Gresch*, 191 Cal. App. 3d 412 (1987))

"Big Joe" Gresch (defendant) is a former football star who played for the Gulf City Maurauders and is now known throughout the community for his philanthropy to youth organizations. He owns residential property at 85 Essendon Street in an upper middle-class neighborhood of Gulf City. On September 19, 1994 he leased property to newcomer Linda Wylie (plaintiff) who moved there with her twelve year-old son, Vincent.

"Bud" and Tammy Lynn Buzzell (not parties to this suit) own and live at the property next door at 83 Essendon Street. The Buzzells own a pit bull dog named "Cuddles," which, according to Ms. Wylie's complaint, "had attacked other dogs and cats in the neighborhood, damaged property and otherwise shown vicious propensities."

Before the Wylies moved in, Cuddles had broken through the fence partitioning the backyards of the two properties. Mr. Gresch repaired the damage by replacing the broken boards with new ones and nailing a small sheet of plywood over a hole. Thus, Mr. Wylie contends that Mr. Gresch had actual knowledge of the dog's "vicious propensities," but nevertheless failed to warn them.

On Saturday, November 10, at about three in the afternoon, Vincent was playing in the front yard of his house when Mr. Buzzell walked by with Cuddles on a leash. Mr. Buzzell asked Vincent if he wanted to play with Cuddles, and Vincent picked up a stick to play fetch. Moments later, Cuddles broke free of his leash and attacked Vincent, biting him on the left side of his head and completely severing his ear. Ms. Wylie, who saw the whole incident from a window, immediately called 911 and then ran to her son's aid. Vincent required eight hours of surgery, an attempt to re-attach the ear was unsuccessful, and he had to stay in the trauma unit for 10 days. Medical bills to date total $18,000. Vincent will soon undergo another surgery in an effort to "reconstruct" the ear as best as possible. The cost of this procedure is $32,000. Since the accident, Vincent has been the subject of jokes and ridicule by other children at school and in the neighborhood, and has been seeing a psychotherapist to help him cope with his handicap, at the cost of $5,200.

Ms. Wylie is very angry that this incident occurred and believes that "someone should pay" for what happened to her son. Accordingly, she has retained the legal services of Tom Ace, an enthusiastic young attorney who is making a name for himself in the legal community as a "go-getter" who wins big verdicts. The complaint includes all past and future medical expenses, and a laundry list of damages for mental anguish, pain and suffering, etc., totaling $500,000.

Mr. Gresch was shocked to learn of the incident, and has deep sympathy for the Wylies, since he works with children on a regular basis. However, he thinks that "everyone knows that pit bulldogs are dangerous," and that he did his duty by repairing the fence. He has retained the legal services of his friend Jane Drebin, a somewhat timid but experienced practitioner.

Mr. Buzzell has testified in deposition to the incident that Cuddles is a "good natured and loving dog." He has never worried about his children playing with the dog, but admits that Cuddles has "gotten into some playful fights with other dogs in the neighborhood" and that he damaged the fence. Mr. Buzzell states that on the date of the incident, Vincent was "swatting and taunting the dog with a stick, and Cuddles was merely defending himself."

A. Introduction

Mediation is facilitated negotiation. The facilitator is neutral. Such a concise statement, of course, oversimplifies, but it is a useful working definition for getting started. A more elaborate definition of mediation is provided in Christopher W. Moore, THE MEDIATION PROCESS: PRACTICAL STRATEGIES FOR RESOLVING DISPUTES 14 (1986).

> Mediation is the intervention into a dispute or negotiation by an acceptable, impartial, and neutral third party who has no authoritative decision-making power to assist disputing parties in voluntarily reaching their own mutually acceptable settlement of issues in dispute.

Professor Kimberlee K. Kovach, MEDIATION: PRINCIPLES AND PRACTICE 17 (1994) offers this descriptive statement about how mediation operates:

> Mediation is a process by which a third party neutral, whether one or more, acts as a facilitator to assist in the resolving of a dispute between two or more parties. It is a non-adversarial approach to conflict resolution where the parties communicate directly. The role of the mediator is to facilitate communication between the parties, assist them on focusing on the real issues of the dispute, and generate options for settlement. The goal of this process is that the parties themselves arrive at a mutually acceptable resolution of the dispute.

These general observations about the nature of mediation provide sufficient background for the reader to begin exploring the mediation process, at least as employed in end-of-the-millennium America.

This introduction is followed by some general reflections about mediation, beginning with a thoughtful study by Lon Fuller that evaluates the forms and functions of mediation. Bush & Folger analyze the modern mediation movement in terms of four "stories" that highlight different views of how the movement has developed and what it means. Dean James Alfini argues that there are three styles of mediation, which he characterizes as trashing, bashing, and hashing.

Section C provides an introduction to mediation as an operative process, as the level of analysis moves from the conceptual to the issues associated with actual mediations. In section D, several experienced mediators offer advice for conducting a successful mediation, and point out pitfalls to avoid. Section E examines the central difficulty that must be addressed in a mediation: impasse. Parties come to a mediation at impasse, not having succeeded in resolving their dispute. Even when a mediation proceeds well, there frequently comes a time when the parties think the dispute cannot be resolved. Dealing effectively with impasse is essential to successful mediations, and particularly to being a successful mediator.

The last section considers mediation as a therapeutic and empowering process. Many people believe there is more to mediation than just serving as an efficient method of dispatching disputes and helping courts with their caseload problems. Mediation permits people to settle their own seemingly intractable problems—to be sure, with the assistance of a third party. Achieving such a settlement often is empowering to the parties, and has therapeutic or healing value for them.

B. Reflections on Mediation in Modern America

1. Lon L. Fuller, *Mediation—Its Forms and Functions*, 44 S. Cal. L. Rev. 305 (1970)*

[Late in his career Professor Lon Fuller, a distinguished student of jurisprudence and contract law, turned his attention to the form and function of various approaches to dispute settlement. Fuller's article on arbitration appears at Chapter 12, section C.]

I have . . . thought it expedient to preface my analysis by putting mediation in the wider context of some assumptions of methodology that appear to shape our efforts to comprehend social phenomena generally.

In every branch of human study that has achieved or aspires to the name of science there seems to repeat itself a fundamental difference in the assumptions men make as to the nature of the thing they are examining. This schism in basic orientations extends over a wide range of subjects. Something of its pervasiveness becomes apparent when we recall the slogan-like terms conventionally employed in describing this opposition of viewpoints: structure versus process, substance versus procedure, statics versus dynamics and—on a more elevated plane—Being and Becoming. As these terms indicate, this recurring difference is not so much thought of as a quarrel about the most profitable posture of the mind as it is about the essential nature of the thing being studied. . . .

[O]ne is tempted to say [mediation] is all process and no structure. Casual treatments of the subject in the literature of sociology tend to assume that the object of mediation is to make the parties aware of the "social norms" applicable to their relationship and to persuade them to accommodate themselves to the "structure" imposed by these norms. From this point of view the difference between a judge and a mediator is simply that the judge orders the par-

---

ties to conform themselves to the rules, while the mediator persuades them to do so. But mediation is commonly directed, not toward achieving conformity to norms, but toward the creation of the relevant norms themselves. This is true, for example, in the very common case where the mediator assists the parties in working out the terms of a contract defining their rights and duties toward one another. In such a case there is no pre-existing structure that can guide mediation; it is the mediational process that produces the structure.

It may be suggested that mediation is always . . . directed toward bringing about a more harmonious relationship between the parties, whether this be achieved through explicit agreement, through a reciprocal acceptance of the "social norms" relevant to their relationship, or simply because the parties have been helped to a new and more perceptive understanding of one another's problems. The fact that in ordinary usage the terms "mediation" and "conciliation" are largely interchangeable tends to reinforce this view of the matter.

But at this point we encounter the inconvenient fact that mediation can be directed, not toward cementing a relationship, but toward terminating it. . . . Thus we find that mediation may be directed toward, and result in, discrepant and even diametrically opposed results. This circumstance argues against our being able to derive any general structure of the mediational process from some identifiable goal shared by all mediational efforts. We may, of course, indulge in observations to the effect that the mere presence of a third person tends to put the parties on their good behavior, that the mediator can direct their verbal exchanges away from recrimination and toward the issues that need to be faced, that by receiving separate and confidential communications from the parties he can gradually bring into the open issues so deep-cutting that the parties themselves had shared a tacit taboo against any discussion of them and that, finally, he can by his management of the interchange demonstrate to the parties that it is possible to discuss divisive issues without either rancor or evasion.

But can we go beyond generalities of this sort? I believe we can, but to accomplish this we shall have to begin by examining in detail the functions mediation can perform in a specific illustrative situation. If this illustrative case is aptly chosen we may then, with appropriate adjustments, extend our conclusions to other situations that vary in specific ways from the model adopted for detailed analysis. The model I propose here is that presented by mediational efforts serving to facilitate the negotiation of a collective bargaining agreement between an employer and a labor union. . . .

I begin, then, by supposing that an employer — say, a corporation engaged in manufacturing — and a labor union representing its production force are about to enter into negotiations concerning the terms of a collective bargaining agreement. I assume that these negotiations will range over a wide variety of issues, either because a collective bargaining agreement is being entered by the parties for the first time, or because an existing agreement has come open for renegotiation and the issues raised by the parties extend over a wide range of subjects, such as rates of pay, seniority provisions, grievance procedures and the timing and length of annual paid vacations.

Now among the characteristics of this relationship that are relevant to our purposes, the first lies in the obvious fact that the parties mediated are two in number, they constitute a dyad, not a triad or more numerous group. To be sure, during the mediational effort some differences of opinion within the union and, less commonly, within the company, may come to the surface, but basically the mediator's efforts are directed toward an ordering of the relations between the company and the union and he will generally be at pains to stay out of quarrels arising within either of the participating groups.

The *second* characteristic of concern here lies in the circumstance that normally neither of the parties, the employer or the union, has any real choice but to reach an agreement with the other. The two parties are locked in a relationship that is virtually one of "bilateral monopoly"; each is dependent for its very existence on some collaboration with the other. . . .

This "tied-in" relation, it should be noted, extends not only to the union as a collective entity, but in some measure to the individual union member as well. If, dissatisfied with what his union has achieved for him, he considers taking a job with another employer he is likely to be reminded that in his new position he will find himself at the bottom of the seniority ladder and vulnerable to lay-off at the first slackening of production. Furthermore, moving into a new employment may forfeit for him any nontransferable "fringe benefits" his union has obtained for him through collective bargaining, these benefits relating to such things as retirement pay, health benefits, paid vacations proportioned to length of service, and the like. We commonly find, then, between the unionized employer, on the one side, and the labor union and its members, on the other, a relationship that may be called one of heavy interdependence: they simply must find some way of getting along with one another.

The *third* characteristic of the relationship that is relevant here lies in the obvious fact that the negotiation of the collective bargaining agreement has elements of an economic trade. This is plainly true, of course, where rates of pay are being negotiated. But it is also true where "non-monetary" provisions of the contract come under discussion. For example, a manufacturer might be willing to accept a revision of the grievance procedure proposed by the union, in return for some expansion of the clause removing certain management decisions from arbitrational review. The question, "Will this help or hurt us?" is one the parties constantly put to themselves as they negotiate the contract—sometimes even when the issue is simply where a comma ought to be inserted. Into every aspect of the negotiations, then, there is likely to enter some calculation of relative "payoff."

The *fourth* characteristic of our illustrative situation stands in some contrast to that just described. The enterprise in which the parties are engaged is not simply one in which each seeks to attain the contractual language that will most favor his immediate interests. The parties are also caught up in the task of drafting a constitution, of putting on paper words by which they can in the future live together successfully. A perception of this aspect of their joint endeavor must temper and often redirect their efforts toward the achievement of their separate goals. A clause with hidden ambiguities that invite endless disputes will carry a heavy price tag for both parties, even though the party securing its adoption may at the time have congratulated himself on having served well his own advantage.

The fact that the actual negotiation of the collective bargaining agreement is conducted, not by principals, but by agents or representatives constitutes a *fifth* characteristic of the situation we are discussing. The employer is an abstract entity called a corporation; those who represent that entity act in a representative capacity and they are by no means commonly the chief executives of the corporation itself. Likewise, of course, the entire membership of the union does not and cannot participate directly in the negotiations; these are commonly conducted on their behalf by an out-of-town expert from the national union headquarters, assisted by a local committee.

The *sixth* and final characteristic of the relationship we are examining lies in the fact that one of the parties, the company, occupies toward the membership of the union a dual role. In the negotiation of the collective bargaining agreement the parties meet each other as equals, with neither having any recognized authority over the other; in the day-to-day management of the plant, however, the company is boss. Its foremen and superintendents, not the labor union, direct the manufacturing process. Indeed, experienced labor leaders exercise a canny reserve about invading this prerogative, for the responsibilities that go with it could be quite inconvenient for them and any sharing of those responsibilities would tend seriously to compromise their role as representatives of the union membership.

These, then, are six characteristics of the collective bargaining situation that have suggested to me it might be useful as a model in analysing the functions of mediation generally. By way of a recapitulation: the parties concerned (1) being two in number, find themselves (2) in a relationship of heavy interdependence exerting a strong pressure to reach an agreement, an agreement that will (3) combine elements of an economic trade with (4) elements of a written charter or constitution for the governance of their future relations; this agreement is (5) negotiated by agents, not principals, and (6) the employer occupies throughout a dual role, being, on the one hand, director of the enterprise and, on the other, a coequal with the union in the negotiation and administration of the collective bargaining agreement.

In what immediately follows I shall attempt an analysis of the ways in which these six characteristics affect the need for, and the functions performed by, a mediator. Following that analysis, I shall attempt to draw some analogies between the situation I have taken as my illustrative model and the uses of mediation in quite different social contexts. . . .

The first question is, then, how the need for a mediator, and the role performed by him, are affected by the fact that the parties whose relations constitute the subject of mediation are two in number. Here Simmel's famous discussion of the dyad and the triad becomes relevant.

Simmel observes that among groups ranked in terms of the number of their members, the group of two, the dyad, is peculiarly handicapped in resolving problems of internal order. Even the triad confronting internal difficulties can be governed openly or tacitly by the majority principle; this is an expedient from which, of course, the dyad is excluded. Then, too, one member of a triad can often undertake to mediate between the other two, having perhaps preserved a posture of detachment precisely in order to assume this role; A seeing trouble brewing between B and C may initially have been inclined to favor B but decided to remain neutral in order to qualify for the role of mediator. This is obviously another resource denied to the dyad.

The dyadic relationship is, then, one eminently suited to mediation and often dependent on it as the only measure capable of solving its internal problems. Indeed, one may ask whether mediation, in the strict sense, is really possible in ordering the internal affairs of any group larger than two. If A, B and C are all at odds with one another, it is extremely difficult for an outsider, say, X, to undertake a mediative role without becoming a participant in the internal maneuvers of the quarreling members. If X asks A's acquiescence in a proposed solution, A may reply that he will give his assent if X will undertake to persuade B to withdraw a concession B made in favor of C. X may thus end by becoming the manipulated tool of those he sought to guide. In this predicament he may face the alternative of retaining the empty title of mediator or becoming, in effect, a fourth member of the group and a participant in its internal games. If he chooses the latter alternative, his accession to membership may not increase, but rather tend to diminish the chance for achieving a functioning order since it introduces for the first time the possibility of a deadlock of two against two, in other words, it impairs an advantage the triad enjoys over the dyad, the capacity to resolve internal difficulties by something like a majority vote.

There is perhaps one situation in which an outsider may, with skill and good luck, serve usefully as a mediator among three. This would be where three different measures are proposed as the solution for some problem faced by the triad. A favors Solution X, B favors Solution Y, while C favors Solution Z. Here the mediator might discuss with each of the parties the grounds upon which, and the degree of conviction with which, he supports his preference for one solution as against the other two. There are thus opened up, in somewhat embarrassing abundance, six separate entries for the mediator's intervention. Exploring these conscientiously he might discover that A's preference for X over Y was based on a mistake of fact; with this mistake corrected A might then be ready to join with B in supporting Y. Or, the mediator might discover that B's preference for Y over Z was very slight and that he was almost indifferent between the two. The mediator might then persuade B to join with C in supporting Z, thus restoring the triad as a functioning entity. These happy outcomes are certainly possible, but it is obvious that the relationships involved are so complex, and the opportunities for misunderstanding so great, that the mediator may find it extremely difficult to maintain the integrity of his role. . . . Certainly if the mediational process can be said to have a home ground, it is to be found in the dyad.

In my analysis of the characteristics of the collective bargaining situation I noted that it involved not only a dyad, but a dyad the members of which stood toward one another in a relation of "heavy interdependence." Perhaps this observation served only to emphasize a characteristic that must be present before a resolution of the internal problems of the dyad becomes a matter of sufficient concern to justify mediative efforts. It is fairly obvious that mediation has scarcely any role to play in human relationships fluidly organized on what may be broadly described as the market principle. If X finds A, B and C all competing to supply his needs through rival contractual arrangements, he may need the services of an expert adviser, but he will scarcely have occasion to call on those of a mediator. Likewise, in a society where transient and freely terminable sexual alliances took the place of marriage it is hardly likely that there would develop any institutional practice comparable to "marriage therapy." Mediation by its very nature presupposes relationships normally affected by some strong internal pull toward cohesion; this is true whether the mediative efforts in question be directed toward the formation, modification or dissolution of such relationships.

Those whose minds are intent on the "structure of authority," rather than on an analysis of social processes, are apt to ask of the mediator not, "What does he do?" but, "Whence comes his capacity or authority to arrange the affairs of others?" In this mood the inquiry is likely to be whether his power rests on a tacit contract with the affected parties, or derives from some charismatic qualities possessed by the mediator himself, or should be attributed to some role or office assigned to him by tradition or higher authority. Now an inquiry along these lines is certainly not meaningless, but taking it too seriously may lead us to ignore the fact that the mediator's "power" may largely derive from the simple fact that he is there and that his help is badly needed. . . . When there is no apparent focal point for agreement the mediator can create one by his power to make a dramatic suggestion. The bystander who jumps into an intersection and begins to direct traffic at an impromptu traffic jam is conceded the power to discriminate among cars by being able to offer a sufficient increase in efficiency to benefit even the cars most discriminated against; his directions have only the power of suggestion, but coordination requires the common acceptance of some source of suggestion. Similarly, the participants of a square dance may all be thoroughly dissatisfied with the particular dances being called, but as long as the caller has the microphone, nobody can dance anything else. The white line down the center of the road is a mediator, and very likely it can err substantially toward one side or the other before the disadvantaged side finds advantage in denying its authority.

A serious study of mediation can serve, I suggest, to offset the tendency of modern thought to assume that all social order must be imposed by some kind of "authority." When we perceive how a mediator, claiming no "authority," can help the parties give order and coherence to their relationship, we may in the process come to realize that there are circumstances in which the parties can dispense with this aid, and that social order can often arise directly out of the interactions it seems to govern and direct.

The third characteristic I found present in the collective bargaining situation lies in the fact that in reaching agreement each party is constantly calculating the relative advantage or disadvantage to him of any particular proposal. There is, in other words, a pervasive evaluation of "payoffs"; this evaluation extends even to provisions of the contract that seem unrelated in any direct way to monetary costs. In terms of the mediator's function, this means that the mediator participates in a bargaining situation where each party seeks to get as much for himself as he can at as small a cost as possible, the "cost" involved being, of course, that entailed in some concession to the opposing party. . . .

But if it is relatively easy to see that an apt exchange can yield advantages to both parties, it is much more difficult to discern the actual processes of discussion and negotiation that will maximize these gains of reciprocity. Suppose, for example, that one party reveals, intentionally or inadvertently, that he is desperately eager to secure some particular concession from his opposing number. It happens that granting this concession would visit very little disadvantage on the party from whom it is demanded. Does he at once reveal this fact, or does he hold back his concession as a resource on which to draw when he wants something badly that the other party is reluctant to give? Which course of action will, in fact, serve ultimately to maximize the gains of reciprocity for both parties? In judging this last question it should be recalled that gratuitous concessions falling outside the frame of normal bargaining are apt to arouse suspicions as to their motivation and may be interpreted as requiring the benefited party to volunteer some counter-concessions, which may itself be unguided by any accurate understanding of its value to the other party—the "exchange" of Christmas presents is notoriously a poor example of maximizing utilities.

An obvious, but mistaken expedient would be to have both parties at once disclose to each other their internal evaluations of all the items under discussion. [T]here are many difficulties with this. . . . the values may be extremely intangible; there is no yardstick that can convert them into numbers. Furthermore, the items on a negotiating agenda may be interrelated in various complex ways. For example, suppose that one party, A, asks for concessions X, Y, and Z. Now it might be that if Y and Z were granted, X would become wholly unnecessary. On the other hand, if the other party were willing to concede both X and Y this concession might yield a return much higher than the value of X alone, say, roughly its double, although Y taken by itself would produce only a small fraction of the value that a grant of X by itself would yield, etc., etc.

Where the bargaining process proceeds without the aid of a mediator the usual course pursued by experienced negotiators is something like this: the parties begin by simply talking about the various proposals, explaining in general terms why they want this and why they are opposed to that. During this exploratory or "sounding out" process, which proceeds without any clear-cut offers of settlement, each party conveys — sometimes explicitly, sometimes tacitly, sometimes intentionally, sometimes inadvertently — something about his relative evaluations of the various items under discussion. After these discussions have proceeded for some time, one party is likely to offer a "package deal," proposing in general terms a contract that will settle all the issues under discussion. This offer may be accepted by the other party or he may accept it subject to certain stipulated changes.

Now it is obvious that the process just described can often be greatly facilitated through the services of a skillful mediator. His assistance can speed the negotiations, reduce the likelihood of miscalculation, and generally help the parties to reach a sounder agreement, an adjustment of their divergent valuations that will produce something like an optimum yield of the gains of reciprocity. These things the mediator can accomplish by holding separate confidential meetings with the parties, where each party gives the mediator a relatively full and candid account of the internal posture of his own interests. Armed with this information, but without making a premature disclosure of its details, the mediator can then help to shape the negotiations in such a way that they will proceed most directly to their goal, with a minimum of waste and friction.

The fourth characteristic of the collective bargaining situation to be examined here lies in what I have called its "constitution-drafting" aspect — It should be kept in mind that the collective bargaining agreement serves, in effect, as the charter of a miniature government; it assigns functions, establishes procedures for the presentation of claims, and, in its provisions relating to arbitration, institutes what amounts to a private judiciary. Drafting such a document is a demanding exercise, not only in the accurate and unambiguous use of language, but in the apt design of institutional arrangements.

When I first mentioned this aspect of the collective bargaining situation I remarked that it stood in some contrast to what we have just examined at length. When the parties have reached the point where they are ready to express their future relationship in written words, their efforts will generally be directed toward an achievement of shared objectives, rather than toward a workable compromise of divergent aims. However, it is obvious that some elements of trade-off are likely to reappear when the parties undertake to reduce to numbered paragraphs an oral agreement previously reached "in principle." . . .

[N]uance of thought and a clause overloaded with qualifications may forfeit its meaning as a clear guidepost for human interaction. In the drafting of any complex agreement there is often an inescapable compromise between what can be simply expressed and what might be abstractly desirable. The mediational process plainly has a place in dealing with such problems.

There is another service that a mediator can render when the parties' efforts toward a formal agreement have reached the drafting stage. The mediator can bring to problems of drafting a third-party perspective; in George Herbert Mead's famous phrase he can serve as "the generalized other." This is important because the generalized other may in fact shortly appear on the scene in the person of Mr. X; six months after the contract is signed Mr. X may become personnel manager of the company in succession to the man who actually negotiated the contract on behalf of the employer and who was familiar with all the considerations that entered into its phrasing. The negotiators must keep in mind, not only what the words mean to them, but what they may mean to one who was not a participant in their deliberations and tacit adjustments. The mediator can help to supply that perspective.

We reach now the fifth aspect of the collective bargaining situation having some significance for the role of the mediator and the contribution he can make to a successful contract. This aspect lies in the circumstance that the contract is negotiated, not by principals, but by representatives or agents. My first observation here relates to limitations, real or pretended, on the agent's authority. Let us suppose that the representative of one of the parties opens the first bargaining session by stating that he has been instructed by his principal that he may not, under any circumstances, make certain specified concessions. The excluded concessions will naturally relate to matters that might reasonably be expected to fall within the scope of the negotiations; the agent is hardly likely to warn the opposite party that his principal will sign no contract requiring him to commit a capital offense. In the collective bargaining situation the limitation on the agent's authority might, in the case of the employer, exclude a provision granting any version of the closed shop, or, in the case of the union, anything like a "management prerogative" clause.

Obviously the mediator will usually serve the cause of effective bargaining by freeing the negotiations from shackles imposed before any discussion of issues has begun and in abstraction from what the negotiations may later reveal about the actual posture of the two parties' interests. If the limitations on the agent's authority are feigned, the mediator can more readily and gracefully penetrate the pretense than can the opposing party. If the limitations have in fact been imposed by the principal, the mediator may induce the agent to ask for their removal and assist him in bringing about that result. None of this means, of course, that in the contract finally signed the principal will inevitably concede things he hoped to prevent from becoming subjects of bargaining; it simply means that the issues sought to be excluded will, in fact, enter into the discussions and be considered as possible ingredients in the final settlement, where, if included, they may of course undergo some modification.

The exploitation of feigned incapacities for the purpose of securing a bargaining advantage has been analysed at some length in "game theory." Long before the device was subjected to any such sophisticated treatment it was familiar to lawyers and businessmen as the technique of "the wicked partner." A and B are discussing the terms of a contract. B demands some concession of A. A replies, "I wish very much I could let you have this. But my partner, who is in Europe and unfortunately cannot be reached, is dead set against it." In analysing the implications of this bargaining stratagem, it is important to realize that it becomes a serious problem only in situations I have described as those of "heavy interdependence," where the needs of the parties and the intertwining of their interests creates a strong pressure toward some sort of accommodation between them. It should also be noted that even in such situations it is a device that may miscarry and disserve the interest of the party who attempted to exploit it. When A refuses in advance even to consider making a particular concession he will realize that he might receive something in return for this concession, but he thinks he has grounds for believing that this counterconcession could not possibly compensate him for what he gave to secure it. This judgment may be misinformed for it has been reached before the internal structure of the other party's interests has been exposed through an open-ended exploration of the different ways in which the parties' diverse interests can be fitted together. But even if the party exploiting the wicked-partner technique is correct in his assumption that he will gain by forestalling in advance any granting of the concession, the bargaining process itself is distorted and it becomes impossible to secure the general and uninhibited exploration of diverse interests essential to a realization of the maximum gains of reciprocity. The scars left by this distortion may affect adversely the future relations between the parties.

All of this means that where the agent pleads in advance a lack of power to grant certain concessions and where the granting of these concessions would normally form an appropriate subject for bargaining between the parties, the mediator, by securing the removal of such restrictions, may make a substantial contribution, not only to the interests of the immediate parties, but to the integrity of the bargaining process considered as an essential in a functioning society.

So much for limitations, real or pretended, on the agent's power. There is a second and quite different implication for the mediator's role deriving from the fact that the parties to the negotiations are represented by agents. This lies in the observation that if there is no mediator the parties' agents may be forced, in effect, to join together in assuming the mediational role.

The negotiation of a collective bargaining agreement is commonly opened by a general session attended by delegations of persons representing both sides. On behalf of the union there may appear an attorney, a field representative from national headquarters and a committee of the local. Management may be represented by an attorney, the personnel manager, the treasurer and perhaps several other officers concerned with labor relations. Plainly, this wide and miscellaneous audience constitutes a very poor human milieu in which to conduct the delicate sounding-out procedures by which the two parties' interests are revealed and gradually fitted together into some workable pattern. Spokesmen for both sides may be deterred, for example, from making anything like definite proposals by the fear of audible or visible dissents coming from their associates in the audience. The result is that the general opening session normally serves only a ceremonial and ritualistic purpose.

What is the next step? If a mediator is available, this is not difficult. Each of the two groups will, in turn, meet alternately with the mediator out of the presence of the other. At these repeated meetings each side will make, perhaps with some initial hesitancy but by degrees more openly, a relatively candid disclosure of the posture of its interests and preferences. Any differences within the ranks that may come to the surface during these meetings need not be damaging; on the contrary, some insight into these differences may furnish the mediator useful guidance as he works his way toward an accommodation of the parties' interests that will furnish a workable charter for their future relations.

What happens in the absence of a mediator? As I have previously expressed it, what not uncommonly occurs is that the two opposing agents join to take over the mediational function. This means that they meet together privately, explore possible ways of bringing to some workable accommodation the diverse interests of their principals, interrupt their discussions to secure advice from their colleagues, return to their joint sessions, and finally agree on the outlines of a settlement which they will propose for acceptance by their respective principals.

Obviously this procedure requires a degree of trust and mutual respect between the two negotiating agents. A good agent does not antagonize his opposite number, but is at pains to keep on good terms with him. When a lawyer representing industry has occasion over time to deal repeatedly and in different contexts with the same labor representative, a certain camaraderie will normally and quite usefully develop between them. This intimacy may, however, easily drift into a tacit reciprocity in the granting of favors that may in time become detached from the interests of the particular clients being represented. Thus, if a lawyer representing industry was forced by the intransigence of his client to deal rather harshly with his opposite number in Centerville, the question may arise, should he make up for this when the two representatives next meet in Zenith, where the employer is quite generous toward labor and ready to grant any reasonable concession recommended by his lawyer? I once heard an employer express himself in terms that left no doubt as to how he thought the lawyer would answer that question. He said, "You lawyers that represent industry and the labor people are like professional wrestlers. You travel around together and when you're in one town you agree on who'll take the fall in the next."

This was a harsh judgment, but it points to a real problem, a problem that the services of a mediator may do much to alleviate. The mediator can, by his explicit assumption of the mediational role, help those purporting to act as representatives remain what they offer themselves as being.

It should be noted that the problem here suggested is not a new one; it is by no means a sordid by-product of our complex modern industrial age. It was some one hundred and eighty years ago that Edmund Burke wrote the following lines:

> The world is governed by go-betweens. These go-betweens influence the persons with whom they carry on the intercourse, by stating their own sense to each of them as the sense of the other; and thus they reciprocally master both sides.

Burke's remarks contain important implications for the ethos of the mediator's office as well as for that of the agent; indeed, Burke seems to have in mind primarily the man who openly assumes the role of "go-between." Is it in fact a common practice of mediators, in communicating the positions of the parties back and forth, to state "their own sense to each of them as the sense of the other?" Certainly when he receives from one party a statement of his position, the mediator, before conveying it to the other party, will normally strip it of vituperation and recrimination; his duty is to convey the substance of what was said, not its tone or the facial expression that accompanied it. But it is not always easy to effect this separation, especially since the depth with which a party feels about an issue is something that enters into the valuations that shape the final adjustment of diverse interests. At the same time an agreement obtained through an outright misrepresentation of the parties' own reasons for their proposals will certainly furnish an insecure basis for future relations, if indeed it does not lead to an immediate collapse of the agreement as soon as the false ground on which it was accepted becomes evident.

Like everyone else concerned with the mediational process, the mediator needs to reflect on his proper role and on the sources of his power. . . .

The sixth and final aspect of the collective bargaining situation requires only brief mention. This aspect lies in the fact that the employer occupies toward the union a dual role, being, on the one hand, director of an economic enterprise employing the union membership and, on the other, confronting the union as a coequal in negotiating and administering the collective bargaining agreement. . . .

Elaborate as the analysis just concluded has been, it has dealt only inferentially and indirectly with what may be said to be the central quality of mediation, namely, its capacity to reorient the parties toward each other, not by imposing rules on them, but by helping them to achieve a new and shared perception of their relationship, a perception that will redirect their attitudes and dispositions toward one another.

This quality of mediation becomes most visible when the proper function of the mediator turns out to be, not that of inducing the parties to accept formal rules for the governance of their future relations, but that of helping them to free themselves from the encumbrance of rules and of accepting, instead, a relationship of mutual respect, trust and understanding that will enable them to meet shared contingencies without the aid of formal prescriptions laid down in advance. Such a mediational effort might well come into play in any of the various forms of mediation between husband and wife associated with "family counseling" and "marriage therapy." In the task of reestablishing the marriage as a going concern the mediator might find it essential to break up formalized conceptions of "duty" and to substitute a more fluid sense of mutual trust and shared responsibility. In effect, instead of working toward achieving a rule-oriented relationship he might devote his efforts, to some degree at least, in exactly the opposite direction.

Because it does not bring this aspect of mediation into relief the illustrative model to which I have just devoted so many pages may seem inaptly chosen. The negotiation of an elaborate written contract, such as that embodied in a collective bargaining agreement between an employer and a labor union, does indeed present a special set of problems for the mediator. But in defense of the choice of this model, it may be observed that complexity and formality of the processes involved may enable us to discern distinctive aspects of the mediator's task which, though present in more informal contexts, would have been blurred and resistant to separate analysis.

Furthermore, it should be remembered that the primary function of the mediator in the collective bargaining situation is not to propose rules to the parties and to secure their acceptance of them, but to induce the mutual trust and understanding that will enable the parties to work out their own rules. The creation of rules is a process that cannot itself be rule-bound; it must be guided by a sense of shared responsibility and a realization that the adversary aspects of the operation are part of a larger collaborative undertaking. The primary task of the [mediator] is to induce this attitude of mind and spirit, though to be sure, he does this primarily by helping the parties to perceive the concrete ways in which this shared attitude can redound to their mutual benefit.

It should also be noted that the benefits of a collective bargaining agreement do not lie simply in the aptness of the numbered paragraphs that appear over the parties' signatures, but derive also from the mutual understanding produced by the process of negotiation itself. . . .

I have suggested that in one aspect the collective bargaining agreement is like a constitution; it must serve as a charter of government, if not for "generations as yet unborn," at least for a period that will in all likelihood extend beyond changes in the personnel administering the agreement. Since those who may have to administer the contract will not have had a chance to participate in the unverbalized understandings and expectations that went into its construction, I suggested that the mediator might usefully bring the perspective of "the generalized other" to the task of drafting the instrument. In this connection it should be observed that it may, paradoxically, sometimes be fortunate if disputes arise promptly under the new contract so that they may be resolved by those who participated in the negotiation of it and shared the perceptions that went into, and at the same time came out of, that process. . . .

One might have been inclined to assume that as, in the course of history, the various forms of social ordering and dispute-settlement became separated in practice, they would become the subject of an earnest discussion among scholars as to their distinctive functions and their most appropriate applications. Instead of this, however, we find the substitution of one simplifying obfuscation for another. Now the tendency is to convert every form of social ordering into an exercise in the authority of the state or, among sociologists, into a projection of "norms" by an abstract entity called "society." Legislation, adjudication, and administrative direction, instead of being perceived as distinctive interactional processes, all are seen as unidirectional exercises of state power. Contract is perceived, not as a source of "law" or social ordering in itself, but as something that derives its whole significance from the fact that the courts of the state stand ready to enforce it. Custom is passed over in virtually complete silence by sociologists and is viewed by legal scholar as becoming worthy of attention only when it has been recognized by the courts and thus been convered into "law." Only mediation seems to resist this tendency to subsume every kind of ordering under the rubric of "power" or "authority." Perhaps the attempt made in this essay . . . to analyse the form and functions of mediation may help in some small measure to stimulate a more general interest in the analysis and comparison of the competing forms of social ordering.

2. Robert A. Baruch Bush & Joseph P. Folger, The Promise of Mediation: Responding to Conflict Through Empowerment and Recognition 15-27 (1994)*

The Mediation Movement: Four Diverging Views

While the growth of mediation in the past two decades is remarkable, what is even more striking is the extraordinary divergence of opinion about how to understand that growth and how to characterize the mediation movement itself. This divergence is so marked that there is no one accepted account of how the mediation movement evolved or what it represents. Instead, the literature of the field reveals several very different accounts or "stories" of the movement, told by different authors and stressing different dimensions of the mediation process and its societal impacts. Thus, the movement is portrayed by some as a tool to reduce court congestion and provide "higher-quality" justice in individual cases, by others as a vehicle for organizing people and communities to obtain fairer treatment, and by still others as a covert means of social control and oppression. And some, including ourselves, picture the movement as a way to foster a qualitative transformation of human interaction. Indeed, these are the four main accounts of the mediation movement that run through the literature on mediation. We call them, respectively, the Satisfaction Story of the movement, the Social Justice Story, the Oppression Story, and the Transformation Story.

The fact that there are four distinct and divergent stories of the movement suggests two important points. On one level, it suggests that the mediation movement is not monolithic but pluralistic—that there are in fact different approaches to mediation practice, with varied impacts. The stories represent these different approaches. On a deeper level, the existence of divergent stories suggests that, while everyone sees the mediation movement as a means for achieving important societal goals, people differ over what goal is most important. The stories thus also represent and support different goals, each of which is seen by some people as the most important one for the movement to fulfill.

Recounting the different stories of the movement is therefore a good way both to illustrate the diversity of mediation practice and also to identify the value choices implicit in varying approaches to practice. The following summary of the four stories presents each one as it might be told by its authors and adherents.

The Satisfaction Story

According to this story: "The mediation process is a powerful tool for satisfying the genuine human needs of parties to individual disputes. Because of its flexibility, informality, and consensuality, mediation can open up the full dimensions of the problem facing the parties. Not limited by legal categories or rules, it can help reframe a contentious dispute as a mutual problem. Also, because of mediators' skills in dealing with power imbalances, mediation can reduce strategic maneuvering and overreaching. As a result of these different features, mediation can facilitate collaborative, integrative problem solving rather than adversarial, distributive bargaining. It can thereby produce creative, 'win-win' outcomes that reach beyond formal rights to solve problems and satisfy parties' genuine needs in a particular situation. The mediation movement has employed these capabilities of the process to produce superior quality solutions to disputes of all kinds, in terms of satisfaction of parties' self-defined needs, for *all* sides.

"Furthermore, in comparison to more formal or adversary processes, mediation's informality and mutuality can reduce both the economic and emotional costs of dispute settlement. The use of mediation has thus produced great private savings for disputants, in economic and psychic terms. Also, by providing mediation in many cases that would otherwise have gone to court, the mediation movement has also saved public expense.It has freed up the courts for other disputants who need them, easing the problem of delaying access to justice. In sum, the movement has led to more efficient use of limited private and public dispute resolution resources, which in turn means greater overall satisfaction for individual "consumers" of the justice system.

"This holds true for all the various contexts in which mediation has been used. Child custody mediation, for example, has produced better-quality results for both children and parents than litigated rulings. Small-claims mediation has resulted in higher party satisfaction with both process and outcome, and higher rates of compliance than litigation. Environmental and public policy mediation have produced creative and highly praised resolutions, while avoiding the years of delay and enormous expense that court action would have entailed. Moreover, mediation in these areas has reduced court caseloads and backlogs, facilitating speedier disposition of those cases that cannot he resolved without trial in court. In these and other kinds of disputes, mediation has produced more satisfaction for disputing parties than could have been provided otherwise."

The next two interpretations of the mediation movement, the Social Justice Story and the Transformation Story, differ somewhat from the Satisfaction Story. The Satisfaction Story claims to depict what has generally occurred in the use of mediation thus far, while the other two describe something that has admittedly occurred only in part thus far. In effect, these are "minor" stories of the movement, but each is still seen by its adherents as representing the movement's most important potential.

The Social Justice Story

According to this story: "Mediation offers an effective means of organizing individuals around common interests and thereby building stronger community ties and structures. This is important because unaffiliated individuals are especially subject to exploitation in this society and because more effective community organization can limit such exploitation and create more social justice. Mediation can support community organization in several ways. Because of its capacity for reframing issues and focusing on common interests, mediation can help individuals who think they are adversaries perceive a larger context in which they face a common enemy. As a result, mediation can strengthen the weak by helping establish alliances among them.

"In addition, by its capacity to help parties solve problems for themselves, mediation reduces dependency on distant agencies and encourages self-help, including the formation of effective 'grass-roots' community structures. Finally, mediation treats legal rules as only one of a variety of bases by which to frame issues and evaluate possible solutions to disputes. Therefore, mediation can give groups more leverage to argue for their interests than they might have in formal legal processes. The mediation movement has used these capacities of the process, to some extent at least, to facilitate the organization of relatively powerless individuals into communities of interest. As a result, those common interests have been pursued more successfully, helping ensure greater social justice, and the individuals involved have gained a new sense of participation in civic life.

"This picture applies to many, if not all, of the contexts in which mediation is used. Interpersonal neighborhood mediation has encouraged co-tenants or block residents, for example, to realize their common adversaries, such as landlords and city agencies, and to take joint action to pursue their common interests. Environmental mediation has facilitated the assertion of novel (and not strictly legal) claims by groups that have succeeded in redressing imbalances of power favoring land developers. Even mediation of consumer disputes has helped strengthen consumers' confidence in their ability to get complaints addressed, which has led to other forms of consumer self-help and increased consumer power. In short, mediation has helped organize individuals and strengthen communities of interest in many different contexts—and could be used more widely for this purpose."

The Social Justice Story of the mediation movement has been told for a long time, though by a relatively small number of authors, usually people with ties to the tradition of grass-roots community organizing. While the numbers of its adherents are few, this story has been told consistently from the earliest stages of the movement.

The third story, the Transformation Story, focuses on some of the same features of the mediation process as the first two. However, it characterizes them, and especially their consequences, in distinct and quite different terms than the other stories.

The Transformation Story

According to this story: "The unique promise of mediation lies in its capacity to transform the character of both individual disputants and society as a whole. Because of its informality and consensuality, mediation can allow parties to define problems and goals in their own terms, thus validating the importance of those problems and goals in the parties' lives. Further, mediation can support the parties' exercise of self-determination in deciding how, or even whether, to settle a dispute, and it can help the parties mobilize their own resources to address problems and achieve their goals. The mediation movement has (at least to some extent) employed these capabilities of the process to help disputing parties strengthen their own capacity to handle adverse circumstances of all kinds, not only in the immediate case but in future situations. Participants in mediation have gained a greater sense of self-respect, self-reliance, and self-confidence. This has been called the empowerment dimension of the mediation process.

"In addition, the private, nonjudgmental character of mediation can provide disputants a nonthreatening opportunity to explain and humanize themselves to one another. In this setting, and with mediators who are skilled at enhancing interpersonal communication, parties often discover that they can feel and express some degree of understanding and concern for one another despite their disagreement. The movement has (again, to some extent) used this dimension of the process to help individuals strengthen their inherent capacity for relating with concern to the problems of others. Mediation has thus engendered, even between parties who start out as fierce adversaries, acknowledgment and concern for each other as fellow human beings. This has been called the recognition dimension of the mediation.

"While empowerment and recognition have been given only partial attention in the mediation movement thus far, a consistent and wider emphasis on these dimensions would contribute powerfully—incrementally and over time—to the transformation of individuals from fearful, defensive, and self-centered beings into confident, empathetic, and considerate beings, and to the transformation of society from a shaky truce between enemies into a strong network of allies.

"This picture captures the potential of all branches of the mediation movement, not just certain areas in which human relationships are considered important (implying that elsewhere they are not). Consumer mediation can strengthen and evoke mutual recognition between merchants and consumers, transforming both the individuals involved and the character of commercial transactions and institutions. Divorce mediation can strengthen and evoke recognition between men and women (even if as childless ex-spouses they will have no further contact), changing both the people involved and the character of male-female interaction generally. Personal injury mediation can strengthen and evoke recognition between individuals who work for loss-coverage institutions and individual accident victims, transforming both the persons involved and the character of compensation processes and institutions in our society. In every area, mediation could, with sufficient energy and commitment, help transform both individuals and society."

The Transformation Story of the mediation movement is not widely told in the published literature of the field. Nevertheless, beyond the world of the printed word, this story is given voice in informal discussions among both academics and mediation practitioners. It is, as it were, the underground story of the movement, often the motivating force behind practitioners' involvement. Perhaps it goes unstated because it is not easy to articulate, or perhaps people are hesitant to articulate (or enact) it for fear of seeming too idealistic and impractical. Yet whenever the story is told, it generates a remarkably enthusiastic response, which suggests that it has much more currency than its published expressions would indicate.

Here, then, are three very different accounts of the mediation movement. Each of them expresses two different kinds of messages about the movement. On one level, each story is a description, purporting to recount what the mediation movement has actually done and what its actual character is today (in whole or in part). On another level, each story is a prescription, suggesting what the movement should do to fulfill what the story's authors see as the most important societal goal or value that mediation can help achieve.

The final story of the movement differs from all the others. The first three all see positive effects or potentials in the movement, although each sees them differently. The fourth, by contrast, sees only negative effects or potentials. It presents not a prescription for the movement but a warning against it. We call it the Oppression Story.

The Oppression Story

According to this story: "Even if the movement began with the best of intentions, mediation has turned out to be a dangerous instrument for increasing the power of the strong to take advantage of the weak. Because of the informality and consensuality of the process, and hence the absence of both procedural and substantive rules, mediation can magnify power imbalances and open the door to coercion and manipulation by the stronger party. Meanwhile, the posture of 'neutrality' excuses the mediator from preventing this. Therefore, in comparison to formal legal processes, mediation has often produced outcomes that are unjust, that is, disproportionately and unjustifiably favorable to stronger parties. Moreover, because of its privacy and informality, mediation gives mediators broad strategic power to control the discussion, giving free rein to mediators' biases. These biases can affect the framing and selection of issues, consideration and ranking of settlement options, and many other elements that influence outcomes. Again, as a result, mediation has often produced unjust outcomes.

"Finally, since mediation handles disputes without reference to other, similar cases and without reference to the public interest, it results in the 'dis-aggregation' and privatization of class and public interest problems. That is, the mediation movement has helped the strong to 'divide and conquer.' Weaker parties are unable to make common cause and the public interest is ignored and undermined. In sum, the overall effect of the movement has been to neutralize social justice gains achieved by the civil rights, women's, and consumer's movements, among others, and to help reestablish the privileged position of the stronger classes and perpetuate their oppression of the weaker.

"This oppressive picture is found in all the movement's manifestations. Divorce mediation removes safeguards and exposes women to coercive and manipulative 'bargaining' that results in unjust property and custody agreements. Landlord-tenant mediation allows landlords to escape their obligations to provide minimally decent housing, which results in substandard living conditions and unjust removals for tenants. Employment discrimination mediation manipulates victims into accepting buy-offs and permits structural racism and sexism to continue unabated in businesses and institutions. Even in commercial disputes between businesses, mediation allows the parties to strike deals behind closed doors that disadvantage consumers and others in ways that will never even come to light. In every area, the mediation movement has been used to consolidate the power of the strong and increase the exploitation and oppression of the weak."

The Oppression Story is clearly a different kind of story than the other three. Rather than offering a description of and prescription for the mediation movement, it sounds a warning against it. This story is almost as widely told as the Satisfaction Story, but by very different authors. In general, many—although not all—writers and thinkers concerned with equality tend to interpret the mediation movement through the Oppression Story and to see it as a serious threat to disadvantaged groups.

3. James J. Alfini, *Trashing, Bashing, and Hashing It Out: Is this the End of "Good Mediation"?*, 19 Fla. St. U. L. Rev. 47, 66-73 (1991)*

C. Mediator Styles and Strategies

[Most of Professor Alfini's article is devoted to court-annexed mediation in Florida, particularly in the circuit courts, but his alliterative typology of mediation styles has general applicability.] Our interviews with the circuit mediators and lawyers revealed three distinct styles. These three approaches to the mediation process are characterized as (1) trashing, (2) bashing, and (3) hashing it out.

1. Trashing

The mediators who employ a trashing methodology spend much of the time "tearing apart" the cases of the parties. Indeed, one of these mediators suggested the "trasher" characterization: "I trash their cases. By tearing apart and then building their cases back up, I try to get them to a point where they will put realistic settlement figures on the table."

To facilitate uninhibited trashing of the parties' cases, the overall strategy employed by these mediators discourages direct party communication. Following the mediator's orientation and short (five to ten minutes) opening statements by each party's attorney, the mediator puts the parties in different rooms. The mediator then normally caucuses with the plaintiff's attorney and her client in an effort to get them to take a hard look at the strengths and weaknesses of their case.

2. Bashing

Unlike the trashers, the mediators who use a bashing technique tend to spend little or no time engaging in the kind of case evaluation that is aimed at getting the parties to put "realistic" settlement figures on the table. Rather, they tend to focus initially on the settlement offers that the parties bring to mediation and spend most of the session bashing away at those initial offers in an attempt to get the parties to agree to a figure somewhere in between. Their mediation sessions thus tend to be shorter than those of the trashers, and they tend to prefer a longer initial joint session, permitting direct communication between the parties.

Most of the bashers interviewed were retired judges who draw on their judicial experience and use the prestige of their past judicial service to bash out an agreement. . . .

3. Hashing It Out

The third circuit mediation style can best be described as one involving a hashing out of a settlement agreement because it places greater reliance on direct communication between the opposing attorneys and their clients. The hashers tend to take a much more flexible approach to the mediation process, varying their styles and using techniques such as caucusing selectively, depending on their assessment of the individual case and the needs and interests of the parties. When asked to describe the mediator's role in one sentence, a hasher responded, "Facilitator, orchestrator, referee, sounding board, scapegoat."

The hasher generally adopts a much less directive posture than the trashers and bashers, preferring that the parties speak directly with one another and hash out an agreement. However, if direct communication appears counterproductive, the hasher acts as a communication link. . . .

Flexibility apparently is the hallmark of the hasher style of mediation. Although hashers prefer to adopt a style that encourages direct party communication to hash out an agreement, they are willing to employ trasher or basher methodologies if they believe it to be appropriate in a particular case.

C. Basics of the Mediation Process

1. Christopher W. Moore, Mediation 1-7, 10-16 (U.S. Army Corps of Engineers 1991) (IWR Pamphlet 91-ADR-P-3)

What is Mediation?

Mediation is a dispute resolution process in which a neutral and impartial third party assists the people in conflict to negotiate an acceptable settlement of contested issues. Mediation is frequently used to avoid or overcome an impasse when parties have been unable to negotiate an agreement on their own. Most disputes are resolved by informal conversations, some form of cooperative problem solving, or negotiation. Involved parties reach an acceptable settlement of their differences through direct unassisted interaction. But not all conflicts can be resolved in this manner.

Some conflicts, which involve strong emotions, significant differences in the ways that data is interpreted, perceived or actual conflicts of interest or extreme bargaining positions, result in impasse. The parties are deadlocked and are either unable to start negotiations, or where negotiations have been initiated, they are stalled and no progress is possible. In conflicts characterized by the above conditions, the parties may need the assistance of a third party to reach an acceptable negotiated settlement. Mediation is one of the major procedures which can be used to aid parties in the resolution of intractable disputes. . . .

Mediation involves the intervention of a third person, or mediator, into a dispute or negotiation to assist the parties to voluntarily negotiate a jointly acceptable resolution of issues in conflict. The mediator is neutral in that he or she does not stand to personally benefit from the terms of the settlement, and impartial in that he or she does not have a preconceived bias about how the conflict should be resolved.

The mediator is asked by the disputing parties to assist them to voluntarily reach an agreement. The mediator has no decision-making authority and cannot impose a decision. The parties maintain all control over the substantive outcome of the dispute. However, the mediator does have influence in that he or she may provide procedural assistance or possible settlement options to the parties that can assist them in reaching agreement. Mediation assistance involves working with the parties to improve their bargaining relationship and communications, clarifying or interpreting data, identifying key issues to be discussed, uncovering hidden interests, designing an effective negotiation process, generating possible settlement options and helping to identify and formulate areas of agreement.

Here is what a mediated assistance in a negotiation or dispute looks like:

- Two or more individuals or organizations are involved in a dispute. Negotiations may not have been initiated, or may have started and the parties reached an impasse. Each party believes that the other is badly motivated, is hiding information, isn't communicating and is making unreasonable demands. There are no good settlement options "on the table." The parties see their positions on the issues as being far apart and perceive little chance of reaching an agreement.
- One or more parties assesses its procedural and substantive alternatives to reaching a negotiated agreement ignoring the conflict and maintaining the status quo, pursuing a third party settlement or escalating the conflict and decides that a negotiated settlement may be more acceptable than its best alternative procedure or outcome, such as avoidance and stalemate, or a legal suit and judicial decision. The party decides to explore whether mediation assistance might promote successful negotiations.
- One or more parties proposes mediation to the other party, both agree to proceed, and a mediator or mediation organization is contacted to set up a mediation session. If an organization is contacted, the parties may have a choice in the selection of the mediator who will work with them.
- At the beginning of mediation, the mediator will usually meet with each of the disputing parties, either jointly or separately, to explain the mediation process. He or she will clarify the voluntary nature of mediation and describe how the mediator will assist the parties to negotiate more effectively. The mediator may also establish some procedural and behavioral guidelines which will foster more productive negotiations. These include guidelines on who talks, limits of confidentiality, how relevant data will be exchanged, and a description of the mediation process itself.
- At the first joint meeting, the parties will each be asked to outline in an opening statement, the key issues which they wish to discuss and to identify some of the interests which they must have addressed or met to reach an acceptable agreement. This educational process assures that all of the parties and the mediator understand the issues and some of the underlying interests.
- The mediator may propose or will work with the parties to develop an acceptable negotiation agenda, the sequence of issues and procedures to be used to address each item.
- The mediator may assist the parties to handle strong emotions, misperceptions, stereotypes, or miscommunication by listening and legitimizing (but not necessarily agreeing with) feelings, clarifying communications, summarizing statements, and proposing more effective communication structures.
- The mediator will ask the parties to jointly discuss each of the issues, and to identify the various interests or needs to be satisfied. Mediators will usually reframe or define issues to be addressed in terms of meeting the parties' joint interests.
- Many disputes are caused by the inability of a team or organization to reach internal agreements on a negotiation strategy or acceptable settlement options. Mediators often assist a team or spokesperson to build an internal consensus or approach to negotiations.
- The mediator will assist the parties to back off of extreme or hard line positions, preferred solutions which are advocated by each of the parties; and to generate alterna-

tive settlement options. Option generation may occur either in joint meetings or in separate caucuses where the mediator meets in private with each of the parties.
- Impasse commonly occurs because parties dislike and dismiss options on the negotiation table, but fail to assess the benefits and costs of alternative resolution procedure and potential outcomes that may result from their use. Mediators often help parties to evaluate the merits of settlement by means of negotiations in contrast to non-negotiated alternatives.
- The mediator helps prepare the parties to make "yesable" proposals that will be more acceptable or readily agreed to by the other party or parties. They do this by assisting parties to make offers which meet both their own and others' interests, and by improving the form or manner in which offers are communicated.
- As parties make offers, the mediator may translate or interpret them to the other side. He or she may do this by "shuttle mediation," where the mediator travels between private meetings with the parties; or directly in a joint session.
- The mediator assists parties to identify and define areas of agreement by "testing" for consensus. The mediator listens for and restates common or overlapping views. Since parties in dispute often talk past an agreement, the mediators' assistance is often invaluable in identifying areas of agreement.
- As the parties reach agreements, the mediator may act as a scribe who captures the settlement in a Memorandum of Understanding (MOU). This MOU, where appropriate, may later be drafted in the form of a contract or other legal document.

Why Use Mediation?

What are the advantages of using mediation over other means of resolving disputes, such as litigation or formal administrative procedures? There are a number of advantages:

- Protection of the Relationship
  In a significant number of conflicts, the parties have or will have an ongoing relationship. Adversarial or win/lose forms of dispute resolution often result in damaged relationships which may preclude the parties working together in the future. Mediation generally results in a settlement that both parties can accept and support, promotes better communications between them, and encourages a respectful and cooperative relationship.
- Time Savings
  Mediation assistance is generally available on short notice. The speed and schedule of settlement is entirely dependent on the parties' willingness to address and reach agreement on the issues.
- Cost Savings
  Mediation involves direct negotiations between the parties. While legal advisors may be present and offer assistance, key managers are the decision makers and are usually the main actors. This means that legal costs are generally lower in the mediation process. Also, since the parties share the cost of hiring the mediator, the expense is kept down.
- Greater Flexibility in Possible Settlements
  Traditional litigation or administrative procedures are generally constrained as to the range of possible settlement options by the law or contract limitations. This means that

the types of issues which can be raised or addressed by the parties is often rather narrow. Structural constraints often force parties to address "relationship" or "personality" issues, or issues not covered under the contract, indirectly using an unsuitable forum or procedure. Mediation, because of its more flexible format and lack of structural constraints, allows the parties to address relationship, procedural and substantive issues. It allows people to get to the "root of the problem" without having to "force-fit" a problem into an inappropriate process. Mediation also allows parties to develop customized creative solutions which are tailored to meet specific concerns or interests.

- Keeps the Decision-Making Authority in the Hands of the Parties
  Procedures such as litigation, administrative hearings and binding arbitration, rely on third party decision makers to break deadlocks and render a decision. These procedures remove decision-making authority and responsibility from the parties who often are the most informed about the issues and options. Mediation keeps the decision-making authority with the people who best know the problems and it preserves both individual and organizational authority.

Initiating and Participating in Mediation

How do you initiate and plan for participation in mediation? This section provides guidance on the specifics of preparing for mediation. The basic steps of initiating and planning for participation in mediation are as follows:

1) Determine whether or not a mediation procedure may assist the parties to resolve a particular dispute.
2) Obtain any needed management commitments to participate in the process.
3) Approach other parties and gain their agreement to participate, or approach a mediator or mediation organization and request that the intermediary discuss with the other party or parties the option of mediation.
4) Identify the key individuals or groups that should participate in the mediation process for a settlement to be reached.
5) Select an acceptable mediator. The parties should identify the expertise that they want the third party to provide, and then jointly select an acceptable third party or ask a reputable mediation or referral agency to appoint one.
6) Prepare for the mediation by clearly identifying facts to be presented, issues to be discussed, interests that must be met and potential settlement options. Parties should also assess their best alternative to a negotiated agreement.
7) Discuss with the mediator and all parties the format, ground rules and process that will be used in the mediation session or sessions. Agreements should be reached on the above points before proceeding.
8) Conduct the mediation session or sessions.
9) Document any agreement reached.

Further information on several of these steps is provided below:

When is Mediation Appropriate?

The key criteria for the appropriateness of mediation is the parties' willingness to participate in the process. Generally, prior to the initiation of mediation, one or more parties will evaluate internally, or possibly with the other party or parties, to determine if the mediation process is the appropriate means for resolving a conflict. Mediation may be appropriate when:

- Parties have tried to initiate negotiations but have been unable to reach agreement on how to begin discussions. In this instance the mediator may play a "convening" role and will help the parties design an acceptable negotiation process. In large public disputes, the mediator may also play a role in identifying the potential parties that should be involved in the mediation process.
- Parties are having difficulties negotiating because of lack of process, poor process, the wrong process or the right process being used in an inefficient manner. The mediator can help by clarifying productive steps for problem solving or by providing a new process for negotiations.
- Parties have engaged in negotiations and have reached an impasse. Mediators are often able to assist parties to break a deadlock by providing procedural assistance, helping to overcome psychological barriers to settlement, suggesting new and creative option generation procedures or identifying potential trade-offs or packages.
- When there are strong psychological or relationship barriers to negotiating a resolution. Mediators can play an intermediary and conciliatory role between the parties. Mediators are trained to handle emotional barriers to settlement, problems of misperception, or poor communications.
- When parties will not, or are reluctant to, meet face-to-face. Mediators can engage in "shuttle diplomacy" carrying messages between the parties and helping them to build an agreement.
- When a matter of legal principle is not involved and the parties do not want to create a legal precedent.
- When each of the parties believes that it has some flexibility in its position and a negotiated settlement with the assistance of a mediator is either more efficient, timely, cost effective or psychologically satisfying than a third party decision by a judge or administrative tribunal.
- When the preservation of a working relationship is important. Many conflicts develop in the context of an ongoing relationship. A negotiated agreement to a dispute is often preferable to a command decision because the parties maintain control of the outcome and "own" the decision. The mediation process often repairs or builds new working relationships that are critical to the success of ongoing work. Are there circumstances where mediation is not appropriate? Generally, cases where one or more parties is acting in bad faith, information necessary for a fair and informed settlement is being withheld or distorted, one or more parties want to lay blame on another or want their "day in court," or where a legal precedent is desirable are not appropriate for mediation.

Who Proposes Mediation?

Any party involved in a dispute may propose mediation as a means to reach a settlement. One party may contact another and propose the process, or a party may contact a mediator or mediation firm and request that the intermediary act in their behalf and contact the other parties. . . . Several approaches can be used to avoid [being perceived as having a weak position]. First, the initiating party can inform the other side, either directly or through an intermediary, that they would like to attempt one last good-faith effort at negotiating a settlement prior to moving to a more adversarial process. The party should also inform the other party that they are preparing to go to an administrative hearing or trial at the same time that they are mediating, so that if mediation fails, no time or advantage for legal action will be lost. This approach clarifies willingness to use adversarial means and be tough, while keeping the door open to a negotiated settlement.

A second approach is for an individual or agency that normally processes a number of disputes to announce before a particular dispute arises, that they will use mediation as a routine step, after unassisted negotiations, in an institutionalized dispute resolution process. By indicating that these two steps will routinely be used prior to moving to more adversarial means, a party can avoid any appearance of weakness on any single case.

Who Participates in Mediation?

Generally the participants in mediation are people who are well informed about contested issues and have the authority to make a decision. In most cases these will be key individuals or decision makers in an organization. Frequently decision makers may be advised by legal counsel or other technical experts, and on occasion a "side" may be represented by a lawyer or negotiating team.

Mediation is a forum where key decision makers can talk directly with each other, without the encumbrance of having to talk through representatives. Face-to-face talks by decision makers often result in productive exchanges and settlements.

How Should a Mediator be Selected?

There are four major considerations in selecting a mediator: 1) the kinds of process assistance that are needed, 2) the degree of substantive assistance which is desirable, 3) the mediator's prior experience in cases of similar complexity or content, and 4) the relationship or personal chemistry between the mediator and the parties.

Mediators vary in how directive they are in providing procedural assistance to parties. Some mediators are "orchestrators" in that they make general process suggestions, "chair" meetings and basically back-up competent and skilled negotiators who need a structured forum to negotiate a settlement. Other mediators are "deal makers." They are much more directive regarding the negotiating approaches or procedures parties should use, may control the agendas of the meetings, may do extensive work in caucuses or private meetings between the mediator and each of the parties, and may provide substantive advice.

Parties selecting a mediator should clarify in their own minds and with the third party which kind of procedural assistance is desired. A mediator's substantive expertise or knowledge may be another consideration in selecting a mediator. Some parties want a mediator with some substantive knowledge of issues in dispute so that he or she can advise them on possible settlement options or packages. A mediator with some knowledge of the issues may also be more able to conduct "reality testing" of proposals that are unreasonable or untenable.

On the other hand, if a mediator has significant substantive knowledge of contested issues, he or she may also have a strong opinion about how the issue should be settled. This knowledge may encourage the third party to lead the parties to his or her preferred settlement rather than facilitate the parties' development of their own solutions. Substantive knowledge and strong opinions on the part of the mediator may also compromise the parties' perception of the mediator's neutrality and thus make the intervenor ineffective in providing future assistance.

Another school of thought is that the mediator does not have to possess specific substantive knowledge of the issues in dispute to be of assistance to the parties. Parties, and intervenors who advocate this approach to mediation argue that the parties themselves have the requisite knowledge to settle the dispute and what is needed from the third party is procedural leadership or relationship building assistance, not specific substantive expertise. The premise to this approach is that the intervenor will learn from the parties any substantive expertise that may be required to settle a case.

Experience is another criteria in the selection of a mediator. It is advisable that the mediator has experience in handling issues of similar complexity as the ones to be negotiated. Parties considering a mediator should investigate the intervenor's track record, range of experiences and references before contracting for services.

Relationship, rapport and "personal chemistry" are rather intangible criteria for the selection of a mediator, but they are often key factors in how effective the intervenor will be. Parties have to trust the intervenor, be able to talk freely with him or her, and believe that the third party is working in good faith to help them develop the best settlement possible, if the third party is to be most effective.

How Can A Party Prepare for Mediation?

Mediation is assisted negotiations. The best way to prepare for mediation is to prepare well for negotiations. The first step in preparing for mediation is for each party to clearly identify what interests must be addressed or met for a satisfactory agreement to be reached. This means clearly identifying the substantive, procedural and relationship interests for each of the involved parties. Substantive interests are objective needs such as money, performance or time which a party wants to have satisfied. Procedural interests are needs about the way that a dispute is resolved. They may include such needs as efficiency, timeliness, an opportunity to present one's case, or preference for cooperative rather than adversarial proceedings.

Relationship or psychological interests are needs related to trust and respect, and expectations for how one is treated in the dispute resolution process itself, or in a future relationship.

Once a party has identified its own interests, it is advisable for him/her to try and identify the needs of the other party or parties who are involved. If others have been explicit about their interests, this will be an easy task. If not, it may require some speculation.

Often a party's interests can be decoded from a position statement, a preferred solution that a party has advocated to meet its needs. By examining a position, it is often possible to identify the underlying interests or needs that the party wants to have satisfied. In some cases, it may not be possible to discern what another party's interests are. In this case, the mediation meeting may have to be used to discover them.

Once the interests for each of the parties have been identified, it is always advisable to generate some potential settlement options. In some negotiations options may have been publicly announced or put on the table in the form of positions. In other cases, where the parties have not begun negotiating, each will have to generate a range of options which would be acceptable to them. This range of options will be used by the mediator and negotiators to craft an agreement which is mutually acceptable to all parties.

Before entering into mediation, it is always wise for the parties to assess what their best alternative to a negotiated agreement, or "BATNA" is. The best alternative refers to both possible settlement options and alternative procedures. Explicitly understanding what non-negotiated alternatives are available, provides a party with a basis to compare settlement options developed at the table. This comparison will assist a party in deciding when to settle and when to stop negotiating and pursue another means of dispute resolution.

Finally, before beginning mediation, each party should think about what his/her relationship expectations are both during and after the negotiations. Some of the questions which should be considered include: Do the parties want an adversarial relationship or would they prefer a more cooperative one? Will the parties have to work together? Will there be future contacts? What impacts will a win/lose settlement have on the relationship? If it is important that the parties settle and maintain some kind of amicable relationship, each party should consider what measures need to be taken to "clear the air" and minimize any unnecessary damage to the relationship in the process of resolving the dispute. The negotiators should decide individually or as a team what they can do to create as positive a negotiation climate as possible. This does not mean side-stepping strong emotions, but it does mean thinking about how feelings of anger or frustration can be expressed without further damaging the relationship.

Finally, each party should meet with the mediator, either in pre-mediation information exchange sessions, or at the beginning of the first joint session, to clarify the role of the mediator and to gain a thorough understanding of the mediation process which will be used.

In the mediation session, there are a variety of actions that parties can take which will enhance the possibility of a successful outcome and which will help the mediator work more effectively. Generally mediators make a series of process suggestions, such as behavioral ground rules or ways to approach a particular issue. It is helpful if the parties work with the mediator and do not fight the process. Also mediators may want to meet with each of the parties separately to help develop settlement options, evaluate a proposal or do some reality or feasibility testing with a party. It is helpful if the parties work with the mediator in these sessions to develop realistic options or appraise potential settlements.

What Happens in a Mediation Session?

Mediation sessions usually begin with introductions if the participating parties have never met face-to-face. The mediator will usually outline the issues that have brought the parties to the session and will gain agreement on the purpose of the meeting. Many mediators may also suggest some procedural ground rules such as a non-interruption agreement, clarification of the limits of confidentiality, an agreement on time limits and a commitment from the parties to bargain in good faith. Often a mediator will outline the process for the negotiations including a description of how issues and interests will be identified, the use of caucuses or private meetings, a description of how possible settlement options will be developed and what happens when an agreement is reached (or not reached).

At this point the mediator will usually ask the initiating party to begin with an opening statement that details the issues to be discussed, the interests to be met and possibly a preferred settlement option. The mediator may ask questions during the opening statement to clarify an issue or interest. At the conclusion of the first party's opening statement, the mediator will usually summarize what he or she has heard. It is then the other party's turn to make an opening statement.

With the completion of the opening statements, the mediator will assist the parties to order the issues into a workable agenda. Often the mediator will look for an easy item to start with, one he believes the parties will be able to settle in a fairly brief period of time. An early settlement of at least one issue creates momentum in the negotiations and demonstrates to the parties that agreements can be reached.

The mediator may assist the parties to work through the issues one at a time or may help them to link and trade issues in a package arrangement. Settlement options may be generated by the parties through structured discussion in joint session, or may be developed through conversations with the mediator in caucuses.

How are the Results of the Meeting Documented?

Meeting documentation can be accomplished in several ways. The mediator may take notes and draft a memorandum of understanding, or MOU, that summarizes the results of the meeting. It may detail the agreements and any areas of disagreement which may remain. If appropriate, this document may be referred to each of the parties' legal advisors to be turned into a formal contract or legally binding agreement.

An alternative to the above procedure is for the parties to take their own notes and to agree at the conclusion of the meeting as to who will draft the final settlement document.

In either of these cases, the parties may need or desire a final meeting to sign a formal document. If parties do not believe that there will need to be any final modifications, the final agreement may be circulated by mail for final signatures. . . .

2. Eric Galton, Representing Clients in Mediation 25-53 (1995)*

[Galton addresses his remarks to counsel for the parties in a mediation, but the discussion and advice are useful for anyone interested in mediation.] Mediation . . . is a process. While a skilled and fully trained mediator is essential, the process itself is what makes things work. The following illustration is a linear model of the mediation process. My purpose is not to create or imply a rigid model or form, but rather to provide you with a series of reference points so that you, the advocate for a party in mediation, may understand every facet of this process. . . .

1. Mediator Introduction

Typically, all parties and their counsel will initially assemble in the same room and the proceedings will commence with the mediator making an introduction. If the mediator is following good form, her introduction usually takes no more than 15 minutes.

1. Explaining the process. Specifically, the mediator in her introduction is attempting to accomplish the following:

(1) Provide some information on her background, expertise, and credentials. The purpose of this part of the mediator's introduction is to humanize the mediator and to help her establish control of the process.
(2) Explain the role of the mediator. The mediator will emphasize her neutrality, will explain that she is not the judge or jury, will assure the parties that she will not offer absolute opinions, and will describe her role as a facilitator.
(3) Explain fully the confidentiality aspects of the mediation process.

---

*Reprinted with permission.

(4) Generally outline the sequence of events that will occur during the day. The mediator will explain the various phases of the mediation process, just as a trial lawyer will tell a jury during voir dire how the trial will unfold. The mediator will also explain the special aspects of the separate caucus during this part of the introduction.

(5) Obtain several commitments from the parties. The mediator will ask the parties if they are willing to allocate whatever time is necessary to permit the process to work, whether they possess the requisite authority to resolve the dispute, and whether they are willing to make a good faith effort to resolve the dispute.

More globally, the mediator's introduction is designed to make the parties and their counsel as familiar and comfortable with the mediation process as is possible. Many lawyers, and most clients, have not been through a mediation. As a result, the mediator must assist the participants in fully understanding what is about to take place and to appreciate that the mediation process is a protected, confidential, and safe environment. The mediator will not be able to have the parties open up and participate if the parties have any doubts or fears about the process itself, confidentiality, or the mediator's neutrality.

2. Pre-mediation issues. Good mediation practice requires that the mediator and all counsel attempt to resolve several important issues prior to the mediation itself. These issues may be handled by a pre-mediation conference call or an exchange of correspondence. The issues that should be resolved prior to the mediation are as follows:

(1) The authority to settle issue must be resolved before the mediation. The issue of who has the authority to settle a case for the party is a thorny one, . . . but to summarize the issue for purposes of this chapter: All parties should confer, agree on who will attend the session, and be comfortable that the persons who will attend the session have authority to resolve the dispute. If the proper parties or representatives are not present, the mediation process likely will not work. The mediation may have to be postponed or rescheduled. Parties or representatives may have had to travel great distances to attend a session. A mediation that breaks down because the necessary parties or representatives are not present may further heighten tensions and animosity. Therefore, the authority issue and who should attend the mediation should be fully discussed before the session itself.

(2) All mediation participants should make realistic travel plans before the session. A mediator never knows how long the mediation process itself will take. Some disputes may be resolved in four hours or less. Most disputes seem to require five to eight hours for the process to run its course. Some complex disputes may even require several days of mediation. . . .

2. Opening Statements by Counsel

The opening statement by counsel is one of the most important facets of the mediation process; yet, in my experience, talented and highly skilled counsel routinely ignore the great opportunity associated with their opening remarks. To be sure, counsel's opening remarks are in part designed either to educate the mediator about the dispute or to educate the mediator further in the event a confidential pre-mediation submission has already been provided. But the second and most important aspect of the opening statement is that it permits each party a direct opportunity to set out for the other party (*not* the other party's lawyer) how counsel sees the case and the basis for such view. Rarely in the litigation process does counsel ever have an opportunity for such direct contact.

We are now crossing into the territory I call "mediation advocacy"; i.e., effective representation of a client in the mediation process. Certainly, mediation is not the courtroom. But how does the experienced attorney (be she a litigator, transactional lawyer, or other) translate her skills into the mediation forum? This is a list of my do's and do not's:

1. Do not address your opening statement to the mediator. The mediator is not the judge or the jury. And, if you have provided the mediator with a confidential pre-mediation submission, the mediator already knows how you see the case.

2. Do not address your remarks to opposing counsel. Opposing counsel has already read your pleadings, read your written discovery, heard your questions at depositions, and probably has spoken to you at length about the case. . . .

3. Do not discuss legal issues in "law talk"—if you discuss issues of law specifically as issues of law at all. You do not discuss issues of law in "law talk" to a jury. Do not do so at a mediation.

4. Do address your remarks to the opposing party. In a mediation . . . the jury is the other party—be she the claimant, the insurance adjuster, the corporate executive, etc.

5. Do not engage in personal attacks on the other party. You are making a good faith appeal. No one who is insulted will listen, re-evaluate, consider your position, or be inclined to negotiate.

6. Do use charts, blow-ups, and well-presented handouts. Impress with preparation and organization—not harsh words.

7. Do acknowledge you understand how the other side feels. Understanding does not equal agreement.

8. Do acknowledge that you are present to listen and are willing to do so. People have two fundamental interests in a mediation—to be listened to and to be understood. Most people feel "no one listens" or "understands" in the litigation process.

9. Do emphasize your good faith participation in the mediation process and your hope for resolution. This is not an expression of weakness; rather, you are expressing open-mindedness and a desire for a sensible solution.

10. Do not address sensitive issues. Prior to the mediation, consider what sensitive issues or "nerves" exist on the other side. Do not address such issues; rather, permit the mediator to do so in a separate caucus.

11. Do express or extend sympathy or concern to those who have either been hurt or experienced a loss. Such an expression is not an admission of liability.

12. Do introduce yourself. Provide some background on who you are. Humanize yourself.

13. Do acknowledge your belief in and support of the mediation process.

14. Do emphasize why you believe resolution will be in everyone's best interest.

15. Do explain your role as an advocate on behalf of your client.

16. Do explain that in anticipation of the mediation, you have thoroughly and objectively re-reveiwed the case and that you have had your client do so as well.

17. Do not ever discuss money in your opening statement. Money cuts to the heart. Money is cold. And your reference to money will be the only thing remembered.

18. Do not ever use absolute words. Words like "never" and "won't" only get in the way. . . .

In mediation, you are not selling the other side on the correctness of your position. The other side, regardless of your legal abilities or oral skills, will always rule against you. Instead, you are communicating your integrity as a human being, your preparedness, your willingness to listen and understand, your good faith participation in the mediation process and your interest in a sensible resolution.

3. Initial Collective Session

I rarely hold a collective session immediately after the lawyers' opening statements. For some mediators, the concept of having the parties "vent" and express their thoughts and feelings is a critical element of the mediation process. The thinking, of course, is that with such feelings vented and therefore "out of the way," the parties will be predisposed towards more rational thought regarding resolution of the dispute.

I am . . . too nervous to permit such an exchange. I would much prefer to allow such venting to occur in separate caucus outside the presence of the other side. . . . If the feelings need to be expressed to the other side, the mediator is able to deliver the message in a "kinder and gentler" way. Also, putting on my negotiator's hat, I do not believe that invectives put people in the mood to negotiate constructively.

As an experienced trial lawyer, I do not see mediation as ESP, voodoo, or a group therapy session. Anything told to me as a mediator in the privacy of the separate caucus is fine because only I hear it and it won't hurt my feelings. Further, despite the confidentiality of mediation, lawyers may be leery that their clients' candid statements in mediation may be used against them if the case does not resolve. For these reasons, I omit the collective session and move into the separate caucus except in the following situations:

1. When little or no discovery has been done. Mediation should never be transformed into a deposition or an adversarial hearing. However, the collective session may be useful in exchanging otherwise discoverable evidence for purposes of evaluation.
2. When the parties have a long-standing business relationship or friendship. . . . [T]he parties in such situations have a great need to communicate directly with each other before going into the separate caucus. Sometimes the parties may not be prepared to negotiate until such direct words are exchanged. . . .
3. It may be appropriate to discuss the procedural posture of the case, what discovery is remaining to get the case ready for trial, the length of the trial, the likelihood of appeal, and the remaining costs. The parties may benefit from a candid discussion of both the time and costs associated with the continuation of the dispute.
4. When an acknowledgment of the negotiation posture may be appropriate. In some instances, the issue of who made the last offer, the amount of the offer, and the like needs to be clarified. A party virtually never will bid against herself. The parties should agree whose court the ball is in.
5. When the party has a real interest in "public shaming" as a pre-condition to resolution. Of course, mediation is a private, confidential proceeding. But a party with such an interest may view the mediator as a member of the public. The party may have an absolute need. . . . Such situations are explosive. And, fortunately, most claimants may fulfill this need by expressing such feelings to the mediator in separate caucus. But in a small group of cases . . . the party will not be able to begin to resolve the dispute until

this public shaming interest is met. The mediator, recognizing such a situation, may engage in some damage control. The mediator . . . should advise all parties that candid expressions, no matter how harsh, are appropriate and better stated under the aura of the confidentiality of a mediation. The mediator may also encourage the parties that such candid expressions should, if at all possible, be stated constructively. The mediator, in essence, is attempting to lessen the degree of rancor expressed or to prepare the other party for what is about to occur.

6. When a party needs to express grief. Some litigants feel that "no one cares" or that the other party does not fully understand the extent of their hurt or loss. A party who feels this way may not be able to consider resolution without having the opportunity to express such feelings directly to the other party.

4. The Separate Caucus

[T]he separate caucus is the essence of mediation. The parties and their counsel are placed in separate quarters and the mediator goes from room to room meeting privately with each side. Everything said in each separate caucus is confidential, save and except for what a party authorizes the mediator to communicate to a party in another room. The mediator must communicate only authorized communications and must take whatever precaution necessary to avoid any unauthorized disclosures. The mediator will separately caucus with each party several times. In complex cases, I may have nine or ten separate caucuses with each party.

While every mediation is different and the mediator may vary protocol in a particular case, the separate caucus usually has three general phases: the initial strength/weakness, objective evaluation caucus; the preliminary negotiation caucus; and the closing/resolution caucus.

The initial separate caucus with each party is typically the most lengthy phase of the mediation process. The mediator usually will visit with each party for at least 30 minutes, and sometimes as long as an hour. Because of the mediator's goals in the initial caucus, the mediator may, especially in a difficult case, have to hold two (and sometimes more) strength/weakness caucuses with each party. . . . The mediator has several goals in the initial caucus and it is indeed a highly critical phase of the process.

1. Bonding with the parties. A mediator will initially make an effort to obtain the trust and confidence of the party. The party already may have confidence in the mediator, but the party may need to get to know the mediator better (and vice versa) before she is willing to "open up." The party needs to be reminded of the confidentiality of the caucus and the mediator's impartiality. The mediator is also looking for insights into the personality of the party and to identify some of her interests unrelated to the dispute; i.e., children, golf, basketball, travel, music, etc. The purpose of this, of course, is for the mediator to "bond" a bit more with the party. Bonding results in a party feeling more relaxed with the process and more comfortable with the mediator. . . .

The mediator bonds with the party not through any tactical plan, but by demonstrating that she has listened, is willing to listen, and is willing to understand (not agree). The mediator bonds with the party by demonstrating preparedness, professionalism, neutrality, and compassion. . . .

2. Venting. Many parties really do need to vent their feelings to the mediator. And most people want to do so right away. Parties feel—correctly—that the dispute belongs to them, and they are often tired of all the "lawyer talk."

Good mediators understand that a party wants such an immediate opportunity to speak. A good mediator may walk into the caucus, look at the party, and simply ask, "Mr. Williams, how do you feel about this dispute?" Typically, the question triggers a flood of information, often emotionally charged, and the party begins to feel more a part of the process itself. The party comes to understand quickly that the mediator is listening and not sitting in judgment.

In the separate caucus, venting occurs with no destructive consequences. But venting, beyond the relief it affords the party, also usually identifies many of the party's interests and needs. Often, a venting party repeats important words or thoughts, which is not accidental. Good mediators write down key words or phrases and recognize that while the dispute may be about money, such words are often the emotional matter that fuels the dispute. . . .

Parties in mediation sometimes tell me that no one, including their own lawyers, ever asked them what the case was really about. . . . For the lawyer, regardless of how caring she may be, the client's problem becomes a "case" or a "file." For the client, the problem may be her entire life. Lawyers speak in terms of issues and positions. Beneath the line of issues and positions is the realm of interests. More often than not, the client's motivations are in the realm of interests and often the keys to resolution are found in this territory as well.

3. Identification of the decision-maker. At this critical stage, the mediator is also attempting to identify who the decision-maker or decision-makers are in each room. . . . In most instances, the party and the party's lawyer will make the decision. . . . In some disputes, the party may be the only decision-maker and in other disputes the party's lawyer may be the only real decision-maker. In certain disputes, the party and the party's lawyer may have very different views of the dispute and its resolution.

Identification of the decision-maker(s) is critical because it is the decision-maker's negotiating style and interests that need to be identified and met if resolution is to occur. . . . If uncertain, the mediator should ask who is going to make the decision. . . .

4. The lawyer as decision-maker. . . . [I]t is not surprising that in certain cases the party's lawyer is going to make the decision — "I'll do whatever my lawyer says." In the great majority of cases, the lawyer functioning as the decision-maker is no problem. The fact that a lawyer has control over her client is usually a great help in a mediation. But, what happens when a lawyer puts her interests ahead of the client's interest and obstructs the mediation process? . . . [In such instances] the mediator may wish to hold a private meeting with the client's counsel to discuss such issues openly and diplomatically.

5. When the lawyer and client are at odds. A more common, and less troublesome, situation is when the mediator perceives that an attorney and client are at odds with each other. In fact, many lawyers suggest mediation because they have lost control over their clients. In such instances, the client is the decision-maker, but she may not be listening to her counsel and often has unrealistic expectations and goals. Typically, a lawyer will cue in the mediator at the first caucus that such a situation exists, or the dynamics in the room will make the problem strikingly obvious.

The mediator's role in such situations is not to dispense legal advice or to play the "second lawyer." Rather, by posing specific and appropriate questions, the mediator should attempt to focus the party on the objective realities of the case so that the party will see both the weaknesses and strengths of her position.

6. Identification of negotiating style. Everyone has a different negotiating style. Some negotiators are very aggressive. Other negotiators are very conciliatory. Some negotiators wish to exploit; others fear being exploited. Many negotiators have done little formal study on the negotiation process. Often, a person's negotiation style is reflective of her personality. As such, a mediator rarely can change the negotiating style of a party to a mediation and probably should not even try.

But from the mediation perspective, . . . the negotiating "pace" of the decision-makers [not their negotiating style] is the critical issue. . . . Some parties to a mediation want to get down to business quickly; others may want to settle in a bit before getting into serious negotiations. Certain parties need to be dragged into the negotiations. Fortunately, very, very few people are unwilling to negotiate at all.

Many times the parties' pace is the same—all parties want to get right down to serious discussions or all parties want a slow, deliberate negotiation. But the more challenging situation, which often occurs, is when each party has a different (sometimes radically different) negotiating pace—one party wants to "cut to the chase" and the other party wants to go slow and be deliberate. This stylistic pace clash may damage any chance of resolution unless it is identified and addressed at the outset. . . .

In separate caucus, the mediator . . . should openly discuss with each party these stylistic differences and encourage each party to respect the style of the other and not to become frustrated. If the mediator sews together such an agreement in the first caucus, the parties' stylistic differences will not, in themselves, create a fatal impasse.

7. The "winner's curse." Many mediations, especially personal injury matters, involve one party agreeing to pay the other side money. The issue is how much. A claimant never wants to leave something on the table. An insurance adjuster never wants to pay too much. An interesting phenomenon based on this premise explains many of the initial rounds of negotiation in mediation. Consider the following story, which I first heard from Professor B. Randolph Lowery of the Pepperdine University School of Law:

Suppose we find ourselves magically transported to the Neiman Marcus department store in Houston—a rather pricey place to shop. You walk into the leather goods section and see a briefcase that you really like. You can just imagine walking into the courtroom proudly holding the briefcase. But your daydream abruptly ends when you look at the price tag and see $500. Even if you have the money, you know you are very hard on your briefcases and are unwilling to pay $500 for an item you will shortly beat into a pulp. So you don't buy the briefcase.

The next week you find yourself in Mexico. You are walking through the shopping area and enter a leather goods store. You see a briefcase in the very back that looks very much like the one you saw at Neiman Marcus. You closely inspect and touch the briefcase. If the briefcase is not identical to the one you saw at Neiman's, it is very, very similar. This briefcase, however, has one unique characteristic. It has no price tag.

You begin to get very excited. You think about the $500 price tag at Neiman's. You think about negotiation. You think about Mexico and the negotiating culture you find yourself in, and you come to a command decision. You take the briefcase from the display counter, you walk over to the sales clerk, you hand her the briefcase, and with utter conviction in your voice you say, "I'll give you $200 for this briefcase." The sales clerk says only one word: "Sold."

How do you feel? Five steps away you think you could have bought the briefcase for $170.

Ten steps away you think $130. You are at the door and think $100. By the time you are outside the shop, you are upset with yourself and have totally forgotten the $300 you saved by not buying the briefcase at Neiman Marcus.

This phenomenon is often referred to as "the winner's curse." And "the winner's curse" often explains the initial bids exchanged during the mediation process; that is, until the defendant says "no" to $1 million or the plaintiff says "no" to $50,000, the "real" negotiation cannot commence. . . . [A]fter the winner's curse bids are exchanged, who will be the one to make the first "credible" proposal? . . .

In a negotiation, what is a "credible" number? A credible number is not a number a party may be willing to pay or accept, but is instead one that encourages a party to perceive that the negotiation is moving into the realm of reason. Interestingly, most cases resolve at the midpoint between the first two credible proposals. . . .

Back to the issue of who makes the first credible proposal. Interestingly, I have observed the opposite of what you may have thought or still think. My observation is that the party who makes the first credible proposal controls the negotiation. . . . [T]he party who makes the first credible proposal, instead of demonstrating weakness, scores a lot of points with the other side and subsequent, more de minimus proposals are excused or tolerated. . . .

6. Strength/Weakness Analysis

Another essential aspect of the initial caucus is a strength/weakness analysis. In this regard, the mediator does not render ultimate opinions; i.e., who will win or lose the lawsuit, whether an absolute limitations defense bars recovery, or whether a witness' credibility is subject to an absolute challenge, etc.

Remember, the mediator's job is not to determine the legal issues but to assist the parties in identifying potential weaknesses as well as obvious strengths. [M]ost litigants have little difficulty identifying their strong points. The mediator simply plays the role of devil's advocate by asking "what if," "what about," "do you think," or "why do you believe" questions.

Generally, the mediator is asking open-ended questions designed to permit the party to identify weaknesses on her own. Weaknesses may involve specific issues in the case, such as whether a jury will accept or believe an expert witness' testimony, whether a defendant will be able to attribute negligence fully to a third party, whether a certain piece of evidence will be admissible, etc. Weaknesses may also involve a more global assessment of the case, such as whether the claim has more limited value in the county in which the case will be tried, whether proof problems may be ignored because of the nature of the injuries or sympathy, whether a party may not desire a public trial for personal reasons, etc.

Because of the mediator's neutrality, most parties are willing participants in the strength/weakness analysis. Most lawyers are eager players in this phase as well because they are interested in a neutral perspective of their case. Advocates, as we all know, may become too close to a case and lose their objectivity. And, . . . a lawyer may have some weaknesses in a case that he identified to the client, but may need the mediator's help in getting the client to understand them. Also, the opening statements and information exchange prior to the initial caucus may produce new information or evidence that may require a re-evaluation of the case. More often than not, however, the opening statements do not produce significant new evidence; rather the opening statements produce a more clear, coherent, and full understanding of the other party's position. Also, the opening remarks are usually the first time the client has heard a complete characterization of the other side's position. . . .

The strength/weakness analysis is therefore critical to the negotiations themselves. Parties come to a mediation with an opening offer that is usually inflated or deflated for negotiating purposes, but that also reflects to some extent their sense of the value of the case. . . .

A party does not re-assess or change value for no reason. Of course, reasons outside of the [dispute itself] may result in value changing; *i.e.*, unwillingness to accept any risk, a desire to avoid delay, avoidance of litigation expenses, a desire for confidentiality, etc. But beyond such factors that a mediator may identify in her introductory remarks, re-evaluating the case with the mediator's help is how the essential change occurs.

[P]arties often do not fully appreciate risk, the other side's position, or the defects in their case without the direct interaction the process affords. The neutral's strength/weakness questions are accepted and welcomed *because* she is a neutral and is not contaminated; that is, the neutral is not the other side.

I would make one final, strong statement regarding the strength/weakness phase of the first caucus. The mediator should *never, never, never* attempt to impose her view of a facet of the case or the whole case on a party. In fact, a mediator should rarely even suggest her view. A mediator who is skilled in good questioning techniques does not even need to suggest her view of an issue. In countless mediations, I have heard a party respond to my question by saying, "You know, I haven't really thought of this before." . . .

7. Money, Expectations, Hopes, Dreams and Motivations

As you probably realize by now, the initial caucus is a critical aspect of the mediation process. Consider mediation to be like building a house. The initial caucus is like building a good foundation.

Ultimately, most resolutions involve the payment of money. In the initial caucus, the mediator will explore monetary issues and attempt to obtain each party's first monetary proposal. Good mediators will go through the strength/weakness analysis before monetary discussions. And good mediators will attempt to identify the non-monetary interests that are motivating the party and that are affecting the party's monetary values.

We all have expectations in life — some of which are realistic and some of which regrettably are not. . . . In the first caucus, a mediator may take the following approach regarding monetary expectations:

1. What are your monetary expectations?
2. Why do you have such monetary expectations?
3. Are these expectations realistic?
4. What are your monetary needs?
5. What do you realistically expect the other side to offer?

Monetary values are in part objective and in part subjective. Value may be claimed in non-monetary ways, but money is often more convenient and is something everyone understands. Ultimately, in any negotiation, the situation boils down to what someone is willing to pay and what someone is willing to accept.

The mediator's goal is to have credible monetary negotiations occur as soon as is practical. The five questions listed above, obviously framed a bit differently by each mediator, will be asked in either the initial caucus or the second caucus. . . .

8. Subsequent Caucuses

The strength/weakness analysis, which is part of the initial caucus, occurs continuously, albeit in a more focused form, throughout all caucuses. Typically, one or two issues, out of an initial potpourri of many issues, become the primary focus of subsequent evaluation. A facet of liability, including the issue of causation, may become the essence of subsequent evaluation. More often than not, though, damages become the major focus of the subsequent caucus.

Damages, whether liability is virtually conceded or not, relate most particularly to the ongoing monetary proposals or counter-proposals. The mediator in second, third, and fourth caucus rounds is making a determined effort to get the monetary negotiations going, to move the parties off their "winner's curse" opening, and to encourage one of the parties to make the first, credible significant move. Needless to say, depending upon the negotiating styles of the parties, this is not an easy process. Ostensible impasse usually occurs during these subsequent caucus rounds, which the mediator must be able to break.

You probably would guess that impasse is the bane of most mediators. Although mediators are trained how to avoid impasse, some live their lives dreading it. In my opinion, mediators should learn to live for impasse. After all, ostensible impasse will occur in every mediation, often several times, and if the parties could resolve their dispute by themselves a mediator would not be needed.

[A]ll declared impasses are not real impasses at all. Mediators become used to parties declaring "I will never" or "I will not." Mediators, not disrespectfully, learn to ignore or discount such declarations. The mediator must keep pushing through such barriers—after all, if the mediator does not try to, who will? If they use good form, mediators will push on without being coercive by constantly re-visiting issues and maximizing communication. When everyone else feels they are "wasting their time," mediators maintain optimism and encourage the parties to continue on. I cannot tell you how many times I have heard "we are wasting our time" in the seventh hour and had the case resolve in the ninth hour. Style, pace, tempo, and re-evaluation explain this. . . .

[T]he mediator must be especially careful in all caucuses to preserve confidentiality and make only authorized disclosures. . . . If a mediator walks into a second or third caucus with you and states "I know I shouldn't tell you this, but," you should consider terminating the session. If the mediator is divulging the other side's confidences, the mediator is probably divulging your confidences.

Good mediators are obsessively meticulous about maintaining confidential information, but mediators are, like everyone else, human beings and on rare occasion capable of mistakenly divulging a piece of confidential information. Should a mediator make such a mistake, she should visit immediately with the party whose confidential information she has inadvertently disseminated and admit the mistake. Most of the time, a party will appreciate such candor, admire the mediator's integrity, and wish to continue with the process. On the other hand, if a party's belief in the process or the mediator is fatally contaminated by the admission, the mediator should consider closing the session. Perhaps another mediator will have a better chance to succeed.

The mediation advocate should feel free to make suggestions like the ones below to the mediator in subsequent caucus rounds. The mediator is the captain of the ship and will make the final call, but she should always be interested in hearing any idea that will increase the chances for a successful resolution.

1. The advocate might suggest that the mediator might get together with the parties without the lawyers present.
2. The advocate might suggest a lawyer caucus to review a point of law with opposing counsel or to discuss a particularly sensitive issue.
3. The advocate might wish to have the mediator present a document or an appellate decision to opposing counsel.
4. The advocate might suggest that a more direct, expedited negotiation would be more helpful.

9. Mediation Advocates' Opinions — What to Tell

Confident mediators, sure of their own skills, may even ask the mediation advocates what they think will work or admit to being a little lost and in need of direction. Such confessions are signs of strength, not weakness. The mediator may be sensing that an unidentified issue or interest is blocking progress, but the only way she will find out is by asking for help. Many mediators have strong intuitive skills. Some mediators have uncanny intuitive skills. But mediators are not psychics and cannot read minds. [O]ne of the greatest tools in the mediator's toolbox is the same as the litigator's most important tool—the ability to ask the right question.

From the mediation advocate's point of view, especially in the later caucuses, a constant tension revolves around the issue of how much information to give away. In modern discovery times, very few secrets exist. But the other side may not have done his homework. Or the other side may have failed to identify a witness. Or the other side may have a real limitations problem of which it is unaware. Does the mediation advocate save such matters for trial? Or does the mediation advocate give such information out to increase the probabilities of resolution?

Because it is the mediator's job to move matters towards resolution, she will always want authority to disclose such information, and you should not blame a mediator for being persistent. But such a decision is clearly the mediation advocate's call. . . . So how does the mediation advocate make this call? I would suggest the following analysis:

1. Is the information likely to be discovered?
2. If a pleading or discovery deadline has been missed, how likely, if such information is disclosed, is your opponent to cure the problem?
3. Just how devastating is your opponent's error? Does the mistake blow your opponent out of the water? Seriously hurt your opponent? Or does the mistake create just a slight degree of discomfort?
4. How are the negotiations going? Has progress been made? If so, will disclosure push things to conclusion? Has no progress been made? If not, will such disclosure get things going?
5. Consider the timing of the disclosure. Do you make all the progress you can make and use the disclosure as your final blast? Do you set your depth charge early and use it as a basis of an aggressive negotiating posture?
6. Ask the mediator her impression of the information itself and the potential impact of such disclosure, not whether you should disclose the information. . . .

Returning to the monetary aspects of the subsequent caucus, the mediation advocate must accept one fundamental principle—each party bears responsibility for the proposals it makes and should not be surprised or angered by an in-kind counterproposal. In other words, minimal increases in an offer usually result in minimal decreases in a demand. Ultimately, if the parties continue to negotiate in such a fashion, a considerable gap will remain and an impasse may well occur. The mediator, as her role requires, is continuously attempting to get both sides to negotiate on a credible basis.

10. Lawyer Caucuses

Lawyer caucuses sometimes are called because a resolution is stalled by a legal issue. Of course, the mediator is not the judge and will not rule on a point of law. But the mediator may believe that counsel are not fully understanding each other's legal positions and that additional discussion would be beneficial. Typically "law talk" sails over clients' heads and sometimes mediation advocates feel they cannot fully discuss points of law in the initial group setting. A lawyer caucus provides a forum for a more expanded discussion of legal issues. Admittedly, a mediation that gets bogged down in extended legal debates may be doomed to failure, but in certain instances, focusing or clarifying the legal issues may be helpful. A lawyer caucus may be useful in breaking a negotiation impasse. . . .

In other circumstances, a mediation advocate may wish to suggest a lawyer caucus in order to have a private meeting with the mediator. Typically a mediation advocate may make such a request when she wishes to let the mediator know she is having a problem with her client. Mediators . . . must never come between an attorney and her client. But, . . . an attorney may believe her client has an exaggerated or incorrect view of the case and would like the mediator's assistance in helping the client better understand things. Often mediators are intuitively aware of such situations, but sometimes a mediator may be uncertain and will hold back so as not to interfere with the attorney-client relationship. A private meeting with the mediator permits the mediation advocate to explain fully those areas in which her client may need some additional reality checking.

I need to make one caveat about lawyer caucuses: Lawyer caucuses should be used sparingly and selectively, and should be brief. The dispute, of course belongs to the parties. Parties may become apprehensive and concerned if too many lawyer caucuses occur or if such caucuses take too long. The parties will wonder what is going on behind their backs and may begin to feel disenfranchised from the process.

11. Additional Collective Sessions

One of the inherent advantages of mediation is its flexibility. As the mediation evolves, a mediator must always be thinking of ways to maximize communication and thereby increase the chances of a successful resolution. The mediation process in fact improves communication and assists parties who had no desire or ability to understand each other's positions in engaging in a meaningful dialogue. Further the mediation process unearths interests, feelings, and motivations that may not have been known or expressed prior to the mediation.

As participants settle into and become comfortable with the mediation process, they may become more willing and able to have a helpful and constructive discussion later in the day. Additionally, a party may indicate to the mediator in caucus a real need to communicate something to the other side. The mediator may assist the party in considering the most constructive way of getting such a message across. Consider the following examples in which such subsequent collective meetings might be useful:

1. A mediator in private caucus learns that the plaintiff's primary motivation in filing a medical malpractice complaint was his feeling that the physician didn't care and never expressed regret. The mediator obtains authorization to tell that to the physician and her counsel. In caucus with the physician, the mediator learns that the physician, while denying liability, wanted to express regret, but did not do so out of fear that such expression would be misconstrued as an admission of liability. The mediator then may wish to reconvene the parties so that the physician, under the safety of mediation, may communicate regret and concern for the family.
2. In a partnership dispute, the mediator in caucus learns that a matter unrelated to the business issues was the real genesis of the current dispute. The mediator also learns that this matter has never been communicated to the other partner and the other partner has no idea that his former associate was angry about the matter. The mediator may decide to bring the parties back together so that such issue may be directly communicated and discussed.
3. The mediator may feel that both sides are not negotiating in a manner likely to obtain resolution, and therefore may elect to re-assemble all the participants in order to suggest that if negotiating progress is not made that an impasse will result and no resolution will be reached. In many instances, the participants will elect to continue the negotiations as opposed to declaring an impasse.

12. Memorandum of Agreement

Assuming the mediation results in a resolution of the dispute, a memorandum of agreement should be prepared and signed by all parties and their counsel. Most mediators have standard memorandum of agreement forms.

Of course, the memorandum of agreement is not the final release, and dismissal documents will be prepared by counsel after the mediation. The memorandum of agreement, however, should be clear and specific enough to avoid any post-mediation controversy as to what was agreed to at the mediation session.

In most cases, the memorandum of agreement will simply set out that the claimant will release any and all claims and dismiss the suit with prejudice in exchange for a specified sum of money. In complex business disputes, the memorandum of agreement will likely include numerous other specific items.

While the memorandum of agreement should be clear and specific, the parties should not attempt to create the final release documents at the session. In one mediation I conducted, an agreement almost fell apart because counsel attempted to draft the final agreement at the session.

I also think it is better practice for the mediator to draft the memorandum of agreement, as opposed to counsel for the parties. A memorandum of agreement drafted by an attorney for one of the parties may be subject to question. If counsel insist upon drafting the memorandum of agreement, all counsel should collaborate on its preparation. After all parties and counsel have executed the agreement, the mediator should provide copies to all participants.

3. James P. Groton, Getting the Mediation Process Started, in Alan E. Harris, Charles M. Sink & Randall W. Wulff, ADR: A Practical Guide to Resolve Construction Disputes 77-86 (1994)*

Why Should Disputants Use Mediation?

Mediation is a private, informal, voluntary procedure in which disputants are assisted by one or more neutral third parties in their efforts toward settlement of their controversy. It essentially represents an extension of the process of negotiation, the principal difference merely being the neutral third party. . . .

Mediation offers a number of advantages to disputants who are interested in resolving their differences:

- It is inexpensive. The cost of a mediation is usually an infinitesimal fraction of the expenses of full-blown litigation or even of arbitration.
- It requires a relatively small investment of time, and usually can be conducted promptly.
- It is non-binding. There is no risk in trying mediation. The mediator's only role is to try to guide the parties toward a settlement. The mediator has no authority to render a decision on the merits. Either party can withdraw at any time.
- Mediation is private and confidential. It obviates the risk that a binding, unfavorable precedent may be publicly established against a party.
- It is flexible, limited only by the imagination, ingenuity, and resourcefulness of the mediator and the parties; the resolution of the claims may well involve subjects extending beyond the limits of the original dispute.
- It focuses on common interests, with intent to achieve "win-win" solutions.
- Because they have participated mutually in the resolution process and they have created the solution, the parties generally have pride in the outcome they authored.
- Resolutions arrived at in this manner make it easier for the parties to continue to do business with each other.
- Mediation usually works. About 80% of cases submitted to mediation settle. . . .

Mediation facilitates communication; gets the necessary information into the process; gets the right people to the table; overcomes emotional blockages; puts the negotiation process back on track; focuses the parties on the problems; and helps the parties reassess their legal predictions.

The mediator can serve as a scapegoat who helps the parties detach from their entrenched positions; serves as a lightning rod; invents options; keeps the door open; presides over an agenda; documents agreements; and helps to implement the agreement.

Executives should approach dispute settlement with the same spirit that they bring to every other aspect of their business. Mediation puts disputes on an express track towards settlement, through the intervention of a third party. It supercharges the negotiations. Mediation can be particularly helpful when corporations want to expedite the resolution of their business disputes.

---

*Reprinted with permission.

What Cases Are Suitable for Mediation, and When Is a Case Ripe for Mediation?

Almost any dispute can be settled at some point by mediation, however, not every problem is ready immediately for resolution. For an effective mediation, the parties and counsel first should have a fairly good, common understanding of the basic facts.

If there are big gaps in either party's factual knowledge, the parties may be too much in the dark for fruitful negotiations. Accordingly, the actual mediation should not begin before the parties at least have initiated a process for obtaining this common background, by agreeing to exchange essential documents, or by asking a mediator to assist them in developing the basic facts. This is not to say that initiation of the mediation proceeding should be delayed; often early assistance from a mediator can help to resolve discovery disputes and to develop the foundational information.

If, despite a common knowledge of the facts, both parties still strongly hold diametrically opposed views about the impact of those facts, then some step may be necessary to inject an element of reality into the process before conventional mediation begins. The parties should consider trying a more evaluative process, such as obtaining a neutral advisory opinion, or setting up a mini-trial or non-binding arbitration, before proceeding with mediation.

In a multi-party case, the number of parties and a disparity of interests can act as obstacles to mediation. However, depending upon the nature of the claims, this may be more of a case management problem than a permanent deterrent to mediation. With proper management by a mediator, mutual interests among groups of parties can be identified. Various issues can be sorted out and mediated, conceivably by a series of mediators. If a party cannot fund a settlement, mediation may appear pointless. However, the goal of some mediations may be merely to agree on liability and have a party admit a debt.

Two relatively rare situations make mediation pointless. If one side approaches a mediation only as an attempt at discovery or to cause delay, that ultimately will sabotage the process. The other clear case in which mediation is not feasible arises from a compelling need to establish a binding legal precedent. . . .

How do You Get Disputing Parties into the Mediation Process?

The most important ingredient in mediation is getting parties to the negotiating table. Mediation cannot occur unless both parties have agreed to try it. This first and most important hurdle can be accomplished in a variety of ways.

Including a mediation clause in a business agreement. The simplest, most direct, and most common way to initiate mediation is for the parties, at the inception of their transaction or business agreement, to agree that any dispute arising out of the business relationship that cannot be resolved, upon the request of either party, will be submitted in good faith to the mediation process. Agreements of this sort are becoming more common in the construction industry. In 1987 the American Institute of Architects (AIA) proposed as optional language for its most commonly-used standard forms of agreement, a clause by which the parties agree to mediate, before resorting to arbitration or any other binding form of dispute resolution. In recent years, all Associated General Contractors' (AGC) documents have included a similar agreement. The joint AIA-AGC Construction Management document issued in 1992 contains such a clause as a part of the basic form, and the AIA has undertaken to include mediation as a part of all future agreements which it issues.

Mutual pledges to mediate. There is a growing movement to encourage businesses, as a matter of company policy, to pledge that if they ever become involved in a dispute with another organization which has signed the same agreement, they will undertake to resolve the problem by mediation before resorting to binding dispute resolution procedures. The recent prevalence of such pledges provides a matrix of cooperation which is conducive to the mutual submission of disputes to mediation.

A policy or institutionalized commitment to mediate. Many companies and organizations simply have declared as a realistic aspect of organizational policy that whenever they are involved in a dispute, they first will seek to negotiate and mediate any disputes. The U.S. Army Corps of Engineers, probably the country's largest construction contractor, forthrightly has declared such an official principle. Even where only one party has adopted a mediation program, the other side, without loss of face, can say it wishes to take advantage of this general policy. In any event, the party that already has adopted such a course of action, without any sign of weakness, can invite the other side to participate in mediation.

The three approaches mentioned above have the advantage of avoiding a problem which frequently impedes even the most tentative efforts toward resolving existing disputes, that is: the perception among many people that the first party to suggest mediation automatically is admitting weakness. [Remember] . . . John F. Kennedy's aphorism, made in a somewhat different context: "Civility is not a sign of weakness. . . . let us never negotiate out of fear, but let us never fear to negotiate."

Direct contact between lawyers. Lawyers for opposing parties have many opportunities to communicate, and it should be relatively easy for one attorney to suggest that, despite both lawyers' confidence in their respective cases, there is always the possibility that they have overlooked something and perhaps it would be useful to both sides to have an impartial mediator help to explore their differences.

Encouraging a reluctant client. Sometimes a lawyer representing an angry client may fear that a suggestion of mediation may cause the client to question the attorney's zeal. In such a situation, even if there is not yet a specific ethical requirement that lawyers make their clients aware of the availability of alternative methods of dispute resolution, attorneys nevertheless should inform their clients that it is a part of their professional obligation to consider with the client the most cost-effective means of dispute resolution available. Lawyers should educate their clients about the availability of mediation as an inexpensive method of dispute resolution which has virtually no risks. This approach would enable a lawyer to discuss frankly with the client the advantages of mediation.

Indirect approach to the other party. Any number of ways exist to suggest mediation without either party carrying the perceived burden of having been the first to suggest it. For example, either party may encourage a third person to make a suggestion to both or all of them that they should try mediation before resorting to a more expensive method of dispute resolution. This third person could be another participant in the construction project, or a representative of a professional or business association to which both disputants belong. If the dispute has gone to arbitration, the American Arbitration Association, as a matter of established policy, will contact both sides and offer mediation facilitated by the AAA as an alternative, without any additional cost. This may be accelerated simply by confidentially asking the AAA case administrator to make such a suggestion to both parties. If the case already is in litigation, many courts have institutionalized programs for referring cases to mediation.

Similarly, an increasing number of statutes require disputants in certain fields first to submit their claims to mediation or conciliation of some kind.

Direct contact between clients. Often disputants have their own channels for communicating with each other, and it may be feasible for one party to mention to the other that although he or she is confident about the case, nevertheless both sides are incurring considerable legal expense, and it might be good business for both of them to consider some less expensive resolution than litigation.

Pre-mediation conference. If one party forthrightly wants to mediate, but the other side is less willing or is less informed about the availability and advantages of mediation and therefore is reluctant to enter into the process, a "premediation" process may help break the ice. In pre-mediation, one side (or both) hires a neutral simply to provide information about the characteristics and advantages of mediation, and to help the parties to decide whether it would be useful in resolution of the dispute. Often the neutral can be the person who contacts the other side and convenes the parties. At a pre-mediation conference, the neutral can familiarize the parties with how the process works, how to prepare for mediation, the timing of mediation, and the function of a mediator. Such a conference often establishes the confidence of both parties not only in the concept of mediation, but also in this particular neutral.

One party underwriting some costs of mediation. Sometimes a party who wants to mediate may try to encourage the other side to enter into mediation by offering to underwrite some or all of the costs. For example, a party may say: "I have such confidence in the process of mediation as a cost-effective way to achieve an agreed upon resolution of disputes, that I am willing to gamble the costs of initiating a mediation, just to get both of us to the negotiating table to see whether there is a potential for constructive resolution of the dispute." Perhaps such an offer would provide for a joint evaluation after a certain number of hours as to whether to proceed with the mediation on an equally shared basis. Or, one party could agree to pay all of the mediation expenses unless the mediation produced a settlement, in which case the parties would share the costs. . . .

How Do You Agree on the Ground Rules for the Mediation?

Because the process is informal and non-binding, the rules for a . . . mediation can accommodate the parties' specific requirements (such as location or timing) and need not be rigid. A pre-existing mediation provision typically will specify a set of ground rules. . . . If there has been no such pre-dispute agreement, then the parties must adopt some procedures. The AAA Construction Industry Mediation Rules have become so commonly accepted that they usually are selected. Alternatively, the disputants could ask the mediator to suggest or prescribe a simple set of ground rules.

How Do You Agree on Who Should Be Present at the Mediation?

In all cases, the parties or their counsel should discuss in advance with the mediator who should be present at the mediation proceedings. Because mediation is a negotiation process which is entirely consensual, the parties themselves absolutely must be present, regardless of whether they are represented by counsel. Whether lawyers should attend depends on the degree of sophistication and the preferences of the parties themselves. If both sides have experienced and articulate executives present, it may not be necessary to bring lawyers to the mediation proceeding. In some instances, the absence of lawyers can help lower the degree of controversy and actually facilitate the negotiations. In any event, ground rules should be established so that each party knows in advance whether the other side proposes to bring a lawyer.

Consideration also should be given to bringing to the mediation hearing representatives who are not necessarily decision makers, but who might be able to contribute fresh ideas about innovative settlement possibilities, and who might suggest ways in which the parties can preserve a continued relationship after a settlement of the immediate dispute.

The parties and the mediator also should consider whether expert witnesses will facilitate the proceedings. Sometimes expert witnesses can help with difficult technical questions. If the experts' opinions are likely to be totally opposed to each other, the mediator and the parties should consider arranging for the simultaneous appearance and questioning of the opposing experts by both the mediator and the parties, to see where their opinions agree, and what the differences are. Typically, fact witnesses rarely help in a mediation.

D. Strategies for Success in Mediation

1. Eric Galton, Representing Clients in Mediation 69-72 (1994)*

Preparing the Client For Mediation

[Y]ou would never permit your client to sit for a deposition without adequate preparation. Yet I routinely preside over mediations in which clients have been prepared badly or not at all. If the goal of the mediation is a final resolution of the dispute, the mediation is one of the three most important aspects of the litigation process, along with the deposition and trial. As such, a client must be fully and completely prepared. I would envision that you would meet with your client the day before (or a few days before) the mediation, have an extended conference to prepare for the mediation, and cover the following topics:

1. Who the mediator is, the mediator's background, and the mediator's practice experience.
2. The personality of the mediator, if you know him.
3. Where and when the mediation will be held.
4. Your best guess as to how long the mediation will last.
5. Who will be attending the mediation and for what purpose.
6. The mediator's role. Include the following:
   (a) The mediator is impartial/neutral and will remain so throughout.
   (b) The mediator is not the judge or jury and will not render a decision or judgment.
   (c) The mediator is attempting to facilitate a discussion geared towards a final resolution.
   (d) Mediation is binding only if the parties reach a final agreement. If not, the parties proceed with the litigation.
   (e) The mediation, by statute or written agreement, is a confidential proceeding.
   (f) The mediator, because of confidentiality, may never be a witness.
   (g) The mediator will play devil's advocate in separate caucus and will have the parties identify their strengths and weaknesses.

---

*Reprinted with permission.

7. The mediation process. In this regard, explain and outline the following:
   (a) The mediator's introduction.
   (b) The lawyers' opening statement.
   (c) The initial separate caucus.
   (d) Subsequent caucuses.
   (e) Lawyer caucuses.
   (f) Subsequent collaborative sessions.
   (g) The memorandum of agreement.
8. The lawyer's role at mediation. Include the following:
   (a) Your role is different than your role will be at trial.
   (b) You will not be objecting to evidence.
   (c) You will not be putting on your full case or even a large part of your case.
   (d) You will present an opening statement, which will be aimed at getting a favorable resolution for your client.
   (e) You will assist your client and the mediator with the negotiations.
   (f) You will participate in caucus in an objective strength/weakness analysis.
   (g) You will listen to what is said at mediation for purposes of any re-evaluation.
   (h) You will talk openly and candidly with the mediator in caucus.
   (i) You will make all decisions as to what is disclosed at mediation.
   (j) You understand the dispute belongs to the client.
   (k) You will permit the client to make the final decision, subject to your advice and counsel.
   (l) Your role, by its very nature, will be much more conciliatory than it would be at trial.
   (m) You may express understanding or empathy with the other side in order to effectuate a positive resolution. Such understanding does not mean agreement and you are not selling out your client.
   (n) If a resolution is reached, you will assist with the preparation of the memorandum of agreement.
   (o) You may choose to avoid sensitive issues that may adversely affect the chances of resolution.
   (p) Your approach may well be different at trial if a resolution is not reached.
   (q) You will be respectful towards the mediator and the process.
9. The client's role at mediation. Include the following:
   (a) The client is there to listen.
   (b) The client is there to evaluate and re-evaluate his case.
   (c) The client is there to participate directly in the negotiations and discussions.
   (d) At the request of the mediator, the client may be asked to make a statement in the collective session. If so, the client should prepare his remarks and express his feelings, but attempt to do so in the most constructive fashion.
   (e) In separate caucus and because of the confidentiality of the process, the client should speak freely and openly to the mediator.
   (f) The client should expect and want the mediator to play devil's advocate in separate caucus. The client should desire an objective review and analysis and not consider it to be a breach of neutrality.

(g) If an agreement is reached, a memorandum of agreement that will be reviewed by the client will be prepared and executed.

(h) The client should enter the mediation process with an open mind and give the process a chance to work.

Client preparation for mediation that covers these topics ensures several things. First, the client will be more comfortable with the mediation process. Second, the client will understand, appreciate, and be more comfortable with the mediator's role. Third, because the client understands the process, the client will be a better, more helpful participant. Finally, a case is more likely to resolve if the client is fully and completely prepared.

2. Stephen P. Morrell & William Baker, Succeeding in Mediation, in Alan E. Hanes, Charles M. Sink & Randall W. Wulff 101-114 ADR: A Practical Guide to Resolve Construction Disputes (1994)*

Introduction

This chapter reviews strategies and techniques for succeeding at a mediation conference. Topics include fact exchanges, caucusing (with an emphasis on negotiations), and procedures for finalizing settlements.

What is "success" in the context of mediation? Success is "closing" the "sale" of an economically acceptable settlement. It is achieved by reaching a bargain that cannot be refused because the alternative, usually litigation, ultimately would provide no better result. Settlements are sold by convincing the other parties to the mediation that they will win by accepting the proposed settlement, and may lose if they reject it.

An Overview of the Mediation Conference

A mediation conference usually starts with a discussion or exchange of facts underlying the matter in dispute. This initial meeting for fact exchanges is attended by the mediator, decision makers (persons with authority to settle) their lawyers or other advocates, and any witnesses. Thereafter, the mediator meets privately or "caucuses" with each side to discuss positions candidly, assessing strengths, weaknesses, and offers. These caucusing sessions should generate movement to the point where the parties' positions converge, at which time the mediator will call for a joint meeting, announce a settlement, and have the parties confirm the settlement in writing. . . .

How then, can a party obtain the consent of its adversaries to a proposed settlement? Much depends on overcoming emotional obstacles to settlement. Decision makers regularly reject good settlements for solely emotional reasons, notwithstanding sound financial considerations dictating the contrary. For example, settlements sometimes are rejected from animosity, at other times for principle ("Millions for defense, but not a cent for tribute"). Such "principle" often is animosity cloaked in rhetoric. Whatever the reason, to be successful at mediation, a party must address the emotional needs of the adversaries.

Exchanging Facts

Typically, the initial exchange of facts includes an opening statement from each party, fol-

---

*Reprinted with permission.

lowed by a more detailed discussion of the facts in dispute. Because this initial exchange sets the tone, it is extremely important to the success of the mediation.

The first issue to be considered is the question: "What are the issues in dispute?" In a surprising number of cases (including those with experienced counsel), the parties do not have a clear understanding of the issues. The mediator addresses this concern by working to identify issues of real consequence to the resolution of the dispute. As they are identified, the parties are directed to focus on the matters that really make a difference.

A primary additional function of a fact exchange is dissemination of enough information to permit decision makers to analyze the merits of their own positions. A decision maker is less likely to agree to a settlement if he or she believes that all the facts have not been sufficiently considered and therefore the issue has not been evaluated objectively.

Unlike exchanges in trial, a fact exchange at a mediation conference is conducted in a non-adversarial environment, one that should not be perceived as hostile or threatening. Mediators almost invariably start by telling the parties that everything they say is off the record and cannot be used for any purpose outside the mediation conference. The parties should feel free to speak openly, which will increase the chances that all significant facts will be disclosed and considered. The mediator will facilitate the free exchange by keeping a tight rein on the proceedings. Parties are allowed to speak freely, but only one at a time and only when it is their turn. The mediator will immediately cut off any objectionable conduct, such as hostile questions or interruptions.

It is important, at the initial meeting, to identify facts that are not in dispute. This saves time, and allows the mediator to obtain early "agreements" from the parties concerning some matters. These agreements help to create goodwill by conditioning the parties to the act of agreeing. Later, when they grapple with more difficult issues, the goodwill may help. A full exploration of the facts also allows the parties to feel that they have had their "day in court", with someone who listens sympathetically to their stories. Emotions vented at the beginning of the process may eliminate impediments to agreement later.

Success at mediation comes from recognizing the importance of practical and psychological aspects of factual communication. All conduct is directed to creating the open, non-hostile atmosphere which facilitates the free flow of information. In this context, each side should be prepared to take the time necessary to fully complete the process, without rushing it. Only by devoting time can the parties obtain the maximum practical (fact gathering) and psychological (elimination of emotional obstacles) benefits of the exchange.

Party Objectives

To convince the opposition of the merits of one's case is a primary objective in the initial meeting. The opponents probably have not heard a comprehensive recitation of the facts and law in support of the "other side's" case. This meeting to exchange "facts" represents a unique chance to talk directly to the adversary and to bypass lawyers or other representatives. Those who have been through the procedure know how effective it can be in imparting to opposing decision makers the real nature of the dispute.

Pressure for settlement is another objective of the fact exchange. In making their presentations, each party should demonstrate full commitment to prosecute or defend the case if the mediation fails. The lawyer for each side should appear as a skillful advocate who will be a force to be reckoned with if the matter goes to trial. This should be done, however, within the context of a climate of cooperation and mutual respect. A contentious atmosphere only angers opposing parties and encourages them to be stubborn and unwilling to settle.

Who Presents the Facts: Decision Maker or Witnesses?

In preparing for a fact exchange one of the first questions which must be addressed is who will present the facts to support the case. Will it be the attorney or decision maker only, or will witnesses be used? The answer, as lawyers like to say, is "it depends."

The attorney may prefer to do all the talking, because this will enable him or her to control tightly which facts and legal arguments are presented. Such exclusive control avoids the risks of inadvertently exposing an unfavorable fact and of using a poor witness. The disadvantage is that the strategy may be perceived as impeding the free flow of information. This may move the other parties to be less candid.

A decision maker may want to present his or her own case even though represented by an attorney. This might work if the speaker is articulate, straightforward, and dispassionate. A decision maker with a forceful personality may be able to convince opposing parties of the need to make a serious offer. But if the issues are more legal than factual, the attorney should lead.

Use of percipient and expert witnesses should be considered seriously. Opposing decision makers may view an attorney's presentation as "lawyer talk" a good line, but far from the whole story. On the other hand, testimony by credible witnesses, who would testify if the matter goes to trial, can be very effective in convincing opposing decision makers of the merits of their opponent's case. They know most cases stand or fall on such testimony.

One consideration in deciding whether to use witnesses is the complexity of the case. In a simple case, an attorney or other advocate can marshal the facts easily. In a complex case (particularly where the amount at issue is small), it may be more cost-effective to have a percipient witness explain the facts, rather than for an attorney to spend hours (or, more likely, days) learning all the details. This is especially true in cases involving specialized knowledge or training. While the lawyer may be able to credibly present the basics of the matter, he or she will have difficulty responding to unanticipated technical questions. Using critical expert witnesses assures that technical matters will be fully addressed.

Cost is the final consideration. If the parties are trying to save money by mediating, the use of several witnesses may defeat the purpose, when others can summarize their information. However, since the case is likely to settle at the mediation, money spent on making a credible and convincing fact presentation will maximize the chances of getting a favorable result.

The Presentation

Often, the exact format for fact exchanges and presentations is determined by the mediator at the mediation conference. For example, if several matters are disputed, the mediator may decide at the conference to conduct a series of mini-mediations, in which each issue is to be presented and negotiated separately, starting with the matters considered easiest to resolve, and working through the more difficult ones.

Since there are no rules governing fact exchanges and each case is different, a party determines how to present the facts and law on a case-by-case basis, always working within the framework established by the mediator. Each party is free to be creative in conveying the story clearly, accurately, and persuasively.

Generally, the best presentations are narratives, as simple and straightforward as possible. The narrative can be enhanced by well-organized use of witnesses and exhibits. In one very effective format, the attorney starts with a short opening statement, continues with a detailed narration of the dispute: thoroughly prepared witnesses, both expert and lay, take over the lawyer's narrative at critical points, and then give the lead back to the attorney, to keep the flow and to state a conclusion. During the presentation, the attorney is free to ask questions (if appropriate, calling for a narrative-type answer) of his or her witnesses, to help clarify their presentations. Exhibits should be presented and addressed at appropriate points. Overhead projectors, charts, photographs, models, or a video can be quite convincing, if carefully prepared and presented.

Questioning or Engaging in a Dialogue with Opposing Parties

When listening to an adversary's presentation, a party inevitably will have a burning question which must be answered for full understanding of the dispute (or to demonstrate the weakness of the other party's position). Depending on how they are handled, questions or dialogues can promote or disrupt the mediation process. They disrupt when questions or comments are perceived as argumentative or breaking the free flow of information, and the mediator will prohibit any questioning or commentary which is perceived as disruptive. On the other hand, engaging in a dialogue or asking questions can be helpful in furthering understanding of the dispute, if comments and questions are handled with tact. One favored approach is to make note of any points or concerns as they arise, but hold them until completion of the opposing presentation. They then can be addressed, with the mediator's consent (and perhaps through the mediator), to the adverse party.

Questions and commentary may reduce emotional obstacles to settlement. This is achieved by asking or talking in a manner that shows respect for the other party and some understanding of that party's position. The adversary then will begin to feel that progress is being made, sensing that other parties understand, although don't necessarily agree.

Because a mediation conference often is the first face-to-face meeting of the parties, it may be the first time that one party learns of an alleged fact that is critical to the adversary's case. Unfortunately, lack of advance knowledge will hinder full exploration of the underlying dispute during the fact exchange meeting. Postponing the mediation conference to investigate the new matter is counterproductive because, among other things, it disrupts the psychological impetus toward settlement that develops in an uninterrupted mediation. When a critical allegation arises for the first time at the conference, the only practical response is to work around it and do a quick fact investigation, either by telephone during a break or between sessions, if the mediation takes more than one day.

Because of its frequency, this problem should be anticipated by anyone who intends to participate in a mediation. Persons with background knowledge, who for tactical reasons will not be attending the conference, should be available by telephone for consultation. Their accessibility will allow an unanticipated matter to be investigated quickly and immediately addressed. Prompt investigation maintains the momentum toward settlement.

Acrimonious or Nonproductive Exchanges

Mediation works, in part, because it creates a psychological environment conducive to settlement. In theory, in being less combative and more cooperative, the parties will develop a sense of trust and mutual respect which will allow them to work toward the common goal of settlement.

Because of experiences giving rise to the dispute or legal proceedings, the parties and their advocates may have developed bitter feelings toward one another. Even if there is no acrimony, some advocates treat mediation as an adversarial proceeding because they lack familiarity with the more cooperative process. Parties and their advocates deal with this in the first instance by making sure that they refrain from doing or saying things that might antagonize adversaries or members of the negotiating teams. Careful thought should be given to how sensitive areas can be discussed in a way that will not anger others. Hotheads should be left at the office even if they are important witnesses. The goal is to convince both adversaries that the other side is considerate and reasonable (if possible, likeable), so they will feel good about working toward a resolution. The importance of tact and interpersonal skills cannot be overstated.

Aside from curbing their own antagonistic impulses, each party and advocate may have to deal with undesirable behavior by adverse decision makers, witnesses, or attorneys. The best approach is to avoid responding in kind. Each side should acknowledge an understanding of the adversaries' points of view. This restraint will help all parties to move beyond emotion to a more rational approach to settlement. After all, more often than not, settlement is the most rational resolution of a dispute.

Caucusing

After the initial fact exchange, the mediator will meet privately, or "caucus," with each party, to generate movement toward a settlement. . . . [I]n an effort to convince the parties to be candid the mediator will advise them that he or she will not disclose caucus discussions unless authorized to do so. While caucusing, the mediator will apply pressure to one or more parties, to obtain enough concessions to reach a settlement. To this end, the parties will be required to re-evaluate their positions in view of any perceived weaknesses. The mediator also will explore alternative remedies (such as the value of monetary payment versus continuing a business relationship). Finally, the mediator will convey most offers and counteroffers, as opposed to having the parties communicate them directly to each other. Caucusing typically takes a number of rounds with each party, and may be broken up by joint caucusing or negotiating sessions attended by more than one, if not all, of the parties.

Pre-Mediation Preparation for Negotiating and Caucusing

To negotiate effectively, a party should develop a negotiating strategy before starting the mediation conference. Attending the conference without a plan or improvising may result in making unnecessary or untimely concessions. In advance, each party should determine a "real bottom line." This figure represents the farthest that the party can go: the highest amount that can be paid, or the lowest amount to be accepted.

Each party also should prepare an estimate of the adversaries' bottom lines. To develop this, the party must evaluate the case from the points of view of the adversary. For instance, in a construction case, a party might consider the following factors: Is an adversary busy, so that tying up key personnel in litigation would interfere with business activities? Is an adversary in a weak financial condition, needing cash immediately and unable to afford extensive litigation? How much of the claim is for out-of-pocket costs (that is, labor and materials) and how much is for "soft" costs (that is, fixed overhead and profit)? A skillful and experienced negotiator often can predict accurately how far an opposing party would be willing to go to settle.

After the bottom lines are determined and estimated, the negotiating goal should be set: that is, the figure to seek during negotiations. Typically, this will exceed the bottom line, but will remain within the range of what is economically acceptable and realistic based on the estimate of the adversary's bottom lines. The amount of the initial offer should be set after the beginning of caucusing. Each party also should develop a plan for the timing and amounts of concessions to be made when moving from the initial offer to the negotiating goal.

The negotiating plan should be discussed fully with, and agreed upon by all, members of the negotiating team. Although the plan undoubtedly will change during the mediation conference, team knowledge of a general plan will minimize the chance of unnecessary or untimely concessions. The team will be better able to structure negotiations when everyone understands what the party wants and expects to achieve.

Negotiating Through Caucus

In the first round of caucuses, the parties should focus on (a) telling the mediator about the merits of the dispute; (b) discussing alternative remedies; and (c) examining the strengths and weaknesses of each party's case. At this stage, formulating offers and counteroffers should not be a primary concern.

Telling the mediator what a party actually thinks (as opposed to simply reiterating an "official" position) will allow the mediator to determine, among other things, how far apart the parties are. Often, they are much closer than their "official" positions would indicate, so that only small compromises are needed. Knowing true positions will permit the mediator, in subsequent caucuses, to move toward those positions, a necessary step in obtaining a settlement.

Discussing alternative remedies assists the mediator in developing a settlement. For instance, does one of the parties just want out of the contract? Or does one of the parties just want the problem fixed? From the answers to these questions, the mediator may conclude that the desire for money is not the motive. The mediator then may be able to fashion a settlement that both meets the needs of the parties and is obtained more easily because it involves little or no money.

Examining strengths and weaknesses is critical to the function of helping the parties to evaluate their cases realistically. For that reason, all weaknesses of its adversaries' cases should be set before the mediator by the party in caucus. This will allow the mediator, when caucusing with the other side, to expose weaknesses under a "bright, white light," and may result in appropriate softening of positions.

Should a party disclose to the mediator weaknesses of that party's own case? The authors believe so. No real risk arises because the mediator is sworn to secrecy and, absent the party's consent, will not disclose such information to adversaries. And there is a benefit. The mediator can evaluate a position to determine if it needs to be adjusted. This "reality check" may convince the party, upon further reflection, that the position is untenable. Surely it is better to make a reality adjustment at the mediation conference than to have a judge or jury make it.

It generally is not a good idea to start talking dollars and cents in the first round of caucuses. The matter of offers and counteroffers should be approached slowly and delicately because, if not handled properly, it could cause the parties to prematurely harden their positions. After talking with all parties, the mediator is in the best position to determine the optimal time for making monetary offers:

1. When the socializing seems to be over or repetitive.
2. When the facts are clear.
3. When all possible stipulations have been made.
4. When the mediator senses the parties are anxious to get moving.

Each party will be asked to construct a rationale for the first offer. The decision makers should be confident that there are sound reasons for their offer, and should not feel that they are just throwing out a dollar figure. After each initial offer is conveyed to the other side, unless the offers overlap, the most difficult part of the process begins. It is during this stage that the parties must generate enough movement from their adversaries to secure an acceptable settlement.

The key to negotiations after the first offers is: patience, patience, patience. It takes time, often big chunks of it, to generate enough movement for the parties to reach a settlement. Negotiating for a better amount, each party will hold out as long as possible before making the bottom-line offer.

At this stage, what will generate the requisite movement? While numerous answers come to mind, the authors believe the primary focus of caucus discussions, after the initial round of offers is made and rejected, should be on facts underlying the dispute. Facts generally are the best ammunition for convincing adversaries to settle, because they usually determine the outcome of the case if it does not settle. . . .

What if the facts do not support one's case, or, if they do, what if arguments based on fact are not achieving the desired result? In this event, the authors suggest urging a review of the following additional matters in caucusing sessions with adversaries:

- Costs unrelated to the merits, such as the expenses the parties might not recover even if they win at trial. What are the legal fees of litigation? What is the value of the time of company personnel involved in preparing for and participating in trial? . . .
- The benefit of getting money today as opposed to waiting several years (or longer in the event of an appeal) if the matter is adjudicated. The funds offered certainly could be put to good use for current business opportunities. Can a party really afford to lose those business opportunities?
- The relative economic strengths of the parties. One party may be able to afford extensive litigation regardless of the cost, while another party may not have the resources to reach or survive the ultimate battle.
- Non-traditional remedies. For example, if the parties can reach agreement on the major dispute over a delay damage claim, they may be willing to submit minor disputes regarding pricing of extra work to arbitration. In a case involving defective construction, the parties might agree to fix the problem within a specified period of time and if the repair is successful, consider the dispute resolved. . . .
- The necessity of making a realistic compromise offer to obtain similar concessions from the other parties to the mediation.
- The risk in giving the matter to a judge or jury for decision. How will a jury understand whether the contractor's inability to fit the mechanical systems into the ceiling space

> was the result of poor coordination among the trades or poorly coordinated structural, architectural, and mechanical drawings? Litigation is like rolling dice, you never know what is going to happen. A party should limit its risk by making some concessions that take into consideration this element of chance. . . .

In the final analysis, whether a party succeeds at the caucusing stage depends on negotiating skills, the nature of the case, and the personalities of the decision makers and their advocates.

Reducing Agreements to Writing

It is quite typical for a mediation conference to run late into the night, with an oral settlement reached at the eleventh hour. As much as the parties would like to call it a day, a mediation is not a success until all matters agreed upon are confirmed in writing.

The parties should not leave the mediation conference without a binding written settlement agreement, if possible. The conclusion of the mediation conference is psychologically the best time to finalize a settlement. Goodwill between the parties is maximum then. After the parties leave the conference, the goodwill dissipates rapidly. Moreover, decision makers often are criticized by their associates back at the office, who weren't present at the mediation conference and can't understand the basis of the proposed settlement. A settlement agreement signed at the conference usually is handwritten by the mediator, the neutral party. This minimizes the chances that the parties will get into an argument about perceived fairness of the agreement, as having been drafted by one party or its attorney.

A party should prepare for settlement by bringing to the conference a short written checklist of terms to be included in any settlement agreement. To minimize any friction which might jeopardize the settlement, all proposed terms should be as evenhanded as possible. Additionally, because any term is a potential dealbreaker, the checklist should contain as few terms as possible.

It may not be possible to obtain a final, written settlement agreement at the conference. Occasionally, decision makers do not have the authority to execute a settlement agreement. [A] large corporation or public agency usually requires board approval of settlements. Also, a party might insist on a formal agreement that is much more detailed than could reasonably be prepared at a mediation conference.

Even if it is not possible to execute a binding settlement agreement at the conference, the parties should not leave without a written confirmation of the terms. If nothing else, this confirms that there has been an actual meeting of minds on those issues described and helps to insure that all significant areas have been addressed. More importantly, executing such a document at the mediation conference will create psychological pressure which deters later reneging on the deal. To maximize such deterrence, the following items should be considered for a "non-binding settlement agreement" to be signed by all parties attending a mediation conference:

- A statement of all matters upon which the parties have agreed, conditionally or otherwise.
- A statement of all conditions (for instance, approval by a board of directors) which must be performed to finalize the settlement and a schedule of deadlines. The "non-binding settlement agreement" should be drafted so that performance of the conditions will result in a binding agreement without additional writing. . . .

- A statement that the responsible person will exercise his or her best efforts to insure that the settlement is finalized. If approvals are necessary, decision makers should represent that they will recommend the proposed settlement.

3. Tom Arnold, *Twenty Common Errors in Mediation Advocacy*, ADR TODAY, Spring 1995, at 2*

Advocacy in mediation tends to be poor to unsophisticated. Trial lawyers often don't know how they foul their own nest or miss important persuasions. And so I here present a quickie list of twenty common errors in mediation advocacy.

1. Wrong Client in the Room

CEOs settle a strikingly larger percentage of cases than any VP and/or house counsel or other agent. Why? Any lesser agent than the CEO, even with explicit "authority," but who is to some degree concerned about review or criticism back at the office by a constituency which was not a participant in the give and take of the mediation, is not the best "client" to settle the case. That may be the best "client" rep available, but it is not the best that exists. No more so than an aggressive, critical, unforgiving, hot head, bellicosely self-righteous personality.

An interesting mix of personality traits, charity towards others and their mistakes, conciliatory attitude, creativity, flexibility, and authority with immunity from fear of criticism by a constituency, is the preferred client representative for a mediation. Of course she should know the subject. But when feasible, be biased against a corporate representative who will inherently be defending her own actions.

2. Wrong Lawyer in the Room

First, some trial lawyers will not prepare themselves or their client for good mediation advocacy. In the small case this is understandable. The process can tolerate a lot of unpreparedness when it must, as in small cases.

Second, many of the better trial lawyers are so arrogantly confident that they can persuade a jury of anything, anything at all (after all, they've done it before), and are so militant of personality, that they cannot be sensitive to the importance of preserving relationships or the exorbitant costs and emotional drain of litigation. Why no sensitivity? Because they can smell a "win" in the court room, and that is what drives them.

[O]n average, it could be that, if reasonable compromise of good faith differences is the business goal, transaction lawyers are on average better mediation counsel than some of the most successful jury trial lawyers. The transaction lawyer's lack of confidence in what they can do in the court room contributes to a willingness to compromise and get a disposal of the dispute quickly and cheaply.

At the least, parties should look for a sensitive, understanding personality, no matter his job experience. Not a limp wet rag, lest he give away the store; even so, prefer an intelligent, flexible and understanding personality who will do his homework, over inflexible arrogance.

---

*Reprinted with permission.

3. Wrong Mediator in the Room

Some mediators bring nothing to the table but the loan of their conference room. Some arrogantly determine their view of the case and urge the parties to accept that view without exploring likely win-win alternatives.

There is a continuum of mediation styles, continuum from the mediator focusing only on narrowly defined issues and those who are totally facilitative, to those whose imagination brings in a broad scope of party interests and those who fully evaluate the case and become directive of the parties rather than merely facilitative. The best mediators move around in the continuums from narrow to broad, from purely facilitative to evaluative and somewhat directive and back again—to fit the mediation to the case and the parties before them.

But while mediators who are masters of the process can render valuable services in any subject matter, whether they know the subject or not, many cases or the parties involved need an expert's suggestive evaluation, want a directive mediator, need someone experienced in the technology, the finances of the business, or the law that is in issue, need a person to help cast lights and shadows on the merits of the case and alternative settlements. Its tough to know and evaluate a mediator and fit the choice of mediator to your case. It may be impossible. But the wrong mediator may fail to get a settlement another mediator might have effectively contributed to.

4. Wrong Case

Contrary to popular thought, almost every type of case from antitrust or patent infringement to unfair competition and employment disputes, is a likely candidate for mediation — mediation which, unlike arbitration, is an essentially safe procedure costing usually no more than perhaps two or three days of depositions of an expert.

But some few cases don't fit the mold. It is not the legal topic (tax law, professional malpractice, etc.) which renders mediation inapposite; it is the value that is not on the table. By way of example: a case where the franchisor, for reasons not related to the case at hand, critically needs a legal precedent by way of construction of a clause found in 3,000 franchise contracts, or a binding legal precedent construing some statute her way, is an unlikely case for mediation settlement. Why? Because the major value one party seeks and essentially must have is not on the table in the mediation room. Any case where major value is involved in the precedent generated, should be looked at carefully as a case where mediation likely is inapposite.

5. Omitting the Client Prep

For good mediation client's need to know and understand a good deal about the mediation process and the particular dispute.

a. the process;
b. what his own best interests are by contrast with his legal or postured positions (often neither the client nor the lawyer have ever really explored the clients true interests);
c. the variety of options and possible alternative arrangements that might settle the case;

d. the strengths and weaknesses of their own case, based on objective independent standards of evaluation;
e. realism as to what may be seen as fair under the circumstances;
f. the importance of apology and empathy;
g. the importance of open-minded listening and reevaluation;
h. their own BATNA and WATNA;
i. the adversary's BATNA and WATNA;
j. the law and strategies and obligations of confidence and disclosures of confidential information;
k. "the dance" (discussed below);
l. the importance of not poisoning the well from which they must drink in order to get a settlement;
m. in most cases, how to make a strong and sympathetic opening statement to the other party with very little, if any, lawyer participation; and
n. the answers to the types of questions the mediator is likely to ask .

Sadly, counsel rarely prepare their clients well for the process Better preparation produces more and better settlements.

6. Failure to Use Advocacy Tools Effectively

Advocacy includes the proper use of advocacy tools: e.g., exhibits, charts, copies of relevant cases or contracts with key phrases highlighted. Visiting mindlessly or in generality about the many admissions the adversaries' various witnesses have made in video depositions and documents has none of the impact of a 90 second video clip where witness A makes his admission in living color, followed by witness B making her admission, followed by witness C making his admission, followed by the readable size copy of the February 29 letter with the key admission highlighted. Putting them together effects power.

Further, the client and senior lawyer whose juniors took the depositions, on the other side, likely never appreciated that all those admissions had been made, much less evaluated their impact. Prepare your materials for persuasive impact. Use the good tools of advocacy. Too few do in mediations.

7. Opening Statements to the Mediator as to a Judge or Jury, Rather than to the Other Party and Counsel

Most lawyers begin a mediation opening statement addressing the mediator, telling his side of the case in language laced with righteous indignation and as adversarial as though to a jury whose mind the lawyer seeks to poison toward the adversary. The lawyer shows no interest in, much less understanding of, the emotional hurt being inflicted upon the adversary, nor the plight the other party perceives herself to be in and which gave rise to the dispute.

In its disrespect for the other people, in its sometimes outright charges of gross impropriety by the adversary, this opening is a terrible poisoning of the well from which the party must drink in order to get his settlement.This is an often tragic abandonment of a marvelous opportunity to persuade and get together with the other party. You see, the "judge or jury" you want to persuade in a mediation is not the mediator, but the adversary. It is the other party you want to persuade to be sympathetic to your cause. So don't hurt him.

Adversary parties arrive at a mediation with much distrust of the opposing lawyer, which means they won't hear much of what is said. Turn them even further off with accusations and you copper rivet failure to settle.

In plenary sessions simply do not address inflammatory issues beyond a neutral statement of facts and how client X feels. Why? Because the mediator can discuss the inflammatory points in his private-caucus "realty checks" more effectively and with less "poisoning" effect than the adversary in his opening statements or the like. In plenary sessions the lawyer/client should rather show their own humanity, respect, warmth, apologies and sympathy.

It continues to surprise me to see the shocking degree that a good sympathetic opening by a well-rehearsed and skillful lawyer (or better yet, by his client) directed to the adversary party rather than the mediator, can so often set the stage for a good settlement. Persuasion addressed to the "jury", which in mediation means the adverse party and his/her counsel, always aids the process of settlement.

8. The Lawyer Instead of the Client at Center of the Process; Show Off a Good Witness

Let any articulate client be the center of the process. Prepare him to speak to and be spoken to by the mediator and the adversary as he explains his plight, and to extend empathy to the other party while explaining why he feels the way he does, or why the responsibility is not his or, why the damages caused by what he did are only peanuts or are great.

The lawyer should not try to explain every word the client utters, or to protect the client from herself. The insurance adjuster or defendant's vice president has not attended depositions, does not know the plaintiff. If the plaintiff comes across as an appealing witness, prep her and show her off to the adjuster by having her talk. People pay more to appealing plaintiffs. If the client presents a negative appeal, of course the lawyer should do the talking for the client.

9. Failure to Let a Sympathetic Client Open for Herself

Many lawyers are arrogant, or feel they are not doing their job if they don't "plead" or "argue" the case, or they feel their client expects them to deliver the opening. Hogwash. At least as often as not, letting the properly coached client do most or even all of the opening, tell why she feels the way she does, induces more and better settlements more quickly than the typical adversarial lawyer opening.

10. Time for Mediation; Flexibility in Needed Discovery

Not too early. Get and give the core, critical discovery first. And not too late. Don't spend exorbitant time or sums in discovery and trial prep before seeking mediation. The mediation process can climb over a lot of non-discovery, and can precipitate a limited bit of critically necessary discovery and resumption of mediation, when the counsel and mediator are flexible and alert to the need.

When both parties were relying on the testimony of a certain Vice President, I picked up the phone, called him, introduced myself and my mediator role, said "You appear to be a key witness in a dispute of some importance. Could you give us a one hour deposition in the morning?" "No", said he, "I've got a Board meeting at 10:00." I responded, "How about 7:30 a.m., one hour limit. It really is pretty important that this decision not be delayed." The deposition was taken with me present to control it, and the case was settled before the Board meeting at 10:00.

11. Failure to Listen to the Other Side

Many lawyers and clients come in so loaded with their own arguments they are incapable of giving open minded attention to what is being expressed from across the table. It is sad to lose a settlement out of such stupidity.

12. Perceptions, Motivations

Brainstorm and determine the other party's motivations and perceptions by preparing a chart of how he sees the relevant things. Seek first to understand, only then to be understood. Understanding the other party's perceptions will make you more realistic. If his perceptions make sense they will make you also more charitable and hence will help induce a fair settlement. If they make no sense, they will make you more firm and hence help induce you to persevere for a more favorable settlement.

13. Hurt, Humiliate the Adversary, Threaten and Deliver Ultimatums? Of Course Not

Don't poison the well from which you must drink to get a settlement. Rather humanize yourself to the adversary. You can be firm and strong on your facts, and still a descent human. That means you don't hurt, humiliate or ridicule the other folks. No pejoratives like "maligner," "fraud," "cheat," "liar." Essentially all settlements are based in some degree upon trust, lawyer to lawyer trust, client to client trust, and client to lawyer trust. If you anger them with ridicule or with pejorative terms like "crook", and "stealing", if you seek to extort from them with threats, if you attack their integrity, they won't trust you and anyway they won't settle with you.

Ultimatums. Ultimatums destroy the process, destroy credibility. Yes there is a time in mediation to walk out whether or not with intent to return, but a series of ultimatums, or often even one ultimatum, is tremendously counterproductive. The same can be said for threats, like a threat to get the other lawyer's law license for urging such a frivolous cause as he has here, or for his grossly inaccurate pleadings, or whatever. Threats are not usually conducive to compromise settlements. Rather let the objective balanced recitation of facts project any threat you use in a mediation.

14. Close Too Fast to the Bottom Line: "The Dance"

If a party opens at $1 million and moves immediately to $500,000, she has telegraphed that there is more give to be obtained. Right or wrong the other side will believe it, and likely will never come to a $500,000 offer. By contrast, a move from $1 million to $750,000, to $650,000, to $600,000, $575,000 to $560,000, to $550,000 telegraphs a different story, and is likely to beget a counter offer of $500,000 that then can be accepted.

In 80 percent of mediations "the dance" is a necessary part of communicating. Sorry about that, but it usually is true. To skip the dance is to risk losing a settlement that could be obtained. Rather, plan your dance to convey the subliminal messages you want to be understood.

15. The Backwards Step

A party which before the mediation offered to pay $300,000, then at the mediation says it is willing to offer only $200,000, without some clear and dramatic reasons for the reduction in the offer, has injured its own credibility, caused animosity and a feeling of bad faith on the other side, and has otherwise interfered with the progress of the process. It is likely to take the better part of a day to overcome the deleterious effect of such a maneuver.

The backwards step is a powerful card to play at the right time, a walk away without yet walking out. But powerful devices are also dangerous devices. The times and circumstances for its productive use are few. Its use should be reserved for the true negotiation experts with vast experience. The general instruction must be: Don't do it.

16. Too Many People

Advisors, people to whom the decision maker must display respect and courtesy, people who feel that since they are there they must put in their two bits worth, all delay a mediation immeasurably while they state and restate the obvious as well as the nonobvious. A caucus that with only one lawyer and VP would take 20 minutes, with five people will take an hour and 20 minutes, or some such. The nominally one-day mediation stretches to two or three, but only if the folks have more patience for the stretch than usually they do. And if it doesn't stretch, an available settlement is lost.

Moreover, the advisors by natural instinct all seem to advise through their own rose-colored-glasses view of the issues, feeding resistance to yielding on a perhaps five to one ratio over feeding confidence in a particular yielding. Whereby, five people per side (*e.g.*, VP in charge of, Marketing Manager, Chief Engineer, house counsel, trial counsel) will only rarely settle a typical commercial case that almost any two people per side would certainly have settled.

This is one of the contexts where I use the "one martini lunch"—send out the two adversary principals alone after X hours of mediation, when all the issues are understood by all, to negotiate on their own with no advice from anybody. The percentage of oral settlements in principal occurring within three hours or less would appall most folks. Of course, there often is need for some brush ups on details they overlooked, and there is need for writing up and signing of the deal before the day is over, but usually those finishing touches don't queer the deal the two principals have made.

17. Failure to Truly Close the Deal

It is important to close the agreement before breaking up from the mediation, with a written, signed, enforceable contract. Too often, when left to think overnight and draft tomorrow, new ideas occur that preclude finalizing the agreement as discussed before parties went home. Unless parties have strong reasons to sleep on it, to need a further evaluation of the deal or a further check on what may have been forgotten, enough so to risk loss of the settlement, it is much better to get some sort of enforceable contract written and signed before the parties separate.

18. Confidentiality

Mediation parties have been known unthinkingly, or irresponsibly, to disclose in open court information disclosed only in confidence in a mediation. Where the information is highly sensitive, consider keeping it confidential. Or if revealed in a mediation where the case did not settle, consider moving before the trial begins for an order in limine with respect to it.

19. Patience; Perseverance

The process takes time. The "dance" takes time. With time people will change their mind when they will not change it without time. The six most important qualities of good advocacy in mediation, are (1) patience, (2) perseverance, (3) patience, (4) perseverance, (5) patience, and (6) perseverance.

20. What is a dispute?

A dispute is a problem to be solved together, not a combat to be won.

4. Eileen Miggins Hohlt, Effective Use of Caucus (1993)*

A successful mediation relies heavily on the candid cooperation of the disputants. But, humans in dispute typically do not deal with each other candidly or cooperatively. In addition, they sometimes hire lawyers. Then, the attorney-client privilege is created, which also discourages candor and cooperation. Further, upon hiring a lawyer, a disputant gets the protection of the rules of evidence and procedure. And, the lawyer has advocacy skills. All these are additional disincentives to candor and cooperation. How does the mediator cut through these layers of insulation to get to the dispute? [One answer is to use] private confidential meetings (caucuses).

Sometime after joint session, the mediator meets independently with one party and its counsel, in a room separate from the other mediation participants. It is here that the mediator sets about initially to:

1. Promote honesty and candor;
2. Establish a bond of trust with a party and an attorney;
3. Identify hidden needs and interests;
4. Encourage parties and attorneys to be actively involved in all phases of the process;
5. Assist parties in clarifying needs and interests;
6. Allow parties to vent to the mediator;
7. Plan negotiation movements and responses; and
8. Test the legal and factual adequacy of positions articulated at joint session or in pleadings.

After having met initially with one party and counsel, the mediator then meets with the other party and counsel. The discussion below outlines how you as a mediator might structure the initial caucus and the subsequent caucuses to maximize the settlement opportunities in a given case.

One of your primary goals in the initial caucus is to establish trust and build rapport as a mediator with the party and counsel. How this is done is, in part, a matter of personal style. Attorney-mediators should fight the strong temptation to begin the initial caucus by talking to the lawyers. The party/client will feel double-teamed by the lawyers and may not participate

*Reprinted with permission.

as fully as is needed. You may need to draw out the party, particularly if the party was relatively quiet in joint session. Keep in mind that the party may have been under strict lawyer's instruction not to speak at joint session. The party undoubtedly has a lot to say. Draw the party out by asking something like: "Joe, I noticed you did not say much in the joint session, is there something you would like to add to what was said?" or "Joe, tell me about yourself/your company." If met with resistance, add "the reason I ask is because you/your company are an important witness/party in this case, and it helps me to understand the case better if I know something about you/your company."

People will generally start to open up when given a chance to talk about themselves. If you are successful in opening up the party, you will likely hear some venting, anger etc. from the party. It is best, at this time, not to react too strongly to it, but rather to let it flow as the party purges. Listen actively as the party speaks because the party will reveal hidden agendas, motivations, needs and interests. However, save the challenges for later, after you have established trust and rapport.

In the initial caucus, you should turn eventually to the attorney to ask specific questions about the case and the risk factors. While this discussion may not be in a rigid order, it should cover:

1. Discussion of the causes of action pled, defenses, and counterclaims;
2. Identification of the elements of each and the evidence to support each element;
3. Range of outcomes at trial;
4. Probability of those outcomes;
5. Assessment of what the opponent(s) might settle for and why; and
6. Formulation of an opening offer/demand and a rationale for same that you, the mediator, can disclose to the other side.

Be sure to remind the caucusing party and attorney that everything said in caucus is confidential and does not leave the room unless they give you permission to disclose information. Then, ask if there is any information you can share with the other side at this time.

When you go into the room for the initial caucus with the second party, start from scratch: bond with the party, get the required information from the attorney etc. Do not assume that you know the whole story after having met with only one side. Further, do not indulge the second caucusing party's suspicions by appearing to have been "brainwashed" already by the first caucusing party.

After the first round of initial caucuses, you may keep each party and counsel unit separated from the other(s) and operate a "shuttle" form of mediation — conveying offers, counter offers and rationales to and from each party. Keep in mind that you as a mediator control the process, but the participants control the content. Plan what you are going to say before you enter each room. During the subsequent caucuses, you as mediator play "Devil's Advocate" with the party and the attorney by asking the hard questions and getting the parties to confront the factual and legal realities of their cases. You will have the chance to:

1. Address hidden needs and interests;
2. Test the validity of party's or attorney's position;
3. Test the reality of a party's or attorney's position;
4. Problem solve in a creative way;
5. Maintain neutrality by not appearing to side with one party or another;

6. Continue to assist parties in clarifying needs and interests;
7. Plan further negotiation movements and responses;
8. Protect the confidential information entrusted to the mediator but reveal certain information with permission; and
9. Continue to test the legal and factual adequacy of positions articulated at joint session or in pleadings.

MISCELLANEOUS POINTERS

Be sure to take accurate notes in the caucuses and protect your notes from accidental viewing by the other side. Carefully keep track of the confidential information. If you do not understand something that is said, have the attorney/party repeat or expand on the idea so you will understand it. How can you communicate something you don't understand? Resist the temptation to tell your war stories regarding a "similar" case. The party involved is not interested in anyone else's lawsuit. Remain neutral. Take a break when you need to.

5. Kimberlee K. Kovach, MEDIATION: PRINCIPLES AND PRACTICE 108-10 (1994)

Restating and Reframing

Restatement of what one party has said, or reframing the way a party has related a problem, is one of the most effective tools mediator uses. Not only does this let the party know that she has been heard and understood by the mediator, it may also assist the others at the table in hearing another point of view. Reframing can also cause the author of the statement to look at the problem in a different light. By using more neutral language, the mediator also begins to refocus the language used by the participants. After they hear statements made a different way, the parties may subsequently choose different words to explain themselves. Reframing is also used to identify the main issues and points, and make a transition to the problem solving stage of the process. By hearing neutral language, and a broad view of the issues, the parties may become open to a more creative problem solving approach. . . .

Some mediators will also ask the parties themselves to do some restating and reframing. The theory behind this approach is that the parties will better understand the other side, and begin to acknowledge another view of the situation if they are required to restate it. Use of this method will depend primarily on the nature of the relationship between the parties and how comfortable they are with the idea. In some cases, after the mediator has restated some of the issues, he may ask each of the parties to restate [the position of the other party]. . . .

E. Impasse — And What to Do About It

1. Christopher W. Moore, *Techniques to Break Impasse*, in Jay Folberg & Ann Milne, DIVORCE MEDIATION 251-75 (1988)*

People who divorce request the assistance of a mediator because they have been unable to negotiate a settlement of issues that divide them. The couple have reached an impasse — a

*Reprinted with permission.

psychological, procedural, or substantive block — that prevents them from moving toward an agreement. . . . This chapter examines some of the causes of impasse, identifies the times in divorce and custody negotiation when impasse is more likely to occur, and describes interventions or techniques commonly used by mediators to overcome impasse and promote agreement. . . .

CAUSES OF CONFLICT AND IMPASSE

In examining the causes of impasse it is important to understand first what is producing the conflict itself. . . . Conflicts (or impasses) often have complex causality. Often a variety of interventions or moves will be initiated by a mediator to respond to the diverse causes of the dispute or impasse.

While the variables causing impasse are all intertwined in actual disputes, it is helpful for the sake of analysis to separate various causal factors of both conflicts in general and impasses in particular. [T]here are five major variables that influence the dynamics and potential deadlock of a conflict: (1) relationship factors, (2) data problems, (3) competing or incompatible interests, (4) the structure of the relationship, and (5) diverse values. Each of these can cause impasse. . . .

Relationship Conflict

Relationship factors refer to a specific set of emotions and behaviors that promote or detract from the positive regard or interaction between two or more people. Four variables tend to produce or influence the development of relationship conflict: strong negative emotions, misperceptions or stereotypes, poor communication, and repetitive negative behavior.

Emotions

Emotions or feelings are complex physiological and psychological reactions based on a person's encounter with the world. Strong negative emotions . . . may be caused by the immediate interaction . . . in the process of negotiating over perceived or actual incompatible interests, or may be the result of restimulation, the surfacing of feelings that remind a person of past interpersonal relations or events not necessarily directly related to the present situation. . . . The conditions that cause immediate emotions can often be handled by direct intervention of the mediator in the negotiating process. By restructuring the communication or behavior patterns of either spouse, the mediator may be able to limit or eliminate the cause of the immediate negative feelings.

Restimulated feelings, may be harder to handle and overcome because they are the result of past interaction. For a disputant to deal with restimulated feelings, he or she must be able to distinguish the current situation and the emotions it produces from past events that originally initiated the negative feelings. . . .

Misperceptions and Stereotypes

Misperceptions and stereotypes are the inaccurate images that disputants have of each other. Misperception and stereotypes may be related to the personality, motivation, predicted or expected behavior, or goals of another party. For negotiators to move toward an acceptable settlement, misperceptions and stereotypes must be identified, checked for accuracy, revised, or have their impact minimized.

Communications

Communication problems are some of the major causes of relationship conflict. By communications we mean verbal or nonverbal signals that are sent and received by disputing parties. Communication problems are the result of inaccurate or inappropriate messages that are sent from one person to another, or problems in listening to or interpreting the messages that are received. Because verbal messages are the major medium by which parties convey messages about what they want and expect from each other, poor verbal communications cause unnecessary conflicts where the parties' interests are in fact the same. For this reason, the intervenor may make a significant effort to improve the quality and, if necessary, the quantity of communication, as a means of managing unnecessary conflict.

Repetitive Negative Behavior

Some conflict in relationships is caused by specific repetitive behavior, by one or both parties, that hinders productive negotiations. Conflicting negative behaviors are often related to conflict style. . . . One party will often start an interaction cycle with a behavior that the other party dislikes. The behavior initiates an escalatory spiral of patterned behavior that is reciprocated by the other person. Managing repetitive negative behavior is crucial if parties are to de-escalate their conflict and reach agreement.

Data Conflict

Data conflict arises from differences in the information used by parties to make a decision. Data conflicts are caused by lack of information, misinformation, diverse views as to what data is relevant, conflicting interpretation of the same data, or differing procedures to assess information. Before a husband and wife can reach an agreement on any substantive question, they must have a common view of relevant data or information and have coordinated their means of assessing its accuracy.

Interest Conflict

Interests are needs or benefits that a party expects to be met or satisfied at the termination of a dispute. Most divorce or custody suits are characterized by a combination of compatible and incompatible interests. The goal of each spouse in negotiations is to maximize the satisfaction of his or her interests, but not to the extent that the other receives so little that they are induced to pursue other means of dispute resolution (i.e., litigation). The effective negotiator attempts to build on compatible interests and to minimize the negative impacts of competing interests. Interest-based conflicts usually occur over a combination of three different categories of interests: substantive benefits, procedural dynamics, and psychological needs. . . .

Substantive Benefits or Interests

Divorcing couples with children must usually reach an agreement on five substantive issues: (1) distribution of marital property, (2) spousal support, (3) child custody, (4) visitation, and (5) child support. Both partners expect to receive at the conclusion of the negotiation some tangible resource — legal rights, money, time with the child, and so forth — by which they can measure the success of the negotiation. Substantive conflicts occur because of perceived or actual incompatibility of substantive needs.

Procedural Interests

Each party to a negotiation has preferences as to the process or way the decisions about the divorce will be handled. Criteria often used to measure or assess procedural interests or satisfaction include fairness to all the parties, lack of coercion in reaching an agreement, and opportunity to participate in the decision-making process.

Psychological Interests

Couples also negotiate over psychological issues and expect interests to be met in this area too. Spouses do not want to be psychologically degraded or debased in the negotiation process. They want to be respected as parents and want to believe that the other spouse is negotiating in good faith. If these needs are not met, agreement and psychological settlement may not be possible. Mediation is not another form of therapy, but the mediation intervention may involve moves to assist the parties to negotiate psychological closure.

Structural Conflict

Structural conflict refers to disputes that develop because of the way a relationship is organized and the patterns of interdependence (independence-dependence) that emerge. Structural conflict is often related to power—its sources, its forms, and the issues over which it is exercised.

Structural variables that influence the dynamics of conflict in a couple include:

- *exploitation:* the degree to which the resources are asymmetrically distributed for the amount of work or energy (the spouses contribute).
- *penetration:* how far the stronger party has been able to penetrate the consciousness of the weaker and create an underdog form of consciousness.
- *fragmentation:* whether the weaker party is structurally separated from people or institutions that would support or empower him or her.
- *marginalization:* the degree to which decision-making power has been concentrated in the hands of one spouse and removed from the other so that the decisions are made unilaterally and without consensus.

Value Conflict

Value conflicts arise over the beliefs and criteria that husbands and wives use for evaluating behavior or differences in intrinsically valuable goals, such as ideologies or religion. Value disputes are extremely difficult to resolve where there is no consensus on appropriate behavior or ultimate goals.

Parents may differ as to how they value each other's sexual behavior or orientation, how much they tell the children about the causes of the divorce, or what an "equal" settlement means. They may also differ about how to achieve intrinsically valuable goals such as economic security or parental relationships with the children. One may define economic security as living luxuriously while the other values comfort but not opulence. One parent may believe that a young child should always stay with his or her mother, while the other wants equal time "because we are both parents."

Values relating to life-style, politics, and religion may also cause conflict. Can the child live with a father who has a gay lover? What kind of religious education should the child have if the father is Jewish and the mother a fundamentalist Christian?

Unnecessary and Genuine Conflict

. . . The division of the causes of conflict into unnecessary and genuine is a key concept for disputants and mediators. The goal in productive conflict management is to eliminate the unnecessary relationship and data causes of conflict, so that the parties can focus on genuine issues in contention—interests, structure, and values.

STAGES OF NEGOTIATION AND MEDIATION AND THE OCCURRENCE OF IMPASSE

. . . I prefer a 10-stage theory of negotiation. . . . The stages include (1) searching for an approach and arena; (2) conciliation; (3) determining a negotiation strategy; (4) defining dispute parameters; (5) defining issues and establishing an agenda; (6) identifying interests; (7) generating settlement alternatives; (8) assessing options; (9) final bargaining; and (10) implementing, monitoring, and formalizing the settlement.

The stages of mediation, with a few exceptions, follow the stages of negotiation. The job of the mediator is to assist the parties to move through the stages and accomplish the required tasks. Impasse can occur at a variety of locations along the stages of negotiation and may be caused by multiple factors. It has been noted that impasse is most likely to occur when the parties are making the transition from one stage or task to another.

In the next section, we will explore each of the five major causes or influences on the dynamics of conflict (relationship, data, interests, structure, and values), describe where they are most likely to occur in the stages of negotiation, and detail some of the mediator moves that may be initiated to respond to the particular type of impasse. . . .

HANDLING RELATIONSHIP PROBLEMS

It is fair to say that every negotiation over marital issues will have some emotional content. There are, however, specific times in the negotiation process when the presence or expression of strong emotions will be more likely to cause an impasse. The stages in negotiation where these strong feelings most often occur include searching for an approach and area, where the presence or expression of strong feelings may block the parties from individually or jointly considering a coordinated procedure; conciliation, where the parties are psychologically preparing for negotiations; defining the dispute parameters, where the parties try to convince each other of the general boundaries of issues to be discussed and may test each other's emotional limits; defining issues and establishing an agenda, where the parties identify specific topics and order them for discussion; identifying interests, where the parties attempt to convince each other of specific needs; and final bargaining, where the parties initiate trade-offs, make concessions, or form integrated solutions to their mutual problems and where they attempt to reach psychological settlement.

Yelling or tears are usually not hard to recognize as possible preconditions for emotional deadlock. Emotional impasse, however, may also be expressed in more subtle terms, such as nonverbal withdrawal, failure to talk, constant recycling of the same message, or rhetorical argument. The mediator, upon observing any of the above behaviors, must decide if the parties' feelings are causing impasse. If this is the case, the mediator can initiate moves that respond to the disputant's emotions.

Responses to Emotional Causes of Impasse

There are three general mediator interventions or responses to current or restimulated emotions when they appear to be influencing the dynamics of the conflict: allow expression of emotions, escalate their expression to promote venting or tension release, or limit their expression.

The mediator may consider the expression of feelings to be productive and may choose not to intervene (1) when the parties are expressing strong feelings about issues that divide them but are not degrading the person who holds an opposing view; (2) when the expression of an emotion is serving an educational function in that it explains how intensely a party feels about an issue; or (3) when the expression of the feelings appears to be helpful for cathartic release of tension for one spouse and does not seem to have a detrimental effect on the other. Under the above conditions, the mediator may choose not to intervene and may allow the feelings to be directly expressed. . . .

Misperceptions and Stereotypes

Misperceptions and stereotypes are most common in the early stages of negotiations when the parties are attempting to test and break down negative images of each other and to build trust in the good-faith bargaining of the other party. Misperceptions also occur in mid-negotiations when one party initiates activities that restimulate past hurts or other emotions in the other and that shift the parties into stereotyped or patterned negative behavior. . . . If the intervenor believes the parties are operating from a basis of misperception or stereotype, he or she has several options for intervention.

First, the intervenor may establish a situation where the parties can question and check out their perceptions about the other. This can be done by requesting that the spouses talk about their perceptions of each other or certain issues and explaining the accuracy or inaccuracy of the perception.

Second, the mediator can describe the stereotyping dynamic and explain how it affects negotiations. By educating the parties about a dynamic that is common to many conflicts, the intervenor can indirectly or directly suggest that the parties evaluate their own dispute in a new light.

Third, the mediator can directly or indirectly challenge the misperception of one or more of the parties and raise doubts about their perceptions. Often the introduction of the view of another party whom a disputant trusts (the mediator) causes enough cognitive dissonance in the mind of the disputant to shift his or her view of the opponent. The mediator can point out how an opponent's behavior is not consistent with the perception or stereotype held by the other party. This mediator move, however, is riskier than focusing the parties on the topic of perception and allowing them to check out views on their own. Direct challenges of a party's perceptions are most often initiated in caucus, where the mediator's challenge is less likely to be perceived as an alliance with an opponent.

Finally, the mediator may encourage a party to initiate moves that will tend to break stereotypes or modify perceptions held by another party. Often the mediator suggests these moves in caucus. A spouse may express appreciation of the other's parenting abilities . . .; accept a negotiation procedure proposed by the other party; grant small concessions to indicate that cooperation and trust is possible; or initiate symbolic acts . . . that jar the perceptions of the other party and encourage him or her to revise negative stereotypes. . . .

Repetitive Negative Behavior

Repetitive negative behavior involves repeated actions that trigger escalatory responses from the other party. Often this behavior is patterned interaction that has developed over the duration of the relationship and is subconscious on the part of both parties. Repetitive negative behavior is most likely to result in impasse during the first five stages of negotiation and in the final bargaining stage. Mediator interventions to handle repetitive negative behavior may be divided into two levels: direct and indirect interventions.

Direct interventions are mediator moves that overtly identify what is happening and then modify the structure. Often, when the mediator overtly identifies and labels behavior, it makes it more difficult for the parties to repeat since everyone will recognize what is happening and no one wants to be held responsible for a damaging action.

Indirect moves require the mediator to recognize patterns and cycles of repetitive behavior and then to structure the negotiation session so that there is no opportunity for them to occur. . . .

DATA CONFLICT

Data conflicts are differences that arise over information used by the parties to make a decision. Data conflicts occur at several stages in the negotiation process. In the early stages — defining dispute parameters, identifying issues and establishing an agenda, and identifying interests — the most common data problems are lack of information, misinformation, and discrepancies in data the parties believe are relevant to deciding the issues. Data, it should be noticed, can refer to concrete substantive information (such as the amount of money needed to feed and clothe two children), procedural information (such as the sequence of filing papers with the court), or psychological data (such as information on a child's increased bedwetting). . . .

The primary task of the mediator is to assist the parties in identifying the additional information needed and to aid them in developing appropriate data collection procedures. Occasionally parties cannot agree on a piece of data. A "data mediator," an independent and mutually acceptable third party who is not the mediator and who is a substantive expert in the area of question, may be consulted to break the deadlock. . . . Assessors, stockbrokers, investment counselors, jewelers, and so forth, can all perform this role. . . .

INTEREST CONFLICTS

. . . Interests are specific needs, benefits, or conditions that a party must have met if a settlement is to be considered satisfactory. Interests may refer to the content or substantive outcomes of negotiations (money, time, or other forms of compensation), procedural preferences for the way that negotiations are carried out, or psychological needs (safety, respect, trust, etc.) In most conflicts, the interests are not all mutually exclusive because the satisfaction of one spouse's needs is not always dependent on the denial of the other's needs. This is especially true in marital disputes where couples often have cross-cutting and common interests, such as the well-being of their children, as well as competing needs. . . .

Psychological Interest Conflict

Parties also have psychological interests or needs that they would like to have met in a negotiated settlement. Psychological interests include not only a need for positive feelings such as respect, caring, or safety, but also a termination of negative feelings that may bind the couple into the dynamics of negative intimacy.

Mediators assist parties to satisfy their psychological needs by making spouses aware that this type of interest exists and by providing procedures that enable them to attain desired ends. Mediators may assist spouses to make statements that meet each other's psychological needs and make settlement more acceptable, request time-out to enable a party to reconcile his or her feelings with the substantive settlement, or assist in a total restructuring of the relationship so that psychological interests become less important. One of the most difficult transitions for spouses and parents to make is the shift from an intimate relationship to that of a businesslike one. Intimate relationships involve high personal disclosure, are informal, and are characterized by implicit expectations. As long as a person remains in an intimate relationship with an ex-spouse, he or she will not make the psychological transition to independence and autonomy. Psychological closure in a divorce requires this transition. Mediators assist spouses to become aware of the need for a new structure for the relationship and to shift their intimate interests to businesslike ones — formality, high personal privacy, low self-disclosure, explicit expectations, and written agreements.

STRUCTURAL CONFLICT

Structural conflict is caused by the way that a spousal or parenting relationship is organized and the patterns of interdependence that emerge. Some of the variables that affect the structure of a relationship include resources to be distributed between the couple, time, patterns of spousal involvement with each other and the children, physical space, and power relationships. . . . Power is the capability of one party to affect the other's rewards or the outcome of a dispute. The range of outcomes in marital disputes may be either positive or negative, depending upon the spouses' exercise of power.

The outcome of a conflict depends upon the exercise by a disputant of various means of influence which either close off or open the way to different settlement options. There are a variety of means of influence that may be used by spouses in relationship disputes: rewards, coercion, claims to authority, association with powerful allies (i.e., attorneys), expertise, and information.

Power is not a characteristic of a person but rather an attribute of a relationship. In other words, one spouse's power is directly related to the power of the other spouse. Power relations are either symmetrical or asymmetrical. A symmetrical power relationship exists when each spouse controls a range of outcomes for the other that are relatively equal. Symmetrical power is characterized by similar capabilities to affect the outcome for the other. An asymmetrical power relationship occurs when one spouse has a greater capacity to control the outcomes for the other. This type of relationship often results in unilateral attempts to change the conflict outcome.

Parties With Symmetrical Power Relations

Social-psychological experiments and practical experience indicate that when negotiators have equal or symmetrical power, they behave in a more cooperative manner, function more effectively, and behave in a less exploitive or manipulative manner than when they are in an asymmetrical power relationship. Furthermore, the smaller the amount of power, particularly coercive power, that is exercised in the negotiations, the more effectively the parties seem to function. . . .

When spouses have different quantities or types of power, an assessment problem often develops. This often results in a breakdown of negotiations. Spouses may return to negotiations only after they have exercised and tested their power and developed a more accurate assessment of the power of the other party. For example, many spouses attempt to negotiate issues in dispute, fail, hire lawyers, and take the case to court. A large number of these cases settle on the courthouse steps. The act of testing the strength and will of an opponent may be an important step in developing an accurate perception of the other disputant's power. Power often has to be tested before the actual degree of influence can be verified. Unfortunately, this testing, which involves the exercise of power, may have a negative impact on the couple's ability to cooperate and negotiate. Even in symmetrical relations, exercise of power may lead to an irreversible breakdown of negotiations.

Mediators in disputes where spouses have symmetrical power relationships but where the equality is hard to determine because of different power bases or measures, generally attempt to change the parties' perceptions of each other's power without encouraging them to resort to coercion. Perception can be changed by increasing the perception of spouses that their opposite has more potential power in relation to themselves than was originally calculated, or by convincing spouses that they have less power in relationship to their opposite than they originally expected. Changing perspectives about power, especially where the parties have symmetrical relationships, is generally an exercise in developing an accurate assessment mechanism. Mediators usually encourage a party to list his or her sources or bases of power and then identify the costs and benefits of exercising it. The same procedure is then followed for the other spouse. A cross-reference of costs and outcomes usually moves the spouses toward a mutual recognition of symmetrical power relations.

Parties With Asymmetrical Power Relations

While symmetrical power relations between spouses seem to be the optimum relationship for effective bargaining, this type of relationship is not the norm for a large number of family disputes. . . . Mediators work with both weaker and stronger parties to minimize the negative effects of asymmetrical power relationships on the negotiation process. . . .

When a mediator encounters a situation where one spouse is bluffing about his or her power and the other is being drawn into the illusion, the mediator, usually in private, attempts to educate the bluffer about the potential costs of being either found out or called upon to carry out the bluff. On one hand discovery that one has been the victim of a deception often leads to a deterioration of the couple's relationship and may, if the victim of the bluff is the stronger party, lead to retaliation. On the other hand, if a bluff regarding power held by a weaker party is believed by a stronger one, and the stronger party decides to resist the demand, the weaker party may be forced to follow through on a course of action that will lead to the bluff's demise. In an effort to respond to this situation, the mediator generally raises questions with the weaker spouse regarding the potential cost of bluffing. If the intervenor is successful in convincing the spouse that the costs of bluffing are too high, the mediator and that spouse jointly search for a way to back away from the bluff or minimize the importance of power dynamics in the context of the negotiations. Backing off from a bluff or minimizing the effects of bluff can often be achieved by ceasing threatening statements or false promises and blurring the explicitness of statements describing the consequences of disagreement. A shift to a general description of outcomes rather than explicit coercive moves leaves all parties more maneuvering room to cope with an impasse. The mediator and the bluffing spouse work jointly to minimize the impact of an ill-timed or inappropriate bluff.

In power situations where spouses appear to have an asymmetrical relationship and where their basis of power is very different, the mediator may attempt to blur or obscure the asymmetry of the disputants' power. Mediators pursue this strategy as a way of creating doubt about the actual power of the parties. This move is often referred to as keeping the parties off balance. . . . The mediator may destabilize the accuracy of the power assessment of the parties in order to promote cooperation based on doubt.

A second mediator strategy, where the parties do not have a symmetrical relationship and the difference in power is not too great, is to stress the costs to a spouse in pursuing a manipulative or competitive win-lose outcome. Although the stronger spouse may ultimately win, the costs of exercising power may be extremely high and the duration of the contest may be prolonged. In asymmetrical situations where the spouses' powers are close to equal, the mediator may urge the parties to treat the relationship as a symmetrical one in order to maximize benefits and lower costs.

By far the most difficult problem faced by mediators regarding disputants' power relationships is an asymmetrical situation where the discrepancy between the means of influence is extremely great. The mediator, because of his or her commitment to neutrality and impartiality, is ethically barred from being a direct advocate for the weaker spouse. Yet the intervenor is also ethically obligated to assist the couple to reach a fair and acceptable agreement that will hold over time.

Wall argues that the mediator's job is to manage the power relationship of the disputants. In asymmetrical power relationships the mediator attempts to balance the power between the dominant and weaker party. The mediator initiates moves to assist the weaker party to mobilize the power he or she currently possesses. The mediator does not, however, directly act as an organizer to develop new power for the weaker disputant unless the mediator has gained approval of the stronger party for such activity. To act as a secret advocate risks the mediator's impartiality and, therefore, effectiveness.

Empowering moves may include aiding the weaker party to obtain, organize, and analyze data and identify and mobilize his or her means of influence; assisting and educating the party to plan an effective negotiation strategy; aiding in the development of financial support so that the spouse can continue to participate in negotiations; and encouraging the party to make realistic concessions. Surprisingly enough, stronger spouses often welcome a mediator's involvement. Mediators may assist weaker parties who are unorganized and unable to negotiate to prepare to engage in a productive exchange.

VALUE CONFLICTS

A value is an enduring belief that specific behaviors or goals for existence are personally or socially preferable. Values usually imply a comparison in that one set of values is preferred over another. Researchers have identified two levels of values, operational and terminal. Operational values are general day-to-day guidelines, such as truth, honesty, respect, and so forth, while terminal values are often systems such as religious beliefs, views on parenting, lifelong goals, or political values. Because both levels of values tie into a person's self-concept, it may appear that negotiating over values is an impossible task. Although value-based conflicts are difficult, they are not impossible to handle. Mediators can be of great assistance to parties in resolving this type of dispute.

Value conflicts are most prominent in the following stages of negotiation: searching for an approach and arena, defining dispute parameters, defining issues and forming an agenda, and identifying interests. The following five procedures are often used by mediators to handle value-based disputes: (1) avoiding value-based issues, (2) agreeing to disagree, (3) translating a value dispute into an interest conflict, (4) searching for superordinate goals, and (5) creating in a party cognitive dissonance between one set of values and another.

Avoidance

Endless bickering about values often results in a deterioration of the couple's relationship and a decline in the spouses' abilities to negotiate. Personal values rarely change in the brief time during which a couple are negotiating a divorce. For this reason, many mediators assertively guide parties away from value-laden issues and focus them on behavioral issues that are more easily resolved. Avoidance of value disputes is often the best way to handle them.

Agreeing to Disagree

On occasion, a couple may not accept avoidance of value-laden issues. They may want to discuss and confront them head-on. Mediators often stress that the couple may have to agree to disagree about value-based issues. For example, a couple who were divorcing had different religious values. One was a fundamentalist Christian and the other an agnostic. The individuals involved had very different expectations about how they wished the other to live and believe. The mediator convinced them that while the spouses were in the couple relationship, parallel values were important. However, since they were divorcing and would no longer be engaged in intimate interaction, common religious beliefs would not be as important as in the previous relationship. Now they should be able to live their lives as each of them wished. . . .

Translating A Value Dispute Into an Interest Conflict

Some value disputes, especially those involving terminal values, many not be resolved in the manners described above. This is especially the case where the parties must continue to interact as parents, and still hold opposing beliefs. Individual beliefs, however, may sometimes be operationalized so that the behavior of the parties (or their children) is deemed to be mutually acceptable.

The process that best illustrates this procedure is reframing a value dispute into an interest conflict. For example, a husband and wife are negotiating over visitation. The husband has an alcohol problem that the wife absolutely abhors. Her father had been an alcoholic, and she hates people who drink. She refuses to allow the child to visit his father. From all appearances this is a nonnegotiable, value-based conflict. . . . The parties then begin a joint search for a solution that meets the father's needs for visitation and the mother's needs for safety and psychological well-being of the child. They settle on a 6-month schedule of visitation in which the father can see the child for several hours each week under the supervision of a local hospital program. In this dispute, a difference of values has been translated into an interest conflict.

Searching for Superordinate Goals or Values

The search for superordinate goals has long been known to be a way to minimize value conflicts. [T]he mediator assesses the parties' beliefs and searches to find a superordinate goal or value that bridges either their operational or terminal values.

For example, a couple were fighting over the religious upbringing of their children. One parent wanted one kind of religious training, and the other wanted another. From all appearances the values of the parents seemed to be irreconcilable. The mediator did not attempt to have the parties argue on the basis of their particular religious beliefs but instead asked how each other's religious values would translate into value-based behavior as displayed by the children. The couple talked about general values they would like their children to have — charity, cheerfulness, forgiveness, honesty, compassion — and then discussed how these values were or were not manifest in their children's lives. The couple proceeded to talk about ways, aside from religion, that they could promote these values and behaviors in their offspring. The particular kind of religious training became less important once overarching values had been identified by the couple.

Creating Cognitive Dissonance

The fifth, and final, means of handling value conflict is to create cognitive dissonance between one value and another within an individual. Cognitive dissonance as a means of dispute resolution is based on balance theory. Balance theory postulates that people like to maintain internal consistency between their attitudes, perceptions, and beliefs about important events or issues and will attempt to modify these beliefs if there is incongruity between two or more important values. Incongruity in an individual's own beliefs or values is catalyzed by the mediator when he or she contrasts one set of a disputant's values against another. This produces strain on the individual's belief system and promotes efforts to reattain congruity. In the search for a superordinate goal, the mediator looks for bridging beliefs or principles that would unify the two disputants. In the cognitive dissonance approach, the mediator searches for a superordinate value held by an individual and contrasts it with a lower value that is causing the conflict.

In a case example, Phillip and Rita have decided to separate after an extremely painful break-up of their marriage. Rita has been involved with another man, and this provided the trigger event for the separation. Phillip is "morally opposed" to Rita's "sleeping around" with other men while their young daughter Sheila is living with Rita. He has stated his values very strongly: "I don't want you to see other men while Sheila is with you." His statement provoked a very angry response from Rita. The mediator switched the topic away from the particular moral value in question and encouraged the parties to discuss their principles of fairness. What did a fair settlement mean to them? Both stressed the fairness meant reasonableness, equal treatment for both partners, taking into consideration the needs of those involved, and so forth. The mediator asked Phillip if he intended to date other women some time in the future. Phillip answered that he did. The mediator then asked Phillip if it was out of the question that he might wish to sleep with them. He answered that it was not. The mediator posed a hypothetical question to Phillip, "If you developed a strong relationship with another woman, would you want to live with her prior to marriage?" Phillip answered, "Possibly." The mediator asked Phillip if he would want his child to know about, and have a friendship with, this new woman who was an important person in Phillip's life. Phillip answered in the affirmative. The mediator then asked Phillip if his desire to live with the woman and his desire to have his daughter know her would mean that the daughter might realize that they were sleeping together. Phillip said, "Yes." The mediator asked Phillip if he thought that this knowledge might be detrimental to Sheila. He responded that if it was an ongoing, loving relationship, it probably would not. The mediator asked Phillip whether he thought that he should be allowed to make this decision to expose his daughter to such information. Phillip adamantly stated that he did. The mediator returned to the principle of fairness and asked whether this right should apply to Rita's decision about whom she had relationships with and how she presented her friends to their daughter.

Phillip, after considering the previous discussion of fairness, reluctantly agreed and backed off his hard-line, value-based position. He stated that he merely wanted to assure that Sheila was not presented with information that she could not handle. Rita agreed that this was an important principle that they could build an agreement around. The couple proceeded to work out the details about how they would relate to others after the divorce and how they would present and explain their relationships to Sheila. In this case the mediator was successful in generating cognitive dissonance between the higher values of love, desire for a meaningful relationship, and fairness, and Phillip's lower operational value regarding sexual behavior in relationships.

CONCLUSION

This chapter reviewed some of the causes of conflict and impasse, analyzed the times when impasse is most likely to occur in a negotiation process, and described a variety of interventions or techniques that may be initiated by a mediator to break impasse. We have explored relationship-based disputes in which strong emotions, misperceptions, stereotypes, poor communication, and repetitive negative behaviors have blocked the ability of the couple to agree. We have also examined data disputes where lack of information, misinformation, differing assessment procedures, and differing viewpoints of what data are relevant tended to produce unnecessary conflict between the disputants. Our analysis indicates that mediators should first handle relationship and data disputes, which may be unnecessarily provoking conflict, before dealing with interests, values, and the structure of the relationship, which may be causing genuine conflict.

Interest disputes in a divorce may be over substantive content, such as child custody, visitation, . . . and property division. Interest conflicts may also be due to differing opinions or desires about negotiation procedures. . . . Of particular concern in procedural disputes is the tendency of couples to initiate positional bargaining as opposed to interest-based bargaining. [O]ne of the major tasks of a mediator is to assist parties to make the transition from positional bargaining to interest-based bargaining.

Finally, interest disputes may be caused by differing psychological needs. In order to achieve a psychological settlement, the mediator must assist the parties to break out of negative intimacy and move toward a more businesslike relationship.

Structural conflicts are often caused by an imbalance of the power relationship within a couple. We have reviewed different kinds of intervention techniques that mediators can use depending on whether the power relationship between the parties is symmetrical or asymmetrical.

Value disputes are perhaps one of the most difficult kinds of conflict to resolve. [W]e have reviewed five different mediation techniques to handle value disputes: (1) avoiding, (2) agreeing to disagree, (3) reframing a value dispute into an interest conflict, (4) searching for superordinate goals or values held by the parties, and (5) creating internal cognitive dissonance between a set of lower operational values and a higher terminal value in a single party. . . .

2. Eric Galton, Representing Clients in Mediation 104-112 (1995)*

1. What an Impasse Is

In mediation and negotiation circles, "impasse" is an often used word, but "impasse" is rarely defined. *Webster's Dictionary* defines "impasse" as a "predicament affording no obvious escape; a deadlock." But, as you will readily conclude, "impasse" has a strong subjective component.

Who thinks that an impasse exists? The parties? The lawyers? The mediator? And how and when does one conclude that a "deadlock" has occurred and that all "less than obvious escapes" have been explored? A declaration of impasse by a party may in fact be a thinly disguised negotiating strategy.

[N]ew mediators, in varying degrees, fear an impasse occurring despite their passionate belief in the mediation process. Mediators wonder, "What do I do when things get stuck? How do I keep things moving and get the negotiations back on track?" The feeling, more candidly stated, is best described by one word: "Help!"

In my view, mediators must become skilled at impasse avoidance techniques and must emotionally and mentally look forward to impasse situations. A mediator's art is in part defined by the ability to work parties out of ostensible impasses.

I would like to provide a word of warning: Each mediation is different and unique. Each mediation has its own feel, its own players, and its own tempo. Some of the impasse breaking or avoidance techniques I have listed below may be perfect for a particular mediation, but wholly inappropriate in a different one. This is an attempt to provide you with an extensive laundry list of options for impasse situations or impasse avoidance. The designation (C) after a listed item is my suggestion that the technique be used only in the separate caucus.

2. Impasse Prevention

Obviously, the ideal situation is to prevent an impasse from occurring at all. And while recognizing that prevention is not always successful, the following list . . . is useful in helping avoid impasses.

1. Teach negotiation in the caucuses (C). A mediation, in a way, is a supervised negotiation. And, unfortunately, many lawyers have not had much training in negotiation or have limited negotiation skills. Parties in each room have to consider that they must accept responsibility for the proposals they make. . . .

---

*Reprinted with permission.

2. Case evaluation (C). Case evaluation (strength/weakness analysis), at least for me, begins before the very first caucus with the preparation of the confidential pre-mediation submissions. . . . Case evaluation helps avoid impasses and to break impasses when they occur. . . .

3. Control. The mediator must gain control of the proceedings from the onset and keep control.

4. Preparation. The mediator, the parties, and counsel must be prepared for the mediation session. Preparation for mediation is every bit as important as preparation for trial. Pre-mediation submissions and client pre-mediation preparation are essential.

5. Authority to settle. Authority to settle issues must be resolved prior to the mediation. An authority to settle issue that surfaces during a mediation will probably create fatal impasse, or worse, further polarize the parties.

6. Constructive participation. During the mediation itself, the parties should commit to constructive participation in the process. I am *not* suggesting that the parties promise to settle, but rather that they promise to give the process a chance.

7. Interest identification. The mediator must identify the interests of the parties early on. Some interests are obvious. Other interests are not.

8. Appropriate environment. The mediation environment must be appropriate. Pre-arrangement for adequate rooms and food must be made. Further, everyone must plan to allocate adequate time for the process.

9. Listening. The parties and their counsel should be encouraged to listen. The mediator, as much as anyone, must listen.

10. Flexibility. The parties, in separate caucus, should be discouraged from using "bottom line" language. Flexibility is the key to success.

3. Impasse Breaking and Impasse Avoidance

1. People moving. Mediators are in the people-moving business. Sometimes you may have the wrong people together. Sometimes new and different combinations of people produce a better chemistry, which generates intriguing options. The mere physical act of motion suggests progress. New combinations create the perception that a new chapter is being started and renews hope. In his introduction, the mediator should preview and explain the possibility of people involved in the mediation being put together in different combinations. As a result, parties will be less intimidated when it happens and perceive such changes as part of the process.

2. Change the scenery. Mediators lose sight of the fact, particularly in the separate caucus phase, that parties may feel stuck or claustrophobic in their room. Sometimes, especially in an impasse situation, I may take one room "for a walk." . . . People get to move their legs, look out the window, and feel more energized. In several mediations, I have taken one room outside and caucused with them on a park bench. Be especially vigilant of this if your caucus rooms don't have windows. Imagine how you would feel after eight hours in such a room.

3. Food. If an impasse occurs at, for example, 4:00 p.m., I often send out for snacks. Food changes moods. Food energizes. Food keeps people going. Food is something new and different. Food implies we are going to continue to work. Many people can't think if they are hungry. Some people, in this non-smoking age, use food to relax. For whatever reason, people become more agreeable when they are eating. As an interesting side note, observe who is eating and who is not eating. You can get a good read on the participants' temperatures through such an observation.

4. Humor—please be careful. Something you think might be terribly funny may be terribly unfunny to the listener or perceived as demeaning. On the other hand, I have used humor to break tense moments, which has served on several occasions to break an impasse. The safest form of humor is self-deprecating humor. If you can demonstrate that you don't take yourself all that seriously and can laugh at yourself, perhaps the listeners may begin not to take themselves so seriously.

5. Lawyer caucus. When things get stuck, I sometimes find it useful to call a lawyer caucus. In my introduction, I advise the parties and their counsel that I may do so. . . .

6. Recess. Most mediators, myself included, believe that progress made in a mediation is cumulative and that momentum towards resolution is created. However, in certain situations, the parties may be too tired to continue or need some time to reflect. A party may also feel pressured. Fatigue or feeling pressured should never become a basis of a fatal impasse. A mediator should consider calling a recess and setting up a time to continue the mediation.

7. Reconvene the group. The impasse may suggest the parties need more direct interaction. A feeling may need to be expressed. The parties may be more inclined to talk later in the day than they were at the beginning of the mediation. Additionally, the mediator is more aware of the interests and feelings at this point and may be in a better position to facilitate the discussion.

8. Confess being stuck. Mediators must be willing to check their egos at the door. At some later phase of the mediation, a mediator may need to advise the parties that he has "run out of ideas" and that if the matter is to be resolved the parties should consider providing him with some ideas. . . . Also, in the wake of such a confession, the parties may come up with some excellent ideas.

9. Suggest the possibility of fatal impasse. The mediator's confidence and belief that resolution will happen is critical. If the mediator does not believe in resolution, no one else will. But late in a mediation, the mediator may suggest that unless some progress occurs, a fatal impasse may result. Most parties do not want a fatal impasse and will work to overcome the possibility.

10. Re-review litigation costs. Undoubtedly, the mediator has discussed costs in the group session and initial caucus. But in the heat of a mediation, parties may forget. Review the future costs again, but not in a coercive manner.

11. Re-review risks (C). Again, the mediator has already discussed risk in the initial caucus. But re-assessing risk late in a mediation may be very effective. As always, re-assessment of risk should not be coercive or heavy-handed.

12. The value of today. Most parties want to achieve closure. In most matters, the trial date (even when set) is uncertain and the possibility of appeal may exist. The problem may not be resolved for . . . years. The parties have a window of opportunity to resolve their problems today. . . . "Today" has a great deal of value.

13. Re-trace the parties' progress. After five or six hours, the parties may have forgotten the progress that has been made. The mediator must remind the parties of where each was at the beginning of the mediation and where they are now.

14. Solicit disagreement by the party's counsel (C). In a separate caucus, ask the party's counsel whether he seriously disagrees with an identified weakness in the other party's position. The party may need to hear that his lawyer disagrees with him. The mediator, however, must never come between the party and his counsel or humiliate the party's counsel. To do so would be unethical, coercive, and just plain wrong.

15. Review the party's initial goals. During the first caucus, the parties should have identified their goals and interests. But during the mediation, a party may have changed his goals. The mediator should review with the party his initial goals and discuss whether these goals have changed and why.

16. Declare a goal unattainable (C). While it is not appropriate for the mediator to criticize a party's goals, it may become apparent during the mediation that the other side simply will not meet one of the party's goals — and the mediator may choose to make this declaration. Certainly such a declaration risks fatal impasse, but much more often, a party may welcome knowing what is not possible.

17. Focus on future relationships. When the parties may have future relationships beyond the particular problem, the mediator should discuss with the parties how the resolution of this problem will affect future relationships or the possibility of future relationships.

18. Acknowledge that everyone is trying. While the mediator must never be coercive, he may occasionally need to be a "cheerleader" for resolution. The parties may need to be reminded that while a log jam exists, everyone is trying hard to work through it.

19. Have the party's lawyer describe what will happen at trial (C). Sometimes a party may need to hear what the trial will be like, the nature of cross-examination, and what issues may be covered in cross-examination.

F. Mediation as Healing/Therapy and Empowerment

1. Comments and Questions

a. This section addresses the perception that the mediation process itself is beneficial. In terms of the mediation "stories" related by Bush & Folger, (see section B, above), this is the transformation story.

b. Can the transformation story exist independent of the success story? That is, can there be transformation if the price is a nontrivial reduction in the rate of settled disputes? Is there a place for healing or empowerment in commercial disputes?

c. Other pieces in this book that support the empowerment and therapy approach are Leonard Riskin's study of farmer-lender mediation (Chapter 9, section D) and Arbitral Therapy (Chapter 12, section D).

2. Lois Gold, *Influencing Unconscious Influences: The Healing Dimension of Mediation*, 11 MEDIATION QUART. 55 (1993)*

To a significant extent the role of the mediator is constrained by the limitations of the negotiating structure and language. We work primarily on a cognitive level, yet 93 percent of all communication is nonverbal, and significant psychological change usually occurs outside conscious awareness.

Beginning with the assumption of divorce negotiations as a multilevel experience, this article will explore the potential for healing in the noncognitive experience of the mediation process. Drawing on the healing arts, Ericksonian hypnotherapy's model of the unconscious as a creative resource, and our own spiritual centers, I will describe how we can augment the healing elements inherent in a collaborative dispute resolution process.

From this perspective, the focus will be threefold: (1) an examination of the concept of mediator "presence," (2) a consideration of mediation within a healing paradigm, and (3) a discussion of indirect interventions and techniques that promote self-healing.

Mediator "Presence"

How we use ourselves and what we bring of our own personal being has largely been neglected in the mediation literature. Narrow role parameters have defined practice without taking into account the relationship between client and mediator or the "presence" the mediator brings to the negotiation session. While this may have been necessary in the nascence of the profession in order to carve a professional identify, develop skills as negotiators, and guard neutrality, we have not had permission to consider our own unique personas in our work. It is almost as though being a "neutral" implies significant constraints on being a person. Mediation is task oriented; for this reason, we have rarely explored the skills and interventions that do not bear directly on negotiating and bargaining. . . .

Four elements of presence can increase our effectiveness as mediators: (1) being centered; (2) being connected to one's governing values and beliefs and highest purpose; (3) making contact with the humanity of the clients; and (4) being congruent.

1. Being centered. Being centered or grounded refers to the state of physical and mental alignment in which people experience an almost transcendental connection to their being or to the larger universe or cosmos. There is a feeling of harmony, as if boundaries disappear. People empty their mind and simply focus on "what is," observing present experience without interfering with it. A shift of consciousness occurs that makes it possible to see things not ordinarily seen because the focus is outside of the self and thinking and judgement are suspended.

Being centered . . . is an altered state of consciousness. In mediation, we usually operate in the linear, analytical mode. However, we shift consciousness all the time, and each state of consciousness produces new opportunities for problem solving, because the mechanisms that operate within it organize experience differently. Working from the center draws from the creative side of our brain, frequently generating new perceptions and perspectives on the problem. At any time during or before a mediation session, the mediator can momentarily shift consciousness by taking a few deep breaths, emptying the mind of all thought, and simply centering on the awareness of the present moment.

When the mediator is centered, this attitude of self-acceptance and self-respect translates into an appreciation of the clients' humanity, enabling the mediator to see them apart from the context of the dispute. A mediator who is centered can inspire trust and allow others to reflect their own truth. When the mediator projects a sense of reverence for what is sacred in this work, is willing to view the clients from the heart, and can speak to the clients' soul, this work will be healing.

2. Being connected to one's governing values and beliefs and highest purpose. The more emotionally connected we are to our highest intention in choosing to become a mediator, the more the power of that intention will be expressed in our work. Because the decision to become a mediator for many represented a radical shift in goals and often grew out of a desire to bring about change, this profession is characterized by a sense of purpose and mission. The more the highest intention in making that choice is clarified, made conscious, and amplified, the more it becomes a guiding force. Intention organizes behavior at the unconscious level. Centering on intention, on why we answered the "calling," is empowering and affects the presence we project. To the extent that we convey the highest possibilities of this work, we enable our clients to recognize and clarify their highest possibilities.

A short meditation before a session can be used to clarify and connect to one's central and governing values and highest purpose. Sit comfortably, close your eyes, take several slow deep breaths, and review your belief in mediation, the skills and resources you have acquired as a negotiator, what you respect most about how you work, why you chose to become a mediator, and what you sense are the deepest concerns and hopes of the clients you are about to see.

3. Connecting with the humanity of the clients. The third element of "presence" is the ability to connect with the client. Some experts suggest that connection is the key to helping and that the quality of the relationship is what makes the difference in enabling others to bear their pain and garner strength. . . .

This kind of connection comes from being able to acknowledge and simply "be with what is"—the loss, sorrow, pain—and to not need to do anything about it. There is a healing power in just being there. By the very act of entering the world of others and acknowledging experiences they may not have been able to communicate and making these experiences more understandable and real to them, something transformational occurs. A profound feeling of intimacy is created when people feel they have been understood at the deepest level. Rapport is lost if the mediator focuses only on the substantive issues and ignores the body language or other signs of stress in the person.

It is easy to become so absorbed in the negotiation process or caught up in the conflict that the individual person becomes invisible. The mediator should try to step back and look at both parties in their human struggle to survive—seeing the lost hopes, spent dreams, and pain. The compassionate acceptance of each person's humanity that the mediator expresses enables the clients to feel more compassion for themselves and possibly for their partners.

It is interesting to compare mediation cases in which the issues were competently resolved and those in which a real feeling of connection between mediator and clients existed. The difference can be seen in the good-bye. It is in the hug instead of the handshake. Mediators are invited to review their cases and examine what characterized the cases in which they felt an emotional connection with clients. What was that connection rooted in? What part of the mediator's self was allowed into the mediation process? I suspect that these are the couples who were helped at the deepest level.

4. Being congruent. A fourth element of presence is congruence. Being congruent is the condition of being emotionally honest, being who you are, and not allowing your anxiety, pride, or ego to be a mask. It is being authentic, not having to be perfect and have all the answers. Carl Rogers has said that "there is something I do before a session. I let myself know that I am enough. Not perfect. Perfect wouldn't be enough. But that I am human, and that is enough." The power of congruence comes from the permission to be who you are, unencumbered by "shoulds" and self-consciousness.

A Healing Paradigm

As mediators, it is not our goal to heal our clients, and we do not typically think of ourselves as healers. However, I believe that we could actualize the healing potential inherent in a cooperative process by thinking about mediation in terms of a healing paradigm as well as within a conflict resolution context. Healing is a complex phenomenon that has physical, spiritual, and emotional components. . . . I would like to draw on the elements of the healing arts that relate to what we do as mediators.

One of the healer's fundamental roles is to help individuals tune into their own healing capacities. People are healed by different kinds of healers and systems because the real healer is within. Different techniques merely activate the inner healer.

Many diverse techniques in the healing arts exist. The threads that unite the various approaches to healing are universals that can be applied to any helping relationship to make it more healing. . . . [T]he major elements of any healing experience [include] (1) the role of unconditional love and caring, (2) the nature of the relationship—rapport, connection, emotional support—since healing does not occur in isolation, (3) the importance of the return to wholeness, (4) the desirability of listening to innate wisdom—helping clients find and listen to their higher intelligence, (5) the need to develop a healing attitude—believing change is possible and working toward a better future, and (6) the realization that healing is our natural state, since the organism strives toward health and restoration.

Love is the uniting principle in all healing approaches. Healing's opposite is judgement, and any system or practitioner loses effectiveness in becoming judgmental. The true healer merely gives the gift of healing but does not watch over the patient to say what form it should be received in. This frees the healer to heal unhampered by anxiety over the possible results. The common denominator in all healing methods is unconditional love that respects the uniqueness of each individual and empowers clients to take responsibility for their own well-being. One aspect of the healer's love is to help clients overcome the fear of change and to align themselves with the process of transformation. Healing arises out of compassion. Compassion is a genuine concern for another's pain. Suffering is a soulless state. Part of the role of ritual is to coax the soul into participating in a time of need. The compassionate healer whose soul is present awakens the other's soul. Empathy, nonpossessive warmth, and genuineness create a sense of being "present" with the client . . . genuinely listening to what is occurring at the moment and putting aside any preconceived notions of what needs to be done. The way we stand in relationship to each other fosters healing. My woundedness allows me to connect to you in your woundedness and creates trust. I know what suffering is. I know of your feeling of isolation, loss, and fright. My woundedness allows me to be with you in a nonjudgmental way, and my presence facilitates something. In a true healing relationship, both heal and are healed.

Although our work does not typically have healing as a focus, the mediation process shares the fundamental principles just outlined. While we describe what we do differently, mediation, like other helping professions, operates within this core framework. We see ourselves as caring individuals who believe that clients have the inner capacity to find their own solutions. We activate the hope that life can be better, that solutions are possible. We value self-determination and empowerment. We are oriented toward the future, supporting clients in moving forward and in constructively coping with change. We help them work toward the higher good for themselves and their families.

Disputes that are honorably resolved open the way for any wounds to mend. A process that is respectful of each person and that encourages the expression of mutual respect and courtesy heals the ravages of hateful and angry diatribes. A process that supports people in retaining control of the awareness of mutual needs, mutual losses, and shared concerns reduces feelings of victimization and blame. A civilized parting in which the parties retain their integrity honors the marriage and the life that was shared. All this is healing. . . . [A]t its best, the mediation process itself, independent of particular interventions or techniques, has considerable healing potential. Perhaps the unrealized potency of mediation lies in the experience of a collaborative, constructive process, which as a whole, has an integrity and healing power that is greater than the benefits derived in any given session.

As an experiment, imagine how your work might be affected if you saw yourself as someone who could help others activate their own healing energies, or if you believed that one of the goals of mediation was to help people heal. How might it change your "presence"? How might you interact with clients differently? How might your interventions be different?

Indirect Interventions and Techniques That Promote Self-Healing

By having a more open and compassionate heart and by making healing part of our consciousness, we can evoke the desire to heal, help create movement toward a healing path, and participate in healing that arises naturally. If we operate from a healing paradigm as well as from a dispute resolution model, we will intuitively bring this dimension into our work more often. This might appropriately be termed *holistic* mediation.

In addition to being aware of the quality of the relationships we establish with our clients and the "presence" we bring to our work, we can use a number of strategic techniques that foster self-healing. The unconscious mind is particularly receptive to suggestions at times of emotional crisis on both a conscious and unconscious level. The indirect references or suggestions the mediator make can have a powerful effect on the subconscious.

1. Frame mediation as a healing process. You can frame mediation in healing terms in many ways. In your informational "monologue," when the clients' attention is usually riveted to you, you can describe how mediation can pave the way for healing by helping parties lay aside old grievances, increase understanding, build trust, become less angry, begin to forgive each other, and so on. Telling an anecdote about other clients or casually stating that other people have experienced mediation as healing can plant a seed without challenging the defenses when there are high levels of conflict. With more receptive clients, you can suggest that if they make healing one of their personal goals, they might find that negotiations go more smoothly. Whenever you refer to the potential for healing in the mediation process, you set the stage for cooperative, healing behaviors.

It is important to remember that while people come to mediation primarily to get matters resolved, a part of them often seeks something more—to be acknowledged, affirmed, have the marriage honored, or say goodbye with dignity. Whenever I describe mediation in terms of these unspoken universals or in terms of paving the way for wounds to heal, I know I have touched a responsive chord. The mediation session is a rare opportunity to respectfully acknowledge profound human concerns at a point where the parties are together, with *both* capable of listening. We speak to the part of the psyche that . . . recognizes the sorrow, loss, and broken spirit and longs (in even the angriest clients) to be whole. Do not underestimate the power of tapping into the universal desire for wellness that exists in even the bitterest disputes. You can suggest that clients make self-healing a guiding principle in interacting with each other—that is, that they constantly ask themselves the question, Will this action promote my healing or make things worse?

2. *Reinforce the choice of mediation as a healing choice.* Committing to a cooperative resolution process and moving in the direction of what seems right promotes healing. Help clients to appreciate the full significance of the choice they have made in using mediation. . . . The act of choosing a peaceful path is a healthy choice. Choice changes us in the quality and direction of the choice. Reinforce the importance of the peaceful choice as a commendable effort toward the higher moral ground.

3. *Clarify the highest intentions.* The more you can help clients become aware of their highest intentions in making positive choices, the more they will be guided by those intentions. Embedded in the choice to mediate are unspoken hopes that can be powerful forces in helping clients get the most out of this process. By helping them clarify their highest intentions and goals in choosing mediation, those intentions become more concrete, visible, and attainable. In the opening discussion of what they hope to achieve from mediation, probe to help them articulate their highest purpose. To each response, ask questions like the following: "What else?" "What would that be like?" "What are your highest hopes for the family or for the future?" Restate or reframe what has been said, to mirror back and anchor what they have each stated as their most important concerns.

4. *Generate awareness of the sacred in divorce.* In divorce, things that should be held in reverence are often treated like bartered commodities. Couples in conflict can become so narrowly focused on their dispute that they lose all awareness of the larger, more important context. The act of bringing children into the world is a privilege, the creation of life sacred; nothing is ever permanent, we are always having to face change. Help clients relate their experience to the larger contexts that govern life. Perspective comes with seeing our small experience in relationship to the overall human experience. Put divorce in its proper context—the undoing of what were once sacred vows. Help clients remember their dreams for the children, recognize that the love that once existed between them is carried on by the children, and accept the lifelong family connection through these children.

5. *Create a spiritual reframe for grief.* It is helpful to share information about the grieving process with couples who seem locked in anger and battle. The mediator can offer direct information about stages of grieving, a simple preemptive statement about the fact that the rage and blame of intense conflict are often a manifestation of grief, or that sometimes intense grief at the loss in divorce carries within it the loss and grief of the past. The mediator can also allude to wider metaphysical contexts—that no life is without suffering; pain is a great teacher; honoring one's grief can open one's heart to greater levels of compassion; a person's own woundedness can make it possible to appreciate a spouse's woundedness. The goal is to help the clients unlock their isolated identification with their pain and shift the frame that locks them in the dispute by referencing it to larger metaphysical contexts about pain and suffering.

6. *Make indirect or embedded suggestions about healing.* Indirect or embedded suggestions address change at an unconscious level. They are effective when there are high levels of conflict, resistance to cooperation, or strong positional arguing. These interventions enable shifts in perception or attitudes to take place without challenging the person's defenses.

You can embed suggestions about healing by posing questions that contain a presuppposition about healing that must be accepted in order to answer the question. Examples include the following: "What is the most healing way you know to handle this parenting dispute?" "How do you see yourselves healing the family?" "How do you want the divorce process to honor what was good in your marriage?" These questions contain a presupposition about the clients' ability to act in healing ways and require parties to search internally for positive solutions without having the opportunity to resist being positive. Even angry clients can be asked, "What would your higher intelligence say about this dilemma?" (The client cannot logically resist this question and is required to draw on personal strengths in order to respond.)

7. *Reframe negotiations in language associated with healing.* Questions framed in terms of healing words, like harmony, wholeness, peaceful, healthy, or mending, require the answer to be organized around these principles. They alter the accessibility of information consistent with these principles and require parties to reorganize responses in terms of mutual benefits rather than individual posturing. Examples might include the following: "How can this misunderstanding be mended?" "How can you bring more harmony into the transitions between households?" Questions or potential impasses can be framed in terms of what would be the most healing solution. A concession can be reframed as a healing gesture or as a gift for the "higher good of the family."

8. *Connect with clients' higher intelligence.* The emotional overload of divorce hampers the capacity for rational, mature reasoning. Impulse control is diminished. To the extent that mediation helps shore up rational functioning by the rules and structure it provides, we can specifically address the more resourceful part of the person—the "higher intelligence." For example, a client who was a college professor regularly launched into a diatribe of "I can't believe you are doing this to me" whenever his wife brought an issue to the bargaining table. When I asked if, as a favor, his higher intelligence could address the issue on the table, he understood immediately and offered a reasonable proposal.

In divorce, we are working with a duality of the personality; the part that wants to act out, and the part, however buried, that wants to do the right thing, that longs for healing and wholeness. Often, both parts need to be acknowledged by the mediator, especially with clients who frequently erupt emotionally in the mediation session. You can help clients find and listen to their higher intelligence by posing questions that require them to hypothetically put aside their angry, mistrustful, or other negative feelings and think of a solution as if these feelings did not exist. As an example, you could ask the following question: "If he hadn't had the affair, what solutions do you think could be found for the disagreement about overnight visits?" You can pose questions directly to the "higher intelligence" while acknowledging the feelings and wishes of the angry or hurt side. Ask clients to operate from this part, and be "unconditionally constructive," acting in the direction of good regardless of whether the other reciprocates.

9. *Increase hope and the belief in the potential for success.* Hope operates to energize and organize a person's resources. The client's confidence and beliefs about the help to be received affect healing. . . . This may account for the frequent reports of improvement between initial phone calls and the first appointment that has been found in a variety of helping professions. Even on the telephone, be encouraging about the potential for success. Conveying your faith increases theirs. Create pictures of positive future expectancies. Tell stories of other success. Help them see how far they have come. Describe the behaviors and attitudes most associated with success in mediation.

10. Make the most of the introductory "monologue." During times of emotional crisis or life transition, the unconscious mind is looking for information to help resolve developmental demands and ease psychological pain. People are more suggestible and are likely to be deeply receptive to suggestions. The introductory informational "monologue" can be strategically used to convey information conducive to negotiating success, cooperation, and healing, because the unconscious is paying close attention. You can embed suggestions about healing and higher purpose as discussed earlier, preempt potential roadblocks by describing a set of behavioral norms associated with successful outcomes, or describe future possibilities for family life after divorce. You may notice times when the clients' rapt attention to your words is almost trancelike. The intensity of their absorption in what you are saying allows your words to enter their subconscious. In this sense, the introductory "monologue" can be used as an induction into a healing and cooperative process.

11. Utilize postmediation suggestion. The unconscious receptivity and search for helpful information are similarly operative at the end of mediation. The mediator can use the closure phase of the last session to seed future growth and healing. In hypnosis, this is referred to as posthypnotic suggestion—the suggestion that clients can continue to learn from the experience in a variety of ways. In a closure monologue, you can suggest how the knowledge clients have gained in mediation may help them handle conflict better in the future; how they may find, as time goes on, that this experience has allowed old wounds to heal; or that the mediation experience may enable them to relate to each other differently in the future. By describing the possibilities for future success or change, you create a future expectancy that may increase the likelihood of unconscious behavior supporting that expectancy.

12. Prescribe leave-taking rituals. The last strategy is to suggest to clients that at some point in time, they may want to consider a ritual or ceremony allowing them to say goodbye to the old relationship and acknowledge a new basis for relating in the future. It is best to let clients design the ceremony, because the symbols and action they choose tend to have more meaning than what you could prescribe. You can describe an example of a basic structure for leave-taking rituals or ceremonies as follows:

Clarifying the purpose—honoring, letting go, burying (what or whom).

Choosing key symbols—representing the other person, the old or new relationship, or the future (wedding rings, memorabilia, photos, heirlooms held for the children).

Deciding on a symbolic act—treasured possession exchange; peace offering; burying the hatchet or burning a symbol of the past; exchanging farewell letters; casting objects out to sea.

Conclusion

There is no rigid prescription for using the ideas described in this article, nor do I offer a unified model based on these concepts. Instead, I have tried to present ideas about how mediation can be more healing and to raise awareness about how the quality of the relationships we establish with our clients can foster a more profound experience. Mediation has the potential to be an ever greater healing force than I have suggested here. Future progress is in the hands of each individual practitioner. However, I do believe there is room for us, as a profession, to consider a more holistic approach to mediation. The ideas in this article will hopefully continue to stimulate the creative unconscious of readers who are mediators about their role in the mediation process.

3. Robert A. Baruch Bush, *Efficiency and Protection, or Empowerment and Recognition?: The Mediator's Role and Ethical Standards in Mediation*, 41 Fla. L. Rev. 253, 267-86 (1989)*

A. The Empowerment-and-Recognition Conception

Thoughtful mediation theorists and practitioners have given much consideration to identifying mediation's unique powers. In their comments, two points consistently are expressed regarding the capacities of the mediation process.

The first special power of mediation, and what some call "[t]he overriding feature and . . . value of mediation," is that "it is a consensual process that seeks self-determined resolutions." Mediation places the substantive outcome of the dispute within the control and determination of the parties themselves; it frees them from relying on or being subjected to the opinions and standards of outside "higher authorities," legal or otherwise. Further, mediation not only allows the parties to set their own standards for an acceptable solution, it also requires them to search for solutions that are within their own capacity to effectuate. In other words, the parties themselves set the standards, and the parties themselves marshall the actual resources to resolve the dispute. When agreement is reached, the parties have designed and implemented their own solution to the problem. Even when the parties do not reach an agreement, they experience the concrete possibility, to be more fully realized in other situations, that they can control their own circumstances. They discover that they need not be wholly dependent on outside institutions, legal or otherwise, to solve their problems. I call this the empowerment function of mediation: its capacity to encourage the parties to exercise autonomy, choice, and self-determination.

Some authorities explicitly recognize empowerment as a unique value of mediation, while others do so implicitly. For example, the value of empowerment certainly is one of the implied premises of Professor Stulberg's cogent argument against requiring mediators to control the "fairness" or "efficiency" of agreements. Concern for empowerment also underlies what could appear to be a distinct view of the special power of mediation, which stresses its capacity to "foster unique and creative solutions that respond to the parties' needs." While this could be seen as a separate power of mediation, I believe that its value ultimately is connected to the concern for individual empowerment. That is, self-determination and empowerment are furthered through outcomes that are designed by and for the parties, rather than outcomes designed by and (at least in part) for outsiders. Mediated outcomes empower parties by responding to them as unique individuals with particular problems, rather than as depersonalized representatives of general problems faced by classes of actors or by society as a whole.

The second special power of mediation was described classically by Professor Lon Fuller: "The central quality of mediation [is] its capacity to reorient the parties to each other . . . by helping them to achieve a new and shared perception of their relationship, a perception that will redirect their attitudes and dispositions toward one another." What Fuller describes here is not just a technique to produce agreements, but an inherently valuable accomplishment uniquely attainable through mediation. Fuller sees mediation as evoking in each party recognition and acknowledgment of, and some degree of understanding and empathy for, the other party's situation, even though their interests and positions may remain opposed. Of course,

*Reprinted with permission.

such mutual recognition often will help produce concrete accommodations and an ultimate agreement. But even when it does not, evoking recognition is itself an accomplishment of enormous value: the value of escaping our alienated isolation and rediscovering our common humanity, even in the midst of bitter division. Professor Riskin observes accordingly that one of the great values of mediation is that it can "encourage the kind of dialogue that would help . . . [the disputants experience] a perspective of caring and interconnection." Others also have stressed this special power of mediation to "humanize" us to one another, to translate between us, and to help us recognize each other as fellows even when we are in conflict. I call this the recognition function of mediation.

B. What Mediators Can Do—And Others Cannot

Here, then, are the special powers of mediation: It can encourage personal empowerment and self-determination as alternatives to institutional dependency, and it can evoke recognition of common humanity in the face of bitter conflict. Both powers involve restoring to the individual a sense of his own value and that of his fellow man in the face of an increasingly alienating and isolating social context. These are valuable powers indeed. Further, they are unique to mediation. These are functions mediation can perform that other processes cannot.

As for evoking empathetic recognition of the other fellow, adjudication and arbitration at best treat such recognition as irrelevant. More often, they destroy the very possibility of empathy by encouraging strong, frequently extreme, adversarial behavior. While in negotiation, recognition may occur, but only haphazardly, for no one stands above the fray to encourage and help the parties rise above their own positions and acknowledge those of their opponents. As for empowerment, it is almost by definition impossible in adjudication and arbitration. Both disempower the parties in differing degrees, whether by their authoritative and legalistic character, or by their heavy reliance on advice and representation by professional advocates. Although empowerment is more of a possibility in negotiation, the difficulty of reaching settlement in unassisted negotiations often frustrates this possibility, and negotiation through professional advocates again involves disempowerment in its own way.

Thus, what mediation can do that other processes cannot, is to encourage empowerment of the parties and evoke recognition between them. These are its unique and valuable capacities. The mediator's role is to act so as to fulfill these unique capacities. Accordingly, in general terms, the mediator's role is: (1) to encourage the empowerment of the parties—i.e., the exercise of their autonomy and self-determination in deciding whether and how to resolve their dispute; and (2) to promote the parties' mutual recognition of each other as human beings despite their adverse positions. I emphasize here that this role can and should be performed successfully whether or not the parties reach an agreement, and whether or not any agreement reached satisfies some external standard of right or fairness. In other words, it is not the mediator's job to guarantee a fair agreement, or any agreement at all; it is the mediators job to guarantee the parties the fullest opportunity for self-determination and mutual acknowledgment. Mediators who ignore this job have not fulfilled their professional responsibilities, even if the parties reach an agreement. Conversely, mediators who do this job have fulfilled their responsibilities, even if the parties reach no agreement.

C. Is Anyone Really Interested in This?

Before analyzing the concrete dimensions of the empowerment-and-recognition conception of the mediator's role, consider the following question: Could such a conception possibly appear realistic and viable to those involved in developing mediator standards, especially in relation to court-connected mediation? In many states, trial judges are the ones who decide whether to refer cases to mediation. Lawyers also are deeply involved, both as mediators and as participants in the development of mediator standards. Is it realistic to expect judges to accept this view of the mediator's role rather than the efficiency conception, when conservation of court resources is supposedly a major reason for the judicial interest in mediation? Further, will lawyers accept this view rather than the protection-of-rights conception, when their professional identity is so tied to advocating clients' rights? What follows is a brief but hopeful answer to these questions.

First, the notion that judges see the value of mediation primarily in terms of efficiency has been seriously challenged of late. At a recent conference, one federal judge said that he would use alternative processes like mediation "even if I had no docket problem at all." The reason, echoed by other judges in explaining their practice of encouraging and even mediating settlements, is not administrative convenience but superior quality. "In most cases, the absolute result of a trial is not as high a quality of justice as the freely negotiated, give a little, take a little settlement." In short, judges may be motivated more by quality concerns than efficiency concerns. If so, then the quality focus of the empowerment-and-recognition conception of the mediator's role should appeal to them.

As for lawyers, they too are probably far from unanimous in seeing mediation in terms of protection-of-rights values. Many of the pioneers of humanistic mediation—in divorce and community mediation and elsewhere—have been veteran lawyers disillusioned with the quality of justice in the adversary system and searching for "higher quality" alternatives. One can safely say that many lawyers still working in the adversary system share this outlook. To these lawyers, at least, the empowerment-and-recognition conception should be attractive.

Other professionals involved in mediation, as well as disputing parties themselves, are even more likely to favor the empowerment-and-recognition conception. Professionals such as counselors, therapists and the like, a large part of whose work involves helping clients to understand themselves and others better and to "take responsibility" for their responses to problems, should find the empowerment-and-recognition conception an appropriate extrapolation of their usual professional role, albeit in a new context. As for disputing parties themselves, the high rates of party satisfaction with mediation that researchers report seem directly related to the opportunities mediation presents for self-determination and mutual acknowledgment. If so, then adopting the empowerment-and-recognition conception should be very responsive to the factors that make mediation desirable to the parties in the first place.

I do not mean by the above argument to understate the problem of persuading legal professionals to accept the empowerment-and-recognition conception. Conferences of judges and court administrators, for example, regularly emphasize efficiency and economy as the most important advantages of mediation to the court system. Much less, if any, attention is paid to the questions of self-determination and recognition. Nevertheless, one of the major reasons for judges' interest in ADR is plainly their concern for public satisfaction with the system of justice they administer. Judges see ADR as a means to dispel dissatisfaction with the formal adjudication process. As noted above, however, the public favors mediation precisely because of its capacity to promote self-determination and recognition, and not necessarily because of its speed or economy. Thus, if adequately educated on the issue, judges should eventually see that adopting the empowerment-and-recognition conception is the best way to realize the capacity of mediation to increase public satisfaction with the justice system.

Finally, while the empowerment-and-recognition conception of the mediator's role may stem from the idealistic strain of mediation theory and practice, I believe that it is strongly implied in the language of recent state legislation. For example, according to Florida Statute section 44.301(1):

"Mediation" means a process whereby a neutral third party acts to encourage and facilitate the resolution of a dispute without prescribing what it should be. It is an informal and nonadversarial process with the objective of helping the disputing parties reach a mutually acceptable agreement.

This statutory language, which is more precise than that of many proposed mediation standards, stresses empowerment and recognition in a number of ways. First, it specifies that the mediator should not prescribe the resolution, suggesting the empowerment function. Second, it specifies that the process should be nonadversarial, suggesting the recognition function. Finally, while it certainly contemplates agreement as the aim of the process, it qualifies that objective with the requirements of mutuality and acceptability.

These are not superfluous terms. Each connotes one of the special values mediation can achieve. Mutuality suggests the value of promoting mutual recognition; acceptability suggests the value of encouraging self-determination and individual choice. That similar language frequently is used to describe mediation should not deprive it of its real meaning. Honoring that meaning, I suggest, requires us to read the Florida law, and others like it, as much closer to adopting the empowerment-and-recognition conception of the mediator's role than either of the alternatives discussed above. This is but one more reason to rest the development of mediator standards on this conception of the mediator's role.

IV. CONCRETE IMPLICATIONS

I began this article with the premise that we cannot establish specific standards for mediators without first adopting some governing conception of the mediator's role. This crucial first step has been my primary focus thus far. We must now move from the general conception of the mediator's role to the more concrete question of what we should actually expect (and not expect) the mediator to do in fulfilling this role. . . In this final section, I do this both positively, suggesting some specific implications that follow from adoption of the empowerment-and-recognition conception, and negatively, criticizing provisions common to several recently proposed codes of mediation practice.

Discussing concrete implications will help clarify what kind of specific standards for qualification, training, and practice should be established. This discussion also will begin to meet a crucial need of mediators themselves, one that often is missing in the world of practice: a clear indicator of what is expected of a mediator. Other dispute-resolution professionals—judges, arbitrators, advocates—operate under fairly clearly defined expectations. Mediators and those they serve deserve no less.

Again, I stress here that I am concerned with the specific responsibilities of the mediator as mediator, rather than, for example, the separate responsibilities of lawyer-mediators under their own code of professional responsibility. For no matter what separate standards they may have to abide by as members of other professions, all mediators also must fulfill their responsibilities as mediators. If they fail in this regard, the special capacities of mediation for empowerment and recognition cannot be realized in practice.

A. What We Should Expect of the Mediator

The empowerment-and-recognition conception of the mediator's role relieves the mediator of any sense of obligation to produce agreements or to ensure against "unfair" agreements; for the definition of success in this role is neither reaching agreements nor protecting rights. However, the empowerment-and-recognition conception by no means frees mediators entirely from a sense of professional obligation; it merely redirects the concern. Now the mediator will feel obligated to do everything possible to ensure that the parties are empowered to exercise their autonomy and self-determination, and that on some level they acknowledge and recognize each other's common humanity. Yet this question still remains: How do mediators know whether they have fulfilled these obligations responsibly? In other words, what specific expectations should mediators strive to satisfy?

I suggest first that both empowerment and recognition require, so to speak, a "pushy" mediator. This means a mediator willing and able to "push" the parties, not in an antagonistic or hostile sense, but in the positive sense of inviting, supporting, encouraging, motivating, and urging the parties to work through the processes of self-determined choice and mutual acknowledgment. Both of these processes are typically so difficult, especially in the midst of disputes, that many individuals may give up (or not even try) for lack of confidence that they can accomplish anything of value. In fact, with some skilled support and guidance, they often can accomplish wonders. Therefore, fulfilling the empowerment-and-recognition role requires the mediator to push the parties in this positive and supportive sense. To put it another way, and to avoid the possible misimpression that I am simply arguing for an aggressive *style* of mediation, mediators must push for the parties to engage in self-determined choice and mutual acknowledgment, using whatever style and strategies they find most effective. Style is a matter of choice and judgment; pushing for self-determination and acknowledgment is a matter of duty.

With this understanding of what I mean by "pushing" in general let me be more specific about what kind of pushing the mediator should do. Fulfilling the empowerment role requires the mediator to ensure that the parties act with full information and understanding in making their decisions. In the absence of such knowledge and comprehension, autonomous choice and self-determination are illusory. Therefore, the mediator should push for the parties to disclose and otherwise marshall all information relevant to resolving the dispute. Alternatively, if significant pieces of information cannot be known, the mediator should push for the parties to carefully assess the importance of the missing pieces in deciding whether and how to proceed in their absence.

Apart from the marshalling of information, the mediator should push for the parties to fully comprehend all the information before them, including the range of issues presented and each party's positions. Therefore, the mediator should summarize, clarify, question, and test for comprehension before allowing decision-making to proceed. On another level, and in light of the information marshalled, the mediator should push for the parties to fully identify and consider all possible options for resolving the issues, before they focus on specific options and actually make decisions.

Perhaps most important, as the process begins either producing the terms of an agreement or moving toward impasse, the mediator should push for the parties to consider and understand fully the consequences of *either* outcome, before they decide for or against agreement. Phrased in the negative, the mediator should make every effort to prevent the parties from either reaching or failing to reach an agreement on the basis of inaccurate or incomplete information or understanding, including failures of either side to understand the other's positions.

The empowerment role also defines the mediator's obligation with respect to law and legal advice. On one hand, the empowerment role is based on the premise that the law need not control the parties' decision regarding how to resolve the dispute; some recent legislation is quite clear about this. On the other hand, the empowerment role assumes the importance of ensuring that decisions are based on all available information. Clearly, information about the law may be relevant to the parties "as an indication of what is obtainable from the legal marketplace, . . . as an indication of societal standards, . . . [or] as an expression of underlying principles . . . which the parties might want to consider in approaching their own resolution." Accordingly the mediator's obligation here must be two-sided. The mediator should push for the parties to obtain and consider independent legal advice before committing themselves to an agreement. However, the mediator also should push for the parties not to abdicate their autonomous judgment and power of choice by mechanically deferring to legal experts and law, but rather to assess their own best interests independently, and make independent decisions in light of all considerations. These obligations should apply whether or not the mediator directly provides the parties with information about the law.

Turning now to the recognition role, fulfilling this role requires the mediator to make every effort to evoke mutual acknowledgement and recognition between the parties. Therefore, the mediator should first of all push for the parties to articulate their positions and the reasons behind them as clearly, forcefully, and yet as respectfully as possible. This will help ensure that each party's views are accessible and therefore able to evoke acknowledgment from the other. Second, as recognition rarely is automatic, the mediator should go further and affirmatively translate and explain each party's positions and reasons to the other, in terms most likely to evoke the other's recognition and empathy. Finally, the mediator should push for each party to hear and understand the other's position without feeling threatened, to the point where each can feel, and if possible somehow express, a measure of recognition of the other party's situation.

The above description of specific obligations flowing from the empowerment-and-recognition role is illustrative, not exhaustive. Yet it includes some of the most important elements of what we should expect mediators to do. One crucial element not mentioned above is the obligation of impartiality, which is necessary to fulfill both aspects of the empowerment-and-recognition role. What I mean by impartiality, however, goes beyond the usual connotation of disclosure of conflicts and neutrality regarding outcome. In reading my description of the "pushy" mediator's job, one might ask how mediators can do so much pushing without alienating one or both parties. Apart from my earlier caveat regarding the positive meaning of "pushy" and "pushing for," the answer lies in an expanded conception of the obligation of impartiality.

Mediators should be visibly evenhanded or two-sided in their pushing. In other words, they should direct their invitations, support, encouragements, challenges, and urgings toward each party in turn and each should see clearly that the other is receiving similar treatment. If necessay, mediators should explicitly assure the parties that they intend to behave identically toward each side, and of course they should always fulfill this assurance. Mediators whose pushing is positive in character, and who adhere to the requirement of *active* impartiality, can serve for each side as translator to the other and also serve each side as devil's advocate for the other. And they can do so without ever losing the trust and confidence of both sides that is necessary to fulfilling both aspects of the mediator's role. I should note, however, that this may be much easier to do if the mediator does at least some of this pushing while meeting separately with each side, a point I return to below.

One other aspect of the obligation of active impartiality is also quite important in fulfilling both aspects of the empowerment-and-recognition role. The impartiality of mediators means not only that they are allied with neither side, but that because of a lack of personal investment, they have more distance and perspective on the parties' discussions. This position "above the fray" should not be a passive listening post. Rather, it should be the basis for what I call the mediator's job of narration. The mediator can impartially hear, and impartially report to the parties, many crucial parts of their own dialogue that they themselves may not have grasped fully or even heard because of their closeness to the situation. Offers, counteroffers, new options for resolution, actual agreements on issues, and statements of acknowledgment and recognition all are presented frequently in mediation sessions without one or both parties even realizing what has occurred. To fulfill both the empowerment and recognition functions, the mediator can and should be an actively impartial *narrator* who lets no relevant exchange between the parties go unheard or ignored.

To conclude this discussion, I must emphasize the fact that almost all the obligations I have described as flowing from the empowerment-and-recognition conception are affirmative obligations, not constraints or restrictions. The reason for this is, as suggested above, that this conception of the mediator's role stems from a positive view of mediation as *seeking* something good in itself, namely empowerment and recognition. The negative view of mediation as *avoidance* of trial or unprincipled bargaining, and the efficiency and protection-of-rights conceptions that derive from this view, tend to produce negative or restrictive definitions of the mediator's obligations (or none at all). Because I reject these conceptions, I also reject the negative approach of several recent "codes" of mediation practice that stem from them. While my purpose here is not to delve into detail, I want to add some final critical comments on some of the common provisions of those codes. These comments indicate what I think should be avoided in moving from the general conception of the mediator's role to setting specific standards.

B. What We Should *Not* Expect of the Mediator

A good deal of commonality exists among the codes of mediator practice proposed or adopted in recent years. My comments here are directed to certain types of provisions that appear in most of these codes or proposals. My criticism derives from my previous argument regarding the importance of the empowerment-and-recognition conception, and from my sense that the provisions in question are inconsistent with responsible fulfillment of that conception.

Consider first provisions imposing a duty on the mediator to advise and "urge" the parties to obtain outside legal advice throughout the mediation process, especially before signing or even "reaching an emotional commitment" to an agreement. Even codes addressed to lawyer-mediators impose this duty. As argued above, the empowerment role obliges the mediator to push for the parties to acquire and consider legal advice. But these provisions go further and seem by their tone to require (or at least allow) the mediator to encourage parties to follow the legal advice they receive without first fully and independently assessing the matter for themselves. This is inappropriate, for it implicates the mediator in disempowering the parties by allowing or encouraging them to submit to legal experts and the law. These provisions simply reflect the protection-of-rights conception, and make little sense once that conception is rejected.

Next, consider provisions imposing a duty on the mediator to ensure the fairness of the agreement, or a duty to "terminate" mediation if the process will result in an unfair or "unreasonable" agreement. Beyond the fact that they compromise impartiality and therefore impair the mediator's effectiveness, such provisions again derive from the protection-of-rights conception and are antithetical to the premise of self-determination inherent in the empowerment conception. This is not to say that mediators have no right to voice concerns about fairness. In one sense, doing so forms part of their obligation to push for full understanding. If the mediator senses real unfairness in an agreement with which the "exploited" party seems satisfied, the mediator should consider testing that party's comprehension of the terms and consequences of the agreement, especially those aspects the mediator considers "unfair." If, however, the party is fully aware of the implications, and still satisfied, then the mediator's "termination" of the process is simply an act of disempowerment.

Mediator concerns for fairness also may relate to the recognition function, for severe unfairness may indicate an absence of recognition on one side, and may toll the mediator's duty to push more with that party to evoke acknowledgment of the other party's situation. Nevertheless, I see no justification for terminating mediation if recognition is absent. The only circumstance that would toll a duty to terminate is when it appears clear that a party lacks the capacity to participate in the process or make self-determined choices because of his or her mental, emotional, or physical condition. Of course, as Professor Stulberg has noted, the mediator may certainly choose to withdraw from a mediation because of personal moral qualms, but this differs greatly from imposing an actual duty to terminate.

I turn now to provisions that require the mediator to prevent intimidation, assure "balanced dialogue," and terminate the mediation if a party acts in "bad faith." What is striking about these provisions is their negative and restrictive character. They say that the mediator should prevent and control intimidation, imbalance, and bad faith. But they say nothing about the mediator's positive capacity, and obligation, not only to balance but to enrich the dialogue: to translate, explain, evoke, and thereby arouse the parties to mutual recognition. Mediators can do much more than balance and control the dialogue, and they should do more. Unfortunately, these provisions ignore any such positive obligation. In effect, they totally ignore the recognition value of mediation, and the mediator's role in realizing that value.

Finally, and worth special note, consider the provisions restricting the mediator from meeting separately with the parties without prior consent from both sides. As discussed above, the empowerment-and-recognition role requires the mediator to do considerable pushing with both parties. The separate meeting or caucus is, in the view of many mediators, an invaluable tool for this work. For numerous reasons, it is neither possible nor desirable to push as strongly with either party when the other is present. As a result, the mediator accomplishes less, both in pushing for full understanding and consideration of all information and options, and in pushing for recognition of the other party. Restricting the mediator's access to this tool might help protect rights, but it greatly hinders fulfillment of both the empowerment and recognition aspects of the mediator's role. As for the potential concern for impartiality noted above, the mediator certainly can maintain active impartiality by caucusing with both parties in an evenhanded way.

To conclude this brief critique, I note that what is remarkable about the existing codes is not only how many provisions they contain of negative and restrictive character, like those criticized here, but how few provisions they contain of positive and directive character. They tell mediators in great detail what not to do, but give them much less guidance about what to do. Ultimately, these codes reveal a stunted picture of the mediator's role. By focusing primarily on the negative, they miss the point, which is the enormous positive opportunity for empowerment and recognition inherent in mediated dialogue, and the need to dedicate the mediator to the fullest possible realization of that opportunity. That is the mediator's role and professional obligation.

V. CONCLUSION: CRUCIAL CHOICES

The choices made in the coming years regarding the governing conception of the mediator's role, and the standards of practice that follow from that role, will determine whether mediation simply becomes another tool for administrative efficiency or protection of individual rights, or whether it fulfills its unique capacities for promoting personal empowerment and interpersonal acknowledgment. The recent state legislation on court-connected mediation possesses the clear potential to lead us in the latter direction. For the reasons discussed herein, I urge all those involved to weigh the options carefully and to transform that potential into the reality of the mediator's role. Doing so may make mediation more, rather than less, controversial, but at least it will be controversial for the right reasons.

G. Closing Considerations

1. Eric R. Galton, MEDIATION CHECKLIST (1995)*

I. Seven Keys to a Successful Mediation

1. ________ Select a qualified mediator
2. ________ A mediator who uses the case evaluation/separate caucus method
3. ________ Prepare for the mediation
4. ________ Select a mediator who requires premediation submissions (confidential)
5. ________ Resolve authority to settle issues prior to the mediation
6. ________ Select a mediator who encourages lawyer participation at the mediation
7 ________ Use mediation as soon as is practical

II. Selecting the Mediator/Questions to Ask

1. ________ At least six years litigation experience or at least six years practical experience in an area in which there is some exposure to litigation matters

*Reprinted with permission.

2. ________ At least forty (40) hours of mediation/arbitration training
3. ________ Actual mediation experience
4. ________ Use of case evaluation/separate caucus method
5. ________ Willing to discuss fee structure
6. ________ Able to provide neutral site for mediation
7. ________ Requires pre-mediation submissions
8. ________ Encourages lawyer participation
9. ________ Willing to reserve adequate time to mediate matter
10. ________ Absence of any conflict

III. Premediation Submission Outline

1. ________ Concise statement of issues and positions
2. ________ Identify strengths and possible weaknesses
3. ________ Provide a chronology
4. ________ Outline negotiations and proposals to date
5. ________ Specify who will be present at the mediation
6. ________ Provide copies of current pleadings
7. ________ Provide copies of pertinent appellate decisions
8. ________ Provide copies of key articles, critical excerpts from depositions, copies of key medical or expert witness reports
9. ________ Tab and index submission
10. ________ Place submission in a three-ring binder
11. ________ Mark submission as confidential

IV. Client Preparation for Mediation

1. ________ Explain mediation process
2. ________ Explain mediator's role
3. ________ Provide copy of premediation submission
4. ________ Explain your role at mediation and how it will be different
5. ________ Explain that client will actively participate
6. ________ Explain that mediator may ask client questions
7. ________ Explain separate caucus
8. ________ Explain benefits of mediation
9. ________ Anticipate initial unrealistic negotiating positions
10. ________ Anticipate sensitive issues and formulate strategies to deal with such issues
11. ________ Provide client with background of mediator
12. ________ Objectively evaluate strengths and weaknesses of case with client
13. ________ Encourage patience, flexibility, open-mindedness, listening
14. ________ Encourage polite, constructive approach
15. ________ Anticipate impasses and need to work through impasses
16. ________ Discuss authority issues

V. ADR Order

1. ________ Obtain prior to session
2. ________ Include confidentiality reference

3. ________ Include pursuant to ADR statute
4. ________ Include identity of mediator
5. ________ Include date, place, and time for mediation
6. ________ Include allocation of mediation costs
7. ________ Include non-binding

VI. Who Should Attend/Authority to Settle

1. ________ Counsel should attend
2. ________ Party should attend except in rare instances and only if agreed to in advance by all parties
3. ________ Insurance representative with authority to settle
4. ________ Preferable to have insurance representative with full authority to settle present
5. ________ Should logistical or economic factors make it impractical to have insurance representative with full authority able to attend:
    A. ________ Discuss matter with opposing counsel
    B. ________ Have local representative with limited authority attend
    C. ________ Agree that representative with full authority shall be available by telephone during the session
    D. ________ Reduce such agreement to writing
6. ________ In exceptional cases, a critical expert witness may attend
7. ________ In cases in which a structured settlement is anticipated, the structure specialists should attend

VII. Objecting to a Motion to Refer or Overcoming Objections to a Motion to Refer

1. ________ Written objections must be filed within ten (10) days after receiving a notice of referral
2. ________ Court must find a reasonable basis for an objection to a referral
3. ________ "Reasonable basis" is not defined
4. ________ Standard is discretionary
5. ________ "I don't like ADR" is probably not a reasonable basis
6. ________ "Mediation will not work" is probably not a reasonable basis
7. ________ Significant economic hardship might be a reasonable basis
8. ________ Proof that referral is for delay purposes only might be a reasonable basis
9. ________ Proof that the referral is designed for abusive discovery purposes might be a reasonable basis
10. ________ If the Court has assigned a mediator, proof that the mediator may not be impartial or has a possible conflict might be a reasonable basis as to the referral to that mediator

VIII. Lawyer's Role at Mediation

1. ________ Power of persuasion and negotiating skills very much apply
2. ________ Rare opportunity to communicate directly to other party
3. ________ Lawyer's role at mediation is different than at trial
4. ________ Lawyer should not cross-examine other party

5. ________ Lawyer should not permit his client to be cross-examined
6. ________ Lawyer should not showboat for his client or other side
7. ________ Lawyer should emphasize at mediation in good faith
8. ________ Lawyer should appear open-minded and reasonable
9. ________ Lawyer should be firm, but diplomatic
10. ________ Lawyer should be a good listener
11. ________ Lawyer should repeat back what he has heard to demonstrate he has listened

IX. Lawyer's Opening Statement

1. ________ Introduce yourself
2. ________ Humanize yourself
3. ________ Introduce your clients and explain who they are
4. ________ Acknowledge your belief in the mediation process
5. ________ Emphasize you and your client are present in good faith
6. ________ Emphasize you are prepared to listen and work through problems
7. ________ Emphasize your belief that a resolution will be in everyone's best interest
8. ________ If strong feelings or emotions are present, acknowledge that you are aware that such feelings exist and that it is not your intention or desire to embarrass, humiliate, or inflame the other party
9. ________ If the other side is injured or a death has occurred, express your sentiments
10. ________ Explain your role on behalf of your client
11. ________ Explain to the other party that you have thoroughly and objectively evaluated the case
12. ________ Outline to the other party your position, the basis of your position, and the fact that you have a good faith disagreement on such issues
13. ________ Close by emphasizing your willingness to listen, your willingness to work through problems, and your hope that with effort and patience on both sides an agreement may be reached
14. ________ Never discuss money in your opening statement
15. ________ Never personalize matters in your opening statement
16. ________ Avoid absolute words; i.e., "won't", "never", etc.

X. Things You Should Never Do During a Mediation

1. ________ Never discuss money in the presence of the other party. Communicate offers through the mediator in the separate caucus phase of the mediation
2. ________ Never refer to the other party by first name unless you have asked for permission to do so
3. ________ Never insult or criticize the mediator . . . especially in the other side's presence
4. ________ Anticipate volatile issues and never make comments to the other party which will trigger strong emotional responses
5. ________ Never undermine the other party's or other lawyer's dignity
6. ________ Never engage in theatrics; i.e., getting up to leave, etc.

XI. Collective Session Considerations (After Opening Statements by Lawyers)

1. ________ Have your client prepared to respond to mediator's questions
2. ________ Have your client prepared to discuss his feelings
3. ________ Have your client prepared to speak in constructive, respectful terms
4. ________ Have your client prepared to express hope that the session will produce an agreement
5. ________ Have your client prepared to express his willingness to listen and work through problems
6. ________ Come prepared to exchange material which is otherwise discoverable

XII. Separate Caucus Phase

1. ________ Parties and counsel are placed in separate rooms and caucus privately with mediator
2. ________ All communications are confidential save and except what the mediator is authorized to disclose to the party in the other room
3. ________ Initial caucus round typically lasts thirty minutes
4. ________ Subsequent caucus rounds last ten to twenty minutes
5. ________ Negotiating process typically begins after second round
6. ________ In the initial caucus, the mediator is attempting the following:
    - A. ________ Getting to better know the parties (bonding)
    - B. ________ Assessing who is the decision-maker (or makers)
    - C. ________ Assessing the personality/negotiating styles of the parties
    - D. ________ Mining for economic and non-economic issues
    - E. ________ Permitting the expression of strong feelings
    - F. ________ Identifying sensitive issues
7. ________ In the second caucus, the mediator is attempting the following:
    - A. ________ Leading the parties in an objective evaluation of their case
    - B. ________ Having the parties identify the strengths of their case on their own
    - C. ________ Having the parties identify the weaknesses of their case on their own
    - D. ________ Playing devil's advocate with the parties and assisting the parties in understanding or acknowledging possible weaknesses that the parties may not have listed on their own
8. ________ In caucus round three and thereafter, the mediator is attempting the following:
    - A. ________ To get the parties "to dance"; i.e., begin the negotiations
    - B. ________ To motivate the parties to negotiate reasonably and constructively
    - C. ________ To work through impasses
    - D. ________ To persistently force the parties to objectively look at their case

E. ________ To communicate proposals and messages; i.e., the mediator as shuttle diplomat

F. ________ To elect to re-convene the parties if appropriate to work through particular problems

G. ________ To hold a lawyer's caucus if special legal issues arise out of separate caucus

H. ________ To minimize negative reactions to proposals, to identify interests, and to keep the parties working through impasses

XIII. Memorandum of Agreement

1. ________ While not the final settlement documents, the agreement should clearly and specifically outline all terms of the agreement
2. ________ Agreement should be jointly drafted by all counsel so that it is not "one side's" agreement and so that the written agreement clearly reflects the agreement reached
3. ________ Should be signed by all counsel and parties
4. ________ All counsel and parties should receive copies of the fully executed agreement

XIV. Economic and Non-Economic Interests in Litigation

1. ________ Avoidance of risk
2. ________ Avoidance of delay
3. ________ Avoidance of cost
4. ________ Party's ability to decide his own destiny
5. ________ Need to be listened to
6. ________ Need to be understood
7. ________ Integrity
8. ________ Reputation
9. ________ Possible future relationships
10. ________ Acknowledgement of responsibility
11. ________ Apology
12. ________ Sympathy
13. ________ Closure

XV. Impasses

1. ________ Present, often many times, in every mediation
2. ________ Often reflects limited or different negotiating styles of parties
3. ________ Ask "why questions" to overcome impasses; i.e., explain the basis of the proposal and the needs that are reflected in a proposal
4. ________ Encourage the other party to categorize needs
5. ________ If at an impasse, forge a new and agreed negotiating pattern
6. ________ Re-visit the other side's weaknesses with the mediator
7. ________ Determine if non-economic interests, if met, will help resolve the impasse
8. ________ Be patient. Some negotiators dance fast. Some negotiators dance more slowly

9. ________ Candidly express your frustration and concern regarding impasse to the mediator

XVI. Special Factors in Medical Malpractice Mediation

1. ________ Dysfunctional communication plays a part in almost every medical malpractice lawsuit
2. ________ Profound injury or death has occurred in many malpractice lawsuits. The plaintiff is often still in the grieving process. Emotional levels are at their peak
3. ________ Physicians, because of the potential of a medical malpractice claim, have not expressed their feelings about what has happened to the other side
4. ________ Physicians feel their reputation, competency, and integrity have been challenged
5. ________ Patients often perceive the physician to be aloof and uncaring
6. ________ Medicine, regrettably, is not an exact science
7. ________ If a physician has been negligent, the physician may have exacerbated matters by offering an implausible explanation
8. ________ A physician may have offered a valid explanation which the patient, because of the emotional aspects of the matter, has not been able to understand
9. ________ The physician's explanation may be perceived as a rationalization
10. ________ The case may involve an act of negligence; but there may be no causation or serious problems regarding causation
11. ________ The physician may not have a good "bedside manner"
12. ________ In certain cases, the plaintiff's conduct may have caused the harm. Because of "denial", such issues may be extremely volatile and must be handled carefully

XVII. Outline of the Mediation Process

1. Selecting the Mediator
2. Enter Mediation Order
3. Pre-mediation Submission
4. Mediator Introduction
5. Lawyers' Opening Statement
6. Collective Session/Brainstorming
7. Separate Caucus
8. Possible Second Joint Session
9. Possible Lawyers' Caucus
10. Drafting the Agreement

2. Recent Developments in the States

State mediation statutes are cited and reprinted in Appendix C of Nancy H. Rogers & Craig A. McEwen, MEDIATION: LAW & POLICY (2d ed. 1994), which is supplemented annually. Appendix B is a subject matter guide to the state laws. The topics are:

1. Labor;
2. Family;
3. Automobile Warranty;
4. Agricultural Debt;
5. Civil Rights;
6. Environment;
7. Confidentiality;
8. Mediator Liability;
9. Mandatory Use;
10. Effect of Statutes of Limitations on Proceedings;
11. Enforcement of Mediated Agreements;
12. Qualifications of Mediators; and
13. Administration of Program/Funding.

Much officially sanctioned mediation activity, particularly that initiated by the judicial branch of government or a unified state bar, is not reflected in state legislation. Reliance on legislation alone to provide a picture of what is being done by state goernment in the mediation area is analogous to reliance on appellate cases alone to provide a picture of what is being done by the courts. The brief survey from selected states that follows is drawn from Peter S. Chantilis, *Mediation U.S.A.*, 26 MEMPHIS L. REV. 1031 (1996), and is used with the permission of the author. This article reports on mediation developments in all fifty states, plus the District of Columbia and Puerto Rico, based on information provided by the bar association in each jurisdiction.

> Arizona lacks comprehensive ADR legislation, but the Supreme Court has been active in promoting use of ADR and many superior courts have offered mediation programs for more than a decade. There are community mediation programs in Tucson and Phoenix. Phoenix boasts the "world's first Self-Service Center for Domestic Relations and Probate cases," where disputants may pick a mediator from a court approved list and "do it yourself." The program will shortly be expanded to include other civil cases.
>
> In California, the state bar has produced a survey of the ADR and settlement programs used by the courts in every county. The bar publishes a directory of existing programs, and provides technical assistance to local bars, courts, and ADR programs. The state bars has established an arbitration system for fee disputes between attorneys and their clients.
>
> Colorado has a statutory Office of Dispute Resolution, with administrative responsibility for programs throughout the state. It handled some 2,000 mediations in 1995. The Colorado Rules of Professional Conduct states that lawyers "should" advise clients about ADR options that might reasonably be used to resolve a dispute short of litigation.
>
> New York lacks legislatively mandated mediation, and does not provide for court-annexed mediation. The courts do refer cases on a voluntary basis to Community Dispute Resolution Centers (established by the Office of Court Administration). A task-force established by Chief Judge Judith Kaye is studying ADR needs in the state.
>
> Pennsylvania does not mandate mediation, but a mediator privilege law was enacted in 1996. A mandatory mediation program for custody disputes is under consideration in the legislature, as is the creation of a statewide office of idpsute resolution and conflict

management. This office is envisioned as addressing all aspects of ADR from serving as an information clearinghouse to creating peer mediation programs in schools to providing dispute resolution services to government entities for public policy controversies.

Puerto Rico provides for voluntary mediation of certain disputes (criminal, domestic violence, and child abuse cases are excluded) through the Conflict Mediation Center of the San Juan Judicial Center, and on a more limited basis in four other judicial districts. Some 4,700 cases were mediated from 1983 through 1994, with an 84 percent success rate. During this same period, an additional 26,000 matters were referred to various governmental agencies. The mediators for referred disputes are government employees.

Chapter 8

Divorce and Family Mediation

CASE STUDY

(Adapted from *Stanard v. Bolin*, 565 P.2d 94 (Wash. 1977))

Ms. Stanard and Mr. Bolin were introduced to each other by mutual friends in October of 1974. Shortly thereafter their courtship developed. During the course of the courtship, Bolin told Stanard that he was worth in excess of $2 million, was planning to retire within two years, and that they would travel after his retirement. Bolin also promised that Stanard would never have to work again, and that her two teenage sons and her mother would be taken care of and never be in need.

On September 22, 1975, Stanard accepted Bolin's marriage proposal. The couple then went to purchase an engagement ring and matching wedding rings. Soon after, the parties located a suitable home for their residence and signed the purchase agreement as husband and wife. At Bolin's insistence, Stanard placed her home on the market for sale and sold most of her furniture at a public auction. December 13, 1975 was set as the wedding date. The church was reserved and a minister was engaged to perform the service. Dresses were ordered for the bridal party, and a reception was arranged. Wedding plans were formally announced to their circle of friends. Stanard even went so far as to quit her job.

Bolin informed Stanard on November 13, 1975 that he would not marry her. This news came as a great shock to Stanard and caused her to become ill, and lose sleep and weight. Stanard had to seek medical treatment. She also had to take her home off the market and repurchase furniture at a cost in excess of that which she received for her "old" furniture. Stanard was forced to cancel the wedding plans and explain to all her friends and neighbors that she was not going to get married. Finally, she had to return the wedding gifts.

[Legal History: Stanard brought a breach-of-marriage-promise action against Bolin. In her first claim of relief, she seeks damages to compensate her for her pain, impairment to health, humiliation, and embarrassment. Her second claim seeks damages to compensate her for her loss of expected financial security.]

A. Introduction

This entire chapter is devoted to family mediation, with a focus on one specific situation: divorce by parents with minor children. This context is particularly difficult and therefore particularly interesting to students of mediation. People who can no longer live together must nevertheless continue to deal with one another in a cooperative fashion. By contrast, multimillion dollar commercial disputes are easier for both the mediator and the parties to settle, and the settlements are far more likely to work as planned, because subsequent cooperation on that transaction is not necessary (beyond a few days, or occasionally a few months). Not only are the personal consequences of divorce so serious for both children and parents, the economic consequences are very important for all but the wealthiest families. Important decisions must be made by persons at an emotionally vulnerable time, about a subject (divorce) with which most parties have no prior experience. In any decision context, inexperience plus emotional distress are worrisome factors.

Section B provides an introduction to the major issues associated with divorce and child custody. (See also the Mnookin & Kornhauser article about bargaining in the shadow of the law, at Chapter 4, section C.) There follows an extended consideration of whether women are disadvantaged in the use of mediation, whether voluntary or mandatory. (The related topic of women as negotiators is considered at Chapter 4, Section E.) The leading articles in the legal literature only date back to 1991, and this debate is still very much alive.

The authors of an excellent study of divorcing in Maine concludes that use of lawyers is the best solution to fairness problems in divorce mediation, one that is certainly preferable to sending divorcing families to litigation, and also preferable to abandoning mandatory mediation. The final topic is the duty of divorce mediators to promote "fair" or "equitable" outcomes. "Fairness" concerns can arise in any type of mediation but it is particularly likely to occur in divorce cases due to different knowledge and power of the parties. To the extent one subscribes to the "women are likely to be taken advantage" school of thought, there is an additional concern for mediators to counteract.

B. How Family Mediation Works

1. Phyllis Gangel-Jacob, *Some Words of Caution About Divorce Mediation*, 23 Hofstra L. Rev. 825 (1995)

[As a prelude to a discussion of divorce mediation, Judge Gangel-Jacob offered a thumbnail sketch of three cases that were before her when she wrote this article.]

a. A forty-three year marriage is coming to an end because the husband, a performer of worldwide reputation, has at age seventy-eight found another life; this obsession is not so uncommon as one might imagine and is frequently referred to by matrimonial lawyers as "life before death syndrome."

b. I have also before me a case of a traditional homemaker (or at least that which a decade ago was considered traditional) who, at age fifty, suddenly discovered that she has been "oppressed" for thirty years, deprived of her true potential, and determined to strike out on her own. Her weeping and understandably distraught husband believes that this is a temporary aberration and that she should be kept from this self-destruction. He may be correct.

c. And there is the case of the young mother, still nursing her third child, who has been told that her husband has found a new and true love in his religious studies class—a yearning for his roots which includes a demand for joint custody of the children.

None of these three people can fathom what has happened to them—they need time to heal and they need powerful allies in the form of skilled, professional, competent counsel to put the brakes on the tsunami wave that is about to sweep them away.

2. Comments and Questions

a. The three examples given by Judge Gangel-Jacob graphically illustrate what devastation a divorce situation often visits on one or both of the spouses, and on the children.

b. Might many people who are not lawyers, and even a few who are, see something else needed by the parties in these three situations than two skilled (and expensive) lawyers per marriage?

c. Divorce mediators (and family law judges) must be able to work with situations similar to those described by Judge Gangel-Jacob on a regular basis. Many people do not have the patience or temperament needed for divorce mediation, and even those who are wonderful at it sometimes get "burned out" by the misery that passes before them on a regular basis.

d. Divorce mediation is extraordinarily difficult, because the mediator must possess, in addition to dispute resolution skills, knowledge of family economics (including tax law), psychology, and the needs of children. Decisions about family dissolution with important long term consequences must be made by stressed individuals who usually lack any experience with the issues that must be resolved.

e. The remaining material in this section is designed to provide an introduction to divorce mediation, where the divorcing couple has minor children.

3. John M. Haynes, The Fundamentals of Family Mediation (1994)*

Changing the Language

[In negotiations about child custody,] mediators avoid terms such as failed marriage, broken home, custody and visitation. They prefer nonjudgmental terms such as ending the relationship, mom's house and dad's house, parenting, access, and residence.

The legal adversarial vocabulary refers to visitation. Most mediators prefer the term access. In that way they reframe the question from when does dad get to visit the kids, to when will the children have access to their dad? The terms custody and visitation are legal terms. As such each has a winner-loser connotation and speaks about ownership of the children rather than supporting future parenting goals. . . .

4. Alison Taylor, *A General Theory of Divorce Mediation*, in Jay Folberg & Ann Milne, Divorce Mediation 61-82 (1988)**

THE MEDIATION PROCESS

The mediation process can best be described as a set of stages. Each stage in the mediation process has its goals and tasks, as well as methodology and skills. The mediator must often

---

change the dimension of his or her role within any given stage of the mediation process. Progress from session to session may include minor variations from the universal process, because of the unique circumstances of the case. Participants may not be ready emotionally to move from one stage to the other. They may need to return to earlier stages or may reverse the stages because of preexisting conditions, the requirements of the particular jurisdiction in which they reside, or the policies and procedures of the agency or individual serving the parties. Despite tailoring to individual needs, all stages should be addressed, since each is necessary for completion of the mediation process.

Stage 1: Introduction—Creating Structure and Trust

The introductory stage is vital to the establishment of a relationship that will facilitate the rest of the mediation process. Creating a therapeutic relationship is not a goal of this stage, as it is with counseling. Sufficient confidence and rapport between the mediator and participants, however, is necessary to successful mediation. Because divorce issues and conflict cut across a participant's self-concept as a sexual being, an economic provider, a parent, and a member of a larger community, most of the information the mediator elicits and helps order is very threatening. If the mediator has enough rapport and has gained enough trust, the participants will be better able to bring out and discuss these very personal issues.

This stage is used to gather relevant information about the participants' perceptions of the conflict, their goals and expectations, and the conflict situation. Data that should be gathered includes:

1. the participants' motivation to use mediation
2. the immediate background and precipitating event(s) to the conflict
3. the interactional and communication styles of the participants
4. the present emotional state of the participants
5. the arrangements for attorney involvement and/or legal formalization of the agreement
6. the present problem or conflict as opposed to the hidden agenda or underlying conflicts
7. immediate safety and security concerns for participants and their dependents

The following sequence helps elicit the needed information and serves as a guide to the mediator for facilitating this first stage.

Sequence

Brief introductions and seating
Preparatory statement by mediator
Confirm case data
Review guidelines
Handover of communication to participants
Discuss expectations
Review and sign an agreement to mediate and pay fees
Distribute and discuss financial worksheets or handouts
Trade mutual assurances
Homework of additional data, tasks

Data Obtained

Nonverbal impression
Present emotional state of participants and legal processes
Immediate past and precipitating events
Extra-participant involvement
Interactional style; emotional state
Interactional and communication styles; emotional state
The presenting problem or conflict versus any hidden agendas and conflicts
The participants' motivation
Immediate safety and security concerns
Needs and willingness to provide concrete help
Abilities to carry through

As can be seen from this chart, the mediator is both acting and presenting, and receiving and evaluating the participants' responses. The participants begin to understand the structure of the mediation process and determine that the mediator is trustworthy and neutral when the mediator limits small talk, ensures a comfortable physical setting for mediation with appropriate spatial arrangements and reviews the explicit expectations for participants and the mediator in the session. It is important to allow adequate time for each participant to present his or her view of the situation. A definitive verbal signal from the mediator, termed here a *handover* to the participant, indicates a need for that participant to become an active part of the communication patterns.

In this beginning stage, most conversation will flow between the mediator and each participant, forming a V-shaped pattern of communication. To ensure that participants have adequate time to present their sides of the situation, some mediators rely on a protocol that requires that the complainant (the person who brought the issue to mediation) should be the first one to tell the story. Other mediators prefer to start off involving the least active participant, the one with whom they have had less contact, or the one who has been coerced or mandated to the mediation process. By starting with the complainant, the mediator reassures that person that they will be heard. Starting with the least active or lesser known person confirms lack of bias created by prior contact or intimidating style. Allowing the first statement to come from the mandated participant can diffuse the usual mixture of anger and sullen resentment that person often feels.

The mediator's preparatory statement or discussion of the mediation rules or guidelines should make clear to the participants that the mediator will not make substantive decisions but that he or she is responsible for control of the session. In this stage of mediation, such information is conveyed not only by written rules, contracts, and verbal discussion, but also through judicious use of nonverbal indicators of authority and control. This stage is over when the mediator's picture of the nature of the manifest and underlying issues in the case is complete. The participants should now have a clear understanding of mediation and be able to determine if they wish to commit to the process. For most private practitioners, this commitment is in the form of an employment agreement or an agreement to mediate.

Stage 2: Fact-Finding and Isolation of Issues

Before good decisions can be reached, both participants must have equal information and must fully understand which issues are open to being resolved or managed. The mediator helps the participants find out where the conflicts really lie and which areas have yet to be discussed. Divorce requires decisions about the future, including finances, property, plans for the children, support, legal processes, and relationships. The specific content and issues in these areas must be organized and discussed.

Factors that can help the mediator organize and discuss issues can be divided into four categories: (I) the immediacy of the conflictual issue, (2) the duration of the conflictual issue, (3) the intensity of feelings about the conflictual issue, and (4) the expressed and perceived rigidity of positions.

The intrapersonal and interpersonal dimensions of these conflicts must be separated at this point. The task of this stage of mediation is to provide a safe place for the participants to set aside personal defenses and for the underlying issues to surface. Often this requires that the mediator reframe the dispute to explore the underlying interests or fracture the dispute into smaller, manageable pieces that can form the components for later agreements and plans. The participants must raise the issues. The mediator helps raise issues and more clearly define, reframe, and redirect them.

The mediator can assist by using communication skills such as open-ended questions, summary, prioritizing, reflection, and clarification.

Because mediators may be held legally and ethically responsible for the assurance of complete disclosure and discussion, it is advisable for the mediator to use a worksheet to write the participants' starting positions on issues and, in later stages, mutually made decisions. The mediator must take the raw information the participants provide and form this into a constructive, usable concept or coherent set of concerns. This requires that the mediator connect disparate bits of information into a comprehensive package of disputes and agreements. To accomplish this, the mediator must use an associative, rather than a linear, thought process. For example, if a participant is telling why he must have custody and then seems to switch into a discussion of transportation, the associatively thinking mediator will pursue a line of questioning to help clarify in what way these two things are connected for the participants rather than just redirecting and dealing only with one subject until it is done. Since the major task at this stage is the reduction of information into definable issues, the mediator must use all the available skills and techniques in order to keep the participants involved.

Forcing the participants to divulge underlying conflicts is anxiety producing for them and hard work for the mediator. The mediator is likely to encounter some level of resistance from one or both of the participants during this stage of the mediation process. Participants may become defensive and resist, stating to the mediator that all the problems and conflicts have been resolved, that they cannot or will not discuss the past, that they have supplied complete information (although they are actually withholding some), and that their attorney will handle the issue. Often this resistance is not expressed openly but surfaces as a specific action or inaction by the participants during the session. Examples of these actions are emotional and verbal withdrawal, verbal battles for dominance, unexpected rescheduling or cancellation of a session, arriving late or inebriated, and refusing or failing to do an assigned task, such as completing a worksheet.

The resistance a mediator sees is only a mirror of the issues that must be resolved or managed during all stages of the mediation process. The mediator should not allow resistant behaviors to evoke an emotional response or take them as a sign of personal failure. As a general rule, such resistance should be discussed openly in private session before returning to the other substantive conflicts. By doing this, mediators directly confront the participant in a way that the other participant has never felt capable of doing. Because it is done at this time, the person may be more receptive to changing, or at least acknowledging, the resistant behaviors. Meanwhile, the other person is able to see an effective model of confrontation that helps rather than makes the situation worse. The outcome is more discussion of underlying issues. If the resistance continues, the mediator should adhere strictly to any previously accepted rules about impasses and termination. The mediator should try to refocus the discussion, whenever possible, rather than call an impasse. A decision to suspend mediation and declare an impasse may be made at this time, should one or both of the participants remain adamant despite good efforts by the mediator to reduce resistance. Allowing mediation to continue if one participant remains obstructive is an unproductive waste of time and money for both participants, and frustrating for the one who is active and open. Stage 2 ends when the mediator knows where the disagreements and conflicts lie, what the underlying and manifest conflicts are, and what each participant wants or will not accept under any circumstance. Before moving to the next stage, the mediator should ask, "Is my understanding of the issues complete?" This stage may take several sessions or only part of a session, depending upon the openness of the participants, the amount of personal threat to the self-concept inherent in the underlying conflict, and the skill of the mediator.

In addition to completeness, the mediator must also assess realistic, case specific goals. Although the goal of mediation is the resolution or management of the manifest conflicts, a case-specific goal may be to bring about a personal awareness of internal, underlying conflicts that impinge on the mediation process. Other appropriate case-specific goals might include cognitive consensus on a certain point and the reduction of certain self-defeating affective or emotional responses.

The goal of a couple disputing custody might be the reduction or cessation of behaviors that continue to disrupt the child's life. The case-specific goal might be to create limits, to stop an overbearing attitude and verbal intimidation, or to create a more equal power structure between the parents during the mediation session, which will carry over into their future parenting of the child. Another case-specific goal might be to reduce the amount of disruption to the child's education through agreeing by conceptual consensus that the parents will not move during a school year or during the remainder of high school.

Such case-specific goals should not be based upon the mediator's value structure. They should be taken from the participants' desires and perceptions that have been communicated to the mediator, often indirectly, during each participant's opening statements and later discussion of the issues. The mediator must know by this time which goals are consistent with each participant's worldview and personality structure. Mediation during this stage can dissolve into rather random questions and answers, unstructured and unguided, unless a knowledgeable mediator helps the participants see the areas of agreement and individual priorities.

Stage 3: Creation of Options and Alternatives

Stage 3 asks the basic question, "How can you do what you want to do in the most effective way?" Both participants must be actively involved in finding the answers to this question. After going over the worksheets or notes made during the earlier stages, the mediator needs to review the open issues. Sometimes the answer to the above question rests upon the solution to the most basic or highest priority issue. For example, how to divide property such as a house may depend on the higher priority issue of the custody plan for the children. The "domino effect" created by ordering priorities can be maximized by a skillful mediator who brings the participants to an awareness of which issue is the stumbling block. When a stumbling block is identified, the mediator must focus both participants' attention on creating realistic and workable options for resolving or managing that issue. Mediation skills are the same for all stages: well-timed questions and reflections.

The tasks of Stage 3 are (1) to help the participants articulate the options they know or want and (2) to develop new options that may be more satisfactory. The mediator's role must reflect this duality: the mediator must be a facilitator for the first task and a creator or synthesizer for the second. It is important to keep both in balance, since a mediator who produces too many new options too fast will inhibit the expression of the participants' views. To reduce this task, some mediators find it helpful to list all the options that come to the attention of the participants before brainstorming additional options. Brainstorming, either during the mediation session or as homework, can be a useful tool for accomplishing the first task of this stage. Some mediators use forms to list the most likely options, for visual evaluation by participants. These help clients evaluate different options on the basis of criteria and the gain or loss for themselves or others if the option were selected. Mediators may want to use their own adaptation of such decision-making forms. To help participants who have become confused by possible options and alternatives, each option can be written onto each form; then the discussion can be limited to each form separately and sequentially.

After a brief review of the open issues, any options that have been mentioned during a participant's opening statements should be listed. The mediator should remind the participants of the criteria that might be used to evaluate options. . . . [S]ome general criteria for developing and evaluating the effectiveness of options and alternatives are: . . . .

1. needs of the participants and others who will be affected by the decision;
2. projections of the past into the future (likely predictions);
3. general economic and social forecasts that may affect an option;
4. legal and financial roadblocks and limitations;
5. anticipations of new people and new situations; and
6. predictable changes in any of the above.

Mediators may want to suggest criteria and help the participants use them effectively in developing options. Rephrasing these criteria into "what if's" scenarios may be helpful to participants in evaluating options. Mediators help participants project themselves into the future by using this technique.

When the participants are emotionally and psychologically ready, a trial period can be used to determine the practicality of a particular option, before a final decision is made. When trial periods are used, both participants are able to experience the consequences of that option. This is particularly effective when one participant has rejected an option because he or she believes that it will not work. The terms of a trial period should be written, including the starting and ending dates, the specific contingencies for continuation, and most important, that implementation of the trial period will not prejudice any future decisions.

Stage 3 of the mediation process is the most creative and active stage for the mediator. The mediator's role during this stage is vastly different from the nondirective, nonauthoritarian role espoused by many counselors, and the highly authoritarian role of a traditional attorney acting as advocate for the client. The mediator is a resource person, an expert who suggests new options based on more extensive knowledge of the subject in conflict. The mediator may also offer information regarding the availability or statistical success of certain options. In states where custody laws require a presumption or preference for joint custody, the mediator may want to provide information about various joint custody arrangements and the success and family satisfaction of such options. Options offered by the mediator must be delivered in a manner that participants can comfortably accept or reject. The participants should not be pressured by the mediator to consider any particular option, nor should they be persuaded to use a trial period that they do not see as beneficial.

The mediator often feels a strong need for completion and closure. The mediator who ties self-worth to the selection of a particular option will be an ineffective facilitator. Coercion, favoritism, and bias should not be allowed. A mediator should be aware of the ethical responsibilities of the role when providing new insight and guiding the participants.

Mediation proceeds to the next stage when there has been full exploration of all options, without prejudice and judgmental attitudes. Options and alternatives are often conglomerate; they pull together several issues. High-priority issues, such as legal and physical custody, to some extent determine other issues, such as child support or visitation plans; decisions made on priority issues can prefigure other contingent issues. Saying yes to one thing automatically means saying no to something else. It is important for mediators to make participants aware of the connections between issues.

Stage 4: Negotiation and Decision Making

At this point in the mediation process participants select one or more options from those generated earlier. The option selected must be something both participants can live with, even if it is not what either participant originally wanted. Mediators must encourage the participants to take the risky step to decide, to make choices, and to compromise or give in on some of the smaller items. This cooperative effort is more likely to bring about the final outcome that the participants want. If the mediator has helped the participants deal successfully with each case-specific goal, the overall goal of resolution of conflict will be reached.

Having several options that seem workable will not necessarily help the participants make a selection. Often the development of several options during stage 3 only confuses the participants. Most people can mentally manipulate only a small number of variables. One way the participants can try to get closer to making a decision is by bargaining, a simple form of negotiation. This can take the form of horse-trading or "this for that," simple exchanges of desirable features or options, similar to what a person does in the marketplace or in economic bargaining. The basic messages conveyed during bargaining are, "What is it you want (or don't want) the most?" or "What is it worth to you to have X?"

Most people in mediation, when confronted with a display of options, need to reduce them to a smaller number. Participants in mediation often do not have a preset start position, comedown position, and final limit, as they would if they were involved in traditional negotiation. Indeed, part of the function of the mediator during this stage is to help the participants avoid positional bargaining and use a softer negotiation style. . . . Often participants can rule out certain options immediately, based on their perception of what is necessary or what is practical.

They are left with some options that cannot be ruled out but that must be negotiated between them.

If one participant cannot get the other to agree to a favored option, mutual agreement may eliminate both persons' preferred option, since they realize that neither will select the other's. This reduction leaves the couple with those options developed during Stage 3. Sometimes this elimination process is not as easy as the sequence implies. The mediator's task is to reframe this bargaining and negotiation into a question to ask each participant, "Which option will best meet everyone's needs?" Mediators should move the participants from a competitive negotiation process to a more cooperative interaction. This is often done by getting cognitive consensus on fundamental principles that are then applied to the particular situation.

During Stage 4 the mediator must reduce his or her involvement and change the communication pattern. Instead of responding primarily to the mediator, the participants must now communicate directly with each other. To accomplish this conversational switch, the mediator can make specific suggestions to the participants to help them evaluate an option. The mediator can clarify the goal and remind the participants of the procedures they can follow to get to that goal. The mediator supplies the technique, but the participants should be doing the conversing and exploration. During this stage of mediation, the mediator's role is an agent of reality, someone who makes the participants doubt the assumptions and firmness of their original positions or perceptions.

Instead of undermining or blocking this "talking-out," the mediator amplifies it through reflection, clarification, and simple questions. The mediator listens and acts as a process observer and monitor who periodically intervenes in the exchange, to question the practicality or advisability of the option and to prevent coercion during negotiations. During this stage, the mediator must be aware of the content being discussed and the process being used by the participants to arrive at a decision. The mediator should help the participants by drawing them back to their fears, hopes, and expectations, which were originally stated shortly after the handover in Stage 1. These can also be brought out by techniques of reflection, summary, and clarification. The mediator starts the interchange between the participants and monitors it so that each person has a chance to talk, can make offers and consider them, and can communicate without undue pressure, coercion, or harassment. Each participant must have the opportunity to understand the other's perspective in evaluating the importance of a certain option. Each must feel that his or her perspective is understood by the other.

To help the participants carry on this principled style of negotiation, as opposed to positional bargaining, the mediator must direct them away from their original opening statements and help the parties develop objective criteria for decisions. Deciding to take the average of two independent appraisals is a principled way of reaching a decision, as compared to arguing over what the price should be. The mediator should point out gains made by the participants in agreeing to a fair standard and procedure and may reiterate the consequence of delay in decision making.

Maintaining some sort of equality in communication during this important negotiation stage is essential, so that a verbose participant does not stifle the expression or preference of a more quiet or passive participant. In this way, decision making is protected from becoming self-defeating or manipulative; decisions are made by an active, cognitive process rather than out of frustration or a need for emotional closure. In order to equalize communication, the mediator may have to be quite controlling and may want to use directive statements such as,

"Tell us what you think, Jim," or reflections such as, "Elaine, you've said all along how happy you'd feel if you could find a way out of this problem." Verbally reinforcing the participants is also helpful.

Another method that often works to explain a participant's resistance to a particular option is to highlight the objection and acknowledge the right to have such conflicts. Using this method, the mediator can ask each participant to imagine the worst possible scenario that could happen, should the couple select that particular option. This is then scrutinized with help from the mediator's role as agent of reality. For example, a custody dispute may be stalled after developing three options: sole custody for the father, sole custody for the mother, or joint legal and physical custody. If the mother is violently opposed to the father's sole custody, she should be encouraged to project the negative consequences of this option, since it will allow her to say her underlying fears and give the mediator a chance to question her projections.

Direct confrontation by the mediator is sometimes necessary to activate decisions. The mediator can acknowledge the block to decision making and give his or her view of the resistance to such a decision. Confrontational techniques must be used in such a way that the participant clearly understands them to be directed toward the lack of progress in the mediation process, not toward the people. Guilt and shame should not be used to motivate movement during a session; a realistic assessment of resistances and consequences is a more productive approach. Another method that sometimes works to motivate a decision is arbitrarily withdrawing the power to choose from the resistant participant. The mediator may pretend to deny access to the decision by declaring an impasse or suggesting that the matter must go to arbitration or to the court because the participants cannot decide. Since the mediation process provides far more empowerment for the participants, they will often jump to recover their right to choose for themselves if they fear its loss.

Another variation of this method is to normalize the participant's right to block decision making. A paradoxical intervention by the mediator provides the participant with a rationale for the indecision. The mediator could say, "You shouldn't try to make a choice right now. You should wait until you are sure, and continue as you are currently doing until then." The paradox is that suggesting or even demanding that no choice be made yet legitimizes the person's right to be ambivalent and therefore gives him or her reverse permission, as well as a needed sense of control. Most participants will voluntarily move toward a choice when this method is used; they need to feel that control before they give it away by accepting an option they perceive as belonging to the other participant. It is important, however, that mediators use such paradoxical interventions cautiously, only as a last resort.

Throwing the weight and responsibility for a decision back on the participants can temporarily block progress, even if the participants are willing to make a choice. Yet it is important to reconfirm that it is the participants who must not only make, but live with, the choices. A way of softening this often overwhelming responsibility is to remind the participants that they have already determined a process for future conflict resolution, should their current decisions not work. They can and should change their agreements when those decisions are no longer useful, with the exception of certain legal decisions, such as property division, that cannot be changed after the divorce is finalized.

Often participants during Stage 4 will ask the mediator's opinion or advice on which option to select. This is a difficult moment for mediators, who should not tell participants what to do. While mediators cannot make decisions for participants, they can remind participants of the sociological and statistical data about the options. Mediators in this situation have often reminded disputants of community norms or values; however, this must be done in a non-judgmental manner. The response to such an inquiry can either augment or break down rapport between the mediator and the participants. Mediators should avoid responses such as "I'm sorry I can't advise you on this, you must make your own choice," which tend to break down rapport and support of the participants. It is far better to say, "Well, I remember you saying earlier that you wanted to [minimize disruption, maintain contact, etc.], and it seems as if this option [could, could not] promote that."

Readiness for decision making is an important and personal thing. Sometimes it requires the reduction of perceptual errors or internal conflicts, sometimes merely an added bit of cognitive information, and sometimes just enough time to create a change in individual development and maturation. Before proceeding with this stage, mediators should assess and evaluate the readiness of each participant to make decisions and should be aware of the alternatives for dealing with participants who are not yet ready. A referral to counseling or other community resource may be needed. Often concurrent services, such as counseling or career development programs, can ease the decision-making process. The question that must be answered affirmatively by the participants is

Have all choices been made for all issues?

If the answer to that question is no, . . . [f]our options are available to the mediator: return to an earlier stage, referral for adjunctive services, declaration of impasse, or termination of the case. It is hoped that mediators will be skilled in reducing resistance so that most mediations move into the next stage and that mediators lacking in skill will not blame the clients for an impasse. By this stage all but the most manipulative or unwilling participants will have invested enough time and energy in the mediation process to motivate them to continue. It is the mediator's responsibility to determine under what conditions that process will continue.

Stage 5: Clarification: Writing a Plan

Most participants will be able to make choices and select options during Stage 4. The function of Stage 5 is to produce a document, a mediated plan, that clearly outlines the participants' intentions and decisions. This document should define the current decisions and anticipated behavior. It should be drawn up in a written form that the participants can easily read and review and should constitute a working document for the participants' purposes. It should he complex enough to cover most probable contingencies. This document can be used by the participants in the next stage of the mediation process. It can be modified in response to the inevitable changes that occur over time.

Usually the mediator organizes, records, and accurately reflects the decisions reached during the mediation sessions. The participants, separately or jointly, may need to use their own words so that the agreement accurately reflects their understanding of the verbal agreement. This should be submitted to the mediator before writing the mediated plan or can be discussed during a session. Using the participants' own wording makes the document more meaningful and relevant. When participants are highly motivated and literate, the mediator may want to supply a model that they can use for the agreement. Allowing participants to write their plan separately will forestall passive aggressive behaviors and many revisions. Writing their own plan may not, however, be appropriate for participants who want to "wrap it up quickly" as a way of ending their internal tension and conflict. It is also not appropriate to request this type of cooperation and responsibility when one or more of the participants would be overwhelmed because of lack of skills or when the power dynamics between the participants are such that they would compete with each other over whose version is acceptable.

Copies of the proposed mediated plan should be given to the participants to review before the next session. Underlying conflicts that have not been adequately resolved in earlier stages of mediation often surface when the mediated plan is discussed; they are often presented as a manifest conflict over the wording of a section that addresses the underlying conflict. Getting the participant to articulate the specific objection to the wording and at the same time determining the underlying conflict are hard work for the mediator. It requires the use of such skills as reflection, summary, and open-ended questions.

Most participants feel relieved at this stage and need verbal reassurance that they have produced an accurate document that reflects their needs. Participants may need to make word changes to feel a sense of ownership of the document. The mediator should be prepared to revise the document immediately upon the parties' review or have the proposed mediated plan retyped and ready for signing within a day or two of the session. Participants as well as mediators often have a strong urge for closure at this point. Mediators, however, must not take on the responsibility for producing the final synthesis. The participants themselves must see that the mediator has no interest in the outcome of mediation beyond a professional duty to facilitate the session.

The signing of the mediated plan or agreement is a symbolic act that carries great meaning for the participants. Mediators may want to mark and enrich this by using some ritual or special behavior. A toast to the hard work and success of the participants in coming to consensual resolution may be appropriate and can start their living the agreement on a positive note. The mediated plan is a symbol of cooperation and closure and should reflect the present and the future. If one of the participants is still involved in the grief loss process and is mourning the demise of the marital relationship, the mediated plan should be framed positively, but less joyfully; that participant may need referral to a support group.

Stage 6: Legal Review and Processing

The legal process is necessary when the conflicts being mediated must be connected to larger social systems and institutions, as occurs with divorce. Stages 6 and 7 are contingent upon forces external to the mediation process; power, control, and responsibility are no longer entirely in the hands of the participants and the mediator. Legal review or processing serves as a watchdog to the earlier stages by passing the agreements through socially accepted processes that check and sanctify the mediated agreement. This provides the participants with a stronger sense of closure and commitment. It also allows a brief respite form the stressful task of developing options and making choices. It gives participants a chance to gain useful input from others who will critique the agreement's completeness and feasibility.

Divorce mediation cases are subject to two types of legal review: by a private attorney before submission to the court and by a judge with a request that the mediated plan be made a part of the decree of dissolution, so that it can more easily be enforced by the court should either of the participants violate the terms of the mediated agreement. Review by either or both sources can help identify new issues or options that can be handled by further mediation or by more traditional legal processes. In other words, if a participant's attorney advises reconsideration on a specific issue, that issue can be mediated again while leaving the other items as agreed and written. This is preferable, from the participants' standpoint, to litigating the issue, which usually halts any acceptance of other agreements that have been mediated.

Legal review by independent counsel may be conducted at any point during the mediation process. Many private attorneys prefer to see any proposed mediated plan before their clients sign it. Some lawyers prefer that their clients leave all financial issues for attorney-assisted negotiation or litigation but are pleased to have their clients mediate custody issues and schedules. Mediators should make it clear, in any case, that legal review can add to the participants' understanding of the relevant issues and options. . . .

If the mediator (or a member of the mediation team) is an attorney, the function and role that mediator will take regarding legal review should be clarified in Stage I and reconfirmed in the agreement to mediate. The participants should understand clearly whether the attorney-mediator is advising both of them and whether he or she can later represent either of the participants in a related matter.

Review by the court adds dimension to legal review. Submitting the mediated plan to the court for its ratification and approval lends additional support and enforceability of the mediated plan. Mediators should check local state laws and court rules regarding the formal requirements for submission of mediated plans as part of a total marital settlement agreement. . . .

Any decisions that participants reach regarding the legal review and processing of their mediated plan should be stated within the mediated plan itself. These need not be commitments but may be intentions, such as, "It is Jim's intention to hire a lawyer to review the mediated plan before its signing." Mediators may want to educate local judges and lawyers regarding the dimension and limitation of the mediated plans. Mediators can protect themselves against charges of unauthorized practice of law by clarifying to attorneys and participants the difference between a mediated plan, which is usually not in legal form, and a marital settlement agreement, which conforms to the requirements of the court and which the participants may submit to the court.

Stage 7: Implementation, Review, and Revision

During the final stage of mediation the participants are trying to implement the terms of the mediated plan. As with Stage 6, this stages takes place outside the confines of the mediation session and does not demand the active, continuous involvement of the mediator. Although this stage relies on the participants, the mediator has a dynamic, though indirect, role. The important process of follow-up begins, initiated either by the mediator or by the participants, who may need further help.

During the first few weeks and months following the signing of the mediated plan, the participants are trying to actualize what was only conjectured and idealized before. It is a difficult time at best. Although they may intend to follow the agreement as it was written, the participants' abilities to match those intentions may have been suddenly and drastically altered. Unforeseen problems may arise, stemming either from the fluidity of the divorce context or from the introduction of external factors beyond the parties' control. Additionally, some families are in the process of further reconstruction when remarriage, cohabitation, or residence with the participants' parent affects the extended family. Participants who have been receiving additional counseling and therapy services may be making personal growth which directly affects their ability or desire to live by the previously agreed-upon terms. Similarly, unresolved underlying conflicts may threaten the mediated plan during the implementation stage.

Printed materials that educate the participants about common problems and difficulties can be provided when the mediated plan is signed. These can prevent or alleviate some predictable problems. The mediator is the only professional many participants will see about the issues, either because of their limited time, money, or attitudes. When problems occur during implementation, many participants prefer to talk to the mediator rather than starting over with another helping professional.

Routine follow-up initiated by the mediator at specific intervals can put out brushfires of discontent and provide positive reinforcement for the continuation of the mediated plan. Follow-up can take the form of phone calls, letters, or personal contact initiated by the mediator. A participant experiencing some level of discontent with the mediated plan can also initiate follow-up procedures. Follow-up contacts can help the participants clarify the meaning and reality of the mediated plan by adding the perspective of time. Enough time must elapse in the implementation stage to make such follow-up useful. Generally, follow-up should start no sooner than 1 month after the signing of the mediated plan. The next intervals for follow-up could be at 6 months and 1 year after the signing of the agreement. If, however, an earlier or later date is directly related to the issues involved in the mediation, it should be substituted. Follow-up not only gives the participant a chance to ventilate and achieve support, but also can provide mediators with useful information regarding the effectiveness of certain options and techniques during mediation.

A helpful, generic follow-up sheet should ask questions regarding the general trends for the agreement, subsequent legal and nonlegal processes used, evaluation of the helpfulness and satisfaction with mediation, and what needs the participants continue to have. It should use open-ended questions with easily tabulated, multiple-choice answers. This worksheet not only organizes the discussions during the follow-up but also provides data for later statistical evaluation of mediation. Whether such follow-up is initiated by the calendar, the client, or the mediator, the content should be handled with warmth and reassurance. If the problems are multitudinous or complicated, or if the contacts are frequent, the mediation participants should be invited to return for additional mediation services or referred to appropriate community resources.

Things change, children grow, new situations are encountered, structures and institutions switch their procedures, and new alliances are formed. Mediation is unique among conflict resolution processes because it can create a process for future review and revision. Mediators can choose either to include a short review session into their schedule of sessions and fee structure or to make it clear that review sessions will be provided only upon request of one or both of the participants with payment of additional fees. The mediator should clarify who will attempt to contact the other participants. Noncooperation or nonattendance according to the terms of the review process outlined in the mediated plan may hold negative consequences, such as invalidation of the entire document or a breach of contract. Including one review session as part of the original mediation fee is probably preferred for family mediation cases because the participants are more likely to use it when they need it.

Unlike the follow-up contact, usually done by phone or individually in private session, a review session is a "mini-version" of the earlier mediation process and usually encompasses the first six stages in one marathon session. Both participants should be present, with the mediator inviting exploration of any current or impending issues, options, and needed choices. When decisions have been made by the participants, the mediator can write them up, have a quick discussion of the wording, and have signed copies of revisions attached to the mediated plan. These amendments should be submitted to the court and made a matter of record if the original mediated plan was so submitted.

In summary, the implementation stage is the time when participants in mediation try to live the terms of the plan. Some level of involvement by the mediator, either through a follow-up evaluation and feedback mechanism or through a review session to make revisions in the original mediated plan, is desirable in divorce mediation. Although a follow-up contact is most often initiated by a mediator, a review session, which usually includes Stages 1 through 6 of the mediation process in a single session, is usually started by the participants because of substantial problems or desired changes.

CONCLUSION

Knowing the stages of mediation can help the mediator plan the pace of sessions. The following is a generic overview of a six-session mediation case. Six sessions seem to be about average for most divorce cases involving money as well as child-related issues. Integrating the stages with the sessions helps define a beginning, a middle, and an end.

First Session: Stage One, Stage Two

If joint:

1. Complete forms as usual for a first interview, meeting briefly with each participant individually to augment rapport and collect data.
2. If participants are ready, sign the Agreement to Mediate/Contract in joint session. If not, show it to them; let them take it home.

If individual:

1. Complete interview guidelines for the one participant; explain letters of invitation and mediation checklist that may be sent.
2. Show the Agreement to Mediate/Counsel; explain that it will be the first thing to be done in the first joint session.
3. Get an idea of areas of agreement, conflict, and general positions, and the flexibility of each.

If finances are involved, consider handing out financial forms. Are clients ready for this as homework? Go over how you want forms filled out.

Second Session: Stage Two, Stage Three

1. If not done already, get signed Agreement to Mediate/ Counsel as commitment to mediation process.
2. Select the most immediate (or easiest) issues and do fact-finding, isolate issues, reframe and reflect, and see if options are available, develop them.

3. Determine readiness for decision making: If they are ready, see if agreement is forthcoming.
4. Record any decisions on Mediation Worksheet, or send out as Memorandum of Understanding.

Third Session: Stage Three, Stage Four

1. Continue as before for each topic or issue listed on the Agreement to Mediate/Counsel.

Fourth Session: Stage Four

1. If one party is very resistant, use individual session to explore concerns, fears.
2. By now, most fact-finding should be complete, and each should be able to negotiate from equal base of information.
3. Make referrals as needed for side issues.

Fifth Session: Stage Five

1. Start summing up progress, giving strokes for hard work; encourage.
2. Act as agent of reality; point out how parties skirt issues and financial needs and what could be done.
3. Start foreshadowing end of series: limited time.
4. Write up draft of Mediated Plan for review next session.

Sixth Session: Stage Five. Referral for Stage Six, Preparation for Stage Seven

1. Review draft of Mediated Plan (if ready), and determine and explain what is left to do (if anything).
2. Explain how other processes work (going to court, attorney negotiation, arbitration) and the likely consequences of each.
3. Determine need/commitment to continue, and for how many more sessions.
4. Confirm terms on a new Agreement to Mediate/Contract if needed; make sure fees for first series are being paid or payment plan is in place. If not needed: confirm Mediated Plan, notify attorneys judges, make referrals if needed, and close case.

5. Robert Tompkins, *Parenting Plans: A Concept Whose Time Has Come*, 33 Family & Conciliation Courts Review 286 (1995)*

Child custody law, both in its conceptual basis and in its reality of practice, is clearly an evolutionary process that reacts to the changing landscape of contemporary families. It reflects the collective thoughts of the legal and psychological communities. Reactive in nature and a product of the legislative process of compromise, child custody laws typically lag behind the changing needs of the families they are designed to serve. Positively stated, child custody laws and the ability to change them provide us with a rare opportunity to impact families in a beneficial manner as families go about the business of reorganizing their roles and responsibilities.

One opportunity that lies before us has evolved into a concept known as The Parenting Plan. It is an idea being explored in a growing number of forums, including legislative bodies, judiciaries, law societies, mental-health associations, and advocacy groups. It is an idea that has become a reality in scattered jurisdictions, most notably in the state of Washington. It is an idea that may be the future, in one form or another, because it provides the operational reality to the conceptual progression that has brought us from fault to no-fault divorce, from sole to joint custody, and from parental rights to parental responsibilities.

Before discussing the concept of parenting plans in detail, we should first explore the limitations and shortcomings of current law and practice concerning child custody. In other words, what is wrong with the status quo? What family needs are not being met by the current system? First a true story, and then some observations. The following story is an example of an opportunity lost:

> A woman was seen in the halls of the courthouse recently by someone who overheard her conversation with a casual acquaintance. The woman had gone through a custody battle with her former husband a couple of years before and was now back in court over a post-divorce dispute regarding the children. After explaining to the acquaintance why she was back in court, the woman was asked how the custody arrangement was working out. She responded, "not great," to which the acquaintance replied, "I don't understand; I thought you won custody rights."

The woman answered, "Yeah, I won alright! I won the right to take the kids to all their doctor and dentist appointments. To get all the calls at work when the kids get sick or into trouble at school. To go to all the parent-teacher conferences. To drive the kids to all their activities. To make, then carry out, all the decisions about discipline. To rush home every day from work to pick up the kids from wherever and then cook every supper. If I supposedly won, why do I feel like the loser?"

This story is an excellent example of the limitations of the child custody laws that exist in most jurisdictions. It elucidates, on a variety of levels, the inability of the present systems to address, let alone meet, the needs of families.

The parents in this case were fairly typical. The mother initiated the divorce, having been dissatisfied for many years in the marital relationship. She felt she grew beyond her husband. He felt she changed under the influence of friends and coworkers at her new job into someone who put her own needs above those of her children. They were both angry and both wanted custody of the children. In the custody dispute each was critical of the other's parenting. In the final analysis, there were no major issues of child abuse, neglect, or substance abuse. In reality, each parent was capable.

Like so many other situations, the issue of custody became the contest with the children as the prize or the "award." The custody contest became the vehicle for the parents to act out their anger—hers built up over years of frustration and his crystallized by sudden rejection. The court process and ultimately the trial became the stage for this tragic opportunity to fulfill the parents' needs for vindication and validation as the "wronged" party. . . .

Although certainly not condoning the hurtful and harmful actions of divorcing parents, it is unrealistic to expect parents to totally submerge and control their own intense emotions of fear, confusion, hurt, and anger. This is a time in one's life when perfectly normal, reasonable, and controlled people find themselves acting in ways they cannot believe. The abnormal becomes normal. Reason is replaced by the ridiculous, and control is only something one spouse wants to exert over the other. These are people who are at their absolute worst. They are not bad parents. They are simply parents having a bad time of it, in need of a service system that is designed to assist them as they struggle internally and externally to reorganize their lives as best they can. We should be careful to resist the temptation to judge them too harshly, to expect too much. As the saying goes, "until you have walked in his shoes."...

What a wonderful opportunity was lost—an opportunity to meet the needs of all family members! Mom, as she reorganized her life around pursuing the satisfaction she missed in her marriage, needed some space and relief from unrelenting child-care responsibilities. Dad, in his struggle to rediscover meaning and direction in his life, would have benefited from the satisfaction of a strengthened connection to his children. And most importantly, the children, in their adjustment to the changes in their lives, needed the nurturance of two parents neither overburdened nor disenfranchised. . . .

It is a sad commentary that the vast majority of the legal energy expended in most divorce cases is in the area of financial or property matters. Either in the lawyer's office, over the phone, or in the courtroom far more time and expense is devoted to issues other than parenting. Whether this is reflective of the priorities or preferences of the parents or the professionals is irrelevant. What is relevant for us all is that the first priority be the needs of the children, not who gets which car or the time-share in Florida. The vehicle that can transport us to a more humanistic, family based system of family law is the concept that has become known as The Parenting Plan.

Simply put, a parenting plan is a detailed articulation of post-divorce parenting responsibilities. It goes far beyond the usual, basic custody order that specifies which parent will have custody and when the other parent will have access to the children. It addresses the specific functions of parenting and distributes responsibility for those functions to either one parent or the other, or both. Before we examine the concept of parenting plans in detail and how they operate, we should enumerate the assumptions behind the concept.

First, parenting plans assume that for the majority of children it is best to promote the substantial and continued participation of both parents in post-divorce child rearing. To this end, parenting plans should not include the word *custody*. Instead, they should use language such as *parental responsibility* and allocate times for *residential care*. In those situations that are inappropriate for shared parental responsibility due to safety concerns, the law needs to provide appropriate protections.

Second, there is the assumption that divorcing parents need encouragement to devote increased levels of thought and consideration to the task of post-divorce parenting. Parents need a divorce process that helps them focus on their children at a time when they are overwhelmed with issues pertaining to their own survival. Thus a parenting plan should mandate that parents consider the variety of functions that constitute parenting and allocate responsibility for those functions. Under the current system, parents too often simply agree to the basic parameters of a parenting arrangement without giving full consideration to its implications or future contingencies.

Third, it is assumed that future conflicts are mitigated if all concerned have shared expectations regarding future events and relationships. When parents have anticipated future occurrences and scenarios and then clarified roles and responsibilities accordingly, the potential for conflict has been reduced significantly. Therefore, a parenting plan should include provisions that address future needs.

Fourth, there is the assumption parents enter the divorce process ill prepared for what lies ahead of them. Most of their knowledge about divorce comes from horror stories from their friends or coworkers, or from the movies. Most have had little or no contact with either the legal system or lawyers. The language is unintelligible, the rules are mystifying, and for most their hired representative and advisor is intimidating. Add to this the fact that they have little knowledge about what their children are experiencing and how to help them, and you have two parents who are virtually powerless to assume positive control of their own and their children's lives. If, as has been asserted so often, "education is power," then the concept of parenting plans should include an educational opportunity for parents to obtain the information they lack. These programs should focus on both the legal and emotional divorce and should include information about a variety of dispute-resolution alternatives.

These four assumptions form the conceptual basis for a new era of divorce law pertaining to the relationship among and between ex-spouses and their children. They sound good in theory, but will they translate into the real world? As mentioned earlier, the state of Washington brought these assumptions and concepts into reality in The Parenting Act in 1987. Its ideological predecessor was Florida's Shared Parental Responsibility Act, enacted in 1982 and followed shortly thereafter by similar legislation in Maine. Although both of these states broke new ground in eliminating the detrimental language of "custody" from court orders, it was Washington that put teeth into the concept by affirmatively asserting the need for divorcing spouses to plan their future parenting relationship in detail. The following is a summary of how Washington has put The Parenting Plan concept into operation.

First, the law eliminates the legal terminology of *custody* and *visitation* or *access*, replacing it with *residential care* and *decision making*. The benefits of this have been discussed previously. However, the law also provides protection in the form of limitations on both shared parenting arrangements and future dispute-resolution options. Those limitations are designed to protect a parent or children who might be placed in a vulnerable position by certain shared parenting arrangements or dispute-resolution mechanisms. The law, in fact, goes on to list the circumstances that would result in vulnerability. They are situations where there is evidence of neglect, willful abandonment, abuse (physical, sexual, or pattern of emotional), or domestic violence.

Second, the law mandates that parents, either individually or jointly, file with the court a proposed parenting plan. Initially, it was mandated that this be filed shortly after the filing of the divorce suit. However, it was determined that this was poor timing. Experience shows that the period surrounding the divorce filing is usually the most emotionally charged and unfocused period for divorcing parents. Proposed parenting plans devised and exchanged so early in the process tended to polarize parents and were somewhat ill conceived. The law now mandates that they be filed 30 days before trial or within 180 days from the filing of the divorce, whichever first occurs.

Third, the law prescribes the minimal details of acceptable parenting plans, thus promoting that appropriate levels of thought, planning, and attention be given to the issues involved in future parenting. This is accomplished through mandated use of a standard parenting-plan form that must be completed in full. This form forces parents to establish in detail parental responsibility in terms of residential care, including the school year, school vacations, holidays, birthdays, and other major events. It also prescribes that parental responsibility be designated for transportation and decision making in the areas of education, religion, and medical decisions—as well as any other areas important to that specific family.

Last, parents must designate the choice of dispute-resolution options should future conflicts arise. Parents can choose from a variety of options, such as the court process, mediation, counselling, and so on. Also, regarding certain options, they are encouraged to name the specific person or agency.

Having looked at how the concept of parenting plans can be made operational at least in one form, we are left with the question of effectiveness. Does it work? Does it produce the desired effects? Again, we have to look to the Washington experience. Because it is such a new idea, there has been little opportunity to study these questions and begin to develop some answers. There has been one study of the Washington law that provides us with some initial helpful information. This was conducted by Jane Ellis and associates and reported in the *University of Michigan Journal of Law Reform* in 1990 (Volume 24-1). The following questions were explored, with the following results:

Do parenting plans promote more individualized post-divorce parenting arrangements, reflective of the unique circumstances and interests of each family? It was found that over half the families studied addressed the issue of decision making beyond the minimum areas prescribed by the standardized form. Specified decision making in the area of child care was added most frequently (52%). Also written in were such areas as recreational activities and teenage driving decisions.

Do parenting plans foster the substantial and consistent participation of both parents in the lives of their children? In terms of decision making, 56% of the parenting plans studied revealed shared decision making, 35% sole decision-making responsibility to mothers, and 9% sole decision making to fathers. The study also found that in comparing primary residences of children before and after the Washington law went into effect, primary residence with the mother dropped from 79% to 70%. For fathers, it dropped from 18% to 10%. However, shared residency on a somewhat equal basis rose from 3% to 20%.

Are parenting plans helpful in reducing the adversarial nature of post-divorce parental relationships? The study found that only 16% of the couples choose the court process as their future dispute-resolution forum. Mediation was the clear preference at 58%, with counselling chosen by 7% of the parents. In fact, 29% of the couples went on to name a specific person or agency including religious leaders, relatives, and the tribal court.

Do parenting plans help parents focus on their children and reduce parental conflict concerning their children? To answer this question, the researchers went to the family lawyers. The answer was "no" for 40%, who felt the same levels of parental conflict existed between parents using parenting plans as did under the old scheme. However, 60% of the lawyers surveyed felt there was improvement and the parenting plans did help parents focus on the needs of their children. Those that felt it was helpful pointed out parenting plans were an opportunity to discuss specific challenges of parenting such as dividing parenting tasks more equitably when both parents work, addressing the particular needs of teenagers who do not want structured arrangements, or meeting the needs of young children who may have trouble with frequent switching of residences.

These views expressed by the lawyers are particularly meaningful. With 60% of the lawyers feeling that parenting plans are a positive change and 40% feeling there was no change, this seems to suggest we have an opportunity to enact a change that does not worsen a situation and in 60% of the cases produces a positive and significant improvement. Also, one would suspect the views expressed by lawyers are, to a certain degree, reflective of their lawyering style or mind set. If they view their role and practice their craft from an adversarial perspective, it would seem that the idea of parenting plans would neither be welcomed nor supported. If it is not among your goals to promote positive post-divorce adjustment of children, then any system can be subverted or circumvented.

Clearly, no system is a panacea, curing all the ills that exist. Parenting plans will not eliminate conflicts regarding children, although they might lessen the intensity and frequency. There will always be a small percentage of highly conflicted, dysfunctional parents that no amount of litigation, counselling, or enlightened divorce laws will help. Conversely, there will also be a small percentage of couples who, no matter what the divorce process entails, will need no assistance in maximizing the positive adjustment of their children.

It is the majority of parents who fall between those extremes that would benefit from the advantages of parenting plans. Those parents are the cases that seldom go to trial, that usually reach a negotiated settlement for a variety of reasons. Either they cannot afford a trial or they trade off concessions, or they simply get worn out. These are parents who, caught up in the legal and emotional tide of divorce, have given little real thought to the particulars of post-divorce child rearing. The children of this silent majority would benefit from a system that encouraged increased attention to parenting issues.

Such a system would change the art of family lawyering. Lawyers, as well as mental-health professionals, have a role as counsellors in assisting clients to understand and accept their responsibilities as parents during and after the divorce process. The family lawyer of the future will have to roll up his or her sleeves and spend time with clients, reviewing the various parenting functions and developing a plan that allocates those functions in a manner that is beneficial to the entire family. The family lawyer of the future will realize that supporting a client in either hoarding or abdicating parental responsibility is usually a disservice to the entire family in general, and the client in particular. The family lawyer of the future will need to be as knowledgeable about the intricate implications of post-divorce parenting as she or he is about tax implications. . . .

C. Are Women Disadvantaged in Family Mediation

1. Trina Grillo, *The Mediation Alternative: Process Dangers For Women*, 100 Yale L.J. 1545 (1991)*

INTRODUCTION: THE PROMISE OF MEDIATION

The western concept of law is based on a patriarchal paradigm characterized by hierarchy, linear reasoning, the resolution of disputes through the application of abstract principles, and the ideal of the reasonable person. Its fundamental aspiration is objectivity, and to that end it separates public from private, form from substance, and process from policy. This objectivist paradigm is problematic in many circumstances, but never more so than in connection with a marital dissolution in which the custody of children is at issue, where the essential question for the court is what is to happen next in the family. The family court system, aspiring to the

*Reprinted by permission of The Yale Law Journal Company and Fred B. Rothman & Company from The Yale Law Journal, Vol. 100, pages 1545-610.

ideal of objectivity and operating as an adversary system, can be relied on neither to produce just results nor to treat those subject to it respectfully and humanely.

There is little doubt that divorce procedure needs to be reformed, but reformed how? Presumably, any alternative should be at least as just, and at least as humane, as the current system, particularly for those who are least powerful in society. Mediation has been put forward, with much fanfare, as such an alternative. The impetus of the mediation movement has been so strong that in some states couples disputing custody are required by statute or local rule to undergo a mandatory mediation process if they are unable to reach an agreement on their own. Mediation has been embraced for a number of reasons. First, it rejects an objectivist approach to conflict resolution, and promises to consider disputes in terms of relationships and responsibility. Second, the mediation process is, at least in theory, cooperative and voluntary, not coercive. The mediator does not make a decision; rather, each party speaks for himself. Together they reach an agreement that meets the parties' mutual needs. In this manner, the process is said to enable the parties to exercise self-determination and eliminate the hierarchy of dominance that characterizes the judge/litigant and lawyer/client relationships. Third, since in mediation there are no rules of evidence or legalistic notions of relevancy, decisions supposedly may be informed by context rather than by abstract principle. Finally, in theory at least, emotions are recognized and incorporated into the mediation process. This conception of mediation has led some commentators to characterize it as a feminist alternative to the patriarchally inspired adversary system.

Whether mandatory mediation, required as part of court proceedings, fulfills these aspirations, or instead substitutes another objectivist, patriarchal, and even more damaging form of conflict resolution for its adversarial counterpart, is the subject of this Article. Many divorcing couples seem pleased with their mediation experiences. Indeed, studies have shown that mediation clients are more satisfied with their divorce outcomes than persons using the adversary system. . . .

Nonetheless, I conclude that mandatory mediation provides neither a more just nor a more humane alternative to the adversarial system of adjudication of custody, and, therefore, does not fulfill its promises. In particular, quite apart from whether an acceptable result is reached, mandatory mediation can be destructive to many women and some men because it requires them to speak in a setting they have not chosen and often imposes a rigid orthodoxy as to how they should speak, make decisions, and be. This orthodoxy is imposed through subtle and not-so-subtle messages about appropriate conduct and about what may be said in mediation. It is an orthodoxy that often excludes the possibility of the parties' speaking with their authentic voices.

Moreover, people vary greatly in the extent to which their sense of self is "relational"—that is, defined in terms of connection to others. If two parties are forced to engage with one another, and one has a more relational sense of self than the other, that party may feel compelled to maintain her connection with the other, even to her own detriment. For this reason, the party with the more relational sense of self will be at a disadvantage in a mediated negotiation. Several prominent researchers have suggested that, as a general rule, women have a more relational sense of self than do men, although there is little agreement on what the origin of this difference might be. Thus, rather than being a feminist alternative to the adversary system, mediation has the potential actively to harm women.

Some of the dangers of mandatory mediation apply to voluntary mediation as well.

Voluntary mediation should not be abandoned, but should be recognized as a powerful process which should be used carefully and thoughtfully. Entering into such a process with one who has known you intimately and who now seems to threaten your whole life and being has great creative, but also enormous destructive, power. Nonetheless, it should be recognized that when two people themselves decide to mediate and then physically appear at the mediation sessions, that decision and their continued presence serve as a rough indication that it is not too painful or too dangerous for one or both of them to go on.

Although this Article cautions against mediation's dangers, I should emphasize at this juncture that mediation is the work I most like to do. Few professional experiences can compare to the moment when the world of possibilities seems to expand for a couple, and hope and optimism coexist, at least temporarily, with pain and anger. It is from my experiences mediating and listening to the stories of those who have been participants in the mediation process, and out of concern for the integrity of that process, that this Article has been written.

Part I of this Article describes the rise of child custody mediation, focusing on the version currently required by California law. . . . Part II describes the promises of mediation: reliance on context rather than exclusively on abstract rules; the inclusion of emotions along with rational self-interest; and the introduction of self-determination in the place of an outside decisionmaker. Part III discusses the particular dangers to women of mandatory mediation's requirement of direct engagement with their adversary. Part IV suggests alternatives to a system of mandatory mediation. While the focus of my discussion is mandatory mediation, many of the observations in the Article also have implications for voluntary mediation, which in many cases also fails to fulfill its promise to be a gentler alternative to the adversarial system.

I. THE RISE OF MANDATORY CUSTODY MEDIATION IN CALIFORNIA

. . . California's mandatory mediation law, which first became effective in 1981, requires that all custody and visitation disputes be mediated prior to being considered by the county Superior Court. The mediation is intended to "reduce acrimony" between the parties and lead to an agreement that assures the children "close and continuing contact with both parents." The court is required to appoint a mediator, who may be a member of the professional staff of a family conciliation court, probation department, or mental health services agency, or some other person or agency the court decides is appropriate. Mediators must have a master's degree in psychology, social work, or another behavioral science; experience in counseling or psychotherapy; knowledge of the California court system and family law procedure; and knowledge of adult and child psychology, including the effects of divorce on children.

In practice, the qualifications of mediators provided by the California courts vary widely. In some urban counties, there are large professional staffs of mediators, all of whom are experienced mental health professionals; in other counties, there may be only one mediator with little professional training. Similarly, some counties have extensive office facilities in which to house their mediation program and provide the opportunity to have several meetings with the mediators; in others, mediation takes place in the twenty minutes before court in a hallway. . . .

In California, mediations are held in private and communications to the mediator from the parties are deemed "official information" protected from disclosure by the Evidence Code. The mediator has discretion to exclude counsel from the mediation, whether or not the parties wish to have them present.

Local courts have the option of requiring mediators to make a recommendation to the court regarding custody or visitation. If the parties do not reach an agreement, the mediator may also make a recommendation that an investigation be conducted or mutual restraining orders be issued. More than half of California counties have opted to require mediators to make such recommendations. In these counties, a mediator meets with the parties and, having assured them of confidentiality, attempts to help them reach an agreement. Should they not reach an agreement, however, the mediator uses what happened in the mediation session to make a recommendation to the court. . . .

II. THE BETRAYAL OF MEDIATION'S PROMISES

A. The Informal Law of Mediation

. . . In even the most mundane settings there develops a type of informal law, shared expectations that there is a right way of acting, that departures from this way are wrong, and that an offender should be sanctioned. The "law" that develops in these "microsocial" settings is often both complex and necessary for human interaction to proceed. Where norms appropriate for a situation are not prescribed or made clear, interaction is impeded and perceived as awkward. The normative components of microsocial settings may be thought of as microlegal systems. . . .

Persons in the midst of a divorce often experience what seems to them a threat to their very survival. Their self-concepts, financial well-being, moral values, confidence in their parenting abilities, and feelings of being worthy of love are all at risk. They are profoundly concerned about whether they are meeting their obligations and continuing to be seen as virtuous persons and respectable members of society. They are especially vulnerable to the responses they receive from any professional with whom they must deal. Against this backdrop, mediation must be seen as a relatively high-risk process. To begin with, for most people it is a new setting. Its norms are generally not understood by the parties in advance, with the result that the parties are extremely sensitive to cues as to how they are supposed to act; they will look to the mediator to provide these cues. Mediators are often quite willing to give such cues, to establish the normative components of the mediation, and to sanction departures from the unwritten rules. The informal sanctions applied by a mediator can be especially powerful, quite apart from whatever actual authority he might have. These sanctions might be as simple as criticizing the client for not putting the children's needs first, or instructing her not to talk about a particular issue. That these informal sanctions might appear trivial does not mean they will not be as influential in changing behavior as sanctions that might on their face appear more severe. . . .

In the following Section, I discuss the mediation process as a microlegal setting characterized by certain normative components. I examine the "law" of that setting with respect to the parties' relationship and emotions, and the informal sanctions that may be applied by the mediator for departures from the approved way of handling these issues.

B. The Promise to Contextualize Decisionmaking

1. Principles Versus Context as the Basis for Decisionmaking

. . . Where child custody is being determined, a system that ostensibly brings context—this mother, this father, these children—into the process of dispute resolution, and renders a decision based on the lives of those actually involved in the dispute rather than on the basis of a general rule, has much to offer. There is, however, a cost to this change in emphasis; for although the language of legal rights may divert public consciousness away from the real roots of anger, the assertion of rights may also clarify and elucidate those roots. The process of claiming rights, by itself, can be empowering for people who have not shared societal power. Thus the risk of mediation is that if principles are abandoned, and context is not effectively introduced, we end up with the worst of both worlds.

a. Principles and Fault in the Adversary System

A series of attempts has been made to make the court system more responsive to the actual situation of persons undergoing a divorce and to their children by deemphasizing claims of right and principle. The first of these attempts consisted of reduced reliance on the notion of fault. . . . It is now typical for states to allow divorce on grounds that do not require fault by either spouse. For the most part, one spouse need only show that the marital relationship is irreparable. These changes have increased the individual autonomy of married persons and given husbands and wives freedom to extricate themselves from unhappy relationships. They have reduced the oppressiveness of principles which, although written into the law, did not fit the manner in which many persons choose to lead their lives.

But there have been other consequences of these changes. For example, results were once much more predictable than they are now, both in terms of the availability of support and the likelihood of the father's being able to obtain custody of the children. This lack of predictability generally harms the party who has the lesser amount of power in the relationship, or who is most risk averse. Moreover, to a certain extent community values have been eliminated from the process by which the state recognizes marriage and its end. While the principles that formerly controlled the process were outmoded and sexist and resulted in much unnecessary pain for persons whose marriages were ending, they were not replaced by different principles based on different values. . . .

b. Principles and Fault in Mediation

The introduction of mediation into family court processes was another part of the effort to make the adversary system fit the realities of divorce more closely. Mediators stepped into the increasingly uncertain legal world of dissolution with a new process which minimized the role of principles and fault. Mediation appeared to provide the opportunity to bring the lessons of context and subjective experience to dissolution proceedings. In mediation, the parties' legal rights would not be central. Instead of relying solely on abstract principles and rules, parties and mediators could attend to the reality of complex relationships. Precedent, legal rules and a legalized formulation of the facts might be seen as irrelevant to the mediation process and an unnecessary constraint on the mediator. Individuals could be seen in relation to one another, and morality treated as "a question of responsibilities to particular people in particular contexts."

The informal law of the mediation setting requires that discussion of principles, blame, and rights, as these terms are used in the adversarial context, be deemphasized or avoided. Mediators use informal sanctions to encourage the parties to replace the rhetoric of fault, principles, and values with the rhetoric of compromise and relationship. For example, mediators typically suggest that the parties "eschew the language of individual rights in favor of the language of interdependent relationships." They orient the parties toward reasonableness and compromise, rather than moral vindication. The conflict may be styled as a personal quarrel, in which there is no right and wrong, but simply two different, and equally true or untrue, views of the world. . . .

2. The Destroyers of Context: Prospectivity and Formal Equality

a. Prospectivity

. . . The chief means by which mediators eliminate the discussion of principles and fault is by making certain types of discussion "off-limits" in the mediation. Mediation experts Jay Folberg and Alison Taylor propose the following as one of the "shared propositions" upon which nearly all mediators agree:

Proposition 5. In mediation the past history of the participants is only important in relation to the present or as a basis for predicting future needs, intentions, abilities, and reactions to decisions.

It is typical for mediators to insist that parties waste no time complaining about past conduct of their spouse, eschew blaming each other, and focus only on the future. For example, one of the two essential ground rules mediator Donald Saposnek suggests a mediator give to the parties is the following:

> There is little value in talking about the past, since it only leads to fighting and arguing, as I'm sure you both know . . . Our focus will be on your children's needs for the future and on how you two can satisfy those needs. . . . [U]nless I specifically request it, we will talk about plans for the future.

Thus, while one of the principal justifications for introducing mediation into the divorce process is that context will be substituted for abstract principles, in fact, by eliminating discussion of the past, context—in the sense of the relationship's history—is removed. The result is that we are left with neither principles nor context as a basis for decisionmaking. . . .

b. Prospectivity and the Assertion of Rights

Felstiner, Abel and Sarat note that some people are apparently able to tolerate substantial amounts of distress and injustice. This "tolerance," they posit, comes from a failure to perceive that they have been injured. They describe a three-step process by which (1) injurious experiences are perceived (naming), (2) are transformed into grievances (blaming), and, (3) ultimately, become disputes (claiming). "Naming" involves saying to oneself that a particular experience has been injurious. . . . "Blaming" occurs when a person attributes fault to another (rather than to an impersonal force, such as luck or the weather). One cannot arrive at "claiming," that is, the assertion of rights, without passing through "blaming." By making blaming off-limits, the process by which a dispute is fully developed—and rights are asserted—cannot be completed. Short-circuiting the blaming process may fall most heavily on those who are already at a disadvantage in society. . . .

The cultural commitment to access to justice has focused on the last stage of disputing—claiming. The more critical place at which inequality is manifested, however, is before experiences are transformed into disputes, that is, at the naming and blaming stages. One adverse consequence of de-emphasizing discussion of principle and fault is that some persons may be discouraged from asserting their rights when they have been injured. Even more troubling, some persons may cease to perceive injuries when they have been injured, or will perceive injuries but those injuries will remain inarticulable, because the language to name them will not be easily available. . . . To the extent that there is something to be gained by the assertion of rights, especially for women and minorities, this is unacceptable.

Many writers have debated recently whether legal rights have some intrinsic value, especially in the context of rights that define the boundaries of state power. Some Critical Legal Studies theorists have suggested that rights claims perpetuate dichotomies such as individual and community, self and other, and family and market, and thus do not promote social reconstruction. . . . Feminist critiques of rights have been based on the characterization of rights claims as formal and hierarchical and, therefore, patriarchal. Both critiques emphasize the ways in which discussion of rights can lead to increased alienation and passivity.

In recent years, a number of women and minority scholars have challenged these critiques of rights, suggesting that rights claims may in fact help enhance and develop individual and political growth. Although the debate usually focuses on "rights" in a very different sense from those at stake when, for example, a mother wants sole rather than joint custody, the debate is useful in considering what the consequences might be of making discussion of principles and fault off-limits in the context of custody. In particular, the literature suggesting that the assertion of rights may have a transformative function applies in this context.

For example, Elizabeth Schneider has demonstrated that assertion of rights can aid in the development of individual and group consciousness among women. She notes that Carol Gilligan describes the developmental challenges of maturity as very different for men and for women. Men must learn connection and care for others; women must learn to care for themselves. The assertion of rights can aid women in this development, as "[t]he essential notion of rights [is] that the interests of the self can be considered legitimate." Thus, assertion of rights can help women distinguish self from other, and ultimately give them a sense of collective identity. . . . Whatever the other limitations of Gilligan's work, her suggestion that assertion of rights can be transformative for many women merits careful attention. To the extent that the mediation process makes it difficult to assert rights, the positive implications of rights-assertion for women, the poor, and minorities of either sex will be lost. . . .

C. The Promise to Include Emotion and the Suppression of Anger

Another criticism of the traditional adversary method of dispute resolution is that it does not provide a role for emotion. Decisions by adversarial parties are posited as rational, devoid of emotion, self-interested, and instrumental (result-oriented). Some proponents of mediation and other methods of alternative dispute resolution believe these characteristics should be retained in mediation to the extent they permit parties to serve their self- interests efficiently. Others have argued that mediation and other forms of alternative dispute resolution provide an opportunity to bring intuition and emotion into the legal process. This latter group of proponents points out that family conflicts in particular often involve a combination of emotional and legal complaints, so that the "real" issues are often obscured in the adversarial setting. Thus, "there may be a great need for an open-ended, unstructured process that permits the disputants to air their true sentiments."

Although mediation is claimed to be a setting in which feelings can be expressed, certain sentiments are often simply not welcome. In particular, expressions of anger are frequently overtly discouraged. This discouragement of anger sends a message that anger is unacceptable, terrifying and dangerous. For a person who has only recently found her anger, this can be a perilous message indeed. This suppression of anger poses a stark contrast to the image of mediation as a process which allows participants to express their emotions.

Women undergoing a divorce, especially ones from nondominant cultural groups, are particularly likely to be harmed by having their anger actively discouraged during the dissolution process. Women have been socialized not to express anger, and have often had their anger labelled "bad." A woman in the throes of divorce may for the first time in her life have found a voice for her anger. As her early, undifferentiated, and sometimes inchoate expressions of anger emerge, the anger may seem as overwhelming to her as to persons outside of it. And yet this anger may turn out to be the source of her energy, strength, and growth in the months and years ahead. An injunction from a person in power to suppress that anger because it is not sufficiently modulated may amount to nothing less that an act of violence.

1. Anger in Adversary Adjudication

People are necessarily angry at divorce, in two senses. First of all, anger is inevitable in ending a marriage; almost everyone who obtains a divorce becomes angry sooner or later. This anger may have many different causes: it may be a result of anticipated losses, wrongful treatment, or the myriad compromises of self that may have been made along the way to the marriage's end. Second, some anger is necessary for the disengagement which is essential to the completion of the divorce. It is thus critical that any system of marital dissolution take anger into consideration and establish a means by which it is permitted to enter into the divorce process. . . .

The manner in which anger is expressed in the adversary system is not, however, without its imperfections. Frequently it is not the party's actual anger that is being expressed, but rather the anger the party is expected to have. Lawyers handling dissolutions under the adversary system may exacerbate or even create conflicts, and fan the flames of anger—real or manufactured—that arise from them. Mediation has been put forth as an alternative forum in which parties can express their sentiments directly and ensure that only their sentiments are expressed.

2. Anger in Mediation

. . . Some mediation literature suggests that mediators should proceed by discouraging the expression of anger. This literature evinces a profound lack of respect for the anger that divorcing spouses feel. For example, Donald Saposnek suggests that "[i]n many ways, the mediator must act as a parent figure to the parents, since their struggles are often not unlike those of siblings squabbling over joint possessions." Saposnek's depiction of divorcing parents suggests that their struggles are devoid of content. He characterizes their anger and conflict as "squabbling" rather than as arising from substantively important conflicts or as a necessary and important step in the divorce process. . . .

Even when mediation literature does approve of bringing anger into the process, it often recommends doing so in a way that subtly undercuts the legitimacy of the anger. Mediators are encouraged, where necessary, to permit parties to "vent" their anger, after which the parties can move on to discuss settlement. This view does not take anger seriously enough. Because it treats expressed anger as having no long-range impact on the party who is exposed to it, it is not necessarily seen as objectionable to require one party to be present and endure the other party's "venting"—even where the party enduring the venting has been the subject of abuse in the marriage. The effects of exposure to anger in such a case can be devastating. If the privilege of expressing anger has not been distributed equally in the relationship prior to mediation, then the mediator should not grant that privilege equally during the mediation.

Second, and equally critically, the view of anger as something to be "vented" does not take anger seriously as a path to clarity and strength. Anger that is merely vented has lost its potential to teach, heal, and energize; it is ineffective anger, anger that "maintains rather than challenges" the status quo. . . .

At the same time, there are other forces which may intensify this dynamic of suppression. Mediators working under time pressures recognize that it takes time to express anger, and its full expression might, indeed, jeopardize a quick settlement. More significantly, there are substantial societal taboos against the expression of anger by women, taboos which have particular force when the disputant is a woman of color. For a woman who has just found her anger, anger which has enabled her to free herself from an oppressive relationship and involve herself and her family in a divorce proceeding, the suppression of the very force that has driven her forward is a devastating message. . . .

D. Mandatory Mediation and the Promise of Self-Determination

Mediation permits persons to speak for themselves and make their own decisions. This self-determination can be empowering. Patterns of domination characteristic of adversary adjudication are challenged in two ways: no outside decisionmaker is present, and the client need not be the passive recipient of a lawyer's advice and decisionmaking. Instead, he can explore alternatives, create options, and make decisions. In private, voluntary mediation, I have found that many say that they have chosen mediation so that they, and not a lawyer, will be in charge of their own destinies. In this very immediate way, mediation can challenge the hierarchical, professionalized way that family law is usually practiced.

This dynamic is fundamentally altered when mediation is imposed rather than sought or offered. When mandatory mediation is part of the court system, the notion that parties are actually making their own decisions is purely illusory. First, the parties have not chosen or timed the process according to their ability to handle it. Second, they are not allowed to decide themselves how much their lawyers should participate, but instead are deprived of whatever protection their lawyers have to offer. Finally, they are not permitted to choose the mediator, and they often cannot leave without endangering their legal position even if they believe the mediator is biased against them.

1. Choice of Process

Several writers have noted that most clients do not understand what mediation is and, therefore, absent coercion, are reluctant to enter into it. For example, mediation is almost never represented in the popular culture, whereas television shows which represent the court system are numerous. It has been argued that because of the general ignorance that surrounds mediation, it makes sense to require people to try mediation before their case is heard by the court, so that they can see whether it works for them: "No law is mandating an agreement, but it is requiring a process, however extensive or minimal it may turn out to be in a particular instance." Proponents of this view seldom recognize that, even though an agreement might not be required, a person might agree to something because of the pressures of the situation; or that, even if no agreement is reached, the process itself might be traumatic.

It is presumptuous to assume that the state has a better idea than the parties themselves about whether mediation will work in their particular case. A party may know something the mediator does not: that her spouse is a pathological, but convincing, liar; that years of living with a man have resulted in a pattern in which the woman consistently accommodates him, even when she does not want to; that the woman will lose sight of her own needs in the attempt to appear a cooperative female; or that the woman will sacrifice many of her interests in order to end what may be a psychologically painful process. In sum, there may be an internal wisdom, one that needs to be honored, that mediation is inappropriate in a particular situation.

It is true that mandatory mediation may serve the interests of women who do not wish to enter the adversary process; if opting out of mediation is permitted, some women (as well as some men) will be forced to litigate when their preference would have been to mediate. There is no way around this unfortunate situation. Either some women will be forced to litigate against their will, or some women will be forced to mediate against their will. Mediation poses such substantial dangers, and provides so few benefits to unwilling female participants, however, that to my mind it is indefensible to require mediation, notwithstanding that such a requirement would help women who do want to mediate. In addition, the woman who participates in the mediation process with a reluctant spouse may have gained little. . . .

Mediation where abuse has occurred is troubling even when mediation is voluntary. Mandatory mediation programs, however, do not always permit abused parties to opt out. Moreover, even where such an exception to the mediation requirement exists, the abused spouse might have trouble showing she is entitled to it; to be relieved from participating in mediation in some jurisdictions, a woman must come forward with more than her word. In some jurisdictions, then, a woman who has been subject to abuse may finally attempt to take a stand against it, have her word doubted, and then be required to meet face to face with the abuser to decide child custody.

Finally, a person might not want to participate in mediation because the timing is wrong. She might be willing to mediate in the future, but might feel for the present too vulnerable, angry, hurt or fragile to use anything but a formal process with built-in distancing mechanisms. Mandatory mediation takes this crucial decision out of her hands.

2. Choice of Mediator: Partiality and Unacknowledged Perspective

Typically in mandatory mediation, the participants cannot choose their mediator or, at best, have a very limited choice of mediators. Some agencies have policies which make it difficult to change mediators when one or both of the parties are dissatisfied with the mediator's handling of the case. Mediators . . . exert a great deal of power. . . . There is much room for, but little acknowledgment of, the possibility of the mediator's exhibiting partiality or imposing a hidden agenda on the parties. . . .

b. Mediators and Judges: The Importance of Form

Mediators are not supposed to be judges, at least in states that do not permit them to make recommendations to the court. It is assumed, however, that mediators as well as judges can and should be impartial. In the context of judging, Judith Resnik has shown how impartiality among judges is an aspiration, not a reality. Rather, a demonstrable "picture of partiality, of prejudgment, of judges ready to translate racial and sexist views into law" emerges. Even among well-intentioned judges who try to be impartial, the twin dangers of unacknowledged perspective and unrecognized partiality are always present. . . .

These dangers, serious enough in the context of judging, are exacerbated in mediation. There are numerous restrictions on the way the decisionmaker ordinarily relates to parties in the adversarial setting that simply do not apply to mediation. . . .

Many formalities of the judicial process serve to maintain this distance. At the most mundane level, judges sit apart from the parties. Ordinarily, they speak to the parties' attorneys rather than directly to the parties. When they do address the parties directly, it is often in a formal manner, and on the record. Judges also do not ordinarily communicate with one side separately. . . .

By contrast, because the mediator views her role as one of understanding and helping the parties rather than judging them, judicial forms of distancing are dispensed with. Mediators sit close to the parties and speak directly to them. They frequently meet with the parties separately, often without subsequently telling the opposing party what transpired. The session with the mediator is rarely entered on the record or even informally recorded. Finally, no attempt is made to limit the sort of material that may be considered in the session on grounds of privilege or relevancy; something may be considered relevant for the purposes of mediation because it is emotionally—even though not logically—connected to the proceedings. In sum, a mediator establishes what may be a risky relationship of informality and apparent intimacy with the parties.

The informal nature of the mediation setting may make it an environment in which prejudices can flourish. Richard Delgado and his coauthors have shown that people who hold prejudicial attitudes are most prone to act on those attitudes in an intimate setting. . . . [See Chapter 5, section C.]

Mediation literature has addressed the problem of unequal bargaining power between the parties by suggesting that the mediator use a variety of techniques to "balance the power." These techniques entail empowering or supporting the less powerful party or disempowering the more powerful party. For example, a mediator might provoke a conflict, forbid the discussion of certain issues, or advise a party who seems to be at an economic disadvantage to see a financial counselor. These suggestions share the premise that the mediator can recognize power disparities when they occur and intervene to lessen their impact.

But, as I have attempted to show, benign intervention may not always be possible. When a mediator analyzes and attempts to correct a power imbalance, she can no longer claim to be simply a facilitator of the couple's process; rather, she is taking an active role in affecting the outcome of that process. But the mediator, due to her own internal processes, may not in fact have a sufficiently clear vision of the interaction between the divorcing spouses to make a considered decision about if and how the power needs to be balanced. The existence of partiality, countertransference, and projection on the part of mediators explains why mediators' attempts to redress imbalances cannot necessarily be relied upon to meet the problem of unequal bargaining power. . . .

3. Joint Custody

Many mediators state unabashedly that they attempt to steer their clients toward joint custody, regardless of what the clients want. Some go so far as to tell a parent that her refusal to request joint custody may result in an award of custody to the other spouse as the "friendlier" parent. This position is justified on the ground that the mediator should be an advocate for the children. Mediators who take this view do so despite the lack of convincing evidence that joint custody is in fact better for children than sole custody. This position also ignores the disturbing reality that a father may request joint custody to obtain financial concessions from his wife in exchange for permitting her to have sole custody; in fact, some lawyers routinely recommend this tactic. . . .

4. Exclusion of Lawyers

In California, lawyers typically are excluded from mediation sessions, and the parties are required to speak for themselves, whether or not they wish to do so. Some argue that exclusion of lawyers contributes to client empowerment. In evaluating whether their exclusion actually furthers client empowerment, it is useful to consider the reasons why a person engaged in a divorce might want the services of a lawyer. First, and most obviously, lawyers are hired for their expertise, particularly their expertise in protecting their clients' rights. Of equal importance, however, is the fact that lawyers are hired to provide a buffer, a layer of insulation, between the client and her spouse. Neither of these rationales for the presence of an attorney disappears in the context of mediation.

a. Lawyers as Protectors of Rights

A lawyer who is excluded from the mediation sessions may be hampered in protecting her client's rights, particularly if custody is ultimately to be litigated in court. For example, privileged or irrelevant material, which the lawyer does not believe should be disclosed, may mistakenly be revealed in mediation. Once such privileged information is disclosed, it is often impossible to keep it out of a later court proceeding.

In states with an evidentiary privilege protecting mediation, a party would not be able to use in court any documents obtained in mediation. In many instances, however, he could obtain the documents in some other manner, once he knows of their existence. Moreover, even if the information is not introduced formally, it may nonetheless subtly influence the proceedings at a later date.

Nor does a provision for consulting with attorneys before an agreement is reached, or for stopping the mediation to allow consultation with an attorney, ensure that a client will be adequately protected. Apart from the possibility of harmful disclosure of information, a party may agree to something because he is nervous, intimidated, exhausted, or frightened. Even if the agreement is not final until it has been presented to the attorneys, it will be difficult for a disempowered party to disavow an agreement already tentatively reached. Moreover, the attorneys themselves may be reluctant to be perceived as sabotaging an agreement.

In jurisdictions in which mediators are permitted to make recommendations to the court, the problem of protecting disempowered parties is even more acute. Under California Civil Code section 4607(e), if no agreement is reached in mediation, a mediator "may, consistent with local court rules, render a recommendation to the court" based on information acquired during the mediation. Where such a recommendation is lawful, it may well seem a futile gesture to fail to "agree" to a proposal that the mediator favors or to disavow the agreement before it is approved by the court—especially in a jurisdiction where mediators' recommendations are almost always accepted. . . .

b. Lawyers as Providers of Insulation

Lawyers serve another function in the divorce process, that of insulating the parties from the hand-to-hand combat and self-help that the rule of law is intended to avoid. The presence of a lawyer means that a party does not have to face his adversary directly if he does not wish to do so. Mediation is often put forward as a method of empowering the parties to a dispute, but the words "Don't call me, call my lawyer" are sometimes the most empowering words imaginable. Mandatory mediation, even absent the pressure to reach an agreement that exists when a recommendation to the court can be made, prevents lawyers from performing this protective function.

The usual view is that mediation is at its best where the parties have a close relationship, and one that is likely to continue in some form. The danger of being deprived of the insulation provided by a lawyer is at its greatest, however, under those precise circumstances. At the time of divorce, the hiring of an attorney can be the first step to disengagement, to seeing oneself as separate from one's spouse; the attorney can keep the party from experiencing directly the hostility, pain, or fear of the other party. An attorney may provide a further type of insulation as well. In mediation it is easy for a woman to feel she is being characterized as greedy, selfish, controlling, or unfeminine. Even if the mediator does not mean to do so, many women may be ready to hear those words, or worse, may be using them internally. An attorney can carry the banner for the proposition that there is nothing wrong with the client's wanting what she wants, and that she is entitled, at a minimum, to survive.

It is interesting to contemplate why a mandatory system of mediation should encourage the exclusion of lawyers. Perhaps some believe that lawyers cannot be relied on to be cooperative and will disrupt the mediation process. In any event, the exclusion of lawyers renders the parties more vulnerable to the exercise of authority—often veiled authority—by the mediator.

III. MANDATORY MEDIATION AND THE DANGERS OF FORCED ENGAGEMENT

. . . While some of mandatory mediation's dangers affect men and women equally, others fall disproportionately on women. A study that compared people who chose to mediate with those who rejected the opportunity found that 44% of the reasons given by women who rejected mediation services offered to them centered around their mistrust of, fear of, or desire to avoid their ex-spouse. In contrast, those men who rejected mediation appeared to do so because they were skeptical of the mediation process or convinced they could win in court. Thus, the requirement of mandatory mediation that the parties meet personally with one another, usually without a lawyer present, presents troubling issues for women. Feminist analyses, looked at alone and together, clarify why this is so.

A. The Ethic of Care in Mediation

[S]everal feminist scholars have suggested that women have a more "relational" sense of self than do men. The most influential of these researchers, Carol Gilligan, describes two different, gendered modes of thought. The female mode is characterized by an "ethic of care" which emphasizes nurturance, connection with others, and contextual thinking. The male mode is characterized by an "ethic of justice" which emphasizes individualism, the use of rules to resolve moral dilemmas, and equality. Under Gilligan's view, the male mode leads one to strive for individualism and autonomy, while the female mode leads one to strive for connection with and caring for others. Some writers, seeing a positive virtue in the ethic of care, have applied Gilligan's work to the legal system. But her work has been criticized by others for its methodology, its conflation of biological sex with gender, and its failure to include race and class differences in its analysis. (Indeed, it is not likely that the male/female differences Gilligan notes are consistent across racial and class lines.) The "ethic of care" has also been viewed as the manifestation of a system of gender domination. Nevertheless, it is clear that those who operate in a "female mode"—whether biologically male or female respond more "selflessly" to the demands of mediation.

Whether the ethic of care is to be enshrined as a positive virtue, or criticized as a characteristic not belonging to all women and contributing to their oppression, one truth emerges: many women see themselves, and judge their own worth, primarily in terms of relationships. This perspective on themselves has consequences for how they function in mediation. . . .

Some commentators have identified mediation as a way to incorporate the ethic of care into the legal system and thereby modify the harshness of the adversary process. And, indeed, at first glance, mediation in the context of divorce might be seen as a way of bringing the woman-identified values of intimacy, nurturance, and care into a legal system that is concerned with the most fundamental aspects of women's and men's lives.

If mediation does not successfully introduce an ethic of care, however, but instead merely sells itself on that promise while delivering something coercive in its place, the consequences will be disastrous for a woman who embraces a relational sense of self. If she is easily persuaded to be cooperative, but her partner is not, she can only lose. If it is indeed her disposition to be caring and focused on relationships, and she has been rewarded for that focus and characterized as "unfeminine" when she departs from it, the language of relationship, caring, and cooperation will be appealing to her and make her vulnerable. Moreover, the intimation that she is not being cooperative and caring or that she is thinking of herself instead of thinking selflessly of the children can shatter her self-esteem and make her lose faith in herself. In short, in mediation, such a woman may be encouraged to repeat exactly those behaviors that have proven hazardous to her in the past. . . .

B. Sexual Domination and Judicial Violence

Women who have been through mandatory mediation often describe it as an experience of sexual domination, comparing mandatory mediation to rape. Catharine MacKinnon's work provides a basis for explaining why, for some women, this characterization is appropriate. MacKinnon has analyzed gender as a system of power relations, evidenced primarily with respect to the control of women's sexuality. While MacKinnon recognizes the sense in which women are fundamentally connected to others, she does not celebrate it. Rather, she sees the potential for connection as invasive and intrusive. It is precisely the potential for physical connection that permits invasion into the integrity of women's bodies. It is precisely the potential for emotional connection that permits intrusion into the integrity of women's lives.

Men do not experience this same fear of sexual domination, according to MacKinnon; they do not live in constant fear of having the very integrity of their lives intruded upon. Men may not comprehend their role in this system of sexual domination any more than women may be able to articulate the source of their feeling of disempowerment. Yet both of these dynamics are at work in the mediation setting. It may seem a large leap, from acts of physical violence and invasion to the apparently simple requirement that a woman sit in a room with her spouse working toward the resolution of an issue of mutual concern. But that which may be at stake in a court-ordered custody mediation—access to one's children—may be the main reason one has for living, as well as all one's hope for the future. And because mandatory mediation is a forced engagement, ordinarily without attorneys or even friends or supporters present, it may amount to a form of "psychic breaking and entering" or, put another way, psychic rape.

There is always the potential for violence in the legal system: "A judge articulates her understanding of a text, and as a result, somebody loses his freedom, his property, his children, even his life . . . . When interpreters have finished their work, they frequently leave behind victims whose lives have been torn apart by these organized, social practices of violence."

The reality of this background of judicial violence cannot be discounted when measuring the potential trauma of the mandatory mediation setting. Although the mediation system is purportedly designed in part to help participants avoid contact with the violence that must come from judicial decisions, in significant ways the violence of the contact is more direct. Since the parties are obliged to speak for themselves in a setting to which the culture has not introduced them and in which the rules are not clear (and in fact vary from mediator to mediator), the potential violence of the legal result, combined with the invasiveness of the setting, may indeed end up feeling to the unwilling participant very much like a kind of rape.

Moreover, in judging, it is understood that the critical view of the quarrel is that of the judge, the professional third party. Mediation is described as a form of intervention that reflects the disputants' view of the quarrel. But having the mediation take place on court premises with a mediator who might or might not inject her prejudices into the process may make it unlikely that the disputants' view will control. Thus, a further sense of violation may arise from having another person's view of the dispute characterized and treated as one's own.

That many reportedly find mediation helpful does not mean everyone does. Consensual sex may take place in a certain setting in one instance but that does not make all sex in that setting consensual; sometimes it is rape. And sometimes it may only seem to be consensual because forced sex is considered par for the course—that is, it is all we know or can imagine.

When I have suggested to mediators that even being forced to sit across the table and negotiate, unassisted, with a spouse might be traumatic, their reaction has been almost uniformly dismissive. Some mediators have denied that this could possibly be the case. Even mediators who acknowledge the possibility of trauma have said, in effect, "So what?" A few hours of discomfort seems not so much to ask in return for a system that, to their mind, serves the courts and the children much better than the alternative. But a few hours of discomfort may not be all that is at stake; the trauma inflicted upon a vulnerable party during mediation can be as great as that which occurs in other psychologically violent confrontations. As such, it should not be minimized. People frequently take months or years to recover from physical or mental abuse, rape, and other traumatic events. Given the psychological vulnerability of people at the time of a divorce, it is likely that some people may be similarly debilitated by a mandatory mediation process.

Moreover, because the mandatory mediation system is more problematic for women than for men, forcing unwilling women to take part in a process which involves much personal exposure sends a powerful social message: it is permissible to discount the real experience of women in the service of someone else's idea of what will be good for them, good for their children, or good for the system.

IV. ALTERNATIVES TO MANDATORY MEDIATION

It has been said that "[d]isputes are cultural events, evolving within a framework of rules about what is worth fighting for, what is the normal or moral way to fight, what kinds of wrongs warrant action, and what kinds of remedies are acceptable." The process by which a society resolves conflict is closely related to its social structure. Implicit in this choice is a message about what is respectable to do or want or say, what the obligations are of being a member of the society or of a particular group within it, and what it takes to be thought of as a good person leading a virtuous life. In the adversary system, it is acceptable to want to win. It is not only acceptable, but expected, that one will rely on a lawyer and advocate for oneself without looking out for the adversary. The judge, a third party obligated to be neutral and bound by certain formalities, bears the ultimate responsibility for deciding the outcome. To the extent that women are more likely than men to believe in communication as a mode of conflict resolution and to appreciate the importance of an adversary's interests, this system does not always suit their needs.

On the other hand, under a scheme of mediation, the standards of acceptable behavior and desires change fundamentally. Parties are to meet with each other, generally without their lawyers. They are encouraged to look at each other's needs and to reach a cooperative resolution based on compromise. Although there are few restrictions on her role in the process, the mediator bears no ultimate, formal responsibility for the outcome of the mediation. In sum, when mediation is the prototype for dispute resolution, the societal message is that a good person—a person following the rules— cooperates, communicates, and compromises.

The glories of cooperation, however, are easily exaggerated. If one party appreciates cooperation more than the other, the parties might compromise unequally. Moreover, the self-disclosure that cooperation requires, when imposed and not sought by the parties, may feel and be invasive. Thus, rather than representing a change in the system to accommodate the "feminine voice," in actuality, mandatory mediation overrides real women's voices saying that cooperation might, at least for the time being, be detrimental to their lives and the lives of their children. Under a system of forced mediation, women are made to feel selfish for wanting to assert their own interests based on their need to survive.

There are, then, many good reasons why a party might choose not to mediate. While some argue that mediation should be required because potential participants lack the information about the process which would convince them to engage in it voluntarily, this is not a sufficient justification for requiring mediation. If the state were committed only to making sure that disputants become familiar with mediation, something less than mandatory mediation—such as viewing a videotaped mediation or attending an orientation program—could be required, and mediators would certainly not be permitted to make recommendations to the court. That more than the simple receipt of information is required under a statutory mediation scheme demonstrates a profound disrespect for the parties' ability to determine the course of their own lives. Perhaps intrusion on the parties' lives might be justified if, in fact, children were demonstrably better off as a result of the process. There is no credible evidence, however, that this is so. The legislative choice to make mediation mandatory has been a mistake.

The choice presented today in California . . . is between an adversary process with totally powerful legal actors, in which clients never speak for themselves (and often do not know what is going on), and a mediation process in which they are entirely on their own and unprotected. The adversary system admittedly works poorly for child custody cases in many respects. There are, however, some ways to avoid damaging custody battles under an adversary system, such as enacting presumptions that make outcomes reasonably clear in advance, court-sponsored lectures on settlement, and joint negotiation sessions with lawyers and clients present. When in court, lawyers could be held to higher standards with respect to communicating with their clients, and judges could refrain from speaking to lawyers when their clients are not present. (It is difficult to imagine how a client can know whether to trust his lawyer when significant parts of the proceedings take place out of earshot).

The only reason to prefer mediation to other, more obvious alternatives is that the parties may, through the mediation process, ultimately benefit themselves and their children by learning how to communicate and work together. Whether this will happen in the context of a particular mediation is something only the parties can judge.

Any reform proposals, of the adversarial system or of a mediation alternative, should be rejected if they result in further disempowerment of the disempowered. Reform must operate on two simultaneous levels: first, by changing the institutions and rules that govern custody mediation, and second, by encouraging the respect of each mediator for the struggles and lives of the individuals involved in mediation. Any reforms should evince a concern for the personhood of the mediation clients, a concern that is lacking under current mediation practices.

With respect to institutional changes, an adequate mediation scheme should not only be voluntary rather than mandatory, but should also allow people's emotions to be part of the process, allow their values and principles to matter in the discussion, allow parties' attorneys to participate if requested by the parties, allow parties to choose a mediator and the location for the mediation, allow parties to choose the issues to mediate, and require that divorcing couples be educated about the availability and logistics of mediation so as to enable them to make an intelligent choice as to whether to engage in it.

The second aspect of reform represents more of a personal dynamic, one which is harder to institutionalize or to regulate. But the mediator must learn to respect each client's struggles, including her timing, anger, and resistance to having certain issues mediated, and also must learn to refrain, to the extent he is capable, from imposing his own substantive agenda on the mediation.

CONCLUSION

Although mediation can be useful and empowering, it presents some serious process dangers that need to be addressed, rather than ignored. When mediation is imposed rather than voluntarily engaged in, its virtues are lost. More than lost: mediation becomes a wolf in sheep's clothing. It relies on force and disregards the context of the dispute, while masquerading as a gentler, more empowering alternative to adversarial litigation. Sadly, when mediation is mandatory it becomes like the patriarchal paradigm of law it is supposed to supplant. Seen in this light, mandatory mediation is especially harmful: its messages disproportionately affect those who are already subordinated in our society, those to whom society has already given the message, in far too many ways, that they are not leading proper lives.

Of course, subordinated people can go to court and lose; in fact, they usually do. But if mediation is to be introduced into the court system, it should provide a better alternative. It is not enough to say that the adversary system is so flawed that even a misguided, intrusive, and disempowering system of mediation should be embraced. If mediation as currently instituted constitutes a fundamentally flawed process in the way I have described, it is more, not less, disempowering than the adversary system—for it is then a process in which people are told they are being empowered, but in fact are being forced to acquiesce in their own oppression.

2. Comments and Questions

a. Professor Grillo argues that it is "presumptuous to assume that the state has a better idea than the parties themselves about whether mediation will work in their particular case." Do you agree? Does this argument prove too much? Would the same arguments apply to mandatory participation in other nonbinding ADR procedures, such as medical malpractice review panels and summary jury trials?

b. Much of law reflects "presumptuous" assumptions about people, even in contravention of the democratic process (e.g., minimum ages in the U.S. Constitution for Representatives, Senators, and the President).

c. Professor Grillo expresses concern that in a mediation: "something may be considered relevant for the purposes of mediation because it is emotionally— even though not logically— connected to the proceedings." Chief Justice Yazzie suggests that such an approach is a strength on the Navajo system, rather than a weakness. Anthropologists, including Laura Nader, a fan of the Grillo article (see Chapter 3, section F) commonly fault judicial trials for their narrow view of relevant evidence.

d. Professors Grillo and Rosenberg (author of the next article) are colleagues at the University of San Francisco. As Rosenberg states, at footnote four, "Professor Grillo is my colleague in the best sense of the word. She introduced me to mediation and got me excited about the area. We have co-taught a course, and she has helped me teach the mediation clinic at USF Law School. She has taught me much about mediation, and she continues to do so."

3. Joshua D. Rosenberg, *In Defense of Mediation*, 33 ARIZ. L. REV. 467 (1991)*

In her recent article on mandatory mediation, my colleague Trina Grillo points out several pitfalls mediators should watch for and explains some ways in which court-annexed mediation can be improved. This effort is a good one and, I hope, will be welcomed by the mediation community. Nonetheless, I believe that a response is necessary; hence, this piece. Essentially, my response is motivated by three concerns:

(1) Many of Professor Grillo's statements and stories do not represent what actually happens at a typical mediation session. Instead, they effectively capture and magnify only the worst possible abuses of the process. Because many potential users of mediation and many policymakers are either unfamiliar or only marginally familiar with mediation, it is dangerous to allow these misrepresentations and distortions to go unchallenged;

(2) To the extent that mandatory mediation presents some real problems, society may be better served by attempting to correct those problems than by abandoning mandatory mediation in areas where it has already proved to be very helpful. Although Professor Grillo does not adequately explore that possibility, many states that have mandatory mediation have already enacted legislation that addresses her concerns; and

(3) Professor Grillo's article suggests that mediation may be dangerous for women. While anything can be dangerous to anyone at some time, mandatory mediation is generally helpful both to women and to men, and an overwhelming number of the women and men who have been through mandatory mediation approve of it strongly.

OVERVIEW

Professor Grillo's article paints a very effective and very dramatic picture of mediation as a misguided and destructive process. As both a teacher and a student of mediation, I have found that the process is supportive, empowering and enlightening to the participants. Helping parties to feel better about themselves and their interests is one of the most important and most valued of skills among mediators. Studies regularly show that people who go through mandatory mediation are pleased with the process.

How does my colleague's picture of mediation as a monster emerge? Professor Grillo's article distorts the mediation process in four ways: (1) the article tells stories about mediation that are the equivalent of using a series of stories about physicians' rape of patients to paint a picture of the practice of medicine in this country; (2) the article subjects mediation to a series of doublebinds, in which anything a mediator does is characterized as bad; (3) mediation is blamed for problems which existed long before mediation and which will continue with or without mandatory mediation; and (4) the article portrays mediation as being both more powerful and more dangerous than it really is. . . .

Professor Grillo's stories tell about mediators who appallingly misapply family systems theory; mediators who dismiss as irrelevant important family history; mediators who make unsubstantiated assumptions that one parent is or is not an appropriate caretaker; mediators who make their own "determinations" and rulings rather than let the parties decide with respect to child custody; mediators who make parties feel guilty and bad about themselves; and mediators who are rude, insensitive, stupid and otherwise incompetent. I do not doubt that such mediators exist. Similarly, some physicians have raped and murdered their patients, judges have knowingly sentenced innocent men to death, presidents have lied and cheated, and schoolteachers have exhibited racial bias towards their students. Nonetheless, we require parents to subject their children to both school and medical care, and we are all required to live according to the rules established by politicians and courts. We do not judge these necessary aspects of our everyday lives by focusing only on various worst case scenarios. It would be unfortunate if we were to use that standard to judge mandatory mediation.

Indeed, most of Professor Grillo's mediation horror stories are not from mediation at all.

Instead, they involve mediation/evaluation, a process in which the "mediator" also functions as an evaluator and quasi- decisionmaker. This process is often more like an informal arbitration or settlement conference than like mediation, a process in which the mediator has no decision-making authority at all. An overwhelming percentage of the mandatory participants (especially the women) prefer even mediation/evaluation to litigation. Nonetheless, it is significantly different from mediation.

Unfortunately, while it is this hybrid mediation/arbitration process that produces most of Professor Grillo's stories, it is all kinds of mandatory mediation that bear the brunt of her criticism. Aside from being criticized for many events that occur only in this nonmediation process, regular mediation is subjected to a "damned if you do, damned if you don't" approach in numerous ways: when formal equality is talked about as something bad, mediation has it; when formal equality is talked about as something good, all of a sudden mediation does not have it. If a mediator either prevents or allows the expression of anger, she has made a mistake. If a mediator either corrects or fails to correct a power imbalance between the parties, she has erred again. If a mediator either discusses or does not discuss the issue of fairness, she is wrong. Finally, if a mediator either asserts or does not assert societal values, it was the wrong thing to do.

In addition, Professor Grillo seems to hold mediation accountable for numerous "problems" for which, it is true, mediation offers no cure. The truth, however, is that mediation did not cause these "problems" and the elimination of mandatory mediation would not alleviate them. Among these "problems" are the elimination of fault-based divorce and child custody determinations; the adoption of no-fault divorce and child custody determinations based on the best interests of the child; the fact that courts do not require fathers to stay with children if the fathers do not want to; societal constraints on women's expression of anger; and societal race and gender bias.

Professor Grillo suggests that so much about mediation is bad and dangerous because mediation is very powerful in an unconscious way. People in the midst of divorce are at an extremely vulnerable time of life. They are profoundly concerned about being seen as good, and will be significantly damaged if they do not receive approval. These people are likely to be even more sensitive in an unfamiliar setting. A mediator, goes the argument, carries enormous potential to do damage, so much so that, according to Professor Grillo, whatever the mediator does is likely to be damaging. Of course, if people are subject to being damaged by exposure to unfamiliar settings, much in life has the potential to do great damage. The truth is that any person or program that has enough impact to do good has the potential to do harm. Unlike most other professionals, however, mediators are trained to be especially sensitive to and understanding of people's feelings and stress. Their entire training is geared towards helping people in conflict and distress.

Professor Grillo's criticisms of mediation can be made about any public service, or indeed any contact between the state and individuals going through a difficult period. Teachers in public schools, physicians, nurses and aides in public hospitals, workers in public benefit programs, employees in legal services programs, clerks at city hall and numerous other public service personnel all deal with individuals at particularly vulnerable times, and all have the ability to do great harm. Unlike a mediator, who has the ability to grant or withhold nothing other than her personal approval, all of these individuals have, additionally, the ability to grant or withhold important rights and benefits. I shudder to imagine the variety of true horror stories one could find about all of these programs, were one to make the effort. We should view mandatory mediation from the same kind of reasonably balanced perspective from which we examine these other public programs.

Rather than compare the worst harm that a grossly incompetent and insensitive mediator could cause with a distorted picture of the "benefits" of going to court, it would be more helpful to compare what a competent mediator would do with what might happen in a competently run court. . . . Between the time Professor Grillo wrote her article and the time it was published, California enacted legislation designed to solve some of the most difficult problems she raises within the mandatory mediation framework.

SUMMARY OF PROFESSOR GRILLO'S POINTS

Basically, Professor Grillo suggests that mandatory mediation of child custody disputes is inappropriate both as a process and because of the substantive results it might produce. Her main process arguments are: (1) mediation can deprive a woman of an opportunity to have her perceptions validated by a judge, and, indirectly, by society; (2) the damaging influence of a mediator is subtle but powerful. The mediator is likely to make a mother feel guilty, selfish, and unacceptable as a human being unless the mother does just what the mediator wants; (3) the process of mediation may encourage undetected race or gender bias; and (4) the very act of attempting to come to an agreement with her former spouse may be intolerable for a woman who is in the midst of extricating herself from a relationship with that same man.

On the substantive level, Professor Grillo suggests that: (1) the best interest of the child standard for custody determination in California is vague and unsatisfactory, and mediation is to blame; (2) a woman in mediation may be unable to stand up to her former spouse for what she thinks is best for herself or her children, so that requiring mediation may result in agreements that are both unfair and unhealthy; and (3) mediators are more likely than courts to engage in behavior that is race or gender biased.

I believe that an honest evaluation of mandatory mediation, even in light of Professor Grillo's criticisms, will reveal that: (1) the process of mediation is generally more validating of both the perceptions and the feelings of those participating in it than is litigation (and, perhaps more importantly, women going through mandatory mediation feel significantly more validated); (2) whatever problems may exist with the substantive law of child custody are separate from a determination of what is the best procedure to implement that law. Complaints about the substantive standard do not translate into problems with a particular procedure; (3) bias against the economically disadvantaged, women and persons of color is more likely in a courtroom than it is in mediation, and even when present, race and gender biases are less likely to influence the outcome of mediation than they are to influence the outcome of litigation; (4) people of either gender are much more likely to find litigation intolerable than they are to find mediation intolerable; and (5) mediation actually helps participants clarify and stand up for what they want, and it is those who settle without the benefit of mediation who are more likely to sacrifice their own interests.

WHAT IS MANDATORY MEDIATION

. . . While the use of mediation in general has a long, cross-cultural history, professionals in this country (lawyers and psychotherapists) have become involved in mediating divorce disputes only relatively recently. This involvement resulted from an almost universal agreement that litigation of divorce cases is bad for the parents, worse for the children, and brings about results that are often both unfair to and ignored by the parties. Unlike court hearings, mediation allows the parties to deal with all the issues brought up by the divorce, whether legal, practical or emotional. Unlike court orders, mediated agreements give parents the opportunity to participate in the decisionmaking regarding their children, and to fashion custody and visitation arrangements that take into account the parents' intimate knowledge of their children's interests, as well as the parents' own special needs and interests.

As divorcing couples began to mediate their divorces, they were generally very pleased with the results. Nonetheless, knowledge about the process and the availability of mediation were not widespread. Attorneys who knew about mediation could be hesitant to recommend to their clients a process that might well eliminate the need for their own services in the case, and parties not represented by counsel had no way at all to learn about the process. California was among the first states to conclude that the best way to educate spouses about the benefits of mediation, as well as the best way to prevent one spouse from immediately forcing the entire family into litigation by refusing to mediate, was to mandate mediation prior to any court hearing for divorcing parents unable to reach agreement on their own concerning the custody and visitation of their minor children. If the parties are unable to resolve their dispute in mediation, the mediation results remain confidential and the judicial process continues.

The results of studies of mandatory mediation have pleased the process' proponents. Parents who participate in mandatory mediation of child custody disputes are twice as likely to be satisfied with both the process and the results as are parents who go to court without mediation. Mediated agreements are more likely to be complied with than are court orders. A vast majority of parents who participate in mandatory mediation of child custody disputes believe that mediation also helps them focus attention on the needs of the children and helps them feel better about themselves. Mediation is twice as likely as court to improve relationships between the parties. Mandatory mediation saves money for both the parties and the state over court hearings, while also allowing the parties significantly more time to address their problems. In addition, requiring parents to mediate prior to allowing them to invoke the power of the court is thought to be consistent with the societal view that, to the extent possible, parents, rather than the state, should make parenting decisions.

Of course, mandatory mediation is not perfect. Some have complained that abused spouses may be unable to hold their own during the process, and that, in any event, requiring victims of abuse to negotiate head-to-head with their abusers may be inappropriate. As a result, in any case where a restraining order is in effect because of actual or threatened spousal abuse, the mediator is directed to see the parties separately, in a kind of shuttle diplomacy. Courts are instructed to develop local rules to respond to requests for a change of mediator or to general problems relating to mediation, and several counties permit spouses who allege abuse to bring a support person to be with them at the mediation.

California law also permits courts to enact local rules requiring mediators to make recommendations to the court regarding custody in the event that mediation is not successful; and some counties have enacted such rules. The grant of this quasi-coercive power results in a mediation/evaluation process that differs substantially from mediation. This process allows the mediator to encourage and reward cooperation, and it may also tempt the mediator to be less patient with and understanding of the parties, because she has at her disposal other ways of "helping" the parties reach what she considers to be the right result. In addition, if the mediator's recommendation holds sway with the judge, the parties may view the mediator as an arm of the court and be guarded in what they reveal in the process.

Research indicates that parties to mandatory mediation/evaluation, including those who would have opted out if given the opportunity, significantly prefer that process over court, both because of the substantive results and because the process was more supportive and helpful. Nonetheless, I personally believe that mediation is preferable to mediation/evaluation. In this paper, I defend only mandatory mediation rather than mediation/evaluation. I do so because the mediation/evaluation process is entirely defensible in its own right, while it is a very different process from "pure" mandatory mediation, and confusion of the two might do justice to neither.

RIGHTS AND BLAMING

Professor Grillo's first major criticism of mediation stems from her suggestion that many women going through a divorce need to be told by a higher authority that they are right and that their husbands are wrong. They need "vindication" from a third party who can tell them that they are morally superior to their husbands. Unlike courts, mediators may attempt to "orient the parties towards reasonableness and compromise, rather than moral vindication," thereby denying women the court's imprimatur on the blame they seek to attach to their husbands.

It is probably true that many people going through a difficult divorce (or just getting out of a difficult marriage) can use some affirmation. It is also true that mediators, at least in California, generally focus not on the parties' relative moral rectitude, but on the interests of the parents and the future best interests of the child. If the parties end up in court rather than in mediation, the substantive legal standard the court will apply in determining child custody is also "the best interests of the child." In determining which parent should have primary responsibility for parenting, the substantive law directs the court to take into account factors such as each parent's willingness to allow substantial visitation to the other parent, but it specifically does not take into account the moral superiority of one parent over the other. The "best interests of the child" standard was in effect prior to the adoption of mandatory mediation, and it has been adopted by many states that still do not have mandatory mediation. As a result, to the extent that a woman seeks to have either a mediator or a court tell her husband "what sort of behavior is not to be tolerated," she is simply barking up the wrong tree. Absent some sort of emotional or physical abuse or other behavior affirmatively detrimental to the child, that kind of determination is not within the purview of child custody courts. . . .

Aside from the fact that the child custody courts are not in the business of making moral pronouncements, if a woman nonetheless wants to ask the court to make those judgments, mandatory mediation does not stand in her way. The statute requires only that the parents participate in mediation. California law imposes no penalties for participating badly or for participating only briefly. The person who is determined to use the court for her own personal vindication may simply refuse to reach an agreement in mediation, and the courtroom door will swing wide open. Once in court, the person looking for personal vindication is likely to be both sorely disappointed by the results and severely chided for having made the effort. . . . These results are neither the fault nor the province of mandatory mediation. . . .

Professor Grillo also implies that there is something inherent in the mediation process that necessarily makes mediation less affirming to a woman than is litigation. The problem, she suggests, is that the family systems approach used by some mediators "imposes a value-free universe," with the result that "a person who has been a victim of violence can be seen as deserving her fate because of self-defeating patterns of behavior." The implication appears to be that mediators do not really refrain from "blaming," but that they simply blame the wrong party. . . .

Professor Grillo points out that this value-free perspective "can deprive a divorcing spouse of the opportunity to appear virtuous in society's eyes and her own." This conclusion seems to rest on the following assumptions: (1) a court will, in fact, blame the husband and praise the woman; (2) having a court blame her husband and praise the woman will be an effective means of helping the woman; and (3) a mediator will not act in a way that will allow the woman to feel good about herself. . . . [T]hese assumptions . . . are inaccurate.

Having a mediator side with a mother in blaming the father is neither necessary nor necessarily helpful to the parent who needs affirmation. Instead, such a response is more likely to sidetrack the angry woman and raise the resistance of the man than it is to either help anyone feel better or facilitate a parenting agreement. It is important to note that a mediator's role is to assist the parties in working with each other to reach agreement. Because the mediator has no actual or threatened external force to employ to change the parties' behavior, she relies on earning the parties' trust and respect as the primary tool to enable her to gain some influence. To the extent that the mediator tells one of the parties that he is blameworthy and bad, she is not likely to win that party's confidence, and is not likely to be effective in helping to change that party's behavior. In addition, every mediator knows that the best way to help people to resolve disputes is to first help them understand what the dispute is about. Until a party feels that her perceptions, feelings and interests are understood and acknowledged, she will probably not feel ready to decide how to act on those perceptions, feelings and interests, and the dispute is not likely to be resolved.

But what if one parent really is bad and wrong? If one parent abuses the children or threatens their physical or emotional health, should such behavior escape comment and be treated with the same respect accorded the kind, nurturing parent's actions? While mediators do not hold themselves out as arbiters of morality, they do not treat all behavior similarly. When one or both parents engage in dangerous or illegal behavior with children, a mediator will explore that behavior. She will do her best to see to it that both parents understand the possible emotional, physical, and legal consequences for the parent and the child. If the child is abused, she will notify the appropriate state agency without delay. She will explore whether the parents understand the consequences of the behavior, and if so, whether they are willing to accept those consequences or whether they are willing to change the behavior. The mediator is not likely, however, to tell one parent that he is "bad," because such accusations are likely to bring nothing but defensive counter-attacks. The mediator is likely to act in ways that will be effective in bringing about more appropriate behavior.

Enabling the parties both to develop trust and to ultimately be willing to examine their behavior and its impact on themselves, their spouses and their children may be the best way to facilitate change in the "bad" spouse's behavior; but Professor Grillo's concern is that this approach will sacrifice the feelings and self respect of the "good" spouse. The idea is that the woman needs to have someone agree with her judgments that her husband is bad in order to feel good about herself. This idea is only slightly off the mark. In order to help someone feel better about herself, her feelings and her perceptions, it is important that a third party understand, accept and appreciate those feelings and perceptions.

Any semi-competent mediator knows that empathy and understanding of the parties' feelings and perceptions is essential. For example, if a woman has sacrificed her career in order to be the primary caretaker, and is also angry at her husband for his past refusal to participate in the day-to-day care of the children, a mediator will acknowledge, accept, and understand the woman's anger and appreciate how the woman might well not trust that the husband will act differently. If the woman also wants to withhold the children from their father in order to punish him for his past behavior, a mediator will also understand, appreciate, and accept that feeling and desire. Indeed, the mediator might well point out that many women would feel the same way. The mediator is not likely to join in the woman's judgment that her husband is therefore bad, nor is she likely to encourage the woman to actually use the child for her revenge. The mediator does not need to join in that judgment (or in the planning for revenge) in order for the woman to feel understood, accepted and validated.

Psychological and legal literature is replete with statements to the effect that accurate empathy, rather than sympathy, is necessary to help a person feel better about herself. While the difference between sympathy and empathy may seem minimal, it is a key aspect in the training of those in the helping professions. In light of its relevance to Professor Grillo's point, this difference is worth some exploration. Essentially, person A is sympathetic to person B if A sees things from a vantage point similar to B's—if she makes the same moral judgments and evaluations. Empathy, on the other hand, requires A to understand and appreciate B's perception of, and reaction to, the world. Rather than making the same judgments as does B, A suspends her own judgment and concentrates on understanding and accepting B. . . .

A very real, but subtle, danger in Professor Grillo's argument on this point is that it seems to support the idea that women, and often women of color, somehow ought to rely on a family court judge for vindication of their moral values. First of all, it is just as likely that the judge will withhold the sought-after approval. More important, however, is the suggestion that it is good for women to ask for the approval of a (probably) white male judge so that they can feel morally adequate. The very process would seem to reinforce a woman's sense of herself as somehow morally inferior to, or at best morally less knowledgeable than, the judge.

Finally, Professor Grillo suggests that women may be both more in need of and more worthy of support around the time of divorce because they are more relational; they are willing to communicate and to engage in problem-solving, addressed to the concerns of the children, with the other parent. It might, in fact, be helpful for the woman's self esteem if the court took the time to praise the parent who engages in this kind of behavior and to condemn the parent who does not. Study after study, however, has shown that the strongest support for a particular behavior is not the presence of a third party verbally praising that behavior, but the presence of a respected third party actually modeling that behavior in the presence of the affected person. What this means is that the best way to support the person who wants to communicate and plan for the best interests of the child is for the state, or its representative, to actually engage with the parents in that kind of behavior. Such is the essence of mediation. It is, of course, quite different from criticizing or blaming people who do not engage in that behavior or who are very angry. In this same regard, to the extent that one is concerned with the impact of either litigation or mediation on women of color, who often are forced to bear the worst of society's burdens, it is well worth pointing out that the woman of color is much more likely to gain increased self-esteem if she sees other women of color, and not just white males, in positions of authority or importance. In Alameda, California, where I worked as a mediator, there are twenty-one mediators employed by the court. Thirteen are women, and six are persons of color. The family court judges are all white males.

ANGER AND CONTEXT

Professor Grillo's next major criticism of mediation results from her observation that many mediators do their best to ultimately help parties focus on planning for future success rather than on assigning blame for past failures. . . . Professor Grillo suggests that this focus prevents women from standing up for themselves, and, along the way, devalues and betrays women. Essentially, the idea seems to be that there can be no assertion of rights without a corresponding assertion that the other party is wrong, and mediation fails to focus on those past wrongs. In addition, because women in mediation will be encouraged not to blame and condemn their husbands, they will be forced to make decisions without any appropriate context; they will be prevented from ever asserting their rights; and they will be forced to blame themselves for their husbands' failures. . . .

The preferred alternative, and that encouraged by mediators, is for the party to realize that she does not like what has been done, that she is entitled to her feelings and perceptions, and that she can and will do something about it (such as standing up for herself and her children). As mentioned earlier, a person's sense of self or of self-legitimacy simply does not depend on finding fault with someone else. Instead, a person's sense of self and of self-legitimacy depends on that person feeling self-worth, which in turn depends on feeling understood and accepted by another—an empathic response. People who need to develop a healthy sense of self and of entitlement specifically ought not to be taught to base that sense of entitlement on a belief that someone else is bad, wrong, or worthy of blame. They need to be helped to develop a sense that they themselves are worthy and valuable, so that their sense of self-worth does not depend on a belief that someone else is somehow inferior. In his seminal work on assertion of self, Boszormenyi-Nagy pointed out the difference between "constructive entitlement," which is the sense of entitlement that individuals may have, independent of any need to attach fault or blame to others, and "destructive entitlement," which fosters a sense of self that is less secure, weaker, and both less healthy and less effective, than that fostered by constructive entitlement.

Fortunately, mediation generally works as intended. Available data indicates that both men and women who have gone through mandatory mediation felt that they had the opportunity to fully express their own views and that because of mediation they were more confident about standing up for themselves. Women felt this to be true even more strongly than did men. . . .

ANGER

Professor Grillo next suggests that mediation necessarily deals badly with women's anger. Either mediators will encourage women to express their anger or they will not encourage them to express their anger, and either alternative is bad for women. If mediators do not encourage women's expression of anger, goes the argument, the mediator thereby "sends a message that anger is unacceptable, terrifying and dangerous. . . . This is a message that their worst fears are true: You are, indeed, they are told, threatening your own children by expressing your anger." Alternatively, if mediators encourage the expression of anger, that anger will be simply vented, and by being vented will lose its potential to teach and will become ineffective. This is a classic double-bind.

According to Professor Grillo, litigation apparently allows the parties to express their anger through their attorney surrogates, in a way that keeps that anger from being either delegitimated or denied expression. The implication that the discovery process and court hearings somehow permit a legitimate expression of anger and thereby do not, as does mediation, impact badly on women, is farfetched. The party who goes into a court hearing angry is likely to come away from that hearing feeling humiliated, controlled, and furious. The issues addressed at the hearing may not be what she wants to discuss, but are likely to be the issues framed by the court and the attorneys. The party is permitted to speak only when spoken to, and to speak only enough to answer the specific questions put to her. She may be prevented from raising issues most relevant for her and required to answer questions she believes are irrelevant and designed only to embarrass or humiliate her. She may be treated abruptly by opposing counsel, as well as by the court, with no alternative but to accept it.

Essentially, the message that comes from the court is: "your wants and needs are irrelevant except to the extent that we say otherwise, and you are either too worthless or too dangerous for us to even let you speak for yourself." A woman's expression of anger may be met by judicial reprimands, intolerance, contempt, and, perhaps worst of all, a ruling against her on the merits. . . .

LACK OF MEDIATOR NEUTRALITY

In the next part of her article, Professor Grillo suggests that any particular mediator (1) may not be able to separate truth from lies, and (2) may be biased against one of the parents. It is difficult to dispute either of these possibilities, but it is also difficult to conclude that these possibilities represent serious problems with mediation. . . .

TRANSFERENCE AND COUNTERTRANSFERENCE

. . . Professor Grillo suggests that both transference and countertransference may occur during mediation, with the result that the mediator may act inappropriately towards a party, or vice versa. This suggestion is undoubtedly accurate. Indeed, transference "is an everyday phenomenon . . . that appears in peoples' every act." Some people may feel coerced to accept a mediator's bias, despite the lack of external coercion. We all know people who feel compelled to do things that are not in their best interests, and if we wish to speak psychoanalytically, we can attribute that unexplained compulsion to transference. Labeling this behavior as transference does nothing to change the fact that the influences of bias are much more dangerous in a courtroom than in a mediation session. The person who is likely to have her competence undercut by the mediator's bias is that much more likely to be injured by the same bias coming from the supposedly all-powerful and all-knowing judge, who speaks with the full authority of the state. Professor Grillo suggests that a party to mediation may be more vulnerable to a mediator than to a judge because the party believes, going into the mediation, that the mediator is on her side. It is doubtful, however, that a woman going into mandatory mediation with her ex- (or soon to be ex-) spouse is likely to let her guard too far down in anticipation of a friendly experience. . . .

Professor Grillo suggests that voluntary mediation is a preferable alternative, but that process offers no more protection against bias than does mandatory mediation. It is true that in voluntary mediation the parties can choose their own mediator, but the same can be true of mandatory mediation. All that is mandated is the mediation, not any particular mediator. In addition, to the extent that mediator bias is subtle and, as Professor Grillo suggests, unconscious, no party can really learn about that bias until she gets to know the mediator quite well. Most people do not know mediators, and have little available guidance in choosing mediators, whether the decision to mediate is one they make for themselves or is made by the state. To the extent that parties feel compelled to accept the mediator's pronouncements because of transference, the problem is likely to be most severe when the mediation is voluntary and the mediator is one the parties have chosen themselves.

GIVING IN

Another criticism of mediation stems from Professor Grillo's assertion that women are more "relational" than men. In essence, Professor Grillo asserts that women are more concerned with relating to and working with people, while men are often more concerned with dominating other people. . . . The truth of this proposition, however, does not lead, directly or indirectly, to the conclusion that mandatory mediation should be abandoned. . . .

FORCED ENGAGEMENT AS HORROR

Professor Grillo's final criticism of mandatory mediation is that the very experience of sitting in a room with her former husband may be awful for some women, and the state ought not to require women to go through that experience. Women would have to negotiate with their husbands over the future of their children even in the absence of state intervention, but they might not otherwise have to come in close physical proximity to them in a setting in which they are encouraged to be open and honest, so that mandatory mediation does, in this respect, affirmatively create a problem for some women. The problem, suggests Professor Grillo, is that women are expected to sit across from their husbands, expose their desires, needs and feelings, and listen to the desires, needs and feelings of their husbands. They are also expected to absorb an assortment of judgments from their husbands and the mediator about their ways of being inside and outside the mediation process.

Indeed, goes the argument, some women will find mediation traumatic and will experience it as being as terrible as rape. . . . The analogy of mandatory mediation to rape is somewhat less than compelling.

First of all, while mandatory mediation may require a woman to sit in the same room as her husband, it cannot be merely the physical proximity that makes the session feel like rape. If it were, a judicial hearing with the parties present would have the same result. What makes the situation so oppressive, according to Professor Grillo, is that the woman may subject herself to listening to and absorbing her husband's concerns and may feel guilty about standing up for her own desires. The choices available to the woman, according to Professor Grillo, are to either stand up for herself and feel intolerably guilty, or to give in and thereby give up what is most important to her—another classic double-bind. Fortunately, much more appealing alternatives are not only available, but are likely. The woman who cooperates for the good of the children is likely to feel good about herself for being concerned with her children and their best interests. She may, for the first time in her life, find her more relational stance being validated and even adopted, and her husband's competitive and noncommunicative stance being rejected by the mediator, a representative of the state. She may be encouraged, for the first time in her life, to stand up to her husband for the good of herself and her children. Her assertion (as opposed to watching someone else attempt to stand up for her) may be a transformative experience. Indeed, if the mediator is any good, the woman will find that she can stand up for herself and have her relational stance validated at the same time. If the mother is angry, the mediation is likely to allow her to feel justified in being angry and to encourage her to protect herself in the future.

Even if the mediation session is a complete disaster, and the woman leaves feeling that she gave in too much or feels guilty for not giving in even more, the comparison of the mediation session to rape goes too far. Mediation differs substantially from forced sexual activity. Mediation does not involve physical coercion and invasion. If, after the mediation session, the woman is unhappy with the tentative agreement that has been reached, she may, either on her own or after consultation with friends or her lawyer, repudiate that agreement. . . .

Most people who might find mediation to be an uncomfortable experience will find the courtroom to be worse. On the other hand, there will be some for whom the experience of mediation will be worse than a courtroom hearing might be. For the vast majority of people, neither experience will have disastrous long-term effects (other than a court hearing making some people abhor the judicial system). For a very small number of people, either experience might be as bad as rape.

Professor Grillo claims that the fact that many people experience mediation as helpful is, at best, only marginally relevant to the question of whether mandatory mediation is appropriate. On that issue I again disagree. Apparently, Professor Grillo believes that in determining whether or not to mandate mediation, we ought to act to protect the very small minority of people who may be traumatized by the process. Unfortunately, it is difficult to do that without creating a situation that will allow one party who does not want mediation to dictate to his spouse that there will be no mediation and that the case will proceed directly to trial. It is likely that allowing one spouse to force the case directly to trial would traumatize more people than does mandatory mediation. Indeed, forcing a party to go through discovery and trial may be the most effective way to traumatize an ex-spouse, both emotionally and financially.

Put simply, the problem is that the absence of mandatory mediation does not result in the presence of voluntary mediation. It results, instead, in the process being governed by whichever spouse decides to choose that process which has caused so many problems in the past. Nonetheless, at least two states with mandatory mediation allow a party to petition the court to be excused from that process. Many courts will grant waivers if the party shows that severe emotional distress is likely, or if other good cause is shown. . . . Others have suggested a limited exception from mandatory mediation in cases of spousal abuse. Clearly, the complete elimination of mandatory mediation is unnecessary to protect even those about whom Professor Grillo is most concerned. . . .

ALTERNATIVES

Professor Grillo suggests changes in the law that might be helpful, but these are not, in any real sense, substitutes for mandatory mediation. She suggests changes in the substantive standard for courts faced with making custody determinations, and she suggests that courts might limit communications between judges and attorneys outside of the earshot of clients. Of course, changing the substantive standard does not eliminate the need for a procedure to implement that standard. Furthermore, making some minor changes in courtroom procedure does little to ameliorate the problems with the procedure previously described. The other alternatives suggested are court-sponsored lectures on settlement, and negotiations attended by both parties and their lawyers. Court sponsored lectures may be helpful, at least to the extent that attorneys are not, in explaining settlement possibilities. Under current law parties may and should be encouraged to have group settlement negotiations with all the parties and their lawyers present. They are not, however, substitutes for, but preliminaries to, mandatory mediation. Mediation is mandatory only for those who cannot find a different way to reach agreement.

None of this refutes the contentions that (1) poorly conducted mediation, like any process done poorly, is not likely to be either helpful or effective, and (2) some people will find mediation extremely distasteful. Correspondingly, however, neither of these assertions refute the contention that mandatory mediation is beneficial. . . .

While a small number of people might experience extreme discomfort in the mediation session, the unfortunate truth is that every law ever enacted changes some preexisting relationships and makes some people unhappy. Mandatory mediation . . . . helps a far greater number of people of both genders than it hurts, and its repeal would hurt a far greater number of people than would its retention. Still, every effort should be made to identify problems with mandatory mediation, and to make the adjustments needed to correct those problems. The states that have adopted mandatory mediation seem to be doing just that. . . .

4. Diane Neumann, *How Mediation Can Effectively Address the Male-Female Power Imbalance in Divorce*, 9 MEDIATION QUART. 227 (1992)*

I have been a mediator and a committed proponent of divorce mediation for ten years. But I have been an ardent feminist even longer. To an outsider, my roles as a divorce mediator and as a feminist often appear mutually hostile and unbridgeable. But fellow mediators and feminists simply do not understand the basic realities of negotiation, divorce, gender, and power. In this article I will describe how these two seemingly diverse roles can be reconciled, how one can acknowledge power imbalance based primarily on gender, and yet, because of the underlying dynamics of the divorce crisis, simultaneously intervene and adequately address the power imbalance between divorcing spouses.

Is There a Power Difference Between Traditional Divorcing Spouses?

What is power? Most of us define power as "the ability to get what one wants." John Haynes . . . defines power as "control of or access to emotional, economic, and physical resources desired by the other person." Haynes believes that power is derived from the ability to influence the actions of others. I think that most people would agree with these general definitions of power. But to really understand power, one needs a more specific definition. I believe that power has four defining features: (1) power is composed of many factors; (2) it is relative, situational, and shifting; (3) everyone has some degree of power; and (4) power is only effective when it is used. For divorce mediation I would add a fifth feature: not every power difference between the spouses affects the mediation.

The first feature, that power is comprised of many factors, provides a foundation for the discussion that follows. It is important to recognize that power is not one factor in the same way that blue eyes, a high I.Q., or a voracious appetite is a single characteristic. Power arises from a complex interplay of myriad factors. The following ten factors all contribute to an individual's power:

1. Belief system—a belief that one is on the side of right.
2. Personality—the image one projects, how powerful one acts.
3. Self-esteem—the internalized image of oneself, how powerful one feels.
4. Gender—Western society grants men greater power than women.
5. Selfishness—consistently putting oneself before others is a form of power.
6. Force—willingness to use coercion or threats and the fear engendered in others is a form of power.
7. Income/assets—power increases with income and the accumulation of assets.
8. Knowledge—possessing information is a form of power.
9. Status or age—increased status confers increased power, and power usually increases with age.
10. Education—higher levels of education are associated with higher levels of power.

Second, power is relative, situational, and can shift. . . . An individual has power only relative to another person. Power is also situational, which means that an individual's power is defined by particular circumstances. An individual has varying degrees of power in each of his or her roles. For example, a woman typically differs in the degree of power she has in her roles as mother, wife, supervisor, and volunteer committee member, while a man may have varying degrees of power in his roles as father, husband, CEO, and member of the Elks club. Degrees of power shift according to circumstance. For example, at the workplace, the chief executive officer of the company has far more power than does his assistant. However, on a weekend trip to Maine, where both men participate in a whitewater rafting trip, the CEO's greater power in relation to his assistant will not transfer to the new situation if the assistant is an expert white-water rafter and the CEO is on the rapids for the very first time.

Third, even if one person has more power than another, each person has some degree of power. The traditional couple displays power differences. Typically, a male spouse has greater power than his wife. But because women as a class have less power than men does not necessarily mean that a woman in mediation has no power, or too little power to engage in meaningful negotiations. She has some degree of power. A woman may feel that she has no power, yet she chooses the food her husband eats, decides how to prepare it, determines when to serve it, and later rules about, whether to save the leftovers and what to do with them. Within a mediation context, at tax time, an unemployed wife may suddenly find herself in a powerful position when her husband requests her to sign the joint income tax form.

Fourth, degree of power, awareness of having power, and exercise of that power are three separate things. An individual who has power may or may not be aware that she or he has power, and may or may not use that power. More often than not, the individual must be aware of her or his power in order to use it, but this is not always the case. Mediators must remember that a client can be helped to use his or her power. An example may shed some light. During a mediation session with Greg and Judy, I began by providing background information concerning alimony. I then asked, "How do you each feel about paying or receiving alimony?" Greg quickly replied, "I won't pay it." I reframed his statement to "You prefer not to make alimony payments?" He nodded his head vigorously. I turned to Judy, who responded to my inquiring expression by replying, "Well, what can I say? You heard him "say that he won't pay alimony." I explained that Greg had stated his preference in response to my question, and then said, "What is your preference?"; Judy then said "Well, maybe I do want support from Greg." In this manner, a client can be helped to use the power that she has. Judy exercised the power that she had to state her choice for alimony. She was empowered by the mediator.

Fifth, not every power difference between spouses affects the divorce settlement. Often in divorce mediation I see couples in which one parent is especially concerned that a child continue to be brought up in a particular faith. That parent has a great degree of power regarding a specific issue, the religious upbringing of the child, but usually this kind of specific power imbalance does not affect other issues.

Many feminists have expressed the belief that the female spouse in a traditional couple has less power than the male spouse, and that this power imbalance remains unchanged during the mediation process, with the result that women receive less than their fair share of assets, and so forth. Joanne Schulman, a staff attorney with the National Center on Women and Family Law, cautions women against the use of mediation: There are any number of factors which can create inequality between the parties. Overwhelmingly, they are factors which tend to favor men over women. She lists the following as garnering more power for men: greater income, greater career mobility, more knowledge of family finances, thinking that earnings or assets are "his," more experience at bargaining, and willingness to use power and control tactics. . . .

[I]n answer to my first question, "Is there a power imbalance between traditional divorcing spouses?," I would respond "Yes." The male spouse does have more power than the female spouse. How, then, can the mediation process result in a fair settlement for this couple?

If a Power Imbalance Between Men and Women Exists, How Can Mediation Be Fair?

Despite disparities in spousal power, divorce mediators can help clients reach fair agreements. The mediation process, the role of the mediator, and the nature of the divorce crisis itself combine to produce fair agreements.

The Mediation Process. The mediation process is a short-term, goal-oriented procedure based on the principle of informed decision making by each individual. A client in mediation must be able to listen, to understand information, and to make decisions. The goal is to reach a fair and mutually satisfactory settlement. Clients typically report that they feel that the process was fair.

The mediation framework emphasizes a cooperative approach. The mediator usually ensures active participation by the clients by employing task oriented tools. The mediator might use budgets, for example, to help clients understand finances as a step in the process of financial negotiations. When necessary, the mediation may involve other professionals, such as attorneys, tax and financial consultants, appraisers, and child psychologists.

The mediator creates a framework for the divorce negotiations. The mediation procedure allows the mediator to take steps to ensure reasonable equality. The structure of the mediation process allows the neutral mediator to balance spousal power by controlling the procedure, determining the course of the negotiations, and reaching the final settlement.

Role of the Mediator. The issue of power does not end with an examination of the clients' power. Analysis of the power dynamics within the mediation process must include examination of the mediator's power. Though the mediator is impartial, his or her impartiality should not be construed as a lack of power. The power of the court-appointed mediator is readily apparent: she or he clearly has the authority of the official court behind her or him. The power of the private mediator is not so apparent, but it is very real.

A mediator's power derives from his or her control of the entire process. This control manifests itself in nine ways:

1. Creating the ground rules
2. Choosing the topic
3. Deciding who may speak
4. Controlling the length of time each person may speak
5. Allowing and timing a person's response
6. Determining which spouse may present a proposal to the other
7. Presenting an interpretation of what the spouse said
8. Ending the discussion
9. Writing down the agreement

Note that every element of power listed is controlled by the mediator. The mediator actually has the most power in the room.

The mediator must recognize the power dynamics between the clients in order to address the power imbalance between spouses. Clients express power in mediation in a number of ways. A basic indicator of power is nonverbal behavior, which is often more indicative of power than is verbal expression. Careful observation of nonverbal expression is an important key to assessing power disparity. . . .

Sometimes the signs of greater power are blatant, yet many times the exercise of significant power is subtle. If I order you to "Get me my coat" and you obey, I obviously have power over you. But if I do not order you to fetch my coat, and without a word or even a glance from me, you run and fetch me my coat, I probably have a greater degree of power over you. The mediator's recognition and assessment of the subtle indications of power arc crucial to a successful mediation.

Effect of Crisis. Divorce, the experts agree, is a crisis. "Crisis" denotes severe instability, a world blown apart. The separation and divorce transition differs markedly from the relative stability of the intact marriage. As Yahm notes of divorcing clients, "the very structure of their lives is often undone." Two important aspects of divorce mark it as different and more stressful than other forms of life crisis. First, divorce is not a single event; it is a transitional process that begins before the actual points of physical separation or legal termination and ends long after both of those points. Second, divorce, unlike many other crises that are caused by external forces, is caused by behavior, by one or both of the spouses. Spouses can join together in an "us" against "them" stand in many crises, but divorce is a crisis that divides the spouses. What was a strength, the nature of a couple's relationship, now becomes a weakness.

The crisis of divorce affects the power balance between the spouses in two critical ways: first, the crisis directly impacts upon the interaction between the partners, and second, the crisis causes a change in the degree of power held by each individual spouse. As a result, each individual is more open to outside intervention. This means that the power dynamics between the spouses are more open to the mediator's interventions.

An example of crisis fostering change is evident in what I term the "moral" issues of power between spouses. Gilligan found that women's morality typically involves judgment of behavior according to the needs of others, while men's morality involves judgment of behavior according to concern for rights. Men make their moral decisions based on the rights or interests of others, while women make their decisions based on the needs of others. Gilligan notes that "conventional feminine morality, because it endorses making decisions in terms of other's needs, functions to reduce women's power."

I propose that the male/female difference in morality that Gilligan observed undergoes a major reversal during the divorce crisis. During the divorce transitional, women are encouraged to satisfy their own needs, and not to make decisions according to the needs of their husbands. The desire to please the husband is neither expected nor encouraged by others; indeed, society now commands the wife to put aside her caretaking role and assume an adversarial role. Those who give advice to the divorcing, and there are many, are unanimous in warning that "divorce is war." Indeed, "aggressive behavior is encouraged by the country's legal system." Because of this change in expected behavior, the wife's established, relative powerlessness in relation to her husband can be transformed into relative powerfulness as she looks to her own self-interest. Meanwhile, the male spouse tends to cling more firmly to his moral standard, as the legal system supports the rights-based model. It is not a coincidence that our legal system is based on the male model of morality; indeed, feminists recognize and define our legal system as "male." And, historically, of course, women have not fared well under the legal system.

Marital Role. In order to explore the effect of the crisis of the divorce upon the individual spouse, we must begin with an examination of the significance of the marital role. . . . [A] role [is] "the rights, responsibilities and normatively prescribed behaviors expected of an individual in a given status or position." A role tells us how we should act toward someone. The importance of a role is determined by its importance to the individual. It is commonly assumed that the loss of the marital role for the wife is more profound than is the loss of the marital role for her husband. I do not believe that this difference is inevitable or even likely.

According to cultural myth, men run away from marriage, while women seek and thrive in a marital relationship. Thus, it is frequently concluded that the loss of the role of a wife is traumatic. Yet studies consistently show that married women experience more stress than married men or single women. . . . [T]he role of wife is "often associated with psychological distress." However, the failure of the role to correlate highly with the well-being of a woman does not diminish the impact of the loss of her marital role. This contradiction, that the role of wife does not create well-being, and that the loss of this role is profoundly upsetting, has significant consequences for divorcing women.

Upon divorce, women in traditional marriages suffer a profound loss for three major reasons. First, society has conditioned women to believe that they cannot be a whole person without a man. Second, women feel more responsible for the marital relationship, and therefore have a greater tendency to see divorce as a sign of personal failure. Third, women tend to have a stronger identification with the role of wife than men have with the role of husband. If the woman identifies more strongly with a role other than wife, such as worker or mother, her loss may not be as traumatic as when she sees herself primarily as a wife. A former client of mine, Theresa Rossi, had been a homemaker for thirty-two years prior to her divorce. On the day she returned from divorce court, she received a letter addressed to "Mrs. Frank Rossi." This incident caused her to remark, "That wasn't me anymore. I felt as if I didn't exist. If I'm not Mrs. Frank Rossi, then who am I?"

Society expects men to react differently than women to their loss of the marital role as husband. Cultural myth suggests that men do not invest much of themselves in marriage. A man's role as husband may not be central to his identification. Indeed, cultural myths would have us believe that the only important roles for men are work and earning money, rather than the role of husband. Yet married men experience less stress than unmarried men. Indeed, studies show that single men experience the greatest stress out of the four possible groups: married men, unmarried men, married woman, and unmarried woman. Bernard concludes that "Marriage is distinctly beneficial for the vast majority of husbands."

. . . Barnett and Grace found that "In contrast to the almost exclusive emphasis on men's work roles as determinate of male stress and well-being, the data from several studies suggest that men's family roles are very important and have significant direct and indirect effects on emotional and physical well-being." Recent studies indicate that the marital role is central to the mental and physical health of men. So what happens when that role ends? Barnett and Grace state that "loss of the marriage role will be more devastating for men than for women."

My own practice reveals that the spouse who suffers the most is almost always the spouse who is being left, regardless of gender. It is hard to measure such pain, and I have not found that one gender always or even primarily suffers greater loss or pain in divorce. A favorite book of mine, Crazy Times by Abigail Trafford, sums up the effect of a breakup for both men and women: "Divorce puts you right on the edge of sanity. . . . You don't have to commit suicide or murder your spouse to know how crazy you feel."

Redefinition of Self. Divorce disrupts the degree of power held by an individual. The primary impetus for this change is the divorce itself. The divorce crisis precipitates a sense of loss of identity, even by the spouse who initiates the end of the relationship. Within the emotional calamity, however, one can trace predictable patterns of emotional responses. Diane Vaughn, a sociologist and the author of Uncoupling (1986), provides a valuable insight into this apparent contradiction of emotional calamity and predictable emotional patterns: "Uncoupling is perceived by those who experience it as woefully chaotic and disorderly. Yet, despite the dubious gifts of confusion, anger, sorrow and pain bestowed on both partners, there is an underlying order that appears across all experiences."

Vaughn defines the central issue of uncoupling as the dilemma for each partner to define him- or herself in the absence of the other person. The question each spouse must ask is, "Who am I?" Every divorcing individual seeks to redefine, or is forced to redefine, herself or himself. The magnitude of this personal struggle cannot be understated. Implicit in the redefinition of self is a breakdown of defenses and an openness to other ways of being. A personal crisis offers the opportunity for significant adult change. The individual change affects the interactions between the spouses, though one or both will usually try to reassert the established interactive spousal patterns. During the crisis, the spousal levels of power are in flux.

Divorce creates a breakdown in the usual personality defenses. The clients' increased vulnerability allows the mediator to effectively use her or his power to strategically intervene in the power dynamics between them. In other words, the divorce crisis causes confusion about one's identity, and undermines one's usual personal defense system. But this confusion and lack of defenses actually works to help the mediator affect significant change.

Power During Divorce. During the crisis of separation and divorce, many of the broad categories of power become more narrowly focused and specific factors emerge by which one spouse gains additional degrees of power. During the divorce transition, more power is gained by the individual who:

1. Wants the divorce.
2. Does not want the divorce, and is willing to pay, emotionally and financially, to slow or stop the divorce.
3. Has legitimate power, which is each person's moral or cultural perception of who should have the power.
4. Has legal favor. In mediation jargon, this individual benefits from "the shadow of the law."
5. Feels guilt concerning the termination of the marriage. Two common reasons for feelings of guilt are initiating the divorce and having an affair.
6. Makes promises or threats that the other spouse believes. The threat or promise may not necessarily concern an issue that is part of the settlement.
7. Develops the divorce settlement options or proposals.
8. Has a strong representative, such as a lawyer, and/or support people in his or her life.

In addition to these elements of power, three other major foundations of power, which, though continuously present, gain significant influence during the divorce process. First, whoever has the greater income and/or financial assets has a source of power. Second, whoever has greater knowledge of financial issues, especially if the issues are part of the negotiated settlement, can assert more power. Third, whoever has used, is using, or is threatening to use physical force or violence toward the other spouse has a source of power.

Conclusion

Divorce mediators recognize the degree of power held by their clients, assess the effect of the imbalance of power upon the negotiations, and employ techniques to intervene in the balance of power to provide a forum in which to have fair negotiations. A divorce mediator can assist clients to reach a fair resolution because of a number of interwoven factors, but three are particularly important: the mediation process, the power of the mediator, and the effect of the divorce crisis. Significant power differences between male and female clients can be addressed within the mediation process because of the specifics of the situation. Significant power disparity between divorcing spouses is evident. The patriarchal structure of society does not have to be abolished before a mediator can address the power dynamics of the divorcing couple, although such a dramatic change would make the mediator's job much easier. A professional mediator, because of the three conditions described in this article, can address the power imbalance in most divorcing couples sufficiently to allow the "magic" of mediation to occur.

I think that the final question skeptics are bound to ask is "What if the mediator fails to do her job?" The failure of a professional to do her job is always a serious problem, in the same way that the failure of a lawyer, therapist, appraiser, or tax consultant results in a serious problem for the client. We must make the profession of mediation accountable in the same manner as other professions. This process is already taking place; mediators at both the state and national levels are creating credentialing and licensing procedures that will make mediators accountable in the same manner as other professionals are accountable.

What is important for me, as a mediator and as a feminist, is that mediation offers clients the opportunity to become empowered. Empowerment is immensely valuable for a divorcing individual, for it is the sense of competency and the ability to take control of your own life during the process of divorce that enables each person to successfully move ahead with her life.

5. Anne Field, *Divorce Mediation and Other (Cheap) Ways to Split*, COSMOPOLITAN, August 1995 at 136*

At their first meeting with a mediator, Dorothy and Jack Walter sat nose-to-nose, hurling obscenities and battling over money, sex, their suburban home, her affair with the gardener, his with his secretary. Both their decibel and resentment levels were soaring. Thirty acrimonious sessions later, the pair miraculously cobbled out a treaty to end their ten-year marital war. They also credited the mediation process with literally saving their lives; one more plate-throwing, eardrum-shattering incident and they'd have lunged at each other's throats.

The number of miserably married couples who, like the Walters, are turning to mediation when it's finally time to call it quits is growing exponentially, according to Susan Snow, a Chicago divorce-court judge. These ex-spouse wanna-bes, she notes, avoid the out-of-control expenses, lengthy delays, and emotional trauma of traditional divorce litigation.

Compare the price tags: An uncontested, amicable divorce may cost $5,000 per partner and drag on for more than a year. And that's for mates who still like each other. A warring duo like Dorothy and Jack could wind up spending $30,000 apiece, and their case might span an entire Presidential administration! Mediation, on the other hand, is fast and relatively inexpensive: $100 to $250 per session. If children are an issue, the process usually takes six to twelve weeks; if not, perhaps only three or four weeks. The tab for the Walters' seven-month marathon? Only $3,000.

"The legal system is designed so that the more couples fight, the more money their lawyers earn," says Lynn Jacob, president of the Academy of Family Mediators. "But we get them to work together, so both win!"

The Process

The basic philosophy of divorce mediation is that even two people who despise each other can reach an accord if they're guided by a neutral third party, someone trained in the intricacies of negotiation. A divorce mediator, usually a lawyer or therapist, asks incisive questions, cuts through anger and hurt, and facilitates rational decision making. Consider Debbie and Michael White, both thirty-six-year-old journalists, facing the finale of their fifteen-year mar-

*Reprinted with permission.

riage. Disturbed by his wife's workaholic schedule and jealous of her higher-profile career, Michael left Debbie and their two small children and moved in with his eighteen-year-old girlfriend.

In a mediator's presence, Debbie twisted in the chair so she faced away from Michael and, her voice quivering, refused ever to let him see their kids again. Then she paused, wept, and confessed her true feelings: Although Michael had devastated her, she still loved him and really wanted to welcome him back into her home, bed, life.

With a few carefully worded questions, the mediator prompted Debbie to face facts: Her marriage was kaput, and Michael's young girlfriend was merely a symptom, not a cause. He also forced her to focus not on emotional wounds but on the matter of immediate concern: child-visitation rights. One hour later, a compromise was reached: The toddlers would see their dad on weekends, but his girlfriend was persona non grata, and her home was off-limits.

Mediation is most useful when children are involved, because even though husbands and wives are parting, they'll still have to communicate and cooperate as moms and dads. "In the adversarial system, anything goes," says pioneering mediator John Haynes. "But mediation is conducted to preserve the parental relationship, not destroy it." As a result, courts in twenty-five states now require child-custody disagreements to go through mediation.

Sessions are usually one hour long. Partners are asked to bring pertinent information: tax returns, a list of assets, bank records. When they reach an equitable agreement, their attorneys file official documents with the court. Although decisions made in mediation aren't binding, up to 90 percent of cases are successfully settled, says Haynes. "People realize it's better to have something they've both created than a decision handed down by a judge."

That's certainly true for Vivian and Bill Berstein, spouses and business partners for twelve years. Together, they built a multimillion-dollar mail-order company, which neither wanted to give up when their marriage fell apart. Continuing as co-owners was out of the question; every business discussion devolved into a screamfest.

Without lawyers, judges, or formal courtroom rules to get in the way, the mediator first got Vivian and Bill to agree on a general plan whereby one spouse would keep the business, buy out the other, and lend him or her enough money to start a new venture. Then he instructed them to calculate their company's not worth. Finally, the mates realized on their own that Vivian, who'd had more contact with overseas suppliers, should keep the business; Bill, who was more aggressive, would do better taking the loan and launching a new product line.

Simple Solutions

The biggest advantage of divorce mediation is that it affords couples the chance to explore myriad options, no matter how idiosyncratic. As a bonus, they can consider developments that might arise years after their divorce becomes final. A joint-custody plan agreed upon when a child is three probably won't be practical five years later, when she's in school; remarriage or relocation of an ex-spouse may also affect terms of their agreement.

In addition, divorcing couples are often so blinded by rage they're unable to see even the most obvious solutions to their disputes. When Brad Heller announced he and wife Natalie couldn't afford to pay the security deposits and rent on two separate apartments, the mediator reviewed the couple's investments and asked, "Isn't there anything you could liquidate?" The answer was so simple. "We could sell our time-share condo in the Bahamas," declared

Brad. "And split the profit," said Natalie. They shook hands, paid the mediator, and went home to plan their lives apart.

Similarly, after five years of nonstop bickering, Jennifer and Artie Bartwell could no longer bear living together. Without children or joint property, their divorce should have been a cinch. The one sticking point: how to break up their sterling silver and darkroom equipment, all of which had been wedding gifts from mutual friends. After three unproductive sessions, a breakthrough came when the mediator asked Jennifer, "Forget about monetary value; which would you *prefer?*"

"The silver." she replied.

"And I'd like the darkroom stuff," said Artie.

Conflict resolved.

The Downside

Women's-rights advocates urge victims of domestic violence to skip mediation and go directly to court. Battered wives, they contend, are too intimidated to defend themselves, especially when husband-tormentors are sitting by their sides.

Critics also charge that the process can backfire even when abuse isn't an issue. "Women tend to be more accommodating than men, and that works to our disadvantage," says Joan Zorza, a senior attorney with the National Center on Women and Family Law in New York City. Plus, a wife who's less money-smart than her husband may not be aware of investments and expenses or able to grasp the future significance of every small decision she makes now.

Getting What You Deserve

A good mediator, however, uses the process to educate. When a contentious couple presents financial information, he may put the data on a big chart. If either party seems confused, he'll clarify. "This is empowering for women," says Diane Neumann, a mediator in Framingham, Massachusetts. "We may walk in having never focused on money issues and leave with a thorough understanding of personal finance."

Meet housewife Susan Swanson. Her husband, Charles, an orthopedic surgeon whose annual income exceeds two hundred thousand dollars, was seeking a divorce. During mediation, Charles presented his plan: He'd keep his sizable pension, and his wife would get the house. This seemed reasonable to Susan until the mediator explained that a wife is legally entitled to half of her husband's retirement savings. What's more, if Susan kept the house, she'd struggle to make the mortgage payments for the next twenty-five years, while Charles's pension would be worth millions.

Shocked, Susan threatened to stop the mediation and hire renowned divorce attorney Raoul Felder. With the specter of legal action looming, Charles withdrew his original proposal and offered to share not only his pension but also his stock portfolio and African art collection. The sweetest part of this deal, says Susan, is she crafted it herself, with a little help from the mediator.

6. Comments and Questions

This article is presented not for the truth of the matters asserted therein, but because it appeared in a leading women's magazine. Its intended audience, according to Editor-in-Chief

Helen Gurley Brown, is "the Cosmo girl." (page 17)

> You love men and children but don't want to get your identity from somebody else. You want to achieve on your own. . . . (Y)ou care about your looks and try to make them even better. You have a job. . . . You are a wonderful "work in progress" — learning, striving, growing, and becoming the person you want and were meant to be.

An article in Cosmopolitan almost certainly has a greater influence on the behavior of reasonably sophisticated and educated adult women than the scholarly publications that are excerpted or cited throughout this book.

D. Lawyer Participation in Divorce Mediation

1. Comments and Questions

a. Recall that the issue addressed by Trina Grillo was not family mediation in general, but **mandatory** mediation. (Some of her critics argue that much of her critique is inapplicable to voluntarily undertaken family mediation.) The next article argues that the presence of lawyers for both parties at mediation achieves the benefits of mandatory mediation without the attendant problems pointed out by Professor Grillo. McEwen, Rogers & Maiman support this conclusion with serious empirical research, something only too rare in the world of law. In addition, the authors provide a sound commentary on many important issues in divorce mediation.

b. The authors note that "Maine mediation may thus seem more like facilitated pretrial settlement conferences and less like mediation sessions." What does this mean?

c. Note that mediators in Maine serve virtually on a pro bono basis — they receive $50 per party for the entire mediation. Would the system be workable if mediators were paid an amount that approached market rates?

2. Craig A. McEwen, Nancy H. Rogers, & Richard J. Maiman, *Bring In the Lawyers: Challenging the Dominant Approaches to Ensuring Fairness in Divorce Mediation*, 79 Minn. L. Rev. 1317 (1995)*

INTRODUCTION

Mandatory divorce mediation is under attack. According to some critical commentators, divorce mediation reinforces bargaining imbalances between parties and places women at a disadvantage. . . . Mediation proponents respond that mandatory mediation can produce results as fair as or more fair than those achieved through a traditional divorce system, and they praise mediation's benefits as compared to litigation. To insure fairness, however, proponents sometimes advocate regulation. . . . This "regulatory" approach to mandated mediation often includes mediator duties to assure fairness . . .; exemption of some cases from compulsory mediation; limitation . . . to custody and visitation issues; [qualifications] for mediators; requirement that the parties' lawyers and the court review mediated agreements; and prohibitions against the mediator making recommendations to the court.

---

*Reprinted with permission.

This "regulatory" approach to assuring fairness in divorce mediation contrasts with the "voluntary participation" approach often favored by those most critical of mediation. Unlike the "regulatory" approach, the "voluntary participation" approach leaves courts without authority to compel the parties to attend mediation sessions. Under this approach, the parties presumably decide whether to go to mediation based upon how well they believe they will fare. The assurance of fairness then rests on their ability to choose. Thus, the "voluntary participation" approach sometimes entails very little regulation of the mediation process.

In this Article, we argue that the debate about fairness in divorce mediation, as well as the resulting legal schemes based on either the "regulatory" or "voluntary participation" approaches, results from the view that one must choose between a "lawyered" process ending in the courtroom, and an informal, problem-solving process involving parties but not lawyers in the mediation room. In our view, this dichotomy has unnecessarily narrowed the policy choices underlying mediation schemes, because it assumes that lawyers either cause conflict or act as mouthpieces for clients with a cause; that the divorce process is one in which, absent mediation (where lawyers do not appear), aggressive lawyers contest custody cases at hearings; and that mediators either protect parties' interests or pressure them toward a particular (and sometimes unjust) settlement.

We challenge these assumptions and . . . argue that the mediation scheme in Maine, where attorneys participate regularly and vigorously in mandated divorce mediation, provides a third avenue — one we call the "lawyer-participant" approach. . . . In Part II, we examine the merits and weaknesses of the two primary contending approaches in mediation statutes, the "regulatory" and "voluntary participation" approaches. In Part III, we identify in detail the four "myths" that confine the debate to the two dominant approaches, and, in Part IV, we examine the perceptions and experiences of Maine divorce lawyers in an effort to challenge these myths. Ultimately, in Part V, we reject as flawed both the "regulatory" and the "voluntary participation" approaches to protecting fairness in divorce mediation and instead advocate Maine's "lawyer-participant" approach. In doing so, we side with the mediation critics in their skepticism about the capacity of the regulatory approach to insure fairness, but we also side with mediation advocates who believe that mediation holds promise for improving the divorce negotiation process without sacrificing fairness.

I. THE "FAIRNESS" DEBATE

Mediation critics claim that mandatory mediation, even if regulated, is less fair than trial. In contrast, mediation proponents contend that the judicial system is itself destructive and thus introduces an unfairness of sorts. For instance, mediator John Haynes begins his book, Divorce Mediation, with the assertion, "The pain, anger, and frustration of divorce are frequently exacerbated by the legal process as it presently works." Furthermore, he argues, "[m]uch of the decision making is taken out of the hands of the clients, as the attorneys engage in battle within the legal system." Similarly, Dean Jay Folberg argues that family law and court procedures are often used "coercively to supplant family self-determination." He states, by contrast, that mediation enhances "self determination," and public support for it affirms "the dignity and importance of the family."

What do mediation critics and proponents mean by "fairness" in the context of divorce mediation? They seem to refer to several aspects of procedural fairness, and appear to link them to outcome fairness. Procedural aspects of fairness in divorce mediation commonly include balanced bargaining between parties; a "level playing field" in the mediation process; self-determination by parties without undue settlement pressures or imposition of a mediator's values; and consideration of the children's interests. Commentators on divorce mediation seem especially concerned with those bargaining imbalances that may reflect differences in power between men and women, because these may lead to negotiated results that favor men. Bargaining imbalances thus produce "unfair results" unless mediators can overcome them. If mediators intervene too strongly to balance differences between parties, however, they may actually tilt the "level playing field" that "neutral" mediators arguably establish. When the circumstances of mediation permit a mediator to impose his or her preferences for an outcome on the parties — as when mediators make recommendations to the triers of fact — settlement pressures not only violate the principle of self-determination, but also may destroy a "level playing field" and produce unfair results, at least when these pressures affect parties differently. Court procedures that penalize the recalcitrant party or that impose costs that one party can bear with more ease than the other can also lead to . . . pressures to capitulate. . . .

Sometimes, commentators include "party empowerment" as another aspect of fairness, but they differ on how to achieve it. For mediation critics, legal advocacy and court hearings equalize power and diminish pressures for settlement. They view lawyers particularly as buffers between demanding spouses and intimidated clients. Lawyers insure that parties understand the alternatives to settlement. For some mediation advocates, however, legal advocacy and decision making diminish party autonomy and freedom — and thus "empowerment" — by allowing lawyers and courts to shape decisions using legal rules in a way that may have little relationship to the parties' priorities, needs, and interests.

At the extremes, these two views of outcome fairness and empowerment lead mediation critics to advocate against settlement and mediation proponents to oppose trials. An intermediate position, typically supported by commentators from both camps, involves determining how far a settlement departs from one that informed, unpressured parties would have reached absent mediation. . . .

Clearly, fairness in divorce mediation concerns both critics and advocates. Most embrace a comparable notion for fairness — that is, mediation should approximate the results achieved in lawyer-to-lawyer negotiation. Even when they embrace this mainstream definition of fairness, however, their commentary about how best to insure fairness in mediation has been constrained by common assumptions about the absence of lawyers, the similarity of all mediation programs, the role that lawyers would play if present, and the role of trial as the alternative to mediation. The same faulty assumptions have also confused the analysis of the dominant "regulatory approach," to which we now turn.

II. EVALUATING THE TWO DOMINANT STATUTORY APPROACHES

The two dominant statutory schemes of mediation — the "regulatory" approach and the "voluntary participation" approach — reflect the debate over fairness in divorce mediation. The "regulatory" approach requires divorcing parents to attend an introductory session on mediation or mediation itself, and the process is highly regulated in an effort to make it fair, despite the usual absence of lawyers at mediation sessions. The "voluntary participation" approach enables the parties to choose whether to participate in an introductory session or mediation session. Because lawyers will not attend mediation sessions, parties should opt not to participate if they anticipate conditions that will lead to unfairness. . . .

A. The "Regulatory" Approach

. . . Under the dominant regulatory scheme, mediation is a negotiation that the mediator guides. The lawyers usually will not attend the mediation session or will attend in silence. Statutes in California, Kansas, and Wisconsin permit exclusion of lawyers from mediation sessions. . . . In some other jurisdictions, parties have a right to bring their lawyers, although in Florida the lawyers may be instructed to speak only privately to their clients. . . .

The typical rationale for excluding lawyers is that they "spoil" mediation: lawyers will interfere with candid expressions by the parties and thwart a problem-solving style of negotiation. Statutes reflect this by highlighting problem solving by the parties and emphasizing that the parties themselves should speak in mediation.

[M]ost commentators would not find such extensive regulation necessary to ensure fairness if lawyers attended and participated in mediation, because the process then would become the equivalent of lawyer-to-lawyer negotiation in terms of fairness. To obviate potential unfairness in the absence of attorney representation, commentators have advocated regulating the mediator and the mediation procedures. . . .

1. Mediator Duties Regarding Fairness

Some statutes and court rules make the mediator accountable for the fairness of the mediation process and result. Mediators often must encourage the parties to consult with their lawyers before signing a mediated agreement. . . . In Iowa, the mediator must "assure a balanced dialogue," and in Florida a "balanced process," although these terms are left undefined. In California, the mediator must be "vigilant" about power imbalances, "conducting negotiations in such a way as to equalize power relationships between the parties." . . . In addition, the mediator commonly must assess and sometimes advocate for the best interests of the children. . . .

Because provisions of mediator accountability are unlikely to be effective, and because they are unnecessary if the parties bring their lawyers to the session, it is important to examine the costs of mediator duties. By analogy, one can examine commentary on the cost of defensiveness in the medical field, which argues that warnings, disclosures, and additional tests result in expenses for the patient and government and physician unwillingness to accept certain cases. If the threat of accountability is taken seriously, mediators may react in similar fashion, issuing warnings, insisting on written acknowledgements, and taking only "low-risk" cases. In this event, the spontaneity, simplicity, and availability of the mediation process will likely fade, a particularly dear cost because these aspects of mediation make it more effective than traditional court processes in engaging parties actively and assisting in identifying creative solutions. . . .

2. Case Selection

If one accepts that unfairness in lawyerless mediation stems in part from bargaining imbalances, it follows that the process becomes more fair if courts exclude cases from mediation that are likely to involve such imbalances. Presumably, fairness would also be enhanced if the courts similarly excluded cases involving parties who are particularly susceptible to mediator pressures. Mediation statutes identify several classes of parties who might be subject either to imbalances or mediator pressure: victims of domestic violence; persons with substance abuse or mental health problems; and persons who fit in a more general category of bargaining disadvantages. Domestic violence exclusions have been the primary subject of debate and regulation. The problem with exclusion as a means to achieve fairness is the difficulty in predicting whether and how power imbalances will appear or when the mediator will pressure a party to settle. . . .

Even if one focuses only on imbalances stemming from domestic violence, the problems arising in implementing case selection by statute or court rule become apparent. Statutes employ three primary means to exclude domestic violence cases from mediation: categorical prohibition, case-by-case screening by the court, and exclusion by the court upon a party's motion and special showing. Each of these methods proves problematic. . . .

3. Issue Limitations

Commentators state that bargaining imbalances are more likely to cause harm if parties discuss economic as well as child status issues during the mediation. Justifications for this assertion vary. One commentator contends that an aggressive parent will demand economic concessions in exchange for allowing the other parent more access to or rights concerning the children. Separating economic issues from child custody and visitation issues in the mediation process presumably averts these inappropriate trade-offs. Other commentators add that the legally-naive party faces the greatest disadvantage in the negotiation of economic issues, where legal advice, higher education, and experience make choices more informed. One also argues that lawyers will resist mediation if non-lawyer mediators "handle" economic issues. Most statutes authorize mandatory mediation only for contested custody and visitation issues, probably to prevent linking these to economic issues, to reduce bargaining imbalances, and to avoid resistance from the bar. In two states [California and Michigan], separate mediation programs, staffed by attorney-mediators, are authorized for economic issues.

The statutes that purport to separate economic from custody/visitation issues probably do not succeed in actually severing these issues or in preventing parties from linking them. Dean Folberg suggests that we must "romanticize" to believe these issues are not considered together. In fact, despite statutory language limiting mediation to custody and visitation issues, a recent national survey indicates that, in a substantial number of programs, mediators are likely to discuss child support. . . .

Issue limitations thus do not seem to solve the problem for which they were designed — avoiding linkage between economic and custody issues. They may be based on faulty premises of custody blackmail. They tend to discourage lawyer attendance, thus eliminating a promising fairness protection. Furthermore, they are costly in terms of party expenditures, party satisfaction, and compliance.

4. Mediator Qualifications

In the early days of divorce mediation, there were few, if any, legal qualifications for divorce mediators. For example, mediators could be court employees or volunteer retirees who had impressed a court administrator as fit for the job. Like negotiators — and, indeed, like judges — mediators were thought to vary in ability, but not in easily quantifiable terms. . . .

Enhanced educational qualifications may carry a variety of costs. . . . [H]igh educational qualifications may produce a contracting pool of mediators who lack diversity and who charge higher fees. Already, there is anecdotal support for this. For example, private mediators in Florida receiving court referrals usually charge $125 per hour for several hours of mediation. Florida requires advanced degrees. In Maine, by contrast, mediators are paid $50 per mediation. Maine does not have such educational requirements. Furthermore, some rural counties may be unable to operate mediation programs, because no one in the community meets the educational qualifications. In addition, varying qualifications may restrict mediators from handling cases in other jurisdictions.

In sum, mediator qualifications can be costly. They may serve other purposes, but they are not needed to preserve fairness if lawyers attend mediation sessions, and they are probably ineffective at insuring fairness if lawyers do not attend.

5. Lawyer and Court Review of Mediated Agreements

Mediated agreements regarding children do not become final until the court approves them. In some jurisdictions, mediators must also advise the parties to seek attorney review of the settlement before execution of the mediation agreements. Court review has traditionally been viewed as a check on only the most egregious and obvious unfairness, because the judge receives only the written result of negotiations and has no advocate for non-signature. [T]he sheer quantity of cases that a judge must oversee makes it impractical for a judge to attend to cases prone to injustice.

While providing limited help in assuring fairness, post-mediation lawyer review is a costly process. The more thorough the review, the more costly it will be. Lawyers who are uncertain about whether the agreement represents the best possible result may recommend against execution, perhaps unnecessarily scuttling the client's best option. Even the possibility of frequent lawyer consultation does not seem to avert rejections of tentative agreements. In fact, mediators view lawyer recommendations against signing tentative mediation agreements as a significant problem. Thus, the cost and effort of the mediation may be lost when lawyers do not participate. In sum, required lawyer review is a costly and less effective alternative to lawyer attendance.

6. No Recommendation by the Mediator to the Court

Some of California's domestic relations courts allow the mediator to make a recommendation to the court if the parties fail to reach a settlement during mediation. This procedure enables the mediator to threaten a recalcitrant party with a negative report. . . .

The prohibitions against mediator recommendations remove a potential source of pressure to settle and, thus, of unfairness. As such, these laws serve a valuable function, regardless of whether lawyers attend the mediation sessions, and we strongly support them. They do not, however, address bargaining imbalances that may exist even in jurisdictions where the mediators do not provide recommendations.

The "regulatory" approach attempts to insure fairness in the absence of lawyer participation in mediation sessions. Only one type of regulatory provision — judicial review — is relatively low in cost. Only one type of provision — prohibition of mediator reports on the merits — seems likely to increase the fairness of divorce mediation. The others — issue limitations, case selection procedures, high mediator qualifications, mediator duties, and lawyer review —

threaten to make mediation more expensive and, in some cases, more rigid and less effective, with little prospect of positive effects on fairness. In short, substituting regulation for lawyer-participation threatens to undermine important qualities of mediation without doing much to insure fairness.

In addition, regulation fails to address the deepest concerns of critics of mediation — that even the best mediators can never be "neutral" and will play a powerful role in shaping outcomes that may create disadvantages for the parties. Lawyers who participate in mediation can address these concerns. Lawyer representation does not guarantee equity, but critics of mediation tend not to criticize as unfair divorce outcomes resulting from lawyer negotiations. Their confidence in lawyer-negotiated outcomes suggests a general agreement that attorney representation provides the best insurance of fairness that we know. The research in Maine, discussed below, indicates that in practice, lawyers play just such a role in protecting client interests in mediation.

B. The "Voluntary Participation" Approach

Some commentators argue that mediation will be more fair if legislators or courts simply eliminate the compulsion to participate. Presumably, if parties choose to use mediation, those who do will be informed, and their rights will not be jeopardized, even though lawyers generally will not attend the mediation sessions. These commentators thus advocate against mandatory participation. . . .

Under the voluntary approach, parties would rarely use mediation and would have little assistance of counsel when they did. Requiring the divorcing parties to attend a mediation session at which their lawyers actively participate would seem to promote fairness more effectively. Regulators and commentators, however, assume that this would destroy mediation. Furthermore, those advocating voluntary mediation often assert that trial will obviate fairness concerns, assuming trial is the alternative to attending mediation sessions.

Such assumptions as these have artificially limited the examination of alternatives for promoting fairness in divorce mediation. . . . We turn now to evidence showing that the assumptions that the two dominant approaches present are myths. This opens up a third policy choice — the "lawyer-participant" approach.

III. ASSUMPTIONS UNDERLYING THE DOMINANT APPROACHES

Four assumptions are implicit in the two dominant statutory approaches to assuring fairness in mediation, and also in the commentary for and against mandatory mediation: (1) lawyers do not attend mediation sessions but do attend trials; (2) divorce mediation sessions are all alike; (3) lawyers spoil mediation if they attend and participate in the sessions; and (4) trial represents the typical alternative to mediation. We address the assumptions in turn, and . . . show them to be myths.

A. The Disappearing Lawyer

Critics and proponents of mediation alike see the absence of lawyers as a defining aspect of divorce mediation. . . . Case summaries of "ideal" mediations by a number of commentators describe sessions without lawyers present. A diminished role for lawyers is indeed one of the goals of some divorce mediation advocates. . . . Under the dominant view, the parties' lawyers may consult before or after the session, perhaps even by phone during it, but they disappear when the parties sit down with the mediator. . . .

Critics of mediation also assume that lawyers do not participate in mediation. They see the results, however, as bad rather than good. For them, lawyers who protect clients from domination at all other points in the divorce process disappear into the shadows during mediation except to advise clients on the wisdom of agreements reached.

B. Mediation as Monolith

Much commentary treats mediation generically, as if all mediation was alike. Many critics of mediation offer as prototypical the mediation programs of one jurisdiction. Professor Grillo, for instance, draws her examples from a county in California that follows the minority rule of permitting the mediator to make disposition recommendations to the court if the parties fail to reach agreement. . . .

Supporters of mandatory mediation also treat mediation generically in their aspiration to a world of uniformly "good" mediators. They argue that "bad mediation" is an aberration that training and tighter or better regulation can cure.

C. Lawyers as Spoilers

Laws that regulate mandatory mediation seem designed to protect the parties' interests in the absence of their lawyers. This regulatory approach implies that the easy solution — encouraging lawyer presence — must be avoided because lawyers negatively affect mediation. . . . Critics of mediation also assume that lawyers would "spoil" the mediation process. Because they see the virtues of a lawyered process, but believe that lawyers and mediation are incompatible, they give little attention to lawyer presence as a protection against unfairness.

D. Mandated Mediation Versus Trial

Much of the current debate about the fairness of mediation presupposes a choice between trials and mediations, although . . . most divorce cases settle. Thus, Professors Grillo and Rosenberg debate whether judges or mediators are more biased and whose biases are more consequential. Proponents sell mediation as a way for parties to control their own fate. By contrast, critics deride mediation because it removes the opportunity to have a judge find on behalf of a weaker party. . . .

In sum, the four assumptions underlying the dominant regulatory approaches . . . are myths. In fact, lawyers can and do participate in mediation sessions more often than they appear in trial; mediation can look very different from state to state and mediation to mediation; lawyers can and do assume constructive roles in mediation as advocates without undermining the party-centered goals of mediation; and mediation can, and in some places does, complement negotiation more often than it substitutes for trials. [W]e turn now to a detailed case study of the experience of lawyers who play an active role in mandated divorce mediation.

IV. THE ASSUMPTIONS UNDERLYING THE DOMINANT APPROACHES ARE MYTHS: A CASE STUDY OF MAINE'S MANDATORY DIVORCE MEDIATION INVOLVING LAWYERS

A. The Study of Divorce Lawyers and Mediation in Maine

In Maine, divorce mediation has been mandatory since 1985. Maine's regulation of divorce mediation differs in key respects from the dominant regulatory model, and the practice of mediation in Maine differs from the mediation schemes that many of the critics of divorce mediation eschew. First, mandated mediation in Maine encompasses economic and other issues of the divorce, rather than solely custody and visitation. Second, any case involving children under eighteen and any contested issue — not just one regarding custody or visitation — triggers compulsory participation. Third, lawyers usually attend the mediation sessions. Fourth, Maine does not regulate mediation as heavily as many other states. Maine has no statutory qualifications for mediators, no required assessments of cases to determine "fitness" for mediation, no mediator duties regarding bargaining imbalances, no mandatory exclusions of particular cases, no limitation on issues, and no authorizations for the mediator to exclude lawyers. . . .

B. The Assumptions Prove to Be Myths in Maine

1. The Disappearing Lawyer

a. Lawyer Participation in Maine Mediation Sessions and Divorce Cases

Before examining whether lawyers disappear in Maine mediation, we must recognize that frequently in divorce cases attorneys never appear at all. In Maine — as in New Hampshire and elsewhere in the United States — lawyers typically represent fewer than half of divorcing parties. In our sample of nearly 5,000 Maine divorce cases, docketed between 1979 and 1988, neither party was represented in sixteen percent of the cases, only the plaintiff was represented in another forty-four percent, and only the defendant was represented in less than two percent. Both parties had attorneys in thirty-eight percent of the cases.

Contested divorce cases, however, are the ones that may be ordered to mediation, and are far more likely to involve two lawyers. Eighty percent of the mediated cases in our post-mandate docket sample involved two attorneys, and another seventeen percent involved one lawyer. Thus, in examining mandatory divorce mediation in Maine, we are largely, although not exclusively, looking at that minority of divorce cases in which both sides have legal representation.

In Maine, lawyers usually attend mediation sessions. Seventy-eight percent of the attorneys we interviewed reported that they "almost always" attended mediation sessions involving their clients and another seventeen percent reported they "usually" did so. Thus, in Maine, lawyers do not disappear when mediation occurs. Nor do they disappear within the mediation sessions. Instead, Maine divorce attorneys actively participate as advisors and, when necessary, as advocates throughout the mediation process.

b. Lawyer Advocacy in Maine Divorce Mediation

Maine lawyers believe that their primary role in mediation is to provide a check on unfairness. According to one attorney:

> I'm there to protect [my client] if I think things are not being run fairly and to watch out for their interests, but primarily, it's them, the mediator and the other spouse.

[V]irtualy every Maine lawyer interviewed described a similar role for themselves. Those lawyers who elaborated identified two aspects of the potential for unfairness. First, "Mediation is like a crucible and bad decisions can be made." As a result, attorneys believe they need to attend mediation to prevent clients from being swept into accepting an inappropriate settlement. . . .

Experienced divorce lawyers understand that even good mediation — or, perhaps, especially, good mediation — can create a momentum toward settlement that prompts some parties to lose perspective on their needs, interests, rights, and options. Unfairness results. Attorneys participate in divorce mediation to prevent that from happening.

Maine divorce lawyers see themselves as protecting against mediator pressures or unfair bargaining advantages that the other party may have. . . .

2. Mediation as Monolith

Both critics and advocates of mediation too frequently assume that "mediation" or "divorce mediation" can be described generically. Generic discussions, however, miss the enormous variation in the structure and processes of mediation programs. . . . Both advocates and critics need to situate their commentaries carefully within this diverse terrain of mediation programs. . . .

3. Lawyers as Spoilers

Commentators suggest that lawyer participation would adversely affect the quality of mediation in three ways. First, lawyer advocacy would reduce settlement rates. Second, lawyers would create an "adversarial" atmosphere. Third, lawyers would "take over," so that clients had little opportunity to participate. This view of lawyers as spoilers of mediation has proven to be inaccurate in Maine. Also, the picture emerging in Maine resembles research elsewhere on lawyers as negotiators.

a. Settlement and Lawyer Participation

The participation of Maine lawyers in mediation does not spoil mediation's capacity to promote settlement, even in the relatively short sessions used in Maine. Maine's Court Mediation Service reports that roughly one-half of all mediation sessions conclude with an agreement. The remaining sessions conclude without settlement, although about twenty percent are rescheduled for further mediation. . . . A 1985 study of Maine mediations concluded that only one percent of the cases in which the parties reached agreements in mediation later went to trial.

The effectiveness of Maine mediation in promoting settlement—even with lawyer participation—should not be surprising. Rather than exacerbating conflict, lawyers report that they and other attorneys typically try to reduce it. The professional norm among the divorce attorneys we interviewed is that of the "reasonable lawyer" who limits client expectations, resists identifying emotionally with the client, avoids substantially inflating demands, understands the likely legal outcome, asserts the client's interests, responds to new information, and seeks to reach a divorce settlement. "Reasonable lawyers" in Maine facilitate rather than resist settlement.

Maine, however, is not unique in this regard. Many researchers have highlighted the attorney's central role in settling contentious divorce negotiations. . . . Kressel estimates that a relatively small percentage of divorce lawyers fit the popular image of a conflict escalator in divorce negotiations, a finding replicated by Canadian research. . . .

Maine lawyers were significantly more willing to endorse "reaching a settlement fair to both parties" as the goal of negotiation—compared with "getting as much as possible for their client"— than a comparable group of New Hampshire lawyers who had never participated in court mandated mediation. In addition, the volume of motions filed per divorce case dropped by twenty percent in Maine following the introduction of mandatory mediation. In neighboring New Hampshire, which has no such mandate, the incidence of motions increased by twenty percent to thirty percent over the same period. One plausible interpretation of these changes and differences is that individual Maine lawyers have learned in mediation to assist clients achieve their goals in a more cooperative fashion. Moreover, the collective experience of the Maine divorce bar altered expectations about appropriate attorney conduct in family law cases. . . .

The Maine data indicates that most lawyers do not employ competitive and disruptive styles of negotiation, that experience with mediation tends to moderate competitive tendencies, and that lawyers tone down aggressive negotiation styles in mediation sessions. Given the evidence of general interest on the part of divorce lawyers in achieving settlement, mediation and lawyer representation are compatible.

b. Encouraging Reasonable Positions and Behavior in Mediation

Despite most lawyers' general orientation toward reasonableness, unreasonable lawyers do exist and unreasonable clients do push their attorneys to advocate unrealistic positions. Mediation, however, diminishes some of these acrimonious tendencies. Mediation modestly challenges the conduct of these occasional "pit bull" or "Rambo" attorneys and provides "reasonable" lawyers increased leverage with difficult clients. The dignified and structured character of the mediation process itself can moderate the most outrageous conduct of both clients and lawyers. . . . The mediation process demands civility and a sense of decorum that may have been lacking in the private interchanges between lawyers and clients. Not only do the norms of mediation diminish the most aggressive conduct by attorneys, but seeing the other side makes posturing more difficult. In mediation, parties also find themselves accountable to the other party and the mediator for their positions. They cannot simply assert a position without justifying it.

Mediation may help diminish client rigidity because it helps clients overcome their suspicions of the opposing side, suspicions that are reinforced by a lack of direct contact. The exposure of lawyers and parties to the otherwise unseen people on the other side of the case provides opportunities to test the degree of consensus between lawyers and clients and to challenge misconceptions.

Mediation with lawyers present also promotes settlement. It enables lawyers to reinforce their own "reality testing" with clients who may be unrealistic in their expectations or demands. In their role as partisans and advocates, lawyers often find it difficult to challenge clients to relinquish unrealistic positions and claims. By highlighting the reactions of mediators, however, attorneys can persuasively reinforce their own advice. Over one-half of the Maine lawyers whom we interviewed spontaneously described mediation as advantageous for this reason. Only by participating in mediation can the lawyer make use of these moderating effects on "unreasonable" demands. At the same time, lawyer participation permits attorneys to encourage client resistance to any overtures from the mediator or other side to abandon positions already viewed as reasonable. Lawyer participation then can simultaneously serve settlement and fairness.

Active participation in the mediation process offers a way to moderate the unreasonable conduct or demands of parties and lawyers. In this fashion mediation adds a dimension to the settlement process that is otherwise unavailable even to "reasonable" lawyers. For these and other reasons, divorce attorneys in Maine tend to view mediation not so much as an alternative to trial, but as an improvement on negotiation. We return below to this issue.

c. *Spoiling Mediation for Clients*

Mediation proponents often express that lawyer participation spoils mediation for their clients by replicating a courtroom environment in which attorneys dominate. The evidence from Maine suggests otherwise. Even with lawyers present, clients reportedly participate actively in mediation sessions, speak and listen to a spouse in a controlled setting, and find an outlet for emotions such as anger.

Maine lawyers recognize that mediation generally requires them to recede into the background, serving as client-advisors and supporters and only occasionally as outspoken advocates. They almost universally report encouraging their clients to take the lead role in mediation sessions, while reserving for themselves the right to intervene when necessary or to confer privately with their clients.

With five mediation participants rather than three, one would reasonably expect some reduction in the parties' speaking time. That, however, may not be problematic. Research in the community mediation setting indicates that the level of client satisfaction relates most directly to whether the clients participate rather than the quantity of participation.

Mediation also permits the expression of emotions. Roughly one quarter of the Maine lawyers spontaneously remarked upon this role of mediation for their clients. Thus, from the viewpoint of attorneys, mediation in Maine — even with lawyers present — enables parties to express their feelings and to participate actively in the divorce process.

Are the lawyers accurate in their description of client participation? With such unanimity of opinion, the inaccuracy would seem to be a matter of degree only; certainly clients were not completely silenced. The picture that lawyers paint of party participation is entirely consistent with one of the authors' observations of mediation sessions. The current director of Maine's Court Mediation Service confirmed that Maine lawyers encourage their clients to speak during sessions. Apparently lawyers do not "spoil" mediation, but instead permit mediation to accomplish many of the goals surrounding party participation and empowerment. . . .

5. Conclusions: The Myths and Maine Mediation

Many advocates of divorce mediation assume that lawyers create conflict and persist in legal argument and positional negotiation so that problem-solving negotiation cannot occur when they are present. Lawyers, presumably, speak in place of their clients and resist settlement. Under this view, if lawyers remind clients of legal rights, any negotiations will focus exclusively on these issues, and lawyers will dominate discussions. In order to preserve party participation and enable problem-solving negotiation, these advocates assume that mediation must take place without lawyers. To protect rights under these circumstances, these advocates argue that well-regulated mediation will balance bargaining inequalities and insure uniformly high-quality mediation. As a consequence, they argue, such mediation offers better resolution of cases than does a trial.

Critics of mandatory mediation similarly assume that mediation precludes discussion of rights and presupposes the absence of lawyers. They conclude, however, that mediators cannot effectively protect weaker parties and regularly insert their own biases in pressuring for settlements. As a consequence, parties lose out in mediation, faring less well than they would in court. All mediation systems share these qualities and thus mandatory mediation — perhaps all mediation — is generically bad, especially for women.

What has occurred under Maine's mandatory mediation scheme challenges these assumptions. First, lawyers who appear at negotiation sessions or trial typically appear at mediation sessions as well. Second, mandatory divorce mediation is highly variable. The existence of a program like Maine's — and similar programs elsewhere — challenges the assumption that all mandatory mediation systems are identical. Operating under few regulations and with the active participation of lawyers, Maine's divorce mediation differs strikingly from the versions portrayed by critics and advocates.

Differentiation does not end with the structure of the system. Mediators and mediation sessions also vary substantially within any system. Because of its dependence on relatively unguided participation of parties, mediation varies substantially with the interests, attributes, and relationships of the participants, as well as the issues at play in a divorce. Mediators must interpret, innovate, and improvise. It is too much to expect that even the best-trained and most perceptive mediators will always understand fully the range of issues and priorities of each party. Inevitably, mediation sessions unfold differently.

Furthermore, the participation of attorneys in Maine mediation helps to assert the rights of and provide support for parties at a disadvantage. It also provides for considerable levels of client involvement, expression of feeling, and personal control. Lawyers see themselves protecting clients against choosing a result because of the pressure of the process, the other party, or the mediator. Yet lawyer attendance does not interfere with settlement rates or with substantial client participation. The active roles of lawyers "spoil" neither advocacy nor the mediation process.

Finally, mandatory mediation in Maine does not usually replace trial. Instead, its major role is to structure and formalize negotiation and to place parties at the center of those negotiations.

The evidence from Maine thus challenges the myths implicit in much of the debate about how best to protect fairness in divorce mediation. Recognizing that mandatory mediation programs vary, that lawyers can participate actively in mediation without either spoiling mediation or neglecting advocacy, and that mandatory mediation serves largely as an adjunct to negotiation rather than as a substitute for trial, we examine anew the alternatives for achieving fairness in divorce mediation.

V. BRING IN THE LAWYERS

Absent the faulty assumptions discussed above, one can look anew at a regulatory scheme in which lawyers participate in mandatory mediation. This scheme achieves fairness primarily by encouraging lawyers to attend and participate. Legislators could accomplish this result by prohibiting exclusion of lawyers from mediation sessions and, in fact, broadening the issues covered in mediation to include matters of real property, alimony, and other financial issues that stimulate lawyer participation. This scheme includes only two other key regulatory provisions — court review of mediated agreements and a prohibition against the mediator's recommendation to the court. It is possible that some extra provision for domestic violence cases, such as the right to refuse joint sessions with the attacker, ought to be included as well. . . .

C. Concerns About the "Lawyer-Participant" Approach

Critics of mandatory mediation will still question what requiring parties to participate in mediation adds to a lawyer-guided settlement or trial process. Mediators may still question whether the lawyer-participant approach, although fair, provides worthwhile benefits for the parties. At base, these reactions stem from the myths discussed and dismissed above. The remaining concerns of mediation critics and advocates about this third regulatory model can be summarized in five questions. First, does mediation add anything to the lawyer-to-lawyer negotiation that usually would otherwise occur? Second, does requiring participation undermine self-determination in the litigation process? Third, does lawyer participation increase the cost of the mediation process? Fourth, what happens in cases in which both sides are not represented by counsel? Fifth, and finally, does lawyer-participant mediation constitute "real mediation"? The research in Maine provides a basis for answering these questions.

1. Mediation Versus Negotiation

One might ask whether lawyer-participant mediation differs from lawyer-to-lawyer negotiation. As described below, Maine divorce attorneys believe that mediation improves negotiation because, in their view, it increases efficiency, decreases communication problems, enhances client involvement and understanding of the process, increases information for attorneys, and dignifies the divorce process for many clients. Unlike many of the theoretical models of negotiation, actual negotiations over divorce cases are discontinuous and fragmented.

Mediation also provides direct communication between the two lawyers and the two parties, and thus insures that nothing will be "lost in the translation." At the least, the mediation process alters the dynamics of the communication in negotiation. Instead of a process in which client A talks to lawyer A who talks to lawyer B who talks to client B and then back again, all actors are present to listen and to speak to one another. This benefit, of course, would exist if lawyers and clients met without the assistance of a mediator, but in practice such four-way talks do not occur frequently unless scheduled through mediation. . . .

Apart from inefficiency and inaccuracy in communication, a lawyer-run negotiation can also create tension in the relationship between lawyer and client. Almost every attorney whom we interviewed attempted to keep clients fully informed of the progress of their cases by sending them copies of all or most correspondence and informing them of any offers received. Yet, lawyers frequently reported that clients felt left out and uninformed. In the episodic, lawyer-run negotiation, clients who play a passive and consultative role may believe that their lawyers are doing little and resent the diminished participation in and control over their case. The direct engagement of parties and concentrated attention to negotiation that mediation provides can thus improve lawyer-client relationships as well as efficiency and communication.

Lawyers also report that participation in mediation permits them to glean additional information that increases their capacity to serve as advisors to and advocates for clients. First, mediation provides attorneys an opportunity for contact with and first-hand assessment of the other party, something that rarely occurs otherwise. Over one-third of the Maine divorce attorneys whom we interviewed commented on this value of the mediation process, often characterizing it as "discovery."

The exposure of lawyers to the other spouse in mediation also helps each attorney to assess that person independent of the potentially inaccurate reports of both their client and the opposing lawyer. The conventional insulation from the other spouse may at times contribute to contentiousness or compromise the capacity of a lawyer to advise her client well. When attorneys cannot "size up" the other party directly, they may be less effective in assessing the other spouse's priorities and needs, a practice widely viewed as essential to effective negotiation.

Typically, arm's-length negotiation leaves little room for divorcing husbands and wives to hear each other out in a relatively safe setting. Either lawyers take over the communication, or direct interactions between the parties are heated and unproductive. Mediation provides a setting for communication between parties that settlement does not, a setting in which parties can and do discuss and explain needs and problems and express anger and disappointment with the other party, not just exchange demands and positions.[345]

Mediation, unlike negotiations, is a dignified process that engages the divorcing parties and gives them a chance to tell their story, not only to their spouse but to someone "official."

A central conclusion from the research about procedural justice is that people value highly the opportunity to voice their grievances and to be heard in a dignified setting. Many Maine lawyers see divorce mediation not only as a way of improving efficiency in negotiation, but also as a way of formalizing and dignifying the process for clients. Lawyer-participation in mediation thus appears to add substantial "value" to lawyer-to-lawyer negotiation.

A by-product of lawyer participation is its effect on lawyers even when not in mediation. By changing the structure for negotiation through the addition of mediation involving parties and attorneys, lawyer behavior may change over time. As discussed above, there is some evidence that Maine lawyers, for example, are significantly more willing to endorse "reaching a settlement fair to both parties" as the goal of negotiation — compared to "getting as much as possible for their client" — than a comparable group of New Hampshire lawyers who had no experience participating in court mandated mediation. Furthermore, the use of the formal legal process — such as discovery requests and motions to compel — declined significantly in Maine after the introduction of mediation while increasing in neighboring New Hampshire. One plausible interpretation of these changes and differences is that Maine

---

[345]Professor Grillo has suggested that anger is best expressed through the lawyer as surrogate or "mouthpiece." Grillo, supra note 2, at 1573 ("The parties' anger is expressed in a formal, contained way through the ritualized behavior of the lawyers.") Neither the typical divorce trial nor the even more typical divorce negotiation, however, provides much room for the lawyer to deliver for the client. Few avenues exist in negotiation — except nasty letters — because a lawyer cannot talk directly with the other spouse if he or she is represented. In addition, our interviews suggest that divorce lawyers generally try to resist voicing client anger themselves because it diminishes their ability to be "reasonable lawyers.". . .Under these circumstances, mediation provides a more likely outlet for expression of anger than either trial or negotiation.

lawyers have learned in mediation to assist clients in achieving their goals in a more cooperative fashion.

2. Mandated Lawyered Mediation and Self-Determination

Maine mandates mediation. Lawyers may not simply select mediation voluntarily to enhance the negotiation process. Requiring lawyer participation in Maine might appear to burden substantially both lawyers and clients. In practice, however, mandatory divorce mediation in Maine permits considerable flexibility and does not appear to undermine free choice regarding settlement.

The general practice in the use of mediation varies from court to court. In some courts, lawyers routinely request mediation soon after filing, while in others local culture encourages mediation requests only when initial efforts at negotiation reveal problems in achieving settlement. Because of its costs, lawyers are less likely to routinely request mediation in cases where the parties have few resources.

From the perspective of clients, mediation in Maine simply appears as another step in the divorce process — often described by lawyers as an important opportunity — rather than as a special burden. In fact, having incorporated mediation into their practices, Maine divorce lawyers report that they typically describe the process, seriously examine settlement options and approaches, and preach mediation's virtues to clients in preparing them to undertake the process. Belief in mediation's potential assistance in negotiation leads eighty-five percent of the Maine divorce lawyers whom we interviewed to request mediation even in cases not involving children. In their vital role as translators and interpreters of the legal process, lawyers convey to their clients a realistic view of the process, but one which emphasizes the opportunities mediation provides rather than the burdens it imposes.

The slight imposition, as perceived by the parties' lawyers, seems even less significant compared with the benefits. Without mandatory mediation, settlement discussions are unlikely to occur as frequently, because both sides — rather than one — have to agree to participate. By requesting mediation in Maine's mandatory system, one side can bring a reluctant party to the negotiation table.

Furthermore, compulsion to participate removes one tactical concern of the party requesting mediation. With mandated mediation, the other side will not view a proposal that the parties seek mediation as a sign of weakness or as a rush to settle. Rather, parties will view such requests as either routine or as a sign that the requesting party wants to proceed to trial and needs to get past the mediation stage.

In addition, lawyers indicate that mandated mediation focuses the lawyers and parties to settle earlier than would otherwise occur. The pressures of managing a law practice, of handling a heavy caseload, and of responding to court deadlines make it difficult for lawyers to pursue sustained efforts to settle a single case. By scheduling mandated mediation, lawyers create a settlement event and deadline. The mediation event may also move indecisive clients to make decisions they have been reluctant to make. Lawyers often request mediation quite early in the case. The scheduled mediation date then prompts case preparation and serious involvement in negotiation.

Finally, required participation brings cases to mediation that profit from the process but would not have gone to mediation in a voluntary system. In fact, the experience of many

Maine lawyers challenge the argument that the parties may know something that the "state" does not about the value of mediation.[368] Attorneys report that they were often mistaken in their predictions about the uselessness of mediation for particular cases. . . .

3. Cost and Lawyer Presence

Does lawyer presence make mediation more costly? Research done in programs without lawyer presence indicates that, on the average, the parties save if they settle through mediation and do not pay more if they attend mediation and do not settle. Some might argue that lawyer presence changes the calculus by making mediation more costly. The Maine lawyers whom we interviewed were almost evenly split on the question of whether mediation increased the costs of divorce.

We think there is a sound argument that the cost on average is about the same for those who undergo mediation under either the "regulatory" approach or the "lawyer-participant" approach. With lawyers present, the sessions can take place early in the case and can address all issues in the divorce. Research in Canada indicates that parties in programs mandating mediation of all issues save costs, whereas no such savings result in programs that mediate only custody issues. Pearson's review of fifteen divorce mediation studies concludes that private programs offering mediation of all divorce issues achieve the greatest cost saving for the parties.

Furthermore, even with lawyers absent, parties incur substantial legal fees connected with mediation. Presumably, fees for consultation before, during, and after mediation (a mean fee of about $1500 per person in one California study) should be lower if lawyers attend.

Mediators are not required to have substantial educational qualifications in Maine, and the mediator's fee is therefore likely to be low. Court mediator fees of $60 per party for the entire mediation in Maine (with the mediator paid $50) compare favorably with fees of about $125 per hour (paid directly to the mediator) in those Florida jurisdictions that refer parties to private mediators who must meet higher qualifications. One private mediation center in California charged an average mediation fee of $2,224 in the late 1980s.

Other cost-related factors deserve mention. When lawyers attend, courts do not need to hold special conferences to assess the case before assignment to mediation, eliminating attendant costs to parties, perhaps including attorney costs. Lawyer attendance renders unnecessary the post-mediation agreement review by the attorney, and the lawyers will not need to advise against signature, thus requiring a costly reconvening of mediation. Attorney presence in mediation may reduce the need for discovery and may narrow the issues, even if the parties do not settle. In Maine, the use of discovery requests and motions to compel for contempt and for temporary support declined significantly after mandatory mediation involving lawyers began. In other words, there is reason to believe that mediation does not simply add a step to an otherwise unaltered litigation or settlement process; instead, mediation involving lawyers changes those processes substantially, making them more efficient and less costly.

---

[368]Grillo: "It is presumptuous to assume that the state has a better idea than the parties themselves about whether mediation will work in their particular case." If settlement rates drop or if the expense of mediation climbs, mandatory mediation may not be worth it, on balance. Thus, courts should monitor their mandatory mediation programs and should change or abandon them when they are not a net benefit or when their cost constitutes a barrier to trial for some parties.

It also seems likely that mediation with lawyers can occur more expeditiously than mediation without them. Lawyers assist in clarifying information, consult with and advise clients on the spot, and help identify unaddressed issues. Absent lawyer participation, mediation experts advise a series of sessions with time for consultation between them. By contrast, Maine divorce cases typically require only a single session.

In sum, the research in Maine offers promise that mandatory mediation, even with lawyers attending, on average does not increase costs and that mandatory mediation does not decrease the possibility of affordable trials.

4. Fairness for Unrepresented Parties

The typical party to a divorce proceeding is represented only if the case is contested. The courts mandate mediation only in contested cases. Because parties are usually represented in contested cases, mediated cases are particularly likely to involve parties with lawyers. A study of three urban domestic relations courts in Ohio indicated that in 247 contested custody cases, about ninety-five percent of the parties had lawyers. In Maine, we estimate from docket records that eighty percent of all mediation cases involved two lawyers. Thus, the nature of selection into mandatory mediation insures that disproportionate numbers of cases involve counsel when compared to the total population of divorce cases. But not all do.

A system for insuring fairness that rests largely on the participation of lawyers, of course, would appear to fall short when parties are unrepresented. Clearly, when lawyers are not representing parties to mediation, they cannot be present to assist them and protect their rights. Although we lack research on this point, we suspect that problems of inequity in bargaining power would be more pronounced and the potential for unfairness greater in negotiations conducted in the absence of a mediator. The mediator can set ground rules, prevent interruption, serve as a drafter, and in other ways moderate the effects of aggressive negotiation on a weaker party. Thus, even weak mediation may be better than leaving the parties alone to work out a settlement, perhaps with one party negotiating, pro se, with the other party's lawyer.

In addition, the regular presence of lawyers in mediation sessions may provide training, education, and a regular check on inappropriate mediator conduct that may in turn improve the quality and fairness of mediation in cases where attorneys are not present. Lawyers might effectively contribute to a system of supervision and quality control of mediators that would be far more effective than rules and qualifications in rooting out ineffectiveness. As experienced users of many mediators, lawyers' confidential judgments of mediator competence could be a far better device for assessing quality than a collection of responses from divorcing parties who only have the one experience to judge.

Still, the research provides little guidance about whether the greater prospect of unfairness for pro se litigants argues in favor of giving those litigants an opportunity to "opt out" of mandatory mediation. The pro se party who opts out would be left to his or her own devices. Because the most likely alternative to mediation is negotiation, those who opt out would presumably face negotiating with the other party's lawyer or directly with the other party. If they are not permitted to opt out, however, the "regulatory" approach is not likely to assure fair mediation. Furthermore, the regulation is likely to be costly for the bulk of the mediation parties who have lawyers. Thus, an "opt out" provision for pro se parties may be the best alternative for the present.

5. Is This "Real Mediation"?

To the divorce mediation traditionalists, lawyers attend judicially-hosted settlement conferences but not mediation sessions, and Maine mediation may thus seem more like facilitated pretrial settlement conferences and less like mediation sessions. These traditionalists may say that sessions involving lawyer participation do not constitute "real mediation.". . .

Ultimately, the needs of divorcing families and the indicia of fairness in the process ought to be key factors in defining mediation procedures. Lawmakers should discard traditional mediation, even if it seems more "real" or satisfying to the mediator, if it fails to serve the families' needs or ensure fairness. The courts call upon mediators to serve these aims rather than to create satisfying professional goals for themselves. Thus, the value of the procedures should not depend on whether mediation professionals view them as producing "real mediation."

CONCLUSION

Critics and proponents of mandatory divorce mediation recognize potential for unfairness in its use. They should also realize that the remedy is that lawyers should participate, along with their clients, in mandatory divorce mediation. Alternative approaches — the "voluntary participation" and "regulatory" approaches — are ineffective and costly. Furthermore, the assumptions underlying these dominant approaches are myths.

With lawyers present and participating, the concern for fairness no longer justifies heavy regulation or confining mediation to voluntary participants. Lawyer participation in the mediation sessions permits intervention on behalf of clients and buffers pressures to settle. Lawyers may also counsel clients to moderate extreme demands. In addition, once lawyers become accustomed to mediation, lawyer involvement in mandated mediation does not appear to prevent the meaningful participation of parties or inhibit emotional expression between spouses.

With mediation covering a broad scope of issues and with lawyers in attendance, the parties probably will pay more for lawyers and less for mediators. Overall costs, however, will probably remain unchanged because settlements are more likely to be comprehensive and less likely to fall victim to negative reviews by a non-participating lawyer. In addition, mediation with lawyers may reduce discovery costs. What the parties will get is likely to be a fair process in which lawyers intervene to protect against pressures from the other party, the process, or the mediator. They are also likely to get a more spontaneous mediation, unfettered by a web of regulation or defensive mediators. They will enjoy, as compared with parties in a system without mandatory mediation, a greater likelihood of having the opportunity to express themselves and to listen to discussions regarding matters of utmost concern. About one-half the time, they can expect to secure a settlement earlier in the process than would otherwise be the case.

Bringing the lawyers into mandatory mediation will permit the repeal of numerous statutes and a reduction in court rules. Furthermore, it will ease fairness concerns as a reason not to compel participation in mediation. The revised regulatory approach preserves the widespread use and flexibility of the mediation process without undue risk of unfairness.

E. Duty of Mediators to Promote Fair Results

1. Scott H. Hughes, *Elizabeth's Story: Exploring Power Imbalances in Divorce Mediation*, 8 Geo. J. Legal Ethics 553, 584-595 (1995)*

. . . [H]ave any cogent and coherent statutes, court rules, or ethical standards emerged to guide mediators in dealing with power imbalances in divorce mediation? Although the voices are many, they infrequently deal with the issue of power imbalance and, when they do, treat it only vaguely, thus providing little or no guidance. . . . In addition to statutes and rules authorizing mediation, ethical standards have been promulgated by the American Bar Association (ABA), the Society of Professionals in Dispute Resolution (SPIDR), the Association of Family and Conciliation Courts, and the Academy of Family Mediators. More recently, a committee composed of representatives of the ABA, SPIDR, and the American Arbitration Association released a set of standards for all types of mediation.

The first questions that should be asked when examining these statutes, rules, and guidelines is whether they create a duty on the part of the mediator to deal with power imbalances. Only the California Family Code addresses this issue directly. It provides that the mediator conduct negotiations "in such a way as to equalize power relationships between the parties." One other rule and two standards require "balanced" dialogue but provide little context or meaning. In Iowa, attorneys acting as family mediators have a duty to assure a "balanced dialogue and must attempt to diffuse any manipulative or intimidating negotiation techniques utilized by either of the participants." This language is echoed by the standards from the ABA and the Conciliation Courts.

It is not clear if these requirements for balanced dialogue are merely procedural requirements or if they lead to some substantive standard. If the duty is procedural, the mediator can fulfill the duty by providing roughly equal time for each participant to speak, by preventing interruptions, and so forth. Any substantive effect that the fulfillment of this procedural duty has on the mediated agreement would be purely coincidental. The Iowa Rules and the ABA Standards, however, are prefaced with the mediator's duty to suspend or terminate the mediation whenever continuation of the process would harm one or more of the participants. Of course, harm could result if the process were to go awry, but limiting this prefatory language to a procedural protection would impose an unnecessarily narrow definition on the phrase "continuation of the process." In that phrase, "process" is equivalent to "mediation," thereby containing both a procedural and a substantive dimension. This reading results in a substantive standard for the balancing of the power between the parties.

This first group of standards and rules provide the only language relating directly to the issue of power imbalances. The California Family Code provides a seemingly uniform duty that spreads across the entire continuum of power imbalances even though the means for implementing the duty are not delineated. Several criticisms can be leveled at the California provision: it provides no guidance on how much balancing is required, on what is necessary should balancing not be possible, and on what should be done if the parties are headed toward

---

an unfair agreement resulting from a severe power imbalance. More specifically, it calls upon mediators to work toward a general balance of power between the parties no matter what the relative balance of power. A power balancing effort is all that is necessary no matter what the results. All parties are benefitted equally, even those in the greatest predicament who need much more help than others. All weaker parties are benefitted to the extent that the power balancing is successful but are prejudiced to the extent that the power balancing is unsuccessful. It does not require termination if the parties are headed toward an unfair agreement. For all of this criticism, it is the best provision relating to the problem of power imbalances in divorce mediation. Unfortunately, it is just not as complete as it could be.

On the other hand, the Iowa Rules, the ABA, and the Conciliation Court Standards, although requiring termination for unconscionable agreements, imply that only minimum effort which will move the parties away from an unfair agreement is necessary and, when that has been accomplished, the duty has been fulfilled. Under these rules, two sets of weaker parties are severely prejudiced: those that are only minimally capable of protecting themselves and those that are incapable of protecting themselves, but through the efforts of the mediator, are rendered minimally capable. The first set, for which no duty exists, ends up with an agreement that, although not unfair, is very nearly so. For the second set, the mediator leads them away from an unfair agreement and then abandons them. To these poor souls, an eye-awakening termination may be the brighter prospect.

Although no specific language concerning power imbalances exists beyond the California statute, the indirect references in the Iowa Rules, and the ABA and Conciliation Courts Standards, the existence of a duty to deal with power imbalances can be extrapolated from both general and specific provisions found in other statutes, rules, and standards. This is so even though the strength of mediation is based upon the self-determination of the participants and the fact that the mediator should not coerce either party, make a substantive decision for any participant, or "direct the decision of the mediation participants based upon the mediator's interpretation of the law as applied to the facts of the situation."

With regard to general provisions, the standards promulgated by the Joint Committee and SPIDR recognize an obligation that extends beyond self-determination and the pure self-interests of the participants. The Preface written by the Joint Committee states that the "Standards of Conduct for mediators are intended [among other things] to promote public confidence in mediation as a process for resolving disputes." While SPIDR, in a section entitled "The Settlement and Its Consequences," stated that the mediator "must be satisfied that agreements in which he or she has participated will not impugn the integrity of the process." Both of these provisions create an obligation to the community or society as a whole. The SPIDR provision looks to the end result of the mediation, the agreement, as the sine qua non from which integrity will be derived.

If the keystone to this new portal to dispute resolution was the process alone, there would be no reason to examine the substance of the agreement or to be concerned with the public confidence. The process alone could be examined, and from it integrity and public confidence could be derived. If the parties reached an agreement, so be it. The sum and substance of it would not be of concern to the public if the process remained intact. However, by looking at mediation as a whole and at the process in particular through the lens of the agreement, the mediator is forced to examine the quality of the agreement in order to judge mediation and the process of mediation. The language contained in the Joint Committee and the SPIDR

Standards require it. If the agreement is to be examined, then some attention must be paid to power imbalances between the parties.

We now turn our attention from general, prefatory language to specific provisions contained in the statutes, rules, and standards. The specific language focuses on three areas: (1) capacity of the parties to mediate; (2) impact of the mediation on the parties; and (3) the nature of any agreement resulting from the mediation. The first two, by aiming at the parties, only indirectly create a duty to focus on the substantive agreement reached, while the third creates such a duty directly.

Concerning the capacity of the parties, the mediator is often called upon to assess the status of the participants and to terminate the mediation if the parties lack the ability to participate in the mediation in a meaningful manner, or in good faith, or if one party is simply not "capable in participating in informed negotiations." Also, the mediator shall terminate the proceeding for certain types of incapacities, such as intoxication, or when a participant is irrational or exhibits impaired judgment.

Baruch Bush, in his Proposed Standards of Practice for Mediators, examines the capacity of the parties in order to make a determination concerning mediability of the dispute:

> Where a party appears to be acting under complete coercion or fear, or without capacity to comprehend the process and issues and make decisions, the mediator is obligated to explore this question and, unless the party in question objects, discontinue the mediation. If that party insists on continuing, the mediator may do so, but should continue to raise the question and check for willingness to proceed.

This provision presents two problems. First, by requiring "complete coercion or fear" before a response is sanctioned, it presents an unreasonably high, but still unnecessarily vague standard for measuring capacity. What is the definition of that phrase? How is a mediator to implement this provision? Second, this provision allows the party to trump the determination of the mediator by objecting, thereby preventing the mediator from discontinuing the mediation. That is followed by the contradictory provision that, if the party "insists on continuing, the mediator may do so."

All of the provisions that measure the capacity of the parties to mediate result from an altruistic vision of mediation similar to the prohibition against mediating abuse cases. The intent is to protect parties who are unable to fend for themselves. Unfortunately, they create a measure that is extremely hard to define and implement. Beyond "complete coercion," asking the mediator to determine "meaningful" or "good faith" participation requires nothing less than speculation for a mediator who has just met or has extremely limited exposure to the parties. This is especially true for attorney-mediators who are singularly unqualified to make a determination of this kind.

With regard to the impact of the mediation upon the parties, under the ABA Standards and provisions from Indiana, Iowa, and Oklahoma, the mediator shall terminate the mediation if he or she believes that it will result in "harm" to a participant. Under the Wisconsin statutes governing family mediation, the mediator may terminate if there is "evidence which indicates one of the parties' health or safety will be endangered if mediation is not terminated."

Like the determination of capacity, the measuring of harm to a party suffers from similar criticisms of vagueness and speculation. Who should be the one to determine fairness? Should the mediation agreement be fair to the mediator or need it be fair only to the parties themselves? The principle of self-determination has already been stated in the guidelines. If the parties to the mediation were the only judges of the fairness of the agreement, this would be nothing more then a redundant statement of self-determination. If procedural fairness was the responsibility of the mediator, and substantive fairness was the responsibility of the parties, there would be no reason to identify the need for self-determination. Fairness, especially when listed co-equally with self-determination, must represent substantive fairness as determined by the mediator.

The third and final category of specific language relates to the agreement and not to the parties themselves. The ABA, Conciliation Courts, and the Academy of Family Mediator Standards all contain identical language: "If the mediator believes that . . . a reasonable agreement is unlikely, the mediator may suspend or terminate mediation and should encourage the parties to seek appropriate help." Only two states have adopted any statutes or rules of this nature.

The SPIDR Standards combine an examination of the agreement with a determination of the impact on the parties: "If the neutral is concerned about the possible consequences of a proposed agreement, and the needs of the parties dictate, the neutral must inform the parties of that concern. In adhering to this standard, the neutral may find it advisable . . . to withdraw from the case." Although the "needs of the parties" would clearly refer to some examination of the capacities of the parties or the impact of an agreement, this phrase, unfortunately, has been left undefined.

Finally, Florida has created a grab-bag of items to monitor, including capacity and impact concerns along with contract terms: "The mediator shall not knowingly assist the parties in reaching an agreement which for reasons such as fraud, duress, overreaching, the absence of bargaining ability, or unconscionability would be unenforceable."

Unfortunately, most statutes and rules are so general that the mediator receives no guidance as to his or her proper role concerning power imbalances. As an example, Delaware defines a mediator as one who shall "assist[] and facilitate[] two or more parties to a controversy in reaching a mutually acceptable resolution of the controversy." In Maine, a workers compensation mediator "is not bound by the rules of evidence or procedure, but shall make inquiry in the manner best calculated to ascertain the substantial rights of the parties and carry out the [spirit of the act]." These statutes not only fail to consider any potential power imbalances, but they place few other constraints (other than confidentiality) upon the mediator. Further, in Delaware, the only language about termination states that the mediator may terminate if there is no agreement. Does this imply that the mediator may not terminate if there is movement toward an agreement, no matter what its nature? This is unclear. Under the Minnesota Civil Mediation Act, an agreement is not binding unless it contains a statement that "the mediator has no duty to protect their [the parties'] interests or provide them with information about their legal rights [and] signing a mediated settlement agreement may adversely affect their legal rights. . . ."

In answer to the question posed at the beginning of this section, no cogent or coherent standards have emerged to guide mediators in dealing with power imbalances. The California Family Code comes the closest by clearly creating a duty to deal with power imbalances but suffers from many other infirmities. As a beginning, the duty created by the California provision should be combined with the language from the standards of the ABA, Conciliation Courts, and the Academy of Family Mediators, which calls upon mediators to take some action if the parties are not headed toward a reasonable agreement. This combination would create a uniform duty to balance power across the continuum and also require termination should the parties, despite the power balancing efforts of the mediator, be headed toward an unfair agreement. The task then remains to explore the frontier of fairness and chart its borders.

VI. FULFILLING THE DUTY

Several conclusions can be drawn from the foregoing discussion. First, mediation is most effective in situations in which ongoing relationships need to be preserved. Second, without some drastic changes to mediation, "[e]ven where settlement is possible, it will likely preserve the relative balance of power between the parties." Third, mediation may be inappropriate between parties of unequal bargaining power. Fourth, mediation is most appropriate in divorce cases with only a moderate level of conflict between parties possessing reasonable negotiating skills. Finally, the problem of power imbalances may be especially acute in divorce, thereby calling for its exclusion from mediation in certain circumstances.

The first conclusion is the most damning. While mediation works best to preserve relationships, the arena of divorce mediation is constructed around the dismantling of the marital relationship. The parties must divide assets originally obtained with no thought of degree of ownership. They must establish separate homes after spending the length of the marriage joined in one. They must deal with a variety of other issues in a manner diametrically opposed to the previous orientation. This is all overlaid with the emotional difficulties entailed in any divorce.

Divorce mediation represents the single area of mediation in which power imbalances are the most prevalent. Spouses are often dysfunctional, and the greater the dysfunctionality, the greater the potential for severe power imbalances. In this arena, we are dealing with quintessential power imbalances. Without more, mediation will likely preserve the relative imbalances of power.

When spouses divorce, they are disentangling themselves from the single, most predominant relationship our society has to offer. For each party, the relationship has been the biggest presence in his or her life. At the same time they are breaking up their relationship, divorcing spouses must deal with societally imprinted images that sanction marriage and subtly condemn divorce. The purposes of other forms of mediation are to repair existing ties of an ongoing relationship or to increase the number of ties that will lead to a stable and lasting agreement. Divorce mediation drastically reduces or, in the case of childless couples or where ongoing support will not be an issue, eliminates existing ties altogether. This can only have a destabilizing effect. It tends to reduce mediation to relying on altruism of the powerful party, the results of which can hardly be depended upon. Competitive bargainers will have no compunction not to take advantage of the situation. This points strongly towards a conclusion that divorce mediation is inappropriate in many instances. . . .

2. Comments and Questions

a. Fairness concerns are particularly acute in the divorce context because non-economic factors are far more important than in other circumstances where mediation is used. (A possible exception is victim-offender mediation, discussed at chapter 9, section C.) To what extent is Hughes' discussion of general applicability, and to what extent are his arguments specific to the divorce context?

b. The best way to think about "fair" or "equitable" results is in terms of their opposites; *i.e.*, the avoidance of "unfair" or "inequitable" results. This approach provides more useful guidance for the working mediator, whose assigned task is to serve as a neutral assisting (apparently competent) parties in reaching a result acceptable to both of them.

This argument is analogous to that made regarding the meaning of "good faith" as being the absence of "bad faith." See Chapter 16, section D. Of course, any time one establishes a standard there will be cases that are close to the line, and reasonable people can differ about what should be done in specific instances.

c. Note that the McEwen, Rogers & Maiman divorce mediation article in section D argues that the best way to ensure fairness is to have counsel for both parties present at the mediation, which at the same time should improve the mediation process by freeing the mediator from fairness concerns. (Of course, there will remain many mediations where neither or only one party is represented by counsel.) Does the fairness problem in divorce mediation present an additional reason for the presence of counsel?

Chapter 9

Mediation Applications

CASE STUDY

In January of 1980, Walter Salmon and Michael Meinhard crêated a joint venture to rent prime real estate on Fifth Avenue in New York. The joint venture agreement provided that Meinhard and Salmon would each contribute $3,000,000 to lease property from Louis Berry for fifteen years. They used the property to run a hotel called the Fitz Carlton. Salmon and Meinhard each collected 50% of the net profits during the entire term of the lease. Similarly, the agreement provided that each party was to equally bear the burden of losses.

During the first five years of the joint venture both Salmon and Meinhard managed the property. Unfortunately, the Fitz Carlton sustained significant losses, and each party paid out of his own pocket equally in order to cover those losses and to continue running the property. Later, when Meinhard stepped out of his managing role, the profits became large, producing a rich return for both Meinhard and Salmon. With Salmon as the manager, the two joint ventures were happy.

In 1994, near the end of the fifteen year lease, Louis Berry, the lessor of the property, became interested in releasing the property. Berry, a New York real estate legend, also owned property adjacent to both sides of the Fitz Carlton. He had a plan to lease the entire tract for a long term to someone who would destroy the buildings then existing, and put up another in their place.

In September 1994, with less than four months of the lease to run, Berry approached the defendant Salmon. Berry and Salmon cut a deal. That deal created a new lease to Salmon individually for the entire tract of land for twenty years. This combined property would be used to create a new shopping mall called, "the Galleria." As a hotel, the leased property brought Salmon and Meinhard $55,000 a month; however, as "the Galleria," the property would bring in $350,000 to $500,000 a month.

Even though Salmon and Berry's negotiations took place before the first lease (and therefore joint venture) expired, Salmon had told Meinhard nothing about this new deal with Berry. Neither Berry or Salmon informed Meinhard of even the bare existence of a project. Meinhard did not discover the deal between Salmon and Berry until February of 1995, when the new lease was an accomplished fact. Meinhard then made a demand on Salmon that the new lease be held in trust as an asset of the joint venture. Salmon rejected Meinhard's demand and Meinhard filed this suit for breach of partnership duty.

A. Introduction

This chapter presents a series of discrete examples of the mediation process in action. The purpose is to consider the use of mediation in a wide variety of settings. These settings for the use of mediation are the following:

1) bioethical disputes (Montefiore Hospital);
2) criminal offenders and their victims;
3) farmer-debtors and their creditors; and
4) major commercial disputes.

You should look for commonalites and differences among these topics, for they will teach you about what is fundamental to mediation and what depends upon setting and circumstances. One of the truly fundamental things to know about mediation is that much depends on setting and circumstances. The chapter closes with a consideration of need and value government regulation of mediators by Nancy Rogers and Craig McEven (respectively, a lawyer and a social scientist), two of the leading ADR thinkers and scholars. This topic is examined further in Chapter 19, section B.

B. Mediation of Bioethical Disputes

1. Comments and Questions

a. The Montefiore model for mediating bioethical disputes that follows is the result of a process of creating an initial model, using it, and then refining the model based on this experience. It will continue to be a work in progress, with adjustments and improvements made to reflect further knowledge and changing circumstances. The design of dispute resolution systems is the topic of Chapter 21.

b. Notice the emphasis on accurate observation of facts, and that facts change over time. Note also that the same facts may be subject to quite different interpretations by differently situated individuals or interests — patients and their families on the one hand, and medical personnel on the other.

c. How does the mediation process address the knowledge imbalance about medical matters between patients and physicians? Is the mediator an educator as well as a neutral? Are there lessons to be learned here that will allow mediation to work well even when there are power imbalances between the parties?

CASE STUDY

Emily K. is an 80 year old widow who was diagnosed with Alzheimer's disease four years ago. The Alzheimer's has progressed to the point where Emily is bedridden and unable to meaningfully communicate or control her bodily functions. There is no effective treatment for Alzheimer's disease and Emily's condition is expected to gradually worsen over the course of the next several years. Before the onset of the disease, Emily was known as proud woman, proper, and fiercely independent.

The severity of Emily's condition makes it impossible for her to feed herself or to be fed by mouth. Because of this, her son Scott gave Emily's doctor consent to insert a feeding tube into Emily's stomach so that she could receive nutrition and hydration. Emily is expected to live for several more years with the feeding tube in place. Her other child, Rick, who lives out of town, was not consulted about inserting the feeding tube. Because he feels that his mother would rather "die with dignity" than remain in her present state Rick feels that she should not be given nutrition and hydration through the tube. Rick has pointed out to Scott that before their mother was diagnosed, she told both of them that if she were ever in a terminally unconscious state she would want to die. Although Scott feels uncomfortable with his mother's present condition, he feels a duty to keep her alive and does not want to take responsibility for "killing" her.

Emily is expected to remain bedridden, uncommunicative, and completely dependent for many years. Scott continues to visit and support her care. Rick is becoming increasingly frustrated by the situation and is seeking legal counsel to be named his mother's guardian. Rick hopes that if he is named his mother's guardian he can then fulfill his mother's wishes to die with dignity.

2. Nancy N. Dubler & Leonard J. Marcus, MEDIATING BIOETHICAL DISPUTES 33-58 (1994) (United Hospital Fund of New York)*

The Stages of Mediation: The Montefiore Model

What follows are process guidelines for management of disputes and conflicts. As we analyzed actual cases and developed our model, we found it helpful to divide the process into three stages.

I. Assessment

1. Discuss the broad contours of the case with the person requesting the consultation.
2. Convene a meeting of all involved medical staff to establish the medical facts.
3. If necessary, trigger an ancillary process to assist in reaching consensus.
4. Once there has been relative agreement on the medical facts, proceed to discuss the options for care.

*Reprinted with permission.

II. Development
1. Determine whether or not the patient is decisionally capable.
2. Ensure that the patient and the family understand the medical facts, including the concept of medical uncertainty.
3. Establish the decision history of the case.
4. Identify the salient legal and ethical principles that are relevant to a resolution of the case and begin a discussion with the staff, patient, and family.

III. Resolution
1. Identify finally who has the authority to decide.
2. Determine whether the patient or the family needs other supports in order to reach a conclusion.
3. Identify the principled solution that has emerged from the discussion.
4. Make certain that the solution agreed upon actually happens.

The most important tasks of the mediator at the three stages of mediation are, in the assessment phase, to investigate and characterize the conflict, identify the parties, and reach agreement on the medical facts; in the development phase, to distinguish and clarify the relevant ethical and legal principles, and ensure that all the parties understand the facts of the conflict and the rights of the parties in the same way; and, in the resolution phase, to assist the patient and family in thinking through the medical options, help them to articulate their values and preferences to caregivers, and ensure that the agreed-upon solution is in fact carried out according to the agreement.

Although these stages appear to be distinct and sequential, they may, in the complex reality of a case, be occurring in some other order, or even simultaneously. Establishing the facts may proceed at the same time as some of the early contacts with the patient and the family, for example, and staff education can take place at any stage of the mediation. These stages should therefore be considered a somewhat artificial disaggregation of the whole.

During all stages of mediation, however, the mediator has certain overriding obligations that arise from the intimidating nature of the medical setting and the tremendous imbalance of power and education that separates patients and families from staff. The mediator must "manage the negotiation"; prevent the staff from "ganging up" on the patient and the family; provide the "time out" and "decisionally neutral space" that permit a principled resolution to emerge; and act in a neutral fashion regarding the resolution. The mediator can do this by not being invested in the outcome, by facilitating the discussion among all of the parties, and by identifying the sources of the conflict and maximizing the options for resolution.

The Assessment Stage

Step 1. Discuss the broad contours of the case with the person requesting a consultation. This initial discussion should identify the patient, elicit a preliminary notion of the patient's decisional capacity (or at least identify the fact that capacity is at issue), determine the existence or nonexistence of family and the family's level of involvement, and explore the disputed issue as perceived by the referring staff member.

Step 2. Convene a meeting of all involved medical staff to establish the medical facts, that is, determine whether there is consensus about the medical history, present condition, and possible prognoses.

There is some controversy about the sequencing and feasibility of this step. In some nonacademic institutions where physicians are only sporadically present on the hospital premises, it may be difficult to schedule a time for all of the medical staff to meet. Nonetheless, the general agreement of the project participants was that the task of establishing the facts is so critical to the next stages of the process, and to any intelligent discussion with the patient and family, that the mediator should expend substantial efforts in pursuit of this initial caregiver meeting.

Although many clinical ethics consultants regard an early meeting with the patient or family as equally important, in our experience a preliminary meeting with the staff is essential to understanding the history and present condition of the patient, and a necessary precondition to discussing the medical and ethical options. We maintained this sequential staging of fact finding even as our practice evolved to a more self-conscious dispute resolution model. If the first meeting is with the caregiving staff, however, a meeting with the patient and family should follow shortly.

Some caregivers will be so uncomfortable with medical uncertainty that they will react with hostility to patients and family members. If the mediator chooses to meet separately with the parties, he or she should explain the reasons to both, label the separate meetings as the start of the mediating-consultation process, and alert both parties to the need to meet together as soon as possible to begin to talk face-to-face about the resolution.

At this first meeting of the care team the mediator should:

- ask the attending physician, primary nurse, and most involved social worker to present the case;
- identify the parties to the conflict from among the staff;
- begin to gather data on whether the patient is perceived as decisionally capable or whether surrogate decision making is contemplated;
- if family members are involved, determine who has been most involved until the time of the consultation;
- if no family members are involved, and if the patient is not capacitated, determine whether the particular service has special provisions for identifying the interests and protecting the rights of incapacitated patients who are without surrogates.

Sometimes establishing the medical facts requires gathering information about the patient that is missing from the medical file and unknown to the staff. It may require special tests or examinations. For example, determining that a patient is brain dead requires that attending neurologists conduct particular examinations according to a preestablished protocol. If these tests have not been done, the staff's general opinion that the patient is brain dead does not establish this as a fact.

Establishing the medical facts requires as much of a process as constructing an intervention plan. Issues of hierarchical standing among and within departments in the medical center come into play here. In the attempt to establish the medical facts, the mediator must try to understand the underlying tensions among the staff and the dynamics of the particular medical service. Medical centers are composed of a series of separate freestanding fiefdoms, all with particular histories and working styles that affect how the "facts of the case" will be established. And who arrives at the facts makes a difference as well. The patient's current condition may appear in one way when the physician reviews the tests and numbers, and quite another when the nurses are surveyed.

"Medical facts" can be defined, therefore, as consensus agreements among the staff regarding the meaning of the narrative medical history, the present data, and the observations of staff regarding the patient's improvement or deterioration. For the purposes of mediation, a medical fact is an interpretation of data in a moment of time that considers the patient in light of the overall history of the illness. Thus, the shorthand for a medical fact may be, "If all agree, call it a fact." This may be an unsatisfactory epistemological explanation, but it must suffice in medicine, where uncertainty is often unresolvable.

The identification of facts also permits the identification of areas of uncertainty, unresolvable areas of disagreement, and points on which more data could be dispositive. Always note, however, that medical situations (unless the patient is dead) are always evolving; facts are always changing. New stages of mediation must always begin, therefore, by establishing the salient medical facts that have emerged since the last meeting and interpreting these facts in the context of the patient's present medical status.

Step 3. If necessary, trigger an ancillary process to assist in reaching consensus. Sometimes the level of disagreement about the medical facts is extreme, or different readings of the same data produce opposing interpretations. In these cases, the mediator must take additional action to help reach consensus. Interventions that project participants identified as helpful include:

1. Assembling the bioethics committee, or a subset of the committee, to see whether new players in a multidisciplinary setting can open new avenues of questioning and agreement.
2. Involving the medical director or some other medical or administrative authority who might convene all of the parties and impose an administrative reading of the medical facts; as a variant, the consultant-mediator might ask that the case be referred to the Serious Incident Committee, or some other committee within the institution, which would be empowered to arrive at a working set of facts for the case. (Both of these solutions demonstrate arguably the failure of the mediative process, but the obligation of the mediator to reach a timely solution may demand such immediate action in this realm in order to facilitate the rest of the process.)
3. If the relevant service has regularly scheduled rounds or conferences, asking for the patient to be presented as the basis for discussion by the full staff.
4. Asking for a literature search.

These initial stages of the mediation process vary enormously in their intellectual and administrative complexity. Project participants found that in many mediations, simply bringing the staff together or arranging a meeting among the staff, the patient, and the family permitted the identification and resolution of disagreements. Only the most difficult cases, often those with long histories, required the addition of administrative deciders for this limited purpose. In any case, however, the involved staff, either by itself or with other individuals or committees, must decide on the facts before the process can proceed.

Step 4. Once there has been relative agreement on the medical facts, the two sides can proceed to discuss the options for care.

The medical facts, supplemented and interpreted by the medical provider's training, skill, and judgment, provide the basis for prognosis; prognosis forms the basis for identifying options for care; and the specific options form the basis for mediating various approaches to the appropriate plan of care for the patient.

At this juncture, the issue of patient capacity—the patient's ability to consent to or refuse care—becomes critical. For patients without such capacity the issues are particularly complex, as the appropriate surrogate and the approved process must both be identified.

Finally, before moving on to the next stage, the mediator must:

1. Determine whether or not there are time constraints in the case. If, for example, one of the treatment options requires an immediate decision in order to preclude some medical catastrophe, the usual process of mediation might be truncated by the demand of the intervention. . . .
2. Determine whether it is the personal philosophy of one of the caregivers, most likely but not always one of the physicians, that is generating the conflict. Some physicians have principled personal positions that preclude certain types of medical actions. . . .
3 Decide how to begin the mediation. . . .

The Development Stage

In this stage, the mediator/ethicist begins to work intensively both with the staff and with the patient and family, if they have not been involved before. In a variation of the caucus procedure, the mediator may work, either initially or over time, with both groups separately as a way of lowering the intimidation factor for the patient and family. It is at this stage that the expertise of the mediator in the bioethical, legal, and ethical literature, and in the concepts and process of bioethical analysis becomes central. . . .

Step 1. Determine whether or not the patient is decisionally capable. (This process should actually begin in the first stage but may carry over to the second.)

If the patient is capable, the patient has the legal right to decide about his or her own care. The patient has the right to make wise or foolish decisions. The mediator should be aware, however, that among the reasons for patient refusals of recommended care intervention is misunderstanding about the nature and cause of the condition and about the quality of the intervention. Although capable adult patients have the right to choose whether to consent to or refuse care, many patients cede this authority to others in their family. The fact that a patient possesses a right does not necessarily mean that he or she will choose to exercise it alone without the consultation, support, and participation of loved ones. . . .

Step 2. Ensure that the patient and the family understand the medical facts, the implications of those facts, the options for future intervention, and the likely result of non-intervention.

Again, the use of caucuses and private discussions may be necessary to help the family or patient to articulate their questions, their positions, and their values and preferences. The overwhelming phalanx of white-coated professionals who ordinarily confront patients and families is always intimidating and often disempowering. Providing the patient and family with space and room for quiet contemplation may permit them to regain emotional composure; better understand the facts, implications, and options (diagnosis, prognosis, and alternatives); decide which of their family members are central to the discussions and decisions and arrange for them to be present; and establish how they are going to proceed with the process of decision making.

Ensure that the patient and family understand the concept of medical uncertainty. The notion of medical uncertainty is central to all medical decision making and to discussions of prognosis. Non-providers, however, are unaccustomed to the concept, and little is done to acquaint them with the central place of uncertainty in the practice of medicine. Many providers present the options for care as if each one were as clear and unambiguous as following a major highway on a road map. Project participants stressed that one of the mediator's most important tasks is to help patients and families understand the uncertainty that surrounds diagnosis and treatment as a precondition to considering options in the decisions about care. . . .

Step 3. Establish the decision history of the case. This is a particularly important step if the conflict is a mature one that has been going on for some time and that has a history of its own. This is most likely to occur with patients transferred from long-term care, or with those for whom discharge planning has been especially difficult or who have had a difficult and lengthy course of care in the hospital.

Step 4. Identify the salient legal and ethical principles that are relevant to a resolution of the case and begin a discussion with the staff, patient, and family.

The notion of bioethics consultation-mediation developed in this report sees individual mediation efforts as a part of the ongoing education program for the staff of a medical center. The goal of any mediation is to provide a principled solution for the case at hand and to provide the basis for like solutions in similar cases in the future. It is critical that the staff understand the reasons for the resolution and that they agree to the wisdom and the justice of the outcome or at least understand the remaining disagreements. . . .

The training of some of the permanent staff in the principled resolution of bioethical conflicts is particularly important. The special characteristics of most medical centers, the sensitive nature of their functioning, the general fear of strangers and of malpractice suits, and the delicate nature of any particular dilemma discourage the possibility of many outsiders gaining access to or being retained by the medical center as mediators. Thus, training of existing staff should be ongoing. . . .

The Resolution Stage

The overriding goal of bioethics mediation, and the characteristic that partially distinguishes it from other sorts of alternative dispute resolution, is that the outcome in any particular case is constrained by the relevant legal and ethical principles, making bioethics mediation a variation of rights-based rather than interest-based mediation. . . .

Step 1. Identify finally who has the authority to decide. In many cases identifying the family as the "decider" and helping the family to process the decision may be the guts of the mediation. Sometimes the family's power will be demonstrated by a health care power of attorney or proxy. Most often, however, the state law on surrogate choice will turn to the family when the patient is no longer capable. . . .

Step 2. If the patient or the family is the identified decider, determine whether the patient or the family needs other supports in order to reach a conclusion. For example, the patient or family might need additional social service support or assistance from the psychiatry consultation liaison service or the bioethics committee. . . .

Step 3. Identify the "principled solution" that has emerged from the discussion. Whereas the mediator must always remain neutral regarding the actual outcome of any case, the boundaries of the inquiry must be set by certain ethical principles and legal rules. There is a finite catechism that contains most of the invariable rules, including the following:

- Patients who are capable of making health care decisions are free to consent to or to refuse care even when the result of that refusal is death.
- Surrogate decisions for patients who do not have the capacity to decide for themselves must proceed according to the law of the state; ethical guidelines for surrogate deciders generally indicate that they should follow explicit directives, then be guided by concepts of substituted judgment, and finally appeal to notions of best interest if information relevant to the particular patient is lacking.
- Parents are free to consent to care for their children but are not equally free to refuse care; parental attempts to refuse care that providers state is vital to the well-being of the child may be presented to a court based on the doctrine of medical neglect. . . .

The fact that "the answer" can be assumed or intuited at the outset does not abrogate the need for the process or dictate the particular configuration of any individual solution. Preexisting notions of appropriate outcome are only part of the final resolution for a number of reasons. Even if fixed rules were held to determine outcome, the massive ambiguity and uncertainty that surround many care situations effectively preclude any judgment before specific investigation. . . . Simple cases tend to grow complex as they unfold. The process of mediating bioethical disputes provides the opportunity for staff, patients, and family members to vent their fears, articulate their concerns, and share their sorrows, all pieces of a principled resolution.

As important as any of these considerations is the commitment of the mediator to neutrality as "fairness of process" as well as neutrality as "unpredetermined outcome." The first requires that all parties be permitted a fair forum for expressing personal positions—a forum that is not dominated by any member of the administrative or medical staff. This commitment to procedural justice can be as determinative as the relevant ethical principles and legal rules in reaching any particular resolution.

Step 4. Make certain that the solution agreed upon actually happens. This may require as little as a note in the medical chart setting forth the substance of the mediation and the bioethical consultation. It may, however, require some further supervision by the mediator. Especially in a dynamic case, it may require the mediator to be in touch with the care team to help it and the patient or family address the changing ethical contours of the case.

Establishing the Medical Facts

All bioethics consultants, no matter what their preferred process, agree that "good ethics begins with good facts." Medical "facts," in general, are difficult to establish. The very concept of "differential diagnosis" implies multiple possible explanations for the etiology of certain conditions. Often there is disagreement about the origin of a medical condition, the present meaning, and the likely prognosis. So, for example, the patient's kidney function may be less than optimal but may either be improving or worsening. It may be that a new medication has caused the problem and that when the medication has been stopped, the ability of the kidney to function more or less normally will return. Or it may be that the kidney itself is damaged, or that its lack of function reflects problems with other organ systems. The reason for kidney failure will determine how the failure relates to the patient's condition and prognosis.

The complexity of this process means that "determining the facts" may involve a lengthy and uncertain chain of discussions over some period of time. How the issues are "framed" reflects a number of problematic assumptions too often unconfronted in bioethical discussions. First, it assumes that all is known that needs to be known when the hint of a dispute first appears. And second, it assumes that the rules and principles that apply will inexorably lead to a single conclusion. But the medical facts, especially the prognosis, and an accurate medical and psychosocial history are often difficult to uncover. Thus, for example, a patient who refuses care may be responding to his relative penury, or his lack of trust in the provider, or his misunderstanding of the risks and benefits of the proposed intervention. Only knowledge of the context and investigation of the actual circumstances can produce a fair and just result in an individual case. Consider, for example, the following case:

> A patient with multi-drug-resistant tuberculosis refused to remain in his room in the hospital wandered into the hall, and was finally restrained to prevent him from endangering the other patients and staff.

Contrast this set of "facts" with the following:

> A patient with infectious multi-drug-resistant tuberculosis was put in a negative-pressure room to ensure maximum protection for the other patients and staff. The room was cold, and the patient was denied extra blankets. He was provided with neither a radio nor a television and he had nothing to read. There was no telephone in his room and he ventured into the hall periodically to use the telephone there.

In the first statement of the facts, the staff would be entirely within its rights to restrain a dangerous patient to prevent harm to others. In the second, the right answer is less certain. The staff might still need to act to protect others, but it would also need to meet the needs of the patient and satisfy the demands of a just solution.

C. Victim-Offender Mediation

1. Jennifer Gerarda Brown, *The Use of Mediation to Resolve Criminal Cases: A Procedural Critique*, 43 Emory L.J. 1247, 1248-1266, 1308-1309 (1994)*

INTRODUCTION

In the ancient days of Western legal systems, criminal offenders could settle with victims and their families to avoid prosecution. For some criminal offenders in the United States, privatized criminal law survives: Victim-Offender Mediation ("VOM") allows offenders to avoid public prosecution or punishment by mediating criminal cases with their victims. An offender may be given the opportunity to participate in VOM at various stages in the criminal justice process. VOM may even divert cases from the criminal justice system, with little or no involvement by state officials unless the mediation fails to resolve the case. Today, more than 100 VOM programs exist in the United States. In 1993, U.S. programs disposed of 16,500 cases involving 12,931 victims and 14,059 offenders.

Offenders participate in VOM in order to reduce their expected punishment. An offender

*Reprinted with permission.

who participates may be rewarded by dismissal of charges or reduction of penalties. An offender who refuses to participate or fails to reach an agreement with the victim, on the other hand, returns to the criminal justice system for possible prosecution or sentencing. The outcome of the mediation can influence judges, parole boards, and prosecutors as they decide how to charge or punish the offender. And the outcome of the mediation turns in large part upon the victim's satisfaction.

Thus, VOM transforms the criminal justice paradigm by placing victims at the center, rather than on the periphery, of the criminal process. In effect, VOM transfers the power to resolve all or part of a criminal case from the state to a private party—the victim. As a result, VOM represents a return to an earlier model of criminal justice. In VOM, as in ancient criminal practice, the victim controls the offender's fate.

The thesis of this Article is that placing such control in the hands of the victim is inconsistent with the character and purpose of the criminal law as it has evolved since ancient times. As currently structured, VOM's relationship to the criminal justice system disserves the interests of victims, offenders, and the state.

VOM disserves the interests of victims by stressing forgiveness and reconciliation before victims have the vindication of a public finding that the offender is guilty. In addition, VOM suppresses victims' outrage and loss by assuming that these negative feelings can be expressed and resolved in the course of a few hours spent meeting with the offender.

VOM disserves offenders in three ways: by using selection criteria that are not clearly related to the goals of the program; by eliminating procedural protections such as the right to counsel or rules of evidence; and by using the leverage of pending criminal process to gain advantages for the victim, a private party. If offenders believe that they will be worse off in the ordinary criminal justice system should they fail to reach a mediated agreement satisfactory to their victims, the offenders may have an unduly strong incentive to mediate and reach agreement, no matter what the psychological or monetary cost.

VOM characterizes many crimes as private disputes that fracture relationships between individuals; the state's interest in these disputes is minimal. The structure of VOM often belies this assumption, however, because the mediation occurs before a backdrop of state involvement and coercion. Victims of crime negotiate not only with their own individual bargaining strength, but also with the threat of enhanced state punishment should the parties fail to reach agreement. The victim appropriates some of the state's leverage over the offender because both the victim and the offender know that the offender is more likely to be prosecuted or incarcerated if the victim is not satisfied with the negotiation.

VOM disserves the interests of the state because it devalues the substantive and procedural norms observed in public processes. Despite proponents' claims that VOM can resolve criminal cases according to the substantive standards of the "community" in which the crime occurred, such a community rarely exists in the United States today apart from the state itself. When centralized rules of criminal law are rejected in the name of a "community" that may not even exist, any standard may fill the vacuum to resolve individual cases. Success is measured by the victim's satisfaction with the outcome rather than consistency with substantive legal rules. VOM programs ignore procedural norms because the end (the parties' ability to reach agreement) often justifies the means (lack of counsel for the offender, coercion prior to and during the mediation).

This Article calls for a decoupling of mediation from the criminal justice system: the success or failure of the mediation should have no impact on the offender's prosecution or punishment. The Article suggests several procedural rules to effect such a separation. A "Chinese wall" between VOM and the criminal justice system is necessary to protect the integrity of the system and the integrity of mediation as a fundamentally voluntary process.

A Chinese wall would address the dangers of VOM to victims, because it would preserve an independent process and the opportunity for catharsis that a public process could offer. The dangers to offenders would be decreased if a Chinese wall were in place because the separation would reduce incentives for prosecutors and program administrators to coerce offender participation. The dangers of VOM to the state would be reduced if the process were separated from the criminal justice system because the Chinese wall would preserve the public forum for public purposes.

These conclusions are subject to an important qualification: If VOM proponents and prosecutors could show that VOM does promote deterrence or rehabilitation, then it might be reintegrated into the criminal justice system. This qualification is consistent with a larger theme: public coercion should only be used to vindicate public interests. To the extent that mediation is shown to further the goals of rehabilitation or specific deterrence, conditioning prosecution on mediation and its results is appropriate.

But the standard for proving that VOM promotes the traditional goals of the criminal law should be rigorous. And even if the system incorporates victim-offender mediation to resolve criminal cases, additional process is required to insure that selection criteria are fair, that the process and its outcomes are as noncoercive as possible (within an admittedly coercive system), and that the public is afforded some opportunity to monitor mediation and its results through regular judicial review. This Article suggests various procedural guidelines that might reduce the dangers, including the provision of counsel for indigent offenders who participate in VOM, court monitoring of mediation agreements, and strict enforcement of rules that exclude from trial and sentencing any evidence of failed mediation attempts.

By proposing a separation between mediation and the criminal justice system, I intentionally seek to eliminate one of the stated goals of most VOM programs: to serve as an alternative to incarceration. Allowing offenders to buy their way out of prison with monetary and nonmonetary compensation to victims unacceptably confounds the private goals of mediation and the public goals of criminal law. If a jurisdiction is serious about creating alternatives to incarceration, then the state, rather than crime victims or private administrators of VOM programs, ought to decide whether offenders are entitled to such alternatives. And the state should place these alternatives in the hands of private parties only after they have fully accounted for the "process dangers" of such a change.

I. BACKGROUND AND HISTORY

A. Criminal Law Evolved to Reduce the Role of Victims

. . . Although we tend now to think of the criminal law as inherently public, in the early days of Western legal systems, private individuals prosecuted criminals and meted out punishment. The criminal law was primarily concerned with victims' compensation or revenge. Criminal law became a matter of public interest with the close of the Anglo-Saxon period in English history and the rise of feudalism. In the Middle Ages, the system of "composition" combined public punishment with private damages so that crime victims and their families could collect satisfaction from wrongdoers. Increasingly, however, intentionally harmful acts were considered offenses against the monarch's peace rather than individual victims, and a structured court system developed to redress these public wrongs.

As the state established a monopoly on punishment, the rights of crime victims were gradually severed from the criminal law. . . . [T]he transformation of the criminal law from private to public enforcement was a mixed blessing for offenders: " [I]f the kindred be no longer allowed to avenge themselves, the corresponding right of the offender to make peace with the kin is also withdrawn. A crime is now a public affair."

In Colonial America, crime remained a private matter, and victims were responsible for apprehending and punishing criminals. Victims could arrest offenders themselves, or pay sheriffs to make the arrests. Victims would hire private attorneys to prosecute cases, and they could collect damages from the convicted defendants, bind them to servitude, or pay for their incarceration by public authorities. By the early 1800s, however, imprisonment became the most prevalent form of criminal punishment and the victim's role diminished dramatically. The rise of imprisonment occurred as crime came to be considered more a breach of the general peace than a private injury to the victim. The state set out to punish and deter, shifting its focus to the offender and concentrating less on compensation to the victim.

B. VOM is a Product of the "Victims' Rights" Movement

Although the state achieved its monopoly in criminal law enforcement centuries ago, in recent years activists have worked to swing the pendulum back toward greater involvement by victims in the criminal process. . . . The movement to amend state constitutions to include some provisions for victims' rights began in the early 1980s, when President Reagan's Task Force on Victims of Crime recommended that the Sixth Amendment to the U.S. Constitution be changed to guarantee that "the victim, in every criminal prosecution, shall have the right to be present and to be heard at all critical stages of judicial proceedings." Soon after that, California became the first state to grant constitutional status to a Victims' Bill of Rights. Rhode Island followed with a constitutional amendment granting victims the right to restitution, to submit victim impact statements at sentencing, and to be treated "with dignity and respect." According to the National Victim Center, thirteen states have enacted constitutional amendments recognizing victims' rights.

In addition to their work on constitutional measures, advocates have sought to make procedural rules more sensitive to the needs of victims. Though varied, these proposals often are designed to: (1) keep suspects in custody following arrest; (2) reduce delay between arrest, preliminary hearing, and trial; (3) eliminate plea bargaining or give victims greater input in that process; (4) minimize or eliminate cross-examination of victims by defense counsel; (5) discard the exclusionary rule; (6) allow victims to participate in sentencing; (7) guarantee that victims receive full restitution; and (8) grant victims a right to mediate with the offender.

C. VOM Seeks to Include Victims When Resolving Criminal Cases

. . . In this Section, I provide some descriptive background on VOM and one influential type of victim-offender mediation called Victim-Offender Reconciliation Programs ("VORP"). VORP ideology and agendas have had tremendous influence on the development of victim-offender mediation, even in programs that do not use the VORP label.

1. A Short History of VOM

One night in 1974, two young men in Kitchener, Ontario vandalized the property of twenty-two people: They broke windows, slashed tires, and damaged churches, stores, and cars. They pled guilty to twenty-two charges. The offenders did not pay restitution to the court clerk's office, however. Instead, in an experiment jointly administered by the probation department's volunteer program and the Mennonite Central Committee, the two young offenders met with each victim. It was hoped that meeting with the victims would help the offenders to see the restitution payments less as fines and more as compensation to real people for the losses they had suffered. Within six months, the young men had fulfilled their restitution obligations in full. Many see this case as the birth of VOM, because the success of this experiment encouraged others to continue to develop the program.

In the mid-1970s similar programs were developing in the United States. The Minneapolis Restitution Center, for example, offered criminal offenders the opportunity to live and work outside the prison setting in order to make restitution payments to the victims of their crimes. As part of the program, offenders would meet with their victims in the presence of a program counselor to discuss the terms of restitution payment. A comparable program in the state of Oklahoma began to require juvenile offenders to make contact (in person or by letter) with the victims to whom they owed restitution.

VOM programs have multiplied dramatically. Today, more than 100 VOM programs exist in the United States. In 1993, U.S. programs disposed of 16,500 cases, involving 12,931 victims and 14,059 offenders. The growth of victim-offender mediation parallels an increased interest in restitution for victims of crime. VOM is seen as a cheap, informal way to determine the amount of restitution to be paid, while at the same time allowing for some interaction between victim and offender. The expectations for that interaction vary highly from one program to another. Some victim-offender mediation programs strive not just to establish restitution agreements, but actually to effect some "reconciliation" between the victim and the offender, resolving conflict that the crime has created. These more ambitious goals are frequently found in mediation programs that operate under the name "VORP"—Victim-Offender Reconciliation Programs.

2. Victim-Offender Reconciliation: the Christian Roots of VOM

VORP is an important root of victim-offender mediation. Even many programs that do not publicly broadcast a VORP orientation continue internally to follow a VORP-directed agenda of "reconciliation." This agenda permeates many VOM programs that are administered by state officials and community organizations, and is not limited to church-based programs.

Initiated by Mennonite reformers in Canada and the United States—principally in the Midwest—VORP programs generally aspire to different goals than the criminal justice system. The Justice Fellowship, a research and policy institute based in Washington D.C. that promotes victim-offender mediation, has declared its aspirations for criminal justice reform:

1. To provide victims and offenders in every community with opportunities for reconciliation through church-based programs;

2. To offer victims of crime in every community crisis intervention services through local churches;
3. To sentence nondangerous offenders to reparative sanctions rather than to prison; and
4. To grant victims a formal role in the criminal justice system, including the right to participate (with legal representation) in criminal cases to pursue restitution.

Although VORP proponents assert that the methodology of the process is consistent with a variety of criminal justice goals—such as rehabilitation, crime prevention, and restitution—the "primary" goal of VORP is "reconciliation." The writers of one guide to VORP explain:

> We recognize that this is an unusual goal in criminal justice circles, and that [it] is a difficult goal to define and measure. However it is defined, though, we mean that our first priority is on relationships: we focus on the relational aspects of crime. Attitudes, feelings and needs of both victims and offender[s] must be taken very seriously. Healing is important.

VORP programs are driven by a strong Christian theological foundation. Indeed, Howard Zehr, who has written extensively on restorative justice and VORP, says that the church should play a "critical" role in maintaining and nurturing VORP: "VORP embodies a vision of justice that is inherently biblical and thus provides an arena where the church can implement its vision." The VORP Book, a kind of operations manual for victim-offender mediation programs, states that " [t]he VORP concept is deeply rooted in Judeo-Christian concepts and is uniquely suited to the ministry of the church." That vision, according to Zehr, includes an understanding of justice radically different from the "retributive" perspective adopted by the existing criminal justice system. . . .

D. How VOM Programs Work

Most VOM programs involve face-to-face meetings between crime victims and offenders in the presence of trained mediators. Beyond this basic description, VOM programs defy generalization. The programs vary in two important ways: They aspire to different goals and they exploit different degrees of state coercion. The differences are significant because they affect the extent to which VOM serves the interests of victims, offenders, and the state.

VOM programs aspire to various ends. Sometimes their goals are not articulated explicitly, but are reflected in operational details of the programs, such as the criteria used to select cases for mediation. Some VOM programs focus on cases involving misdemeanors—mostly nonviolent property crimes. Some programs limit their cases to felonies. Most programs mediate some combination of misdemeanors and felonies. Some proponents of VOM even encourage its use in select cases of violent felonies, including homicide, armed robbery, and rape. Selection criteria reflect the different program goals. The more serious the crimes a program is willing to mediate, the more that program probably aspires to serve as an alternative to incarceration. In addition, programs that mediate more serious crimes reflect a willingness to displace some of the state's authority, since states presumably take a greater interest in resolving more serious cases.

The diverse goals of programs involving victim-offender mediation are also reflected in their relative entanglement in the criminal justice system. Most VOM programs are distinguishable from standard community mediation programs (even though community mediation programs may also handle cases involving technically criminal conduct) because the VOM programs mediate cases in which the participants' roles as victim and wrongdoer are more clearly determined. Indeed, community mediation programs receive referrals primarily from civil, rather than criminal, courts. Community mediation programs provide an alternative to the adversary system altogether, diverting cases before they even enter the criminal justice system. Referrals to VOM, in contrast, are usually made by law enforcement or criminal court personnel after an offender has entered the criminal justice system; often the adversary system takes the case to the point of conviction (following adjudication or a plea).

A final way in which the goals of VOM programs differ is the degree of importance placed on "reconciliation of the conflict (i.e., the expression of feelings; greater understanding of the event and each other; closure)." While many programs concern themselves primarily with hammering out restitution agreements, others also seek to address emotional issues surrounding the crime. This difference can have an especially strong effect on victims. While the potential benefits of "reconciliation" may be great, a program's strong emphasis on this goal could harm victims who are not ready or willing to forgive their offenders.

In addition to different goals, VOM programs display a varying willingness to exploit state coercion. The timing of the mediation can have a tremendous effect on the level of coercion experienced by an offender. VOM programs conduct mediation at various points in the criminal justice process: on the early side, some mediations occur after arrest and before any charges are filed; on the late side, some mediations follow an offender's conviction and sentencing. As an offender's case progresses through the system, the offender may gather information about the evidence, the severity of the charges, and the likelihood of conviction. The fear of state punishment may lead offenders to agree both to mediation generally and to a victim's demands specifically.

Programs that conduct mediation early in the criminal process, when the offender still lacks information about the likely outcome of the case, can more effectively exploit the offender's fear of state punishment in order to secure the offender's cooperation. A VOM program appears to lack some of the state's coercive power, because the offender can refuse to mediate. But the offender's freedom to reject mediation can be constrained if the offender fears indirect punishment for the refusal to mediate (this could occur if the offender's failure to cooperate in mediation is taken into account at the time of sentencing). Even if the VOM program does not actively exercise coercive power, it can exploit the offender's fear of state coercion by scheduling mediation at a time when the offender's uncertainty is greatest.

The differences among VOM programs, outlined above, make it difficult to formulate a "typical" model for VOM. For the sake of discussion and argument in this article, let us assume a VOM program that exclusively takes adult offenders. The program receives most of its case referrals from courts and probation officers before the offenders enter a formal guilty plea or receive their sentence. Once referred, each case is assigned to a mediator—in most programs, a volunteer from the community—who contacts the victim and offender individually. If the parties agree to mediate, the mediator sets a time and place for the mediation to be held and conducts the mediation. If the parties reach agreement, they enter into a written contract outlining the provisions of their agreement, both monetary and nonmonetary. The mediator returns a written report of the mediation and a copy of the contract to the VOM program office, and the administrator of the program forwards the contract (often with a copy of the report as well) to the referring agency.

In most programs, VOM program staff monitor performance of the contract; in some systems, the probation office will also check to insure that the restitution is paid if it is a condition of probation. If, on the other hand, one of the parties refuses to mediate or the parties cannot resolve the case in mediation, the case is returned to the referring agency—the prosecutor's office, the court, or the probation office. There, the offender will be subject to state prosecution and sentencing. Sometimes the mediator will report back to the referring agency about the case. If the offender was somehow responsible for the failure to resolve the case (by refusing to mediate or agree to the victim's demands), the case will return to the system with the mediator's report and "the judge will have to decide whether to order restitution or alter the sentence in some way." Similarly, if the victim's uncooperative attitude prevented the parties from mediating or reaching agreement, a judge subsequently setting a restitution amount could also be made aware of the victim's actions. . . .

CONCLUSION

In June of 1992, I attended a conference about victim-offender mediation. . . . Reflecting on the conference, I had conflicting reactions to VOM. I hoped that the programs might facilitate compensation for victims and rehabilitation for offenders, but feared that VOM might involve dangerous levels of coercion. Hope and fear may be reasonable reactions to VOM's maddeningly middle ground. VOM advances neither of the parties' positions as fully as the adversarial system. Instead, it establishes its own normative scheme for the parties at the outset, based more upon an agenda of "reconciliation" than on the real interests of the victim, offender, or community. VOM assumes a compromise of all parties' needs before their interactions have even begun. . . .

VOM straddles the private and public spheres: It characterizes cases as private disputes affecting individuals rather than the state, and it rejects the state's substantive legal rules for resolution of criminal cases. At the same time, however, VOM uses the state's coercive power to distort parties' choices about participation, agreement, and performance. This Article seeks to shift VOM firmly into the private sphere, and calls for a decoupling of mediation from the criminal justice system. The mediation should not affect public proceedings against the offender. A Chinese wall is necessary to protect the integrity of the criminal justice system and the integrity of mediation as a fundamentally voluntary process.

To achieve this decoupling, I have suggested several procedural reforms. Ideally, the occurrence and result of mediation should be hidden from the prosecutor, the judge, and the jury in the criminal proceedings. Inevitably, however, the prosecutor is likely to know that mediation has occurred. Any evidence regarding the mediation or matters discussed in it should be deemed irrelevant at trial and sentencing. To insulate the criminal justice system further, any victims who wish to participate in VOM could be deposed prior to the mediation to insure that their testimony does not change in the wake of the mediation.

These recommendations are premised on VOM's failure to promote the traditional goals of criminal law. If additional study demonstrates to the satisfaction of policy makers that VOM does promote deterrence or rehabilitation, then mediation might be more formally integrated into the criminal justice system. Should that occur, however, additional formality would facilitate several goals: Selection criteria would be more objective and more clearly tailored to the goals of the mediation programs; the parties would receive complete information—including legal advice—about likely adjudicative outcomes and the various alternatives to any agreement they might negotiate; and the public would be afforded some opportunity to monitor mediation results through regular judicial review. With such safeguards in place, the integration of mediation into the criminal justice system could be achieved in a manner consistent with my general thesis—public power should be used only to vindicate public interests.

2. Mark S. Umbright, Mediating Interpersonal Conflicts: A Pathway to Peace 135-163 (1995)

The field of victim offender mediation in the United States is most often associated with the development in 1978 of the first Victim Offender Reconciliation Program (VORP), in Elkhart, Indiana. This joint effort of the Mennonite Central Committee and the Prisoner and Community Together (PACT) organization was modeled after the initial VORP, in Kitchener, Ontario, that began in 1974. The VORP tradition remains the most clearly articulated and documented expression of victim-offender mediation and has greatly influenced the larger field, particularly private community-based agencies, including some church-related organizations. . . .

Today there are approximately 125 such programs in the United States and nearly 30 in Canada. Most are operated by private nonprofit correctional agencies working closely with the local courts. Some are sponsored directly by probation departments or state departments of corrections, as in Oklahoma. Nearly all work with nonviolent property offenses and minor assaults, with some programs processing a small number of more violent offenses. An even larger number of programs operate in Europe, where the field began developing in the mid-1980s, largely based upon the Victim Offender Reconciliation Program (VORP) model in Canada and the United States, and is now growing more rapidly than in North America. England has established 18 programs; Germany, 25; France, 40; Belgium, 8; Norway, 54; and Finland, 20. Austria recently adopted a policy to promote the use of victim-offender mediation for young offenders nationally.

3. Comments and Questions

a. If you were a victim of a crime, would you want to participate in a mediation with the perpetrator? Ask a few of your friends for their views on this question.

b. Who is the likely beneficiary of such a mediation? Are both parties likely to benefit with some frequency?

c. What personal characteristics associated with the people and the crime point toward or away from participation in victim offender mediation?

d. Suppose a crime victim wants to meet with the offender, but the offender is unwilling. Should the victim be entitled to a mediation?

e. Should a victim ever be required to meet with the perpetrator, to advance rehabilitative goals? Society commonly requires the victim of brutal crimes, notably rape, to relive the event in open-court, and then be subjected to demeaning public cross-examination.

f. The parents of a murdered child in Texas recently were permitted to watch the execution of the person who had murdered their child. Both found doing so to be a worthwhile experience that brought closure to their grief and loss.

D. Farmer-Lender Mediation

1. Leonard L. Riskin, *Two Concepts of Mediation in the FmHA Farmer-Lender Mediation Program*, 45 ADMIN. L. REV. 21 (1993)*

This article concerns just one mediation program conducted by one federal agency, but it has, I hope, significant implications for mediation efforts in other contexts. In 1988, the Farmers Home Administration launched a massive effort, mandated by Title V of the Agricultural Credit Act of 1987, to mediate between farmers and their creditors over delinquent loans. The effort's most striking aspect is that it embraced two radically different forms of mediation. This development has significance beyond the farmer-lender mediation program. The federal government is moving swiftly to employ alternative methods of resolving disputes, due in part to recent legislation such as the Administrative Dispute Resolution Act of 1990, which may portend a vast expansion in the use of alternative methods of dispute resolution (ADR) by federal agencies, and the Civil Justice Reform Act of 1990, which provides encouragement and authorization for federal district courts to use alternative methods of dispute resolution.

Part I of this article describes the background of the program and Part II its implementation. Part III explains the two kinds of mediation; Part IV deals with the significance of these developments for organizations and individuals outside the FmHA.

I have avoided excessive detail about the FmHA loan programs or the FmHA's implementation of the farmer-lender mediation program, and this for two reasons. First, this program was large and diverse, including thousands of mediations conducted by hundreds of mediators in at least thirty states. Seventeen of these states created mediation programs for which the FmHA provided matching funds. In more than a dozen other states, the FmHA arranged for mediation services through contracts. In some states FmHA used its own employees to conduct "voluntary meetings of creditors." The circumstances facing mediation participants varied not only state-to-state but also by region within states and by time periods. Every farm family had its unique set of personalities and circumstances—legal, economic, social, psychological, and interpersonal—and so did every mediator and every lender. Moreover, the mediations often were set in an elaborately complex system of loans and loan servicing options. Accordingly, it seemed impossible to describe or analyze this program in any detailed way.

Second, a more detailed description—though it might have been useful to a small number of officials concerned with the program under study or very similar programs—would be of limited interest and utility to others charged with carrying out different kinds of dispute resolution efforts. Therefore, I have attempted to provide just enough texture for the reader to understand the program and its implementation and to focus on the feature of the program.

I. BACKGROUND

A. The Farmers Home Administration

The FmHA is the successor to the Resettlement Administration, which was created in 1935, and the Farm Security Administration. Its "current mission statement directs [it] to serve as a temporary source of supervised credit and technical support for rural Americans for improving their farming enterprises, housing conditions, community facilities, and other busi-

*Reprinted with permission.

ness endeavors until they are able to qualify for private sector resources." The Agency's 11,558 full-time employees operate numerous loan programs through forty-six state offices, 264 district offices, and 1,904 county offices. The Agency often is called a "lender of last resort" because it generally makes loans to persons who can secure no other financing.

B. The Farm Crisis

The farm sector enjoyed a boom in the 1970s. In 1972-73 farm income rose greatly. Because of the widespread expectation that income would continue to climb, the price of farmland increased dramatically. As a result, many farmers borrowed to purchase machinery and to develop their land, a practice that was highly profitable during boom times. In the early 1980s, however, a rise in interest rates was accompanied by a precipitous decline in the prices of land and machinery. Consequently, many farmers were unable to service their debt, and delinquencies on loans to major farm lenders—principally banks, the Farm Credit System, life insurance companies, and the Farmers Home Administration—grew substantially. Because the FmHA is a lender of last resort, large numbers of farmers who were denied credit assistance by other sources turned to the FmHA for help, and the FmHA responded by increasing its portfolio. In the first six months of 1985, FmHA made $763 million in new loans to over 7,000 farmers who were technically insolvent. It also made new loans to over 12,000 farmers who had extreme financial difficulties. Because FmHA borrowers tend to be greater risks than other borrowers, FmHA's delinquencies peaked earlier than those of the other major sources of farm lending. The FmHA was slower than other lenders to liquidate, because it is a public entity with a quasi-social function. During each of the years 1980, 1981, and 1982 the FmHA charged off less than $50 million, but the charge off figures were $100 million in 1983 and 1984, $300 million in 1985, and $400 million in 1986. All four major sources of loans experienced heavy losses.

In the economic downturn afflicting the agricultural sector, FmHA borrowers were hit particularly hard. FmHA, in turn, began to exercise frequently its right to accelerate loans and foreclose on property securing those loans. Borrowers filed numerous lawsuits challenging the FmHA's procedures, with some success. And a widely seen motion picture, Country, starring Jessica Lange and Sam Shepard, dramatized the plight of a family treated roughly by the FmHA.

Accompanying the economic decline in the farm sector was a deterioration in family structures and the social fabric in many rural areas, especially in the midwest. Rates of divorce, child abuse, depression, suicide, and drug abuse escalated, and many rural communities suffered community-wide depression marked by a feeling of hopelessness, exacerbated by a shortage and lack of coordination of social services. . . .

C. Pre-1988 Farm Credit Mediation Programs

Iowa and Minnesota responded early to these conditions. The cornerstone of the efforts in both states was successful mediation programs that have greatly affected the development of farmer-lender mediation efforts in other states. Although these two programs were created in very different ways and have very different structures, they share, and have promoted, a common philosophical approach to farmer-lender mediation.

The Minnesota program grew from the work of a task force that was initiated by the Minnesota Department of Agriculture in 1984 and included both public and private agencies that provided services to farmers. It subsequently added bankers, farm advocates, church groups, educators, economists, and farmers. As the crisis deepened, some farm advocates pressed for a one-year moratorium on foreclosures. In November 1985, bankers agreed—at the Governor's request—to a voluntary ninety-day moratorium on foreclosures on agricultural property and the creation of a farmer-lender mediation program under which the University of Minnesota Extension Service offered farmer-lender mediation to parties who requested it. In short order, the Service located and trained over 300 mediators, and by December 1985 they began to conduct mediations.

During the "moratorium" period, some lenders continued foreclosures. As a result, many legislators viewed the moratorium effort as a failure. In May 1986, the Minnesota legislature, "[i]n a remarkable bipartisan effort," enacted a statute to address the farm crisis. Among other things, the statute established a farmer-lender mediation program that was "mandatory" in the sense that it prohibited persons from moving to enforce interests in farm property securing debts of more than $5,000 without first serving the debtor with a notice of the availability of mediation. The statute also provided that the creditor may not move against the property until ninety days after the debtor files a mediation request, and it required the Agricultural Extension Service to train and provide mediators, as well as credit analysts (to help the farmer prepare for mediation). . . .

By its terms, the Minnesota statute applies to the FmHA as a creditor. But the FmHA refused to participate in mediations or to restructure loans in connection with mediations. . . . [A]ccording to one commentator, "farmers began filing for bankruptcy because then FmHA would be forced to participate in bankruptcy proceedings."

The Iowa program also began with voluntary mediation, which legislation turned into a program that required farm lenders to participate in mediation requested by borrowers before proceeding against farm property. A broad-based working committee under the leadership of Lieutenant Governor Bob Anderson, with help from the Conflict Clinic, Inc., held forums to discuss mediation. This group rejected the notions of locating the mediation service in a government agency, as had been done in Minnesota, or in a private organization, out of a concern that the providers would appear biased. It decided to create a non-profit corporation that "represented farmers, creditors, mediators, attorneys, educators and business executives," to operate the Iowa Farmer-Creditor Mediation Service. The principal goal of the program was to build commitment to the mediation process, rather than seek specific outcomes, such as keeping farmers on the land.

In the early days of the program, an FmHA employee served on the board of the corporation, and the FmHA participated in mediations until August 1987. At that time, according to Michael Thompson, Executive Director of the Iowa Mediation Service, the FmHA General Counsel became aware of the discrepancy between FmHA's practices in Iowa and in other states and called a halt to such participation. . . .

D. The Agricultural Credit Act of 1987

In response to these and related events, Congress passed the Agricultural Credit Act of 1987, a massive attempt to deal with problems in the agricultural credit realm . Title VI established the mediation program. Much of Title VI was intended to respond to court-ordered changes in FmHA's treatment of delinquent borrowers, and it has actually given more rights to FmHA borrowers than was required by the court.

1. Mediation

Title V propelled the Department of Agriculture (USDA) into mediation by requiring the Secretary to certify and provide matching grants to state mediation programs that met certain criteria; to participate in state mediation programs; and to make "a reasonable effort" to contact and encourage creditors to take part in a restructuring plan. To fulfill this last requirement, the FmHA included in its rules on restructuring a requirement that delinquent borrowers be offered a chance to participate in mediation or a voluntary meeting of creditors; in addition, it began a program to contract for mediation services in some states that lacked certified mediation programs.

Title V requires the Secretary to provide states that have "qualified" mediation programs with matching funds, limited to 50 percent of the cost of each program and to $500,000 per year for each state. The Secretary must certify a state mediation program as "qualified" if the program:

(1) provides for mediation services to be provided to producers, and their creditors, that, if decisions are reached, result in mediated, mutually agreeable decisions between parties under an agricultural loan mediation program;
(2) is authorized or administered by an agency of the State government or by the Governor of the State;
(3) provides for the training of mediators;
(4) provides that the mediation sessions shall be confidential; and
(5) ensures that all lenders and borrowers of agricultural loans receive adequate notification of the mediation program.

Section 503 requires that [for each USDA] program . . . that makes, guarantees, or insures agricultural loans, the Secretary [shall]:

(A) prescribe rules requiring that each such program shall participate in good faith in any state agricultural loan mediation program;
(B) participate in agricultural loan mediation programs;
(C) cooperate in good faith with requests for information or analysis of information made in the course of mediation under any agricultural loan mediation program; . . . and
(D) present and explore debt restructuring proposals advanced in the course of such mediation.

[Similar standards apply to . . . the Farm Credit Administration (FCA), an independent regulatory agency of the executive branch charged with regulating the Farm Credit System. . . .

The Act included significant changes in the functioning of the FCA as well as the FmHA. The most important of these, for present purposes, were requirements that these lenders restructure loans where restructuring is in the government's financial interests and would help keep the farmer on the farm. . . .

To be eligible for such assistance "the delinquency must be due to circumstances beyond the control of the borrower," and "the borrower must have acted in good faith . . . and must present a preliminary plan . . . that contains reasonable assumptions that demonstrate that the borrower will be able to (A) meet the necessary family living and farm operating expenses; and (B) service all debts, including those of the loans restructured." In addition, "(4) the loan, if restructured, must result in a net recovery to the Federal Government, during the term of the loan as restructured, [at least] equal to the net recovery to the Federal Government from an involuntary liquidation or foreclosure on the property securing the loan. . . .

Mediation is awarded a major role in the decision to restructure. The Secretary is to give priority to principal and interest write-down only if creditors (other than those creditors who are fully collateralized) representing a substantial portion of the total debt of the borrower held by such creditors, agree to participate in the development of the restructuring plan or agree to participate in a state mediation program. Further, the Secretary is required to "make a reasonable effort" to contact and encourage the creditors to take part in the development of a plan of restructuring, a notion that later became known as a "voluntary meeting of creditors."

II. FmHA IMPLEMENTATION

As the FmHA began to implement this program in January 1988, it faced a daunting situation: 85,000 delinquent Farmer Program borrowers and another 33,000 in an "inactive" status, such as bankruptcy or foreclosure. The loan portfolio of delinquent FmHA farmer program borrowers totaled $11.4 billion (out of the total FmHA farm loan portfolio of $26 billion, which represented fifteen percent of total farm debt); $9.6 billion of the $11.4 billion in payments were overdue.

In addition, and to make matters more difficult for the FmHA, it was operating under both federal court injunctions forbidding it to take further adverse actions until it revised the forms used to advise delinquent borrowers of servicing options and appeal rights and Agricultural Credit Act requirements to revise substantially its procedures for dealing with delinquent borrowers.

The statute not only called for the USDA to certify state mediation programs and to participate in those programs that it certified, but also required that it make "a reasonable effort" to contact and encourage creditors to take part in a plan of restructuring. This led the FmHA both to encourage FmHA offices in states that lacked certified mediation programs ("noncertified states") to contract for mediation services and to provide, in its rules, that delinquent borrowers in such states would have a chance to request mediation or a voluntary meeting of creditors.

After explaining the promulgation of rules by the FmHA, I will review the progress it made in both certified and noncertified states.

A. Rulemaking

1. Mediation

A. Certified State Mediation Programs

The final rule establishing the certification process provided that the FmHA will participate in mediations conducted under a State agricultural loan mediation program "under the same terms and conditions applicable to agricultural creditors generally, and will cooperate in good faith in such mediations by complying with requests for information and analysis, and in presenting and exploring debt restructuring proposals, wherever feasible, when that State is . . . a qualifying State.". . .

In setting out the requirements for certification of state programs, the rule imposed standards identical to those set forth in the statute. The FmHA rejected suggestions that the certification requirements be made more restrictive. Some comments on the proposed rule had urged that the FmHA impose minimum numbers of hours for training of mediators and detailed provisions as to "brochures, broadcast announcements, and notification of the mediators' names, addresses and phone numbers on foreclosure notices." The FmHA rejected these proposals that it "micro-manage," stating that such provisions were not contemplated by the statute, and that varying local conditions could call for different activities in the states. These decisions to defer to the state programs in the details of their activities seem not only consistent with the statute but also quite sensible. State programs, on the whole, appear to have carried out their tasks well. . . .

B. Contract Mediation in Noncertified States

The rule also establishes mediation, or something approaching mediation, in states that do not have certified programs. It requires the state director to "provide the means of conducting a voluntary meeting of creditors, either with a mediator or a designated FmHA representative," encourages the state directors to "contract for qualified mediators within their jurisdictional areas," and states that the "National Office will provide the State a list of qualified mediators for contracting purposes. " The rule goes on to provide that when a mediator is available, the County Supervisor will help the mediator schedule a meeting with the "borrower and all of the borrower's undersecured creditors holding a substantial part of the borrower's debt and encourage them to participate in such a meeting. The mediator will be responsible for conducting the meeting in accordance with accepted mediation practices and to develop an Agreement to assist the farmers in resolving their financial difficulties.

The rule also provides that when a mediator is not available, the State Director will designate an FmHA employee "to conduct a meeting of creditors and attempt to develop a plan with borrowers and their creditors that will assist the borrowers to resolve their financial difficulty. This FmHA representative must not have been previously connected with the borrower's account and must "have demonstrated good human relations skills and ability to resolve problems and settle disputes." The State Directors are to provide the training needed.

2. The Place of Mediation in the Loan Servicing Process

The original interim rules on how the FmHA would take part in mediation, restate that the FmHA will participate in certified state mediation programs " under the same terms and conditions as other creditors. These rules also explain debt servicing, which they describe as "a continuing process, not a single event," with two objectives:

(1) To help the farmers manage credit so they can return to private sector credit sources; and
(2) To minimize costs to the Government of providing this opportunity to farmers in financial difficulty, borrowers' accounts must be managed with an overall objective of keeping the farmer in business and at the same time, minimizing loan costs and losses.

There are two basic kinds of loan servicing actions: primary loan servicing and preservation loan servicing. Primary loan servicing includes: consolidation; rescheduling and/or reamortization; deferral of principal and interest payments; reducing the interest rate; writing down (reducing) amount of the debt; or a combination of these. Preservation loan servicing may be available to borrowers who are ineligible for primary loan servicing. Preservation loan servicing includes: leaseback/buyback and homestead protection.

The rules explain that the FmHA will send a notice describing these options and the methods of applying for them to farmer program borrowers whose loans were accelerated between November 1, 1985, and May 7, 1987, to all other farmer program borrowers whose loans have been accelerated, to borrowers with pending bankruptcy proceedings whose accounts had not been foreclosed or liquidated, to borrowers who were 180 days delinquent, and to borrowers who were less than 180 days delinquent and who the FmHA had determined were ineligible for primary loan servicing.

The farmer who wishes to apply for servicing must complete numerous forms, the most important of which is the "farm-home plan," on which the farmer is to set forth all information relevant to his cash flow situation. Once this is done, the FmHA will determine whether the farmer is eligible for any of the primary loan servicing options.

The farmer will be considered eligible for a servicing option if he is unable to pay his debts to the FmHA for reasons beyond his control; has acted in good faith; and has a feasible plan. A "feasible plan" means that the farm-home plan shows a cash flow that allows the farmer to: pay necessary family living and farm operating expenses; pay all debts, including the restructured debt to FmHA; and pay FmHA an amount worth more than the "net recovery value" of the loan.

Such criteria demand very complex computations. To aid its county offices in making the determination of eligibility for primary loan servicing, the FmHA has developed DALR$, the Debt and Loan Restructuring System, a computer program operated on the FmHA County Office computer systems. The program assists the FmHA loan officer in making a decision "about whether any combination of primary loan servicing options will make it possible for the borrower to develop a feasible plan and thus stay on the farm and avoid loss to the government." DALR$ considers the primary loan servicing options in the order listed above, that is, from the least to the most extreme. The borrower is not eligible for debt write off if he is eligible for any of the less drastic options.

The county supervisor makes decisions as to the input, based on the farm-home plan submitted by the borrower and other factors, and the DALR$ program then quickly performs mathematical calculations which, if performed manually, would take a great deal of time and would run the risk of mathematical error. The DALR$ program provides a printout for the FmHA and the borrower.

If the DALR$ program shows that the borrower has a feasible plan, the FmHA will offer the primary loan servicing option for which the farmer is eligible. If, however, the DALR$ program shows that the borrower is ineligible for primary loan servicing, the FmHA will send a notice, along with a printout of the DALR$ program. This notice advises the farmer of the FmHA's conclusion that the farmer has been unable to develop a feasible plan because of debts to "lenders other than the FmHA." It also includes one of the following two paragraphs:

(If a Certified State Mediation program is available)

> We are requesting mediation under the (Name) State Certified Mediation Program. We will work with you and your creditors to determine if your debts can be adjusted sufficiently to permit you to develop a feasible plan of operation. If, with the adjustment of your debt, you are able to develop a feasible plan of operation which shows that you can make an annual payment to FmHA of at least $ ____, FmHA will reconsider your application for primary loan servicing.

(If a certified State Mediation program is not available)

We will schedule a meeting with you and your other creditors in an effort to reach agreements with them to adjust your debts sufficiently to permit you to develop a feasible plan of operation. The FmHA State Director will contract for a mediator or appoint an FmHA representative not previously involved in servicing of your account upon your written request to participate in the meeting with creditors.

Notice that under these rules, the FmHA does not request mediation until after it has determined that the borrower is ineligible for primary loan servicing. In addition, the notice seems to suggest that the only purpose of the mediation is to seek to have the lenders other than FmHA adjust their debts so that the borrower can have a feasible plan under the DALR$ program. . . . [T]his limitation has helped foster an inappropriately narrow focus in some mediations.

If the mediation produces debt adjustments that will permit the DALR$ program to show a feasible plan, the FmHA will offer the primary loan servicing option for which the borrower is eligible. If, however, the mediation does not produce those adjustments, the FmHA will send the borrower a notice that the FmHA intends to accelerate the loan and proceed against the property; this notice also explains that the borrower has appeal rights and an opportunity to purchase the land at its "net recovery value."

If the farmer does not appeal or does not win the appeal and does not elect the "net recovery buyout," the FmHA will automatically consider the farmer for the two preservation loan servicing options—homestead protection and leaseback/buyback. Homestead protection allows the farmer to either obtain homestead protection, which allows the farmer to purchase the homestead (the house and up to 10 acres) or get a lease with an option to buy the homestead. Under the leaseback/buyback program, the farmer leases the property with an option to buy. . . .

B. State Mediation Programs

1. Funding and Structure

The statute provides minimal and sparse standards for certification of state mediation programs. The FmHA adopted these same standards in its rulemaking and implementation, deciding not to control the details of the mediations or the mediation training in the certified state mediation programs. For that reason, and because of variations in local conditions, there are vastly different programs among the certified states. For example, the programs in Iowa and Minnesota, which predated the federal legislation, are mandatory in the sense that the farmer has the option of requiring certain creditors to participate in mediation before they may foreclose. These two programs also provide the farmer with much more extensive preparation services than some of the other certified programs.

There is also much variety among the other certified programs. Only two of these—South Dakota and Arkansas—are mandatory. Many provide the farmers with significant support services, but they do so in different ways. In Kansas, an elaborate support service network called Farmers Assistance Counseling and Training (FACTS), a unit of the Kansas Board of Agriculture, helps the farmers prepare for mediation. Both the Texas and the North Dakota programs assign negotiators to help the farmers prepare for the mediations and to represent the farmers during the mediation.

The programs were started in many different ways and are organized differently. [T]he

Minnesota Program is operated by the University of Minnesota Extension, and the Iowa program by a non-profit corporation created for this purpose. The Nebraska program is conducted jointly by the Nebraska Legal Aid Society and the Interchurch Ministries of Nebraska under contract with the Nebraska Department of Agriculture. In Texas, the program is conducted by Texas Tech University. In Kansas, the program was originally operated by a non-profit corporation and then transferred to the State Board of Agriculture. The Oklahoma Department of Agriculture contracted with the Oklahoma Conference of Churches to operate its certified program. Several programs, including those in Alabama, North Dakota, South Dakota and Utah, are conducted directly out of state offices. . . .

Notwithstanding these differences, these programs have something in common besides federal matching funds: They share a philosophy of mediation that differs from that which informs the mediation practitioners in some noncertified states, a matter discussed more fully below.

2. Benefits and Costs

A. Numbers of Mediations

The FmHA farm-credit mediation program plainly has accomplished a great deal and produced enormous cost savings to both the federal government and the states. Unfortunately, however, it is extremely difficult . . . to give details to support that statement. The FmHA currently is unable to produce an accurate report or a good estimate of the numbers of cases that have been mediated in either certified or noncertified states. Accordingly, it is difficult to estimate financial savings. Of course, it is virtually impossible to put the very important intangible benefits into a cost-benefit analysis.

B. Financial Costs and Savings

Using the assumption described above, that 4,608 mediations were conducted by certified state programs as of November 30, 1989, the FmHA has estimated that the average cost to the government per mediation in the certified states was $651, a conclusion reached by dividing 4,608 into $3 million the amount of matching grant funding received by certified states in fiscal year 1989.

The FmHA also has attempted to calculate benefits. The FmHA predicted that the net savings to states during fiscal year 1989 would be between $18 million and $37 million, and that the federal government would save between $7 million and $15 million. For the federal government, this means gross benefits of between $3 and $6 for each matching dollar. One can quarrel with the assumptions and methodology underlying these calculations, of course, but it is clear that the program has resulted in substantial savings to states, to the U.S. Department of Agriculture, and to private lenders.

There are other financial savings. Every mediation that prevents litigation also saves money for taxpayers and creditors, including the expense of loan administration, and in the case of a government lender, handling appeals. When a mediation results in a restructured loan or another outcome that keeps a farmer on the farm, there are many benefits to the local community or economy. Each job lost causes a "ripple effect" in the community and reduces the tax base. [Economisist usually speak of the "multiplier effect."]

C. Other Benefits

Other savings are impossible to measure but valuable nonetheless. Participants in farmer lender mediation in North Dakota and in Texas report high degrees of satisfaction with the process, though generally borrowers were more positive about the program than were lenders.

Studies in Minnesota have confirmed the beliefs of many mediators that farm credit mediations have restored disrupted communications between farmers and lenders, helped farmers avoid personal crises, and promoted peaceful change in farm communities. In addition, mediation has improved farmer's decisionmaking, not just in the mediation, but also afterwards, and, most fundamentally, helped keep farmers on their farms.

Other possible benefits of mediation are difficult to identify or measure. For instance, through mediation, farm families might learn of counseling or educational services that could reduce stress or lead to additional income. When mediation helps a farmer better understand his options, it may produce a resolution that is more satisfying and workable to the farmer, even if that means getting off the farm.

This program also fostered the development in 1989 of an important organization, the Coalition of Agricultural Mediation Programs (CAMP). It "provides a framework for people to work together on: (1) common legislative goals; (2) expansion of USDA's use of mediation beyond FmHA farm debt restructuring; and (3) representing and promoting rural/agricultural mediation."

Extending mediation services to rural matters other than farm credit is an explicit goal of CAMP. At CAMP meetings, the conventional wisdom is that both CAMP and FmHA should address not only the crisis in the farm sector, but also a chronic condition in rural America marked by a deterioration in the social fabric in many rural communities. . . .

In some states, farm-credit mediation programs have begun to mediate other kinds of matters connected to rural communities. In Kansas, for instance, farm-credit mediators have started a program to mediate with extended families that are coping with passing a farm from one generation to another. And the Iowa legislature recently extended the Farm Mediation Service, which was subject to a 1990 "sunset" provision, and expanded its mandate to include other disputes involving farmers, such as care and feeding contracts and . . . conservation matters.

C. Contract Mediation in Noncertified States

Numerous FmHA offices in states without certified programs . . . awarded contracts for mediation services to private individuals or organizations. . . . In 1989, the FmHA contracted with the Federal Mediation and Conciliation Service (FMCS) to provide pilot mediation services in Georgia, Maine, and New York. In some states the FmHA arranged for its own employees to preside at "voluntary meetings of creditors." . . .

D. Implementation Problems

This program has encountered three major problems: The first two—an absence of reliable data on numbers of mediations and a lack of participation in mediation by some other creditors, including other federal agencies are covered elsewhere. The third the development of, and tension between, two different notions of the nature and purposes of mediation is discussed in Part III of this article.

III. TWO CONCEPTS OF MEDIATION

The farmer-lender mediation effort is infused with a tension between two different conceptions which I will call "broad" and "narrow" of the goals, purposes and, perhaps, very nature of mediation. I define these conceptions as follows:

The broad approach assumes that the goal of farmer-lender mediation is to reach a wise agreement that deals with the underlying interests of the parties. There are any number of possible outcomes, and the process is open to discussion of whatever seems to be relevant.

The narrow approach rests on the assumption that the only appropriate focus of a farmer-lender mediation is to discuss the possibility that creditors other than FmHA will adjust the borrower's debts sufficiently to allow a rerun of the DALR$ program that will allow the farmer to "cash flow," which will permit the FmHA to offer the farmer primary loan servicing. A mediation so conceived allows only two possible outcomes: (1) The non-FmHA creditors make sufficient reductions and the FmHA offers primary loan servicing to the farmer; or, (2) the creditors do not make sufficient adjustments and, subsequently not at the mediation session the FmHA informs the borrower of his other options, such as net recovery buyout, preservation financing, and voluntary conveyance of the land.

Speaking generally, the certified state mediation programs employ a broad approach. Among the noncertified programs of which I have knowledge, the narrow approach seems most common, but I have found illustrations of both approaches and of mixtures of the two approaches in the work of individual contract mediators. In addition, some FmHA representatives involved in farmer-lender mediation take the broad view and others the narrow. The dichotomy is observable also in the FmHA literature.

A. Manifestations of the Two Concepts

1. "Broad" Mediation

The essence of the "broad" approach is an openness to dealing with whatever issues are important to the resolution of the difficulties between the borrower and the lenders. Often this means searching for and dealing with the underlying interests of the parties through a problem-solving process that could include explicit attention to developing and understanding options. Thus, the mediator might encourage the parties to think about alternatives in addition to primary loan servicing, such as net recovery buyout and lease/buyback. The mediator might help a farmer consider, or reconsider, whether to make additional changes in the farm operation or in off-farm employment, which could change the farm-home plan. It also means, of course, that a mediation could deal with barriers to negotiation, such as: (1) emotional problems within the family (which could be addressed directly or through referral); (2) communication problems between borrower and lenders; and (3) disputes between lenders.

This broad conception of mediation was well developed in the first two farm-credit mediation programs those in Minnesota and Iowa. The Minnesota program includes goals of improving "communication and relationships between farmers and lenders;" encouraging "full discussion of debt restructuring options;" and improving "the relationship among agencies and organizations working with farm families to increase profitability in agriculture." . . .

The financial condition of the farmer is only one side of the problem. Most farmers have families that are directly affected by the problems. The emotional issues tend to be kept secret within the walls of the family home, and are often far more complex than the finances. The fact that the family problems are not discussed within or outside of the immediate family makes the burden sometimes unbearable for the farmer and/or his wife. The children feel the tension, and when they are not told what is happening, are left to their fantasies. They fear the loss of the family farm which includes the home, and become less attentive and uninterested in school. They may fear that their parents will divorce. It is not unusual for the wives to be kept totally in the dark about the problems, though they feel the stress of their husbands and also fear the worst. The husbands are proud and believe that they should be able to handle everything, for them to be unable to manage is admitting failure. Hence, there have been suicides of farmers, divorces, depression, and possibly delinquency or at least psychological dropping out of school by the children.

It is important to realize that the lender may also experience emotional stress. The lender is often the person who helped the farmer to obtain the loans in the first place, and may feel some responsibility or guilt about the present state of affairs. The lender is usually a well respected member of the community, and may be plagued with depression about what is happening to the entire community, his friends, and those with whom he worships in the same church on Sundays. Some lenders have found themselves ostracized by those close to them because of his role in the rural finance crisis.

The mediator of farm issues needs to understand the emotional side of the problem. Both the farmer and the lender may be experiencing the anticipation of a loss, be it the farm or close friends. Their process of dealing with the loss is similar to that of grieving a death.

In the broad view of mediation, the "emotional side" has at least two aspects. First, a mediator must be able to help the parties deal with their emotional difficulties to the extent necessary to allow them to make decisions required to; resolve their financial problems and to enable them to operate the farm profitably so as to fulfill loan obligations. . . . At the other extreme, the mediator might help the participant (normally the farmer) think through whether he needs other assistance, say, from a counselor (psychological, financial, agricultural) or a divorce lawyer. . . .

The broad approach generally emphasizes encouraging and empowering the participants to make their own decisions. Accordingly, programs using a broad approach tend to provide extensive help to farmers in preparing for and, in some states, participating in, mediations. Thus, both mediators and participants normally spend more time in preparing for and participating in these mediations than their counterparts in narrow mediations. . . .

2. "Narrow" Mediation

Under a "narrow" view of the purposes of farmer-lender mediation, the principal—and sometimes the exclusive—issue is whether the creditors will adjust their debts so that a rerun of the DALR$ program would show a feasible plan. A feasible plan would allow the FmHA to provide primary loan servicing so that the borrowers could continue farming, and owning, the land. A number of directors of certified state mediation programs have indicated that some of the FmHA representatives in their states held this narrow view so strongly that it severely limited FmHA's participation in mediations. In some noncertified programs, this narrow view of mediation not only dominated FmHA's participation, but also controlled the outlook of the mediators. The mediations under these programs tended to be much shorter and more formulaic than under certified state programs.

One example of the narrow approach in noncertified states is the mediation model developed and promoted by Ted W. Spiegel, Executive Director of United States Arbitration and Mediation Midsouth, Inc., of Louisville, Kentucky (U.S.A.&M. Midsouth). U.S.A.&M. Midsouth has had contracts with the FmHA to provide mediation in Kentucky, North Carolina, and Tennessee and operates under contracts with FmHA in Kentucky and Tennessee.

The process was limited to debt reduction by non-FmHA creditors. It employed a highly structured format that allowed significantly less room than would a broad approach for problem-redefinition, option development, or direct communications between the borrower and the lenders. Spiegel believed, understandably, . . . that mediation between the farmer and the FmHA is "prohibited by the regulations." Under this format, before each mediation, the mediator obtains the DALR$ program and sets a goal for debt reduction by non-FmHA creditors that would allow the farmer to qualify for primary loan servicing. In contrast, mediators using a broad approach in Iowa would often mediate over what figures should be used in the DALR$ program. In other words, under Spiegel's narrow approach the mediator accepts the outcome of the DALR$ program, but under the broad approach used in Iowa the mediator allows the farmer and the FmHA representative to negotiate over the appropriate input into the DALR$ program.

The mediator—either Spiegel or a person he had trained—begins with an opening statement and does not allow the farmer to "say anything to all the people in the beginning" because he "does not want to embarrass the farmer, does not want him to appear to be begging." Everyone knows what the farmer wants. After the opening statement, the mediator meets with each non-FmHA creditor privately. In these sessions, he stresses compassion and confidentiality. He keeps the creditors separate and asks them to give concessions, not knowing what the other creditors will do. "If that fails," Spiegel says, "I ask them to give contingent concessions." When Spiegel develops "something that looks like it might work," he calls the farmer back in. Spiegel allocated two hours for each mediation, but some were completed in just 15 minutes.

Other units of U.S.A.&M. won contracts with FmHA to provide mediation in other states. And Spiegel's model, which is consistent with U.S.A&M., Inc.'s approach to mediation in personal injury insurance claims, has influenced the conduct of mediation by at least some of these other units. For instance, mediators in local affiliates of U.S.A.&M., Inc. that secured mediation contracts with the FmHA in Missouri in 1988 were highly influenced by the model developed by Spiegel; thus, they believed, for example, that two hours typically was ample time for a mediation. One of the mediators almost always completed mediations in less than an hour and was able to conduct some mediations in just a few minutes each. Another, who conducted about 30 mediations—all but one of which resulted in restructuring—generally spent 45-60 minutes in mediations, following roughly 30 minutes of telephone contacts with non-FmHA creditors. Both of these mediators believed that all parties generally left mediations feeling pleased. It is important to recognize that although narrowly focused mediations generally pay less explicit attention to interpersonal aspects of the situations they are dealing with, such processes may have the effect of improving feelings and relations.

The emphasis on gaining concessions from the non-FmHA creditors shown in these mediations leads me to question whether either the farmer or the FmHA are really "participating" in such mediations or are just attending them. . . . Although the narrow approach generally has an ideological base, sometimes mediators who begin with such an approach will broaden it in response to perceived needs of the parties. . . .

Another example of a narrow approach was that employed by the Federal Mediation and Conciliation Service (FMCS). Although its training programs apparently included a problem-solving orientation, which is almost synonymous with a broad approach to mediation, in conducting mediations in several noncertified states the FMCS seemed to accept unquestioningly severe limits on the scope of mediation. But the FMCS mediators apparently went a step further than their counterparts at U.S. Arbitration and Mediation. After determining that the non-FmHA creditors could not make sufficient adjustments, the FMCS mediators tried to persuade the farmer to sell the land. . . .

3. Effects of the Divergence in Approaches to Mediation

The divergence in views on the proper approach to mediation has manifested itself in several ways. First, as already indicated, the mediations typically conducted under certified programs differ greatly from those conducted in at least some contract mediation programs. Second, in some certified states, at some times, while mediators yearned or pushed for a broad approach, FmHA representatives at mediations clung to the narrow view, believing or maintaining that they had no authority to discuss options other than primary loan servicing, and that the DALR$ program was the only avenue toward that approach. At CAMP meetings, directors of state certified mediation programs have reported difficulties resulting from such restricted participation by FmHA, including resentment by other creditors of FmHA's inflexibility. They stressed that the mediation process could be improved if more discretion were vested in FmHA representatives. However, some of these state program directors also reported that many FmHA representatives were willing, sometimes "with some nudging," to interpret their mandates generously.

Third, in noncertified states, some contractors who were imbued with a broad mediation vision may have spent much more time as mediators—in preparing, conducting, and following up—than they or the FmHA anticipated. . . .

4. Advantages and Disadvantages of Each Approach

Each approach to farmer-lender mediation has its own internal logic and advantages and disadvantages. The narrow approach accepts the definition of the problem that is implicit in FmHA rules: will non-FmHA creditors adjust their debts sufficiently to allow primary loan servicing? The broad approach seeks out underlying interests and works with the parties to define the problems and identify options as broadly as they wish. Thus, the narrow approach is more predictable and, in a sense, efficient. The objective is clear, the types of outcomes limited. It demands less involvement of the participants. All concerned spend less time, so the costs to the government and to participants should be lower. . . . If the burdens of participation are lower in narrow mediations, perhaps some borrowers and lenders would find participation more appealing.

On the other hand, the narrow approach may cause all concerned to miss opportunities to develop solutions that will meet the needs of the parties and to improve relationships and communications. It can provide a convenient myopia for a FmHA representative who has decided against primary loan servicing.

The broad approach offers the opportunity to develop a diverse array of problem-solving solutions that better meet the parties' actual needs. Where this is effective, it produces superior results. In such cases, the broad approach has a bigger payoff than the narrow. It also has an important educational function and can lead to problem-solving approaches to community-wide problems. Potential disadvantages of the broad approach are that it can demand more of the time and energy of all concerned and may call for some interpersonal skills in the mediation that are less necessary in the narrow approach.

B. Why the Two Concepts Developed

1. The Disparity Between Certified and Contract Mediation Programs

It is easy to see why the broad mediation conception developed more readily in certified state mediation programs than in some of the mediation programs that were created in non-certified states through contracts with FmHA state offices. The two kinds of programs were created and developed quite differently. Many of the certified programs were launched before FmHA began participating in farm credit mediation in 1988. Creditors with whom the programs dealt did not have the kind of rigid requirements for adjusting loans that govern the FmHA. The programs often grew out of efforts that had strong community and high level political support. Many of the people who became mediators in such programs did so on a semi-volunteer basis, i.e., for small fees, and had strong connections to the agricultural sector and to rural communities.

Thus, many of the leaders of these programs began with concerns not just to keep farmers on the land, but also to help farmers—and rural communities—cope with economic and social deterioration. These concerns, as well as the mediation philosophies of the leaders of these groups, helped shape a broad concept of mediation. The Iowa and Minnesota mediation programs, the first and probably the largest, became prototypes for most of the other certified programs, though all of the certified programs differed from them in significant ways.

Thus, the certified programs developed their own concepts of mediation in response to concerns such as those listed above, and the Agricultural Credit Act of 1987 directed the FmHA to participate in those programs.

In contrast, in the noncertified states, the FmHA set the terms for mediation. And in doing so, the FmHA has shown a deep and understandable ambivalence. Recall that the Agricultural Credit Act of 1987 requires the FmHA to participate only in the mediations offered by certified state programs. It does not direct FmHA to offer or participate in mediation in other states. The statutory basis for the contract mediation program is a requirement that the FmHA make "a reasonable effort" to contact and encourage creditors to take part in a restructuring plan. In addition, implementation of a broad form of mediation is more time consuming and expensive, and the certified programs generally were better funded.

2. Within the FmHA

One reason why a narrow concept of mediation evolved in some FmHA offfices is the place assigned to mediation in the FmHA's procedures for reviewing the status of delinquent borrowers. Under the FmHA's rules, the delinquent borrower is officially notified of the mediation option only after the FmHA has determined—normally through the DALR$ program—that the farmer is ineligible for primary loan servicing. Many FmHA officials apparently feel that, at this stage, their only option is to attempt to arrange for other creditors to adjust their debts, and to do this through a mediation or a voluntary meeting of creditors, both of which they see as limited to such narrow purposes.

[T]he FmHA located mediation late in the loan servicing process for two reasons: (1) Comments from farm advocacy groups that feared that if mediation occurred earlier, the FmHA might use mediation to delay carrying out its obligation to restructure if the borrower met the statutory criteria, and (2) FmHA's perception that some lenders would not want to participate in a mediation if they thought there was still a chance that the farmer's situation could be improved by FmHA restructuring. . . .

Yet the narrow vision is reinforced by several official FmHA pronouncements, including the notice sent to the farmer, which suggests just one purpose for the mediation, an attempt to persuade other creditors to adjust the farmer's debts:

> If you cannot show a feasible farm plan because you owe too much to other creditors and suppliers, FmHA will help you try to get your other creditors to adjust your debts. This will be done by FmHA asking for mediation if your state has a mediation program approved by the United States Department of Agriculture. If there is no state mediation program, FmHA will try to set up a meeting with your other creditors and suppliers if it can be shown that a reduction in these debts can provide a feasible farm plan.

On the other hand, some FmHA statements appear to acknowledge a reasonably broad notion of mediation.

C. Addressing the Dichotomy

How should the Department of Agriculture and FmHA react to the problems created by the existence of these two alternative views of farmer-lender mediation? . . . I believe that the broad approach is generally preferable—that it is more congenial and usually produces superior outcomes. But I have no empirical data to back up that conclusion, either from this program or another, and so I am relying on my own experience and discussions with others, both of which are filtered through my own values.

Choosing one of these approaches may boil down to a question of values. However, the choice could be aided by research into such issues as the extent to which mediators put these philosophical approaches into practice and the extent to which these approaches—as practiced produce different outcomes. The results of such studies would help officials improve the farmer-lender mediation program and other government efforts in dispute resolution.

1. In Certified States

In states that have certified programs, the FmHA should do what is necessary to ensure that its representatives are willing and able to participate in broad mediations. When Congress enacted Title V of the Agricultural Credit Act of 1987, mandating "good faith" participation by agencies of the Department of Agriculture, the only existing state mediation programs were based on the broad approach; thus, to the extent that a congressional intent on this point could be inferred, that intent must have been to require the department to participate in a broad type of mediation.

2. In Noncertified States

I believe that the FmHA also should promote broad mediation in noncertified states, though the case for this proposition is less clear. In addition to the likelihood of better outcomes, one reason for doing so is to provide services in the noncertified states that approximate those provided in certified state programs. To achieve such parity, the FmHA would have to take steps to ensure that contractors understand and are capable of delivering broad services. In addition, to compensate contractors reasonably for their services might require significantly more than is currently paid by the FmHA in some states.

I must also note, however, that the FmHA could choose not to pursue the goal of providing equivalent services. As mentioned above, the FmHA is not required by law to participate in or offer mediation services in states that do not have certified programs. Second, providing equivalent services in noncertified states might work against another important DOA objective—encouraging such states to develop mediation programs that will qualify for matching funds. Thus, it may be advisable for the FmHA to consider other options. One is the possibility of simply ensuring that the personnel in the FmHA state offices are sufficiently familiar with the differences between and advantages and disadvantages of the two approaches so that they can make an intelligent choice about the type of mediation services they wish to procure; and announce that to potential contractors.

3. Moving Toward Broad Mediation

Moving uniformly toward broad mediation will not be simple. Each model of mediation has its own values and internal logic. Yet in practice, it may sometimes be difficult to distinguish one approach from the other. Good mediators are sensitive to the participants' needs. Accordingly, sometimes a mediator who starts with a narrow approach will broaden it, and one who starts with a broad approach will narrow it in response to developments in the mediation.

In my experience, however, persons who are drawn to one model often have trouble recognizing the strengths of, or the need for, the other; what one sees depends upon what one is seeking. In addition, the narrow model of mediation has the virtue of simplicity, whereas the broad model may call upon FmHA personnel to exercise judgment and to develop new and innovative solutions. Some government officials might fear that this sort of endeavor—requiring the exercise of greater discretion—could jeopardize their careers. Moreover, the FmHA's farm lending programs are very large and require hundreds of people in their administration. Therefore, the need for efficiency, fairness, uniformity, and order makes understandable the allure of a narrow approach to mediation, sometimes with exclusive reliance on the DALR$ program. For all these reasons, there may be a great deal of internal resistance to change in the direction I am proposing. . . .

IV. IMPLICATIONS FOR OTHERS

The development of two radically different types of mediation in the FmHA's program bears several implications for other organizations and individuals who participate in mediation or other alternative forms of dispute resolution. What is most remarkable is not that two forms of mediation developed, but that this seemed to happen without anyone within the FmHA desiring such bifurcation or trying to foster it. In seeking to procure "mediation services" through local contracts, the FmHA apparently either intended to procure the same broad kind of mediation that was provided in the certified programs or had no idea that there were different types of mediation.

The same sort of mixup can occur elsewhere: in other government agencies, as they develop and implement alternative dispute resolution policies under the Administrative

Dispute Resolution Act of 1990 or Executive Order No. 12,778; federal district courts, many of which will develop and implement alternative dispute resolution projects under the Judicial Improvements Act of 1990; and in countless private organizations and law offices around the country, as they search for alternative ways to resolve disputes. In all these organizations, individuals at every level need education and training so they can appreciate the flexibility of mediation and other dispute resolution processes. . . .

What does all of this imply for the lawyers, judges, and executives who will be educated or trained in mediation and other forms of dispute resolution because of the new legislative and executive initiatives described above?

I mean to suggest that they need to know something more than the differences between broad and narrow forms of mediation. Indeed, I identified broad and narrow forms of mediation in the farmer-lender mediation program only because these categories seemed most useful in understanding this program; other systems of categorization may work better in other mediation efforts. Moreover, in my view, the most generally useful distinction is not that between narrow and broad conceptions of mediation but between adversarial and problem-solving approaches to defining and resolving a dispute or planning a transaction.

Lawyers, judges, and others who participate in or foster mediation or other dispute resolution efforts must understand that they have choices among various goals and processes that they can employ in a mediation. The same holds for other dispute resolution mechanisms. The idea of a mini-trial, for instance, is that the procedure is designed to fit the specific situation in each case. And even arbitration, the most established of the alternatives, can be customized or combined with other procedures to address the circumstances.

ADR should not stand for "alternative dispute resolution" but "appropriate dispute resolution." The participants in the dispute, with the help of their lawyers, should select the most appropriate method for resolving a dispute. But in selecting that method, it is not enough to chose a generic process, such as mediation or arbitration. The parties and their lawyers can, and should, customize any of these processes to meet their needs. But first, they must understand the possibilities.

2. Comments and Questions

a. What is Professor Riskin's perception about the scope and role of the ideal mediator in farmer-lender mediations? Is a "straight business" approach more appropriate for commercial disputes? Riskin's views about the appropriate role for mediators are further explored in Chapter 20, section F.

b. Compare Riskin's approach to those suggested for bioethical disputes and victim-offender mediation, as discussed in the two previous sections.

c. A brush with bankruptcy often causes severe personal as well as financial problems for farm families. Various helping professionals might explore these needs, and address such problems as they arise. Why is the mediator of a creditor-debtor dispute the right person to become the family counsellor? Is the reason that the mediator may be the only free assistance that is available? Is it that farm families are stoic, and unlikely to ask for help? Are there other reasons? How well equipped is the typical farmer-creditor mediator to address psychological and family breakdown issues?

E. Commercial Disputes

1. American Arbitration Association, Mediation Rules For Commercial Financial Disputes (1993)*

1. Agreement of Parties

Whenever, by stipulation or in their contract, the parties have provided for mediation or conciliation of existing or future Commercial Financial Disputes under the auspices of the American Arbitration Association (AAA) or under these rules, they shall be deemed to have made these rules, as amended and in effect as of the date of the submission of the dispute, a part of their agreement.

2. Initiation of Mediation

Any party or parties to a dispute may initiate mediation by filing with the AAA a submission to mediation or a written request for mediation pursuant to these rules, together with the appropriate filing fee. If there is no submission to mediation or any contract providing for mediation, a party may request the AAA to invite another party to join in a submission to mediation. Upon receipt of such a request, the AAA will contact the other parties involved in the dispute and attempt to obtain a submission to mediation.

3. Requests for Mediation

A request for mediation shall contain a brief statement of the nature of the dispute and the names, addresses, and telephone numbers of all parties to the dispute and those who will represent them, if any, in the mediation. The initiating party shall simultaneously file two copies of the request with the AAA and one copy with every other party to the dispute.

4. Appointment of the Mediator

Upon receipt of a request for mediation, the AAA will appoint a qualified mediator to serve. Normally, a single mediator will be appointed unless the parties agree otherwise or the AAA determines otherwise. If the agreement of the parties names a mediator or specifies a method of appointing a mediator such as the submission of names of qualified persons to the parties for their selection, that designation or method shall be followed.

5. Qualifications of the Mediator

No person shall serve as a mediator in any dispute in which that person has any financial or personal interest in the result of the mediation, unless approved by the written consent of all parties. Prior to accepting an appointment, the prospective mediator shall disclose any circumstance likely to create a presumption of bias or prevent a prompt meeting with the parties. Upon receipt of such information, the AAA shall either replace the mediator or immediately communicate the information to the parties for their comments. In the event that the parties disagree as to whether the mediator shall serve, the AAA will appoint another mediator. The AAA is authorized to appoint another mediator if the appointed mediator is unable to serve promptly.

---

*Reprinted with permission.

6. Vacancies

If any mediator shall become unwilling or unable to serve, the AAA will appoint another mediator, unless the parties agree otherwise.

7. Representation

Any party may be represented by persons of the party's choice. The names and addresses of such persons shall be communicated in writing to all parties and to the AAA.

8. Date, Time, and Place of Mediation

The mediator shall fix the date and the time of each mediation session. The mediation may be held at the appropriate regional office of the AAA, or at any other convenient location agreeable to the mediator and the parties, as the mediator shall determine.

9. Identification of Matters in Dispute

At least ten days prior to the first scheduled mediation session, each party shall provide the mediator with a brief memorandum setting forth its position with regard to the issues to be resolved. At the discretion of the mediator, such memoranda may be mutually exchanged by the parties.

At the first session, the parties will be expected to produce all information reasonably required for the mediator to understand the issues presented. The mediator may require any party to supplement such information.

10. Authority of the Mediator

The mediator does not have the authority to impose a settlement on the parties but will attempt to help them to reach a satisfactory resolution of their dispute. The mediator is authorized to conduct joint and separate meetings with the parties and to make oral and written recommendations for settlement. Whenever necessary, the mediator may also obtain expert advice concerning technical aspects of the dispute, provided that the parties agree and assume the expenses of obtaining such advice. Arrangements for obtaining such advice shall be made by the mediator or the parties, as the mediator shall determine.

11. Privacy

Mediation sessions are private. The parties and their representatives may attend mediation sessions. Other persons may attend only with the permission of the parties and with the consent of the mediator.

12. Confidentiality

Confidential information disclosed to a mediator by the parties or by witnesses in the course of the mediation shall not be divulged by the mediator. All records, reports or other documents received by a mediator while serving in that capacity shall be confidential. The mediator shall not be compelled to divulge such records or to testify in regard to the mediation in any adversary proceeding involving one of the parties in any judicial forum.

The parties shall maintain the confidentiality of the mediation and shall not rely on, or introduce as evidence in any arbitral, judicial, or other proceeding:

(a) views expressed or suggestions made by a party with respect to a possible settlement of the dispute;
(b) admissions made by a party in the course of the mediation proceedings;
(c) proposals made or views expressed by the mediator; or
(d) the fact that another party had or had not indicated a willingness to accept a proposal for settlement made by the mediator.

13. No Stenographic Record

There shall be no stenographic record of the mediation process.

14. Termination of Mediation

The mediation shall be terminated:

(a) by the execution of a settlement agreement by the parties;
(b) by a written declaration of the mediator to the effect that further efforts at mediation are no longer worthwhile; or
(c) by a written declaration of a party to the effect that the mediation proceedings are terminated.

15. Exclusion of Liability

Neither the AAA nor any mediator is a necessary party in judicial proceedings relating to the mediation. Neither the AAA nor any mediator shall be liable to any party for any act or omission in connection with any mediation conducted under AAA rules or procedures.

16. Interpretation and Application of Rules

The mediator shall interpret and apply these rules insofar as they relate to the mediator's duties and responsibilities. All other rules shall be interpreted and applied by the AAA.

17. Expenses

The expenses of witnesses for either side shall be paid by the party producing such witnesses. All other expenses of the mediation, including required travel and other expenses and fees of the mediator and expenses of representatives of the AAA, and the expenses of any witness and the cost of any proofs or expert advice produced at the direct request of the mediator, shall be borne equally by the parties unless they agree otherwise.

Administrative Fees

The case filing fee is $300. This fee is to be borne equally or as otherwise agreed by the parties. The parties are charged a supplemental fee based on the number of hours or days of mediator time. The fee is for the compensation of both the mediator and the AAA and varies according to region. Check with your local office for specific availability and rates.

There is no charge to the filing party where the AAA is requested to invite other parties to join in a submission to mediation. If a case settles after AAA involvement but prior to dispute resolution, the filing party will be charged a $150 filing fee. The expenses of the AAA and the mediator, if any, are borne equally by the parties unless they vary this arrangement by agreement.

If the parties have attempted mediation under these rules but have failed to reach a settlement, the AAA will apply the administrative fee of the mediation toward subsequent AAA arbitration, when filed with the AAA within 90 days of the termination of the mediation. . . . Once the parties agree to mediate, no refund of the administrative fee will be made.

2. Comments and Questions

a. As evidenced by the existence of the above rules, the AAA has expanded beyond arbitration, and now offers mediation services as well. (You will learn much more about arbitration in Part IV.) The AAA arbitration rules are found in Chapter 10, section C.

b. The AAA rules provide a convenient catalogue of the major matters to consider in commercial financial arbitration.

c. There are a variety of hybrid procedures that combine mediation and arbitration. These are addressed in Chapter 13, section C. The last paragraph of these mediation rules expressly contemplates "med-arb," where the parties first mediate but if that does not succeed they proceed to arbitration. The knowledge that arbitration will follow impasse provides an incentive to settle the dispute.

F. Regulating Mediation: Analysis and Proposal

1. Nancy H. Rogers & Craig A. McEwen, MEDIATION LAW, POLICY & PRACTICE §§ 13:02 to 13.03 (2d ed. 1994)*

§ 13:02. Cost-Benefit Analysis of Current Regulation of Mediation.

Mediation laws . . . can be roughly divided by their relationship to: enforceability of the mediated agreement, compulsion to participate and pressures to settle, enforceability of predispute mediation clauses, confidentiality, mediator qualifications, liability and immunity for mediators, mediator certification and continued accountability, other means to promote fairness of the process, and funding and administration. The provisions in each of these types of law differ significantly among states and even for different types of mediation within a given state.

At the same time, there is substantial uniformity in the apparent goals reflected by these laws, including:

1. To promote effectiveness in terms of increased use of mediation and higher settlement of cases, especially in those cases in which its use reduces transaction costs for the parties or resolves disputes that disrupt the lives of persons other than the parties;
2. To preserve fairness, defined as consent by parties who retain the option of rejecting settlement and securing legal advice;
3. To enhance quality, in terms of a public perception that the mediation programs and broader justice system are fair and responsive to the parties' needs; and
4. To maintain access to courts and other public institutions as well as to mediation.

*Reprinted with permission.

Recently, some have argued that the laws also ought to serve other goals, including:

5. To promote productive careers for mediators;
6. To create a single set of expectations about the manner in which "true mediation" is conducted;
7. To bring about reconciliation among the parties;
8. To promote public values; and
9. To increase respect for mediation as a profession.

Occasionally, some of the goals listed in 5 through 9 are reflected in legislation. For example, requiring mediators to have graduate-level degrees, certified training, and years of experience in another profession seems to serve goals 5, 6, and 9. Arguably, however, regulation should not serve these goals. Enhancing an emerging profession is less important than enhancing quality, effectiveness, fairness, and access as reflected in goals 1 through 4 above. The regulation created makes it less likely that more essential goals will be reached since it tends to narrow the field of mediators, decreases diversity, and probably increases the cost of mediation.

An interesting report by a commission in New South Wales, Australia, responds to a similar mediator advocacy for high entry credentials and accreditation:

> "There is some concern that regulation confers benefits on members of an occupation when they themselves request it. There is concern that in the process of setting standards of practice and ethical codes which have State sanction, rules to eliminate unqualified and unscrupulous practitioners, to protect clients and to emphasize the service ideal, will be accompanied by rules to reduce competition and artificially enhance the status of practitioners to the detriment of the public. Clearly, the individual practitioners recognized by the State will be advantaged. They are more likely to be employed, have enhanced professional reputations and potentially higher incomes because the pool of competitors is limited. The occupational group will most probably enjoy communal benefits with enhanced reputation or credibility by curbing those whose performance lowers the reputation of the practice as a whole."

The report concludes that the effects of such regulations in order to protect consumers are speculative at this point and that the costs of regulation are likely to outweigh any benefits.

[Here] we assume the validity of the first four primary goals set out above and assess the effectiveness of regulation in reaching them. We recognize, however, that even the four primary goals present difficult issues of definition and may compete with each other. The other goals (listed as 5. through 9. above), though legitimate, seem subordinated in importance. They can appropriately be viewed as objectives for program administration, but it seems unwise to use them as a justification for costly legal regulation. . . .

Mandatory participation provisions are obviously effective in promoting greater use of mediation. People are more likely to participate in mediation if directed to do so by a court, administrative agency, or a previously agreed to contract clause. Research on mediation indicates that settlement rates are roughly comparable in mandatory and voluntary mediation programs.

There remains a question of whether laws requiring participation in mediation will ultimately leave such a bad taste in the mouths of participants that they will not voluntarily seek mediation for disputes outside of the court or agency context. Still, empirical research indicates that the immediate reaction is typically not negative; parties ordered to participate are as likely to be satisfied with the process as those who choose it. In addition, there is new evidence that those who are ordered to participate in mediation will find ways to increase voluntary use. In response to a national survey of corporate counsel, lawyers who had participated in court-ordered mediation were much more likely (77% versus 44% of the entire pool) to report that they had voluntarily increased their use of nonbinding processes such as mediation in their disputes with other companies.

These positive results in terms of increasing participation both within the compulsory programs and outside that context must be counterbalanced by potential negative aspects. When participation is compelled, the concerns about fairness and quality increase. Also, there is concern that some parties will be so burdened by the extra step that they cannot afford to continue the court or agency process.

The statutes regarding mandatory mediation are very different, reflecting serious policy disagreements about these issues. First, the statutes and courts construing them take different approaches to what constitutes adequate participation. We [believe] . . . that requirements should be limited in scope and clearly drawn—requiring attendance for a specified time and exchange of certain information rather than good faith bargaining. Requiring more does little to increase settlement rates, interferes with the confidentiality of the process, and promotes unnecessary litigation about compliance.

Second, the over one hundred statutes authorizing mandatory participation create different types of referral schemes: some dictate a blanket mandate for all cases of a given type, with delineated exceptions; others authorize a judge or other official to designate certain cases for compulsory participation; still others require the parties to select a type of dispute resolution process. Most statutes now authorize the case by case selection process. This permits court officials to accumulate evidence on which cases are best handled through mediation and to make selective referrals that will reduce wasted time. For example, if research shows that mediation is less likely to produce settlement if dispositive motions are pending, the case by case approach permits the courts to choose the optimal moment in each case. In addition, it reduces the need for party motions to raise exceptions. For example, the judge may initially avoid assigning to mediation a case apparently involving domestic violence, eliminating the need for a party to move exclusion and prepare documentation sufficient to persuade the court that the violence occurred.

In some contexts, courts or agencies can order the parties to participate in mediation without specific statutory authorization. However, where the authorization is needed, it seems useful to provide it in the uniform statute. In crafting the authorization, the statute should defer to a local official for the selection of cases and should define compliance clearly and simply.

Only a few states have statutes governing *predispute mediation clauses.* Several statutes require inclusion of such a clause in settlement agreements that will be approved by the court. Others provide for enforceability of the clauses. There is little outcry for a statute that would provide courts with the summary enforcement powers accorded arbitration clauses. Early court decisions appear to be enforcing these clauses by dismissing or staying litigation based on the contract. In short, statutory provisions regarding enforcement of predispute mediation clauses appear unnecessary.

Funding schemes are also geared toward increasing participation in mediation. The more than 200 such statutes affect whether and how much the parties will be charged and how many cases can be mediated. In terms of their effectiveness, a few conclusions are clear. First, when mediation is voluntary and the parties must pay for it, voluntary use is low. Second, in some areas volunteer mediators are plentiful enough that little funding is needed in order to encourage broad participation. For example, courts in 13 Ohio counties make mediation available for over a thousand cases a year through the use of volunteer "Settlement Week" mediators. The program is offered free without statutory authorization or special funding. Third, statutes authorizing the courts to require the parties to pay for mediation even if they are required to participate in it enable the courts to quickly create high volume use of mediation. This has been the recent experience of both Texas and Florida. At the same time, . . . such approaches to funding present issues of fairness and access that ultimately lead us to advocate against their use for routine cases.

Although it is possible to generalize about statutory funding schemes and their effectiveness in promoting use of mediation, it may be counterproductive to include these schemes in a uniform mediation statute. There may be jurisdictional and subject matter differences in the ability to attract good volunteers, to add to court filing fees or fines in order to fund programs, or to secure general revenues. Thus, we omit funding from our proposal for uniform laws. At the same time, funding a program by routinely imposing the expense on the parties presents such compelling fairness and access problems that this avenue ought to be eliminated in a uniform statute.

Ironically, laws facilitating settlement pressures both have the greatest track record for increasing settlement rates and present the greatest concerns in terms of other goals for laws regulating mediation. Authorization for the mediator to recommend findings to the judge if the parties fail to settle in mediation, for example, produces significantly higher settlement rates. As effectiveness for that purpose increases, so too does the argument that the process lacks guarantees of fairness, since some parties will feel precluded from rejecting a recommended settlement and proceeding to trial. Settlement pressures also reduce access to trial and other processes. If the settlement pressures include monetary sanctions, the laws have a more severe impact on those with fewer resources. [F]airness and access arguments seem to outweigh arguments about effectiveness in terms of settlement rates. Thus, settlement pressure authorization should be omitted from the uniform law.

Confidentiality provisions are also designed to increase frankness in mediation sessions and thus both participation and settlement. Legislators have largely been persuaded of their merit; more than 200 statutes add confidentiality protection to mediation. Despite their popularity, little evidence exists to verify that confidentiality legislation increases settlement rates in mediation. In fact, settlement rates resemble each other from state to state in similar Settlement Week mediation programs despite the fact that some states have a mediator privilege and others do not. Broad confidentiality provisions have caused fairness concerns, because they sometimes eliminate crucial evidence or cloak matters of public importance. At the same time, narrowly drawn mediation privilege statutes seem to present few concerns in terms of fairness or access. . . .

Mediator qualifications present different issues. The likely costs of substantial qualifications seem high in terms of the goals of access. Nonetheless, legislators and judges seem to assume that some entry level qualifications should be required for mediators who receive referrals from publicly supported programs. These statutes and rules set widely varying standards, combining education, experience, training, and screening in different ways.

If one looks solely at the effectiveness of mediator qualifications in promoting settlement, the evidence that mediator qualifications make a difference in settlement rates is limited. Empirical evidence does not verify effects on settlement rates for any qualifications except previous mediation experience. Anecdotal evidence provides no dramatic evidence that higher educational qualifications promote settlement. Settlement rates are roughly the same in domestic mediation programs in Maine and California, despite requirements of mental health education in California and no similar requirement in Maine. Further, mediation skills training seems to make little difference in the ability of attorney mediators to settle cases in Settlement Week, despite the fact that the mediators' mediation skills training varied from none to over 80 hours.

The commentary on mediator qualifications provides little help. Even blue ribbon task forces shun specifics, noting that qualifications should vary according to the amount of choice accorded the parties, the substantive area of the dispute, and the availability of talent. Moreover, there is reason to read the commentary by those in the field with more cynicism than usual, because mediators who profit from a narrower pool and an expanded market for training may be tempted to recommend high qualifications.

In other words, mediator qualifications, like confidentiality provisions, come with little to support their effectiveness in terms of promoting settlement. At the same time, the qualifications present greater risks than posed by mediator privileges in terms of the accompanying goals of preserving access to court and guarding against unfairness. One would assume that mediation costs will go up as the mediator pool decreases. As a result, use of mediation may be reduced or parties may be asked to pay substantial costs, thereby raising concerns about access. If the qualifications also decrease the diversity of the mediator pool, additional fairness concerns arise. Further, to the extent that mediator qualifications are offered as a way to insure fairness in mediation, the effort is misplaced; ensuring lawyer participation in mediation sessions is more likely to protect against unfairness.

In light of uncertainty about effectiveness and likely costs, what should legislators do about qualifications in a model statute? Perhaps the best approach is to start with qualifications that are not likely to decrease substantially the size or diversity of the mediator pool. Local program administrators can impose their own requirements if the statutory qualifications are insufficient to produce an appropriate settlement rate. At the same time, referring parties to a pool of mediators provides a superior approach to reference to mediator by name. Reference to particular private mediators may create a perception of cronyism by the court and lower public regard for the justice system.

Provisions that create *immunity for mediators* decrease their insurance costs and arguably encourage them to be more flexible and creative. At the same time, liability may protect against unfairness in certain situations. This results in a dilemma, because fairness is one of those goals that may often trump all others. Few would advocate an unfair process, even if it was less costly and faster than other processes. Otherwise, a coin toss would become the predominant dispute resolution process. At the same time, these fairness-directed provisions should not be off limits in terms of assessing their cost-effectiveness. Even well-intentioned fairness provisions ought to be omitted from a proposed uniform law if they offer little promise of success in protecting against unfairness, and they decrease participation, settlement, or access to trial.

In the case of immunity, one might argue that there is little evidence either that liability is needed to ensure fairness or that statutory immunity is needed to reduce costs. The courts seem likely to protect their own appointed mediators and elsewhere insurance costs have remained low. Thus, at this point, it seems better to err on the side of the fairness concerns and omit an immunity provision.

[W]e [earlier] reviewed a number of other provisions for mediator accountability through certification and other provisions for assuring quality, fairness, and effectiveness and concluded that they offer little promise. At the same time, in the face of compulsory participation, the court or agency ought to *monitor the mediation process* and stand ready to remove mediators from the list or stop mandating that particular kinds of cases participate in mediation. In short, they ought to be required to monitor the process.

§ 13:03. Uniform Mediation Statute.

It is time to begin the dialogue on a uniform mediation statute that would regulate mediation procedures but would leave funding or administration of mediation programs to be established independently. In a state with few mediation statutes, such a uniform mediation statute might contain a provision that it preempts other more complex mediation statutes which deal with something other than administration and funding. However, such an approach might be risky in a state like California; it would be important first to study the one hundred or more mediation laws to determine the effect of a preemptive statute.

The proposed statute omits as unnecessary or inappropriate provisions for enforceability of the mediated agreement, authorization for pressures to settle, enforcement of predispute mediation clauses, mediator liability and immunity, mediator accountability, and mediator certification. It is a simpler statute, designed to be applicable in a variety of contexts. The time has come to develop a leaner, clearer, and more uniform approach to regulating mediation. . . . We offer this draft statute to stimulate the dialogue that we hope will result in a uniform statute, one that will improve upon the complex, intrusive, and unclear regulatory scheme that now exists.

Mediation

Mediation Defined. Mediation is a nonbinding process in which a mediator(s), who is not a party to the dispute, assists the parties in negotiating their dispute.

Mandatory Mediation. A court or administrative agency may direct the parties and their lawyers in a proceeding pending before it to participate in a mediation session. Alternatively, the court or administrative agency may make participation in mediation a prerequisite to filing particular motions in which urgent disposition is not needed. In making such an order, the judge or hearing officer shall consider the likelihood of settlement through mediation, whether attendance will be unduly burdensome to any party, including whether the cost is more than the party can afford and more than is justified by the nature of the case, and whether attendance will permit intimidation of one party by another. The parties and their lawyers will meet the requirements for participation by appearing for the period required and by submitting the documents required by the order. Parties directed to attend mediation should not also be required to pay a mediation fee, except for extraordinary cases in which the parties' ability to pay and the importance of the issues justify appointment of a special master mediator.

Mediator Qualifications. A court or administrative agency should make a mandatory reference to a pool of mediators only if it has established requisite qualifications for effective mediators and if the person or persons meet those qualifications. The court or administrative agency should endeavor to establish qualifications that create a broad pool of mediators. Reference to a particular private mediator should occur only in an extraordinary case.

Monitoring. A court or administrative agency that regularly requires the parties to participate in mediation should develop a means to monitor the quality of the mediation in terms of settlement rates, perceptions of fairness, cost for the parties, and access to trial or hearing in the event that settlement is not reached.

Mediation Privilege. Evidence of discussions during a mediation session shall be protected from disclosure during a civil action or administrative proceeding, if the mediation occurred pursuant to court or administrative agency directive or by written agreement of the parties. An exception will be made to this privilege if: (1) all parties to the mediation waive the privilege, (2) necessary to prevent commission of a crime or physical harm to a person, or (3) a court orders disclosure after making a finding that the harm caused to the administration of justice by nondisclosure outweighs the purposes served by the privilege. This provision does not preempt public meetings laws.

Lawyers. The parties should be permitted to bring their attorneys to mediation sessions.

Uniformity. Whenever reference is made to mediation in statutes or rules of procedure, these provisions shall regulate the process, unless otherwise indicated.

2. Comments and Questions

a. Many of the topics introduced here will be revisited later, notably in various mediation processes, hybrids that include mediation, and the material on professionalism in Chapters 19 and 20.

b. Do you like the brief and general approach taken by the model statute, or would you prefer a longer and more detailed statute? If you drafted such a statute, what would you add to the Rogers-McEwen model, and what would you leave out?

Part IV

Arbitration

Chapter 10

The Arbitration Process

CASE STUDY

Bob Jones, age 48, and Sara Smith, age 31, are neighbors in the Brentwood apartment Complex in the small town of Melville, New Olympia. Bob lives in a spacious two bedroom apartment overlooking the golf course while Sara lives in a small interior efficiency apartment. They both work in the local machine parts manufacturing plant. Bob is a high ranking manager and Sara is a senior assembly line worker in the quality control section. Bob has worked at the plant for over twenty years while Sara has worked there for seven. Bob drives a two door foreign luxury car. Sara drives a late model domestic utility vehicle. They were introduced to each other the day Sara started at the plant and have grown to be good friends.

On the day of Friday, September 1, 1995, Sara asked Bob for a ride to and from work because her car was in the shop. Bob said, "Ok, but we will have to leave work a little early because I'm going on a trip over the long weekend and I need to hurry home to finish packing." Sara indicated that she should not have a problem leaving early. They agreed to meet in the front foyer of the plant at 4:45 p.m. Bob was there on time. He waited for five minutes and looked around for Sara, but there was no sign of her. He decided to go down to the assembly line to see if Sara was there. Sure enough she was there, working away. As soon as Sara saw Bob she realized she had forgotten that they were going to leave early. She apologized to Bob and quickly got her things together. They left the plant at 4:55 p.m. To make up time Bob was speeding. Bob is a conservative driver who rarely speeds, but in this case he believed he had to in order to get home in time to finish packing and drive to the regional airport to catch his plane.

They were about half way home when they approached the intersection of Elm street and Broadway Boulevard. They were traveling on Broadway. Bob saw that the traffic signal was yellow so he hit the accelerator in order to speed through the intersection. Unfortunately, there was an anxious teenager named Jimmy Wilson, revving his engine to the Rolling Stones, waiting on Elm Street for the light to turn green. As soon as the light turned green Jimmy raced into the intersection without first looking to see if the intersection was clear. He did not see Bob's car until it was too late. Jimmy hit the brakes, but could not avoid smashing into Bob's car on the passenger side between the door and the rear bumper.

Police and ambulances soon came to the scene and rushed Bob, Jimmy, and Sara to the hospital. Bob and Jimmy were wearing their seatbelts. Sara was not. Bob sustained minor injuries that were remedied with stitches, pain killers, and some light physical therapy. He was released from the hospital within 24 hours. Jimmy suffered some soft tissue injuries, bruised ribs, and a mild concussion. He was released from the hospital within 48 hours. Sara was severely injured. She sustained lacerations on her face and upper body, three broken ribs, back injuries, and internal bleeding. She was in the hospital for close to a month.

Once she was released from the hospital Sara was ordered to home rest and to attend strenuous physical therapy three times a week for the next six months. The doctors have stated that she will not be able to return to work for approximately 9 to 12 months. Furthermore, the doctors have expressed little hope that she will be able to perform the same assembly line activities she was performing prior to the accident without incurring chronic back pain. Since the accident Bob has called Sara only once and has failed to visit her on a single occasion. On Monday, October 30, 1995, Sara filed suit to recover damages for personal injury, medical expenses, loss of wages, and pain and suffering sustained from the accident.

New Olympia has a guest passenger statute (prohibiting passengers in the car from suing the driver); however, the state Supreme Court (five to four decision) recently held that the statute is invalid because it is excessively broad. Members of the state legislature are currently divided on whether or not to enact a more narrow guest passenger statute. New Olympia recognizes comparative fault doctrines and allows the submission of evidence regarding the failure to wear a seat belt. For the sake of simplicity, ignore any possible claims that Sara might have other than the claims against Bob.

A. Introduction

We now turn to arbitration, the last of the three primary ADR procedures. The defining characteristic of arbitration is that the third party neutral, the arbitrator, renders a decision about the issue(s) under arbitration. The decision often is binding on the parties, but this is not a necessary attribute of arbitration, and sometimes the parties seek only a nonbinding decision. Private parties usually want a binding decision, but nonbinding arbitration is the form used by courts and government.

To the maximum extent possible, we have selected articles and cases that illustrate arbitration issues and problems from three substantive areas: commercial dealings between merchants, contracts between businesses and consumers, and labor management relations. By limiting our examination of arbitration to a few substantive topics, we hope to provide the student with a better understanding of the subject. Whenever faced with a choice, we selected depth over breadth.

The basis for requiring parties to participate in arbitration is commonly said to be contractual; i.e. because the parties have entered an agreement to arbitrate. Agreement at the time of arbitration is not required, as once was true, but absent such agreement arbitration will be ordered only if there was a prior promise to arbitrate — this particular dispute, or future disputes in general. Accordingly, it can sensibly be said that the basis for arbitration is consent even though one of the parties subsequently wants the dispute adjudicated before a court. To say that arbitration is a contractual relationship is a large generalization, and general principles do not decide hard questions. The reader should consider the "nature" of arbitration to be an open question that is considered and reconsidered throughout the materials in the ensuing three chapters.

Arbitration, as discussed here, is limited to situations where the parties "selected" arbitration. (The enforcement of mandatory arbitration clauses in contracts of adhesion, where there is a significant disparity of bargaining power between the parties, is considered in several contexts in Chapters 11 and 12.) Typically the parties to an arbitration agreement are "private" individuals or entities, as opposed to units of government or parastatal organizations.

The voluntariness aspect of participation in an arbitration becomes important in "court annexed arbitration," a procedure where a court orders litigants to participate in nonbinding arbitration as a precondition to trial. This topic is discussed in Chapter 16. Administrative agencies also employ nonbinding arbitration (they lack authority to mandate binding arbitration), and sometimes participation is required for program beneficiaries or parties contracting with the government. This topic is discussed in Chapter 15. Various hybrid procedures that include elements of arbitration, notably mediation and arbitration combinations, are discussed in Chapter 13. The law of arbitration is covered in Chapter 11, and Chapter 12 examines the application of arbitration in the commercial, consumer, and labor contexts.

This chapter provides an introduction to the workings of the arbitration process. While these materials focus on problems, the reader should remember that arbitration nearly always works as planned. The vast majority of contracts are performed without incident, so there is no need for resort to arbitration (or any other dispute resolution process). Where disputes do arise, most are shrugged off (sometimes called "lumping it"), or quickly settled through informal negotiations. Where a dispute that the parties agreed to arbitrate cannot be settled, whether before or after the dispute arose, the arbitration proceeding nearly always is completed without incident and the matter ends there.

Exploration of the arbitration process commences with two articles about major commercial disputes. Next, the American Arbitration Association (AAA) administered arbitration and the Center for Public Resources (CPR) nonadministered arbitration procedures are considered in detail. After a discussion of non-binding arbitration, Chapter 10 concludes with materials on the drafting of arbitration clauses, including standard provisions for most situations that the student is likely to encounter.

A private not-for-profit organization, the American Arbitration Association (AAA) has been a central force in the arbitration area for many decades. Until recently, it was the only arbitration organization of consequence in America. With the growth of ADR since the 1970s, the AAA has expanded into mediation, and other ADR organizations have become important providers of arbitration services. The AAA has developed extensive standardized procedures, forms, and model contract provisions, some of which are reproduced here.

Arbitration may be conducted by a single person, or by a multiple member panel. While a panel could consist of any number of persons, in practice the panel is always composed of three members. The use of an odd number of arbitrators is designed to avoid a tie vote. (Recall that co-mediation by two persons is common, often by persons with different skills or professional backgrounds. Because mediators facilitate a settlement by the parties, and do not render a decision, there is no tie vote problem.) The vast majority of arbitration proceedings are conducted by a single arbitrator; the use of three member panels is reserved for situations where large sums of money or questions of great importance to the parties are at issue. We use the term the term "arbitrator," except where otherwise noted, as referring to both single arbitrators and multi-member panels.

B. Arbitration of Commercial Disputes

1. Soia Mentschikoff, *Commercial Arbitration*, 61 COLUM. L. REV. 846 (1961)*

I. INTRODUCTION

B. Setting For Arbitration

. . . The first thing to be noted is that although commonly thought of as a single type phenomenon, both the structure and the process of commercial arbitration are determined by the different institutional contexts in which it arises. There are three major institutional settings in which commercial arbitration appears as a mechanism for the settlement of disputes.

The simplest is when two persons in a contract delineating a business relationship agree to settle any disputes that may arise under the contract by resort to arbitration before named arbitrators or persons to be named at the time of the dispute. In this, which can be called individuated arbitration, the making of all arrangements, including the procedures for arbitration, rests entirely with the parties concerned. . . . [W]e believe that the chief moving factors here are: (1) a desire for privacy as, for example, in certain crude oil situations where such arrangements exist; (2) the availability of expert deciders; (3) the avoidance of possible legal difficulties with the nature of the transaction itself; and (4) the random acceptance by many businessmen of the idea that arbitration is faster and less expensive than court action.

A second type of arbitration arises within the context of a particular trade association or exchange. The group establishes its own arbitration machinery for the settlement of disputes among its members, either on a voluntary or compulsory basis, and sometimes makes it available to nonmembers doing business in the particular trade. A particular association may also have specialist committees, which are investigatory in character, with the arbitration machinery handling only the private disputes involving nonspecialist categories of cases. Occasionally, when the volume of arbitration in a particular trade association is not large enough to warrant the maintenance of its own machinery, or when the relevant trade association consists only of one segment of an entire industry, the association joins with other related associations in the organization of a confederated trade association system under which a single machinery for compulsory or voluntary use by persons in the related industries or trades is provided.

The third setting for commercial arbitration is found in administrative groups, such as the American Arbitration Association (AAA), the International Chamber of Commerce, and various local chambers of commerce, which provide rules, facilities, and arbitrators for any persons desiring to settle disputes by arbitration. Many trade associations with insufficient business to warrant separate organizations make special arrangements with one of these groups to process disputes that arise among their members.

---

*This article originally appeared at 61 COLUM. L. REV. 846 (1961). Reprinted by permission.

In a survey of trade associations in which we received 547 relevant responses, 34 per cent of the associations indicated that their members made individual arrangements for arbitration; 29 per cent indicated that they used some type of organized machinery, including the AAA; and 26 percent reported that their members never arbitrate. [Another 150 or so of the responses indicated that the trade associations were mere clearing houses of information.] These differential responses from trade associations as to the utilization of arbitration was not on a random basis, but indicated instead that these were rational reasons for the existence of these differences.

C. Factors Determining the Need for Arbitration

At this point it is useful to distinguish between those factors that can be said to produce a need for arbitration machinery in commercial groups and those factors that merely make it desirable. The reasons commonly given for arbitration — speed, lower expense, more expert decision, greater privacy — are appealing to all businessmen, and yet not all utilize arbitration. It seems reasonably clear, therefore, that for some trades these factors are of greater importance than for others, and that for some trades there must be countervailing values in not resorting to arbitration. We postulated three factors as being theoretically important in determining whether or not a particular trade needed institutionalized use of arbitration, and incorporated questions relating to these factors in our trade association questionnaire.

The first factor was the nature of the economic function being performed in relation to the movement of the goods by the members of the association. We postulated that persons primarily buying for resale, that is merchants in the original sense of the term, were much more likely to be interested in speed of adjudication, and that since price allowance would be a central remedy for defects in quality or, indeed, for nondelivery, the speed and low cost characteristics of arbitration would be particularly attractive to them, thus leading to the creation of institutionalized machinery. The trade associations in which such merchants constitute all or part of the membership reported as follows: 48 per cent use institutionalized machinery, 34 per cent make individual arrangements for arbitration, and only 18 per cent never arbitrate. These figures are to be contrasted with the reports from those trade associations that stated that their memberships did not include any merchants. In those groups 23 per cent reported the existence of institutionalized arbitration, 44 per cent reported individual arrangements, and 33 per cent reported no arbitration whatever.

The second major factor that we thought would be important in determining the need for arbitration was the participation of the members of the association in foreign trade. Apart from the enhanced possibility of delay inherent in transnational law suits, when the parties to a transaction are governed by different substantive rules of law, resort to the formal legal system poses uncertainty and relative unpredictability of result for at least one of the parties. This uncertainty and unpredictability is increased by the fact that the very rules governing the choice of the applicable law are themselves relatively uncertain and are not uniform among the nations of the world. Faced with such an uncertain formal legal situation, any affected trade group is apt to develop its own set of substantive rules or standards of behavior as the controlling rules for its members. Obviously, when a trade group develops its own rules of law, it requires as deciders of its disputes persons who are acquainted with the standards it has developed. Since knowledgeability does not reside in the judges of any formal legal system, the drive toward institutionalized private machinery is reinforced.

So far as American foreign trade associations are concerned, it is necessary to distinguish between associations whose members are primarily importers, and associations whose members are primarily exporters. The important thing to be noticed about this distinction is that in all cases of dispute other than those involving pure nondelivery, the documents or goods will be in the buyer's country when the dispute arises. Although the existence of an operative private law governing trade in particular commodities, with consequent administration by private adjudicatory machinery, means that such machinery can exist either in the buyer's or the seller's country, we postulated that in view of the normal location in the buyer's country of the documents or goods at the time of the dispute, a rule of convenience of forum would tend to place the situs of arbitration in the buyer's country. It seemed reasonable to expect, therefore, that trade associations whose members included importers would show a higher incidence of organized arbitration than those that did not. Of the groups reporting an import relationship to foreign trade, 67 per cent did have organized machinery, 25 per cent made individual arrangements, and only 8 per cent reported they were arbitrated. Of groups that had both an import and export connection, 37 per cent reported that they had organized machinery, 45 per cent made individual arrangements, and 18 per cent never arbitrated. Of the groups which reported that the members dealt only in domestic trade or only in export, 25 per cent reported their own organized machinery, 40 per cent reported individual arrangements, and 35 per cent reported no arbitration.

The third factor that we thought would bear on the need for arbitration machinery relates to the kind of goods dealt with by the members of the association. One of the major areas of dispute among businessmen centers on the quality of the goods involved. If, therefore, the goods are such as not to be readily susceptible of quality determination by third persons, arbitration or, indeed, inspection, is an unlikely method of settling disputes. If goods are divided into raws, softs, and hards, the differences in their suitability for third party adjudication becomes relatively clear. On the whole, raws are a fungible commodity, one bushel of #1 wheat being very much like another bushel of #1 wheat. On the other hand, hards, which consist of items like refrigerators and automobiles, are not viewed by their producers as essentially fungible, however they may appear to the layman. We did not believe that Ford would like to have General Motors' sitting on disputes involving the quality of Ford cars, or viceversa. Moreover, quality differentials in raws can normally be reflected by price differentials, but defects in hard goods frequently affect their usefulness and therefore price differential compensation is not feasible. Thus, the normal sales remedy for raws has come to be price allowance, whereas the normal sales remedy for hard goods has come to be repair or replacement. Raws, involving fungibility and ease of finding an appropriate remedy, are therefore highly susceptible to third party adjudication, whereas hard goods tend to move away from such adjudication. Soft goods, which are the intermediate category and range from textiles to small hardware, we thought would constitute a neutral category.

In our survey of exchanges dealing in grain and livestock, 100 per cent of those responding [61] reported the use of institutionalized arbitration. There are, of course, other reasons for such a unanimous response by the exchanges, but the nature of the goods involved is a very important one. The trade association survey showed that of all the reporting associations dealing in raws, 46 per cent had machinery, 29 per cent made individual arrangements, and only 25 per cent never arbitrated. On the other hand, only 4 per cent of those reporting hards as their basic goods had machinery, 46 per cent made individual arrangements, and 50 per cent never arbitrated. Of the soft goods associations reporting, 33 per cent had machinery, 41 per cent made individual arrangements, and 26 per cent never arbitrated.

To the extent that the factors leading to institutionalized machinery reinforce each other, as, for example, in the case of an association reporting that its members have an import relationship to foreign trade, deal in raws, and consist of merchants, the existence of arbitration machinery rises to approximately 100 per cent. When the contrary report is made, that is, that the membership consists of manufacturers of hard goods engaged only in domestic business, the percentage drops off to about 8 per cent.

D. Relation of Arbitration to Other Formalized Procedures

Since commercial arbitration normally arises out of contracts between the parties to the dispute, and since the major issue is usually one of either interpretation of the contract or the measurement of performance, it is obvious that one of the factors enhancing predictability of result is the extent to which the arbitrator is aware of the trade meaning of the contract terms and the significance of the various aspects of performance under it. One would therefore expect that trades in which arbitration was a normal institutional way of life would realize rather early the prophylactic importance of generally understood and agreed upon standard contract clauses and quality specifications. Of the 117 groups reporting institutionalized arbitration, 68 per cent reported that standard form contracts were used. This 68 per cent constituted 48 per cent of the total group reporting the use of standard form contracts. On the other hand, of the 114 groups reporting that they never used arbitration only 36 per cent reported that they used standard form contracts. In other words, trade groups having institutionalized adjudicatory machinery do tend to develop standardization of contract terms.

They also move towards standardization of quality and specialized provisions for adjudicating questions of quality. Seventy-six per cent of the 121 associations reporting institutionalized arbitration have such standardization on at least some of the goods they trade in, while the comparable figure for 113 never-arbitrate groups is 63 per cent. Sixty per cent of 120 institutionalized arbitration groups also provide special inspection machinery for quality adjudications, moving that area of dispute from the adversary to the umpire systems. Only 34 per cent of 113 never-arbitrate groups provide such umpire machinery; Examined in detail, we find that 52 per cent of institutionalized arbitration groups studied have both quality standardization and special inspection machinery, whereas only 25 per cent of the never-arbitrate groups have that combination. Furthermore, only 15 per cent of the institutionalized arbitration groups lack both quality standardization and inspection machinery, whereas 30 per cent of the never-arbitrate groups lack both.

Finally, groups having institutionalized arbitration also show a tendency to have other important self-regulation committees, such as those on ethics and disciplinary proceedings, rules, form contracts, and the like. Sixty per cent of these groups report the existence of such committees, while only 26 per cent of the never-arbitrate group report the existence of such committees. If we put together the existence of form contracts and special committees we find that 46 per cent of the institutionalized arbitration groups have both, while only 14 per cent have neither. However, in the never-arbitrate groups the percentages are virtually reversed; 49 per cent have neither and only 11 per cent have both.

We can thus say that the presence of institutionalized arbitration is a strong index of the existence of a generally self-contained trade association having its own self-regulation machinery and that the forces leading to institutionalized arbitration also, therefore, tend to lead to creation of self-contained, self-governing trade groups.

In addition to the institutionalized arbitration that takes place in the context of the trade associations, a great deal also occurs inside commodity and stock exchanges. The exchanges, of course, are much more tightly organized than are the trade associations and, in addition to an arbitration committee, frequently maintain various specialist committees among whose functions are the deciding of disputes arising out of contracts for commodities traded in the exchange under specific trade rules. For example, in the New York Produce Exchange, there is an arbitration committee with residual jurisdiction, but the trade committees that sit in arbitration most frequently are Animal Oils and Fats Committee, Cottonseed Products Committee, Flour Committee, Grain Committee, Pepper Committee, Soybean Oil Committee, Steamship Committee, and Vegetable Oils, Waxes, and Fats Committee. In exchange groups, not only is resort to arbitration on the whole compulsory for members, but failure to abide by an award is frequently considered grounds for disciplinary proceedings against the recalcitrant party. In addition, the particular norms or standards by which such disputes are judged are frequently spelled out by special committees with a degree of particularity that is rarely matched by our statutes and only occasionally by regulations of administrative agencies. . . .

III. THE AMERICAN ARBITRATION ASSOCIATION

The AAA was the American response to the delays and difficulties that could result from procedural defects in the arbitration process in situations where the economic sanctions of some of the trade groups were not available. This organization from its beginning held itself out as an expert in matters that went to the enforceability of an award and set up its rules and regulations with the primary aim of rendering awards that would not be set aside by the courts. It has succeeded greatly in the accomplishment of this goal, and as a result, it is now one of the most important forums for the determination of commercial disputes by arbitration.

Of the 128 trade associations reporting existence of institutionalized arbitration machinery, 73 per cent indicated that the machinery was organized and serviced either by the trade association itself or by one of the four federated associations. [These are the General Arbitration Council, The National Federation of Textiles, Association of Food Distributors of New York, and the Uniform Plan of the National Canners Association.] The other 27 per cent indicated that they had made special arrangements with the American Arbitration Association; some allowed members a choice between their own and AAA machinery; and others used only the AAA. The AAA thus handles up to 27 per cent of the institutionalized arbitration of trade associations as well as a large variety of individual arrangements for arbitration.

A. Comparison with the Self-Contained Trade Group Arbitration

Arbitration at the AAA differs substantially from arbitration at the self-contained trade groups. The first and most significant difference between the two systems lies in the use of precedent. The decisions that are rendered by the arbitration committees of self-contained trade associations do have precedential value. This is achieved in two ways: in some associations opinions are written and circulated to the membership; in others awards can be appealed or referred to other committees for the establishment of general standards. Most important, however, in all of these associations there is a continuity in the membership of the deciders, which means that the system of precedent operates automatically, for a question decided in one case on the basis of consideration of competing norms is unlikely to be decided differently in the next case by the same people. However, the casual system of arbitration used by the AAA is designed to discourage the use of precedent. The AAA puts enormous pressure on its arbitrators not to write opinions but to merely state the award in dollar amounts. . . .

The second significant difference is that of the self-contained trade association groups, 40 per cent explicitly discourage or forbid the use of attorneys, and in the remaining 60 per cent attorneys very rarely appear. The AAA, on the other hand, encourages the parties to use attorneys. This difference reflects the basic proposition that in the self-contained trade groups the norms and standards of the group itself are being brought to bear by the arbitrators, and the incursion of lawyers with their potential emphasis on general legal norms and standards is viewed as a factor deflecting expeditious hearing and wise decision. At the AAA, theoretically, substantive legal rules are welcome as norms for decision, and therefore attorneys are welcome. In fact, however, relatively few arbitrators or counsel feel bound by the substantive rules of law, although most feel it should be "considered."

The third difference between self-contained trade association systems and the casual arbitration at the AAA lies in the methods by which awards are enforced. The ultimate sanction in many of the self-contained associations and in almost all of the exchanges is a disciplinary proceeding and thus, potential legal problems with respect to procedure are not seriously considered in these groups. The ultimate sanction at the Association is the rendering of judgment on the award by a court of competent jurisdiction, and therefore problems of procedure are always uppermost in the minds of the tribunal clerks, who are charged with the duty of policing the arbitrators sufficiently, so that the award rendered will be legally enforceable. . . .

C. Personnel

1. Use of Lawyers. . . . In almost all self-contained trade associations and exchanges lawyer participation in the arbitration proceedings is either forbidden or discouraged, and very few of the arbitrators are lawyers or law-trained. The emphasis in these groups is on the utilization of norms and standards of the trade for deciding without regard to their similarity to or difference from the norms or standards that would be imposed by substantive rules of law. We frequently heard, both orally and in writing, that lawyer participation was not desired for two reasons: (1) lawyers did not understand the business usages and practices that were typically involved in adjudicating the dispute and were therefore not helpful; and (2) lawyers made the proceedings unduly technical and tended to create unnecessary delays. . . . When both parties were represented by attorneys, 43 per cent of the cases were decided in less than 90 days and 21 per cent in less than 60 days. When neither party brought an attorney, 78 per cent of the cases were decided in less than 90 days and 49 per cent in less than 60 days. Of course, the figures also showed that attorneys were more likely to be employed as the amount involved in the case became larger.

Personal observation at the Association leads me to the reluctant conclusion that in the great majority of the cases observed, lawyer participation not only failed to facilitate decision but was so inadequate as to materially lengthen and complicate the presentation of the cases. Nonetheless, the Association encourages lawyer participation. Lawyers represent one or more of the parties in 80 per cent of the cases, and serve as arbitrators in about 30 per cent. The availability of legal norms or standards for utilization in the disposition of particular arbitrations at the Association is therefore theoretically present.

2. Use of Expert Deciders. Court actions are typified by the absence of expertise as to the particular business or trade involved, on the part of both the judge and the jury, but in the self-contained trade group arbitration mechanisms, the arbitrators all have this expertise. Although in 45 per cent of the cases at the Association, at least one of the arbitrators was a person from the trade or business in which the dispute arose, the use of such an expert varied from a high of 73 per cent for sales cases involving quality determination to a low of 25 per cent for cases involving employment or agency contracts, royalties, leases, and the like. . . .
3. Role Attitudes. The most important similarity of AAA arbitration to the formal legal system . . . is found in the attitudes with which the arbitrators come to the proceedings. First and perhaps most significant, the Association explicitly urges its arbitrators to adopt a judicial attitude that will lead to decision on the merits rather than to a compromise award. "Compromise" is used here in its invidious sense of arriving at decision by, as one arbitrator expressed it, "giving a little and taking a little." It does not mean that legitimate clashes of interest are not resolved in a way that seems fairest to both sides, a process that lies at the foundation of any attempt to evolve a rule of law. . . .

Although almost 100 per cent of the arbitrators polled thought that both parties should share the burden of proof to some extent, 75 per cent of them believed that in the ultimate analysis the burden should rest on the claimant. Again, the parallel to the formal legal structure is striking. This view of allocation of burden of proof is not an empty one; some cases in our field study were ultimately decided on this basis.

Finally, almost 70 per cent of the experimental arbitrators believed that they should decide the case "on the basis of the evidence available to them and not try to supplement the evidence by their own efforts." This attitude of course, does not mean that the arbitrators believe that they may not request the parties to provide any additional information necessary to clear up ambiguous points. As to this, over 90 per cent believed that they were justified in making such a request.

4. Prior Knowledge of Case. At the AAA the arbitrators, with rare exceptions, know no more about the dispute than can be told by an examination of the written claim of the petitioner and the answer of the respondent. Frequently, these are read immediately prior to the commencement of the arbitration. The elaborate pretrial techniques of the formal legal system are of doubtful availability in arbitration and are not in fact used. The equivalent of the pretrial conference that can be found in the sifting operations of many of the trade associations is not present, except as the arbitrators, after the commencement of hearings, may attempt to get the parties to agree on which issues are to be arbitrated. . . .

D. Proceedings Prior to Hearings

Proceedings at the AAA have three phases. The first deals with the filing of the case, the selection of arbitrators, and the setting of the hearing date. The second phase consists of the hearings themselves. The third phase consists of the deliberations among the arbitrators.

1. Selection of Arbitrators. The standard method of appointing arbitrators is for the

Association to provide the parties with lists of names chosen from its panel of commercial arbitrators. The original lists reflect any wishes the parties may have concerning particular occupations or kinds of persons. The parties then indicate the names to which they object on the list and express an order of preference for the others. The Association then selects the arbitrators from the names not objected to and, when possible, follows the preference of the parties.

2. The Hearings. . . . Following the opening statements, the claimant calls his witnesses. Each witness is sworn in by the clerk unless the parties waive the necessity for swearing in. Any written evidence is marked as an exhibit by the clerk, who also compiles a witness list. In the absence of a transcript, the arbitrators assume the task of making their own notes on what is said or of seeking to remember without notes. In the absence of an early delineation of issues, testimony that is deemed important and relevant for one side can be and is overlooked by one or more of the arbitrators. This can have serious consequences if such evidence is not noted by some other arbitrator, for the overlooked evidence can not then enter into the decision-making process. . . . Although some arbitrators believe that they should participate very little in the proceedings, most arbitrators frequently ask questions, particularly of the parties. Lawyer arbitrators tend to participate most actively and to treat the proceedings as highly informal, while lay arbitrators have a tendency to treat the proceedings as relatively formal.

Once the evidence is in, the parties or their counsel are permitted to sum up, and sometimes the arbitrators ask for additional data or for permission to send the disputed article to some outside source for testing or examination. Any attempt by the arbitrators to seek conciliation or mediation is immediately stopped by the tribunal clerk, who carefully explains to them that the arbitrator's function is to decide the dispute on the merits and not to seek a settlement. This attitude of the Association toward settlement, of course, differs significantly from the attitude of the courts, for judges have frequently been known to call the parties into chambers for the purpose of seeing whether a settlement can be effected.

3. Deliberations. After the hearings are declared closed, the arbitrators, possibly on the same day, meet to reach a decision. Briefs are sometimes requested, but this is not the usual practice. The tribunal clerk, who has sat through the hearings and who frequently is consulted by the arbitrators as to appropriate procedure, sometimes sits with the arbitrators during deliberations, but more commonly, he is simply available to answer questions. His major task at this point is to draft the award in a legally perfect manner and to prevent the arbitrators from issuing an opinion.

E. The Decision-Making Process

. . . The basic task of arbitrators at the Association is to decide with fairness to the parties the merits of a controversy that arose in the past and is presented to them for the first time by the parties or their counsel. They do not have the two further tasks that are present both in the judicial organs of the self-contained trade groups and in the courts: because their decision is not intended to have precedential value, they are not compelled to either ascertain or judge the generalized situation that is typified by the particular case or to issue a rule that will have guiding value for parties in similar situations. The institutional drive by the Association against the addition of these tasks, which is exemplified by the pressure put on the arbitrators not to write opinions, simplifies the arbitrator's job and in one important sense makes that job somewhat parallel to the job allotted to the jury by our formal legal system. For both the jury and Association arbitrators, institutional pressure converge toward the production of a simple final product. In the case of the jury the product is the verdict; in arbitration it is called the award. Typically the product is limited in form to a "yes" or "no" answer or to a dollar amount. This, of course, makes it possible for both jurors in a court and commercial arbitrators at the Association to reach an agreed upon decision without reaching agreement on the reasons for the decision.

2. Comments and Questions

a. As is true for many areas of the law, there is a dearth of empirical studies about how commercial parties make use of arbitration, when, and for what type of issues.

b. Professor Mentschikoff, a distinguished commercial lawyer before she became a law school professor, was shocked by the low quality of legal practice that she observed in arbitrations. She stated (at page 859):

> Personal observation at the AAA leads me to the reluctant conclusion that in the great majority of the cases observed, lawyer participation not only failed to facilitate decision but was so inadequate as to materially lengthen and complicate the presentation of the cases.

Regarding presentations at arbitration hearings, an obvious place for legal skills to shine, Mentschikoff concluded (at page 864):

> Although lawyers are supposed to be skilled in presentation of cases and in the delineating of issues, our observation disclosed that on the whole they were not significantly better than ordinary laymen. In fact, the extent to which issues in the cases failed to be delineated at an early stage in the proceedings was utterly extraordinary.

c. Professor Mentschikoff concluded that the participation of lawyers delayed the arbitration process. A review of AAA records demonstrated that arbitrations proceedings between represented parties consumed more time than those where the parties were unrepresented. It seems probable that lawyers are employed more frequently in relatively complex disputes, or when larger sums are at issue, which could account for some or even most of the additional time consumed in arbitrations where the parties are represented by counsel. Since delay is an expected concomitant of any increase in the number of persons that participate in an arbitration, it would be surprising if the addition of lawyers did not result in lengthened proceedings.

d. The next article addresses the use of arbitration in complex commercial disputes. It was written by a distinguished and experienced practitioner. While simple and smaller disputes are not necessarily complex disputes writ small, it is generally true that if you learn about all the problems that arise in complex disputes you will be well equipped to handle simpler ones.

3. William L.D. Barrett, *Arbitration of a Complex Commercial Case: Practical Guidelines for Arbitrators and Counsel*, ARBITRATION J., December 1986, at 15*

Arbitration is increasingly being used to resolve large and complex commercial cases. Its expert panels, informal procedures, and speed offer many advantages over trial by judge or

*Reprinted with permission.

jury. Judges dislike tying up a court for the days or weeks that such a case requires, and a lay jury can have difficulty in assimilating a considerable amount of evidence, often of a highly technical approach to damages, which they feel is foreign to the commercial spirit of bargain and compromise. . . .

There is now general agreement among arbitrators and counsel that large and complex cases must be managed. The purpose of case management is to define the issues in dispute, and to assemble and present the proof necessary to decide them as efficiently as possible. All of the various procedural steps should be seen as a part of this process; all procedural rulings should be based on advancing it.

What is a complex case? While the size of the amount in controversy does not itself make a case complex, it can, because of the high stakes, induce counsel to look for issues that must be disposed of before the core questions can be addressed. The result is simple cases that have been made complex.

In a "made complex" case, draconian measures . . . could be entirely appropriate: if lawyers are forced to present a case in a short time, they must simplify—and, in the process, jettison—any issues raised only to confuse or delay or that are pressed more in hope than on hard evidence. Lawyers are understandably conservative about discarding issues. At the outset, at least, lawyers almost instinctively believe that anything that can be claimed or contested should be. Typically, however, as a case progresses, reality begins to assert itself. As lawyers gain confidence that they know which issues are important, they become more willing to simplify.

This writer's experience suggests that it is rare for parties to present completely frivolous issues or to raise issues solely to obscure matters or to put off the day of reckoning. Counsel recognize that once the case begins, the arbitrators have the power of ultimate decision. Just as in a court case with a single judge presiding from its inception, attorneys are reluctant to antagonize the panel, to appear to have made foolish arguments, or to be considered obstructionist. Experienced lawyers know that their credibility is a precious asset—one that they preserve with care and risk only with great deliberation. It follows that most complex cases are inherently so.

An inherently complex case is one where there is an involved factual situation, perhaps of a highly technical nature, or one where the facts and law are mixed, or where, because the situation existed for a long time great volume of proof is necessary. In such a case, even if both sides are completely professional and cooperate in good faith, it can still be far from easy to frame the issues, organize the proof, and present the case in an orderly way. Even arbitrators who are expert in the subject matter can find that their experience bears on only a fraction of the issues.

In such a case, the old prescription of patience, patience, and most patience is probably best. If experienced counsel have difficulty in proving facts in a simple way, it is probably unwise for arbitrators to assume that they know better, at least at first. In finding out what proof is important, what issues will be dispositive and how to hold a hearing both sides will feel has been fair, the arbitrator and counsel must work together. Given mutual trust and respect, many of these problems will solve themselves.

The guidelines that follow are not rules of procedure. They simply describe the way in which many matters that commonly arise in large cases are handled. Each case presents unique problems. One of the advantages of arbitration is that the procedures can be tailored to suit the specific requirements of each case. In appropriate cases, the parties or the arbitrators will suggest procedures different from those presented here. In the absence of special circumstances, however, it can be assumed that these guidelines will indicate normal practice and provide a general idea of what can be expected as the case progresses.

NOTICE OF ARBITRATION AND RESPONSES

The rules of the American Arbitration Association (AAA) require only a brief statement of the claim, and a response is not mandatory. Frequently, when the parties meet at a prehearing conference or preliminary hearing, the respondent claims to have insufficient information to answer the claim or to predict what proofs and witnesses he or she will want to offer. Claimants can expedite the case by providing the respondents with more detail about their claims before these meetings. When thus informed, respondents can reasonably be asked at the preliminary hearing what elements of the claim they dispute and what defenses they will assert. Throughout these guidelines, suggestions regarding claims will apply with equal force to counterclaims asserted by the respondent.

THE PRELIMINARY CONFERENCE

A preliminary conference is often called by the AAA soon after a case is commenced. At such a conference, the parties confer with the tribunal administrator, who attempts to resolve as many of the procedural problems as possible. Under current practice, such a conference is off the record. The arbitrators will see some of the results of the conference, but only those upon which there was agreement.

The topics covered are specification of claim, document requests, stipulation of uncontested facts, witness lists, estimates of length of the case, and logistical matters such as the size of the hearing room, such special facilities as an interpreter, and whether there should be a transcript.

A preliminary conference is a useful way to expedite a case because preliminary matters and those which are agreed upon can progress while the panel is being selected. When the parties finally appear before the arbitrators, it will be assumed by the panel that all agreements reached at the preliminary conference have been carried out, and that no valuable hearing time need be devoted to them.

THE PANEL

The panel usually meets for the first time immediately before the preliminary hearing. At that time, they should choose a chairperson, who will preside at all hearings. In addition, the chair usually acts as the liaison with the AAA for handling such procedural matters as scheduling. Normally, the parties agree that the chairperson may handle incidental matters such as discovery problems that arise between hearings, and that, in the chairperson's discretion, counsel can be heard by conference call, with the rest of the panel included only when necessary. It should be noted that the rules only require that evidence be taken in the presence of all arbitrators and parties. Procedural and discovery matters not involving evidence can, with the parties' agreement, be handled by any one of the arbitrators. All contact with the arbitrators is made through the tribunal administrator at the AAA.

HEARINGS IN GENERAL

Evidentiary hearings are the main event in arbitration. All of the other devices—preliminary hearings, conferences, discovery, and procedural matters in the hearings themselves—have but one purpose: the orderly examination and evaluation of each party's proof. None of these is an end in itself and none will alone be dispositive of a complex case.

Arbitration of a large case places different burdens on counsel than does litigation. Probably the major difference is the speed with which the case will actually go to "trial." Attorneys who are accustomed to a year or two of discovery might be unprepared for evidentiary hearings within one or two months of the filing of the claim. The arbitrators will generally schedule a preliminary hearing as soon as they have been appointed, and they will expect the evidentiary hearings to begin promptly thereafter.

Arbitrators recognize that the parties have not had the benefit of months of discovery to learn about the other's case or to refine the issues. There is inevitably some simplification of the case as it proceeds through hearings to the point where the real dispute comes into focus. One reason for having a prompt start to the evidentiary hearings is to allow this process of definition and clarification to get under way. The arbitrators recognize that they know far less about the dispute than do the parties, and, until the testimony begins to show them what the case is about, they are usually reluctant to take a very active role. Once the form of dispute becomes clear, however, counsel should expect the panel members to want more testimony on the questions they will need to answer and less on such formal and collateral matters as reputation and credibility.

PRELIMINARY HEARINGS AND CONFERENCES DURING HEARINGS

A preliminary hearing is desirable and is usually held as soon as possible after the panel has been appointed. Counsel should regard the preliminary hearing as a valuable opportunity to present an outline of the case and should prepare accordingly. The arbitrators will be trying to form an idea of the number of hearing days that will have to be scheduled, and counsel should be prepared to be as specific as possible about the witnesses to be called and the estimated length of direct testimony. The purpose of all preliminary hearings and conferences is to provide structure to the evidentiary hearings and to see that the latter are used as much as possible for testimony.

Ideally, a preliminary hearing will accomplish all of the objectives of a pretrial conference under federal practice. Because the first hearing generally takes place as soon as the panel has been appointed and before the parties have completed their preparation, it is not realistic to expect that all procedural matters can be definitively settled at that time. The parties should, however, include as much of the following as possible in prehearing memoranda exchanged and filed with the AAA reasonably far in advance of the preliminary hearing.

The claimant's memorandum should include (1) a brief statement of the facts; (2) a complete statement of each claim, including a summary of the applicable law; (3) a statement of damages in as much detail as possible, giving the basis for any estimates and the reason for using them; and (4) an outline of the proof that will be presented in support of each claim and item of damages, including the names of all expected witnesses, a brief summary of their anticipated testimony, and an estimate of the amount of hearing time, exclusive of cross-examination.

The respondent's memorandum should include (1) a brief statement of the facts, with specific mention of those asserted by the claimant which the respondent disputes; (2) a response to each claim, including a summary of the applicable law and a statement as to whether or not the respondent agrees with the summary of the law provided by the claimant; (3) respondent's position regarding the claimant's damages, with a list of any unprovided back-up material that will be needed; (4) a statement of how much cross-examination is anticipated for each witness of the claimant; and (5) an outline of the responding proof, including proof regarding any affirmative defenses, with names of anticipated witnesses, a summary of their anticipated testimony, and an estimate of the amount of hearing time, exclusive of cross-examination.

If the respondent asserts counterclaims, he or she should provide the same information as is set forth above for the claimant. The claimant should submit a response to each counterclaim covering the material set forth above for the respondent.

The foregoing represents an ideal. Only rarely will all of this material be ready shortly after a complex case has begun. Most arbitrators would agree that it is probably not desirable to delay the case while every item is assembled. The material available at the preliminary hearing is generally sufficient to begin the evidentiary hearings.

It is often impossible and even inadvisable to schedule more than the first group of three or four hearing days at the preliminary hearing. After the first few days of testimony, when the issues dividing the parties become more focused, it is usually much easier to make accurate predictions of the remaining needs.

Discovery requests should be made at the preliminary hearing if discovery has not already been completed on an informal basis. An exchange of documents is normally directed to be complete by some reasonable time before the first evidentiary hearing. The practice is to have conferences throughout the evidentiary hearings, at counsel's request or at the request of the panel, for the purpose of narrowing issues and organizing the order of testimony.

DISCOVERY

Limited discovery is especially desirable in a large case. The arbitrators recognize that one of the reasons the parties have chosen to arbitrate their dispute is to avoid the expense, disruption, and delay that extensive discovery often entails. On the other hand, evidentiary hearings are frequently less focused than they would be if the parties had been able to clarify through discovery what is actually in dispute.

In the ordinary case, the arbitrators will allow discovery of essential documents. While a broad request for documents will not normally be allowed, at a minimum the parties should expect to exchange the documents they intend to introduce as exhibits and other documents that may reasonably be necessary for cross-examination with respect to them. Documents that form the basis of a summary or chart should always be made available to the other side, as should all records necessary to support a claim for damages.

The scope and timing of documentary requests should initially be discussed by counsel and, if counsel cannot agree, may again be taken up at a preliminary hearing. Intervals between evidentiary hearings are often used for additional document exchanges. Depositions are discouraged, except in unusual cases, as when an important witness is unable to appear at a hearing.

Failure of the parties to cooperate with one another will be a burden on the arbitrators, who will have to decide peripheral issues, and will often cause delay. The arbitrators might feel that they have no choice but to grant an adjournment if a party cannot continue in the absence of material that could reasonably have been furnished by the other side. Delays of this sort are a costly nuisance, and counsel working together in a professional manner should be able to avoid them.

Material claimed to be privileged can be submitted to the panel in camera—that is, off the record. If the panel sustains the privilege, the material is not considered and does not enter the record. In the unusual case where a party wishes to challenge the panel's determination, the materials can be marked for identification and submitted for an appropriate judicial ruling.

COMMUNICATION BETWEEN REPRESENTATIVES

Since there are no formal procedures in arbitration, counsel must make informal requests of one another. Representatives are expected to arrange between themselves convenient times for exchange and inspection of documents and other materials. Hearing time should not be wasted on such matters.

STIPULATIONS

While counsel might be unwilling to admit facts not in dispute, particularly when it is still early in the process, an issue should, whenever possible, be considered undisputed unless the other party intends to submit proof to contest it. Stipulations that are impossible at the outset of a case can often be agreed to after the case has progressed and the issues have been clarified.

CONDUCT OF HEARINGS

It is the responsibility of counsel to see that witnesses are available and documents and other evidence are ready so that the scheduled hearings proceed as smoothly and rapidly as possible. The arbitrators will have planned on a full day for each scheduled hearing, and it is important that all available hearing time be employed. Counsel should, if necessary, be prepared to put on witnesses out of order if a scheduled witness is unable to appear. It is a common practice to take up such housekeeping matters as scheduling and discovery at the opening of each morning session. All such matters take time, however, and should, if possible, be resolved by counsel outside of the hearing. Arbitrators will expect counsel to confer privately about unusual evidentiary problems and attempt to resolve them before bringing them up at a hearing.

In a large and complex case, opening statements are generally of only limited usefulness. They can be helpful if they outline the main factual contentions, give the proposed order of witnesses, and show how their testimony will establish the factual contentions. The opening statement can also alert the arbitrators to unusual evidence or the need for an on-site inspection. Arbitrators are interested in hearing testimony and will not appreciate argument.

Examination and cross-examination of witnesses take place as at any trial, except that the arbitrators may ask questions of their own. Arbitrators respect each party's right to present the case as it thinks best and avoid asking questions that will be covered in further examination by counsel. Counsel should welcome questioning by the arbitrators because it provides an indication of which points are troubling the panel.

Objections should be kept to a minimum. Arbitrators who are not lawyers are easily annoyed by objections they consider overly technical and beside the point, since the technical rules of evidence do not apply. Counsel should not hesitate, however, to object to the form of a question where it is misleading, ambiguous, or otherwise improper or unfair.

The scope of cross-examination is at least as generous as under the Federal Rules of Evidence. Cross-examination should be directed at the credibility of witnesses' testimony on direct. Strings of rhetorical questions, argument with the witness, and similar theatrics, however proper they might be in a courtroom, are usually out of place in the more relaxed and intimate setting of an arbitration hearing.

WITNESSES

To avoid wasting time on introductory background testimony, biographies of witnesses should be supplied. Counsel should give each other in advance of hearings the expected order of witnesses so that cross-examination can proceed without delay and the materials necessary for cross-examination can be made available.

AFFIDAVITS

Affidavits can be offered for any purpose under the rules. In a large case, however, their use is generally confined to matters of authenticity of documents preparation of materials, summaries, routine practice, and other issues not likely to be disputed. Affidavits can be essential when a witness cannot attend a hearing. Because the arbitrators recognize that affidavits have been prepared by counsel and cannot be cross-examined, they are necessarily of less weight than live testimony where controversial matters are involved. The lawyer's affidavit-brief, often seen in state court motion practice and containing arguments and case citations, would be inappropriate in arbitration. On the other hand, a short affidavit by a witness stating that he or she did not see an incident, or has searched a file and found no relevant document, could save an hour's time at a hearing.

DOCUMENTARY EVIDENCE

In most cases, documentary proof is submitted in the form of copies. Unless there are questions about authenticity or legibility, the originals are generally not needed. Authenticity and similar matters relating to documents—such as that each document is what it purports to be, was sent at about the time of preparation, and was received in the ordinary course—will be assumed.

Normally no proof is required on any of these points, unless a party raises an issue about one. Objections relating to best evidence, hearsay (except as to weight), and similar matters will usually be overruled and should not be made unless there is a genuine problem or prejudice regarding the document in question.

Normally, it makes no difference which side offers a document, and a single book containing topics of the documents both sides intend to introduce, arranged in chronological or other suitable order, is probably easiest to use at a hearing. Documents should be prenumbered and would be well presented in a single joint binder with numbered tabs. One set should be available for each arbitrator and for use by witnesses as required.

Where a large number of documents is involved, counsel should make arrangements to have them available at each hearing and stored between hearings. At the close of the case, each party should be sure that all documentary materials that have been offered are available to the panel for its deliberation.

EXPERTS

The party calling an expert should furnish to the other side, in advance, summaries of the expert's qualifications and proposed testimony, with the basis of conclusions given in reasonable detail. Unless there is a question about it, no testimony should be necessary at the hearing about the expert's qualifications.

SUMMARIES AND CHARTS

Voluminous or repetitious proof should be summarized in some form. A good chart or summary can often give a clear perspective on an issue than hours of testimony or hundreds of documents, and counsel will normally be expected to provide such material. Summaries and charts should be constructed with care, since sloppy presentation and mistakes reflect poorly on a party's preparation. It should be possible to eliminate introduction of the data underlying a chart or summary unless there is a genuine question about them. Summaries and charts must be accompanied by an explanation of how and by whom they were prepared: the other side must be given access to the underlying material and fair opportunity to verify its accuracy. This verification should be completed in advance of the hearing at which the chart or summary is offered.

DAMAGES

The claimant should prepare a complete schedule of damages of every category. If damages are consequential or continuing, they should be estimated and the basis for the estimate provided. All books and records that form the basis for damage calculations should be made available to the opposing side for inspection. The damage schedule should be available not later than the first evidentiary hearing. The same procedure would apply to counterclaims, if any.

BRIEFS AND CLOSING ARGUMENTS

After the close of evidentiary hearings, the parties are normally expected to provide post-hearing briefs and an oral argument. A post-hearing brief should be focused on the important issues and should explain why the record supports the position presented.

A complex case will often generate hundreds of exhibits and several thousand pages of testimony. It is imperative that each brief summarize the record with accurate citations, showing what the parties claim the record establishes regarding their factual contentions. It is unrealistic to assume that arbitrators will have the time to sit through a mass of evidence without guidance from counsel.

An important distinction must be made between briefs in arbitration and briefs in a court proceeding; many arbitrators, and a majority of commercial panelists, are not lawyers. Lay arbitrators do not have access to reports of cases cited in a brief and are not likely to be persuaded by a string of citations. Even arbitrators who are lawyers do not have clerks to summarize authorities and check citations. It follows that legal authorities should be kept to a minimum and that they should be discussed with enough of the flavor of the principal cases that their significance can be appreciated without reading the case itself. Strings of citations are generally useless. If the cases are important, copies should be furnished with the brief.

In other respects, a good post-hearing brief is not different from a post-trial brief. It should argue the party's position forcefully. Above all it should provide guidance to the arbitrators. Unlike judges, arbitrators do not usually write opinions; indeed, they are discouraged from doing so. Nevertheless they, like judges, must reason the case out. They must feel that their award is firmly rooted in the record and is legally sound. Matters not related to law or evidence can be appropriate in an arbitration brief. Arguments addressed to business sense, the equities, and commercial realities, for example, will be appropriate in certain cases.

At a post-closing argument, counsel should above all be prepared to answer questions. The arbitrators will usually have read the record and briefs, and will often have discussed the case on a preliminary basis. Counsel should expect a "hot bench": that is, the arbitrators will be well prepared. The arbitrators are often interested in testing the soundness of their preliminary views while counsel argue their positions.

CONCLUSION

A large and complex case will inevitably take on a life of its own. The personalities of the participants and the special issues of the case will have much more to do with its progress than these guidelines. It will often be found that even with goodwill and efficient management, there is simply no short and expeditious way for complex proof to be presented. Nevertheless, it is hoped that these suggestions will assist counsel and arbitrators to arrive at the conclusion of their cases more rapidly, with more time spent on consideration of the genuine issues and less spent on peripheral matters.

C. American Arbitration Association: Administered Arbitration

1. Comments and Questions

a. The next two sections set forth the rules and procedures used by the AAA and the CPR Institute for Dispute Resolution for arbitration of complex commercial disputes. These readings explain how arbitration proceedings work, and the pressure points in the arbitration of disputes. The AAA and CPR rules are designed to address all the major issues and problems that will arise in a commercial arbitration.

b. What are the differences between AAA administered and CPR non-administered arbitration? What are the costs and benefits of the two approaches? Which one do you prefer, and why? Consider both qualitative and economic factors. What suggestions do you have for improving the AAA or the CPR rules for commercial disputes? To what extent are the rules specific to complex commercial transactions, and to what extent are they useable for arbitration generally? (You should revisit this question after studying the labor arbitration materials in Chapter 12.)

2. American Arbitration Association, Arbitration Rules for Commercial Disputes [with AAA Commentary] (1993)*

1. Agreement of Parties

The parties shall be deemed to have made these rules a part of their arbitration agreement whenever they have provided for arbitration by the American Arbitration Association (hereinafter AAA) or under its Commercial Arbitration Rules. These rules and any amendment of them shall apply in the form obtaining at the time the demand for arbitration or submission agreement is received by the AAA. The parties, by written agreement, may vary the procedures set forth in these rules.

A. Arbitrability—Issues and/or claims frequently arise in arbitration that one or the other party deems not to be subject to arbitration. Such issues are generally raised by the

*Reprinted with permission.

respondent, as one might expect, and are called "issues of arbitrability." As a neutral administrative agency, the AAA has no authority to make determinations on issues of arbitrability. The role of the AAA in such instances is to identify such issues when they arise and advise the parties of the avenues available for resolution of such issues. Primarily, issues of arbitrability may be decided either by an arbitrator or the courts.

In its conduct of an arbitration, it is the AAA's position that, once an issue of arbitrability has been identified, the AAA proceeds with the administration of the case and has the issue heard and determined by the arbitrator unless the parties agree otherwise. In other words, under a broad arbitration clause, the arbitrator decides the issue of arbitrability unless the parties can resolve it on their own or the issue is put before the courts.

B. Motions to Stay Arbitration—The mere filing of a motion to stay arbitration does not automatically act to stay the arbitration. In the absence of a stay (either temporary or permanent) from a court and upon the request of a party that the arbitration proceed, the AAA continues with its administration of the case. As a practical matter, if a party (usually the respondent) files a motion to stay arbitration, the other party (usually the claimant) often agrees to hold the case in abeyance until the court rules on the respondent's motion.

C. Motions to Compel Arbitration—Reasons to file motions to compel vary but they are typically filed either by a defendant in a lawsuit where the parties' contract contains an arbitration provision or by a claimant to an already filed arbitration in response to a respondent's motion to stay arbitration. The former would necessarily happen prior to the case being filed with the AAA. The latter would occur after the case is filed with the AAA and where the claimant requests the arbitration be held in abeyance (usually without objection from the respondent) pending the court's ruling.

D. Consolidation—Generally speaking, consolidation of two or more separately filed arbitrations may only occur with the consent of all parties or, if the contract so provides, or by a court order.

E. Section 47 of the rules provides that the AAA is not a necessary party in judicial proceedings relating to the arbitration. As a neutral administrative agency, the AAA promptly abides by a court order directed against any party.

2. Name of Tribunal

Any tribunal constituted by the parties for the settlement of their dispute under these rules shall be called the Commercial Arbitration Tribunal.

3. Administrator and Delegation of Duties

When parties agree to arbitrate under these rules, or when they provide for arbitration by the AAA and an arbitration is initiated under these rules, they thereby authorize the AAA to administer the arbitration. The authority and duties of the AAA are prescribed in the agreement of the parties and in these rules, and may be carried out through such of the AAA's representatives as it may direct.

If the parties want any aspect of the arbitration to be conducted in a manner different than provided for in the rules, they must so specify in their arbitration agreement or by subsequent stipulation. Absent mutual consent to the contrary, the AAA administers the arbitration in accordance with the rules.

Working with the AAA Staff

A. Cases filed with the AAA are assigned to various staff members called case administrators. Case administrators manage every aspect of the arbitration from the filing of a case to its final disposition. In some respects, their duties are similar to that of a trial-court administrator, although their responsibilities are usually far greater and more involved.
B. Section 29 of the rules prohibits any direct communication, either oral or written, between the parties and a neutral arbitrator other than at the oral hearing, unless the parties and the arbitrator agree otherwise. In cases where no direct communication is allowed (which are most cases), all communication must be funneled through the AAA, specifically the case administrator.
C. The case administrator is your source for up-to-date information on all aspects of your case. The administrator's job is to help the parties and the arbitrators get through the arbitration as fairly, expeditiously, and economically as possible. This person is a valuable resource.

4. National Panel of Arbitrators

The AAA shall establish and maintain a National Panel of Commercial Arbitrators and shall appoint arbitrators as provided in these rules. . . .

5. Regional Offices

The AAA may, in its discretion, assign the administration of an arbitration to any of its regional offices.

6. Initiation under an Arbitration Provision in a Contract

Arbitration under an arbitration provision in a contract shall be initiated in the following manner.

(a) The initiating party (hereinafter claimant) shall, within the time period, if any, specified in the contract(s), give written notice to the other party (hereinafter respondent) of its intention to arbitrate (demand), which notice shall contain a statement setting forth the nature of the dispute, the amount involved, if any, the remedy sought, and the hearing locale requested, and
(b) shall file at any regional office of the AAA three copies of the notice and three copies of the arbitration provisions of the contract, together with the appropriate filing fee. . . .

The AAA shall give notice of such filing to the respondent or respondents. A respondent may file an answering statement in duplicate with the AAA within ten days after notice from the AAA, in which event the respondent shall at the same time send a copy of the answering statement to the claimant. If a counterclaim is asserted, it shall contain a statement setting forth the nature of the counterclaim, the amount involved, if any, and the remedy sought. If a counterclaim is made, the appropriate fee . . . shall be forwarded to the AAA with the answering statement. If no answering statement is filed within the stated time, it will be treated as a denial of the claim. Failure to file an answering statement shall not operate to delay the arbitration. Applying the following recommendations will help you get your case off to the best start possible.

Prior to Filing a Demand for Arbitration

A. Contact your local regional office to obtain the latest copy of the rules applicable to your dispute and current Demand for Arbitration forms (a list of the regional offices can be found at the end of this brochure). The rules are revised and amended on a continuing basis. Procedures and costs change over time.

B. Review the arbitration clause in the contract. Be sure that it provides for administration by the American Arbitration Association. This is usually done by specifying that the arbitration will be conducted under the rules of the AAA. The AAA can only function as the administrator if both parties agree.

C. Additionally, in your cover letter transmitting the demand to the AAA, highlight unusual or special provisions—e.g., locale, number and selection method of arbitrators, time limits, etc.— contained in the arbitration clause.

Filing a Demand for Arbitration

A. Using the AAA's Demand for Arbitration form for filing your case will ensure that the AAA has all of the information necessary to initiate your case promptly. Specifically, the following information is vital.

1. The Name of the Respondent—Be sure that this is the legal name of the responding entity and that that entity is the one with which you have the contract/agreement containing the arbitration provision.
2. The Name of the Individual Representing the Respondent—For corporate entities, this could be an officer—e.g., president, CEO, etc.—or an attorney. Providing the AAA with a specific person's name helps expedite receiving an initial response to your demand. If you know that the respondent is represented by an attorney and you know the name of that attorney, please indicate it on the demand so that our initial contact on the case can be with the attorney.
3. Addresses and Telephone Numbers (and Fax Numbers if Applicable) of Both the Respondent and Its Representative.
4. A Copy of the Arbitration Clause—This must be provided in order for the AAA to confirm it has jurisdiction to administer the case and to ensure that we adhere to special provisions relevant to the conduct of the arbitration.
5. The Nature of the Dispute—Additional sheets may be used if you run out of room on the demand form. Simply stating "breach of contract" is insufficient. While this information need not be detailed, it should specifically and clearly outline the major issues involved in the dispute. Three reasons why this is important are as follows:
   a. The list of arbitrators proposed by the AAA is compiled based on the information provided here. The better the information, the better the list of arbitrators.
   b. An arbitrator selected to serve on the case will, in part, base his decision on whether or not to accept the appointment on what type of dispute he is being asked to hear and resolve. Without clear information, such a decision might be difficult to make.
   c. If the claimant's statement of the nature of the dispute is unclear, the respondent will, in all likelihood, have some difficulty in responding to it. That would only serve to delay the arbitration process.

6. The Claim or Relief Sought—This is usually stated in monetary terms and/or requests for specific performance. When possible, the statement of claim should specify the total claim accompanied by an itemization and quantification; i.e., specific amounts for each category of claim; examples—a contract balance in the amount of $25,000 plus extras in the amount of $5,000 for total claim of $30,000 or payment of royalty fees in the amount of $150,000 and determination that the respondent is in violation of a no-competition clause with an accompanying directive to cease competitive practices.

[I]f a party files an undetermined or undisclosed claim or counterclaim prior to the hearing, the AAA asks the arbitrator to have the party specify the amount of its claim or counterclaim as soon as the hearing commences. The party is then billed the appropriate additional filing fee based on the arbitrator's information. Please do not leave the arbitrator in the position of having to guess what you want!

7. The Hearing Locale Requested—To keep expenses to a minimum, the AAA attempts to select arbitrators within the vicinity of the hearing. Failing to request a specific hearing locale unduly delays the initiation of your case.
8. Names, Addresses, Telephone and Fax Numbers of the Claimant and the Claimant's Representative—The claimant's representative may sign the demand form on behalf of the claimant. Again, failing to provide this complete information and/or failing to sign the form delays initiation of the case.

B. File three copies of the demand with the AAA with the appropriate filing fee. . . . A case is not considered filed unless accompanied by the filing fee.
C. Send the original of the demand, with attachments, to the respondent or its designated representative.

Filing an Answering Statement and/or a Counterclaim

A. Upon receiving a Demand for Arbitration, the AAA initiates the case by sending a joint "initiating" letter to the parties. That letter (i) advises the parties of the formal case caption, including the case number, (ii) acknowledges the AAA's authority to act as the administrator for the proceeding, (iii) states the claimant's requested hearing locale, (iv) gives the respondent ten days (from the date of the letter) to file an answering statement and to object to the requested hearing locale, and (v) describes what must be done in order to file a counterclaim.

The initiating letter might also contain a list of arbitrators and a calendar form for soliciting hearing dates. If that is the case, both parties have the same ten-day period within which to return the list and calendar.

B. If the AAA does not hear from the respondent within ten days from the date of the initiating letter, the AAA assumes that the claim is denied, that the respondent has no objection to the hearing locale requested by the claimant and proceeds with the next step in the administration of the case. While not required by the rules, the AAA does, however, usually attempt to contact the respondent by telephone to verify receipt of both the Demand for Arbitration and the AAA's initial correspondence.

C. If a counterclaim is going to be asserted, it is best to do so together with and within the time limit set for filing the answering statement. There is no set time limit within which a counterclaim must be asserted. However, Section 8 of the rules states in part that, "After the arbitrator is appointed . . . no new or different claim may be submitted except with the arbitrator's consent." The general rule of thumb is to file a counterclaim as soon as possible. Additionally, when inviting an arbitrator to serve on a case, the AAA likes to be able to provide statements of both claims and counterclaims for the arbitrator's information when considering whether or not to take the case.

D. There is no counterclaim form used by the AAA. The form of the counterclaim may be as formal or as informal as the respondent wishes; e.g., a letter form, a brief narrative, the same form used for an answer and counterclaim in civil litigation, etc. If the case had its genesis in court and an answer and/or counterclaim was already filed in that forum, such papers may be used as the answer and/or counterclaim to the Demand for Arbitration. Regardless of form, the counterclaim should specifically and clearly state the nature of all counterclaims being asserted with an accompanying itemization and quantification wherever possible.

E. Two copies of the answering statement and/or counterclaim, accompanied by the appropriate filing fee as provided in the fee section of the rules, must be filed with the AAA and simultaneously sent to the claimant. A counterclaim is not considered filed unless accompanied by the required filing fee.

F. No response to the answering statement and/or the counterclaim is required by the rules. Such a response may, however, be filed at the claimant's option.

7. Initiation under a Submission

Parties to any existing dispute may commence an arbitration under these rules by filing at any regional office of the AAA three copies of a written submission to arbitrate under these rules, signed by the parties. It shall contain a statement of the matter in dispute, the amount involved, if any, the remedy sought, and the hearing locale requested, together with the appropriate filing fee. . . .

A. Submissions to arbitration are used when there is no contract between the parties providing for arbitration. Forms for Submission to Dispute Resolution may be obtained by contacting your local regional office.

B. When initiating cases filed by submission, the AAA submits a list of arbitrators and calendar forms to solicit hearing dates with its opening letter. The parties then have ten days within which to return those forms to the AAA.

C. There are many similarities between filing a submission and a demand. For additional guidance in filing a submission, refer to the prior section on Filing a Demand for Arbitration.

8. Changes of Claim

After filing of a claim, if either party desires to make any new or different claim or counterclaim, it shall be made in writing and filed with the AAA, and a copy shall be mailed to the other party, who shall have a period of ten days from the date of such mailing within which to file an answer with the AAA. After the arbitrator is appointed, however, no new or different claim may be submitted except with the arbitrator's consent.

A. Once an arbitrator has been appointed to your case, you run the risk of not being able to file a new claim/counterclaim or make a different claim/counterclaim. However, most arbitrators are generally sympathetic in allowing such changes if they arise from the same contract and the same set of facts; such allowance is, however, discretionary.
B. Procedurally, if either party files a change of claim, different claim, or new claim after the arbitrator has been appointed, the AAA acknowledges receipt of the change and asks the other party to provide a written response thereto within ten days. After the due date for the response, the AAA provides the arbitrator with the requested claim change and any response for a ruling as to whether or not the change will be allowed.
C. On rare occasions, changes in claims are made at the last minute just prior to the beginning of the hearing. In such instances, presentation and comments on the change are made at the opening of the hearing. The arbitrator will rule at that time.
D. In instances when claims change during the hearing, the arbitrator hears both sides' positions and makes a ruling at that time.

9. Applicable Procedures

Unless the AAA in its discretion determines otherwise, the Expedited Procedures shall be applied in any case where no disclosed claim or counterclaim exceeds $50,000, exclusive of interest and arbitration costs. Parties may also agree to using the Expedited Procedures in cases involving claims in excess of $50,000. The Expedited Procedures shall be applied as described in Sections 53 through 57 of these rules, in addition to any other portion of these rules that is not in conflict with the Expedited Procedures.

All other cases shall be administered in accordance with Sections 1 through 52 of these rules. If an expedited case has or develops the features of a regular case (multiple arbitrators, multiple hearings, transcripts, briefs, etc.), the AAA has the authority under the rules to move the case to the regular arbitration track.

10. Administrative Conference, Preliminary Hearing, and Mediation Conference

At the request of any party or at the discretion of the AAA, an administrative conference with the AAA and the parties and/or their representatives will be scheduled in appropriate cases to expedite the arbitration proceedings. There is no administrative fee for this service.

In large or complex cases, at the request of any party or at the discretion of the arbitrator or the AAA, a preliminary hearing with the parties and/or their representatives and the arbitrator may be scheduled by the arbitrator to specify the issues to be resolved, to stipulate to uncontested facts, and to consider any other matters that will expedite the arbitration proceedings. Consistent with the expedited nature of arbitration, the arbitrator may, at the preliminary hearing, establish (i) the extent of and schedule for the production of relevant documents and other information, (ii) the identification of any witnesses to be called, and (iii) a schedule for further hearings to resolve the dispute. There is no administrative fee for the first preliminary hearing.

With the consent of the parties, the AAA at any stage of the proceeding may arrange a mediation conference under the Commercial Mediation Rules, in order to facilitate settlement. The mediator shall not be an arbitrator appointed to the case. Where the parties to a pending arbitration agree to mediate under the AAA's rules, no additional administrative fee is required to initiate the mediation.

Administrative Conferences

A. Administrative conferences are available to all cases. In some the conferences are done over the telephone and are arranged by the case administrator. Administrative conferences usually involve only the parties' representatives and the case administrator.
B. Typical issues addressed during an administrative conference are (i) the status of settlement discussions, (ii) specifications of claims and counterclaims, (iii) estimated number of hearing days, (iv) dates, times, and the place of hearing, (v) the number and qualifications of arbitrators and terms of compensation, (vi) stipulation of uncontested facts, (vii) requests for production of documents, (viii) stenographic records, (ix) necessity of a site inspection, and (x) the possibility of mediation.

Preliminary Hearings

A. The only discovery available in arbitration is what is mutually agreed by the parties. However, if any party feels that it has serious discovery needs, a preliminary hearing is the best forum in the arbitration process for seeking relief.
B. An arbitrator's subpoena authority is limited to issuing subpoenas for witnesses and documents at scheduled hearings only. If necessary, however, a party that has been unsuccessful in getting documents from another party might want to request that the arbitrator issue a subpoena to have them brought to a preliminary hearing, which is, after all, a scheduled hearing.
C. Preliminary hearings are primarily used in large or complex cases and are almost always conducted in person, although they may be conducted by telephone. In determining what is a "large or complex" case, the AAA considers the number of parties, the number of issues involved, the complexity of those issues, and the monetary size of the claims.
D. Typical issues addressed in a preliminary hearing are (i) specification of claims and counterclaims, (ii) identities of affiliated, related, or successor persons or entities, (iii) stipulation of uncontested facts, (iv) information to be exchanged and a schedule for the exchange (including reports from experts), (v) lists of witnesses with outlines of testimony (including biographies and reports of expert witnesses), (vi) advance filing and advance identification of exhibits (schedules for filing of affidavits or conducting depositions), (vii) estimated length of the case, (viii) a schedule of evidentiary hearings, (ix) the number of copies of exhibits to be made, (x) whether or not briefs (post- or prehearing) will be necessary, and (xi) the form of the award.
E. A preliminary hearing is beneficial for getting large, complex cases on the right course at an early stage in the process. It provides both the parties and the arbitrators an opportunity to get to know each other before the evidentiary hearing. Additionally, the case administrator assigned to the case might attend to offer procedural guidance. The administrator prepares and distributes written confirmation of all arrangements agreed during the preliminary hearing.

Mediation Conferences

A. Mediation has been called a "no-lose" or "win-win" option. Mediation is a settlement device. In contrast to arbitration and litigation, which are retrospective in that they seek to look backward in an attempt to find fault and assess blame, mediation is prospective in that it looks forward to how the parties can jointly create a settlement that is mutually acceptable.

B. In order for a mediation conference to have a reasonable chance of resulting in a settlement, (i) both parties must have a strong desire and/or motivation to settle, (ii) both parties must be flexible in their positions, and (iii) someone with absolute settlement authority from both sides must attend. . . .

11. Fixing of Locale

The parties may mutually agree on the locale where the arbitration is to be held. If any party requests that the hearing be held in a specific locale and the other party files no objection thereto within ten days after notice of the request has been mailed to it by the AAA, the locale shall be the one requested. If a party objects to the locale requested by the other party, the AAA shall have the power to determine the locale and its decision shall be final and binding.

A. When filing a Demand for Arbitration, the claimant states its preference for a hearing locale. When a case is filed by submission, the parties have usually already agreed on a locale. When the parties to a submission cannot agree, the AAA determines the locale.

B. If the arbitration provision in the parties' contract specifies a particular locale, the AAA conducts the hearing in that locale unless the parties subsequently agree otherwise.

C. When initiating a case filed by a Demand for Arbitration, the AAA's initiating letter gives the respondent ten days to object to the claimant's requested hearing locale. If no objection is filed, the locale shall be the one requested. If an objection is filed, the AAA asks the parties to file written argument as to why their particular locale should be selected. After considering the parties' positions, the AAA makes a determination that is final and binding. . . .

12. Qualifications of an Arbitrator

Any neutral arbitrator appointed pursuant to Section 13, 14, 15, or 54, or selected by mutual choice of the parties or their appointees, shall be subject to disqualification for the reasons specified in Section 19. If the parties specifically so agree, in writing, the arbitrator shall not be subject to disqualification for those reasons.

Unless the parties agree otherwise, an arbitrator selected unilaterally by one party is a party-appointed arbitrator and is not subject to disqualification pursuant to Section 19. The term "arbitrator" in these rules refers to the arbitration panel, whether composed of one or more arbitrators and whether the arbitrators are neutral or party appointed.

13. Appointment from Panel

If the parties have not appointed an arbitrator and have not provided any other method of appointment, the arbitrator shall be appointed in the following manner: immediately after the filing of the demand or submission, the AAA shall submit simultaneously to each party to the dispute an identical list of names of persons chosen from the panel.

Each party to the dispute shall have ten days from the transmittal date in which to strike any names objected to, number the remaining names in order of preference, and return the list to the AAA. In a single-arbitrator case, each party may strike three names on a peremptory basis. In a multi-arbitrator case, each party may strike five names on a peremptory basis. If a party does not return the list within the time specified, all persons named therein shall be deemed acceptable. From among the persons who have been approved on both lists, and in accordance with the designated order of mutual preference, the AAA shall invite the acceptance of an arbitrator to serve. If the parties fail to agree on any of the persons named, or if acceptable arbitrators are unable to act, or if for any other reason the appointment can not be made from the submitted lists, the AAA shall have the power to make the appointment from among other members of the panel without the submission of additional lists.

A. The parties may appoint as arbitrators anyone on whom they mutually agree. Arbitrators need not come from the AAA's National Panel of Arbitrators.
B. If the arbitration provision of the parties' contract specifies the method for arbitrator selection and/or the qualifications that arbitrators must have, the AAA follows that method unless the parties subsequently agree otherwise.
C. When the arbitrator is to be selected from the AAA's national panel, the AAA compiles a list from members of its panel who are knowledgeable in the subject matter of the dispute. The list is accompanied by a biographical sketch for each proposed arbitrator. The biographies provide information on the arbitrators' current employment, employment history, areas of technical expertise, educational background, practical career experiences, and professional-association memberships. Additional information on arbitrators can be obtained by contacting an AAA regional office.
D. For one-arbitrator cases, the AAA's list contains ten names. For three-arbitrator panels, the list contains fifteen names.
E. The number of strikes permitted is limited but which names are struck is purely discretionary. The parties' selections should be made without consultation with one another. When returning the lists to the AAA, it is unnecessary to provide a copy to the other side. . . .

14. Direct Appointment by a Party

If the agreement of the parties names an arbitrator or specifies a method of appointing an arbitrator, that designation or method shall be followed. The notice of appointment, with the name and address of the arbitrator shall be filed with the AAA by the appointing party. Upon the request of any appointing party, the AAA shall submit a list of members of the panel from which the party may, if it so desires, make the appointment.

If the agreement specifies a period of time within which an arbitrator shall be appointed and any party fails to make the appointment within that period, the AAA shall make the appointment.

If no period of time is specified in the agreement, the AAA shall notify the party to make the appointment. If within ten day thereafter an arbitrator has not been appointed by a party, the AAA shall make the appointment.

A. Arbitrators selected under this section are called "party-appointed" arbitrators. When the parties have agreed to party appointed arbitrators, either by contract or submission, they are free to designate whomever they wish to act in this capacity. There is no restriction and such arbitrators are not subject to the provisions set forth in Section 19 of the rules. Party-appointed arbitrators may be either "neutral" or "advocate" arbitrators.

Neutral Party-Appointed Arbitrators—Although selected and designated by a party, such arbitrators are neutral in that they have no preconceived bias in favor of the appointing party's position and have no unilateral contact with that party during the course of the arbitration.

Advocate Party-Appointed Arbitrators—Such arbitrators are not only selected and designated by a party, they have unlimited communication with that party and act in concert with that party throughout the course of the arbitration, advocating the merits of that party's position.

B. When considering use of advocate party-appointed arbitrators, it is good to remember that, when it comes to the final award, the net result is virtually the same as having the case heard by a single arbitrator; for, in the vast majority of cases, the neutral chairperson ends up casting the deciding "vote." From a practical standpoint, advocate party-appointed arbitrators might add an additional level of comfort to the parties who appointed them but rarely add to the effectiveness of the process.

C. The terms of compensation for party-appointed arbitrators are usually negotiated directly with the appointing party. Such arrangements may, however, be made through the AAA.

15. Appointment of Neutral Arbitrator by Party-Appointed Arbitrators or Parties

If the parties have selected party-appointed arbitrators, or if such arbitrators have been appointed as provided in Section 14, and the parties have authorized them to appoint a neutral arbitrator within a specified time and no appointment is made within that time or any agreed extension, the AAA may appoint a neutral arbitrator, who shall act as chairperson.

If no period of time is specified for appointment of the neutral arbitrator and the party-appointed arbitrators or the parties do not make the appointment within ten days from the date of the appointment of the last party-appointed arbitrator, the AAA may appoint the neutral arbitrator, who shall act as chairperson.

If the parties have agreed that their party-appointed arbitrators shall appoint the neutral arbitrator from the panel, the AAA shall furnish to the party-appointed arbitrators, in the manner provided in Section 13, a list selected from the panel, and the appointment of the neutral arbitrator shall be made as prescribed in that section.

16. Nationality of Arbitrator in International Arbitration

Where the parties are nationals or residents of different countries, any neutral arbitrator shall, upon the request of either party, be appointed from among nationals of a country other than that of any of the parties. The request must be made prior to the time set for the appointment of the arbitrator as agreed by the parties or set by these rules. . . .

17. Number of Arbitrators

If the arbitration agreement does not specify the number of arbitrators, the dispute shall be heard and determined by one arbitrator, unless the AAA, in its discretion, directs that a greater number of arbitrators be appointed.

A. The choices for the number of arbitrators on a case are either one or three. If the parties' arbitration clause or agreement does not specify the number of arbitrators and the amount claimed in a commercial or construction dispute is $250,000 or less, one arbitrator will be appointed to hear the case.

B. In determining the appropriate number of arbitrators for a particular case, the AAA considers (i) the number of parties, (ii) the number of issues, (iii) the complexity of those issues, and (iv) the size of monetary claims.

18. Notice to Arbitrator of Appointment

Notice of the appointment of the neutral arbitrator, whether appointed mutually by the parties or by the AAA, shall be sent to the arbitrator by the AAA. . . .

19. Disclosure and Challenge Procedure

Any person appointed as neutral arbitrator shall disclose to the AAA any circumstances likely to affect impartiality, including any bias or any financial or personal interest in the result of the arbitration or any past or present relationship with the parties or their representatives. Upon receipt of such information from the arbitrator or another source, the AAA shall communicate the information to the parties and, if it deems it appropriate to do so, to the arbitrator and others. Upon objection of a party to the continued service of a neutral arbitrator, the AAA shall determine whether the arbitrator should be disqualified and shall inform the parties of its decision, which shall be conclusive.

A. The duty to disclose any pertinent information relative to an arbitrator's appointment to a case rests first and foremost with that arbitrator. However, if a party or its representative has information relative to a particular arbitrator's service, it should be made known to the AAA.

B. As soon as an arbitrator advises the AAA of a disclosure, it is sent to the parties in writing. The parties are given a period of time, usually ten days, within which to provide the AAA with their responses to the disclosure.

C. If a party objects to an arbitrator's continued service based on a disclosure, the AAA advises the other party of the objection and get its comments. After considering both parties' positions, the AAA decides whether the arbitrator should be removed or affirmed.

20. Vacancies

If for any reason an arbitrator is unable to perform the duties of the office, the AAA may, on proof satisfactory to it, declare the office vacant. Vacancies shall be filled in accordance with the applicable provisions of these rules.

In the event of a vacancy in a panel of neutral arbitrators after the hearings have commenced, the remaining arbitrator or arbitrators may continue with the hearing and determination of the controversy, unless the parties agree otherwise.

In cases with three arbitrators, a vacancy will only be filled if all parties agree. In other words, if a vacancy occurs and one party wants the vacancy filled and another party does not, the arbitration proceeds with the two remaining arbitrators, assuming that the remaining arbitrators agree.

21. Date, Time, and Place of Hearing

The arbitrator shall set the date, time, and place for each hearing. The AAA shall mail to each party notice thereof at least ten days in advance, unless the otherwise agreed by the parties.

A. In the normal administration of an arbitration, these details are generally arranged by the case administrator after consultation with the parties and the arbitrator.
B. Date—When the case administrator submits the list of arbitrators to the parties, a calendar for the upcoming two-month period is also sent. The parties are asked to strike all unavailable dates, estimate the number of days required to hear the case, and return the calendar to the AAA with the list of arbitrators. The case administrator then advises the arbitrator of the parties' mutually available dates. The hearing is then scheduled for the first date(s) also open on the arbitrator's calendar. An official Notice of Hearing is then mailed to the parties and the arbitrator.
C. Time—Pursuant to the rules, the arbitrator sets the time of hearings. That is generally done after the case administrator has consulted the parties and shared their responses with the arbitrator.
D. Place—Hearings are often conducted at the regional office administering the case. Rooms are available on a rental basis. Check with your local office for availability and rates.

22. Representation

Any party may be represented by counsel or other authorized representative. A party intending to be so represented shall notify the other party and the AAA of the name and address of the representative at least three days prior to the date set for the hearing at which that person is first to appear. When such a representative initiates an arbitration or responds for a party, notice is deemed to have been given.

A. If a party who was previously unrepresented appears at the hearing with counsel (without notifying the other party at least three days in advance) and the other party is not represented by counsel, the arbitrator will adjourn the hearing if requested to do so by the unrepresented party in order to afford that party an opportunity to obtain counsel. . . .

23. Stenographic Record

Any party desiring a stenographic record shall make arrangements directly with a stenographer and shall notify the other party of these arrangements in advance of the hearing. The requesting party or parties shall pay the cost of the record. If the transcript is agreed by the parties to be, or determined by the arbitrator to be, the official record of the proceeding, it must be made available to the arbitrator and to the other parties for inspection, at a date, time, and place determined by the arbitrator.

24. Interpreters

Any party wishing an interpreter shall make all arrangements directly with the interpreter and shall assume the costs of the service.

25. Attendance at the Hearing

The arbitrator shall maintain the privacy of the hearings unless the law provides to the contrary. Any person having a direct interest in the arbitration is entitled to attend the hearing. The arbitrator shall otherwise have the power to require the exclusion of any witness, other than a party or other essential person, during the testimony of any other witness. It shall be discretionary with the arbitrator to determine the propriety of the attendance of any other person.

Persons directly concerned in an arbitration have the right to attend hearings. The arbitrator may permit others to attend, with due regard to the right of privacy. The arbitrator may also require the retirement of a witness from the hearing room during the testimony of other witnesses.

26. Postponements

The arbitrator for good cause shown may postpone any hearing upon the request of a party or upon the arbitrator's own initiative, and shall also grant such postponement when all parties agree.

A. If a party finds itself needing to postpone a hearing, for whatever reason, it should first contact the other side to see whether it has any objection. If the other party has no objection, the requesting party need only notify the AAA, by telephone or in writing, of its request and the other party's concurrence. The AAA, of course, places a courtesy call to the other side to confirm its agreement to postpone the hearing.

If the other side objects to the postponement request, the AAA transmits the parties' respective positions to the arbitrator for a ruling. The arbitrator's ruling is final.

B. If the parties present to the AAA a joint request to postpone, the arbitrator is so notified and has no authority to overrule it. . . .

27. Oaths

Before proceeding with the first hearing, each arbitrator may take an oath of office and, if required by law, shall do so. The arbitrator may require witnesses to testify under oath administered by any duly qualified person and, if it is required by law or requested by any party, shall do so.

A. Arbitrators are always sworn when they execute their Notice of Appointment.
B. The arbitrator generally administers oaths to witnesses. If present, a stenographer may execute this function.

28. Majority Decision

All decisions of the arbitrators must be by a majority. The award must also be made by a majority unless the concurrence of all is expressly required by the arbitration agreement or by law.

An arbitration award executed by only two concurring arbitrators is valid, unless the arbitration agreement or applicable law requires that the award be signed by all three. Any dissenting arbitrator may sign the award with a notation of dissent.

29. Order of Proceedings and Communication with Arbitrator

A hearing shall be opened by the filing of the oath of the arbitrator, where required; by the recording of the date, time, and place of the hearing, and the presence of the arbitrator, the parties, and their representatives, if any; and by the receipt by the arbitrator of the statement of the claim and the answering statement, if any.

The arbitrator may, at the beginning of the hearing, ask for statements clarifying the issues involved. In some cases, part or all of the above will have been accomplished at the preliminary hearing conducted by the arbitrator pursuant to Section 10.

The complaining party shall then present evidence to support its claim. The defending party shall then present evidence supporting its defense. Witnesses for each party shall submit to questions or other examination. The arbitrator has the discretion to vary this procedure but shall afford a full and equal opportunity to all parties for the presentation of any material and relevant evidence.

Exhibits, when offered by either party, may be received in evidence by the arbitrator. The names and addresses of all witnesses and a description of the exhibits in the order received shall be made a part of the record.

There shall be no direct communication between the parties and a neutral arbitrator other than at oral hearing, unless the parties and the arbitrator agree otherwise. Any other oral or written communication from the parties to the neutral arbitrator shall be directed to the AAA for transmittal to the arbitrator. . . .

30. Arbitration in the Absence of a Party or Representative

Unless the law provides to the contrary, the arbitration may proceed in the absence of any party or representative who, after due notice, fails to be present or fails to obtain a postponement. An award shall not be made solely on the default of a party. The arbitrator shall require the party who is present to submit such evidence as the arbitrator may require for the making of an award.

A. When a party fails to respond to the AAA's communications or has indicated that it will not be participating in the arbitration, the AAA sends all Notices of Hearing, a letter affording the nonparticipant an opportunity to file documents or evidence on its behalf, and the award to the nonparticipant via regular first-class mail and certified mail-return receipt requested.
B. When a party fails to be present at the hearing, the AAA will try to reach the party by telephone to determine the cause for their not being present. All information is relayed to the arbitrator. Based on the information provided, the arbitrator may either proceed with the hearing or grant a postponement. If the arbitrator elects to proceed, he or she may afford the absent party additional time to either submit evidence in writing or to request a new hearing.

31. Evidence

The parties may offer such evidence as is relevant and material to the dispute and shall produce such evidence as the arbitrator may deem necessary to an understanding and determination of the dispute. An arbitrator or other person authorized by law to subpoena witnesses or documents may do so upon the request of any party or independently.

The arbitrator shall be the judge of the relevance and materiality of the evidence offered, and conformity to legal rules of evidence shall not be necessary. All evidence shall be taken in the presence of all of the arbitrators and all of the parties, except where any of the parties is absent in default or has waived the right to be present.

A. The rules of evidence and the rules of civil procedure need not apply in an arbitration proceeding.
B. As a general rule, arbitrators are fairly liberal in allowing whatever evidence and/or testimony the parties wish to present. Objections to evidence may be made, but usually serve only to let the arbitrator know of the objecting party's concerns and rarely result

in exclusion of any evidence. As a practical matter, an arbitrator usually acknowledges the objection and allows the evidence, stating that it will be given whatever weight he or she deems appropriate under the circumstances.

C. Subpoenas—Subpoena power in arbitration is limited to subpoenaing witnesses and documents for an oral hearing only. Since the rules of civil procedure do not apply, discovery is purely voluntary and, therefore, no subpoena may be issued for discovery purposes. . . .

D. Requesting a Subpoena—The AAA has its own subpoena forms for both documents and witnesses. They may be obtained from your local regional office. Attorneys authorized by law may issue subpoenas for AAA arbitrations. If a party wants a subpoena to be issued by an arbitrator, a request must be made through the AAA since there can be no direct communication between the parties and a neutral arbitrator. . . .

Enforcement of subpoenas issued by an arbitrator lies with the courts, not the arbitrator or the AAA. Arbitrators may, however, draw "negative inferences" about a party's failure to abide by a subpoena.

32. Evidence by Affidavit and Posthearing Filing of Documents or Other Evidence

The arbitrator may receive and consider the evidence of witnesses by affidavit, but shall give it only such weight as the arbitrator deems it entitled to after consideration of any objection made to its admission.

If the parties agree or the arbitrator directs that documents or other evidence be submitted to the arbitrator after the hearing, the documents or other evidence shall be filed with the AAA for transmission to the arbitrator. All parties shall be afforded an opportunity to examine such documents or other evidence.

After the hearing has ended, the case administrator contacts the arbitrator to determine whether the hearing was closed or whether the parties will be submitting additional documents or other evidence. If so, the case administrator confirms such arrangements with the parties and arbitrator, in writing. Such arrangements generally provide deadlines for both the original filing and responses thereto, if any.

33. Inspection or Investigation

An arbitrator finding it necessary to make an inspection or investigation in connection with the arbitration shall direct the AAA to so advise the parties. The arbitrator shall set the date and time and the AAA shall notify the parties. Any party who so desires may be present at such an inspection or investigation. In the event that one or all parties are not present at the inspection or investigation, the arbitrator shall make a verbal or written report to the parties and afford them an opportunity to comment.

A. Most requests for inspections or investigations come from a party, not the arbitrator. As a practical matter, such arrangements as date, time, and who will attend are made at the hearing.

B. The parties may, by stipulation, have an inspection or investigation conducted however they choose but all must be given an opportunity to attend. Some options are (i) to have the arbitrator make the inspection or investigation unaccompanied, (ii) to have only the parties' representatives accompany the arbitrator or, (iii) to have the parties' principals and their representatives accompany the arbitrator. As a general rule, the fewer the participants the better. Inspections and investigations have the potential to turn easily into shouting matches. This can be avoided by carefully selecting and preparing the participants.

34. Interim Measures

The arbitrator may issue such orders for interim relief as may be deemed necessary to safeguard the property that is the subject matter of the arbitration without prejudice to the rights of the parties or to the final determination of the dispute.

The extent of the arbitrator's authority under this section is subject to varying court interpretation. Some examples of interim relief include:

1. a directive from the arbitrator that a party not sell or otherwise dispose of real or personal property pending a final determination by the arbitrator;
2. a directive from the arbitrator that a party cease and desist from engaging in a certain business or other activity until a final determination from the arbitrator;
3. a directive from the arbitrator that a party perform under a contract pending a final determination; and
4. a directive from the arbitrator that books and records from a partnership be made available to a party pending a final determination.

35. Closing of Hearing

The arbitrator shall specifically inquire of all parties whether they have any further proofs to offer or witnesses to be heard. Upon receiving negative replies or if satisfied that the record is complete, the arbitrator shall declare the hearing closed.

If briefs are to be filed, the hearing shall be declared closed as of the final date set by the arbitrator for the receipt of briefs. If documents are to be filed as provided in Section 32 and the date set for their receipt is later than that set for the receipt of briefs, the later date shall be the date of closing of the hearing. The time limit within which the arbitrator is required to make the award shall commence to run, in the absence of other agreements by the parties, upon the closing of the hearing.

A. If documents, other evidence, and briefs are to be submitted subsequent to the conclusion of the oral hearing, the hearing remains open until the due date of the submission. When considering whether or not such filings are necessary, it is good to keep in mind that they will delay the issuing the award by the arbitrator.
B. Briefs are generally discouraged since they delay the issuing of the award. The filing of briefs is discretionary with the arbitrator. The arbitrator may also determine the length and format of briefs.

36. Reopening of Hearing

The hearing may be reopened on the arbitrator's initiative, or upon application of a party, at any time before the award is made. If reopening the hearing would prevent the making of the award within the specific time agreed on by the parties in the contract(s) out of which the controversy has arisen, the matter may not be reopened unless the parties agree on an extension of time. When no specific date is fixed in the contract, the arbitrator may reopen the hearing and shall have thirty days from the closing of the reopened hearing within which to make an award.

37. Waiver of Oral Hearing

The parties may provide, by written agreement, for the waiver of oral hearings in any case. If the parties are unable to agree as to the procedure, the AAA shall specify a fair and equitable procedure.

A. Arbitration laws usually provide that parties be afforded an oral hearing. Under the AAA rules, parties have the right to waive an oral hearing and proceed by another method. Generally, the parties prescribe this other method themselves. It may be by correspondence, conference calls, samples of goods, or any other method that satisfies the parties. In the absence of any such prescribed method, the procedure to be used, when oral hearings have been waived, is to conduct the arbitration by the submission of written documents.
B. Waiving an oral hearing and proceeding under the rules do not waive the remainder of the rules. All other rules are effective, except where they are inconsistent with waiver of oral hearings.

38. Waiver of Rules

Any party who proceeds with the arbitration after knowledge that any provision or requirement of these rules has not been complied with and who fails to state an objection in writing shall be deemed to have waived the right to object.

39. Extensions of Time

The parties may modify any period of time by mutual agreement. The AAA or the arbitrator may for good cause extend any period of time established by these rules, except the time for making the award. The AAA shall notify the parties of any extension.

A. A party finding it necessary to request an extension of time should first contact the other side to see whether it has any objection and, if not, agree on the length of the extension. The requesting party need only advise the AAA of these arrangements. The case administrator, of course, places a courtesy call to the other side to confirm its agreement.
B. Generally speaking, when the AAA grants extensions of time, the period of the extension is seven days, although, depending on the circumstances, such extensions may be for any period of time that the AAA deems appropriate. Prior to an arbitrator's being appointed to the case, the AAA determines all contested requests for time extensions. Once an arbitrator is appointed, such requests are submitted to him for a ruling.
C. No extension of time may be granted for the award due date except by mutual agreement of the parties.

40. Serving of Notice

Each party shall be deemed to have consented that any papers, notices, or process necessary or proper for the initiation or continuation of an arbitration under these rules; for any court action in connection therewith; or for the entry of judgment on any award made under these rules may be served on a party by mail addressed to the party or its representative at the last known address or by personal service, in or outside the state where the arbitration is to be held, provided that reasonable opportunity to be heard with regard thereto has been granted to the party.

The AAA and the parties may also use facsimile transmission, telex, telegram, or other written forms of electronic communication to give the notices required under these rules.

41. Time of Award

The award shall be made promptly by the arbitrator and, unless otherwise agreed by the parties or specified by law, no later than thirty days from the date of closing the hearing, or, if oral hearings have been waived, from the date of the AAA's transmittal of the final statements and proofs to the arbitrator.

42. Form of Award

The award shall be in writing and shall be signed by a majority of the arbitrators. It shall be executed in the manner required by law.

A. The parties may agree and require that the award be in a specific form.
B. Unless required by the parties' arbitration agreement, the arbitrator's award will not contain findings of fact or conclusions of law.
C. Since arbitrators are not required to give reasoning for their awards, most awards are very brief and to the point. For example, "The Claimant shall pay to the Respondent the net sum of $67,894.32. The arbitrator's fee and expenses shall be borne equally by the parties and the administrative fees and expenses of the American Arbitration Association shall be borne as incurred."

43. Scope of Award

The arbitrator may grant any remedy or relief that the arbitrator deems just and equitable and within the scope of the agreement of the parties, including, but not limited to, specific performance of a contract. The arbitrator shall, in the award, assess arbitration fees, expenses, and compensation as provided for in Sections 48, 49, and 50 in favor of any party and, in the event that any administrative fees or expenses are due the AAA, in favor of the AAA.

44. Award upon Settlement

If the parties settle their dispute during the course of the arbitration, the arbitrator may set forth the terms of the agreed settlement in an award. Such an award is referred to as a consent award.

45. Delivery of Award to Parties

Parties shall accept as legal delivery of the award the placing of the award or a true copy thereof in the mail addressed to a party or its representative at the last known address, personal service of the award, or the filing of the award in any other manner that is permitted by law.

A. Once an arbitrator has made his decision, he notifies the case administrator. The administrator transcribes the decision into a standard format and mails the award to the arbitrator to be signed, dated, and notarized or affirmed, depending on the law of the state in which the award is rendered. The arbitrator sends the award back to the administrator for transmittal to the parties via first-class mail.

B. The AAA must transmit the award to all parties simultaneously via the same method. If one party wants it sent by facsimile, the AAA will do so if the others agree. Likewise, if mutually requested, the case administrator will read the award over the telephone on a conference call.

46. Release of Documents for Judicial Proceedings

The AAA shall, upon the written request of a party, furnish to the party, at its expense, certified copies of any papers in the AAA's possession that may be required in judicial proceedings relating to the arbitration.

47. Applications to Court and Exclusion of Liability

(a) No judicial proceeding by a party relating to the subject matter of the arbitration shall be deemed a waiver of the party's right to arbitrate.
(b) Neither the AAA nor any arbitrator in a proceeding under these rules is a necessary party in judicial proceedings relating to the arbitration.
(c) Parties to these rules shall be deemed to have consented that judgment upon the arbitration award may be entered in any federal or state court having jurisdiction thereof.
(d) Neither the AAA nor any arbitrator shall be liable to any party for any act omission in connection with any arbitration conducted under these rules.

48. Administrative Fees

As a not-for-profit organization, the AAA shall prescribe filing and other administrative fees and service charges to compensate it for the cost of providing administrative services. The fees in effect when the fee or charge is incurred shall be applicable.

The filing fee shall be advanced by the initiating party or parties, subject to final apportionment by the arbitrator in the award. The AAA may, in the event of extreme hardship on the part of any party, defer or reduce the administrative fees.

49. Expenses

The expenses of witnesses for either side shall be paid by the party producing such witnesses. All other expenses of the arbitration, including required travel and other expenses of the arbitrator, AAA representatives, and any witness and the cost of any proof produced at the direct request of the arbitrator, shall be borne equally by the parties, unless they agree otherwise or unless the arbitrator in the award assesses such expenses or any part thereof against any specified party or parties.

A. The arbitrator has no authority to assess the expenses associated with producing witnesses unless the parties agree otherwise.
B. All of the arbitrator's expenses are reimbursed 100%. Such costs include but are not limited to mileage, car rental, airfare, and hotel rooms. Based on the number of arbitrators on the case and the parties' estimated number of hearing days, the case administrator estimates the amount of anticipated expenses and the cost of arbitrator compensation. Unless they agree otherwise, the parties are billed equally for those anticipated costs and expenses. Section 51 provides that monies billed in this regard are put on deposit with the AAA. If the AAA's estimate for expenses is too low, addi-

tional billings are made. Conversely, if the estimate is in excess of what was used, surpluses are refunded.

C. While all AAA and arbitrator expenses are billed equally, the arbitrator has wide latitude in determining how those expenses will ultimately be assessed. The arbitrator's assessment of expenses is a part of the award. Therefore, be sure to let the arbitrator know how you think such expenses ought to be borne.

50. Neutral Arbitrator's Compensation

Unless the parties agree otherwise, members of the National Panel of Commercial Arbitrators appointed as neutrals will serve without compensation for the first day of service.

Thereafter, compensation shall be based on the amount of service involved and the number of hearings. An appropriate daily rate and other arrangements will be discussed by the administrator with the parties and the arbitrator. If the parties fail to agree, . . . an appropriate rate shall be established by the AAA and communicated in writing to the parties.

Any arrangement for the compensation of a neutral arbitrator shall be made through the AAA and not directly between the parties and arbitrator.

A. Arbitrators serving on AAA cases are volunteers. As such, they generally serve with no compensation for the first day of hearing on each case for which they are selected. Occasionally, an arbitrator requests that the parties waive this "free" day and compensate him from the first day of hearing. Any such waiver must be unanimous.

B. Beginning with the second hearing day of each case, arbitrators receive compensation at a daily rate negotiated between the arbitrator and the parties by the AAA. . . .

C. "Study Time"—It is not unusual for arbitrators to request compensation for time spent in preparation for the case and for review and deliberation for the award. Such time is called "study time."

D. When the parties are unable to agree on terms of arbitrator compensation, the AAA has the authority to establish an appropriate rate.

E. Once the terms of compensation have been finalized, the case administrator sends two copies of a Compensation Stipulation to each party for signature acknowledging their obligation in this regard. One copy is to be returned to the AAA. The other is for the party's file.

51. Deposits

The AAA may require the parties to deposit in advance of any hearings such sums of money as it deems necessary to cover the expense of the arbitration, including the arbitrator's fee, if any, and shall render an accounting to the parties and return any unexpended balance at the conclusion of the case.

52. Interpretation and Application of Rules

The arbitrator shall interpret and apply these rules insofar as they relate to the arbitrator's powers and duties. When there is more than one arbitrator and a difference arises among them concerning the meaning or application of these rules, it shall be decided by a majority vote. If that is not possible, either an arbitrator or a party may refer the question to the AAA for final decision. All other rules shall be interpreted and applied by the AAA.

Expedited Procedures

53. Notice by Telephone

The parties shall accept all notices from the AAA by telephone. Such notices by the AAA shall subsequently be confirmed in writing to the parties. Should there be a failure to confirm in writing any notice hereunder, the proceeding shall nonetheless be valid if notice has, in fact, been given by telephone.

54. Appointment and Qualifications of Arbitrator

(a) Where no disclosed claim or counterclaim exceeds $50,000, exclusive of interest and arbitration costs, the AAA shall appoint a single arbitrator, from the National Panel of Commercial Arbitrators, without submission of lists of proposed arbitrators.
(b) Where all parties request that a list of proposed arbitrators be sent, the AAA upon payment of the service charges . . . shall submit simultaneously to each party an identical list of five proposed arbitrators, drawn from the National Panel of Commercial Arbitrators, from which one arbitrator shall be appointed. Each party may strike two names from the list on a peremptory basis. The list is returnable to the AAA within seven days from the date of the AAA's mailing to the parties.
(c) If for any reason the appointment of an arbitrator cannot be made from the list, the AAA may make the appointment from among other members of the panel without the submission of additional lists.
(d) The parties will be given notice by telephone by the AAA of the appointment of the arbitrator, who shall be subject to disqualification for the reasons specified in Section 19. Within seven days, the parties shall notify the AAA, by telephone, of any objection to the arbitrator appointed. Any objection by a party to the arbitrator shall be confirmed in writing to the AAA with a copy to the other party or parties.

55. Date, Time, and Place of Hearing

The arbitrator shall set the date, time, and place of the hearing. The AAA will notify the parties by telephone, at least seven days in advance of the hearing date. A formal Notice of Hearing will be sent by the AAA to the parties.

56. The Hearing

Generally, the hearing shall be completed within one day, unless the dispute is resolved by submission of documents under Section 37. The arbitrator, for good cause shown, may schedule an additional hearing to be held within seven days.

57. Time of Award

Unless otherwise agreed by the parties, the award shall be rendered not later than fourteen days from the date of the closing of the hearing.

AAA SCHEDULE OF FEES AND CHARGES*

Administrative Fees

The AAA's administrative charges are based on filing and service fees. Arbitrator compensation, if any, is not included. Unless the parties agree otherwise, arbitrator compensation and administrative fees are subject to allocation by the arbitrator in the award.

Filing Fees

A nonrefundable filing fee is payable in full by a filing party when a claim, counterclaim, or additional claim is filed, as provided below.

Amount of Claim or Counterclaim	**Fee**
Up to $20,000	$ 500
Above $20,000 to $50,000	$ 750
Above $50,000 to $250,000	$2,500
Above $250,000 to $500,000	$3,000
Above $500,000 to $5,000,000	$4,000
Above $5,000,000	$5,000

When no amount can be stated at the time of filing, the filing fee is $2,500, subject to adjustment when the claim or counterclaim is disclosed. When a claim or counterclaim is not for a monetary amount, an appropriate filing fee will be determined by the AAA. The minimum filing fee for any case having three or more arbitrators is $2,500.

Expedited Procedures, outlined in Sections 53-57 of the rules, are applied in any case where no disclosed claim or counterclaim exceeds $50,000, exclusive of interest and arbitration costs. Under those procedures, arbitrators are directly appointed by the AAA. Where the parties request a list of proposed arbitrators under those procedures, a service charge of $250 will be payable by each party.

A. Filing fees are calculated on claims for affirmative relief only. No fee is due on amounts claimed as offsets.

B. Filing fees are calculated on the amount that a party is seeking to recover, not on the amount actually awarded. Therefore, make certain that the affirmative claims being asserted are reasonable and not inflated.

C. Undetermined and Undisclosed Claims—Such claims can run anywhere from several thousand to several million dollars. When claims of this nature are filed, the AAA seeks a quantification of claim amounts early and often. The inability, and in some cases the unwillingness, of a party to specify and quantify its claim could negatively impact the arbitration in several ways. Remember, if a party does not know what it seeks, the arbitrator will not know what to award.

Hearing Fees

For each day of hearing held before a single arbitrator, an administrative fee of $150 is

*__Authors Note.__ These AAA charges are, of course, subject to change, and may have changed since the publication of this book. We included them to provide the reader with a rough guide to the costs associated with major arbitration proceedings.

payable by each party. For each day of hearing held before a multi-arbitrator panel, an administrative fee of $200 is payable by each party. There is no hearing fee for the initial hearing in cases administered under the Expedited Procedures.

Postponement/Cancellation Fees

A fee of $150 is payable by a party causing a postponement of any hearing scheduled before a single arbitrator. A fee of $200 is payable by a party causing a postponement of any hearing scheduled before a multi-arbitrator panel.

A. If a postponement request is unilateral and the other party agrees to the request, the party initiating the request pays the postponement fee.
B. If a postponement request is unilateral and the other party objects to the postponement, the request is submitted to the arbitrator for a ruling. If the arbitrator rules to allow the postponement, the party making the request pays the fee.
C. If a postponement request is mutual, the fee is split equally between the parties.
D. There is no postponement fee when a hearing is postponed at the request of an arbitrator.

Processing Fees

On single-arbitrator cases, a processing fee of $150 per party is payable 180 days after the case is initiated, and every 90 days thereafter, until the case is withdrawn or settled or the hearings are closed by the arbitrator.

On multi-arbitrator cases, a processing fee of $200 per party is payable 180 days after the case is initiated, and every 90 days thereafter, until the case is withdrawn or settled or the hearings are closed by the arbitrators.

Suspension for Nonpayment

If arbitrator compensation or administrative charges have not been paid in full, the AAA may so inform the parties in order that one of them may make the required payment. If such payments are not made, the arbitrator may order the suspension or termination of the proceedings. If no arbitrator has yet been appointed, the AAA may suspend.

Hearing Room Rental

The Hearing Fees described above do not cover the rental of hearing rooms, which are available on a rental basis. Check with our local office for availability and rates.

D. CPR Institute for Dispute Resolution, CPR Non-Administered Arbitration Rules and Commentary (1995)*

The Rules are intended in particular for use in complex commercial arbitrations and are designed to assure the expeditious and economical conduct of proceedings. . . .

---

*Copyright ©1995, CPR Institute for Dispute Resolution, 366 Madison Avenue, New York, NY 10017. Reprinted with permission. The CPR Institute for Dispute Resolution is a nonprofit initiative of 500 general counsel of major corporations, leading law firms and prominent legal academics in support of private alternatives to the high costs of litigation. Organized in 1979 as the Center for Public Resources/CPR Legal Program, CPR develops new methods to resolve business and public disputes by alternative dispute resolution (ADR).

A. General and Introductory Rules

Rule 1. Scope of Application

1.1 Where the parties to a contract have provided for arbitration under the Rules, they shall be deemed to have made these Rules a part of their arbitration agreement, except to the extent that they have agreed in writing, or on the record during the course of the arbitral proceeding, to modify these Rules. These Rules, and any amendment thereof adopted by CPR, shall apply in the form obtaining at the time the arbitration is commenced.

1.2 These Rules shall govern the arbitration except that where any of these Rules is in conflict with a mandatory provision of applicable law, that provision of law shall prevail.

Rule 2. Notices

2.1 Notices shall be given in writing at the address specified in writing by the recipient or, if no address has been specified, to the then business or residence address of the recipient. Notices may be given by mail, telex or facsimile transmission. Notices shall be deemed to have been received on the date of delivery.

2.2 Time periods specified by these Rules or established by the Arbitral Tribunal (the "Tribunal") shall start to run on the day a notice is received, unless the Tribunal shall specifically provide otherwise.

Rule 3. Commencement of Arbitration

3.1 The party commencing arbitration (the "Claimant") shall address to the other party (the "Respondent") a notice of arbitration.

3.2 The arbitration shall be deemed commenced on the date on which the notice of arbitration is received by the Respondent.

3.3 The notice of arbitration shall include in the text or in attachments thereto:

(a) The full names, descriptions and addresses of the parties;

(b) A demand that the dispute be referred to arbitration pursuant to the Rules;

(c) The verbatim text of the arbitration clause or the separate arbitration agreement that is involved;

(d) A statement of the general nature of the claimant's claim;

(e) The relief or remedy sought; and

(f) The name and address of the arbitrator appointed by the Claimant, unless the parties have agreed that neither shall appoint an arbitrator.

3.4 Within twenty days after receipt of the notice of arbitration, the Respondent shall deliver to the Claimant a notice of defense. Failure to deliver a notice of defense shall not delay the arbitration; in the event of such failure, all claims set forth in the demand shall be deemed denied.

3.5 The notice of defense shall include:

(a) Any comment on items (a), (b), and (c) of the notice of arbitration that the Respondent may deem appropriate;

(b) A statement of the general nature of the Respondent's defense; and

(c) The name and address of the arbitrator appointed by the Respondent, unless the parties have agreed that neither shall appoint an arbitrator.

3.6 The Respondent may include in its notice of defense any counterclaim within the scope of the arbitration clause. If it does so, the counterclaim in the notice of defense shall include items (a), (b), (c), (d) and (e) of Rule 3.3.

3.7 If a counterclaim is asserted, within twenty days after receipt of the notice of defense, the Claimant shall deliver to the Respondent a reply to counterclaim which shall have the same elements as provided in Rule 3.5 for the notice of defense.

3.8 Claims or counterclaims may be freely added or amended prior to the establishment of the Tribunal and thereafter with the consent of the Tribunal. Notices of defense or replies to amended claims or counterclaims shall be delivered within twenty days after the addition or amendment.

3.9 If a dispute is submitted to arbitration pursuant to a submission agreement, Rule 3 shall apply to the extent that it is not inconsistent with the submission agreement.

Rule 4. Representation

4.1 The parties may be represented or assisted by persons of their choice.

4.2 Each party shall communicate the name, address and function of such persons in writing to the other party and to the Tribunal.

B. Rules with Respect to the Tribunal

Rule 5. Selection of Arbitrators by the Parties

5.1 Unless the parties have agreed in writing on a Tribunal consisting of a sole arbitrator or of three arbitrators not appointed by parties, the Tribunal shall consist of two arbitrators appointed by the parties and a third arbitrator, who shall chair the Tribunal, selected as provided in Rule 5.2. Unless otherwise agreed, any arbitrator not appointed by a party shall be a member of the CPR Panels of Neutrals.

5.2 As soon as possible after the appointment of two party-appointed arbitrators and delivery of the notice of defense provided for in Rule 3.4 and in any event within fifteen days thereafter, the party-appointed arbitrators shall discuss potential candidates for the third arbitrator and shall proceed to select the third arbitrator. They shall attempt to make their selection within twenty days of their initial discussion, but they may extend their selection process until one or both of them have concluded, and have so advised the appointing parties, that a deadlock has been reached. In this event, the third arbitrator shall be selected as provided in Rule 6.

5.3 If the parties have agreed on a Tribunal consisting of a sole arbitrator or of three arbitrators none of whom shall be appointed by either party, as soon as possible after delivery of the notice of defense provided for in Rule 3.4 and in any event within twenty days thereafter, the parties' representatives shall discuss potential candidates for the arbitrator(s) and shall proceed to select the arbitrator(s). They shall attempt to make their selection within twenty days of their initial discussion, but they may extend their selection process until one or both of them have concluded that a deadlock has been reached. In this event, the arbitrator(s) shall be selected as provided in Rule 6.

Rule 6. Selection of Arbitrator(s) by CPR

6.1 Whenever (i) a party has failed to appoint the arbitrator to be appointed by it; (ii) the parties have failed to appoint the arbitrators to be appointed by them acting jointly; (iii) the party appointed arbitrators have failed to appoint the third arbitrator; or (iv) the parties have provided that one or more arbitrators shall be appointed by CPR, the arbitrator(s) required to complete the Tribunal shall be selected as provided in Rule 6, and either party may request CPR in writing, with copy to the other party, to proceed pursuant to Rule 6.

6.2 The written request may be made as follows:

(a) If a party has failed to appoint the arbitrator to be appointed by it, or the parties have failed to appoint the arbitrator(s) to be appointed by them through agreement, at any time after such failure has occurred.

(b) If the party-appointed arbitrators have failed to appoint the third arbitrator, as soon as the procedure contemplated by Rule 5.2 has been completed.

(c) If the arbitrator(s) are to be appointed by CPR, as soon as the arbitration has been commenced.

6.3 The written request shall include complete copies of the notice of arbitration and the notice of defense or, if the dispute is submitted under a submission agreement, a copy of the agreement supplemented by the notice of arbitration and notice of defense if they are not part of the agreement.

6.4 CPR shall then proceed as follows:

(a) Promptly following receipt by it of the request provided for in Rule 6.3, CPR shall convene the parties in person or by telephone one or more times to attempt to select the arbitrator(s) by agreement of the parties.

(b) If the procedure provided for in (a) does not result in the selection of the required number of arbitrators, CPR shall submit to the parties a list, from the CPR Panels of Neutrals, of not less than five candidates if one arbitrator remains to be selected, and of not less than seven candidates if two or three arbitrators are to be selected. Such list shall include a brief statement of each candidate's qualifications. Each party shall number the candidates in order of preference, shall note any objection it may have to any candidate, and shall deliver the list so marked to CPR. Any party failing without good cause to return the candidate list so marked within ten days after receipt shall be deemed to have assented to all candidates listed thereon. CPR shall designate as arbitrator(s) the nominee(s) willing to serve for whom the parties collectively have indicated the highest preference and who does not appear to have a conflict of interest. If a tie should result between two candidates, CPR may designate either candidate. If this procedure for any reason should fail to result in designation of the required number of arbitrators, CPR shall appoint a person or persons whom it deems qualified to fill any remaining vacancy.

Rule 7. Qualifications, Challenges and Replacement of Arbitrators

7.1 Each arbitrator shall be independent and impartial.

7.2 By accepting appointment, each arbitrator shall be deemed to be bound by these Rules and any modification agreed to by the parties, and to have represented that he or she has the time available to devote to the expeditious process contemplated by these Rules.

7.3 Each arbitrator shall promptly disclose in writing to the Tribunal and the parties any circumstances that might cause doubt regarding the arbitrator's independence or impartiality. Such circumstances include bias, interest in the result of the arbitration, and past or present relations with a party or its counsel.

7.4 Any arbitrator may be challenged if circumstances exist or arise that give rise to justifiable doubt regarding that arbitrator's independence or impartiality, provided that a party may challenge an arbitrator whom it has appointed only for reasons of which it becomes aware after the appointment has been made.

7.5 A party may challenge an arbitrator only by a notice in writing to the Tribunal, with copy to the other party, given no later than fifteen days after (i) the parties have been notified that the Tribunal has been constituted, or (ii) the challenging party has become aware of the circumstances specified in Rule 7.4, whichever shall last occur. The notice shall state the reasons for the challenge with specificity.

7.6 When an arbitrator has been challenged by a party, the other party may agree to the challenge or the arbitrator may voluntarily withdraw. Neither of these actions implies acceptance of the validity of the challenge.

7.7 If neither agreed disqualification nor voluntary withdrawal occurs, the challenge shall be decided as follows:

(a) By unanimous vote of the remaining members of the Tribunal;

(b) If the Tribunal consists of a sole Arbitrator, or fails or refuses to decide the challenge, by the President of CPR.

7.8 In the event of death, resignation or successful challenge of an arbitrator not appointed by a party, a substitute arbitrator shall be selected pursuant to the procedure by which the arbitrator being replaced was selected. In the event of the death, resignation or successful challenge of an arbitrator appointed by a party, that party may appoint a substitute arbitrator; provided, however, that should that party fail to notify the Tribunal and the other party of its appointment within twenty days from the date on which the opening arose, that party's right of appointment shall lapse and the Tribunal shall promptly request CPR to appoint a substitute arbitrator forthwith.

7.9 In the event that an arbitrator fails to act or is *de jure* or *de facto* prevented from duly performing the functions of an arbitrator, the procedures provided in Rule 7.8 shall apply to the selection of a replacement. If the Tribunal consists of a sole arbitrator and the parties do not agree on whether the arbitrator has failed to act or is prevented from performing the functions of an arbitrator, either party may request CPR to make that determination forthwith. If the Tribunal consists of three arbitrators and the parties do not so agree, such determination shall be made by a majority of the Tribunal.

7.10 If the sole arbitrator or the chairman of the Tribunal is replaced, the successor shall decide the extent to which any hearings held previously shall be repeated. If any other arbitrator is replaced, the Tribunal in its discretion may require that some or all prior hearings be repeated.

Rule 8. Challenges to the Jurisdiction of the Tribunal

8.1 The Tribunal shall have the power to hear and determine challenges to its jurisdiction.

8.2 The Tribunal shall have the power to determine the existence, validity or scope of the contract of which an arbitration clause forms a part, and/or of the arbitration clause itself. For the purposes of challenges to the jurisdiction of the Tribunal, the arbitration clause shall be considered as separable from any contract of which it forms a part.

8.3 Any challenges to the jurisdiction of the Tribunal, except challenges based on the award itself, shall be made not later than the notice of defense or, with respect to a counterclaim, the reply to the counterclaim.

C. Rules with Respect to the Conduct of the Arbitral Proceedings

Rule 9. General Provisions

9.1 Subject to these Rules, the Tribunal may conduct the arbitration in such manner as it shall deem appropriate. The chairman shall be responsible for the organization of arbitral conferences and hearings and arrangements with respect to the functioning of the Tribunal.

9.2 The proceedings shall be conducted in an expeditious manner. The Tribunal is empowered to impose time limits it considers reasonable on each phase of the proceeding, including without limitation the time allotted to each party for presentation of its case and for rebuttal. In setting time limits, the Tribunal should bear in mind its obligation to manage the proceeding firmly in order to complete proceedings as economically and expeditiously as possible.

9.3 Except as otherwise provided in these Rules or permitted by the Tribunal, no party or anyone acting on its behalf shall have any *ex parte* communication with any arbitrator with respect to any matter of substance relating to the proceeding, or on any matter with the arbitrator it appointed, except that a party and the arbitrator it appointed may confer regarding the selection of the chairman of the Tribunal.

9.4 As promptly as possible after the selection of the Tribunal, the Tribunal shall hold an initial pre-hearing conference for the planning and scheduling of the proceeding. The objective of this conference shall be to discuss all elements of the arbitration with a view to planning for its future conduct. Matters to be considered in the initial pre-hearing conference may include, *inter alia,* the following:

(a) Procedural matters such as setting specific time limits for, and manner of, any required discovery; the desirability of bifurcation or other separation of the issues in the arbitration; the scheduling of conferences and hearings; the scheduling of pre-hearing memoranda; the need for and type of record of conferences and hearings, including the need for transcripts; the amount of time allotted to each party for presentation of its case and for rebuttal; the mode, manner and order for presenting proof; the need for expert witnesses and how expert testimony should be presented; and the necessity for any on-site inspection by the Tribunal;

(b) The early identification and narrowing of the issues in the arbitration;

(c) The possibility of stipulations of fact and admissions by the parties solely for purposes of the arbitration, as well as simplification of document authentication; and

(d) The possibility of the parties engaging in settlement negotiations, with or without the assistance of a mediator.

After the initial conference, further pre-hearing or other conferences may be held as the Tribunal deems appropriate.

9.5 In order to define the issues to be heard and determined, the Tribunal may *inter alia* make pre-hearing orders for the arbitration and instruct the parties to file more detailed statements of claim and of defense and pre-hearing memoranda.

9.6 Unless the parties have agreed upon the place of arbitration, the Tribunal shall fix the place of arbitration. The award shall be deemed made at such place. Hearings may be held and the Tribunal may schedule meetings, including telephone meetings, wherever it deems appropriate.

Rule 10. Discovery

The Tribunal shall permit and facilitate such discovery as it shall determine is appropriate in the circumstances, taking into account the needs of the parties and the desirability of making discovery expeditious and cost-effective. The Tribunal may issue orders to protect the confidentiality of proprietary information, trade secrets and other sensitive information disclosed in discovery.

Rule 11. Evidence and Hearings

11.1 The Tribunal shall determine the manner in which the parties shall present their cases. Unless otherwise determined by the Tribunal, the presentation of a party's case shall include the submission of a pre-hearing memorandum including the following elements:

(a) A statement of facts;

(b) A statement of each claim being asserted;

(c) A statement of the applicable law upon which the party relies;

(d) A statement of the relief requested, including the basis for any damages claimed; and

(e) A statement of the evidence to be presented, including the name, capacity and subject of testimony of any witnesses to be called and an estimate of the amount of time required for the witness' direct testimony.

11.2 Evidence may be presented in written or oral form as the Tribunal may determine is appropriate. The Tribunal is not required to apply the rules of evidence used in judicial proceedings, *provided, however,* that the Tribunal shall apply the lawyer-client privilege and the work product immunity. The Tribunal shall determine the applicability of any privilege or immunity and the admissibility, relevance, materiality and weight of the evidence offered.

11.3 The Tribunal, in its discretion, may require the parties to produce evidence in addition to that initially offered. It may also appoint experts whose testimony shall be subject to cross examination and rebuttal.

11.4 The Tribunal shall determine the manner in which witnesses are to be examined. The Tribunal shall have the right to exclude witnesses from hearings during the testimony of other witnesses.

Rule 12. Interim Measures of Protection

12.1 At the request of a party, the Tribunal may take such interim measures as it deems necessary with respect to the subject matter of the dispute, including measures for the preservation of assets, the conservation of goods or the sale of perishable goods. The Tribunal may require security for the costs of such measures.

12.2 A request for interim measures by a party to a court shall not be deemed incompatible with the agreement to arbitrate or as a waiver of that agreement.

Rule 13. The Award

13.1 The Tribunal may make final, interim, interlocutory and partial awards. An award may grant any remedy or relief which the Tribunal deems just and equitable and within the scope of the agreement of the parties, including but not limited to specific performance of a contract. With respect to any interim, interlocutory or partial award, the Tribunal may state in its award whether or not it views the award as final for purposes of any judicial proceedings in connection therewith.

13.2 All awards shall be in writing and shall state the reasoning on which the award rests unless the parties agree otherwise. When there are three arbitrators, the award shall be made and signed by at least a majority of the arbitrators; and if the award decides a number of issues, the part of the award relating to each issue shall be made and signed by at least a majority of the arbitrators.

13.3 A member of the Tribunal who does not join in an award may file a dissenting opinion. Such opinion shall not constitute part of the award.

13.4 Executed copies of awards and of any dissenting opinion shall be delivered by the Tribunal to the parties.

13.5 Within fifteen days after receipt of the award, either party, with notice to the other party, may request the Tribunal to correct in an award any errors in computation, any clerical or typographical errors, or any errors of a similar nature.

Within thirty days after the delivery of an award to the parties, the Tribunal may make corrections on its own initiative and corrections requested by either party. All such corrections shall be in writing, and the provisions of Rule 13 shall apply to them.

13.6 After expiration of the thirty-day period provided in Rule 13. 5, awards shall be final and binding on the parties, and the parties will undertake to carry out awards without delay.

13.7 The dispute should in most circumstances be submitted to the Tribunal for decision within six months after the initial pre-hearing conference required by Rule 9.4. The final award should in most circumstances be rendered within one month thereafter. The parties and the arbitrators shall use their best efforts to comply with this schedule.

D. Miscellaneous Rules

Rule 14. Failure to Comply with Rules

Whenever a party fails to comply with these Rules in a manner deemed material by the Tribunal, the Tribunal shall fix a reasonable period of time for compliance and, if the party does not comply within said period, the Tribunal may impose a remedy it deems just, including an award on default. Prior to entering an award on default the Tribunal may require the non-defaulting party to produce evidence and legal argument in support of its contentions, which the Tribunal may receive without the defaulting party's presence or participation.

Rule 15. Costs

15.1 Each arbitrator shall be compensated at an hourly rate determined at the time of appointment for all time spent in connection with the proceeding and shall be reimbursed for any travel and other expenses.

15.2 The Tribunal shall fix the costs of arbitration. The costs of arbitration include:
(a) The fees and expenses of members of the Tribunal;
(b) The costs of expert advice and other assistance engaged by the Tribunal;
(c) The travel and other expenses of witnesses to such extent as the Tribunal may deem appropriate;
(d) The costs for legal representation and assistance and experts of the successful party to such extent as the Tribunal may deem appropriate;
(e) The charges and expenses of CPR with respect to the arbitration;
(f) The costs of a transcript; and
(g) The costs of meeting and hearing facilities.

15.3 Subject to any agreement between the parties to the contrary, the Tribunal may apportion the costs of arbitration between or among the parties in such manner as it deems reasonable taking into account the circumstances of the case, the conduct of the parties during the proceeding, and the result of the arbitration.

15.4 The Tribunal may request each party to deposit an equal amount as an advance for the costs referred to in Rule 15.2, except those specified in subparagraph (d), and, during the course of the proceeding, it may request supplementary deposits from the parties. Any such funds shall be held and disbursed in such a manner as the Tribunal may deem appropriate.

15.5 If the requested deposits are not paid in full within twenty days after receipt of the request, the Tribunal shall so inform the parties in order that jointly or severally they may make the required payment. If such payment is not made, the Tribunal may suspend or terminate the proceedings.

15.6 After the award has been rendered, the Tribunal shall return any unexpended balance from deposits made to the parties as may be appropriate.

Rule 16. Confidentiality

The parties and the arbitrators shall treat the proceedings, any related discovery and the decisions of the Tribunal, as confidential, except in connection with a judicial challenge to, or enforcement of, an award, and unless otherwise required by law.

Rule 17. Settlement and Mediation

17.1 Either party may propose settlement negotiations to the other party at any time. The Tribunal may suggest that the parties explore settlement at such times as the Tribunal may deem appropriate and shall suggest that they do so at or before conclusion of the hearing. The Tribunal shall give such assistance in settlement negotiations as the parties may request and the Tribunal may deem appropriate.

17.2 With the consent of the parties, the Tribunal at any stage of the proceeding may arrange for mediation of the claims asserted in the arbitration by a mediator acceptable to the parties. The Mediator shall be a person other than a member of the Tribunal, unless the parties request and the Tribunal agrees that a member of the Tribunal designated by the parties may serve as Mediator. The Tribunal may provide the Mediator with whatever factual and legal material developed in the arbitration it deems appropriate and may permit the Mediator to attend conferences and hearings held in connection with the arbitration. Unless the parties agree otherwise, any such mediation shall be conducted under the *CPR Model Mediation Procedure for Business Disputes.*

Rule 18. Actions against CPR or Arbitrators

Neither CPR nor any arbitrator shall be liable to any party for any act or omission in connection with any arbitration conducted under these Rules.

Rule 19. Waiver

A party knowing of a failure to comply with any provision of these Rules and neglecting to state its objections promptly waives any objection thereto.

GENERAL COMMENTARY

The CPR Institute for Dispute Resolution ("CPR") brings a distinct viewpoint to the field of business dispute resolution. Its tenets:

1. Most business disputes are best resolved privately and by agreement.
2. Executives should play a key role in business dispute resolution and should approach a dispute as a problem to be solved, not a contest to be won.
3. A skilled and respected neutral third party can play a critical role in bringing about agreement.
4. Efforts should first be made to reach agreement by unaided negotiation.
5. If such efforts are unsuccessful, resolution by a non-adjudicative procedure, such as mediation or the minitrial, should next be pursued. These procedures remain available even while litigation or arbitration is pending.
6. If adjudication by a neutral third party is required, a well-conducted arbitration proceeding usually is preferable to litigation.
7. During an arbitration proceeding, the door to settlement should remain open; arbitrators should encourage the parties to discuss settlement; if appropriate, employing a mediator.
8. Arbitration proceedings often can be conducted efficiently by the Arbitral Tribunal without administration by a neutral organization, or limiting the role of such an organization to assistance in arbitrator selection, if required.

Features of Well-Managed Arbitration Proceedings

Primary objectives of arbitration are to arrive at a just and enforceable result, based on a private procedure that is:

- fair,
- expeditious,
- economical, and
- less burdensome and adversarial than litigation.

The above objectives are most likely to be achieved if the parties and their attorneys:

- adopt well-designed rules of procedure;
- select skilled arbitrators who are able and willing to actively manage the process;
- limit the issues to focus on the core of the dispute; and
- cooperate on procedural matters even while acting as effective advocates on substantive issues.

General Commentary on the Rules

The Rules reflect CPR's view that disputants should make all reasonable efforts to resolve their dispute by agreement. Rule 16 requires the Arbitral Tribunal (the "Tribunal") to suggest at or before conclusion of the hearing that the parties engage in settlement negotiations, and authorizes the Tribunal to arrange mediation with the consent of the parties.

The standard arbitration clauses in the Rules have been drafted to make proceedings under the Rules subject to the United States Arbitration Act, 9 U.S.C. § 1 et seq. If parties desire a different law, or if the federal law does not apply (where, for example, the underlying transaction is not "in commerce"), another law should be specified.

Every disputant wants to have a reasonable opportunity to develop and present its case. Parties that choose arbitration over litigation do so in large part out of a need or desire for a proceeding that is also speedy and economical—factors which tend to go hand in hand. The Rules were designed with each of these objectives in mind. . . .

Counsel are expected to cooperate fully with the Tribunal and with each other to assure that the proceeding will be conducted with civility in an efficient, expeditious and economical manner. Rule 15 empowers the arbitrators in apportioning costs to take into account "the circumstances of the case." This broad power is intended to permit the arbitrators to apportion a greater share of costs than they otherwise might to a party which has employed tactics the arbitrators consider dilatory, or in other ways has failed to cooperate in assuring the efficient conduct of the proceeding.

The Rules may be modified by written agreement. The Rules are designed for an arbitration between two parties but may be amended to provide for a proceeding among three or more parties. . . .

Administered vs. Non-Administered Arbitration

The principal functions normally performed by an organization administering arbitration proceedings are to: provide a set of rules which the parties can adopt in a pre-dispute agreement or for an existing dispute; provide administrative staff to render impartial services required for smooth case handling and to insulate arbitrators from parties;

- provide lists of persons from which arbitrators may be chosen;
- appoint the arbitrator(s) if necessary;
- decide arbitrator conflict of interest challenges if necessary;
- determine arbitrator fees and bill the parties for such fees;
- schedule hearings and send notices of hearings;
- provide hearing rooms;
- distribute documents;
- review awards for procedural comments.

The charges of administering organizations typically are related to the amount in dispute, but rates vary.

Many arbitration practitioners and arbitrators see a need for administered arbitration, but others favor non-administered or "ad hoc" arbitration, particularly for large or complex cases. They believe that the arbitrator(s) and the parties' advocates are capable of performing most of the functions generally performed by the administering organization, and that the arbitrator(s) and advocates often may be better able to control the conduct of the proceeding than such an organization. The fees charged by an administering organization may also be a factor.

The assistance of a neutral third party may be needed in selecting the Tribunal or deciding a conflict of interest challenge to an arbitrator. Under the Rules, CPR is available to perform these limited functions.

Over ninety percent of arbitrations take place pursuant to the parties' binding commitment in their business agreement to submit possible future disputes to arbitration in accordance with specified rules. Once a dispute has arisen, it is usually much more difficult for the parties to agree on any alternative to litigation. Our Committee recommends the inclusion of a dispute resolution clause in most business agreements. The parties should also consider whether to provide for administered or non-administered arbitration. Rules for administered arbitration have long been available for incorporation by reference. The availability of rules well-designed for the efficient conduct of a non-administered proceeding will facilitate the choice between these alternative procedures.

The Rules are intended primarily for disputes between responsible parties who will not attempt to obstruct the process. However, the Rules do permit the process to go forward even if a respondent fails to deliver a notice of defense, fails to participate in selection of the Tribunal, or ultimately fails to appear at a hearing.

Salient Features of the Rules

The Rules differ in numerous respects from arbitration rules promulgated by other organizations. Features which our Committee considers particularly significant are:

1. The Rules call for non-administered arbitration.
2. The Rules require the expeditious conduct of the proceeding, empowering the arbitrator(s) to establish time limits for each phase of the proceeding (Rule 9.2), and to penalize a party engaging in dilatory tactics (Rule 15.3).
3. All arbitrators, including those appointed by either party, are required to be independent and impartial (Rule 7.1). Such a requirement enhances the acceptability of the arbitration process, albeit a departure from existing U.S. practice.
4. The parties are given ample opportunity to select a sole arbitrator or a panel of three arbitrators without intervention of CPR. If they fail, either party may request CPR's assistance (Rule 5).
5. CPR will first convene the parties to attempt to select the arbitrator(s) by agreement of the parties. Only if that attempt fails will CPR submit a list of candidates to the parties for ranking (Rule 6.4).
6. The Tribunal may decide challenges to its jurisdiction (Rule 8). This should allow arbitrators to decide all issues, including arbitrability questions, without the necessity for court intervention.
7. The chairman of the Tribunal is assigned responsibility for the organization of conferences and hearings and arrangements with respect to the functioning of the Tribunal (Rule 9.1).
8. The Tribunal is required to hold at least one pre-hearing conference to plan and schedule the proceeding (Rule 9.4). Such conference should result in the smooth scheduling of the case, and may aid possible settlement.
9. The Tribunal is given great leeway in matters of procedure. The Tribunal is specifically empowered, for instance, to:
    - establish time limits for each phase of the proceeding (Rule 9.2);

- limit the time allotted to each party for presentation of its case (Rule 9.2);
- make pre-hearing orders (Rule 9.5);
- permit such discovery as it deems appropriate (Rule 10);
- require the submission of pre-hearing memoranda (Rule 11 .1);
- require evidence to be presented in written form (Rule 11.2).

10. The Tribunal is empowered to appoint neutral experts (Rule 11.3).

11. The Tribunal may take interim measures for the preservation of assets or other interim measures (Rule 12.1).

12. The Tribunal is required to state the reasoning on which its award rests unless the parties agree otherwise (Rule 13.2). Our Committee believes the parties are entitled to know how the decision was reached.

13. Each arbitrator is to be fully compensated at an hourly rate determined at the time of appointment for all time spent in connection with the proceeding (Rule 15.1).

14. The Tribunal is empowered to apportion costs, including attorneys' fees and other costs incurred by the successful party, between the parties, taking into account the circumstances of the case, the conduct of the parties during the proceeding and the result (Rule 15.3).

15. The proceedings are confidential (Rule 16).

16. The Tribunal may suggest at any time that the parties engage in settlement negotiations and shall make that suggestion at or before conclusion of the hearing (Rule 17.1).

17. The Tribunal may arrange for mediation of the dispute at any time with the consent of the parties (Rule 17.2).

E. Non-Binding Arbitration

1. Lester Edelman et al., Non-Binding Arbitration 1-5, 8-12 (U.S. Army Corps of Engineers 1990) (IWR Pamphlet 90-ADR-P-2)

NON-BINDING ARBITRATION

"Non-binding arbitration," [is] a private dispute resolution process in which a dispute is submitted to an impartial and neutral person or panel who provides a written, non-binding opinion used as a guide for negotiations towards a settlement. . . .

What is Non-Binding Arbitration?

Have you ever been in the midst of a conflict and longed for just one person who could be fair and objective? The people representing each side may have fixed or biased viewpoints. People's perceptions are often skewed by self-interest. In addition, both sides tend to be aware only of the facts which support their positions. More than that, there are often organizational pressures not to "give in." Acknowledging that the other side may have a legitimate point often implies a criticism of those people within your own organization who played a role in creating the impasse. So it's hardly surprising that the people involved in a lingering conflict have trouble seeing each other's point of view. But how would a person not involved in the conflict view the dispute? What would such a person think was a fair resolution of the conflict?

This idea of finding out what a fair, impartial person would feel about the dispute is at the heart of non-binding arbitration. Essentially the two parties present their facts and positions to a qualified neutral person (or a panel) selected jointly, and this person advises the parties as to what he or she believes are the facts and what would be a fair settlement. In non-binding arbitration this opinion is just advisory. But normally it carries a great deal of weight because the parties should have confidence in the arbitrator they selected. Also, both parties recognize that if they completely ignore the arbitrator's opinion, it will probably mean that the dispute will be resolved only through costly litigation. So, both sides are not inclined to stray too far from the arbitrator's opinion. Of course, in the final analysis, when non-binding arbitration is used, any settlement is a negotiated agreement entered into freely by both parties.

Why Use Non-Binding Arbitration?

Why would you use non-binding arbitration? There are several reasons:

- **Technical Fact-finding**

One of the features that makes nonbinding arbitration attractive is the ability to select a technically respected expert who will be able to give an informed opinion based on the critical technical facts in the dispute. By using a technical expert, the parties will be assured that complex technical issues will be given due consideration, from an informed person. After litigation it's not unusual to hear people complain that "the Judge didn't have the technical background to decide this case." In non-binding arbitration, the parties can select an arbitrator with the specific knowledge to understand complex technical facts and issues.

- **Impartial Opinion**

Since all parties participate in selecting the arbitrator, presumably all sides believe the arbitrator's conclusions will be fair and unbiased. The acknowledged need for a neutral party implies, of course, that you have already decided that the controversy should be resolved. An arbitrator, not having any history of involvement or stake in the outcome, can see the merits (or weaknesses) of both sides' positions in a way that they may not be able to do.

- **Avoid Problems of Litigation**

Even if the sides are polarized, it would still be possible to resolve the controversy in a court of law. Why not let the judge decide the case? There can be a number of reasons: (1) there are significant costs associated with litigation; (2) litigation may delay resolution for several years; (3) judges, who likely do not have technical backgrounds, will be asked to resolve technical disputes; (4) a judicial decision may be an all-or-nothing decision (a risk both parties must bear), while an arbitrator in non-binding arbitration has greater flexibility to recommend a settlement based on his or her perception of fairness; and (5) a negotiated agreement, even if achieved through non-binding arbitration, is more likely to maintain a favorable working relationship between the parties.

- **Overcomes Internal Pressure**

Not infrequently negotiators face pressures from people within their own organization to "hang tough" or "not let those guys get away with it." This may so tie negotiators' hands that they are unable to negotiate a reasonable agreement for fear of losing face within their own organizations. When an arbitrator issues a report with a recommendation, the negotiators can accept the arbitrator's recommendation without having "sold out" the organization to the other side. Because the arbitrator is presumed to be "fair and reasonable," there's less danger of appearing too "soft" if you accept a settlement proposed by the arbitrator. The arbitrator's analysis and recommendation provides a valid and reasoned basis for settlement.

- **Encourages a Decision**

Even though an arbitrator's recommendation (in non-binding arbitration, at least) does not "decide" the issue, it creates considerable impetus for a decision. It pushes the parties to make a decision, and get the dispute resolved. After the arbitrator's recommendation, any party avoiding a decision will be clearly seen as "foot-dragging" or "unwilling to bite the bullet." During negotiation, this failure to make a hard decision might be disguised for some time in the by-play of negotiation.

- **Timely Decision**

Non-binding arbitration is a way to get a timely answer to a difficult question, without the delay of litigation. Whether a single arbitrator or a panel is used, the parties are galvanized into action by the recommendation. . . .

Concerns about the Use of Non-binding Arbitration

Some people are concerned that arbitrators will use a "split the difference" approach. Their concern is that, rather than really make hard judgments about the relative merits of the positions, the arbitrator will recommend a settlement which is midway between the two positions.

If there is a concern, the remedy is for the parties to agree on specific limiting instructions to the arbitrator. Since the arbitrator's role is defined by the parties, the arbitrator can be instructed to make judgments as to the technical facts of the case. Or, the arbitrator could be instructed not to recommend a specific dollar amount, but instead recommend the principles or process by which the dollar figure should be calculated. Once the arbitrator recommends a principle or process for settlement, the parties may then be able to negotiate the actual price, and it would not be based on simply splitting the difference.

Another concern is that arbitration may not be suitable for all cases. This is entirely true. The Corps of Engineers confines the use of non-binding arbitration and other ADR techniques to cases where the law is established and where settlement turns on the facts of the case. Interpretations of a new law or regulations, for example, would not be an appropriate issue for non-binding arbitration. They would be resolved better by a judge.

Why Not Binding Arbitration?

In non-binding arbitration, the arbitrator's recommendation is not final. The parties choose whether to accept it, and if they don't like the recommendation, the dispute will continue. In situations where getting a prompt resolution is a prime consideration, it might be preferable to use binding arbitration, where both parties commit in advance to accept the arbitrator's recommendations as binding and final.

Planning to Use Non-Binding Arbitration

How do you actually go about initiating and conducting non-binding arbitration? This section provides guidance on the specifics of preparing for and conducting non-binding arbitration.

The basic steps in conducting non-binding arbitration are:

1) Approach the other parties to assess willingness to use an ADR technique.
2) Determine, by mutual agreement with the other parties, that non-binding arbitration is the most suitable technique.
3) Negotiate an agreement governing the procedures to be followed during the non-binding arbitration proceedings.
4) Select an arbitrator or arbitration panel.
5) Exchange exhibits or position papers prior to the presentation.
6) Hold an informal presentation at which all parties present their facts and positions to the arbitrator.
7) Review the arbitrator's report and assess whether to accept the recommendations.
8) Conduct negotiations. . . .

Developing a Procedural Agreement

Once there is an agreement in principle to use non-binding arbitration, the next step is to negotiate an agreement on the exact procedures to be followed. Typically this is negotiated by attorneys for the Corps and the other parties. . . . When you are developing your agreement you should be certain to consider:

- How the arbitrator will be selected
- The nature of the recommendations desired from the arbitrator
- Where the presentation will be held
- The schedule of activities
- When and in what form exhibits or other documents will be exchanged (and what occurs if documents are submitted late)
- How the presentation itself will be structured, including:
  —How formal the presentations will be
  —Whether presentations will be made by attorneys or technical people
  —Who will be present during the presentations
  —How long each party will have to present its case
  —Whether there will be cross-examination
  —The total time for the presentation
- The confidentiality of materials and presentations in the event no settlement is reached
- How the costs of the proceedings, including legal fees, will be allocated
- When the arbitrator's report is due
- How the arbitrator's report is structured
- The process for acceptance/non-acceptance of the arbitrator's position
- Termination of ADR

Selecting an Arbitrator or Panel

The first step in selecting an arbitrator is to determine what kind of arbitrator you want. In one case, for example, the decision was made to select a technical expert, fully qualified in the construction practices which were at the heart of the dispute. In another case, the arbitrator was an attorney. In a third case, an arbitration panel was established, with both technical and legal expertise. It is entirely up to the parties to determine what kind of arbitrator they want, considering the issues in the dispute.

Another factor to consider is what kind of report you want from the arbitrator. Do you want just a dollar figure? Do you want to know what entitlement the arbitrator believes each party has? Do you want a proposed basis for settlement, but not an actual dollar figure? Answering these questions may also influence the selection of the arbitrator.

Once you're in agreement on what kind of arbitrator and report you want, the next step is the actual selection. This is often done by having each side submit a list of acceptable arbitrators to the other parties, and finding a name on those lists that everyone can agree upon.

Schedule of Activities

It is important for both sides to understand when each activity in the ADR process is to take place, and the importance of maintaining these schedules. ADR is a cooperative process; if one side thinks the other is seeking an advantage by missing deadlines or hiding information, the ADR effort may be crippled. Set realistic deadlines for all milestones in the ADR process (e.g. completing discovery, exchanging position papers, or delivering witness lists) and then stick to the schedule.

Exchanging Exhibits or Position Papers

The ADR agreement should describe what kinds of documents will be exchanged prior to the formal presentation. This might include the nature of the materials to be exchanged, the length of the materials exchanged (sometimes this is limited to a maximum number of pages, to hold down the amount of material which must be mastered before the presentation), and the deadline for exchange of information. The deadline issue is important. In some of the [Army Corps of Engineers] cases, . . . important papers were not exchanged until the last minute, making it difficult to prepare.

The Format of the Presentation

Normally, non-binding arbitration is quite informal, though the arbitrator will have some influence on the procedure. The formal rules of evidence are not applied and objections to testimony or materials are not permitted. Witnesses are allowed to testify in the narrative. Usually, a transcript is not made. The arbitrator may ask questions of the witnesses, to clarify their testimony.

The key point is that you have considerable flexibility in how you wish to structure the actual presentation to the arbitrator. The procedural agreement is an opportunity to establish a common understanding of who makes the presentation, how much time is available, whether cross-examination is permitted, whether time taken to answer questions from the arbitrator is taken from each parties' time limit, etc. The best advice is simply to design the presentation to meet your specific needs, rather than assume there is a single right way to do it.

How the Arbitrator's Report is Structured

The philosophy that procedures should be designed to meet your specific needs also prevails in determining what kind of report you want from the arbitrator, the timing of this report, and to whom this report should be given. The arbitrator's report may be a fact-finding report or a recommendation for settlement which includes a detailed justification for the amounts recommended. Of course, any settlement agreement must be based on reasonable and articulate criteria if it is to be approved as in the best interests of the government.

Negotiating Final Agreement

Normally there are time limits placed on how many days the parties may take to decide whether to accept the arbitrator's recommendations. You may also want to specify whether a negotiation session will be held prior to this decision, or whether each party makes this decision in isolation. Experience has shown that it is difficult to "tinker" with an arbitrator's decision and negotiate a different agreement, because upsetting the balance within the recommendations may cause the entire package to become unacceptable. . . .

2. Comments and Questions

a. The very use of "binding" and "non-binding" arbitration as defining categories reflects a legal viewpoint. In practice, the distinction is not so dramatic. Most "non-binding" arbitrations produce results that are substantially if not exactly followed by the parties. Conversely, where "binding" arbitration produces a dramatically negative result that one party, that party is likely to so something to improve its position. That something might be further negotiations, resort to judicial process, claim a set-off based on other claims, or exert whatever other form of pressure is available. At least where the "winning" party wants to keep doing business with the "losing" party, a common situation in commercial disputes, some form of "settlement" is likely even though the arbitration produced a "binding" decision.

b. Neither federal administrative agencies nor the courts may require the use of binding arbitration, but they can and sometimes do order persons to participate in nonbinding arbitration. Nonbinding arbitration in the administrative context is discussed in Chapter 14. Court annexed arbitration is discussed in Chapter 16.

c. The Corps of Engineers uses a form of nonbinding arbitration called "disputes review panels" on major construction projects, to prevent disputes from reaching the stage where litigation might be required. An arbitration panel is selected jointly by the Corps and the contractor before construction begins. The panel reviews disputes as they arise and recommends solutions, while work progresses. Experience shows that these panels have been effective in preventing disputes from halting work, and permit the Corps and the contractor to maintain a solid working relationship.

F. Drafting of Provisons Related to Arbitration

1. Comments and Questions

a. Lawyers who need to draft contracts, wills, or other documents do not begin by writing on a blank computer screen (or, if they are old fashioned, a clean piece of paper). Rather, they use an existing document, usually a form, and adapt it to meet their particular needs. Often, adaption amounts to nothing more than filling in blanks with information about the parties to and subject matter of a transaction.

b. Two dangers must be considered in drafting arbitration language (and legal documents generally). The commonly offered warning is that the mindless use of standardized forms, without considering whether the form provisions meet the particular needs and circumstances of your client in this transaction, is a disservice to the client (and might even provide the basis for a malpractice claim). The opposite danger should also be borne in mind: quality model provisions (such as those set out below) have been created by experienced experts, and changed periodically to reflect experience with their use. Do not change forms just for the sake of originality. Before making any changes in standard language be certain that you understand what was intended by the drafters, else you risk inadvertently harming the interests of your client (which also might provide the basis for a malpractice claim).

2. CPR Institute for Dispute Resolution, Standard Arbitration Clauses (1995)*

A. Pre-dispute Clause

"Any controversy or claim arising out of or relating to this contract, or the breach, termination or validity thereof, shall be settled by arbitration in accordance with the *CPR Non-Administered Arbitration Rules,* by (a sole arbitrator) (three arbitrators, of whom each party shall appoint one) (three arbitrators, none of whom shall be appointed by either party). The arbitration shall be governed by the United States Arbitration Act, 9 U. S.C. § 1-16, and judgment upon the award rendered by the Arbitrator(s) may be entered by any court having jurisdiction thereof. The place of the arbitration shall be (city, state)."

B. Existing Dispute Submission Agreement

"We, the undersigned parties, hereby agree to submit to arbitration in accordance with *CPR's Non-Administered Arbitration Rules* (the "Rules") the following controversy:

> [Describe briefly]
>
> We further agree that the above controversy shall be submitted to (a sole arbitrator) (three arbitrators, of whom each party shall appoint one) (three arbitrators, none of whom shall be appointed by either party). We further agree that we shall faithfully observe this agreement and the Rules and that we shall abide by and perform any award rendered by the arbitrator(s). The arbitration shall be governed by the United States Arbitration Act, 9 U.S.C. § 1-16, and judgment upon the award may be entered by any court having jurisdiction thereof. The place of the arbitration shall be (city, state)."

The Rules are designed to provide a procedural basis for the settling of disputes. They are not intended to change substantive provisions of applicable law. Therefore, it is recommended that parties consider the inclusion in their agreement of specific clauses as to the law governing the contract and the arbitration. It is also advisable to state whether or not the Tribunal is empowered to award punitive damages.

---

*Copyright ©1995, CPR Institute for Dispute Resolution, 366 Madison Avenue, New York, NY 10017. Reprinted with permission. The CPR Institute for Dispute Resolution is a nonprofit initiative of 500 general counsel of major corporations, leading law firms and prominent legal academics in support of private alternatives to the high costs of litigation. Organized in 1979 as the Center for Public Resources/CPR Legal Program, CPR develops new methods to resolve business and public disputes by alternative dispute resolution (ADR).

3. American Arbitration Association, Drafting Dispute Resolution Clauses: A Practical Guide (1993)*

STANDARD ARBITRATION AGREEMENTS

It is not enough to state that "disputes arising under the agreement shall be settled by arbitration." While that language indicates the parties' intention to arbitrate and may authorize a court to enforce the clause, it leaves many issues unresolved. Issues such as to when, where, how, and before whom a dispute will be arbitrated are subject to disagreement, with no way to resolve them except to go to court.

The standard arbitration clause suggested by the American Arbitration Association addresses those questions. It has proven highly effective in over a million disputes. The parties can provide for arbitration of future disputes by inserting the following into their contracts.

STD 1 • Any controversy or claim arising out of or relating to this contract, or the breach thereof, shall be settled by arbitration administered by the American Arbitration Association in accordance with its [applicable] rules and judgment on the award rendered by the arbitrator may be entered in any court having jurisdiction thereof.

Arbitration of existing disputes may be accomplished by use of the following.

STD 2 • We, the undersigned parties, hereby agree to submit to arbitration administered by the American Arbitration Association under its [applicable] rules the following controversy [cite briefly]. We further agree that we will faithfully observe this agreement and the rules, that we will abide by and perform any award rendered by the arbitrator(s) and that a judgment of the court having jurisdiction may be entered upon the award.

The preceding clauses, which refer to the time-tested rules of the AAA, have consistently received judicial support. The standard clause is often the best to include in a contract. By invoking the AAA's rules, those clauses meet the following requirements of an effective arbitration clause.

1. It makes clear that all disputes are arbitrable. Thus, it minimizes dilatory court actions to avoid the arbitration process.
2. It is self enforcing. Arbitration can continue despite an objection from a party, unless the proceedings are stayed by court order or by agreement of the parties.
3. It provides for a complete set of rules and regulations. This feature eliminates the need to spell out rules and regulations in the parties' agreement.
4. It provides for the appointment of an impartial neutral. Arbitrators are selected by the parties from a large pool of available experts. Under the AAA rules, a procedure is available to disqualify an arbitrator for bias.
5. It settles disputes over the locale of proceedings. When the parties disagree, locale determinations are made by the AAA as the administrator, alleviating need for direction from the courts.
6. It can provide for administrative conferences. If the clause provides for AAA Commercial Arbitration Rules, Construction Industry Arbitration Rules, or related

*Reprinted with permission.

rules for resolving business disputes, there is a provision for an administrative conference with the parties' representatives and an AAA staff member to expedite the arbitration proceedings.

7. It can provide for preliminary hearings. If the clause provides for the AAA's various commercial arbitration rules, a preliminary hearing can be arranged in large and complex cases to specify the issues to be resolved, clarify claims and counterclaims, provide for an exchange of information, and consider other matters that will expedite the arbitration proceedings.
8. Mediation is available. If the clause provides for the AAA's various commercial arbitration rules, mediation conferences can be arranged to facilitate a mutual settlement, without additional administrative cost to the parties.
9. It establishes time limits to assure prompt disposition of disputes. An additional feature of the AAA's various commercial arbitration rules is the Expedited Procedures, which are used to resolve smaller claims.
10. It insulates the arbitrator from the parties. Under the vast majority of rules that provide for resolution of business disputes, the AAA channels communications between the parties and the arbitrator, which serves to protect the continued neutrality of the arbitrator and the process.
11. It establishes a procedure for serving of notices. Depending on the rules used and the type of the case, notices may be served by regular mail, addressed to the party or its representative at the last known address. Under most of the rules, the AAA and the parties may use facsimile transmission, telexes, telegrams, or other written forms of electronic communication to give the notices required by the rules.
12. It gives the arbitrator the power to decide matters equitably and to fashion any appropriate relief, including specific performance. The AAA rules allow the arbitrator to grant any remedy or relief that the arbitrator deems just and equitable and within the scope of the agreement of the parties, including, but not limited to, specific performance of a contract.
13. It allows ex-parte hearings. A hearing may be held in the absence of a party who was given due notice. Thus, a party cannot avoid an adverse award by merely refusing to appear.
14. It provides for enforcement of the award. The award can be enforced in any court having jurisdiction, with only limited grounds for resisting the award.

CUSTOMIZED ARBITRATION AGREEMENTS

The standard clause does not always meet the mutual needs of the parties. Arbitration being a consensual process, the parties are free to design their arbitration agreement in whatever manner they choose.

To assist in drafting arbitration clauses that modify or add to the standard clause, the following examples of arbitration clauses used by parties to accomplish a variety of purposes have been compiled. Although the AAA does not specifically recommend these clauses, they illustrate some of the choices made by parties in addressing the various areas described.

One important "drafting pointer" should be noted here. If, in a domestic transaction as distinguished from an international transaction, the parties desire that the arbitration clause be final and binding and subject to enforcement in a court of appropriate jurisdiction, it is essential that the clause contain an "entry of judgment" provision, such as that found in the standard arbitration clause ("and judgment on the award rendered by the arbitrator may be entered in any court having jurisdiction thereof").

MINITRIAL

The minitrial is a structured dispute resolution method in which senior executives of the parties involved in a dispute meet in the presence of a neutral advisor and, after hearing presentations of the merits of each side of the dispute, attempt to formulate a voluntary settlement. A clause providing for minitrial might read,

MT 1

- Any controversy or claim arising from or relating to this contract shall be submitted to the American Arbitration Association under its Minitrial Procedures.

NEGOTIATION

The parties might wish to attempt to resolve their disputes through negotiation prior to arbitration. A sample of a clause which provides for negotiation follows.

NEG 1

- In the event of any dispute, claim, question, or disagreement arising from or relating to this agreement or the breach thereof, the parties hereto shall use their best efforts to settle the dispute, claim, question, or disagreement. To this effect, they shall consult and negotiate with each other in good faith and, recognizing their mutual interests, attempt to reach a just and equitable solution satisfactory to both parties. If they do not reach such solution within a period of sixty days, then, upon notice by either party to the other, disputes, claims, questions, or differences shall be finally settled by arbitration administered by the American Arbitration Association in accordance with the provisions of its [applicable] rules.

MEDIATION

The parties might wish to attempt mediation before submitting their dispute to arbitration. This can be accomplished by making reference to mediation in the arbitration clause. To be most effective, the mediation clause can specify the AAA's Commercial or Construction Industry Mediation Rules. Examples of such language follow.

MED 1

- If a dispute arises out of or relates to this contract, or the breach thereof, and if the dispute cannot be settled through negotiation, the parties agree first to try in good faith to settle the dispute by mediation administered by the American Arbitration Association under its Commercial Mediation Rules before resorting to arbitration, litigation, or some other dispute resolution procedure.
- The parties hereby submit the following dispute by mediation administered by the American Arbitration Association under its Commercial Mediation Rules [the clause may also provide for the qualifications of the mediator(s), the method of payment, the locale of meetings, or any other item of concern to the parties].

MEDIATION—ARBITRATION

A clause can be inserted into a contract that first provides for mediation under the AAA's mediation rules. If the mediation is unsuccessful, the dispute would then go to arbitration under the AAA's arbitration rules. This process is sometimes referred to as "Med-Arb." Samples of med-arb clauses follow.

MEDARB 1 • If a dispute arises from or relates to this contract or the breach thereof and if the dispute cannot be settled through direct discussions, the parties agree to endeavor first to settle the dispute in an amicable manner by mediation administered by the American Arbitration Association under its Commercial Mediation Rules before resorting to arbitration. Thereafter, any unresolved controversy or claim arising from or relating to this contract or breach thereof shall be settled by arbitration administered by the American Arbitration Association in accordance with its Commercial Arbitration Rules and judgment on the award rendered by the arbitrator(s) may be entered in any court having jurisdiction thereof.

MEDARB 2 • Any other claim, dispute, or other matter in question arising from or related to this agreement or the breach thereof shall be settled in accordance with Article 4 of AIA Document A201, except that, in addition to and prior to arbitration, the parties shall endeavor to settle disputes by mediation in accordance with the Construction Industry Mediation Rules of the American Arbitration Association currently in effect unless the parties mutually agree otherwise. Any mediation arising under this Paragraph shall be conducted in accordance with the provisions of Subparagraphs 9.1.2 and 9.1.3.**

MEDARB 3 • If a monetary dispute arises from or relates to this contract, the parties agree first to submit it to mediation administered by the American Arbitration Association under its Commercial Mediation Rules and, if unable to agree on a settlement amount, to submit their dispute to a neutral person appointed by the AAA who shall select between their final negotiated positions, that selection being binding on the parties.

ARBITRATION—MEDIATION

Parties can also provide for arbitration-mediation, which works as follows. The arbitration proceeds along the traditional track, with the arbitrator rendering an award. The decision is then sealed for a period certain, during which the parties attempt to mediate. If the dispute is successfully settled in mediation, the award is destroyed or transmitted to the parties, pursuant to the terms of the parties' agreement. If the mediation does not produce a settlement, the award is issued and is fully enforceable and binding.

ARBMED 1 • Any controversy or claim arising from or relating to this contract or the breach thereof shall first be submitted to arbitration administered by the American Arbitration Association in accordance with its [applicable] rules. The award rendered by the arbitrator under the rules shall be sealed for [a

**Reprinted from AIA Document A121/CMc and AGC Document 565, Standard Form of Agreement Between Owner and Construction Manager—the 1991 Edition. The AIA/AGC should be contacted for instructions on the use of its Form Documents.

specified number] days while the parties attempt to mediate the dispute. The mediation shall be administered by the American Arbitration Association under its [applicable] mediation rules. The mediator shall not be the arbitrator previously appointed to hear the dispute. If the mediation is successful, the parties agree that the award of the arbitrator shall be [destroyed/transmitted to the parties for their information]. If the mediation is unsuccessful, the award of the arbitrator shall be transmitted to the parties and judgment on the award may be entered in any court having jurisdiction thereof.

NOTES

GOVERNING LAW

It is not uncommon for parties to specify the law that will govern the contract and/or the arbitration proceedings. Some examples follow.

- . . . shall be resolved by arbitration in accordance with Title 9 of the US Code (United States Arbitration Act) and the Commercial Arbitration Rules of the American Arbitration Association.
- This contract shall be governed by the laws of the state of [specify].
- . . . shall be settled by arbitration in accordance with [state] Arbitration Law and administered by the American Arbitration Association under its [applicable] rules.
- In rendering the award, the arbitrator shall determine the rights and obligations of the parties according to the substantive and procedural laws of [state].
- The parties acknowledge that this agreement evidences a transaction involving interstate commerce. The United States Arbitration Act shall govern the interpretation, enforcement, and proceedings pursuant to the arbitration clause in this agreement.

In international cases, where the parties have not provided for the law applicable to the substance of the dispute, the AAA's International Arbitration Rules contain specific guidelines for arbitrators regarding applicable law. See the discussion of international disputes on page 36.

PROVISIONAL REMEDIES

While the AAA's rules give the arbitrator the authority to grant interim relief, the parties might wish to make this power explicit or give themselves the option of applying to court for provisional remedies, in conjunction with the arbitration process. This can be accomplished as follows.

PROV 1 • Any provisional remedy that would be available from a court of law shall be available from the arbitrator to the parties to this agreement pending arbitration.

PROV 2 • Either party may make an application to the arbitrator seeking injunctive relief to maintain the status quo until the arbitration award is rendered or the controversy is otherwise resolved.

PROV 3 • Either party may, without inconsistency with this agreement, seek from a court any interim or provisional relief that is necessary to protect the rights or property of that party, pending the establishment of the arbitral tribunal (or pending the arbitral tribunal's determination of the merits of the controversy).

PROV 4 • Either party may apply to any court having jurisdiction hereof and seek injunctive relief to maintain the status quo until the arbitration award is rendered or the controversy is otherwise resolved.

Note that the AAA's rules also provide for interim relief by the arbitrator upon application of a party.

CONDITIONS PRECEDENT TO ARBITRATION

Under an agreement of the parties, certain conditions might have to occur before a dispute is ready for arbitration. Examples of conditions precedent include written notification of claims within a fixed period of time and exhaustion of other contractually established procedures. These kinds of provision may, however, be a source of delay. Examples of "condition precedent" language follow.

CONPRE 1 • If a dispute arises from or relates to this contract, the parties agree that senior management will try in good faith to settle the dispute within thirty days thereafter before resorting to arbitration administered by the American Arbitration Association under its [applicable] rules.

CONPRE 2 • Any controversy or claim arising out of or related to the contract, or the breach thereof, shall be settled by arbitration in accordance with the Construction Industry Arbitration Rules of the American Arbitration Association, and judgment upon the award rendered by the arbitrators may be entered in any court having jurisdiction thereof, except controversies or claims relating to aesthetic effect and except those waived as provided for in Subparagraph 4.3.5. Such controversies or claims upon which the Architect has given notice and rendered a decision as provided in Subparagraph 4.4.4 shall be subject to arbitration upon written demand of either party. Arbitration may be commenced when 45 days have passed after a claim has been referred to the Architect as provided in Paragraph 4.3 and no decision has been rendered.*

Under a broad arbitration clause—i.e., one that encompasses "any claim arising from or relating to" a contract—the question of whether a claim has been asserted within an applicable time limit is generally regarded as an arbitrable issue.

ESCROW PROVISIONS

Pending the outcome of the arbitration, parties may agree to hold in escrow money, a letter of credit, goods, or the subject matter of the arbitration. A sample of a clause providing for such escrow follows.

ESC 1 • Pending the outcome of the arbitration [name of party] shall place in escrow with [law firm, institution, or AAA] as the escrow agent, [the sum of, a letter of credit, goods, or the subject matter in dispute]. The escrow agent shall be entitled to release the [funds, letter of credit, goods, or subject matter in dispute] as directed by the arbitrator(s) in the award, unless the parties agree otherwise in writing.

---

*Reprinted from AIA Document A201, General Conditions of the Contract for Construction—1987 Edition. The AIA should be contacted for instructions on use of its Form Documents.

LOCALE PROVISIONS

Parties might want to add language specifying the place of the arbitration. Examples of locale provisions that might appear in an arbitration clause follow.

LOC 1 • Any controversy relating to this agreement or any modification or extension of it shall be resolved by arbitration in the city of [specify], administered by the American Arbitration Association under the then prevailing [applicable] rules.

LOC 2 • Any controversy or claim arising from or relating to this agreement or the breach thereof will be settled by arbitration administered by the American Arbitration Association in accordance with its [applicable] rules then in effect, and judgment on the award rendered by the arbitrator may be entered in any court having jurisdiction. Any such arbitration will be conducted in the city nearest the customer's main US office having an AAA regional office.

LOC 3 • The arbitration proceedings shall be conducted in [city], [state].

LOC 4 • The site of the arbitration shall be [city], [state].

LOC 5 • The arbitration shall be held in [city], [state], or at any other place selected by mutual agreement.

LOC 6 • . . . shall be settled by arbitration in [city], [state] under the [applicable] Rules then obtaining of the American Arbitration Association.

In specifying a locale, parties also should consider (1) the convenience of the location (e.g., availability of local counsel, transportation, hotels, meeting facilities, etc.); (2) the available pool of qualified arbitrators within the geographical area; and (3) the applicable procedural and substantive law. Of particular importance in international cases are the applicability of a convention providing for recognition and enforcement of arbitral agreements and awards and the arbitration regime at the chosen site.

LANGUAGE

In matters involving multilingual parties, the arbitration agreement often specifies the language in which the arbitration will be conducted. An example of such language follows.

LANG 1 • The language(s) of the arbitration shall be [specify].

LANG 2 • The arbitration shall be conducted in the [specify] language but, at the request and the expense of a party, documents and testimony shall be translated into [specify language].

LANG 3 • The arbitration shall be conducted in the language in which the contract was written.

Such arbitration clauses could also deal with selection and cost allocation of an interpreter.

BIFURCATION

Parties can provide in their arbitration clause for a bifurcated proceeding. For instance, the parties can agree that evidence and testimony will first be given on the issue of liability. If liability is found, the proceedings would continue on the issue of damages. If liability is not found, the matter might be declared closed and a final award issued against the claimant. Such a clause might read,

BIF 1 • The parties agree that the arbitrator shall rule as to liability prior to receiving evidence or testimony on any damage claim. In the event that liability is found, the arbitration proceeding shall continue before the same arbitrator to resolve all damage issues.

ARBITRATOR SELECTION

Under the AAA's arbitration rules, arbitrators are generally selected using a listing process. The AAA administrator provides each party with a list of proposed arbitrators who are generally familiar with the subject matter involved in the dispute. Each side is provided ten days to strike all names deemed unacceptable, number the remaining names in order of preference, and return the list to the AAA. The AAA then invites arbitrators to serve from the names remaining on the list, in the designated order of mutual preference.

The parties may use other arbitrator appointment systems, such as the party-appointed method in which each side designates one arbitrator and the two thus selected appoint the chair of the panel. This method is not recommended by the AAA because use of partisan arbitrators can delay the process and produce compromise awards or deadlocks. One way to address those problems is to agree that party appointed arbitrators serve in a neutral capacity.

The parties' arbitration clause can also specify by name the individual whom the parties want as their arbitrator.

All of these issues and others can be dealt with in the arbitration clause. Some illustrative provisions follow.

ARBSEL 1 • In the event that arbitration is necessary, [name of specific arbitrator] shall act as the arbitrator.

ARBSEL 2 • The arbitrator selected by the claimant and the arbitrator selected by respondent shall, within ten days of their appointment, select a third neutral arbitrator. In the event that they are unable to do so, the parties or their attorneys may request the American Arbitration Association to appoint the third neutral arbitrator. Prior to the commencement of hearings, each of the arbitrators appointed shall take an oath of impartiality.

ARBSEL 3 • Within fifteen days after the commencement of arbitration, each party shall select one person to act as arbitrator and the two selected shall select a third arbitrator within ten days of their appointment. If the arbitrators selected by the parties are unable or fail to agree upon the third arbitrator, the third arbitrator shall be selected by the American Arbitration Association.

When providing for direct appointment of the arbitrator(s) by the parties, it is best to specify a time frame within which it must be accomplished. Also, in many jurisdictions, the law permits the court to appoint arbitrators where privately agreed means fail. Such a result may be time consuming, costly, and unpredictable. Parties who seek to establish an ad-hoc method of arbitrator appointment might be well advised to provide a fallback, such as, should the particular procedure fail for any reason, "arbitrators shall be appointed as provided in the AAA Commercial Arbitration Rules."

NUMBER AND QUALIFICATIONS OF ARBITRATORS

Parties often have very definite ideas about the qualifications of an arbitrator appointed to a dispute. The qualification requirements may include specific educational, professional, or training experience. Parties concerned about the number of arbitrators appointed in a case can predetermine whether the dispute shall be heard by one arbitrator or by a panel of three arbitrators. Typical additions to an arbitration clause dealing with such matters follow.

QUAL 1 • The arbitrator shall be a certified public accountant.

QUAL 2 • The arbitrator shall be a retired judge of the [specify] Court.

QUAL 3 • The arbitration proceedings shall be conducted before a panel of three neutral arbitrators, all of whom shall be members of the bar of the state of [specify], actively engaged in the practice of law for at least ten years.

QUAL 4 • The panel of three arbitrators shall consist of one contractor, one architect, and one construction attorney.

QUAL 5 • Arbitrators must be members of the [specify] state bar actively engaged in the practice of law with expertise in the process of deciding disputes and interpreting contracts in [the particular field of law involving the subject controversy].

QUAL 6 • The arbitrators will be selected from a panel of persons having experience with and knowledge of electronic computers and the computer business and at least one of the arbitrators selected will be an attorney.

QUAL 7 • One of the arbitrators shall be a member of the bar of the state of [specify], actively engaged in the practice of law, or a retired member of the state or federal judiciary.

QUAL 8 • The arbitration shall be before one neutral arbitrator to be selected in accordance with the Commercial Rules of the American Arbitration Association and shall proceed under the Expedited Procedures of those rules, irrespective of the amount in dispute.

QUAL 9 • In the event that any party's claim exceeds $1 million, exclusive of interest and attorneys' fees, the dispute shall be heard and determined by three arbitrators.

NATIONALITY OF ARBITRATORS

Parties might wish to specify that the arbitrator should or should not be a national or citizen of a particular country. The following examples can be added to the arbitration clause to deal with this concern.

NATLY 1 • The arbitrator appointed to hear and decide disputes under this provision shall be a citizen of [country].

NATLY 2 • The arbitrator shall be a national of [country].

NATLY 3 • The arbitrator shall not be a national of either country of the parties to the dispute.

CONSOLIDATION

Where there are multiple parties with disputes arising from the same transaction, complications can often be reduced by the consolidation of all disputes. Parties can provide for the consolidation of two or more separate arbitrations into a single proceeding or permit the intervention of a third party into an arbitration. In a construction dispute, consolidated proceedings may eliminate the need for duplicative presentations of claims and avoid the possibility of conflicting rulings from different panels of arbitrators. Conversely, consolidating claims might be a source of delay and expense. Examples of language that can be included in an arbitration clause follow.

CONSOL 1 • The owner, the contractor, and all subcontractors, speciality contractors, material suppliers, engineers, designers, architects, construction lenders, bonding companies, and other parties concerned with the construction of the structure are bound, each to each other, by this arbitration clause, provided that they have signed this contract or a contract that incorporates this contract by reference or signed any other agreement to be bound by this arbitration clause.

CONSOL 2 • Arbitration proceedings under this agreement may be consolidated with arbitration proceedings pending between other parties if the arbitration proceedings arise from the same transaction or relate to the same subject matter. Consolidation will be by an order of the arbitrator in any of the pending cases or, if the arbitrator fails to make such an order, the parties may apply to any court of competent jurisdiction for such an order.

CONSOL 3 • No arbitration arising out of or relating to the Contract Documents shall include, by consolidation or joinder or in any other manner, the Architect, the Architect's employees or consultants, except by written consent containing specific reference to the Agreement and signed by the Architect, Owner, Contractor and any other person or entity sought to be joined. No arbitration shall include, by consolidation or joinder or in any other manner, parties other than the Owner, Contractor, a separate contractor as described in Article 6 and other persons substantially involved in a common question of fact or law whose presence is required if complete relief is to be accorded in arbitration. No person or entity other than the Owner, Contractor or a separate contractor as described in Article 6 shall be included as an original third party or additional third party to an arbitration whose interest or responsibility is unsubstantial. Consent to arbitration involving an additional person or entity shall not constitute consent to arbitration of a dispute not described therein or with a person or entity not named or described therein. The foregoing agreement to arbitration and other agreements to arbitrate with an additional person or entity duly consented to by parties to the Agreement shall be specifically enforceable under applicable law in any court having jurisdiction thereof.*

REMEDIES

Under a broad arbitration clause and most AAA rules, the arbitrator may grant "any remedy or relief that the arbitrator deems just and equitable" within the scope of the parties' agreement. Sometimes, parties want to specifically include or exclude certain remedies. Particular care, however, should be given to this type of arbitration provision, to avoid unnecessary litigation about which issues are arbitrable. Samples of clauses dealing with remedies follow.

---

*Reprinted from AIA Document A201, General Conditions of the Contract for Construction—1987 Edition. The AIA should be contacted for instruction on the use of its Form Documents.

REM 1 • The arbitrator shall have the authority to award any remedy or relief that a court of this state could order or grant, including, without limitation, specific performance of any obligation created under the agreement, the awarding of punitive damages, the issuance of an injunction, or the imposition of sanctions for abuse or frustration of the arbitration process.

REM 2 • The arbitrators will have no authority to award punitive or other damages not measured by the prevailing party's actual damages and may not, in any event, make any ruling, finding, or award that does not conform to the terms and conditions of the agreement.

REM 3 • Arbitration shall be conducted in [state], under the auspices of the American Arbitration Association, in accordance with its Commercial Arbitration Rules before a partner of [specify the name of an accounting firm], an independent public accounting firm. The scope of the arbitration shall be limited to whether the Closing Financial Statements and/or the Statement of the Seller's [specify year] sales were true and complete and were prepared in accordance with Generally Accepted Accounting Principles consistently applied.

REM 4 • Arbitrators shall be empowered to impose sanctions and to take other actions with regard to the parties that the arbitrators deem necessary to the same extent that a judge could, pursuant to the Federal Rules of Civil Procedure, the [state] Rules of Civil Procedure, and applicable law.

CONFIDENTIALITY

While the confidentiality of the hearings is protected by AAA rules and the arbitrators are expected to adhere to ethical standards concerning confidentiality (see the AAA-ABA Code of Ethics for Arbitrators in Commercial Disputes, Canon VI), parties might also wish to impose limits on themselves as to how much information regarding the dispute may be disclosed outside the hearing. The following language might serve this purpose.

CONF 1 • Neither a party nor an arbitrator may disclose the existence, content, or results of any arbitration hereunder without the prior written consent of both parties.

The preceding language could also be modified to restrict only disclosure of certain information (i.e., "trade secrets").

AWARD PROVISIONS

The arbitration clause can be specifically worded to limit the remedial power of the arbitrator, even if the evidence indicates that greater relief might be warranted. For example, the clause can establish high and low figures beyond which the arbitrator may not award. This is called "high-low" arbitration. In some agreements, the arbitrator is made aware of the high-low figures; in others, that information is not provided to the arbitrator but is contained in a separate "control contract" between the parties. Another variation is "last best offer" arbitration, also known as "baseball" arbitration. In that system, the parties negotiate to their final positions and the arbitrator is compelled to select the figure of one party or the other—nothing between, above, or below the two. While provisions such as these are permissible and sometimes appropriate, they have the potential to produce results that are unusual or unintended. Such provisions should only be adopted with careful forethought and negotiation. Examples of such arbitration clauses follow.

A High-Low or Control Clause; with the Arbitrator Uninformed of Limits

AWARD 1

- . . . In the event that the arbitrator denies the claim or awards an amount less than the minimum amount of [specify], then this minimum amount shall be paid to the claimant. Should the arbitrator's award exceed the maximum amount of [specify], then this maximum amount shall be paid to the claimant. It is further understood between the parties that, if the arbitrator awards an amount between the minimum and the maximum stipulated range, then the exact awarded amount will be paid to the claimant. The parties further agree that this agreement is private between them and will not be disclosed to the arbitrator.

A High-Low Clause, with the Arbitrator Informed of Limits

Award 2

- Any award of the arbitrator in favor of [specify party] and against [specify party] shall be at least [specify a dollar amount] but shall not exceed [specify a dollar amount]. [Specify a party] expressly waives any claim in excess of [specify a dollar amount] and agrees that its recovery shall not exceed that amount. Any such award shall be in satisfaction of all claims by [specify a party] against [specify a party].

A Last-Best-Offer or "Baseball" Clause

AWARD 3

- . . . Each party shall submit to the arbitrator and exchange with each other in advance of the hearing their last best offers. The arbitrator shall be limited to awarding only one or the other of the two figures submitted.

AWARD 4

- The parties agree that the arbitration to be employed by the panel shall be "baseball arbitration." Each party shall present to the panel, for each taxable year at issue, the total income amount that Apple Singapore would have earned at arm's length relating to the PCBN and system manufacture/assembly, taking into account all sales, service, and use of intangible property transactions, if any, between Apple and Apple Singapore, respectively. The parties are specifically limited to presenting to the panel only one amount for each taxable year in dispute. For each taxable year in dispute, the panel shall select one of the amounts presented by the parties for that specific tax year.*

DISCOVERY

Discovery frequently is time consuming and expensive. While full-blown discovery is seldom recommended in arbitration, information exchange can be beneficial in large, complex cases. For such cases, the AAA's various commercial arbitration rules provide for an administrative conference with the AAA staff and/or a preliminary hearing with the arbitrator. The purposes of such meetings are to (1) clarify the issues to be resolved; (2) specify the claims of

*Reproduced from Apple Computer Inc. and Consolidated Subsidiaries v. Commissioner of Internal Revenue, *United States Tax Court,* Docket No. 21781-90.

each party; (3) identify any witness to be called; and, at a preliminary hearing, (4) establish the extent of and a schedule for production of relevant documents and other information.

In addition to the information exchanges facilitated by the provisions of the AAA rules, some parties favor traditional discovery. The following language can serve this purpose.

DISC 1 • The arbitrator shall have the discretion to order a prehearing exchange of information by the parties, including, without limitation, production of requested documents, exchanging of summaries of testimony of proposed witnesses, and examination by deposition of parties.

DISC 2 • The parties shall allow and participate in discovery in accordance with the Federal Rules of Civil Procedure for a period of ninety days after the filing of an answer or another responsive pleading. Unresolved discovery disputes may be brought to the attention of the chair of the arbitration panel and may be disposed of by the chair of the panel.

DISC 3 • Limited civil discovery shall be permitted for production of documents and taking of depositions. All discovery shall be governed by the [specify] Rules of Civil Procedure. All issues regarding compliance with discovery requests shall be decided by the arbitrator. If the parties do agree to discovery, they might include time limitations as to when all discovery should be completed. The parties also should provide for resolution of outstanding discovery issues by the arbitrator.

JUDICIAL REFERENCE

Under the laws of some states, courts may refer all or some issues of a pending litigation to a referee, who is authorized to issue a report on certain issues of the dispute. Toward that end, the AAA has developed special Juridical Reference Procedures. Parties may also stipulate to use the judicial reference process, either after or before a dispute arises, by use of a contractual clause. Model language for these purposes follow.

JUDREF 1 • Any controversy or claim arising from or relating to this contract or the breach thereof shall be determined, at the request of either party, by a general reference conducted by a referee appointed pursuant to the provisions of [specify] and administered by the American Arbitration Association in accordance with its Judicial Reference Procedures. The parties intend this general reference agreement to be specifically enforceable in accordance with [specify].

JUDREF 2 • It is hereby stipulated by the parties hereto, through their respective undersigned counsel, that trial by jury is waived as to [specify] herein; that [the issue or cause] be referred to [name] as referee to hear and determine [the issue or all issues in this case whether of fact or law] and to report his or her statement of decision to the [court} within twenty days after testimony and argument are concluded and that judgment may be entered thereon as if the action had been tried by the court; that the costs of the referee be borne [as the parties agree or the court determines at time of appointment]; and that an order to this effect may be entered accordingly without further notice. This general reference shall be administered by the American Arbitration Association under its Judicial Reference Procedures.

WRITTEN OPINIONS

With the exception of international and labor cases, arbitrators in business disputes customarily render a brief decision without an opinion. The AAA does not encourage commercial arbitrators to write opinions that give reasons for the award in domestic cases. A lengthy written opinion can prolong a proceeding and might open avenues for attack by the losing party. Often, an itemized award can eliminate need to render an opinion. However, in some situations, parties might desire an award with written findings. In such cases, the following language can be written into their agreement.

OPIN 1 • The arbitration award shall be in writing and shall specify the factual and legal bases for the award.

OPIN 2 • The award of the arbitrators shall be accompanied by a reasoned opinion.

OPIN 3 • Upon the request of a party, the arbitrator's award shall include findings of fact and conclusions of law.

OPIN 4 • The award shall be in writing, shall be signed by a majority of the arbitrators, and shall include a statement regarding the disposition of any statutory claim.

APPEALS

Experienced parties and their attorneys rarely write arbitration clauses that allow for appeals of the arbitrator's award. Parties generally appreciate the advantage of arbitral finality and recognize that appeals will delay the ultimate resolution of the dispute. However, the parties may provide for an appeal of the arbitrator's award. Parties may also provide for appeals of court decisions, in lieu of appellate-court review, by slightly modifying the clause. An example of such language is

APP 1 • Either party may appeal the arbitration panel's award to an appellate arbitrator by filing with the AAA, within twenty days after transmittal of the award, a written brief, not to exceed twenty pages, stating the reasons why the panel's decision should be reversed or modified. The opposing party shall file with the AAA and serve on the appealing party, within twenty days after receiving the appeal brief, an opposition brief, not to exceed twenty pages.

The appellate arbitrator shall be appointed directly by the AAA, without submission of lists of proposed arbitrators, and shall be a retired judge of a court of record in the state in which the arbitration was held.

Either party may request oral argument, which must be conducted within fourteen days following the submission of the final brief. The appellate arbitration shall be based only on the record of the initial hearing and oral argument, if any. The appellate arbitrator shall render a written decision affirming, reversing, modifying, or remanding the arbitral panel's decision within twenty days after receiving the final appellate submissions. The appellate arbitrator may reverse, modify, or remand the matter for further proceedings by the arbitral panel only on one of the following grounds:

1. any ground specified in 9 USC sections 10 or 11;
2. if the award contains material errors of applicable law; or
3. if the award is arbitrary or capricious.

The appellate arbitrator may render a final decision on the appeal or remand the matter for further proceedings by the arbitral panel.

FEES AND EXPENSES

The rules generally provide that the administrative fees be borne as incurred and that the arbitrators' compensation be allocated equally between the parties but this can be modified by agreement of the parties. Fees and expenses of the arbitration, including attorneys' fees, can also be dealt with in the arbitration clause. Some typical language dealing with fees and expenses follow.

FEE 1 • All fees and expenses of the arbitration shall be borne by the parties equally. However, each party shall bear the expense of its own counsel, experts, witnesses, and preparation and presentation of proofs.

FEE 2 • The prevailing party shall be entitled to an award of reasonable attorney fees.

FEE 3 • The arbitrator is authorized to award any parties sum deemed proper for the time, expense, and trouble of arbitration, including arbitration fees and attorneys' fees.

FEE 4 • The arbitrators shall award to the prevailing party, if any, as determined by the arbitrators, all of its costs and fees. "Costs and fees" mean all reasonable preaward expenses of the arbitration, including the arbitrators' fees, administrative fees, travel expenses, out-of-pocket expenses such as copying and telephone, court costs, witness fees, and attorneys' fees.

FEE 5 • Each party shall bear its own costs and expenses and an equal share of the arbitrators' and administrative fees of arbitration.

FEE 6 • The arbitrators shall award costs and expenses of the arbitration proceeding in accordance with the provisions of the loan agreement, promissory note, and/or other loan documents relating to the credit that is the subject of the arbitrated claim or dispute.

THE LARGE, COMPLEX CASE PROGRAM

The Large, Complex Case Dispute Resolution Program has been designed primarily for business disputes involving claims of at least $1,000,000, although parties are free to provide for their use in other disputes. The key elements of the program are (1) selection of arbitrators who satisfy rigorous criteria to insure that the panel is an extremely select one and training, orientation, and coordination of those arbitrators in a manner designed to facilitate the program; (2) establishment of new procedures for administration of those cases that elect to be included in the program; (3) flexibility of those parameters so that parties can more speedily and efficiently resolve their disputes; and (4) administration of large, complex cases by trained, senior AAA staff.

The AAA has established the following criteria for arbitrators serving in the program.

1. Experience and Competence
   a. Fifteen-year Business or Professional Practice Involving Complex Legal or Business Matters
   b. Extensive Experience in Dispute Resolution
   c. Preferably, Strong Academic Background and Professional/Business Credentials
   d. Preferably, Scholarship and Continuing Education

2. Neutrality
   a. Commitment to Impartiality and Objectivity
   b. Freedom from National or Cultural Prejudice
   c. Independence and Open Mindedness
3. Judicial Capacity
   a. Dispute-Management Skills
   b. Judicial Temperament—Impartiality, Patience, and Courtesy
   c. Talent for Adjudication, Negotiation, and Conciliation
4. Reputation
   a. Highest Respect of the Bar and/or Business Community
   b. Integrity, Patience, and Courtesy
5. Commitment and Availability
   a. A Willingness to Serve if Nominated and General Availability to Serve in Accordance with the Needs of the Parties
   b. Ability to Devote Time and Effort to Major Disputes
   c. Successful Completion of an Advanced AAA Panelist Training Course
6. Quality Control
   a. Careful Attention to Selecting Panelists to Meet the Needs of the Particular Dispute and the Desires of the Parties
   b. Periodic Review of the Panel

The Supplementary Procedures for Large, Complex Disputes have been designed to be extremely party driven. They will be used upon the agreement of the parties or where a court or another authorized body directs their application.

The procedures provide for an early administrative conference with the AAA, and a preliminary hearing with the arbitrators. Documentary exchanges and other essential exchanges of information are facilitated. The procedures also provide that a statement of reasons may accompany the award, if requested by the parties. The procedures are meant to supplement the applicable rules that the parties have agreed to use. They include the possibility of the use of mediation to resolve some or all issues at an early stage. Parties might also wish to include other provisions, contained in this guide, in their dispute resolution procedures. The parties can provide for future application of the procedures by including the following arbitration clause in their contract.

LCCP 1 • Any controversy or claim arising from or relating to this contract or the breach there of shall be settled by arbitration administered by the American Arbitration Association under its [applicable] Arbitration Rules and the Supplementary Procedures for Large, Complex Disputes and judgment on the award rendered by the arbitrator(s) may be entered in any court having jurisdiction thereof.

A pending dispute can be referred to the program by the completion of a Submission to Arbitration if the underlying contract documents do not provide for AAA administration.

LCCP 2 • We, the undersigned parties, hereby agree to submit to arbitration administered by the American Arbitration Association under its [applicable] Arbitration Rules and the Supplementary Procedures for Large, Complex Disputes the following controversy [cite briefly]. We further agree that we will faithfully observe this agreement and the rules, that we will abide by and perform any award rendered by the arbitrator(s), and that a judgment of the court having jurisdiction may be entered on the award.

INTERNATIONAL DISPUTES

The American Arbitration Association administers international commercial cases under various arbitration rules either within or outside the United States. The AAA administers cases under its own International Arbitration Rules, as well as under the International Arbitration Rules of the Asia/Pacific Center for Resolution of International Business Disputes and the UNCITRAL Arbitration Rules. Following are samples of arbitration clauses that relate to international disputes.

INTL 1 • Any controversy or claim arising out of or relating to this contract shall be determined by arbitration administered by the American Arbitration Association under its International Arbitration Rules.

INTL 2 • Any controversy or claim arising from or relating to this contract shall be determined by arbitration administered by the Asia/Pacific Center for Resolution of International Business Disputes under its International Arbitration Rules.

INTL 3 • Any dispute, controversy, or claim arising out of or relating to this contract, or the breach, termination, or invalidity thereof, shall be settled by arbitration under the UNCITRAL Arbitration Rules in effect on the date of this contract. The appointing authority shall be the American Arbitration Association. The case shall be administered by the American Arbitration Association under its Procedures for Cases under the UNCITRAL Arbitration Rules.

INTL 4 • The arbitration proceedings shall be conducted in [city], [country].

INTL 5 • The language(s) of the arbitration shall be [specify].

INTL 6 • The arbitrator appointed to hear and decide disputes under this provision shall be a citizen of [country].

The parties might wish to expand any of these clauses by adding a requirement regarding the number of arbitrators appointed to the dispute.

The parties may also submit an international dispute under the AAA's commercial and other specialized arbitration rules, as supplemented by the Supplementary Procedures for International Commercial Arbitration. Those procedures do not supersede any provision of the applicable rules but merely codify various procedures customarily used in international arbitration. Included among them are provisions specifying the neutrality of arbitrators, consecutive hearing days, the language of hearings, and opinions. The thrust of the procedures is to expedite international proceedings and keep them as economical as possible.

Enforcement of international awards is addressed by the 1958 UN Convention on the Recognition and Enforcement of Foreign Arbitral Awards, which has been ratified by more than 80 nations, and in this hemisphere by the recently adopted Inter-American Convention on International Commercial Arbitration.

4. Tom Arnold, A VOCABULARY OF ALTERNATIVE DISPUTE RESOLUTION PROCEDURES, footnote 37 (1995)*

Arbitration Clause Check List

(1) Ad hoc vs. administered arbitration.

(2) Identity of administering agency.

(3) Description of issues submitted to arbitration, including, recite that a construction of the contract to arbitrate and the scope of arbitration shall itself be an issue to be arbitrated. E.g.,"Any controversy, dispute or claim arising out of or relating to this contract or the performance, enforcement, breach, termination or validity thereof, including the determination of the scope of the contract to arbitrate, shall be determined by arbitration."

(4) Governing law provision; statute of limitations. Expressly authorize or negate "amiable compositeur", "ex aequo et bono," or "natural justice and equity" on the one hand, or such as the "law of Delaware (or where ever)". Don't trust the complex of statutes of limitations and related conflicts rules: Put your own limitation period into the contract — particularly if you are permitting amiable compositeur/natural justice and equity which will induce many arbitrators to disregard the statute of limitations.

If you want the dispute to be arbitrated to be the same dispute that would be handled by a court and with the same remedies, be sure the choice of law clause is not limited to "This contract shall be construed under . . ." That designates no law for the statute of limitations or the extraordinary remedies like seizure of property and punitive damages. Rather use a more generic clause like "All disputes referred to arbitration and the statute of limitations and the remedies for any wrongs that may be found, shall be governed by the law of . . ." Why? Because the statute of limitations is likely regarded as adjectival law, and it and remedies like seizure of property and punitive damages law that are otherwise sometimes not allowable in arbitration, are almost always regarded as not "a construction of the contract," and so such law is not adopted by a construction-of-the-contract clause and indeed may not be adopted by adoption of "the substantive law of . . ."

Often, particularly in international contracts, you will want two or three choices of law for different things, like substantive law and statute of limitations of Connecticut, the procedural law and lex arbitri of the arbitration forum, and arbitration law solely of the Federal Arbitration Act as supplemented by the Texas (or California) International Arbitration Act (which, modeled after the UNCITRAL Model law, fills in some voids in the federal act.) But in some forums, there must be some sort of rational connection between the substantive law selected and the dispute or disputants, while in others the right of the parties to choose a "neutral" law is honored.

But be careful, especially in intellectual property cases. Some jurisdictions have procedural law that there be no discovery and substantive law that the accused infringer of a method patent has the burden of proving non-infringement, as an offset. The substantive patent law and related procedural law are often interrelated, so if you select a patent law you must know the procedural law that goes with it or you risk serious entrapment.

---

*Reprinted with permission.

(5) Review provisions if any (constrast para. 23, below). Both the finality of the arbitrator's award without review, and the power of the arbitrator to fashion creative procedures and remedies, are often the greatest merits of the process, in terms of both economics and equity.

But in a big case an arbitrator running wild with creativity is also a legitimate fear, a possibility you may wish to restrain or guard against. One partial protection is three arbitrators rather than one, expensive as that is.

Another protection is court review of the arbitrator's law; another is court determination of whether there was "substantial evidence" for his/her findings. These reviews are themselves burdensome and costly in time and money and command the expense of transcripts and reasoned awards with findings and conclusions and sacrifice the prompt finality of the award addressed in (23) below, but they tend to keep the arbitrators more disciplined in response to law.

(6) Process for interim or provisional remedies. To be heard by the court or only by the arbitrator(s), and under what circumstances heard by each.

(7) The place of hearing. "The place of arbitration shall be [city and country]" or "If the parties do not agree the arbitrator shall select the place(s) for hearings after consultation with the parties." I strongly urge the first form, coupled with a personal jurisdiction clause to the effect, "The parties consent to the personal jurisdiction of the state and Federal courts of [that city] with respect to any dispute arising out of or otherwise related to this arbitration agreement or the arbitration it provides for or the enforcement of the Award."

In international arbitration the choice of site usually also is a choice of law governing the hearing process of the arbitration and the confirmation or modification of the award (possibly the enforcement as well), whereby site can be very important. I suggest also: Choose a site which is a signatory to the New York Convention.

(8) A set of administrative rules. Consider, by way of example:

> "Any controversy, dispute or claim arising out of or relating to this contract or the performance, enforcement, breach, termination or validity thereof, shall be determined by arbitration and a judgement of the court may be entered upon the award upon request by either party within one year of the award. The arbitration shall be in accordance with the arbitration rules of ICA (International Centers for Arbitration, Houston), WIPO (World Intellectual Property Organization, Geneva), AAA Commercial, Patent or International Rules, ICC, or Uncitral Rules in force at the time of the contract." If the appointing or administering agency is different from the agency whose rules are adopted, "The appointing (or "administering agency") shall be [name the institution or person]."

Be advised that the AAA rules have buried in them an adoption of the AAA as case administrator, so don't adopt AAA rules without negativing that recitation unless you are also of a mind to use AAA case administration and pay the fees for that—which do not tend to be exorbitant.

The AAA will act as appointing authority and administer cases either under AAA rules or under the UNCITRAL Arbitration Rules which in my judgement are much better in a few particulars. So, consider, for example:

"Any controversy, dispute or claim arising out of or relating to this contact or the performance, enforcement, breach, termination, or validity thereof, shall be determined by arbitration in accordance with the Uncitral Arbitration Rules in effect on the date of this contract. The American Arbitration Association shall be the arbitrator appointing authority and shall administer the arbitration in accordance with its Procedures For Cases Under the Uncitral Arbitration Rules." A judgement of the court may be entered upon the award upon request by either party within one year of the award.

(9) Rules should be subject to personally drafted modifications of your choice — for a patent or trademark case you will likely modify several of the adopted rules.

(10) Procedures for appointment of arbitrators, and sometimes of setting arbitrator(s)' fees.

(11) The number of arbitrators. "The number of arbitrators shall be [one, two or three]."

(12) Recitation of whether the arbitration can proceed or must start over when one arbitrator ceases to serve, and perhaps under what timing and conditions.

(13) The qualifications of the arbitrators, in panels perhaps different for the Chairman and other arbitrators. Some need not be lawyers. Give explicit consideration to a recitation that the arbitrators have time to expedite the arbitration and commit to give a priority of claim upon their time sufficient to conclude the arbitration in X days. Consider reciting that the arbitrators shall stay together and work continuously after the close of evidence, until their award is completed. Consider specifying nationality of arbitrators.

(14) Third-party claims; joinder of third-party respondents.

(15) Evidence rules. Arbitration's "cure" for the various burdens, problems and injustice resulting from court evidence exclusionary rules is essentially to "let it all in", but that practice carries with it a sometimes equal or worse mischief. There is law many places that one ground for overturning an award is refusal of the arbitrator to consider relevant evidence, and arbitrators have need for social acceptance by counsel —particularly when they were named by counsel. So counsel are prone to offer prejudicial material and rounds of responses to it, effectively trying the immaterial issues, and arbitrators are prone not to cut it off. Not infrequently this results in a run-away arbitration, months (sometimes years) of time and related costs sometimes in the hundreds of thousands of dollars. To avoid the risk of this booby-trap there should be a contract clause authorizing and instructing the arbitrator to indulge evidence exclusion and waiving the right to have an award overturned by reason of evidence exclusion, and essentially to the effect:

The arbitrator shall have the authority to exclude evidence deemed to be irrelevant, redundant or prejudicial beyond its probative value, and is instructed to exercise that authority consistently with expediting the proceeding reasonably. The parties explicitly agree that exclusion of evidence by the arbitrator on grounds of irrelevance, redundance, or prejudicial beyond its probative value, shall not be grounds of failure to confirm and enforce the award.

The strong bias of most arbitrators is to let in too much, so the risk from such a clause is small. In that context if you trust your arbitrator with your case on the merits, you must trust him also to rule out time consuming evidence or you risk experiencing one of the arbitrator horror stories we have all heard about.

(16) Language of the hearings. "The language to be used in the arbitral proceedings shall be [language]." Who pays for interpretation? If a live witness needs interpretation, adverse parties likely want their own interpreter as check or back-up where the value at risk justifies the expense.

(17) How fees and costs are to be controlled and borne.

(18) May attorneys' fees be awarded? Usually, yes, awarded as part of "costs" in foreign cases, and the arbitrators have wide discretion not limited to specific evidence as to costs and fees. In U.S. specific statutes like 35 USC § 285 govern.

(19) Prejudgment interest? Now universally accepted in the U.S. But, at what rate?

(20) May multiplied damages or punitive awards be granted? Not normally permissible in international arbitration, never in foreign law arbitration unless spelled out in the contract to arbitrate.

(21) May injunctive remedies be awarded? Now quite widely accepted in the U.S., but in some international arbitration the arbitration award of an injunction is far from settled. And apparently the courts in some countries do not enforce injunctions effectively, so this possibility must be checked out.

(22) Currency in which the award is to be paid. Official exchange rate or black market exchange rate?

(23) An award enforcement provision: If it be an international dispute within the ultimate control of the "New York Convention," this clause is necessary only if a potential country of enforcement of the award has not signed the "New York" 1958 Convention On the Recognition and Enforcement of Foreign Arbitral Awards. If the dispute is not international, however, it is desirable (perhaps necessary) under the Federal Arbitration Act to have an explicit clause to the effect that the award may be enforced by any court having jurisdiction over the dispute or arbitration of it.

(24) Provisions concerning discovery and discovery management. Under many rules there is in arbitration no discovery by way of depositions, written interrogatories or requests for admission common to U.S.court practice; in many Continental countries there may be an inquisition by the arbitrators but of unpredictable scope. In the U.S. the arbitrator can issue a subpoena to a witness and to produce documents; in England a court will issue a subpoena in aid of arbitration; in most countries there is no subpoena in arbitration so discovery and final-hearing testimony is limited to party discovery the arbitrator can persuade the parties to yield—which is usually all identifiable relevant documents but often little else. How is a subpoena enforced? Who may subpoena a witness or documents?

To avoid surprises and resulting unfairness the parties need to agree on the scope of discovery. E.g., limiting discovery to a specified window of time; authorizing depositions but limiting deposition time to X hours or certain witnesses; providing that there shall be no objections recited during depositions except X, perhaps the deposition to be presided over by the neutral; affording a limited number of interrogatories or requests for admission; controlling document requests and production. Those provisions are often tough stuff to arrive at even after the parameters of the dispute are known, and are even tougher in a commercial contract before any dispute is definable.

(25) Neutrality of arbitrators. Perhaps, "Each arbitrator shall be neutral, independent, disinterested, impartial and shall abide by the Canons of Ethics of the American Bar Association for neutral, independent arbitrators. An arbitrator shall be subject to disqualification if an appointing party, either before or after the appointment, asks for the views of the arbitrator or makes an ex parte disclosure of significant facts or themes of the dispute beyond what is appropriate for the arbitrators' conflict check and revelation of his qualifications for the case. There shall be no ex parte communications with an arbitrator either before or during the arbitration, relating to the dispute or the issues involved in the dispute or the arbitrator's views on any such issues [or in cases using party appointed arbitrators to appoint a third arbitrator, a party-appointed arbitrator's choice of a third arbitrator].

(26) Various devices for controlling procrastination and for expediting the case, such as:
   (a) Clause reciting that the prompt resolution of the dispute is important to the parties.
   (b) Commitment from arbitrator(s) and perhaps counsel as well that t(he)y have time and commit priority of claim on their time by which to expedite the case.
   (c) "Instruction, direction and command" to arbitrator or the chairman of the panel to assume "case management initiative and control" to schedule the case early and reasonably to expedite the case toward full resolution within X weeks—whatever is reasonable for the case.
   (d) Commitment by the arbitrator(s) to render the award within X days of close of evidence or any post-evidence briefing.
   (e) Rewards to the arbitrator if the dispute is resolved by a first target date, penalties if not resolved in defined timely fashion including specifically, X days after close of evidence or post-evidence briefing.
   (f) Requirement that arbitrators remain together working upon the award, after the close of evidence, until they complete their award.
   (g) Use naked award or limit reasons to not more than five or so pages and to only those issues necessary to support the award.
   (h) For expediting purposes be biased to one arbitrator rather than three — strongly so.
   (i) Limiting each party at final hearing time to X hours for all of its arguments, presentation of case, cross examination, etc. — usually selected something like 20% longer than responsible pre-hearing estimates of time needed.

(27) Award final and binding and not subject to appeal. (A common clause in some few countries, unnecessary in others.)

(28) The award subject to interest payments or other penalties from the date of the award.

(29) Compulsory negotiation or mediation prior to a binding arbitration. I strongly urge a day of mediation early in an intellectual property dispute, prior to an arbitration. Further, "baseball" or "last offer" binding arbitration has much to recommend it as the form of follow-on after a mediation.

(30) Consent to personal jurisdiction of a given court where the arbitration is to be held and enforcement is deemed likely to be necessary.
(31) Consent to proceed with an ex parte hearing when a party, having notice of the hearing, fails to appear.

Chapter 11

The Law of Arbitration

CASE STUDY

Everyone knew Lawrence "Heads-Up" Hammond. He was the star quarterback for the NFL's San Antonio Seagulls through the mid-1970s. Twenty years after his career ended, he was a 55-year old divorced businessman. In truth, he had struggled as a businessman—always seemingly undercapitalized. People tended to forget, Hammond always thought, that he was an NFL star at a time when the league's MVP probably earned less than a million dollars for a season, a bit short of the multi-million dollar bonuses merely above average players now received for just switching teams. This time, though, Hammond knew he had come across the deal of a lifetime; all he needed was a few investors to kick in about a million dollars total. The deal? Ostrich farming. He could even take the money in some installments because he could buy the ostriches a few at a time.

Frank Fanning had been an admirer of Hammond during his football years. Fanning, a successful investor and owner of a large meat packing company in Austin, had come to know Hammond personally over the past few years because—both being good golfers—they had been paired in some celebrity-type golf tournaments. Without investigating as prudently as he normally did when presented a business opportunity, Fanning jumped at the chance to be in the ostrich business with Hammond. He invested $500,000 in cash in return for stock in the newly-formed ostrich-farming company and told Hammond that in return for additional stock in the company he would sign a promissory note six months later for another $500,000 that Hammond could use for collateral in borrowing the rest of the funds needed to be fully in business. The note simply would be canceled once the loan using it as collateral had been paid off.

As time went by, however, Fanning began to realize that perhaps he should have used his usual prudence in deciding whether to become a minority shareholder in a closely held corporation operating a highly-speculative business (Hammond was the majority shareholder at 75%; Fanning had 25% and was to receive another 24% in return for the note). Fanning, with nearly six months of hindsight, was still confident that Hammond would be ultimately successful in the venture, but Fanning was not as enamored of the business venture (or his relationship with Hammond, who hadn't seemed to have much time to play golf with Fanning) as he initially had been. While a close call, Fanning decided not to throw good money after what might be bad by signing the promissory note.

Fanning notified Hammond of this decision by routine mail sent to the ostrich farm near San Antonio, encouraging him to seek other investors for the additional money. At his Austin office several days later, Fanning received an overnight package from Hammond. The package contained a copy of a promissory note for $500,000 in favor of the ostrich farm corporation signed by "Frank Fanning." The package also contained documents indicating the note had been sold by the ostrich farm to Notes 'R' Us Corporation on a discounted basis, and the package contained a stock certificate transferring the additional stock to Fanning. The date on the note and on the stock certificate was about two weeks before the date of Fanning's letter to Hammond, and the date on the contract conveying the note was the previous day. The package also contained a letter from Hammond, which read:

Dear Frank:

Since, several weeks ago, you executed the note represented in this letter by the enclosed photocopy, I cannot tell you the degree of consternation I felt upon receipt of a letter from you yesterday indicating that you did not intend to execute such a note. If you have changed your mind, I can understand that, but I cannot understand your letter. It makes no sense. As agreed six months ago, you executed this note recently so that I could use it to obtain the remainder of the funds needed to bring our ostrich-farming business into the black.

As contemplated, I have sold the note. I sold it to Notes 'R' Us, a large national company that buys promissory notes for cash at discounted rates. I have enclosed copies of the documents that were used to consummate this transaction. As you can see, Notes 'R' Us paid our corporation $350,000 for the note.

Please contact me at your first opportunity to explain what must obviously be some form of miscommunication. The farm is doing well. I am using the proceeds of the discounted note to buy the remainder of the birds we will need. We should be in the black, on schedule, in about two years.

Please call me soon so we can get to the bottom of this mystery. Looking forward to hearing from you, I send my

Warmest personal regards,

Lawrence Hammond
President and CEO
Heads-Up Ostrich Farm, Inc.

A. Introduction

This Chapter sets out the legal structure for arbitration in America, with an emphasis on the issues that have reached the courts in recent years. We begin with an historical introduction to American arbitration law, and its roots in English law. Early arbitration law was entirely state or territorial law so the statutory law was not uniform, and the law in action varied considerably from place to place.

Arbitration law today is statutory law, at both the federal and state level, so the place to begin is with the statutes. The Federal Arbitration Act (FAA) was adopted in 1925, and it remains largely unchanged to this day. Provisions for the enforcement of foreign arbitral awards were added in 1970 and 1990. Like the U.S. Constitution, the FAA is short and general. This approach allows flexibility, but also generates litigation about the meaning and application of the Act.

The traditional problem with state arbitration law, whether statutory or common law, was not one of inconsistency, but rather a quite consistent hostility toward arbitration. The basis for state legislation favorable to arbitration is the Uniform Arbitration Act (UAA), adopted by the Commissioners on Uniform State Laws and endorsed by the ABA in 1955. Thirty-five states have adopted the UAA, and the law in most of the remaining states is generally similar. Even if states have identical arbitration statutes, however, other laws that create "rights" for consumers and others will differ, so the legal treatment of similarly situated persons still can differ dramatically between states.

The FAA and the UAA enshrine several basic principles that encourage agreements to arbitrate by providing serious judicial backing for arbitration. These include:

1. Agreements to arbitrate are specifically enforced — a striking contrast to the usually limited availability of specific relief for breaches of contract.
2. Courts will refuse access to the courts when the parties have agreed to arbitrate.
3. Arbitration awards are judicially enforced.
4. Judicial review of arbitration awards is very limited.

The scope and limitations of these principles are among the central topics considered in this Chapter.

The threshold question about arbitration is arbitrability: whether the parties have agreed to submit the type of dispute at hand to an arbitrator, or whether one party can select a judicial forum. The appropriate forum depends on the agreement of the parties, a principle that is easy to state but often difficult to apply in practice. The key issues are whether a court or an arbitrator is to determine arbitrability, and what standards are to be applied in making that decision. A subsidiary question is, what standards are to be used by appellate courts in reviewing lower court decisions on arbitrability? (The term arbitrability does NOT cover situations where the parties agree to arbitrate but their agreement is unenforceable for public policy reasons; that topic is covered later.)

The next topic is the law to be applied, specifically whether federal law preempts state law. Prominent examples of state law from recent litigation include determining arbitrability, public policy against requiring arbitration of certain classes of disputes, the limitations period, stays of arbitration, counterclaims, and the authority of arbitrators to award punitive damages.

The remedial powers of arbitrators, and the standards for judicial review of arbitral awards, are frequent subjects of litigation, if for no other reason than that large amounts of money (or other remedial consequences) are at stake. The primary focus here is on the arbitration damages law of New York, as developed by the Court of Appeals (the highest state court). We take this approach for both substantive and pedagogical reasons. The substantive reason is the importance of New York arbitration law, notably the prohibition of punitive damages awards by arbitrators. The pedagogical reason is that teaching materials almost always consist of cases from several jurisdictions, in order to present interesting cases or to highlight differences between jurisdictions. Practicing lawyers and their clients are interested in the law in a particular jurisdiction, not the "majority rule" or the latest theories of professors. After the New York cases, we present two complex arbitration damages cases, from the highest courts of California and New Jersey.

Next we consider the difficulties that can arise due to multiple contracts, claims, issues, and parties. In the simple arbitration scenario, there are two parties who have a dispute about a discrete issue. In other instances, however, there may be multiple disputes that arose at different times, multiple contracts between the same parties, multiple interested persons who are not all parties to the same contract, or multiple issues, some of which the parties agreed to arbitrate while others may be litigated. Where persons have litigated or arbitrated one dispute, they may be precluded from subsequently raising issues that could have been decided in the earlier proceeding. Among the fancy labels frequently used by courts are res judicata, claim preclusion, issue preclusion, and collateral estoppel. Serious consideration of these complexities would require an entire course; here we can do no more than introduce some of the problems that commonly arise.

The last topic covered in this Chapter is the enforcement of agreements to arbitrate when a party seeks access to the courts because a claim is based on violation of federal law. (State law claims are likely to be preempted by federal law. See the 1995 Supreme Court decision in *Allied-Bruce,* reprinted in Section C.) The Supreme Court has held that securities claims are subject to arbitration, as are civil racketeering (RICO) claims. The same is true of at least some alleged antitrust law violations. The submission to arbitration of employment discrimination claims is covered in Chapter 12, together with other materials on labor arbitration.

In closing this introduction, it is important to remind readers that a focus on litigation presents a distorted picture of reality. It cannot be emphasized enough that nearly all arbitration agreements are carried out according to their terms without difficulty, without litigation, and the parties are entirely satisfied with the process (if not necessarily the substantive outcome). Furthermore, most litigation is brought by parties who are dissatisfied with the result or expected result of arbitration, rather than with concerns about the process.

B. Early Anglo-American Arbitration Law

1. Comments and Questions

a. The next two excerpts, written by Judge Jerome Frank and Professor Soia Mentschikoff, both of whom were distinguished legal practitioners and thinkers, summarize the early attitude of the English and American courts. See also the Bruce Mann article in Chapter 1, section E.

b. The final article, by John Van Winkle, discusses the early arbitration experience in Indiana. Prior to the enactment of the Federal Arbitration Act in 1925 there was no national law of arbitration, although there was fair uniformity in the earlier hostility toward arbitration.

2. *Kulukundis Shipping Co., S/A v. Amtorg Trading Corp.*, 126 F.2d 978, 982-985 (2d Cir. 1942) (Judge Jerome Frank)

It has been well said that "the legal mind must assign some reason in order to decide anything with spiritual quiet." And so, by way of rationalization, it became fashionable in the middle of the 18th century to say that agreements [to arbitrate] were against public policy because they "oust the jurisdiction" of the court. But that was a quaint explanation, inasmuch as an award under an arbitration agreement, enforced both at law and at equity, was no less an ouster; and the same was true of releases and covenants not to sue, which were given full effect. Moreover, the agreement to arbitrate was not illegal, since suit could be maintained for its breach. [This "right" was of little practical effect, however, because only nominal damages were awarded for such a breach. Equity would not grant specific performance of the agreement, and the courts would not bar a suit despite an arbitration agreement.] . . .

An effort was made to justify this judicial hostility to the executory arbitration on the ground that arbitrations, if unsupervised by the courts, are undesirable, and that legislation was needed to make possible such supervision. But if that was the reason for unfriendliness to such executory agreements, then the courts should also have refused to aid arbitrations after they ripened into awards. . . .

That English attitude was largely taken over in the 19th century by most courts in this country. . . . An executory agreement to arbitrate would not be given specific performance or furnish the basis of a stay of proceedings on the original cause of action. Nor would it be given effect as a plea in bar, except in limited instances, i.e., in the case of an agreement expressly or impliedly making it a condition precedent to litigation that there be an award determining some preliminary questions of subsidiary fact upon which any liability was to be contingent. *Hamilton v. Liverpool etc. Ins. Co.*, 136 U.S. 242 (1890). In the case of broader executory agreements, no more than nominal damages would be given for a breach.

Generally speaking, then, the courts in this country were unfriendly to executory arbitration agreements. . . . Effective state arbitration statutes were enacted beginning with the New York statute of 1920. The purpose of [the FAA] was deliberately to alter the judicial atmosphere previously existing. The report of the House Committee stated, in part:

> Arbitration agreements are purely matter of contract, and the effect of the bill is simply to make the contracting party live up to his agreement. . . . The need for the law arises from an anachronism of our American law. Some centuries ago because of the jealousy of the English courts for their own jurisdiction, they refused to enforce specific agreements to arbitrate upon the ground that the courts were thereby ousted from their jurisdiction. This . . . principle became firmly embedded in the English common law and was adopted with it by the American courts. The courts have felt that the precedent was too strongly fixed to be overturned without legislative enactment, although they have frequently criticized the rule and recognized its illogical nature and the injustice which result from it. The bill declares simply that such agreements for arbitration shall be enforced, and provides a procedure in the Federal courts for their enforcement. . . . It is particularly appropriate that the action should be taken at this time when there is so much agitation against the costliness and delays of litigation. These matters can be largely eliminated by agreements for arbitration, if arbitration agreements are made valid and enforceable.

3. Soia Mentschikoff, *Commercial Arbitration*, 61 Colum. L. Rev. 846 (1961)*

Mercantile disputes have been decided by merchants in the Anglo-American world since at least the thirteenth century. In the early period the decision of mercantile cases was assigned to courts staffed by merchants such as the piepowder courts or the staple courts, and the town courts, or merchant juries were utilized; the guilds and trading companies had their own tribunals. In the Tudor period, the Privy Council, a major forum for commercial matters, solved its mercantile cases by reference to merchant arbitrators. . . . Chancery referred its mercantile cases to arbitration, while the common law courts seemed to be using merchant juries. The Mayor's Court of London . . . handled mercantile cases. . . . The trading companies emerged and had as a common feature provisions for resolution of disputes between members by the organization itself. Following the Restoration, the prerogative courts lost jurisdiction, but the common law courts seem not to have been used extensively by merchants. The guilds and trading companies continued, as did the city and borough courts. In 1697 an arbitration statute was enacted to render the awards of arbitrators "the more effectual in all cases." Forms for arbitration bonds and awards became readily available and legal textbooks on arbitrators were published. Clearly, it was the accepted method of resolving disputes arising out of accounts.

In the colonies, arbitration existed as a form of dispute settlement from the earliest period. In 1768 the New York Chamber of Commerce was founded with one of its purposes being the arbitration of disputes among its members. It was the sole civil tribunal to operate during the British occupation at the time of the revolution. In the nineteenth century, as trade became more specialized, exchanges were organized with arbitration provisions for their members. Later, trade associations come into the picture. Side-by-side with these self-contained trade group arbitrations were individual arrangements and court references of matters to arbitration which was sometimes conducted with the aid of local chambers of commerce. Always, however, merchants were involved as deciders, and always there were the two basic institutions—the self-contained trade groups and the forums open to everyone.

The development of arbitration in England and the United States was not completely parallel. The law of arbitration in the United States took a significantly different turn from the one it took in England. In England, the Common Law Procedure Act of 1854 specifically permitted arbitrators to refer matters for decision on the law to the courts by stating the arbitration [as a special case]. The Arbitration Act of 1889 permitted such submission of a special case to the court whenever the arbitrators were empowered to do so by the parties in their original submissions, or whenever the arbitrators felt it desirable. To this day English arbitrators can and do submit awards in the form of a special case to the courts for final adjudication as to the substantive rules of law.

In the United States, however, if we take the law of New York as the most "progressive" example, it is clear that there was no similar development. The New York Legislature never provided a method by which arbitrators could have the aid of the courts in the disposition of a case on a substantive rule of law. In fact, the first of the so-called modern arbitration statutes, the New York Arbitration Act of 1920, made it clear that errors of law were not grounds for

*This article originally appeared at 61 Colum. L. Rev. 846 (1961). Reprinted by permission.

setting aside an arbitration award. This general position that the courts are not available for final determination of the legal issues in an arbitration was reemphasized by the Federal Arbitration Act of 1925 and is supported today by the Uniform Arbitration Act. The effect of this difference in law was that in England it was virtually impossible to develop the process that is known as "ad hoc" arbitration, that is to say, arbitration without any precedential value. On the other hand, in the United States, except for the self-governing trade groups, the formal legal machinery made it difficult for anything other than ad hoc arbitration to develop.

The most pressing legal questions concerning the enforceability of an arbitration award in the United States thus became questions of procedure. If the procedure followed by the arbitrators was correct, the award would be enforced. In England both the procedure and the substance were subject to review.

4. John R. Van Winkle, *An Analysis of the Arbitration Rule of the Indiana Rules of Alternative Dispute Resolution*, 27 IND. L. REV. 735 (1994)*

A. Common Law of Arbitration

Common law arbitration and statutory arbitration have coincided in Indiana since its statehood.[3] At common law, any person competent to enter into a contract could agree to submit a dispute or controversy, or even a difference of opinion, to arbitration. Common law arbitration, however, had two significant limitations. First, although both existing and future disputes could be submitted to arbitration, the arbitrator's decision was only binding or conclusive as to existing disputes and not future ones. Secondly, under common law arbitration, if no lawsuit was pending, the arbitrator's decision did not become a judgment enforceable in court. Rather, the defaulting party was liable on the bond which each party to the arbitration was required to provide. Some of the early arbitration statutes were enacted to address these deficiencies in common law arbitration.

Just as the common law concerning arbitration preceded statehood, so did statutory provisions concerning arbitration. . . .

B. The Indiana Arbitration Act

The Indiana Arbitration Act . . . was enacted in 1852 and has been changed little since that time. The first section of the original Act provided as follows:

> All persons, except infants, married women and insane persons, may, by an instrument in writing, submit to the arbitration or umpirage of any person or persons, to be by them mutually chosen, any controversy existing between them, which might be the subject of a suit at law, except as otherwise provided in the next section, and may agree that such submission be made a rule of any court of record designated in such instrument.

The comments to that Act referred to [prior case law] and stated:

---

[3]Common law arbitration refers to the cumulative decisions of the Courts of England and the Acts of the English Parliament in aid of that common law, in existence prior to the fourth year of James I, which common law decisions and parliamentary enactments are of a general and not specific or local nature and which are not inconsistent with the Constitution of the United States, the Constitution of the State of Indiana or Acts of the United States Congress or the Indiana Legislature. Shroyer v. Bash, 57 Ind. 349, 353 (1877).

> When a cause is pending it may be referred to arbitration by consent of parties, and such submission made a rule of court. At common law, however, if no suit were pending, and any matter in controversy were submitted to arbitration, such submission could not be made a rule of court; but the party was left to his action on the award or arbitration bond. The object of the statute is to give the parties the same remedies that the common law gives in cases referred after the commencement of a suit.

Although the statute extended common law arbitration by providing that arbitration of disputes not yet in litigation could nevertheless be enforced after award as a judgment (or "rule of any court"), the statute perpetuated the previous deficiency in the common law in that it provided that only existing, and not future, disputes could be submitted to arbitration. As indicated above, section 1 is clear that parties were free to submit to arbitration "any controversy **existing** between them."

The 1852 Indiana Arbitration Act has been amended infrequently. . . . [A] 1939 amendment deleted married women from the first sentence of Section 1. The 1852 statute contained 26 sections, most of those remaining unchanged to this date. Section 2 excepts certain real estate matters from the category of cases which can be arbitrated.

Section 3 of the 1852 Act required the parties, at the time of the agreement to arbitrate, to execute mutual bonds to secure performance of the arbitration award. Section 3 also provided that the parties must agree to make the agreement or submission a rule of court, thereby enabling the parties to execute either on the judgment created by the award or to institute an action on the bond. Under the current statute, as in the 1852 Act, either party can appoint or designate a time and place for the arbitrator or arbitrators to meet. Witnesses can be required to attend by issuance subpoenas and, unless the parties agree otherwise, the award of a majority of arbitrators is valid.

The Indiana Arbitration Act provided that if either party failed to comply with an award, it could be filed in the court named in the submission. The award had to be entered of record and a rule granted to show cause before judgment could be entered.

Upon a rule to show cause, an adverse party was provided with three grounds to object to the rendition of a judgment: that the award was obtained by fraud, that the arbitrators were guilty of misconduct or that the arbitrators exceeded their power. The 1852 Indiana Arbitration Act also provided, and current law provides today, that any party to a submission can move the court to modify or correct an award on three bases: an evident miscalculation of figures, a decision on a matter or matters not submitted to arbitration, and a clearly defective award.

In summary, the 1852 statute (the Indiana Arbitration Act) empowered parties to enter into irrevocable contracts to submit existing disputes to binding arbitration, the awards from which could be entered and enforced as judgments. The obvious, and commercially important, deficiency . . . was that it did not allow parties to enter into written agreements to submit future disputes to arbitration. This deficiency was addressed by the adoption of the Indiana Uniform Arbitration Act [in 1970].

C. The Federal Arbitration Act [United States Code Title 9]

1. Comments and Questions

a. The story of modern arbitration law begins with the New York legislation in 1920, which in turn served as a model for the Federal Arbitration Act of 1925 (FAA). 43 Stat. 883 (1925).

b. The FAA has remained largely unchaged to the present day. Provisions for the enforcement of foreign arbitral awards were added in 1970 and 1990. Like the U.S. Constitution, the FAA is short and lacking in specifics. This approach permits flexibility and adjustment to changing conditions, but also generates litigation about the meaning and application of the Act.

2. The FAA [Unabridged]

a. General Provisions

§ 1. "Maritime transactions" and "commerce" defined; exceptions to operation of title

"Maritime transactions", as herein defined, means charter parties, bills of lading of water carriers, agreements relating to wharfage, supplies furnished vessels or repairs to vessels, collisions, or any other matters in foreign commerce which, if the subject of controversy, would be embraced within admiralty jurisdiction; "commerce", as herein defined, means commerce among the several States or with foreign nations, or in any Territory of the United States or in the District of Columbia, or between any such Territory and another, or between any such Territory and any State or foreign nation, or between the District of Columbia and any State or Territory or foreign nation, but nothing herein contained shall apply to contracts of employment of seamen, railroad employees, or any other class of workers engaged in foreign or interstate commerce.

§ 2. Validity, irrevocability and enforcement of agreements to arbitrate

A written provision in any maritime transaction or a contract evidencing a transaction involving commerce to settle by arbitration a controversy thereafter arising out of such contract or transaction, or the refusal to perform the whole or any part thereof, or an agreement in writing to submit to arbitration an existing controversy arising out of such a contract, transaction, or refusal, shall be valid, irrevocable, and enforceable, save upon such grounds as exist at law or in equity for the revocation of any contract.

§ 3. Stay of proceedings where issue therein referable to arbitration

If any suit or proceeding be brought in any of the courts of the United States upon any issue referable to arbitration under an agreement in writing for such arbitration, the court in which such suit is pending, upon being satisfied that the issue involved in such suit or proceeding is referable to arbitration under such an agreement, shall on application of one of the parties stay the trial of the action until such arbitration has been had in accordance with the terms of the agreement, providing the applicant for the stay is not in default in proceeding with such arbitration.

§ 4. Failure to arbitrate under agreement; petition to United States court having jurisdiction for order to compel arbitration; notice and service thereof; hearing and determination

A party aggrieved by the alleged failure, neglect, or refusal of another to arbitrate under a written agreement for arbitration may petition any United States district court which, save for such agreement, would have jurisdiction under Title 28, in a civil action or in admiralty of the subject matter of a suit arising out of the controversy between the parties, for an order directing that such arbitration proceed in the manner provided for in such agreement. Five days' notice in writing of such application shall be served upon the party in default. Service thereof shall be made in the manner provided by the Federal Rules of Civil Procedure. The court shall hear the parties, and upon being satisfied that the making of the agreement for arbitration or the failure to comply therewith is not in issue, the court shall make an order directing the parties to proceed to arbitration in accordance with the terms of the agreement.

The hearing and proceedings, under such agreement, shall be within the district in which the petition for an order directing such arbitration is filed. If the making of the arbitration agreement or the failure, neglect, or refusal to perform the same be in issue, the court shall proceed summarily to the trial thereof. If no jury trial be demanded by the party alleged to be in default, or if the matter in dispute is within admiralty jurisdiction, the court shall hear and determine such issue. Where such an issue is raised, the party alleged to be in default may, except in cases of admiralty, on or before the return day of the notice of application, demand a jury trial of such issue, and upon such demand the court shall make an order referring the issue or issues to a jury in the manner provided by the Federal Rules of Civil Procedure, or may specially call a jury for that purpose. If the jury find that no agreement in writing for arbitration was made or that there is no default in proceeding thereunder, the proceeding shall be dismissed. If the jury find that an agreement for arbitration was made in writing and that there is a default in proceeding thereunder, the court shall make an order summarily directing the parties to proceed with the arbitration in accordance with the terms thereof.

§ 5. Appointment of arbitrators or umpire

If in the agreement provision be made for a method of naming or appointing an arbitrator or arbitrators or an umpire, such method shall be followed; but if no method be provided therein, or if a method be provided and any party thereto shall fail to avail himself of such method, or if for any other reason there shall be a lapse in the naming of an arbitrator or arbitrators or umpire, or in filling a vacancy, then upon the application of either party to the controversy the court shall designate and appoint an arbitrator or arbitrators or umpire, as the case may require, who shall act under the said agreement with the same force and effect as if he or they had been specifically named therein; and unless otherwise provided in the agreement the arbitration shall be by a single arbitrator.

§ 6. Application heard as motion

Any application to the court hereunder shall be made and heard in the manner provided by law for the making and hearing of motions, except as otherwise herein expressly provided.

§ 7. Witnesses before arbitrators; fees; compelling attendance

The arbitrators selected either as prescribed in this title or otherwise, or a majority of them, may summon in writing any person to attend before them or any of them as a witness and in a proper case to bring with him or them any book, record, document, or paper which may be deemed material as evidence in the case. The fees for such attendance shall be the same as the fees of witnesses before masters of the United States courts. Said summons shall issue in the name of the arbitrator or arbitrators, or a majority of them, and shall be signed by the arbitrators, or a majority of them, and shall be directed to the said person and shall be served in the same manner as subpoenas to appear and testify before the court; if any person or persons so summoned to testify shall refuse or neglect to obey said summons, upon petition the United States district court for the district in which such arbitrators, or a majority of them, are sitting may compel the attendance of such person or persons before said arbitrator or arbitrators, or punish said person or persons for contempt in the same manner provided by law for securing the attendance of witnesses or their punishment for neglect or refusal to attend in the courts of the United States.

§ 8. Proceedings begun by libel in admiralty and seizure of vessel or property

If the basis of jurisdiction be a cause of action otherwise justiciable in admiralty, then, notwithstanding anything herein to the contrary, the party claiming to be aggrieved may begin his proceeding hereunder by libel and seizure of the vessel or other property of the other party according to the usual course of admiralty proceedings, and the court shall then have jurisdiction to direct the parties to proceed with the arbitration and shall retain jurisdiction to enter its decree upon the award.

§ 9. Award of arbitrators; confirmation; jurisdiction; procedure

If the parties in their agreement have agreed that a judgment of the court shall be entered upon the award made pursuant to the arbitration, and shall specify the court, then at any time within one year after the award is made any party to the arbitration may apply to the court so specified for an order confirming the award, and thereupon the court must grant such an order unless the award is vacated, modified, or corrected as prescribed in sections 10 and 11 of this title. If no court is specified in the agreement of the parties, then such application may be made to the United States court in and for the district within which such award was made. Notice of the application shall be served upon the adverse party, and thereupon the court shall have jurisdiction of such party as though he had appeared generally in the proceeding. If the adverse party is a resident of the district within which the award was made, such service shall be made upon the adverse party or his attorney as prescribed by law for service of notice of motion in an action in the same court. If the adverse party shall be a nonresident, then the notice of the application shall be served by the marshal of any district within which the adverse party may be found in like manner as other process of the court.

§ 10. Same; vacation; grounds; rehearing

(a) In any of the following cases the United States court in and for the district wherein the award was made may make an order vacating the award upon the application of any party to the arbitration—
  (1) Where the award was procured by corruption, fraud, or undue means.
  (2) Where there was evident partiality or corruption in the arbitrators, or either of them.
  (3) Where the arbitrators were guilty of misconduct in refusing to postpone the hearing, upon sufficient cause shown, or in refusing to hear evidence pertinent and material to the controversy; or of any other misbehavior by which the rights of any party have been prejudiced.
  (4) Where the arbitrators exceeded their powers, or so imperfectly executed them that a mutual, final, and definite award upon the subject matter submitted was not made.
  (5) Where an award is vacated and the time within which the agreement required the

award to be made has not expired the court may, in its discretion, direct a rehearing by the arbitrators.

(b) The United States district court for the district wherein an award was made that was issued pursuant to section 580 of title 5 may make an order vacating the award upon the application of a person, other than a party to the arbitration, who is adversely affected or aggrieved by the award, if the use of arbitration or the award is clearly inconsistent with the factors set forth in section 572 of title 5.

§ 11. Same; modification or correction; grounds; order

In either of the following cases the United States court in and for the district wherein the award was made may make an order modifying or correcting the award upon the application of any party to the arbitration—

(a) Where there was an evident material miscalculation of figures or an evident material mistake in the description of any person, thing, or property referred to in the award.

(b) Where the arbitrators have awarded upon a matter not submitted to them, unless it is a matter not affecting the merits of the decision upon the matter submitted.

(c) Where the award is imperfect in matter of form not affecting the merits of the controversy.

The order may modify and correct the award, so as to effect the intent thereof and promote justice between the parties.

§ 12. Notice of motions to vacate or modify; service; stay of proceedings

Notice of a motion to vacate, modify, or correct an award must be served upon the adverse party or his attorney within three months after the award is filed or delivered. If the adverse party is a resident of the district within which the award was made, such service shall be made upon the adverse party or his attorney as prescribed by law for service of notice of motion in an action in the same court. If the adverse party shall be a nonresident then the notice of the application shall be served by the marshal of any district within which the adverse party may be found in like manner as other process of the court. For the purposes of the motion any judge who might make an order to stay the proceedings in an action brought in the same court may make an order, to be served with the notice of motion, staying the proceedings of the adverse party to enforce the award.

§ 13. Papers filed with order on motions; judgment; docketing; force and effect; enforcement

The party moving for an order confirming, modifying, or correcting an award shall, at the time such order is filed with the clerk for the entry of judgment thereon, also file the following papers with the clerk:

(a) The agreement; the selection or appointment, if any, of an additional arbitrator or umpire; and each written extension of the time, if any, within which to make the award.

(b) The award.

(c) Each notice, affidavit, or other paper used upon an application to confirm, modify, or correct the award, and a copy of each order of the court upon such an application.

The judgment shall be docketed as if it was rendered in an action. The judgment so entered shall have the same force and effect, in all respects, as, and be subject to all the provisions of law relating to, a judgment in an action; and it may be enforced as if it had been rendered in an action in the court in which it is entered.

§ 14. Contracts not affected

This title shall not apply to contracts made prior to January 1, 1926.

§ 15. Inapplicability of the Act of State doctrine

Enforcement of arbitral agreements, confirmation of arbitral awards, and execution upon judgments based on orders confirming such awards shall not be refused on the basis of the Act of State doctrine.

§ 16. Appeals

(a) An appeal may be taken from—
  (1) an order—
    (A) refusing a stay of any action under section 3 of this title,
    (B) denying a petition under section 4 of this title to order arbitration to proceed,
    (C) denying an application under section 206 of this title to compel arbitration,
    (D) confirming or denying confirmation of an award or partial award, or
    (E) modifying, correcting, or vacating an award;
  (2) an interlocutory order granting, continuing, or modifying an injunction against an arbitration that is subject to this title; or
  (3) a final decision with respect to an arbitration that is subject to this title.
(b) Except as otherwise provided in section 1292(b) of title 28, an appeal may not be taken from an interlocutory order—
  (1) granting a stay of any action under section 3 of this title;
  (2) directing arbitration to proceed under section 4 of this title;
  (3) compelling arbitration under section 206 of this title; or
  (4) refusing to enjoin an arbitration that is subject to this title.

b. Convention on the Recognition and Enforcement of Foreign Arbitral Awards [New York Convention]

§ 201. Enforcement of Convention

The Convention on the Recognition and Enforcement of Foreign Arbitral Awards of June 10, 1958, shall be enforced in United States courts in accordance with this chapter.

§ 202. Agreement or award falling under the Convention

An arbitration agreement or arbitral award arising out of a legal relationship, whether contractual or not, which is considered as commercial, including a transaction, contract, or agreement described in section 2 of this title, falls under the Convention. An agreement or award arising out of such a relationship which is entirely between citizens of the United States shall be deemed not to fall under the Convention unless that relationship involves property located abroad, envisages performance or enforcement abroad, or has some other reasonable relation with one or more foreign states. For the purpose of this section a corporation is a citizen of the United States if it is incorporated or has its principal place of business in the United States.

§ 203. Jurisdiction; amount in controversy

An action or proceeding falling under the Convention shall be deemed to arise under the laws and treaties of the United States. The district courts of the United States (including the courts enumerated in section 460 of title 28) shall have original jurisdiction over such an action or proceeding, regardless of the amount in controversy.

§ 204. Venue

An action or proceeding over which the district courts have jurisdiction pursuant to section 203 of this title may be brought in any such court in which save for the arbitration agreement an action or proceeding with respect to the controversy between the parties could be brought, or in such court for the district and division which embraces the place designated in the agreement as the place of arbitration if such place is within the United States.

§ 205. Removal of cases from State courts

Where the subject matter of an action or proceeding pending in a State court relates to an arbitration agreement or award falling under the Convention, the defendant or the defendants may, at any time before the trial thereof, remove such action or proceeding to the district court of the United States for the district and division embracing the place where the action or proceeding is pending. The procedure for removal of causes otherwise provided by law shall apply, except that the ground for removal provided in this section need not appear on the face of the complaint but may be shown in the petition for removal. For the purposes of Chapter 1 of this title any action or proceeding removed under this section shall be deemed to have been brought in the district court to which it is removed.

§ 206. Order to compel arbitration; appointment of arbitrators

A court having jurisdiction under this chapter may direct that arbitration be held in accordance with the agreement at any place therein provided for, whether that place is within or without the United States. Such court may also appoint arbitrators in accordance with the provisions of the agreement.

§ 207. Award of arbitrators; confirmation; jurisdiction; proceeding

Within three years after an arbitral award falling under the Convention is made, any party to the arbitration may apply to any court having jurisdiction under this chapter for an order confirming the award as against any other party to the arbitration. The court shall confirm the award unless it finds one of the grounds for refusal or deferral of recognition or enforcement of the award specified in the said Convention.

§ 208. Chapter 1; residual application

Chapter 1 applies to actions and proceedings brought under this chapter to the extent that that chapter is not in conflict with this chapter or the Convention as ratified by the United States.

c. Inter-American Convention on International Commercial Arbitration [Panama Convention]

§ 301. Enforcement of Convention

The Inter-American Convention on International Commercial Arbitration of January 30, 1975, shall be enforced in United States courts in accordance with this chapter.

§ 302. Incorporation by reference

Sections 202, 203, 204, 205, and 207 of this title shall apply to this chapter as if specifically set forth herein, except that for the purposes of this chapter "the Convention" shall mean the Inter-American Convention.

§ 303. Order to compel arbitration; appointment of arbitrators; locale

(a) A court having jurisdiction under this chapter may direct that arbitration be held in accordance with the agreement at any place therein provided for, whether that place is within or without the United States. The court may also appoint arbitrators in accordance with the provisions of the agreement.

(b) In the event the agreement does not make provision for the place of arbitration or the appointment of arbitrators, the court shall direct that the arbitration shall be held and the arbitrators be appointed in accordance with Article 3 of the Inter-American Convention.

§ 304. Recognition and enforcement of foreign arbitral decisions and awards; reciprocity

Arbitral decisions or awards made in the territory of a foreign State shall, on the basis of reciprocity, be recognized and enforced under this chapter only if that State has ratified or acceded to the Inter-American Convention.

§ 305. Relationship between the Inter-American Convention and the Convention on the Recognition and Enforcement of Foreign Arbitral Awards of June 10, 1958

When the requirements for application of both the Inter-American Convention and the Convention on the Recognition and Enforcement of Foreign Arbitral Awards of June 10, 1958, are met, determination as to which Convention applies shall, unless otherwise expressly agreed, be made as follows:

(1) If a majority of the parties to the arbitration agreement are citizens of a State or States that have ratified or acceded to the Inter-American Convention and are member States of the Organization of American States, the Inter-American Convention shall apply.

(2) In all other cases the Convention on the Recognition and Enforcement of Foreign Arbitral Awards of June 10, 1958, shall apply.

§ 306. Applicable rules of Inter-American Commercial Arbitration Commission

(a) For the purposes of this chapter the rules of procedure of the Inter- American Commercial Arbitration Commission referred to in Article 3 of the Inter-American Convention shall, subject to subsection (b) of this section, be those rules as promulgated by the Commission on July 1, 1988.

(b) In the event the rules of procedure of the Inter-American Commercial Arbitration Commission are modified or amended in accordance with the procedures for amendment of the rules of that Commission, the Secretary of State, by regulation in accordance with section 553 of title 5, consistent with the aims and purposes of this Convention, may prescribe that such modifications or amendments shall be effective for purposes of this chapter.

§ 307. Chapter 1; residual application

Chapter 1 applies to actions and proceedings brought under this chapter to the extent chapter 1 is not in conflict with this chapter or the Inter-American Convention as ratified by the United States.

3. Scope of the Federal Arbitration Act

a. *Allied-Bruce Terminix Companies, Inc. v. Dobson*, 115 S. Ct. 834 (1995)

Justice BREYER delivered the opinion of the Court.

This case concerns the reach of § 2 of the Federal Arbitration Act. That section makes enforceable a written arbitration provision in "a contract evidencing a transaction involving commerce." Should we read this phrase broadly, extending the Act's reach to the limits of Congress' Commerce Clause power? Or, do the words "involving" and "evidencing" significantly restrict the Act's application? We conclude that the broader reading of the Act is the correct one; and we reverse a State Supreme Court judgment to the contrary.

I

In August 1987 Steven Gwin, a respondent, who owned a house in Birmingham, Alabama, bought a lifetime "Termite Protection Plan" (Plan) from the local office of Allied-Bruce Terminix Companies, a franchise of Terminix International Company. In the Plan, Allied-Bruce promised "to protect" Gwin's house "against the attack of subterranean termites," to reinspect periodically, to provide any "further treatment found necessary," and to repair, up to $100,000, damage caused by new termite infestations. Terminix International "guarantee[d] the fulfillment of the terms" of the Plan. The Plan's contract document provided in writing that "any controversy or claim . . . arising out of or relating to the interpretation, performance or breach of any provision of this agreement shall be settled exclusively by arbitration."

In the Spring of 1991 Mr. and Mrs. Gwin, wishing to sell their house to Mr. and Mrs. Dobson, had Allied-Bruce reinspect the house. They obtained a clean bill of health. But, no sooner had they sold the house and transferred the Termite Protection Plan to Mr. and Mrs. Dobson than the Dobsons found the house swarming with termites. Allied-Bruce attempted to treat and repair the house, but the Dobsons found Allied-Bruce's efforts inadequate. They therefore sued the Gwins, and (along with the Gwins, who cross-claimed) also sued Allied-Bruce and Terminix in Alabama state court. Allied-Bruce and Terminix, pointing to the Plan's arbitration clause and § 2 of the Federal Arbitration Act, immediately asked the court for a stay, to allow arbitration to proceed. The court denied the stay. Allied-Bruce and Terminix appealed.

The Supreme Court of Alabama upheld the denial of the stay on the basis of a state statute making written, predispute arbitration agreements invalid and "unenforceable." To reach this conclusion, the court had to find that the Federal Arbitration Act, which preempts conflicting state law, did not apply to the termite contract. It made just that finding. The court considered the federal Act inapplicable because the connection between the termite contract and interstate commerce was too slight. In the court's view, the Act applies to a contract only if "at the time [the parties entered into the contract] and accepted the arbitration clause, they contemplated substantial interstate activity." Despite some interstate activities (e.g., Allied-Bruce, like Terminix, is a multistate firm and shipped treatment and repair material from out of state), the court found that the parties "contemplated" a transaction that was primarily local and not "substantially" interstate. . . .

II

Before we can reach the main issues in this case, we must set forth three items of legal background.

First, the basic purpose of the Federal Arbitration Act is to overcome courts' refusals to enforce agreements to arbitrate. The origins of those refusals apparently lie in ancient times, when the English courts fought for extension of jurisdiction—all of them being opposed to anything that would altogether deprive every one of them of jurisdiction. American courts initially followed English practice, perhaps just standing upon the antiquity of the rule prohibiting arbitration clause enforcement, rather than upon its excellence or reason. Regardless, when Congress passed the Arbitration Act in 1925, it was motivated, first and foremost, by a desire to change this antiarbitration rule. It intended courts to enforce arbitration agreements into which parties had entered, and to place such agreements upon the same footing as other contracts.

Second, some initially assumed that the Federal Arbitration Act represented an exercise of Congress' Article III power to "ordain and establish" federal courts. In 1967, however, this Court held that the Act "is based upon and confined to the incontestable federal foundations of control over interstate commerce and over admiralty." *Prima Paint Corp. v. Flood & Conklin Mfg. Co.*, 388 U.S. 395 (1967). The Court considered the following complicated argument: (1) The Act's provisions (about contract remedies) are important and often outcome-determinative, and thus amount to "substantive" not "procedural" provisions of law; (2) *Erie R. Co. v. Tompkins*, 304 U.S. 64, 71-80 (1938), made clear that federal courts must apply state substantive law in diversity cases; therefore, (3) federal courts must not apply the Federal Arbitration Act in diversity cases. This Court responded by agreeing that the Act set forth substantive law, but concluding that, nonetheless, the Act applied in diversity cases because Congress had so intended. The Court wrote: "Congress may prescribe how federal courts are to conduct themselves with respect to subject matter over which Congress plainly has power to legislate."

Third, the holding in *Prima Paint* led to a further question. Did Congress intend the Act also to apply in state courts? Did the Federal Arbitration Act preempt conflicting state antiarbitration law, or could state courts apply their antiarbitration rules in cases before them, thereby reaching results different from those reached in otherwise similar federal diversity cases? In *Southland Corp. v. Keating*, 465 U.S. 1 (1984), this Court decided that Congress would not have wanted state and federal courts to reach different outcomes about the validity of arbitration in similar cases. The Court concluded that the Federal Arbitration Act preempts state law; and it held that state courts cannot apply state statutes that invalidate arbitration agreements.

We have set forth this background because respondents, supported by 20 state attorneys general, now ask us to overrule Southland and thereby to permit Alabama to apply its antiarbitration statute in this case irrespective of the proper interpretation of § 2. . . . Nothing significant has changed in the 10 years subsequent to Southland; no later cases have eroded Southland's authority; and, no unforeseen practical problems have arisen. Moreover, in the interim, private parties have likely written contracts relying upon Southland as authority. Further, Congress, both before and after Southland, has enacted legislation extending, not retracting, the scope of arbitration. *See, e.g.*, 9 U.S.C. § 15 (eliminating the Act of State doctrine as a bar to arbitration); 9 U.S.C. §§ 201-208 (international arbitration). For these reasons, we find it inappropriate to reconsider what is by now well-established law. . . .

III

The Federal Arbitration Act, § 2, provides that a "written provision in any maritime transaction or a contract evidencing a transaction involving commerce to settle by arbitration a controversy thereafter arising out of such contract or transaction . . . shall be valid, irrevocable, and enforceable, save upon such grounds as exist at law or in equity for the revocation of any contract." The initial interpretive question focuses upon the words "involving commerce." These words are broader than the often-found words of art "in commerce." They therefore cover more than only persons or activities within the flow of interstate commerce. But, how far beyond the flow of commerce does the word "involving" reach? Is "involving" the functional equivalent of the word "affecting?" That phrase—"affecting commerce"—normally signals a congressional intent to exercise its Commerce Clause powers to the full. We cannot look to other statutes for guidance for the parties tell us that this is the only federal statute that uses the word "involving" to describe an interstate commerce relation.

After examining the statute's language, background, and structure, we conclude that the word "involving" is broad and is indeed the functional equivalent of "affecting." For one thing, such an interpretation, linguistically speaking, is permissible. The dictionary finds instances in which "involve" and "affect" sometimes can mean about the same thing. V Oxford English Dictionary 466 (1st ed. 1933) (providing examples dating back to the mid-nineteenth century, where "involve" means to "include or affect in . . . operation"). For another, the Act's legislative history, to the extent that it is informative, indicates an expansive congressional intent; *see also* 9 U.S.C. § 1 (defining the word "commerce" in the language of the Commerce Clause itself).

Further, this Court has previously described the Act's reach expansively as coinciding with that of the Commerce Clause. *See, e.g., Perry v. Thomas,* 482 U.S. 483, 490 (1987) (the Act "embodies Congress' intent to provide for the enforcement of arbitration agreements within the full reach of the Commerce Clause"). Finally, a broad interpretation of this language is consistent with the Act's basic purpose, to put arbitration provisions on "the same footing" as a contract's other terms. Conversely, a narrower interpretation is not consistent with the Act's purpose, for (unless unreasonably narrowed to the flow of commerce) such an interpretation would create a new, unfamiliar, test lying somewhere in a no-man's land between "in commerce" and "affecting commerce," thereby unnecessarily complicating the law and breeding litigation from a statute that seeks to avoid it. . . .

IV

Section 2 applies where there is "a contract evidencing a transaction involving commerce." The second interpretive question focuses on [this phrase]. Does "evidencing a transaction" mean only that the transaction (that the contract "evidences") must turn out, in fact, to have involved interstate commerce? Or, does it mean more?

Many years ago, Second Circuit Chief Judge Lumbard said that the phrase meant considerably more. He wrote: "The significant question . . . is not whether, in carrying out the terms of the contract, the parties did cross state lines, but whether, at the time they entered into it and accepted the arbitration clause, they contemplated substantial interstate activity. Cogent evidence regarding their state of mind at the time would be the terms of the contract, and if it, on its face, evidences interstate traffic . . ., the contract should come within § 2. In addition, evidence as to how the parties expected the contract to be performed and how it was performed is relevant to whether substantial interstate activity was contemplated." *Metro Industrial Painting Corp. v. Terminal Constr. Co.*, 287 F.2d 382, 387 (2d Cir. 1961) (Lumbard, C.J., concurring).

The Supreme Court of Alabama, and several other courts, have followed this view, known as the "contemplation of the parties" test. We find the interpretive choice difficult, but for several reasons we conclude that the first interpretation ("commerce in fact") is more faithful to the statute than the second ("contemplation of the parties"). First, the "contemplation of the parties" interpretation, when viewed in terms of the statute's basic purpose, seems anomalous. That interpretation invites litigation about what was, or was not, "contemplated." Why would Congress intend a test that risks the very kind of costs and delay through litigation (about the circumstances of contract formation) that Congress wrote the Act to help the parties avoid?

Second, the statute's language permits the "commerce in fact" interpretation. That interpretation, we concede, leaves little work for the word "evidencing" (in the phrase "a contract evidencing a transaction") to perform, for every contract evidences some transaction. But, perhaps Congress did not want that word to perform much work. The Act's history, to the extent informative, indicates that the Act's supporters saw the Act as part of an effort to make arbitration agreements universally enforceable. They wanted to "get a Federal law" that would "cover" areas where the Constitution authorized Congress to legislate, namely "interstate and foreign commerce and admiralty." They urged Congress to model the Act after a New York statute that made enforceable a written arbitration provision "in a written contract." Early drafts made enforceable a written arbitration provision "in any contract or maritime transaction or transaction involving commerce." Members of Congress, looking at that phrase, might have thought the words "any contract" standing alone went beyond Congress's constitutional authority. And, if so, they might have simply connected those words with the later words "transaction involving commerce," thereby creating the phrase that became law. Nothing in the Act's history suggests any other, more limiting, task for the language. . . .

Finally, we note that an amicus curiae argues for an "objective" ("reasonable person" oriented) version of the "contemplation of the parties" test on the ground that such an interpretation would better protect consumers asked to sign form contracts by businesses. We agree that Congress, when enacting this law, had the needs of consumers, as well as others, in mind. Indeed, arbitration's advantages often would seem helpful to individuals, say, complaining about a product, who need a less expensive alternative to litigation. *See, e.g.*, H.R.Rep. No. 97-542, p. 13 (1982) ("The advantages of arbitration are many: it is usually cheaper and faster than litigation; it can have simpler procedural and evidentiary rules; it normally minimizes hostility and is less disruptive of ongoing and future business dealings among the parties; it is often more flexible in regard to scheduling of times and places of hearings and discovery devices . . ."). And, according to the American Arbitration Association (also an amicus here), more than one-third of its claims involve amounts below $10,000, while another third involve claims of $10,000 to $50,000 (with an average processing time of less than six months).

We are uncertain, however, just how the "objective" version of the "contemplation" test would help consumers. Sometimes, of course, it would permit, say, a consumer with potentially large damage claims, to disavow a contract's arbitration provision and proceed in court. But, if so, it would equally permit, say, local business entities to disavow a contract's arbitration provisions, thereby leaving the typical consumer who has only a small damage claim (who seeks, say, the value of only a defective refrigerator or television set) without any remedy but a court remedy, the costs and delays of which could eat up the value of an eventual small recovery.

In any event, § 2 gives States a method for protecting consumers against unfair pressure to agree to a contract with an unwanted arbitration provision. States may regulate contracts, including arbitration clauses, under general contract law principles and they may invalidate an arbitration clause "upon such grounds as exist at law or in equity for the revocation of any contract." What States may not do is decide that a contract is fair enough to enforce all its basic terms (price, service, credit), but not fair enough to enforce its arbitration clause. The Act makes any such state policy unlawful, for that kind of policy would place arbitration clauses on an unequal "footing," directly contrary to the Act's language and Congress's intent.

For these reasons, we accept the "commerce in fact" interpretation, reading the Act's language as insisting that the "transaction" in fact "involve" interstate commerce, even if the parties did not contemplate an interstate commerce connection.

V

The parties do not contest that the transaction in this case, in fact, involved interstate commerce. In addition to the multistate nature of Terminix and Allied-Bruce, the termite-treating and house-repairing material used by Allied-Bruce in its (allegedly inadequate) efforts to carry out the terms of the Plan, came from outside Alabama.

Consequently, the judgment of the Supreme Court of Alabama is reversed and the case is remanded for further proceedings consistent with this opinion. It is so ordered.

Justice O'CONNOR, concurring.

The reading of § 2 adopted today will displace many state statutes carefully calibrated to protect consumers, *see, e.g.*, Mont. Code Ann. § 27-5-114(2)(b) (1993) (refusing to enforce arbitration clauses in consumer contracts where the consideration is $5,000 or less), and state procedural requirements aimed at ensuring knowing and voluntary consent, *see, e.g.*, S.C. Code Ann. § 15-48-10(a) (Supp.1993) (requiring that notice of arbitration provision be prominently placed on first page of contract). I have long adhered to the view, discussed below, that Congress designed the Federal Arbitration Act to apply only in federal courts. But if we are to apply the Act in state courts, it makes little sense to read § 2 differently in that context. In the end, my agreement with the Court's construction of § 2 rests largely on the wisdom of maintaining a uniform standard.

I continue to believe that Congress never intended the Federal Arbitration Act to apply in state courts, and that this Court has strayed far afield in giving the Act so broad a compass. . . . Yet, over the past decade, the Court has abandoned all pretense of ascertaining congressional intent with respect to the Federal Arbitration Act, building instead, case by case, an edifice of its own creation. I have no doubt that Congress could enact, in the first instance, a federal arbitration statute that displaces most state arbitration laws. But I also have no doubt that, in 1925, Congress enacted no such statute.

Were we writing on a clean slate, I would adhere to that view and affirm the Alabama court's decision. But, as the Court points out, more than 10 years have passed since *Southland*, several subsequent cases have built upon its reasoning, and parties have undoubtedly made contracts in reliance on the Court's interpretation of the Act in the interim. After reflection, I am persuaded by considerations of stare decisis, which we have said "have special force in the area of statutory interpretation," to acquiesce in today's judgment. Though wrong, *Southland* has not proved unworkable, and, Congress remains free to alter what we have done.

Today's decision caps this Court's effort to expand the Federal Arbitration Act. Although each decision has built logically upon the decisions preceding it, the initial building block in *Southland* laid a faulty foundation. I acquiesce in today's judgment because there is no "special justification" to overrule *Southland.* It remains now for Congress to correct this interpretation if it wishes to preserve state autonomy in state courts.

Justice SCALIA, dissenting.

[O]ne of respondents' central arguments is that *Southland* was wrongly decided, and their request for its overruling has been supported by an amicus brief signed by the attorneys general of 20 States. . . . I agree with the respondents (and belatedly with Justice O'Connor) that Southland clearly misconstrued the Federal Arbitration Act.

I do not believe that proper application of stare decisis prevents correction of the mistake. Adhering to *Southland* entails a permanent, unauthorized eviction of state-court power to adjudicate a potentially large class of disputes. Abandoning it does not impair reliance interests to a degree that justifies this evil. Primary behavior is not affected: no rule of conduct is retroactively changed, but only (perhaps) the forum in which violation is to be determined and remedied. I doubt that many contracts with arbitration clauses would have been forgone, or entered into only for significantly higher remuneration, absent the *Southland* guarantee. Where, moreover, reliance on *Southland* did make a significant difference, rescission of the contract for mistake of law would often be available. Restatement (Second) of Contracts § 152 (1979).

I shall not in the future dissent from judgments that rest on *Southland.* I will, however, stand ready to join four other Justices in overruling it, since *Southland* will not become more correct over time, the course of future lawmaking seems unlikely to be affected by its existence, and the accumulated private reliance will not likely increase beyond the level it has already achieved (few contracts not terminable at will have more than a 5-year term).

Justice THOMAS, with whom Justice SCALIA joins, dissenting.

I disagree with the majority at the threshold of this case, and so I do not reach the question that it decides. In my view, the Federal Arbitration Act (FAA) does not apply in state courts. I respectfully dissent. . . .

II

Rather than attempting to defend *Southland* on its merits, petitioners rely chiefly on the doctrine of stare decisis in urging us to adhere to our mistaken interpretation of the FAA. In my view, that doctrine is insufficient to save *Southland.*

The majority and Justice O'CONNOR properly focus on whether overruling *Southland* would frustrate the legitimate expectations of people who have drafted and executed contracts in the belief that even state courts will strictly enforce arbitration clauses. I do not doubt that innumerable contracts containing arbitration clauses have been written since 1984, or that arbitrable disputes might yet arise out of a large proportion of these contracts. Some of these contracts might well have been written differently in the absence of *Southland.* Still, I see no reason to think that the costs of overruling *Southland* are unacceptably high. Certainly no reliance interests are involved in cases like the present one, where the applicability of the FAA was not within the contemplation of the parties at the time of contracting. In many other cases, moreover, the parties will simply comply with their arbitration agreement, either on the theory that they should live up to their promises or on the theory that arbitration is the cheapest and best way of resolving their dispute. In a fair number of the remaining cases, the party seeking to enforce an arbitration agreement will be able to get into federal court, where the FAA will apply. And even if access to federal court is impossible (because § 2 creates no independent basis for federal-question jurisdiction), many cases will arise in States whose own law largely parallels the FAA. Only Alabama, Mississippi, and Nebraska still hold all executory arbitration agreements to be unenforceable, though some other States refuse to enforce particular classes of such agreements.

b. Comments and Questions

1. *Allied-Bruce* makes it clear that the reach of the FAA is very broad indeed. The Supreme Court decided three important arbitration cases in 1995 — *Allied Bruce, First Options,* and *Mastrobuono* — each of which is reproduced in this Chapter. While the substantive issues vary, the overall sense conveyed by the Court is one of generous receptiveness toward arbitration, and an expansive reading of the FAA.

2. One commentator concludes that the Allied-Bruce decision is "a death knell" for state consumer protection legislation that limits the use of arbitration, and that arbitration clauses in form contracts will be enforced against consumers. Janet M. Grossnickle, Allied-Bruce Terminex Cos. v. Dobson: *How the Federal Arbitration Act Will Keep Consumers and Corporations Out of the Courtroom,* 36 B.C. L. REV. 769, 789-790 (1995).

3. In the philosophical debate between advocates of national uniformity and supporters of decentralized government (notably Justice O'Connor, a former state legislator in Arizona), it appears that the national uniformity approach has the upper hand in the arbitration arena. Of course, this could change, either through new opinions by the Supreme Court or by amendments to the FAA.

4. Often state "consumer protection" laws turn out to be nothing more than historical anomalies. As Justice Thomas pointed out, the only states that do not enforce predispute agreements to arbitrate are Alabama, Mississippi, and Nebraska. Would the argument for state law be more persuasive if a state had recently enacted legislation limiting arbitration?

5. Giving greater deference to state law often does not lead to local control, but the export of the law of a distant state throughout the country. Many businesses attempt to use New York law, which is discussed later in this Chapter, notably because New York prohibits arbitrators from awarding punitive damages (even when expressly authorized by contract). This trend can be observed in the securities industry, where a customer of a brokerage firm living in Florida, and doing business only with a local office of a national firm, will find the entire agreement subject to New York law, and even be required to litigate in New York courts. Before concluding that this scenario is improbably, read the *Luckie* decision later in this Chapter (section

F) — and note that *Luckie* is not some relic of the bad old days or an aberrant decision of a lower court, but the considered judgment of the New York Court of Appeals (the highest state court) in 1995.

6. One has to admire the principled position taken by Justice O'Connor in sticking to *stare decisis* on the preemption issue even when she originally took the opposite position, and clearly has not changed her mind on the merits. Too often judges use the doctrine of precedent instrumentally to further their desired conclusion, rather than as a principle to be adhered to whatever the result. When "liberal" judges were in the ascendancy, "conservatives" criticized them for failing to adhere to precedent, but when the "conservatives" gained a majority on the Supreme Court they often have done the same thing. Or, as Gordon Crovitz, the legal editor of the Wall Street Journal crowed, it's "payback time." As for "liberal" concerns about *stare decisis,* Crovitz observed that "the hypocrisy is impressive."

7. The extent to which federal arbitration law preempts state law is considered at length later in this Chapter, in section F.

D. State Arbitration Legislation

1. Comments and Questions

a. The first modern arbitration was adopted in New York in 1920, and that statute served as a model for the FAA. The National Conference of the Commissioners on Uniform State Laws adopted a model arbitration statute in 1925, but it was withdrawn in 1943 after being adopted by only six states (Nevada, North Carolina, Pennsylvania, Utah, Wisconsin, and Wyoming).

b. The second attempt by the Commissioners was far more successful. The Commissioners promulgated the Uniform Arbitration Act (UAA) in 1955. 7 U.L.A. 1 (1955). The American Bar Association House of Delegates promptly approved the effort, an imprimatur that no doubt promoted the wide adoption of the UAA. The UAA has been adopted in thirty-five states and the District of Columbia, and there are provisions similar to parts of the UAA in the laws of additional states. Every state has adopted some form of arbitration legislation, with Vermont being the last to join the fold in 1987. Peter H. Berge, *The Uniform Arbitration Act: A Retrospective on Its Thirty-Fifth Anniversary,* 14 HAMLINE L. REV. (1991) discusses the background of the UAA, and also examines the history of arbitration in Minnesota. The predecessors of the UAA are discussed in Maynard Pirsig, *Some Comments on Arbitration Legislation and the Uniform Act,* 10 VAND. L. REV. 685 (1957).

In general, the provisions of the UAA are parallel to the FAA. Of course, "in general" will not do in the context of a particular issue or dispute. Nevertheless, the overall pattern of national similarity, if not uniformity, is worth noting. The extensive federal preemption of state arbitration law, a matter that is discussed in section F of this Chapter, adds to uniformity.

c. The full text of the UAA is followed by an article by John Van Winkle about arbitration in Indiana, which melds the UAA, prior arbitration legislation, local rules, and adaption to local conditions. The end result is a body of arbitration law that is less uniform than that in most UAA states.

2. The Uniform Arbitration Act [Unabridged]

§ 1. Validity of Arbitration Agreement.

A written agreement to submit any existing controversy to arbitration or a provision in a written contract to submit to arbitration any controversy thereafter arising between the parties is valid, enforceable and irrevocable, save upon such grounds as exist at law or in equity for the revocation of any contract. This act also applies to arbitration agreements between employers and employees or between their respective representatives [unless otherwise provided in the agreement].

§ 2. Proceedings to Compel or Stay Arbitration.

(a) On application of a party showing an agreement described in Section 1, and the opposing party's refusal to arbitrate, the Court shall order the parties to proceed with arbitration, but if the opposing party denies the existence of the agreement to arbitrate, the Court shall proceed summarily to the determination of the issue so raised and shall order arbitration if found for the moving party, otherwise, the application shall be denied.

(b) On application, the court may stay an arbitration proceeding commenced or threatened on a showing that there is no agreement to arbitrate. Such an issue, when in substantial and bona fide dispute, shall be forthwith and summarily tried and the stay ordered if found for the moving party. If found for the opposing party, the court shall order the parties to proceed to arbitration.

(c) If an issue referable to arbitration under the alleged agreement is involved in an action or proceeding pending in a court having jurisdiction to hear applications under subdivision (a) of this Section, the application shall be made therein. Otherwise and subject to Section 18, the application may be made in any court of competent jurisdiction.

(d) Any action or proceeding involving an issue subject to arbitration shall be stayed if an order for arbitration or an application therefor has been made under this section or, if the issue is severable, the stay may be with respect thereto only. When the application is made in such action or proceeding, the order for arbitration shall include such stay.

(e) An order for arbitration shall not be refused on the ground that the claim in issue lacks merit or bona fides or because any fault or grounds for the claim sought to be arbitrated have not been shown.

§ 3. Appointment of Arbitrators by Court.

If the arbitration agreement provides a method of appointment of arbitrators, this method shall be followed. In the absence thereof, or if the agreed method fails or for any reason cannot be followed, or when an arbitrator appointed fails or is unable to act and his successor has not been duly appointed, the court on application of a party shall appoint one or more arbitrators. An arbitrator so appointed has all the powers of one specifically named in the agreement.

§ 4. Majority Action by Arbitrators.

The powers of the arbitrators may be exercised by a majority unless otherwise provided by the agreement or by this act.

§ 5. Hearing.

Unless otherwise provided by the agreement:

(a) The arbitrators shall appoint a time and place for the hearing and cause notification to the parties to be served personally or by registered mail not less than five days before the hearing. Appearance at the hearing waives such notice. The arbitrators may adjourn the hearing from time to time as necessary and, on request of a party and for good cause, or upon their own motion may postpone the hearing to a time not later than the date fixed by the agreement for making the award unless the parties consent to a later date. The arbitrators may hear and determine the controversy upon the evidence produced notwithstanding the failure of a party duly notified to appear. The court on application may direct the arbitrators to proceed promptly with the hearing and determination of the controversy.

(b) The parties are entitled to be heard, to present evidence material to the controversy and to cross-examine witnesses appearing at the hearing.

(c) The hearing shall be conducted by all the arbitrators but a majority may determine any question and render a final award. If, during the course of the hearing, an arbitrator for any reason ceases to act, the remaining arbitrator or arbitrators appointed to act as neutrals may continue with the hearing and determination of the controversy.

§ 6. Representation by Attorney.

A party has the right to be represented by an attorney at any proceeding or hearing under this act. A waiver thereof prior to the proceeding or hearing is ineffective.

§ 7. Witnesses, Subpoenas, Depositions.

(a) The arbitrators may issue (cause to be issued) subpoenas for the attendance of witnesses and for the production of books, records, documents and other evidence, and shall have the power to administer oaths. Subpoenas so issued shall be served, and upon application to the Court by a party or the arbitrators, enforced, in the manner provided by law for the service and enforcement of subpoenas in a civil action.

(b) On application of a party and for use as evidence, the arbitrators may permit a deposition to be taken, in the manner and upon the terms designated by the arbitrators, of a witness who cannot be subpoenaed or is unable to attend the hearing.

(c) All provisions of law compelling a person under subpoena to testify are applicable.

(d) Fees for attendance as a witness shall be the same as for a witness in the .... Court.

§ 8. Award.

(a) The award shall be in writing and signed by the arbitrators joining in the award. The arbitrators shall deliver a copy to each party personally or by registered mail, or as provided in the agreement.

(b) An award shall be made within the time fixed therefor by the agreement or, if not so fixed, within such time as the court orders on application of a party. The parties may extend the time in writing either before or after the expiration thereof. A party waives the objection that an award was not made within the time required unless he notifies the arbitrators of his objection prior to the delivery of the award to him.

§ 9. Change of Award by Arbitrators.

On application of a party or, if an application to the court is pending under Sections 11, 12 or 13, on submission to the arbitrators by the court under such conditions as the court may order, the arbitrators may modify or correct the award upon the grounds stated in paragraphs (1) and (3) of subdivision (a) of Section 13, or for the purpose of clarifying the award. The application shall be made within twenty days after delivery of the award to the applicant. Written notice thereof shall be given forthwith to the opposing party, stating he must serve his objections thereto, if any, within ten days from the notice. The award so modified or corrected is subject to the provisions of Sections 11, 12 and 13.

§ 10. Fees and Expenses of Arbitration.

Unless otherwise provided in the agreement to arbitrate, the arbitrators' expenses and fees, together with other expenses, not including counsel fees, incurred in the conduct of the arbitration, shall be paid as provided in the award.

§ 11. Confirmation of an Award.

Upon application of a party, the Court shall confirm an award, unless within the time limits hereinafter imposed grounds are urged for vacating or modifying or correcting the award, in which case the court shall proceed as provided in Sections 12 and 13.

§ 12. Vacating an Award.

(a) Upon application of a party, the court shall vacate an award where:
  (1) The award was procured by corruption, fraud or other undue means;
  (2) There was evident partiality by an arbitrator appointed as a neutral or corruption in any of the arbitrators or misconduct prejudicing the rights of any party;
  (3) The arbitrators exceeded their powers;
  (4) The arbitrators refused to postpone the hearing upon sufficient cause being shown therefor or refused to hear evidence material to the controversy or otherwise so conducted the hearing, contrary to the provisions of Section 5, as to prejudice substantially the rights of a party; or
  (5) There was no arbitration agreement and the issue was not adversely determined in proceedings under Section 2 and the party did not participate in the arbitration hearing without raising the objection; but the fact that the relief was such that it could not or would not be granted by a court of law or equity is not ground for vacating or refusing to confirm the award.

(b) An application under this Section shall be made within ninety days after delivery of a copy of the award to the applicant, except that, if predicated upon corruption, fraud or other undue means, it shall be made within ninety days after such grounds are known or should have been known.

(c) In vacating the award on grounds other than stated in clause (5) of Subsection (a) the court may order a rehearing before new arbitrators chosen as provided in the agreement, or in the absence thereof, by the court in accordance with Section 3, or if the award is vacated on grounds set forth in clauses (3) and (4) of Subsection (a) the court may order a rehearing before the arbitrators who made the award or their successors appointed in accordance with Section 3. The time within which the agreement requires the award to be made is applicable to the rehearing and commences from the date of the order.

(d) If the application to vacate is denied and no motion to modify or correct the award is pending, the court shall confirm the award.

§ 13. Modification or Correction of Award.

(a) Upon application made within ninety days after delivery of a copy of the award to the applicant, the court shall modify or correct the award where:
   (1) There was an evident miscalculation of figures or an evident mistake in the description of any person, thing or property referred to in the award;
   (2) The arbitrators have awarded upon a matter not submitted to them and the award may be corrected without affecting the merits of the decision upon the issues submitted; or
   (3) The award is imperfect in a matter of form, not affecting the merits of the controversy.

(b) If the application is granted, the court shall modify and correct the award so as to effect its intent and shall confirm the award as so modified and corrected. Otherwise, the court shall confirm the award as made.

(c) An application to modify or correct an award may be joined in the alternative with an application to vacate the award.

§ 14. Judgment or Decree on Award.

Upon the granting of an order confirming, modifying or correcting an award, judgment or decree shall be entered in conformity therewith and be enforced as any other judgment or decree. Costs of the application and of the proceedings subsequent thereto, and disbursements may be awarded by the court.

§ 15. Judgment Roll, Docketing.

(a) On entry of judgment or decree, the clerk shall prepare the judgment roll consisting, to the extent filed, of the following:
   (1) The agreement and each written extension of the time within which to make the award;
   (2) The award;
   (3) A copy of the order confirming, modifying or correcting the award; and
   (4) A copy of the judgment or decree.

(b) The judgment or decree may be docketed as if rendered in an action.

§ 16. Applications to Court.

Except as otherwise provided, an application to the court under this act shall be by motion and shall be heard in the manner and upon the notice provided by law or rule of court for the making and hearing of motions. Unless the parties have agreed otherwise, notice of an initial application for an order shall be served in the manner provided by law for the service of a summons in an action.

§ 17. Court, Jurisdiction.

The term "court" means any court of competent jurisdiction of this State. The making of an agreement described in Section 1 providing for arbitration in this State confers jurisdiction on the court to enforce the agreement under this Act and to enter judgment on an award thereunder.

§ 18. Venue.

An initial application shall be made to the court of the [county] in which the agreement provides the arbitration hearing shall be held or, if the hearing has been held, in the county in which it was held. Otherwise the application shall be made in the [county] where the adverse party resides or has a place of business or, if he has no residence or place of business in this State, to the court of any [county]. All subsequent applications shall be made to the court hearing the initial application unless the court otherwise directs.

§ 19. Appeals.

(a) An appeal may be taken from:

(1) An order denying an application to compel arbitration made under Section 2;

(2) An order granting an application to stay arbitration made under Section 2(b);

(3) An order confirming or denying confirmation of an award;

(4) An order modifying or correcting an award;

(5) An order vacating an award without directing a rehearing; or

(6) A judgment or decree entered pursuant to the provisions of this act.

(b) The appeal shall be taken in the manner and to the same extent as from orders or judgments in a civil action.

§ 20. Act Not Retroactive.

This act applies only to agreements made subsequent to the taking effect of this act.

§ 21. Uniformity of Interpretation.

This act shall be so construed as to effectuate its general purpose to make uniform the law of those states which enact it.

§ 22. Constitutionality.

If any provision of this act or the application thereof to any person or circumstance is held invalid, the invalidity shall not affect other provisions or applications of the act which can be given effect without the invalid provision or application, and to this end the provisions of this act are severable.

§ 23. Short Title.

This act may be cited as the Uniform Arbitration Act.

§ 24. Repeal.

All acts or parts of acts which are inconsistent with the provisions of this act are hereby repealed.

§ 25. Time of Taking Effect.

This act shall take effect ....

3. John R. Van Winkle, *An Analysis of the Arbitration Rule of the Indiana Rules of Alternative Dispute Resolution*, 27 IND. L. REV. 735 (1994)*

Rule 1.3(B) of the Rules for Alternative Dispute Resolution [adopted in November, 1991] defines arbitration as a "process in which a neutral third person or a panel, called an arbitrator or an arbitration panel, considers the facts and arguments which are presented by the parties and renders a decision." Arbitration cannot be ordered by a court and will only occur under the rules as a result of an agreement between the parties. That agreement by the parties may also provide that the arbitration decision be binding or non-binding.

Once an agreement to arbitrate is reached, the court enters an order and names a panel of three arbitrators from which the parties can, absent an agreement, strike. A hearing is scheduled by the arbitrator or the chair of the arbitration panel. Although traditional rules of evidence need not apply to the presentation of testimony, the rules of discovery are applicable to the arbitration process and the regular judge of the court retains jurisdiction to rule on discovery matters and other disputes. If the parties agreed that the arbitration was to be binding, the decision of the arbitrator or the arbitrators is entered as a judgment. If the arbitration is not binding, and one of the parties disagree with the arbitrator's decision, the parties may proceed to trial.

I. HISTORICAL BACKGROUND OF THE ADR ARBITRATION RULE

Rule 3 must be read in conjunction with the common law and statutory provisions relating to arbitration which existed prior to the enactment of the ADR Rules. The ADR Arbitration Rules do not repeal or replace either the common law applicable to arbitration, [or] . . . previously enacted arbitration statutes. . . .

II. UNIFORM ARBITRATION ACT

[T]he "Uniform Arbitration Act," was approved by the American Bar Association in 1955. Fifteen years elapsed before Indiana adopted the Act. Prior to that time, Indiana's businessmen and women were without a significant commercial weapon. Although both at common law and under the Indiana Arbitration Act, parties could agree to submit existing disputes to arbitration, commercial contract provisions requiring future disputes between the parties to a transaction or a contract to be submitted to arbitration were not enforceable.

For reasons that are not clear, when the Indiana General Assembly adopted the Indiana Uniform Arbitration Act, the first section of the Uniform Act was changed significantly. The Uniform Act, as approved by the National Conference of Commissioners on Uniform State Laws, provided as follows:

> A written agreement to submit any existing controversy to arbitration or a provision in a written contract to submit to arbitration any controversy thereafter arising between the parties is valid, enforceable and irrevocable, save upon such grounds as exists at law or in equity for the revocation of any contract. This Act also applies to arbitration agreements between employers and employees or between their respective representatives [unless otherwise provided in the agreement].

Indiana changed that section however, as follows:

> A written agreement to submit to arbitration is valid, and enforceable, an existing controversy or a controversy thereafter arising is valid and enforceable, save upon such grounds as exist at law or in equity for the revocation of any contract. If the parties to such an agreement so stipulate in writing, the agreement may be enforced by designated third persons, who shall in such instances have the same rights as a party under this chapter. This chapter also applies to arbitration agreement between employers and employees or between their respective representatives [unless otherwise provided in the agreement].

No explanation is found for the changing of this language, which, it is submitted, renders nonsensical the first section of the Indiana Uniform Arbitration Act. It must be assumed that the meaning and intent is the same as that of the general Uniform Arbitration Act.

Under the Indiana Uniform Arbitration Act, arbitration is "initiated by a written notice by either party, mailed by registered or certified mail, or delivered to the other party, briefly stating a claim, the grounds for the claim, and the amount or amounts. Issues are joined by a written notice of admissions or denials and counterclaims or set-offs shall also be mailed and delivered." Upon the application of a party demonstrating an opposing party's refusal to arbitrate, the court has the authority under the Indiana Uniform Arbitration Act to order the parties to proceed with arbitration. If the opposing party denies the existing agreement to arbitrate, a summary determination of this issue is made by the court without further pleading. Parties may apply to the court for a stay of arbitration, demonstrating that no agreement to arbitrate exists. This issue is also to be summarily determined without further pleadings.

As is true with many aspects of the Indiana Uniform Arbitration Act, the parties are given the opportunity to determine in the arbitration agreement many of the terms and conditions which will guide and bind the parties in the arbitration. Parties have, for example, the right to determine the manner in which the arbitrators are appointed. One important provision of the Indiana Uniform Arbitration Act, however, provides that the court has the authority to stay an arbitration proceeding upon a showing that the method of appointment of arbitrators is likely to, or has, resulted in the appointment of arbitrators who are partial or biased. If the arbitration agreement does not provide a method of appointment of arbitrators, and if the parties cannot agree on any method, the court is given the authority to appoint one or more arbitrators.

The parties can also provide in the arbitration agreement for the details of the arbitration hearing. If the agreement does not so provide, the arbitrators are required under the Act to appoint a time and place for the hearing. The Indiana Uniform Arbitration Act makes clear that the arbitrators have the authority to issue subpoenas for the attendance of witnesses and for the production of books, records, documents and other evidence. The arbitrators may also "order depositions to be taken for use as evidence, and not for discovery, if the witness cannot be subpoenaed or is unable to attend the hearing."

Upon an award in arbitration, the parties have ninety days after the mailing of the award to apply to the court to vacate the arbitrator's award. The court has the authority to vacate an award when (1) the award was procured by corruption or fraud; (2) the award demonstrates evident partiality; (3) the arbitrators exceeded their powers; (4) the arbitrators refused to postpone the hearing upon sufficient cause shown or refused to hear material evidence; or (5) no arbitration agreement existed. If the award is not vacated and, after the expiration of ninety days from the date of the mailing of the copy of the award, either party may apply to the court to confirm the arbitrator's award. Upon such confirmation, the court shall enter a judgment consistent with the arbitration award and cause the judgment to be docketed as if rendered in an action decided by the court.

In addition to the procedures for vacation of an award, parties may also apply within ninety days after the mailing of a copy of the award for "modifications or corrections" of the award. The court has the authority to modify or correct the award where (1) there was an evident miscalculation of figures; (2) the arbitrators made an award upon a matter not submitted; or (3) the award was imperfect in a matter of form which did not affect the merits of the controversy. . . .

The Indiana Uniform Arbitration Act provides for limited appeals. Appeals may be taken from (1) an order denying an application to compel arbitration; (2) an order granting application to stay arbitration; (3) an order confirming or denying confirmation of an award; (4) an order modifying or correcting an award; (5) an order vacating an award without directing a rehearing; or (6) a judgment or decree entered pursuant to the Act. All appeals shall be taken in the same manner and to the same extent as orders or judgments in any civil action. It is against this statutory and common law arbitration background that the ADR Arbitration Rule must be examined.

III. ADR ARBITRATION RULE

A. Relationship of Arbitration Under the Common Law, the Indiana Arbitration Act, the Indiana Uniform Arbitration Act and the ADR Arbitration Rules

Arbitration under the ADR Arbitration Rules may occur if a lawsuit has already been instituted and if all parties to the lawsuit agree to arbitration. In contrast, under the Indiana UAA if the parties to the dispute had entered into a contract or agreement to submit all future disputes to arbitration before the dispute actually arose then arbitration of the subsequent dispute would occur under the Indiana UAA and a general civil suit would not have been filed (unless the parties waived arbitration).

[T]he primary purpose of the 1852 Indiana Arbitration Act was to provide enforcement by judgment for arbitration awards entered in arbitration conducted where no lawsuit was pending. At common law, if a lawsuit was pending, the parties could agree to submit the dispute to arbitration and the result would be enforceable as a judgment.

Section 22 of the 1852 statute provided (and provides today) as follows:

If the subject-matter of any suit pending in any court might originally have been submitted to arbitration, the parties to such suit, their agent or attorney-at-law, may consent, by rule of court, to refer the matters in controversy to certain persons mutually chosen by them in open court.

While it appears that this section would allow parties to agree after a law suit is filed to submit the matter to arbitration, it is probably limited to submission of the case to referees and not to arbitration. The 1852 Act has "referees" as a headnote for section 22 . . . Rather, an agreement attempted under the 1852 code will be treated as and controlled by common law arbitration principles. Such an agreement under this statute could not be revoked by the parties without the approval of the trial judge.

Even though the right to submit issues in pending litigation existed at common law, the ADR Arbitration Rules do provide one significant difference. If the parties in litigation, at common law, agreed to subject issues to arbitration, either party could revoke the agreement to arbitrate at any time before the arbitration award is actually rendered. Clearly, under Rule 3.1 of the ADR Arbitration Rules, the agreement to arbitrate could only be revoked by consent of both parties and, probably, only with the approval of the court. . . . The ADR Arbitration Rules have no application (as of this date) to disputes where no litigation is pending. . . .

B. Initiation of Arbitration Under the ADR Arbitration Rules

Under Rule 3.1 of the ADR Arbitration Rules, arbitration is initiated by the filing of an agreement to arbitrate ("Arbitration Agreement"). Clearly, the agreement requires the consent of all parties but it is not as clear whether the trial court can refuse to accept an Arbitration Agreement. Rule 3.1 provides that upon approval, the Arbitration Agreement "shall be noted on the Chronological Case Summary of the Case and placed in the Records of Judgments and Orders for the court." . . . Another uncertainty inherent in ADR Arbitration Rule 3.1 is whether two or more parties, in multi-party lawsuits, can agree to arbitrate issues unique to them, without the agreement of the remaining parties. It is submitted that because arbitration can be limited to certain issues, parties to a cross-claim should be free to submit that cross-claim to arbitration even over the objection of other parties.

C. Arbitration Agreement

The ADR Arbitration Rules are extraordinary in that they allow the parties to make the most fundamental decisions concerning the arbitration process. The parties can decide:

1. whether the arbitration process is binding or non binding;
2. whether all or part of the issues in the case will be arbitrated;
3. whether one or more arbitrators shall decide the case;
4. what procedural rules are to be followed during the mediation process. . . .

Although Rule 3.1 provides that the parties may include in the Arbitration Agreement the procedural rules to be followed, the scope and extent of that right is limited by the specific procedural requirements of the remaining sections of Rule 3. Rule 3.4, for example, provides that upon accepting the appointment to serve, the arbitrator or chair of the panel "shall meet with all attorneys of record to set a time and place for any arbitration hearing." Other provisions of the rule are subject to an "unless otherwise agreed by the parties" condition; one relating to the amount of the fee and the other relating to whether papers must be filed and exchanged.

D. Case Status During Arbitration

Rule 3.2 provides that cases submitted to arbitration "shall remain on the regular docket and trial calendar of the court." . . . Rule 1.7 provides that "during the course of any alternative dispute resolution proceeding, the case remains within the jurisdiction of the court" and that, "[f]or good cause shown and upon hearing," the court can terminate any ADR process. . . .

E. Assignment of Arbitrators

The court's order approving the arbitrator and decreeing that the selection and arbitration is pursuant to Rule 3 is important to ensure that the immunity, confidentiality and other rule provisions will be applicable. If the parties have agreed that the arbitration is to be conducted by a panel, they can agree on the panel members, not to exceed three. If the parties have agreed to a panel but cannot agree on its members, Rule 3.3 provides that each party shall select one arbitrator and the court shall select the third. . . .

One question raised . . . by the ADR court rules, is whether the decision of a panel of arbitrators must be unanimous or majority. At common law, if the agreement of the parties was silent, the award of the arbitrators had to be unanimous. The Indiana Arbitration Act provides that the award of a majority of the arbitrators is valid, unless otherwise provided in the submission or agreement. Similarly, the Indiana UAA provides that unless otherwise provided by the agreement, the powers of the arbitrators may be exercised by a majority.

There is no specific provision indicating that those parts of the Indiana Arbitration Act and the Indiana Uniform Arbitration Act not in conflict with the ADR Rules apply to arbitrations under the ADR Arbitration Rules. The ADR Court Rules do, however, encourage the parties to use the provisions of those rules to the extent possible and appropriate. . . .

F. Arbitration Procedures

Rule 3.4(C) . . . specifically provides that the discovery rules of the Rules of Civil Procedure apply to arbitration proceedings. Rule 3.2 provides that the trial court retains jurisdiction to rule on discovery matters. By providing that discovery rules are applicable to arbitration, the Indiana Supreme Court has significantly changed the manner in which arbitration will proceed, as well as how it will be perceived. The right to take depositions and to require the production of documents will provide many Indiana trial lawyers with the "security" or the comfort level necessary for an agreement to arbitrate. At the same time, discovery in the arbitration process will move arbitration closer to a more "formal" process. . . .

Rule 3.4(D) provides that traditional rules of evidence need not apply with regard to the presentation of testimony. . . .

Rule 3.4(b) provides that in the case of binding arbitration, parties can object to the admissibility of documents under traditional rules of evidence. This would seem to indicate that in non-binding arbitration proceedings, the parties have no such right of objection. . . .

Upon accepting the appointment to serve, the arbitrator or the chair of the arbitration panel is required to meet with all attorneys of record to set a time and place for an arbitration hearing. . . . In the absence of an agreement, the place of the hearing is in the discretion of the arbitrator or chair of the arbitration panel. The Rules provide that courts are encouraged to allow access to regular courtroom facilities when use is not anticipated. Clearly, arbitrations can be held anywhere that the parties and the arbitrators find reasonable, including law office conference rooms, public meeting rooms and other such facilities.

The Rule specifically provides that arbitration proceedings shall not be open to the public. Presumably, part of the reason for a closed hearing is the fact that arbitration proceedings are considered to be settlement negotiations and subject to the same confidential restrictions as mediation proceedings. Any evidence tending to indicate the willingness to accept or offer any valuable consideration to settle a claim is not admissible to prove liability for or in validity of the claim or its amount. Further, evidence of conduct or statements made during the arbitration process is not admissible in any subsequent proceeding. Clearly, the confidentiality provisions and the provision requiring arbitration proceedings to be closed to the public are in part necessitated by the fact that the arbitration process may not dispose of all the issues. . . .

Although Rule 3.4 provides that arbitration proceedings are to be considered settlement negotiations, there are important restrictions on the confidentiality provisions. Using Federal Rule of Evidence 408 as a reference, it should be noted that that rule only protects offers of compromise regarding the "validity or amount" of a "disputed" claim. . . .

G. Pre-Arbitration Brief

Five days prior to the arbitration hearing, each party may file with the arbitrator or chair a pre-arbitration brief. The brief should set forth the factual and legal positions concerning the issues being arbitrated. If filed, Rule 3.4(D) provides that the arbitration briefs are to be served upon the opposing party or parties. Further, the parties in the arbitration agreement can alter the filing deadlines for the briefs.

H. Arbitration Determination

The ADR Arbitration Rules provide that the arbitrator or chair shall file a written determination or award within twenty days after the hearing. The filing shall be made in the pending litigation and a copy of the determination or award is to be served on all parties participating in the arbitration.

Clearly, significant differences occur depending upon whether the arbitration is binding or non-binding. If the parties had agreed that the arbitration was binding as to all issues, the determination or award is to be entered by the court as a judgment.

If the arbitration was binding on part of the issues, but not all, the court shall file and accept the arbitrator's award or determination as a "joint stipulation by the parties" and proceed with the litigation on the remaining issues.

If the arbitration was non-binding on any or all issues, each party is required to affirmatively reject (in writing) the arbitration determination or award within twenty days from the filing of the written determination. If the arbitration award or determination is not rejected within that twenty day period, the award or determination becomes binding and shall be entered as a judgment, if it is on all of the issues or accepted as a joint stipulation if on part of the issues.

In the event that a non-binding arbitration determination is rejected, all documentary evidence introduced at the arbitration is to be returned to the parties and the determination and acceptances and rejections sealed and filed in the case file.

I. Arbitrability of Punitive Damages

The Indiana UAA provides that the fact that the relief granted was such that it could not or would not be granted by a court of law or equity is not a ground for vacating or refusing to confirm an arbitration award. Indiana courts have nevertheless held that arbitrators may not award punitive damages.

J. Scope of Arbitrator's Authority

Prior to the ADR Arbitration Rules, Indiana courts joined courts of other jurisdictions in granting to arbitrators wide discretion in the remedies and results that arbitrators could reach. The arbitrators were not restricted by provisions of substantive law but rather could exercise a general sense of equity or fairness.

The scope of authority of arbitrators under the ADR Arbitration Rules is delineated both by the issues framed in the lawsuit and by the Arbitration Agreement. Parties to litigation can agree to submit to arbitration not only all the issues in the lawsuit but also issues between them which might not have been included within the scope of the litigation. The arbitrator has the discretion under the ADR Arbitration Rules (as existed at common law and under prior statutory arbitration) to resolve the issues in a manner that the arbitrator decides is "equitable," even if that manner is not necessarily within the confines or restrictions of substantive law provisions. . . .

K. Subpoenas

ADR Arbitration Rule 3 does not make any provision for the issuance of subpoenas. Presumably, the provisions of the Indiana Arbitration statute and the Indiana UAA will be applicable. . . .

The Indiana Arbitration Act provides that parties may be required to attend hearings before arbitrators upon the issuance of subpoenas issued by any justice of the peace on behalf of either party. The Indiana UAA also provides that arbitrators may issue subpoenas for the attendance of witnesses and for the production of books, records, documents and other evidence. Because the right to present testamentary evidence in arbitration could be illusory without subpoena power, it is presumed that the Indiana Supreme Court will provide access to pre-existing statutes providing the power to issue subpoenas in arbitrations.

L. Post Determination Proceedings: Appeals from ADR Arbitration

The ADR Arbitration Rules do not make any provision for appeals or post-determination proceedings. Clearly, if the parties have elected non- binding arbitration, the parties will either accept the arbitration determination or proceed with the litigation.

Rule 3.4(E) provides that the arbitration award or determination shall be made within 20 days after the hearing and, that after the rendering of the award, "the court shall enter judgment on the determination." In contrast, the Indiana UAA specifically provides that judgment should not be entered by the court until at least ninety days after the rendering of the arbitration award. During this ninety day waiting period, parties have the right to file either an application to vacate the award or an application to modify or correct an award. Under the Indiana UAA, after the expiration of the 90 days and after the entry of judgment, parties then have limited rights of appeals.

M. Scope of Appellate Review of Arbitration Awards

Indiana courts have followed the majority of jurisdictions in holding that the purpose of arbitration generally (and the specific purpose of the UAA) is to allow parties to reach resolution of their disputes by earlier and quicker methods. Strict and limited judicial review is necessary to avoid frustration of these goals.

Several general principles should be found applicable to issues of review of arbitration awards under the ADR Arbitration Rule:

1. The award will be presumed to be based on proper grounds.
2. The fact that arbitrator did not "follow the law" will not be a ground for review, unless the Arbitration Agreement specifically so limited the arbitrator's authority.

3. Courts can review arbitration award on the basis of fraud and corruption, or if the arbitrators have ordered that an illegal act be done.
4. Courts can refuse to enforce arbitration awards when enforcement of the award would violate public policy.
5. Awards can be voided if the arbitrator or arbitrators were clearly not impartial.
6. Courts can review arbitration awards on the grounds that the Arbitration Agreement was not followed. . . .

4. Comments and Questions

This article illustrates several matters of interest, quite apart from the law of Indiana.

a. The limitations on arbitration, and the enforcement of arbitration awards, is a common tale among the states, with the Uniform Arbitration Act being a national response that has been adopted in most states.

b. New laws (such as the UAA) and court rules do not exist in a vacuum. Other legislation, regulations, and case law may have a major impact on how the new legal standards are applied in practice.

c. In adopting uniform laws, such as the UAA, states often make some additions, deletions, and changes. Since uniform laws do not take account of existing local law, the old and the new may not mesh well. Efforts to address such problems have the effect of reducing uniformity. Life is full of trade-offs.

d. As a recent and carefully considered approach to the use of arbitration, the Indiana ADR rules are entitled to serious consideration by other jurisdictions that address similar issues.

e. The move to engraft legal standards onto arbitration is interesting. Do you agree with this approach? Is it a harbinger of the future for the rest of the country?

E. Who Determines Arbitrability, And by What Standard?

1. *AT&T Technologies, Inc. v. Communications Workers of America*, 475 U.S. 643 (1986)

White, J., delivered the opinion for a unanimous Court.

The issue presented in this case is whether a court asked to order arbitration of a grievance filed under a collective bargaining agreement must first determine that the parties intended to arbitrate the dispute, or whether that determination is properly left to the arbitrator.

I

AT&T Technologies, Inc. (AT&T or the Company), and the Communications Workers of America (the Union) are parties to a collective-bargaining agreement which covers telephone equipment installation workers. Article 8 of this agreement establishes that "differences arising with respect to the interpretation of this contract or the performance of any obligation hereunder" must be referred to a mutually agreeable arbitrator upon the written demand of either party. This Article expressly does not cover disputes "excluded from arbitration by other provisions of this contract." Article 9 provides that, "subject to the limitations contained in the provisions of this contract, but otherwise not subject to the provisions of the arbitration clause," AT&T is free to exercise certain management functions, including the hiring and placement of employees and the termination of employment "When lack of work necessitates Layoff." Article 20 prescribes the order in which employees are to be laid off.

[T]he Union filed a grievance challenging AT&T's decision to lay off 79 installers from its Chicago base location. The Union claimed that, because there was no lack of work at the Chicago location, the planned layoffs would violate Article 20 of the agreement. Eight days later, however, AT&T laid off all 79 workers, and soon thereafter, the Company transferred approximately the same number of installers from base locations in Indiana and Wisconsin to the Chicago base. AT&T refused to submit the grievance to arbitration on the ground that under Article 9 the Company's decision to lay off workers when it determines that a lack of work exists in a facility is not arbitrable. The Union then sought to compel arbitration by filing suit in federal court pursuant to § 301(a) of the Labor Management Relations Act, 29 U.S.C. § 185(a). . . .

Plaintiffs interpret Article 20 to require that there be an actual lack of work prior to employee layoffs and argue that there was no such lack of work in this case. Under plaintiffs' interpretation, Article 20 would allow the union to take to arbitration the threshold issue of whether the layoffs were justified by a lack of work. Defendant interprets Article 20 as merely providing a sequence for any layoffs which management, in its exclusive judgment, determines are necessary. Under defendant's interpretation, Article 20 would not allow for an arbitrator to decide whether the layoffs were warranted by a lack of work but only whether the company followed the proper order in laying off the employees." Finding that the union's interpretation of Article 20 was at least arguable, the court held that it was "for the arbitrator, not the court to decide whether the union's interpretation has merit," and accordingly, ordered the Company to arbitrate.

The Court of Appeals for the Seventh Circuit affirmed. . . .
The court acknowledged the "general rule" that the issue of arbitrability is for the courts to decide unless the parties stipulate otherwise, but noted that this Court's decisions . . . caution courts to avoid becoming entangled in the merits of a labor dispute under the guise of deciding arbitrability. From this observation, the court announced an "exception" to the general rule, under which "a court should compel arbitration of the arbitrability issue where the collective bargaining agreement contains a standard arbitration clause, the parties have not clearly excluded the arbitrability issue from arbitration, and deciding the issue would entangle the court in interpretation of substantive provisions of the collective bargaining agreement and thereby involve consideration of the merits of the dispute." All of these factors were present in this case. . . .

We now vacate the Seventh Circuit's decision and remand for a determination of whether the Company is required to arbitrate the Union's grievance. The principles necessary to decide this case are not new. They were set out by this Court [in 1960] in a series of cases known as the Steelworkers Trilogy. These precepts have served the industrial relations community well, and have led to continued reliance on arbitration, rather than strikes or lockouts, as the preferred method of resolving disputes arising during the term of a collective-bargaining agreement. We see no reason either to question their continuing validity, or to eviscerate their meaning by creating an exception to their general applicability.

The first principle gleaned from the Trilogy is that "arbitration is a matter of contract and a party cannot be required to submit to arbitration any dispute which he has not agreed so to submit." This axiom recognizes the fact that arbitrators derive their authority to resolve disputes only because the parties have agreed in advance to submit such grievances to arbitration.

The second rule, which follows inexorably from the first, is that the question of arbitrability—whether a collective bargaining agreement creates a duty for the parties to arbitrate the particular grievance—is undeniably an issue for judicial determination. Unless the parties clearly and unmistakably provide otherwise, the question of whether the parties agreed to arbitrate is to be decided by the court, not the arbitrator. . . .

The third principle derived from our prior cases is that, in deciding whether the parties have agreed to submit a particular grievance to arbitration, a court is not to rule on the potential merits of the underlying claims. Whether "arguable" or not, indeed even if it appears to the court to be frivolous, the union's claim that the employer has violated the collective bargaining agreement is to be decided, not by the court asked to order arbitration, but as the parties have agreed, by the arbitrator. "The courts, therefore, have no business weighing the merits of the grievance, considering whether there is equity in a particular claim, or determining whether there is particular language in the written instrument which will support the claim. The agreement is to submit all grievances to arbitration, not merely those which the court will deem meritorious."

Finally, it has been established that where the contract contains an arbitration clause, there is a presumption of arbitrability in the sense that "[a]n order to arbitrate the particular grievance should not be denied unless it may be said with positive assurance that the arbitration clause is not susceptible of an interpretation that covers the asserted dispute. Doubts should be resolved in favor of coverage." Such a presumption is particularly applicable where the clause is as broad as the one employed in this case, which provides for arbitration of "any differences arising with respect to the interpretation of this contract or the performance of any obligation hereunder. . . ." In such cases, "[i]n the absence of any express provision excluding a particular grievance from arbitration, we think only the most forceful evidence of a purpose to exclude the claim from arbitration can prevail."

This presumption of arbitrability for labor disputes recognizes the greater institutional competence of arbitrators in interpreting collective-bargaining agreements, "furthers the national labor policy of peaceful resolution of labor disputes and thus best accords with the parties' presumed objectives in pursuing collective bargaining." The willingness of parties to enter into agreements that provide for arbitration of specified disputes would be "drastically reduced," however, if a labor arbitrator had the "power to determine his own jurisdiction. . . ." Cox, *Reflections Upon Labor Arbitration,* 72 HARV. L. REV. 1482, 1509 (1959). Were this the applicable rule, an arbitrator would . . . be empowered "to impose obligations outside the contract limited only by his understanding and conscience." . . .

With these principles in mind, it is evident that the Seventh Circuit erred in ordering the parties to arbitrate the arbitrability question. It is the court's duty to interpret the agreement and to determine whether the parties intended to arbitrate grievances concerning layoffs predicated on a "lack of work" determination by the Company. If the court determines that the agreement so provides, then it is for the arbitrator to determine the relative merits of the parties' substantive interpretations of the agreement. It was for the court, not the arbitrator, to decide in the first instance whether the dispute was to be resolved through arbitration.

The Union does not contest the application of these principles to the present case. Instead, it urges the Court to examine the specific provisions of the agreement for itself and to affirm the Court of Appeals on the ground that the parties had agreed to arbitrate the dispute over the layoffs at issue here. But it is usually not our function in the first instance to construe collective bargaining contracts and arbitration clauses, or to consider any other evidence that might unmistakably demonstrate [whether] a particular grievance was . . . subject to arbitration. . . .

Justice BRENNAN, with whom THE CHIEF JUSTICE and Justice MARSHALL join, concurring.

I join the Court's opinion and write separately only to supplement what has been said in order to avoid any misunderstanding on remand and in future cases. The Seventh Circuit's erroneous conclusion that the arbitrator should decide whether this dispute is arbitrable resulted from that court's confusion respecting the "arbitrability" determination that we have held must be judicially made. . . .

The Court of Appeals was mistaken insofar as it thought that determining arbitrability required resolution of the parties' dispute with respect to the meaning of Articles 9 and 20 of the collective bargaining agreement. In *Warrior & Gulf,* the Union challenged management's contracting out of labor that had previously been performed by Company employees. The parties failed to resolve the dispute through grievance procedures, and the Union requested arbitration; the Company refused, and the Union sued to compel arbitration. The collective bargaining agreement contained a standard arbitration clause similar to Article 8 of the AT&T/CWA contract, i.e., providing for arbitration of all differences with respect to the meaning or application of the contract. We held that, in light of the congressional policy making arbitration the favored method of dispute resolution, such a provision requires arbitration "unless it may be said with positive assurance that the arbitration clause is not susceptible of an interpretation that covers the asserted dispute. Doubts should be resolved in favor of coverage."

The Company in *Warrior & Gulf* relied for its argument that the dispute was not arbitrable on a "Management Functions" clause which, like Article 9 of the AT&T/CWA agreement, excluded "matters which are strictly a function of management" from the arbitration provision. We recognized that such a clause "might be thought to refer to any practice of management in which, under particular circumstances prescribed by the agreement, it is permitted to indulge." However, we also recognized that to read the clause this way would make arbitrability in every case depend upon whether management could take the action challenged by the Union; the arbitrability of every dispute would turn upon a resolution of the merits, and "the arbitration clause would be swallowed up by the exception." Therefore, we held that, where a collective bargaining agreement contains a standard arbitration clause and the "exception" found in the Management Functions clause is general, "judicial inquiry . . . should be limited to the search for an explicit provision which brings the grievance under the cover of the [Management Functions] clause. . . ." "In the absence of any express provision excluding a particular grievance from arbitration, . . . only the most forceful evidence of a purpose to exclude the claim from arbitration can prevail. . . ."

The Seventh Circuit misunderstood these rules of contract construction and did precisely what we disapproved of in *Warrior & Gulf*—it read Article 9, a general Management Functions clause, to make arbitrability depend upon the merits of the parties' dispute. As *Warrior & Gulf* makes clear, the judicial inquiry required to determine arbitrability is much simpler. The parties' dispute concerns whether Article 20 of the collective bargaining agreement limits management's authority to order layoffs for reasons other than lack of work. The question for the court is "strictly confined" to whether the parties agreed to submit disputes over the meaning of Article 20 to arbitration. Because the collective-bargaining agreement contains a standard arbitration clause, the answer must be affirmative unless the contract contains explicit language stating that disputes respecting Article 20 are not subject to arbitration, or unless the party opposing arbitration—here AT&T—adduces "the most forceful evidence" to this effect from the bargaining history. Under *Warrior & Gulf*, determining arbitrability does not require the court even to consider which party is correct with respect to the meaning of Article 20. . . .

2. Comments and Questions

a. Are you persuaded by the unanimous Supreme Court? Can you make a persuasive argument for the 7th Circuit's decision? Would adoption of the 7th Circuit approach "eviscerate" the Steelworkers trilogy?

b. Why do you think Justice Brennan wrote a concurring opinion in this unanimously decided case?

3. *Shearson Lehman Hutton, Inc. v. Wagoner*, 944 F.2d 114 (2d Cir. 1991)

CARDAMONE, Circuit Judge:

After opening an account with a leading brokerage firm, the principal . . . sold worthless notes and loan agreements to fellow church members, and used the proceeds to make stock trades in the name of his wholly-owned corporation, which subsequently went bankrupt. Among the issues we must decide is whether the trustee in bankruptcy, standing in the corporation's shoes, is attempting to assert the noteholders' claims in an arbitration forum against the brokerage house.

In July 1982 Herbert M. Kirschner, a member of Jehovah's Witnesses, formed HMK Management Corporation and, as its sole stockholder, director, and president, he managed, directed, and controlled its trading and business activities. HMK opened . . . [several accounts] with plaintiff Shearson/American Express (Shearson Lehman Hutton's predecessor) in Greenwich, Connecticut. . . . HMK used these accounts to execute trades on which Shearson took commissions. Because they were not discretionary accounts Shearson had no authority to execute trades on behalf of HMK, absent Kirschner's express order. When HMK opened these accounts it signed Customer Agreements with Shearson that contained arbitration clauses.

HMK's trading was quite active, and since Kirschner was a trusted customer Shearson agreed to his use of a spare desk and a video monitor on the fourth floor of its offices. Shearson's main office was on the ground floor of the same building. The rules of the New York Stock Exchange permit such use of a broker's equipment by its experienced and trusted customers. While trading as HMK, Kirschner was issuing HMK Notes and HMK Loan Agreements to fellow Jehovah's Witnesses and using the proceeds of the loans to make trades in the HMK accounts. . . .

In February and March, 1983 HMK experienced losses, and Shearson attempted to give Kirschner advice in order to minimize them. During these conversations, a Shearson manager asked Kirschner if he had any partners in HMK or was trading with the money of others. Kirschner represented orally, and later affirmed in writing, that he was the sole owner of HMK and was trading only with his own funds. In July, 1984 the manager of the Greenwich office became aware that Kirschner might be using loan proceeds derived from others to trade in the HMK accounts. After meeting with Kirschner on August 6, the manager closed the HMK accounts, and terminated Kirschner's use of Shearson's fourth floor office and equipment. Later in 1984 HMK filed for bankruptcy.

In 1985, HMK noteholders brought suits in federal court against Shearson. In June, 1988 the Trustee in Bankruptcy for the Estate of HMK, Walter Wagoner, Jr., filed a demand for arbitration with the arbitration division of the New York Stock Exchange. The demand stated that it was asserting contractual claims stemming from the Customer Agreements on behalf of HMK, as well as claims that Shearson had breached its fiduciary duty to HMK . . . thereby gaining for itself "extraordinarily high" commissions. Finally, it accused Shearson of churning the HMK accounts.

Shearson asked the New York Stock Exchange to decline to accept the arbitration, but the Exchange refused. Shearson then moved for a temporary restraining order and a preliminary injunction in the United States District Court for the District of Connecticut. The magistrate issued a proposed ruling denying the motion for a preliminary injunction, holding that though it was difficult to discern precisely what the trustee was alleging, it appeared to be a "breach of contract claim" properly brought within New York's six-year statutory period. The proposed ruling also noted that the claims bordered on being frivolous, but stated that this determination should be left to the arbitrators.

On reconsideration, the magistrate reversed himself, and ruled that HMK's claims in fact sounded in tort and did not adequately allege a breach of contract. Applying the Connecticut three-year statute of limitations on tort claims, the magistrate recommended that the district court grant Shearson's motion for an injunction because the statute of limitations had expired. On . . . that basis [the District Court] granted a permanent injunction barring the trustee from instituting or pursuing arbitration of its claims against Shearson. The trustee appeals.

DISCUSSION

II. Statute of Limitations

Having decided [in Part I, omitted] that the trustee has standing to bring only the churning claim, we next consider whether the district court erred in granting summary judgment in Shearson's favor as to this claim on the grounds that it is time-barred. The district court's opinion on this point is somewhat unclear. It decided the claim sounded in tort and that the statute of limitations had therefore expired, but failed to state how it arrived at that conclusion. It could have done so in one of two ways. Either it assumed it had power to determine the statute of limitations question—without first examining the scope of the arbitration agreement to see whether the trustee's claim fell within it—and adopted the three-year limitations period because it believed the causes of action sounded more in tort than contract; or, alternatively, it implicitly found that the claim fell outside the scope of the arbitration agreement because it asserted a cause of action sounding in tort, and then went on to decide as a matter of law that they were time-barred. On either basis, we think the district court erred.

We address the two possible interpretations of its holding. If we take the view that the trial court decided the statute of limitations question itself—before examining the scope of the agreement—that conflicts with the rule that it is up to the arbitrators, not the court, to decide the validity of time-bar defenses. . . . [I]f the churning claim falls within the scope of the arbitration clauses in the Customer Agreements, the district court went beyond its authority in addressing the statute of limitations issue.

If, on the other hand, we assume the trial court first decided that the churning claim fell outside the scope of the arbitration agreement before reaching the statute of limitations question, then it also erred. We have said that a court asked to stay arbitration has four tasks: [F]irst, it must determine whether the parties agreed to arbitrate; second, it must determine the scope of that agreement; third, if federal statutory claims are asserted, it must consider whether Congress intended those claims to be nonarbitrable; and fourth, if the court concludes that some, but not all, of the claims in the case are arbitrable, it must then determine whether to stay the balance of the proceedings pending arbitration. *Genesco, Inc. v. T. Kakiuchi & Co.*, 815 F.2d 840, 844 (2d Cir. 1987). Only the scope of the agreement is at issue here, and we review the district court's determination of the scope of an arbitration agreement de novo.

The arbitration clauses in the three Customer Agreements all read as follows:

> "Unless unenforceable due to federal or state law, any controversy arising out of or relating to my account, to transactions with you for me or this authorization or the breach thereof, shall be settled by arbitration in accordance with the rule, then in effect, of the National Association of Securities Dealers, Inc. or the Boards of Directors of the New York Stock Exchange, Inc. and/or the American Stock Exchange, Inc. as I may elect, and shall be governed by the laws of the State of New York."

In determining the scope of this clause, "any doubts concerning the scope of arbitrable issues should be resolved in favor of arbitration, whether the problem at hand is the construction of the contract language itself or an allegation of waiver, delay, or a like defense to arbitrability." The scope of the arbitration clause implicates the intent of the parties, but doubts regarding that intent must also be resolved in favor of arbitrability. Again, when the contract contains a "broad" arbitration clause, as the one at issue here, that purports "to refer all disputes arising out of a contract to arbitration," the strong presumption in favor of arbitrability applies with even greater force.

Here the trustee's allegation that Shearson churned HMK accounts clearly arises out of or relates to the HMK account. The arbitration clause does not limit claims to tort or contract. Rather, given that the arbitration clause in each of the Customer Agreements states that all controversies "arising out of or relating to" the accounts are arbitrable, the churning allegation does "touch matters" covered by these Agreements.

III. Waiver

Finally, Shearson asserts that the trustee waived his rights to arbitration through delay and by obtaining pretrial discovery from the other federal actions. Shearson reasons that because the trustee has retained the same counsel as the noteholders who brought the federal actions, he therefore has access through counsel to substantially all the discovery obtained in these prior federal cases. In addition, Shearson argues, the trustee knew of the arbitration provision in the contract as early as 1985, but failed to file a demand for arbitration until over three years later. . . . [A]ll of the pretrial discovery and merits litigation at issue occurred during the cases the noteholders brought, and that the trustee's claims, while overlapping, are distinct from those cases. . . .

Delay due to litigation of issues going to the merits rises to the level of waiver in some instances. Yet, in light of the strong federal policy favoring enforcement of agreements to arbitrate disputes, waiver through participation in previous litigation may be found only when the party seeking to avoid arbitration is able to demonstrate some resulting prejudice.

. . . Shearson's arguments are based on the assumption that the trustee and the noteholders are one and the same. Yet, as was critical to our holding regarding standing, legally they are not the same parties and do not present the same claims. Consequently, there is no prejudice to Shearson demonstrated from any action taken by the trustee, and we are left only with the fact that the trustee delayed seeking arbitration for more than three years. But delay standing alone is an insufficient basis to support waiver. Under these circumstances, the right to arbitration has not been waived.

4. *First Options of Chicago v. Kaplan,* 115 S. Ct. 1920 (1995)

Justice BREYER delivered the opinion for a unanimous Court.

In this case we consider two questions about how courts should review certain matters under the Federal Arbitration Act, (1) how a district court should review an arbitrator's decision that the parties agreed to arbitrate a dispute, and (2) how a court of appeals should review a district court's decision confirming, or refusing to vacate, an arbitration award.

I

The case concerns several related disputes between, on one side, First Options of Chicago, Inc., a firm that clears stock trades on the Philadelphia Stock Exchange, and, on the other side, three parties: Manuel Kaplan; his wife, Carol Kaplan; and his wholly owned investment company, MK Investments, Inc. (MKI), whose trading account First Options cleared. The disputes center around a "workout" agreement, embodied in four separate documents, which governs the "working out" of debts to First Options that MKI and the Kaplans incurred as a result of the October 1987 stock market crash. In 1989, after entering into the agreement, MKI lost an additional $1.5 million. First Options then took control of, and liquidated, certain MKI assets; demanded immediate payment of the entire MKI debt; and insisted that the Kaplans personally pay any deficiency. When its demands went unsatisfied, First Options sought arbitration by a panel of the Philadelphia Stock Exchange.

MKI, having signed the only workout document (out of four) that contained an arbitration clause, accepted arbitration. The Kaplans, however, who had not personally signed that document, denied that their disagreement with First Options was arbitrable and filed written objections to that effect with the arbitration panel. The arbitrators decided that they had the power to rule on the merits of the parties' dispute, and did so in favor of First Options. The Kaplans then asked the Federal District Court to vacate the arbitration award, and First Options requested its confirmation. The court confirmed the award. Nonetheless, on appeal the Court of Appeals for the Third Circuit agreed with the Kaplans that their dispute was not arbitrable; and it reversed the District Court's confirmation of the award against them.

We granted certiorari to consider two questions regarding the standards that the Court of Appeals used to review the determination that the Kaplans' dispute with First Options was arbitrable. First, the Court of Appeals said that courts "should independently decide whether an arbitration panel has jurisdiction over the merits of any particular dispute." First Options asked us to decide whether this is so (i.e., whether courts, in "reviewing the arbitrators' decision on arbitrability," should "apply a de novo standard of review or the more deferential standard applied to arbitrators' decisions on the merits") when the objecting party "submitted the issue to the arbitrators for decision." Second, the Court of Appeals stated that it would review a district court's denial of a motion to vacate a commercial arbitration award (and the correlative grant of a motion to confirm it) "de novo." First Options argues that the Court of Appeals instead should have applied an "abuse of discretion" standard.

II

The first question—the standard of review applied to an arbitrator's decision about arbitrability—is a narrow one. To understand just how narrow, consider three types of disagreement present in this case. First, the Kaplans and First Options disagree about whether the Kaplans are personally liable for MKI's debt to First Options. That disagreement makes up the merits of the dispute. Second, they disagree about whether they agreed to arbitrate the merits. That disagreement is about the arbitrability of the dispute. Third, they disagree about who should have the primary power to decide the second matter. Does that power belong primarily to the arbitrators (because the court reviews their arbitrability decision deferentially) or to the court (because the court makes up its mind about arbitrability independently)? We consider here only this third question.

Although the question is a narrow one, it has a certain practical importance. That is because a party who has not agreed to arbitrate will normally have a right to a court's decision about the merits of its dispute (say, as here, its obligation under a contract). But, where the party has agreed to arbitrate, he or she, in effect, has relinquished much of that right's practical value. The party still can ask a court to review the arbitrator's decision, but the court will set that decision aside only in very unusual circumstances. Hence, who—court or arbitrator—has the primary authority to decide whether a party has agreed to arbitrate can make a critical difference to a party resisting arbitration.

We believe the answer to the "who" question (i.e., the standard-of-review question) is fairly simple. Just as the arbitrability of the merits of a dispute depends upon whether the parties agreed to arbitrate that dispute, so the question "who has the primary power to decide arbitrability" turns upon what the parties agreed about that matter. Did the parties agree to submit the arbitrability question itself to arbitration? If so, then the court's standard for reviewing the arbitrator's decision about that matter should not differ from the standard courts apply when they review any other matter that parties have agreed to arbitrate. That is to say, the court should give considerable leeway to the arbitrator, setting aside his or her decision only in certain narrow circumstances. If, on the other hand, the parties did not agree to submit the arbitrability question itself to arbitration, then the court should decide that question just as it would decide any other question that the parties did not submit to arbitration, namely independently. These two answers flow inexorably from the fact that arbitration is simply a matter of contract between the parties. . . .

[A] fair and complete answer to the standard-of-review question requires a word about how a court should decide whether the parties have agreed to submit the arbitrability issue to arbitration. And, that word makes clear that the Kaplans did not agree to arbitrate arbitrability here.

When deciding whether the parties agreed to arbitrate a certain matter (including arbitrability), courts generally (though with a qualification we discuss below) should apply ordinary state-law principles that govern the formation of contracts. The relevant state law here, for example, would require the court to see whether the parties objectively revealed an intent to submit the arbitrability issue to arbitration.

This Court, however, has (as we just said) added an important qualification, applicable when courts decide whether a party has agreed that arbitrators should decide arbitrability: Courts should not assume that the parties agreed to arbitrate arbitrability unless there is "clea[r] and unmistakabl[e]" evidence that they did so. In this manner the law treats silence or ambiguity about the question "who (primarily) should decide arbitrability" differently from the way it treats silence or ambiguity about the question "whether a particular merits-related dispute is arbitrable because it is within the scope of a valid arbitration agreement"—for in respect to this latter question the law reverses the presumption.

But, this difference in treatment is understandable. The latter question arises when the parties have a contract that provides for arbitration of some issues. In such circumstances, the parties likely gave at least some thought to the scope of arbitration. And, given the law's permissive policies in respect to arbitration, one can understand why the law would insist upon clarity before concluding that the parties did not want to arbitrate a related matter. On the other hand, the former question—the "who (primarily) should decide arbitrability" question—is rather arcane. A party often might not focus upon that question or upon the significance of having arbitrators decide the scope of their own powers. And, given the principle that a party can be forced to arbitrate only those issues it specifically has agreed to submit to arbitration, one can understand why courts might hesitate to interpret silence or ambiguity on the "who should decide arbitrability" point as giving the arbitrators that power, for doing so might too often force unwilling parties to arbitrate a matter they reasonably would have thought a judge, not an arbitrator, would decide.

On the record before us, First Options cannot show that the Kaplans clearly agreed to have the arbitrators decide . . . the question of arbitrability. First Options relies on the Kaplans' filing with the arbitrators a written memorandum objecting to the arbitrators' jurisdiction. But merely arguing the arbitrability issue to an arbitrator does not indicate a clear willingness to arbitrate that issue, i.e., a willingness to be effectively bound by the arbitrator's decision on that point. To the contrary, insofar as the Kaplans were forcefully objecting to the arbitrators deciding their dispute with First Options, one naturally would think that they did not want the arbitrators to have binding authority over them. This conclusion draws added support from (1) an obvious explanation for the Kaplans' presence before the arbitrators (i.e., that MKI, Mr. Kaplan's wholly owned firm, was arbitrating workout agreement matters); and (2) Third Circuit law that suggested that the Kaplans might argue arbitrability to the arbitrators without losing their right to independent court review. . . .

We conclude that, because the Kaplans did not clearly agree to submit the question of arbitrability to arbitration, the Court of Appeals was correct in finding that the arbitrability of the Kaplan/First Options dispute was subject to independent review by the courts.

III

We turn next to the standard a court of appeals should apply when reviewing a district court decision that refuses to vacate, or confirms, an arbitration award. Although the Third Circuit sometimes used the words "de novo " to describe this standard, its opinion makes clear that it simply believes . . . that there is no special standard governing its review of a district court's decision in these circumstances. Rather, review of, for example, a district court decision confirming an arbitration award on the ground that the parties agreed to submit their dispute to arbitration, should proceed like review of any other district court decision finding an agreement between parties, i.e., accepting findings of fact that are not "clearly erroneous" but deciding questions of law de novo.

One Court of Appeals, the Eleventh Circuit, has said something different. Because of federal policy favoring arbitration, that court says that it applies a specially lenient "abuse of discretion" standard (even as to questions of law) when reviewing district court decisions that confirm (but not those that set aside) arbitration awards. First Options asks us to hold that the Eleventh Circuit's view is correct.

We believe, however, that the majority of Circuits is right in saying that courts of appeals should apply ordinary, not special, standards when reviewing district court decisions upholding arbitration awards. For one thing, it is undesirable to make the law more complicated by proliferating review standards without good reasons. More importantly, the reviewing attitude that a court of appeals takes toward a district court decision should depend upon "the respective institutional advantages of trial and appellate courts," not upon what standard of review will more likely produce a particular substantive result. . . . [C]ourts grant arbitrators considerable leeway when reviewing most arbitration decisions; but that fact does not mean that appellate courts should give extra leeway to district courts that uphold arbitrators. First Options argues that the Arbitration Act is special because the Act, in one section, allows courts of appeals to conduct interlocutory review of certain antiarbitration district court rulings (e.g., orders enjoining arbitrations), but not those upholding arbitration (e.g., orders refusing to enjoin arbitrations). 9 U.S.C. § 16. But that portion of the Act governs the timing of review; it is therefore too weak a support for the distinct claim that the court of appeals should use a different standard when reviewing certain district court decisions. The Act says nothing about standards of review.

We conclude that the Court of Appeals used the proper standards for reviewing the District Court's arbitrability determinations. The judgment of the Court of Appeals is affirmed.

F. When Does Federal Law Preempt State Law?

1. *Perry v. Thomas*, 482 U.S. 483 (1987)

Justice Marshall delivered the opinion of the Court.

In this appeal we decide whether § 2 of the Federal Arbitration Act, which mandates enforcement of arbitration agreements, pre-empts § 229 of the California Labor Code, which provides that actions for the collection of wages may be maintained "without regard to the existence of any private agreement to arbitrate."

Thomas brought this action . . . against his former employer, Kidder, Peabody & Co. (Kidder, Peabody), and two of its employees, appellants Perry and Johnston. His complaint arose from a dispute over commissions on the sale of securities. Thomas alleged breach of contract, conversion, civil conspiracy to commit conversion, and breach of fiduciary duty, for which he sought compensatory and punitive damages. After Thomas refused to submit the dispute to arbitration, the defendants sought to stay further proceedings in the Superior Court . . . [and] sought arbitration under the authority of the Federal Arbitration Act.

The demands for arbitration were based on a provision found in a Uniform Application for Securities Industry Registration form, which Thomas completed and executed in connection with his application for employment with Kidder, Peabody. That provision states: "I agree to arbitrate any dispute, claim or controversy that may arise between me and my firm, or a customer, or any other person, that is required to be arbitrated under the rules, constitutions or by-laws of the organizations with which I register. . . ." Rule 347 of the New York Stock Exchange, Inc. (1975), with which Thomas registered, provides that "[a]ny controversy between a registered representative and any member or member organization arising out of the employment or termination of employment of such registered representative by and with such member or member organization shall be settled by arbitration, at the instance of any such party. . . ." Kidder, Peabody sought arbitration as a member organization of the New York Stock Exchange (NYSE). Perry and Johnston relied on Thomas' allegation that they had acted in the course and scope of their employment and argued that, as agents and employees of Kidder, Peabody, they were beneficiaries of the arbitration agreement. . . .

"Section 2 is a congressional declaration of a liberal federal policy favoring arbitration agreements, notwithstanding any state substantive or procedural policies to the contrary. The effect of the section is to create a body of federal substantive law of arbitrability, applicable to any arbitration agreement within the coverage of the Act." Enacted pursuant to the Commerce Clause, this body of substantive law is enforceable in both state and federal courts. *Southland Corp. v. Keating,* 465 U.S. 1 (1984), held [section 2] to pre-empt a provision of the California Franchise Investment Law that California courts had interpreted to require judicial consideration of claims arising under that law. As we stated in *Keating,* "[i]n enacting § 2 of the federal Act, Congress declared a national policy favoring arbitration and withdrew the power of the states to require a judicial forum for the resolution of claims which the contracting parties agreed to resolve by arbitration." . . . Section 2 embodies a clear federal policy of requiring arbitration unless the agreement to arbitrate is not part of a contract evidencing interstate commerce or is revocable "upon such grounds as exist at law or in equity for the revocation of any contract." We see nothing in the Act indicating that the broad principle of enforceability is subject to any additional limitations under state law. . . . This clear federal policy places § 2 of the Act in unmistakable conflict with California's § 229 requirement that litigants be provided a judicial forum for resolving wage disputes. Therefore, under the Supremacy Clause, the state statute must give way.

The judgment of the California Court of Appeal is reversed, and the case is remanded for further proceedings not inconsistent with this opinion. It is so ordered.

Justice STEVENS, dissenting.

Despite the striking similarity between this case and *Merrill Lynch, Pierce, Fenner & Smith, Inc. v. Ware,* 414 U.S. 117, 94 S.Ct. 383, 38 L.Ed.2d 348 (1973), the Court correctly concludes that the precise question now presented was not decided in Ware. Even though the

Arbitration Act had been on the books for almost 50 years in 1973, apparently neither the Court nor the litigants even considered the possibility that the Act had pre-empted state-created rights. It is only in the last few years that the Court has effectively rewritten the statute to give it a pre-emptive scope that Congress certainly did not intend. *See Southland Corp. v. Keating,* 465 U.S. 1, 18-21 (1984). The dicta in some of these recent cases are admittedly broad enough to cover this case, but since none of our prior holdings is on point, the doctrine of stare decisis is not controlling. Accordingly, because I share Justice O'CONNOR'S opinion that the States' power to except certain categories of disputes from arbitration should be preserved unless Congress decides otherwise, I would affirm the judgment of the California Court of Appeal.

Justice O'CONNOR, dissenting.

The Court today holds that § 2 of the Federal Arbitration Act (Act), 9 U.S.C. § 1 et seq., requires the arbitration of appellee's claim for wages despite clear state policy to the contrary. This Court held in *Southland Corp. v. Keating,* 465 U.S. 1 (1984), that the Act applies to state court as well as federal court proceedings. Because I continue to believe that this holding was "unfaithful to congressional intent, unnecessary, and in light of the [Act's] antecedents and the intervening contraction of federal power, inexplicable," I respectfully dissent.

Even if I were not to adhere to my position that the Act is inapplicable to state court proceedings, however, I would still dissent. We have held that Congress can limit or preclude a waiver of a judicial forum, and that Congress' intent to do so will be deduced from a statute's text or legislative history, or "from an inherent conflict between arbitration and the statute's underlying purposes." *Shearson/American Express Inc. v. McMahon,* 482 U.S. 220, 227 (1987). As Justice STEVENS has observed, the Court has not explained why state legislatures should not also be able to limit or preclude waiver of a judicial forum: "We should not refuse to exercise independent judgment concerning the conditions under which an arbitration agreement, generally enforceable under the Act, can be held invalid as contrary to public policy simply because the source of the substantive law to which the arbitration agreement attaches is a State rather than the Federal Government. I find no evidence that Congress intended such a double standard to apply, and I would not lightly impute such an intent to the 1925 Congress which enacted the Arbitration Act."

Under the standards we most recently applied in *Shearson/American Express Inc. v. McMahon, supra,* there can be little doubt that the California Legislature intended to preclude waiver of a judicial forum; it is clear, moreover, that this intent reflects an important state policy. Section 229 of the California Labor Code specifically provides that actions for the collection of wages may be maintained in the state courts "without regard to the existence of any private agreement to arbitrate." Cal.Lab.Code Ann. § 229 (West 1971). The California Legislature thereby intended "to protect the worker from the exploitative employer who would demand that a prospective employee sign away in advance his right to resort to the judicial system for redress of an employment grievance," and § 229 has "manifested itself as an important state policy through interpretation by the California courts."

In my view, therefore, even if the Act applies to state court proceedings, California's policy choice to preclude waivers of a judicial forum for wage claims is entitled to respect. Accordingly, I would affirm the judgment of the California Court of Appeal.

2. *In the Matter of Smith Barney, Harris Upham & Co. v. Luckie*, 647 N.E.2d 1308 (N.Y. 1995)

TITONE, Judge.

These two appeals arise from controversies concerning separate securities transactions undertaken by two securities brokers on behalf of two unrelated investors. The common issue presented is whether the Appellate Division in each case properly held that the timeliness of claims sought to be arbitrated pursuant to an agreement governed by the Federal Arbitration Act (FAA) is a question reserved to the arbitrators, notwithstanding the facts that each arbitration agreement contained a New York choice of law provision, and that, under New York law, Statute of Limitations questions are properly resolved by the courts. In light of the United States Supreme Court's decision in *Volt Information Sciences v. Leland Stanford Jr. Univ.*, 489 U.S. 468 (1989), we conclude that a determination by the court on the Statute of Limitations question offends neither the language of the FAA nor its underlying policies where the parties have mutually agreed that New York law shall govern the dispute. Accordingly, we reverse in each case and remit . . . for a determination on the previously unaddressed Statute of Limitations questions.

I

In 1989, respondent Doris Kahn commenced arbitration against petitioner Smith Barney, Harris Upham & Co., a national securities broker-dealer having its principal executive offices in New York, alleging Federal and State claims of fraudulent and unsuitable sale of certain securities. Kahn, a Florida resident, made her Smith Barney investments exclusively through petitioner's Florida offices. . . .

The governing customer agreement between Smith Barney and Kahn refers to and incorporates a Securities Account Agreement, which in turn contains an arbitration clause. The parties' arbitration clause provides that "[a]ny controversy between Smith Barney and [Kahn] arising out of or relating to this contract or the breach thereof shall be settled by arbitration" and specifies the available arbitration fora. The arbitration clause is directly followed in the securities account agreement by New York choice of law provision, which states that "[t]his agreement and its enforcement shall be governed by the laws of the State of New York."

The parties subsequently engaged in extensive State and Federal litigation to determine both the appropriate forum for arbitrating their dispute, and whether the arbitration is barred by the Statute of Limitations. In 1989, by special proceeding, petitioner Smith Barney sought an order in New York Supreme Court staying the arbitration before the National Association of Securities Dealers (NASD)[2] pursuant to CPLR 7503 and moved to dismiss Kahn's claims pursuant to CPLR 7502(b) on the ground, among others, that they were time-barred. Supreme Court granted a temporary stay of arbitration pending determination of the petition. The court ultimately denied the petition for a stay, ruling that Kahn's claims were governed by New York's six-year Statute of Limitations for fraud, and were timely filed. The Appellate Division affirmed the denial of the stay of arbitration on different grounds. The Court ruled

[2]Arbitration was held in the fall of 1994 [before the NASD], and respondent was awarded $360,098.62 plus costs.

that the Statute of Limitations question is one to be resolved by the arbitrators rather than the courts. Relying on the fact that "[t]he parties' intention to resolve all disputes by arbitration [was] clear," the Court reasoned that "dismissal of respondent's claims pursuant to CPLR 7502(b) would defeat the policies of the Federal Arbitration Act." Thus, the Court concluded that "the arbitrators should decide the Statute of Limitations issue, including whether New York or Florida law applies." This Court granted Smith Barney's motion for leave to appeal, but denied its motion for a stay of arbitration pending resolution of this appeal. . . .

II

. . . In enacting the FAA, Congress established a Federal policy favoring arbitration agreements, which is to be advanced by rigorous judicial enforcement of arbitration agreements, and by resolution of any ambiguities as to the scope of the arbitration clause itself in favor of arbitration. Notwithstanding the Federal policy favoring liberal enforcement of agreements to arbitrate, . . . arbitration is manifestly a matter of contract. . . . [T]he policy established by the FAA is to ensure that private agreements to arbitrate are enforced according to their terms. Accordingly, the parties are at liberty to include a choice of law provision in their agreement, and the parties' choice will be honored unless the chosen law creates a conflict with the terms of, or policies underlying, the FAA. . . .

The question we must resolve is whether New York arbitration law conflicts with the FAA on the question of the arbitrability of these Statute of Limitations disputes such that its application must be preempted.

Generally, under New York statutory and case law, a court may address three threshold questions on a motion to compel or to stay arbitration: (1) whether the parties made a valid agreement to arbitrate; (2) if so, whether the agreement has been complied with; and (3) whether the claim sought to be arbitrated would be time-barred if it were asserted in State court. Clearly, under New York law, statutory time limitations questions such as those presented on these two appeals—as opposed to contractual time limitations agreed upon by the parties—are for the courts, not the arbitrators.

Undeniably, in the absence of an explicit choice of law provision, governing Federal law would have precluded the courts in the appeals before us from addressing the Statute of Limitations issue, or from issuing stays under our arbitration act. However, the parties' choice that New York law would govern "the agreement and its enforcement" indicates their "intention to arbitrate to the extent allowed by [this State's] law," even if application of the State law—and an adverse ruling on a Statute of Limitations claim—would relieve the parties of their responsibility under the contract to arbitrate. Although the parties broadly agreed to arbitrate "any controversy" arising from the customer agreements, that clause—like all other provisions in the contract—was subject to the parties' additional qualification that New York State law provides the basis of decision for questions concerning not only the agreement, but more critically, its enforcement. Accordingly, we conclude that under this agreement the parties agreed to refer questions of timeliness to the courts by incorporating New York law.

In light of our conclusion that the parties intended that New York law govern the arbitration, the dispositive question for resolution of these appeals becomes whether . . . the FAA's compulsory arbitration provisions and its underlying policies require that even those questions normally reserved to the courts pursuant to New York law must be resolved by the arbitrators, notwithstanding the presence of a New York choice of law provision in the agreement to arbitrate.

[T]he provisions of CPLR 7502(b) and 7503 authorizing the courts to consider a time limitation asserted as a bar to arbitration in connection with an application to compel or stay arbitration do not expressly conflict with any provision of the FAA. Additionally, Congress did not intend "to occupy the entire field of arbitration" in enacting this statutory scheme. In the absence of any express conflict between the provisions of the FAA and New York's arbitration law or some express congressional intent to occupy the entire field of arbitration in commercial disputes, the FAA will be found to preempt State law only to the extent that the State law stands as an obstacle to the accomplishment and execution of the full purposes and objectives of Congress. Accordingly, the dispositive inquiry before us is whether application of New York arbitration law in this context "undermine[s] the goals and policies of the FAA." We conclude that it does not.

Our point of departure on this aspect of the preemption analysis is the United States Supreme Court's decision in *Volt Information Sciences v. Leland Stanford Jr. Univ.*, 489 U.S. 468, 109 S.Ct. 1248, *supra.* In *Volt,* the Supreme Court held that a California statute permitting a court to stay arbitration pending resolution of related litigation was not preempted by the FAA where the parties included a clause in their arbitration agreement stating that the agreement will be governed by California law. . . . The Court concluded that "[t]here is no federal policy favoring arbitration under a certain set of procedural rules; the federal policy is simply to ensure the enforceability, according to their terms, of private agreements to arbitrate." The Court went on to note that "[i]nterpreting a choice-of-law clause to make applicable state rules governing the conduct of arbitration—rules which are manifestly designed to encourage resort to the arbitral process—simply does not offend . . . any policy embodied in the FAA."

Turning its focus to preemption, the Supreme Court addressed whether the State law, which authorized a stay of arbitration where no Federal counterpart was available, created a conflict with Federal law which "would undermine the goals and policies of the FAA." Concluding that it would not, the Court reasoned that the FAA "simply requires courts to enforce privately negotiated agreements to arbitrate, like other contracts, in accordance with their terms." Applying ordinary contract principles, the Court concluded that parties are not only free to limit by agreement the issues to be arbitrated, but also to "specify by contract the rules under which that arbitration will be conducted." Finally, in key language, the Court explained that where "the parties have agreed to abide by state rules of arbitration, enforcing those rules according to the terms of the agreement is fully consistent with the goals of the FAA, even if the result is that arbitration is stayed where the Act would otherwise permit it to go forward."

In the aftermath of *Volt,* the courts have divided on whether New York's rule permitting the court to address a statute of limitations question conflicts with the compulsory arbitration provisions of the FAA and is thus preempted. [W]e conclude that this State's body of arbitration law—including the rule that courts may consider threshold Statute of Limitations claims—is not inimical to the policies of the FAA. . . . New York's rule permitting the courts to address Statute of Limitations defenses to arbitration where the parties so choose in no way interferes with the parties' contractual freedom to choose arbitration. . . . In fact, by honoring the parties' selection of New York law to govern their agreement and its enforcement, our holding advances the Federal policy of "ensur[ing] the enforceability according to their terms, of private agreements to arbitrate."

[P]etitioners attempt to distinguish *Volt* on the grounds that the California law at issue there merely permitted imposition of a temporary stay of the arbitration, while an adverse ruling on the Statute of Limitations issue by the courts in these cases would result in a permanent stay of arbitration. . . . Contrary to petitioners' position, the Supreme Court did not rest its decision on the fact that the Court-issued stay in Volt was only temporary. . . . Accordingly, the potential permanency of the stay granted pursuant to New York law does not alter our conclusion that application of New York law to permit court determination of statutory timeliness issues does not conflict with the underlying policies of the FAA.

III

When making a threshold Statute of Limitations determination under New York law, the courts must apply the same period of limitations in arbitration that would govern if an action were brought on the claim being arbitrated. *Matter of SCM Corp. [Fisher Park Lane Co.].* Under the New York borrowing statute (CPLR 202), a securities fraud claim arising outside this State is subject to the limitations periods of the jurisdiction where the injury occurred—generally, the place where the investors resided and sustained the economic impact of the loss. In borrowing the foreign statute, "[a]ll the extensions and tolls applied in the foreign state must be imported with the foreign statutory period, so that the entire foreign statute of limitations . . . applie[s], and not merely its period." Since the Appellate Division in each case before us did not address the Statute of Limitations arguments, including applicability of the borrowing statute, relevant accrual dates, tolls and extensions by virtue of each panel's conclusion that the question was for the arbitrators, we remit in each case for such a determination.

KAYE, Chief Judge (concurring).

I concur in the Court's opinion and conclusion that because the form arbitration agreements at issue plainly provide that New York law governs the "agreement and its enforcement "the parties can fairly be understood to have agreed that all of New York arbitration law (including the provisions of CPLR article 75 which allow a party to first litigate Statute of Limitations issues in court) would apply. I write separately, however, to make two somewhat related points concerning what I fear may be the continuing erosion of the pro-arbitration policy originally expressed by Congress in the Federal Arbitration Act (FAA).

First, I remain troubled by the practical effect for respondents — residents of the States of Florida and Virginia — who now have to litigate the brokerage firms' Statute of Limitations defenses in New York State court before ever reaching the arbitrators' door. Because of the Supreme Court's direction in *Volt Information Sciences v. Leland Stanford Jr. Univ.*, that "private agreements to arbitrate [be] enforced according to their terms," and the explicit terms of the agreements before us, however, I feel compelled to join the Court in reversing here.

Second, I think it useful to underscore the distinctly different interpretive choices made by the Court in this case and in *Salvano v. Merrill Lynch, Pierce, Fenner & Smith,* [decided today]. In the present case, the Court concludes that the express language of the parties' agreements contemplated that the whole of New York arbitration law would apply, and following *Volt* we give force to the parties' agreement. In *Salvano,* by contrast, the arbitration agreements and New York Stock Exchange rules are silent as to the availability of expedited arbitration. Nonetheless, the majority concludes that the parties, by their silence, implicitly agreed that an expedited process was not permissible and thus, the Court lacked the authority to expedite the arbitration. As my dissent reflects, since the applicable agreements and rules in Salvano were silent as to the issue of expedition, it is incumbent upon the Court to vindicate the underlying policy of the FAA and affirm the issuance of an order expediting the arbitration during the pendency of the preliminary injunctions. The difference between my vote to reverse in the present case and my dissenting vote to affirm in *Salvano* thus results from the difference between the agreements themselves.

3. Comments and Questions

a. In what sense did the parties select New York law? In particular, in what sense do residents from all over America (Florida and Virginia, in the main case) "choose" to litigate statute of limitations questions in the New York courts, instead of having them heard before an arbitrator? How many customers do you think understand the arbitration rules that the New York Court of Appeals says they "agreed" to follow?

b. As an experiment, try negotiating the arbitration terms of the standard brokerage form contract with a broker. Before doing so, state your hypothesis about the expected negotiation process and the ultimate result.

c. Courts in other states, and the federal courts in New York, have interpreted the same language in brokerage agreements differently from the New York state court. *See Merrill Lynch, Pierce, Fenner & Smith v. Shaddock,* 822 F. Supp. 125 (S.D.N.Y. 1993) (time-bar defenses are for arbitrators, despite New York choice of law clause); *Merrill Lynch, Pierce, Fenner & Smith v. Gregg,* 1993 WL 616691 (M.D. Fla. 1993) (same); *Victor v. Dean Witter Reynolds,* 606 So.2d 681 (Fla. App. 1992) (same), *review denied,* 614 So.2d 502 (Fla. 1993). Those courts opting for preemption generally rely on *Shearson Lehman Hutton v. Wagoner,* 944 F.2d 114 (2d Cir.1991), reprinted in section E of this Chapter.

d. One view of the *Smith Barney* decision is that it reflects the parochial view of a state wanting to retain local power over the decision of disputes arising all over America. Even Chief Justice Kaye is troubled by this aspect of the reach of New York law. It is hardly surprising that courts outside New York, and the federal courts even in New York, take a different view of the matter. Of course, the interpretation of New York law by the highest court of that state is NOT binding on courts in other states, although such an interpretation certainly can be cited as persuasive authority.

4. *Mastrobuono v. Shearson Lehman Hutton, Inc.*, 115 S. Ct. 1212 (1995)

STEVENS, J., delivered the opinion of the Court, in which REHNQUIST, C.J., and O'CONNOR, SCALIA, KENNEDY, SOUTER, GINSBURG, and BREYER, JJ., joined.

New York law allows courts, but not arbitrators, to award punitive damages. In a dispute arising out of a standard-form contract that expressly provides that it "shall be governed by the laws of the State of New York," a panel of arbitrators awarded punitive damages. . . . The question presented is whether the arbitrators' award is consistent with the central purpose of the Federal Arbitration Act to ensure "that private agreements to arbitrate are enforced according to their terms."

I

In 1985 petitioners, Antonio Mastrobuono, then an assistant professor of medieval literature, and his wife Diana Mastrobuono, an artist, opened a securities trading account with respondent Shearson Lehman Hutton, Inc. (Shearson), by executing Shearson's standard-form Client's Agreement. Respondent Nick DiMinico, a vice president of Shearson, managed the Mastrobuonos' account until they closed it in 1987. In 1989, petitioners filed this action in the United States District Court for the Northern District of Illinois, alleging that respondents had mishandled their account and claiming damages on a variety of state and federal law theories.

Paragraph 13 of the parties' agreement contains an arbitration provision and a choice-of-law provision. Relying on the arbitration provision and on §§ 3 and 4 of the Federal Arbitration Act (FAA), 9 U.S.C. §§ 3, 4, respondents filed a motion to stay the court proceedings and to compel arbitration pursuant to the rules of the National Association of Securities Dealers. The District Court granted that motion, and a panel of three arbitrators was convened. After conducting hearings in Illinois, the panel ruled in favor of petitioners.

In the arbitration proceedings, respondents argued that the arbitrators had no authority to award punitive damages. Nevertheless, the panel's award included punitive damages of $400,000, in addition to compensatory damages of $159,327. Respondents paid the compensatory portion of the award but filed a motion to vacate the award of punitive damages. The District Court granted the motion, and the Court of Appeals for the Seventh Circuit affirmed. Both courts relied on the choice-of-law provision in Paragraph 13 of the parties' agreement, which specifies that the contract shall be governed by New York law. Because the New York Court of Appeals has decided that in New York the power to award punitive damages is limited to judicial tribunals and may not be exercised by arbitrators, *Garrity v. Lyle Stuart, Inc.*, the District Court and the Seventh Circuit held that the panel of arbitrators had no power to award punitive damages in this case. . . . We now reverse.

II

Earlier this Term, we upheld the enforceability of a predispute arbitration agreement governed by Alabama law, even though an Alabama statute provides that arbitration agreements are unenforceable. *Allied-Bruce Terminix Cos. v. Dobson.* Writing for the Court, Justice Breyer observed that Congress passed the FAA "to overcome courts' refusals to enforce agreements to arbitrate." After determining that the FAA applied to the parties' arbitration agreement, we readily concluded that the federal statute pre-empted Alabama's statutory prohibition.

Petitioners seek a similar disposition of the case before us today. Here, the Seventh Circuit interpreted the contract to incorporate New York law, including the *Garrity* rule that arbitrators may not award punitive damages. Petitioners ask us to hold that the FAA pre-empts New York's prohibition against arbitral awards of punitive damages because this state law is a vestige of the ancient judicial hostility to arbitration. Petitioners rely on *Southland Corp. v. Keating* and *Perry v. Thomas,* in which we held that the FAA pre-empted two California statutes that purported to require judicial resolution of certain disputes. In *Southland,* we explained that the FAA not only "declared a national policy favoring arbitration," but actually "withdrew the power of the states to require a judicial forum for the resolution of claims which the contracting parties agreed to resolve by arbitration."

Respondents answer that the choice-of-law provision in their contract evidences the parties' express agreement that punitive damages should not be awarded in the arbitration of any dispute arising under their contract. Thus, they claim, this case is distinguishable from *Southland* and *Perry,* in which the parties presumably desired unlimited arbitration but state law stood in their way. Regardless of whether the FAA pre-empts the *Garrity* decision in contracts not expressly incorporating New York law, respondents argue that the parties may themselves agree to be bound by *Garrity,* just as they may agree to forgo arbitration altogether. In other words, if the contract says "no punitive damages," that is the end of the matter, for courts are bound to interpret contracts in accordance with the expressed intentions of the parties—even if the effect of those intentions is to limit arbitration.

We have previously held that the FAA's pro-arbitration policy does not operate without regard to the wishes of the contracting parties. *Volt Information Sciences, Inc. v. Leland Stanford Junior University*. . . . After referring to the holdings in Southland and Perry, which struck down state laws limiting agreed-upon arbitrability, we added: "But it does not follow that the FAA prevents the enforcement of agreements to arbitrate under different rules than those set forth in the Act itself. Indeed, such a result would be quite inimical to the FAA's primary purpose of ensuring that private agreements to arbitrate are enforced according to their terms. Arbitration under the Act is a matter of consent, not coercion, and parties are generally free to structure their arbitration agreements as they see fit. Just as they may limit by contract the issues which they will arbitrate, so too may they specify by contract the rules under which that arbitration will be conducted."

Relying on our reasoning in *Volt,* respondents thus argue that the parties to a contract may lawfully agree to limit the issues to be arbitrated by waiving any claim for punitive damages. On the other hand, we think our decisions in *Allied-Bruce, Southland,* and *Perry* make clear that if contracting parties agree to include claims for punitive damages within the issues to be arbitrated, the FAA ensures that their agreement will be enforced according to its terms even if a rule of state law would otherwise exclude such claims from arbitration. Thus, the case before us comes down to what the contract has to say about the arbitrability of petitioners' claim for punitive damages.

III

Shearson's standard-form "Client Agreement," which petitioners executed, contains 18 paragraphs. The two relevant provisions of the agreement are found in Paragraph 13. The first sentence of that paragraph provides, in part, that the entire agreement "shall be governed by the laws of the State of New York." The second sentence provides that "any controversy" arising out of the transactions between the parties "shall be settled by arbitration" in accordance with the rules of the National Association of Securities Dealers (NASD), or the Boards of Directors of the New York Stock Exchange and/or the American Stock Exchange. The agreement contains no express reference to claims for punitive damages. To ascertain whether Paragraph 13 expresses an intent to include or exclude such claims, we first address the impact of each of the two relevant provisions, considered separately. We then move on to the more important inquiry: the meaning of the two provisions taken together.

The choice-of-law provision, when viewed in isolation, may reasonably be read as merely a substitute for the conflict- of- laws analysis that otherwise would determine what law to apply to disputes arising out of the contractual relationship. Thus, if a similar contract, without a choice-of-law provision, had been signed in New York and was to be performed in New York, presumably "the laws of the State of New York" would apply, even though the contract did not expressly so state. In such event, there would be nothing in the contract that could possibly constitute evidence of an intent to exclude punitive damages claims. Accordingly, punitive damages would be allowed because, in the absence of contractual intent to the contrary, the FAA would pre-empt the *Garrity* rule.

Even if the reference to "the laws of the State of New York" is more than a substitute for ordinary conflict-of-laws analysis and, as respondents urge, includes the caveat, "detached from otherwise-applicable federal law," the provision might not preclude the award of punitive damages because New York allows its courts, though not its arbitrators, to enter such awards. In other words, the provision might include only New York's substantive rights and obligations, and not the State's allocation of power between alternative tribunals. Respondents' argument is persuasive only if "New York law" means "New York decisional law, including that State's allocation of power between courts and arbitrators, notwithstanding otherwise applicable federal law." But, as we have demonstrated, the provision need not be read so broadly. It is not, in itself, an unequivocal exclusion of punitive damages claims.

The arbitration provision (the second sentence of Paragraph 13) does not improve respondents' argument. On the contrary, when read separately this clause strongly implies that an arbitral award of punitive damages is appropriate. It explicitly authorizes arbitration in accordance with NASD rules; the panel of arbitrators in fact proceeded under that set of rules. The NASD's Code of Arbitration Procedure indicates that arbitrators may award "damages and other relief." NASD Code of Arbitration Procedure P 3741(e) (1993).[6] While not a clear authorization of punitive damages, this provision appears broad enough at least to contemplate such a remedy. Moreover, as the Seventh Circuit noted, a manual provided to NASD arbitrators contains this provision:

> "The issue of punitive damages may arise with great frequency in arbitrations. Parties to arbitration are informed that arbitrators can consider punitive damages as a remedy."

Thus, the text of the arbitration clause itself surely does not support— indeed, it contradicts—the conclusion that the parties agreed to foreclose claims for punitive damages.[7]

At most, the choice-of-law clause introduces an ambiguity into an arbitration agreement that would otherwise allow punitive damages awards. As we pointed out in Volt, when a court interprets such provisions in an agreement covered by the FAA, "due regard must be given to the federal policy favoring arbitration, and ambiguities as to the scope of the arbitration clause itself resolved in favor of arbitration."

Moreover, respondents cannot overcome the common-law rule of contract interpretation that a court should construe ambiguous language against the interest of the party that drafted it. Respondents drafted an ambiguous document, and they cannot now claim the benefit of

---

[6]. . .[O]ne NASD rule is not before us, namely Rule 21(f)(4) of the NASD Rules of Fair Practice, which reads: "No agreement [between a member and a customer] shall include any condition which . . . limits the ability of a party to file any claim in arbitration or limits the ability of the arbitrators to make any award." Brief for United States et al. 6. Rule 21(f)(4) applies only to contracts executed after September 7, 1989. Notwithstanding any effect it may have on agreements signed after that date, this rule is not applicable to the agreement in this case, which was executed in 1985.

[7]"Were we to confine our analysis to the plain language of the arbitration clause, we would have little trouble concluding that a contract clause which bound the parties to "settle all disputes" through arbitration conducted according to rules which allow any form of "just and equitable" remedy of relief was sufficiently broad to encompass the award of punitive damages. . . .

the doubt. The reason for this rule is to protect the party who did not choose the language from an unintended or unfair result.[10] That rationale is well-suited to the facts of this case. As a practical matter, it seems unlikely that petitioners were actually aware of New York's bifurcated approach to punitive damages, or that they had any idea that by signing a standard-form agreement to arbitrate disputes they might be giving up an important substantive right. In the face of such doubt, we are unwilling to impute this intent to petitioners.

Finally the respondents' reading of the two clauses violates another cardinal principle of contract construction: that a document should be read to give effect to all its provisions and to render them consistent with each other. We think the best way to harmonize the choice-of-law provision with the arbitration provision is to read "the laws of the State of New York" to encompass substantive principles that New York courts would apply, but not to include special rules limiting the authority of arbitrators. Thus, the choice-of-law provision covers the rights and duties of the parties, while the arbitration clause covers arbitration; neither sentence intrudes upon the other. In contrast, respondents' reading sets up the two clauses in conflict with one another: one foreclosing punitive damages, the other allowing them. This interpretation is untenable.

We hold that the Court of Appeals misinterpreted the parties' agreement. The arbitral award should have been enforced as within the scope of the contract. The judgment of the Court of Appeals is, therefore, reversed.

Justice THOMAS, dissenting.

Because the choice-of-law provision here cannot reasonably be distinguished from the one in *Volt,* I dissent. [I]n *Volt* . . . we concluded that the FAA does not force arbitration on parties who enter into contracts involving interstate commerce. Instead, the FAA requires only that "arbitration proceed in the manner provided for in [the parties'] agreement." Although we will construe ambiguities concerning the scope of arbitrability in favor of arbitration, we remain mindful that "as with any other contract, the parties' intentions control. . . . Thus, if the parties intend that state procedure shall govern, federal courts must enforce that understanding.

In this case, as in *Volt,* the parties agreed to mandatory arbitration of all disputes. As in Volt, the contract at issue here includes a choice-of-law clause. Indeed, the language of the two clauses is functionally equivalent. . . . New York law forbids arbitrators from awarding punitive damages, and permits only courts to award such damages. As in *Volt,* petitioners here argue that the New York rule is "anti-arbitration," and hence is pre-empted by the FAA. In concluding that the choice-of-law clause is ambiguous, the majority essentially accepts petitioners' argument. Volt itself found precisely the same argument irrelevant, however, and the majority identifies no reason to think that the state law governing the interpretation of the parties' choice-of-law clause supports a different result.

The majority claims that the incorporation of New York law "need not be read so broadly"

[10]"Where one party chooses the terms of a contract, he is likely to provide more carefully for the protection of his own interests than for those of the other party. He is also more likely than the other party to have reason to know of uncertainties of meaning. Indeed, he may leave meaning deliberately obscure, intending to decide at a later date what meaning to assert. In cases of doubt, therefore, so long as other factors are not decisive, there is substantial reason for preferring the meaning of the other party." Restatement (Second) of Contracts § 206, Comment a (1979).

as to include both substantive and procedural law, and that the choice of New York law "is not, in itself, an unequivocal exclusion of punitive damages claims." But we rejected these same arguments in *Volt,* and the *Garrity* rule is just the sort of "state rule governing the conduct of arbitration" that *Volt* requires federal courts to enforce. "Just as [the parties] may limit by contract the issues which they will arbitrate, so too may they specify by contract the rules under which that arbitration will be conducted." To be sure, the majority might be correct that *Garrity* is a rule concerning the State's allocation of power between "alternative tribunals," although *Garrity* appears to describe itself as substantive New York law. Nonetheless, *Volt* makes no distinction between rules that serve only to distribute authority between courts and arbitrators (which the majority finds unenforceable) and other types of rules (which the majority finds enforceable). Indeed, the California rule in *Volt* could be considered to be one that allocates authority between arbitrators and courts, for it permits California courts to stay arbitration pending resolution of related litigation.

5. Comments and Questions

a. Is Justice Thomas correct that Volt has been limited, emasculated, or even overruled sub silentio? (The text of *Volt* is found at section H of this Chapter.)

b. *Mastrobuono* is discussed in *The Supreme Court — Leading Cases,* 109 HARV. L. REV. 269-279 (1995).

c. After *Mastrobuono,* how would the Supreme Court decide the *Smith Barney* case, and why?

6. Preemption Under the Railway Labor Act: *Hawaiian Airlines, Inc. v. Norris,* 114 S. Ct. 2239 (1994)

BLACKMUN, J., delivered the opinion for a unanimous Court.

This case involves the scope of federal pre-emption under the Railway Labor Act (RLA). The RLA, which was extended in 1936 to cover the airline industry, 45 U.S.C. §§ 181-188, sets up a mandatory arbitral mechanism to handle disputes "growing out of grievances or out of the interpretation and application of agreements concerning rates of pay, rules, or working conditions." The question in this case is whether an aircraft mechanic who claims that he was discharged for refusing to certify the safety of a plane that he considered unsafe and for reporting his safety concerns to the Federal Aviation Administration may pursue available state law remedies for wrongful discharge, or whether he may seek redress only through the RLA's arbitral mechanism. We hold that the RLA does not pre-empt his state law causes of action. . . .

On February 2, 1987, respondent was hired by petitioner Hawaiian Airlines, Inc. (HAL). Many of the terms of his employment were governed by a collective-bargaining agreement (CBA) negotiated between the carrier and the International Association of Machinists and Aerospace Workers. Under the CBA, respondent's duties included inspecting and repairing all parts of a plane and its engine. On July 15, 1987, during a routine preflight inspection of a DC-9 plane, he noticed that one of the tires was worn. When he removed the wheel, respondent discovered that the axle sleeve, which should have been mirror-smooth, was scarred and grooved. This damaged sleeve could cause the landing gear to fail. Respondent recommended that the sleeve be replaced, but his supervisor ordered that it be sanded and returned to the plane. This was done, and the plane flew as scheduled. At the end of the shift, respondent refused to sign the maintenance record to certify that the repair had been performed satisfactorily and that the airplane was fit to fly. The supervisor immediately suspended him pending a termination hearing. Respondent immediately went home and called the FAA to report the problem with the sleeve. [In response, the FAA initiated a comprehensive investigation, and ultimately settled all charges for a substantial fine.]

Respondent then invoked the grievance procedure outlined in the CBA. . . . Petitioner HAL accused respondent of insubordination, claiming that his refusal to sign the record violated the CBA's provision that an aircraft mechanic "may be required to sign work records in connection with the work he performs." Respondent relied on the CBA's guarantees that an employee may not be discharged without just cause and may not be disciplined for refusing to perform work that is in violation of health or safety laws. The hearing officer terminated respondent for insubordination.

Still conforming to the CBA procedures, respondent appealed his termination, seeking a "Step 3" grievance hearing. Before this hearing took place, HAL offered to reduce respondent's punishment to suspension without pay. . . . Respondent did not respond to this offer, nor, apparently, did he take further steps to pursue his grievance through the CBA procedures.

On December 18, 1987, respondent filed suit against HAL. His complaint included two wrongful-discharge torts—discharge in violation of the public policy expressed in the Federal Aviation Act and implementing regulations, and discharge in violation of Hawaii's Whistleblower Protection Act. He also alleged that HAL had breached the collective-bargaining agreement. HAL removed the action to the United States District Court for the District of Hawaii, which dismissed the breach of contract claim as pre-empted by the RLA, and remanded the other claims to the state trial court. The trial court then dismissed respondent's claim of discharge in violation of public policy, holding that it, too, was pre-empted by the RLA's provision of exclusive arbitral procedures. . . .

In the meantime, respondent had filed a second lawsuit in state court, naming as defendants three of HAL's officers who allegedly directed, confirmed, or ratified the claimed retaliatory discharge. He again sought relief for, among other things, discharge in violation of public policy and of the Hawaii Whistleblower's Protection Act. The Hawaii trial court dismissed these two counts as pre-empted by the RLA. . . . The Supreme Court of Hawaii reversed in both cases, concluding that the RLA did not pre-empt respondent's state tort actions.

II

Whether federal law pre-empts a state law establishing a cause of action is a question of congressional intent. Pre-emption of employment standards "within the traditional police power of the State" "should not be lightly inferred." Congress' purpose in passing the RLA was to promote stability in labor-management relations by providing a comprehensive framework for resolving labor disputes. To realize this goal, the Act establishes a mandatory arbitral mechanism for "the prompt and orderly settlement" of two classes of disputes. The first class, those concerning "rates of pay, rules or working conditions," are deemed "major" disputes. Major disputes relate to "the formation of collective bargaining agreements or efforts to secure them." The second class of disputes, known as "minor" disputes, "gro[w] out of grievances or out of the interpretation or application of agreements covering rates of pay, rules, or working conditions." Minor disputes "involve controversies over the meaning of an existing collective bargaining agreement in a particular fact situation." Thus, "major disputes seek to create contractual rights, minor disputes to enforce them." Petitioners contend that the conflict over respondent's firing is a minor dispute. If so, it must be resolved only through the RLA mechanisms, including the carrier's internal dispute-resolution processes and an adjustment board established by the employer and the unions. Thus, a determination that respondent's complaints constitute a minor dispute would pre-empt his state law actions. . . .

[T]he RLA's mechanism for resolving minor disputes does not pre-empt causes of action to enforce rights that are independent of the CBA. More than 60 years ago, the Court rejected a railroad's argument that the existence of the RLA arbitration scheme pre-empted a state statute regulating the number of workers required to operate certain equipment. Not long thereafter, the Court rejected a claim that the RLA pre-empted an order by the Illinois Commerce Commission requiring cabooses on all trains; the operative collective-bargaining agreement required cabooses only on some of the trains. . . .

In a case remarkably similar to the case before us now, this Court made clear that the existence of a potential CBA-based remedy did not deprive an employee of independent remedies available under state law. In *Lingle v. Norge Division of Magic Chef, Inc.*, 486 U.S. 399, 108 S. Ct. 1877, 100 L. Ed.2d 410 (1988), an employee covered by a labor agreement was fired for filing an allegedly false worker's compensation claim. After filing a grievance pursuant to her collective-bargaining agreement, which protected employees against discharge except for "proper" or "just" cause, she filed a complaint in state court, alleging that she had been discharged for exercising her rights under Illinois worker's compensation laws. The state court had held her state-law claim pre-empted because "the same analysis of the facts" was required in both the grievance proceeding and the state-court action. This Court reversed. . . .

While recognizing that "the state-law analysis might well involve attention to the same factual considerations as the contractual determination whether Lingle was fired for just cause," the Court disagreed that "such parallelism render[ed] the state-law analysis dependent upon the contractual analysis." . . . [E]ven if dispute resolution pursuant to a collective-bargaining agreement, on the one hand, and state law, on the other, would require addressing precisely the same set of facts, as long as the state-law claim can be resolved without interpreting the agreement itself, the claim is "independent" of the agreement for . . . pre-emption purposes.

Given this convergence in the pre-emption standards under the two statutes [LMRA and RLA], we conclude that *Lingle* provides an appropriate framework for addressing pre-emption under the RLA, and we adopt the *Lingle* standard to resolve claims of RLA pre-emption. . . . [9]

III

[9] Returning to the case before us, the question under *Lingle* is whether respondent's state-law wrongful discharge claims are independent of the collective-bargaining agreement. Petitioners argue that resort to the agreement is necessary to determine whether respondent, in fact, was discharged. This argument is foreclosed by *Lingle* itself. *Lingle* teaches that the issue to be decided in this case—whether the employer's actions make out the element of dis-

[9]It is true, as petitioners observe, that the RLA and the LMRA are not identical in language, history, and purpose. The LMRA, unlike the RLA, does not mandate arbitration, nor does it prescribe the types of disputes to be submitted to arbitration under bargaining agreements. Nonetheless, the common purposes of the two statutes, the parallel development of RLA and LMRA pre-emption law, and the desirability of having a uniform common law of labor law pre-emption, support the application of the Lingle standard in RLA cases as well.

charge under Hawaii law—is a "purely factual question."

Nor are we persuaded by petitioners' contention that the state tort claims require a determination whether the discharge, if any, was justified by respondent's failure to sign the maintenance record, as the agreement required him to do. Although such a determination would be required with regard to respondent's separate allegation of discharge in violation of the agreement, the District Court dismissed that count as preempted by the RLA, and respondent does not challenge that dismissal. The state tort claims, by contrast, require only the purely factual inquiry into any retaliatory motive of the employer.

Accordingly, we agree with the Supreme Court of Hawaii that respondent's claims for discharge in violation of public policy and in violation of the Hawaii Whistleblower Protection Act are not pre-empted by the RLA, and we affirm that court's judgment.

G. Judicial Review of Remedies Ordered by an Arbitrator

1. Remedial Authority of Arbitrators Under New York Law [As Viewed by the New York Court of Appeals]

a. Why Focus on New York Law?

The cases in this section all were decided by the Court of Appeals, the highest court in New York. (Contrary to the terminology used in other states, the Supreme Court is the middle level appellate court.) New York has long been a leader in commercial arbitration, and its law has had a major impact on American arbitration law. (The New York arbitration statute was the direct precursor of the FAA.) While the importance of New York City as the commercial hub has diminished, New York law continues to have a disproportionate influence because it is incorporated into many contracts with arbitration provisions. Also, New York City is the hub of the the securities industry, and many of the important recent arbitration cases have been based on securties disputes. There is also a pedagogicial value to analysis of a series of cases from a single jurisdiction about a particular topic. This is what lawyers commonly do when they consult case law, but it is something that almost never happens in law school.

b. *In the Matter of the Arbitration between Stanley J. Staklinski and Pyramid Electric Co.*, 160 N.E.2d 78 (N.Y. 1959)

DESMOND, Judge.

We see nothing illegal about this arbitration award and no reason for vacating it. Petitioner was for years appellant's president and in charge of its production and engineering and one of its directors and largest stockholders. In 1954 appellant entered into an 11-year contract employing petitioner as manager in charge of production and engineering at a large salary plus a percentage of net profits. Included was a covenant that, if petitioner should be declared permanently disabled, he would receive reduced compensation for the next three years and then the contract would end. The contract provided that any controversy arising out of it should be settled by arbitration in accordance with American Arbitration Association rules and the rules of that Association in so many words authorized an arbitrator to grant equitable relief including "specific performance of a contract."

In June, 1956 the corporation's directors made a determination that appellant was permanently disabled and that his services should be terminated. Petitioner disputed the finding of permanent disability. The resulting difference of opinion was just such a controversy as the parties had agreed to submit to arbitration and to arbitration it went. The arbitrators held in favor of petitioner on the issue and ordered petitioner's reinstatement. That, of course, put beyond reach of the courts the question thus conclusively determined by arbitration as to whether petitioner was in fact permanently disabled. It is now asserted, however, that it is against public policy to compel a corporation to continue the services of an officer whose services are unsatisfactory to the directors. But we must remember that this corporation made a valid long-term employment contract with this man and agreed that any disputes would go to arbitrators who would be empowered to order specific performance. Since the contract was indisputably valid, so is the arbitration award. The power of an arbitrator to order specific performance in an appropriate case has been recognized from early times (*see* Justice Story in *McNeil v. Magee,* 1829, Fed. Cas. No. 8,915).

In *Matter of Ruppert* (Egelhofer), we upheld the grant by arbitrators of an injunction against a strike in a labor dispute, and we cited a number of precedents therefor. A supposed public policy against such an injunction was urged on us in *Ruppert* since there we had a specific statute (Civil Practice Act, § 876-a) which would have made it impossible for a court to grant that same injunction. However, we held in *Ruppert* that the parties had agreed not only to submit their controversies to arbitration but had validly authorized the arbitrators to issue an injunction. The same is true here. Whether a court of equity could issue a specific performance decree in a case like this is beside the point. There is no controlling public policy which voids an arbitration agreement like this one and the courts are not licensed to announce a new public policy to fit the supposed necessities of the case.

FROESSEL, Judge (concurring).

I concur for affirmance. It do not, however, read the arbitrator's award or the judgment entered thereon as directing "specific performance" of a personal service contract.

The only dispute submitted to arbitration was whether petitioner was "permanently disabled," so as to entitle the corporation to terminate its liability to him after making specified payments for three years from the date of disability. All the arbitrators decided was that petitioner was not "permanently disabled," and hence was improperly discharged under the "permanent disability" clause of the contract. In directing the corporation to reinstate him in his position, the arbitrators awarded the natural and logical relief called for by the nature of the dispute submitted to them.

Future performance will depend upon future events which cannot now be foreseen. The board of directors of the corporation may discharge petitioner for good cause, and any discharge without good cause will be at the peril of damages.

BURKE, Judge (dissenting).

. . . In this case the mandatory injunction exceeded the powers of the arbitrator and the decree enforcing it violates both the statutory policy confiding to directors the management of public corporations and the principles of equity barring injunctive relief of this nature. We do not believe that, under a general grant of equitable powers, arbitrators may disregard equitable principles and issue an award not possible either at law or equity. . . .

Cases involving collective bargaining agreements are inapposite here. The reason for this conclusion was stated by the United States Supreme Court in *J. I. Case Co. v. National Labor*

Relations Board: "Collective bargaining between employer and representatives of a unit, usually a union, results in an accord as to terms which will govern hiring and work and pay in that unit. The result is not, however, a contract of employment except in rare cases; no one has a job by reason of it and no obligation to any individual ordinarily comes into existence from it alone. The negotiations between union and management result in what often has been called a trade agreement, rather than a contract of employment." . . .

However, the reasons compelling the courts and arbitrators to grant both specific performance and injunctive relief in collective bargaining agreements do not apply to contracts such as the one in question. A decree for the reinstatement of a nonresident manager in a public corporation is subject to all the obstacles and objections equity has always recognized, and is not justified by the special considerations that make this type of relief desirable in the collective bargaining area.

Matter of Ruppert (Egelhofer), *supra,* involving a collective bargaining agreement, is cited as upholding an arbitrator's award of equitable relief (injunction) where a court, under the same circumstances, would be powerless to act. However, as we view *Ruppert,* it is neither determinative nor controlling of the issues here.

Implicit in the *Ruppert* decision was a finding that not only had the parties authorized the imposition of equitable relief but that "nothing short of an injunction would have accomplished the evident intent of the parties that there be a speedy and immediately effective relief against strikes, lockouts and slowdowns."

Even if the agreement here authorizes specific performance of this contract, we are still of the opinion that the injunctive relief should not have been granted by the arbitrators. To hold otherwise is to state in effect that under this agreement the corporation itself could seek specific performance of a recalcitrant employee and that arbitrators could award specific performance compelling the employee to work for the corporation. Such a result would be clearly undesirable.

c. *In the Matter of the Arbitration between Grayson-Robinson Store Inc. and Iris Construction Corp.,* 8 N.Y.2d 133, 168 N.E.2d 377, 202 N.Y.S.2d 303 (1960)

DYE, FULD and FROESSEL, JJ., concur with Desmond, C. J.; VAN VOORHIS, J., dissents in an opinion in which BURKE and FOSTER, JJ., concur.

DESMOND, Chief Judge.

Again, as in *Matter of Stakliski* (Pyramid Elec. Co.), the courts are called upon to confirm an arbitration award which, conformably to the express powers given by the parties to the arbitrators, directed specific performance of a contract. Appellant, defaulting in performance and losing its case before the arbitrators, now argues to the courts . . . that enforcement of this award would be contrary to public policy. Specific performance of a contract to construct a building, argues appellant, is never ordered by courts of equity because of the necessity of continuous judicial supervision and control of performance. Therefore, so the argument runs, the same courts will not confirm and enforce an arbitration award which decrees specific performance of the same kind of agreement. We disagree. There is no hard and fast rule against applying the remedy of specific performance to such contracts, especially when the parties have by agreement provided for just that remedy.

In 1955 appellant Iris, owner of vacant land in Levittown, Nassau County, entered into a written agreement with respondent Grayson . . . whereby Iris undertook to erect on the Iris tract a building (part of a shopping center) to be rented by Iris to Grayson for use as a retail department store for a term of 25 years after completion with certain optional provisions for renewals of the term. Possession was to be turned over to Grayson "on or before September 1, 1957, time being of the essence." The agreement called for arbitration of all disputes and incorporated the rules of the American Arbitration Association which in terms empower the arbitrator in his award to grant any just or equitable remedy or relief "including specific performance."

There were several amendments and extensions of the original contract, but none of these are relevant to our discussion. The plans and specifications for the building were completed or practically completed, a public ground-breaking ceremony was held and excavation commenced, then Iris notified Grayson that because of difficulties in getting mortgage money, Iris could not go further unless Grayson agreed to increase the agreed rent. The tenant declined to pay more. The building has never been completed. . . .

At the arbitration and in the courts Iris has argued impossibility but the arbitrators disposed of that issue by ordering Iris to proceed forthwith with the improvements of the leased premises in accordance with the terms of the said lease, as amended. There was no proof before the arbitrators of any physical or actual impossibility as distinguished from difficulty of financing or additional expense of construction. . . .

The only ground suggested for such a refusal [to enforce the arbitration award] is that confirmation would involve the court in supervision of a complex and extended construction contract. We hold that this apprehension or speculation is no deterrent to confirmation by the courts.

There is, of course, an old tradition or approach according to which courts have been reluctant to enforce Contracts which require the performance of varied and continuous acts, or the exercise of special skill, taste, and judgment because the execution of the decree would require such constant superintendence as to make judicial control a matter of extreme difficulty. . . . There is no universal rule that courts of equity never will enforce a contract which requires some building to be done. They have enforced such contracts from the earliest days to the present time. On varying facts our New York decisions take one or the other position. Modern writers think that the difficulty of enforcement idea is exaggerated and that the trend is toward specific performance. Clearly there is no binding rule that deprives equity of jurisdiction to order specific performance of a building contract. At most there is discretion in the court to refuse such a decree. And here we do not even have an equity suit but a motion made as of right to confirm a completely valid arbitration award conforming in all respects to the express conferral of authority on the arbitrators and meeting all statutory requirements for confirmation. . . .

Arbitration is by consent and those who agree to arbitrate should be made to keep their solemn, written promises. . . . The courts should follow a liberal policy of promoting arbitration both to accord with the original intention of the parties and to ease the current congestion of court calendars. The judgment should be affirmed, with costs.

Van Voorhis, Judge (and two others), dissenting.

. . . The decision in the present case lends the enforcement machinery of the courts, to implement specific performance directed by arbitration that extends beyond any equitable relief which the courts have heretofore granted either on arbitrations or after trial. The mechanism for enforcement of this award of specific performance of a complicated construction contract for the erection of a building estimated to cost $5,000,000, is a judgment to be entered following confirmation of the award under section 1466 of the Civil Practice Act which provides that "The judgment so entered has the same force and effect, in all respects as, and is subject to all the provisions of law relating to, a judgment in an action; and it may be enforced as if it had been rendered in an action in the court in which it is entered." This signifies not that the arbitrators but that the court is the agency which will be called upon to supervise the construction of this elaborate and expensive building, and which will be required to do so by the very inappropriate remedy of punishment as for contempt of court. The plans and specifications, whether they have been finally approved by the parties or not, are not before the court and have been materially changed since the contract was made. They have been the subject of long and acrimonious disputes between the parties which are not likely to end with the entry of a judgment on this award for specific performance. . . .

These problems are neither solved nor diminished by the circumstance that this responsibility of supervision of the construction of this building has to be undertaken by the court as the result of an arbitration. If the arbitrators were to remain upon the scene and supervise and enforce the building operations which courts are not created to handle, the result might be different. Once the award has been confirmed and judgment of specific performance entered, the arbitrators depart and the court has to enforce the building contract by contempt proceedings against the appellant and the persons of its officers and agents. The court cannot look to the arbitrators to resolve disputes arising in the erection of this building, either of interpretation of the building contract, plans or specifications, or concerning performance. The theory on which judgment will be entered is that the award is final and definite so that the acts to be performed can be clearly ascertained and the court determine whether or not the performance rendered is in accord with the contractual duty assumed. In order to punish deviation from the specific performance directed, or to decide whether or in what respects there has been performance, substantial performance or nonperformance, the court will be unable to call in the arbitractors to interpret its decree or subrogate them to vindicate its dignity if its decree is violated.

The court cannot appoint a receiver as an arm of the court to take possession of the property and cause the work to be done. The unsatisfactoriness of contempt of court as the means of enforcement of transactions of this kind is augumented by the inability of the court to punish defaults that are not willful or deliberate.

While there is no universal rule that courts of equity never will enforce a contract which requires some building to be done, the question is practical rather than a matter of precedent and specific performance of construction projects can be decreed . . . where the possible differences between the parties over the performance of the undertaking are such as lie within a narrow compass, and which can be adjusted by the court. . . . But because this can be done in some instances does not mean that it can be done in all, nor does equitable jurisdiction in arbitrators signify that the courts will enforce anything that arbitrators may do especially if it is of a nature that has been held to be unenforcible by judicial decree.

The board of arbitration, without doubt, would have had jurisdiction to award damages to petitioners for any breach of this construction contract which has occurred but they were not asked to award damages. Petitioners told the arbitrators that they did not want damages but specific performance, which it is evident that the arbitrators granted pro forma . . . without considering whether the construction of this building by appellant had become impossible. They appear not to have understood that specific performance is not granted mechanically, that equity does not enforce idle ceremonies, that before making an award of this kind they had to rule upon whether performance had become impossible, and that if it was impossible petitioners would be relegated to damages.

The record before us indicates that appellant applied unsuccessfully to 27 different lending institutions in order to obtain the necessary mortgage money with which to erect this building. Petitioners appear to recognize that for this reason the building may not be constructed by appellant even after the entry of a specific performance decree. They profess an intention of suing for damages by the recovery of a fine to be imposed on appellant under section 773 of the Judiciary Law in case appellant is adjudged in contempt. This contention presents a double anomaly in that (1) if it is impossible for appellant to construct the building, its failure to do so would not be willful and, therefore, would not subject it to punishment for contempt, and (2) the board of arbitration is deprived of its function to assess damages which should have been claimed and awarded in the first instance in case they found specific performance by appellant to be impossible.

Therefore, even if confirmation were not denied to the specific performance award on account of difficulty in enforcement, the award should be vacated and the matter remitted to the arbitrators to rule upon whether specific performance by appellant is possible and, if they find it is not, to decide upon the question of damages.

d. Comments and Questions

1. Does the dissent question the power of the courts to proceed as the majority decides, or only the wisdom of doing so?

2. Before granting specific performance, should arbitrators be required to determine that specific performance is likely to occur without further recourse to the courts? If an affirmative finding is made, what should be the standard of review by the courts?

e. *Garrity v. Stuart*, 353 N.E.2d 793 (1976)

JASEN, FUCHSBERG and COOKE, JJ., concur with BREITEL, C.J.

GABRIELLI, J., dissents and votes to affirm in a separate opinion in which JONES and WACHTLER, JJ., concur.

BREITEL, Chief Judge.

Plaintiff author brought this proceeding under CPLR 7510 to confirm an arbitration award granting her $45,000 in compensatory damages and $7,500 in punitive damages against defendant publishing company. . . .

An arbitrator has no power to award punitive damages, even if agreed upon by the parties. Punitive damages is a sanction reserved to the State, a public policy of such magnitude as to call for judicial intrusion to prevent its contravention. Since enforcement of an award of punitive damages as a purely private remedy would violate strong public policy, an arbitrator's award which imposes punitive damages should be vacated.

Arbitrators generally are not bound by principles of substantive law or rules of evidence, and thus error of law or fact will not justify vacatur of an award. It is also true that arbitrators generally are free to fashion the remedy appropriate to the wrong, if they find one, but an authentic remedy is compensatory and measured by the harm caused and how it may be corrected. These broad principles are tolerable so long as arbitrators are not thereby empowered to ride roughshod over strong policies in the law which control coercive private conduct and confine to the State and its courts the infliction of punitive sanctions on wrongdoers.

The court will vacate an award enforcing an illegal agreement or one violative of public policy. Since enforcement of an award of punitive damages as a purely private remedy would violate public policy, an arbitrator's award which imposes punitive damages, even though agreed upon by the parties, should be vacated.

Matter of Associated Gen. Contrs., N.Y. State Chapter (Savin Bros.), is inapposite. That case did not involve an award of punitive damages. Instead, the court permitted enforcement of an arbitration award of treble liquidated damages, amounting to a penalty, assessed however in accordance with the express terms of a trade association membership agreement. The court held that the public policy against permitting the awarding of penalties was not of such magnitude as to call for judicial intrusion. In the instant case, however, there was no provision in the agreements permitting arbitrators to award liquidated damages or penalties. Indeed, the subject apparently had never ever been considered.

Even if the so-called malicious breach here involved would permit of the imposition of punitive damages by a court or jury, it was not the province of arbitrators to do so. Punitive sanctions are reserved to the State, surely a public policy of such magnitude as to call for judicial intrusion. The evil of permitting an arbitrator whose selection is often restricted or manipulatable by the party in a superior bargaining position, to award punitive damages is that it displaces the court and the jury, and therefore the State, as the engine for imposing a social sanction. The trouble with an arbitration admitting a power to grant unlimited damages by way of punishment is that if the court treated such an award in the way arbitration awards are usually treated, and followed the award to the letter, it would amount to an unlimited draft upon judicial power. . . .

Actual damage is measurable against some objective standard — the number of pounds, or days, or gallons or yards; but punitive damages take their shape from the subjective criteria involved in attitudes toward correction and reform, and courts do not accept readily the delegation of that kind of power. Where punitive damages have been allowed for those torts which are still regarded somewhat as public penal wrongs as well as actionable private wrongs, they have had rather close judicial supervision. If the usual rules were followed there would be no effective judicial supervision over punitive awards in arbitration.

Parties to arbitration agree to the substitution of a private tribunal for purposes of deciding their disputes without the expense, delay and rigidities of traditional courts. If arbitrators were allowed to impose punitive damages, the usefulness of arbitration would be destroyed. It would become a trap for the unwary given the eminently desirable freedom from judicial overview of law and facts. It would mean that the scope of determination by arbitrators, by the license to award punitive damages, would be both unpredictable and uncontrollable. It would lead to a Shylock principle of doing business without a Portia-like escape from the vise of a logic foreign to arbitration law.

In imposing penal sanctions in private arrangements, a tradition of the rule of law in organized society is violated. One purpose of the rule of law is to require that the use of coercion be controlled by the State. In a highly developed commercial and economic society the use of private force is not the danger, but the uncontrolled use of coercive economic sanctions in private arrangements. For centuries the power to punish has been a monopoly of the State, and not that of any private individual. The day is long past since barbaric man achieved redress by private punitive measures.

The parties never agreed or, for that matter, even considered punitive damages as a possible sanction for breach of the agreement. Here there is no pretense of agreement, although plaintiff author argues feebly that the issue of punitive damages was "waived" by failure to object originally to the demands for punitive damages, but only later to the award. The law does not and should not permit private persons to submit themselves to punitive sanctions of the order reserved to the State. The freedom of contract does not embrace the freedom to punish, even by contract. On this view, there was no power to waive the limitations on privately assessed punitive damages and, of course, no power to agree to them by the failure to object to the demand for arbitration.

Under common-law principles, there is eventual supervision of jury awards of punitive damages, in the singularly rare cases where it is permitted, by the trial court's power to change awards and by the Appellate Division's power to modify such awards. That the award of punitive damages in this case was quite modest is immaterial. Such a happenstance is not one on which to base a rule.

Accordingly, the order of the Appellate Division should be modified, without costs, to vacate so much of the award which imposes punitive damages, and otherwise affirmed.

GABRIELLI, Judge (dissenting).

[T]he majority reaches a result favoring a guileful defendant and voids a just and rational award of punitive damages to a wholly innocent and deserving plaintiff. Stripped to its essence the defendant, by willful and fraudulent guises, refused to pay plaintiff royalties known to be due and owing to her; forced her to commence actions claiming fraudulent acts and to enforce arbitration to redress the wrongs done to her and to collect the sums rightfully due; and, finally, defendant waived any objection to the claim for punitive damages, deliberately refused to participate in the arbitration hearing and abruptly left the hearing without moving against the claim for punitive damages or even so much as offering any countervailing evidence or argument on the merits of plaintiff's claims. I cannot, therefore, join with the majority and conclude, as they now do, that the ultimate limit of the damages awardable to plaintiff is that sum which was unquestionably due and owing to her in any event under the royalty agreement.

The basic issue presented for our determination is whether, in an arbitration proceeding brought pursuant to a contract containing a broad arbitration clause, an award of punitive damages is violative of public policy. . . . The agreements contained identical, broad arbitration clauses which provide:

> "Any controversy or claim arising out of this agreement or the breach or interpretation thereof shall be determined by arbitration in accordance with the rules then obtaining of the American Arbitration Association, and judgment upon the award may be entered in the highest court of the forum, State or Federal, having jurisdiction." . . .

I would reject the notion that this award of punitive damages is violative of public policy. We have only recently treated with a somewhat similar argument in *Matter of Associated Gen. Contrs., N.Y. State Chapter* (Savin Bros.). There we considered the effect of a public policy argument against penalty awards with respect to an arbitration commenced by a national trade association in the construction industry against one of its employer-members pursuant to the provisions of a broad arbitration clause contained in the association agreement. Specifically at issue was whether an arbitration award of treble liquidated damages, assessed in accordance with the express terms of the agreement, was enforceable. We held that since the arbitration was in consequence of a broad arbitration clause and concerned no third-party interests which could be said to transcend the concerns of the parties to the arbitration, there was present no question involving public policy of such magnitude as to call for judicial intrusion. . . .

The case at bar falls within the rationale and rule of the *Associated Gen. Contrs.* case. Controlling here, as there, is the fact that the arbitration clause is broad indeed; there are no third-party interests involved; and the public policy against punitive damages is not so commanding that the Legislature has found it necessary to embody that policy into law, especially one that would apply to all cases involving such damages irrespective of the amount sought, the relative size of the award, or the punishable actions of the parties. Or, put another way, the public policy which favors the peaceful resolutions of disputes through arbitration outweighs the public policy disfavoring the assessment of punitive damages in this instance, where the unjustifiable conduct complained of is found to be with malice. I would conclude, therefore, that any public policy limiting punitive damage awards does not rise to that level of significance in this case as to require judicial intervention.

The majority would distinguish the *Associated Gen. Contrs.* case upon the thin ground that the enforcement of a treble liquidated damages clause which was applicable to numerous nationwide contracts that conceivably could have amounted to astronomical sums is not the equivalent of the enforcement of an award of penalty damages. . . . *Associated Gen. Contrs.* is not only apposite but is controlling. . . .

An affirmance here would do no violence to precedents in this court. In at least two varied circumstances we have held that although public policy would bar a civil suit for relief, that same public policy was not of such overriding import as to preclude confirmation of an arbitration award. *Matter of Staklinski* (Pyramid Elec. Co.); *Matter of Ruppert* (Egelhofer). In Ruppert was permitted the enjoining of a work stoppage in a labor dispute by arbitration despite the fact that the issuance of such relief by a court was prohibited by statute. Similarly, in *Staklinski*, citing *Ruppert*, we upheld an arbitration award of specific performance of an employment contract in the face of the public policy against compelling a corporation to continue the services of an officer whose services were unsatisfactory to the board of directors. The rule to be distilled from these cases, therefore, is that only where the public interest clearly supersedes the concerns of the parties should courts intervene and assert exclusive dominion over disputes in arbitration. . . .

f. Comments and Questions

1. Note that the contract at issue in *Garrity v. Stuart* (to be precise, two contracts with identical arbitration provisions) was silent about punitive damages. Would you favor a rule that permitted an arbitrator to award punitive damages when expressly authorized by the underlying contract, but not otherwise?

2. In most jurisdictions, and under the FAA, arbitrators are empowered to award punitive damages. Where that is the rule, should effect be given to a contract provision that expressly prohibits the awarding of punitive damages? New York continues to follow *Garrity v. Stuart*, notwithstanding that this is the minority position, and that the original case was a 4-3 decision.

3. Concerns often are expressed about excessive awards of punitive damages but the usual culprits are juries not arbitrators. Can you recall reading or hearing of any instance where an arbitrator awarded inappropriately high punitive damages? The award in *Garrity v. Stuart* was actual damages of $45,000 plus punitive damages of $7,500.

4. Does the majority or the dissent have the better of the argument regarding the *Associated General Contractors* case?

5. The majority opinion notes that a party with superior bargaining power might be able to obtain punitive damages, pursuant to a contract provision, when it would be unlikely to get punitives from a court. Is this or the obverse the likely scenario in *Garrity v. Stuart?* In dealings between authors and publishers, who typically has the greater bargaining power? Whose contract forms are commonly used?

6. What groups or classes of persons benefit from rules that permit or prohibit punitive damages? Which have the power to retain counsel to draft form agreements, and then require their use by others?

g. *In the Matter of the Arbitration between SCM Corp. and Fisher Park Lane Co.*, 358 N.E.2d 1024 (N.Y. 1976)

BREITEL, C.J., and JASEN and WACHTLER, JJ., concur with JONES, J.

FUCHSBERG, J., concurs in result in a separate opinion.

COOKE, J., dissents and votes to reverse in another separate opinion in which GABRIELLI, J., concurs.

JONES, Judge.

We hold that, for purposes of applying the Statute of Limitations, a landlord's counterclaim to the tenant's demands for recovery of overpayment of rent (where that counterclaim is based on the assertion that the lease between them should be reformed) does not arise "from the transactions, occurrences, or series of transactions or occurrences" upon which the tenant's claim for overpayment of rent depends. Accordingly in this instance, the landlord's attempted supplemental submission to arbitration of its claim for relief in the nature of reformation was properly stayed, on timely application of the tenant, as being barred by the six-year Statute of Limitations. We also hold that, were the landlord's counterclaim to be reached, an arbitrator would have power under a broad arbitration clause to grant appropriate relief including that similar to the remedy of reformation in equity. It was thus error below to grant the stay of arbitration on the alternative ground that the specific relief sought therein would not have been available.

In June, 1966 the parties entered into an agreement by which the tenant leased several floors of a commercial building from the landlord for a term of 50 years commencing February 28, 1968. The agreement provided a fixed rent, made subject in section 2.02 to annual adjustments equal to 17.73% of changes in real estate taxes and expenses incurred on the building over "Base Taxes" and an "Expense Base Factor" as those terms were defined. Also included was an arbitration clause by which the parties agreed that "if there be any dispute between Landlord and Tenant with respect to the provisions of this Section 2.02, the issue shall be expeditiously submitted to the American Arbitration Association for determination."

After the tenant had entered upon the premises it was advised on August 6, 1969 of a rent escalation due to an increase in taxes for the 1969-1970 tax year and on September 21, 1970 of an escalation resulting from an increase in operating expenses during the fiscal year ended

November 30, 1969. The requested payments were made without objection as were increases for each due for expense increases for the tenant included a reservation of its right to year ended November 30, 1972 and for tax increases for the 1973-1974 tax year the tenant included a reservation of its right to disagree with the escalations imposed.

On February 15, 1974 the tenant served a demand for arbitration of claims that the landlord's calculation of the "Expense Base Factor" and the annual increments in expenses through 1972 had been improper and that the landlord had violated section 2.02 of the lease insofar as taxes on the property were concerned. Arbitration was postponed during settlement negotiations and after their collapse until it was judicially determined that the landlord was barred by lapse of time from making an application for a stay of arbitration. Shortly before the first arbitration hearing, scheduled for January 19, 1976, the landlord filed an amended answer in the arbitration proceedings in which it asserted a "Fifth Defense" by which it sought for the first time in effect to have the lease rewritten so as to raise the tenant's liability for increases in electricity expense from 17.73%, as specified in the agreement, to 24.98%, asserted to be the tenant's proportionate share of such expenses. The tenant then promptly instituted the present proceeding for a stay of arbitration of the alleged defense asserting that the reformation sought was beyond the power of the arbitrators and in any event, not having been sought until almost 10 years after the execution of the lease, was barred by the Statute of Limitations. . . .

By virtue of CPLR 7503 (subd. (b)) the tenant is entitled to a stay of arbitration of the landlord's claim for relief if "the claim sought to be arbitrated would have been barred by limitation of time had it been asserted in a court of the state." The landlord's counterclaim falls precisely within this description. . . . The particular form of remedy sought by what is denominated the fifth defense stated in respondent's answer is a rewriting of the terms of the lease agreement with a concurrent determination of liability on the part of the tenant for additional rent in consequence of such revision of the instrument. Were the landlord to seek such relief in a judicial proceeding, it would be barred by the six-year limitation provided by CPLR 213 (subd. 1) for an action for which no other limitation is fixed by law. . . .

What the landlord asserts in this present instance is not a defense—that is, a bar to the claim asserted by the tenant—but is in the nature of a counterclaim, i.e., a statement of circumstances which in and of themselves may form the basis of an adjudication of affirmative relief in favor of the landlord on its claim, irrespective of the tenant's success or failure on the latter's cause of action. The landlord's repeated insistence that it seeks relief on its request for reformation only in the event that the arbitrator considers the tenant's claim for refund of overpayment of rent serves simply to make the assertion of its demand for relief contingent; it does not vary the nature of the remedy pursued.

Nor is the landlord's reliance on CPLR 203 well founded. That section excludes from the bar of limitations, but only to the extent of plaintiff's claim, counterclaims even if they would have been barred at the time of the commencement of the action, provided that the counterclaim be one that "arose from the transactions, occurrences, or series of transactions or occurrences, upon which a claim asserted in the complaint depends." Here, however, respondent's claim for reformation is not in the nature of recoupment, the equitable doctrine in which the statutory provision is grounded. It does not seek a recovery-back predicated on some act or fact growing out of the matter constituting the cause or ground of the action brought, but is instead a setoff—a separate and distinct claim in favor of the landlord. The tenant's demand for refund of rent overpayment is predicated on acts of the landlord related to, or by which it computed and assessed, escalations of rent after the term of the lease commenced in February, 1968; the landlord's demand for reformation is grounded on allegations as to the intention of the contracting parties prior to and at the time the lease was executed with respect to the proportionate share of electrical expense to be borne by the tenant. The tenant's claim relates to performance under the contract; the landlord's relates to the negotiation and articulation of the agreement made between the parties prior to its execution. While in a most general sense both might be said to be associated with the lease, in the language of CPLR 203, the claims do not arise out of the same transactions or occurrences.

Since the landlord's counterclaim for relief in the nature of reformation of the 1966 contract, if asserted in a law action in 1974, would have been barred by the Statute of Limitations, the tenant has properly been granted a stay of arbitration under CPLR 7503.

We find no merit in the landlord's contentions that the tenant by initiating arbitration authorizing that remedy and by participating therein for two years has waived any right to challenge respondent's demand that the arbitrator reform the lease. First, it may be observed that there has been no participation in arbitration of respondent's demand for reformation by petitioner, which moved promptly after receipt of the amended answer to stay arbitration of that claim. Neither may petitioner be said to have waived its right to challenge the arbitrability of the claim for reformation by virtue of the fact that it initiated the arbitration process. On timely application and absent participation in arbitration proceedings without challenge to the matters introduced, there is no basis for barring a party who has sought arbitration from thereafter seeking judicial determination as to arbitrability of matter set forth in an answer which would expand the scope of the arbitration.

Finally, because the issue has been briefed and argued expansively by the parties in this action, was explicitly addressed by the court below, and is one on which lower courts have differed, we take this occasion to express our disagreement with the position articulated by the Appellate Division that arbitrators have no power under a broad arbitration clause to grant what we would think of as the remedy of reformation. Arbitrators have power to fashion remedies appropriate to the resolution of the dispute between the parties before them. To the extent that relief in the nature of reformation might be deemed an appropriate remedy for the controversies existing between this tenant and this landlord, the award of such a remedy would fall within the authority of arbitrators acting under a broad arbitration clause. "It is customary and appropriate for arbitrators to pass upon claims for reformation for mutual mistake, often applying principles more liberal than judicial equity." The function of arbitrators is to "find a just solution" to the controversy between the parties; to that end it will be for them to "fashion the remedy appropriate to the wrong." Moreover, the rules of the American Arbitration Association adopted by the parties now before the court expressly provide that "(t)he Arbitrator may grant any remedy or relief which he deems just and equitable and within the scope of the agreement of the parties."

In arbitration parties seek the resolution of differences which have arisen between them in concrete factual settings free from the requirements and expectations familiar to judicial proceedings with respect both to the formulation of pleadings and causes of action and to historical and current legal theories as to the availability of remedies. The awards of arbitrators are not subject to judicial review for errors of law or of fact. Nor should there be the control which would flow from the exercise of such power of review. Submissions are for determinations based on the ad hoc application of broad principles of justice and fairness in the particular instance. Reliance is not placed on continuity of tribunal personnel or operation. Predictability is not an objective and awards do not have, nor is it intended that they should have, the precedential value that we attach to judicial determinations. Thus analytical structure and synthesis take on a different function. In the present context, for instance, it would be unimportant whether an arbitrator were to formulate his resolution of the landlord's claim for increased additional rent in a conclusion that the initial intent of the parties was that the percentage figure in the lease be higher and accordingly that the lease should be rewritten to manifest that intent, or, on the other hand, in a determination that in all the circumstances justice dictated that the differences between the parties should be disposed as though the percentage figure had been higher. This is not to suggest that awards are not based on analysis, logic and experience. It is to say that the channels of legal procedure and thought understandably may often be found to be lacking, or at least not determinative.

We hold that in the absence of contrary public policy *(cf., Garrity v. Lyle Stuart, Inc.)* or an express provision in the arbitration agreement otherwise limiting his authority, the arbitrator of the disputes between these parties would have the power to grant relief which in the courts would be called reformation by rewriting the provisions of the lease. Because, however, the claim of the landlord for which such relief is sought is barred by the Statute of Limitations, the order staying arbitration of that claim should be affirmed.

FUCHSBERG, Judge, concurring.

I too vote for affirmance; however, I cannot concur with the majority's suggestion that reformation is an arbitral issue. . . .

[R]eliance upon prior decisions of this court holding that arbitrators may "fashion the remedy appropriate to the wrong" begs the question of whether the claim to be arbitrated is within the scope of the arbitration clause. Only if the claim is encompassed by the clause do the arbitrators have discretion to grant the relief they deem proper. Thus, rule 42 of the American Arbitration Association provides that the arbitrator may "grant any remedy or relief which he deems just and equitable and within the scope of the agreement."

"(G)iven the eminently desirable freedom from judicial overview of law and facts" prevailing in arbitration, the caution against making the proceedings a trap for the unwary, recently expressed by this court in holding that arbitrators lack the power to award punitive damages *(Garrity v. Lyle Stuart, Inc.)* is equally applicable here. The power of reformation would likewise "mean that the scope of determination by arbitrators . . . would be both unpredictable and uncontrollable."

COOKE, Judge, dissenting.

I concur in the reasoning of the majority to the extent that it holds that, were it to reach the landlord's counterclaim, an arbitrator would have the power under a broad arbitration clause to grant the landlord's claim for reformation. I dissent, however, because, I submit, the Statute of Limitations should not be applied to bar the landlord's Fifth Defense in arbitration.

With respect to counterclaims, the relevant portion of the statute provides: "if the defense or counterclaim arose from the transactions, occurrences, or series of transactions or occurrences, upon which a claim asserted in the complaint depends, it is not barred to the extent of the demand in the complaint notwithstanding that it was barred at the time the claims asserted in the complaint were interposed." (CPLR 203)

The above-quoted portion of the statute codifies the doctrine of equitable recoupment. The doctrine could be invoked under prior law, but the CPLR has expanded its application. . . . [A] counterclaim of recoupment is permitted on any claim arising out of the same transaction. Moreover, recoupment does not depend upon any distinctions between defense, counterclaim, setoff and recoupment

The majority states that the landlord's claim is not in the nature of recoupment, that it does not seek a recovery predicated on the same act or fact growing out of the tenant's claim, but rather is "a separate and distinct claim." In support of its position, the majority adds that the tenant's claim relates to "performance under the contract," but the landlord's claim relates to "negotiation and articulation . . . prior to its execution." From this, the majority concludes that the claims do not arise out of the same transactions or occurrences. It is precisely this type of conceptualism that CPLR 203 was intended to eliminate.

The words "same transaction or occurrence" should be broadly construed. The majority's construction is too narrow. The tenant's claims relate to whether the landlord computed additional rent in accordance with the lease; the landlord's counterclaim relates to the question of what were the correct percentages to be used in computing such rent. Contrary to the view expressed by the majority, both claims arose from the same transaction—the negotiation of the terms of the lease. That the tenant claims overpayment resulting from the landlord's acts after execution of the lease does not alter the fact that both claims relate to what the parties intended in their negotiations. The landlord's claim is thus one for equitable recoupment and, if found valid by the arbitrators, should be allowed to the extent of the tenant's claim. Accordingly, the Statute of Limitations should not be held to bar the landlord's counterclaim in the arbitration proceeding.

2. Remedial Authority of Arbitrators in General

a. Comments and Questions

1. Based on the cases and disputes considered so far, the reader might be excused for concluding that the substantive issues presented to arbitrators for decision are pretty straight forward, and that sensible results can be rendered easily. The next two cases demonstrate that complex comercial cases commonly raise very difficult problems for arbitrators.

2. As you read the *Tretina* case, try to determine precisely what the arbitrator decided.

3. The contractual basis of arbitration extends to choice of remedies. Remedial provisions in an arbitration agreement might be so one-sided as to be unconscionable, make provision for an illegal remedy (*e.g.*, punitive damages in New York), or be so extreme as to preclude enforcement. Apart from such limitations, the parties are free to contract for a particular type or set of remedies.

4. A well-known example of specialized and limited remedial provisions is "baseball arbitration." In disputes between major league baseball teams and players eligible for arbitration, each party picks a salary figure to be paid to the player for the next season. The arbitrator must select one of these numbers. Unlike with most arbitrations, no compromise is permitted.

b. *In re Arbitration Between Tretina Printing, Inc. v. Fitzpatrick & Assocs., Inc.*, 640 A.2d 788 (N.J. 1994)

CLIFFORD, J., filed concurring opinion; STEIN, J., filed dissenting opinion, in which HANDLER and O'HERN, JJ., joined.

Per Curiam.

This appeal and cross-appeal arise out of an arbitrator's award in a construction-management-contract dispute. The Chancery Division modified and confirmed the award. The Appellate Division reversed and vacated the award. We . . . now reverse the judgment of the Appellate Division and reinstate the arbitrator's award. Moreover, the Court adopts as a rule governing judicial review of private-contract arbitration awards the standard set forth in the Chief Justice's concurring opinion in *Perini v. Greate Bay Hotel & Casino, Inc.*, 129 N.J. 479, 610 A.2d 364 (1992).

I

Fitzpatrick & Associates, Inc. (Fitzpatrick) entered into a contract with Tretina Printing Corporation (Tretina) for the design and construction of a printing plant and office building. The parties agreed to a "guaranteed maximum price" (GMP) of $2,566,050, which reflected a guarantee by Fitzpatrick that the total cost of the project, including any corrective work and a construction-management fee, would not exceed that sum. The contract provided that Tretina would pay Fitzpatrick a $200,000 construction-manager's fee (provided that Fitzpatrick did not breach the contract) as part of the total cost. If the cost of the completed project exceeded the GMP, Fitzpatrick would absorb those costs itself. If the total cost turned out to be less than the GMP, then Tretina would turn over to Fitzpatrick thirty percent of the savings as well as the construction-management fee.

In addition, the contract contained a provision for "retainage," under which Tretina was entitled to withhold payment to Fitzpatrick of a sum equal to 150% of the estimated cost of completing any unfinished or unsatisfactory work. On completion of that work, Tretina would become obligated to pay Fitzpatrick the amount it had retained to cover the potential cost. Lastly, the contract specifically provided that "all claims, disputes, and other matters . . . arising out of, or relating to, this Agreement or the breach thereof . . . shall be decided by arbitration" and that the arbitrator's decision "shall be final. . . ."

When Tretina failed to pay one of Fitzpatrick's requisitions, Fitzpatrick filed a claim for arbitration; Tretina cross-claimed because of Fitzpatrick's allegedly deficient and incomplete work in several areas of the construction. By that time, Tretina had paid Fitzpatrick $2,119,819. Thus, under the contract terms, at the time that the parties began arbitration, Tretina was liable for up to $446,231 of all of the remaining construction costs, including the cost of corrective work and Fitzpatrick's construction management fee of $200,000.

The arbitrator, appointed by the American Arbitration Association, conducted twenty-two arbitration sessions over a one-year period, heard twenty-one witnesses, and reviewed 222 exhibits before issuing his written award. The award contained two lists consisting of Fitzpatrick's claims and Tretina's claims. Next to each item on the list the arbitrator either assigned a dollar amount, directed Fitzpatrick to complete or to pay for the cost of completing the claimed deficiency, or denied the claim. The "TOTAL AWARD TO FITZPATRICK" was $269,912.34 and the "TOTAL AWARD TO TRETINA" was $520,180.00, leaving a "TOTAL NET AWARD TO TRETINA" of $260,267.66.

Tretina moved for an order confirming the award and Fitzpatrick moved for an order vacating or modifying it. In a written decision, the Chancery Division modified the award and confirmed it as modified. Although the trial court made a few minor changes, it deferred to the arbitrator's judgment on all but one issue, namely, retainage. The arbitrator had listed

Fitzpatrick's fourth claim as: 4. Retainage: Construction management fee, $100,000; interest at 10% for 33 months, $27,500. Total of $127,500.

As the trial court observed, the construction-management fee is entirely different from retainage. In addition, the court explained that retainage was not a separate claim; rather, it was a fund held by Tretina, who was required to pay it to Fitzpatrick "only if [Fitzpatrick] did not breach its contract and only to the extent that approved work did not require repair or redoing." Thus, according to the court, after the arbitrator calculated the damages that Fitzpatrick owed Tretina, he should have treated the retainage as a credit against those damages because Tretina has never paid over the retained money. The court reasoned that the arbitrator had either overlooked the retainage claim or had assumed that Tretina's award would be offset by the retainage amount to which Fitzpatrick was entitled. Thus, after reducing somewhat the arbitrator's net award to Tretina, the trial court reduced that award by $201,148, the "accumulated retainage" claimed by Fitzpatrick, bringing Tretina's net award down to $61,369.66.

Tretina appealed to the Appellate Division, claiming that the trial court had mistakenly exercised its discretion in modifying the award and in not requiring the arbitrator to clarify his award. Fitzpatrick cross-appealed, arguing that the award was so defective that the Chancery Division should have vacated it. The Appellate Division, after conducting a detailed analysis of the contract and of the arbitration proceedings, concluded that of the two judicial remedies, modification or vacation of the award, provided by the [New Jersey] Arbitration Act (the Act), modification was not available because "the award ignores the basic contours of the parties' contract, decides some submitted disputes contrary to the evidence, and completely fails to decide others." The court therefore vacated the award. Id. at 53, 619 A.2d 1037. In reaching that decision the Appellate Division relied on Perini.

II

The Act provides that once an arbitrator issues an award, any party to the arbitration may seek confirmation of that award in the Superior Court within three months of the arbitrator's decision. If the trial court does not confirm the award, it can either vacate the award, or modify or correct it. However, the statute narrowly defines the circumstances under which a court may resort to those remedies.

Under the Act a court shall vacate an arbitration award: a. Where the award was procured by corruption, fraud or undue means; b. Where there was either evident partiality or corruption in the arbitrators, or any thereof; c. Where the arbitrators were guilty of misconduct in refusing to postpone the hearing, upon sufficient cause being shown therefor, or in refusing to hear evidence, pertinent and material to the controversy, or of any other misbehaviors prejudicial to the rights of any party; d. Where the arbitrators exceeded or so imperfectly executed their powers that a mutual, final and definite award upon the subject matter submitted was not made. When an award is vacated and the time within which the agreement required the award to be made has not expired, the court may, in its discretion, direct a rehearing by the arbitrators.

The Act also provides that a court shall modify or correct an award: a. Where there was an evident miscalculation of figures or an evident mistake in the description of a person, thing or property referred to therein; b. Where the arbitrators awarded upon a matter not submitted to them unless it affects the merits of the decision upon the matter submitted; and c. Where the award is imperfect in a matter of form not affecting the merits of the controversy. The court shall modify and correct the award, to effect the intent thereof and promote justice between the parties.

The Chancery Division confirmed and modified this arbitrator's award [as] . . . "imperfect in a matter of form not affecting the merits of the controversy." In reversing, the Appellate Division relied on [the requirement that] a court must vacate any award that has been procured by "corruption, fraud, or undue means," or in which the arbitrator "so exceeded or imperfectly executed [his] powers" that his award on the matter submitted was not "mutual, final, and definite." . . . The Appellate Division vacated the award under what it termed "the Perini standard," and the parties' arguments revolve around whether that "standard," which today we reject, has been met in this case.

Perini involved a contract dispute between Perini Corporation as construction manager and Greate Bay Hotel & Casino as owner. Perini contended that the arbitrators had failed to observe "settled principles of contract law" in the calculation of the owner's lost profits from its hotel and casino business. Perini alleged that the arbitrators had erred by including delay damages in the owner's award. It argued that the damages had not been contemplated by the parties, that they included lost profits based on delays that had been experienced after substantial completion of the project, and that the damages were speculative and disproportionate. It urged that those mistakes of law constituted a sufficient basis on which to vacate the award. Although the plurality opinion acknowledged the persuasiveness of Perini's arguments, it nevertheless concluded that the arbitrators' calculation of the award could find a basis in the evidence. Even though the plurality members were troubled by the magnitude of the award, they were satisfied that the arbitrators had not manifestly disregarded any undebatable principle of law, and thus they upheld the award.

In reviewing the narrow circumstances in which a court can vacate an arbitration award, the Perini plurality concluded that the "undue means" and "exceeded their powers" provisions of the statute embraced egregious mistakes of law; thus, a court could vacate an arbitrator's award on that basis. The plurality members emphasized, however, that they did not intend "that the arbitrators be judges or that their decisions be subject to the same appellate supervision as those of judges." Rather, the scope of judicial review should be limited. "Thus, in private-sector arbitration an arbitrator's determination of a legal issue should be sustained as long as the determination is reasonably debatable." The plurality opinion concluded that the purpose of a court's review is to guard against arbitrator errors that on their face are undebatable, unmistakable, gross, or in manifest disregard of the applicable law. Thus, the plurality in Perini would allow a court to vacate an award when an arbitrator makes a mistake in respect of an undebatable point of law. The plurality opinion articulated the appropriate standard of judicial review as follows: Whether the arbitrators are viewed as having acted with "undue means" or having "exceeded their powers," the judicial inquiry must go beyond a search for mere mistakes of law. Were we to decide otherwise, arbitration would simply become another form of private non-jury trial. . . . That formulation requires that the arbitrators must have clearly intended to decide according to law, must have clearly mistaken the legal rule, and that mistake must appear on the face of the award. In addition, the error, to be fatal, must result in a failure of intent or be so gross as to suggest fraud or misconduct.

The Chief Justice, concurring in the judgment in *Perini,* would have even further restricted the courts' role in reviewing voluntary private-sector arbitration awards. (Wilentz, C.J., concurring). His concurring opinion argued that "[a]rbitration awards should be what they were always intended to be: final, not subject to judicial review absent fraud, corruption, or similar wrongdoing on the part of the arbitrators." Thus in most cases the Chief Justice would not vacate an award even though it might be based on a mistake of law. The concurrence urged that the statute reflected that interpretation of the law, and that the Court should overturn precedent that was inconsistent with the rule that the Chief Justice advocated.

Finally, the dissenters in *Perini* agreed with the plurality's standard but disagreed with the result that should be reached by applying that standard to the parties' claims. (Stein, J., concurring in part and dissenting in part).

Therefore, although a majority of those who sat in *Perini* agreed on the controlling standard, they could not agree on its application to the circumstances of that case. In this case as well we do not achieve unanimity in respect of the correct standard of review or in the result; but a majority of the Court now agrees that the correct standard of review is not that adopted by five members who sat in *Perini* (Justices Clifford, Handler, O'Hern, and Stein, and Judge Keefe, temporarily assigned), but rather the standard set forth in the Chief Justice's opinion concurring in the judgment in *Perini,* in which Judge Arnold Stein, temporarily assigned, joined.

That standard is as follows: Basically, arbitration awards may be vacated only for fraud, corruption, or similar wrongdoing on the part of the arbitrators. [They] can be corrected or modified only for very specifically defined mistakes. . . . If the arbitrators decide a matter not even submitted to them, that matter can be excluded from the award. For those who think the parties are entitled to a greater share of justice, and that such justice exists only in the care of the court, I would hold that the parties are free to expand the scope of judicial review by providing for such expansion in their contract; that they may, for example, specifically provide that the arbitrators shall render their decision only in conformance with New Jersey law, and that such awards may be reversed either for mere errors of New Jersey law, substantial errors, or gross errors of New Jersey law and define therein what they mean by that. I doubt if many will. And if they do, they should abandon arbitration and go directly to the law courts.

Because the record before us contains not even a hint of misconduct by the arbitrator, and because no statutory ground exists for invalidating or modifying the award, we uphold the arbitrator's award. In doing so, we need not confront the parties' arguments that focus on the *Perini* plurality opinion, given our rejection of the standard announced therein. Nor need we rehash the extensive treatment that the pertinent authorities were given in the contesting opinions in *Perini,* for we cannot improve on the arguments included therein. Three members now join the Chief Justice in the views expressed in his *Perini* concurrence, which therefore requires reinstatement of the arbitrator's award. We announce our adoption of the new standard governing review of arbitration awards so that parties who resort to private-party arbitration may be guided accordingly, not because the outcome in this appeal turns on which standard we apply. It does not. We are satisfied that under either standard the result would be the same.

III

Which brings us to the dissent. A decent respect for our dissenting colleague's thoughtful opinion, which would lead to a remand to the arbitrator for clarification (a result both parties resisted at oral argument before us), impels us to explicate our differing view in some detail.

The dissent's reliance on [the miscalculation provision of the Act] as a basis for a remand is misplaced. That section . . . covers cases in which the award contains "an evident miscalculation of figures or an evident mistake in the description of a person, thing or property referred to therein." The clear purpose of that section is to enable the court to correct simple arithmetical errors, such as 2 + 2 = 5, or obvious mistakes in identification, such as 14 Hill Street instead of 41 Hill Street.

The dissent argues that the arbitration award in this case is ambiguous. We agree. The perceived ambiguity in the award arises from the arbitrator's allocation of the retainage sum allegedly due Fitzpatrick. Our dissenting colleague suggests that the retainage issue presents an "evident miscalculation of figures" requiring judicial action. Yet as the dissent explains, the arbitrator did not make a simple mistake in his addition or subtraction; rather the contention is that he omitted entirely one of the party's claims. Although we cannot determine from the face of the award whether the arbitrator erred in his dealing with the retainage, we are confident that any such error does not constitute a mere "miscalculation" and is by no means "evident." We refuse to shoehorn this case into a category in which it clearly does not fit simply because we discern either an absence of specificity in the arbitrator's analysis or an ambiguity in the arbitrator's treatment of that claim.

Moreover, [the Act] directs a court to correct errors; it does not provide for a remand to the arbitrator. In addition, [the Act] directs a court to modify an award only if those changes will not affect the merits of the controversy. The clear implication is that the Legislature intended that courts correct mistakes that are obvious and simple—errors that can be fixed without a remand and without the services of an experienced arbitrator. Thus, even if the alleged error in this case did constitute an "evident miscalculation," the proper action for the court would be to correct it, not to remand to the arbitrator.

Beyond that, we disagree as well with the dissent's contention that the power of courts to resubmit ambiguous awards to arbitrators for clarification is "well-settled." On the contrary, in the absence of a statutory provision or an authorization in the arbitration agreement, a court that is asked to vacate, modify, or confirm an award usually has no power, except by the consent of the parties, to recommit the matter to the arbitrator. Resubmission is foreclosed because with the rendering of an award, an arbitrator exhausts his or her commission. In fact, our research discloses only one case in which a court relied exclusively on its inherent power to resubmit an ambiguous award to the arbitrator, *La Vale Plaza, Inc. v. R.S. Noonan, Inc.*, 378 F.2d 569 (3d Cir.1967), and that case is readily distinguishable from the one before us. . . .

Nor are the federal labor-law cases persuasive authority here. As did the Illinois Supreme Court in *Rauh v. Rockford Products Corp.*, 574 N.E.2d 636 (1991), we decline to follow those cases on review of a commercial arbitration award. The Illinois court looked instead to the Illinois Uniform Arbitration Act, which specifies the grounds for vacating or modifying an award.

Moreover, the federal labor-law cases address the federal courts' authority under § 301 of the Labor-Management Relations Act, 29 U.S.C.A. § 185, to enforce collective-bargaining agreements that contain arbitration clauses. The United States Supreme Court has interpreted that section as conferring on the federal courts broad latitude for fashioning a body of substantive law from the policy of the national labor laws. The fundamental goal of those labor laws is to curtail industrial strife and work stoppages through the arbitration of grievances.

Arbitration in the context of a labor dispute differs from private-contract arbitration in important ways. Parties enter commercial contracts voluntarily. They act without any compulsion to deal with each other instead of with some other party. The arbitration clause in their contracts represents a way to settle disputes informally should any arise. In a labor agreement, however, the parties must deal with each other. They have no choice. In that circumstance the agreement to arbitrate is vital to keeping the relationship between the parties afloat and guided by a set of agreed-to rules. In a commercial contract, arbitration is produced by a breakdown in the parties' agreement. The parties use it as a last resort. In the labor arena, arbitration serves as the machinery under a collective-bargaining agreement that is "at the very heart of the system of industrial self-government." Accordingly, the decisions of the federal courts reflect a strong preference for settling all aspects of labor disputes through the arbitration process. Therefore, if a union and management cannot agree on the scope of an arbitration award or on the method of enforcing the award, courts, seeking to defer to the arbitration process, may resubmit the issue to the arbitrator for clarification. Resubmission is based not on any explicit provision in a federal statute but rather on the underlying policy of advancing industrial peace.

We acknowledge that in limited circumstances a court can remand to an arbitrator for reconsideration or clarification. For example, in *Jersey City Police Officers Benevolent Ass'n v. City of Jersey City,* the Appellate Division properly directed the trial court to resubmit one issue to the arbitrator where it "had been neither submitted to nor decided by the arbitrator" in the initial proceedings. The arbitrator had not exercised his powers relating to that issue, so his authority had never expired. Likewise, if the obligations under an award are unclear to the parties, a court may resubmit the question to the arbitrator for clarification. The purpose of those types of resubmissions is to allow the arbitrator to settle all the issues without judicial encroachment on the arbitration process, not to explain how the arbitrator arrived at the conclusions contained in the award.

In the case before us, however, the arbitrator has settled all the disputed issues. We may remain uncertain about the analysis that led to the stated result on one discrete issue, the retainage question; but asking an arbitrator to explain his or her reasoning works against the very goals of arbitration: finality and expedition. Remands for reconsideration or further explanation threaten the reliability of arbitration awards. Moreover, requiring an arbitrator to justify a decision reflects a lack of faith in the arbitration process and is inconsistent with our commitment to maintaining arbitration as an alternative to litigation in the courts.

In this case, the parties' obligations could not be clearer: one owes the other a sum of money. No one contends that the arbitrator never considered retainage. The parties presented evidence on that issue and the award has a retainage section. We conclude that an ambiguity in how the arbitrator calculated one part of a multi-claim, complex contract dispute provides no basis for resubmitting the award to the arbitrator for clarification.

IV

Finally, and but distantly related to the foregoing discussion, we add our recognition that in rare circumstances a court may vacate an arbitration award for public-policy reasons. For example, in *Faherty v. Faherty,* 97 N.J. 99, 477 A.2d 1257 (1984), we held that "whenever the validity of an arbitration award affecting child support is questioned on the grounds that it does not provide adequate protection for the child, the trial court should conduct a special review of the award." That heightened judicial scrutiny is required because of the courts' traditional role as *parens patria.* Similarly, in a public-sector arbitration setting, a court can properly vacate an award because of a mistake of law. That exception is necessary because public policy demands that a public-sector arbitrator, who must consider the effect of a decision on the public interest and welfare, issue a decision in accordance with the law.

Additionally, in *Faherty*, we concluded that a combination of public-policy reasons and a mistake of law warranted judicial vacation of the arbitration award. We vacated a portion of the arbitration award because it granted one spouse alimony after she had remarried, and because, unlike the contract in this case, the parties in *Faherty* had agreed that the arbitrator would decide legal issues in accordance with New Jersey law. Because the alimony allowance in *Faherty* represented a fundamental error of New Jersey law, the court properly vacated that portion of the award.

CLIFFORD, J., concurring.

In *Perini Corp. v. Greate Bay Hotel & Casino, Inc.*, 129 N.J. 479, 610 A.2d 364 (1992), I voted with the plurality opinion and agreed with a majority of the members on the standard of judicial review that courts should apply to private-contract arbitration awards. Today I provide the fourth vote for the quite different test set forth in the Chief Justice's opinion concurring in the judgment in that case, having succumbed to the persuasive force of that opinion. Unlike me, the others in today's majority have no explaining to do, being either already on record as favoring the *Perini* concurrence or not hitherto committed to any position on the subject because they did not participate in the *Perini* deliberations or decision. Although this new alignment of the Court on the *Perini* issue does not affect the result of this appeal—nor would it have produced a different result in *Perini*—I have emerged from the closet only so that those who count heads can keep an accurate score and be guided henceforth accordingly.

Given the tenuous nature of *Perini* as precedent, I prefer to view my defection more as a demi-pirouette—not particularly graceful or elegant, I admit, but something less than a full-fledged about-face. . . . Much as I would prefer to announce that my change of position is attributable to some epiphany, to some deeply moving event that produced a sudden startling cerebral awakening, to some lightning bolt of cognitive awareness and intellectual enrichment, the plain truth of the matter is that I have thought more about it and have changed my mind. My awakening, however belated, puts me squarely in the Chief Justice's camp. For whatever ambivalence that progression demonstrates I refuse to commit myself to the psychiatrist's couch, content instead to resurrect—as apparently I must every couple of decades—that reassuring old turkey, "The matter does not appear to me now as it appears to have appeared to me then." Bramwell, B., in *Andrews v. Styrap*, 26 L.T.R. (n.s.) 704, 706 (Ex.1872).

STEIN, J., dissenting. . . .

Although the difference between the standard now adopted by the majority and the standard adhered to by the plurality in *Perini* is of enormous importance to parties contemplating the use of private-contract arbitration, the distinction is entirely irrelevant to the only issue that divides the Court in this case: whether we should confirm or remand for clarification an arbitration award that appears to have disregarded or overlooked an item of "retainage" in the amount of $201,148.

The source of law that authorizes modification of arbitration awards to correct miscalculations or mistakes is statutory, not judicial. . . . [T]he critical inquiry before us turns on the meaning of the award and requires an essentially factual determination whether [as provided by the New Jersey Arbitration Act] "there was an evident miscalculation of figures or an evident mistake in the description of a person, thing or property" in the award itself. . . .

I

. . . I agree with the majority's conclusion that what the Appellate Division identified as flaws and omissions in the award do not constitute a basis adequate to justify disturbance of the award.

[T]he Appellate Division noted that the arbitrator made no award with respect to various claims by the contractor for delay damages and interest. In addition, the Appellate Division concluded that the arbitrator's award to the owner was excessive in respect of a concrete loading dock and was inconsistent with the contract in respect of awards for replacement of glass and repair of cables. The Appellate Division concluded that the defects in the award it had identified were "gross, unmistakable, undebatable, or in manifest disregard of the applicable law and leading to an unjust result." The majority concludes that, notwithstanding the defects identified by the Appellate Division, "no statutory ground exists for invalidating or modifying the award." Except for the retainage item, I concur with the majority's disposition. . . .

The retainage item, however, has nothing to do with errors of law on the part of the arbitrator. The arbitrator's award was divided into two sections. The first summarized the claims of Fitzpatrick & Associates, Inc. (Fitzpatrick), the contractor. The second summarized the claims of Tretina Printing Corporation (Tretina), the owner. Under the heading "Fitzpatrick Claims," the arbitrator had designated "Retainage" as the fourth numbered category of claims. The contract authorized the owner to retain an amount equal to 150% of the cost of completion of unfinished items; as each unfinished item was completed, the owner was to pay the related amount of retainage to the contractor. Fitzpatrick claimed that the retainage withheld was $201,148, a figure disputed by Tretina. . . .

In determining to modify the award, the Chancery Division noted that the arbitrator's inclusion of an award for part of the construction-management fee under the heading "Retainage" is a non sequitur. The contract provided in Article 7 for a Construction Manager's Fee of $200,000, a provision separate from the retainage provision in Article 11. The arbitrator's award of $100,000, plus interest, as a construction manager's fee under the heading of "Retainage" affords no explanation for the arbitrator's apparent mistake in failing to account for the retainage either under that heading or elsewhere in the award. As the Chancery Judge observed: It is unclear how the arbitrator handled the item of retainage. During the course of Fitzpatrick's work some $201,148 had been retained by Tretina in accordance with the terms of the contract. These were monies held out of payments authorized as a reserve to cover any deficiencies which later turned up regarding that approved work. Had the contract been satisfactorily completed, Fitzpatrick would have been entitled to the retainage—in whole or in part.

However, the monies have always been, and are today, held by Tretina. The arbitrator in making his net award of $260,267.66 in favor of Tretina either overlooked or assumed that the parties would recognize the offset that Fitzpatrick was entitled to for the retainage. It is clear as one reads the award that the retainage did not enter into his computation. Under his disposition of the Fitzpatrick claims the arbitrator lists as #4 "Retainage" but then proceeds to discuss the construction management fee (an entirely different matter) under that heading. Retainage was not a separate claim. It was a liquidated fund to be turned over to Fitzpatrick in whole or in part only if it did not breach its contract and only to the extent that approved work did not require repair or redoing. Tretina prevailed on its claim of breach by Fitzpatrick. The arbitrator liquidated all of its damage claims (save the ones involving the sewer pipe, sprinklers, clip meters and loading dock clearance). The retainage then must be treated as a credit on the amount due, since Tretina has never paid over that money. I will modify the arbitrator's award in that regard as I am permitted to do.

Following the Chancery Division's modification of the award to credit Fitzpatrick with the omitted amount of retainage, Tretina sought reconsideration of that determination, relying on its attorney's certification to support its contention that a remand to the arbitrator was the appropriate and authorized mechanism for resolving any ambiguity in the award. . . .

[T]he certification of Tretina's attorney states: If this be so, then the matter should have been remanded to the arbitrator for a clarification as to how, if at all, he handled the issue of retainage. At the oral argument . . . the [c]ourt indicated it was inclined to send the parties back to the arbitrator for just that purpose. Both parties agreed that, if the [c]ourt thought the award to be ambiguous, they would not object to such a procedure. . . . I believe it is unlikely that Klausner overlooked that figure in his award. Rather, it is just as likely, if not more probable, that the arbitrator combined the construction management fee being withheld with the retainage and made a lump-sum adjusted award for the two items of $100,000. . . . [Tretina proposed that the arbitrator be subpoenaed] "for oral testimony only for the limited purpose of ascertaining what he did with the retainage claim. Note that Tretina is not requesting the arbitrator to re-evaluate the award, or even to inquire into the merits, but simply tell us what he did in forming the award on the issue raised by Judge McGann."

The principle is well-settled that the power of courts to modify arbitration awards to correct evident mistakes includes the power to remand to the arbitrator in order to obtain clarification of the award. In *La Vale Plaza, Inc. v. R.S. Noonan, Inc.*, 378 F.2d 569 (1967), the Third Circuit addressed the inherent power of federal courts to remand an arbitration award to the arbitrator to clarify its meaning, under circumstances strikingly similar to those before us. Noonan, a general contractor, had demanded arbitration concerning the amount due it in respect of a contract to construct a shopping center. The arbitrators rendered an award in favor of Noonan for $30,861.64. Shortly thereafter La Vale filed suit to recover the difference between the amount of the award and the sum of $56,429.66 that it had paid to Noonan while the arbitration was pending. Noonan asserted that that payment was overdue and had been taken into account by the arbitration award. The district court remanded the matter to the arbitrator to clarify whether the arbitrator had taken into account the payment made by La Vale while the arbitration was pending.

In affirming the District Court's order, the Third Circuit explained that the remand did not have the effect of reopening the arbitration: Where the award, although seemingly complete, leaves doubt whether the submission has been fully executed, an ambiguity arises which the arbitrator is entitled to clarify. The resolution of such an ambiguity is not within the policy which forbids an arbitrator to redetermine an issue which he has already decided, for there is no opportunity for redetermination on the merits of what has already been decided. Instead, the clarification of an ambiguity closely resembles the correction of a mistake apparent on the face of the award and the determination of an issue which the arbitrators had failed to decide. Thus, in the present case the arbitrators will act only to remove the cloud of doubt as to whether they considered the payment of $56,429.66 in making their award and will in no way reopen the merits of the controversy.

Other courts similarly have recognized the appropriateness of a remand to the arbitrators in order to clarify an apparent ambiguity in the award. In explaining the relationship between the purposes of arbitration and the desirability of remanding to clarify ambiguous awards, the Ninth Circuit in *Hanford,* observed: We share the view of the district court that the opinion required clarification and interpretation. We also share the view of the district court that this was a task to be first performed by the arbitration committee and not the court, and that the court properly remanded the matter to the arbitration committee for such clarification and interpretation. It is appellant's position that once the arbitrators have acted, it is the duty of the court to interpret and enforce the award, rather than to send the matter back to the arbitrators, to the end that the further delay involved in sending the matter back can be avoided. We think, however, that all of the foregoing cases accept the philosophy that where the parties have elected to submit their disputes to arbitration, they should be completely resolved by arbitration, rather than only partially resolved. In some cases the carrying out of this philosophy will require remanding the matter to the arbitrators, and we think that this is such a case.

I perceive no inconsistency at all between the deferential standard for sustaining arbitration awards today adopted by the Court, and the settled and accepted practice of resubmission of ambiguous awards to arbitrators for clarification. To the contrary, the Legislature's specific requirement that in case of "an evident miscalculation of figures or an evident mistake in the description of a person, thing or property . . . [t]he court shall modify and correct the award, to effect the intent thereof," reflects the Legislature's intention that mistaken or ambiguous arbitration awards should not be rubber-stamped by a reviewing court. Because an ambiguous award, such as the one before us, can be clarified by the simple and pragmatic expedient of resubmission to the arbitrator for that singular purpose, the majority's insistence on confirming the award in its present form is unsettling. We need not elevate our interest in the finality of arbitration awards over a court's ability to "promote justice between the parties," particularly where, as here, the objectives are compatible.

II

I consider this case to be an entirely inappropriate occasion to revisit the holding in *Perini.* Because that view obviously has not prevailed, I hasten to adopt the majority's view that no purpose would be served in revisiting the underlying arguments that divided the Court in *Perini.* Nevertheless, I adhere to the views expressed in the *Perini* plurality opinion concerning the appropriate standard for judicial review of arbitration awards, as well as with the view I expressed in *Perini* that "[t]he reliability of arbitration as an alternative method of dispute resolution mandates judicial intervention in extreme cases . . . in which a settled legal principle and industry practice have been repudiated by the arbitrators' award."

c. *Advanced Micro Devices, Inc. v. Intel Corp.,* 885 P.2d 994 (Cal. 1994)

WERDEGAR, Justice. LUCAS, C.J., and ARABIAN and GEORGE, JJ., concur.

California law allows a court to correct or vacate a contractual arbitration award if the arbitrators "exceeded their powers." In *Moncharsh v. Heily & Blase,* 832 P.2d 899 (1992), we held arbitrators do not exceed their powers merely by erroneously deciding a contested issue of law or fact; we did not, however, have occasion there to further delineate the standard for measuring the scope of arbitrators' authority. This case requires us to decide the standard by which courts are to determine whether a contractual arbitrator has exceeded his or her powers in awarding relief for a breach of contract.

An arbitrator determined the Intel Corporation (Intel) had breached portions of its 1982 technology exchange agreement with Advanced Micro Devices, Inc. (AMD), including the implied covenant of good faith and fair dealing. The superior court confirmed the award, but the Court of Appeal, holding the arbitrator had exceeded his authority in awarding AMD the right to use certain Intel intellectual property, ordered the award corrected by eliminating the disputed relief.

We conclude that, in the absence of more specific restrictions in the arbitration agreement, the submission or the rules of arbitration, the remedy an arbitrator fashions does not exceed his or her powers if it bears a rational relationship to the underlying contract as interpreted, expressly or impliedly, by the arbitrator and to the breach of contract found, expressly or impliedly, by the arbitrator. The remedy fashioned by the arbitrator here was within the scope of his authority as measured by that standard. We therefore reverse the contrary judgment of the Court of Appeal.

FACTS AND PROCEEDINGS

AMD and Intel are both engaged in the creation, design, production and marketing of complex integrated circuits, also known as computer chips. In the period 1978–1981 both AMD and Intel were pursuing strategies for producing and marketing 16-bit microprocessors and the 32-bit microprocessors that were expected to follow. AMD was attempting to secure entry into this market through an agreement with a third chip maker, Zilog, while Intel had developed its own 16-bit microprocessor, the 8086. Intel, needing another producer to "second source"[2] the 8086, approached AMD.

Intel hoped to establish the 8086's basic architecture, known as iAPX, as the market standard, guaranteeing future sales of the 8086's expected progeny as well. AMD, having had what it saw as a bad experience in a previous second-source agreement with Intel, wanted to be sure it would not be cut off from second sourcing future generations of the 8086 family. In addition, reaching an agreement with Intel would mean abandoning AMD's relationship with Zilog; AMD therefore sought a long-term arrangement.

The parties entered into the contract at issue in February 1982. According to its preamble the agreement was intended "to establish a mechanism for exchanging technical information so that each party acquires the capability to develop products suitable for sale as an alternate source for products developed by the other party." During the ten-year term of the contract (cancelable after five years on one year's notice by either party), either company could elect to be a second source for products offered it by the other. The nondeveloping company would receive technical information and licenses needed for it to make and sell the part. The developing company would receive a royalty. In addition, the developing company would earn the right to be a second source for products developed by the other party. The terms of exchange—the respective value of the products—were to be calculated by a specified equation from the complexity and size of the parts.

[2]The chip makers' customers, computer manufacturers, frequently prefer a product be made by more than one source, as this helps ensure competition and a reliable supply. Hence the common practice of second sourcing, in which the company developing a product licenses to another company the right, for a royalty, to make and sell it.

The parties had fundamentally different views of the contract. AMD believed the agreement created a partnership or joint venture under which the two companies would agree in advance on products to be developed by each of them, avoiding duplicative research expenditures and guaranteeing each a more complete product line. Intel, on the other hand, saw the agreement as "little more than an armed truce," in which each proposed second-source agreement was to be the subject of combative bargaining with no continuing obligations from episode to episode. The arbitrator rejected both extremes, finding that, "while a party was not obligated to act substantially against its self interest in deciding to transfer or accept a part, there was an implied covenant to make the relationship work which obligated a party to consider in good faith . . . the purposes of the contractual relationship . . . and to negotiate reasonably to accomplish this purpose. If it could not do this it should terminate the arrangement—as Intel finally did." The purposes of the agreement, according to the arbitrator, were expansion of product line and savings on research and development.

The contract provided for arbitration of "disagreements aris[ing] under this Agreement. . . ." Arbitration was to be by a single arbitrator, whose decision would be considered "a final and binding resolution of the disagreement." Disagreements over product exchanges led AMD to petition the superior court to compel arbitration in April 1987. The parties agreed on an arbitrator and to the rules he would follow, including section 42, entitled "Scope of the Award," which provided: "The Arbitrator may grant any remedy or relief which the Arbitrator deems just and equitable and within the scope of the agreement of the parties, including, but not limited to, specific performance of a contract." Section 41 further instructed the arbitrator to "interpret and apply these Rules insofar as they relate to his powers and duties." After hearings in superior court, a temporary judge (who was also the chosen arbitrator) made an order of reference stating the issues for arbitration and providing, as to each issue, that "the Arbitrator is authorized to fashion such remedy as he may in his discretion determine to be fair and reasonable but not in excess of his jurisdiction."

The arbitration lasted four and one-half years and included three hundred and fifty-five days of hearings. As the current dispute focuses narrowly on two items of relief awarded, only a small portion of the arbitrator's extensive findings need be summarized here.

Under the contract AMD could initially obtain second-source rights to Intel's 8086 chip and other specified products for cash. After 1985, AMD would have open access to Intel's product line if Intel accepted AMD products of sufficient value, as determined from the complexity-size formula. In 1984 the parties negotiated an amendment to the contract, under which AMD was to second source the successors of the 8086—the 80186 and 80286—in exchange for substantial royalties to Intel. Intel also agreed at that time to accept certain AMD products then in development, conditional in some instances on final specifications. The arbitrator found that "[i]f Intel took all these products, or even some of them, AMD would have access to the Intel line of products without restriction—and no royalties."

The arbitrator found Intel extensively breached its obligations to act in good faith and deal fairly. Beginning in mid-1984 Intel, anxious to be the sole source for the 80386 (its 32-bit chip, which was to prove vastly successful) and convinced the contract was to its disadvantage, decided to frustrate the operation of the contract by taking no more products from AMD. Intel also resolved to keep this decision from AMD and the public, leaving AMD and others in the industry with the belief AMD would be a second source for the 80386. This "ke[pt] AMD in the Intel competitive camp" and avoided public knowledge of Intel's sole-source strategy for the 80386, a strategy Intel feared could limit its market if known. The plan succeeded: AMD continued for about two years to believe, incorrectly, its agreement with Intel "had a future."

One concrete example of Intel's failure to negotiate in good faith was its treatment of AMD's Quad Pixel Display Manager (QPDM), a graphics chip. Although Intel promised in 1984 to accept the QPDM from AMD provided the parties agreed on its specifications, the arbitrator found Intel made no actual attempt to negotiate the remaining differences as to specifications. Instead, partly in order to avoid having both to give AMD the 80386 and to eliminate royalties on other products, Intel summarily rejected the QPDM. In doing so, the arbitrator found, Intel breached the implied covenant of good faith and fair dealing as well as "its implied covenant to negotiate reasonably to further the goals of the relationship between the parties. . . ."

The arbitrator also found, however, Intel was not obliged under the contract to accept the QPDM or other products that would have earned AMD the 80386 rights. Apart from Intel's breach, moreover, the arbitrator found AMD had unnecessarily delayed in seeking alternative ways to enter the 32-bit chip market. Having inferred by mid-1985 that Intel was not going to accept the AMD parts that could earn AMD the 80386, AMD should have sought arbitration at that time or immediately begun reverse engineering the 80386 when it became available in July 1986. Instead, AMD did not begin reverse engineering the 80386 until a later time and did not produce its own 80386 chip—known as the Am386—until March 1991. "In short, Intel's plan succeeded . . . because of AMD's inertia." For this reason, the arbitrator declined to award AMD the hundreds of millions of dollars it sought in lost 80386 profits.

Despite AMD's delay, the arbitrator found AMD had actually been damaged by Intel's breach: "One knows that AMD lost some goodwill as the result of the Intel conduct; one knows that AMD lost some profits from not having the 80386 as the result of the Intel conduct. . . . The actual damages are immeasurable; and nominal damages only are inequitable." The proper remedy, the arbitrator decided, was to relieve AMD from "legal harassment by Intel over AMD's alleged use of Intel intellectual property in the reverse engineered AMD 386."

The arbitrator therefore awarded AMD a permanent, nonexclusive and royalty-free license to any Intel intellectual property embodied in the Am386. He also awarded AMD a further two-year extension of certain patent and copyright licenses, insofar as they related to the Am386, that originated in a 1976 agreement between the parties, which had been extended under the 1982 contract to 1995. The arbitrator designated these items as remedies for breach of the covenant of good faith and fair dealing, as well as for failure to negotiate in good faith over the QPDM specifications and for other breaches.

The superior court confirmed the award, but the Court of Appeal reversed. Although it recognized the scope of judicial review did not extend to redeciding the merits of the controversy, the court believed the extent of the arbitrator's remedial powers was reviewable "de novo." The Court of Appeal found itself unable to locate a "rational nexus" between the award and the contract itself. Therefore, the court concluded, the arbitrator had improperly "rewr[itten] the parties' agreement."

I. STANDARD OF REVIEW OF THE REMEDIES FASHIONED BY A PRIVATE ARBITRATOR

A. Review of Arbitrability

Although this court has not previously articulated a detailed standard for review of the remedies fashioned by an arbitrator, we have considered the related question how to review determinations of arbitrability, that is, whether an arbitrator exceeded his or her authority by deciding a particular issue. On that point, our decisions teach that courts should generally defer to an arbitrator's finding that determination of a particular question is within the scope of his or her contractual authority.

Code of Civil Procedure section 1283.4 provides the arbitrator's written award shall determine all submitted questions "necessary in order to determine the controversy." Construing that section in *Morris v. Zuckerman* (1968) 69 Cal. 2d 686, 690, 72 Cal. Rptr. 880, 446 P.2d 1000 this court held it is for the arbitrators to determine what issues are "necessary" to the ultimate decision. We continued: "Likewise, any doubts as to the meaning or extent of an arbitration agreement are for the arbitrators and not the court to resolve."

Although section 1286.2 permits the court to vacate an award that exceeds the arbitrator's powers, the deference due an arbitrator's decision on the merits of the controversy requires a court to refrain from substituting its judgment for the arbitrator's in determining the contractual scope of those powers.

Giving substantial deference to arbitrators' own assessments of their contractual authority is consistent with the general rule of arbitral finality we recently reaffirmed in *Moncharsh*. As we stated there, parties to private, nonjudicial arbitration typically expect their dispute will be resolved without necessity for any contact with the courts. The decision to arbitrate disputes is motivated in part by the desire to avoid the delay and cost of judicial trials and appeals. "Ensuring arbitral finality thus requires that judicial intervention in the arbitration process be minimized." A rule of judicial review under which courts would independently redetermine the scope of an arbitration agreement already interpreted by the arbitrator would invite frequent and protracted judicial proceedings, contravening the parties' expectations of finality.

B. Review of Remedies

Intel contends that even if California precedents require deference to an arbitrator's assessment of arbitrability, a different, less deferential rule applies to an arbitrator's choice of remedies. Intel's position is neither logically persuasive nor supported by precedent. In providing for judicial vacation or correction of an award, our statutes do not distinguish between arbitrators' power to decide an issue and their authority to choose an appropriate remedy; in either instance the test is whether arbitrators have "exceeded their powers." . . .

Deference to the arbitrator is also required by the character of the remedy decision itself. Fashioning remedies for a breach of contract or other injury is not always a simple matter of applying contractually specified relief to an easily measured injury. It may involve, as in the present case, providing relief for breach of implied covenants, as to which the parties have not specified contractual damages. It may require, also as in this case, finding a way of approximating the impact of a breach that cannot with any certainty be reduced to monetary terms. Passage of time and changed circumstances may have rendered any remedies suggested by the contract insufficient or excessive. . . .

The choice of remedy, then, may at times call on any decision maker's flexibility, creativity and sense of fairness. In private arbitrations, the parties have bargained for the relatively free exercise of those faculties. Arbitrators, unless specifically restricted by the agreement to following legal rules, may base their decision upon broad principles of justice and equity. As early as 1852, this court recognized that, "The arbitrators are not bound to award on principles of dry law, but may decide on principles of equity and good conscience, and make their award ex aequo et bono [according to what is just and good]." . . .

Independent reevaluation by a court, moreover, is unlikely to be either expeditious or accurate. Arbitrations may, as this case demonstrates, be lengthy and complicated. The proceedings may be informal and a complete stenographic record may not be prepared. A reviewing court is thus not in a favorable position to substitute its judgment for that of the arbitrators as to what relief is most just and equitable under all the circumstances. Further, independent review of remedies, no less than of other arbitrated questions, would tend to increase the cost and delay involved. . . .

We do not, by the above, intend to suggest an arbitrator's exercise of discretion in ordering relief is unrestricted or unreviewable. Such an extreme position enjoys no support in our statutes or cases. The powers of an arbitrator derive from, and are limited by, the agreement to arbitrate. Awards in excess of those powers may, under sections 1286.2 and 1286.6, be corrected or vacated by the court. . . .

The principle of arbitral finality, the practical demands of deciding on an appropriate remedy for breach, and the prior holdings of this court all dictate that arbitrators, unless expressly restricted by the agreement or the submission to arbitration, have substantial discretion to determine the scope of their contractual authority to fashion remedies, and that judicial review of their awards must be correspondingly narrow and deferential.

C. Standard of Review

Having rejected the extremes of "de novo" review on the one hand, and complete unreviewability on the other, we must attempt to articulate a standard capturing the middle ground of deferential yet meaningful review. We begin by surveying similar efforts in the Courts of Appeal and in other jurisdictions.

Recent decisions in the Courts of Appeal have employed two formulas to determine whether an arbitrator's award exceeded his or her powers. The courts have asked whether the award rests on a "completely irrational" construction of the contract or whether it amounts to an "arbitrary remaking" of the contract. These tests were combined in *Southern Cal. Rapid Transit Dist. v. United Transportation Union,* into a single formula: "Generally, a decision exceeds the arbitrator's powers only if it is so utterly irrational that it amounts to an arbitrary remaking of the contract between the parties."

These statements of the standard tend to focus the inquiry on the arbitrator's construction of the contract. Useful as such an examination may sometimes be, it is incomplete as a test of whether arbitrators have exceeded their powers in awarding a particular item of damages or other relief. The critical question with regard to remedies is not whether the arbitrator has rationally interpreted the parties' agreement, but whether the remedy chosen is rationally drawn from the contract as so interpreted. This case illustrates the distinction; Intel argues not that the arbitrator misconstrued the contract, but that the remedy he fashioned bore an insufficient relationship to the agreement as he interpreted it.

In contrast to the California cases, decisions from the federal courts applying the "essence" test announced in *Steelworkers v. Enterprise Corp.,* (hereafter *Enterprise*) properly focus on the source of the arbitrators' chosen remedy. In *Enterprise,* a labor arbitrator ordered several workers reinstated with backpay upon finding their dismissal improper. The collective bargaining agreement authorizing the arbitration, however, had expired after the workers' dismissal but before the award. The company argued the award of reinstatement, and of backpay after expiration of the agreement, was therefore unenforceable. The high court held the award could not be refused enforcement on this ground. If the arbitrator was relying solely on statutory requirements extraneous to the contract, he exceeded his powers under the submission. But if the award derived from the arbitrator's construction of the agreement, even an erroneous construction, it was within his authority. Ambiguity on this point, which the court found to exist, was insufficient grounds to refuse enforcement.

In reaching its holding the high court explained the limits on an arbitrator's authority to fashion remedies as follows: "[A]n arbitrator is confined to interpretation and application of the collective bargaining agreement; he does not sit to dispense his own brand of industrial justice. He may of course look for guidance from many sources, yet his award is legitimate only so long as it draws its essence from the collective bargaining agreement. When the arbitrator's words manifest an infidelity to this obligation, courts have no choice but to refuse enforcement of the award."

Judicial review of remedies as outlined in the *Enterprise* decision thus looks not to whether the arbitrator correctly interpreted the agreement, but to whether the award is drawn from the agreement as the arbitrator interpreted it or derives from some extrinsic source. As the court explained in a later labor case, where an arbitrator is authorized to determine remedies for contract violations, "courts have no authority to disagree with his honest judgment in that respect. . . . [A]s long as the arbitrator is even arguably construing or applying the contract and acting within the scope of his authority, that a court is convinced he committed serious error does not suffice to overturn his decision." *United Paperworkers v. Misco, supra,* 484 U.S. at p. 38, 108 S.Ct. at p. 371 (hereafter Misco).

The dissent argues the *Enterprise/Misco* standard should not be applied in the commercial context, apparently on the ground commercial arbitrators do not have the same need for flexibility in fashioning remedies as labor arbitrators. The dissent, we think, overstates the difference: while many commercial arbitrations involve single transactions in which a finding of breach suggests well-defined contractual damages, others—including the present one—involve lengthy and complicated dealings between the parties, in which the breaches are numerous, extended or repeated, and monetary damages are either indeterminable or inadequate. We nonetheless recognize differences do exist, and our employment of the *Enterprise/Misco* formulation does not, as the dissent suggests, incorporate the entire body of labor arbitration law applying that test. . . .

We recognize certain aspects of labor arbitration may be unique, and not all rules established for resolution of disputes over collective bargaining agreements are applicable to commercial contracts. On the issues discussed here, however, *Enterprise* and other federal labor decisions have been influential in the commercial arbitration context because they are grounded on "considerations of judicial policy" equally applicable to review of commercial arbitration awards. In both labor and commercial arbitrations, the choice of remedies calls on the arbitrator's flexibility and informed judgment; in both areas, independent judicial reevaluation of remedies would tend to defeat the contractual intent to resolve disputes efficiently and by private mechanisms.

Although the *Enterprise* test emphasizes the source from which the arbitrator drew the award, it nevertheless is objective. The arbitrator cannot shield his decision from scrutiny "simply by making the right noises—noises of contract interpretation. . . ." Rather, the question is whether the award is "so outre that we can infer that it was driven by a desire to do justice beyond the limits of the contract." . . .

Local 120 v. Brooks Foundry, Inc., 892 F.2d 1283 (6th Cir.1990) is particularly instructive, as it deals with the difficult problem of choosing remedies for a real but unquantifiable injury. After the union agreed to a wage concession for all workers, the company improperly protected one favored employee from the reduction. In the arbitrated grievance, the union requested an award of $130,000, the aggregate amount of the wage concession for all employees. The arbitrator found such a massive award would be inappropriate and beyond the company's ability to pay and instead awarded 10 percent of the amount, $13,000, which he stated was intended as "damages" to "cushion" the harm to the union from the company's breach.

The Court of Appeals reversed the district court's ruling vacating the award. Acknowledging the amount of the award was not drawn directly from measurement of the injury done the union the court held it was nonetheless within the arbitrator's powers. "[D]etermining damages appropriate for an inchoate injury is not always an exact exercise, susceptible to strict logical explication." The arbitrator did not abuse his authority in taking into account "the economic facts of life which prompted the pay cut provision" or in viewing it in "the realistic light of the history that brought it about." The court concluded the award, although "unusual and even bizarre," drew its essence from the contract because it was "related to arguably proper compensatory damages. . . ."

We distill from these cases what we believe is a meaningful, workable and properly deferential framework for reviewing an arbitrator's choice of remedies. Arbitrators are not obliged to read contracts literally, and an award may not be vacated merely because the court is unable to find the relief granted was authorized by a specific term of the contract. The remedy awarded, however, must bear some rational relationship to the contract and the breach. . . . The award will be upheld so long as it was even arguably based on the contract; it may be vacated only if the reviewing court is compelled to infer the award was based on an extrinsic source. In close cases the arbitrator's decision must stand.

D. Relationship of Relief to Rights Under Contract

Intel maintains that, whatever the general standard, the cases establish one "bright-line" rule: "arbitrators may not award a remedy that conflicts with express terms of the arbitrated contract." To the extent this means arbitrators may not award remedies expressly forbidden by the arbitration agreement or submission, the point is well taken. To the extent Intel is advocating a broader rule—that arbitrators may not award a party benefits different from those the party could have acquired through performance of the contract—the cases do not support its position. No exact correspondence is required between the rights and obligations of a party had the contract been performed and the remedy an arbitrator may provide for the other party's breach.

[A]rbitrators, unless expressly restricted by the agreement of the parties, enjoy the authority to fashion relief they consider just and fair under the circumstances existing at the time of arbitration, so long as the remedy may be rationally derived from the contract and the breach. . . . Because parties to arbitration agreements do have the power to limit possible remedies in this manner, we do not believe our holding will, as the dissent speculates, discourage arbitration.

II. Application to This Case

[S]ection 42 of the rules of arbitration agreed upon by the parties authorized the arbitrator to grant "any remedy or relief which the Arbitrator deems just and equitable and within the scope of the agreement. . . ." [I]t . . . is identical . . . to Rule 43 of the AAA Commercial Arbitration Rules. . . . The AAA rule has been described as "a broad grant of authority to fashion remedies."

Paragraph 6 of the award, which extends for two years (insofar as they related to the Am386) certain licenses to Intel patents and copyrights originally granted AMD in 1976 and extended to 1995 under the 1982 agreement, bears a clear and rational relationship to the contract and the effects of Intel's breach. Having found Intel succeeded in keeping AMD in the Intel camp for about two years through its bad-faith conduct, the arbitrator extended for that same period rights that AMD had enjoyed under the contract and that could be useful to it in recovering from the breach's effects.

Paragraph 5 awards AMD a nonexclusive, royalty-free license to any Intel copyrights, patents, trade secrets or maskwork rights contained in the Am386. Because the question whether AMD had appropriated any Intel intellectual property in creating the Am386 was apparently one of the issues between the parties in federal litigation at the time this award was made, Intel contends the arbitrator went outside the scope of the arbitration in fashioning paragraph 5 of the award. Intel points to language the arbitrator used that suggests extrinsic concerns. In the award itself the arbitrator stated he intended paragraph 5 to provide AMD a defense in the pending federal litigation. In the accompanying opinion he explained paragraphs 5 and 6 were intended to end "the incessant warfare" between the parties. . . .

Intel emphasizes paragraph 5 gave AMD rights it had not earned in performance of the contract. As we have explained, however, a valid award for breach of contract does not require exact correspondence with the particular benefits the injured party would have received had the contract been fully performed. The arbitrator acted within his powers by fashioning a remedy rationally designed to alleviate the unfair results of Intel's breach, a breach that was not specifically anticipated in the parties' agreement. . . .

That the arbitrator found AMD had not "earned" the Intel 80386 is, under the circumstances, not significant. The award sought not to implement a technology exchange required by the contract, but to alleviate the effects of Intel's breach of the contract's implied covenants. . . .

The dissent, while accepting the principle an award must be rationally linked to the contract or breach, would hold in addition that "the potential remedies available to an arbitrator are limited to those that a court could award on the same claim." . . . We believe this approach is inconsistent with the principles of contractual arbitration and with the agreement of the parties in this case. . . . [P]arties who submit their disputes to arbitration "may expect not only to reap the advantages that flow from the use of that nontechnical, summary procedure, but also to find themselves bound by an award reached by paths neither marked nor traceable and not subject to judicial review." . . .

The test proposed by the dissent would impermissibly embroil the courts in reviewing the legal correctness of an arbitrator's decision on submitted issues. To determine whether a remedy is within the range a court could award on the same claim, a reviewing court would inevitably have to interpret the contract and resolve factual and legal disputes on questions such as the nature of the breach and the extent of the cognizable injury to the nonbreaching party. Reference to "normal contract remedies" is not sufficient, because what remedies are legally and equitably available for breach of contract may depend on the nature of the contract, the breach and the injury. Consequently, the dissent's approach would require judicial reexamination of the award's legal and factual sufficiency, an enterprise we disapproved in *Moncharsh.* In addition, to measure the award of an arbitrator, who may have been chosen for practical experience or technical expertise rather than legal training, strictly against the legal limits of contract damages is, we believe, unrealistic and contrary to the parties' expectations. . . .

KENNARD, Justice, dissenting. MOSK and SPENCER, JJ., concur.

. . . Under the majority's decision an arbitrator in a commercial contract dispute may award an essentially unlimited range of remedies, whether or not a court could award them if it decided the same dispute, so long as it can be said that the relief draws its "essence" from the contract and not some other source. This standard, taken from the far different realm of federal labor law, imposes only the most minimal scrutiny on an arbitration award. . . .

In particular, it permits an arbitrator to award a remedy that a court would be prohibited from awarding. In my view, an arbitrator's award must both fall within the range of remedies that a court could award for the same claim and, in the case of a contract dispute, bear a rational relationship to the contract. Because the arbitrator's award in this case does not meet either test, I dissent. . . .

In my view, there are two sources of limitations on the remedial powers of an arbitrator deciding a contract dispute. First, because our arbitration statutes merely establish a different procedure for resolving disputes, and do not create new substantive claims or remedies, an arbitrator lacks the power to award a remedy outside the scope of those that a court could award for the same claim. Second, an arbitrator deciding a contract dispute lacks the power to make an award that has no rational linkage to the agreement or its breach.. . .

[B]oth a scope-of-available-remedies test and a rational relationship test are necessary to assess whether a remedy exceeds the arbitrator's powers. Either alone is incomplete. For example, an award of attorney fees may be a completely rational remedy for breach of a contract that is silent as to them, yet exceed the arbitrator's powers because the governing law precludes attorney fees as a remedy for breach of contract. Conversely, an award of compensatory damages may be within the scope of the potential remedies available for a breach of contract claim, yet lack any rational relationship to the arbitrator's interpretation of the contract if the arbitrator interprets the contract to find that there was no breach. . . .

The majority holds that arbitration awards in commercial contract disputes should be judicially reviewed under the "essence" test of federal labor arbitration law. Under this extremely deferential test, the only requirement is that "[t]he remedy awarded . . . must bear some rational relationship to the contract and the breach." "The award will be upheld so long as it was even arguably based on the contract; it may be vacated only if the reviewing court is compelled to infer the award was based on an extrinsic source."

For the following reasons, the majority's "essence" test is an inadequate test for reviewing whether an arbitration award is within the arbitrator's remedial powers. First, it is incomplete because it does not address whether the arbitration award is within the range of remedies authorized by law or by agreement for the claim decided by the arbitrator. Second, the "essence" test is an unsatisfactory measure of arbitration awards in commercial contract disputes because the degree of relationship it requires between an arbitrator's award and the contract giving rise to the dispute is about the most minimal imaginable.

As it has evolved in the field of labor law, however, the "essence" test is a broad grant of power to arbitrators that provides only the barest scrutiny of the relationship between an arbitrator's award and the collective bargaining agreement on which it is based. The "essence" test authorizes any arbitration award, no matter how "unusual and even bizarre," unless it can be said with assurance that "the arbitrator must have based his award on some body of thought, or feeling, or policy, or law that is outside the contract."

Like the commercial contract arbitration cases from other jurisdictions on which it relies, the majority has uncritically adopted the "essence" test as the standard of review for commercial contract dispute arbitration awards, and thereby imported wholesale the specialized body of labor arbitration law interpreting that test, without rigorously analyzing whether the reasons that gave rise to the "essence" test in labor arbitration also hold true in the quite different world of commercial contract arbitration. . . . [T]he policy reasons that led to the adoption and broad scope of the "essence" test in the collective bargaining arena do not support its use in the commercial contract context. . . .

One policy reason why arbitrators in the collective bargaining context are given extraordinarily broad remedial powers is the impossibility of reducing to writing all aspects of a collectively bargained employment relationship between an employer and what may be hundreds or thousands of employees in numerous job classifications at numerous locations. "The collective bargaining agreement is more than a contract; it is a generalized code to govern a myriad of cases which the draftsmen cannot wholly anticipate. . . . A collective bargaining agreement is an effort to erect a system of industrial self-government."

Another policy reason supporting the "essence" test in the collective bargaining context is the difference in function between labor arbitration and commercial contract arbitration. . . . Labor arbitration is typically an ongoing process during the life of a collective bargaining agreement that adjusts and modifies the agreement to meet the changing conditions of the workplace. "[A]rbitrators under these collective agreements are indispensable agencies in a continuous collective bargaining process." . . .

"Courts and arbitration in the context of most commercial contracts are resorted to because there has been a breakdown in the working relationship of the parties; such resort is the unwanted exception. But the grievance machinery under a collective bargaining agreement is at the very heart of the system of industrial self-government. Arbitration is the means of solving the unforeseeable. The processing of disputes through the grievance machinery is actually a vehicle by which meaning and content are given to the collective bargaining agreement. . . . The grievance procedure is, in other words, a part of the continuous collective bargaining process." . . .

The AAA's instructions to arbitrators describe only three categories of remedies for a breach of contract: money damages, specific performance, or an injunction enjoining breach. (A Guide for Commercial Arbitrators, at pp. 23-24.) The AAA has provided a helpful example showing that arbitrators are not authorized to award equitable relief going beyond these categories: "For instance, ruling on a claim by a building owner against a contractor who failed to do certain work according to specifications, you might award monetary damages or direct the contractor to do the work over again. You might also dismiss the claim. An award directing the contractor to reimburse the owner by landscaping the property would be improper, however, where landscaping was not contemplated in the contract." Section 42 therefore does not authorize any additional remedies not otherwise authorized by the parties' agreement or by the substantive law underlying the claim.

In this case, the relief awarded in paragraphs 5 and 6 is unauthorized by section 42 because it is not within the scope of the remedies otherwise authorized by contract law or by the parties' agreement and because it is a benefit "not contemplated in the contract." To use the AAA example just mentioned, it is the equivalent of awarding landscaping as a remedy for faulty construction of a building. Thus, paragraphs 5 and 6 exceed the arbitrator's powers and should be vacated. . . .

[P]aragraphs 5 and 6 are not a remedy that is rationally related to Intel's breach of the covenant of good faith, given the lack of causation that the arbitrator found between Intel's breach and the damage claimed by AMD. . . . Instead, paragraphs 5 and 6 are plainly the arbitrator's attempt to give AMD "something" by solving a dispute (the federal court patent and copyright litigation between AMD and Intel over the Am386) outside the scope of the AMD-Intel contract and outside the scope of the arbitration agreement. The arbitrator's stated purpose for paragraphs 5 and 6 was to provide AMD with a complete defense to Intel's federal court litigation against AMD over the Am386. In place of paragraphs 5 and 6 the arbitrator initially proposed directly enjoining Intel from litigating its federal intellectual property claims, and only substituted paragraphs 5 and 6 when AMD informed him that his proposed injunction was an unconstitutional interference with the federal court litigation. Because in making paragraphs 5 and 6 of the award the arbitrator was attempting to resolve a dispute that did not arise under the AMD-Intel contract and that was not submitted to him for decision, paragraphs 5 and 6 lack any rational relationship to the AMD-Intel contract. . . .

Moreover, paragraphs 5 and 6 fail even under the majority's "essence" test. The gist of the arbitrator's decision in those paragraphs was that although AMD, independent of Intel's breach, had failed to comply with the conditions precedent for earning the right to the 80386, it was nevertheless equitable to give AMD the rights to the Am386. Even under the "essence" test used to review labor arbitrations, a remedy fails to draw its essence from the contract if it awards a contractual benefit subject to a condition precedent to a party that, for reasons unrelated to the breach, has failed to comply with the condition precedent.

Although in this case the Court of Appeal correctly determined that the arbitrator had exceeded his powers in his choice of remedies in paragraphs 5 and 6 of the award, the court erred in deciding that rather than being vacated, the award could be corrected and then confirmed by deleting paragraphs 5 and 6. Under Code of Civil Procedure section 1286.2, subdivision (d), when an arbitrator's award exceeds the arbitrator's powers, the award must be vacated unless it can be "corrected without affecting the merits of the decision upon the controversy submitted." Here, the arbitrator did find that Intel had breached the covenant of good faith; deleting the only remedies the arbitrator awarded for that breach necessarily affects the merits of the arbitrator's decision on that issue. . . .

d. Comments and Questions

1. If a modern day Charles Dickens wanted to skewer arbitration by focusing on a single awful instance of the process gone beserk, the writer could hardly do better than *AMD v. Intel.* Compare Dickens' memorable presentation of *Jarndyce v. Jarndyce* in BLEAK HOUSE (1854). It is not inevitable that arbitration produce a prompt, (relatively) inexpensive, and final decision.

2. To the extent that the dissent in *AMD v. Intel* suggests that American or California law limits arbitrators to awarding such remedies as could be awarded by a court, the opinion is simply incorrect. Do you think arbitrators should be limited to granting relief that a court has the power to award?

3. The dissent would uphold the decision of the arbitrator on the merits, but vacate the damages award. What would happen then? Even if the parties are inclined to pay the arbitrator to conduct further proceedings, the arbitrator may be unavailable. Among the causes for unavailability might be refusal to serve, retirement, death, incapacity, disappearance, other work commitments, or a conflict of interest. The risk of arbitrator unavailability is much greater where the arbitration was conducted by a three member panel. The use of such panels is normally limited to particularly complex or contentious disputes, the very ones where major problems are most likely to arise.

4. The referral of an arbitration proceeding back to the arbitrator, a possibility that was also discussed in *Tretina Printing*, presents conceptual difficulties because the arbitrator is not subject to the supervision of a court in the same way that lower courts are, and arbitrators do not have an institutional existance. Even to speak of a lower court assumes an institutional arrangement created by law. A court exists quite apart from the persons who are the temporary role incumbents who serve as judges on that court. An arbitrator is a person who is vested with temporary authority to arbitrate a dispute between the parties. The arrangent is ad hoc, and based on contract.

H. Mixture of Arbitrable and Nonarbitrable Claims

1. *Dean Witter Reynolds v. Byrd*, 470 U.S. 213 (1985)

Justice MARSHALL delivered the opinion of the Court.

The question presented is whether, when a complaint raises both federal securities claims and pendent state claims, a Federal District Court may deny a motion to compel arbitration of the state-law claims despite the parties' agreement to arbitrate their disputes.

I

In 1981, A. Lamar Byrd sold his dental practice and invested $160,000 in securities through Dean Witter Reynolds Inc., a securities broker-dealer. The value of the account declined by more than $100,000 between September 1981 and March 1982. Byrd filed a complaint against Dean Witter in the United States District Court California, alleging violations the Securities Exchange Act of 1934, and of various state law provisions. Federal jurisdiction over the state law claims was based on diversity of citizenship and the principle of pendent jurisdiction. In the complaint, Byrd alleged that an agent of Dean Witter had traded in his account without his prior consent, that the number of transactions executed on behalf of the account was excessive, that misrepresentations were made by an agent of Dean Witter as to the status of the account, and that the agent acted with Dean Witter's knowledge, participation, and ratification.

When Byrd invested his funds with Dean Witter in 1981, he signed a Customer's Agreement providing that "[a]ny controversy between you and the undersigned arising out of or relating to this contract or the breach thereof, shall be settled by arbitration." Dean Witter accordingly filed a motion for an order severing the pendent state claims, compelling their arbitration, and staying arbitration of those claims pending resolution of the federal court action. It argued that the Federal Arbitration Act, which provides that arbitration agreements "shall be valid, irrevocable, and enforceable, save upon such grounds as exist at law or in equity for the revocation of any contract," § 2, required that the District Court compel arbitration of the state-law claims. The Act authorizes parties to an arbitration agreement to petition a federal district court for an order compelling arbitration of any issue referable to arbitration under the agreement. Because Dean Witter assumed that the federal securities claim was not subject to the arbitration provision of the contract and could be resolved only in the federal forum, it did not seek to compel arbitration of that claim. The District Court denied in its entirety the motion to sever and compel arbitration of the pendent state claims, and on an interlocutory appeal the Court of Appeals for the Ninth Circuit affirmed. 726 F.2d 552 (1984).

II

Confronted with the issue [of] whether to compel arbitration of pendent state law claims when the federal court will in any event assert jurisdiction over a federal-law claim, the Federal Courts of Appeals have adopted two different approaches. Along with the Ninth Circuit in this case, the Fifth and Eleventh Circuits have relied on the "doctrine of intertwining." When arbitrable and nonarbitrable claims arise out of the same transaction, and are sufficiently intertwined factually and legally, the district court, under this view, may in its discretion deny arbitration as to the arbitrable claims and try all the claims together in federal court. These courts acknowledge the strong federal policy in favor of enforcing arbitration agreements but offer two reasons why the district courts nevertheless should decline to compel arbitration in this situation. First, they assert that such a result is necessary to preserve what they consider to be the court's exclusive jurisdiction over the federal securities claim; otherwise, they suggest, arbitration of an "intertwined" state claim might precede the federal proceeding and the factfinding done by the arbitrator might thereby bind the federal court through collateral estoppel. The second reason they cite is efficiency; by declining to compel arbitration, the court avoids bifurcated proceedings and perhaps redundant efforts to litigate the same factual questions twice.

In contrast, the Sixth, Seventh, and Eighth Circuits have held that the Arbitration Act divests the district courts of any discretion regarding arbitration in cases containing both arbitrable and nonarbitrable claims, and instead requires that the courts compel arbitration of arbitrable claims, when asked to do so. These courts conclude that the Act, both through its plain meaning and the strong federal policy it reflects, requires courts to enforce the bargain of the parties to arbitrate, and "not substitute [its] own views of economy and efficiency" for those of Congress.

We agree with these latter courts that the Arbitration Act requires district courts to compel arbitration of pendent arbitrable claims when one of the parties files a motion to compel, even where the result would be the possibly inefficient maintenance of separate proceedings in different forums. Accordingly, we reverse the decision not to compel arbitration.

III

. . . By its terms, the Act leaves no place for the exercise of discretion by a district court, but instead mandates that district courts shall direct the parties to proceed to arbitration on issues as to which an arbitration agreement has been signed. Thus, insofar as the language of the Act guides our disposition of this case, we would conclude that agreements to arbitrate must be enforced, absent a ground for revocation of the contractual agreement.

It is suggested, however, that the Act does not expressly address whether the same mandate—to enforce arbitration agreements—holds true where, as here, such a course would result in bifurcated proceedings if the arbitration agreement is enforced. Because the Act's drafters did not explicitly consider the prospect of bifurcated proceedings, we are told, the clear language of the Act might be misleading. Thus, courts that have adopted the view of the Ninth Circuit in this case have argued that the Act's goal of speedy and efficient decision-making is thwarted by bifurcated proceedings, and that, given the absence of clear direction on this point, the intent of Congress in passing the Act controls and compels a refusal to compel arbitration. . . .

The legislative history of the Act establishes that the purpose behind its passage was to ensure judicial enforcement of privately made agreements to arbitrate. We therefore reject the suggestion that the overriding goal of the Arbitration Act was to promote the expeditious resolution of claims. The Act, after all, does not mandate the arbitration of all claims, but merely the enforcement—upon the motion of one of the parties—of privately negotiated arbitration agreements. . . . [P]assage of the Act was motivated, first and foremost, by a congressional desire to enforce agreements into which parties had entered, and we must not overlook this principal objective when construing the statute, or allow the fortuitous impact of the Act on efficient dispute resolution to overshadow the underlying motivation. . . .

IV

It is also suggested, however, and some Courts of Appeals have held, that district courts should decide arbitrable pendent claims when a nonarbitrable federal claim is before them, because otherwise the findings in the arbitration proceeding might have collateral estoppel effect in a subsequent federal proceeding. This preclusive effect is believed to pose a threat to the federal interest in resolution of securities claims, and to warrant a refusal to compel arbitration. Other courts have held that the claims should be separately resolved, but that this preclusive effect warrants a stay of arbitration proceedings pending resolution of the federal securities claim. In this case, Dean Witter also asked the District Court to stay the arbitration proceedings pending resolution of the federal claim, and we suspect it did so in response to such holdings. . . .

We conclude that neither a stay of proceedings, nor joined proceedings, is necessary to protect the federal interest in the federal-court proceeding, and that the formulation of collateral estoppel rules affords adequate protection to that interest.

Initially, it is far from certain that arbitration proceedings will have any preclusive effect on the litigation of nonarbitrable federal claims. The full-faith-and-credit statute requires that federal courts give the same preclusive effect to a State's judicial proceedings as would the courts of the State rendering the judgment, and since arbitration is not a judicial proceeding, we held that the statute does not apply to arbitration awards. The same analysis inevitably would apply to any unappealed state arbitration proceedings. We also declined, in *McDonald,* to fashion a federal common-law rule of preclusion, in part on the ground that arbitration cannot provide an adequate substitute for a judicial proceeding in protecting the federal statutory and constitutional rights that § 1983 is designed to safeguard. We therefore recognized that arbitration proceedings will not necessarily have a preclusive effect on subsequent federal-court proceedings.

[C]ourts may directly and effectively protect federal interests by determining the preclusive effect to be given to an arbitration proceeding. Since preclusion doctrine comfortably plays this role, it follows that neither a stay of the arbitration proceedings, nor a refusal to compel arbitration of state claims, is required in order to assure that a precedent arbitration does not impede a subsequent federal court action. The Courts of Appeals that have assumed collateral estoppel effect must be given to arbitration proceedings have therefore sought to accomplish indirectly that which they erroneously assumed they could not do directly.

2. *Volt Information Sciences, Inc. v. Stanford University*, 489 U.S. 468 (1989)

Chief Justice REHNQUIST delivered the opinion of the Court.

Unlike its federal counterpart, the California Arbitration Act, contains a provision allowing a court to stay arbitration pending resolution of related litigation. We hold that application of the California statute is not pre-empted by the Federal Arbitration Act, in a case where the parties have agreed that their arbitration agreement will be governed by the law of California.

Appellant Volt Information Sciences, Inc. (Volt), and appellee Board of Trustees of Leland Stanford Junior University (Stanford) entered into a construction contract under which Volt was to install a system of electrical conduits on the Stanford campus. The contract contained an agreement to arbitrate all disputes between the parties "arising out of or relating to this contract or the breach thereof." The contract also contained a choice-of-law clause providing that "[t]he Contract shall be governed by the law of the place where the Project is located." During the course of the project, a dispute developed regarding compensation for extra work, and Volt made a formal demand for arbitration. Stanford responded by filing an action against Volt in California Superior Court, alleging fraud and breach of contract; in the same action, Stanford also sought indemnity from two other companies involved in the construction project, with whom it did not have arbitration agreements. Volt petitioned the Superior Court to compel arbitration of the dispute. Stanford in turn moved to stay arbitration pursuant to Cal. Civ. Proc. Code Ann. § 1281.2(c) (West 1982), which permits a court to stay arbitration pending resolution of related litigation between a party to the arbitration agreement and third parties not bound by it, where "there is a possibility of conflicting rulings on a common issue of law or fact." The Superior Court denied Volt's motion to compel arbitration and stayed the arbitration proceedings pending the outcome of the litigation on the authority of § 1281.2(c).

The California Court of Appeal affirmed. The court acknowledged that the parties' contract involved interstate commerce, that the FAA governs contracts in interstate commerce, and that the FAA contains no provision permitting a court to stay arbitration pending resolution of related litigation involving third parties not bound by the arbitration agreement. However, the court held that . . . the parties had incorporated the California rules of arbitration, including § 1281.2(c), into their arbitration agreement. Finally, the court rejected Volt's contention that, even if the parties had agreed to arbitrate under the California rules, application of § 1281.2(c) here was nonetheless pre-empted by the FAA because the contract involved interstate commerce.

The court reasoned that the purpose of the FAA was not to mandate the arbitration of all claims, but merely the enforcement of privately negotiated arbitration agreements. While the FAA pre-empts application of state laws which render arbitration agreements unenforceable, "[i]t does not follow, however, that the federal law has preclusive effect in a case where the parties have chosen in their [arbitration] agreement to abide by state rules." To the contrary, because "[t]he thrust of the federal law is that arbitration is strictly a matter of contract," the parties to an arbitration agreement should be "at liberty to choose the terms under which they will arbitrate." Where, as here, the parties have chosen in their agreement to abide by the state rules of arbitration, application of the FAA to prevent enforcement of those rules would actually be "inimical to the policies underlying state and federal arbitration law," because it would "force the parties to arbitrate in a manner contrary to their agreement." The California Supreme Court denied Volt's petition for discretionary review.

Appellant acknowledges, as it must, that the interpretation of private contracts is ordinarily a question of state law, which this Court does not sit to review. But appellant nonetheless maintains that we should set aside the Court of Appeal's interpretation of this particular contractual provision for two principal reasons.

Appellant first suggests that the Court of Appeal's construction of the choice-of-law clause was in effect a finding that appellant had "waived" its "federally guaranteed right to compel arbitration of the parties' dispute," a waiver whose validity must be judged by reference to federal rather than state law. This argument fundamentally misconceives the nature of the rights created by the FAA. The Act was designed "to overrule the judiciary's longstanding refusal to enforce agreements to arbitrate," and place such agreements "upon the same footing as other contracts." . . .

[Section] 4 of the FAA . . . confers only the right to obtain an order directing that "arbitration proceed in the manner provided for in [the parties'] agreement." Here the Court of Appeal found that, by incorporating the California rules of arbitration into their agreement, the parties had agreed that arbitration would not proceed in situations which fell within the scope of § 1281.2(c). This was not a finding that appellant had "waived" an FAA-guaranteed right to compel arbitration of this dispute, but a finding that it had no such right in the first place, because the parties' agreement did not require arbitration to proceed in this situation. Accordingly, appellant's contention that the contract interpretation issue presented here involves the "waiver" of a federal right is without merit.

Second, appellant argues that we should set aside the Court of Appeal's construction of the choice-of-law clause because it violates the settled federal rule that questions of arbitrability in contracts subject to the FAA must be resolved with a healthy regard for the federal policy favoring arbitration. . . . [W]e do not think the Court of Appeal offended [this] principle by interpreting the choice-of-law provision to mean that the parties intended the California rules of arbitration, including the § 1281.2(c) stay provision, to apply to their arbitration agreement. There is no federal policy favoring arbitration under a certain set of procedural rules; the federal policy is simply to ensure the enforceability, according to their terms, of private agreements to arbitrate. Interpreting a choice-of-law clause to make applicable state rules governing the conduct of arbitration—rules which are manifestly designed to encourage resort to the arbitral process—simply does not offend . . . any policy embodied in the FAA.[5]

The question remains whether . . . application of § 1281.2(c) is nonetheless pre-empted by the FAA to the extent it is used to stay arbitration under this contract involving interstate commerce. It is undisputed that this contract falls within the coverage of the FAA, since it involves

[5]Unlike the dissent, we think the California arbitration rules. . . generally foster the federal policy favoring arbitration. . . . [T]he FAA itself contains no provision designed to deal with the special practical problems that arise in multiparty contractual disputes when some or all of the contracts at issue include agreements to arbitrate. California has taken the lead in fashioning a legislative response to this problem, by giving courts authority to consolidate or stay arbitration proceedings in these situations in order to minimize the potential for contradictory judgments.

interstate commerce, and that the FAA contains no provision authorizing a stay of arbitration in this situation. . . .

The FAA contains no express pre-emptive provision, nor does it reflect a congressional intent to occupy the entire field of arbitration. But even when Congress has not completely displaced state regulation in an area, state law may nonetheless be pre-empted to the extent that it actually conflicts with federal law—that is, to the extent that it "stands as an obstacle to the accomplishment and execution of the full purposes and objectives of Congress." The question before us, therefore, is whether application of § 1281.2(c) to stay arbitration under this contract in interstate commerce, in accordance with the terms of the arbitration agreement itself, would undermine the goals and policies of the FAA. We conclude that it would not. . . .

[T]he FAA does not require parties to arbitrate when they have not agreed to do so, nor does it prevent parties who do agree to arbitrate from excluding certain claims from the scope of their arbitration agreement. It simply requires courts to enforce privately negotiated agreements to arbitrate, like other contracts, in accordance with their terms.

In recognition of Congress' principal purpose of ensuring that private arbitration agreements are enforced according to their terms, we have held that the FAA pre-empts state laws which "require a judicial forum for the resolution of claims which the contracting parties agreed to resolve by arbitration." *Southland Corp. v. Keating*, 465 U.S. 1 (1984) (finding pre-empted a state statute which rendered agreements to arbitrate certain franchise claims unenforceable); *Perry v. Thomas* (finding pre-empted a state statute which rendered unenforceable private agreements to arbitrate certain wage collection claims). But it does not follow that the FAA prevents the enforcement of agreements to arbitrate under different rules than those set forth in the Act itself. Indeed, such a result would be quite inimical to the FAA's primary purpose of ensuring that private agreements to arbitrate are enforced according to their terms. . . . Where, as here, the parties have agreed to abide by state rules of arbitration, enforcing those rules according to the terms of the agreement is fully consistent with the goals of the FAA, even if the result is that arbitration is stayed where the Act would otherwise permit it to go forward. [In so doing], we give effect to the contractual rights and expectations of the parties, without doing violence to the policies behind by the FAA.

Justice BRENNAN, with whom Justice MARSHALL joins, dissenting.

The litigants in this case were parties to a construction contract which contained a clause obligating them to arbitrate disputes and making that obligation specifically enforceable. The contract also incorporated provisions of a standard form contract prepared by the American Institute of Architects and endorsed by the Associated General Contractors of America; among these general provisions was § 7.1.1: "The Contract shall be governed by the law of the place where the Project is located." When a dispute arose between the parties, Volt invoked the arbitration clause, while Stanford attempted to avoid it (apparently because the dispute also involved two other contractors with whom Stanford had no arbitration agreements).

The Federal Arbitration Act (FAA) requires courts to enforce arbitration agreements in contracts involving interstate commerce. The California courts nonetheless rejected Volt's petition to compel arbitration in reliance on a provision of state law that, in the circumstances presented, permitted a court to stay arbitration pending the conclusion of related litigation. Volt, not surprisingly, suggested that the Supremacy Clause compelled a different result. The

California Court of Appeal found, however, that the parties had agreed that their contract would be governed solely by the law of the State of California, to the exclusion of federal law. In reaching this conclusion the court relied on no extrinsic evidence of the parties' intent, but solely on the language of the form contract. . . .

I have no quarrel with the general proposition that the interpretation of contracts is a matter of state law. By ending its analysis at that level of generality, however, the Court overlooks well-established precedent to the effect that, in order to guard against arbitrary denials of federal claims, a state court's construction of a contract in such a way as to preclude enforcement of a federal right is not immune from review in this Court as to its "adequacy." . . . Where "the existence or the application of a federal right turns on a logically antecedent finding on a matter of state law, it is essential to the Court's performance of its function that it exercise an ancillary jurisdiction to consider the state question. Federal rights could otherwise be nullified by the manipulation of state law." I agree with the Court that "the FAA does not require parties to arbitrate when they have not agreed to do so." . . .

The substantive question in this case is whether or not they have done so. And that question, we have made clear in the past, is a matter of federal law. . . . Not only does the FAA require the enforcement of arbitration agreements, but we have held that it also establishes substantive federal law that must be consulted in determining whether (or to what extent) a given contract provides for arbitration. . . . I agree fully with the Court that "the federal policy is simply to ensure the enforceability, according to their terms, of private agreements to arbitrate," but I disagree emphatically with its conclusion that that policy is not frustrated here. Applying the California procedural rule, which stays arbitration while litigation of the same issue goes forward, means simply that the parties' dispute will be litigated rather than arbitrated.

Construction of a contractual provision is, of course, a matter of discerning the parties' intent. It is important to recall, in the first place, that in this case there is no extrinsic evidence of their intent. We must therefore rely on the contract itself. But the provision of the contract at issue here was not one that these parties drafted themselves. Rather, they incorporated portions of a standard form contract commonly used in the construction industry. That makes it most unlikely that their intent was in any way at variance with the purposes for which choice-of-law clauses are commonly written and the manner in which they are generally interpreted.

It seems to me beyond dispute that the normal purpose of such choice-of-law clauses is to determine that the law of one State rather than that of another State will be applicable; they simply do not speak to any interaction between state and federal law. A cursory glance at standard conflicts texts confirms this observation: they contain no reference at all to the relation between federal and state law in their discussions of contractual choice-of-law clauses. The same is true of standard codifications. *See* Uniform Commercial Code § 1-105(1); Restatement (Second) of Conflict of Laws § 187. Indeed the Restatement of Conflicts notes expressly that it does not deal with "the ever-present problem of determining the respective spheres of authority of the law and courts of the nation and of the member States." *Id.*, § 2, Comment c. Decisions of this Court fully bear out the impression that choice-of-law clauses do not speak to any state-federal issue. . . .

Moreover, the literal language of the contract—"the law of the place"—gives no indication of any intention to apply only state law and exclude other law that would normally be applicable to something taking place at that location. By settled principles of federal supremacy, the law of any place in the United States includes federal law. As the dissenting judge below noted, "under California law, federal law governs matters cognizable in California courts upon which the United States has definitively spoken." Thus, "the mere choice of California law is not a selection of California law over federal law. . . ." In the absence of any evidence to the contrary it must be assumed that this is what the parties meant by "the law of the place where the Project is located."

Most commercial contracts written in this country contain choice-of-law clauses, similar to the one in the Stanford-Volt contract, specifying which State's law is to govern the interpretation of the contract. Were every state court to construe such clauses as an expression of the parties' intent to exclude the application of federal law, as has the California Court of Appeal in this case, the result would be to render the Federal Arbitration Act a virtual nullity as to presently existing contracts. I cannot believe that the parties to contracts intend such consequences to flow from their insertion of a standard choice-of-law clause. Even less can I agree that we are powerless to review decisions of state courts that effectively nullify a vital piece of federal legislation. I respectfully dissent.

3. Comments and Questions

a. Several of the cases in the chapter present dispute that ended up being subject to both arbitration and litigation. See, e.g. the *Coors* and *Mitsubishi* cases in section I.

b. The FAA is silent about the duplication that can occur from arbitration and litigation, which led the *Byrd* Court to conclude that it was required to "compel arbitration of pendent arbitrable claims when one of the parties files a motion to compel, even where the result would be the possibly inefficient maintenance of separate proceedings in different forums."

c. The California approach, described in the *Volt* decision, has the great merit of addressing the inefficiency problem in at least a limited way. It is likely that a modest amount of thought could produce a better system, at least in theory. Try to design amendments to the FAA and the UAA that provide for a better approach to the inefficiency problem. Can the courts effectively and inexpensively implement your system?

I. Arbitration of Antitrust Claims

1. *Mitsubishi Motors Corp. v. Soler Chrysler-Plymouth, Inc.*, 473 U.S. 614 (1985)

Justice BLACKMUN delivered the opinion of the Court.

The principal question presented by these cases is the arbitrability, pursuant to the Federal Arbitration Act, 9 U.S.C. § 1 et seq., and the Convention on the Recognition and Enforcement of Foreign Arbitral Awards (Convention) of claims arising under the Sherman Act, and encompassed within a valid arbitration clause in an agreement embodying an international commercial transaction.

I

Mitsubishi Motors Corporation (Mitsubishi) is a Japanese corporation which manufactures automobiles and has its principal place of business in Tokyo, Japan. Mitsubishi is the product of a joint venture between, on the one hand, Chrysler International, S.A. (CISA), a Swiss corporation registered in Geneva and wholly owned by Chrysler Corporation, and, on the other, Mitsubishi Heavy Industries, Inc., a Japanese corporation. The aim of the joint venture was the distribution through Chrysler dealers outside the continental United States of vehicles manufactured by Mitsubishi and bearing Chrysler and Mitsubishi trademarks. Soler Chrysler-Plymouth, Inc. (Soler), is a Puerto Rico corporation with its principal place of business in Pueblo Viejo, Guaynabo, Puerto Rico.

On October 31, 1979, Soler entered into a Distributor Agreement with CISA which provided for the sale by Soler of Mitsubishi-manufactured vehicles within a designated area, including metropolitan San Juan. On the same date, CISA, Soler, and Mitsubishi entered into a Sales Procedure Agreement (Sales Agreement) which, referring to the Distributor Agreement, provided for the direct sale of Mitsubishi products to Soler and governed the terms and conditions of such sales. Paragraph VI of the Sales Agreement, labeled "Arbitration of Certain Matters," provides: "All disputes, controversies or differences which may arise between [Mitsubishi] and [Soler] out of or in relation to Articles I-B through V of this Agreement or for the breach thereof, shall be finally settled by arbitration in Japan in accordance with the rules and regulations of the Japan Commercial Arbitration Association."

Initially, Soler did a brisk business in Mitsubishi-manufactured vehicles. . . . In early 1981, however, the new car market slackened. Soler ran into serious difficulties in meeting the expected sales volume, and by the spring of 1981 it felt itself compelled to request that Mitsubishi delay or cancel shipment of several orders. About the same time, Soler attempted to arrange for the transshipment of a quantity of its vehicles for sale in the continental United States and Latin America. Mitsubishi and CISA, however, refused permission for any such diversion, citing a variety of reasons, and no vehicles were transshipped.[1] Attempts to work out these difficulties failed.

. . . Mitsubishi brought an action against Soler in the United States District Court for the District of Puerto Rico under the Federal Arbitration Act and the Convention. Mitsubishi sought an order, pursuant to 9 U.S.C. §§ 4 and 201, to compel arbitration in accord with the Sales Agreement. Shortly after filing the complaint, Mitsubishi filed a request for arbitration before the Japan Commercial Arbitration Association.

Soler denied the allegations and counterclaimed against both Mitsubishi and CISA. It alleged numerous breaches by Mitsubishi of the Sales Agreement, raised a pair of defamation claims, and asserted causes of action under the Sherman Act; the federal Automobile Dealers' Day in Court Act; the Puerto Rico competition statute; and the Puerto Rico Dealers' Contracts Act. In the counterclaim premised on the Sherman Act, Soler alleged that Mitsubishi and CISA had conspired to divide markets in restraint of trade. To effectuate the plan, according to Soler, Mitsubishi had refused to permit Soler to resell to buyers in North, Central, or South America vehicles it had obligated itself to purchase from Mitsubishi; had

[1]The reasons advanced included concerns that such diversion would interfere with the Japanese trade policy of voluntarily limiting imports to the United States; that the Soler-ordered vehicles would be unsuitable for use in certain proposed destinations because of their manufacture, with use in Puerto Rico in mind, without heaters and defoggers; that the vehicles would be unsuitable for use in Latin America because of the unavailability there of the unleaded, high octane fuel they required; that adequate warranty service could not be ensured; and that diversion to the mainland would violate contractual obligations between CISA and Mitsubishi.

refused to ship ordered vehicles or the parts, such as heaters and defoggers, that would be necessary to permit Soler to make its vehicles suitable for resale outside Puerto Rico; and had coercively attempted to replace Soler and its other Puerto Rico distributors with a wholly owned subsidiary which would serve as the exclusive Mitsubishi distributor in Puerto Rico.

After a hearing, the District Court ordered Mitsubishi and Soler to arbitrate each of the issues raised in the complaint and in all the counterclaims save two and a portion of a third.[7] With regard to the federal antitrust issues, it . . . held that the rights conferred by the antitrust laws were "of a character inappropriate for enforcement by arbitration." The District Court held, however, that the international character of the Mitsubishi-Soler undertaking required enforcement of the agreement to arbitrate even as to the antitrust claims.

The Court of Appeals for the First Circuit affirmed in part and reversed in part. It first rejected Soler's argument that Puerto Rico law precluded enforcement of an agreement obligating a local dealer to arbitrate controversies outside Puerto Rico.[8] It also rejected Soler's suggestion that it could not have intended to arbitrate statutory claims not mentioned in the arbitration agreement. Assessing arbitrability "on an allegation-by-allegation basis," the court then read the arbitration clause to encompass virtually all the claims arising under the various statutes, including all those arising under the Sherman Act.

Finally, after endorsing the doctrine . . . precluding arbitration of antitrust claims, the Court of Appeals concluded that neither this Court's decision in Scherk nor the Convention required abandonment of that doctrine in the face of an international transaction. Accordingly, it reversed the judgment of the District Court insofar as it had ordered submission of "Soler's antitrust claims" to arbitration. Affirming the remainder of the judgment, the court directed the District Court to consider in the first instance how the parallel judicial and arbitral proceedings should go forward.

We granted certiorari primarily to consider whether an American court should enforce an agreement to resolve antitrust claims by arbitration when that agreement arises from an international transaction.

II

At the outset, we address the contention raised in Soler's cross-petition that the arbitration clause at issue may not be read to encompass the statutory counterclaims stated in its answer

---

[7]The District Court found that the arbitration clause did not cover the fourth and sixth counterclaims, which sought damages for defamation, or the allegations in the seventh counterclaim concerning discriminatory treatment and the establishment of minimum-sales volumes. Accordingly, it retained jurisdiction over those portions of the litigation. In addition, because no arbitration agreement between Soler and CISA existed, the court retained jurisdiction, insofar as they sought relief from CISA, over the first, second, third, and ninth counterclaims, which raised claims under the Puerto Rico Dealers' Contracts Act, the federal Automobile Dealers' Day in Court Act, the Sherman Act, and the Puerto Rico competition statute. . . . These aspects of the District Court's ruling were not appealed and are not before this Court.

[8]Soler relied on P.R. Laws Ann., Tit. 10, § 278b-2 (Supp.1983), which purports to render null and void "[a]ny stipulation that obligates a dealer to adjust, arbitrate or litigate any controversy that comes up regarding his dealer's contract outside of Puerto Rico, or under foreign law or rule of law." The Court of Appeals held this provision pre-empted by 9 U.S.C. § 2, which declares arbitration agreements valid and enforceable "save upon such grounds as exist at law or in equity for the revocation of any contract." Soler does not challenge this holding in its cross-petition here.

to the complaint. In making this argument, Soler does not question the Court of Appeals' application of the Sales Agreement to the disputes involved here as a matter of standard contract interpretation. Instead, it argues that as a matter of law a court may not construe an arbitration agreement to encompass claims arising out of statutes designed to protect a class to which the party resisting arbitration belongs "unless [that party] has expressly agreed" to arbitrate those claims, by which Soler presumably means that the arbitration clause must specifically mention the statute giving rise to the claims that a party to the clause seeks to arbitrate. Soler reasons that, because it falls within the class for whose benefit the federal and local antitrust laws and dealers' Acts were passed, but the arbitration clause at issue does not mention these statutes or statutes in general, the clause cannot be read to contemplate arbitration of these statutory claims.

We do not agree, for we find no warrant in the Arbitration Act for implying in every contract within its ken a presumption against arbitration of statutory claims. . . . The "liberal federal policy favoring arbitration agreements" manifested by this provision and the Act as a whole, is at bottom a policy guaranteeing the enforcement of private contractual arrangements: the Act simply "creates a body of federal substantive law establishing and regulating the duty to honor an agreement to arbitrate." . . . "The preeminent concern of Congress in passing the Act was to enforce private agreements into which parties had entered," a concern which "requires that we rigorously enforce agreements to arbitrate." *Dean Witter Reynolds Inc. v. Byrd,* 470 U.S. 213, 221 (1985).

Accordingly, the first task of a court asked to compel arbitration of a dispute is to determine whether the parties agreed to arbitrate that dispute. The court is to make this determination by applying the "federal substantive law of arbitrability, applicable to any arbitration agreement within the coverage of the Act." . . . The Arbitration Act establishes that, as a matter of federal law, any doubts concerning the scope of arbitrable issues should be resolved in favor of arbitration, whether the problem at hand is the construction of the contract language itself or an allegation of waiver, delay, or a like defense to arbitrability. Thus, as with any other contract, the parties' intentions control, but those intentions are generously construed as to issues of arbitrability.

There is no reason to depart from these guidelines where a party bound by an arbitration agreement raises claims founded on statutory rights. . . . [W]e are well past the time when judicial suspicion of the desirability of arbitration and of the competence of arbitral tribunals inhibited the development of arbitration as an alternative means of dispute resolution. Of course, courts should remain attuned to well-supported claims that the agreement to arbitrate resulted from the sort of fraud or overwhelming economic power that would provide grounds "for the revocation of any contract." But, absent such compelling considerations, the Act itself provides no basis for disfavoring agreements to arbitrate statutory claims by skewing the otherwise hospitable inquiry into arbitrability.

. . . . By agreeing to arbitrate a statutory claim, a party does not forgo the substantive rights afforded by the statute; it only submits to their resolution in an arbitral, rather than a judicial, forum. It trades the procedures and opportunity for review of the courtroom for the simplicity, informality, and expedition of arbitration. We must assume that if Congress intended the substantive protection afforded by a given statute to include protection against waiver of the right to a judicial forum, that intention will be deducible from text or legislative history. Having made the bargain to arbitrate, the party should be held to it unless Congress itself has evinced an intention to preclude a waiver of judicial remedies for the statutory rights at issue. Nothing, in the meantime, prevents a party from excluding statutory claims from the scope of an agreement to arbitrate.

In sum, the Court of Appeals correctly conducted a two-step inquiry, first determining whether the parties' agreement to arbitrate reached the statutory issues, and then, upon finding it did, considering whether legal constraints external to the parties' agreement foreclosed the arbitration of those claims. We endorse its rejection of Soler's proposed rule of arbitration clause construction.

III

We now turn to consider whether Soler's antitrust claims are nonarbitrable even though it has agreed to arbitrate them. We find it unnecessary to assess the legitimacy of . . . agreements to arbitrate arising from domestic transactions. [W]e conclude that concerns of international comity, respect for the capacities of foreign and transnational tribunals, and sensitivity to the need of the international commercial system for predictability in the resolution of disputes require that we enforce the parties' agreement, even assuming that a contrary result would be forthcoming in a domestic context. [The Court then proceeded to explain at length why antitrust claims are appropriately heard by arbitrators.]

There is no reason to assume at the outset of the dispute that international arbitration will not provide an adequate mechanism. To be sure, the international arbitral tribunal owes no prior allegiance to the legal norms of particular states; hence, it has no direct obligation to vindicate their statutory dictates. The tribunal, however, is bound to effectuate the intentions of the parties. Where the parties have agreed that the arbitral body is to decide a defined set of claims which includes, as in these cases, those arising from the application of American antitrust law, the tribunal therefore should be bound to decide that dispute in accord with the national law giving rise to the claim.[19] And so long as the prospective litigant effectively may vindicate its statutory cause of action in the arbitral forum, the statute will continue to serve both its remedial and deterrent function.

Having permitted the arbitration to go forward, the national courts of the United States will have the opportunity at the award-enforcement stage to ensure that the legitimate interest in the enforcement of the antitrust laws has been addressed. The Convention reserves to each signatory country the right to refuse enforcement of an award where the "recognition or

[19]In addition to the clause providing for arbitration before the Japan Commercial Arbitration Association, the Sales Agreement includes a choice-of-law clause which reads: "This Agreement is made in, and will be governed by and construed in all respects according to the laws of the Swiss Confederation as if entirely performed therein." The United States raises the possibility that the arbitral panel will read this provision not simply to govern interpretation of the contract terms, but wholly to displace American law even where it otherwise would apply. . . . At oral argument, however, counsel for Mitsubishi conceded that American law applied to the antitrust claims and represented that the claims had been submitted to the arbitration panel in Japan on that basis. . . . We therefore have no occasion to speculate on this matter at this stage in the proceedings, when Mitsubishi seeks to enforce the agreement to arbitrate, not to enforce an award. Nor need we consider now the effect of an arbitral tribunal's failure to take cognizance of the statutory cause of action on the claimant's capacity to reinitiate suit in federal court. We merely note that in the event the choice-of-forum and choice-of-law clauses operated in tandem as a prospective waiver of a party's right to pursue statutory remedies for antitrust violations, we would have little hesitation in condemning the agreement as against public policy.

enforcement of the award would be contrary to the public policy of that country." While the efficacy of the arbitral process requires that substantive review at the award-enforcement stage remain minimal, it would not require intrusive inquiry to ascertain that the tribunal took cognizance of the antitrust claims and actually decided them.[20]

As international trade has expanded in recent decades, so too has the use of international arbitration to resolve disputes arising in the course of that trade. The controversies that international arbitral institutions are called upon to resolve have increased in diversity as well as in complexity. Yet the potential of these tribunals for efficient disposition of legal disagreements arising from commercial relations has not yet been tested. If they are to take a central place in the international legal order, national courts will need to "shake off the old judicial hostility to arbitration," and also their customary and understandable unwillingness to cede jurisdiction of a claim arising under domestic law to a foreign or transnational tribunal. To this extent, at least, it will be necessary for national courts to subordinate domestic notions of arbitrability to the international policy favoring commercial arbitration.

Justice STEVENS, with whom Justice BRENNAN joins, and with whom Justice MARSHALL joins except as to Part II, dissenting.

. . . This Court agrees with the Court of Appeals' interpretation of the scope of the arbitration clause, but disagrees with its conclusion that the clause is unenforceable insofar as it purports to cover an antitrust claim against a Japanese company. This Court's holding rests almost exclusively on the federal policy favoring arbitration of commercial disputes and vague notions of international comity arising from the fact that the automobiles involved here were manufactured in Japan. Because I am convinced that the Court of Appeals' construction of the arbitration clause is erroneous, and because I strongly disagree with this Court's interpretation of the relevant federal statutes, I respectfully dissent. In my opinion, (1) a fair construction of the language in the arbitration clause in the parties' contract does not encompass a claim that auto manufacturers entered into a conspiracy in violation of the antitrust laws; (2) an arbitration clause should not normally be construed to cover a statutory remedy that it does not expressly identify; (3) Congress did not intend § 2 of the Federal Arbitration Act to apply to antitrust claims; and (4) Congress did not intend the Convention on the Recognition and Enforcement of Foreign Arbitral Awards to apply to disputes that are not covered by the Federal Arbitration Act. . . .

In my opinion, the elected representatives of the American people would not have us dispatch an American citizen to a foreign land in search of an uncertain remedy for the violation of a public right that is protected by the Sherman Act. This is especially so when there has been no genuine bargaining over the terms of the submission, and the arbitration remedy provided has not even the most elementary guarantees of fair process. Consideration of a fully developed record by a jury, instructed in the law by a federal judge, and subject to appellate review, is a surer guide to the competitive character of a commercial practice than the practically unreviewable judgment of a private arbitrator.

---

[20]We note, for example, that the rules of the Japan Commercial Arbitration Association provide for the taking of a "summary record" of each hearing; for the stenographic recording of the proceedings where the tribunal so orders or a party requests one; and for a statement of reasons for the award unless the parties agree otherwise. Needless to say, we intimate no views on the merits of Soler's antitrust claims.

Unlike the Congress that enacted the Sherman Act in 1890, the Court today does not seem to appreciate the value of economic freedom. I respectfully dissent.

2. Comments and Questions

a. The majority opinion ended its complex opinion by stating "it is so ordered." Precisely what was ordered by each of the courts that decided the case with respect to each of the claims for which arbitration was sought? What would you have ordered, and why? To what extent should avoidance of multiple fora be a consideration?

b. The multiple fora issue appears again in the next case, fought by two large breweries. The ruling of the court was that one issue will be arbitrated, one will be litigated, and one will proceed to discovery subject to the possibility that it will later be sent to arbitration. What would you have ordered?

c. Justice Stevens points out that "the greatest risk" is not that violations of the Sherman Act will go unremedied, but that "the arbitrator will condemn business practices under the antitrust laws that are efficient in a free competitive market." 473 U.S. at 657. Do you agree?

d. The implicit assumption in all the arguments against arbitration of statutory claims is that the public objective sought by the statute will be inadequately addressed. Stevens suggest the opposite — that arbitrators will be too sympathetic to statutory goals. This "overprotection hypothesis" should be considered in evaluating other claims that arbitration is inadequate to vindicate public policy goals.

e. One may well conclude from the cases presented in this and Chapter 12 that Justices Brennan, Marshall, and Stevens oppose arbitration of issues with an important pulic policy element such as antitrust, securities fraud, and employment discrimination claims. (Interestingly, civil racketeering claims do not present a similar concern.) If, however, the dissent's concern about dispatching Americans to seek vindication of public rights protected by the Sherman Act in a foreign jurisdiction, they should have less concern about domestic arbitration of antitrust issues.

3. *Coors Brewing Co. v. Molson Breweries*, 51 F.3d 1511 (10th Cir. 1995)

HENRY, Circuit Judge.

Defendant Molson appeals the decision of the district court denying its motion to stay plaintiff Coors's antitrust suit pending contract arbitration. We have jurisdiction pursuant to 9 U.S.C. § 16. . . .

Coors Brewing Company (Coors) is a Colorado corporation engaged in the business of brewing, marketing, and distributing beer. In 1985, Coors entered into a licensing agreement with Molson Breweries of Canada Limited (Molson), a Canadian corporation also in the beer industry. Coors and Molson agreed that Molson would brew and distribute Coors products in Canada. Under the terms of the agreement, Coors gave Molson access to Coors trademarks, brewing processes, and marketing information. Molson, in turn, agreed to use its best efforts to distribute Coors products in Canada and to keep marketing and product information confidential. The agreement further provided that either party could terminate the agreement for cause under a specified procedure, or without cause by giving the other party ten years notice of termination. The agreement also contained an arbitration clause: "Any dispute arising in connection with the implementation, interpretation or enforcement of this Agreement, . . .

shall be finally settled under the Rules of the American Arbitration Association. . . ."

In 1993, Miller Brewing Company (Miller), a Wisconsin corporation also in the business of brewing and marketing beer, entered into a partnership with Molson. [T]he agreement gave Miller one seat on Molson's board of directors and created a reciprocal licensing arrangement. Under the reciprocal licensing arrangement, Miller is the exclusive distributor of Molson products in the United States and Molson is the exclusive distributor of Miller products in Canada.

Coors filed a Notice of Arbitration with Molson, alleging that Molson breached its contract with Coors, and seeking injunctive relief, damages, and termination of the licensing agreement. Coors also filed the instant complaint in United States District Court against Molson and Miller alleging antitrust violations of the Clayton and Sherman Acts. In its exhaustive complaint, Coors makes allegations that we divide into three general categories. First, Coors alleges that the Miller-Molson alliance is a combination in restraint of trade, lessening competition in the United States and North American beer markets. Second, Coors alleges that Miller will have access to Coors's confidential product and marketing information. Third, Coors alleges that Miller will control the distribution and marketing of Coors brands in Canada. Molson brought a motion to stay the antitrust proceedings against both Molson and Miller pending the resolution of the contract arbitration. The district court denied the motion, and Molson sought expedited appeal. . . .

1. Molson v. Coors

Molson argues that Coors has dressed up its contract claims in antitrust clothes to avoid its own agreement to arbitrate. Specifically, Molson argues that a valid arbitration agreement exists between Coors and Molson, that arbitration will settle factual issues important to the antitrust claims, and that a stay is appropriate even if the factual grounds for the contract arbitration and antitrust suit are different.

Coors, on the other hand, argues that the contract and antitrust claims are separate. It claims two distinct interests: protecting its contractual rights, which it concedes are subject to arbitration, and protecting its interest in competition in the United States and North American beer markets, which it argues is not subject to arbitration. In short, Coors argues that it should be able to pursue an antitrust suit unrelated to the contract just as any other beer manufacturer or consumer could. This court reviews the underlying arbitrability of a contract de novo. *O'Connor v. R.F. Lafferty & Co.*, 965 F.2d 893, 901 (10th Cir. 1992).

The Federal Arbitration Act (FAA), 9 U.S.C. § 3, requires a district court to stay judicial proceedings where a written agreement provides for the arbitration of the dispute that is the subject of the litigation. There is a strong federal policy favoring arbitration for dispute resolution. The policy basis of this statute is particularly strong in the context of international transactions. All doubts are to be resolved in favor of arbitrability. In addition to the general policy favoring arbitration, Molson argues that *Mitsubishi Motors Corp. v. Soler Chrysler-Plymouth* stands for the proposition that antitrust claims within the scope of a contract can be subject to arbitration, even if the arbitration clause does not specifically mention antitrust disputes.

Coors argues that the FAA and Mitsubishi do not control this dispute for two reasons: First, Coors argues that the arbitration clause in the Coors-Molson license agreement is a narrow arbitration clause and that it does not include antitrust disputes. [The court concluded that the "any dispute arising in connection with the implementation, interpretation, or enforcement" language in the Coors-Molson arbitration term included antitrust disputes.] Second, Coors argues that even if the arbitration clause includes antitrust disputes, its antitrust claims are outside the scope of the contract and thus not subject to the contractual arbitration clause. . . .

2. Scope of Contract

Having concluded that the Coors-Molson arbitration clause encompasses antitrust disputes, we turn to Coors's second argument and determine whether Coors's claims are within the scope of the contract. Coors argues that its claims are unrelated to the contract and that the antitrust dispute is therefore not subject to the contractual arbitration agreement. We hold that some of Coors's antitrust causes of action are within the scope of the Coors-Molson licensing agreement and that some of Coors's claims are outside the scope of that contract.

Although the Supreme Court in *Mitsubishi* reversed the First Circuit's holding that public policy prohibited the involuntary arbitration of antitrust claims, it adopted and affirmed the First Circuit's determination that the antitrust claims were within the scope of that contract. The First Circuit's discussion of the contract in *Mitsubishi* emphasized that the antitrust claims were closely related to the contract because they turned upon specific contractual provisions. . . . The First Circuit concluded that because *Mitsubishi* based its refusal to deal on concerns about trademarks, reputation, and goodwill — considerations that the contract specifically addressed — the antitrust claims were within the scope of the contract. . . .

An arbitration clause "does not extend to all disputes of any sort . . . but only to disputes touching specified provisions of the agreement." The First Circuit's basis for holding the antitrust claims to be within the scope of the contract thus logically limits the Supreme Court's holding in *Mitsubishi* to antitrust claims that have a reasonable factual connection to the contract. We therefore hold that Coors's antitrust claims that do not implicate the contract are litigable.

In addition . . . there are practical reasons to read *Mitsubishi* in a more limited way than Molson suggests. As Molson's counsel acknowledged at oral argument, its interpretation of Mitsubishi is that every brewer in America except Coors may bring an antitrust action against Molson. Although Mitsubishi allowed parties to a contract to compel the arbitration of their antitrust disputes, it did not proclaim that all disputes between parties who include an arbitration clause in their contracts are subject to arbitration. A dispute within the scope of the contract is still a condition precedent to the involuntary arbitration of antitrust claims.

Coors's claims regarding market concentration are not related to the licensing agreement, and Coors may therefore litigate those claims. Coors's claims regarding confidentiality and proprietary information involve the Coors-Molson licensing agreement. Like the First Circuit in Mitsubishi, we conclude that the contractual arbitration clause controls this dispute. Molson gained access to the Coors information because of the parties' contractual relationship. Also under the terms of their contract, both parties agreed to arbitrate claims arising from this contract. Coors must keep its promise to arbitrate its allegations involving confidential product and marketing information.

Coors's least developed and most novel claim is that Miller's control over Molson will have an anti-competitive effect on the United States and North American beer markets. Coors argues that Miller holds a seat on Molson's board of directors, that Molson's bylaws require a unanimous vote of all directors, and that Miller may thus be in a position to control the distribution of Coors products. . . . Coors has not specifically stated how Miller's control over

Molson will create anti-competitive effects. . . . [W]e conclude that Coors has presented a sufficient factual outline to suggest that it might develop a theory unrelated to the Coors-Molson licensing agreement. Coors is therefore entitled to conduct discovery and refine its theories. However, we do not make a final judgment on any control theory because the record before us is insufficient to allow it. At a later point in this litigation, Molson may again challenge Coors's claims, with respect to both their relation to the licensing agreement and their legal sufficiency.

4. Antitrust Arbitration in America

a. *Nghiem v. NEC Electronics, Inc.*, 25 F.3d 1437 (9th Cir. 1994)

O'SCANNLAIN, Circuit Judge:

Peter Nghiem, an American citizen of Vietnamese heritage, was employed by NEC Electronics, Inc. in California from August 31, 1989 until he was fired in June 1990. Nghiem brought suit against NEC . . . alleging, inter alia, wrongful termination, race discrimination, and an antitrust violation. Nghiem claims that NEC had represented that it would provide a long-term management position to Nghiem if he accepted its employment offer.

On August 31, 1989, Nghiem signed an employment contract which did not contain an arbitration clause. . . . Nghiem claims that he did not sign a modified version of NEC's employment contract because it contained a clause for binding arbitration. On September 5, 1989 and May 7, 1990, Nghiem signed acknowledgments for receipt of NEC's company handbook. The handbook explained that NEC had a four-step "Problem Resolution Process" for employee complaints. Nghiem claims that he felt compelled to use this process because the language of the handbook said that this was the only process for resolving employee complaints. Step Four of the process is "final and binding arbitration." Nghiem followed the four-step process, including initiating arbitration pursuant to Step Four.

Through the spring of 1991, Nghiem presented evidence and argument in the arbitration hearings, including a fifty-page closing brief. On November 18, 1991, the arbitrator rendered a decision in favor of NEC. Meanwhile, on June 10, 1991, Nghiem had filed suit in state court on substantially the same issues. NEC removed to federal district court on March 6, 1992. [T]he district court granted NEC's motion for confirmation of the arbitration award and dismissed Nghiem's suit in its entirety, including the statutory claims of employment discrimination and an antitrust violation.

Nghiem points out that the contract he signed does not have an arbitration clause and that he did not sign a proposed subsequent contract which did. Although Nghiem claims that NEC told him he had to pursue arbitration, that is inconsistent with his claim that he consciously avoided signing any agreement which would require him to pursue arbitration. The district court found that Nghiem voluntarily initiated binding arbitration and this finding is not clearly erroneous. . . . In addition to the employee handbook, which provides for binding arbitration and which Nghiem acknowledges receiving, on September 21, 1990, Nghiem wrote a letter to NEC's Human Resource Director, Denny Mitchell, requesting to proceed with Step Four of NEC's problem resolution process—final and binding arbitration. This constitutes a writing memorializing an agreement to arbitrate.

Once a claimant submits to the authority of the arbitrator and pursues arbitration, he cannot suddenly change his mind and assert lack of authority. Nghiem is bound by the arbitrator's decision. . . . Furthermore, Nghiem's voluntary initiation of arbitration can be interpreted as waiver of any objection he may have had over the authority of the arbitrator. Finally, the Supreme Court has held that "as a matter of federal law, any doubts concerning the scope of arbitrable issues should be resolved in favor of arbitration, whether the problem at hand is the construction of the contract language itself or an allegation of waiver, delay, or a like defense to arbitrability." *Mitsubishi Motors Corp. v. Soler Chrysler-Plymouth Inc.*

Even if the arbitration is valid, Nghiem nevertheless claims that his employment discrimination complaint cannot be settled through such process and must be adjudicated in federal court. Although the earlier Supreme Court cases precluded Title VII cases from being subjected to compulsory arbitration, *Alexander v. Gardner-Denver Co.*, 415 U.S. 36, 94 S. Ct. 1011, 39 L. Ed. 2d 147 (1974), the Court has recently opened the door to arbitration of these claims. *Gilmer v. Interstate/Johnson Lane, Corp.*, 500 U.S. 20, 111 S. Ct. 1647, 114 L. Ed. 2d 26 (1991). Before *Gilmer*, this court read *Alexander* as holding "that an employee's statutory right to trial de novo under Title VII is not foreclosed by prior submission of her claim to final arbitration under a collective-bargaining agreement." *Perugini v. Safeway Stores, Inc.*, 935 F.2d 1083, 1086 (9th Cir. 1991). Although "the Supreme Court [did] not overrule *Alexander* in *Gilmer*, it [did] reject a reading of *Alexander* as prohibiting the arbitration of employment discrimination claims."

Nghiem rather argues that Gilmer does not apply because the 1991 amendments to Title VII provide for jury trial. We conclude, however, that establishing a right to jury trial for Title VII claims does not evince a congressional intent to preclude arbitration; it merely defines those procedures which are available to plaintiffs who pursue the federal option, as opposed to arbitration. Title VII claims are clearly subject to arbitration and Nghiem's argument, therefore, fails.

Nghiem further contends that his antitrust claims should be heard in federal court because antitrust claims are not subject to arbitration. Nghiem relies on *American Safety Equipment Corp. v. J.P. Maguire & Co.*, 391 F.2d 821 (2d Cir. 1968). In *American Safety*, the Second Circuit held that antitrust claims cannot be arbitrated because of the public interest in enforcing antitrust laws, the potential bias and limited expertise of arbitrators, the complexity of antitrust law, and the procedural differences between trials and arbitrations. Until now, this circuit has followed the holding and reasoning of *American Safety*.

In light of more recent Supreme Court decisions, however, we must review whether it is appropriate to continue to follow *American Safety*. We are bound by decisions of prior panels unless an en banc decision, Supreme Court decision or subsequent legislation undermines those decisions." In *Mitsubishi Motors*, however, the Supreme Court has indeed undermined the reasoning behind *American Safety*. In *Mitsubishi*, the Court held that an antitrust claim could be submitted to an international arbitral tribunal.

Although *Mitsubishi* found "it unnecessary to assess the legitimacy of the *American Safety* doctrine as applied to agreements to arbitrate arising from domestic transactions," we are persuaded that the decision is not restricted to the international context. . . . [T]he Supreme Court has subsequently cited *Mitsubishi* for the general proposition that antitrust claims can be arbitrated. *Gilmer*, 500 U.S. at 26-27. . . . We hold that *Mitsubishi* effectively overruled *American Safety* and its progeny, including *Lake Communications*.

Mitsubishi may be seen as evidence of the Supreme Court's desire to make statutory rights subject to arbitration. In holding that claims brought under section 10(b) of the Exchange Act of 1934, and RICO, 18 U.S.C. § 1961, can be subject to arbitration, the Supreme Court noted that the "federal policy favoring arbitration" established by the FAA "is not diminished when a party bound by an agreement raises a claim founded on statutory rights." *Shearson/American Express v. McMahon,* 482 U.S. 220, 226 (1987). One scholar summed up the situation concisely: The reasoning used by the Court in *McMahon* to support its holding regarding the arbitrability of 1934 Act and RICO claims . . . suggests that domestic antitrust disputes are likewise subject to arbitration. . . . The *McMahon* Court made no distinction between the international and domestic arbitral forums, but rather stated that domestic and international arbitrators are equally able to handle complex statutory schemes involving treble damage remedies. Such reasoning, in combination with the FAA can only mean the judicially implied antitrust exemption to the FAA no longer exists. G. Richard Shell, *Res Judicata and Collateral Estoppel Effects of Commercial Arbitration,* 35 UCLA L. Rev. 623, 624 n. 7 (1988). . . .

b. *Kotam Electronics, Inc. v. JBL Consumer Products, Inc.*, 59 F.3d 1155 (11th Cir. 1995)

Hatchett, Circuit Judge:

In this appeal, the sole issue we address is whether the holding in *Cobb v. Lewis,* 488 F.2d 41 (5th Cir. 1974), that antitrust claims are non-arbitrable, remains controlling precedent in this circuit in light of intervening decisions of the United States Supreme Court. We affirm the district court's ruling that Cobb controls.

From 1984 to 1992, Kotam Electronics, Inc. (Kotam), a dealer and distributor of consumer electronics products, entered into annual dealer and distributor contracts with JBL Consumer Products, Inc. (JBL). These contracts contained identical provisions requiring the parties to submit claims asserting violations of the antitrust laws to binding arbitration. . . .

The district court's denial of JBL's motion to stay judicial proceedings pending arbitration involved only a question of law. Therefore, we review the district court's decision de novo. In *Cobb,* the former Fifth Circuit . . . concluded that "as a general matter, antitrust claims are not appropriate subjects of arbitration." In reaching this holding, the *Cobb* court followed the reasoning of . . . *American Safety Equipment Corp. v. J.P. Maguire & Co.,* 391 F.2d 821 (2d Cir. 1968).

In *Bonner v. City of Prichard, Ala.,* 661 F.2d 1206, 1207 (11th Cir.1981) *(en banc),* this court adopted as binding precedent all decisions of the former Fifth Circuit rendered prior to October 1, 1981. This court also adopted the rule that a prior decision of the circuit (panel or en banc) could not be overruled by a panel but only by the court sitting en banc. . . . The Supreme Court has not expressly overruled *Cobb,* and neither has an en banc court of this circuit.

At the same time, however, according to both Eleventh and Fifth Circuit precedent this panel may not overlook decisions by the Supreme Court which implicitly overrule a binding circuit decision, or undercut its rationale. JBL contends that the Supreme Court has substantially undercut the rationale of *Cobb* in *Mitsubishi Motors Corp. v. Soler Chrysler-Plymouth, Inc.* In its analysis, the Supreme Court rejected the *American Safety* considerations endorsed in *Cobb.*

[W]e do not believe that *Mitsubishi* has undermined *Cobb.* In *Mitsubishi,* the Court stated . . . that: "We find it unnecessary to assess the legitimacy of the *American Safety* doctrine as applied to agreements to arbitrate arising from domestic transactions. . .." . . . None of the cases the Supreme Court has decided subsequent to *Mitsubishi* compel us to change this conclusion. No question exists that the Court has relied on *Mitsubishi* to expand the scope of statutory claims subject to arbitration [citing *Gilmer, McMahon,* and *Rodriguez de Quijas*]. In none of these cases, however, did the Court speak directly to the propriety of arbitrating domestic antitrust claims. Accordingly, they do not change our view that *Cobb* remains controlling precedent in this circuit.

JBL's reliance on *Nghiem v. NEC Electronic, Inc.,* 25 F.3d 1437 (9th Cir.), *cert. denied,* 115 S.Ct. 638 (1994) does not persuade us to change our position either. In *Nghiem,* a panel of the Ninth Circuit, subject to a similar "prior panel rule" as this court, relied on *Mitsubishi* to overrule *Lake Communications, Inc. v. ICC Corp.,* 738 F.2d 1473 (9th Cir. 1984), a decision that endorsed the American Safety reasoning and holding. The Nghiem court provided three reasons to support its holding. First, the court noted that in *Gilmer* "the Supreme Court . . . cited *Mitsubishi* for the general proposition that antitrust claims can be arbitrated." Second, the court stated that "*Mitsubishi* . . . specifically refuted the analysis of *American Safety.*" Third, the court indicated that "*Mitsubishi* may be seen as evidence of the Supreme Court's desire to make statutory rights subject to arbitration." Our analysis has already revealed that we disagree with the Ninth Circuit's second and third reasons in support of its outcome in *Nghiem.* With regard to the first reason, we believe that the best source for deciding what *Mitsubishi* held is the *Mitsubishi* decision itself, and not a phrase in a subsequent case summarizing (imprecisely, we believe) the *Mitsubishi* holding. *See Gilmer,* 500 U.S. at 26. In any event, given the precise issue in this case, JBL's reliance on authority outside of the Supreme Court or this circuit is misplaced.

JOHN R. GIBSON, Senior Circuit Judge, dissenting:

Mitsubishi makes plain that it deals only with arbitration of antitrust cases in an international setting and, on several occasions, disavows that it applies to domestic transactions. Nevertheless, *Mitsubishi* devotes nearly four pages to analyzing *American Safety* . . . . The Court considers and rejects the four ingredients supporting *American Safety*'s conclusion that antitrust cases may not be arbitrated. Only one of the four ingredients in *American Safety,* the proposition that an arbitration panel will threaten business conduct because of innate hostility to antitrust law, reflects any difference between a domestic and international case. In turn, *Cobb* is based on *American Safety.* I conclude that *Mitsubishi* deals a death blow to *Cobb. Mitsubishi* either overruled *Cobb,* or at least, destroyed circuit authority refusing to enforce arbitration agreements in domestic antitrust disputes. Thus, I believe that the circuit operates on a clean slate, and that it would be wise to directly consider the issue. If we did so, I would conclude, like the Ninth Circuit and several other district courts, that agreements to arbitrate domestic antitrust disputes are enforceable. . . .

c. Comments and Questions

1. It will not have escaped the attention of even the most casual reader that the *Ngiem* and *Kotam* courts reached opposite conclusions on the same issue. What would you have decided, and why?

2. What do you think the Supreme Court will decide when directly confronted with an antitrust arbitration claim? Does it matter whether the arbitration agreement expressly covers antitrust claims?

3. In *Gilmer v. Interstate/Johnson Lane Corp.*, reprinted in Chapter 12, the Supreme Court cited Mitsubishi in support of the proposition that Sherman Act claims are subject to arbitration, without mentioning the international limitation. 500 U.S. 20, 26 (1991).

4. Judge Frank Easterbrook, a noted antitrust scholar as well as a respected jurist, has expressed (in dicta) the following view about the arbitrability of antitrust claims: "Producers may agree to arbitrate their antitrust disputes — certainly so for international transactions and likely so for domestic transactions." *San Juan v. American Board of Psychiatry and Neurology, Inc.*, 40 F.3d 247 (7th Cir. 1995).

J. Predispute Agreements to Arbitrate Securities Claims

1. *Shearson/American Express, Inc. v. McMahon*, 482 U.S. 220 (1987)

Justice O'CONNOR delivered the opinion of the Court.

This case presents two questions regarding the enforceability of predispute arbitration agreements between brokerage firms and their customers. The first is whether a claim brought under § 10(b) of the Securities Exchange Act of 1934 must be sent to arbitration in accordance with the terms of an arbitration agreement. The second is whether a claim brought under the Racketeer Influenced and Corrupt Organizations Act (RICO) must be arbitrated in accordance with the terms of such an agreement.

I

Between 1980 and 1982, respondents Eugene and Julia McMahon, individually and as trustees for various pension and profit-sharing plans, were customers of petitioner Shearson/American Express Inc. (Shearson), a brokerage firm registered with the Securities and Exchange Commission (SEC or Commission). Two signed customer agreements . . . provided for arbitration of any controversy relating to the accounts the McMahons maintained with Shearson. The arbitration provision provided in relevant part as follows: "Unless unenforceable due to federal or state law, any controversy arising out of or relating to my accounts, to transactions with you for me or to this agreement or the breach thereof, shall be settled by arbitration in accordance with the rules, then in effect, of the National Association of Securities Dealers, Inc. or the Boards of Directors of the New York Stock Exchange, Inc. and/or the American Stock Exchange, Inc. as I may elect."

In October 1984, the McMahons filed an amended complaint against Shearson and petitioner Mary Ann McNulty, the registered representative who handled their accounts, in the United States District Court for the Southern District of New York. The complaint alleged that McNulty, with Shearson's knowledge, had violated § 10(b) of the Exchange Act and Rule 10b-5 by engaging in fraudulent, excessive trading on respondents' accounts and by making false statements and omitting material facts from the advice given to respondents. The complaint also alleged a RICO claim, and state law claims for fraud and breach of fiduciary duties. Relying on the customer agreements, petitioners moved to compel arbitration of the McMahons' claims pursuant to § 3 of the Federal Arbitration Act, 9 U.S.C. § 3.

II

The Federal Arbitration Act, 9 U.S.C. § 1 et seq., provides the starting point for answering the questions raised in this case. The Act was intended to "revers[e] centuries of judicial hostility to arbitration agreements," by "plac[ing] arbitration agreements upon the same footing as other contracts." The Arbitration Act accomplishes this purpose by providing that arbitration agreements "shall be valid, irrevocable, and enforceable, save upon such grounds as exist at law or in equity for the revocation of any contract." 9 U.S.C. § 2. The Act also provides that a court must stay its proceedings if it is satisfied that an issue before it is arbitrable under the agreement, § 3; and it authorizes a federal district court to issue an order compelling arbitration if there has been a "failure, neglect, or refusal" to comply with the arbitration agreement, § 4.

The Arbitration Act thus establishes a "federal policy favoring arbitration," requiring that "we rigorously enforce agreements to arbitrate." This duty to enforce arbitration agreements is not diminished when a party bound by an agreement raises a claim founded on statutory rights. . . .

To defeat application of the Arbitration Act in this case, therefore, the McMahons must demonstrate that Congress intended to make an exception to the Arbitration Act for claims arising under RICO and the Exchange Act, an intention discernible from the text, history, or purposes of the statute. We examine the McMahons' arguments regarding the Exchange Act and RICO in turn.

III

When Congress enacted the Exchange Act in 1934, it did not specifically address the question of the arbitrability of § 10(b) claims. The McMahons contend, however, that congressional intent to require a judicial forum for the resolution of § 10(b) claims can be deduced from § 29(a) of the Exchange Act, which declares void "[a]ny condition, stipulation, or provision binding any person to waive compliance with any provision of [the Act]."

. . . [W]e reject the McMahons' argument that § 29(a) forbids waiver of § 27 of the Exchange Act, [which] provides in relevant part: "The district courts of the United States . . . shall have exclusive jurisdiction of violations of this title or the rules and regulations thereunder, and of all suits in equity and actions at law brought to enforce any liability or duty created by this title or the rules and regulations thereunder." . . . What the antiwaiver provision of § 29(a) forbids is enforcement of agreements to waive "compliance" with the provisions of the statute. But § 27 itself does not impose any duty with which persons trading in securities must "comply." . . . Because § 27 does not impose any statutory duties, its waiver does not constitute a waiver of "compliance with any provision" of the Exchange Act under § 29(a).

We do not read *Wilko v. Swan*, 346 U.S. 427 (1953), as compelling a different result. In *Wilko*, the Court held that a predispute agreement could not be enforced to compel arbitration of a claim arising under § 12(2) of the Securities Act, 77l(2). The basis for the ruling was § 14 of the Securities Act, which, like § 29(a) of the Exchange Act, declares void any stipulation "to waive compliance with any provision" of the statute. At the beginning of its analysis, the *Wilko* Court stated that the Securities Act's jurisdictional provision was "the kind of provision that cannot be waived under § 14 of the Securities Act." This statement, however, can only be understood in the context of the Court's ensuing discussion explaining why arbitration was inadequate as a means of enforcing "the provisions of the Securities Act, advantageous to the buyer." The conclusion in *Wilko* was expressly based on the Court's belief that a judicial forum was needed to protect the substantive rights created by the Securities Act: "As the protective provisions of the Securities Act require the exercise of judicial direction to fairly assure their effectiveness, it seems to us that Congress must have intended § 14 . . . to apply to waiver of judicial trial and review." *Wilko* must be understood, therefore, as holding that the plaintiff's waiver of the "right to select the judicial forum," was unenforceable only because arbitration was judged inadequate to enforce the statutory rights created by § 12(2). . . . *Wilko* must be read as barring waiver of a judicial forum only where arbitration is inadequate to protect the substantive rights at issue. . . . [W]here arbitration does provide an adequate means of enforcing the provisions of the Exchange Act, § 29(a) does not void a predispute waiver of § 27 . . ..

The second argument offered by the McMahons is that the arbitration agreement effects an impermissible waiver of the substantive protections of the Exchange Act. Ordinarily, "[b]y agreeing to arbitrate a statutory claim, a party does not forgo the substantive rights afforded by the statute; it only submits to their resolution in an arbitral, rather than a judicial, forum." The McMahons argue, however, that § 29(a) compels a different conclusion. Initially, they contend that predispute agreements are void under § 29(a) because they tend to result from broker overreaching. They reason . . . that *Wilko* is premised on the belief "that arbitration clauses in securities sales agreements generally are not freely negotiated." According to this view, Wilko barred enforcement of predispute agreements because of this frequent inequality of bargaining power, reasoning that Congress intended for § 14 generally to ensure that sellers did not "maneuver buyers into a position that might weaken their ability to recover under the Securities Act." The McMahons urge that we should interpret § 29(a) in the same fashion.

We decline to give *Wilko* a reading so far at odds with the plain language of § 14, or to adopt such an unlikely interpretation of § 29(a). The concern that § 29(a) is directed against is evident from the statute's plain language: it is a concern with whether an agreement "waive[s] compliance with [a] provision" of the Exchange Act. The voluntariness of the agreement is irrelevant to this inquiry: if a stipulation waives compliance with a statutory duty, it is void under § 29(a), whether voluntary or not. Thus, a customer cannot negotiate a reduction in commissions in exchange for a waiver of compliance with the requirements of the Exchange Act, even if the customer knowingly and voluntarily agreed to the bargain. Section 29(a) is concerned, not with whether brokers "maneuver[ed customers] into" an agreement, but with whether the agreement "weaken[s] their ability to recover under the [Exchange] Act." The former is grounds for revoking the contract under ordinary principles of contract law; the latter is grounds for voiding the agreement under § 29(a).

The other reason advanced by the McMahons for finding a waiver of their § 10(b) rights is that arbitration does "weaken their ability to recover under the [Exchange] Act." That is the heart of the Court's decision in *Wilko*, and respondents urge that we should follow its reasoning. *Wilko* listed several grounds why, in the Court's view, the "effectiveness [of the Act's provisions] in application is lessened in arbitration." First, the *Wilko* Court believed that arbitration proceedings were not suited to cases requiring "subjective findings on the purpose and knowledge of an alleged violator." *Wilko* also was concerned that arbitrators must make legal determinations "without judicial instruction on the law," and that an arbitration award "may be made without explanation of [the arbitrator's] reasons and without a complete record of their proceedings." Finally, *Wilko* noted that the "[p]ower to vacate an award is limited," and that "interpretations of the law by the arbitrators in contrast to manifest disregard are not subject, in the federal courts, to judicial review for error in interpretation." Wilko concluded that in view of these drawbacks to arbitration, § 12(2) claims "require[d] the exercise of judicial direction to fairly assure their effectiveness."

As Justice Frankfurter noted in his dissent in *Wilko,* the Court's opinion did not rest on any evidence, either "in the record . . . [or] in the facts of which [it could] take judicial notice," that "the arbitral system . . . would not afford the plaintiff the rights to which he is entitled." Instead, the reasons given in *Wilko* reflect a general suspicion of the desirability of arbitration and the competence of arbitral tribunals—most apply with no greater force to the arbitration of securities disputes than to the arbitration of legal disputes generally. It is difficult to reconcile *Wilko*'s mistrust of the arbitral process with this Court's subsequent decisions involving the Arbitration Act. *See, e.g., Mitsubishi Motors Corp. v. Soler Chrysler-Plymouth, Inc., Dean Witter Reynolds Inc. v. Byrd.*

Indeed, most of the reasons given in *Wilko* have been rejected subsequently by the Court as a basis for holding claims to be nonarbitrable. . . . Thus, the mistrust of arbitration that formed the basis for the *Wilko* opinion in 1953 is difficult to square with the assessment of arbitration that has prevailed since that time. This is especially so in light of the intervening changes in the regulatory structure of the securities laws. Even if *Wilko*'s assumptions regarding arbitration were valid at the time *Wilko* was decided, most certainly they do not hold true today for arbitration procedures subject to the SEC's oversight authority.

In 1953, when *Wilko* was decided, the Commission had only limited authority over the rules governing self-regulatory organizations (SROs)—the national securities exchanges and registered securities associations—and this authority appears not to have included any authority at all over their arbitration rules. Since the 1975 amendments to § 19 of the Exchange Act, however, the Commission has had expansive power to ensure the adequacy of the arbitration procedures employed by the SROs. No proposed rule change may take effect unless the SEC finds that the proposed rule is consistent with the requirements of the Exchange Act, and the Commission has the power, on its own initiative, to "abrogate, add to, and delete from" any SRO rule if it finds such changes necessary or appropriate to further the objectives of the Act. In short, the Commission has broad authority to oversee and to regulate the rules adopted by the SROs relating to customer disputes, including the power to mandate the adoption of any rules it deems necessary to ensure that arbitration procedures adequately protect statutory rights.

In the exercise of its regulatory authority, the SEC has specifically approved the arbitration procedures of the New York Stock Exchange, the American Stock Exchange, and the NASD, the organizations mentioned in the arbitration agreement at issue in this case. We conclude that where, as in this case, the prescribed procedures are subject to the Commission's § 19 authority, an arbitration agreement does not effect a waiver of the protections of the Act. While *stare decisis* concerns may counsel against upsetting *Wilko*'s contrary conclusion under the Securities Act, we refuse to extend Wilko's reasoning to the Exchange Act in light of these intervening regulatory developments.

IV

Unlike the Exchange Act, there is nothing in the text of the RICO statute that even arguably evinces congressional intent to exclude civil RICO claims from the dictates of the Arbitration Act. This silence in the text is matched by silence in the statute's legislative history.

The private treble-damages provision codified as 18 U.S.C. § 1964(c) was added to the House version of the bill after the bill had been passed by the Senate, and it received only abbreviated discussion in either House.

Because RICO's text and legislative history fail to reveal any intent to override the provisions of the Arbitration Act, the McMahons must argue that there is an irreconcilable conflict between arbitration and RICO's underlying purposes. Our decision in *Mitsubishi Motors Corp. v. Soler Chrysler-Plymouth, Inc.*, 473 U.S. 614 (1985), however, already has addressed many of the grounds given by the McMahons to support this claim. . . . Not only does *Mitsubishi* support the arbitrability of RICO claims, but there is even more reason to suppose that arbitration will adequately serve the purposes of RICO than that it will adequately protect private enforcement of the antitrust laws. Antitrust violations generally have a widespread impact on national markets as a whole, and the antitrust treble-damages provision gives private parties an incentive to bring civil suits that serve to advance the national interest in a competitive economy. RICO's drafters likewise sought to provide vigorous incentives for plaintiffs to pursue RICO claims that would advance society's fight against organized crime. But in fact RICO actions are seldom asserted "against the archetypal, intimidating mobster." Only 9% of all civil RICO cases have involved allegations of criminal activity normally associated with professional criminals. The special incentives necessary to encourage civil enforcement actions against organized crime do not support nonarbitrability of run-of-the-mill civil RICO claims brought against legitimate enterprises. The private attorney general role for the typical RICO plaintiff is simply less plausible than it is for the typical antitrust plaintiff, and does not support a finding that there is an irreconcilable conflict between arbitration and enforcement of the RICO statute.

In sum, we find no basis for concluding that Congress intended to prevent enforcement of agreements to arbitrate RICO claims. The McMahons may effectively vindicate their RICO claim in an arbitral forum, and therefore there is no inherent conflict between arbitration and the purposes underlying § 1964(c). Moreover, nothing in RICO's text or legislative history otherwise demonstrates congressional intent to make an exception to the Arbitration Act for RICO claims. Accordingly, the McMahons, "having made the bargain to arbitrate," will be held to their bargain. Their RICO claim is arbitrable under the terms of the Arbitration Act.

Justice BLACKMUN, with whom Justice BRENNAN and Justice MARSHALL join, concurring in part and dissenting in part.

I concur in the Court's decision to enforce the arbitration agreement with respect to respondents' RICO claims and thus join Parts I, II, and IV of the Court's opinion. I disagree, however, with the Court's conclusion that respondents' 10(b) claims also are subject to arbitration.

Both the Securities Act of 1933 and the Securities Exchange Act of 1934 were enacted to protect investors from predatory behavior of securities industry personnel. In *Wilko v. Swan* the Court recognized this basic purpose when it declined to enforce a predispute agreement to compel arbitration of claims under the Securities Act. Following that decision, lower courts extended *Wilko*'s reasoning to claims brought under § 10(b) of the Exchange Act, and Congress approved of this extension. In today's decision, however, the Court effectively overrules *Wilko* by accepting the Securities and Exchange Commission's newly adopted position that arbitration procedures in the securities industry and the Commission's oversight of the self-regulatory organizations (SROs) have improved greatly since *Wilko* was decided. The Court thus approves the abandonment of the judiciary's role in the resolution of claims under the Exchange Act and leaves such claims to the arbitral forum of the securities industry at a time when the industry's abuses towards investors are more apparent than ever.

II

There are essentially two problems with the Court's conclusion that predispute agreements to arbitrate § 10(b) claims may be enforced. First, the Court gives *Wilko* an overly narrow reading so that it can fit into the syllogism offered by the Commission and accepted by the Court, namely, (1) *Wilko* was really a case concerning whether arbitration was adequate for the enforcement of the substantive provisions of the securities laws; (2) all of the *Wilko* Court's doubts as to arbitration's adequacy are outdated; (3) thus *Wilko* is no longer good law. Second, the Court accepts uncritically petitioners' and the Commission's argument that the problems with arbitration, highlighted by the *Wilko* Court, either no longer exist or are not now viewed as problems by the Court. This acceptance primarily is based upon the Court's belief in the Commission's representations that its oversight of the SROs ensures the adequacy of arbitration. . . .

Even if I were to accept the Court's narrow reading of *Wilko*, as a case dealing only with the inadequacies of arbitration in 1953, I do not think that this case should be resolved differently today so long as the policy of investor protection is given proper consideration in the analysis. Despite improvements in the process of arbitration and changes in the judicial attitude towards it, several aspects of arbitration that were seen by the *Wilko* court to be inimical to the policy of investor protection still remain. Moreover, I have serious reservations about the Commission's contention that its oversight of the SROs' arbitration procedures will ensure that the process is adequate to protect an investor's rights under the securities Acts. . . .

Even those who favor the arbitration of securities claims do not contend, however, that arbitration has changed so significantly as to eliminate the essential characteristics noted by the *Wilko* Court. Indeed, proponents of arbitration would not see these characteristics as "problems," because, in their view, the characteristics permit the unique "streamlined" nature of the arbitral process. As at the time of *Wilko*, preparation of a record of arbitration proceedings is not invariably required today. Moreover, arbitrators are not bound by precedent and are actually discouraged by their associations from giving reasons for a decision. Judicial review is still substantially limited to the four grounds listed in § 10 of the Arbitration Act and to the concept of "manifest disregard" of the law.

The Court's "mistrust" of arbitration may have given way recently to an acceptance of this process, not only because of the improvements in arbitration, but also because of the Court's present assumption that the distinctive features of arbitration, its more quick and economical resolution of claims, do not render it inherently inadequate for the resolution of statutory claims. Such reasoning, however, should prevail only in the absence of the congressional policy that places the statutory claimant in a special position with respect to possible violators of his statutory rights. . . . [T]he arbitral process at best places the investor on an equal footing with the securities-industry personnel against whom the claims are brought.

Furthermore, there remains the danger that, at worst, compelling an investor to arbitrate securities claims puts him in a forum controlled by the securities industry. This result directly contradicts the goal of both securities Acts to free the investor from the control of the market professional. The Uniform Code provides some safeguards but despite them, and indeed because of the background of the arbitrators, the investor has the impression, frequently justified, that his claims are being judged by a forum composed of individuals sympathetic to the securities industry and not drawn from the public.[21] . . . Accordingly, it is often possible for the "public" arbitrators to be attorneys or consultants whose clients have been exchange members or SROs. *See* Panel of Arbitrators 1987-1988, CCH American Stock Exchange Guide 158-160 (1987) (71 out of 116 "public" arbitrators are lawyers). The uniform opposition of investors to compelled arbitration and the overwhelming support of the securities industry for the process suggest that there must be some truth to the investors' belief that the securities industry has an advantage in a forum under its own control.

Justice STEVENS, concurring in part and dissenting in part.

Gaps in the law must, of course, be filled by judicial construction. But after a statute has been construed, either by this Court or by a consistent course of decision by other federal judges and agencies, it acquires a meaning that should be as clear as if the judicial gloss had been drafted by the Congress itself. This position reflects both respect for Congress' role, and the compelling need to preserve the courts' limited resources. . . . For this reason, I respectfully dissent from the portion of the Court's judgment that holds *Wilko* inapplicable to the 1934 Act. Like Justice Blackmun, however, I join Parts I, II, and IV of the Court's opinion.

2. Racketeering [RICO] Claims

In all the contentiousness about the appropriate role of arbitration in the securities field, it should not be overlooked that the Supreme Court in *McMahon* unanimously, and with little debate, held that civil RICO claims are subject to arbitration. This holding allows for the following *a fortiori* argument whenever a question arises about whether public policy should limit arbitration of a particular matter: since agreements to arbitrate racketeering claims are enforced, surely the courts should also enforce agreements to arbitrate __________ [the matter at hand].

3. *Rodriguez de Quijas v. Shearson/American Express, Inc.*, 490 U.S. 477 (1989)

KENNEDY, J., delivered the opinion of the Court, in which REHNQUIST, C.J., and WHITE, O'CONNOR, and SCALIA, JJ., joined. STEVENS, J., filed a dissenting opinion, in which BRENNAN, MARSHALL, and BLACKMUN, JJ., joined.

Justice KENNEDY delivered the opinion of the Court.

The question here is whether a predispute agreement to arbitrate claims under the Securities Act of 1933 is unenforceable, requiring resolution of the claims only in a judicial forum.

---

[21]The Uniform Code mandates that a majority of an arbitration panel, usually composed of between three to five arbitrators, be drawn from outside the industry. Each arbitrator, moreover, is directed to disclose "any circumstances which might preclude such arbitrator from rendering an objective and impartial determination." In addition, the parties are informed of the business associations of the arbitrators, and each party has the right to one peremptory challenge and to unlimited challenges for cause. The arbitrators are usually individuals familiar with the federal securities laws.

I

Petitioners are individuals who invested about $400,000 in securities. They signed a standard customer agreement with the broker, which included a clause stating that the parties agreed to settle any controversies "relating to [the] accounts" through binding arbitration that complies with specified procedures. The agreement to arbitrate these controversies is unqualified, unless it is found to be unenforceable under federal or state law. The investments turned sour, and petitioners eventually sued respondent and its broker-agent in charge of the accounts, alleging that their money was lost in unauthorized and fraudulent transactions. In their complaint they pleaded various violations of federal and state law, including claims under § 12(2) of the Securities Act of 1933, 15 U.S.C. § 771(2), and claims under three sections of the Securities Exchange Act of 1934.

The District Court ordered all the claims to be submitted to arbitration except for those raised under § 12(2) of the Securities Act. It held that the latter claims must proceed in the court action under our clear holding on the point in *Wilko v. Swan,* 346 U.S. 427 (1953). The Court of Appeals reversed, concluding that the arbitration agreement is enforceable because this Court's subsequent decisions have reduced *Wilko* to "obsolescence."

II

The *Wilko* case, decided in 1953, required the Court to determine whether an agreement to arbitrate future controversies constitutes a binding stipulation "to waive compliance with any provision" of the Securities Act, which is nullified by § 14 of the Act. 15 U.S.C. § 77n. The Court considered the language, purposes, and legislative history of the Securities Act and concluded that the agreement to arbitrate was void under § 14. But the decision was a difficult one in view of the competing legislative policy embodied in the Arbitration Act, which the Court described as "not easily reconcilable," and which strongly favors the enforcement of agreements to arbitrate as a means of securing "prompt, economical and adequate solution of controversies."

It has been recognized that *Wilko* was not obviously correct, for the language prohibiting waiver of "compliance with any provision of this title" could easily have been read to relate to substantive provisions of the Act without including the remedy provisions. The Court did not read the language this way in *Wilko,* however, and gave two reasons. First, the Court rejected the argument that "arbitration is merely a form of trial to be used in lieu of a trial at law." The Court found instead that § 14 does not permit waiver of "the right to select the judicial forum" in favor of arbitration, because "arbitration lacks the certainty of a suit at law under the Act to enforce [the buyer's] rights." Second, the Court concluded that the Securities Act was intended to protect buyers of securities, who often do not deal at arm's length and on equal terms with sellers, by offering them "a wider choice of courts and venue" than is enjoyed by participants in other business transactions, making "the right to select the judicial forum" a particularly valuable feature of the Securities Act.

We do not think these reasons justify an interpretation of § 14 that prohibits agreements to arbitrate future disputes relating to the purchase of securities. The Court's characterization of the arbitration process in Wilko is pervaded by what Judge Jerome Frank called "the old judicial hostility to arbitration." That view has been steadily eroded over the years, beginning in the lower courts. The erosion intensified in our most recent decisions upholding agreements to arbitrate federal claims raised under the Securities Exchange Act of 1934, see *Shearson/American Express Inc. v. McMahon,* 482 U.S. 220 (1987), under the Racketeer Influenced and Corrupt Organizations (RICO) statutes, and under the antitrust laws, see *Mitsubishi Motors Corp. v. Soler Chrysler-Plymouth, Inc.*, 473 U.S. 614 (1985). The shift in the Court's views on arbitration away from those adopted in *Wilko* is shown by the flat statement in *Mitsubishi:* "By agreeing to arbitrate a statutory claim, a party does not forgo the substantive rights afforded by the statute; it only submits to their resolution in an arbitral, rather than a judicial, forum." To the extent that *Wilko* rested on suspicion of arbitration as a method of weakening the protections afforded in the substantive law to would-be complainants, it has fallen far out of step with our current strong endorsement of the federal statutes favoring this method of resolving disputes.

Once the outmoded presumption of disfavoring arbitration proceedings is set to one side, it becomes clear that the right to select the judicial forum and the wider choice of courts are not such essential features of the Securities Act that § 14 is properly construed to bar any waiver of these provisions. Nor are they so critical that they cannot be waived under the rationale that the Securities Act was intended to place buyers of securities on an equal footing with sellers. *Wilko* identified two different kinds of provisions in the Securities Act that would advance this objective. Some are substantive, such as the provision placing on the seller the burden of proving lack of scienter when a buyer alleges fraud. Others are procedural. The specific procedural improvements highlighted in *Wilko* are the statute's broad venue provisions in the federal courts; the existence of nationwide service of process in the federal courts; the extinction of the amount-in-controversy requirement that had applied to fraud suits when they were brought in federal courts under diversity jurisdiction rather than as a federal cause of action; and the grant of concurrent jurisdiction in the state and federal courts without possibility of removal.

There is no sound basis for construing the prohibition in § 14 on waiving "compliance with any provision" of the Securities Act to apply to these procedural provisions. Although the first three measures do facilitate suits by buyers of securities, the grant of concurrent jurisdiction constitutes explicit authorization for complainants to waive those protections by filing suit in state court without possibility of removal to federal court. These measures, moreover, are present in other federal statutes which have not been interpreted to prohibit enforcement of predispute agreements to arbitrate.

Indeed, in *McMahon* the Court declined to read § 29(a) of the Securities Exchange Act of 1934, the language of which is in every respect the same as that in § 14 of the 1933 Act, compare 15 U.S.C. § 77v(a) with § 78aa, to prohibit enforcement of predispute agreements to arbitrate. The only conceivable distinction in this regard between the Securities Act and the Securities Exchange Act is that the former statute allows concurrent federal-state jurisdiction over causes of action and the latter statute provides for exclusive federal jurisdiction. But even if this distinction were thought to make any difference at all, it would suggest that arbitration agreements, which are "in effect, a specialized kind of forum-selection clause," should not be prohibited under the Securities Act, since they, like the provision for concurrent jurisdiction, serve to advance the objective of allowing buyers of securities a broader right to select the forum for resolving disputes, whether it be judicial or otherwise. And in *McMahon* we explained at length why we rejected the *Wilko* Court's aversion to arbitration as a forum for resolving disputes over securities transactions, especially in light of the relatively recent expansion of the Securities and Exchange Commission's authority to oversee and to regulate those arbitration procedures. We need not repeat those arguments here.

Finally, in *McMahon* we stressed the strong language of the Arbitration Act, which declares as a matter of federal law that arbitration agreements "shall be valid, irrevocable, and enforceable, save upon such grounds as exist at law or in equity for the revocation of any contract." 9 U.S.C. § 2. Under that statute, the party opposing arbitration carries the burden of showing that Congress intended in a separate statute to preclude a waiver of judicial remedies, or that such a waiver of judicial remedies inherently conflicts with the underlying purposes of that other statute. But as Justice Frankfurter said in dissent in *Wilko,* so it is true in this case: "There is nothing in the record before us, nor in the facts of which we can take judicial notice, to indicate that the arbitral system . . . would not afford the plaintiff the rights to which he is entitled." Petitioners have not carried their burden of showing that arbitration agreements are not enforceable under the Securities Act.

The language quoted above from § 2 of the Arbitration Act also allows the courts to give relief where the party opposing arbitration presents "well-supported claims that the agreement to arbitrate resulted from the sort of fraud or overwhelming economic power that would provide grounds for the revocation of any contract." This avenue of relief is in harmony with the Securities Act's concern to protect buyers of securities by removing "the disadvantages under which buyers labor" in their dealings with sellers. Although petitioners suggest that the agreement to arbitrate here was adhesive in nature, the record contains no factual showing sufficient to support that suggestion.

III

. . . We now conclude that *Wilko* was incorrectly decided and is inconsistent with the prevailing uniform construction of other federal statutes governing arbitration agreements in the setting of business transactions. Although we are normally and properly reluctant to overturn our decisions construing statutes, we have done so to achieve a uniform interpretation of similar statutory language, and to correct a seriously erroneous interpretation of statutory language that would undermine congressional policy as expressed in other legislation. Both purposes would be served here by overruling the *Wilko* decision.

It also would be undesirable for the decisions in *Wilko* and *McMahon* to continue to exist side by side. Their inconsistency is at odds with the principle that the 1933 and 1934 Acts should be construed harmoniously because they "constitute interrelated components of the federal regulatory scheme governing transactions in securities." . . . [T]he inconsistency between *Wilko* and *McMahon* undermines the essential rationale for a harmonious construction of the two statutes, which is to discourage litigants from manipulating their allegations merely to cast their claims under one of the securities laws rather than another. For all of these reasons, therefore, we overrule the decision in *Wilko.* The judgment of the Court of Appeals is Affirmed.

Justice STEVENS, with whom Justice BRENNAN, Justice MARSHALL, and Justice BLACKMUN join, dissenting.

. . . In the final analysis, a Justice's vote in a case like this depends more on his or her views about the respective lawmaking responsibilities of Congress and this Court than on conflicting policy interests. Judges who have confidence in their own ability to fashion public policy are less hesitant to change the law than those of us who are inclined to give wide latitude to the views of the voters' representatives on nonconstitutional matters. . . . [T]here are valid policy and textual arguments on both sides regarding the interrelation of federal securities and arbitration Acts. None of these arguments, however, carries sufficient weight to tip the balance between judicial and legislative authority and overturn an interpretation of an Act of Congress that has been settled for many years.

I respectfully dissent.

4. Comments and Questions

a. It is striking that the dissenting opinion (including the excised parts) has not a single favorable word to say about *Wilko v. Swan* on the merits.

b. In *Rodriguez de Quijas* (1989), the Supreme Court spoke of the value of parallel interpretations of the 1933 and 1934 Acts (as it has on many other occasions) as a reason for following *McMahon* rather than adhering to *Wilko.* One may be forgiven for wondering why the majority failed to make use of this argument when the Court decided *McMahon* (1987) just two years earlier.

Chapter 12

Arbitration Applications

CASE STUDY

Mr. Dingle answered an ad placed in the paper by Ms. Bean in which Ms. Bean offered to set up a specialty store, engaging in the retail sale of cartoon character-type merchandise. She represented that she would generate a business plan, help secure financing, find a location, complete the planning and layout of the store, contract for the build out of the store, order and stock the inventory, hire personnel to operate the store, and consult and train Mr. Dingle in the development of his store. Basically, Ms. Bean was to start a business ready to open its doors, then hand it over to Mr. Dingle to run. Ms. Bean was to receive $100,000 in exchange for her services.

The two parties signed a contract setting forth each party's obligations. The contract was signed in January, and the store was scheduled to be opened in June. Mr. Dingle alleges that Ms. Bean was unable to perform many of the contractual obligations herself, and contracted out to various independent contractors, such as: two outside consultants who were hired to generate business plans, two people who were hired to purchase the merchandise, and three architects hired to design the layout of the store. The first architect was hired once Ms. Bean had represented to Mr. Dingle that she had obtained space for the store. After Mr. Dingle had paid the architect $6,000 for the design, it was discovered that the space for the store had been rented to someone else, thus leaving the architectural plans useless. Ms. Bean caused this to occur on two separate occasions, resulting in a total loss of over $20,000 in architecture expenses. Mr. Dingle was forced to procure a space for his store on his own, despite the fact that the contract stated that it was Ms. Bean's obligation to do so.

In October, the store was still not completed. Feeling that Ms. Bean had not fulfilled her obligations under the contract, Mr. Dingle terminated her employment, and paid her $10,000 for her services. Ms. Bean felt that she had fulfilled her obligations under the contract up until the time of her termination. In retaliation, Ms. Bean allegedly refused to give Mr. Dingle the merchandise she had purchased for the store on Mr. Dingle's credit card. Ms. Bean also allegedly wrote letters to the Small Business Administration and Mr. Dingle's bank, directing them not to approve Mr. Dingle's loan.

Since the letters written by Ms. Bean were damaging Mr. Dingle's business, and because Ms. Bean continued to take actions to harm his reputation, Mr. Dingle filed suit requesting a temporary injunction. His suit also brought action for Libel and Breach of Contract. Ms. Bean responded by counter-suing for Breach of Contract and Slander, claiming that Mr. Dingle had called her a thief and damaged her business reputation.

A. Introduction

This Chapter is the third and last to examine arbitration. Chapter 10 focused on how the arbitration process works, and planning for its use in the event of disputes. The primary focus there was on commercial disputes. Chapter 11 covered the law of arbitration, largely through U.S. Supreme Court and New York cases. The substantive topics were commercial disputes, and a large number of securities industry cases. The materials in this Chapter complete the picture, covering important topics that have not yet been fully considered.

Consumer protection concerns arise when contracts between businesses and their consumer customers require the use of arbitration to settle disputes between the parties. These issues are addressed in the contexts of disputes between banks and their consumer customers. The rapidly expanding use of arbitration terms by banks means that most adult Americans either are or soon will be participants in contracts requiring arbitration. People with brokerage accounts already have agreed to arbitration, perhaps unknowingly.

The largest topic in the Chapter, both in terms of pages and importance, is labor arbitration. Several of the cases in the previous chapter looked to labor arbitration rules by way of analogy, but all recognized that arbitration in the workplace is different, even unique. How large these differences are, and the extent to which they are material in the resolution of particular arbitration issues, are questions that you should keep asking yourself as you consider these materials.

Arbitration has been a central feature of contracts between organized labor and management since Congress enacted the National Labor Relations Act in the wake of the Great Depression, so arbitration law developed in the labor context earlier than in other areas. The basic structure was firmly established in 1960 by three Supreme Court decisions known collectively as the "Steelworkers Trilogy." Thus the contours of labor arbitration were firmly established years before the birth of the modern ADR Movement.

The most important and contentious current topic in labor arbitration is the enforcement of agreements to arbitrate fair employment practices complaints. These can arise under a large (and growing) array of federal and state statutes. The leading cases, their potential impact, and important open issues are examined. The issues surrounding arbitration of fair employment complaints are similar to those considered in Chapter 11, in the context of alleged violations of the antitrust and securities laws. Again, the question arises of whether work place disputes are different in important ways for purposes of arbitration.

Because labor arbitration takes place in the context of a continuing relationship — even in the extreme case where an employee is dismissed, the labor-management contract remains in force — arbitration can be a therapeutic process. Accordingly, we consider the potential benefits (and limitations) of promoting therapeutic values in labor arbitration. The idea that a dispute settlement process can be empowering to the parties and promote healing between the parties is common in the mediation literature, but far less so for arbitration.

Finally, this chapter examines the arbitration of disputes between broker-dealers and their customers. While many of the issues considered in Chapter 11 arose in the securities context, we did not consider the overall relationship between securities firms and their customers. The major vehicle for this consideration is the report of a "blue ribbon" panel chaired by Professor David Ruder, former Chair of the Securities & Exchange Commission. The recommendations on important arbitration issues, such as the awarding of punitive damages by arbitrators, will be influential in all areas of arbitration, particularly regarding agreements between businesses and their consumer customers.

B. Enforcement of Arbitration Clauses in Contracts Between Businesses and Their Consumer Customers: Banking Institutions

1. Comments and Questions

a. The full text of the arbitration terms employed by two of the banks discussed in the Budnitz article, Bank of America and Zions First National Bank, are reproduced after the article.

b. Since arbitration provisions in contracts between securities firms and their customers are clearly enforceable, even when violations of the federal securities laws are alleged, it is important for Professor Butnitz to distinguish between bank and brokerage customers. The securities cases are *McMahon* and *Rodriguez de Quijas,* which are found in Chapter 11. Arbitration in the securities industry is considered at length in the Report of the National Association of Securities Dealers Taskforce on Securities Arbitration (1996) portions of which are reprinted in Section E of this Chapter.

c. Professor Budnitz argues that mandatory arbitration provisions of disputes between banks and their consumer customers are incompatible with appropriate norms of consumer protection. Do the same arguments apply to both deposit and loan customers? Would you reach the same result, based on the same analysis, with respect to credit card customers?

d. Separation of commercial banking and investment banking was a product of the 1930s, one of the many responses to the Great Depression. The "wall" between the two categories is full of holes and exceptions. Many banks offer brokerage services to their customers. The cash management or similarly named accounts offered by securities firms are a transaction account in all but name, and one that pays a better rate of return on the funds therein than similar accounts offered by banking organizations.

e. Assuming the customer is a "conumer," however defined, should the nature of the protection afforded the consumer depend on the type of product or the institution that offers the product?

2. Mark E. Budnitz, *Arbitration of Disputes Between Consumers and Financial Institutions: A Serious Threat to Consumer Protection,* 10 OHIO ST. J. ON DISP. RESOL. 267 (1995)*

I. INTRODUCTION

Financial institutions increasingly are requiring consumers to arbitrate disputes rather than resort to litigation. They have done so at a time when arbitration is exceedingly popular as a means of ameliorating the excessive costs and delays of litigation.

This Article examines in detail several of the arbitration contracts currently in use. Several findings emerge from this review. . . . [T]he contracts typically cover far more than potential lender liability claims. [A major theme of Budnitz's article, discussion of which is omitted here, is that the use of arbitration in the banking context arose as a response to lender liability litigation.] Indeed, some contracts purport to include disputes of any kind regardless of when

*Reprinted with permission.

they arise. The Article then reviews the state and federal arbitration statutes and case law governing arbitration contracts, and the attacks which consumers can make to challenge their validity. The Article next questions this type of arbitration as a matter of public policy. Finally, the Article discusses legislative approaches to safeguard consumer interests and recommends a course of action for lawmakers. . . .

III. THE SOLUTION: ARBITRATION

This section will analyze the arbitration contracts used by four financial institutions with their customers. In addition, this section will analyze a variety of selected arbitration clauses used by financial institutions, whether in consumer or commercial transactions, in order to explore the variety of options available to these institutions, and the problems they may pose if required in consumer transactions. Finally, this section will analyze those contracts in light of federal and state arbitration statutes in order to understand the significance of the provisions drafted by the institutions.

A. Arbitration Provisions Used by Four Financial Institutions

[The four] . . . institutions [are] Bank of California, Bank of America, Marathon Bank, and Zions First National Bank. These financial institutions have taken a variety of approaches to arbitration, illustrating the many choices available to them and the different types of difficulties consumers may encounter.

For example, Marathon Bank and the Bank of California impose mandatory arbitration upon the consumer and the institution whenever there is a dispute. In contrast, the Bank of America and Zions require arbitration only if either party requests it. There may not be any practical difference in the two types of provisions. Presumably, if both of the parties to a dispute subject to the contracts drafted by Marathon and Bank of California agreed they did not want the dispute decided by arbitration, no one would trigger the arbitration process and the dispute would be decided by some other formal or informal dispute resolution mechanism.

Bank of California, Marathon, and Zions employ broad "dragnet" clauses which subject to arbitration not only disputes arising out of or relating to the agreement the parties executed, but also to any other dispute among the parties. Bank of America's contract confines the scope of arbitration to disputes arising out of or relating to the agreement. One reviewer of that contract noted that by limiting itself in this fashion, Bank of America was allowing many types of disputes to escape arbitration. The Marathon contract specifically states what may be implicit in the contracts of Bank of California and Zions, namely, that the obligation to arbitrate extends to any "past, present or future transactions, agreements or relationships."

All four banks specify that the arbitration contract considers alleged torts within its scope. . . . Despite the breadth of these scope provisions, the contracts carve out of arbitration either party's right to foreclose on real or personal property, exercise self-help, or maintain a court action for provisional or ancillary remedies. Such provisions may favor financial institutions. It is the lender who would use the rights granted in the provision; consumers would rarely, if ever, use them.

Except for the Bank of America, the banks' contracts specify that the arbitrations are to be governed by the Federal Arbitration Act (FAA). In contrast, the Bank of America's contract provides that arbitrations shall be pursuant to California law. Bank of America apparently believes California's arbitration law is more favorable than the FAA. Conversely, one reason

Marathon prefers the FAA is its preemption of "conflicting state law theories such as contracts of adhesion."

All four financial institutions state in their contracts that disputes are to be decided pursuant to the rules of the American Arbitration Association (AAA). Bank of California and Zions incorporate the Commercial Arbitration Rules of the AAA. Marathon incorporates both those rules, as well as the Supplemental Procedures for Financial Institution Disputes.

The four banks provide for the selection of arbitrators according to the methods employed by the AAA. There are differences, however, in their approaches. The contracts used by Bank of California and Zions are silent on selection of arbitrators, but contain general provisions which incorporate the AAA Commercial Arbitration Rules. Consequently, those rules govern selection. Bank of America's contract provides that selection is to be made in the same manner as the AAA uses in its proceedings, but there is no reference to the Commercial Arbitration Rules. Marathon directs the parties to follow the Commercial Arbitration Rules of the AAA and the Supplemental Procedures for Financial Institution Disputes. But, in a significant departure from the other banks, its contract also provides that either party may require that arbitrators be retired judges. Selection of a retired judge substantially increases the cost of arbitration by $200 to $300 per hour. The provision has been justified in three ways. First, the prevailing party may be able to recover its arbitration costs—including the arbitrator's fee. Second, the provision ensures "important protection on the quality of the decision maker." Third, the clause provides an incentive for the parties to be "reasonable" in their approach to resolving the dispute.

Only the Zions contract specifically provides for the location of the arbitration hearings. That contract specifies that all proceedings will be held in Salt Lake City, Utah. Because the other contracts are silent, the location of hearings held in disputes involving the other banks are determined in accordance with the AAA rules. These rules provide that the parties may agree on the locale for the hearing. Alternatively, one party may request a specific locale; the opposing party has ten days to object. If that party does object, the arbitrator has authority to decide on the locale.

All four contracts use traditional "legalese," much of which presumably would be incomprehensible to most consumers. Examples include: "setoff . . . provisional or ancillary remedies . . . receiver." Probably more crucial is the omission in the contracts used by three of the banks of an explanation of the arbitration contract's significance and what rights the consumer is surrendering. In stark contrast, the Zions contract includes "plain English" disclosures. The first disclosure states that arbitration is "usually final and binding and subject to only very limited review by a court." There is no explanation of what final and binding arbitration means, and the contract does not discuss the circumstances under which a court may review an arbitrator's order. The next disclosure, however, goes a long way towards remedying the obscurity of the first disclosure by explaining that the parties are waiving their rights to litigate the dispute in court, and that this includes waiver of their rights to a jury trial. Next, the Zions contract warns that discovery in arbitration is more limited and different than in court proceedings. There is no explanation of what "discovery" includes. The fourth disclosure informs the parties that the arbitrator is not required to issue an opinion containing findings of fact or "legal reasoning." In addition, this disclosure again cautions that the right to appeal the arbitrator's award is limited, but does not explain in what way it is limited. Finally, the contract tells the parties that one of the arbitrators may be affiliated with the banking industry. Zions also provides a brochure which goes into greater detail to explain in "plain English" what arbitration entails. . . .

[Ed. Supreme Court in *Allied-Bruce Terminix Cos. v. Dobson* adopted a broad reading of the FAA's preemptive effect where a transaction involves interstate commerce, and strongly reaffirmed *Southland.* Justice O'Connor, concurring, expressed the concern that the majority's decision would "displace many state statutes carefully calibrated to protect consumers . . . and state procedural requirements aimed at ensuring knowing and voluntary consent." In apparent response, the majority stated that states could still protect consumers by applying general contract law principles. In addition, the Court noted that Section 2 of the FAA authorizes a court to invalidate an arbitration clause if grounds exist for doing so under the rules for revoking contracts. The next section of this article discusses state arbitration law and should be read in the context of the expansive reach of the FAA as constured in *Allied-Bruce.*]

D. Applicable State Arbitration Law

The persons promoting the UAA were motivated by their belief that it would encourage increased use of arbitration in commercial transactions. Thirty-five states have adopted the UAA. The UAA is substantially similar to the FAA. For purposes of this article, it is instructive to examine UAA case law for the lessons that case law can teach banks and consumers concerning problem areas. Bank of America's contract provides that California arbitration law applies rather than the FAA, and other financial institutions may follow its example. . . .

Several aspects of the arbitration contract have been explored in cases decided under the UAA. These cases are also relevant to litigation decided under the FAA because state law applies to questions involving the validity of contracts under the federal Act. The Florida Court of Appeals has established minimum requirements for arbitration contracts which provide guidance to institutions drafting those agreements. The court stated that an arbitration contract must be definite enough to give the parties some idea of what matters are to be submitted to arbitration. The court warned that it would construe ambiguous provisions in favor of the party seeking a ruling that the arbitration contract is invalid. [T]his may present problems for the wide-ranging "dragnet" clauses used by some banks. In addition, the court required arbitration contracts to provide some detail as to the arbitration procedure which will apply. [T]his requirement raises the issue of whether simply referring to AAA procedures in a contract with a consumer is adequate.

The burden is on the party seeking to enforce an arbitration agreement to show that the opposing party "knowingly, intelligently, and voluntarily" waived his or her right to a trial in court. Missouri attempted to assure this by enacting a non-uniform amendment to its UAA which requires arbitration contracts to include the following disclosure in ten point capital letters: THIS CONTRACT CONTAINS A BINDING ARBITRATION PROVISION WHICH MAY BE ENFORCED BY THE PARTIES. Michigan goes even further, requiring that patients be furnished brochures describing the arbitration procedure they are subjecting themselves to by signing an agreement to arbitrate malpractice claims.

Contracts subject to the UAA have been attacked as unconscionable, with results varying depending upon the facts. In one case, the contract provided that insureds were bound by arbitration awards, but the insurance company was bound only if it consented in writing. The court declared the contract unconscionable because it was "unfairly structured." [I]n a medical malpractice case, a court rejected an unconscionability claim based on the argument that the AAA's fees were oppressive. The court pointed out that the fees were much less than the cost of litigating the claim. Moreover, the AAA Commercial Arbitration Rules provide that "in the event of extreme hardship" the administrative fee can be deferred or reduced.

The Delaware Supreme Court has held that certain insurance arbitration contracts are against public policy. The contract in Worldwide provided that if the arbitration award exceeded the state financial responsibility limits, either party could appeal the decision for a judicial trial de novo. If the award was below those limits, however, the award was not appealable. Noting that the practical effect was to provide the insurance company with the right to appeal while denying that right to the insured, the court struck down the contract and declared that it "promotes litigation, circumvents the arbitration process and provides an escape device in favor of the insurance company."

Some states have dealt with claims that the arbitration contract should be struck down because it provides for a forum inconvenient to one of the parties. A Michigan statute declares unenforceable arbitration clauses in franchise agreements requiring arbitration outside Michigan unless, at the time of arbitration, the franchisee agrees to arbitrate outside the state. Oregon's arbitration statute invalidates contracts that provide for arbitration outside the state. Courts have interpreted Florida's law as rendering agreements calling for out of state arbitration unenforceable.

The arbitrator obviously is a key player in the arbitration process. . . . Whereas judges are subject to careful public scrutiny prior to appointment or election, neither the public nor any governmental body has input into the process private arbitration organizations use to determine whether arbitrators are qualified. . . . The parties can only prevent their case being heard by an arbitrator they consider unqualified or biased by not selecting that arbitrator. A "repeat player" such as a lender which determines the arbitration organization and uses arbitration frequently, however, has a decided advantage over the "one shot" player such as the consumer. The repeat player is far more likely to know the persons in the arbitration pool. Moreover, the pool may be severely limited. A GAO report found that most arbitrators in employment discrimination cases involving the securities industry were white males with an average age of 60. . . .

Courts, however, generally have been unsympathetic to challenges to the selection of the arbitrator. When a brokerage employee objected to the arbitration tribunals established by the New York Stock Exchange to hear employee grievances, the Second Circuit refused to side with the employee absent evidence of actual unfairness in the way the tribunals operated. The court expressed its appreciation for those willing to serve as arbitrators, for it believed arbitration is a "generally thankless task" and those agreeing to be arbitrators are performing a service. The California Supreme Court has shown somewhat more of an inclination to entertain challenges to the selection of arbitrators where the arbitration agreement is an adhesion contract where the possibility of overreaching is present.[231] The court insisted upon a standard of "minimal levels of integrity." The objective of this standard was to ensure that the weaker party would have a "realistic and fair opportunity to prevail in a dispute." . . .

The state courts have supported the doctrine allowing arbitrators to decide based on what is fair and just rather than what the law requires. . . . The courts refuse to consider "even gross errors of judgement in law" unless they are apparent on the face of the award. This precludes

---

[231]Graham v. Scissor-Tail, Inc., 623 P.2d 165 (Cal. 1981). *See also* Neaman v. Kaiser Found. Hosp., 11 Cal. Rptr. 2d 879, 883 (Ct. App. 1992) (improper for arbitrator to fail to disclose that he served as the party-chosen arbitrator for one of the parties to the instant action).

most challenges based on an erroneous application of the law because the arbitrator is not required to give reasons for the award. The Michigan Supreme Court is somewhat more inclined to consider an arbitrator's error of law where the arbitration contract provides that the arbitration award may be entered as a judgment in that state's courts. That court rejected the manifest disregard standard and held that the arbitrator cannot "ignore controlling principles of law, either intentionally or unintentionally, even with the consent of the parties, and expect ultimate judicial imprimatur as well." . . .

The California Supreme Court, often a bellwether, held that an arbitrator's decision is binding and final and therefore cannot be reviewed on the basis of an error of law. [T]he court noted that although California had not adopted the UAA, its statutory provisions on judicial review "largely mirror" those of the UAA. Those provisions list the grounds for review; no other grounds are permissible. Therefore, the court would not consider the contention that the arbitrator committed an error of law which appeared on the face of the decision. The court justified its ruling, inter alia, on the basis that the parties had agreed to arbitrate their dispute; consequently, they decided a possible non-reviewable error of law was an "acceptable cost" in light of the benefits of arbitration. Furthermore, the court stated that even if the arbitration agreement had not demonstrated the parties' intent that the arbitrator's decision be final and binding, this intent is implied in every arbitration contract. The court left only one loophole. A court could consider a claim that the entire underlying transaction was illegal. . . .

The courts deciding cases under the UAA are split on whether the arbitrator has the authority to award punitive damages. . . . [S]ome banks have drafted very broad arbitration contracts. While these have the advantage of preventing consumers from seeking judicial redress for a wide variety of claims, ironically those broadly drafted contracts also may prompt some courts to hold that the arbitrator has authority to award punitive damages. . . .

IV. CONSUMER CHALLENGES TO ARBITRATION CONTRACTS

Some consumers may welcome arbitration of their disputes with financial institutions. Generally, arbitration is faster and less expensive than litigation. The arbitrator may have greater expertise than a judge. The arbitration contract may allow the consumer to force the institution to arbitrate its collection action, which may make such actions more costly and time-consuming than a summary action in court.

Other consumers may decide to challenge the arbitration contracts into which they have entered with financial institutions. Perhaps they object to the structural features of arbitration such as the loss of a jury trial and a judge, the limited right of discovery and appeal, the unlikelihood of class relief, or the lack of publicity. Or perhaps they object to specific provisions in the contracts drafted by their creditor. Finally, they may have a generalized hostility to arbitration because they or someone they know about had a bad experience with lender arbitration or with other types of ADR. . . .

Section 2 of the FAA provides that arbitration contracts are valid, enforceable, and irrevocable, except insofar as "grounds . . . exist at law or in equity for the revocation of any contract." Pursuant to this provision, arbitration contracts can be challenged as unconscionable. A lawsuit filed as a class action [*Patterson*] successfully attacked ITT's arbitration contract on the grounds of unconscionability. The contract stated that any dispute would be resolved "by the National Arbitration Forum, Minneapolis, Minnesota." . . . [However, a U.S. District

Court upheld the same ITT provision.] Despite the consumer's success in *Patterson*, California cases subsequent to Patterson, not involving distant forum clauses, have rejected challenges based on unconscionability. . . .

To the extent that contracts include terms reproduced in fine print on the reverse side of a document and use excessive "legalese," they are subject to attack. Also, if the consumer challenging the clause is non-English speaking, poor, or unsophisticated, a court is more likely to find procedural unconscionability. While the typical bank consumer may be a relatively sophisticated and well-educated middle class person, more and more low income consumers are becoming customers as states mandate basic banking. In addition, courts which view banking services as necessities are more likely to be sympathetic to arbitration challenges based on unconscionability. . . .

Finally, bank arbitration contracts may be subject to challenge in those states which have "plain language" statutes. For example, New York law requires every contract in a consumer transaction to be "[w]ritten in a clear and coherent manner using words with common and every day meanings; [and] [a]ppropriately divided and captioned by its various sections." In 1993, Pennsylvania enacted a plain language law which excludes documents used by financial institutions. While this evidently excludes banks, the law may nevertheless apply to finance companies and mortgage companies. The boilerplate language employed by many banks may fail to comply with these requirements.

Presumably, financial institutions will learn how to draft arbitration contracts which will sustain legal challenges brought by consumers against them. They will draft contracts in plain language or will prepare accompanying brochures which clearly and comprehensively explain the arbitration procedure and compare the advantages and disadvantages of arbitration and adjudication. They will draft contracts which evenly balance the rights and obligations of both parties and avoid provisions which seem to give the institutions an advantage, such as distant forum clauses. They will develop, perhaps in conjunction with the AAA, procedural rules designed specifically for consumer disputes and will establish panels of arbitrators specially trained to deal with these types of disputes. Even if financial institutions are able to accomplish all of this, however, the question remains whether arbitration is an appropriate mechanism to deal with consumer disputes.

V. THE APPROPRIATENESS OF ARBITRATION OF CONSUMER DISPUTES WITH FINANCIAL INSTITUTIONS

This section explores the issue of whether arbitration of consumer disputes with financial institutions is appropriate in the sense of whether it is wise social and legal policy. The legality of arbitration of these disputes is assumed, even if the consumer's claim is based on a federal statute providing for suit in a state or federal district court. If a bank's arbitration contract is drafted so as to withstand the challenges discussed in Part IV, it is quite certain the Supreme Court will look favorably upon the arbitrability of any type of dispute pursuant to the contract, unless Congress has clearly stated otherwise. The effectiveness of arbitration is assumed: it is assumed that for the most part arbitration of these disputes can be done in a prompt, inexpensive manner. This section asks whether, even if legal and effective, arbitration of these disputes represents a public policy which should be encouraged and promoted. . . .

[Since arbitration between broker-dealers and customers in the securities industry is so well established, it is essential for the author to distinguish the bank-customer relationship.]

In the [securities] instance, there is a dispute "between an industry and outsiders pursuant to standard form contracts . . . [in which] arbitration is being imposed by an industry on another interest group that knows little of the industry's form of arbitration and understands less of the industry's customs."

Arbitration between financial institutions and consumers bears a strong resemblance to . . . arbitration between brokers and investors. Like securities arbitration, it is not accurate to view this as arbitration between an individual financial institution and an individual consumer who happened to have agreed to arbitrate their disputes. Rather, . . . this is a carefully planned strategy by influential members of the financial services industry to resolve . . . claims made by consumers as a group. . . .

Along with these similarities, there are three major differences between securities arbitration and bank-consumer arbitration, two of which lend support to critics of arbitration in bank-consumer disputes. First, investors generally are more sophisticated than many consumers. People who deal with brokers have discretionary income which generally means they have higher incomes and better education than the general public. Consumers deal with banks and other financial institutions because they offer essential services. In fact, as banks increase their outreach with low-cost, no-frills basic banking services as a result of legislative mandate or voluntary practice, their customer base will include persons of ever more modest means. The lower level of sophistication of consumers coupled with the use of standard form contracts likely means consumers understand arbitration less than investors.

Another major difference between securities arbitration and consumer arbitration with financial institutions is the lack of government oversight in the [later]. In *Shearson/American Express, Inc. v. McMahon,* the Court justified its holding in part by pointing out that the S.E.C. carefully supervised securities arbitration. No supervisory agency has this role in regard to consumer arbitration with financial institutions.

The third difference between securities arbitration and consumer arbitration cuts the other way by ameliorating the negative impact which arbitration may have on consumers. Although arbitration contracts are universal for margin and option accounts in the securities industry, they are far from being so in the financial services industry. Consequently, consumers still have a viable option: they can take their business to a financial institution which does not require arbitration. This option is subject to two significant qualifications, however. First, unless consumers are provided with an adequate description of the advantages and disadvantages of both litigation and arbitration, they cannot fully appreciate the need to consider finding a financial institution which does not require arbitration. As described above, most arbitration contracts do not provide such a description. Second, it is likely that in the future, financial institutions increasingly will require arbitration, leaving the consumer with no choice but to accept arbitration or stop doing business with financial institutions altogether. This absence of alternatives is especially possible in rural or low income areas where few financial institutions may provide services. . . .

VI. PROPOSALS FOR REFORM

The preceding sections have discussed concerns in the arbitration of disputes between financial institutions and consumers. This section sets forth several legislative proposals for dealing with these concerns, analyzing the benefits and drawbacks of each. The reference to the legislature in this discussion refers to both Congress and state legislatures, unless otherwise noted.

A. The Laissez Faire Approach: Hear No Evil, See No Evil, Do Nothing

One possible approach is for the legislature to do nothing. Inaction can be justified on several bases. First, there is not as yet evidence that many consumers have been seriously abused by arbitration proceedings with financial institutions. It is better to wait until problems emerge. First, perhaps no problems will emerge. Second, legislative solutions can best be designed in light of the problems which do arise. With actual problems before it, the legislature can tailor solutions which deal with whatever abuses actually occur. Also, legislatures can avoid overbroad treatment, addressing only those issues which need legislative tinkering. This in turn can help consumers as well as financial institutions. For example, actual experience may indicate the consumer has a good understanding of how arbitration differs from litigation. Therefore, a consumer does not need a brochure describing those differences. The consumer, who arguably is already confused by information overload, is benefitted by not requiring unnecessary disclosures. . . .

Consumer advocates are reluctant to wait until they, government agencies, or legislative committees have documented substantial abuses involving many consumers and financial institutions. First, most consumers do not complain. Second, it is always uncertain how much evidence will be necessary to attract the attention of the legislature. Even if overwhelming evidence is gathered, in any given year, a legislature may be preoccupied with other matters such as a budget deficit. Once the legislature turns its attention to the need for legislation, there probably will be a substantial time lag before any legislation will pass. The consumer financial services lobby is certain to oppose strong measures. . . . Finally, it is better to act now, while consumer arbitration with financial institutions is in its formative stages. If legislatures postpone action until adequate documentation of actual consumer harm is available, many more financial institutions probably will have adopted arbitration, drafted contracts, and instituted procedures. If legislation subsequently is proposed, these institutions will complain about the cost and disruption new laws will cause. . . .

Finally, the consumer advocates decry the impact arbitration has on the comprehensive scheme of consumer protection laws which have been enacted. It deprives the consumer of the laws which their elected representatives passed for the consumer's benefit. It deprives the system of case law which is needed to interpret and apply consumer protection statutes in those transactions not covered by arbitration, and deprives regulatory and enforcement agencies of needed data.

B. The Consumer Protection Approach: Minimum Standards

[T]his section proposes that if a legislature decides to amend its laws to protect consumers from the adverse consequences of arbitration, a statute should contain the following standards, as an absolute minimum.

The very essence of arbitration is that it is a voluntary agreement between two parties. Given the disparity of power and knowledge between consumers and financial institutions, the often necessitous circumstances under which a consumer seeks financial services, and the potentially all-encompassing scope of the arbitration contract, legislation should require that a consumer is not bound unless the arbitration contract is signed. Several states already impose this requirement.

The legislature should consider whether or not to impose format requirements on the contract. Examples include: requiring the contract to be on a separate page from any other contract, requiring the contract to be written in plain language, and requiring the contract to be printed in at least ten point type. An alternative approach is to delegate to a government agency the task of issuing format guidelines. Examples of appropriate agencies are the Federal Trade Commission or Federal Reserve Board on the federal level, and departments of consumer affairs and consumer protection divisions of offices of the Attorney General on the state level.

Financial institutions may object that this will impose tremendous administrative and cost burdens upon them. They will argue that the burden will be especially severe in regard to current customers. . . . The institution's problem is less severe in regard to new customers. They will be presented with an arbitration contract at the time they are signing up for the institution's services, and probably will sign the arbitration contract with the same lack of attention they are paying to the numerous other forms they are signing. It would be easy to keep a record of those few new customers who refuse to sign the contract. . . .

Requiring financial institutions to obtain customer signatures on arbitration contracts raises issues related to persons who do not sign these agreements. The preceding discussion assumes that a current customer cannot be denied service due to the failure to sign. That customer agreed to purchase services at a stated price, and the institution should not be able to unilaterally impose a modification which fundamentally alters the agreement. The position of a new customer may be more precarious. If the consumer refuses to sign the arbitration contract, can the financial institution refuse to provide services? At first glance, it appears refusal is a legitimate course of action. . . . The legislature may wish to require banks to serve a new customer under those circumstances, even where arbitration contracts are not signed. . . .

Every consumer should receive a brochure accompanying the arbitration contract. Without a brochure explaining the consequences of signing the agreement, a consumer cannot intelligently and knowingly waive his or her right to access to the judicial process. At least one bank, Zions First National Bank, has voluntarily produced a brochure. It describes the arbitration procedure and points out the benefits of arbitration. Unfortunately, it does not compare the advantages and disadvantages of both arbitration and litigation. . . .

A third minimum standard should be legislation which prohibits clauses providing for hearings in distant forums. . . .

Fourth, the legislation should limit the costs of arbitration to the consumer. . . . A financial institution could easily make arbitration infeasible to a consumer by requiring use of an arbitration organization whose filing and arbitrator fees are excessive in relation to the amount of the consumer's claim or the consumer's resources. Legislation restricting costs would not unduly burden consumer arbitration.

Fifth, legislation should require financial institutions to forward the results of arbitrations to a central repository. This information would serve as a data base for regulatory and enforcement agencies. The information also should be open to the public so every consumer and the media can monitor consumer arbitration and spot institutions to avoid. The securities industry has established such a system.

The minimum standards legislation proposed in this part would be appropriate both for Congress and state legislatures because they affect arbitration under both the FAA and state arbitration statutes. One problem, however, can be solved only by Congress. [D]ecisions of the Supreme Court have made unclear the power of states to prohibit the arbitration of disputes arising out of certain types of transactions. Congress should amend the FAA to permit states to do so, at least in consumer transactions. . . .

C. The Consumer Protection Approach: Alternative I—Base Safeguards On Type Of Claim

In regard to consumer claims based on common law theories, in addition to the minimum standards discussed above, a consumer may need more liberal discovery rules in order to prove each case. Banks will oppose this, arguing that such departures from traditional arbitration procedure destroy its benefits. New Jersey's Alternative Procedure for Dispute Resolution Act, however, represents a measured compromise which retains most of the advantages of arbitration while permitting depositions and the inspection and copying of documents. Interrogatories are permitted when authorized by the decisionmaker, called an "umpire." Discovery must be completed within 60 days, but the umpire can extend that time and can limit or terminate discovery. The umpire's discovery decisions are subject to appeal. Legislatures may want to adopt these discovery rules for all consumer cases based on common law claims.

In regard to consumer claims based on consumer protection statutes, legislatures should consider two alternatives. . . . Arbitration ignores the legislature's overall regulatory and enforcement scheme, to balance the interests of consumers and financial institutions. Arbitration eviscerates the judiciary's role in interpreting and applying statutes with major public policy implications.

The second alternative is to allow arbitration of disputes in which the consumer's claims are based on consumer protection statutes, but to require substantial safeguards. . . . The New Jersey Alternative Procedure for Dispute Resolution Act requires that the umpire decide the case "in accordance with applicable principles of substantive law." The arbitration rules of the Center for Public Resources [CPR] clearly contemplate a "legal" award rather than a broad, unfettered exercise of equitable discretion.

The only way to know if the arbitrator followed the law is to require a "reasoned" decision which includes findings of fact and determinations of law. The New Jersey law provides for this type of award. Reasoned awards are the norm in international commercial arbitration and arbitration administered by the Society of Maritime Arbitrators and are required by the arbitration rules of the Center for Public Resources. Because of the breadth and complexity of consumer protection statutes, legislation also should require a training program in consumer protection for arbitrators. It makes no sense to require the arbitrator to follow the law if there is no assurance the arbitrator is familiar with it.

The legislature should consider whether to allow judicial review of an arbitration award on the grounds that the arbitrator did not correctly apply the applicable law. New Jersey permits this. Financial institutions can be expected to oppose it, arguing that judicial review on that basis obliterates one of arbitration's chief advantages for them. Courts may balk as well, because judges see arbitration as a means of reducing dockets. Consumer advocates will argue that judicial review is the only method by which a consumer can be assured that arbitration awards do indeed preserve consumer rights. Furthermore, it is reasonable to expect that the number of actual appeals would be very small since the typical consumer does not complain when dissatisfied.

A legislature that wishes to prevent arbitration from obliterating the public policy objectives of consumer protection statutes must consider what remedies to preserve in arbitration. Consumer protection statutes typically authorize the court to award a successful consumer costs and attorney's fees and provide for minimum statutory damages. This recognizes that the consumer acts as a private attorney general promoting the common good when the consumer successfully brings actions under these statutes, and it is therefore appropriate to provide incentives to encourage such actions. The incentives are necessary due to the fact that the amount of money often involved in these cases, while very significant to the average consumer, is not enough to justify these actions. This feature is especially crucial to preserve in arbitration where the consumer's share of the arbitrator's fee may make arbitration more expensive for the consumer than litigation.

Punitive damages are important to deter companies from engaging in outrageous conduct. Consumer advocates therefore argue that legislation should provide the arbitrator with the authority to award punitive damages in appropriate cases. Class actions are sometimes a highly efficient way to correct violations of consumer protection statutes, especially where the violation is a defect in standard form contracts which affect every consumer who signed those contracts. Therefore, consumer advocates argue the arbitrator should have the authority to treat the case as a class action where appropriate and feasible.

Financial institutions likely would oppose the above proposals, contending that they incorporate so much of the elements of litigation in the judicial forum that they lose the benefits of arbitration. Consumer advocates would counter that without these safeguards, consumers stand to lose the rights these laws guarantee them. In addition, these laws are part of the legislature's overall financial institution regulatory scheme. These laws help not only the consumer, but also the business community because they prohibit conduct which allows a firm engaging in socially undesirable conduct to gain an unfair advantage over firms which do not. Consumer advocates also could point out that even with the above safeguards incorporated into arbitration, it is nevertheless advantageous to financial institutions compared to litigation. For example, cases would be heard and decided more quickly because the arbitrator does not have to compete with a criminal court docket. Even if discovery is allowed to the extent proposed here, it is more limited than discovery in a court case. Arbitrators do not adhere to strict rules of evidence, so both sides can more easily present their proof and argue their positions. Financial institutions would still be able to determine the scope of disputes covered by arbitration, whether to follow the AAA's procedures or other procedures on selection of arbitrators and many other items. In other words, even with the suggested safeguards, the financial institution remains in the driver's seat to a large extent, unlike its position in the judicial forum.

Finally, the legislature should consider requiring that arbitration in cases involving consumer protection statutes be nonbinding. . . . If consumer arbitration of disputes with financial institutions was nonbinding, the legislature would not be as concerned about the need to incorporate litigation safeguards into arbitration. . . .

Financial institutions also may oppose this proposal based on the fear that those who do go to court after nonbinding arbitration will be precisely those for whom the institutions most want binding arbitration: consumers with class action claims or those seeking punitive damages or both. Nevertheless, legislatures may find nonbinding arbitration an attractive solution because it preserves traditional arbitration while providing access to the judicial forum.

D. Consumer Protection Approach: Alternative II—Across The Board Rules To Govern Consumer Disputes

The proposal discussed above sets up a two-tiered system, with one set of arbitration rules for cases where the consumer's claims are based on common law theories and another set of stricter rules for those cases based on consumer protection statutes. Even if one agrees legislatures should adopt laws to safeguard the consumer in arbitration, one can question the advisability of this two-tiered system. In such a system, the consumer will be tempted to make claims based on consumer protection statutes in order to gain the advantages of the attendant safeguards. The financial institution and consumer consequently will become engaged at the outset in a battle over whether the consumer has a legitimate basis for making that type of claim. Furthermore, some might argue that a claim based on a common law cause of action such as fraud may be far more significant to the public interest than one based on a technical violation of a disclosure requirement in a consumer credit statute.

For these reasons, the legislature should consider an alternative approach. If the legislature does not wish to make distinctions between types of claims, the legislature could instead treat all claims alike. The legislature that wants to protect the consumer in arbitration could simply provide that arbitration of consumer disputes is prohibited. This solution eliminates any confusion. It eliminates any need for the legislature to decide what types of safeguards to incorporate into arbitration.

On the other hand, the legislature may want to preserve the arbitration option while treating all consumer arbitration alike. This could be done by retaining consumer arbitration but building in some or all of the safeguards suggested above. How many and which safeguards is a function of how serious the legislature is about preserving consumer rights. As in most human endeavors, every benefit to one group may result in a cost to another group. Every consumer safeguard built into arbitration makes arbitration somewhat less "efficient" for financial institutions. On the other hand, allowing financial institutions to avoid judicial forums by means of adhesion contracts when their actions violate statutes which specifically provide consumers with those forums is a serious deprivation of consumer rights and an evisceration of legislative purpose.

3. Arbitration Provisions: Bank of America

(a) Mandatory Arbitration. Any controversy or claim between or among the parties, including but not limited to those arising out of or relating to this Agreement or any agreements or instruments relating hereto or delivered in connection herewith and any claim based on or arising from an alleged tort, shall at the request of any party be determined by arbitration. The arbitration shall be conducted in accordance with the United States Arbitration Act (Title 9, U.S. Code), notwithstanding any choice of law provision in this Agreement, and under the Commercial Arbitration Rules of the American Arbitration Association ("AAA"). The arbitrators shall give effect to statutes of limitation in determining any claim. Any controversy concerning whether an issue is arbitrable shall be determined by the arbitrators. Judgment upon the arbitration award may be entered in any court having jurisdiction. The institution and maintenance of an action for judicial relief or pursuit of a provisional or ancillary remedy shall not constitute a waiver of the right of any party, including the plaintiff, to submit the controversy or claim to arbitration if any other party contests such action for judicial relief.

(b) Real Property Collateral. Notwithstanding the provisions of subparagraph (a), no controversy or claim shall be submitted to arbitration without the consent of all parties if, at the time of the proposed submission, such controversy or claim arises from or relates to an obligation to Bank which is secured by real property collateral. If all parties do not consent to submission of such a controversy or claim to arbitration, the controversy or claim shall be determined as provided in subparagraph (c).

(c) Judicial Reference. At the request of any party a controversy or claim which is not submitted to arbitration as provided and limited in subparagraphs (a) and (b) shall be determined by a reference in accordance with California Code of Civil Procedure Sections 638 et seq. If such an election is made, the parties shall designate to the court a referee or referees selected under the auspices of the AAA in the same manner as arbitrators are selected in AAA-sponsored proceedings. The presiding referee of the panel, or the referee if there is a single referee, shall be an active attorney or retired judge. Judgment upon the award rendered by such referee or referees shall be entered in the court in which such proceeding was commenced in accordance with California Code of Civil Procedure Sections 644 and 645.

(d) Provisional Remedies, Self-Help and Foreclosure. No provision of this Paragraph shall limit the right of any party to this Agreement to exercise self-help remedies such as setoff, to foreclose against or sell any real or personal property collateral or security, or obtaining provisional or ancillary remedies from a court of competent jurisdiction before, after, or during the pendency of any arbitration or other proceeding. The exercise of a remedy does not waive the right of either party to resort to arbitration or reference. At Bank's option, foreclosure under a deed of trust or mortgage may be accomplished either by exercise of power of sale under the deed of trust or mortgage or by judicial foreclosure.

4. Arbitration Provisions: Zions First National Bank

ARBITRATION DISCLOSURES:

1. ARBITRATION IS USUALLY FINAL AND BINDING ON THE PARTIES AND SUBJECT TO ONLY VERY LIMITED REVIEW BY A COURT.
2. THE PARTIES ARE WAIVING THEIR RIGHT TO LITIGATE IN COURT, INCLUDING THEIR RIGHT TO A JURY TRIAL.
3. PRE-ARBITRATION DISCOVERY IS GENERALLY MORE LIMITED AND DIFFERENT FROM COURT PROCEEDINGS.
4. ARBITRATORS' AWARDS ARE NOT REQUIRED TO INCLUDE FACTUAL FINDINGS OR LEGAL REASONING AND ANY PARTY'S RIGHT TO APPEAL OR TO SEEK MODIFICATION OF RULINGS BY ARBITRATORS IS STRICTLY LIMITED.
5. A PANEL OF ARBITRATORS MIGHT INCLUDE AN ARBITRATOR WHO IS OR WAS AFFILIATED WITH THE BANKING INDUSTRY.

ARBITRATION PROVISIONS:

(a) Any controversy or claim between or among the parties, including but not limited to those arising out of or relating to this Agreement or any agreements or instruments relating hereto or delivered in connection herewith, AND including but not limited to a claim based on or arising from an alleged tort, shall at the request of any party be determined by arbitration in accordance with the Commercial Arbitration Rules of the American Arbitration Association. The arbitration proceedings shall be conducted in Salt Lake City, Utah. The arbitrator(s) shall have the qualifications set forth in subparagraph (c) hereto. All statutes of limitations which would otherwise be applicable in a judicial action brought by a party shall apply to any arbitration or reference proceeding hereunder.

(b) In any judicial action or proceeding arising out of or relating to this Agreement or any agreements or instruments relating hereto or delivered in connection herewith, including but not limited to a claim based on or arising from an alleged tort, if the controversy or claim is not submitted to arbitration as provided and limited in subparagraph (a) hereto, all decisions of fact and law shall be determined by a reference in accordance with Rule 53 of the Federal Rules of Civil Procedure or Rule 53 of the Utah Rules of Civil Procedure or other comparable, applicable reference procedure. The parties shall designate to the court the referee(s) selected under the auspices of the American Arbitration Association in the same manner as arbitrators are selected in Association-sponsored arbitration proceedings. The referee(s) shall have the qualifications set forth in subparagraph (c) hereto.

(c) The arbitrator(s) or referee(s) shall be selected in accordance with the rules of the American Arbitration Association from panels maintained by the Association. A single arbitrator or referee shall be knowledgeable in the subject matter of the dispute. Where three arbitrators or referees conduct an arbitration or reference proceeding, the claim shall be decided by a majority vote of the three arbitrators or referees, at least one of whom must be knowledgeable in the subject matter of the dispute and at least one of whom must be a practicing attorney. The arbitrator(s) or referee(s) shall award recovery of all costs and fees (including attorneys' fees, administrative fees, arbitrators' fees, and court costs). The arbitrator(s) or referee(s) also may grant provisional or ancillary remedies such as, for example, injunctive relief, attachment, or the appointment of a receiver, either during the dependency of the arbitration or reference proceeding or as part of the arbitration or reference award.

(d) Judgment upon an arbitration or reference award may be entered in any court having jurisdiction, subject to the following limitation: the arbitration or reference award is binding upon the parties only if the amount does not exceed Four Million Dollars ($4,000,000); if the award exceeds that limit either party may commence legal action for a court trial de novo. Such legal action must be filed within thirty (30) days following the date of the arbitration or reference award; if such legal action is not filed within that time period, the amount of the arbitration or reference award shall be binding. The computation of the total amount of an arbitration or reference award shall include amounts awarded for arbitration fees, attorneys' fees, and all other related costs.

(e) At the Bank's option, foreclosure under a deed of trust or mortgage may be accomplished either by exercise of a power of sale under the deed of trust or mortgage or by judicial foreclosure. The institution and maintenance of an action for judicial relief or pursuit of a provisional or ancillary remedy shall not constitute a waiver of the right of any party, including the plaintiff, to submit the controversy or claim to arbitration if any other party contests such action for judicial relief.

(f) Notwithstanding the applicability of other law to any other provision of this Agreement, the Federal Arbitration Act, 9 U.S.C. § 1 et seq., shall apply to the construction and interpretation of this arbitration paragraph.

5. Comments and Questions

a. The New Jersey legislation discussed by Budnitz is found at N.J. Stat. Ann. §§ 2A:23A-1 et. seq. *See also* John O'Hare, *The New Jersey Alternative Dispute Resolution Act: Vanguard of a Better Way?*, 136 U. PA. L. REV. 1723 (1988).

b. At what point (decisions based on law, written opinions, judicial review, training for arbitrators, etc.) does arbitration cease to be a serious option? Legislative strategists for any given position might want to prohibit a practice. Where doing so is unrealistic, a practical (and perhaps even preferred) alternative is to permit the practice but hedge it in with so many restrictions as to greatly limit or even to abolish it *sub silentio.*

c. Professor Budnitz characterizes bank customers as often being low and moderate income, but the definition used in many state "consumer" protection statutes is far more inclusive. For example, the Texas Deceptive Trade Practices Act defines a consumer as any individual, person or an organization with assets up to $25 million — that's right, MILLION.

d. Imagine a town with three banks, with no other banks for fifty miles in any direction: one bank requires arbitration for all disputes; the second mandates non-binding arbitration; and the third has no arbitration provision in its customer contract. What role is the arbitration variable likely to play in the selection of a bank by persons who move to the town?

Inducing consumers to switch from one bank to another is more difficult than attracting a person new to an area who wants to open an account at some bank, because of the transaction costs associated with switching institutions. And, because the initial choice was the best one for the [rational maximizer] consumer, it will take a considerable incentive to cause the person to switch banks. Assume that one bank imposes the worst imaginable arbitration provision on its consumer customers, while another bank located across the street imposes the best possible arbitration provision, in each instance as defined by the consumer in question. (Transaction account agreements between banks and their customers commonly allow the bank to alter the agreement, and the customer "accepts" this "offer" by continuing to use the account after receiving notice from the bank.) How many customers do you think would move their accounts from the bank with the worst arbitration option to the one with the best arbitration option? Of those who do switch, do you think they will be predominantly the poorer customers about whom consumer protection advocates (including your authors) are primarily concerned, or will they be the wealthier (and more educated) customers?

e. A further problem for consumers in the evaluation of any arbitration provision is that arbitration is a contingent event; the arbitration term will come into effect only if there is a dispute between the bank and the customer, and then only if a negotiated settlement proves impossible. (The same problem arises with other contingent contract terms such as limitation of warranties, liquidated damages, and attorney's fees.) A common term in sales contracts is that the limitations period is reduced to one year from the Uniform Commercial Code's default position of four years. This approach is expressly authorized in section 2-725. How does a sophisticated business, that has access to the finest economists, probabilty theorists, and lawyers evalute the one and four year limitations provisions? To reduce the issue to money, how much will a rational enterprise pay for a preferred limitations term or arbitration provision? If sophisticated business organizations cannot make this calculation, what can be expected of consumers, particularly those with limited wealth and education who are most in need of protection?

f. Suppose that a bank (or two banks that provide identical services at adjacent locations) offer the following options for checking accounts. The best possible arbitration terms for the customer and 5 percent interest on deposits, or the worst possible arbitration term for the bank and 6 percent interest. (Best and worst are defined from the viewpoint of the customer in question.) Theory and common sense produce the same result — take the money.

g. There is a considerable literature about how and why people select banks. The answer to the "how" question is that people talk to friends or relatives, and are sometimes affected by advertising. Only an extreme masochist would select a bank by acquiring the contracts of the conveniently located institutions and reading them — even when these materials are written in simple English. The three leading factors in the selection of a bank are location, location, and location. Economic factors (loan charges, interest paid on deposits) are a consideration, and particular service features (ATM, credit cards, Saturday hours) are important to some potential customers.

h. Can you construct an argument that mandatory, binding arbitration, with no requirement of adherence to law by the arbitrator, is the best option for bank customers — particularly those with low or modest income?

i. The type of analysis presented by Budnitz can be used for other consumer transactions of consequence, notably claims related to the purchase (or lease) of insurance, motor vehicles, computers, and major appliances.

j. As discussed in Chapter 11, and noted by Professor Budnitz, federal preemption of state laws regarding arbitration is quite broad. For contracts between consumers and businesses engaged in interstate commerce, can state arbitration law survive federal preemption? Consider, in particular, the Supreme Court's 1995 *Allied-Bruce* decision (Chapter 11, section C). Even where the apparent answer is no, remember that state officials, including judges, are often quite partial to local law, and strongly object to "interference" by a distant federal government that does not understand local conditions.

C. Arbitration of Employment Disputes

1. The Steelworkers Trilogy

In 1960 the Supreme Court decided three cases that set the ground rules for the relationship between the judiciary and the labor arbitrations. *United Steelworkers v. American Mfg. Co.*, 363 U.S. 564 (1960); *United Steelworkers v. Warrior & Gulf Navigation Co.*, 363 U.S. 574 (1960); *United Steelworkers v. Enterprise Wheel & Car Corp.*, 363 U.S. 593 (1960). As the United States Steelworkers union was a name party in each instance, the cases are known collectively as the Steelworkers trilogy. Simply stated, the Supreme Court adopted the following principles:

a. The courts should enforce a contractual promise to arbitrate, and should use a presumption of arbitrability in determining whether the parties agreed to arbitrate a type or class of disputes.

b. The courts should order arbitration without inquiring into the merits of the underlying grievance.
c. The courts should enforce an arbitation award so long as it can be said to have "drawn its essence" from the terms of the agreement.

These standards are highly deferential to aritration agreements entered into by labor and management and the decisions of arbitrators made purusant to such agreements. The literature on labor arbitration makes frequent reference to "the Steelworkers trilogy." The trilogy is discussed in *AT&T Technologies, Inc. v. Communications Workers of America* (Chapter 11, section E). The "essence" test is discussed in both the majority and dissenting opinions of *Advanced Micro Devices v. Intel* (Chapter 11, section G).

2. Role of the Arbitrator in Labor Disputes

a. Comments and Questions

1. The author of the piece that follows, Lon Fuller, was a distinguished law professor who is best known for his work in Jurisprudence and Contracts. Late in his career Fuller turned his attention to different forms of dispute settlement. His best known article is *The Forms and Limits of Adjudication,* 82 HARV. L. REV. 353 (1978). Related works are *Mediation — Its Forms and Functions,* 44 S. CAL. L. REV. 305 (1971), excerpted in Chapter 7, section B, and the article excerpted here. While the focus is on arbitration in the collective bargaining context, many of his observations are applicable to arbitration generally. Taken together, Fuller's articles represent an early effort at "fitting the forum to the fuss."

2. Professor Fuller addresses two issues that are central to labor arbitration: What is the proper role of the arbitrator, and how should contracts be interpreted. To what extent can Fuller's observations be generalized from the collective bargaining context to arbitration of other types of disputes?

b. Lon L. Fuller, *Collective Bargaining and the Arbitrator,* 1963 WIS. L. REV. 3*

The purpose of this paper is to discuss two controversies about labor arbitration. These controversies have surrounded the institution almost from its inception. They touch on what may be called its permanent problems. . . .

The first of these controversies relates to the proper role of the arbitrator — how he should conceive his function, how he should conduct the hearings, what limits he should impose on himself. The second related to the principles he should follow in interpreting the collective bargaining agreement and in applying its provisions to the controversy before him. As this statement of the second issue implies, my concern here is primarily with arbitration arising under an existing agreement, and not with arbitration conducted to set the terms of a new contract.

One conception of the role of the arbitrator is that he is essentially a judge. His job is to do justice according to the rules imposed by the parties' contract, leaving the chips to fall where they may. He decides the controversy entirely on the basis of arguments and proofs presented to him "in open court" with the parties confronting one another face to face. He does not attempt to mediate or conciliate, for to do so would be to compromise his role as an adjudicator. . . . The opposing conception expects the arbitrator to adapt his procedures to the case at hand. Indeed, in its more extreme form it rejects the notion that his powers for good should be restrained at all by procedural limitations. By this view the arbitrator has a roving commission to straighten things out, the immediate controversy marking the occasion for, but not the limits of, his intervention. . . .

The other major controversy . . . relates to the interpretation of the collective bargaining agreement. By one view a labor contract is like any other legal document and ought to be subject to the same principles of interpretation. If, as it commonly does, it states that the arbitrator shall have no power to add to or to detract from its terms, the arbitrator must accept this limitation. . . . The opposing view stresses the unique quality of the collective bargaining agreement. . . . It is at once a constitution and the written record of an economic trade. . . . From the curiously mixed nature of the collective bargaining agreement there is derived (by a logic that is certainly not obvious) the conclusion that it must be construed freely. . . .

In presenting these two controversies I have purposely thrown the contending sides into a sharper opposition than commonly exists in practice. In reality the matter is never so black and white as I have just painted it. . . . The two controversies I have outlined are to some extent two aspects of a single dispute. One can generally predict that the arbitrator with strong instincts toward mediation will also be likely to favor free principles of contract construction. . . .

II.

[After an extensive discussion of contract interpretation, Fuller summarizes.] First, there is nothing ineffably peculiar about the job of interpreting collective bargaining agreements. Such agreements are complicated and they contain specialized legal documents. Such documents may also involve what may be called constitutional aspects, establishing a private system of adjudication and providing procedures for accommodating the contract to changing circumstances. Second, intelligent interpretation of collective bargaining agreements requires an understanding of a complex and changing body of industrial practice. This understanding is not as a practical matter accessible to courts through ordinary procedures of proof. Third, in most cases there is and can be no sharp distinction between testimony bearing on the merits of a dispute and testimony bearing on the arbitrator's jurisdiction to hear the dispute. For this reason to determine the question of arbitrability on the basis of a fraction of the facts relevant to the case as a whole is to take a shot in the dark, a proceeding all the more dangerous when the marksman mistakenly thinks, as he often does, that he sees the target clearly. . . .

III.

Let me now turn to the other major controversy surrounding labor arbitration, that of the proper role of the arbitrator himself. Is his office essentially judicial, with all the restraints that term implies? Or shall we assign to him a freer role, something like that suggested by the term "labor-relations physician?"

Here we encounter the difficulty of defining the restraints of the judicial role in the case of one who does not hold public office in the ordinary sense of the word. . . . The problem then becomes that of defining in some more general sense what it means to act like a judge.

At this point one is tempted to discern the essence of the judicial function in a requirement that the decision reached be *informed* and *impartial.* This will not do, however. The expectation that judgments should be informed and impartial applies to many social roles: that of supervisors toward those under their direction, of teachers toward pupils, of parents toward children, and so forth. The essence of the judicial function lies not in the substance of the conclusion reached, but in the procedures by which that substance is guaranteed. One does not become a judge by acting intelligently and fairly, but by accepting procedural restraints designed to insure, so far as human nature permits, an impartial and informed outcome of the process of decision.

I believe there is open to us a relatively simple way of defining the procedural restraints to which the judicial role is subject. We can do this by looking at adjudication, not through the eyes of the judge, but through the eyes of the affected litigant. Adjudication we may define as a social process of decision which assures to the affected party a particular form of participation, that of presenting proofs and arguments for a decision in his favor.

Viewed in this light, adjudication is only one form of social decision in which the affected party is afforded an institutionally guaranteed participation. Elections grant to the affected party participation through voting; contracts grant to him participation through negotiation, either in person or through representatives. No procedure of decision guarantees any particular outcome and least of all an outcome favorable to any particular participant. But the essence of the rule of law lies in the fact that men affected by the decisions which emerge from social processes should have some formally guaranteed opportunity to affect those decisions.

[A]djudication is a process of decision in which the affected party—"the litigant"—is afforded an institutionally guaranteed participation, which consists of the opportunity to present proofs and arguments for a decision in his favor. Whatever protects and enhances the effectiveness of that participation, advances the integrity of adjudication itself. Whatever impairs that participation detracts from its integrity. When that participation becomes a matter of grace, rather than of right, the process of decision ceases to deserve the name of adjudication.

From the analysis just presented can be derived, I believe, all of the restraints usually associated with an adjudicative role. Thus, interest or bias on the part of the adjudicator constitutes an obvious impairment of the interested party's participation through presenting proofs and arguments. So does the holding of private conferences, for the party not included in such a conference cannot know toward what he should be directing the presentation of his case. Matters are not squared when both parties are separately consulted, for then both are dependent on the candor and intelligence of the adjudicator in learning what the other side is saying, not to mention the more usual objections, such as the lack of an opportunity to cross-examine.

The test here suggested by no means coincides with popular prejudice concerning the judicial role. In this country there is a strong inclination to identify judicial behavior with passiveness, the judge being viewed as an umpire over a game in which he takes no active part until called upon by one of the parties to do so. The test here proposed renders a quite different judgment. If the arbiter of a dispute judges prematurely without hearing what both sides have to say, he obviously impairs the effectiveness of the parties' participation in the decision by proofs and arguments. On the other hand, that participation may be equally impaired if the parties are given no inkling at any time as to what is happening in the arbiter's mind. One cannot direct an effective argument into a vacuum. Accordingly it is the part of the wise arbitrator at some time, usually toward the end of the hearing, to convey to the parties some notion of the difficulties he finds in supporting or in answering certain of the arguments that have been addressed to him. He may find it useful also to summarize the arguments on each side, asking the parties to make corrections or additions so that he may be sure he fully grasps what each is contending for. Such discussions, initiated by the arbitrator himself, take him out of a purely passive role. It is plain, however, that they enhance meaningful participation by the parties in the decision and thus enhance the integrity of adjudication itself.

Perhaps the crassest infringement of adjudicative integrity consists in what has been called the "rigged award." In its most extreme form this means that although the affected parties think their case is being submitted to arbitrational decision, in fact their representatives have already agreed on the outcome to be incorporated in the award. It might seem that this procedure involves not so much an abuse of arbitration as a fraud by representatives on their constituents. But it should not be forgotten that the object of the whole manipulation is to secure the moral force of adjudication for what is in fact not adjudicated at all. The apparent participation of the affected party—through proofs and arguments presented on his behalf—is an empty sham. This problem of the "rigged," or more politely, the "informed" award deserves some analysis. Such an analysis will reveal that, while in some cases to clothe an agreement with the trappings of an award will constitute a plain abuse of adjudicative power, in other instances the appraisal is less obvious.

Let me take two extreme cases, beginning with an instance where the practice is presented in its most innocent form. Six grievances are scheduled for hearing over a three-day period. These grievances are all closely related, involving, let us say, a series of work-load or machine-assignment problems. Late on the third day the sixth case has still not been heard. If it is to be heard at all, a new hearing will have to be scheduled and this will be difficult. Though the arbitrator has as yet rendered no formal award in any of the cases heard, the drift of his mind has become apparent during the hearing of the first five cases, and the disposition of the sixth is not hard to predict. The parties' representatives agree on a solution of it and ask the arbitrator to incorporate their settlement in an award. If the first five cases were reported to the membership as settled by arbitration, while the sixth was reported as settled by agreement, quite unjustified suspicions and doubts would be aroused. Hence the arbitrator is willing to put the agreed settlement "in series," as it were, with its five companions. It would take a purist indeed to discern any real wickedness in this action.

At the other extreme is the case where an arbitrator is paid handsomely to hold extended hearings, where a parade of witnesses is heard, where lawyers plead with heart-stirring eloquence, when all the while the whole thing has been rigged and fixed from the beginning and the whole hearing is a farce from start to finish. [E]ven if awards rendered in cases like this always produced a short-run advantage judged from the standpoint of public welfare, the long-run cost would be too high to pay. Such an arbitrational practice is essentially parasitic. It takes advantage of the fact that most awards are honest, for if all awards were known to be fixed there would be no point in masquerading an agreement as the decision of an arbitrator. . . .

In deciding what he should do the arbitrator is not entitled to take the easy way out by saying, "After all, the purpose of arbitration is to promote good labor relations. If I can head off an unjustified and futile strike by issuing as an arbitrator's decision what is really an agreed settlement, then my conscience is clear." Before taking this escape the arbitrator should reflect that he is trustee for the integrity of the processes of decision entrusted to his care. He should ask himself whether the argument for bending his powers for good is not like that of the man who, in order to give to a worthy charity, embezzles funds entrusted to his care for an undeserving nephew. In practice the temptation to take short cuts in order to do good is a much greater threat to the integrity of arbitration than the temptation to use its forms for evil purposes. . . .

There remains the difficult problem of mediation by the arbitrator, who instead of issuing an award, undertakes to persuade the parties to reach a settlement, perhaps reinforcing his persuasiveness with "the gentle threat" of a decision. Again, there is waiting a too easy answer: "Judges do it." Of course, judges sometimes mediate, or at least bring pressure on the parties for a voluntary settlement. Sometimes this is done usefully and sometimes in ways that involve an abuse of office. In any event the judiciary has evolved no uniform code with respect to this problem that the arbitrator can take over ready-made. Judicial practice varies over a wide range. If the arbitrator were to pattern his conduct after the worst practices of the bench, arbitration would be in a sad way.

Analysis of the problem as it confronts the arbitrator should begin with a recognition that mediation or conciliation, the terms being largely interchangeable, has an important role to play in the settlement of labor disputes. There is much to justify a system whereby it is a prerequisite to arbitration that an attempt first be made by a skilled mediator to bring about a voluntary settlement. . . .

Mediation and arbitration have distinct purposes and hence distinct moralities. The morality of mediation lies in optimum settlement, a settlement in which each party gives up what he values less, in return for what he values more. The morality of arbitration lies in a decision according to the law of the contract. The procedures appropriate for mediation are those most likely to uncover that pattern of adjustment which will most nearly meet the interests of both parties. The procedures appropriate for arbitration are those which most securely guarantee each of the parties a meaningful chance to present arguments and proofs for a decision in his favor. Thus, private consultations with the parties, generally wholly improper on the part of an arbitrator, are an indispensable tool of mediation.

Not only are the appropriate procedures different in the two cases, but the facts sought by those procedures are different. There is no way to define "the essential facts" of a situation except by reference to some objective. Since the objective of reaching an optimum settlement is different from that of rendering an award according to the contract, the facts relevant in the two cases are different, or, when they seem the same, are viewed in different aspects. If a person who has mediated unsuccessfully attempts to assume the role of arbitrator, he must endeavor to view the facts of the case in a completely new light, as if he had previously known nothing about them. This is a difficult thing to do. It will be hard for him to listen to proofs and arguments with an open mind. If he fails in this attempt, the integrity of adjudication is impaired.

These are the considerations that seem to me to apply where the arbitrator attempts to mediate before hearing the case at all. This practice is quite uncommon, and would largely be confined to situations where a huge backlog of grievances seemed to demand drastic measures toward an Augean clean-up. I want now to pass to consideration of the case where the arbitrator postpones his mediative efforts until after the proofs are in and the arguments have been heard. In doing so I pass over the situation where the arbitrator interrupts the hearing midway in order to seek a voluntary settlement. The standards properly applicable to this intermediate situation may be derived from those governing the two cases that lie on either side of it.

One might ask of mediation first undertaken after the hearing is over, what is the point of it? If the parties do not like the award, they are at liberty to change it. If there is some settlement that will effect a more apt adjustment of their interests, their power to contract for that settlement is the same after, as it is before, the award is rendered. One answer would be to say that if the arbitrator undertakes mediation after the hearing but before the award, he can use "the gentle threat" of a decision to induce settlement, keeping it uncertain as to just what the decision will be. . . .

There is, however, a more convincing argument for mediative efforts after the hearing and before the award. This lies in the peculiar fact — itself a striking tribute to the moral force of the whole institution of adjudication — that an award tends to resist change by agreement. Once rendered it seems to have a kind of moral inertia that puts a heavy onus on the party who proposes any modification by mutual consent. Hence if there exists the possibility of a voluntary settlement that will suit both parties better than the award, the last chance to obtain it may occur after the hearing and before the award is rendered. This may in fact be an especially propitious moment for a settlement. Before the hearing it is quite usual for each of the parties to underestimate grossly the strength of his adversary's case. The hearing not uncommonly "softens up" both parties for settlement.

What, then, are the objections to an arbitrator's undertaking mediative efforts after the hearing and before rendering the award, this being often so advantageous a time for settlement? Again, the objection lies essentially in the confusion of role that results. In seeking a settlement the arbitrator turned mediator quite properly learns things that should have no bearing on his decision as an arbitrator. For example, suppose a discharge case in which the arbitrator is virtually certain that he will decide for reinstatement though he is striving to keep his mind open until he has a chance to reflect on the case in the quiet of his study. In the course of exploring the possibilities of a settlement he learns that, contrary to the position taken by the union at the hearing, respectable elements in the union would like to see the discharge upheld. Though they concede that the employee was probably innocent of the charges made by the company, they regard him as an ambitious trouble maker the union would be well rid of. If the arbitrator fails to mediate a settlement, can he block this information out when he comes to render his award?

It is important that an arbitrator not only respect the limits of his office in fact, but that he also *appear* to respect them. The parties to an arbitration expect the arbitrator to decide the dispute, not according to what pleases the parties, but by what accords with the contract. Yet as a mediator he must explore the parties' interests and seek to find out what would please them. He cannot be a good mediator unless he does. But if he has then to surrender his role as mediator to resume that of adjudicator, can his award ever be fully free from the suspicion that it was influenced by a desire to please one or both of the parties?

Finally, in practice, the settlement mediated after the hearing will seldom be free from some taint of being "rigged." Indeed, when an agreement is reached under the express or implied threat of an award, the distinction between agreement and award is lost; the "rigged award" blends into the coerced settlement, and it may at a given time be uncertain which will emerge from the discussions. During these discussions it is most unusual for all affected to know at all times just what is going on.

These, then, are the arguments against the arbitrator's undertaking the task of mediation. They can all be summed up in the phrase, "confusion of role." Why, then, should any arbitrator be tempted to depart from his proper role as adjudicator? In what follows I shall try to analyze the considerations that sometimes press him toward a departure from a purely judicial role. I shall also offer suggestions as to how these considerations can be met without that departure — by methods that keep the arbitrator within the proper limits of his role.

IV

The most obvious case where an arbitrator is tempted to mediate is where the decision dictated by the terms of the contract is plainly less advantageous to the parties than one that lies within their powers of agreement. Suppose, for example, the following situation. Certain employees called out in an emergency, occurring outside their regular shifts and on a holiday, claim triple pay for the work done. Though the arbitrator has no personal fondness for pyramided overtime, it seems clear to him that under the relevant provisions of the contract the grievants are entitled to triple pay. The company advances as one of its arguments that if triple pay is allowed, the employees may connive to make available in emergencies only those whose shift schedules are such as to qualify them for triple pay. The union offers during the hearing to work out an agreement by which any such practice would be forestalled.

In such a case the arbitrator will be strongly tempted to propose private consultations, during which he could explain to the company that if the case goes to an award, he will have to grant triple pay and that he will have no way of qualifying his award so as to avoid the abuse about which the company is concerned. I think, however, that there is no need for the arbitrator thus to step down from the bench. He may, for example, explain toward the end of the hearing that he finds it useful to request each party to state how he would write an opinion in his own favor. He then asks the company representative to give in outline form an opinion that would justify a refusal of triple pay. He may thus bring home to the company the plight he has in writing his award. He may further at this point ask the union to clarify its proposal for avoiding abuses. Thus without abandoning his role as judge of the dispute he may open the way for a voluntary settlement. . . .

It may be objected that this procedure is an hypocrisy and constitutes mediation from the bench. In a sense this is true. But the procedure suggested avoids what is always undesirable and suspicion-arousing: private consultations with the parties. The procedure in no way impairs the integrity of adjudication, for each party has his full chance to present his proofs and arguments in open court and each knows every consideration that the other is advancing for a decision in his favor.

A second situation where an arbitrator may be moved to undertake mediation is presented by a case where there is really no intelligible standard of decision. . . . One cannot join issue in an intellectual void. Unless there is some standard by which the relevance of proofs can be judged and the cogency of arguments measured, the litigant's participation in the process of decision becomes an empty form.

In actual practice I don't think the arbitrator tempted to mediate can find much justification in considerations like those just outlined. . . . In comparison with contracts generally, labor agreements are tolerably well drafted. The fact that crucial provisions are sometimes drafted at 4 a.m. by tired and angry men does not make them as different from other contracts as labor negotiators are likely to suppose. The difficult problems of interpretation are those common to contracts generally: overlooked situations, apparent or real inconsistencies, carelessness of thought and language, passages drafted by one party in his own terms and never closely examined by the other, provisions knowingly left vague or ambiguous either for later resolution through arbitration or simply through an inability to find an apt verbal solution for the problem addressed. . . . In labor contracts a high specificity of standards often impedes justiciability instead of advancing it. I think most arbitrators would rather decide discharge cases under a simple provision requiring "just cause" than under an elaborate table of detailed offenses. Such a table, because of the limitations of human foresight, usually does more harm than good. . . .

The procedural limitations that surround the adjudicative function are designed to insure as rational a decision as possible. The essential open-endedness of all human arrangements makes it impossible to guarantee that every dispute that arises *will* find waiting for it a rule conclusively dictating its decision. Every system of rules yields occasional cases that could be decided either way with equal persuasiveness. This is as true of labor arbitrations as it is of other adjudicative processes, but no more so. . . .

The problem of finding appropriate standards of decision may seem somewhat more difficult in the case of arbitrations to set the terms of a new contract—almost invariably, of course, wage terms. Here the problem is not so much a lack of standards as a multiplicity of standards—all, curiously, of a conservative nature, being directed toward the restoration of a disturbed balance of some sort. George W. Taylor has suggested a procedure by which the arbitrator may in such cases secure a firmer basis for decision. This consists in requesting the parties to include in their agreement of submission a stipulation of the criteria by which judgment should be rendered. Even in the absence of such an agreement, however, the arbitrator will generally find himself compelled to do the best he can. Arbitration being usually a last resort in such cases, the chances of agreement have usually been sufficiently explored to make mediation pointless. If there is any hope that mediation could result in a settlement, it ought to be conducted by someone other than the arbitrator.

I come now to a third kind of situation of much more fundamental importance than those I have so far discussed. An understanding of this situation is, I believe, essential not only for an understanding of labor arbitration, but of adjudication generally. The point I wish now to develop is this: There are certain kinds of problems that by their nature are unsuited to solution by the adjudicative process.

Let me return to the starting point. I have defined adjudication as a process of decision characterized by a particular form of participation accorded to the affected party, that of presenting proofs and arguments for a decision in his favor. The question then becomes, in what kinds of cases can this participation be meaningful? At this point I am no longer concerned with the availability of standards of decision. I am raising the more basic question of the kinds of problems that are amenable to solution by the adjudicative process. The question I have in mind is the counterpart of that which can be raised about elections. An election, too, is a method of decision in which the interested party is accorded a particular form of participation, in this case, that of voting. A good many questions can be decided by voting: who shall be president, whether a bond issue shall be authorized, and so forth. But there are other questions that do not lend themselves to such a decision: how troops shall be employed to meet an enemy attack, what is the cheapest way to build a bridge, and so forth. There are, in other words, intrinsic limits to the kinds of questions that can be resolved by elections. I want now to discuss whether the method of decision known as adjudication is subject to similar limits.

Let me begin with typical cases that fall neatly within the competence of the adjudicative process. One such case is that which calls for a yes-or-no decision between parties with opposed interests, no other interests being directly affected by the outcome. The claim is made that a particular employee is entitled to a week's vacation. The company argues that under a proper construction of the contract the employee is entitled to no vacation at all. The decision of such a case can be reached entirely within the limits of normal adjudicative propriety, each party advancing his proof and arguments in the presence of the other. . . .

A second kind of case that normally puts no strain on the forms of adjudication may be called the more-or-less case. In a law suit a party asks for $10,000 damages. The possible decisions run from zero to $10,000. The plaintiff of course argues for $10,000, the defendant for zero, the actual judgment may lie somewhere in between. The important thing is that all of the possible decisions may be represented within a single dimension, as points along a straight line.

In practice more-or-less questions are normally compounded with yes-or-no questions: does the defendant owe anything, and if so, how much? Thus, in a discharge case the arbitrator may be asked to decide, yes or no, whether the employee shall be reinstated. If he is reinstated, the arbitrator may then have to decide how much back pay, more or less, he is entitled to. Though this makes the issues more complex, there is nothing in the nature of the case as a whole that makes it unsuitable for decision within the adjudicative frame.

Now let me present a case in which the question is not simply yes or no, more or less, or a combination of the two. To emphasize that the problem is a general one, I shall begin with a case falling completely outside the field of labor relations.

[Deceased] left a collection of paintings valued at millions of dollars. The pictures were drawn from different periods, different nations, different schools of art. Her will devised the collection to the Metropolitan Museum and the National Gallery of Art "in equal shares." The will prescribed no apportionment and set up no procedure for accomplishing any apportionment.

Here obviously the problem of effecting a division "in equal shares" does not permit of a yes-or-no answer. Similarly the available solutions do not lie along a straight line of more-or-less, but are scattered in an irregular pattern across a checkerboard of possibilities. One can imagine an optimum solution, yielding the greatest utility to both donees, that might lie only a few moves away from the worst possible solution. If one were to seek the best solution by a series of approximations, the movement of a single picture across the line might call for a host of compensatory adjustments in the allotment of other pictures. For it should be remembered that the problem here is not merely that of giving to the two museums collections that might produce an equal dollar return if offered for sale a conjectural standard in any event — but also that of giving to each those pictures that will most effectively supplement the extensive collection it already has. . . .

What difficulty would have been encountered in attempting to effect an equal division of the paintings within the usual adjudicative frame? The difficulty lies in the fact that meaningful participation by the litigants through proof and arguments would become virtually impossible. There is no single solution, or simple set of solutions, toward which the parties meeting in open court could address themselves. If an optimum solution had to be reached through adjudicative procedures, the court would have had to set forth an almost endless series of possible divisions and direct the parties to deal with each in turn. . . .

Returning now to labor arbitration: . . . Union and management agree that the internal wage structure of the plant is out of balance—some jobs are paid too little in comparison with others, some too much. A kind of wage fund (say, equal to a general increase of five cents an hour) is set up. Out of this fund are to be allotted, in varying amounts, increases for the various jobs that will bring them into better balance. In case the parties cannot agree, the matter shall go to arbitration. . . . Since in the allotment every job is pitted against every other, any tentative agreements reached as to particular jobs will have to lapse if the parties fail in the end to reach an agreement on the reorganization of the wage structure as a whole. In short, the arbitrator will usually have to start from scratch and do the whole job himself. . . .

What modifications of his role will enable the arbitrator to discharge this task satisfactorily? The obvious expedient is a resort to mediation. After securing a general education in the problems involved in reordering the wage scale, the arbitrator might propose to each side in turn a tentative solution, inviting comments and criticisms. Through successive modifications a reasonably acceptable reordering of rates might be achieved, which would then be incorporated in an award. Here the dangers involved in the mediative role are probably at a minimum, precisely because the need for that role seems so obvious. Those dangers are not, however, absent. . . . Prolonged involvement in an attempt to work out a settlement agreeable to both parties obscures the arbitrator's function as a judge and makes it difficult to reassume that role. Furthermore, a considerable taint of the "rigged" award will in any event almost always attach to the final solution. The very fact that this solution must involve a compromise of interests within the union itself makes this virtually certain.

There is one device that may sometimes meet the demands of a problem like this while keeping the arbitrator's role within the strictest limits of judicial propriety. This lies in the tentative award. After hearing the arguments and proofs, the arbitrator issues a tentative award with an order to both parties to show cause why it shall not become final. If the arguments on the show cause order reveal mistakes, they can then be corrected. The difficulties with this solution are: (1) it will often be too simple, for in a complicated case a whole series of tentative awards with repeated corrections might be needed; (2) the release of a tentative award may arouse expectations that will resist later adjustment, however essential that adjustment may be from the standpoint of the total solution; and (3) because of the consideration just mentioned there may, again, appear some taint of the "fixed" award. The argument at the hearing on the tentative award may become indistinguishable from proposals of settlement, and the case may thus in effect be negotiated before a very restricted audience.

The use of a tripartite board of arbitration is a third way of adjusting arbitration to such problems as the reordering of a wage scale. By the tripartite form I mean, of course, the arrangement by which a neutral chairman is flanked by two "arbitrators" appointed by the interested parties. . . .

The pros and cons of tripartite arbitration are fairly familiar. Those who may be called the partisan arbitrators are cast in a difficult and subtle role that is seldom performed adequately. They cannot be wholly advocates, running back and forth to inform their constituents of every turn in the discussion among the arbitrators. They cannot be wholly judges, for their function is to represent a point of view, a posture of interests. If a majority decision is required, a proceeding that has the facade of arbitration is converted into a continuation of negotiation in an inept and distorted form, as the impartial umpire turns from side to side in an effort to induce one of the flanking arbitrators to join with him.

Here one variant form deserves mention, that is, where by the terms of the collective bargaining agreement, or by a kind of tacit agreement expressed in practice, the decision is to be rendered by the impartial umpire with his co-arbitrators serving merely as advisers and warners. This variant form relieves the impartial chairman from the necessity for bargaining, and eliminates the confusion implicit in a merging of roles. But now the objection is that the two advisers are given a deceptive title. If they are not in fact arbitrators they ought not to be given a title that calls to mind, or should call to mind, a distinctive social role which in fact they do not perform.

This suggests a rather simple solution for the kind of problem we have been considering. Why not try the case before a single arbitrator with a clear written understanding that before making his award final he must submit it . . . to two persons named in advance, each to represent the interests of one side? It should be clearly understood that the two advisers are advisers merely, and that the arbitrator is free to disregard their advice. This solution would combine the advantages of the three procedures I have passed in review. It would formalize the post-hearing conference and reduce the temptation to pretense. In comparison with the tentative award, by making it clear who should be privileged to advise the arbitrator, it would reduce the embarrassment (and with it, again, the temptation to dissimulation) in deciding who should attend the argument on the tentative award. Finally, it would eliminate the ambiguities of role implicit in tripartite arbitration. The difficulties of the solution lie in the judgment, discretion, and courage demanded of the two partisan advisers. But these are difficulties that should in any event be openly faced. If they are not present in the other solutions, it is largely because they are dodged or are concealed by various subtle and unsubtle forms of hypocrisy.

These, then, are the methods by which arbitration may be adjusted to the solution of polycentric problems. . . . A candid analysis of the problems of arbitration cannot, I believe, neglect cases of the kind I have just described. They are significant and important. Nevertheless, they constitute only a small portion of the cases going to arbitration. I want to urge that we analyze carefully the nature of the cases where ordinary adjudicative forms are demonstrably inadequate, that for these cases we adopt, in an open way, those modifications that seem to meet their special needs and to entail a minimum sacrifice of procedural due process, and that, finally, for all other cases (which constitute the great bulk of those going to arbitration) the usual restraints of the adjudicative office be preserved. . . .

In what has preceded I have tried to identify those situations in which some modification of the strict judicial role is essential if an intelligent decision is to be reached. I have not . . . been describing what happens in fact. The line that in actual practice divides arbitrational purism from its opposite follows a more haphazard pattern. Many human motives, worthy and unworthy, combine to set it.

There is one general consideration that may incline the arbitrator to resolve any doubts presented by particular cases in favor of assuming a mediative role. This lies in a conviction . . . that all labor arbitrations involve to some extent polycentric elements. The relations within a plant form a seamless web; pluck it here, and a complex pattern of adjustments may run through the whole structure. A case involving a single individual, say, a reclassification case, may set a precedent with implications unknown to the arbitrator, who cannot see how his decision may cut into a whole body of practice that is unknown to him. . . .

That there is much truth in this observation it would be foolish to deny. The integrity of the adjudicative process can never be maintained without some loss, without running some calculated risk. Any adjudicator—whether he be called judge, hearing officer, arbitrator, or umpire—who depends upon proofs and arguments adduced before him in open court, with each party confronting the other, is certain to make occasional mistakes he would not make if he could abandon the restraints of his role. The question is, how vital is that role for the maintenance of the government—in this case a system of industrial self-government—of which he is a part?

In facing that question as it arises in his practice the arbitrator ought to divest himself, insofar as human nature permits, of any motive that might be called personal. It has been said that surgeons who have perfected some highly specialized operation tend strongly to favor a diagnosis of the patient's condition that will enable them to display their special skills. Can the arbitrator be sure he is immune from a similar desire to demonstrate virtuosity in his calling? It is well-known in arbitrational circles that combining the roles of arbitrator and mediator is a tricky business. The amateur who tries it is almost certain to get in trouble. The veteran, on the other hand, takes an understandable pride in his ability to play this difficult dual role. He would be less than human if he did not seek out occasions for a display of his special talents, even to the point of discerning a need for them in situations demanding nothing more than a patient, conscientious judge, able to put a sensible meaning on the words of the contract.

In practice departures from the strict judicial role are most common in the case of the so-called permanent umpire, who may preside over disputes between the same parties for many years. In such a situation success in combining the role of arbitrator with that of mediator attests not only to the arbitrator's professional skill, but to the depth of trust imposed in him by the parties. The role of arbitrator-mediator thus becomes doubly satisfying and the temptation to assume it correspondingly greater. Furthermore, with the permanent umpire, departures from the judicial role tend to become cumulative. As the parties discover his willingness to resolve all controversies including those unsuited to decision within the restraints of a judicial role they are likely to become more and more dependent upon him. He becomes in effect a kind of super-manager. In the short run this role can relieve both union and management of many inconvenient responsibilities. The cost in the long run is that the moral force of the judicial role has been forfeited. It is no longer available as a reserve for meeting an eventual crisis. Meanwhile, the parties' capacity for unaided self-government may have suffered a serious decline through disuse.

The picture just drawn may lean a little toward the dismal. At the same time it is vitally important, I believe, that the apparent successes of mediative arbitration by permanent umpires be appraised with a full understanding of the situations in which they have occurred. Was the industry in question, for example, economically sick? Sick industries may need, not judges, but physicians, though, as with individuals, a sign of returning health would be a restored capacity to dispense with medical care. Again, did the apparent successes of mediative arbitration entail hidden costs not revealed in reports that confine themselves to the disposition of disputes? . . .

Sometimes judgment on the issues here under discussion is influenced by a kind of slogan to the effect that an agreed settlement is always better than an imposed one. As applied to disputes before they have gone to arbitration this slogan has some merit. When the case is in the hands of the arbitrator, however, I can see little merit in it, except in the special cases I have tried previously to analyze. After all, successful industrial self-government requires not only the capacity to reach and abide by agreements, but also the willingness to accept and conform to disliked awards. It is well that neither propensity be lost through disuse. Furthermore, there is something slightly morbid about the thought that an agreement coerced by the threat of decision is somehow more wholesome than an outright decision. It suggests a little the father who wants his children to obey him, but who, in order to still doubts that he may be too domineering, not only demands that they obey but insists that they do so with a smile. After having had his day in court, a man may with dignity bend his will to a judgment of which he disapproves. That dignity is lost if he is compelled to pretend that he agreed to it.

The ad hoc arbitrator, called in to decide a single case, will usually be most strongly moved to undertake mediation when it becomes apparent to him that what the parties really need is not someone to judge their dispute, but a labor relations adviser. For example, a company, inexperienced in collective bargaining and perhaps generally inept in labor relations, may be insisting on its pound of flesh — which, to be sure, it is entitled to under the contract — without being aware of the price it will pay for its victory in worsened labor relations. There is no easy way out of such a predicament for the arbitrator. In most cases he will do well to proceed with his assigned role, consoling himself with the thought that there is no better teacher than experience. He should think long and hard before employing the written opinion as an outlet for his pedagogical inclinations. Perhaps later on, after the award has been rendered, some discussion might be in order if his relationship with the party concerned seems to suggest it might be useful.

Throughout this paper I have asserted that adjudication is a social process of decision. This is true not only in the sense that it is a process of decision in which the affected party is afforded an institutionally guaranteed form of participation. It is also true in the sense that the success of adjudication, and the maintenance of its integrity, depend not only on the arbitrator, but on everyone connected with the process as a whole. It has been said that it is impossible for a judge to rise above the level of the bar practicing before him. So it may become virtually impossible for the arbitrator to perform his proper role if the parties — through ignorance, ineptness or selfish interest — are constantly pushing him out of that role. . . .

A viable system of law requires that parties be willing to settle the great bulk of disputes out of court. It requires not only a willingness to settle cases that are reasonably certain to be decided against the conceding party, but also to settle at least some cases he could be quite certain of winning if they were taken to litigation. The decision of a dispute by law is not always the same thing as a wise disposition of it. People who are always demanding their "rights" can be a menace to any society. One of the responsibilities of the parties to a collective bargaining agreement is to ease the strains on arbitration by not litigating cases where there is an obvious tension between the result demanded by the terms of the contract and that which accords with practical wisdom in labor relations.

I have just been asserting that a large part of the responsibility for maintaining the integrity of arbitration rests with the parties. I do not wish to be understood as suggesting, however, that the arbitrator is entitled to thrust on the parties the whole responsibility for his role. I emphatically reject the contention . . . that in appraising such practices as meeting with the parties separately the dangers envisaged with respect to judges and other governmental personnel are not equally applicable to the arbitrator, for, the parties' control of the process and their individual power to continue or terminate the services of the arbitrator are adequate safeguards against these dangers. . . . The democratic principle does not require us . . . to indulge in the fiction that whatever institutions develop in a particular situation must be viewed as approved by those affected by them.

Industrial self-government in this country may be said to rest on four distinct procedures: (1) those by which the bargaining unit is defined, (2) those by which bargaining representatives are chosen and their authority delimited, (3) those of negotiation by which the terms of the collective agreement are set, and (4) those of arbitration. These four procedures stand in a relation of interdependence. A failure of function in one of them will inevitably affect the others.

Successful arbitration obviously depends upon successful collective bargaining. It is from the collective bargaining agreement that arbitration derives its standards. If those standards are clearly and properly set, they will shape the award toward the needs of industrial self-government as seen by those most directly in contact with its problems. . . . Carelessly drawn agreements invite, may indeed demand, a departure by the arbitrator from his proper role. In this case the damage done becomes cumulative, since arbitration is almost certain to become overloaded if there are no standards to govern the settlement of grievances short of arbitration.

Conversely, the institution of collective bargaining can be undermined if the arbitrator casts off all restraints, assumes a variety of discordant roles, and presides generally over a process of decision from which may emerge, almost indifferently, a half-coerced agreement or a half-agreed award. In any such procedural chaos the guideline of the agreement is inevitably forfeited. When the agreement ceases to play a significant role in arbitration, the incentive to draft it carefully and fairly is lost.

The institution of voluntary arbitration, soundly administered, is an essential of industrial self-government. The danger of an extension of judicial control over arbitration lies, not only in the delays, costs and formalities it would entail, but in the kinds of interpretation it would produce. The whole purpose of a collective bargaining agreement can be frustrated by unresponsive interpretations. A collective bargaining agreement may be viewed as a series of answers to a series of problems. The answers cannot be understood without understanding the problems. If an adjudicator (whether he be judge or arbitrator) attempts to read answers out of the agreement without understanding the problems to which those answers are addressed, all the processes of industrial self-government are upset and thrown out of balance.

The mediating form-free arbitrator and his opposite number, the stiffly literal judge, are equally threats to effective collective bargaining. The first may dissipate the benefits of careful negotiation and draftsmanship by disregarding the contract in the resolution of disputes. The second may dissipate those benefits by projecting into the agreement incongruent meanings, foreign to the thinking of those who created it.

Successful collective bargaining is also dependent on the application of proper principles of representation on both sides of the table. The most common curse on the side of the employer lies in absentee management. Head office policy often requires certain stands by the negotiators of an agreement that violate the needs of the immediate situation. Reaching agreement on a decent framework for the parties' future relations becomes difficult under these conditions. The result is often a contract full of incongruities, with the head of a giraffe and the body of an elephant. Needless to say, such contracts impose serious strains on the process of arbitration.

Being essentially political organizations, unions are less subject to the evils of absentee management, though certainly not immune from them. More commonly in the case of unions the inner tensions that reflect themselves into the processes of bargaining and arbitrating are those that arise from the deficiencies of the majority principle as a means of resolving conflicting interests within the bargaining unit. I have already observed that unions often resort to arbitration as a method of resolving these internal difficulties. The same difficulties often produce imperfect and ambiguous contracts.

It is important to recall that both the majority principle and adjudication represent processes of decision that are subject to inherent limitations in the kinds of problems they can resolve. One problem that majority vote cannot easily solve is that of effecting an optimum rearrangement of relations within the voting group itself. In practice such reorderings usually come about through some process of internal bargaining. This is not necessarily an unwholesome thing. If fifty-one percent of an electorate slightly prefer one situation, while forty-nine percent very strongly prefer another, a "deal" may make everyone better off. . . .

The purpose of these rather scattered observations is to drive home the point that the procedures of industrial self-government whether they be formal or informal, stand in a relation of interdependence. They are all parts, one of another. The right functioning of the system as a whole depends upon the right functioning of each of its components.

Taking the system as a whole, and viewing it across considerable periods of time, I should say that it works remarkably well. Indeed I believe that our system of industrial self-government is one of the finest expressions of the American genius for political arrangements. Writing more than a century ago John Stuart Mill declared:

> What the French are in military affairs, the Americans are in every kind of civil business; let them be left without a government, every body of Americans is able to improvise one, and to carry on that or any other public business with a sufficient amount of intelligence, order and decision. This is what every free people ought to be.

If the first branch of Mill's comparison has become somewhat dated, I hope this is not equally true of the second, and that Americans do still in fact retain some of the capacity in the design of social architecture they displayed so prominently during an earlier and more creative period. The success of our system of industrial self-government encourages me to think they do. . . .

3. Arbitration of Employment Discrimination Claims

a. *Alexander v. Gardner-Denver Co.*, 415 U.S. 36 (1974)

Mr. Justice POWELL delivered the opinion of the Court.

This case concerns the proper relationship between federal courts and the grievance-arbitration machinery of collective-bargaining agreements in the resolution and enforcement of an individual's rights to equal employment opportunities under Title VII of the Civil Rights Act of 1964. Specifically, we must decide under what circumstances, if any, an employee's statutory right to a trial de novo under Title VII may be foreclosed by prior submission of his claim to final arbitration under the nondiscrimination clause of a collective-bargining agreement.

I

In May 1966, petitioner Harrell Alexander, Sr., a black, was hired by respondent Gardner-Denver Co. (the company) to perform maintenance work at the company's plant in Denver, Colorado. In June 1968, petitioner was awarded a trainee position as a drill operator. He remained at that job until his discharge from employment on September 29, 1969. The company informed petitioner that he was being discharged for producing too many defective or unusable parts that had to be scrapped.

On October 1, 1969, petitioner filed a grievance under the collective-bargaining agreement in force between the company and petitioner's union, Local No. 3029 of the United Steelworkers of America (the union). The grievance stated: "I feel I have been unjustly discharged and ask that I be reinstated with full seniority and pay." No explicit claim of racial discrimination was made.

Under Art. 4 of the collective-bargaining agreement, the company retained the right to hire, suspend or discharge (employees) for proper cause. Article 5, § 2, provided, however, that there shall be no discrimination against any employee on account of race, color, religion, sex, national origin, or ancestry, and Art. 23, § 6(a), stated that no employee will be discharged, suspended or given a written warning notice except for just cause. The agreement also contained a broad arbitration clause covering "differences aris(ing) between the Company and the Union as to the meaning and application of the provisions of this Agreement" and "any trouble aris(ing) in the plant."[3] Disputes were to be submitted to a multistep grievance procedure, the first four steps of which involved negotiations between the company and the union. If the dispute remained unresolved, it was to be remitted to compulsory arbitration. The company and the union were to select and pay the arbitrator, and his decision was to be "final and binding upon the Company, the Union, and any employee or employees involved." The agreement further provided that "(t)he arbitrator shall not amend, take away, add to, or change any of the provisions of this Agreement, and the arbitrator's decision must be based solely upon an interpretation of the provisions of this Agreement." The parties also agreed that there "shall be no suspension of work" over disputes covered by the grievance arbitration clause. [These terms, and the multi-step grievance procedure, are still in common use today.]

The union processed petitioner's grievance through [this] machinery. In the final pre-arbitration step, petitioner raised, apparently for the first time, the claim that his discharge resulted from racial discrimination. The company rejected all of petitioner's claims, and the grievance proceeded to arbitration. Prior to the arbitration hearing, however, petitioner filed a charge of racial discrimination with the Colorado Civil Rights Commission, which referred the complaint to the Equal Employment Opportunity Commission on November 5, 1969.

At the arbitration hearing on November 20, 1969, petitioner testified that his discharge was the result of racial discrimination and informed the arbitrator that he had filed a charge with

[3]. . .Grievances shall be taken up in the following manner. . . Step 1. An attempt shall first be made by the employee with or without his assistant grievance committeeman (at the employee's option), and the employee's foreman to settle the grievance. The foreman shall submit his answer within one (1) working day and if the grievance is not settled, it shall be reduced to writing, signed by the employee ans his assistant grievance committeeman, and the foreman shall submit his signed answer of such grievance. Step 2. If the grievance is not settled in Step 1, it shall be presented to the Superintendent, or his representative, within two (2) working days after the Union has received the Foreman's answer in Step 1. The Superintendent or his representative shall submit his signed answer two (2) working days after receiving the grievance. Step 3. If the grievance is not settled in Step 2, it shall be presented to the manager of Manufacturing oı his representative within five (5) working days after the Union has received the Superintendent's answer in Step 2. The Manager of Manufacturing or his representative shall meet with the representatives of the Union to attempt to resolve the grievance within five (5) working days following the presentation of the grievance. The Manager of Manufacturing or his representative shall submit his signed answer within three (3) working days after the date of such meeting. Step 4. If the grievance is not settled in Step 3, it shall be referred to the Personnel Manager, and/or his representatives, and the International representative and chairman of the grievance committee within five (5) working days after the Union has received the Step 3 answer. Within ten (10) working days after the grievance has been referred to Step 4, the above-mentioned parties shall meet for the purpose of discussing such grievance. Within five (5) working days following the meeting, the Company representatives shall submit their signed answer to the Union. The Union representatives shall signify their concurrence or nonconcurrence and affix their signatures to the grievance. Step 5. Grievances which have not been settled under the foregoing procedure may be referred to arbitration by notice in writing within ten (10) calendar days after the date of the Company's final answer in Step 4.

the Colorado Commission because he "could not rely on the union." . . . [T]he arbitrator ruled that petitioner had been "discharged for just cause." He made no reference to petitioner's claim of racial discrimination. The arbitrator stated that the union had failed to produce evidence of a practice of transferring rather than discharging trainee drill operators who accumulated excessive scrap, but he suggested that the company and the union confer on whether such an arrangement was feasible in the present case.

On July 25, 1970, the EEOC determined that there was not reasonable cause to believe that a violation of Title VII of the Civil Rights Act of 1964 had occurred. The Commission later notified petitioner of his right to institute a civil action in federal court within 30 days. Petitioner then filed the present action . . . alleging that his discharge resulted from a racially discriminatory employment practice in violation of the Act.

The District Court granted respondent's motion for summary judgment and dismissed the action. The court found that the claim of racial discrimination had been submitted to the arbitrator and resolved adversely to petitioner. It then held that petitioner, having voluntarily elected to pursue his grievance to final arbitration under the nondiscrimination clause of the collective-bargaining agreement, was bound by the arbitral decision and thereby precluded from suing his employer under Title VII. The Court of Appeals for the Tenth Circuit affirmed. . . . We reverse.

II

Congress enacted Title VII of the Civil Rights Act of 1964 to assure equality of employment opportunities by eliminating those practices and devices that discriminate on the basis of race, color, religion, sex, or national origin. Cooperation and voluntary compliance were selected as the preferred means for achieving this goal. To this end, Congress created the Equal Employment Opportunity Commission and established a procedure whereby existing state and local equal employment opportunity agencies, as well as the Commission, would have an opportunity to settle disputes through conference, conciliation, and persuasion before the aggrieved party was permitted to file a lawsuit. In the Equal Employment Opportunity Act of 1972 Congress amended Title VII to provide the Commission with further authority to investigate individual charges of discrimination, to promote voluntary compliance with the requirements of Title VII, and to institute civil actions against employers or unions named in a discrimination charge.

Even in its amended form, however, Title VII does not provide the Commission with direct powers of enforcement. The Commission cannot adjudicate claims or impose administrative sanctions. Rather, final responsibility for enforcement of Title VII is vested with federal courts. The Act authorizes courts to issue injunctive relief and to order such affirmative action as may be appropriate to remedy the effects of unlawful employment practices. Courts retain these broad remedial powers despite a Commission finding of no reasonable cause to believe that the Act has been violated. Taken together, these provisions make plain that federal courts have been assigned plenary powers to secure compliance with Title VII. . . .

III

Title VII does not speak expressly to the relationship between federal courts and the grievance-arbitration machinery of collective-bargaining agreements. . . . There is no suggestion in the statutory scheme that a prior arbitral decision either forecloses an individual's right to sue or divests federal courts of jurisdiction. . . . Moreover, the legislative history of Title VII manifests a congressional intent to allow an individual to pursue independently his rights under both Title VII and other applicable state and federal statutes. . . . In sum, Title VII's purpose and procedures strongly suggest that an individual does not forfeit his private cause of action if he first pursues his grievance to final arbitration under the nondiscrimination clause of a collective-bargaining agreement.

In reaching the opposite conclusion, the District Court relied in part on the doctrine of election of remedies. That doctrine, which refers to situations where an individual pursues remedies that are legally or factually inconsistent, has no application in the present context. In submitting his grievance to arbitration, an employee seeks to vindicate his contractual right under a collective-bargaining agreement. By contrast, in filing a lawsuit under Title VII, an employee asserts independent statutory rights accorded by Congress. The distinctly separate nature of these contractual and statutory rights is not vitiated merely because both were violated as a result of the same factual occurrence. And certainly no inconsistency results from permitting both rights to be enforced in their respectively appropriate forums. . . .

We are also unable to accept the proposition that petitioner waived his cause of action under Title VII. To begin, we think it clear that there can be no prospective waiver of an employee's rights under Title VII. It is true, of course, that a union may waive certain statutory rights related to collective activity, such as the right to strike. These rights are conferred on employees collectively to foster the processes of bargaining and properly may be exercised or relinquished by the union as collective-bargaining agent to obtain economic benefits for union members. Title VII, on the other hand, stands on plainly different ground; it concerns not majoritarian processes, but an individual's right to equal employment opportunities. Title VII's strictures are absolute and represent a congressional command that each employee be free from discriminatory practices. Of necessity, the rights conferred can form no part of the collective-bargaining process since waiver of these rights would defeat the paramount congressional purpose behind Title VII. In these circumstances, an employee's rights under Title VII are not susceptible of prospective waiver.

The actual submission of petitioner's grievance to arbitration in the present case does not alter the situation. Although presumably an employee may waive his cause of action under Title VII as part of a voluntary settlement, mere resort to the arbitral forum to enforce contractual rights constitutes no such waiver. . . .

IV

The District Court and the Court of Appeals reasoned that to permit an employee to have his claim considered in both the arbitral and judicial forums would be unfair since this would mean that the employer, but not the employee, was bound by the arbitral award. . . . But in instituting an action under Title VII, the employee is not seeking review of the arbitrator's decision. Rather, he is asserting a statutory right independent of the arbitration process. . . .

V

. . . Arbitral procedures [are] . . . a comparatively inappropriate forum for the final resolution of rights created by Title VII. This conclusion rests first on the special role of the arbitrator, whose task is to effectuate the intent of the parties rather than the requirements of enacted legislation. Where the collective-bargaining agreement conflicts with Title VII, the arbitrator must follow the agreement. To be sure, the tension between contractual and statutory objectives may be mitigated where a collective-bargaining agreement contains provisions facially similar to those of Title VII. But other facts may still render arbitral processes comparatively inferior to judicial processes in the protection of Title VII rights. Among these is the fact that the specialized competence of arbitrators pertains primarily to the law of the shop, not the law of the land.[18] Parties usually choose an arbitrator because they trust his knowledge and judgment concerning the demands and norms of industrial relations. On the other hand, the resolution of statutory or constitutional issues is a primary responsibility of courts, and judicial construction has proved especially necessary with respect to Title VII, whose broad language frequently can be given meaning only by reference to public law concepts.

Moreover, the fact-finding process in arbitration usually is not equivalent to judicial fact-finding. The record of the arbitration proceedings is not as complete; the usual rules of evidence do not apply; and rights and procedures common to civil trials, such as discovery, compulsory process, cross-examination, and testimony under oath, are often severely limited or unavailable. And as this Court has recognized, arbitrators have no obligation to the court to give their reasons for an award. Indeed, it is the informality of arbitral procedure that enables it to function as an efficient, inexpensive, and expeditious means for dispute resolution. This same characteristic, however, makes arbitration a less appropriate forum for final resolution of Title VII issues than the federal courts. . . .

We think, therefore, that the federal policy favoring arbitration of labor disputes and the federal policy against discriminatory employment practices can best be accommodated by permitting an employee to pursue fully both his remedy under the grievance-arbitration clause of a collective-bargaining agreement and his cause of action under Title VII. The federal court should consider the employee's claim de novo. The arbitral decision may be admitted as evidence and accorded such weight as the court deems appropriate. Reversed.

b. *Gilmer v. Interstate/Johnson Lane Corp.*, 500 U.S. 20 (1991)

Justice WHITE delivered the opinion of the Court.

The question presented in this case is whether a claim under the Age Discrimination in Employment Act of 1967 (ADEA) can be subjected to compulsory arbitration pursuant to an arbitration agreement in a securities registration application. The Court of Appeals held that it could, and we affirm.

I

Respondent Interstate/Johnson Lane Corporation (Interstate) hired petitioner Robert Gilmer as a Manager of Financial Services in May 1981. As required by his employment, Gilmer registered as a securities representative with several stock exchanges, including the New York Stock Exchange (NYSE). His registration application, entitled "Uniform Application for Securities Industry Registration or Transfer," provided, among other things, that Gilmer "agree[d] to arbitrate any dispute, claim or controversy" arising between him and Interstate "that is required to be arbitrated under the rules, constitutions or by-laws of the organizations with which I register." NYSE Rule 347 provides for arbitration of "[a]ny controversy between a registered representative and any member or member organization arising

[18]Significantly, a substantial proportion of labor arbitrators are not lawyers. This is not to suggest, of course, that arbitrators do not possess a high degree of competence with respect to the vital role in implementing the federal policy favoring arbitration of labor disputes.

out of the employment or termination of employment of such registered representative."

Interstate terminated Gilmer's employment in 1987, at which time Gilmer was 62 years of age. After first filing an age discrimination charge with the Equal Employment Opportunity Commission (EEOC), Gilmer subsequently brought suit . . . alleging that Interstate had discharged him because of his age, in violation of the ADEA. In response to Gilmer's complaint, Interstate filed . . . a motion to compel arbitration of the ADEA claim. In its motion, Interstate relied upon the arbitration agreement in Gilmer's registration application, as well as the Federal Arbitration Act (FAA). The District Court denied Interstate's motion, based on this Court's decision in Alexander v. Gardner-Denver Co., 415 U.S. 36 (1974), and because it concluded that "Congress intended to protect ADEA claimants from the waiver of a judicial forum." The United States Court of Appeals for the Fourth Circuit reversed, finding "nothing in the text, legislative history, or underlying purposes of the ADEA indicating a congressional intent to preclude enforcement of arbitration agreements."

II

The FAA . . . states that "[a] written provision in any maritime transaction or a contract evidencing a transaction involving commerce to settle by arbitration a controversy thereafter arising out of such contract or transaction . . . shall be valid, irrevocable, and enforceable, save upon such grounds as exist at law or in equity for the revocation of any contract." 9 U.S.C. § 2. The FAA also provides for stays of proceedings in federal district courts when an issue in the proceeding is referable to arbitration, § 3, and for orders compelling arbitration when one party has failed, neglected, or refused to comply with an arbitration agreement, § 4.[2]

It is by now clear that statutory claims may be the subject of an arbitration agreement, enforceable pursuant to the FAA. Indeed, in recent years we have held enforceable arbitration agreements relating to claims arising under the Sherman Act; § 10(b) of the Securities Exchange Act of 1934; the civil provisions of the Racketeer Influenced and Corrupt Organizations Act (RICO); and § 12(2) of the Securities Act of 1933. In these cases we recognized that "[b]y agreeing to arbitrate a statutory claim, a party does not forgo the substantive rights afforded by the statute; it only submits to their resolution in an arbitral, rather than a judicial, forum."

Although all statutory claims may not be appropriate for arbitration, "[h]aving made the

[2]Section 1 of the FAA provides that "nothing herein contained shall apply to contracts of employment of seamen, railroad employees, or any other class of workers engaged in foreign or interstate commerce." 9 U.S.C. § 1. Several amici curiae in support of Gilmer argue that that section excludes from the coverage of the FAA all "contracts of employment." Gilmer, however, did not raise the issue in the courts below; it was not addressed there; and it was not among the questions presented in the petition for certiorari. In any event, it would be inappropriate to address the scope of the § 1 exclusion because the arbitration clause being enforced here is not contained in a contract of employment. The FAA requires that the arbitration clause being enforced be in writing. See 9 U.S.C. §§ 2, 3. The record before us does not show, and the parties do not contend, that Gilmer's employment agreement with Interstate contained a written arbitration clause. Rather, the arbitration clause at issue is in Gilmer's securities registration application, which is a contract with the securities exchanges, not with Interstate. The lower courts addressing the issue uniformly have concluded that the exclusionary clause in § 1 of the FAA is inapplicable to arbitration clauses contained in such registration applications. We implicitly assumed as much in Perry v. Thomas, where we held that the FAA required a former employee of a securities firm to arbitrate his statutory wage claim against his former employer, pursuant to an arbitration clause in his registration application. . . . Consequently, we leave for another day the issue raised by amici curiae.

bargain to arbitrate, the party should be held to it unless Congress itself has evinced an intention to preclude a waiver of judicial remedies for the statutory rights at issue." In this regard, we note that the burden is on Gilmer to show that Congress intended to preclude a waiver of a judicial forum for ADEA claims. . . .

III

Gilmer concedes that nothing in the text of the ADEA or its legislative history explicitly precludes arbitration. He argues, however, that compulsory arbitration of ADEA claims pursuant to arbitration agreements would be inconsistent with the statutory framework and purposes of the ADEA. Like the Court of Appeals, we disagree.

[T]he ADEA, among other things, makes it unlawful for an employer "to fail or refuse to hire or to discharge any individual or otherwise discriminate against any individual with respect to his compensation, terms, conditions, or privileges of employment, because of such individual's age." This proscription is enforced both by private suits and by the EEOC. In order for an aggrieved individual to bring suit under the ADEA, he or she must first file a charge with the EEOC and then wait at least 60 days. An individual's right to sue is extinguished, however, if the EEOC institutes an action against the employer. Before the EEOC can bring such an action, though, it must "attempt to eliminate the discriminatory practice or practices alleged, and to effect voluntary compliance with the requirements of this chapter through informal methods of conciliation, conference, and persuasion."

As Gilmer contends, the ADEA is designed not only to address individual grievances, but also to further important social policies. We do not perceive any inherent inconsistency between those policies, however, and enforcing agreements to arbitrate age discrimination claims. It is true that arbitration focuses on specific disputes between the parties involved. The same can be said, however, of judicial resolution of claims. Both of these dispute resolution mechanisms nevertheless also can further broader social purposes. The Sherman Act, the Securities Exchange Act of 1934, RICO, and the Securities Act of 1933 all are designed to advance important public policies, but, as noted above, claims under those statutes are appropriate for arbitration. "[S]o long as the prospective litigant effectively may vindicate [his or her] statutory cause of action in the arbitral forum, the statute will continue to serve both its remedial and deterrent function."

We also are unpersuaded by the argument that arbitration will undermine the role of the EEOC in enforcing the ADEA. An individual ADEA claimant subject to an arbitration agreement will still be free to file a charge with the EEOC, even though the claimant is not able to institute a private judicial action. Indeed, Gilmer filed a charge with the EEOC in this case. In any event, the EEOC's role in combating age discrimination is not dependent on the filing of a charge; the agency may receive information concerning alleged violations of the ADEA "from any source," and it has independent authority to investigate age discrimination. Moreover, nothing in the ADEA indicates that Congress intended that the EEOC be involved in all employment disputes. Such disputes can be settled . . . without any EEOC involvement. Finally, the mere involvement of an administrative agency in the enforcement of a statute is not sufficient to preclude arbitration. For example, the Securities Exchange Commission is heavily involved in the enforcement of the Securities Exchange Act of 1934 and the Securities Act of 1933, but we have held that claims under both of those statutes may be subject to compulsory arbitration.

In arguing that arbitration is inconsistent with the ADEA, Gilmer also raises a host of challenges to the adequacy of arbitration procedures. [W]e have already rejected most of these arguments as insufficient to preclude arbitration of statutory claims. Such generalized attacks on arbitration "res[t] on suspicion of arbitration as a method of weakening the protections afforded in the substantive law to would-be complainants," and as such, they are "far out of step with our current strong endorsement of the federal statutes favoring this method of resolving disputes." Consequently, we address these arguments only briefly.

Gilmer first speculates that arbitration panels will be biased. However, "[w]e decline to indulge the presumption that the parties and arbitral body conducting a proceeding will be unable or unwilling to retain competent, conscientious and impartial arbitrators." In any event, we note that the NYSE arbitration rules, which are applicable to the dispute in this case, provide protections against biased panels. The rules require, for example, that the parties be informed of the employment histories of the arbitrators, and that they be allowed to make further inquiries into the arbitrators' backgrounds. In addition, each party is allowed one peremptory challenge and unlimited challenges for cause. Moreover, the arbitrators are required to disclose "any circumstances which might preclude [them] from rendering an objective and impartial determination." The FAA also protects against bias, by providing that courts may overturn arbitration decisions "[w]here there was evident partiality or corruption in the arbitrators." 9 USC § 10(b). There has been no showing in this case that those provisions are inadequate to guard against potential bias.

Gilmer also complains that the discovery allowed in arbitration is more limited than in the federal courts, which he contends will make it difficult to prove discrimination. It is unlikely, however, that age discrimination claims require more extensive discovery than other claims that we have found to be arbitrable, such as RICO and antitrust claims. Moreover, there has been no showing in this case that the NYSE discovery provisions, which allow for document production, information requests, depositions, and subpoenas will prove insufficient to allow ADEA claimants such as Gilmer a fair opportunity to present their claims. Although those procedures might not be as extensive as in the federal courts, by agreeing to arbitrate, a party "trades the procedures and opportunity for review of the courtroom for the simplicity, informality, and expedition of arbitration." Indeed, an important counterweight to the reduced discovery in NYSE arbitration is that arbitrators are not bound by the rules of evidence.

A further alleged deficiency of arbitration is that arbitrators often will not issue written opinions, resulting, Gilmer contends, in a lack of public knowledge of employers' discriminatory policies, an inability to obtain effective appellate review, and a stifling of the development of the law. The NYSE rules, however, do require that all arbitration awards be in writing, and that the awards contain the names of the parties, a summary of the issues in controversy, and a description of the award issued. In addition, the award decisions are made available to the public. Furthermore, judicial decisions addressing ADEA claims will continue to be issued because it is unlikely that all or even most ADEA claimants will be subject to arbitration agreements. Finally, Gilmer's concerns apply equally to settlements of ADEA claims, which, as noted above, are clearly allowed. . . .

It is also argued that arbitration procedures cannot adequately further the purposes of the ADEA because they do not provide for broad equitable relief and class actions. (H)owever, arbitrators do have the power to fashion equitable relief. Indeed, the NYSE rules applicable here do not restrict the types of relief an arbitrator may award, but merely refer to "damages and/or other relief." The NYSE rules also provide for collective proceedings. Rule 612(d). But "even if the arbitration could not go forward as a class action or class relief could not be granted by the arbitrator, the fact that the [ADEA] provides for the possibility of bringing a collective action does not mean that individual attempts at conciliation were intended to be barred." Finally, it should be remembered that arbitration agreements will not preclude the EEOC from bringing actions seeking class-wide and equitable relief.

An additional reason advanced by Gilmer for refusing to enforce arbitration agreements relating to ADEA claims is his contention that there often will be unequal bargaining power between employers and employees. Mere inequality in bargaining power, however, is not a sufficient reason to hold that arbitration agreements are never enforceable in the employment context. Relationships between securities dealers and investors, for example, may involve unequal bargaining power, but we nevertheless held in *Rodriguez de Quijas* and *McMahon* that agreements to arbitrate in that context are enforceable. [T]he FAA's purpose was to place arbitration agreements on the same footing as other contracts. Thus, arbitration agreements are enforceable "save upon such grounds as exist at law or in equity for the revocation of any contract." 9 U.S.C. § 2. . . . There is no indication in this case, however, that Gilmer, an experienced businessman, was coerced or defrauded into agreeing to the arbitration clause in his registration application.

IV

In addition to the arguments discussed above, Gilmer vigorously asserts that our decision in *Alexander v. Gardner-Denver Co.* and its progeny preclude arbitration of employment discrimination claims. Gilmer's reliance on these cases, however, is misplaced.

In *Gardner-Denver*, the issue was whether a discharged employee whose grievance had been arbitrated pursuant to an arbitration clause in a collective-bargaining agreement was precluded from subsequently bringing a Title VII action based upon the conduct that was the subject of the grievance. In holding that the employee was not foreclosed from bringing the Title VII claim, we stressed that an employee's contractual rights under a collective bargaining agreement are distinct from the employee's statutory Title VII rights.[5]

There are several important distinctions between the *Gardner-Denver* line of cases and the case before us. First, those cases did not involve the issue of the enforceability of an agreement to arbitrate statutory claims. Rather, they involved the quite different issue whether arbitration of contract-based claims precluded subsequent judicial resolution of statutory claims. Since the employees there had not agreed to arbitrate their statutory claims, and the labor arbitrators were not authorized to resolve such claims, the arbitration in those cases understandably was held not to preclude subsequent statutory actions. Second, because the arbitration in those cases occurred in the context of a collective-bargaining agreement, the claimants there were represented by their unions in the arbitration proceedings. An important concern therefore was the tension between collective representation and individual statutory rights, a concern not applicable to the present case. Finally, those cases were not decided under the

[5]The Court in Alexander v. Gardner-Denver Co. also expressed the view that arbitration was inferior to the judicial process for resolving statutory claims. That "mistrust of the arbitral process," however, has been undermined by our recent arbitration decisions. "[W]e are well past the time when judicial suspicion of the desirability of arbitration and of the competence of arbitral tribunals inhibited the development of arbitration as an alternative means of dispute resolution." Mitsubishi Motors Corp. v. Soler Chrysler-Plymouth, Inc., 473 U.S. 614, 626-627 (1985).

FAA. . . . Therefore, those cases provide no basis for refusing to enforce Gilmer's agreement to arbitrate his ADEA claim.

V

We conclude that Gilmer has not met his burden of showing that Congress, in enacting the ADEA, intended to preclude arbitration of claims under that Act.

Justice STEVENS, with whom Justice MARSHALL joins, dissenting.

Section 1 of the Federal Arbitration Act (FAA) states: "[N]othing herein contained shall apply to contracts of employment of seamen, railroad employees, or any other class of workers engaged in foreign or interstate commerce." 9 U.S.C. § 1. The Court today, in holding that the FAA compels enforcement of arbitration clauses even when claims of age discrimination are at issue, skirts the antecedent question whether the coverage of the Act even extends to arbitration clauses contained in employment contracts, regardless of the subject matter of the claim at issue. In my opinion, arbitration clauses contained in employment agreements are specifically exempt from coverage of the FAA, and for that reason respondent Interstate/Johnson Lane Corporation cannot, pursuant to the FAA, compel petitioner to submit his claims arising under the Age Discrimination in Employment Act of 1967 (ADEA) to binding arbitration.

Petitioner did not, as the majority correctly notes, raise the issue of the applicability of the FAA to employment contracts at any stage of the proceedings below. Nor did petitioner raise the coverage issue in his petition for writ of certiorari before this Court. It was amici who first raised the argument in their briefs in support of petitioner prior to oral argument of the case. Notwithstanding the apparent waiver of the issue below, I believe that the Court should reach the issue of the coverage of the FAA to employment disputes because resolution of the question is so clearly antecedent to disposition of this case. . . .

The Court, declining to reach the issue for the reason that petitioner never raised it below, nevertheless concludes that "it would be inappropriate to address the scope of the § 1 exclusion because the arbitration clause being enforced here is not contained in a contract of employment. . . . Rather, the arbitration clause at issue is in Gilmer's securities registration application, which is a contract with the securities exchanges, not with Interstate." In my opinion the Court too narrowly construes the scope of the exclusion contained in § 1 of the FAA. . . .

Given that the FAA specifically was intended to exclude arbitration agreements between employees and employers, I see no reason to limit this exclusion from coverage to arbitration clauses contained in agreements entitled "Contract of Employment." In this case, the parties conceded at oral argument that Gilmer had no "contract of employment" as such with respondent. Gilmer was, however, required as a condition of his employment to become a registered representative of several stock exchanges, including the New York Stock Exchange (NYSE). Just because his agreement to arbitrate any "dispute, claim or controversy" with his employer that arose out of the employment relationship was contained in his application for registration before the NYSE rather than in a specific contract of employment with his employer, I do not think that Gilmer can be compelled pursuant to the FAA to arbitrate his employment-related dispute. Rather, in my opinion the exclusion in § 1 should be interpreted to cover any agreements by the employee to arbitrate disputes with the employer arising out of the employment relationship, particularly where such agreements to arbitrate are conditions of employment. . . .

Not only would I find that the FAA does not apply to employment-related disputes between employers and employees in general, but also I would hold that compulsory arbitration conflicts with the congressional purpose animating the ADEA, in particular. . . .

c. Comments and Questions

1. Are *Gardner-Denver* and *Gilmer* consistent decisions? How might you distinguish the two cases? Having done so, are you persuaded? If so, what are the key differences between the two cases?

2. Even if the results in *Gardner-Denver* and *Gilmer* can be reconciled, can the approaches taken by the Court in these two cases be reconciled? Compare the attitude toward mandatory arbitration of the Supreme Court in 1974 and 1991.

3. Is *Gardner-Denver* still good law today? What will happen the next time a similar EEO case is decided by the Supreme Court? Does the answer depend in part on how the composition of the Court has changed since 1991?

4. The next two articles provide an indication of the impact of *Gilmer* on federal and state courts.

d. Christine Godsil Cooper, *Where Are We Going With* Gilmer? — *Some Ruminations on the Arbitration of Discrimination Claims*, 11 St. Louis U. Pub. L. Rev. 203, 237-40 (1992)*

The cast of opposing characters filing amici briefs in the *Gilmer* case consisted of the regular suspects. Those favoring arbitration were management interests (the Chamber of Commerce, the Equal Employment Advisory Council, and the Securities Industry Association). Those opposing arbitration were employee interests (the American Association of Retired Persons, the Lawyers Committee for Civil Rights Under Law, and the AFL-CIO). Why the assumption that arbitration is good for management and bad for employees?

Most advocates, though certainly not all, assume that arbitration saves employers time because it is quicker than litigation, in part because of its severe limitations on discovery, and because of the shorter limitations periods often contained in arbitration systems. This time savings, if real, obviously translates into cost savings to employers.

In 1990, the average civil rights employment case was disposed of by a federal district court in twelve months from the date of federal court filing. The average arbitration handled by the NYSE was disposed of within ten . . . months. Thus far, the time frames for both litigation and arbitration are similar. However, the one year period for litigation does not account for the time the case spent at the EEOC before the court filing. Both Title VII and ADEA claimants must file a charge of discrimination with the EEOC before proceeding in court. Title VII claimants must await a right to sue letter, and ADEA claimants cannot file court cases until sixty days after filing a charge with the EEOC.

As of January, 1991, the average age of an open charge at the EEOC was two hundred sixty days. Thus, the twelve month figure for litigation must be increased by the average two hundred sixty days spent at the EEOC, making the litigation average about twenty-one months. Now the time advantage of arbitration is clearer. But the comparisons are rough, and it must

---

*Reprinted with permission.

be remembered that the comparison is only with the NYSE data. Commercial arbitration systems, like labor arbitration systems, can contain whatever configuration of dates and procedures the drafters desire. Consideration of limitations periods under statute and through arbitration complicates the comparison.

Even if arbitration saves a lot of time—and it could—that time is also saved by both sides. Thus the time factor alone cannot be why management wants arbitration but employees do not. Management must believe that it will do better in arbitration than before a judge or jury. Is this belief correct?

In a study completed shortly after *Gardner-Denver*, Professors Hoyman and Stallworth concluded that judges and arbitrators usually decide cases the same way. More specifically, they found that "a very small fraction of all discrimination arbitration findings are subsequently reversed." The chance that an arbitration award would be reversed in court was one in a hundred. A number of empirical studies have concluded that arbitration awards in discrimination disputes look like judicial decisions in discrimination disputes. The fear that juries will award unreasonable amounts based on visceral reactions is one frequently voiced by management. While this belief is difficult to test, it is very real. Management is well protected by law, by jury instructions, and by juror attitudes that are more conservative than commonly believed. The average employment discrimination claimant loses. But the management attorney is not worried about the average case so much as the extreme case. One can describe the task of the management attorney as protecting the client from a "big hit". How could the management attorney resist the feeling that lay jurors would behave more emotionally and award higher damages than professional arbitrators or others drawn from managerial ranks?

Yet there are some stunning reported decisions of arbitrators that suggest they offer no haven to employers. In a recent case [*Fahnestock & Co. v. Waltman*, 935 F.2d 512 (2d Cir. 1991)], a panel of arbitrators in a securities industry arbitration awarded a terminated employee $56,000 for wrongful discharge, $100,000 for defamation, $14,700 for attorneys' fees, and $100,000 for punitive damages. There is no indication in the case that the employee was wrongfully terminated; it seems that he was justifiably terminated because the company closed his division. After the termination, a nasty dispute ensued over ownership of certain files in the possession of the former employee. The employer then changed the termination form to suggest that the employee had been guilty of fraud, the wrongful taking of property, and other irregularities. . . .

Arbitration could offer a hearing to employees who could have one no other way. The NYSE system arbitrates any and all employment disputes. This would encourage complaints of discriminatory (or even unfair) terms and conditions, as well as claims of failure to promote—the kinds of claims that are less likely to be pressed in litigation.

With the time factor seeming to have the same effect for employers as for employees, and with the results factor indeterminate—particularly with the possibility of fomenting claims in arbitration—why is there such a battle between employer groups and employee groups over *Gilmer*? One part of the answer is the speculation on results, with plaintiffs' lawyers loving and defendants' lawyers loathing juries. But I think a bigger part of the answer is control. What management must want is the right unilaterally to design the arbitration system. Plaintiffs' lawyers see in that the potential for construction of an arbitration system that is ostensibly fair but that in fact acts to favor management.

e. Stephen L. Hayford & Michael J. Evers, *The Interaction Between the Employment-at-Will Doctrine and Employer-Employee Agreements to Arbitrate Statutory Fair Employment Practices Claims: Difficult Choices for At-Will Employers*, 73 N.C. L. Rev. 443 (1995)*

I. INTRODUCTION

Among the major developed countries, only the United States permits private sector nonunionized employers, not otherwise contractually constrained, to discharge employees for virtually any reason or for no reason at all. Instead of a single statute that prohibits unjust dismissals, American employers face a patchwork of statutory bars on certain types of conduct deemed unacceptable because it discriminates against various insular groups on the basis of race, color, national origin, gender, religious beliefs and practices, disability, age, or other status.

The employment-at-will doctrine (EAWD), which provides the rationale for giving employers broad discretion to discharge employees, has served as the touchstone for the legal dimension of the American employer-employee relationship for some one hundred years. The thesis of this Article is that recent changes in the law of commercial arbitration, and the concomitant move toward the increased use of arbitration to resolve employer-employee disputes, may, over time, render hollow this once impregnable and indispensable doctrine. . . .

Anxiety over the costs, complexity, and consternation associated with traditional civil litigation has propelled employers to search for alternatives to litigation to achieve prompt, cost-effective, and accurate resolutions of employees' statutory FEP claims. The use of alternative dispute resolution (ADR) methods, especially binding arbitration, significantly accelerated after the 1991 opinion of the United States Supreme Court in *Gilmer v. Interstate/Johnson Lane Corp.*, which expressly approved employer-employee agreements to arbitrate statutory FEP claims. . . .

Can at-will employers secure the purported benefits of arbitrating statutory fair employment practices claims without inadvertently limiting — or completely surrendering — the discretion they presently enjoy under the EAWD? The answer lies in an evaluation of both the specific and broader effects resulting from the interaction between the EAWD and employer-employee agreements to arbitrate statutory FEP claims. . . .

The Article will detail the specific, obvious effects of the interaction between the modern EAWD and employer-employee agreements to arbitrate statutory FEP claims, focusing on the interplay between the three primary limitations on the modern EAWD (the implied covenant of good faith, the implied-in-fact contract terms/enforceable promises doctrine, and the public policy exception) and employer efforts to formulate and implement a binding arbitration device.

Subsequently, the Article discusses three broader results of the interaction between the EAWD and FEP arbitration. These results, which will be referred to as the "broad interaction effects," are particularly significant because their impact will become apparent only with the widespread use of arbitration as an alternative means for adjudicating employee statutory FEP claims. The Article illustrates how the EAWD/FEP interaction will, first, obligate at-will employers to arbitrate virtually all challenged discharges of members of traditionally protected groups; second, result in the imposition of a de facto just cause standard that will greatly constrain the discretion of at-will employers to discharge protected-group members

*Reprinted with permission.

for illegitimate reasons not proscribed by the various FEP statutes; and third, impede the ability of at-will employers to refuse to arbitrate the discharges of nonprotected-group members. The Article concludes with a look at the full scope of the ramifications for at-will employers inherent in the decision to arbitrate statutory FEP claims.

II. *GILMER* AND THE CHANGING LAW OF EMPLOYMENT ARBITRATION

Prior to *Gilmer,* the conventional wisdom was that the federal judiciary would never deem arbitration a suitable surrogate for judicial enforcement of statutory bars on employment discrimination. That view was based on *Alexander v. Gardner-Denver Co.* . . .

Gilmer is a watershed case. Since it was handed down, four circuit courts of appeals have enforced contractual agreements between individual employees and their employers to compel the arbitration of an employee's Title VII charges. In addition, the Ninth Circuit held that an employee's claim of an employer violation of the Employee Polygraph Protection Act of 1990 was subject to arbitration under the same type of contractual agreement at issue in *Gilmer.* Significantly, the D.C. Circuit recently held that nothing in the Civil Rights Act of 1991 suggests that Congress intended to modify or undermine the rule of *Gilmer.*

Given the resonant nature of the Supreme Court's endorsement of the arbitration of statutory FEP claims as articulated in *Gilmer,* there is every reason to believe that the above-framed general rule — that agreements to arbitrate statutory claims are enforceable, absent proof of contrary congressional intent — will also control in the sphere of employment dispute resolution. This inference is further supported by the congressional endorsement of arbitration and other ADR devices in the Civil Rights Act of 1991 and the ADA, which was enacted in 1990. . . .

IV. THE MODERN EAWD RULE

The modern EAWD provides that, absent a legal rule to the contrary, either party to an employment relationship for an indefinite (unspecified) term can terminate the relationship at will, despite the employee's length of service, with or without cause or notice, and without giving any explanation or reason, unless the freedom to terminate is constrained by contract. Conversely, where employment is for a definite term based on a contract, an employer can terminate only for cause. This general conceptualization of the EAWD notwithstanding, the modern rule recognizes that the employer's freedom to terminate at will can be, and often is, restrained by statutory employment standards or limitations of the common law.

A. Legislative Limitations on the Modern EAWD

. . . [Instead of a general limitation on dismissal without cause,] our legislatures have chosen to enact a number of more narrowly drawn statutory bars to unequal treatment (including discharge) based on a person's race, color, sex, national origin, religion, age, disability, or union-related activity. The first of these prohibitions was set forth in the National Labor Relations Act (NLRA) of 1935. Section 8(a)(3) of the NLRA bars private-sector employers from discriminating against employees (or applicants for employment) on the basis of their union activity or affiliation. . . .

Today, Title VII of the Civil Rights Act of 1964 effectively precludes at-will employers from terminating employees based on their race, color, national origin, sex, or religion. The ADA, in concert with the Vocational Rehabilitation Act, similarly protects qualified individuals with disabilities. The ADEA effectively prohibits age-based discharges of workers age 40 and over.

In the same manner, the Fair Labor Standards Act, which imposes minimum standards for wages and hours, the Occupational Safety and Health Act of 1970, which imposes standards for worker safety and protects workers from unreasonable risk of injury or death, and the Equal Pay Act of 1963, which proscribes gender-based wage discrimination, all prevent employers from discharging employees in retaliation for exercising or enforcing their statutory rights. Subject to limited exceptions, the Employee Polygraph Protection Act of 1988 protects employees from discharge for refusing to submit to a polygraph examination. Although not a substantive bar to termination, the Worker Adjustment and Retraining Notification Act requires subject employers to give workers advance notice of plant closings and related layoffs before terminating the employment relationship. These congressional initiatives have incrementally restricted employers' discretion to terminate at will. State and municipal legislatures also have enacted an array of statutes and ordinances that parallel and supplement the protections provided by federal law. . . .

V. THE INTERACTION BETWEEN THE EAWD AND EMPLOYER-EMPLOYEE AGREEMENTS TO ARBITRATE STATUTORY FAIR EMPLOYMENT PRACTICES CLAIMS

The analysis now returns to the central question posited at the outset of this article: Can at-will employers secure the purported benefits of arbitrating statutory fair employment practices claims without inadvertently limiting, or completely surrendering, the remaining discretion to terminate employees presently enjoyed under the modern EAWD?

Of the two categories of limitations imposed on the EAWD during the course of the last sixty years—legislative and judicially fashioned—those imposed by the judiciary without the benefit of explicit legislative direction are the grist of this analysis. . . . [I]t is easy to ascertain the result of the interaction between the EAWD and the substantive protections of the several FEP statutes when statutory FEP claims are submitted to arbitration. The EAWD simply does not shield discharges by at-will employers that abrogate the statutorily guaranteed FEP rights of terminated protected-group members. The statutory FEP protections trump the EAWD.

Uncertainty arises, however, when the focus shifts to the likely effects of the interaction between the several judicially fashioned exceptions to the EAWD and employer-employee agreements to arbitrate statutory FEP claims. . . . The potential impact of the three common-law doctrines used by judges to constrain the EAWD—the implied covenant of good faith, the implied-in-fact contract terms/enforceable promises doctrine, and the public policy exception—is uncertain when the doctrines are applied within the milieu of contractual agreements to arbitrate statutory FEP claims. Each of the probable specific interaction effects will be examined in turn.

A. Arbitration Agreements and the Implied Covenant of Good Faith

By agreeing with its employees to arbitrate unresolved statutory FEP claims, an employer introduces a contract into an otherwise contract-free employment relationship. In doing so, the employer raises the possibility that the arbitration agreement will form the basis for a judicial attribution to both parties of an implied, enforceable obligation to deal with one another fairly and in good faith within the context of the agreement to arbitrate. Disclaimers, either general in nature or specifically directed toward the implied covenant of good faith, may not be an effective barrier to invocation of the covenant, because the usual rule is that the obligation to conduct contractual relations in good faith cannot be waived. . . .

B. Arbitration Agreements and the Implied-In-Fact Exceptions to the EAWD

[T]he interaction between employer-employee agreements to arbitrate statutory FEP claims and the implied-in-fact exceptions to the EAWD. . . . will arise where a court finds that the manner in which the employer promulgates, articulates, and implements the arbitration procedure for statutory FEP claims constitutes an implied contract . . . term, or an enforceable tacit promise, to terminate employees only for just cause. Here, the critical tasks for employers will be careful drafting of the arbitration agreement and consistent application and implementation of its terms. . . .

In explaining the arbitration agreement to employees, employers must describe clearly the limited scope of the appeals procedure it creates. They must avoid speaking in broad terms of guarantees of "fairness," "workplace justice," and "workplace due process." Forthrightness and accuracy is critical. Employees must not be given any reasonable basis to believe that they are agreeing to anything more than a procedure for arbitrating employer actions claimed to be in violation of the explicit protections and rights secured to them by the FEP statutes expressly embraced by the arbitration procedure. . . .

Further caution should be exercised if, as frequently is the case, the arbitration mechanism is linked to a prearbitration grievance procedure or mediation step. An implied contract term or enforceable promise may be created by any statement, action, or representation by a front-line supervisor, higher level manager, or employee relations official which implies that disputes, other than those linked directly to a bona fide claim of a statutory FEP violation, will be arbitrated. Thus, when an employee attempts to join a statutory FEP claim with collateral matters not within the reach of the arbitration procedure, the employer must make clear that only the facts and circumstances pertinent to the statutory FEP claim will be arbitrated. . . .

One of the primary pitfalls to which employers must remain alert will arise if the arbitration procedure proves to be an efficient method for expeditiously achieving satisfactory resolutions to statutory-based disputes. If it does, there will be substantial temptation to utilize the arbitration mechanism to resolve other, nonstatutory employer-employee disputes that the employer does not want to litigate in court. If the employer succumbs to that temptation routinely, or even occasionally, the implied-in-fact doctrine will materialize to furnish a court with a sound basis for inferring an employer commitment to arbitrate all employment disputes. This danger will be most discernible in tough, high-stakes discharge cases that normally would fall within the purview of the EAWD. . . .

C. Arbitration Agreements and the Public Policy Exception to the EAWD

There are two dimensions to the interface between employer-employee agreements to arbitrate statutory FEP claims and the public policy exception to the EAWD. First, the previously discussed premise of the public policy exception establishes that otherwise permissible at-will terminations of employees running afoul of a clear public policy are not shielded by the EAWD. The second dimension is the rule of *Gilmer* that, as a separate public policy pertaining to the arbitration of statutory FEP claims under the FAA, arbitration is a suitable surrogate for litigation only if the arbitration procedure itself provides adequate procedural and substantive due process safeguards.

Few public policies relating to the employer-employee relationship are more significant or far reaching than the two identified above. In evaluating the conduct of employers in the administration and implementation of these arbitration procedures, the courts undoubtedly will act quickly to remedy employer conduct found to have abridged the right of claimant employees to have their statutory FEP claims arbitrated fairly. The signal sent to employers by the intersection of these two public policies is unmistakable. If employers want arbitration to function as a substitute for traditional litigation, they must ensure that it is a truly fair procedure providing employees with a full opportunity to challenge discharges and other personnel actions on a level playing field. . . .

VI. THE BROAD INTERACTION EFFECTS: THE COMPULSION TO ARBITRATE; THE DE FACTO JUST CAUSE STANDARD; AND DIFFERENTIAL TREATMENT OF NONPROTECTED-GROUP MEMBERS

. . . .

C. At-Will Discharges of Ostensively Nonprotected Group Members: When the Employer Refuses to Arbitrate

A troubling concern will arise if implementation of employer-employee agreements to arbitrate statutory FEP claims does indeed afford individuals who are clearly protected-class members the right to challenge all discharges through arbitration under a de facto just cause standard. Under this scenario, only those individuals falling outside the traditional protected groups—nondisabled Caucasian males under forty years of age—will be denied the opportunity to take issue with terminations they believe to have been unfair. . . .

At-will employers cannot ignore the potential ramifications of a workplace due process regime that draws so clear a distinction between the discharge appeals rights of protected-group members and their nonprotected-group member peers. The question for contemplation is whether at-will employers will be able to continue to discharge nonprotected-group members for any reason and then refuse to arbitrate their challenges to termination, when they are obligated to arbitrate under a de facto just cause standard virtually all challenged discharges of protected-group members. . . .

VII. CONCLUSION: ARBITRATION OR THE EAWD — A HOBSON'S CHOICE FOR AT-WILL EMPLOYERS

. . . At-will employers that wish to take advantage of the benefits of arbitrating FEP claims must do so with a clear understanding of the rigor and good faith that will be required to avoid inadvertently piercing the EAWD shield through either imprecise framing of the arbitration mechanism, or inept or untoward administration of its terms. Despite these substantial risks, properly motivated at-will employers guided by competent counsel and represented by an adequately trained supervisory and management corps have little reason to fear that these first-level, specific interaction effects will inadvertently expand the scope of the contemplated arbitration procedure beyond the reach of employee statutory FEP claims.

The broader, more complex interaction effects are farther reaching and present a more sobering proposition for at-will employers. Since these three broad interaction effects will arise as a matter of law and not as the result of any careless or pernicious management conduct, at-will employers that choose to arbitrate employee statutory FEP claims will have little control over their impact. Thus, an implied obligation to arbitrate all challenged discharges of traditional protected-group members will inevitably emerge, over time, from application of the law of commercial arbitration pertaining to matters of substantive arbitrability. This implied obligation, and the de facto just cause standard for protected-group members inherent in the disparate treatment order and allocation of proof paradigm, will become apparent to at-will employers (and their employees) who regularly arbitrate statutory FEP claims.

The impact of the third category of broad interaction effects, those arising when at-will employers refuse to arbitrate the discharge of Caucasian males, is less certain, but of significantly greater potential consequence. If at-will employers that desire to arbitrate statutory FEP claims in fact find themselves effectively obliged to arbitrate and justify all challenged terminations of non-Caucasians, women, ethnic and religious minority group members, the disabled, and those over forty years of age, only Caucasian males will be left within the effective reach of the EAWD. They alone will be without just cause protection.

Setting aside the not insubstantial question of whether Caucasian males would tolerate being denied the same de facto just cause guarantee and right to challenge unfair discharges afforded their fellow employees, there is substantial reason to doubt the legality under Title VII and section 1981 of an employment policy that draws such a distinction in employment conditions on the basis of employees' race, color, national origin, and gender. . . .

The message for at-will employers is clear. The price for securing the benefits of arbitrating statutory FEP claims may prove to be a partial or total surrender of the EAWD shield. At-will employers that adopt the binding arbitration device as the vehicle for adjudicating the statutory FEP claims of their employees must do so with full knowledge of the risk inherent in taking that step. At the very least, at-will employers that choose to arbitrate statutory FEP claims will be compelled to arbitrate and defend, under a de facto just cause standard, all challenged discharges of traditional FEP protected-group members. If the third category of broad interaction effects conceptualized by the authors materializes, at-will employers will be forced to arbitrate and defend the challenged discharges of all employees, protected and nonprotected-group members alike, thereby eviscerating the EAWD completely. Therefore, at-will employers choosing to arbitrate statutory FEP claims must be at least implicitly willing to relinquish the remaining vestiges of the EAWD and embrace a just cause standard that applies to all of their employees. . . .

f. Comments and Questions

1. Are you persuaded? Prediction is a dangerous endeavor, as Yogi Berra observed, particularly when you are talking about the future.

2. There is an important point to the Hayford and Evers article that quite transcends the particular issues discussed, which is that dispute settlement procedures may have important and not easily forseen impacts quite beyond the handling of particular disputes.

g. Michele M. Buese, *Contracting Employment Disputes Out of the Jury System: Analysis of the Implementation of Binding Arbitration in the Non-Union Workplace and Proposals to Reduce the Harsh Effects of a Non-Appealable Award*, 22 Pepp. L. Rev. 1485 (1995)*

The main issue of concern for employers and employees contemplating contracting for

*Reprinted with permission.

arbitration, left unresolved by Gilmer, is whether the FAA applies to contracts of employment. If the FAA is found to apply to employment contracts (as it was found to apply to registration contracts), then the Gilmer decision, and cases following its reasoning, will be binding precedent in the situation where an employee signs an employment contract containing an arbitration clause. If the FAA is found not to apply to employment contracts, then Gilmer will not be binding precedent on employment related statutory disputes and employees will retain the right to litigate these claims. Since Gilmer did not resolve this "contracts of employment" issue, potential statutory claim litigants can only examine how courts have applied Gilmer to employment contracts containing arbitration clauses thus far to gain insight into the applicability of the FAA to these contracts.

Most courts have found that only contracts of employment relating specifically to those workers mentioned in the statute, and those workers in similar positions who actually transport goods interstate or internationally are excluded from the arbitration provisions of the FAA.[126] The rationale behind these cases is that if Congress had intended to exclude all contracts of employment, it would have been unnecessary to have specifically named certain classes in the statute as examples; since such classes were enumerated, clearly only these types of workers were meant to be excluded. Despite a limited number of decisions classifying employment contracts outside the securities industry, most courts have indicated that employment contracts will not fall within the contracts of employment exception of the FAA.

Gilmer did not conclusively decide which statutory rights can be contracted out of the jury system by opting for arbitration in an employment agreement. When the coverage of statutory rights is at issue (usually because the contract states nothing about their inclusion or exclusion), the Supreme Court held that the burden is on the party opposing arbitration to show that Congress intended to preclude the waiver of judicial remedies for those rights at issue. Therefore, if an employment contract says nothing as to the arbitration of statutory claims, arbitration of these claims will be allowed unless judicial intent not to have them arbitrated can be shown.

While federal policy as to the arbitration of statutory claims is becoming more clear, the states have not conclusively established whether arbitration of statutory claims will be compelled under the states' arbitration statutes when the FAA is inapplicable. However . . . arbitration clauses not covered by the FAA will likely be enforceable under state law. . . . [M]ost state arbitration statutes do not contain the contracts of employment exception. . . . In addition, several state courts have relied on Gilmer in upholding agreements to arbitrate. Therefore, whether by federal statute or by state provision, most employment related contracts requiring arbitration of claims cover statutory claims normally guaranteed a jury trial.

---

[126]*See, e.g.*, Miller Brewing Co. v. Brewery Workers Local Union No. 9, 739 F.2d 1159, 1162 (7th Cir. 1984), *cert. denied*, 469 U.S. 1160 (1985) (FAA did not exclude contracts of employment of brewery workers because they are not involved in the transportation industry); Stokes v. Merrill Lynch, Pierce, Fenner & Smith, Inc., 523 F.2d 433, 436 (6th Cir. 1975); Erving v. Virginia Squires Basketball Club, 468 F.2d 1064, 1069 (2d Cir. 1972) (FAA did not exclude contract of professional basketball player); Dickstein v. DuPont, 443 F.2d 783, 785 (1st Cir. 1971) (account executive's contract covered by the FAA); Tenney Eng'g v. United Elec. Radio & Mach. Workers of Am. Local 437, 207 F.2d 450, 451-53 (3d Cir. 1953) (FAA excludes only those workers actually involved in moving goods interstate).

h. Comments and Questions

1. It may strike the reader as quite astonishing that such a fundamental question about the scope of a federal statute adopted in 1925 is still so wide open. How do you think the FAA's employment limitation should be interpreted on this issue, and why?

2. What weight, if any, should be given to Congressional inaction? What weight should be given to the views of the Congress that enacted the FAA? What account, if any. should be taken of the dramatic differences in the American economy, labor relations, and other differences between 1925 and today?

4. Use of ADR Procedures, Notably Arbitration, for Equal Employment Opportunity Claims

a. General Accounting Office, Health, Education, & Human Services Division, B-257171, July 5, 1995

In fiscal year 1994, the Equal Employment Opportunity Commission (EEOC) received over 90,000 discrimination complaints from employees, almost twice the number filed in 1981 and 10 times the number in 1966. The number of employment law cases filed in the federal courts has increased similarly. In resolving these complaints, employers have become more and more concerned about the costs—in time, money, and good employee relationships. In response, some employers have adopted internal alternative dispute resolution (ADR) approaches, including arbitration. . . . Some require their employees to agree to mandatory, binding arbitration of discrimination complaints as a condition of their employment, forcing employees to waive the right to sue. . . .

To determine the extent of the use of ADR approaches, we sent a questionnaire to a stratified, random sample of 2,000 businesses that had (1) filed equal employment opportunity (EEO) reports with the EEOC in 1992 and (2) reported having more than 100 employees. ADR approaches include negotiation, fact finding, peer review, internal mediation, external mediation, and arbitration.

To obtain more detailed information on ADR approaches, we telephoned those employers who had reported using arbitration and asked each of them to send us a description of the arbitration policies used. As part of our assessment of the policies, we compared the policies' provisions with the key quality standards proposed by the Commission on the Future of Worker-Management Relations as standards for a private arbitration system that ensures employees a fair and full airing of their complaints. . . .

Background

If workers believe that they have been discriminated against in an employment matter, they may generally file a charge with EEOC, one of several federal agencies responsible for enforcing equal employment opportunity (EEO) laws and regulations. Under title VII of the Civil Rights Act of 1964, EEOC investigates—and may litigate, on its own behalf or on behalf of the charging party—charges of employment discrimination because of race, color, religion, sex, or national origin. EEOC has similar responsibility under the Age Discrimination in Employment Act of 1967, which prohibits employment discrimination against workers aged 40 and older; under the Equal Pay Act of 1963, which prohibits payment of different wages to men and women doing the same work; and under the Americans With Disabilities Act, which prohibits employment discrimination against workers with physical or mental disabilities.

In April 1995, EEOC announced changes in the way it processes private-sector employment discrimination charges. As soon as guidance and implementation instructions are issued, EEOC will begin categorizing charges according to three priorities. The first category is for charges that appear more likely than not to involve discrimination, and these charges will be fully investigated. The second category includes charges that appear to have some merit but will require additional evidence to determine whether a violation occurred. The third category includes charges that can be immediately dismissed without investigation. EEOC also announced that it will initiate a voluntary ADR program using mediation to handle some of its workplace discrimination charges. Under this planned program, some employees filing charges and their employers will work with a neutral mediator to settle discrimination disputes, rather than go through EEOC's traditional investigative procedures. If the employer and employee fail to reach a resolution, the charge will be returned to EEOC's regular caseload.

If EEOC investigates the charge, it notifies the employer of the charge and requests information from the employer and any witnesses with direct knowledge of the incident that led to the discrimination charge. If the evidence obtained by the EEOC investigator does not show reasonable cause to believe discrimination occurred—for example, the employee was terminated for poor performance and not due to discrimination—EEOC dismisses the case after issuing a "no cause" finding and a right-to-sue letter. When the evidence shows that reasonable cause exists to believe discrimination occurred, EEOC tries conciliation. If conciliation attempts fail, EEOC may go to court on behalf of the employee, although it rarely chooses to do so. EEOC officials have said that the Commission lacks sufficient legal staff to significantly increase the number of cases it can litigate effectively. When EEOC decides not to go to court, it issues the employee a right-to-sue letter, which allows the employee to sue.

While charges filed with EEOC may lead to legal relief for employees with valid claims, each charge results in costs to the employer, even though most are found to be in compliance with the law. Although the employee does not pay for the EEOC investigation, he or she may incur psychological costs while pursuing the claim, the average time of which was 328 days in fiscal year 1994. The federal government also incurs costs for each charge investigated.

ADR approaches are being considered by employers because "almost any system is quicker, cheaper, and less harrowing than going to court," according to an official of the Equal Employment Advisory Council, an employers' group. Their concerns have recently increased as a result of (1) multimillion dollar jury awards to employees and (2) the provision in the Civil Rights Act of 1991 that permits punitive damages in cases of intentional discrimination under title VII of the Civil Rights Act of 1964 and the Americans With Disabilities Act. In addition, a 1991 U.S. Supreme Court decision upholding mandatory arbitration for statutory claims concerning employment disputes in the securities industry has led to consideration of arbitration in particular. Finally, some employers feel that ADR approaches can minimize the adversarial relationship between employer and employee resulting from such complaints.

Commission Appointed to Address Worker-Management Relations

The Commission was appointed at the request of the President by the Secretary of Commerce and the Secretary of Labor to address three questions:

- What (if any) new methods or institutions should be encouraged, or required, to enhance workplace productivity through labor-management cooperation and employee participation?

- What (if any) changes should be made in the present legal framework and practices of collective bargaining to enhance cooperative behavior, improve productivity, and reduce conflict and delay?
- What (if anything) should be done to increase the extent to which workplace problems are directly resolved by the parties themselves, rather than through recourse to state and federal courts and governmental bodies?

In researching this third question, the Commission considered the range of federal and state laws regulating the workplace, including those ensuring minimum wages and maximum hours; a safe and healthy workplace; secure and accessible pension and health benefits; adequate notice of plant closings and mass layoffs; unpaid family and medical leave; and bans on wrongful dismissal, as well as those outlawing discrimination on the basis of race, sex, religion, age, or disability.

According to the Commission's December 1994 report, both employers and employees agree that, if private arbitration is to serve as a legitimate form of private-sector enforcement of public employment law, arbitration policies must provide a neutral arbitrator who knows the laws in question and understands the concerns of the parties:

- a fair and simple method by which the employee can obtain the necessary information to present his or her claim,
- a fair method of cost-sharing between the employer and employee to ensure affordable access to the system for all employees, the right to independent representation if the employee wants it, a range of legal remedies equal to those available through litigation,
- a written opinion by the arbitrator explaining his or her rationale for the decision, and sufficient judicial review to ensure that the result is consistent with employment laws.

The Commission noted, however, that most experts who had testified before it agreed that imposition of fairness standards must not turn arbitration into a second court system.

Some Existing Arbitration Policies Would Not Meet Commission's Recently Proposed Standards

In our review of employers' arbitration policies, we found that some do not meet the fairness standards recently proposed by the Commission on the Future of Worker-Management Relations. Using the Commission's six standards, we evaluated dispute resolution policies provided by 26 employers that reported using arbitration to resolve discrimination complaints by employees not covered under collective bargaining agreements. Most of these policies, which are discussed below, are recent: 15 had been implemented in the past 5 years.

Almost All Employers Reported Using ADR Approaches, but Few Use or Plan to Use Arbitration

Almost 90 percent of employers that had more than 100 employees and filed EEO reports with EEOC in 1992 use at least one ADR approach to resolve discrimination complaints. The reported use of these approaches ranges from about 80 percent for fact finding to about 9 percent for external mediation. Almost 40 percent of these employers use a trained mediator from within the company to help resolve disputes. Only about 10 percent of employers use arbitration. Arbitration was mandatory for all covered employees for about one-fourth to one-half of the employers using this approach. . . .

Arbitration Is Frequently the Final Step in a Policy Including Other ADR Approaches

A dispute resolution policy frequently has a series of steps, such as those discussed below, that can be linked to different ADR approaches. Usually, a policy that includes arbitration has it as the final step.

Steps 1 and 2: Negotiation

In step 1, an employee with a complaint is encouraged to discuss the matter with his or her immediate supervisor. The employee and supervisor should make sincere, good faith efforts to resolve the matter. If the employee prefers not to present the matter directly to the immediate supervisor or if they cannot resolve the matter the employee then discusses the matter with a representative of the establishment's human resources department and decides whether to proceed to the next step.

In step 2, the employee may request that a representative of the establishment's human resources department conduct an assessment of the dispute and help the employee and supervisor reach a resolution.

Step 3: Fact Finding

If resolution has not been reached, an employee may proceed to step 3 and request an investigation by a representative of the establishment's human resources department. The results of the investigation are discussed with the appropriate senior manager and the employee. The senior manager decides how the complaint should be resolved. A decision letter is sent to both—the employee and supervisor—at the end of this step.

Step 4: Review Board

An employee who is dissatisfied with the senior manager's decision may request that the problem be reviewed by a review board, which is composed of an executive, a manager, and a representative from the corporate human resources office. The employee may request the help of an executive adviser in preparing for this step. At the end of step 4, the board will make a final company decision on the dispute's merits, including corrective action, if appropriate.

Step 5: Arbitration

If an employee is dissatisfied with the board's decision, he or she may submit the complaint to binding arbitration, which is step 5 of this company's dispute resolution policy. An employee must give notice within 20 working days of the date the board reached its decision. The arbitration is to be administered in accordance with the procedures of the American Arbitration Association (AAA), a nonprofit organization that trains arbitrators and maintains lists of arbitrators who can be used to resolve different types of disputes, including labor-management and employment disputes. The arbitration will be heard by an arbitrator who is licensed to practice law in the state in which the arbitration takes place. Under [one] company's policy, the employer and the employee share equally the fees and costs of the arbitrator, although the arbitrator may order the company to pay the employee's costs in excess of 2 weeks' salary if the employee demonstrates a continuing inability to pay his or her entire share.

Smaller Businesses Are as Likely to Report Using Arbitration as Larger Ones

Larger employers with larger human resource and legal staffs might be assumed to be more likely to use arbitration. However, we found no statistically significant difference in use of arbitration based on business size.

Firms With Some Workers Covered by Collective Bargaining Agreements Are More Likely to Report Using Arbitration

Since arbitration has long been a feature of grievance procedures in the collective bargaining arena, employers that have collective bargaining agreements with some of their workers might be more likely to use arbitration with those not covered by collective bargaining. . . . [B]usinesses with some union workers are nearly three times as likely as those with no union workers to use arbitration, lending credence to this notion.

Selection of Arbitrator Usually Involves Both Employer and Employee

In its final report, the Commission states that the arbitrator selection process should allow both the employer and the affected employee(s) to participate. The arbitrator should be selected from a roster of qualified arbitrators who have training and experience in the area of law covering the dispute being arbitrated and are certified by professional associations specializing in such dispute resolution. The process should ensure that rosters include significant numbers of women and minorities. Neither party should be able to limit the roster unilaterally to avoid the possibility the arbitration selected will be biased in favor of that party.

While we did not evaluate the qualifications or demographics of the panels from which arbitrators would be chosen, we noted that in 22 of the 26 policies we examined, both the employee and employer are directly involved in selecting the arbitrator. In 12 policies, this is done with the help of AAA. Immediately after the complaint is filed, AAA simultaneously sends an identical list of people chosen from its panel of employment arbitrators to both the employer and the employee. The employer and the employee (1) strike any names they object to and (2) number the remaining names in order of preference. In a single arbitrator case, the employer and the employee may each strike up to three names. AAA chooses an arbitrator from among those approved on both lists in accordance with the designated order of preference. If no agreement is reached on any of the names, AAA makes the appointment from other members of the panel. In seven policies we reviewed, the employer and employee alternate striking names from a list One policy rather vaguely calls for selection "based on the parties' preferences." In two policies, the employer selects the names on the list, but the employee is involved in selecting the arbitrator. In one of the remaining four policies, the employer unilaterally selects the arbitrator, while the other three do not discuss arbitrator selection.

Employee Access to Information Is Rarely Discussed

According to the Commission, employees should have the opportunity to gather the relevant information they need to support their legal claims. Employees pursuing a discrimination complaint, for example, should be granted access to their personnel files. Broader access to personnel files should also be available to employees bringing systemic discrimination claims. During arbitration, an employee with a complaint should be allowed at least one deposition, with a company official of the employee's choosing. The arbitrator should be empowered to expand discovery (pretrial or prehearing procedure by which one party gains information held by the other) to include any material he or she finds valuable for resolving the dispute.

Only three policies we reviewed discuss access to information. One policy states that discovery will be allowed and governed under the discovery rules of the state code of civil procedure unless otherwise agreed to by the parties; one policy provides for 2 days of depositions; and the remaining policy limits the taking of depositions to one company representative, two other persons, and one expert witness named by the company but also allows requests for documents related to the complaint.

Both Employer and Employee Usually Share Payment of Arbitrator

To ensure impartiality of the arbitrator, the Commission proposes that both the employee and the employer contribute to the arbitrator's fee. Ideally, the employee contribution should be capped in proportion to the employee's salary to avoid discouraging claims by low-wage workers.

Seven policies do not address cost sharing. In four policies, the employer pays for all arbitration costs; costs are to be shared equally in nine policies; and the employee share is either capped or limited to less than half the costs in the remaining six policies. For example, one employer pays all costs in excess of $50. Another firm pays 80 percent of the arbitration costs, while the employee is responsible for 20 percent.

Right to Independent Counsel Generally Permitted

According to the Commission, both employers and employees agree that fairness requires the right of independent representation if the employee wants it. AAA rules state that "any party may be represented by counsel or by any other representative."

Twenty-one of the policies we reviewed permit the employee to be represented by an attorney during arbitration. Four policies do not address representation. Only one policy specifically states that representation by an attorney will not be permitted.

Remedies Rarely Addressed, but Not Specifically Limited by Policies

The Commission states that the introduction of a workplace arbitration system should not curb substantive employee protections. This means that private arbitration should offer employees the same array of remedies available in court. Arbitrators should be allowed to award whatever relief—including reinstatement, back pay, additional economic damages, punitive awards, injunctive relief, and attorney's fees—would be available in court under the law in question.

Eighteen of the 26 policies do not address legal remedies available to the arbitrator. Of the eight remaining policies, seven state that the arbitrator can use any remedy available under law, while one policy prohibits the arbitrator from assessing damages beyond those required to compensate for actual losses.

Final Arbitrator Decision Is Sometimes in Writing

The Commission states that the arbitrator should issue a written opinion that states the findings of fact and reasons that led to his or her decision. This opinion need not correspond in style or length to a court opinion. However, it should set out, in understandable terms, the basis for the arbitrator's ruling.

Ten policies do not address the form of the arbitrator's decision. The remaining 16 policies require the arbitrator to provide a written ruling, but specific provisions of these policies vary considerably. For example, one policy requires the decision to "contain findings of fact and conclusions of law supporting the decision and the award," while another states that the written opinion should not include findings of fact and conclusions of law unless requested by both the employer and the employee.

Judicial Review Is Not Addressed in Policies

According to the Commission, judicial review of an arbitrator's ruling must ensure that the ruling reflects an appropriate understanding and interpretation of the relevant legal doctrines. A reviewing court should defer to an arbitrator's findings of fact as long as it has substantial evidentiary basis. However, the reviewing court's authoritative interpretation of the law should bind arbitrators much as it now binds administrative agencies and lower courts. For example, if an arbitration decision on a sexual harassment complaint disregards the standard set for such claims by the Supreme Court, the reviewing court should have the power to overturn the arbitration decision as inconsistent with current law.

No policies require that the arbitration decision reflects an appropriate understanding and interpretation of relevant legal doctrines and be reviewable by a court on that basis. Sixteen policies call for the arbitration results to be "final and binding." However, none of these policies specifically provide for judicial review. The remaining 10 policies do not address reviewing the arbitrator's opinion.

b. Comments and Questions

1. The data collected by the GAO about the use of ADR in the processing of employment discrimination complaints is far from definitive, but it is the best available information. Based on the case law from the Supreme Court, do you expect there to be a dramatic increase in the use of mandatory, binding arbitration of employment disputes generally, and discrimination claims in particular? Does your answer depend on how the Supreme Court resolves still open legal issues? If so, what are these issues?

2. The GAO evaluated current employment arbitration programs against criteria established by a Commission on the Future of Worker-Management Relations. Are these the best or most useful standards to use in evaluating employee arbitration programs? What standards would you add, subtract, or alter? How are the standards proposed by the Commission different from current law, as expressed in the Federal Arbitration Act and the Uniform Arbitration Act?

D. Therapeutic Values of Arbitration

1. Comments and Questions

a. We have seen earlier that ADR procedures often have a therapeutic aspect, compared with litigation, because people have a greater rule in the settlement of "their" dispute. Usually, the therapeutic value of ADR is seen as beneficial. However, therapy sometimes is regarded negatively, as a substitute for power that is obtained from the victory achievable in litigation. Examples of this perspective are found in the Laura Nader article in Chapter Three, and the

Trina Grillo article in Chapter 8. The work of Professors Robert Baruch Bush and Leonard Riskin (see the articles in Chapter 19) treats the participatory and therapeutic aspects of mediation as important benefits.

b. The next article examines the therapeutic aspects of labor arbitration. Note that the authors regard therapy as an appropriate and useful aspect of labor arbitration, but that this role is limited and should continue to be so. Do you agree with the authors about the appropriate place of therapy in labor arbitration? To what extent are the costs and benefits of arbitral therapy discussed by the authors unique to the labor and collective bargaining context? Is there a place for therapeutic values in arbitration between banks and their customers? What about securities brokers and their customers? Do therapeutic values have any place in the arbitration of complex commercial disputes?

2. Roger I. Abrams, Frances E. Abrams & Dennis R. Nolan, *Arbitral Therapy*, 46 Rutgers L. Rev. 1751 (1994)*

I. INTRODUCTION

[In 1960] the Supreme Court issued its famous Steelworkers Trilogy decisions that set the ground rules for the relationship between the courts and the labor arbitration process. In *United Steelworkers v. American Manufacturing Co.* the first of the Trilogy, Justice William Douglas posited therapeutic effects for the labor arbitration process. The Court held that a trial court should order arbitration even of claims the trial judge believes meritless. "The processing of even frivolous claims may have therapeutic values of which those who are not part of the plant environment may be quite unaware." In footnote 6, Justice Douglas quoted at length from an article by Professor Archibald Cox referring to the "cathartic value" of arbitration and explaining the value to the parties of arbitrating even frivolous claims:

> Frivolous cases are often taken, and are expected to be taken, to arbitration. What one man considers frivolous another may find meritorious, and it is common knowledge in industrial relations circles that grievance arbitration often serves as a safety valve for troublesome complaints. Under these circumstances it seems proper to read the typical arbitration clause as a promise to arbitrate every claim, meritorious or frivolous, which the complainant bases upon the contract. The objection that equity will not order a party to do a useless act is outweighed by the cathartic value of arbitrating even a frivolous grievance and by the dangers of excessive judicial intervention.

Many participants in labor arbitration sense that the process may have therapeutic effects. The literature on labor arbitration and later Supreme Court decisions repeat Justice Douglas's dictum. There is a consensus that the therapeutic effect is a valuable, although not primary, goal of the arbitration process.

It is thus surprising that no one has ever examined the bases of Justice Douglas's claim. Is labor arbitration really therapeutic? If so, for what types of problems? What elements of the arbitration process make it therapeutic? How does the therapy work?

Psychologists examine therapeutic relationships. The psychology literature discusses the elements of therapeutic relationships that foster positive benefits for clients. The legal literature, in contrast, pays little attention to the therapeutic aspects of the formal legal process. In

*Reprinted with permission.

this Article, we apply insights from psychology to understand better the possible therapeutic value of the labor arbitration process.

II. THE ARBITRATION MODEL

Labor arbitration is an informal mechanism for resolving grievance disputes arising during the term of a collective bargaining agreement. Over the past century, both the parties to collective bargaining agreements and the labor arbitrators have shaped the arbitration process. Without judicial or legislative prescriptions, labor and management have incrementally created a widely-accepted model of labor arbitration.

Employers and unions initially try to resolve their differences through a contractual grievance procedure. If they cannot resolve a dispute, the union may invoke arbitration. At the arbitration stage, a single neutral arbitrator, jointly selected by the parties, resolves the dispute.

Arbitrators hear the case at a mutually convenient site. Lawyers often represent the parties, but more commonly non-lawyers represent one or both. The typical labor arbitrator is a white male in his sixties, about half have law degrees, and most are educators who arbitrate part-time. The arbitrator holds an informal but orderly hearing, not bound by the rules of evidence, to gather evidence and hear arguments. Arbitrator (and former Secretary of Labor) W. Willard Wirtz stated that arbitrators:

> have established the pattern of ordered informality; performing major surgery on the legal rules of evidence and procedure but retaining the good sense of those rules; greatly simplifying but not eliminating the hearsay and parole evidence rules; taking the rules for the admissibility of evidence and remolding them into rules for weighing it; striking the fat but saving the heart of the practices of cross-examination, presumptions, burden of proof, and the like.

The arbitrator hears testimony from sworn witnesses on direct and cross-examination and receives pertinent documents. One or both parties may order a transcript. Most hearings last a single day, often only a few hours.

After the hearing, parties may submit written briefs. The arbitrator reviews the record in the case and within a month or two issues a written opinion containing reasons for the award. The collective bargaining agreement normally provides that the arbitrator's award is final and binding on the parties. Some public sector contracts still provide for advisory arbitration. As a labor-management relationship matures, parties usually develop confidence in the arbitration process and move toward a binding procedure.

All unionized sectors of the economy follow this arbitration model. Virtually all collective bargaining agreements contain arbitration provisions. These provisions cover all types of workers-unskilled, skilled, and professional.

III. IS ARBITRATION THERAPEUTIC?

Psychologists define [therapeutic] in various ways. Therapy is a process "through which one person helps another to find relief from emotional pain." A therapeutic process is curative. Individuals who believe a helper or counselor has "curative" powers often experience relief from their problems or emotional disorders. Therapy is a verbal interaction that lessens anxiety, thereby leading to tension reduction. Simply telling one's story may prove helpful.

The therapeutic experience requires the development of a relationship between a client and therapist aimed toward ameliorating emotional symptoms. Although there are many therapeutic orientations, they share common characteristics, including "comfort, support, guidance, reassurance, guilt-reduction through confession, and hope." As the therapeutic relationship develops, a client experiences an atmosphere free of criticism and judgment. . . . To understand the therapeutic aspects of labor arbitration, we will use insights developed in group, family, couples, and brief psychotherapy, techniques most similar to arbitration. . . .

The essence of the therapeutic experience in a group setting lies in "increasing people's knowledge of themselves and others, assisting people to clarify the changes they most want to make in their life, and giving people some of the tools necessary to make these desired changes." Psychological studies suggest that the therapeutic process is useful to many professions and to all human relationships.

Justice Douglas cites Professor Cox's article referring to labor arbitration as "cathartic." Catharsis is free expression, a simple release of feelings, sometimes accompanied by an emotional expression such as tears, anger, or shouting. Following catharsis, a person is calmer. Labor relations professionals will easily recognize the accuracy of Professor Cox's description.

A. The Problems for Which Arbitration Might Be Therapeutic

Justice Douglas's brief reference to therapeutic and cathartic values does not explain how arbitration produces these results or even what problems the process might redress. Before we explore the possible therapeutic effects of arbitration, we must identify its possible beneficiaries and the possible problems it might solve. Arbitration might address both individual and organizational problems.

The individual grievant may have demonstrable economic and psychological problems as a result of the employer's alleged contract breach. Deprived of contract benefits or even of a job, the aggrieved individual feels constrained by an internal labor relations system. A purely internal dispute-resolution system may inhibit expression and may not afford a remedy. The lack of a satisfactory procedure may depress the grievant, leaving him or her suffering from low self-esteem, resentment toward his employer, and stress. Although management might admit its error within the grievance procedure, in some cases relief—both economic and psychological—requires invoking the arbitration process.

The union representing the grievant might have concerns of its own. These are most likely to be economic or political, but might also be psychological. The union as an institution may have no remedy other than to demand relief from management. During the term of the collective bargaining agreement, the union may not lawfully use its economic power. Although a union may win some grievances through logical persuasion, at times management will not yield to the merits of the case. For example, the employer might deny a facially meritorious grievance to show support for its supervisors or for other "political" or tactical reasons. The union as an institution may as a result feel enervated and powerless. (Without an effective dispute-resolution mechanism, it may actually become so.)

Management officials also may experience psychological problems for which arbitration might be therapeutic. Although able to resist union claims through the grievance procedure, individual officials may feel that the employees do not respect them or their positions. Power does not necessarily mean comfort. In some cases, management officials might even experience guilt for their actions affecting the grievant.

B. How Arbitration Might Resolve These Problems

We might posit several ways in which arbitration might lessen or eliminate the psychological problems of the participants. For the individual grievant, arbitration provides the opportunity to explain to a neutral party the basis for the complaint. The arbitrator listens to the grievant and has the authority to grant relief. The arbitrator-grievant relationship may relieve the grievant's depression while enhancing self-esteem.

Arbitration might not relieve the grievant's resentment towards management. In an adversarial proceeding, both management and union may appeal less to reason than to partisanship. Similarly, arbitration is not a stress-free activity. Successful establishment of the arbitrator-grievant relationship may reduce the grievant's stress but may not eliminate it. Nevertheless, the employee may gain some comfort. Arbitrator and Professor Benjamin Aaron has suggested that the grievant's presence at the hearing watching management's witnesses subjected to "searching and often embarrassing cross-examination" may result in "a kind of catharsis that helps to make even eventual defeat acceptable" to the grievant.

Arbitration can also reduce the union's psychological concerns. By participating in arbitration, the union shows its power and ability to represent its members' interests. It also proves its power to force management to justify its actions before a third party. The union may or may not win the particular grievance. Win or lose, however, the opportunity to challenge management's decision before an outside authority improves the union's image and self-image. Moreover, by depriving the employer of unilateral authority, the union strengthens its hand in future negotiations. Finally, arbitration serves as an acceptable source of difficult decisions the union may not be able, politically, to make on its own. An arbitrator can tell an influential grievant that he or she is wrong a lot easier than an elected union leader can.

Similarly, management officials have the opportunity to confirm their positions by explaining them to the neutral arbitrator. Like union officials, managers may value the outsider's ability to decide issues that are politically difficult. A labor relations manager may be in no position to tell the company's chief executive that a change in policy violates the contract; an arbitrator is.

C. Evidence of Arbitration's Therapeutic Effects

Unfortunately it is virtually impossible to design an empirical test of arbitration's vaunted therapeutic effects. The problems are practical, not theoretical. . . . Fortunately, though, ample anecdotal evidence supports Douglas's assertions. Union representatives tell arbitrators that they appreciate the opportunity to present a case in arbitration even when they lose. The cathartic effect is sometimes clear. . . . Arbitration appears in some instances to soothe and relieve a grievant's pain.

The arbitration hearing . . . is a special time set aside for participants to tell their stories. Arbitrator William Simkin described the beneficial results:

> One of the fundamental purposes of an arbitration hearing is to let people get things off their chest, regardless of the decision. The arbitration proceeding is the opportunity for a third party, an outside party, to come in and act as a sort of father confessor to the parties, to let them get rid of their troubles, get them out in the open, and have a feeling of someone hearing their troubles. Because I believe so strongly that that is one of the fundamental purposes of arbitration, I don't think you ought to use any rules of evidence. You have to make up your own mind as to what is pertinent or not in the case. Lots of

> times I have let people talk for five minutes, when I know all the time that they were talking it had absolutely nothing to do with the case—just completely foreign to it. But there was a fellow testifying, either as a worker or a company representative, who had something that was important for him to get rid of. It was a good time for him to get rid of it.

The hearing serves as a form of psychodrama. Arbitration's ritualized ceremonies allow the actors to express important events from their work lives on a stage before an audience of their colleagues and an arbitrator.

D. The Limits of the Therapeutic Value of Arbitration

While a successful arbitration may be therapeutic and cathartic, that is not its primary goal. Labor and management agree to arbitration because it is a comparatively efficient and inexpensive method of resolving disputes with finality. An arbitration that does not resolve a dispute fails to achieve its primary goal, even if it helps the participants to feel better about themselves. The arbitrator is not a "labor relations physician." Arbitrators rule on the merits based on the terms of the parties' collective bargaining agreement and the existing body of arbitral common law, not on how the losing party will feel about the outcome. Thus arbitration's therapeutic effects are collateral by-products of the decision-making process.

The therapeutic values of arbitration may be important nonetheless. They explain, at least in part, why parties might choose to arbitrate even frivolous matters. As political organizations, unions must sometimes arbitrate cases they know they will lose. Although they might welcome arbitration's therapeutic value to the grievants, they may really want to have a third party deny the grievance. By doing so, they may avoid potential liability for breach of their duty of fair representation and yet will bear no blame for the result.

Arbitration's therapeutic values may also explain, at least in part, why the Supreme Court would order a reluctant party to arbitrate even a frivolous grievance. The Trilogy's principle of ordering the arbitration of even frivolous matters runs contrary to the traditional equity maxim that a court should not order parties to perform a futile act. If a grievance is frivolous, arbitrating the case would be a waste of time but for other benefits such as a therapeutic effect. The Court's decision might rest on any of several grounds. First, the Court might have believed that it was carrying out the intentions of the parties to the agreement, an appropriate goal in a contract case. The parties contracted for arbitration of all arbitrable matters, not merely the meritorious ones. Second, the Court might simply have decided as a matter of federal labor policy that arbitration is preferable to litigation or self-help measures, even if that policy obliges a court to order a futile act. Third, the Court might have recognized that courts are institutionally incapable of determining whether a grievance is frivolous. The risk of "false positives" is too high, especially when the parties have provided an alternative system for that decision. Finally, the Court might have favored arbitration because of judicial economy and institutional capabilities. When parties have their own system for resolving disputes, they should use it without unnecessary delay. This keeps the courts free for business only the courts can do.

IV. ARBITRATION'S THERAPEUTIC ELEMENTS

What aspects of arbitration might make it therapeutic? We can identify a series of the characteristics of the arbitration model that enhance its therapeutic value.

A. An Employee-Initiated Process

Even before the arbitration process begins, the parties' grievance procedure may offer therapeutic values. An aggrieved employee begins the grievance procedure by contacting a supervisor to complain about a contract violation. A union steward may or may not participate at this stage. This first step of the grievance procedure might be oral, although some collective bargaining agreements require a written grievance. By filing a grievance, the employee can command the attention of the supervisor. The employee exerts some control over his or her work life, even without getting immediate relief.

In the psychological counseling context, a client usually seeks help for a problem by contacting a therapist. Some therapists may require the client to write out the problem on a form, much like a grievance form. . . . By beginning the healing process, the client feels a sense of relief and hope even before meeting the counselor. It is helpful to know that something is happening. In both the counseling and the grievance situations, beginning the process is therapeutic in itself. That is so even if the party contacted cannot or will not solve the underlying problem. Of course, the grievant's supervisor does not act as a therapist. The therapeutic value of the grievance stage flows from the process of filing a grievance, not from the conduct of the supervisor.

Typically, the union, not the individual grievant, decides whether to arbitrate an unresolved dispute. The question whether to arbitrate arises, however, only because the aggrieved employee filed the grievance in the first instance. Using the grievance process, the employee moves from helplessness to seeking a remedy for an economic concern.

Clients seek therapy when faced with unresolved problems affecting their daily lives. Unions seek arbitration for the same reason. A grievance festers in the workplace unless resolved in negotiation or arbitration. It may affect the morale of union members. The union must prove to its members that it will press their concerns even at the risk of losing.

The ability to file a grievance and to begin a counseling relationship gives the grievant and the client a sense of power and personal value. They can force others to pay attention to their problems. They learn how to call upon others for help. Thus, even if a grievance never goes to arbitration, the grievant gets attention. Even if therapy does not assuage all problems, the client learns how to seek help. Processing and arbitrating grievances also gives the union a chance to promote the best interests of the persons it represents.

B. Arbitrator Selection

Under the typical arbitration model, the union and the employer jointly select the arbitrator. Control over selection of the decision-maker may have a positive therapeutic influence. Although the grievant usually does not participate in the selection, his or her representative does. Even indirect participation will enhance the grievant's trust in the arbitrator. For the union, of course, an equal say in selecting the adjudicator empowers the organization. . . .

Parties select an arbitrator based on prior experiences, on recommendations, and on their review of published awards and other data. These are good sources upon which to base a choice. Both parties are likely to seek someone who understands the therapeutic potential of the arbitration process, although they might not use those terms. . . . Arbitrator Richard Bloch recently noted the impact of the arbitrator's conduct of the hearing on the arbitrator's acceptability. The same may be true for other aspects of an arbitrator's conduct affecting therapeutic values. References within the industrial relations community will report whether the arbitrator "runs a good hearing" by controlling the proceeding. For therapeutic reasons among others, parties want a fair, well-managed proceeding.

Similarly, a client normally selects a therapist based on prior experience and on recommendations from doctors or friends. This client information may be incomplete or inaccurate, but even so the client believes the person selected will fulfill the therapeutic function. Choosing one's own therapist is an important step toward recovery. The selection processes for therapists and arbitrators raise the positive expectations of clients and grievants and their unions. Someone the affected persons helped select — either directly or indirectly — will listen to the problem and work toward a resolution. That alone bodes well for the processes to come and their curative effects.

C. The Site of the Arbitration Hearing

Parties normally hold arbitration hearings in hotel meeting rooms or conference rooms at the workplace. A neutral, non-threatening location may enhance the therapeutic values of the process to the participants. Were the hearing held in a courtroom, for example, the formal surroundings might inhibit witnesses and thus dampen the potential therapeutic effect. A hearing held in the employer's office could be a chilling experience for employees. An unfriendly environment would likely inhibit the testimony of the grievant and co-workers, perhaps keeping them from frankly stating their recollections and expressing their views and emotions. Certain places promote candor; others do not. The arbitrator is independent of the parties, although employed by both. A neutral site reflects this independence.

The setting for a client-therapist relationship is similarly important. The therapist must provide an environment suitable for exploring problems. The decor and arrangement of furniture in a therapist's office is an aspect of proxemics, the study of environmental or personal space. The setting varies depending on the therapist's orientation. The therapist, however, will choose a setting to enhance the therapeutic effect. Most psychologists believe that an informal setting relaxes the client and encourages exchange of necessary information. Others suggest that the setting should be nondescript, allowing the client to focus attention inward.

In a counseling relationship, the distance a therapist sits from the client influences the therapeutic effect. A client will feel discomfort if the therapist sits too near or too far. A space of three to four feet best promotes communication. This distance diminishes anxiety and allows the client to focus on internal rather than external issues.

Most psychologists try to design a therapeutic environment that is mildly stimulating. This allows the client to be alert but able to focus on issues without distraction. To benefit from counseling, the client must feel comfortable in the surroundings. Distracting furniture, colors and pictures might inhibit the interchange between therapist and client.

Arbitration requires a greater degree of formality. Sitting around on soft chairs and couches discussing the workplace problem would not encourage the orderly collection of the data needed to adjudicate the dispute. A little formality silently conveys the importance of the proceeding. That, in turn, encourages truthfulness and mutual respect. The setting of the hearing also affects the legitimacy of the process. The arbitrator's decision will affect the employees' work lives. A completely informal environment might suggest that the arbitrator will not give the decision the proper attention.

The arrangement of tables in the arbitration hearing room may be important. The arbitrator sits on the same level as the parties, but at a separate table. This signifies a suitable detachment without the distancing effect of a judge's raised bench. Witnesses sit directly before or beside the arbitrator, allowing eye contact and an evaluation of demeanor. Some arbitrators insist on a U-shaped series of connected tables. Space between the arbitrator and the parties increases formality without helping fact-gathering.

The setting of arbitration and counseling is important to the therapeutic mix. Both are informal, although arrangement of the arbitration hearing room must emphasize efficient data collection over good feelings. Grievants and clients must feel comfortable in their respective settings. Neither procedure should tolerate artificial barriers to communication.

D. An Informal Hearing Not Bound by the Rules of Evidence

Arbitration hearings are orderly but informal. The atmosphere of informality at the hearing enhances the therapeutic value of the proceeding by encouraging those concerned to speak freely. The arbitrator wears business clothes, not a robe. Informal discussion may precede the hearing. The parties and the arbitrator relate to one another. The arbitrator normally introduces himself or herself to the parties and meets the grievant before the hearing.

On the other hand, the arbitration process demands some formality to demonstrate its importance, its seriousness, its distinctiveness, and its legitimacy. Thus the arbitrator does not wear casual clothes, follows a ritualized procedure, sits apart, and addresses (and is addressed by) the advocates and witnesses by honorific titles ("Arbitrator Jones," "Ms. Smith").

A similar situation occurs in counseling, most particularly in family therapy which usually begins with a social stage of mutual introductions. The therapist tries to make the family feel comfortable in the office while maintaining a professional distance.

During the arbitration hearing, the arbitrator gets the information needed to resolve the dispute. Through testimony and documents, the parties inform the arbitrator about their work relationship and the facts of the grievance. Parties can cross-examine witnesses to test their testimony and elicit additional information for the arbitrator. The arbitrator normally seeks to reduce conflict between the parties at the hearing because conflict may interfere with data collection.

A particularly important facet of arbitration is the opportunity for participants to explain events directly to an outside authority. The rules of the arbitration hearing foster the collection of this unfiltered data. Representatives of the parties may try to interfere with this process by lodging evidentiary objections. The experienced arbitrator will not permit objections to thwart introduction of this pertinent evidence.

Often one party uses a lawyer while the other does not. If evidentiary rules applied, the party lacking a lawyer would be at a great disadvantage in presenting its story to the arbitrator. Some traditional court rules of evidence designed to keep prejudicial information from the jury have no place in arbitration. An arbitrator is not an untutored juror. The skilled arbitrator, like a judge, can give evidence the weight it deserves.

It may be therapeutic for the grievant to tell the story through his or her testimony. For best results, the grievant must perceive the hearing as more than a continuation of the employer-controlled grievance procedure. Evidentiary rules foreign to the participating workers should not inhibit the grievant's ability to tell the "truth" as he or she sees it. Similarly, a therapist encourages the client to share information that will help the therapist better understand the client, from the client's frame of reference. No procedural "rules" inhibit this information transmittal, although some may help it. For example, therapy usually occurs at a set time and place. Moreover, confidentiality is an underlying principle of psychotherapy which encourages full and frank communication.

One therapeutic advantage of an arbitration hearing is that the grievant expects a prompt resolution of the problem. The hearing itself normally lasts only a few hours. Either by contract or appointing agency rule, the arbitrator's award is normally due in 30 or 60 days. Arbitration is thus more like time-limited or brief psychotherapy than Freudian psychoanalysis, which often takes years. A client facing a few therapeutic sessions will expect improvement. Brief psychotherapy focuses on specific symptoms or identified issues, much as arbitration focuses on particular alleged contract breaches rather than the whole bargaining relationship.

One essential step in developing a brief psychotherapeutic relationship is fostering the client's emotional safety. Clients need to know the therapist will respect rather than ridicule them. Similarly, in arbitration grievants must feel their concerns are important to the arbitrator. In contrast to their status at work, grievants in arbitration have special recognition. They deserve the attention of all the people gathered in the arbitration hearing room, especially that of the arbitrator. In brief therapy, the client often feels that the simple act of talking about the problem can be helpful, even if the discussion is only superficial. Much the same occurs in arbitration.

Within the limits of an orderly proceeding, informality is an essential therapeutic aspect of labor arbitration. Beyond the necessary order, formality will likely decrease the proceeding's therapeutic value. This "ordered informality" also fosters the arbitrator's information-gathering because witnesses find it easy to convey their evidence and opinions. That in turn helps the arbitrator to complete the assigned task of resolving the dispute on the merits. Similarly, informality engenders trust and openness within the client-therapist relationship. It helps the client to speak freely and allows the therapist to understand the nature of the client's problem. Only then, with the therapist's help, can the client begin to resolve the problem.

E. The Grievant-Arbitrator Relationship

Of the many possible therapeutic aspects of arbitration, the most important to the individual grievant is the potential relationship with the arbitrator. The grievant's initial and final perceptions of the arbitrator will critically affect therapeutic values. The therapeutic key is the creation of a relationship between the grievant and the arbitrator within which the grievant trusts the arbitrator. The arbitrator's personal characteristics—expertise, openness, and the ability to control the proceeding, among others—foster this trust. The grievant-arbitrator relationship also resembles the relationships developed in group and family therapy.

During the grievance procedure, the grievant could not help but notice that management controlled the process. After all, management could, and did, deny the grievant's claim. At the arbitration hearing, in contrast, the grievant finds a new power, the arbitrator. The grievant sees how the arbitrator controls the proceeding. The arbitrator's control places the union and the employer on the same plane, thus raising the grievant's relative position. (For the same reason, arbitration enhances the union's position in the eyes of its members and in the eyes of the company.) . . .

Carl Rogers explains that a therapist's personal characteristics and attitudes are essential to the development of the therapeutic relationship. The therapist must show "congruence,"

(Rogers's term for genuineness); "unconditional positive regard;" and "empathy." These aspects of a client-therapist relationship contribute to the therapeutic effect.

A labor arbitrator who exhibits the same characteristics also will promote therapeutic values. This does not require partisanship favoring the grievant. A therapist's focus in individual therapy is the client's well-being, but the arbitrator's primary concern is the relationship between the employer and the union. At times the arbitrator must sacrifice a full therapeutic effect for the grievant to maintain the stability of the collective relationship. The arbitrator can listen and empathize without showing bias toward the grievant. Therapeutic effect does not depend upon partiality. It is enough for the arbitrator to treat the grievant with respect and listen to his or her story. . . .

Research by psychologists on group process suggests that the group leader's personal characteristics can determine the effectiveness of the process. A series of leadership elements are important to therapeutic effectiveness: Courage, Willingness to Model, Presence, Goodwill and Caring, Belief in Group Process, Openness, Nondefensiveness in Coping with Attacks, Personal Power, Stamina, Willingness to Seek New Experiences, Self-Awareness, Sense of Humor, and Inventiveness.

The best arbitrators exhibit the same characteristics. They face difficult cases courageously, without concern for personal self-interest. They model appropriate behavior for the parties and their representatives. They involve themselves in the hearing and exhibit respect and caring for the parties. They believe in the process, approach the hearing without preconceptions, and remain open to new ideas and different lifestyles. Finally, they put aside personalities in dealing with the hearing's inevitable tensions.

Moreover, arbitrators are in control throughout the hearing, directing the proceeding in an efficient and productive manner. Arbitration can be exhausting, and arbitrators need stamina. Venturing to small towns and strange plants to hear disputes, arbitrators must be willing to experience the unknown. Throughout the proceeding, arbitrators must respect arbitration's goals while seeking the information necessary for a fair and informed decision. Arbitrators must maintain a sense of humor to keep the process in perspective. Successful arbitrators must creatively respond to unforeseen events at the hearing. They must also creatively draft an opinion that will meet the parties' needs while staying true to the contract. . . .

F. The Opportunity to Address the Arbitrator

At the close of the hearing, many arbitrators offer grievants a chance to speak freely on the record. This . . . hearing fulfills the grievant's expectation about the relationship with the arbitrator. By offering the grievant a chance to speak, the arbitrator shows concern, empathy, and understanding of the grievant's turmoil and discomfort.

This may be the most therapeutic moment of the arbitration hearing. Unencumbered by management or the union, the employee can speak freely. Sometimes the statements are very revealing. They may convince the arbitrator that a grievant cannot return to the workplace. Other employees show contrition and rehabilitation. Even if grievants say nothing, they are likely to appreciate the offer.

Carl Rogers stresses the importance of the client's expression of feelings. The therapist elicits these expressions by showing an understanding of the individual's problem and a willingness to listen. Other therapeutic models insist that simply releasing unexpressed feelings is not enough to produce a therapeutic effect. There must be a cognitive element present, a knowing appreciation, and an understanding of the problem. A grievant who accepts the arbitrator's offer of a chance to speak freely may accomplish both exposition and understanding. On the other hand, the grievant may only feel a cathartic release. In either case, the experience is psychologically helpful. . . .

The entire therapist-client session is a direct conversation between the two persons. In contrast, only a small part of the arbitration hearing involves a direct interchange between arbitrator and grievant. In this brief period, however, the arbitrator can learn a lot about the grievant. In addition, the interchange reinforces the grievant's perception of the process as fair, open, and curative.

G. The Opinion

The arbitration process is not over until the arbitrator issues an opinion explaining the basis of the award. The opinion explains a loss to the losing party. Thus, the arbitrator should write the opinion in language the affected employees can understand. Employees may not agree with the outcome, but a well-written opinion can convince them that the arbitrator at least heard and understood their positions. . . .

The arbitration opinion completes the therapeutic process. Even when the arbitrator denies the grievance, the grievant at least learns the reasons for the loss. The careful arbitration opinion therefore reinforces arbitration's therapeutic values. . . .

V. THERAPEUTIC VALUES AND ARBITRAL LEGITIMACY

. . . We have tried to suggest how and when arbitration might be therapeutic. Therapy, however, is only one of several arbitral values, others of which deserve at least as much protection. The arbitrator should therefore try to accomplish the therapeutic goals of arbitration without losing sight of the other goals. A purely therapeutic approach would not be desirable, nor would it fulfill the parties' needs and expectations. To the contrary, it could destroy the very legitimacy essential to arbitration's success. . . . Here are a few examples.

A. Insufficient Formality

An unstructured, completely informal proceeding might be the best way to solve an individual's psychological problems. Nevertheless, it might destroy the parties' respect for arbitration as a quasi-judicial process. Arbitration requires more than a helpful chat with a counselor about a workplace problem. Arbitrators who are too informal and too familiar with the parties may raise significant doubts about the legitimacy of their awards. . . . Because of the importance of the results to the participants, arbitration should have sufficient formality to provide the dignity and respect appropriate to the issue.

B. Insufficient Finality

The ultimate result of the arbitration process must be a binding resolution of the dispute. A purely therapeutic model might leave some substantive issues for the parties to resolve after the arbitrator's intervention is complete. A psychologist, for example, will try to encourage the client to develop remedial strategies to deal with difficult situations. Therapy teaches clients to exercise self-control. Although arbitrators commonly leave the back pay calculation to the parties for final resolution, they must address the merits with finality. Parties also may learn something about problem solving that would be useful in the future. This might be a collateral benefit of the process, but it is not its central focus. The most important task for the arbitrator is to resolve the dispute with finality.

C. Failure to Exercise Judgment

A therapist might avoid telling a client bluntly that he or she is wrong. An arbitrator may have to do so in an opinion. Failing to exercise judgment would be neither honest nor "legitimate." Judgment is what the parties wanted when they agreed to arbitration and selected a neutral to judge the dispute.

D. Lack of Impartiality

A therapist might try to assure a client that he or she is on the client's side. The arbitrator, on the other hand, must maintain strict impartiality. The arbitrator's relationship with the grievant must not be misread as favoring the union's case. It is a difficult line for the arbitrator to walk between openness and taking sides.

E. Deciding the Particular Dispute

A therapist might decide to extend and expand treatment to help the client resolve many outstanding issues. By comparison, an arbitrator should seek a speedy resolution of the submitted dispute. A therapist offers advice; an arbitrator must decide the issue. A therapist often operates on subjective feelings; an arbitrator should strive to decide a case on the record. Thus, while there are parallels between arbitration and therapy, there are differences in purpose and process. . . .

VI. THREATS TO THERAPEUTIC VALUES

Since the Trilogy, changes in the legal environment have tested arbitration's therapeutic values. Statutory changes have threatened to make labor arbitration more court-like. Many parties now take statutory disputes to arbitration rather than to court because it is cheaper and more efficient. The growth of public-sector arbitration has aggravated the problem because government employee cases normally involve laws and regulations. The infusion of legal terms and concepts into labor arbitration has made the process more like a court. These developments jeopardize arbitration's therapeutic values.

A dispute based on the reading of a statute is likely to be more formal than one that requires interpreting a privately-written contract. A swarm of lawyers descending on the local Holiday Inn conference room for an arbitration hearing brings with it legalisms and court-like trappings. This is especially true if the attorneys are unschooled in the ways of alternative dispute resolution. Federal sector arbitration, burdened by statutory review procedures, can be excessively formal.

Fortunately, most arbitration cases remain unaffected by external law. There is no sign that arbitrators have changed the way they conduct hearings in a typical case. A just cause determination in a simple discharge case, a seniority case involving bumping rights in a layoff, a subcontracting case involving unit work — none of these requires much formality. The essential therapeutic nature can remain strong. Statutes need not require abandoning arbitration's therapeutic values.

VII. CONCLUSION

There is a solid basis for Justice Douglas's assumption that labor arbitration may be therapeutic. Many elements of the arbitration process resemble traditional psychotherapy. Of course, many aspects of psychotherapy have no role in arbitration. Parties apparently find arbitration valuable even when they lose. If they did not find it useful, labor and management would not include an arbitration clause in virtually every collective bargaining agreement.

Arbitrators may not see themselves as performing a therapeutic function. It is clearly not their primary duty. They are "creature(s) of the parties" appointed to interpret and apply the collective bargaining agreement, not labor relations physicians. The better arbitrators, however, do understand their role is multi-faceted. They must resolve particular disputes. They also have important obligations to the continuing relationship between labor and management. Finally, though, they also fulfill Justice Douglas's promise in the Trilogy by serving a therapeutic function.

Labor and management should worry about the developments in labor arbitration that jeopardize its therapeutic values. Arbitration can accommodate a broad spectrum of issues, but it cannot maintain its therapeutic nature if court-like formality replaces ordered informality, if the rules of evidence strictly govern hearings, or if the employees cannot tell their stories to an informed neutral. . . . Excessive legalism endangers labor arbitration's procedural values. . . . If we are to maintain arbitration's positive role in the workplace, we must protect those elements that help employees reach a better understanding of themselves and their behaviors.

E. Arbitration in the Securities Industry

1. Comments and Questions

a. The National Association of Securities Dealers (NASD) report that follows presents a picture of securities arbitration, both as presently practiced and with improvements recommended by the NASD Taskforce. (The report of this blue ribbon panel is often referred to as the Ruder Report, after its distinguished chair, former SEC Chair David Ruder.)

b. Many of the arbitration issues presented in Chapter 11 arose in the securities context, so it is important to consider the working of securities arbitration.

c. While the NASD recommendations focus on disputes between securities dealers and customers, consider whether the same ideas should be adopted for labor, commercial, and other arbitration.

2. National Association of Securities Dealers, Report of the Arbitration Policy Taskforce (1996)

SUMMARY OF RECOMMENDATIONS

Although the Task Force found securities arbitration to be a relatively efficient, fair, and less costly forum for resolution of disputes involving public investors, member firms, and firm employees, it believes that many areas for improvement of the system exist. . . . In summary form, the following are the most significant of our recommendations:

1. The securities industry should be permitted to continue to include predispute arbitration agreements in customer contracts, but disclosure should be improved.
2. The NASD six year eligibility rule should be suspended for three years during which time recommended procedures for early resolution of statute of limitations issues should be firmly applied.
3. Parties should be prohibited from bringing actions in court raising procedural arbitrability issues before an arbitration award has been entered.
4. Punitive damages should be permitted in all jurisdictions (determined by the investor's domicile) where available in a judicial forum for the same types of claims, subject to a cap of the lesser of two times compensatory damages or $750,000.
5. The NASD should expand its voluntary mediation program and institute a two year pilot program in early neutral evaluation.
6. The NASD should continue to offer an arbitration system with three tiers: simplified, standard, and complex, and the ceiling for the simplified procedures should be raised from $10,000 to $30,000.
7. Automatic production of essential documents should be required for all parties, and arbitrators should play a much greater role in directing discovery and resolving discovery disputes.
8. Arbitrator selection, quality, training, and performance should be improved by various means, including adoption of a list selection method, earlier appointment of arbitrators, enhancement of arbitrator training, and increased compensation.
9. Employment disputes, including statutory discrimination claims, should continue to be subject to arbitration, but with the enhancements recommended for customer disputes.
10. NASD pilot rules for injunctions in member-member disputes are beneficial and should be closely monitored.
11. Non-lawyers should be allowed to continue representing parties in arbitration, subject to certification; the NASD should conduct a study to examine whether to continue to permit non-lawyer representation.
12. The staffing and budget of the NASD Arbitration and Mediation Department should be increased.
13. The NASD should provide budgetary and operational autonomy for the arbitration system, which should be administered either as a unit of the newly created NASD regulation subsidiary or as a separate unit reporting directly to the NASD parent holding company.
14. Procedures for monitoring the implementation of the recommendations of this Report should be established by the NASD.

THE NASD ARBITRATION PROCESS: CURRENTLY AND UNDER THE TASK FORCE'S RECOMMENDATIONS

I. THE CURRENT NASD ARBITRATION PROCESS

Most customers are first exposed to the concept of securities arbitration when they are asked to sign a predispute arbitration clause in a contract with a broker-dealer. If a dispute subsequently arises between the customer and the broker-dealer, the customer is obligated to submit the dispute to arbitration.

The predispute arbitration agreement may give the customer a choice of which arbitration forum will hear the dispute. In almost all cases, this choice will be limited to two or more of the SRO [self-regulatory organizations] arbitration forums. The American Arbitration Association (AAA) is not frequently included as an option. If the customer does not choose which forum will hear the dispute, the broker-dealer may select the forum.

If the investor chooses to bring the claim to NASD arbitration, he or she will initiate arbitration proceedings by filing a statement of claim with the NASD Director of Arbitration and Mediation, describing the controversy in dispute and the remedies sought. The party initiating an arbitration is referred to as the "claimant." The claimant must transmit a filing fee based on the amount in controversy and a deposit to cover the cost of hearings.

As a threshold consideration, the claimant must state a claim that arises out of his or her business relationship with the broker-dealer. The claim must also involve member broker-dealers or persons associated with them, typically firm employees.

A claim may not be eligible for NASD arbitration if more than six years have elapsed since the occurrence or event giving rise to the dispute. A claim's "eligibility," as it is referred to, may be decided in some cases by the Director of Arbitration. In many cases, however, the eligibility of a claim for arbitration is decided by the arbitrators later in the process. Often, determining whether six years have passed since the events giving rise to the claim requires consideration of relevant facts. If a customer alleges that a broker-dealer engaged in unauthorized trading, for example, the customer's claim may not accrue until the customer learned of the unauthorized trading, rather than on the date of the transaction.

The Director of Arbitration serves the statement of claim on the party or parties against whom the claim has been brought, known as the respondent(s). In most cases the respondent is a broker-dealer, an employee of a broker-dealer, or both. The respondent then has twenty days to answer the claim, setting forth any defenses and facts that it will rely upon at the arbitration hearing. The respondent may also bring its own claim against the claimant, known as a counterclaim, or it may bring a claim against a third party to be heard in the same arbitration, known as a cross-claim.

At this stage, the case may proceed in one of three ways, depending on the amount of damages alleged. If the claim is for $10,000 or less, the matter will be resolved through special "simplified arbitration" procedures. Under simplified arbitration, a single arbitrator is appointed to decide the case, usually based solely upon the parties' claims and answers, along with any attached exhibits. Under these rules, the customer may request that the arbitrator hold a hearing, but the broker-dealer may not.

Alternatively, the case may proceed under newly established rules for large and complex cases if the amount in controversy is at least $1 million, or if the parties mutually agree to submit the claim under these enhanced and more flexible procedures. These rules incorporate elements of civil litigation not usually available in SRO arbitration, such as permitting arbitrators to rule on motions that would dismiss all or part of the case before a merits hearing is held ("dispositive" motions). Under these rules, upon the parties' mutual agreement, the arbitrators' final decision may be accompanied by a statement of reasons.

Unless the case is handled under the simplified arbitration procedures or the large and complex case rules, the claim will proceed under the standard procedures. After the answer has been filed, the parties may request documents and other information relevant to the issue, a process known generally as "discovery." Any party may request information or documents from another party, and the party from whom discovery is sought must either respond to the request or raise appropriate objections within thirty days. Depending on what stage in the proceedings an objection has been raised, the dispute will be resolved either by the Director of Arbitration or an arbitrator who has been selected to hear the case.

Sometime after the answer has been filed, and usually well after discovery is underway, the process of selecting arbitrators and setting hearing dates will begin. Potential arbitrators are designated as either "public arbitrators" or "industry arbitrators." An industry arbitrator is one who has been associated with a broker-dealer within the previous three years, or is retired from such a position. Attorneys, accountants, and other professionals who have devoted 20 percent or more of their professional time to providing services to members of the securities industry within the previous two years also are considered industry arbitrators. A public arbitrator is one who is not an industry arbitrator. Public arbitrators come from a wide variety of backgrounds, and may or may not have significant experience with the securities industry.

All arbitration panels in standard arbitration involving public customers are comprised of two public arbitrators and one industry arbitrator. The chair of the panel is, in almost all cases, one of the public arbitrators. If the amount in controversy does not exceed $30,000, a single public arbitrator may be appointed to hear the case, unless either one of the parties requests a panel of three. Arbitrators are initially chosen by the Director of Arbitration, who provides the parties with the names of the arbitrators and a statement of their backgrounds. This statement includes the arbitrator's professional background and a list of NASD arbitration panels on which the arbitrator has served. The arbitrators also are required to disclose any financial or personal interest in the controversy that may bias their judgment.

After these names have been provided, parties may challenge selected arbitrators "for cause." The moving party must demonstrate to the Director of Arbitration that the selected arbitrator has some conflict of interest or is otherwise ineligible to participate (e.g., because an arbitrator considered "public" should actually have been classified as "industry"). If the Director agrees, the arbitrator will be replaced by another arbitrator. There is no limit to the number of cause challenges a party can make. In addition, each party may remove one of the arbitrators from the list without providing any reason. This is known as a "peremptory challenge." If an arbitrator is removed through a peremptory challenge, another arbitrator is appointed to that position by the Director of Arbitration.

Once an arbitration panel has been selected, the Director of Arbitration schedules one or more dates for a hearing. At some point prior to the first hearing, the Director of Arbitration may schedule a pre-hearing conference. The purpose of a pre-hearing conference is to resolve discovery disputes, identify witnesses and documents that will be presented at the hearing, decide upon stipulations, and narrow the scope of disputed facts.

The arbitration hearing itself may last one day, or it may last as long as several weeks, or indeed months in very complex cases. If a hearing extends beyond more than a few days, hearing sessions are often scheduled on non-consecutive days, sometimes stretching over several months. Sessions are typically held at NASD offices, conference facilities, or the offices of one of the arbitrators. The hearings are tape-recorded.

The arbitration hearing begins with an introduction of the arbitrators, a statement of any disclosures made by the arbitrators relating to their interest in the case, and a final oral confirmation of the parties' acceptance of the panel's composition. Parties may be represented at all stages by legal counsel or any other representative, and any such representations are also noted at this time. The arbitrators then take an oath of impartiality and fairness.

The proceedings begin with an opening statement by each party, starting with the claimant. After these statements, the claimant presents his or her case through witnesses and documentary evidence. The arbitration hearing is not subject to the same rules of evidence that govern courtroom proceedings, and the parties may present whatever evidence the arbitrators consider relevant. Witnesses are sworn before testifying, and are subject to cross-examination by adverse parties. Arbitrators also may ask questions of the witnesses. After the claimant has finished his or her presentation of witnesses and evidence, the respondent may do the same. Each side then presents a closing argument summarizing what has been proven.

After the closing arguments, the arbitrators deliberate in a closed session and attempt to reach consensus on a final decision, known as the "award." All decisions are made by majority vote. As arbitration is an equitable proceeding, arbitrators are not bound by the same statutes and case law that would be applied in a court. Although arbitrators may not disregard controlling case law and should make an effort to conform their decision to its general principles, they may ultimately decide the case based on whatever equitable principles they consider appropriate.

Arbitrators are not required to provide reasons or a written opinion explaining the award. The arbitrators provide only a written report of the final award, specifying the amount awarded to the prevailing party and any non-monetary relief. The award is final and is only subject to review in a court of law for very narrowly defined reasons, such as fraud, arbitrator partiality, or manifest disregard for the law. Arbitration of the dispute also precludes subsequent litigation over the same dispute or issues decided in the resolution of the claim.

As a final matter, it is important to note that the process described here may be interrupted at various stages by "collateral" litigation in civil courts. Collateral litigation occurs when one of the parties goes to court — prior to the entry of an award, for example — to challenge the authority of the arbitral panel to hear the dispute. One of the parties, for example, may go to court to challenge the eligibility of a claim for arbitration, or ask the court to declare that the arbitral panel has no power to award punitive damages. Depending on several different factors, including the state in which the collateral litigation is brought and the terms of the predispute arbitration clause signed by the customer, these challenges will be met with varying degrees of success.

II. THE NASD ARBITRATION PROCESS UNDER THE TASK FORCE'S RECOMMENDATIONS

As under the present system, most customers' first exposure to the securities arbitration process would be a predispute arbitration clause contained in an account agreement with a member firm. This clause would contain certain uniform provisions and disclosures relating to the arbitration process. The NASD also would enforce its rules prohibiting member firms from imposing certain limitations on the types of claims and awards that a party may seek in arbitration.

The filing of a claim would proceed as it does under the present system. Claims would proceed under one of three different sets of rules according to the amount in controversy: simplified, standard, or complex.

Punitive Damages

Under any set of rules, parties could seek awards of punitive damages for egregious behavior, subject to a cap of the lesser of two times compensatory damages or $750,000. Punitive damages would be permitted for any claim for which the investor's home state would allow an award of punitive damages in court. Any award including a grant of punitive damages would specify what portion of the award is for compensatory damages and what portion is for punitive damages. At the request of a party against whom punitive damages had been awarded, the arbitrators would prepare a written document describing the conduct that gave rise to the award.

Simplified Arbitration

All claims alleging damages of $30,000 or less, including amounts claimed for punitive damages, would be heard under the simplified arbitration procedures (an increase from the current ceiling of $10,000). Claims in this category would be heard by a single arbitrator, as with the present rules. The parties would select the arbitrator within 45 days of the respondent's answer, according to the list selection process described below. As further described below, parties would have an early opportunity to seek dismissal of claims on the basis of statutes of limitations.

As under the current simplified procedures, the investor could request a hearing, or the arbitrator could order one. If no hearing is held, the arbitrator would decide the claim based on the parties' written pleadings, and any exhibits attached to the claim and response.

Discovery would be discouraged in simplified arbitration. The documents upon which the arbitrator would rely in reaching a decision would include the pleadings and exhibits. Unless the parties agree to voluntary discovery, discovery would be permitted only at the discretion of the arbitrator, who would review proposed document requests and their justification. The arbitrator would look for guidance, in exercising his or her discretion, to the lists prepared for early automatic document production in the standard arbitration process. Depositions would not be permitted.

Under the simplified rules, parties could voluntarily submit the case to either mediation or early neutral evaluation. No cases in the simplified category would be subject to mandatory early neutral evaluation (ENE) during the pilot period, described below.

Standard Arbitration

The standard arbitration procedures would include all claims in excess of $30,000, except cases in which the parties have either chosen the complex rules or agreed to have the case heard under the simplified arbitration procedures. For claims not exceeding $50,000, a single public arbitrator would be selected by the parties to hear the case, unless one of the parties requested a panel of three arbitrators.

At an early stage in the proceedings, parties would be encouraged to submit to voluntary, non-binding mediation of the dispute. In addition, during a two year pilot period, 25 percent of all claims in excess of $30,000 would be submitted to an alternative dispute resolution mechanism known as early neutral evaluation. In ENE, a skilled evaluator with experience in the subject matter of the dispute provides a candid assessment of the merits of each party's position after reading the pleadings and listening to brief presentations by the parties. Both mediation and ENE would be entirely confidential; nothing that the parties disclose in these sessions could be used in subsequent arbitral or court proceedings. Arbitrators would be authorized to impose sanctions against any party or counsel who violates the confidentiality rule.

Parties would select the arbitration panel early in the arbitration process, usually within 45 days of the service of the respondent's answer. In general, the arbitration panel, and especially the panel chair, would play a much greater role in managing the pre-hearing arbitration process, for example, by resolving statute of limitations motions and overseeing the discovery process.

The parties would select arbitrators according to a "list selection process" similar to one employed by the AAA. Under this system, the NASD would send each party three lists of names: (1) a list of public arbitrators; (2) a list of public arbitrators qualified to serve as panel chairs; and (3) a list of industry arbitrators. Each party would then strike from the lists any arbitrator that it did not want to appear on the panel, and rank any remaining arbitrators by order of preference. If mutually agreeable arbitrators were not selected in each category, new lists would be provided for each category in which agreement was not reached. This process would continue for no more than three rounds until an industry and two public arbitrators, one qualified to serve as a panel chair, had been selected. In the unlikely event that positions on the arbitration panel remained vacant after three rounds, the NASD would appoint any remaining arbitrators. Arbitrators selected by the NASD could be challenged only for cause.

Claims filed in NASD arbitration would no longer be subject to the six year eligibility rule described above. Instead, any claim, counterclaim, or cross-claim would have to satisfy the statute of limitations applicable to that claim. All parties would have an opportunity to file dispositive motions seeking to dismiss claims on statute of limitations grounds. The arbitrators would decide these motions by applying the relevant state or federal statute of limitations, as it would be applied in court. Arbitrators would resolve these motions at the earliest opportunity, in most cases before the hearing on the merits. If necessary, arbitrators could hold hearings to resolve any questions of fact related to the motion. Arbitrators would provide written reasons for their decision to grant or deny a motion to dismiss on statute of limitations grounds, and would include reference to the law on which they relied in reaching a determination.

In addition to motions to dismiss on statute of limitations grounds, parties could file other dispositive motions, which also would be resolved by the arbitration panel prior to the hearing, when possible.

The cornerstone of the discovery process in cases proceeding under the standard rules would be a system of early automatic document production. Under this system, the parties would exchange certain essential documents early in the arbitration process, normally within 45 days of the filing of the respondent's answer. The particular documents to be exchanged would depend on the types of claims and defenses asserted in the case. To facilitate early automatic document production, each party asserting a claim or defense would be required to indicate on a form which types of claims or defenses were being raised.

Arbitrators would retain the discretion to authorize document requests beyond the initial production requirements, as well as information requests, if the parties could not agree to additional discovery on a voluntary basis. Additional document and information requests would be permitted upon a showing that the additional documents and information are reasonably likely to be relevant and important to the resolution of particular issues in dispute. Information requests would be permitted only for specific factual information not available in documents produced by the parties, and would be limited to a set number unless the arbitrators set aside the limit. In addition, depositions would be permitted only in exigent circumstances, such as to preserve the testimony of a witness who is dying.

Discovery disputes would be resolved by the arbitrators as expeditiously as possible. As described above, arbitrators will be selected and appointed much earlier in the process for this purpose. Arbitrators would be encouraged to exercise their broad powers to sanction misconduct in the discovery process. In cases of egregious misconduct, the arbitrators would be authorized to refer member firms or associated persons to the NASD disciplinary authorities at the end of the arbitration, or, in the case of misconduct by an investor's counsel or representative or a firm's outside counsel, to a new NASD review process that will be established for this purpose.

Arbitration hearing dates would be scheduled by the arbitrators, not by the NASD staff, early in the arbitration process, in consultation with the parties and counsel. Whenever possible, the arbitrators would schedule consecutive hearing dates, and any postponements or reschedulings would be granted by the arbitrators only upon a showing of cause, such as an impending settlement or a compelling personal reason on the part of one of the participants.

Large and Complex Cases

The pilot large and complex case rules would remain available for claims of $1 million or more, claims raising complex issues, or any other claim for which the parties agree to use these rules. . . . These rules allow the parties voluntarily to adopt special procedures for how the case will be heard.

Part V

Additional ADR Approaches

Chapter 13

Hybrids and Other ADR Procedures

CASE STUDY

Daubert v. Merrell Dow was a class action brought by Jason Daubert and Eric Schuller on behalf of themselves and a group of similarly situated minors born with limb reduction birth defects. While pregnant, the mothers of these children had been prescribed Bendectin, a prescription anti-nausea drug marketed by Merrell Dow. The children claimed that their birth defects resulted from their mothers' ingestion of this drug.

Merrell Dow moved for summary judgement stating first, that Bendectin did not cause birth defects in humans and second, that the children would be unable to find evidence supporting their settlement. The company produced a physician/epidemiologist expert who testified that there were no studies that found Bendectin to cause malformations in fetuses, thus concluding that the drug had not been shown to be a risk factor for birth defects.

The children contested this evidence with eight experts whose studies showed that there was a link between Bendectin and limb reduction birth defects. These data were from in vitro studies, in vivo studies, and reanalysis of previously published epidemiological studies.

Summary judgement was granted in 1989 by the district court for Merrell Dow, stating that "scientific evidence is admissible only if the principle upon which it is based has general acceptance in the field." The court ruled that the opinion of the children's eight experts, which was not based on epidemiological evidence, was not admissible to establish causation, and further that the reanalysis was inadmissible because it had not been subjected to peer review.

This case reached the Supreme Court, in 1992, which agreed to hear the case in light of the divisions among lower courts on the question of admissibility of this expert testimony. The Supreme Court decided to vacate the rule of "general evidence" as the standard for admissibility of scientific evidence and ultimately determined that they would send the case back to the lower courts for further proceedings.

A. Introduction

The "big three" ADR processes—negotiation, mediation, and arbitration—were examined at length and in depth over the last nine chapters. The ensuing six chapters address other ADR procedures, many of which are hybrids or variants of the primary processes.

This chapter opens with a taxonomy of ADR procedures, along with variants thereof. Mediation and arbitration hybrids are of sufficient importance to receive separate treatment. As the focus of the subsequent chapters is the use of ADR by government (administrative agencies and the judiciary), two important forms of private ADR are discussed in this chapter: Mini-Trial and Ombudsman.

The denomination "mini-trial" is at best misleading, because this process is a species of settlement and not even remotely related a judicial proceeding. The type of ombudsman discussed here is that of a dispute settlement official in a corporate or university setting, rather than the government ombudsman whose role is to facilitate dealings between individuals and a government agency.

B. A Taxonomy of ADR Procedures

1. Comments and Questions

a. There are numerous recognized forms of ADR, several of which go by different names, and particular ADR procedures may have several variations. What is a separate procedure and what is a variant of a single procedure may be a matter of taste or definition. In addition, individuals or organizations often customize processes for particular needs or circumstances.

b. The next article, by Tom Arnold, canvasses a large number of ADR processes. The purpose is both descriptive and evaluative: what process is useful in what circumstances.

c. Usages may vary among countries and also within the United States. Where ADR takes place pursuant to an agreement of the parties, the named process means what the parties have defined it to mean.

d. Several procedures are discussed in greater detail elsewhere in this book. In those instances, only a brief description is provided here, plus a citation to the extended discussion.

2. Tom Arnold, A Vocabulary of Alternative Dispute Resolution Procedures (1995)*

No vocabulary of ADR is uniformly used by all people or in all nations. And the assumed characteristics of a given process for one nation are commonly in error for another. Even "alternative" as used in Alternative Dispute Resolution has different meanings in various places — in Europe mostly meaning alternative to adjudicative processes and hence not including binding arbitration which is adjudicative, but in the U.S. mostly meaning alternative to court processes and hence including binding arbitration. Here I use the U.S. idiom, inclusive of arbitration.

Apparently, to some cultures, the translation of "arbitration" includes an initial try at conciliation, which is antithetical to many Anglo disputants' intent in their contract for "binding arbitration." Further, Anglo-American practice puts a much heavier focus on oral argument and hearings than is common in either Continental European or Oriental practice. English courts/arbitrators tend not to receive and study written law briefs to the degree that is routine in U.S. court/arbitration practice, but rather to rely more on oral presentations. All these fac-

*Reprinted with permission.

tors introduce confusion into the use of the words of ADR procedures.

We should start this effort at definitions with appreciation of the fact that there are three primary processes for dispute resolution:

1. party negotiation (in several forms);
2. mediated or facilitated negotiation (in several forms); and
3. adjudication (also in several forms including both private adjudication or arbitration, and court trials).

Surely it is fair to observe that with a very few categories of exceptions, the appropriate first dispute resolution process is in the negotiation/mediation portion of the spectrum—usually the least expensive and most likely to preserve relationships, and surely the safest from explosion into a horror story.

Only after mediation, should parties normally move to any form of adjudication, which is more costly, more painful, and more divisive of relationships. Commonly binding arbitration, often in the "last offer arbitration" style, is best following a mediation; but arbitration, like court litigation in the U.S., is laced with booby traps for the unwary, particularly in complex cases, and needs much more careful and informed attention to fitting its architecture to the dispute than it usually gets.

We need at the outset also to make some observations about the three significant approaches at dispute resolution: (l) interests, (2) rights, and (3) power. These three often get mixed up and intermingled, but there is a continuum from interests through rights to power, and being sufficiently attuned to those differences to recognize what mode is dominating or might be best for a particular dispute, is important. . . .

Some disputes need a measure of power based resolution, and/or a measure of rights based resolution. But as a general . . . proposition, the burdens in terms of painful turmoil, time and money, increase sharply as you move through that continuum from interests to rights to power. [A]s you approach the question of what dispute resolution process to select for any given situation, you should be aware of the three approaches, interest, rights and power, and the very high likelihood that things get worse as you move through that continuum.

Against the background of the differences between interest, rights and power approaches to dispute resolution, let us now set some framework about different modes of ADR in at least one vocabulary defining some of the infinitely variant procedures. The better known forms and names of ADR are commonly though not uniformly referred to by the terms as follows:

I. NEGOTIATION/"WISE MEN" OR "WISE PEOPLE"

Typically meaning:

Negotiation:

Parties exchange views and proposals either personally, by mail or both, often with at least the early rounds being not by counsel, hopefully leading toward an agreement by way of compromise of the controversy.

"Wise Men/women"

Nickname for higher officials of corporations joint-venturing a major project, to whom expected disputes are referred for negotiated solution with an order, "Resolve the dispute!" Not "if you can," but simply "Do it." You know what? They usually do.

Direct negotiation of course should be the first approach at resolution of any dispute.

But, either by reason of inattention or tactics, disputants, particularly in the U.S., tend to disregard this fact and file suit. A clause in a business contract that some argue ought to be used as frequently as an arbitration or mediation clause, is a clause binding the parties to good faith negotiation of settlement before suit is filed, i.e., before animosities are inflamed by the filing. Construction contracts and other situations where the dispute is likely to be one commanding interim relief, like a Temporary Restraining Order, require an exemption for such remedies.

As between businesses this negotiation preferably should be at some level above that of the individuals who generated the dispute in the first place, and these are sometimes nicknamed "wise men" or "wise people."

For example, in several major commercial contract areas including the oil and gas and major construction industries: when there is some sort of joint venture or partnership and ongoing contract administration and relationships are both important and expected, disputes are commonly handled in a three step process:

- First by reference to a "Partnership Committee" (typically non-lawyer representatives from both parties, usually with background in the commercial contract and/or the dispute area) whose determination, if they reach one, is conclusive.
- If they fail to agree, the dispute is referred to senior officials of the joint venturing parties, hopefully removed from the nitty gritty of the dispute—and these are called the "wise people" who have not been directly involved in the dispute and who hopefully will be able to resolve the dispute.
- If the "wise people" fail to agree, then typically the dispute is submitted to binding arbitration. I wonder, why not mediation first?. . . .

II. NEUTRAL (EXPERT?) FACT FINDER

Typically meaning:

(1) a neutral;
(2) appointed to be architect/performer of an investigation into a critical fact or facts;
(3) often him/herself being an expert in the subject technology, or working with the aid of economists, accountants, scientists, engineers, or public officials and their studies as needed;
(4) the subject facts being such that when once determined they are likely to decide the dispute in the minds of the parties or the public, or at least be very important to the decisions; and
(5) his/her findings may be binding or nonbinding.

A key scientific determination (e.g., is there an oxide on the catalyst or not?) has itself disposed of more than a few big disputes with more reliability than, and at a small fraction of the cost of, a court determination of the same fact intermixed usually with many other factual and legal contentions.

This function can take the form of a special master appointed by the court for specific fact finding, or a scientific expert doing tests to determine facts (like, is this blood stain Joe Jones' blood?), or an appraiser doing studies of comparables to determine value of a property, etc.

In the context of public interest disputes, like firemen's or air traffic controllers' salaries, or whether a police shooting was justified or was an act of police brutality and a civil rights' violation, the "neutral fact finder" takes on the role also of advisor to the body-politic: What should we the public believe, unjustified police brutality or proper police firmness, in response to a thug setting up or threatening police?

III. OMBUDSMAN

See section E of this Chapter.

Typically meaning:

(1) a third party fact finder/adjuster;
(2) perhaps salaried but still largely neutral;
(3) selected to investigate complaints or grievances from an institution's constituents, employees or clients;
(4) who makes nonbinding advisory recommendations to senior management about how to resolve the dispute;
(5) in a voluntary, private, informal process;
(6) wherein, although salaried by the institution, his/her duty is not to management but to the facts and to natural justice and equity for the constituents.

IV. EARLY NEUTRAL EVALUATION, MODERATED SETTLEMENT CONFERENCE, ADVISORY OPINIONS

See Chapter Fifteen, Section B.

Typically meaning:

(1) an informal, mostly oral case presentation;
(2) without much by way of evidence, witnesses or affidavits or much reference to documents. . . .

This procedure is similar to nonbinding arbitration, but with no evidence rules or consideration, no cross examination, attorneys and clients communicating (unlike litigation), and often with no formality in the neutral's conclusion or "award" or its communication.

Moderated settlement conferences before lawyer panels are advantageous in cases heavy in application-of-law content wherein the reaction of lawyers/judges may dominate any court decision (like the summary jury trial is advantageous in cases low on disputed law and where the jury's evaluation of the damages is influential in settlement). The participation of CEOs or near CEOs is not commonly thought of as "required" to the usage "moderated settlement conference," as is common with the procedure normally termed a "mini-trial." . . .

V. SUMMARY JURY TRIAL

See Chapter Fifteen, Section C.

Typically meaning:

(1) a fairly formal case presentation;
(2) primarily by argument of counsel rather than by client or witnesses;
(3) using primarily affidavit evidence and lawyer arguments — jury considers it all with only the most obvious evidence objections made or sustained unless handled by motions in limine;
(4) presented to a regular jury impaneled and presided over by a magistrate or judge;
(5) wherein the jury hears and decides the case in a nonbinding decision; and

(6) commonly, wherein the jurors are available for interview by the parties afterward whereby their responses and reactions can be learned by the parties.

This procedure is in notable contrast to binding "hi-low" summary jury trial, discussed in the next section.

Summary jury trials are advantageous in cases heavy on facts and/or damages speculation where the response of a typical jury is likely to influence settlement—an interesting parallel to the Moderated Settlement Conference held before lawyers, who can coach as to how the legal issues play to them.

VI. BINDING HI-LOW SUMMARY JURY TRIAL

Typically meaning:

(1) a Summary Jury Trial as discussed in section V;
(2) which is binding;
(3) wherein the parties have negotiated an agreed cap on the low and high recovery to assure that plaintiff gets something, but not too much.

VII. FACILITATIVE OR "CLASSIC" MEDIATION

See Chapters Seven to Nine.

VIII. "CONCILIATION" OR EVALUATIVE MEDIATION

Typically meaning:

Facilitative mediation with a Neutral Evaluation add-on.

[There is a] continuum, from narrow to broad relevant party interests, and from pure facilitation to what I call the "closet arbitrator" who evaluates, decides and directs the parties, all sometimes practiced under the name "mediation." . . . [S]ometimes . . . the more clearly evaluative and directive processes are called "Conciliation" or "Evaluative Mediation" in contrast to classic facilitative mediation. In procedures properly under this name, the neutral forms a conclusion as to what the case is worth and advises how (s)he thinks it should be settled. . . . If the parties don't like the neutral's recommendation, they have the self-service protection of walking away without an agreement. Many parties want and ask for mediator evaluations — that is what they expect out of the process. . . . This method where the neutral makes a non-binding recommendation, sub nomine "Conciliation", is increasing in popularity in international dispute resolution.

And this method is commonly practiced particularly by some retired judges, and can be both fair and efficient at least if reserved until the very end of a facilitative mediation process and used with reservation and care only in cases where the neutral has himself tried a dozen essentially duplicate cases or otherwise really does know all the arguments on both sides and the value of the likely tradeouts for fair resolution of the dispute.

Yet another model is that propounded by James C. Freund of New York, who is very experienced in the business transactions where he practices. . . . After the openings by the two parties and often some clarification discussion, he breaks the parties into private caucuses, and either then or after a first caucus with each party, arrives at his own judgement "X" of what the settlement should be. He does not undertake to be a messenger engaged in shuttle diplomacy and negotiations between the two parties. Rather, he then undertakes an essentially independent negotiation in sequence with each party, seeking to get party A to agree to a position toward B from his position X, and to get party B to agree to a position toward A from his position X. When he gets them to overlap, usually at or near X, he has got a settlement. This is a sophisticated approach not available to mediators who do not know very well the territory where they are working. . . .

IX. CASE-MANAGED, HYBRID MEDIATION

This is my phrase for:

(1) selecting neutral(s) who are highly sophisticated in the technology and law of the controversy;
(2) using mostly prehearing party briefs and evidence referred to therein and consultations with counsel;
(3) using also mini-discovery and neutral investigation as the neutrals feel their own need for it on key points prior to any hearing;
(4) the neutral(s) study the merits of the case to the degree of arriving (tentatively, even before opening statements) at their own dispute resolution proposal; [I've heard of one case where the neutral studied and conferred ex parte for three days at the claimant's place of business, then three days at the respondent's place of business, with the mediation commencing immediately thereafter with the presentation of each party's opening statements to a by-then well-informed mediator.]
(5) the neutral(s) also hearing opening statements by all parties and revising their proposal as appropriate;
(6) the neutral(s) then assuming administrative management of the dispute resolution process and advocating the neutral(s)'settlement proposal—a leadership role uniquely important in complex multi-party cases;
(7) high flexibility likely including the postponement of resolution of some important issues (like how the plaintiffs will divide the recovery among themselves);
(8) quite probably after opening statements, the parties being kept apart throughout many rounds of shuttle diplomacy/neutral(s)-advocacy until the final-confirmation-of-agreement-by-the-parties-stage; and
(9) quite possibly some heavy pressure from the judge presiding over the case to convince the parties that he is going to force a settlement and he has the power to make it stick.

X. MED-ARB

See section C of this Chapter.

XI. NONBINDING ARBITRATION

See chapter 10, Section E and Chapter 14, section E.

—A variant of "neutral evaluation" or "Early Neutral Evaluation" (ENE), discussed in Section IV above.

Typically meaning:

(1) a moderately formal case presentation;
(2) normally primarily by counsel with client inputs;
(3) with affidavit, deposition and/or documentary evidence received and relied upon;

(4) rarely hearing live witnesses;
(5) presentation to one or sometimes three arbitrators who initially preside as judge over the proceedings, hearing evidence primarily in a passive role, like a judge, though also cross-examining points here and there;
(6) wherein the arbitrator(s) render a decision or opinion (perhaps, an "award") which hopefully will beget further settlement conversations in light of the neutral'(s) opinion and story on how the case "played" to him;
(7) wherein the neutral(s) often evolves after the award into a partially or fully performing mediator;
(8) wherein private communications between a party and the arbitrators are not normally contemplated unless explicitly provided for in the agreement to arbitrate (except perhaps in AAA Rules arbitrations with two party-appointed arbitrators who are sometimes not true neutrals), but that point is in need of explicit contract determination;

Nonbinding arbitration is referred to in Texas statutes and some other places, simply as "arbitration", but it is not to be confused with binding arbitration which is vastly different.

Note the absence here of any real focus on CEOs or top officers being present as is a heavy focus in what is commonly called a "mini-trial." But for that thin and sometimes nonexistent difference, "mini-trial" is merely another name for a nonbinding arbitration before neutrals knowledgeable in the subject, hybridized with follow-on mediation to beget party-settlement, wherein the "trial" commonly is of a somewhat summary character. . . . The term "mini-trial" for nonbinding arbitration followed by conciliation or mediation, developed its popularity in the context of commercial dispute resolution procedures where a nonbinding arbitration and a post-award mediation involve a neutral knowledgeable in the subject matter and the presence and participation of CEOs or other very high corporate officials with full and independent authority to settle the case.

XII. BINDING ARBITRATION

See Chapters Ten to Twelve.

In the idiom of some countries apparently including oriental, Muslim and a couple of northern European countries, "arbitration" may be construed as inclusive of conciliation, and unless the contract is extremely explicit that only adjudicative arbitration has been agreed to, the performing neutral may initiate a conciliatory process first, or indeed may even be substantially disinclined ever to decide the case. But as used herein, "arbitration" refers only to the adjudicative process. A key feature of arbitration is absence of the classic rules of evidence—which can be both merit and gross mischief. Affidavits may be received and relied upon with respect to essentially uncontested issues, but should be considered inadequate proof of contested issues unless corroborated by other evidence or by surrounding circumstances or at least subject to live witness cross-examination. Clarification of the arbitrator's approach to evidence, at a prehearing conference, is important.

Oriental and continental Europe users of ADR attach much less importance to oral hearings and oral examination of witnesses than does the Anglo-American tradition. Further, rather that a preparatory period pointing toward a final "trial hearing" as in Anglo-American practice, arbitration tribunals in those countries are likely to have a series of hearings in one place or another, addressing issues in phases. Continental European arbitrators, reflecting the culture of their court practice, are prone to do the cross examination themselves perhaps even in lieu of counsel cross examination as expected in any Anglo-American arbitration. Confusion over who has the duty or privilege of cross examination needs to be clarified in an early preliminary hearing or correspondence.

XIII. COURT ANNEXED ARBITRATION

See Chapter Fifteen, section D.

Typically meaning:

(1) a court ordered arbitration to an award;

(2) perhaps totally nonbinding or perhaps the award being subject to a timely request for court trial de novo;

(3) settlement conversations and/or mediation diversions along the way being common;

(4) commonly, wherein the appealing party pays for costs and attorney fees if he does not do better (by a specified percentage) in the court than in the arbitration. . . .

And while I give it no separate title, court-ordered mediation is more common than arbitration in many jurisdictions. The experience in Texas [since 1988] has seen a virtual abandonment of most court-annexed ADR except mediation which is extremely widely used.

XIV. CAUCUS ARBITRATION

A rarely used, but in employee trade secret cases a highly useful, variation on the arbitration theme is arbitration with private caucuses between each party and the neutral as in mediation. (This process has been used in both binding and nonbinding arbitration formats.) The trade secrets are revealed and discussed in the private caucuses where the neutral assumes the role of active cross-examiner. He may caucus with the other party in aid of getting ideas for the cross examination. . . . Of course, this is much more palatable to many in the nonbinding format where a party retains the privilege of walking away, than in the binding format.

XV. "BASEBALL" OR "FINAL-OFFER" ARBITRATION

Typically meaning a binding arbitration, wherein

(1) the arbitrator(s) hear(s) the case as in regular binding arbitration;

(2) each party then writes out his/her own proposal for a settlement agreement or award and presents it to the arbitrator;

(3) the arbitrator(s) picks the party's proposal which he thinks most appropriate and fair, on balance, having no authority to render any award other than an award proposed by one of the two parties.

[T]he parties usually are strongly biased to propose reasonable compromises, lest the arbitrator take the other party's proposal.

It is important to recognize the circumstances where this proposition may not hold. A baseball or football player, by the history of the last three years and a good year just completed, and by the recitations of the negotiations leading up to the arbitration, is confident management cannot offer him less than $1 million which is really OK, and if management did offer less the arbitrators would surely take his high demand; so why not "go for broke" and ask the arbitrators for his full original demand of $5 million instead of a compromise figure in between. . . .

"Night baseball" is a variation wherein the neutral writes up his own proposed settlement before seeing what the parties proposed, with the settlement then being on the terms of the party-offer closest to the mediator's proposal.

XVI. MEDALOA, (ALTERNATIVES A AND B)

See section C of this Chapter.

XVII. MINI-TRIAL

See section D of this Chapter.

XVIII. NEUTRAL AS CONSULTING ARCHITECT OF ADR PROCESS

> Meaning:
> The parties jointly (or separately) employing an experienced neutral to be a consulting architect of a dispute resolution process tailored to the dispute at hand, often with flexibility planned in, e.g., with expectation that after a mediation stage they will move into binding arbitration on some point, jury trial on another, etc.

It is important that the "experienced neutral" have . . . the breadth of experience to be an architect. [Otherwise] . . . he is likely to recommend process X, merely because that is the one he knows.

Often the best procedure is for the parties jointly to employ an experienced neutral and let him, in consultation with the parties, be the principal architect for the hybridization of these various procedures into a detailed process unique to the particular dispute, likely a process not completely or precisely within any of the definitions recited here, and wherein the neutral is explicitly instructed to assume case management initiative and control. . . . Of course many parties like to employ an experienced neutral privately as their own advisor, whether or not the disputants jointly employ a consulting architect neutral.

A fascinating example of this is the *IBM v. Fujitsu* case involving computer software. The two neutrals were given considerable leeway in structuring the dispute resolution process, and ended up using:

— some neutral expert fact investigation,
— some mediation,
— some mini-trial,
— some binding arbitration,
— significant discovery by tutorials not known in court procedure, and
— retention of jurisdiction after the award to assess the amount of royalties payable after the market bloom and use could be accurately observed.

XIX. RENT-A-JUDGE OR "PRIVATE JUDGING"

A court-annexed process available when statutes or local court rules permit court referral of cases to neutral third parties for formal trials, typically meaning:

(1) a fairly formal case presentation as in a court trial commonly following traditional formalities and procedural and evidentiary rules;
(2) presented by counsel, witnesses, and documentary evidence essentially as in regular trial;

(3) to a privately selected and privately paid neutral, usually a retired judge, who presides over the proceedings as a judge, and who has the same powers as a trial judge;
(4) wherein a record of the proceedings is usually made by a privately retained court reporter;
(5) wherein the private judge reports his decision to the referring court and judgment is entered on the decision as if the action had been decided by a court; and
(6) wherein the parties' rights to appellate review and enforcement of the decision are the same as if the judgment had been entered by a district court.

In many respects, Rent-a-Judge is akin to fully formal binding arbitration where the parties have provided for appellate review of the arbitrator's award. However, because "Rent-a-Judge" procedures are usually controlled by statute and often require a court referral, it is not clear whether the parties can agree in advance to submit a case to a private judge under some of these statutes.

For the most part it is retired judges who are neutrals in this procedure—hence the nickname "Rent-a-Judge." Partly because of this the process closely resembles traditional litigation in form, although the expertise of the judge, the speed of decision, and the flexible rules and procedures may be quite different from those found in the courthouse with its backlogs.

One item, more significant than non-trial lawyers can ever understand: Court trial settings are much more commonly vacated and reset than held onto, which makes it very difficult to plan a major trial with witnesses from far away, etc., etc. Usually, a Rent-a-judge setting can be depended upon — no small value.

Although the presentation is usually made according to traditional procedural and evidentiary rules, the parties may agree to relax or change these rules. Under the Texas statute, a private judge has the powers of a district court judge except he may not hold for contempt persons who are not witnesses before him.

Unlike awards obtained in ADR procedures (except perhaps a court-confirmed arbitration award), the award rendered by the neutral in this process becomes, in essence, a judgment of the court. As such, it is subject to the same processes (e.g., appeal, motion for a new trial) as a trial court decision.

XX. SPECIAL MASTER UNDER FRCP 53 OR STATE LAW

Many of the functions recited under the titles above, can also be performed by a Special Master appointed under Rule 53 of the Federal Rules of Civil Procedure, and parallel state rules.

XXI. PARTNERING

See Chapter Twenty-One, Section C.

XXII. MEETINGS FACILITATION

Typically meaning:

A neutral presiding over a conference of any modest number of people, usually working with flip charts, who clarifies statements, keeps the discussion outline, directs the topics, assures that even shy people are heard and participate as much as the outspoken dominating personalities.

Mediation is a form of facilitation; conference facilitation is a form of mediation. Facilitation is a marvelous device for the many committee and board meetings when they address difficult, emotionally charged issues and when they involve both bully, dominating personality types and shy hesitant personality types.

XXIII. JOB SITE ADR

Typically meaning:

In construction contracts between subcontractors, between sub and general contractors, etc. The driving force is saving time on minor disputes as well as money and delay. A characteristic of these clauses is the low level of detail in the contract — assign the dispute resolution to somebody, whomever, and get it done pronto, is the theme.

XXIV. KEY CAVEATS CONCERNING THE ABOVE "VOCABULARY"

Two key understandings about the foregoing *Vocabulary of ADR:*

- The nicknames and their definitions are neither cast in stone nor uniformly accepted. They are often not statutorily defined. Some are statutorily defined but often in a manner different from other statutes or usage.
- Thus, to use any one of these terms without further definition is likely to be vague and indefinite to other people or courts accustomed to a different parlance. Hence such use is poor contract practice, lest an intent to do one thing be either uncertain or construed as a contract to do another.

Further, excepting for certain "public interest" or "public order" limitations on enforceability, the parties can contract for whatever procedure, evidence practice, discovery, injunctive or attorney fee remedies, court review, etc., that they want, and can call it whatever they want to as long as they make the substance of their contract explicit and clear. People often do label their procedures differently from what is outlined above.

C. Mediation and Arbitration Hybrids

1. Comments and Questions

a. Of the many hybrid ADR procedures, those that combine variants of mediation and arbitration are the most important, and so receive closer consideration here.

b. For form clauses that provide for Med-Arb or Arb-Med, see the AAA model clauses, found in Chapter 10, section F.

2. Tom Arnold, A Vocabulary of Alternative Dispute Resolution Procedures (1995)*

I. MED-ARB

Often meaning:

Almost any mix of mediation and arbitration. [But remember, nonbinding arbitration followed by mediation, carries its own name, "mini-trial." See section D of this Chapter.]

*Reprinted with permission.

Such mixes are often in danger of losing the morality of arbitration (where a neutral assumes ownership of the responsibility to make it right, often in accord with some designated law) and also the morality of classic mediation (where the parties by their agreement assume the responsibility to make it acceptably fair).

In a perhaps more preferred context "Med-Arb" means,

(1) facilitative mediation followed by
(2) binding arbitration:

Alternative A, before different neutrals;
Alternative B, before the same neutral.

Alternative B, before the same neutral, procedure creates the circumstance that some of the unanswered, unchecked, irresponsible statements in private mediation caucuses may influence the arbitration award—a worrisome circumstance worthy of consideration but the importance of which is often grossly exaggerated. The assumed difficulty has been found to be grossly overstated on many occasions where the sophistication and balance of the neutral can be trusted, and where the parties in private causes tend toward objective non-slanderous recitations of essentially admitted facts.

This gives rise to the question: How much trust do you have in the adversary not to lie in caucus? How much trust do you have in the mediator/arbitrator? If not much, then let the arbitration proceed before a neutral different than the mediator. If the facts are substantially admitted except as to points well presented on both sides in the opening statement and/or if there is a lot of trust, then ask the mediator to base his conclusion on the formal evidence in the arbitration presentation and proceed to arbitrate—you are likely to like the result.

There is an important further step that can be used with Med-Arb and also with MEDALOA discussed below, namely an intermediate facilitated negotiation of the arbitration process to fit the process to the size, value, risks, and other natures of the dispute. . . . I am biased often to design a "final offer" or " baseball" arbitration step, with defined limits on discovery, discovery time, witnesses, hearing time, etc. as discussed with "MedALOA" (**MED**iation **A**nd **L**ast **O**ffer **A**rbitration). . . .

II. MEDALOA, (ALTERNATIVES A AND B)

MEDALOA is the name assigned in 1993 by Bob Coulson, then president of the AAA, to . . . the hybrid process of **MED**iation **A**nd **L**ast **O**ffer **A**rbitration. It comes in two alternative varieties for two different situations:

Alternative A: Small Value at Risk

In cases where relatively little is at risk or where the impasse has occurred with the parties not far apart by comparison with the burdens of a separate and independent arbitration, and where the party trust of the mediator is high:

(1) Classic mediation and if no settlement occurs then,

(2A) This step may be in the original agreement for ADR, or after impasse the mediator or a party may propose and the parties accept and then agree: each party to present a court-trial type summation argument of their case to the mediator-now-turned-arbitrator or to a new arbitrator if the parties so elect; each party to prepare a written final or "last offer" and present it to the arbitrator; the arbitrator to pick the last offer which seems the most just of the last offers and that last offer becomes a binding arbitration award.

Alternative B: Big Value at Risk

In cases, particularly complex cases, where much is at risk and/or the separation of the parties at impasse is great,

(1) Classic mediation and if no settlement occurs then,

(2B) After the mediation,

- the mediator on the merits turns into a mediator/ facilitator of a facilitated negotiation of the architecture of a binding arbitration process—not necessarily but preferably a "baseball" or "last offer" arbitration style as defined in (2-A) above,
- whereby a binding arbitration can be tailored to the now-well-understood dispute and circumstance in dozens of truly important ways.

Alternative A: Small Value at Risk

The Alternative A approach uses last offer arbitration before the same neutral merely as a means of breaking impasse in a mediation. It is the quick, cheap, easy road to final disposition—very attractive in low value cases and in cases where the parties are already so close together that it would be a crime to lose settlement over so little a difference.

Often the disputed facts are well aired in joint sessions and there is little exposure to the judgement of the neutral being poisoned in private caucuses; often parties trust the mediator they've come to know and who has shown neutrality and familiarity with the subject matter. Assuredly, those who "have been there" have found value in the mediator-turned-arbitrator sufficiently to justify the thought that theoreticians whose judgement is only intuitive, run too afraid of the mediator-turned-arbitrator in these cases.

But often a party wants an arbitrator not at risk of having his/her judgement poisoned by private caucus recitations the party hasn't heard and hence has not checked or answered, or a party wants an arbitrator to whom he entrusts a final decision in the case, to have more expertise in the subject matter than the mediator has demonstrated.

Sometimes the mediator knows (s)he doesn't know enough about the subject matter or has had his/her judgement so poisoned by private caucus information or the development of a dislike for a party that (s)he may decline the arbitrator role. Perhaps more often the mediator feels uncomfortable assuming the role of "decider" in context of the background by which (s)he induced the parties to trust him/her—for his/her decision may seem to one of them to be a breach of the trust they felt.

If anybody is uncomfortable with the mediator turned arbitrator, the mediator can likely in 15 minutes on the phone find an arbitrator the parties will agree to for this case, who can give it half a day within a week so the dispute can be disposed of while it is still on the parties and counsel's minds.

Note that the net effect of this process may be that of a hi-lo arbitration, because the offers pending at impasse time during the mediation, by the psychology of the process, tend to constitute the "hi" and the "lo" of what the arbitrator will have submitted to him as "last offers". If you don't like the gamesmanship of not being sure, then explicitly contract that those are hi-lo offers. The parties nearly always move closer together in this process than they were at mediation impasse, making the value to be decided even less than it was then. The event of the yield being sufficient that the offers overlap, is discussed under Alternative B, below. This is a tool of efficient compromise, not a process by which to get the extreme result.

Alternative B: Big Value at Risk

Unlike mediation which inherently is essentially safe, arbitration is not inherently safe; rather it is laced with booby traps for the unwary that can make a horror story out of an apparently routine arbitration. In complex cases the risk of such a horror story may be one-in-five to one-in-ten. When a commercial contract is entered into the parties usually don't know such things as:

(1) the complexity or value of the ultimate dispute or its need for discovery, and hence what level of resources are reasonable for this dispute;
(2) the degree of imperative for a quick decision;
(3) the plus and minus values of one vs. three arbitrators or of having some arbitrators be non-lawyers with technical background from the subject industry;
(4) the plus and minus values for or against non-neutral party-appointed arbitrators as under AAA rules for party-appointed arbitrators;
(5) the plus and minus values of one administrator or another, or of ad hoc arbitration in lieu of administered arbitration;
(6) the plus and minus values of reasoned awards (required for enforcement of the award in some countries) vs. naked awards as AAA rules advocate and use in domestic U.S. cases;
(7) the plus and minus values of explicit limits on party-time in discovery or final hearing;
(8) the differences in different arbitration rules and the significance of those differences;
(9) the value of arbitrator and counsel commitment that they have time and will give a priority claim upon their time to this dispute sufficient for its final resolution by a recited target date;
(10) the value of explicit arbitrator authority to reject evidence deemed prejudicial and either redundant or immaterial without risking a court setting the award aside for refusal to consider evidence;
(11) what appellate review, if any, the parties contemplate, or whether to have finality of the arbitrator's award;
(12) et cetera, et cetera, et cetera.

Not knowing these and dozens of other things, the parties at the time of a commercial transaction cannot tailor a potential arbitration to the nature of the dispute, cannot discern the necessary trade-outs to render the process both appropriately efficient and appropriately thorough and still free of risk of the process exploding into a horror story of time and expense as too many commercial arbitrations do.

But after a mediation both the parties and the mediator know the various parameters of the dispute and have time to look at arbitration practice and its booby traps—booby traps that are easily avoided but only if you know where they are. With aid of an experienced arbitrator (hopefully, the mediator) and/or arbitration counsel for this exercise, the parties ought to be able in the facilitated negotiation to design an arbitration process that is safe, expeditious and that provides for a better quality consideration than is typical from a jury or a judge with an overly crowded docket.

When fitting a complex dispute into an appropriate arbitration budget, the ideas must include addressing each of the things parties usually don't know at commercial transaction time, and at least the following additional ideas:

(1) Explicitly reciting that no objections shall be made during discovery depositions — sometimes a savings of thousands of dollars.
(2) Explicitly limiting discovery to a window of X weeks, and discovery deposition time to a total of perhaps 50 hours per side.
(3) Explicitly limiting final hearing time to perhaps 48 hours per side—some figure perhaps 20% longer than realistic early estimates—and then by stop watch holding the parties to that time (this to protect against exploding arbitration hearings such as the recent case estimated to the court at six weeks but which ended up taking four and a half years, 300 actual hearing days, producing 42,000 pages of transcript, an award that was appealed and vacated in significant part).
(4) Explicitly authorizing, instructing and directing the arbitrator or chairman of a panel to assume case management initiative and control by which to expedite the case toward a final conclusion and disposition by target date X.

Why arbitration of the "last offer" type? During the mediation phase each party has made concessions and has developed some sort of feel for the other party's concessions and views. The psychology of last-offer arbitration usually (not always) is to bias parties toward further concession, lest they risk the arbitrator selecting the other party's proposal as the award. Often the offers come so close together that the arbitrator's choice is of no real importance—you get what in effect is a mediated compromise.

If in the last offers presented to the arbitrator the parties yield so far toward the other party as to overlap a small amount, the arbitrator reports that fact to the parties and suggests a split of the difference. If the overlap of each party's concession to the other is great, the arbitrator can suggest a return to mediation (known as "extra innings baseball")— where settlement is always promptly reached, the parties knowing they offered more than they needed to but not knowing how much.

This little-known and little-used process, mediation followed by last offer arbitration (with or without the intermediate facilitated arbitration architecture negotiation, depending on the case) is the process of choice in the vast majority of commercial cases.

D. Mini-Trial

1. Jethro K. Lieberman & James F. Henry, *Lessons From the Alternative Dispute Resolution Movement*, 53 U. Chi. L. Rev. 424, 427-429 (1986)*

The mini-trial is not in fact a trial at all, but a highly-structured settlement process. Because it is a flexible device that can be tailored to the precise needs of the parties, no single procedural model of the mini-trial has yet prevailed. But in general, the known mini-trials share many of the following characteristics:

---

*Reprinted with permission.

1. The parties negotiate a set of procedural ground rules (a protocol) that will govern the nonbinding mini-trial.
2. The time for preparation is relatively short—between six weeks and three months—and the amount of discovery is relatively limited.
3. The hearing itself is sharply abbreviated—usually no more than two days.
4. The hearing is often conducted by a third-party neutral, typically called the "neutral advisor.
5. The case is presented to representatives of the parties with authority to settle; there is no judge or jury.
6. The lawyers present their "best"' case; they do not have time to delve into side issues.
7. Immediately after the hearing, the party representatives meet privately to negotiate a settlement.
8. If they cannot reach a settlement, the neutral advisor may render an advisory opinion on how he thinks a judge would rule if the case were to go to court.
9. The proceedings are confidential: the parties generally commit themselves to refrain from disclosing details of the proceedings to any outsider.

Several observations are in order about the trust-building capacity of the mini-trial. First, the very process of negotiating the protocol tends to foster trust.[20] Second, by concentrating on their best possible case, the lawyers usually feel constrained to discuss the central issues. Third, the kind of lawyerly hairsplitting, namecalling, and pettifogging that might delight courtroom regulars would leave the business executives to whom mini-trials are presented singularly unamused. Finally, the presence at the hearing of a neutral advisor, to whom both parties have consented, enhances the prospect that they will credit any advisory opinion that he renders. . . .

In a mini-trial held by Texaco and Borden, for example, the parties resolved a breach-of-contract claim and antitrust counterclaim totaling in the hundreds of millions of dollars by renegotiating the entire contract for the supply of natural gas. Both parties claimed a net gain. No court could have ordered the parties to renegotiate; at best a judge or jury could only have compromised on the amount of damages it awarded the "winner."

2. Tom Arnold, A Vocabulary of Alternative Dispute Resolution Procedures (1995)*

[The typical characteristics of a mini-trial are the following]:

(1) a moderately formal case presentation more like a binding arbitration than any other, though typically held in a hotel or office conference room or even a borrowed courtroom, usually in a somewhat summary fashion with limits on witnesses and/or examination time or whatever;

(2) usually presented solely by counsel though the parties are free to agree to use witnesses;

[20]It might be objected that this prospect is circular: only if the parties trust each other at least to a limited extent will they agree to conduct a mini-trial at all. But experience suggests that they need not trust each other very much at the outset. Their need to negotiate in order to gain access to the forum tends to foster trust, and their desire to save further litigation costs might simply overwhelm the distrust.

(3) with affidavit, deposition and documentary evidence normally received and relied upon to the extent of its inherent credibility but without following strict Rules of Evidence; sometimes including one or two key witnesses live and subject to cross-examination though more often attorney's argument without live witnesses;
(4) presented to party CEO-type representatives with hopefully unlimited decision making authority;
(5) and presented also to a neutral (or three), usually expert in the subject area (e.g., patent lawyer in a patent case) who initially presides over the proceedings and hears evidence partially in a passive role like an Anglo-American judge though also cross-examining points and commenting on evidence and arguments here and there to put them in perspective, and who presents a conclusion without prior private conversations with any party or party representative (on this point, different from mediation);
(6) wherein the neutral(s) may ask questions and comment on evidence and arguments along the way, to give perspective to the business people,
(7) where at the conclusion of this arbitration-typoe hearing the neutral(s) makes a non-binding ruling normally with reasons orally presented, which ruling (revealing as it does how the case "played") is intended as an aid to the parties' further negotiation toward settlement;
(8) and, wherein it is planned that after the ruling the neutral(s) shall become a fully performing conciliator, preferably (when so trained) a regular facilitative mediator, in some but not all definitions including shuttle diplomacy between the parties, as in the section above on "Mediation" (a role for which he must be trained and prepared).

Presentation to a CEO-type official is the first key difference between of this procedure and what is often termed "nonbinding arbitration," where any authorized decision maker can be present. And I might add, it is an important difference. The mediation step is the second differentiation over pure nonbinding arbitration.

In terms of purpose — to induce the parties to settle — reciting conditions in the award regarding areas of weak proof, tightness or looseness with respect to fair notice of issues in adherence to pleadings, and receiving possibly irresponsible evidence, the more typical nonbinding "mini-trial" is essentially the same as a nonbinding arbitration or the moderated settlement conference. But the term "mini-trial" has usually been applied to proceedings with a very high focus on:

(1) having experts as neutrals, and
(2) having CEO-type principals present and committed:
    (a) to hear the case through the mouth of the adversary;
    (b) to see their own counsel perform by comparison with the adversary;
    (c) to pick up an evaluation of the resources and effort that carrying the case to trial will require if there is no settlement; and
    (d) to settle the case if it can be settled.

Further, while the traditional use of "mini-trial" is with respect to fully nonbinding processes, there is no reason that high and low limits on recovery might not be agreed upon in advance as in the commonly used "hi-lo arbitration", with the panel's two party-reps and the neutral advisor commissioned to produce a binding decision by a majority of the panel (effectively meaning by the neutral advisor alone but with inputs from his fellow panelists) if no agreement is reached between the party-representatives.

3. Lester Edelman et. al., *The Mini-Trial* 1-6, 9-17 (U.S. Army Corps of Engineering 1989) (IWR Pamphlet 89-ADR-P-1)*

What is a Mini-Trial?

First of all, a mini-trial isn't a trial. There's no judge or lengthy procedures. Decisions are reached quickly and made by managers who have managerial and, often, technical skills, not by third parties such as judges. In fact, the mini-trial is a structured form of negotiated settlement. All parties enter into a mini-trial voluntarily, and any party can drop out when it wants to. A mini-trial is successful when there is a mutual agreement. Here's what a mini-trial might look like:

- Two or more organizations involved in a dispute would agree to use a mini-trial as an alternative to going to court, a contract appeals board, or some other judicial body.
- Each participating organization would designate a senior manager to represent the organization and to make binding commitments on behalf of the organization. Ideally this manager would not have had any substantial previous involvement in the dispute.
- The management representatives and their attorneys would then jointly develop a mini-trial agreement. Since the mini-trial is to help them make decisions, they need to define what they want to happen before and during the mini-trial. . . .
- Attorneys for the participating organizations would then go about preparing their case, advocating the position of their organizations. One unique thing about these preparations, though, is that the attorneys know that they will have only a few hours, or at most several days, to present their case.
- Normally the mini-trial agreement will specify that both parties will prepare short position papers outlining their case. These papers will be exchanged at an agreed-upon time before the mini-trial so that management representatives will be able to read them prior to the mini-trial itself.
- At the agreed-upon date, attorneys for the participating organizations will present their cases in front of the management representatives of the organizations.
- In many mini-trials, the management representatives are assisted by an impartial neutral advisor. This is optional.
- Following the presentations and any questions, the management representatives would then move to another room, without their staffs, and attempt to resolve the dispute.
- The results of the mini-trial are then documented as carefully as any other negotiated settlement which could be subjected to review by whoever has an interest in whether the negotiated settlement is fair.
- The mini-trial agreement will also include a provision that statements made by participants during the mini-trial can't be used against participants in court if no agreement is reached during the mini-trial. This means that concessions made in the relatively informal mini-trial conference can't be dragged up later on in court. . . .

*Reprinted with permission.

Why Use a Mini Trial?

What are the advantages of a mini-trial over more traditional ways of resolving disputes, such as litigation or formal administrative procedures? There are a number of advantages:

- Puts the Decision Back in the Hands of Managers
- Greater Flexibility in Possible Settlements
- Protect the Relationship
- Time-Savings
- Cost Savings
- Protect Management Time

Concerns Expressed About Mini-Trials

Every dispute resolution technique has its strengths and weaknesses, and mini-trials are no exception. Some concerns expressed about mini-trials are not, however, well-founded. Here's a list which includes both very real limitations of mini-trials, and concerns expressed by people who have not used the technique:

- Not Appropriate for Some Issues
- Extra Work for Managers
- Cost of Preparation
- Is It the Best Possible Deal
- Protection Against Lying
- To Offer to Use a Mini-Trial Says We Have a Weak Case
- It's Not Supporting the Field

Selecting the Management Representatives

The senior management people who will represent each organization are normally selected before the mini-trial agreement is developed. This is done so that they can participate in developing the agreement.

While the mini-trial is a structured negotiation process, there is considerable latitude in how the mini-trial is conducted. The management representatives need to ensure that the procedures described in the agreement will serve their needs.

There are two basic criteria for selection of the senior managers to represent the organizations:

- Not Previously Associated with the Issue
- Able to Bind the Organization

Selecting the Neutral Advisor. . . .

Although it is not mandatory that a neutral advisor be selected, there are distinct advantages in using a neutral advisor. The advantage of early selection of the neutral advisor is that the neutral advisor may be able to assist in developing the agreement. There may still be some suspicion or even hostility between the parties, and suggestions coming from the neutral advisor may be treated with more openness than those coming from the other side. The neutral advisor can also provide a communication link, if communication between the parties becomes difficult. The neutral advisor can encourage the management representatives to take charge of the mini-trial agreement, to make sure it meets their needs.

The exact role of the neutral advisor can be agreed upon beforehand, or it can be covered in the mini-trial agreement. The original idea of the neutral advisor was to introduce both an impartial opinion and an element of mediation into the proceedings. The history of mini-trials suggests that the negotiation period can be rocky, and the neutral advisor may be able to keep the negotiations moving.

Among the roles which the neutral advisor can play are:

- Point out the strengths and weaknesses of each organization's position.
- Advise the management representatives on how a judge might apply the law.
- Help devise new compromises or redefine the issues in ways which lend themselves to resolution.
- Help bring the parties to the table, and help keep them there.
- Chair the conference and help set the proper procedural ambience for negotiation.
- Help the parties clarify the worth of various claims and derive reasonable prices.
- Deflate unreasonable claims and break down entrenched positions.
- Articulate the rationale for a solution, making it easier for both sides to buy-in than if the rationale were proposed by one of them.

As can be seen from this list, there are several aspects to the neutral advisor's role. The neutral advisor can act like a technical expert or consultant. The neutral advisor can act like an arbitrator in a non-binding arbitration, suggesting what a reasonable outcome might be, but with no authority to bind the parties. Finally, the neutral advisor can act like a facilitator or mediator, helping to keep communication open, clarifying positions, and seeking out new compromises. Clearly the role you decide upon will influence your selection of a mini-advisor.

To date, most neutrals have been retired judges, or law professors with special expertise in the issues under discussion. Technical experts have also been used, where management representatives primarily wanted advice on technical rather than legal issues. In at least one mini-trial, there was a small panel of neutral advisors including an attorney, and two technical experts. Some organizations have also talked of using a mediator as a neutral advisor, putting the emphasis on helping the negotiation process. Since neutral advisors are to be neutral, employees of either of the parties, or anybody else standing to gain from the manner in which the dispute is resolved, cannot be considered.

Among the questions which should be addressed before you decide what kind of neutral advisor you want are:

- Will the neutral advisor assist in developing the mini-trial agreement?
- Will the neutral advisor hold any meetings (formal or informal) between the management representatives prior to the conference?
- Will the neutral advisor preside over the conference?
- What kinds of information do you want from the neutral advisor, and at what point in the conference or negotiation process?
- Do you want the neutral advisor to make recommendations or suggest possible rationales for compromise?
- Will the neutral advisor be present during the negotiations?
- Do you want the neutral advisor to assist with negotiations, or just respond when asked questions?
- Does the neutral advisor play any further role if the initial negotiations are not successful?

Developing a Mini-Trial Agreement

The mini-trial agreement spells out all the procedures and ground-rules which will be followed during the mini-trial. While the attorneys representing each organization will be very involved in developing the mini-trial agreement because it includes a number of procedural issues which affect them very directly, it is important for senior managers to view the mini-trial agreement as serving their purposes. If you're a senior manager, the mini-trial agreement spells out how you want the information to be gathered and presented for you to make a decision. Topics to be covered in the mini-trial agreement include:

- Discovery
- Date, Time, and Place
- Participant's Obligation to Present Best Case and Negotiate
- The Role of the Neutral Advisor
- The Name of the Neutral Advisor, (or the Process Which will be Used to Select the Neutral Advisor)
- The Exchange of Position Papers
- Confidentiality of Statements
- Allocation of Expenses
- Pending Litigation
- The Roles of People to be Present During the Mini-Trial
- The Number of People in the Room
- Schedule/Agenda
- Neutral Advisor's preliminary opinion
- Termination
- Other Procedures the Management Representatives Want

The Mini-Trial Proceeding

- Preliminary Meeting with Neutral Advisor
  Some neutral advisors like to have a meeting, or dinner, attended by both management representatives, prior to the mini-trial conference. The purpose of this meeting is not to discuss the content of the issues, but to get to know each other and discuss the procedures which will be followed. Most of all, the meeting allows these key figures in the mini-trial to begin to get comfortable with each other and the procedure before the mini-trial conference.
- Conduct the Mini-Trial Conference
  The mini-trial conference will follow the agenda shown in the mini-trial agreement, except that it can be changed at any time by mutual agreement of the management representatives. The attorneys are given great leeway in how they make their presentations. They may choose to make the entire presentation themselves, or present experts or witnesses. They may choose to use visuals, slides, exhibits, or even movies. The whole idea is that each attorney gets a chance to make his best case, anyway he wants within the limited time available to him.
- The Negotiation Process
  Once the conference is over, and the management representatives have asked all their questions, the management representatives adjourn to another room to begin negotiations. Depending on the role defined for him, they may be accompanied by the neutral advisor. No other attorneys or staff are normally present for the negotiations. Once in the negotiation room, the management representatives may conduct the negotia-

tions any way they want. Usually the negotiations are relatively informal. Either representative can leave the room to request information of his own staff, or review legal points. If both management representatives decide they want to hear additional presentations on specific points, they can request it.

It is not necessary to resolve the issue in a single session. Some mini-trials have resulted in agreements in principle within 30 minutes, while others have involved several negotiation sessions, spread over several days.

- Documentation

  Frequently the management representatives will develop an agreement in principle, then request the attorneys to prepare more detailed agreements implementing the agreement. This agreement in principle should be put in writing, with copies given to both parties, to be used as guidance by the attorneys. The management representatives' agreement in principle also can be referred to in case there are later questions about the intent of the formal agreement.

4. CPR Institute for Dispute Resolution, CPR Minitrial Model Procedure and Commentary (1995)*

Introduction

Most bona fide disagreements or disputes between reputable companies are best regarded as business problems to be resolved promptly through business-oriented negotiations. If such negotiations become deadlocked, the parties should consider a non-adjudicative dispute resolution process designed to facilitate settlement.

The informal procedure known as a minitrial, consisting of an adversarial "information exchange" followed by management negotiations, has become a highly successful form of private business dispute resolution. The procedure is private, informal, expeditious and far less expensive or disruptive of business relationships than litigation or arbitration. The procedure does not result in an adjudication. The parties fashion their own solution. Experience shows that the chances of arriving at a solution are very high. The procedure serves to penetrate impasses caused by good faith disagreements on the merits of each party's position. Administrative involvement of an institution is not required.

The business executives, who have the best understanding of their underlying interests and have settlement options not available to adjudicators or attorneys, play a central role in the process. The solution they develop is likely to be more creative and business-oriented than the win-lose decision of a tribunal. The procedure is particularly suitable when difficulties arise out of complex, long-term undertakings, such as take-or-pay contracts, joint ventures, major construction projects or technology arrangements. Such difficulties are best resolved amicably and rapidly, with the least damage to the business relationship. Minitrials also have been successful in one-shot situations in which no business relationship exists, such as securities fraud, wrongful termination, partnership dissolution, antitrust and product liability disputes. . . .

---

*Copyright © 1995, CPR Institute for Dispute Resolution, 366 Madison Avenue, New York, New York 10017-3122. Reprinted with permission. The CPR Institute for Dispute Resolution is a non-profit initiative of 500 general counsel of major corporations, leading law firms and prominent legal academics in support of private alternatives to the high costs of litigation. Organized in 1979 as the Center for Public Resources/CPR Legal Program, CPR develops new methods to resolve business and public disputes by alternative dispute resolution (ADR).

The model procedure is not self-executing, but is to be invoked through execution of an "initiating agreement". A party may withdraw from the process at any time before its conclusion. The procedure is without prejudice to the rights and remedies of the parties should the settlement efforts fail.

Model Minitrial Procedure

1. Institution of Proceeding

The parties will commence the proceeding by entering into a written agreement (the "initiating agreement"), substantially in the form attached hereto as Appendix A [omitted]. The date of the initiating agreement is called the "commencement date."

2. The Minitrial Panel

2.1. The minitrial panel shall consist of one member of management from each party (the "management representative"), who shall have authority to negotiate a settlement on behalf of the party represented, and a neutral advisor (the "Neutral Advisor").

2.2. If the management representatives are not designated in the initiating agreement, each party shall name its management representative within thirty days from the commencement date by written notice to the other party and the Neutral Advisor. Each party thereafter may designate a different management representative by written notice to the other party and the Neutral Advisor.

3. The Neutral Advisor

3.1. The Neutral Advisor, who shall be independent and impartial, will perform the functions stated in this procedure and any additional functions on which the parties may hereafter agree.

3.2. If the Neutral Advisor is not named in the initiating agreement, the parties will attempt to select a Neutral Advisor by mutual agreement.

3.3. If the parties have not agreed on a Neutral Advisor within fifteen days from the commencement date, either party may request CPR in writing, with copy to the other party, to assist in the selection of a Neutral Advisor. A copy of the initiating agreement shall be attached to such request.

CPR shall then proceed as follows:

(a) Promptly following receipt by it of the request, CPR shall convene the parties in person or by telephone one or more times to attempt to select the Neutral Advisor by agreement of the parties.

(b) If the procedure provided for in (a) does not result in the selection of the Neutral Advisor, CPR shall submit to the parties a list of not less than three candidates. Such list shall include a brief statement of each candidate's qualifications. Each party shall strike from the list any candidate it finds unacceptable, shall number the remaining candidates in order of preference, and shall deliver the list so marked to CPR. CPR shall designate as Neutral Advisor the nominee willing to serve for whom the parties collectively have indicated the highest preference and who does not have a conflict of interest (see paragraph 3.4.). If a tie should result between two candidates, CPR may designate either candidate. If this procedure for any reason should fail to result in designation of the Neutral Advisor, the parties may request CPR to repeat the procedure, proposing a list of not less than three new candidates.

3.4. Each party shall promptly disclose to the other party any circumstances known to it which would cause justifiable doubt regarding the independence or impartiality of an individual under consideration or appointed as Neutral Advisor. Any such individual shall promptly disclose any such circumstances to the parties. If any such circumstances have been disclosed, the individual shall not serve as Neutral Advisor unless all parties agree.

3.5. No party, nor anyone acting on its behalf, shall unilaterally communicate with the Neutral Advisor on any matter of substance, except as specifically provided for herein or agreed between the parties.

3.6. The parties will promptly send to the Neutral Advisor such materials as they may agree upon for the purpose of familiarizing the Neutral Advisor with the facts and issues in the dispute. The parties shall comply promptly with any requests by the Neutral Advisor for additional documents or information relevant to the dispute.

3.7. The parties may jointly seek the advice and assistance of the Neutral Advisor or CPR in interpreting this procedure and on procedural matters.

3.8. The Neutral Advisor's per diem or hourly charge will be established at the time of appointment. Unless the parties otherwise agree, (a) the fees and expenses of the Neutral Advisor, CPR's time charges, and any other expenses of the proceeding will be borne equally by the parties; and (b) each party shall bear its own costs of the proceeding.

4. Discovery

4.1. If either or both parties have a substantial need for discovery to prepare for the information exchange, the parties shall attempt in good faith to agree on a plan for strictly necessary, expeditious discovery. Should they fail to agree, either party may request a joint meeting with the Neutral Advisor, who shall assist the parties in formulating a discovery plan.

4.2. Should the minitrial not result in a settlement of the dispute, discovery taken in the proceeding may be used in any pending or future proceeding between the parties relating to the dispute unless the parties otherwise agree. Such discovery shall not restrict a party's ability to take additional discovery in any such proceeding.

5. Briefs and Exhibits

Before the information exchange, the parties shall exchange, and submit to the Neutral Advisor, briefs, as well as all documents or other exhibits on which the parties intend to rely during the information exchange. The parties shall agree upon the length of such briefs, and on the date on which such briefs, documents and other exhibits are to be exchanged.

6. The Minitrial Information Exchange

6.1 The minitrial information exchange shall be held before the minitrial panel at a place and time stated in the initiating agreement or thereafter agreed to by the parties and the Neutral Advisor.

6.2. During the information exchange each party shall make a presentation of its best case, and each party shall be entitled to a rebuttal. The order and permissible length of presentations and rebuttals shall be determined by agreement between the parties, or failing such agreement, by the Neutral Advisor.

6.3. The Neutral Advisor will moderate the information exchange.

6.4. The presentations and rebuttals of each party may be made in any form, and by any individuals, as desired by such party. Presentations by fact witnesses and expert witnesses shall be permitted.

6.5. Presentations may not be interrupted, except that during each party's presentation, and following such presentation, any member of the panel may ask clarifying questions of counsel or other persons appearing on that party's behalf. No member of the panel may limit the scope or substance of a party's presentation. No rules of evidence, including rules of relevance, will apply at the information exchange, except that the rules pertaining to privileged communications and attorney work product will apply.

6.6. Members of the panel, and if the parties so agree, each party and counsel, may ask questions of opposing counsel and witnesses during scheduled, open question and answer exchanges and during that party's rebuttal time.

6.7. The information exchange shall not be recorded by any means. However, subject to Section 8, persons attending the information exchange may take notes of the proceedings.

6.8. In addition to counsel, each management representative may have advisors in attendance at the information exchange, provided that the other party and the Neutral Advisor shall have been notified of the identity of such advisors at least five days before commencement of the information exchange.

7. Negotiations Between Management Representatives

7.1. At the conclusion of the information exchange, the management representatives shall meet one or more times, as necessary, by themselves, and shall make all reasonable efforts to agree on a resolution of the dispute. By agreement, other members of their teams may be invited to participate in the meetings.

7.2. At the request of either management representative, the Neutral Advisor will meet with the management representatives jointly or separately at his or her discretion, and will give an oral opinion as to the issues raised during the information exchange and as to the likely outcome at trial of each issue. Thereupon, the management representatives will again attempt to resolve the dispute. If either management representative requests a written opinion on such matters, the Neutral Advisor shall promptly render such an opinion. Thereupon, the management representatives will again attempt to resolve the dispute. At the request of the management representatives, the Neutral Advisor may at any time mediate the negotiations and may propose settlement terms.

7.3. The terms of any settlement are to be set out in a written agreement which is to be signed by the management representatives as soon as possible after conclusion of the negotiations and will, once signed, be legally binding on the parties.

8. Confidentiality

8.1. The entire process is a compromise negotiation. All offers, promises, conduct and statements, whether oral or written, made in the course of the proceeding by any of the parties, their agents, employees, experts and attorneys, and by the Neutral Advisor are confidential. Such offers, promises, conduct and statements are privileged under any applicable mediation privilege, and are subject to FRE 408 and any state counterpart rules or doctrine and are inadmissible and not discoverable for any purpose, including impeachment, in litigation between the parties to the minitrial or other litigation. However, evidence that is otherwise admissible or discoverable shall not be rendered inadmissible or non-discoverable as a result of its presentation or use at the minitrial. The Neutral Advisor is the parties' joint counsel, or agent if not an attorney.

8.2. The Neutral Advisor will be disqualified as a witness, consultant, or expert for any party, and as an arbitrator between the parties, and his or her oral and written opinions will be inadmissible for all purposes in this or any other dispute involving the parties hereto.

9. Court Proceedings

9.1. If on the commencement date no litigation is pending between the parties with respect to the subject matter of the minitrial, no party shall commence such litigation until the minitrial proceedings have terminated in accordance with Section 10 hereof. Execution of the initiating agreement shall toll all applicable statutes of limitation until the minitrial proceedings have terminated. The parties will take such other action, if any, required to effectuate such tolling.

9.2. If on the commencement date litigation is pending between the parties with respect to the subject matter of the minitrial, the parties may promptly (a) present a joint motion to the court to request a stay of all proceedings pending conclusion of the minitrial proceedings; and (b) request the court to enter an order protecting the confidentiality of the minitrial and barring any collateral use by the parties of any aspect of the minitrial in any pending or future litigation. The grant of such stay and protective order shall not be a condition to the continuation of the minitrial proceeding.

10. Termination of Proceeding

The proceeding shall be deemed terminated if and when (a) the parties have not executed a written settlement of their dispute on or before the thirtieth day following conclusion of the information exchange (which deadline may be extended by mutual agreement), or (b) either party serves on the other party and on the Neutral Advisor a written notice of withdrawal from the proceeding.

11. Actions Against the Neutral Advisor or CPR

Neither the Neutral Advisor nor CPR shall be liable to any party for any act or omission in connection with the minitrial proceeding.

Commentary on Model Minitrial Procedure

Length of Proceeding. The simplicity of the procedure permits rapid completion. The period from signing the initiating agreement to settlement might be about ninety days. Of course, the length of the process will vary from case to case. The information exchange frequently can be completed in one day.

Discovery. Discovery, if any, should be limited to that for which each party has a substantial need for purposes of the minitrial information exchange. As a rule, such discovery would be far less extensive and less formal than discovery conducted in preparation for a trial. The objective is to enable the parties, through limited discovery on the merits, in a short period to define the issues and to learn the principal strengths and weaknesses of their cases. If litigation between the parties is pending, any prior discovery in that litigation should be taken into account in determining the need for additional discovery. The principal form of discovery normally should be the production of relevant documents. Interrogatories generally are not appropriate. Depositions, if any, should be taken only of one or a few key witnesses, and should be confined in scope to the minimum necessary to prepare for the information exchange.

The Information Exchange. A key feature of this procedure is the information exchange. Why hold such an exchange? Executives often lack a thorough understanding of the adversary's side of a dispute and each party is best able to present its own position in a persuasive manner. The information exchange leads each party to focus on the most important issues in presenting its case to the management representative of the other party. Such a presentation usually gives each executive a much better understanding of the dispute and leads to a more realistic position in the settlement negotiations which follow. Participation in the process also tends to defuse hostility and to strengthen the resolve of both management representatives to find a solution. The tone of the minitrial should be one of businesslike problem-solving. Nevertheless, counsel are expected to vigorously advocate their positions during the information exchange.

The Management Representatives. The negotiations are more likely to succeed if the negotiators have not been directly involved in the dispute and therefore do not feel a need to defend past actions. The settlement may well entail a new business deal in which neither party loses. The more senior the management representatives, the greater the range of options they are likely to perceive for a constructive solution. In some circumstances negotiations will be more productive if more than one representative of each party participates.

The prospects for success of the process are likely to be enhanced if the management representatives are evenly matched and command the respect of the other party. Therefore, the parties should consult on the selection of their management representatives.

The Neutral Advisor. A highly qualified Neutral Advisor, in whose impartiality and judgment the parties have confidence, can significantly enhance the prospects for success. It may well be desirable to select as the Neutral Advisor a respected former judge, senior lawyer or legal scholar with a thorough knowledge of the applicable law and the ability to facilitate the conduct of the process including, if necessary, mediation between the parties. Such a person can give the executives educated, objective views on the legal issues and on the likely outcome of a lawsuit or arbitration. The Neutral Advisor could also be a person experienced in the field to which the dispute relates.

With the concurrence of the executives, the Neutral Advisor can also play a mediating role in their negotiations and make settlement proposals. If need be, CPR can assist in the selection of a Neutral Advisor. The parties have the option of dispensing with a Neutral Advisor.

The parties should enter into an agreement with the Neutral Advisor by which the latter agrees to be bound by the provisions of Section 8 (Confidentiality) of the procedure, and covering the Neutral Advisor's fee or time charges and such other matters as the parties and the Neutral Advisor see fit.

Neutral Expert. If the parties need independent expert advice on critical technical or legal issues, and the Neutral Advisor does not possess the required expertise, they may agree on the selection of a neutral expert or empower the Neutral Advisor to select one.

Termination. Section 10 of the model procedure permits either party to withdraw from the proceeding at any time by notice to the other party and the Neutral Advisor. The parties may wish to modify this provision to call for a notice period or to impose a monetary sanction on a party that withdraws before the proceeding has run its course.

Business Agreement Clauses. Persons drafting a business agreement are urged to incorporate the model procedure by reference. The following contract clause is suggested:

> "The parties will attempt in good faith to resolve any controversy or claim arising out of or relating to this agreement in accordance with the CPR Model Minitrial Procedure and will enter into an initiating agreement in the form annexed to such Procedure."

The above clause may not be legally enforceable. Moreover, the minitrial procedure is terminable at will. However, between reputable companies an expression of intent, enforceable or not, carries considerable weight. If a dispute arises, the above contract clause would substantially increase the likelihood that the parties will make a serious effort to arrive at a compromise through this process, rather than seeking an adjudicative solution.

The business agreement could provide that if a controversy arises, negotiations between executives would be the first step in attempting resolution; this procedure, the second step. The agreement also could provide that if the minitrial should not result in a settlement, the dispute will be settled by arbitration in accordance with the CPR Non-Administered Arbitration Rules & Commentary.

E. Ombudsman

1. Tom Arnold, A Vocabulary of Alternative Dispute Resolution Procedures (1995)*

Ombudsman

Typically meaning:

(1) a third party fact finder/adjuster;
(2) perhaps salaried but still largely neutral;
(3) selected to investigate complaints or grievances from an institution's constituents, employees or clients;
(4) who makes nonbinding advisory recommendations to senior management about how to resolve the dispute;
(5) in a voluntary, private, informal process;
(6) wherein, although salaried by the institution, his/her duty is not to management but to the facts and to natural justice and equity for the constituents.

Good ombudsmen are as true neutrals as humans can be; . . . abuse of their duty to be neutral causes them to forfeit the trust and respect of the constituency they serve.

---

*Reprinted with permission.

2. Mary B. Rowe,* *Options, Functions, and Skills: What an Organizational Ombudsman Might Want to Know*, 11 NEGOTIATION J. 103 (1995)**

The ombuds profession is expanding rapidly. With this expansion comes ever-increasing interest, and sometimes confusion, about the profession. Generally speaking, there are two common kinds of ombudsperson today—the classical ombudsperson and the organizational ombudsperson. My focus here is the organizational ombuds practitioner, the more numerous of the two categories in North America.

An organizational ombudsperson is a confidential and informal information resource, communications channel, complaint-handler and dispute-resolver, and a person who helps an organization work for change. Organizational ombudspeople are employed by public and private institutions, agencies and corporations. Their purpose is to foster values and decent behavior—fairness, equity, justice, equality of opportunity, and respect. The ombudsperson often will be especially concerned with respect for those who are—or who see themselves as—less powerful than others in a given situation. The organizational ombudsperson is a designated neutral within an organization and usually reports at or near the top of that organization, outside ordinary management channels. An *outside* organizational ombudsperson works on contract as an ombuds service provider and may report to the chief executive officer or to the head of the division that is contracting with the practitioner. Outside ombudspeople work under the same precepts as internal ombudspeople.

Some ombudspeople serve more or less by themselves as dispute resolution practitioners, or side-by-side with a traditional, single grievance channel. However organizations are increasingly moving toward integrated conflict management systems of which the ombuds function is one part.

There are several basic changes implicit in this evolution. The first is the idea of a system that deals with all persons in the workplace and all kinds of problems—rather than a single grievance procedure, which is typically solely for workers grieving against management, and solely for resolution of a limited list of disputes. The second is the idea of conflict management as a goal for everyone in the organization. This may include such ideas as teaching all managers and members of teams how to use constructive dissent for continuous improvement, as well as training managers in traditional "complaint handling." A third idea is that of integrating conflict management options and structures—-with each other—and with the organization's overall human resource strategy.

In my view, an effective, integrated conflict management system might have these characteristics: There are multiple access points for people with concerns and problems, and there are multiple options for managing conflict which are often available in parallel rather than as designated steps of one procedure. The options are initially available for complainant choice for most problems rather than solely at supervisory choice. These options may be interest-based, rights-based, based option to a rights and power-based option, or loop back from a rights-based option to an interest-based option.

The system is open to managers with concerns, as well as employees. The system will deal with virtually every kind of concern of interest to people in the organization, including for

* The author is the Ombuds at Massachusetts Institute of Technology.

**Reprinted with permission of Plenum Publishing Corporation.

example, disputes between coworkers and between fellow managers, teammates, and groups, as well as the classic concerns about conditions of employment and termination. There is a set of principles about conflict management, and these principles are embedded in the organization's human resource strategy, and backed by top managers.

Both the designation of neutrality and direct access to the chief executive officer help to preserve the independence and contribute to the effectiveness of ombudspeople. The ethic—and strict practice—of confidentiality help to preserve the possibility that people who contact the ombudsperson can decide themselves how to deal with their concerns. Organizational ombudspeople typically will not answer questions from anyone, including senior management, about those with whom they may have had contact—and they maintain the privacy of everyone with whom they have spoken—unless they have permission to speak for the purpose of informal problem resolution.

Even with "permission to speak," ombudspeople typically will not appear in formal proceedings inside or outside their organizations. In order to safeguard both the appearance and practice of neutrality and confidentiality, they do not keep case records for the employer and they resist appearing as witnesses in judicial or quasi-judicial proceedings. Ombudspeople maintain that there is (or should be) a privilege which belongs to the office and not to any visitor to the office—thus no visitor to the office may waive privilege to ask an ombudsperson to testify. In support of this practice, many ombudspeople have an agreement with their employers that the employer will not call the ombudsperson in its own defense. Ombudspeople may, of course, serve managers, but the ombuds practitioner does not represent or act formally on behalf of a manager (or of the employer or any employee).

Organizational ombuds practitioners are different in some significant ways from "pure" or classical ombudspeople, who are created by law and generally appointed by legislative bodies. Classical ombudspeople receive complaints about the administrative acts of government agencies. They may have jurisdiction over all agencies of a local or state government or only over certain agencies. Outside of the United States, some are national ombudspeople with powers to investigate many agencies throughout the given country. Some classical ombudspeople, in North America and elsewhere around the world, are "specialty ombudspeople" who deal with the needs of a defined population such as children or crime victims. Classical ombudspeople are also designated neutrals, and have many of the functions I shall describe in this article. However, they also serve an important additional role for citizens as formal investigators and fact-finders with subpoena power and strong legal safeguards for their independence and for the confidentiality of their records. In addition, they can—and do—publish public reports that make findings on whether a complaint was justified and they may also offer recommendations to an agency they have investigated. Like organizational ombudspeople, they have no power to enforce their findings or recommendations.

An organizational ombudsperson may serve internal staff (employees and managers) or *clients of the organization*[4] (such as students, franchisees, newspaper readers, retirement plan

[4]There is much confusion about the use of the term "client." I do not use the term client to refer to a person who comes to my office or calls me—lest it appear that I am an advocate for that person—as distinguished from being an advocate for a fair process with respect to that person and with respect to others involved in the concern. (I do use the term client to refer to people who are clients of the organization—by the same token, a client ombudsperson is a person who serves the clients of the organization.)

participants, banking customers, etc.) or *both internal staff and clients of the organization*. Some organizational ombudspeople who serve the employer's clients do so in a manner similar to that of classical, statutory ombudspeople. That is, some client ombudspeople may on occasion look into a problem and issue a written report. Common examples include newspaper ombudspeople and others who serve customers of the employer. However, many ombuds practitioners do all their work informally, and put almost nothing on paper. Most ombudspeople who deal with internal staff, and many of those who deal with students, do no formal investigations and write no case reports.

In general, in referring to people who contact me, I refer to "visitors" or "callers." If a person brings a complaint I may use the term "complainant." Other practitioners use terms like "inquirer" or simply "people in contact with the office."

By tradition, an ombudsperson may neither make, change, nor set aside a law or management policy or decision. An ombudsperson may agree or not agree to help a person who contacts him or her. Ombuds practitioners often prefer not to deal with third party complaints, that is complaints from people who are outsiders to a dispute. However, at their own judgment, they may agree to listen to a third party, and in certain cases like whistle blowing, this service may be important to the organization By tradition, an ombudsperson may act on his or her own motion (or initiative) if he or she perceives a problem that appears to need attention.

Acting in this fashion, the ombuds practitioner should try not to run the risk—or give any impression—of violating the confidentiality of any visitor to the office. Acting on one's own initiative would be most likely when the practitioner personally observes some problem like a safety hazard—or a management document that seems indecipherable and needs to be rewritten. It might also happen if the practitioner sees multiple problems of the same sort arising within the organization, and finds a way to surface a pattern to the attention of management without disclosing the identity of any visitor.

People who call upon an organizational ombudsperson typically need options and usually can be offered a number of different options from which to choose. In fact, the customary practice of offering options, rather than choosing for a complainant how a complaint will be handled, helps to define the profession of ombudsmanry within organizations. Many managers think of options for conflict management as options for the manager. An ombudsperson, by contrast, in most instances thinks of options to offer to the *person* who contacts the practitioner. Most organizational ombudspeople, by their codes of ethics, will not act without permission unless a situation seems potentially catastrophic and there seems no other responsible option and no time to develop a responsible option. For this reason, organizational ombuds practitioners assert that speaking to an ombudsperson does not put the employer on notice. Typically, an ombudsperson who hears a concern that does not appear to pose an imminent risk of harm will simply continue to work to see that the issue gets raised in a responsible fashion.

In addition to serving as mediators, counselors, and third party intervenors, ombudspeople have a variety of other functions. In practice, organizational ombudspeople have most of the functions that any dispute resolution practitioner can have. The exceptions are that organizational ombudspeople typically do not investigate formally for management for the purpose of adjudication; do not keep case records for the employer; and do not make management decisions. The multiplicity of functions—and the fact that organizational ombudspeople typically do not do formal investigations for adjudication and do not adjudicate—also helps to define the ombuds profession.

Ombudspeople need certain knowledge and need to learn a variety of skills to pursue their basic functions. Skills and knowledge may be acquired through experience, academic courses, reading, self-reflection, workshops at professional conferences, discussions with other ombudspeople, and through training courses like Ombudsman 101, 202, 303.[6]

The information that follows covers all three subjects simultaneously: the basic options and alternatives open to an inquirer/visitor/complainant, *the functions* of complaint-handlers (all but *two* of which are practiced by ombudspeople) and a basic outline of *skills* that an ombudsperson should acquire. This information comes from four national surveys of organizational ombudspeople, presentations by many practitioners at national conferences, and hundreds of discussions with practitioners for which I am greatly indebted.

It is important, however, to note that ombudsmanry is a profession in evolution, and that probably no statement about ombudspeople is true for all practitioners. This article derives from an attempt by other practitioners and myself to describe and set forth some standards of practice—it is not an assertion of consensus about or within the profession.

Basic Options, Functions, and Skills

Listening. The first option that a caller or visitor may choose is just to talk, and for the ombudsperson to listen, in an active and supportive fashion. The ombudsperson may affirm the feelings of the individual but should be an impartial person with respect to the facts of a situation. In many cases, "being heard" is all that a caller wants. Listening and being gently questioned may help put a problem into perspective. It may help a person to deal with rage or grief or uncertainty or fear. It may help people deal with stress so they can take the time that they need to figure out what is happening to them. Listening impartially is a special skill and requires constant thought and discipline.

Providing and Receiving Information. Often a caller needs information on a one-to-one basis. For example, a caller may not know what information or which records are by law available to him or her. The ombuds practitioner might provide a copy of a policy or obtain clarification of the meaning of a policy, so a complainant under stress need not search or read through dozens of pages of a manual. The ombudsperson may be able to provide (or help to find) information that resolves a problem in one or two contacts. An ombudsperson also may serve an important role in receiving information. A person who perceives unsafe work conditions, discrimination, or other unethical or criminal behavior, may be able to surface information through an ombudsperson in a way that protects the observer.

Reframing Issues and Developing Options. An ombudsperson may be able to help a visitor or complainant develop new options. Often people come to an ombudsperson's office believ-

[6]The Ombudsman Association (TOA) offers Ombudsman 101, 202, 203 for ombudspeople, a *Handbook*, a *Bulletin*, a *Newsletter*, regular surveys, a mentoring program, and a national conference. There are several active organizations of academic ombudspeople: ACCUO (The Association of Canadian College and University Ombudspeople), The California Caucus of Ombudsmen, and UCOA (The University and College Ombuds Association), which offer annual conferences, excellent journals and papers, support for new and experienced academic practitioners, and a forthcoming *UCOA Handbook*. The United States Ombudsman Association brings together classical ombudspeople, and the Canadian Public Sector Ombudsmen bring together the classical practitioners in Canada. The National Society of Patent Representatives serves those who work with patents; and the National Association of State Long-Term Care Ombudsman in Programs serves those who work with nursing home residents.

ing they have no options or only bad ones. The ombuds practitioner can often help frame or reframe the issues, identify or develop new and different perspectives, and describe additional, responsible and effective paths from which the visitor may choose. This function is often especially useful to managers in a quandary—for themselves or with respect to supervisory problems—as well as to employees.

Referral. Many visitors and complainants need more than one helping resource; in effect, they need a helping network. Some need the help of a person such as a social worker or an accompanying person who can act as an advocate. And sometimes the ombuds practitioner is not the best person to help but knows who would be more appropriate. An ombudsperson should understand the other resources within the organization which are available for people with problems, should bc able to refer callers and complainants to others, and should be able to work with others on behalf of a visitor or complainant when given permission to do so.

Helping People Help Themselves In a Direct Approach. An ombuds practitioner may help a visitor or complainant to deal directly with the perceived source of a problem. Through discussion, support and role-playing, a visitor may develop the skills and self-confidence to work on an issue without third party intervention.

This option includes A (the complainant) choosing to deal directly with B (the apparent offender or the perceived source of a problem) in any of several ways:

- A could choose (to learn how) to write a private note or letter to B, laying out the facts as A sees them, A's feelings about these facts, and the remedies proposed by A.
- A could choose (to learn how) to go talk directly with B, with or without presentation of a note or letter. A may decide to go back to B alone, or accompanied by a friend or colleague.

If an ombudsperson knows that a direct approach is being chosen by A, then he or she would typically follow up with A—asking if the situation is resolved with no apparent reprisal, or "just checking in."

Drafting a private letter . . . is often the most helpful first step for a visitor to take, in deciding what to do next. This is especially true if the visitor is angry and upset. Thus, preparing a private letter, whether or not it is sent, is almost always helpful in choosing an option—and in pursuing any option. If the complainant wishes help in drafting a letter, an ombudsperson may ask questions, offer editing suggestions, offer ideas about an effective tone for the intended message of the letter, suggest reorganization of points, etc. The practitioner typically would not write, nor keep a copy of, notes or a letter for a complainant, though it is important for the writer to keep a copy. The ombudsperson typically will explain that it is the responsibility of a complainant to document and preserve evidence that he or she has, and to make sure that his or her evidence is in safekeeping in the files of responsible line or staff managers, if the complainant wishes such evidence to "be on record."

Sending a private letter—in the cultural contest of North America—may be a good approach for a complainant whose concerns are (at least in part) a matter of perception, as in the case of arguments over who should get credit for a good idea. These personal communications often work. But the writer should keep a copy in case the private letter does not succeed. In a subsequent formal complaint of harassment, for example, the complainant's letter might help to demonstrate that offensive behavior actually occurred and that it was unwelcome—which would be essential in making a finding of sexual harassment. In some cultures, the direct approach may not be considered appropriate and in some cultures a direct approach should only be in a note—or, conversely, only in person.

Informal Third-Party Intervention and Shuttle Diplomacy. A visitor or complainant may choose to ask a third party to be a shuttle diplomat—to go back and forth between A and B, or bring A and B together informally, to resolve the problem. The third party could be the ombuds practitioner himself or herself. On the other hand, after consultation with the ombudsperson, the visitor might choose to ask someone else to intervene—a colleague, housemaster, student dean, or faculty member in an academic institution, an administrative officer, a personnel officer, an impartial line supervisor or department head, or some other appropriate person. Or the ombudsperson might agree to take a concern directly to a supervisor or even a very senior manager for review and informal problem solving.

An ombudsperson should be sensitive to fairness in such approaches. She or he should be prepared to communicate that there should be no formal disciplinary action taken by a third party without a process which is fair to an alleged offender. (For example, moving someone or reassigning duties is not by itself defined as disciplinary action, where these are customary management responsibilities—although the employer should carefully consider the fairness of moving a complainant or respondent—but a formal letter of reprimand would be defined as disciplinary action which requires a fair investigatory process.) The ombudsperson will often follow up, to see if informal intervention solved the problems and to check about possible reprisal.

"Looking Into" the Problem. Organizational ombudspeople typically have access to all or to almost all of the data kept by an employer. Some organizational ombudspeople may occasionally agree to look into a problem on a fairly exhaustive basis and write a report. Some such practitioners refer to this practice as "investigation," as a classical ombudsperson might do. However, this function is typically at the request of someone in the organization other than the employer, and is typically not for disciplinary purposes.[7] The written reports of some organizational ombudspeople (for example, in Canada) may occasionally be introduced in formal hearings, though in these cases the ombudsperson typically will refuse to identify his or her sources of information, unless names have been included with permission as part of the report.

Client ombudspeople (who serve clients of the employer, such as readers of a newspaper, customers of a bank, vendors, franchisees of a franchiser) also may agree to look into a problem and submit a written report. Sometimes this report is submitted in draft to a relevant manager before being issued, allowing for discussion and perhaps remedy of a problem—or revision of the draft. Sometimes the report is simply issued without such a step. The findings of an ombudsperson may be accepted in whole or in part, ignored, or rejected by the employer and its managers. By tradition, the findings are not binding on the employer.

It appears that most organizational ombudspeople who serve internal staff and students look into problems much less formally, and never or almost never write a case report. They usually will report their findings directly to a relevant manager or the findings become part of

[7]Individual ombudspeople do occasionally act outside their ordinary role and agree to do formal investigations for the employer for the purpose of adjudication. Some ombudspeople have served as formal observers of the fairness of an adversarial hearing process. On the basis of consultations with several hundred practitioners, I believe that in such circumstances ombudspeople should write a memo to file noting the exception from ordinary practice. With respect to such exceptions practitioners should not necessarily expect to be shielded from a summons to testify in formal hearings inside or outside the organization, although they should attempt to preserve the privacy of anyone who has given information, to the extent possible.

the work of shuttle diplomacy and informal intervention. If the informal findings of an ombuds practitioner indicate the need for formal investigation (for example, by the audit department, ethics office, safety office, security department, campus police, or line management) the practitioner will typically endeavor to see the matter turned over to the appropriate fact finder.

Classic Mediation. This option is offered by ombudspeople in many (though not all) organizations. In classic mediation, A and B are helped by an ombudsperson (or another person who is a trained mediator) to find their own settlement in a process that is rather formal and well defined. A and B may meet with each other and the mediator, or may deal with each other indirectly, with the mediator going back and forth between them. Classic mediation is purely voluntary for A and B and for the mediator. This option must therefore be chosen by both disputants, and agreed to by the ombudsperson or other trained mediator, if it is to occur. Settlements often are put into writing, and may be on- or off-the-record, depending on the wishes of the parties. Formal mediation is still relatively rarely chosen as an option but is becoming somewhat more common. Many 30-to-40 hour training programs are available to teach mediation, and most offer a certificate of completion.

Some ombudspeople also have training and expertise in intergroup and intragroup mediation and conflict management. They find themselves occasionally working with groups, or called in to advise managers who are interested in mediation techniques to manage dissent and disputes. Some ombudspeople are called upon to support the work of teams—especially self-managed teams—that are experiencing tension.

Generic Approaches. A visitor may choose a generic approach which is intended to change a process in the workplace—or to alert possible offenders to their inappropriate behavior without identifying them or the visitor—in such a way that the alleged problem disappears. For example, an ombuds practitioner might be given permission to approach a department head about a given problem without using any names. The department head might then choose to distribute and discuss copies of the appropriate employer policy—for instance, to stop supervisors from requiring uncompensated overtime from nonexempt staff. Or a department head who was informed about possible harassment might encourage harassment training, in such a way as to stop and prevent inappropriate behavior. Generic approaches may be effective in stopping a specific offender and may help to prevent similar problems. These approaches typically do not affect the privacy or other rights of anyone in the organization.

Systems Change. Ombudsman Association surveys indicate that about a third of the working time of organizational ombudspeople is spent on systems change—that is, working with line and staff managers to improve the supervision, human services, and conflict management systems of the organization. A practitioner might notice a problem new to the organization and surface it in a timely fashion, thus serving as an early warning channel for new issues. The practitioner might notice a pattern, or multiple incidents of the same kind, which would indicate the need for employer attention—or the need for a new policy or procedure or structure in the organization. She or he might also hold focus groups on current issues to supply information to decision makers. In addition, some ombudspeople produce annual reports, including statistical data, and some also summarize or highlight problems of concern. These practices must be pursued in a manner consistent with the confidentiality of ethical ombuds practice. Many ombudspeople teach or facilitate in training programs to help prevent certain kinds of problems and to help teach principles of ethical management relevant to the given organization. Some are especially active with respect to diversity training.

Following Through. Often an ombuds practitioner will undertake some action as requested by a visitor. In other cases the visitor will act directly. Ombuds practitioners may thereafter "follow through" on the problems brought to them—in a wide variety of ways. For example, the ombudsperson may simply ask the visitor to call back in a month, to see if all is well—or the practitioner might call back a year later to see how things are going. The ombudsperson might follow up on an administrative action to see that it was effective—or might decide to track problems in a given area or of a given type with an eye toward further consultation with management.

A Custom Approach. Where none of the options above seem exactly right, a caller or visitor may ask for or need unusual help. A typical example would be action with a long or short time lag that is appropriate to the situation. If all options temporarily seem inappropriate, and especially if the concern seems serious, an ombuds practitioner may simply commit to continuing to look for a responsible approach that is tailor-made for a particular situation.

Investigation and Adjudication and Formal Appeals. There are two formal complaint-handling functions that an ombuds practitioner docs not have but should know about. As distinguished from an ombudsperson, a supervisor, department head, personnel officer, formal factfinder or other appropriate staff person may investigate and/or adjudicate a concern in a formal fashion, or deal with an appeal in a formal grievance channel. A practitioner functioning as an ombudsperson is, by contrast, not part of the due process or compliance structure of an organization. He or she does not require testimony from others, does not provide testimony, or do formal investigations, or keep formal case records for the employer. (Some ombudspersons do play a neutral role in convening or supporting peer review grievance channels.)

An ombuds practitioner should, however, understand the formal grievance process. Disciplinary action and adverse administrative action require a fair investigatory process, including notice to the alleged offender and a reasonable opportunity for that person to respond to complaints against him or her. The ombudsperson should be able, if asked, to help others to learn how to investigate and adjudicate fairly, and to support managers to deal with appeals effectively and fairly. The ombudsperson typically would not need to learn the particulars of a formal grievance, but might be able to advise on fair process in dispute resolution—perhaps offering pros and cons for consideration. The ombudsperson should also be able to describe and offer the formal grievance option to complainants for consideration. Some ombudspeople accept concerns and complaints about apparently unfair formal procedures.

Additional Skills and Knowledge

An ombudsperson needs additional skills and knowledge. These include maintaining confidentiality and neutrality, maintaining statistical records and using them appropriately, and using data—in a fashion consonant with confidentiality—to inform management of new problems. The practitioner should know how to inform senior managers of exemplary management and employee practices that deserve commendation or emulation.

Developing new skills on a continuous basis and teaching skills to other practitioners are important both for the practitioner and for building the profession. Ombudspeople should practice self-reflection and self evaluation of their function. Ombudspeople should foster continuous evaluation—through surfacing the concerns and commendations of users—of the employer's conflict management system, and, as appropriate, of other human services in the organization. The cost effectiveness of good communications, of raising problems on a timely basis, and of fair conflict management, should be understood and communicated by ombuds practitioners.

One hopes that the ombudsperson will show common sense, and continually strive for good judgment, respect, and compassion. An ombudsperson should learn how to use inoffensive humor to defuse stress and tension. Mentoring and teaching mentoring are important skills. An ombudsperson should continually try to learn more about preventing and dealing with reprisal, and how to help people who fear reprisal. Dealing with senior managers who are themselves a problem for the organization, and dealing with difficult and possibly dangerous people are vital skills to learn and to continue to learn. An ombudsperson should learn when and how to seek consultation when he or she needs help.

An ombudsperson needs to know such guidelines as the Code of Ethics and Standards of Practice for his or her professional organization. The practitioner should know how and where ombudspeople practice, how ombudspeople meet together professionally, how the profession is organized, and how to keep improving professional skills on a continuous basis. An ombudsperson should understand and practice thoughtful confidentiality, with respect to discussions with other ombudspeople, to protect the privacy of those whose concerns are discussed and to protect the privacy of other ombuds practitioners and their employers.

The ombudsperson should know his or her employer's values and ethics, policies and procedures, and the structure and processes of the employer's organization. The practitioner should have general knowledge of laws relevant to the given organization, and of laws related to major client groups that will be served. Examples of such knowledge might include employment law, the Federal Sentencing Guidelines, laws governing access to records, etc. The ombudsperson should have reasonable knowledge of cross-cultural, ethnic, and gender issues and facts.

Functions Organizational Ombudspeople Should Not Have

There is much discussion in the profession about functions that organizational ombudspeople do not or should not have. In addition, there is much discussion among practitioners who perform multiple roles in their organization about roles where there is or may be role conflict. Accordingly, I present what I see as a growing consensus about functions that organizational ombudspeople should not perform when they are in the role of ombudsperson.

Practitioners should not—in the role of ombudsperson—write formal reports at the request of management for decision making by management. For example, organizational ombudspeople should not provide formal risk assessment with respect to formal grievances, or factfinding for formal grievances, or keep case records with names for the employer. Ombudspeople ought not be compliance officers in any domain—for example, with respect to equal opportunity, safety, or ethics functions—nor should they be inspectors general. Ombudspeople should not be human resource/employee relations/industrial relations officers, nor serve as internal counsel.

In the role of ombudsperson, they should not make binding decisions for the employer or serve as arbitrators. Ombudspeople should not be advocates for any party in a formal process or accompany visitors or give testimony in a formal grievance process. They should not be part of any formal due process structure, though they may be mediators or neutral conveners attached to such a structure. Ombudspeople should not negotiate with lawyers on behalf of any party. Part-time ombudspeople should not serve as ombuds practitioners in any area where they arc also line managers.

Conclusion

In this article I have tried to outline the present day practice of organizational ombudsmanry in North America, as I understand it thus far. I have drawn on very generous contributions from others in the profession, from my own experience, and from research. Probably no ombudsperson lives up, every day, to the standards he or she has set for good judgment, fairness, compassion, neutrality, respect for others—for true and ethical professionalism.

3. Comments and Questions

a. The corporate ombuds discussed by Mary Rowe is a recent innovation. Ombudsman is a Swedish word, and it describes an official whose job is to provide assistance to persons having a problem with a federal government agency. The ombusdman cannot direct an agency to take action, or to refrain from doing so, but she can exert moral persuasion. Variants on the public ombuds model have been adopted in other small countries, but there is no functional equipment for the U.S. government. Inspectors General (IG) at agencies exercise oversight to avoid fraud, waste and abuse, a role that certainly benefits the public, but IG's are not a conduit for assisting persons who are having difficulty with the agency. Some states have established an ombudsman's office to promote appropriate assistance from the government. (Often the problem is that the agency lacks authority to do what has been requested of it, whereupon the task of the ombuds it to explain the situation to the person seeking help.)

b. Mary Rowe regards it as important that the corporate ombuds has direct access to the Chief Executive Officer. Do you agree, or is this simply special pleading for a particular form of one category of senior staff (as opposed to line). The same sorts of arguments are made on behalf of the general counsel, the chief auditor, and others. There is an obvious power basis for this approach since reporting directly to the CEO, rather than through a senior vice president, is a major indicia of importance within the organization.

c. Do you expect that the ombuds "profession" will seek to be regulated by government, probably via certification? The purpose would be to protect the public against inappropriate ombudsing, which activity would then constitute the unauthorized practice of ombudsmanny. You may want to reconsider your answer after reading the materials in Chapter 19, section B.

Chapter 14

Dispute Resolution by Administrative Agencies

CASE STUDY

Mrs. S. was an 83 year old widow who had been living alone for the last several years. At the beginning of each month, she received her Social Security check in the amount of $863.42. Due to deteriorating health conditions caused by cancer, Mrs. S. was taken to the local hospital by her daughter (Party A) on November 31, 1993 at approximately 10:00 p.m. Unfortunately, there was nothing the doctor could do other than try to make Mrs. S. as comfortable as possible. She was pronounced dead by the physician on call at 11:59 p.m. on November 31, 1993. Party A was responsible for the financial affairs of her mother and used some of the funds from the Social Security check to cover funeral costs.

Approximately four weeks after the death of Mrs. S., Party A received a letter from a representative of the Office of Social Security Benefits (Party B) asking for the return of the check issued to Mrs. S. for the month of November, 1993. The policy of the Social Security agency was that, in order to be eligible for benefits, the recipient must survive the month. In this case, time of death (TOD) was recorded one minute short of a full month. Therefore, the representative maintains she was strictly following procedure when she sent the letter requesting the return of the check.

A. Introduction

The Chapter deals with three distinct but related topics: the government as provider **of** ADR services, administrative agencies **as** ADR, and the use of ADR **by** administrative agencies. The discussion is limited to federal agencies, and even then only a small part of the administrative landscape is examined.

The Administrative Procedure Act (APA), 5 USC §§ 551 et. seq., governs the procedures used by federal agencies in taking formal action (unless the agency's organic statute specifically provides otherwise). Formal agency action can take either of two forms: adjudication or rulemaking. The product of rulemaking is a "rule," while the result of adjudication is an "order."

Many important activities of administrative agencies do not fit within the APA definitions of either category, and these are commonly called "informal action." In terms of separation of powers analysis, most of these activities would be characterized as "executive." One of the central facts about the administrative state is that the separation of powers is largely inapplicable to agency activities.

Adjudication is the administrative analogue of trials in the judicial system. Among the most significant differences are that juries are absent in adjudication, rules of evidence usually are much relaxed, and the decider of fact is a subject-matter expert. Do these features make administrative adjudication similar to ADR procedures in important ways?

Rulemaking is the administrative analogue of legislation, except that the scope of an agency's authority is defined by Congress. The English employ the illuminating term "subordinate legislation" for what the APA calls a "rule." The one important use of ADR in this area is negotiated rulemaking, commonly known as "reg-neg," which is the last topic covered in this Chapter. Reg-neg procedures are detailed in The Negotiated Rulemaking Act of 1990.

The other materials in the Chapter all deal with settlement of disputes. In some instances, federal agencies provide ADR services to the public, notably in the context of emergencies and labor disputes. An assortment of ADR procedures have been used to settle disputes between an agency and contractors, notably by the Army Corps of Engineers.

Section C addresses the availability of judicial review from administrative adjudication. Short of constitutional challenges, the authority of Congress to eliminate judicial review, and to substitute agency procedures including ADR, is almost without limits. Detailed consideration is given to dispute resolution at the Veterans Administration (VA). Binding arbitration in certain Federal Insecticide, Fungicide, and Rodenticide Act (FIFRA) proceedings has been upheld by the Supreme Court.

There are few constitutional restrictions on the use of ADR by and at agencies. Only mandatory arbitration might raise some problems. Congress has adopted general legislation that governs the use of ADR by administrative agencies, the Administrative Dispute Resolution Act (ADRA).

While most of this Chapter discusses the use of ADR by administrative agencies, Section E focuses on agencies as ADR—specifically, public benefits agencies that process a massive number of applications and disputes. These programs include Aid to Families with Dependent Children (AFDC), Social Security, and Veterans Administration benefits. These agencies alone decide far more disputed cases per year than the entire federal judicial system.

B. ADR Services Provided by Federal Agencies

1. Comments and Questions

a. This section examines the federal agencies that now provide mediation services in the labor area, and those that have been used during emergencies.

b. Mediation has played an important role in the settlement of disputes during times of war. The material that follows deals with the American experience during World War II, the Korean War, and the Vietnam War. When next the United States becomes involved in a major war, it is likely that some variant of the procedures discussed below will be used.

2. William E. Simkin & Nicholas A. Fidandis, MEDIATION AND THE DYNAMICS OF COLLECTIVE BARGAINING 37-39, 195-207 (1986)*

a. *Mediation of Emergency Disputes*

National Defense Mediation Board

An upsurge of strikes in the late fall and winter of 1940-41 and the probability of early involvement of the United States in World War II led to the establishment of the National Defense Mediation Board (NDMB) by a presidential executive order, dated March 19, 1941. The NDMB was a tripartite agency with three public members, four labor members, and four industry members. Alternate members and a small staff-assisted in the handling of a total of 118 cases over which the board assumed jurisdiction during its life of approximately 10 months.

It is apparent that President Roosevelt concluded that the United States Conciliation Service (USCS), then an agency within the Department of Labor, was inadequate to handle all mediation responsibilities with a war around the corner. Rather than attempt to make fundamental changes within the existing agency, the decision was made to expand the USCS mediation staff and hope for as many settlements as possible at that level but at the same time to superimpose a new agency for the more difficult cases.

The NDMB assumed jurisdiction only in cases that were referred to it by the secretary of labor after conciliators had not secured settlements. All NDMB cases were disputes at plants involving military production. In more than half the cases, strikes were in progress when the disputes were certified by the secretary.

The executive order contained no ban on strikes or lockouts, and no general no-strike, no-lockout pledge had been secured from labor and management. An early major policy of the NDMB was to decide that it could function effectively and accomplish its intended purposes only if strikes were not in progress while it was active in a case. Accordingly, it required a commitment not to strike during mediation, or the suspension of any strike already in progress, before it would begin to mediate. As a part of this process, the board developed a practice of securing from the employer a voluntary commitment to make wage increases retroactive, thereby assuring employees that the delay in settlement would not be at their expense. This retroactive-pay policy could only have been effectuated under near-war conditions and in disputes affecting war production.

Initially the NDMB had no sanctions other than public opinion. It usually made recommendations which were released to the public and were accepted by both parties. In some instances it was not even necessary to make public recommendations. However, the board came to grief over union security issues.

In a case involving the Federal Shipbuilding and Drydock Corporation and the Industrial Union of Marine and Shipbuilding Workers (CIO), the board recommended a maintenance-of-membership clause. The company rejected that recommendation, and the union called a strike on August 6, 1941. This was the first instance of a strike directly attributable to rejection of a board recommendation. On August 23, 1941, the secretary of the navy seized the shipyard under a directive issued by the president. Employees returned to work, but the union

---

*Reprinted with permission from *Mediation and Dynamics of Collective Bargaining (2d ed.)* by William E, Simkin and Nichlos A Fidnadis. Copyright ©1986 by The Bureau of National Affairs, Inc., Washington, D.C. 20037.

security controversy was not resolved and became an early legacy to the National War Labor Board.

Thus, even though it was seldom used, plant seizure of a war production facility became recognized as a potential backstop to NDMB recommendations. The obvious conclusion is that the government decided it could not then afford the luxury of rejection of a mediation recommendation at a vital war production facility. Mediation with the potential sanction of plant seizure clearly is different from [conventional] mediation. . . . It was acceptable only because of the special prewar circumstances.

A second major union security issue arose soon thereafter in a captive-mine case, when the steel companies owning the mines refused to grant the union shop in response to a demand by the United Mine Workers. A strike started but was terminated when the NDMB assumed jurisdiction. A panel of the board then recommended arbitration. The union rejected the board's recommendation and again went on strike. The president intervened, the second strike was terminated, and the parties agreed to submit the issues to the full NDMB for a recommendation on the merits. By a vote of 9-2, with CIO members dissenting, the board recommended against the union shop. Thereupon a strike began for the third time. The CIO members resigned from the board and requested that action be discontinued on all other pending cases involving CIO unions.

Although the NDMB continued in existence until January 12, 1942, and acted on a number of non-CIO cases, it was apparent that the withdrawal of the CIO had all but ended its usefulness, at least temporarily. The attack on Pearl Harbor and the active entry of the United States into the war created a more urgent situation.

Perhaps the greatest achievement of the NDMB was its experimentation with tripartite mediation. Labor and industry representatives had learned to work together with public representatives to solve many extremely difficult problems in a near-war atmosphere. The effective termination of the usefulness of the NDMB created the almost immediate necessity for a new agency: the National War Labor Board (NWLB). . . .

National War Labor Board

With the National Defense Mediation Board in disarray and the December 7, 1941, attack on Pearl Harbor, the almost immediate declaration of war dictated that something be done about labor disputes—and quickly. . . . President Roosevelt convened a group of high industry and labor officials . . . in Washington . . . [in] December 1941. The basic report to the president was simple. Its conclusions were:

(1) There shall be no strikes or lockouts.
(2) All disputes shall be settled by peaceful means.
(3) The president shall set up a War Labor Board to handle these disputes.

The conferees reached complete agreement at a fairly early stage of their deliberations on all but one issue: the union security issue that had plagued the NDMB. . . . Management representatives insisted that union security be excluded from "all disputes," and union representatives insisted that it be included. Upon receiving this report, the president advised the conference that: "The three points agreed upon cover of necessity all disputes that may arise between labor and management." The employer representatives accepted this judgment with some reluctance, and the conference was adjourned.

Thus the War Labor Board to be named by the president was based on a no-strike, no-lockout agreement among representatives selected by the most prominent management and labor organizations. In substance, the new board was created as a voluntary mediation and arbitration agency. Critics have challenged the word "voluntary" on the ground that no 24 individuals had the authority to bind thousands of companies and the many union officials not present at the conference. The absence of legal authority to bind companies and unions not represented directly did not detract from the moral and psychological effect of the conference's decision. The prestigious character of the 24 members and the widespread support for the war created an atmosphere in which open approval of the agreement was voiced promptly by many companies, employer groups, and unions. The wounds caused by the CIO defection from the NDMB had been healed. Most groups and organizations that did not officially approve the agreement accepted it tacitly.

President Roosevelt issued Executive Order 9017 on January 12, 1942, creating the National War Labor Board and transferring to it the staff and unfinished business of the National Defense Mediation Board. The NWLB included 12 regular members (four public, four industry, and four labor). Alternate industry and labor members were named at the outset. The public members originally had no alternates, but several associate public members soon were named who acted principally as mediators. . . .

The executive order spelled out the basic procedural guides. It provided, first, that agreements should be reached by direct negotiations. Failing that, the next step was to call in conciliators from the United States Conciliation Service. If conciliation failed, the secretary of labor would certify the case to the NWLB. Unlike prior NDMB procedures, the NWLB could also intervene on its own motion after consulting with the secretary of labor. Having taken jurisdiction, according to the executive order, the Board shall finally determine the dispute, and for this purpose may use mediation, voluntary arbitration, or arbitration under rules established by the Board.

Especially during the first year of board operation, a substantial proportion of cases were settled by mediation without the necessity of official board action. Mediation continued as the primary procedural process of the board throughout its life, but the percentage of cases so settled diminished considerably as time went on. In the more important cases, regular board members frequently acted as the mediators. In a larger number of cases, associate public members and sometimes staff members worked with alternate or substitute industry members. Except for the occasional use of single hearing officers, most mediation was performed by a tripartite team (one public, one industry, and one labor member).

The "voluntary arbitration" provision of the executive order was effectuated occasionally in new contract disputes by persuading the disputants to agree to arbitration. The arbitrator was selected directly by the parties or was appointed by the board. However, the principal development of voluntary arbitration occurred in grievance disputes. In that era, grievance arbitration had been practiced in a few industries (notably apparel and printing) but was not widely used in the newly organized mass production industries. A major achievement of the NWLB was its promotion of grievance arbitration. This developed in large part out of public members' belief in the process and gradual industry and labor acceptance of the concept. Pragmatically, it was furthered by early acquisition by the board of a heavy workload of contract disputes. It was necessary to find other means of handling the large number of grievance disputes, some of which tended to erupt in the form of strikes or threatened strikes.

The final means of settlement, "arbitration under rules established by the Board," were formal recommendations by the board itself in the form of "directive orders." If a board panel or one of its mediation panels failed to achieve a complete settlement by mediation, a majority recommendation of all remaining disputed issues was made to the board. The board considered the recommendations, adopted or modified them, and issued a directive order.

During the early months, the board was concerned almost solely with the settlement of disputes and avoidance of strikes. However, inflationary trends soon became evident, and in April 1942 the president publicly called for wage and price restraint. On July 16 1942, the board announced what became known as the Little Steel Formula. Developed specifically for a disputed case involving four steel companies, it established a pattern for decisions on general wage increase issues. On October 2, 1942, the Congress amended the Emergency Price Control Act, and on the following day the president issued Executive Order 9250, delegating wage stabilization authority to the NWLB.

Thereafter the board functioned in two capacities. It retained its responsibility to resolve all disputes. It acquired the responsibility to approve, disapprove, or modify all wage increases, including those agreed to voluntarily by the parties. To accomplish this dual purpose, the board revamped its structure and procedures. A Disputes Division and a Stabilization Division were created. However, the full board retained control and supervision over both disputes and wage stabilization.

The tremendous increase in work load caused by wage stabilization and an accelerating volume of disputes required decentralization. The Washington, D.C., offices simply could not handle the load. Moreover, the board favored decentralization in order to keep the decision-making process as close as possible to the parties. Accordingly, 12 regional war labor boards and a board for Hawaii were established to decide most cases on a regional basis. It also developed that some industries could be handled best by industry commissions or panels. Beginning in September 1942 and at various times thereafter until the end of 1944, a total of 17 commissions or panels were created.

All regional boards, the commissions, and the panels were tripartite (public, industry, and labor) and functioned in essentially the same manner as the national board. They were delegated authority to issue directive orders, except that some of the panels were limited to making recommendations to the national board. Directive orders of board agencies could be appealed, thereby reserving final authority to the national board. While the national board retained original jurisdiction in a few major disputes, its work load increasingly became that of a policy-making agency, including action on appeals.

The NWLB and its subsidiary agencies decided 17,650 disputes during the period from January 12, 1942, to August 18, 1945. A substantial number of dispute cases were closed between then and December 31, 1945, when the board was terminated. The four-year total was about 20,000 cases. . . .

How did the board and its agencies mediate? It should be recognized at the outset that this was mediation with reserve powers not normally available in peacetime mediation. The reserve power held by a tripartite mediation panel was the certainty of recommendations to the national board or to a regional board and a subsequent directive order if the parties did not agree. The final reserve power of the national board was plant seizure.

At the risk of repetition, it is most important to recognize that the tripartite composition of the mediation panels was a most valuable asset. The industry member normally had the confidence of the company negotiators and spent much time with them. The labor member was similarly regarded by the union negotiators. The public member talked to both sides, jointly and separately, but performed his most important mediation functions in executive sessions of the tripartite panel. Thus, the mediation sessions were a combination of (1) direct negotiation between the parties in the presence of the full panel, (2) sessions of the mediators with the parties separately and (3) mediation within the panel.

With the advent of the War Labor Board, conciliators in the United States Conciliation Service faced a difficult role. The existence of the board was both a challenge and a menace to the proud and able conciliators of the service. The challenge was to assist in securing a settlement before it became necessary to certify the dispute to the board. The menace was the probability that one or both of the parties would not give the conciliator a chance but would seek to use him as a certifying agent to get the dispute before the board as quickly as possible. Many competent and conscientious conciliators were frustrated and hamstrung by this situation. If they refused to recommend certification, a union could force the issue by calling a strike. The less able and less insistent conciliators often gave up the battle and did not really try to mediate; they washed their hands of the case by immediate certification. Despite these problems, the Conciliation Service did succeed in a surprising number of cases and there were many voluntary settlements without any mediation. . . .

Wage Stabilization Boards

After the National War Labor Board was terminated, Congress passed the Taft-Hartley Act in 1947, . . . [which] created a mechanism for handling emergency disputes. It also replaced the United States Conciliation Service with the Federal Mediation and Conciliation Service. . . .

President Truman's decision to send troops to Korea in mid-1950 was the beginning of the next war emergency. A threat of inflation caused the Congress to pass the Defense Production Act in September of that year. On September 9, 1950, the president issued Executive Order 10161 establishing an Economic Stabilization Agency, within which was created the Wage Stabilization Board (WSB). The WSB was a tripartite agency (three public, three industry, and three labor members). The agency was given no power or authority with respect to labor disputes; it was only a stabilization agency. It will be noted that this was the opposite of the World War II sequence. The National Defense Mediation Board and the National War Labor Board operated for more than a year as disputes agencies before the NWLB was given important stabilization responsibilities.

This 1950 Wage Stabilization Board, like the first World War II agency, collapsed [in February 1951] when all labor members withdrew. The immediate occasion for defection was the issuance of General Wage Regulation No. 6, a cost-of-living general wage increase adjustment formula from which the labor members dissented. A major contributing factor was the absence of any disputes function in the board's jurisdiction.

The president then created a National Advisory Board, on which labor representatives agreed to serve. . . . The Advisory Board's report to the president proposed the reconstitution of the Wage Stabilization Board with labor dispute responsibilities of a much more limited character than had been the case with the NWLB. A no-strike, no-lockout pledge was not obtained. On April 21, 1951, the president issued Executive Order 10233 establishing a reconstituted Wage Stabilization Board of 18 members (six public, six labor, and six industry members). Its authority was as recommended by the Advisory Board.

The Wage Stabilization Board utilized regional boards and a few other subordinate agencies. However, these were concerned almost solely with stabilization. The limited disputes functions were handled by the 18-member board in Washington.

On March 20, 1952, the WSB issued recommendations in a hotly disputed steel industry case. Those recommendations, affecting wages, other cost items, and the perennial union security issue, had significant repercussions. . . . Soon [thereafter], the Congress amended the Defense Production Act to strip the WSB of any effective disputes jurisdiction. Moreover, the board was required again to be reconstituted, this time with Senate confirmation of the members of a new 18-member tripartite board. The third WSB was short-lived. In the late fall of 1952 it modified downward a wage increase that had been negotiated by the coal operators and John L. Lewis. The miners went on strike. During his lame duck period in office, President Truman overruled the board and, on December 3, 1952, approved the full amount that had been negotiated. Thereupon, Chairman Archibald Cox and all the industry members resigned. Soon after assuming office, President Eisenhower issued an executive order terminating all activities of the board.

The War in Vietnam

The Vietnam War was the next occasion for testing the efficacy of collective bargaining when a substantial proportion of the nation's resources and manpower have been diverted to military action. A feature of the Vietnam War was the absence of any special wartime labor disputes procedure. Several Taft-Hartley injunctions were due directly to defense preparation for participation in the war. Similarly, activity by some nonstatutory boards was traceable to the war. However, resort to such measures was not appreciably more frequent than during the period prior to Vietnam. How is this to be explained?

One reason is that the Kennedy and Johnson administrations, and also initially the Nixon administration, made a conscious decision to avoid *mandatory* wage and price controls. While no additional disputes-settling procedures were established during this period the Nixon Administration unexpectedly instituted a wage and price controls program in late 1971 to combat rising inflation. After some initial problems with compliance, a revised tripartite program, the Cost of Living Council, was set up under the direction of John Dunlop. Although it had no official authority to settle labor disputes federal mediators worked closely with the controls agency until the stabilization program was ended by Congress in 1974, the last full year of the Vietnam War. . . .

A major reason why a War Labor Board was not proposed was a firm policy decision at the highest levels of government and within civilian leadership at the Pentagon. Briefly stated, it was to give collective bargaining every possible opportunity to work. Direct and frequent liaison between the Defense Department and the Federal Mediation and Conciliation Service resulted in frank and candid appraisal of maximum strike time that could be accommodated by military needs on the one hand and the best prognosis as to whether a strike would occur and, if so, its expected duration on the other hand. Time and again, initial gloomy Pentagon estimates as to criticality were softened after more thorough checking. In short, the Defense Department did not push the panic button in its final informal reports to the FMCS unless there was a real and pressing urgency. Effective civilian control at the Pentagon tempered the normal military reaction to labor disputes in wartime. At most war production plants the FMCS was thereby able to utilize the full collective bargaining pressures of a contract deadline and a possible strike threat. And even if a strike started, the absence of official hysteria permitted hard-hitting mediation in lieu of government decision making.

The FMCS sought to gear its mediation policies and performance to meet the specific needs of each important defense production dispute. Defense cases generally were given priority, and, where necessary, more aggressive mediation tactics were used than in otherwise comparable nondefense disputes. The FMCS was not always successful, as evidenced by the Taft-Hartley injunctions and nonstatutory boards. . . . But in many instances settlements were achieved by collective bargaining, assisted by intensive mediation, that would unquestionably have gone the War Labor Board route if such a board had been in existence. Many disputes that can be characterized as "near misses" were settled when the alternative was a Taft-Hartley injunction. . . .

The strike record during the Vietnam War was not as good as during the National War Labor Board's three most active years. However, the absence of a no-strike, no-lockout pledge and the fact that the Vietnam War was never accorded the same popular support as World War II suggest that the record of the 1960s was remarkably good. If the comparison of Vietnam is with the Korean War period, the evidence is even stronger. The Korean conflict was more palatable to the American public than Vietnam, but the strike record during the Korean War was not as good.

b. Federal Mediation and Conciliation Service

The Federal Mediation and Conciliation Services (FMCS), the largest mediation agency, was established as an independent agency in 1947. It succeeded the United States Conciliation Service which had been a part of the Department of Labor for many years. At various times . . . from 1961 through 1981, it has employed from a low of 214 to a high of 350 full-time labor mediators in addition to other personnel. The average for these 21 years was 292 mediators.

The central office of the FMCS is in Washington D.C. It is organized geographically into regional and district offices. Mediators work in and out of these offices and a majority work out of field offices situated in most large cities throughout the United States. . . .

The principal functions of the FMCS are to mediate in private sector crisis bargaining, to assist in noncrisis bargaining (formerly called preventive mediation and now known as technical assistance), to act in federal public sector labor disputes under the Civil Service Reform Act, to do mediation work under the special federal program related to health care, and to mediate in state and local public sector labor disputes in states that do not have their own mediation agencies. An additional important function . . . is FMCS assistance to parties in the selection of labor arbitrators for grievance disputes.

c. National Mediation Board

The National Mediation Board (NMB) was established in its present form in 1934. . . . Its jurisdiction is limited to railroads and airlines. The principal functions of the NMB are to mediate railroad and airline disputes, to assist the parties in those two industries in the selection of labor arbitrators for grievance disputes, and to act in railroad and airline representation (a function performed elsewhere by the NLRB). . . .

The NMB headquarters are in Washington D.C. and, unlike the FMCS, it has no administrative or mediation offices elsewhere. It is headed by three board members, appointed by the president and confirmed by the Senate for three-year staggered terms. Only two of the three board members may be from one political party. . . .[There is] a relatively small full-time mediator staff (approximately twenty members). . . . They come within the province of civil service regulations.

d. Atomic Energy Labor-Management Relations Panel

The Atomic Energy Labor-Management Relations Panel was created in 1949 by Presidential action. . . . All members serve on a part-time basis. The primary function of the panel is to serve in the mediation of disputes having direct relevance to atomic energy matters.

3. Comments and Questions

a. The next piece discusses dispute resolution assistance by the U.S. Army Corps of Engineers Board of Contract Appeals (BCA). The BCA is an internal review body within the Corps of Engineers. The Board is not a court, although its members are called judges and its operations parallel those of courts in many ways. In separation of powers terms, the Board is part of the Executive rather than the Judicial branch of government.

b. The Army Corps of Engineers has been the leader within the federal government in making innovative use of ADR. The examples in the subsequent article indicate the range of ADR procedures that have been used by the Corps. One reason for this record of innovation is that the Corps is in the construction business, where ADR has long been widely used. *See* generally, Alan E. Harris, Charles M. Sink & Randall W. Wulff [eds.], ADR: A PRACTICAL GUIDE TO RESOLVE CONSTRUCTION DISPUTES (1994). As these authors observe in their preface, "ADR methods are particularly well-suited to the construction industry." Why is ADR "particularly well-suited" to construction disputes? Within the realm of construction, is ADR especially well-suited for large projects, such as those regularly undertaken by the Corps?

4. Reba Page & Wesley C. Jockisch, *The Corps of Engineers Board of Contract Appeals Use of Alternative Dispute Resolution*, 24 PUBLIC CONTRACT L.J. 453 (1995)*

This article provides information regarding several appeals processed by the U.S. Army Corps of Engineers Board of Contract Appeals using ADR procedures. . . . It is interesting to note the progression of ADR procedures used and the adoption of less structured approaches as the parties have become more trusting of the ADR process. While ADR was only initially considered for appeals already docketed at the Board, the Board [now] is prepared to assist parties in a series of related claims under the same contract that range from docketed appeals to disputes that have not been the subject of a decision by the Contracting Officer. In this instance the parties have agreed that the Board's successful resolution of the disputes will preclude any further action including further appeal. Following are the various judges' comments on the procedure and processing of key ADR proceedings each handled:

1. Nonbinding Mediation: *Park Constr. Co.*

Park Construction Company was awarded a contract for Stage 1B-3 of the Rochester Flood

---

*Reprinted with permission.

Control Project in the amount of $9,843,000. The work included construction and excavation of flood control structures and a pedestrian bridge throughout the approximately one-mile project on the South Fork of the Zumbro River near Rochester, Minnesota.

[T]he Contracting Officer denied Parks claim of $430,000 for constructive acceleration and for extension of the contract time of performance for weather delays. Park appealed to the Board the denial of its claim in the revised amount of $420,000.

During the preliminary conference, the presiding Board member set the hearing date for November 14, 1994, with discovery concluding on August 12, 1994. Based on the parties request to use a settlement judge to resolve their dispute, Judge Jockisch as Chairman of the Board agreed to assign Administrative Judge Ketchen to serve as a neutral to conduct the mediation. However, Judge Jockisch also directed the parties to complete the negotiation process by September 30, 1994, prior to the scheduled trial date and indicated that the hearing would proceed on the scheduled date if the parties did not resolve the appeal by settlement.

Judge Ketchen assisted the parties in the mediation process. The parties agreed to several elements of the mediation that would govern the negotiating process. Importantly, the settlement judge would not make a binding decision, but would function as a mediator to assist the parties in attempting to negotiate a resolution.

Each party had a principal with settlement authority present during the negotiations and each principal participated fully in the mediation process. Both parties agreed that the process would begin in a joint session with both parties representatives and the mediator present.

The initial joint session gave representatives of both parties several hours for presenting and discussing their respective positions on the first mediation day. Following that, as agreed by the parties, the mediator conducted a number of individual sessions on an alternating basis with each party's representatives.

During these individual sessions with each party, the judge discussed with each its position on the facts and issues in an effort to narrow the gap between the parties positions toward possible settlement. He discussed the strengths and weaknesses of their positions with each party. He attempted to establish areas of agreement on the facts and issues, and to more clearly define areas of disagreement in order to aid in devising a strategy to facilitate negotiations. The process took place in a conference room in offices provided by appellant's counsel; other rooms were provided for each party's use to confer when not meeting in individual session with the judge.

Toward the end of the second day of the mediation, following an impasse, significant progress was made toward settlement when a breakthrough began with each party making several offers and counteroffers. However, a second impasse occurred. Although the judge and the parties attempted to overcome the blockage, the parties did not reach agreement and the appeal did not settle.

At the close of the mediation, Judge Ketchen informed the parties that he would preserve the confidentiality of the mediation and would not participate further in Board proceedings involving this appeal. He also advised the parties that he would not be subject to being called as a witness in any proceeding by either party.

Without fear of breaching the confidentiality of the mediation, Judge Ketchen opined that the process worked successfully, although the benefits of a settlement were not realized. Because the elements necessary for a successful negotiation were present, a great potential existed during the mediation at differing times and in different degrees for resolving the matter to the satisfaction of both parties with a considerable savings of time and money to all. The parties were able to narrow the issues later heard on appeal and better focus their arguments. In short, the mediation process was clearly useful, even though immediate resolution was not achieved.

2. Minitrial with Nonbinding Decision: *Newell Enterprises, Inc.*

Newell Enterprises, Inc. (NEI), sought $2,100,000 in additional compensation under a Corps construction contract for a levee within the Mississippi River flood control system. In accordance with a Memorandum of Understanding (MOU), the parties filed a joint request to engage in ADR. That process called for the use of an administrative judge from the BCA to serve as a settlement judge. As required by the Board's "Notice Regarding Alternative Methods of Dispute Resolution," the Board's Chairman approved the parties' joint request and assigned Administrative Judge Ketchen to serve as the settlement judge. The role of the settlement judge was to observe summary presentations by the parties, evaluate the parties respective presentations, issue a nonbinding bench decision, and assist the parties in their attempt to resolve the dispute.

The MOU stated these basic requirements and procedures:

(1) Delivery of . . . documents submitted to the settlement judge seven days before the scheduled joint session at the Board's offices in Washington, D.C.;

(2) Summary abbreviated presentations to the settlement judge in one day, including optional opening statements, the presentation of witnesses, cross-examination of witnesses, the offering of evidence and other documents as desired, and closing arguments;

(3) No transcription of proceedings and waiver of briefs;

(4) Consideration of liability (entitlement) only;

(5) A nonbinding, summary bench decision of no precedential value by the settlement judge on the second day to include discussion with the parties of the settlement judges findings, also nonbinding, as would be any of the settlement judges rulings and orders;

(6) Actions or statements by the settlement judge or the parties representatives neither constituted admissions nor could be offered in evidence in other proceedings. The disputes resolution procedure did not render evidence otherwise admissible before the Board inadmissible because of its use during the dispute resolution procedure;

(7) Negotiations to commence between the parties immediately after the summary bench decision, discussion with or without the settlement judges presence or assistance at the parties discretion;

(8) The MOU neither constituted an arbitration agreement nor would it be construed so as to waive any contract rights, the Board's rules, or rights under the CDA or other law;

(9) The settlement judge would be disqualified as a trial witness, consultant, or expert, and would not take part in subsequent proceedings regarding the appeal or the decision;

(10) The parties summary presentations and their negotiations would he confidential. All presentations and discussions in connection with the negotiation proceedings among the parties representatives and the settlement judge would be inadmissible as evidence by the parties in subsequent proceedings before the Board or in judicial proceedings.

In accordance with the agreement, the minitrial took place on September 2 and 3, 1992, with the parties making presentations to the judge. Judge Ketchen advised the parties of his nonbinding bench decision on the second day and discussed with them the basis for his decision. Afterward, the parties did not immediately enter into negotiations as had been agreed; instead, the proceedings were adjourned and the parties' representatives left Washington.

Although the appeal eventually settled a few months before going to hearing, Judge Ketchen believed that the ADR procedure would have settled the matter more expeditiously had the parties been clear on the requirement that each party have a principal having full settlement authority physically present during the minitrial presentations and the nonbinding bench decision and discussion afterward. The Government interpreted the MOU as not requiring its principal's presence. This would have enabled the parties to conduct discussions immediately following issuance of the judge's decision and discussion of the findings, with the presentations fresh in everyone's minds, and might have enabled far quicker resolution.

3. Summary Binding Trial: *Anthony J. Bertucci Constr. Co., Inc.*

Bertucci Construction had entered into a contract with the Corps for Bank Restoration of Southwest Pass, in Plaquemines Parish, Louisiana. Bertucci's claim exceeded $600,000, and turned primarily upon surveying methodology.

Following a final decision by the Contracting Officer, the parties elected to use ADR to resolve the dispute. The parties agreed to submit their appeal to a single judge for a summary binding trial on the issue of whether the contractor had encountered a differing site condition because of the Government's alleged failure to provide a readily recoverable baseline. A key provision of the agreement was that the judge's decision would be final and conclusive, neither appealable under the CDA nor subject to collateral attack by either party, and could not be set aside except for fraud.

There are several points raised by Judge Peacock that are well worth considering. First, the issue presented involved gray areas in the law of surveying procedures. The case could have established a useful new precedent. Nevertheless, use of a less costly and time-consuming method for achieving a binding resolution of their dispute was of paramount importance to the parties.

Second, whether the use of ADR meaningfully shortened the overall time for the trial is questionable. The pretrial schedule was shortened, but the parties reserved up to three days for trial. The length and character of the trial was essentially the same as would have been required under non-ADR procedures. Given the large dollar amount involved, the length of the trial was well justified. Scheduling requirements should be tailored to the need of each case, as determined by the parties, with suggestions from the Board member. Nevertheless, the fact that the judge provided a decision within the ten-day time frame as planned following trial was of value because a fully paneled Board decision may take considerably longer.

Third, Judge Peacock's prehearing preparation for trial was more extensive than in a non-ADR case. It is critical for the judge to define and understand the disputed issues before trial, and essential to ensure that key factual issues are adequately addressed during the trial. This may require extensive questioning of witnesses from the bench, in contrast to the traditional hearing practice relying more on questioning by counsel.

Unlike other ADR procedures, the Board's decision in a summary binding trial concludes the case. Judge Peacock recommends that the ADR judge should be permitted to discuss the merits of the case with other Board members prior to issuance of the decision. The parties need not be concerned that other judges will be prejudiced by such discussions, since the proceedings are binding and there is no residual involvement for other Board members. Judge Peacock opined that the summary trial procedure is preferable to binding or nonbinding arbitration both now permitted under the ADRA. Once a decision is issued the case is concluded; neither party may opt out and neither party may appeal. Unlike outside arbitrators, extensive concerns about selection, expertise, and impartiality are generally eliminated. No payment of fees of nongovemment personnel are involved. Unlike some arbitrations, the parties can select the degree of formality, discovery and procedural due process that they desire. There are no set rules. The parties should be creative in following procedures that best satisfy the unique dictates of their case. A further advantage over arbitration is that the outcome of a summary trial is more predictable. Although unpublished, the decisions are read and discussed by other Board members. With such peer review, significant deviations from Federal procurement law are unlikely.

4. Mediation: *Maecon, Inc.* and *The Travelers Indemnity Co.*,

This case is especially interesting from the ADR proponents perspective for the unusual form of process agreed upon and the flexibility displayed by the participant as the ADR process unfolded. The project involved coastal marine construction; it called for an experimental sand pumping system to accommodate natural littoral dynamics on the coast of California, assist in keeping a channel navigable, and replenish beach sand. The contact was in the original amount of over $5.4 million.

The "heart" of the project was a large, barge-mounted engine and pump assembly to be procured, installed, and extensively tested by the contractor. Maecon, the original contractor terminated for default, alleged delays and design defects which it said hampered progress and caused additional costs. The Government unilaterally allowed some price increases, but issued two "cure notices," which asserted that Maecon had failed to make adequate progress toward completion. Maecon made additional claims of changes, differing site conditions, and delays.

After several unsuccessful attempts to run and test the engine and pump assembly, a third cure notice was issued. The contractor's right to proceed with the contract work was later terminated for default. The surety reviewed the project's status and agreed to complete the contract work.

More claims were filed by the surety completing contractor. The total of all contractor and surety claims was over $7.5 million. The Corps had allowed about $1.6 million in contract modifications issued to the original contractor and to the surety/completing contractor. The termination for default of the original contractor had not been resolved.

Pleadings were filed and discovery commenced under the Board's Rules. In 1991, the parties jointly petitioned the Board for a suspension of the processing of the appeals by the Board to allow for the presentation of additional monetary claims to the contracting officer and to allow the parties to engage in unassisted negotiation. The appeals were dismissed without prejudice for that purpose, the parties were given three years in which to reinstate the appeals. Following that dismissal, a final "global" claim was prepared and presented to the Corps' contracting officer. Two years and 364 days after the appeal was dismissed without prejudice, the appellant asked that the initial appeals be returned to the Board's active docket. At the same time, the "global" claim was appealed.

The appellant suggested that ADR be used to attempt resolution, which was readily accepted by the respondent and the Board. An agreement, quickly and easily reached, generally provided for a three day settlement conference to be attended by principals for both parties. Five days prior to the conferences, each party was allowed to submit a brief to the settlement judge. The ADR process was set up in the following manner:

Day 1: Each party was allocated a half day to make its best summary presentation of the facts, analyses, claims, and defenses to the other party and to that settlement judge.

Day 2, Morning: A general "roundtable" discussion of any and all issues would be conducted among all attendees with the settlement judge acting as a participant and mediator.

Day 2, Afternoon: The settlement judge was to meet independently, then with both parties together, to offer suggestions and recommendations.

Day 3, Morning: The parties would meet to attempt settlement without the settlement judge being present.

Day 3, Afternoon: If the Parties had not settled both would meet with the settlement judge for a nonbinding decision in the nature of arbitration.

On Day 1, proceedings occurred substantially as planned. Some discussion, such as was scheduled for the Day 2 roundtable, was conducted during Day 1 because the settlement judge asked questions and followed up with requests for responses from the other side. At the conclusion of Day 1, each party was asked by the settlement judge to prepare a brief clarification of certain points to be presented at the start of Day 2 and to determine for itself whether the Day 1 presentations translated into a change in its position on settlement in terms of damages.

At the start of Day 2, the surety/contractor presented a two page outline of significant settlement issues. The outline, plus follow-up presentations project scheduling, tended to focus the roundtable discussions. At mid-day on Day 2, the ADR proceedings departed from the planned format. The roundtable continued into the afternoon. The parties then asked for the settlement judge's evaluation in open session. Each party then met separately with the settlement judge. During these sessions, the settlement judge elaborated on the evaluation and implications for damages calculations as well as termination for default of the original contractor. Each party was asked by the settlement judge to be prepared to make its best opening offer at the start of Day 3.

Day 3 was taken up with separate conferences during which each party presented its offer and discussed its basis with the settlement judge, followed by formulation of an accompanying message for the settlement judge to take to the other side. Throughout these negotiations, the settlement judge acted as a neutral broker, conveying the point of view of one side to the other.

Both principals reported satisfaction. Several of the "witnesses" and consultants found the mediation remarkably efficient. Counsel were relieved that settlement was achieved. Having a settlement judge with experience in resolution of federal construction contract disputes, considerable previous exposure to engineering and construction technology and terminology, and a good familiarity with Corps of Engineers project management and business processes, was very helpful and kept the mediation moving apace.

There is no doubt that much time and money were saved compared with the investment which would have been required for full preparation, hearing, and briefing by the parties and counsel. The Board saved time that would have been required for hearing preparation, the hearing, and decision writing, not to mention time and effort possibly resolving preliminary issues related to discovery and other prehearing matters.

Last but not least, the parties are not billed for the settlement judge's time and Board conference facilities. The bottom line is that the Board is prepared to foster informal, inexpensive, and expeditious dispute resolution whenever wherever appropriate.

C. Adjudication: Judicial Review

1. *Johnson v. Robison*, 415 U.S. 361 (1974)

Mr. Justice BRENNAN delivered the opinion of the Court.

A draftee accorded Class I—O conscientious objector status and completing performance of required alternative civilian service does not qualify under 38 U.S.C. § 1652(a)(1) as a "veteran who . . . served on active duty" (defined in 38 U.S.C. § 101(21) as "full-time duty in the Armed Forces"), and is therefore not an "eligible veteran" entitled under 38 U.S.C. § 1661(a) to veterans' educational benefits provided by the Veterans' Readjustment Benefits Act of 1966. Appellants, the Veterans' Administration and the Administrator of Veterans' Affairs, for that reason, denied the application for educational assistance of appellee Robison, a conscientious objector who filed his application after he satisfactorily completed two years of alternative civilian service. . . . Robison thereafter commenced this class action . . . seeking a declaratory judgment that 38 U.S.C. §§ 101(21), 1652(a)(1), and 1661(a), read together, violated the First Amendment's guarantee of religious freedom and the Fifth Amendment's guarantee of equal protection of the laws. Appellants moved to dismiss the action on the ground . . . that the District Court lacked jurisdiction because of 38 U.S.C. § 211(a) which prohibits judicial review of decisions of the Administrator.

We hold . . . that § 211(a) is inapplicable to this action and therefore that appellants' motion to dismiss for lack of jurisdiction of the subject matter was properly denied. On the merits, [all of plaintiff's theories were rejected]. . . .

Plainly, no explicit provision of § 211(a) bars judicial consideration of appellee's constitutional claims. That section provides that "the decisions of the Administrator on any question of law or fact under any law administered by the Veterans' Administration providing benefits for veterans . . . shall be final and conclusive and no . . . court of the United States shall have power or jurisdiction to review any such decision. . . ." The prohibitions would appear to be aimed at review only of those decisions of law or fact that arise in the administration by the Veterans' Administration of a statute providing benefits for veterans. A decision of law or fact "under" a statute is made by the Administrator in the interpretation or application of a particular provision of the statute to a particular set of facts, Appellee's constitutional challenge is not to any such decision of the Administrator, but rather to a decision of Congress to create a statutory class entitled to benefits that does not include I—O conscientious objectors who performed alternative civilian service. Thus, as the District Court stated: "The questions of law presented in these proceedings arise under the Constitution, not under the statute whose validity is challenged." . . .

Nor does the legislative history accompanying the 1970 amendment of § 211(a) demonstrate a congressional intention to bar judicial review even of constitutional questions. No-review clauses similar to § 211(a) have been a part of veterans' benefits legislation since 1933. . . . [T]he Administrator, in a letter written in 1952, comprehensively explained the policies necessitating the no-review clause and identified two primary purposes: (1) to insure that veterans' benefits claims will not burden the courts and the Veterans' Administration with expensive and time-consuming litigation, and (2) to insure that the technical and complex determinations and applications of Veterans' Administration policy connected with veterans' benefits decisions will be adequately and uniformly made.

The legislative history of the 1970 amendment indicates nothing more than a congressional intent to preserve these two primary purposes. . . . Nothing whatever in the legislative history of the 1970 amendment, or predecessor no-review clauses, suggests any congressional intent to preclude judicial cognizance of constitutional challenges to veterans' benefits legislation. Such challenges obviously do not contravene the purposes of the no-review clause, for they cannot be expected to burden the courts by their volume, nor do they involve technical considerations of Veterans' Administration policy. . . .

2. Comments and Questions

a. Does *Johnson v. Robison* stand for the proposition that, under our system of separation of powers, the legislature cannot preclude constitutional challenges to agency actions? The separation of powers is enshrined in the constitutions of all fifty states, as well as the United States Constitution.

b. *Johnson v. Robison* also illustrates the usual result in constitutional claims cases—the government wins.

c. Absent a constitutional dimension, Congress may prohibit judicial review of agency decisions, as it has done with the veterans' benefits claims.

3. Access to the Federal Court System

a. *Walters v. National Association of Radiation Survivors*, 473 U.S. 305 (1985)

Justice Rehnquist delivered the opinion of the Court.

Title 38 U.S.C. § 3404(c) limits to $10 the fee that may be paid an attorney or agent who represents a veteran seeking benefits for service-connected death or disability. The United States District Court for the Northern District of California held that this limit violates the Due Process Clause of the Fifth Amendment, and the First Amendment, because it denies veterans or their survivors the opportunity to retain counsel of their choice in pursuing their claims. We . . . now reverse.

I

Congress has by statute established an administrative system for granting service-connected death or disability benefits to veterans. See 38 U.S.C. § 301 et seq. The amount of the benefit award is not based upon need, but upon service connection—that is, whether the disability is causally related to an injury sustained in the service—and the degree of incapacity caused by the disability. A detailed system has been established by statute and Veterans' Administration (VA) regulation for determining a veteran's entitlement, with final authority resting with an administrative body known as the Board of Veterans' Appeals (BVA). Judicial review of VA decisions is precluded by statute. 38 U.S.C. § 211(a); Johnson v. Robison, 415 U.S. 361 (1974). The controversy in this case centers on the opportunity for a benefit applicant or recipient to obtain legal counsel to aid in the presentation of his claim to the VA. Section 3404(c) of Title 38 provides: "The Administrator shall determine and pay fees to agents or attorneys recognized under this section in allowed claims for monetary benefits under laws administered by the Veterans' Administration. Such fees—(2) shall not exceed $10 with respect to any one claim. . . ." Section 3405 provides criminal penalties for any person who charges fees in excess of the limitation of § 3404.

Appellees here are two veterans' organizations, three individual veterans, and a veteran's widow. The two veterans organizations are the National Association of Radiation Survivors, an organization principally concerned with obtaining compensation for its members for injuries resulting from atomic bomb tests, and Swords to Plowshares Veterans Rights Organization, an organization particularly devoted to the concerns of Vietnam veterans. Appellees did not seek class certification. . . .

Congress began providing veterans pensions in early 1789, and after every conflict in which the nation has been involved Congress has, in the words of Abraham Lincoln, "provided for him who has borne the battle, and his widow and his orphan." The VA was created by Congress in 1930, and since that time has been responsible for administering the congressional program for veterans' benefits. In 1978, . . . approximately 800,000 claims for service-connected disability or death and pensions were decided by the 58 regional offices of the VA. Slightly more than half of these were claims for service-connected disability or death, and the remainder were pension claims. Of the 800,000 total claims in 1978, more than 400,000 were allowed, and some 379,000 were denied. Sixty-six thousand of these denials were contested at the regional level; about a quarter of these contests were dropped, 15% prevailed on reconsideration at the local level, and the remaining 36,000 were appealed to the BVA. At that level some 4,500, or 12%, prevailed, and another 13% won a remand for further proceedings. . . .

As might be expected in a system which processes such a large number of claims each year, the process prescribed by Congress for obtaining disability benefits does not contemplate the adversary mode of dispute resolution utilized by courts in this country. It is commenced by the submission of a claim form to the local veterans agency, which form is provided by the VA either upon request or upon receipt of notice of the death of a veteran. Upon application a claim generally is first reviewed by a three-person "rating board" of the VA regional office — consisting of a medical specialist, a legal specialist, and an "occupational specialist." A claimant is "entitled to a hearing at any time on any issue involved in a claim. . . ." Proceedings in front of the rating board "are ex parte in nature," no Government official appears in opposition. The principal issues are the extent of the claimant's disability and whether it is service connected. The board is required by regulation "to assist a claimant in developing the facts pertinent to his claim," and to consider any evidence offered by the claimant. In deciding the claim the board generally will request the applicant's Armed Service and medical records, and will order a medical examination by a VA hospital. Moreover, the board is directed by regulation to resolve all reasonable doubts in favor of the claimant.[2]

After reviewing the evidence the board renders a decision either denying the claim or assigning a disability "rating" pursuant to detailed regulations developed for assessing various disabilities. Money benefits are calculated based on the rating. The claimant is notified of the board's decision and its reasons, and the claimant may then initiate an appeal by filing a "notice of disagreement" with the local agency. If the local agency adheres to its original decision it must then provide the claimant with a "statement of the case"—a written description of the facts and applicable law upon which the board based its determination—so that the claimant may adequately present his appeal to the BVA. Hearings in front of the BVA are subject to the same rules as local agency hearings—they are ex parte, there is no formal questioning or cross-examination, and no formal rules of evidence apply. The BVA's decision is not subject to judicial review [except for constitutional claims].

The process is designed to function throughout with a high degree of informality and solicitude for the claimant. There is no statute of limitations, and a denial of benefits has no formal res judicata effect; a claimant may resubmit as long as he presents new facts not previously forwarded. Although there are time limits for submitting a notice of disagreement and although a claimant may prejudice his opportunity to challenge factual or legal decisions by failing to challenge them in that notice, the time limit is quite liberal—up to one year—and the VA boards are instructed to read any submission in the light most favorable to the claimant. Perhaps more importantly for present purposes, however, various veterans' organizations across the country make available trained service agents, free of charge, to assist claimants in developing and presenting their claims. These service representatives are contemplated by the VA statute, 38 U.S.C. § 3402, and they are recognized as an important part of the administrative scheme. Appellees' counsel agreed at argument that a representative is available for any claimant who requests one, regardless of the claimant's affiliation with any particular veterans' group.[4]. . .

III

. . . Appellees' first claim, accepted by the District Court, is that the statutory fee limitation, as it bears on the administrative scheme in operation, deprives a rejected claimant or recipient of "life, liberty or property, without due process of law," U.S. Const., Amdt. 5, by depriving him of representation by expert legal counsel. Our decisions establish that "due process" is a flexible concept—that the processes required by the Clause with respect to the termination of a protected interest will vary depending upon the importance attached to the

---

[2]Title 38 CFR § 3.102 (1984) states:. . . "When, after careful consideration of all procurable and assembled data, a reasonable doubt arises regarding service origin, the degree of disability, or any other point, such doubt will be resolved in favor of the claimant. By reasonable doubt is meant one which exists by reason of the fact that the evidence does not satisfactorily prove or disprove the claim, yet a substantial doubt and one within the range of probability as distinguished from pure speculation or remote possibility. . . . The reasonable doubt doctrine is also applicable even in the absence of official records, particularly if the basic incident allegedly arose under combat, or similarly strenuous conditions, and is consistent with the probable results of such known hardships."

[4]The VA statistics show that 86% of all claimants are represented by service representatives, 12% proceed pro se, and 2% are represented by lawyers. Counsel agreed at argument that the 12% who proceed pro se do so by their own choice.

interest and the particular circumstances under which the deprivation may occur. In defining the process necessary to ensure "fundamental fairness" we have recognized that the Clause does not require that "the procedures used to guard against an erroneous deprivation . . . be so comprehensive as to preclude any possibility of error," and in addition we have emphasized that the marginal gains from affording an additional procedural safeguard often may be outweighed by the societal cost of providing such a safeguard.

These general principles are reflected in the test set out in Mathews v. Eldridge, 424 U.S. 319 (1976), which test the District Court purported to follow, and which requires a court to consider the private interest that will be affected by the official action, the risk of an erroneous deprivation of such interest through the procedures used, the probable value of additional or substitute procedural safeguards, and the government's interest in adhering to the existing system. In applying this test we must keep in mind, in addition to the deference owed to Congress, the fact that the very nature of the due process inquiry indicates that the fundamental fairness of a particular procedure does not turn on the result obtained in any individual case; rather, "procedural due process rules are shaped by the risk of error inherent in the truth-finding process as applied to the generality of cases, not the rare exceptions."

The Government interest, which has been articulated in congressional debates since the fee limitation was first enacted in 1862 during the Civil War, has been this: that the system for administering benefits should be managed in a sufficiently informal way that there should be no need for the employment of an attorney to obtain benefits to which a claimant was entitled, so that the claimant would receive the entirety of the award without having to divide it with a lawyer. This purpose is reinforced by a similar absolute prohibition on compensation of any service organization representative.

While Congress has recently considered proposals to modify the fee limitation in some respects, a Senate Committee Report in 1982 highlighted that body's concern that "any changes relating to attorneys' fees be made carefully so as not to induce unnecessary retention of attorneys by VA claimants and not to disrupt unnecessarily the very effective network of nonattorney resources that has evolved in the absence of significant attorney involvement in VA claims matters." S.Rep. No. 97-466, p. 49 (1982). Although this same Report professed the Senate's belief that the original stated interest in protecting veterans from unscrupulous lawyers was "no longer tenable," the Senate nevertheless concluded that the fee limitation should with a limited exception remain in effect, in order to "protect claimants' benefits" from being unnecessarily diverted to lawyers.

In the face of this congressional commitment to the fee limitation for more than a century, the District Court had only this to say with respect to the governmental interest: "The government has neither argued nor shown that lifting the fee limit would harm the government in any way, except as the paternalistic protector of claimants' supposed best interests. To the extent the paternalistic role is valid, there are less drastic means available to ensure that attorneys' fees do not deplete veterans' death or disability benefits."

It is not for the District Court or any other federal court to invalidate a federal statute by so cavalierly dismissing a long-asserted congressional purpose. If "paternalism" is an insignificant Government interest, then Congress first went astray in 1792, when by its Act of March 23 of that year it prohibited the "sale, transfer or mortgage . . . of the pension . . . [of a] soldier . . . before the same shall become due." Acts of Congress long on the books, such as the Fair Labor Standards Act, might similarly be described as "paternalistic"; indeed, this Court once opined that "[s]tatutes of the nature of that under review, limiting the hours in which grown and intelligent men may labor to earn their living, are mere meddlesome interferences with the rights of the individual. . . ." *Lochner v. New York*, 198 U.S. 45, 61 (1905). That day is fortunately long gone, and with it the condemnation of rational paternalism as a legitimate legislative goal. . . .

A necessary concomitant of Congress' desire that a veteran not need a representative to assist him in making his claim was that the system should be as informal and nonadversarial as possible. This is not to say that complicated factual inquiries may be rendered simple by the expedient of informality, but surely Congress desired that the proceedings be as informal and nonadversarial as possible. The regular introduction of lawyers into the proceedings would be quite unlikely to further this goal.

Describing the prospective impact of lawyers in probation revocation proceedings, we said in *Gagnon v. Scarpelli*, 411 U.S. 778, 787-788 (1973): "The introduction of counsel into a revocation proceeding will alter significantly the nature of the proceeding. If counsel is provided for the probationer or parolee, the State in turn will normally provide its own counsel; lawyers, by training and disposition, are advocates and bound by professional duty to present all available evidence and arguments in support of their clients' positions and to contest with vigor all adverse evidence and views. The role of the hearing body itself . . . may become more akin to that of a judge at a trial, and less attuned to the rehabilitative needs of the individual. . . . Certainly, the decisionmaking process will be prolonged, and the financial cost to the State—for appointed counsel, . . . a longer record, and the possibility of judicial review—will not be insubstantial." . . .

Thus, even apart from the frustration of Congress' principal goal of wanting the veteran to get the entirety of the award, the destruction of the fee limitation would bid fair to complicate a proceeding which Congress wished to keep as simple as possible. It is scarcely open to doubt that if claimants were permitted to retain compensated attorneys the day might come when it could be said that an attorney might indeed be necessary to present a claim properly in a system rendered more adversary and more complex by the very presence of lawyer representation. It is only a small step beyond that to the situation in which the claimant who has a factually simple and obviously deserving claim may nonetheless feel impelled to retain an attorney simply because so many other claimants retain attorneys. And this additional complexity will undoubtedly engender greater administrative costs, with the end result being that less Government money reaches its intended beneficiaries.

We accordingly conclude that under the *Mathews v. Eldridge* analysis great weight must be accorded to the Government interest at stake here. The flexibility of our approach in due process cases is intended in part to allow room for other forms of dispute resolution; with respect to the individual interests at stake here, legislatures are to be allowed considerable leeway to formulate such processes without being forced to conform to a rigid constitutional code of procedural necessities. It would take an extraordinarily strong showing of probability of error under the present system—and the probability that the presence of attorneys would sharply diminish that possibility—to warrant a holding that the fee limitation denies claimants due process of law. We have no hesitation in deciding that no such showing was made out on the record before the District Court. . . .

Passing the problems with quantifying the likelihood of an erroneous deprivation, however, under *Mathews* we must also ask what value the proposed additional procedure may have in reducing such error. In this case we are fortunate to have . . . unchallenged statistics [that] chronicle the success rates before the BVA depending on the type of representation of the claimant. . . .

ULTIMATE SUCCESS RATES BEFORE THE BOARD OF VETERANS' APPEALS BY MODE OF REPRESENTATION

Mode of representation	Success rate
American Legion	16.2%
American Red Cross	16.8%
Disabled American Veterans	16.6%
Veterans of Foreign Wars	16.7%
Other nonattorney	15.8%
No representation	15.2%
Attorney/Agent	18.3%

The District Court opined that these statistics were not helpful, because . . . lawyers were retained so infrequently that no body of lawyers with an expertise in VA practice had developed, and lawyers who represented veterans regularly might do better than lawyers who represented them only pro bono on a sporadic basis. The District Court felt that a more reliable index of the effect lawyers would have on the proceedings was a statistical study showing success of various representatives in appeals to discharge review boards in the uniformed services—statistics that showed a significantly higher success rate for those claimants represented by lawyers as compared to those claimants not so represented.

We think the District Court's analysis of this issue totally unconvincing, and quite lacking in the deference which ought to be shown by any federal court in evaluating the constitutionality of an Act of Congress. We have the most serious doubt whether a competent lawyer taking a veteran's case on a pro bono basis would give less than his best effort, and we see no reason why experience in developing facts as to causation in the numerous other areas of the law where it is relevant would not be readily transferable to proceedings before the VA. Nor do we think that lawyers' success rates in proceedings before military boards to upgrade discharges—proceedings which are not even conducted before the VA, but before military boards of the uniformed services—are to be preferred to the BVA statistics which show reliable success by mode of representation in the very type of proceeding to which the litigation is devoted.

The District Court also concluded . . . (1) that the VA processes are procedurally, factually, and legally complex, and (2) that the VA system presently does not work as designed. . . . The District Court's opinion is . . . short on definition or quantification of "complex" cases. If this term be understood to include all cases in which the claimant asserts injury from exposure to radiation or agent orange, only approximately 3 in 1,000 of the claims at the regional level and 2% of the appeals to the BVA involve such claims. Nor does it appear that all such claims would be complex by any fair definition of that term: at least 25% of all agent orange cases and 30% of the radiation cases, for example, are disposed of because the medical examination reveals no disability. What evidence does appear in the record indicates that the great majority of claims involve simple questions of fact, or medical questions relating to the degree of a claimant's disability; the record also indicates that only the rare case turns on a question of law. There are undoubtedly "complex" cases pending before the VA, and they are undoubtedly a tiny fraction of the total cases pending. . . .

Even if the showing in the District Court had been much more favorable, appellees still would confront the constitutional hurdle posed by the principle enunciated in cases such as Mathews to the effect that a process must be judged by the generality of cases to which it applies, and therefore, process which is sufficient for the large majority of a group of claims is by constitutional definition sufficient for all of them. But here appellees have failed to make the very difficult factual showing necessary.

Reliable evidence before the District Court showed that claimants represented by lawyers have a slightly better success rate before the BVA than do claimants represented by service representatives, and that both have a slightly better success rate than claimants who were not represented at all. . . . Neither the difference in success rate nor the existence of complexity in some cases is sufficient to warrant a conclusion that the right to retain and compensate an attorney in VA cases is a necessary element of procedural fairness under the Fifth Amendment. . . .

Justice STEVENS, with whom Justice BRENNAN and Justice MARSHALL join, dissenting.

The Court does not appreciate the value of individual liberty. It may well be true that in the vast majority of cases a veteran does not need to employ a lawyer, and that the system of processing veterans benefit claims, by and large, functions fairly and effectively without the participation of retained counsel. Everyone agrees, however, that there are at least some complicated cases in which the services of a lawyer would be useful to the veteran and, indeed, would simplify the work of the agency by helping to organize the relevant facts and to identify the controlling issues. What is the reason for denying the veteran the right to counsel of his choice in such cases? The Court gives us two answers: First, the paternalistic interest in protecting the veteran from the consequences of his own improvidence; and second, the bureaucratic interest in minimizing the cost of administering the benefit program. I agree that both interests are legitimate, but neither provides an adequate justification for the restraint on liberty imposed by the $10 fee limitation. . . .

At the time the $10 fee limitation was enacted, Congress presumably considered that fee reasonable. The legal work involved in preparing a veteran's claim consisted of little more than filling out an appropriate form, and, in terms of the average serviceman's base pay, a $10 fee then was roughly the equivalent of a $580 fee today. At its inception, therefore, the fee limitation had neither the purpose nor the effect of precluding the employment of reputable counsel by veterans. Indeed, the statute then, as now, expressly contemplated that claims for veterans benefits could be processed by "agents or attorneys."

The fact that the statute was aimed at unscrupulous attorneys is confirmed by the provision for criminal penalties. Instead of just making an agreement to pay a greater fee unenforceable—as an anticipatory pledge of an interest in future pension benefits is unenforceable—the Act contains a flat prohibition against the direct or indirect collection of a greater fee, and provides that an attorney who charges more than $10 may be imprisoned for up to two years at hard labor. Thus, an unscrupulous moneylender or merchant who might try to take advantage of an improvident veteran might have difficulty collecting his bill, but the unscrupulous lawyer might go to jail. . . .

II

The Court's opinion blends its discussion of the paternalistic interest in protecting veterans from unscrupulous lawyers and the bureaucratic interest in minimizing the cost of administration in a way that implies that each interest reinforces the other. Actually the two interests are quite different and merit separate analysis.

In my opinion, the bureaucratic interest in minimizing the cost of administration is nothing but a red herring. Congress has not prohibited lawyers from participating in the processing of claims for benefits and there is no reason why it should. . . .

The informality that the Court emphasizes is desirable because it no doubt enables many veterans, or their lay representatives, to handle their claims without the assistance of counsel. But there is no reason to assume that lawyers would add confusion rather than clarity to the proceedings. . . .

The fact that a lawyer's services are unnecessary in most cases, and might even be counterproductive in a few, does not justify a total prohibition on their participation in all pension claim proceedings. . . . The interest in efficient administration plainly does not justify a total prohibition on representation by counsel. Nor can it justify a rule that indirectly accomplishes that result by discouraging their participation in all cases.

The paternalistic interest in protecting the veteran from his own improvidence would unquestionably justify a rule that simply prevented lawyers from overcharging their clients. Most appropriately, such a rule might require agency approval, or perhaps judicial review, of counsel fees. It might also establish a reasonable ceiling, subject to exceptions for especially complicated cases. In fact, I assume that the $10 fee limitation was justified by this interest when it was first enacted in 1864. But time has brought changes in the value of the dollar, in the character of the legal profession, in agency procedures, and in the ability of the veteran to proceed without the assistance of counsel. . . .

The fundamental error in the Court's analysis is its assumption that the individual's right to employ counsel of his choice in a contest with his sovereign is a kind of second-class interest that can be assigned a material value and balanced on a utilitarian scale of costs and benefits. It is true that the veteran's right to benefits is a property right and that in fashioning the procedures for administering the benefit program, the Government may appropriately weigh the value of additional procedural safeguards against their pecuniary costs. It may, for example, properly decide not to provide free counsel to claimants. But we are not considering a procedural right that would involve any cost to the Government. We are concerned with the individual's right to spend his own money to obtain the advice and assistance of independent counsel in advancing his claim against the Government. . . .

b. Jerry L. Mashaw, Due Process in the Administrative State 264-267 (1985)

Not since *Goldberg v. Kelly* has the Supreme Court been willing to model the due process hearing rights deemed essential to security of welfare state entitlements explicitly and extensively on the elements of civil trial. [This trend] could in the end permit the development of a Kafkaesque welfare state monster that is the antithesis of the liberal ideal. In our darkest moments we might even imagine that substantive judicial review of entitlements might be foreclosed, and lawyers will be barred from representing claimants within the administrative process.

Indeed such an administrative welfare system already exists. Its processes are almost entirely informal, nonadversary, and insulated from the courts and the private bar. It is the Veterans Administration (VA). It is the most competent and humane social services agency since King Solomon dispensed charity and justice to his adoring subjects. A monstrous bureaucracy the VA may be, but it is more like Puff the Magic Dragon than Frankenstein.

VA examiners are bound to obtain for the veterans every benefit to which they are entitled, not only those for which application is initially made. Outreach programs begin before service personnel leave active duty and continue through multiple media and institutions to alert needy veterans of their potential rights. Congressional oversight is active, and congressional case work is ubiquitous, both overwhelmingly directed at ensuring that reasonable expectations of assistance are not disappointed.

This combination of participation, information, representation, and counseling reduces appeals at the final stage to a minuscule, less than two percent of disappointed applicants. The VA bureaucracy is orderly, humane, comprehensible, and supportive. It has achieved these characteristics without constitutional due process adjudication; and within a statutory scheme that proscribes judicial review and fends off the bar by limiting fees to $10 per case.

c. Lawyers and Judicial Review to the Rescue

In 1988 Congress adopted legislation that created the Court of Veterans Affairs (CVA). 38 U.S.C. §§ 4051 to 4092. The CVA is an Article I court staffed by judges appointed by the President with the advice & consent of the Senate for 15 year terms. The President's power of removal is limited to "misconduct, neglect of duty, engaging in the practice of law, or physical or mental disability." Prior to removal, the judge must be given a "full specification" of the reasons for removal, and "an opportunity to be heard."

The CVA has exclusive jurisdiction to review decisions of the Board of Veterans Affairs (BVA). The VA Administrator may **not** appeal a BVA decision, only the veteran. The standard for CVA review is similar to that found in the APA. Finding of fact will be upheld unless "clearly erroneous." Other findings will be upheld unless "arbitrary capricious, an abuse of discretion, or otherwise not in accordance with law." The jurisdiction of the CVA regarding the schedule of ratings for disabilities is expressly limited.

Private parties may be represented at the BVA level by members of bar and other persons that meet standards of proficiency specified by the CVA. (The VA is represented by its general counsel.) The fee arrangement must be filed with the CVA, which body may, sua sponte, review the agreement, and order a reduction if the fee is found to be "excessive or unreasonable." The maximum permitted contingent fee is 20 percent. The CVA may levy a registration fee of $30 per year on persons admitted to practice before it.

Decisions of the CVA are subject to review at the behest of "any party" by the Court of Appeals for the Federal Circuit. The scope of review is limited to the validity of statues, regulations, and the interpretation thereof relied on by the CVA. The legislation is silent regarding the availability of Supreme Court review.

d. *Thomas v. Union Carbide Agricultural Products Co.*, 473 U.S. 568 (1985)

Justice O'CONNOR delivered the opinion of the Court.

This case requires the Court to revisit the data-consideration provision of the Federal Insecticide, Fungicide, and Rodenticide Act (FIFRA), which was considered last Term in *Ruckelshaus v. Monsanto Co.*, 467 U.S. 986 (1984). *Monsanto* examined whether FIFRA's data-consideration provision effects an uncompensated taking in violation of the Fifth Amendment. In this case we address whether Article III of the Constitution prohibits

Congress from selecting binding arbitration with only limited judicial review as the mechanism for resolving disputes among participants in FIFRA's pesticide registration scheme. We conclude it does not and reverse the judgment below.

I

. . . As a precondition for registration of a pesticide, manufacturers must submit research data to the Environmental Protection Agency (EPA) concerning the product's health, safety, and environmental effects. . . . Congress enacted the original data-compensation provision in 1972 because it believed "recognizing a limited proprietary interest" in data submitted to support pesticide registrations would provide an added incentive beyond statutory patent protection for research and development of new pesticides. The data submitters, however, contended that basic health, safety, and environmental data essential to registration of a competing pesticide qualified for protection as a trade secret. With EPA bogged down in cataloging data and the pesticide industry embroiled in litigation over what types of data could legitimately be designated "trade secrets," new pesticide registrations "ground to a virtual halt."

The 1978 amendments were a response to the "logjam of litigation that resulted from controversies over data compensation and trade secret protection." Congress viewed data-sharing as essential to the registration scheme, but concluded EPA must be relieved of the task of valuation because disputes regarding the compensation scheme had "for all practical purposes, tied up their registration process" and "[EPA] lacked the expertise necessary to establish the proper amount of compensation." Legislators and the Agency agreed that "[d]etermining the amount and terms of such compensation are matters that do not require active government involvement [and] compensation payable should be determined to the fullest extent practicable, within the private sector."

Against this background, Congress in 1978 amended [FIFRA] to clarify that the trade secret exemption from the data-consideration provision did not extend to health, safety, and environmental data. In addition, the 1978 amendments granted data submitters a 10-year period of exclusive use for data submitted after September 30, 1978, during which time the data may not be cited without the original submitter's permission.

Regarding compensation for use of data not protected by the 10-year exclusive use provision, the amendment substituted for the EPA Administrator's determination of the appropriate compensation a system of negotiation and binding arbitration to resolve compensation disputes among registrants. Section 3(c) authorizes EPA to consider data already in its files in support of a new registration, permit, or new use, but "only if the applicant has made an offer to compensate the original data submitter." If the applicant and data submitter fail to agree, either may invoke binding arbitration. The arbitrator's decision is subject to judicial review only for "fraud, misrepresentation, or other misconduct."

The concept of retaining statutory compensation but substituting binding arbitration for valuation of data by EPA emerged as a compromise. This approach was developed by representatives of the major chemical manufacturers, who sought to retain the controversial compensation provision, in discussions with industry groups representing follow-on registrants, whose attempts to register pesticides had been roadblocked by litigation since 1972.

Appellees are 13 large firms engaged in the development and marketing of chemicals used to manufacture pesticides. . . . As a threshold matter, we must determine whether appellees'

Article III claims demonstrate sufficient ripeness to establish a concrete case or controversy. [The Court answered yes, and then turned to the merits.] . . . .

Appellees contend that Article III bars Congress from requiring arbitration of disputes among registrants concerning compensation under FIFRA without also affording substantial review by tenured judges of the arbitrator's decision. Article III, § 1, establishes a broad policy that federal judicial power shall be vested in courts whose judges enjoy life tenure and fixed compensation. These requirements protect the role of the independent judiciary within the constitutional scheme of tripartite government and assure impartial adjudication in federal courts.

. . . "[N]either this Court nor Congress has read the Constitution as requiring every federal question arising under the federal law . . . to be tried in an Art. III court before a judge enjoying life tenure and protection against salary reduction." Instead, the Court has long recognized that Congress is not barred from acting pursuant to its powers under Article I to vest decisionmaking authority in tribunals that lack the attributes of Article III courts. *See, e.g., Walters v. National Assn. of Radiation Survivors*, 473 U.S. 305 (1985) (Board of Veterans' Appeals). Many matters that involve the application of legal standards to facts and affect private interests are routinely decided by agency action with limited or no review by Article III courts. *See, e.g., United States v. Erika, Inc.*, 456 U.S. 201, 206 (1982) (no review of Medicare reimbursements); Monaghan, *Marbury and the Administrative State*, 83 COLUM. L. REV. 1, 18 (1983) (administrative agencies can conclusively adjudicate claims created by the administrative state, by and against private persons).

Appellees contend that their claims to compensation under FIFRA are a matter of state law. We disagree. Any right to compensation from follow-on registrants under § 3(c) for EPA's use of data results from FIFRA and does not depend on or replace a right to such compensation under state law. As a matter of state law, property rights in a trade secret are extinguished when a company discloses its trade secret to persons not obligated to protect the confidentiality of the information. Therefore registrants who submit data with notice of the scheme established by the 1978 amendments, and its qualified protection of trade secrets as defined in § 10, can claim no property interest under state law in data subject to § 3(c). *Cf.* 21 CFR § 171.1(h) (1984) (data submitted under Food, Drug, and Cosmetic Act is in public domain and follow-on registrants need not submit independent data). Nor do individuals who submitted data prior to 1978 have a right to compensation under FIFRA that depends on state law. To be sure, such users might have a claim that the new scheme results in a taking of property interests protected by state law. Compensation for any uncompensated taking is available under the Tucker Act. For purposes of compensation under FIFRA's regulatory scheme, however, it is the "mandatory licensing provision" that creates the relationship between the data submitter and the follow-on registrant, and federal law supplies the rule of decision. . . .

Looking beyond form to the substance of what FIFRA accomplishes, we note several aspects of FIFRA that persuade us the arbitration scheme adopted by Congress does not contravene Article III. First, the right created by FIFRA is not a purely "private" right, but bears many of the characteristics of a "public" right. Use of a registrant's data to support a follow-on registration serves a public purpose as an integral part of a program safeguarding the public health. Congress has the power, under Article I, to authorize an agency administering a complex regulatory scheme to allocate costs and benefits among voluntary participants in the program without providing an Article III adjudication. It also has the power to condition issuance of registrations or licenses on compliance with agency procedures. Article III is not so inflexible that it bars Congress from shifting the task of data valuation from the agency to the interested parties.

The 1978 amendments represent a pragmatic solution to the difficult problem of spreading the costs of generating adequate information regarding the safety, health, and environmental impact of a potentially dangerous product. Congress, without implicating Article III, could have authorized EPA to charge follow-on registrants fees to cover the cost of data and could have directly subsidized FIFRA data submitters for their contributions of needed data. Instead, it selected a framework that collapses these two steps into one, and permits the parties to fix the amount of compensation, with binding arbitration to resolve intractable disputes. Removing the task of valuation from agency personnel to civilian arbitrators, selected by agreement of the parties or appointed on a case-by-case basis by an independent federal agency, surely does not diminish the likelihood of impartial decisionmaking, free from political influence.

We note as well that the FIFRA arbitration scheme incorporates its own system of internal sanctions and relies only tangentially, if at all, on the Judicial Branch for enforcement. The danger of Congress or the Executive encroaching on the Article III judicial powers is at a minimum when no unwilling defendant is subjected to judicial enforcement power as a result of the agency "adjudication." *See e.g.*, L. JAFFE, JUDICIAL CONTROL OF ADMINISTRATIVE ACTION 385 (1965) (historically judicial review of agency decisionmaking has been required only when it results in the use of judicial process to enforce an obligation upon an unwilling defendant). . . .

In any event, under FIFRA, the only potential object of judicial enforcement power is the follow-on registrant who explicitly consents to have his rights determined by arbitration. See 40 CFR § 162.9-5(b) (registration application must contain a written offer to pay compensation "to the extent required by FIFRA").

Finally, we note that FIFRA limits but does not preclude review of the arbitration proceeding by an Article III court. We conclude that, in the circumstances, the review afforded preserves the "appropriate exercise of the judicial function." FIFRA at a minimum allows private parties to secure Article III review of the arbitrator's "findings and determination" for fraud, misconduct, or misrepresentation. This provision protects against arbitrators who abuse or exceed their powers or willfully misconstrue their mandate under the governing law. Moreover, review of constitutional error is preserved. . . . For purposes of our analysis, it is sufficient to note that FIFRA does provide for limited Article III review, including whatever review is independently required by due process considerations. . . .

e. Comments and Questions

1. The Court points out that Congress may require a prospective registrant to provide data, make such submissions available to the public (notably competitors) without paying any compensation, and allow follow-on registrants to make use of such data without charge. Precisely this approach is used in the Food, Drug and Cosmetics Act. Since Congress could require FIFRA registration applications to allow "their" data to be used by follow-on registrants without compensation, what is the problem with adopting a compensation plan that incorporates mandatory binding arbitration?

2. In these circumstances, why isn't Union Carbide thrilled at obtaining compensation under the FIFRA scheme, since Congress could have adopted the FDCA approach and not provided for compensation from follow-on registrants? Any why would Union Carbide prefer a long and expensive judicial proceeding to a faster and cheaper arbitration? Does *Carbide* suspect some sort of systematic bias against agribusiness giants?

3. The key to understanding the *Union Carbide* case is found in that most basic rule for understanding capitalism and politics: follow the money. Carbide of course preferred compensation to the no compensation alternative faced by the large drug companies, but this is a second best solution. If the arbitration system was declared unconstitutional the compensation system would be thrown out too, but something else would happen too. Carbide could, on the basis of trade secret law, deny competitors access to their filings. Congress might enact a drug filings type system, but Carbide (along with other giant agribusiness firms) had already won that battle, and thus had some confidence of winning again. If competitors could not use the (paid for) Carbide research data, they would have to replicate that research at great expense. This is good for Carbide, but socially wasteful. All but the largest competitors would be driven from the field entirely because of the large research costs—which must be paid "up front" before even going through the FIFRA application process approval, let alone the start of a cash flow from sales.

D. Agency Adjudication as ADR: Public Benefits Cases

1. Comments and Questions

a. Vast numbers of disputes that could be assigned to judicial bodies — Article I, Article III, and state courts—are instead decided by administrative agencies. Therefore, it makes sense to consider agencies themselves as a form of ADR.

b. A few numbers graphically illustrate the importance of adjudication by federal agencies. In 1981, some 2.3 disability claims were filed with the Social Security Administration, and 250,000 contested claims were heard by administrative law judges. SOCIAL SECURITY ADMINISTRATION, ANNUAL REPORT TO CONGRESS (1982). The 250,000 figure exceeds the number of cases decided annually by the entire federal court system.

c. Administrative agencies have no constitutional status, notwithstanding the frequent reference to agencies as the "fourth branch of government." Agencies are created by statute, and can be abolished or reformed by the legislature. Agency authority to adjudicate disputes is also statutory, and many agencies are not granted this power.

d. The common theme of the cases in this section is that all arose in benefits programs, where the agency must process a huge volume of claims. The *Walters* case (veterans), presented in the previous section, also fits in this category.

2. *Goldberg v. Kelly*, 397 U.S. 254 (1970)

Mr. Justice BRENNAN delivered the opinion of the Court.

The question for decision is whether a State that terminates public assistance payments to a particular recipient without affording him the opportunity for an evidentiary hearing prior to termination denies the recipient procedural due process in violation of the Due Process Clause of the Fourteenth Amendment. [The Court's answer is yes.] . . .

A caseworker who has doubts about the recipient's continued eligibility must first discuss them with the recipient. If the caseworker concludes that the recipient is no longer eligible, he recommends termination of aid to a unit supervisor. If the latter concurs, he sends the recipient a letter stating the reasons for proposing to terminate aid and notifying him that within seven days he may request that a higher official review the record, and may support the request with a written statement prepared personally or with the aid of an attorney or other person. If the reviewing official affirms the determination of ineligibility, aid is stopped immediately and the recipient is informed by letter of the reasons for the action. Appellees' challenge to this procedure emphasizes the absence of any provisions for the personal appearance of the recipient before the reviewing official, for oral presentation of evidence, and for confrontation and cross-examination of adverse witnesses. However, the letter does inform the recipient that he may request a post-termination "fair hearing." This is a proceeding before an independent state hearing officer at which the recipient may appear personally, offer oral evidence, confront and cross-examine the witnesses against him, and have a record made of the hearing. If the recipient prevails at the "fair hearing" he is paid all funds erroneously withheld. A recipient whose aid is not restored by a "fair hearing" decision may have judicial review. The recipient is so notified. . . .

Appellant does not contend that procedural due process is not applicable to the termination of welfare benefits. Such benefits are a matter of statutory entitlement for persons qualified to receive them. Their termination involves state action that adjudicates important rights. . . .

It is true, of course, that some governmental benefits may be administratively terminated without affording the recipient a pre-termination evidentiary hearing. But . . . when welfare is discontinued, only a pre-termination evidentiary hearing provides the recipient with procedural due process. . . . [T]ermination of aid pending resolution of a controversy over eligibility may deprive an eligible recipient of the very means by which to live while he waits. Since he lacks independent resources, his situation becomes immediately desperate. His need to concentrate upon finding the means for daily subsistence, in turn, adversely affects his ability to seek redress from the welfare bureaucracy. . . .

[T]he interest of the eligible recipient in uninterrupted receipt of public assistance, coupled with the State's interest that his payments not be erroneously terminated, clearly outweighs the State's competing concern to prevent any increase in its fiscal and administrative burdens. As the District Court correctly concluded, "(t)he stakes are simply too high for the welfare recipient, and the possibility for honest error or irritable misjudgment too great, to allow termination of aid without giving the recipient a chance, if he so desires, to be fully informed of the case against him so that he may contest its basis and produce evidence in rebuttal." . . .

[T]he pre-termination hearing need not take the form of a judicial or quasi-judicial trial. We bear in mind that the statutory "fair hearing" will provide the recipient with a full administrative review. Accordingly, the pre-termination hearing has one function only: to produce an initial determination of the validity of the welfare department's grounds for discontinuance of payments in order to protect a recipient against an erroneous termination of his benefits. Thus, a complete record and a comprehensive opinion, which would serve primarily to facilitate judicial review and to guide future decisions, need not be provided at the pre-termination stage. We recognize, too, that both welfare authorities and recipients have an interest in relatively speedy resolution of questions of eligibility, that they are used to dealing with one another informally, and that some welfare departments have very burdensome caseloads. These considerations justify the limitation of the pre-termination hearing to minimum procedural safeguards, adapted to the particular characteristics of welfare recipients, and to the limited nature of the controversies to be resolved. . . .

"The fundamental requisite of due process of law is the opportunity to be heard." The hearing must be "at a meaningful time and in a meaingful manner." In the present context these principles require that a recipient have timely and adequate notice detailing the reasons for a proposed termination, and an effective opportunity to defend by confronting any adverse witnesses and by presenting his own arguments and evidence orally. These rights are important in cases such as those before us, where recipients have challenged proposed terminations as resting on incorrect or misleading factual premises or on misapplication of rules or policies to the facts of particular cases. . . .

The opportunity to be heard must be tailored to the capacities and circumstances of those who are to be heard. It is not enough that a welfare recipient may present his position to the decision maker in writing or second-hand through his caseworker. Written submissions are an unrealistic option for most recipients, who lack the educational attainment necessary to write effectively and who cannot obtain professional assistance. Moreover, written submissions do not afford the flexibility of oral presentations; they do not permit the recipient to mold his argument to the issues the decision maker appears to regard as important. Particularly where credibility and veracity are at issue, as they must be in many termination proceedings, written submissions are a wholly unsatisfactory basis for decision. The second-hand presentation to the decisionmaker by the caseworker has its own deficiencies; since the caseworker usually gathers the facts upon which the charge of ineligibility rests, the presentation of the recipient's side of the controversy cannot safely be left to him. Therefore a recipient must be allowed to state his position orally.

In almost every setting where important decisions turn on questions of fact, due process requires an opportunity to confront and cross-examine adverse witnesses. The right to be heard would be, in many cases, of little avail if it did not comprehend the right to be heard by counsel. We do not say that counsel must be provided at the pre-termination hearing, but only that the recipient must be allowed to retain an attorney if he so desires. Counsel can help delineate the issues, present the factual contentions in an orderly manner, conduct cross-examination, and generally safeguard the interests of the recipient. We do not anticipate that this assistance will unduly prolong or otherwise encumber the hearing.

Finally, the decisionmaker's conclusion as to a recipient's eligibility must rest solely on the legal rules and evidence adduced at the hearing. To demonstrate compliance with this elementary requirement, the decision maker should state the reasons for his determination and indicate the evidence he relied on, though his statement need not amount to a full opinion or even formal findings of fact and conclusions of law. And, of course, an impartial decision maker is essential. . . . [P]rior involvement in some aspects of a case will not necessarily bar a welfare official from acting as a decision maker. He should not, however, have participated in making the determination under review.

Mr. Justice Black, dissenting.

In the last half century the United States, along with many, . . . other nations of the world, has moved far toward becoming a welfare state, that is, a nation that for one reason or another taxes its most affluent people to help support, feed, clothe, and shelter its less fortunate citizens. The result is that today more than nine million men, women, and children in the United States receive some kind of state or federally financed public assistance in the form of allowances or gratuities, generally paid them periodically. . . . [T]he list of recipients is not static, and some people go off the lists and others are added from time to time. These ever-changing lists put a constant administrative burden on government and it certainly could not have reasonably anticipated that this burden would include the additional procedural expense imposed by the Court today. . . .

The more than a million names on the relief rolls in New York, and the more than nine million names on the rolls of all the 50 States were not put there at random. The names are there because state welfare officials believed that those people were eligible for assistance. Probably in the officials' haste to make out the lists many names were put there erroneously in order to alleviate immediate suffering, and undoubtedly some people are drawing relief who are not entitled under the law to do so. Doubtless some draw relief checks from time to time who know they are not eligible, either because they are not actually in need or for some other reason. Many of those who thus draw undeserved gratuities are without sufficient property to enable the government to collect back from them any money they wrongfully receive. But the Court today holds that it would violate the Due Process Clause of the Fourteenth Amendment to stop paying those people weekly or monthly allowances unless the government first affords them a full "evidentiary hearing" even though welfare officials are persuaded that the recipients are not rightfully entitled to receive a penny under the law. . . . I do not believe there is any provision in our Constitution that should thus paralyze the government's efforts to protect itself against making payments to people who are not entitled to them. . . .

The Court apparently feels that this decision will benefit the poor and needy. In my judgment the eventual result will be just the opposite. While today's decision requires only an administrative, evidentiary hearing, the inevitable logic of the approach taken will lead to constitutionally imposed, time-consuming delays of a full adversary process of administrative and judicial review. . . . While this Court will perhaps have insured that no needy person will be taken off the rolls without a full "due process" proceeding, it will also have insured that many will never get on the rolls, or at least that they will remain destitute during the lengthy proceedings followed to determine initial eligibility. . . .

The operation of a welfare state is a new experiment for our Nation. . . . [N]ew experiments in carrying out a welfare program should not be frozen into our constitutional structure. They should be left, as are other legislative determinations, to the Congress and the legislatures that the people elect to make our laws.

3. Comments and Questions

a. *Goldberg v. Kelly,* decided by a 5 to 4 vote, represents the high water mark of individualized due process hearings for large public benefits programs such as social security, veterans, and welfare. (This is a statement of fact, not a value judgment.) While often ignored or distinguished, *Goldberg* has not been overruled and it provides a convenient citation for a court that seeks to require expansive due process requirements.

b. The case that best exemplifies the retreat from *Goldberg* is *Mathews v. Eldridge,* 424 U.S. 319 (1976). Plaintiff was a recipient of disability payments pursuant to the Social Security

Act. He was subsequently terminated as no longer disabled, and payments ceased immediately. The issue presented was whether payments could be terminated prior to a hearing. The district court and the court of appeals both thought that *Goldberg* governed this situation, and decided for the plaintiff, only to be reversed by the Supreme Court. Of course, the *Eldridge* Court did not overrule *Goldberg* explicitly, but rather went to great lengths to distinguish the two cases—excellent evidence that the situations are not easily distinguishable. Justice Brennan, the author of the majority opinion in *Goldberg* dissented in *Eldridge*.

Even if one is persuaded by the reasons for distinguishing *Goldberg* (termination based on medical examinations, disability not based on financial need, availability of public assistance, and others), *Eldridge* clearly evinces a different calculus. The *Eldridge* Court notes the administrative burden of pre-termination hearings, the dollar losses to government from improper payments that cannot be recouped, and that more process is likely to mean less benefits for those who are disabled. These very concerns were pointed out in *Goldberg*—by Justice Black in the dissent.

c. The specific facts of *Eldridge* were compelling: due to the loss of the disability income, the family's house was foreclosed upon, and their furniture was repossessed. In evaluating the need for pre-termination hearings, should the due process calculus be based on disability claimants generally, or on the circumstances of individual claimants?

4. *Richardson v. Perales*, 402 U.S. 389 (1971)

Mr. Justice BLACKMUN delivered the opinion of the Court.

In 1966 Pedro Perales, a San Antonio truck driver, then aged 34, filed a claim for disability insurance benefits under the Social Security Act. [The Act] provides that the term "disability" means "inability to engage in any substantial gainful activity by reason of any medically determinable physical or mental impairment. . . . Section 205(g), relating to judicial review, states, "The findings of the Secretary as to any fact, if supported by substantial evidence, shall be conclusive. . . ."

The issue here is whether physicians' written reports of medical examinations they have made of a disability claimant may constitute "substantial evidence" supportive of a finding of nondisability, within the § 205(g) standard, when the claimant objects to the admissibility of those reports and when the only live testimony is presented by his side and is contrary to the reports. [The Court's answer is yes.] . . .

[Despite treatment and an operation,] Mr. Perales continued to complain, but [two physicians] . . . were unable to find any objective neurological explanation for his complaints. [The primary physician] advised that he return to work. In April 1966, Perales consulted Dr. Max Morales, Jr., a general practitioner of San Antonio. Dr. Morales hospitalized the patient from April 15 to May 2. His final discharge diagnosis was: "Back sprain, lumbo-sacral spine."

Perales then filed his claim. As required by the Act, the claim was referred to the state agency for determination. The agency obtained the hospital records and a report from Dr. Morales. The report set forth no physical findings or laboratory studies, but the doctor again gave as his diagnosis: "Back sprain, lumbosacral spine," this time "moderately severe," with "Ruptured disk not ruled out."

The agency arranged for a medical examination, at no cost to the patient, by Dr. John H. Langston, an orthopedic surgeon. This was done May 25. Dr. Langston's ensuing report to the

Division of Disability Determination was devastating from the claimant's standpoint. . . . "He may have a very mild chronic back sprain associated with the congenital anomalies as seen on x-ray, but it has been a long time since I have been so impressed with the obvious attempt of a patient to exaggerate his difficulties by simply just standing there and not moving — not even the uninvolved upper extremities. . . .

The state agency denied the claim. Perales requested reconsideration. Dr. Morales submitted a further report to the agency and an opinion to the claimant's attorney. This outlined the surgery and hospitalizations and his own conservative and continuing treatment of the patient, the medicines prescribed, the administration of ultrasound therapy, and the patient's constant complaints. The doctor concluded that the patient had not made a complete recovery from his surgery that he was not malingering, that his injury was permanent, and that he was totally and permanently disabled. . . .

The state agency then arranged for an examination by a board-certified psychiatrist with a sub-specialty in neurology. The agency again reviewed the file. The Bureau of Disability Insurance of the Social Security Administration made its independent review. The report and opinion of Dr. Morales, as the claimant's attending physician, were considered, as were those of the other examining physicians. The claim was again denied.

Perales requested a hearing before a hearing examiner. The agency then referred the claimant to [another physician] for electromyography studies [who found some back problems but far short of qualifying as disability]. . . .

The requested hearing was set for January 12, 1967, in San Antonio. Written notice thereof was given the claimant with a copy to his attorney. The notice contained a definition of disability, advised the claimant that he should bring all medical and other evidence not already presented, afforded him an opportunity to examine all documentary evidence on file prior to the hearing, and told him that he might bring his own physician or other witnesses and be represented at the hearing by a lawyer.

At the two hearings oral testimony was submitted by claimant Perales, by Dr. Morales, by a former fellow employee of the claimant, by a vocational expert, and by Dr. Lewis A. Leavitt, a physician board-certified in physical medicine and rehabilitation, and chief of . . . the Department of Physical Medicine at Baylor University College of Medicine. Dr. Leavitt was called by the hearing examiner as an independent "medical adviser," that is, as an expert who does not examine the claimant but who hears and reviews the medical evidence and who may offer an opinion. The adviser is paid a fee by the Government. The claimant, through his counsel, objected to any testimony by Dr. Leavitt not based upon examination or upon a hypothetical. Dr. Leavitt testified over this objection and was cross-examined by the claimant's attorney. He stated that the consensus of the various medical reports was that Perales had a mild low-back syndrome of musculo-ligamentous origin.

The hearing examiner, in reliance upon the several medical reports and the testimony of Dr. Leavitt, observed in his written decision, "There is objective medical evidence of impairment which the heavy preponderance of the evidence indicates to be of mild severity. Taken altogether, the Hearing Examiner is of the conclusion that the claimant has not met the burden of proof." . . .

The claimant then made a request for review by the Appeals Council and submitted as supplemental evidence a judgment dated June 2, 1967, in Perales' favor against an insurance company for workmen's compensation benefits aggregating $11,665.84, plus medical and related expenses, and a medical report letter dated December 28, 1966, by Dr. Coyle W. Williams, apparently written in support of a welfare claim made by Perales. In his letter the doctor noted an essentially negative neurological and physical examination except for tenderness in the lumbar area and limited straight leg raising. He observed, "I cannot explain all his symptoms on a physical basis. I would recommend he would recondition himself and return to work. My estimation, he has a 15% permanent partial disability of the body as a whole." The Appeals Council ruled that the decision of the hearing examiner was correct. . . .

We therefore are presented with the not uncommon situation of conflicting medical evidence. The trier of fact has the duty to resolve that conflict. We have, on the one hand, an absence of objective findings, an expressed suspicion of only functional complaints, of malingering, and of the patient's unwillingness to do anything about remedying an unprovable situation. We have, on the other hand, the claimant's and his personal physician's earnest pleas that significant and disabling residuals from the mishap of September 1965 are indeed present.

The issue revolves, however, around a system which produces a mass of medical evidence in report form. May material of that kind ever be "substantial evidence" when it stands alone and is opposed by live medical evidence and the client's own contrary personal testimony? [The Court's answer is yes.]

The Social Security Act has been with us since 1935. . . . The system's administrative structure and procedures, with essential determinations numbering into the millions, are of a size and extent difficult to comprehend. But, as the Government's brief here accurately pronounces, "Such a system must be fair—and it must work." . . .

Section 205(b) directs the Secretary to make findings and decisions; on request to give reasonable notice and opportunity for a hearing; and in the course of any hearing to receive evidence. It then provides: "Evidence may be received at any hearing before the Secretary even though inadmissible under rules of evidence applicable to court procedure." In carrying out these statutory duties the Secretary has adopted regulations that state, among other things: "The hearing examiner shall inquire fully into the matters at issue and shall receive in evidence the testimony of witnesses and any documents which are relevant and material to such matters." . . . There emerges an emphasis upon the informal rather than the formal. . . .

The vast workings of the social security administrative system make for reliability and impartiality in the consultant reports. We bear in mind that the agency operates essentially, and is intended so to do, as an adjudicator and not as an advocate or adversary. This is the congressional plan. We do not presume on this record to say that it works unfairly.[7]

One familiar with medical reports and the routine of the medical examination, general or specific, will recognize their elements of detail and of value. The particular reports of the physicians who examined claimant Perales were based on personal consultation and personal examination and rested on accepted medical procedures and tests. . . . These are routine, standard, and unbiased medical reports by physician specialists concerning a subject whom they had seen. That the reports were adverse to Perales' claim is not in itself bias or an indication of nonprobative character.

The reports present the impressive range of examination to which Perales was subjected. A specialist in neurosurgery, one in neurology, one in psychiatry, one in orthopedics, and one

---

[7][I]n fiscal 1968, 320,164 consultant examinations were obtained [by the Social Security Administration].

in physical medicine and rehabilitation add up to definitive opinion in five medical specialties, all somewhat related, but different in their emphases. It is fair to say that the claimant received professional examination and opinion on a scale beyond the reach of most persons and that this case reveals a patient and careful endeavor by the state agency and the examiner to ascertain the truth. So far as we can detect, there is no inconsistency whatsoever in the reports of the five specialists. Yet each result was reached by independent examination in the writer's field of specialized training. . . .

Courts have recognized the reliability and probative worth of written medical reports even in formal trials and, while acknowledging their hearsay character, have admitted them as an exception to the hearsay rule . . . and in so doing, relied on the Business Records Act, 28 U.S.C. § 1732. . . .

Mr. Justice DOUGLAS, with whom Mr. Justice BLACK and Mr. Justice BRENNAN concur, dissenting.

This claimant for social security disability benefits had a serious back injury. The doctor who examined him testified that he was permanently disabled. His case is defeated, however, by hearsay evidence of doctors and their medical reports about this claimant. Only one doctor who examined him testified at the hearing. Five other doctors who had once examined the claimant did not testify and were not subject to cross-examination. But their reports were admitted in evidence. Still another doctor testified on the hearsay in the documents of the other doctors. All of this hearsay may be received, . . . [b]ut this hearsay evidence cannot by itself be the basis for an adverse ruling. . . .

Cross-examination of doctors in these physical injury cases is, I think, essential to a full and fair disclosure of the facts.

One doctor whose word cast this claimant into limbo never saw him, never examined him, never took his vital statistics or saw him try to walk or bend or lift weights. He was a "medical adviser" to HEW. The use of circuit-riding doctors who never see or examine claimants to defeat their claims should be beneath the dignity of a great nation. Three other doctors who were not subject to cross-examination were experts retained and paid by the Government. . . .

5. *Heckler v. Campbell*, 461 U.S. 458 (1983)

Justice POWELL delivered the opinion of the Court.

The issue is whether the Secretary of Health and Human Services may rely on published medical-vocational guidelines to determine a claimant's right to Social Security disability benefits. The Social Security Act defines "disability" in terms of the effect a physical or mental impairment has on a person's ability to function in the work place. It provides disability benefits only to persons who are unable "to engage in any substantial gainful activity by reason of any medically determinable physical or mental impairment." 42 U.S.C. § 423(d)(1)(A). And it specifies that a person must "not only [be] unable to do his previous work but [must be unable], considering his age, education, and work experience, [to] engage in any other kind of substantial gainful work which exists in the national economy, regardless of whether such work exists in the immediate area in which he lives, or whether a specific job vacancy exists for him, or whether he would be hired if he applied for work."

In 1978, the Secretary of Health and Human Services promulgated regulations implementing this definition. The regulations recognize that certain impairments are so severe that they prevent a person from pursuing any gainful work. . . . If a claimant suffers from a less severe impairment, the Secretary must determine whether the claimant retains the ability to perform either his former work or some less demanding employment. If a claimant can pursue his former occupation, he is not entitled to disability benefits. If he cannot, the Secretary must determine whether the claimant retains the capacity to pursue less demanding work.

The regulations divide this last inquiry into two stages. First, the Secretary must assess each claimant's present job qualifications. The regulations direct the Secretary to consider the factors Congress has identified as relevant: physical ability, age, education and work experience. Second, she must consider whether jobs exist in the national economy that a person having the claimant's qualifications could perform.

Prior to 1978, the Secretary relied on vocational experts to establish the existence of suitable jobs in the national economy. . . . Although this testimony often was based on standardized guides, vocational experts frequently were criticized for their inconsistent treatment of similarly situated claimants. To improve both the uniformity and efficiency of this determination, the Secretary promulgated medical-vocational guidelines as part of the 1978 regulations.

These guidelines relieve the Secretary of the need to rely on vocational experts by establishing through rulemaking the types and numbers of jobs that exist in the national economy. They consist of a matrix of the four factors identified by Congress — physical ability, age, education, and work experience — and set forth rules that identify whether jobs requiring specific combinations of these factors exist in significant numbers in the national economy. Where a claimant's qualifications correspond to the job requirements identified by a rule, the guidelines direct a conclusion as to whether work exists that the claimant could perform. If such work exists, the claimant is not considered disabled.

In 1979, Carmen Campbell applied for disability benefits because a back condition and hypertension prevented her from continuing her work as a hotel maid. After her application was denied, she requested a hearing de novo before an Administrative Law Judge. He determined that her back problem was not severe enough to find her disabled without further inquiry, and accordingly considered whether she retained the ability to perform either her past work or some less strenuous job. He concluded that even though Campbell's back condition prevented her from returning to her work as a maid, she retained the physical capacity to do light work. In accordance with the regulations, he found that Campbell was 52-years old, that her previous employment consisted of unskilled jobs and that she had a limited education. He noted that Campbell, who had been born in Panama, experienced difficulty in speaking and writing English. She was able, however, to understand and read English fairly well. Relying on the medical-vocational guidelines, the Administrative Law Judge found that a significant number of jobs existed that a person of Campbell's qualifications could perform. Accordingly, he concluded that she was not disabled.

This determination was upheld by both the Social Security Appeals Council, and the District Court. . . . The Court of Appeals for the Second Circuit reversed. It accepted the Administrative Law Judge's determination that Campbell retained the ability to do light work. . . . The court noted, however, that it "has consistently required that the Secretary identify specific alternative occupations available in the national economy that would be suitable for the claimant," and that these jobs be supported by "a job description clarifying the nature of the job, [and] demonstrating that the job does not require exertion or skills not possessed by the claimant." . . . The court concluded that because the Secretary had failed to introduce evidence that specific alternative jobs existed, the determination that Campbell was not disabled was not supported by substantial evidence.

The Secretary argues that the Court of Appeals' holding effectively prevents the use of the medical-vocational guidelines. By requiring her to identify specific alternative jobs in every disability hearing, the court has rendered the guidelines useless. An examination of both the language of the Social Security Act and its legislative history clearly demonstrates that the Secretary may proceed by regulation to determine whether substantial gainful work exists in the national economy.

The Court of Appeals held that "[i]n failing to show suitable available alternative jobs for Ms. Campbell, the Secretary's finding of not disabled is not supported by substantial evidence." It thus rejected the proposition that "the guidelines provide adequate evidence of a claimant's ability to perform a specific alternative occupation," and remanded for the Secretary to put into evidence "particular types of jobs suitable to the capabilities of Ms. Campbell." The court's requirement that additional evidence be introduced on this issue prevents the Secretary from putting the guidelines to their intended use and implicitly calls their validity into question. Accordingly, we think the decision below requires us to consider whether the Secretary may rely on medical-vocational guidelines in appropriate cases.

The Social Security Act directs the Secretary to "adopt reasonable and proper rules and regulations to regulate and provide for the nature and extent of the proofs and evidence and the method of taking and furnishing the same" in disability cases. As we previously have recognized, Congress has "conferred on the Secretary exceptionally broad authority to prescribe standards for applying certain sections of the [Social Security] Act." Where, as here, the statute expressly entrusts the Secretary with the responsibility for implementing a provision by regulation, our review is limited to determining whether the regulations promulgated exceeded the Secretary's statutory authority and whether they are arbitrary and capricious.

We do not think that the Secretary's reliance on medical-vocational guidelines is inconsistent with the Social Security Act. It is true that the statutory scheme contemplates that disability hearings will be individualized determinations based on evidence adduced at a hearing, . . . but this does not bar the Secretary from relying on rulemaking to resolve certain classes of issues. The Court has recognized that even where an agency's enabling statute expressly requires it to hold a hearing, the agency may rely on its rulemaking authority to determine issues that do not require case-by-case consideration. . . .

[I]n determining whether a claimant can perform less strenuous work, the Secretary must make two determinations. She must assess each claimant's individual abilities and then determine whether jobs exist that a person having the claimant's qualifications could perform. The first inquiry involves a determination of historic facts, and the regulations properly require the Secretary to make these findings on the basis of evidence adduced at a hearing. We note that the regulations afford claimants ample opportunity both to present evidence relating to their own abilities and to offer evidence that the guidelines do not apply to them. The second inquiry requires the Secretary to determine an issue that is not unique to each claimant — the types and numbers of jobs that exist in the national economy. This type of general factual issue may be resolved as fairly through rulemaking as by introducing the testimony of vocational experts at each disability hearing.

As the Secretary has argued, the use of published guidelines brings with it a uniformity that previously had been perceived as lacking. To require the Secretary to relitigate the existence of jobs in the national economy at each hearing would hinder needlessly an already overburdened agency. We conclude that the Secretary's use of medical-vocational guidelines does not conflict with the statute, nor can we say on the record before us that they are arbitrary and capricious. . . .

6. Comments and Questions

a. Does it bother you that HHS has not presented a scintilla of evidence to suggest that Ms. Campbell can in fact find employment? Given her resume—52 year old female immigrant from Panama, lacking skills or education, with minimal English language ability, and a history of back problems—how would you assess Ms. Campbell's job prospects in your area?

b. Suppose that Ms. Campbell presented a daily log that shows six months of dedicated but unsuccessful job searches—replete with a listing of the firms applied to (including names and telephone numbers of persons contacted at each firm), a slew of rejection letters, and whatever additional evidence you would find persuasive. Must HHS even consider this material, let alone give it any weight?

E. Agency-Mandated ADR

1. Comments and Questions

a. In the next article, Professor Harold Bruff, a leading administrative law scholar, leads us through some quite complex doctrinal developments relating to limitations on adjudication of disputes by administrative agencies, and the scope of judicial review. As you consider these difficulties, do not lose sight of Bruff's conclusions:

1. He focuses on arbitration because it is the only ADR procedure that even might raise constitutional concerns; and
2. "This Article concludes that if certain safeguards are adopted, arbitration in federal programs can surmount all of these [constitutional] obstacles."

b. In considering the use of various ADR procedures by administrative agencies, you should not be unduly impressed that there are no constitutional infirmities. To say that a statute or rule is constitutional is only a flimsy argument in its favor, and says nothing about its wisdom, vel non, as public policy.

2. Harold H. Bruff, *Public Programs, Private Deciders; The Constitutionality of Arbitration in Federal Programs*, 67 Tex. L. Rev. 441 (1989)*

I. INTRODUCTION

The "administrative state" evolved from the constitutional branches' desire to shift many decisions to administrative agencies, which were to apply expert judgment through use of

*Published originally in 67 *Texas Law Review* 441 (1989). Copyright 1989 by the Texas Law Review Association. Reprinted by permission.

speedy and informal procedures. Eventually, however, increasing formality beset the administrative process. To reverse this trend, agencies began experimenting with alternative dispute resolution (ADR), a diverse group of informal procedures that typically employ private parties to resolve legal controversies. Federal agencies rely on these procedures to make decisions that would otherwise be assigned to courts or executive officers. The use of private deciders in public programs, however, raises fundamental constitutional concerns, for the very legitimacy of the administrative state rests on the nature and strength of the relationships between federal agencies and the constitutional branches. The use of ADR techniques may lead to constitutional infirmities by overly attenuating the ties between private decision makers and constitutional officers.

In a series of recommendations, the Administrative Conference of the United States (ACUS) has urged the use of ADR techniques in federal programs. Many ADR procedures, such as negotiated rulemaking and mediation to help settle litigation, avoid serious constitutional challenge, because although private parties influence the agencies' decisions, government officers retain final authority. These procedures do not differ sharply enough from other avenues of private influence on public policy making to justify constitutional distinctions. Alone among the recommended procedures, arbitration delegates decision making to private individuals and allows only limited governmental review. . . .

Existing law authorizes or requires federal agencies to employ arbitration in a variety of contexts, which fall into three broad categories for analytical purposes. The first is money claims by or against the government. For example, private insurance carriers arbitrate claims of Medicare beneficiaries for reimbursement of certain medical expenses. The second encompasses disputes between the government and its employees, including both the resolution of grievances under an existing law or contract and the determination of future contractual relations. The third is disputes between private parties related to program administration. Examples include claims against the "Superfund" for cleanup of toxic wastes, the ascertainment of employers' liability for withdrawal from pension plans overseen by the Pension Benefit Guaranty Corporation, and the determination of compensation that a pesticide manufacturer must pay for the use of another's data in obtaining federal registration.

. . . The use of private deciders may violate separation of powers principles associated with the grant of judicial power to the federal courts. Alternatively, the informality of arbitral schemes may result in an unacceptable threat to the due process rights of persons affected by arbitration. Finally, delegation of decision-making authority may improperly intrude on executive prerogatives. This Article concludes that if certain safeguards are adopted, arbitration in federal programs can surmount all of these obstacles.

IV. AN APPROACH TO THE CONSTITUTIONAL ISSUES

Several principles guide the analysis of the constitutionality of arbitration in federal programs. . . . [T]he optimal specificity of constitutional rules that regulate the organization of government is low. The size and diversity of government and the use of arbitration in a wide range of programs means that no single set of detailed constitutional criteria can readily be crafted to fit them all. Moreover, predicting the effects of rules on institutions is hazardous, even in the short run. Arbitration in government is still experimental; courts should not shackle evolving procedures with rigid constitutional doctrine.

Second, courts should defer to administrative or legislative choice of procedure, whether the issue is statutory authorization or constitutionality. The acceptability of a procedure is a function of the particular issues to be decided, and both Congress and administrative agencies are capable of evaluating the factors relevant to choosing a procedure.

Finally, . . . powers granted to private deciders must be structured so that both internal incentives and outside supervision conform their decisions to the public interest. This judgment is necessarily specific to each particular program. . . .

V. GRANTING JUDICIAL POWER TO AGENCIES AND ARBITRATORS

To what extent may adjudicative authority that could be assigned to the federal courts be placed in other hands, including those of arbitrators? Article III creates the "judicial Power of the United States," but the federal courts are not its sole repository. State courts also decide federal questions and cases within federal diversity jurisdiction. This distribution of business results partly from Congress' disinclination to vest exclusive jurisdiction in the federal courts and partly from parties' selection of state courts. The FAA also shifts business away from the federal courts by fostering the use of private arbitrators for many cases within the federal judicial power. Not surprisingly, clear limits to congressional power over federal jurisdiction have never emerged, resulting in confusion over limits in particular contexts. . . .

A. Delegation of Adjudicative Power in Administrative Law

Even within the federal government, no obvious theory underlies the distribution of adjudicative business among the available fora. Variations appear in both institutional characteristics and procedural formality. The catalogue includes article III district courts, article III adjuncts (such as bankruptcy courts), "legislative" courts (such as the Tax Court), administrative agencies employing the full adjudicative procedures of the Administrative Procedure Act (APA), and agencies employing more informal procedures. The last category, informal executive adjudication, includes much case-by-case decision making. Hence it includes a vast number and range of decisions, such as personnel promotions and contract awards. Agencies often conduct this adjudication without any statutorily specified procedure, but in many instances the results are subject to meaningful judicial review.

The federal courts could conceivably adjudicate many of these kinds of cases under federal question jurisdiction, but a vastly bloated judiciary and an equally shrunken executive would result. More importantly, some functionally adjudicative activities are "executive" in the constitutional sense and may not be transferred to the courts. An obvious example is the President's exercise of law-applying judgment pursuant to responsibilities conferred on him by the Constitution or by statute. . . . [T]he Supreme Court, in delineating the boundary between legislative and executive responsibilities, has noted that "[i]nterpreting a law enacted by Congress to implement the legislative mandate is the very essence of execution of the law." Yet this definition also describes a principal activity of the federal courts. Plainly, a simple formalist distinction will not suffice for separation of powers purposes.

The Court has struggled to identify adjudictive functions that must remain in federal courts, those that may be placed in the executive, and those that must be placed in the executive. Despite these uncertainties, the legitimacy of administrative adjudication bears on the constitutionality of arbitration in federal programs. Theories that justify transferring judicial power to agencies may also provide support for the further step of delegating it to arbitrators.

Crowell v. Benson [285 U.S. 22 (1932)] established the constitutionality of delegating adjudicative power to administrative agencies. Congress had created a workers' compensation scheme for longshoremen and had authorized an agency to decide claims under procedures resembling those later codified in the APA. The Court rejected a due process assault on administrative fact-finding, because judicial review could assure the presence of substantial evidence for the award. Article III did not require that the subject matter, which was within the federal judicial power, be allocated to the courts. It sufficed that reviewing courts retained power to decide issues of law. . . . *Crowell* evinced concern about the fairness of adjudication performed outside court. Modern administrative law responds partly through structure, partly through procedure. Ostensibly pursuing expertise, many agencies draw their membership from regulated groups. Typically, such agencies both investigate and adjudicate. This combination aids policy making but also gives rise to problems of bias and interest that the organizational separation of investigative and adjudicative staffs attempts to solve. For similar reasons, administrative law judges enjoy statutory guarantees of their independence and must normally follow APA procedures that attempt to balance informality and accuracy.

The Supreme Court has upheld this general arrangement against due process attack because of the protections flowing from the separation of functions and procedural guarantees. Moreover, the Court tolerates some loss of neutrality as the cost of obtaining the policy-making advantages of combined functions at the top of an agency. Notwithstanding the Court's general approval, however, the characteristics of a particular scheme can present unacceptable dangers of bias or interest.

[A]dministrative law displays a basic ambivalence about the deciders' neutrality—the benefits of obtaining knowledgeable or autonomous decision making inure at the risk of introducing unacceptable levels of bias or interest. Arbitration can ameliorate these problems. Its central premise is that consent to the process and practical guarantees of deciders' neutrality justify an informal and final procedure. . . .

B. Public Rights, Private Rights, and Federal Arbitration

. . . In *Thomas v. Union Carbide Agricultural Products Co.*, the Court upheld the mandatory arbitration requirements of the Federal Insecticide, Fungicide, and Rodenticide Act (FIFRA). Under the Act, manufacturers wishing to register and market a pesticide must give the Environmental Protection Agency (EPA) their research data on the product's effects. The EPA considers the data for both the initial registration and later filings for similar products submitted by other manufacturers. Later registrants must compensate the earlier ones for use of the data, in amounts determined by arbitration if the manufacturers cannot agree. A federal court can set aside an arbitrator's award only for "fraud, misrepresentation, or other misconduct."

Writing for the majority in *Thomas*, Justice O'Connor rejected "doctrinaire reliance on formal categories" as a guide to article III and instead favored an analysis focusing on the right at issue and the congressional purposes behind the scheme. The majority characterized FIFRA as creating a compensatory right with many public characteristics. It concluded that Congress could authorize an agency to "allocate costs and benefits among voluntary participants" in a regulatory program without providing an Article III adjudication.

Justice O'Connor interpreted *Northern Pipeline* as holding only that Congress could not give a non-Article III court power to decide state-law contract actions without the litigant's consent and subject only to ordinary appellate review. She rejected an argument that FIFRA had created a "private right," explicitly disapproving the definition advanced by the *Northern Pipeline* plurality insofar as it turned on whether "a dispute is between the Government and an individual." Justice Brennan, Marshall, and Blackmun concurred, abandoning any implication that public rights cases are restricted to those in which the government is a party and explaining that their *Northern Pipeline* position focused on the state law nature of the claims at issue.

In passing, the Court squelched the *Northern Pipeline* plurality's threat to the structure of the administrative state. The Court stated that *Crowell* fell within mandatory Article III jurisdiction because it concerned a statute that replaced a common-law action. . . .

Turning to the use of arbitration, the Court noted Congress's need to streamline compensation controversies. It perceived a close nexus between the use of arbitration and effective administration of the pesticide registration program. The Court also emphasized the existence of consent by the affected firms; it considered the danger of encroachment on the judiciary's central role to be "at a minimum when no unwilling defendant is subjected to judicial enforcement power."

The Court accepted the statute's limitations on judicial review, which it read to allow reversal of arbitrators "who abuse or exceed their powers or willfully misconstrue their mandate under the governing law." The concurring Justices, like the majority, echoed the traditional "manifest disregard for the governing law" standard of review. The Court also held that review for constitutional error was available, alleviating any due process concerns about the extent of review.

Thomas demonstrates the absence of clear distinctions between public and private rights in federal programs. Congress had a substantial "public" purpose in choosing arbitration in FIFRA—to relieve the executive of tangled administrative adjudications. Congress, however, could have shifted the compensation controversies into federal court without offending article III. Aware of that alternative and its consequence for judicial case loads, the Court embraced arbitration and accorded the courts a minimal supervisory role.

Although some of the language in Justice O'Connor's opinion in *Thomas* suggests that Article III courts must hear common-law claims, the Court has since modified its stance. In *Commodity Futures Trading Commission v. Schor,* [478 U.S. 833 (1986)] the Court upheld the authority of the Commodity Futures Trading Commission (CFTC) to entertain state-law counterclaims in reparation proceedings when disgruntled customers seek redress for brokers' violation of statutes or regulations. The Commodity Exchange Act authorized CFTC adjudicators to decide counterclaims arising out of transactions properly alleged in a complaint. Schor filed a claim for reparations, and the defendants counterclaimed for debt.

Justice O'Connor's opinion for seven Justices relied in part on consent—Schor chose the CFTC's "prompt" and "inexpensive" procedure instead of a lawsuit. Indeed, the Court compared this option to arbitration and concluded that the voluntary choice of informal procedures minimized separation of powers concerns. The Court then asked whether the new forum exercised the "range of jurisdiction and powers normally vested only in Article III courts" and whether the latter retained the "essential attributes of judicial power." Only the jurisdiction over counterclaims differed from the usual agency model. The Court saw no reason to deny agencies all pendent jurisdiction and found federalism concerns minimal, because federal courts could have entertained the claims. Thus, *Schor* suggests that agencies may resolve any state-law claim closely related to a federal issue within their jurisdiction. Agencies' exercise of pendent jurisdiction reduces federal court case loads by resolving potential diversity cases; arbitration accompanied by minimal judicial supervision maximizes this benefit.

In both *Thomas* and *Schor*, as in the FAA cases, the Court emphasized the consent of the participants as a justification for nonjudicial processes. *Schor* was an easy case, because the plaintiff could choose between a lawsuit and agency adjudication. *Thomas*, however, was another matter. The Court strained to characterize FIFRA registrations as "voluntary"—the choice available to a chemical company is to forgo marketing a pesticide it does not register. . . . *Thomas*, then, perhaps heralded a looser standard of consent for federal regulatory programs, allowing public values to offset concern for the autonomy of the regulated party. The subject matter of a dispute certainly should affect the stringency of judicial scrutiny of consent to arbitration. The schemes in both *Thomas* and *Schor* promoted the original purpose of Article III's protections: to guarantee the independence of adjudication from political pressure emanating from the executive or Congress. In *Thomas*, the Court remarked that shifting from agency adjudicators to private arbitrators "surely does not diminish the likelihood of impartial decision-making, free from political influence." Similarly, in *Schor* it noted that Congress had placed adjudication in an independent agency, which would be "relatively immune from the political winds that sweep Washington." Arbitration is superior to agency adjudication in this regard, because it increases the decider's independence. . . .

Today it seems unlikely that Congress will run afoul of *Northern Pipeline* unless the subject matter involves prized judicial responsibilities. . . . On the other hand, when expeditious process clearly serves non-Article III functions, such as ordinary program administration, the courts are not likely to insist that Congress increase their already heavy case loads. Therefore arbitration should be safe from a successful Article III assault as long as Congress confines it to specialized subject matter in federal programs with related executive functions.

C. Limiting Judicial Review

Judicial review of arbitration has always been more limited than review of administrative adjudication. Nevertheless, a minimum level of oversight of awards should be preserved. Thomas suggests that courts will review at least the facial consistency of an arbitral award with statutory criteria and constitutional norms. These inquiries require only a brief statement of the basis for an award. They also accord with the FAA's general criteria for review of arbitration and would not require probing the factual basis of awards. More intensive review would destroy the informality that accounts for the virtues of arbitration.

In general, courts seem most likely to reach issues that concern the overall structure and validity of a statutory scheme rather than its application to particular facts. Thus, courts routinely permit constitutional inquiry of statutes that appear to preclude all review. Judges thereby avoid reaching troubling issues about the power of Congress to insulate administrative action completely. . . .

By deferring to agency review of arbitrator's decisions, courts can further reduce the burden on their dockets. Because arbitration is inappropriate for elaborating public-law norms, most arbitrations should be free of substantial constitutional or statutory issues. . . .

Forgoing judicial review of some aspects of arbitration in federal programs is consistent with the tradition that courts do not review all law-applying decisions that occur within the executive branch. The aspects of arbitration that would escape judicial review would resemble some kinds of executive functions that courts presently decline to review. Like arbitration programs, these functions feature needs for expertise, informality, and expedition; a large volume of potentially appealable actions; and the presence of methods other than judicial review for preventing abuses of discretion.

VI. DUE PROCESS

. . . Voluntary arbitration should usually satisfy due process criteria. In general, a party's consent to a particular procedure is the best guarantee of fairness, if the alternatives are also acceptable. (Here, the alternative would be ordinary administrative process.) Of course, there are limits to what a citizen may bargain away for the benefits of an expeditious decision. To steer clear of those limits, Congress should avoid authorizing arbitration for disputes in which constitutional or statutory rights are evolving and need the special contributions of both administrators and judges. . . .

The fairness of arbitration derives partly from the specificity of the governing standard. A standard should be specific enough to meet the primary needs of the parties, the arbitrator, and the reviewing entities. The parties need enough information to exercise meaningful consent to the use of arbitration and to present their cases. The arbitrators need enough guidance to make awards that will be consistent with each other. The reviewing entities must be able to judge the facial validity of awards. In *Thomas,* arbitrators were to provide "compensation" to pesticide registrants for the use of their data. The vagueness of this standard raised fundamental questions: for example, does it mean the cost of creating the data or the value to the later registrant? An agency presented with such a vague statutory directive should elaborate it through rulemaking before asking arbitrators to apply it.

Provisions for review by an agency or a court under the standards of the FAA also help to ensure the accuracy of arbitrations. Review focuses on the two most important ways in which arbitration can go awry—loss of neutrality in the decider, and an award exceeding the bounds of the ex ante expectations of the parties. It would be difficult to provide added checks without radically formalizing the process.

The strength of the government's interest in informality varies. It is relatively great in high volume, small dollar contexts, such as Medicare, in which fact questions predominate. When expeditious processes are available, it is possible to devote more resources to the formal processes needed for resolution of policy or formation of precedent. Insofar as the government's fiscal interest concerns payment of awards as well as provision of process, however, the government's advantage is not a simple matter of minimizing procedural costs. Instead, the government should seek a process that optimally balances accuracy and cost. Such a balance is a peculiarly executive function, and . . . the agency's choice of process is entitled to deference by a court weighing the dictates of due process.

VIII. CONCLUSION

To satisfy the due process and separation of powers concerns emanating from Articles II and III of the Constitution, arbitral schemes must have certain relationships with federal courts and agencies. Agencies are responsible for the composition of the arbitral pool, the method of selecting arbitrators in particular cases, and the articulation of the governing norm. When arbitration does not have the full consent of private parties, agencies have a special responsibility to assure its fairness by supervising the conduct of arbitration in ways consistent with its neutrality. Agencies must review awards in the limited ways that are familiar in private arbitration, and also for their consistency with the agency's law and policies. Federal courts can then defer to agencies for review of individual awards, while retaining their traditional function of deciding statutory and constitutional challenges to the scheme as a whole. . . .

3. Stephen K. Huber, *Administrative Dispute Resolution Act of 1990* (1996)

General ADR Provisions

The Administrative Dispute Resolution Act (ADRA) of 1990 covers the use ADR of procedures in lieu of adjudication "to resolve issues in controversy, including, but not limited to, settlement negotiations, conciliation, facilitation, mediation, factfinding, minitrials, and arbitration, or any combination thereof." [§ 571(d)] Congress sought not simply to clarify the authority of agencies to make use of ADR, but also to promote the use of voluntary alternative means of dispute resolution.

Agencies are given plenary authority to use ADR in lieu of adjudication, "if the parties agree to such proceeding." The statute advises agencies to *"consider"* not using ADR in the following circumstances: [§ 572(b), emphasis supplied]

1. an authoritative precedent is needed;
2. uniformity of result is important for policy reasons, and the use of ADR might result in different decisions;
3. the matter significantly affects persons or groups that are not parties to the proceeding;
4. a full public record is important; and
5. the matter is one over which the agency will maintain continuing jurisdiction, with authority to alter the disposition in the light of changed circumstances.

The ADRA does not prohibit the use of ADR in these circumstances, and the agency decision is not subject to collateral attack. Party acquiescence is not a concern, since consent is a condition precedent to the use of ADR pursuant to the ADRA in lieu of agency adjudication.

The decision of an agency to use or not use ADR, or to choose one ADR procedure over another, is "committed to the discretion of the agency and shall not be subject to judicial review." Judicial review of arbitration awards is available pursuant to the FAA, which is to say only on the very limited grounds. [§ 581]

The ADRA contains interesting and expansive confidentiality provisions. These are discussed in Chapter 17, section E. The Act "does not prevent the discovery or admissibility of any evidence that is otherwise discoverable, merely because the evidence was presented in the course of a dispute resolution proceeding," and it does not constitute a state specifically exempting disclosure under the Freedom of Information Act. [§ 553(b)(3)]

4. Cynthia B. Dauber, *The Ties That Do Not Bind: Nonbinding Arbitration in Federal Administrative Agencies*, 9 Admin. L.J. Am. U. 165 (1995)*

. . . Acknowledging the need for ADR within the federal agencies, Congress enacted the Administrative Dispute Resolution Act (the ADR Act or the Act) in 1990. The ADR Act both

*Reprinted with permission.

authorizes and encourages agencies to use these techniques voluntarily. The provisions give agencies a framework within which ADR proceedings are acceptable. . . .

The Act requires every federal agency to: (1) adopt an agency policy on the use of ADR; (2) designate a senior official as the agency's ADR specialist; (3) provide training on ADR methods; and (4) review all contracts and agreements for possible implementation of ADR methods. The Act also extends the use of ADR to existing agency mechanisms with amendments to the Federal Torts Claims Act and the Contract Disputes Act. In addition, the amendments enlarged discretionary settlement amounts to give the agencies greater latitude when using ADR methods. . . . [The author discusses a variety of issues related to the ADRA. Only her discussion of agency implementation is reproduced here.]

A year after enactment of the ADR Act, the Bush administration indicated its strong support for ADR within the executive branch by issuing a corresponding executive order. The Order on Civil Justice Reform emphasized the need for more efficient resolution of disputes to decrease the number of litigated civil cases. The Order directs government attorneys to make reasonable efforts to settle disputes before commencing civil litigation.

Agencies appeared willing to experiment with new conflict resolution concepts. More than seventy percent of disputes submitted to ADR processes reach a settlement. Mere discussion of possible ADR techniques often will lead to agreement between parties.

Even before the Act, which gave statutory authority to agencies to use ADR, some agencies had implemented pilot programs to perform mini-trials, arbitration, mediation, and negotiated rulemaking. In one successful example of ADR, the Federal Deposit Insurance Corporation implemented ADR techniques to solve disputes about creditor claims, valuation issues, and professional liability. The changes resulted in less litigation and lower attorney fees.

The Act prompted several agencies confronted with equal employment opportunity (EEO) claims to implement mediation [programs]. Mediation of EEO disputes at the Air Force Civilian Appellate Review Agency has worked with more than fifty percent of all complaints settled. Also, starting with a pilot program at the Federal Aviation Administration, the Department of Transportation intends to use mediation as a tool for solving EEO claims throughout the agency. Even the House of Representatives adopted a plan that calls for the resolution of bias-related claims through ADR methods. . . .

Some agencies have settled contract disputes using nonbinding arbitration. Moreover, specific statutory authority permits several agencies to implement binding arbitration. Agencies have begun to understand that settlement of disputes through ADR methods has major benefits over litigation. . . .

Because the ADR Act is designed only to encourage ADR, it did not compel any major or widespread changes in . . . handling disputes involving the government. A general reluctance in the agencies to try new methods stems from fear of reprisal for errors and the refusal to relinquish decision-making power. . . . Without a cooperative and flexible agency atmosphere, alternative dispute resolution will not succeed in the federal government . . . .

2. Arbitration Provisions

The ADRA authorizes the use of arbitration by federal agencies. [§ 575] The required party consent "may be obtained either before or after an issue in controversy has arisen." However, agencies "may not require any person to consent to arbitration as a condition of entering into a contract or obtaining a benefit." Agreements to arbitrate are enforceable under the Federal Arbitration Act [see Chapter 11, section C].

Provisions for the selection of an arbitrator, neutrality, and how arbitration proceedings are to be conducted parallel those in general use for private arbitration. [§§ 577-579] The arbitrator may consider "any oral or documentary evidence, except that irrelevant, immaterial, unduly repetitious, or privileged evidence may be excluded by the arbitrator." [§ 579(c)(4)] Ex parte communications with the arbitrator by any "interested person" are subject to the same sort of restrictions that apply in agency adjudication and court proceedings (i.e., almost never). [§ 579(d)] With the consent of the parties, the arbitration proceeding may be conducted, in whole or in part, "by telephone, television, computer, or other electronic means. . . ." [§ 579(c)(2)]

The decision of the arbitrator need not be lengthy, but it must do more than state the result. The award "shall include a brief, informal discussion of the factual and legal basis for the award, but formal findings of fact or conclusions of law" are not required. [§ 580(a)]

An arbitrator's award becomes final after thirty days, but the agency can extend this period to sixty days by notifying the other party to the dispute. [§ 580(b)] Once the award becomes final, it can be enforced under the FAA. [§ 580(d)] The award may not be used as a precedent, and "may not be serve as an estoppel in any other proceeding. . . ." [§ 580(e)]

The most striking aspect of this arbitration system is that the agency, but not the private party, can reject the decision of the arbitrator "before the award becomes final by serving on all other parties a written notice to that effect, in which case the award shall be null and void." [§ 580(c)] A vacated arbitral award is not admissible in any proceeding that raises the same or related issues. [§ 580(f)] The prevailing party in a vacated proceeding may apply for reimbursement of costs and fees incurred in connection with the arbitration proceeding. The agency "shall award the petitioning party those fees and expenses that would not have been incurred in the absence of such arbitration proceeding, unless the agency head or his or her designee finds that special circumstances make such an award unjust." [§ 580(g)] A decision to terminate an arbitration proceeding or vacate an arbitral award shall be committed to the discretion of the agency and shall not be subject to judicial review. [§ 581(b)(2)] While agencies are granted apparently unfettered power to vacate arbitral awards (apart from paying the other party's expenses), resort to this power except in the rarest of circumstances will result in a refusal to enter into arbitration with the agency.

5. U.S. Department of Justice, Order No. 1160.1 (1995), Subject: Promoting the Broader Appropriate Use of Alternative Dispute Resolution Techniques

1. PURPOSE. The purpose of this order is to promote the broader use of alternative dispute resolution (ADR) in appropriate cases to improve access to justice for all citizens and to lead to more effective resolution of disputes involving the government.
2. SCOPE. The provisions of this order shall apply to all Departmental litigating divisions and to all U.S. Attorneys. This order is applicable to civil matters only. It is not intended to affect criminal matters, including enforcement of criminal fines or judgments of forfeiture. . . .

4. AUTHORITY. In addition to the general authority conferred upon the Attorney General by law, specific authority to provide ADR guidance is provided by section 3 of the Administrative Dispute Resolution Act of 1990, 104 Stat. 2736-37.
5. DEFINITION. As used in this order, "formal ADR techniques" include, but are not limited to, arbitration, mediation, early neutral evaluation, neutral expert evaluation, mini-trials and summary jury trials.
6. CREATION OF POSITION OF SENIOR COUNSEL FOR ALTERNATIVE DISPUTE RESOLUTION. There shall be created within the Department of Justice, the position of "Senior Counsel for Alternative Dispute Resolution" . . . [who] shall:
   a. Assist senior management in developing policies for the use of ADR. . . .
   b. Assist with the design and execution of ADR-related training, recordkeeping, program evaluation and reporting functions.
   c. Provide advice and assistance to Department supervisors and employees on selecting appropriate cases for using ADR and on the application of particular ADR techniques. . . .
7. COMPONENT ADR GUIDANCE. Each litigating division and the Executive Office for United States Attorneys, acting on behalf of the United States Attorneys, shall provide its attorneys with the following ADR guidance:
   a. A policy statement by the head of the component indicating that attorneys are expected to use ADR in appropriate cases as an alternative to litigation and are to cooperate with court-annexed or court-sponsored ADR programs and with efforts to develop and evaluate such programs.
   b. A set of criteria to be used in identifying specific cases appropriate for resolution through settlement negotiations or the use of a formal ADR technique. . . .
   c. A requirement that . . . attorneys handling civil matters be required to participate in periodic supplemental ADR training. . . .
8. FURTHER RESPONSIBILITIES OF PERFORMING COMPONENTS. . . . The components subject to this order shall review their ADR guidance at least annually, and . . . shall make any necessary changes. The components . . . shall designate a person or persons with primary responsibility for coordinating the component's ADR efforts so that a network of individuals with ADR expertise is established throughout the Department.
9. NO PRIVATE RIGHTS CREATED. This order is intended only to improve the internal management of the Justice Department in resolving disputes and conducting litigation. This order shall not be construed as creating any right or benefit, substantive or procedural, enforceable at law or in equity, by a party against the United States, its agencies, its officers, or any other person. This order shall not be construed to create any right to judicial review involving the compliance or noncompliance of the United States, the Justice Department, its officers, or any other person with this order. Nothing in this order shall be construed to obligate the United States to offer funds to settle any case, accept a particular settlement or resolution of a dispute, to alter its standards for accepting settlements, to submit to binding arbitration, or to alter any existing delegation of settlement or litigating authority.

F. Rulemaking

1. Stephen K. Huber, *The Negotiated Rulemaking Act of 1990* (1996)

Congress enacted the Negotiated Rulemaking Act of 1990 to establish a framework for the use of "reg-neg" in federal rulemaking proceedings, and to encourage agencies to employ reg-neg when it enhances the notice and comment rulemaking process. Congress made a point of disclaiming any intention "to limit innovation and experimentation with the negotiated rulemaking process or with other innovative rulemaking procedures otherwise authorized by law." [§ 561] No change was made in the rulemaking standards enunciated in the APA. [§ 553]

The initiative to undertake a negotiated rulemaking rests entirely with the responsible agency. Others are free to suggest the use of reg-neg for a proceeding, but a negative decision is not subject to review. To use reg-neg, the agency must determine that doing so is "in the public interest," and that: [§ 563]

1. there are a limited number of identifiable interests that will be significantly affected by the rule;
2. it appears likely that a committee can be convened with a balanced representation of these interests;
3. it appears likely that a committee will reach consensus on the proposed rule within a fixed period of time;
4. the reg-neg proceeding will not unduly delay the notice of proposed rulemaking and the issuance of the final rule;
5. the agency is willing to commit adequate resources and technical assistance, to the committee; and
6. the agency expects, consistent with the legal obligations of the agency, to use the committee consensus as the basis for the rule proposed by the agency for notice and comment.

Specific procedures are stated for the announcement of a proposed reg-neg proceeding, the submission of comments by interested persons, and nomination of members for the reg-neg committee. [§ 564] Agencies are authorized to employ a "convenor" to determine the feasibility of undertaking a reg-neg proceeding. [§ 563]

After evaluating this information the agency may decide to terminate the process, in which case it must publish a notice, with reasons, in the Federal Register. If the agency decides to proceed with the negotiated rulemaking, it establishes a committee of up to twenty-five members, with balanced representation of "the interests that will be significantly affected by a proposed rule." Each committee must include at least one person "representing the agency." [§ 565] Reg-neg committees and their members are subject to the Federal Advisory Committee Act (FACA).

The chair of the reg-neg committee is the "facilitator," nominated by the agency, with committee approval "by consensus." If the agency nominee is not approved, the committee selects a person, again "by consensus." No provision is made for an impasse, presumably on the theory that if the committee cannot agree on a facilitator, it certainly will not be able to produce a widely acceptable proposed rule. The facilitator may not be the agency representative. [§ 566]

The legislation defines "consensus" to mean "unanimous concurrence among the interests represented," unless a committee (unanimously) adopts a "general but not unanimous concurrence" standard. [§ 562(c)] Where consensus is thwarted by a single interest, the agency might promulgate a proposed rule that tracks the dominant but not unanimous position, and use that broad agreement as a reason for its position. (Remember that an agency can propose a rule without consulting with anyone, but that is not an approach designed to win friends or support for the agency.)

It is contemplated that the facilitator will be paid — at the usual low government rate for consultants. [§ 568] The members normally are not compensated, and do not even receive reimbursement of expenses. Reasonable compensation and expenses are paid if the member "certifies a lack of adequate financial resources to participate in the committee," and the agency determines that the member's participation "is necessary to assure an adequate representation of the member's interest."

Upon reaching a consensus, the committee submits a report to the appointing agency that contains its recommendations, which will take the form of a proposed rule if one is agreed upon. If a proposed rule is not agreed upon, the committee may submit a report that specifies areas where the committee did reach a consensus. Any committee member is entitled to "include as an addendum to the report additional information, recommendations, or materials." [§ 566]

This legislation does not provide a basis for judicial review of agency action related to a negotiated rulemaking. A final rule that results from a reg-neg proceeding is subject to judicial review in the same manner as a rule which is the product of other rulemaking procedures. [§ 570]

2. David M. Pritzker, *The Blossoming of Reg-Neg*, NIDR News, August 1995, at 6*

Since the early 1980's, a growing number of government agencies have been using negotiated rulemaking in an effort to improve the way they draft regulations. Recent initiatives of the Clinton Administration, as well as some legislative prodding, have led to more widespread, serious consideration and use of the process than ever before.

Negotiated rulemaking, or "reg-neg," provides a means of resolving regulatory problems through the effective application of mediation among the interests affected by a regulatory program. The goal is to reach agreement on regulatory issues through procedures that foster cooperative efforts rather than the more customary adversarial approach.

To use the reg-neg process, the regulatory agency assembles a committee consisting of representatives of the various interests and a representative of the agency. With the assistance of a skilled mediator or facilitator, the committee members engage in negotiations aimed at reaching consensus on the text of a proposed regulation. If consensus is achieved, then the agency publishes the text in the Federal Register and invites public comment, as required by the Administrative Procedure Act.

Throughout the period of development and application of reg-neg, the concept has enjoyed bi-partisan support. The first attempts to use the process were based on a 1982 recommendation of the Administrative Conference of the United States (ACUS), an independent fed-

*Reprinted with permission.

eral agency created to study issues of administrative procedure and to recommend ways to improve the fairness, efficiency, or effectiveness of federal agency programs. The first uses of reg-neg occurred in 1983, under the Reagan Administration, at the Federal Aviation Administration and the Environmental Protection Agency (EPA). (Of the approximately 50 negotiated rulemaking proceedings undertaken by federal agencies, about one third have been at the EPA.) Other agencies continued the experiment, including the Department of Labor's Occupational Safety and Health Administration (OSHA), Nuclear Regulatory Commission (NRC), Federal Trade Commission (FTC), and the Department of Agriculture's Animal and Plant Health Inspection Service (APHIS).

By 1990, Congress added its endorsement through the Negotiated Rulemaking Act, passed with bi-partisan support and signed by President Bush. . . . [T]he Act recognized the apparent value of consensual processes and actually encouraged agencies to experiment and innovate with these ideas. The Clinton Administration also encouraged this approach through recommendations of the National Performance Review and the provisions of Executive Order 12866, which addressed procedures for regulatory planning and review. On the same day in September 1993 that the President signed the executive order, he also issued a directive to agency heads to choose at least one candidate rule for development through reg-neg. . . .

The earliest reg-negs addressed environmental issues and conditions applying to particular kinds of workplaces. More recently, interest has broadened to include a variety of financial and funding formulas (HCFA, Education, HUD, and the Farm Credit Administration), protection of animals (APHIS), technical issues in communications (FCC), and valuation of resources (Interior). The scope of coverage has ranged from the relatively narrow focus of the Coast Guard's reg-neg on drawbridges along the Chicago River to EPA's reformulated gasoline regulation, which will affect millions of drivers across the United States.

Congress has on several occasions, required that negotiated rulemaking be used in particular situations. These have included education assistance programs, public housing funding, and implementation of legislation on Native American self-determination. The last of these may be, in some respects, the most challenging effort yet to apply consensus-building procedures to federal regulatory questions. Working together, the Department of the Interior and the Department of Health and Human Services, with the assistance of the Administrative Conference and the Federal Mediation and Conciliation Service (FMCS), have brought together 48 Native American tribal representatives and 15 government officials to try to reach agreement on a range of issues affecting the relationship between the tribes and the federal government. Among the unusual features is the participation of two federal agencies, the size of the committee, and the fact that a new, creative approach is being taken in an area characterized by a long history of mistrust. . . .

In March 1995, President Clinton again focused agency attention on negotiated rulemaking in his "Regulatory Reinvention Initiative" memorandum. Among the steps aimed at increasing public participation in government, the President directed agencies to expand substantially their efforts to promote consensual rulemaking and required each agency to submit to the Office of Management and Budget (OMB) . . . "a list of upcoming rulemakings that can be converted into negotiated rulemakings."

The original goal of negotiated rulemaking was to avoid costly litigation challenging agency regulations. Agency experience suggests that reg-neg has been successful in this respect, even when complete consensus is not achieved. Over a 12-year period, only three lawsuits have been filed involving rules based on negotiated rulemaking, and in none of the cases has there been any challenge to the reg-neg process. Beyond that apparent success, however, there appears to be a widely held view by agencies and other participants in reg-neg that it has resulted in "better" rules, in the sense that the agencies are making rulemaking decisions based on more complete and accurate information that has been subjected to careful review by the negotiating committees. The negotiation process helps ensure that regulatory alternatives. as well as their real-world consequences, are factored into the decisionmaking process. Negotiated rulemaking thus identifies and helps avoid inefficient or costly regulatory choices by the agency, and potentially reduces the cost of implementation to both the government and the private sector.

As interest in reg-neg grows, agencies continue to explore new ways to adapt the consensus building approach to their particular needs. The EPA, for example, considers a variety of techniques of varying degrees of formality. These include "policy dialogues," where the goal may be consensus on principles rather than on regulations, and various kinds of forums. workshops, or roundtables. OSHA and NRC have been experimenting with ways to use modern technology such as electronic bulletin boards to enhance communications among committee members and with the interested public. Agencies are also seeking ways to conserve resources when using negotiated rulemaking, through more efficient contracting procedures to obtain neutrals and better use of staff.

3. Comments and Questions

a. The Negotiated Rulemaking Act of 1990 is codified at 5 USC §§ 561 to 570, as part of the Administrative Procedure Act. The legislative history is found at 1990 U.S. Code Cong. & Admin. News 6697.

b. Members of reg-neg committees are subject to the Federal Advisory Committee Act (FACA). The leading case on FACA is *Association of American Physicians and Surgeons v. Clinton,* 997 F.2d 898 (D.C. Cir. 1993), which litigation grew out of the participation of Hillary Rodham Clinton in the President's Task Force on National Health Care Reform. FACA requires open meetings by advisory committees, subject to an exception for committees composed entirely of full-time government officers or employees of the federal government.

c. Evaluations of reg-neg typically focus on the number of proceedings initiated, and the number that reach a consensus agreement on important issues. (Consensus is a continuum that stretches from total agreement on all relevant issues to an agreement on some important issues.) Arguably, however, the most important indicia of success is the avoidance of judicial review, with only three challenges of negotiated rules in twelve years. In the article that follows, political scientist Shep Melnick persuasively demonstrates that judicial review of rulemaking has been destructive of good government. While Melnick does not discuss reg-neg, his critique certainly would lead one to favor any reasonable approach to rulemaking that results in decreased litigation.

d. Compare reg-neg proceedings to the negotiation of a treaty, a mediation, and legislation. What similarities and differences are there between these processes?

4. R. Shep Melnick, *Administrative Law and Bureaucratic Reality*, 44 ADMIN. L. REV. 245 (1992)*

From the perspective of a political scientist, what is both puzzling and exasperating about the literature on administrative law is how little it has to say about administrators and administration. Administrative law in the United States is almost entirely about courts. Articles abound on judicial doctrines relating to scope of review and rulemaking procedures. But no one pays much attention to the tasks performed by administrators, the agency's sense of mission, the conflicting pressures placed on it, or even what happens after judges hand down their decisions. Others have noticed this lacuna. Peter Schuck and Donald Elliott [recently] wrote,

> Although the study of administrative law started in earnest more than fifty years ago, we still know little about what is perhaps the central question in that field: how does judicial review actually affect agency decisionmaking? This question goes to the fundamental nature and quality of the modern administrative state, yet academic specialists have largely neglected it; the subject remains a matter for uninformed speculation. Despite (or perhaps because of) the lack of data, strong opinions on this question are common.

One such strongly held (but unsubstantiated) opinion is that without "searching and thorough" judicial review, bureaucrats would be running wild, issuing arbitrary and capricious orders with utter abandon. Another view is that without such judicial review agencies would be in the hip pocket of "special interests," captured, we are always told, "by the very interests they are supposed to control." It is bad enough that these two views are incompatible. What is worse is that usually they are both wrong. . . .

In recent years a small group of scholars have taken a closer look at how court decisions have reshaped administrative agencies and their policies. The purpose of this article is to acquaint students of administrative law with some of these findings. As will soon become clear, most of these studies show that judicial intervention has had an unfortunate effect on policymaking. Judicial review has subjected agencies to debilitating delay and uncertainty. Courts have heaped new tasks on agencies while decreasing their ability to perform any of them. They have forced agencies to substitute trivial pursuits for important ones. And they have discouraged administrators from taking responsibility for their actions and for educating the public. . . .

RULEMAKING

Let me start with the most obvious problem, rulemaking delay. In the late 1970s William H. Rodgers, Jr. summed up the conventional wisdom about aggressive judicial review of agency rulemaking by saying, "The hard look doctrine plays no favorites; it is advanced as enthusiastically by industry as it is by environmentalists. Its acceptance is deep." Ten years later many people are having second thoughts.

In retrospect, what happened is quite clear. The courts said, consider all the "relevant" evidence, respond to all "significant" comments, and weigh all "reasonable" alternatives. Who could object to that? The problem was that judges failed to explain what they meant by "relevant," "significant," and "reasonable." Like pornography, they knew it only after they saw it. Since agencies do not like losing big court cases, they reacted defensively, accumulating more and more information, responding to all comments, and covering all their bets. The rulemak-

*Reprinted with permission.

ing record grew enormously, far beyond any judge's ability to review it. As a result, it took longer and longer to complete the rulemaking process. Richard Pierce reports that "the time required to make policy through rulemaking has been stretched to nearly a decade." In some instances the final rules appeared just as the underlying problem had disappeared or changed fundamentally.

Thus began a vicious cycle: the more effort agencies put into rulemaking, the more they feared losing, and the more defensive rulemaking became. Even then, they lost a significant number of cases—it was just too hard to predict what a randomly selected panel of judges would do. Draw two Reagan appointees on a three judge panel and you might well lose because you regulated too much; draw two Carter appointees, you might lose because you regulated too little. Little wonder that many agencies looked for ways to avoid the rulemaking quagmire. Some agencies decided it would be easier to use adjudication to establish agency policy. Others set policy through interpretive rulings or internal enforcement policies. So instead of more rules, we have more discretion; instead of uniformity, we have particularism. Just as water runs downhill, agencies run away from uncertainty, which is what the judicial review often represented.

Jerry Mashaw and David Harfst's recent book presents a particularly graphic example of how a federal agency has responded to "hard look" judicial review by virtually abandoning rulemaking. After the courts rejected its first set of safety rules, the National Highway Traffic Safety Administration replaced rulemaking with a recall strategy. Decisions of other federal courts made this strategy easy to pursue. The only problem was that recalls do little to improve auto safety. In a similar vein, Richard Pierce has shown that the courts made it impossible for the Federal Energy Regulatory Commission to use rulemaking to revise seriously deficient policies on regulation of natural gas.

This does not mean that agencies never engage in rulemaking or win in court. What do we know about the effects of judicial review for the substance of the rules that are issued? In the area of health and safety standards both my research and the work of John Mendeloff indicate that judicial review has decreased the number of standards but increased their stringency. Why? Because at the same time that industry is challenging an agency's evidence, public interest groups are charging that the agency has not sufficiently protected the public health.

Judges on key courts have often insisted that EPA and some other agencies take a "health only" approach to standard-setting, especially when a carcinogen is involved. In *Lead Industries Ass'n. v. EPA,* for example, Judge Skelly Wright announced that the legislative history of the Clean Air Act "shows [that] the Administrator may not consider economic or technological feasibility in setting air quality standards." In another decision involving standards for airborne lead, Judge Wright hearkened back to Judge Bazelon's famous claim about the "special judicial interest in favor of protection of the health and welfare of people."

The courts have hardly been consistent on this. The Supreme Court's rulings on OSHA's statutory mandate are far from doctrinaire—in fact they are incoherent. For many years the Supreme Court's inability to speak clearly on such matters left the lower courts—especially the D.C. Circuit—in control. The D.C. Circuit now appears to be pulling back from its previous absolutist position, but in the 1970s and 1980s the message EPA and other agencies often got was this: If you want a standard to survive, collect lots of information, make the rule very stringent, and then use enforcement discretion to avoid the politically dangerous consequences of this stringency. With so few standards being set, environmentalists insisted that the ones that survived were really tough. Seeing these stringent regulations coming down the pike, business fought them tooth and nail, adding to delay.

Mendeloff convincingly argues that this peculiar combination of under-regulation and over-regulation leads us to get far less safety bang for the buck than European nations, which set more standards, but make them individually more lenient. The courts do not bear sole responsibility for this costly adversarial system, but they surely add to the problem. How is it possible to arrange a grand compromise—more standards for less stringency—if any trade association or environmental group can challenge it in court and have a shot at winning? How is it possible to encourage open horse-trading when the courts are insisting upon "rational" decisionmaking based on the accumulation of enormous amounts of technical information?

ACTION-FORCING LITIGATION

Many of the statutes passed by Congress in the 1970s and 1980s were filled with so-called nondiscretionary duties: deadlines, "hammers," and the like. A 1985 study co-authored by the Environmental Law Institute and the Environmental and Energy Study Institute reports that EPA alone was subject to 328 statutory deadlines. Among the other findings of this study were the following:

1. "Very few statutory deadlines (14 percent) have been met."
2. "Congress imposes more deadlines on EPA than it can possibly meet."
3. "Court-ordered deadlines almost always command top management attention at EPA. Top management takes the threat of contempt quite seriously and personally, even though the threat is not real."
4. "The multiplicity of deadlines reduces EPA's ability to assign priority to anything not subject to a deadline."

What this means is that scores of deadlines and other statutory requirements are lying around, usually unused, but still potential weapons in lawsuits—or threatened lawsuits. Do nondiscretionary duties and court enforcement produce "the rule of law"? Of course not; they produce the rule of those who decide which lawsuits to bring. Or, to put it another way, it transfers responsibility for setting agency priority from top administrators to interest groups. . . . It is hard to imagine a worse way to apportion agency resources.

The study cited above asked former EPA administrators what they thought of deadlines and judicial enforcement of them. One said, "From a real world point of view, they are necessary." But another was much more negative, saying, "Deadlines reinforce the sense that we [EPA] are not getting anywhere, to the detriment of public sense of confidence in government." Surprisingly enough, the negative view came from William Ruckelshaus, one of the most outstanding public administrators we have seen in some time, and the positive view came from Anne Gorsuch Burford, who is probably among the worst.

One example will help explain why Ruckelshaus found the deadline-litigation syndrome so detrimental to environmental protection. The Clean Air Act gives the EPA one year to publish regulations setting standards for pollutants it determines are "hazardous." During the Carter administration, EPA determined that radionuclides are carcinogenic, and therefore listed them as hazardous air pollutants. It failed to take any further action. About one year into the Reagan Administration, the Sierra Club sued in the northern district of California. Several years later the matter finally came to a head when Judge Orrick commanded Administrator Ruckelshaus to issue a standard for radionuclides.

At first Ruckelshaus surprised everyone by refusing to obey the court. Not only was the scientific evidence unclear—it always is—but EPA estimated that the health risks were tiny and the potential cost large. Estimated risk from some facilities was one cancer death every fifty years, from other facilities, one cancer death every thirteen to seventeen years. Ruckelshaus was in the middle of a major effort to educate the American public about the nature of environmental risks—to let them know that there is no such thing as a completely safe environment, and to force the government and the public to be honest about the level of safety they are willing to pay for. He told the court, "Given the inevitable burdens that regulation imposes just by its existence, and the shortage of resources to deal with real health risk both in EPA and the society at large, these risks did not appear to me to be large enough to warrant regulation." The judge responded by calling Ruckelshaus a "scofflaw," describing his actions as "outrageous," and expressing shock that such a "responsible person" (and a lawyer to boot) would so cavalierly disregard an order of the U.S. District Court. After being found in contempt of court, Ruckelshaus published regulations that would have virtually no effect on radionuclide levels. EPA estimated that it spent $7.6 million in contract funds and 150 staff-work years on this regulation.

One might conclude from this story that the bureaucracy is filled with scofflaws like William Ruckelshaus who need to be reined in by federal judges. Let me suggest instead that the problem is that too many administrators are more than willing to hide behind the argument "don't blame me for stupid policy, the courts made me do it." The law reviews are filled with theoretical discussions of a dialogue between courts and agencies, about using judicial review to stimulate "deliberation." In the real world what happens is that judicial review short-circuits real deliberation about what constitutes good policy. Agencies say, "The courts made me do it"; courts say, "Congress made me do it"; and Congress says, "Protect public health, but don't put anyone out of work, and don't question our right to condemn the agency no matter what it does." The political science literature calls this "blame-avoidance." Most people call it passing the buck. Only a law professor could call it "dialogue."

SEPARATION OF POWERS

The legal literature is reticent to admit what everyone knows: that a large number of administrative law cases are the outgrowth of divided government. For the first 180 years of the Republic, divided government—control of the presidency by one party and control of Congress by the other—was a rare event. In 1969, however, it became virtually a permanent condition of the American polity. . . .

Those who read the newspaper have noticed that Democrats and Republicans do not always agree on domestic policy or even on foreign affairs. Agencies often find themselves caught between congressional subcommittees (and their persistent staff) that demand more spending or more regulatory activity and the White House (or, more likely, the Office of Management and Budget) that demands less. With relaxed rules on standing . . . many of these disputes end in court. . . .

Given the importance of the presidency in our constitutional system, it is remarkable how seldom the president is mentioned in the legal literature on administrative law. . . . In many cases, federal judges (not to mention the authors of law review articles) assume the pose of Louis in the movie Casablanca: they are shocked, shocked!, to find politics going on here. (It is appropriate that "Casablanca" means "White House" in Spanish.) This was particularly evident in the famous air bag case. Given the vagueness of the underlying statute and the inability of previous administrations to decide whether to mandate airbags, one must ask what was wrong with allowing the outcome of a presidential election—a landslide, at that—to determine the outcome of the controversy? If Congress wants to require airbags, it can do so by writing a law to that effect. . . .

At the very least, it is time for administrative law to be more honest about the role of the Executive Office of the President and political appointees. We should remember that the Constitution makes the president part of the legislative process and gives the president—not judges—the responsibility to "faithfully execute the laws."

NATIONAL UNIFORMITY

In some policy areas judicial review has substantially reduced the uniformity of federal law. There is no little irony in this. Ever since the days of John Marshall, federal courts have tried (and often succeeded) to strengthen the Union by reining in the states. Now that we have created a large number of federal agencies charged with carrying out nationally uniform programs, extensive court intervention all too often creates different rules for different circuits. As Peter Strauss has pointed out, "[T]he infrequency of Supreme Court review combines with the formal independence of each circuit's law from that of the other circuits to permit a gradual balkanization of federal law." He notes that the legal profession has "yet to come to grips with the problem."

Although the problem has arisen in a variety of areas—tax law, labor law, education of the handicapped, and welfare, to name a few—it became most apparent in the heated confrontation between the courts and the executive branch over disability benefits. The agency charged with carrying out disability reviews, the Social Security Administration (SSA), is the very embodiment of the New Deal's commitment to national uniformity. The SSA's willingness to engage in "non-acquiescence" in order to preserve this uniformity predated the Reagan Administration's attempt to purge the disability rolls in the early 1980s. The heavy-handedness of the Reagan Administration's policies should not blind us to the larger issue. In her recent book on the SSA, Martha Derthick has this to say about the agency's much maligned nonacquiescence policy:

> The underlying premise—that policy must be nationally uniform—was not in the least contrived for the occasion. It was contained in law, Congress having stipulated in 1980 that administration of the disability insurance program be "uniform . . . throughout the United States." Just as important, it had long been at the core of the agency's operating code. . . . [T]his code had been reinforced in the SSA's case by the particular historical circumstance that its programs and administrative style were a reaction against the features of American federalism. For the SSA's programs to develop regional differences would be more than a monumental inconvenience to the agency; it would constitute a humiliating retrogression to the time when state governments dominated domestic functions and citizens were treated differently depending on where they happened to live. The SSA's very existence rested on the belief that such differences were unfair.

Compared with agencies like the SSA, the IRS, or even EPA, the federal judiciary is a highly decentralized institution. Constant intervention by the decentralized judiciary can lead to confusion and unfairness. It can also have a corrosive effect on the sense of mission of an agency like the Social Security Administration—a commitment to national uniformity and to prompt determinations, which has served us well since 1935.

POWER WITHIN THE AGENCY

Aggressive judicial review creates winners and losers within administrative agencies. Clearly the biggest losers are political executives, who are less able to set priorities or to resist demands from congressional committees and interest groups. The biggest winners are lawyers with the agency's Office of General Counsel. Many studies of courts and agencies have come to this conclusion. OGC attorneys are the ones who explain what the courts are likely to accept and reject. Frequently—especially on remand—they end up writing substantial portions of the regulations. At the risk of offending my readers, let me suggest two difficulties with this transfer of power to their "brother" and "sister" attorneys.

First, many of these lawyers work in the agency for a relatively short period of time; they are bright, aggressive young men and women who yearn to "cast a shadow" before moving on to a more lucrative career elsewhere. In that sense they are no different from congressional staffers, law clerks, or many lower-echelon people in the White House. More cocky neophytes with short time horizons is hardly what Washington needs.

Second, few of these lawyers have ever run anything. They seldom have a sense of how hard it is to manage a program at the regional or state level. As Martin Shapiro has put it, the judicial demand for rationality:

> tends to shift power within the agencies from those who are really concerned about making policies that work to those concerned with defending them in court . . . from real administrators responsible for the actual operations of programs to lawyers. And it will often lead to a choice of the alternative that can most easily be made to appear synoptic rather than the one that seems best.

This power shift has contributed to some memorable policy disasters. For example, in the early 1970s the D.C. Circuit ordered EPA to promulgate transportation control plans adequate to meet ambient air quality standards, even in cities like Los Angeles. Top administrators considered this politically suicidal. Regional and technical personnel warned that it would be hard to formulate reasonable plans and virtually impossible to implement them. Hard chargers in the Office of General Counsel, though, saw this as their chance to remake the American system of transportation, to fight highways and automobiles, and promote mass transit. The plans, of course, were a political, technical, and management nightmare. . . .

GET REAL, ADMINISTRATIVE LAW

This article has suggested both that courts often make a mess of policy because they have a poor understanding of administrative agencies and that administrative law has done little to correct judicial misperceptions. What understanding of bureaucracy might be more accurate? Let me propose the following generalization about public bureaucracies in the United States: They are almost always given huge, even utopian, goals and are then saddled with a large number of constraints that prevent them from achieving these goals efficiently—or even at all. We tell EPA, for example, to protect the public heath with an adequate margin of safety, but advise it not to spend too much money or put anyone out of work. We tell them to use the best scientific evidence, but refuse to let them pay enough to recruit top-flight scientists, and then we tell them, "By the way, do it within 90 days." We expect bureaucrats to account for every penny of public money, to record every conversation with a member of an interest group, to show that they have treated everyone equally, and to consider all the relevant information and alternatives—but to stop producing all that red tape and being so damn slow.

Courts are particularly likely to make these conflicting demands because they are so decentralized, their exposure to policymaking is so episodic, and the opportunities for forum-shopping are so apparent to interest groups. Courts are good at responding to complaints, and people have lots of complaints about bureaucracy. The problem is that these complaints often require incompatible responses. Today the D.C. Circuit hears a case brought by environmental groups complaining about unconscionable delay. In two years the Sixth Circuit will hear industry complain about shoddy evidence and exorbitant costs. And two years after that a district court judge in Cleveland will be asked to balance the "equities" in order to keep a particular local factory in operation. Who considers the connection among all these decisions? The Supreme Court? Simply to ask this question is to answer it—no one does. . . .

Part VI

ADR In The Judicial System

Chapter 15

Court-Annexed ADR Procedures

CASE STUDY

The accident out of which this dispute arose was apparently the result of the effervescence and ebullition of Houstonians in their exuberance and joy when the Houston Rockets won their second basketball championship on July 15, 1995.

The Plaintiff, Ima Smith, is an individual. Ms. Smith is a twenty-five year old law student from Dallas. Plaintiff has brought this suit against Defendant for $300,000.00 for injuries resulting from an accident which occurred on the sidewalk adjacent to The Royal Bacchus in Houston.

The Defendant is a corporation operating under the name, The Royal Bacchus. The corporation consists of nine hotels, four of which are located in Texas. The corporation's main headquarters are also in Texas.

The hotel in question occupies an entire block of the well-known party strip of Richmond Street. On the night in question, several police barricades were set up along Richmond Street. This was in anticipation of, and in response to, the previous year's festivities following the Rockets' victory. No motor vehicles were allowed to enter Richmond. The Houston Chronicle, the city's only newspaper, strongly suggested that Richmond vendors, clubs and hotels be on special alert for crime and unruly conduct.

Ima Smith was a guest at The Royal Bacchus for a weekend seminar on Legal Negotiation in the 90's. The seminar was to be held at The Royal Bacchus on Saturday afternoon, July 16, 1995, in the main conference room. Ima needs this last class to graduate from law school this summer. She has a job offer open to begin in September as an associate of Justice & Justice, P.C.

On the evening of Friday, July 15, 1995, at about 10:30 p.m. Ima, while walking on the sidewalk on Richmond Street adjoining The Royal Bacchus hotel, just after stepping out from under the marquee, was struck on the head by a heavy, over-stuffed arm chair, knocked unconscious, and received injuries to her head, neck, back and right shoulder for which she is asking damages from the owners of the hotel.

Although there were a number of persons in the immediate vicinity, no one appears to have seen from whence the chair came, nor to have seen it before it was within a few feet from the plaintiff's head, nor has there been any identification of the chair as belonging to the hotel. However, it is a reasonable inference that the chair came from some portion of the hotel.

A sober passerby, Ms. Abbie Stinent, saw plaintiff unconscious on the sidewalk and rushed to call the ambulance. It has since been discovered that on July 15, 1995 following the Rockets' victory, The Royal Bacchus was hosting a victory party for college students in the main ballroom of the hotel. Tickets were $25.00 with a college I.D. There were more than 600 students who attended the celebration.

Plaintiff cannot prove that the chair which caused the accident belonged to The Royal Bacchus and that the chair was under the exclusive control and management of The Royal Bacchus. Also, Smith was heard, by the hotel's bell boy, Tip Green, to be shouting obscenities to an open window where some of the party attendant's were standing. Mr. Green has agreed to testify in this matter if necessary.

Plaintiff has incurred $25,000.00 in medical bills (ambulance, emergency room services, MRI, and physical therapy provided by her chiropractor.) Plaintiff is also claiming at least $3,000.00 in lost wages and claims $600.00 for her/his registration in the seminar and law school credit. Plaintiff will not be able to graduate and therefore not be able to begin her position with Justice & Justice, P.C. as previously planned.

A. Introduction

This chapter examines in depth several ADR procedures that are commonly employed by courts in dealing with litigation. (The issues surrounding the use of court-annexed ADR is the subject of Chapter 16.) A connection to the judicial process is the common theme that ties together a group of otherwise quite distinct ADR procedures—whence the imprecise appellation, "court-annexed." Even within a single ADR process, practice may differ in important ways from one jurisdiction to another. This is particularly true where the use of an ADR process is based on state statute, as with medical malpractice screening panels.

Early neutral evaluation [ENE] is considered mainly in its court-annexed context, but an identical process can be and is used by disputants quite apart from the judicial process. Summary jury trial (SJT), on the other hand, is a true judicial process that takes place in the courthouse before a real jury. (In general, ENE is best for cases where legal issues predominate, while SJT is best for cases where fact questions predominate.) Court-annexed arbitration (CAA) takes place pursuant to a court order, but a similar (nonbinding) arbitration could be undertaken independently by disputants.

The common use of mediation by appellate courts, as opposed to party-initiated ADR, is a recent development, but one that has achieved considerable success. Appellate mediation graphically demonstrates that ADR has become an integral part of the judicial process, to which it is supposedly the alternative. (Not all students of ADR applaud this development—see the views of Professor Menkel-Meadow, set forth in Chapter 18, section D.)

B. Early Neutral Evaluation

1. Comments and Questions

a. Early Neutral Evaluation (ENE) is a term that can be, and is, used in several senses. ENE began as a private form of ADR, with the names moderated settlement conference and advisory opinion sometimes used to describe similar proceedings. The defining characteristics of private ENE—an early evaluation by a neutral based on a general presentation of the dispute by representatives of each side—are quite flexible. In the wake of the Civil Justice Reform Act of 1990, ENE has become a court-connected process in many federal districts. As such, it is defined with greater specificity in court rules, and is less amenable to being custom designed by disputants.

b. The Rosenberg & Folberg article provides a detailed description and analysis of a court-connected ENE program. Note the problems identified by the authors, and the solutions proposed by them. How did the court-connected context shape the problems that arose in the Northern California ENE pilot project? Are the proposed solutions equally applicable to private ENE?

2. Tom Arnold, A Vocabulary of Alternative Dispute Resolution Procedures (1995)*

Early Neutral Evaluation [Sometime synonyms: Moderated Settlement Conference, Advisory Opinions]

Typically meaning:

(1) an informal, mostly oral case presentation;

(2) without much by way of evidence, witnesses or affidavits or much reference to documents;

(3) in substantial cases, argument commonly presented exclusively by counsel rather than client, perhaps followed by client participation in discussions after the neutral(s)'s evaluation report;

(4) presented to a panel of one or two (then commonly called an "Advisory Opinion" procedure) or to a panel of three neutrals (in some circles then called a "Moderated Settlement Conference"), almost always lawyers, hopefully with some background in the subject matter;

(5) the panel of one to three hears the presentation, reports their evaluation, and participates as facilitator in further settlement discussions influenced by how the case "played" to them;

(6) private communications between a party and the neutrals are usually not contemplated in this process, though the process may evolve into classic mediation with private caucuses . . .;

(7) hopefully the neutral(s) will also coach as to other ADR procedures that appear appropriate to the controversy.

This procedure is similar to nonbinding arbitration, but with no evidence rules or consideration, no cross examination, attorneys and clients communicating (unlike litigation), and often with no formality in the neutral's conclusion or "award" or its communication.

Moderated settlement conferences before lawyer panels are advantageous in cases heavy in application-of-law content wherein the reaction of lawyers/judges may dominate any court decision (like the summary jury trial is advantageous in cases low on disputed law and where the jury's evaluation of the damages is influential in settlement). The participation of CEOs or

*Reprinted with permission.

near CEOs is not commonly thought of as "required" to the usage "moderated settlement conference," as is common with the procedure normally termed a "mini-trial." . . .

3. Joshua D. Rosenberg & H. Jay Folberg, *Alternative Dispute Resolution: An Empirical Analysis*, 46 Stan. L. Rev. 1487 (1994)*

INTRODUCTION

During the past decade, courts at every level have begun to use alternative dispute resolution (ADR) processes. . . . This article adds to the empirical research by reporting on a quantitative and qualitative study of the ADR program of the United States District Court for the Northern District of California. The Northern District is one of six courts designated as demonstration districts in the Civil Justice Reform Act of 1990 (CJRA). Prior to the enactment of the CJRA, the Northern District had generated significant national interest in its design and use of an ADR procedure known as early neutral evaluation (ENE). Pursuant to the CJRA, the court retained the authors to evaluate its mandatory ENE program and suggest improvements.

Our most important findings include the following: (1) Approximately two-thirds of those who participated in the mandatory ADR program felt satisfied with the process and believed it worthy of the resources devoted to it (dissatisfaction with the program resulted primarily from dissatisfaction with the particular neutral assigned to the case); (2) while the percentage of parties who reported saving money approximately equaled the percentage who reported that the process resulted in a net financial cost, the net savings were, on average, more than ten times larger than the cost of an ENE session; (3) approximately half the participants in the program reported that participation decreased the pendency time of their cases; (4) the majority of parties and attorneys reported learning information in the ENE session that led to a fairer resolution of their case; and (5) the ENE process varied significantly from case to case and from neutral to neutral, and the most important factor in determining the success of the process in any one case was the individual neutral involved. Consequently, we focused many of our suggestions for improvement on ensuring the quality of the neutrals. While these findings and suggestions are based on the Northern District's ENE program, we believe that they are likely to be relevant for other court-based ADR.

I. HISTORY AND OPERATION OF EARLY NEUTRAL EVALUATION

A. History of the Program

In 1982, then Chief Judge Robert F. Peckham appointed a task force to develop procedures to reduce pretrial costs and delays for litigants in the Northern District of California. A subcommittee identified the following major sources of pretrial cost and delay: (1) complex and unclear pleading practice that often confuses the real substance of the dispute; (2) lawyers' and parties' failure to assess their case thoroughly and dispassionately at an early stage; (3) clients' and attorneys' unrealistic expectations of success; (4) clients' feelings of alienation from the legal process; (5) poor and indirect communication between the litigation parties; and (6) attorneys' reluctance to raise the possibility of settlement out of fear of being perceived as weak. This subcommittee designed the ENE process to encourage each party to confront and analyze its own situation early in the suit and to enable each litigant and lawyer to hear the other side present its case. The process was also intended to help the parties identify the real areas of agreement and dispute and to help them develop an approach to discovery that would focus immediately on the central issues and disclose the key evidence promptly. In addition, ENE was intended to offer all counsel and litigants a confidential, frank, and thoughtful assessment of the relative strengths of their positions and the overall value of the case. Finally, the committee also hoped that ENE would provide the parties with an early opportunity to try to negotiate a settlement.

The court established a pilot ENE program in 1985. It handled about a dozen cases assigned by Wayne Brazil, the magistrate who administered the program at that time. An early study of the pilot program revealed promising results. In the second phase of the ENE experiment, the court assigned 150 cases in specified subject areas to the program, with sixty-seven actually proceeding through the ENE process. A study of these cases concluded that most ENE participants strongly believed ENE was worthwhile. Based on the apparent success of the experimental program, the court further expanded and refined the ENE program in 1988 and again in 1989.

B. Design of the ENE Session

Absent a waiver granted by the court, every party in a case assigned to ENE must attend the ENE session, together with the attorney who will be lead counsel should the case go to trial. If a party is a corporation, it must be represented at the session by a person (other than outside counsel) who has authority both to enter stipulations and to bind the party to the terms of a settlement. Prior to the ENE session, each side must submit to the neutral a statement identifying session participants, major disputed issues, and any discovery that would be a necessary prelude to meaningful settlement discussions. The session is expected to last approximately two hours, during which the following events are expected to take place:

1. The evaluator explains the purposes of the program and outlines the procedures.
2. Each side in turn presents a 15-minute opening statement, either by counsel, client, or both, without interruption from the evaluator or the other party. The statement presents the side's case and legal theories and describes the supporting evidence.
3. The evaluator may then ask questions of both sides to clarify issues, arguments, and evidence, to fill in evidentiary gaps, and to probe for strengths and weaknesses.
4. The evaluator identifies the issues on which the parties agree (and encourages them to enter stipulations where appropriate) and also identifies the important issues in dispute.
5. The evaluator adjourns to another room to prepare a written case evaluation. The evaluation assesses the strengths and weaknesses of each side's case, determines which side is likely to prevail, and establishes the probable range of damages in the event the plaintiff wins.
6. The evaluator returns to the ENE conference room, announces that she has prepared an informal evaluation of the case, and asks the parties if they would like to explore settlement possibilities before she discloses the evaluation to them. If either party declines the offer to begin settlement discussions, the evaluator promptly discloses her written assessment. If, on the other hand, both sides are interested in working on settlement, the evaluator facilitates these discussions.

7. If the parties do not hold settlement discussions or if discussions do not produce a settlement, the evaluator helps the parties develop a plan for efficient case management. This aid may include scheduling motions or discovery that would put the case in a position for rapid settlement or disposition.
8. After the ENE session, the parties may agree to a follow-up session or other activity. With the consent of the court, the parties may engage the evaluator for additional sessions on a compensated basis.

C. Administration of the Program

. . . Early in the life of the ENE program, the ADR task force required all evaluators to attend a training session lasting approximately two and one-half hours. After the first experimental stage of ENE, program organizers videotaped the training session so that evaluators who were unable to attend could watch the tape. Evaluators also received written materials describing the program generally and suggesting how they could best perform their roles.

II. METHODOLOGY

This study is based on a review of all cases filed from April 1988 through March 1992 that met the subject matter criteria for automatic referral to ENE. Of these, the even-numbered cases constitute the "experimental" (ENE) group, and the odd-numbered cases make up the "control" group. The review also included all cases that went through ENE by one of the two other potential avenues for entry into the process—stipulation or referral by the judge. . . .

III. FINDINGS

A. Overview

Our study revealed an ADR program strongly influenced by the individual assigned as the neutral for a given case. For example, when the evaluator was skilled in mediation, ENE often resembled mediation. When the evaluator was more familiar with hard-nosed settlement tactics, that approach appeared to dominate the ENE session. When the evaluator was interested primarily in discovery, there was often little settlement discussion. We found that the nature and outcome of ENE sessions depended more on variations among evaluators than on any other factor, despite the relatively clear guidelines given to evaluators about how to conduct the sessions.

The creators of ENE intended for the session to take place within 150 days of filing. The timing of ENE sessions varied substantially, however, and some cases were not referred to the process until they had been pending for well over a year.

The ENE process was intended to lie somewhere between mediation, in which a third party with substantial procedural expertise facilitates communication among the parties in the interest of settling some or all of the issues in dispute, and nonbinding arbitration, in which a third party with substantial subject matter expertise reviews the case presented by the litigants and determines an appropriate outcome. As conducted, ENE ran the gamut from one extreme to the other, and sometimes bore little resemblance to any other process. Most evaluators appraised their cases in some respects, but the specificity and directness of these appraisals varied tremendously from actual predictions of jury verdicts to subtle hints about possible weaknesses of a claim or defense. . . .

Despite this variation in the ENE process, about two-thirds of the parties who participated in an ENE session believed that the session was helpful and worth their efforts. Parties and attorneys divided relatively evenly over the questions whether ENE reduced costs and whether it resulted in decreased pendency time. More significant, however, was the fact that those who believed ENE did not make a valuable contribution to their case reported that the process was, at worst, a waste of time with an average cost of about $4000 (including attorneys' fees, preparation time, and transportation). Those satisfied with the ENE process, however, reported earlier disposition of their cases, increased understanding of their cases, and an average savings of over $40,000 per participant. . . .

E. Specific Outcomes

After determining that ENE participants on average saved money and time and were satisfied with the process, we next sought to identify the specific outcomes that produced these results. We found that to a great extent ENE was accomplishing just what its originators had intended: The ENE program organized, streamlined, and generally increased the efficiency of discovery and trial preparation; in many cases, it increased prospects for early settlement; and almost all participants who were satisfied with the ENE process reported gaining a better understanding of both the law and the facts of the case. Moreover, these participants noted that subsequent settlement discussions were informed by, and furthered as a result of, this increased understanding.

Thirty-five percent of the parties and 23 percent of the attorneys reported that their cases settled either in ENE or as a direct result of it. Fifty-four percent of the attorneys and 52 percent of the parties reported that ENE increased the prospects for early settlement of their cases. . . .

Fifty-nine percent of the attorneys and 66 percent of the parties reported that ENE resulted in the identification and clarification of issues. Fifty-four percent of the attorneys and 41 percent of the parties who responded to questions regarding ENE's impact on costs reported that ENE decreased discovery and trial-preparation costs by improving communication between the sides. Forty-five percent of the attorneys reported that fees were reduced in part because they obtained specific, discoverable information in the ENE session. In addition, 29 percent of the attorneys and 49 percent of the parties reported that they agreed on future discovery exchanges in the ENE session, and smaller numbers reported cost savings as a direct result of agreeing to stipulations or to specific motion practice at the sessions. Finally, 16 percent of the attorneys reported that ENE allowed them to "back burner" certain unsettled issues that otherwise might have generated substantial discovery costs.

One way that ENE produced the above outcomes is simply by forcing the participants to give earlier attention to their cases. Approximately 42 percent of the attorneys and 37 percent of the parties reported that ENE required their side to focus on the case earlier than they otherwise would have. In addition, 54 percent of the attorneys and 49 percent of the parties believed that ENE forced the other side to focus on the case earlier. Significantly, in cases that did not go through ENE, 59 percent of the attorneys reported that the other side's failure to focus on the case until a later time posed at least a moderate impediment to the commencement of serious settlement discussions.

In addition to requiring participants to focus on their case earlier, ENE also eliminated another significant obstacle to serious settlement discussions—the fear that initiating settlement discussion would give the other side a strategic negotiating advantage. In cases that did not go through ENE, 27 percent of the attorneys reported that earlier settlement discussions were impeded because neither side wanted to initiate such discussions out of fear of being perceived as weak. By forcing the parties to discuss their case and possible settlement at an early stage, ENE facilitated useful discussions that might never have commenced otherwise.

For many participants, the primary factor improving both settlement prospects and discovery planning was their increased understanding of the case. Thirty-five percent of the attorneys and 51 percent of the parties reported developing a better understanding of the legal issues involved in the case as a result of ENE, 46 percent of the attorneys and 40 percent of the parties reported developing a better understanding of the factual issues, 42 percent of the parties reported developing a better understanding of the litigation process, and 70 percent of the parties reported gaining a better understanding of the other side's perception of the case.

The greater understanding that attorneys and parties developed in ENE also helped them more realistically evaluate their case. Sixty-seven percent of the parties and 52 percent of the attorneys stated that, as a result of the ENE process, they developed a more realistic assessment of the likely outcome of their cases, and that their changed assessment made at least a moderate contribution to improving the prospects for earlier settlement. Of those who did not go through ENE, 41 percent of attorneys reported that their own failure to fully understand the case impeded serious settlement discussions, and 53 percent reported that the other side's failure to understand the case impeded the successful conclusion of settlement discussions. A total of 57 percent of the non-ENE attorneys reported increased costs and fees because one or more sides did not have an adequate understanding of the case early on.

In addition to learning about the law and facts of their cases, ENE participants also gained valuable insights into procedural aspects of the litigation. Fifty-two percent of the parties and 31 percent of the attorneys stated that their development of a more realistic assessment of the costs of continuing litigation through trial improved settlement prospects.

IV. HOW THE ENE PROCESS WORKS IN PRACTICE

H. Key ADR Ingredients and Potential Pitfalls

Overall, our data reveal that the ENE program works. Its designers effectively responded to specific problems that tend to result in increased costs, fees, time, and dissatisfaction with the litigation process. For cases that went through the court system without ENE, those negative factors remained. Although ENE did not eliminate all of these problems in every case, it proved worthwhile in most cases. Participants who went through ENE because they believed, often erroneously, that they had no other choice were pleased with their experience in almost two-thirds of the cases. Over 80 percent said they would participate again voluntarily in other cases. Attorneys and parties reported net savings that exceeded total costs by more than ten to one. The ENE process shortened the pendency time in about half of the cases assigned to the process.

The most important factors influencing the success of ENE are the personal skills and abilities of the individual evaluator. Other important factors are the extent to which the evaluator conducts the session in accordance with the procedure suggested in General Order 26 and the attitude and actions of the judge before whom the case is pending.

In addition to identifying some of the most important ingredients in a successful court-connected ADR program, our research also identified several potential pitfalls. The most important of these are:

Expectations. Participants who expected ENE to be something substantially different from what it actually was were among the most dissatisfied with the process.

Coordination. While we found no apparent correlation between the success of ENE and how early in the litigation process it took place, poor timing did cause some dissatisfaction when it resulted from a lack of coordination between the evaluator and the court.

Participation by parties. Parties' involvement in ENE was an important part of the program's success. Nonetheless, there were times when one party could not or would not participate. When one party appeared in person and the other side did not, the party appearing in person tended to have a lower than average level of satisfaction with the process.

Enforcement of court rules by neutrals. For the most part, ENE evaluators failed to report violations of court rules, as General Order 26 directs them to do. While some wanted more authority and others wished for less, almost all evaluators failed to make a regular practice of simply reporting the violations they observed. Confusion about the appropriate role of neutrals in this regard was distressing to some ENE participants.

Selection of the neutral for each case. On several occasions, delays in selecting a qualified neutral prevented a timely ENE session. Selecting neutrals and checking for conflicts of interest were difficult to conduct efficiently through the mail.

V. RECOMMENDATIONS

Our report to the Task Force on Alternative Dispute Resolution included thirty-five specific recommendations for improving the content and administration of ENE in the Northern District of California. In this article, we discuss and expand on only the most important and universally significant recommendations. Our suggestions anticipate, and to some extent depend on, a pilot case-management program recently adopted by the Northern District of California. Although participation in this program by judges is strictly voluntary, as of April 1, 1994, every full-time judge is participating. Before proceeding with specific recommendations for ENE, we describe this new program.

General Order 34, which implemented the case-management pilot program, calls for a series of meetings to accomplish, without an outside neutral, several of the goals originally envisioned for ENE. It requires lead counsel for each side to meet and confer (in person if separated by less than 100 miles, otherwise by telephone) within 100 days after filing of the complaint in order to accomplish the following: (1) identify the principal factual and legal issues in dispute and the principal evidentiary bases for claims and defenses, (2) identify and plan appropriate discovery and motions, and (3) identify for the court the ADR procedure counsel intend to use, or explain why no such procedure would help resolve the case. Within 110 days after the complaint is filed, attorneys must file a written statement describing the issues, discovery, and motions agreed upon, as well as the ADR process they have selected. If they have not selected an ADR process, they must explain their reasons for failing to do so. Within 120 days of filing the complaint, the court holds a case-management conference in order to do the following: (1) identify the principal factual and legal issues in dispute, (2) determine whether any motions ought to be brought early on, (3) determine a plan for at least the first stage of discovery, and (4) consider submitting the case to an ADR procedure. The court can require parties to accompany their attorneys at the case-management conference.

A. Separate and Refine ADR Processes

At times, flexibility in the ENE session allowed evaluators to structure the process to best suit the case before them. More often than not, however, variations in the structure of ENE sessions resulted from the different personal approaches taken by evaluators rather than the different case characteristics. In fact, different evaluators' approaches to the same kind of case varied more than did individual evaluators' approaches to very different types of cases.

Focus groups and interviews made it clear that certain evaluators focused exclusively on facilitating communication between the parties and never gave their own dollar assessment of the case. Other evaluators held sessions resembling arbitration or, in some cases, mini-trials. Some evaluators focused exclusively on settlement, while others focused primarily on trial preparation. Discrepancies between participants' expectations for ENE and the actual procedure and focus of the session created frustration for many. If left unchanged, the name ENE might come to denote a variety of distinct processes, leaving litigants uncertain about what will actually happen in their sessions. Instead of maintaining this status quo or eliminating some potentially useful processes altogether, we suggest that the court specify separate and distinct processes and select and train different pools of individuals to carry them out. This approach will allow participants to develop a clear, specific, and accurate idea of the process for their case.

B. Require Litigants to Select an ADR Process

Despite the fact that over 80 percent of the attorneys said they would select ENE in other cases if it were available, no attorney whose case was not administratively assigned to ENE requested to participate in the program. Some explained that they did not participate for strategic reasons, but the vast majority of attorneys either misunderstood or did not know about the program.

Similarly, few of those whose cases were assigned to ENE opted out, despite the fact that many expressed serious reservations or a firm desire not to participate. This indicates that litigants and their attorneys often follow the path of least resistance, simply staying on the track into which they were initially slotted regardless of their judgments about the suitability of that track for their case. What may appear to be complete freedom of choice to participate in alternative dispute resolution may actually result in no real choices being made at all.

Another problematic aspect of the role of choice in the ENE program was the absence of any relationship between a litigant's initial interest in pursuing ENE and her ultimate satisfaction with the process. It appears that when parties do make choices concerning ADR, those choices may be ill-informed and incorrect.

1. Choosing ADR at the case-management conference.

We suggest requiring participants to select a particular type of ADR at or before the case-management conference, absent exceptional circumstances, and granting the judge the explicit authority and responsibility to select an appropriate ADR option should the parties fail to agree on one or fail to show why they should be excused from ADR. Litigants should be permitted to select either ENE, arbitration, or mediation. If the litigants agree, they should be permitted to engage in their selected ADR process prior to the case-management conference; otherwise, the conference agenda should include scheduling some form of ADR unless one party demonstrates that ADR is inappropriate.

If attorneys know they will be responsible for discussing and selecting an ADR option for their case, they will likely pay attention to ADR to make the required selection. The process we propose does not require that ADR be used in every case, because any party who explains why ADR is inappropriate in her case will be excused from making a selection. But what is important to establish is the expectation that ADR will be used in every case. Most attorneys now operate under the assumption that ADR is not expected, and, in fact, they rarely select court-sponsored ADR voluntarily. Changing the general expectation would do much to increase the use of ADR.

Requiring litigants to select appropriate ADR for their cases would also eliminate some of the most frequently heard complaints about ADR. If different types of ADR were distinguished from each other and litigants were required to choose one ADR option, they would be less likely to be surprised by or unprepared for the process that actually takes place. In addition, participants would likely have an investment in believing that they had made the best possible choice. That investment would then translate into a greater receptivity to their chosen process and an increased commitment to making it work.

The court has kept the scheduling of ENE and litigation events on two separate and independent tracks. Requiring attorneys to select ADR at the case-management conference would have an additional benefit: The date for the ENE session could be set at the case-management conference (with some flexibility built in to accomodate evaluators' scheduling conflicts), thereby assuring litigants of some compatibility between the ADR schedule and the litigation schedule. ADR could be scheduled at a future date that would allow enough time for ample discovery before ENE and yet ensure that the session occurs early enough to facilitate organization and potential settlement before litigants spend large sums of money.

Using the case-management conference as the focal point for ADR decisionmaking will also increase the involvement of the judge in selecting a process. Of course, just as requiring attorneys to make decisions regarding ADR will not automatically ensure the education of attorneys, involving judges in the decision making process will not ensure that they will act as advocates for ENE or for any other ADR process. What it will do, however, is increase judges' awareness of ADR and its impact on litigation.

2. Opting out of "mandatory ADR."

Since parties may obtain an exemption from ADR in appropriate cases, it would be helpful for them to know in advance what factors might appropriately excuse a case from the general ADR requirement. In order to avoid burdening a litigant's right to a trial, the court should excuse any party who establishes that the costs of ADR are likely to impose an undue burden. The costs of ADR include the party's own time and transportation costs, attorney's fees for preparation and participation in ADR, and any possible payment for the services of the neutral. A litigant ought to be excused from ADR if she establishes that (1) there is a reasonable likelihood that these costs will exceed the value of reasonably foreseeable benefits from ADR (i.e., reduced discovery and trial preparation costs) or (2) she is unable to pay these costs, either because she has few resources or because the costs substantially outweigh the other costs of litigation.

The court may wish to avoid encouraging settlement in some cases. These may include cases where the court prefers to issue a ruling for its precedential value, where the litigation affects individuals not party to the lawsuit, where a full public record of the proceeding is important, or where one or more parties may be unable to negotiate effectively, either because they are appearing pro se or because of some problem with counsel. In excusing these cases from settlement-oriented ADR processes, however, the court should not exclude them from other ENE benefits. In many cases, the court may not want to encourage settlement but may still wish to assist litigants in identifying and clarifying the issues in dispute and in organizing discovery and trial preparation. Rather than excluding these cases from ADR altogether, the court might offer a form of ENE without an evaluation component or settlement discussion, but with an enhanced focus on the identification and efficient adjudication of the important issues. To the extent that the judge would assist the litigants in this way at the case-management conference, a session with another neutral would not be necessary. A full ENE session would be inappropriate if it discouraged the judge from fully attending to responsibilities in the case. Nonetheless, ENE has proven to be an effective supplement to the work of even the most diligent judges in cases that did not settle. Consequently, the court ought not to sacrifice all of the benefits of ENE in the interest of avoiding settlement.

If more judges become strong advocates of ADR, litigants might fear that asking for an exemption from ADR will alienate the judge who will ultimately decide their case. In response to this concern, we strongly recommend that all activity connected with ADR processes remain confidential. To avoid any inadvertent intimidation of parties into ADR, we suggest that parties be permitted to petition a designated ADR judge (other than the judge hearing their case) to remove their case from ADR. The court can prevent unnecessary reliance by the opposing side and unnecessary work by court personnel by requiring the petitioning party to file any removal request within forty-eight hours after the case-management conference, and the court should then rule on this request quickly thereafter. All stages of this petition process, including whether a case went through an ADR process and what transpired in any ADR conference, ought to remain confidential and beyond the knowledge of the adjudicating judge.

C. Educate Attorneys About ADR Processes

Studies have shown that a litigant's attorney is the most significant determinant of the party's attitude toward ADR. If the attorney favors ADR and explains its utility to her client, the client is significantly more likely to appreciate and benefit from the ADR process.

Attorneys' significant role in influencing clients' attitudes, combined with their relative unfamiliarity with ADR, may create two potential problems with requiring ADR in every case. First, some attorneys and, consequently, their clients would make the choice resentfully. Rather than increasing their commitment to a process they selected, the parties might manifest increased resentment towards a judicial system that required them to opt for a process they did not appreciate. Second, because of attorneys' limited experience with ADR, they may provide poor advice to their clients in selecting the appropriate ADR process. Many attorneys are more familiar with arbitration and judicial settlement conferences than with ENE or mediation. Since people tend to choose familiar procedures, many attorneys might select a form of ADR not because that process is inherently superior to ENE, but simply because they are more comfortable with it. In addition, attorneys might opt for arbitration because it is the most adversarial ADR process and, as a result, most like litigation. Finally, both attorneys and parties might not select ENE (or mediation) because they are afraid to risk appearing interested in good faith settlement negotiations, even if they are so interested.

In order for litigants to select an appropriate ADR forum, attorneys and their clients must learn more about available ADR options. We suggest three avenues for educating attorneys about these other options: (1) improving written materials, (2) requiring continuing legal education about ADR for members of the Northern District bar, and (3) increasing the role of the court's professional ADR staff in educating attorneys about their options. . . .

D. Educate Parties About ADR

While attorneys have an undeniably important impact on their clients' decisions, clients themselves must ultimately make the decisions and live with the consequences. Requiring attorneys to inform their clients fully about ADR both reinforces the client's role as the decisionmaker and ensures that she will base her decisions on accurate information. Attorneys should be required to inform their clients about both the general information in the court's written materials and how the specifics of their own case affect an appropriate ADR selection. The court should require attorneys to submit a certification that they have conducted these case-specific ADR discussions early in the case.

E. Guidance Regarding Appropriate ADR

Guidelines for indentifying the optimum ADR process for each case would help litigants select the most appropriate form of ADR for their cases and would help judges assign cases to the most appropriate ADR in the absence of litigant agreements. We hesitate to make specific recommendations in this area for the following reasons: (1) We found relatively few statistically significant outcome differences among the various nature of suit categories; (2) to the extent that litigants in certain kinds of cases might not have been as satisfied with ENE as much as those in other kinds of actions, it is not clear that an alternative ADR process would have been more helpful; and (3) to a great extent, outcome differences, particularly party satisfaction, depended more on individual evaluators than on the type of case.

Despite the above disclaimers, focus groups and interviews revealed certain case characteristics that indicate ENE is likely to be useful. Unlike arbitration, which requires each side to present its case for decision, ENE occurs early in the litigation, encourages and facilitates communication across party lines, and helps parties organize the litigation. Unlike mediation, ENE provides participants with a knowledgeable third party's objective view on the merits and on procedure. As a result, ENE is likely to be particularly useful in cases where: (1) the sides have very different assessments of the case based on different interpretations of the law or on different conclusions drawn from agreed-upon facts; (2) the case involves complex legal questions, requiring considerable subject matter expertise to help clarify the issues for trial, or complex facts, requiring substantial organization and development of discovery plans even after the case-management conference; or (3) the litigants could benefit from the informal discovery provided by the parties' presentations and the evaluator's inquiries.

F. Ensuring the Quality of Evaluators

The court maintains a pool of about 150 evaluators, each of whom has volunteered to perform two sessions per year. The ENE program was limited to even-numbered cases and to certain nature of suit categories primarily because the court has been unwilling to expand the evaluator pool without careful regard to qualifications. Screening potential evaluators takes a significant amount of time and energy, and many of the court's volunteer evaluators were hand-picked by judges, magistrates, and members of the court's ADR task force.

Expansion of the ENE program obviously requires the recruitment of more evaluators. In addition, marked improvement in the ENE program requires improvements in the selection and training of evaluators to ensure that the court retains only those who perform well and that its best evaluators are fully utilized.

We suggest the following steps to ensure an adequate supply of qualified evaluators: (1) impose a fee on litigants who go through ENE, (2) allocate a portion of these fees to pay for administrative and training costs that accompany the ENE program, and (3) use part of the fees collected to pay evaluators for sessions they hold in excess of two per year. The administrative and training costs would include, in addition to those responsibilities currently being performed by the court's ADR director and deputy director, the costs of the following proposed activities: (1) developing performance-based selection criteria for new evaluators; (2) improving evaluators' initial training; (3) establishing an ongoing program of meetings for all evaluators, including smaller meetings within each nature of suit category; (4) establishing a procedure to collect immediate feedback from participants on the performance of evaluators; and (5) using that feedback, together with other relevant sources, to ensure that only the most skilled evaluators are retained.

1. Fees for court-sponsored ADR.

Some ADR supporters fear that charging a fee for mandatory ADR might increase the costs such that they outweigh the benefits of participation. Others are concerned that mandating services that create additional fees might interfere with the right to a jury trial. Still others fear that charging fees for court-sponsored ADR, while providing adjudication without fees, might bias litigants against ADR.

We suggested above that courts should excuse litigants for whom participation in ADR might represent an unreasonable cost or imposition. To the extent that ADR participants must pay fees, the court ought to include those fees with the other costs of participation in determining whether it constitutes an undue burden. In addition, litigants who are entitled to the waiver of other fees due to their financial condition ought to be equally entitled to waiver of any court-imposed ADR fees.

Even if litigants are not required to pay for ADR they cannot afford, to the extent that ADR is a service that ought to be provided by courts, it would be preferable if it, like adjudication services, were provided free of charge. Indeed, to the extent that ADR is desirable, an ideal system would encourage ADR use rather than discourage it by imposing fees. We recommend fees for court-provided ADR only because we are not yet working within that ideal system.

When the evaluators are skilled and the attorneys and litigants have been educated about the process, the satisfaction rate with ENE is very high. On the other hand, the primary reason for dissatisfaction with ENE is an unsatisfactory experience with a particular evaluator. Assuring that participants are educated and participate, and assuring that ENE evaluators are skilled, require resources. If adequate funds are available elsewhere, they ought to be used. If these funds are not available, the court is faced with the options of employing a process that is well-run but costs litigants some money, employing a free process that lacks consistent high quality, or disregarding ADR altogether. We suggest the first approach. . . .

While an ADR fee might bias litigants against the process, a successful encounter with

ADR would provide the strongest pro-ADR message. Conversely, an unsuccessful experience might discourage participants from future ADR use. The benefits of ensuring a consistently high-quality program appear to more than outweigh the cost of imposing fees.

2. Improved selection, training, and retention of evaluators.

Aside from funding some or all of the administrative costs incurred in educating attorneys and parties about ADR, most of the ADR fees would finance improved procedures for selection, training, and retention of evaluators. . . .

Because litigation and advocacy skills differ from the skills required of a good evaluator (other than analytic ability and subject matter expertise), some sort of additional screening procedure is likely to improve the quality of evaluators selected. An attorney's past success as an evaluator or as a mediator is the most obvious relevant criterion. However, the expanded use of evaluators will eventually require recruiting new neutrals, which will in turn require making explicit judgments about qualifications of individuals relatively inexperienced as neutrals. Courts have successfully implemented performance-based selection of neutrals. A selection panel rates candidates' performace in a role-playing scenario. Some courts also give a written test. Alternatively, potential applicants might be asked to view a videotape of an evaluation session and to answer questions or offer appropriate responses in the course of the tape.

There are at least three reasons for initial and continuing training sessions for evaluators. First, the training would ensure that evaluators learn the specific ENE process and employ that process with sufficient uniformity so that participants know what to expect from it. Second, evaluators could maximize the skills and abilities that correlate with successful performance. Third, training would utilize evaluators' growing understanding of the process to continue to develop and refine ENE. In order to accomplish these goals, we suggest a substantial initial training program, as well as ongoing meetings for all evaluators and also within each nature of suit category.

The initial training might include a 2-day workshop in the ENE process and relevant skills. Evaluators already serving and receiving consistently high reviews from participants ought to be exempted from this aspect of training. Ongoing meetings of all evaluators or of all evaluators within each subject area might be scheduled semiannually in order to allow evaluators to compare notes, share successful techniques, and provide suggestions for reforming the ENE process. During the course of our study, evaluators who attended focus groups appreciated the chance to meet together and asked for some ongoing opportunity to do so. If judges attend the initial training sessions and the ongoing evaluator meetings, evaluators would understand the importance of their participation, and the judges would learn about processes into which they may order litigants.

Regardless of how evaluators are selected and trained, the court should regularly assess their performance in order to ensure their continuing suitability for the role. The court should develop a set of brief confidential pre- and post-ENE questionnaires for attorneys and parties that include feedback on the performance of the evaluator. The court should then evaluate neutrals based on these questionnaires and on telephone follow-up where appropriate. Unsatisfactory neutrals should be removed from the court's list. The importance of the evaluator to the success of the process, together with the mandatory nature of the suggested program, demand no less.

3. Retention of evaluators.

The current voluntary service of evaluators allows the court to take maximum advantage of the generosity and energy of many highly skilled and highly paid individuals. The court would increase its chances of maintaining this quality service by involving judges in the program to increase its status and prestige, by compensating those who perform in excess of two sessions per year, and by linking service to the court with other benefits. A compensation program would allow the court to make maximum use of the best evaluators without either taking undue advantage of their generosity or driving them out of the program. We recommend that the court continue to require all evaluators to perform two uncompensated evaluations per year. The court should specify a compensation rate for any additional cases in which an evaluator serves and should fund these payments with a portion of the ADR fees.

4. Selection of the neutral for each case.

. . . While allowing participants' input into the selection of a neutral is likely to increase their commitment to making the process work, it will also increase the complexity of administration of the ENE program. To minimize the additional complexity and to ensure that the court can continue to take advantage of the two free sessions, participant input should be limited. We suggest that the court provide ENE participants with a list of four potential neutrals. The parties may agree on one or more acceptable to both, or each side can strike one name and the court will select from among those remaining. The court will be able to ensure that all neutrals appear on the lists from time to time, and that the workload is spread relatively evenly among them. In addition, even after each side is permitted a strike, there will be enough names remaining on the list to ensure that an acceptable neutral will be available even after unanticipated conflicts.

Some litigants will probably want complete freedom to select a neutral of their choice and will be willing to pay whatever fee that neutral charges. We suggest that if all parties agree, they may retain, at their own expense, any neutral on the court's list so long as they do so prior to being assigned a neutral from the court. Allowing such choice will: (1) increase satisfaction with the program by ensuring that parties can retain their evaluator of choice; (2) better ensure that all evaluators, however selected, are qualified, competent, and adequately trained; (3) minimize complaints of second-class treatment by those unable or unwilling to pay an evaluator's private fee by ensuring that all litigants have access to the identical pool of evaluators; and (4) ensure that only those neutrals who are willing to provide some service to the court on a noncompensated basis can in turn profit from the market for ENE services created by the court's ADR requirement. While this last result may appear monopolistic, the district's mandatory ADR program will create a new market for ENE services, and if neutrals seek to tap into that new market, they will need to join forces with the court. Indeed, to the extent that there is currently a private, for-fee market for ENE services in the Northern District of California, it is solely the result of the district's current success with the program.

G. Improve Communication Between Evaluators and Litigants

1. Prior to the session.

Parties and their attorneys must have a clear and specific understanding of the ENE process in order to properly prepare for and fully participate in it. While some clear and explicit written explanation of ENE for all participants is essential, it is not sufficient. Those evaluators who had telephone conversations with attorneys prior to the session in order to describe what to expect and how to prepare noted that these conversations helped ensure a successful session; and such communication may be essential to help participants develop accurate expectations for the process, regardless of how effective the court's informational material is.

It would be helpful for the evaluator to discuss with each side his own specific view of ENE, what he expects to happen, his view of his role in the process, his expectations of each participant, and how long he expects the process to take. This explanation might be most useful if it took place either in a preplanned conference call or in separate telephone calls between the evaluator and counsel for each side. The ENE process should formally incorporate these calls, so that all participants will expect them to happen, see that they do happen, and will know what to expect from them.

2. Postsession.

Communication between litigants and the evaluator ought to continue after the ENE session. The evaluator should at least learn whether the parties engaged in the actions agreed upon in the ENE session; knowledge that this will happen may help motivate the attorneys to actually take the actions agreed upon in the session.

Even if no specific actions are agreed upon in the ENE session, it may well become evident at a later point that additional contact with the evaluator would be helpful to the litigants. Study participants contacted the evaluator after the conclusion of the ENE session in 21 percent of the cases. However, an additional 21 percent of both attorneys and parties stated that further contact would have been helpful but did not occur. Finally, regardless of its impact on the litigants, follow-up with the evaluator would provide evaluators with information to assess their own performances and to help them identify potential improvements for their handling of subsequent cases.

Within sixty days of the conclusion of the ENE session, the process should require attorneys for each side to submit a brief statement to the evaluator, perhaps in the form of a letter detailing any actions agreed upon in the session and explaining their result. Additionally, such a letter could inform the evaluator whether further sessions or telephone calls would be helpful. Finally, the court ought to take steps to ensure that evaluators receive notice of the final outcomes in all cases in which they serve.

H. Enforcement of ENE Requirements

Several evaluators stated that they were hampered by receiving inadequate written statements prior to the session. Others reported being more severely limited by the absence of at least one important party at the session itself. Of those who did appear at the session, the vast majority participated in the process, but evaluators still complained that more than a few parties refused to take part in a meaningful way.

In response to these problems, several evaluators and attorneys suggested that the court grant evaluators some sort of direct enforcement authority. Others suggested that evaluators be encouraged to ask the court to enforce General Order 26 more vigilantly, although it was not clear how that might happen. Others voiced concern that connecting the evaluator too closely to the power of the court might detract from the evaluator's neutrality, although it appears that many attorneys already believed that the evaluator had some direct enforcement power.

Parties and attorneys should understand that written statements prior to the session and personal presence at the session are required, and that the court will enforce these requirements. At the same time, it is important that the parties perceive the evaluator as a neutral whose main power lies in her knowledge and ability to facilitate communication, and not in her ability to punish the participants. When these facts are clear to all, the parties may be more willing to take advantage of the process, and the neutral will be forced to attend to the interests of the parties she is attempting to serve.

One possible solution that does not put the evaluator in the role of enforcer would be to require each participant in attendance at the ENE session to sign a statement including the name, address, role, and, for party representatives, any limits on their authority either to settle, enter into stipulations, or make major decisions in the litigation. This statement would be forwarded to the ADR section of the court, thereby allowing the court to ensure complete attendance without putting the evaluator in the role of enforcer. This would also provide the court with the names and addresses of attendees in case further follow-up research becomes appropriate. . . .

C. Summary Jury Trial

1. *Strandell v. Jackson County*, 838 F.2d 884 (7th Cir. 1988)

Before Wood and Ripple, Circuit Judges, and Gordon, Senior District Judge.

Ripple, Circuit Judge.

In this appeal, we must decide whether a federal district court can require litigants to participate in a nonbinding summary jury trial. . . . Thomas Tobin, Esquire, appeals from a judgment of criminal contempt for refusing to participate in such a procedure.

Mr. Tobin represents the parents of Michael Strandell in a civil rights action against Jackson County, Illinois. The case involves the arrest, strip search, imprisonment, and suicidal death of Michael Strandell. In anticipation of a pretrial conference on September 3, 1986, the plaintiffs filed a written report concerning settlement prospects. The plaintiffs reported that they were requesting $500,000, but that the defendants refused to discuss the issue. At the pretrial conference, the district court suggested that the parties consent to a summary jury trial. A summary jury trial generally lasts one day, and consists of the selection of six jurors to hear approximations by counsel of the expected evidence. After receiving an abbreviated charge, the jury retires with directions to render a consensus verdict. After a verdict is reached, the jury is informed that its verdict is advisory in nature and nonbinding. The objective of this procedure is to induce the parties to negotiate a settlement. Mr. Tobin informed the district court that the plaintiffs would not consent to a summary jury trial, and filed a motion to advance the case for trial. The district court ordered that discovery be closed on January 15, 1987, and set the case for trial.

During discovery, the plaintiffs had obtained statements from 21 witnesses. The plaintiffs learned the identity of many of these witnesses from information provided by the defendants. After discovery closed, the defendants filed a motion to compel production of the witnesses' statements. The plaintiffs responded that these statements constituted privileged work-product; they argued that the defendants could have obtained the information contained in them through ordinary discovery. The district court denied the motion to compel production . . . [because] defendants had failed to establish "substantial need" and "undue hardship," as required by Rule 26(b)(3) of the Federal Rules of Civil Procedure.

On March 23, 1987, the district court again discussed settlement prospects with counsel. The court expressed its view that a trial could not be accommodated easily on its crowded docket and again suggested that the parties consent to a summary jury trial. On March 26, 1987, Mr. Tobin advised the district court that he would not be willing to submit his client's case to a summary jury trial, but that he was ready to proceed to trial immediately. He claimed that a summary jury trial would require disclosure of the privileged statements. The district court rejected this argument, and ordered the parties to participate in a summary jury trial. . . .

On March 31, 1987, the parties and counsel appeared, as ordered, for selection of a jury for the summary jury trial. Mr. Tobin again objected to the district court's order compelling the summary jury trial. The district court denied this motion. Mr. Tobin then respectfully declined to proceed with the selection of the jury. . . . The court then held Mr. Tobin in criminal contempt for refusing to proceed with the summary jury trial. . . .

[The court ruled that Rule 16, as it then read, did not authorize a district judge to require parties to pacticipate in a summary jury trial.]

In turning to the narrow question before us—the legality of compelled participation in a summary jury trial—we must also acknowledge . . . that a district court no doubt has substantial inherent power to control and to manage its docket. That power must, of course, be exercised in a manner that is in harmony with the Federal Rules of Civil Procedure. Those rules are the product of a careful process of study and reflection designed to take "due cognizance both of the need for expedition of cases and the protection of individual rights." . . . [I]n those areas of trial practice where the Supreme Court and the Congress, acting together, have addressed the appropriate balance between the needs for judicial efficiency and the rights of the individual litigant, innovation by the individual judicial officer must conform to that balance. . . .

2. Comments and Questions

a. Subsequent amendments to the Federal Rules of Civil Procedure provide clear authority for U.S. district courts to order a summary jury trial. See the Ponte article, below. Assuming that the local court rules make explicit provision for the use of SJT, should a court exercise its discretion to order an SJT on the Strandell facts?

b. If the answer to the previous question is no, should an order to partipate in SJT be reversed by the appropriate U.S. court of appeals as an abuse of discretion?

3. *Cincinnati Gas and Electric Co. v. General Electric Co.*, 854 F.2d 900 (6th Cir. 1988)

KEITH, Circuit Judge.

Appellants, The Cincinnati Post, et al., appeal pursuant to 28 U.S.C. § 1291 from orders issued by the district court on September 14, 1987, October 5, 1987, and November 20, 1987, which appellants contend denied them their first amendment right of access to the summary jury trial conducted in the underlying action. For the reasons set forth below, we AFFIRM the district court.

I.

This appeal arises out of a lawsuit involving the design and construction of the William H. Zimmer Nuclear Power Plant ("Plant"). . . . From the outset of this litigation, the parties recognized the need for confidential treatment of much of the material that would be produced in discovery. As a result, the parties negotiated a comprehensive protective order, which the magistrate approved. This order provided varying degrees of protection for documents classified as "Confidential" or "Highly Confidential" by the party producing them. The order restricted the use by nonproducing parties of documents accorded either level of confidentiality to "the prosecution or defense of this action," or to other proceedings arising in connection with the Plant. In addition, the order provided that any reference to "Highly Confidential" documents in motions, briefs, or other court papers or filings had to be accompanied by appropriate markings and separately filed under seal.

[T]he district court issued an order requiring the parties to participate in a summary jury trial. The order included a provision closing the proceeding to the press and public, . . . and stated that "[t]he proceedings, and all results thereof, shall be confidential, and shall not be disclosed other than to the parties, their attorneys, consultants and insurers. The jurors shall be appropriately instructed as to such confidential treatments."

[A]ppellants moved to intervene in the underlying action for the limited purpose of challenging the order closing the summary trial. The district court denied appellants' motion to intervene, holding that they had no right to attend the summary jury trial. The court observed that "[t]he summary jury trial, for all it may appear like a trial, is a settlement technique." Accordingly, the court held that the press had no first amendment right of access because: (1) there is no tradition of access to summary jury trials or to other recognized settlement devices, and (2) public access "does not play a particularly significant positive role" in the functioning of the summary jury trial because "the proceeding is non-binding and has no effect on the merits of the case, other than settlement." . . .

Less than two months after the conclusion of the summary jury trial, the parties reached a settlement. On November 20, 1987, the district court issued an order approving the terms of the settlement and dismissing the action with prejudice. The court continued the gag orders and the sealing of the transcript and jury list, ruling that "all other Orders in this case concerning the confidentiality of documents and the summary jury trial remain in effect."

II.

The precise issue before us is whether the first amendment right of access attaches to the summary jury proceeding in this case. Appellants argue that the district court erred in refusing to allow them to intervene for the purpose of attending the summary jury trial proceeding. Appellants specifically argue that: (1) the summary jury proceeding is analogous in form and function to a civil or criminal trial on the merits, and therefore, the first amendment right of access which encompasses civil and criminal trial and pre-trial proceedings also encompasses the summary jury proceedings; and (2) public access would play a significant positive role in the functioning of the judicial system and summary jury trials.

Appellees contend that the first amendment right of access does not apply to summary jury proceedings. Appellees argue that settlement proceedings are totally lacking in any tradition of public access, and that appellants exalt form over function in arguing that a summary jury trial is no different from a trial on the merits. Appellees further argue that public access would not play a significant positive role in the functioning of summary jury trials. We agree with appellees' arguments and hold that the first amendment right of access does not attach to summary jury trial proceedings. . . .

The Supreme Court has in recent years decided a number of cases dealing with the right of access. *Press-Enterprise Co. v. Superior Court,* 478 U.S. 1 (1986) (*"Press-Enterprise II"*).

In *Press-Enterprise II* the Court held that a qualified right of access applied in criminal proceedings to a preliminary hearing which was conducted before a magistrate in the absence of a jury. The Court held that the analysis of a first amendment claim of access involves two "complimentary considerations." First, the proceeding must be one for which there has been a "tradition of accessibility." This inquiry requires a court to determine "whether the place and process [to which access is sought] has historically been open to the press and general public." Second, public access must play a "significant positive role in the functioning of the particular process in question." Moreover, even if these elements are satisfied, the right of access is a qualified one and must be outweighed by a strong countervailing interest in maintaining the confidentiality of the proceedings.

With regard to the first part of the test, we concur with the district court that "there is no historically recognized right of access to summary jury trials in that this mechanism has been in existence for less than a decade." The summary jury trial is a device that is designed to settle disputes. Settlement techniques have historically been closed to the press and public. Thus, we find that "while the history of the summary jury trial is limited, there is general agreement that historically settlement techniques are closed procedures rather than open."

Appellants argue that summary jury trials are structurally similar to ordinary civil jury trials, which have historically been open to the public. However, it is clear that while the summary jury trial is a highly reliable predictor of the likely trial outcome, there are manifold differences between it and a real trial. In a summary jury proceeding, attorneys present abbreviated arguments to jurors who render an informal verdict that guides the settlement of the case. Normally, six mock jurors are chosen after a brief voir dire conducted by the court. Following short opening statements, all evidence is presented in the form of a descriptive summary to the mock jury through the parties' attorneys. Live witnesses do not testify, and evidentiary objections are discouraged. Thus, some of the evidence disclosed to the mock jury might be inadmissible at a real trial.

Following counsels' presentations, the jury is given an abbreviated charge and then retires to deliberate. The jury then returns a "verdict." To emphasize the purely settlement function of the exercise, the mock jury is often asked to assess damages even if it finds no liability. Also, the court and jurors join the attorneys and parties after the "verdict" is returned in an informal discussion of the strengths and weaknesses of each side's case.

At every turn the summary jury trial is designed to facilitate pretrial settlement of the litigation, much like a settlement conference. It is important to note that the summary jury trial does not present any matter for adjudication by the court.[5] Thus, we find appellants' argument to be unpersuasive and therefore hold that the "tradition of accessibility" element has not been met.

---

[5]Appellants' assertion that the summary jury trial is like an adjudication because the parties are compelled to participate is incorrect. The district court expressly stated that the proceeding was undertaken with the cooperation of the parties.

The second criterion in the Court's public access analysis is whether access "plays a significant positive role in the functioning of the particular process in question." Appellants contend that public access would have community theraputic value because of the importance of the nuclear power and utility rate issues raised. We disagree. . . .

The summary jury trial can play a particularly useful role in facilitating the settlement of complex cases and is typically employed in cases that either will consume significant judicial resources if they proceed to trial, or that are not amenable to settlement through other techniques. However, where a party has a legitimate interest in confidentiality, public access would be detrimental to the effectiveness of the summary jury trial in facilitating settlement. Thus, public access to summary jury trials over the parties' objections would have significant adverse effects on the utility of the procedure as a settlement device. Therefore, allowing access would undermine the substantial governmental interest in promoting settlements, and would not play a "significant positive role in the functioning of the particular process in question."

Appellants' claim of a public "right to know" has no validity with regard to summary jury trials. As the lower court correctly noted, the public would have no entitlement to observe any negotiations leading to a traditional settlement of the case, and the parties would be under no constitutional obligation to reveal the content of the negotiations. Thus, the public has no first amendment right to access to the summary jury trial.

Appellants also argue that the summary jury trial should be open to the public because the facilitation of a settlement between the parties has a final and decisive effect on the outcome of the litigation. To support their argument, appellants rely on the Court's language in *Press-Enterprise II,* that preliminary criminal hearings must be open to the public because of their decisive effect on criminal cases. We disagree.

In contrast to the summary proceedings in this case, the proceeding at issue in *Press-Enterprise II* resulted in a binding judicial determination which directly affected the rights of the parties. Summary jury trials do not present any matters for adjudication by the court. Thus, it is the presence of the exercise of a court's coercive powers that is the touchstone of the recognized right to access, not the presence of a procedure that might lead the parties to voluntarily terminate the litigation. Therefore, we find appellant's argument to be meritless.

GEORGE CLIFTON EDWARDS, Jr., Senior Circuit Judge, concurring in part and dissenting in part.

The proceeding conducted in this case resulted in a settlement and a court decree. It resembled both settlement negotiations and a bench trial. While I join the majority in holding that the negotiations which led to the settlement of this case could properly be conducted in camera, I do not agree that the record can appropriately continue to be sealed after a settlement has been effected. I recognize that the view expressed above might impede some settlements, but I cannot reconcile complete suppression of this record with the First Amendment. . . .

4. Neil Vidmar & Jeffrey Rice, *Jury Determined Settlements, and Summary Jury Trials*, 19 FLA. ST. U. L. REV. 89, 95-103 (1991)*

Courts began early to incorporate ADR devices to resolve disputes. . . . [C]ourts are frequently motivated by objectives not primarily designed for the parties' benefit. Specifically, they are often predominatly interested in court-centered efficiency: saving the court time and money. Many of the court-administered procedures have not been successful when judged by other, and perhaps more appropriate, goals. They certainly have not transformed the disputes to foster better quality solutions and nonadversarial results. In addition, they often do not increase disputant-centered processual efficiency. . . . [W]hat is efficient for the courts is not necessarily efficient for the parties. The end result of many of the courts' attempts at ADR has been processual inefficiencies and injustice such as injection of delay, the obtaining of nondiscoverable evidence, and manipulation of the rules, time, or information.

It is not surprising, therefore, that many disputants view these attempts as unwelcome additional steps in the litigation process. It is also not surprising that adversarial attorneys have turned to litigation to protect their clients' interests. But what if court-caused effects are removed? Is adversary legal culture necessarily hostile to the concept of ADR? We now compare the summary jury trial, a child of the court, and jury-determined settlements, a privately developed and administered voluntary ADR device.

III. THE SUMMARY JURY TRIAL: ITS ASSETS AND LIABILITIES

The summary jury trial (SJT), developed by federal judge Thomas Lambros, is an ADR procedure that aims to achieve settlements without full length trials. The disputants' lawyers present summaries of their respective evidence and arguments to a jury composed of regular veniremen in a hearing limited to one day or less. The jury then renders a verdict, and the lawyers and their clients are encouraged to talk to the jurors about how they perceived the merits of the two positions. The verdict is not binding on the parties, and they can have a regular trial de novo on an expedited calendar if no settlement is forthcoming. The theory of the SJT is that by presenting their positions quickly and efficiently in the abbreviated hearing, the parties can learn about the "probable" verdict if the case is submitted to a regular jury. They can then negotiate a reasonable settlement in light of the predicted verdict to avoid the higher costs associated with a full scale trial. Not only do the parties presumably benefit if a settlement is reached, but the case is removed from the court's trial docket.

Observe that the SJT preserves important aspects of the traditional legal approach to the resolution of conflict. First, the advisory verdict is couched in terms of winning and losing. The outcome, if the plaintiff wins, is limited to the setting of a quantum of damages. Second, it preserves components of [some, but not all, of] the adversary system. . . . Lawyers describe evidence favorable to their client's side and argue why, under the law, their clients should win. Third, and very significantly, it uses judgments—if only advisory—from a group of lay persons rather than a judge (or arbitrators). . . .

Jury decisions are treated as having greater legitimacy than those rendered by professionals. In our own research with ADR in medical malpractice and other personal injury suits, we have found that plaintiff and defense lawyers alike have resisted arbitration procedures on the grounds that they believe a jury would render a fairer outcome. Their clients sometimes prefer a jury resolution on symbolic or emotional grounds. For example, in one case the parents involved in a wrongful death suit stated that they wanted a jury rather than an insurance adjuster or lawyer to say what they should be compensated for the life of their daughter. Nevertheless, despite a preference for resolution by jury, parties often do not want to endure the slow, inefficient, and costly court system to obtain a jury verdict.

Despite its potential assets, the SJT largely fails. First, it is nonbinding. Professor Menkel-

Meadow argues that the fact that court adopted ADR procedures are nonbinding is their saving grace. In an important sense she is correct: it would be unfair to impose ADR on disputants without allowing them a trial de novo so as to exercise their full rights. It is also an imperative, given federal and state constitutional guarantees of jury trials in civil matters. However, the nonbinding nature points up a primary limitation of court-annexed ADR. At minimum, disputants do not get the promise of a termination of their conflict and thus must endure an extra step in the resolution process with the added costs of time and money. At worst, it allows the SJT to be used as an adversarial weapon to force a compromise of strategy or resources that will be used at trial.

The second limitation of the SJT is that it is court-instituted and court-controlled. Legal and political constraints on the court result in compromised procedures, and court-centered efficiency concerns ultimately take precedence over disputant-centered interests. The courts put pressure, sometimes explicit and sometimes implicit, on parties to engage in SJTs. Yet consider what the parties get. The SJT is carefully controlled by the court. The hearing is theoretically limited to a half day or, at most, a full day. Generally, the court keeps a tight rein on jury selection, procedural matters, the form of evidence presented to the jury, and even the instructions to the jury. Thus, live witnesses are usually verboten even though the case may hinge on the credibility of these witnesses. Why is there not more flexibility? The answer, of course, is that court-centered administrative efficiency concerns take priority over disputant-centered processual interests. The court cannot justify devoting more time, space, and judicial resources to a procedure that does not promise to remove the case from the docket.

Thus, courts adopt ADR to relieve pressure on caseloads but are limited by legal constraints to nonbinding procedures. The nonbinding nature not only goes against disputant interests in termination of the case, but it causes the courts to devise the procedure so as to serve the courts' efficiency interests over the disputants' interests. The consequence is litigation by adversary lawyers to protect those interests, which adds to court caseloads. The developing "common law" of ADR that Professor Menkel-Meadow takes note of is not caused by adversariness but rather is a result of the process.

This analysis leads us to the conclusion that court-centered ADR frequently will result in compromised procedures that serve neither the interests of the court nor the interests of the disputants. At best its overall success, measured against either goal, will be marginal. In contrast, the real opportunities for quality justice can be found in the realm of voluntary ADR. Furthermore, we submit that adversarial culture is not necessarily incompatible with ADR when the effects of court-centered interests are removed. Our own research with jury determined settlements helps to illustrate this proposition.

IV. JURY-DETERMINED SETTLEMENTS: VOLUNTARY ADR IN AN ADVERSARY SETTING

Over the past several years, the authors and our colleagues, in association with the Private Adjudication Center, have experimented with an ADR device that we have labelled a Jury-Determined Settlement (JDS). It was originally developed for medical malpractice cases through Duke Law School's Medical Malpractice Research Project. More recently, however, it has been used in other types of personal injury suits.

Like the summary jury trial, the JDS is designed for disputes that are basically binary in nature. JDS is an abbreviated procedure, and uses a jury to decide the outcome. It differs, however, from the summary jury trial in some very key aspects. It is voluntary, the parties and their lawyers retain almost total control over the process, and the jury verdict is binding.

The assumptions underlying the JDS are straightforward. Parties in personal injury disputes often attempt a settlement. They want to settle to decrease transaction costs, avoid the risks of trial, and have a final resolution as early as possible. They may also want to avoid publicity or the emotional trauma of a lengthy trial. The focal point of settlement negotiations involves arguments about how a jury is likely to decide the case. Although both parties may be acting reasonably, impasses occur when there are different interpretations about evidence and jury equities. Often a mindset towards trial overtakes both parties at this point. Additionally, many forms of ADR are viewed as inappropriate to break the deadlock. Mediation is unlikely to change their differing interpretations of how the jury will decide, and arbitration is seen as rendering a less fair result than a jury of laypersons will provide. Even if a court procedure, such as a summary jury trial, is available, the parties may be concerned about compromising key evidence or jeopardizing other legitimate adversary concerns.

The JDS was designed as a process whereby the parties can agree to settle many issues, and agree to disagree on certain issues, but seek to resolve the latter by quasi-traditional means. Specifically, the JDS attempts to satisfy the disputants' interests by providing them with an abbreviated trial decided by a jury, which is binding and which allows the exercise of adversarial control over the procedures. The parties also set limits on the range of the jury's award through a high-low agreement. In cases in which liability is strongly contested, the low may be set at zero. For cases primarily involving damages, the high is typically determined by the least amount plaintiffs assert they will take to settle the dispute, and the low is determined by the most defendants assert they will give to settle. In this latter instance, plaintiffs are guaranteed the amount specified by the low regardless of the verdict, and defendants are protected from an extreme award by the agreement that they will pay no more than the high even if the verdict falls outside that limit.

In JDS "trials" conducted to date, the Center has solicited the cooperation of the local court to provide both jurors and a courtroom, though jurors could be obtained in other ways and the procedure could take place in a private setting. Although the Center provides guidance and advice, the parties negotiate how the rest of the trial will be carried out. Negotiations include: choosing a judge; setting a discovery schedule and trial date; determining length of total proceeding and allocation of time between parties; setting the size of the jury and the length of voir dire; and agreeing on numbers of witnesses and form of testimony, evidentiary rules, and jury instructions. The negotiations over these procedural issues are often intense and adversarial. The end result has been "trials" that lasted as long as two-and-one-half days and included live witnesses who also were cross-examined.

Even though the parties must share the costs of the proceeding and extensive time is spent in negotiations and preparation for the JDS "trial," the parties and their lawyers have generally expressed great satisfaction with the procedure. Plaintiffs receive a verdict rendered by a jury, are guaranteed at least the money provided for in the low agreement, and receive their damages immediately after the trial rather than after lengthy appeals. Defendants and their insurers have been spared the risk of exposure to large damage awards. In the malpractice cases, physicians are spared the days or weeks away from their office practices that regular trials would consume. In addition, the trial is arranged privately and public exposure is reduced. Our interviews with the parties and their lawyers suggest that the most important key to party and lawyer satisfaction is the extent of processual control that is provided by the JDS procedure. The lawyers are encouraged to negotiate creative solutions to procedural road blocks or other matters rather than have them imposed by a judge. On balance, adversarial interests may be better served by the JDS than by traditional legal proceedings.

We do not contend that the JDS is suitable for every dispute, not even every dispute that may be cast in binary terms. Indeed, its applicability may be limited to a class of disputes within the binary category. What we do argue, however, is that the JDS demonstrates that adversarial approaches to dispute resolution are not necessarily incompatible with one of the goals of the ADR movement, namely to provide better quality disputant-centered processual efficiency.

V. SUMMARY AND CONCLUSIONS

Our commentary has involved two main themes. First, we believe more attention needs to be given to assumptions about the mediation and adversary models and about the types of disputes that enter the legal system. Second, by separating court-centered efficiency effects from adversarial approaches to dispute resolution, we conclude that adversarialness is not necessarily incompatible with ADR.

Many ADR proponents seem wedded so strongly to the mediation model as the ideal mode of dispute resolution and to the goal of dispute transformation, that they give short shrift to disputes for which resolution along more traditional legal lines is appropriate. The proponents also ignore the social and psychological limits of disputants' desire for control over the resolution process, and they misconceive legal-adversarial approaches to disputes as incompatible with — indeed, hostile to — ADR.

Although we focused on the Jury-Determined Settlement as a vehicle for illustrating how adversary legal culture and ADR can be compatible, over the past several years our own research has shown highly adversarial lawyers willing to experiment with a number of ADR procedures, including arbitration and mediation as well as the JDS. And this has occurred with what is reputed to be one of the most intractable types of litigation, namely medical malpractice. We ascribe this willingness of lawyers to consider new forms of dispute resolution to the educational effects of the ADR movement. To us, then, the challenge for ADR proponents is to conceptualize disputes so as to recognize legitimate adversary concerns and then devise procedures to accommodate them. Of course, the educational process must also continue.

5. Lucille M. Ponte, *Putting Mandatory Summary Jury Trial Back on the Docket: Recommendations on the Exercise of Judicial Authority*, 63 Fordham L. Rev. 1069 (1995)*

. . . For years, SJT has generated divided federal court opinions and legal critiques on its mandatory use. Some courts and legal commentators have rejected compulsory SJT as violative of the Federal Rules of Civil Procedure (the "Rules") and as exceeding the courts' inherent power to manage case dockets. Other judges and legal analysts have asserted that there is substantial legal support for mandatory SJT under these same Rules and within the courts' inherent authority. The 1993 *In re NLO, Inc.* case [5 F.3d 154 (6th Cir. 1993)] rejecting compulsory SJT, renewed the swirl of controversy over SJT and focused attention once more on this con-

*Reprinted with permission.

tentious legal debate. However, December 1993 changes to the Rules and a closer analysis of earlier Supreme Court decisions have turned the tables again in favor of mandatory SJT.

The Sixth and Seventh Circuits accept only voluntary SJT, asserting that mandatory SJT is allowed neither under the Rules nor as a result of courts' authority to manage their dockets. [See *In re NLO, Inc.*, 5 F.3d 154 (6th Cir. 1993); *Strandell v. Jackson County*, 838 F.2d 884 (7th Cir. 1987).] But in an effort to deal with burgeoning caseloads, some federal courts have approved compulsory SJT use, without the parties' mutual agreement, based on the Rules and the courts' inherent authority. Differing court views hinge primarily on the interpretation of the explicit language of Rule 16 and its underlying policies as stated in the notes of the advisory committee. . . . [Other courts upheld the use of SJT. As indicated in the excerpt below, this debate is now moot.]

B. Statutory Revisions Settle SJT Debate

The case law and critics rejecting mandatory SJT relied heavily on the lack of express authority for SJT under the Rules or other statutory law. . . . [T]he enactment of the Judicial Improvements Act of 1990 (the "Act") . . . directs federal courts to draft a civil justice expense and delay reduction plan. . . . The formulated plan should institute appropriate ADR programs. The Act specifically mentions SJT as a permissible ADR option. [28 USC § 473(a)(6)(B).]

[The Federal Rules were amended in 1993.] These changes have put much of the court debate over mandatory SJT and other forms of mandatory ADR to rest. Although the revision to the Rule may appear to be minor, a major clarification of the Rule's meaning comes from the advisory committee's explanatory notes that the *Strandell* and *In re NLO* courts relied upon to reject SJT. The revised drafters' notes spell out more clearly the varied types of settlement procedures that may be utilized and the court's authority to compel participation in these processes.

"Paragraph (9) is revised to describe more accurately the various procedures that, in addition to traditional settlement conferences, may be helpful in settling litigation. Even if a case cannot immediately be settled, the judge and attorneys can explore possible use of alternative procedures such as . . . summary jury trials . . . that can lead to consensual resolution of the dispute without a full trial on the merits. The rule acknowledges the presence of statutes and local rules or plans that may authorize use of some of these procedures even when not agreed to by the parties."

. . . Not only may courts consider SJT, but courts may compel party participation under statute, local rules or local plans. The Rule 16 drafters' notes that the Sixth and Seventh Circuits relied upon so heavily no longer support their view. The new drafters' notes endorse the use of mandatory SJT as an acceptable settlement device, regardless of party approval. Therefore, SJT is not the unwarranted extension of judicial power previously asserted by the Sixth and Seventh Circuits.

However, the notes leave open the issue of a court's inherent authority to mandate SJT in the absence of statute or local rules. "The rule does not attempt to resolve questions as to the extent a court would be authorized to require such proceedings as an exercise of its inherent powers." Although a Supreme Court case may finally settle this issue, the new Rule 16 notes, coupled with the *Colgrove* case, suggest that innovative settlement mechanisms such as SJT are likely to be viewed as valid exercises of inherent court authority.

Conclusion

SJT is an innovative ADR mechanism aimed at preserving party and judicial resources through more predictive and efficient dispute resolution. Unfortunately, the limited studies of SJT provide inconclusive results on SJT's ability to meet these goals. Despite the lack of definitive evidence to support SJT use, recent amendments to Rule 16 and its explanatory notes clearly support compelled participation in SJT and other ADR processes. The *Colgrove* Supreme Court case provides further support for the courts' inherent authority to mandate SJT. Federal court guidelines on case selection and screening are needed to maximize SJT advantages and minimize SJT disadvantages. In addition, with mandatory SJT in place, courts will be able to establish evaluation procedures to help measure the fairness and efficiency of the process as well as the quality of its outcomes. Mandatory SJT marks an opportunity for courts to assess more accurately whether the theoretical benefits of SJT can be demonstrated in practice.

6. Comments and Questions

a. In *Colgrove v. Battin,* 413 U.S. 149 (1973), the Supreme Court upheld a local federal court rule that reduced a civil trial jury from twelve to six. The Constitution does not deny the courts authority to be flexible and innovative in the face of changing times and needs. "New devices may be used to adapt the ancient institution to present needs and to make of it an efficient instrument in the administration of justice. . . . [Such changes] are essential to the preservation of the right' of trial by jury." *Id.* at 158. Is the reduction in the size of a civil jury from the traditional 12 members more or less significant, either in procedural or constitutional terms, than SJT?

b. SJT has been severely criticized for the use of jurors, and for failing to inform them that their verdict is nonbinding. Most notably, Judge Posner questioned the ethics of withholding this information:

> Never telling the jury worries me. . . . Telling the jurors after they have delivered the summary verdict that the verdict is not legally binding is only a partial anodyne for my concern. . . . The jurors are still being fooled; and they are learning that juries sometimes make decisions and at other times simply referee fake trials. As word spreads, the conscientiousness of jurors could decline; it is almost a detail that the utility of the summary jury trial would also decline.

Richard A. Posner, *The Summary Jury Trial and Other Methods of Alternative Dispute Resolution: Some Cautionary Observations,* 53 U. CHI. L. REV. 366, 386-387 (1986).

The nondisclosure can, of course, be easily eliminated by informing jurors in advance about the SJT and the role of the advisory jurors therein. This disclosure comes at a cost; it may limit the effectiveness of the SJT process because jurors will take the process less seriously, or because the parties think the jurors take the matter less seriously. Attorneys believe that not telling the jurors until after SJT is complete is important to help maintain responsible juror determinations. James J. Alfini, *Summary Jury Trials in State and Federal Courts: A Comparative Analysis of the Perceptions of Participating Lawyers,* 4 OHIO ST. J. ON DISP. RESOL. 213 (1989) (reporting a comparison study of SJT use in Florida state and federal program).

c. Is there a place for mandatory SJT based on inherent court powers, after the adoption of local court rules that do not provide for SJT? That is, if local court rules do not provide for

SJT, would not a purported exercise of inherent power in effect be contrary to the reasoned decision pursuant to established procedures for determining appropriate procedures?

CASE STUDY

(Adapted from *Ahern v. Knecht*, 202 Ill.App3d 709, 563 N.E.2d 787 (1990))

Mr. and Mrs. Joseph Ahern filed suit against James Knecht in small claims court to recover money paid for the repair of their home air conditioner. Mrs. Ahern had contacted Mr. Knecht from an advertisement in the yellow pages. After diagnosing the problem, Mr. Knecht presented Mrs. Ahern with an estimated bill of $762 and demanded payment in advance. Mrs. Ahern wrote the repairman a check, expressing shock at the amount. Mrs. Ahern admitted she knew little of mechanical matters and felt intimidated by Mr. Knecht. When she returned, Mrs. Ahern found the air conditioner not running. Mr. Knecht had left a note stating the compressor was weak. Mr. Knecht refused to replace the compressor or refund the plaintiff's money. Another company serviced the unit and charged $72.

[Legal History: The Court found the terms of the contract unconscionable, holding that the defendant should have charged $150 for the repairs performed. After deducting the $72 paid to the second company, the Court entered judgement for the Aherns in the amount of $684. This was affirmed on appeal.]

D. Court Annexed Arbitration

1. Lisa Bernstein, *Understanding the Limits of Court-Connected ADR: A Critique of Federal Court-Annexed Arbitration Programs*, 141 U. Pa. L. Rev. 2169, 2177-2186 (1993)*

I. THE BASIC FEATURES OF COURT-ANNEXED ARBITRATION PROGRAMS

The Judicial Improvements and Access to Justice Act sets out the basic structure of federal CAA programs, but gives each district the authority to adopt local rules specifying important program features.

Suits for predominantly money damages that fall below a particular amount in controversy, which, depending on the district, ranges from $50,000 to $150,000 and do not involve federal constitutional claims or conspiracies to interfere with civil rights, must be submitted to non-binding arbitration before a trial can be requested. In some districts, the parties or the trial judge may make a motion to exempt the case from arbitration where "the objectives of arbitration would not be realized (1) because the case involves complex or novel legal issues, (2) because legal issues predominate over factual issues, or (3) for other good cause." In most districts the maximum amount in controversy is a jurisdictional limit, not a cap on the damages an arbitrator can award.

Hearings are conducted by either a single arbitrator or a panel of three arbitrators chosen from a volunteer pool of lawyers. Hearings take place 80 to 180 days after the filing of the answer and decisions are rendered shortly thereafter. In some districts, hearings are open to the public, in others, they are closed. The amount of pre-arbitration discovery permitted and the types of pre-trial motions decided prior to the hearing are governed by local rule, subject to certain constraints imposed by Congress.

At the arbitration hearing, the Federal Rules of Evidence do not apply. Arbitrators may permit the introduction of any credible non-privileged evidence, including hearsay. The arbitrators are not required to issue written or oral findings of fact or conclusions of law, and at least one district prohibits them from doing so. A few districts encourage live testimony, while others discourage it, providing by local rule that "the presentation of testimony shall be kept to a minimum, and that cases shall be presented to the arbitrators primarily through the statements and arguments of Counsel." One district bans live testimony altogether and requires that "[a]ll evidence shall be presented through counsel who may incorporate argument on such evidence in his or her presentation." Some programs limit the length of the hearing.

Good faith participation in the arbitration hearing is required of both the parties and their counsel. Most districts require parties to be present at the hearing, and some districts require the presence of a person with full settlement authority. Although the authority of the court to order a person with settlement authority to be present at an arbitration hearing has yet to be definitively established, an *en banc* panel of the Seventh Circuit has upheld a district judge's authority to order a person with full settlement authority to be present at a settlement conference. [*G. Heileman Brewing Co. v. Joseph Oat Corp.*, reprinted in Chapter 16.] In some districts, if either the nonattendance of a party or the preparation and presentation of counsel is deemed not to constitute "participation in a meaningful way" in the arbitration process, the court can impose monetary sanctions and/or strike a party's demand for a trial de novo ("trial"). The court's authority to strike a party's demand for a trial has been upheld by several district courts, but has not yet been considered by any court of appeals.

After the arbitrator has rendered an award, which may, depending on the local rule, include costs, each party has thirty days to request a trial. When a party requests a trial, the case is restored to its original place on the docket and treated as if it had never been arbitrated; neither the record of the hearing, if made, nor the arbitrators' decision are admissible at trial. In the pilot districts, trial de novo request rates range from forty-six to seventy-four percent of arbitrated cases.

Some districts have disincentives to requesting a trial. Most districts require the party requesting a trial to post a bond with the court in the amount of the arbitrators' fees and costs which, depending on the district and the number of arbitrators, can range from $125 to $450 for the typical case. Although complex cases often cost substantially more to arbitrate, most districts put a cap on the amount of the bond a party can be required to post in order to obtain a trial. If the party requesting the trial improves his position at trial, this bond is returned to him; if he fails to do so, it is retained by the court.

In the past, some districts had a rule requiring the party requesting a trial to pay his opponent's post-arbitration attorneys' fees and/or costs if he failed to improve his position at trial. The authority of courts to enact such local rules absent congressional authorization was a question of some dispute. In 1988, Congress decided that pending further study by the

Federal Courts Study Committee, such provisions should not be part of the pilot programs. However, in its 1990 report, the Committee recommended that Congress authorize the pilot districts to experiment with fee and cost-shifting provisions, common features of many state CAA programs. If a trial is not requested within thirty days of the arbitration decision, the decision is entered as the judgment of the court and has the same force and effect as a trial judgment. It cannot, however, be appealed.

The pilot programs also permit litigants in any civil action or in any adversarial bankruptcy proceeding to voluntarily submit their case to arbitration. In some districts, when cases are submitted to the program with the parties' consent and a trial is requested, the court

> may assess costs . . . and reasonable attorney fees against the party demanding trial de novo if . . . such party fails to obtain a judgment, exclusive of interest and costs . . . which is substantially more favorable to such party than the arbitration award, and . . . the court determines that the party's conduct in seeking a trial de novo was in bad faith.

Although all districts permit parties to voluntarily submit disputes to arbitration either for free or at a minimal cost, litigants rarely choose this option. In Michigan, where CAA has been available since 1978 and cases submitted to the program by consent are subject to a post-arbitration fee and cost-shifting rule, only two cases have been submitted to the program by consent. In the Northern District of California where voluntary CAA has also been available since 1978, but cases submitted to the program by consent are not subject to a post-arbitration fee and cost-shifting rule, voluntary participation in the CAA program is also rare.

2. *Firelock, Inc. v. District Court*, 776 P.2d 1090 (Colo. 1989) (*en banc*)

Rovira, Justice.

This case requires us to determine whether the Colorado Mandatory Arbitration Act (Act) violates the Colorado Constitution and the due process and equal protection clauses of the fourteenth amendment to the United States Constitution. . . . In 1988, McGhee Communications, Inc. (McGhee) commenced an action . . . against the petitioner, Firelock Incorporated (Firelock). McGhee claimed that it rendered advertising services to Firelock for which Firelock did not pay. In its complaint, McGhee certified that the probable recovery would not exceed $50,000, exclusive of interest and costs, and that the case was not exempt from mandatory arbitration.

Firelock filed an answer denying that the requested amount was owed, asserted several affirmative defenses, and demanded a jury trial. Firelock also filed a motion to refrain from assignment for mandatory arbitration under the Act. . . . McGhee resisted the motion and requested that the trial court . . . order arbitration to be commenced promptly. . . .

II.

The Act provides a framework of mandatory arbitration in eight pilot judicial districts. . . . In these eight pilot districts, any civil action filed in any court of record except the county court and small claims court after January 1, 1988, and before July 1, 1990, seeking money damages in the sum of $50,000 or less, excluding costs and interest, is to be assigned to mandatory arbitration once the action is at issue.

Pursuant to the Act, the complaint and any applicable counterclaim or cross-claim governed by the Act must contain a certification that the probable amount of recovery exceeds or does not exceed $50,000, the limit imposed for mandatory arbitration. The Act establishes procedures for the selection and compensation of arbitrators, and sets forth an outline of procedures for the arbitration hearing. Arbitrators must be "qualified" and must file a consent to act as an arbitrator in the district in which the court is located, but an arbitrator need not be an attorney. [The Act] provides for a trial de novo for any party dissatisfied with the decision of the arbitrators. The demand for a trial de novo must be filed with the court within thirty days after the filing of the arbitrators' decision. The Act also provides that, unless the trial de novo results in "an improvement of the position of the demanding party by more than ten percent," the demanding party must pay the costs of the arbitration proceeding including arbitrator fees, but not exceeding $1,000.

[The Act] provides that the supreme court, pursuant to its authority under the Colorado Constitution, is empowered to promulgate rules governing the arbitration proceedings established in the Act. Pursuant to this authority, we adopted C.R.C.P. 109.1. C.R.C.P. 109.1 establishes the procedure for certification of the probable amount of recovery and the basis for any exemption from the Act, sets forth sanctions for failure to comply with the certification procedures, and provides for a detailed procedure for the selection of arbitrators. C.R.C.P. 109.1 also provides for the filing of a pre-arbitration "Disclosure Statement," sets forth limited rules for discovery, and establishes the details of the arbitration hearing and the powers of the arbitrators. C.R.C.P. 109.1(q) provides that if neither party demands a trial de novo within thirty days after the filing of the arbitrators' award, then the award becomes final and the trial court must enter judgment on the award. . . .

III.

On appeal, Firelock presents several reasons for finding that the Act is unconstitutional. Firelock argues that the Act violates article III and article VI, sections 1 and 9, of the Colorado Constitution, which provide for the separation of powers; article II, sections 3 and 6, of the Colorado Constitution, which provide for the right of access to courts; article II, section 23, of the Colorado Constitution and C.R.C.P. 38, which provide for the right to trial by jury; article II, section 25, of the Colorado Constitution and the equal protection and due process clauses of the United States Constitution; and article XVIII, section 3, of the Colorado Constitution, which provides the General Assembly with authority over consensual arbitration. We will address each of these arguments in turn.

A.

Firelock asserts that the Act violates the separation of powers provision of the Colorado Constitution because section 13-22-402(2) requires "that the pilot district courts must refrain from exercising their general jurisdiction pending arbitration." Firelock also asserts that the Act "is an unconstitutional delegation of judicial power to unqualified private citizens" because it allows arbitration to be "conducted by persons who are not only not members of the judiciary, but indeed who do not even have to be licensed attorneys."

Article III of the Colorado Constitution provides: The powers of the government of this state are divided into three distinct departments,—the legislative, executive and judicial; and no person or collection of persons charged with the exercise of powers properly belonging to one of these departments shall exercise any power properly belonging to either of the others, except as in this constitution expressly directed or permitted. "The fundamental meaning of the separation of powers doctrine is that the three branches of government are separate, coordinate, and equal." The purpose of article III is to prevent one branch of government from exercising any power that is constitutionally vested in another branch of government. . . . With respect to the authority vested in district courts, article VI, section 9, states that "[t]he district courts shall be trial courts of record with general jurisdiction, and shall have original jurisdiction in all civil, probate, and criminal cases, except as otherwise provided herein."

We must decide, therefore, whether the General Assembly can constitutionally require a district court to refrain from exercising its original jurisdiction in some civil cases while arbitration is proceeding. . . .

Many courts have said that the essence of judicial power is the final authority to render and enforce a judgment or remedy. . . . [T]he arbitrators' decision is not an exercise of the sovereign power of the state because the decision is non-binding, and the arbitrators do not perform a judicial function because they do not possess the final authority to render and enforce a judgment. . . .

[T]he arbitration panel must file its decision with the district court, and if neither party demands a trial de novo within thirty days after the filing, only then will the decision be enforceable. Thus, neither party need be bound by the arbitrators' decision because either party can demand a full and complete trial on the facts and the law by the district court with no effect given to the arbitrators' decision. Furthermore, the district court, not the arbitration panel, enters the judgment. Therefore, we conclude that the arbitration process created by the Act does not vest judicial authority in another branch of government in violation of article III of the Colorado Constitution because the arbitration panels do not perform "a judicial function."

Firelock relies on *Wright v. Central Du Page Hospital Association*, 63 Ill.2d 313, 347 N.E.2d 736 (Ill. 1976), where the Illinois Supreme Court struck down provisions relating to the establishment of medical review panels in medical malpractice cases. The Illinois statute provided for a three member arbitration panel consisting of one circuit judge, one practicing physician, and one practicing attorney. The circuit judge was to preside over the proceeding and decide procedural and evidentiary issues, but as to other issues, both legal and factual, the power and function of the lawyer and physician member of the panel were the same as that of the judge. The determinations of the panel were to be made in a written opinion stating its conclusions of fact and conclusions of law with a dissenting member filing a separate opinion. Either party could reject the panel's decision and proceed to trial as in any other civil case. The expenses of the panel were to be apportioned among the parties equally, except that a party who rejected a unanimous decision of the panel and who failed to prevail at trial could be taxed with the reasonable attorney's fees of the prevailing party, the costs of the panel, and the costs of the trial.

The Illinois Supreme Court held the statute to be unconstitutional because, among other things, the physician and lawyer member of the medical review panel are empowered to make conclusions of law and fact "according to the applicable substantive law" over the dissent of the circuit judge. This, we hold, empowers the nonjudicial members of the medical review panel to exercise a judicial function in violation of [the Illinois] Constitution.

We find this case to be inapposite because, here, the Act does not provide for a member of the judiciary in the arbitration panel with equal authority in the decision. Thus, there is no provision allowing two nonjudicial members of the panel to make conclusions of law and fact over the dissent of a member of the judiciary. Because the Act does not provide a mixed panel of judicial and nonjudicial members whereby the authority of the judiciary is diluted by the presence of laymen, we find *Wright* to be inapposite. [The Coloado Supreme Court noted that Wright is an abberation not generally followed, and that many cases from other jurisdictions support the position of the Court.]

B.

Firelock claims that the Act unconstitutionally impedes the right of access to courts guaranteed by article II, sections 3 and 6, by forcing litigants to arbitrate their claims before access is given to the district court and by requiring a party who requests a trial de novo to pay the arbitration costs up to $1,000 if he does not improve his position by at least 10%.

Article II of the Colorado Constitution is entitled "Bill of Rights." Article II, section 3, provides that "[a]ll persons have certain natural, essential and inalienable rights," including, among others, the right of "enjoying and defending their lives and liberties." Section 6 of article II provides that: "Courts of justice shall be open to every person, and a speedy remedy afforded for every injury to person, property or character; and right and justice should be administered without sale, denial or delay."

Generally, a burden on a party's right of access to the courts will be upheld as long as it is reasonable. "In a proper case . . . the right of free access to our courts must yield to the rights of others and the efficient administration of justice." *People v. Spencer*, 524 P.2d 1084, 1086 (1974) (enjoining a *pro se* plaintiff who filed numerous unfounded lawsuits from proceeding pro se as plaintiff in the courts of this state).

Many other reasonable burdens similar to the one imposed by the Act are present within our system of justice. For example, section 13-32-101, 6A C.R.S. (1987), requires the payment of a docket fee at the time of first appearance in all civil actions and special proceedings in all courts of record. C.R.C.P. 54(d) provides that "[e]xcept when express provision therefor is made either in a statute of this state or in these rules, costs shall be allowed as of course to the prevailing party unless the court otherwise directs." In disputes between landlords and tenants over the return of a security deposit, the willful retention of a security deposit renders the landlord liable for, among other things, reasonable attorney fees and court costs. C.R.C.P. 68 requires a prevailing party to pay costs incurred after the receipt of an offer of settlement when the judgment obtained by the prevailing party is not more favorable than the offer. Although this list is not all inclusive, it is demonstrative of the extent of a permissible burden on the right of access to the courts.

We conclude that the litigants are not denied their right of access to the courts because the Act provides for de novo review of the decision of the arbitration panel. Furthermore, the requirement that a prevailing party pay the costs of arbitration up to $1,000 if the party does not increase his position by at least 10% at trial does not place an unreasonable burden on the right of access to the courts. Therefore, we hold that the Act does not violate article II, section 6, of the Colorado Constitution.

C.

Firelock next asserts that article II, section 23, of the Colorado Constitution establishes a constitutional right to a jury trial in civil actions and the Act impermissibly infringes on this right. Firestone also argues that this court created the right to a jury trial in civil cases when we adopted C.R.C.P. 38 and that the Act violates that right. . . .

The Act provides for *de novo* review by the district court thereby giving either party the opportunity for a jury trial, and the provision for the payment of the costs of arbitration if the party does not increase its position by 10% is not an unreasonable burden on the availability of a jury trial. Reasonable prerequisites to the availability of a jury trial are not unusual. For example, section 13-70-103, 6A C.R.S. (1987), requires the payment of a jury fee "in each cause tried by jury." . . .

D.

Firelock next argues that the Act violates article II, section 25, of the Colorado Constitution and the equal protection clause of the United States Constitution. According to Firelock, the Act creates two classifications which violate the right to equal protection. First, the Act treats litigants in the pilot districts differently than litigants outside the pilot districts. Second, within the pilot districts, the Act treats litigants differently based on the monetary amount of the claim.

The fourteenth amendment to the United States Constitution provides that no state shall "deprive any person of life, liberty or property without due process of law, nor deny to any person within its jurisdiction the equal protection of the laws." U.S. Const. amend. XIV, § 1. The due process clause of article II, section 25, of the Colorado Constitution guarantees the right of equal protection to the citizens of Colorado. In interpreting the equal protection guarantee under the Colorado Constitution, we have followed the analytical mode developed by the United States Supreme Court in construing the equal protection clause of the fourteenth amendment. The equal protection clause guarantees that all persons who are similarly situated will receive like treatment by the law. Statutes facing a constitutional challenge are presumed to be constitutional, and the party challenging the statute bears the burden of proving it to be unconstitutional beyond a reasonable doubt. We must first decide which standard of review applies to a challenge to the Act, and then we must apply that standard.

Firelock argues that a standard of strict judicial scrutiny must be applied in resolving its equal protection challenge because the Act infringes on Firelock's fundamental rights, namely, the right of access to court and the right to a trial by jury. To pass strict scrutiny, the government must establish that the statutory classification is necessarily related to a compelling governmental interest. "In the absence of a statutory infringement on a fundamental right or the creation of a suspect class, . . . equal protection of the laws is satisfied if the statutory classification has a reasonable basis in fact and bears a reasonable relationship to a legitimate governmental interest. When a statutory classification significantly interferes with the exercise of a fundamental right, it cannot be upheld unless it is supported by sufficiently important state interests and is closely tailored to effectuate only those interests." . . .

As discussed in part III.B. regarding the right of access to courts and part III.C. regarding the right to trial by jury, the Act does not unreasonably infringe upon or "significantly interfere with" any fundamental right. Furthermore, neither of the classifications creates a suspect class, such as one based on race or national origin. Therefore, the strict scrutiny standard is not the correct standard to apply. Because the strict scrutiny standard is not appropriate and because there is no classification triggering an intermediate standard of review, the rational basis standard is the applicable standard of review.

We next examine the classifications advanced by Firelock to determine whether they are rationally related to a legitimate governmental interest. First, the General Assembly's decision to examine the success or failure of the Act in eight pilot districts is not a violation of equal protection. "The Fourteenth Amendment does not prohibit legislation merely because it is special, or limited in its application to a particular geographical or political subdivision of the state." Rather, the Equal Protection Clause is offended only if the statute's classification "rests on grounds wholly irrelevant to the achievement of the State's objective." *Holt Civic Club v. City of Tuscaloosa*, 439 U.S. 60 (1978). . . .

It is not unreasonable for the General Assembly to determine that claims below $50,000 should be subject to arbitration while claims above $50,000 are not. In *Bushnell v. Sapp*, 194 Colo. 273, 571 P.2d 1100 (1977), we addressed a similar argument with respect to the Colorado Auto Accident Reparations Act or "No-fault statute." In that case, the appellant argued that the $500 medical expense threshold created an arbitrary classification and thereby denied him equal protection of the laws. We rejected this argument, stating: Where and how to draw the line between major and minor claims of this nature is for the legislature to determine, and not the courts. . . . Here the General Assembly's choice that the Act apply to claims of $50,000 and below is not irrational. Other examples of reasonable monetary classifications include a $5,000 limitation in county court, a $2,000 limitation in the small claims division of county court, and a $50,000 limitation for diversity jurisdiction in federal court.

Arbitration is favored by the law in Colorado. . . . Arbitration promotes quicker resolution of disputes by providing an expedited opportunity for the parties to present their cases before an unbiased third party. By expediting the adversary process, arbitration promotes quicker settlement of cases thereby speeding up access to the courts and decreasing the costs to the parties. Although administrative convenience is not a legitimate governmental purpose, we believe that the governmental interest advanced by arbitration is more than mere administrative convenience. When the governmental interest served by arbitration is considered in light of the burden placed on the parties, we have no trouble concluding that the Act promotes a legitimate governmental interest and the procedures created by the Act are reasonably related to that interest. Accordingly, we hold that the Act does not violate the equal protection guarantee of the United States and Colorado Constitutions.

E.

Firelock next argues that article XVIII, section 3, of the Colorado Constitution prohibits the General Assembly from passing legislation imposing arbitration on employers and employees without their consent. Therefore, according to Firelock, the General Assembly cannot constitutionally impose arbitration on parties without their consent.

Article XVIII, section 3, provides: It shall be the duty of the general assembly to pass such laws as may be necessary and proper to decide differences by arbitrators, to be appointed by mutual agreement of the parties to any controversy who may choose that mode of adjustment. The powers and duties of such arbitrators shall be as prescribed by law.

In *In re Bill Relating to Arbitration*, 21 P. 474 (1886), we stated: We are of the opinion that section 3, art. 18, neither contemplates nor admits of a law providing for the compulsory submission of differences to arbitration. A submission of differences to the decision of arbitrators must be by mutual agreement of the parties to the controversy . . . .

Firelock asserts that this case is dispositive of the issue before us. We disagree. *In re Bill Relating to Arbitration* involved legislatively imposed binding arbitration. Here, on the other hand, the Act provides for non-binding arbitration with de novo review by the district court. Nothing in the language of article XVIII, section 3, speaks to the question of whether the General Assembly can pass laws relating to non-binding arbitration. We conclude that article XVIII, section 3, does not control the dispute before us and, therefore, does not prohibit the General Assembly from enacting the legislation at hand.

We conclude that the Mandatory Arbitration Act, §§ 13-22-401 to 13-22-409, 6A C.R.S. (1987), does not violate the Colorado Constitution or the United States Constitution. Therefore, we discharge the rule to show cause and direct the district court to proceed with the assignment of the case to arbitration.

ERICKSON, Justice, specially concurring:

While I acknowledge that the right of access to the courts is an important one, the burgeoning case load in our courts has itself caused delay and increased costs. Access to the courts for all litigants may be improved by different alternatives for dispute resolution, such as arbitration and mediation.

In my view, the mandatory arbitration pilot project in issue was a legislative method of reducing delay and providing access to the courts by winnowing out those cases that can be resolved by simpler and less costly methods. It is certainly not obvious to me that the method selected by the legislature will prevent some litigants from obtaining access to the courts. Since a number of cases may be satisfactorily resolved before trial, it would appear that arbitration will actually improve access to the courts. . . .

LOHR, Justice, dissenting:

I respectfully dissent. . . . Unlike the majority, I am persuaded that the Mandatory Arbitration Act violates the right of every person to obtain access to the courts as guaranteed by article II, section 6, of the Colorado Constitution. . . . Because I would resolve the case on right of access grounds, I would not reach the other constitutional arguments. . . .

Article II, section 6, of the Colorado Constitution states: Courts of justice shall be open to every person, and a speedy remedy afforded for every injury to person, property or character; and right and justice should be administered without sale, denial or delay. We have previously recognized that this provision "guarantees to every person the right of access to courts of justice in this state." . . . Article II, section 6, "limits very stringently the power to exclude resident plaintiffs from our court system where jurisdiction has otherwise been properly established." *McDonnell-Douglas v. Lohn*, 557 P.2d 373, 374 (1976) (because of article II, section 6, the doctrine of forum non conveniens has only the most limited application in Colorado courts). The lesson of *McDonnell-Douglas* is that we must carefully scrutinize any innovative procedure, however well intended, that interferes with the fundamental right of every person to obtain access to the courts to obtain redress for their legally cognizable grievances.

I do not read the cases cited by the majority as holding that "a burden on a party's right of access to the courts will be upheld as long as it is reasonable." Rather, I view *Spencer* and *Winslow* as holding only that the trial courts of this state are not constitutionally prohibited from enjoining *pro se* appearances in certain extreme cases involving a history of abuse of the judicial process. In reaching this conclusion in *Spencer* and *Winslow*, we acknowledged that under some circumstances a litigant's right of access to the courts "must yield to the interests of other litigants and of the public in general in protecting judicial resources from the deleterious impact of repetitious, baseless *pro se* litigation."...

The cases assigned to mandatory arbitration are not chosen for reasons relating to their deleterious impact on the judicial process. On the contrary, all cases in which a party seeks money damages in the sum of $50,000 or less, and only those cases, are siphoned off from the courts and diverted into the arbitration forum. The special concerns that motivated the issuance of injunctions against pro se litigants in cases such as *Spencer* and *Winslow*—preventing abuse of the judicial process, refusing to allow the judicial process to be used to harass others, and conserving limited judicial resources by not devoting them to the resolution of repetitious, meritless claims—are not present in this case.

The procedure by which a litigant must submit his claim for mandatory arbitration as a condition precedent to trying his case in a court restricts access to the courts in two important ways. First, the litigant may not present his claim to a court until he has undergone the delay and expense attendant to an arbitration proceeding. Second, in order to obtain access to a court after arbitration has been completed, the litigant must accept the consequence that he will be required to pay the costs of the arbitration proceeding, including arbitrator fees, up to a maximum of $1,000 should he fail to improve his position by more than ten percent. These burdens of time and expense are considerable and will likely have the practical effect of preventing litigants with smaller claims from ever obtaining access to the courts to assert them. In short, for some litigants these barriers to access to the courts will not simply burden such access but as a practical matter will bar entry into a judicial forum. The majority does not explain why these obviously important limitations on a litigant's fundamental right of access to the courts are permissible except to analogize them to the collection of docket fees, the award of costs to a prevailing party, and the imposition of certain other incidental costs of litigation applicable in special situations. The majority simply offers the conclusion that the burdens are reasonable. I cannot agree that it is constitutionally permissible to burden the fundamental right of access to the courts in these significant ways.

In sum, I regard the mandatory arbitration process at issue in this case as limiting access to the courts in a manner that conflicts with both the spirit and the letter of article II, section 6, of the Colorado Constitution. See *Aldana v. Holub*, 381 So.2d 231 (Fla. 1980) (medical mediation statute violated due process because application of its rigid jurisdictional periods proved arbitrary and capricious, and enlargement of these periods would effectively deprive claimants of access to the courts); *State ex rel. Cardinal Glennon Memorial Hosp. v. Gaertner*, 583 S.W.2d 107 (Mo. 1979) (statute requiring that medical malpractice claims be referred to medical malpractice review panel before being filed in court held unconstitutional based on fact that it "imposes a procedure" as a precondition to constitutionally established right of access to the courts); *Jiron v. Mahlab*, 659 P.2d 311, 313 (N.M. 1983) (statute requiring medical malpractice claimant to appear before a review commission prior to filing suit deprives plaintiffs of their constitutional right of access to the courts if the review requirement "causes undue delay prejudicing a plaintiff by the loss of witnesses or parties"); *cf. Mattos v. Thompson*, 421 A.2d 190 (Pa. 1980) (striking as unconstitutional a statute giving arbitration panel original jurisdiction over medical malpractice claims where delays involved in statutory procedures oppressively burdened the right to a jury trial so as to "make the right practically unavailable").

In reaching the conclusion that the Mandatory Arbitration Act cannot be squared with the constitutional right of access to the courts, I do not mean to imply that all efforts and methods to resolve disputes outside of the judicial forum violate that constitutional right. I would hold only that the particular mandatory procedure involved in this case imposes constitutionally impermissible burdens on that right.

3. Comments and Questions

a. Many state constitutions are lengthy, detailed, outdated, and full of arcane provisions. In states with such a constitution, the chances increase that some provision will be read by a court to preclude innovative solutions to government problems, even when undertaken pursuant to legislation.

b. CAA is sometimes used in about one-half of the states, and in numerous U.S. district courts. In some states (*e.g.*, Texas), court ordered mediation has largely supplanted all other forms of ADR, including CAA.

c. The next case (*Gullo*) is unusual in that the proposed subsequent use of information from an arbitration proceeding that was arguably "court annexed" is in a criminal proceeding, so the liberty of the subject rather than just money is at issue.

4. *United States v. Joseph Gullo*, 672 F. Supp. 99 (W.D.N.Y. 1987)

ELFVIN, District Judge.

[Defendants] have been charged in a one-count Indictment with participating in the use of extortionate means to collect, or attempt to collect, an extension of credit in violation of 18 U.S.C. §§ 874 and 2. . . .

Gullo's motion to dismiss the Indictment arises out of his participation, as a party, in an arbitration hearing. In January 1986 he received from the Community Dispute Resolution Settlement Center ("the CDR Center") a notice indicating that a complaint or grievance had been lodged against him. The subject matter of the complaint was directly related to the events leading to the present Indictment. The complaint or grievance form identified the grievant, the nature of the dispute and the settlement sought, noted that the grievance had been referred to the CDR Center by the Jamestown (N.Y.) Police Department and described the CDR Center as "a project of the Better Business Bureau Foundation of Western New York . . . ." The grievance form further states that "BY SIGNING THE AGREEMENT, YOU ARE INDICATING YOUR WILLINGNESS TO TRY AND RESOLVE YOUR DISPUTE WITHOUT COURT ACTION. THIS FORM DOES NOT BIND YOU TO THE PROCESS OR GUARANTEE YOUR CASE WILL BE RESOLVED. THE CDR CENTER WILL CONTACT YOU ABOUT ARBITRATION IN THE MATTER." Gullo apparently executed the document and a second document, [which] advises that agreement to arbitrate would result in an attempt by a neutral to reach settlement through mediation and, if mediation failed, in binding arbitration. It further states that the party agreeing to such dispute resolution understood that "the neutral will hold all information received during the hearing as confidential and will not voluntarily divulge that information. [The Parties] agree that the neutral will not be subpoenaed by either party in any subsequent legal proceeding.". . .

During the course of the dispute resolution process Gullo made certain statements. He now claims that those statements were involuntarily made in violation of his rights under the Fifth and Fourteenth Amendments and that the statements should not have been presented to the Grand Jury. He argues that the Indictment should be dismissed for these reasons or, in the alternative, that the statements made and the arbitration result should be suppressed.

The CDR Center operates pursuant to the Community Dispute Resolution Centers Program established July 27, 1981 by sections 849-a to 849-g of New York's Judiciary Law. The statute states in part that there existed a "compelling need for the creation of dispute resolution centers as alternatives to structured judicial settings. Community dispute resolution centers can meet the needs of their community by providing forums in which persons can participate in the resolution of disputes in an informal atmosphere without restraint and intimidation. * * * Community dispute resolution centers can serve the interests of the citizenry and promote quick and voluntary resolution of certain criminal matters." . . .[The Act provides] that the dispute resolution center may not hear certain types of disputes of a more serious criminal nature. . . .

The Fifth and Fourteenth Amendments are implicated . . . only if the arbitration process is found to be government action. "The most outrageous behavior by a private party seeking to secure evidence against a defendant does not make that evidence inadmissible under the Due Process Clause." Here, if the mediation/arbitration proceeding out of which Gullo's statements emanate had been private and not state action, the Fifth and Fourteenth Amendments would not serve as vehicles to dismiss the Indictment or to suppress statements made.

The CDR Center is a private organization staffed by its own personnel. It is under contract to New York to provide certain services and has agreed to abide by the applicable statutory and regulatory requirements. In the present case, the issue for arbitration had assertedly been referred by the Police Department. Charges had not been brought against Gullo and this Court does not know whether such would have been brought absent Gullo's agreement to arbitrate. This Court finds, however, that the CDR Center's contract with New York, its receipt of funding from that state and its resolution of the conflict between Gullo and the complainant fail to establish it as a state actor.

This Court does not find that Gullo's statements had been made involuntarily. Importantly, any compunction or coercion had been promoted by a non-government source. . . . The obtainment and use of Gullo's statements is not found to have violated his constitutional rights.

Gullo also asserts that the privilege established by subdivision 849-b.6 applies and, therefore, the Indictment should be dismissed because confidential material had been divulged to the Grand Jury or, alternatively, that all information obtained from and arising out of the arbitration proceeding should be suppressed. Federal Rules of Evidence rule 501 leaves privileges to statutory and common law development "in the light of reason and experience." To determine whether to recognize specific privileges that are not "firmly embedded in federal law" requires balancing four factors: "first, the federal government's need for the information being sought in enforcing its substantive and procedural policies; second, the importance of the relationship or policy sought to be furthered by the state rule of privilege and the probability that the privilege will advance that relationship or policy; third, in the particular case, the special need for the information sought to be protected; and fourth, in the particular case, the adverse impact on the local policy that would result from non-recognition of the privilege."

As to the first factor, there is a strong policy in favor of full development of facts and admissibility in criminal cases. . . . Suppression here would impinge on such policy.

Secondly, the policy sought to be furthered by the state promulgated privilege is the encouragement of participation in "the resolution of disputes in an informal atmosphere without restraint and intimidation." The confidentiality outlined under subdivision 849-b.6 is core to establishing an atmosphere "without restraint and intimidation." Although it is unclear whether the privilege acts in any primary sense to encourage participation in the program, it directly serves to insure the effectiveness of the program and thereby, secondarily, it serves to promote continued support for and existence of the program. It should be noted that abrogation of the privilege would place funding for the program in jeopardy.

With respect to the third factor, the United States has not shown any particularized need for the evidence. In fact, it concedes that, even without the evidence in dispute, the Grand Jury had more than enough evidence upon which to base its finding of probable cause.

The final factor for consideration concerns the impact on local policy from not recognizing the privilege in this case. The privilege generally serves to foster participation in the program and serves to promote candor by those participating. Although, this Court grants that few potential parties will likely forego participation in the program because of knowledge that evidence adduced therein would be subject to presentation in a federal prosecution, the effectiveness of the program will nonetheless be reduced by compelled disclosure and its very funding will be called into question.

In balance, this Court finds that the privilege afforded by subdivision 849-b.6 must be recognized in proceedings before this Court. All statements made during the dispute resolution process and all terms and conditions of such settlement shall be suppressed.

The revelation of privileged matters to the Grand Jury does not lead inexorably to the conclusion that the defendants have been wrongfully prejudiced or that the Grand Jury's function has been impaired to a degree calling for the very serious step of dismissing the Indictment. The preferable remedy—that chosen in this instance—is to exclude such evidence at trial. . . .

E. Screening Panels: Medical Malpractice Claims

1. Comments and Questions

a. The Macchiaroli article that follows, which includes a model statute, details the experience in various states with medical malpractice screening statutes. Common to all plans is that participation in the state screening panel process is a condition precedent to litigation. Is the malpractice crisis unique, or are there other categories of law suits that might usefully (and constitutionally) be subject to a screening panel process?

b. The question of whether federal courts are bound to apply state screening provisions in diversity cases, discussed in part IV(F) of the Macchiaroli article and section 401 of her proposed statute, is considered at Chapter 16, section E.

2. Jean A. Macchiaroli, *Medical Malpractice Screening Panels: Proposed Model Legislation to Cure Judicial Ills*, 58 GEO. WASH. L. REV. 181, 186-97, 239-60 (1990)*

The device known as the medical malpractice screening panel was among the reform measures initiated by some states during the initial crisis of the mid-1970s. Typically, a screening panel is comprised of members of the legal and medical communities who render an opinion regarding the liability of a health care provider subject to a medical malpractice claim. Some

*Reprinted with permission.

states permit the panel to value damages as well, provided that the panel finds at least one defendant liable. In contrast to arbitration, the decision of a screening panel is nonbinding and, therefore, is not an outright substitute for traditional litigation. Approximately one-half of the states currently have statutory provisions for medical malpractice screening panels, but the requirements and procedures vary considerably.

Notwithstanding this variation, all state legislatures that have created screening panels have done so for essentially identical reasons. The legislative objective was to expedite the process of claim resolution with an aim toward reducing the overall transaction costs of malpractice claims and, accordingly, alleviating the adverse effects of the insurance crisis. To achieve these ends, the screening panel systems were designed to encourage settlement between the adversaries. An incidental goal of the system was to minimize the number of nonmeritorious claims entering the jury trial process. . . .

This Article begins by examining the varieties of medical malpractice screening panels, focusing on the polymorphic provisions among existing statutes. The second part of this Article reviews the various constitutional challenges to screening panels and comments upon areas of constitutional vulnerability in screening panel statutes. Next, this Article addresses the application of state medical malpractice screening panel requirements to federal court diversity actions under the principles of *Erie Railroad v. Tompkins* and its progeny.

Finally, this Article presents various considerations and recommendations for model medical malpractice screening panel legislation and proposes a model statute. This Article argues that a mandatory, pre-action screening panel that provides for the determination of both liability and damages and contains the bilateral threat of cost sanctions for proceeding to a subsequent trial with a baseless claim or defense, is the best conceivable panel statute to achieve the goals of the system. Aside from serving the policy objectives of medical malpractice reform, the proposed model statute is intended to resolve the constitutional questions raised by, and procedural flaws and insufficiencies contained in, earlier and existing screening panel statutes. This Article concludes that in an era of increased judicial and legislative attention to alternative dispute resolution and continued recognition of the need for alternatives in the medical malpractice area, a properly designed screening panel statute can provide needed therapy for an ailing system.

I. CHARACTERISTICS OF MEDICAL MALPRACTICE SCREENING PANELS

Although most screening panels are mandatory, a number of states have established voluntary systems. Other states allow the parties to waive the panel requirement upon agreement of the parties. Nebraska alone permits the plaintiff to waive the panel requirement unilaterally. The states are divided between those that require screening prior to commencement of a medical malpractice action and those that provide for screening after commencement of an action, with most states favoring pre-action panel referral. . . . Commencement of the action places the lawsuit under the auspices of the court and may require investment of substantial judicial and party resources, particularly for motion practice and matters related to discovery, even prior to panel review.

Panels vary in size from three members to as many as six or seven. A significant majority of jurisdictions include at least one attorney and at least one health care provider on their screening panels. Arizona, Maine, Massachusetts, New Hampshire, New Jersey, New York, and Virginia include a sitting or retired judge with the attorney and health care provider components. Further, several states provide that laypersons be included in their screening panels. Typically, panel proceedings are informal and confidential. The power to subpoena witnesses and documents is generally available. The types of evidence that a screening panel may examine vary among the states, with most statutes specifically allowing party statements in oral or deposition form, medical records, and learned treatises. A number of statutes provide that the panel members may consult independent, neutral experts regarding the case before the panel. A few state panels may compel a physical examination of the claimant.

All medical malpractice screening panels have the authority to make a determination regarding liability. The states diverge greatly, however, on whether the screening panel should determine damages. Alaska, Delaware, Indiana, Louisiana, and Virginia permit a determination of the existence and extent of damages suffered by the claimant but do not authorize the panel to assess the actual value of the damages. Florida, Hawaii, Maryland, and New Hampshire expressly authorize screening panels to determine the amount of damages. Idaho authorizes the screening panel to set a settlement figure, but only if the panel is in unanimous agreement on the amount. Montana grants the screening panel the authority to approve settlements and to "recommend an award." In Nevada, if the panel issues a decision favorable to the plaintiff, a mandatory settlement conference must take place with a judge, after which the judge must determine the settlement value of the case.

[M]ost states have set a time limit within which a medical malpractice screening panel must render its decision. The statutory limitations tend to require a decision anywhere from five to thirty days after completion of the hearing, or from thirty to 180 days from the time of selection of the panel. Several states do not specify the period of time for rendering a panel decision. In addition to, or in place of such limitations, some states set a time limitation within which the panel hearing must be held.

A few states provide for limited judicial review of screening panel decisions. Delaware provides for superior court review of panel decisions on motion. Upon such review, the court "shall strike any portion of the panel's opinion which [it] finds to be based on error of law or not supported by substantial evidence." In Maryland, a party may apply to the panel to modify or correct its decision with respect to liability, damages, or costs. The panel's ruling becomes reviewable by the court when a party rejects the panel's award and files an "action in court to nullify the award." If the court does not vacate the award, the award becomes admissible in the ensuing trial on the merits and is "presumed to be correct."

The decisions of medical malpractice screening panels are, by their very nature, nonbinding. If a litigant is displeased with the screening panel's decision, that litigant has the right to proceed to trial. Most state legislation, therefore, has addressed the issue of whether to allow the decision of a medical malpractice screening panel to be admitted in a subsequent trial on the merits of the same claim. Although some division exists, in a majority of states the panel decision is admissible at trial. Connecticut, Maine, New Jersey, and New York permit the panel decision to be admitted at trial only if the decision was unanimous. Although New Hampshire does not permit the panel decision to be admitted at trial, the statute does allow a transcript of the panel proceedings to be used at a subsequent trial in the same manner in which a deposition could be used. Most states treat the panel decision as mere evidence at trial. Accordingly, the trier of fact must not treat the panel decision as conclusive on any issue: the trier must assess the panel decision along with the other evidence presented in the case and determine the weight to accord it. Delaware characterizes the panel decision as "prima facie evidence" at trial, but emphasizes that the trier of fact must not consider the decision conclusive. Only Maryland deviates substantially from the general trend by requiring that the panel decision be accorded a "presumption of correctness" at a subsequent trial.

States have been more reluctant to permit panelists to be called as witnesses at a subsequent trial of the same case. Arizona, Connecticut, and Nevada expressly state that a panelist may not be called as a witness, while permitting the panel decision to be admitted into evidence.

Although all states with a medical malpractice screening panel system recognize the parties' right to a trial de novo subsequent to the panel's decision, a few states impose some form of sanction upon a party who proceeds to trial after having obtained an unfavorable decision from the screening panel. The Massachusetts and Michigan statutes contain bond provisions. In Massachusetts, a plaintiff who does not prevail before the screening panel must post a bond in the amount of $6,000 to proceed to trial. If the plaintiff does not then prevail at trial, the court will assess costs against the plaintiff, including the costs of attorney fees and witness and expert fees.

In Michigan, if the panel unanimously decides that a claim or defense asserted by any party is "frivolous," that party must post a bond in the amount of $5,000 dollars before that party can proceed to trial. If the trial yields a judgment against the party asserting the claim or defense that the panel determined to be frivolous, the bond will apply to the reasonable costs of the other parties, including attorney fees.

Other states have enacted cost-allocation provisions. The Maryland statute contains no bond provision, but does provide for the assessment of costs against any party who seeks a trial de novo and does not ultimately obtain a judgment more favorable than the panel's at trial. The Maryland statute is different from the Massachusetts and Michigan statutes not only with respect to the bond requirement, but also because Maryland requires a party to obtain a more favorable decision after trial. Thus, the Maryland statute affects both plaintiffs and defendants who seek a trial de novo.

Another form of cost allocation relates to panel costs. The Maryland panel statute provides for the assessment of panel costs, including witness fees, expert fees, and reasonable attorney fees, against either a party, the party's attorney, or both for maintaining a position in bad faith before the panel. Similarly, the Alaska panel statute authorizes the imposition of panel cost on either party for asserting a frivolous claim or denial. Colorado provides for the shifting of up to $1,000 of the panel proceeding costs to a party who seeks a trial of the claim if that party did not improve its result by more than ten percent over the panel decision. Furthermore, Hawaii establishes an affirmative duty of parties and insurers to cooperate with the panel. Two types of sanctions are available under the Hawaii provision. First, the court may impose the costs of subsequent litigation on a party or insurer who fails to cooperate with the panel. Second, the court may assess the costs of the panel as a civil penalty, payable to the general fund, against a party or insurer who fails to cooperate with the panel. The Nevada cost sanctions are integrated with that state's requirement of a mandatory settlement conference. A claimant who, following an unfavorable panel decision, proceeds to a trial of the claim must prevail after the trial or be liable for the defendant's reasonable costs and attorney fees. A claimant receiving a favorable panel decision must proceed to a mandatory settlement conference, after which the judge who presided at the conference must value the claim. A defendant who refuses to offer the plaintiff the amount determined by the judge will be liable to the plaintiff for costs and attorney fees if the trial results in a judgment for the plaintiff that is greater than the proposed settlement value. If, however, the defendant offers the plaintiff the amount determined by the judge, but the plaintiff refuses the offer, the plaintiff will be liable for costs and attorney fees if the trial yields an award for the plaintiff that is less than the proposed settlement value. Thus, the Nevada legislature has attempted to impose the threat of costs equitably on both plaintiffs and defendants.

Florida has enacted a comprehensive scheme directed at discouraging the institution of patently nonmeritorious medical malpractice actions. An important feature of the scheme is the requirement of presuit investigation of medical malpractice claims. The plaintiff, prior to application to the screening panel, must conduct an investigation of the merits of the claim with respect to liability and causation and obtain expert verification of the claim. The defendant or the defendant's insurer then must investigate and obtain expert verification of the merits of the defense. Various sanctions are available for a party's failure to undertake the investigation or to present the requisite verification, or for a party's failure to demonstrate that the claim or defense "rests on a reasonable basis." Additionally, the Florida legislature has provided for mandatory settlement conferences in medical malpractice actions. Cost shifting is available in conjunction with an offer of judgment by a defendant or a demand for judgment by a plaintiff. If the judgment after trial is not at least twenty-five percent more favorable to the party rejecting the demand, the court will assess costs against the rejecting party.

States have experienced varying degrees of success with medical malpractice screening panel systems. In Rhode Island . . . a screening panel system proved ineffective and eventually was repealed. During the period of time in which screening panels operated in the state, only approximately one-fifth of the disputes that came before screening panels were actually resolved by them. Similarly, Pennsylvania's voluntary screening panel system had the undistinguished record of only nine panel hearings out of 2,466 claims. Thus, significant practical problems with the operation and utilization of screening panel systems have affected some states. Yet, practical problems notwithstanding, signs of panel success are recurrent.

The diverse and sometimes conflicting provisions contained in the various state screening panel statutes demonstrate the need for close scrutiny in this area. States generally recognize the need for medical malpractice claims screening, but are in considerable disagreement regarding the specific means with which to implement the concept. . . .

IV. CONSIDERATIONS FOR A MODEL SCREENING PANEL STATUTE

A. Framework of the Model Act.

Although only about one-half of the states have some form of medical malpractice screening panel system currently in operation, private commentators, federal agencies, and state-appointed committees and task forces have repeatedly called for screening panel legislation. For reasons of both cost containment and judicial efficiency such legislation is warranted. Existing and repealed statutes represent a hodgepodge of legislative activity and alternative dispute resolution philosophy, and have generated a wealth of litigation on a broad spectrum of issues. Because of contradictory judicial interpretations of screening panel statutes, this legislative and judicial activity has left an ambiguous legacy. Nevertheless, the emerging lesson is that a screening panel statute that is both Constitutionally sound and politically viable is welcome and achievable. . . . Thus, model legislation is especially salutary.

To achieve its purported goals, a medical malpractice screening panel statute should include, at a minimum, the following features: (1) a complete statement of the purposes and goals of the screening process; (2) a definition of covered actions; (3) a provision establishing the panel as a mandatory prerequisite to litigation of the claim; (4) a provision declaring the composition of the panel, featuring attorney and health care provider members; (5) a delineation of panel proceedings; (6) provisions regarding use of panel findings in subsequent litigation of the same case; (7) the threat of costs for proceeding to trial with a baseless claim or defense; and (8) a position statement on the application of the panel requirement in federal diversity actions.

B. Purposes and Goals

Because medical malpractice screening panel statutes came into existence in response to the perceived crisis in medical malpractice liability insurance, the goals of the screening panel statutes uniformly have been (1) to minimize increases in the cost of professional liability insurance for health care providers, (2) to assure the availability of quality health care for the citizens of the state, and (3) to promote judicial efficiency. State legislatures thereby have aimed to discourage frivolous and nonmeritorious actions against health care providers, to encourage settlement of meritorious medical malpractice claims, and to reduce the overall costs of handling medical malpractice claims.

The importance of the legislative intent section of the statute is a direct result of judicial activity in the area of equal protection challenges to screening panel legislation. Most medical malpractice screening panel schemes will withstand an equal protection challenge regardless of whether the examining court applies the rational basis test or an intermediate level of scrutiny. But in some instances, the reviewing court will demand a clearly articulated legislative purpose. Some courts may go even further by requiring the party arguing the validity of the panel statute to produce statistical evidence that the statute has substantially furthered the legislatively articulated goals. In any event, inclusion of a legislative purpose section in the statute should stymie most equal protection challenges and thus is warranted. . . .

At a minimum, therefore, the legislature should set forth its perception of the medical malpractice insurance and claims crises in the state, and should enumerate the specific goals of the legislation. Some indication should exist of the relationship between the procedural aspects of the screening panel statute and the substantive policies of the state. Moreover, a balanced statement of legislative findings should mention the adverse effects of increased claims on medical malpractice plaintiffs. . . . [C]lear evidence of legislative purpose is fundamental to equal protection analysis.

C. Covered Actions and Presentation of Claims

Medical malpractice screening panels should be established for all actions commenced against health care providers within the jurisdiction. The definition of "health care provider" should be sufficiently broad to include individual physicians and surgeons, professional corporations, and hospitals, as well as officers, employees, and agents of such entities. The term "medical malpractice" should encompass all professional conduct of the defendant that is related to the defendant's treatment of the plaintiff. The screening panel statute should encompass all medical malpractice claims against entities practicing medicine within the jurisdiction. The legislature may wish to include within the scope of the statutory scheme dentists and podiatrists, or other health care professionals. Whatever definition is used, it forms the basis for justifying the classification of medical malpractice claims for treatment in a distinct category.

Review by the screening panel should operate as a condition precedent to suit. To best serve the interests of judicial efficiency and economy, the claimant should present the proposed complaint to the panel prior to commencing the action, and the claim should proceed through the screening process autonomously, leaving the judicial system unencumbered. Any action commenced in the courts of the state without compliance with this prerequisite should be dismissed for failure to comply with the statutory requirement. Moreover, administration and overview of the panel by the state department of insurance would remove the process from the typically overburdened judicial system, and reflect the connection between the panel system and the underlying medical malpractice insurance problem. Presumably, the insurance department would have a vested interest in assuring that the screening panel system efficiently serves its goals.

Arguably, requiring referral to the screening panel after commencement of the action, rather than as a precondition to suit would allow for the benefits of continuing judicial supervision of the action. Discovery could proceed during the panel review process, and judicial intervention would be available to resolve disputes between the parties. Ideally, however, a screening panel system should operate to require minimal, if any, intrusion into the judicial system. If the goal of the panel system to achieve early settlement of the claim is attained prior to entry of the claim into the judicial process, the judicial system will have suffered no burden. The later panel review occurs, the more judicial time and resources may be invested in the claim. Pre-action referral to the screening panel theoretically should dispose of virtually all frivolous and nonmeritorious claims prior to entry of the claims into the judicial system. Failure to substantially achieve this goal would indicate either a lapse in the efficiency of panel administration or a lack of sufficient statutory disincentives to litigate the frivolous or nonmeritorious claims in the court system. Accordingly, requiring referral of the claim to the screening panel prior to commencement of the action would best serve the interests of the judicial system.

When panel referral is prior to commencement of the action, the statute should include a provision tolling the applicable limitations period until ninety days following transmission of the decision of the screening panel to the parties. Moreover, the statute should contain strict time limitations for panel selection, hearing, and rendering of the decision. If strict time limitations are incorporated, the toll provision would not unjustly prejudice defendants in extending the statutory period within which medical malpractice plaintiffs may bring their actions. The claim would not become stale and, indeed, the defendant would have been sufficiently notified at the time of presentation of the claim to the medical malpractice screening panel.

[R]eferral to a medical malpractice screening panel should be mandatory and not voluntary. Parties should not be permitted to waive the panel requirement by agreement. Only with a mandatory, non-waivable panel requirement can the system function efficiently. Mandatory panel review may provide a convenient forum for pre-action settlement negotiations in actions that might otherwise proceed far into litigation before settlement becomes a possibility. Because the screening panels, by their very nature, preserve the claimant's right of access to the courts, no impermissible restrictions would be implicated by mandatory panel review. Requiring the processing of all medical malpractice claims through the screening panel should encourage earlier settlements and, thus, lower settlement values and ultimate litigation costs. The logical result of lower average costs per claim would be lower insurance premiums and, ultimately, lower costs for medical services.

D. Panel Composition and Proceedings

The medical malpractice screening panel should be composed of an attorney and two health care providers. Any greater number of panel members would tend to increase the difficulties in panel selection and coordination of schedules and, therefore, would increase delay in the process. The majority of panel members should be health care providers, consistent with the nature of the screening panel as an expert advisory board. In particular, the health care providers can assist the panel in determining the standard of care in the community, and have the expertise to determine difficult medical causation issues. The proposed model statute does not contain a provision for a judicial component of the panel, in keeping with the goal to eliminate intervention of the judicial system at the panel stage. The attorney member, who should sit on the panel and serve as the chairman, should have practiced before the courts of the state in the area of personal injury litigation. This requirement is consistent with the image of the medical malpractice screening panel as an expert advisory panel.

Selection of health care providers to sit on the panel should be made from a list maintained by the state department of insurance and obtained from the state medical licensing board or state medical society. The list should include the health care providers' specialties within the field of medicine. Health care providers who sit on a particular panel should be from the medical specialty related to the subject matter of the claim. When a defendant is a hospital or other health care facility, one of the panels members should be a person involved in administration of a health care facility. The department of insurance, therefore, should maintain a list of individuals involved in administration of health care facilities within the state. The department should obtain the list from the state board of licensing for hospitals and other health care facilities.

The goal in establishing a panel selection process is to provide for the most efficient and speedy administration of the panel system. Accordingly, panel size should be limited to a few individuals whose particular expertise could illuminate the issues presented by the claim. The panel selection should be conducted by the commissioner of insurance or the commissioner's designee. Moreover, a time limit of sixty days from time of presentation of the claim until the scheduled date of the panel hearing should be strictly enforced.

Efficiency should be the goal of the panel statute. Panel proceedings should be informal and confidential, in accordance with the existing screening panel statutes. The panel should have authority to compel evidence related to the claim, which at a minimum should include medical and hospital records, laboratory or other test results, and an independent physical examination of the claimant. The subpoena power should be available to compel witnesses to testify before the panel, as well as for production of records, documents, and other evidence. Furthermore, the panel should have the right to consult independent experts on the subject matter of the claim. Strict observation of the rules of evidence should not be required, although appropriate foundation for evidence, based upon the rules of evidence, should be enforced by the panel. After interviewing the parties, taking testimony from witnesses, and examining the records and other physical evidence relevant to the claim, the panel should issue its decision in writing. The decision should be rendered no later than thirty days after completion of the hearing.

The incorporation of strict time limitations into the model statute serves several purposes. First, allowing the claim to remain a relatively short time before the screening panel assures that undue delay would not infringe upon the plaintiff's constitutional rights. Conversely, the defendant will not be prejudiced by the toll, which operates during panel consideration, provided that the claim is processed rapidly and efficiently through the panel process. Furthermore, the smooth flow of claims through the screening panel system with speedy rendering of panel decisions will encourage parties to enter into settlement negotiations at an early, and less costly, stage of the dispute. At the very least, a well administered and efficient panel process will lend credibility to the panel decision in the eyes of the parties and may encourage more early dispositions of claims without the need for judicial intervention.

The panel first should determine liability, causation, and the existence of damages. If the panel's decision with respect to all three elements is in favor of the claimant, the panel should proceed to set a monetary settlement value on the claim, distinguishing between economic and noneconomic damages. Claimants may object to a provision permitting the panel to value the case by setting a figure on damages as beneficial to health care provider defendants at the expense of claimants. The natural predilection of the health care provider members of the panel may be to set a much lower figure than their juror counterparts would set in a trial on the same claim. Nevertheless, the benefits to the system in allowing the panel to value the claim and establish a ball-park figure for settlement purposes outweighs the effect of any diminished valuation as a result of panelists' professional associations. Indeed, panelists who have sworn an oath to carry out their duties in good faith may compensate by inflating the valuations they otherwise would set in an effort to avoid the semblance of professional prejudice.

If the panel decision, including any dissent, is admissible at a subsequent trial of the claim, as this proposal recommends, the panel's settlement valuation should be excluded. Juries rarely have experience in assigning a money amount to a personal injury, and may tend to view the panel's valuation as an estimation of damages, rather than a settlement figure. Moreover, jurors tend not to have the practical expertise to distinguish between the absolute value of a case and the settlement value of the case. This is particularly true with respect to the often difficult process of determining pain and suffering damages. Although most courts have upheld screening panel admissibility provisions when confronted with a right to jury trial challenge, the opportunity for confusion in interpreting the panel's settlement valuation counsels against the valuation's admissibility. All panel decisions should be rendered promptly in writing, and should be supported by appropriate reference to medical records and professional treatises. A dissenting panel member should be permitted to file an opinion to preserve accurately the true balance of panel expert opinion on the claim.

E. Use of Panel Decisions in Subsequent Litigation

A key feature of the proposed model statute is the provision authorizing the admissibility of the decision of the screening panel in any subsequent litigation of the same claim. The panel decision, with the exception of the panel's settlement recommendation, should be admissible whether or not it was unanimous. The decision should be treated at trial as any other evidence submitted by the parties. A prima facie case may not be established solely on the existence of the panel decision. The aim of the admissibility provision is to encourage early settlement of the action. The panel decision operates, in effect, as a free expert opinion for the party in whose favor the decision is rendered. Such pressure on the party against whom the panel decision is rendered should create a situation in which settlement is at least a viable option.

No panel member should be called to testify at the subsequent trial. Some protection should be afforded the panel members thus encouraging members to express their own opinions fully during the panel deliberation. Some panel members, particularly those in the medical profession, may be unwilling to find in favor of either party if they know that they may be called to defend their views publicly at the subsequent trial. Moreover, the statute should provide for immunity of the panel members for any claim arising out of, and within the scope of, their service on the panel. Ideally, admissibility of the panel decision in a subsequent trial of the same claim should not create an uncomfortable situation for panel members. Furthermore, panel members likely will have spent a considerable amount of time in their official capacity as screening panel members, and a predictable end of their duties should be foreseeable. Allowing members to be called as witnesses at a subsequent trial might be an oppressively burdensome consumption of their time. Any incremental increase in clarity of the panel decision would not merit such burden on panel members. Most likely, the testimony of panel members, if allowed, would only be duplicative.

The state's interest in achieving the ultimate goals of reducing claim costs and relieving trial dockets crowded with medical malpractice actions signals the need for screening panel statutes that impose a threat of sanctions on those parties who, unsuccessful at the panel stage, continue to a trial of the claim, but do not ultimately prevail. Such provisions must be drafted with great care so as not to obstruct the access of the parties to court. Moreover, to truly encourage settlement of the claims at an early stage, any sanction provision should apply with equal force to plaintiffs and defendants.

Two states currently have provisions requiring a bond and imposing costs on a party who does not prevail at trial. Bond provisions, however, have the effect of placing the burdens inherent in rejecting the panel decision solely on the plaintiff. A need exists for imposition of a sanction on a defendant who received an unfavorable panel decision but who refused to make a reasonable offer of settlement. Although the logic of bond provisions is apparently that plaintiffs voluntarily litigate, while defendants are involuntarily forced to defend claims that may or may not have any merit, thus making it the plaintiff's choice whether to proceed to trial following the panel determination, the bond provisions do not create an incentive for defendants to dispose of medical malpractice cases prior to trial. A defendant who does not prevail before the panel may refuse to settle the action, thus forcing the plaintiff to incur the costs of trial. The defendant may take this step with impunity — other than, of course, the risk of a substantial verdict at trial in favor of the plaintiff. In any event, the defendant may be able to take advantage of docket delays to wear down the plaintiff, thus increasing the likelihood of a low settlement figure prior to verdict.

An effective screening panel system must incorporate some form of sanction as a means of deterring those parties with nonmeritorious positions, be they plaintiffs or defendants, from proceeding to trial in the face of an unfavorable panel decision. The proposed model statute contains a tripartite cost-allocation provision designed to impose the threat of litigation costs, including attorney fees, on both parties. First, if the claimant does not prevail before the panel, but proceeds to trial and again does not prevail, the claimant shall be liable for the defendant's litigation costs. If, on the other hand, the claimant received a favorable panel decision, but the defendant refused to make an offer of settlement in at least the amount set by the panel as a reasonable settlement value, the claimant may proceed to trial knowing that the defendant shall become liable for costs if the defendant loses at trial. Finally, if the claimant received a favorable panel decision and the defendant offered the amount set by the panel, but the claimant refused, the claimant will bear the risk of costs to be imposed if the claimant does not receive a verdict at trial that is at least 25 percent higher than the panel amount.

F. Screening Panels in Federal Diversity Actions

For a state screening panel system to achieve its goals, the panel requirement should apply equally to federal courts and state courts. The avoidance of forum shopping and the need for equitable administration of the laws mandate that if a state statute imposes a screening panel requirement on actions brought in state court, that same requirement should apply to actions brought in federal district court on the basis of diversity of citizenship. Nevertheless, some screening panel statutes have encountered Erie doctrine problem resulting in refusal to apply the requirements in federal court diversity actions.

Delaware has recognized the need to serve the goals of Erie and has incorporated into its screening panel statute a provision attempting to accommodate the respective interests of the state and federal courts in the area of medical malpractice screening. The Delaware statute provides . . . for establishment of a screening panel:

> upon request of a Federal District Court Judge sitting in a civil action in the District of Delaware alleging malpractice, in the manner instructed by the said federal court but also in a manner as consistent as possible with the process of selecting such panels provided for in Superior Court actions in this chapter.

The Delaware provision is indicative of a reasonable legislative attempt to set forth a standard for applying medical malpractice screening panels in federal diversity actions, which accommodates the respective interests of the state and federal judicial systems. But the Delaware statute establishes voluntary post-commencement screening and is not directly applicable to a mandatory pre-action screening panel requirement that is advocated by this proposed model statute.

To avoid forum shopping and to provide for the equitable administration of the laws, medical malpractice actions to be filed in federal court on the basis of diversity of citizenship should undergo pre-action screening in the same manner and to the same extent as medical malpractice actions to be commenced in state court. Accordingly, diversity actions sounding in medical malpractice should be referred to state screening panels prior to filing of the actions in federal court. This will assure uniformity in the treatment of state court plaintiffs and federal-court plaintiffs in medical malpractice actions.

The screening panel statute, while not self-executing in this area, should reflect the state of the law and the policy of the state regarding the application of screening requirements to diversity actions in federal district court. This means that in most jurisdictions and as set forth in the model statute, the panel statute should declare that screening panel review shall be a condition precedent to instituting a medical malpractice action in federal district court on the basis of diversity of citizenship, and that the panel decision shall be admissible in a subsequent trial in federal court. . . .

Model Medical Malpractice Screening Panel Act

Legislative Findings and Purpose

Section 101. (a) Findings. The legislature finds that the number of suits and claims for damages and the amount of judgments and settlements arising from health care have increased greatly in recent years. These increases have had the following effects:

(1) The insurance industry has substantially increased the cost of medical malpractice insurance;

(2) Health care cost has increased, both through health care providers passing the cost of premiums to the patient and through the providers practicing defensive medicine to protect against future medical malpractice claims;

(3) Certain health care providers have been discouraged from continuing to provide services because of the high cost and possible unavailability of malpractice insurance;

(4) Increased delays in the progress of medical malpractice cases through the litigation process to trial have delayed recovery by claimants with meritorious cases and have increased the overall costs per claim to parties.

(b) Purpose. The high cost of medical claims in this state can be alleviated by requiring early determination of the merit of claims. The declared purpose of mandatory medical malpractice pretrial screening panels in this state is:

(1) to identify claims of health care professional negligence that merit compensation and to encourage early resolution of those claims prior to trial; and

(2) to encourage early withdrawal or dismissal of nonmeritorious claims of health care professional negligence.

Definitions

Section 102. (a) "Health care provider" means any individual, partnership, corporation, facility or institution licensed by this state to provide health care or medical professional services in the field of medicine, surgery, dentistry, podiatry, optometry, chiropractic, or nursing, including any officer, employee, or agent thereof acting within the scope of his or her employment.

(b) "Medical malpractice" means any action against a health care provider alleging personal injuries arising out of health care rendered, or the failure to render health care, by the health care provider, or any other alleged departure from the accepted standards of health care.

(c) "Health care" means any act, or treatment performed or provided, or which should have been performed or provided, by any health care provider for, to, or on behalf of a patient during the course of the patient's medical diagnosis, care, treatment, or confinement.

(d) "Patient" means a natural person who is under the care of, or has been under the care of, a health care provider.

Jurisdiction of Medical Malpractice Screening Panel

Section 103. (a) Prerequisite to suit. No action against a health care provider may be commenced in any court of this state before the claimant's proposed complaint has been presented to a medical malpractice panel established pursuant to this chapter and an opinion is rendered by the panel. Any action commenced without a determination by the panel shall be dismissed without prejudice for failure to comply with this section.

(b) Tolling of statute of limitations. Submission of a medical malpractice claim for the consideration of the medical malpractice screening panel shall toll the running of the applicable limitation period for that claim, and such limitation period shall not commence to run again until 90 days after the panel's final decision is transmitted to the claimant and the claimant's attorney by certified mail.

Administration of Screening Panel

Section 201. (a) The Commissioner of Insurance shall be responsible for the administration of the procedures for selection of candidates for service on medical malpractice screening panels.

(b) The Commissioner shall adopt and publish such rules and regulations as may be necessary to carry out the provisions of this chapter and to establish the procedures for the selection and operation of malpractice screening panels.

Establishment of Screening Panel

Section 202. (a) Within 10 days of the filing of a notice of medical malpractice claim with the state Department of Insurance together with proof of service on respondent(s), the Commissioner of Insurance shall select a panel composed of two physicians and one attorney from lists maintained by the Department of Insurance. The physicians shall be from the same specialty within the field of medicine as the individual against whom the claim is filed. If a party against whom the claim is filed is a hospital or other health care facility, the panel shall be composed of one hospital administrator, one physician, and one attorney.

(b) The attorney member of the panel shall be a practitioner with experience in the trial of personal injury cases and shall serve as the panel chairperson.

(c) All panel members shall be compensated at the rate of $100 per claim and shall be entitled to reasonable travel and living expenses incurred as a result of the performance of their duties on the panel.

Procedures of Screening Panel

Section 203. (a) Notice of Claim. The notice of claim filed with the Department of Insurance shall contain a brief statement of facts of the case, naming the persons involved, and the dates and the circumstances, so far as they are known, of the alleged act or acts of medical malpractice.

(b) Response. The health care provider or providers named by the claimant in the notice of claim shall respond to the notice of claim within 10 days of service of the notice of claim upon the health care provider. The response shall be served upon the claimant and filed with the Department of Insurance together with proof of service.

(c) Date for Hearing. Upon establishment of the screening panel, the panel shall set a date for a hearing of the claim before the panel which shall be for a date no later than 60 days from the time of initial presentation of the claim to the Department of Insurance.

(d) Submission of Evidence. Within a reasonable time period, and in any event no less than 5 days prior to the date set for the hearing, the parties shall submit to the screening panel all written material, including, but not limited to, medical and hospital reports, X-rays laboratory tests, excerpts of treatises, and other documents relevant to the claim. A copy of all evidence submitted to the panel shall be sent to each party.

(e) Hearing. The hearing shall consist of the testimony of witnesses and presentations by the parties or their counsel or both. The hearing shall be informal and confidential. No stenographic record shall be made of the hearing. All evidence, documents, and exhibits shall, at the close of the hearing, be returned to the parties or witnesses from whom they were obtained.

(f) Subpoena Power. The panel shall have the authority to subpoena witnesses and documents and to administer oaths.

(g) Expert Witness. Upon application of any party or upon its own decision, the panel may request an additional impartial and qualified physician having particular expertise in the medical specialty involved to assist in the determination of the claim. Such physician may conduct a professional or expert physical examination of the claimant upon the request of a party or of the panel. The panel shall determine the fee and expenses to be paid to such physician and the parties to the hearing shall share equally in such fee and expenses.

Decision of Screening Panel

Section 204. (a) Time to Render Decision. The panel shall render its written decision on the claim no later than 30 days after completion of the hearing.

(b) Scope of Decision. (1) The panel shall render one or more of the following opinions:

(A) The evidence does not support a conclusion that the health care provider failed to comply with the appropriate standard of care.

(B) The evidence supports a conclusion that the health care provider failed to comply with the appropriate standard of care and such failure was a proximate cause of the alleged damages.

(C) The evidence supports a conclusion that the health care provider failed to comply with the appropriate standard of care and such failure was not a proximate cause of the alleged damages.

(D) The evidence indicates that there is a material issue of fact, not requiring expert opinion, bearing on liability for consideration by a court or jury.

If the panel's opinion is that set forth in subdivision (b)(l)(B) of this section, the panel may determine whether the claimant suffered any disability or impairment and the extent and duration of the disability or the percentage of the impairment.

(2) If the panel's opinion is that set forth in subdivision (b)(l)(B) of this section, the panel may decide the amount if any, which in its recommendation should reasonably be offered in settlement of the claim. The amount shall specify which portion of the amount recommended is attributable to economic losses and which to noneconomic losses. The panel may not recommend punitive damages.

(c) Form of Decision. The panel's decision shall be in writing. Any member of the panel who does not agree with the panel's decision may file a dissenting opinion.

(d) Effect of Decision. The panel shall sit as an expert advisory board. The panel's decision shall be without administrative or judicial authority and shall not be binding on any party.

Effect of Panel Decision on Subsequent Action: Admissibility of Panel Decision

Section 301. (a) Panel Dension Admitted. Any report of the opinion reached by the screening panel shall be admissible as evidence in any action subsequently brought by the claimant in a court of law on the same claim, provided that any amount recommended by the panel in settlement of the claim shall not be admissible into evidence in such action. The opinion of the screening panel shall not be conclusive.

(b) No Testimony by Panel Members. No members of the panel shall testify by compulsion of subpoena or otherwise, at a subsequent trial of the same claim.

(c) Immunity of Panel Members. Panel members shall have absolute immunity from civil liability for all communications, findings, opinions, and conclusions made in the course and scope of duties prescribed by this Act.

Effect of Panel Decision on Subsequent Action: Assessment of Costs and Fees

Section 302. (a) If the screening panel finds in favor of the claimant and the defendant makes an offer of settlement to the claimant in at least the amount recommended by the panel for settlement of the claim, but such offer is rejected by the claimant, the claimant may file an action in a court of law. If the claimant does not obtain a judgment that is at least twenty-five percent higher than the amount offered in settlement by the defendant, the claimant shall be liable for the defendant's reasonable costs and attorney fees associated with the defense of the court action.

(b) If the screening panel finds in favor of the claimant and the defendant fails to make an offer of settlement to the claimant in at least the amount recommended by the panel for settlement of the claim. the claimant may file an action in a court of law. If the defendant does not obtain a favorable judgment in court, the defendant shall be liable for the claimant's reasonable costs and attorney fees associated with the prosecution of the court action.

(c) If the panel decision is not in favor of the claimant, the claimant may file an action in a court of law. If the claimant does not obtain a favorable judgment in court, the claimant shall be liable for the defendant's reasonable costs and attorney fees associated with the defense of the court action.

Screening Panels in Federal District Court Actions

Section 401. (a) Screening Panel as Condition Precedent. Presentation of a medical malpractice claim to a state screening panel pursuant to this act shall be a condition precedent to commencement of an action on the same claim in federal district court. No such action shall be commenced in federal district court without the screening panel having previously rendered its opinion.

(b) Admissibility of Panel Decision. Any report of the opinion reached by the screening panel shall be admissible as evidence in any action subsequently brought by the claimant on the same claim in federal district court, provided that any amount recommended by the panel in settlement of the claim shall not be admissible.

F. ADR in Appeals Courts: Appellate Mediation

1. Comments and Questions

a. Set out below are discussions of two specific and very different appellate ADR programs, both of which seem to have achieved considerable success. Susan FitzGibbon's article also provides considerable comparative information about other appellate ADR processes.

b. Judge Kaufman's evaluation of the CAMP program is that of a proud parent, not a disinterested scholar. Still, he is not alone in thinking well of CAMP, and the visibility of both Judge Kaufman and the 2d Circuit means that the CAMP model is widely known. The bulk of the article from which the CAMP material is drawn appears in Chapter 18, section B.

c. What factors promote the success of appellate ADR in achieving settlements? After all the parties were unable to settle the case, they went to trial, at least one party refused to accept the judgment of the trial court, post-trial settlement was not achieved, and an appeal was filed. (In the process they have spent considerable sums for costs and attorney fees.)

d. What factors inhibit settlement at the appellate level? Professor FitzGibbon notes that "at the moment of appeal, the parties are likely to be decidedly less friendly than they were before litigation commenced."

2. Irving R. Kaufman, *Reform for A System in Crisis: Alternative Dispute Resolution in the Federal Courts*, 59 Fordham L. Rev. 1 (1990)*

1. The Civil Appeals Management Plan

One of the first programs to institutionalize ADR processes in the federal courts was one I introduced in 1974, my first year as Chief Judge of the Second Circuit. This innovation, the Civil Appeals Management Plan ("CAMP"), injected court-sponsored mediation into appellate litigation. The primary aims of CAMP are to encourage the resolution of appeals short of full-blown appellate proceedings and to expedite the disposition of all civil appeals. Virtually all civil appeals taken in the Second Circuit are referred to CAMP. Within ten days of docketing an appeal, the appellant must submit a brief "Pre-Argument Statement." One of the circuit's two full-time "staff counsel" then issues a schedule including a date for a CAMP conference, deadlines for the filing of briefs and a date for oral argument of the appeal. Because parties are more likely to settle before they have invested large sums in preparing for the appeal, the first conference is scheduled well in advance of the deadline for filing briefs.

At the first conference, counsel discuss in dept the strengths and weaknesses of their cases. In addition, "[a]ttorneys should obtain advance authority from their clients to make such commitments as may reasonably be anticipated." At the conclusion of the conference, a staff attorney is expected to give counsel "the benefit of his [or her] views of the merits," and does not hesitate to point out weaknesses or to predict the outcome of the appeal. To promote honest discussion and to avoid any hint of judicial pressure, all participants are prohibited from advising the court of the detailed discussions at the conference. A party that breaches confidentiality is subject to censure.

In the words of former Chief Judge Feinberg, CAMP's success "has been outstanding." In 1989, the program disposed of 601 appeals without briefs or arguments — nearly twenty percent of the total appeals terminated. In more concrete terms, CAMP settles more cases than two judges would normally handle in a year at one-third the cost of two judicial chambers. Early settlement saves large sums for parties by sparing them the expense of briefs and oral argument.

In short, CAMP has achieved its goals. It "does result in the settlement or withdrawal of appeals that would otherwise have to be considered by three-judge panels." It "almost cer-

*Reprinted with permission.

tainly results in faster disposition" of cases that settle and "probably results in faster disposition of appeals that are argued." By a substantial margin, attorneys enjoyed participating in CAMP. Indeed, this pioneer effort at resolving appeals quickly and cheaply has surpassed its objective.

3. Susan FitzGibbon, *Appellate Settlement Conference Programs: A Case Study*, 1993 J. Dispute Res. 57 (1993)*

I. INTRODUCTION

The 1990s may be the decade in which the courts bring alternative dispute resolution in house. Professor Owen Fiss' nightmare that private settlement will rob courts of cases for the dispensation of justice and the furtherance of societal goals has become Professor Carrie Menkel-Meadow's foreboding that the courts will "co-opt" and drain the life from true alternative dispute resolution (ADR) processes. It may be argued that appellate court-sponsored settlement programs dodge both of these criticisms because parties have had a day in court, the process is a form of mediation, and the settlement is thus final only if the parties agree to settle. . . .

[I]n mediation prompted and conducted by an appellate court, the parties, or at least one of them, had originally decided to resort to court, i.e., had decided against settlement. Generally, the parties have gone through discovery, pretrial preparation, and trial. Rules of evidence were observed and rulings on motions as well as the outcome of trial were dictated by rules of law. One or both parties decided to appeal because they lost. At the moment of appeal, the parties are likely to be decidedly less friendly than they were before litigation commenced. . . .

While the majority of reform plans, studies, and legislation focus on court-annexed alternative to trials, appellate courts face similar problems of increasing caseloads and accompanying delays in case resolutions. A widely used alternative to full appellate review is the settlement conference. In 1976, the year of the Pound Conference, the Missouri Court of Appeals for the Eastern District inaugurated its pre-argument settlement program. This Article will describe and evaluate the Settlement Program of the Missouri Court of Appeals for the Eastern District. It should be stressed at the outset that the settlement rate achieved in the program compels the conclusion that the program has been an unqualified success, particularly given the limited resources allocated to the program and the minimal regulatory constraints of the program. The analysis will use the accepted conceptual framework of mediation as the basis of inquiry into the program.

II. BACKGROUND

The Missouri Court of Appeals for the Eastern District (MCA/ED) is one of three district courts comprising the Missouri Court of Appeals, which has general jurisdiction in all cases except those few cases within the exclusive jurisdiction of the Missouri Supreme Court. Based in one of the state's largest metropolitan centers, St. Louis, the Eastern District has 14 judges responsible for cases appealed from 26 counties with a total population of approximately 2.2 million. Although the MCA/ED is an intermediate court, the decisions it renders are final unless the case is transferred to the Missouri Supreme Court. . . .

---

*Reprinted with permission.

III. SETTLEMENT PROGRAM OVERVIEW

A brief description of the Eastern District's Settlement Program will set the stage for discussion and analysis of its components. An active judge of the court, who is released from one-half to two-thirds of the usual case load, administers the program, conducts the settlement conference, and performs post conference follow-up work. Within approximately one week of the filing of an appeal, the Settlement Judge screens the most recently filed civil cases (with some exceptions) to determine matters appropriate for settlement. The Settlement Judge screens the cases by reviewing a one-page statement of the case and either the motion for new trial or a list of issues to be raised on appeal, all of which the MCA/ED requires the appellant to file with the notice of appeal.

During the screening process, the Settlement Judge evaluates the settlement possibilities of each case and makes notes of his impressions. An underlying assumption of the MCA/ED settlement program is that the trial disposition places the case in a completely new light and that, viewed in this light, new opportunities for settlement exist. For each case selected for settlement, the judge creates and maintains a settlement file, which is kept completely separate from the Court's regular records. In cases selected for the settlement docket, the judge notifies the attorneys of record by letter that the case has been set for a settlement conference in the judge's chambers at court within the subsequent three to four weeks. . . .

While attorneys are invited to bring their clients along, the notice states that clients will not be present during the settlement conference unless all parties agree to their attendance. If a client is not present at the court, he or she should be available by telephone. The notice also explains that the Settlement Judge will be disqualified from any further participation in the case if it does not settle. The notice further advises the attorneys that the court may suspend preparation of the trial transcript. If the transcript has been filed, the court may suspend the deadline for the filing of briefs while the case is in the settlement process.

In the conference, the Settlement Judge serves as mediator to facilitate a settlement between counsel. The Settlement Judge attempts to determine whether room for settlement exists and to generate offers acceptable to the clients. To this end, the Settlement Judge may present a personal evaluation of the issues of the case as well as his view of how the court is likely to decide the case.

Throughout the conference, the Settlement Judge acts to diffuse tension and conflict between the sides and may also explore underlying factors and interests that may help or hinder settlement. The Settlement Judge may "caucus" with the attorneys, i.e., hold separate individual meetings with them for more candid discussion of the case. Most conferences last one-half hour [to] . . . one hour. After the conference, if counsel orally settled during the conference or if the possibility of settlement exists, the Settlement Judge retains the case on the settlement docket. If not, the Judge returns the case to the court's regular active docket.

Subsequently, the Settlement Judge will follow-up on the cases still on the settlement docket to determine whether the attorneys have reduced their agreement to writing (if the case has settled) or to determine the status of the attorneys' progress toward settlement. If a case does not settle eventually, the Settlement Judge decides when to return it to the active docket. With this brief sketch of the process in mind, this Article will now focus on analysis of its individual components.

IV. AUTHORITY FOR THE SETTLEMENT CONFERENCE

Missouri Supreme Court Rule 84 serves as the authority for the settlement conference program. It provides that in civil appeals the courts may hold a conference to explore with the parties the possibility of settlement. The MCA/ED has only one other rule applicable to the settlement program. Local Rule A.01 requires the appellant to file a one-page statement of the case and either a list of issues to be raised on appeal or a copy of the motion for new trial. Furnishing this information facilitates the screening by the Settlement Judge of cases for the settlement program. . . . [T]he MCA/ED did not adopt Local Rule A.01 in conjunction with the establishment of the Settlement Program; rather it implemented the rule to gain information for assigning cases to its accelerated docket.

The decision not to have more formal rules for the settlement program was a conscious one. The absence of additional rules contributes to the flexibility of the process and . . . avoids problems of enforcing such rules for non-compliance. A corollary to the decision to have no rules is the absence of sanctions for attorney non-compliance with the process. . . . [T]he court believes that it has the inherent power to issue an order requiring attendance at a Settlement Conference. Even without rules or express sanctions, the court has enjoyed excellent cooperation in the program from the bar.

The MCA/ED is one of the very few state appellate settlement programs with essentially no formal rules (aside from Rule A.01) governing the process. Settlement conference rules in other states range from simple to elaborate and cover a wide spectrum of topics including the filing of a prehearing statement of the case, the purpose of the conference, the notice and timing of the conferences, how attorneys and/or parties may request or be ordered to the conference, how parties may opt out of the conference, who must or may attend the conference, suspension of the briefing schedule, who presides at the conference, the disqualification of the conference judge from participating in the merits of the appeal, the confidentiality of conference discussions, assessment of costs of the process, and sanctions.

Obviously, written rules which spell out the process may assist attorneys and parties in understanding and preparing for a settlement conference. But, as will be seen, the absence of rules does not mean that certain procedures and safeguards do not exist in the Eastern District of Missouri program. The MCA/ED's lack of rules lends the appearance of simplicity and informality to the program, which is perhaps more inviting to attorneys who are already otherwise restricted by an overwhelming variety of procedural rules. . . .

V. PURPOSE OF THE SETTLEMENT CONFERENCE PROGRAM

The MCA/ED established its Settlement Program in response to the increased number of appeals filed. The program aims only to settle cases, thus reducing the number of cases submitted for full appellate review. . . . [T]he MCA/ED program serves both the court's interest in efficiency and the parties' interest in a fair and efficient resolution of the dispute.

The decision to focus only on facilitating settlement in the MCA/ED program may be driven in part by the fact that an active judge of the court, whose time has been described as the most expensive resource in the courthouse, screens the cases and conducts the conferences and follow-up work. The possibility of completely removing the case from the court's docket compensates for the Settlement Judge's release time from working on active docket appeals, arguably more than the possibility of case simplification would. In view of this and the settlement rate of 41 percent for the period of time studied for this Article, the exclusive goal of settlement appears to be a rational and efficient choice.

VI. CASE COVERAGE AND SELECTION

In the MCA/ED, the Settlement Judge selects cases for the program by category and by screening. Criminal cases, juvenile cases, cases in which child custody is the sole issue, and most pro se matters are automatically excluded from the settlement process. Almost all appellate settlement programs categorically exclude criminal matters, which for due process reasons may be viewed as cases inappropriate for the mediation process. Juvenile matters and cases which only involve child custody are also deemed to require full adversarial appellate review in part because these cases raise the State's concerns for the best interests of the child. Matters in which a party is acting pro se are often automatically excluded from appellate settlement program coverage because that party lacks legal training and thus may not be equipped to participate in the process on the same level as an attorney. In addition, pro se litigants often mistakenly believe that a settlement judge or settlement attorney somehow represents and authoritatively speaks for the court, and this misperception of the role of the neutral mediator completely upsets the balance and purpose of mediation.

The Settlement Judge screens other civil cases by reviewing the Rule A.01 statement of the case and either the motion for new trial or the list of issues to be raised on appeal to determine whether they are appropriate for the settlement program. The value of case screening by the Settlement Judge lies in his unique ability to evaluate settlement possibilities on the basis of substantive and procedural expertise as well as his experience on the bench and in the settlement process. . . . [C]ases routinely (but not categorically) deemed too problematic for the settlement program include: injunctions, zoning cases, cases requiring interpretation of an ordinance or resolution of a legislative or corporate body, and cases brought by attorneys who never settle.

The decision categorically to exclude some cases and to screen the rest also represents a conscious process choice among alternatives by the MCA/ED. Review of other appellate settlement programs reveals that some include all civil cases, while other programs include most civil cases with exceptions for, inter alia, constitutional issues and cases involving administrative agencies. In some programs, cases are assigned at random from all of the civil cases filed. Other programs, like that administered by the MCA/ED, engage in a screening process. . . .

The late Judge Irving R. Kaufman, who pioneered the Civil Appeals Management Plan (CAMP) in the Second Circuit Court of Appeals, criticized the screening of cases for the settlement docket on two grounds: (1) he was not convinced that different types of cases have different settlement rates; and (2) he believed that screening somehow conflicts with the concept of "even-handed administration of justice."

The MCA/ED based the decision to screen cases on the experience of the judges involved in the settlement program who concluded that some cases are less amenable to a mediated settlement. For example, zoning cases may be deemed inappropriate for a mediated settlement because the general public interest in zoning decisions requires a public process and a written, reasoned resolution, while cases requiring an ordinance or resolution of a body are not conducive to mediation because one side essentially lacks authority to settle. In his classic analysis of mediation, Lon Fuller also concluded that, for process reasons, certain types of disputes are appropriate for a mediated resolution while others are not. ADR commentator and

District of Columbia Circuit Judge Harry T. Edwards has similarly asserted that certain cases, such as those raising public law issues, should not be resolved in mediation.

Recent recommendations by the Society of Professionals in Dispute Resolution (SPIDR) further support the decision to screen cases from the process. In its Report on Mandatory Dispute Resolution and Settlement Coercion, SPIDR recommended a case-by case selection procedure for mandatory ADR programs to avoid problems of bringing inappropriate cases to the process. It may be concluded that screening cases provides a workable means for the MCA/ED to exclude from the settlement process cases raising issues better resolved by full appellate review and cases which, for a variety of process reasons, are unlikely to be settled in mediation.

Judge Kaufman's concern that parties will somehow perceive bias or unfairness from the selection for the settlement program is unpersuasive. While a broad rule which includes most civil cases in the settlement program may alleviate fear that cases have been "hand picked" for settlement, the interests of efficiency (particularly in a program administered by an active judge as opposed, e.g., to one administered by staff attorneys), the integrity of the Settlement Judge and the program, as well as the foregoing criticisms of overinclusive settlement programs would seem to outweigh this criticism of the screening procedure. A rule requiring mediation of all civil cases also may create the appearance of "just another mandatory step" in the appellate process, and thus actually detract from both the voluntary nature of the process and from truly active rather than mechanical participation of attorneys in the process.

Judicial selection of cases for the settlement conference conducted by the Settlement Judge and the requirement of attorney participation in the process, which the next section addresses in detail, represent the most visible factors distinguishing the MCA/ED process from private mediation in which the parties agree to attempt to resolve a dispute in mediation.

VII. MANDATORY PROCESS AND PROCEDURAL SAFEGUARDS

Once a case is selected for settlement, the MCA/ED mandates participation of attorneys in the settlement conference. Although the MCA/ED process is in that sense mandatory, . . . Settlement Judges perceive it as an invitation to attorneys which creates an opportunity to settle and as an offer to assist in that effort rather than as an order that suggests that the attorneys must settle or should settle the matter. The Settlement Judges are also mindful of the fact that counsel and the parties have probably tried to settle the case earlier in the process, and they appreciate the cooperation of counsel in making an attempt at settlement. . . . Once the Settlement Judge selects a matter for the settlement docket, attorneys may only "opt out" of the procedure if both (or all) sides convince the Settlement Judge that no possibility of settlement exists and that the conference would simply be a wasted effort. So long as one side is amenable to attending the settlement conference, the other attorney(s) will be required to attend. The availability of an "opt out" procedure comports with SPIDR's recommendation that mandatory court-annexed ADR programs provide "consideration of motions for exclusion.". . .

While the majority of cases processed by the MCA/ED program are there because the Settlement Judge mandates the procedure, the program does permit attorneys to "opt in" to the settlement process. If one attorney is interested in utilizing the settlement process, he or she may request that the case be set for a conference; upon request, the Settlement Judge will refrain from disclosing the fact that only one attorney requested inclusion on the settlement docket. This is significant because it is believed that attorneys may hesitate to suggest settlement because their case may then be perceived as weak.

A number of state appellate settlement programs also employ mandatory procedures with provisions for attorneys to request inclusion in the settlement process. The majority of state programs are mandatory, and very few offer settlement conferences on a purely voluntary basis.

In evaluating any mandatory dispute resolution procedure, one must first distinguish mandatory participation in the process, which occurs in the MCA/ED program, from "coercion to settle once participation has begun." . . . The MCA/ED program merely mandates attendance at the conference; no one is required to settle.

[P]articularly in mandatory settlement programs, concern exists for more subtle forms of pressure to settle which may emanate from the position of the person recommending or conducting the settlement procedure or from the existence of deterrents to participation in the judicial process. . . . The MCA/ED program has no express provision for the imposition of sanctions for noncompliance with the settlement process, imposes no costs, as such, on the parties, and bars the Settlement Judge from communicating with the court about cases on the settlement docket. Thus, these forms of coercion are not issues in the MCA/ED program.

Under other settlement program rules, sanctions, including dismissal of the appeal, may be imposed for failure to attend the settlement conference, for failure to file a conference statement (or other documents), or for failure to comply with the order embodying the results of the parties' agreement at the prehearing conference. In one program "appropriate" sanctions may be assessed against attorneys who are grossly unprepared for or unreasonably uncooperative in the settlement conference.

The MCA/ED decision not to impose sanctions for various types of noncompliance with the Settlement Program conforms to the principle of program flexibility, avoids enforcement problems, and alleviates concerns for coercive process. The absence of express sanctions further demonstrate a certain degree of confidence in and respect for members of the bar (and, impliedly, also for the parties) who are being "invited" to cooperate with the court and to assist in yet another attempt to settle the case. Another possible advantage is that attorneys may view and approach a settlement process without sanctions in a more positive and, therefore, genuinely cooperative manner. This is another feature which the MCA/ED program shares with voluntary ADR processes.

Concern for a different "subtle" form of undue coercion arises from the fact that an active judge of the court mandates attorney attendance and conducts the settlement conference. . . . The MCA/ED program disqualifies the Settlement Judge from participating in any way in the merits of the case, bars any communication concerning the case between the Settlement Judge and other members of the court, and requires maintenance of separate settlement files. Thus, participants in the MCA/ED program should have no fear that either their failure to settle or their settlement discussions will influence the ultimate judicial resolution of their case. . . .

Finally why has the MCA/ED implemented a settlement program which provides for mandatory, albeit "invited," attendance rather than voluntary, party initiated attendance? The answer is clearly related to the main purpose of the settlement program from the point of view of the court — to reduce the number of cases requiring full appellate process. For all of the publicity, popularity, and the alleged superiority of ADR methods, to the large part of the general public and to many attorneys it remains an unknown in comparison with the judicial system. The small number of cases in which the attorneys "opt in" to the MCA/ED program suggests that the settlement program would not be routinely utilized to attempt settlements if the process were available on a purely voluntary basis. . . .

A particular benefit of a mandatory settlement program such as the MCA/ED is that the Settlement Judge initiates the process, thus creating the opportunity for the attorneys to stop thinking like adversaries and to seriously consider settlement while also avoiding the appearance of weakness on the part of the other lawyer. Judicial initiation of the process also offers a "face saving" opportunity to settle for a party or attorney who has previously contended that they would never settle this case. . . . In sum, MCA/ED can only be assured of greater efforts to settle cases if the program is mandatory. . . .

VIII. THE ACTIVE JUDGE AS MEDIATOR

In the MCA/ED, an active judge of the court serves as the Settlement Judge. The role of the Settlement Judge is that of a neutral mediator who assists the parties in reaching a settlement. The Settlement Judge generally follows a procedure, similar to that in private mediation, of explaining the process, allowing each side to present his or her view of the issues on appeal, and finally of exploring with counsel the options for settlement.

Unlike private mediation, in the MCA/ED and in most appellate settlement programs, the parties have no choice as to the mediator. In mandatory mediation programs which designate the mediator, there is no marketplace quality control of the process generated by party selection of the neutral. Consequently, commentators Rogers and McEwen have asserted that additional safeguards to insure fair process are necessary. The MCA/ED safeguards are that the mediator is an active judge of the court who must maintain a reputation for fairness in order for the settlement program to flourish and that the Settlement Judge works primarily with attorneys, who are less likely to be intimidated or coerced in the process than the individual parties might be.

Of course, as with private mediation, judges have varying degrees of skill and develop a reputation which either enhances the process or, in the worst-case scenario, makes it a wasteful part of the litigation process. To date, this worst case scenario has been described in the literature only sporadically and anecdotally and is more associated with a trial judge who pushes settlement in a case which he or she would ultimately try. Finally, it should be stressed that one of the oldest and most successful institutional mediation processes in the country, interest mediation of collective bargaining agreements by the Federal Mediation and Conciliation Service (FMCS), is a mediation process which can be viewed as quasi-mandatory because in practice it prompts the parties who are unable to reach agreement to seek the FMCS mediator's assistance.

In private mediation, selection of a neutral decisionmaker is generally based upon, inter alia, the neutral's experience, personal qualities, subject matter expertise, and "capacity to appreciate the dynamics" of the dispute. At the appellate level, such experience and expertise must include an understanding of and familiarity with appellate procedure. Consequently, any neutral selected would likely be an attorney. This is not necessarily true at the trial level where the real alternative to a mediated settlement is an "unassisted" settlement because less than ten percent of cases filed go to trial. Because the "alternative" to an appellate settlement is more likely to be resolution of the appeal by the court, a judge's assessment of how the case may fare in the appellate process is of particular significance. Arguably, if given a choice of neutrals to conduct the mediation, attorneys seeking to settle an appellate case would choose an active appellate judge for his or her unique experience in the judicial resolution of such matters, and, importantly, in the current thinking and working of this court. . . .

In the MCA/ED, the Settlement Judge may offer a personal evaluation of the case, a prediction as to the outcome of the appeal, and an opinion of how the rest of the court would view the case. In light of the fact that the majority of appellate opinions are unanimous, it would seem that the opportunity to have a case evaluated by an active judge of the court would prove invaluable either to fashion a settlement or to prepare briefs and oral arguments.

Assignment of an active judge to the settlement docket prompts criticism on grounds that the process will be coercive and inefficient. . . . [M]any of these fair process questions are resolved by procedures ensuring the disqualification of the judge from participation in deciding the merits and ensuring the confidentiality of the process. In addition to alleviating concern for coercive process, disqualification of the Settlement Judge from the merits of the case also permits the judge to pursue settlement vigorously with counsel uninhibited by the possibility of having subsequently to rule on the merits.

Aside from fair process concerns relating primarily to cases which do not settle, court-annexed settlement programs raise a different question of fairness within the settlement process: Will the Settlement Judge, motivated by the desire for a caseload reduction and a high percentage of settled cases, exceed the authority of a true mediator and force the parties into settlement? Recognizing this concern, the commentary to the ABA Model Code of Judicial Conduct Canon 3(13)(8) provides: "A judge should encourage and seek to facilitate settlement, but parties should not feel coerced into surrendering the right to have their controversy resolved by the courts." . . .

While this concern is valid, it may be exaggerated. A judge who employed undue pressure in the settlement process would quickly gain a reputation which would make most attorneys wary of and resistant to the settlement efforts of that judge and the process, thus sabotaging the judge's effectiveness and goals of the program. The MCA/ED settlement program emphasis on respect for attorneys and cooperation with the bar, evidenced, inter alia, by the Settlement Judge's admonition that the first step in the conference procedure is to "make the attorneys comfortable," by the absence of express sanctions and by the disqualification and confidentiality procedures, indicates that at the very least the MCA/ED design is that the Settlement Judges are more concerned with fair process and good relations with the bar than settlement rates. Moreover, at the trial level, attorneys may fear judicial retribution in other cases if they fail to accede to a judge's pressure to settle in a particular case. Such fears are diminished at the appellate level because there is far less need for contact with and cooperation from the court (*e.g.*, no discovery). Further, because MCA/ED cases are generally decided by decision of the majority of a three judge panel, the odds are that the actual merits of different appeal will outweigh one judge's possible animosity towards an attorney who refused to settle a previous case in the settlement program. Thus, at the appellate level attorneys who fail to settle should have little fear of retribution in subsequent cases.

Assigning an active judge of the court to manage the settlement program and conduct settlement conferences also prompts efficiency considerations. In the MCA/ED program, the Settlement Judge receives one-half to two-thirds of release time to run the settlement program. If the program yields more settled cases annually than a judge would normally handle in one-half to two-thirds of a year it would then seem to be successful. . . .

Employment of retired judges or staff attorneys are the two main" "efficient" alternatives to assignment of an active judge to settle cases. A settlement program conducted by someone other than an active judge obviates the need for release time and for disqualification of the judge from hearing the case on the merits. But confidentiality concerns must be addressed because the settlement program is sponsored by the court, even if an active judge does not mediate the cases.

Programs employing retired judges to conduct settlement conferences have the advantage of a neutral who . . . has the experience, expertise, and stature of a judge and who is not a drain on the resources of the court. However, the possible disadvantages of a retired rather than an active Settlement Judge is that attorneys may perceive active judges as being more in tune with the current thinking of the court than senior judges are and that the reputations of senior judges tend to fade after they retire from the bench. Thus, it may be argued that because of their judicial status and experience, active judges may be more effective mediators in appellate court-annexed settlement programs.

IX. SETTLEMENT CONFERENCE PROCEDURE AND FOLLOW-UP

. . . In the MCA/ED, the conduct of the settlement conference will depend upon the personal style of the Settlement Judge. After introductions and general explanation of the process, the Settlement Judge will establish his understanding and appreciation of the issues and his familiarity with the case. Starting with the appellant's attorney, the Settlement Judge may ask each side for an evaluation of the case on appeal, focussing primarily on the main issues. The Settlement Judge may then provide a "reality check" for the attorneys by, *inter alia,* giving his own evaluation of each issue and his reading of how other members of the court would view the issues, projecting the likelihood of either side prevailing on appeal and exploring the reality of "victory on appeal." These assessments should cause the parties to question the validity of their respective positions and promote movement toward settlement. This may be loosely described as a rights-based approach to mediation, the goal of which is to provide the attorneys with the non-binding evaluation of an experienced neutral as to the likely outcome of the case on appeal.

The Settlement Judge may also refer counsel to specific opinions of the court which may affect the outcome of the case. Counsel may be unfamiliar with the cited cases or may be unaware of how the court is likely to interpret and apply the cited case to their appeal. This practice offers the benefit of either moving the parties to settlement or helping counsel shape a theory of the case on appeal.

In the alterative, after explaining the program, the Settlement Judge may proceed by immediately working to develop viable offers of settlement from each side rather than focussing on the merits of the appeal. This may be loosely viewed as a type of an "interest-based" approach to mediation which focuses more on the underlying and practical needs of the parties and on the development of an objective rationale to support an offer. This approach avoids the risk of erroneous predictions of the case outcome which may diminish the credibility of the Settlement Judge. If the judge is able to refrain from outcome prediction, he also does not run the risk of alienating the "losing" attorney or of encouraging that attorney to attempt to convince the judge and the other side that the case is a winner. Thus, that attorney will be less likely to engage in posturing or to become entrenched in a position.

It has been suggested that mediation may only be beneficial in interest-based controversies in which the parties have an ongoing relationship. Thus, for example, a medical malpractice case based upon a question of rights stemming from a single encounter between the parties would be deemed inappropriate for mediation. Statistics from the MCA/ED dictate a contrary conclusion because the program has settled a significant number of, e.g., medical malpractice cases. The success of court-annexed mediation at the appellate level in such cases may stem from the fact that the trial court decision provides an objective starting point for settlement negotiations and the fact that after trial or summary judgment the parties share a sufficiently intense interest in avoiding a return to the trial court to motivate them to collaborate in the mediational effort. . . .

Following the stated purpose of the conference, the Settlement Judge will attempt to obtain an agreement by counsel at the settlement conference. If this cannot be achieved, the Settlement Judge will try to have the parties develop offers which may be explored with their clients. Although the attorneys are supposed to participate in the conference with authority to settle and with their client available for consultation, the MCA/ED Settlement Judges realize that if completely new or unexplored offers develop, more time may reasonably be needed to assess them.

In many cases, the real work of the settlement program begins after the conference. In this phase, the Settlement Judge will "follow up" on cases in which settlement was achieved but not reduced to writing and on cases in which settlement is still a possibility. Within two to three weeks and at similar intervals thereafter, the Settlement Judge calls the attorneys or has the attorneys call him to discuss the progress in writing the agreement or in negotiations. By this regular contact with counsel, the Settlement Judges continue to work with counsel to achieve settlement and to create deadlines which may motivate the parties to persevere in or to complete the settlement process. The follow-up calls may also be viewed as "telephone caucuses" because they provide an opportunity for the Settlement Judge to explore settlement progress and possibilities with the attorneys individually. Both the deadline and communication functions of the follow-up calls serve to maintain . . . the momentum to settle. Only in unusual cases will the MCA/ED Settlement Judge hold follow-up in person conferences. . . .

X. SETTLEMENT PROGRAM PARTICIPANTS

. . . The MCA/ED program excludes clients from attending the settlement conference mainly because they are not likely to be as objective and dispassionate as their attorneys, because they lack familiarity with the intricacies of the appellate process, and because counsel may be more guarded in settlement negotiations with their clients present. Perhaps domestic relations matters best exemplify the type of cases in which client participation may be counterproductive to settlement.

State and federal appellate settlement programs have handled the question of who participates in the process in a number of ways: some, like the MCA/ED, generally exclude clients from the process, unless the parties agree to their attendance; some allow clients to attend but not to participate in the process; some urge client attendance; some require client attendance; and some even provide for the attendance and participation of non-parties if they may aid the settlement process.

Contrary to the MCA/ED approach, SPIDR has recommended that mandatory settlement programs allow party and attorney participation in the process. The SPIDR Recommendations generally appear to address pre-trial settlement programs. Obviously, if such pre-trial settlement programs are mandatory and final, they eliminate the trial if there is in fact a settlement. The MCA/ED program may be distinguished on two grounds: (1) while the process requires attorney participation, it is designed not to be coercive toward settlement; and (2) because this is an appellate program the parties already have some ruling from the trial court. In this context, it must be reemphasized that the goal of the MCA/ED program is to devise a settlement acceptable to the clients. As such, exclusion of the client from the settlement conference does not translate somehow into exclusion of the client from the settlement decision. In light of these distinctions and this program goal, SPIDR's recommendations of client participation in court-sponsored settlement programs may be viewed as less compelling in the context of the MCA/ED program.

Nevertheless, the practical exclusion of clients from the conference by the MCA/ED program . . . stands in stark contrast to a model of private mediation and to such institutional mediation as that by FMCS. It is suspected that this difference in approach, although explainable by the very nature of the appellate process, may be rooted in the personal experience of those who design and practice in the particular appellate settlement program. For example, client participation in appellate settlement is strongly recommended by Eighth Circuit Settlement Director, John H. Martin, who believes that client involvement significantly enhances the settlement process by minimizing the posturing of attorneys, by generating additional settlement options, by avoiding the delay of communicating offers, and by educating the client about the process. In sum, Mr. Martin asserts that client participation substantially contributes to building momentum to settle. Mr. Martin's strong views on client involvement reflect his 11 years of experience as Settlement Director, but, in this context, it is still noteworthy that he also has had many years of experience as a labor mediator for the Federal Mediation and Conciliation Service.

Professor Leonard L. Riskin, . . . who is also a mediator, shares this enthusiasm for client participation in court annexed settlement conferences to the extent that he recommends that Settlement Judges should require client attendance and encourage their full participation in the process. In making this recommendation, Professor Riskin catalogues the possible risks and benefits which may flow from client participation in settlement conferences, and he notes that evaluation of the asserted risks and benefits may depend on whether or not the client is viewed as a reasonably intelligent individual capable of standing firm for his or her interests. He argues that a decision to exclude clients from the settlement may reflect a view of the settlement process grounded upon a traditional lawyer-client relationship, adversarial negotiation, and coercive intervention by the judicial host, while a decision to include clients may reflect a view of the settlement process based on a participatory lawyer-client relationship, problem solving negotiation, and facilitative intervention by the judicial host. Professor Riskin believes that the possible benefits of client inclusion outweigh the possible risks, and that clients' interests are best served by allowing them to participate fully in the settlement negotiations. Professor Riskin further asserts that in the conference the Settlement Judges should encourage full client participation and should enhance that participation by focussing on underlying interests, thus providing an opportunity for problem-solving negotiations. . . .

XI. TIMING, PLACE, AND COST OF SETTLEMENT

The MCA/ED initiates the settlement conference procedure early in the appellate process to facilitate settlements and to avoid, as much as possible, costs of transcripts and briefs. . . . There is widespread agreement that more momentum and opportunity exists to settle matters at the earliest possible stage of the case, because the parties have invested less in the process and they and their attorneys tend to be less entrenched in their positions.

As to setting, the vast majority of MCA/ED settlement conferences are conducted in-person in the judge's chambers or, occasionally, in a conference room at the court. In some cases, the Settlement Judge has waived attendance at the conference but has required the attorneys to call and consult with the judge by telephone. The current Settlement Judge allows some conferences to be conducted over the telephone, and they mainly occur in cases involving out-of-state attorneys. . . . [F]ollowing the successful lead of the Sixth Circuit, the Tenth Circuit has implemented a settlement program that holds conferences almost exclusively by telephone. A survey of attorneys in the Sixth Circuit who participated in the settlement program revealed a strong preference for the telephone conference procedure. While this technique would seem to be particularly convenient for attorneys (and clients) who would not have to leave their offices, attorneys in the Tenth Circuits who practice in the court's locale (Denver) have responded in questionnaires that they would prefer an in-person conference. On one hand the telephone conference may be sufficient to provide clues of the thinking of the settlement judge or attorney and so to provide the final "push" for settlement. But it is doubted overall that it can be as effective as face-to-face discussion between the parties or their attorneys and the mediator. The telephone conference method certainly does not draw upon the methods of mediation which precede court annexed ADR and which rely heavily upon interaction among participants.

In line with SPIDR's recommendations, the cost of the settlement process is the same as for the appellate process. No additional charges are assessed so that, in essence, the only cost of the settlement program is the attorney's time preparing for and participating in the settlement conference and follow-up process. Arguably, participation in the program yields a benefit (rather than a cost) even if the case does not settle because the attorneys gain some insight into their case or into the court from the settlement discussions with an active judge of the court. Moreover, participation in the settlement conference program may contribute to settlement between the parties outside of the program. The program is completely administered by the court, thus giving the court full control of the process.

XII. FAIR PROCESS

Fairness in mediation has come to be defined as a process which preserves the parties' choice to settle. . . . The safeguards of the integrity of the MCA/ED Settlement Program provide the answer to a variety of concerns for fairness in mediation in general and in mandatory, court-annexed settlement programs in particular. . . .

XIII. REVIEW OF MCA/ED SETTLEMENT DATA AND FINDINGS

In preparing this Article, the author collected available information from 1,350 cases selected for and processed in the settlement program in order to evaluate how the program works in fact. From the data collected, the author primarily sought to determine whether the MCA/ED Settlement Program was achieving its stated goal of settling cases. The data were also reviewed to determine which types of cases were likely to be chosen for the settlement program, which cases, of those so chosen, were most likely to settle, and the length of time which the settlement process took.

Information and statistics . . . were drawn from the 1,350 cases selected for and processed in the Settlement Program from June 1983 through June 1989. . . . Data concerning these 1,350 cases were collected from the court's docket sheets and from the separately maintained settlement files and settlement notebooks of the two judges who served as Settlement Judge for this period. The judges retained these files and notebooks for the sole purpose of having data for a study of the program. It is noteworthy that these settlement files and notebooks were maintained in the judges' offices and were physically separate from the court's regular active docket files. . . .

In general, the Settlement File for a case contained copies of the notice on appeal, a statement of the case, a list of issues on appeal or the motion for a new trial, as well as copies of the correspondence concerning the settlement program including letters notifying counsel that the case had been selected for a settlement conference, advising the court reporter to stop (or to resume) transcript preparation, advising counsel that the case was being returned to the active docket and specifying a new due date for the transcript, legal file or briefs, or thanking counsel for settling the case. The Settlement Judge's notebooks were maintained in order of settlement conference date on notebook sheets which listed, inter alia, the case caption and docket number, the judge's impressions and description of follow-up work, and whether the case had settled or not. Each judge also maintained a separate listing of settled cases with cases listed according to the month in which the case actually settled. . . . [T]he Settlement Judges only counted as settled cases which settled as a result of the program. The settlement count included settled cases in which attorneys personally attended settlement conferences as well as cases settled by telephone consultation, and excluded cases which ultimately were redocketed.

Subsequent review of the court's regular docket sheets for each of these cases confirmed the filing date of the appeal, and often confirmed or described the case type. The final disposition of unsettled cases and the disposition date for all cases were also taken from the court's docket sheets. The final dispositions of the cases were categorized as follows: settled by the MCA/ED program, disposed of by judicial opinion, transferred to the Missouri Supreme Court, voluntarily dismissed by the parties, remanded to the trial court, or dismissed for procedural default on motion either of the court or of a party. For purposes of this study, a case was counted as settled on the date the court granted whatever motion the parties filed to dismiss the matter (e.g., voluntary dismissal, remand, procedural default, etc). If a case was transferred to the Missouri Supreme Court, the date that the transfer was granted was listed as the date of disposition. For all other dispositions — by opinion, by voluntary dismissal, by remand, by procedural default on motion of the court or of a party — the date of the court's mandate indicating that all activity in the case had ceased was listed as the disposition date.

The cases reviewed were classified by case type. When neither the settlement file nor the docket sheet indicated the case type, the actual opinion was consulted for this information. If no opinion existed, the case type was listed as "none." Cases were assigned to one of . . . six categories: Administrative, Contract, Domestic Relations, Property, Tort, and Other, which includes all other types of cases as well as cases for which case type information could not be found. . . . [Twenty-eight] percent of the cases on the Settlement docket were tort cases, 26 percent of the cases were domestic relations cases, and 23.6 percent of the cases were contract cases. . . .

(T)he Settlement Program settled a total of 554 cases for a settlement rate of 41 percent.

The number and percentage of cases settled demonstrates that the MCA/ED is successfully achieving settlements. The settlement rate may also be viewed as evidence that settlements achieved in the MCA/ED program are voluntary, even though attendance is mandatory. The settlement number and rates are a precise reflection of the program's effect because only those cases actually settled within the program were counted as settled. Some appellate settlement programs count as settled any case which is not disposed of by a judicial opinion. If the MCA/ED figures were so adjusted, the program could boast of a 54.6 percent rate of settlement. It must be noted that the MCA/ED Settlement Conference and follow-up, in fact, may have led to or at least contributed to the number of voluntary dismissals, remands and cases dismissed by procedural default, but when the Settlement Judge finally removed these cases from the Settlement Docket and returned them to the active docket, they were no longer counted as settled by the program.

As to the settlement rate by type of case, it is noteworthy that tort cases had a higher than average settlement rate of 45.2 percent (4.2 points above the average), while domestic relations cases settled at a rate slightly below the average, 38.2 percent, and the contract case settlement rate of 36.1 percent was 4.9 points below the average. The higher-than-average settlement rates of administrative and property cases are not significant because each category represented such a small number and percentage of cases. . . .

The MCA/ED Settlement Conference program . . . processed cases on the Settlement Docket in a timely fashion. On the average, settlement notices setting the case for conference were mailed within 19 days of the filing of the appeal. This is particularly impressive because it means that the Settlement Judge was able to screen all of the eligible cases filed and to dispatch notice of the conference to the parties in less than three weeks. The data further indicate that the Settlement Conferences were held promptly thereafter — on average, within 26 days of the Settlement Notice. Thus, if it could be clearly determined at the Settlement Conference that a case had no chance of settling, the case could be returned to the regular docket with the parties having lost, on average, only 44 days. In view of the fact that the program offers 41 percent of the cases selected the opportunity to completely resolve the dispute in approximately four months, the average 44-day delay for cases which do not settle does not seem burdensome. . . .

(I)t took approximately 64 days for these cases to be returned to the regular appellate process. This figure reflects the additional time which elapsed after conference during which it appeared that the matter still had settlement possibilities.

If this time (64 days) from filing to return to the active docket is deducted from the average time in which settlement program cases were disposed of by opinion (396 days) the average time for case resolution by opinion is 332 days. Even if this figure is somewhat inflated, it still may be inferred that a party may wait as long as ten months for an opinion resolving a case to be issued. By comparison, the Settlement Program offers the opportunity to resolve a case in less than half that time (130 days).

The following comparison demonstrates the success of the MCA/ED Settlement Program from the court's perspective. For fiscal years 1983 through 1989, the average number of appeals disposed of per judge per year was 92.8 in the MCA/ED. For the period studied herein, the settlement judges settled an average of 97.8 cases annually in only two-thirds to one-half of their time. In sum, the statistics show the efficiency and success of the MCA/ED settlement program from the point of view of the parties and the court.

XIV. PROPOSAL OF A NATIONAL REPORTING SYSTEM

In light of the national push for various forms of court-annexed ADR, it is important to establish some measure of the efficiency of these programs. Currently, there are at least 19 active appellate settlement programs in intermediate appellate courts in 12 states. In addition, the majority of federal appellate courts have instituted or are contemplating institution of settlement programs. At least a part of the value of these programs could be demonstrated by establishment of a national reporting system of cases settled by each of these appellate programs. . . .

XV. CONCLUSION

Court-annexed ADR is a simple and predictable response to the increased use of litigation to resolve disputes and to solve societal problems. It builds on proven and traditional methods of extrajudicial settlement; it reflects the fact that parties frequently settle their differences even after they resorted to court and commenced litigation. At the same time, court-annexed ADR alleviates the need for a vast amount of new judges or for new, specialized tribunals, that is, for a wholesale change in the existing system and tradition. . . .

In the current developmental stage of court-annexed ADR, it is quite clear that different forms of ADR are used, including those that fit only the very broad notion of ADR, such as small claims courts. However, when the ADR form used is one which results in a private settlement which is final in the sense that it is enforceable as such, the analysis of that form must follow a two-pronged inquiry. One inquiry is whether the chosen form of the court-annexed ADR is what it is meant to be. In the case of court-annexed mediation, the question is whether it is a process leading to a consensual settlement or whether it is an unstated process of coercion which would deprive the parties either of the right to have a day in court or of the right to dispose freely of their dispute by other means. The other inquiry is whether the court annexed mediation satisfies the stated purpose, i.e., whether it is efficient and results in a fair number of settlements.

The MCA/ED Settlement Program is unquestionably a consensual process which follows a private mediation model in its techniques and in substance and which is free of coercion. It does not compromise the right of parties to proceed with the appeal or to settle the appeal if they wish. It is indeed nothing more and nothing less than mediation, albeit with prominent features of "neutral-expert evaluation." The mandatory aspect of the process—its instigation by the court—does not in its effects differ appreciably from proven mandatory resorts to mediation based on a clause in a contract, or on an institutional initiation of mediation by FMCS based upon the expiration of a collective bargaining agreement. The Settlement Judge's interventions in the process are free of sanctions and do not differ from interventions by private or institutional mediators. To the extent that one may seek to uncover various subtle forms of authority in the judge's initiation of the process or interventions during the process, the wide use of the process, and the increasing familiarity of the bar with the process which functions as it is supposed to function, should eliminate any fears in this respect.

The practical exclusion of clients from participation in the MCA/ED Settlement Process represents a rational component of the MCA/ED program design. It is clear that, in general, client presence during and participation in mediation can substantially contribute to building consensus and achieving settlement. But the MCA/ED experience demonstrates that, at least at the appellate level, the exclusion of clients does not detract from success in the settlement process in part because on appeal the issues are likely to be better defined and to involve more technical legal questions than at the pre-trial stage. Consequently, issues presented may be addressed more expeditiously by the attorney representatives and the Settlement Judge, whose time is a precious commodity. Thus, in the appellate process which deals mostly with issues of law, the attorneys are in fact in a similar position with respect to familiarity with the client's interests and thinking as, for example, middle level managers would be in a typical interest mediation designed to reach a bargain quite different from a bargain about already developed isolated legal issues.

The settlement rate proves the efficiency of the process and accommodates the basic purpose formulated by the court and by the national discussion on court-annexed ADR and is a measure of the objective and significant success of the program. . . . The MCA/ED Settlement Program is a successful program which does not compromise the public interest or the traditional dispensation of justice by the courts or the freedom of parties to resolve their disputes as they wish.

Chapter 16

Court-Annexed ADR: Issues and Options

CASE STUDY

(Adapted from: *MacPherson v. Buick Motor Co.*)

The defendant, Buick Motor Co., is a manufacturer of automobiles. Buick Motor Co. sold an automobile to a retail dealer. The retail dealer resold the automobile to Donald/Donna MacPherson, the plaintiff.

At about 11:00 P.M. on a Wednesday night, the plaintiff was driving the automobile when suddenly, the front driver's side of the vehicle slammed to the ground causing the vehicle to spin out of control and flip over several times landing on its side. Donald/Donna MacPherson was thrown out of the vehicle and injured. When the police came to the scene of the accident they saw, in the distance, the plaintiff walking in a swaying and unsteady manner along the side of the road. He/She was walking away from the scene of the accident. The officers were not sure if the plaintiff was injured so they ran to him/her. As they approached him/her they noticed that his/her head was bleeding and bruised. The officers urged the plaintiff to wait for an ambulance to arrive so that he/she could have his/her injuries treated and, if necessary, he/she could be taken to a hospital. The plaintiff refused and assured the officers that he/she was not in need of medical treatment.

MacPherson told the officers that he/she lived only a few minutes down the road and would walk home. The officers offered to drive him/her home. However, MacPherson laughed and declined the offer, stating that he/she had very nosey neighbors and that if he/she were escorted home in a police car the neighborhood would be abuzz with rumors and gossip.

Before allowing MacPherson to walk home the officers took a statement from him/her regarding the cause of the accident. MacPherson said, "There was a loud "BANG!", as though the tire had exploded and the vehicle slammed to the ground and began to flip over." The officers had a tow truck remove the vehicle from the road and they went to the police station to file their report.

The following Monday, MacPherson contacted an attorney regarding the accident. The attorney had an inspection performed on the vehicle and found that the tire was made of defective rubber. But the inspection also indicated that the rubber probably would have been suitable for the driving conditions encountered by MacPherson on the night of the accident.

A. Introduction

The previous chapter provided an introduction to the major court-annexed ADR procedures. This chapter addresses general questions about the use of such procedures by the courts. The first topic is constitutional constraints on mandatory court-ordered ADR. The one fundamental limitation is that the process must be nonbinding on the parties.

The second topic is judicial settlement conferences, a formal name for what courts have done long before the Federal Rules of Civil Procedure and similar state rules provided formal names for judical efforts to effect case settlements. While the materials in this section focus on judicial settlement conferences, they offer wider application. Judge Wayne Brazil's wise observations and advice about effective lawyering in judicial settlement conferences will be very helpful to attorneys in any form of facilitated negotiation. The duty of parties to appear at a settlement conference, and the authority of representatives to settle a case, has resulted in interesting and important cases.

It is clear that courts can order litigants to participate in various forms of nonbinding ADR. Such an order then presents the question of whether a party can be required to do more than appear, or whether there is a further duty to participate in "good faith." Assuming such a duty exists, how should a court determine noncompliance, and what sanctions are appropriate? Even this brief statement of the issues suggests the absence of easy answers. The chapter closes with an examination of the questions surrounding the application of state law by federal courts in diversity cases.

B. Constitutional Limitation on Compulsory Court-Annexed ADR

1. Dwight Golann, *Making Alternative Dispute Resolution Mandatory: The Constitutional Issues*, 68 Or. L. Rev. 487 (1989)*

This Article covers situations in which statutes or court rules unilaterally impose ADR on disputants, including popular forms of "court-annexed" or "court-related" dispute resolution. . . . [It] deals principally with controversies involving legal causes of action. . . . Because ADR without adjudication cannot result in a mandatory outcome, and because some of the most important constitutional guarantees apply only to civil suits, the use of mandatory ADR in such situations is much less likely to present constitutional problems. [T]he analysis here deals primarily with the application of compulsory ADR to disputes involving civil claims. This Article focuses on three leading forms of dispute resolution: mediation, arbitration, and the summary jury trial.

[T]his Article is organized by constitutional principles rather than by particular forms of ADR. It consists of the following sections: Models of Mandatory ADR, The Right of Jury Trial, Separation of Powers, Due Process and Access to the Courts, The Right to Equal Protection, and Federal-State Relations. . . . The Article concludes by identifying the constitutional boundaries within which ADR designers are free to experiment with new processes to resolve civil disputes.

---

*Reprinted with permission.

THE RIGHT OF JURY TRIAL

One of the most serious constitutional questions raised by proposals to make dispute resolution mandatory is the potential impairment of a litigant's right to a jury trial. Access to a jury in federal civil cases is guaranteed by the seventh amendment to the United States Constitution, which provides that . . . litigants are entitled to have a claim presented to a jury if the claim would have received a jury trial under the common law of England at the time the Constitution was ratified. The seventh amendment also guarantees jury trials to newly created causes of action which closely resemble common law claims. The seventh amendment does not apply to litigation in state courts, but . . . the constitutions of forty-eight states provide generally that the right to jury trial shall be preserved inviolate. . . . The only forms of ADR not likely to involve jury issues are those created to deal with statutory claims. . . . Examples of the latter include mandatory mediation programs for divorce, child custody disputes, and administrative arbitration of claims for government benefits.

A. Analysis of Existing Law

The key factors in analyzing the constitutionality of ADR are, first, whether a process applies to legal causes of action and, second, the extent to which the outcome of the process, as well as participation in it, is mandatory. If a dispute does not involve a legal claim, its diversion to mandatory ADR raises no federal jury issue—the seventh amendment applies by its terms only to suits at common law.

1. Binding ADR

Any form of ADR that applies to civil claims and which has a final and binding outcome on the disputants cannot be applied to jury claims without violating constitutional requirements. This conclusion is true because no form of ADR provides a jury trial. Neither mediation nor arbitration resembles a jury proceeding, and even the mechanism which comes closest, the summary jury trial, does not satisfy constitutional standards.

Because ADR does not provide jury trials, the only way to apply binding dispute resolution to jury claims is to transform those claims so that they no longer carry jury trial rights. For example, the right of an employee to sue his employer in tort for job-related injuries has been abolished in many states and replaced by worker's compensation statutes. Under such laws, an employee no longer needs to prove employer negligence in order to recover, but must submit all other issues concerning his injury claim to binding arbitration by an administrative agency. The traditional jury trial has been eliminated as an option, as courts have held that removal of the element of fault from worker's compensation actions has transformed the actions to such an extent that they need not be tried to a jury. Similarly, no-fault automobile statutes, which abolish the right to sue in tort in certain circumstances, have been held not to violate jury trial guarantees.

2. Nonbinding Processes

[M]ost court-related mandatory ADR programs are nonbinding. Such programs may consist simply of preconditions on access to a jury, or may include penalties designed to discourage the exercise of trial rights. The question is whether such requirements, although theoretically nonbinding, may constitutionally impair litigants' access to juries. . . . The United

States Supreme Court has repeatedly interpreted the seventh amendment to allow innovations in civil procedure unknown to the common law. As Justice Brandeis once observed:

> [T]he Seventh Amendment . . . does not require that old forms of practice and procedure be retained. . . . New devices may be used to adapt the ancient institution to present needs and to make of it an efficient instrument in the administration of justice. Indeed, such changes are essential to the preservation of the right.

[T]he Supreme Court has applied a reasonableness standard to evaluate claims that procedural innovations violate jury rights. Under this test, changes will be upheld even if they somewhat delay or burden a litigant's access to a jury, so long as jury trials remain available to persistent litigants. State courts have interpreted their constitutions to impose tests of historical precedent and reasonableness which are similar to the federal doctrines. . . .

The leading precedent concerning the effect of nonbinding ADR processes on jury rights [is] *Capital Traction v. Hof,* 174 U.S. 1 (1899). *Capital Traction* involved a tort claim against a street railway company. A local statute required such cases to be tried first before a jury and a justice of the peace. After the proceeding was concluded, either party could reject the jury's verdict and obtain a second jury trial presided over by a judge, subject to the requirement that appellants file bonds to secure payment of any awards against them. This early ADR procedure was apparently designed to conserve the time of judges, and perhaps to reduce delay for litigants, by diverting jury trials to justices of the peace. [The Supreme Court upheld this procedure, and observed:]

> [I]t is not "trial by Jury," but "the right of trial by jury," which the Amendment declares "shall be preserved." It does not prescribe at what stage of an action a trial by jury must, if demanded, be had; or what conditions may be imposed upon the demand of such a trial, consistently with preserving the right to it.

[G]iven the fact that no major form of mandatory ADR involves burdens greater than the full-scale preliminary trial format upheld in *Capital Traction,* it is extremely unlikely that an ADR participation requirement without more would violate the seventh amendment. In fact, lower federal courts have sustained various court-related arbitration requirements in reliance on these cases. . . .

Modern civil practice also supports this conclusion. Discovery proceedings can impose delays, legal and personal costs, and stress which exceed most forms of court related ADR, yet discovery has never been considered an impermissible burden on jury trial rights. The Federal Rules of Civil Procedure, for example, allow litigants to require their opponents, and even nonparty witnesses, to participate in depositions that are often as burdensome as involvement in court-annexed arbitration or summary jury trials. Modern rules of procedure also authorize judges to require litigants to participate in settlement negotiations, which may involve time commitments similar to mediation. . . . As long as modern discovery processes are permitted in jury cases, it is difficult to argue that mandatory participation in court-related ADR poses a serious seventh amendment problem.

The most difficult questions concerning impairment of jury trial rights arise from ADR penalties, including cost-shifting provisions, security requirements, and admission of ADR results at trial.

Cost-Shifting Provisions. Cost-shifting provisions discourage disputants from opting for litigation by requiring them to pay, as a condition of appeal, some portion of the cost of ADR or of any subsequent litigation. This expense may take the form of opponents' attorneys' fees or the fees of ADR neutrals. No Supreme Court precedent directly addresses the issue of ADR cost shifting . . . [but] liability for fees formed part of the right to jury trial at English common law. Dozens of modern federal statutes also authorize cost shifting, including attorneys' fees. It seems difficult to argue, therefore, that cost shifting in connection with mandatory ADR violates federally guaranteed jury trial rights. . . .

Security Requirements. . . . The effects of ADR security requirements on jury trial rights are not significantly different from those of other forms of prejudgment security commonly used in state and federal litigation, such as property attachments, trustee process of bank accounts, and wage garnishments. Nothing indicates that such prejudgment security devices raise any serious issue of impairment of jury rights, and ADR security requirements ordinarily should not do so either. . . .

Admission of ADR Results or Testimony at Trial. . . . The use of an auditor's findings at trial most closely resembles the introduction of the results of court-related arbitration, but the reasoning . . . applies by analogy to the introduction of a mediator's opinion or the verdict of a summary jury.

Federal Rule of Civil Procedure 53(e)(3) institutionalizes the admissibility of ADR results in modern litigation, stating explicitly that "[i]n an action to be tried by a jury . . . [the master's] findings upon the issues submitted to [the master] are admissible as evidence of the matters found and may be read to the jury. . . ." Rule 53(e)(3) has withstood seventh amendment challenges in federal courts. Federal Rule of Evidence 706 provides additional support for the use of ADR results at trial, authorizing the court to retain neutral experts to investigate and testify on complex matters. Such testimony is routinely admitted in both bench and jury trials. . . .

Some statutes take the admission of ADR results one step further by imposing a rebuttable presumption that the pretrial finding is correct. Where the ADR expert makes a finding on the merits of a dispute, the effect of such a statute may be to shift the burden of proof. The courts have upheld such shifts in burden against jury trial impairment arguments. It should be stressed that the [judicial] analysis rests on the assumption that if the opinion of an ADR moderator is introduced at trial, opposing parties will be allowed to cross-examine the moderator. Some mandatory programs, however, permit ADR results to be introduced but do not allow the moderator to be called for cross-examination. . . .

SEPARATION OF POWERS

One of the primary goals of ADR is to channel disputes away from courtrooms and, in most instances, away from judges. Doing so raises the question of whether compulsory dispute resolution violates the separation of powers clause of the United States Constitution or its state law counterparts. . . .

The issue of encroachment or aggrandizement typically associated with separation of powers—clashes between branches of government over important political issues is largely absent from the field of ADR. Mandatory dispute-resolution initiatives have resulted less from any desire of Congress to usurp judicial functions or to control the outcome of cases than from a shared legislative and judicial dissatisfaction with the present operation of the court system. . . .

A. The Scope of Article III

. . . The category of claims required to be submitted to article III courts is similar, but not identical, to the class of claims carrying jury trial rights. "Core" claims are to be distinguished from "public rights" litigation, in which the cause of action is premised on a public statute and the government is usually a party. The Supreme Court has held that public claims need not be decided by article III courts, on the theory that Congress could have assigned such decisions to the legislative or executive branches without referring them to traditional adjudication at all. In certain circumstances, however, even traditional "core" claims may be channelled to non-article III courts.

If article III applies to a dispute, it requires that the case be decided by a judge who meets minimum constitutional requirements, including life tenure and protection against diminution of salary. Because article III concerns only "cases [and] controversies," ADR mechanisms that are not applied to civil causes of action do not present any federal separation of powers concern. Most federal court-related dispute resolution programs, however, deal with "core" civil causes of action which are subject to article III, such as state common law tort, contract, and property claims. Furthermore, most ADR neutrals do not meet article III requirements. Thus, separation of powers issues are present in many forms of federal court-related ADR.

B. Federal Processes

1. Binding ADR

ADR mechanisms with binding outcomes consist primarily of forms of arbitration. Such processes typically involve adjudication of cases by administrative law judges and attorneys serving on an ad hoc basis, who plainly do not meet minimum article III tenure and income-protection requirements. The issue, therefore, is whether any principle allows common law claims in federal courts to be channelled to binding arbitration.

One possibility is to characterize the claim as a "public right" not subject to article III protection In *Crowell v. Benson*, the Supreme Court held that a federally administered workmen's compensation program for injured merchant seamen involved public rights rather than common law claims. Cases arising from the program could therefore be sent to binding arbitration before an administrative agency without violating article III.

[I]n *Thomas v. Union Carbide Agricultural Products*, the Court decided that disputes over federally created compensation rights for pesticide makers could also be routed to binding arbitration. Although the actual disputes in *Union Carbide* were between private parties, the Court reasoned that because Congress need not have created compensation rights at all, the use of arbitration to settle such disputes did not violate the separation of powers clause.

The Supreme Court has recognized that even common law disputes may sometimes be diverted to binding processes that do not meet article III standards. In *Commodity Futures Trading Commission v. Schor*, for example, the Court upheld the imposition of binding arbitration on disputes between commodities futures customers and their brokers, although one of the claims sent to arbitration was a "core" state law cause of action. The Court ruled that there was no absolute prohibition on "the adjudication of Article III business in a non-Article III tribunal," stating that the key issue was the "practical effect that the congressional action will have on the constitutionally assigned role of the federal judiciary."

Schor emphasized five factors which minimized article III concerns and permitted the use of binding ADR in that setting: (1) the program dealt with a limited area of the law and did not involve any grant of general jurisdiction to an alternative mechanism; (2) the agency could not implement its orders, but had to apply to a federal court for enforcement; (3) factual findings could be overturned by the reviewing court if they were against the weight of the evidence; (4) all legal rulings were subject to de novo court review; and (5) the agency had no other judicial powers. In essence, the Court allowed disputes in a specialized subject area to be sent to non-article III adjudication, in deference to congressional policy and on the condition that arbitrators' decisions as to law, fact, and remedies would be subject to close judicial review.

Broad-based ADR programs, such as ones which impose arbitration on monetary claims below a defined amount, would probably not meet the limited subject-area criterion of Schor, suggesting that binding outcomes could not be imposed in most existing federal court-related ADR programs. Public rights, however, could be channelled to binding ADR because they are not subject to article III. Even some "core" claims could be sent to binding dispute resolution if the program applied only to a narrow range of cases, allowed courts to scrutinize ADR results on a discretionary basis, and was supported by a strong legislative statement of purpose.

2. Nonbinding Processes

The other major category of compulsory ADR consists of programs that apply to civil claims but have nonbinding outcomes, including most forms of court-related ADR. If a program is truly nonbinding, requiring only that parties participate in it as a condition of access to court, it does not involve the exercise of judicial power, and thus does not pose article III concerns. For example, mediation does not ordinarily result in any decision by the mediator. Advisory arbitration and summary jury trials lead to decisions, but ones which may be rejected by the disputants. These models do not incorporate the kind of compulsion which is implicit in article III adjudication. Mere ADR precondition requirements, therefore, do not appear to pose serious separation of powers issues.

. . . Absent direct precedent, a court should analyze the separation of powers issues raised by ADR penalty clauses in much the same manner as it reviews their impact on jury trial rights. . . . The similar motivations of the separation of powers clause and the seventh amendment suggest that a "reasonableness" analysis similar to that used under the seventh amendment and discussed in the preceding section should also be applied to the separation of powers issues raised by ADR penalty clauses. That analysis supports the forms of penalties commonly used in court-related programs.

DUE PROCESS AND ACCESS TO THE COURTS

. . . [F]orms of ADR designed to provide more efficient adjudication, such as arbitration, usually do so by omitting steps traditionally associated with adjudicatory procedure, while mediative processes reject basic assumptions of the adversarial model of adjudication. Both of these ADR systems raise the question of whether mandatory devices comply with the federal due process clause and corresponding provisions of state law.

The due process clause of the Constitution, which governs state court litigation through the fourteenth amendment, applies to deprivations of "life, liberty or property." Liberty and property interests are involved in most current forms of civil dispute resolution. Significant issues include whether various forms of mandatory ADR cause deprivations significant enough to require compliance with the due process clause, and what due process principles require of ADR in particular circumstances. The discussion which follows is divided into three categories: ADR processes that do not involve civil claims, processes that apply to civil claims and are binding, and processes that apply to claims but the outcomes of which are to some degree nonbinding. The last category includes most forms of court-related ADR.

A. Disputes Not Involving Civil Claims

Disputes, especially in the field of labor relations, are sometimes subjected to forms of mandatory dispute resolution without the further right to adjudicate the controversy if ADR is unsuccessful. Unlike jury trial and separation of powers guarantees, the due process clause may apply to the use of ADR in controversies that do not involve a civil cause of action. The question in such situations is whether mere compelled participation in an ADR procedure can amount to a serious enough deprivation of a liberty or property interest to invoke due process requirements.

In this context, the situation of claimants and that of persons disputing claims should be distinguished. Persons given the right to compel an adversary to participate in ADR, but not to obtain a coercive decision, might argue that the due process clause requires that all civil "rights" be accompanied by guaranteed access to an adjudicatory procedure with a binding result. It is highly unlikely, however, that such a contention would be accepted.

B. Binding ADR

In cases involving arbitration of property rights, the requirements of the due process clause have been interpreted as flexible, if not amorphous. The Supreme Court has characterized the right as "an opportunity to be heard at a meaningful time and in a meaningful manner" which is "appropriate to the nature of the case."

The Court expressed . . . openness to nontraditional decisionmaking in another government benefits decision, *Walters v. National Ass'n of Radiation Survivors*. That case involved a due process challenge to a federal law which effectively barred applicants for veterans' disability benefits from hiring lawyers to assist them. The Veterans' Administration system, in the words of the Court, "does not contemplate the adversary mode of dispute resolution utilized by courts in this country." In lieu of providing attorneys, the system first allowed veterans to file claims with the assistance of a comprehensive system of volunteer agents, and second, gave them the right to an oral hearing before an agency board required to assist them in developing their cases and to resolve any evidentiary doubts in their favor. In a comment applicable to almost any legislatively adopted form of mandatory ADR, the *Walters* Court noted:

> [G]reat weight must be accorded to the [g]overnment interest at stake here. The flexibility of our approach in due process cases is intended in part to allow room for other forms of dispute resolution; with respect to the individual interests at stake here legislatures are to be allowed considerable leeway to formulate such processes without being forced to conform to a rigid constitutional code of procedural necessities.

The Court stressed that because of the government's strong interest in experimenting with dispute resolution, "an extraordinarily strong showing of probability of error under the present system — and the probability that the presence of [additional procedural protections] would sharply diminish that possibility — would be required to justify striking down the challenged statute." It also noted that no single example of error could support a due process attack because "a process must be judged by the generality of cases to which it applies, and therefore, process which is sufficient for the large majority of a group of claims is by constitutional definition sufficient for all of them." The Court concluded that the practical exclusion of lawyers from the veterans' benefits hearing system did not violate due process requirements.

Although the Court has also applied due process principles to private adjudication, it has not described the minimum standards for such processes with any specificity. Due process requirements in the context of public benefits disputes, however, where the state is an interested party as well as the designer or administrator of the mechanism, should be more exacting than the criteria applied to private litigation where the government has no stake in the outcome. Thus, any binding ADR mechanism that meets the criteria used for public benefits decisions should be adequate for private disputes as well. . . .

The [Supreme Court] decisions . . . do not specify the due process elements which must be incorporated in ADR mechanisms, but they contain important themes. First, the cases emphasize that due process is a flexible concept adaptable to the circumstances of particular disputes. Indeed, the Court has been willing not only to streamline the traditional adversary model, but to abandon it entirely in certain circumstances. Second, the policy concerns cited in approving new processes are very similar to those cited by proponents of alternative dispute resolution. For example, the Court has cited the value of expert non-legal decisionmaking, lower litigation costs, speedy decisions, and avoidance of the disruptive effect of adversarial hearings on allied social institutions and on the litigants themselves. Even where the Supreme Court has not endorsed the value of a particular procedure, it has stressed the importance of judicial deference to a legislative decision to experiment with it. . . .

C. Nonbinding Processes

A third analytic category consists of mandatory ADR programs that process civil claims, but do not impose binding outcomes. This category includes most forms of court-related ADR. As noted in the previous section, arbitration can be designed to satisfy due process principles even if a de novo trial is not provided. However, processes such as court-related arbitration, the summary jury trial, and, particularly, mediation do not provide adjudicatory due process. Instead, such mechanisms use a two-step approach to meet constitutional concerns — they require participation in processes that may not meet constitutional standards, but permit dissatisfied disputants to obtain due process through a de novo court hearing. The issue, then, is whether ADR constitutes an unreasonable barrier to disputants' access to court, or unreasonably impairs the quality of the later adjudicative hearing.

1. Preconditions

The due process concern associated with precondition requirements is that engaging in ADR can impose such serious burdens of delay, expense, and stress on disputants as to constitute an unreasonable burden on access to adjudication. The issue presented here is similar to the arguments, discussed earlier, that mandatory participation in ADR burdens the exercise of jury trial rights. For the same reasons that mere participation in ADR does not unreasonably impair access to juries, it should not ordinarily constitute an unreasonable barrier to adjudication. . . .

2. Penalty Provisions

Cost-Shifting Provisions and Security Requirements. Monetary barriers to adjudication, whether in the form of cost-shifting provisions or security requirements, usually pose no significant issues under the due process clause. . . . [A] federal statute imposing filing fees on bankruptcy petitions complied with due process requirements, although the statute had the effect of absolutely barring the plaintiff debtor's access to bankruptcy court. The Supreme Court has also ruled that the due process clause is not violated by requirements that litigants post a bond to secure a preliminary judgment against them as a condition of access either to court or to an appeal.

[T]he impact of ADR cost-shifting provisions on defendants is no worse than the effects of the fee-shifting statutes cited in the discussion of jury rights. Just as the prospect of liability for attorneys' fees is likely to chill a litigant's decision to claim a jury trial, so cost-shifting rules may affect a defendant's decision to reject an ADR award and claim a due process hearing. Neither situation, however, has been held to present constitutional concerns.

There is a special problem with ADR security requirements that are imposed before trial. Arguably, these requirements violate Supreme Court decisions forbidding the imposition of prejudgment security measures, such as property attachments, without a prior hearing. In the case of court-related ADR, however, the imposition of a security requirement is ordinarily based on an opinion by a neutral moderator that the appellant is likely to be held liable for an award or costs in an amount equal to the security. Such findings closely track the requirements imposed by the Supreme Court on pretrial security orders, and the security requirements usually imposed in court-related ADR should therefore satisfy due process standards. . . .

Admission of ADR Result or Testimony in Court. There is little reason to believe that the admission of dispute resolution results or the testimony of ADR neutrals at trial violates the due process clause, as long as cross-examination is provided. . . . Rule 706 of the Federal Rules of Evidence, which provides for testimony by a court-appointed neutral expert, is closely analogous to testimony by an ADR neutral. For the same reasons that the use of such techniques does not violate the right to jury trial, it is even less likely to offend the more flexible standards of due process.

The potential due process problem in this form of penalty is not in the admission of the ADR result, but in restrictions on how it is received. For example, some dispute resolution programs do not permit ADR neutrals, such as arbitrators or mediators, to be called to testify, even for purposes of cross-examination. Such restrictions serve the valid social purposes of preserving the confidentiality of the ADR proceeding itself and lessening the burdens on part time ADR neutrals, many of whom are minimally compensated for their services. But the lack of opportunity to cross-examine violates one of the basic requirements of formal due process models. . . .

THE RIGHT TO EQUAL PROTECTION

Equal protection analysis of compulsory dispute resolution involves three issues: whether ADR programs create "classifications" within the meaning of the equal protection clause of the federal Constitution or its state law counterparts, what the standard of review should be to such classifications, and whether classifications are permissible.

A. ADR Classifications

ADR programs do create classifications for equal protection purposes. . . . For example, court-related arbitration typically covers only monetary claims for less than a specified dollar amount, while other ADR processes apply to cases within a limited subject area, such as child custody disputes, medical malpractice cases, worker's compensation claims, or civil rights complaints.

B. The Standard of Review

The intensity of equal protection analysis depends on the nature of the classification involved. If a classification applies to a "suspect" group or a "fundamental" right, then a strict standard of review will be applied; the classification must serve a "compelling government interest" and must be drawn as narrowly as possible to achieve that interest. All other classifications are tested on a "reasonable" or "rational" relationship standard; there must exist a logical connection between the classification at issue and a legitimate governmental goal. In most cases, the label applied to the classification determines the outcome of the analysis—the rational relationship standard is almost always met, while the strict scrutiny standard is rarely satisfied. No major alternative dispute resolution program employs suspect classifications, nor do ADR programs ordinarily single out fundamental rights. ADR programs that apply only to small monetary claims may have a disparate impact on the poor and minorities, but the impact is not enough to invoke heightened scrutiny.

It does not appear, in any case, that ADR programs create significant discrimination among classes. Although . . . a rule that the results of court-related ADR are admissible at trial assists only one side in a particular case, it does not necessarily harm the class of affected litigants as a whole unless the ADR procedure itself is biased. Thus, one of the premises of equal protection analysis, a disfavored class, is often missing from compulsory dispute resolution programs. . . .

C. Validity of ADR Classifications

1. Binding ADR

The federal government and many state legislatures have created causes of action that can be heard only in binding arbitration by administrative agencies. Leading examples include claims for government benefits and worker's compensation. Such classifications are plainly subject to a "rational relationship" test, and pose no serious equal protection question.

2. Nonbinding ADR

. . . The Supreme Court repeatedly has rejected equal protection challenges to state and federal statutes that impose nonbinding preconditions on civil suits. . . . The most suggestive recent case is *Bankers Life and Casualty v. Crenshaw,* where the Supreme Court . . . [rejected] an equal protection challenge to a Mississippi law imposing a fifteen percent penalty on litigants who unsuccessfully appealed from certain categories of monetary judgments. The statute served ADR goals by discouraging frivolous appeals and the use of exhausting litigation tactics to force favorable settlements, while providing some compensation to parties required to defend valid judgments. . . .

[I]t is unlikely that the Supreme Court would hold that forced participation in the leading forms of nonbinding ADR denies disputants equal protection of the law. . . . State supreme courts that have considered challenges to various forms of nonbinding court-related ADR under equal protection doctrines have reached similar results.

[T]he Fifth Circuit Court of Appeals upheld a Florida statute establishing mandatory screening panels for medical malpractice claims. The court reasoned that the right to pursue a tort claim for malpractice does not implicate a fundamental right and should be judged by the rational relationship test. . . . [A] federal district court rejected an equal protection challenge to a local court rule requiring that civil claims for less than $50,000 go through nonbinding arbitration. The court found that the experiment addressed a valid goal — the promotion of swift, efficient dispute resolution — and that the disparities in treatment which it created were constitutionally acceptable. . . .

[With] two important exceptions . . . penalty provisions . . . raise no serious equal protection issues to the general approval of penalty provisions. Both focus on security requirements . . . . [T]he security [may] not greatly exceed the damages for which the appellant is potentially liable under substantive law. Security provisions lacking a procedure for indigent disputants to petition for a reduction or waiver also raise a second equal protection concern. Challenges to these provisions would be unlikely to prevail under federal equal protection doctrines, but they might well find a receptive hearing under some state constitutions. . . .

CONCLUSION

For purposes of clarity, the discussion in this Article has been organized by constitutional principles. This final section draws together the results of these analyses to provide conclusions about the constitutionality of the leading forms of mandatory ADR.

A. Disputes That Do Not Involve a Cause of Action

The use of mandatory processes in disputes that do not involve a civil claim rarely poses constitutional issues. From the perspective of a coerced participant, mandatory participation in dispute resolution, without more, is the rough equivalent of being subpoenaed as a witness in civil discovery. Participation does not result in a binding outcome or any significant loss of property or liberty and, therefore, rarely poses constitutional concerns.

B. Binding ADR

The only form of mandatory ADR likely to impose a binding outcome is arbitration. Binding arbitration cannot be imposed on jury claims without violating both federal and state constitutional guarantees. Nonjury causes of action, however, including most claims based on statutes, can be channelled to arbitration. Similarly, although the federal separation of powers clause generally bars Congress from diverting "core" common law claims to binding ADR, the rule does not apply to statutory claims or in special circumstances.

Assuming that a particular claim can be sent to binding arbitration, due process and equal protection principles determine how the arbitration process must be designed and conducted. Contrary to statements in some court opinions, binding arbitration is not a per se violation of the due process clause. In fact, popular forms of arbitration generally comply with due process principles, because they provide disputants with an opportunity to be heard at a meaningful time and in a meaningful manner by a neutral decisionmaker. The level of formality and adverseness required by the due process clause varies enormously, however, depending on the circumstances of the dispute.

If due process principles are satisfied, then the diversion of certain types of civil claims to binding ADR rarely will raise a significant issue under the equal protection clause. If, however, the parties to a dispute have signed a prior contract to submit the controversy to private arbitration, or the use of ADR clashes with a strong federal policy, then public dispute resolution processes imposed by state law may well be preempted.

C. Nonbinding and Court-Related ADR

The third general category of compulsory dispute resolution consists of processes that apply to civil claims but have nonbinding outcomes. This category, referred to as court-related ADR, includes the growing number of programs designed to divert civil litigation from the courts. Such programs are only theoretically nonbinding, however, because the programs usually include penalty provisions intended to discourage disputants from demanding their day in court. Court-related mandatory ADR generally complies with state and federal constitutional requirements. However, if the penalties are too heavy, or are imposed rigidly on appellants regardless of the merits of their case, they may be constitutionally invalid.

Participation Requirements. Requirements that disputants participate in ADR as a precondition to obtaining access to a court usually pose no serious constitutional concerns. If, however, the dispute resolution requirement is so poorly designed or administered that claims are denied on a random basis or serious and widespread delays in case resolution result, then the process may be struck down as an unreasonable burden on access to juries, courts (under access-to-court principles), or adjudication generally (under due process doctrines).

Cost-Shifting Provisions. ADR designers often impose fee or cost-shifting rules on disputants who reject ADR results and proceed with conventional litigation. If penalties are applied only to those litigants who reject an ADR outcome but do not obtain a better result at trial, then they should not discourage valid appeals or raise a serious constitutional question.

Monetary penalties, however, are sometimes imposed on disputants who appeal from ADR even if they later prevail in court. Such provisions amount to a blanket penalty on ADR appeals, regardless of their validity. If penalties are significant in size, they, like onerous participation requirements, may be invalidated as unreasonable burdens on access to courts or adjudication generally.

Security Requirements. By requiring that costs or awards be secured (or paid into court) at the time an appeal from ADR is filed, security requirements increase the impact of cost shifting or of the ADR result itself. As a rule, security requirements pose no more constitutional issues than do cost shifting provisions.

If, however, a security requirement is very large, either in absolute terms or in relation to the amount in dispute, it may deter disputants with valid claims from going to court. The constitutional problems created by high security requirements are more significant than those created by cost shifting rules, precisely because of their greater impact on disputants. In particular, indigent litigants may find it hard to post security, regardless of the merits of their appeals. High security requirements, such as a rule that appellants post bonds equal to twice their legal liability, have been struck down as violations of equal protection principles. Security requirements also could be attacked under jury trial or due process doctrines. To deal with this problem, ADR designers should permit disputants to petition for reduction or waiver of security requirements in appropriate cases.

Admission of ADR Result or Testimony in Court. The third major form of penalty used in nonbinding programs permits the results of ADR, or the opinion of the ADR moderator, to be introduced at any subsequent trial of the dispute. Again, this device poses no inherent constitutional problem.

The most serious potential issue that may arise from the use of such a penalty concerns the availability of cross-examination. If the opinion of a mediator or arbitrator about the merits of a case is admitted at trial, but the litigant who lost in ADR is not permitted to cross-examine the ADR neutral to point out weaknesses in the ADR process, then the opposing litigant will be denied formal due process and jury trial rights may be compromised as well.

Subject to the specific comments articulated in this Article, ADR processes with nonbinding outcomes may be applied to almost any kind of civil dispute without violating the provisions of the federal Constitution or most of its state counterparts. The Constitution thus gives ADR designers broad freedom to experiment with and implement mandatory dispute-resolution processes in order to improve the quality of American civil justice.

2. Lucy V. Katz, Compulsory *Alternative Dispute Resolution and Voluntarism: Two-Headed Monster or Two Sides of the Coin?*, 1993 J. Disp. Resol. 1, 22-31*

Constitutional Issues

Most constitutional challenges to ADR involve mandatory arbitration and medical malpractice review panels. . . . Objections to these ADR methods have been based on the following constitutional arguments: the Seventh Amendment right to jury trial in civil cases; the Due Process Clause, as found in the Fifth and Fourteenth amendments; the Equal Protection Clause; Article III on judicial powers; and the First Amendment. State court challenges have been based on analogous provisions in state constitutions, particularly those guaranteeing due process, access to courts, and equal protection. Few of these challenges have been successful. Generally, the U.S. Supreme Court is hospitable to alterations of traditional legal processes, approving such procedures as the appointment of auditors to assist judges in decision-making, the elimination of common law causes of action, the six-person jury, and "nonadversarial" administrative procedures dealing with important rights. . . .

The right to jury trial. The Seventh Amendment right to a jury trial is limited to suits that were triable to a jury at common law. Even in such matters, the amendment has been held to require only that a trial on the merits be available at some point before final determination of the parties' rights. Whether any given procedure violates the Seventh Amendment depends essentially on a reasonableness test: If the procedure is reasonable and does not unduly burden the jury trial right, it is valid. Under this analysis, most departures from traditional litigation have been tolerated by the Supreme Court, as long as the parties have some chance eventually to present their claims to a jury. Even the total elimination of the jury trial, in workers' compensation matters for example, has been upheld as long as the loss of the jury trial right is offset by a substantial benefit.

Compulsory arbitration in civil cases, and other mandatory forms of ADR, does not, therefore, violate the Seventh Amendment so long as a jury trial is available de novo at some point. Penalties imposed for insisting on trial de novo do not, if reasonable, violate the jury trial right. Generally, the benefits of arbitration, such as speed and the elimination of frivolous suits, outweigh the burdens, such as delay in obtaining a jury trial, and so the procedure is deemed reasonable. . . .

---

*Reprinted with permission.

Some state courts have struck down medical malpractice review panels or other arbitration programs as violative of the right to jury trial while others have upheld similar statutes. A few opinions have invalidated medical review panels as applied in specific circumstances in which delays or other procedural roadblocks have been deemed so onerous as to go beyond the limits of reasonableness. Georgia's Supreme Court has upheld a local program for arbitration of claims up to $25,000.

Due process of law. Due process challenges to ADR involve two types of claims: (1) that a procedure deprives a claimant of a due process hearing on the merits; and (2) that particular procedures, such as penalty assessments or sanctions, are administered without adequate due process protections. Like Seventh Amendment claims, due process arguments are rarely successful in the federal courts. The Supreme Court has struck firmly to its pronouncement in *Mathews v. Eldridge* [424 U.S. 319 (1976)] that due process is a flexible concept, that its requirements vary depending on a number of factors, and that a full due process hearing with notice and the right to representation is not required in all cases. Administrative proceedings are valid substitutes for trial as long as there is an opportunity for judicial review of constitutional issues. Under the Due Process Clause, mandatory arbitration is invalid only if the arbitral result is final and binding and parties are deprived of any subsequent judicial hearing. . . .

ADR procedures that are so burdensome as to prevent any access to courts do deprive claimants of a hearing in violation of the due process clause, but such instances usually involve technical restrictions that, through no fault of the claimant, foreclose a trial or hearing. . . . Fees, bonds, or penalties for unsuccessful appeals of arbitral awards do not violate due process rights as long as a judge can modify harsh requirements to permit meritorious appeals. As in the jury trial cases, if the fee is not an absolute bar to a full due process hearing, it is valid.

Particular procedures may violate due process if they fail to provide adequate notice. This is especially relevant in sanctions cases, in which penalties are imposed for failure to attend or to participate in a pretrial settlement conference. Some courts have held that penalties for failure to comply with pretrial orders, including orders to settle by a certain date or to go to trial, are really in the nature of civil or criminal contempt proceedings, and may not be imposed without full due process notice and hearing.

Rules on use at a later trial of testimony or information gained at an ADR proceeding sometimes raise due process concerns. Statutes allowing an arbitrator or mediator opinion to be introduced into evidence at a later trial have been upheld if there is an opportunity to cross examine the opinion's author. However, disclosure and cross examination conflict with the strong policy of confidentiality in ADR, particularly in procedures such as mediation or summary jury trials, and in some circumstances court rules bar examination of mediators. Disclosure of a result in such a case without opportunity for cross examination would arguably be a denial of due process.

Equal protection of the law. Some suits have raised equal protection arguments against ADR procedures that are applied only to certain classes of lawsuits, such as medical malpractice claims, or claims for under a certain dollar limit. Such classifications have been upheld by several courts, usually under the rational-basis test applied by the Supreme Court to social and economic legislation. The states' goals of affording speedier trials, eliminating docket congestion, and alleviating the medical malpractice "crisis" all have been held legitimate, and efforts to channel some cases into speedier procedures, to eliminate frivolous claims early in litigation, or to encourage settlements have been deemed rationally related to those goals.

Moreover, experimental ADR programs, which may be necessarily underinclusive, do not for that reason constitute an equal protection violation.

On the other hand, certain state courts have upheld equal protection claims, particularly in medical malpractice cases. The Supreme Court of Rhode Island held that a medical malpractice screening provision failed even minimum scrutiny under the Equal Protection Clause because, the court found, no malpractice crisis existed when the legislation was enacted and so there was no basis at all to justify the restrictive classification. The Louisiana Supreme Court held that a malpractice damage limit of $500,000, not including medical expenses, constituted discrimination based on physical condition, which is prohibited by the state constitution. Presumably the same would be true of a medical malpractice arbitration panel.

A potentially more serious set of equal protection problems arises when ADR procedures are applied differently to plaintiffs and defendants in the same law suit. In *Lindsey v. Normet*, the Supreme Court struck down as arbitrary and irrational an Oregon requirement that tenants, not landlords, who appeal from an eviction proceeding must post bond for double the rent expected to accrue during the appeal. The Connecticut Supreme Court struck down that state's automobile lemon law because it allowed only consumers, and not manufacturers, to reject an unfavorable arbitration award and to demand a trial de novo. Manufacturers were relegated to limited judicial review under the standards applicable to private, voluntary arbitration awards. . . . Other procedures that give one-sided access to arbitration or mediation, such as the farmer-lender mediation statutes providing for mediation at the option of the farmer, may be vulnerable to equal protection challenges.

Separation of powers. When ADR procedures vest decision-making power in non-judges, questions arise regarding the separation of powers or, generally, the right of access to courts. Many procedures do this: arbitrators are often practicing lawyers; medical malpractice panels may include physicians and community representatives; and mediation is frequently done by lay persons or mental health professionals. Such features arguably violate Article III of the U.S. Constitution, which vests the judicial power in judges appointed by the President and confirmed by the Senate, who serve for life terms on good behavior. Non-Article III judges may not decide disputes within the power of Article III courts. Such disputes include common law and analogous claims. While Congress may delegate jurisdiction over public rights to other bodies such as administrative tribunals, it may not do the same with common law rights. The Court has also held that Article III is violated when an alternative forum threatens the judiciary's independence through undue political domination of the courts.

The mere postponement of judicial consideration does not rise to an Article III violation. Therefore the trial de novo provisions that forestall Seventh Amendment violations in court-annexed arbitration also prevent Article III problems. State courts have upheld mandatory ADR provisions against similar claims. Particularly in nonbinding procedures, courts appear reluctant to invalidate the use of people other than judges to aid in ADR or in decision-making generally, as long as the lay persons do not make binding decisions free of judicial oversight. However, the Illinois Supreme Court has twice held its malpractice legislation invalid because review panels consisting of a judge, a lawyer, and a health care professional held adversary hearings and decided legal and factual issues. The court held that the process violated constitutional language vesting "exclusive and entire judicial power in the courts."

First Amendment claims. The need for confidentiality in mediation and other consensual procedures has generated First Amendment challenges in a few cases. The Sixth Circuit

Court of Appeals held that the press has no right to attend a summary jury trial in an opinion that strongly reflects judicial appreciation of the dynamics of consensual procedures.

3. Comments and Questions

a. The Golann and Katz articles make it clear that whatever concerns and criticisms there are of existing ADR programs, they do not normally present constitutional concerns. A few states have declared particular ADR procedures unconstitutional, notably medical malpractice screening panels, but such decisions are sufficiently rare to be characterized as aberrations. Are there any ADR practices or procedures in common use that you believe should be declared unconstitutional?

b. Even where a state constitution employs language that is materially identical to that in the federal Constitution, a state court sometimes interprets its provision in manner at variance with U.S. Supreme Court decisions. Also, state constitutions often contain limitations that have no federal parallel.

c. The bottom line for all three branches of government is that there are few if any constitutional impediments to carefully crafted and reasonable ADR innovations.

C. Judicial Settlement Conference

1. Succeeding in Settlement Conferences

a. Comments and Questions

1. The author of the next article, Wayne Brazil, is a former law professor, a magistrate judge, an ADR pioneer, and a careful observer of the legal scene. His views on effective lawyering in judicially hosted settlement conferences are based on extensive personal experience, enhanced by thoughtful analysis.

2. The validity of Brazil's observations and suggestions are not limited to settlement conferences; they have wide application to mediated ADR settings generally.

b. Wayne D. Brazil, *Effective Lawyering in Judicially Hosted Settlement Conferences*, 1988 J. Disp. Resol. 1, 22-31*

I. INTRODUCTION

The purpose of this article is to describe in detail the most effective approaches and techniques that I have seen lawyers use in settlement conferences. Having hosted hundreds of negotiations, I have seen many different lawyering styles. In the pages that follow, I share with interested litigators my ideas . . . about what works in the settlement dynamic and what does not. I write informally; the "you" that I address so often are the litigators I hope to reach. . . .

At the outset it is important to emphasize a theme that runs through much of this article: the way counsel behaves during the conference can dramatically affect how the judge and other counsel handle themselves in the negotiation process. Throughout this article I point to examples of how one lawyer's conduct and choices are likely to affect the responses that come

*Reprinted with permission.

from his opponent. . . . [T]oward the end of this article I suggest strategies for breaking negotiation logjams and for maximizing the odds of reaching closure. . . .

III. THE PRINCIPAL TARGETS OF PERSUASION

When deciding on an overall strategy for a given settlement conference, and when responding to specific developments during the course of negotiations, you should keep as close to the front of your mind as possible a very important fact: your persuasive efforts cannot be focused on just one target, but must be designed to reach at least three and sometimes four different people:

(1) opposing counsel,
(2) the opposing party,
(3) the judge who is hosting the conference, and
(4) in some cases, your own client. . . .

[O]ne of your primary objectives in a settlement conference should be to convert the judge into an ally, to so persuade him of the reasonableness of your client's position that he becomes not just a facilitator of communication, but an assertive advocate of a solution that fits your client's needs. . . .

IV. THE PROS AND CONS OF DIFFERENT SETTLEMENT CONFERENCE FORMATS

I have experimented with several different formats for settlement conferences. . . . In the vast majority of cases . . . I begin the conference by meeting privately with one lawyer at a time; later in the conference, if the situation calls for it, I often meet with lawyer and client, one side at a time. In multiparty cases, I usually start by meeting privately with the lawyer or lawyers for one party at a time (rather than meeting with everyone on one side). Thus, I have a series of one-on-one conversations, in private, with the lawyers, learning as much as I can about how each litigant views the situations of *all* the others, not just those formally lined up against it.

It has been my experience that this format — which I refer to as "private caucusing" — usually is the most productive. Compared to the various group meeting formats, this structure offers several advantages. The lawyers tend to be more relaxed and flexible, factors which are conducive to working toward common ground. The lawyers also tend to be more open with me and somewhat more honest, both about the weaker aspects of their client's case and about what offers or demands they would seriously consider. In these one-on-one sessions there is no other lawyer and no party or client to try to impress, so counsel are somewhat less likely to posture. . . .

Another significant advantage of the private caucusing format is that it gives lawyers an opportunity to tell the judge if they have client control problems. . . . A related advantage of the private caucusing system is that it permits lawyers to warn the judge if there are particular subjects or possible components of settlement packages about which their clients are especially sensitive. . . .

The one-on-one format also offers advantages to the judicial host of the conference that can benefit counsel. The judge can move through the analysis more quickly than he or she could if the clients were present (in which case he or she would feel constrained to translate legal concepts into lay terms) and the judge can be more frank in expressing reactions to particular evidence or lines of argument than he or she would be if all counsel were present. . . . This format also reduces the odds that something the judge or one of the lawyers says will embarrass another lawyer, either in front of his peers or in front of his client, or both. . . .

In private meetings with counsel and client, I have asked lawyers *basic* questions (about the evidence or the applicable law) that lawyers have not been able to answer. In a surprising percentage of cases, lawyers have failed to complete key aspects of their case preparation before the settlement conference and when my questions expose this fact, they often are embarrassed. . . . [C]ausing a lawyer this kind of embarrassment can have a disastrous effect on a settlement conference. An embarrassed attorney feels the need to repair his image in the mind of his client or of opposing counsel. Unfortunately, many lawyers try to make such repairs by becoming "tougher," more rigid, more demanding, or more belligerent. Another common reaction to embarrassment in this setting is to attempt to discredit the judge who was the source of the troublesome question or analysis. Both of these reactions tend to interfere with the process of searching for common ground. . . .

In the group setting, lawyers and parties are likely to feel greater pressure to play their cards close to their chests, to posture and to exaggerate. The group setting is also more likely to make the judge feel that he or she must avoid altogether, or at least work gingerly through, subjects about which participants are especially sensitive. . . .

It is important to acknowledge here an argument that cuts in the opposite direction. Some lawyers might contend that the information the participants present to the judge and to each other in a group setting is likely to be more reliable than information presented in private, one-on-one sessions because in the group sessions the presence of opposing counsel or a knowledgeable person representing the opposing party has a tendency to reduce exaggeration and moderate emotions. [Also,] a lawyer or client is less likely to misrepresent the evidence when he speaks in the presence of an opponent who will challenge misstatements, provide additional information, and present a balancing perspective or interpretation.

There are two problems with this line of reasoning. First, it assumes that the private caucusing format offers no opportunities for counsel or parties to balance or challenge presentations by their opponents. . . . The second problem with the argument . . . is that it assumes that the presence of opponents tends to moderate posturing rather than to exaggerate it. My experience, and the experience of other judges who have worked extensively in settlement, does not support this view. On the contrary, our perception is that the presence of other lawyers and parties heightens tensions and encourages everyone to take more extreme positions. . . .

[T]here are two potentially significant advantages to the group format. [It] permits every participant in the conference to know all the bases (in evidence, law, and argument) on which the judge predicates the assessments he or she articulates and the recommendations he or she makes. . . . A second advantage of the group meeting format is that it can be used to assure the judge and counsel that each offer and demand, accompanied by its rationale, is heard by the party (not just its lawyer) to whom it is directed. . . . I also have been concerned on occasion that lawyers may have used non-existent client control problems as excuses for not responding seriously, or more flexibly, to offers or demands that seemed reasonable to me.

In many cases, however, this "solution" is both unnecessary and unwise. There are devices for assuring that offers and the rationales that support the offers are reaching the parties that do not require the wholesale restructuring of the conference. One such device consists of the judge meeting privately with lawyer and client for one side at a time, after a series of one-on-one sessions with counsel, and having the lawyers present to their clients (in the presence of the judge) the offers that are on the table and the reasons behind these offers. Another possibility is for the judge to host a series of private caucuses, then to call a group session that includes all the clients for the purpose of exchanging and explaining offers and demands. As a third possibility, the judge might require each party to submit its offer or demand in writing, along with an outline of its rationale, then require each client to confirm that he reviewed the proposal that was directed to him. . . .

V. KEY CONCEPTUAL PREPARATION JUST BEFORE THE CONFERENCE

[I]t is important to emphasize the key subjects that counsel should review in the hours just before the conference. . . . At this late stage, counsel should not be attempting to develop basic information for the first time, but should be synthesizing and [applying] the last organizational touches. . . .

1. Outline the principal legal theories on which each party is likely to rely, listing every essential element of each claim or defense.
2. For each element of each legal theory, identify the nature and source of the evidence that is likely to be adduced either to support or to challenge the element in question.
3. If any of the legal theories (as opposed to the evidence in support of them) will be challenged, identify the legal authorities (cases, statutes, etc.) on which each side is likely to rely with respect to each theory that will be contested.
4. Systematically compare the parties' real-world situations (outside the litigation) to identify each side's needs and concerns and to isolate the kinds of things each side might be able to do for its opponent that its opponent could not do for itself, or at least could not do as efficiently or effectively.
5. Identify the kinds of concessions that are likely to be least painful for each side. Working with your client, make a list of possible concessions, starting with those that would be least painful and working down to those concessions that your client would least like to make.
6. Develop a series of "hypotheticals" through which you could articulate your client's offers or demands (these might incorporate assumptions about which evidence the trier of fact would find most persuasive, how the judge would rule on pivotal pretrial motions, or specified elements that might be included in an overall settlement package).
7. Decide what role you want the judicial host of the conference to play, then plan your conduct so that it encourages the judge to play this role.
8. Decide which approach or style you want opposing counsel to adopt during the negotiations, then plan your conduct so that it encourages opposing counsel to respond appropriately.
9. Be sure you understand the scope of the relevant confidentiality rules. . . . Make sure that you have clearly in mind those matters you will disclose only to the judge in confidence and that you must remind the judge not to disclose to any other party. . . .

VI. THE MOST EFFECTIVE TONE OR STYLE

. . . The most effective lawyers in this setting do all they can to appear to the judge to be rational, open-minded, flexible, and genuinely interested in seeking a negotiated disposition of the case. If the judge perceives you to be analytical, flexible, and open-minded, he will like you and be interested in working with you. Most important, he will have more confidence in your judgment, and more respect for your professionalism, than he would if he perceived you as approaching settlement as a poker game or as an opportunity to try to manipulate other people. He is also more likely to believe what you tell him, both about your client's position on particular offers or demands and about evidence or law that you cannot show him during the conference. . . .

Settlement conferences are not trials. Good lawyers understand this and make sure that the judge knows they understand it. Good litigators self-consciously change hats for settlement conferences. They abandon their openly adversarial style and adopt a style that is more conciliatory, more flexible, more open, and readier to acknowledge the strengths on the other side and the weaknesses at home. They go out of their way to show the judge they know that this is not an appropriate environment for the emotional intensity and combativeness that sometimes characterize a trial. . . . Before completing my observations about effective "tones" or "styles" for negotiations, it is important to re-emphasize, in a slightly different context, the basic point that belligerence, or playing the role of the tough guy, is counterproductive and inappropriate in a judicially hosted settlement conference. . . .

The generalization that integrates all the thoughts in this section is simple: the lawyers who are most effective in settlement negotiations cultivate a "style" or "tone" that is dominated by careful reasoning, open-minded flexibility, and a manifest interest in vigorously pursuing the possibility of settlement.

VIII. THE ANALYSIS STAGE

For purposes of clarifying this presentation, I have divided the "substantive" aspects of settlement conferences into two principal dimensions: analysis and negotiation. In the real world, these dimensions of the process are inextricably intertwined. In fact, the heart of effective negotiation is careful analysis. Nonetheless, it is helpful to think about "analysis" and "negotiation" separately.

In good settlement conferences, the process, in fact, divides into two stages, the first dominated by analysis of the relevant law and evidence, and the second dominated by exchanges of proposals (possible terms of settlement) that are rationalized by what was presented during the analysis stage. . . . [O]ne reason that I treat the analysis stage separately in this article is to encourage counsel to appreciate that it is only through analysis that they can make the conference an independently significant event, an event capable of producing (rather than simply reporting) real movement.

A good lawyer takes the analytical initiative. She lets the judge know, at the outset, that she expects her private caucus sessions with the judge to begin with and be dominated by analysis. The good lawyer . . . does not wait for the judge to move the discussion into analysis; instead, the lawyer takes the initiative and launches the review of the law and evidence. This is an extremely effective tactic because it communicates two things to the judge: one is that you are a rational, open minded person who expects settlement negotiations to be dominated by reasoning, and the other (just as important) is that you are confident that if reasoning dominates the process, your client will benefit. . . . [B]y appearing to want to reason toward a solution, a lawyer gains real credibility with the judicial host.

The analysis that a good lawyer presents has several distinguishing characteristics. The first is that it is systematic. . . . When I hear a disjointed presentation I assume that the lawyer is poorly prepared, does not really understand the case, or is intentionally skipping points (evidentiary or legal) that favor his opponent. By contrast, when I hear a systematic analysis, I am impressed by both the lawyer's intelligence and his confidence in his client's position.

Systematic analysis begins with an explicit identification of the relevant legal principles. The persuasive lawyer points to authority for each legal principle that might be subject to question. . . . . The best lawyers *never ignore contrary authority,* or sources that seem to support their opponent's position. Instead, they squarely acknowledge such material, then present the authorities that support their client's position and try to show why they are more persuasive. . . .

The lawyer has two objectives: the first is to persuade the judicial host and the second is to give the host the ammunition he or she needs to persuade opposing counsel, who is certain to point to at least some authority or evidence that tends to support his client's position. . . . Since disposition turns on a comparison of the two sides, the effective lawyer forthrightly conducts the comparison for the judge. He does not ignore the strengths in his opponent's case.

The most effective lawyers complement their systematic analysis with a manifest openness of mind. . . . There are several ways to impress the judicial host with your open-mindedness. The first is to listen. I have seen many lawyers who are so preoccupied with arguing their client's side of the case, and with deflecting attention away from its weaknesses, that they appear not even to hear major points made by the judge or by opposing counsel. . . . Many lawyers apparently believe that the judge will not perceive their diversionary tactics or their obfuscating responses. In my experience, however, such tactics are obvious and cost the lawyers who resort to them considerable credibility. . . .

A second way to impress the host of your conference with your open-mindedness is to ask questions, both of the judge and of the other parties. I have been impressed, for example, when a lawyer describes with particularity the evidence his client can muster on an important factual issue, then says:

> I think the evidence I have just described is very persuasive, but I'm not sure that my opponent is convinced. Is there some aspect of my reasoning that you [judge] question, or is there persuasive evidence that points in the opposite direction that I am overlooking or just haven't learned about yet?

I also am impressed when, after a long analytical effort, a lawyer remains unconvinced about his opponent's position and says: "Judge, I just don't understand how [opposing counsel] arrives at her valuation. Am I missing something? Would you go through the reasoning for me?" These kinds of questions serve two purposes: they reinforce the impression that the lawyer asking them is genuinely interested in reasoning toward a settlement and they pressure the judge and the opposition either to acknowledge that there are holes in the other side's case or to expose more fully the evidence that supports it. If there are holes, you want to be sure the judge sees them. If there is evidence you don't know about, you want to learn it. . . .

A lawyer can undermine the good impression that asking questions creates by reacting inappropriately to the answers. If you ask for the judge's views, do not respond with a knee-jerk defensiveness or counterattack if you do not like what you hear. Instead, absorb and digest what you hear. Give the judge the impression that you are thinking about it. If you learn new information, put it in context. Try to articulate to the judge how the new information fits in with the information you already have. If the new information is sufficiently important, tell the judge that you would like some time to discuss it with your client and to analyze its implications. In other words, give the impression that you take the new information seriously and intend to do it analytical justice. This will improve the credibility of whatever response you offer later in the conference or at a follow-up session.

Another way to impress the judge with your open-mindedness is to admit to at least the more obvious weaknesses in your client's case. One cardinal principal of effective lawyering in this environment says that you should never permit the judge to learn the worst things about your client's case from your opponent. If the judge has heard about the case from you (either through your written pre-conference statement or orally at the conference), but then learns for the first time from your opponent about serious problems for your side of the case, you will greatly damage your credibility. . . .

Wise lawyers also know that there are ways to minimize the implications even of concessions they make in private sessions with the settlement judge. For example, a cautious lawyer might elect to articulate his concessions hypothetically or conditionally. . . . The beauty of this [approach] is that it gives away virtually nothing while permitting counsel to indicate what range of figures is likely to be acceptable. This kind of statement gives the judge something to work with but does not commit your client to a particular view of the evidence or law.

Another painless way to earn credibility points with the judge during the analysis stage is to concede that some of your client's legal theories appear to be more difficult than others to carry, or that meeting your burden on some of your numerous affirmative defenses may be problematic. . . . The basic point here is simple: good lawyers use carefully selected concessions both to earn credibility points with the judge and to advance the analytical ball. . . .

IX. THE NEGOTIATION STAGE

Perhaps the most important point to be made about the negotiation stage is that you should not rush into it. . . . One reason is that good lawyers use settlement conferences for many purposes in addition to trying to reach a settlement. For example, you can use a settlement conference to narrow and focus the dispute and to develop a cost effective discovery plan. Many cases (probably most) do not settle at the first conference. Knowing this, it is important to use the first conference to identify the key areas of disagreement, then to devise a plan for generating the information or other sources of leverage that will move the parties' positions closer together. Sometimes this involves taking a few key depositions, or discovering certain documents. Sometimes it involves briefing an important motion, or impleading a new party. The point, of course, is that good lawyers use settlement conferences to identify what separates the parties' positions. If they were to rush to a superficial exchange of numbers, they would squander this learning opportunity.

By rushing to the negotiation stage, a lawyer also loses an opportunity to learn more about the opposing client, what is important to him, how he thinks and reacts, and what kinds of things in addition to money he might find attractive. The more substantial the analysis stage is, the greater the opportunity to learn things that you can use to tailor either the content of your client's offer or the way it is presented so as to fit the needs or personality of the client (or lawyer) on the other side. . . .

There is another, more psychologically subtle reason for not rushing into the negotiation stage. I think the odds go down that an agreement will be reached when the lawyers start exchanging offers and demands early in the conference. To maximize the prospects for settlement counsel not only need to explore the case fully and analytically, but also to create room for a kind of psychological momentum to build up. If lawyers and parties invest a significant amount of time in a settlement conference, they are more likely to want a return on that investment, and the kind of return they are most likely to look for is an agreement. To put it another way, if the parties have invested a lot of time in the conference, they are more likely to build up expectations for it and more likely to feel disappointed if no agreement is reached.

Moreover, the more substantial the analysis stage of the proceedings is, the more likely the parties are to perceive one another as taking the negotiations seriously, proceeding in good faith, and having a genuine interest in refining their understanding of the evidence and law and of adjusting their settlement positions to reflect that evolving understanding. There is a better chance of achieving settlement if the parties perceive one another as willing to listen, flexible, and willing to modify their offers or demands as they learn new things during the course of the discussions. These reasoned adjustments in position can give the participants greater confidence in the process and foster good will between them. These feelings, in combination with the momentum that develops from the fact that the parties make changes in their positions, maximize the odds of settling the case. To rush to a simple-minded exchange of numbers prevents these positive forces from developing.

A. Calculated concessions to create momentum

If he has done his homework well, counsel can begin by making concessions that are on the "significance periphery" of the case or that are least painful for his client. Good lawyers always come prepared with some points they can give away in an effort to generate movement in the negotiations. In virtually all settlement conferences, both sides are called upon to make concessions. One of your goals should be to have made what appear to be a significant number of concessions before the focus of the negotiations moves to the points that most threaten your client's position in the case, and before the judge or the other side ask for the things that would be most painful for your client to give. . . . It is unwise to permit the negotiations to reach crucial matters before you have built up "negotiation credits" by making concessions in less consequential areas.

Another way to generate momentum in the negotiations is to break the case, or possible settlement packages, into component parts and to negotiate about the parts one at a time, starting with those that are least threatening. The goal is to build optimism and to energize the discussion before tackling the most difficult aspects of the negotiations. The likelihood of success is much greater if all participants feel that progress is being made, even if the progress initially is in the areas of least consequence. . . .

On the other hand, I have seen cases in which the opposite strategy works best. Fearing that they will not be able to agree about the value of individual elements of damages, and/or fearing that excessive friction might develop if counsel attempted to negotiate separately about each of many such elements, some lawyers prefer to negotiate about the value of the case as a whole. This strategy permits the parties to disagree, secretly, about the value of individual components of the settlement package but agree about the bottom-line value of the entire suit. . . .

While it is a mistake to insist that the opposition make a concession before your client will, it also is a mistake to make a series of substantial concessions without some reciprocation from the other side. Even when the points are not of great moment, it is important that the whole process include some movement by both sides. Unless the liability picture is very clear (one way or the other), negotiations take on an unhealthy, lopsided cast when one side makes a clearly disproportionate number of the concessions or moves much greater distances than its opponent. . . . If you permit your client to make a whole series of unreciprocated concessions, and if you work up agreements on significant points without requiring your opponent to meet you at least part way, you encourage disrespect for your confidence in your client's position, and tempt your opponent to conclude that you will make even larger concessions without reciprocation. . . .

The most serious mistake, however, would be for counsel to permit these risks to dissuade him from being the first to make "calculated concessions" during negotiations. . . . By being the first to offer calculated concessions, you are more likely to communicate your confidence in your mastery of your case and yourself than any weakness or vulnerability.

My experience suggests that if you are in a situation in which the settlement might consist of a package with components in addition to up-front money, it often is a good idea to discuss the money last. In our society, it is often the money that provokes the most emotion and that is perceived as the center of the deal. If there are other possible elements of a settlement package, you should work on these first. Try to build a sense of momentum, and to develop some trust and good will, before you get to the part of the negotiations that you anticipate will be most highly charged. . . .

In crafting your overall negotiation strategy, you should plan to hold back some modest concessions, and perhaps some non-pivotal arguments, so that later in the process you have ammunition left with which to induce the other side to move or to help it or your own client rationalize movement that is necessary to reach closure. I have seen situations in which a lawyer needed an excuse or a justification to support a recommendation to his own client that he (the client) make a further adjustment in his settlement position. In this situation, you will be much better off if you have saved a point or two that you, the other lawyer, or the judge, can use to help justify a change in position. . . .

X. FROM AGREEMENT IN PRINCIPLE TO AGREEMENT IN FACT: STEPS TO REDUCE THE ODDS OF RUPTURE

. . . Once the parties have reached agreement, counsel should immediately have its terms set out on the record or in a writing signed by all counsel and litigants. You cannot assume that everyone understands, agrees, and will remember all the key terms. There often is a sense of relief, sometimes almost euphoria, when the parties finally agree to terms after a long period of discovery, motions, and negotiations. Counsel and litigants sometimes feel a peak of energy when they reach agreement; there can be a sense of momentum and good will that seems to make it unnecessary to resort to formalities.

To put the terms in writing, or commit them to the record, seems anticlimactic and requires a difficult shifting of emotional gears. There are also cases in which the emotional environment seems so fragile that counsel will be reluctant to risk fracturing it by trying to get the parties to articulate their agreement in a writing and sign it. . . . Good lawyers will realize that they court disaster if they permit the participants in the negotiations to leave with only a vague sense of what has happened. Gently and firmly, counsel must ensure that the key terms of the agreement are put on the record or committed to a signed writing on the spot.

Having the key terms placed on the record or committed to a writing on the spot has two principal purposes, the first of which is to make sure that everyone in fact understands what the substantive terms of the agreement are. Ensuring this understanding reduces the odds that there will be bickering over details, bickering that can increase the cost of closure and jeopardize the deal. The second purpose of committing the terms to a writing (or getting them on the record) is to discourage "settler's remorse" from seriously tempting a party to try to back out of the deal. . . . Counsel also should address all other potentially significant loose ends before leaving the conference. . . .

Counsel also should take care to specify which party will pay any outstanding liens (which might be held by carriers, hospitals, public agencies, etc.). Similarly, it is important to have a clear, articulated understanding about attorneys' fees and costs. Counsel usually attend carefully to the question of fees (how much, from what source, when, etc.), but can be much less careful about costs. I have seen large settlements seriously threatened by disputes over costs that have broken out well after the agreement supposedly had been reached. . . . Counsel should . . . seek approval from the judge if the agreement arguably displaces a court order.

Another matter that counsel should address as part of the closure process is how to handle sensitive documents or other tangible things (e.g., computer chips) that have been produced during discovery. The settlement agreement should specify what kinds of documents or products are to be returned, to whom, and on what schedule. A party who wants his opponent to attest, under oath, that he has returned all originals and has returned or destroyed any copies of sensitive documents should submit a proposed declaration and have an executed version of it attached to the final settlement agreement. In sensitive situations, it can also be a good idea to have the lawyer or party to whom documents are returned sign an acknowledgement, certifying acceptance and indicating that the process of returning materials has been satisfactorily completed.

Counsel should also not leave the settlement conference (or private negotiating session) without reaching an understanding about which lawyer will compose the first draft of the agreement and when she will circulate it for comment. Similarly, there should be a clearly fixed date by which the money will change hands and/or other elements of the bargain will be completed. For example, if products are to be delivered, or a statement is to be released to the press, counsel should fix the date and the place.

If you want a confidentiality provision in the settlement agreement, you should make this clear at the final negotiating session. Occasionally I have seen parties . . . bristle at the idea of entering a settling defendants "secret deal." If there is any possibility that a party will be troubled by a request for confidentiality, it is a good idea to raise the issue of confidentiality early in the negotiations so that the judge can explain that there is nothing untoward . . . about such provisions. Individual litigants may feel more comfortable with confidentiality if, when they first encounter the idea, it has a judge's imprimatur. Occasionally a plaintiff's attorney will also resist a confidentiality provision. If the source of this resistance is the lawyer's desire to use information about the settlement to encourage other potential plaintiffs to file suit, counsel . . . might try to negotiate a compromise whereby the plaintiff or his lawyer would be permitted to disclose the fact of settlement but not the amount, or, perhaps, to use certain negotiated phrases to characterize the settlement.

Counsel who are concerned about the enforceability of confidentiality provisions might consider negotiating a liquidated damages clause under which a fixed sum would be payable if one party proved that the other had disclosed material that he had agreed to keep confidential. A liquidated damages clause like this might put some teeth in the confidentiality provision and permit a party to avoid the difficult problem of proving (with the requisite level of certainty) the magnitude of economic harm caused by a breach. . . .

Whether courts will honor confidentiality agreements in settlement contracts, even when entered by clearly competent institutional litigants of equal bargaining power, is a complex question that does not admit of a simple answer. At this point, it will suffice to point out that counsel may compromise their ability to keep terms of a settlement confidential if they file the settlement contract itself, under seal, in connection with the stipulation that terminates the case (e.g., a stipulated dismissal with prejudice). . . .

XI. CONCLUSION

Lawyers who are good settlement negotiators understand clearly that the hat they wear during negotiations is very different from the hat they might wear at an adversarial hearing or during a trial. They know that effectiveness in the settlement dynamic requires careful preparation (by them and of their clients), tight reasoning, unusual levels of candor about strengths and weaknesses, calm and open-minded exchanges of views, a quiet, understated confidence, flexibility, and the capacity to make controlled concessions. Good settlement lawyers pay attention to the needs (economic and psychological) of others and know that they have an advantage if, by the reasonableness and professionalism of their presentations, they can convert the settlement judge to an advocate of a solution that they can recommend to their client.

2. In Person Appearance of Private Parties

a. *G. Heileman Brewing Co., Inc. v. Joseph Oat Corp.*, 871 F.2d 648 (7th Cir. 1989) (en banc)

KANNE, Circuit Judge.

May a federal district court order litigants—even those represented by counsel—to appear before it in person at a pretrial conference for the purpose of discussing the posture and settlement of the litigants' case? After reviewing the Federal Rules of Civil Procedure and federal district courts' inherent authority to manage and control the litigation before them, we answer this question in the affirmative and conclude that a district court may sanction a litigant for failing to comply with such an order.

I. BACKGROUND

A federal magistrate ordered Joseph Oat Corporation to send a "corporate representative with authority to settle" to a pretrial conference to discuss disputed factual and legal issues and the possibility of settlement. Although counsel for Oat Corporation appeared, accompanied by another attorney who was authorized to speak on behalf of the principals of the corporation, no principal or corporate representative personally attended the conference. The court determined that the failure of Oat Corporation to send a principal of the corporation to the pretrial conference violated its order. Consequently, the district court imposed a sanction of $5,860 upon Oat Corporation pursuant to Federal Rule of Civil Procedure 16(f). This amount represented the costs and attorneys' fees of the opposing parties attending the conference.

II. THE APPEAL

Oat Corporation appeals, claiming that the district court did not have the authority to order litigants represented by counsel to appear at the pretrial settlement conference. Specifically, Oat Corporation contends that, by negative implication, the language of Rule 16(a)(5) prohibits a district court from directing represented litigants to attend pretrial conferences.[1] That is, because Rule 16 expressly refers to "attorneys for the parties and any unrepresented parties" in introductory paragraph (a), a district court may not go beyond that language to devise procedures which direct the pretrial appearance of parties represented by counsel. Consequently, Oat Corporation concludes that the court lacked the authority to order the pretrial attendance of its corporate representatives and, even if the court possessed such authority, the court abused its discretion to exercise that power in this case.

A. Authority to Order Attendance

The language of Rule 16 does not give any direction to the district court upon the issue of a court's authority to order litigants who are represented by counsel to appear for pretrial proceedings. Instead, Rule 16 merely refers to the participation of trial advocates—attorneys of record and pro se litigants. However, the Federal Rules of Civil Procedure do not completely describe and limit the power of the federal courts. . . . The Supreme Court has acknowledged that the provisions of the Federal Rules of Civil Procedure are not intended to be the exclusive authority for actions to be taken by district courts. *Link v. Wabash R.R.*, 370 U.S. 626 (1962).

In *Link*, the Supreme Court noted that a district court's ability to take action in a procedural context may be grounded in inherent power, governed not by rule or statute but by the control necessarily vested in courts to manage their own affairs so as to achieve the orderly and expeditious disposition of cases. This authority likewise forms the basis for continued development of procedural techniques designed to make the operation of the court more efficient, to preserve the integrity of the judicial process, and to control courts' dockets. . . . [T]he mere absence of language in the federal rules specifically authorizing or describing a particular judicial procedure should not, and does not, give rise to a negative implication of prohibition. See . . . Fed. R. Civ. P. 83 ("In all cases not provided for by rule, the district judges and magistrates may regulate their practice in any manner not inconsistent with these rules or those of the district in which they act.").

Obviously, the district court, in devising means to control cases before it, may not exercise its inherent authority in a manner inconsistent with rule or statute. . . . In this case, we are

---

[1]Rule 16(a)(5) provides: (a) Pretrial Conferences: Objectives. In any action, the court may in its discretion direct the attorneys for the parties and any unrepresented parties to appear before it for a conference or conferences before trial for such purposes as . . . (5) facilitating the settlement of the case. FED. R. CIV. P. 16(a)(5).

required to determine whether a court's power to order the pretrial appearance of litigants who are represented by counsel is inconsistent with, or in derogation of, Rule 16. We must remember that Rule 1 states, with unmistakable clarity, that the Federal Rules of Civil Procedure "shall be construed to secure the just, speedy, and inexpensive determination of every action." . . .

The wording of the rule and the accompanying commentary make plain that the entire thrust of the amendment to Rule 16 was to urge judges to make wider use of their powers and to manage actively their dockets from an early stage. We therefore conclude that our interpretation of Rule 16 to allow district courts to order represented parties to appear at pretrial settlement conferences merely represents another application of a district judge's inherent authority to preserve the efficiency, and more importantly the integrity, of the judicial process.

B. Exercise of Authority to Order Attendance

Having determined that the district court possessed the power and authority to order the represented litigants to appear at the pretrial settlement conference, we now must examine whether the court abused its discretion to issue such an order.

At the outset, it is important to note that a district court cannot coerce settlement. In this case, considerable concern has been generated because the court ordered "corporate representatives with authority to settle" to attend the conference. In our view, "authority to settle," when used in the context of this case, means that the "corporate representative" attending the pretrial conference was required to hold a position within the corporate entity allowing him to speak definitively and to commit the corporation to a particular position in the litigation. We do not view "authority to settle" as a requirement that corporate representatives must come to court willing to settle on someone else's terms, but only that they come to court in order to consider the possibility of settlement.

As Chief Judge Crabb set forth in her decision which we now review: There is no indication . . . that the magistrate's order contemplated requiring Joseph Oat . . . to agree to any particular form of settlement or even to agree to settlement at all. The only requirement imposed by the magistrate was that the representative [of Oat Corporation] be present with full authority to settle, should terms for settlement be proposed that were acceptable to [Oat Corporation].

If this case represented a situation where Oat Corporation had sent a corporate representative and was sanctioned because that person refused to make an offer to pay money—that is, refused to submit to settlement coercion—we would be faced with a decidedly different issue—a situation we would not countenance.

The Advisory Committee Notes to Rule 16 state that "[a]lthough it is not the purpose of Rule 16(b)(7) to impose settlement on unwilling litigants, it is believed that providing a neutral forum for discussing [settlement] might foster it." These Notes clearly draw a distinction between being required to attend a settlement conference and being required to participate in settlement negotiations. Thus, under the scheme of pretrial settlement conferences, the corporate representative remains free, on behalf of the corporate entity, to propose terms of settlement independently—but he may be required to state those terms in a pretrial conference before a judge or magistrate.

As an alternative position, Oat Corporation argues that the court abused its discretion to order corporate representatives of the litigants to attend the pretrial settlement conference. Oat Corporation determined that . . . it would be unreasonable for the magistrate to require the president of that corporation to leave his business [in Camden, New Jersey] to travel to Madison, Wisconsin, to participate in a settlement conference. . . . Consequently, Oat Corporation believes that the district court abused its authority.

We recognize, as did the district court, that circumstances could arise in which requiring a corporate representative (or any litigant) to appear at a pretrial settlement conference would be so onerous, so clearly unproductive, or so expensive in relation to the size, value, and complexity of the case that it might be an abuse of discretion. Moreover, "[b]ecause inherent powers are shielded from direct democratic controls, they must be exercised with restraint and discretion." However, the facts and circumstances of this case clearly support the court's actions to require the corporate representatives of the litigants to attend the pretrial conference personally.

This litigation involved a claim for $4 million—a claim which turned upon the resolution of complex factual and legal issues. The litigants expected the trial to last from one to three months and all parties stood to incur substantial legal fees and trial expenses. This trial also would have preempted a large segment of judicial time—not an insignificant factor. Thus, because the stakes were high, we do not believe that the burden of requiring a corporate representative to attend a pretrial settlement conference was out of proportion to the benefits to be gained, not only by the litigants but also by the court.

Additionally, the corporation did send an attorney, Mr. Fitzpatrick, from Philadelphia, Pennsylvania to Madison, Wisconsin to "speak for" the principals of the corporation. It is difficult to see how the expenses involved in sending Mr. Fitzpatrick from Philadelphia to Madison would have greatly exceeded the expenses involved in sending a corporate representative from Camden to Madison. Consequently, we do not think the expenses and distance to be traveled are unreasonable in this case.

We thus conclude that the court did not abuse its authority and discretion to order a representative of the Oat Corporation to appear for the pretrial settlement conference on December 19.

C. Sanctions

Finally, we must determine whether the court abused its discretion by sanctioning Oat Corporation for failing to comply with the order to appear at the pretrial settlement conference. Oat Corporation argues that the instructions directing the appearance of corporate representatives were unclear and ambiguous. Consequently, it concludes that the sanctions were improper.

Absent an abuse of discretion, we may not disturb a district court's imposition of sanctions for failure of a party to comply with a pretrial order. The issue on review is not whether we would have imposed these costs upon Oat Corporation, but whether the district court abused its discretion in doing so. *National Hockey League v. Metropolitan Hockey Club, Inc.*, 427 U.S. 639, 642 (1976) (citations omitted).

Oat Corporation contends that the presence of Mr. Fitzpatrick, as an attorney authorized to speak on behalf of the principals of Oat Corporation, satisfied the requirement that its "corporate representative" attend the December 19 settlement conference. . . . Mr. Possi was present acting in his capacity as Oat Corporation's attorney of record. Mr. Fitzpatrick, who was not an attorney of record in the case, asserted that he was directed to attend the conference and speak on behalf of Oat Corporation's principals.[14]

The distinction is clearly drawn between an attorney representing a corporation and a corporate representative. As we define in this opinion— consistent with the meaning given by the magistrate—a corporate representative is a person holding "a position with the corporate entity." Although Mr. Fitzpatrick was representing the corporate principals and Mr. Possi the corporation, no corporate representative attended as required by the magistrate's order. We therefore conclude that the court properly sanctioned Oat Corporation pursuant to Rule 16(f) for failing to send a corporate representative to the settlement conference. . . . The judgment of the district court is hereby AFFIRMED.

POSNER, Circuit Judge, dissenting.

Rule 16(a) . . . could be thought to carry the negative implication that no represented party may be directed to appear—that was the panel's conclusion—but I hesitate to so conclude in a case that can be decided on a narrower ground. . . .

The question of the district court's power to summon a represented party to a settlement conference is a difficult one. . . . One danger is that it encourages judicial high-handedness ("power corrupts"); several years ago one of the district judges in this circuit ordered Acting Secretary of Labor Brock to appear before him for settlement discussions on the very day Brock was scheduled to appear before the Senate for his confirmation hearing. The broader concern illustrated by the Brock episode is that in their zeal to settle cases judges may ignore the value of other people's time. One reason people hire lawyers is to economize on their own investment of time in resolving disputes. It is pertinent to note in this connection that Oat is a defendant in this case; it didn't want its executives' time occupied with this litigation.

On the other hand, die Not bricht Eisen ["necessity breaks iron"]. Attorneys often are imperfect agents of their clients, and the workload of our district courts is so heavy that we should hesitate to deprive them of a potentially useful tool for effecting settlement, even if there is some difficulty in finding a legal basis for the tool. Although few attorneys will defy a district court's request to produce the client, those few cases may be the very ones where the client's presence would be most conducive to settlement. If I am right that Rule 16(a) empowers a district court to summon unrepresented parties to a pretrial conference only because

---

[14]On December 19, the following dialogue took place between the magistrate and Mr. Fitzpatrick: THE COURT: I made it clear on December 14th, that for purposes of this conference . . . that each party in addition to [being] represented by counsel would have present the party itself for purposes of authorizing or discussing settlement in this case, speaking specifically about the order which is dated December 18th but was entered I think clearly enough on the 14th. That in addition to counsel, each party . . . shall be represented at the conference in person by a representative having full authority to settle the case or make dedcisions relevant to all matters reasonably anticipated to come before the conference. . . . As a matter of fact, Mr. Possi called yesterday to find out from my secretary if that is what I really meant . . . he was informed that it is what I really meant; and I would like to have your explanation as to why no one from Joseph Oat is here. MR. FITZPATRICK: I am here as a representative of Joseph Oat which I understood your order to be. I have discussed this thing thoroughly with the principals of Joseph Oat. They directed me to come to the conference. They directed me that I could speak for them, with authority to speak for them. Their direction was I should make no offer to settle the case. That is their position. That is the position they choose to take and they designated me as the representative to communicate that to the Court.

their presence may be necessary to get ready for trial, we need not infer that the draftsmen meant to forbid the summoning of represented parties for purposes of exploring settlement. The draftsmen may have been unaware that district courts were asserting a power to command the presence of a represented party to explore settlement. We should hesitate to infer inadvertent prohibitions.

The narrowly "legal" considerations bearing on the question whether district courts have the power asserted by the magistrate in this case are sufficiently equivocal to authorize—indeed compel—us to consider the practical consequences for settlement before deciding what the answer should be. Unfortunately we have insufficient information about those consequences to be able to give a confident answer, but fortunately we need not answer the question in this case—so clear is it that the magistrate abused his discretion, which is to say, acted unreasonably, in demanding that Oat Corporation send an executive having "full settlement authority" to the pretrial conference. This demand, which is different from a demand that a party who has not closed the door to settlement send an executive to discuss possible terms, would be defensible only if litigants had a duty to bargain in good faith over settlement before resorting to trial, and neither Rule 16 nor any other rule, statute, or doctrine imposes such a duty on federal litigants. There is no federal judicial power to coerce settlement. Oat had made clear that it was not prepared to settle the case on any terms that required it to pay money. That was its prerogative, which once exercised made the magistrate's continued insistence on Oat's sending an executive to Madison arbitrary, unreasonable, willful, and indeed petulant. This is apart from the fact that since no one officer of Oat may have had authority to settle the case, compliance with the demand might have required Oat to ship its entire board of directors to Madison. . . .

Sufficient unto the day is the evil thereof: We should reverse the district court without reaching the question whether there are any circumstances in which a district court may compel a party represented by counsel to attend a pretrial conference.

EASTERBROOK, Circuit Judge, with whom POSNER, COFFEY and MANION, Circuit Judges, join, dissenting.

Our case has three logically separate issues. First, whether a district court may demand the attendance of someone other than the party's counsel of record. Second, whether the court may insist that this additional person be an employee rather than an agent selected for the occasion. Third, whether the court may insist that the representative have "full settlement authority"—meaning the authority to agree to pay cash in settlement (maybe authority without cap, although that was not clear). Even if one resolves the first issue as the majority does, it does not follow that district courts have the second or third powers, or that their exercise here was prudent.

The proposition that a magistrate may require a firm to send an employee rather than a representative is puzzling. Corporate "employees" are simply agents of the firm. Corporations choose their agents and decide what powers to give them. Which agents have which powers is a matter of internal corporate affairs. Joseph Oat Corp. sent to the conference not only its counsel of record but also John Fitzpatrick, who had authority to speak for Oat. Now Mr. Fitzpatrick is an attorney, which raised the magistrate's hackles, but why should this count against him? Because Fitzpatrick is a part-time rather than a full-time agent of the corporation? Why can't the corporation make its own decision about how much of the agent's time to hire? Is Oat being held in contempt because it is too small to have a cadre of legal employees—because its general counsel practices with a law firm rather than being "in house"?

At all events, the use of outside attorneys as negotiators is common. Many a firm sends its labor lawyer to the bargaining table when a collective bargaining agreement is about to expire, there to dicker with the union (or with labor's lawyer). Each side has a statutory right to choose its representatives. Many a firm sends its corporate counsel to the bargaining table when a merger is under discussion. Oat did the same thing to explore settlement of litigation. A lawyer is no less suited to this task than to negotiating the terms of collective bargaining or merger agreements. Firms prefer to send skilled negotiators to negotiating sessions (lawyers are especially useful when the value of a claim depends on the resolution of legal questions) while reserving the time of executives for business. Oat understandably wanted its management team to conduct its construction business.

As for the third subject, whether the representative must have "settlement authority": the magistrate's only reason for ordering a corporate representative to come was to facilitate settlement then and there. As I understand Magistrate Groh's opinion, and Judge Crabb's, the directive was to send a person with "full settlement authority". Fitzpatrick was deemed inadequate only because he was under instructions not to pay money. . . . On learning that Fitzpatrick did not command Oat's treasury, the magistrate ejected him from the conference and never listened to what he had to say on Oat's behalf, never learned whether Fitzpatrick might be receptive to others' proposals. (We know that Oat ultimately did settle the case for money, after it took part in and "prevailed" at a summary jury trial—participation and payment each demonstrating Oat's willingness to consider settlement.) The magistrate's approach implies that if the Chairman and CEO of Oat had arrived with instructions from the Board to settle the case without paying cash, and to negotiate and bring back for the Board's consideration any financial proposals, Oat still would have been in contempt.

Both magistrate and judge demanded the presence not of a "corporate representative" in the sense of a full-time employee but of a representative with "full authority to settle." Most corporations reserve power to agree (as opposed to power to discuss) to senior managers or to their boards of directors—the difference depending on the amounts involved. Heileman wanted $4 million, a sum within the province of the board rather than a single executive even for firms much larger than Oat. Fitzpatrick came with power to discuss and recommend; he could settle the case on terms other than cash; he lacked only power to sign a check. The magistrate's order therefore must have required either (a) changing the allocation of responsibility within the corporation, or (b) sending a quorum of Oat's Board.

Magistrate Groh exercised a power unknown even in labor law, where there is a duty to bargain in good faith. Labor and management commonly negotiate through persons with the authority to discuss but not agree. The negotiators report back to management and the union, each of which reserves power to reject or approve the position of its agent. . . . [A] judge may not compel a party to make a settlement offer, let alone to accept one. Rule 68, which requires a party who turns down a settlement proposal to bear costs only if that party does worse at trial, implies the same thing. Yet if parties are not obliged to negotiate in good faith, on what ground can they be obliged to come with authority to settle on the spot—an authority agents need not carry even when the law requires negotiation? The order we affirm today compels persons who have committed no wrong, who pass every requirement of Rules 11 and 68, who want only the opportunity to receive a decision on the merits, to come to court with open checkbooks on pain of being held in contempt. . . .

The majority does not discuss these problems. Its approach implies, however, that trial courts may insist that representatives have greater authority than labor negotiators bring to the table. And to create this greater authority, Oat Corp. might have to rearrange its internal structure—perhaps delegating to an agent a power state law reserves to the board of directors. Problems concerning the reallocation of authority are ubiquitous. For example, only the Assistant Attorney General for the Civil Division has authority to approve settlements of civil cases, and his authority reaches only to $750,000; above that the Deputy Attorney General must approve. 28 C.F.R. §§ 0.160(a)(2), 0.161. An attorney for the government, like Fitzpatrick, lacks the authority to commit his client but may negotiate and recommend. Does it follow that, in every federal civil case, a magistrate may require the presence of the Assistant or Deputy Attorney General or insist that they redelegate their authority? If such a demand would be improper for the Department of Justice, is it more proper when made of Joseph Oat Corporation?

These issues will not go away. The magistrate's order was to send a representative with the authority to bind Oat to pay money. What is the point of insisting on such authority if not to require the making of offers and the acceptance of "reasonable" counteroffers—that is, to require good faith negotiations and agreements on the spot? Fitzpatrick had the authority to report back to Oat on any suggestions; he had the authority to participate in negotiations. The only thing he lacked—the only reason Oat was held in contempt of court—was the ability to sign Oat Corp.'s check in the magistrate's presence. What the magistrate found unacceptable was that Fitzpatrick might say something like "I'll relay that suggestion to the Board of Directors", which might say no. Oat's CEO could have done no more. We close our eyes to reality in pretending that Oat was required only to be present while others "voluntarily" discussed settlement.

b. Rule 16, Federal Rules of Civil Procedure (1993 Version)

Rule 16 on Pretrial Conference was amended in 1993. It now reads, in relevant part:

> (c) At any [pretrial] conference under this rule consideration may be given, and the court may take appropriate action, with respect to . . .
>
> (9) settlement and the use of special procedures to assist in resolving the dispute where authorized by statute or local rule; . . .
>
> If appropriate, the court may require that a party or its representative be present or reasonably available by telephone in order to consider possible settlement of the dispute.

Section (f) provides for the imposition of sanctions (costs and attorney fees) for being unprepared at a pretrial conference, failing to participate in good faith, or for not appearing at all. The advisory committee notes about the revised Rule 16 are instructive:

Paragraph (9) is revised to describe more accurately the various procedures that, in addition to traditional settlement conferences may be helpful in settling litigation. Even if a case cannot immediately be settled, the judge and attorneys can explore possible use of alternative procedures such as mini-trials, summary jury trials, mediation, neutral evaluation, and non-binding arbitration that can lead to consensual resolution of the dispute without a full trial on the merits. . . .

> The amendment of paragraph (9) should be read in conjunction with the sentence added at the end of subdivision (c), authorizing the court to direct that, in appropriate cases, a responsible representative of the parties be present or available by telephone

during a conference in order to discuss possible settlement of the case. The sentence refers to participation by a party or its representative. Whether this would be the individual party, an officer of a corporate party, a representative from an insurance carrier, or someone else would depend on the circumstances. Particularly in litigation in which government agencies or large amounts of money are involved, there may be no one with on-the-spot settlement authority, and the most that should be expected is access to a person who would have a major role in submitting a recommendation to the body or board with ultimate decision-making responsibility. The selection of the appropriate representative should ordinarily be left to the party and its counsel. Finally, it should be noted that the unwillingness of a party to be available, even by telephone, for a settlement conference may be a clear signal that the time and expense involved in pursuing settlement is likely to be unproductive and that personal participation by the parties should not be required.

The explicit authorization in the rule to require personal participation in the manner stated is not intended to limit the reasonable exercise of the courts's inherent powers, *e.g. G. Heileman Brewing Co. v. Joseph Oat Corp.*, or its powers to require party participation under the Civil Justice Reform Act of 1990.

c. Comments and Questions

1. In the context of litigation between private parties, is the majority opinion in *Heileman Brewing* or the Easterbrook dissent more persuasive? (Settlement when the government is a party is considered in the next section.)

2. Do the 1993 revisions favor the position of the majority or the dissent in *Heileman Brewing?* On the same facts, how should the case be decided under the present rule?

3. A problem for the courts may be lack of the most modern technology. With the teleconferencing capability available in medium sized law firm, not to mention computers and fast modems that allow for almost instant communication of hard copies of settlement proposals or other documents, it seems positively archaic, not to mention expensive, for courts to mandate in person attendance at meetings that require long-distance travel.

4. The majority is acutely aware that travel from Camden, New Jersey to Madison, Wisconsin may present considerable costs. It responds that Oat Corporation sent a lawyer from Philadelphia, but it could have sent a senior executive instead for about the same price, so cost is not a factor. This approach ignores the opportunity costs of the executive's time, and the harm to the Oat Corporation of having that person not attending to business.

5. At the risk of offending some personal friends, it should be noted that judges with lifetime appointments sometimes have an unduly expansive view about the value of their time, and a more moderate appreciation of the value of other people's time. This point is driven home by the William Brock incident described by Judge Posner.

6. Should it matter that the party objecting to personal attendance at a settlement conference is the defendant, who is an involuntary participant in litigation? Where venue is available in several places, the plaintiff is likely (other things being equal) to select the geographically most convenient court, which probably is the least convenient forum for defendant. This was true in *Heileman Brewing.*

7. *Heileman Brewing* is a troubling and much discussed case. Professor Sherman appears to support the majority, and he favors allowing flexibility to the courts:

> There should be no fixed rule either way as to party representative attendance; the efficiency and proportionality considerations identified by the majority proivde appropriate guidance for case-by-case determinations. . . . Although anti-coercion and litigant-autonomy policies favor honoring the party's choice of a representative, a court should be entitled to dtermine that the day-in-court and promotion-of-ADR-settlement objectives cannot be served by the sole attendance of an attorney.

Edward F. Sherman, *Court-Mandated Alternative Dispute Resolution: What Form of Participation Should be Required?*, 46 SMU L. REV. 2079, 2106 (1993).

8. Professor Riskin, a strong proponent of the healing aspects of mediation, would "routinely require attendance of represented clients, and representatives of organizational clients with full settlement authority, in the absence of suitable and suitably presented objection. . . ." Leonard L. Riskin, *The Represented Client in a Settlement Conference: The Lessons of* G. Heileman Brewing Co. v. Joseph Oat Corp., 69 WASH. U. L.Q. 1059 (1991). In this article, Riskin recounts the following story of a successful mediation:

> [The disputants were] two brothers. The legal issue involved partnership. The case settled and the brothers renewed an old friendship, but only after [the mediator] asked them two pwersonal questions: "What was your relationship as children?" and "What would your parents [who were deceased] think if they saw you [in court]?"

This story wonderfully illustrates the transformative potential of mediation, but what does it have to do with a commercial dispute between two unrelated corporations located half a country apart?

3. Settlement Authority of Government Representatives

a. *In re Stone*, 986 F.2d 898 (5th Cir. 1993)

Before JOLLY, DAVIS, and SMITH, Circuit Judges.

PER CURIAM:

In these petitions seeking writs of mandamus, we decide whether a federal district judge has the power, by a standing order, to direct the federal government to send a representative with full settlement authority to settlement conferences and, if so, whether he abused his discretion by so doing in these routine civil lawsuits involving the United States. In addition to requiring counsel to attend these conferences, the court also requires the attendance of a designated representative of each party with full authority to settle the case; that representative must appear in person—availability by telephone is not sufficient. We conclude that although the district judge possesses the ultimate power to require the attendance at issue, it is a power to be very sparingly used, and here the district judge, albeit with the best of intentions, has abused his discretion.

In each of the petitions before us, the federal government objects to this order as applied to it. By statute, the Attorney General of the United States has the power to conduct all litigation on behalf of the United States, its agencies, and its officers, unless otherwise provided by law. Pursuant to authority given by 28 U.S.C. § 510 the Attorney General has developed a set of regulations delegating settlement authority to various officials. See 28 C.F.R. §§ 0.160 - 0.172.

As we read these regulations, United States Attorneys often will be able to settle a case without approval from a higher authority, as the regulations provide that each local United States Attorney has settlement authority up to $500,000. If the client agency disagrees with the United States Attorney over the terms of the settlement, however, an Assistant Attorney General must approve the settlement. In addition, settlements in various classes of important cases always must be approved by the Deputy Attorney General or one of the Assistant Attorneys General.[1]

Although it is historically reserved for "extraordinary" cases, we have used the writ of mandamus as a "one-time-only device to 'settle new and important problems' that might have otherwise evaded expeditious review." As district courts continue to become more heavily involved in the pretrial process, appellate courts may be asked more often to issue writs of mandamus to protect the asserted rights of litigants. Pretrial orders such as the ones before us raise important issues but are ill-suited for review after final judgment. Because these cases present an important, undecided issue involving the efficient administration of justice, we may appropriately invoke mandamus review.

The district court claims inherent power to issue the order. [T]here are three general categories of inherent powers. The first category delineates powers that are so fundamental to the essence of a court as a constitutional tribunal that to divest the court of absolute command within this sphere is really to render practically meaningless the terms "court" and "judicial power." . . .

The second category of inherent powers encompasses those "necessary to the exercise of all others." For the most part, these powers are those deemed necessary to protect the efficient and orderly administration of justice and those necessary to command respect for the court's orders, judgments, procedures, and authority. . . . Congress may interfere with this category of inherent power within "limits not precisely defined," so long as it does not abrogate or render the specific power inoperative.

Courts have recognized several examples of this type of inherent power. The contempt sanction long has been recognized as among the most important of these powers. In addition, the Supreme Court has recognized the power to levy sanctions in response to abusive litigation practices.

The third category of inherent powers includes those reasonably useful to achieve justice. This category of powers recognizes that the legislature cannot foresee every tool the courts might need to employ to reach a just result in all cases. Where it appears that a court cannot adequately and efficiently carry out its duties without employing some special device, the court has inherent power to do so. This category of inherent power arises from mere necessity and, consequently, can be completely regulated by Congress. As an example of this type of power, the Supreme Court has upheld the power of a district court to appoint an auditor to aid in litigation involving a complex commercial matter.

By employing the above three categories, we may now establish a method for reviewing purported exercises of inherent powers. . . . [W]hile we review the court's exercise of such powers only for abuse of discretion, we define the powers narrowly, as they are shielded from

---

[1]Even if a case is to be settled for not more than $500,000, so that a United States Attorney could settle it under the regulations, his settlement authority disappears upon disagreement over the terms of the settlement by the client agency.

effective democratic control and must be exercised with restraint.

The district court's standing order invokes its inherent power to manage its own docket to achieve the just and efficient disposition of cases. On the basis of our discussion above, we conclude that this power fits most appropriately in the second category.

We are able to conclude, based upon the foregoing, that, subject to the abuse-of-discretion standard, district courts have the general inherent power to require a party to have a representative with full settlement authority present—or at least reasonably and promptly accessible—at pretrial conferences. This applies to the government as well as private litigants. We find no statute or rule that attempts to regulate the court's use of that inherent power. But a district court must consider the unique position of the government as a litigant in determining whether to exercise its discretion in favor of issuing such an order.[5]

. . . The purpose of the structure established by the Attorney General is to promote centralized decisionmaking on important questions. Centralized decisionmaking promotes three important objectives. First, it allows the government to act consistently in important cases, a value more or less recognized by the Equal Protection Clause. Second, centralized decisionmaking allows the executive branch to pursue policy goals more effectively by placing ultimate authority in the hands of a few officials. Third, by giving authority to high-ranking officials, centralized decisionmaking better promotes political accountability.

Given the reasonable policy justifications for the Justice Department's settlement regulations and the insignificant interference with the operation of the courts, the district court abused its discretion in not respecting those regulations. Where the interference with the courts is slight, courts should not risk becoming "monitors of the wisdom and soundness of Executive action." The order at issue here imposes a major inconvenience on at least one of the parties without the showing of a real and palpable need.

The district court contends that the government is not special and should not be treated differently from private litigants. The government is in a special category in a number of respects, however, in addition to its need for centralized decisionmaking. [T]he Government is a party to a far greater number of cases on a nationwide basis than even the most litigious private entity. . . . Obviously, high-ranking officials of cabinet agencies could never do their jobs if they could be subpoenaed for every case involving their agency. As a result, we have held that such subpoenas are appropriate only in egregious cases. *See, e.g., In re Equal Employment Opportunity Comm'n*, 709 F.2d 392, 398 (5th Cir.1983). "[T]he efficiency of the EEOC would suffer terribly if its commissioners were subject to depositions in every routine subpoena enforcement proceeding." In determining whether to require the government (or, for that matter, a private party) to send a representative to a pretrial conference with full authority to settle, a district court should take a practical approach. The court must be permitted to conduct its business in a reasonably efficient manner; it need not allow the parties or counsel to waste valuable judicial resources unnecessarily. On the other hand, the court should recognize that parties have a host of problems beyond the immediate case that is set

[5]Our holding today allows us to avoid deciding whether forcing the Attorney General to alter the settlement regulations would run afoul of the doctrine of separation of powers. The government also relies upon a portion of the Judicial Improvements Act of 1990, 28 U.S.C.A. § 473, which gives district courts the power to adopt local rules to require parties with full settlement authority to attend settlement conferences. This statute does not affect the issue before us, as the district judge did not act pursuant to a local rule passed pursuant to this statute; instead, he primarily asserts inherent powers.

for pretrial conference. This is particularly true of the government. . . .

We conclude that the district court abused its discretion in routinely requiring a representative of the government with ultimate settlement authority to be present at all pretrial or settlement conferences. We do not suggest that the district court can never issue such an order, but it should consider less drastic steps before doing so.

For example, the court could require the government to declare whether the case can be settled within the authority of the local United States Attorney. If so, the court could issue an order requiring the United States Attorney to either attend the conference personally or be available by telephone to discuss settlement at the time of the conference.

According to the government at argument, most of its routine litigation can be settled within the United States Attorney's authority. Where that is not so, and failure of the government to extend settlement authority is a serious, persistent problem, substantially hampering the operations of the docket, the court could take additional action, such as requiring the government to advise it of the identity of the person or persons who hold such authority and directing those persons to consider settlement in advance of the conference and be fully prepared and available by telephone to discuss settlement at the time of the conference. Finally, if the district court's reasonable efforts to conduct an informed settlement discussion in a particular case are thwarted because the government official with settlement authority will not communicate with government counsel or the court in a timely manner, the court, as a last resort, can require the appropriate officials with full settlement authority to attend a pretrial conference.

The measures we outline above are intended to be exemplary, and we express no ultimate view as to such hypothetical situations except to point out that there are many steps that reasonably can be taken, far short of the standing order at issue here. We include these scenarios to demonstrate that the district court, before issuing an order such as the directive under review here, must give individualized attention to the hardship that order will create. The court must then exercise its discretion in light of the circumstances of that case. We believe that such practical measures will enable the courts to administer their dockets efficiently while allowing the Department of Justice to handle effectively the burdensome volume of litigation thrust upon it.

In summary, we conclude that the district court abused its discretion in these cases. We find it unnecessary to issue writs of mandamus, however. The able district judge has indicated that he welcomes this court's exposition of this issue, and we are confident that he will abide by our decision and adjust his directives accordingly. Thus, the petitions for writs of mandamus are DENIED without prejudice.

b. Comments and Questions

1. Should government ever be treated differently from private litigants in the settlement context? If so, in what circumstances, and how should the treatment differ?

2. As noted by the 5th Circuit, Congress has expressly authorized District Courts to adopt local settlement rules, so there appears no need to rely on inherent authority. Why not require District Courts to adopt settlement rules, rather than proceeding on the basis of inherent authority? This approach would inform the public about the law, and prevent apparently arbitrary exercises of authority by individual judges. (In administrative law, this is a standard argument for broad use of rulemaking authority.)

3. Does a U.S. district judge have inherent authority to ignore court settlement rules, where the judge deems it important to do so? Presumably your answer would not change with respect to state judges, a far larger category of government officials.

4. Note the "kid gloves" treatment given to the district judge who was held to have engaged in an abuse of discretion, a truly unusual event. No writ of mandamus is issued, because the appeals court is confident that its suggestions will be followed.

5. Abuse of discretion is rare, in part because the discretion of district judges is so broad. In the event that discretion has been misused, appellate judges do not like to chastise their judicial brethren (all of whom are acquaintances and some are friends). Most misuses of discretion are dealt with informally, if at all. Even when an abuse is so severe that a court has to publicly rebuke a district judge, as in the Stone case, the rebuke is administered gently.

6. Settlement authority problems at the state and local level may be more difficult than those presented in the Stone case. For example, the settlement authority of the city attorney in Houston (the fourth largest city in America) is limited to $5,000. Any larger amount requires the approval of the City Council — and, of course, (supporters of open government will be pleased to know), proposed settlements are considered in public meetings. Would it be crass to suggest that public posturing by the elected members of the council sometimes takes place, and that political factors sometimes play a role?

7. Can a judge, whether state or federal, order the Council to even consider a tentative settlement? The Council sets it own agenda, and by Council rules any one of the fourteen members may table an item for one week. Suppose the Council disapproves a settlement, or authorized a settlement amount significantly lower than the tentative settlement? Would your view of the matter change, depending on the source of the $5,000 limitation? Among the possibilities are custom, written Council policy, local ordinance, state statute, and state constitution.

8. The state constitution possibility is not preposterous; many states have multi-volume constitutions that cover matters of astonishing detail. Consider the following proposed amendments to the Texas constitutions (largely as described on the ballot) that were among the sixteen put before the voters of the entire state in 1993:

Proposition 2 promotes the reduction of pollution and encourages the preservation of jobs by allowing the Legislature to exempt from ad valorem taxation all or part of property used for the control of air, water, or land pollution. (In plain English, this is a corporate tax break.)

Proposition 3 clears up a Mexican land grant matter in Fort Bend and Austin County for 146 families on 144 acres of land.

Proposition 5 allows the Legislature to prescribe the qualifications for sheriffs.

Proposition 6 abolishes the office of county surveyor in Jackson County, and substitutes an official designated by Commissioners Court.

Proposition 7 repeals a provision relating to the issuance of stock adopted by the Constitutional Convention in 1875. (This limitation was in response to concerns about "watered stock" that has become obsolete and an impediment to the issuance of separate classes of stock, stock dividends, and other financing devices.)

Proposition 8 abolishes the office of county surveyor in McLennan County.

Proposition 9 modifies the provisions for redemption of real property sold at a tax sale, reducing the period from two years to six months. (This provision does not apply to land designated for agricultural use, and residence homesteads.)

Proposition 13 adds the Texas State Technical College to the institutions eligible to receive funding under the Higher Education Assistance Fund.

Proposition 15 permits voters of a county to decide whether to abolish the office of county surveyor, at an elections called for that purpose by the County Commissioner's Court.

9. Another type of entity that is a common party to law suits is state universities. Large state universities (*e.g.*, the University of Wisconsin) are separate legal entities governed by a board of regents. The regents are state residents, but they live throughout the state. (Indeed, geographic diversity is a common consideration in the appointment of regents.) Regents serve on a part-time basis, and they usually receive no cash compensation (expenses are reimbursed and there are other rewards). Regents typically are successful (and highly compensated executives) or professionals. Placing such persons at the beck and call of judges all over America would be a severe impediment to recruiting highly capable regents. Boards of Regents hold four to eight regular meetings per year, and these normally are scheduled a full year in advance. Special meetings are held for important issues, but commonly some regents participate by telephone or notational voting.

10. It is easy to understand why public officials, whether elected or appointed, are concerned about the payment of large sums from the public coffers. However, settlement of law suits by government is a two-way street, and the government may win as well as lose. Government should also be concerned that it does not receive too little in settling cases where it prevails.

D. Is There a Duty of Good Faith Participation in Mandatory ADR?

1. *Decker v. Lindsay*, 824 S.W.2d 247 (Tex. Civ. App. 1992)

SAM H. BASS, Justice.

We are faced with two questions today: (1) Can a party be compelled to participate in an alternative dispute resolution (ADR) procedure despite its objections?, and (2) Have relators established their right to mandamus relief?

John and Mary Decker, relators, seek mandamus relief against respondent, Judge Tony Lindsay, who signed an order on October 18, 1991 referring their suit against Jordan Mintz, the real party in interest, to mediation under TEX. CIV. PRAC. & REM. CODE ANN. § 154.021(a)

Judge Lindsay's mediation order was made on her own motion, without any hearing. She consulted with neither party before entering her order. *See* TEX. CIV. PRAC. & REM. CODE ANN. § 154.021(b). However, only relators objected to the referral and they submitted their objections for a ruling without oral argument. Judge Lindsay overruled their objections.

The October 18, 1991, order requires the parties to agree on a mediation date "within the next 30 days," or by November 18, 1991. If no agreed date is scheduled, the order provides that the mediator will select a date within the next 60 days, or by December 18, 1991. The order also reads, "TO BE MEDIATED PRIOR TO TRIAL SETTING OF 1-20-92."

We are concerned primarily with the following provisions of Judge Lindsay's order: Mediation is a mandatory but non-binding settlement conference, conducted with the assistance of the Mediator. . . . Fees for the mediation are to be divided and borne equally by the parties unless agreed otherwise, shall be paid by the parties directly to the Mediator, and shall be taxed as costs. Each party and counsel will be bound by the Rules for Mediation printed on the back of this Order. . . . Named parties shall be present during the entire mediation process . . . . Counsel and parties shall proceed in a good faith effort to try to resolve this case. . . . Referral to mediation is not a substitute for trial, and the case will be tried if not settled.

Two of the Rules for Mediation, affixed to the order, are relevant to our discussion: 2. Agreement of the Parties. Whenever the parties have agreed to mediation they shall be deemed to have made these rules, as amended and in effect as of the date of the submission of the dispute, a part of their agreement to mediate. . . . 6. Commitment to Participate in Good Faith. While no one is asked to commit to settle their dispute in advance of mediation, all parties commit to participate in the proceedings in good faith with the intention to settle, if at all possible.

Mandamus issues only to correct a clear abuse of discretion or the violation of a duty imposed by law when there is no other adequate remedy by law. Mandamus relief may be afforded where the trial court's order is void. However, the order of the trial court must be one beyond the power of the court to enter; it is not enough that the order is merely erroneous. . . .

Relators assert Judge Lindsay's order is void and constitutes a clear abuse of discretion for the following reasons, which they also stated in their objection to mediation filed with the trial court: (1) the lawsuit arises out of a simple rear-end car collision, where the only issues are negligence, proximate cause, and damages; (2) trial is likely to last for only two days; (3) it is relators' opinion that mediation will not resolve the lawsuit, and they have not agreed to pay fees to the mediator; (4) mediation may cause relators to compromise their potential cause of action under the Stowers doctrine; (5) the law does not favor alternative dispute resolution where one of the litigants objects to it and when the litigants have been ordered to pay for it; and (6) court-ordered mediation, over the relators' objection and at their cost, violates their right to due process and their right to open courts under article I, section 13 of the Texas Constitution.

The real party in interest disputes relators' contention that the lawsuit and its issues are simple. The real party in interest has raised the defense of unavoidable accident and asserts that the parties have wide-ranging disagreement over Mr. Decker's claimed economic and medical damages.

Relators contend that trial will last for only two days. Consequently, it will take only slightly more time than the mediation ordered. However, the proposed joint pretrial order, signed by counsel for the relators and counsel for the real party in interest, provides an estimated trial time of three to four days.

While relators assert that mediation will not resolve the lawsuit, the real party in interest suggests that in a day invested in mediation, where communication between the parties is facilitated, relators may change their evaluation of the lawsuit.

Under Tex. Civ. Prac. & Rem. Code Ann. § 154.054(a) the court may set a reasonable fee for the services of an impartial third party appointed to facilitate an ADR procedure. Unless otherwise agreed by the parties, the court must tax the fee as other costs of the suit. No fee was ever set for the mediation in this case. [A]fter this proceeding was filed, the mediator advised the parties that she waived her fee in the case.

We cannot say that Judge Lindsay abused her discretion in impliedly finding the first three reasons advanced by relators were not reasonable objections to court-ordered mediation.

Mediation may be beneficial even if relators believe it will not resolve the lawsuit. The statute certainly allows a reasonable fee to be charged, . . . but now the fee issue is moot.

Concerning relators' remaining objections, Texas law recognizes that an insurer has a duty to the insured to settle a lawsuit if a prudent person in the exercise of ordinary care would do so. *G.A. Stowers Furniture Co.,* 15 S.W.2d at 547. If an ordinarily prudent person would have settled the lawsuit, and the insurer failed or refused to do so, it is liable to the insured for the amount of damages eventually recovered in excess of the policy limits. Relators assert that an insured, for example the real party in interest here, frequently assigns to the plaintiff his *Stowers* rights against his insurer, in return for a covenant that the plaintiff will not execute on the insured's personal assets. Therefore, relators contend that by ordering them to mediation, Judge Lindsay is interfering with their right to preserve a potential cause of action against the liability insurer of the real party in interest.

First, relators have no *Stowers* rights against the liability insurer of the real party in interest. Second, there has been no trial; there has been no judgment; there has been no assignment of the real party in interest's *Stowers* rights to relators; there has been no determination that a reasonably prudent person would have decided, at the time relators made their offer, to settle the litigation for the policy limits. A *Stowers* cause of action does not accrue until the judgment in the underlying case becomes final. We cannot say that Judge Lindsay abused her discretion in impliedly finding that court-ordered mediation would not cause relators to compromise a potential cause of action under *Stowers*.

Relators also argue that chapter 154 of the Texas Civil Practice and Remedies Code presents a "voluntary" procedure, and that mandatory referral to a paid mediator is not within its scope. Section 154.002 expresses the general policy that "peaceable resolution of disputes" is to be encouraged through "voluntary settlement procedures." Courts are admonished to carry out this policy. A court cannot force the disputants to peaceably resolve their differences, but it can compel them to sit down with each other.

Section 154.021(a) authorizes a trial court on its motion to refer a dispute to an ADR procedure. However, if a party objects, and there is a reasonable basis for the objection, the court may not refer the dispute to an ADR procedure. The corollary of this provision is that a court may refer the dispute to an ADR procedure if it finds there is no reasonable basis for the objection. A person appointed to facilitate an ADR procedure may not compel the parties to mediate (negotiate) or coerce the parties to enter into a settlement agreement. A mediator may not impose his or her own judgment on the issues for that of the parties.

Therefore, the policy of section 154.002 is consistent with a scheme where a court refers a dispute to an ADR procedure, requiring the parties to come together in court-ordered ADR procedures, but no one can compel the parties to negotiate or settle a dispute unless they voluntarily and mutually agree to do so. Any inconsistencies in chapter 154 can be resolved to give effect to a dominant legislative intent to compel referral, but not resolution.

However, Judge Lindsay's order does not comport with the scheme set forth in chapter 154. Her order, and the mediation rules that are a part of it, do more than require the parties to come together; they require them to "negotiate" in good faith and attempt to reach a settlement. . . .

[I]n one very important respect, Judge Lindsay's order violates the open courts provision. It requires relators attempt to negotiate a settlement of the dispute with the real party in interest in good faith, when they have clearly indicated they do not wish to do so, but prefer to go to trial. As we noted above, the order does more than refer the dispute to an ADR procedure; it requires negotiation. Chapter 154 contemplates mandatory referral only, not mandatory negotiation.

Having reviewed the arguments of relators, which do not attack the statute, but only the order of referral, and those of the real party in interest and the documents submitted to us, we conclude that Judge Lindsay's order is void insofar as it directs relators to negotiate in good faith a resolution of their dispute with the real party in interest through mediation, despite relators' objections.

2. Edward F. Sherman, *Court-Mandated Alternative Dispute Resolution: What Form of Participation Should be Required?*, 46 SMU L. Rev. 2079 (1993)*

I. THE SETTLEMENT FUNCTION OF [NONBINDING] COURT-MANDATED ADR

In determining what should be required in a court-mandated ADR proceeding, it is useful to consider what its function and objectives are when it is annexed to the litigation system. The primary motivation of court rules and orders incorporating ADR has clearly been the hope of achieving settlement short of trial. Other benefits that ADR can have — such as exploring underlying interests, reconciling the parties, according them emotional closure, or permitting flexibility in the agreement — have been secondary in courts' motivation to institutionalize ADR. . . .

The function of court-mandated ADR, therefore, is efficient and effective settlement, and the procedures that govern its operation should be consistent with the values and objectives of settlement within the context of our trial-based litigation system.

This having been said, it is not to be assumed that court-annexation of an ADR process should transform it into a mirror image of an adversary trial. The very reason for believing that ADR might result in settlement is that it has unique features suited to getting an agreement that are lacking in a trial. These include the dynamics of assisted dialogue and cooperative problem-solving, reality-testing of perceptions and positions, neutral evaluation of strengths and weaknesses, empowering of parties to confront each other's values and the fairness of their positions, searching for mutually beneficial solutions, and flexibility of solutions outside the formal standards of legal rules — all under the protective cloak of confidentiality. These features are essential to the capacity of an ADR proceeding to achieve a settlement, and it would be counterproductive for a court to undermine those attributes and techniques when mandating ADR. The settlement objective of ADR as an integral part of the litigation process is best served by adopting those procedures governing its use that will preserve its settlement-enhancing features, as long as not inconsistent with the values and objectives of the litigation system as a whole.

The objection will undoubtedly be made that the essence of ADR cannot be reconciled with the objectives of the trial-based, adversary litigation system. I think this view fails to appreciate that our litigation system and ADR have a great deal in common — indeed, they are but different points along a spectrum of dispute-resolution processes. Both place a high value on a rational approach to dispute resolution, fairness of process, and the centrality of

---

*Reprinted with permission.

party autonomy. . . . That does not mean that ADR does not utilize some very different approaches to dispute resolution that attempt to overcome dysfunctional adversariness, but, on balance, those techniques can be reconciled with the litigation system.

Concern over a mismatch between ADR and litigation stems in part from the over-selling of ADR as a docket-clearing and cost-saving device. Some judges have embraced mandatory ADR as the solution to their crowded dockets with little sensitivity to the fact that obtaining a settlement is not necessarily a sign of successful ADR. Mediation, for example, seeks a solution through the voluntary cooperation of the parties, and mediator manipulation of the parties in order to achieve a settlement, without concern for the quality of the agreement and how it was achieved, would seriously undermine the objectives of the process. Moreover, empirical evidence as to cost-savings of court-annexed ADR is far from clear. Court-annexed ADR, therefore, should not be seen as simply another docket-control device. If its distinctive process is understood and respected when court-annexed, its values and objectives need not be compromised.

There are obviously procedural differences between a trial and ADR. For example, rules of evidence apply in a trial but not in ADR. That difference does not, however, make ADR inconsistent with ultimate resort to trial unless a party's trial rights would be adversely affected by being forced to participate in ADR conducted without rules of evidence. Sometimes a difference between ADR and trial procedure will require modifying the ADR procedure for greater compatibility with the litigation process. For example, discovery is generally available in litigation but not in ADR. It may be desirable in a particular case to permit discovery in court-mandated ADR, given that it will be allowed in the normal course of litigation and could offer greater efficiency and fairness in the ADR proceeding. There may be other situations when the trial procedure should be modified for greater compatibility with ADR. For example, time-tables established in scheduling conferences for performing various pretrial functions or the time for ruling on pre-trial motions might be modified to enhance the effectiveness and efficiency of a court-ordered ADR proceeding. Thus the integration of ADR into litigation should permit some adjustment of the procedures of either litigation or ADR to prevent incompatibility.

II. VALUES AND OBJECTIVES OF ADR IN THE TRIAL-BASED LITIGATION SYSTEM

Under our legal system, the trial is the paradigm for formal dispute resolution. It is the ultimate legal mechanism to which parties may resort for resolving disputes. Even court-mandated ADR processes are performed "in the shadow" of a trial in the sense that the likely trial result provides a bench-mark for the parties' expectations and demands in the ADR proceeding.

It is fundamental in determining the appropriate role of court-mandated ADR that parties' constitutional rights to a trial by jury cannot be abrogated. Thus binding forms of ADR (such as traditional arbitration) cannot be mandated, and the forms of ADR that courts have adopted are all nonbinding. A corollary of the principle that the ultimate right to trial cannot be abrogated is that if an ADR process is ordered, it must be accomplished in a manner that will not undermine the ultimate right to a trial.

Four basic principles can be distilled from applying the values and objectives of court-mandated ADR in the trial-based litigation system.

A. Avoidance of Coercing Parties into Settling

If a nonbinding ADR proceeding is not to undermine the ultimate right to a trial, parties obviously should not be "coerced" into settling. Judicial encouragement of settlement has long been practiced in federal and many state courts; until the advent of the ADR movement, this was primarily accomplished through a settlement conference with the judge who used a combination of jaw-boning and veiled threats to move the parties towards settlement. The courts have uniformly held that such settlement procedures must not have the effect of coercing the parties into settling.

In a typical case, *Kothe v. Smith,* the Second Circuit reversed sanctions against the defendant after he refused to settle before trial (on the judge's recommendation of a $20,000 to $30,000 settlement figure), but settled for $20,000 after one day of trial. The Second Circuit concluded that an "attorney should not be condemned for changing his evaluation of the case after listening to [the opponent's] testimony during the first day of trial." The process used in Kothe was a judicial settlement conference, authorized by Federal Rule of Civil Procedure 16. The appellate court viewed this rule as "designed to encourage pretrial settlement discussions," but not to "impose settlement negotiations on unwilling litigants." "Pressure tactics to coerce settlement," it said, "simply are not permissible."

Pressure tactics, of course, are often involved in settlement procedures — either in judicial conferences or ADR. The question is when they become so coercive that they are not permissible. The line between "coercion" and "encouragement" of settlement is sometimes difficult to draw, but this distinction is central to resolving the form of participation required of a party in a court-mandated ADR proceeding.

B. A Fair Proceeding that is Equivalent to a Day in Court

If ADR is mandated as an integral part of litigation, the process used should be consistent with the parties' ultimate right to a trial. An ADR process that undermines the basic values of a trial should not be forced on a party even if it might result in settlement. . . .

Compatibility with the trial system does not, of course, require that an ADR proceeding possess all the attributes of a trial. A mediation, for example, encourages consideration of a much broader range of matters than would be admissible in a trial, but this creates no irreconcilable conflict with trial rules. A mediation simply allows the parties to determine their own standards of relevancy in choosing to settle rather than going to a trial where formal rules of evidence would pertain. But if the parties are required to participate in an ADR process, it should at least provide them with the sense of having had their "day in court." Studies indicate that litigants tend to judge the justness of dispute proceedings not so much on whether they win or lose, but on whether they view the process itself to have been fair. Respect for our judicial system can only be maintained if parties who settle in ADR proceedings later feel that they had a fair opportunity to have their say and voluntarily choose to settle rather than going to trial. Therefore, a critical feature of the form of participation required in court-mandated ADR is that it enable the process to provide the parties a sense of having participated in a fair proceeding.

C. A Proceeding Calculated to Achieve Its Purposes

The imposition of any ADR procedures on the parties as a prerequisite to exercising their right to a trial must be calculated to aid in the resolution of the dispute. Parties should not be forced to participate in costly, time-consuming procedures that are futile. Mandatory ADR procedures, therefore, should be suited to developing the facts and law in a way that will enhance the fair and efficient resolution of the case without wasted effort. If court-annexed ADR is to be effective, it should be true to its own process goals and values. Thus, respect for the process objectives of ADR is a necessary principle of its integration into the litigation system. It may be necessary for courts, at times, to alter their usual procedures in order to insure that ADR objectives are not compromised. If, however, the underlying ADR process cannot be reconciled with the objectives of the trial-based litigation system through accommodations in either the court or ADR procedures that do not negate their basic values, then ADR should not be mandated.

D. Respect for Litigant Autonomy

Our trial system accords considerable deference to litigant autonomy over the conduct of litigation. Litigant autonomy is respected in such matters as choice of forum, selection of the parties, shaping of claims and defenses, development of issues, utilization of discovery, preparation of cases, and ultimate presentation before judge or jury. The policy underlying litigant autonomy derives from the conviction that the parties are in the best position to know the facts and appreciate their objectives and that courts are not well-suited to taking over the function of preparing, developing, and presenting cases.

ADR also places a high value on individual autonomy, with special emphasis on the empowerment of the parties to shape their own cases and solutions. ADR processes respect the rights of the parties to shape their arguments, articulate their interests and demands, and ultimately to agree or not to a settlement. The commanding role of the parties in determining their own resolution of the dispute under ADR is an important factor in explaining why there is a greater compliance rate with judgments resulting from settlement than from court-imposed decrees.

ADR that is court-mandated, rather than voluntary, might appear to be inconsistent with litigant autonomy because the parties are forced to participate. However, participation in the process, as opposed to actual agreement, must sometimes be mandated. Experience shows that parties often benefit from ADR even though their participation is not voluntary. Most mediators have encountered the situation where parties announce at the beginning of the process that they are only there because they were ordered to participate by the court or other authority and that they will not compromise their positions in any way. Many of these situations still result in settlements, indicating that freedom of control over the content and presentation of their cases is often more important to the satisfactory operation of ADR than whether the parties were forced initially to participate.

Procedures governing the conduct of ADR generally accord the parties more autonomy [than] that is offered in a trial. In terms of what participation should be required of parties, therefore, party autonomy requires a level of participation consistent with the parties' freedom to present their cases, their interests, and their demands in the manner they choose.

III. FORMS OF PARTICIPATION REQUIRED IN ADR

The four principles just discussed provide guidelines for judging what forms of participation in ADR proceedings are compatible with the values and objectives of the litigation system. I will focus on five frequently encountered forms of participation that may be required to comply with court-ordered ADR: good faith participation; exchange of position papers and objective information; minimum meaningful participation; participation with settlement authority; and obligation to pay the third-party neutral's fee.

A. Good Faith Participation

Over the past several years some judges in ordering parties to participate in ADR proceedings have included a provision that they must participate in good faith. A number of states have also adopted, by statute or rule, a good faith participation requirement for mediation or ADR. A good faith participation requirement is obviously premised on the belief that since ADR is non-binding, it will be a futile exercise unless the parties engage in it with willingness to present their best arguments and to listen to those of the other side with an open mind.

1. Inadequacy of Case Precedents for Policy Guidance

There is remarkably little case law that examines policy issues as to the propriety of a requirement of good faith participation in ADR. A good faith standard first appeared in a 1983 amendment to Rule 16, the pretrial conference rule on which the authority for federal courts' annexation of ADR processes has been based. Rule 16(f) provides for sanctions, upon motion or a judge's own initiative, for a party's or its attorney's failing to obey a scheduling or pretrial order, being "substantially unprepared to participate in the conference," or failing "to participate in good faith." There have been few reported cases on the application of the Rule 16 good faith participation requirement. It is usually failure to appear or lack of preparation, rather than the quality of participation, that has resulted in sanctions. That is not surprising since a settlement conference with a judge is usually informal, leaving both the judge and attorneys considerable leeway in how they will participate. Only recently has there been an emphasis on attendance and participation by the parties themselves, raising a host of new issues about participation. Thus Rule 16 precedents offer little guidance as to the scope of the good faith participation requirement in ADR.

The recent court-annexation of ADR processes has resulted in few decisions in either federal or state courts concerning required participation in ADR, and such decisions provide little policy guidance as to what kind of participation is required. In most cases courts have relied on Rule 16 (or an equivalent in state courts) or on inherent judicial authority for their power to sanction for nonparticipation. The decisions that have addressed the issue tend to rely on narrow questions of a court's authority to make such an order or on the appropriateness of the sanctions imposed for noncompliance. For example, in *Decker v. Lindsey* a Texas appellate court upheld an order to mediate, reasoning that a court "can compel [the parties] to sit down with each other" in a mediation and "to come together in court-ordered ADR procedures." It struck down, however, a part of the order that required participation in good faith, based on an interpretation of the Texas "open courts" statute as forbidding an order that requires negotiation when the parties prefer to go to trial. In *Department of Transportation v. City of Atlanta* the Georgia Supreme Court held that "a trial court has the authority to refer the parties to mediation," but that the order to engage in mediation in good faith would exceed the court's authority if construed as justifying contempt penalties if the mediation failed.

Other cases have determined that the applicable statute did not, in fact, require "good faith participation." *Graham v. Baker* involved an Iowa statute that required participation in a mediation session before a creditor can receive a "mediation release" to undertake forfeiture proceedings in farmer-creditor loan disputes. The creditors' attorney attended the mediation, but "refused to cooperate with the mediator," denied the debtors "any opportunity to put forward their proposals for resolving the situation," was "agitated and belligerent," and was "hostile to the [debtors], the mediator, and the mediation process." The Iowa Supreme Court held that since the statute "does not give the mediation service the power to compel either debtor or creditor to negotiate," the creditor's attendance satisfied the minimal participation required by the statute, even though the creditor stated that his position was not negotiable.

Some cases have simply found that the conduct did not amount to an absence of good faith. In *Halaby, McCrea & Cross v. Hoffman,* the Colorado Supreme Court found that the trial judge had abused his discretion in imposing sanctions on a law firm for failure to participate in a court-ordered settlement conference in good faith. Without questioning the propriety of the order, the court found that the defendant's failure to disclose that his settlement authority was limited to $300 was not acting in bad faith. This conclusion was based on the defendant having submitted a required confidential statement to the judge setting out his position that the plaintiff's claims were without merit and on the plaintiff having failed to ask him at the beginning of the conference about his settlement authority. Again, the decision is of little use in determining the appropriate level of good faith participation in other situations.

2. Inadequacy of the Collective Bargaining Analogy

A possible source for policy guidance in applying the "good faith participation" requirement is collective bargaining. Under the labor laws, unions and management that are required to engage in collective bargaining must bargain in good faith. Is that an apt analogy for ADR? Both ADR and collective bargaining would undoubtedly benefit from the parties' good faith participation. But there are differences in ADR which suggest that such participation is not as critical to the process as in collective bargaining and that the content of "good faith participation" is more difficult to determine.

First, the necessity for demanding good faith participation is less in ADR than in collective bargaining. The failure of an ADR proceeding simply means that the parties are relegated to their basic constitutional right to a trial. Failure of collective bargaining, on the other hand, can have severe social consequences — labor unrest, non-cooperation, and strikes. The fact that there is no reasonable fall-back process after unsuccessful collective bargaining underlines the importance of forcing the parties to meet a certain level of participation.

Second, the labor laws impose positive duties on management and labor to participate in collective bargaining that do not exist in the procedural context of ADR. Negotiation in good faith is viewed as critical to labor's rights to share in the determination of contract provisions. The good faith participation duty in collective bargaining refers to "a bilateral procedure whereby the employer and the bargaining representative jointly attempt to set wages and working conditions for the employees." In effect, the conduct of the collective bargaining process itself is a playing out of the substantive rights guaranteed in the labor laws.

There is no similar substantive entitlement of parties in an ADR proceeding. A party has no right to force another party to accept its participation in shaping a settlement agreement. The authority for ADR in court rules and orders is only procedural, with express limitations on enlarging or modifying substantive rights. If the ADR is not successful, it will be followed by a trial where the parties' substantive rights can be vindicated.

The lack of a substantive entitlement in ADR makes it especially difficult to define the content of good faith participation. Court precedents have set out the parameters of good faith participation in collective bargaining. The parties have an obligation to "participate actively in the deliberations so as to indicate a present intention to find a basis for agreement." This implies "an open mind and a sincere desire to reach an agreement" and "to reach a common ground." Among those factors that may evidence bad faith bargaining can be Boulwarism (adopting a "take-it-or-leave-it" position),[63] surface bargaining (as in rejecting a proposal and tendering one's own without attempting to reconcile the differences), proposals that are predictably unacceptable, failing to offer concessions of value, and demands that are contrary to the spirit of the labor laws (for example, that the union cede most of its rights under the Act or give the management unilateral control of wages, hours, or working conditions).

Many of these same factors are fairly conventional tactics used by negotiators in law suits. Negotiators are not obligated to demonstrate an intent to find a basis for agreement, or to display a sincere desire to reach common ground, or to respond to and counter meaningfully the offers of the other side. ADR offers a process of assisted negotiation where the parties should be able to choose to be forthcoming and make concessions or not. To deny them the right to take strong, or even extreme, positions (for example, that there is no liability or that a certain sum is the only basis on which a settlement is possible) would deprive them of litigant autonomy and the legitimate right to hold out and have those issues determined in a trial. The level of accommodation to the other side required in collective bargaining is clearly unsuitable for ADR.

One further consideration operating against the use of the good faith participation standard in ADR is its inherent ambiguity. Phrased in terms of subjective intent, it seems to require an examination into a party's motives rather than its objective conduct. Its subjectivity raises the spectre of courts having to make complex investigations into the bargaining process of an ADR proceeding upon any party's claim of bad faith participation by another. The possibility of satellite litigation seeking sanctions for bad faith participation could severely undermine its claim to economy and efficiency.

Sanction motions also raise difficult issues of confidentiality. Many jurisdictions accord confidentiality to ADR. Proper determination of a sanction motion for bad faith participation could require the parties and the third party neutral to testify concerning communications made during the ADR proceeding. Courts would thus be faced with either rejecting confidentiality in bad faith participation cases (thereby undermining the need to encourage candor in ADR), or upholding confidentiality (thereby denying the parties access to crucial evidence on the participation issue). A broad good faith participation requirement increases the need for making this difficult confidentiality choice by multiplying the occasions when parties can seek sanctions based on their opponent's statements in the ADR proceeding.

3. Incompatibility with Values and Objectives of Litigation

If the ADR and collective-bargaining precedents provide little policy analysis, they do at least demonstrate that too expansive a "good faith participation" requirement may not be compatible with the four principles underlying the values and objectives of court-mandated ADR. Although in a non-binding ADR proceeding, a broad participation requirement may not be

---

[63]*General Elec. Co.*, 150 NLRB 192 (1964), *enforced,* 418 F.2d 736 (2d Cir. 1969), cert. denied, 397 U.S. 965 (1970). The name comes from a vice-president of General Electric who formulated the strategy of making of a non-negotiable "firm and fair offer," that was held to constitute bad faith bargaining.

coercive in the Kothe sense in which a judge attempts to impose his settlement figure on the parties, the higher the level of participation required, the greater the coercion by forcing a party to present its case in a manner not of its choosing. This shades into an invasion of litigant autonomy by interfering with the party's choice as to how to present its case. A legitimate claim of litigant autonomy can be made as to those matters of case presentation as to which the parties have superior expertise and can best perform in the interests of accuracy and efficiency. Under the principle of providing the equivalent of a day in court, the good faith participation requirement could result in a freer exchange of information and views, but, by requiring the parties to participate as they might not have chosen to do in a trial, it does not necessarily enhance their feeling of having had a fair proceeding. For the equivalent of a day in court, no greater degree of participation should be required than is needed for fairness under the ADR process (which places a high value on litigant autonomy and lack of coercion). This shades into the fourth principle — calculated to achieve its process purposes — which insists that the parties not be required to perform unnecessary or futile acts that are not reasonably likely to result in settlement. Imposing collective-bargaining kinds of good faith requirements on the parties seems as likely to result in satellite litigation over sanctions as to improve the possibility of settlement.

B. Exchange of Position Papers and Objective Information

If a "good faith participation" requirement is undesirable in ADR, there are forms of participation that would enhance the likelihood of success that rely on objective conduct and therefore are more easily enforced by courts. For any form of ADR to succeed, there must be some indication of the parties' positions on the relevant issues and some exchange of basic factual information. Requiring the parties to provide each other and the third-party neutral with position papers and other relevant information lays a basis for meaningful consideration of the case without mandating specific forms of presentation or interaction with the other party. It encourages further oral participation and interaction without having to specify its form, since once having submitted a position paper, parties and counsel are less likely to refuse to discuss their positions at the ADR proceeding.

A reasonable order would be that the parties provide a position paper in advance of the ADR proceeding which would include a plain and concise statement of: (1) the legal and factual issues in dispute, (2) the party's position on those issues, (3) the relief sought (including a particularized itemization of all elements of damage claimed), and (4) any offers and counteroffers previously made. This is a shortened list of the kinds of items that are routinely required by federal courts in proposed pretrial orders under the authority of the Rule 16 pretrial conference rule.

The order might also require the parties to provide to the other side in advance, or to bring to the ADR proceeding, certain documents, such as current medical reports or specific business records. It would thus also serve as a discovery or subpoena order. Such an order may not be necessary if discovery has already been conducted in the normal course of the litigation (although updating of documents, such as medical records, is still often necessary). Courts should be aware of the interplay between on-going discovery in the case and any production provisions contained in an ADR order. The two should be coordinated so as not to conflict. When ADR is ordered early in the litigation before discovery, some form of abbreviated discovery may be necessary if the ADR proceeding is to be meaningful. On the other hand, there is a growing tendency for courts to stay ordinary discovery if a scheduled ADR proceeding could make full discovery unnecessary. Courts should take care to insure that ADR not be used strategically as a vehicle to delay or frustrate normal discovery. If a stay of discovery is granted, the court should require the ADR proceeding to take place within a reasonably short time period.

C. Minimum Meaningful Participation

Although exchange of position papers and objective information often provides an alternative to mandating a specific level of participation in ADR, there can still be a need for a minimal level of oral participation by the parties if the process is to have a genuine hope of success. It is not easy to fashion a term to describe what that minimal level should be because the necessary degree of participation varies with the type of ADR process involved. For want of a better term, I have adopted the language used by some courts that require the parties to participate "in a meaningful manner." Although hardly a model of certainty and precision, a "minimal meaningful participation" standard avoids the subjectivity of "good faith participation" by suggesting that the degree of participation required to be "meaningful" is related to the goal of the ADR procedure. Since the methodology and objectives of ADR processes vary a good deal, the "minimal meaningful participation" standard allows flexibility of participation depending on the particular process involved in each case.

1. Meaningful Participation Varies with Type of ADR

The distinction between "facilitative ADR," on the one hand, and "evaluative" or "trial run" ADR on the other, is useful for judging the degree of participation that is "meaningful" for achieving the ADR goals. "Facilitative ADR," such as mediation, is the least structured process and should require the least amount of formal participation. It is true that mediation works best when the parties interact on all levels, and it has been argued that "the client should be obliged respectfully to consider, and reconsider, with the other parties or the judicial host, the positions and the interests of both sides, and to think about ways to resolve the dispute." The trouble with this definition of the participation requirement is that it trenches deeply on litigant autonomy and, because of its subjectivity, would be difficult for a court to enforce. That is not to say that parties should not be encouraged to undertake such interactive participation as would be conducive to good mediation results, but that courts should not require it of them.

The objective of mediation is to get the parties to communicate in the broad interests of settlement, and thus mediation requires at least briefly indicating one's positions as to the relevant issues, listening to the other side, and reacting to the other side's positions. Unlike "evaluative" and "trial run" ADR processes, a comprehensive presentation of the case is not necessarily required. Assuming that there is no serious disparity between the parties as to opportunity to obtain information, they should be entitled to provide only that information that they choose to reveal. A failure to address or to disclose information as to all issues may suggest weakness to the other party and lower its willingness to make offers, but that is a strategic risk a party should be entitled to take. One objective of mediation is to identify the underlying interests of the parties in the hope of finding a solution that satisfies both sides. Nevertheless, as in any negotiation, disguising of true interests and bottom lines cannot be prohibited, for otherwise the courts would be enmeshed in judging subjective negotiation behavior that could severely abridge litigant autonomy.

The anti-coercion and litigation-autonomy policies underlying court-annexed ADR would also contravene any requirement of affirmative offer behavior, such as collective bargaining-type requirements that a party make an offer or counteroffer, avoid making predictably unacceptable offers or surface bargaining, or refrain from extreme demands or inflexible positions. A proper minimal meaningful participation requirement should be restricted to what is essential for the mediation process, that is, that the parties state their position(s) and listen to the other side's position(s). This might be described in short as a requirement that the parties must "discuss settlement," although no specific content, other than stating and reacting to positions, should be mandated. Thus, a lack of minimal meaningful participation would seem to require something akin to refusal to state one's position as to critical issues (such as the central issues of liability and damages) or to listen to the opposing party's position as to those issues. Imposing any stricter standard of participation would threaten the anti-coercion and litigant-autonomy principles so important to the voluntariness ideal of mediation.

In contrast to mediation, "evaluative" forms of ADR require more participation from a party. For a proper evaluation by a third-party neutral in evaluative processes such as "early neutral evaluation" or "outcome determinative" or "evaluative" mediation, there must be a fairly comprehensive presentation of the issues of fact and law. An evaluation based on a sketchy or incomplete exploration of the case risks inaccuracy and unreliability by the evaluator. It also does a disservice to the parties who might place weight on it, and, if they do appreciate its limitations due to inadequate presentation, it is a waste of their time and money.

Similarly, in a "trial run" ADR proceeding, a good deal more is expected of the parties than just to talk, listen, and respond. Trial run processes contemplate a presentation of each side's case to various third parties so they can make a non-binding decision — to attorney or other expert arbitrators in court-annexed arbitration, to a jury in a summary jury trial, or to the parties' principal decision-makers in a mini-trial. For each of these processes to provide a reasonably accurate picture of how the case might play out if it went to trial, the parties are expected accurately to summarize their evidence and present their best arguments. These objectives may be jeopardized if the two sides do not provide a minimal level of formal presentation.

The one reported decision that has considered the participation requirement in a "trial run" ADR process is unsatisfactory in its analysis of the policy issues. In *Gilling v. Eastern Airlines, Inc.*, [680 F. Supp. 169 (D.N.J. 1988)], a suit by a passenger against an airline, the parties were ordered to participate in a court-annexed arbitration. The defense counsel presented only summaries of her position and read a few passages from deposition testimony and answers to interrogatories. When asked by the arbitrator at the end of the proceeding whether she wanted any damage award that he might make to be broken down into compensatory and punitive damages, she said "Do what you want, or, we don't care what you do, we won't pay it anyway." The arbitrator found that she merely "went through the motions," rendering the proceeding "a sham." In awarding sanctions, the court deferred to the arbitrator's judgment in weighing "the earnestness of the defendants' presentation against the gravity of the plaintiffs' allegations and the defendants' potentially sizeable exposure to liability" and to "his overall assessment of the meaningfulness of their participation."

The defense counsel's refusal to make any presentation as to damages would seem to violate a proper minimal meaningful participation requirement. Damages are central to a trial run form of ADR, and the arbitrator's evaluation could be severely crippled if a party refuses entirely to present its position or any information as to the damages issue. However, the imposition of sanctions because the defense counsel put on only summaries of her positions and read a few portions of depositions and interrogatories is troubling because it involves the court in judging just how much material must be presented. The arbitrator's finding that she merely "went through the motions" is a subjective commentary on the level of motivation behind her presentation. Litigant autonomy should allow counsel a fair degree of selective choice in what she presents. Unless the portions of depositions and interrogatories that she read were irrelevant or failed completely to address the issues in the case, the court should not have determined, on that basis alone, that she did not satisfy the participation standard. Even in a trial run process, a party or his attorney should be allowed to sift and choose what is to be presented without risk of sanction.

It appears that the arbitrator was especially angered by the fact that the defense counsel was contemptuous of the process. However, sanctions based on the attitude of the participant seem highly undesirable. There may be some point at which a party or counsel is so abusive of the other party or the neutral third-party, or so contemptuous in its behavior, that a court's sanction power should be invoked. It does not appear that that point was reached here. Any attempt to tightly monitor the quality and spirit of counsel's participation ultimately undercuts the values and objectives of court-mandated ADR and presents an unsatisfactory prospect of satellite litigation.

2. Required Participation Should Not Interfere with Trial Strategy

Consistency with the objectives of court-mandated ADR requires that a minimal meaningful participation standard not materially interfere with the parties' ultimate ability to present their cases to a jury. Two prominent cases have wrestled with situations where parties refused to comply with ADR orders because they feared that they would jeopardize their strategic position in a trial. These cases demonstrate that such claims are easily made and must be carefully scrutinized by courts. They also indicate that courts can sometimes take procedural steps that will allay a party's strategic concerns with participation.

In *Strandell v. Jackson County, Illinois,* the plaintiff's attorney, in a case involving arrest, strip search, imprisonment, and suicidal death, appeared as ordered for a summary jury trial, but refused to proceed with the selection of the jury. He argued that participation in the trial would force him to disclose privileged attorney work product. He had obtained statements from twenty-one witnesses, which had been denied to the defendants on a motion to compel after discovery had closed on the ground that they had failed to establish the substantial need and undue hardship required to overcome the qualified work product immunity. The Sixth Circuit found that the plaintiff's participation in the summary jury trial would "affect seriously the well-established rules concerning discovery and work-product privilege" and vacated the lower court's judgment of contempt for refusal to participate.

This reasoning does not hold up under scrutiny. The plaintiff's attorney was not required to put on any specific evidence in the summary jury trial. Given due regard for litigant autonomy, he would certainly have been entitled, for example, to hold back the work-product evidence for sole use at trial. Of course, that could mean that he would not do as well with the summary jury as he hoped he would do at trial. But that is a strategic choice he had to make — either hold back his work-product and possibly weaken his case in the summary jury trial, or risk all on the trial. Since the summary jury trial is non-binding, all he risked was an adverse summary jury trial verdict that might conceivably weaken his bargaining position for settlement before trial. Putting him to this choice would not seem unfair given the reasonable settlement objective of the summary jury trial.

The concern in *Strandell* of interfering with discovery privileges is more troubling but also seems misplaced. Because discovery had been closed, plaintiffs claimed a right not to have to disclose the statements prior to trial. But this was only a temporary strategic interest that would come to an end at the latest at trial. . . .

Decker v. Lindsay provides another example of a party's refusal to participate in ADR. Unlike *Strandell,* the appellate court upheld the mandatory order, a decision which, upon analysis, seems to be "the right thing for the wrong reason." The trial judge referred the case to mediation on her own motion. Plaintiff's counsel objected on a number of grounds, including that he could not participate in the mediation because it would jeopardize his Stowers position.[100] The plaintiff had sent a "Stowers letter" to the defendant offering to settle within policy limits, which was refused. Plaintiff maintained that his Stowers position could be jeopardized if he were forced to participate in a mediation. This was apparently based on the concern that any willingness by plaintiff in a mediation to consider lesser offers than his previous policy-limits offer might be used by the insurer to show that its refusal of the policy-limits offer was not unreasonable.

The appellate court rejected this argument on the ground that there had not yet been a trial and plaintiff had not yet established *Stowers* rights. This is a formalistic explanation that ignored the fact that plaintiff did have a genuine legal interest, although future and contingent, that might entitle him to recover above policy limits against the defendant's insurance company. A better justification would have been that although plaintiff had established a potential *Stowers* position (if defendant continued in the future to reject settlement offers within policy limits), this gave him no right to refuse to try to settle the case short of trial. The "*Stowers* doctrine" was directed at an insurance company's failure to settle in good faith, but would not seem to entitle a plaintiff to lock in for all time an early refusal to settle within policy limits as bad faith, with no obligation on plaintiff's part to engage in further negotiations to try to achieve a settlement. Thus a balancing of the policy underlying the Stowers doctrine with the ADR policy of encouraging settlement would justify requiring plaintiff to participate in this case.

One problem with this conclusion is that plaintiff, being forced to attend the mediation, might still be unwilling to make any offers for fear of jeopardizing his Stowers position. If, however, the trial court had been sensitive to the problem, there are procedural steps it might have taken to allay the plaintiff's concerns. First, it could have conditioned its mediation order on the defendant's waiving any objection to plaintiff's *Stowers* position that could result from participation in the mediation. This would have given the plaintiff the incentive to participate freely, without fear of losing his *Stowers* position. Second, the court might have made a deter-

---

[100]Under the Texas Stowers decision, a plaintiff may make an offer to settle within policy limits and if the insurer (which has control over the conduct of the defense) refuses to do so, and an eventual jury verdict against defendant exceeds policy limits, the insurer may be liable to pay the insured the excess of the judgment over policy limits, if an ordinarily prudent person would have settled it. *G.A. Stowers Furniture Co. v. American Indemnity Co.*, 15 S.W.2d 544 (Tex. Comm'n App. 1929, holding approved). The insured frequently assigns his rights against the insurance company to the plaintiff after a judgment in excess of policy limits.

mination that plaintiff's *Stowers* rights would not be at risk because of mediation confidentiality. The broad Texas ADR confidentiality provision forbids disclosure of any communication made in an ADR proceeding, and thus defendant could not have relied on what plaintiff said or did in the mediation to prove that its refusal of the policy-limits offer was not unreasonable. This determination would have allowed the plaintiff to participate in the mediation without risk of jeopardizing his Stowers position if settlement were not achieved. These are the sorts of determinations and accommodations that courts should be willing to consider when ADR participation orders are claimed to trench unduly on parties' strategic interests.

D. Obligation to Attend With Settlement Authority

Court orders that the parties participate in ADR proceedings often provide that they must attend with "full authority to settle the case" and, in the case of a corporate party or governmental body, that a representative attend who has authority to settle. Such orders raise questions, first, as to what persons are included when parties are ordered to attend, and, second, as to what kind of settlement authority the parties and/or attorneys must have. . . . [The omitted discussion focuses on attendance and settlement authority of corporations, notably the *Heileman Brewing* case, and the Government, notably the *Stone* case.]

E. Parties' Obligation to Pay Mediator's Fee

A necessary consideration in court-ordered ADR is who will pay for the third-party neutral. The problem normally arises only with mediation since courts generally pay for the neutrals in court-administered processes such as early neutral evaluation, court-annexed arbitration, and summary jury trial. Most courts do not have funds for payment of mediators and therefore require the parties to bear the cost, analogizing a mediator to special masters and other judicial surrogates like guardians ad litem whose fees are assessed against the parties. The plaintiffs in Decker objected to being ordered to pay for the mediator, but the appellate court observed that the Texas ADR statute allows the court to set a "reasonable fee" for the services of an impartial third party, concluding that it "certainly allows a reasonable fee to be charged." . . .

3. Comments and Questions

a. The leading American articles on good faith in contract law are Friedrich Kessler & Edith Fine, *Culpa in Contrahendo, Bargaining in Good Faith, and Freedom of Contract: A Comparative Study*, 77 HARV. L. REV. 401 (1964) (German and U.S. law); Robert S. Summers, *The General Duty of Good Faith — Its Recognition and Conceptualization*, 67 CORNELL L. REV. 810 (1982); Steven J. Burton, *More on Good Faith Performance of a Contract: A Reply to Professor Summers*, 69 IOWA L. REV. 497 (1984). Burton and Summers have both written extensively on aspects of good faith in contract and commercial law; in each instance the citation is to the latest of a series of articles. *See also* Malcolm Clarke, *The Common Law of Contract in 1993: Is There a General Doctrine of Good Faith*, 23 HONG KONG L.J. 318 (1993) (England and Commonwealth law).

b. It is widely accepted in contract and commercial law that good faith has a negative meaning only — good faith means the absence of bad faith. Put another way, good faith is an "excluder," defined by what is excluded from its ambit. The duty of good faith in bargaining, or in performance of an agreement, is an obligation to avoid bad faith conduct.

"Bad faith" is hardly a self-defining term, and it can only be determined in the context of the circumstances of particlar parties and their dealings with each other. A focus on bad faith does, however, clarify the task at hand: to prevail, a party must allege and prove that specific conduct took place, and that it constituted bad faith (failed to meet the good faith standard).

Both the Restatement Second of Contracts (section 205) and the Uniform Commercial Code (sections 1-201(19), 1-203, and 2-103(b)) impose a general duty of good faith, but they offer little in the way of concrete guidance about what good faith means, or a methodology for applying this general concept to concrete instances.

c. Professor Riskin favors an expansive role for the duty of good faith in mediation, but he also has the good sense to recognize that attempts to enforce such a duty would probably be harmful to use of ADR. In the judical settlement context, where Rule 16(f) establishes an obligation to "participate in good faith," each side should:

> be obliged respectfully to consider, and reconsider, with the other parties or the judicial host, the positions and the interests of both sides, and to think about ways to resolve the dispute. The reader might argue that this is not the sort of a duty that the law can enforce, and the reader would be correct. If, however, we think of the order to attend as an invitation to discuss as much as debate, to converse as much as to convince, to perceive as persuade, we may see more settlements and more "justice" than we expect.

Leonard L. Riskin, *The Represented Client in a Settlement Conference: The Lessons of* G. Heileman Brewing Co. v. Joseph Oat Corp., 69 WASH U. L.Q. 1059, 1114 (1991).

d. Judge Posner's dissenting opinion in the *Heileman Brewing* case states in categorical terms that there is no obligation of good faith bargaining in settlement negotiations. A requirement that Joseph Oat send an executive with full settlement authority to the settlement conference:

> would be defensible only if litigants had a duty to bargain in good faith over settlement before resorting to trial, and neither Rule 16 nor any other rule, statue, or doctrine imposes such a duty on a federal litigant. There is no federal power to coerce settlement.

e. Assuming there is some duty of good faith participation in court-ordered ADR, can the minimum level of compliance be stated in advance with any reasonable degree of specificity?

f. Justice Stewart famously observed of "hard core" pornography: "I shall not today attempt further to define the kinds of material I undestand to be embraced within that shorthand description; and perhaps I could never succeed in intelligibly doing so. But I know it when I see it. . . ." *Jacobellis v. Ohio,* 378 U.S. 184, 197 (1964) (concurring opinion). Should we require of any standard of "good faith" participation in ADR, whether established by courts or legislatures, a test that provides more guidance than Stewart provided about hard core pornography? In a broad sense, this question seems to require philosophical inquiry, but it also is one that is commonly faced by disputants (and their counsel).

E. Conflicts Between State and Federal ADR Policies

1. Comments and Questions

a. To introduce the issue at hand, some breathtaking oversimplification is required. The teaching of *Erie Railroad v. Tompkins,* decided by the Supreme court in 1938, is that federal courts must apply state substantive law in federal suits where jurisdiction is based on diversity of citizenship. In the area of procedure, however, there are separate bodies of state and federal law.

b. The policy basis behind Erie is that results in litigation should not turn on whether a case is decided by a federal or a state court, and "forum shopping" should be discouraged. With respect to procedure, local autonomy is retained. Of course, procedure sometime trenches on substance, and can even be outcome-determinative.

c. Are medical malpractice screening panel and other ADR processes, whose use is required by state law, "substantive" or "procedural"? In most instances, this question could be dismissed as an unhelpful exercise in labeling. In the *Erie* context, the answer to this question matters, as demonstrated by *Woods v. Holy Cross Hospital.* This case is followed by an exploration of other actual and potential problems associated with the application of *Erie* in the ADR context.

2. *Woods v. Holy Cross Hospital*, 591 F.2d 1164 (5th Cir. 1979)

TJOFLAT, Circuit Judge:

In this case we are called upon to examine portions of Florida's Medical Malpractice Law and determine whether its mandate that a medical malpractice claimant participate in a mediation process prior to bringing an action in court must be enforced by a federal district court in a diversity case. For the reasons set forth below, we find that this requirement meets federal constitutional standards and must be applied in such an action.

I

. . . Nellie Woods, a citizen of Ohio and the administratrix of the estate of her late husband, filed an action in federal district court in which she claimed damages pursuant to Florida's Wrongful Death Act for Mr. Woods's death. The alleged cause of death was medical malpractice committed by two physicians and a hospital, all named as defendants. Their malpractice insurers were later added as parties-defendant. Jurisdiction was based upon diversity of citizenship. The defendants separately moved to dismiss Mrs. Woods's complaint, alleging that her failure to abide by the mediation panel requirement of Florida Statutes section 768.44 precluded her action. The district court granted the motions to dismiss on the ground that Mrs. Woods had failed to perform a condition precedent to her suit by not proceeding before a Florida malpractice mediation panel. This appeal was taken by Mrs. Woods from the final judgment dismissing her complaint. . . .

Her major arguments are as follows: (1) the Florida Medical Malpractice Law is procedural rather than substantive and under the rules of *Erie Railroad v. Tompkins* and its progeny is inapplicable in a diversity case; and (2) the Florida Medical Malpractice Law violates federal equal protection, due process, and right to jury trial standards. . . . We will discuss Mrs. Woods's major arguments seriatim after we set forth the relevant Florida statutory scheme.

II

In 1975 the Florida Legislature found as follows: WHEREAS, the cost of purchasing medical professional liability insurance for doctors and other health care providers has skyrocketed in the past few months; and WHEREAS, it is not uncommon to find physicians in high-risk categories paying premiums in excess of $20,000 annually; and WHEREAS, the consumer ultimately must bear the financial burdens created by the high cost of insurance; and WHEREAS, without some legislative relief, doctors will be forced to curtail their practices, retire, or practice defensive medicine at increased cost to the citizens of Florida; and WHEREAS, the problem has reached crisis proportion in Florida . . . Preamble to 1975 Fla.Laws ch. 75-9. Accordingly, it adopted the Medical Malpractice Reform Act of 1975. . . .

Florida Statutes section 768.44 creates a system under which prior to bringing an action against a medical or osteopathic physician, podiatrist, hospital or health maintenance organization in any court of the state a medical malpractice claimant must submit his claim to a medical liability mediation panel by filing the claim on special forms with the clerk of a state circuit court. If he fails so to file he is precluded from bringing any action based on medical malpractice in "any court of (the state of Florida)."

After a claim is properly filed all defendants must answer within twenty days or else a claimant may proceed in court. If answers are timely filed a claim is heard by a mediation panel consisting of a state circuit judge, an attorney, and a licensed physician. The circuit judge is chosen in a "blind" system; the attorney and physician are chosen from lists compiled by the chief judge of each judicial circuit in Florida. The attorney and physician panel members are each paid one hundred dollars for each day they spend on the panel; both parties to a claim are assessed equally for the payment of these fees. A hearing must be held within ten months of the filing of a claim with the circuit court clerk or else the mediation panel's jurisdiction terminates and a normal lawsuit may be filed; any applicable statute of limitations is tolled from the filing of a claim until at least sixty days after a mediation panel either mails its decision to the parties or has its jurisdiction otherwise terminated. Discovery rules of the Florida Rules of Civil Procedure are applied at panel hearings, and procedural and evidentiary rules are less formal than in ordinary civil litigation. Parties may subpoena and cross-examine witnesses at hearings; counsel for the parties may make opening and closing statements. The judge presiding over a hearing is precluded from presiding over any subsequent judicial proceedings arising out of the claim at issue, and other panel members may act as neither counsel nor witnesses at any subsequent trial of the claim.

Within thirty days of the completion of any hearing a panel files a written decision in which, using specified language, it finds the defendant was or was not negligent and accordingly is or is not liable to the plaintiff. A panel member may concur or dissent to the decision in writing. If liability is found and the parties so agree the panel may proceed to help the parties reach a settlement. In this regard, the panel may recommend a reasonable range of damages, but may not recommend punitive damages. Any damage recommendation is not admissible into evidence at any subsequent trial.

Section 768.47 provides that if any party rejects the decision of a mediation panel he may institute litigation based on his claim in an appropriate court. The panel findings are admissible into evidence in any subsequent litigation, but specific findings of fact are inadmissible. Parties may comment upon panel findings in opening statement or closing argument just as on any other evidence introduced at trial. If there was a dissenting opinion to the panel's decision the numerical vote of the panel is also admissible into evidence. If a defendant fails to participate in the mediation panel process the plaintiff may disclose this fact in any subsequent civil action. Panel members may not be called to testify as witnesses concerning the merits of a case. The jury is instructed that a panel's finding is not binding upon it but should be accorded such weight as the jury chooses to ascribe to it. . . .

III

Mrs. Woods's most troublesome argument is that sections 768.44 and .47 are procedural rather than substantive and thus should be inapplicable in a district court diversity case. As a general rule, in a federal diversity case the district court applies the substantive law of the forum state. The test for the application of state as opposed to federal law has been expressed in various ways, whether in a "substance-procedure" test, an "outcome determinative" test, or by reference to the "discouragement of forum-shopping and avoidance of inequitable administration of the laws." Under any of the relevant tests we are convinced that Florida Statutes sections 768.44 and .47 must be applied in federal court.

Section 768.44 provides that a plaintiff whose claim is based on an injury or death allegedly caused by medical malpractice must submit his claim to a medical liability mediation panel before he files an action in court; section 768.47 requires the admission into evidence of the panel's findings at any subsequent trial of such a claim. If federal courts sitting in diversity cases refuse to apply sections 768.44 and .47, Florida's medical malpractice statutory scheme will be inequitably administered. Non-resident plaintiffs will have a substantial advantage over resident ones, as non-resident suitors may avoid the mediation panel provision simply by bringing their actions in federal court; consequently, the worst form of forum-shopping will be encouraged. As we have observed, the Florida Legislature acted in 1975 to avert what it viewed as an impending crisis in the health care field. An integral part of its action was to require malpractice claimants to submit their claims to mediation, "thereby reducing the cost of medical malpractice insurance and ultimately medical expenses." We would do grave damage to the legislative response evidenced by Florida's Medical Malpractice Law if we refused to apply the mediation requirement in diversity cases. We decline to take such a step.[6]

As a result of our holding, before a non-resident plaintiff may bring a Florida-law-based diversity malpractice action he must first follow the steps set forth in section 768.44.[8] If he fails to do so he must face the same result that a resident plaintiff would face in a Florida state court dismissal of his action until he abides by section 768.44. He will incur no undue detriment in abiding by this provision since section 768.44(4) provides for the tolling of any applicable statute of limitations during the mediation process. After the mediation process is completed, a diversity court must permit the admission of panel findings into evidence pur-

[6][A]n important part of the mediation process is the subsequent admissibility of panel findings into evidence. Under *Erie* a federal diversity court must permit such panel findings to be admitted into evidence in a Florida-law-based malpractice action. *See Conway v. Chemical Leaman Tank Lines, Inc.*, 540 F.2d 837 (5th Cir. 1976) (Texas rule that in wrongful death action fact of surviving spouse's subsequent remarriage is admissible as background evidence but inadmissible for mitigation of damages applies in diversity case); Cf. Fed. R. Evid. 302 (effect of presumption regarding state law claim determined by state law); Fed. R. Evid. 501 (rule of privilege concerning state law claim ruled by state law); Fed. R. Evid. 601 (competency of witness concerning state law claim determined by state law). As did the court in *Conway*, "we recognize in (section 768.47) one of those rare evidentiary rules which is so bound up with state substantive law that federal courts sitting in (Florida) should accord it the same treatment as state courts in order to give full effect to (Florida's) substantive policy." . . .

[8][S]ection 768.44(1)(a) requires submission of a malpractice claim to a medical liability mediation panel before suit may be filed in any court in the state of Florida. It would presumably be within the discretion of a federal district judge to stay for a reasonable time an action filed in district court pending compliance with section 768.44's mediation panel requirement rather than to dismiss such an action outright; such a result might be particularly appropriate where the statute of limitations is about to run.

suant to section 768.47 in any subsequent action based upon the malpractice claim. In our view the result of our holding is essential, . . . as otherwise the non-resident plaintiffs would be encouraged to forum-shop in the federal courts, and justice would be inequitably applied between resident and non-resident malpractice claimants.

IV

Having decided that a federal diversity court must apply the mediation panel provisions of Florida law, we turn to Mrs. Woods's federal constitutional arguments. We note at the outset that both the Florida provisions in particular, and the medical malpractice mediation requirements of a number of other states in general, have successfully withstood challenges based on both state and federal constitutional grounds. . . .

The Florida provisions at issue need not be evaluated under the strict scrutiny standard, as neither a suspect class nor a fundamental right is involved in the classifications made by sections 768.44 and .47.[15] Consequently, there need only be a rational basis for the classifications made by them.

In the area of economics and social welfare, a State does not violate the Equal Protection Clause merely because the classifications made by its laws are imperfect. If the classification has some "reasonable basis," it does not offend the Constitution simply because the classification "is not made with mathematical nicety or because in practice it results in some inequality."

When a state provision does not violate a fundamental right "the burden is not upon the state to establish the rationality of its restriction, but is upon the challenger to show that the restriction is wholly arbitrary." We note the special circumstances which gave rise to Florida's Medical Malpractice Reform Act of 1975. As stated in the preamble to this law, the Florida Legislature found that a crisis had developed in Florida's health care industry because of rising malpractice insurance rates. This crisis would cause injury not only to the health care industry but also to the citizenry of Florida; as physicians curtailed their practices, retired, or practiced defensive medicine and other health care providers restricted their services both the quantity and quality of health care in Florida would diminish. One significant factor causing the rising insurance rates was an increase in malpractice litigation, and one way to reduce such litigation was to screen out nonmeritorious claims through the use of liability mediation panels. In addition, such panels could encourage the settlement of meritorious claims, since after a panel found a malpractice defendant negligent he would be encouraged to settle the dispute rather than proceed to a trial in which the panel finding would be introduced into evidence against him. The use of mediation panels, as well as the provision for the subsequent admission of panel findings in evidence, was a reasonable legislative response to the malpractice problem. Moreover, we note that such panels have apparently proved successful in Florida. . . .

The second major constitutional challenge Mrs. Woods raises against sections 768.44 and .47 is a claimed denial of due process. Mrs. Woods argues that the following violations of due

[15]The classifications made by section 768.44 might be viewed in several ways: (1) medical malpractice victims versus victims of other torts, (2) medical malpractice tortfeasors versus other types of tortfeasors, (3) medical malpractice plaintiffs versus medical malpractice defendants, or (4) medical malpractice claims versus other types of claims. . . . While not all of these possible classifications have been challenged by Mrs. Woods, we reject equal protection challenges against the Florida provisions based upon any of them. [T]he Florida Legislature had a rational basis for specially distinguishing any of these potential classifications; consequently such special treatment is constitutional.

process flow from the operation of the Florida Medical Malpractice Law: (1) the denial of access to the courts; (2) the delay in the filing of a court action incident to the mediation process; (3) mandatory arbitration; (4) the admission of panel findings in evidence at a subsequent trial; and (5) a malpractice claimant's inability to voir dire prospective mediation panel members. [The court rejected these due process claims.] . . .

We note that Mrs. Woods did not exhaust the range of potential due process violations which have been raised in the various attacks upon mediation panel requirements. Other supposed violations have included the limitation of a common law right of recovery without providing a quid pro quo to the disadvantaged party, the burdening of a malpractice claimant with the cost of two proceedings, the infringement of the right to a fair hearing before an impartial tribunal because of the presence of physicians on a screening panel, and the denial of the right to present all causes of action in a single proceeding (since a malpractice claim might arise out of circumstances wherein not all potential defendants were health care providers entitled to pretrial mediation).

Mrs. Woods's final attack against sections 768.44 and .47 is her contention that they combine unconstitutionally to restrict her seventh amendment right to a jury trial. Two seventh amendment questions are presented: (1) does making screening a condition precedent to a jury trial unduly burden the right to such a trial; and (2) does the admission into evidence of a mediation panel's finding on liability usurp the function of a jury.

Mrs. Woods argues that the delay incident to the mediation prerequisite unconstitutionally infringes upon her seventh amendment right. This contention is without merit. The seventh amendment "does not prescribe at what stage of an action a trial by jury must, if demanded, be had, or what conditions may be imposed upon the demand of such a trial, consistently with preserving the right to it." Nothing in the seventh amendment requires that a jury make its findings at the earliest possible moment in the course of civil litigation; the requirement is only that the jury ultimately determine the issues of fact if they cannot be settled by the parties or determined as a matter of law. . . .

If a federal court may constitutionally refer a complicated matter to an auditor or special master, it may certainly utilize a medical liability mediation panel without violating the dictates of the seventh amendment. Once the panel has considered the evidence and rendered its decision either party to the claim is free to proceed to a jury trial; the jury will remain the ultimate arbiter of the case. So long as Mrs. Woods's right to have her claim fully and finally determined by a jury is preserved, she cannot be heard to complain that her right to a jury trial has been unconstitutionally restricted.

Mrs. Woods maintains that the presentation of panel findings on liability at a subsequent jury trial will so influence the jury that it will be unable independently to examine the question of liability, particularly since section 768.47 precludes the calling of panel members to testify regarding the merits of the case. We are unable to accept this contention. Section 768.47(2) specifically provides that "(t)he jury shall be instructed that the conclusion of the hearing panel shall not be binding, but shall be accorded such weight as they choose to ascribe to it." . . . [T]he United States Supreme Court has on several occasions approved the admission of expert findings into evidence before a jury and has consistently rejected seventh amendment challenges to such a procedure. In *Meeker v. Lehigh Valley Railroad*, 236 U.S. 412 (1915), the Supreme Court held that a provision in the Interstate Commerce Act providing that findings and orders of the Interstate Commerce Commission were admissible as prima facie evidence of the facts stated therein in a suit brought to enforce a reparation award did not violate the seventh amendment. . . .

RONEY, Circuit Judge, concurring:

I concur in the result reached by Judge Tjoflat on the ground that the Florida plan for handling medical malpractice claims meets the rational relationship standard required for constitutionality, which all parties here agree to be the proper test. Once that standard is met, neither the federal Government nor this Court should concern itself with the wisdom of the plan. . . . The success of a program, or lack thereof, does not provide the key to constitutionality, only rationality or the lack thereof.

3. Comments and Questions

a. Should qualitative evaluations of ADR programs be taken into account by courts in determining constitutionality, or is the matter of quality and success entirely a question for the legislative branch of government?

b. Medical malpractice screeing panel statutes (discussed in Chapter 15, section E) represent the most important area of potential conflict between federal and state ADR policies. Where federal law is silent, as was the case in *Woods v. Holy Cross Hosptial,* the only task for the federal court is to decide whether to give effect to state law.

c. What happens when there are competing or alternative federal ADR policies or procedures in place? With the growing use of ADR in federal courts, this will be an increasingly common situation. Does it matter whether the source is local court rules, as opposed to general legislation? In states with several federal districts, each with its own ADR provisions adopted pursuant to local rules, one can envision the spectre of different results in different federal districts in the application of the same state ADR statute. Different substantive outcomes according to whether a case is decided in a federal or a state court was long ago recognized as intolerable. Now larger states face the possibility of something even worse.

d. The preemptive power of federal law can be extremely broad, as we saw in the arbitration context (Chapter 11, section F). Can you envision situations where federal laws preempts the use of state ADR procedures? Suppose the federal government, as part of health care reform, adopts a national screening system for medical malpractice claims?

4. Lucy V. Katz, *Compulsory Alternative Dispute Resolution and Voluntarism: Two-Headed Monster or Two Sides of the Coin?*, 1993 J. DISP. RESOL. 11

The issue is whether state-mandated ADR must be employed in federal court diversity actions. Under *Erie v. Tompkins,* most courts have applied state ADR requirements in diversity actions, as long as the state practices are in harmony with the Federal Rules of Civil Procedure. The Seventh Circuit Court of Appeals has held that a state requirement of arbitration before filing suit should apply in a diversity case. The requirement, the court held, was an integral part of the rights and obligations established by state law, and, furthermore, arbitration did not interfere with the federal distribution of functions between judge and jury. In Hawaii, a district court imposed a state-mandated penalty in a diversity case [$10,000 in costs and attorney fees], when the plaintiff failed to improve on a prior arbitration award by at least 15 percent.

A different result was reached in a New York district court. In *Seck v. Hamrang*, the court refused to convene a malpractice screening panel prior to trial, as required by state law. The court reasoned that the state panel proceeding conflicted with the underlying spirit of the 1983 amendments to Rule 16 of the Federal Rules of Civil Procedure, which granted courts broad discretion and flexibility in pretrial management. Unlike the New York statute, the federal Rule presumably provided judges a choice among a variety of settlement procedures, including mediation, arbitration, and summary jury trial. The proposed changes in the Federal Rules of Civil Procedure, and the extensive enactment of new local federal rules, many of which enlarge authority for a variety of ADR procedures, make *Seck* a significant decision. The more extensive federal ADR becomes, the more likely it is that courts will find that the federal rules occupy the field to the exclusion of contradictory state law.

5. Dwight Golann, *Making Alternative Dispute Resolution Mandatory: The Constitutional Issues*, 68 Or. Law Rev. 487 (1989)*

. . . Although federal claims are sometimes filed in state court, the more common example of forum shopping is for persons involved in state law controversies to bring their cases to federal court under principles of diversity or pendent jurisdiction. Such cases present difficult problems of federal-state relations.

Since the Supreme Court's 1938 decision in *Erie Railroad v. Tompkins* mandating the use of state substantive law in federal diversity actions, there have been a number of decisions concerning the application of state ADR requirements in diversity litigation. In most cases, state ADR mechanisms have been enforced. This pattern may be changing, however, as state and federal ADR programs proliferate. Thus, for example, in 1949 the Supreme Court ruled that a New Jersey law requiring small corporate shareholders to post a bond as a condition to filing derivative actions, and to pay the defendants' attorneys' fees if they lost in court, should be applied in federal diversity cases. The Court decided that this rudimentary ADR policy, designed to discourage frivolous lawsuits by minority shareholders, embodied a substantive state policy to impose new liabilities on certain plaintiffs. Therefore, it fell within the states' historic role of regulating corporations, and did not conflict with other controls on derivative actions in the Federal Rules of Civil Procedure.

Similarly, in *Bernhardt v. Polygraphic Company of America*, the Court ruled that a state policy permitting certain disputants to revoke agreements to arbitrate should be applied in federal court. The Court found that since "[t]he change from a court of law to an arbitration panel may make a radical difference in ultimate result," the Federal Arbitration Act should not be applied.

Taking guidance from these and other *post-Erie* decisions, federal courts have consistently enforced state medical-malpractice ADR requirements in diversity litigation. Several federal courts of appeal have concluded that the *Erie* doctrine requires federal courts sitting in diversity cases to apply mandatory state screening or arbitration mechanisms to medical malpractice claims, and to stay or dismiss such claims if necessary to enforce compliance with state ADR prerequisites.

This attitude may be changing, however. As federal courts adopt their own ADR procedures, they are increasingly forced to choose between supremacy clause doctrines, which favor federal courts enforcement of their own settlement procedures, and *Erie* principles, which favor deference to state ADR policies in diversity cases. . . . The Supreme Court has ruled that a mandatory state penalty on unsuccessful appeals was preempted in diversity litigation by a federal rule authorizing judges to impose similar penalties on a discretionary basis. This decision, in turn has been interpreted by at least one federal district court to justify disregarding a state screening requirement in a medical malpractice diversity action. That court reasoned that a recent amendment to Federal Rule of Civil Procedure 16, which authorizes federal judges to use a variety of dispute resolution techniques on a discretionary basis, conflicted with the mandatory arbitration mechanism imposed by state law.

Broadly speaking, *Erie* litigation involves at least three conflicting interests: respect for the state policies embodied in substantive rules of decision, concern that litigants' choice of forum not affect the outcome of their case and thus encourage forum shopping, and the principle echoing preemption doctrines that federal courts should be free to manage their own caseloads through appropriate rules of procedure. Based on these principles, some general guidelines can be offered concerning the application of state ADR techniques to federal diversity suits.

First, dispute resolution mechanisms that seek to change the quality of parties' relationships and avoid adversarial litigation altogether, such as mediation and mandatory cooling-off periods, are more likely to be enforced in diversity actions than processes such as court-related arbitration and summary jury trials, which attempt only to make an existing litigation process swifter and more economical. The use of mediative techniques embodies a substantive state policy concerning the ordering of relationships and is intended to produce outcomes different from litigation, rather than simply reaching the same outcome with less delay and expense.

Second, to the extent that an ADR process is invoked before litigation begins, or at least before substantial proceedings have taken place, it will cause less conflict with case management procedures. It is thus more likely to be applied in federal diversity cases than processes used closer to the time of trial when federal judges and magistrates are likely to be actively involved with the litigation. Again, mediation is often imposed at the outset of litigation; summary jury trials are usually invoked by judges close to the time of trial, and arbitration programs may be imposed at varying stages of litigation.

Finally, processes that do not require active judicial intervention are less likely to create federal-state conflict than mechanisms in which judges must play a central role. This factor again favors the enforcement of mandatory mediation and arbitration, as opposed to summary jury trial requirements, in diversity cases.

Among forms of compulsion, precondition requirements should most often be respected in diversity litigation because they usually take effect before or shortly after a case is filed. Monetary penalties imposed by state law, such as cost shifting and security rules, may or may not be applied in federal litigation. Application depends on the strength of the state's policy interest in a particular requirement and the supremacy clause concern of the extent to which it conflicts with federal law or court rules. Provisions that affect the conduct of trials, such as requirements that ADR results or the testimony of an ADR expert be admitted into evidence, are the least likely to be applied in federal court. While a provision that ADR results be admissible in the judge's discretion might not be objectionable, a rule that mandated the admission of such evidence would directly conflict with a federal judge's discretionary authority under the Federal Rules of Evidence.

Chapter 17

Settlement Law and Policy

CASE STUDY

The parties in this case are Bob Jones (Jones) and Home Sweet Home Apartment Complex (Complex). This dispute has arisen because of the towing of a car belonging to a friend of Jones.

Jones had lived at the complex approximately two months. A friend came to visit and unknowingly parked in an assigned space. When Jones' friend was leaving, he and Jones discovered his friend's car was gone. Towing signs were posted in the parking lots so Jones phoned the number on the signs to see if the car had been towed. The towing company said they had not towed the car. Jones then tried to reach Complex but only got an answering service who said they could not give out any information about towing and that Jones would have to wait to speak to the leasing office the following day. Finally, Jones called the Police Tow Line, a phone number which was not provided on the towing signs, by the Complex's answering service, or in Jones' lease. Jones learned that his friend's car had been towed by them, but it could not be picked up until the next morning.

The following morning, Jones picked up his friend's car and paid $108.24 in towing charges because he felt responsible for the situation. The same day Jones contacted Complex's leasing office about the towing. Complex's representative told Jones that Complex accepted no responsibility for the towing of cars. She said the lease authorized residents to have cars towed from their assigned spaces. She said that the name and number of the towing company provided in the lease and on the towing signs is provided only as a courtesy to residents, but actually residents are free to call any towing company.

Jones told the representative that he believed that the Complex was obligated to be sure that if a car was towed that the towing company listed in both the lease and on the signs was the one used. Jones contended that Complex authorized its residents to act as its agents in having cars towed from their assigned parking spaces and that the lease between Complex and its residents dictates the use of a particular towing company. Jones said that by phoning a towing company other than the one listed in the lease, the resident who had the car towed breached the contract between Jones and Complex. Jones' position was that Complex was responsible for the action of its agents and therefore liable to him for the costs of towing. Jones received no response from the leasing office and his communication with the property management company responsible for the Complex also failed.

A. Introduction

The first topic discussed in this chapter is the debate over settlments. Settlement of disputes generally, and of lawsuits in particular, has long been much the most common form of dispute termination. To borrow the title of the article by Galanter & Cahill, "most cases settle." It is a measure of the success of the ADR movement, that a distinguished legal scholar, Owen Fiss, was moved to write an article "Against Settlement," where he cautions against settling too many cases. There followed a lively debate in the legal literature, that has not yet run its course.

After this philosophical consideration of settlement, the remainder of the chapter addresses more narrlowly focused legal issues. A series of Texas cases addresses the enforcement of apparent settlements that are denied or repudiated (the two are commonly pleaded in the alternative) by one of the parties. The most common instance of this scenario is divorce cases, which raises public concerns in additon to the interests of the parties. A related issue is whether any different treatment is warranted for settlements reached by the parties alone, through self-selected mediation, or court-ordered mediation.

Confidentiality is commonly regarded as important, or even essential, for the success of settlement negotiations and of ADR processes in general. Under federal law, notably the Federal Rules of Evidence, the apparent protection for settlement communications is subject to important exceptions. On the merits, Professor Eric Green argues that an expanded privilege for mediation communications is a bad idea. (This is definitely a minority position in the ADR community.) The Administrative Conference concluded that significant protection for disclosures in ADR procedures was appropriate, and Congress took this advice in enacting the Administrative Dispute Resolution Act of 1990.

The final section provides an introduction to the issues associated with the impact of settlements between two parties on other disputes between the same parties, or on nonparties to the settlement. Res judicata and collateral estoppel are the most commonly used legal labels.

B. The Great Settlement Debate

1. Owen M. Fiss, *Against Settlement*, 93 Yale L.J. 1073 (1984)*

In a recent report to the Harvard Overseers, President [and former law professor] Derek Bok called for a new direction in legal education. He decried "the familiar tilt in the law curriculum toward preparing students for legal combat," and asked instead that law schools train their students "for the gentler arts of reconciliation and accommodation." He sought to turn our attention from the courts to "new voluntary mechanisms" for resolving disputes. In doing so, Bok echoed themes that have long been associated with the Chief Justice [Warren Burger], and that have become a rallying point for the organized bar and the source of a new movement in the law. This movement . . . has even received its own acronym—ADR (Alternative Dispute Resolution).

The movement promises to reduce the amount of litigation initiated, and accordingly the bulk of its proposals are devoted to negotiation and mediation prior to suit. But the interest in

---

*Reprinted by permission of the Yale Law Journal Company and Fred B. Rothman & Company.

the so-called "gentler arts" has not been so confined. It extends to ongoing litigation as well, and the advocates of ADR have sought new ways to facilitate and perhaps even pressure parties into settling pending cases. . . . Rule 16 of the Federal Rules of Civil Procedure was amended to strengthen the hand of the trial judge in brokering settlements: The "facilitation of settlement" became an explicit purpose of pre-trial conferences, and participants were officially invited, if that is the proper word, to consider "the possibility of settlement or the use of extrajudicial procedures to resolve the dispute." . . .

The advocates of ADR are led to . . . exalt the idea of settlement . . . because they view adjudication as a process to resolve disputes. They act as though courts arose to resolve quarrels between neighbors who had reached an impasse and turned to a stranger for help. Courts are seen as an institutionalization of the stranger and adjudication is viewed as the process by which the stranger exercises power. The very fact that the neighbors have turned to someone else to resolve their dispute signifies a breakdown in their social relations; the advocates of ADR acknowledge this, but nonetheless hope that the neighbors will be able to reach agreement before the stranger renders judgment. Settlement is that agreement. It is a truce more than a true reconciliation, but it seems preferable to judgment because it rests on the consent of both parties and avoids the cost of a lengthy trial.

In my view, however, this account of adjudication and the case for settlement rest on questionable premises. I do not believe that settlement as a generic practice is preferable to judgment or should be institutionalized on a wholesale and indiscriminate basis. It should be treated instead as a highly problematic technique for streamlining dockets. Settlement is for me the civil analogue of plea bargaining: Consent is often coerced; the bargain may be struck by someone without authority; the absence of a trial and judgment renders subsequent judicial involvement troublesome; and although dockets are trimmed, justice may not be done. Like plea bargaining, settlement is a capitulation to the conditions of mass society and should be neither encouraged nor praised.

THE IMBALANCE OF POWER

By viewing the lawsuit as a quarrel between two neighbors, the dispute-resolution story that underlies ADR implicitly asks us to assume a rough equality between the contending parties. It treats settlement as the anticipation of the outcome of trial and assumes that the terms of settlement are simply a product of the parties' predictions of that outcome. In truth, however, settlement is also a function of the resources available to each party to finance the litigation, and those resources are frequently distributed unequally. Many lawsuits do not involve a property dispute between two neighbors, or between AT&T and the government, . . . but rather concern a struggle between a member of a racial minority and a municipal police department over alleged brutality, or a claim by a worker against a large corporation over work-related injuries. In these cases, the distribution of financial resources, or the ability of one party to pass along its costs, will invariably infect the bargaining process, and the settlement will be at odds with a conception of justice that seeks to make the wealth of the parties irrelevant.

The disparities in resources between the parties can influence the settlement in three ways. First, the poorer party may be less able to amass and analyze the information needed to predict the outcome of the litigation, and thus be disadvantaged in the bargaining process. Second, he may need the damages he seeks immediately and thus be induced to settle as a way of accelerating payment, even though he realizes he would get less now than he might if he awaited judgment. All plaintiffs want their damages immediately, but an indigent plaintiff may be exploited by a rich defendant because his need is so great that the defendant can force him to accept a sum that is less than the ordinary present value of the judgment. Third, the poorer party might be forced to settle because he does not have the resources to finance the litigation, to cover either his own projected expenses, such as his lawyer's time, or the expenses his opponent can impose through the manipulation of procedural mechanisms such as discovery. It might seem that settlement benefits the plaintiff by allowing him to avoid the costs of litigation, but this is not so. The defendant can anticipate the plaintiff's costs if the case were to be tried fully and decrease his offer by that amount. The indigent plaintiff is a victim of the costs of litigation even if he settles.

There are exceptions. Seemingly rich defendants may sometimes be subject to financial pressures that make them as anxious to settle as indigent plaintiffs. But I doubt that these circumstances occur with any great frequency. I also doubt that institutional arrangements such as contingent fees or the provision of legal services to the poor will in fact equalize resources between contending parties: The contingent fee does not equalize resources; it only makes an indigent plaintiff vulnerable to the willingness of the private bar to invest in his case. In effect, the ability to exploit the plaintiff's lack of resources has been transferred from rich defendants to lawyers who insist upon a hefty slice of the plaintiff's recovery as their fee. These lawyers, moreover, will only work for contingent fees in certain kinds of cases, such as personal-injury suits. And the contingent fee is of no avail when the defendant is the disadvantaged party. Governmental subsidies for legal services have a broader potential, but in the civil domain the battle for these subsidies was hard-fought, and they are in fact extremely limited, especially when it comes to cases that seek systemic reform of government practices.

Of course, imbalances of power can distort judgment as well: Resources influence the quality of presentation, which in turn has an important bearing on who wins and the terms of victory. We count, however, on the guiding presence of the judge, who can employ a number of measures to lessen the impact of distributional inequalities. He can, for example, supplement the parties' presentations by asking questions, calling his own witnesses, and inviting other persons and institutions to participate as amici. These measures are likely to make only a small contribution toward moderating the influence of distributional inequalities, but should not be ignored for that reason. Not even these small steps are possible with settlement. There is, moreover, a critical difference between a process like settlement, which is based on bargaining and accepts inequalities of wealth as an integral and legitimate component of the process, and a process like judgment, which knowingly struggles against those inequalities. Judgment aspires to an autonomy from distributional inequalities, and it gathers much of its appeal from this aspiration.

THE ABSENCE OF AUTHORITATIVE CONSENT

The argument for settlement presupposes that the contestants are individuals. These individuals speak for themselves and should be bound by the rules they generate. In many situations, however, individuals are ensnared in contractual relationships that impair their autonomy: Lawyers or insurance companies might, for example, agree to settlements that are in their interests but are not in the best interests of their clients, and to which their clients would not agree if the choice were still theirs. But a deeper and more intractable problem arises from the fact that many parties are not individuals but rather organizations or groups. We do not know who is entitled to speak for these entities and to give the consent upon which so much of the appeal of settlement depends.

Some organizations, such as corporations or unions, have formal procedures for identifying the persons who are authorized to speak for them. But these procedures are imperfect: They are designed to facilitate transactions between the organization and outsiders, rather than to insure that the members of the organization in fact agree with a particular decision. Nor do they eliminate conflicts of interests. The chief executive officer of a corporation may settle a suit to prevent embarrassing disclosures about his managerial policies, but such disclosures might well be in the interest of the shareholders. The president of a union may agree to a settlement as a way of preserving his power within the organization; for that very reason, he may not risk the dangers entailed in consulting the rank and file or in subjecting the settlement to ratification by the membership. Moreover, the representational procedures found in corporations, unions, or other private formal organizations are not universal. Much contemporary litigation, especially in the federal courts, involves governmental agencies, and the procedures in those organizations for generating authoritative consent are far cruder than those in the corporate context. We are left to wonder, for example, whether the attorney general should be able to bind all state officials, some of whom are elected and thus have an independent mandate from the people, or even whether the incumbent attorney general should be able to bind his successors.

These problems become even more pronounced when we turn from organizations and consider the fact that much contemporary litigation involves even more nebulous social entities, namely, groups. Some of these groups, such as ethnic or racial minorities, inmates of prisons, or residents of institutions for mentally retarded people, may have an identity or existence that transcends the lawsuit, but they do not have any formal organizational structure and therefore lack any procedures for generating authoritative consent. The absence of such a procedure is even more pronounced in cases involving a group, such as the purchasers of Cuisinarts between 1972 and 1982, which is constructed solely in order to create funds large enough to make it financially attractive for lawyers to handle the case. . . .

THE LACK OF A FOUNDATION FOR CONTINUING JUDICIAL INVOLVEMENT

The dispute-resolution story trivializes the remedial dimensions of lawsuits and mistakenly assumes judgment to be the end of the process. It supposes that the judge's duty is to declare which neighbor is right and which wrong, and that this declaration will end the judge's involvement (save in that most exceptional situation where it is also necessary for him to issue a writ directing the sheriff to execute the declaration). Under these assumptions, settlement appears as an almost perfect substitute for judgment, for it too can declare the parties' rights. Often, however, judgment is not the end of a lawsuit but only the beginning. The involvement of the court may continue almost indefinitely. In these cases, settlement cannot provide an adequate basis for that necessary continuing involvement, and thus is no substitute for judgment.

The parties may sometimes be locked in combat with one another and view the lawsuit as only one phase in a long continuing struggle. The entry of judgment will then not end the struggle, but rather change its terms and the balance of power. One of the parties will invariably return to the court and again ask for its assistance, not so much because conditions have changed, but because the conditions that preceded the lawsuit have unfortunately not changed. This often occurs in domestic-relations cases, where the divorce decree represents only the opening salvo in an endless series of skirmishes over custody and support.

The structural reform cases that play such a prominent role on the federal docket provide another occasion for continuing judicial involvement. In these cases, courts seek to safeguard public values by restructuring large-scale bureaucratic organizations. The task is enormous, and our knowledge of how to restructure on-going bureaucratic organizations is limited. As a consequence, courts must oversee and manage the remedial process for a long time—maybe forever. This, I fear, is true of most school desegregation cases, some of which have been pending for twenty or thirty years. It is also true of antitrust cases that seek divestiture or reorganization of an industry.

The drive for settlement knows no bounds and can result in a consent decree even in the kinds of cases I have just mentioned, that is, even when a court finds itself embroiled in a continuing struggle between the parties or must reform a bureaucratic organization. The parties may be ignorant of the difficulties ahead or optimistic about the future, or they may simply believe that they can get more favorable terms through a bargained-for agreement. Soon, however, the inevitable happens: One party returns to court and asks the judge to modify the decree, either to make it more effective or less stringent. But the judge is at a loss: He has no basis for assessing the request. He cannot, to use Cardozo's somewhat melodramatic formula, easily decide whether the "dangers, once substantial, have become attenuated to a shadow," because, by definition, he never knew the dangers.

JUSTICE RATHER THAN PEACE

The dispute-resolution story makes settlement appear as a perfect substitute for judgment . . . by trivializing the remedial dimensions of a lawsuit, and also by reducing the social function of the lawsuit to one of resolving private disputes: In that story, settlement appears to achieve exactly the same purpose as judgment—peace between the parties—but at considerably less expense to society. The two quarreling neighbors turn to a court in order to resolve their dispute, and society makes courts available because it wants to aid in the achievement of their private ends or to secure the peace.

In my view, however, the purpose of adjudication should be understood in broader terms. Adjudication uses public resources, and employs not strangers chosen by the parties but public officials chosen by a process in which the public participates. These officials, like members of the legislative and executive branches, possess a power that has been defined and conferred by public law, not by private agreement. Their job is not to maximize the ends of private parties, nor simply to secure the peace, but to explicate and give force to the values embodied in authoritative texts such as the Constitution and statutes: to interpret those values and to bring reality into accord with them. This duty is not discharged when the parties settle.

In our political system, courts are reactive institutions. They do not search out interpretive occasions, but instead wait for others to bring matters to their attention. They also rely for the most part on others to investigate and present the law and facts. A settlement will thereby deprive a court of the occasion, and perhaps even the ability, to render an interpretation. A court cannot proceed (or not proceed very far) in the face of a settlement. To be against settlement is not to urge that parties be "forced" to litigate, since that would interfere with their autonomy and distort the adjudicative process; the parties will be inclined to make the court believe that their bargain is justice. To be against settlement is only to suggest that when the parties settle, society gets less than what appears, and for a price it does not know it is paying. Parties might settle while leaving justice undone. The settlement of a school suit might secure the peace, but not racial equality. Although the parties are prepared to live under the terms they bargained for, and although such peaceful coexistence may be a necessary precondition of justice, and itself a state of affairs to be valued, it is not justice itself. To settle for something means to accept less than some ideal.

I recognize that judges often announce settlements not with a sense of frustration or disappointment, as my account of adjudication might suggest, but with a sigh of relief. But this sigh should be seen for precisely what it is: It is not a recognition that a job is done, nor an acknowledgment that a job need not be done because justice has been secured. It is instead based on another sentiment altogether, namely, that another case has been "moved along," which is true whether or not justice has been done or even needs to be done. Or the sigh might be based on the fact that the agony of judgment has been avoided.

There is, of course, sometimes a value to avoidance, not just to the judge, who is thereby relieved of the need to make or enforce a hard decision, but also to society, which sometimes thrives by masking its basic contradictions. But will settlement result in avoidance when it is most appropriate? Other familiar avoidance devices, such as certiorari, at least promise a devotion to public ends, but settlement is controlled by the litigants, and is subject to their private motivations and all the vagaries of the bargaining process. There are also dangers to avoidance, and these may well outweigh any imagined benefits. . . . Someone has to confront the betrayal of our deepest ideals and be prepared to turn the world upside down to bring those ideals to fruition.

THE REAL DIVIDE

To all this, one can readily imagine a simple response by way of confession and avoidance: We are not talking about those lawsuits. Advocates of ADR might insist that my account of adjudication, in contrast to the one implied by the dispute-resolution story, focuses on a rather narrow category of lawsuits. They could argue that while settlement may have only the most limited appeal with respect to those cases, I have not spoken to the "typical" case. My response is twofold.

First, even as a purely quantitative matter, I doubt that the number of cases I am referring to is trivial. My universe includes those cases in which there are significant distributional inequalities; those in which it is difficult to generate authoritative consent because organizations or social groups are parties or because the power to settle is vested in autonomous agents; those in which the court must continue to supervise the parties after judgment; and those in which justice needs to be done, or to put it more modestly, where there is a genuine social need for an authoritative interpretation of law. I imagine that the number of cases that satisfy one of these four criteria is considerable; in contrast to the kind of case portrayed in the dispute-resolution story, they probably dominate the docket of a modern court system.

Second, it demands a certain kind of myopia to be concerned only with the number of cases, as though all cases are equal simply because the clerk of the court assigns each a single docket number. All cases are not equal. The Los Angeles desegregation case, to take one example, is not equal to the allegedly more typical suit involving a property dispute or an automobile accident. The desegregation suit consumes more resources, affects more people, and provokes far greater challenges to the judicial power. The settlement movement must introduce a qualitative perspective; it must speak to these more "significant" cases, and demonstrate the propriety of settling them. Otherwise it will soon be seen as an irrelevance, dealing with trivia rather than responding to the very conditions that give the movement its greatest sway and saliency.

Nor would sorting cases into "two tracks," one for settlement, and another for judgment, avoid my objections. Settling automobile cases and leaving discrimination or antitrust cases for judgment might remove a large number of cases from the dockets, but the dockets will nevertheless remain burdened with the cases that consume the most judicial resources and represent the most controversial exercises of the judicial power. A "two track" strategy would drain the argument for settlement of much of its appeal. I also doubt whether the "two track" strategy can be sensibly implemented. It is impossible to formulate adequate criteria for prospectively sorting cases. The problems of settlement are not tied to the subject matter of the suit, but instead stem from factors that are harder to identify, such as the wealth of the parties, the likely post-judgment history of the suit, or the need for an authoritative interpretation of law.

The authors of the amendment to Rule 68 make a gesture toward a "two track" strategy by exempting class actions and shareholder derivative suits, and by allowing the judge to refrain from awarding attorney's fees when it is "unjustified under all of the circumstances." But these gestures are cramped and ill-conceived, and are likely to increase the workload of the courts by giving rise to yet another set of issues to litigate. It is, moreover, hard to see how these problems can be avoided. Many of the factors that lead a society to bring social relationships that otherwise seem wholly private (e.g., marriage) within the jurisdiction of a court, such as imbalances of power or the interests of third parties, are also likely to make settlement problematic. Settlement is a poor substitute for judgement; it is an even poorer substitute for the withdrawal of jurisdiction.

For these reasons, I remain highly skeptical of a "two track" strategy, and would resist it. . . . [M]ost ADR advocates make no effort to distinguish between different types of cases or to suggest that "the gentler arts of reconciliation and accommodation" might be particularly appropriate for one type of case but not for another. They lump all cases together. This suggests that what divides me from the partisans of ADR is not that we are concerned with different universes of cases, that Derek Bok, for example, focuses on boundary quarrels while I see only desegregation suits. I suspect instead that what divides us is much deeper and stems from our understanding of the purpose of the civil law suit and its place in society. It is a difference in outlook.

Someone like Bok sees adjudication in essentially private terms: The purpose of lawsuits and the civil courts is to resolve disputes, and the amount of litigation we encounter is evidence of the needlessly combative and quarrelsome character of Americans. Or as Bok put it, using a more diplomatic idiom: "At bottom, ours is a society built on individualism, competition, and success." I, on the other hand, see adjudication in more public terms: Civil litigation is an institutional arrangement for using state power to bring a recalcitrant reality closer to our chosen ideals. We turn to the courts because we need to, not because of some quirk in our personalities. We train our students in the tougher arts so that they may help secure all that the law promises, not because we want them to become gladiators or because we take a special pleasure in combat.

2. Comments and Questions

a. Against Settlement is widely cited and much admired, even by those who disagree with Professor Fiss. Of course, Professor Fiss is not against all private dispute resolution; he just does not want settlement "institutionalized on a wholesale and indiscriminate basis." Conversely, not even the fiercest advocates of ADR propose the elimination of courts.

b. An important aspect of the sentiment favoring settlement is the view that disputing is bad, and the less we have of it the better. A classic statement of this view was made by Professor Grant Gilmore, in closing his 1974 Storrs Lectures:

> Law reflects but in no sense determines the moral worth of a society. The values of a reasonably just society will reflect themselves in a reasonably just law. The better the society the less law there will be. In Heaven there will be no law, and the lion will lie down with the lamb. The worse the society, the more law there will be. In Hell there will be nothing but law, and due process will be meticulously observed.

GRANT GILMORE, THE AGES OF AMERICAN LAW 111 (1977). How might Fiss respond to his former Yale Law School colleague?

c. Fiss points out that officials of organization may settle disputes in a manner that favors personal over organizational interests. This certainly happens, and is another example of the principal-agent problem discussed by Professors Gilson and Mnookin in Chapter 3. In the corporate context, is the solution to limit settlements, or are the best solutions likely to be found in the context of corporate governance—fewer "inside" directors, or a litigation committee dominated by outside directors?

d. Government officials, including judges, also are subject to principal-agent problems. They may promote objectives other than the public good. This is one of the central insights of public choice theory. *See generally* DANIEL A. FARBER & PHILIP P. FRICKEY, LAW AND PUBLIC CHOICE (1991); GLEN O. ROBINSON, AMERICAN BUREAUCRACY: PUBLIC CHOICE AND PUBLIC LAW (1991).

e. Judicial decisions gain legitimacy because judges are, as Fiss states, "public officials chosen by a process in which the public participates." Is it unfair to suggest that public participation in the selection of the U.S. district court is severely attenuated? [We resist the temptation to delve into the political and financial aspects of how state judges are appointed.] Should Fiss favor the election of judges, in the name of increased public participation? Public choice theory suggests that the prospect of future election campaigns will undermine judicial autonomy.

f. Why does Fiss oppose the idea of a "two track" strategy for channeling disputes? After all, as Fiss tells us, the quality of justice already depends on wealth. A multi-track system operated by the courts would no doubt be imperfect, but should not Fiss's approach lead him to prefer a system where the channeling is done by "public officials chosen by a process in which the public participates" rather than by private parties in settlements?

g. If some persons are coerced into settlement by inability to finance litigation, isn't the solution to reform litigation? To blame settlement seems akin to shooting the messenger who delivers the bad news. The faith placed by Professor Fiss in the judicial system to redress imbalances of wealth and power is doubted by many. The best article on point still is Marc Galanter, *Why the "Haves" Come Out Ahead: Speculation on the Limits of Social Change*, 9

LAW & SOC'Y REV. 95 (1974). Professor Galanter's observations about settlement policy—more questions than answers—are presented later in this Chapter.

h. The next piece, by Professors McThenia and Shaffer, looks at settlement through the lens of religion, not a common approach in legal literature. For another religious perspective on law, see Robert Cover, *The Supreme Court 1982 Term — Foreword: Nomos and Narrative,* 97 HARV. L. REV. 4 (1983).

3. Andrew W. McThenia & Thomas L. Shaffer, *For Reconciliation*, 94 YALE L.J. 1660 (1985)*

Professor Owen Fiss, in his recent comment, Against Settlement, weighs in against the Alternative Dispute Resolution (ADR) movement. . . . Fiss attacks a straw man. . . . His understanding that the plea of ADR advocates is based on efficiency reduces the entire question to one of procedures. Fiss's argument rests on the faith that justice—and he uses the word—is usually something people get from the government. He comes close to arguing that the branch of government that resolves disputes, the courts, is the principal source of justice in fragmented modern American society.

Fiss's view that the claims of ADR advocates arise from a popular dissatisfaction with law reduces the issue to one of order. As his first stated understanding reduces justice to statism, this understanding reduces justice (or, if you like, peace) to a tolerably minimum level of violence in the community. In our view, an appropriate engagement of the Fiss attack on ADR must go all the way back to these two characterizations in his argument against ADR and in favor of court-dominated dispute resolution. We are not willing to let him frame the issue.

Certain themes recur in the ADR literature. Many advocates of ADR make efficiency-based claims. And a plea for ending the so-called litigation explosion, and for returning to law and order, runs through the rules-of-procedure branch of the ADR literature. But the movement, if it is even appropriate to call it a single movement, is too varied for Fiss's description. Rather than focusing on the substance of claims made for ADR, Fiss has created a view of the function of courts that he can comfortably oppose. . . .

Fiss . . . understands pleas to consider alternatives to current means of resolving disputes as turning on the inefficiency of traditional adjudication and popular dissatisfaction with it. He equates the ADR movement with those who urge settlement more than judgment and who seek a "truce more than a true reconciliation." He argues that settlement is "a capitulation to the conditions of mass society," a capitulation that "should be neither encouraged nor praised." He assumes that the ADR movement is one that wants peace at any price and treats settlement as "the anticipation of the outcome of trial. . . ."

Fiss is against settlement because he views the matters that come before courts in America, and that are inappropriate for ADR, as including cases in which: (1) there are distributional inequities; (2) securing authoritative consent or settlement is difficult; (3) continued supervision following judgment is necessary; and (4) there is a genuine need for an authoritative interpretation of law. Fiss characterizes disputes in this limited way—as arguments between two neighbors, one of whom has vastly superior bargaining power over the other. It is then easy for him to prefer litigation to settlement, because litigation is a way to equalize bargaining power.

The soundest and deepest part of the ADR movement does not rest on Fiss's two-neighbors model. It rests on values—of religion, community, and work place—that are more vigorous than Fiss thinks. In many, in fact most, of the cultural traditions that argue for ADR, settlement is neither an avoidance mechanism nor a truce. Settlement is a process of reconciliation in which the anger of broken relationships is to be confronted rather than avoided, and in which healing demands not a truce but confrontation. Instead of "trivializing the remedial process," settlement exalts that process. Instead of "reducing the social function . . . to one of resolving private disputes," settlement calls on substantive community values. Settlement is sometimes a beginning, and is sometimes a postscript, but it is not the essence of the enterprise of dispute resolution. . . .

The "real divide" between us and Fiss may not be our differing views of the sorts of cases that now wind their way into American courts, but, more fundamentally, it may be our different views of justice. Fiss comes close to equating justice with law. He includes among the cases unsuited for settlement "those in which justice needs to be done, or to put it more modestly, where there is a genuine social need for an authoritative interpretation of law." We do not believe that law and justice are synonymous. We see the deepest and soundest of ADR arguments as in agreement with us: Justice is not usually something people get from the government. And courts . . . are not the only or even the most important places that dispense justice.[33]

Many advocates of ADR can well be taken to have asked about the law's response to disputes, and alternatives to that response, not in order to reform the law but in order to locate alternative views of what a dispute is. Such alternatives would likely advance or assume understandings of justice (or, if you like, peace) that are also radically different from justice as something lawyers administer, or peace as the absence of violence. They assume not that justice is something people get from the government but that it is something people give to one another. These advocates seek an understanding of justice in the way Socrates and Thrasymachus did in the Republic: Justice is not the will of the stronger; it is not efficiency in government; it is not the reduction of violence: Justice is what we discover—you and I, Socrates said—when we walk together, listen together, and even love one another, in our curiosity about what justice is and where justice comes from.

Most of us who have gone to college know something about Socrates. Many more of us who grew up in the United States know something about Moses and Jesus. It is from Torah and Gospel, more than from Plato, that we are most likely to be able to sketch out radical alternatives to the law's response to disputes. As a matter of fact, our religious culture contains both a theoretical basis for these alternatives and a way to apply theory to disputes.

---

[33]Professor Milner S. Ball, who discussed this comment with us, suggested that Fiss is not arguing so much against religious or community-based ADR as against DR (deregulation). Fiss may, Ball suggests, be asking us to consider whether an overly enthusiastic support of settlement is not another form of the deregulation movement, one that permits private actors with powerful economic interests to pursue self-interest free of community norms. We may, Ball suggests, be reacting to Fiss's overly inclusive statements about ADR; he may have over-stated, and we may have over-reacted. Thus, we may have more common ground than we think. Ball's suggestion is one we will enjoy pursuing. When we do, we will want to tell Ball that the powerful economic interests are as much members of the fragmented but also reconciling commuity as the oppressed are. And we will want to tell Fiss that it may make a general and important difference that, in almost any kind of ADR, (a) the parties talk to one another, rather than to the government; and that (b) the third party, if there is one present, comes not as a resolver of disputes but as a neighbor.

In the Hebraic tradition (as in the Islamic), scripture is normative. Judaism, for example, does not merely seek to follow Torah; it loves Torah, it finds life in Torah, it celebrates Torah as one might celebrate the presence of a lover, or of a loving parent, or of a community that nourishes peace—commitment to common well being, and even a feeling of being well. (Salvation is not too strong a word for it.) Justice is the way one defines a righteous life; justice does involve according other persons their due but, more radically, in the Hebraic view, it involves loving them. Such a justice is the product of piety, to be sure, but not piety alone; it is the product of study, of reason, and of attending to the wise and learning from them how to be virtuous. . . .

The Christian side of the Hebraic tradition has, or should have, all of this. It also has a unique procedure established in St. Matthew's Gospel—a system backed up by stern condemnation of Christians who turn from the Gospel and seek instead the law's response to disputes. In this system—as well as in Judaism— religious community claims authority to resolve disputes and even to coerce obedience. The procedure involves, first, conversation; if that fails, it involves mediation; if mediation fails, it involves airing the dispute before representatives of the community. If the dispute goes so far as judgment, the system—as is also the case in Judaism—permits pressure: "[I]f he refuses to listen to the community, treat him like a pagan or a tax collector. I tell you solemnly, whatever you bind on earth shall be considered bound in heaven; whatever you loose on earth shall be considered loosed in heaven." [Matthew 18: 17-18.]

Thus, the procedure gives priority to restoring the relationship. Hebraic theology puts primary emphasis on relationships, a priority that is political and even ontological, as well as ethical, and therefore legal. And so, most radically, the religious tradition seeks not resolution (which connotes the sort of doctrinal integrity in the law that seems to us to be Fiss's highest priority) but reconciliation of brother to brother, sister to sister, sister to brother, child to parent, neighbor to neighbor, buyer to seller, defendant to plaintiff, and judge to both. (The Judge is also an I and a Thou.) This view of what a dispute is, and of what third parties seek when they intervene in disputes between others, provides an existing, traditional, common alternative to the law's response. The fact seems to be that this alternative has both a vigorous modern history and a suitable contemporary vitality. . . .

Contemporary manifestations of the Hebraic tradition claim adherence to a moral authority that is more important than the government. The Torah is the wisdom of God; the Gospel is the good news that promises a peace the world cannot give. From one perspective, theology makes such religious views of dispute and resolution seem peripheral. That impression is deceptive, though: In the aggregate these views of what a dispute is are consistent with one another and, as such, consistent with the moral commitments of most people in America. The numbers of people in this country who might find them so is not declining; it is increasing. "In the aggregate" is an appropriate consideration, as one assays radical alternatives to the law's response to disputes, because there is substantial commonality among the practitioners of this radical, Hebraic alternative. Religious systems of reconciliation rest on a substantively common theology and on a substantively common argument that, contrary to the implications of Fiss's view of justice, the government is not as important as it thinks it is.

Professor David Trubek ends a recent and pessimistic essay on alternative dispute resolution [*Turning Away From Law?*, 82 MICH. L. REV. 824 (1984)] with a paradox: "[N]o one," he says, "really seems to believe in law any more." The "elites" who complain of a litigation explosion—Chief Justice Warren Burger and others who champion alternatives—question the law's efficacy. But so do those who criticize the law as political and oppressive, most notably scholars in the Critical Legal Studies movement. The elites exalt an informalism they don't believe in, Trubek says; and the radicals exalt a formalism they distrust. Apparently the new legal-process school—or at least one of its eloquent spokesmen, Owen Fiss—still believes in law. Fiss's writing on structural reform is powerful. It may not reflect the way the world actually is, but it is a statement of hope. And that is important in an age of nihilism. But we suspect those who believe in law and in nothing else; we hope Fiss is not among them. Informalism of the Chief Justice's formulation may deserve distrust. But informalism has some contemporary manifestations—many of them resting on the most ancient and deepest of our traditions—that deserve trust and even celebration. These manifestations too are statements of hope. Suggestions for alternatives to litigation need to be critically examined—no doubt many of them are hollow. What they do not need, and what the legal community does not need, is an argument that reduces these alternatives to a caricature.

4. Owen M. Fiss, *Out of Eden*, 94 Yale L.J. 1669 (1985)*

Religion can inspire. It can also distort, and this is precisely what it does for Professors McThenia and Shaffer. It leads them to mistake the periphery for the center.

In my earlier article I tried to come to terms with a movement that seeks alternatives to litigation. . . . Professors McThenia and Shaffer now lend their voices to this movement, but in an unusual way. They add a religious dimension. They emphasize reconciliation rather than settlement, and appear to be moved by a conception of social organization that takes the insular religious community as its model: "Justice is what we discover—you and I, Socrates said—when we walk together, listen together, and even love one another, in our curiosity about what justice is and where justice comes from." McThenia and Shaffer speak out on behalf of social mechanisms that might restore or preserve loving relationships and, not surprisingly, they find the judicial judgment a rather inept instrument for that purpose.

I have no special interest in countering their plea: I am as much for love as the next person. What McThenia and Shaffer say is not wrong, just beside the point: Their reasons for seeking alternatives to litigation are not those of the movement. Chief Justice Burger is not moved by love, or by a desire to find new ways to restore or preserve loving relationships, but rather by concerns of efficiency and politics. He seeks alternatives to litigation in order to reduce the caseload of the judiciary or, even more plausibly, to insulate the status quo from reform by the judiciary. Of course, McThenia and Shaffer are entitled to their own reasons for supporting a social and political movement, but they should not delude themselves that they have given a general account of ADR or explained its saliency and sway within the bar today.

McThenia and Shaffer should also understand that their plea for reconciliation does not respond to the primary social situation to which ADR is addressed. In their search for alternatives to litigation, the advocates of ADR focus on social situations in which interpersonal relationships have been so thoroughly disrupted that there is no chance of reconciliation: People turn to courts when they are at the end of the road. That is why I focused my attention on settlement rather than reconciliation. . . . To be against settlement is not to be against reconciliation but to address another social situation altogether.

Of course, it would be nice if the blacks of Chicago, to take one example, did not have to go to court in order to obtain all that the Constitution promises, and instead were able to work things out with the school board by walking, and talking, and loving. But once they have turned to the courts, it strikes me as absurd for the legal system to create incentives or pressures that force them to settle. It is costly to litigate, as they well know, but it also is costly to settle. To ignore these costs and to disfavor litigation because you hope that social relations between the parties can be restored is like ignoring the dangers of plea bargaining and favoring it over trial because you wish the crime that gave rise to the prosecution had not occurred.

In defending their variant of ADR, Professors McThenia and Shaffer might contest my factual premise about the divided character of our communities. They might argue that the blacks of Chicago who turn to the courts are mistaken in their belief that they cannot get justice on their own. Or McThenia and Shaffer might insist that no matter how improbable, reconciliation is always a possibility, at least as a logical or formal matter, and that one should not be allowed into court unless one first has attempted reconciliation—a miracle is always possible. On this account, ADR emerges as an exhaustion requirement, and at one point McThenia and Shaffer draw on the experience of the ancient Hebrews and Christians to proffer such an idea: "The [preferred] procedure involves, first, conversation; if that fails, it involves mediation; if mediation fails, it involves airing the dispute before representatives of the community." Only if the claimant refuses to heed the advice of the community elders will he or she be allowed to turn to the courts, and then only at the greatest risk: Whatever you lose on earth should be considered lost in heaven.

I am sure that there is much to be learned from the ancient Hebrews and Christians. I am sure that there is much force to the plea for reconciliation when it is addressed to the insular religious communities that still dot the American landscape. But I think Professors McThenia and Shaffer . . . are fundamentally misguided in their effort to model law and the legal system of modern America on these religious communities. Such exercises result in a marvelous display of learning, and one cannot help being moved by the underlying religious commitments. But I must also admit that I am left with the firm impression that such efforts misunderstand the character of our social life and the role that the state and its courts must play in our search for justice today.

From the perspective of an insular religious community, distinguished by its cohesiveness and the devotion of its members to a set of shared values, there may be reason to doubt the claim of those who turn to the courts that reconciliation is not possible. There may even be reason to force the claimant to try those mechanisms that might restore the relationship, for what is at stake is not just a claim of right, but the totality of relationships known as the community. But once we stop thinking about the Anabaptists and start thinking about Chicago, once we stop thinking about the ancient Hebrews and Christians and turn to modern America, we can see that there is no reason in the world to engage such assumptions. There is no reason to assume either that the despair of blacks over getting justice on their own is unwarranted, or that they sue because they want some high class counseling. The more reasonable assumption is that they turn to the courts because they have to.

Moreover, once we change our perspective and consider the modern American community, whether it be a Chicago, or an Evanston, or a Gary, we can understand why an exhaustion requirement of the type Professors McThenia and Shaffer propose is likely only to compound the costs of justice. Society will come to have two (or more) processes where it now has one, because the claimant is not likely to be satisfied with conversation, mediation, or a lecture by the representatives of the community, and thus will eventually turn to the courts. The McThenia-Shaffer proposal is likely to obstruct access to the courts without increasing the chance that the fabric of the community will be restcred.

Milner Ball [THE PROMISE OF AMERICAN LAW: A THEOLOGICAL, HUMANISTIC VIEW OF LEGAL PROCESS (1981)], referred to in . . . the McThenia and Shaffer essay, is a scholar whose work is infused with a religious perspective, and yet he gets the point. He understands that my critique was not aimed at this religion-based strand of ADR, which plays a slight and trivial role in the professional debates of the day. He also understands the more general ADR version of the 1980's for what it is: not a vindication of community, religious or otherwise, but just another assault upon the activist state, "another form of the deregulation movement, one that permits private actors with powerful economic interests to pursue self-interest free of community norms." The force of Ball's observation is not lost on McThenia and Shaffer. They seem genuinely reluctant to defend this more general form of ADR, and in the closing paragraph of their essay specifically disassociate themselves from what they call the "[i]nformalism of the Chief Justice's formulation." They do, however, have something in common with the Chief Justice, namely his distrust of the state, and its courts. McThenia and Shaffer are anti-statists: "Justice is not usually something people get from the government." Apparently people get it from talking and listening to one another.

I believe that people should talk and listen to one another. But sometimes that is not possible, because their relationships have disintegrated, or because the community is fractionated, or because those who have power are not interested in either talking or listening to the weak and disadvantaged. Moreover, even when people are prepared to talk and listen to one another, they might not understand the norms of the community, or, as Professor Ball suggests, they might not be prepared to abide by them. Adjudication is but a response to this predicament. It is a social process that uses the power of the state to require the reluctant to talk and to listen, not just to each other, but also to a judge (and sometimes juries) who must in turn listen and talk to the parties. These public officials are the trustees of the community. They are given the power to decide who is right and who is wrong and, if need be, to bring the conduct of the parties into conformity with the norms of the community. The underlying hope is that if all goes well, justice will be done.

I realize that all might not go well and that adjudication might fail. Justice is not reducible to the law or to the particular decisions of any court: It is an aspiration. The truth of the matter, however, is that all institutions—not just those of the state—stand in jeopardy of failing in this aspiration. And there is no reason whatsoever for believing that adjudication suffers this risk more than any other institution. In fact, given the inequalities and divisions that so pervade our society, and given the need for a power as great as that of the state to close the gap between our ideals and the actual conditions of our social life, adjudication is more likely to succeed in this aspiration. Adjudication is more likely to do justice than conversation, mediation, arbitration, settlement, rent-a-judge, mini-trials, community moots or any other contrivance of ADR, precisely because it vests the power of the state in officials who act as trustees for the public, who are highly visible, and who are committed to reason. What we need at the moment is not another assault on this form of public power, whether from the periphery or the center, or whether inspired by religion or politics, but a renewed appreciation of all that it promises.

5. Jethro K. Lieberman & James F. Henry, *Lessons From the Alternative Dispute Resolution Movement*, 53 U. Chi. L. Rev. 424, 432-435 (1986)*

III. IS ADR SOCIALLY VALUABLE? A RESPONSE TO THE CRITICS

Proponents of ADR suggest that its value lies in reducing the burden on courts and disputants. Alarmed at the ever-increasing numbers of cases filed, the Chief Justice and others see arbitration and other practices as ways of removing large individual cases and even large classes of cases from the courts, thus removing a burden from the shoulders of judges (while shifting it to someone else). To the delight of their critics, they have occasionally forgotten that whether this change is beneficial depends on the relative justice and expense of dispositions through formal in-court adjudication and through less formal out-of-court methods of dispute resolution.

Critics of ADR, like Owen Fiss, suggest that ADR proponents mistake the function of courts as "mere"' dispute resolvers.[35] By diverting cases from courts, society loses the benefit of court sanctioned judgments:

> The advocates of ADR . . . act as though courts arose to resolve quarrels between neighbors who had reached an impasse and turned to a stranger for help. Courts are seen as an institutionalization of the stranger and adjudication is viewed as the process by which the stranger exercises power. . . .The dispute-resolution story makes settlement appear as a perfect substitute for judgment . . . by trivializing the remedial dimensions of a lawsuit, and also by reducing the social function of the lawsuit to one of resolving private disputes: In that story, settlement appears to achieve exactly the same purpose as judgment—peace between the parties—but at considerably less expense to society.

Fiss also argues that advocates of ADR have an unstated political agenda: to keep the activist state from meddling with powerful private economic interests. Finally, Fiss suggests that settlements lack the legitimacy of cases fully adjudicated to judgment.

Four responses to this critique are in order. One short answer to Fiss is that most ADR proponents make no claim for shunting all, or even most, litigation into alternative forums. The ADR movement of the 1980s does not suppose that every legal dispute has a non-judicial solution. Indeed, the ADR literature recognizes that some types of cases are not suited to resolution outside the courtroom, including particularly cases in which the plaintiff seeks a declaration of law by the court. Fiss overlooks this accepted limitation of ADR because he assumes, at least implicitly, that all cases resemble Brown v. Board of Education. But, of course, they do not. It seems obvious that large classes of cases are not so consequential, and do not call for the definitive ruling of a judge or the imprimatur of an official organ of the state. Automobile accidents, uncontested divorces, breaches of contract, and other common types of suits do not cry out to be memorialized in the official reports, and, in any event, most are settled far short of trial.

A second response to Fiss's critique is that his "conspiracy theory" of ADR is dubious. Many people who seek to use ADR are scarcely "powerful" economic interests—ADR is not limited

---

*Reprinted with permission.

[35]We cite Fiss . . . because he is the most articulate opponent of an ADR perspective; hence it is useful to test the propositions of ADR against his critique. We say "a" perspective because, as suggested in the text, Fiss tends to emphasize the perspective of the judge imposing an "alternative" procedure on unwilling litigants, rather than that of the consumer of legal services making a rational choice among available options.

to adoption by Fortune 500 companies. Moreover, ADR does not dispense with community norms. All dispute resolution takes place with an eye toward existing alternatives—including litigation. Finally, the choice to employ ADR is made by parties who have determined that the injustice resulting from delay and the prohibitive costs of pursuing a case through the courts (direct expenditures for lawyers and expenses, as well as significant indirect expenditures, like lost opportunity costs) far outweigh any putative injustice stemming from the decision to forgo judgment by the court.

A third response to Fiss is that not all questions need to be answered. An open society needs the tension of open questions; parties who settle do not thereby foreclose answers at some later time when matters of principle are truly at stake and the issues cannot be compromised. Fiss agrees that avoidance has a value to society, "which sometimes thrives by masking its basic contradictions." He questions, however, whether settlement will result in too much avoidance. But we know of no way to measure the appropriateness of avoidance. Furthermore, Fiss's concern is one-sided. We should be equally concerned to prevent courts from rendering judgment when settlement is more appropriate.

Finally, Fiss's position is seriously weakened by his failure to offer proof that court judgments are more just. He says, for example, that "[a]djudication is more likely to do justice than conversation, mediation, arbitration, settlement, rent-a-judge, mini-trials, community moots or any other contrivance of ADR, precisely because it vests the power of the state in officials who act as trustees for the public, who are highly visible, and who are committed to reason."

Does ADR reach a just result or merely an expedient one? How can one measure the justice of a private settlement? The question is important, but it has not been well discussed in the ADR literature—no doubt because it is so difficult a proposition to test. Whatever the answer, it seems fair to ask the same questions of courts. In theory, courts are committed to reason, but in practice much stands in their way. Some judges are dispassionate and disinterested seekers after justice, but not all are. And all judges are busy; it is a fair assumption that they do not have sufficient time to devote to any single case. Moreover, the maneuvering of partisan lawyers alone is often enough to ensure that justice will not be done.

A perhaps more controversial response to Fiss's argument about the quality of outcomes is that in certain important classes of cases—cases involving public institutions like schools, hospitals, and prisons (the very cases that particularly interest Fiss)—courts themselves invoke processes that are firmly lodged in the ADR arsenal. Stories that describe litigation over unconstitutional prison conditions, inhumane mental hospital conditions, and segregated schools frequently depict the judge acting as mediator, helping the parties to negotiate the remedy the court will impose by consent decree. If the courts themselves find these processes useful or even necessary, chances are good that the same processes can be as beneficial when invoked outside the courts.

6. Marc Galanter & Mia Cahill, *"Most Cases Settle": Judicial Promotion and Regulation of Settlement*, 46 Stan. L. Rev. 1339 (1994)*

V. CONCLUSION

What have we learned . . . [about] the benefits of judicial promotion of settlement? We began by observing that most litigation results in settlement and that the portion of cases settled is increasing. Both the overall context that frames legal disputes and the characteristics of individual disputes make it seem highly unlikely that the portion of disputes ending in settlement will decrease in the near future. Demand for adjudication-backed remedies is increasing faster than the supply of facilities for full-blown adjudication. Much of this remedy-seeking is suffused by a scarcely concealed readiness to compromise, commended by normative and strategic considerations that are more intense in some settings and less in others.

The enlargement of the legal world enhances the opportunities for compromise. As society gets richer, the stakes in disputes become higher, and more organizations and individuals can make greater investments in litigation. Expenditures on one side produce costs on the other. Again, as the law becomes more voluminous, more complex, and more uncertain, costs increase. Virtually every "improvement" in adjudication increases the need and opportunity for greater expenditures. Refinements of due process require more submissions, hearings, and findings; elaborations of the law require research, investigation, and evidence. As transaction barriers (time, resources, uncertainty about recovery and its amount) rise, there is a greater chance of overlap in the bargaining positions of the parties. There is more of a "settlement range" in which both parties are better off than if they had run through the full course of adjudication.

This increase in settlements is largely independent of self-conscious efforts to promote them. Indeed, these promotion efforts are at least as much the result as the cause of settlement activity. As settlement ranges are extended, actors face the problem of how to reach agreement within the settlement range. The recent proliferation of settlement brokers (e.g., private judges, mediators, and special masters) and devices (minitrials and summary jury trials) testifies to the increasing demand for signals to identify points of convergence within the broad settlement ranges created by higher transaction costs.

Settlement is not intrinsically good or bad, any more than adjudication is good or bad. Settlements do not share any generic traits that commend us to avoid them per se or to promote them. This does not mean that some settlements are not preferable to some adjudications—and to other settlements. . . . [T]here is, we would suppose, great variation in the quality of settlements from one disputing arena to another and within such arenas.

When we think about trials, we are concerned that they be of high quality, meeting standards of fair procedure, accurate decision, and beneficial outcome. The occurrence of a settlement is in itself no more an assurance of a quality result than is the occurrence of a trial. (Indeed, it provides somewhat less assurance, since trials are constrained to conform publicly to tested procedural standards and to apply norms that are widely shared and publicly endorsed.) To produce settlements of high quality is not simply a matter of embracing whatever seems to produce more settlements. It is a challenge not only for those who negotiate settlements, but also for those judges and mediators who intervene in them and for those who formulate policy that affects the settlement process.

The task for policy is not promoting settlements or discouraging them, but regulating them. How do we encourage settlements that display desirable qualities? This requires that we have a sense of which qualities we consider important in a particular settlement arena—full disclosure of relevant facts, adequate compensation, fair sharing of the exchange surplus, encouraging future relations between the parties, providing guidelines for future negotiators, or any of the many other features by which we might judge a settlement. When we are evaluating the efficacy of policies to promote settlement, we have to assess their net contribution to the occurrence of desirable (and undesirable) features.

What do we know of the effects of judicial intervention on the number or the quality of settlements? As to number, the available studies provide no basis for thinking judicial promotion leads to a number of settlements that is sufficiently higher than would otherwise occur to compensate for the opportunity costs of the judicial attention diverted from adjudication. Some very effective programs may be hidden among the dismal aggregates, waiting to be revealed by more discriminating research. As to the effects of judicial promotion on the quality of settlements, we simply do not know. Again, there may be some splendid results out there, but so far they have remained unobserved by research. Are settlements arranged by judges less variable, more principled, more reflective of the merits? No one knows.

Developing reliable knowledge of the quality of settlements is fraught with difficulties. The difficulty of assessing this judicial activity is compounded when we enlarge the inquiry to include general effects. We simply don't know about the wider effects of judicial settlement promotion. Are judicially promoted settlements accompanied by more deterrence, by more reinforcement of legal norms, and by other desirable effects on wider audiences than bilateral settlements? (Or, if we have reason to think that a settlement would not have occurred without judicial intervention, than adjudication?) There is some reason to believe that settlement may entail substantial costs in information loss, but it is not clear how much of this loss can be attributed to judicial intervention. Beyond these effects of single instances of judicial intervention, we may ask about the effects of the overall pattern. Does judicial participation affect the style of lawyers in conducting bilateral negotiations? Does it affect the styles of judges when they are trying cases, ruling on motions, and so forth? Once again, we must confess ignorance.

Although there is a lot we don't know about settlement, existing knowledge supplies both useful ideas about things worth trying and valuable cautions against the snares of policy fashion. As we noted earlier, settlement is not an "alternative" process, separate from adjudication, but is intimately and inseparably entwined with it. They are two faces of a single process of strategic maneuvering and bargaining in the (actual or threatened) presence of the adjudicative forum. Because settlement is bound intimately to litigation, settlement outcomes reflect in some measure the potential results and costs of litigation. Substantive and procedural rules, and the practices of courts and lawyers, confer bargaining endowments upon the parties in settlement negotiations. Power to achieve an attractive settlement may be dependent on having adjudication as a viable alternative. Even those who emphasize the power of principle in negotiation recognize that "the relative negotiating power of two parties depends primarily upon how attractive to each is the option of not reaching agreement." So the promotion of quality settlements implies at the least a continuing production of adjudicated outcomes needed to equip deserving parties to achieve such settlements.

But the bargaining endowments produced by the legal rules are not self-implementing. They are translated into outcomes by the features of the particular bargaining arena. Many features of the arena offer possibilities for policy intervention: the skills and styles of the negotiators; the ethical constraints under which they operate; the presence of mediators or other settlement facilitators; the review of negotiation results by third parties (as, for example, in judicial hearings to determine the fairness of settlements in class action lawsuits and in cases involving minors); and requirements about publicity and disclosure.

How do alterations in these features affect the costs of the settlement process? How do they affect the distribution of the "savings" produced by the settlement? How do they affect the "general effects" or "public goods" produced by the settlement? Are settlements in a particular arena improved by detaching them from adjudication—for example, by removing them into different institutions or setting up cost barriers against recourse to de novo adjudication? Or is it better to couple them more closely with adjudication, for example by summary jury trials before the fact or fairness hearings afterward?

Even though we don't know the answers to these questions, the fact that we ask them reflects a change in our understanding of the relation of the courts to civil justice that has profound implications for policy. Once, courts were envisioned as dedicated exclusively to adjudication, so that settlement was seen as the product of a consensual private departure from the public forum. The results were an accidental byproduct for which the court was not accountable. The only instances in which courts had a responsibility for the quality of settlements were in cases involving minors and class actions, where there was a danger of divergent interests between a party and its representative. But now it is common knowledge that most remedy seeking in the vicinity of courts is going to eventuate in settlement. We share an inescapable awareness that courts do more than adjudicate. They preside over a cluster of dispute processes. They project models, sanctions, bargaining chips, categories, and doctrine that support processes of negotiation, mediation, and arbitration, some within the precincts of the courts and some at a distance. Once we see settlements not as a stray byproduct of the judicial process, but as part of the essential core, the responsibilities of courts can no longer be defined as coextensive with adjudication. Once we apprehend the multiplex connection between court and settlement, ensuring the quality of these processes and the settlements they produce is a central task of the administration of justice.

The Civil Justice Reform Act's enlargement of judicial concern to include the promotion of settlements and the fostering of "alternative" devices for resolving cases reflects an important, but still incomplete, reformulation of the responsibilities of courts. Once we recognize that all components of the intricate ecology of disputing are linked in complex and sometimes paradoxical ways to what courts do, it is manifest that the obligation of seeing that justice is done is not discharged by uncritical celebration of settlement (or uncritical condemnation of it). It requires a discriminating appreciation of the complex dynamics of the various species of settlements in different bargaining arenas and an appreciation of the limited capacity of the devices for regulating them. Settlement is not the answer; it is the question.

More generally, ADR, so ardently embraced as a solution, quickly decomposes into a whole new set of questions that courts must address if they are to deliver justice. To answer them requires a body of knowledge of which only scattered patches presently exist. Having abandoned the exclusive focus on adjudication to embrace the whole dispute process, the courts have launched themselves on a voyage over seas that can be charted only with instruments still to be fashioned.

C. Enforcement of Proffered Settlement Agreements

1. Comments and Questions

a. This section addresses the following scenario: What happens when one party to a dispute claims that the parties have reached a settlement, and the other party (a) denies that a settlement was reached, or (b) seeks to disavow an admitted agreement? A closely related scenario is where the parties have agreed on some issues, and one party claims the agreement to be binding while the other party responds that there was no final agreement until all outstanding issues were settled.

b. Should the finality accorded a claimed settlement depend on whether it was the result of a direct negotiation between the parties, or obtained with the assistance of a mediator? What if the settlement resulted from one of the processes discussed in Chapter 15? Should the type of process, or the extent of court connectedness thereof, make a difference?

c. To appreciate the difficulties faced by parties and their counsel in dealing with the enforcement of claimed settlements, consider the next three cases, all recent decisions from a single jurisdiction (Texas). Has the Texas Supreme Court definitively disposed of the settlement problem?

d. As evidenced by the next two cases, divorce proceedings presents a common setting for litigated settlement disputes, because they require court approval.

2. *Ames v. Ames*, 860 S.W.2d 590 (Tex. Civ. App. 1993)

POFF, Justice.

Appellant Raymond K. Ames appeals from the trial court's final decree granting him and his wife Nancy Jo Ames a divorce. . . . Raymond initially argues the settlement agreement is invalid; however, anticipating we might not agree, he alternatively argues that the agreement is inviolable and the court erred in modifying the agreement. His second argument compels us to reverse the judgment and remand the cause to the trial court.

Raymond filed suit to divorce his wife Nancy, appellee. Nancy answered Raymond's petition and filed a counter-petition for divorce. The parties were ordered to mediation which resulted in a community property settlement agreement reached on June 5, 1991. Both parties and their respective attorneys signed the settlement agreement. The record reflects that on June 20, 1991, Raymond attempted to withdraw his consent to the settlement agreement by means of a letter from his attorney to Nancy's attorney. On August 20, 1991, Nancy filed a "Motion For Entry of Decree of Divorce" based on the June 5 settlement agreement. On November 27, 1991, the trial court entered a decree of divorce.

Raymond contends that the trial court erred in entering its decree of divorce on the basis of the settlement agreement because he had repudiated the agreement. We disagree. In its order of mediation, the trial court stated that "[t]his case is appropriate for mediation pursuant to Tex.Civ.Prac. & Rem.Code §§ 154.001 et seq." Chapter 154 of the Texas Civil Practice and Remedies Code is entitled "Alternative Dispute Resolution Procedures." Section 154.071(a) states: If the parties reach a settlement and execute a written agreement disposing of the dispute, the agreement is enforceable in the same manner as any other written contract. We interpret this statute to mean, inter alia, that a party who has reached a settlement agreement disposing of a dispute through alternative dispute resolution procedures may not unilaterally repudiate the agreement.

While parties may be compelled by a court to participate in mediation, "[a] mediator may not impose his own judgment on the issues for that of the parties." Tex.Civ.Prac. & Rem.Code § 154.023(b)). Put another way, a court can compel disputants to sit down with each other but it cannot force them to peaceably resolve their differences. The job of a mediator is simply to facilitate communication between parties and thereby encourage reconciliation, settlement and understanding among them. Hopefully, mediation will assist the parties in reaching a voluntary agreement that will serve to resolve their dispute and avoid the need for traditional litigation.

If voluntary agreements reached through mediation were non-binding, many positive efforts to amicably settle differences would be for naught. If parties were free to repudiate their agreements, disputes would not be finally resolved and traditional litigation would recur. In order to effect the purposes of mediation and other alternative dispute resolution mechanisms, settlement agreements must be treated with the same dignity and respect accorded other contracts reached after arm's length negotiations. Again, no party to a dispute can be forced to settle the conflict outside of court; but if a voluntary agreement that disposes of the dispute is reached, the parties should be required to honor the agreement.

We are aware of the cases in which it has been held that a valid consent judgment cannot be rendered unless consent exists at the time the court undertakes to make the agreement the judgment of the court. These cases are inapplicable to agreements reached pursuant to alternative dispute resolution procedures described in chapter 154 of the Texas Civil Practice and Remedies Code.

Raymond argues strenuously, however, that section 154.071(a) . . . conflicts with Tex.Fam.Code Ann. § 3.631(a) and that the Family Code provision is controlling. Section 3.631(a) states: To promote amicable settlement of disputes on the divorce or annulment of a marriage, the parties may enter into a written agreement concerning the division of all property and liabilities of the parties and maintenance of either of them. The agreement may be revised or repudiated prior to rendition of the divorce or annulment unless it is binding under some other rule of law. Raymond contends that section 3.631(a) controls over section 154.071(a) of the Texas Civil Practice and Remedies Code because section 3.631(a) deals with an agreement incident to divorce while section 154.071(a) concerns agreements in general. Raymond cites the well-known rule that a specific statute should control over a general statute and thus concludes that section 3.631(a) is controlling.

We are not convinced, however, that the two statutes are in conflict. Even though section 3.631(a) is the more specific statute in this case, the Family Code provision expressly states that an agreement may be repudiated prior to rendition of the divorce "unless it is binding under some other rule of law." Pursuant to section 154.071(a) of the Practice and Remedies Code, the settlement agreement is binding. Raymond could not unilaterally repudiate the agreement. The trial court was empowered to consider the settlement agreement. [The decision of the trial court was reversed because that court's division of property "differed significantly from the settlement agreement."]

3. *Cary v. Cary*, 894 S.W.2d 111 (Tex. Civ. App. 1995)

HEDGES, Justice.

In this case, we are asked to decide whether a rule 11 agreement entered into as a result of court-ordered mediation may be the basis of a consent judgment if one party withdraws consent to the rendition of judgment. We hold that it cannot. The issues in this divorce action . . . involve only the division of property.

Culminating a long and tortuous series of legal proceedings, the trial court ordered the parties to mediate the dispute. On April 21, 1994, a rule 11 agreement was signed by both parties as a result of a protracted mediation proceeding. Four days later, wife filed a notice of "possible repudiation" of settlement agreement. Tex.R.Civ.P. 11. [The husband] then filed a motion to render final decree of divorce, based on the rule 11 agreement.

On May 10, 1994, the trial court held a hearing on husband's motion to render final decree of divorce. Wife had repudiated the rule 11 agreement, and withdrew consent to the rendition of judgment. Nevertheless, the trial court ruled that it was a valid agreement under Tex.Civ.Prac. & Rem.Code Ann. ch. 154 (Vernon Supp. 1995) (covering alternative dispute resolution) and announced that it would render a consent decree based on it. . . .

On May 24, 1994, the court reconvened the hearing on husband's motion to render the final decree of divorce. Both parties appeared by attorney, and no objection was made that the proposed decree did not accurately reflect the agreement reached during mediation. Wife did assert her withdrawal of consent. The decree of divorce was rendered over the objection of wife's counsel. . . . [A]ppellant contends that the trial court erred in granting a consent decree because the rule 11 agreement on which it was based lacked wife's consent.

If the parties reach a settlement through alternative dispute resolution procedures and execute a written agreement disposing of the dispute, the agreement is enforceable in the same manner as any other written contract. Tex.Civ.Prac. & Rem.Code Ann. § 154.071(a). Under that section, "a party may enforce the agreement without the other party's consent under contract law."

It has long been the law of this state that a court cannot render a valid consent judgment unless at the time of rendition, all parties consent to the agreement underlying the judgment. "Therefore, a party has the right to revoke his consent at any time before the rendition of judgment." *Quintero v. Jim Walter Homes, Inc.*, 654 S.W.2d 442, 444 (Tex. 1983). Furthermore, the Family Code provides that: [t]o promote amicable settlement of disputes on the divorce or annulment of a marriage, the parties may enter into a written agreement concerning the division of all property and liabilities of the parties and maintenance of either of them. The agreement may be revised or repudiated prior to rendition of the divorce or annulment unless it is binding under some other rule of law. Tex.Fam.Code Ann. § 3.631(a).

Husband contends that because the rule 11 agreement emanated from a court-ordered mediation proceeding, wife cannot withdraw her consent. As authority, he cites *In re Marriage of Ames. Ames* recognizes the line of cases holding that "a valid consent judgment cannot be rendered unless consent exists at the time the court undertakes to make the agreement the judgment of the court." The court held that "[t]hese cases are inapplicable to agreements reached pursuant to alternative dispute resolution procedures described in chapter 154 of the Texas Civil Practice and Remedies Code."

We disagree with the *Amarillo* court and adhere to the concept that consent of the parties is required up to the moment of rendition of the consent judgment, no matter how the agreement was reached. We find nothing in chapter 154 that would confer some sort of heightened dignity to an agreement reached through mediation. We agree with husband that an agreement facilitated by court-ordered mediation is enforceable as a contract. Similarly enforceable are voluntary mediation-inspired agreements and rule 11 agreements. But none of these agreements obviate the necessity of consent at the time of the rendition of judgment.

Husband argues that chapter 154 controls § 3.631(a) of the Family Code, basing his argument on the concluding language "unless [the agreement] is binding under some other rule of law." He would identify "some other rule of law" as the alternative dispute resolution provisions. Our reading of chapter 154 does not persuade us that agreements which are fruits of that process relieve the trial court of the necessity of consent of all parties when a consent judgment is rendered.

Were we to hold otherwise, we would transform mediation into binding arbitration. The Legislature has crafted a distinction between the two procedures and their effects, which we are not authorized to alter. We reject husband's argument that our holding will make mediation meaningless. Mediation will continue to provide an efficient method of dispute resolution, and agreements reached thereby will continue to be enforceable between the parties. We merely decline to elevate mediation to something other than the Legislature declared by statute.

Husband is not totally bereft. He retains a cause of action for breach of contract, which may be tried contemporaneously with his divorce suit. His remedies may include both contract damages and specific performance, where applicable.

4. *Padilla v. LaFrance*, 907 S.W.2d 454 (Tex. 1995)

Phillips, Chief Justice, delivered the opinion of the Court.

The primary issue presented is whether a series of letters between the parties' representatives constituted a written settlement agreement enforceable under Texas Rule of Civil Procedure 11, even though plaintiffs withdrew their consent to the settlement before the letters were filed with the court and before judgment was rendered on the agreement. The court of appeals held that any agreement was unenforceable under Rule 11 because plaintiffs revoked consent before the letters were filed with the court. Because we hold that the letters constituted an enforceable Rule 11 agreement, we reverse the judgment of the court of appeals and remand to the trial court with instructions to enforce the parties' settlement agreement.

I

One member of the LaFrance family was killed and two others were seriously injured when their vehicle collided with that driven by Enrique Padilla. After the LaFrances sued Padilla, his insurer, State Farm Mutual Automobile Insurance Company, assumed defense of the claims. The parties subsequently engaged in settlement negotiations and, as discussed below, vigorously dispute whether an enforceable settlement agreement was consummated.

On April 10, 1991, Jeffrey Steidley, the LaFrances' attorney, mailed a settlement demand to Brian Chandler, Padilla's attorney, providing in pertinent part as follows: Dear Mr. Chandler: You are quite familiar with the facts and circumstances surrounding the above referenced matter. At this time we make demand for policy limits of $40,000 for full and final settlement of this case against the insured that you represent. Payment of this sum should be made on or before Tuesday, April 23, 1991 at 5:00 p.m., by delivery of checks in the appropriate amount to the offices of the undersigned made payable in the following amounts and to the following payees: One check in the amount of $20,000.00 to Madeleine LaFrance As Next Friend of Michelle LaFrance and Olivier & Steidley. One check in the amount of $20,000.00 made payable to Ernest J. LaFrance, Marlene Luther, Marilyn Koenig, Madeleine LaFrance and Olivier & Steidley, their attorneys of record. Please be advised that although I will be more than happy to discuss this case with you or any of your representatives, no oral discussion that we may have will serve to alter the time limits expressed in the correspondence. I look forward to receipt of the checks on or before date specified, failing which this offer to settle will be withdrawn and my clients will proceed to perfect their rights under Texas law, the substance of which I know you are well aware.

Chandler forwarded this letter to Phil Bradshaw, the State Farm adjuster handling the claim, who telephoned Steidley's office on April 15 and spoke with Sherea Carry. Bradshaw informed Carry of an outstanding $1,600 medical lien for treatment to Michelle LaFrance that needed to be cleared up in connection with the settlement. Carry responded that she would have Steidley call Bradshaw to discuss the lien. When Bradshaw did not hear back from Steidley, he called Steidley's office on April 18 and again on the morning of April 23 to discuss the lien. Each time he was able to speak only with Carry, who informed Bradshaw that the lien had not yet been resolved.

When Bradshaw still had not heard from Steidley by the afternoon of April 23, the settlement deadline, he faxed this handwritten letter to Steidley: Dear Mr. Steidley, This will confirm our settlement agreement . . . whereby State Farm agreed to meet the policy limit demands set out in your letter of 4/10/91. The only thing holding up resolution of this is the hospital lien re: Michelle. I await word from you regarding the lien so I know to whom to make drafts payable. . . . Steidley responded before 5:00 p.m. the same day, by fax and regular mail, with this letter: Dear Mr. Bradshaw: This letter will confirm that the above referenced matter has been settled for all applicable policy limits, which have been represented to us to be $40,000. Please forward settlement checks in the above referenced matter. This office will take care of the lien filed by Medical Center Hospital out of the settlement funds forwarded by your office. Your attention to this matter is greatly appreciated. . . . Approximately one week later, Chandler tendered two settlement checks for $20,000 each to Steidley, along with a formal settlement agreement. Steidley, however, refused to accept the checks or sign the agreement, contending that Padilla had not timely accepted the April 10 settlement offer.

Padilla subsequently filed Steidley's April 23 letter with the court, describing it as "an acceptance of a settlement." Padilla then filed a counterclaim in the pending suit, seeking enforcement of the alleged settlement agreement. . . . Padilla argued that the letters between the parties' representatives constituted a written settlement agreement. Although acknowledging that the court could not render a consent judgment incorporating the terms of the settlement, as the LaFrances had revoked consent, he nonetheless contended that the court could enforce the settlement by summary judgment. The LaFrances countered that the parties did not have an enforceable agreement under Texas Rule of Civil Procedure 11, which requires agreements regarding pending suits to "be in writing, signed and filed with the papers as part of the record. . . ." The LaFrances further argued that, even if an otherwise valid Rule 11 agreement existed, it could not be enforced since the LaFrances had revoked consent prior to any judgment being rendered on the agreement.

After a hearing on May 1, 1992, the court orally ruled that an enforceable settlement agreement did not exist, granting the LaFrances' motion for summary judgment and denying Padilla's. . . . [T]he court of appeals concluded that the parties did not have an enforceable settlement agreement under Texas Rule of Civil Procedure 11. The court held that, under Rule 11, consent to the settlement agreement must exist at the time it is filed with the court. Although not expressly deciding whether Steidley's April 23 letter constituted a signed writing sufficient under Rule 11, the court noted that the LaFrances had revoked any consent prior to that letter being filed with the court. The court accordingly affirmed the trial court's summary judgment in favor of the LaFrances. . . .

III

Texas Rule of Civil Procedure 11 provides as follows: Unless otherwise provided in these rules, no agreement between attorneys or parties touching any suit pending will be enforced unless it be in writing, signed and filed with the papers as part of the record, or unless it be made in open court and entered of record. This rule has existed since 1840 and has contained the filing requirement since 1877. The rationale for the rule is straight forward: Agreements of counsel, respecting the disposition of causes, which are merely verbal, are very liable to be misconstrued or forgotten, and to beget misunderstandings and controversies; . . . there is great propriety in the rule which requires that all agreements of counsel respecting their causes shall be in writing, and if not, the court will not enforce them. They will then speak for themselves, and the court can judge of their import, and proceed to act upon them with safety. The rule is a salutary one, and ought to be adhered to whenever counsel disagree as to what has transpired between them. A settlement agreement must comply with Rule 11 to be enforceable.

The LaFrances argue that 1) the writings in this case do not evidence a binding agreement, 2) even if there was an agreement, it did not comply with Rule 11 because the LaFrances withdrew their consent before the writings were filed with the court, and 3) any agreement was further unenforceable because the LaFrances withdrew their consent before judgment was rendered on the agreement. We consider each of these arguments in turn.

A

Rule 11 requires settlement agreements to "be in writing." Although we have never articulated what is necessary to satisfy this "in writing" requirement, we may analogize to the statute of frauds, which requires certain contracts to be in writing. To satisfy the statute of frauds, "there must be a written memorandum which is complete within itself in every material detail, and which contains all of the essential elements of the agreement, so that the contract can be ascertained from the writings without resorting to oral testimony." The written memorandum, however, need not be contained in one document.

These principles apply equally to Rule 11 agreements. Applying them here, we hold that the series of letters between Steidley, Bradshaw and Chandler are sufficient to constitute an agreement in writing satisfying Rule 11. Steidley's initial letter to Chandler offered to settle case for the $40,000 policy limits, making clear that the offer could only be accepted by payment of the money by a specific deadline. It is undisputed that Padilla did not tender the $40,000 within that deadline. Where an offer prescribes the time and manner of acceptance, those terms must ordinarily be complied with to create a contract. However, a different method of acceptance may be effectual where the "original offeror thereafter manifests his assent to the other party." That was the case here. The later writings reflect that Steidley agreed to a modification of the terms of acceptance set out in the original letter.

Bradshaw's letter—faxed to Steidley on the afternoon of April 23—agreed to pay the $40,000 policy limits, specifically confirming a "settlement agreement" between the parties. That letter, however, noted uncertainty as to one detail, payment of the hospital lien, and requested guidance from Steidley. Steidley responded that same day with a letter indicating that plaintiffs would pay the hospital lien out of the settlement funds, specifically stating that "[t]his letter will confirm that the above referenced matter has been settled for all applicable policy limits. . . ." Steidley used this language, indicating a consummated settlement, notwithstanding that no checks had not yet been forwarded by Padilla. Steidley, therefore, assented to Padilla's alteration of the mode of acceptance set out in Steidley's original offer. Rather than requiring actual payment by a particular deadline, Steidley accepted Padilla's agreement to pay the policy limits as acceptance of his earlier offer. Moreover, the letters reflect all material terms of the agreement . . . . We accordingly hold that the parties entered into a binding settlement agreement, evidenced by a writing sufficient to satisfy Rule 11.

B

Rule 11 requires settlement agreements to be filed "with the papers as part of the record." Padilla did not file any of the settlement letters until after the LaFrances had refused to accept the settlement checks tendered by Padilla. The court of appeals accordingly held that the agreement did not comply with Rule 11 because it was not filed until after the LaFrances had revoked their consent.

Although Rule 11 requires the writing to be filed in the court record, it does not say when it must be filed. The purpose of the rule—to avoid disputes over the terms of oral settlement agreements—is not furthered by requiring the writing to be filed before consent is withdrawn. "To require the parties to immediately rush to the courthouse with a signed document in order to quickly comply with the requirements of Rule 11 before the other party reneges on his agreement goes against the grain of the policy in Texas jurisprudence which favors the settlement of lawsuits." The purpose of the filing requirement . . . is to put the agreement before the court so that "the court can judge of [its] import, and proceed to act upon [it] with safety." This purpose is satisfied so long as the agreement is filed before it is sought to be enforced. Padilla met that requirement here by filing each of the settlement letters with his motion for summary judgment on the counterclaim.

C

Finally, the LaFrances argue that the settlement is unenforceable because they withdrew consent before judgment was rendered on the agreement. The LaFrances rely on *Kennedy v. Hyde*, where we held that "notwithstanding a valid Rule 11 agreement, consent must exist at the time an agreed judgment is rendered."

The LaFrances, however, confuse the requirements for an agreed judgment with those for an enforceable settlement agreement. Although a court cannot render a valid agreed judgment absent consent at the time it is rendered, this does not preclude the court, after proper notice and hearing, from enforcing a settlement agreement complying with Rule 11 even though one side no longer consents to the settlement. The judgment in the latter case is not an agreed judgment, but rather is a judgment enforcing a binding contract. . . .

[I]n *Quintero v. Jim Walter Homes, Inc.*, 654 S.W.2d 442 (Tex. 1983), we held that the trial court erred by rendering an agreed judgment of dismissal based on a release signed by plaintiff because plaintiff did not consent to the judgment at the time it was rendered. We noted, however, that "our reversal of the judgment of dismissal is without prejudice to the rights of the Jim Walter Homes in its attempt to plead and prove an enforceable settlement agreement under the release."

An action to enforce a settlement agreement, where consent is withdrawn, must be based on proper pleading and proof. In this case, for example, Padilla filed a counterclaim seeking enforcement of the parties' agreement, and both sides moved for summary judgment on that claim. As previously discussed, the summary judgment evidence established an enforceable settlement agreement as a matter of law. The trial court therefore should have granted Padilla's motion for summary judgment and enforced the agreement.

5. Comments and Questions

a. In *Padilla*, Chief Justice Phillips proceeds to find a settlement agreement by examining the communications between the parties in the same manner as with any other contract, by looking for offer, acceptance, and consideration. Should courts look for settlement agreements in the same manner as any other contractual undertaking, or should they require something closer to a single document that is labeled "Settlement Agreement?" While the facts in *Padilla* are not close to the limiting case, the court did have to construe several documents to find a settlement agreement.

b. The Uniform Commercial Code, section 2-201, and the case law in most states, require dramatically less detail in a writing in order to satisfy the statute of frauds than does the opinion by Chief Justice Phillips. Section 2-201, comment one, states:

> The required writing need not contain all the material terms of the contract and such material terms as are stated need not be stated precisely. All that is required is that the writing afford a basis for believing that the offered oral testimony rests on a real transaction. The only term which must appear is the quantity term. . . . The price, time and place of payment or delivery, the general quality of the goods, or any particular warranties all may be omitted.

Texas has adopted the UCC, so in a case similar to *Padilla*, except that the claim being settled was for the sale of goods instead of a tort, the analysis might be quite different. Few if any other states would apply the statute of frauds as strictly as suggested by Chief Justice Phillips. Should less complete writings be sufficient to establish a settlement agreement?

c. The consequence of finding a binding agreement is not trivial — the unhappy party is denied access to the courts and the jury trial, guaranteed by the U.S. and most state Constitutions. Texas regards jury trials so highly that they are available even in traffic ticket cases.

6. Texas Family Code Amendment

In 1995, the Texas Legislature amended the Family Code, § 153.0071 [Ch. 751, § 27], by adding the following language regarding mediated settlements:

> (d) A MEDIATED settlement agreement is binding on the parties if the agreement:
> (1) provides in a separate paragraph an underlined statement that the agreement is not subject to revocation;
> (2) is signed by each party to the agreement; and
> (3) is signed by the party's attorney, if any, who is present at the time the agreement is signed.
>
> (e) If a MEDIATED settlement agreement meets the requirements of Subsection (d), a party is entitled to judgment on the MEDIATED settlement agreement notwithstanding Rule 11, Texas Rules of Civil Procedure, or any other rule of law.

7. Comments and Questions

a. Does it make sense to have one body of rules for mediated settlement agreements and another for other settlements?

b. Does it make sense to have a separate body of rules for mediated settlement agreements in the family law context? Does it make sense to have separate provisions for mediated and for unmediated divorce or separation agreements?

c. How should state law treat purported settlements by the parties to a dispute? Should it matter if a law suit has been filed? Should it matter if the parties were represented by counsel when the agreement was reached?

d. Is the contract analogy helpful in family dissolution situations, especially where children are involved?

e. Based on the materials that you have just read, write a short essay (about two pages) addressed to Texas lawyers that summarizes settlement law in Texas.

f. Assume that you are a state legislator eager to avoid the uncertainties that have arisen in Texas. What policy recommendations would you make?

D. Discovery of ADR and Settlement Communications

1. Comments and Questions

a. Most ADR professionals, notably mediators, believe that there should be some privilege for information associated with attempts at settlement. This formulation is purposely broad, and allows room for disagreement about the precise contours of the privilege.

b. Should the extent of privilege depend on the type of procedure used, or the type of neutral employed? Should there be greater privilege accorded to persons assisting with a mediated settlement than if the parties settle without the assistance of a third party neutral?

c. Professor Eric Green, a leading ADR thinker, has argued against a special mediation privilege, a view the he quite accurately characterizes as heresy within the ADR movement. Forty-one states have enacted mediation confidentiality statutes, up from fourteen when Professor Green wrote the article that appears next, so it appears that his views have not prevailed. In addition, most court rules adopted pursuant to the Civil Justice Reform Act of 1990 (CJRA) include mediation privileges. These developments are discussed in Michael A. Perino, *Drafting Mediation Privileges: Lessons From the Civil Justice Reform Act*, 26 SETON HALL L. REV. 1 (1995). Similar protection is found in the Administrative Dispute Resolution Act of 1990, considered below.

d. As demonstrated in the excellent article by Wayne Brazil, as updated by Kristina Kerwin, there are still many ways that a determined (and needy) party in litigation can gain access to information about prior settlement negotiations, and the positions taken by various parties.

e. Mediators and other ADR professionals are required to maintain confidences in nearly all circumstances, absent a contrary judicial directive. This duty is an aspect of professional ethics, and is discussed in Chapter 20.

2. *National Labor Relations Board v. Macaluso*, 618 F.2d 51 (9th Cir. 1980)

Before DUNIWAY and WALLACE, Circuit Judges, and JAMESON, District Judge.

WALLACE, Circuit Judge:

The single issue presented in this National Labor Relations Board (NLRB) enforcement proceeding is whether the NLRB erred in disallowing the testimony of a Federal Mediation and Conciliation Service (FMCS) mediator as to a crucial fact occurring in his presence. We enforce the order.

I.

In early 1976 Retail Store Employees Union Local 1001 (Union) waged a successful campaign to organize the employees of Joseph Macaluso, Inc. (Company) at its four retail stores in Tacoma and Seattle, Washington. The Union was elected the collective bargaining representative of the Company's employees, was certified as such by the NLRB, and the Company and Union commenced negotiating a collective bargaining agreement. Several months of bargaining between Company and Union negotiators failed to produce an agreement, and the parties decided to enlist the assistance of a mediator from the FMCS. Mediator Douglas Hammond consequently attended the three meetings between the Company and Union from which arises the issue before us. . . .

During the spring and summer of 1976 the Company engaged in conduct which led the NLRB to charge it with unfair labor practices. Proceedings were held and the NLRB ruled that the Company had violated section 8(a)(1) of the National Labor Relations Act (NLRA) by threatening pro-union employees, and section 8(a)(3) of the NLRA by discharging an employee for union activity. At this unfair labor practice proceeding the NLRB also found that the Company and Union had finalized a collective bargaining agreement at the three meetings with Hammond, and that the Company had violated NLRA sections 8(a)(5) and (1) by failing to execute the written contract incorporating the final agreement negotiated with the Union. The NLRB ordered the Company to execute the contract and pay back-compensation with interest, and seeks enforcement of that order in this court. In response, the Company contends that the parties have never reached agreement, and certainly did not do so at the meetings with Hammond.

The testimony of the Union before the NLRB directly contradicted that of the Company. The two Union negotiators testified that during the first meeting with Hammond the parties succeeded in reducing to six the number of disputed issues, and that the second meeting began with Company acceptance of a Union proposal resolving five of those six remaining issues. The Union negotiators further testified that the sixth issue was resolved with the close of the second meeting, and that in response to a Union negotiator's statement "Well, I think that wraps it up," the Company president said, "Yes, I guess it does." The third meeting with Hammond, according to the Union, was held only hours before the Company's employees ratified the agreement, was called solely for the purpose of explaining the agreement to the Company accountant who had not attended the first two meetings, and was an amicable discussion involving no negotiation.

The Company testimony did not dispute that the first meeting reduced the number of unsettled issues to six, but its version of the last two meetings contrasts sharply with the

Union's account. The Company representatives testified that the second meeting closed without the parties having reached any semblance of an agreement, and that the third meeting was not only inconclusive but stridently divisive. While the Union representatives testified that the third meeting was an amicable explanatory discussion, the Company negotiators both asserted that their refusal to give in to Union demands caused the Union negotiators to burst into anger, threaten lawsuits, and leave the room at the suggestion of Hammond. According to the Company, Hammond was thereafter unable to bring the parties together and the Union negotiators left the third meeting in anger.

In an effort to support its version of the facts, the Company requested that the administrative law judge (ALJ) subpoena Hammond and obtain his testimonial description of the last two bargaining sessions. The subpoena was granted, but was later revoked upon motion of the FMCS. Absent Hammond's tie-breaking testimony, the ALJ decided that the Union witnesses were more credible and ruled that an agreement had been reached. The Company's sole contention in response to this request for enforcement of the resulting order to execute the contract is that the ALJ and NLRB erred in revoking the subpoena of Hammond, the one person whose testimony could have resolved the factual dispute.

II.

Revocation of the subpoena was based upon a long-standing policy that mediators, if they are to maintain the appearance of neutrality essential to successful performance of their task, may not testify about the bargaining sessions they attend. Both the NLRB and the FMCS (as amicus curiae) defend that policy before us. We are thus presented with a question of first impression before our court: can the NLRB revoke the subpoena of a mediator capable of providing information crucial to resolution of a factual dispute solely for the purpose of preserving mediator effectiveness? . . . We must determine . . . whether preservation of mediator effectiveness by protection of mediator neutrality is a ground for revocation consistent with the power and duties of the NLRB under the NLRA.

The NLRB's revocation of Hammond's subpoena conflicts with the fundamental principle of Anglo-American law that the public is entitled to every person's evidence. . . . The facts before us present a classic illustration of the need for every person's evidence: the trier of fact is faced with directly conflicting testimony from two adverse sources, and a third objective source is capable of presenting evidence that would, in all probability, resolve the dispute by revealing the truth. Under such circumstances, the NLRB's revocation of Hammond's subpoena can be permitted only if denial of his testimony "has a public good transcending the normally predominant principle of utilizing all rational means for ascertaining truth." The public interest protected by revocation must be substantial if it is to cause us to "concede that the evidence in question has all the probative value that can be required, and yet exclude it because its admission would injure some other cause more than it would help the cause of truth, and because the avoidance of that injury is considered of more consequence than the possible harm to the cause of truth." 1 Wigmore, Evidence 296 (1940). We thus are required to balance two important interests, both critical in their own setting.

We conclude that the public interest in maintaining the perceived and actual impartiality of federal mediators does outweigh the benefits derivable from Hammond's testimony. This public interest was clearly stated by Congress when it created the FMCS: "It is the policy of the

United States that (a) sound and stable industrial peace and the advancement of the general welfare, health, and safety of the Nation and of the best interests of employers and employees can most satisfactorily be secured by the settlement of issues between employers and employees through the processes of conference and collective bargaining between employers and the representatives of their employees; (b) the settlement of issues between employers and employees through collective bargaining may be advanced by making available full and adequate governmental facilities for conciliation, mediation, and voluntary arbitration to aid and encourage employers and the representatives of their employees to reach and maintain agreements concerning rates of pay, hours, and working conditions, and to make all reasonable efforts to settle their differences by mutual agreement reached through conferences and collective bargaining or by such methods as may be provided for in any applicable agreement for the settlement of disputes. . . ." 29 U.S.C. § 171. [F]ederal mediation has become a substantial contributor to industrial peace in the United States. The FMCS, as amicus curiae, has informed us that it participated in mediation of 23,450 labor disputes in fiscal year 1977, with approximately 325 federal mediators stationed in 80 field offices around the country. Any activity that would significantly decrease the effectiveness of this mediation service could threaten the industrial stability of the nation. The importance of Hammond's testimony in this case is not so great as to justify such a threat. Moreover, the loss of that testimony did not cripple the fact-finding process. The ALJ resolved the dispute by making a credibility determination, a function routinely entrusted to triers of fact throughout our judicial system. . . .

Public policy and the successful effectuation of the Federal Mediation and Conciliation Service's mission require that commissioners and employees maintain a reputation for impartiality and integrity. Labor and management or other interested parties participating in mediation efforts must have the assurance and confidence that information disclosed to commissioners and other employees of the Service will not subsequently be divulged, voluntarily or because of compulsion, unless authorized by the Director of the Service. No officer, employee, or other person officially connected in any capacity with the Service, currently or formerly shall, . . . produce any material contained in the files of the Service, disclose any information acquired as part of the performance of his official duties or because of his official status, or testify on behalf of any party to any matter pending in any judicial, arbitral or administrative proceeding, without the prior approval of the Director. 29 C.F.R. § 1401.2(a), (b) (1979). . . . To execute successfully their function of assisting in the settlement of labor disputes, the conciliators must maintain a reputation for impartiality, and the parties to conciliation conferences must feel free to talk without any fear that the conciliator may subsequently make disclosures as a witness in some other proceeding, to the possible disadvantage of a party to the conference. If conciliators were permitted or required to testify about their activities, or if the production of notes or reports of their activities could be required, not even the strictest adherence to purely factual matters would prevent the evidence from favoring or seeming to favor one side or the other. The inevitable result would be that the usefulness of the (FMCS) in the settlement of future disputes would be seriously impaired, if not destroyed. The resultant injury to the public interest would clearly outweigh the benefit to be derived from making their testimony available in particular cases.

During oral argument the suggestion was made that we permit the mediator to testify, but limit his testimony to "objective facts." . . . We not believe, however, that such a limitation would dispel the perception of partiality created by mediator testimony. In addition to the line-drawing problem of attempting to define what is and is not an "objective fact," a recitation of even the most objective type of facts would impair perceived neutrality, "for the party standing condemned by the thrust of such a statement would or at least might conclude that the (FMCS) was being unfair."

We conclude, therefore, that the complete exclusion of mediator testimony is necessary to the preservation of an effective system of labor mediation, and that labor mediation is essential to continued industrial stability, a public interest sufficiently great to outweigh the interest in obtaining every person's evidence. No party is required to use the FMCS; once having voluntarily agreed to do so, however, that party must be charged with acceptance of the restriction on the subsequent testimonial use of the mediator. We thus answer the question presented by this case in the affirmative: the NLRB can revoke the subpoena of a mediator capable of providing information crucial to resolution of a factual dispute solely for the purpose of preserving mediator effectiveness. Such revocation is consonant with the overall powers and duties of the NLRB, a body created to implement the NLRA goals of "promot(ing) the flow of commerce by removing certain recognized sources of industrial strife and unrest" and "encouraging practices fundamental to the friendly adjustment of industrial disputes. . . ." 29 U.S.C. § 151.

3. Eric D. Green, *A Heretical View of the Mediation Privilege*, 2 Ohio St. J. on Disp. Resol. 1 (1986)*

I. INTRODUCTION

Conventional wisdom among practicing mediators is that the confidentiality of mediation should be protected by a statutory or court-created privilege. The claims for expanded positive law protection of party-party and party-mediator communications is based upon the purported necessity of such confidentiality for the success of mediation, and on claims that the social utility of such a privilege outweighs its costs.

This Article critically examines the arguments for an expanded statutory or common law mediation privilege. I take the heretical position among mediators in arguing that the current campaign to obtain a blanket mediation privilege rests on faulty logic, inadequate data, and short-sighted professional self-interest. Neither the necessity for such a privilege nor the social utility of a general mediation privilege have been demonstrated. Moreover, an adequate degree of confidentiality in mediation can be obtained with only slight changes in current laws. Extension of confidentiality protections through the enactment of a new privilege statute may well be counterproductive to the goal of increased acceptance of private dispute resolution. Such an extension will also frustrate other important social and legal policies, such as the enforcement of restraints on illegal business conspiracies and combinations, the protection of individual rights, and the enforcement of the criminal law. . . .

The term "mediation privilege" is used rather than "mediator's privilege" to emphasize that any privilege that applies to the mediation process should belong to the parties rather than the mediator. It is the parties' interest in private dispute resolution that is the justification for the process in the first place. A persuasive case has yet to be made that an individual mediator's

*Reprinted with permission.

desire to avoid being called as a witness during a trial deserves any greater recognition than the normal desire of any person, whether percipient witness or professional consultant, to avoid being involuntarily drawn into a court battle. On the other hand, the general process of mediation, over the long run, may require that the mediation be separated from and protected against adjudication, so that even if all the parties to mediation are willing to dispense with the confidentiality and inadmissibility of mediation, the law would not permit information from the mediation to be used in court. Recognition of a privilege in this situation is based on an institutional concern for mediation as an important and distinct resolution process, rather than a concern for the mediators' own professional interests. The term "mediation privilege" is broad enough to encompass situations in which the parties seek confidentiality and where the mediation proceeding should be insulated from adjudication or other processes (e.g., investigation, legislation, other mediation).

II. UNPACKING THE PROBLEM OF CONFIDENTIALITY IN MEDIATION

A major problem with current proposals to expand legal protection for mediation confidentiality is their failure to recognize the complexity of the issue. There are at least five different sub-issues, each of which can be resolved in a variety of ways, that greatly affect the scope, validity, and effects of a claim of privilege. In outline form, these sub-issues and their possible resolutions are:

A. What does "confidentiality" mean?

1. Inadmissibility at trial. Confidentiality could mean only that statements or evidence used in mediation and/or the terms of a settlement are inadmissible in a court proceeding (whether between the parties to the mediation or between a mediation party and a third party, or between two third parties). Even though inadmissible as judicial evidence, such statements, documents, or facts may be subject to discovery processes.
2. Insulation from formal discovery processes by third parties. This goes a significant step beyond mere inadmissibility. Most privileges, including attorney-client, doctor-patient, spousal, and self-incrimination, are afforded this degree of protection.
3. Enforcement of legal remedies to prevent or compensate for voluntary disclosure by mediation parties, non-party participants, and the mediator. At the extreme, a legal remedy to prevent disclosure would include the ability to enjoin publication of statements made in mediation, the outcome of the mediation, and the mere acknowledgment that mediation occurred.

B. What is made confidential?

1. The mere fact of settlement.
2. The terms of settlement.
3. Statements made by the parties in the course of settlement discussions.
4. Documents and other evidence disclosed by the parties in the course of settlement discussions.
5. Statements made by or notes of the mediator.
6. The mediator's impressions, opinions, or recommendations.

C. Who can enforce any confidentiality provision?

1. The parties to the mediation.
2. Witnesses or other participants in the mediation.
3. The mediator (any mediator or only certified mediators?).
4. Interested non-participants.
5. Courts and other public agencies.

D. Against whom can confidentiality be enforced?

1. The parties.
2. The mediator.
3. Non-party participants (e.g., witnesses).
4. Private third parties.
5. Public third parties.

E. How absolute should any grant of confidentiality be (what exceptions should there be)?

1. Absolute (no exceptions).
2. One broad exception when the interests of justice or public policy requires it.
3. A list of specific exceptions.

This [listing] exercise has three purposes. The first purpose is to demonstrate the sheer complexity of the issue and hence the inappropriateness of any blanket mediation privilege. The second purpose, related to the first, is to emphasize the difficulties inherent in drafting a privilege statute or exclusionary rule which is precise enough to apply in all cases where it ought to apply, and not apply where it should not. The third purpose is to demonstrate that even though a blanket privilege may be inappropriate, there is a relatively limited core or paradigm situation in which confidentiality is both needed and appropriate. . . .

The paradigm case in support of the enactment of a confidentiality statute is a situation in which (a) one party to a mediation, (b) to advance its own interests, tries to (c) introduce either the (d) statements of another party or the impressions, notes, or opinions of the mediator (e) in subsequent litigation over the same event (f) between the same parties (g) when the interests of third parties and the public are not involved. However, . . . confidentiality in the paradigm case is already adequately provided for under current law in the form of rules of evidence excluding compromises, offers of compromise, and statements made in connection with compromise offers, as well as under rules granting the right of the parties to contract for confidentiality. Moreover, trying to expand a grant of confidentiality beyond this core situation may cause a public backlash against this "secretive" type of dispute resolution. The benefits of a blanket confidentiality privilege are minimal at best, and do not outweigh the tremendous harm that will result from the public perception that a mediation that takes place behind a curtain of confidentiality may produce unfair results. . . .

V. A HARD LOOK AT THE CLAIMS FOR A MEDIATION PRIVILEGE

Can a mediation privilege be justified under traditional privilege analysis? The classic approach is Wigmore's utilitarian calculus. Starting from the premise that "the public is entitled to every man's evidence" and that exemptions from this rule are exceptional and to be discountenanced, Wigmore poses four conditions that must be fulfilled to justify a privilege:

(1) The communications must originate in a confidence that they will not be disclosed.
(2) This element of confidentiality must be essential to the full and satisfactory maintenance of the relation between the parties.
(3) The relation must be one which in the opinion of the community ought to be sedulously fostered.
(4) The injury that would inure to the relation by the disclosure of the communications must be greater than the benefit thereby gained for the correct disposal of the litigation.

This formula contains a dual focus on the instrumental purpose of the communication and the cost/benefit effect on the trial process. Courts are extremely reluctant to recognize new privileges. . . .

VI. CONCLUSION

A blanket mediation privilege is a bad idea. Attempts by the mediation community to obtain a statutory privilege may backfire. If the attempt is successful, an over-inclusive and under-inclusive statute is likely to be enacted, resulting in the unintended implication that some communications that ought to be confidential were not intended to be protected, and that a backlash of public and judicial opinion against secrecy of events should not be confidential. If the attempt at enactment of a mediation privilege is unsuccessful, it may be understood as a rejection of confidentiality protection for all mediations.

Some confidentiality protection for mediation and other forms of alternative dispute resolution is appropriate. There appears to be sufficient protection under current law to permit alternative dispute resolution to flourish. Working for modest amendment to Evidence Rule 408 to make it clear that the Rule excludes evidence of compromises, offers to compromise, and statements made in connection with such offers for substantive as well as impeachment purposes, would be a better legislative agenda for mediators rather than lobbying for a mediation privilege. An expanded Rule 408, coupled with careful drafting of the confidentiality clause in a mediation agreement where such agreements are used, and attention to the public policy generally favoring out-of-court settlements, adequately protects parties to mediation.

4. Wayne D. Brazil, *Protecting the Confidentiality of Settlement Negotiations*, 39 HASTINGS L.J. 955 (1988)*

The wise lawyer takes care to understand the scope of the protection the law affords to statements made and acts done in connection with settlement negotiations. This Article, which focuses on settlement negotiations in federal courts, begins by exploring the scope of Federal Rule of Evidence 408. Rule 408 provides:

> Evidence of (1) furnishing or offering or promising to furnish, or (2) accepting or offering or promising to accept, a valuable consideration in compromising or attempting to compromise a claim which was disputed as to either validity or amount, is not admissi-

ble to prove liability for or invalidity of the claim or its amount.

Evidence of conduct or statements made in compromise negotiations is likewise not admissible. This rule does not require the exclusion of any evidence otherwise discoverable merely because it is presented in the course of compromise negotiations. This rule also does not require exclusion when the evidence is offered for another purpose, such as proving bias or prejudice of a witness, negativing a contention of undue delay, or proving an effort to obstruct a criminal investigation or prosecution. I describe how far this rule's promise of confidentiality extends and the circumstances under which it would permit communications made during settlement negotiations to be admitted into evidence at trial.

Second, this Article discusses other possible sources of protection against admissibility, especially Federal Rule of Evidence 403. Federal Rule of Evidence 403 provides:

> Although relevant, evidence may be excluded if its probative value is substantially outweighed by the danger of unfair prejudice, confusion of the issues, or misleading the jury, or by considerations of undue delay, waste of time, or needless presentation of cumulative evidence.

[Also considered are] statutes that several states have recently enacted to encourage to use of mediation. This state legislation is significant because it erects a protective shield around mediations that appears to be more difficult to penetrate than the shields that Federal Rules of Evidence 408 and 403 erect around settlement communications. Thus, counsel might want to take into account before filing a lawsuit or selecting the court in which to file it the extent of the protection that is available for communications whose purpose is to resolve the dispute before trial. When it is especially important to preserve the confidentiality of such communications, lawyers might consider mediation, as opposed to party-to-party settlement negotiations or even a judicially hosted settlement conference, because of the greater protection that some state laws seem to offer to mediation proceedings.

Third, this Article examines the circumstances under which settlement communications might be subject to pretrial discovery. It by no means follows that material from settlement negotiations is protected from discovery just because a rule of evidence would make that material inadmissible for certain purposes at trial. In fact, the weight of authority suggests that there is no generalized "privilege" for settlement communications and that they are discoverable, at least after a showing of substantial need. Lawyers who conduct settlement negotiations on behalf of or with public entities face an additional peril: there are a number of reported cases in which the press or parties who were not involved in the negotiations have been able to use the Freedom of Information Act, or a state law equivalent to the Act, such as the California Public Records Act, to force disclosure of settlement documents.

Finally, this Article examines the effectiveness of alternative methods for enhancing protection of settlement communications including protective or sealing orders and side agreements. . . .

The bottom line of this Article's analysis will be disheartening to some: despite the policy that inspires rule 408, there are many circumstances in which the things that lawyers and clients say and do during settlement negotiations will not be protected from disclosure or barred from use at trial. Thus, the prudent lawyer must think carefully about what she communicates in the settlement context and about selecting the safest possible environment for these communications. . . . [T]he state of the law in this area may offer an extra incentive to parties who are especially interested in confidentiality to conduct their negotiations through a judicially hosted settlement conference that is structured around private caucuses. . . .

I. FEDERAL RULE OF EVIDENCE 408: FAILURE TO FULFILL ITS PROMISE OF CONFIDENTIALITY

Federal courts had afforded an uneven and limited protection to settlement proposals prior to the adoption of the Federal Rules of Evidence in 1975. The principal source of limitation on the scope of the common law doctrine applied prior to 1975 was the policy rationale that gave birth to it: for most courts, the reason not to admit offers of compromise lay in the notion that they were irrelevant. According to Wigmore, an offer to settle evidences only a party's desire to terminate the litigation; it could not support any reliable inference about the merits of the claim or the amount of damages.

While the "irrelevance rationale" could support exclusion of the parties' offers or demands, the courts had considerable difficulty using this rationale to exclude statements made by the parties or their conduct while they were trying to negotiate a settlement. As a result, most courts would not exclude from evidence admissions of fact that parties made during settlement discussions unless the author explicitly made the statement hypothetical, or incanted the prophylactic words "without prejudice," or unless the words constituting the admission were "so connected with the offer as to be inseparable from it."

In drafting rule 408, the Advisory Committee decided that the common-law rationale for exclusion of offers of compromise was too narrow. The Committee (and, eventually, the Supreme Court and Congress) concluded that another rationale, recognized earlier by some courts, was "more consistently impressive." This rationale recognized that it was in the public interest, and in the interest of individual litigants, to encourage consensual resolution of disputes. Thus, the Committee made "compromise and settlement of disputes" the principal purpose of Federal Rule of Evidence 408. To promote that purpose, the Committee reconstructed the law so as to expand considerably the zone of "freedom of communication with respect to compromise." Most significantly, the new rule offered protection not just to offers or demands, but also to "conduct or statements made in compromise negotiations." Thus, in adopting this rule, the Supreme Court and Congress in effect reversed a long line of federal cases that refused to protect unqualified (e.g., not in hypothetical form) statements of fact or admissions that were made during the course of settlement talks.

The importance of the principal rationale for rule 408 cannot be overemphasized. As articulated by the District Court in Minnesota shortly after the rule was adopted, "[t]he purpose for the privilege surrounding offers of compromise is to encourage free and frank discussion with a view toward settling the dispute." Counsel should use this rationale to enhance the protections the law affords their and their clients' words and deeds in settlement negotiations. Counsel should preface letters and direct or telephonic oral communications that are designed to contribute to prospects for settlement with an express statement that their purpose is to explore possible bases for settlement or to promote settlement negotiations. Lawyers who find themselves trying to dissuade a court from admitting evidence involving settlement negotiations should argue vigorously that a ruling in favor of admission would pose a grave threat to the policy objective that is at the heart of the rule. That policy objective is vital to the survival of our court system, for if a large percentage of our cases did not settle, the backlog in our courts would become totally intolerable.

The language of rule 408 unfortunately leaves a great deal of uncertainty about the scope of the rule. Trial judges must make judgments on a relatively unguided basis in many gray areas. It is in these areas that resort to the primary purpose of the rule is most important. . . .

II. THE PRINCIPAL LIMITATIONS ON THE SCOPE OF RULE 408

Unfortunately for lawyers and clients who want "free and frank discussion" to maximize the odds of achieving settlement, limits on the scope of rule 408 result in many circumstances in which courts may admit into evidence even communications that clearly were part of good faith negotiations, the sole purpose of which was to settle claims that already have been filed in court.

The primary reason counsel cannot safely assume that their communication will be protected by rule 408, however, is not the possibility that courts might construe narrowly the threshold requirements that there be a "claim" and that it be "disputed." The more consequential limit on the rule's scope is the proviso that it applies only when the purpose of admitting evidence from the negotiations is "to prove liability for or invalidity of the claim or its amount." Thus, by its own terms, rule 408 does not preclude admission of offers of compromise, or statements made in negotiations, when admitting the evidence would serve any purpose other than directly proving or disproving liability for or the amount of the claim. Because there are so many other purposes for which such evidence might be admitted, because it is impossible to forceast the likelihood that any such purpose will surface at trial, and because the outcome of any given judge's balancing analysis under rule 403 is not predictable, the wise lawyer has no choice but to be circumspect when negotiating directly with the opposition. . . .

There are many purposes for which settlement negotiation evidence might be offered that would not be within the scope of rule 408. The most significant of these are (1) to impeach a witness; (2) to negative a contention of undue delay; (3) to prove wrongful acts during negotiations; (4) to prove the existence of or to block enforcement of an alleged settlement contract; and (5) to show the state of mind of a party. The principal impression created by most of the cases . . . is that the scope of rule 408 is indeed limited and that many courts appear to be quite comfortable permitting parties to brush past the thin veil of confidentiality that surrounds settlement negotiations. . . .

III. RULE 403: AN ADDITIONAL SOURCE OF PROTECTION

Rule 408 does not purport to compel courts to admit evidence of settlement whenever that evidence is offered for some purpose other than to prove liability or damages. Rather, in such situations the rule simply does not compel exclusion of the evidence. Rule 408 also does not purport to prevent counsel from invoking other rules of evidence to attempt to block admission of settlement material. When rule 408 does not compel exclusion, counsel should look to Federal Rule of Evidence 403 as an independent potential source of protection.

It is important to emphasize at the outset that the Advisory Committee's note to this rule states that the other rules in article IV, which include rule 408, "reflect the policies underlying" rule 403 and consist of "concrete applications evolved for particular situations." Thus, rule 408 is a sub-species of rule 403, and the kind of analysis required by rule 403 is appropriate to decide whether evidence from settlement negotiations should be excluded under rule 403 even though it is not barred by rule 408.

[I]t is important to describe a strong argument by analogy from rule 404(b). Rule 404(b), also in article IV, is one of the "concrete applications [of the kind of balancing generally called for in rule 403] evolved for particular situations." The structure of rule 404(b) parallels the structure of rule 408. Both begin by prohibiting admission of specified kinds of evidence for a specified purpose, then go on to announce that courts are not required to exclude the kind of evidence the rule covers if it is offered for a purpose other than the one proscribed. Rule 404(b) prohibits admission of evidence of "other crimes, wrongs, or acts . . . to prove the character of a person in order to show that he acted in conformity therewith." In its second sentence rule 404(b) states that such evidence "may . . . be admissible for other purposes, such as proof of motive, opportunity, intent, preparation, plan, knowledge, identity, or absence of mistake or accident." Explaining how courts should proceed when the rule does not require that the evidence be excluded because it is offered for a purpose that is not prohibited, the Advisory Committee's note declares:

> No mechanical solution is offered. The determination must be made whether the danger of undue prejudice outweighs the probative value of the evidence in view of the availability of other means of proof and other factors appropriate for making decisions of this kind under Rule 403.

Thus, for a rule that also is in article IV, and that is structured just like rule 408, the Advisory Committee makes it clear that courts should conduct an independent analysis under rule 403 after they conclude that the concrete application provided for in a particular rule does not require exclusion. . . .

IV. DISCOVERABILITY VS. ADMISSIBILITY: IS THERE A "PRIVILEGE" FOR SETTLEMENT COMMUNICATIONS?

Attorneys must be careful to distinguish pretrial discoverability from admissibility at trial. Litigators cannot safely assume that statements made during settlement negotiations that would not be admitted at trial (by virtue of rule 408, or rule 403, or simply because they would be irrelevant) are also immune from discovery. Courts attempting to resolve the discoverability question must face issues and conduct analyses that are quite different from the issues and analyses relevant when ruling on the question of admissibility. Unfortunately for counsel, who would like to be able to predict the likelihood that settlement communications will remain confidential, the published opinions on discoverability of settlement negotiations do not reflect a consensus about basic issues in this area. As the paragraphs that follow make clear, some courts are sympathetic with the need to preserve confidentiality even as against discovery, while many others have ruled that settlement communications are discoverable despite the policies that inform rule 408.

Whether or not communications made during settlement negotiations are discoverable may depend, in part, on whether courts will recognize a "privilege" for settlement communications under rule 408 or federal common law. This question is important because the scope of discovery is defined as "any matter, not privileged, which is relevant to the subject matter involved in the pending action." It follows that if communications made in connection with settlement are privileged, they will fall outside the scope of discovery, even if they are relevant. While no appellate court in the federal system has addressed this question directly, several district court opinions express or imply views on this matter. The majority view seems to be that settlement communications are not "privileged" within the meaning of the rules that define the scope of discovery. The same question arises under analogous state statutes. . . .

C. A Test for Discoverability that Appropriately Reflects the Policy Objectives

Although it may be fair to say that rule 408 does not create a privilege, the rule clearly reflects a significant federal policy in favor of promoting settlements by encouraging freedom of communication that is not implicated by most discovery requests. This policy would be seriously jeopardized if courts routinely permitted discovery of communications made in settlement discussions. Counsel seeking to protect settlement materials from discovery should argue vigorously that courts should order disclosure only after conducting a balancing analysis in which the federal policy of promoting settlement is given the full weight it deserves. Case law supports this balancing approach. . . .

D. Settlements with Public Entities: Public Right of Access

Lawyers who represent public entities in settlement negotiations, or private parties who decide to enter a settlement agreement with a public entity, must be aware of the possibility that interested persons could use the Freedom of Information Act (FOIA) [5 USC § 552], or a state law equivalent . . . to force disclosure of both the terms of a settlement agreement and other documents related to settlement negotiations.

FOIA contains no exemption that explicitly mentions materials generated in connection with settlement negotiations. Because of this, and the general admonition that courts are to construe FOIA's exemptions narrowly and to resolve doubts in favor of disclosure, there are circumstances in which citizens can use FOIA to force governmental agencies to disclose documents generated in connection with settlements. The reported decisions suggest that documents related to settlement negotiations will be deemed exempt from FOIA if they have not been disclosed to or received from an adversary. These decisions also suggest, however, that documents disclosed to or received from an adversary during confidential settlement negotiations are vulnerable to a FOIA request, regardless of the nature of the interest that inspires the request.

Among the nine exemptions from FOIA, the one that seemed most promising to lawyers trying to preserve the confidentiality of settlement documents was number five, which covers "inter-agency or intra-agency memoranda or letters which would not be available by law to a party other than an agency in litigation with the agency." This exemption protects government generated documents whose confidentiality the government has maintained and which satisfy the criteria for any clearly established privilege. For example, this exemption would prevent use of FOIA to compel disclosure of a document the government generated in connection with settlement negotiations if the document satisfied the criteria for the attorney-client privilege or the work product doctrine. Similarly, the fifth exemption applies to documents that would be protected from disclosure in civil litigation by the "deliberative process" privilege.

On several occasions government lawyers have tried unsuccessfully to persuade courts that there is a separate "settlement privilege" in civil litigation and that materials that would qualify for it also should fall within the protections of the fifth exemption. The seminal case is *County of Madison, New York v. United States Department of Justice* [641 F.2d 1036 (1st Cir 1981)]. In that opinion, Chief Judge Coffin, writing for a unanimous panel, ordered the government to disclose documents generated in connection with settlement negotiations in an earlier, related matter. The documents in question had either been sent by the party opponent to the government or by lawyers for the government to opposing counsel during the course of the negotiations. The appellate court refused to categorize these documents as "intra-agency" memoranda or letters.

The court also rejected an argument that FOIA empowers federal courts, under the guise of exercising equitable discretion, to decide whether considerations of "public policy" justify adding exemptions to FOIA for categories of documents not specifically exempted by Congress on the face of the statute. The court acknowledged the importance of the government's ability to resolve disputes by settlement and conceded that the government's ability to reach consensual agreements with adversaries in litigation would be impaired if parties knew that under FOIA "written settlement communications will be available to anyone, irrespective of the merit of his or her need to know." The *County of Madison* panel felt constrained, nonetheless, to honor the letter and spirit of FOIA, which they emphasized "is not a withholding statute but a disclosure statute." The court ruled that the public policy favoring settlement simply cannot justify distorting FOIA's language and giving courts discretionary power to limit the statute's disclosure mandate by carving out an exemption that is not even intimated in that language. The effect of *County of Madison* is clear: exemption five will not protect documents related to settlement that were generated by or shared with a party opponent, even if both the government and its opponent intended all such documents to remain confidential. . . .

V. ALTERNATIVE METHODS OF ENHANCED PROTECTION OF SETTLEMENT NEGOTIATIONS

In light of the numerous threats to the confidentiality of settlement communications previously discussed, the following section presents a number of alternative approaches counsel can consider in order to protect settlement negotiations from disclosure. [The discussion of protective orders or sealing orders; side agreements under seal; and private contracts between settling parties to ensure confidentiality is omitted.]

C. Federal Rule of Civil Procedure 68 and State Mediation Statutes

Attorneys who are especially concerned about preserving the confidentiality of offers or demands, or of statements made during negotiations, should consider proceeding under Federal Rule of Civil Procedure 68, or a state law analogue, like section 998 of the California Code of Civil Procedure, or turning to a "mediation" process that enjoys special state statutory protection.

The bar to admissibility that is articulated in Federal Rule of Civil Procedure 68, and in section 998 of the California Code of Civil Procedure, is virtually unqualified, in sharp contrast to the limited protection offered by Federal Rule of Evidence 408. Rule 68 flatly declares that evidence of an unaccepted offer that was made under the rule is "not admissible except in a proceeding to determine costs." The language of section 998 of the California Code of Civil Procedure is similarly sweeping: "If such offer is not accepted . . . it . . . cannot be given in evidence upon the trial." These prohibitions seem operative regardless of the purpose for which the evidence would be proffered at trial and thus avoid the limitations on the scope of rule 408. Since neither rule 68 nor section 998 purports to extend protection to evidence of "conduct or statements made in compromise negotiations," counsel cannot be sure to what extent these rules of procedure can be invoked to protect communications that accompany and explain protected offers. Moreover, by their express terms, these rules apply only to offers that are not accepted. It is unlikely that these rules would offer any protection in a case in which a person who was not a party to a settlement agreement is attempting to compel disclosure of settlement communications or terms.

As an alternative to simple two-party settlement negotiations, counsel could proceed with private mediations that are covered by recently enacted state confidentiality statutes with much greater confidence in the scope of the protection they afford. As one commentator has noted, recent "legislative enactments in several states have provided near-absolute protection for communications made in mediation, [thus greatly enhancing] the protection available to mediation under the traditional rules of evidenced and contract." Some of the most populous states in the country, including California, New York, and Florida, have enacted such laws.

The California version of these statutes appears as section 1152.5 of the Evidence Code, which was added in 1985. Except for certain family law matters that are covered by other confidentiality provisions, this statute applies to any kind of civil dispute. When parties "agree to conduct and participate in a mediation for the purpose of compromising, settling, or resolving a civil dispute," and when, before the mediation begins, they agree in writing to invoke the protections of the statute after setting forth the provisions of the statute in their agreement, the law prohibits admitting evidence "of anything said or . . . any admission made in the course of the mediation" or any "document prepared for the purpose of, or in the course of, or pursuant to, the mediation."

The Law Revision Commission's comment to the 1985 addition makes clear that parties can waive their confidentiality rights under this section either by failing to object to a proffer at the time of trial or by mutual consent. . . . [T]he purpose of this section is "to encourage this alternative to a judicial determination of the action" and that the justification for the confidentiality provision is the same as the justification for the much narrower provision contained in section 1152, which renders offers of compromise "inadmissible to prove . . . liability for the loss or damage or any part of it." The Law Revision Commission's comment emphasizes that instead of attempting to limit the applicability of the statute through a definition of the term "mediation," the legislature decided that it would make the statutory protections available only when "the persons who will participate in the mediation (including the mediator) execute a written agreement before the mediation begins stating that Section 1152.5 of the Evidence Code applies to the mediation' and only when their agreement sets "out the full text of subdivisions (a) and (b) of Section 1152.5."

Thus, California practitioners who want to take advantage of the broad protections available through this statute should develop forms that recite all the relevant provisions of the statute and that expressly articulate the commitments to confidentiality that all parties and the mediator make. When they follow the proper procedure, California lawyers should be able to use this statute to fill virtually any gap left by section 1152 of the California Evidence Code, which applies only to "offers to compromise."

There is no reason to believe that because a dispute is already the subject of litigation the protections of section 1152.5 are rendered inaccessible. There is reason to believe, however, that this more generous section would not apply to negotiations between the parties that did not involve a neutral third party. While the new statute does not purport to define "mediation," it clearly contemplates a process that involves the participation of a neutral person who must sign the confidentiality agreement. Counsel cannot simply change the label of direct settlement negotiations to "mediation" and assume that they will enjoy the protections of the new statute, but must involve a neutral person from the outset.

Before deciding to proceed under section 1152.5, counsel should consider the disadvantages that might derive from the breadth of its protections. As a commentator has pointed out concerning comparable statutes enacted in other states, proceeding under statutes that on their face bar use of evidence from mediations regardless of the purpose for which the evidence would be used could create extra difficulties for a party who subsequently seeks either (1) to enforce an agreement that resulted from the mediation or (2) to resist enforcement of an agreement that was the product of duress, fraud, mutual mistake, or overreaching. Similarly, the broad language of a statute like section 1152.5 could impair efforts to redress wrongs arising out of violation of some specific duty relating to the conduct of negotiations, such as the duty to bargain in good faith in labor disputes, or the duty of an insurance carrier to consider in good faith reasonable settlement proposals.

Apparently anticipating this problem, the Minnesota legislature explicitly provided that the promise of confidentiality that extends generally to communications made in connection with mediations does not apply when a party applies to a court "to have a mediated settlement agreement set aside or reformed." Even though they acted a year later than their counterparts in Minnesota, California legislators failed to add any such caveat or qualifier to the promise of confidentiality in section 1152.5. Thus, counsel cannot be sure how California courts will respond when a party attempts to use material or statements made in connection with a mediation to enforce or to defeat a mediated settlement agreement. Given this uncertainty, counsel must assess separately the needs and risks presented by each specific situation that calls for some effort to reach a settlement, then either (1) choose from the pre-existing procedures the one that best fits that situation or (2) attempt to create, through private contract, a mini-trial process that is specially tailored to meet the needs of the parties.

D. Private Caucus Settlement Conferences

A private caucus settlement conference hosted by a judge or magistrate offers two sources of protection for communications. In conferences structured on this model the parties have virtually no direct interaction. The person to whom they present the reasoning that supports their offers or demands, and to whom they divulge how far they might be willing to go in an effort to compromise differences, is the judge—not opposing counsel. Furthermore, the parties can ask the judge to keep secret the admissions or concessions about which they are most sensitive, or the most potentially damaging reasons for the positions they are taking. An opponent who does not learn these things cannot attempt to introduce them at trial.

The second source of protection for communications made during judicially hosted settlement conferences is the difficulty an opponent would have compelling a judge who had hosted such a conference to testify at trial about what a party said to her in confidence during the negotiations. There may be circumstances under which this kind of testimony could be compelled, but the judicial community is likely to require a compelling showing before permitting a party to penetrate this sensitive arena. . . .

Conclusion

Despite commonly made assumptions, and the apparent promise of Federal Rule of Evidence 408, there are many circumstances in which many courts would permit both the discovery and the admission at trial of confidential settlement communications. Given the unpredictability of judicial rulings in this area, and the unforeseeability of events that could result in disclosure or admission at trial of settlement communications, good lawyers have no choice but to proceed with caution in this area. If confidentiality is their client's paramount concern, counsel should not rely on the rules of evidence for protection and should consider taking some of the extra precautions described in the latter sections of this Article.

5. Kristina M. Kerwin, "*The Discoverability of Settlement and ADR Communications: Federal Rule of Evidence 408 and Beyond*, 12 Rev. Litig. 665 (1993)*

B. Recent Case Law Affirming the "No Privilege" View

Since the July 1988 publication of Brazil's article, several cases have affirmed the view that settlement communications are discoverable, at least under certain circumstances.

In 1988, the court in *Morse/Diesel, Inc. v. Fidelity and Deposit Co*, 122 F.R.D. 447 (S.D.N.Y. 1988), allowed discovery of settlement documents. In a suit by a contractor against its subcontractor's surety, the subcontractor, as a third-party defendant, sought and was allowed discovery of settlement documents in possession of the contractor. First, the court addressed the contractor's argument that the documents were protected by Rule 408. . . . [T]he court made the familiar point that Rule 408 "only applies to the admissibility of evidence at trial and does not necessarily protect such evidence from discovery." Further, District Judge Leisure wrote that "[t]his view has been uniformly adopted by the courts in dealing with the provision." . . . The court found that the subcontractor, as a third-party defendant, had made the requisite "particularized showing" that the requested discovery would lead to admissible evidence.

Along a different line of reasoning, the court in *Guy Gannett Publishing Co. v. University of Maine*, 555 A.2d 470 (Me. 1989), interpreted Maine Rule of Evidence 408(a), which is substantially similar to Rule 408, as allowing discovery of a settlement agreement between the university and a former basketball coach. In granting the plaintiff's request to discover the settlement agreement between the defendant and nonparty coach, the court rejected the defendant's argument that the agreement was protected by a privilege created by Maine Rule 408(a). Unlike the preferred rationale for Rule 408, the court in *Guy Gannett* explained that Maine Rule 408(a) "represents a policy choice to exclude evidence relating to settlements as irrelevant on the issue of liability. It does not make such evidence privileged." The court went on to note that the policy of encouraging settlements is not threatened by merely allowing discovery of such an agreement, as long as it may not be used at trial against one of the settling parties. . . .

In *American Society of Composers v. Showtime*, 912 F.2d 563 (2d Cir. 1990), . . . the court actually upheld the admission of evidence by the plaintiff concerning the settlement offer the plaintiff received from HBO, another defendant in an identical claim, clearly implying that discovery of settlement information is permissible. The opinion reiterates the common rejection of the relevance argument to keep out settlement information in favor of the policy encouraging settlement as a better justification for Rule 408. The court explained that "[t]he implication of this policy for our case is that settlement offers or agreements are not automatically inadmissible—even as to liability or the amount of damages—if they are offered

---

*Reprinted with permission.

against a party who was not a participant in the settlement discussions or agreement." The court emphasized that use of the evidence in this case against Showtime would not threaten the underlying policy as would use of the offer against the settling party, HBO. . . .

IV. THE MIXED BAG OF PROTECTION FROM DISCOVERABILITY AFFORDED BY STATE STATUTES

Although protection for communications made during informal, unassisted settlement negotiations is minimal, concerned practitioners may have alternatives under various state and federal statutes that provide extra protection to statements made during formal ADR proceedings, especially mediation. As with the case law interpreting Rule 408, the trend in this legislation seems to be driven by a desire to increase the confidentiality of settlement proceedings. However, the actual statutes are a mixed bag containing varying degrees of protection. Although a few states seem to provide almost absolute protection, most of the statutes have either restrictions on applicability or the same type of exceptions as Rule 408.

A. Statutes Affording Near-Absolute Protection

The few state statutes that seem to provide absolute protection for settlement information do so only for communications made during formal mediation. Oklahoma's Dispute Resolution Act defines mediation as follows: "[T]he process of resolving a dispute with the assistance of a mediator outside of a formal court proceeding." The Act further provides that:

> A. Any information received by the mediator [or his agent] . . . is privileged and confidential. . . .
>
> B. No part of the proceeding shall be considered a matter of public record.
>
> C. No mediator, initiating party, or responding party . . . shall be subject to administrative or judicial process requiring disclosure of any matters discussed or shall disclose any information obtained during any part of the mediation proceedings.

The protection in this Act seems nearly absolute because the only exception to the no-disclosure rule is for an action for damages against a mediator arising out of mediation.

The confidentiality provision of Michigan's Community Dispute Resolution Act provides equally comprehensive protection: "The work product and case files of a mediator or center are confidential and not subject to disclosure in a judicial or administrative proceeding. Communications relating to the subject matter of the resolution during the resolution process by a party, mediator, or other person shall be a confidential communication."

The protection granted here may be even greater than that of the Oklahoma Act as the Michigan provision does not even specify an exception for claims against the mediator. One possible problem with the Michigan Act, however, is that it is unclear whether the confidentiality provision is limited to mediation conducted through the dispute resolution centers established by the Act, thereby providing no protection to independent mediation.

Almost identical to the Michigan law is New York's Community Dispute Resolution Centers Program Act. The coverage of this statute, however, is not quite so broad as the Oklahoma and Michigan statutes because it introduces its confidentiality provision with the following disclaimer: "Except as otherwise expressly provided in this article. . . . "Additionally, the Act stipulates that only communications "relating to the subject matter of the resolution" are protected. Like the Michigan statute, the New York Act suffers from the ambiguity of whether the protection applies only to mediation conducted pursuant to the authority of a Dispute Resolution Center established by the Act.

Finally, the California Evidence Code also provides broad protection to communications made during mediation. The California law provides complete protection for both statements and documents that were part of the mediation, but only if all parties sign a written agreement setting out the text of these statutory provisions prior to the proceeding. The law also provides the exception that otherwise protected information may be admitted in evidence if all parties consent. Because this statute is part of the California Evidence Code, and not a separate dispute resolution act like the Michigan and New York provisions, it should apply to all mediation.

B. Big Exceptions Lead to Only Moderate Protection

Many state statutes purport to establish a privilege for settlement communications made during some type of formal ADR proceeding, but contain exceptions similar to those in Rule 408 so that the ultimate protection is minimal. Utah's Alternative Dispute Resolution Providers Act probably gives the broadest protection of statutes in this category; the only significant exception is for evidence "otherwise subject to discovery, [and] . . . not prepared specifically for use in and actually used in the ADR procedure." Although the "otherwise subject to discovery" provision is potentially very broad, the Act does exclude all "statements, memoranda, materials, and other tangible evidence" specifically prepared for the proceeding, which could cover a significant amount of information "otherwise discoverable." Other exceptions in this act include consent in writing by all parties, an action against the ADR provider, a matter invoking the child abuse reporting requirements, and an immediate threat of physical violence against a readily identifiable victim. The Utah Act, unlike the statutes discussed in the previous section, applies to all ADR proceedings, not just mediation.

On the other hand, many states' confidentiality provisions include the "otherwise discoverable" exception standing alone or in conjunction with even more exceptions, thereby greatly diminishing the protection given, just as that clause does in Rule 408. Statutes fitting this description include Florida's Citizen Dispute Settlement Centers Act, Colorado's Dispute Resolution Act, and Texas' Alternative Dispute Resolution Procedures Act. Similarly, many states have evidence rules nearly identical to Rule 408. . . .

E. ADR, Confidentiality, and Federal Administrative Law

1. Administrative Conference of the United States, Encouraging Settlements by Protecting Mediator Confidentiality, Recommendation 88-11, 1 CFR § 305.88-11 (1988)

This recommendation seeks to encourage agency use of alternative means of dispute resolution by affording appropriate protection to communications between the parties and the neutral in settlement negotiations. The Conference, of course, recognizes the principle that decisions affecting the public welfare ought to be made in the open and subject to public and judicial scrutiny. Nevertheless, since settlements are essential to administrative agencies, a careful balance must be struck between the openness required for the legitimacy of many agency agreements and the confidentiality that is critical if sensitive negotiations are to yield agreements. This recommendation attempts to strike that balance, without thwarting open decisionmaking. . . .

[M]any of the benefits of ADR can be achieved only if the proceedings are held confidential. Confidentiality assures the parties that what is said in the discussions will be limited to the negotiations alone so they can be free to be forthcoming. This need extends to the neutral's materials, such as notes and reports, which are produced solely to assist the neutral in the negotiation process and which others could misconstrue as indicating a bias against some party or interest. This is why many mediators routinely destroy their personal notes and drafts and return all other materials to the parties. Moreover, if the neutral were to testify in a subsequent proceeding as to what went on during the negotiations, his neutrality might be destroyed. The ADR process could be jeopardized because one party or another is likely to feel disadvantaged. Also, the parties would justifiably feel their confidences might be threatened. All this would certainly inhibit future participation by parties and neutrals. . . .

The Administrative Conference takes the view that maintaining confidentiality of settlement discussions is consistent with the principle underlying the FOIA, Rule 408 of the FRE, Rule 26(b)(3) of the FRCP, and the work product doctrine. To encourage the use of ADR in negotiations, the recommendation contains a model rule seeking to protect the communications between the neutral and the parties or other participants in the course of the negotiations as well as the neutral's own notes and impressions. It does so in recognition that the mediator will virtually never have information or evidence that is not shared by at least one other person, excepting of course the neutral's own notes, recollections, and judgments. The rule does not address (1) when meetings or negotiations should be held in public session, (2) what justification should be prepared to support any agreement reached, or (3) what information should be available from a party to the negotiations.

The rule covers oral communications or actions that are related to a settlement proceeding, as well as documents that are created specifically for the negotiations or other, previously existing documents that are furnished to the neutral in confidence by a participant in the negotiation. The restrictions on the neutral's disclosing information from the negotiation are not categorically absolute, being subject to several narrow exceptions that deal with extraordinary cases. Finally, the model rule does not attempt to impose its terms on all parties for all issues; they would be free to vary the terms for their particular negotiations.

RECOMENDATION

1. Agencies that use the services of neutrals in settlement proceedings:
   (a) should explicitly indicate that as a matter of policy they will not seek to discover or otherwise force disclosure of a neutral's notes, memoranda or recollections or of documents provided to the neutral in confidence in the course of settlement negotiations;
   (b) in arranging with an individual or organization to serve as a neutral in settlement proceedings, should include a provision in any agreement with the neutral that (i) the agency makes no claim to the neutral's notes, memoranda or recollections or to documents provided to the neutral in confidence in the course of the settlement negotiations and (ii) that such material is outside the scope of the agency's right to any data developed pursuant to the agreement; and

(c) should adopt a procedural rule, consistent with the model rule contained in the appendix below, for all cases where the agency itself is a party to the negotiations or where private parties are negotiating the resolution of an issue in controversy concerning a statute, regulation, or policy administered by the agency.

2. The neutral, including a neutral (as defined in the model rule) who serves as a presiding officer, should carefully segregate, and identify as settlement documents, all materials received or developed during the course of a settlement proceeding, including any retained following its conclusion, so they will be used solely to assist the neutral in working to settle the issues in controversy.
3. Agencies should interpret the FOIA, Rule 408 of the Federal Rules of Evidence, Rule 26(b)(3) of the Federal Rules of Civil Procedure, and the work product doctrine to avoid disclosure of settlement communications by neutrals serving in administrative settlement proceedings.

Model Rule [for adoption by administrative agencies]

§ xxx.1 Introduction; Encouraging Settlement; ADR Techniques

§ xxx.2 Definitions

As used in this rule:

(a) "Issue in controversy" means a question that is material to a decision involving a statute, regulation, or policy administered by [the agency] about which persons who would be substantially affected or the agency disagree.

(b) "Settlement proceeding" means any process, such as facilitation, mediation, minitrial, factfinding, or non-binding arbitration, that is used to resolve issues in controversy by agreement of the parties in which a neutral serves, whether or not administrative or judicial proceedings have been instituted.

(c) "Neutral" means an individual who with respect to the issues in controversy—

(1) is not a party;

(2) does not have any official, financial, or personal conflict of interest unless such interest has been fully disclosed in writing and all parties agree that the individual may nevertheless serve as a neutral; and

(3) works to aid the parties in arriving at settlement of the issues in controversy through agreement.

(d) "Settlement communication" means any oral or written communication or conduct made in confidence and in connection with a settlement proceeding by any party, neutral, non-party participant, or other source of information relevant to the proceeding.

(e) "Settlement document" means any written material that is—

(1) prepared for the purpose of, in the course of, or pursuant to a settlement proceeding, including memoranda, notes, and work product of the neutral and the parties, or

(2) provided to the neutral in confidence for purposes of the settlement proceeding.

An agreement reached as a result of a settlement proceeding is not a settlement document unless the parties agree in writing, and the law allows, that it shall be regarded as such.

(f) "In confidence" means with the expressed desire of the source that the information be kept confidential or provided under circumstances that would create the reasonable expectation that it will not be disclosed.

(g) "Party" means a person or entity whose dispute is the subject of the settlement proceeding, including representatives of such a party.

(h) "Non-party participant" means a person or entity who is not a party to the dispute but who participates in the settlement proceeding, such as by providing information, analysis, advice, or views.

§ xxx.3 Applicability of the Rule

(a) This rule applies to any settlement proceeding whether or not [the agency] is a party if the parties communicate with the neutral under circumstances that reasonably imply that the parties expect that the communications will be held confidential. Prior to beginning substantive negotiations, the parties may (1) agree that this rule does not apply to their negotiations or (2) modify the terms of this rule by agreement in which case that agreement will prevail to the extent it is authorized by law or is otherwise consistent with this rule. So that the neutral can decide whether he wishes to serve under those conditions, the parties shall so inform the neutral otherwise prior to commencing settlement proceedings. If they fail to do so, this rule shall apply.

(b) The provisions of the rule take effect when —

(1) a person has been specifically requested or accepted by at least one party to (i) serve as the neutral in the settlement proceeding, or (ii) discuss the potential of conducting a settlement proceeding, or (iii) contact other potential parties to determine whether it would be appropriate to convene a settlement proceeding to resolve the issues in controversy;

(2) the other parties with whom the neutral has contact knows that he or she is occupying the role of a neutral; and

(3) they communicate with the neutral in that capacity.

(c) The rule does not address—

(1) the extent to which a party may disclose settlement documents and communications either voluntarily or in response to discovery or legal process; or,

(2) the information that is required to support a decision or agreement reached in a settlement proceeding.

§ xxx.4 Neutral Impartiality and Confidentiality of Settlement Negotiations

(a) A neutral shall not voluntarily or through compulsory process disclose or testify concerning settlement communications or settlement documents, unless—

(1) all parties to the settlement proceeding and the neutral consent in writing, and if the settlement communication or document was provided by a non-party participant, that participant also consents in writing;

(2) the request is for a settlement document that was provided to the neutral in a public meeting or is otherwise already in the public domain;

(3) the settlement document is required by law to be made public, but only if it is not available from the person who prepared it or from any other source;

(4) a court determines that there is a need for such testimony or disclosure. The agency takes the position that any such determination should be pursuant to a finding that the need for disclosure to—(i) prevent a manifest injustice, (ii) reveal a violation of law, or (iii) protect the public health or safety—is of sufficient magnitude

in the particular case to outweigh the integrity of settlement proceedings in general by reducing the confidence of parties in future cases that their communications will remain confidential; or

(5) the settlement document or communication is relevant to the resolution of a dispute between the neutral and a party or participant, but only to the extent that the document or communication is used for purposes of resolving that dispute and not any issue in controversy in the settlement proceeding.

(b) If a demand, by way of discovery request or other legal process, is made for disclosure by the neutral of a settlement document or communication, the neutral shall make reasonable efforts to notify the parties and any affected non-party participant so that countermeasures may be taken if desired.

§ xxx.5 Agency Records

(a) The agency makes no claim of control or ownership over the notes, memoranda, and other work product prepared by a neutral or by his or her staff in connection with a settlement proceeding.

(b) The agency takes the position that settlement documents and communications are not agency records solely on account of their having been received by the neutral during a settlement proceeding; a document or other material that is otherwise an agency record remains as such.

2. Comments and Questions

a. As with many proposed or enacted statutes, it is essential to understand the definitions. They do not simply tell an unknowing reader what terms mean; they define the scope of the legislation. Although the title of the Administrative Conference recommendation refers to "protecting mediator confidentiality," the model act covers a far wider range of activity aimed at the settlement of disputes by and with administrative agencies.

b. Do you favor adoption of the ACUS proposal? If not, does it contain features that could usefully be incorporated in confidentiality statutes or agency regulations?

c. Compare the ACUS approach to that taken by Congress in the Administrative Dispute Resolution Act. (Other aspects of this legislation are considered in Chapter 14.) Which do you prefer, and why?

3. Administrative Dispute Resolution Act of 1990, 5 USC §§ 571, 574

§ 571. Definitions.

For the purposes of this subchapter, the term —

. . . (7) "in confidence" means, with respect to information, that the information is provided

(A) with the expressed intent of the source that it not be disclosed; or

(B) under circumstances that would create the reasonable expectation on behalf of the source that the information will not be disclosed[.]

§ 574. Confidentiality.

(a) Except as provided in subsections (d) and (e), a neutral in a dispute resolution proceeding shall not voluntarily disclose or through discovery or compulsory process be required to disclose any information concerning any dispute resolution communication or any communication provided in confidence to the neutral, unless —

(1) all parties to the dispute resolution proceeding and the neutral consent in writing, and, if the dispute resolution communication was provided by a nonparty participant, that participant also consents in writing;

(2) the dispute resolution communication has already been made public;

(3) the dispute resolution communication is required by statute to be made public, but a neutral should make such communication public only if no other person is reasonably available to disclose the communication; or

(4) a court determines that such testimony or disclosure is necessary to —

(A) prevent a manifest injustice;

(B) help establish a violation of law; or

(C) prevent harm to the public health or safety, of sufficient magnitude in the particular case to outweigh the integrity of dispute resolution proceedings in general by reducing the confidence of parties in future cases that their communications will remain confidential.

(b) A party to a dispute resolution proceeding shall not voluntarily disclose or through discovery or compulsory process be required to disclose any information concerning any dispute resolution communication, unless —

(1) the communication was prepared by the party seeking disclosure;

(2) all parties to the dispute resolution proceeding consent in writing;

(3) the dispute resolution communication has already been made public;

(4) the dispute resolution communication is required by statute to be made public;

(5) a court determines that such testimony or disclosure is necessary to —

(A) prevent a manifest injustice;

(B) help establish a violation of law; or

(C) prevent harm to the public health and safety, of sufficient magnitude in the particular case to outweigh the integrity of dispute resolution proceedings in general by reducing the confidence of parties in future cases that their communications will remain confidential;

(6) the dispute resolution communication is relevant to determining the existence or meaning of an agreement or award that resulted from the dispute resolution proceeding or to the enforcement of such an agreement or award; or

(7) the dispute resolution communication was provided to or was available to all parties to the dispute resolution proceeding.

(c) Any dispute resolution communication that is disclosed in violation of subsection (a) or (b), shall not be admissible in any proceeding relating to the issues in controversy with respect to which the communication was made.

(d) The parties may agree to alternate confidential procedures for disclosures by a neutral. Upon such agreement the parties shall inform the neutral before the commencement of the dispute resolution proceeding of any modifications to the provisions of subsection (a) that will govern the confidentiality of the dispute resolution proceeding. If the parties do not so inform the neutral, subsection (a) shall apply.

(e) If a demand for disclosure, by way of discovery request or other legal process, is made upon the neutral regarding a dispute resolution communication, the neutral shall make reasonable efforts to notify the parties and any affected nonparty participants of the demand. Any party or affected nonparty participant who receives such notice and within 15 calendar days does not offer to defend a refusal of the neutral to disclose the requested information shall have waived any objection to such disclosure.

(f) Nothing in this section shall prevent the discovery or admissibility of any evidence that is otherwise discoverable, merely because the evidence was presented in the course of the dispute resolution proceeding.

(g) Subsections (a) and (b) shall have no effect on the information and data that are necessary to document an agreement reached or order issued pursuant to a dispute resolution proceeding.

(h) Subsections (a) and (b) shall not prevent the gathering of information for research or educational purposes, in cooperation with other agencies, governmental entities, or dispute resolution programs, so long as the parties and the specific issues in controversy are not identifiable.

(i) Subsections (a) and (b) shall not prevent the use of a dispute resolution communication to resolve a dispute between the neutral in a dispute resolution proceeding and a party to or participant in such proceeding, so long as such dispute resolution communication is disclosed only to the extent necessary to resolve such dispute.

(j) This section shall not be considered a statute specifically exempting disclosure under section 552(b)(3) of this title [the Freedom of Information Act].

4. Comments and Questions

a. Congress passed the ADR Act to encourage federal agencies to use mediation and other forms of ADR. The objective of the ADR Act was to "enable parties to ADR proceedings to be forthcoming and candid, without fear that frank statements may later be used against them."

b. This approach is praised in Michael A. Perino, *Drafting Mediation Privileges: Lessons from the Civil Justice Reform Act*, 26 SETON HALL L. REV. 1 (1995). A sensible approach is adopted for serious application of the general goal of confidentiality, and allowing disclosure in specific circumstances. "A court is permitted to order both neutrals and parties to disclose . . . communications if . . . necessary to: (i) prevent a manifest injustice; (ii) help establish a violation of law; or (iii) prevent harm to the public health or safety. Disclosures sought for these reasons are subject to a balancing test: the alleged necessity for the disclosure must be of sufficient magnitude in the particular case to outweigh the integrity of dispute resolution proceedings in general by reducing the confidence of parties in future cases that their communications will remain confidential."

F. Multiple Forums, Multiple Parties, Nonparties

1. Comments and Questions

a. For most analytical purposes it is useful to deal with disputing in terms of a discrete dispute between two clearly identified parties, be they individuals or large organizations. The world is not so simple, however, and disputing can involve multiple forums; multiple interested persons; multiple parties: multiple issues; subsequent claims involving issues similar to those decided in a prior proceeding, etc. Such problems are commonly faced by courts, and there is a rich body of doctrine to draw upon. Legal labels commonly associated with these issues are collateral estoppel (issue preclusion) and res judicata (claim preclusion). The two ADR cases that follow, one based on a minitrial and the other an arbitration, are merely suggestive of the vast array of complexities that can and do arise.

b. The law of res judicata and collateral estoppel law is complex and, because so much is at stake, is a common issue in litigation. The application of these doctrines in the context of commercial arbitration is the subject of Shell, *Res Judicata and Collateral Estoppel Effects of Commercial Arbitration*, 35 UCLA L. REV. 623 (1988).

c. In many instances, a party will be concerned about proceeding to arbitration of a claim because related parties or transactions (in a factual not a legal sense) are not subject to inclusion in the arbitration proceeding. *Volt Information Sciences v. Stanford University*, considered in Chapter 11, presents this scenario.

d. The next case, *Flynn v. Gorton* is of real importance, if for no other reasons than that the facts are so commonplace (automobile accident, multiple claims).

2. *Flynn v. Gorton*, 255 Cal. Rptr. 768 (Cal. App. 1989)

SCOVILLE, Presiding Justice.

John Flynn and Achilda Gorton were involved in an automobile accident in 1983. Flynn was turning left and Gorton was entering the intersection when their cars collided. Kim Blackburn was a passenger in Gorton's car. Gorton brought a personal injury suit against Flynn, alleging his negligence caused the collision. Flynn generally denied the allegation and claimed Gorton's negligence contributed to the accident.

Gorton elected to submit the case to arbitration and agreed that any award would not exceed $25,000. The arbitrator awarded her $20,281.08 in full settlement of her claims. The award became a final judgment which Flynn satisfied in full. Blackburn then filed a personal injury complaint against Flynn and Gorton, alleging both were negligent. Flynn cross-complained against Gorton for implied indemnity, contribution and declaratory relief. He alleged Blackburn's injuries resulted from Gorton's negligence in causing the accident and he was entitled to a determination of each party's comparative negligence and an apportionment of damages.

Gorton demurred to Flynn's cross-complaint, arguing it was barred under the doctrine of res judicata because it presented the same claim decided in the judicial arbitration action. She asked the court to take judicial notice of the court files, the arbitrator's award, and his cover letter explaining the award. The award was silent as to the arbitrator's reasons for the decision. However, in the arbitrator's cover letter, he stated: ". . . the issue of liability was no issue at all, and very clearly in favor of the plaintiff." . . .

On appeal Flynn argues the issue raised in his cross-complaint, i.e. whether Gorton was partially responsible for her passenger's injuries, was not addressed in the arbitration action. He contends the arbitration award did not resolve whether: (1) under comparative fault principles, Gorton was responsible in part for the collision and thus for Blackburn's injuries; and (2) whether Gorton otherwise contributed to her passenger's injuries, e.g. by failing to have seat belts or by somehow aggravating Blackburn's injuries after the collision. Flynn asserts the arbitration award and court file are silent on the issue of the parties' comparative fault in causing the collision, and it may be that the approximately $20,000 award to Gorton reflected an offset for her contributory negligence. He argues under these circumstances his action was not barred by res judicata.

The doctrine of res judicata is composed of two parts: claim preclusion and issue preclusion. Claim preclusion prohibits a party from relitigating a previously adjudicated cause of action; thus, a new lawsuit on the same cause of action is entirely barred. Issue preclusion, or collateral estoppel, applies to a subsequent suit between the parties on a different cause of action. Collateral estoppel prevents the parties from relitigating any issue which was actually litigated and finally decided in the earlier action. The issue decided in the earlier proceeding must be identical to the one presented in the subsequent action. If there is any doubt, collateral estoppel will not apply. Res judicata and collateral estoppel share common goals. Both prevent inconsistent results and promote finality and judicial economy by bringing an end to litigation.

Judicial arbitration was enacted by the Legislature in 1978 to serve similar ends. Due to the cost, complexity and delay involved in court adjudication, the Legislature declared that arbitration should be encouraged or required as "an efficient and equitable method for resolving small claims." Under the statute, court-ordered arbitration is mandatory in certain courts for civil actions in which the amount in controversy does not exceed a specified amount. Such arbitration can also be elected by stipulation of the parties or by the unilateral decision of the plaintiff if he or she agrees that any award will not exceed the statutory amount.

Unlike commercial or true arbitration, judicial arbitration is not binding, since any party dissatisfied with an award may elect trial de novo. The Legislature, however, seeking to encourage finality of judicial arbitration awards, enacted disincentives to trial de novo. For example, if a party requesting trial de novo does not obtain a more favorable judgment, he or she is liable for significant costs and fees.

Discouraging trial de novo is essential to the proper functioning of the judicial arbitration system. Along with its goal of resolving small claims efficiently and affordably, judicial arbitration is intended to ease court caseloads. The success of judicial arbitration in achieving these goals is dependent on a small incidence of trial de novo election.

If trial de novo is not requested within the statutory period, a judicial arbitration award becomes final and is not subject to appeal. There is no question the Legislature intended the award, once final, to be a binding resolution of the particular cause of action. [A] final award shall have "the same force and effect as a judgment in any civil action or proceeding," except that it shall not be subject to appeal and generally may not be attacked or set aside. Accordingly, a final judicial arbitration award, if clear and unambiguous, is res judicata in any subsequent proceeding on the same cause of action.

In the instant case, Flynn's indemnity action would have been barred if it had stated the same cause of action as Gorton's arbitrated negligence claim. The two proceedings, however, did not involve the same cause of action. Gorton's negligence claim involved her primary right to be free of personal injury, whereas this action concerns Flynn's right to equitable indemnity against third party damages. Thus, Flynn's action was not barred under the cause preclusion aspect of res judicata.

Collateral estoppel is equally inapplicable here, but for different reasons. It would be unfair and unwise to give collateral estoppel effect to judicially arbitrated resolutions of issues. To begin with, as this case well illustrates, there are practical difficulties. No record is made of arbitration proceedings and generally no findings of fact or conclusions of law are required. Thus, it is difficult to determine from the award alone what issues were actually litigated and how they were resolved.

Even if this difficulty could be surmounted, it is unfair to bind the parties to judicially arbitrated resolutions of issues. The doctrine of collateral estoppel is based on the premise that a thorough fact-finding process was completed in the first proceeding. However, in judicial arbitration, the low monetary amount in controversy and the option of trial de novo can leave parties without a serious incentive to litigate. Because the stakes involved are low, the parties may be willing to accept a compromise position without much of a fight.

Moreover, it is unlikely parties would expect a judicial arbitration award to have collateral estoppel effect in other proceedings where the stakes may be higher than they were in the arbitration proceeding. If they did, the result might be intensified litigation, delays and costs, as well as an increased rate of trial de novo election. Such a development would be directly contrary to the purposes underlying judicial arbitration legislation.

In summary, we hold that judicial arbitration awards should be accorded claim preclusion, but not issue preclusion, effect.

3. *Haworth, Inc. v. Steelcase, Inc.*, 12 F.3d 1090 (Fed. Cir. 1994)

MICHEL, Circuit Judge.

Appellant, Herman Miller, Inc. (HMI), appeals the decision of the district court denying HMI's motion to intervene. Because we determine that the court did not abuse its discretion in so ruling, we affirm.

In 1985, Haworth, Inc. (Haworth) filed suit against Steelcase, Inc. (Steelcase) in the U.S. District Court for the Western District of Michigan, alleging that electrified wall panel systems made and sold by Steelcase infringed Haworth's patents. In April 1989, Steelcase sued Haworth in the same court for infringement of certain Steelcase patents. Eventually, the district court ruled in the first lawsuit that Haworth's patents were valid, enforceable and infringed. Before completion of the liability phase of the second suit, the two cases were consolidated, and the parties agreed . . . to submit the remaining issues, including damages, to a Special Master for resolution by settlement or mini-trial (hereinafter "the ADR proceeding"). Both parties agreed to relinquish any right to appeal any decision by the Special Master or any judgment entered thereon by the district court. . . . They also agreed that all . . . information produced in or in connection with the ADR proceeding would be kept confidential, and that neither party could disclose any information concerning the proceeding without the express written permission of the other.

In January 1992, Haworth sued HMI for infringement of the same patents asserted against Steelcase. In that case, pursuant to Fed.R.Civ.P. 45, HMI subpoenaed Steelcase, a third party, for the production of all documents relating to the Haworth-Steelcase litigation, including the ADR proceeding. After Steelcase objected to the subpoena, HMI filed a motion to intervene in the Haworth-Steelcase litigation simply for the purpose of obtaining those same documents. HMI argued that it should be permitted to intervene because of, among other things: (1) HMI's need for access to sworn testimony to prevent Haworth or its witnesses from taking inconsistent positions in the two suits; (2) the efficiency of not duplicating in the Haworth-HMI suit discovery already taken in the Haworth-Steelcase litigation; and (3) the judicial economy served by the issue-preclusive effect that may be accorded to the Special Master's findings. . . .

Magistrate Judge Rowland denied HMI's motion to intervene and issued a thorough, well-reasoned, twenty-two page opinion explaining the reasons for his decision. HMI appealed the Magistrate's decision to the District Court for the Western District of Michigan, and the court upheld the denial. HMI now appeals.

This appeal involves a procedural matter not unique to patent law, namely the denial of a motion to intervene [so] . . . Sixth Circuit law controls, and the standard of appellate review for a motion for permissive intervention is an abuse of discretion. . . . In the present case, HMI has failed to establish any such abuse of discretion. . . . Accordingly, we affirm the district court's denial of HMI's motion to intervene.

On appeal, HMI argues that the district court abused its discretion because it: (1) gave undue weight to the agreement to keep the ADR proceeding secret, while ignoring the countervailing public policy interest of maintaining open access to court records; (2) overlooked HMI's compelling need for the information; and (3) incorrectly concluded that issue preclusion would not likely apply to the Special Master's findings.

HMI contends that the district court abused its discretion by improperly focusing on the private concerns of Haworth and Steelcase, while de-emphasizing the public policy favoring open judicial proceedings. [The court distinguished *Meyer Goldberg, Inc. v. Fisher Foods, Inc.*, 823 F.2d 159 (6th Cir. 1987), because] . . . (1) the proceeding was "public" unlike the private ADR proceeding here; (2) the underlying case had terminated, whereas the ADR proceeding in the present case is still ongoing; (3) only a modification of a protective order after trial was sought, rather than intervention which, at this stage of the proceedings, would essentially permit, though not require participation in, or at least presence at, the evidentiary proceedings and perhaps even settlement negotiations; and (4) the appellate court did not direct intervention, but only remanded for reconsideration, because the record did not reflect the district court's consideration of the tradition of open records, whereas in the present case HMI asks the court to direct the district court to grant HMI's motion to intervene.

Even if the cases were indistinguishable, however, the district court judge did not disregard the legal rule outlined in *Meyer Goldberg*. By agreeing with Magistrate Judge Rowland that "the parties to the ADR process had a legitimate secrecy interest," that "this interest would be harmed if HMI were allowed to intervene," and that "HMI's need for information does not outweigh existing privacy concerns," the district judge considered the factors enumerated in and which formed the principal bases for the remand in *Meyer Goldberg*—namely the parties' legitimate secrecy interests weighed against the movant's need for the information and the public's interest in having access to the records. . . . [T]he court . . . concluded that public access interests should not, in this case, override the ADR agreement, which also fosters strong public policies in favor of judicial economy and private resolution of disputes. . . .

Magistrate Judge Rowland further added that [a]llowing intervention would jeopardize the settlement of not one but two lawsuits which were filed in the Western District of Michigan and later consolidated, as well as the resolution of other disputes between these parties. Furthermore, it is unlikely future elaborate alternative dispute resolution methods, such as the one fashioned in this case, would be utilized if confidentiality could not be maintained.

In short, the allowance of HMI's intervention, over the opposition of both parties to the ADR proceeding, poses a threat to the continuation and successful completion of the ADR proceeding. At minimum, intervention might chill Haworth's willingness to cooperate in the ADR proceeding. . . . Rule 24(b) of the Federal Rules of Civil Procedure, which governs permissive intervention, specifically states that "[i]n exercising its discretion the court shall consider whether the intervention will unduly delay or prejudice the adjudication of the rights of the original parties."

Next, HMI contends that the district court abused its discretion by overlooking HMI's compelling need for the information contained in the ADR documents. HMI asserts that it needs deposition transcripts and other sworn testimony given in the ADR proceeding to prevent Haworth and its witnesses from taking inconsistent positions in the HMI litigation. HMI also argues that the Special Master can be expected to determine Haworth's production costs, its profits and its ability to make additional sales otherwise made by the accused infringers [as well as the other factors relevant to determining damages]. . . .

Magistrate Judge Rowland found, however, and the district court agreed, that HMI could not "identify any instance where [Haworth] was taking inconsistent positions in its cases. . . ." Moreover, HMI already had access to all information relating to the *Haworth v. Steelcase* public liability trial and appeal, as well as discovery of all Haworth documents and information which antedated or existed apart from the ADR proceeding itself. . . . Taking all factors into consideration, HMI has not shown that the district court judge abused his discretion in concluding that the privacy concerns outweigh the need for the requested documents. Therefore, we affirm insofar as HMI relies on its alleged need for the information.

HMI also argues [for intervention] because of the potential issue-preclusive effect of some of the Special Master's expected findings. . . . Because the judgment from the Haworth-Steelcase litigation is potentially binding upon Haworth, HMI contends that it has a per se right to intervene.

We disagree. First, . . . we know of no authority, aside from Rule 24(a) upon which HMI did not rely, to support a per se right. Moreover, that HMI may argue that Haworth is bound by findings of the Special Master and may not relitigate such issues does not mean HMI therefore must be allowed to intervene. After all, issue-preclusive effect could still be derived from findings of the Special Master since presumably HMI might be able to obtain access to them after the ADR proceeding concludes even though under the ADR agreement the Special Master's opinion is to be under seal. Therefore, HMI is not being denied potential benefits, but merely required to await the event.

Second, the district court properly predicted that little issue-preclusive effect or collateral estoppel should be or likely will be accorded to the findings of the Special Master as to Haworth because the ADR proceeding is different from "just another patent case in the federal courts" . . . [so] the specter of collateral estoppel does not loom as large in this situation as it might in others. [A]s a condition of participating in ADR, each party has surrendered [its] right to appeal the decisions of the special master. More importantly, the ethic of ADR is often different than that of litigation. There is an emphasis on compromise, of each side softening their positions in order to meet in the middle. Each concession must be understood in the context of those of the other party. The series of positions each party takes and the decisions of the special master must be looked at as an integrated whole. Therefore, the rationale which drives issue-by-issue collateral estoppel is not wholly applicable in this situation. Generally speaking, we agree.

Third, even if the Special Master's ruling does create some risk of issue preclusive effect against Haworth, this risk must be weighed against other factors in determining whether to grant HMI's motion to intervene. The district court did so and did so reasonably. In this case, judicial economy is best served by promoting ADR and shielding it from unwarranted intrusions. [T]he successful completion of the ADR proceeding between Haworth and Steelcase will resolve the infringement disputes involving six patents without using any additional judicial time or resources. . . . Even if it were shown that intervention would save resources, because of the interests of the ADR parties, HMI's motion could still be properly denied. Therefore, affirmance of the district court's denial of HMI's motion to intervene is appropriate in view of these considerations as well.

Chapter 18

ADR and Adjudication: Policy Implications

CASE STUDY

This case is a wrongful death and survival action grounded in strict products liability and negligence. The plaintiffs are the two minor children, husband, and parents of the late Jerrian Smith. Mrs. Smith died of massive liver failure on April 8, 1988. She was twenty-eight years of age. The plaintiffs contend the liver failure, called fulminant hepatic necrosis, was brought on by Mrs. Smith's occupational exposure to an animal anesthetic called Halothane. Until March 10, 1988, Mrs. Smith was a veterinary technician at the Treetop Animal Hospital in Burrville, Arkansas. Dr. Bill Barker, the sole veterinary practitioner at Treetop, employed Halothane to anesthetize the animals who underwent surgery at the clinic. Mrs. Smith regularly assisted in the small operating room during these procedures.

On March 10, 1988, Jerrian Smith noted that she had become jaundiced and immediately visited her personal physician, Dr. Ben Hart. After further discussions with Mrs. Smith, Dr. Hart diagnosed the patient as having early symptoms of hepatitis brought on by toxic exposure. Dr. Hart referred her to the emergency room at the medical center in Burrville, where she was re-examined. On March 23, Mrs. Smith was admitted to the hospital as her condition was rapidly deteriorating. By March 30, Mrs. Smith had lapsed into a coma from which she never recovered. Mrs. Smith was transferred to Episcopal Hospital in Megatropolis, Arkansas where she died a few days later, never regaining consciousness.

The anesthesia machine used at the Clinic employed a Halothane vaporizer and, as installed, the machine vented waste anesthetic gases into the operating room. The clinic was centrally air conditioned but no gas exhaust system was used to prevent the waste anesthetic gases from circulating in the air of the room where Mrs. Smith worked.

The defendants in this case are the manufacturer of the anesthesia machine, OHMEDA, and Mrs. Smith's employer, Treetop Animal Hospital. The plaintiffs contend that OHMEDA failed to properly warn the users of its machine. Treetop has been accused of negligently using the machine after it had become common knowledge in the industry that halothane exposure could be fatal to humans.

A. Introduction

The previous three chapters examined numerous specific ADR procedures related to the settlement of actual or potential law suits prior to trial. In this chapter we seek to present a more general perspective on the intersection of ADR and the judicial system. While there is some reference to specific ADR procedures, the objective here is to consider the larger issues associated with the use of ADR in the courts, particularly the federal courts. Our goal is to raise the major issues associated with court-connected ADR, and to provide you with a set of questions to assist you in thinking seriously about these issues.

We begin with the view from the judiciary. Judge Irving R. Kauffman reminds us yet again about the litigation explosion in the federal courts, and argues that ADR is an important part of the solution. A paper from the federal judicial center sets out the issues for the courts. While the situation in individual states will vary, the analytic approach presented by Stienstra and Willging is generally applicable in the state context.

Professor Longan addresses the use of judges or judicial adjuncts to mediate federal civil cases. A similar analysis could be applied to evaluate the judicial use of other ADR procedures. Longan focuses on mediation by federal magistrates, and concludes that this is a salutary development.

Professors Resnik and Menkel-Meadow both examine the use of ADR by the courts, and each comes to a pessimistic conclusion. Menkel-Meadow, a leader in the ADR movement, laments the cooptation of ADR into the legal system. Resnik, a critic of the extensive use of ADR by the courts, laments that ADR has been only too successful in replacing judicial contests. In each instance, however, the articles are worthy of our attention because of the high quality of the analysis, and the interesting issues presented.

B. Courts in Crisis: Is ADR a Solution?

1. Irving R. Kaufman, *Reform for A System in Crisis: Alternative Dispute Resolution in the Federal Courts*, 59 Fordham L. Rev. 1 (1990)*

In its third century, the federal court system has entered a period of crisis. Faced with ever-burgeoning caseloads and essentially static resources, the nation's courts fall further and further behind the promise of the Federal Rules of Civil Procedure: "the just, speedy, and inexpensive determination of every action." . . . The problem is not merely one of harried judges. Litigants, people with grievances, are being denied meaningful access to the courts. Delay prevents the courts from doing their job—resolving people's disputes at reasonable costs so that they may return to their normal lives.

After more than forty years on the federal bench, I am convinced that a decisive moment is at hand for the federal courts. The problem has grown beyond the reach of tinkering with the periphery of the judicial system. Flexibility, experimentation and a willingness to innovate are essential if the administration of justice is to keep up with the society we serve. What follows is a brief examination of proposed changes in judicial administration, stressing those that hold the greatest promise to reduce the major costs of justice—expense and delay. . . .

---

*Reprinted with permission.

I. SCOPE OF THE PROBLEM AND SOME CAUSES

. . . As daunting as the cost of litigation may be, the monster of delay might be more imposing to litigants. In even our smaller urban jurisdictions, a delay of over two and a half years from filing of suit to trial has become routine. The median time from issue to civil trial in federal district court is a year and a half, though the more difficult cases usually take far longer. Since 1986, the number of civil cases that have been on federal dockets for more than three years has grown by a third, to 22,391.

This growth in backlog and delay is in part attributable to the absolute growth in federal caseloads—an increase of which I am painfully aware. In 1949, the year in which I was appointed to the Southern District of New York, 53,421 cases were brought in the district courts. By 1989, that number had grown to 233,293, an increase of over 430 percent. In 1961, the year President Kennedy elevated me to the Second Circuit, 4,204 cases were filed in the United States Courts of Appeals. This past year, 39,734 appeals were taken.

Of course, forty years has made for a faster, more complex and harder world in many respects, and the public might agree with David Copperfield that the courts might be improved if we judges "got up early in the morning, and took off our coats to the work." I am second to none in my admiration of hard work, but that particular ointment has already been liberally applied. In 1989, on average, federal district court judges were responsible for 485 filed cases, 407 of which were civil filings. In human terms, this is a crushing burden that translates into a need to dispose of more than a case a day or face an ever-growing backlog. When I began as a district judge, the workload was a third of its present prodigality. . . .

II. AVERTING THE FLOOD WITH ADR

Short of learning to live together with greater comity, we must find a way to settle disputes more efficiently. Reallocating judicial business by the varied methods of "alternative dispute resolution," or ADR, holds out great promise of accomplishing this goal. Because ADR has only recently developed all the trappings of a "movement," including an acronym, specialized journals and think tanks, we sometimes forget that there has been a long history of alternatives to formal adjudication. Most familiar are extrajudicial mechanisms such as voluntary, binding arbitration. Indeed, such arbitration has been practiced in North America since colonial times. . . .

The focus [here], however, is on . . . judicial ADR mechanisms, those used in connection with court proceedings. The nascent trend toward including ADR mechanisms within the judicial system might well develop into a major wave of judicial reform, one capable of restoring meaningful access to the courts. This assimilation has great potential, but it is not a panacea for all that ails the administration of justice. As we consider institutionalizing ADR within the federal courts, we must take care to embrace only those mechanisms that promise to reduce litigation's cost while increasing its pace. Above all, we must ensure that the programs implemented meet our standards of justice. The challenge for the federal courts is to reap the benefits of ADR while minimizing the risks. . . . [A discussion of particular court-annexed ADR programs is omitted.]

CONCLUSION

Seven hundred seventy-five years ago, King John, in the Magna Carta, promised "[T]o no one will we deny or delay right or justice." That promise has proven devilishly difficult to keep.

It has yet to be completely fulfilled. . . .

[Court-connected ADR programs] . . . bring the encouraging news that there are judicial innovators willing to take courageous steps. As with any experiment, questions arise just as some problems are solved. But given the dire situation in which our courts find themselves and the encouraging results that these procedural innovations achieved, I feel confident in urging an expansion in court-annexed ADR.

I caution that ADR is not a magic potion. It is not a panacea for all the problems facing the federal courts. The problems of caseloads, delays and costs are simply too great. But all the evidence to date indicates that ADR can make a valuable contribution to easing access to the courts. To take advantage of that potential, Congress should act:

(1) to authorize mandatory arbitration in all federal district courts; and

(2) to make explicit the authority of all federal courts to refer cases to mandatory nonbinding ADR, including early neutral evaluation, court-annexed arbitration, and summary jury trials.

This enabling legislation should be general enough to allow continued local diversity. These reforms will take root only if district courts can adapt them to particular local needs. In addition, participation by the local bar in the drafting of court rules will give them greater acceptability. Exploring alternative procedures will furnish us with experience and knowledge. Using the district courts as laboratories will help us learn what works best. . . .

For the federal courts to function efficiently, an essential reform that must be pursued is perfecting our ability to remove from the calendar, early in the litigation process, those cases that are destined to settle after clogging a court's docket for years. Many cases are frivolous, brought out of a notion that litigation should be a first resort and not a last recourse. Indeed, some are brought to extort settlement. It is important to weed out these cases, the sooner the better, through motion or settlement. They pollute the whole process of meting out justice and thus deny access to other litigants. Even in meritorious cases, however, we must consider whether parties, if given the assistance of the courts, might not arrive at a mutually agreeable solution relatively quickly and inexpensively. . . .

2. Comments and Questions

a. The explosion in federal civil litigation is hardly news, but its reiteration by one of the most respected and longest serving federal judge seems worthy of note. In addition, the dramatic growth of federal criminal cases, which take precedence under the Speedy Trial Act, has further increased the difficulty of obtaining a civil trial in federal court. These problems tend to be particularly severe in major urban areas.

b. Courts are intrinsically conservative institutions—the very nature of precedent is backward-looking. Court of appeals judges are not radicals, and certainly Judge Kaufman would not be so characterized. He would not speak out on behalf of experiments absent very severe problems. Note that his high hopes for ADR as part of the solution is tempered by a warning against regarding ADR as a panacea.

c. The article that follows presents the major issues related to use of ADR in the federal courts. You should think about them—both now and before the final examination in this course.

3. Donna Stienstra & Thomas E. Willging, Alternatives to Litigation: Do They Have a Place in the Federal Courts (Federal Judicial Center 1995)

Introduction

In this paper we examine the place of court-based, presumptively mandatory, nonbinding alternative dispute resolution (ADR) in the federal district courts. By its nature, the inquiry involves . . . a debate about the role of the courts in society. . . . Although the current rapid implementation of ADR in the federal courts may seem to make these issues moot, that very implementation is prompting policy makers—whether at the level of the individual court, the Judicial Conference, or Congress—to take note of the phenomenon, to ask basic questions about its value and effects, and to distinguish between the different kinds of ADR with their different procedures and objectives.

We address the questions about the role of the courts and ADR's value and effects through a series of arguments in support of and in opposition to court-based ADR programs. The purpose of the paper is not to come to a conclusion on the value of court-based ADR, but to inform the reader and policy maker through a fair summary of the points that can be made on each side of the issue.

The arguments for and against providing alternative dispute resolution methods in the federal courts are the heart of the paper. Before turning to those arguments, we first define the object of our discussion, court-based alternative dispute resolution, and describe the context in which the ADR debate is taking place today.

Definitions and Context

The first formal recognition of ADR's role was stated in the 1983 amendments to Federal Rule of Civil Procedure 16(b)(7), which provided for the use of "extra-judicial procedures to resolve the dispute." Adoption of this language followed by several years the federal courts' initial experimentation with court-based ADR, in the form of mediation and nonbinding mandatory arbitration programs. Since then a number of other forms of ADR have been established as court-based programs. It is this segment of ADR, the court-based programs, that we argue for and against in this paper. . . .

In 1990, the Report of the Federal Courts Study Committee urged Congress to make clear the authority of district courts to establish ADR programs, including presumptively mandatory procedures. Two years later, a survey of all federal district judges showed that many supported, at least in principle, the use of ADR procedures in the federal courts: 66% disagreed with the proposition that courts should resolve litigation through traditional procedures only; 86% disagreed with the proposition that ADR should never be used in the federal courts; and 56% said that ADR should be used in the federal courts because in some cases it produces a fairer outcome than traditional litigation. . . .

Passage of the Civil Justice Reform Act of 1990 (CJRA) undoubtedly quickened the pace of federal district court ADR development. The CJRA, as part of its effort to reduce civil litigation cost and delay, requires thirteen district courts to implement alternative dispute resolution procedures, ten "pilot" districts and three "demonstration" districts, and instructs all other district courts to "consider" adopting ADR procedures. At least two-thirds of the district courts now authorize use of one or more forms of ADR, and perhaps as many as a third of the courts have in place or intend to establish court-based programs.

The context in which the federal courts are now debating ADR's merits has also been changed by growing receptivity to ADR outside the federal courts. Consider, for example, the following developments:

- Programs are proliferating in state courts, and a number of states are moving beyond general authorization to comprehensive state-wide programs that provide litigants with a range of ADR options.
- The 1990 Administrative Dispute Resolution Act requires each federal agency to consider ADR for resolving disputes, and a 1991 executive order directs agencies to consider ADR as one of a number of methods for improving civil justice. A number of agencies, many with the assistance of the Administrative Conference of the United States, have developed ADR programs for internal as well as external disputes.
- In 1984, the Legal Program of the Center for Public Resources (now known as the CPR Institute for Dispute Resolution), a nonprofit organization established to publicize ADR, initiated a program to seek corporate pledges to use ADR. By 1994, almost 700 of the nation's largest companies and more than 2,000 of their subsidiaries had signed the pledge. A similar program begun in 1991 to seek law firm pledges to counsel clients about ADR had garnered 1,500 signatories by the end of 1993.
- In 1993, the American Bar Association Standing Committee on Dispute Resolution became a full-fledged ABA section. . . .

These developments have been driven by a variety of goals and circumstances, among them a search for lower costs and quicker dispositions in civil cases, the changing economics of legal practice, the demands imposed on judge time—particularly trial time—by a rising criminal caseload, and a conviction that ADR can, in some cases, provide a better process and a better outcome.

This substantial incorporation of ADR into the dispute resolution process, both inside and outside the courts, presents the federal court system with many questions, such as:

- Should ADR have a role at all in the federal courts?
- What should that role be?
- How can ADR fulfill that role most effectively?
- What weight should be given to the preferences of the public and the bar?
- How will adoption of ADR change the role of the courts?
- How will it change the role of the judge?

Embedded in these questions is a far more basic one: What is a court and what values does it serve? This paper will not answer these questions, but it will, we hope, provide arguments and information that will inform the debate. The arguments and responses in this paper debate the merits of the following proposition:

> To fulfill their mission while using both litigant and court resources wisely, each federal district court should at an early point in each civil case help litigants identify the procedure most appropriate for managing and resolving the case. The procedures available to litigants should include, in addition to traditional litigation procedures, an array of court-based, publicly funded, nonbinding processes, such as mediation, arbitration, and early neutral evaluation. There should be a presumption that parties in appropriate cases will use one of these processes, but the right to trial must be preserved in every case.

More specifically, we consider the following questions:

1. Given that a core function of the courts as public institutions is to serve individual litigants and thus maintain public confidence in society's capacity for peaceful dispute resolution, does ADR:
   - enhance that function by meeting litigant needs through a wider variety of dispute resolution methods, or frustrate it by diverting resources from the declaration and application of the law to programs designed solely to aid parties in settling their disputes?
   - enhance that function by providing litigants with greater opportunities to tell their story to a neutral, or compromise the courts' role and resources by substituting court-based programs for functions properly carried out by litigants' own counsel?
2. In respect to the courts' responsibility to use their own and litigants' resources wisely:
   - should courts use ADR to provide additional forums for pretrial preparation and settlement explorations, or should such activities be limited to judges under Federal Rule of Civil Procedure 16?
   - does ADR have the potential to save litigants, or courts themselves, time, money, or both, or are such savings illusory and achievable only at the expense of the trial by jury?
3. Should ADR be available through publicly funded, court-based programs as a means of providing all litigants with access to these procedures and of guaranteeing the procedural protections litigants rightfully expect from courts, or would ADR develop better through private-sector experimentation with flexible rules and practices?
4. Should federal courts have the authority to mandate that litigants in appropriate cases participate in ADR, or do mandatory programs distort the benefits of ADR?

In the course of debating the proper role of ADR in the federal courts, we identified several points of agreement:

- Although there is considerable evidence about user perceptions of ADR, research findings are currently insufficient on the cost and time consequences of ADR and cannot fully inform that part of the debate that revolves around cost and time. Research should not in any case displace other sources of guidance, such as logical analyses, individual and social values, and intuitions, but where the debate about the proper role of ADR can be informed by empirical analyses, that research should be undertaken promptly.
- ADR provides substantial benefits to litigants by satisfying their need to tell their story to a neutral. Courts should be responsive to the importance litigants place on a meaningful and fair forum, whether they provide that forum through ADR or in some other way.
- Efficiency should not be the overriding principle when a court considers whether to implement an ADR program.
- Fair procedures and case outcomes as well as litigant and public satisfaction with the courts require that any court-based ADR programs provide high-quality service. Essential to that quality is the effective training and performance of the attorneys who serve as mediators, arbitrators, and early neutral evaluators. Ensuring such quality requires resources.
- The use of multiple ADR procedures in a single case can be duplicative and unnecessarily costly and should not generally be imposed on parties.

- There appears to be value in an early screening process to determine case needs and party preferences and to educate attorneys and litigants about their case processing and dispute resolution options.
- The outcomes of court-based ADR procedures, particularly mandatory procedures, must be nonbinding and must preserve access to trial without penalty, unless the parties voluntarily agree to a binding outcome.

One additional point of agreement—that district judges should not serve as neutrals in court-based ADR programs—deserves slightly more discussion because many will disagree with our position. A district judge's involvement as the ADR neutral poses a serious risk—or at least an appearance of risk—to that judge's independence and neutrality by exposing the judge to the parties' private pretrial assessments of their case and to their negotiating postures. This is particularly true in cases that, if tried, will be tried by the judge (this risk arises also when judges participate in settlement conferences in cases they, rather than a jury, will decide). Can a judge who places a value on a case as a neutral evaluator, or a judge who learns the details of each party's situation and concerns as a mediator, serve as the impartial decision maker at trial—or perhaps even when deciding other matters in the case? Although judges may insist that they can remain neutral, parties may justifiably be worried that they cannot. As a consequence, litigants may be reluctant to participate fully in the ADR process. These concerns can be set aside, of course, if a judge serves as the mediator or evaluator in another judge's cases, but is such an approach a wise use of the justice system's scarcest resource? We believe the answer is no. . . .

C. Court Bureaucracy, Civil Cases, and ADR

1. Patrick E. Longan, *Bureaucratic Justice Meets ADR: The Emerging Role For Magistrates as Mediators*, 73 Neb. L. Rev. 712 (1994)*

I. INTRODUCTION

Many federal judges do not have time for their civil dockets. The amount of time the average district judge devotes to civil trials has declined steadily in the last ten years. Simultaneously, the criminal dockets have grown too large and become too complex for the district judges to spend sufficient time tending to civil cases which by law have lower priority. The Speedy Trial Act imposes deadlines on the indictment and trial of federal criminal defendants, but there is no comparable statute for civil cases. 18 U.S.C. § 3161. According to the Administrative Office of the United States Courts, the number of new criminal cases increased from 27,968 in 1980 to 47,467 in 1992. The "weighted" criminal filings per judgeship, which is a measure of the number and complexity of the criminal cases, increased from 47 to 54 in the same time period.

Congress continues to create more federal crimes despite urgent entreaties not to do so. The President and Senate have moved slowly to fill district court vacancies, and many believe that adding more judges is an unacceptable solution.

The ever-increasing pressures on the district judges have resulted in two trends in the handling of civil cases. The first is the increasing use of judicial "adjuncts" such as magistrates,

*Reprinted with permission.

bankruptcy judges, law clerks, staff attorneys, interns, externs, and the other ingredients of "bureaucratic justice." The second development, more aptly called a movement, has been to direct civil cases away from adjudication to alternative forms of dispute resolution such as arbitration, mediation, early neutral evaluation, and summary jury trials. Each of these developments attempts to cope with the logjam in the district judge's courtroom. Each has its supporters and its critics.

The two developments converge when judicial adjuncts, particularly magistrates, mediate civil cases. Using magistrates to assist in settlement is not a new idea. Magistrates preside over tens of thousands of pretrial conferences each year, and one of the topics appropriate for such conferences is settlement. Some magistrates have become settlement "specialists" with little other responsibility. Other magistrates report having presided over hundreds of settlement conferences. . . .

In 1990, Congress passed the Civil Justice Reform Act and charged each district court with the responsibility for devising plans to reduce cost and delay in the civil dockets. Thirty-four districts implemented plans by the end of 1991. Four of these incorporate magistrate mediation into their plans while another eight provide for settlement conferences to be presided over by magistrates. Among the recommendations in other districts are at least three that involve magistrate settlement conferences. Also, a committee of the Judicial Conference approved a long-range plan in 1993 that forecast expanded use of magistrates for alternative dispute resolution. . . .

The magistrate system was designed to be flexible so that it can adapt to changing needs and possibilities. The nature of federal civil litigation has changed and continues to change in ways that permit and, indeed, require magistrates to assume a greater role in settling cases. This Article explains why magistrates can and should mediate more civil cases.

II. OBSTACLES TO UNASSISTED SETTLEMENT

Alternative dispute resolution techniques exist because parties and lawyers need help in settling cases. The first problem with which they need help is the problem of divergent expectations about the outcome of trial. The second type of problem concerns the nature of the forum for settlement. This section discusses each of these needs as a prelude to comparing how well different forms of mediation meet them. . . .

The economic model of settlement assumes that each party will come to a bottom-line figure by predicting the outcome and extra expense of continued litigation and comparing that expected value with settlement. The plaintiff's expected outcome of trial, E, is the probability of victory multiplied by the plaintiff's estimate of the amount of the judgment if there is one. The plaintiff's expected net return from continued litigation is this figure minus the cost, C, that the plaintiff will incur to obtain it. The plaintiff will settle if the settlement offer is at least equal to the expected return from trial, E - C. Any lower offer would be unacceptable because the plaintiff expects to do better at trial.

Similarly, the defendant compares settlement to the expected outcome of the trial. The expected loss of the defendant, E, is the probability assigned by the defendant to a plaintiff victory multiplied by the defendant's estimate of the judgment if there is one. The defendant must also consider the cost of continuing to litigate, C, and compare any settlement demand with the expected total loss if the defendant does not settle, E + C. Only if the settlement demand is less than or equal to this figure will the defendant settle.

The condition for settlement is that the plaintiff's minimum demand, E - C, must be less than or equal to the defendant's maximum settlement offer, E + C. An equivalent formulation is that settlement will occur if E - E < C + C. The settlement decision thus depends upon the parties' expectations and the costs of litigation.

Cases will be difficult to settle if the parties have divergent expectations about the outcome of trial. If the plaintiff assigns a significantly greater probability to victory or a significantly higher damage award if there is a judgment than the defendant does, then the plaintiff's expectation, E, will be much different than the defendant's expectations, E. The higher E - E is, the less likely settlement is to occur. The algebraic result confirms common sense. The plaintiff with high hopes is hard to pacify. The defendant with no fear is less likely to pay a large settlement. Divergent expectations make settlement unlikely.

On the other hand, settlement should occur if the parties have convergent expectations. The closer their expectations are, the more likely the parties are to reach agreement and to split the savings of not litigating to a foregone conclusion. If E - E approaches zero, the condition for settlement is more likely to be satisfied. It is easy to see why. If the parties know what the outcome of trial will be, they can settle and save the cost of going forward with the litigation. Convergent expectations are the primary reason that ninety percent of all disputes never reach litigation. . . .

The economic model of settlement tells us when settlement is rational, but it is not always enough for a settlement to be rational. Settlement involves people, litigants and lawyers, and the indisputable theorems of algebra and probability do not satisfy the human needs that can impede settlement. Process, as well as substance, matters. What those human needs are, and how mediation can assist in satisfying them, is the subject of this section. . . .

Litigants usually feel wronged or wrongly accused. Those feelings must be dealt with before the parties will be ready psychologically to accept even the most rational settlement. What the litigant needs is a catharsis, the chance to express his or her position about the events that led to the dispute. Litigants "must be allowed to tell their stories to a sympathetic listener who is not attempting to ignore or minimize their tragic circumstances. . . . They have at least been provided with the opportunity to explain." When the settlement process makes such a catharsis possible, settlement often follows quickly.

Another frequent problem is that clients either do not receive or do not believe reliable information from their counsel about the likely outcome of the case. Lawyers do raise false hopes about cases, especially early in litigation, and they may be reluctant to share with their clients their revised, more realistic assessment, later in the case. Clients, of course, have the final word with respect to settling cases. If the lawyers filter the information about the case and do not assist the clients with realistic predictions, settlement opportunities will be missed.

Sometimes the client simply does not believe the lawyer and needs to have his optimism doused by someone else. Try as the lawyer might, the lawyer cannot convince the party that things are as bleak as they really are, either because the lawyer's earlier advice was different or because the client is simply bull-headed. The settlement process that relies on convergent expectations cannot settle such a case until the client, who retains the power to settle or not to settle, is convinced of the calculation.

Often the lawyers are the ones who need a mediator. Because litigation practice has become uncivil and unprofessional, even bitter, many lawyers on opposite sides of a case cannot bring themselves to speak to one another, let alone work cooperatively toward a settlement. Reflections of this problem appear in the numerous professionalism codes that courts and bar associations have promulgated in an attempt to remedy this problem. Many of the codes deal with the problem of lawyers who cannot, or refuse to, discuss amicable resolution of their dispute. One example is the civility code of the Seventh Circuit which imposes a duty on counsel to "endeavor to confer early with other counsel to assess settlement possibilities" and recognizes that "[c]onduct that may be characterized as uncivil, abrasive, abusive, hostile, or obstructive impedes the fundamental goal of resolving disputes rationally, peacefully, and efficiently." The Tenets of Professional Courtesy of the Kansas City Metropolitan Bar Association states that: "A Lawyer Should Maintain a Cordial and Respectful Relationship With Opposing Counsel." The comment to this tenet recognizes that "effective and open communication between lawyers aids the resolution of the conflict." Perhaps the saddest commentary is that lawyers need official reminders of such obvious facts. . . .

At the root of the problem is the combination of three facts about American civil litigation. First, the process is adversarial, meaning that the development of the case is in the hands of the lawyers. Second, virtually all of pretrial practice occurs outside the direct supervision of any judicial authority. Any lawyer who is inclined to be combative has some rein. Third, the litigation bar has grown so dramatically, particularly in urban areas, that the lawyers have less fear that they will face the same adversary in a series of cases over their careers. One is more apt to misbehave when one is unlikely to encounter the victim again. Each of these facts contribute to the "Rambo" approach to litigation. Rambo does not settle. Rambo kicks adversaries and takes names. That attitude impedes even a rational resolution, and settlement simply cannot occur if the lawyers will not talk to each other.

The informational and procedural needs of the parties and lawyers impede unassisted settlement. Mediation can help, but the question is what type of mediation can help the most. The next section discusses three candidates.

III. THREE TYPES OF MEDIATION COMPARED

There are three types of mediation. The first is referral mediation. Here, the district court refers the case to a non-judicial mediator either in private practice or, more rarely, as part of a full-time court-annexed mediation service. The second type is mediation by the trial judge. The third is mediation by the magistrate. How well each can assist the parties and lawyers in overcoming the obstacles to unassisted settlement is the measure of its value.

A. Referral Mediation

Non-judicial mediators can contribute to convergent expectations if their evaluations are credible. The mediator assesses the case in light of his or her experience and frankly shares that assessment. For this reason, non-judicial mediation programs routinely employ only very experienced lawyers as mediators.

The risk with referral mediation is not that the mediator will fail to bring the parties to agree upon the likely outcome of the case but rather that the mediator may be too good at doing so. A mediator determined to settle a case may manipulate the settlement process to see that cases settle regardless of the fairness of the result. A settlement is unfair to the extent that it is based upon factors other than the underlying rights and obligations of the parties. Referral mediators are in a position to settle cases without regard to those underlying rights, and they have incentive to do so. Both of these facts should cause attorneys to hesitate to overcome the barriers to settlement with such a system.

Evidence of lawyers' susceptibility to manipulation comes from the Civil Appeals Management Plan (CAMP) of the United States Court of Appeals for the Second Circuit. Since 1974, the Second Circuit has employed staff counsel whose job it is to settle cases or at least narrow the issues for the court. Several lawyers surveyed regarding CAMP expressed the concern that "inexperienced advocates . . . might take as gospel staff counsel's analysis of the chances for success in the Second Circuit." . . . The inexperienced lawyer, the one most in need of guidance from the mediator, is the most vulnerable.

The risk of manipulation is especially great because most mediators use a "caucus" method in which they meet with each side outside the presence of the others. A mediator who is determined to settle the case may simply evaluate the case differently for each party, hoping to make at least one side significantly less optimistic. The case will settle if that process is successful, albeit without regard to whose case truly is weaker. One study of mediator behavior described this process of "trashing" each side's case . . . .

Another study concluded that mediators who use caucuses do emphasize different things to each side. If the mediator is trashing both sides, he or she is not working to overcome the inexperience of counsel by providing an experienced perspective, but rather playing on that inexperience and the timidity that comes with it to achieve a settlement, any settlement. . . .

[T]he mediator's financial incentive is to settle cases. Although the mediator does not operate on a contingent fee, the private mediator who mediates to make money relies on repeat business. The institutional mediator needs to justify the expense of his or her office. Because the judges who make the referrals are usually interested in dispositions, the mediator's incentive is to have a high "batting average" for cases settled. That batting average will justify the repeat business or the budget required by the mediator. Indeed, it is hard to imagine by what other criterion they would be evaluated. The judge or the court administrator is not likely to take an independent look at the underlying fairness of each settlement achieved. They will rely on the convenient assumption that the result must be fair because the parties agreed to it, in turn ignoring the one reason why mediation is necessary: the parties through their . . . lawyers are incapable of judging what is fair. . . . The incentives are to see that cases settle on any terms, without regard to the fairness of the particular terms. Referral mediation must be judged with this fundamental flaw in mind.

Referral mediators can help to a limited extent with the procedural obstacles to settlement. Referral mediation can help to achieve a catharsis first by involving the parties directly in the settlement process. The parties will feel unburdened because they have the chance to tell their story to a neutral figure. A distinguished private mediator may also be able to convince the stubborn client of the realities of the case, and the prospect of such a conversation may persuade the reluctant lawyer to come clean on the likely outcome of the case. This is one reason why the personal presence of the client at the mediation session is crucial. Private mediation also provides a forum where combative lawyers must meet and talk settlement in the presence of a third party. The procedural problem with referral mediation, however, is not that it cannot work but that it is inferior in every respect to judicial mediation.

The problem with the referral mediator is that he or she is just another lawyer. The parties already have a lawyer, and they need someone with more legitimacy, while the lawyers need someone with more authority to overcome the procedural obstacles to settlement. A judge will better serve the parties' needs. A catharsis will occur much more often when a judicial officer is involved. . . .

Judges are better mediators because litigants can express themselves to someone who embodies "the prestige and power of the judicial system." The deflation effect is also easier to achieve with a judge. Clients believe judges more than lawyers and are more likely to be persuaded by hearing how a judge views their case than by hearing how another lawyer views it. The lawyers who need to level with their clients are much more likely to do so ahead of time if they know that the rosy expectations they have created are about to be punctured by the judge. The lawyer will not want either the client's wrath or the judge's disdain and, instead, will give reliable information about the case. A mediation session with a judge also gives the lawyer authoritative ammunition with which to persuade a recalcitrant client that settlement is the best course. One judge has reported that his practice of telling the lawyers what the case is worth and telling them to tell the clients that he said so was popular with counsel because "[t]hey want to be able to go back to their clients and have some of the load taken off their shoulders. They say, This is what I think, but the judge says this."

The mediation session is also an opportunity for the judge to attempt to overcome hostility between lawyers. In attempts to create a cooperative, working climate, some judges have arranged for lunch with the lawyers and their clients and invited them to social evenings together. Another attempts to overcome the "intractable belligerence" of counsel by holding conferences in a local coffee shop or while strolling together in a local park. If such tactics are not effective, the judicial mediator is also much more likely to adjust the attitude of combative trial lawyers. The presence of the judge improves the civility of lawyers and can keep them talking. With a judicial officer, they know they are dealing with someone who has the authority to enforce, and will enforce, appropriate standards of professional conduct. No longer is the lawyer free to misbehave, secure in the knowledge that the judge is not watching. The judge is there. Furthermore, the lawyer will be constrained by the likelihood that he or she will have repeated interactions with the judge. In an urban trial practice today, one can alienate other lawyers with little fear of retaliation in future cases. This is not so with the judge. Civility becomes the order of the day, and settlement is more likely.

Thus, referral mediation is not a full solution to either the informational or the procedural needs of the parties and lawyers. The fear of manipulation and the lack of legitimacy and authority in a non-judicial mediator both must raise doubts about the efficacy of this process. A judicial officer, without the financial incentive to manipulate parties and with the legitimacy and authority of office, is needed. The question is who that judicial officer should be.

B. Trial Judge Mediation

The first judicial option is to have the district judge mediate his or her own cases. The discussion of settlement as part of the Rule 16 pretrial conference is the most frequently used form of mediation in the federal courts. It overcomes many of the problems of referral mediation but creates others. It is better than referral mediation, but it is not the answer.

Experienced lawyers can help settle cases, but experienced judges enjoy a special ability and credibility in assessing cases and therefore have a unique ability to bring the parties' expectations together. Many have processed thousands of cases and thus their view on the value of a case is entitled to, and will receive, extra respect. Especially today, in an era of few civil trials, the trial judge will have more experience with the results of trial than even the most experienced lawyer. Their evaluations of a case are likely to be quite accurate. They have no financial incentive to manipulate those predictions, and lawyers rightly believe that the involvement of a judge makes a fair settlement more likely.

The trial judge is also more likely to bring the parties' expectations together because the judge's evaluation has more credibility than that of a non-judicial mediator. That credibility arises both from the reputation of the individual judge and the status of the judge's office. As one retired judge-mediator in Florida told a researcher, "If you're a retired judge you bring much more prestige to the mediation table than just an attorney because the people look at this attorney and say, I have an attorney; what do I need this guy for? A judge they listen to."

The trial judge, however, can bring the parties together for reasons other than the judge's expertise in assessing cases. The judge can coerce as well as inform. Although judges, unlike referral mediators, have no financial incentive to coerce settlement, they have other reasons to do so. They have too much to do. They face peer pressure among their fellow judges to keep their docket moving and to keep their dispositions high. The fear of coercion is what leads lawyers overwhelmingly to prefer a judge other than the judge who will preside over the trial if a settlement conference is to occur.

Some judges succumb to the pressure to coerce settlements, although detection of such activity in chambers is difficult. One survey of trial judges revealed that one-tenth of those surveyed described their typical practice as "interven[ing] aggressively through the use of direct pressure." For example, Judge Weinstein of the Southern District of New York had enormous success in settling the Agent Orange litigation, but his tactics were considered coercive by some. Another judge took the direct approach and sanctioned a party for refusing to settle, despite the fact that the law is clear that parties cannot and should not be forced to settle against their will. The exasperation of the overworked trial judge with the positions parties take can and does lead to inappropriate pressure.

A trial judge determined to settle a case has enormous power to coerce a settlement. The court can threaten to remove a case from the trial docket. The court can instill in the parties a fear of retaliation which makes a trial an unappealing alternative to almost any settlement. The court can create that fear by intimating how the court will rule on particular matters such as admissibility of crucial evidence, choice of law, or immunity. The judge can play on the fears of the lawyers who have other cases to come before that judge and fear alienating the court. A judge simply has countless ways to use his or her discretion to nudge a reluctant party toward making a deal.

The possibility of coercion by the trial judge, like the possibility of manipulation by the referral mediator, means that cases may settle on terms and for reasons other than the underlying justice of the dispute. Such settlements are unacceptable. The parties need to obtain the information about the value of the case from someone without the incentive to manipulate or the power to coerce them.

As discussed above, judicial mediation is much preferable to referral mediation as a procedural matter. The parties' needs for a catharsis and deflation, and the lawyers' needs for an authoritative third party, are better served when a judge is involved. There are significant problems, however, with the process of trial judge mediation. In addition to the obvious problem that a truly vindictive judge may tilt the scales of justice against a party who refuses to settle, there are two other problems: preconceptions of the merits of a case and disclosure to the court of information that is irrelevant to the trial.

Settlement discussions will involve the disclosure of information about the merits of the case and the information that will be presented at trial. Although necessary, this disclosure will not be in the full glory of adversarial trial. The lawyers will summarize evidence but not be permitted to cross-examine witnesses during a mediation. The trial judge who participates in mediation may, indeed must, form judgments about the case and how it should come out and share those with the lawyers. Although one would hope that those judgments are reliable, they cannot be permitted to become self-fulfilling. The judge may become psychologically committed to one view of the case — the view he or she expresses in the privacy of chambers during the court-sponsored mediation — and be unable to shake that conception even in the face of evidence to the contrary.

One district judge, in describing a hypothetical case, "quoted" himself as suggesting to a plaintiff in a settlement conference that a jury verdict in the amount sought might require a remittitur or new trial. That is precisely the kind of information necessary for the predictive settlement conference to work: the lawyer has received some valuable information from a reliable source about the likely damages in the case. However, if the case does not settle, can the judge objectively evaluate after hearing all the evidence whether a total victory for the plaintiff should be reduced or set aside? The risk that the judge will be wedded to his or her preconception, or feel compelled to carry out the implied threat of a new trial in order not to be perceived as weak, is real. Even if this judge waited to make up his or her mind, the appearance of impartiality may have been compromised. Yet a motion to recuse on this basis will fail. Someone other than the judge who will preside over trial needs to conduct the mediation.

Another problem with the use of the trial judge to perform the mediation is that mediation requires the parties to negotiate and exchange information. Often, information relevant to settlement is irrelevant to adjudication, and parties justifiably fear that revelations that might help settlement will taint a later trial if mediation is unsuccessful. Precisely this concern excludes from evidence at trial statements made in the course of settlement. Parties may not be candid with the trial judge in a settlement conference. To permit the judge who will officiate at trial to conduct the mediation risks either unproductive negotiations because the parties withhold their true interests or a tainted trial process because the judge knows information he or she should not, or both.

In summary, trial judges are better situated than referral mediators to overcome the informational and procedural obstacles of settlement. Yet using the trial judge as a settlement officer creates additional risks of coercion and of a tainted process not present when the mediator is uninvolved in the trial if settlement does not occur. The ideal settlement officer would combine the expertise, legitimacy, and authority of the trial judge with the distance of the referral mediator. The magistrate's position is evolving in ways that make that combination possible.

C. Magistrate Mediation

. . . The Federal Magistrates Act of 1968 left largely undefined what duties the magistrates could undertake. Their duties were defined by the district judges in each district, resulting in differing authority from district to district. Some districts authorized magistrates to hold civil trials upon the consent of the parties. To remove any controversy about the practice, Congress amended the Magistrates Act in 1979. Today, magistrates have the undoubted authority to conduct complete civil trials upon consent of all parties.

Magistrates are trying more civil cases. Magistrates conducted 825 civil trials in 1982. In 1992, magistrates held 1,368 consensual civil trials. . . . As the magistrates try more cases, they gain greater insight into the likely impact of evidence, theories, and recovery on a judge or jury. They bring increasing expertise to the settlement conference. . . .

Those assessments will also improve because the office of magistrate is becoming more attractive to more qualified individuals. In 1981, magistrates earned seventy-six percent of what district judges made. In recent years, Congress has pegged magistrates salaries at ninety-two percent of the salary for an Article III judge. This tie to the Article III judiciary is an important step for magistrates as a demonstration of their importance to the judicial system. In addition, with recent changes in the compensation for Article III judges, magistrate compensation has increased to $120,000 per year. . . .

Another important recent development that will give the magistrates increased credibility has been the magistrates' successful effort to secure the title "Judge." . . . No longer can there be any doubt that magistrates are entitled to the important status of being called judge. Accordingly, their assessments of cases in settlement conferences will be given more weight. They are better equipped to help parties settle cases on fair terms.

Fears of manipulation and coercion are much less necessary with magistrates than with referral mediators and trial judges. The magistrate can help the parties' expectations to converge without encountering the problems of the referral or institutional mediator who relies upon a "batting average" of settled cases to justify repeat business or continued funding of institutionalized mediation. The magistrate is in a position to seek only just settlements. The magistrate has the security of a definite term of office — eight years for full-time magistrates — and so is not dependent for continued livelihood of a record of dispositions. Furthermore, to the extent that magistrates are subject to non-renewal at the end of their term, settlement is only one of many tasks performed by them and thus is unlikely to be a source of overwhelming pressure to settle cases at the cost of justice. The temptation to manipulate the settlement process to justify one's place in it is not as great when there is a definite term of office and other bases for defending one's place.

Furthermore, unlike the trial judge mediator, the magistrate will not be able to coerce settlements when the parties have not consented to trial before the magistrate. Magistrate mediation insulates the trial from the settlement discussions. The parties always have the resort of trial. The magistrate thus can feel free to become deeply involved in settlement in innovative ways. A survey of lawyers concluded, not surprisingly, that they believed that settlement conferences should be conducted by judges other than the trial judge, and their worries "about the propriety of judicial participation in settlement all but evaporates . . . when the judicial officer who hosts the settlement conference is not the judge to whom the case has been assigned for trial."

Thus, of the three types of mediation, magistrate mediation is superior in overcoming the informational obstacles to settlement. Magistrates are gaining in experience and prestige. Magistrates bring their new-found ability and credibility to the table and will be better able to guide parties to realistic, convergent expectations. Furthermore, their evaluations will be believed. In addition, there is less fear of manipulation or coercion. There remains, however, the evaluation of the ability of magistrates to assist with the procedural obstacles to settlement.

As discussed above, what parties need from the settlement process is a catharsis and a deflation. Magistrates are now in a better position than ever to provide both. The litigant who unburdens himself to the magistrate is talking not only to a disinterested third party but also to someone with the trappings and the title of judicial office. It is one thing for a party to tell her story to her lawyer or to an another lawyer appointed or employed to mediate the case. It is quite another to walk into the chambers of a judicial officer with the title of judge and the accoutrements of office and tell that same story. The satisfaction of participating in the resolution of the dispute in this official and impressive setting is significantly different and much more likely to lead to settlement. The catharsis is dependent upon the party's perception of the legitimacy of the forum, and the magistrate, as judge, has become more legitimate. Deflation also is more likely. As discussed above, a client who is out of control may see reason if the bad news comes from a judge. A lawyer who is reluctant to deliver the bad news will know that he or she will have many other occasions to interact with the magistrate and thus will have an incentive to give realistic advice before the magistrate does so. The key is that the magistrate is a judicial officer and now is more likely to be perceived as one.

The increasing status of the magistrate also lends increasing authority to the mediation process. Magistrates are in an excellent position to control attorney incivility. First, the magistrates are probably the judicial officers who are most likely to be familiar with the phenomenon, having fought in the trenches of discovery warfare for years. Second, such behavior is usually best controlled when a judicial officer is present to referee. One conference observed by Professor Christopher Smith began to degenerate when a lawyer sarcastically accused another lawyer of misrepresenting the facts of an earlier dispute. The magistrate scolded the attorney with the desired effect. The fact that the lawyers will have repeat business with the magistrate will also help keep them under control. In fact, they probably will have more frequent interaction with the magistrate than with the district judge and thus will have more incentive to appear reasonable in front of the magistrate. . . .

IV. THE USES OF JUDICIAL TIME

One solution to the problems of trial judge mediation is to have trial judges swap cases. Mediation under such a system has the virtues of judicial mediation without the baggage of coercion or a tainted process. There are other problems, however, and not all of them can be solved by a buddy system. The brutal fact of the matter is that federal trial judges do not have time to devote to assisting settlement negotiations at the level of detail required to do any good. . . .

It may be that "the best that judges can do to promote good settlements is to adjudicate as many cases as possible to make clear the alternative to consensual agreement." One trial judge who spent considerable time in settlement conferences concluded that the same results would have followed from setting a firm trial date. Many other judges and observers have reached much the same conclusion. One prominent federal judge, the late Robert Peckham, concluded that judges who spend time on settlements are actually less productive than judges who keep their cases moving toward trial. Taking the trial judges out of settlement conferences will leave them more time to try cases. Once the word gets out that trial has become a more likely alternative, the lawyers and parties may find it easier to settle more cases without assistance. Trial is a better use of the district judge's time than settlement.

One of the most vigorous supporters of alternative dispute resolution in the federal courts has opposed using magistrates as mediators because of the burden of other activities such as pretrial disputes. Magistrate mediation in at least one magistrate's experience has averaged two to three hours per case. That figure probably is conservative. There is room for hope, however, that magistrates may be able to make a significant contribution to mediation efforts because the primary source of docket pressure does not affect them as much as it affects district judges, and recent changes in the discovery rules have the potential of lifting some of the burden of discovery disputes from the magistrates' shoulders. . . .

V. CONCLUSION

Magistrates are in a unique position to assist in settlement of civil cases. In large part, this position is the result of recent trends in federal civil litigation, some of which are desirable and others of which are regrettable. Magistrates are enjoying new status and are exercising their trial authority with increasing frequency. Both trends assist the magistrate in making settlement discussions more realistic, more satisfying, and more productive. Some of the attractiveness of magistrate mediation, however, arises from more negative developments. The inability of lawyers to form realistic trial expectations requires the intervention of experienced lawyers or judges. The habitual incivility of lawyers toward each other requires the presence of a judicial officer to keep counsel in line. Magistrates can perform both roles.

None of these trends, good or bad, shows any sign of abating soon. Ultimately, the success or failure of magistrate mediation may depend upon whether the other duties of magistrates permit them to spend sufficient time in mediations. If they do, their unique position in the federal judicial system will serve the process of settlement well.

2. Comments and Questions

a. The increased salary for magistrates ($120,000 per year) may be assumed to have a positive impact on their job skills, but it also increases the opportunity costs of using magistrates as court-annexed mediators.

b. There is a considerable literature on the expanding use of judicial adjuncts. *See, e.g.*, RICHARD A. POSNER, THE FEDERAL COURTS 102-19 (1985); Wade H. McCree, Jr., *Bureaucratic Justice: An Early Warning*, 129 U. PA. L. REV. 777 (1981); Owen Fiss, *The Bureaucratization of the Judiciary*, 92 YALE L.J. 1442 (1983); Linda Silberman, *Judicial Adjuncts Revisited: The Proliferation of Ad Hoc Procedure*, 137 U. PA. L. REV. 2131 (1989); J. Clifford Wallace, *Tackling the Caseload Crisis*, AM. BAR ASS'N J., June 1994, at 88. See also the influential series of articles by Judith Resnik, cited in the comments after her article later in this Chapter.

c. Do not lose sight of the point made by Professor Longan at the beginning of his article about the dominance of criminal cases in many U.S. district courts, and the concomitant delays for civil cases. This factor has an enormous impact in promoting settlements, whether by negotiation, voluntary mediation, or some form of court-ordered process. In addition, increased mandatory minimum sentences and "three strikes laws" (automatic life sentence for third felony) increase the number of criminal cases at both the federal and state level by making plea bargaining a less attractive option.

CASE STUDY

John Slacker was a day laborer at Texon, a major oil company. His job consisted of using hydraulic hoses to clean out barrels that had contained crude oil in order to prepare them for future use. On one particular occasion, John was cleaning barrels when a nauseous odor started to make him dizzy. Crude barrels are not harmful to persons, however, in this case a toxic barrel was accidently unloaded in the area designated for crude barrels, Texon posted warning signs everywhere instructing workers to immediately leave the area and breathe the oxygen provided in the emergency area if they became faint or dizzy. John also had extensive training by Texon on what to do in a situation such as that. However, John continued to clean the barrel and ultimately passed out. John fell into a coma for one week.

Thereafter, John sued Texon for negligently exposing him to hazardous chemicals. The damages claimed consisted of hospital costs for two weeks, loss of past and future wages, mental anguish, and punitives. Texon paid nothing.

The exposure to the hazardous chemical caused 10% permanent lung damage to John. However, doctors all agree that a person only uses 85% of their full lung capacity unless he is a competitive runner. John had 90% of his full lung capacity. Ironically, John had been a track star in high school and had been offered scholarships to major universities for his accomplishments. Therefore, John claimed that because he lost his full lung capacity, Texon had denied him the opportunity to ever run competitively again, which was his key to a college education and thereafter higher wages.

Texon pointed out that it had been three years since John had graduated from high school. He had turned down all prior opportunities to go to college on scholarship and no college was recruiting him any longer. Therefore, his loss of 10% lung capacity was not as significant as John had made it out to be.

John also complained that he had been out of work for five months. Since the accident, he had not been able to obtain the same salary he had been making before. However, John had been cleared by doctors as being fully healed and capable of the same type of work after two months. In discovery, John admitted that he had not attempted to immediately go back to work after those two months because he was having fun with his friends and enjoyed staying home playing Nintendo. John also admitted that he really did not like how hard he had to work in his previous position and therefore decided to take a different position at Texon. It just so happened that without working as hard, John did not get the same compensation level as he had previously received.

D. Cooptation of ADR Into the Legal System

1. Carrie Menkel-Meadow, *Pursuing Settlement in an Adversary Culture: A Tale of Innovation Co-opted or "The Law of ADR,"* 19 Fla. St. U. L. Rev. 1, 1-5, 39-45 (1991)*

In this Article I tell a tale of legal innovation co-opted. Put another way, this is a story of the persistence and strength of our adversary system in the face of attempts to change and reform some legal institutions and practices. In sociological terms, it is an ironic tale of the unintended consequences of social change and legal reform. A field that was developed, in part, to release us from some—if not all—of the limitations and rigidities of law and formal legal institutions has now developed a law of its own. With burgeoning developments in the use of nonadjudicative methods of dispute resolution in the courts and elsewhere, issues about alternative dispute resolution (ADR) increasingly have been "taken to court." As a result, we are beginning to see the development of case and statutory law and, dare I say, a "common law" or "jurisprudence" of ADR. . . .

As a proponent of a particular version of ADR—the pursuit of "quality" solutions—I am somewhat troubled by how a critical challenge to the status quo has been blunted, indeed co-opted, by the very forces I had hoped would be changed by some ADR forms and practices. In short, courts try to use various forms of ADR to reduce caseloads and increase court efficiency at the possible cost of realizing better justice. Lawyers may use ADR not for the accomplishment of a "better" result, but as another weapon in the adversarial arsenal to manipulate time, methods of discovery, and rules of procedure for perceived client advantage. Legal challenges cause ADR "issues" to be decided by courts.

An important question that must be confronted is whether forcing ADR to adapt to a legal culture or environment may be counterproductive to the transformations proponents of ADR would like to see in our disputing practices. . . . Here are some of the issues that are raised by these recent developments:

1. What are the values of settlement and of adjudication?
2. When is a court not a court? What makes a court a "special" institution and what should it be doing? Related to these concerns are issues of legal authority for the variations on court adjudication—when can a court "order" someone to settle, require a juror to serve a nonjuror function, or exclude the public from a proceeding?
3. What values should a court-institutionalized ADR device serve? Who should pay?" Who should have access? What are the consequences of using ADR devices for the rest of the system? When should a "public" system "subsidize" private agreements?
4. What are the politics of ADR? Are there patterns of usage? Do particular kinds of clients choose different processes? Are there differences between big cases and small cases, or in the choices of wealthy clients and poorer clients?
5. What should be the system or values implicated in case allocation—should it be a free market? Should there be restrictions or regulations of case types? Should these programs be voluntary or mandatory?
6. How can we measure the effects of different allocations or assignments to particular processes? How should we measure the "quality" of justice?
7. What processes are appropriate within our system of dispute resolution? When is adversarialness appropriate, and when is it not? What other processes can be used while preserving our long tradition of process-fairness and rights protections?
8. On what bases should cases be settled, decided, or tried—by considering only legal rules, personal needs, or economic expediency?

. . . The major question I wish to explore here is whether new forms of dispute resolution will transform the courts or whether, in a more likely scenario, the power of our adversarial system will co-opt and transform the innovations designed to redress some, if not all, of our legal ills. Can legal institutions be changed if lawyers and judges persist in acting from traditional and conventional conceptions of their roles and values?

* * *

C. Issues, Proposals, and Reforms for Innovation and Evaluation of ADR in the Courts

In a sense, we are at a second stage in the development of alternative dispute resolution innovations. The bloom on the rose has faded as some experiments have been tried and now present their own problems or dilemmas. Some of us still aim for consciousness transformation and creative solutions to problems; others are more focused on the institutionalized forms of ADR and what can be done to make them work. Many of the issues raised by these developments require policy judgments for which we have an inadequate empirical data base; others require us to make normative choices based on what we value in a procedural system. If ADR is to meet the basic levels of fairness, then the following questions must be addressed, and the following data must be collected to prevent ADR from becoming totally swallowed by the adversarial system:

1. To what extent will courts lose their legitimacy as courts if too many other forms of case-processing are performed within their walls? If the "other" processes are not considered legitimate within public institutions, they will be legally challenged and transformed so that they will no longer be "alternatives, " but only watered-down versions of court adjudication. These watered-down versions may be violative of the legal rights and rules our courts are intended to safeguard. Are theorists, practitioners, and citizens capable of changing our views of what courts should do?
2. Should some case types be excluded from alternative treatment?
3. What are the purposes for using particular forms of alternative dispute resolution? Caseload management and docket reduction may suggest entirely different processes than a search for a better quality solution which might be quite costly and time-consuming. If the goals and purposes of particular ADR institutions are clarified now, future problems based on overly abstract goals may be avoided.
4. What forms of ADR should be institutionalized? Not all ADR devices are the same. There is a tendency in the literature and in the rhetoric to homogenize widely different approaches to dispute resolution. A more thorough and careful consideration of each of the devices might lead to different conclusions about the utility and legitimacy of these devices. Mandatory settlement conferences, for example, may become quite acceptable if the judicial officer attending the conference will not also be ruling on the evidence at trial. Similarly, we might feel differently about summary jury trials if they were as accessible to the public as any other activity conducted in open court and if jurors were told about what they were doing. These distinctions implicate all of the legal policy issues in drafting the rules of procedure. How much regulation of each process should there be? How clear should the rules be before parties can elect different processes or before they can be "ordered" to attend? . . .
5. What are the politics of ADR? Does ADR serve the interests of particular groups? This is not an easy question to answer. Many have argued that "minor" disputes have been siphoned out of the public legal system, while "major" disputes have continued to

receive the benefits of the traditional court system. Large corporations are also removing their cases from the court system. Through their increased use of private ADR, the economics of dispute resolution are more subtle. Some may be "forced" out while others choose to opt out. What will this mean for payment and subsidies of dispute resolution? Will "free market" forces decide the fate of ADR? Who will control decision-making about ADR—judges, lawyers, clients, or legislators? If those with the largest stake in the system exit, who will supply the impetus and resources for court and rule reform? At the level of institutional decision-making, are these issues for individual judges, for the Congress, or for the United States Supreme Court to decide?

6. What are the cultural forces producing these legal changes at these particular times? Has the larger culture around us changed since particular legal innovations were adopted? If attempts to incorporate party participation in disputing were made in the "participatory" 1960s and 1970s, then does the 1980s [and 1990s] era of privatization of public services dictate other considerations in the use of ADR? How has the rhetoric of quality justice been transformed into a rhetoric of quantity and case processing?
7. How are different forms of ADR actually functioning? This is the evaluation question. We need to know more about how these processes actually work in terms of processes used and outcomes achieved, as well as the more common measures of party satisfaction.

In my view, alternative dispute resolution and the pursuit of settlement in the courts will, and should, continue. The courts will deal with these issues as they experiment with different formats and as they continue to rule on the legal issues presented by ADR. In order for ADR to develop in a way that enhances our trust in the American legal system, several important reforms should accompany our experimentation.

First, some forms of ADR should remain mandatory, but not binding. At first blush, it is easier to suggest that ADR should be used only consensually to preserve the kind of settlement culture that is motivated to reach voluntary and consensual agreement without the "taint" of coercion and unproductive adversarialness. But in my own experience as both a mediator and a litigator, I have seen many good settlements emerge through the skilled intervention or facilitation of the parties by skilled negotiators or third parties, even in cases where settlement seemed impossible. . . . In addition, in order to rigorously evaluate some of these alternative processes, we will have to study them as they are used on a wide variety of cases without choices about opting in or out.

Second, if some settlement processes are to be made mandatory, certain essential legal protections may have to flow from those processes. If they do not, then processes may have to be chosen consensually or voluntarily. I would recommend records of proceedings—stenographic proceedings of both summary jury trials and mandatory settlement conferences—in order to provide a record for appeals or challenges for "coercive settlement" conduct. Such coercion would violate legal standards of abuse of judicial discretion for those settlement practices involving judicial officers. I would still preserve the confidentiality of some forms of settlement to facilitate candor. Records should be available to parties in the event of challenges as judges may be called upon to rule about whether particular hearings should be conducted *in camera* or opened to the public and whether documents should be sealed. In all other settlement processes, like arbitration or mediation led by attorneys, decisions should be nonbinding with right of trial de novo to protect the parties' constitutional rights, and to provide an alternative to an inappropriate arbitration process.

Third, if settlement processes are to be conducted within the courts, they should be facilitated by those who will not be the ultimate triers of fact. Because I believe that good settlement practice frequently depends on the revelation of facts that would be inadmissible in court, the facilitator of settlement cannot be the same person who will ultimately find facts or decide the outcome of the case. In some courts this will mean the use of magistrates, and in others it will mean rotating judges through cases on other dockets.

Fourth, settlement facilitators must be trained to conduct settlement proceedings, particularly those that depart from conventional adjudication models. In its current format, the summary jury trial operates much like a regular trial. Therefore, it requires few skills different from those we assume judges currently possess. Because it uses mediation techniques, a settlement conference draws on other skills and therefore requires specialized training.

Fifth, we must provide the evidence for systematic evaluation of alternative dispute resolution devices. To accomplish this goal, I recommend the recording of proceedings, as well as more sophisticated data collection at the court level. With the advent of computer technology, it should be possible to create data sets of case treatments that would permit the kind of systematic analysis necessary to compare outcomes and processes of greater variety and in greater depth. These data sets could be supplemented by qualitative research, including party satisfaction measures.

Sixth, different forms of ADR should be unbundled and separately evaluated. Summary jury trials may work best in fact-intensive cases, or in cases likely to take a great deal of trial time. Evaluation and consideration of the advantages and disadvantages of summary jury trial can be distinguished from the pros and cons of mandatory settlement conferences, and from early neutral evaluation and other case management devices. We must be more precise about what we call "alternative" and what we label "adjudication." Both of these concepts have become so abstract, undifferentiated, and homogeneous that we no longer know what is being measured against what. "Shadow verdicts" may not be the same as "shadow bargains," and in order to evaluate these processes, we need to understand the baseline comparisons. It might be instructive to determine how important it is to parties, as well as scholars, that settlements track legal entitlements.

Finally, categorical judgments about particular processes are likely to be unhelpful. Mediation or summary jury trials per se do not violate our procedural rules or jurisprudential norms. More often, the issue is whether a particular process is carried out sensitively or "coercively." Because of the range of human variation in how these proceedings are conducted, it makes more sense at this point to allow judicial experimentation and legal challenges to be handled in each case. Standards, like abuse of discretion, should protect against the abuses of those who do not adequately protect the parties' rights to fair process. Furthermore, the amendment process to the Federal Rules of Civil Procedure provides another opportunity for regulation.

I offer these simple suggestions to encourage the flowering of alternatives to expensive and limited court adjudication, while at the same time seeking to preserve that which characterizes the good in both adjudication and settlement. Both authoritative rulings and consensual agreements have their place in our dispute resolution system. These should be monitored and managed so that they preserve what is good about each without "infecting" the other. I am as unhappy with "coerced compromises" as settlements as I am with limited adversarial solutions to polycentric problems.

2. Comments and Questions

a. In a book review excerpted in Chapter 3, Professor (of anthropology) Sally Merry suggested that those associated with the ADR movement failed to recognize the historical pattern in America of oscillation between formal and informal patterns of dispute resolution.

> [S]imilar developments have arisen during the twentieth century. There seems to be an historical pattern of oscillation between formal systems of dispute resolution and informal reforms that gradually became more formalized, leading to new calls for informal reforms of the now calcified older reforms. . . . The ADR movement seems to be the most recent manifestation of this historical pattern, an effort to create informal systems outside the legal system that eventually come to incorporate many of its characteristics. As each alternative gradually comes to look more like the legal system it has replaced, routine treatment, delay, and impersonality are likely to reemerge. This transformation is already occurring in the ADR movement. . . . It is assuming more legalistic, formal characteristics as it becomes more closely integrated into the courts. We should not be surprised.

Do you agree with Merry that the transformation discussed (and worried about) by Professor Menkel-Meadow, or some variant thereof, was to be expected? Menkel-Meadow tells us a "tale of unintended consequences of social change and legal reform." Merry responds, "we should not be surprised." This juxtaposition of viewpoints does not mean either one is right or wrong. Rather, they are two different perspectives on ADR in America, and both can increase our knowledge and understanding.

b. Thinking carefully about the probing questions raised by Professor Menkel-Meadow would be an excellent way to prepare for the final examination in this course.

c. Professor Menkel-Meadow, a leader in the ADR movement, laments that ADR has been co-opted into the adversary culture—at best, a partial success. In the article that follows, Professor Resnik, a doubter about the expanding use of ADR, laments that ADR has swept the field so completely that the "preservation of adjudicatory forms, with judges in distinctive roles" is in doubt. No doubt, each hopes the other is right. What do you think, and how would you characterize the present situation?

E. Too Much ADR, Too Little Adjudication?

1. Judith Resnik, *Many Doors? Closing Doors? Alternative Dispute Resolution and Adjudication*, 10 Ohio St. J. on Disp. Resol. 211 (1995)*

I. INTRODUCTION: THE STATE'S ATTITUDES TOWARD ALTERNATIVES TO ADJUDICATION

As the title for this lecture forecasts, my review prompts me to be less optimistic than others about the array of options that are and will be available to litigants seeking decision making from the state. The assumption of many proponents, that ADR will increase the options available to litigants within the publicly financed system, may not be borne out. As the state makes alternative dispute resolution its own, both ADR and adjudication are being reconcep-

*Reprinted with permission.

tualized. . . . In this interaction, we may soon find ourselves with a narrower, not a richer, range of forms of dispute resolution. . . .

II. THE CALL FOR MANY DOORS

I turn back less than two decades, to 1976 and the Pound Conference, a meeting of some 250 judges, lawyers, court administrators, law professors, and non-lawyers at which Professor Frank Sander called for a "multi-doored" courthouse. Reviewing his published comments is useful, for what was written not yet twenty years ago seems like it was aimed at a group of people removed from us by many more than two decades.

Professor Sander took as his burden the need to explain the "significant characteristics of various alternative dispute resolution mechanisms." He assumed his readership's familiarity with adjudication; his task was to educate his readers on what else there was and then to persuade his readers of the desirability and utility of those "alternative dispute resolution forms." His purpose was to suggest "promising avenues to explore."

Professor Sander's key move was to focus the discussion not on substantive areas (i.e., should tax cases go to a specialized court?) but rather on process. He urged that across a wide variety of disputes, the process should be elaborated, and a mediation, conciliation, or alternative phase be incorporated into it. Professor Sander pointed to some experiments with these processes, labeled "alternative dispute resolution," as evidence of the plausibility of his proposals.

Pause to consider the metaphor that has come to encapsulate his ideas: a "multi-doored courthouse." The image has a good deal of appeal, stemming in part from its implicit reliance on the phrase "access to justice" to posit a structure with several doors of entry. In his reprinted speech, Frank Sander actually described a "lobby" in which a litigant could be "channelled through a screening clerk" to one of six doors, comprising "a diverse panoply of dispute resolution processes." Specifically, one might be sent to "mediation, arbitration, fact finding, malpractice screening panel, superior court, or an ombudsperson."

While "flexible," this model also assumed something presumably stable: the courthouse was a known, readily conjured-up entity. In fact, one of the doors in the Sander lobby was to something called the "superior court." Moreover, one of Professor Sander's goals was to "reserve the courts for those activities for which they are best suited and to avoid swamping and paralyzing them with cases that do not require their unique abilities." Whatever the number of doors, the call was for access to and preservation of the courthouse.

It is fair to say that, within a very short time period, . . . Frank Sander's call has been heard. It is worth mapping that shift, from disinterest and some hostility toward ADR to the embrace of it as a mode of responding to disputes.

III. ADR AS A GENERIC FORM

Before detailing the shift, both in practice and in ideology, to show the markers in law and doctrine that delineate the state's endorsement of ADR, a definitional framework for alternative dispute resolution is needed. Thus far, my shorthand phrase "ADR" has assumed a uniformity of activity unfair to the complexity and richness of the ADR arena. I will not detail all its array here, but I do not want to be heard as blurring distinctive aspects of the many modes of dispute resolution under the ADR umbrella. . . . I will group the various methods into modes that are delineated by the nature of the work of that third party.

A first mode is quasi-adjudicatory; this form of ADR offers a truncated, abbreviated fact-finding process that yields an outcome, decided by a third party, in the hopes that with that result, the parties will conclude their dispute. Both private contractual and court-annexed arbitration fit this mode. The difference is that under contractual arbitration, individuals or entities have an agreement . . . to arbitrate, and that agreement also specifies the mechanism for selection of arbitrators. In contrast, under many court-annexed arbitration programs, litigants are sent to arbitration without such prior agreements and have varying amounts of control over the selection of arbitrators. Court-annexed arbitration typically permits parties to reject the arbitrator's decision and litigate, albeit sometimes with penalties and disincentives. However, if the parties do not object, the judgment of the arbitrator functions as a judgment of the court.

Under both court-annexed and contractual arbitration, the assumption is that information, provided to an outsider, will enable that outsider to render a fair outcome. What makes this process not adjudication is that the proceeding is not conducted by a state-employed individual who bears the title "judge," formal evidentiary rules do not apply, and opinions are often not written. It is, however, important to keep in mind that this process shares with adjudication a commitment to a case-specific outcome made by a third party and predicated upon an inquiry into the claims of fact made by disputants.

A second mode of ADR also relies upon some third party intervention but for a different purpose. A third party is introduced not to make a decision, but rather to inform the disputants of how outsiders view the dispute and how these outsiders would decide, were they asked to do so. The hope is that with such information, the disputants themselves will obviate the need for third party intervention by settling their differences. That settlement, however, is presumed to have been shaped in light of the views of the outsiders. The views of those outsiders, in turn, are presumed to have been shaped by the information that the parties' provided in a format akin to adjudication. In both "summary jury trials" and "minitrials," information comes either from witnesses or with arguments by lawyers or litigants.

A third form of ADR moves further away from formal modes of information development. Conversation (sometimes called mediation, sometimes called a conference, sometimes called evaluation) is employed to elicit agreement by the parties. Judge-run settlement conferences are an example of this genre of ADR, as are "early neutral evaluations" ("ENE"). In this form of ADR, the relationship between information and outcome may be obscure, in part by virtue of the absence of formal articulation by the third party of its views of the respective positions of the disputants. Reaching agreement is one goal, as is the narrowing of the dispute, should further proceedings or adjudication be needed. When settlements take place, it is because of parties' consent, which may or may not track their legal rights.[37]

Some commentators have attempted to limit the use of the term ADR and resist its application. For some, settlement programs or judicial management are not properly classified as ADR; for others, criteria are imposed to qualify a program as ADR. The impulse to constrain the vocabulary stems from a variety of concerns, including that too much is being packaged as ADR, confusing the analysis, and that certain forms of intervention, such as judicial engage-

[37]A vivid example of a settlement expressly detached from legal right comes from Judge Jack Weinstein's work in the Agent Orange litigation. His efforts produced a $180 million settlement for the class, which he then approved. Thereafter, Judge Weinstein dismissed the claims of those who had "opted out"—on the grounds that these individuals had no legal claim, that as far as he could then tell, dioxin did not cause their injury.

ment with the parties to search for settlement, would be better described as "creative judicial management" ("CJM") or settlement efforts, and separately considered, rather than subsumed within the ADR framework.

The effort to peel settlement programs away from ADR is, in my view, hard to sustain. Settlement remains a central purpose of many forms of ADR, including those not styled "settlement conferences." Even those forms of ADR closely resembling adjudication, such as court-annexed arbitration, rely on parties' acceptance of the outcomes (a form of settlement) rather than parties' insistence on adjudication. Moreover, many within the legal community include settlement efforts as part of their own descriptions of the reasons for ADR, or link various forms of ADR to court management and settlement. Hence, the discussion that follows considers settlement programs as a species of ADR.

The concern about the way in which an overflowing "ADR basket" can make mushy an analysis is a different kind of criticism, one well taken in many contexts. Were this essay an inquiry into the quality of outcomes or processes of ADR, it would be necessary to consider each form individually and not to speak of ADR as a "generic." However, my interest here is in the relationship between ADR in its generic form, as an idea of an alternative regime (much as Professor Sander sought) to state-based adjudication. Because the legal establishment's promotion of the variety of forms of ADR has generally been as a package, it is appropriate within the confines of this lecture to consider ADR as an undifferentiated set of processes. . . .

IV. THE CONTOURS OF THE NEW FRAMEWORK

Over the past decades, the proposals for ADR have turned, with the assistance of many federal and state judges, into law. Below, I delineate some of the ways in which ADR has become "legalized" and institutionalized. As I develop the discussion of the "law of ADR," I will also begin my discussion of the attitudes toward and claims made about the nature and quality of both alternative dispute resolution and adjudication.

A. Supreme Court Doctrine: Revising Rules on the Legality of Contracts to Arbitrate

Opinions of the United States Supreme Court, separated by almost three decades, offer a first set of comparisons. The context is court enforcement of contracts to arbitrate disputes, involving federal statutory rights, outside the courts. My subsequent discussion is about alternative dispute resolution within the courts. While that distinction is important in terms of legal doctrine, the changes in the Supreme Court's descriptions of the function of both private alternatives to adjudication and adjudication itself provide insight into the legal establishment's contemporary acceptance of court-based ADR.

In 1953, in *Wilko v. Swan,* the United States Supreme Court held that a customer of a brokerage firm who claimed he had been fraudulently "induced" to buy stock had a right to litigate a claim of violation of the Securities Act of 1933, notwithstanding that the customer had signed a contract to arbitrate future disputes. The Court rested its decision on an interpretation of Congress—that the Securities Act itself precluded such agreements.

Two concerns influenced this reading of the securities statute in Justice Reed's opinion for the Court. The first was the Court's fear of arbitrators' potential arbitrariness: that unlike a person who bore the name "judge," an arbitrator was potentially lawless. While an arbitrator might, at some level, be governed by law, the arbitration itself was not a process obliged to enforce federal law. The trial court in *Wilko* had used the phrase "looser approximations" of rights to capture this concern.

A second concern that animated the Court's refusal to enforce an agreement to arbitrate was anxiety about the adequacy of negotiations between parties. The Court noted that, while courts and legislatures might find arbitration a reasonable mode of dispute resolution, parties could be coerced into turning to arbitration; as a consequence, the "validity" of the agreement to arbitrate was in issue. Justice Reed spoke of the "surrender" of rights and of the "advantages" provided by federal law. In the Court's view, a security buyer's "surrender," prior to a claimed violation, would necessarily have been made at a time when the buyer was "less able to judge the weight of the handicap" of ceding a place in the litigation queue than would the adversary, the brokerage firm.

Three assumptions, central to *Wilko,* were key to its intellectual framework. First, arbitration was assumed to be something different from and less loyal to law than adjudication. Second, public judgments rendered by federal trial courts on factual questions, such as the claim of fraudulent inducement of a client by a firm to purchase stock, in individual cases, were viewed as desirable mechanisms of social regulation. Third, the judiciary viewed with skepticism the agreements of parties; parties' agreements were insufficient, in and of themselves, to valorize all the decisions embodied in those agreements.

For almost thirty years, these assumptions formed something called a "public policy" objection to arbitration of federal statutory claims—an objection that became embedded in the case law and that moved from the securities context to the antitrust context and then to other federal statutory regimes. The arbitrator as dispute resolver was posited as a potential hazard to the state, as lawmaker. As a consequence, when litigants sought to avoid agreements to arbitrate federal statutory claims, they were able to persuade judges of the necessity of permitting adjudication, not arbitration, to ensure that principles of federal law would guide the outcome of the dispute. Implementation of this position took two forms; one approach permitted litigants to avoid the arbitration itself, while another permitted litigants who had been to arbitration to avoid the preclusive effect of those decisions and to litigate federal statutory claims.

During the 1980s, however, the Supreme Court changed its mind. The Court, once again describing itself as interpreting congressional intent, reached a different understanding of that intent. On rereading, it turned out that Congress was for, rather than against, arbitration in the context of federal regulatory regimes. Initially, *Wilko* was narrowed; . . . Then, *Wilko* was flatly overruled. Public policy no longer prohibits arbitration; rather, public policy welcomes arbitration of federal statutory claims.

Along the path of this doctrinal shift, the three assumptions embodied in *Wilko* were revised as well. Recall the first, a view of arbitration as different from adjudication and potentially lawless. From the vantage point of the 1980s, the prior generation's emphasis of difference was cast in a negative light, as "suspicious" and "mistrust[ful]," and properly to be replaced with a "healthy regard for the federal policy favoring arbitration." The current assumption is that arbitration is sufficiently similar to adjudication so as to serve as its equal. "Arbitral tribunals" (as they came to be named) are now lauded for their capacity to handle "complexities," such as antitrust law. Moreover, attributes of arbitration (its relative informality, its reduced use of discovery, its disinterest in precedent) that were formerly perceived to be undesirable became the very elements now lauded as "streamlined," "flexible," "prompt", and "efficient". The tone in some contemporary opinions is that opponents or skeptics of arbitration are outmoded, "far out of step" with current thinking.

The second assumption that *Wilko* exemplified was that adjudication was a mechanism for regulation and rights pronouncement. This assumption has also been revised. No longer are the regulatory goals of the state of paramount interest in adjudication. "[I]mportant incidental policing function[s]" take a back seat to the goal of responding to individual claims of the need for compensation. Arbitration and adjudication are again equated: both are interested in the resolution of individual disputes and, with such resolution, both "further broader social purposes."

And finally, no longer are parties' agreements to arbitrate to be scrutinized by the courts, nervous about inequality of bargaining and suspicious of "surrender." Rather, once having made a bargain, the parties "will be held to their bargain." "Mere inequality in bargaining power" does not often undermine the agreements forged. . . .

C. Congressional Promotion of ADR and ADR's Use in Administrative Agencies

The Federal Rules of Civil Procedure are largely the work product of the judiciary, acting through its special committees. These rules come into being by virtue of congressional inaction. But Congress has not been silent in the ADR conversation. Over the past few years, many members of Congress have also voiced enthusiasm for ADR, and some of their views have become part of legislation. The Civil Justice Reform Act of 1990 reiterated by statute the aspiration that district courts use ADR. This legislation is the major statement by Congress on civil processes of the last decade. Its stated purposes are to reduce delay and expense, and alternatives to trial and adjudication are important aspects of the legislation.

A related piece of legislation is the Administrative Dispute Resolution Act of 1990 ("ADRA") which requires each federal agency to "adopt a policy that addresses the use of alternative means of dispute resolution and case management." The act instructs agencies to consider using ADR at all phases of their work, from rulemaking and enforcement actions to agency adjudication. The ADRA is predicated upon congressional "findings" of ADR's desirability. Congress believed ADR to be "faster, less expensive, and less contentious," and that ADR could generate "more creative, efficient, and sensible outcomes" than does "litigation in the Federal courts." This legislation represents a "government-wide emphasis" on ADR. Like ADR in the federal courts, programs existed in agencies before legislation authorized their use. Like ADR in the courts, commentators report uneven implementation, but the aspiration for expansive use remains strong.

ADR within the courts remains on the congressional agenda. In 1993 and 1994, some members of Congress urged mandating that each district court provide court-annexed arbitration programs. The Judicial Conference of the United States objected and argued that such programs should be optional with district courts. A second issue is not whether to mandate that courts offer such programs but whether, if such programs exist, to mandate that litigants whose cases qualify be required to use court-annexed arbitration before being permitted to return to the "traditional" adjudicatory mode. Congress's current, interim response has been to continue the authorization of twenty districts, ten of which may only provide voluntary nonbinding court-annexed arbitration and ten of which may, at their option, mandate participation in such programs. Congress has thus accommodated the judiciary's concerns and reauthorized the current court-annexed programs without requiring that all districts put such activities into place.

D. The Executive and ADR

Civil justice reform efforts have also been the focus of the Executive branch. The Bush Administration promulgated an Executive Order [No. 12,778] that required government attorneys to seek to settle cases. That Executive Order also called for increased use of ADR. Although there is dispute about both what animated the Executive's interest in this area and the degree to which the Executive actually committed itself by this Order to do anything specific, there is no question about the Executive's rhetorical posture, which joined its co-branches of government in praising ADR. Members of the Clinton Administration have also adopted a pro-ADR stance. Vice President Al Gore's report, *Creating a Government that Works Better & Costs Less: Improving Regulatory Systems,* acknowledged the propriety of litigation at times, but also praised alternatives as sometimes generating "better results than might otherwise occur."

E. The Legalization and Institutionalization of ADR

Let me pause to summarize. In 1976, Frank Sander called for more modalities of dispute resolution—based in the courts. His call has been more than heard; it has become law. Via legislation, national and local rule making, and executive proclamation, every branch of the federal government has signalled its support of ADR. While the pattern of implementation is varied and the discussion of it encompasses a range of procedures, approval in theory of ADR has become commonplace.

The current legal issues are not whether ADR is a desirable mode for courts and agencies to adopt or whether courts should play a role in encouraging parties to settle and to explore a variety of procedures to help them achieve an agreement. Rather, today's issues are what forms of ADR should be adopted, what kinds of settlement programs are acceptable, what kinds of disputes are appropriate to which forms of ADR, whether ADR providers are (like judges) immune from suits and the reach of their jurisdiction, and how to increase use of ADR procedures. Discussion centers about the permissible and impermissible incentives to settle. . . .

V. THE INTERRELATIONSHIP BETWEEN CLAIMS MADE FOR ADR AND VIEWS OF ADJUDICATION

. . . [T]he discussion below maps differing kinds of benefit perceived to be conferred by ADR and the relationship between that benefit and what adjudication is supposed to afford. Because ADR's success is often marked by distinguishing ADR from adjudication, attitudes about what adjudication does and does not do can be found, sometimes explicitly and other times implicitly, in discussions of ADR.

A. Explanations Supporting ADR and Their Reflections on Adjudication

One could read the rules and statutes on ADR as a national referendum, standing for the proposition that the conclusions reached by ADR in general and by settlement in particular are either equal to or better than those achieved by adjudication by either judge or jury. What is particularly interesting is that some of the prominent proponents of this claim are themselves judges, whom we might have thought would be adjudication loyalists. What are the elements for the stature of ADR? Below I identify some of the (often overlapping or interrelated) themes.

1. ADR as a Default Position

A major premise of one strand of ADR advocacy is that current adjudicatory procedures are simply inadequate to the task. ADR functions not so much as a good, in and of itself, but rather as a good because the system is in "crisis" and something is needed to fix it. ADR is one of many techniques of managing this crisis, and might be on an equal footing with other proposed curative measures, such as curtailing discovery rights or controlling abusive attorneys. When ADR is proposed on these grounds, it is seen as a useful alternative because of the claim that ADR is cheaper and quicker than trial, which is the baseline often used in the discussion. . . .

The claim that ADR is less expensive than adjudication may also entail the claim that litigation is unnecessarily expensive and wasteful. Sometimes an ADR form is preferable because it is provides a quicker, cheaper quasi-adjudication (*i.e.* court-annexed arbitration), and sometimes an ADR form is preferable because it eschews adjudication altogether. Under this view, ADR moves out from under; ADR is no longer a default position, but a practice preferred to adjudication, for it is a way to make the world "better."

2. ADR as More Congenial than Adjudication

A second form of praise for ADR is about its potential for kindness as contrasted (sometimes explicitly) with nastiness, which is associated with adjudication. ADR is perceived to be friendly, flexible, and nicer than the uncivil exchanges that characterize litigation. This congenial theme contains a bundle of claims, which is worth sorting through.

One means by which ADR is believed to achieve a congenial tone is because some forms of ADR have the potential to reduce the role of attorneys. Less lawyering is not only a way to minimize fees and thus make the process less expensive and speedier. . . . A world with fewer lawyers is imagined to be less rigid and more inventive. The assumption is that, without lawyers, the disputants are empowered to act, and with that empowerment, can shape solutions more responsive to their needs than third parties, in role as adjudicators, would impose.

The ADR-as-congenial set of claims is not wholly dependent upon the elimination of lawyers. Rather, ADR is also seen as beneficial when lawyers are present—to educate and civilize lawyers by focusing them on the needs of their clients. Some forms of ADR aspire to teach lawyers that initiating settlement negotiations and engaging in various forms of compromise are not signs of weakness. Other forms of ADR hope to provide clients with information directly, enabling clients to better monitor their lawyers who may not always be loyal agents. While adjudicatory modes increase parties' dependence on lawyers, ADR may, under this view, both lessen parties' dependence on lawyers and focus lawyers' attention more directly on parties' needs and interests. . . .

The vision of ADR as communicative and congenial comes with a frank critique of many of the attributes of adjudication. The formality of adjudication is perceived as undermining open communication. The procedural requirements of adjudication are described as roadblocks to communication and to fairness. The rights of public access and information are seen as intrusive on private parties, who might otherwise respond to the state in its role as facilitator of agreements. Adjudication is seen as a process that often brings out the worst in its participants, either because it distorts their abilities to pursue self-interest or because it defines self-interest in such a fashion that requires inflicting losses, rather than maximizing gains.

3. ADR as More Efficient than Adjudication

For those forms of ADR that are focused on settlement, three assumptions result in efficiency: first, settlements by parties are voluntary; second, the parties have better information than adjudicators; third, with information and volition, parties have the control to achieve outcomes that are better than those imposed by adjudicators. Settlement-oriented ADR thus becomes a more efficient way to resolve disputes than adjudication. . . .

Efficiency claims on behalf of ADR forms that are quasi-adjudicatory rest not on consent as much as on speed, accessibility, and on the quantum of procedure provided. Court-annexed arbitration is described as a quicker, shorter, less formal trial. Because efficiency is not simply equated with economy but also entails accuracy (or sufficient accuracy in light of reduced costs), claims made for scaled-down adjudication embody a serious critique of adjudication. The point made is that the outcomes are just as good, or good enough, with less process, less cost, less delay.

4. ADR as Fairer than Adjudication

The efficiency arguments for ADR are sometimes turned into or related to arguments about fairness. Both arguments . . . share a view that parties have superior access to and actual possession of information than do third party decision makers. From this vantage point, adjudication is seen as a technique that can both distract and confuse. Legal rules operate to frame debates in a fashion that obscures parties' goals and that results in either wins or losses, rather than a richer set of possible resolutions. In contrast, ADR is seen as focusing on issues, relaxing the law, and thus providing more "just" results. . . .

The perceived fairness of ADR may, like the other claims detailed above, vary with the kind of program used. For example, proponents of ADR as more fair may cite litigant reports of more satisfaction with court-annexed ADR than with judicially run settlement conferences at which they are not present, and argue for court-annexed arbitration but not other forms of ADR. Moreover, not only may proponents argue on behalf of a particular form of ADR (such as mediation), they may also believe that those processes are inappropriate for particular kinds of cases. . . .

VI. CONCLUSION: CHANGES TO BE WELCOMED?

Before concluding, I want to be sure that I am not heard as putting forth too pat a story; our legal culture is not unitary or without nuance. . . . ([M]y task here is not to elaborate a structural analysis of why procedural forms have been transformed over the last three decades. Rather, I have considered the changes in the ways in which adjudication and ADR have been framed and discussed by members of the legal establishment. . . .

I turn now toward the future. I believe we are approaching a time when many a civil trial will be characterized as a "pathological event." One possibility is that this development is to be welcomed as an appropriate correction to what John Langbein calls the "too trial-centered" Anglo-American tradition. From this perspective, one must recall that a strong source of pressure for ADR comes from the judiciary. Judicial endorsement of ADR is a demonstration from individuals with firsthand knowledge of the weakness of adjudication, its failures and limitations. To the extent judicial support of ADR affects our understanding of the value of adjudication, judges may wisely be participating in a societal shove that will result in the demise of civil adjudication as it is currently understood. Further, the decline of civil adjudication in law courts, and its shift to governmental agencies, claims facilities, and private dispute resolution centers may be the appropriate denouement of this cycle of procedural reform.

Alternatively, anxiety about the triumph of ADR can come from across the spectrum, from those perceived to be proponents of ADR as well as from those styled proponents of adjudication. Proponents of ADR have succeeded in making it "an integral part of our federal judicial system." In the process, they have helped to change both "our federal judicial system" and ADR.

For those who envisioned ADR as the blossoming of something different and generative, they should worry (as scholars such as Carrie Menkel-Meadow . . . do) about its institutionalization and its transformation into the very adversarial processes that they had hoped to avoid. As courts make ADR their own, that formalization may well undermine the very attributes of ADR that prompted its praise. Further, as courts compel ADR, the relationship between ADR and volition weakens, pushing it ever closer to a state-imposed mode of resolution. On the other hand, when ADR mimes adjudication, the critique of ADR as a lawless or factless process loses strength.

Similarly, those who think adjudication has something to offer had better start explaining why one would aspire to a preserve for adjudication, and why relatively highly paid government officials (to wit federal and state judges) should be empowered to do some of it. If there is an important and affirmative, if not a cheerful, story to be told for the preservation of adjudicatory forms, with judges in distinctive roles, and why a culture would value, cherish, fund, encourage, and sometimes insist on adjudication, then those who believe so had better speak up soon, for it is becoming increasingly hard to hear those claims. . . .

2. Comments and Questions

a. Professor Resnik insists on a broad and inclusive definition of ADR procedures. Is this approach essential to her analysis? Does this characterization provide her with an easier target for criticism?

b. Compare the views expounded by Judith Resnik with those of Laura Nader (Chapter 5, section F), Richard Delgado (Chapter 5, section C), and Owen Fiss (Chapter 17, section B). Would you expect that these authors share common perceptions about the American legal system, other than their concerns about ADR?

c. Professor Resnik's widely respected views about the decline of courts as institutions for the decision of cases are set out at length in several superb articles. *See, Managerial Judges,* 96 HARV. L. REV. 374 (1982); *Failing Faith: Adjudicatory Procedures in Decline,* 53 U. CHI. L. REV. 494 (1986); *The Domain of Courts,* 137 U. PA. L. REV. 2219 (1989)

Part VII

Dispute Resolution Professionals

Chapter 19

Professional Qualifications, Professional Liability

CASE STUDY

(Adapted from *James Baird Co. v. Gimbel Bros., Inc.* 64 F.2d 344 (2d Cir. 1933))

This dispute began on the 24th of December, when defendant submitted two different price listings of linoleum (varied in quality type) to contractors that might submit bids to the Department of Highways in Pennsylvania for construction of a public building in Philadelphia. Due to an arithmetic error, the employee that the defendant sent to examine and compute the needed amount of linoleum, under-estimated the measurements by about one-half. The plaintiff, who received the defendant's offer by mail on the 27th of December, submitted their bid on December 28, based on the defendant's inaccurate quote. Two more things happened later on the 28th: first, the defendant learned of its error; second, defendant telegraphed all contractors it had previously written to, revoked the initial offer and said their final price would be double that of the first offer.

A timeline for this case goes: 12/30, the public authorities in Philadelphia accept plaintiff's bid; 12/31, the plaintiff receives defendant's formal withdrawal in the mail; and on 1/2, the plaintiff accepts the public authority's offer, even though the wording of the contract was ambiguous and defendant continually refused to recognize or fulfill the contract. Plaintiff then brought suit for damages based on breach of contract.

A. Introduction

The topic of this chapter is (minimum) professional qualifications and professional liability. These two topics are closely related because they are two aspects of what it means to be a professional. One cost of being a recognized professional with special skills is a higher duty of care toward clients, and a greater likelihood of legal liability.

While much of the chapter focuses on actual or proposed qualifications, and asks the reader to evaluate them on their merits, the consideration of qualifications begins with the source of authority, and whether government should mandate qualifications. There is a vast difference between government established minimum qualifications, and a private organization (e.g, American Arbitration Association, Association of Family Mediators, SPIDR) requiring adherence by its members to the identical standard. Government regulation of ADR providers is already well established, either directly or because so many ADR providers are also members of licensed professions.

Government regulation of occupations is a topic that has been widely studied by economists, political scientists, sociologists, and others. It is commonly observed by outsiders that the primary beneficiaries of such regulation are the group being regulated rather than the public, for whose benefit and protection the regulation is supposedly undertaken. A typology of government regulation of occupations is followed by an article by Walter Gellhorn that discusses abuses of occupational licensure. Then, Rogers and McEwen discuss regulation of mediators.

The next topic is substantive qualifications for neutrals. Alison Taylor discusses standards for practitioners of family mediation, and Barbara Diamond reviews the qualifications and standards employed in various states. The Report of the NASD's Arbitration Policy Taskforce addresses the recruitment, selection, training, and evaluation of securities arbitrators focuses on a specific subject area and ADR procedure, but the issues and analysis are of general applicability. (Ethical standards for dispute resolution professionals is the topic of Chapter 20.)

Malpractice, an amalgam of tort and contract theories, is the primary basis for liability of professionals, including persons involved in dispute resolution. The ADR professional who works in the context of a court-related proceeding may be the beneficiary of (absolute) quasi-judicial immunity, or at least qualified immunity. In addition to protection for individual ADR professionals, the availability of immunity lends prestige to dispute resolution activities.

B. Should Government Regulate Dispute Resolution Professionals?

1. Typology of Approaches to Professional Regulation

The licensure or other government regulation of dispute resolution professionals is just one instance of the general category of professional regulation. In order to think sensibly about professional qualifications it is useful to adopt a widely accepted set of labels. Moving from the least to the most restrictive, these are registration, certification, and licensure. The discussion omits the often important revenue raising aspects of professional regulation.

a. Registration

Under a registration system, anyone who fits within a certain category must notify the state, and provide relevant individual and activity information. Often identifying information must be publicly displayed. Examples from the professions are difficult to find, because demonstrated competence and licensure are among the hallmarks of a profession. Taxi drivers commonly are required to have a registration, with a picture and identifying number, prominently displayed at a specified place in the taxi. Owners of automobiles are required to register them with the state, and to display an identifying plate supplied (sold) by the state. Firms without a permanent place of business might be required to register with the state, and provide information about who the owners are and where they can be found. In each instance, the basis for registration is to promote the general welfare by facilitating the recovery of lost property, preventing fraud, and identifying wrongful activity.

b. Certification

Under a certification system, government certifies that people have specified skills, but identical activities may be performed by uncertified persons. (This definition excludes non-government assertions of quality such as a "best buy" rating from Consumers Report, Newsweek's ranking of professional schools, or membership in exclusive professional organizations that admit only people with specified qualifications.)

Anyone may engage in the business of helping people with the design of a house, but in most states the title of "architect" is reserved for individuals who have met state certification standards. As with accountants and appraisers, this example is not a pure one because in each instance some work — typically the most complex, prestigious, and remunerative work — is open only to licensed professionals.

c. Licensure

Under a licensing scheme, the practice of activities ranging from law and medicine to barbering and cosmetology is limited to persons who have met the standards for licensure established by state law. While there may be questions at the outer limits of what constitutes the practice of law or barbering, it is clear that enchroachment on core activities by the unlicensed constitutes the unauthorized practice of law or barbering. The explosion of professional licensure in America, mostly at the state level, is detailed in the article by Walter Gellhorn that follows.

In many states, there is a system for lawyers to become specialists, which typically requires experience, passing a test, and then continuing education to maintain specialist status. Attorneys who meet these specialist standards may so identify themselves to the public, but other attorneys are not precluded from undertaking the same work as recognized specialists. The person who meets the state's standards for specialists is often said to be a "licensed" specialist, but that usage in inaccurate under the definitions used here. Such a specialist is *licensed* to be an attorney, an exclusionary category, but is *certified* as a specialist, because other attorneys are not excluded from doing the same work as specialists.

2. Walter Gellhorn, *The Abuse of Occupational Licensure*, 44 U. Chi. L. Rev. 6 (1976)*

[L]iterally hundreds of occupations are subject to licensing laws in one or more states. Possibly the founding fathers knew of restrictions in some of the new American states on the practices of law and medicine. They would, however, have been aghast to learn that in many parts of this country today aspiring bee keepers, embalmers, lightning rod salesmen, septic tank cleaners, taxidermists, and tree surgeons must obtain official approval before seeking the public's patronage. After examining the roster of those who must receive official permission to function, a cynic might conclude that virtually the only people who remain unlicensed in at least one of the United States are clergymen and university professors, presumably because they are nowhere taken seriously.

A consideration of the proliferation of occupational license requirements is especially timely because it may help in evaluating two contemporary currents of public policy. First,

---

*Reprinted with permission.

prominent politicians and public officials assert that too much economic activity is subject to regulation; they urge "regulatory reform," a code phrase meaning the reduction of regulation. Second, within the legal profession demand is mounting for some formal means of identifying "specialists" among lawyers.

I. THE BEGINNINGS OF "LEARNED PROFESSIONS"

At one time the learned professions were those of theology, law, and medicine. . . . The American legal profession has been regarded as unassailably "learned" since the early immigrants set foot on Plymouth Rock more than 350 years ago. In actuality, the expounders of law in those distant times were small farmers and craftsmen who acted upon vagrant memories of local customs believed to have been enforced in England by some anonymous magistrate, coupled with notions of propriety derived from the Bible. When the colonists in 1636 codified their laws, their compilation was, as the late Julius Goebel has said, a "crude imitation of inaccurately remembered things." The same characterization can fairly be applied to legal developments throughout the colonies, but the crude imitators and inaccurate rememberers nevertheless maintained their status as learned. . . .

II. THE PROLIFERATION OF LEARNED PROFESSIONS OR REASONABLE FACSIMILES THEREOF

In recent decades occupational licensing has grown explosively. One consequence has been a debilitation of the concept of a "profession" and a distortion of the idea that licensing should serve primarily as an instrument of social control to protect the public against unfit or unscrupulous practitioners.

If occupational licensing resulted simply in downgrading the word "profession" or in enlarging the ranks of the "learned," one would have small cause for alarm. After all, the complexities of modem life have created new demands for special training and perceptions. As long ago as 1956 a former Surgeon General of the United States noted that nurses and other health aides are called on to "master a body of knowledge greater in extent and usefulness for the care of the sick than all of the medical knowledge of a century ago. In addition, they have codes of ethics and possess techniques as exact as those of the brain surgeon." So one can understand why what had once been thought of as differences in kind between occupational levels are now often regarded as mere differences in degree; precisely defining the word "profession" is by no means easy.

Licensing has done far more than simply gratify the understandable status-longing of semi-skilled or specialized workers who, in Professor Merton's words, "want to acquire at least the outer appearance and preferably the inner substance of professional standards, values and education." It has also badly eroded the right to work, one of man's most precious liberties.

Licensing has only infrequently been imposed upon an occupation against its wishes. Unwelcomed licensure has indeed occurred, as when stockbrokers were brought under federal regulation in response to the financial scandals of 1929. In many more instances, however, licensing has been eagerly sought—always on the purported ground that licensure protects the uninformed public against incompetence or dishonesty, but invariably with the consequence that members of the licensed group become protected against competition from newcomers. That restricting access is the real purpose, and not merely a side effect, of many if not most successful campaigns to institute licensing schemes can scarcely be doubted. Licensing, imposed ostensibly to protect the public, almost always impedes only those who desire to enter the occupation or "profession;" those already in practice remain entrenched without a demonstration of fitness or probity. The self-interested proponents of a new licensing law generally constitute a more effective political force than the citizens who, if aware of the matter at all, have no special interest which moves them to organize in opposition.

The restrictive consequence of licensure is achieved in large part by making entry into the regulated occupation expensive in time or money or both. In Iowa, for example, a person who aspires to ease the pains of those who suffer from bunions and corns must have graduated from "a school of podiatry approved by the board of podiatry examiners" and must then be examined, according to the statute, "in the subjects of anatomy, chemistry, dermatology, diagnosis, pharmacy and materia medica, pathology, physiology, histology, bacteriology, neurology, . . . foot orthopedics, and others, as prescribed by the board." This does indeed sound imposing. One suspects, however, that the verbiage is of more benefit to bunion removers than to bunion sufferers.

In California a license to cut hair can be won only after the completion of a long apprenticeship, graduation from a barber college, and success in an examination that in past years has demanded knowledge of such esoteric things as the chemical composition of the bones and the name of the muscle that is inserted in the hyoid bone. Illinois purportedly tests a would-be barber's knowledge of, among other things, physiology, electricity, anatomy, and barber history. Fifty years ago not a single American state required a barber to attend a tuition-demanding "college" for the equivalent of an academic year. Now most of the states insist that new recruits to the hair-cutting profession receive institutionalized instruction in bacteriology; histology of the hair, skin, nails, muscles, and nerves; diseases of the skin, hair, glands, and nails; and other matters about which one may venture to guess few barbers are consulted. Most of the barber examining boards apparently draw their tests from a small booklet published by Milady Publishing Company, which also produces the textbook most barber colleges use because that single volume apparently reveals everything their students need to know to pass the examination. Plainly, a barber need not overburden his mind with scientific or theoretical profundities. The costly and time-consuming acquisition of artificial learning in a pseudo profession nevertheless blocks an occupational choice that might otherwise be available to the impecunious.

III. OCCUPATIONAL LICENSING AND COMPETITION

A. Irrelevancies as Barriers to Competition

Barbering has been used as a horrible example, but irrelevancies are by no means confined to any one of the new "professions." Years ago a Wisconsin legislator, after examining some of that state's occupational requirements, exclaimed sadly that as a practical matter, her child could no longer aspire to become a watchmaker, but fortunately could still qualify to seek the presidency of the United States. In some states virtually the only "profession" open to a once-convicted felon is that of burglar; he is barred from other activities because he is presumed to be a person of bad moral character, regardless of the nature of the felony or its relevance to his intended occupation. Until the courts finally called a halt, becoming a master plumber in Illinois took just a bit longer than becoming a Fellow of the American College of Surgeons.

Some restrictions on occupational choice are blatant absurdities. For example, Georgia insists that those who seek to be commercial photographers must pass with flying colors a Wasserman test for syphilis. At one time the Indiana Athletic Commission insisted that boxers and wrestlers take a loyalty oath before being allowed to enter the ring. Silliness like this is probably not motivated by anything so rational as a desire to discourage competition.

More often, however, the statutory constraints have had truly exclusionary intent and effect. These constraints include requirements that licensees be citizens or residents of a locality. Although these restrictions are probably unconstitutional, they are enforced until challenged. Some states insist that only an American citizen can qualify to become, for instance, a pharmacist, chiropodist, tree surgeon, embalmer, bill collector, or osteopath—evidencing a type of xenophobia which reached a fever pitch in state legislatures in the late 1930s when European refugees began arriving in large numbers during a time of job scarcity. Other laws provide that, regardless of national citizenship, a licensee must have been a resident of the license-issuing state for a substantial period of time—although the relationship between prior residence and occupational qualifications may be undiscoverable, as in the case of optometrists, accountants, masseurs, and dentists. One would suppose that lenses are ground and teeth are cleaned in essentially the same manner in different states, but the statutes pretend that one must have lived within the license-issuing state in order to understand its citizenry's needs. Occupational licenses have also been conditioned upon residency in political subdivisions smaller than a state. Twenty-eight states provide for the licensing of plumbers, but in most of these states the plumbers have managed to prevent licensing on a statewide basis. Instead, licenses are issued by the cities, which impose municipal residence requirements aimed at excluding "outsiders" from the local job market. Some state laws authorize counties and cities to say who may become an auctioneer, plumber, fortune teller, lawn-sprinkler installer, and stationary engineer, among other "professions" for which residence is made a sine qua non. Outsiders, no matter how highly skilled or experienced, are barred by reason of not being able to claim a narrowly localized experience.

Americans have traditionally thought themselves free to pursue happiness wherever it might be found. Mobility . . . has been a characteristic of our society, and most of us think it has made for a healthier country, one in which parochialism has yielded to the inflow of new populations, new ideas, new techniques. Local licensure tends in the opposite direction, toward enclosure within fixed boundaries. Requirements unrelated to suitability and proficiency probably will not withstand judicial scrutiny, but until a frustrated applicant chooses to take a case to court—or until conscientious legislators repeal obnoxiously discriminatory statutes—the bad laws remain as threats to occupational freedom.

All reasonably sophisticated persons know that a well-knit special interest group is likely to prevail over an amorphous "public" whose members are dispersed and, as individuals, are not in sharp conflict with the organized interest. Of course many special interests perceive themselves as nurturers of the public interest rather than as self-seekers. The line between the common weal and one's own is not always easily drawn. But occupational licensing has typically brought higher status for the producer of services at the price of higher costs to the consumer; it has reduced competition; it has narrowed opportunity for aspiring youth by increasing the costs of entry into a desired occupational career; it has artificially segmented skills so that needed services, like health care, are increasingly difficult to supply economically; it has fostered the cynical view that unethical practices will prevail unless those entrenched in a profession are assured of high incomes; and it has caused a proliferation of official administrative bodies, most of them staffed by persons drawn from and devoted to furthering the interests of the licensed occupations themselves.

Moreover . . . members of ethnic minorities are systematically discouraged from becoming licensees by irrelevant requirements. Licensing tests are often administered solely in English, so that Spanish-speaking citizens and foreign-born residents encounter special difficulty. In some instances, indeed, written tests may be altogether inapposite means of determining whether an applicant possesses a requisite degree of skill. Many economically deprived young people cannot easily meet the qualifications demanded of applicants, such as paying tuition to pseudo-professional schools or undergoing needlessly prolonged periods of apprenticeship. Recent years have seen hard won progress in overcoming racial discrimination in private employment. Discrimination, as the courts have found, has been strongly reinforced by ostensibly objective tests which are actually unrelated to successful job performance, and employers have been ordered to abandon this kind of testing. The time is ripe for those who care about social justice to attack licensing regulations which, with all the force of government, authorize similarly obnoxious entry examinations and thus achieve discrimination behind the facade of protecting the public.

B. Limits of Antitrust Remedies

Present antitrust laws may be ineffective in overcoming the significant anticompetitive consequences of laws that make access to an occupation burdensome and impose restraints upon those who have managed to gain a license. In 1943 the Supreme Court held [in *Parker v. Brown,* 317 U.S. 341] that the antitrust statutes are aimed at private, not state, action, and ruled that a California statute constricting the competitive marketing of raisins immunized behavior the antitrust laws would otherwise have forbidden. . . . [T]he state action defense should not, however, bar the use of antitrust laws against restrictive practices adopted voluntarily within a licensed occupation. The antitrust laws may not reach an anticompetitive economic policy embedded in a state's statute, but they can and do reach anticompetitive policy choices made by licensees, perhaps without a state's opposition and yet not by its direction. A state must command, not merely permit, a restraint of trade in order to immunize it against federal antitrust laws.

This lesson was taught the legal profession in 1975, when the Supreme Court in *Goldfarb v. Virginia State Bar* [421 U.S. 773] held that a bar association's minimum fee schedule violated the Sherman Act's prohibition of combinations in restraint of trade. How often the lesson may have to be taught to others remains to be seen. The occupational licensing statutes to which this article has been addressed tend to reduce competition, but they rarely acknowledge this to be their purpose—and even less often do they direct licensees to submit to explicitly anticompetitive controls for monopolistic purposes. The restrictive practices of licensed groups are usually designed within the groups, rather than imposed on them from the outside. To the extent that this is so, *Parker v. Brown* gives no protection against the antitrust laws, for the Supreme Court has differentiated between state action and private action wearing a mask.

IV. LAWYERS, SPECIALIZATION, AND CONTINUING LEGAL EDUCATION

The prudence as well as the legality of recent proposals to categorize lawyers and to require their periodic participation in formal educational programs may be questioned. The specialization issue is likely to prove difficult. As a result of the *Goldfarb* case and controversy concerning other groups' restraints upon the advertising of services and costs, the legal profession has cautiously modified its traditional insistence that speaking about oneself in a tone louder than a whisper is unethical. In 1976 for the first time the American Bar Association voted that a lawyer should be permitted to indicate "in dignified form" in professional announcements and in the yellow pages of telephone directories his preferred areas of practice and his educational background. The Association frowns upon a lawyer's identifying himself as a "specialist" unless he has met the requirements of a state program of certification.

Whether, when, and how lawyers should be allowed to assert that they have special qualifications are still unresolved questions. Genuinely high-minded and disinterested persons have urged that formal identification of specialists is needed to protect uninformed laymen against incompetent, inefficient, or inadequately experienced lawyers who may disserve their clients' best interests. They think that lawyers should emulate doctors in drawing more distinct lines than now separate specialists and general practitioners.

Thirty-three varieties of medical specialists can now be recognized because they have achieved "board certification." A licensed physician who wishes to be formally identified as equipped to practice in one of these thirty-three areas of specialization must complete additional training and survive an examination by the certifying agency, composed of persons already certified. To be sure, certification is not a prerequisite of a generalist's performing a specialist's task. Many hospitals, however, make their facilities available only to those who possess board certification, and thus the incentive to gain board approval has been strong in the medical profession.

Everyone within the legal profession knows that specialization exists. Attorneys are frequently and familiarly identified, by their colleagues in the profession and by themselves, as tax lawyers or commercial lawyers or corporate lawyers or labor lawyers or communications lawyers or criminal lawyers or divorce lawyers—the list could be elongated far beyond the thirty-three specialists the doctors have proclaimed. A question of lively interest to the profession is whether the de facto specialization of today, acquired freely either by explicit design or simply through the vicissitudes of practice, should in the future be attested through certification. Tension exists between the laudable desire to ensure the efficient rendition of professional services to clients and the not necessarily intended likelihood that certification will reduce competition among lawyers, discourage well qualified but uncertified persons from performing functions within the zone of a "specialization," and thus increase the costliness of legal services. Were no lawyer permitted to identify himself as equipped to engage in a special type of practice until he had been certified, exclusivity would be powerfully stimulated. This seems the probable outcome if formal certification spreads widely.

The legal profession must take great care not to emulate the many occupational groups that have managed to convert licensure from a sharp weapon of public defense into a blunt instrument of self-enrichment. Perhaps instead of continuing toward specialist certification, the bar should permit each member to inform the public, if the member chooses, about the kinds of legal service he or she is prepared to render. Misrepresentation of qualifications or demonstrated incompetence should of course be deemed cause for disciplinary action. Proceedings aimed at individual malefactors or bumblers might more meaningfully protect the public than would the creation of clusters of self-anointed specialists. In the past lawyers have been backward about taking steps against unworthy members of their own profession. This seems to be characteristic of professional people in general; they criticize one another's shortcomings in private, but are rather resistant to disciplining the unfit and the unscrupulous in public proceedings. If, however, the professions are to continue to enjoy the autonomy they so highly prize, they will have to accept more fully the responsibility implicit in a privileged status.

The advocacy of mandatory continuing legal education, sometimes linked with proposals concerning specialist certification, has also become clamorous. [Many] states have already approved mandatory systems intended (as their proponents say) to maintain high levels of professional competence; similar plans are said to be under serious consideration in more than half the states. A common feature of the plans is that all licensed lawyers must annually enroll for a stated number of hours in formal course work, in programs approved by a state supervisory body.

The efficacy of this kind of compulsory education is dubious. Advocates of forced schooling have at times ignored the expense involved, have overlooked the reality that sitting in lecture halls for say, fifteen hours a year may not be a highly productive mental exercise, and have made assumptions about the cause and cure of professional inadequacies without verifying them by empirical studies. Moreover, mandatory continuing legal education involves large hidden social costs. . . . Obviously, costliness does not show worthlessness. Still, lawyers should be closely attentive to the experience of other licensees lest they end by disserving the public interest they purportedly safeguard.

V. CONCLUSION

If men were angels, as has been remarked, external controls over their conduct would be superfluous. Since the most recent census fails to disclose a significant increase in the angelic population, I do not join those who advocate ending occupational licensing altogether. Painful economic experiences might ultimately lead consumers of services to locate the most efficient, most trustworthy suppliers. Meanwhile, however, many persons would suffer avoidable wounds to person or purse. The anonymity of a largely urbanized American society prevents the kind of informed choice which may have been possible when clients, patients, and customers could rely with reasonable confidence upon neighbors' opinions of professionals and tradesmen. For that reason I accept the view that in some occupations some kind of quality control may be needed to protect the uninformed against blatant incompetents, wily charlatans, and persons whose past delinquencies suggest the probability of future corrupt conduct.

Everything is, however, a matter of degree. I am comforted by the thought that surgeons and structural engineers must pass scrutiny by somebody more knowledgeable than I am or am likely to become about their qualifications. On the other hand, I think it absurd to set up elaborate mechanisms as precautions against my being dissatisfied with the way my hair has been cut, my toenails trimmed, my muscles kneaded, my hearing aid fitted, or my drains unclogged. Only the credulous can conclude that licensure is in the main intended to protect the public rather than those who have been licensed or, perhaps in some instances, those who do the licensing.

To say that licensing has been abused and overused is not to say that prophylactic administration should be abandoned. I do not advocate reviving the doctrine of caveat emptor, nor do I, as a realist, suppose for a minute that customers and clients who have been ill served can be made whole by lawsuits against their miscreant servitors. Litigation is too unwieldly to meet the needs of those who have suffered minor injuries. What are needed are measures that will provide protection against those demonstrably deficient in capability or integrity without in the process creating artificial limitations upon career choices, work opportunities, and stimuli to provide superior service at lesser cost. Among these protective measures are permissive certification and mandatory registration.

Permissive certification may be suitable when a program of prior training or a demonstration of an objectively measurable degree of skill can be regarded as a genuine precondition of a person's claiming an occupational status. For example, some state laws provide that before a person identifies himself as an "architect," he must have been certified as one who deserves that title because he has given proof of his education and capability. These laws do not, however, bar others from engaging in the work architects do; those who are uncertified may not call themselves "architects," but they may do work of an architectural nature without risking prosecution for engaging in the "unauthorized practice" of a licensed occupation. Certification of this kind permits pertinently defined expectations, so that the consuming public can differentiate between a self-styled expert and a person whose qualifications have been passed on by a state authority. Yet, unlike licensure, this control mechanism does not wholly withdraw occupational opportunity from persons who, though unable to meet all the requirements of certification (for example, formal education), may be competent.

A far more comprehensive regulatory device is the simple registration of anyone who desires to receive a particular occupational license, with the automatic issuance of the license upon registration. Engaging in the occupation without a license, or obtaining it by misrepresentation, would be made a serious offense, in order to stimulate prompt and accurate registration. An appropriate state agency, not linked with an occupational group, would be created to receive complaints against licensees, investigate them, and, if objectionable conduct is found, initiate proceedings looking toward revocation, suspension, or other appropriate discipline by a court or a special tribunal.

A plan of this nature would, I believe, end the present abuse of licensure that serves selfish interests by constricting occupational freedom. It would recapture the public power now delegated to multiple licensing boards whose members are drawn from and owe allegiance to the occupations they supposedly regulate in the public interest. It would require that licensees be subject to stern discipline, but only after carefully formulated charges, fair hearings, and impartial determinations, untainted by suspicion that the determiners' self-interest has influenced their judgment. It would take away the eligibility of those whose occupational unworthiness could be demonstrated, but would not, as so many licensing laws now do, place artificial roadblocks in the path of work opportunities or squelch career aspirations by treating predictive opinions as final judgments.

3. Comments and Questions

a. Walter Gellhorn is perhaps the leading administrative law teacher and scholar in America over the last fifty years (which is to say, from the inception of modern administrative law). He clearly is not reflexively opposed to government regulation or intervention in economic activity.

b. A common criticism of professional licensure is that the real beneficiaries are not the public but the profession, because it limits entry and thus results in higher prices. Licensure also provides a form of group organization, what in other contexts might be called a trade union, which also helps to raise the income of the profession and the costs to the public that is supposedly being protected.

c. None of these ideas are new. Over 200 years ago, Adam Smith observed: "People of the same occupation seldom meet together, even for merriment and diversion, but the conversation ends in a conspiracy against the public, or in some contrivance to raise prices."

d. Occupational licensure is not simply a matter of economic policy, but also a fundamental limitation on individual freedom. As Milton Friedman, himself an economist, noted:

> The overthrow of the medieval guild system was an indispensible early step in the rise of freedom in the Western world. It was a sign of the triumph of liberal ideas, and widely recognized as such. . . . [B]y the mid-nineteenth century . . . [individuals] could pursue whatever trade or occupation they wished without the by-your-leave of any governmental or quasi-governmental authority.

Milton Friedman, CAPITALISM AND FREEDOM 137 (1962).

4. Nancy H. Rogers & Craig A. McEwen, MEDIATION LAW, POLICY & PRACTICE §§ 11:04 to 11:07 (2d ed. 1994)*

§ 11:04. Mediator Certification and Continuing Accountability

Those who see value in holding the mediator accountable for the fairness, quality, and effectiveness of the process have sometimes advocated a continuing oversight of mediators. For example, the Standards for Court-Connected Mediation Programs recommend continued monitoring with a possibility of removing mediators from a mediator roster.

Although mediators remain unlicensed, several states do certify mediators in some contexts. In 1989 New Hampshire created statutory procedures for certifying marital mediators and mediation programs and a certification board to discipline those in violation of standards set by that board. The benefits of certification for the mediators and programs include the ability to use the title "certified mediator," to avoid subpoena under some circumstances, and to have court recognition for marital mediations. Florida now certifies a variety of types of mediators, who then may receive court referrals. Utah has created a voluntary certification program for dispute resolution pronders. A new North Carolina statute combines this oversight with stringent educational requirements for mediators, eliminating all but those with a master's degree in a human relations discipline from the pool of custody and visitation mediators. Voluntary associations, such as the Society of Professionals in Dispute Resolution, are also creating certification programs to enforce association standards.

Although such efforts precede agreement in the field as to what constitutes malfeasance or lack of competence, they have a positive aspect, compared to qualifications, because they do not dramatically restrict entry into the field for those capable persons seeking to become mediators.

§ 11:05. Procedural Requirements.

The forms of regulation described thus far focus on the mediator. They are based on a view that, if one can weed out all but the good mediators and provide incentives for them to perform well, then mediation programs will be effective, fair, and of high quality. A different, perhaps complementary, approach, is to focus regulation on the procedures surrounding the

*Reprinted with permission.

mediations themselves. A number of states have taken a procedural approach. For example, case selection procedures may remove cases for which mediation is unlikely to be helpful or might result in unfairness. Requirements that parties be permitted to bring counsel or that unrepresented parties may opt out of mediation are also geared to fairness of the process. Further, parties are sometimes informed about the limitations of mediation and sometimes are given an advocate.

These and other procedural provisions neither narrow the pool of mediators nor interfere with the flexibility provided the mediator. Thus, they seem less likely to be costly than qualifications, malpractice liability, and certification. Still, they, like other regulatory approaches, have only a short track record and have been given little systematic study.

§ 11:06. Criteria for Public Funding and Other Quality Control Measures.

A few other regulatory approaches have been employed. For example on rare occasions, regulation, beyond civil liability, certifications, and qualifications, is provided by a variety of criminal penalties for mediators. Thus, for example, the U.S. Community Services mediator who unlawfully discloses mediation information is criminally liable. This drastic penalty may be designed to assure parties that information will not be disclosed to its institutional home, the U.S. Justice Department. In a more novel statute, the individual who acts for compensation as a mediator pursuant to the Minnesota Civil Mediation Act may be held criminally liable for failing to provide the parties with a written statement of "educational background and relevant training and experience in the field." In each case, the criminal penalties are unnecessarily severe for acts which seem unlikely to cause serious harm.

Another method of enforcing standards in mediation is through criteria for funding or court referrals. For example, funding may be limited to programs whose mediators are supervised in certain ways and who monitor the quality of the mediation provided. The criteria are set variously by statute or court rule. Still another approach has been to set aside the mediated agreement in "substandard" mediations. A New York trial court did just that, where the conduct of a landlord-tenant mediation made informed consent unlikely.

§ 11:07. Conclusion.

Recent statutes related to publicly funded or court annexed mediation have preserved the federal labor concept of a high quality mediation that requires the mediator to be free from conflict of interest, maintain confidentiality to the extent permitted by law, assist in settlement only when it is the parties' free choice, and act with integrity. Moreover, some of these laws have codified the practices existing in labor programs to be attentive to the training of mediators. However, the recent enactments have sometimes restricted entry to the field and added duties for the mediator in an effort to assure higher quality, fairness, and effectiveness.

Caution is warranted in creating new regulation of mediators. Placing unclear and inconsistent duties in laws may lead mediators to worry unnecessarily about the risk of liability and dissuade able people from acting as mediators. The imposition of required warnings may diminish mediation's informality. Some mediator qualifications may unduly raise expenses and reduce the diversity of the mediator pool. If they contribute little to the quality of mediation, this form of regulation is not justified.

These standard-setting laws may have less impact on the quality of mediation than do other legal provisions not thought to relate to quality. For example, funding schemes that put a premium on settlement rates reduce the likelihood that the mediator will take time to be certain all parties evaluate potential settlements carefully. Similarly, limitations on practice of law by mediators may prevent them from providing information useful in the evaluation of the settlement, even if they are inclined to do so. Thus, lawmakers should be attentive to how mediation laws affect the quality of mediation, even when the laws are not focused on establishing mediation standards.

5. Comments and Questions

a. Most federal government employees are potentially subject to criminal sanctions for improper disclosure of confidential information. At the Internal Revenue Service and enforcement agencies these standards are of real importance, but criminal sanctions are almost never imposed. How many FMCS or other federal employees do you think have spent even one night in jail for improper disclosure of information?

b. Do you favor government regulation of mediation? If so, what form should that regulation take? Should the federal government establish minimum standards for mediators that it hires, either as employees or consultants? If so, to what extent should these standards be uniform, and to what extent should they be determined at the agency level?

c. Serious professional standards require a bureaucracy to test for initial competence, monitor continuing competence, and enforce professional standards. Preventing unauthorized practice is another common undertaking of professional regulation. Is the primary beneficiary the public or the profession? Typically the state agency created for professional regulation is controlled by persons who are members of the regulated profession. Is this an example of what the public administration and administrative law literature calls "the capture thesis?" (The hypothesis is that agencies are to an important extent "captured" by the interests they were supposedly created to regulate.)

C. Qualifications for Neutrals

1. Alison Taylor, *The Four Foundations of Family Mediation: Implications for Training and Certification*, 12 Mediation Quarterly 77 (1994)*

Imagine for a moment a grand building supported by a pillar at each of the four corners, with several doors through which people are entering. All of these doors lead into a central room where people are conversing intensely. The entire edifice is supported by the four massive pillars of its foundation. If any one of these foundational supports were missing, the entire building would be skewed, unsteady, and able to collapse at any moment.

Now imagine that there are rulemakers who are placing restrictions about who can come into the building, and what they need to bring with them as proof that they belong. The rulemakers have installed gatekeepers at each of the doors, who are to make sure that everyone who gains access to the room has the same set of proof. Everyone in the room is supposed to have done the same things before the gatekeepers will allow them into the room.

Let us also imagine that the gatekeepers and rulemakers are disagreeing about what proof is needed, and which door is the best through which to enter, since each doorway represents a different background and different set of experiences and knowledges. There is a struggle among the rulemakers and the gatekeepers about which will be the only door that opens for entry.

Inside the common room, there are rumors that each person must now prove his or her right to be there, even though all of them showed the right proof to the gatekeepers in order to enter. Some of the conversations we hear in the room and even outside the doors sound like this: "Will we be thrust out of the room if we are not found to be competent?" "Who will determine our competency?" "Do we really need to have our competency measured if we met all of the official requirements that the rulemakers set and showed proof to the gatekeepers?" "If we are going to have to prove our competency now that we are in, why did we even need to show our proof to enter?" "Shouldn't we make the rules tougher, so fewer get in?"

Now imagine that outside the building are officers of the state, who are examining the rules used to get into the building to see if they are adequate. Some of the officers are proposing a different set of rules, and some of these require more things to be shown, because the officers do not want too many people in the building. Some of the proposed new rules require fewer things to do for entry, because the officers are afraid that some people will not be able to obtain the necessary proof and will be excluded from the building. Most of these officers of the state have never done the work that those inside the building have done and may not be listening to what the rulemakers, the gatekeepers, or the people inside the building have to say. They are only speaking to other officers from other states, comparing and making their proposal different from those of the other states. Some are proposing a uniform set of rules.

Now let us look at the crowd outside the doors. Some want into the room because they believe that it will strengthen their ability to make money, since then they can advertise that they have shown their proof and are special members, having done all that was required at the time. Others want access to the room because they want to be able to carry on a dialogue with the others in the room who came in through a different door and path and who therefore have a different view of the work they all do. Some want into the building because they fear if they do not get in now they will not be able to get in later. Others do not know why they want in, but they heard about the rules and thought they would see if it made any difference to be in the room.

Outside the building, some people are looking around for the next road show to go by, offering to teach them in one week all they need to know to get in the door. Some have heard that there are other places where they can get what is needed for entry through the door, but there is no list posted anywhere, and so there is a long line at the telephone to call around for that information.

Others see the building, see how long the line is, look at the rules, and decide that they do not want to go into the room, or feel that they cannot comply with all of the requirements to secure the proof to show the gatekeepers, so they walk away from the building. Others are talking with the officers of the state to try to change the rules so that they do not have to go in at all. Some find out they do not need to go in. In fact, they can open up a shop right now and offer their services with little or no training, as long as they are not hired by the state to do the work. Some are trying to build another building with another set of rules to enter. There is no identifiable place where they can find out what it is really like inside the building.

In my view this situation is analogous to the current state of family mediation, our professional society, and the ongoing dialogue within the Association of Family Mediation (AFM) about the education and training requirements for practitioner member status and the proposed voluntary certification. Family mediation is the building, and the AFM practitioner members are inside.

Current Rules

Recently, the AFM newsletter published the rules for practitioner member status, what people must do to get in the door, and what they show to the gatekeepers. Under these rules, a mediator must have documented training that includes "a substantive knowledge base," unspecified except for the requirement of five hours each on the following topics: psychological issues of separation, divorce, and family dynamics; issues and needs of children in divorce; family economics; and conflict resolution theory and mediation process. While these seem like perfectly adequate rules to ensure that everyone in the room can talk to one another about these topics, no matter which path they took to get there or which door they entered, these requirements seem to ignore the fact that the entire building rests on foundations that include more than five hours of information and skill for each of these topics.

Competency Certification, and State Licensure

None of the current AFM practitioner member requirements entail a demonstration of competency, yet the proposed voluntary certification process we have started will require it. Competency is based on both knowledge and skill, and yet we have not yet as a group articulated the essential knowledge or the depth of those topics. We cannot articulate what every family mediator knows or should know. We have not yet solidified all the skill-based interventions and techniques used by family mediators. While there are books and tapes that try to explain the specific techniques that individual mediators use, there is not yet a consensus that all mediators, given the same case and clients, would be expected to handle the case the same way. Our standards of practice from AFM, Association of Family and Conciliation Courts, and other groups are so general that they give no guidance on the actual practice of family mediation. Some of us are hoping that professional psychometrists can help us by standardizing these items in ways generally accepted as valid and reliable in our society. But we cannot teach, nor can we expect people to produce for evaluation of their competency, that which we cannot or have not yet articulated, named, or categorized. Until we all recognize with some certainty the process or technique of choice, rather than of personal style or preference, we cannot compile a comprehensive set of expectations that translates into personal and professional competency.

Voluntary certification through AFM at this point in time may be seen as a stamp-of-approval process from one's peers, showing that one can function similarly and adequately compared to everyone else in the room. Such peer review may become standardized and its input worthwhile, both for the mediator undergoing it as well as for the perception of the profession as self-regulating, consistent, and capable of quality assurance. It is like testing each car at the end of the assembly line to see if it runs. The test will tell us if it meets the standard, but this process will not tell us which car works better than another.

In order for a review of competency to be effective for the family mediator who is experiencing it, and for the profession in general, the criteria need to be well defined and taught as part of the training and apprenticeship process. Because competency is only relative to that of others within the building, it may not relate to the larger knowledge bases on which it rests, and it will evolve over time, as the sophistication level in the room develops. In some ways, a competency review is like asking all the people already in the room to show why they should not be thrown out, despite the fact that they complied with all the requirements to come in.

Voluntary certification through AFM, even though available to non-AFM members, will not touch the issue of those outside the room who reject it or cannot qualify to be in the room. It will not necessarily protect the consumer of mediation services, as perhaps the officers of the state may wish, since it may not be required of all mediators who practice family mediation within a jurisdiction or state, even though some hiring authorities and states may require it. As a voluntary process, it will only appeal to those who have enough ethical or business sense to subject themselves to it. It in many ways is like preaching to the enlightened.

Voluntary certification is causing ripples of discontent and anxiety and the program will be slow to implement. Unless it is envisioned as a final stage of teaching, comparing one person's production to another's, rather than as a regulatory mechanism, voluntary certification is likely to fall short of its promise. If we view it as a final learning tool, or as a quality check, then we will allow people several chances, give them specific feedback for improvement, and provide training opportunities to see others at a level of competence from which we can derive the criteria of competence we are seeking as a group. If, however, we allow voluntary certification to become another hoop, a regulatory process, a personal marketing tool, or a process that is redundant, it will discourage growth and development of this field.

For these reasons, if we plan to test mediators by using certain criteria, the trainers of mediators need to know what the criteria are so that all AFM approved trainings and trainings used to meet AFM requirements will teach to those criteria. This is clearly planned once there is specification of criteria. The current rate of approved AFM trainings does not ensure this, since there are wide disparities between the content and process used to teach current AFM-approved trainings, and many applicants for practitioner member status have received their training in programs that are not related to the AFM requirements. In many ways, the more we concentrate on rulemaking and gatekeeping to get in the door (the practitioner member requirements), and the need to double check our own skills by testing those who are already in the room (voluntary certification), the more we lose track of the foundations on which this building rests — foundations that should be part of the full education and training process for anyone wishing to do this work.

Four Pillars of Knowledge

Mediation is an interdisciplinary field and is most often a second career for practitioners. We each start from a different profession or origin and bring unique knowledge and skills to our work. Each one of those sets of knowledge and skills is a pillar of our own, which supports our own mediation practice. But a building that rests on one central pillar is a building that can be toppled easily. It is incumbent on us all to complete our personal foundations by gaining the other pillars of knowledge that were missing in our education process. There is more than one knowledge base we need to master in order to practice family mediation at the level of expertise necessary to work adequately for all clients.

- Mediation, conflict resolution, and negotiation processes;
- Legal and financial knowledge and processes;
- Adult, child, and family development (historical, normal, and assessment);

- Helping professional skills (communications, interviewing, referral, case management, collaboration with other professionals, and strategic case planning).

Problems in Education and Training of These Foundations

From my experience as a trainer in an AFM-approved course, as an individual supervisor of many professional interns, and as an AFM-approved consultant who has worked with both new and experienced mediators who have "been in the room for a while" and as a mediator who has worked in both public and private practice, I know that effective competent family mediators need all four of these knowledge-skill bases in order to construct their own practices. I also realize each time I train a new cadre of potential mediators how very limited the knowledge and skill training can be in a setting of forty, fifty-four, or sixty hours, or even as a comprehensive internship program consisting of three terms of content and nine months of experience with supervision. While some aspects of family mediation training can be accomplished in the short format, in most forty- to sixty-hour trainings the knowledge bases are only approached in a cursory way, even when augmented with extensive reading assignments. The skill development is disadvantaged by the lack of experimental learning with direct supervision, since most forty- to sixty-hour trainings do not include actual case experience with direct feedback. Unless these components are added after the training, the training is inadequate to produce true competency for independent practice.

It is true that short training is inadequate no matter what the profession of origin of the mediator prior to training. I have worked with mediators who were highly skilled professionals in the areas of law, family therapy, communications, social work, counseling, psychology, and education, all of which brought a richness to their work with families and individuals needing mediation for disputes. Until they became deeply involved in, not just conversant with, all four pillars, they were not able to respond appropriately to family mediation cases. We need to be cross-training ourselves, without having to take multiple master's degrees, as some mediators have done. We need to have long-term learning in these foundations, not just short-term "smorgasbord" tastes that get us in the door but do not help us with the work. Pretending that we can know, for example, child development, family law, communication techniques, and assessment of individuals in forty to sixty hours belies our development of disciplines that require years of study in order to meet their views of sufficiency in knowledge and skill.

Yet out of the voiced concern of the Society of Professionals in Dispute Resolution for equity, parity, inclusion, and other noble concepts and the belief that no one entity, discipline, or education curriculum should become the exclusive path through the door of this building, we have tried to set the standards for inclusion at such a low level as to deny the depth of the foundation. Some people lacking these foundations have been seen walking through the door. This is why we now feel the need to check everyone in the room with the voluntary certification process, and why legislators have provided licensure, certification, or approval in some states to protect the public against those who would try to do this work unprepared for its complexity.

Potential mediators who need initial training are the last group to call for increased standards for training, education, and skill competence. Where there is a potential market with an economic interest there are many who will have something to sell. If with minimal cost and energy people can hang out a new shingle and receive customers, it serves their interests to keep the standards low and the availability high. When one learns that a new source of income in hard economic times may be attainable with minimal retraining and personal investment in acquiring the foundational concepts and skills, it is natural to promote the minimization of rules in order to personally qualify.

No single discipline currently taught as an organized program duplicates the foundations of knowledge and skill necessary to be a family mediator who is adequately equipped to handle all cases that could walk through the door. Even such excellent, creative new programs as the Conflict Resolution Program of Antioch rely on the students to secure adequate instruction by selecting or creating options within their area or ability to travel, rather than create a set of core courses available at one site for those who wish to use mediation in this family mediation path. While some graduate programs in law, sociology, social work, and conflict resolution have added family mediation courses to their offerings, one such course in a degree program will not give the student the depth necessary in all four foundations.

For example, a law school may offer a family mediation course yet not require as a prerequisite a course on child development. That single course may lull students into believing that they are now qualified to offer family mediation as part of their law practices. Such mediators often do not voluntarily join AFM or become practitioner members. Nor are any restrictions imposed on them in states where mediation in the private sector is yet unregulated. For example, in the state of Oregon, there are no minimum qualifications or certification or licensure of anyone doing family mediation in the private sector. The minimum qualifications in Oregon for receiving court referrals as a listed domestic relations mediator under the new civil mediation administrative rules are the standard training and observation or participation in only three cases, or thirty hours, related to children; in contrast, the minimum qualifications for a court-connected domestic relations mediator working with the same kinds of cases, are significantly higher in education, training, experience, and continuing education expectations. This triple standard not only confuses potential mediators but also encourages people to meet the lowest, rather than the highest possible standards. Legally trained mediators may be able to practice family mediation in the public and private sectors, and may have excellent "people work" from the pillar of helping professional skills, but they often need more information and greater skill in human development and assessment.

Similar career transitions from family therapy can leave human services mediators without sufficient knowledge of their own states' rules on child support, financial division, and legal process. Mediators from family therapy backgrounds usually have been trained extensively in the helping professional skills and the human development foundations, but they lack the pillar of law and finance as well that of negotiation and conflict resolution. Practitioners who come from education and communication backgrounds usually need additional knowledge and skill in conflict resolution, negotiation, and law and finance. Everyone needs it all.

In many states, cosmetologists, food handlers, barbers, and butchers must go through more hours of training than are required of family mediators and must demonstrate their competency through testing and undergo certification, licensure, and inspection. Plumbers and other tradespersons must go through apprenticeships, but family mediators can start to practice without any apprenticeship or mentoring. How can we continue to insist that short term training is adequate? How does this serve the public interest, the needs of this field, and most important, the needs of the families with whom we work? How can AFM, as one of the professional organizations directly interested in and affected by this condition, offer only voluntary certification, someday, as a solution? How can we expect psychometrists to adequately prepare a valid, reliable paper-and-pencil qualifying test when we cannot yet state with certainty the foundational concepts, skills, and techniques needed when applied to given client-situation types?

Recommendations

While general mediation skills are life skills, transferable to many settings, disputes, and job descriptions, acquisition of the knowledge and skills necessary to be an effective family mediator in helping children and adults with issues that profoundly impact their families depends on more than cursory training. Whether or not this field becomes a "real" profession (which has as its hallmarks a body of knowledge in which all members are educated, a recognized way of transmitting this body of knowledge, and a way of evaluating practitioners of the profession), we need at least to work together as an organization representing the most professional among us to delimit and develop these three hallmarks for family mediation.

Define Core Knowledge and Skills. Instead of trying to guard the AFM door, or set up new practitioner member entry requirements, or look over one another's shoulders once we are inside and develop voluntary certification, we as a professional-level body whose members are among the most knowledgeable about the work should outline what every family mediator really needs to know and do, and what background information we all need in order to be effective in our work. We need more than a set of requirements to be in our group. We need to delineate our field, before we are told by legislators and others with little practical experience what is necessary and sufficient, and what constitutes competency. We need to solicit our own membership to secure vital information that comprehensively covers our knowledge and skill. We need to collate and define our approaches so that we can teach them to others and use them as the criteria for evaluation of competence, prior to instituting a competency-based voluntary certification process. We are really the only ones who can do these tasks well, not the legislators, the psychometrists, the trainers, or the educators.

Create Comprehensive Training and Experience. We must create educational opportunities for ourselves and for potential family mediators. We have historically supported annual conferences that bring new ideas and skills to practitioners, but not all of us can attend, and potential mediators need a more stable, defined curriculum than what is decided on by our conference committee. We should take it as a central task for our organization to work with universities and existing programs to create the kind of course work in all four foundational areas where potential mediators and current mediators can secure what they need by tapping into extension courses, continuing education departments and the disciplines of law, social work, counseling and psychology, sociology, and marriage and family therapy, we can utilize the existing resources of graduate schools and make them more accessible to us. For example, courses usually taught as upper-level selections for counselors, social workers, educators, and psychologists can and should be audited by those who know they need additional study in the pillar of human development.

Instead of trying to fold into our mediator training five hours of "the issues and needs of children in divorce," we should be finding or developing comprehensive courses on child development. We should also develop specialized courses that speak to our unique knowledge base, such as child support calculations and divorce research. We need to help universities create comprehensive programs to meet all the requirements for competency, knowledge, and experience. Such programs could be set up with a core set of family mediation courses, with access to needed additional courses and with a mediation experience under direct supervision that would help the potential mediator achieve the kind of personal competency we are seeking.

Upgrade Our Own Knowledge and Skills. We should reexamine our personal knowledge and skill assets and deficits and try to strengthen areas of weakness through supplementary supervision, continuing education, and directed reading. If I assess that I do not know all I should about a particular topic, or my knowledge base is out of date, I should be reading good quality texts, even if I cannot find continuing education offerings or classes to take. The AFM bookstore is a boon to finding resources; but if time and money are limited, I would like my professional society to compile a list of recommended books that the majority of mediators have read and found helpful or that seem fundamental in each of the four major topic areas. Finding this level of consensus will help us continue to develop our field.

In addition, to broaden our foundations, those of us who find journal articles in other disciplines that seem noteworthy should suggest them to others in an effort to create more interdisciplinary exchange. AFM could also be instrumental in providing videotapes of presentations worthy of dissemination as national continuing education material and making these tapes available to members without an entrepreneurial economic incentive. In this way we could create a better sense of common thought.

Create a National Standard for Family Mediators. We should eliminate the practitioner member status and make the certification process a combination of competency, experience, and adequate knowledge. We should not be allowing a specialized status of practitioner member that implies competency if we cannot reasonably ensure it. We should stop thinking of training by the hour and require documentation of adequate course work in all four foundational bases. If someone passes a graduate-level course on child development, or on conflict resolution, negotiation, or family law we should accept that as meeting the requirement rather than require an arbitrary number of training hours.

If we accept that competence is made up of what one knows and what one can do, we should make sure that certification includes both components. Members wishing to be certified should submit not only documentation of attendance at courses and training on the outlined body of knowledge but also a videotape for review by three AFM-approved consultants, to be evaluated on predetermined objective criteria. If two agree that it demonstrates competency, the practitioner member should be given certification by the AFM. A current practitioner member might be given two years to complete adequate courses to match the new standard. If courses are impractical or unavailable, the practitioner member should be able to discuss the required reading list with an approved consultant, who could then determine completion of an adequate knowledge base.

Future AFM mediators would only have either member or certified mediator standing. They would have another member assigned to them to discuss which courses and training would complete their unique backgrounds but still provide them with all necessary foundational knowledge. The membership committee would be the final arbitrator of completeness when accepting applications for certification. This level of mentorship would change the character of our organization from paid subscribers to members helped into a profession by other members.

Experience under supervision would be required before anyone could practice family mediation. A mediator could start to practice after direct supervision of three cases or thirty hours, which would be available through co-mediation with any certified mediator or approved consultant. Eligibility to apply for certification would require a mediator to document ten cases or one hundred hours of direct client contact.

We should actively work to implement the AFM-certified family mediator requirements as the basis of all state certification or licensure in both the private and public sectors. By making these standards applicable in all sectors, and by making sure that legislation requires adequate knowledge, competency, and experience, we could prevent families from experiencing inadequate or destructive family mediation services. If the requirements of certification are necessary to the adequate performance of our job, they should apply to all those doing the work. If all plumbers and cosmetologists must be licensed according to one standard of knowledge, adequacy, and proficiency, then all family mediators should also be licensed or certified to one standard, no matter the state in which they reside. After all, a poorly made drain or a bad haircut is the same in all states, and incomplete or incompetent mediation is the same no matter where it happens.

We should not tolerate a double standard for public and private mediators. We should not allow poorly trained practitioners to pass themselves off to the public as the same as those who have spent time, energy, and money securing professional-level skills, making us and our profession different if we work for a county or for ourselves. While the populations that come to private sector services may be different, our repertoires can be customized to match the populations with whom we work, but our essential knowledge and skills, the basics of competency, do not change. If it is in the public's best interest to have public sector mediators who are adequately trained and competent, is it not also in the public interest to have private practitioners, to whom clients pay more with at least the same level of competency, or even higher?

Certainly all other professional bodies have answered analogous questions in the affirmative. Attorneys do not allow nonattorneys to practice law, and doctors, no matter where they practice, must be competent to perform at a level of adequacy determined not by the state alone but by their professional bodies and academic institutions. Why should AFM not be the primary body to determine professional-level practice and the body of skills and knowledge necessary for family mediation?

No other profession, with perhaps the exception of counselors, allows those who have not passed the requirements of competency to use the name of the profession. Individuals cannot lawfully practice as doctors if they have not done and do not know what actual doctors have done and know, as reflected in their rules for licensure, and individuals cannot lawfully practice as attorneys if they are not accepted by the state bar. Yet any individuals at this point in time can call themselves family mediators and become "healers" of families without any assurance that they are adequately prepared or competent compared to others according the current standards. After we, as AFM members, have determined our knowledge base, our skill base, and our practice dimensions, we should require name protection of the term family mediator to refer to our standards of education, skill, and competency in any subsequent state licensure or certification.

Future Image

If these recommendations were realized, the picture of the edifice of family mediation that opens this article would be very different. Let us project these recommendations to a possible future. Now the building on the four foundations would have the pillars' names and compositions clearly written on them, so that aspiring mediators could go out and find that information, and there would be agreement within the common room as to what they are and how much knowledge and how many skills are necessary. Everyone in the room would have comparable knowledge of all four of those pillars. There would now be one door and one line, and people within the room would come out to greet and help support those trying to come in rather than guard the door. The application line would start and go through another edifice, the school, where with one year's time an interested person could secure adequate knowledge, skills, and experience to get into line. Having gone through the school, each individual would be assured that he or she meets the requirements to get into the building and is able to do the work inside.

Outside, the officers of the state would have listened to those inside the building, allowing them to determine what it takes to do the job and to set up the new rules: In order to set up a shop of any sort, one needs to go to school and be found competent by those in the room. There would be some assurance that those who were not acting competently could be restrained, admonished, or prevented from practicing by those in the room.

2. Barbara Diamond, *ADR Programs in Other States* (July 12, 1994) (Memo to the Structure and Finance Subcommittee, State Bar of Massachusetts Standing Committee on Dispute Resolution)

II. STATE RULES REGARDING QUALIFICATION AND SELECTION OF NEUTRALS

Virtually all of the states where courts make referrals to ADR impose some requirements as to the qualifications of neutrals who receive referrals and provide a mechanism for selecting the neutral. The most common requirement for service as a neutral is a prescribed amount of training. The most common approach to selection is to direct the parties to agree on a neutral from among those who are qualified, and, if they cannot agree, to direct the court to decide.

A. Qualifications of Neutrals

Qualifications for mediators have been implemented in California, Florida, Minnesota, New York, Oklahoma, Texas, Nebraska, North Carolina, Oregon, Utah and Hawaii. In some states, the qualifications are established by court rule, with or without a statutory directive, and in others the qualifications are completely statutory. The states also vary as to whether the qualifications are enforced through a process of certifying the neutral or the training program, applied locally, or left to be self-enforcing.

California exemplifies court-generated credentialling and a combination of local and state control. The California Judicial Council suggests, but does not require, that local programs establish education and experience criteria for dispute resolution providers to whom the court makes referrals. As a result, the credentialling programs for civil mediation are completely local, although, for example, the San Diego center offers a comprehensive credentialling program available to anyone. The only statewide qualifications for mediators in California apply to mediators in the mandatory child custody mediation programs, who must hold an M.A. in counselling or a related field, have two years clinical experience, and participate in annual continuing education. These standards are part of general standards of practice which were developed and are "implemented" by the Statewide Office of Family Court Services in the Administrative Office of the Courts. The Judicial Council adopted the standards. Most of the California family mediators are court employees, and local court rules in some places are more demanding than the state rules, requiring five years experience and a clinical license.

Minnesota is another court-based credentialling system in which the key factor is the certification of the training program. The Minnesota Supreme Court rules provide for the state court administrator to assemble a roster of qualified neutrals, defined as those who meet specified training and continuing education requirements, which vary according to the ADR process in which they wish to participate. The state court administrator is directed to certify those training programs which meet the training qualifications of the rule. Neutrals selected by the parties because of their expertise need not satisfy the training requirements. Practicing neutrals as of the date the rules were adopted had one year to be placed on the roster without satisfying the training rules, through an application to a temporary Supreme Court ADR Review Board which reviewed their education, training and experience. The rules also allow neutrals to apply to the Supreme Court for a waiver of the training requirements after the Board disbands.

New York and Texas have statutory credentialling systems in which training programs are certified. The New York statute creating community dispute resolution centers requires the centers to use mediators who have received 25 hours of training. The Office of Court Administration has established curriculum guidelines for the training, including an apprenticeship component and quality control, and established a review process for training manuals and potential trainers. The Office monitors training sessions and certifies trainers. In Texas, the statute sets forth required hours of training to qualify for court appointment as an "impartial third party," to be provided by approved ADR organizations. The statute also allows the court to appoint a non-qualifying person who has particular legal or other professional training or experience.

North Carolina has a similar approach under court rules. The rules for its Superior Court pilot mediated settlement conference programs set forth qualifications of mediators, and provide for the Administrative Office of the Courts to certify mediators and mediator training programs.

Utah takes the unique approach of delegating certification to an executive branch agency. The Utah statute permits court referrals only to dispute resolution providers certified by the Division of Occupational and Professional Licensing in the Department of Commerce according to standards set jointly by the Division and an Alternative Dispute Resolution Providers Board. Utah is also one of the few states that provides for decertification of providers in prescribed circumstances (including unlawful or unprofessional conduct, revocation of license to practice another profession, or conviction of a crime).

Oklahoma, Oregon and Nebraska provide for local enforcement of state court-imposed credentialling requirements. The Oklahoma Rules and Procedures for the Dispute Resolution Act establish minimum state credentialling requirements for mediators, and require each agency receiving state funds to provide the Administrative Director of the Courts with an annual report listing its agency sponsored mediators, who must meet these requirements in order to qualify for the benefits and protection of the Act. The Rules also provide for the Administrative Director to certify training programs. Oklahoma also has adopted a Code of Professional Conduct for Mediators, but without any apparent enforcement mechanism.

Oregon requires all recipients of state grants for dispute resolution programs to insure that its mediators have received basic mediation training in a program which addresses specified issues from a trainer who has extensive training and experience. Nebraska imposes similar requirements on approved centers.

Hawaii's state Center for Alternative Dispute Resolution maintains a panel of qualified neutrals who must mediate under the "Standards for Private and Public Mediators in the State of Hawaii." A unique form of quality control is provided through the supervision afforded by the practice of having mediators generally work in teams. No other means of enforcing the standards of practice is evident.

The most extensive credentialling and quality control of neutrals takes place in Florida, where the Supreme Court is directed by statute to establish minimum standards for qualification, certification, professional conduct, discipline and training for mediators and arbitrators appointed by the courts. The standards require all mediators to show good moral character, but impose separate qualifications for county court mediators (20 hours training and four observation sessions), family mediators (40 hours training, a relevant advanced degree or CPA or eight years' experience, two observation sessions, and two supervised family mediation), and circuit court mediators (40 hours training, bar membership, two observation sessions, and two supervised circuit mediations). Mediators are certified by the Florida Supreme Court through the Florida Dispute Resolution Center (a joint creation of the Supreme Court and the Florida State University College of Law). Standards of professional conduct are enforced through disciplinary rules by a Mediator Qualifications Board comprised of judges, mediators and attorneys and staffed by the Dispute Resolution Center. The Center also certifies mediator training programs.

In addition to the foregoing 12 states, at least ten other states . . . have imposed or [are] in the process of developing qualifications for practice as a mediator: Iowa, Michigan, Virginia, Wisconsin, Kansas, Louisiana, Montana, Nevada, New Hampshire, and North Dakota.

B. Selection of Neutrals

State rules for the selection of neutrals in court-connected programs fall along a spectrum of different methods of balancing the advantages of giving parties a choice in the selection of a neutral against the need for court oversight to ensure quality control. At one end of the spectrum, the court selects the neutral. At the other end, the rule provides an opportunity for the parties to have completely free choice in selecting the neutral, but this approach is rarely used. In the middle, the parties select from a court-approved roster. In fact, most states use a hybrid approach, giving judges discretion to consult the parties or allowing the parties a choice in the first instance but providing a means to choose if the parties cannot agree. Other states appear to lack any state rule on this issue, while still others make referrals to ADR centers which are responsible for the selection of the mediator.

Texas is an example of a state where the assigned judge has the authority to select the neutral, who in general is required to have completed a course of training but who may instead possess different, appropriate qualifications. The judge is permitted but not required to appoint a neutral who is agreed on by the parties. Utah also gives the judge a fairly free hand, by permitting the judge either to appoint a certified ADR provider or to appoint certified ADR providers who are agreed upon by the parties. Florida started with a rule under which the judge made the appointment, but in 1991, based on considerations of propriety, changed its rule to a hybrid approach: the parties have ten days to select a neutral from the court-certified roster or a mediator who is otherwise approved by the court, but if they cannot agree, the court makes an appointment from the roster according to a rotation or by other procedures in a local administrative order.

States such as Minnesota and Indiana occupy the middle ground. In Minnesota, the preferred method is for the parties to agree on a qualified neutral from the state roster. If they cannot agree, the judge makes the appointment. In Indiana, the options are set forth in more detail: the parties first have a choice, and the court steps in if they cannot agree. The parties have 15 days after referral to select a mediator from the court's approved list or from another court's list, or to choose a nonlisted mediator who must be approved by the court. If the parties cannot agree, the court lists three mediators from court-approved lists for alternate striking by the parties, with the plaintiff striking first.

Oregon is at the opposite end of the spectrum, where it is possible for the parties to have the greatest involvement. The basic rule in Oregon is a middle ground system, but there is liberal opportunity to use a different system. The usual procedure, set by statute, is for the clerk to select three mediators from the court's panel from whom the parties may choose, for the court to make the appointment if they object to all three, and for the clerk to make the appointment from among the three if the parties neither object nor make a choice. The clerk observes this procedure "unless instructed otherwise by the court." The statute also provides that the parties may "choose, at their own expense, mediation services other than those suggested by the court," without losing the protection of the statute as to confidentiality and protection from liability. Hawaii's system reflects the central role of the state Center for Dispute Resolution: the Center appoints a neutral who must be acceptable to the parties. If the parties object, the Center then prepares a strike list and administers a strike off procedure to make the selection. In Oklahoma, the court refers the case to a local mediation center, which confirms the referral through an initial interview and then assigns a mediator. Mediators are assigned by the director of the local Dispute Resolution Center to which the case is referred in New York.

3. National Association of Securities Dealers, Report of the Arbitration Policy Taskforce 88-112 (1996)

G. MANAGEMENT OF THE ARBITRATOR POOL: TIMING OF APPOINTMENT AND SCHEDULING OF HEARINGS; SELECTION, BACKGROUND INFORMATION AND EVALUATION; RECRUITMENT AND COMPENSATION; AND QUALITY AND TRAINING.

Traditionally, arbitrators have been regarded as well informed peers who serve for nominal compensation to render a prompt and equitable resolution of a dispute, drawing upon their experience and judgment. The increased complexity and litigiousness of securities arbitration, as well as demands on arbitrators to perform a wider and more challenging array of duties, have created a tension between the traditional role of arbitrators and the rising demand for professionalization.

With the changes in securities arbitration noted above and documented throughout this report, the traditional model of arbitration has become difficult to sustain. The demands upon securities arbitrators in terms of training, expertise, responsibilities, and time commitment have grown dramatically. Many believe that the inevitable result will be a cadre of professional, full time arbitrators, not unlike the judiciary. This professionalization already has occurred in other arbitration settings, including labor relations, large commercial disputes, and family law, and has been fueled by an explosion in the field of alternative dispute resolution (ADR). In fact, many private neutrals now offer a wide range of ADR services, including arbitration, mediation, early neutral evaluation, and mini-trials.

In considering recommendations for improvement of the arbitration system, such as recommendations for additional training requirements and prehearing responsibilities for arbitrators, the Task Force was presented directly with the choice between the traditional and professional models of arbitration. The Task Force struggled with the question of whether to professionalize the arbitrator pool or to retain the concept of the predominantly lay arbitrator. There are factors that favor each model. A body of professional arbitrators could enhance the quality and procedural consistency of NASD arbitration, and could be called upon to perform a wider range of functions necessary to expedite the dispute resolution process. At the same time, however, complete professionalization could undercut the essentially informal and equitable characteristics of securities arbitration.

To the extent that the recommendations, if effected, will require increased training and time and financial commitments from prospective arbitrators, it will become increasingly difficult to attract arbitrators who have other significant vocational responsibilities. An attorney with an active practice might commit a few days a year to participate on an arbitration panel, but might be deterred by the prospect of extensive required training, pre-hearing responsibilities, and a series of hearings that may continue for several weeks. An industry arbitrator, still actively employed as a registered representative or trader, might be even less likely to be able to commit to participation on panels of several weeks duration. Thus, since our recommendations impose greater burdens on NASD arbitrators, it is possible that employed professionals whose occupations are not in the ADR field will withdraw from the pool. Despite the possibility of these developments, the Task Force believes that the improvements suggested are salutary and should be implemented, and that such additional professionalism as may result from these steps is both inevitable and desirable.

Recognizing the measured requirements on arbitrators may tend to professionalize the arbitrator pool, the Task Force nevertheless has sought to obtain many of the benefits of a pool of professional arbitrators while retaining the essential characteristics of lay arbitration. The recommendations that we offer to enhance the arbitrator pool are designed to accomplish these two objectives.

Below we consider and make recommendations to improve the arbitration pool in each of the following areas: timing of appointment and scheduling of hearings, selection, background information and evaluation, recruitment and compensation, and quality and training.

TIMING OF ARBITRATOR APPOINTMENT AND SCHEDULING OF HEARINGS

1. Issues
    a. Arbitrators are selected too late in the arbitration proceedings.

One of the most frequently heard complaints with respect to arbitrators is that they are selected too late in the proceedings to guide the pre-hearing conduct of the arbitration effectively. . . . [M]any commentators proposed either earlier appointment and involvement of panel members, or earlier appointment of a skilled panel chair who could resolve pre-hearing issues, or appointment of a special discovery magistrate.

b. Hearing sessions are often non-consecutive and frequently postponed.

Under current practice, arbitrators generally are recruited to serve on particular dates previously agreed upon by the parties with the NASD staff. If, as frequently occurs, counsel for the parties either are not ready to present their cases on the dates scheduled or have underestimated the number of hearing sessions required to present their cases, it becomes necessary for the arbitrators and the parties to schedule new and/or additional hearing dates. When this occurs, it is often difficult or impossible to find consecutive dates on which all parties, their counsel, and the three arbitrators can meet. If a hearing lasts longer than one or two days, as many hearings now do, the arbitrators must often schedule non-consecutive hearing dates that may be separated by weeks or months in order to accommodate their schedules and those of the parties and their counsel. . . .

The result often is to prolong resolution of the dispute. If there is a hiatus between hearings, it is also more difficult for the parties to present, and the arbitrators to follow, a coherent case. Delayed or disjointed scheduling also usually increases costs to the parties. Another negative result of the disruptions and reschedulings may be that arbitrators are less willing to serve again. One of the primary complaints we received from arbitrators about the process was their inability to determine their other commitments with certainty and to make efficient use of their time because of frequent postponements of scheduled hearing dates.

2. Recommendations
   a. The Task Force recommends that arbitrators be appointed within 45 days of the service of the respondent's answer. . . .
   b. The Task Force recommends that hearing sessions be scheduled consecutively whenever possible; that flexibility in hearing times be encouraged: and that rescheduling be permitted by the panel only upon a showing of cause. . . .

ARBITRATOR SELECTION

1. Issues
   a. Participants are concerned that the selection process reflects staff bias and prejudgment.

Presently, the NASD arbitration staff attempts to select panel members who are well suited to the nature of the case they will hear. For example, the staff might seek arbitrators who are familiar with the financial product at issue in the case, or who have some expertise in an area of law that is likely to arise. Selecting arbitrators in this way also permits the staff to reject arbitrators with obvious conflicts of interest and to consult with potential arbitrators about their availability.

Many observers, however, feel that this attempt to select suitable panel members results in bias and inappropriate prejudgments by the arbitration staff. As parties generally may exercise only one peremptory strike, and thereafter may challenge arbitrators only for cause, the Arbitration Department's selections have a significant impact on the composition of the panel. This concern is heightened because challenges for cause also, are decided by the staff until the commencement of the hearing.

b. Additionally, the participants have limited input on the choice of arbitrators.

Apart from the perception of bias in the selection process, the parties have little opportunity to participate in the choice of arbitrators. For a three person panel in customer arbitrations, the parties are given a slate of only three names: two public members (one of whom will be the chair), and one industry member. . . . [E]ach party generally may exercise only one peremptory challenge, after which the NASD staff selects a replacement. Thereafter, the party may challenge an arbitrator only for cause. The criteria for a successful cause challenge are not easily met, particularly for pro se parties who may have little access to information concerning potential arbitrators.

Thus, under the present selection system, parties on both sides share the feeling that they have little impact or control on the composition of the arbitration panel. For investors and their counsel, the current procedure further reinforces their perception that the arbitration process is industry controlled.

c. Arbitrators complain that they are not selected frequently enough to justify the time and expense of the training sessions. . . .

2. Recommendations

a. The Task Force recommends that the NASD adopt a list selection method for choosing the arbitration panel.

The selection of arbitrators for a case should avoid even the appearance of impropriety. Judging from the volume and intensity of the comments received, the NASD's current procedures for arbitrator selection and disqualification in customer—firm disputes do not meet this test.

We therefore recommend that the NASD adopt a variant of the AAA's method of selecting arbitrators. Under this system, the parties would be provided with three lists of candidates: (i) a list of public arbitrators qualified to be panel chairs to contain no fewer than three names, (ii) a list of other public arbitrators, to contain no fewer than five names; and (iii) a list of industry arbitrators, to contain no fewer than five names. Each party could strike names from any of the lists and would then rank the remaining names on each list in order of preference. If mutually agreeable arbitrators are not selected, new lists would be provided for each category in which agreement was not reached. This process would continue for no more than three rounds. If, at the end of three rounds, an industry and two public arbitrators, one qualified as a panel chair, had not been chosen, the NASD Arbitration Department would appoint the remaining arbitrator or arbitrators. Arbitrators selected by the staff could be challenged only for cause. The Task Force recognizes that in some geographical areas the process will have to be modified because of the shortage of eligible arbitrators.

b. The Task Force recommends that greater flexibility be permitted in designating individuals as "public" or "industry" arbitrators. . . .

c. The Task Force recommends that arbitrators be placed on the selection lists on a rotating basis to promote more frequent selection of arbitrators who complete the training programs.

We also recommend that arbitrators who have invested the time and financial resources to undergo arbitrator training be placed on arbitrator selection lists on a regular rotating basis. Thus, the NASD should monitor the frequency with which individual arbitrators are listed and selected. We recognize that the selection of an arbitrator ultimately rests with the parties, especially under the list selection method that we have recommended. Nonetheless, the NASD should attempt to offer qualified arbitrators as candidates on a rotating basis.

ARBITRATOR BACKGROUND INFORMATION AND EVALUATION

1. Issues
    a. Information provided to the parties on the arbitrator's background and experience may not be complete.

[P]arties and their counsel usually want to obtain copies of awards previously rendered by a potential arbitrator. The parties can obtain the awards from the NASD, but they must expressly request them. . . . In addition, the Securities Arbitration *Commentator* provides a service whereby parties can obtain copies of past arbitrator awards for a fee. Securities arbitration awards rendered since 1989 also are available on Westlaw. None of these sources is easily available to all parties, however, and may require substantial cost. Thus, some parties may lack critical information needed to assess whether to challenge an arbitrator.

    b. Evaluations of the arbitrators are not routinely made.

At the end of every arbitration, the NASD asks all parties and their counsel to fill out evaluations of the arbitrators and the arbitration process generally. Unfortunately, very few parties or their counsel complete these evaluations. The NASD staff has tried different methods to induce the parties to complete the evaluations, including making the evaluations easier to fill out, but it has had little success. Apparently, some parties are concerned that a negative evaluation could affect a subsequent arbitral award, despite assurances that an evaluation is not shared with the arbitrators if the evaluator requests that it not be disclosed.

The NASD also asks arbitrators to evaluate the other arbitrators on their panel. Again, the rate of return is very low. When members of the NASD arbitration staff attend a hearing session, which they do in less than 50 percent of all hearing sessions, they submit evaluations of the arbitrators.

2. Recommendations

Under the list selection process recommended above, parties will play a much greater role in the selection of arbitrators. In order for the parties to take full advantage of this process, the NASD should significantly improve the quality and quantity of available information concerning potential arbitrators.

    a. The Task Force recommends that the NASD database of arbitrator information be expanded significantly and regularly updated.

The Task Force recommends that the NASD automated database of arbitrator information be significantly expanded and made available to the parties on-line. Hard copies also should be available. The database should include a fuller statement of the arbitrator's employment history, professional activities, and other areas that could reveal potential biases or conflicts of interest. The database also should include a detailed record of awards that the arbitrator has rendered in all SRO arbitrations, also available on-line. . . .

    b. The Task Force recommends that arbitrators be required to provide written disclosures of circumstances that might create a reasonable impression of possible bias.
    c. The Task Force recommends that evaluations by participants remain voluntary. but that innovative steps be taken to encourage a greater number of responses. . . .
    d. The Task Force recommends that arbitrators be required to evaluate co-panelists before they are asked to serve again and before they receive their honoraria.

While we recognize that a "carrot" approach might produce more thoughtful evaluations than a "stick" approach, the NASD has been stymied in the past in obtaining evaluations.

Thus, we reluctantly recommend that arbitrators should be required to evaluate their co-panelists before they are asked to serve again and before they receive their honoraria for their participation in the case. Arbitrator evaluations should be required even if the case settles before the award is granted.

ARBITRATOR RECRUITMENT AND COMPENSATION

1. Issues

a. There is a shortage of qualified arbitrators.

The NASD is encountering a serious challenge in recruiting qualified arbitrators to meet the rapidly growing caseload. There are currently approximately 4,600 arbitrators in the NASD arbitration pool, conducting arbitrations in 43 cities. The size of the pool was dramatically reduced in 1993, when the NASD required, for the first time, all new arbitrators and all arbitrators who had not decided a case prior to January 1, 1993, to attend an arbitrator training session. Because many arbitrators in the pool at that time had never heard a case through grant of an award, the number of eligible arbitrators was reduced from 7,000 to approximately 2,600.

Simultaneously, the number of new cases filed with the NASD increased from approximately 4,400 cases in 1992 to slightly more than 6,000 cases in 1995. In addition, the number of challenges to arbitrators selected by the staff has increased, necessitating the consideration of more than three arbitrators for many of the claims.

In response to this shortage, the NASD established a nationwide program to identify, recruit, and train potential arbitrators in all of the cities in which it conducts arbitrations. Since the mandatory training requirement was instituted in 1993, the NASD Arbitration Department has conducted over 150 introductory arbitrator training sessions around the country. As a result, the pool of eligible arbitrators increased significantly to its current level of close to 5,000 arbitrators.

Despite impressive progress in recruiting and training new arbitrators, there remains a shortage of available arbitrators in many areas. . . . The shortage of arbitrators is largely regional. Some areas, including New York, have a sufficient number of available arbitrators, while other areas, including Los Angeles, Las Vegas, and Salt Lake City, are facing an urgent shortage. Moreover, the need for public arbitrators is several times greater than the need for industry arbitrators. . . .

b. The level of compensation for NASD arbitrators is a factor in the reduced arbitrator pool.

One cited cause of the shortage of qualified arbitrators is the level of compensation. NASD arbitrators currently are paid an honorarium of $225 per day, with the panel chair receiving an additional $50. These relatively low amounts reflect a view that serving as an arbitrator is a form of public service. . . .

c. The level of compensation for NASD arbitrators also affects the composition and quality of the arbitrator pool.

Over time, the low level of arbitrator compensation also has had an affect on the composition of the arbitrator pool. As the demands on arbitrators increase, the most likely to be deterred from serving are those for whom the opportunity costs are highest—working professionals. Those who remain in the pool are more likely to be either retired persons or those who work as full-time, professional securities arbitrators. Both of these groups bring a body of experience to NASD arbitration whose value cannot be underestimated. At the same time, however, it is important to attract arbitrators from a wide range of backgrounds and professions. Serving as an arbitrator should remain a viable opportunity for people with active careers in other areas.

Additionally, the low levels of compensation have an adverse impact on the quality of available arbitrators. Highly skilled arbitrators whose services are in demand in other forums, where compensation is often substantially higher, are likely to eschew lower paying NASD arbitration. Thus, the NASD risks losing the opportunity to recruit experienced arbitrators because it is not competitive in the compensation it offers.

2. Recommendations
   a. The Task Force recommends that arbitrator compensation be raised to a level that will attract well qualified arbitrators and create incentives for training.

We are aware that many of the recommendations that we make with respect to arbitrator training and the arbitrator's pre-hearing duties will only further exacerbate the problem of recruiting new arbitrators. Imposing new requirements and time commitments on potential arbitrators necessarily involves this trade-off. Nonetheless, we believe that it is essential for the NASD to improve the overall quality, training, and effectiveness of NASD arbitrators while continuing the effort to expand the arbitrator pool. For these two objectives to be met, arbitrator compensation should be raised.

   b. The Task Force recommends that the NASD examine various factors in establishing competitive levels of compensation. . . .
   c. The Task Force recommends that compensation for panel chairs be raised. and that the differential between panel chairs and other arbitrators be increased. . . .

ARBITRATOR QUALITY AND TRAINING

1. Issues
   a. The performance of NASD arbitrators is inconsistent and, overall, not as high as it could be.

The most frequently expressed concern was that the skills and training of NASD arbitrators are not always adequate to meet the challenges of contemporary securities arbitration. We also were told of widely varying levels of skills and experience among NASD arbitrators.

In particular, the advent of "new" types of claims in securities arbitration, including punitive damages, RICO, and employment discrimination, has led some participants in the securities arbitration process to question whether the typical securities arbitrator is equipped to handle all issues. Moreover, claims involving complex financial instruments such as derivatives may prove challenging even to an arbitrator otherwise familiar with the securities industry.

There is, as noted above, a divergence of opinion on the question of to what degree the arbitrator pool should be professionalized. Nevertheless, it is clear that the overall performance of NASD arbitrators is not as high as it could be. Surveys commissioned by the NASD Arbitration Department reveal concern by arbitration participants about NASD arbitrator quality. When asked how the NASD arbitration process could be improved, 20 percent of the respondents in a 1993 survey indicated "better quality arbitrators." In a follow-up study in 1994, 15 percent of the respondents chose "better quality arbitrators" — second only to "quicker scheduling for hearings." The two characteristics for which arbitrators received the lowest ratings in both the 1993 and 1994 surveys were "ability to cope with complex material" and "ability to analyze problems and identify key issues." By contrast, arbitrators received high ratings for their professional conduct and their ability to listen to the parties.

b. The NASD has made extensive efforts to improve arbitrator performance.

In response to these concerns, the NASD has made significant efforts to improve the quality and frequency of arbitrator training. Most importantly, as noted above, the NASD has required all new arbitrators to receive mandatory arbitration training since 1993. The mandatory program is typically a day long program and provides a basic overview of the securities arbitration process. More than 2,100 arbitrators have now completed this program.

In addition to the introductory training, the NASD offers a training program for panel chairs. Unlike the initial arbitrator training session, however, this program is not required for arbitrators who are to serve as panel chairs. Approximately 270 arbitrators have completed this one day course. The NASD also has started to offer specialized training in particular areas of substantive law and arbitration practice, including employment discrimination, discovery issues, and remedies. The NASD conducted 83 such programs in 1994 and 12 in 1995. These programs are typically offered in cities that have the highest volume of cases, and provide arbitrators with an opportunity to learn about specialized topics and to share experiences in an informal setting.

c. The NASD has worked with other SROs and the AAAs to co-sponsor arbitrator training programs.

Since 1993, the NASD has co-sponsored training programs with the AAA, Amex, NYSE, and other SROs. These organizations also have agreed to recognize each other's training programs on a reciprocal basis. Thus, an arbitrator trained in the NYSE program is eligible to serve on an NASD arbitration panel. . . .

Many commentators question the necessity and cost effectiveness of maintaining separate SRO arbitrator training programs. Many believe that the SROs should consolidate their arbitrator recruitment, training and selection functions — in short, maintain a single pool of securities arbitrators.

2. Recommendations

a. The Task Force recommends that the scope and frequency of mandatory arbitrator training be expanded.

We recommend that the scope and frequency of arbitrator training be expanded even further. In particular, we believe that there should be a continuing education requirement beyond the introductory session presently required of new arbitrators. Appropriate programs should be available for all levels of experience, emphasizing arbitration procedure, arbitration techniques, and relevant areas of substantive law. These programs also should take a variety of forms, as appropriate, including lectures, seminars, role playing exercises, and discussion groups.

The NASD might also wish to experiment with new training approaches. For example, some of the more experienced arbitrators may agree to serve as mentors to less experienced arbitrators. The NASD might also keep its eligible pool of arbitrators current on developments with a newsletter or other similar publication.

b. The Task Force recommends that panel chairs receive more extensive training.

As we have recommended throughout, the Task Force believes that panel chairs should play a greater role in the arbitration process. The early appointment of a skilled, experienced arbitrator who can help to resolve and expedite the pre-hearing process is a critical element of our attempt to streamline the arbitration process and to provide firmer control over the parties' conduct. The skilled, experienced arbitrator also will be important to our effort to assure greater consistency in the conduct of arbitral proceedings and the rendering of awards.

Accordingly, panel chairs should be required to demonstrate a strong command of NASD arbitration procedure and general arbitration techniques, as well as familiarity with industry practices and substantive law. We believe that panel chairs, unlike other arbitrators, should undergo a qualification process involving evaluation of their training and experience.

To prepare arbitrators to serve as panel chairs, the NASD should develop an extensive training program and should aggressively recruit experienced arbitrators to participate. Arbitrators who believe that they already possess the requisite skills should be subject to a thorough evaluation of their background and experience to determine whether they qualify as panel chairs. Ultimately, we envision a pool of trained and experienced panel chairs serving along with panelists from the larger pool of lay arbitrators. [The concept is not unlike certain European systems in which a professional judge sits with two or more lay judges in civil cases.]

c. The Task Force recommends that the NASD continually evaluate the quality and effectiveness of its training programs.

We recommend that the NASD continually evaluate the effectiveness of its existing training program in order to determine whether improvements or changes are required. While we have not examined the arbitrator training program in detail, a recent analysis commissioned by the NASD has identified several shortcomings in the program. We note, in particular, the report's observation that new arbitrators are not currently required to demonstrate any sort of proficiency prior to sitting on a panel. While we do not believe that a testing requirement need be established at this time, the NASD must make a greater effort to ensure some minimum standard of arbitrator preparedness. The NASD also should consider whether a testing program would be useful, practical, and cost efficient.

CASE STUDY

(Adapted from *Jackson v. Show Show Drugs*)

Show Show Drugs (SSD) is a Japanese company that makes various pharmaceuticals. In early 1980, SSD realized that there was a huge, untapped market in the U.S. for enhanced vitamin E pills. At that time, the "health craze" was just beginning. There were also reports from Europe that vitamin E, in very concentrated doses, taken in the evening, would have beneficial effects and reduce insomnia.

SSD began production of a concentrated "Super E" pill in early 1982. The U.S. market was larger than expected. Every fitness guru began recommending Super E for athletes to increase stamina. *Redbook* even ran several articles on the "athletic" benefits to spice up marriage. Physicians began prescribing Super E to recovering alcoholics to help with sleep difficulty. Between 1982 and 1984, SSD sales to the U.S. tripled. Even though used for medicinal purposes, USDA approval was not required because Super E was sold as a "dietary supplement." There were no federal purity standards developed in this country. During this time, SSD also began selling Super E in France for "endurance" purposes. France, however, required purity testing of all Super E.

Between 1984 and 1986, SSD ran their production facilities 24 hours a day, 365 days a year, but still couldn't keep up with the demand. SSD hired Japanese chemists and microbiologists to help solve the problem. These scientists determined that by genetically altering the bacteria used to make Super E, they could increase production with no additional expense. By 1992, the bacteria had been genetically altered five (5) times. The bacteria used in 1992 existed solely in SSD labs and production facilities.

On January 12, 1994, the French importer of Super E rejected a shipment and informed SSD the product contained an unidentifiable contaminant. On February 3, 1994, SSD sent a shipment of Super E to its wholly owned distributor, Show Show America (SSA). Both shipments were from the same production lot. On February 19, 1994, SSA sent the Super E to Greatfoods in Houston, Texas. That same day, Jan Jackson bought and took some of this Super E.

Jan Jackson was an executive assistant to a senior vice president of a large oil company headquartered in Houston. Her annual income exceeded $125,000. Jan loved her job and was expected to remain at the company. Since she rose to the top in such a short time, there were rumors of an affair with her boss. Jan was generally in good health, except she liked Vodka and chain smoked Camel cigarettes. With the exception of her grandmother, who had a neurological condition that left her blind, all Jan's family was healthy.

In March 1994, Jan developed a serious medical condition. She became weak, had terrible muscle spasms in her hands and legs, and now seems confused often. In September 1994, she had a sudden and unexplainable black-out while driving. She can no longer work. Jan has undergone extensive and painful testing. Her current medical bills, since March 1994, total over $150,000. Her doctors have diagnosed Jan as having a rare, new medical syndrome and had never seen anything like it before early 1994. They contacted the Centers for Disease Control (CDC) about Jan's condition. CDC had reports of 15 other cases in Houston. All 16 have similar, though not exactly the same symptoms. The only link CDC has been able to uncover is that 12 of the 16 bought Super E from Greatfoods in early 1994. The CDC is calling the condition "Super E Syndrome."

Jan's condition is getting worse. However, since Super E Syndrome is new, there is no generally accepted treatment. Physicians caring for the 16 patients can not agree on how to stop the progress of the disease. There is also infighting over who should receive the grant money to conduct research. Jan's doctor has begun using chemotherapy to treat her condition. This has been criticized by another faction of doctors on the east coast who are in competition for research funds.

[Legal History: Jan and her husband filed a lawsuit against SSD and SSA on January 17, 1995 seeking recovery for medical expenses, emotional distress, pain and suffering, and loss of consortium. Jan's husband also seeks recovery for loss of consortium and loss of household services. SSD has entered a special appearance and challenges jurisdiction. SSA has answered and claims no liability. Both SSD and SSA have conducted extensive paper discovery. Jan's attorney has received answers to interrogatories and requests for admission. SSD has claimed privilege to all documents requested in requests for production.]

D. Liability for Professional Negligence: Malpractice

1. Nancy H. Rogers & Craig A. McEwen, MEDIATION LAW, POLICY & PRACTICE § 11.03 (2d ed. 1994)*

Section 11.03 Mediator Liability

The new form of legal assistance by the lawyer-mediator also represents a new school of thought and thus perhaps a new standard for liability. Professor Leonard Riskin suggests that the conduct of the mediator he calls the "neutral lawyer" be assessed for purposes of malpractice "in terms of whether he exercised reasonable care in assisting the participants toward fairness or maximization" of joint gains. However, [others] . . . contend that an approach which requests clients to waive the usual standard of care is equivalent to asking the client to waive the right to sue for malpractice a route which is unethical and unenforceable. Even if not a lawyer, the mediator who provides legal assistance may be held liable for negligence in that assistance and, if promising to act like a lawyer, may even be held to the standard of the reasonably prudent lawyer. [The authors do not cite a single actual instance where a mediator has been held liable on this theory.]

In either case, a major obstacle to recovery against a mediator may be the required showing of damage resulting from the mediator's negligence. In *Lange v. Marshall*, a Missouri court of appeals reversed a $74,000 legal malpractice judgment against a lawyer claiming to be a mediator. The lawyer, Marshall, had represented the plaintiff and her husband in a dissolution proceeding. Following Marshall's advice, plaintiff signed a settlement agreement, which she said had been executed while she was hospitalized and sedated for emotional problems. She later repudiated the settlement, persuading the court not to enter judgment based on it. She obtained a new lawyer, entered a second settlement, and sued Marshall. Marshall's claim that he was a mediator, and therefore not subject to legal malpractice liability, was unavailing in the trial court. [In short, it appears that the theory of liability was LEGAL malpractice, not MEDIATOR malpractice.]

On appeal, Marshall convinced the court that plaintiff had not proved she was damaged by the earlier settlement, because she had not provided evidence upon which a reasonable jury could find that her husband would have agreed to the second settlement at an earlier point if she had been advised by competent and independent counsel. Professor Arthur Chaykin has criticized the appellate court's ruling, arguing that other courts require the malpractice plaintiff merely to show that damages were reasonably likely to have resulted from the mediator's malfeasance. Further, he points out that other plaintiffs may use expert testimony to establish the likelihood of settlement and thus meet even the *Lange* court's standard. A number of cases finding damages as the result of malfeasance in settlement discussions support Chaykin's position. [None of the cited cases appear to involve liability on the basis of being a mediator.]

Other bases for liability: Because mediators frequently promise confidentiality, their implicit or explicit breach of this promise may be a source of liability based on a theory other than mediator malpractice. Applying variously breach of contract and invasion of privacy doctrines, in addition to malpractice, the courts have found liability for breaches of confidence by various professionals. Of course, a legal mandate or urgent public policy reason for disclosure

---

*Reprinted with permission.

will probably preclude liability. However, the Supreme Court has ruled that First Amendment interests in dissemination of news by the media constitute insufficient reason to block a plaintiff from recovering damages for a newspaper's breach of a promise of confidentiality, given in exchange for information. The mediator may have to weigh a countervailing duty to nonparties to the mediation. Some jurisdictions recognize a duty to exercise reasonable care to protect (including sometimes to warn) persons the defendant knows are in serious danger of physical harm. Such liability generally is premised upon a finding of greater expertise to assess the danger and a closer relationship to the person who poses the danger than exists in most mediations, except perhaps those by certain specialized mediators, such as environmental or family cases.

Beyond negligence and breach of confidence or contract, commentators have listed a variety of other sources of possible mediator liability. For example, Folberg and Taylor suggest that the mediator may be liable for fraud, false advertising, defamation, and outrageous conduct. Chaykin suggests that breach of fiduciary duty and tortious interference with contract or business relations are other possible theories of recovery against mediators.

Of course, most of this analysis is based on doctrines applied to other professions. Few mediators have been sued. In part, the paucity of suits also may be explained by the fact that few parties are significantly damaged, since particularly egregious practices in mediation may provide the basis for defenses in suits to enforce the mediated agreements.

Mediator negligence: [T]he courts have not yet recognized mediator malpractice. At the same time, rulings affecting other services providers indicate that certain acts . . . are likely to subject the mediator to liability. Further, mediators who agree to offer the special skill of another profession, such as law or clinical psychology, may be liable under malpractice standards for the second profession.

One theory of negligence liability against mediators would be that the mediator was inept—that the mediator failed to have or exercise the special skills, knowledge, or training of mediators. Admittedly, it is not easy to identify the special qualifications to support the argument. Sometimes mediators are required to satisfy certain educational qualifications, but the qualifications in a single statute may vary widely. For example, one family court mediation rule requires that the mediator be an attorney, certified public accountant, psychiatrist, or have a specified graduate level degree, meaning that two mediators in the same program may have widely divergent skills. . . . Required mediator qualifications vary even more widely from state to state. What is added in the way of specific mediation training is brief (usually forty hours of training or less)—much less substantial than those for professions typically liable for malpractice. . . .

If mediator malpractice is recognized as a tort, a breach of ethical requirements created to protect the parties, such as maintenance of confidentiality, forthrightness about qualifications, and disclosure of interests that preclude neutrality, may be considered as persuasive evidence of negligence. Further, under some circumstances, violation of statutory provisions enacted to protect the parties may be ruled a basis for recovery in negligence.

If the mediator agrees to provide legal services as well, it is more likely that legal malpractice standards would be applied. If hired as a lawyer for the parties, the mediator must exercise the care and skill of a reasonably prudent attorney. The standard may be higher if the mediator claims a specialty, but the standard of the reasonably prudent attorney may not be lower as the result of a disclaimer. If not hired as a lawyer, the attorney is arguably relieved of the standard of care. Suppose that the lawyer-mediator is hired (generally at a higher fee) because of legal expertise but specifically states that he is not representing either party. This lawyer-mediator is permitted, under ethical interpretations in a number of jurisdictions, to give legal advice to both parties in the midst of the mediation. However, it is less likely that the lawyer-mediator will stop the mediation to research legal doctrines which the lawyer-mediator does not know but are readily discoverable, as required of the lawyer advocate.

Thus, assuming the lawyer did not research the issue and gave bad advice, causing harm to the parties, the lawyer-mediator would be negligent unless the courts adopt a new standard for malpractice liability, one which recognizes that the parties are relying on the legal expertise of the mediator but also that the reliance is limited.

2. Comments and Questions

a. Specific examples of malpractice liability being imposed on mediators or other neutrals are almost nonexistent, but this does not keep dispute resolution professionals from worrying about the possibility. This concern is not limited to talk. The insurance industry sells separate errors and omissions policies for mediation and for arbitration. Usually, this coverage is acquired as a rider on a professional liability policy.

b. Many of the potential claims discussed by Rogers & McEwen (e.g., fraud, false advertising tortious interference with business relations, and defamation) constitute actionable claims that could be raised even in a jurisdiction that refused to recognize malpractice actions against mediators.

c. The actual damages resulting from mediator negligence would almost certainly be modest, if not nominal. Still, the consequence of a successful malpractice claim is far greater than the money damages, due to loss of reputation. Professionals provide personal services, and a strong reputation is an important intangible asset — "good will" in accounting parlance.

E. Immunity from Suit by Association with Judicial Process

1. *Butz v. Economou*, 438 U.S. 478 (1978)

Mr. Justice WHITE delivered the opinion of the Court.

This case concerns the personal immunity of federal officials in the Executive Branch from claims for damages arising from their violations of citizens' constitutional rights. Respondent filed suit against a number of officials in the Department of Agriculture claiming that they had instituted an investigation and an administrative proceeding against him in retaliation for his criticism of that agency. . . . The complaint presented 10 "causes of action," some of which purported to state claims for damages under the United States Constitution. . . .

The defendants moved to dismiss the complaint on the ground that "as to the individual defendants it is barred by the doctrine of official immunity. . . ." The defendants relied on an affidavit submitted earlier in the litigation by the attorney who had prosecuted the original administrative complaint against respondent. He stated that the Secretary of Agriculture had had no involvement with the case and that each of the other named defendants had acted "within the course of his official duties." . . .

[T]he decision in *Bivens* [*v. Six Unknown Named Agents of Federal Bureau of Narcotics*, 403 U.S. 388 (1971)] established that a citizen suffering a compensable injury to a constitutionally protected interest could invoke the general federal question jurisdiction of the district courts to obtain an award of monetary damages against the responsible federal official. . . . The barrier of sovereign immunity is frequently impenetrable. Injunctive or declaratory relief is useless to a person who has already been injured. For people in Bivens' shoes, it is damages or nothing. . . .

The extension of absolute immunity from damages liability to all federal executive officials would seriously erode the protection provided by basic constitutional guarantees. . . . This is not to say that considerations of public policy fail to support a limited immunity for federal executive officials. We consider here the need to protect officials who are required to exercise their discretion and the related public interest in encouraging the vigorous exercise of official authority. . . . We therefore hold that, in a suit for damages arising from unconstitutional action, federal executive officials exercising discretion are entitled only to the qualified immunity . . . subject to those exceptional situations where it is demonstrated that absolute immunity is essential for the conduct of the public business. . . .

Although a qualified immunity from damages liability should be the general rule for executive officials charged with constitutional violations, our decisions recognize that there are some officials whose special functions require a full exemption from liability. In each case, we have undertaken "a considered inquiry into the immunity historically accorded the relevant official at common law and the interests behind it."

In *Bradley v. Fisher*, the Court analyzed the need for absolute immunity to protect judges from lawsuits claiming that their decisions had been tainted by improper motives. The Court began by noting that the principle of immunity for acts done by judges "in the exercise of their judicial functions" had been "the settled doctrine of the English courts for many centuries, and has never been denied, that we are aware of, in the courts of this country." The Court explained that the value of this rule was proved by experience. Judges were often called to decide "[c]ontroversies involving not merely great pecuniary interests, but the liberty and character of the parties, and consequently exciting the deepest feelings." . . . If a civil action could be maintained against a judge by virtue of an allegation of malice, judges would lose "that independence without which no judiciary can either be respectable or useful." Thus, judges were held to be immune from civil suit "for malice or corruption in their action whilst exercising their judicial functions within the general scope of their jurisdiction." In *Pierson v. Ray*, 386 U.S. 547 (1967), we recognized that state judges sued on constitutional claims pursuant to § 1983 could claim a similar absolute immunity.

The principle of *Bradley* was extended to federal prosecutors through the summary affirmance in *Yaselli v. Goff*, 275 U.S. 503 (1927). The Court of Appeals in that case discussed in detail the common-law precedents extending absolute immunity to parties participating in the judicial process: judges, grand jurors, petit jurors, advocates, and witnesses. Grand jurors had received absolute immunity "lest they should be biased with the fear of being harassed by a vicious suit for acting according to their consciences (the danger of which might easily be insinuated where powerful men are warmly engaged in a cause and thoroughly prepossessed of the justice of the side which they espouse)." The court then reasoned that "[t]he public prosecutor, in deciding whether a particular prosecution shall be instituted or followed up, performs much the same function as a grand jury." The court held the prosecutor in that case immune from suit for malicious prosecution and this Court affirmed. . . .

Despite these precedents, the Court of Appeals concluded that all of the defendants in this case — including the Chief Hearing Examiner, Judicial Officer, and prosecuting attorney — were entitled to only a qualified immunity. The Court of Appeals reasoned that officials within the Executive Branch generally have more circumscribed discretion and pointed out that, unlike a judge, officials of the Executive Branch would face no conflict of interest if their legal representation was provided by the Executive Branch. The Court of Appeals recognized that "some of the Agriculture Department officials may be analogized to criminal prosecutors, in that they initiated the proceedings against [respondent], and presented evidence therein," but found that attorneys in administrative proceedings did not face the same "serious constraints of time and even information" which this Court has found to be present frequently in criminal cases. We think that the Court of Appeals placed undue emphasis on the fact that the officials sued here are from an administrative perspective, employees of the Executive Branch. Judges have absolute immunity not because of their particular location within the Government but because of the special nature of their responsibilities. This point is underlined by the fact that prosecutors—themselves members of the Executive Branch—are also absolutely immune. It is the functional comparability of their judgments to those of the judge that has resulted in both grand jurors and prosecutors being referred to as quasi-judicial officers, and their immunities being termed quasi-judicial as well.

The cluster of immunities protecting the various participants in judge-supervised trials stems from the characteristics of the judicial process rather than its location. Absolute immunity is thus necessary to assure that judges, advocates, and witnesses can perform their respective functions without harassment or intimidation.

At the same time, the safeguards built into the judicial process tend to reduce the need for private damages actions as a means of controlling unconstitutional conduct. The insulation of the judge from political influence, the importance of precedent in resolving controversies, the adversary nature of the process, and the correctability of error on appeal are just a few of the many checks on malicious action by judges. Advocates are restrained not only by their professional obligations, but by the knowledge that their assertions will be contested by their adversaries in open court. Jurors are carefully screened to remove all possibility of bias. Witnesses are, of course, subject to the rigors of cross-examination and the penalty of perjury. Because these features of the judicial process tend to enhance the reliability of information and the impartiality of the decisionmaking process, there is a less pressing need for individual suits to correct constitutional error.

We think that adjudication within a federal administrative agency shares enough of the characteristics of the judicial process that those who participate in such adjudication should also be immune from suits for damages. The conflicts which federal hearing examiners seek to resolve are every bit as fractious as those which come to court. . . . Moreover, federal administrative law requires that agency adjudication contain many of the same safeguards as are available in the judicial process. The proceedings are adversary in nature. . . . There can be little doubt that the role of the modern federal hearing examiner or administrative law judge within this framework is "functionally comparable" to that of a judge. . . . Those who complain of error in such proceedings must seek agency or judicial review.

We also believe that agency officials performing certain functions analogous to those of a prosecutor should be able to claim absolute immunity with respect to such acts. The decision to initiate administrative proceedings against an individual or corporation is very much like the prosecutor's decision to initiate or move forward with a criminal prosecution. An agency official, like a prosecutor, may have broad discretion in deciding whether a proceeding should be brought and what sanctions should be sought. . . . The discretion which executive officials exercise with respect to the initiation of administrative proceedings might be distorted if their immunity from damages arising from that decision was less than complete. . . .

We believe that agency officials must make the decision to move forward with an administrative proceeding free from intimidation or harassment. Because the legal remedies already available to the defendant in such a proceeding provide sufficient checks on agency zeal, we hold that those officials who are responsible for the decision to initiate or continue a proceeding subject to agency adjudication are entitled to absolute immunity from damages liability for their parts in that decision.

We turn finally to the role of an agency attorney in conducting a trial and presenting evidence on the record to the trier of fact. We can see no substantial difference between the function of the agency attorney in presenting evidence in an agency hearing and the function of the prosecutor who brings evidence before a court. In either case, the evidence will be subject to attack through cross-examination, rebuttal, or reinterpretation by opposing counsel. Evidence which is false or unpersuasive should be rejected upon analysis by an impartial trier of fact. If agency attorneys were held personally liable in damages as guarantors of the quality of their evidence, they might hesitate to bring forward some witnesses or documents. . . .

Mr. Justice REHNQUIST, with whom THE CHIEF JUSTICE, Mr. Justice STEWART, and Mr. Justice STEVENS join, concurring in part and dissenting in part.

I concur in that part of the Court's judgment which affords absolute immunity to those persons performing adjudicatory functions within a federal agency, those who are responsible for the decision to initiate or continue a proceeding subject to agency adjudication, and those agency personnel who present evidence on the record in the course of an adjudication. I cannot agree, however, with the Court's conclusion that in a suit for damages arising from allegedly unconstitutional action federal executive officials, regardless of their rank or the scope of their responsibilities, are entitled to only qualified immunity even when acting within the outer limits of their authority. . . .

The critical inquiry in determining whether an official is entitled to claim immunity is not whether someone has in fact been injured by his action; that is part of the plaintiff's case in chief. The immunity defense turns on whether . . . the official was acting within the outer bounds of his authority. Only if the immunity inquiry is approached in this manner does it have any meaning. That such a rule may occasionally result in individual injustices has never been doubted, but at least until today, immunity has been accorded nevertheless. As Judge Learned Hand said in *Gregoire v. Biddle*, [177 F.2d 579 (2d Cir. 1948)]:

> "The justification for doing so is that it is impossible to know whether the claim is well founded until the case has been tried, and that to submit all officials, the innocent as well as the guilty, to the burden of a trial and to the inevitable danger of its outcome, would dampen the ardor of all but the most resolute, or the most irresponsible, in the unflinching discharge of their duties. Again and again the public interest calls for action which may turn out to be founded on a mistake, in the face of which an official may later find himself hard put to it to satisfy a jury of his good faith. There must indeed be means of punishing public officers who have been truant to their duties; but that is quite

> another matter from exposing such as have been honestly mistaken to suit by anyone who has suffered from their errors. As is so often the case, the answer must be found in a balance between the evils inevitable in either alternative. In this instance it has been thought in the end better to leave unredressed the wrongs done by dishonest officers than to subject those who try to do their duty to the constant dread of retaliation." . . .

The steady increase in litigation, much of it directed against governmental officials and virtually all of which could be framed in constitutional terms, cannot escape the notice of even the most casual observer. From 1961 to 1977, the number of cases brought in the federal courts under civil rights statutes increased from 296 to 13,113.

The ultimate irony of today's decision is that in the area of common-law official immunity, a body of law fashioned and applied by judges, absolute immunity within the federal system is extended only to [officials] functioning in the judicial system. . . . If one were to hazard an informed guess as to why such a distinction in treatment between judges and prosecutors, on the one hand, and other public officials on the other, obtains, mine would be that those who decide the common law know through personal experience the sort of pressures that might exist for such decisionmakers in the absence of absolute immunity, but may not know or may have forgotten that similar pressures exist in the case of nonjudicial public officials to whom difficult decisions are committed. But the cynical among us might not unreasonably feel that this is simply another unfortunate example of judges treating those who are not part of the judicial machinery as "lesser breeds without the law."

2. *Davis v. Scherer*, 468 U.S. 183 (1984)

[Qualified immunity was held sufficient to defeat a claim based on the official's violation of state law. The Court, in an opinion by Justice Powell explained its decision.] The qualified immunity doctrine recognizes that officials can act without fear of harassing litigation only if they reasonably can anticipate when their conduct may give rise to liability for damages, and only if unjustified lawsuits are quickly terminated. . . . Nor is it always fair, or sound policy, to demand official compliance with statute and regulation on pain of money damages. [O]fficials . . . who enjoy only qualified immunity routinely make close decisions in the exercise of the broad authority that necessarily is delegated to them. These officials are subject to a plethora of rules, often voluminous, ambiguous, and [even] contradictory. . . . [O]fficials should not err always on the side of caution. [O]fficials with a broad range of duties and authority must often act swiftly and firmly at the risk that action deferred will be futile or constitute virtual abdication of office.

3. Comments and Questions

a. The eponymous Butz in *Butz v. Economou* was Secretary of Agriculture Earl Butz. It does not strike everyone as obvious that junior lawyers should receive absolute immunity, while Cabinet members receive only limited immunity. Do you subscribe to Justice Rehnquist's closing comment in his *Butz* dissent?

b. Has absolute immunity become an unduly expansive (and protective) category? Remember that the alternative is not no immunity, but "qualified" immunity? Should that be sufficient for all public officials? For mediators?

c. Assuming absolute immunity is appropriate for judges, should it also apply to persons who perform "quasi-judicial" tasks? Should it matter if the task is performed on a private contract basis or pursuant to a court order? Keep this apparently bright line distinction in mind as you read *Howard v. Drapkin.*

4. *Howard v. Drapkin*, 271 Cal. Rptr. 893 (Cal. App. 1990)

CROSKEY, Associate Justice.

Plaintiff Vickie Howard ("plaintiff") appeals from a dismissal entered after a demurrer to her second amended complaint was sustained without leave to amend. The instant case evolved from a family law matter in which child custody and visitation were in dispute (the "underlying action"). Defendant Robin Drapkin ("defendant"), a psychologist, performed an evaluation of plaintiff and her family and plaintiff now claims that defendant acted improperly in carrying out that task.

In this appeal we are asked to determine whether the alleged wrongful actions of which plaintiff complains were performed in such a context that defendant can claim (1) common law immunity as a quasi-judicial officer participating in the judicial process or (2) statutory privilege under Civil Code section 47(2) for a publication in a judicial proceeding. We conclude that defendant, acting in the capacity of a neutral third person engaged in efforts to effect a resolution of a family law dispute, is entitled to the protection of quasi-judicial immunity for the conduct of such dispute resolution services. We also find that the litigation privilege provided for in section 47(2) applies to the facts of this case. We therefore affirm the dismissal of plaintiff's complaint.

FACTUAL AND PROCEDURAL BACKGROUND

This case arises in the context of a family law dispute over custody and visitation rights with respect to the minor son of the plaintiff and her former husband, Robert. The dispute was one of a series and involved charges of physical and sexual abuse. Plaintiff initiated family law proceedings in which she sought to have Robert's custody and visitation rights terminated. Prior to any court hearing, plaintiff and Robert entered into a stipulation which provided that the defendant, as an independent psychologist, would evaluate the facts and circumstances and render non-binding findings and recommendations. This stipulation was ultimately signed by the court and converted into an order.

Plaintiff's claims against defendant apparently arise from (1) a single six-hour session between plaintiff and defendant, conducted pursuant to the aforesaid stipulation, in which plaintiff alleges that defendant was abusive, (2) defendant's report which plaintiff claims was negligently prepared, included false statements and omitted crucial information and (3) defendant's alleged failure to disclose certain conflicts of interest and lack of expertise in child abuse matters. The pleading before us is plaintiff's second amended complaint in which she had pled causes of action for professional negligence, intentional infliction of emotional distress, negligent infliction of emotional distress and fraud.

Defendant is a psychologist licensed by the State of California who was hired in that capacity in early February 1987 by plaintiff and Robert. She was hired to perform a family evaluation of plaintiff, Robert and their nine-year-old child. Such evaluation was necessary because the child had accused Robert of physical, emotional and sexual abuse. Defendant was to evaluate what contact Robert would have with the child, if any.

The agreement to hire defendant was put into the form of a stipulation and was signed by plaintiff and Robert and by their respective attorneys in the underlying action. (It was entitled "STIPULATION AND ORDER FOR CHILD CUSTODY EVALUATION.") The family law judge had not required the stipulation, did not participate in drafting it and did not supervise defendant's work. Eventually, however, the "order" portion of the stipulation was signed by the court on August 12, 1987, approximately six months after the parties had signed it. Defendant's written report, made after her evaluation was finished, states that her evaluation began March 18, 1987 and ended September 3, 1987.

By the terms of the stipulation, defendant was authorized to provide written reports, but only to plaintiff and to Robert, not to the court. Plaintiff or Robert could call defendant to testify in the custody hearings but the court could not. Defendant was obligated to complete her evaluation, to prepare a written report and to participate in the proceedings or in a deposition only if her fees for such activity were paid in advance.

Plaintiff alleges that her final evaluation meeting with defendant was scheduled for the evening before the order to show cause hearing. Defendant represented to plaintiff that this meeting would only last an hour and a half. It lasted over six hours—from 5:30 p.m. to 11:50 p.m. For five of those six hours, defendant personally attacked plaintiff, screamed at her, ridiculed her, accused her of lying and fabricating evidence, threatened she would lose custody of her son if she persisted in believing his allegations about his father, and misrepresented that the child's doctors and other experts involved in the case did not believe the child had been abused. Plaintiff claims that defendant did this to induce plaintiff to abandon her belief that Robert had abused their child.

With respect to defendant's alleged non-disclosures, plaintiff asserts that defendant (1) failed to divulge her lack of expertise in the area of child and sexual abuse, (2) failed to disclose that she and Robert had a prior professional relationship in that they had spoken and participated together in professional seminars and (3) failed to disclose that she was a close personal friend of the wife of one of the partners in the law firm which represented Robert in the underlying action.

Plaintiff alleges that in defendant's written report, she neglected to state that a September 1979 hospital examination of the child resulted in the examining doctor (1) finding evidence of "irritation of [the child's] scrotum glans [sic], penis and shaft of penis" and (2) stating that "It seemed like somebody had been chomping on his penis." Besides omitting this and other material information in the written report, plaintiff claims that defendant failed to investigate certain other relevant matters.

Finally, plaintiff asserts that defendant acted with the intent to circumvent the judicial process and to cause plaintiff severe humiliation, mental anguish, and emotional and physical distress. Plaintiff claims that defendant's acts were willful, wanton, malicious and oppressive and she seeks both compensatory and punitive damages.

Defendant filed a general demurrer to the second amended complaint, contending that she has quasi-judicial, quasi-arbitral and/or arbitral immunity as well as immunity as an expert witness. She also claimed entitlement to the "judicial proceeding" or litigation privilege set out in section 47(2). In opposing the demurrer, plaintiff argued that defendant was not a quasi-judicial officer or an arbitrator, having been hired as a private evaluator, and that case law imposes an "interest of justice" limitation upon the section 47(2) privilege which would work in this case to defeat defendant's reliance on such defense. . . .

DISCUSSION

Defendant asserts both of these grounds and we have concluded that both arguments are meritorious. For the historical and policy reasons discussed below, we believe that absolute quasi-judicial immunity is properly extended to neutral third persons who are engaged in mediation, conciliation, evaluation or similar dispute resolution efforts. As to defendant's second argument, the issue of section 47(2) privilege has, since the filing of the briefs herein, been resolved in defendant's favor by the Supreme Court's decision in *Silberg v. Anderson*, 786 P.2d 365 (Cal. 1990).

1. Common Law Immunity

. . . Under the concept of "quasi-judicial immunity," California courts have extended absolute judicial immunity to persons other than judges if those persons act in a judicial or quasi-judicial capacity. Thus, court commissioners "acting either as a temporary judge or performing subordinate judicial duties ordered by the appointing court" have been granted quasi-judicial immunity. So also, quasi-judicial immunity from civil suits for acts performed in the exercise of their duties has been given to grand jurors; administrative law hearing officers; arbitrators; organizations sponsoring an arbitrator; and prosecutors. Additionally, the State Bar and the Committee of Bar Examiners, as arms of the Supreme Court, and their officials, as officers of the Supreme Court, have been afforded quasi-judicial immunity from civil suits for acts performed in the exercise of their duties. As with the reason for granting judicial immunity, quasi-judicial immunity is given to promote uninhibited and independent decisionmaking. . . .

Plaintiff seeks to establish that California's version of common law judicial and quasi-judicial immunity is applied only to public officials (judges, grand jurors, prosecutors, commissioners, etc.). If that were so, then arbitrators would not be protected by common law quasi-judicial immunity. . . . It just so happens, that with the exception of arbitrators, and sometimes referees, such functions have usually been performed by public officials. . . .

[D]efendant and amicus ask this court to go beyond California's apparently heretofore limited application of the "persons connected with the judicial processes" analysis and apply common law quasi-judicial immunity like the federal courts have applied it—to people connected with the judicial process who are not "public officials," arbitrators or referees, such as (1) mediators, guardians ad litem, therapists, receivers, bankruptcy trustees and other persons appointed by the courts for their expertise and (2) persons whose work product comes into the judicial process to be used by the court even though they were not court-appointed, such as social workers and probation department employees. Defendant and amicus also argue that immunity should be extended even further to a third category of people—those persons involved in alternative methods of dispute resolution, such as mediators and "neutral fact-finders," who function apart from the courts, as did the defendant in the instant case.

Such an extension of quasi-judicial immunity would find persuasive support in a number of federal cases. The federal courts have held that immunity applies to such court-appointed persons as a trust officer employed by the Oregon Department of Veterans Affairs which was acting (by court appointment) as the conservator of plaintiff's estranged husband; a receiver appointed by a court to manage property of a marital estate during a dissolution of the marriage; a child protective services worker acting pursuant to a court order to take a child into custody; and guardians ad litem, psychologists and attorneys for children in child abuse actions.

With respect to nonappointed persons whose work product comes into the judicial process, the courts have held that immunity was properly given to probation officers who prepare pre-sentencing reports for the use by the courts, and workers at the Michigan Department of Social Services and psychiatrists who were involved in terminating plaintiffs' parental rights. *Kurzawa v. Mueller*, 732 F.2d 1456 (6th Cir.1984). The *Kurzawa* court stated that in order to protect the well-being of children, the defendants must be able to perform their jobs "without the worry of intimidation and harassment from dissatisfied parents."

We are persuaded that the approach of the federal courts is consistent with the relevant policy considerations of attracting to an overburdened judicial system the independent and impartial services and expertise upon which that system necessarily depends. Thus, we believe it appropriate that these "nonjudicial persons who fulfill quasi-judicial functions intimately related to the judicial process" should be given absolute quasi-judicial immunity for damage claims arising from their performance of duties in connection with the judicial process. Without such immunity, such persons will be reluctant to accept court appointments or provide work product for the courts' use. Additionally, the threat of civil liability may affect the manner in which they perform their jobs.

Extension of Immunity to Persons Engaged in Neutral Dispute Resolution Is Appropriate

In arguing for extensions of immunity to the category of persons who function apart from the courts in an attempt to resolve disputes, defendant and amicus emphasize that in this day of excessively crowded courts and long delays in bringing civil cases to trial, more reliance is being placed by both parties and the courts on alternative methods of dispute resolution. Along traditional lines, the provisions of article VI, section 22 of the Constitution, which allow the Legislature to provide for the appointment by trial courts of officers such as commissioners, references and masters are becoming ever more important. We have court commissioners and voluntary and mandatory referees. In addition, contracts for binding arbitration and provisions for non-binding arbitration help relieve court congestion. So also does Civil Code section 4607's provision for mandatory mediation of child custody and visitation disputes.

More recently, other aspects of alternative dispute resolution efforts are being used with greater frequency. There are voluntary settlement conferences which are conducted by volunteers working with the court through, for example, local bar associations. In addition, if it is necessary, the parties can choose a mediator or neutral fact-finder with the expertise to facilitate a resolution of their particular dispute. As amicus notes, mediation is traditionally a non-binding dispute resolution alternative. While most mediation is voluntary, some is compulsory, like that provided for in Civil Code section 4607. Besides relieving court congestion and speeding up the conclusion of cases, these less-traditional alternative dispute resolution procedures are often less expensive and less stressful than seeing a case through its normal trial path. Like the more formal dispute resolution procedures, they are critical to the proper functioning of our increasingly congested trial courts.

We agree with defendant and amicus that the justification for giving judicial and quasi-judicial immunity to judges, commissioners, referees, court-appointed persons (such as psychologists, guardians ad litem and receivers), and nonappointed persons (such as those who prepare probation reports and handle child abuse cases) applies with equal force to these neutral persons who attempt to resolve disputes. Although they are not "law connected," as are judges, commissioners and court-appointed experts, neither are non-judicial arbitrators. Similarly, referees, although appointed by the courts, may or may not be employees or officers of the court and they may be paid by the parties.

Plaintiff notes that attorneys can be held liable to their clients for professional negligence because they have a specific duty to their clients. Using a "duty to the public" vs. "duty to a client" approach, plaintiff seeks to distinguish the federal "court appointment" cases from the instant case. She argues that "It is . . . the absence of a public responsibility, and the presence of a duty to private clients, which distinguishes the instant case from the various authorities defendant cited . . . for the proposition that court-appointed mental health professionals are immune from civil liability. . . . In each of the cases relied upon by the defendant, the psychologist or psychiatrist was either acting as an agent of the court pursuant to a court appointment in order to provide an opinion to the court itself [citations] or was a government official who owed a direct duty to the public at large or was appointed by the court and had the responsibility of reporting to a governmental agency."

However, in reviewing the issue of immunity, we think that the focus is more correctly placed on a non-advocate vs. advocate analysis. Thus, while the criminal defense attorney who is paid with public funds has a duty to the public not to waste those funds, it is his or her job as an advocate for the defendant which makes him or her responsible and liable to the defendant and susceptible to a later civil action.

In contrast, the psychologist who is mediating a child custody dispute, whether by court appointment or not, is not an advocate for either parent, even if paid by them. The job of third parties such as mediators, conciliators and evaluators involves impartiality and neutrality, as does that of a judge, commissioner or referee; hence, there should be entitlement to the same immunity given others who function as neutrals in an attempt to resolve disputes. In a sense, those persons are similar to a judge who is handling a voluntary or mandatory settlement conference, no matter whether they are (1) making binding decisions (such as referees acting pursuant to Code Civ. Proc., § 638, subd. (1), and arbitrators), (2) making recommendations to the court (such as referees acting under Code Civ. Proc., § 639 or mediators acting under Civ.Code, § 4607), or (3) privately attempting to settle disputes, such as the defendant here.

We therefore hold that absolute quasi-judicial immunity is properly extended to these neutral third-parties for their conduct in performing dispute resolution services which are connected to the judicial process and involve either (1) the making of binding decisions, (2) the making of findings or recommendations to the court or (3) the arbitration, mediation, conciliation, evaluation or other similar resolution of pending disputes. As the defendant was clearly engaged in this latter activity, she is entitled to the protection of such quasi-judicial immunity.

2. Statutory Privilege

The second ground for demurrer raised by defendant is based on the provisions of section 47(2). . . . *Silberg v. Anderson* mandates that in spite of the nature of the behavior which plaintiff's allegations attribute to defendant, the defendant is protected from the tort liability claimed by plaintiff. [*Silberg* also was an action against a psychologist retained in the context of a divorce proceeding.]. . . .

In discussing the privilege given by section 47(2), the Silberg court noted that (1) the privilege has been given application "to any communication, whether or not it amounts to a publication"; (2) it applies to all torts except malicious prosecution; (3) "it applies to any publication required or permitted by law in the course of a judicial proceeding to achieve the objects of the litigation, even though the publication is made outside the courtroom and no function of the court or its officers is involved"; and (4) it applies "to all publications, irrespective of their maliciousness."

In setting out the "test" for application of the section 47(2) privilege, the Silberg court stated: "The usual formulation is that the privilege applies to any communication (1) made in judicial or quasi-judicial proceedings; (2) by litigants or other participants authorized by law; (3) to achieve the objects of the litigation; and (4) that has some connection or logical relation to the action. . . .

. . . The *Silberg* court rejected the "interest of justice" requirement, saying that endorsement of such a requirement "would be tantamount to the exclusion of all tortious publications from the privilege, because tortious conduct is invariably inimical to the interest of justice." The court stated that even though well-intentioned, the interest of justice requirement "is wholly inconsistent with the numerous cases in which fraudulent communications or perjured testimony have nevertheless been held privileged."

. . . All of the causes of action in plaintiff's second amended complaint allege tortious conduct. Thus, the four-part test for section 47(2) immunity which is set out in *Silberg* is applicable to each. Plaintiff apparently concedes, as she must, the existence here of the second and the fourth elements of the section 47(2) test, i.e., that the communications were made by a participant in the litigation and that the publications have some connection or logical relation to the case. Defendant was an invited, and ultimately court-approved, participant in the dissolution matter and her communications were obviously related to a portion of the issues in the dissolution action—custody and visitation.

Although it seems that plaintiff should also concede the existence of the first element (that the defendant's alleged wrongful communications were made in a judicial or quasi-judicial proceeding), plaintiff argues in her reply brief that defendant's communications were "collateral" because they were not made during the course of and as a part of the judicial proceeding. That contention has no merit. The court in *Silberg* stated that the section 47(2) privilege applies "even though the publication is made outside the courtroom and no function of the court or its officers is involved."

As for the third element, i.e. that the communication be made to achieve the objects of the litigation, we find that this element is clearly met. Defendant's alleged wrongful communications (whether express or implied and whether screamed or simply stated) were "not . . . extraneous to the action" but rather had a "logical relation" to it. Defendant's acts were part of a process undertaken by the husband and wife to aid the court in its decision on an important matter in the dissolution. Defendant's "motives, morals, ethics or intent" are not in issue when asking whether her acts were in furtherance of the objects of the dissolution proceedings. Thus, we conclude that section 47(2)'s privilege serves to protect defendant from her alleged wrongful conduct.

CONCLUSION

The absolute immunity and privilege to which defendant is entitled must protect her from suit. Such doctrines are not mere defenses to liability. If such protection is to be meaningful it must be effective to prevent suits such as this one from going beyond demurrer. Avoiding the expense and burden of having to defend an action such as this one is precisely the goal which the principles of absolute immunity and privilege were intended to achieve. In order to best protect the ability of neutral third parties to aggressively mediate or resolve disputes, a dismissal at the very earliest stage of the proceedings is critical to the proper functioning and continued availability of these services.

DANIELSON, Associate Justice, concurring and dissenting.

I concur in the result reached in the foregoing decision, but emphatically dissent and disassociate myself from the reasoning and the holding of the majority opinion which would create, by judicial legislation, a "quasi-judicial immunity" in persons whom it vaguely designates as "neutral third party participants in the judicial process."

In the first place, the majority simply designates those upon whom it would confer this newly-created quasi-judicial immunity as "neutral," and assumes that they are, in fact, neutral. Whether or not they are truly neutral presents a very substantial question of fact, one which would not have to be decided if this appeal were decided under existing law. The litigation privilege of Civil Code section 47, subdivision (2) (hereafter section 47(2)) provides a broad privilege which will protect participants in litigation from the consequences of their communications. Thus, the immunity which the majority would create serves no recognizable useful purpose.

The Majority's Holding is Judicial Legislation

[D]efendant has asked this court to "go beyond" California's heretofore limited application of immunity and apply it to others (1) appointed by courts for their expertise, and (2) persons whose work product comes into the judicial process to be used by the court, even though they were not court appointed, such as social workers. The majority has granted that request. The majority holds "that absolute quasi-judicial immunity is properly extended to neutral third party participants in the judicial process." . . . By that act of "extending" they have created a new immunity, a new exemption from accountability, which has not existed in the laws of this state.

The Majority's Holding is Gratuitous

The majority's creation of a new quasi-judicial immunity is wholly gratuitous. In deciding the central issue presented by this appeal the court could have, and should have, decided it on the basis of existing law. The litigation privilege of section 47(2) disposes of that issue fully, completely, and quickly. . . . The disposition under section 47(2) is correct and, standing alone, fully supports the result reached.

Judicial Immunity Is Very Limited In Scope

[J]udicial immunity, even for judges, is limited to those judicial acts which are adjudicatory in nature, i.e. decision making, dispositive, and the immunity does not otherwise extend to acts which simply happen to be done by judges. It is the function of adjudication of an issue, the decision making function, which requires and is the basis for judicial immunity. . . . It is important that this limitation be kept in mind, since the effect of the majority opinion is to extend judicial immunity, termed "quasi-judicial immunity," to persons who do not adjudicate but who are, at most, "neutral third-party participants in the judicial process."

The Majority's Reasoning Does Not Support Its Holding

The majority discourse at length on their perceived need for creating their new quasi-judicial immunity. The examples they cite as demonstrating a need for such immunity do not support their conclusion. Where immunity is granted to the categories of persons which they mention, that immunity is based upon the function such person is performing at the particular time, not on his or her calling or profession. Even the act of a judge, in the performance of his duties as a judge, which is not adjudicatory in nature, is not clothed with judicial immunity. *Forrester v. White*, 484 U.S. 219 (1984). The many categories of professionals referred to by the majority are granted immunity for their acts as adjuncts to a judge in aid of the judge's performing an adjudicatory act; they are the extension, so to speak, of the judge in those circumstances.

The Creation Of Immunity Is A Legislative Function

When it is necessary, or desirable, as a matter of public policy, to extend judicial immunity to persons who would otherwise probably not enjoy it the Legislature has the power and the right to do so. Thus the Legislature has extended such immunity to arbitrators when acting in the capacity of arbitrators. The Legislature also has the constitutional power to provide for the appointment of persons other than judges to perform some judicial duties. . . .

In 1985 the Legislature granted judicial immunity to arbitrators by enacting Code of Civil Procedure section 1280.1, which provides, in part: "An arbitrator has the immunity of a judicial officer from civil liability when acting in the capacity of arbitrator under any statute or contract." If there had been any need to extend judicial immunity to those encompassed in the new immunity created by the majority opinion the Legislature could have met that need by similar legislation at that time, or if such need now exists the Legislature is the correct branch of government, and has the power and the right to do so now. . . .

5. *Wagshal v. Foster*, 28 F.3d 1249 (D.C. Cir. 1994), *cert. denied*, 115 S. Ct. 1314 (1995)

STEPHEN F. WILLIAMS, Circuit Judge:

This case presents the issue of whether a court-appointed mediator or neutral case evaluator, performing tasks within the scope of his official duties, is entitled to absolute immunity from damages in a suit brought by a disappointed litigant. The district court found such immunity and we agree.

In June 1990, appellant Jerome S. Wagshal filed suit in D.C. Superior Court against Charles E. Sheetz, the manager of real property owned by Wagshal. In October 1991 the assigned judge, Judge Richard A. Levie, referred the case to alternative dispute resolution pursuant to Superior Court Civil Rule 16 and the Superior Court's alternative dispute resolution program. While the program does not bind the parties (except when they agree to binding arbitration), participation is mandatory.

Judge Levie chose "neutral case evaluation" from among the available ADR options, and appointed Mark W. Foster as case evaluator. Pursuant to the order of appointment, the parties signed a "statement of understanding" providing (among other things) that the proceedings would be confidential and privileged, and that the evaluator would serve as a "neutral party." Moreover, the parties were not allowed to subpoena the evaluator or any documents submitted in the course of evaluation, and "[i]n no event [could the] mediator or evaluator voluntarily testify on behalf of a party." Wagshal signed in January 1992. . . .

After Foster held his first session with the parties, Wagshal questioned his neutrality. Foster then asked that Wagshal either waive his objection or pursue it; if Wagshal made no response waiving the objection, Foster would treat it as a definite objection. Receiving no response by the deadline set, and later receiving a communication that he regarded as equivocal, Foster wrote to Judge Levie in February 1992, with copies to counsel, recusing himself. The letter also reported to the judge on his efforts in the case and recommended continuation of ADR proceedings. In particular, Foster said that the case was one "that can and should be settled if the parties are willing to act reasonably," and urged the court to order Wagshal, "as a pre-condition to any further proceedings in his case, to engage in a good faith attempt at mediation." He also urged Judge Levie to "consider who should bear the defendant's costs in participating" in the mediation to date.

Judge Levie then conducted a telephone conference call hearing in which he excused Foster. Wagshal's counsel voiced the claim that underlies this suit—that he thought Foster's withdrawal letter "indicates that he had certain feelings about the case." . . . On that subject, Judge Levie said, "I don't know what his opinions are and I'm not going to ask him because that's part of the confidentiality of the process." Neither Wagshal nor his counsel made any objection or motion for Judge Levie's own recusal.

Judge Levie soon after appointed another case evaluator, and Wagshal and the other parties settled the *Sheetz* case in June 1992. In September 1992, however, Wagshal sued Foster . . . in federal district court, claiming that Foster's behavior as mediator had violated his rights to due process and to a jury trial under the Fifth and Seventh Amendments, and seeking injunctive relief and damages under 42 U.S.C. § 1983. . . . His theory is that Foster's conduct as case evaluator forced him to settle the case against his will, resulting in a far lower recovery than if he had pursued the claim. . . .

Foster's first line of defense against the damages claim was the assertion of quasi-judicial immunity. The immunity will block the suit if it extends to case evaluators and mediators, so long as Foster's alleged actions were taken within the scope of his duties as a case evaluator.

Courts have extended absolute immunity to a wide range of persons playing a role in the judicial process. These have included prosecutors, law clerks, probation officers, a court-appointed committee monitoring the unauthorized practice of law, a psychiatrist who interviewed a criminal defendant to assist a trial judge, persons performing binding arbitration, and a psychologist performing dispute resolution services in connection with a lawsuit over custody and visitation rights. On the other hand, the Supreme Court has rejected absolute immunity for judges acting in an administrative capacity, court reporters charged with creating a verbatim transcript of trial proceedings, and prosecutors in relation to legal advice they may give state police. The official claiming the immunity "bears the burden of showing that such immunity is justified for the function in question."

We have distilled the Supreme Court's approach to quasi-judicial immunity into a consideration of three main factors: (1) whether the functions of the official in question are comparable to those of a judge; (2) whether the nature of the controversy is intense enough that future harassment or intimidation by litigants is a realistic prospect; and (3) whether the system contains safeguards which are adequate to justify dispensing with private damage suits to control unconstitutional conduct.

In certain respects it seems plain that a case evaluator in the Superior Court's system performs judicial functions. Foster's assigned tasks included identifying factual and legal issues, scheduling discovery and motions with the parties, and coordinating settlement efforts. These obviously involve substantial discretion, a key feature of the tasks sheltered by judicial immunity and the one whose absence was fatal to the court reporter's assertion of immunity in *Antoine*. Further, viewed as mental activities, the tasks appear precisely the same as those judges perform going about the business of adjudication and case management.

Wagshal protests, however, that mediation is altogether different from authoritative adjudication. . . . However true his point may be as an abstract matter, the general process of encouraging settlement is a natural, almost inevitable, concomitant of adjudication. Rule 16 of the Federal Rules of Civil Procedure, for example, institutionalizes the relation, designating as subjects for pre-trial conferences a series of issues that appear to encompass all the tasks of a case evaluator in the Superior Court system: "formulation and simplification of the issues," "the possibility of obtaining admissions of fact and of documents," " the control and scheduling of discovery," and a catch-all, "such other matters as facilitate the just, speedy, and inexpensive disposition of the action." Wagshal points to nothing in Foster's role that a Superior Court judge might not have performed under Superior Court Rule 16(c), which substantially tracks the federal model. Although practice appears to vary widely, and some variations raise very serious issues, see, *e.g., G. Heileman Brewing Co. v. Joseph Oat Corp.*, 871 F.2d 648 (7th Cir. 1989) (*en banc*), it is quite apparent that intensive involvement in settlement is . . . common among federal district judges.

Wagshal does not assert that a case evaluator is performing a purely administrative task. . . . Because the sort of pre-trial tasks performed by a case evaluator are so integrally related to adjudication proper, we do not think that their somewhat managerial character renders them administrative for these purposes.

Conduct of pre-trial case evaluation and mediation also seems likely to inspire efforts by disappointed litigants to recoup their losses, or at any rate harass the mediator, in a second forum. *Cf. Butz v. Economou*, 438 U.S. at 512 ("The loser in one forum will frequently seek another, charging the participants in the first with unconstitutional animus."). Although a mediator or case evaluator makes no final adjudication, he must often be the bearer of unpleasant news—that a claim or defense may be far weaker than the party supposed. Especially as the losing party will be blocked by judicial immunity from suing the judge, there may be great temptation to sue the messenger whose words foreshadowed the final loss.

The third of the Supreme Court's criteria, the existence of adequate safeguards to control unconstitutional conduct where absolute immunity is granted, is also present. Here, Wagshal was free to seek relief from any misconduct by Foster by applying to Judge Levie. Alternatively, if he thought Foster's communications might prejudice Judge Levie, he could have sought Levie's recusal under Superior Court R.Civ.P. 63-I, Bias or Prejudice of a Judge. The avenues of relief institutionalized in the ADR program and its judicial context provide adequate safeguards.

Wagshal claims that even if mediators may be generally entitled to absolute immunity, Foster may not invoke the immunity because his action was not taken in a judicial capacity, and because he acted in complete absence of jurisdiction.

Wagshal's argument . . . rests simply on his claim that Foster's letter to Judge Levie, stating that he felt he "must recuse" himself and giving his thoughts on possible further mediation efforts and allocation of costs, breached Foster's obligations of neutrality and confidentiality. We assume such a breach for purposes of analysis. But "if judicial immunity means anything, it means that a judge will not be deprived of immunity because the action he took was in error . . . or was in excess of his authority." Accordingly "we look to the particular act's relation to a general function normally performed by a judge." Applying the same principle to case evaluators, we have no doubt that Foster's announcing his recusal, reporting in a general way on the past course of mediation, and making suggestions for future mediation were the sort of things that case evaluators would properly do.

Wagshal finally argues that Foster cannot be immune for the statements in his letter made after he stated that he "must recuse" himself. This is frivolous. Even if the letter alone effected a recusal (which is doubtful—Judge Levie clearly saw himself as later excusing Foster from service), the simultaneous delivery of an account of his work was the type of act a case evaluator could properly perform on the way out. In fact, we doubt very much if a modest gap in time between effective recusal and recounting of the events would take the latter out of the immunity. . . .

We hold that absolute quasi-judicial immunity extends to mediators and case evaluators in the Superior Court's ADR process, and that Foster's actions were taken within the scope of his official duties.

6. Nancy H. Rogers & Craig A. McEwen, Mediation Law, Policy & Practice § 11.03, Mediator Immunity (2d ed. 1994)*

Reflecting a policy judgment that the importance of encouraging people to act as mediators exceeds the significance of permitting mediator liability as a means to compensate injured parties or ensure quality in mediation, a minority of states have enacted statutory mediator immunities. The immunities apply to specific programs under specified conditions. For example, in Colorado, mediators in the court-annexed mediation program may be held liable only for "willful or wanton misconduct."

In contrast to the approach taken in the states adopting statutory mediator immunities, the New Jersey Supreme Court Task Force on Dispute Resolution declined to recommend mediator immunity because of the absence of other quality control measures for mediation. In its 1989 report, the Task Force stated:

> "It is . . . difficult to anticipate all situations in which harm may befall those who so participate in [dispute resolution] . . . programs. . . . Limiting liability now would run a serious risk of exposing the public to harm."

Instead, the Task Force recommended that mediators in court-annexed programs be accorded state-provided defense and indemnification. Reflecting reluctance for broad-reaching immunity, a 1989 California provision permits liability, but provides a cap ($10,000), for violations of provisions regarding agricultural mediation.

Many other mediators may be shielded from liability for certain acts under common law protection accorded judges, prosecutors, arbitrators, witnesses, and governmental officials. The courts recognize judicial immunity in order to permit judges to render decisions without concern for later liability and to foreclose an avenue to relitigate a matter already decided. Normally, a party aggrieved by the judge's actions can appeal. Further, the judge is publicly accountable for decisions. Absolute immunity has also been accorded to judicial acts which are not public or appealable, such as hosting judicial settlement conferences, since judicial acts are those normally performed by a judge when the parties are under the expectation that the

*Reprinted with permission.

judge is dealing with them in a judicial capacity. At the same time, the immunity has not been extended to legislative, administrative, or executive functions of the judge.

Covering judicial acts rather than judges, the common law judicial immunity has been applied to others appointed or employed by the court, if these persons are performing an act normally performed by the judge. Thus, judicial immunity has been applied to clerks, a physician appointed to give an opinion on the mental health of the defendant, a court-appointed therapist, and a court-appointed guardian ad litem for a child. The Massachusetts Supreme Judicial Court held that absolute judicial immunity applied to a psychiatrist designated by the probation department, which had been ordered by the court to conduct a visitation and psychiatric evaluation of a family for a child custody and visitation hearing. The court emphasized that the psychiatrist testified and was available for cross-examination and further that the parties could appeal the ruling based in part on his testimony. Therefore, there was no undue risk to the parties in the event that the evaluation was not properly performed. Even with a court appointment, however, those whose activities are principally investigatory are sometimes ruled outside judicial immunity, since investigation is not a judicial act, nor is it a judicial act to serve as an advocate for a party.

If other courts follow lower federal courts in their rulings that holding a settlement conference is a judicial rather than an investigatory act, court-appointed and court-employed mediators may be covered by judicial immunity. In a case of first impression, a federal district court held that a volunteer, court-appointed mediator was entitled to judicial immunity. Another federal district court ruled that judicial immunity applied to a private lawyer who acted as a case evaluator. In addition, the Court of Appeals for the Ninth Circuit ruled that court-employed social workers who acted as conciliators were "performing a judicial function at the direction of a court" and thus entitled to quasi-judicial immunity.

One would not expect that judicial immunity would protect the mediator who acts independently of the court. Although judicial immunity has generally been limited to persons acting at the court's direction, a California Court of Appeals in *Howard v. Drapkin* applied quasi-judicial immunity to acts of a private psychologist employed by domestic court parties. Taking what may be a minority view, the court indicated that the immunity covered the period before, as well as after, the court appointed the psychologist. In dicta, the court extended its rationale to private mediators who are "connected to the judicial process." Key considerations for the nonappointed persons were that their work product comes into the judicial process and that it was integral to the judicial process. Regarding dispute resources, the court stated:

> "Besides relieving court congestion and speeding up the conclusion of cases, these less-traditional alternative dispute resolution procedures are less expensive and less stressful than seeing a case through its normal trial path."

Other common law immunities may cover particular acts of mediators. For example, when the court requests the mediator to testify, the mediator might come within witness immunity, which protects those who testify from defamation liability. If the mediator becomes an arbitrator by the agreement of the parties, the common law arbitral immunity may protect the mediator-turned-arbitrator in a decision-making capacity. In addition, a qualified immunity is afforded public officials performing discretionary functions. However, because the qualified immunity is grounded in the need to afford protection to policy-makers, it might cover the administrator of a public mediation program when making a policy decision about a particular use of mediation, but not normally a mediator engaged in mediating a specific case.

If not protected by an existing statutory or common law immunity, it seems unlikely that the courts will recognize a new common law immunity for mediators. The Supreme Court recently emphasized that it has been "quite sparing" in recognition of absolute immunity, reasoning that "the official seeking absolute immunity bears the burden of showing that such immunity is justified for the function in question." The mediator does not need protection against reprisals for decision-making or testimony and thus does not fit the usual rationale for immunity. Further, mediators closely resemble counselors, lawyers, and other service providers whose primary activities of adjusting and counseling have not received common law immunity protection. Nonetheless, a California appellate court, in dicta, distinguished court-connected private mediators from lawyers by virtue of their neutrality.

Chapter 20

Professional Responsibility: Ethical Issues in ADR

CASE STUDY

(Adapted from *Dennard Enterprises v. Wings 'N' Curls of Florida, Inc.*)

In August 1986, Mark Dennard (plaintiff) heard about purchasing a franchise from Wings 'N' Curls (defendant) and was presented a written prospectus concerning the purchase of the franchise. This prospectus set out the rights and obligations of both the franchisor and franchisee. Later in March 1987, Mark Dennard purchased a franchise from Wings 'N' Curls to be located in Houston, Texas. Wings 'N' Curls promised to provide professional expertise, support, goods and services to assist Mr. Dennard in building a successful business. The franchise was purchased pursuant to a written contract executed on March 12, 1987. Under this contract, Dennard Enterprises, Inc. paid $15,000 as a franchise payment for the Houston franchise and was to make monthly payments of 5% of the weekly gross sales, less sales tax, to Wings 'N' Curls.

In the spring of 1988, Mr. Dennard was interested in opening a second franchise. So, after receiving a prospectus (similar to the first one), Mr. Dennard signed a contract for a second franchise to be located in College Station, Texas in August, 1988. The terms for the second franchise were identical to the terms for the first franchise.

Mr. Dennard sued Wings 'N' Curls for negligence and breach of contract, misrepresentation and Deceptive Trade Practices Act violations. His basis for these allegations was that Wings 'N' Curls failed to perform duties as provided by provisions in the franchise agreement. These duties included providing professional expertise, training, advertising, special hot sauce, blue cheese dressing and special yellow chicken wings. Additionally, Mr. Dennard withheld royalty payments from Wings 'N' Curls for the months of January to May, 1989 which totaled $3,147.57. His reason was that Wings 'N' Curls, by not following the provisions provided by the franchise agreement, injured Mr. Dennard and substantially lowered the value of both the Houston franchise and the College Station franchise. Mark Dennard wants (1) to have the franchise agreements declared null and void; (2) damages and attorney fees; and (3) keep the two franchises without any participation by Wings 'N' Curls.

A. Introduction

Many of the matters discussed in this Chapter should be familiar to readers from the earlier consideration of specific ADR processes. The topics covered here overlap with those in Chapter 19, because there often is no clear line between quality practice and professional standards. Matters like maintaining confidences, basic integrity, and careful stewardship of funds are fundamental to quality job performance as a dispute resolution professional.

Section B provides an overview of professional ethics rules and issues, largely through an assortment of professional codes for ADR providers. These are divided into codes applicable to all neutrals, those addressed to mediators, and standards for arbitrators. The remainder of the chapter is devoted to an examination of a few important professional ethics issues.

The first of these topics is an examination of the extent to which a person, particularly a lawyer, may dissemble in a negotiation. The reader should think about the issues presented not simply in terms of rules, but also in terms of societal norms about appropriate behavior.

The rules applicable to maintaining confidentiality about settlement negotiations, including mediation, were examined in Chapter 17, section D. Here the focus is on a moral assessment of confidentiality, and the circumstances when other values ought to permit disclosure.

Getting business is a standard topic of professional codes of behavior, and often of state law, even though it would not be regarded as an ethics issue by most people. Finally, Professor Riskin explains how codes of "ethics" prohibit attorneys from adopting the role of "neutral lawyer" in mediation. He shows how norms of professional ethics actually hinder lawyers from serving as a "neutral lawyer" in mediation—even with full disclosure to, and informed consent by, the parties.

B. Overview of Professional Responsibility Issues

1. Comments and Questions

a. As you read the codes of ethics in this section, you should make a list of the issues covered in each, and notice the similarities between them. To the extent there are differences, the usual next question is why?

b. Some of the codes address the conduct of neutrals generally, while others govern only mediation. The arbitration code is the most specific of all, being limited to commercial arbitration and including special rules for party-appointed arbitrators. What are the costs and benefits of a very general, a specific, and an intermediate approach?

2. Standards for All Neutrals

a. Ethical Standards of Professional Conduct for Members of the Society of Professionals in Dispute Resolution [SPIDR] (1987)*

Application of the Standards

Adherence by SPIDR members to these standards is basic to professional conduct. SPIDR members commit themselves to be guided in their professional conduct by these standards.

*Reprinted with permission.

The SPIDR Board of Directors is available to advise members about interpretation of these standards. Other neutral practitioners and organizations are welcome to follow these standards.

It is recognized that SPIDR members resolve disputes in various sectors within the disciplines of dispute resolution and have their own codes of professional conduct. These standards have been developed as general guidelines of practice for neutral disciplines represented in the SPIDR membership. Ethical considerations relevant to some, but not all, of these disciplines are covered by these standards.

A. General Responsibilities

Neutrals have a duty to the parties, to the profession, and to themselves. They should be honest and unbiased, act in good faith, be diligent, and not seek to advance their own interests at the expense of the parties.

Neutrals must act fairly in dealing with the parties, have no personal interest in the terms of the settlement, show no bias toward individuals and institutions involved in the dispute, be reasonably available as requested by the parties, and be certain that the parties are informed of the process in which they are involved.

B. The Neutral's Responsibilities to the Parties

1. Impartiality — The neutral must maintain impartiality toward all parties. Impartiality means freedom from favoritism or bias either by word or by action, and a commitment to serve all parties, as opposed to a single party.
2. Informed Consent — The neutral has an obligation to assure that all parties understand the nature of the process, the procedures, the particular role of the neutral, and the parties' relationship to the neutral.
3. Confidentiality — Maintaining confidentiality is critical to the dispute resolution process. Confidentiality encourages candor, a full exploration of the issues and a neutral's acceptability. There may be some types of cases, however, in which confidentiality is not protected. In such cases, the neutral must advise the parties, when appropriate in the dispute resolution process, that the confidentiality of the proceedings cannot necessarily be maintained. Except in such instances, the neutral must resist all attempts to cause him or her to reveal any information outside the process. A commitment by the neutral to hold information in confidence within the process also must be honored.
4. Conflict of Interest — The neutral must refrain from entering or continuing in any dispute if he or she believes or perceives that participation as a neutral would be a clear conflict of interest. The neutral also must disclose any circumstance that may create or give the appearance of a conflict of interest and any circumstance that may reasonably raise a question as to the neutral's impartiality. The duty to disclose is a continuing obligation.
5. Promptness — The neutral shall exert every reasonable effort to expedite the process.
6. The Settlement and its Consequences — The dispute resolution process belongs to the parties. The neutral has no vested interest in the terms of a settlement, but must be satisfied that agreements in which he or she has participated will not impugn the integrity of the process. The neutral has a responsibility to see that the parties consider the terms of a settlement. If the neutral is concerned about the possible consequences

of a proposed agreement, and the needs of the parties dictate, the neutral must inform the parties of that concern. In adhering to this standard the neutral may find it advisable to educate the parties, to refer one or more parties for specialized advice, or to withdraw from the case. In no case, however, shall the neutral violate section 3, Confidentiality, of these standards.

C. Unrepresented Interests

The neutral must consider circumstances where interests are not represented in the process. The neutral has an obligation, where in his or her judgment the needs of the parties dictate, to assure that such interests have been considered by the principal parties.

D. Use of Multiple Procedures

The use of more than one dispute resolution procedure by the same neutral involves additional responsibilities. Where the use of more than one procedure is initially contemplated, the neutral must take care at the outset to advise the parties of the nature of the procedures and the consequences of revealing information during any one procedure which the neutral may later use for decision making or may share with another decision maker. Where the use of more than one procedure is contemplated after the initiation of the dispute resolution process, the neutral must explain the consequences and afford the parties an opportunity to select another neutral for the subsequent procedures. It is also incumbent upon the neutral to advise the parties of the transition from one dispute resolution process to another.

E. Background and Qualifications

A neutral should accept responsibility only in cases where the neutral has sufficient knowledge regarding the appropriate process and subject matter to be effective. A neutral has a responsibility to maintain and improve his or her professional skills.

F. Disclosure of Fees

It is the duty of the neutral to explain to the parties at the outset of the process, the bases of compensation, fees, and charges, if any.

G. Support of the Profession

The experienced neutral should participate in the development of new practitioners in the field and engage in efforts to educate the public about the value and use of neutral dispute resolution procedures. The neutral should provide pro bono services, as appropriate.

H. Responsibilities of Neutrals Working on the Same Case

In the event that more than one neutral is involved in the resolution of a dispute, each has an obligation to inform the others regarding his or her entry in the case. Neutrals working with the same parties should maintain an open and professional relationship with each other.

I. Advertising and Solicitation

A neutral must be aware that some forms of advertising and solicitation are inappropriate and, in some conflict resolution disciplines, such as labor arbitration, may be impermissible. All advertising must honestly represent the services to be rendered. No claims of specific results or promises which imply favor of one side over another for the purpose of obtaining business should be made. No commissions, rebates, or other similar forms of remuneration should be given or received by a neutral for the referral of clients.

b. Draft Ethical Standards for Neutrals Providing ADR Services to State Trial Courts in Massachusetts (1995)*

I. INTRODUCTION

These Ethical Standards are designed to promote honesty, integrity and impartiality by all neutrals and other individuals involved in providing court-connected dispute resolution services. These standards seek to assure the courts and citizens of the Commonwealth that such services are of the highest quality, and to promote confidence in these dispute resolution services.

These Ethical Standards address issues of impartiality, informed consent, disclosure of fees, conflict of interest, responsibility to non-participating parties, advertising by neutrals, confidentiality, and withdrawing from the dispute resolution process. In addition, these standards are intended as a foundation on which court departments can build their dispute resolution policies, programs and procedures to best serve the public.

These Standards apply to all neutrals as defined in these Standards who are involved in providing court-connected dispute resolution services for the Trial Court including those who are state or other public employees. [The Committee is considering whether these Standards should apply to neutrals who provide services in court-connected programs when they are providing similar services in non-court-connected programs.] State and other public employees are subject to the Massachusetts Conflict of Interest Law, M.G.L. c. 268A, and therefore, to the extent that these standards are in any manner inconsistent with M.G.L. c. 268A, the statute shall govern.

All courts providing dispute resolution services and all court-connected dispute resolution programs shall provide the neutrals with a copy of these Ethical Standards. These Standards shall be made a part of all training and educational programs for providers of court-connected dispute resolution services, and shall be available to the public.

II. DEFINITIONS

The following are three definitions that we have developed in connection with the draft Ethical Standards. We envision that the following definitions will be part of a separate comprehensive section on definitions which will be applicable to the full Committees report.

"Court-connected dispute resolution services" means dispute resolution services (1) provided by a person approved by or under the control of the Court, whether a paid employee or volunteer, (2) paid for with funds under the control of the Court, or (3) provided by a person or organization independent of the Court but as a result of a specific court referral, whether to a for profit or not-for-profit provider.

"Immediate family" means the individual's spouse, domestic partner, guardian, ward, parents, children, and siblings.

"Neutral" means all individuals providing court-connected dispute resolution services, including but not limited to mediators, arbitrators, case evaluators, conciliators, and adminis-

*Reprinted with permission.

trators of court-connected dispute resolution programs. "Neutral" also includes masters, clerks, clerk-magistrates, registers, family service officers, housing specialists, probation officers, dispute intervention specialists, other court employees when they are providing court-connected dispute resolution services. These Standards apply to all of the above-listed individuals except to the extent that the Standards are inconsistent with duties imposed by statute or Court rule.

Commentary: There are certain court employees (e.g., family service officers and housing specialists) whose duties may conflict with these Standards in certain situations—for example conducting mediations in which the Court may require disclosure of otherwise confidential communications. In those situations the applicable Court rule or statute will govern.

III. STANDARDS

A. IMPARTIALITY: **A neutral shall provide dispute resolution services in an impartial manner. Impartiality means freedom from favoritism and bias in word, action, and/or appearance.**

1. A neutral shall provide dispute resolution services only for those disputes where she or he can be impartial with respect to all of the parties and the subject matter of the dispute.
2. If at any time prior to or during the dispute resolution process the neutral is unable to conduct the process in an impartial manner, the neutral shall so inform the parties and shall withdraw from providing services, even if the parties express no objection to the neutral continuing to provide services.
3. No neutral or any member of the neutral's immediate family or his or her agent shall request, solicit, receive, or accept any in-kind gifts or any type of compensation other than the court-established fee.

B. INFORMED CONSENT: **The neutral shall make every reasonable effort to ensure that each party to the dispute resolution process (a) understands the nature and character of the process, and (b) in consensual processes, understands and voluntarily consents to any agreement reached in the process.**

1. A neutral shall make every reasonable effort to ensure at every stage of the proceedings that each participant understands the dispute resolution process in which he or she is participating. The neutral shall explain (a) the respective responsibilities of the neutral and the parties, and (b) the policies, procedures and guidelines applicable to the process.
2. If at any time the neutral believes that any party to the dispute resolution process is unable to understand the process or participate fully in it—whether because of mental impairment, emotional disturbance, intoxication, language barriers, or other reasons — the neutral shall (a) limit the scope of the dispute resolution process in a manner consistent with the party's ability to participate, and/or recommend that the party obtain appropriate assistance in order to continue with the process, or (b) terminate the dispute resolution process.
3. Where a party is unrepresented by counsel and where the neutral believes that independent legal counsel and/or independent expert information or advice is needed to reach an informed agreement or to protect the rights of one or more of the participants, the neutral shall so inform the participant(s).

Commentary: This Standard is ordinarily not applicable in arbitration.

4. A neutral may use his or her knowledge to inform the parties' deliberations, but shall not provide legal advice, counseling, or other professional services in connection with the dispute resolution process.

Commentary: The provision in this Standard permitting a neutral to use his or her knowledge to inform the parties' deliberations is ordinarily not applicable in arbitration.

5. The neutral shall inform the participants of their right to withdraw from the process at any time and for any reason, except as is provided by law or court rule.

Commentary: In arbitration, the parties may not have the right to withdraw from the proceedings.

6. In mediation, case evaluation, and other non-adjudicative processes, the neutral shall not coerce the parties in any manner to continue the process or to reach agreement.

C. FEES: **A neutral shall disclose to the parties the fees that will be charged, if any, for the dispute resolution services being provided.**

Commentary: For purposes of this Standard, fees may include the neutral's fees, administrative fees, and related expenses. . . .

1. A neutral shall inform each participant in a court-connected dispute resolution process in waiting, prior to the start of the process, of (a) the fees, if any, that will be charged for the process, (b) if there will be a fee, whether it will be paid to the neutral, court, and/or the program, (c) whether the parties may apply for a fee-waiver or other reduction of fees, and (d) whether the services are being provided by volunteers.
2. If a fee is charged for the dispute resolution process, the neutral shall enter into a written agreement with the parties, before the dispute resolution process begins, stating the fees and time and manner of payment.
3. Fee agreements may not be contingent upon the result of the dispute resolution process or amount of the settlement.
4. Neutrals shall not accept, provide, or promise a fee or other consideration for giving or receving a referral of any matter, except for a standardized contribution for serving on a referral list, which contribution shall be disclosed to the parties and the program administering the process.
5. If the Court has established fees for its dispute resolution services, no neutral shall request, solicit, receive, or accept any payment in any amount greater than the court-established fees when providing court-connected dispute resolution services.

D. CONFLICT OF INTEREST. **A neutral shall disclose to all parties participating in the dispute resolution process all actual or potential conflicts of interest, including circumstances that could give rise to an appearance of conflict. A neutral shall not serve as a neutral in a dispute resolution process in which he or she has such a conflict, unless the parties, after being informed of the actual or potential conflict, give their consent and the neutral has determined that the conflict is not so significant as to cast doubt on the integrity of the dispute resolution process and/or central.**

1. As early as possible and throughout the dispute resolution process, the neutral shall disclose to all parties participating in the process, all actual or potential conflicts of interest, including but not limited to the following:
   (a) any known current or past personal or professional relationship with any of the parties or their attorneys; or
   (b) any financial interest, direct or indirect in the subject matter of the dispute or a financial relationship (such as a business association or other financial relationship) with the parties, their attorneys, or immediate family member of any party or their attorney, to the dispute resolution proceeding; and
   (c) any other circumstances that could create an appearance of conflict of interest.
2. Where the neutral determines that the conflict is so significant as to cast doubt on the integrity of the dispute resolution process and/or neutral, the neutral shall withdraw from the process, even if the parties express no objection to the neutral continuing to provide services.
3. Where the neutral determines that the conflict is not significant, the neutral shall ask the parties whether they wish the neutral to proceed. The neutral shall obtain consent from all parties before proceeding.
4. A neutral must avoid even the appearance of a conflict of interest both during and after the provision of services.
   (a) A neutral shall not use the dispute resolution process to solicit, encourage or otherwise procure future service arrangements with any party.
   (b) A neutral may not subsequently act on behalf of any party to the dispute resolution process, nor represent one such party against the other, in any legal proceeding related to the subject of the dispute resolution process.
   (c) A neutral may not subsequently act on behalf of any party to the dispute resolution process, nor represent one such party against the other, in any legal proceeding unrelated to the subject of the dispute resolution process [for a period of one year] [or] [unless the parties to the process consent to such action or representation]. [Policy question: should this disqualification apply to all individuals with whom the neutral is in business, such as other lawyers in the neutral's firm, or other mental health professionals in a neutral's group practice? Should the disqualification be waivable by the parties? If a period of time must elapse, what is a reasonable period?]
5. A neutral shall avoid conflicts of interest in recommending the services of other professionals.

E. RESPONSIBILITY TO NON-PARTICIPATING PARTIES: **A neutral should consider, and where appropriate, encourage the parties to consider, the interests of persons affected by actual or potential agreements and not participating or represented in the process.**

1. If a neutral believes that the interests of parties not participating or represented in the process will be affected by actual or potential agreements, the neutral should ask the parties to consider the effects of including or not including the absent parties and/or their representatives in the process. This obligation is particularly important when the

interests of children or other individuals who are not able to protect their own interests are involved.

F. ADVERTISING, SOLICITING, OR OTHER COMMUNICATIONS BY NEUTRALS: **Neutrals shall be truthful in advertising, soliciting or other communications regarding the provision of dispute resolution services.**

1. A neutral shall not make untruthful or exaggerated claims about the dispute resolution process, its costs and benefits, its outcomes, or the neutral's qualifications and abilities.
2. A neutral shall not make claims of specific results, benefits, outcomes, or promises which imply favor of one side over another.

G. CONFIDENTIALITY: **A neutral shall maintain the confidentiality of all oral and/or written information disclosed during the course of dispute resolution proceedings, subject only to the exceptions listed in this section.**

1. The information disclosed in dispute resolution proceedings that shall be kept confidential by the neutral includes, but is not limited to:
   (a) The identity of the parties;
   (b) The nature and substance of the dispute;
   (c) The neutral's impressions, opinions, and recommendations;
   (d) Statements made by or notes of the neutral;
   (e) Any statements made by or documents or other physical evidence disclosed by any party or witness in the dispute resolution process; and
   (f) The terms of any settlement, award, or other resolution of the dispute, unless the parties consent to such disclosure, or disclosure is required by law or court rule.
2. A neutral shall not reveal information obtained in a private session with one or more of the parties in a dispute resolution process without prior permission from the party from whom the information was received.
3. The following are exceptions to the neutral's duty to maintain the confidentiality of all disclosures made in the course of dispute resolution proceedings:
   (a) When, based upon information disclosed in dispute resolution proceedings, a neutral has reasonable cause to believe that a minor or other person who the neutral believes is incapable of protecting his/her own interests has been subjected to abuse or neglect, or is at substantial risk of such abuse or neglect in the future, the neutral shall to the extent permitted by law, disclose that information to appropriate authorities.

Commentary: Such disclosure may not be currently permitted under G.L. ch 233, § 23C.

   (b) When, based upon information disclosed in dispute resolution proceedings, a neutral has reasonable cause to believe that a person poses a danger of physical harm to himself/herself or to another person(s), the neutral shall to the extent permitted by law, disclose that information to the person in danger of harm or to appropriate authorities.

Commentary: Such disclosure may not be currently permitted under G.L. ch 233, § 23C.

   (c) A neutral shall not be required to maintain the confidentiality of any oral or written information disclosed in dispute resolution proceedings (i) where such information is necessary for the defense of any person in a criminal prosecution and where a subpoena has been issued to the neutral for the information sought, (ii) in any other case where the neutral is required by law to disclose such information, or (iii) where the information is offered by the neutral in order to defend himself or herself in a civil action regarding his or her conduct in the dispute resolution process.

4. Neutrals shall maintain the confidentiality of all records of dispute resolution proceedings. Any information or materials disclosed by the neutral for research, training, or statistical compilation shall be adapted by the neutral so as to render anonymous any identifying information contained therein. The disclosure for such purposes of any material rendered anonymous shall not be a violation of the confidentiality obligation of this section.
5. Neutrals may discuss confidential information with individuals who administer the court-connected dispute resolution program in which they obtained the confidential information.
6. A neutral shall not use information obtained in dispute resolution proceedings for his or her personal advantage.
7. Prior to the commencement of dispute resolution proceedings, the neutral shall explain to all parties the provisions concerning confidentiality, and the exceptions to confidentiality, contained in these Standards.

Commentary: The obligation of the parties to maintain the confidentiality of communications made in the course of a mediation is governed by Mass. Gen. Laws ch 233, § 23C. As it now stands, § 23C prohibits disclosure of communications made in the course of a mediation (as defined in the statute) even if those communications relate to child abuse or neglect. Therefore, the provisions in these Standards permitting disclosure of certain communications (see sections 3(a)-(c), above), do not apply in every case to mediations, but do apply to other dispute resolution proceedings, such as arbitration or case evaluation. Other statutes, such as ch 119, § 51A (the mandated reporting statute) may also govern the obligation to disclose, or maintain confidentiality of, communications relating to child abuse and neglect. [The Committee is considering whether § 23C should be amended to permit disclosure of communications relating to child abuse or neglect, planned commission of a crime, and certain other communications.]

H. WITHDRAWING FROM THE DISPUTE RESOLUTION PROCESS. **Under certain circumstances, a neutral shall or may withdraw from the dispute resolution process.**

1. A neutral shall withdraw from the dispute resolution process when:
    a) the neutral is unable to conduct the process in an impartial manner (see section A.2, above);
    b) in an appropriate case (as described in section B.2, above), the neutral believes that a party to the dispute resolution process is unable to understand the process or participate fully in it;
    c) the neutral determines that a conflict of interest is so significant as to cast doubt on

the integrity of the dispute resolution process and/or neutral (see section D.2, above); or

d) the neutral believes that the parties' agreement is illegal or involves the commission of a crime.

2. The neutral may withdraw from the dispute resolution process when the neutral believes that:

   a) she or he lacks the expertise or resources necessary to handle the case, and the necessary expertise or resources are not available to the parties or the neutral;

   b) continuing the dispute resolution process would give rise to an appearance of impropriety or impugn the integrity of the process;

   c) in a non-adjudicative process, one or more of the parties is not participating in good faith;

   d) in a non-adjudicative process, continuing with the process would cause severe harm to one or more of the parties, a non-participating party, or the public;

   e) one or more of the parties threatens to harm the neutral or another party or engages in other conduct which undermines the fairness or integrity of the process;

   f) continuing discussions would not be productive, would result in unwarranted cost to the parties, and/or would result in an unwarranted use of the resources of the dispute resolution program; or

   g) the parties' agreement violates public policy.

Commentary: These Standards provide for discretionary withdrawal when it may be possible for the neutral to overcome the problems described in 2(a) - (g) above, or where the neutral determines that the problem may not be severe enough to warrant termination of the process.

3. Standards for Mediators

a. AAA/ABA/SPIDR, Standards of Conduct for Mediators (1994)*

Introductory Note

The initiative for these standards came from three professional groups: the American Arbitration Association, the American Bar Association, and the Society of Professionals in Dispute Resolution (SPIDR). The standards are intended to apply to all types of mediation. . . . The standards draw on existing codes of conduct for mediators and take into account issues and problems that have surfaced in mediation practice. . . .

I. Self-Determination: A Mediator Shall Recognize that Mediation is Based on the Principle of Self-Determination by the Parties.

Self-determination is the fundamental principle of mediation. It requires that the mediation process rely upon the ability of the parties to reach a voluntary, uncoerced agreement. Any party may withdraw from mediation at any time.

COMMENTS:

- The mediator may provide information about the process, raise issues, and help parties explore options. . . .

---

*Reprinted with permission.

II. Impartiality: A Mediator Shall Conduct the Mediation in an Impartial Manner.

The concept of mediator impartiality is central to the mediation process. A mediator shall mediate only those matters in which she or he can remain impartial and evenhanded. If at any time the mediator is unable to conduct the process in an impartial manner, the mediator is obligated to withdraw.

COMMENTS:

- A mediator shall avoid conduct that gives the appearance of partiality toward one of the parties. . . .
- When mediators are appointed by a court or institution, the appointing agency shall make reasonable efforts to ensure that mediators serve impartially. . . .

III. Conflicts of Interest: A Mediator Shall Disclose all Actual and Potential Conflicts of Interest Reasonably Known to the Mediator. After Disclosure, the Mediator Shall Decline to Mediate Unless all Parties Choose to Retain the Mediator. The Need to Protect Against Conflicts of Interest Also Governs Conduct that Occurs During and After the Mediation.

A conflict of interest is a dealing or relationship that might create an impression of possible bias. The basic approach to questions of conflict of interest is consistent with the concept of self-determination. The mediator has a responsibility to disclose all actual and potential conflicts that are reasonably known to the mediator and could reasonably be seen as raising a question about impartiality. If all parties agree to mediate after being informed of conflicts, the mediator may proceed with the mediation. If, however, the conflict of interest casts serious doubt on the integrity of the process, the mediator shall decline to proceed.

A mediator must avoid the appearance of conflict of interest both during and after the mediation. Without the consent of all parties, a mediator shall not subsequently establish a professional relationship with one of the parties in a related matter, or in an unrelated matter under circumstances which would raise legitimate questions about the integrity of the mediation process.

COMMENTS:

- The mediator's commitment must be to the parties and the process. Pressures from outside of the mediation process should never influence the mediator to coerce parties to settle.

IV. Competence: A Mediator Shall Mediate Only When the Mediator Has the Necessary Qualifications to Satisfy the Reasonable Expectations of the Parties.

Any person may be selected as a mediator, provided that the parties are satisfied with the mediator's qualifications. Training and experience in mediation, however, are often necessary for effective mediation. A person who offers herself or himself as available to serve as a mediator gives parties and the public the expectation that she or he has the competency to mediate effectively. In court-connected or other forms of mandated mediation, it is essential that mediators assigned to the parties have the requisite training and experience.

COMMENTS:

- Mediators should have available for the parties information regarding their relevant training, education and experience.

- The requirements for appearing on a list of mediators must be made public and available to interested persons.
- When mediators are appointed by a court or institution, the appointing agency shall make reasonable efforts to ensure that each mediator is qualified for the particular mediation.

V. Confidentiality: A Mediator Shall Maintain the Reasonable Expectations of the Parties with Regard to Confidentiality.

The reasonable expectations of the parties with regard to confidentiality shall be met by the mediator. The parties' expectations of confidentiality depend on the circumstances of the mediation and any agreements they may make. The mediator shall not disclose any matter that a party expects to be confidential unless given permission by all parties or unless required by law or other public policy.

COMMENTS:

- . . . Since the parties' expectations regarding confidentiality are important, the mediator should discuss these expectations with the parties.
- If the mediator holds private sessions with a party, the nature of these sessions with regard to confidentiality should be discussed prior to undertaking such sessions.
- A mediator should avoid communicating information about how the parties acted in the mediation process, the merits of the case, or settlement offers. The mediator may report, if required, whether parties appeared at a scheduled mediation.
- Where the parties have agreed that all or a portion of the information disclosed during a mediation is confidential, the parties' agreement should be respected by the mediator.
- Confidentiality should not be construed to limit or prohibit the effective monitoring, research, or evaluation, of mediation programs by responsible persons. . . .

VI. Quality of the Process: A Mediator Shall Conduct the Mediation Fairly, Diligently, and in a Manner Consistent with the Principle of Self-Determination by the Parties.

A mediator shall work to ensure a quality process and to encourage mutual respect among the parties. A quality process requires a commitment by the mediator to diligence and procedural fairness. There should be adequate opportunity for each party in the mediation to participate in the discussions. The parties decide when and under what conditions they will reach an agreement or terminate a mediation.

COMMENTS:

- A mediator may agree to mediate only when he or she is prepared to commit the attention essential to an effective mediation. . . . A mediator should not allow a mediation to be unduly delayed by the parties or their representatives. . . .
- Mixing the role of a mediator and the role of a professional advising a client is problematic, and mediators must strive to distinguish between the roles. A mediator should therefore refrain from providing professional advice. . . .
- A mediator shall withdraw from a mediation when incapable of serving or when unable to remain impartial.
- A mediator shall withdraw from the mediation or postpone a session if the mediation

is being used to further illegal conduct, or if a party is unable to participate due to drug, alcohol, or other physical or mental incapacity.

- Mediators should not permit their behavior in the mediation process to be guided by a desire for a high settlement rate.

VII. Advertising and Solicitation: A Mediator Shall Be Truthful in Advertising And Solicitation for Mediation.

Advertising or any other communication with the public concerning services offered or regarding the education, training, and expertise of the mediator shall be truthful. Mediators shall refrain from promises and guarantees of results.

COMMENTS:

- In an advertisement or other communication to the public, a mediator may make reference to meeting state, national, or private organization qualifications only if the entity referred to has a procedure for qualifying mediators and the mediator has been duly granted the requisite status.

VIII. Fees: A Mediator Shall Fully Disclose and Explain the Basis of Compensation, Fees, and Charges to the Parties.

The parties should be provided sufficient information about fees at the outset of a mediation to determine if they wish to retain the services of a mediator. If a mediator charges fees, the fees shall be reasonable, considering, among other things, the mediation service, the type and complexity of the matter, the expertise of the mediator, the time required, and the rates customary in the community. The better practice in reaching an understanding about fees is to set down the arrangements in a written agreement.

COMMENTS:

- A mediator who withdraws from a mediation should return any unearned fee to the parties.
- A mediator should not enter into a fee agreement contingent upon the result or the dollar amount of the settlement.
- Co-mediators who share a fee should hold to standards of reasonableness in determining the allocation of fees.

IX. Obligations to the Mediation Process: Mediators have a duty to improve the practice of mediation.

b. Robert B. Moberly, *Ethical Standards For Court-Appointed Mediators and Florida's Mandatory Mediation Experiment*, 21 Fla. St. U. L. Rev. 701 (1994)*

II. MEDIATOR COVERAGE AND CHOICE

[In 1992, the Florida Supreme Court promulgated the Florida Rules for Certified and Court-Appointed Mediators.] The standards "apply to all mediators who are certified or participate in court-sponsored mediation." Certification requirements vary, depending on whether the mediator will be conducting county, family, or circuit court mediations.

*Reprinted with permission.

Additionally, the parties are free to select a mediator who does not meet the certification requirements but who is qualified by training or experience to mediate all or some of the issues in the particular case. For example, mediators from outside the state are not likely to become certified in Florida, yet the parties may wish to select such a person for reasons of expertise or outside viewpoint. Similarly, the parties may wish to select a prominent person from within the state who has not sought or obtained certification.

A national study recently concluded that parties should have "the greatest possible choice" in selecting such mediators. Where choice exists, it is not necessary to impose restrictive qualification (that is, certification) requirements. Rather, "a free market should be relied on," so long as the parties are provided with complete and accurate information about the mediator. Of course, it should be recognized that the standards of conduct discussed in this Article apply to all court-appointed mediators, whether or not they are certified, and regardless of whether they are selected by the parties or by the judge.

III. MEDIATOR STANDARDS OF PROFESSIONAL CONDUCT

The overall structure of the standards emphasizes a mediator's duties to the public, to the parties, to the court, and to the mediation process. Some of the standards reflect a tension between a desire to set aspirational goals and the need for black-letter principles that can be easily understood and enforced. Moreover, the establishment of court-annexed mediation ethics is a new endeavor. For this reason, mediation standards should properly be considered as organic in nature, with a recognition that such standards are likely to change and evolve with the growth of court-sponsored mediation.

A. General Mediator Standards

A mediator holds a unique position of trust. For mediation to succeed, the mediator must maintain the parties' trust while moving them toward a suitable solution. This requires mediators to adhere to the highest standards of integrity, impartiality, and professional competence in their service.

People of varying professions and personalities serve as mediators. For example, social workers, psychologists, and lawyers could be qualified to serve as mediators in Florida legal disputes, depending on the nature of the dispute. . . . The mediator standards of conduct neither replace nor eliminate the relevant ethical standards of the mediator's profession. Rather, they run concurrently with other applicable standards which do not conflict with them. If a conflict arises between the mediator standards of conduct and another professional ethical code of conduct in Florida court-annexed mediation, the mediator standards will apply.

B. Responsibilities to Courts

Court-affiliated mediators, by definition, mediate pursuant to court appointment. Thus, the mediator is responsible to the court for the propriety of his or her activities as a mediator. The mediator must be "candid, accurate, and fully responsive to a court concerning the mediator's qualifications, availability, and all other pertinent matters." The mediator also must agree to follow all administrative policies, rules, and statutes. Further, the mediator must refrain from activities that have "the appearance of improperly influencing a court to secure placement on a roster or appointment to a case, including gifts or other inducements to court personnel."

C. Mediation Process

Many mediation participants will be unfamiliar with the process, so the mediator should clarify several matters at the outset. The mediator should inform the parties that mediation is consensual, that the mediator is an impartial facilitator, and that the mediator may not impose or force any settlement on the parties. In addition, the mediator may need to establish some ground rules and explain the process. The mediator also should discuss at the outset such questions as whether there will be individual caucuses or whether all activity will take place in front of the other party; and whether the mediator will suggest alternatives or simply referee the parties' discussion.

Some actions may not be referred to mediation except upon petition of all parties. These include: appeals from rulings of administrative agencies; bond estreatures; forfeitures of seized property; habeas corpus and extraordinary writs; bond validation; declaratory relief; and other matters as may be specified by administrative order of the chief judge in the circuit.

Additionally, the mediator should help the parties determine if mediation is the best method to solve their problem by evaluating the benefits, risks, and costs of mediation, and other available methods of problem solving. The mediator should not prolong a mediation session if it becomes apparent that the case is unsuitable for mediation or that one of the parties cannot or will not meaningfully participate in mediation.

D. Self-Determination

An important standard provides that "[a] mediator shall assist the parties in reaching an informed and voluntary settlement," but that "[d]ecisions are to be made voluntarily by the parties themselves." . . . Because the parties to a mediation have the right to decide their settlement, it follows that mediators are prohibited from coercing a settlement. Moreover, a mediator may not make any substantive decisions for a party.

However, the mediator is not simply a referee. Depending upon the problem and the parties involved, the mediator's best course of conduct may fall in various places along a continuum ranging from passive neutrality to intervention. . . . [T]he standards direct the mediator to promote a balanced process and to encourage the parties to conduct the mediation sessions in a non-adversarial manner.

Occasionally, a settlement affects not only the lives of the mediating parties, but also the rights of third parties, such as children. The mediator has a responsibility to "promote consideration of the interests" of unrepresented persons who may be affected by an agreement. The mediator must also "promote mutual respect among the parties throughout the mediation process." Mutual respect, however, is a fairly intangible concept. Although the mediator's goal is not necessarily to create a friendship where there was none before, the mediator may want to consider emphasizing future relations and trust in a settlement. . . .

E. Impartiality

A mediator must be impartial, which is defined as freedom from favoritism in word, action, and appearance. "Impartiality implies a commitment to aid all parties, as opposed to an individual party, in moving toward an agreement." Thus the impartiality requirement prohibits the mediator from accepting or from giving gifts or other items of value to persons involved in any mediation. Additionally, the mediator should withdraw "if the mediator believes the mediator can no longer be impartial."

Disclosure of any possible bias is prudent. . . . First, "any current, past, or possible future representation or consulting relationship with any party or attorney involved in the mediation" must be disclosed, as well as "any pertinent pecuniary interest." . . . [Second], close personal ties and other circumstances that may put the mediator's impartiality in question.

Mediators also must maintain their impartiality by refraining from certain activities. A mediator may not provide counseling or therapy to any party during the mediation. Future counseling or representation is not expressly prohibited; however, in a limited effort to deal with this potential conflict, mediators are prohibited from using the mediation process to solicit or encourage future professional service with either party.

F. Confidentiality

[E]ach party has a privilege to refuse to disclose communications made during a mediation. Such communications, other than an executed settlement agreement, are confidential and inadmissible, unless all parties agree otherwise. Mediators are obliged to maintain this confidentiality, except where required by law to disclose information. The principle of confidentiality also applies to information obtained in individual caucuses, unless the party to the caucus permits disclosure. In addition, the mediator must maintain confidentiality in the storage and disposal of records, and must render anonymous all identifying information when materials are used for research, training, or statistical compilations.

G. Professional Advice

There may be times during mediation when the mediator is asked about such things as possible outcomes if the dispute went to trial. The pertinent distinction the mediator must make here is between giving . . . information and . . .advice. The mediator may give legal information, provided that he or she is qualified by training or experience to provide it. This allows the mediator to advise all parties of laws that are common knowledge and may be applicable to the dispute. For example, it would seem that an experienced family mediator would know of, and could provide, court-established child support guidelines. On the other hand, mediators should avoid giving legal advice, such as how an agreement might affect the participants' legal rights or obligations.

Allowing a mediator to give either legal information or advice is controversial. Some commentators believe that if a mediator is allowed to comment at all, personal bias may enter the process in deciding which laws to reveal. Other commentators believe that a mediator may inquire about legal issues, but should direct the parties to independent counsel for their resolution. Still other commentators are concerned that too many restraints will severely limit a mediator's ability to move the parties to an informed settlement. These commentators would allow a mediator to define all the legal issues without directly applying the law to the immediate facts. . . .

H. Fees and Expenses

The rules seek equitable billing by mediators. . . . Prior to mediation, a mediator must give all parties a written explanation of the fees and costs. The written explanation must contain the basis and amount of charges for the following: mediation sessions, preparation for sessions, travel time, postponement or cancellation of the mediation session by the parties, preparation of the written mediation agreement, and all other items to be charged by the mediator. The explanation also should include the parties' pro rata share of mediation fees and costs, if previously determined by the court or agreed to by the parties. Further, the mediator must keep adequate records to support charges for services and expenses, and make an accounting to the parties or the court upon request.

Some billing practices are impermissible. First, no commission, rebate or similar remuneration may be given or received by a mediator for referral of clients for mediation or related services. Second, a mediator may not be compensated on a contingency fee basis. Third, when calculating fees and costs, the mediator may not charge in excess of actual time spent or allocated, or costs incurred. . . .

I. Concluding Mediation

Under the mediation procedural rules, the parties are obliged to reduce any agreement to writing. The mediator must discuss with the participants how to formalize and implement the agreement, including "caus[ing] the terms . . . to be memorialized appropriately . . . ." However, mediators are not themselves required to write the agreement. Even if the parties have not come to a full agreement, the mediator may advise the parties to formalize what has been agreed upon and direct the parties toward procedures available for resolving the remaining issues. A mediator must not knowingly assist in forming an agreement that would be denied judicial enforcement because of fraud, duress, overreaching, the absence of bargaining ability, or unconscionability. . . .

J. Training and Education

. . . Upon request, the mediator must disclose the extent and nature of his or her mediation training and experience. . . . [A] mediator is encouraged to participate in continuing education activities to maintain professional competence. Further, an experienced mediator has a duty to "cooperate in the training of new mediators, including serving as a mentor." Under an administrative order of the Florida Supreme Court, every certified mediator must allow a minimum of two mediator trainees per year to observe mediation sessions.

K. Advertising and Soliciting

Mediators are not prohibited from advertising their services if the information in the advertisement honestly represents the services to be rendered. In addition to personal qualifications, the mediator must accurately represent in the advertisements the mediation process, as well as its costs and benefits. The mediator may not claim that settlements always will be reached, nor may the mediator make promises that imply favoritism to one side to obtain business.

L. Relationships With Other Professionals

A mediator should respect the professional integrity of other mediators. When more than one mediator is involved with the same dispute, each mediator has a duty to keep other participating mediators informed. "The wishes of the parties supersede the interests of the mediators." A mediator should not mediate any dispute that is assigned to another mediator without first consulting that person. . . .

IV. ENFORCEMENT OF MEDIATOR STANDARDS OF CONDUCT

. . . Florida is the first state to adopt a procedure to enforce mediator standards of conduct. The procedure involves mediators, as well as judges and attorneys, in the discipline process. The enforcement mechanism uses a Mediator Qualifications Board (Board), complaint committees, and the staff of the Florida Dispute Resolution Center (Center). In short, a complaint committee investigates complaints. If the committee finds probable cause, a panel of the Board will hear and decide the case. The mediator may appeal an adverse decision to the Florida Supreme Court. The Center provides staff support in processing complaints.

V. ATTORNEY OBLIGATION TO ADVISE CLIENTS OF ALTERNATIVE DISPUTE RESOLUTIONS

Should attorneys be responsible for considering or advising clients of alternative dispute resolution procedures such as mediation? . . . Florida has perhaps the most comprehensive system of statewide and state-controlled court mediation in the country. Thus it would seem incumbent upon Florida attorneys to advise their clients of the availability of mediation and its potential benefits. Failure to do so could result in charges of a violation of professional responsibility, malpractice, or both. . . .

c. National Association of Social Workers, STANDARDS OF PRACTICE FOR SOCIAL WORK MEDIATORS

INTRODUCTION

Social workers sit at the center of many social conflicts. In their role as facilitator of . . . interactions [among individuals and institutions], social workers face the issue of conflict resolution as a normal part of their professional activities. The role of social worker in these conflicts has been variously described as advocate, negotiator, and mediator.

Increasingly, social workers and other professionals have chosen or been asked to play the formal role of mediator, that is, a neutral third party who helps people or groups in conflict arrive at mutually acceptable solutions. Social workers mediate issues such as divorce and postdivorce disputes, parent-child conflicts, child welfare issues, and disagreements concerning care of the elderly. In addition, they mediate neighborhood disputes, community conflicts, and personnel issues. As the use of mediators in a variety of circumstances has increased, a concomitant development has taken place regarding the conceptual framework and skills set within which mediators function. Mediation increasingly is viewed as a powerful intervention tool distinct from, albeit informed by, other approaches to client services.

These developments have led the National Association of Social Workers (NASW) to develop and adopt a set of standards that are intended to guide the practice of social workers who function as neutral third parties. These standards were developed to complement the NASW *Code of Ethics* and to be consistent with the standards of major mediation organizations. . . .

STANDARDS FOR THE PRACTICE OF MEDIATION BY SOCIAL WORKERS

Standard 1: Social work mediators shall function within the ethics and stated standards and accountability procedures of the social work profession.

Interpretation: All social workers have a fourfold responsibility: to clients, to the profession, to self, and to society. Social work mediators should identify themselves as members of the social work profession. NASW members shall be familiar with and adhere to the NASW *Code of Ethics* and shall cooperate fully and in a timely fashion with the adjudication procedures of the committee of inquiry, peer review, and appropriate state regulatory boards. They should be aware of and adhere to relevant stated professional standards for social work practices.

Standard 2: Social work mediators should remain impartial and neutral toward all parties and issues in a dispute.

Interpretation: Social work mediators should enter into a dispute as a mediator only when they can maintain a stance of impartiality and neutrality. . . . An impartial mediator acts without bias in word and action and is committed to helping all parties rather than to advocating for any single person.

Neutrality relates to the mediator's relationship to the parties and the issues involved. A mediator should have no relationship with parties or vested interests in the substantive outcome that might interfere or appear to interfere with the ability to function in a fair, unbiased, and impartial manner.

It is important that the mediator continue to maintain a neutral stance after the mediation is completed to avoid casting doubt on the legitimacy of the mediation that occurred and to ensure continued availability for future interventions as appropriate.

Standard 3: The social work mediator shall not reveal to outside parties any information received during the mediation process.

Interpretation: As with . . . other social work methods, the success of mediation depends largely on the confidentiality of the process. The mediator should not reveal to other parties any information received during private sessions or caucuses without the express permission of the parties from whom the mediator received the information.

Mediators should be aware of any legal or statutory limits placed on mediation in the jurisdiction in which they practice. Exceptions to confidentiality and any other exceptions that may arise because of the circumstances, legal framework, or institutional structure within which mediation occurs should be disclosed to the parties before or during their initial meeting with the mediator.

The mediator should inform the parties of the possibility that the mediator might be compelled to testify in court or in other ways reveal information gathered during the mediation process. Confidentiality applies to the mediator and the mediator's records.

Standard 4: Social work mediators shall assess each conflict and shall proceed only in those circumstances in which mediation is an appropriate procedure.

Interpretation: Mediation is not appropriate for all types of conflict. Mediators should assess whether each party has the capacity to engage in mediation and has the support necessary to be an effective participant. . . .

[T]he mediation process should address a potential imbalance of power that might exist between the parties. In those situations in which legal advice or other expert consultation is necessary or would serve parties better, the mediator should make the appropriate referrals. The role of mediator should not be confused with that of an attorney, psychotherapist, or evaluator, even if the mediator also has expertise in one or more of those areas.

Standard 5: The social work mediator shall seek at all times to promote cooperation, to prevent the use of coercive tactics, to foster good-faith bargaining efforts, and to ensure that all agreements are arrived at on a voluntary and informed basis.

Interpretation: . . . Although it is not always possible to ensure that all parties are negotiating in good faith, it is the mediator's responsibility to promote and expect good-faith behavior. The mediator should not allow coercive or bad-faith tactics to continue during the mediation process. If the mediator is aware that these tactics are being used and cannot stop their use, the mediation process should be discontinued.

Standard 6: The social work mediator shall recommend termination of the process when it appears that it is no longer in the interest of the parties to continue it.

Interpretation: . . . Occasionally, it is in the interest of one party to prevent an agreement from being reached. At other times parties are simply unable to agree, and they reach an impasse. The mediator should not continue with the mediation if these situations occur. The mediator should, however, exert every effort to promote the successful conclusion of mediation and should not abandon the effort prematurely.

Standard 7: The social work mediator is responsible for helping the parties arrive at a clearly stated, mutually understood, and mutually acceptable agreement.

Interpretation: The mediator's role is to conduct a fair process, not to promote a particular outcome. The mediator should try to ensure that the agreement, whether partial or full, reflects a fair and good-faith negotiation effort. If the mediator feels that the agreement is illegal, grossly unfair to a participating or unrepresented party, the result of bad-faith bargaining, or based on inaccurate information, the mediator has the obligation to make this known to the parties involved and to try to correct the problem. When parties agree to an unconscionable outcome, an illegal agreement, or one based on dishonesty or misrepresentation, mediators should disassociate themselves from the agreement in accordance with standards of confidentiality.

Standard 8: The social work mediator shall develop an unbiased written agreement that specifies the issues resolved during the course of mediation.

Interpretation: The written agreements should, to the extent possible, be in the language of the parties themselves, and should be clearly understood by them. . . . [I]t is important for parties to know that any agreement may be legally binding and should not be finalized without the appropriate legal advice.

Standard 9: Social work mediators shall have training in both the procedural and substantive aspects of mediation.

Interpretation: Social workers should mediate disputes only in those areas for which they are qualified by training or experience. . . . Occasionally, mediators will be asked to mediate a dispute in which they do not have substantive expertise. If a mediator skilled in that specialty is not available, the mediator either should work with a co-mediator or consultant who is familiar with the substantive area or take the time to become familiar enough with the area to be able to help parties explore their interests and options in an informed manner.

Standard 10: A social work mediator shall have a clearly defined and equitable fee structure.

Interpretation: The fee structure should be presented to all parties at the outset of the mediation. . . . All compensation mediators receive for their services should be known to all involved parties, and mediators should accept no side payments or fees based on the outcome of the mediation process. . . . Under no circumstances should the fee structure give the mediator a vested interest in a particular outcome. Fees should therefore not be contingent on the nature of the agreement or even on the achievement of an agreement.

Standard 11: The mediator shall not use any information obtained during the mediation process for personal benefit or for the benefit of any group or organization with which the mediator is associated.

Interpretation: Mediators are often given access to information that could be used for personal or organizational benefit. It is inappropriate for the mediator to compromise the mediation process by using this information outside the mediation process.

Standard 12: Social work mediators shall be prepared to work collaboratively as appropriate with other professionals and in conformance to the philosophy of social work and mediation.

Interpretation: The mediator should not separately mediate any dispute that already is being mediated. If another mediator has been involved in the case, the mediator should ascertain that this relationship has been terminated before agreeing to become involved. . . . Mediators should respect the involvement of legal, mental health, social services, and other professionals involved in the dispute or with the parties and should work with them in a cooperative and respectful manner.

4. Standards for Arbitrators

a. AAA/ABA, The Code of Ethics for Arbitrators in Commercial Disputes

Arbitrators, like judges, have the power to decide cases. However, unlike full-time judges, arbitrators are usually engaged in other occupations before, during, and after the time that they serve as arbitrators. Often, arbitrators are purposely chosen from the same trade or industry as the parties in order to bring special knowledge to the task of deciding. This code recognizes these fundamental differences between arbitrators and judges.

In some types of arbitration, there are three or more arbitrators. In such cases, it is sometimes the practice for each party, acting alone, to appoint one arbitrator and for the other arbitrators to be designated by those two, by the parties, or by an independent institution or individual. The sponsors of this code believe that it is preferable for parties to agree that all arbitrators should comply with the same ethical standards. However, it is recognized that there is a long-established practice in some types of arbitration for the arbitrators who are appointed by one party, acting alone, to be governed by special ethical considerations. Those special considerations are set forth in the last section of the code, headed "Ethical Considerations Relating to Arbitrators Appointed by One Party."

CANON I. An Arbitrator Should Uphold the Integrity and Fairness of the Arbitration Process.

B. It is inconsistent with the integrity of the arbitration process for persons to solicit appointment for themselves. However, a person may indicate a general willingness to serve as an arbitrator. . . .

D. After accepting appointment and while serving as an arbitrator, a person should avoid entering into any financial, business, professional, family or social relationship, or acquiring any financial or personal interest, which is likely to affect impartiality or which might reasonably create the appearance of partiality or bias. For a reasonable period of time after the decision of a case, persons who have served as arbitrators should avoid entering into any such relationship, or acquiring any such interest, . . . that might create the appearance that they had been influenced in the arbitration by the anticipation or expectation of the relationship or interest. . . .

G. An arbitrator should make all reasonable efforts to prevent delaying tactics, harassment of parties or other participants, or other abuse or disruption of the arbitration process.

H. The ethical obligations of an arbitrator begin upon acceptance of the appointment and continue throughout all stages of the proceeding. . . . [C]ertain ethical obligations [as specified in this Code] begin as soon as a person is requested to serve as an arbitrator and certain ethical obligations continue even after the decision in the case has been given to the parties.

CANON II. An Arbitrator Should Disclose any Interest or Relationship Likely to Affect Impartiality or Which Might Create an Appearance of Partiality or Bias.

These provisions of the code are intended to be applied realistically so that the burden of detailed disclosure does not become so great that it is impractical for persons in the business world to be arbitrators, thereby depriving parties of the services of those who might be best informed and qualified to decide particular types of case.

This code does not limit the freedom of parties to agree on whomever they choose as an arbitrator. When parties, with knowledge of a person's interests and relationships, nevertheless desire that individual to serve as an arbitrator, that person may properly serve. . . .

E. In the event that an arbitrator is requested by all parties to withdraw, the arbitrator should do so. In the event that an arbitrator is requested to withdraw by less than all of the parties because of alleged partiality or bias, the arbitrator should withdraw unless . . . an agreement of the parties, or arbitration rules agreed to by the parties, establishes procedures for determining challenges to arbitrators, [and] then those procedures should be followed. . . .

CANON III. An Arbitrator in Communicating With the Parties Should Avoid Impropriety or the Appearance of Impropriety.

A. If an agreement of the parties or applicable arbitration rules referred to in that agreement, establishes the manner or content of communications between the arbitrator and the parties, the arbitrator should follow those procedures

B. [A]rbitrators should not discuss a case with any party in the absence of each other party. [A listing of exceptions is omitted.]

C. [W]henever an arbitrator communicates in writing with one party, the arbitrator should at the same time send a copy of the communication to each other party. Whenever the arbitrator receives any written communication concerning the case from one party which has not already been sent to each other party, the arbitrator should do so.

CANON IV. An Arbitrator Should Conduct the Proceedings Fairly and Diligently.

D. Unless otherwise agreed by the parties, . . . an arbitrator should accord to all parties the right to appear in person [or by counsel] and to be heard after due notice of the time and place of hearing. . . .

G. When an arbitrator determines that more information than has been presented by the parties is required to decide the case, it is not improper for the arbitrator to ask questions, call witnesses, and request documents or other evidence.

H. It is not improper for an arbitrator to suggest to the parties that they discuss the possibility of settlement of the case. However, an arbitrator should not be present or otherwise participate in the settlement discussions unless requested to do so by all parties. An arbitrator should not exert pressure on any party to settle.

I. Nothing in this code is intended to prevent a person from acting as a mediator or conciliator of a dispute in which he or she has been appointed as arbitrator, if requested to do so by all parties or where authorized or required to do so by applicable laws or rules. . . .

CANON V. An Arbitrator Should Make Decisions in a Just, Independent and Deliberate Manner.

A. An arbitrator should, after careful deliberation, decide all issues submitted for determination. An arbitrator should decide no other issues. . . .

D. In the event that all parties agree upon a settlement of issues in dispute and request an arbitrator to embody that agreement in an award, an arbitrator may do so, but is not required to do so unless satisfied with the propriety of the terms of settlement. . . .

CANON VI. An Arbitrator Should be Faithful to the Relationship of Trust and Confidentiality Inherent in that Office.

A. An arbitrator is in a relationship of trust to the parties and should not, at any time, use confidential information acquired during the arbitration proceeding to gain personal advantage or advantage for others, or to affect adversely the interest of another.

B. Unless otherwise agreed by the parties, or required by applicable rules or law, an arbitrator should keep confidential all matters relating to the arbitration proceedings and decision.

. . . [Extensive provisions regarding payment are omitted.]

CANON VII. Ethical Considerations Relating to Arbitrators Appointed by One Party.

Introductory Note

In some types of arbitration in which there are three arbitrators, it is customary for each party, acting alone, to appoint one arbitrator. The third arbitrator is then appointed by agreement either of the parties or of the two arbitrators, or, failing such agreement, by an independent institution or individual. In some of these types of arbitration, all three arbitrators are customarily considered to be neutral and are expected to observe the same standards of ethical conduct. [In other instances] . . . it has been the practice that the two arbitrators appointed by the parties are not considered to be neutral and are expected to observe many, but not all, of the same ethical standards as the neutral third arbitrator. For the purposes of this code, an arbitrator appointed by one party who is not expected to observe all of the same standards as the third arbitrator is called a "nonneutral arbitrator." Canon VII describes the ethical obligations that nonneutral party-appointed arbitrators should observe and those that are not applicable to them. . . .

It should be noted that, in cases conducted outside the United States, the applicable law might require that all arbitrators be neutral. Accordingly, in such cases, the governing law should be considered before applying any of the following provisions relating to nonneutral party-appointed arbitrators.

A. Obligations under Canon I

Nonneutral party-appointed arbitrators should observe all of the obligations of Canon I [except]:

(1) Nonneutral arbitrators may be predisposed toward the party who appointed them but in all other respects are obligated to act in good faith and with integrity and fairness. For example, nonneutral arbitrators should not engage in delaying tactics or harassment of any party or witness and should not knowingly make untrue or misleading statements to the other arbitrators.

(2) The provisions of Canon I.D relating to relationships and interests are not applicable to nonneutral arbitrators.

B. Obligations under Canon II

Nonneutral party-appointed arbitrators should disclose . . . all interests and relationships which Canon II requires be disclosed. Disclosure . . . is for the benefit not only of the party who appointed the nonneutral arbitrator, but also for the benefit of the other parties and arbitrators so that they may know of any bias which may exist or appear to exist. However, this obligation is subject to the following provisions.

(1) Disclosure by nonneutral arbitrators . . . need not include as detailed information as is expected from persons appointed as neutral arbitrators.

(2) Nonneutral arbitrators are not obliged to withdraw if requested to do so by the party who did not appoint them, notwithstanding the provisions of Canon II.E.

C. Obligations under Canon III

Nonneutral party-appointed arbitrators should [comply with] . . . Canon III concerning communications with the parties, subject only to the following provisions.

(1) [If] . . . the two party-appointed arbitrators are expected to appoint the third arbitrator, nonneutral arbitrators may consult with the party who appointed them concerning the acceptability of persons under consideration for appointment as the third arbitrator.

(2) Nonneutral arbitrators may communicate with the party who appointed them concerning any other aspect of the case, provided they . . . inform the other arbitrators and the parties that they intend to do so. [It is] . . . sufficient to disclose at any time the intention to follow the procedure of having such communications in the future and there is no requirement [of] . . . disclosure before each separate occasion on which such a communication occurs.

(3) When nonneutral arbitrators communicate in writing with the party who appointed them concerning any matter as to which communication is permitted under this code, they are not required to send copies of any such written communication to any other party or arbitrator.

E. Obligations under Canon V

Nonneutral party-appointed arbitrators should observe . . . Canon V [except:] Nonneutral arbitrators are permitted to be predisposed toward deciding in favor of the party who appointed them.

F. Obligations under Canon VI

Nonneutral party-appointed arbitrators should observe . . . Canon VI [except:] Nonneutral arbitrators are not subject to the provisions of Canon VI with respect to any payments by the party who appointed them.

b. Nonneutral Neutrals: Party-Appointed Arbitrators

The provisions regarding party-appointed arbitrators in the AAA\ABA Code of Ethics for Commercial Arbitrators (there is a separate code of ethics for labor arbitrators) merit careful consideration. At one level, there is simply a variant set of rules for a special situation. More fundamentally, however, the party-appointed arbitrator is, to an important extent, not a neutral. Put more starkly, in some instances two of the three arbitrators are nonneutral neutrals.

The dominant view is that party-appointed arbitrators are an unfortunate aberration, but one that is too well established to be eradicated. Another possibility that merits consideration, however, is that this hybrid approach has something to teach us about dispute resolution. Surely the reason that this hybrid approach has became so well established is that parties in labor and commercial disputes find it useful. The objective, after all, is to settle disputes, not to maintain purity of forms.

C. Puffing, Deception and Lying in Negotiations

1. James J. White, *Machiavelli and the Bar: Ethical Limitations on Lying in Negotiation*, 1980 American Bar Foundation Research J. 921*

Upon the enactment of the Model Rules of Professional Conduct, published ethical norms will for the first time give explicit consideration to the lawyer's behavior in the process of negotiation. Rules 4.1, 4.2, and 4.3 deal with negotiation. Although the Canons, the interpretations of the Canons, and the Disciplinary Rules and Ethical Considerations gave tangential consideration to negotiating none of the Disciplinary Rules or Ethical Considerations explicitly considered negotiation apart from the process of litigation or counseling. The mere recognition of negotiation as a separate process worthy of unique rules is a large step. The purpose of this paper is to address the general question of truthfulness as that question is faced in Rule 4.2.

The difficulty of proposing acceptable rules concerning truthfulness in negotiation is presented by several circumstances. First, negotiation is nonpublic behavior. If one negotiator lies to another, only by happenstance will the other discover the lie. If the settlement is concluded by negotiation, there will be no trial, no public testimony by conflicting witnesses, and thus no opportunity to examine the truthfulness of assertions made during the negotiation. Consequently, in negotiation, more than in other contexts, ethical norms can probably be violated with greater confidence that there will be no discovery and punishment. Whether one is likely to be caught for violating an ethical standard says nothing about the merit of the standard. However, if the low probability of punishment means that many lawyers will violate the standard, the standard becomes even more difficult for the honest lawyer to follow, for by doing so he may be forfeiting a significant advantage for his client to others who do not follow the rules.

The drafters appreciated, but perhaps not fully, a second difficulty in drafting ethical norms for negotiators. That is the almost galactic scope of disputes that are subject to resolution by negotiation. One who conceives of negotiation as an alternative to a lawsuit has only scratched the surface. Negotiation is also the process by which one deals with the opposing side in war, with terrorists, with labor or management in a labor agreement, with buyers and sellers of goods, services, and real estate, with lessors, with governmental agencies, and with one's clients, acquaintances, and family. By limiting ones consideration to negotiations in which a lawyer is involved in his professional role, one eliminates some of the most difficult cases but is left with a rather large and irregular universe of disputes. Surely society would tolerate and indeed expect different forms of behavior on the one hand from one assigned to negotiate with terrorists, and on the other from one who is negotiating with the citizens on behalf of a governmental agency.

The difference between those two cases illustrates the less drastic distinctions that may be called for by differences between other negotiating situations. Performance that is standard in one negotiating arena may be gauche, conceivably unethical, in another. More than almost any other form of lawyer behavior, the process of negotiation is varied; it differs from place to place and from subject matter to subject matter. It calls, therefore, either for quite different rules in different contexts or for rules stated only at a very high level of generality.

A final complication in drafting rules about truthfulness arises out of the paradoxical nature of the negotiator's responsibility. On the one hand the negotiator must be fair and truthful; on the other he must mislead his opponent. Like the poker player, a negotiator hopes that his opponent will overestimate the value of his hand. Like the poker player, in a variety of ways he must facilitate his opponent's inaccurate assessment. The critical difference between those who are successful negotiators and those who are not lies in this capacity both to mislead and not to be misled.

Some experienced negotiators will deny the accuracy of this assertion, but they will be wrong. I submit that a careful examination of the behavior of even the most forthright, honest, and trustworthy negotiators will show them actively engaged in misleading their opponents about their true positions. That is true of both the plaintiff and the defendant in a lawsuit. It is true of both labor and management in a collective bargaining agreement. It is true as well of both the buyer and the seller in a wide variety of sales transactions. To conceal one's true position, to mislead an opponent about one's true settling point, is the essence of negotiation.

Of course there are limits on acceptable deceptive behavior in negotiation, but there is the paradox. How can one be "fair" but also mislead? Can we ask the negotiator to mislead, but fairly, like the soldier who must kill, but humanely?

Truthtelling in General

The obligation to behave truthfully in negotiation is embodied in the requirement of Rule 4.2(a) that directs the lawyer to "be fair in dealing with other participants." Presumably the direction to be fair speaks to a variety of acts in addition to truthfulness and also different from it. At a minimum it has something to say about the threats a negotiator may use, about the favors he may offer, and possibly about the extraneous factors other than threats and favors which can appropriately be used in negotiating. As I have suggested elsewhere, each of these issues has important ramifications, and each merits independent consideration by the drafters of the Model Rules and by lawyers. In this paper I ignore those questions and limit my consideration to the question of truth telling.

The comment on fairness under Rule 4.2 makes explicit what is implicit in the rule itself by the following sentence: "Fairness in negotiation implies that representations by or on behalf of one party to the other party be truthful." Standing alone that statement is too broad. Even the Comments contemplate activities such as puffing which, in the broadest sense, are untruthful. It seems quite unlikely that the drafters intend or can realistically hope to outlaw a variety of other nontruthful behavior in negotiations. Below we will consider some examples, but for the time being we will consider the complexity of the task.

Pious and generalized assertions that the negotiator must be "honest" or that the lawyer must use "candor" are not helpful. They are at too high a level of generality, and they fail to appreciate the fact that truth and truthful behavior at one time in one set of circumstances with one set of negotiators may be untruthful in another circumstance with other negotiators. There is no general principle waiting somewhere to be discovered, as Judge Alvin B. Rubin seems to suggest in his article on lawyer's ethics. [Alvin B. Rubin, *A Causerie on Lawyers' Ethics in Negotiation,* 35 LA. L. REV. 577 (1975).] Rather, mostly we are doing what he says we are not doing, namely, hunting for the rules of the game as the game is played in that particular circumstance.

The definition of truth is in part a function of the substance of the negotiation. Because of the policies that lie behind the securities and exchange laws and the demands that Congress has made that information be provided to those who buy and sell, one suspects that lawyers engaged in SEC work have a higher standard of truthfulness than do those whose agreements and negotiations will not affect public buying and selling of assets. Conversely, where the thing to be bought and sold is in fact a lawsuit in which two professional traders conclude the deal, truth means something else. Here truth and candor call for a smaller amount of disclosure, permit greater distortion, and allow the other professional to suffer from his own ignorance and sloth in a way that would not be acceptable in the SEC case. In his article Rubin recognizes that there are such different perceptions among members of the bar engaged in different kinds of practice, and he suggests that there should not be such differences. Why not? Why is it so clear that one's responsibility for truth ought not be a function of the policy, the consequences, and the skill and expectations of the opponent?

Apart from the kinds of differences in truthfulness and candor which arise from the subject matter of the negotiation, one suspects that there are other differences attributable to regional and ethnic differences among negotiators. Although I have only anecdotal data to support this idea, it seems plausible that one's expectation concerning truth and candor might be different in a small, homogeneous community from what it would be in a large, heterogeneous community of lawyers. For one thing, all of the lawyers in the small and homogeneous community will share a common ethnic and environmental background. Each will have been subjected to the same kind of training about what kinds of lies are appropriate and what are not appropriate.

Moreover, the costs of conformity to ethical norms are less in a small community. Because the community is small, it will be easy to know those who do not conform to the standards and to protect oneself against that small number. Conversely, in the large and heterogeneous community, one will not have confidence either about the norms that have been learned by the opposing negotiator or about his conformance to those norms.

The differences that may result in perceptions about "truth and candor" often come to the surface in my negotiations seminar at the Michigan Law School, where there will be students from all parts of the country, from large and small cities, and from a variety of ethnic backgrounds. One such seminar involved a discussion between two students who had engaged in a mock negotiation that had been heated and had resulted in an unsatisfactory outcome for both. Each student had grown up in Manhattan; one was black, the other was Jewish. Their discussion in the seminar about their personal reactions to negotiation, about their experience as children and young adults in the art of negotiation, and about their personal reactions to it was illuminating. The Jewish student, one of the best in the class, was more at ease with the negotiation process, more comfortable with the ambiguity it produced, and more experienced as a negotiator. The black student, also a good student, reported that an extended negotiation without some event to relieve the tension caused him tremendous anxiety. He reported that his youthful negotiations' were short and often concluded in explosive behavior. For example, if there were an argument about where two groups would play baseball (on my lot or yours), the typical negotiation would last a few minutes and, if it were not quickly resolved, would be concluded by a fight. At the conclusion of that fight the game would be played on the winner's lot. Although the anecdote does not show systematic ethical differences between the two students, it does reveal systematically different attitudes about the negotiation process as a whole, and there is no reason to believe that there are not similar and systematic differences about the appropriate level of candor and honesty among the various ethnic and regional subgroups in our society. That is not to say that one norm is correct, only that the rules of the game played by one group are not the same as the rules played by another.

If the Comments or the body of the Model Rules are to refer to truthfulness, they should be understood to mean not an absolute but a relative truth as it is defined in context. That context in turn should be determined by the subject matter of the negotiation and, to a lesser extent, by the region and the background of the negotiators. Of course, such a flexible standard does not resolve the difficulties that arise when negotiators of different experience meet one another. I despair of solving that problem by the promulgation of rules, for to do so would require the drafters of these rules to do something that they obviously could not wish to do. That is, unless they wish to rely on the norms in the various subcultures in the bar to flesh out the rules, they will have to draft an extensive and complex body of rules.

Five Cases

Although it is not necessary to draft such a set of rules, it is probably important to give more than the simple disclaimer about the impossibility of defining the appropriate limits of puffing that the drafters have given in the current Comments. [Comment 4.2 states: "The precise contours of the legal duties concerning disclosure, representation, puffery, over-reaching, and other aspects of honesty in negotiations cannot be concisely stated."] To test these limits, consider five cases. Easiest is the question that arises when one misrepresents his true opinion about the meaning of a case or a statute. Presumably such a misrepresentation is accepted lawyer behavior both in and out of court and is not intended to be precluded by the requirement that the lawyer be "truthful." In writing his briefs, arguing his case, and attempting to persuade the opposing party in negotiation, it is the lawyer's right and probably his responsibility to argue for plausible interpretations of cases and statutes which favor his client's interest, even in circumstances where privately he has advised his client that those are not his true interpretations of the cases and statutes.

A second form of distortion that the Comments plainly envision as permissible is distortion concerning the value of one's case or of the other subject matter involved in the negotiation. Thus the Comments make explicit reference to "puffery." Presumably they are attempting to draw the same line that one draws in commercial law between express warranties and "mere puffing" under section 2-313 of the Uniform Commercial Code. While this line is not easy to draw, it generally means that the seller of a product has the right to make general statements concerning the value of his product without having the law treat those statements as warranties and without having liability if they turn out to be inaccurate estimates of the value. As the statements descend toward greater and greater particularity, as the ignorance of the person receiving the statements increases, the courts are likely to find them to be not puffing but express warranties. By the same token a lawyer could make assertions about his case or about the subject matter of his negotiation in general terms, and if those proved to be inaccurate, they would not be a violation of the ethical standards. Presumably such statements are not violations of the ethical standards even when they conflict with the lawyer's dispassionate analysis of the value of his case.

A third case is related to puffing but different from it. This is the use of the so-called false demand. It is a standard negotiating technique in collective bargaining negotiation and in some other multiple-issue negotiations for one side to include a series of demands about which it cares little or not at all. The purpose of including these demands is to increase one's supply of negotiating currency. One hopes to convince the other party that one or more of these false demands is important and thus successfully to trade it for some significant concession. The assertion of and argument for a false demand involves the same kind of distortion that is involved in puffing or in arguing the merits of cases or statutes that are not really controlling. The proponent of a false demand implicitly or explicitly states his interest in the demand and his estimation of it. Such behavior is untruthful in the broadest sense; yet at least in collective bargaining negotiation its use is a standard part of the process and is not thought to be inappropriate by any experienced bargainer.

Two final examples may be more troublesome. The first involves the response of a lawyer to a question from the other side. Assume that the defendant has instructed his lawyer to accept any settlement offer under $100,000. Having received that instruction, how does the defendant's lawyer respond to the plaintiff's question, "I think $90,000 will settle this case. Will your client give $90,000?" Do you see the dilemma that question poses for the defense lawyer? It calls for information that would not have to be disclosed. A truthful answer to it concludes the negotiation and dashes any possibility of negotiating a lower settlement even in circumstances in which the plaintiff might be willing to accept half of $90,000. Even a moment's hesitation in response to the question may be a nonverbal communication to a clever plaintiff's lawyer that the defendant has given such authority. Yet a negative response is a lie.

It is no answer that a clever lawyer will answer all such questions about authority by refusing to answer them, nor is it an answer that some lawyers will be clever enough to tell their clients not to grant them authority to accept a given sum until the final stages in negotiation. Most of us are not that careful or that clever. Few will routinely refuse to answer such questions in cases in which the client has granted a much lower limit than that discussed by the other party, for in that case an honest answer about the absence of authority is a quick and effective method of changing the opponent's settling point, and it is one that few of us will forego when our authority is far below that requested by the other party. Thus despite the fact that a clever negotiator can avoid having to lie or to reveal his settling point, many lawyers, perhaps most, will sometime be forced by such a question either to lie or to reveal that they have been granted such authority by saying so or by their silence in response to a direct question. Is it fair to lie in such a case?

Before one examines the possible justifications for a lie in that circumstance, consider a final example recently suggested to me by a lawyer . . . [who] represented three persons who had keen charged with shoplifting. Having satisfied himself that there was no significant conflict of interest, the defense lawyer told the prosecutor that two of the three would plead guilty only if the case was dismissed against the third. Previously those two had told the defense counsel that they would plead guilty irrespective of what the third did, and the third had said that he wished to go to trial unless the charges were dropped. Thus the defense lawyer lied to the prosecutor by stating that the two would plead only if the third were allowed to go free. Can the lie be justified in this case?

How does one distinguish the cases where truthfulness is not required and those where it is required? Why do the first three cases seem easy? I suggest they are easy cases because the rules of the game are explicit and well developed in those areas. Everyone expects a lawyer to distort the value of his own case, of his own facts and arguments, and to deprecate those of his opponent. No one is surprised by that, and the system accepts and expects that behavior. To a lesser extent the same is true of the false demand procedure in labor-management negotiations where the ploy is sufficiently widely used to be explicitly identified in the literature. A layman might say that this behavior falls within the ambit of "exaggeration," a form of behavior that while not necessarily respected is not regarded as morally reprehensible in our society.

The last two cases are more difficult. In one the lawyer lies about his authority; in the other he lies about the intention of his clients. It would be more difficult to justify the lies in those cases by arguing that the rules of the game explicitly permit that sort of behavior. Some might say that the rules of the game provide for such distortion, but I suspect that many lawyers would say that such lies are out of bounds and are not part of the rules of the game. Can the lie about authority be justified on the ground that the question itself was improper? Put another way, if I have a right to keep certain information to myself, and if any behavior but a lie will reveal that information to the other side, am I justified in lying? I think not. Particularly in the case in which there are other avenues open to the respondent, should we not ask him to take those avenues? That is, the careful negotiator here can turn aside all such questions and by doing so avoid any inference from his failure to answer such questions.

What makes the last case a close one? Conceivably it is the idea that one accused by the state is entitled to greater leeway in making his case. Possibly one can argue that there is no injury to the state when such a person, particularly an innocent person, goes free. Is it conceivable that the act can be justified on the ground that it is part of the game in this context, that prosecutors as well as defense lawyers routinely misstate what they, their witnesses, and their clients can and will do? None of these arguments seems persuasive. Justice is not served by freeing a guilty person. The system does not necessarily achieve better results by trading two guilty pleas for a dismissal. Perhaps its justification has its roots in the same idea that formerly held that a misrepresentation of one's state of mind was not actionable for it was not a misrepresentation of fact.

In a sense rules governing these cases may simply arise from a recognition by the law of its limited power to shape human behavior. By tolerating exaggeration and puffing in the sales transaction, by refusing to make misstatement of one's intention actionable, the law may simply have recognized the bounds of its control over human behavior. Having said that, one is still left with the question, Are the lies permissible in the last two cases? My general conclusion is that they are not, but I am not nearly as comfortable with that conclusion as I am with the conclusion about the first three cases.

Taken together, the five foregoing cases show me that we do not and cannot intend that a negotiator be "truthful" in the broadest sense of that term. At the minimum we allow him some deviation from truthfulness in asserting his true opinion about cases, statutes, or the value of the subject of the negotiation in other respects. In addition some of us are likely to allow him to lie in response to certain questions that are regarded as out of bounds, and possibly to lie in circumstances where his interest is great and the injury seems small. It would be unfortunate, therefore, for the rule that requires "fairness" to be interpreted to require that a negotiator be truthful in every respect and in all of his dealings. It should be read to allow at least those kinds of untruthfulness that are implicitly and explicitly recognized as acceptable in his forum, a forum defined both by the subject matter and by the participants.

Mandatory Disclosure

Model Rule 4.2(b) requires the lawyer "to disclose a material fact known to the lawyer, even if adverse, when disclosure is . . . necessary to correct a manifest misapprehension of fact or law resulting from a previous representation made by the lawyer or known by the lawyer to have been made by the client. . . ." Elsewhere the rules make clear that one must make such a disclosure even though he is disclosing facts that would otherwise be privileged and that he would otherwise be prohibited from disclosing because of Rule 1.7. The rule is clear and explicit; it unequivocally resolves conflict between client confidentiality and disclosure. For that the drafters should be commended. More important, the drafters are right.

To those who value the privilege more highly than the drafters and who think it sacrilegious to suggest that a lawyer should disclose his client's confidence, consider the anomalies that result if the lawyer is not required to speak up. Assume, for example, that the lawyer for a tenant has negotiated a $2,000 settlement with the landlord's lawyer. Assume that the dispute arose when the tenant's apartment was burglarized and that the settlement was based on the assertion by the tenant that the landlord was negligent in maintaining the locks. Assume, however, that the settlement was based on figures that had been relayed orally by the tenant client to his lawyer. Subsequently the tenant brings a receipt showing that a missing stereo was purchased for $200, although the tenant has now altered the receipt to show a $1,500 purchase price. The $2,000 settlement offer was based on that altered price. Obviously the landlord's lawyer would not have offered a $2,000 settlement had he known that the stereo was worth only $200 and not $1,500. It is a material misrepresentation that would allow any agreement to be overturned on the grounds of fraud or mistake. Would it not be anomalous, then, if the rule said to the lawyer, "You must accept this settlement or at most you can resign, but because these were privileged documents and privileged information you may not disclose them to the other side"? Such a rule would require a lawyer to facilitate an agreement that, if the facts were known, would be unenforceable. Rule 4.2 would require the lawyer to come forward and to tell the other side the stereo's true price.

Consider two other cases where the rule will come into play. One is the situation in which a client has stated certain facts on a deposition and then concedes to his lawyer that they are not true, or it comes to the lawyer's attention by other means that they are not true. In such circumstances the lawyer would have to disclose that to the opposing party. The same rule would apply if at an early stage in a negotiation one party had relied on a case that was subsequently overruled or on a statute that was repealed.

There are two difficulties with the rule; one of them may be a major difficulty. First and least important is to determine how to measure when a "manifest misapprehension" has occurred. Consider, for example, the case widely used in mock negotiation by lawyers and law students in which a mechanic testifies in the deposition that his customer (the father of a child who was killed in an auto accident after the mechanic worked on the car) did not request that the mechanic check the brakes but asked only for a "general checkup" of the car. Subsequently the mechanic comes to his lawyer and states that he "remembers" that the father of the dead child did tell him to check the brakes. To me that has always seemed a straightforward case for this rule, one in which the witness lied initially, subsequently was overcome with remorse, and confessed to his lawyer.

There is another plausible hypothesis that has been suggested to me by my colleague Andrew S. Watson, whose specialty is psychiatry and law, and by various lawyers who have negotiated the problem. That is the hypothesis that the mechanic testified truthfully the first time that he had in fact not been ordered to check the brakes, but that his sense of guilt at being even remotely connected with the death of the child caused him subsequently to believe incorrectly and to state inaccurately that he had been instructed to check the brakes. How is the lawyer to behave in such a case? If he adopts the latter interpretation, there is no misrepresentation and he need not come forward. If he adopts the former interpretation, the case falls squarely within 4.2(b). The rule will present a series of other linedrawing problems in determining whether or not the fact was "material" and in determining whether it "resulted" from a previous representation by the lawyer or his client. Finally, as in the hypothetical case, there will be the question of what is a manifest misapprehension. Doubtless these difficulties are inherent in any rules of the kind proposed, and if we are to have such a rule, we will have to tolerate substantial deviation in its application and use by lawyers based on their individual interpretations of these words.

A more troublesome difficulty with the rule, and one related to the first, is that it may be so widely violated that it ought not be enacted. It is my hypothesis that it is better to have no rule than to have one so widely violated as to be a continuing hypocrisy that may poison the application of the remaining rules. It is conceivable that Rule 4.2(b) is such a rule. In the first place the rule runs up against the traditional and deep-seated idea that the lawyer has a single-minded commitment to his client's case. Like many of the rules it also conflicts with the lawyer's desire to win, with his own identification with his client's case. Of course, lawyers who are so bound up with their clients' cases are not exemplars, but the rules are designed to deal with the mine run as well as the exemplary lawyer. Thus the rule calls on the lawyer not only to squeal on his client but, worse, to destroy a winner for himself and his client.

Of course, it is in the nature of compliance with ethical norms that one's self-interest is often injured, but there must be a trade-off between compliance and injury to one's self-interest. If the latter is too great, few will follow the rules. If any significant part of the rules is routinely violated by a majority of the bar, that in turn weakens the structure of all the rules and makes it difficult to sustain a commitment of the organized bar to following and enforcing those rules. Whether the proposed rule concerning revelations of clients' misstatements and misrepresentations is a rule that would be so widely violated that it should not be enacted I cannot say. From presenting the problem I described above to several hundreds of lawyers and discussing that problem afterward, I am confident that a majority of the lawyers operating under today's rules would not reveal the fact that the client had recanted his deposition in a negotiation with the other party. My observation of those lawyers suggests that the most common position is one in which the lawyer will no longer use the mechanic's assertion affirmatively but will not admit that the mechanic has recanted the position he took on the deposition.

Do these anecdotal data suggest that lawyers in general will not follow the rule? At least it should give pause. It is conceivable that lawyers would change their attitude if a rule as explicit and straightforward as the one proposed were enacted and if there were an effective means to inform the bar at large about such a rule.

In summary, I support Rule 4.2(b), but I think the drafters need to realize that by enacting that rule together with some of the others that are proposed we are asking lawyers to deviate from the traditional American attitude that the lawyer is identified with his client's interest and is obliged to protect privileged information. Because such a rule asks the lawyer not only to act contrary to his selfish interests but also to violate the important psychological association with his client and his client's case, the drafters are undertaking a difficult chore. In their consideration of this rule, the drafters must take account of that question and of the probability that lawyers will be willing to conform to such a rule. If they conclude that a substantial minority of the lawyers who know such a rule will nevertheless violate it, that alone is sufficient basis for not enacting such a rule.

2. Walter W. Steele, *Deceptive Negotiating and High-Toned Morality*, 39 Vand. L. Rev. 1387 (1986)*

I. PREVALENT AMBIGUITIES

. . . From a lawyer's perspective, an advantage of negotiation over other forms of dispute resolution is that negotiation usually is done by lawyers. Litigators and negotiators are usually the same lawyers, and many lawyers negotiate more than they litigate. But consider the following points: (1) lawyers study litigation as an art and frequently attend courses about litigation; but lawyers seldom study negotiation as an art, and courses about negotiation are relatively rare; (2) litigators operate under sophisticated rules of procedure that prevent abuse and exploitation of one litigator by another, stronger litigator, but negotiators operate under

*Reprinted with permission.

primitive and obtuse rules of professional responsibility and under an amorphous set of professional mores common among lawyers. . . .

[E]xplicit negotiation rules are controversial and value laden, while explicit rules of procedure for courts are pervasive and normative. Studying a negotiating rule brings forth remarkably varying opinions, but considering a rule of procedure for courts evokes little controversy. The adversary system unifies thinking about rules of procedure for courts, but no well-understood, commonly accepted unifying philosophy for negotiating exists. This lack of an underlying premise about negotiation may account in part for the fact that standards for negotiation are called "ethics," while standards for procedure in court are called "rules." . . .

Much of the ambiguity surrounding standards of negotiation centers around trustworthiness. Unfortunately, trustworthiness and its outward manifestation—truth telling—are not absolute values. . . . [N]o one tells the truth all of the time, nor is perpetual truth telling expected in most circumstances. To tell the truth in some social situations would be rude. . . . [A] person considered trustworthy and a truth teller actually is a person who tells the truth at the right or necessary time. That person is adept at determining when the proper time for truth has come and perhaps even signals to the opposite party that now that person may be reliable. Reliance is a significant factor in trustworthiness. . . .

Another aspect of the controversy over negotiating standards is abuse of power. Rules of procedure and, to some extent, rules of evidence help prevent one lawyer in a court controversy from taking unreasonable advantage of the other lawyer. . . . But there are no rules of procedure or rules of evidence governing the negotiating process, only ill defined rules of ethics. Consequently, the tactic of bullying and abuse of position has free reign in negotiation. . . .

II. LET'S DANCE: CONVENTIONAL NEGOTIATING ETHICS

. . . As practiced by many attorneys, deception is the spirit of negotiation. Negotiating lawyers misstate facts, willfully mislead by manipulating known facts, or fail to correct an opponent's ignorance or misconception about matters central to the negotiation. These tactics vary in sophistication from merely putting on a false face to expressly lying about the extent of settlement authority. In a broad sense, justifications exist for this less than honest standard for negotiating. A lawyer's devotion to the client's interest is so compelling that some lawyers feel justified, if not compelled, to employ some deception when negotiating. . . .

Another justification for less than honest and straight-forward negotiating is the belief that a convention exists among lawyers to mislead during negotiations. This viewpoint, when carried to its logical conclusion, means that lawyers expect to negotiate with one another much like the proverbial used car salesperson. . . . A final justification for less than honest and straight-forward negotiating is that deceit is inherent to negotiation. . . .

None of these rationalizations for deceptive negotiating is fully satisfactory. As a consequence, each prevaricating negotiator relies upon one or some combination of them. . . . Obviously, what is missing is a specific and reasonably thorough set of standards for negotiating.

III. A REVIEW OF THE CONVENTIONAL RULES

The existing standards for negotiating include statements in the Model Code of Professional Responsibility; statements in the new Model Rules of Professional Conduct; a few cases based largely on principles of contract law, not principles of ethics; and a few statutes criminalizing lawyer deceit. . . .

Under the Model Rules of Professional Conduct, a lawyer with a client who is recalcitrant about revealing information during a negotiation is in a dilemma. Rule 4.1 states: "In the course of representing a client a lawyer shall not knowingly:

(a) make a false statement of material fact or law to a third person; or

(b) fail to disclose a material fact to a third person when disclosure is necessary to avoid assisting a criminal or fraudulent act by a client, unless disclosure is prohibited by rule 1.6.

Within the context of negotiating, Rule 4.1 leads one to several postulates. First, a lawyer cannot disclose a confidence, even though material to a negotiation, if the client instructs the lawyer not to reveal it, unless failure to reveal would result in the client's committing a criminal act that the lawyer believes is likely to result in imminent death or substantial bodily harm—a very unlikely scenario. Second, if not limited by a client's instructions, a lawyer must reveal a fact material to the negotiation if necessary to avoid a fraud by the client.

The older Model Code did not define "fraud." The newer Model Rules define "fraud" as conduct having a purpose to deceive, not mere failure to apprise another of relevant information. Because a client with a purpose to deceive (i.e. fraud) invariably will expressly forbid the lawyer to reveal material facts, this second postulate is of little practical value. Third, a lawyer cannot make a false statement of material fact or law. This particular postulate should come as no surprise. After all, a profession aspiring to be high-toned would not tolerate its members making false statements, a fortiori materially false statements. Consequently, confidentiality between lawyer and client is not a justification for a lawyer declaratively lying about a material fact or law during a negotiation.

Finally, a brief caveat might be added. Deceitful or not, lies about price, value, and some other matters are practically sacrosanct to conventional negotiation. If lawyers were forbidden from engaging in these lies, they would be at a tremendous disadvantage when negotiating with any nonlawyer. Consequently, lawyers are permitted to lie about these matters during negotiation. In summary, we can say that Rule 4.1 does little to guide a lawyer during negotiation when the lawyer's concern is how much, if any, confidential client information can be revealed. In fact, Rule 4.1 says more about what deceit is permitted in the name of confidentiality than it says about what deceit is not permitted. . . .

V. THE IMPACT OF FAIRNESS ON LOYALTY TO THE CLIENT

. . . Among the many objections to the movement toward fairness as a standard for negotiating between lawyers, the objection that a fairness standard may detract from a lawyer's paramount obligation to the client is the most worthy of serious and concerned study. Indeed, if a single principle unifies the legal profession, it is paramount loyalty to the client's cause. Lord Brougham summarized the issue as only an English barrister could in his renowned defense of the Queen in 1820.

> To save that client by all means and expedients, and at all hazards and costs to other persons, and, amongst them, to himself, is his first and only duty; and, in performing this duty he must not regard the alarm, the torments, the destruction which he may bring upon others.

Eloquence aside, Lord Brougham is quite simply wrong. To postulate that the value of loyalty to client is higher than all other values not only does not comport with reality; it does not conform with the requirements of professional ethics. Although loyalty to client is sometimes put forward by lawyers as an absolute value, a noticeable shift has occurred over the years in the approach taken by codified professional ethics. The original Canons of Professional Ethics stated in Canon 15:

> The lawyer owes entire devotion to the interest of the client, warm zeal in the maintenance and defense of his rights and the exertion of his utmost learning and ability, to the end that nothing be taken or be withheld from him, save by the rules of law, legally applied.

Later, when the ABA adopted the Code of Professional Responsibility, the corresponding idea was located in DR 7-101(A)(3), which states: "A lawyer shall not intentionally . . . prejudice or damage his client during the course of the professional relationship. . . ." Currently, under the new Model Rules, Rule 1.3 simply states: "A lawyer shall act with reasonable diligence and promptness in representing a client." Apparently, the excessively ambitious verbiage in the original canon has given way over the years as the obligation of the legal profession to the public good has increased. . . .

The curious anomaly is that while lawyers continue to use loyalty to client as a stalking horse for maintaining the status quo in negotiating ethics, they also create specific exceptions to client loyalty when mandated by this second level of abstraction. Examples in the Model Rules abound: (1) A lawyer shall not counsel or assist a client in fraud or a criminal act; (2) a lawyer may reveal confidences to prevent a client from committing a crime likely to result in substantial bodily harm; (3) a lawyer may reveal confidences to establish a claim or to assert a defense in a controversy between lawyer and client; (4) a lawyer may withdraw if a client insists upon pursuing an objective that the lawyer considers repugnant or imprudent; (5) in rendering advice a lawyer may take into account moral factors; (6) a lawyer may disclose matters as required in connection with a report of an evaluation to the public; (7) a lawyer shall be candid with a tribunal, including revealing law adverse to his client, and if a proceeding is ex parte, a lawyer must reveal facts adverse to his client; (8) a lawyer shall not violate the legal rights of third persons to obtain evidence; (9) a lawyer may engage in public interest activity that may adversely affect the private interests of a client; (10) a lawyer may not engage in conduct prejudicial to administration of justice. In each of these instances the Model Rules permit, and in many instances require, a lawyer to do something that benefits the public good to the likely detriment of the client. Why, then, is the notion that negotiation should achieve a fair result through forthrightness a repugnant notion to so many lawyers?

VI. IS NORMALIZING A STANDARD OF FAIRNESS REALISTIC?

We have noted that categorical rules about negotiation are always controversial and frequently ignored. We have noted that some form of deceit, at least in the broadest sense of the word, is inherent in all negotiations and that a lawyer with an obligation to obtain the best result for a client cannot be expected, realistically, to negotiate outside the context of everyday convention. We have explored the rationalization that part of a lawyer's professional socialization is realizing the extent to which deceit and abuse of power may be employed during negotiations. Finally, we have explored the effect of several professional norms, such as confidentiality, on the prospects for candor and fairness in a negotiation between attorneys. Taken together, all of these factors seem to doom any hope of interposing fairness as a new, enforceable standard for the negotiating process. Nevertheless, some lawyers speculate and dream about a new approach to negotiation. Perhaps no better example of this plea for high-toned morality can be found than in the words of Judge [Alvin] Rubin:

> Client avarice and hostility neither control the lawyer's conscience nor measure his ethics. Surely if its practitioners are principled, a profession that dominates the legal process in our law-oriented society would not expect too much if it required its members to adhere to two simple principles when they negotiate as professionals: Negotiate honestly and in good faith; and do not take unfair advantage of another—regardless of his relative expertise or sophistication.

Posed against Rubin and those of like mind is another group of lawyers with the view that lawyer negotiators must have explicit and detailed commandments if they are to break free from the conventional, professional norms that now seem to compel deceitful negotiating practices. In the words of Professor White:

> Pious and generalized assertions that the negotiator must be "honest" or that the lawyer must use "candor" are not helpful. They are at too high a level of generality, and they fail to appreciate the fact that truth and truthful behavior at one time in one set of circumstances with one set of negotiators may be untruthful in another circumstance with other negotiators.

To admit that changing current standards of negotiating practice among lawyers is difficult is not to admit that it is impossible.

Many practicing lawyers now openly concede, at least at the intellectual level, the need to bring some sort of uplifting modifications to the practice of negotiating. Proof of this view can be found in the legislative history of Rule 4.2 of the new Model Rules of Professional Conduct. The 1980 Discussion Draft of Rule 4.2(a) stated: "In conducting negotiations a lawyer shall be fair in dealing with other participants." Without more in the way of text or explanation, adoption of that rule, relying as it did on the nebulous concept of "fair" as the key descriptive phrase, probably would have done more harm than good. As proposed the rule could have become a vehicle for lawyers with one set of values to characterize other, honest lawyers with different values as "unfair" and in violation of the rule.

As if anticipating such unintended and undesirable results, the drafters of the proposed rule added an explanation of fairness within the context of negotiation. Their approach is conservative. One part of the explanation of "fairness" stated:

> Fairness in negotiation implies that representations by or in behalf of one party to the other party be truthful. This requirement is reflected in contract law, particularly the rules relating to fraud and mistake. A lawyer involved in negotiations has an obligation to assure as far as practicable that the negotiations conform to the law's requirements in this regard.

In reality, that commentary does little more than ask lawyers to follow existing case precedents concerning truth, concealment, fraud, and mistake.

For the benefit of lawyers who might be especially concerned about the impact of fairness on their attorney-client confidences, the drafters of the proposed Comment added this statement:

> A lawyer could properly be regarded as having a professional responsibility to see that negotiations under his or her auspices are informed on all sides. However, to make a lawyer responsible for an opposing party's information about the matter in negotiation exposes the lawyer to charges of misfeasance that can be easily contrived, and exposes the transaction to additional risk of being legally avoided on the ground of mistake.

Whether intentional or not, that statement can be interpreted as an innovative way to avoid the controversy, discussed earlier, about the tensions surrounding a lawyer's client-related duty to keep confidences and a lawyer's society-related duty to achieve fair results. Instead of confronting the issue of when a lawyer should reveal a client confidence because it promotes fairness in negotiations, the drafters deftly shifted the focus from fairness to allegations of lawyer misfeasance if fair disclosure becomes the norm. One might speculate whether a rationale for lack of candor based on self-interested protection from accusations of misfeasance is more palatable than the conventional rationale based on a lawyer's duty to his client.

If lawyers adopted fairness as an explicit standard as proposed, questions would be raised about the inherently deceitful aspects of negotiation, such as overstating of price or value. The drafters of the proposed rule dealt with that issue quite candidly.

> The precise contours of the legal duties concerning disclosure, representation, puffery, overreaching, and other aspects of honesty in negotiations cannot be concisely stated. They have changed over time and vary according to circumstances. They also can vary according to the party's familiarity with transactions of the kind involved. Thus, the modern law of commercial transactions places duties of disclosure on sellers that go well beyond the classic rule of caveat emptor, and modern securities transactions often must conform to elaborate disclosure rules. It is a lawyer's responsibility to see that negotiations conducted by the lawyer conform to applicable legal standards, whatever they may be.

As mentioned previously, because the Model Rules drafters proposed fairness as a standard, a group of lawyers in fact do join with Judge Rubin's call for honest and candid negotiating practice. Admittedly, the wording of proposed Rule 4.1 left room for legitimate concern about interpretation. Instead of embracing the idea of a new high-toned morality for negotiating practice and attempting to lessen the vagueness of the proposed standard, however, the drafters voted for an entirely different version of Rule 4.1—one that totally ignores fairness. As adopted Rule 4.1 states:

> In the course of representing a client a lawyer shall not knowingly: (a) make a false statement of material fact or law to a third person; or (b) fail to disclose a material fact to a third person when disclosure is necessary to avoid assisting a criminal or fraudulent act by a client, unless disclosure is prohibited by Rule 1.6.

That lawyers should not deceive, should not mislead, or should not overreach is too much a part of the common morality to be ignored much longer. Normative negotiating conduct between lawyers cannot survive as a set of values distinct from values held by society at large. Fairness and honesty as concepts are too ingrained in the American mentality to be disregarded even by the legal profession. For now, each lawyer must decide on an individual basis, and perhaps even on a negotiation by negotiation basis, whether he will adopt a high-toned moral approach or a car salesman approach to negotiations, but one wonders how long the absence of specific standards for honesty and candor in negotiation will be tolerated.

VII. A CONCLUDING PROPOSAL FOR A FAIRNESS STANDARD

As a starting point the following proposed rule is offered:

Obligation of Fairness and Candor in Negotiation. When serving as an advocate in court a lawyer must work to achieve the most favorable outcome for his client consistent with the law and the admissible evidence. However, when serving as a negotiator lawyers should strive for a result that is objectively fair. Principled negotiation between lawyers on behalf of clients should be a cooperative process, not an adversarial process. Consequently, whenever two or more lawyers are negotiating on behalf of clients, each lawyer owes the other an obligation of total candor and total cooperation to the extent required to insure that the result is fair.

Like other explicit statements this rule is value laden and provocative. Perhaps the best single answer to criticism of the proposal is to point out that the rule is not designed for specific situations; instead, the rule points toward an ethos of high-toned morality among negotiating lawyers. . . .

The price of high-toned negotiation among lawyers is some lessening of the confidentiality of communication between lawyer and client. Ultimately, some clients will receive less from a settlement negotiated under the standard of fairness than they would have received before the change to the fairness standard. These losses, however, both in confidentiality of information and in settlement result, are losses that come about because lawyers are fairer negotiators. A loss paid for in fairness cannot be described properly as a loss. . . .

Of course, fair negotiation practices require more effort from the legal profession. But lawyers in negotiating situations have an adequate idea of what is fair, and many negotiators strive to reach fair results now. All that the proposed rule suggests is that a lawyer not do that which his conscience and his experience tell him is unfair. The time for change has come.

3. Comments and Questions

a. Do you support Professor Steele's proposal? If not, how would you improve it?

b. Steele's proposal speaks to fair results, and also to total candor by attorneys. Is total candor sufficient, or is there a further duty to promote an "objectively fair" outcome?

c. Steele suggests that a lower standard of candor is required in communications in court than in negotiations outside the judicial context? Does this put the priorities backwards?

d. Many do not accept the idea that a mediator is required to pursue an objectively "fair" settlement. How would mediation, which is no more than a special form of negotiation, be altered if counsel for both parties but not the mediator had a duty to pursue a fair settlement?

e. Does "fair" have any objective meaning, even in the context of a specific fact situation, or is it best regarded as an excluder, with fairness being the absence of unfairness?

D. Confidentiality

1. Comments and Questions

a. Much has already been said about confidentiality in the context of the legal rules regarding discoverability of ADR communications. See Chapter 17, section D. The article by Professor Kevin Gibson, a philosopher, examines the circumstances under which mediators ought to breach confidentiality. His arguments are based on moral principle, and what he thinks the rules for conduct should be, and they should be evaluated on that basis. Gibson is not counselling disobedience of existing rules, or refusing to comply with court orders.

b. The responsibility of dispute resolution (and other) professionals to maintain confidentiality extends far beyond circumstances where disclosure is required by law or court order. The operating rule is simple: never make an unnecessary disclose of information received in a professional context—not to your friends, not to your family, not to anyone! And, when in doubt, err on the side of not making disclosures, absent the explicit consent of all necessary parties.

2. Kevin Gibson, *Confidentiality in Mediation: A Moral Reassessment*, 1992 J. Disp. Resol. 25*

. . . In this article, I will examine confidentiality by looking at the present state of mediation, and some of the legal justifications that are presented. . . . I will argue that there should be many more cases where confidentiality may be broken, and there should be greater provision for external review. I contend that for mediation to be effective some degree of confidentiality may be required, but it is wrong to assume that mediation needs absolute confidentiality. . . .

In order to keep the discussion as broad and inclusive as possible, I will use "mediation" to refer to any organized intervention by an impartial third party and to any part of that process. Although some may consider this term to be too broad, I believe that my conclusions apply extensively. . . .

To encourage openness and to give clients a degree of protection, a mediator will promise to uphold confidentiality. Although such a promise may expedite any particular negotiation, there are nevertheless two strong reasons why the details of a mediation session should not be kept completely confidential. First, if the process is allowed to go on without any sort of review, then it lacks public accountability. Unfair procedures may lead to unfair outcomes, applicable rights may be infringed, and a client may come away from the mediation far worse off than if he or she had gone to court. Secondly, if there are unrepresented but concerned parties who have a right to know or a duty to be warned about something introduced in mediation, then there is a pull towards breaking confidentiality. . . .

IX. THE DUTY TO BREAK CONFIDENTIALITY

Usually, the only clear reference to a mediator's duty to actively break confidentiality is the duty to warn of imminent harm and the duty to report child abuse.

A. The Duty to Warn

The landmark case of Tarasoff v. Regents of the University of California [551 P.2d 334 (1976)] serves as precedent in cases where confidentiality is in conflict with a duty to warn third parties. Tarasoff concerned a patient, Prosenjit Poddar, who told his therapist during psychotherapy that he would kill an unnamed, but clearly identifiable, young woman. The therapist, who worked for the University of California, believed the threats were real and informed the campus police, requesting their assistance in confining Poddar. The police took Poddar into custody, but released him shortly afterwards since they considered him rational. Tatania Tarasoff, the potential victim, was not warned. Poddar ended therapy, and killed Tarasoff roughly two months after making his initial declaration. . . .

The Tarasoff ruling . . . requires psychotherapists to disclose information needed to protect the public from violent patients, even when doing so breaches confidentiality. Tarasoff is a significant precedent in that it places upon the professional the "duty to warn." It should be noted that Tarasoff is more than a passive removal of immunity from testimony; it imposes an active duty to disclose without prompting. The "duty to warn" has been upheld in similar cases.

Currently, the duty to warn has not been specifically imposed on mediators, although the analogy seems to be strong enough to support a parallel duty to that of therapists and coun-

---

*Reprinted with permission.

selors. Like therapists, mediators are in a position where they are likely to become aware of the intentions of a client because of their special relationship to the parties. Thus, a potentially violent husband in a divorce proceeding may only disclose his intentions to hurt his wife's lover because he is in a setting which encourages the sharing of his feelings about the divorce by someone trained in perceptive listening.

The Tarasoff precedent brings with it several problems. For example, Tarasoff is based on a threat and it is left to the professional to gauge the seriousness of that threat. It is not clear whom the mediator would contact: the victim directly, the police, or some superior in the mediation center. Moreover, the mediator is left to decide what exactly constitutes "serious psychological or physical harm."

Asking whether it is likely that a crime will be committed unless mediation confidentiality is broken simplifies this question. However, such a simple rule fails in that there could be reportable cases which are not crimes, and cases which are crimes but may not warrant disclosure. The Tarasoff case itself deals only a very serious sort of crime—premediated murder —and therefore its application may be very narrow. It does not give guidance on other sorts of serious crime, nor does it offer help on acts which may be either illegal but morally justifiable, like the environmental protest, or cases which are legal but immoral, like a cartel agreement.

An example of a threatened crime where it is unclear whether there might be "serious physical harm" sufficient to warrant disclosure is a case where an environmental group suggests during a private caucus with the mediator that one planned "event" will be to splash blood over a furrier's stock. The group is seeking publicity and will acknowledge the act and offer to pay for any damage. The damage would be to property which is susceptible to restitution. In the absence of strict rules, the mediator is again forced to rely on his or her personal judgment.

Nevertheless, it appears incumbent on the mediator to know the appropriate area of law and judge the severity of any admission. However mere knowledge in advance of a crime seems insufficient to warrant a presumed duty to warn.

B. Child Abuse

Child abuse is assumed by many mediators to be the sole justified exception to mediation confidentiality, and they tell their clients at the outset that they will halt the process and report any revealed incidents. The law generally imposes a duty to report by a "caring professional . . . having cause to believe that a child's physical or mental health or welfare has been or may be adversely affected by abuse or neglect." The set of professionals who must report abuse includes physicians, nurses, social workers, teachers, psychologists, chiropractors, public officials, law enforcement personnel, attorneys, clergy and dentists, but not mediators.

Although most mediators assume a duty to report, and would seem to be included in the group by analogy, there is no general legal requirement for them to report. Most reporting laws also state that no one shall be relieved of the duty to report because of the privileged or confidential nature of their communications. There are questions about whether the abuse is actual or potential, and whether mediators need to have heard about the abuse from the child. . . . [T]he requirements may vary for each profession. In Oregon, for example, "attorneys, psychiatrists, psychologists, and clergy need not report child abuse if their suspicion is based solely on confidential communications with adults; they must have direct contact with the child or a non-confidential source of suspicion before reporting is required." Social workers and physicians in Oregon, however, must report a suspicion of child abuse if there is reasonable cause gained from any source. Some commentators have interpreted the Oregon requirements to mean that "[s]ocial workers and physicians . . . must report any suspicion of child abuse."

Where the duty of mediators has been addressed, legal opinion has been notoriously non-committal. For example, the Attorney General of New York was asked to rule on the obligation of mediators to report child abuse. He noted that the statutes mandated reports from health care professionals such as physicians, surgeons, coroners, dentists, osteopaths, and Christian Science practitioners, as well as social workers, school officials, day care workers, peace officers, law enforcement officers, and then concluded [that]:

> [T]he confidentiality provisions of the Community Dispute Resolution Program do not bar Program mediators from reporting evidence of child abuse which is not contained in the memoranda, work products or case files of a mediator and which is not the subject matter of the resolution process. Nor are Program mediators, when acting as such, required to report such evidence as are other officials or professionals specified in section 413 of the Social Services Law.

Barring judicial ruling, mediators do not appear to be members of the group required to report.

The suffering involved and the inability of the victim to alter his or her situation are significant moral distinctions in reportable abuse cases. I see no moral reason why child abuse should be held as unique, since the degree of suffering that an elderly person may endure may be effectively similar, and both the child and the elderly person may be equally inarticulate or find it difficult to have themselves taken seriously. The policy that underlies reporting child abuse appears to support other types of reports as well, and hence I believe that more forms of abuse should be reportable by mediators. . . .

X. CONFIDENTIALITY AND ETHICS

B. Appropriate Cases For Breaching Confidence

There are four cases where I believe that the assessment of moral duty by a mediator will indicate that he or she should break with the present code of conduct and breach confidentiality. A common element in all the cases is that the mediator is acting outside the strictures of the present codes of professional conduct and is required to make a conscious moral deliberation to determine the appropriate role-behavior.

1. Accountability

The most common case is one where there is no good reason to breach confidentiality, except for a claim that it is in the public interest that the process be accountable. Parties will bargain and make disclosures in the course of negotiation. There may be an appeal for openness of the process, so that we can ensure that individual rights are not compromised by parties bargaining in bad faith or that there is incompetence on the part of the mediator. . . .

2. Threats

Consider the hypothetical case of The Threatening Husband: where during the course of a divorce mediation the ex-husband makes a threat. The marriage broke up because the wife became involved with someone else. During a one-on-one discussion with the mediator about child custody, the ex-husband, a security guard, becomes agitated and yells that if he sees his children with his wife's lover he will shoot him. The mediator asks the husband if the threat is real or an expression of anger. The husband replies that he has a temper and the thought of seeing his children accompanied by another man makes him "real mad." The mediator is left wondering whether the statement constitutes a real threat, and whether the threat invokes a duty to warn. One difference between this case and Tarasoff is the vagueness of the threat and the consequent uncertainty on the part of the mediator about whether it constitutes a case of "imminent harm."

There are several possible courses of action open to the mediator: (1) ask the husband to repeat the threat to the wife; (2) ask permission from the husband to restate the threat; (3) tell the wife anyway; (4) break off the mediation; or (5) report the threat to "the authorities"—presumably the police. Present practice, as governed by codes of conduct, might suggest that the mediator should ask permission to repeat in the joint session what was said privately in caucus. If permission is not given, the mediator has the discretion to end the mediation. However, as the threat was neither specific nor imminent there appears to be no duty to warn. . . .

I contend that just as the present sort of introductory remarks that a mediator makes at the beginning of a joint session contain qualification clauses which announce that child abuse will be reported do not appear to deter clients in general, there would be few negative effects from a clause which tells disputants that threats will also result in the breach of confidentiality. A possible consequence of this kind of introductory remark will be to discourage those who know that they are likely to make threats.

Once a threat has been made, I feel that the mediator has a responsibility to the potential victim to let him or her know about it, and allow the potential victim to then choose what to do with the information. Thus, a threat made in the presence of a mediator will most likely result in a breach of confidentiality, whether the report is made to the victim directly, or to a responsible agency. This conclusion allows the mediator greater discretion than he or she has at present by slavishly following a code—the mediator may report a greater range of cases, but only after conscious moral deliberation.

3. Reports of Crime or Abuse

In discussions between joint owners of a family business, one brother intimates that he suspects that the mother, who is in a private nursing home, is being neglected, perhaps because she is left unattended for long periods of time and has bed sores. Although the allegations are not material to the negotiations, the allegation has been made in the presence of the mediator, and the mediator is presented with the issue of the Neglected Mother.

Strictly speaking, the allegations do not concern the mediator, since they refer to a person not represented and not affected by the mediation. The mediator might suggest, without any ethical conflict, that the case be investigated by the parties to the mediation. However, we can imagine that some individuals would not take the allegation seriously, or might not agree to an investigation for other reasons.

Even if the parties themselves wish to ignore the allegation, the mediator may think that a particular case ought to be investigated, and it appears that he or she is foreclosed from pursuing the allegation under the codes of conduct. This is not to say that the mediator should have an obligation to follow through on every rumor that surfaces in mediation. Rather, it suggests that the mediator should be able to make considered judgments about the substance of the allegation and initiate an investigation if he or she believes it to be appropriate.

Such an investigation need not be performed by the mediator personally, rather, the allegations need to be substantiated and then a report made. Ideally, the mediator would give the responsibility of dealing with the allegation back to the party who made it. However, if the party is unwilling or unable to take the responsibility, then the mediator would have to take it upon him or herself to report the allegation, initially to a supervisor, and if necessary to appropriate outside agencies like the social services.

Essentially, what I am advocating here is nothing more or less than treating allegations of serious harm similarly to the way that child abuse is presently treated in mediation. The rationale is that the overall greatest welfare will come about if mediators are willing to break confidentiality, even on behalf of someone not in, or affected by, the mediation itself. . . .

We can contrast the position of the mediator in this incident with that of the attorney. . . . Under their canons of professional responsibility, attorneys should not break client confidences for the advantage of a third party, unless the client consents after full disclosure. Thus, in the present case the brothers may not give permission for an attorney to follow through on the allegation, perhaps because it would involve embarrassing revelations. If permission is not granted, then the attorney has no right to reveal what was imparted during a confidential session. Even though an attorney may disclose information about an imminent crime, he or she may only reveal sufficient information to prevent a crime that his or her client intends to commit. . . .

4. Whistleblowing

A mediator is involved in negotiations between a supplier and contractor. During the talks, the mediator discovers that there will be some toxic chemicals which need disposal and the clients agree to use a contact of the manufacturer who has a way of dealing with toxics "no questions asked." This hypothetical is the case of Suspicious Waste Disposal. The mediator announces that she cannot be party to anything illegal and complicity in any illegal dumping would be equivalent to betraying the public trust in the mediation process. She is assured that she should not worry, since although the public might not approve, the contact will do nothing illegal. The supplier and contractor further hint that the waste will be "going south."

In this case, the mediator faces the conflict between retaining confidentiality in mediation and letting the public know about a deal that may be legal, but is probably unfair to unrepresented parties. To break confidentiality would effectively be a form of "whistleblowing," or calling a foul upon one's own enterprise for the general good. It is sometimes argued that mediators should be indifferent to the settlements that parties may come to. However, I believe that given careful consideration, there may be cases where whistleblowing is appropriate.

The balance which the mediator must determine is the same that any whistleblower must gauge—the utility of his or her product in local and general terms. Here the mediator is helping to produce an agreement that may be in the interests of his or her employers—the disputants—but against the public interest.

Claims that whistleblowing is inappropriate to mediation have two elements: one that suggests that the merits in any individual case are outweighed by the potential damage to the process in general, and an associated claim that a mediator has a duty to preserve the mediation process. The belief that revelations from one particular case damages mediation has been popularized by the wording in Tomlinson [an NLRB decision] which suggests that the benefit in particular cases would be outweighed because testimony by a mediator would "seriously impair," or even "destroy" the usefulness of the Conciliation Service. . . .

The second argument suggests that a mediator should remain loyal to the mediation process. Yet, using this form of words is nothing more than hypostatization, where an abstract entity is treated as concrete. Thus, although grammatically correct, it makes no sense to speak of "loyalty to a process." What the phrase means, properly interpreted, is that mediators are dedicated to the ends of the mediation process, things like wise, efficient settlements which allow a continuing relationship. Given this interpretation, there is no reason for a mediator to hold confidentiality as sacred, but rather it should be seen as a means to an end. Consequently, if mediation is likely to result in an unfair agreement, there should be no compulsion to hang on to confidentiality as an end-in-itself. . . .

Codes of conduct do not provide neat algorithms for all cases in any circumstances and so they are necessarily indeterminate. Even within a code, there will be latitude for personal decisions. Obligatory disclosure is a function of the codes of ethics that are established for mediation. Permissible disclosure is a function of the beliefs and values of the individual mediator and it is incumbent on the mediator to inform his or her clients of the approach and standards that will be used in the mediation process.

A concern is that clients who live immoral lives may come to mediation to sort out a dispute that is, in itself, innocent. Perhaps the operators of two "crack houses" have a dispute about their property line. By my analysis the clients are at risk of being reported by the mediator, and thus immoral disputants may be driven to other means of resolving their differences, like violence. I see this as a genuine difficulty. One possible solution is that the mediator may whistle-blow but is not obliged to do so. We can imagine some mediators having a professional speciality in resolving disputes between unsavory characters with the understanding that only imminent harm and abuse will be reported.

From the mediator's perspective, we find the number of possible cases where confidentiality may be breached has enlarged. Nevertheless, special considerations apply, and as with whistleblowing cases in general there is an expectation that the cases would be exceptional and the potential harm serious and of immediate concern to the public. Moreover, mediators will have differing attitudes about which cases are sufficiently harmful and therefore requiring reporting. Even though we cannot expect mediators to give a before-the-fact listing of such cases, it is nevertheless possible for them to give general statements about their particular approach and attitudes which would indicate their personal values.

I believe these factors would make whistleblowing cases sufficiently unusual so that ordinary potential mediation clients would not be discouraged from using the process. Still, the whistleblowing provision does give the mediator a set of conditions where breaching confidentiality would be acceptable, whatever the letter of the law might be. . . .

E. Seeking Business: Advertising and Solicitation

1. Comments and Questions

a. Advertising and solicitation are illustrative of provisions in professional codes that are concerned with business getting and limiting competition. For an explication of this theme see Stephen K. Huber, Competition at the Bar and the Proposed Code of Professional Standards, 57 N.C. L. Rev. 559 (1979).

b. Why should advertising and solicitation of business by dispute settlement or any other professionals be governed by a separate body of rules and requirements? There already exists a formidable array of statutory protection at both the federal and state level, agencies that will prosecute persistent offenders (e.g., Federal Trade Commission, Attorneys General), and state common law remedies (e.g., fraud, misrepresentation, breach of warranty). The most serious concern, that of in-person solicitation (commonly if inaccurately referred to as "ambulance chasing"), can be handled through the law of duress, or the provision of a "cooling off" period. Statutes and regulations regarding door-to-door sales offer a promising analogy.

c. The article that follows summarizes the advertising rules applicable to Texas lawyers. Would you recommend the adoption of a similarly complex and detailed set of rules for dispute resolution professionals?

d. Advertising rules are being overtaken by modern technology, such as "Web pages." These are subject to the advertising rules, but the State Bar Advertising Review Committee is far behind in its review process. In an interview, Mr. Hile confessed that he does not know how to access the Internet, and he apparently lacks a teenage child or neighbor to show him the way. A proposal to simply require lawyers to file their Web address, plus a statement of compliance with the rules, was rejected even after the Committee, even after it was explained to them that Web pages can be, and commonly are, changed daily.

2. Richard C. Hile, *Rules Regulating Advertisements and Written Solicitation Communications: An Overview*, 58 Texas Bar Journal 595 (1995)*

The passage of the amendments to Part VII of the Texas Rules of Disciplinary Procedure . . . marks a new era in lawyer advertising in Texas. Not only are there sweeping changes in the substantive provisions concerning public media advertisements and written solicitation communications, but Texas lawyers for the first time will be required to file advertisements and writings which are not exempt with the State Bar Advertising Review Committee. This committee will have the task of reviewing these advertisements and writings to ensure compliance with the rules, and where questions arise to require substantiation of . . . claims made therein. The following outline summarizes the rules. . . .

I. False or misleading communications.
   A. A lawyer shall not make a false or misleading communication about the qualifications or the services of *any* lawyer or firm. A communication is false or misleading if it:
      1. contains misrepresentation of fact or facts or omits a fact necessary to make a statement considered as a whole not materially misleading;
      2. creates an unjustified expectation about results a lawyer can achieve, or states or implies that a lawyer can achieve results by means that violate these rules or other law;
      3. compares the lawyer's services with other lawyer services, unless such can be substantiated by verifiable objective data;
      4. states or implies that the lawyer is able to influence improperly or upon irrelevant grounds any tribunal, legislative body, or public official; or
      5. designates one or more specific areas of practice in an advertisement in the public

*Reprinted with permission.

media or in a written solicitation unless the advertising lawyer is competent to handle legal matters in each such areas of practice.

B. [These rules] do not require a lawyer to be certified by the Texas Board of Legal Specialization to advertise a specific area of practice; however, certification satisfies this requirement as to such an area of practice.

II. Information required and/or prohibited in public media advertisements.

A. Required information:

1. Name of lawyer who is responsible for ad content;
2. Statement reflecting either board certification or disclaimer of noncertification by the Texas Board of Legal Specialization;
3. Any person who portrays a lawyer or narrates an advertisement as if he or she was such a lawyer shall be one or more of the lawyers whose services are being advertised;
4. If contingent fees is advertised. the advertisement must state whether the client is obligated to pay all or a portion of the court costs and/or related expenses. If a specific percentage or range of fees is disclosed, the advertisement must also disclose whether the percentage is computed before or after expenses are deducted;
5. If specific fees are advertised, they shall be followed for the period during which the advertisement is reasonably expected to be effective, unless the advertisement specifies a shorter period, but in no instance shall the fees be binding for more than one (1) year after date of publication;
6. The geographic location of lawyer's or firm's principal office. More than one (1) office may be advertised if
   a. staffed by a lawyer at least three (3) days a week;
   b. the advertisement discloses times during which a lawyer will be present at that and other offices; or
   c. states meetings with lawyers are by appointment only;
7. If a lawyer or law firm pays all or a part of the costs of an advertisement in the public media for a lawyer not in the same firm, then the advertisement must disclose the name and address of the financing lawyer, the relationship between the advertising lawyer and financing lawyer, and whether the lawyer is likely to refer cases received through the advertisement to the financing lawyer;
8. If a lawyer knows or should know at the time of an advertisement that a case or matter will likely be referred to other lawyers or firms, a statement of such fact shall be conspicuously included in such advertisement;
9. Cooperative ads require:
   a. statement that advertisement is paid by cooperating lawyers;
   b. names of each cooperative lawyer;
   c. special competency [claims] for each lawyer shall be disclosed;
   d. shall not state or imply that lawyers participating in cooperative ad possess professional superiority, or [are] able to perform services in superior method, except to the extent that information permitted by [these Rules];
   e. shall not otherwise violate Texas Disciplinary Rules of Professional Conduct.

B. Information or matters prohibited in public media advertisements.

1. False or misleading communications;

2. Mottos, slogans or jingles that are false or misleading;
3. A lawyer's association with a lawyer referral service unless such meets the requirements of [Texas law].

III. Written solicitation to prospective clients.

A. Written solicitations shall:
1. be reviewed and either signed by or approved in writing by the lawyer or a lawyer in the firm;
2. contain the appropriate disclaimer information required by and [satisfying] the requirements of [these Rules];
3. be plainly marked "ADVERTISEMENT" on the first page of the communication and also on the face of the envelope. "ADVERTISEMENT" shall be in a color contrasting sharper with the background color and at least 3/8ths inch vertically, or three (3) times the vertical height of the letters in the body of the communication, whichever is larger;
4. contain a statement disclosing how the lawyer obtained the information prompting such written communication if such resulted from a specific occurrence;

B. Written solicitation shall not:
1. involve coercion, duress, fraud, overreaching, intimidation, undue influence, or harassment;
2. contain a false, fraudulent, misleading, deceptive, or unfair statement or claim;
3. resemble legal pleadings or other legal documents;
4. reveal on the envelope the nature of the legal problem of the prospective client or nonclient.

C. The requirements in Paragraphs A and B hereinabove do not apply to written solicitations that:
1. are directed to family members or a person with whom the lawyer has or had an attorney-client relationship;
2. are not motivated by or concerned with a particular past occurrence or event or a prospective client's specific existing legal problem;
3. the lawyer's use of the communication to secure professional employment was not significantly motivated by desire or by the possibility of obtaining pecuniary gain (Example: legal service lawyers).

F. Professional Ethics and the Neutral Lawyer

1. Comments and Questions

a. Professor Riskin's article grew out of the discovery that an important potential role for lawyer neutrals was at best discouraged, and perhaps even a basis for sanctions, under codes of professional responsibility. The traditional view is that a lawyer may serve as a neutral or an advocate, but a hybrid role is impermissible.

b. Should there be a place for the "impartial advising attorney" in codes of legal ethics? What about psychologists and other experts or licensed professionals that participate in mediation? Do the professional codes of any other group prohibit such a role?

2. Leonard L. Riskin, *Toward New Standards for the Neutral Lawyer in Mediation*, 26 ARIZ. L. REV. 329 (1984)*

INTRODUCTION

. . . This Article focuses upon one method of providing legal services: . . . placing one lawyer in a neutral position, as either a mediator who uses his legal skills along with other techniques of helping others resolve a dispute or plan a transaction or an "impartial advisory attorney," who gives legal advice but generally does not try explicitly to facilitate an agreement. These are new forms of lawyering that hold enormous potential for extending mediation services while according adequate protection to the disputants' legal rights. Thus, neutral lawyering can enable lawyers and the bar to fulfill what Justice Burger has called their traditional function of "healing human conflict."

But simply putting a lawyer in a neutral position does not always eliminate the danger that adversarial perspectives will dominate the mediation and reduce or destroy mediation's potential for enhancing relationships and providing satisfying solutions to problems. Much depends on how the neutral lawyer conceives of his task. This perception, in turn, depends importantly upon the impression the legal profession gives its members in regulating the activity of neutral lawyering.

The work of psychologist Carol Gilligan is illuminating in this regard. She has identified two different modes of thinking or "voices" used in addressing moral issues. One "voice" stresses independence and autonomy: it operates primarily through rational processes and relies heavily on rules. The other is grounded in relationships; it emphasizes interdependence and caring. In all people, both voices are present. In men, however, the voice of autonomy tends to be stronger and clearer, while in women, on the whole, the voice of caring dominates.

A hierarchical image of human relationships informs the masculine mode; a web-like image informs the feminine. The import of this dichotomy to dispute resolution is quite direct. The perspective of autonomy dominates the judicial and adversary processes. The perspective of caring and interconnection finds mediation much more hospitable. In fact one of the great values of mediation is that it can make it possible for disputants to hear the voice of caring. [B]oth voices are essential in most mediations. . . .

There is much validity and value, of course, in both modes of thinking about human relations. If mediation is to be extended appropriately, maintaining flexibility, informality and openness while adequately protecting interests normally fostered by adversary processes, it must at least permit, and perhaps encourage, everyone involved to hear and respond to both voices. The central focus of this Article is how — through regulating the neutral lawyer — to allow both voices to be expressed harmoniously in mediation.

A number of bar associations have issued ethics opinions that seek to regulate neutral lawyering. Some of these adopt a highly adversarial perspective. They respond strongly to the voice of autonomy and rights, and they threaten to "legalize" mediation just as arbitration was legalized earlier in this century. . . . Fortunately, another cluster of opinions has evolved; these embody a better integration of the conflicting impulses toward autonomy and interdependence.

Part I describes the need for legal services in mediation and the use of neutral lawyers to answer that need. Part II contains an analysis of existing and proposed professional ethics

---

guidelines and concludes that some are too restrictive and others insufficiently instructive. In Part III, I proffer standards of conduct that would provide appropriate guidance for lawyers and would accommodate their interests as well as those of the bar and the public. . . .

I. LEGAL SERVICES AND THE NEUTRAL LAWYER IN MEDIATION

This Article centers on the duties of the neutral lawyer in situations in which involvement of lawyers for individual parties is either in doubt or is not extensive. When adversary lawyers do not participate in the mediation or do not provide extensive review or advice, when the parties do not know whether they will consult adversary lawyers, when the parties choose against consulting adversary lawyers — when any of these things happen, the neutral lawyer must decide whether and how to accommodate interests normally protected by independent counsel.

The legal services supplied by neutral lawyers in mediation fall along a continuum. At one extreme is the so-called "impartial advisory attorney" who meets with the parties jointly to answer legal questions or to incorporate the decisions they have reached into a written contract. Such lawyers normally do not function as mediators, i.e., they do not try explicitly to help the parties reach an agreement. In an intermediate position on the continuum is the lawyer who performs the same kind of service as an impartial advisory attorney, but does so as part of a team with a mediator, ordinarily a psychotherapist. Finally, some lawyers serve explicitly as mediators.

These lawyer-mediators differ in the extent to which they emphasize law. For some, the substance of the law and the respective rights of the participants form the foundation for decision-making. For others, the law plays a supporting role to the participants' own senses of fairness.

Lawyer-mediators vary also in the type of legal services they provide. Some advise the parties of their rights, explain what is likely to happen if the matter is litigated, and prepare an agreement in what could be final form. Some of these lawyer-mediators urge the parties to have such agreements reviewed by independent counsel; others insist. . . .

A larger group of lawyer-mediators are willing only to prepare a memorandum of agreement that is not in final form, i.e., one that must be redrafted by a lawyer in order to be capable of having legal effect. Within this group, some mediators tell the parties about their legal positions and what would happen in court, and some do not. Of those who do not, some disclaim, or even hide, any identification with the legal profession; these do not fall within my concept of the neutral lawyer.

Neutral lawyering can enhance the mediation process by giving people access to law in a way that diminishes the likelihood that law will dominate their decision-making. The neutral lawyer can reduce the need for and influence of lawyers on the individual parties. This may enable the parties to reach their own agreement. . . .

Moreover, the neutral lawyer can convey legal information in a non-adversarial fashion. This is not an easy task, of course. It is often difficult for lawyers to make clear predictions of what courts would do. Even where the neutral lawyer can make clear predictions, the parties may have difficulty perceiving her as neutral. In some cases, the best way for the neutral lawyer to inform the parties of their rights is to tell them what she thinks they would be told by individual lawyers. Often this will satisfy the needs of the parties, thus saving legal fees and, perhaps, avoiding unnecessary conflict.

The neutral lawyer who serves as a mediator, or who is otherwise deeply involved in the mediation process, offers additional benefits. Because he is an expert on law, he can help free the parties from dependence upon legal norms so that they may reach for a solution that peculiarly suits them. He can do this by helping them understand their legal positions, including the uncertainties, and by explaining that they have a choice about whether to follow legal norms. If experienced, he can offer a variety of arrangements to fulfill the parties' objectives and, more readily than adversary counsel, help integrate these into the decision-making process in ways that will be responsive to the parties unique needs. And he can do a better job than a non-lawyer mediator of identifying essential issues, pressing the parties for decisions, and incorporating these into the resulting agreement. . . .

I do not mean to suggest that lawyers should dominate . . . mediation activity or that it is . . . better to have a lawyer than a non-lawyer mediator. . . . [M]ost lawyers are ill-suited, by training and inclination, to the mediator's role. . . . At the same time, those lawyers who can serve in neutral capacities in mediation and employ their legal skills offer a unique and valuable service to the parties and have a chance to enable themselves and the bar. But they need guidance and encouragement.

II. EXISTING AND PROPOSED GUIDELINES

In determining the extent and nature of their work as neutrals in mediation, lawyers will look for guidance to professional ethics and to malpractice law. Malpractice law, in turn, will draw heavily upon professional ethics pronouncements in establishing standards. The problem is that neither existing nor proposed professional ethics declarations provide appropriate guidance or encouragement. . . .

Professional ethics promulgations dealing explicitly with the work of a neutral attorney in mediation have arisen almost exclusively in divorce mediation, and in the last few years. I divide these opinions into two groups in accordance with whether they conceive of the neutral lawyer as "representing" the parties (the "traditional" approach) or as "not representing" the parties (the "progressive" approach). The traditional opinions stress independence and separation, thus seeming to respond to the "masculine" mode described by Gilligan. The progressive opinions, on the whole, show a better integration of the impulses toward separation and connection.

A. The Traditional Approach

Bar ethics opinions have invoked a number of canons from the Model Code of Professional Responsibility to restrict the activities of lawyers as neutrals. . . . Canon 3 is designed to protect both clients and the bar and commands the lawyer to help prevent the unauthorized practice of law. Canon 9 is meant primarily to protect the bar and individual lawyers by ordering lawyers to avoid even the appearance of professional impropriety. Three other canons are intended mainly to ensure the lawyer's loyalty to her client by enjoining the lawyer to protect the client by preserving his confidences (Canon 4); exercising independent judgement on the client's behalf (Canon 5); and representing him "zealously within the bounds of the law" (Canon 7). These last two canons are the most troublesome in relation to neutral lawyering because they are inconsistent with the expectations of most parties in mediation, most mediators, and many neutral lawyers. In some of the ethics opinions discussed below, these Canons tend to overshadow Ethical Consideration 5-20, the statement in the Code that has the most potential for encouraging neutral lawyering. It provides:

> A lawyer is often asked to serve as an impartial arbitrator or mediator in matters which involve present or former clients. He may serve in either capacity if he first discloses such present or former relationships. After a lawyer has undertaken to act as an impartial arbitrator or mediator, he should not thereafter represent in the dispute any of the parties involved.

The traditional ethics opinions conceive of the neutral lawyer as engaging in "multiple representation." They see a lawyer-client relationship as the sine qua non for giving legal advice and limit the lawyer's authority to represent more than one party by his ability to adequately protect each. Thus, in these opinions, the impulse toward autonomy overshadows the impulse toward connection.

Two opinions dealt with situations in which an attorney-client relationship was deemed to exist between the mediator and both parties. The Washington State Bar and the New Hampshire State Bar committees ruled that, because of this relationship, the lawyer could not ethically engage in certain activities connected with mediation because he would be unable, in so doing, to adequately protect the individual interests of his clients.

Disciplinary Rule 5-105(C) permits multiple representation only "if it is obvious that [the lawyer] can adequately represent the interests of each and if each consents to the representation after full disclosure of the possible effect of such representation on the exercise of his independent professional judgment on behalf of each." The Washington State Bar committee found that this provision was violated by a "Cooperative Divorce Program," under which a lawyer "represented both parties" in reaching and drafting a separation agreement, and apparently filing it with the court. For similar reasons, the New Hampshire committee opined that a lawyer could not ethically mediate a divorce between present clients. . . .

The New Hampshire committee had additional concerns: the inability of the lawyer-mediator to invoke the attorney-client privilege to keep revelations confidential, and the Canon 9 injunction that the lawyer avoid even the appearance of impropriety. The committee's opinion does not apply to other arrangements which might have adequate ethical safeguards or where no previous attorney-client relationship existed.

The Maryland State Bar's Ethics Committee has been more lenient with lawyers who served as "impartial advisory attorneys" in "structured" divorce mediation programs. The committee stressed various dangers: the risk of aiding in the unauthorized practice of law (a violation of Disciplinary Rule 3-101(A)); the risk of creating "the impression that the agreement was the product of negotiation between lawyers [which may preclude the clients] from going behind the agreement to explain their original intentions"; and, the inherent delicacy of the drafting. The committee obligated the lawyer himself to make the determination whether multiple, representation was permissible in a given case. . . .

[T]he Maryland committee decided that the lawyer might appropriately serve in this capacity, but only if he could provide such protection. The Maryland committee felt that a lawyer-mediator who does not have a lawyer-client relationship with the parties may not give legal advice because he would not have a duty of loyalty. But a lawyer who has such a relationship with the parties may function as an impartial advisory attorney if he complies with Disciplinary Rule 5-105(C). He may even represent one of the parties in the subsequent divorce litigation if, in so doing, he could comply with Disciplinary Rule 5-105(C), and requirements in Disciplinary Rule 5-102 as to the lawyer's obligation to withdraw as counsel when he may be called as a witness.

The central idea that pervades these opinions — that the lawyer may represent more than one client in the same matter only if he or she can adequately protect their interests — is embraced by the . . . Model Rules of Professional Conduct, in Rule 2.2.

This traditional approach is not helpful to the development of neutral lawyering in mediation. First, it saddles the lawyer with the burdens of the notion of representation. The idea of undivided loyalty to an individual client is inconsistent with a neutral posture toward all the parties. The vision of a lawyer working for the self-conceived interests of a client, usually in opposition to the interests of others, contrasts starkly with the actual and appropriate orientation of a lawyer who acts as mediator or impartial advisory attorney. Second, because the traditional approach is informed by such a limited notion of what lawyers do, it is of no help whatever in encouraging or guiding neutral lawyers who do not have lawyer-client relationships with the parties. Moreover, it fails to recognize that there are ways to accommodate the disputants' interests in protection from one another without imposing the full burden of doing so on the neutral lawyer.

A recent opinion of the Oregon State Bars offers some hope of mild relief, within the traditional approach, from the restrictions of the notion of "representation." . . . Like the other traditional opinions, this one obligated the mediating attorney to comply with the protective requirements of Disciplinary Rule 5-105(C). It went further, however, and defined a limited representational role for the neutral lawyer:

> A lawyer-mediator, however, does not (and may not) act in an adversarial role but must limit his or her services to providing informational assistance to the parties in a neutral fashion. Any representation by an attorney as an advocate must be rendered by independent counsel, and a lawyer-mediator should advise the parties to have their respective attorneys review any agreement that results from the mediation process.

B. The Progressive Approach

Happily, some ethics opinions and proposed rules do regulate the role of the neutral lawyer in mediation in a fashion that could facilitate the appropriate development of this activity. The authors of these opinions clearly envisioned the need to protect participants, but understood that such protection can be afforded without placing the entire responsibility on the neutral lawyer through the notion of "representation." To the contrary, in this perspective, the neutral lawyer does not represent the parties and must tell them so.

Unhappily, in freeing the neutral lawyer from some of the baggage associated with the idea of representation, these ethics opinions leave too much ambiguity about the neutral lawyer's remaining obligations, and the proposed rules lean too heavily upon adversarial assumptions.

Opinions expressing a better integration of impulses toward autonomy with those toward interdependence have issued recently from bar associations or their ethics committees in Boston, Connecticut, and New York City. These opinions recognized the value of neutral lawyers in mediation and permitted them to perform certain legal services. The Boston opinion, relating to a lawyer who mediated, centered on what legal services the lawyer could ethically perform as part of the mediation. The Connecticut opinion dealt with a lawyer who was described as part of an interdisciplinary team with a counselor and who seemed to function much as an "impartial advisory attorney." The New York opinion concerned a lawyer functioning as either mediator or impartial advisory attorney in a "structured mediation" program.

These opinions each held that a lawyer in the roles that they considered does not "represent" the parties and must so advise them; that he may give legal advice and prepare the separation agreement; but that he may not "represent" either or both parties in subsequent legal proceedings. . . . Each of the opinions imposed additional requirements. They directed that the lawyer make certain explanations of the limitations on his protective role and of the advantages of independent counsel. The New York opinion insisted that such lawyers "give legal advice only to both parties in the presence of the other," and such practice was an implicit assumption of the other two opinions. Under all three opinions the parties' intelligent [and informed] assent to mediation is important. . . .

Although these opinions recognize the value of the neutral lawyer in mediations they leave too much ambiguity about such a lawyer's obligations. Given that she does not "represent" the parties, just how protective of them must she be? The Connecticut opinion did not address this issue. The Boston and New York City opinions relied heavily upon the notion of informed consent to protect both disputants and lawyers. . . .

Such approaches contain two flaws. First, they do not clearly establish what the neutral lawyer is obligated to say. The injunction to explain "all applicable considerations" . . . is difficult to comprehend in the absence of an understanding of the overall obligations that the neutral lawyer discharges by doing so. Second, even if experts could adequately describe what the neutral lawyer is to say, there is a fatal defect in an approach that relies upon regulating disclosures; it tends to ignore both the interactive process between professional and client and the client's understanding of the information.

Both flaws result from the failure of the progressive opinions to articulate the overall objectives of the mediation process or of the neutral lawyer. According to these opinions, the neutral lawyer has an obligation to explain things to the disputants. And though the obligation is unclear, its existence plainly creates a risk that he will be charged with professional misconduct or malpractice. This risk may dissuade lawyers from undertaking neutral roles in mediation or may influence the manner in which they participate. Thus, the "progressive" opinions do not provide the potential neutral lawyer a sufficient basis for either guiding his conduct or overcoming fears of malpractice liability or professional censure. . . .

III. TOWARD NEW STANDARDS

. . . The profession and the public need new standards, ones that will encourage appropriate involvement of lawyers in neutral roles by properly accommodating their interests as well as those of the participants, society, and the bar. To accomplish this, the standards must be informed by a clear sense of the neutral lawyer's duties, and these duties must be formulated so as to encourage the kind of behavior we wish to foster.

When people enter mediation using a neutral lawyer, and when the role of independent counsel for the participants is unclear or minimal, all interested parties — participants, neutral lawyers, the bar, and society — take on certain risks in exchange for possible benefits. The participants face a risk of winding up with an unfair agreement or an agreement which, though fair as between the parties, gives them less than they could have achieved through other processes. Neutral lawyers face a perceived risk of professional censure or malpractice liability. By authorizing this activity, the bar encounters a threat to its institutional integrity. There are risks to society as well. With the diminished involvement of lawyers and courts, a danger arises that societal needs or norms embodied in law or procedure will not be respected, and the rights of third parties might thereby be prejudiced.

Any standards promulgated should respond to these dangers. In addition, they should foster behaviors in neutral lawyers that would make it possible for the participants to hear the voice of caring and interconnection and that can help produce processes and agreements more responsive to the human needs of the participants and affected third parties.

In the remainder of this Article, I will propose and explain two interrelated standards designed to do these things. One is based upon a duty to foster a fair agreement and the other upon a subsidiary duty to "maximize" interests. . . . Their principal uses should be by bar ethics committees in the promulgation or interpretation of "progressive" ethics opinions, by courts in malpractice actions, and by lawyers in determining their own course of conduct. In addition, the standards could be adopted by other organizations that have developed or are developing guidelines to govern the activities of neutral lawyers in mediation. . . .

These standards, finally, also could be employed in situations or jurisdictions where the neutral lawyer is deemed to represent both or all of the participants either because the facts compel it or because of orientation of the decision-maker. In such contexts, they could help continue the process, commenced with the Oregon State Bar Opinion, of defining a new notion of the idea of neutral "representation" in mediation.

A. Fairness

The neutral lawyer in mediation should have a duty to assist participants toward an agreement, and through a process, that 1) meets the participants' own senses of fairness; 2) does not violate minimal societal notions of fairness between persons who make agreements; and 3) does not violate minimal standards of fairness toward unrepresented third parties.

The first part of the standard is aspirational. . . . [I]t could . . . encourage the kind of dialogue that would help make a perspective of caring and interconnection available to participants. This subjective aspect of the standard points the mediator in a direction.

The other parts of the standard are more objective and set the outer limits of the kind of agreements toward which the mediator should be assisting the participants. Under the second part of the standard, the agreement toward which the mediator helps the disputants must not be one which a court would refuse to enforce because of fraud, duress, overreaching, the absence of bargaining ability, or because of substantive unconscionability. Under the third part, the agreement and the process must not offend societal notions of fairness to third parties and other interests.

This fairness standard is supported by some significant currents in the literature on mediation, and it cuts across others. Some writers on negotiation or mediation in general have identified fairness as an important goal. . . . My view is that the neutral lawyer should be obligated to do what is reasonable under the circumstances to enhance these interests.

There are doubtless situations where the mediator need not do much to promote either fairness or maximization — where the parties are evenly matched, for instance, and are represented or advised by capable legal counsel, and where the dispute will not have a significant impact on third parties. In the situations I am addressing, however: first, the involvement of independent legal counsel is either non-existent, minimal or uncertain; second, neutral lawyers may be giving legal advice; and third, the participants lack some of the protections associated with adversary processes. Society and unrepresented third parties or interests also lack the kind of protection that courts can provide through reliance upon and establishment of precedent and through procedures to protect the interests of third parties. Accordingly, it is essential that the neutral lawyer be responsible for fostering these fairness interests.

The most important and most difficult part of the fairness standard is the subjective fairness notion. Use of this standard would produce better agreements . . . by affecting the process in two different ways. First, and obviously, the standard would encourage innovation and flexibility, as opposed to the rigidity that the rule oriented approaches discussed above would foster. Second, and not so obviously, the fairness standard would tend to produce more appropriate attitudes in the neutral lawyer and the participants and thus would markedly affect both the mediation process and the resulting agreement.

The mediator's attitude will reflect the conditions under which his profession permits him to function. The atmosphere in the mediation, in turn, will be highly dependent upon the mediator's attitude. Thus, if the mediator feels constricted or defensive, the entire endeavor may be narrowed.

For instance, the lawyer-mediator who is obligated to impose a three-day cooling off period between the agreement to mediate and the start of mediation might tend to see such a requirement as protective not only of the participants but also of himself. Such reliance on formalities for protection could easily foster an adversarial, formal orientation between the participants and the mediator and, consequently, among the participants. The cooling off period could interfere with such tasks as searching for a true commitment to mediate or determining each participant's idea of fairness. And the adversarial atmosphere could markedly affect all aspects of the process.

More broadly, mediation thrives on trust, and trust requires risk-taking. Participants can exchange some of the protections associated with adversarial/representational processes for a "warmer way of disputing" and the opportunity for a better agreement and relationship. Adversarial rules could potentiate an individualistic perspective, which is already present in most lawyers, and would undercut the cooperative attitude that the lawyer should be cultivating. In contrast, the use of a subjective fairness standard should incline neutral lawyers to join the parties in taking risks.

The subjective fairness standard removes the certainty or illusion of certainty that flows from fixed rules, and it encourages a constant focus on what really should matter. Accordingly, the neutral lawyer would be encouraged for reasons both of self-protection and of service to the participants, to probe deeply into the parties' actual senses of fairness, rather than to rely on the apparent safety of procedural devices that are thought, ordinarily, to serve fairness. . . . The uncertainty created by the subjective fairness standard, on the other hand, would enhance the impulse, based on a perspective of caring and interconnection, toward achieving the best outcome for the clients; it would encourage the participants and the neutral lawyer to keep talking until all are satisfied with the fairness of the agreement.

The fairness standard would bring about better outcomes for another reason: it would assist and encourage the mediator and the parties to see law in its proper relation to mediation. In order to decide whether they would be willing to mediate or agree to a particular resolution, most persons would like to know what disposition a court might make of their case. But one of the chief values of mediation is its ability to free participants from the dominance of an adversarial perspective, which tends to keep their ideas of possible solutions closely moored to their legal rights and thus limits their imagination. With fairness as the overriding goal, the participants can choose to see law as occupying a subsidiary position. Thus the mediator can help bring in law, not to govern and define relationships — unless the participants want it to

— but to inform and test the participants' own senses of fairness under the subjective fairness standard and, under the objective aspects of the standard, to set limits. . . .

Fairness may not be enough. An agreement that is fair between the participants and is not unfair to third parties could be a bad deal for both (or all) of the participants. And all those concerned — disputants, lawyers, the bar, and society — have an interest in preventing such a result. This is the burden of my other standard—the topic of the following section.

B. Maximization

Leading writers on negotiation and mediation recognize that an important goal of these processes should be to identify and exploit joint gains. The neutral lawyer in mediation should be under a duty, subsidiary to the fairness obligation, to help the participants do this.

Unlike most adjudicative procedures, mediation does not ordinarily begin with the notion that there is a fixed pie that the parties must slice up. Instead, the idea is that, by working cooperatively, they can enlarge the pie and perhaps share an entire dinner. If such a process is working, the mediatees, although they retain their individual interests, soon take on the characteristics of a group, with a common interest in working out the most satisfactory solution for everyone. This maximization process has at least two aspects. One is to help the parties enlarge whatever will be available to share or divide. The other is to identify and exploit value differences among the participants. . . .

Part of the maximization process is to help the participants recognize and acknowledge the value of non-material interests, such as mutual respect, caring, and trust. This enriches the pie as well as enlarging it. The neutral lawyer who is responsive to the fairness and maximization standards will be inclined to make available to the participants perspectives under which this can occur.

In other cases, however, the challenge will be to enlarge the number of issues, identify differences in the way participants value certain items or issues, and exploit those differences through trade-offs leading toward the most "efficient" contract, i.e., one that will not permit further joint gains. Sometimes the problem is solved simply by encouraging the participants to focus upon and disclose their true interests. Fisher and Ury tell of the "proverbial two sisters who quarreled over an orange. After they finally agreed to divide the orange in half, the first sister took her half, ate the fruit and threw away the peel, while the other threw away the fruit and used the peel from her half in baking a cake."

In the "real world," participants in mediation may wish to conceal their true valuations in order to enhance their bargaining positions. . . . [T]he mediator must try to help them reveal their actual interests, while the pie is being enlarged, in such a way as not to be vulnerable when it is divided.

C. Malpractice

For purposes of malpractice liability, the neutral lawyer would not be a guarantor of either fairness or maximization. His conduct would be assessed in terms of whether he exercised reasonable care in assisting the participants toward fairness or maximization. The reasonableness of his care would generally be measured by a standard of what the "prudent neutral lawyer" would have done under the circumstances.

The fairness standard . . . would have implications for the way in which a neutral lawyer decided whether and how to give legal advice. It would encourage dialogue about whether the agreement at issue meets the participants' own senses of fairness and societal notions of fairness. The discussions should include attention to whether each participant can adequately form a subjective understanding of fairness without consulting outside counsel.

Such a dialogue would produce better agreements than those which would result from mediations governed by a rule that compels a neutral lawyer to repeat admonitions and threats about the advisability of independent legal counsel. They would also make malpractice actions exceedingly unlikely. Participants who have exhaustively explored how their own senses of fairness, and society's, are expressed in an agreement are unlikely to sue the neutral lawyer. First, they probably will not see unfairness later. Second, they will have formed a significant bond with the neutral lawyer. Even if a malpractice suit were brought, it probably would be unsuccessful.

Violations of the first part of the fairness standard, which obligates the neutral lawyer to assist the participants toward an agreement that meets their own senses of fairness, would almost never give rise to liability. The standard itself is highly subjective. Even if a violation could be shown, it would be difficult to prove resulting damages.

Violations of the second part of the fairness standard, which is grounded on societal notions of fairness in agreements between persons, are more likely to result in liability, but still are not apt to do so. It would be possible to show that an agreement was unconscionable, that the neutral lawyer did not exercise reasonable care in failing to avoid it, and that damages resulted. Such cases would be quite unusual and quite appropriate bases for liability.

The third part of the fairness standard, which deals with societal conceptions of fairness to unrepresented third parties, also would rarely produce liability. The neutral lawyer's duty to the parties should be seen as higher than that owed to outsiders. Egregious cases would give rise to liability, however, and that consideration should impel the neutral lawyer to keep these third party interests in the forefront of the participants' consideration.

Certain kinds of violations of the maximization standard could give rise to liability, while others probably would not. Many of the interests and values at stake in a mediation — such as trust, respect, and cooperation — are not subject to quantification or valuation. Failure to act reasonably to foster such values, even if it could be established, could not be readily associated with measurable damages in a malpractice action.

It is easier to envision how a neutral lawyer might be held liable for failing to adequately foster material interests. A neutral lawyer who failed to tell the couple about the tax advantages of alimony over child support, and instead concurred in their plans to make all payments child support, probably would have breached his duty to exercise reasonable care to help the participants maximize their assets — unless . . . he reasonably believed that outside counsel or a competent accountant would be consulted and would cover this matter. Whether such belief was reasonable would depend upon the [particular facts].

If the neutral lawyer failed to discharge this duty, it would be extraordinarily difficult for the participants to prove individual injuries. In a complex negotiation, so many trade-offs occur that it would be hard to demonstrate how the participants would have incorporated this kind of tax-saving device into their agreement. Yet it could be shown that, collectively, they lost a good deal of money, and that amount could be estimated. [F]or purposes of establishing the neutral lawyer's maximization obligation and assessing damages, it seems best to view the group that comprises all mediation participants as if it were a legal entity. The obligations of the neutral lawyer to this entity are very close to those owed to an individual client.

These risks are relatively easy for the neutral lawyer to contain. He can either know the relevant techniques for maximizing such group interests or take reasonable care to see that the participants learn of these techniques.

Techniques for uncovering and exploiting value differences to achieve joint gains may be less familiar to lawyers. A crucial objective would be to encourage participants to adopt a cooperative problem-solving mode instead of a competitive one. Many techniques are available, but none is sure-fire. In addition, attempts at building trust are likely to engender good relations between neutral lawyer and participant . . ., [so] it seems unlikely that neutral lawyers would be sued or held liable for violation of the maximization duty.

IV. CONCLUSION

The fairness and maximization standards proposed in this Article seem appropriate for all mediators, not just neutral lawyers. Lawyers and non-lawyers might discharge their obligations under these standards differently, however. It would be proper, for instance, for a neutral lawyer, but not a non-lawyer, to supply directly certain information about law.

In maintaining that these standards should govern the activities of neutral lawyers in mediation, I am really suggesting a mechanism by which neutral lawyers can integrate themselves into the mediation process in a fashion that will respect, and not disrupt, mediation's potential for enhancing human relationships, and at the same time will give adequate recognition to the individualistic interests that the law normally protects.

The regulation of neutral lawyering is a test of the bar's ability to help blend the individualistic perspective with views based more upon caring and interconnection. In so doing, it must be concerned not only with serving its constituencies and maintaining its independence and institutional integrity, but also with fulfilling its higher purposes.

Adoption of the proposed standards would lead to disciplined experimentation with neutral lawyering, allowing participants, neutral lawyers, and the bar to reach for and express the highest parts of their natures while protecting their more individualistic interests. It would give lawyers a chance to participate, fully and creatively, in a great adventure that could offer exceptional benefits for lawyers and society. Lawyers who work as neutrals under the fairness and maximization standards could broaden their perspectives and give increased attention to the voice of caring and connection. Some will find ways to employ this fuller perspective in their adversarial work. And that could be the true promise of neutral lawyering.

3. Comments and Questions

Note that Professor Riskin sees his prescriptions as valuable for all mediators. The reason for focusing on lawyers is that their professional codes are an obstacle to filling the role of third party neutral in the way Riskin deems most appropriate.

Chapter 21

Planning For and Avoiding Disputes: Systems Design

CASE STUDY

(Adapted from *Coleman v. Zatechka*, 824 F. Supp. 1360 (D. Neb.1993))

Plaintiff is Kristy Coleman, a 21 year-old student at the University of Nebraska, a public institution, in Lincoln. Defendant is Douglas Zatechka, Director of Housing for the University. Ms. Coleman brought suit against the university alleging that university policies on roommate assignment were in violation of the Americans With Disabilities Act and Section 504 of the Rehabilitation Act.

Ms. Coleman is a victim of cerebral palsy and requires the use of a wheelchair to assist with her mobility and the services of a personal attendant for help with her personal needs. She applied for admission to the university in the summer of 1991 and was accepted for the 1991-92 school year. Wishing to be as much a part of the college community as possible, Ms. Coleman submitted a residence housing contract for dormitory housing. Her application stated that she wanted a room in Selleck Hall and preferred a non-smoking roommate. Her choice of Selleck Hall was based on the modifications that had been made to the dormitory that made it accessible to mobility-impaired students. Selleck Hall is a coed dorm and has a 24-hour open visitation policy. According to the procedures of the university, when an applicant requested a double room but did not stipulate a specific roommate, the university would place the name in a roommate pool and randomly assign a roommate. When Ms. Coleman arrived on campus for the beginning of the Fall term, she found that she had been assigned a room in the dormitory she had requested but she had not been assigned a roommate. She was informed that university policy prohibits the random assignment of a roommate with disabilities who requires a personal attendant care. This is an over all policy and no individual investigation is made into the application of a student with disabilities as to the nature or scope of the disability. The university believed that the policy was in the best interest of all students. In implementing the policy originally, the university took into account the opinions of disabled students who reported feeling uncomfortable with an assigned roommate in the room when the personal attendant was there. The university further felt that the policy would head off the requests for room changes from students randomly assigned to a room with a disabled student. They hoped to avoid what they saw as chaos if students had to be moved around after the beginning of the term.

A formal complaint was filed against the university alleging that the university did not provide equal housing opportunities to disabled students, but the complaint was dropped when the university promised to find a roommate for Ms. Coleman for the 1992-93 school year. She completed her application and submitted it to the university, but again, her name was not put into the roommate pool. Instead, the university sent out a letter to the women students who had residence contracts for the 1992-93 school year asking that anyone interested in sharing a room with a student needing a wheelchair and attendant care contact the housing department. Ms. Coleman was not aware of this letter nor was she aware of an attempt of the university to offer $550 to any student willing to share a room with Ms. Coleman. Neither attempt was successful in finding a roommate for Ms. Coleman.

[Relevant Legal Information: The ADA of 1990 states that:

"No qualified individual with a disability shall, by reason of such disability, be excluded from participation in or be denied the benefits of services, programs, or activities of a public entity, or be subjected to discrimination by any such entity." 42 U.S.C. 12132

Section 504 of the Rehabilitation Act (29 U.S.C. 794) offers the same protection:

"No otherwise qualified individual with handicaps . . . shall solely by reason of her or his handicap, be excluded from the participation in, be denied the benefits of, or be subjected to discrimination under any program or activity receiving Federal financial assistance."

Under both acts, in the educational context, a "qualified" person with a disability is one who meets the academic and technical standards required for admission into the school or program.]

A. Introduction

The second best thing to do about disputes is to settle them in an amicable manner that allows relationships to continue. The best thing to do about disputes is to prevent them from happening. This basic truth has long been apparent, and it is easily stated, but attaining reasonable (let alone excellent) relations often proves to be an elusive goal. System design is planning for disputes, both to prevent disputes and to ameliorate their impact when disputes do occur.

The chapter begins with an examination of designing systems for the avoidance and resolution of disputes. An important and related approach to achieving organizational success is total quality management (TQM). The next topic is labor-management relations, and planning for the departure of professional employees from their organizations—especially law firms. The final subject is partnering a dispute process for high dollar or long-term relationships between organizations. Partnering has been confined to major construction projects, but it could be used much more broadly and frequently for inter-organization relationships.

Before turning to these topics, something needs to be said about contract planning for the use of ADR in the event disputes occur. This is an easy matter—just do it. No imagination or drafting skill is required. Indeed, the temptation to use a "home-made" dispute resolution clause should be avoided. Standardized language for inclusion in contracts is easily available. See Chapter 10, section F for a wide variety of ADR form clauses. Of course, you can borrow these or other standardized terms without making use of the drafting organization.

The message of this chapter is to plan ahead, but doing so is hard work. Consider in this regard the cautionary tale of *Aluminum Company of America, Inc. v. Essex Group, Inc.*, 499 F. Supp. 53 (W.D. Pa. 1980). Alcoa and Essex entered a long-term contract whereby Alcoa agreed to smelt alumina supplied by Essex, and to return it as aluminum. The amount to be paid by Essex was determined by a complex formula based on three factors (national construction costs, local labor costs at the Alcoa facility to be used, and wholesale prices for industrial commodities). This contract was performed for some years, to the profit of Alcoa and the apparent satisfaction of both parties. Then the price of nonlabor costs, notably the price of electricity (vast amounts of which is consumed in the smelting process) rose considerably more than the wholesale price for industrial commodities, an index that was suggested by Alcoa because its expenses for smelting alumina at the plant to be used closely tracked the fluctuations of this index.

Alcoa had gone to considerable trouble to assess possible risks, and to design a pricing formula that would protect it from major cost increases. As part of that process it hired an expert economic consultant, one Dr. Alan Greenspan—the same person who in 1996 was appointed to a third consecutive term as Chairman of the Federal Reserve System Board of Governors. The moral is not that Greenspan was insufficiently clairvoyant, but that the injunction to engage in careful planning is far easier to state than to execute.

B. Main Elements of an ADR System Design

1. E. Wendy Trachte-Huber, ADR System Design: The Pre-Litigation Option (The Attorney As Consultant) (1993)*

I. INTRODUCTION

All organizations experience conflict of some sort. Often this conflict is handled in inefficient or outdated ways. In an effort to assist organizations in resolving their conflicts, experts are being called on to develop "systems designs." A common premise of dispute systems design is that shifting from a power or rights-based system to an interests-based dispute resolution system is desirable. This paper will provide an overview of the systems design process and will examine some current trends in systems design. . . .

II. ALTERNATIVE DISPUTE RESOLUTION SYSTEMS DESIGN

ADR Systems Design involves the use of an ADR professional to develop a comprehensive plan for the resolution of conflict, both internal and external, in an organization. This systematic and institutionalized approach is more desirable than ad hoc efforts for several reasons:

1. A coordinated and systematic approach is the most efficient and cost effective;
2. The systems design approach will generally increase the range of dispute resolution

---

*Reprinted with permission.

options available to an organization; and

3. The coordinated approach allows for an evaluation process which can be fed back to the organization in order to continually evaluate the efficacy of the newly implemented system.

The System Design process generally involves four basic phases: assessment, development, implementation and evaluation.

1. Assessment. During this phase, the organization is examined and inspected for current methods of conflict resolution. The dispute resolution professional gathers data on the organization and meets with key decision makers within the organization. Techniques used in assessment include individual interviews, questionnaires, and personal observation. Working teams are developed to assist in the development of a comprehensive conflict resolution system for the organization.

2. Development. During this phase, the dispute resolution professional and members of the working teams develop a plan to resolve conflicts within the organization. The dispute resolution professional provides expertise in alternative methods of conflict resolution, and the working teams provide expertise on the organization itself. Procedures are developed for the implementation of the conflict resolution system.

3. Implementation. During this phase, the newly-created system is put into operation within the organization. Often there are policy changes which must be implemented, as well as key players who must be trained and educated on the use of the system. The persons who will be affected by the new system, the target population, are educated and trained where necessary. For instance, if peer mediation is to be a component of the conflict resolution system, a mediation training program is provided.

4. Evaluation. After the system has been implemented, some mechanism must be provided for quality control. Often ongoing training is necessary, and changes in the original design may be required. The conflict resolution system design is dynamic rather than static, and may need to change due to shifts in the type of disputes or shifts in the disputants. As with any new process, experience often results in useful suggestions for improvements.

A well-designed conflict resolution system should provide for continual monitoring of the output (the conflicts that pass through the system) to see how it is working. By including a mechanism for feedback, the system can be fine tuned to exactly meet the needs of the users.

It is important to avoid the temptation to consider the newly designed and implemented system a finished and unchangeable product. By providing methods in the initial design by which a continual flow of information can be directed to the designers and implementers of the system, the feedback needs will be met. . . .

IV. THE ROLE OF THE ATTORNEY IN ADR SYSTEMS DESIGN

Attorneys often take a reactive rather than a proactive approach towards problems. It is a shift in this attitude which will allow attorneys the vision to assist clients with ADR systems design. Rather than react to the actions of others, an attorney may assist a client in developing methods to deal with conflict when it arises, and to prevent it from arising. This proactive approach will ultimately save the client time and money.

One type of consultant is a person from outside the organization. Outside consultants bring a fresh perspective to the organization. As outside consultants, attorneys may work with existing clients in the development of ADR Systems Designs. The working team approach, with the attorney as a member of the team, will allow the attorney an opportunity to advise his or her long-term clients about methods to resolve conflict.

In-house counsel may also act as a consultant if they have the necessary expertise in systems design. This strategy will allow for a comprehensive, systematic approach to handling disputes in-house. Many corporations are moving to an in-house approach to systems design. Methods being used include implementing ADR Committees to develop contract clauses, as well as methods to evaluate cases for ADR techniques. Of course, the in-house and outside approaches can be combined, with the outsider taking the lead in the design stage, and the insider taking the lead during implementation. At least part of the evaluation phase should be conducted by someone not associated with the design and implementation of the System, in order to avoid bias. An independent evaluator also can provide valuable advice about improving the current System.

2. Cathy A. Costantino & Christina Sickles Merchant, Designing Conflict Management Systems — A Guide to Creating Productive and Healthy Organizations 19-32, 117-33 (1995)*

The design or improvement of conflict management systems derives many of its practices and principles from well-established organization development (OD) concepts and techniques. We suggest that OD can be thought of as the who, what, and why of organizational action and change, addressing how organizations, their leaders, and their members seek and sustain change: considering, planning, managing, and measuring. These core tasks are also essential to the effective design or improvement of conflict management systems. In general terms, OD is about discovering the need for change, is planned and intentional in nature, and is as durable as possible over time. We suggest that conflict management systems designers need to pursue similar goals in order to achieve a measure of effectiveness in their efforts, and that many OD principles are relevant when exploring conflict management as a system. . . .

Conflict management design extends and applies many OD concepts to the specific area of organizational conflict—the whether and how of dealing with systemic conflict in organizations. Conflict management design draws from the full range of OD theory and practice, particularly systems thinking, change intervention design, search processes, relationship building, strategic redesign and implementation, and action learning for improved conflict management systems development. Moreover, the core values associated with organization development—openness, tolerance of diversity, learning, involvement, appreciation of and management of differences, generation of valid data, and the search for feedback—are particularly critical for successful work with conflict itself and for the systemic management of it in any organization. We examine several of these OD principles, practices, and values here in more detail as they relate particularly to the design of organizational conflict management systems.

When the principles of OD (the who, what, and why) are combined with the principles of conflict management design (the whether and how), a more complete and holistic approach to effective organizational conflict management emerges. OD encourages recognition and understanding of the crucial components of organizations: purpose, structure, leadership, culture, and relationships with internal and external environments. Perhaps one of the reasons that there has been increased dissatisfaction with many of the traditional methods of resolv-

---

ing disputes is their frequent failure to take into account organizational dynamics: how organizations function, how they learn, how they know whether they are performing well, how they adjust to new information and the need for any change, and how they go about the business of changing. We believe that with a grounding in OD values, principles, and processes, practitioners and managers can be more effective in assisting organizations to move away from case-by-case dispute resolution programs and toward more comprehensive, even "global," identification and management of conflict in their systems. . . .

Whole and Open Systems Thinking

[O]rganizations are commonly viewed today as open systems: arrangements of parts dynamically interrelated with each other and with the influences in their environment. Anyone who works with or within organizations is well aware of the following prevailing practice: organizations are structured into functional components such as production operations, sales divisions, customer service offices, human resources departments, legal departments, and the like. Each component has its distinctive purpose, population, role, and culture, and each relies to a greater or lesser extent on the other components to achieve overall organizational performance.

Further, each component of the organization is related to the whole system in a broader sense, with the need to move across or span the functional boxes or boundaries of offices, departments, and divisions in order to accomplish organizational purposes. Thus, each structural and functional component of the organization contributes to and adopts organization-wide characteristics with respect to many subsystems. Examples of such subsystems include the human system (how and which individuals are recruited, selected, mentored, and retained), the work system (how the primary mission of the organization is actually accomplished), the reward system (how the organization rewards and recognizes service and accomplishment of objectives), the financial management system (how the organization allocates and accounts for resource use), and the information system (how data is collected, managed, and disseminated within and outside the organization). What we propose is that conflict management also be viewed as a subsystem within a larger system.

A systems approach to working with organizations encourages the identification of those subsystems that make up the whole and the examination of how well they collectively interact in order to discover how to improve them. . . . [I]mproving the systemic functioning of organizations requires focusing attention on the social systems by which organizational members interact to produce results and on the technical systems that advance output and productivity in the workplace. . . . [T]hese "sociotechnical" aspects of the workplace and its improvement need to be examined and improved collectively rather than segmentally, for when systems interact dynamically with each other within the core of the whole of the organization, it is difficult to identify which is cause and which is effect.

Conflict Management as a System

As one of the many "systems" in organizations, conflict management has been one of the last to be directly recognized and developed. It seems obvious that any organization must have a system, consciously or otherwise, by which it exposes and resolves dissatisfaction, yet this concept of conflict as a system has only recently come into focus. Even more interesting is the relatively new notion that the adequacy and effectiveness of the conflict management system has an effect on the successful operation of other systems within the organization and of the organization as a whole. Perhaps these concepts have not been recognized because organizational conflict management systems have usually been housed in discrete components (legal and human resource departments) that have the responsibility to provide conflict management services to the rest of the organization. Characteristically, these departments' specialized knowledge about the rules, processes, and techniques for handling conflict becomes a matter of job security and, as a result, is tightly held onto in order to increase the department's value to the rest of the organization. In a broader sense, the topic of conflict often makes people uneasy, and individuals, groups, and organizations will therefore conspire to avoid facing it directly. . . .

Traditionally, dispute resolution functions have been housed in two locations within an organization: the legal department (dealing primarily with external disputes) and the human resources and/or personnel department (dealing primarily with internal disputes). Typically, separation of these functions is amplified and strengthened by mission, structure, staff qualifications, and reporting relationships separate and apart from the service, sales, or production components (the technical core) of the organization. In practice, it is often the case that the legal and human resource departments of many organizations are viewed as a necessary evil that must be tolerated to handle the conflicts that others neither like nor believe they are equipped to handle.

Looking at conflict management as but one of many systems within the larger organizational constellation permits an enhanced understanding of conflict as it arises and a sharpened recognition of the opportunities for action in managing such conflict. In this way, the OD systemic perspective aids in the process of observing how organizational units interact and produce to achieve organizational goals, including the collateral and ever-present generation and management of conflict and its costs. The adoption of OD's "helicopter perspective" allows one to metaphorically hover in the air and take a look at what is happening on the ground with respect to conflict management and how it affects other systems. The development of the ability to gain a whole systems perspective of the existing causes, costs, and resolutions of conflict is a crucial link and the common ground between OD and conflict management systems design.

Characteristics of Conflict Management Systems

Like other systems within an organization, conflict management systems have certain characteristics:

• *Boundaries.* These borders, some tangible and some intangible, separate one system from another. In the case of the conflict management system, its internal management boundaries are often clearly defined as the human resource and legal components of any organization. It is in these components that disputes arising from within or outside the organization's overall boundaries are received, processed, and resolved.

• *Purpose.* All systems have a goal or mission that is their reason for being. As long as it meets the expectations and requirements of the external environment regarding products and services, the system can continue to operate in pursuit of its purpose or goal. In the case of the conflict management system, its purpose is the resolution of various types of disputes between the organization and internal or external claimants. Explicitly or implicitly, its purpose within the larger organizational context is to reflect the dominant view of preferred responses to conflict and its resolution (for example, fight or flight).

• *Inputs.* Systems absorb multiple resources in anticipation of fulfilling their purpose: they take in ideas, people, dollars, and raw materials. The conflict management system does this as well by staffing and otherwise funding and supporting organizational components intended to perform the multitude of conflict resolution tasks; the raw materials of the system are the disputes to be resolved.

• *Transformation.* The staff, funding, and other inputs taken into the organization from the external environment are transformed or changed in some manner by the people and technology of the system. This happens at the technical core of the organization, whether by transforming raw materials into saleable products or by providing services to clients. Typically, these core task processes, which fulfill the system's overall purpose, are accomplished by individuals, in roles, organized into groups with a defined function. Such is the case in the organizational conflict management system where staff work to transform disputes into resolutions and impasse into results through processes such as dispute and case intake, information gathering, investigation and fact finding, meetings, oral and written arguments, negotiations, litigation, and court appearances.

• *Outputs.* A system's products or services are then exported to the external environment, which, ideally, finds them useful and acceptable. The outputs of the conflict management system, which are provided internally to the organization or externally to the environment, are the "endings" of disputes, such as withdrawals of cases, decisions, agreements, and settlements.

• *Feedback.* Determining whether a system has fulfilled its purpose is accomplished through feedback. The external environment expects that the system will use feedback either to improve the products or services delivered or to revise goals and objectives in order to bring them into line with expectations. The environment, external to the subsystem (but still within the organization) or external to the organization as a whole, is thus critical to the continued viability of any open system, for it not only supplies the input of people, material, and energy, but also receives and evaluates the output. Organizational conflict management systems receive feedback from their customers, constituents, and employees regarding the adequacy, quality, cost, and perception of fairness about dispute resolutions and results.

We find that thinking of conflict management as an open system operating within a larger organizational system and within an external environment provides a useful framework for approaching conflict management system design and intervention. . . . Operating from an open systems perspective in managing organizational conflict leads to at least two significant results: (1) identification of key areas for inquiry regarding potential change (that is, within the input, transformation, and/or output processes of the organization's current conflict management system) and (2) uncovering dissonance, dysfunction, and dissatisfaction. The conflict management system gathers this information through assessment, feedback, and other participative methods. Those who need to participate in such processes are most easily identified as internal and external "customers" and stakeholders of the organization's dispute resolution program. The assessment is done by looking at the way the organization currently deals with disputes, since that is actually its current conflict management system. . . .

Conflict Management as a Change Intervention

OD intervenors seek to develop open, empowering, and collaborative relationships with the client systems they serve. . . . Most OD intervenors are aware of and use the "self as instrument" perspective during all aspects of the change intervention process. . . . Self-knowledge about bias, blind spots, vulnerability to certain influences, and sensitivity to conflict is of critical importance to anyone seeking to influence others and to guide change in organizational systems dealing with conflict. . . .

Design Architecture: Constructing Conflict Management Models

In contrast to organizational assessment, which looks at the big picture and the "macro" aspects of the design effort, architectural construction focuses on disputes themselves and methods of resolution, which is the "micro" part of managing conflict. Organizational assessment is concerned with the why, what, and who of the current dispute resolution system; design architecture looks at the whether, when, and how of any new conflict management system.

In exploring design architecture, we focus on alternative dispute resolution (ADR) as one possible enrichment of an organization's capacity to manage conflict in its system. More specifically, we look at architectural considerations: whether, when, and how to use ADR. In exploring each of these issues, we offer six key principles to guide the design architecture process. The first two principles address "whether," the next two focus on "when," and the last two concern "how." . . .

Whether, When, How

The first question of design architecture is whether to use ADR at all. Perhaps it is not better, cheaper, faster, more durable. Perhaps the current methods of dispute resolution are working just fine, and there is no need for change. Here, the design architects, the organization and its stakeholders ask the following questions in determining whether to use ADR:

- What, if anything, is missing in these disputes?
- Do stakeholders express dissatisfaction and frustration with all or only part of existing dispute resolution processes?
- How do stakeholders express this dissatisfaction?
- Is an ADR process a possible and appropriate way to address the concerns expressed?
- If so, what type(s) of ADR is/are appropriate?
- Would such ADR steps or processes be a good "fit" with the goals of the organization (mission) and the technology of doing its work (culture)?

If it is decided that ADR is appropriate, the next inquiry for the design team, the organization, and the stakeholders is when to use ADR:

- At what stage of the dispute is there a gap or complaint?
- Can an interest-based process be introduced at that point in the existing procedure?
- Would such an addition address the concern expressed?
- If an ADR step is introduced at that time, what is the likely effect on subsequent stages of the existing dispute resolution system? Would ADR enhance or diminish the possibility of satisfactory resolution?
- Have preventive forms of ADR (such as partnering, ADR clauses, joint problem solving) been attempted with regard to these disputes—before they arise?
- For both prevention and new ADR steps, will disputants have the necessary skills and knowledge to use ADR effectively to resolve the disputes at that stage?

The *how* stage of design architecture is then a blend of the answers to the above questions (whether and when) with the spectrum of ADR options, a continuum from preventive to imposed methods. . . .

Six Principles

The whether, when, how paradigm for design architecture can be translated into practical guiding principles that can help frame any design architecture effort:

1. Develop guidelines for whether ADR is appropriate.
2. Tailor the ADR process to the particular problem.
3. Build in preventive methods of ADR.
4. Make sure that disputants have the necessary knowledge and skill to choose and use ADR.
5. Create ADR systems that are simple to use and easy to access and that resolve disputes early, at the lowest organizational level, with the least bureaucracy.
6. Allow disputants to retain maximum control over choice of ADR method and selection of neutral wherever possible.

PRINCIPLE 1: Develop guidelines for whether ADR is appropriate.

Although ADR is an acronym for alternative dispute resolution, many practitioners engaging in design architecture find it useful to think of ADR as "appropriate" dispute resolution: is ADR appropriate for this *type of conflict,* and if so, what *type* of ADR? This involves helping the organization choose the dispute resolution mechanism that is most tailored to the particular stage or category of dispute—the least costly, most timely, most satisfactory, and most durable methods to employ in seeking resolution. ADR is not an off-the-shelf, one-size-fits-all product. . . .

Organizations are made up of people, culture, technology, and mission, and it is important to ensure that the ADR design is congruent with all of these. Based on an organizational assessment, design architects (as a team or as individuals) critically evaluate whether ADR is understood and viewed as useful by employees and disputants, whether it could further the organization's mission, and whether it fits with the organization's culture. For example, an organization that has a "warrior" culture—a preference for adversarial methods of resolution—may be more likely to accept and use imposed methods of ADR (binding arbitration) than to relinquish disputes to facilitated methods (mediation). The same may be true of organizations whose mission is to enforce some regulatory scheme or ensure compliance with a particular set of standards. Conversely, an organization whose mission is to foster international or community relations may be more prone to use facilitated methods of ADR, such as negotiation and consensus building. . . .

In some cases, however, ADR may not be appropriate at all. For example, where an organization wants to establish a rights-based precedent that can be used in other cases, the court system, rather than ADR, may be the most appropriate forum for resolution. Similarly, if the government has a significant policy that it wants to test, it may be inappropriate to use ADR. In fact, the Administrative Dispute Resolution Act of 1990 provides that an agency should consider not using ADR if one of the following six factors is present: the need to establish precedent; a question of significant public policy that requires additional procedures before a final resolution can be made; the desire to create an established body of policy and decision; the necessity for a public record, which cannot be provided by ADR; the need to maintain ongoing supervision or jurisdiction for compliance, and ADR would interfere with that requirement; or the matter significantly affects absent persons or organizations who are not parties to the ADR process. The considerations for determining whether ADR is appropriate are applicable to the private and nonprofit sectors as well. For example, a company may decide that it wants to push the edge of the law in a particular area, such as patent infringement or the use of noncompete clauses. A nonprofit organization bringing a class action suit on behalf of disabled students in a school district may decide that it needs ongoing supervision by the court to monitor and enforce any consent decree. Even here, it may still be possible to reach a resolution through some form of ADR, such as mediation, if the parties can petition the court at a later date to enforce the settlement or appoint a master. . . .

PRINCIPLE 2: Tailor the ADR process to the particular problem.

Aside from the organizational fit, there should also be a process fit: the ADR process should be appropriate for the particular problem at hand. Choosing mediation as the ADR process when in fact the nuances of a particular case and the interests of the disputants indicate that neutral expert fact finding would be more appropriate (and possibly more successful) can lead to a conclusion by disputants and organizational leadership that ADR does not make sense. For example, in a dispute involving technical or quantitative issues—the value of a real estate parcel, the amount of soil to fill a hole, or the average life expectancy of certain insureds—fact finding or advisory methods may in some instances be more useful than facilitative methods. In a dispute involving how certain franchisee disputes will be resolved, it may be more appropriate to use a form of joint problem solving, which improves the ongoing business relationship, as opposed to a more imposed method of resolution such as arbitration, which may have a chilling effect on the ongoing relationship, reducing it to a matter of winners and losers.

Are there really dangers inherent in selecting an "inappropriate" ADR method? If it fails to work, why not just go back and pick a different method and hope to get it right the second time? The danger in constructing a design built on inappropriate ADR methods is that unsuccessful ADR experiences lead to the impression on the part of managers, resource allocators, disputants, and critics that all forms of ADR are unsuccessful or meaningless exercises: "ADR didn't work here, so why should it work somewhere else?" . . .

PRINCIPLE 3: Build in preventive methods of ADR.

It may be useful to think of developing a range of preventive methods of ADR that are applicable in a variety of contexts, such as the individual, group, organization, community, and global environments. . . . For example, methods of prevention at the individual level may include increasing one's tolerance for and acceptance of conflict or improving interpersonal communication and active listening skills; prevention methods at the level of the group may involve practicing consensus decision making, engaging in team building, and generating problem resolution options through brainstorming; prevention methods at the level of the organization could entail circulating ongoing employee feedback surveys, developing strategic visions collectively (search conferences), and involving constituents in change processes on an ongoing basis; prevention methods at the level of the community might include creating multicultural educational programs and forums, as well as conducting search conferences to establish a community vision and direction; prevention methods at the level of nations could include offering assistance, training, and support to emerging nations in the development of institutional dispute resolution processes as well as in training dispute resolvers. . . .

To date, not much attention has been focused on preventive methods of ADR. As organizations continue to adopt "best practices" in their day-to-day operations and relationships—to compete, to control costs, and to maximize resources—dispute prevention becomes increasingly important. Furthermore, organizations will come to expect design architects to be familiar with ADR methods of prevention and to include them in their recommendations for the furtherance of the systemic management of conflict.

PRINCIPLE 4: Make sure that disputants have the necessary knowledge and skill to choose and use ADR.

Determining when to use ADR depends in large measure on whether the affected disputants have the necessary knowledge to choose ADR and the skills to use it once they have chosen it. People are unlikely to choose a procedure about which they know nothing. Thus, labor and management need to know how to engage in interest-identification processes, brainstorming, and consensus decision making in order to use interest-based negotiation. A dissatisfied customer needs to know what mediation is and how to participate in it before she can choose it and participate as an informed ADR user. An unhappy claimant needs to know what nonbinding arbitration is before he can decide to submit his claim to such a process. Whether and when ADR is used is often determined by the ADR knowledge and skill levels of those choosing the method.

Practitioners know that disputants, more often than not, are only ready to resolve disputes in their own time. Disputants have to be assured that they have standing and that their complaint has been heard. Further, they need information about their dispute before they can consider possible choices for resolution, especially the more unfamiliar forms of ADR. For example, it may be difficult for claimants to choose early neutral evaluation or a mini-trial if they have not assessed their case or they do not have a basic understanding of the facts to be presented to a neutral. It would be hard for claimants to use the services of an ombudsperson without first identifying the issue or being able to articulate the particular grievance. Some practitioners have seen ADR fail because disputants were unfamiliar or uncomfortable with the facts of their case or had not yet assessed their options; they were thus not only unable to commit to a solution but also unable to commit to a process. Conversely, sometimes practitioners see disputants and organizations delay ADR use to the point where the dollars and time already expended in overdeveloping the facts require them to justify such use of resources to the point of litigation. In this way, the optimal time for the use of ADR in a particular dispute is intimately tied to the organization's culture of dispute development and its tolerance of conflict and risk.

PRINCIPLE 5: Create ADR systems that are simple to use and easy to access and that resolve disputes early, at the lowest organizational level, with the least bureaucracy.

Effective design architects embrace the KISS principle (keep it simple, stupid"). They make ADR simple to use, easy to access, and readily available, with a minimum of delay. In order for disputants to actually choose ADR, it must be easier to use than the current dispute resolution system. . . .

In most instances, resolving disputes as early as possible decreases costs and increases satisfaction. As noted above, early resolution may be impeded by the disputants' own understanding and knowledge (or the lack thereof) of their case. More often, early resolution is impeded by organizational constraints, such as cultural attitudes toward conflict or risk, the need for lengthy review and approval processes, or the failure to make ADR simple to use and easy to access.

Many organizations require the use of multiple levels of the bureaucracy to study, dissect, and review the merits of a dispute before it can be resolved. Thus, although the disputants may want to resolve the dispute as quickly and as early as possible, organizational practices and procedures may constrain them. This is where the principle of "subsidiarity" arises: designing conflict management systems that resolve disputes at the lowest organizational level possible. As an architectural design principle, subsidiarity is often difficult to implement in highly stratified, vertically organized institutions that take pride in their review and approval procedures. Some organizations, for example, bifurcate the review and approval processes: they require review and approval through several chains of command to engage in ADR and then a second review and approval (often through the same chain of command) to commit to a resolution reached through ADR. . . . However, some practitioners have found it helpful to work with such an organization's leadership to point out the benefit and wisdom of designing more streamlined approval procedures for particular divisions, offices, or clusters of cases.

PRINCIPLE 6: Allow disputants to retain maximum control over choice of ADR method and selection of neutral wherever possible.

Not surprisingly, practitioners have found that disputants are likely to be more resistant to an ADR process if they are not involved in selecting it and even more resistant if they have little or no voice in determining who the neutral will be. Consistently attempting to build on the values of participation, openness, and feedback requires that selection of ADR methods be derived rather than imposed. . . .

3. William R. Potapchuk et. al., *Getting to the Table: A Guide for Senior Managers* (1990), U.S. Army Corps of Engineers Working Paper No. 3 [IWR Working Paper 90-ADR-WP-3], Appendix A

A GUIDE TO SITUATION ASSESSMENT

When you are involved in a difficult situation, ongoing assessment of the actors, issues, and other dynamics is essential to developing effective strategy and making wise choices. Broad participation in an analysis and assessment process by all the parties will help build a shared perspective on the problem and the steps necessary to move forward. Indeed, joint analysis is often a key step in bringing parties to the table.

The following guide offers a series of questions to help you identify useful information. The commentary is specifically focused on data from the analysis that will impact the building of a forum and the getting-to-the-table stage of disputes.

Assessment also is useful for developing and clarifying your interests in preparation for negotiations. While this task is not emphasized here, we encourage you to be well prepared as you enter negotiations.

I. THE PARTIES, THEIR RELATIONSHIPS, AND THEIR NEEDS

A. Who Are The Parties?

- Who is responsible for making the decision?

- Who may be affected by potential solutions?
- Who may be able to block or ensure a particular decision?

Understanding the broad set of stakeholders can help you begin to assess how many persons or organizations will need to be involved, and how much narrowing can be accomplished.

B. How Is Each Party Organized?

- Are the parties primarily organizational entities?
- What is their structure — hierarchical? collective?
- Does each organization have identified leadership?
- What is the relationship between the leadership and others?

If each party is well organized and will vest responsibility in its leadership, ascertaining representatives will be easier.

C. What Is The Power Base Of Each Of The Parties?

Of the parties who do not have formal authority for the decision, but seek to influence the decision:

- Does any party have the capacity to block decisions they do not approve?
- Does any party have an incentive to escalate the conflict?
- What is the capacity of each party to sustain its involvement over time?
- Does any party need another party in order to accomplish its goals? Does interdependence exist between these parties and the decision makers?
- Does any party have past experience with joint decision-making processes?
- Would any party need specific assistance to effectively participate in a joint decision-making process?

If some parties have the capacity to block decisions, they will certainly need to be involved in the process. If parties have the capacity to sustain activities, they may be able to effectively participate in a joint decision-making process, and stalling by decision makers will not be effective. If the parties need each other to accomplish their objectives, joint decision-making may be appropriate.

Of the parties who do have formal authority for the decision:

- Can the parties make and implement any decision they please?
- Can the parties protect their essential interests in the decision no matter how the decision is made? How?
- Are the parties constrained by previous decisions or decisions made by others (e.g., legislative bodies, precedent)?
- Can the parties sustain their involvement over time in any kind of process (e.g., legal, negotiated)?
- Do the parties need other parties to accomplish their goals?
- Do the parties have any experience with joint decision-making processes?

If the parties can make and implement any decision they please, reasons for entering joint decision-making will be for other than their substantive interests. If they cannot, they may seek a process where they can protect their essential interests and sustain their involvement over time.

D. How Has Power Been Used In The Situation?

- Have any of the parties used their power such that other parties have felt it has been to prevent them from reaching their goals?
- Have any of the parties used their power to help other parties?

If one of the parties has systematically used its power in a direct attempt to injure other parties, those parties will be distrustful and be very wary of joint decision-making processes.

E. What Do Each Of The Parties Want?

- What are the stated positions of each party?
- What are the stated goals of each party?
- What are the underlying interests of each party?
- What are the dominant values that appear to guide the actions of each party? Are they mutually exclusive?
- Do any of the positions, goals, interests, values, or issues of any party challenge the identity of other parties?
- Does this situation represent high stakes for any party?
- Are there common interests which might provide the basis for an agreement?

Knowing what motivates each of the parties and whether there are overlapping interests can help predict whether the parties will see any value in coming to the table. Parties involved in identity or high stakes conflicts will need a table where each party believes their essential interests are protected.

F. Past Relationships

- Do any of the parties have a history of relationships with other parties?
- Has that history been productive or conflictual?
- Were the relationships characterized by trust and respect?
- Have any of the parties avoided other parties because they believed working relationships would be difficult?

Past relationships that worked well can be the basis for developing joint decision-making efforts. Difficult relationships, especially those characterized by distrust, may need to be addressed directly for joint decision-making to be productive.

G. Current Status Of Relationships

- Has the nature of the relationships between the parties changed over time?
- Are there existing working relationships?
- How are the parties communicating with each other?

If they are not communicating directly, are there any trusted intermediaries?

- Do the parties accept each other's role in developing a joint agreement?

If the current relationships are healthy joint decision making will help maintain strong relationships. If current relationships are contentious or characterized by lack of trust, a strong past relationship, a desire for a future relationship, or high levels of interdependence can mitigate current difficulties.

H. Desire For Future Relationships

- Do any of the parties desire a future working relationship with other parties?
- Will the parties need to work together on implementing an agreement?
- Are the parties forced to interact regularly because of the nature of their work or networks?

A desire for a future working relationship can be a strong impetus for using joint decision-making processes.

I. Who Are The Primary Stakeholders?

- Who are the primary stakeholders? Why?
- Who are the secondary stakeholders?

Primary stakeholders will probably need to be directly involved in joint decision making. Secondary stakeholders may need to be kept informed or participate only at key points in the process.

II. THE SUBSTANCE

A. What Are The Issues?

- How does each party describe its own central issues?
- Do the issues differ between those who have authority for the decision and those who seek to influence the decision?
- Can all the issues be addressed in a joint decision-making process?
- Is resolution of the issues likely to be precedential?
- Are there secondary issues that may have an impact on the process or the outcome?
- Is there a framing of the issues that will address the concerns of all the parties?

Once the issues are clear, some determination can be made about how they can be approached. Some issues may be addressed only through one approach. Others may be addressed through a range of approaches. Putting some issues on the table or taking others off may be a prerequisite for some parties agreeing to come to the table.

B. Are The Issues Framed As Integrative, Distributive, Or Redistributive?

- Are the issues either-or?
- Can distribution or redistributive issues be reframed as integrative?
- Can the resources be increased?

Integrative issues — which by definition are those that can be resolved by meeting everyone's needs — are the easiest to negotiate and promote cooperative approaches. Distributive issues "such as how shall this new money be allocated — often produce competitive orientations. Redistributive issues — such as how shall the city's agencies respond to a 10 percent budget cut — promote adversarial approaches. Either—or issues — such do we build the highway or not? — also promote adversarial approaches. Reframing the issues or increasing the resources available can help promote cooperative approaches.

C. How Does Each Party See The Available Options For Each Issue?

- Have options been developed for each central issue? For secondary issues?
- Are the options well defined?
- Have all the potential options been explored by all the parties?
- Do any of the options seem to meet the needs of all the parties?
- Does any party feel that none of the options meets its needs?
- If new options are generated, will extensive or expensive further study be required?

If all the potential options have been generated and none seems to meet the needs of the parties, joint decision making may be difficult. If new options can be created that better meet the needs of the parties, joint decision-making processes may be appropriate. If new options require extensive or expensive study, pre-negotiation protocols should address the group's ability to generate new options.

D. What Are The Data And Information Needs?

- Do each of the parties believe sufficient data is available?
- Are the data and their analysis considered trustworthy by the parties?
- Will each party feel comfortable working with a common body of data?

Developing a common understanding of the problem may require further data collection or additional analysis. Each party must feel comfortable with the data.

III. BACKGROUND, CONTEXT, AND FORMAL PROCESS

A. What Is The History Of The Situation?
- Have there been several stages (e.g., latent, emerging, litigation)?
- Have external events influenced the situation? How? Will they affect a decision-making process or the outcomes?
- The history of the situation may be a guide to future action for disputants and the third party.

B. Are There Any Parameters Set Externally That Must Be Followed?
- Are there any statutes or regulations that govern action in this situation? Is there any flexibility?
- Have there been any similar situations whose outcome will influence what happens here?

The external context may limit what is possible or what the parties believe is possible.

C. Is There A Formal Process Typically Used For Resolving These Issues?
- Can all the stakeholders use the formal process?
- Is the formal process adjudicative, administrative, consensual or legislative in nature?

The formal process often helps define the informal process. Joint decision-making processes may only be able to produce advisory outcomes if formal legislative or judicial action is needed. If all of the primary stakeholders cannot participate in the formal process, they may seek to sabotage the formal process or engage in alternatives.

IV. STRATEGIC ISSUES

A. Are There Any Likely Existing Forums For Resolving The Issues?
- Are there any forums which have been used to resolve similar situations in the past? Have they been perceived as productive?
- Do some of the issues require a certain kind of forum (i.e., constitutional issues may require court involvement)?

The existence of several forums may allow some parties to go forum shopping. Sometimes the choice of forum is limited by the issues.

B. How Does Each Party See Its Alternatives?
- How does each party see its best alternative to a negotiated agreement? Its worst alternative? Its most likely alternative?
- Do any of the forums lack credibility from the perspective of any party?

If the parties have superior strategic alternatives to a joint process, they may pursue those alternatives. Some forums may be particularly difficult to "sell" to some of the parties.

4. Comments and Questions

a. How does an organization develop the expertise to undertake a system design, and the "in-house" training of employees? The basic options are to hire someone, to send some employees for training, and to hire an outside organization to design and implement the process. (All sorts of hybrids are possible, that combine elements of the three basic alternatives.)

b. Assume that a firm has chosen to adopt an "out house" approach to system design. What are the key factors in selecting a system design provider? Should that provider organization be used subsequently to mediate or arbitrate organization disputes?

c. What are the key considerations for an organization in determining the optimum approach to implementing a dispute prevention and resolution system?

C. Total Quality Management (TQM)

1. Comments and Questions

a. This section provides a brief overview of total quality management (TQM), a well-established approach to management. The leading practitioner, W. Edward Deming, was honored in Japan long before his work was recognized in the United States. Deming's ideas helped to drive the Japanese economic miracle.

b. There are a vast array of differently named quality improvement ideas and programs, many accompanied by a formidable special vocubulary. Many of the suggestions of the TQM movement strike outsiders as glorified common sense. Success depends not on intellectual knowledge but effective implementation.

c. Prevention of disputes, and minimizing the impact of those disputes that do occur, is an important aspect of TQM. One effective resolution strategy for organization is to appoint an ombudsperson. See the materials in Chapter 13, section D.

2. E. Wendy Trachte-Huber, ADR System Design: The Pre-Litigation Option (The Attorney As Consultant) (1993)

III. THE TOTAL QUALITY MANAGEMENT MOVEMENT

The business community has known about total quality management (TQM) for many years, but the legal community has embraced TQM only recently. The TQM approach emphasizes customer service and employee teamwork to improve products and service to customers. TQM has found a new application in the design of conflict management systems.

W. Edwards Deming, management consultant and leader of the TQM movement, has distilled the core principles underlying TQM into his Fourteen Points. These are:

1. Create constancy of purpose for improvement of product and service;
2. Adopt a new philosophy;
3. Cease dependence on mass inspection;
4. End the practice of awarding business on price tag alone;
5. Improve constantly and forever the system of production and service;
6. Institute training;
7. Institute leadership;
8. Drive out fear;
9. Break down barriers between staff areas;
10. Eliminate slogans, exhortations, and targets for the work force;
11. Eliminate numerical quotas;
12. Remove barriers to pride of workmanship;

13. Institute a vigorous program of education and retraining; and
14. Take action to accomplish the transformation.

A fifteenth point could well be, "Develop and implement a dynamic dispute resolution system." Many of these points reflect the importance of a comprehensive, systematic approach to conflict resolution within an organization. It is important to recognize that even though Deming directs his remarks to the business community, attorneys may also benefit from the recognition that clients are their customers. Providing a full range of services to clients should be the main objective of the legal profession. ADR systems design provides another important client service to add to the armory of the full service law firm or an in-house legal department.

D. Labor-Mangement Relationships

1. Comments and Questions

a. Shorn of the language of system design and TQM, dealing with disputes has long been a central feature of collectively bargained contracts, which commonly include a complex framework for addressing labor management disputes. Over a period of years, the resolution of many specific disputes produces a "common law" of the unit, factory or industry. See generally the materials in Chapter 12, section C, and the Abrams et. al. article in Chapter 12, section D.

b. The U.S. Government has adopted a systems design approach to labor relations, backed up by an Executive Order. The Army Corps of Enginners has been a leader in this area. A leading example in the private sector is provided by the large engineering firm, Brown & Root.

2. Executive Order No. 12,871 (October 1, 1993) (President Clinton), 58 Fed. Reg. 52,201 (1993)

Labor-Management Partnerships

The involvement of Federal Government employees and their union representatives is essential to achieving the National Performance Review's Government reform objectives. Only by changing the nature of Federal labor-management relations so that managers, employees, and employees' elected union representatives serve as partners will it be possible to design and implement comprehensive changes necessary to reform Government. Labor-management partnerships will champion change in Federal Government agencies to transform them into organizations capable of delivering the highest quality services to the American people. . . . [I]n order to establish a new form of labor-management relations throughout the executive branch to promote the principles and recommendations adopted as a result of the National Performance Review, it is hereby ordered:

Section 1. The National Partnership Council.

(a) There is established the National Partnership Council ("Council"). The Council shall comprise the following members appointed by the President:
  (1) Director of the Office of Personnel Management;
  (2) Deputy Secretary of Labor;
  (3) Deputy Director for Management, OMB;
  (4) Chair, Federal Labor Relations Authority;

(5) Federal Mediation and Conciliation Director;
(6) President, American Federation of Government Employees;
(7) President, National Federation of Federal Employees;
(8) President, National Treasury Employees Union;
(9) Official, Public Employees Department, AFL-CIO; and
(10) [Officers from two other executive agencies.]

(b) Responsibilities and Functions. The Council shall advise the President on matters involving labor-management relations in the executive branch. Its activities shall include:

(1) supporting the creation of labor-management partnerships and promoting partnership efforts in the executive branch, to the extent permitted by law;
(2) proposing to the President statutory changes necessary to achieve the objectives of this order, including legislation consistent with the National Performance Review's recommendations for the creation of a flexible and responsive hiring system and the reform of the General Schedule classification system;
(3) collecting and disseminating information about, and providing guidance on, partnership efforts in the executive branch, including results achieved, to the extent permitted by law;
(4) utilizing the expertise of individuals both within and outside the Federal Government to foster partnership arrangements; and
(5) working with the President's Management Council toward reform consistent with the National Performance Review's recommendations throughout the executive branch.

(c) Administration. (1) The President shall designate a member of the Council who is a full-time Federal employee to serve as Chairperson. The responsibilities of the Chairperson shall include scheduling meetings of the Council.

(2) The Council shall seek input from nonmember Federal agencies, particularly smaller agencies. It also may, from time to time, invite experts from the private and public sectors to submit information. The Council shall also seek input from companies, nonprofit organizations, State and local governments, Federal Government employees, and customers of Federal Government services, as needed.
(3) To the extent permitted by law and subject to the availability of appropriations, OPM shall provide such facilities, support, and administrative services to the Council as the Director of OPM deems appropriate.
(4) Members of the Council shall serve without compensation for their work on the Council, but shall be allowed travel expenses, including per diem in lieu of subsistence, as authorized by law, for persons serving intermittently in Government service.
(5) All agencies shall, to the extent permitted by law, provide to the Council such assistance, information, and advice as the Council may request.

(d) General. (1) I have determined that the Council shall be established in compliance with the Federal Advisory Committee Act, as amended (5 U.S.C. App. 2).

(2) [T]he functions of the President under the Federal Advisory Committee Act, as amended, except that of reporting to the Congress, that are applicable to the Council, shall be performed by the Director of OPM, in accordance with guidelines and procedures issued by the Administrator of General Services. . . .

Section 2. Implementation of Labor-Management Partnerships Throughout the Executive Branch. The head of each agency shall:

(a) create labor-management partnerships by forming labor-management committees or councils at appropriate levels, or adapting existing councils or committees if such groups exist, to help reform Government;

(b) involve employees and their union representatives as full partners with management representatives to identify problems and craft solutions to better serve the agency's customers and mission;

(c) provide systematic training of appropriate agency employees (including line managers, first line supervisors, and union representatives who are Federal employees) in consensual methods of dispute resolution, such as alternative dispute resolution techniques and interest-based bargaining approaches;

(d) negotiate over the subjects set forth in 5 U.S.C. 7106(b)(1), and instruct subordinate officials to do the same; and

(e) evaluate progress and improvements in organizational performance resulting from the labor-management partnerships.

Section 3. No Administrative or Judicial Review. This order is intended only to improve the internal management of the executive branch and is not intended to, and does not, create any right to administrative or judicial review, or any other right, substantive or procedural, enforceable by a party against the United States, its agencies or instrumentalities, its officers or employees, or any other person.

3. U.S. Army Corps of Engineers, *Partnership Councils: Building Successful Labor-Management Relationships*, IWR Working Paper 94-ADR-WP-5 (1994)

INTRODUCTION

In most organizations, the establishment of a Partnership Council institutes a dramatic change from a traditional adversarial culture to a new cooperative relationship. The quality of this new relationship will stem from mutual trust, honest communications, and teamwork. The effort the partners put into the relationship will be reflected in the lasting results achieved. Building an effective relationship takes understanding and time, but most of all it takes commitment to the mutual goals and vision of the partnership. . . . Creating a successful Partnership Council is a collaborative endeavor that involves labor and management focusing on their common interests. This pamphlet is intended to be a blueprint for all partners to use in establishing a new labor-management partnership for their organization. . . .

EXECUTIVE ORDER No. 12,871: "LABOR-MANAGEMENT PARTNERSHIPS"

Acting on the National Performance Review (NPR) partnership recommendation, the President issued Executive Order 12,871 on October 1, 1993. The order states that the involvement of federal employees and their union representatives in a partnership is essential to achieving the NPR's reform objectives. As partners in the design and implementation of comprehensive change, federal employees will transform agencies "into organizations capable of delivering the highest quality services to the American people." To do this, agencies are directed to do the following: create labor-management partnerships by forming councils;

involve employees and their union representatives as full partners with management; provide training in consensual methods of dispute resolution and interest-based bargaining; negotiate over the subjects in 5 U.S.C. § 7106 (b)(1); and evaluate progress in organizational performance.

[Section 7106 is titled Management Rights, but (b)(1) specifically permits an agency to negotiate about "the numbers, types, and grades of employees or positions assigned to any organizational subdivisions, work project, or tour of duty, or on the technology, methods, and means of performing work."]

1. Why a Partnership?

The simple answer to the question, "Why form a partnership?" is that it is necessary to comply with the National Performance Review and President Clinton's Executive Order. But beyond meeting these requirements, creating a labor-management partnership makes good business sense. It is logical to involve all parties in reshaping the organizational culture, finding better ways to prevent and resolve differences, and establishing a relationship to meet the needs of the partners and the American people.

2. What Is a Partnership Council?

A Partnership Council is an internal group composed of labor and management officials and reflecting a new relationship among the partners. In an organization that has several bargaining units, the organization may have more than one Partnership Council or a single Partnership Council with several bargaining unit members. Regardless of how many Partnership Councils are established, the partners decide the way that an individual partnership develops and the final form that it takes. Each partnership will be different and should be tailored to meet the needs of the partners and satisfy their common interests. Specific details such as the number of members, the level of membership, and the formality of the meetings will depend on the partners.

PREPARATION FOR SUCCESS

1. Make It a Joint Design

The Partnership Council should be collaboratively designed by labor and management. When the partnership is being established, there should be no one-sided objectives or hidden agendas. The partners need to work together to create a Partnership Council to better serve the organization and its employees and to meet the organization's mission. . . .

2. Form the Partnership Design Team

One way to create a Partnership Council is to begin by forming a design team that consists of representatives from labor and management. Full participation by each partner on the design team will significantly increase the chances of success for the Partnership Council since the partners will share ownership in the new relationship that results from their joint endeavor. The members of the design team may be the same individuals who will initially serve on the Partnership Council and may include union members and officers, senior managers, human resources officials, and an attorney. The level of representation for management will depend on the extent of bargaining unit representation in the activity.

3. Consider Partnership Characteristics

The Partnership Design Team should incorporate the following characteristics of successful partnerships when designing the Partnership Council:

Attitude – Each partner adopts a positive attitude that reflects the change in attitude from confrontational to cooperative.

Commitment – Each partner pledges to act and fulfill all duties necessary to make the partnership successful.

Respect – The partners recognize and acknowledge that individual personalities and organizational structures can differ, yet are entitled to respect.

Communications – The partners dedicate themselves to open and honest communications that involve speaking freely and frankly and listening actively.

Sharing – Each partner is willing to share necessary information voluntarily without engaging in positional bargaining.

Trust – Trust is earned over time by the partners' actions being consistent with their words.

Goals – Mutual goals are jointly established by the partnership, which also sets objectives to reach those goals.

Consensus – Solutions to issues are jointly developed by all partners, are acceptable to all partners, and are supported by all partners.

Responsibility – All partners accept responsibility for the change in the relationship, feel responsible for the success or failure of the partnership, and act accordingly.

Synergy – All partners work together to achieve a synergistic partnership in which the totality is greater than the sum of the individual parts.

WORKING FOR SUCCESS

The Partnership Design Team can use a facilitated workshop to develop the partnership. The development workshop should establish open communications, create a team spirit, and enhance commitment to the partnership. To ensure success at the development workshop, the Partnership Design Team should meet for several days soon after the team is formed in order to design the development workshop. During the workshop, the following steps can be useful.

a. **Assess Current Relationship.** An important activity for the design team is learning from the past. The team should recognize positive and negative aspects of their existing relationship. Specifically, they should identify sources of past conflict that caused disputes and created barriers between the partners, as well as sources of agreement that fostered better relationships. This assessment requires an honest evaluation of the relationship.

b. **Discuss Partner Expectations.** The partners need to put their expectations for the Partnership Council on the table. Expectations need to be discussed in order to set realistic limits and avoid disappointment and frustration.

c. **Identify Common Interests.** The workshop can help the partners identify their common interests in a partnership. These interests are often expressed in simple statements such as "reducing tension," "building better communications," "creating a safer workplace," or "improving relationships." By taking the time at the beginning of the workshop to identify common interests, the partners will establish the foundation for a successful Partnership Council.

d. **Establish Partnership Functions.** The partners need to clarify what they want the Partnership Council to accomplish. The general functions can be to share information, prevent disputes, build consensus, and identify training opportunities.
e. **Commit to Bargain Over Discretionary Items.** These negotiations should be well-planned and use interest-based bargaining principles.
f. **Designate Action Teams.** Identify action items that can assist in preventing or resolving problems and designate joint Action Teams to solve those problems. Action items may include traditional subjects such as collective bargaining negotiations, or new areas such as training opportunities, and workplace partnership activities. Action Teams that focus on these subjects should consist of subgroups of the Partnership Council.
g. **Develop Future Vision.** The partnership should have a joint vision that articulates what the organization will be like in the future as a result of the Partnership Council's positive relationship.
h. **Set Mutual Goals.** Setting mutual goals establishes what the partners want to accomplish within their vision for the partnership. To achieve these goals, the partners also need to establish performance measures to indicate progress that can be reviewed at future Partnership Council meetings.
i. **Fix Meeting Procedures.** The Partnership Council should have simple, fair, and efficient procedures. Establishing procedures early during the process prevents later disputes over process. Procedures can cover subjects such as: establishing membership on the Partnership Council, selecting meeting locations, setting schedules, establishing the agenda format, and recording meeting minutes.
j. **Create Partnership Charter.** At the conclusion of the development workshop, the design team needs to create a charter to guide the partnership throughout its relationship. The charter is not a contractual agreement between labor and management, nor does it affect or change any collective bargaining agreements. Rather, the charter expresses the intent of the Partnership Council to work together in a cooperative relationship.

The charter should be a concise written document that consists of the partnership vision and a list of jointly developed goals. Typically, the charter comprises one or two pages and is signed by all members of the design team as an expression of their commitment to the partnership.

MAINTAINING SUCCESS

After the design team has conducted the development workshop, signed a charter, and formed the Partnership Council, it is time to initiate the follow-up program. This program consists of regularly scheduled meetings of the Partnership Council and special meetings of the Action Teams. Additionally, partnership training should be part of the program.

a. **Partnership Council Meetings.** Partnership Council meetings are essential to sustaining a cooperative relationship. Meetings should be held as needed, but at the beginning of the partnership they should probably be held frequently, perhaps monthly at first and later quarterly. The matter of scheduling is an item for the partners to decide. The meetings should be flexible and encourage full participation by the partners. At the meetings, the partners can introduce new members, share information, discuss training needs, review Action Team reports, identify new problems, and evaluate the relationship. These sample agenda items are explained below.

b. Agenda Items. Introducing a new member to the partnership can be done easily. In addition to a simple introduction at the meeting, the new member needs to be provided a copy of the charter and the opportunity to sign it. Sharing information is the responsibility of all partners. Management needs to share information that can impact bargaining unit employees. Similarly, labor must share the attitudes of bargaining unit members on issues. Discussing training needs is necessary to provide the partners with the tools required to build the relationship. Training needs and the opportunities to satisfy those needs will be discussed in a later publication. Reviewing Action Team reports ensures that problems are being addressed in a timely manner. The partners can review what has been done and offer suggestions on plans for resolution.

Identifying new problems is a responsibility of all partners. Recognizing that the identification of issues is a joint responsibility brings problems into the open, permits statements to be made on interests, and allows the partners to form Action Teams if necessary. Evaluating the relationship may be the most important function of the Partnership Council meetings. The evaluation process can be expedited by developing a checklist of partnership characteristics for each partner to rate.

c. Meeting Minutes. Since the Partnership Council will be involved in a number of diverse activities, minutes of the meetings will be valuable to record what happened and also to set the agenda for the next meeting. The responsibility for recording the minutes can be rotated among the partners.

d. Action Team Meetings. Action Team meetings are separate meetings for the members of the Action Team and others that the team decides to include. The meetings provide the members with the opportunity to focus their full attention on a particular issue. The Action Team will normally engage in a fact-finding process and then make recommendations in a report to the Partnership Council. The frequency and length of the meetings depend upon the difficulty of the problem and the desires of the members.

e. Training. In most Partnership Councils, the partners will need training. The partners should actively participate in these joint exercises. The main training areas will probably concern relationships and consensual methods of dispute resolution. Relationship training may include instruction in communication skills and team building. Training in consensual methods of dispute resolution should center on interest-based bargaining and the techniques of alternative dispute resolution (ADR). After the Partnership Council decides that training is needed, the activity training officer should be contacted to assist in finding training resources.

CONCLUSION

The time has arrived to develop better labor-management relationships. The creation of a Partnership Council is a giant step in this direction. To establish a successful Partnership Council within an organization requires considerable preparation and careful planning. Although the task may see formidable, it does not have to be. This pamphlet provides a practical approach to accomplish it. By forming a Partnership Design Team and using a development workshop, a foundation for success can be built for the Partnership Council. . . .

APPENDIX C: CHARTER FOR PARTNERSHIP COUNCIL

We, the partners to this Charter, have a vision that working together in a trusting cooperative partnership will greatly improve our relationship and will significantly benefit bargaining unit employees, the Army Corps of Engineers, and the American public. To implement this vision, the partners will seek to:

1. Make partnership part of the organizational culture.
2. Respect each partner.
3. Accept responsibility and accountability for the success of the partnership.
4. Meet regularly as agreed by the partners.
5. Share information of interest with all partners.
6. Identify partnership training opportunities.
7. Reach solutions to problems through consensus decision-making.
8. Use interest-based bargaining principles.
9. Establish dispute resolution alternatives.
10. Ensure appropriate resources are available to address action items.

4. William L. Bedman, *From Litigation to ADR: Brown & Root's Experience*, Dispute Res. J., Vol. 50, Oct.-Dec.1995, at 8*

As Brown & Root's in-house labor counsel for approximately the last 20 years, I have had the benefit of experiencing many changes in the workplace and in employment law. Brown & Root is a service company whose principal products are construction, maintenance and engineering services. Accordingly, our employees and their employment relationships with the company are the organization's most important assets.

Beginning about five years ago, it became clear to me that there was something inherently wrong with the litigation process as it was applied to employment cases. Like most major companies, Brown & Root won most of the employment cases filed against it or settled the claims for modest amounts. The amounts we spent on outside lawyers exceeded several times what we paid out in settlement. However, the money Brown & Root spent for the privilege of winning most of its cases had little tangible impact on the company or its employees. Most of the cases were litigated years after the events giving rise to the cases occurred. By that time, the terminated employee was usually working somewhere else, many of the managers and co-employees were gone and there was little institutional value in the events that transpired in the litigation.

What brought about the real need for change in the process was a sexual harassment and tort claim trial which took place in 1992. The case had been around as an EEOC charge or lawsuit for almost five years by the time it reached trial. The company obtained favorable verdicts for the sexual harassment and state tort claims. However, the case cost almost $450,000 in legal fees and permanently altered the careers of several employees and former employees including the plaintiff. Apparently, she believed she would be hitting the lottery right up until the time the jury came back and gave her nothing. The financial and human cost associated with that kind of litigation was so high that we began a concerted effort to examine alternatives to the litigation system for resolving employment matters.

---

*Reprinted with permission.

At that time, we did have some prior ADR experience, as in 1990 we had implemented a binding arbitration program for our ERISA benefit plans which was also tied to a more formalized appeals process. One thing that was observed after we adopted this arbitration program, is that the incidence of litigation dropped close to zero. More matters were actually being brought to and resolved in the internal administrative process than previously, largely because the employees were now aware that there was a more formal structure in place for their complaints.

Building on this experience, in the summer of 1992, a series of task forces were established to study and evaluate existing systems within Brown & Root Co., handling employment problems. These task forces were given the responsibility of reviewing options and concepts which ranged from no change to radical change. The task forces included senior operations management, representatives of the Legal and Employee Relations Departments, outside legal experts, representatives from the American Arbitration Association, outside consultants in conflict management design, and experts in employee relations communications. As part of the development process, about 300 Brown & Root employees from all levels of the company were interviewed individually and in focus groups to determine their opinions and impressions of the existing company attitude on conflict in the workplace. Additionally, their reactions to different design concepts were catalogued.

The program [which started in 1993] is a comprehensive employment dispute resolution program for all employees in the United States from the chief executive officer to the entry level employee. The key features of the dispute resolution program (DRP) are:

- The DRP was designed with input from employees at all levels from field employees to senior management.
- The DRP is a four-option program: it provides multiple processes, both inside and outside the company, for resolving disputes.
- In keeping with employee input and expert opinion, the DRP encourages collaborative approaches to dispute resolution by offering multiple channels for direct talk, or negotiation, and for both informal and formal mediation.
- The DRP promotes the resolution of disputes at the lowest possible level through in-house options. This is in keeping with the views of those we surveyed. Most disputes are resolved within a month through in-house options.
- The DRP provides some options that offer very high standards of confidentiality, and prohibits retaliation for use of the system.
- As an employee benefit designed to ensure fairness, the DRP offers to each employee access to legal counsel of the employee's choosing.
- To ensure its independence, the DRP reports to a dispute resolution policy committee composed of senior executives, rather than to a department or a single individual.
- Brown & Root routinely collects and analyzes data in order to evaluate utilization, cost benefit and employee satisfaction.

Cause and Effect

In the process of developing the dispute resolution program, we spent some time trying to understand how the litigation-based system evolved and the nature of the main factors causing its inefficiency and negative effects when it is applied to employment matters. The present heavy dependence on the judicial system to resolve employment disputes is probably the result of convergence of a number of factors. These factors include the civil rights movement and the expansion of tort law. . . .

[T]he labor litigation system and federal agencies set up to assist in the investigation and adjudication of labor matters are becoming unmanageably slow, expensive and cumbersome. The Equal Employment Opportunity Commission now has the highest backlog it has had in many years. The creation of new rights and the passage of federal legislation has done nothing to ease this burden. A simple employment dispute, involving no more than $5,000 in lost wages and benefits, can easily cost several times this much to resolve — no matter who prevails. Furthermore, administrative investigation and litigation may take years to complete. By the time of trial, the perceptions of the parties and witnesses have been irreversibly colored and polarized by years of conflict. Relatively cost-free remedies, such as reinstatement, have often become impossible. Emotional and economic damages which did not exist at the time of the dispute have accumulated, compounded, and assumed an importance far out of proportion to the nature of the dispute.

To a significant degree, these economic and emotional costs are products of the system itself. An employee who has recently been terminated may be shocked and depressed. These conditions are directly related to the termination. However, these difficulties are normally neither devastating nor permanent. But, a former employee who has spent several years in the litigation system is in an altogether different position. This individual has spent years building mistrust and suspicion, locked in conflict and absorbing the financial and emotional impacts of litigation. Quite often, because of the long-term alienation from former co-workers, he or she has lost an important part of the network of acquaintances that support any career. Further, he or she may become strongly focused on past wrongs, at the expense of present and future career. Naturally, the larger the potential damage award, the more this is likely to occur. Inevitably, earning capacity and employment skills suffer.

Such economic losses are not a natural result of the wrong suffered. They are a natural result of a litigation-based dispute resolution system. What converts this from a highly arbitrary tax on employers to an economic tragedy is that employees do not obtain substantial recoveries with any great frequency. Reliable statistics are not readily available, but practical experience shows that, in the great majority of cases, the employees lose or must settle for far less than what they think they are entitled to receive. Actual large recoveries are quite rare. This is not a defect in law or procedure. It simply reflects a fact of life: The judicial system does not provide ordinary employees who must work for a living any real hope of obtaining significant economic relief in any time period that is realistic from the employee's standpoint.

In short, litigation, as a system of employment dispute resolution, is highly inefficient, both economically and morally. It wastes time, money and careers. This is true even if, as assumed here, the end result is always correct. To the extent that the results through litigation are wrong, the social loss can only be greater.

These observations do not prove that contractually resolved disputes are better decided, or even that contractual dispute resolution is more efficient. However, this discussion should dispel any illusion that private litigation has any automatic claim to historical, legal, moral or economic merit. Before turning to existing alternatives in detail, including Brown & Root's experience, it is worth describing the policy framework for other types of dispute resolution.

Policy Implications of ADR

The Federal Arbitration Act (FAA) has carved out a relatively litigation-free zone around arbitration that has, particularly in recent years, allowed arbitration to develop and flourish. The "halo effect" of the FAA has also tended to protect other forms of dispute resolution which are probably not "arbitration" under the FAA. This trend has been hastened by recent, strong state legislative and judicial initiatives toward alternative dispute resolution of litigated matters. The trend has also been reinforced by experience with the EEOC and analogous state agencies, whose principal function has been to attempt to "conciliate" (mediate) employment disputes. Indeed, this is one of the ironies of the resistance to employer-initiated dispute resolution procedures. If the case is litigated, one of the first steps the court or agency is likely to take is to pressure the parties to undertake an alternative means of resolution. This procedure, typically mediation, is likely to be less well adapted to the particular employment environment than the system the employer would have adopted if left to its own devices.

This versatility is one of the principal advantages of a private dispute resolution mechanism. The particular method adopted can be adapted to fit each individual corporate structure. Indeed, Brown & Root's DRP looks unlike other systems, although many of them share common features. In addition to avoiding the one-size-fits-all approach typical of litigation, . . . private mechanisms avoid most of the other inherent problems with the litigation system. Even the most complex private dispute resolution systems are usually substantially faster than litigation, and are almost always cheaper, at least for the employee. Because the principal social costs of litigation derive from its delay and expense, private systems offer a greater advantage.

Litigation is, or at least is assumed to be, extremely good at finding the truth. However, important as this function may be to resolving disputes, it is also a weakness. Litigation's single-minded search for complete disclosure and legal correctness short changes other, equally valid goals of a dispute resolution system.

One of these objectives is reconciliation, which is best achieved by early mediation where each party retains some level of credibility with the other. Another is the opportunity to "tell one's story" to an outside decision-maker. Many social scientists believe that this is an important act of catharsis, even if the teller loses. In litigation, the opportunity comes only years later and is hemmed in by elaborate and expensive trial procedures. The litigation process is also largely inscrutable to the average citizen. Americans have always felt that even a confessed criminal is entitled to understand what is happening to him and why he is being punished. Yet, litigated employment matters are governed by procedural and substantive rules which are rarely understood by the parties, other than the most sophisticated employers and litigants. Arbitration cannot completely avoid substantive complexity, but it can radically simplify the procedural rules of the road.

Despite these advantages, arbitration and other dispute resolution mechanisms are sometimes criticized for denying employees important substantive rights. We believe these criticisms to be unfounded as applied to a properly designed and managed dispute resolution system which preserves the substantive employment rights of the employees while providing increased procedural benefits through expedited resolution and cost efficiency. This allows the parties to reach closure on the matter while the events are fresh and the employee can still pursue his career. By a properly designed and managed system, we mean one that includes such features as the key characteristics of our system listed above. It is critical to note that under a system with such characteristics, few disputes reach adjudicatory mechanisms such as arbitration or the courts; the vast majority are resolved by the mutual agreement of the parties, achieved through collaborative processes.

Ultimately, the greatest beneficiary of a private employment dispute resolution system, if it is allowed to flourish, may be the court system itself. Many federal courts are today awash in paper generated by relatively small cases. . . . The greatest contributors to the problem are federal drug cases and prisoner habeas petitions. However, federal employment cases probably run a close third. The courts have responded to this crisis by restricting and formalizing discovery, pressuring settlements, placing arbitrary limits on trial time, and developing ever more rigid and complex procedures designed to increase paper flow and decrease the time judges (but not lawyers) spend on each case.

In short, the court system, with regard to employment cases, is being stifled by overload. Its primary virtue, careful and deliberate reconstruction of the past, is becoming a quality of the pressing need for judicial efficiency. Yet, unlike private dispute resolution, the sacrifice is not offset by any substantial progress toward other legitimate objectives of the litigants, for example, reconciliation, catharsis, closure or comprehension. Certainly there are more settlements of litigated cases than in times past. But these settlements are not driven by reconciliation. They are, as often as not, driven by the litigants' dawning realization that one's day in court may be too long in coming, too short to tell the story, too expensive to afford, and too hard to understand.

Brown & Root's Four-Option System

Private employment dispute resolution has enormous promise. There is every reason to believe that it will deliver superior justice, superior speed, and reduced cost. Yet the field is quite new. Not only are employers just beginning to implement ambitious, sophisticated systems of dispute resolution, but dispute resolution, as a field of serious academic study, is in its infancy. The hard data have yet to be gathered, and perhaps the hard questions has yet to be asked—about both litigation and private methods.

A few observations can be made with a high degree of certainty. First, the litigation system has no special claim to delivering justice, or even both. Second, the litigation system is, even assuming perfect efficiency in achieving the "right" result, an extremely slow, expensive device imposing heavy monetary and non-monetary costs on the participants. If another system is available, it ought to be given a chance to succeed. Third, as stated above, we have little concrete information on the vast array of alternatives. The existing studies do not contain sufficient statistical data from which to draw reliable conclusions.

In its first two years, almost 1,000 employees utilized some aspect of the Brown & Root Program. Of these 1,000 matters, over 75% were resolved within eight weeks of the employee's contact. The vast majority were resolved within the company. The overwhelming majority of these cases were resolved through collaborative, in-house processes such as informal or formal mediation. About 50 have gone to outside mediation, slightly fewer than that have gone to internal mediation and about 15 have gone to outside arbitration. While the company has not prevailed in all the arbitrations, its win/loss record is comparable to its previous experience in the litigation forum with similar cases.

Even with an employee benefit plan which compensates employees for their legal expenses, fewer than 80 employees have requested the assistance of counsel over the first two years. In two-thirds of the arbitrations which have occurred, the employees have elected to proceed without the use of legal counsel.

While the total cost of this program is still being analyzed, it is clear that the annual expense for this type of program is substantially less than what a large, litigated employment case can cost both Brown & Root and the employee in legal expenses, while doing a much better job of delivering justice in the workplace to the average employee.

The Brown & Root DRP provides the employee four options for the resolution of a dispute. These options may be employed or bypassed for another option at the employee's discretion. The options are:

A. *The Company's Open Door Policy:* Under this option, the employee may speak to his or her immediate supervisor or to a higher level manager in the chain of command.

B. *Conference:* Under this option, the employee meets with a company representative from the DRP of choice to talk about the dispute and to choose a method for resolving it. One method available is an internal, informal mediation involving the use of a Brown & Root advisor.

C. *Formal Mediation:* This option involves the use of . . . an AAA mediator.

D. *Formal Arbitration:* This option involves the use of the AAA's arbitration program.

One of the most utilized and cost-effective parts of the Brown & Root's DRP is the advisor program. In some corporations this is called an ombudsmen program. Regardless of its title, the program is generally structured to provide a confidential outlet for current and former employees who have employment-related problems, primarily through informal mediation.

All of the Brown & Root advisors are volunteers who receive 50 hours of training in mediation and collaboration skills. Our volunteers are selected on the basis of interest and natural ability. Brown & Root constantly seeks to add to its pool of mediators and advisors in order to honor its commitment to diversity in its DRP. Since all of the employees are employed in full-time positions, the cost effectiveness of this DRP is readily apparent. While a portion of their attention is directed towards terminated employees, about two-thirds of advisor matters relate to incumbent employees, with a resolution rate of 50%. The basic goal of preserving the employment relationship is realized to a much greater degree through this process than almost any other within the DRP.

The actual task the advisors perform varies greatly from one case to the other. They may act as mediators, as fact-finders, or both, or may practice collaborative techniques all in an effort to obtain resolution at the earliest phase of the dispute in some cases they may give advice to the employee as to what avenues may be opened within the organization to assist them. They never serve as an advocate for the employee, and in many situations never actually contact anyone within the company.

Along with the advisor program, the DRP places a heavy emphasis on mediation. In the first two years, the resolution rate of mediated disputes exceeded 80%. Resolutions reached in the mediations ranged from a simple apology to reinstatement and substantial monetary damages. The mediators' common link is confidentiality, consistent with the expectations of the parties. Furthermore, the resolutions come very rapidly when compared to either litigated determinations, or even mediated resolutions after matters go to litigation.

The timely resolution of the disputed matter is one of the most powerful attributes of the advisor and mediation functions of the Brown & Root Dispute Resolution Program.

Conclusion

Even though the Brown & Root Program has been in effect for over two years, it still remains somewhat unique because of its comprehensive scope in applying to virtually all employment disputes (except workers' compensation and unemployment claims), and binding all employees from senior executives to entry level employees. We have also developed several training programs for supervisors which provide them with conflict management skills to try to handle employment problems at the lowest possible level. We believe that the equitable and uniform nature of our program, together with reinforcement of its conflict management purpose through comprehensive and consistent management training, are keys to the long-term success and viability of any dispute resolution program. Additionally, the Brown & Root program was developed largely by employees of Brown & Root with appropriate external help, but the principal focus was to integrate a new system into into existing processes while maintaining organizational cultural values and norms. [T]he program has succeeded in both bringing quicker resolution to problems and substantially reducing the company's transaction expenses and legal fees while preserving employment relationships.

5. Mobility of Lawyers and Other Professionals

Whether a professional employee, be it an associate or a partner, leaves a firm on good terms or in a blizzard of disputes often depends on sound planning. A smooth transition is important for both the firm and the person who is leaving. Movement among law firms, or to other jobs, is sufficently common in the legal profession that there is a treatise on the subject. *See* ROBERT W. HILLMAN, LAWYER MOBILITY: THE LAW OF PARTNER WITHDRAWALS AND LAW FIRM BREAKUPS (1994). *See also* Barbara B. Buchholz, *Graceful Exits: Careful Planning in a Partnership Agreement Can Take the Acrimony Out of Firm Defections,* AM. BAR ASS'N J., August 1995, at 76.

Issues that can arise include the return of capital, rights to earned but uncollected billings, contacting firm clients, and duties to assume obligations such as a lease or expected losses.

Noncompete clauses generally are not enforceable, and a financial penalty term may be treated as a disguised noncompete term. ADR clauses in contracts between individual professionals and their firms are an obvious way to reduce disputes, and to minimize the impact of those disputes that do occur.

E. Partnering

1. Tom Arnold, A Vocabulary of Alternative Dispute Resolution Procedures (1995)*

Partnering:

Typically meaning:

A collaborative contracting and contract-administration process which includes:

(1) an agreement to partner including goals of the partnering relationship, necessary organizational involvement, and necessary individual relationship development and involvement;

*Reprinted with permission.

(2) a partnering retreat, immediately after the contract is let, where key decision makers from each of the contracting parties:
(3) develop open communications, friendship, trust, a willingness to work through problems, explore options and create solutions;
(4) possibly use a neutral facilitator to explore contract concerns as well as the respective partner's needs and interests in a non-threatening manner;
(5) discuss concerns that they may have with the project and explore potential solutions;
(6) commit themselves jointly to create and sustain a quality project, on time, on budget;
(7) draft and sign-off on a project charter which commits the parties together to broad project goals and working relationships; and
(8) develop an implementation plan, including objective criteria to measure against performance and evaluation forms to be used at monthly meetings, to measure success in reaching performance standards and manage incipient disputes away.

It could be argued that partnering is not alternative dispute resolution (ADR), but rather an effective management process using ADR methodology. Indeed, the primary focus of partnering is dispute prevention, as opposed to dispute resolution. Because the partnering process takes time, money, and commitment, its use to date has been limited to large, long-term contracts and projects.

2. Lester Edelman et. al., *Partnering* 1-5, 7-10, 17-20 (U.S. Army Corps of Engineering 1991) (IWR Pamphlet 91-ADR-P-4)

Partnering [is] designed to create a positive, disputes prevention atmosphere during contract performance. Partnering uses team-building activities to help define common goals, improve communication, and foster a problem-solving attitude among a group of individuals who must work together throughout contract performance.

A central objective of Partnering is to encourage contracting parties to change from their traditional adversarial relationships to a more cooperative, team-based approach and to prevent disputes. The Partnering concept, therefore, is significant because it offers the most efficient form of dispute resolution: dispute prevention. Indeed, the benefits of successful owner/contractor relations go beyond preventing disputes and include improved communication, increased quality and efficiency, on-time performance, improved long-term relationships, and a fair profit and prompt payment for the contractor.

What is Partnering?

How many times have you reached the end of a construction project only to be faced with a number of unresolved conflicts? There is a way to prevent these conflicts during construction by establishing a partnering relationship between the owner and the contractor. Partnering lays the foundation for better working relations on a project including better dispute resolution. By taking steps before construction begins to change the adversarial mindset, to recognize common interests, and to establish an atmosphere of trust and candor in communications, Partnering helps develop a cooperative management team. This team has the ability to appreciate the roles and responsibilities each will have in carrying out the project.

Partnering is the creation of an owner-contractor relationship that promotes achievement of mutually beneficial goals. It involves an agreement in principle to share the risks involved in completing the project, and to establish and promote a nurturing partnership environment. Partnering is not a contractual agreement, however, nor does it create any legally enforceable rights or duties. Rather, Partnering seeks to create a new cooperative attitude in completing government contracts. To create this attitude, each party must seek to understand the goals, objectives, and needs of the other—their "win" situation—and seek ways that these objectives can overlap.

Why Use Partnering?

From the beginning of a typical construction project, the structure of the relationship promotes an adversarial attitude between the parties. There are two distinct management teams, each making independent decisions with the intent of reaching their own goals for the project. These decisions directly affect the path each party chooses to achieve its goals—but they are often made in a vacuum, without regard for the other party's interests and expectations. Communication may be limited—or non-existent! Conflicts are inevitable as paths diverge and expectations are not met. The worst stereotypes of the other side are remembered, and they seem to block the way to our goals. An adversarial management style takes over and the goals each party had for the project get lost in preparation for litigation. The stage is set for future conflict and, often, litigation.

It's as if two people are planning to travel together to a common destination, but each has his own map and refuses to show it to his traveling companion!

The bottom line is clear: The adversarial management relationship jeopardizes the ability of either side to realize its expectations. The result is increased costs for the taxpayer and declining profit margins for the contractor. This is truly a lose-lose outcome for all.

Both parties have recognized that there needs to be a better way of doing business. Efficiency and productivity must be increased. Neither the government nor contractors can afford the costly posturing that the present adversarial climate promotes. Partnering offers the chance to change from an adversarial style to a more cooperative, synergistic relationship that takes full advantage of the strengths of all team members. . . .

[One Corps official described the benefits of Partnering in the following terms.] The end result of . . . "adversary management" is a continuing upward spiral of risk and cost: risk of the contractor going broke, risk of projects taking much longer than necessary for completion, and risk of significant cost overruns. These costs do not go to productive facilities, but instead to overhead, litigation, and contesting experts. Partnering seemed to offer the opportunity of harnessing the capabilities, talents, and positive energies of both owner and contractor groups and focusing them on mutually agreed-upon goals. It offered the opportunity for all parties to change preconceived attitudes in order for both to win in the long run.

How Does Partnering Work?

Partnering creates a climate for success by building a cooperative management team dedicated to a win-win atmosphere. To do this, the members of the team must undergo a change in mindset and discover how it is in their best interest to cooperate. The concepts of principled negotiation, where solutions are sought that serve the fundamental interests of both negotiating parties, are introduced.

There are three basic steps involved in establishing the Partnering relationship. Since Partnering is an attitude change aimed at building a new relationship, it is important as a first step to establish the new relationship through personal contact. Success in a Partnering arrangement depends on the personal commitment of the management team. This commitment is built through personal relationships that must be formed early and reinforced throughout the project. The second step in Partnering is crafting a joint statement of goals and establishing common objectives in specific detail for reaching the goals. Achieving these intermediate objectives will lead to success for both the owner and the contractor. Finally, Partnering identifies specific disputes prevention processes designed to head off problems, evaluate performance, and promote cooperation.

Although these basic steps create the Partnering relationship, teamwork is essential to instill the Partnering spirit. Through a series of joint workshops, guided by facilitators, Partnering builds team spirit. The emphasis in the workshops is on identifying shared interests and focusing on cooperative effort.

There are other factors to consider in establishing a Partnering relationship. Here's a list of some of the considerations:

- prepare early for Partnering;
- secure top management support and commitment to Partnering;
- identify Partnering "champions;"
- choose participants for the Partnering workshop;
- select neutral facilitators for the Partnering workshop;
- conduct the joint workshop;
- create a Partnering Charter;
- arrange regular follow-up sessions
- plan combined activities.

Establishing cooperative processes for evaluating progress and solving problems is another feature of successful Partnering. Evaluation mechanisms should be specific in measuring the achievement of the objectives that will make the project a success. A system for problem-solving, which will provide for expedited decisions, should be established.

Another essential feature of Partnering is committed people. Partnering needs "champions" at a high management level, and other champions throughout the organization who are willing to take risks, use professional judgment, and make management decisions in a new cooperative environment. Partnering is people who believe in cooperation, rather than confrontation, as the most effective and efficient way to achieve their goals.

How Do We Know It's Working?

When Partnering is working, old adversarial patterns change and a new spirit pervades the working relationship. This new spirit has many indicators. Look for these signs of successful Partnering.

- Sharing—The partners share a common set of goals.
- Clear Expectations—Each partner's expectations are clearly stated, up front, and provide the basis for working together.
- Trust and Confidence—Partners actions are consistent and predictable. Trust is earned when one's actions are consistent with one's words. We must "walk the talk."
- Commitment—Each partner must be willing to make a real commitment to participate in the partnership.
- Responsibility—Responsibility is recognizing and accepting the consequences of our

choices. Partners are accountable to each other and should agree up front on measures for mutual accountability.

- Courage—Partners have the courage to forthrightly confront and resolve conflict.
- Understanding and Respect—Partners understand and respect each other's responsibilities, authorities, expectations and boundaries, as well as any honest differences between them.
- Synergy—The partnership is more than the sum of the individual partners. The relationship is more powerful than any of the partners working alone because it is based on the collective resources of the partners.
- Excellence—Partners expect excellence from each other and give excellence in return.

These are the positive indicators of a successful Partnering effort. If you look closely at the list again, it's clear that most of these indicators are based on the ability of the partners to communicate and solve problems.

What Concerns Are There About Partnering?

Some people have expressed a concern that Partnering may place the owner and the contractor "too close," and that there is a need for distance between the parties to maintain objectivity and proper oversight. Unfortunately, this adversarial attitude leads to some very expensive and counterproductive actions. Not only is the climate of trust and communication hindered, but distance between the parties can allow room for an expensive "wall of paper" to rise between the parties. Documents are exchanged to begin building a case for litigation.

Another concern is the view that contract requirements will be relaxed in the interest of Partnering. This concern, however, is based on a misconception about the nature of Partnering. Partnering does not mean that the public interest takes a back seat to the interests of the parties. All federal procurement laws and regulations must be complied with by the parties. But this does not mean that the government and the contractor have to avoid cooperation to comply with laws and regulations. In a Partnering relationship, the contractor should understand and appreciate government regulatory requirements; and the government should understand and appreciate the contractor's expectations.

Some individuals have said that Partnering is all relationships and no substance, that the benefits are intangible and not worth the extra effort and expense. Experience has shown others that there are benefits, both tangible as well as intangible. This experience is detailed in this pamphlet. And the expense is not great, even where a facilitated initial workshop and follow-up sessions are used. Costs are shared by the government and the contractor.

Perhaps the most telling comment, however, may be that no matter what the tangible advantages, Partnering represents the fair way of doing business. One Corps manager wrote: "I have field employees who say it's a pleasure to come to work and not be afraid to advise the contractor of any perceived problem and be proud of working on the project as a team member.". . .

PARTNERING PROCESS

A successful Partnering program starts with an understanding of the important elements of the process and careful planning of each step. Essentially, the important elements are 1) early preparation, 2) management commitment to the concept, 3) a joint workshop, 4) a team charter, and 5) follow-up meetings and evaluation processes.

1. Early Preparation: Introduce the Concept to Bidders

After an internal commitment has been made to use Partnering in a contract, the Corps should state its intent to use the concept in its solicitation for bids. This will introduce the concept to the bidders. The point to be stressed is that Partnering is a voluntary relationship designed to improve cooperation and communications during construction.

2. Management Commitment

- Secure Top Management Support and Commitment

Partnering requires a personal commitment between contracting parties to accept a new relationship and a senior management decision to commit resources to the effort. Top management of both the Corps and the contractor must be supportive.

Visible top management commitment sends the vital message that Partnering is acceptable and will be supported. Management support, instilling enthusiasm and overcoming obstacles, empowers people to act. Top managers can most visibly show their support by attending the Partnering workshop and introducing the concept in person.

A Partnering program can be implemented without a huge commitment of resources. The additional costs (for the workshop and facilitators) are relatively small and are shared by the parties. There is a commitment of management time, and there must be a willingness to "go the extra mile" for the benefit of the team.

- Identify Partnering "Champions" for the Project

Partnering needs "champions" to foster the new relationship. There are two kinds of champions that an effective Partnering program needs: a top management champion who will instill the Partnering ethic within the organization, and a "managing partner" champion who will carry out the nurturing of the Partnering relationship throughout the course of the contract. Top management support is vitally important to provide the favorable environment for Partnering to grow. Operational level champions for Partnering are important in the day-to-day managing of the process by providing administrative and logistical support, encouraging communication, and promoting problem-solving. The Resident Engineer is the natural choice for operational level champion.

3. The Joint Partnering Workshop

- Choose Participants for the Partnering Workshop

A Partnering workshop is the starting point for the new relationship. The participants in the Partnering workshop should be key stakeholders in the success of the project. On construction projects, the Corps Area or Resident Engineer, the contractor project manager, and their principal assistants are key stakeholders. The personal involvement of key stakeholders is vitally important. Other considerations for the Partnering workshop are the size and complexity of the project, since these factors will control the number and specialties of participants at the workshop. Also consider including Corps District and home office personnel.

In large projects, before the Partnering workshop, the Resident Engineer and the Project Manager may attend a training center that specializes in principle-centered leadership training. This is an opportunity for these two key leaders to establish a respectful, trusting relationship and plan for the Partnering workshop.

- Select Neutral Facilitators for the Workshop

Partnering depends on developing relationships and committing to cooperation toward common goals. The change in mindset from the adversarial to the cooperative does not come automatically, simply by talking about it. An effective way to develop this new attitude is to use a neutral facilitator to guide the workshop.

A neutral facilitator is a third party who manages the process of the workshop and who can guide the participants to discover for themselves the benefits of cooperative action. Professional facilitators provide expertise in organizational development, communications, group dynamics, and team building. As an outsider, the facilitator can devote attention to guiding the workshop in developing the Partnering structure. Because the facilitator has no association with either party, the impartial status allows the facilitator to be the focus of comments or criticism from one side to the other without the resentment or conflict that may be the result of a direct confrontation.

A facilitated workshop is recommended for larger projects. However, it may not always be possible to employ a professional facilitator. As an alternative, consider a facilitator from another District to serve at the Partnering workshop. Remember it is important that the facilitator should not be directly or indirectly involved in the project. The parties should develop their own goals with the impartial facilitator assisting.

- Conduct the Workshop

The Partnering workshop helps participants establish open communications, develop a team spirit, set long range Partnering goals for the project, and gain commitment to the implementation plan. A combination of group activities, lectures, and experiential learning exercises has been effective in helping groups reach these goals in the workshop setting.

Suggestions for a successful Partnering workshop include conducting the workshop as soon as possible after contract award; scheduling the workshop for several days since new working relationships take time to develop; using a location away from the office or project site to allow participants the chance to get away from their daily duties and concentrate on Partnering.

The Partnering workshop should mold a single-minded joint management team for the project. To build an effective team, the workshop must strengthen the ability of the participants to communicate as a team. Team members must also develop and practice the skills and attitudes required of teamwork. At the workshop, one of the important activities will be to learn from the past and create for the future. This involves an honest evaluation of the strengths and weaknesses of past experiences and the strengths and weaknesses of the project team. The team then makes a group decision about positive strategies.

Since no project can be completed without the need to solve problems and resolve conflicts, conflict management and problem-solving skills should be a part of the workshop as well. The team must develop a problem-solving strategy that enables managers to address problems quickly and efficiently. "No action" on a problem is not an option! Problems that are not addressed sow the seeds of discord and division for the team. Expedited negotiations and alternative dispute resolution (ADR) techniques offer methods for successful resolution of problems.

4. The Partnering Charter

- Define Goals and Objectives

At the conclusion of the Partnering workshop, the parties need to create a blueprint for their new relationship, which can be summed up in a Charter. The Partnering Charter defines the long-term goals and objectives for the project. This is a win-win charter. It is a collaborative effort written at the workshop by all participants and therefore includes the overlapping goals of the project team. Common goals are: a quality project carried out safely, in a timely and cost effective manner. To achieve these goals, the team must transform them into concrete objectives and action items which can be measured at follow-up sessions. If all the goals and objectives are achieved, both contracting parties will win.

The Partnering Charter should include objectives that will provide measurable milestones for success on the project. These objectives should be specific and should be the framework for a Partnering implementation plan. As an example, the following is a list of some project objectives:

- meet the design intent;
- encourage a maximum amount of value engineering savings;
- limit cost growth;
- cause no impact to follow-on projects;
- lose no time due to job-related injuries;
- encourage a fair sharing of contract risks;
- use ADR methods;
- avoid litigation;
- finish ahead of schedule;
- include an implementation plan.

The implementation plan fills out these objectives by including measurable details. For example, the implementation plan can call for a specific number of value engineering submittals or a target dollar amount of savings; a specified cost growth percentage; or a joint safety awareness program. These are just a few examples of how specifics can be added to the objectives to make them part of a viable plan for ensuring project success.

5. Follow-up Meetings and Evaluation

- Arrange Regular Follow-up Meetings

The importance of following up on the initial Partnering workshop cannot be stressed enough. The lessons of Partnering need continued reinforcing so they do not fade with time or under the stress of the job. On-going evaluation of Partnering goals and objectives is essential. The best method is to conduct regularly scheduled follow-up sessions between the key leaders.

- Develop Evaluation Processes

To evaluate performance, successful Partnering efforts have included a jointly developed evaluation form. The evaluation form assigns weights to the Partnering objectives relative to the overall project. Ratings are determined for each evaluation period, and then compared to an agreed-upon standard. Corps and contractor leaders jointly rate performance. The result is a numerical score as well as a narrative evaluation. Such an evaluation can be the focus for a team meeting where problems are addressed and the values of partnership are encouraged and reinforced. Evaluation is important for good management of a project and encouragement of Partnering values.

- Plan Combined Activities

There are other ways to advance the Partnering relationship through combined activities. Follow-up workshops could be scheduled to nurture the lessons and skills of Partnering.

Debriefing sessions following significant milestones in the project could be the occasion for review of achievement. Awards ceremonies jointly conducted could recognize and reinforce cooperative effort. Professional development programs such as lectures, workshops, and breakfast seminars could be scheduled to emphasize job skills as well as team work.

3. Partnering Experiences: Oliver Lock and Dam Replacement

The Corps of Engineers has used Partnering in a number of construction contracts with positive results and valuable lessons learned. This section will describe one of the Corps' experiences with Partnering, and will also consider how Partnering can be applied to improve management of other kinds of contracts.

A $110 million replacement lock and dam is being constructed on the Black Warrior Tombigbee Waterway at Tuscaloosa, Alabama, to replace an old undersized lock. The new lock chamber will be 110 feet by 600 feet with a 28 foot lift, and the dam will be 800 feet long and 45 feet high. More than three million cubic yards of excavation will be required, along with 290,000 cubic yards of concrete and 1,750 tons of steel. This work comprises the major portion of the total replacement work, the actual lock and dam construction, at a cost of $70 million. The contractor for the project is FRU-CON Construction Corp. of Baldwin, Missouri. The Notice to Proceed was provided to FRU-CON on 1 April 1988, with the new lock scheduled to open in the fall of 1991.

Dan Burns, then Chief of Construction at Mobile, had been considering using the Partnering concept on a Corps project for some time. When Mr. Burns approached FRU-CON management within days of the contract award to suggest Partnering, they enthusiastically agreed. As described earlier, top management commitment is a key to Partnering success.

Initial Workshop

Key individuals met for a four day facilitated team building workshop in Mobile. To further emphasize management commitment to the process, the president of FRU-CON and the Mobile District Engineer addressed the group, adding their support to the Partnering effort.

Professional facilitators were used at the workshop to develop teamwork, trust and communication through specific activities and participatory exercises. The activities and efforts were:

- experiential learning exercise on the value of cooperation vs. self-interest;
- nominal group exercise to identify strengths and potential problems;
- group development of action plans;
- exercise on problem-solving styles and their effects on interaction;
- exercise on leadership styles and effects;
- theory building discussion on conflict management;
- experiential exercise on applying theories of principled negotiation.

Specific products of the Partnering workshop addressed goals and objectives for the project, procedures for handling problems and evaluating success, and promoting team spirit:

- a Partnering agreement signed by all participants;
- a cooperatively-developed, structured team process for dealing with unexpected problems;
- a plan to employ Alternative Dispute Resolution options, if necessary;
- a project evaluation methodology, including specific ways to measure the achievement of team objectives;

- a team name and logo: "The Million Dollar Team";
- a plan for follow-up workshops to maintain and reinforce the partnership.

Changed Attitudes, Behaviors, Processes

The Oliver Partnering experience is being evaluated in part by using surveys of the participants to keep an on-going record of attitudes and perceptions. The first such survey was taken before the initial workshop and repeated after the conclusion of the workshop. Similar questionnaires have been used at each follow-up session. Since the project is not complete, no final conclusions can be made. However, some general observations from the preliminary results can be made, and they indicate a positive response to Partnering.

The preliminary results show positive improvements in communications and teamwork on the Oliver project. This was especially true in comparing the surveys before and after the initial workshop, when all answers showed positive improvement. Later surveys show that team members continue to have a positive attitude toward the project, rating it well above the "typical" public construction project.

Participants were asked to assess changes in behavior patterns that could be attributed to Partnering. These questions addressed perceptions of how the parties acknowledge and face concerns and problems, the degree of cooperation, and response to issues. In each case, they were asked to assess their own behavior as well as the other partner's. Expectations were raised at the initial workshop and have lessened somewhat in later surveys. The overall rating remains good, however; and the evidence of successful problem-solving is positive.

The final evaluation factor deals with Partnering procedural issues. Questions on these issues were presented after follow up sessions but not after the initial workshop since none of the participants had any experience at that time with Partnering processes. Topics covered in these questions include the value of the problem-solving and monthly evaluation procedures that were developed at the initial Partnering workshop; an assessment of how much project progress was due to applying partnering concepts; and an assessment of the usefulness of follow-up sessions. Although Partnering has not solved all problems, the participants seem to agree that the process is an improvement over the adversarial approach to construction projects. Responses to a survey question asking whether Partnering was detrimental or helpful to their organization's effectiveness were overwhelmingly positive.

Experience with Partnering

The Oliver project has not been without its problems. There have been controversies including difficult technical issues, one of which remains at issue. There have also been notable successes in problem-solving. Three examples indicate how the Partnering experience can pay dividends:

Miter Gates: Early in the contract, the contractor discussed with the government's resident engineer the contractor's alternatives for miter gate fabrication. The result of this collaborative discussion was the contractor's not selecting the low bidder in order to get more quality and schedule reliability. This has proven to be a sound decision contributing to overall project quality and a "critical path" item done well within the allotted time.

Sand Suppliers: This key material, sand, has presented problems throughout the heavy concrete production period. However, where the government would normally take an "it's your problem" attitude, the Partnering ethic has encouraged a joint effort to solve the problem. After extensive discussion and analysis, the government felt satisfied in allowing a different technical specification and, ultimately, a slightly different design mix for the concrete. Also, the government has assisted in trying to identify alternative sand suppliers and in determining their production capacity. The result has been a win-win solution. The resolution of a difficult problem in a technically sound manner allowed the project to proceed on schedule without cost to the government.

Left Bank Design: The contract required that the contractor prepare a structural design for a braced cofferdam on the left abutment, facing downstream. The contractor, after reviewing the criteria and their field data, felt that it was questionable if not impossible to perform as the specifications intended. Instead of the defensive exchange of documents, a list of some of the contractor's considerations was provided and a joint meeting to discuss the issue was scheduled. At the meeting, the design of the braced cofferdam was discussed professionally and satisfactorily, rather than defending the details and 'intent' of the specifications. This was very productive for both parties and sped resolution of a difficult problem.

Lessons Learned

The Oliver Lock and Dam project is a pioneering effort for the Corps of Engineers. As with any new effort, there are lessons to be learned for the future in carrying out the project. Mobile leadership has concluded that the Partnering concept does make a positive difference in project outcome, and has identified a number of lessons which will be included in the project evaluation:

- an enduring commitment with real involvement of management is essential;
- the partnership must have constant reinforcement to avoid "traditional" behavior;
- care must be exercised to assure realistic expectations, goals, and objectives early in the partnership. Set sights high, but make the targets achievable so they can endure throughout the project;
- Partnering can be applied successfully on single projects of fixed or limited duration, characteristic of government contracts;
- it is highly desirable to include engineering and design personnel in Partnering activities and follow-up;
- the Partnering attitude can become pervasive if extended further into the participating organizations, to the level of foreman and superintendents, perhaps in phases as the project progresses.

APPENDIX

Role Plays

Role Play Number and Title	Type Dispute
1. "Bicycle Bedlam"	Consumer/Small Business
2. "Someones in the Kitchen"	Contractor/Home Repair
3. "Terri's Timepiece"	Employer/Employee
4. "That's Not My Cat"	Roommate/Landlord/Tenant
5. "Roommate, Put Yourself In My Shoes"	Roommate
6. "Making the Grade to Wrongful Termination"	Employer/Employee
7. "It's in the Car(d)s"	Consumer/Car Dispute
8. "Employee/Employer-Wrongful Termination"	Employer/Employee
9. "Rift Over a Raise"	Employer/Employee
10. "No, I Want The..."	Divorce/Property Division
11. "The Home Repair Contract"	Contractor/Home Repair
12. "Homeowner's Association Dispute"	Multi-Party Association
13. "The Recording Contract"	Contract
14. "Shaky Building"	Contract
15. "Grandpa's Agreement"	Property
16. "Marriage Not! Made in Heaven"	Divorce
17. "BMW Gone Mad"	Contract Dispute
18. "Helping Hands"	Employment Dispute
19. "Construction Contract Case"	Contract Dispute
20. "Undue Influence"	Will Contest
21. "Unwanted Exposure"	Invasion of Privacy Dispute
22. "Booby" Doesn't Play Nice	Sports Dispute
23. "Zaruba v. Zaruba	Zaruba Divorce Dispute
24. "Sexual Harassment"	Sexual Harassment Dispute
25. "The Unpoppy-lar Drug Test"	Employment Dispute
26. "Fishing for Trouble"	Employment/Contract Dispute
27. "Mutually Acceptable Roommate"	ADA Dispute
28. "Too Old for Generation X"	Employment Dispute
29. "Dust Gets in my Eyes"	Property Nuisance Dispute
30. "Boroff v Boroff"	Divorce Custody Dispute
31. "Four Brothers Owned a Mill"	Small Business/Family Dispute
32. "The Case of the Broken Smile"	Personal Injury
33. "Clean-It-Right"	Neighborhood/Nuisance Dispute
34. "My Supervisor Makes Me Sick!"	Employment Dispute
35. "Watch Your Step"	Landlord/Tenant/PI Dispute
36. "The Case of the Wrongful Cremation"	Personal Injury Dispute

Role Play 1.

BICYCLE BEDLAM

(Adapted from Role Play developed by Louis A. Vetrano, Jr. for the A.A. White Dispute Resolution Institute—Used with Permission.)

General Facts

Larry is a novice cyclist who has been cycling on a recreational basis for the past six years. He owns an expensive Italian bicycle with precision parts. He was preparing for a cross country bicycle trip and wanted his bicycle in top working order. He took the bicycle to the shop where it was originally purchased. While in the shop, Larry commented that he "was a better cyclist than a mechanic" and was already nervous about the trip so he wanted a "professional" to do the tuneup. He asked that the spokes be tightened, the gear shifters adjusted, and the chain replaced. He asked if the repairs could be done quickly because the trip was to begin in only two days. The shop owner said that the total cost of these repairs would be $32.00 and that the bicycle would be ready as promised. Larry agreed and left the bicycle for repairs.

Larry picked up his bicycle on schedule and left on his trip the next day. On the first day of the trip, the chain broke and wrapped around the spokes of the rear wheel and in the process, destroyed the entire shifter system, as well as the wheel itself. Because replacement parts were unavailable in the small towns the tour passed through, Larry spent the rest of the trip riding in the support vehicle.

When he returned from the trip, Larry went to the bike shop and threatened to file a complaint with the Better Business Bureau if the bike shop did not fix the damages and pay for the loss of the trip. The total damages requested are:

$217.00 replacement parts for bicycle (retail)
$750.00 cost of the trip
$967.00 grand total

Larry and the shop owner have agreed to try alternative dispute resolution.

Role Play 2.

SOMEONE'S IN THE KITCHEN WITH DINAH

(Adapted from Role Play developed by Louis A. Vetrano, Jr. for the A.A. White Dispute Resolution Institute—Used with Permission.)

General Facts

Dinah had just purchased a new house and wanted to have the kitchen remodeled. She contacted one of the local do-it-yourself companies to have the work done. Dinah met with Dan, a representative of Squared Up Builders. After going through several versions of kitchen layouts, the two of them agreed on a design, price, appliances and accessories. The work was to begin immediately and be completed within six weeks. One week passed without any work starting, so Dinah called Dan to determine the cause for the delay. He said that there was a problem with some of the materials, that the problem would be corrected, and the project would be back on schedule. From that day on the work progressed at a very slow rate. Workers would not show up at the appointed time or they would not have the correct appliances. Each time there was a delay, Dinah would call the manager of Squared Up Builders and each time she was told that the delays would end. Nine weeks later she received a bill for the total job but only 90% of the job was complete. Dinah paid 50% of the bill. She attached a letter stating that she was unhappy with all the delays, and that she wanted the job finished before she would pay the remainder.

Two weeks later the job was finished, but not to Dinah's satisfaction. Much of the work was poor quality. Dinah had many phone conversations with the installation department but was unable to get someone to look at the work. To date, the remaining 50% of the bill has not been paid. Squared Up Builders has threatened to report Dinah to the credit bureau and Dinah has threatened to report Squared Up Builders to the Better Business Bureau. They have agreed to utilize ADR to resolve the dispute.

Role Play 3.

TERRI'S TIMEPIECE

(Adapted from Role Play developed by Louis A. Vetrano, Jr. for the A.A. White Dispute Resolution Institute—Used with Permission.)

General Facts

Terri has been a chauffeur in this fair city for many years. She has gained the respect of many of her colleagues as a result of her excellent driving abilities. Her duties as a chauffeur include keeping the car on schedule. In order to keep her car on schedule Terri is required to wear a reliable watch while on duty. One day a passenger accidentally knocked her briefcase against Terri's watch causing the watch to break. Consequently, Terri's car ran behind schedule for the rest of the day. Her supervisor noticed the delay at the end of the day and questioned Terri. The supervisor wrote a report on the incident and told Terri to get another watch before her next shift. As it was late in the day, Terri was unable to buy another watch before returning to work, besides, she thought the company should replace the watch.

The next morning when Terri arrived for work, her supervisor noticed that she was not wearing her watch. Her supervisor did not allow Terri to drive that day. Terri has threatened to file a complaint with the chauffeur's union. She has agreed to utilize alternative dispute resolution before filing a formal complaint.

Role Play 4.

THAT'S NOT MY CAT

General Facts

This dispute involves Chris and Pat, who have been friends since high school. They moved to this college town together and have been roommates since their freshman year. The landlord for their apartment is also a party to the dispute. Things were going very well for Chris and Pat until last semester when Chris started hanging around with some new fraternity/sorority friends.

Since that time Chris has been staying out late, skipping classes and is always asking Pat to lie for him/her when parents call. When Spring Break finally came, Pat went home alone. Shortly after Pat's return to campus, he/she came home to find he/she had been locked out of the apartment for non-payment of rent, and for a violation of the no pet covenant in the lease. There are eight months remaining on the one year lease that Chris and Pat signed. Pat gave Chris the money for rent before leaving on Spring Break and is very upset because they have never missed the rent.

The landlord has not brought an action yet, but has acted upon the landlord's lien set out in the lease agreement. The next day, Chris returned and told Pat that he/she left the key for one the fraternity/sorority friends to use the apartment while they were out of town. The friend has a cat and the landlord must have seen it in the apartment. (S)he knows nothing about the rent money.

Pat is so upset. (S)he wants an opportunity to pay the rent and fulfill the obligation. The landlord wants the tenants out and full payment for all twelve months. Rent is $500 per month, with a $20.00 late fee and Pat paid the deposit of one-months rent.

Role Play 5.

"ROOMMATE, PUT YOURSELF IN MY SHOES"

General Facts

This dispute involves roommates, Jo(e) and Sean, who were introduced to each other last year by a mutual friend. When they realized Jo(e)'s current roommate was graduating and Sean was looking for a place near campus, they decided to arrange for Sean to move into Jo(e)'s condo.

Things are going very well for Jo(e) and Sean in their new arrangement. Sean loves being a block from campus. Jo(e) is happy with the new roommate arrangement also. Sean is much neater than his/her previous roommate. Jo(e) is very picky about such things, (s)he expects the same from roommates.

Shortly after moving in to Jo(e)s condo, Sean's sister Sally and her dog Max come for a visit. Sally is very upset because her husband Hank took off on the rodeo circuit when it came through town last month and she has not heard from him since. Sean tries to comfort Sally. A week after their arrival, Sally locates Hank in Montana and decides to leave to follow him. Because she can't take Max, she leaves him with Sean, knowing (s)he will take very good care of the pet.

The next day, Jo(e) is granted an interview with a prestigious high-tech company, the place he/she has dreamed of working since starting at the university. The big day arrives and Jo(e) is unable to find his/her black dress shoes to go with the grey power suit. Further, many of his/her ties are not in his/her hanging rack. After further investigation, he/she finds the shoes and ties in Sean's room chewed to shreds. Sean and Max are no where to be found.

Jo(e) ends up going to the interview dressed in his/her grey suit with an outdated, purple tie and brown shoes. (S)he is so upset, that the interview does not go well, and Jo(e) becomes angry all over again. Afterward, Jo(e) tells Sean (s)he must get rid of Max immediately or be out by the end of the week. Jo(e) then goes to the Student Attorney's office to find out his/her rights in kicking out Sean.

Role Play 6.

MAKING THE GRADE TO WRONGFUL TERMINATION

(Developed by Deborah Henshaw Urbanski for the AA White Dispute Resolution Institute—Used with Permission.)

General Facts

This dispute involves a wrongful termination claim against the University and Professor Pocatella by his teaching assistant Sandy Morris.

The employee/claimant, Sandy was Prof. Pocatella's T.A. for two years before (s)he was terminated for re-writing Prof. Pocatella's final exam and other alleged insubordinate actions.

The employee contends (s)he has not done anything that is not done by all other T.A.'s in the department and that his/her evaluations have always been exceptionally high. (S)he has not been able to find another position since the termination action three months ago.

The University and Prof. Pocatella want to end this matter and do not want to be sued. While a suit has not been filed, a demand letter has been sent by an attorney, however, no attorney's are present at this dispute resolution session.

Role Play 7.

"IT'S IN THE CAR(D)S"

(Adapted from a Role Play developed by Louis A. Vetrano, Jr. for the A.A. White Dispute Resolution Institute—Used with Permission)

General Facts

Sam is the owner of a small used car dealership. Sam sold a car to Mary. Mary has had the car in twice for repairs since she bought the car. Sam has a part time mechanic who does the repair work. Mary has refused to pick up the car after the last repair and quit making payments on the car. She is now five payments behind. She has now filed a lawsuit against Sam trying to get her money back. Sam and Mary have not talked for several weeks. Both have agreed to try a dispute resolution procedure.

Role Play 8.

EMPLOYEE/EMPLOYER WRONGFUL TERMINATION

General Facts

This dispute involves employment at a medical center. The employee claimant was a bookkeeper at a ten physician general practice clinic. The employee worked for about eight months, and was terminated by the employer, We Are Doctors. All employment related communication, including this termination was through the managing partner, Dr. Sam. The stated reasons for the employment termination included alleged continuous tardiness and carelessness on the job. The employee contends that s/he has not been late any more than most of the other employees, and that s/he takes great care in all work. In fact, the employee's one evaluation was exceptionally high. It took place after six months on the job. The termination occurred a month ago, and the claimant has not yet been able to find employment.

The management committee of We Are Doctors wants to end this silly matter, and wants nothing more to do with the employee; yet, it does not want to be sued. The employee wants the job back, the missed month's salary, and a written acknowledge of the wrongful actions which s/he believes to have occurred. While suit has not been filed, a demand letter has been sent by the employee's attorney; however, no attorneys are present at the mediation hearing.

The exact nature of the relationship between the parties, as well as the salary is left up to the role players.

Role Play 9.

RIFT OVER A RAISE

(Adapted from a Role Play Developed by Laura Vickers for A.A. White Dispute Resolution Institute—Used with Permission)

General Facts

Sally Martin has worked as an administrative secretary for the university for seven years. She is very efficient and is always on top of her work. In seven years, she has received many favorable reviews from her boss, Dean Higgins. Dean Higgins gave Sally a 7% raise in her salary four years ago. Sally feels that she deserves another raise. Sally asked Dean Higgins to raise her salary an additional 5% six months ago. Since then, she has noticed that Dean Higgins has become increasingly demanding. Sally finds it difficult to talk to Dean Higgins. Last month, Sally received her first unfavorable work review from the Dean. Sally cannot imagine what caused the change in the evaluation of her work. When she asks Dean Higgins for an explanation, he just says she's not working hard enough. The Dean also says he has had cuts in the office budget, and can't afford to give Sally a raise. Sally asked Dean Higgins if he would go to mediation to discuss the problems.

Role Play 10.

"NO, I WANT THE ...."

(Adapted from a Role Play Developed by Laura Vickers for A.A. White Dispute Resolution Institute—Used with Permission)

General Facts

Bobby and SueAnn Spillers have been married for twenty-two years. The Spillers are getting a divorce. SueAnn worked as a manicurist to put Bobby through dental school. Bobby has been in practice for fourteen years, and is a very successful dentist. SueAnn has not worked in twelve years. SueAnn has stayed home to take care of their ten year old daughter, Jessica. The Spillers wish to divide their community property and debts.

Bobby drives a 1996 Mazda RX 7 on which the Spillers owe $7,500. SueAnn drives a 1996 Suburban that is paid for. The family home was custom-built and is worth $327,000. The Spillers owe $85,000 on the mortgage of the home. The family owns a beach house valued at $175,000. The beach house is paid for. The Spillers have a thirty-five foot deep sea fishing boat worth $32,000. They owe $8,250 on the boat. Bobby and SueAnn have a joint checking account with a balance of $69,000. They also have a rare and valuable collection of 19th century dental tools appraised at $17,500. They owe American Express $5,750 and Visa $3,875.

Role Play 11.

THE HOME REPAIR CONTRACT

General Facts

Lanelle is a home owner. She recently hired Bob to repair her roof. After the roof was repaired there was a heavy rain. The roof leaked around the chimney and damaged the ceiling. Lanelle called Bob to repair the leak around the ceiling. Bob made a trip out to repair the roof, but not the chimney. The next time it rained, the roof leaked around the chimney again. Lanelle called Bob again — to fix the roof and the ceiling. Now Bob will not return Lanelle's calls. The receptionist in Bob's office keeps telling Lanelle that what she really needs to do is get someone in to fix the chimney. The receptionist refuses to discuss the replacement of the ceiling. Lanelle decides to try mediation since the dollar amount involved in this case is relatively small.

Role Play 12.

HOMEOWNERS ASSOCIATION DISPUTE

(Adapted from a Role Play Developed by Laura Vickers Legal Intern
©1995 A. A. White Dispute Resolution Institute—Used With Permission)

General Facts

The homeowners' association of Deerwood Village has a problem. Three factions of the association are in disagreement over how to spend a good part of the yearly membership fees, $10,000. One faction is headed by Tom Gross. Tom and his group think that the Deerwood Village swimming pool is in a state of disrepair.

The second group is led by Sadie Raskin. She and her associates believe that the membership fees would be best spent building a park for the neighborhood kids to play safely. The third faction is headed by Julia Westin. Julia and her association members want to spend the money on neighborhood landscaping. They believe this would benefit the environment and make Deerwood Village a more beautiful place to live. The three groups cannot seem to reach a compromise. They have come to mediation to try to agree on how the money should be spent.

Role Play 13.

THE RECORDING CONTRACT

General Facts

In 1992, the Texas alternative rock band "Speakeasy" recorded their first album called "1st Song." In order to record this album, the four members recruited the help of Lou Diamond, a friend of theirs for many years. Diamond created a record company called Bulldog Records, completely funded with his own money, and orally contracted with Speakeasy for its first recording deal. Since the members of Speakeasy and Diamond were close friends, many terms of the arrangement were not discussed.

"1st Song" was recorded and released in a few short weeks and a single pressing (a pressing is 10,000 copies) of the CD was produced and delivered to regional radio stations and local music stores. The band aggressively promoted their CD with club dates, regional tours and college radio promotions. Before they knew it, Speakeasy was taking off. Their success was primarily due to their live shows and a song that was on "1st Song" called "Home." Album sales were rising, but they were not making a great deal of money. Late in 1993, only 4,000 copies of "1st Song" remained on the shelves. At this point, Diamond and Speakeasy decided that it would not be prudent to invest the money to produce another pressing and Speakeasy and Diamond ended their business relationship and eventually all copies of "1st Song" disappeared from the shelves.

Speakeasy continued to promote the CD in the local clubs and were eventually approached by Jim Weitz of Superscope Records, one of the music industries newest major labels that had made its mark by signing some of the best up and coming new bands. Superscope offered Speakeasy three record deals and immediately sent them into the studio to record their second CD, "2nd Song." The form contract they signed with Superscope contained a clause that assigned to Superscope all rights to any recorded material the band has produced. It is Superscope's position that this clause assigns the rights to "1st Song" over to them.

Since the song "Home" was such a success, Superscope insisted that Speakeasy include it on "2nd Song." Superscope aggressively promoted the band and the song, sending copies of the CD to all of the major radio stations in the nation and sending Speakeasy on tours across the U.S. and Canada with some of their more established bands. The result was that the song "Home" was climbing the charts and Speakeasy had become an overnight sensation.

While on tour in New York, approximately one year after Superscope and Speakeasy signed their contract, Speakeasy's drummer was in a record store and saw several copies of "1st Song" in the bins behind the copies of "2nd Song." This struck him as odd since the first CD was released only in Texas and because all copies had been sold over a year ago. He discussed this with the store manager and discovered that the store had received a shipment of 100 copies only the week before from Bulldog Records. The CD was marked with a label stating "Featuring the new hit song . . . Home!"

The drummer promptly reported his finding to Weitz. Upon further investigation, Weitz discovered that Diamond and Bulldog had sent over 200,000 copies of "1st Song" to various record stores in the U.S. and Canada. Superscope's attorney immediately filed an application for injunctive relief, and the injunction was granted until the rights of the parties can be established. The injunction prohibits Bulldog Records from further distribution and the 175,000 copies of "1st Song" that remained on the shelves were returned to Bulldog Records. The injunction also prohibits Superscope from producing and marketing "1st Song."

Superscope and Speakeasy then filed this action against Bulldog Records seeking $2 million in damage for copyright infringement, unauthorized sales and intentional interference with a contractual relationship. Bulldog Records denies that Superscope or Speakeasy have any rights in "1st Song" because Diamond produced the CD entirely with his own funds and because Speakeasy told him that "they did not care what he did with 1st Song." It is Bulldog's position that Speakeasy surrendered it's rights to the CD with that statement.

Role Play 14.

SHAKY BUILDING

(Adapted from Role Play developed by KENNETH J. LANE from Lonergan, et al. v. San Antonio Loan & Trust Co., 104 S.W. 1061 (Tex. 1907)—Used with Permission)

General Facts

Sally Trusco contracted with a builder, Thomas Lonergan & Co., Inc. (TLCO), to construct a building in accordance with plans and specifications made by Sally's architect, Alfred Giles. Upon completion of the construction, the building fell. Ms. Trusco contends TLCO failed to perform its contract to complete and deliver the structure. Sally has sued TLCO for $200,000 for the cost of clearing the construction site and rebuilding the structure.

It is undisputed that the reason the building which TLCO erected fell was not because of defective material or work, nor because of negligence by the contractor, but solely because of fatal defects inherent in the plans and specifications. TLCO has filed a countersuit for $100,000 in damages and the unpaid amount on the original contract, claiming it complied with the contract and built the structure in accordance with the plans provided by the owner.

Upon substantial completion but prior to final inspection of the building, Sally Trusco proceeded to move equipment into the second story in violation of the terms of the agreement. Thomas Lonergan, President of TLCO, was injured when the second story collapsed and has sued for $500,000 in damages for personal injuries.

The parties have been informed that the architect's insurance company is willing to pay the $200,000 policy maximum in damages. It has defenses against both actions; however, it is likely it will lose one or both claims. The insurance company doesn't care who it pays as long as all parties sign a release.

Role Play 15.

GRANDPA'S AGREEMENT

(Adapted from Role Play developed by Alexandra Prentice—Used with Permission)

General Facts

In 1957, Mr. Newton and Mr. Gillan bought a large plot of land on Lake Michigan. They divided the land in half, and each built a house on his half of the property. At the time, Mr. Newton and Mr. Gillan orally agreed to split the costs of developing the property: they put in a septic tank, built a boat dock, and made a gravel driveway that they could share for access to the road. The septic tank was placed underneath Gillan's property, and the dock was built on Newton's land. The costs of these improvements was divided 50-50, and use of each was to be shared 50-50. There is no written evidence of the 1957 agreements.

Each house has lake-front property, but as the dock is located on the Newton's property, the Gillans must walk across the Newton's front yard in order to use the dock. This arrangement suited both families for years. In 1982, the Gillans built their own boat dock on their property, but they continued to use the original dock, for sunbathing and picnicking. The Newton's did not object or complain to the Gillans.

In 1989, Grandpa Gillan died, leaving the lake house jointly to his children and grandchildren. They use the house on weekends, and occasionally have large parties.

Last year it became apparent that the septic tank needed to be repaired. The septic tank is underground directly behind the Gillan's house, but the Newton's use the tank, too. One of the Gillans went over to Jim Newton's house to discuss the repairs, and asked if Newton would pay for his share. Jim Newton agreed to pay for half of the repairs. However, the tank was leaking beyond repair, and had to be replaced. The cost was $11,000. Jim Newton refuses to pay.

Role Play 16.

MARRIAGE NOT MADE IN HEAVEN

(Adapted from Role Play developed by Ronique J. Bastine—Used with Permission)

General Facts

Paula and Michael have been married for five years. Prior to the marriage they had a son together named Geoff. One year ago they separated and Paula moved about 500 miles away, leaving Michael and Geoff in the small town in which they lived. Michael was a sales representative with a major company and made a good salary and some months he had very good bonus and commission checks. When Paula left, Michael had to quit his job and find one that, paid less but, was more conducive to providing for Geoff. Paula did not call or write. She worked but did not provide any type of child support or assistance. Michael used his savings to hire a private investigator to find Paula at a cost of $250.00 dollars a day. The investigator had no leads on how to find Paula and really milked Michael for all he could get, his billed totaled more than $5000.00. He did finally locate Paula and set up a surveillance to determine what kind of lifestyle she was living. He found out Paula was going to different night clubs every night and coming home at very early hours of the morning. The investigator reported to Michael that Paula was living a loose life and he believed she was working as a topless dancer. He provided pictures of Paula coming in and out of the different clubs with different gentlemen. Michael tried to contact Paula to plead with her to return to her family but his letters went unanswered. He even made a tape of Geoff asking for his Mommy, but she still did not respond.

Recently Paula has returned to their small town and has asked Michael if she could see Geoff, he refused and also refused to communicate with her. Feeling distraught she spoke with her new roommate who advised her to seek the help of an attorney, she told her she had just as much right to see her child as her husband. Paula was short on cash and found Quickie Turner who told her I'll have you rid of that man and back with your son in no time, TRUST ME.

When Michael received the divorce papers he was outraged, "How dare she divorce me!", so he hired Killer Jackson. Killer assured him, Paula didn't have a chance after the life she lived, she would be lucky if she even got visitation. With the two lawyers involved the divorce turned very nasty very quickly and several motions, depositions and hearings later they were ordered to mediation.

Role Play 17.

BMW GONE MAD

(Adapted from Olga Anzaldua from *BMW of North America, Inc. v. Ira Gore*, Jr, 646 So. 2d 619 (Ala. 1994)—Used with Permission)

General Facts

Dr. I. Doolittle bought a new 1990 BMW 535i automobile from German Auto, Inc., a Birmingham automobile dealership, for $40,000. German Auto buys its cars from BMW of North America (BMW NA), the only distributor authorized to import BMW's into the United States.

Dr. Doolittle, a graduate of Harvard College and Duke Medical School, is a local pediatrician in Birmingham. At the time of the sale, Dr. Doolittle signed a "Retail Buyer's Order" and an "Acknowledgement of Disclosure" form. The disclosure form required Dr. Doolittle to acknowledged that the automobile might have sustained damage at some point and that he had inspected it and had agreed to accept it. However, no repairs or known damage was listed on the disclosure form.

Dr. Doolittle drove the car for approximately nine months before taking it to "Slick Finish," an independent automobile detailing shop, to make the car look "snazzier than it would normally appear," even though he was not unsatisfied with the car's appearance and had not noticed any flaws in the finish of the car. The detailer informed Dr. Doolittle that the car had been partially refinished.

After confronting German Auto, Dr. Doolittle determined that the car's paint had been refinished because of acid rain damage sustained during transit from BMW's manufacturing plant in Germany to BMW NA, the distributor. As it turns out, BMW NA had adopted a company policy that it would not disclose any damage to either the dealer or to the customer if the cost of repairing such damage was less than 3% of the manufacturer's suggested retail price (MSRP). The cost to the distributor for refinishing Dr. Doolittle's car was approximately $650. Consequently, BMW NA did not disclose to the dealer that the automobile it sold to Dr. Doolittle had been refinished.

Dr. Doolittle has sued German Auto and BMW NA in an Alabama district court on the theory that failure to disclose the refinishing constituted fraud, suppression of a material fact, and breach of contract. Dr. Doolittle is suing for actual and punitive damages.

Role Play 18.

HELPING HANDS

(Adapted from a Role Play developed by Gilbert M. Piette—Used with Permission)

General Facts

Lena Cavazos is a middle-age woman who works for Helping Hands, a large 501(c)(3) organization (tax-exempt) providing counseling and educational services. The Helping Hands corporation is active throughout the United States with national, regional and city offices. Lena became involved with Helping Hands years ago on a volunteer basis. Later, she took an entry level salaried position and quite a few years later, entered a two year training program to qualify for the intermediate level salaried position she now holds.

Lena has worked in a city office in Chisme as an intermediate staff member for about five years. She is a spirited individual who believes strongly in social justice ideals and has been an outspoken advocate for the underprivileged both in her role with Helping Hands as well as in her private life. It is not uncommon for her to take part in marches and demonstrations for causes she supports.

At times Lena's commitment to her ideals has been a source of friction within the organization. She will refuse to assist the Helping Hands staff if she believes a particular office decision or procedure is not "just" or equitable. Her former manager/boss (top position in the city office) found her to be aggressive, divisive and belligerent if she did not personally agree with the approach taken by Helping Hands in addressing various issues. As time progressed, her unwillingness to cooperate if she did not personally share the accepted view of the Helping Hands management earned her the reputation of a "loose cannon." Nonetheless, she definitely had talents in administration, management and could be quite effective, if she agreed with you. Unfortunately, in recent years, the working relationship with her former boss had deteriorated and the staff had split into opposing camps.

About a year ago, her former boss let his personal problems get out of hand. He had been an effective manager for many years but as personal problems mounted his professionalism at the office began to suffer as well. Regional management received complaints of sexual harassment from some clients of the Chisme office. Aside from possible civil suits, management was concerned about bad publicity which would have a deleterious impact on the tax free donations which provided the bulk of income for Helping Hands as a 501(c)(3) organization. When regional management confronted the boss he recognized his problem and quietly resigned from his position in the Chisme office. Regional management asked Lena Cavazos to help manage day to day operations of the office under the direction of a temporary manager until another qualified permanent manager could be found. She was not qualified for the manager's position and would not be able to obtain the necessary qualifications. During this interim period, friction between her and the interim manager broke out into open confrontation. Upon his departure he recommended to the regional office that they terminate Lena Cavazos' position.

Ernest, an experienced city office manager, was transferred to take over the Chisme office. He hoped to develop a team approach and bring in some new, young staff members. He has been fully informed of the prior history of the office and is concerned that Lena Cavazos's history of uncooperative behavior could impair development of the team approach. At the same time he recognized her abilities, her long history with the organization and her numerous contacts in the community. Aware that regional management is considering the recommendation to "move her out," Lena hires an attorney and threatens to go public with "what she knows" about the sexual harassment situation with her former boss.

The Helping Hands organization has an ombudsman. In the past, use of an ombudsman has avoided the potential of bad publicity by settling matters internally. The Policy Handbook requires Conciliation, Mediation or Arbitration prior to legal action. Lena is open to mediation but fears getting railroaded. She is still threatening to "go public" if things don't go well and to follow up with legal action if she is terminated.

Role Play 19.

CONSTRUCTION CONTRACT CASE

(Adapted by Patricia A. Meier from the *Board of Regents of the University of Texas v. S & G Construction Company* 529 S.W.2d 90 (1975)—Used with Permission)

General Facts

The State University Board of Regents (State) and S & G Construction Company (S&G) entered into a contract to build additional married student housing. The project involved building eighteen new multistoried apartment units, remodeling of two older units, and construction of the necessary streets, parking lots, curbing, drainage facilities, sidewalks, utilities, landscaping, and recreational facilities. The topography of the construction site was very uneven.

Immediately after work began, it was discovered that the topography information on the site plans was inaccurate and unusable. The parties discussed the problems and proceeded on a piecemeal basis. However, S&G's president advised State's project architect that the piecemeal directions were not adequate and serious problems with the project would develop if they were not given a correct, overall site plan detailing the relationship of the various improvements. The State University project architect acknowledged the inadequacy of the few supplemental plans furnished.

Upon discovery of the error S&G could have refused to perform the contract. However, they choose to perform at the original price as long as revised plans and specifications were provided. The project continued with State's Chief of Construction providing partial plans and verbal instructions. However, no overall new plans were furnished, despite repeated requests by S&G for a completely revised overall site plan.

The lack of corrected plans caused a lot of extra work for the contractor. Every improvement was located and relocated between three to five times. Many of the changes had to be made without aid of any written supplemental plans. Eventually, the project was completed to the satisfaction of both parties.

Both parties agree that the contractor is due additional compensation for the additional work. However, the parties disagree on how to measure or calculate the amount. Currently, the State has paid the contract amount plus extra compensation for approved written change orders, minus $12,000 for liquidated damages for late completion of the project. Selected provisions from the contract's general conditions are as follow:

17. Changes in Work
No changes in the work covered by the approved contract documents shall be made without prior written approval of the Owner.

18. Extras
Without invalidating the contract, the Owner may order extra work or make changes by altering, adding to or deducting from the work, the contract sum being adjusted accordingly, and the consent of the Surety being first obtained where necessary or desirable. All the work of the kind bid upon shall be paid for at the price stipulated in the proposal, and

no claims for any extra work or materials shall be allowed unless the work is ordered in writing by the Owner or its Architect/Engineer, acting officially for the Owner, and the price is stated in such order.

22. Claims for Extra Costs
No claim for extra work or cost shall be allowed unless the same was done in pursuance of a written order of the Architect/Engineer approved by the Owner, as aforesaid, and the claim presented with the first estimate after the changed or extra work is done. When work is performed under the terms of subparagraph 17(c) of the General Conditions, the contractor shall furnish satisfactory bills, payrolls and vouchers covering all items of cost and when requested by the Owner, give the Owner access to accounts relating thereto.

In addition the contract provided:
The contractor will be furnished additional instructions and detail drawings as necessary to carry out the work included in the contract. The additional drawings and instructions thus supplied to the Contractor will coordinate with the contract documents, and will be so prepared that they can be reasonably interpreted as part thereof. The contractor shall carry out the work in accordance with the additional detailed drawings and instructions.

Role Play 20.

UNDUE INFLUENCE*

***Adapted from the Seward Johnson Will Contest written about in David Margolick's book, UNDUE INFLUENCE: THE EPIC BATTLE FOR THE JOHNSON & JOHNSON FORTUNE (1993). (Adapted from a role play developed by Amy B. Whitworth—Used with Permission)**

General Facts

In 1968, Barbara Piasecka (nicknamed Basia — BAH-sha), secured a job as a cook at the New Jersey estate of J. Seward Johnson, the incredibly rich heir to the Johnson & Johnson Company fortune. As a cook, Basia failed miserably, but Essie Johnson, Seward's wife, took pity on her and made her an upstairs maid, where she later caught the eye of Essie's randy septuagenarian husband, Seward, who nearly ran his yacht aground when he spotted her sunning in a bikini. He hired Basia as his personal art curator (she had studied art history in Poland), made her his scuba partner, took her traveling abroad, and set her up in a fancy Manhattan apartment. Seward lavished gifts on her — a $500,000 trust fund, a house on the Mediterranean, art work, furs, and jewels — making her so rich that she needed a will, and a lawyer of her own. Instead of sending Basia to his personal lawyer, Robert Myers, Seward sent her to a prestigious New York firm, where the trust and estates partner there assigned the task of drafting Basia's will to Nina Zagat, a recent Yale graduate.

Essie Johnson, not terribly unhappy to be rid of the philandering Seward, agreed to a divorce for $20 million and a couple of houses. Eight days later, in 1971, Seward, age 76, and Basia, age 34, married. In 1972, Seward had Myers revise his will to increase Basia's trust to $50 million. The bulk of his estate went to Harbor Branch Foundation, an oceanographic research center he had set up. Seward left nothing to his six children.

In the Spring of 1973, Seward decided that his interests and Basia's were identical, and executed a new will using Nina as his attorney as well. In the years following, Nina became Basia's best friend. She served the Johnson's and their foundation loyally, reliably and honestly. She traveled with them on vacations and oversaw the legal work they generated. Over the next several years, various wills were executed, each transferring more of the estate to Basia and allowing Nina to serve as executor and trustee. The final will was signed in 1983 while Seward was dying from cancer. It left Basia almost everything tangible: the artwork, the airplane, the houses, jewelry, boats, and livestock. Some $225 million went to a trust from which Basia could draw income and a limited amount of principal during her lifetime. The rest of the estate approximately $75 million — would be in a separate trust, whose interest went to Basia for life, then, depending on her direction, either to charity, Harbor Branch, or Seward's kin. Harbor Branch was, thus, effectively written out of the will unless Basia chose to make a remainder bequeath.

Seward passed away a month later leaving an estate of $402,824,972. The six Johnson children and Harbor Branch Foundation filed a will contest, alleging that Seward Johnson lacked the capacity to make a will and that it had been produced by the undue influence of his widow, Basia, acting in concert with her lawyer, Nina Zagat.

---

*Reprinted with permission.

Role Play 21.

UNWANTED EXPOSURE

(Adapted by Sara Bird Perro from *Barber v. Time*, 159 S.W.2d 291 (Mo. 1942)—Used with Permission)

General Facts

The parties are Burt Williams, the plaintiff, in an invasion of privacy case, represented by his/her attorney, Lee Keller, and Star Lyons, the editor/owner of *The American Inquirer*, and his/her attorney Mary Jones. The case is an action for damages based on a violation of plaintiffs right of privacy. *The American Inquirer* published an article (with Burt's picture) about a physical ailment for which he/she was being treated in a hospital. The article read as follows:

Starving Glutton

> One night last week, Burt Williams grabbed a candy bar, packed up some clothes, and walked to General Hospital "I want to stay here," Burt said between bites. "I want to eat all the time. I can finish a normal meal and be back in the kitchen in ten minutes eating again." Dr. Bower immediately packed Burt off to a ward and ordered a big meal from the hospital kitchen while he questioned Burt. The doctor found that although Burt had eaten enough in the past year to feed a family of four, Burt had lost 25 pounds. After a preliminary examination, Dr. Bower thought Burt's pancreas might be functioning abnormally. He thought it might be burning up too much sugar in Burt's blood causing an excessive flow of digestive juices, which can sharpen the appetite. While the doctor made painstaking laboratory tests and discussed the advisability of a rare operation, Burt Williams lay in bed and ate.

[This article was accompanied by a picture of an enormously obese Burt Williams clad in a longsleeved hospital gown. It was a close-up picture showing Burt's face, head and arms, with the bedclothes covering Burt's chest.]

Burt Williams did not consent to the publication of any article or picture in connection with the illness. Burt protested against any publicity at all to the reporters who interviewed him/her. In fact, Burt's picture was only taken because one of the reporters was distracting Burt by begging for his consent, while the reporter's assistant snapped a shot. *The American Inquirer* picked up the story and the photo from a news service and verified it with local papers. Star Lyons made the mistaken assumption that Burt Williams had given consent to the other news services to publish the story and the photograph. It is undisputed that this consent was not given.

The story was published less than one year ago. Burt Williams has been extremely humiliated and embarrassed by comments from family and strangers about his unusual disorder. However, since publication of the article, Dr. Bower has developed a weight-loss serum from the study of Burt Williams' pancreas. Burt has lost 137 pounds and is in excellent health.

Burt Williams has settled with the other three publishers of the eating disorder story. This lawsuit is pending in 12 weeks.

Role Play 22.

"BOOBY" DOESN'T PLAY NICE

(Adapted from a Role Play by Timothy Reilley from *Hackbart v. Cincinnati Bengals. Inc.*, 601 F.2d 516 (10th Cir.), *cent. denied,* 444 U.S. 931, 100 S.Ct. 275, 62 L.Ed. 2d 188 (1979).

General Facts

The Plaintiff, Dale Hackbart is a football player for the Denver Broncos. While playing for Denver, Dale was injured during a game with the Cincinnati Bengals in 1973. During this game, a player for the Bengals, Charles "Booby" Clark, slammed his right forearm into the back of Dale's head with sufficient force to throw him to the ground. This hit occurred after the play was over and while Dale was on his knees.

Dale has filed a lawsuit for assault and battery and negligence against Charles "Booby" Clark individually and against the Cincinnati Bengals under the theory of vicarious liability.

"Booby" has admitted that the blow to Dale's head was intentional, but he did not mean to injure him. It is also common knowledge that intentional striking of a player in the face or from the rear is prohibited by the rules of football as well as the general customs of the game.

Dale was hospitalized as a result of this incident and it is believed that his playing ability will be impaired. Dale is seeking reimbursement for his medical expenses and is also seeking damages for his physical and mental pain and suffering.

Charles "Booby" Clark is a player of modest ability and is paid the league minimum. He does not have insurance and will not be able to pay any substantial amount. "Booby" has agreed to cooperate with Dale in his case against the Bengals in exchange for a release. (Ignore the legality of this arrangement.) The remaining claims asserted are limited to those against the Bengals franchise.

The Commissioner of the N.F.L. has requested that these parties attend a mediation before proceeding further with this lawsuit.

Role Play 23.

ZARUBA V. ZARUBA

(Adapted from a Role Play Developed by Donna Woodruff from *Zaruba v. Zaruba*, 498 S.W.2d 695 (Tex. Civ. App.—Corpus Christi 1973, writ dism'd w.o.j.)— Used With Permission)

General Facts

Anthony Zaruba and Mildred Novak Zaruba were married to each other on November 18, 1980. At the time of marriage, the wife was 25 years old and the husband was 44 years old. Neither party had been previously married. Both parties want a divorce. They have lived apart without cohabitation for the past three years. Anthony and Mildred have two children, Paul and Diane, ages seven and three, respectively. Prior to the birth of their daughter, Anthony moved out of the family home. After the birth of Diane, Anthony refused to live as husband and father with Mildred and the two children. He has remained separated from them. The children have always lived with Mildred in the Zaruba family home, which Anthony and Mildred bought ten years ago. At the present time, the market value of the home is approximately $225,000.

Although Anthony had substantial income and net worth throughout the marriage, he contributed a relatively small amount per month to support his wife, son, and daughter. The first two years after he left Mildred he visited the kids approximately every two weeks. During the last year, he has visited them every Sunday.

Anthony received both B.A. and M.B.A. degrees from the University of Houston when he was in his twenties. He is an astute businessman who is well trained in the operation of automobile dealerships and in making financial investments. He is thus able to generate substantial income. On the other hand, Mildred received no formal education after high school. She has no experience or training in any profession or trade and as a result, is unable to generate substantial income.

Anthony owned two Chevrolet dealerships at the time of marriage. The large majority of the inventory in the two Chevrolet dealerships acquired after marriage was purchased with community credit. Anthony did not regularly withdraw the profits arising from the operation of the Chevrolet dealerships from his business bank account. Instead, the profits were mixed and commingled with the original separate capital in the businesses. The dealerships' profits significantly increased during their marriage.

Anthony also works as a financial consultant for Anderson Consulting and has worked there for the past 25 years. His current salary is $50,000 per year. In five years, his yearly salary will likely be around $56,000. He has a defined benefit pension plan with Anderson. He is eligible to receive retirement benefits at age 65. Anderson Consulting uses the following formula to determine Anthony's monthly payment under the plan: (.02) x (average of highest three years of earnings) x (number of years of service with the employer).

During the marriage, Anthony and Mildred purchased a mini-van, a Mercedes, and a condo in Puerto Vallarta, Mexico. The mini-van has a fair market value of $17,000 whereas the Mercedes has a fair market value of $30,000. The present market value of the condo in Puerto Vallarta is $125,000.

Role Play 24.

SEXUAL HARASSMENT

(Adapted from a Role Play Developed by Gerrie Zhang—Used with Permission)

General Facts

Linda Morgan, a Chemical Engineer and Sales Manager with Chemco, a large corporation, recently resigned due to a sexual harassment dispute in the workplace. She has filed an EEOC complaint and a discrimination action. Ms. Morgan claims that Mr. Ned Olson, the Division Manager and her immediate supervisor, insulted her because of her gender and often made her the target of unwanted sexual innuendos. She resigned after Mr. Olson suggested, in the presence of several of Ms. Morgan's co-workers, that she must have promised sexual favors to a customer in order to secure an account. She claims that Olson's conduct created an abusive and hostile work environment for her because of her gender and that she was constructively discharged because of that hostile environment. Chemco and Mr. Olson claim that Ms. Morgan resigned from her job because Chemco terminated its business relationship with Ms. Morgan's husband, and that her job performance was not satisfactory. The parties have agreed to participate in non-binding mediation.

Ms. Morgan worked for Chemco for ten years. She was hired as a Chemical Engineer and, after receiving sales and management training provided by Chemco, Ms. Morgan made the transition to management. As Sales Manager, Ms. Morgan worked directly for Mr. Olson, the Division Manager.

Mr. Olson has been employed by Chemco for twenty years. He began his employment with Chemco as an Associate Engineer and was promoted to Chemical Engineer. He has been a manager for five years. As Division Manager, Mr. Olson was Ms. Morgan's immediate supervisor for approximately one year.

Role Play 25.

THE UNPOPPY-LAR DRUG TEST

(Adapted from a Role Play Developed by Elizabeth Harris based on *SmithKline Beecham Corp. v. Jane Doe*, 903 S.W.2d 347 (Tex. 1995)—Used with Permission)

General Facts

Sativa Stone, a 24-year-old graduate student studying business administration at the University of Houston, was offered a job by Harris Industries as a Marketing Assistant shortly before her graduation. In accordance with Harris company policy, Stone's offer was contingent upon satisfactory completion of a drug screening examination. Harris Industries' policy regarding the screening was on the employment application, and it read: "Any individual whose test results are positive and who did not disclose current medications will not be eligible for hire." Earlier that same year, Harris Industries had contracted with Positive Proof Laboratories to perform all employee/applicant drug screening. Positive Proof Laboratories got the contract with Harris Industries by designing a comprehensive drug-testing system for the company, from specimen "pick-up" by its specially trained assistants through proper reporting of test results and long-term retention of test records. Positive Proof advertised itself as a "responsible, quality-conscious laboratory that offers a complete, correct drug screening analysis for potential employees." Since Positive Proof had taken over Harris' testing, Harris' personnel office had developed a complete reliance on Positive Proof' s expertise, in that all the Harris personnel office had to do was give the potential employee the address of the lab. There, a Positive Proof employee would test the applicant and process the results.

After reviewing Sativa's resume and application, Harris' personnel office told Sativa she would be hired if her drug screening came back with a satisfactory result. Harris gave Sativa the lab's address. When Sativa arrived at the lab, she completed an information form for Positive Proof Lab, which asked her to list all the medications she was currently taking. Sativa listed birth control pills as the only medication she was taking.

After performing the drug test, Positive Proof Laboratories sent Sativa' s results to Harris Industries, who in turn called Sativa to inform her that she would not be hired because she did not pass her drug test, which had shown positive results for opiates. Sativa told Harris Industries that she couldn't believe it because she was not on drugs. In an excited and panicked state, Sativa told Harris personnel that she had taken her roommate's prescription drugs and forgotten to write that on the information sheet. Harris personnel said that if that was the case, she would not be eligible for employment because she had lied on her information sheet. Sativa was adamant that she was not taking illicit drugs and asked Harris Industries who had performed the drug test. She was told that Positive Proof had done the testing. Sativa immediately contacted the lab and told them that she had no idea how her test could have come up positive because she had not taken any drugs, other than her birth control pills. Positive Proof told Sativa that she had tested positive for opiates and that their results were 100% accurate, and furthermore, they only gave the company the results and they weren't responsible for the consequences of her actions.

Sativa was so distressed that she called her father, a chemist. He told her that recent research had shown that some every day substances, such as poppy seeds, could cause a positive reading for illegal substances. Sativa remembered that she had eaten several poppy seed muffins at breakfast on the day before her drug test. Sativa immediately called Positive Proof and told them that she had eaten the muffins the day before her drug test and that is probably why her exam came up positive for opiates. Sativa demanded that Positive Proof call Harris personnel and inform them about that. Positive Proof told Sativa that their results were 100% accurate and that they were not responsible for her employment problems.

Sativa then went directly to an employment lawyer, Cindy Sue, who filed suit against Positive Proof for negligence. Sativa claims that Positive Proof was negligent for: (1) failing to inform her before she undertook the urinalysis drug test that poppy seeds are a known cause of positive test results and could lead to her failing the drug test; (2) failing to inform prospective employers and/or test recipients that poppy seeds are a known cause of positive test results and could lead to a positive test result for opiate use; and (3) failing to ask applicants whether they have ingested any poppy seed foods within a reasonable period before their test was administered; and (4) failure to report the level of opiates found in her drug test and failing to inform third persons, including the prospective employer, that this level was consistent with poppy seed ingestion and not illicit drug use.

She had also sued Positive Proof for breach of good faith and fair dealing; defamation; and tortious interference with a prospective contract. Sativa also sued Harris Industries separately for defamation, and they entered into a confidential settlement with Sativa last month. Sativa has asked Positive Proof Laboratories for $2 million in damages.

Role Play 26.

FISHING FOR TROUBLE

(Adapted from a Role Play Developed by Kyle W. Sanders—Used with Permission)

General Facts

Bubba Hebert and Lance Fisher have been friends for twenty years. Currently, Bubba is working for Lance in his construction business. While they have had a business relationship before, it has never affected their friendship.

In August of 1990, Bubba and Lance joined together to purchase a fishing boat. The purchase price of the boat was $10,000. Bubba and Lance co-signed on a loan for this amount. The loan term was for six years during which time each party was to pay $100.00 a month. Three years into this term, Lance put the boat into storage and denied Bubba access. At this point, Bubba stopped paying on the note. Lance, fearful of a poor credit rating, took out a second loan to pay off the full amount owing on the first loan. Bubba now contends that since Lance paid off the full amount, he wants to keep the boat. Since it is now Lance's boat, Bubba wants the money he paid on the boat for the first three years of the term. Lance refuses to pay Bubba, so Bubba filed this cause of action to recover the money paid.

There appears to also be an underlying issue concerning a truck that Lance allowed Bubba's son to use temporarily. He offered to sell it to the son if he finished high school. The son failed to finish high school and Lance thus took the truck back. Some of the emotions in this case could very well derive as much from this incident as the boat business.

Role Play 27.

MUTUALLY ACCEPTABLE ROOMMATE

(Adapted from Role Play Developed by Robin Lowenkron from *Coleman v . Zatechka*, 824 F. Supp. 1360 (D. Neb. 1993)—Used with permission)

General Facts

This is a dispute between Ms. Coleman, and the University of Nebraska. Plaintiff Coleman filed a complaint with the United States Department of Education's Office for Civil Rights charging that the University did not provide students with disabilities with housing comparable to that provided other students.

Coleman has cerebral palsy. As a result she is confined to a wheelchair and requires the services of a personal attendant to assist her with dressing, showering and toileting. When she filled out her housing application, she requested a double room with a non-smoking roommate. Under the schools normal policies, her name should have been placed in a pool with all the others who did not request a specific roommate. However, the school did not assign her a roommate.

After Coleman filed her complaint, the school made some attempts to find her a "mutually acceptable" roommate. The school never put Ms. Coleman's name in the pool with all the other students. The school was not able to locate someone willing to room with Ms. Coleman. As a result, Ms. Coleman spent two years in a double room without an assigned roommate. Ms. Coleman then initiated this suit against the University.

Role Play 28.

TOO OLD FOR GENERATION X

(Adapted from a Role Play Developed by Cindy Lange based on *McKennon v. Nashville Banner Publishing Co.*, 115 S.Ct. 879 (1995)—Used With Permission)

General Facts

Mary Oldie, a 60 year old woman, began her employment with Newsy Publishing Company 25 years ago as a receptionist. Through hard work and dedicated service, Mary had advanced to the position of Vice President of Sales for the Southwest Region at the time of her termination, which was 2 months ago. Newsy allegedly terminated Mary due to a reduction in force program. Mary, however, believes that she was terminated because of her age in violation of the Age Discrimination in Employment Act (ADEA).

Newsy is a publishing company located and incorporated in the state of Yoakum. Up until about one year ago, Newsy, was in the business of publishing and selling magazines and books targeted at middle aged and elderly people. However, approximately one year ago management decided to change the company's strategy and primarily target the younger "Generation X" market which is comprised mostly of people in their twenties. Although these younger readers would now be Newsy's largest target audience, Newsy intended to continue to publish many of the magazines and books it had always published. Newsy anticipated that its new customer mix would be 65% "Generation X" readers and 35% middle aged to elderly readers. Rumors around the office were that upper management was concerned that some of the older employees who had contact with the public would not project the hip image that the company was now attempting to convey. Mary believes that the reduction in force program was just a pretext to get rid of her because she was too old for Newsy's new image. The sales territory which Mary had been responsible for now constituted the largest "Generation X" market. As a Vice President of Sales, Mary had extensive contact with the public in carrying out her job duties.

Another thing that leads Mary to believe her termination was age-based was the fact that an executive secretary of one of the officers told Mary that "she was just too old for the company's new youthful image, and besides, a grandma couldn't get the kind of sales that the top dogs want."

Mary filed a complaint with the State of Yoakum's Equal Employment Opportunity Commission which issued her a right to sue letter. Mary has not yet filed suit. However, her attorney, Liz Litigator, has sent the company a notice of her intent to bring a claim against it for age discrimination unless the parties could work out some sort of settlement. Mary has told Newsy that she would never want to be reinstated after the way the company treated her, instead she wants them to pay her damages! ! ! Mary's son suggested that she and Newsy attempt to mediate the case.

Mary can make out the first three elements of a prima facie case of age discrimination in that she was over 40, qualified to do the job, and was terminated. However, since she was allegedly terminated due to a reduction in force plan, she also has to prove that Newsy either refused to retain or relocate her *because of age,* or regarded her age as a negative factor in its *decision* to lay her off. The problem with proving this last element is that Mary has no direct evidence that she was terminated because of her age. In all likelihood the secretary's remarks will not be admissible evidence on this point because the case law holds that derogatory statements made by someone not involved in the termination decision are "stray remarks" which are not admissible to prove discriminatory intent on the part of the party making the adverse employment decision.

Even if Mary could establish her prima facie case, which raises the presumption of discrimination, Newsy can rebut this presumption by offering one legitimate nondiscriminatory reason for its decision to terminate Mary. Newsy contends it can win on this point because it terminated Mary pursuant to a reduction in force plan which was necessitated by the company's faltering financial situation. If Newsy did convince the fact finder that this reduction in force plan was the real reason for Mary's termination, Mary would have one last chance to win by proving that the reduction in force plan was merely a pretext for Newsy's firing her because of age.

Newsy's lawyer, Denny Defender, says the company will litigate because it can easily prove that Mary was legally terminated pursuant to the company's legitimate reduction in force plan. Under this plan, the company had determined that it was necessary to terminate two people, and it picked the two people it would terminate by looking at the past year's sales records. Mary and the other laid off person had the lowest sales records for the previous year. The other employee terminated was a 50 year old man. Newsy concedes that in previous years, Mary had received numerous awards for her outstanding sales record.

Mary had been willing to take another position, but the company did not consider such an option. If a Plaintiff wins a case under the ADEA, possible remedies include: back pay, front pay, reinstatement, injunctive relief and other equitable relief the court deems necessary. Additionally, if an employer is found to have willfully discriminated, the employee can get punitive damages.

Role Play 29.

DUST GETS IN MY EYES

(Adapted from a Role Play Developed by Candace Kaiser from *Boomer v. Atlantic Cement Company*—Used With Permission)

General Facts

Atlantic Cement Co. commenced production at the Portland Cement plant in Coeymans, New York, in Albany County three years ago. Mr. Boomer is a landowner with land adjacent to the plant. He is seeking an injunction to restrain the Atlantic Cement Co. from conducting operations which cause the emission of dust and smoke and from conducting excessive blasting in the operation of the plant.

Role Play 30.

BOROFF V. BOROFF

(Adapted from a Role Play Developed by Elizabeth Hollas from *Boroff v. Boroff*, 197 Neb. 641, 250 N.W.2d 613 (1977)—Used with Permission)

General Facts

Both the husband and wife want a divorce after 14 years of marriage. They have one son who is 14 years old and one daughter who is 12 years old.

The wife, Patricia is currently employed at a cafe in Herman, Nebraska, and earns $60 in net income each week. She works from 5:30 a.m. until 1 p.m., 3 days a week, and from 5:30 a.m. until 2 p.m., 2 days a week. She has a high school education, and has previously worked for Western Electric, wiring PBX machines.

The husband, Eugene, is the postmaster at Herman, Nebraska, and earns $14,489 per year. With his deductions, he receives a monthly take-home pay of approximately $790.

The house which the Boroffs' own is worth approximately $12,000 and they owe a loan company $3,900.20 on the house, which is paid off at the rate of $61 per month, including real estate taxes and insurance. Other assets of the Boroffs total $3,144. Eugene listed current debts such as oil bills, hospital bills, service station bills, mastercharge, etc. . . . as being in the amount of approximately $600.

Role Play 31.

FOUR BROTHERS OWNED A MILL

(Adapted from a Role Play Developed by Walter Dean from *Dreifuerst v. Dreifuerst*, 280 N.W. 2d 335 (1979)—Used With Permission)

General Facts

The Dreifuerst brothers have been business partners for many years, but lately things have not been going as smoothly as when they first began. The four brothers now get into shouting matches over minor disagreements that they would have laughed off a couple of years ago. There is a general feeling that maybe 25 years is long enough and the brothers should dissolve the partnership.

Though they started with nothing, they now have so much, it is hard to figure out who should get what. The property consists of two grain mills. One is located in Clearview, and the other in Cyprus.

The suit was brought by Bob, one of the four brothers. He is trying to get the partnership assets divided up without a sale. The others want to sell the assets and divide the money between the partners, with each partner receiving an equal share.

The two sides have long stopped being civil, and it is taking a toll on their family life. The four have always been brothers first and partners second. Their families have socialized almost every weekend for as long as anyone can remember. Lately, Bob and his wife have not been invited to do anything with the rest of the family, and when everyone else gets together they just end up grumbling about what a jackass Bob has become.

Role Play 32.

THE CASE OF THE BROKEN SMILE

(Adapted from a Role Play Developed by Heather Simone—Used With Permission)

General Facts

Susan Moses was driving home from work in stop and go traffic. As she stopped, she glanced in her rear view mirror and saw a car, driven by Glen Walsh coming towards her. Glen was unable to stop in time and rear ended Susan. Susan called 911 to report the accident then exited her car to check out the damage to her 1993 Camaro. Glen also checked his car, a 1989 Honda. Both cars were damaged in the accident. The police officer arrived a short time later and prepared a police report of the incident. When asked if she was injured, Susan complained of a headache but said she was otherwise okay. Glen was not injured in the accident.

Later that evening, Susan began feeling worse and went to the emergency room, where the doctor took x-rays and examined her. He told her she had a neck sprain and sent her home. The next day, her headache had worsened and her face and jaw also hurt, so she went to another doctor who felt something might be wrong with her jaw and referred her to a dentist. The dentist referred her to a maxillofacial specialist who diagnosed her with temporomandibular joint disorder (TMJ). The dentist believes that the TMJ was caused by the accident and will testify to his conclusions.

The dentist treated her for the TMJ by using splints and physical therapy. The treatment alleviated the TMJ symptoms but ruined her bite. As a result, Susan had to have her jaw broken to repair her bite. Because of the surgery, she had to have her mouth wired shut for six weeks. Although her bite is now repaired, she still has symptoms from the TMJ which will necessitate Susan wearing a splint for at least the next two years to prevent the TMJ from worsening. She may have to wear the splint for the rest of her life.

Susan and Glen were both insured by the same insurance carrier. Susan filed a claim with Glen's insurance company. However, because she had filed two previous claims in the past three years on her own insurance, the insurance company refused to pay any of her medical expenses. The insurer did pay the repair costs for the damage to her car.

Susan consulted an attorney, Vincent Fairlane, who filed suit for Susan. The petition alleged that Glen's negligence proximately caused the accident and her injuries. She prayed for damages totalling $250,000 for past and future medical expenses, lost wages, disfigurement, and pain and suffering. Susan's actual damages are as follows:

Medical Expenses	$25,000
Lost Wages	$ 4,700

The remaining $220,000 encompasses future medical expenses, which her dentist estimates at $30,000 over the rest of her life, and damages for her pain and suffering and disfigurement.

Glen's attorney, Larry McMahon, filed an answer denying any responsibility for the accident. The answer alleged that Susan was contributorily negligent in that her brake lights were not on and that she cut in front of him and slammed on her brakes.

Much of the discovery has been completed, including depositions of the parties and their expert witnesses. Both sides have been negotiating and have made alternating settlement offers but they are still very far apart. Glen's only offer of settlement was $25,000. Susan's only offer was $200,000. Neither party has budged from those offers in two months, and trial is set for June. In an attempt to settle the case without the necessity of a trial, both parties have agreed to mediation.

Role Play 33.

CLEAN-IT-RIGHT

(Adapted from a Role Play Developed by Cipriano Romero from *Graceland Cors. v. Consolidated Laundries Coro.*, 7 A.D.2d 89, 180 N.Y.S.2d 644, aff'd 6 N.Y.2d 900, 190 N.Y.S. 2d 708, 160 N.E.2d 926 (1959)— Used With Permission)

General Facts for Mediator and Parties

Clean-it-Right dry cleaners and laundry service is located at the corner of First Avenue and East 94th Street. It is owned by Mrs. Dennis Jennings who inherited the business five years ago upon her husband's death. Clean-it-Right parks and stores its four trucks on the pedestrian sidewalk on the East 94th Street side of its own building. The laundry trucks obstruct the north pedestrian sidewalk of East 94th Street between First and Second Avenue. The loading area is located on that side of the building.

Valley Brite is a small three apartment unit that has been recently renovated by the owner, Mr. Thomas Burke. Before Mr. Burke's purchase of the building, the apartments were abandoned for eight years. Mr. Burke made a large investment in renovating and now is trying to turn a profit on the venture. The apartments are adjacent to the laundry along East 94th. The apartments have a controlled access gate surrounding the building. The entrance to the property is located on East 94th Street about ten feet from the side of the laundry. Residents use the sidewalk along East 94th to reach the apartments' entrance.

Mr. Burke is complaining that the parked trucks substantially block the access by residents to the apartments. The noise of trucks backing up early in the morning has also drawn complaints from residents. Mr. Burke claims the situation with the trucks is costing him money. Mr. Burke is considering a nuisance action with damages against the cleaners.

Role Play 34.

MY SUPERVISOR MAKES ME SICK!

(Adapted from a Role Play Developed by Deborah Edwards Based on *Sherrylen Weiler v. Household Finance Corp.*—Used With Permission)

General Facts

Sherrylen Weiler was employed by Household Finance Corp. (HFC) beginning in 1987. In 1991, she was transferred to the position of Manager of Branch Accounting. Her supervisor was Terrence Skorupka (a defendant in this case). During Sherrylen's annual performance evaluation in 1993, Terrence made some remarks concerning Sherrylen's attitude towards her subordinates, advising her that she should work on her interpersonal skills. Sherrylen became very upset, experiencing, as she puts it, severe stress and anxiety because of his criticism.

Two weeks after her evaluation, Sherrylen requested a transfer to another supervisor. She was told by Human Resources (HR) that there were no openings at present, but that she should apply for a transfer through the internal hiring procedure when a suitable job became vacant.

Less then three weeks after her visit to HR, Sherrylen's psychologist, Dr. Neil Mahoney, contacted HR to notify them that Sherrylen was under his care for depression and anxiety and as a consequence would not be able to return to work at that time. Sherrylen was placed on short term disability until her leave expired six months later. Sherrylen then applied for long-term disability but this was denied because she was able to work.

HR contacted Sherrylen and provided her with a list of open vacancies, prompting her to apply for transfer. Sherrylen's only response to this letter was a letter sent by her attorney, Mr. Peter Barron, advising HFC that his client was not able to return to work at that time.

Shortly thereafter, Sherrylen filed a claim with the Equal Employment Opportunity Commission, charging discrimination under the Americans with Disabilities Act against HFC and her supervisor, Skorupka. The EEOC issued Sherrylen a right to sue letter and she proceeded to file a claim in civil court under Title I of the ADA. Sherrylen is seeking back pay and compensatory damages for emotional pain and suffering, mental anguish, inconvenience and loss of enjoyment of life. HFC retained outside counsel, Ms. Jane Kalk to represent them in this matter.

Role Play 35.

WATCH YOUR STEP

(Adapted from a Role Play Developed by Michael A. Federico *from Goldstein v. L.F. Corrigan*, 405 S.W.2d 425 (Tex. Civ. App.—Waco, 1966)—Used With Permission)

General Facts

Zola Goldstein was a tenant in Apartment A, 6432 Bandera Street. The lease was for a term of twelve months. Mrs. Goldstein and her brother had originally leased the apartment for $115 per month. After living in the apartment for less than a month, she slipped and fell on the floor. She slipped as a result of a warped or irregular condition in the floor of the apartment between the dining room and the living room. There were no other factors which contributed to her accident. As a result, she broke her wrist and suffered minor bruises to various parts of her body.

In the lawsuit, Mrs. Goldstein alleged that the landlord was guilty of negligence which proximately caused her injuries. Specifically, she alleged the landlord was negligent: 1) in failing to keep the floor in a safe condition; 2) failing to repair the floor; 3) permitting a structural defect to exist; 4) permitting the floor to become warped; 5) failing to make inspections; 6) failing to repair after acquiring knowledge; 7) and in failing to properly light the area. She sought damages for medical expenses, pain and suffering. She also sought damages for the cost to repair the floor, so as to have a safe apartment to live in for the remaining term of the lease.

Role Play 36.

THE CASE OF THE WRONGFUL CREMATION

(Adapted From a Role Play Developed by Dino Ioannides from *Culpepper v. Pearl St. Bldg., Inc.*, 877 P.2d 877 (Colo. 1994)—Used With Permission)

General Facts

David and Betty Masterson are the parents of the deceased, Kevin Masterson. Kevin was found alone in his apartment about a week after his death. Kevin was a diabetic and was insulin dependent. He had been suffering from health problems for about six months before his death. However, strange circumstances surrounded his death and the police could not rule out foul play. The investigators told the family that there was very little evidence to go on until such time as the coroner completed the autopsy.

At the county coroner's office, Kevin's body was placed in a refrigeration unit next to another decedent, Bob Berrydew, who had died of an accidental shotgun wound to the head. The bodies were easily distinguishable and had also been tagged for identification purposes. The coroner's office had made arrangements for the We Toast-You Crematorium to pick up Bob Berrydew's body for cremation. Drivers for the crematorium unfortunately picked up the wrong body (i.e. Kevin's body). The body was taken to the crematorium where the cremation process was initiated. In the meantime, the county coroner discovered the crematorium's mistake and phoned the crematorium. On discovering the facts, the crematorium stopped the cremation process.

The remains, which included primarily Kevin's skeleton (the skin had been mostly cremated), were returned to the coroner's office. The coroner proceeded with the autopsy to the extent possible; the coroner's final report listed the cause of death as "unknown." The remains were subsequently transferred to Kevin's parents, who arranged for completion of the cremation.

The Mastersons have filed an action in state court against the crematorium. The Mastersons' argument is that the wrongful cremation of their son's body prevented them from learning the cause of his death, and especially prevented them from learning whether Kevin was murdered. Their claims include conversion and destruction of property, and negligent infliction of emotional distress.

INDEX

INDEX

A.A. White Dispute Resolution Institute, Appendix
Abel, Richard, 134, 217, 405
Abrams, Francis, 782
Abrams, Roger, 782
Academy of Family Mediators, 460
Administered arbitration, 532, 566
Administrative Conference, 883, 1091
Administrative Dispute Resolution Act of 1990, 500, 892, 890, 1095
Administrative Law
  See generally, Chapter 14
  arbitration, 869, 883
  benefits programs, 860
  capture thesis, 1153
  confidentiality, 1091
  internal review, 854
  judicial review, 860, 861
  nonbinding arbitration, 890
  professional regulation, 1142
  reg-neg, 895
  rulemaking, 894, 897
Advertising, 1240, 1241
Advisory opinions, 806, 908
Agency theory, 97, 189
Agent Orange, 1118, 1131
Agreements to settle, 1064
Alfini, James, 293, 935
American Arbitration Association, 458, 501, 520, 526, 532, 1171, 1205, 1216
American Bar Association, 5, 458, 1205, 1216
Anthropology, 123
Antitrust, 699, 708, 1146
Appellate mediation, 980
Arbitration
  See generally Chapters 10-12. *See also,* American Arbitration Association, Federal Arbitration Act, Uniform Arbitration Act, 599, 620
  administered, 533
  administrative agencies, 873, 883
  agreements, 574, 591
  antitrust, 699, 708
  appeals, 587
  arbitrability, 633
  banking, 725
  baseball, 585, 814

caucus, 814
commercial disputes, 516, 525
complex cases, 525
confidentiality, 584, 945
Connecticut, 30
consumers, 727
court annexed, 935
discovery, 86
discrimination, 758
employment, 742, 756, 775
England, 30
ethics, 1216
mandatory, 883, 934
New York cases, 657
non-administered, 556
non-binding, 568, 808, 890
party-appointed arbitrators, 1220
preemption, 643, 655
remedies, 584, 663, 671
securities, 636, 639, 645, 650, 713, 794, 1165
standard clauses, 573, 574
statute of limitations, 645
therapy, 781
Arbitration-mediation, 578
Architect (of ADR proces), 816
Arnold, Tom, 329, 591, 806, 816, 821, 833, 909, 1286
Association of Family Mediators, 1153
Atomic Energy Labor Relations Panel, 854
Auerbach, Jerold, 5, 6, 205, 218

Baker, William, 321
Ball, Milner, 1053, 1057
Banking arbitration, 725
Bargaining
competitive, 149, 171
cooperative, 149, 173
divorce, 159
integrative, 149, 175
shadow of law, 152
Barrett, William, 524
Baseball arbitration, 585, 813
Bedman, William, 1280
Bernstein, Lisa, 935
Berra, Lawrence (Yogi), 148, 775
Bierman, H. Scott, 83, 94

Bioethical disputes, 467
Bleak House, 691
Blumberg, Abraham, 253
Board of Contract Appeals, 854
Body language, *see* communication
Brazil, Wayne, 995, 1080
Brown, Jennifer, 474
Brown & Root, 1280
Bruff, Harold, 883
Budnitz, Mark, 725
Buese, Michelle, 773
Burger, Warren, 23, 131, 106
Bush, Robert Baruch, 288, 361
Business disputes, *see* Commercial disputes, Consumer disputes

Cahill, Mia, 1061
California, 402, 458, 908, 1084, 1088, 1097, 1182
Campbell, Joseph, 121
Caucus, 335, 814
Certification, *see* Dispute resolution professionals
Cheyenne Way, 8, 141, 142
Chicken, 68
Children, *see* Family disputes
Choice of law, 578
Civil Justice Reform Act of 1990, 1137
Cognitive disonance, 112
Colorado, 937, 1095
Commercial disputes, 245, 247, 501, 516, 525
Communication
  See generally, Chapter 2
  dysfunctional, 48
  facilitators, 44
  gender differences, 47
  impression management, 72, 74, 75
  inhibitors, 41
  nonverbal, 40
  questions, 49, 51
Compulsory court annexed ADR, 400, 449, 980
Conciliation, *see* Mediation
Confidentiality, 584, 945, 1077, 1080, 1151, 1235
Connecticut, 30
Constitution, *see* U.S. Constitution
Construction (ADR in)
  Army Corps of Engineers, 854
  generally, 854

job site, 816
partnering, 1286
Consumer disputes, 725
Continuing education, 1153
Cooper, Christine, 766
Cooperation, 110,
Corps of Engineers, *see* U.S. Army Corps of Engineers
Cosmopolitan, 436
Costantino, Cathy, 1259
Court mandated ADR, 1019, 1022
Court annexed ADR, 935, 980, 1019, 1112, 1123
CPR Institute for Dispute Resolution, 556, 827
Craver, Charles, 193
Criminal law, 252, 259, 474, 945, 1108, 1112
Cross-cultural disputing
See generally Chapter 5
anthropology, 125
Arusha (Tanzania), 147
form clauses, 590
Japan, 234
Korean-Americans, 205
Navajo Peacemaking, 224
prejudice, 215
Custody, *see* Family disputes

Dauber, Cynthia, 890
Decision theory, 93
Delgado, Richard, 215, 410, 1137
DeMente, Boye Lafayette, 239
Department of Justice, 892
Diamond, Barbara, 1162
Dickens, Charles, 693
Disability claims, 861, 877, 880
Discovery, 101, 1073
Discrimination, 215, 756, 775
Dispute resolution professionals
see generally, Chapters 19-20
arbitrators, 1216
certification, 1143, 1151
continuing education, 1153
court-connected, 1199
ethical codes, 1196, 1208
family mediators, 1153
immunity, 1177, 1192
licensing, 1143

malpractice, 1254
mediators, 504, 1153, 1244
quasi-judicial immunity, 1177
registration, 1142
securities arbitrators, 1165
social workers, 1213
state requirements, 1162
training, 1153
Dispute settlement continuum, 4
Divorce, *see* Family disputes
Dubler, Nancy, 467
Dunlop, John, 151, 854
Dunung, Sanjyot, 238

Early neutral evaluation, 811, 911, 1128
Easterbrook, Frank, 101, 713
Economics, 79, 83, 94, 161, 178
Edelman, Lester, 567, 823, 1287
Edwards, Harry, 20
Ellis, Jane, 399
Emergency mediation, 846
Empirical data
employment, 775
family, 439
litigation, 1061, 1106
negotiation, 193
Employment, 741, 756, 768, 775, 1273
Employment-at-will doctrine, 768
Empowerment, 361, 782
England (law of), 30, 153, 601, 602
Equal employment opportunity, *see* Discrimination, Employment
Ethics, *see* Professional Standards
Evaluative mediation, 810
Evers, Michael, 768
Executive Orders
No. 9017, 849
No. 9250, 850
No. 12778, 500, 1133
No. 12871, 1273, 1276, 1284
Expert fact finding, 808

Facilitation, 815
Fair employment practices, *see* Discrimination, Employment
Fair results, 457
Family disputes, 108

See generally, Chapter 8
anger/emotion in, 406, 425, 453
bargaining, 152
fair results, 457
impasse, 338
lawyers, 439
mediation process, 381
parenting plans, 395
women, 400, 429
Farmer-lender mediation, 483
Federal Advisor Committee Act, 897
Federal Arbitration Act
purpose, 601
principles, 599
scope of, 612
text, 605
Federal Mediation & Conciliation Service, 11, 854, 1073
Federal Rules of Civil Procedure
Rule 16, 1012, 1035, 1041, 1189
Rule 24, 1100
Rule 26, 1089
Rule 45, 1098
Rule 68, 1083
Federal Rules of Evidence
Rule 403, 1080
Rule 408, 1080, 1089
Felstiner, William, 405
Fernandez, Luis, 83, 94
Festinger, Lyonel, 112, 118
Fidandis, Nicholas, 847
Field, Anne, 436
FIFRA, 872
Financial institutions, 725
Final offer arbitration, 813
Fish, Stanley, 67
Fisher, Glen, 235
Fisher, Roger, 150, 175, 179, 182
Fiss, Owen, 1046, 1057, 1123, 1137
FitzGibbon, Susan, 963
Florida, 461, 1035, 1088, 1208
Folberg, Jay, 338, 381, 405, 440, 910
Folger, Joseph, 288
Form ADR clauses, 573, 574
Foster, Dean Allen, 236
Freedom of Information Act, 1082, 1091

Friedman, Milton, 1150
Friedman, Lawrence, 223
Fuller, Lon, 277, 742

Galanter, Marc, 1061
Galton, Eric, 302, 319, 350, 369
Game theory, 82, 93, 94, 95
Gangel-Jacob, Phyllis, 380
Gellhorn, Walter, 1143
General Accounting Office, 775
Getting to Yes, 150, 175, 179, 183, 188
Gibson, Kevin, 1235
Gifford, Donald, 170, 259
Gilligan, Carol, 47, 195, 406, 413, 433, 1243
Gilmore, Grant, 1053
Gilson, Ronald, 97
Goffman, Erving, 75
Golann, Dwight, 980, 1042
Gold, Lois, 353
Goldberg, Stephen, 124
Good faith, 462, 1019, 1034
Great Britain, *see* England
Green, Eric, 123, 1077
Grillo, Trina, 134, 400, 418, 453
Groton, James, 315
Gulliver, P.H., 146

Hardin, Garrett, 80
Harmony restoration process, 205
Harris, Alan, 315, 321
Harris, Philip, 241
Hayford, Stephen, 768
Haynes, John, 49, 381, 440
Henry, James, 27, 820, 1060
Hille, Richard, 1241
Hoebel, E. Adamson, 141, 142
Hohlt, Eileen, 335
Hughes, Scott, 458

Ifugao go-between, 140
Impasse, 338, 350
Indiana, 603, 625
Information gathering, 49, 51
International disputes, 590
International Chamber of Commerce, 516

Iowa, 484

Japan (negotiating in), 234
Jockisch, Wesley, 854
Judicial Improvements Act of 1990, 500
Judicial settlement conference, 995
Judicial review, 862
Jury determined settlements, 928
Justice Department, 892

Kahneman, Daniel, 190
Kantor, Rosabeth, 47
Katz, Lucy, 992, 1041
Kaufman, Irving, 962, 1106
Kerwin, Kristina, 1089
Kornhauser, Lewis, 152
Kovach, Kimberlee, 276, 337
Kpelle moot, 140
Kritek, Phyllis, 119

Labor disputes, *see* Employment
Law Enforcement Assistance Administration, 10
Lax, David, 151, 168, 178, 188
Leff, Arthur, 245
Legislative bodies, 74, 264
LeReche, Diane, 205
Licensing, *see* Dispute resolution professionals
Lieber, Franz, 68
Lieberman, Jethro, 27, 820, 1060
Limitations, *see* Statute of Limitations
Listening, 40
Llewellyn, Karl, 6, 139, 141, 142
Longan, Patrick, 1112
Lying/dissembling/puffing, 1220, 1228

Macchiaroli, Jean, 947
Machiavelli, Nicco, 182, 1220
MacKinnon, Catherine, 413
Magistrates as mediators, 994, 1112
Maiman, Richard, 439
Maine, 439
Malpractice by mediators, 1174, 1254
Malpractice screening, 14, 138, 928, 945, 1035
Mandatory ADR, 400, 439, 1019
Mann, Bruce, 30

March, Robert, 237
Marcus, Leonard, 467
Mashaw, Jerry, 868
Massachusetts, 1205
McEwen, Craig, 439, 504, 1151, 1175, 1192
McThenia, Andrew, 1054
Med-arb, *see* Mediation-arbitration
Mediation
See generally, Chapters 7-9
AAA rules, 501
anger/emotion in, 406, 425, 453
appellate, 961
bioethical issues, 467
business-getting, 1240
caucus, 335
checklist, 370
clients, 319
conciliation, 812
confidentiality, 1234
court annexed, 980, 1112
ethics standards, 1199, 1205, 1208
examples, 854
fair results, 457
family, 49, 400, 439, 1153
farmer-lender, 483
federal v. state law, 1035
forms and function, 277, 493
good faith participation, 1019
healing dimension, 354
impasse, 338, 350
Korean-Americans, 205
lying/dissembling/puffing, 1220, 1228
magistrates, 1112
malpractice, 1175, 1254
mandatory, 412, 421
neutral lawyer, 1243
privilege, 1077
process, 294, 315, 381
regulation of, 504, 1151
social workers, 1213
standard clauses, 577
stories, 288
styles, 293
victim-offender, 474
women, 400, 429

MEDALOA, 816
Mediation-arbitration, 577, 816
Medical malpractice, *see* malpractice screening
Melling, Tom, 265
Melnick, Shep, 898
Menkel-Meadow, Carrie, 139, 151, 222, 930, 1123, 1136
Mennonites, 478, 482
Mentschikoff, Soia, 516, 602
Merchant, Christina, 1259
Merry, Sally, 123
Metaphors, 120
Milne, Ann, 338, 381
Mini-trial, 15, 576, 820, 823, 827, 854
Minnesota, 484
Missouri, 961
Montefiore Hospital, 467
Moore, Christopher, 276, 294, 337
Mnookin, Robert, 97, 152, 186
Moberly, Robert, 1208
Moderated settlement conference, 806, 908
Moran, Robert, 241
Morgenstern, Oskar, 93
Morrell, Stephen, 321
Multi-door court house, 16, 1128
Murray, John, 149
Myths, 121

Nader, Laura, 6, 131, 139, 219, 1137
Nader, Ralph, 139
Naipaul, Shiva, 241
National Defense Mediation Board, 846
National Mediation Board, 854
National War Labor Board, 847
Navajo peacemaking, 224
Negotiated Rulemaking Act of 1990, 894, 897
Negotiation
  See generally, Chapters 4-6
  assessment, 1267
  barriers to settlement, 187
  criminal cases, 252, 259
  family, 387
  legislation, 264
  lying/dissembling/puffing, 1220, 1228
  managers, 151
  models, 146, 149, 151, 341

plea bargaining, 252, 259
stages, 146
standard clauses, 576
strategy, 171, 259, 995
women, 193
Negotiator's dilemma, 179
Neighborhood justice centers, 12
Neumann, Diane, 429
Neutral fact finding, 806
Neutral lawyer (mediation), 1244
New York (arbitration), 602, 604, 657
New York Convention (foreign arbitral awards), 609
Nolan, Dennis, 782
Non-administered arbitration, 556, 566
Non-binding arbitration, 568, 812, 890
Nonverbal communication, *see* Communication

Occupational regulation, 1142
Ombudsman, 833

Page, Reba, 854
Panama Convention (international arbitration), 611
Parable of the Commons, 80, 177
Parenting plans, 395
Partnership Councils, 1275
Partnering, 1287
Party-appointed arbitrators, 1220
Perino, Michael, 1097
Pin factory, 178
Plea bargaining, 252, 259
Ponte, Lucille, 932
Posner, Richard, 67, 937, 1007, 1034, 1122
Potapchuk, William, 1267
Pound Conference, 5, 6, 9, 16, 133, 1128
Preemption (of state law), 642, 641, 654, 1035
Principal-agent problem, 97, 189
Prisoner's dilemma, 81, 98, 177, 196
Prisoner grievances, 13
Pritzker, David, 895
Private judging, 816
Privileged communications, 1077, 1080
Professional Standards
see generally, Chapters 19-21, *see also* Dispute resolution professionals
confidentiality, 584, 1077, 1080
fair results, 457

mediators, 361
Pruitt, Dean, 175
Psychology, 112, 114, 190, 191
Public choice theory, 96, 1053
Punitive damages, 663

Questions, *see* Communication

Racketeering [RICO], 728
Raiffa, Howard, 95, 101
Railway Labor Act, 654
Reactive devaluation, 123, 191, 308
Redman, Eric, 272
Registration, *see* Dispute resolution professionals
Reg-neg, 890, 892, 895
Regulation, *see* Dispute resolution professionals
Rent-a-judge, 15, 140, 815
Resnik, Judith, 1128, 1137
Rice, Jeffrey, 928
Riordan, Kathleen, 48
Riskin, Leonard, 483, 1014, 1035, 1174, 1244
Rogers, Nancy, 188, 439, 504, 1151, 1175, 1192
Rosenberg, Joshua, 136, 417, 910
Ross, Lee, 191
Rowe, Mary, 834
Rubin, Alvin, 1220
Rulemaking, 894, 897

Sander, Frank, 8, 123, 1128
Sansom, William, 73
Santayana, George, 74
Saposnek, Donald, 407
Sarat, Austin, 405
Sartre, Jean Paul, 74
Screening panels, *see* Malpractice screening
Sebenius, James, 151, 168, 178, 188
Securities arbitration, 636, 639, 645, 795, 1165
Separation of powers, 869, 898
Settlement of Cases
against settlement, 1046, 1057, 1128
agreements, 1064
authority to settle, 1005
discovery of communications, 1073
for reconciliation, 1054
judicial, 995

most cases settle, 1060
U.S. Government, 1014
Settlement communications, 1073
Settlement conference, 995
Shaffer, Thomas, 1054
Shavell, Steven, 83
Sherman, Edward, 1014, 1022
Simkin, William, 847
Sink, Charles, 315, 321
Smith, Adam, 79, 178
Socrates, 122
Social Security Administration, 873, 992
Social work mediators, 1213
Society for Professionals in Dispute Resolution (SPIDR), 458, 1196
Solicitation of business, 1212, 1241
Solomon, 29, 869
Special master, 816
Speedy Trial Act, 1106, 1108
SPIDR, *see* Society for Professionals in Dispute Resolution
Statute of limitations, 645, 741
Staw, Barry, 114
Steele, Walter, 1228
Steelworkers Trilogy, 741
Stienstra, 1109
Strategic behavior, 162
Strategies (for bargaining)
competitive, 149, 171
cooperative, 149, 173
integrative, 149, 175
Summary jury trial, 810, 924, 928, 932
Systems design
see generally, Chapter 21
architect of ADR process, 815
assessment, 1267
attorneys, 1257
conflict management, 1259
elements of, 1257
facilitation, 816
labor-management relations, 1273
organization development, 1259
partnering, 1286
total quality management, 1272

Tannen, Deborah, 47
Taylor, Alison, 381, 405, 1153

Texas, 482, 1019, 1065, 1066, 1068, 1072, 1241
Tompkins, Robert, 395
Total quality management, 1272
Trajedy of the Commons, 80
Transaction costs, 161
Transformation, 291
Tversky, Amos, 190
Twining, William, 6, 139

Umbright, Mark, 482
UNCITRAL, 590, 593
Uniform Arbitration Act
  principles, 599
  text, 620
Uniform Commercial Code, 8, 204, 247, 742, 1034, 1072, 1220
U.S. Arbitration & Mediation, 495
U.S. Army Corps of Engineers, 568, 823, 854, 1267, 1275, 1287
U.S. Conciliation Service, 854
U.S. Constitution (and ADR)
  delegation, 883
  due process, 877, 980, 995
  equal protection, 937, 980, 995
  jury trial, 980, 995
  separation of powers, 871, 898, 980, 995
U.S. Department of Justice, 892
Ury, William, 150, 175, 179
Utah, 265

VanWinkle, John, 603, 625
Vaughn, Diane, 434
Veterans' claims, 861, 869
Victim-offender mediation, 474, 482
Vidmar, Neil, 928
Von Neumann, John, 93

Wage stabilization boards, 852
Weber, Max, 141, 203
Weinstein, Jack, 1112, 1128
A.A. White Dispute Resolution Institute, Appendix
White, James, 179, 1220
Willging, Thomas, 1109
Wilson, Woodrow, 272
Winner's curse, 191, 308
Win-win solutions, 177

Women
  see also Family disputes
  mediation, 400, 429
  negotiators, 193
Wulff, Randal, 315, 321
Yazzie, Robert, 224